MATCH OF THE

FOOTBALL YEARBOOK

2008/2009

RONALDO
7
SAMSUNG
SAMSUNG

unicef

Transfer talk: Ronaldinho, Silva, Podolski, Arshavin

First published 2008

Data collation by Warner Leach Ltd

ISBN 978-0-9558588-0-2

Published by Interact Publishing Limited
www.footballyearbook.co.uk

Editor: Terry Pratt

Data interpretation: Tony Warner, Stephen Hall

Production: Jamie Stamper and Martin Richardson

Data management: Peter Watts, Tim Tyler

Programming: Jonathan Proud, Paul Ward

Additional writing: Jamie Stamper, Tim Spiers, Tom Bennett

Printed and bound by Lego in Italy.

By arrangement with the BBC

THE PREMIER IS A STAGE FOR STARS

Recent Champions Leagues suggest the Premier League has gained ascendancy over the traditional giants of Europe; AC Milan, Inter and Juvé of Italy and Real Madrid and Barca from Spain.

The big wages, the opportunity for silverware and the power of our top clubs is attracting the best in Europe. Players want to make their name, as

Turkish fans, whose national team and clubs sprang some surprises in 2007-08

Roque Santa Cruz, Dimitar Berbatov and Emmanuel Adebayor have done; improve their chances of winning trophies, as Michael Ballack and Fernando Torres yearn to do; or sharpen their edge in the most demanding football environment as Cristiano Ronaldo and Cesc Fabregas can claim to have done.

Ronaldo dominating the scoring tables and headlines across the continent, Fabregas supplying Spain's creativity as well as Arsenal's, Torres moving up a gear from mid-table Atletico to 30+ goals in a season only adds to the lustre of the Premier League.

While an increasing number of overseas stars want to play on our shores, so the high profile strugglers make club managers more discerning. For every Santa Cruz and Didier Drogba, there's a Juan Sebastian Veron, or Mateja Kezman. Picking the winners has never been harder; landing the failures, never more expensive.

Increasingly every blogger, fantasy league manager and computer games-player thinks they can spot the budding stars from the likely failures. Of course *we* don't have a network of European scouts to pick the probables from the possibles, but hopefully this book is a good place to start seeing how players measure up. Villarreal must contain some gems and has players topping our charts; France has a sprinkling of talent shining out from some of its lesser clubs; Klaas Jan Huntelaar's instinct for goal will be put to a greater test soon.

The shop window of the African Nations Cup and Euro 2008 found the display lights picking out some unexpected talents. We hope you pick your way through and discover not just which foreign talents are glittering but also get some insights into where your own club has hidden strengths.

A big thank you to all those who have worked so hard through the season and during the frenetic period at its end to make this book possible, especially: Jamie Stamper, Martin Richardson, Steve Hall, Jonathan Proud, Tony Warner and Peter Watts.

Terry Pratt

306

Juve are back...

And with the likes of Del Piero, Buffon, Nedved and Camoranesi filling the Serie A charts, it's like they've never been away

Alessandro Del Piero celebrating a top scoring performance in Serie A

ABN·AMRO

348

Dutch hot-shots

Huntelaar lighting up the Dutch league and still topping the scoring charts as Ajax show the rest of Europe the way to the back of the net

Still in striking form, Klaas jan Huntelaar

adidas

386

Ribery revels in Bundesliga

Bayern go looking for foreign stars to get back to the top and pinch a French gem from under the nose of Arsenal

Franck Ribery; a target for Wenger, a revelation for Bayern

424

Benzema - the French Rooney?

Lyon pull new stars Karim Benzema and Hatem Ben Arfa out of their reserves to reclaim the French title

Karim Benzema; worth £20m plus claims Lyon president

THE CLUBS

104

'Harry's a legend now isn't he?'

Pompey shows there's life in the FA Cup outside of the 'Big Four' and Spurs leave Chelsea without a trophy to their name

Kanu believe it?

466

Champions League

The Premier League lays claim to being the best in the world with three out of four semi-finalists for the second year in-a-row

John Terry's tears fall in Moscow

484

Uefa Cup

The Russians are coming and Zenit and Andrei Arshavin are already here. Their top clubs now have the money to compete with the best in Europe

Rangers find final a game too far

492

Euro 2008, African Nations Cup

At last, we have two international football tournaments where goals are flying in and the attacking sides, such as Spain, flourish

A Ghana fan gets behind the Black Stars

CHARTING PERFORMANCE

Goalkeepers

Brad Friedel - 'Mr Consistency'

United went to Ewood Park in April knowing a win would make them all but bullet-proof in their title defence. Santa Cruz scored after 21 minutes and then it was all about United's famed forward line; Tevez, Ronaldo, Rooney, Giggs, Scholes *et al* against **Brad Friedel**. The remarkably consistent keeper was having one of those games when he seemed unbeatable. Here's his season's record: -

Goals Conceded in the League

Friedel played every minute of every game for Rovers and conceded **48** goals in the **3420** minutes he played in league matches.

Goals Conceded in all competitions

Add in the eight European and domestic cup games he played in and he conceded another 11, making it 59 goals in total.

KEY GOALKEEPER

Brad Friedel	
Goals Conceded in the League Number of League goals conceded while the player was on the pitch	48
Goals Conceded in all competitions Total number of goals conceded while the player was on the pitch	59
League minutes played Number of minutes played in league matches	3420
Clean Sheets In games when player was on pitch for at least 70 minutesmins	8
Goals to Shots Ratio The average number of shots on target per each League goal conceded	5,54
Defensive Rating Ave mins between League goals conceded while on the pitch	71

Clean Sheets

In league games he prevented the opposition from scoring in **8** games. If a keeper is subbed or sent off, he must have played for at least 70 minutes (a Counting Game) *and* the opposition finished goalless.

Defensive Rating

This is the key statistic we use to compare keepers, how often a team scores against them in league games. Friedel only let in a goal every **71** minutes on average - the ninth best record in the Premier League.

Goals to Shots Ratio

Of course a keeper needs protection from his colleagues. In the Premier League, we record how many saves a keeper makes per goal conceded. We use the Shots on Target stats and by this measure Friedel faced 266 Shots on Target, saving **5.54** of them for every goal he conceded.

That's a better record than fellow American Kasey Keller (who of course played far less games), who finished ahead of Friedel on Defensive Rating but only saved **3.81** Shots on Target per goal conceded.

Edwin van der Sar has the best Defensive Rating in the league, a goal conceded only every **142** minutes on average and the best Goals to Shots Ratio, saving **8.72** Shots on Target per goal conceded.

Midfielders

Cahill shows his all-round worth

Tim Cahill is the scoring star of Everton's midfield. Even in an injury-hit season he can finish second in the club's overall scoring charts. However, he adds more than just fire-power as he seems to bring an all-round balance to the side as Everton's midfield chart shows.

Goals in the League

Cahill managed a return of **7** league goals from just 18 appearances and scored **10** goals in total in the season - only Yakubu scored more.

Assists

He laid on just **2** goals for colleagues in the league, where Mikel Arteta is a better provider of scoring passes.

Defensive Rating

However, his work rate, tackling back and possession also helped to keep opposition goals down. Everton only conceded a goal every **150** minutes on average when Cahill was on the pitch. That's nearly 40 minutes better than any of his colleagues.

Contribution to Attacking Power

This is where Cahill's value really shows through. Everton were a far more dangerous outfit when he was adding to the goal threat. They scored a goal every **48** minutes when he was on the pitch. Without him their average was a goal every 80 minutes. Cahill has easily the best Attacking Power at the club with even Yakubu rating only a goal every 55 minutes

KEY PLAYERS - MIDFIELDERS

Tim Cahill	
Goals in the League	7
Goals in all competitions	10
Assists League goals scored by a team mate where the player delivered the final pass	2
Defensive Rating Average number of mins between League goals conceded while on the pitch	150
Contribution to Attacking Power Average number of minutes between League team goals while on pitch	48
Scoring Difference Defensive Rating minus Contribution to Attacking Power	102

	PLAYER	GOALS LGE	GOALS ALL	ASSISTS	DEF RATE	POWER	SC DIFF
1	Tim Cahill	7	10	2	150	48	102 mins
2	Mikel Arteta	1	4	5	111	59	52 mins
3	Leon Osman	4	7	3	110	59	51 mins

Scoring Difference

This measure is like a personal goal difference for a midfield player and we use it as a rough guide to compare top performers. It is found by taking away a player's Attacking Power from their Defensive Rating. With Cahill it is **150** minus **48**, which makes his Scoring Difference **+102**. That's the sixth best Scoring Difference in the whole league. A positive figure means the team is more likely to score than concede when a player is on the pitch. Negative results show the opposite.

Goalscorers

Harry rings the changes in attack

Portsmouth's best ever season saw a mix of striking partnerships at Fratton Park. **Benjani Mwaruwari** never looked prolific before this season when he lead the league charts early on before being transfered in favour of **Jermain Defoe**. The skills of **Kanu** was an inspiration in the FA Cup and Harry added **Milan Baros** in the January transfer window.

KEY PLAYERS - GOALSCORERS

Jermain Defoe	
Goals in the League	8
Goals in all competitions	8
Assists League goals scored by a team mate where the player delivered the final pass	1
Contribution to Attacking Power Average number of minutes between League team goals while on pitch	88
Player Strike Rate Average number of minutes between League goals scored by player	133
Club Strike Rate Average minutes between League goals scored by club	71

	PLAYER	GOALS LGE	GOALS ALL	ASSISTS	POWER	S RATE
1	Jermain Defoe	8	8	1	88	133 mins
2	Benjani Mwaruwari	12	12	1	65	152 mins
3	Nwankwo Kanu	4	7	4	114	344 mins

Goals in the League

Mwaruwari scored most for Pompey with **12** league goals, not including his three for City. Kanu scored 4 in the league plus 3 vital cup goals giving him a total of **7** in All Competitions.

Assists

Defoe creates goals for himself but not many for colleagues while Kanu laid on as many league goals as he scored with **4** Assists.

Contribution to Attacking Power

This measures how potent Pompey's attack is when each player is on the pitch. Here the creativity and pace of John Utaka adds to the overall goal threat; Pompey score every **62** minutes when he plays.

Player Strike Rate

This is the main measure we use to rank Strikers. It shows how regularly they score. By this measure Defoe is the pick of the trio. He scored a league goal every **133** minutes on average. Add in his four league goals for Spurs and it's still a 133 Strike Rate; that's the fourth best in the Premier League and just outside the top 20 in Europe.

Club Strike Rate

This gives Pompey's Attacking Power as a club for the season. They scored **48** goals in the season (that's 3420 league minutes) or a goal every **71** minutes on average. When compared to a player's Attacking Power it shows whether they added to their team's potency. Taken over the league season, Kanu certainly didn't but - even worse - neither Baros nor David Nugent troubled the league scorers at all.

Defenders

Ramos beefs up Spurs' defence

Juande Ramos identified Spurs' defence as his side's main weakness and used the January transfer window to bring in a number of defenders. With Ledley King injured, Jonathan Woodgate was bought to replace Younes Kaboul and Alan Hutton from Rangers joined at fullback.

Goals Conceded in the League

Both players made an improvement to the team, although Spurs still conceded **16** league goals in 12 games with Woodgate on the pitch.

Goals Conceded in all competitions

He conceded another 4 in 5 cup appearances to make **20** in total.

Clean Sheets

We only measure Clean Sheets in league games where the player has influenced a game for at least 70 minutes. These we call Counting Games. There were **4** Clean Sheets in Woodgate's 12 Counting Games.

Defensive Rating

This is the key measurement on which we compare Defenders. It shows how regularly a side concedes a goal when a particular defender is on the pitch. Spurs conceded a goal every **66** minutes on average when Woodgate was playing. However, with one of the worst five defensive records in the Premier League they conceded a goal every 48 minutes when he didn't play. Woodgate is Spurs best defender on this showing. Alan Hutton enjoyed a similar record to Woodgate and had the second best Defensive Rating of 60. Pascal Chimbonda and Younes Kaboul didn't get in Spurs' top four ratings.

KEY PLAYERS - DEFENDERS

Jonathan Woodgate	
Goals Conceded in the League Number of League goals conceded while the player was on the pitch	16
Goals Conceded in all competitions Total number of goals conceded while the player was on the pitch	20
League minutes played Number of minutes played in league matches	1066
Clean Sheets In games when the player was on pitch for at least 70 minutes	4
Defensive Rating Average number of mins between League goals conceded while on the pitch	66
Club Defensive Rating Average number of mins between League goals conceded by the club this season	56

	PLAYER	CON LGE	CON ALL	MINS	C SHEETS	DEF RATE
1	Jonathan Woodgate	16	20	1066	4	66 mins
2	Alan Hutton	20	21	1215	4	60 mins
3	Michael Dawson	39	50	2195	5	56 mins

Club Defensive Rating

This provides a quick check on whether a defender is tightening his club's defence. Woodgate's Rating is 10 minutes higher than the club average of a goal conceded every 56 minutes, so he is. United's Nemanja Vidic has a Defensive Rating 50 minutes higher than his club's average and is in the top three in Europe.

Squad Appearances

Now with injuries and suspensions

This season we've started to keep track of injuries and suspensions to help get a better view of a Premiership manager's selection policy. It helps show how a player has been used over a season.

Squares

A dark green square ■ shows the player was in the starting XI and finished the game. A light green square ■ shows he was on the bench but didn't get subbed on. A faint blank square □ shows they didn't make it to the bench. A dark edged blank square □ means the player was *reported* injured.

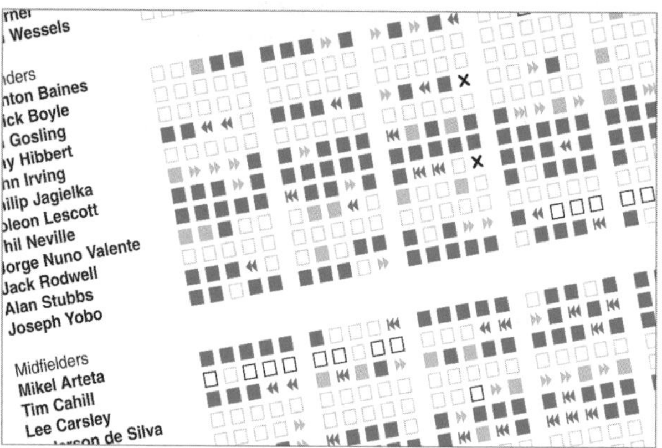
Wessels
Jorge Nuno Valente
Jack Rodwell
Alan Stubbs
Joseph Yobo
Midfielders
Mikel Arteta
Tim Cahill
Lee Carsley

Arrows

A dark green arrow « shows the player started the game but was subbed off or sent off. A light green arrow » shows they started on the bench but were subbed on. Still paler arrows show the player was subbed on but still didn't complete the 90 minutes.

Counting Games

A player registers a Counting Game when they play for 70 minutes or more in a particular game. Managers often take a view around the 70 minute mark and will rest key players. A dark green arrow with a small line before it ⏮ means they were subbed off *after* 70 minutes and it counts as a Counting Game. A light green arrow with a small line after it means they were subbed on in the first 20 minutes and played a full 70 minutes after that – also a Counting Game.

Crosses

A black cross **X** shows a player was suspended for that game and not eligible for selection.

Competition Key

A quick guide to the Competition, Venue and Result is shown at the top of the Squad Appearances Chart. **H** or **A** in Venue refer to **H**ome and **A**way. The result is W, L or D and shown in the appropriate colour. The Competitions are: **L** = League; **F** = FA Cup; **C** = Champions League; **E** = Uefa Cup; **W** = the League Cup in the English divisions; **O** = Other, for example a Play-Off match. Finally the numbers along the top refer to the game number and can be checked against the team's Results Chart for more details. There's more information of how squads are used in the Premier League round up pages.

Team of the Season

Selecting the top performers

The club XI

Each club has a team of the season generated by our computers. The computer selects first from players who have played at least 12 Counting Games, or CG. We sometimes reset this to lower to include a particularly strong performance but then we mark it with an asterisk.

TEAM OF THE SEASON
REINA
CG 38 DR 122
FINNAN
CG 21 DR 130
SKRTEL
CG 13 DR 119
HYYPIA
CG 21 DR 135
CARRAGHER
CG 33 DR 126
GERRARD
CG 31 SD +60
MASCHERANO
CG 24 SD +66
ALONSO
CG 15 SD +99
BENAYOUN
CG 13 SD +51
VORONIN
CG 12 AP 62
TORRES
CG 27 SR 106

KEY: DR = Defensive Rate, SD = Scoring Difference AP = Attacking Power SR = Strike Rate, CG=Counting games – League games playing at least 70 minutes

Defence

If there is a choice of Keeper, it chooses the one with the best (highest) Defensive Rating **DR**. It then selects the best four Defensive Ratings among the club's Defenders. They will be the defenders who concede goals least often, regardless of whether they are central or full backs.

Midfield

The computer chooses its midfield based on the highest Scoring Differences **SD**. Positive figures mean the team has scored more often than it conceded when that individual played. **Yossi Benayoun** just qualifies for Liverpool's Team of the Season as he tallied **13** Counting Games, but he had one of the best Attacking Powers at the club and a better Scoring Difference than **John Arne Riise**, who played more games in all but misses out. **Xabi Alonso** shares the same Attacking Power as Benayoun but brings far more defensive stability and therefore has the best Scoring Difference at the club.

Attack

In most divisions the computer selects the two best Strike Rates among the club forwards. In the Premiership, we give it more leeway. If a club plays with a withdrawn forward or advanced midfield player, we look at their Attacking Power. Liverpool's **Andrey Voronin** has a better Strike Rate and Attacking Power than Dirk Kuyt, so the computer chooses him for second spot alongside **Fernando Torres**, who is one of only three Premier Players in the European Top 20 Goalscorers.

Occasionally we find a team that has chopped and changed so much we can't find a full 4-4-2 that has played sufficient Counting Games. Then the Computer selects on the next highest Counting Games or advances a utility player into the gap. We mark these with an asterisk.

Divisional Teams of the Season

The most effective players in each division are sorted into top 15-20 charts of Goalkeepers, Defenders, Midfielders or Goalscorers. The most effective 4-4-2 across a division is selected the same way with one difference – no team is allowed to have more then one of its players in any position. This means that **Vidic** gets into the Premier XI Defence team, so Ferdinand and Evra miss out. The most any club can supply to the divisional team is therefore four players.

Goal Attempts

United make van der Sar work

Shots For

We record Goal Attempts in Premiership League games. The Goal Attempts FOR chart details the featured side's attacking prowess. Shots On Target are split into Home and Away records and the overall Total is shown before being turned into an Average per League game. We do the same for Shots Off Target and note the total of all shots struck.

You would expect **United** to hit most shots on Average and at **16.2** per game they do. However, they hit more Shots On Target per goal scored

GOAL ATTEMPTS

FOR Goal attempts recorded in League games	HOME	AWAY	TOTAL	AVE
shots on target	195	147	342	9.0
shots off target	150	125	275	7.2
TOTAL	345	272	617	16.2
Ratio of goals to shots Average number of shots on target per League goal scored				4.3
Accuracy rating Average percentage of total goal attempts which were on target				55.4

AGAINST Goal attempts recorded in League games	HOME	AWAY	TOTAL	AVE
shots on target	95	120	215	5.7
shots off target	80	105	185	4.9
TOTAL	175	225	400	10.5
Ratio of goals to shots Average number of shots on target per League goal scored				9.8
Accuracy rating Average percentage of total goal attempts which were on target				53.8

than either Arsenal or Chelsea. While lower league sides tend to hit far less shots but with more accuracy; Birmingham get over 60% on target. Along with most sides United are more adventurous at home with 56% of shots being hit at Old Trafford.

Shots Against

You may not expect United to be only fifth best at keeping shots at bay. Liverpool's defence lets far fewer shots through, while both Chelsea and Everton are better at keeping opponents from shooting on target. Where United are way ahead is in keeping those shots from turning into goals. Only around one shot in every ten on target find their way into the net, which says a lot for **Edwin van der Sar** and **Tomasz Kuszczak**. It also suggests that United's opponents were shooting under pressure - less than **54%** of the opponents' shots were on target.

Disciplinary Records

Wigan's bad boys

Red and Yellow cards are shown for all clubs. **Boro** have the worst disciplinary record in the Premier League. Wigan are only 12th in our bad boys table but are used as our example. Strikers can earn a lot of bookings and **Emile Heskey**'s five yellows at a card every 414 minutes on average is not unusual. **Josip Skoko** tops this table with a card every **167** minutes on average. Michael Brown picked up the most cards, **11** and his average of one every **224** minutes is also among the worst 20 in the league.

BOOKINGS

Josip Skoko	
League Yellow	4
League Red	0
All competitions Yellow	4
All competitions Red	0
League Average	167 mins between cards

	PLAYER	LEAGUE Y	LEAGUE R	TOTAL Y	TOTAL R	AVE
1	Josip Skoko	4	0	4	0	167
2	Michael Brown	11	0	11	0	224
3	Wilson Palacios	5	1	6	1	231
4	Ryan Taylor	4	0	4	0	278
5	Emile Heskey	5	0	5	0	414
6	Titus Bramble	5	0	6	0	468
7	Luis A Valencia	5	0	5	0	542
8	Paul Scharner	6	0	7	0	552
9	Marlon King	1	0	1	0	667
10	Kevin Kilbane	3	1	3	1	740
	TOTAL	58	4	61		4

Top Point Earners

The knack of turning draws into wins

Average points

Fulham skipper **Brian McBride** was injured in the act of scoring in the third game of the season. He returned in time to help his club complete a great escape from relegation. In games when McBride played at least 70 minutes, they averaged **1.58** points.

TOP POINT EARNERS

Brian McBride	
Counting Games League games when player was on pitch for at least 70 minutes	12
Average points Average League points taken in Counting games	1.58
Club Average points Average points taken in League games	0.95

	PLAYER	GAMES	PTS
1	Brian McBride	12	1.58
2	Paul Stalteri	12	1.42
3	Jimmy Bullard	15	1.40
4	Brede Paulsen Hangeland	15	1.40
5	Kasey Keller	13	1.38
6	Clint Dempsey	26	1.08
7	Aaron Hughes	29	1.07
8	Danny Murphy	27	1.04
9	Paul Konchesky	32	0.97
10	Simon Davies	35	0.97

Club Average Points

Overall Fulham gained 36 points, an average of **0.95** - just under a point per game. While McBride was injured, they managed just 17 points from 26 games compared to 19 from the 12 Counting Games he played. Paul Stalteri (a late loan acquisition) and Jimmy Bullard (return from long-term injured) were also way ahead of the club average.

Most Missed Players

The Premiership Round-up notes players who are badly missed by their clubs. Had McBride kept his record and played all Fulham's games, the side would have finished level with Villa.

THE PREMIERSHIP ROUND-UP

The Premier League again dominates our Top Leagues in Europe chart at the back of the book. No foreign team was able to knock out any Premier side in the Champions League. Cristiano Ronaldo has the best Strike Rate in Europe with a goal every 88 minutes but team-mate Wayne Rooney seems to be United's catalyst – they score every 34 minutes when he is on the pitch. Rooney is third in the league Assists chart behind Villa's Ashley Young and chart-topping Cesc Fabregas, who has 17. Chelsea may have the new Claude Makelele already in their ranks in John Obi-Mikel as Chelsea's defensive resilience rockets whenever he is on the pitch. Edwin van der Sar and Petr Cech are in Europe's top three keepers and neck-and-neck in terms of shots-on-target saved to goals conceded. Brian McBride and Tim Cahill are the two 'Most Missed' players, their teams performing over a point a game better on average when either is on the pitch. Roque Santa Cruz is just behind Ronaldo in the Share of Goals chart, hitting 38% of Blackburn's total. Joleon Lescott and Martin Laursen are the two scoring defenders you want in your fantasy league teams.

CLUB STRIKE FORCE

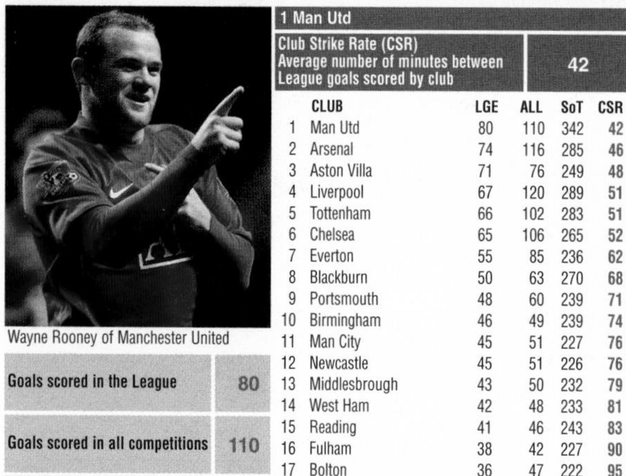

Wayne Rooney of Manchester United

Goals scored in the League	80
Goals scored in all competitions	110
Shots on target (SoT) Shots on target hit by the team recorded in League games	342

1 Man Utd

Club Strike Rate (CSR) Average number of minutes between League goals scored by club	42

	CLUB	LGE	ALL	SoT	CSR
1	Man Utd	80	110	342	42
2	Arsenal	74	116	285	46
3	Aston Villa	71	76	249	48
4	Liverpool	67	120	289	51
5	Tottenham	66	102	283	51
6	Chelsea	65	106	265	52
7	Everton	55	85	236	62
8	Blackburn	50	63	270	68
9	Portsmouth	48	60	239	71
10	Birmingham	46	49	239	74
11	Man City	45	51	227	76
12	Newcastle	45	51	226	76
13	Middlesbrough	43	50	232	79
14	West Ham	42	48	233	81
15	Reading	41	46	243	83
16	Fulham	38	42	227	90
17	Bolton	36	47	222	95
18	Sunderland	36	36	212	95
19	Wigan	34	38	207	100
20	Derby	20	26	194	171

CLUB DEFENCES

1 Man Utd

Club Defensive Rate (CDR) Average number of minutes between League goals conceded by club	155

	CLUB	LGE	ALL	CS	SoT	CDR
1	Man Utd	22	33	21	215	155
2	Chelsea	26	44	21	201	131
3	Liverpool	28	51	18	177	122
4	Arsenal	31	53	15	204	110
5	Everton	33	47	14	208	103
6	Portsmouth	40	43	16	239	85
7	Blackburn	48	59	8	266	71
8	West Ham	50	55	8	234	68
9	Wigan	51	54	12	253	67
10	Aston Villa	51	54	9	229	67
11	Man City	53	58	11	267	64
12	Middlesbrough	53	58	8	234	64
13	Bolton	54	64	12	244	63
14	Fulham	60	64	7	259	57
15	Sunderland	59	65	7	228	57
16	Tottenham	61	79	9	253	56
17	Birmingham	62	68	3	298	55
18	Newcastle	65	71	8	299	52
19	Reading	66	73	8	303	51
20	Derby	89	98	3	309	38

Rock solid Van der Sar and Ferdinand

Goals conceded in the League	22
Goals conceded in all competitions	33
Clean Sheets (CS) Number of league games where no goals were conceded	21
Shots on Target Against (SoT) Shots on target conceded by team in League games	215

PLAYER NATIONALITIES

Overseas country with the most player appearances in the Premiership - France

In the squad	747	Percentage of League action	6.33
Appearances in League games	661	Caps for France this season	2
Most appearances	Clichy	Percentage of time on pitch	97.4

	COUNTRY	PLAYERS	IN SQUAD	LGE APP	% LGE ACT	CAPS	MOST APP	APP
	England	234	4394	3752	37.51	153	Robert Green	100.0
1	France	38	747	661	6.33	57	Gael Clichy	97.4
2	Rep of Ireland	30	707	626	6.03	86	Stephen Kelly	100.0
3	Spain	15	330	302	3.20	33	Jose Reina	100.0
4	Holland	15	325	305	3.08	74	Wilfred Bouma	95.4
5	Wales	22	378	290	2.81	57	Simon Davies	93.8
6	Scotland	19	338	293	2.62	49	Craig Gordon	89.5
7	N Ireland	14	249	233	2.53	55	George McCartney	94.3
8	Nigeria	11	288	273	2.38	22	Joseph Yobo	76.3
9	United States	9	249	220	2.35	19	Brad Friedel	100.0
10	Brazil	15	297	260	2.24	18	Blumer Elano	71.4
11	Ivory Coast	8	199	185	1.90	33	Habib Kolo Toure	75.0
12	Australia	12	244	181	1.88	0	Mark Schwarzer	89.5
13	Senegal	10	223	200	1.88	20	El Hadji Diouf	77.2
14	Portugal	11	196	148	1.44	28	Cristiano Ronaldo	80.5
15	Sweden	9	169	134	1.33	47	Olof Mellberg	86.7
16	Finland	7	159	133	1.23	27	Jussi Jaaskelainen	73.7
17	Norway	7	137	128	1.22	17	Morten G Pedersen	84.0
18	Iceland	6	115	109	1.18	11	Ivar Ingimarsson	87.8
19	Argentina	5	123	113	1.10	12	Carlos Tevez	78.321
20	Czech Republic	7	144	112	1.06	36	Petr Cech	67.6

CLUB MAKE-UP – HOME AND OVERSEAS PLAYERS

1 Arsenal

Overseas players in the squad	28	Home country players	7
Percent of overseas players	80.0	Percent of League action	100.00
Most appearances	Clichy	Appearance percentage	97.4

	CLUB	OVERSEAS	HOME	% OVERSEAS	% LGE ACT	MOST APP	APP %
1	Arsenal	28	7	80.0	100.00	Gael Clichy	97.4
2	Fulham	29	10	74.4	85.54	Simon Davies	93.8
3	Birmingham	21	12	63.6	79.62	Stephen Kelly	100.0
4	Blackburn	21	6	77.8	79.10	Brad Friedel	100.0
5	Liverpool	24	7	77.4	78.60	Jose Reina	100.0
6	Chelsea	22	10	68.8	76.18	Nicolas Anelka	75.3
7	Man City	23	11	67.6	74.10	Richard Dunne	91.9
8	Reading	23	12	65.7	70.39	M Hahnemann	100.0
9	Portsmouth	21	10	67.7	69.94	Sylvain Distin	93.4
10	Man Utd	22	14	61.1	69.88	Patrice Evra	82.5
11	Bolton	29	13	69.0	69.08	Andy O'Brien	82.5
12	Everton	20	12	62.5	65.65	Tim Howard	94.7
13	Newcastle	21	11	65.6	65.44	Habib Beye	72.3
14	Sunderland	26	9	74.3	63.47	Craig Gordon	89.5
15	Tottenham	19	15	55.9	62.11	Dimitar Berbatov	87.3
16	Middlesbrough	17	15	53.1	58.42	Mark Schwarzer	89.5
17	Wigan	17	12	58.6	57.31	Paul Scharner	96.9
18	Derby	22	17	56.4	55.63	Kenny Miller	75.1
19	West Ham	15	17	46.9	41.09	George McCartney	94.3
20	Aston Villa	9	14	39.1	40.41	Martin Laursen	98.5

CLUB STARTING FORMATIONS

1 Blackburn	
Most used starting formation	
Number of different formations used	

How often the club used its most frequently used formation	97.4%

	CLUB	Formation	Number	Used %
1	Blackburn	442	2	97.4
2	Arsenal	442	2	94.7
3	Everton	442	2	94.7
4	Wigan	442	3	94.7
5	Tottenham	442	2	92.1
6	Fulham	442	3	92.1
7	Birmingham	442	2	92.1
8	Man Utd	442	3	92.1
9	Middlesbrough	442	2	92.1
10	Reading	442	3	92.1
11	Derby	442	3	84.2
12	West Ham	442	3	81.6
13	Portsmouth	442	3	78.9
14	Sunderland	442	3	78.9
15	Liverpool	442	3	76.3
16	Man City	442	3	76.3
17	Chelsea	433	2	73.7
18	Newcastle	442	4	65.8
19	Aston Villa	442	2	65.8
20	Bolton	442	3	47.4

Four-four-two is still the English formation with all but Chelsea and Bolton using it over 50% of the time.

Chelsea are the only club with a preferred starting formation – 4-3-3, which they used in 74% of their games.

On average sides used around three different starting formations during the season.

Average number of different formations used by Premiership clubs	2.7

FINAL LEAGUE TABLE

	HOME						AWAY					TOTAL			
	P	W	D	L	F	A	W	D	L	F	A	F	A	DIF	PTS
Man Utd	38	17	1	1	47	7	10	5	4	33	15	80	22	58	87
Chelsea	38	12	7	0	36	13	13	3	3	29	13	65	26	39	85
Arsenal	38	14	5	0	37	11	10	6	3	37	20	74	31	43	83
Liverpool	38	12	6	1	43	13	9	7	3	24	15	67	28	39	76
Everton	38	11	4	4	34	17	8	4	7	21	16	55	33	22	65
Aston Villa	38	10	3	6	34	22	6	9	4	37	29	71	51	20	60
Blackburn	38	8	7	4	26	19	7	6	6	24	29	50	48	2	58
Portsmouth	38	7	8	4	24	14	9	1	9	24	26	48	40	8	57
Man City	38	11	4	4	28	20	4	6	9	17	33	45	53	-8	55
West Ham	38	7	7	5	24	24	6	3	10	18	26	42	50	-8	49
Tottenham	38	8	5	6	46	34	3	8	8	20	27	66	61	5	46
Newcastle	38	8	5	6	25	26	3	5	11	20	39	45	65	-20	43
Middlesbrough	38	7	5	7	27	23	3	7	9	16	30	43	53	-10	42
Wigan	38	8	5	6	21	17	2	5	12	13	34	34	51	-17	40
Sunderland	38	9	3	7	23	21	2	3	14	13	38	36	59	-23	39
Bolton	38	7	5	7	23	18	2	5	12	13	36	36	54	-18	37
Fulham	38	5	5	9	22	31	3	7	9	16	29	38	60	-22	36
Reading	38	8	2	9	19	25	2	4	13	22	41	41	66	-25	36
Birmingham	38	6	8	5	30	23	2	3	14	16	39	46	62	-16	35
Derby	38	1	5	13	12	43	0	3	16	8	46	20	89	-69	11

CLUB GOAL ATTEMPTS FOR

Thunderous volley by Carlos Tevez

Shots on target	342
Shots off target	275
Ratio of shots on target to goals	4.3
Accuracy Rating	55.4

1 Man Utd	
Total shots	617

	CLUB	SoT	Soff	Tot	SG	AR
1	Man Utd	342	275	617	4.3	55.4
2	Liverpool	289	283	572	4.3	50.5
3	Arsenal	285	247	532	3.9	53.6
4	Chelsea	265	249	514	4.1	51.6
5	Portsmouth	239	255	494	5.0	48.4
6	Tottenham	283	207	490	4.3	57.8
7	Blackburn	270	198	468	5.4	57.7
8	Aston Villa	249	212	461	3.5	54.0
9	West Ham	233	221	454	5.5	51.3
10	Everton	236	203	439	4.3	53.8
11	Middlesbrough	232	199	431	5.4	53.8
12	Newcastle	226	203	429	5.0	52.7
13	Fulham	227	193	420	6.0	54.0
14	Wigan	207	212	419	6.1	49.4
15	Sunderland	212	206	418	5.9	50.7
16	Reading	243	166	409	5.9	59.4
17	Man City	227	181	408	5.0	55.6
18	Bolton	222	173	395	6.2	56.2
19	Birmingham	239	154	393	5.2	60.8
20	Derby	194	151	345	9.7	56.2

CLUB GOAL ATTEMPTS AGAINST

1 Derby	
Total shots against	564

	CLUB	SoT	Soff	Tot	SG	AR
1	Derby	309	255	564	3.5	54.8
2	Birmingham	298	236	534	4.8	55.8
3	Reading	303	231	534	4.6	56.7
4	Newcastle	299	218	517	4.6	57.8
5	Fulham	259	239	498	4.3	52.0
6	Man City	267	220	487	5.0	54.8
7	Portsmouth	239	237	476	6.0	50.2
8	Wigan	253	208	461	5.0	54.9
9	Aston Villa	229	229	458	4.5	50.0
10	Blackburn	266	183	449	5.5	59.2
11	West Ham	234	212	446	4.7	52.5
12	Tottenham	253	186	439	4.1	57.6
13	Bolton	244	195	439	4.5	55.6
14	Middlesbrough	234	203	437	4.4	53.5
15	Sunderland	228	208	436	3.9	52.3
16	Everton	208	224	432	6.3	48.1
17	Chelsea	201	205	406	7.7	49.5
18	Man Utd	215	185	400	9.8	53.8
19	Arsenal	204	159	363	6.6	56.2
20	Liverpool	177	155	332	6.3	53.3

Yet more despair for Derby keeper Carroll

Shots on target against	309
Shots off target against	255
Ratio of shots on target to goals	3.5
Accuracy Rating	54.8

STADIUM CAPACITY AND HOME CROWDS

	TEAM	CAPACITY	AVE	HIGH	LOW
1	Arsenal	60432	99.4	60161	59442
2	Man Utd	76212	99.3	76013	75055
3	Tottenham	36236	99.26	36178	35504
4	Portsmouth	20288	98.18	20556	17180
5	Newcastle	52387	97.96	52307	49948
6	Reading	24200	97.43	24374	21379
7	West Ham	35657	97.04	34980	33629
8	Fulham	24600	96.64	25357	20774
9	Derby	33597	96.53	33087	30048
10	Chelsea	42522	96.12	41837	31683
11	Liverpool	45362	95.97	44459	42308
12	Aston Villa	42573	94.89	47938	32288
13	Everton	40565	90.99	40049	31885
14	Man City	47500	88.96	47321	38261
15	Sunderland	49000	88.46	47802	37369
16	Birmingham	30009	87.24	29252	22089
17	Blackburn	31367	77.03	30316	19316
18	Wigan	25000	76.18	25133	14007
19	Middlesbrough	35120	76.05	33952	22920
20	Bolton	27879	74.97	25414	17014

Key: Average. The percentage of each stadium filled in League games over the season (AVE), the stadium capacity and the highest and lowest crowds recorded.

AWAY ATTENDANCE

	TEAM	AVE	HIGH	LOW
1	Liverpool	97.98	76000	20388
2	Man Utd	97.7	60161	20510
3	Newcastle	95.3	75965	20304
4	Arsenal	94.78	75985	19676
5	Sunderland	94.33	75648	18637
6	Man City	93.8	75970	18614
7	West Ham	93.27	76013	20525
8	Chelsea	92.85	75663	19011
9	Derby	92.5	75725	17014
10	Tottenham	92.22	75696	18673
11	Everton	91.59	75749	18820
12	Bolton	91.33	75467	17055
13	Wigan	91.15	75300	18623
14	Aston Villa	91.13	75932	18413
15	Birmingham	90.98	75459	17926
16	Blackburn	90.81	75710	16489
17	Fulham	90.42	75055	16973
18	Middlesbrough	90.1	75720	14007
19	Reading	89.83	75655	19043
20	Portsmouth	87.86	75145	17695

Key: Average. How close each club has come to filling grounds in its away league matches (AVE) and the highest and lowest crowds recorded.

CHART-TOPPING MIDFIELDERS

1 John Obi Mikel - Chelsea	
Goals scored in the League	0
Assists in league games	0
Defensive Rating Av number of mins between League goals conceded while on the pitch	244
Contribution to Attacking Power Average number of minutes between League team goals while on pitch	54
Scoring Difference Defensive Rating minus Contribution to Attacking Power	190

	PLAYER	CLUB	GOALS	ASS	DEF R	POWER	SCORE DIFF
1	John Obi Mikel	Chelsea	0	0	244	54	**190 mins**
2	Cristiano Ronaldo	Man Utd	31	7	161	40	**121 mins**
3	Luis Anderson	Man Utd	0	2	165	46	**119 mins**
4	Michael Carrick	Man Utd	2	3	157	42	**115 mins**
5	Paul Scholes	Man Utd	1	5	153	47	**106 mins**
6	Tim Cahill	Everton	7	2	150	48	**102 mins**
7	Tomas Rosicky	Arsenal	6	3	148	47	**101 mins**
8	Frank Lampard	Chelsea	10	11	143	43	**100 mins**
9	Xabi Alonso	Liverpool	2	2	146	47	**99 mins**
10	Nani	Man Utd	3	13	131	36	**95 mins**
11	Owen Hargreaves	Man Utd	2	3	139	52	**87 mins**
12	Joe Cole	Chelsea	7	5	137	51	**86 mins**
13	Florent Malouda	Chelsea	2	5	154	69	**85 mins**
14	Shaun Wright-Phillips	Chelsea	2	4	149	65	**84 mins**
15	Michael Ballack	Chelsea	7	3	128	48	**80 mins**
16	Ryan Giggs	Man Utd	3	10	131	51	**80 mins**
17	Javier Mascherano	Liverpool	1	2	119	53	**66 mins**
18	Mathieu Flamini	Arsenal	3	2	110	46	**64 mins**
19	Alexander Hleb	Arsenal	2	11	110	47	**63 mins**
20	Francesc Fabregas	Arsenal	7	20	105	45	**60 mins**

The Divisional Round-up charts combine the records of chart-topping keepers, defenders, midfield players and forwards, from every club in the division.. The one above is for **the Chart-topping Midfielders**. The players are ranked by their Scoring Difference although other attributes are shown for you to compare.

CHART-TOPPING GOALSCORERS

1 Cristiano Ronaldo - Man Utd	
Goals scored in the League (GL)	31
Goals scored in all competitions (ALL)	42
Contribution to Attacking Power Average number of minutes between League team goals while on pitch	40
Player Strike Rate (S Rate) Average number of minutes between League goals scored by player	88
Club Strike Rate (CSR) Average minutes between League goals scored by club	42

	PLAYER	CLUB	GOALS: LGE	ALL	POWER	CSR	S RATE
1	Cristiano Ronaldo	Man Utd	31	42	40	42	**88 mins**
2	Fernando Torres	Liverpool	24	33	44	51	**106 mins**
3	Emmanuel Adebayor	Arsenal	24	30	45	46	**122 mins**
4	Jermain Defoe	Portsmouth	8	8	88	71	**133 mins**
5	Ayegbeni Yakubu	Everton	15	21	55	62	**143 mins**
6	Benjani Mwaruwari	Portsmouth	12	12	65	71	**152 mins**
7	Nicolas Anelka	Bolton	10	11	73	95	**160 mins**
8	Roque Santa Cruz	Blackburn	19	23	70	68	**167 mins**
9	Wayne Rooney	Man Utd	12	18	34	42	**181 mins**
10	Robbie Keane	Tottenham	15	23	50	51	**181 mins**
11	Mikael Forssell	Birmingham	9	9	62	74	**186 mins**
12	Didier Drogba	Chelsea	8	15	52	52	**190 mins**
13	Carlos Tevez	Man Utd	14	19	42	42	**191 mins**
14	John Alieu Carew	Aston Villa	13	13	51	48	**196 mins**
15	Michael Owen	Newcastle	11	13	72	76	**197 mins**
16	Dimitar Berbatov	Tottenham	15	23	54	51	**199 mins**
17	Frank Lampard	Chelsea	10	20	43	52	**200 mins**
18	Dean Ashton	West Ham	10	11	74	81	**200 mins**
19	Michael Ballack	Chelsea	7	9	48	52	**201 mins**
20	Benni McCarthy	Blackburn	8	9	76	68	**210 mins**

The Chart-topping Goalscorers measures the players by Strike Rate. They are most likely to be Forwards but Midfield players and even Defenders do come through the club tables. It is not a measure of the number of League goals scored - although that is also noted - but how often on average they have scored.

CHART-TOPPING DEFENDERS

1 Juliano Belletti - Chelsea	
Goals Conceded in the League The number of League goals conceded while he was on the pitch	8
Goals Conceded in all competitions The number of goals conceded while he was on the pitch in all competitions	17
Clean Sheets In games when he played at least 70 mins	14
Defensive Rating Average number of minutes between League goals conceded while on pitch	239
Club Defensive Rating Average mins between League goals conceded by the club this season	131

	PLAYER	CLUB	CON: LGE	ALL	CS	CDR	DEF RATE
1	Juliano Belletti	Chelsea	8	17	14	131	**239 mins**
2	Nemanja Vidic	Man Utd	13	20	19	155	**205 mins**
3	Patrice Evra	Man Utd	16	22	16	155	**176 mins**
4	Rio Ferdinand	Man Utd	20	28	19	155	**152 mins**
5	John Terry	Chelsea	13	25	12	131	**145 mins**
6	Wes Brown	Man Utd	21	30	17	155	**144 mins**
7	Alex	Chelsea	15	21	13	131	**138 mins**
8	Sami Hyypia	Liverpool	15	31	10	122	**135 mins**
9	Ricardo Carvalho	Chelsea	13	26	13	131	**134 mins**
10	Steve Finnan	Liverpool	15	27	9	122	**130 mins**
11	Jamie Carragher	Liverpool	24	45	15	122	**126 mins**
12	Philippe Senderos	Arsenal	10	24	7	110	**124 mins**
13	Martin Skrtel	Liverpool	10	16	7	122	**119 mins**
14	Bacary Sagna	Arsenal	21	28	11	110	**117 mins**
15	Ashley Cole	Chelsea	21	30	14	131	**114 mins**
16	Gael Clichy	Arsenal	30	36	15	110	**111 mins**
17	Emmanuel Eboue	Arsenal	15	23	4	110	**110 mins**
18	Philip Jagielka	Everton	24	36	12	103	**110 mins**
19	Alvaro Arbeloa	Liverpool	21	33	12	122	**108 mins**
20	Phil Neville	Everton	30	40	13	103	**107 mins**

The Chart-topping Defenders are resolved by their Defensive Rating, how often their team concedes a goal while they are playing. All these rightly favour players at the best performing clubs because good players win matches. However, good players in lower-table clubs will chart where they have lifted the team's performance.

CHART-TOPPING GOALKEEPERS

1 Edwin van der Sar - Man Utd	
Goals conceded in the League	18
Goals conceded in all comps (ALL)	24
Counting Games (CG) League games when he played at least 70 minutes	28
Clean Sheets (CS) In games when he played at least 70 mins	14
Goals to Shots Ratio (GSR) The average number of shots on target per each League goal conceded	8.72
Defensive Rating Average number of minutes between League goals conceded while on pitch	142

	PLAYER	CLUB	CG	CON: LGE	ALL	CS	GSR	DEF RATE
1	Edwin van der Sar	Man Utd	28	18	24	14	8.72	**142 mins**
2	Petr Cech	Chelsea	25	17	27	14	8.76	**136 mins**
3	Jose Reina	Liverpool	38	28	41	18	6.32	**122 mins**
4	Tim Howard	Everton	36	30	40	14	6.7	**108 mins**
5	Manuel Almunia	Arsenal	29	24	33	11	6.63	**108 mins**
6	David James	Portsmouth	35	36	39	16	6.28	**87 mins**
7	Radek Cerny	Tottenham	13	14	23	4	6.14	**83 mins**
8	Kasey Keller	Fulham	13	16	18	5	3.81	**73 mins**
9	Brad Friedel	Blackburn	38	48	59	8	5.54	**71 mins**
10	Scott Carson	Aston Villa	34	45	47	9	4.69	**69 mins**
11	Joe Hart	Man City	26	34	39	7	5.47	**68 mins**
12	Robert Green	West Ham	38	50	53	8	4.68	**68 mins**
13	Chris Kirkland	Wigan	37	49	51	12	5.08	**67 mins**
14	Mark Schwarzer	Middlesbrough	34	47	50	8	4.26	**65 mins**
15	Steve Harper	Newcastle	19	28	28	6	5.07	**64 mins**
16	Jussi Jaaskelainen	Bolton	28	42	46	8	4.43	**60 mins**
17	Maik Taylor	Birmingham	34	54	56	3	5.04	**56 mins**
18	Craig Gordon	Sunderland	34	55	58	6	3.67	**55 mins**
19	M Hahnemann	Reading	38	66	66	8	4.59	**51 mins**
20	Antti Niemi	Fulham	22	39	41	2	4.38	**50 mins**

The Chart-topping Goalkeepers are positioned by their Defensive Rating. We also show Clean Sheets where the team has not conceded and the Keeper has played all or most (at least 70 minutes) of the game. Only the top keeper for each team is included in this chart.

GOALS

	PLAYER	TEAM	LGE	SR
1	Ronaldo	Man Utd	31	88
2	Torres	Liverpool	24	106
3	Adebayor	Arsenal	24	122
4	Santa Cruz	Blackburn	19	167
5	Yakubu	Everton	15	143
6	Keane	Tottenham	15	181
7	Berbatov	Tottenham	15	199
8	Tevez	Man Utd	14	191
9	Carew	Aston Villa	13	196
10	Mwaruwari	Portsmouth	12	152
11	Rooney	Man Utd	12	181
12	Owen	Newcastle	11	197
13	Gerrard	Liverpool	11	258
14	Agbonlahor	Aston Villa	11	298
15	Anelka	Bolton	10	160
16	Lampard	Chelsea	10	200
17	Ashton	West Ham	10	200
18	Kitson	Reading	10	252
19	Forssell	Birmingham	9	186
20	Martins	Newcastle	9	228
21	Young	Aston Villa	9	365
22	Barry	Aston Villa	9	368
23	Downing	Middlesbrough	9	379
24	Defoe	Portsmouth	8	133
25	Drogba	Chelsea	8	190
26	McCarthy	Blackburn	8	210
27	Tuncay Sanli	Middlesbrough	8	276
28	Elano	Man City	8	305
29	Lescott	Everton	8	421
30	van Persie	Arsenal	7	153

GOALS – MIDFIELDERS

	PLAYER	TEAM	LGE	SR
1	Ronaldo	Man Utd	31	88
2	Gerrard	Liverpool	11	258
3	Lampard	Chelsea	10	200
4	Barry	Aston Villa	9	368
5	Downing	Middlesbrough	9	379
6	Elano	Man City	8	305
7	Ballack	Chelsea	7	201
8	Cahill	Everton	7	214
9	Cole, J	Chelsea	7	353
10	Fabregas	Arsenal	7	408
11	Harper	Reading	7	478
12	Rosicky	Arsenal	6	222
13	Essien	Chelsea	6	348
14	Larsson	Birmingham	6	444
15	Bentley	Blackburn	6	553
16	Kapo	Birmingham	5	403
17	Murphy	Fulham	5	494
18	Nolan	Bolton	5	553
19	Petrov	Man City	5	594
20	Davies	Fulham	5	641

GOALS – DEFENDERS

	PLAYER	TEAM	LGE	SR
1	Lescott	Everton	8	421
2	Laursen	Aston Villa	6	561
3	Gallas	Arsenal	4	681
4	Scharner	Wigan	4	828
5	Taylor	Wigan	3	370
6	Bikey	Reading	3	456
7	Kaboul	Tottenham	3	535
8	Higginbotham	Sunderland	3	630

TEAM OF THE SEASON

VAN DER SAR
MAN UTD
CG 28 DR 142
BELLETTI
CHELSEA
CG 21 DR 239
VIDIC
MAN UTD
CG 29 DR 205
HYYPIA
LIVERPOOL
CG 21 DR 135
JAGIELKA
EVERTON
CG 29 DR 110
RONALDO
MAN UTD
CG 28 SD +121
MIKEL
CHELSEA
CG 18 SD +190
CAHILL
EVERTON
CG 17 SD +102
ROSICKY
ARSENAL
CG 14 SD +101
ADEBAYOR
ARSENAL
CG 32 AP 45
TORRES
LIVERPOOL
CG 27 SR 106

The Premiership Team of the Season shows a 4-4-2 of the best players in the Premiership based upon the selection criteria used for the chart-toppers. The players selected are taken from the lists for each club except that to get into a Divisional Team of the Season you must have played at least 17 Counting Games in the league (roughly half the league season) and not 12 as is the case in the club lists. The other restriction is that we are only allowing one player from each club in each position. So the maximum number of players one club can have in the divisional team is four.

- **The Divisional team's goalkeeper** is the player with the highest *Defensive Rating*
- **The Divisional team's defenders** are also tested by *Defensive Rating*, i.e. the average number of minutes between league goals conceded while on the pitch.
- **The Divisional team's midfield** are selected on their *Scoring Difference*, i.e.their *Defensive Rating* minus their *Contribution to Attacking Power* (average number of minutes between league goals scored while on the pitch. It takes no account of Assists.
- **The Divisional team strikeforce** is made up of the striker with the highest *Strike Rate* (his average number of minutes between league goals scored while on the pitch) together with the striker with the highest *Contribution to Attacking Power.*

ASSISTS

	PLAYER	TEAM	LGE	ALL
1	Fabregas	Arsenal	17	20
2	Young	Aston Villa	16	16
3	Rooney	Man Utd	12	13
4	Berbatov	Tottenham	11	12
5	Kalou	Chelsea	11	11
6	Barry	Aston Villa	10	10
7	Gerrard	Liverpool	9	13
8	Nani	Man Utd	9	13
9	Lampard	Chelsea	9	11
10	Bentley	Blackburn	9	9
11	Elano	Man City	9	9
12	Shorey	Reading	9	9
13	Santa Cruz	Blackburn	8	8
14	Petrov	Man City	8	8
15	Jones	Sunderland	8	8
16	Cole	West Ham	8	8
17	Hleb	Arsenal	7	11
18	Kuyt	Liverpool	7	8
19	Davies	Fulham	7	7
20	Aliadiere	Middlesbrough	7	7
21	Geremi	Newcastle	7	7
22	Huddlestone	Tottenham	7	7
23	Pienaar	Everton	6	8
24	Jenas	Tottenham	6	8
25	Roberts	Blackburn	6	7
26	Drogba	Chelsea	6	7
27	Ronaldo	Man Utd	6	7
28	Tevez	Man Utd	6	7
29	Agbonlahor	Aston Villa	6	6

SHARE OF GOALS

	PLAYER	TEAM	% LGE GOALS
1	Ronaldo	Man Utd	38.75
2	Santa Cruz	Blackburn	38.00
3	Torres	Liverpool	35.82
4	Adebayor	Arsenal	32.43
5	Anelka	Bolton	27.78
6	Yakubu	Everton	27.27
7	Mwaruwari	Portsmouth	25.00
8	Owen	Newcastle	24.44
9	Kitson	Reading	24.39
10	Ashton	West Ham	23.81
11	Berbatov	Tottenham	22.73
12	Keane	Tottenham	22.73
13	Downing	Middlesbrough	20.93
14	Bent	Wigan	20.59
15	Miller	Derby	20.00
16	Martins	Newcastle	20.00
17	Forssell	Birmingham	19.57
18	Jones	Sunderland	19.44
19	Tuncay Sanli	Middlesbrough	18.60
20	Carew	Aston Villa	18.31
21	Elano	Man City	17.78
22	Tevez	Man Utd	17.50
23	Harper	Reading	17.07
24	Defoe	Portsmouth	16.67
25	Chopra	Sunderland	16.67
26	Gerrard	Liverpool	16.42
27	McCarthy	Blackburn	16.00
28	Dempsey	Fulham	15.79
29	Viduka	Newcastle	15.56

PREMIERSHIP CHART-TOPPING POINT EARNERS

1 Carvalho - Chelsea

Counting Games Played at least 70mins.	19
Total Points Taken in Counting Games	51
Average Taken in Counting Games	2.68

	PLAYER	TEAM	GAMES	POINTS	AVE
1	R Carvalho	Chelsea	19	51	2.68
2	W Rooney	Man Utd	23	61	2.65
3	Luis Anderson	Man Utd	14	37	2.64
4	S Kalou	Chelsea	21	53	2.52
5	J Obi Mikel	Chelsea	18	45	2.50
6	T Rosicky	Arsenal	14	33	2.36
7	Nemanja Vidic	Man Utd	29	68	2.34
8	P Senderos	Arsenal	12	28	2.33
9	Martin Skrtel	Liverpool	13	30	2.31
10	Tim Cahill	Everton	17	39	2.29
11	M Flamini	Arsenal	30	67	2.23
12	F Torres	Liverpool	27	60	2.22
13	E van der Sar	Man Utd	28	62	2.21
14	Xabi Alonso	Liverpool	15	33	2.20
15	M Almunia	Arsenal	29	61	2.10
16	Petr Cech	Chelsea	25	50	2.00
17	D Hamann	Man City	22	42	1.91
18	Yakubu	Everton	23	42	1.83
19	Tim Howard	Everton	36	65	1.81
20	Sean Davis	Portsmouth	16	29	1.81

For the Top Point Earners we have applied the same rule of only allowing one player per position for each club, the same as the Team of the Season. The most one club can have in the top 20 is four players, one keeper, one defender, one midfielder and a forward.

PREMIERSHIP MOST MISSED PLAYERS

	PLAYER	TEAM	AVERAGE	CLUB	DIFF
1	B McBride	Fulham	1.58	0.95	0.63
2	Tim Cahill	Everton	2.29	1.71	0.58
3	Geremi Njitap	Newcastle	1.71	1.13	0.58
4	O Martins	Newcastle	1.65	1.13	0.52
5	Paul Stalteri	Fulham	1.42	0.95	0.47
6	D Hamann	Man City	1.91	1.45	0.46
7	Jimmy Bullard	Fulham	1.40	0.95	0.45
8	R Carvalho	Chelsea	2.68	2.24	0.44
9	Kasey Keller	Fulham	1.38	0.95	0.43
10	G McSheffrey	Birmingham	1.33	0.92	0.41
11	Daryl Murphy	Sunderland	1.44	1.03	0.41
12	M Etherington	West Ham	1.69	1.29	0.40
13	W Rooney	Man Utd	2.65	2.29	0.36
14	Luis Anderson	Man Utd	2.64	2.29	0.35
15	T Huddlestone	Tottenham	1.53	1.21	0.32
16	Sean Davis	Portsmouth	1.81	1.50	0.31
17	Martin Skrtel	Liverpool	2.31	2.00	0.31
18	B Gunnarsson	Reading	1.25	0.95	0.30
19	Emile Heskey	Wigan	1.35	1.05	0.30
20	Steve Harper	Newcastle	1.42	1.13	0.29

The Most Missed Players we have applied the same rule of only allowing one player per position for each club, the same as the Team of the Season. The most one club can have in the top 20 is four players, one keeper, one defender, one midfielder and a forward.

1 McBride - Fulham

Average points	1.58
Club average	0.95
Difference	0.63

MANAGERS - SUBSTITUTIONS USED

Club with the highest percentage of subs used - Man City		Sven-Goran Eriksson	
Matches where no subs were used	0	Matches where one sub was used	0
Matches where two subs were used	6	Matches where three subs were used	32
Total subs used in season	108	Percentage of possible subs used	94.74

Club	Manager	0 SUBS	1 SUB	2 SUBS	3 SUBS	TOTAL	%
Man City	Sven-Goran Eriksson	0	0	6	32	108	94.74
Sunderland	Roy Keane	0	0	6	32	108	94.74
West Ham	Alan Curbishley	0	1	4	33	108	94.74
Man Utd	Sir Alex Ferguson	0	1	8	29	104	91.23
Liverpool	Rafael Benitez	0	3	5	30	103	90.35
Derby	Paul Jewell	0	1	10	27	102	89.47
Chelsea	Avram Grant	0	1	11	26	101	88.60
Tottenham	Juande Ramos	0	3	8	27	100	87.72
Arsenal	Arsene Wenger	2	2	6	28	98	85.96
Birmingham	Alex McLeish	0	3	11	24	97	85.09
Fulham	Roy Hodgson	0	2	14	22	96	84.21
Reading	Steve Coppell	0	3	13	22	95	83.33
Newcastle	Kevin Keegan	0	4	11	23	95	83.33
Blackburn	Mark Hughes	0	4	13	21	93	81.58
Middlesbrough	Gareth Southgate	0	5	14	19	90	78.95
Bolton	Gary Megson	2	4	11	21	89	78.07
Everton	David Moyes	0	9	11	18	85	74.56
Wigan	Steve Bruce	0	9	13	16	83	72.81
Aston Villa	Martin O'Neill	0	8	16	14	82	71.93
Portsmouth	Harry Redknapp	0	10	12	16	82	71.93

MANAGERS - SUBSTITUTION TIMES

Club with the highest percentage of subs used - Sunderland		Roy Keane	
Substitutes made during first half	5	Substitutes made between 46 and 69 minutes (mainly tactical)	51
Substitutes made between 70-85 mins	44		
Substitutes made after 86 mins	8	Total subs used in season	108

Club	Manager	0-45 MINS	46-69	70-85	86+	TOTAL
Sunderland	Roy Keane	5	51	44	8	108
Derby	Paul Jewell	10	50	35	7	102
Man Utd	Sir Alex Ferguson	4	46	46	8	104
Tottenham	Juande Ramos	3	46	45	6	100
Man City	Sven-Goran Eriksson	6	42	46	14	108
West Ham	Alan Curbishley	6	41	50	11	108
Bolton	Gary Megson	4	39	39	7	89
Birmingham	Alex McLeish	3	38	45	11	97
Liverpool	Rafael Benitez	1	36	51	15	103
Fulham	Roy Hodgson	3	36	47	10	96
Chelsea	Avram Grant	6	36	41	18	101
Blackburn	Mark Hughes	3	34	33	23	93
Newcastle	Kevin Keegan	5	32	46	12	95
Middlesbrough	Gareth Southgate	5	32	38	15	90
Arsenal	Arsene Wenger	4	31	45	18	98
Portsmouth	Harry Redknapp	2	31	38	11	82
Aston Villa	Martin O'Neill	5	30	34	13	82
Wigan	Steve Bruce	7	29	32	15	83
Everton	David Moyes	5	23	38	19	85
Reading	Steve Coppell	4	21	58	12	95

LEAGUE PENALTY TAKERS

32RED
Villa's Gareth Barry steps up to take the pen

Penalties scored - Gareth Barry	5
Penalties saved	0
Penalties missed	1
League total	6
Percentage scored	83.3
% of all League penalties taken	5.4

1 - Barry - Aston Villa; McCarthy - Blackburn

Penalties Taken Total number of penalties taken in the league	6

PLAYER	CLUB	TOTAL	Sc	Sa	Mi	%Scored
Barry	Aston Villa	6	5	0	1	83.33
McCarthy	Blackburn	6	5	1	0	83.33
Ronaldo	Man Utd	5	4	0	1	80.00
Keane	Tottenham	5	3	1	1	60.00
Lampard	Chelsea	4	4	0	0	100.00
Adebayor	Arsenal	3	3	0	0	100.00
McSheffrey	Birmingham	3	3	0	0	100.00
Gerrard	Liverpool	3	3	0	0	100.00
Defoe	Portsmouth	3	2	1	0	66.67
Murphy	Fulham	3	2	1	0	66.67
van Persie	Arsenal	3	2	1	0	66.67
Noble	West Ham	2	2	0	0	100.00
Kuyt	Liverpool	2	2	0	0	100.00
Saha	Man Utd	2	2	0	0	100.00
Hunt	Reading	2	2	0	0	100.00
Downing	Middlesbrough	2	2	0	0	100.00
Ballack	Chelsea	2	2	0	0	100.00
McFadden	Birmingham	2	2	0	0	100.00
Elano	Man City	2	2	0	0	100.00
Owen	Newcastle	2	2	0	0	100.00
TOTAL PENALTIES		88	68	15	5	77.27

CLUB - LEAGUE SQUAD USAGE

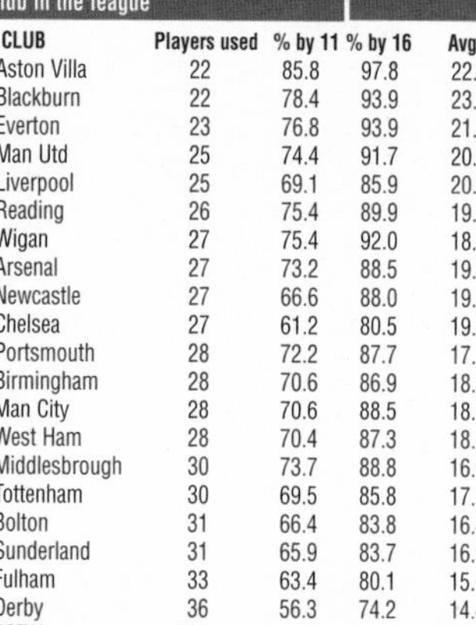

1 Aston Villa

Players used Total number of players used by the club in the league	22

CLUB	Players used	% by 11	% by 16	Avge
Aston Villa	22	85.8	97.8	22.7
Blackburn	22	78.4	93.9	23.2
Everton	23	76.8	93.9	21.9
Man Utd	25	74.4	91.7	20.9
Liverpool	25	69.1	85.9	20.8
Reading	26	75.4	89.9	19.7
Wigan	27	75.4	92.0	18.6
Arsenal	27	73.2	88.5	19.1
Newcastle	27	66.6	88.0	19.0
Chelsea	27	61.2	80.5	19.2
Portsmouth	28	72.2	87.7	17.9
Birmingham	28	70.6	86.9	18.4
Man City	28	70.6	88.5	18.8
West Ham	28	70.4	87.3	18.8
Middlesbrough	30	73.7	88.8	16.9
Tottenham	30	69.5	85.8	17.3
Bolton	31	66.4	83.8	16.4
Sunderland	31	65.9	83.7	16.9
Fulham	33	63.4	80.1	15.6
Derby	36	56.3	74.2	14.4
TOTAL	554			

Villa players team talk before the game

% of games played by leading 11 players	85.8
% of games played by leading 16 players	97.8
Average number of appearances per player	22.7

LEADING APPEARANCES

DEFENDERS

	PLAYER	GAMES	TIME
1	Stephen Kelly	38	3420
2	Joleon Lescott	38	3375
3	Martin Laursen	38	3368
4	Gael Clichy	38	3330
5	Paul Scharner	37	3313
6	Stephen Warnock	37	3284
7	Wilfred Bouma	38	3262
8	Phil Neville	37	3239
9	George McCartney	38	3226
10	Nicky Shorey	36	3220
11	Sylvain Distin	36	3194
12	Luke Young	35	3109
13	Liam Ridgewell	35	3105
14	Lucas Neill	34	3060
15	Rio Ferdinand	35	3047
16	Daniel Lewis Collins	36	3045
17	Richard Dunne	36	3041
18	Jamie Carragher	35	3040

MIDFIELDERS

	PLAYER	GAMES	TIME
1	Stewart Downing	38	3416
2	James Harper	38	3349
3	David Bentley	37	3320
4	Gareth Barry	37	3319
5	Stephen Hunt	37	3314
6	Simon Davies	37	3208
7	Fabrice Muamba	37	3199
8	Nigel Reo-Coker	36	3103
9	Nicky Butt	35	2998
10	Martin Petrov	34	2973
11	Kevin Kilbane	35	2962
12	Morten Gamst Pedersen	37	2872
13	Lee Carsley	34	2866
14	Niko Kranjčar	34	2857
15	Francesc Fabregas	32	2856
16	Steven Gerrard	34	2839
17	Steed Malbranque	37	2839
18	Hayden Mullins	34	2805

FORWARDS

	PLAYER	GAMES	TIME		PLAYER	GAMES	TIME
1	Ashley Young	37	3285	10	Clint Dempsey	36	2674
2	Gabriel Agbonlahor	37	3278	11	Kevin Davies	32	2642
3	Roque Santa Cruz	37	3189	12	El Hadji Diouf	34	2640
4	Kevin Doyle	36	3010	13	Kenny Miller	30	2567
5	Dimitar Berbatov	36	2987	14	John Alieu Carew	32	2552
6	Emmanuel Adebayor	36	2929	15	Fernando Torres	33	2549
7	Kenwyne Jones	33	2819	16	David Kitson	34	2524
8	Robbie Keane	36	2718	17	Alan Smith	33	2396
9	Carlos Tevez	34	2677	18	Marcus Bent	31	2331

FIRST SCORERS

SCORED FIRST

CLUB	MATCHES	WON	DRAWN	LOST
Man Utd	29	25	3	1
Chelsea	26	21	5	0
Arsenal	24	19	3	2
Everton	24	19	3	2
Liverpool	24	18	6	0
Tottenham	23	11	8	4
Aston Villa	18	13	2	3
Man City	17	13	3	1
West Ham	17	9	7	1
Middlesbrough	17	9	4	4
Bolton	15	9	2	4
Birmingham	15	7	6	2
Fulham	15	5	5	5
Portsmouth	14	14	0	0
Wigan	14	10	2	2
Blackburn	14	9	4	1
Newcastle	14	9	2	3
Reading	13	10	1	2
Sunderland	12	9	3	0
Derby	9	1	5	3

CONCEDED FIRST

CLUB	MATCHES	WON	DRAWN	LOST
Man Utd	8	2	2	4
Chelsea	9	4	2	3
Liverpool	9	3	2	4
Everton	11	0	2	9
Arsenal	12	5	6	1
Tottenham	14	0	4	10
Man City	17	2	3	12
Portsmouth	18	2	3	13
Aston Villa	19	3	9	7
Bolton	19	0	4	15
Blackburn	20	6	5	9
West Ham	20	4	2	14
Fulham	20	3	4	13
Middlesbrough	20	1	7	12
Newcastle	21	2	5	14
Wigan	21	0	5	16
Birmingham	22	1	4	17
Reading	22	0	2	20
Sunderland	25	2	2	21
Derby	27	0	1	26

CLUB DISCIPLINARY RECORDS

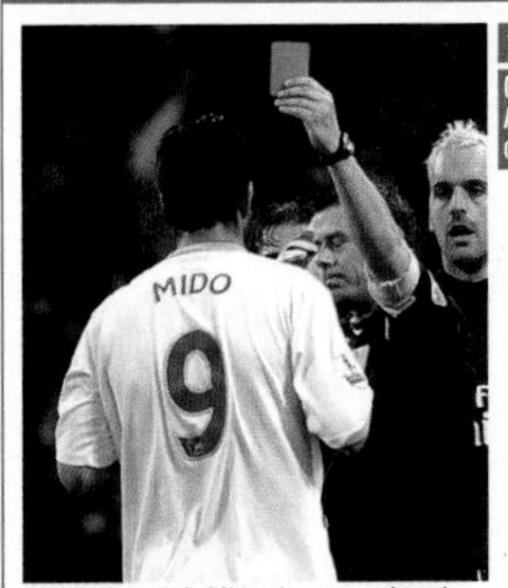
MIDO
9
Middlesbrough's Mido shown a red card

League Yellow	86
League Red	2
League Total	88
All Competitions Yellow	102
All Competitions Red	2
TOTAL	104

1 Middlesbrough

Cards Average in League
Average number of minutes between a card being shown of either colour: **38**

	CLUB	LEAGUE Y	LEAGUE R	TOTAL Y	TOTAL R	AVE
1	Middlesbrough	86	2	102	2	38
2	Blackburn	74	6	87	6	42
3	Bolton	76	0	107	0	45
4	Chelsea	65	5	97	7	48
5	Birmingham	68	3	72	3	48
6	Sunderland	67	4	71	5	48
7	West Ham	66	2	73	2	50
8	Reading	61	5	72	6	51
9	Fulham	60	6	67	7	51
10	Derby	63	1	71	2	53
11	Newcastle	63	1	66	2	53
12	Wigan	60	4	65	4	53
13	Portsmouth	58	3	71	3	56
14	Arsenal	57	3	89	5	57
15	Aston Villa	56	4	56	4	57
16	Man City	51	4	60	4	62
17	Tottenham	52	1	89	4	64
18	Man Utd	51	2	75	3	64
19	Liverpool	46	1	78	3	72
20	Everton	40	3	69	3	79

PLAYER DISCIPLINARY RECORD

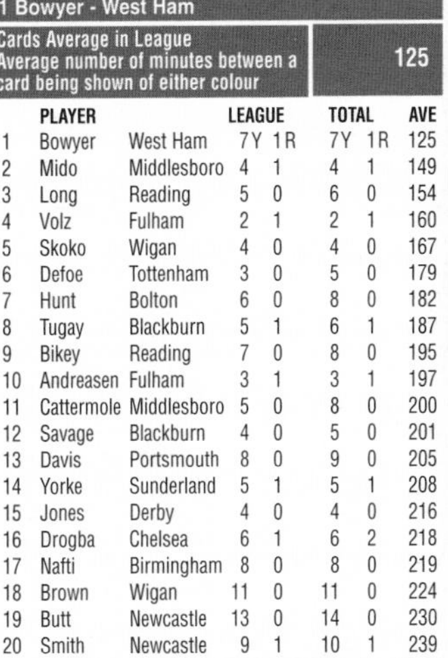

1 Bowyer - West Ham

Cards Average in League
Average number of minutes between a card being shown of either colour: **125**

	PLAYER		LEAGUE Y	LEAGUE R	TOTAL Y	TOTAL R	AVE
1	Bowyer	West Ham	7	1	7	1	125
2	Mido	Middlesboro	4	1	4	1	149
3	Long	Reading	5	0	6	0	154
4	Volz	Fulham	2	1	2	1	160
5	Skoko	Wigan	4	0	4	0	167
6	Defoe	Tottenham	3	0	5	0	179
7	Hunt	Bolton	6	0	8	0	182
8	Tugay	Blackburn	5	1	6	1	187
9	Bikey	Reading	7	0	8	0	195
10	Andreasen	Fulham	3	1	3	1	197
11	Cattermole	Middlesboro	5	0	8	0	200
12	Savage	Blackburn	4	0	5	0	201
13	Davis	Portsmouth	8	0	9	0	205
14	Yorke	Sunderland	5	1	5	1	208
15	Jones	Derby	4	0	4	0	216
16	Drogba	Chelsea	6	1	6	2	218
17	Nafti	Birmingham	8	0	8	0	219
18	Brown	Wigan	11	0	11	0	224
19	Butt	Newcastle	13	0	14	0	230
20	Smith	Newcastle	9	1	10	1	239

air asia
Lee Bowyer receives a warning from the ref

League Yellow	7
League Red	1
League Total	8
All Competitions Yellow	7
All Competitions Red	1
TOTAL	8

REFEREES - PENALTIES

1 M. A. Riley

Penalties Average
Average number of minutes between penalties awarded: **180**

	REF	Home	Away	Total	Avge
1	M. A. Riley	5	1	6	180.00
2	R. Styles	3	2	5	180.00
3	M. L. Dean	4	0	4	247.50
4	M. R. Halsey	2	2	4	270.00
5	S. Tanner	3	0	3	180.00
6	P. Dowd	1	2	3	180.00
7	M. Clattenburg	1	2	3	330.00
8	M. Atkinson	2	0	2	495.00
9	A. Marriner	2	0	2	315.00
10	C. J. Foy	2	0	2	450.00
11	H. M. Webb	2	0	2	450.00
12	P. Walton	1	0	1	720.00
13	S. G. Bennett	1	0	1	1,260.00

Mike Riley awarded 6 penalties this season

Games	12
Penalties awarded to home side	5
Penalties awarded to away side	1
Total	6

REFEREES - CARDS

REFEREE
FIFA
Mike Dean dishes out another card

Games	11
Yellow	56
Yellow/Red	3
Straight reds	1

1 Phil Dowd

Cards Average
Average number of cards per match of either colour: **5.45**

	REF	Games	Y	Y/R	R	AVE
1	M. L. Dean	11	56	3	1	5.45
2	Howard Webb	1	5	0	0	5
3	M. A. Riley	12	52	0	1	4.42
4	R. Styles	10	40	1	2	4.3
5	Steve Tanner	1	4	0	0	4
6	K. Stroud	2	8	0	0	4
7	S. G. Bennett	14	50	3	1	3.86
8	H. M. Webb	10	38	0	0	3.8
9	M. Clattenburg	11	36	0	3	3.55
10	P. Walton	8	27	0	1	3.5
11	A. G. Wiley	13	43	1	0	3.38
12	C. J. Foy	10	31	1	0	3.2
13	M. R. Halsey	12	35	0	2	3.08
14	M. Atkinson	11	32	1	0	3
15	A. Marriner	7	19	1	1	3
16	L. Mason	3	8	0	0	2.67
17	S. Tanner	7	19	0	0	2.5
18	P. Dowd	6	10	0	3	2.17
	TOTALS	156	529	11	15	3.56

CLUB - LEAGUE PENALTIES AWARDED

AIG
United's Ronaldo appeals for a penalty

Awarded at home	4
Awarded away	4
Number scored	6
Number saved	2
Number missed	0
% of League penalties awarded	9.1
Number of takers	3

1 Man Utd

Penalties Awarded
Total number of penalties awarded to the club in the league: **8**

CLUB	H	A	Total	Sc	Sa	M	%	No
Man Utd	4	4	8	6	2	0	9.1	3
Aston Villa	4	3	7	6	1	0	8.0	2
Blackburn	5	2	7	5	2	0	8.0	2
Chelsea	4	3	7	7	0	0	8.0	3
Portsmouth	6	1	7	4	2	1	8.0	6
Tottenham	4	3	7	4	2	1	8.0	3
Arsenal	5	1	6	5	1	0	6.8	2
Birmingham	4	2	6	6	0	0	6.8	3
Liverpool	3	2	5	5	0	0	5.7	2
Wigan	3	2	5	4	1	0	5.7	5
Newcastle	2	2	4	4	0	0	4.5	3
Reading	2	2	4	2	1	1	4.5	3
Fulham	2	1	3	2	1	0	3.4	1
Bolton	1	1	2	0	1	1	2.3	2
Man City	0	2	2	2	0	0	2.3	1
Middlesbrough	2	0	2	2	0	0	2.3	1
Sunderland	0	2	2	1	1	0	2.3	2
West Ham	1	1	2	2	0	0	2.3	1
Derby	1	0	1	0	1	0	1.1	1
Everton	1	0	1	1	0	0	1.1	1
TOTALS	54	34	88	68	16	4		47

CLUB - LEAGUE PENALTIES CONCEDED

1 Sunderland

Penalties Conceded
Total number of penalties conceded by the club in the league: **9**

CLUB	H	A	Total	Sc	Sa	M	%
Sunderland	2	7	9	9	0	0	10.2
Birmingham	3	5	8	8	0	0	9.1
Reading	4	3	7	3	3	1	8.0
Blackburn	3	3	6	4	2	0	6.8
West Ham	4	2	6	2	3	1	6.8
Bolton	1	4	5	5	0	0	5.7
Fulham	2	3	5	5	0	0	5.7
Liverpool	1	4	5	4	1	0	5.7
Arsenal	1	3	4	3	0	1	4.5
Aston Villa	2	2	4	2	2	0	4.5
Derby	1	3	4	3	0	0	4.5
Everton	3	1	4	4	0	0	4.5
Man City	1	3	4	2	2	0	4.5
Portsmouth	2	2	4	2	2	0	4.5
Wigan	2	2	4	2	1	1	4.5
Chelsea	1	2	3	3	0	0	3.4
Middlesbrough	0	2	2	2	0	0	2.3
Newcastle	0	2	2	2	0	0	2.3
Man Utd	0	1	1	1	0	0	1.1
Tottenham	1	0	1	1	0	0	1.1
TOTAL	34	54	88	67	16	4	

14
Higginbotham handles to concede a penalty

Conceded at home	2
Conceded away	7
League Total	9
Number scored	9
Number missed	0
% of League penalties conceded	10.2

PREMIERSHIP - AUGUST

LEAGUE PERFORMANCE FOR THE MONTH

		HOME					AWAY					TOTAL			
	P	W	D	L	F	A	W	D	L	F	A	F	A	DIF	PTS
Chelsea	4	2	0	0	4	2	1	1	0	3	2	7	4	3	10
Man City	4	2	0	0	2	0	1	0	1	2	1	4	1	3	9
Wigan	4	2	0	0	4	0	0	1	1	2	3	6	3	3	7
Liverpool	3	0	1	0	1	1	2	0	0	4	1	5	2	3	7
Everton	4	1	1	0	3	2	1	0	1	3	2	6	4	2	7
Arsenal	3	2	0	0	3	1	0	1	0	1	1	4	2	2	7
Newcastle	3	0	1	0	0	0	1	1	0	5	3	5	3	2	5
Portsmouth	4	1	1	0	4	2	0	1	1	2	3	6	5	1	5
Blackburn	3	0	1	0	1	1	1	1	0	3	2	4	3	1	5
Man Utd	4	1	1	0	1	0	0	1	1	1	2	2	2	0	5
Aston Villa	3	1	0	1	3	3	0	1	0	0	0	3	3	0	4
Birmingham	4	0	1	1	2	3	1	0	1	4	4	6	7	-1	4
Middlesbrough	4	0	1	1	3	4	1	0	1	2	2	5	6	-1	4
West Ham	3	0	1	1	1	3	1	0	0	1	0	2	3	-1	4
Reading	4	1	0	1	2	2	0	1	1	0	3	2	5	-3	4
Sunderland	4	1	0	1	1	2	0	1	1	2	5	3	7	-4	4
Tottenham	4	1	0	1	5	3	0	0	2	0	2	5	5	0	3
Bolton	4	1	0	1	4	3	0	0	2	2	5	6	8	-2	3
Fulham	4	1	0	1	3	3	0	0	2	2	4	5	7	-2	3
Derby	4	0	1	1	3	4	0	0	2	0	5	3	9	-6	1

GOAL OF THE MONTH

MATCH OF THE DAY

Charles N'Zogbia
Middlesboro v *Newcastle*

Charles N'Zogbia cuts inside from the left leaving several Boro defenders for dead and just as it looks as though all he can do is cross, the Frenchman unleashes a curling drive that beats Schwarzer and smashes into the top corner of the net.

THE MONTH'S TOP GOALSCORERS

	GOALS IN THE MONTH		THE SEASON TO END OF MONTH		
Bolton	Anelka	3	Anelka	3	50%
Chelsea	Lampard	3	Lampard	3	42.90%
Wigan	Sibierski	3	Sibierski	3	50%
Birmingham	Jerome	2	Jerome	2	33.30%
Arsenal	van Persie	2	van Persie	2	50%
Blackburn	Santa Cruz	2	Santa Cruz	2	50%
Derby	Oakley	2	Oakley	2	66.70%
Everton	Osman	2	Osman	2	33.30%
Fulham	Healy	2	Healy	2	40%
Man City	Geovanni	2	Geovanni	2	50%
Middlesboro	Mido	2	Mido	2	40%
Newcastle	Martins, N'Zogbia	2	Martins, N'Zogbia	2	40%
Portsmouth	Mwaruwari, Utaka	2	Mwaruwari, Utaka	2	33.30%
Sunderland	Chopra	2	Chopra	2	66.70%
Tottenham	Malbranque	2	Malbranque	2	40%
Aston Villa	Barry, Maloney, Young	1	Barry, Maloney, Young	1	33.30%
Liverpool	Gerrard, Sissoko, Torres, Voronin	1	Gerrard, Sissiko, Torres, Voronin	1	20%
Man Utd	Nani, Scholes	1	Nani, Scholes	1	50%
Reading	Bikey, Hunt	1	Bikey, Hunt	1	50%
West Ham	Bowyer, Noble	1	Bowyer, Noble	1	50%

BARCLAYS PLAYER OF THE MONTH

Micah Richards - Manchester City

Thomas Cook.com

BARCLAYS MANAGER OF THE MONTH

Sven-Goran Eriksson - Manchester City

PREMIERSHIP - SEPTEMBER

LEAGUE PERFORMANCE FOR THE MONTH

		HOME					AWAY					TOTAL			
	P	W	D	L	F	A	W	D	L	F	A	F	A	DIF	PTS
Arsenal	4	2	0	0	8	1	2	0	0	4	1	12	2	10	12
Man Utd	4	2	0	0	3	0	2	0	0	2	0	5	0	5	12
Liverpool	4	1	1	0	6	0	1	1	0	1	0	7	0	7	8
Portsmouth	4	1	1	0	7	4	1	0	1	2	3	9	7	2	7
Man City	4	2	0	0	4	1	0	1	1	3	4	7	5	2	7
Blackburn	4	1	0	1	1	1	1	1	0	2	1	3	2	1	7
West Ham	4	1	0	1	3	1	1	0	1	4	3	7	4	3	6
Aston Villa	3	2	0	0	4	0	0	0	1	0	1	4	1	3	6
Newcastle	4	2	0	0	4	1	0	0	2	1	4	5	5	0	6
Everton	4	1	0	1	2	1	1	0	1	2	3	4	4	0	6
Fulham	4	0	2	0	6	6	0	2	0	1	1	7	7	0	4
Sunderland	4	1	0	1	3	3	0	1	1	2	3	5	6	-1	4
Birmingham	4	1	0	1	1	1	0	1	1	0	2	1	3	-2	4
Middlesbrough	4	1	1	0	4	2	0	0	2	0	5	4	7	-3	4
Derby	4	1	1	0	2	1	0	0	2	0	11	2	12	-10	4
Reading	4	1	0	1	2	4	0	0	2	5	9	7	13	-6	3
Tottenham	3	0	0	1	1	3	0	2	0	4	4	5	7	-2	2
Bolton	4	0	1	1	2	3	0	1	1	1	2	3	5	-2	2
Chelsea	4	0	2	0	0	0	0	0	2	0	4	0	4	-4	2
Wigan	4	0	1	1	1	2	0	0	2	1	3	2	5	-3	1

GOAL OF THE MONTH

MATCH OF THE DAY

Emmanuel Adebayor (2nd goal)
Tottenham v *Arsenal*

Deep into stoppage time, the tireless Adebayor receives a high ball from a long pass but takes the ball in his stride, controls with his chest and rockets a sensational volley from the edge of the box into the top corner leaving the Spurs keeper with no chance.

THE MONTH'S TOP GOALSCORERS

	GOALS IN THE MONTH		THE SEASON TO END OF MONTH		
Arsenal	Adebayor	6	Adebayor	6	37.50%
Man City	Petrov	3	Petrov	3	27.30%
Portsmouth	Mwaruwari	3	Mwaruwari	5	33.30%
Reading	Kitson	3	Kitson	3	33.30%
Aston Villa	Agbonlahor	2	Agbonlahor	2	28.60%
Bolton	Anelka	2	Anelka	5	55.60%
Derby	Miller	2	Miller, Oakley	2	40%
Everton	Lescott	2	Lescott	3	30%
Fulham	Dempsey	2	Dempsey	3	25%
Liverpool	Alonso, Torres	2	Torres	3	25%
Man Utd	Saha	2	Saha	2	28.60%
Middlesboro	Downing	2	Downing	3	33.30%
Newcastle	Viduka	2	Martins, N'Zogbia, Viduka	3	30%
Sunderland	Leadbitter	2	Chopra, Leadbitter	2	25%
Tottenham	Bale	2	Bale, Malbranque	2	20%
West Ham	Ashton, Etherington	2	Ashton, Bowyer, Etherington	2	22.20%
Birmingham	Kapo	1	Jerome, Kapo	2	28.60%
Blackburn	Bentley, McCarthy, Santa Cruz	1	Santa Cruz	3	42.90%
Wigan	Bent, Koumas	1	Sibierski	3	37.50%
Chelsea		0	Drogba, Essien, Malouda, Pizarro	1	14.30%

BARCLAYS PLAYER OF THE MONTH

Cesc Fabregas - Arsenal

Fly Emirates

BARCLAYS MANAGER OF THE MONTH

Arsene Wenger - Arsenal

PREMIERSHIP – OCTOBER

LEAGUE PERFORMANCE FOR THE MONTH

	HOME						AWAY					TOTAL			
	P	W	D	L	F	A	W	D	L	F	A	F	A	DIF	PTS
Man Utd	3	2	0	0	8	1	1	0	0	4	1	12	2	10	9
Chelsea	3	1	0	0	6	0	2	0	0	3	0	9	0	9	9
Blackburn	3	2	0	0	6	3	1	0	0	2	1	8	4	4	9
Portsmouth	3	0	1	0	0	0	2	0	0	4	0	4	0	4	7
Arsenal	3	2	0	0	5	2	0	1	0	1	1	6	3	3	7
Newcastle	3	2	0	0	6	3	0	0	1	1	2	7	5	2	6
Reading	3	2	0	0	3	1	0	0	1	2	4	5	5	0	6
Man City	3	2	0	0	4	1	0	0	1	0	6	4	7	-3	6
Liverpool	3	0	2	0	3	3	1	0	0	2	1	5	4	1	5
Aston Villa	4	1	0	1	2	4	0	2	0	5	5	7	9	-2	5
West Ham	3	1	0	0	3	1	0	1	1	0	1	3	2	1	4
Everton	3	0	0	1	1	2	1	0	1	4	3	5	5	0	3
Birmingham	3	1	0	0	3	2	0	0	2	1	3	4	5	-1	3
Fulham	3	0	1	1	0	2	0	1	0	1	1	1	3	-2	2
Tottenham	4	0	1	1	5	6	0	1	1	3	5	8	11	-3	2
Sunderland	3	0	1	0	1	1	0	0	2	3	6	4	7	-3	1
Bolton	3	0	1	1	1	2	0	0	1	0	2	1	4	-3	1
Derby	3	0	0	1	0	2	0	1	1	0	1	0	3	-3	1
Middlesbrough	3	0	0	1	0	2	0	0	2	2	7	2	9	-7	0
Wigan	3	0	0	1	0	2	0	0	2	2	7	2	9	-7	0

GOAL OF THE MONTH

MATCH OF THE DAY

Carlos Tevez (1st goal)
Man Utd v Middlesbrough

The ball is played into Tevez on the edge of the Boro box, who directs it to Rooney who has his back to goal, the England striker returns the favour and a delightful back-heel frees the Argentinian on the penalty spot for a simple finish. Great teamwork!

THE MONTH'S TOP GOALSCORERS

	GOALS IN THE MONTH		THE SEASON TO END OF MONTH		
Tottenham	Keane	5	Keane	6	33%
Blackburn	McCarthy	4	McCarthy	5	33.30%
Man Utd	Rooney	4	Rooney, Tevez	4	21%
Chelsea	Drogba	3	Drogba	4	25%
Man City	Elano	3	Elano	4	27%
Reading	Doyle	3	Kitson	4	28.60%
Sunderland	Jones	3	Jones	4	33%
Arsenal	van Persie	2	Adebayor	6	27%
Aston Villa	Agbonlahor, Gardner, Laursen	2	Agbonlahor	4	28.60%
Birmingham	Kapo	2	Kapo	4	36%
Liverpool	Kuyt	2	Torres	4	24%
Portsmouth	Mwaruwari	2	Mwaruwari	7	37%
Wigan	Bent	2	Bent, Sibierski	3	30%
Bolton	Anelka	1	Anelka	6	60%
Everton	Arteta, Johnson, Yakubu	1	Lescott	3	20.00%
Fulham	Davies	1	Dempsey	3	23%
Middlesboro	Aliadiere, Hutchinson	1	Downing	3	27.30%
Newcastle	Butt, Cacapa, Emre, Martins, Milner, Owen	1	Martins	4	23.50%
West Ham	Bellamy, Cole	1	Ashton, Bellamy, Bowyer, Etherington	2	17%
Derby		0	Miller. Oakley	2	40.00%

BARCLAYS PLAYER OF THE MONTH

Wayne Rooney - Manchester United

AIG

BARCLAYS MANAGER OF THE MONTH

Mark Hughes - Blackburn Rovers

PREMIERSHIP – NOVEMBER

LEAGUE PERFORMANCE FOR THE MONTH

	HOME						AWAY					TOTAL			
	P	W	D	L	F	A	W	D	L	F	A	F	A	DIF	PTS
Aston Villa	4	1	0	0	2	0	3	0	0	9	1	11	1	10	12
Everton	3	2	0	0	10	2	0	1	0	1	1	11	3	8	7
Portsmouth	3	0	1	0	0	0	2	0	0	6	1	6	1	5	7
Liverpool	3	1	0	0	2	0	1	1	0	3	0	5	0	5	7
Arsenal	3	1	1	0	4	2	1	0	0	3	1	7	3	4	7
Chelsea	3	0	1	0	1	1	2	0	0	4	0	5	1	4	7
Man City	3	2	0	0	3	1	0	1	0	0	0	3	1	2	7
West Ham	3	0	2	0	2	2	1	0	0	5	0	7	2	5	5
Tottenham	3	1	0	0	4	0	0	2	0	2	2	6	2	4	5
Bolton	3	1	1	0	1	0	0	1	0	1	1	2	1	1	5
Man Utd	3	1	0	0	2	0	0	1	1	2	3	4	3	1	4
Fulham	3	1	1	0	5	3	0	0	1	0	2	5	5	0	4
Middlesbrough	3	0	1	1	1	4	0	1	0	0	0	1	4	-3	2
Blackburn	4	0	1	1	0	4	0	1	1	2	4	2	8	-6	2
Newcastle	3	0	0	2	1	7	0	1	0	1	1	2	8	-6	1
Sunderland	3	0	1	0	1	1	0	0	2	1	8	2	9	-7	1
Reading	3	0	0	1	1	3	0	0	2	2	5	3	8	-5	0
Birmingham	3	0	0	2	1	4	0	0	1	1	3	2	7	-5	0
Wigan	3	0	0	1	0	2	0	0	2	0	6	0	8	-8	0
Derby	3	0	0	2	0	7	0	0	1	0	2	0	9	-9	0

GOAL OF THE MONTH

MATCH OF THE DAY

Luke Young
Middlesbrough v Tottenham

O'Neil's ball is cleared well by the Tottenham defence but it drops to Luke Young 35-yards out and he ambitiously unleashes a shot at goal but much to everyone's surprise it is a thunderbolt that flies into the top corner leaving Paul Robinson with no chance.

THE MONTH'S TOP GOALSCORERS

	GOALS IN THE MONTH		THE SEASON TO END OF MONTH		
Everton	Cahill, Yakubu	3	Yakubu	5	19.20%
Man Utd	Ronaldo	3	Ronaldo	6	26.10%
Arsenal	Gallas	2	Adebayor	7	24.10%
Aston Villa	Agbonlahor, Carew, Young	2	Agbonlahor	6	24%
Liverpool	Gerrard	2	Torres	5	22.70%
Man City	Ireland	2	Elano, Petrov	4	22.20%
Portsmouth	Kranjcar	2	Mwaruwari	8	32%
Tottenham	Bent, D, Jenas	2	Keane	6	25%
West Ham	Bowyer	2	Bowyer	4	21.10%
Birmingham	Forssell, Kapo	1	Kapo	5	38.50%
Blackburn	Emerton, Warnock	1	McCarthy	5	29.40%
Bolton	Anelka, Nolan	1	Anelka	7	58.30%
Chelsea	Belletti, Drogba, Kalou, Lampard, W-Phillips	1	Drogba	5	23.80%
Fulham	Davies, Dempsey, Healy, Kamara, Murphy	1	Dempsey	4	22.20%
Middlesboro	Young	1	Downing	3	25.00%
Newcastle	Milner	1	Martins	4	21.10%
Reading	Doyle, Harper, Shorey	1	Doyle, Kitson	4	24%
Sunderland	Higginbotham, Yorke	1	Jones	4	29%
Derby		0	Miller, Oakley	2	40%
Wigan		0	Bent, Sibierski	3	30.00%

BARCLAYS PLAYER OF THE MONTH

Gabriel Agbonlahor - Aston Villa

32RED
.com

BARCLAYS MANAGER OF THE MONTH

Martin O'Neill - Aston Villa

31
32RED
.com

PREMIERSHIP – DECEMBER

LEAGUE PERFORMANCE FOR THE MONTH

		HOME					AWAY					TOTAL			
	P	W	D	L	F	A	W	D	L	F	A	F	A	DIF	PTS
Man Utd	6	3	0	0	8	2	2	0	1	6	2	14	4	10	15
Arsenal	7	2	0	0	3	1	2	2	1	8	5	11	6	5	14
Chelsea	6	3	1	0	9	5	1	0	1	1	1	10	6	4	13
Tottenham	6	3	0	1	15	9	1	0	1	2	2	17	11	6	12
Liverpool	6	2	0	1	8	2	1	1	1	3	4	11	6	5	10
Everton	6	2	0	1	6	4	1	1	1	3	2	9	6	3	10
West Ham	6	1	1	1	3	4	2	0	1	3	2	6	6	0	10
Middlesbrough	6	1	0	1	3	3	2	1	1	3	4	6	7	-1	10
Reading	6	2	1	0	6	3	0	2	1	6	8	12	11	1	9
Birmingham	6	1	2	0	5	2	1	0	2	4	7	9	9	0	8
Wigan	6	2	1	1	8	6	0	1	1	2	5	10	11	-1	8
Newcastle	7	1	2	0	5	4	1	0	3	3	6	8	10	-2	8
Man City	6	1	2	0	6	4	0	2	1	3	4	9	8	1	7
Blackburn	6	1	0	2	3	3	1	1	1	7	8	10	11	-1	7
Sunderland	6	2	1	1	5	6	0	0	2	1	4	6	10	-4	7
Aston Villa	6	0	1	2	3	6	1	2	0	7	6	10	12	-2	6
Bolton	6	2	0	0	7	1	0	0	4	3	13	10	14	-4	6
Portsmouth	6	0	2	2	0	2	1	0	1	4	5	4	7	-3	5
Fulham	6	0	1	1	1	2	0	1	3	2	11	3	13	-10	2
Derby	6	0	0	3	2	5	0	1	2	3	7	5	12	-7	1

MATCH OF THE DAY

GOAL OF THE MONTH

Tuncay Sanli
Derby v *Middlesbrough*

GARMIN
SAT-NAV
GARMIN
SAT-NAV

Stewart Downing's fantastic first-time cross from the left is inch-perfect and finds the in-form Tuncay Sanli who gets on the end of it and makes no mistake as he brilliantly sweeps it home on the volley that gives Bywater no chance for Tuncay's third goal in as many games.

THE MONTH'S TOP GOALSCORERS

	GOALS IN THE MONTH		THE SEASON TO END OF MONTH		
Everton	Yakubu	3	Yakubu	8	28%
Man Utd	Ronaldo	3	Ronaldo	9	31%
Arsenal	Adebayor	2	Adebayor	9	27.30%
Birmingham	Jerome	2	Jerome, Kapo	5	29.40%
Blackburn	Bentley	2	McCarthy	5	25%
Liverpool	Gerrard	2	Gerrard, Torres	6	22%
Middlesboro	Tuncay Sanli	2	Downing	4	26.70%
Newcastle	Martins	2	Martins	6	26.10%
Portsmouth	Muntari	2	Mwaruwari	8	29%
Tottenham	Keane	2	Keane	8	29%
Aston Villa	Barry, Gardner	1	Agbonlahor	6	22.20%
Bolton	Anelka, Davies, Nolan	1	Anelka	8	50%
Chelsea	Cole, J, Lampard, Shevchenko	1	Drogba, Lampard	5	21%
Derby	Howard	1	Miller, Oakley	2	33%
Man City	Bianchi, Geovanni	1	Petrov	4	20%
Reading	Doyle, Harper, Hunt, Kitson	1	Doyle, Kitson	5	24%
Sunderland	Stokes	1	Jones	4	26.70%
West Ham	Ashton	1	Ashton, Etherington	3	15.00%
Wigan	Landzaat, Scharner	1	Bent	3	25%
Fulham		0	Dempsey	4	22.20%

BARCLAYS PLAYER OF THE MONTH

Roque Santa Cruz - Blackburn Rovers

bet
24

BARCLAYS MANAGER OF THE MONTH

Arsene Wenger - Arsenal

PREMIERSHIP – JANUARY

LEAGUE PERFORMANCE FOR THE MONTH

		HOME					AWAY					TOTAL			
	P	W	D	L	F	A	W	D	L	F	A	F	A	DIF	PTS
Man Utd	4	3	0	0	9	0	1	0	0	2	0	11	0	11	12
Chelsea	4	2	0	0	3	0	2	0	0	3	1	6	1	5	12
Arsenal	4	2	1	0	6	1	1	0	0	3	0	9	1	8	10
Everton	4	1	1	0	1	0	2	0	0	4	1	5	1	4	10
Aston Villa	4	2	1	0	6	3	0	1	0	2	2	8	5	3	8
Blackburn	4	1	1	0	2	1	1	1	0	3	2	5	3	2	8
West Ham	4	2	0	0	3	1	0	1	1	1	3	4	4	0	7
Sunderland	4	2	0	0	4	0	0	0	2	0	3	4	3	1	6
Portsmouth	4	1	0	0	3	1	1	0	2	2	4	5	5	0	6
Man City	4	0	1	0	1	1	1	1	1	3	2	4	3	1	5
Bolton	4	1	1	1	2	2	0	1	0	0	0	2	2	0	5
Middlesbrough	4	1	1	1	2	3	0	1	0	1	1	3	4	-1	5
Tottenham	4	1	0	0	2	0	0	1	2	1	4	3	4	-1	4
Wigan	4	0	0	1	1	2	1	1	1	2	2	3	4	-1	4
Liverpool	4	0	2	0	3	3	0	1	1	1	2	4	5	-1	3
Derby	4	0	1	1	1	2	0	0	2	1	4	2	6	-4	1
Birmingham	4	0	0	1	0	1	0	1	2	1	4	1	5	-4	1
Fulham	4	0	0	2	1	5	0	1	1	1	2	2	7	-5	1
Newcastle	4	0	1	1	0	2	0	0	2	0	9	0	11	-11	1
Reading	4	0	0	2	0	4	0	0	2	1	4	1	8	-7	0

MATCH OF THE DAY

GOAL OF THE MONTH

Cristiano Ronaldo (2nd Goal)
Man Utd v Portsmouth

The Portuguese wizard conjures up yet another moment of magic when he lines up a free-kick from 30 yards out. Ronaldo lashes the ball with incredible pace and power into the very top corner making it look so easy and after the winger describes it as his best goal ever.

THE MONTH'S TOP GOALSCORERS

	GOALS IN THE MONTH		THE SEASON TO END OF MONTH		
Man Utd	Ronaldo	6	Ronaldo	19	40%
Arsenal	Adebayor	5	Adebayor	16	33%
Portsmouth	Mwaruwari	3	Mwaruwari	12	35%
Aston Villa	Carew, Laursen	2	Agbonlahor	7	16%
Chelsea	Ballack	2	Drogba, Kalou	5	14%
Everton	Johnson, Lescott	2	Yakubu	9	22.50%
Liverpool	Torres	2	Torres	11	30%
Sunderland	Richardson	2	Jones	5	20.80%
Birmingham	O'Connor	1	Jerome, Kapo	5	21.70%
Blackburn	Derbyshire, McCarthy, Roberts, Samba, S Cruz	1	Santa Cruz	11	34.40%
Bolton	Giannakopoulos, Nolan	1	Anelka	10	42%
Derby	Nyatanga	1	Miller, Oakley	3	25.00%
Fulham	Davies, Murphy	1	Dempsey	6	26%
Man City	Elano, Fernandes, Sturridge, Vassell	1	Elano	5	16.10%
Middlesboro	Aliadiere, Boateng, Wheater	1	Downing, Tuncay	4	19%
Reading	Harper	1	Kitson	8	27%
Tottenham	Defoe, Keane, Lennon	1	Keane	11	25.00%
West Ham	Ashton, Cole, Ferdinand, Noble	1	Ashton	5	17%
Wigan	Bramble, Sibierski	1	Bent	7	30.40%
Newcastle	Ameobi	0	Martins	6	22%

BARCLAYS PLAYER OF THE MONTH

Cristiano Ronaldo - Manchester United

AIG

BARCLAYS MANAGER OF THE MONTH

Sir Alex Ferguson - Manchester United

PREMIERSHIP – FEBRUARY

LEAGUE PERFORMANCE FOR THE MONTH

	HOME						AWAY					TOTAL			
	P	W	D	L	F	A	W	D	L	F	A	F	A	DIF	PTS
Arsenal	3	1	0	0	2	0	1	1	0	5	3	7	3	4	7
Liverpool	3	2	0	0	6	2	0	1	0	0	0	6	2	4	7
Everton	3	1	0	0	1	0	1	1	0	2	0	3	0	3	7
Portsmouth	3	1	1	0	2	1	1	0	0	1	0	3	1	2	7
Aston Villa	3	1	0	0	4	1	1	0	1	3	3	7	4	3	6
Wigan	3	2	0	0	3	0	0	0	1	0	2	3	2	1	6
Man Utd	3	0	0	1	1	2	1	1	0	6	2	7	4	3	4
Tottenham	2	0	1	0	1	1	1	0	0	3	0	4	1	3	4
Blackburn	3	1	1	0	4	1	0	0	1	0	2	4	3	1	4
Middlesbrough	3	1	0	0	1	0	0	1	1	3	4	4	4	0	4
West Ham	3	0	1	0	1	1	1	0	1	1	1	2	2	0	4
Birmingham	3	0	2	0	3	3	0	1	0	1	1	4	4	0	3
Fulham	3	1	0	1	2	2	0	0	1	0	1	2	3	-1	3
Bolton	3	0	0	1	0	1	1	0	1	3	4	3	5	-2	3
Sunderland	3	1	0	0	2	0	0	0	2	0	4	2	4	-2	3
Man City	3	0	0	2	1	5	1	0	0	2	1	3	6	-3	3
Chelsea	2	0	1	0	0	0	0	1	0	1	1	1	1	0	2
Derby	3	0	0	1	0	3	0	1	1	1	3	1	6	-5	1
Newcastle	3	0	1	1	2	6	0	0	1	1	4	3	10	-7	1
Reading	3	0	0	2	1	4	0	0	1	0	1	1	5	-4	0

MATCH OF THE DAY

GOAL OF THE MONTH

Daryl Murphy
Sunderland v Wigan

The Republic of Ireland international collected a superb pass from substitute Andy Reid just outside the Wigan penalty area before stepping in from the right and unleashing an unstoppable left-foot drive that leaves Chris Kirkland stunned by the strike.

THE MONTH'S TOP GOALSCORERS

	GOALS IN THE MONTH		THE SEASON TO END OF MONTH		
Liverpool	Torres	4	Torres	15	35%
Arsenal	Adebayor	3	Adebayor	19	33.90%
Aston Villa	Carew	3	Carew	9	18%
Birmingham	McFadden	3	Jerome, Kapo	5	18.50%
Blackburn	McCarthy	2	Santa Cruz	11	31%
Man Utd	Ronaldo, Rooney	2	Ronaldo	21	38.20%
Newcastle	Owen	2	Martins	6	20%
Portsmouth	Defoe	2	Muntari, Utaka	4	10.80%
Tottenham	Berbatov	2	Keane	12	25%
Bolton	Davies, Helguson, Nolan	1	Nolan	5	19%
Chelsea	Anelka	1	Drogba, Kalou, Lampard	5	13%
Derby	Villa	1	Miller	3	23%
Everton	Jagielka, Lescott, Yakubu	1	Yakubu	10	23%
Fulham	Bullard, Davies	1	Dempsey	6	24.00%
Man City	Fernandes, Mwaruwari, Vassell	1	Elano	5	14.70%
Middlesboro	Aliadiere, Downing, Huth, Tuncay	1	Downing, Tuncay	5	20.00%
Reading	Shorey	1	Kitson	8	26%
Sunderland	Etuhu, Murphy	1	Jones	5	19.20%
West Ham	Ljungberg, Solano	1	Ashton	5	16%
Wigan	Kilbane, Scharner, Valencia	1	Bent	7	26.90%

BARCLAYS PLAYER OF THE MONTH

Fernando Torres - Liverpool

BARCLAYS MANAGER OF THE MONTH

David Moyes - Everton

PREMIERSHIP – MARCH

LEAGUE PERFORMANCE FOR THE MONTH

	HOME						AWAY					TOTAL			
	P	W	D	L	F	A	W	D	L	F	A	F	A	DIF	PTS
Chelsea	6	3	0	0	9	2	2	1	0	9	4	18	6	12	16
Man Utd	5	3	0	0	9	0	2	0	0	4	0	13	0	13	15
Liverpool	6	4	0	0	10	1	1	0	1	3	4	13	5	8	15
Reading	5	2	1	0	4	1	1	0	1	2	2	6	3	3	10
Portsmouth	5	3	0	0	8	2	0	0	2	1	5	9	7	2	9
Blackburn	5	1	1	0	4	2	1	1	1	2	2	6	4	2	8
Birmingham	5	2	1	0	8	3	0	0	2	3	6	11	9	2	7
Newcastle	5	1	0	1	2	1	1	1	1	5	5	7	6	1	7
Everton	5	1	1	0	4	2	1	0	2	1	2	5	4	1	7
Sunderland	5	1	0	2	2	3	1	1	0	1	0	3	3	0	7
Tottenham	6	2	1	1	11	8	0	0	2	2	6	13	14	-1	7
Arsenal	5	0	2	0	2	2	1	1	1	4	4	6	6	0	6
Middlesbrough	5	1	0	1	1	1	0	2	1	2	3	3	4	-1	5
Man City	5	1	1	0	2	1	0	1	2	1	5	3	6	-3	5
Wigan	5	1	1	0	1	0	0	1	2	1	5	2	5	-3	5
Fulham	5	1	0	1	1	3	0	2	1	3	5	4	8	-4	5
West Ham	6	1	0	1	2	5	0	1	3	2	11	4	16	-12	4
Derby	5	0	2	1	2	3	0	0	2	1	7	3	10	-7	2
Aston Villa	5	0	1	1	1	2	0	1	2	1	7	2	9	-7	2
Bolton	5	0	1	2	3	6	0	0	2	0	3	3	9	-6	1

MATCH OF THE DAY

GOAL OF THE MONTH

Cristiano Ronaldo
Man Utd v Aston Villa

Ronaldo scores for United with an outrageous back heel from a corner. The ball dropped behind him in the box and, as he realised that he would be unable to turn with the ball, he improvised and simply flicked it goalwards with his heel, megging one player and beating Carson.

THE MONTH'S TOP GOALSCORERS

	GOALS IN THE MONTH		THE SEASON TO END OF MONTH		
Liverpool	Torres	6	Torres	21	38%
Portsmouth	Defoe	6	Defoe	8	17.40%
Chelsea	Lampard	5	Lampard	10	17.90%
Man Utd	Ronaldo	5	Ronaldo	26	38%
Birmingham	Forssell, Zarate	3	Forssell	7	18%
Blackburn	Santa Cruz	3	Santa Cruz	14	33.30%
Everton	Yakubu	3	Yakubu	13	27.10%
Newcastle	Owen	3	Martins, Owen	7	18.90%
Tottenham	Bent, D, Berbatov	3	Keane	14	23.00%
Bolton	Taylor	2	Nolan	5	17%
Derby	Villa	2	Miller, Villa	3	19%
Reading	Bikey	2	Kitson	9	24.30%
West Ham	Ashton	2	Ashton	7	20%
Arsenal	Bendtner, Gallas, Sagna, Toure, van Persie	1	Adebayor	19	31%
Aston Villa	Barry	1	Carew	9	17.30%
Fulham	Bullard, Kamara, McBride	1	Dempsey	6	21%
Man City	Elano, Ireland, Onuoha	1	Elano	6	16%
Middlesboro	Aliadiere, Downing, Tuncay	1	Downing, Tuncay	6	21%
Sunderland	Chopra, Jones, Reid	1	Jones	6	21%
Wigan	Heskey, King	1	Bent	7	25.00%

BARCLAYS PLAYER OF THE MONTH

Cristiano Ronaldo - Manchester United

BARCLAYS MANAGER OF THE MONTH

Sir Alex Ferguson - Manchester United

PREMIERSHIP - APRIL

LEAGUE PERFORMANCE FOR THE MONTH

	HOME						AWAY					TOTAL			
	P	W	D	L	F	A	W	D	L	F	A	F	A	DIF	PTS
Aston Villa	4	2	0	0	9	1	1	1	0	8	2	17	3	14	10
Chelsea	4	1	1	0	3	2	2	0	0	3	0	6	2	4	10
Newcastle	4	2	0	0	5	0	0	2	0	2	2	7	2	5	8
Liverpool	4	1	0	0	3	1	1	2	0	5	3	8	4	4	8
Arsenal	4	1	1	0	3	1	1	0	1	7	4	10	5	5	7
Bolton	4	1	0	0	1	0	1	1	1	2	5	3	5	-2	7
Wigan	4	1	2	0	3	1	0	1	0	1	1	4	2	2	6
Man City	4	1	0	2	5	6	1	0	0	2	1	7	7	0	6
Sunderland	4	1	0	1	4	4	1	0	1	3	3	7	7	0	6
Fulham	4	0	0	2	1	5	2	0	0	5	2	6	7	-1	6
Man Utd	4	1	0	0	2	1	0	2	1	4	5	6	6	0	5
Everton	4	1	1	1	3	3	0	1	0	1	1	4	4	0	5
Blackburn	4	0	2	0	2	2	1	0	1	2	3	4	5	-1	5
Tottenham	4	0	2	0	2	2	0	2	0	2	2	4	4	0	4
West Ham	4	1	1	1	4	4	0	0	1	0	1	4	5	-1	4
Portsmouth	4	0	1	1	0	1	1	0	1	2	3	2	4	-2	4
Middlesbrough	4	0	1	1	2	3	0	1	1	3	4	5	7	-2	2
Birmingham	4	0	2	0	3	3	0	0	2	1	7	4	10	-6	2
Reading	4	0	0	1	0	2	0	1	2	0	5	0	7	-7	1
Derby	4	0	0	2	2	12	0	0	2	1	3	3	15	-12	0

MATCH OF THE DAY

GOAL OF THE MONTH

Stiliyan Petrov
Derby v *Aston Villa*

Stiliyan Petrov wouldn't have believed that he would have been able to beat Roy Carroll from 45 yards! However, when the keeper's clearance went straight to the Villa man on the halfway line, he simply stepped forward to float the ball over the stricken goalkeeper!

THE MONTH'S TOP GOALSCORERS

	GOALS IN THE MONTH		THE SEASON TO END OF MONTH		
Arsenal	Adebayor	5	Adebayor	24	33.30%
Aston Villa	Agbonlahor, Carew	4	Carew	13	18.80%
Blackburn	Santa Cruz	3	Santa Cruz	17	37.00%
Liverpool	Crouch	3	Torres	22	34.40%
Middlesboro	Alves	3	Downing, Tuncay	7	21%
Newcastle	Owen	3	Owen	10	22.70%
Birmingham	Forssell	2	Forssell	9	21%
Chelsea	Ballack, Essien	2	Lampard	10	16%
Fulham	Kamara	2	Dempsey	6	17.10%
Man City	Mwaruwari, Vassell	2	Elano	7	15.90%
Man Utd	Ronaldo, Rooney	2	Ronaldo	28	38%
Sunderland	Chopra	2	Jones	7	19.40%
Tottenham	Berbatov	2	Berbatov	15	23%
Wigan	Heskey, Taylor	2	Bent	7	22%
Bolton	Davies, Giannakopoulos, McCann	1	Nolan	5	15.20%
Derby	Earnshaw, McEveley, Mears	1	Miller, Villa	3	16%
Everton	Lescott, Neville, Osman, Yobo	1	Yakubu	13	25.00%
Portsmouth	Kranjcar, Utaka	1	Defoe	8	17%
West Ham	Ashton, Cole, Noble, Zamora	1	Ashton	8	21%
Reading	Bikey	0	Kitson	9	24%

BARCLAYS PLAYER OF THE MONTH

Ashley Young - Aston Villa

32RED

BARCLAYS MANAGER OF THE MONTH

Avram Grant - Chelsea

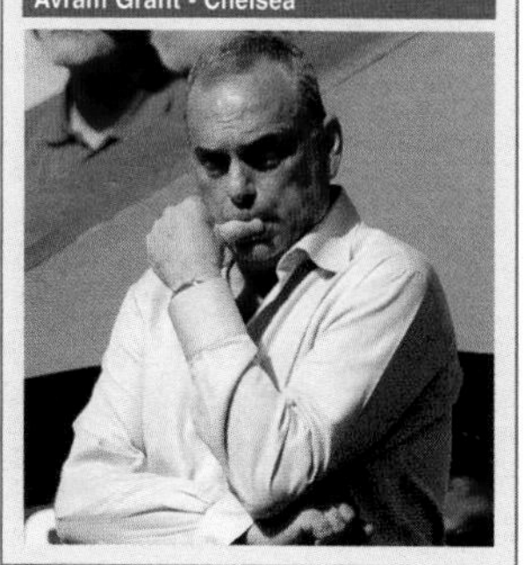

PREMIERSHIP - MAY

LEAGUE PERFORMANCE FOR THE MONTH

	HOME						AWAY					TOTAL			
	P	W	D	L	F	A	W	D	L	F	A	F	A	DIF	PTS
Middlesbrough	2	2	0	0	10	1	0	0	0	0	0	10	1	9	6
Man Utd	2	1	0	0	4	1	1	0	0	2	0	6	1	5	6
Fulham	2	1	0	0	2	0	1	0	0	1	0	3	0	3	6
Liverpool	2	1	0	0	1	0	1	0	0	2	0	3	0	3	6
Arsenal	2	1	0	0	1	0	1	0	0	1	0	2	0	2	6
Bolton	2	1	0	0	2	0	0	1	0	1	1	3	1	2	4
Chelsea	2	0	1	0	1	1	1	0	0	2	0	3	1	2	4
Reading	2	0	0	1	0	1	1	0	0	4	0	4	1	3	3
Birmingham	2	1	0	0	4	1	0	0	1	0	2	4	3	1	3
Everton	2	1	0	0	3	1	0	0	1	0	1	3	2	1	3
Wigan	2	0	0	1	0	2	1	0	0	2	0	2	2	0	3
Blackburn	2	1	0	0	3	1	0	0	1	1	4	4	5	-1	3
Tottenham	2	0	0	1	0	2	1	0	0	1	0	1	2	-1	3
Aston Villa	2	0	0	1	0	2	0	1	0	2	2	2	4	-2	1
West Ham	2	0	1	0	2	2	0	0	1	1	4	3	6	-3	1
Portsmouth	2	0	0	1	0	1	0	0	1	0	2	0	3	-3	0
Sunderland	2	0	0	1	0	1	0	0	1	0	2	0	3	-3	0
Newcastle	2	0	0	1	0	2	0	0	1	1	3	1	5	-4	0
Derby	2	0	0	1	0	4	0	0	1	1	3	1	7	-6	0
Man City	2	0	0	0	0	0	0	0	2	1	9	1	9	-8	0

MATCH OF THE DAY

GOAL OF THE SEASON

Emmanuel Adebayor
Tottenham v *Arsenal*

The Arsenal striker's superb volley against Spurs is a deserved winner. Adebayor collects high from a long ball and comfortably controls with his chest before smashing a sensational volley from the edge of the box into the top corner leaving the Spurs keeper with no chance.

THE MONTH'S TOP GOALSCORERS

	GOALS IN THE MONTH		THE SEASON TO END OF MONTH		
Man Utd	Ronaldo	3	Ronaldo	31	38.80%
Middlesboro	Alves	3	Downing	9	21%
Birmingham	Jerome	2	Forssell	9	19.60%
Blackburn	Santa Cruz	2	Santa Cruz	19	38.00%
Everton	Yakubu	2	Yakubu	15	27%
Liverpool	Torres	2	Torres	24	35.80%
West Ham	Ashton	2	Ashton	10	24%
Wigan	Valencia	2	Bent	7	21%
Arsenal	Bendtner, Walcott	1	Adebayor	24	32.40%
Aston Villa	Barry, Young	1	Carew	13	18.30%
Bolton	Diouf, Taylor	1	Nolan	5	14%
Chelsea	Ballack, Malouda, Shevchenko	1	Lampard	10	15.40%
Derby	Miller	1	Miller	4	20%
Fulham	McBride, Murphy, Nevland	1	Dempsey	6	15.80%
Man City	Elano	1	Elano	8	18%
Newcastle	Owen	1	Owen	11	24%
Reading	Doyle, Harper, Kitson, Lita	1	Kitson	10	24%
Tottenham	Keane	1	Berbatov, Keane	15	23%
Portsmouth	Ashdown	0	Defoe	8	16.70%
Sunderland	Chopra	0	Jones	7	19.40%

BARCLAYS PLAYER OF THE SEASON

Cristiano Ronaldo - Manchester United

BARCLAYS MANAGER OF THE SEASON

Sir Alex Ferguson - Manchester United

A chance to create and keep a unique record of the forthcoming season

MY FOOTBALL YEAR

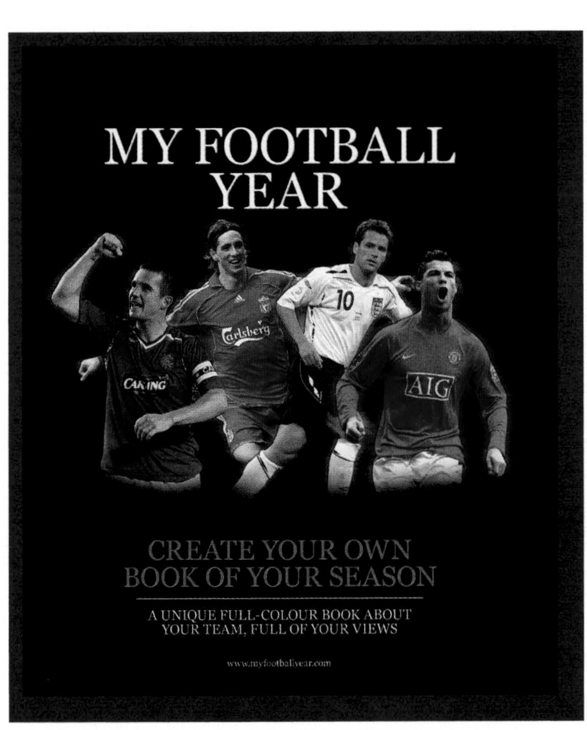
MY FOOTBALL YEAR
CREATE YOUR OWN BOOK OF YOUR SEASON
A UNIQUE FULL-COLOUR BOOK ABOUT YOUR TEAM, FULL OF YOUR VIEWS

ONLY £19.99
APRIL

For supporters of the Premier League, top Scottish teams and international sides

This is a completely new kind of book where we help you to create a record of your season, featuring your favourite teams.

My Football Year provides you with all the match reports, stats, star player marks and top quality action pictures from the games. You use our designs and reports or create your own using our simple intuitive software.

At the end of the season you press the PRINT button and we'll print it out and send it to you – all in the price.

It's a completely unique book with your name as author and editor.

Thousands of fans created their own fantastic books covering the 2007-08 season, and we've added more teams and more features for 2008-09. You can buy My Football Year for £19.99 from good book shops for the start of the season.

Find out more at:

www.myfootballyear.com

interact publishing

MANCHESTER UNITED

Fifty years on from the Munich air disaster and 40 years after European football pioneer Sir Matt Busby engineered United's first Champions of Europe team, they have done it again. As Sir Alex Ferguson said, "Even John Terry slipping as he took the penalty might have been fate." It was an emotional night in Moscow, which saw Sir Bobby Charlton, a survivor of the Busby Babes crash and a two goal hero when they beat Benfica in 1968, lead the team up the stairs to the Champions League trophy. Sir Bobby had just seen another great servant of the club, **Ryan Giggs**, score the goal that ensured United reclaimed their Premier League title and then overtake Charlton's own United appearance record in the Champions League final. It wasn't just John Terry who looked emotional on the night.

NICKNAME: RED DEVILS

KEY: Won / Drawn / Lost

1	facs	**Chelsea**	N	W	3-0*	Giggs 34 (*on penalties)
2	prem	**Reading**	H	D	0-0	
3	prem	**Portsmouth**	A	D	1-1	Scholes 15
4	prem	**Man City**	A	L	0-1	
5	prem	**Tottenham**	H	W	1-0	Nani 68
6	prem	**Sunderland**	H	W	1-0	Saha 71
7	prem	**Everton**	A	W	1-0	Vidic 84
8	ecgpf	**Sp Lisbon**	A	W	1-0	Ronaldo 62
9	prem	**Chelsea**	H	W	2-0	Tevez 45, Saha 89 pen
10	ccr3	**Coventry**	H	L	0-2	
11	prem	**Birmingham**	A	W	1-0	Ronaldo 51
12	ecgpf	**Roma**	H	W	1-0	Rooney 70
13	prem	**Wigan**	H	W	4-0	Tevez 54, Ronaldo 59, 76, Rooney 82
14	prem	**Aston Villa**	A	W	4-1	Rooney 36, 44, Ferdinand 45, Giggs 75
15	ecgpf	**Dinamo Kiev**	A	W	4-2	Ferdinand 10, Rooney 18, Ronaldo 41, 68 pen
16	prem	**Middlesbrough**	H	W	4-1	Nani 3, Rooney 33, Tevez 55, 85
17	prem	**Arsenal**	A	D	2-2	Gallas 45 og, Ronaldo 82
18	ecgpf	**Dinamo Kiev**	H	W	4-0	Pique 31, Tevez 37, Rooney 76, Ronaldo 88
19	prem	**Blackburn**	H	W	2-0	Ronaldo 34, 35
20	prem	**Bolton**	A	L	0-1	
21	ecgpf	**Sp Lisbon**	H	W	2-1	Tevez 61, Ronaldo 90
22	prem	**Fulham**	H	W	2-0	Ronaldo 10, 58
23	prem	**Derby**	H	W	4-1	Giggs 40, Tevez 45, 60, Ronaldo 90 pen
24	ecgpf	**Roma**	A	D	1-1	Pique 34
25	prem	**Liverpool**	A	W	1-0	Tevez 43
26	prem	**Everton**	H	W	2-1	Ronaldo 22, 88 pen
27	prem	**Sunderland**	A	W	4-0	Rooney 20, Saha 30, 86 pen, Ronaldo 45
28	prem	**West Ham**	A	L	1-2	Ronaldo 14
29	prem	**Birmingham**	H	W	1-0	Tevez 25
30	facr3	**Aston Villa**	A	W	2-0	Ronaldo 81, Rooney 89
31	prem	**Newcastle**	H	W	6-0	Ronaldo 49 , 70, 88, Tevez 55, 90, Ferdinand 85
32	prem	**Reading**	A	W	2-0	Rooney 77, Ronaldo 90
33	facr4	**Tottenham**	H	W	3-1	Tevez 38, Ronaldo 69 pen, 88
34	prem	**Portsmouth**	H	W	2-0	Ronaldo 10, 13
35	prem	**Tottenham**	A	D	1-1	Tevez 90
36	prem	**Man City**	H	L	1-2	Carrick 90
37	facr5	**Arsenal**	H	W	4-0	Rooney 16, Gallas 20 og, Nani 38, Fletcher 74
38	eckl1	**Lyon**	A	D	1-1	Tevez 87
39	prem	**Newcastle**	A	W	5-1	Rooney 25, 80, Ronaldo 45, 56, Saha 90
40	prem	**Fulham**	A	W	3-0	Hargreaves 15 , Park 44, Davies 72 og
41	eckl2	**Lyon**	H	W	1-0	Ronaldo 41
42	facqf	**Portsmouth**	H	L	0-1	
43	prem	**Derby**	A	W	1-0	Ronaldo 76
44	prem	**Bolton**	H	W	2-0	Ronaldo 9, 20
45	prem	**Liverpool**	H	W	3-0	Brown 34, Ronaldo 79, Nani 81
46	prem	**Aston Villa**	H	W	4-0	Ronaldo 17, Tevez 33, Rooney 53, 70
47	ecqfl1	**Roma**	A	W	2-0	Ronaldo 39, Rooney 66
48	prem	**Middlesbrough**	A	D	2-2	Ronaldo 10, Rooney 74
49	ecqfl2	**Roma**	H	W	1-0	Tevez 70
50	prem	**Arsenal**	H	W	2-1	Ronaldo 53 pen, Hargreaves 72
51	prem	**Blackburn**	A	D	1-1	Tevez 88
52	ecsfl1	**Barcelona**	A	D	0-0	
53	prem	**Chelsea**	A	L	1-2	Rooney 56
54	ecsfl2	**Barcelona**	H	W	1-0	Scholes 14
55	prem	**West Ham**	H	W	4-1	Ronaldo 3, 24, Tevez 26, Carrick 59
56	prem	**Wigan**	A	W	2-0	Ronaldo 33 pen, Giggs 80
57	ecfin	**Chelsea**	N	W	6-5*	Ronaldo 26 (*on penalties)

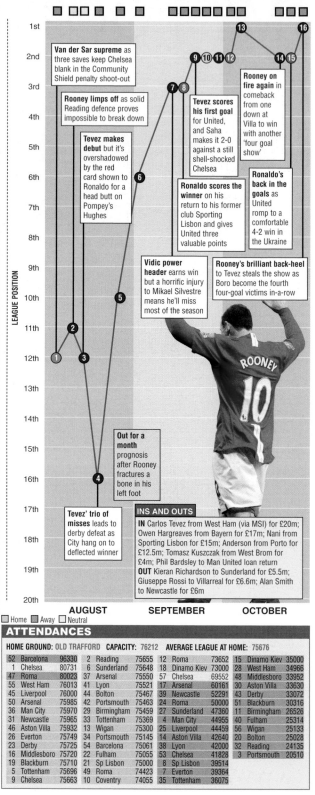

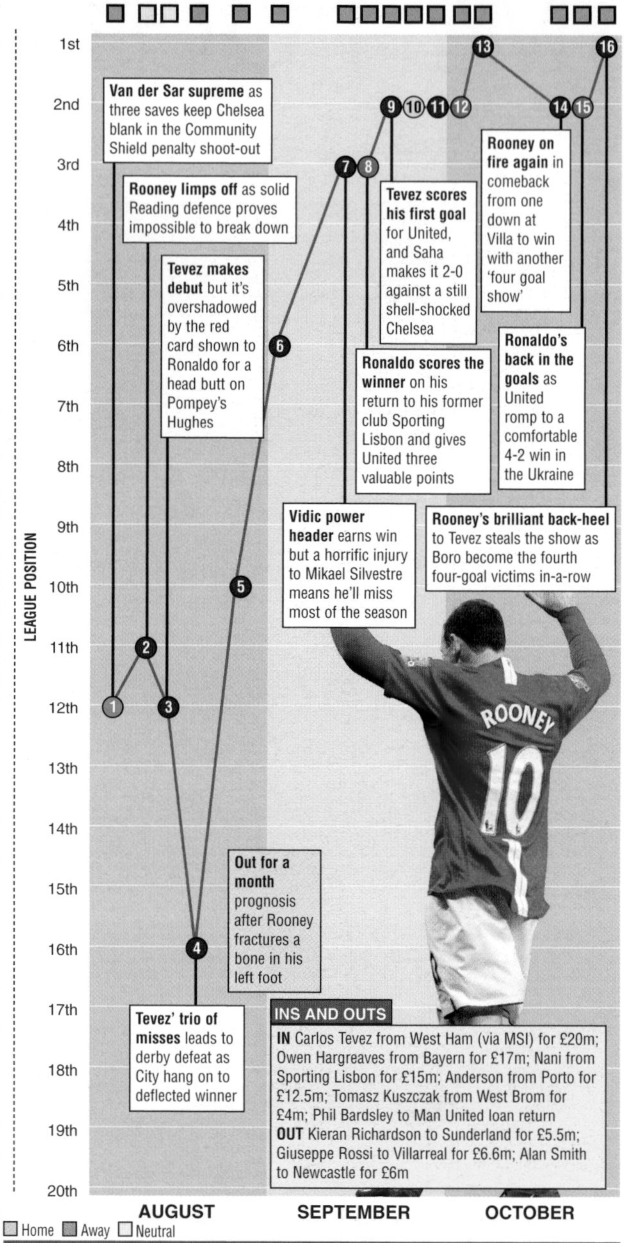

LEAGUE POSITION: 1st, 2nd, 3rd, 4th, 5th, 6th, 7th, 8th, 9th, 10th, 11th, 12th, 13th, 14th, 15th, 16th, 17th, 18th, 19th, 20th

AUGUST SEPTEMBER OCTOBER

Home / Away / Neutral

Van der Sar supreme as three saves keep Chelsea blank in the Community Shield penalty shoot-out

Rooney limps off as solid Reading defence proves impossible to break down

Tevez makes debut but it's overshadowed by the red card shown to Ronaldo for a head butt on Pompey's Hughes

Out for a month prognosis after Rooney fractures a bone in his left foot

Tevez' trio of misses leads to derby defeat as City hang on to deflected winner

Vidic power header earns win but a horrific injury to Mikael Silvestre means he'll miss most of the season

Tevez scores his first goal for United, and Saha makes it 2-0 against a still shell-shocked Chelsea

Ronaldo scores the winner on his return to his former club Sporting Lisbon and gives United three valuable points

Rooney on fire again in comeback from one down at Villa to win with another 'four goal show'

Ronaldo's back in the goals as United romp to a comfortable 4-2 win in the Ukraine

Rooney's brilliant back-heel to Tevez steals the show as Boro become the fourth four-goal victims in-a-row

INS AND OUTS

IN Carlos Tevez from West Ham (via MSI) for £20m; Owen Hargreaves from Bayern for £17m; Nani from Sporting Lisbon for £15m; Anderson from Porto for £12.5m; Tomasz Kuszczak from West Brom for £4m; Phil Bardsley to Man United loan return

OUT Kieran Richardson to Sunderland for £5.5m; Giuseppe Rossi to Villarreal for £6.6m; Alan Smith to Newcastle for £6m

ATTENDANCES

HOME GROUND: OLD TRAFFORD **CAPACITY:** 76212 **AVERAGE LEAGUE AT HOME:** 75676

52	Barcelona	96330	2	Reading	75655	12	Roma	73652	15	Dinamo Kiev	35000
1	Chelsea	80731	6	Sunderland	75648	18	Dinamo Kiev	73000	28	West Ham	34966
47	Roma	80023	37	Arsenal	75550	57	Chelsea	69552	48	Middlesboro	33952
55	West Ham	76013	41	Lyon	75521	17	Arsenal	60161	30	Aston Villa	33630
45	Liverpool	76000	44	Bolton	75467	39	Newcastle	52291	43	Derby	33072
50	Arsenal	75985	42	Portsmouth	75463	24	Roma	50000	51	Blackburn	30316
36	Man City	75970	29	Birmingham	75459	27	Sunderland	47360	11	Birmingham	26526
31	Newcastle	75965	33	Tottenham	75369	4	Man City	44955	40	Fulham	25314
46	Aston Villa	75932	13	Wigan	75300	25	Liverpool	44459	56	Wigan	25133
26	Everton	75749	34	Portsmouth	75145	14	Aston Villa	42640	20	Bolton	25028
23	Derby	75725	54	Barcelona	75061	38	Lyon	42000	32	Reading	24135
16	Middlesboro	75720	22	Fulham	75055	53	Chelsea	41828	3	Portsmouth	20510
19	Blackburn	75710	21	Sp Lisbon	75000	8	Sp Lisbon	39514			
5	Tottenham	75696	49	Roma	74423	7	Everton	39364			
9	Chelsea	75663	10	Coventry	74055	35	Tottenham	36075			

Ronaldo's goals bring historic double

Final Position: **1st**

KEY: League, Champions Lge, UEFA Cup, FA Cup, League Cup, Other

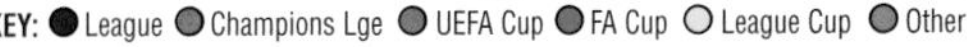

Frustrated at the Reebok as Anelka nets only goal and Ferguson misses Ronaldo and Rooney

Four scored for a fifth time as Kiev crumble after Pique nets his first goal

So close in six pointer at the Emirates but Ronaldo's late goal is answered in stoppage time by Gallas

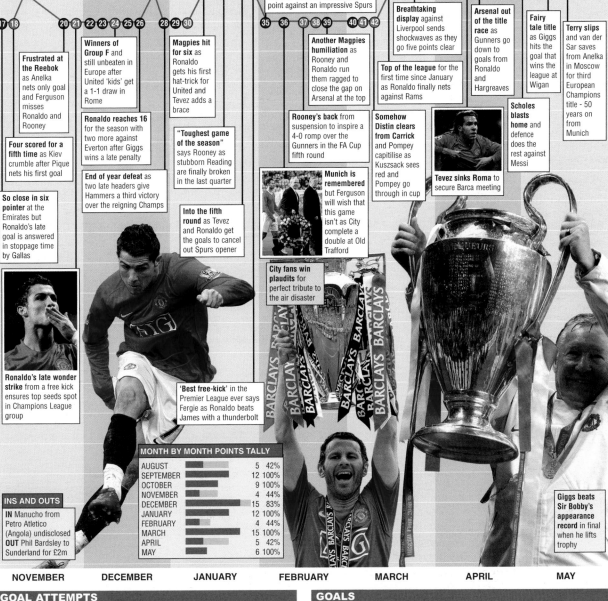

Ronaldo's late wonder strike from a free kick ensures top seeds spot in Champions League group

Winners of Group F and still unbeaten in Europe after United 'kids' get a 1-1 draw in Rome

Ronaldo reaches 16 for the season with two more against Everton after Giggs wins a late penalty

End of year defeat as two late headers give Hammers a third victory over the reigning Champs

Magpies hit for six as Ronaldo gets his first hat-trick for United and Tevez adds a brace

"Toughest game of the season" says Rooney as stubborn Reading are finally broken in the last quarter

Into the fifth round as Tevez and Ronaldo get the goals to cancel out Spurs opener

'Best free-kick' in the Premier League ever says Fergie as Ronaldo beats James with a thunderbolt

Tevez is the hero salvaging a point against an impressive Spurs

Another Magpies humiliation as Rooney and Ronaldo run them ragged to close the gap on Arsenal at the top

Rooney's back from suspension to inspire a 4-0 romp over the Gunners in the FA Cup fifth round

Munich is remembered but Ferguson will wish that this game isn't as City complete a double at Old Trafford

City fans win plaudits for perfect tribute to the air disaster

Breathtaking display against Liverpool sends shockwaves as they go five points clear

Top of the league for the first time since January as Ronaldo finally nets against Rams

Somehow Distin clears from Carrick and Pompey capitilise as Kuszsack sees red and Pompey go through in cup

Arsenal out of the title race as Gunners go down to goals from Ronaldo and Hargreaves

Tevez sinks Roma to secure Barca meeting

Fairy tale title as Giggs hits the goal that wins the league at Wigan

Scholes blasts home and defence does the rest against Messi

Terry slips and van der Sar saves from Anelka in Moscow for third European Champions title - 50 years on from Munich

Giggs beats Sir Bobby's appearance record in final when he lifts trophy

MONTH BY MONTH POINTS TALLY

Month	Points	%
AUGUST	5	42%
SEPTEMBER	12	100%
OCTOBER	9	100%
NOVEMBER	4	44%
DECEMBER	15	83%
JANUARY	12	100%
FEBRUARY	4	44%
MARCH	15	100%
APRIL	5	42%
MAY	6	100%

INS AND OUTS

IN Manucho from Petro Atletico (Angola) undisclosed
OUT Phil Bardsley to Sunderland for £2m

NOVEMBER DECEMBER JANUARY FEBRUARY MARCH APRIL MAY

GOAL ATTEMPTS

FOR — Goal attempts recorded in League games

	HOME	AWAY	TOTAL	AVE
shots on target	195	147	342	9.0
shots off target	150	125	275	7.2
TOTAL	345	272	617	16.2

Ratio of goals to shots — Average number of shots on target per League goal scored: **4.3**

Accuracy rating — Average percentage of total goal attempts which were on target: **55.4**

AGAINST — Goal attempts recorded in League games

	HOME	AWAY	TOTAL	AVE
shots on target	95	120	215	5.7
shots off target	80	105	185	4.9
TOTAL	175	225	400	10.5

Ratio of goals to shots — Average number of shots on target per League goal scored: **9.8**

Accuracy rating — Average percentage of total goal attempts which were on target: **53.8**

GOALS

Ronaldo

League	31
FA Cup	3
League Cup	0
Europe	8
Other	0
TOTAL	42

League Average **88** mins between goals

	PLAYER	LGE	FAC	LC	Euro	TOT	AVE
1	Ronaldo	31	3	0	8	42	88
2	Tevez	14	1	0	4	19	191
3	Rooney	12	2	0	4	18	181
4	Saha	5	0	0	0	5	148
5	Nani	3	1	0	0	4	524
6	Giggs	3	1	0	0	4	744
7	Ferdinand	2	0	0	1	3	1523
8	Hargreaves	2	0	0	0	2	764
9	Carrick	2	0	0	0	2	1102
10	Scholes	1	0	0	1	2	1836
11	Pique	0	0	0	2	2	
12	Park	1	0	0	0	1	630
13	Vidic	1	0	0	0	1	2668
14	Brown	1	0	0	0	1	3029
15	Fletcher	0	1	0	0	1	
	Other	0	0	0	0	0	
	TOTAL	78	9	0	20	107	

SQUAD APPEARANCES

Match	1 2 3 4 5	6 7 8 9 10	11 12 13 14 15	16 17 18 19 20	21 22 23 24 25	26 27 28 29 30	31 32 33 34 35	36 37 38 39 40	41 42 43 44 45	46 47 48 49 50	51 52 53 54 55	56 57
Venue	N H A A H	H A A H H	A H H A A	H A H H A	H H H A A	H A A H A	H A H H A	H H A A A	H H A H H	H A A H H	A A A H H	A N
Competition	O L L L L	L L C L W	L C L L C	L L C L L	C L L C L	L L L L F	L L F L L	L F C L L	C F L L L	L C L C L	L C L C L	L C
Result	W D D L W	W W W W L	W W W W W	W D W W L	W W W D W	W W L W W	W W W W D	L W D W W	W L W W W	W W D W W	D D L W W	W W

Goalkeepers
Ben Foster
Tom Heaton
Tomasz Kuszczak
Edwin van der Sar

Defenders
Phillip Bardsley
Wes Brown
Richard Eckersley
Jonny Evans
Patrice Evra
Rio Ferdinand
Gary Neville
John O'Shea
Gerard Pique
Mikael Silvestre
Danny Simpson
Nemanja Vidic

Midfielders
Luis Anderson
Michael Carrick
Chris Eagles
Darren Fletcher
Darron Gibson
Ryan Giggs
Owen Hargreaves
Sam Hewson
Lee Martin
Nani
Ji-Sung Park
Cristiano Ronaldo
Paul Scholes

Forwards
Febian Brandy
Fraizer Campbell
Dong Fanghuo
Wayne Rooney
Louis Saha
Carlos Tevez
Danny Wellbeck

KEY: ■ On all match ■ On bench ⏮ Subbed or sent off (Counting game) « Subbed or sent off (playing less than 70 mins) ⏭ Subbed on from bench (Counting Game) » Subbed on (playing less than 70 mins) » Subbed on and then subbed or sent off (Counting Game) » Subbed on and then subbed or sent off (playing less than 70 min □ Not in 16 □ Injured ✕ Suspended

KEY PLAYERS - GOALSCORERS

Cristiano Ronaldo

Goals in the League	31
Goals in all competitions	42
Assists League goals scored by a team mate where the player delivered the final pass	7
Contribution to Attacking Power Average number of minutes between League team goals while on pitch	40
Player Strike Rate Average number of minutes between League goals scored by player	88
Club Strike Rate Average minutes between League goals scored by club	42

	PLAYER	GOALS LGE	GOALS ALL	ASSISTS	POWER	S RATE
1	Cristiano Ronaldo	31	42	7	40	88 mins
2	Wayne Rooney	12	18	13	34	181 mins
3	Carlos Tevez	14	19	7	42	191 mins
4	Nani	3	4	13	36	524 mins

KEY PLAYERS - MIDFIELDERS

Cristiano Ronaldo

Goals in the League	31
Goals in all competitions	42
Assists League goals scored by a team mate where the player delivered the final pass	7
Defensive Rating Average number of mins between League goals conceded while on the pitch	161
Contribution to Attacking Power Average number of minutes between League team goals while on pitch	40
Scoring Difference Defensive Rating minus Contribution to Attacking Power	121

	PLAYER	GOALS LGE	GOALS ALL	ASSISTS	DEF RATE	POWER	SC DIFF
1	Cristiano Ronaldo	31	42	7	161	40	121 mins
2	Luis Anderson	0	0	2	165	46	119 mins
3	Michael Carrick	2	2	3	157	42	115 mins
4	Paul Scholes	1	2	5	153	47	106 mins

PLAYER APPEARANCES

	AGE (on 01/07/08)	IN NAMED 16	APPEARANCES	COUNTING GAMES	MINUTES ON PITCH	APPEARANCES	MINUTES ON PITCH	THIS SEASON	HOME COUNTRY
Goalkeepers									
Ben Foster	25	4	1	1	90	1	90	-	England
Tom Heaton	22	6	0	0	0	0	0	-	England
Tomasz Kuszczak	26	37	9	8	765	16	1210	-	Poland
Edwin van der Sar	37	29	29	28	2565	44	3845	4	Holland
Defenders									
Phillip Bardsley	23	0	0	0	0	1	45	-	England
Wes Brown	28	36	36	34	3029	52	4400	4	England
Richard Eckersley	19	0	0	0	0	0	0	-	England
Jonny Evans	20	0	0	0	0	3	163	5	N Ireland
Patrice Evra	27	35	33	29	2820	48	4198	2	France
Rio Ferdinand	29	35	35	34	3047	51	4517	7	England
Gary Neville	33	0	0	0	0	1	10	-	England
John O'Shea	27	36	28	8	1144	38	1813	5	Rep of Ireland
Gerard Pique	21	17	9	4	480	13	822	-	Spain
Mikael Silvestre	30	5	3	1	186	6	343	-	France
Danny Simpson	21	6	3	0	130	8	411	-	England
Nemanja Vidic	26	32	32	29	2668	45	3810	2	Serbia
Midfielders									
Luis Anderson	20	28	24	14	1485	38	2265	1	Brazil
Michael Carrick	26	32	31	22	2204	49	3611	1	England
Chris Eagles	22	6	4	0	133	6	313	-	England
Darren Fletcher	24	21	16	5	650	24	1169	5	Scotland
Darron Gibson	20	1	0	0	0	0	0	1	Rep of Ireland
Ryan Giggs	34	31	31	21	2232	43	2893	-	Wales
Owen Hargreaves	27	25	23	15	1529	34	2214	2	England
Sam Hewson	19	0	0	0	0	0	0	-	England
Lee Martin	21	0	0	0	0	1	45	-	England
Nani	21	29	26	13	1572	41	2505	5	Portugal
Ji-Sung Park	27	14	12	3	630	18	1149	-	South Korea
Cristiano Ronaldo	23	34	34	28	2747	49	4121	8	Portugal
Paul Scholes	33	24	24	17	1836	34	2557	-	England
Forwards									
Febian Brandy	19	0	0	0	0	0	0	-	England
Fraizer Campbell	20	1	1	0	18	2	63	-	England
Dong Fanghuo	23	1	0	0	0	2	109	-	China PR
Wayne Rooney	22	27	27	23	2182	43	3404	4	England
Louis Saha	29	19	17	5	741	24	1114	-	France
Carlos Tevez	24	36	34	29	2677	48	3476	4	Argentina
Danny Wellbeck	17	0	0	0	0	0	0	-	England

KEY: LEAGUE | ALL COMPS | CAPS | (MAY FIFA RANKING)

TEAM OF THE SEASON

VAN DER SAR

CG 28 DR 142

BROWN

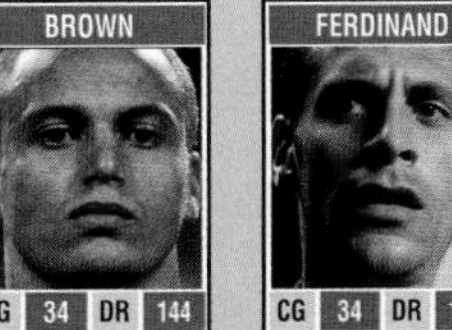

CG 34 DR 144

FERDINAND

CG 34 DR 152

VIDIC

CG 29 DR 205

EVRA

CG 29 DR 176

RONALDO

CG 28 SD +121

CARRICK

CG 22 SD +115

SCHOLES

CG 17 SD +106

ANDERSON

CG 14 SD +119

TEVEZ

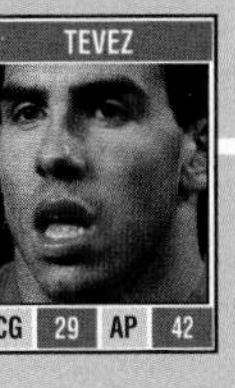

CG 29 AP 42

ROONEY

CG 23 SR 181

KEY: DR = Defensive Rate, SD = Scoring Difference AP = Attacking Power SR = Strike Rate, CG=Counting games – League games playing at least 70 minutes

TOP POINT EARNERS

Wayne Rooney

Counting Games League games when player was on pitch for at least 70 minutes	23
Average points Average League points taken in Counting games	2.65
Club Average points Average points taken in League games	2.29

	PLAYER	GAMES	PTS
1	Wayne Rooney	23	2.65
2	Luis Anderson	14	2.64
3	Carlos Tevez	29	2.41
4	Nani	13	2.38
5	Cristiano Ronaldo	28	2.36
6	Nemanja Vidic	29	2.34
7	Patrice Evra	29	2.28
8	Michael Carrick	22	2.23
9	Rio Ferdinand	34	2.21
10	Wes Brown	34	2.21

KEY PLAYERS - DEFENDERS

Nemanja Vidic

Goals Conceded in the League Number of League goals conceded while the player was on the pitch	13
Goals Conceded in all competitions Total number of goals conceded while the player was on the pitch	20
League minutes played Number of minutes played in league matches	2668
Clean Sheets In games when the player was on pitch for at least 70 minutes	19
Defensive Rating Average number of mins between League goals conceded while on the pitch	205
Club Defensive Rating Average number of mins between League goals conceded by the club this season	155

	PLAYER	CON LGE	CON ALL	MINS	C SHEETS	DEF RATE
1	Nemanja Vidic	13	20	2668	19	205 mins
2	Patrice Evra	16	22	2820	16	176 mins
3	Rio Ferdinand	20	28	3047	19	152 mins
4	Wes Brown	21	30	3029	17	144 mins

KEY GOALKEEPER

Edwin van der Sar

Goals Conceded in the League Number of League goals conceded while the player was on the pitch	18
Goals Conceded in all competitions Total number of goals conceded while the player was on the pitch	24
League minutes played Number of minutes played in league matches	2565
Clean Sheets In games when the player was on pitch for at least 70 minutes	14
Goals to Shots Ratio The average number of shots on target per each League goal conceded	8.72
Defensive Rating Ave mins between League goals conceded while on the pitch	142

BOOKINGS

Wayne Rooney

League Yellow	8
League Red	0
All competitions Yellow	12
All competitions Red	0

League Average 272 mins between cards

	PLAYER	LEAGUE		TOTAL		AVE
1	Wayne Rooney	8Y	0R	12Y	0R	272
2	Wes Brown	8	0	8	0	378
3	Cristiano Ronaldo	5	1	7	1	457
4	Nani	2	1	4	1	524
5	Nemanja Vidic	5	0	6	0	533
6	Paul Scholes	3	0	4	0	612
7	Darren Fletcher	1	0	3	0	650
8	Patrice Evra	4	0	7	0	705
9	Luis Anderson	2	0	3	0	742
10	Rio Ferdinand	4	0	6	0	761
11	Owen Hargreaves	2	0	4	0	764
12	Michael Carrick	2	0	3	0	1102
13	John O'Shea	1	0	1	0	1144
14	Edwin van der Sar	2	0	3	0	1282
15	Ryan Giggs	1	0	1	0	2232
	Other	1	0	3	1	
	TOTAL	51	2	75	3	

CHELSEA

John Terry's tears will summarise the season when Roman Abramovich's five-year strategy to win the Champions League, came within three inches of coming true. It seemed the script was written when Avram Grant delivered Chelsea, bang on schedule, to the final - in Moscow of all places. They delivered a hard-fought come-back against a United side, they hit the woodwork twice and here was Terry, striding confidently up to place the ball for the trophy-winning spot-kick. He slipped and the ball thudded against the post. The season should be remembered for the character of this club. It imploded at the start of the season, losing its charismatic manager, then it suffered a multitude of key injuries, survived the African Cup exodus and came back to reach two finals and create the closest Premier title race ever but ran out of luck.

NICKNAME: THE BLUES

KEY: Won / Drawn / Lost

1	facs	**Man Utd**	N	L	0-3*	Malouda 45 (*on penalties)
2	prem	**Birmingham**	H	W	3-2	Pizarro 17, Malouda 30, Essien 49
3	prem	**Reading**	A	W	2-1	Lampard 47, Drogba 50
4	prem	**Liverpool**	A	D	1-1	Lampard 62 pen
5	prem	**Portsmouth**	H	W	1-0	Lampard 31
6	prem	**Aston Villa**	A	L	0-2	
7	prem	**Blackburn**	H	D	0-0	
8	ecgpb	**Rosenborg BK**	H	D	1-1	Shevchenko 53
9	prem	**Man Utd**	A	L	0-2	
10	ccr3	**Hull City**	A	W	4-0	Sinclair 37, Kalou 48, 81, Sidwell 52
11	prem	**Fulham**	H	D	0-0	
12	ecgpb	**Valencia**	A	W	2-1	J.Cole 21, Drogba 71
13	prem	**Bolton**	A	W	1-0	Kalou 41
14	prem	**Middlesbrough**	A	W	2-0	Drogba 8, Alex 57
15	ecgpb	**Schalke**	H	W	2-0	Malouda 5, Drogba 47
16	prem	**Man City**	H	W	6-0	Essien 17, Drogba 31, 55, J.Cole 60, Kalou 75, Shevchenko 90
17	ccr4	**Leicester**	H	W	4-3	Lampard 20, 29, 90, Shevchenko 87
18	prem	**Wigan**	A	W	2-0	Lampard 11, Belletti 18
19	ecgpb	**Schalke**	A	D	0-0	
20	prem	**Everton**	H	D	1-1	Drogba 70
21	prem	**Derby**	A	W	2-0	Kalou 17, Wright-Phillips 73
22	ecgpb	**Rosenborg BK**	A	W	4-0	Drogba 7, 20, Alex 40, J.Cole 73
23	prem	**West Ham**	H	W	1-0	J.Cole 76
24	prem	**Sunderland**	H	W	2-0	Shevchenko 23, Lampard 75 pen
25	ecgpb	**Valencia**	H	D	0-0	
26	prem	**Arsenal**	A	L	0-1	
27	ccqf	**Liverpool**	H	W	2-0	Lampard 59, Shevchenko 90
28	prem	**Blackburn**	A	W	1-0	J.Cole 22
29	prem	**Aston Villa**	H	D	4-4	Shevchenko 45 pen, 50, Alex 66, Ballack 88
30	prem	**Newcastle**	H	W	2-1	Essien 28, Kalou 87
31	prem	**Fulham**	A	W	2-1	Kalou 54, Ballack 61 pen
32	facr3	**QPR**	H	W	1-0	Camp 28 og
33	ccsfl1	**Everton**	H	W	2-1	Wright-Phillips 26, Lescott 90 og
34	prem	**Tottenham**	H	W	2-0	Belletti 19, Wright-Phillips 81
35	prem	**Birmingham**	A	W	1-0	Pizarro 79
36	ccsfl2	**Everton**	A	W	1-0	J.Cole 69
37	facr4	**Wigan**	A	W	2-1	Anelka 53, Wright-Phillips 82
38	prem	**Reading**	H	W	1-0	Ballack 32
39	prem	**Portsmouth**	A	D	1-1	Anelka 55
40	prem	**Liverpool**	H	D	0-0	
41	facr5	**Huddersfield**	H	W	3-1	Lampard 18, 60, Kalou 70
42	eckl1	**Olympiakos**	A	D	0-0	
43	cccf	**Tottenham**	N	L	1-2	Drogba 39
44	prem	**West Ham**	A	W	4-0	Lampard 17 pen, J.Cole 20, Ballack 22, A.Cole 64
45	eckl2	**Olympiakos**	H	W	3-0	Ballack 5, Lampard 25, Kalou 48
46	facqf	**Barnsley**	A	L	0-1	
47	prem	**Derby**	H	W	6-1	Lampard 27 pen, 57, 66, 72, Kalou 42, J.Cole 64
48	prem	**Sunderland**	A	W	1-0	Terry 10
49	prem	**Tottenham**	A	D	4-4	Drogba 3, Essien 20, J.Cole 52, 79
50	prem	**Arsenal**	H	W	2-1	Drogba 73, 81
51	prem	**Middlesbrough**	H	W	1-0	Carvalho 5
52	ecqfl1	**Fenerbahce**	A	L	1-2	Deivid 13 og
53	prem	**Man City**	A	W	2-0	Dunne 6 og, Kalou 53
54	ecqfl2	**Fenerbahce**	H	W	2-0	Ballack 4, Lampard 87
55	prem	**Wigan**	H	D	1-1	Essien 55
56	prem	**Everton**	A	W	1-0	Essien 41
57	ecsfl1	**Liverpool**	A	D	1-1	Riise 90 og
58	prem	**Man Utd**	H	W	2-1	Ballack 45, 86 pen
59	ecsfl2	**Liverpool**	H	W	3-2	Drogba 33, 105, Lampard 98 pen
60	prem	**Newcastle**	A	W	2-0	Ballack 60, Malouda 82
61	prem	**Bolton**	H	D	1-1	Shevchenko 62
62	ecfin	**Man Utd**	N	L	5-6*	Lampard 45 (*on penalties)

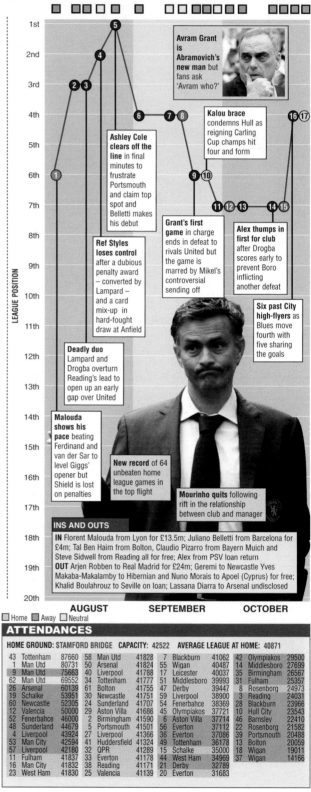

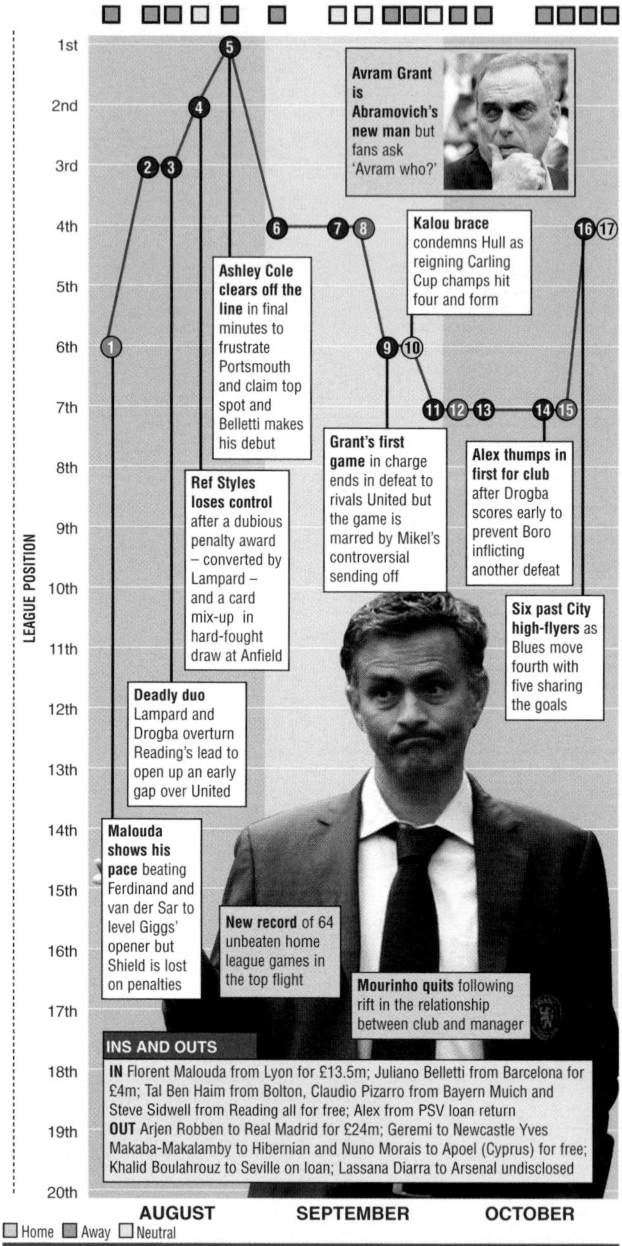

LEAGUE POSITION

1st 2nd 3rd 4th 5th 6th 7th 8th 9th 10th 11th 12th 13th 14th 15th 16th 17th 18th 19th 20th

AUGUST SEPTEMBER OCTOBER

Avram Grant is Abramovich's new man but fans ask 'Avram who?'

Kalou brace condemns Hull as reigning Carling Cup champs hit four and form

Ashley Cole clears off the line in final minutes to frustrate Portsmouth and claim top spot and Belletti makes his debut

Grant's first game in charge ends in defeat to rivals United but the game is marred by Mikel's controversial sending off

Alex thumps in first for club after Drogba scores early to prevent Boro inflicting another defeat

Ref Styles loses control after a dubious penalty award – converted by Lampard – and a card mix-up in hard-fought draw at Anfield

Six past City high-flyers as Blues move fourth with five sharing the goals

Deadly duo Lampard and Drogba overturn Reading's lead to open up an early gap over United

Malouda shows his pace beating Ferdinand and van der Sar to level Giggs' opener but Shield is lost on penalties

New record of 64 unbeaten home league games in the top flight

Mourinho quits following rift in the relationship between club and manager

INS AND OUTS

IN Florent Malouda from Lyon for £13.5m; Juliano Belletti from Barcelona for £4m; Tal Ben Haim from Bolton, Claudio Pizarro from Bayern Muich and Steve Sidwell from Reading all for free; Alex from PSV loan return
OUT Arjen Robben to Real Madrid for £24m; Geremi to Newcastle Yves Makaba-Makalamby to Hibernian and Nuno Morais to Apoel (Cyprus) for free; Khalid Boulahrouz to Seville on loan; Lassana Diarra to Arsenal undisclosed

Home / Away / Neutral

ATTENDANCES

HOME GROUND: STAMFORD BRIDGE **CAPACITY:** 42522 **AVERAGE LEAGUE AT HOME:** 40871

43	Tottenham	87660	58	Man Utd	41828	7	Blackburn	41062	42	Olympiakos	29500
1	Man Utd	80731	50	Arsenal	41824	55	Wigan	40487	14	Middlesboro	27699
9	Man Utd	75663	40	Liverpool	41788	17	Leicester	40037	35	Birmingham	26567
62	Man Utd	69552	34	Tottenham	41777	51	Middlesboro	39993	31	Fulham	25357
26	Arsenal	60139	61	Bolton	41755	47	Derby	39447	8	Rosenborg	24973
19	Schalke	53951	30	Newcastle	41751	59	Liverpool	38900	3	Reading	24031
60	Newcastle	52305	24	Sunderland	41707	54	Fenerbahce	38369	28	Blackburn	23966
12	Valencia	50000	29	Aston Villa	41686	45	Olympiakos	37721	10	Hull City	23543
52	Fenerbahce	46000	2	Birmingham	41590	6	Aston Villa	37714	46	Barnsley	22410
48	Sunderland	44679	5	Portsmouth	41501	56	Everton	37112	22	Rosenborg	21582
4	Liverpool	43924	27	Liverpool	41366	36	Everton	37086	39	Portsmouth	20488
53	Man City	42594	41	Huddersfield	41324	49	Tottenham	36178	13	Bolton	20059
57	Liverpool	42180	32	QPR	41289	15	Schalke	35000	18	Wigan	19011
11	Fulham	41837	33	Everton	41178	44	West Ham	34969	37	Wigan	14166
16	Man City	41832	38	Reading	41171	21	Derby	32789			
23	West Ham	41830	25	Valencia	41139	20	Everton	31683			

Terry's tears end a season of so nears...

Final Position: **2nd**

KEY: ● League ● Champions Lge ● UEFA Cup ● FA Cup ○ League Cup ● Other

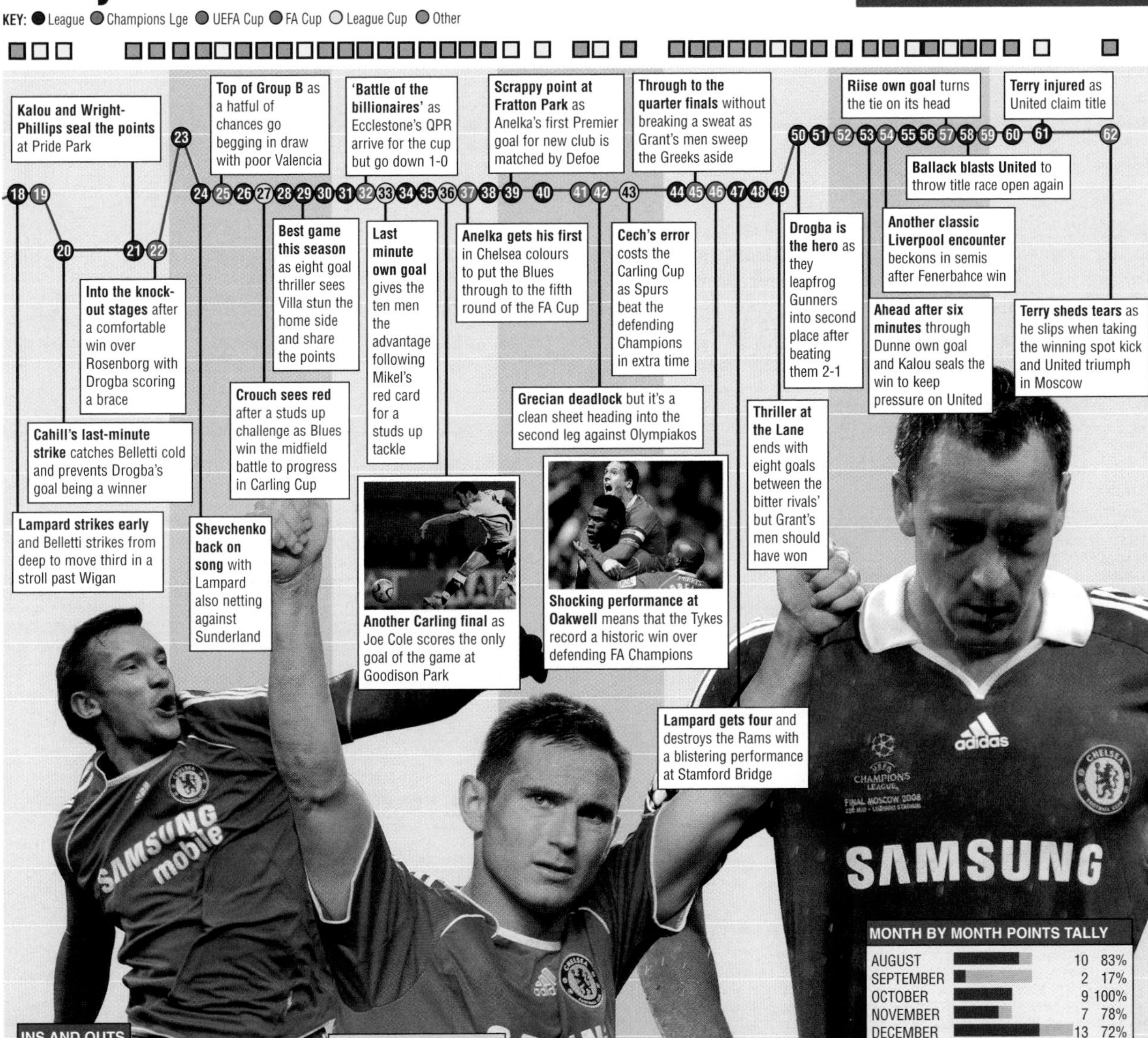

Kalou and Wright-Phillips seal the points at Pride Park
Top of Group B as a hatful of chances go begging in draw with poor Valencia
'Battle of the billionaires' as Ecclestone's QPR arrive for the cup but go down 1-0
Scrappy point at Fratton Park as Anelka's first Premier goal for new club is matched by Defoe
Through to the quarter finals without breaking a sweat as Grant's men sweep the Greeks aside
Riise own goal turns the tie on its head
Terry injured as United claim title
Ballack blasts United to throw title race open again
Best game this season as eight goal thriller sees Villa stun the home side and share the points
Last minute own goal gives the ten men the advantage following Mikel's red card for a studs up tackle
Anelka gets his first in Chelsea colours to put the Blues through to the fifth round of the FA Cup
Cech's error costs the Carling Cup as Spurs beat the defending Champions in extra time
Drogba is the hero as they leapfrog Gunners into second place after beating them 2-1
Another classic Liverpool encounter beckons in semis after Fenerbahce win
Into the knock-out stages after a comfortable win over Rosenborg with Drogba scoring a brace
Ahead after six minutes through Dunne own goal and Kalou seals the win to keep pressure on United
Terry sheds tears as he slips when taking the winning spot kick and United triumph in Moscow
Cahill's last-minute strike catches Belletti cold and prevents Drogba's goal being a winner
Crouch sees red after a studs up challenge as Blues win the midfield battle to progress in Carling Cup
Grecian deadlock but it's a clean sheet heading into the second leg against Olympiakos
Thriller at the Lane ends with eight goals between the bitter rivals' but Grant's men should have won
Lampard strikes early and Belletti strikes from deep to move third in a stroll past Wigan
Shevchenko back on song with Lampard also netting against Sunderland
Another Carling final as Joe Cole scores the only goal of the game at Goodison Park
Shocking performance at Oakwell means that the Tykes record a historic win over defending FA Champions
Lampard gets four and destroys the Rams with a blistering performance at Stamford Bridge
Anelka signs for £15m from Bolton to lift attack while Drogba's on African duty
SAMSUNG

INS AND OUTS

IN Nicolas Anelka from Bolton for £15m; Branislav Ivanovic from Lokomotiv Moscow for £9m; Franco di Santo from Audax Italiano (Chile) for £3.4m

MONTH BY MONTH POINTS TALLY

Month	Points	%
AUGUST	10	83%
SEPTEMBER	2	17%
OCTOBER	9	100%
NOVEMBER	7	78%
DECEMBER	13	72%
JANUARY	12	100%
FEBRUARY	2	33%
MARCH	16	89%
APRIL	10	83%
MAY	4	67%

NOVEMBER DECEMBER JANUARY FEBRUARY MARCH APRIL MAY

GOAL ATTEMPTS

FOR – Goal attempts recorded in League games

	HOME	AWAY	TOTAL	AVE
shots on target	141	124	265	7.0
shots off target	143	106	249	6.6
TOTAL	**284**	**230**	**514**	**13.5**

Ratio of goals to shots – Average number of shots on target per League goal scored: **4.1**

Accuracy rating – Average percentage of total goal attempts which were on target: **51.6**

AGAINST – Goal attempts recorded in League games

	HOME	AWAY	TOTAL	AVE
shots on target	78	123	201	5.3
shots off target	87	118	205	5.4
TOTAL	**165**	**241**	**406**	**10.7**

Ratio of goals to shots – Average number of shots on target per League goal scored: **7.7**

Accuracy rating – Average percentage of total goal attempts which were on target: **49.5**

GOALS

Lampard

League	10
FA Cup	2
League Cup	4
Europe	4
Other	0
TOTAL	20

League Average **200** mins between goals

	PLAYER	LGE	FAC	LC	Euro	TOT	AVE
1	Lampard	10	2	4	4	**20**	200
2	Drogba	8	0	1	6	**15**	190
3	Kalou	7	1	2	1	**11**	304
4	Cole, J	7	0	1	2	**10**	353
5	Ballack	7	0	0	2	**9**	201
6	Shevchenko	5	0	2	1	**8**	148
7	Essien	6	0	0	0	**6**	348
8	Malouda	2	1	0	1	**4**	696
9	Wright-Phillips	2	1	1	0	**4**	823
10	Alex	2	0	0	1	**3**	1035
11	Pizarro	2	0	0	0	**2**	344
12	Belletti	2	0	0	0	**2**	959
13	Anelka	1	1	0	0	**2**	967
14	Carvalho	1	0	0	0	**1**	1745
15	Terry	1	0	0	0	**1**	1895
	Other	1	0	2	0	3	
	TOTAL	**64**	**6**	**13**	**18**	**101**	

SQUAD APPEARANCES

Match	Venue	Competition	Result
1 2 3 4 5	N H A A H	O L L L L	L W W D W
6 7 8 9 10	A H H A A	L L C L W	L D D L W
11 12 13 14 15	H A A A H	L C L L C	D W W W W
16 17 18 19 20	H H A A H	L W L C L	W W W D D
21 22 23 24 25	A A H H H	L C L L C	W W W W D
26 27 28 29 30	A H A H H	L W L L L	L W W D W
31 32 33 34 35	A H H H A	L F W L L	W W W W W
36 37 38 39 40	A A H A H	W F L L L	W W W D D
41 42 43 44 45	H A N A H	F C W L C	W D L W W
46 47 48 49 50	A H A A H	F L L L L	L W W D W
51 52 53 54 55	H A A H H	L C L C L	W L W W D
56 57 58 59 60	A A H H A	L C L C L	W D W W W
61 62	H N	L C	D L

Goalkeepers
- **Petr Cech**
- **Carlo Cudicini**
- **Henrique Hilario**
- **Rhys Taylor**

Defenders
- **Alex**
- **Juliano Belletti**
- **Tal Ben Haim**
- **Wayne Bridge**
- **Ricardo Carvalho**
- **Ashley Cole**
- **Paulo Ferreira**
- **Glen Johnson**
- **John Terry**
- **Harry Worley**

Midfielders
- **Michael Ballack**
- **Joe Cole**
- **Lassana Diarra**
- **Michael Essien**
- **Frank Lampard**
- **Claude Makelele**
- **Florent Malouda**
- **John Obi Mikel**
- **Lee Sawyer**
- **Steven Sidwell**
- **Shaun Wright-Phillips**

Forwards
- **Nicolas Anelka**
- **Didier Drogba**
- **Salomon Kalou**
- **Claudio Pizarro**
- **Ben Sahar**
- **Andriy Shevchenko**
- **Scott Sinclair**

KEY: ■ On all match ■ On bench ⏮ Subbed or sent off (Counting game) « Subbed or sent off (playing less than 70 mins) ⏭ Subbed on from bench (Counting Game) » Subbed on (playing less than 70 mins) » Subbed on and then subbed or sent off (Counting Game) » Subbed on and then subbed or sent off (playing less than 70 min □ Not in 16 □ Injured ✕ Suspended

KEY PLAYERS - GOALSCORERS

Didier Drogba

Goals in the League	8
Goals in all competitions	15
Assists League goals scored by a team mate where the player delivered the final pass	7
Contribution to Attacking Power Average number of minutes between League team goals while on pitch	52
Player Strike Rate Average number of minutes between League goals scored by player	190
Club Strike Rate Average minutes between League goals scored by club	52

	PLAYER	GOALS LGE	GOALS ALL	ASSISTS	POWER	S RATE
1	Didier Drogba	8	15	7	52	**190 mins**
2	Frank Lampard	10	20	11	43	**200 mins**
3	Michael Ballack	7	9	3	48	**201 mins**
4	Salomon Kalou	7	11	11	44	**304 mins**

KEY PLAYERS - MIDFIELDERS

John Obi Mikel

Goals in the League	0
Goals in all competitions	0
Assists League goals scored by a team mate where the player delivered the final pass	0
Defensive Rating Average number of mins between League goals conceded while on the pitch	244
Contribution to Attacking Power Average number of minutes between League team goals while on pitch	54
Scoring Difference Defensive Rating minus Contribution to Attacking Power	190

	PLAYER	GOALS LGE	GOALS ALL	ASSISTS	DEF RATE	POWER	SC DIFF
1	John Obi Mikel	0	0	0	244	54	**190 mins**
2	Frank Lampard	10	20	11	143	43	**100 mins**
3	Joe Cole	7	10	5	137	51	**86 mins**
4	Florent Malouda	2	4	5	154	69	**85 mins**

PLAYER APPEARANCES

	AGE (on 01/07/08)	IN NAMED 16	APPEARANCES	COUNTING GAMES	MINUTES ON PITCH	APPEARANCES	MINUTES ON PITCH	THIS SEASON	HOME COUNTRY
Goalkeepers									
Petr Cech	28	26	26	25	2313	40	3618	4	Czech Republic
Carlo Cudicini	34	32	10	10	900	19	1600	-	Italy
Henrique Hilario	32	16	3	2	207	6	452	-	Portugal
Rhys Taylor	18	2	0	0	0	0	0	-	Wales
Defenders									
Alex	26	34	28	22	2070	39	2972	1	Brazil
Juliano Belletti	32	25	23	21	1918	38	3037	-	Brazil
Tal Ben Haim	26	26	13	10	1019	23	1657	5	Israel
Wayne Bridge	27	13	11	9	818	22	1774	3	England
Ricardo Carvalho	30	22	21	19	1745	38	3365	4	Portugal
Ashley Cole	27	27	27	27	2413	41	3577	5	England
Paulo Ferreira	29	22	18	13	1291	28	1972	6	Portugal
Glen Johnson	23	2	2	1	149	3	226	-	England
John Terry	27	23	23	20	1895	37	3245	4	England
Harry Worley	19	0	0	0	0	0	0	-	England
Midfielders									
Michael Ballack	31	20	18	14	1411	30	2349	2	Germany
Joe Cole	26	37	33	26	2475	55	4017	9	England
Lassana Diarra	23	0	0	0	0	1	24	4	France
Michael Essien	25	27	27	23	2093	46	3580	6	Ghana
Frank Lampard	30	24	24	22	2009	40	3367	5	England
Claude Makelele	35	20	18	12	1223	34	2605	7	France
Florent Malouda	28	21	21	15	1393	38	2555	5	France
John Obi Mikel	21	29	29	18	1952	39	2590	4	Nigeria
Lee Sawyer	18	0	0	0	0	0	0	-	England
Steven Sidwell	25	16	15	3	517	25	1092	-	England
Shaun Wright-Phillips	26	29	27	14	1647	41	2584	7	England
Forwards									
Nicolas Anelka	29	14	14	9	967	24	1439	6	France
Didier Drogba	30	20	19	17	1526	32	2699	7	Ivory Coast
Salomon Kalou	22	31	30	21	2134	48	3070	5	Ivory Coast
Claudio Pizarro	29	23	21	1	689	32	1276	4	Peru
Ben Sahar	18	0	0	0	0	0	0	2	Israel
Andriy Shevchenko	29	24	17	5	742	25	1100	5	Ukraine
Scott Sinclair	19	3	1	0	15	7	397	-	England

KEY: LEAGUE ALL COMPS CAPS (MAY FIFA RANKING)

TEAM OF THE SEASON

CECH — CG 25 DR 136

BELLETTI — CG 21 DR 239

CARVALHO — CG 19 DR 134

TERRY — CG 20 DR 145

ALEX — CG 22 DR 138

J.COLE — CG 26 SD +86

MIKEL — CG 18 SD +190

LAMPARD — CG 22 SD +100

MALOUDA — CG 15 SD +85

KALOU — CG 21 AP 44

DROGBA — CG 17 SR 190

KEY: DR = Defensive Rate, SD = Scoring Difference AP = Attacking Power SR = Strike Rate, CG=Counting games – League games playing at least 70 minutes

TOP POINT EARNERS

Ricardo Carvalho

Counting Games League games when player was on pitch for at least 70 minutes	19
Average points Average League points taken in Counting games	2.68
Club Average points Average points taken in League games	2.24

	PLAYER	GAMES	PTS
1	Ricardo Carvalho	19	2.68
2	Salomon Kalou	21	2.52
3	John Obi Mikel	18	2.50
4	Shaun Wright-Phillips	14	2.50
5	Michael Ballack	14	2.43
6	Frank Lampard	22	2.41
7	John Terry	20	2.30
8	Didier Drogba	17	2.24
9	Paulo Ferreira	13	2.23
10	Florent Malouda	15	2.20

KEY PLAYERS - DEFENDERS

Juliano Belletti

Goals Conceded in the League Number of League goals conceded while the player was on the pitch	8
Goals Conceded in all competitions Total number of goals conceded while the player was on the pitch	17
League minutes played Number of minutes played in league matches	1918
Clean Sheets In games when the player was on pitch for at least 70 minutes	14
Defensive Rating Average number of mins between League goals conceded while on the pitch	239
Club Defensive Rating Average number of mins between League goals conceded by the club this season	131

	PLAYER	CON LGE	CON ALL	MINS	C SHEETS	DEF RATE
1	Juliano Belletti	8	17	1918	14	239 mins
2	John Terry	13	25	1895	12	145 mins
3	Alex	15	21	2070	13	138 mins
4	Ricardo Carvalho	13	26	1745	13	134 mins

KEY GOALKEEPER

Petr Cech

Goals Conceded in the League Number of League goals conceded while the player was on the pitch	17
Goals Conceded in all competitions Total number of goals conceded while the player was on the pitch	27
League minutes played Number of minutes played in league matches	2313
Clean Sheets In games when the player was on pitch for at least 70 minutes	14
Goals to Shots Ratio The average number of shots on target per each League goal conceded	8.76
Defensive Rating Ave mins between League goals conceded while on the pitch	136

BOOKINGS

Didier Drogba

League Yellow	6
League Red	1
All competitions Yellow	6
All competitions Red	2
League Average	218 mins between cards

	PLAYER	LEAGUE		TOTAL		AVE
1	Didier Drogba	6Y	1R	6Y	2R	218
2	Ricardo Carvalho	6	1	12	1	249
3	Michael Ballack	5	0	6	0	282
4	John Terry	6	0	8	0	315
5	John Obi Mikel	5	1	8	2	325
6	Michael Essien	5	1	9	1	348
7	Juliano Belletti	5	0	8	0	383
8	Ashley Cole	4	1	5	1	482
9	Joe Cole	5	0	6	0	495
10	Frank Lampard	4	0	5	0	502
11	Tal Ben Haim	2	0	4	0	509
12	Alex	4	0	6	0	517
13	Steven Sidwell	1	0	2	0	517
14	Claudio Pizarro	1	0	1	0	689
15	Florent Malouda	2	0	2	0	696
	Other	4	0	9	0	
	TOTAL	65	5	97	7	

ARSENAL

Arsene Wenger has challenged the old Alan Hansen adage that 'You'll never win anything with kids'. The young stars who were chasing Carling Cups two seasons ago are now giving footballing lessons to the likes of Milan on their home turf and getting within four points of the league title. There is much to admire about Wenger's Arsenal: their thrilling brand of fast ground-hugging passing, the fact that they nurture promise rather than buy established stars and their willingness to back their academy graduates. In the end injuries to influential players such as **Rosicky**, **Sagna**, **van Persie** and **Eduardo** caused the team to stumble but, having thrown down a marker this season; it will be fascinating to see if **Fabregas** and the rest can kick-on from here.

NICKNAME: THE GUNNERS

KEY: Won / Drawn / Lost

1	prem	**Fulham**	H	W	2-1	van Persie 83 pen, Hleb 90
2	ecql1	**Sparta Prague**	A	W	2-0	Fabregas 72, Hleb 90
3	prem	**Blackburn**	A	D	1-1	van Persie 18
4	prem	**Man City**	H	W	1-0	Fabregas 80 60,114
5	ecql2	**Sparta Prague**	H	W	3-0	Rosicky 7, Fabregas 82, da Silva 89
6	prem	**Portsmouth**	H	W	3-1	Adebayor 8 pen, Fabregas 35, Rosicky 59
7	prem	**Tottenham**	A	W	3-1	Adebayor 65, 90, Fabregas 80
8	ecgph	**Sevilla**	H	W	3-0	Fabregas 27, van Persie 60, da Silva 90
9	prem	**Derby**	H	W	5-0	Diaby 10, Adebayor 26, 50 pen, 79, Fabregas 70
10	ccr3	**Newcastle**	H	W	2-0	Bendtner 83, Denilson 89
11	prem	**West Ham**	A	W	1-0	van Persie 13
12	ecgph	**S Bucharest**	A	W	1-0	van Persie 76
13	prem	**Sunderland**	H	W	3-2	van Persie 7, 80, Senderos 14
14	prem	**Bolton**	H	W	2-0	Toure 68, Rosicky 80
15	ecgph	**Slavia Prague**	H	W	7-0	Fabregas 5, 58, Hubacek 24 og, Walcott 41, 55, Hleb 51, Bendtner 89
16	prem	**Liverpool**	A	D	1-1	Fabregas 80
17	ccr4	**Sheff Utd**	A	W	3-0	da Silva 8, 50, Denilson 69
18	prem	**Man Utd**	H	D	2-2	Fabregas 48, Gallas 90
19	ecgph	**Slavia Prague**	A	D	0-0	
20	prem	**Reading**	A	W	3-1	Flamini 44, Adebayor 52, Hleb 78
21	prem	**Wigan**	H	W	2-0	Gallas 83, Rosicky 85
22	ecgph	**Sevilla**	A	L	1-3	da Silva 11
23	prem	**Aston Villa**	A	W	2-1	Flamini 24, Adebayor 36
24	prem	**Newcastle**	A	D	1-1	Adebayor 4
25	prem	**Middlesbrough**	A	L	1-2	Rosicky 90
26	ecgph	**S Bucharest**	H	W	2-1	Diaby 8, Bendtner 42
27	prem	**Chelsea**	H	W	1-0	Gallas 45
28	ccqf	**Blackburn**	A	W	3-2	Diaby 6, da Silva 29, 104
29	prem	**Tottenham**	H	W	2-1	Adebayor 48, Bendtner 75
30	prem	**Portsmouth**	A	D	0-0	
31	prem	**Everton**	A	W	4-1	da Silva 47, 58, Adebayor 78, Rosicky 90
32	prem	**West Ham**	H	W	2-0	da Silva 2, Adebayor 18
33	facr3	**Burnley**	A	W	2-0	da Silva 9, Bendtner 75
34	ccsfl1	**Tottenham**	H	D	1-1	Walcott 79
35	prem	**Birmingham**	H	D	1-1	Adebayor 21 pen
36	prem	**Fulham**	A	W	3-0	Adebayor 19, 38, Rosicky 81
37	ccsfl2	**Tottenham**	A	L	1-5	Adebayor 70
38	facr4	**Newcastle**	H	W	3-0	Adebayor 51, 84, Butt 89 og
39	prem	**Newcastle**	H	W	3-0	Adebayor 40, Flamini 72, Fabregas 80
40	prem	**Man City**	A	W	3-1	Adebayor 9, 88, da Silva 26
41	prem	**Blackburn**	H	W	2-0	Senderos 4, Adebayor 90
42	facr5	**Man Utd**	A	L	0-4	
43	eckl1	**AC Milan**	H	D	0-0	
44	prem	**Birmingham**	A	D	2-2	Walcott 50, 55
45	prem	**Aston Villa**	H	D	1-1	Bendtner 90
46	eckl2	**AC Milan**	A	W	2-0	Fabregas 84, Adebayor 90
47	prem	**Wigan**	A	D	0-0	
48	prem	**Middlesbrough**	H	D	1-1	Toure 86
49	prem	**Chelsea**	A	L	1-2	Sagna 59
50	prem	**Bolton**	A	W	3-2	Gallas 62, van Persie 68 pen, Samuel 90 og
51	ecqfl1	**Liverpool**	H	D	1-1	Adebayor 23
52	prem	**Liverpool**	H	D	1-1	Bendtner 54
53	ecqfl2	**Liverpool**	A	L	2-4	Diaby 13, Adebayor 84
54	prem	**Man Utd**	A	L	1-2	Adebayor 48
55	prem	**Reading**	H	W	2-0	Adebayor 30, Gilberto Silva 38
56	prem	**Derby**	A	W	6-2	Bendtner 25, van Persie 39, Adebayor 59, 81, 90, Walcott 78
57	prem	**Everton**	H	W	1-0	Bendtner 77
58	prem	**Sunderland**	A	W	1-0	Walcott 24

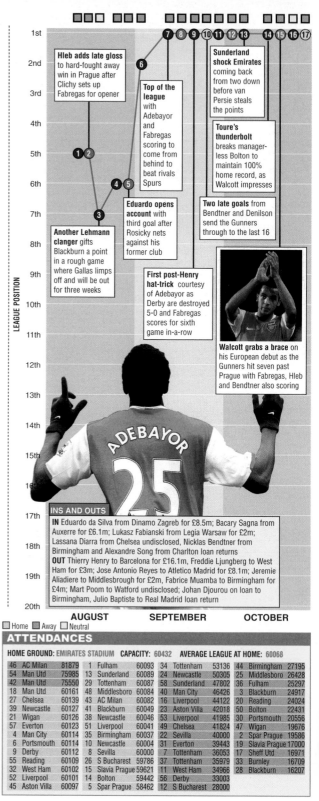

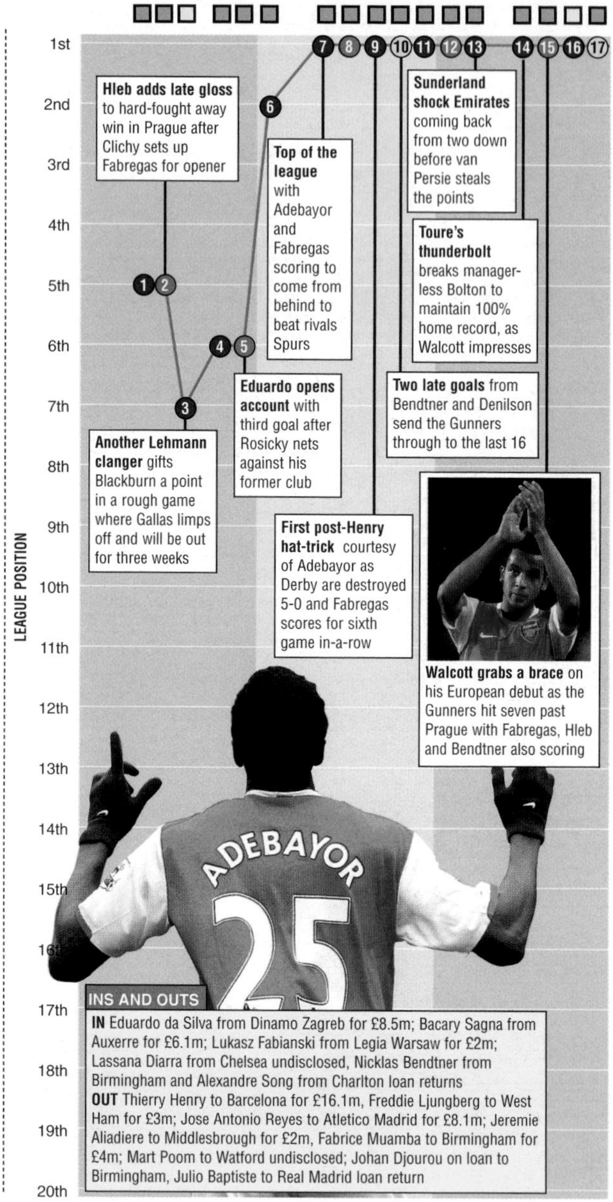

LEAGUE POSITION
1st
2nd
3rd
4th
5th
6th
7th
8th
9th
10th
11th
12th
13th
14th
15th
16th
17th
18th
19th
20th
AUGUST
SEPTEMBER
OCTOBER
Home Away Neutral
Hleb adds late gloss to hard-fought away win in Prague after Clichy sets up Fabregas for opener
Top of the league with Adebayor and Fabregas scoring to come from behind to beat rivals Spurs
Sunderland shock Emirates coming back from two down before van Persie steals the points
Toure's thunderbolt breaks manager-less Bolton to maintain 100% home record, as Walcott impresses
Eduardo opens account with third goal after Rosicky nets against his former club
Two late goals from Bendtner and Denilson send the Gunners through to the last 16
Another Lehmann clanger gifts Blackburn a point in a rough game where Gallas limps off and will be out for three weeks
First post-Henry hat-trick courtesy of Adebayor as Derby are destroyed 5-0 and Fabregas scores for sixth game in-a-row
Walcott grabs a brace on his European debut as the Gunners hit seven past Prague with Fabregas, Hleb and Bendtner also scoring
ADEBAYOR 25

INS AND OUTS

IN Eduardo da Silva from Dinamo Zagreb for £8.5m; Bacary Sagna from Auxerre for £6.1m; Lukasz Fabianski from Legia Warsaw for £2m; Lassana Diarra from Chelsea undisclosed, Nicklas Bendtner from Birmingham and Alexandre Song from Charlton loan returns

OUT Thierry Henry to Barcelona for £16.1m, Freddie Ljungberg to West Ham for £3m; Jose Antonio Reyes to Atletico Madrid for £8.1m; Jeremie Aliadiere to Middlesbrough for £2m, Fabrice Muamba to Birmingham for £4m; Mart Poom to Watford undisclosed; Johan Djourou on loan to Birmingham, Julio Baptiste to Real Madrid loan return

ATTENDANCES

HOME GROUND: EMIRATES STADIUM **CAPACITY:** 60432 **AVERAGE LEAGUE AT HOME:** 60068

46	AC Milan	81879	1	Fulham	60093	34	Tottenham	53136	44	Birmingham	27195
54	Man Utd	75985	13	Sunderland	60089	24	Newcastle	50305	25	Middlesboro	26428
42	Man Utd	75550	29	Tottenham	60087	58	Sunderland	47802	36	Fulham	25297
18	Man Utd	60161	48	Middlesboro	60084	40	Man City	46426	3	Blackburn	24917
27	Chelsea	60139	43	AC Milan	60082	16	Liverpool	44122	20	Reading	24024
39	Newcastle	60127	41	Blackburn	60049	23	Aston Villa	42018	50	Bolton	22431
21	Wigan	60126	38	Newcastle	60046	53	Liverpool	41985	30	Portsmouth	20556
57	Everton	60123	51	Liverpool	60041	49	Chelsea	41824	47	Wigan	19676
4	Man City	60114	35	Birmingham	60037	22	Sevilla	40000	2	Spar Prague	19586
6	Portsmouth	60114	10	Newcastle	60004	31	Everton	39443	19	Slavia Prague	17000
9	Derby	60112	8	Sevilla	60000	7	Tottenham	36053	17	Sheff Utd	16971
55	Reading	60109	26	S Bucharest	59786	37	Tottenham	35979	33	Burnley	16709
32	West Ham	60102	15	Slavia Prague	59621	11	West Ham	34966	28	Blackburn	16207
52	Liverpool	60101	14	Bolton	59442	56	Derby	33003			
45	Aston Villa	60097	5	Spar Prague	58462	12	S Bucharest	28000			

Fabregas leads youngsters over 80 points

Final Position: **3rd**

KEY: League · Champions Lge · UEFA Cup · FA Cup · League Cup · Other

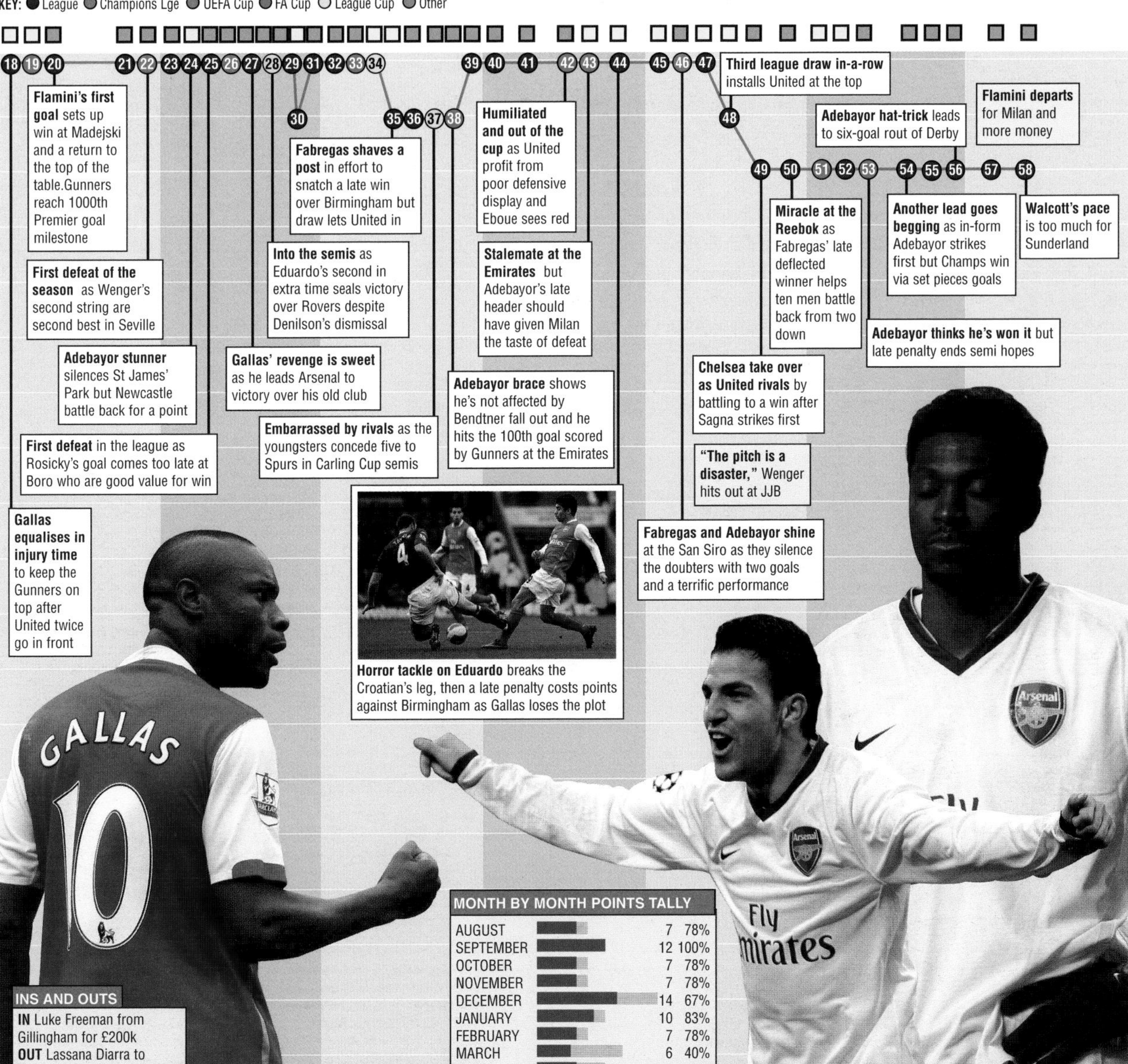

Flamini's first goal sets up win at Madejski and a return to the top of the table.Gunners reach 1000th Premier goal milestone
First defeat of the season as Wenger's second string are second best in Seville
Adebayor stunner silences St James' Park but Newcastle battle back for a point
First defeat in the league as Rosicky's goal comes too late at Boro who are good value for win
Gallas equalises in injury time to keep the Gunners on top after United twice go in front
Fabregas shaves a post in effort to snatch a late win over Birmingham but draw lets United in
Into the semis as Eduardo's second in extra time seals victory over Rovers despite Denilson's dismissal
Gallas' revenge is sweet as he leads Arsenal to victory over his old club
Embarrassed by rivals as the youngsters concede five to Spurs in Carling Cup semis
Humiliated and out of the cup as United profit from poor defensive display and Eboue sees red
Stalemate at the Emirates but Adebayor's late header should have given Milan the taste of defeat
Adebayor brace shows he's not affected by Bendtner fall out and he hits the 100th goal scored by Gunners at the Emirates
Horror tackle on Eduardo breaks the Croatian's leg, then a late penalty costs points against Birmingham as Gallas loses the plot
Third league draw in-a-row installs United at the top
Adebayor hat-trick leads to six-goal rout of Derby
Flamini departs for Milan and more money
Miracle at the Reebok as Fabregas' late deflected winner helps ten men battle back from two down
Another lead goes begging as in-form Adebayor strikes first but Champs win via set pieces goals
Walcott's pace is too much for Sunderland
Adebayor thinks he's won it but late penalty ends semi hopes
Chelsea take over as United rivals by battling to a win after Sagna strikes first
"The pitch is a disaster," Wenger hits out at JJB
Fabregas and Adebayor shine at the San Siro as they silence the doubters with two goals and a terrific performance
GALLAS
10
Fly Emirates

INS AND OUTS

IN Luke Freeman from Gillingham for £200k
OUT Lassana Diarra to Portsmouth for £5.5m; Mark Randall to Burnley on loan

MONTH BY MONTH POINTS TALLY

Month	Points	%
AUGUST	7	78%
SEPTEMBER	12	100%
OCTOBER	7	78%
NOVEMBER	7	78%
DECEMBER	14	67%
JANUARY	10	83%
FEBRUARY	7	78%
MARCH	6	40%
APRIL	7	58%
MAY	6	100%

NOVEMBER DECEMBER JANUARY FEBRUARY MARCH APRIL MAY

GOAL ATTEMPTS

FOR — Goal attempts recorded in League games

	HOME	AWAY	TOTAL	AVE
shots on target	145	140	285	7.5
shots off target	134	113	247	6.5
TOTAL	279	253	532	14.0

Ratio of goals to shots Average number of shots on target per League goal scored: 3.9

Accuracy rating Average percentage of total goal attempts which were on target: 53.6

AGAINST — Goal attempts recorded in League games

	HOME	AWAY	TOTAL	AVE
shots on target	100	104	204	5.4
shots off target	67	92	159	4.2
TOTAL	167	196	363	9.6

Ratio of goals to shots Average number of shots on target per League goal scored: 6.6

Accuracy rating Average percentage of total goal attempts which were on target: 56.2

GOALS

Adebayor

League	24
FA Cup	2
League Cup	1
Europe	3
Other	0
TOTAL	30

League Average 122 mins between goals

	PLAYER	LGE	FAC	LC	Euro	TOT	AVE
1	Adebayor	24	2	1	3	30	122
2	Fabregas	7	0	0	6	13	408
3	da Silva	4	1	4	3	12	240
4	van Persie	7	0	0	2	9	153
5	Bendtner	5	1	1	2	9	187
6	Rosicky	6	0	0	1	7	222
7	Walcott	4	0	1	2	7	314
8	Gallas	4	0	0	0	4	681
9	Diaby	1	0	1	2	4	716
10	Hleb	2	0	0	2	4	1215
11	Flamini	3	0	0	0	3	887
12	Senderos	2	0	0	0	2	622
13	Toure	2	0	0	0	2	1282
14	Denilson	0	0	2	0	2	
15	Gilberto Silva	1	0	0	0	1	1189
	Other	1	0	0	0	1	
	TOTAL	73	4	10	23	110	

SQUAD APPEARANCES

Match	1	2	3	4	5	6	7	8	9	10	11	12	13	14	15	16	17	18	19	20	21	22	23	24	25	26	27	28	29	30	31	32	33	34	35	36	37	38	39	40	41	42	43	44	45	46	47	48	49	50	51	52	53	54	55	56	57	58
Venue	H	A	A	H	H	H	A	H	H	H	A	A	H	H	H	A	A	H	A	A	H	A	A	A	A	H	H	A	H	A	A	H	A	H	H	A	A	H	H	A	H	A	H	A	H	A	A	H	A	A	H	H	A	A	H	A	H	A
Competition	L	C	L	L	C	L	L	C	L	W	L	C	L	L	C	L	W	L	C	L	L	C	L	L	L	C	L	W	L	L	L	L	F	W	L	L	W	F	L	L	L	F	C	L	L	C	L	L	L	L	C	L	C	L	L	L	L	L
Result	W	W	D	W	W	W	W	W	W	W	W	W	W	W	W	D	W	D	D	W	W	L	W	D	L	W	W	W	W	D	W	W	W	D	D	W	L	W	W	W	W	L	D	D	D	W	D	D	L	W	D	D	L	L	W	W	W	W

Goalkeepers
Manuel Almunia
Lukasz Fabianski
Jens Lehmann
Vito Mannone

Defenders
Gael Clichy
Johan Djourou
Emmanuel Eboue
William Gallas
Kerrea Gilbert
Gavin Hoyte
Justin Hoyte
Bacary Sagna
Philippe Senderos
Habib Kolo Toure
Armand Traore

Midfielders
Nacer Barazite
Denilson
Vassiriki Diaby
Lassana Diarra
Francesc Fabregas
Mathieu Flamini
Gilberto Silva
Alexander Hleb
Henri Lansbury
Francisco Merida Perez
Mark Randall
Tomas Rosicky
Alexandre Song
Theo Walcott

Forwards
Emmanuel Adebayor
Nicklas Bendtner
Eduardo da Silva
Kieran Gibbs
Robin van Persie

KEY: On all match · On bench · Subbed or sent off (Counting game) · Subbed or sent off (playing less than 70 mins) · Subbed on from bench (Counting Game) · Subbed on (playing less than 70 mins) · Subbed on and then subbed or sent off (Counting Game) · Subbed on and then subbed or sent off (playing less than 70 min · Not in 16 · Injured · ✕ Suspended

KEY PLAYERS - GOALSCORERS

Emmanuel Adebayor

Goals in the League	24
Goals in all competitions	30
Assists League goals scored by a team mate where the player delivered the final pass	5
Contribution to Attacking Power Average number of minutes between League team goals while on pitch	45
Player Strike Rate Average number of minutes between League goals scored by player	122
Club Strike Rate Average minutes between League goals scored by club	46

	PLAYER	GOALS LGE	GOALS ALL	ASSISTS	POWER	S RATE
1	Emmanuel Adebayor	24	30	5	45	122 mins
2	Robin van Persie	7	9	5	53	153 mins
3	Tomas Rosicky	6	7	2	47	222 mins
4	Francesc Fabregas	7	13	20	45	408 mins

KEY PLAYERS - MIDFIELDERS

Tomas Rosicky

Goals in the League	6
Goals in all competitions	7
Assists League goals scored by a team mate where the player delivered the final pass	2
Defensive Rating Average number of mins between League goals conceded while on the pitch	148
Contribution to Attacking Power Average number of minutes between League team goals while on pitch	47
Scoring Difference Defensive Rating minus Contribution to Attacking Power	101

	PLAYER	GOALS LGE	GOALS ALL	ASSISTS	DEF RATE	POWER	SC DIFF
1	Tomas Rosicky	6	7	2	148	47	101 mins
2	Mathieu Flamini	3	3	2	110	46	64 mins
3	Alexander Hleb	2	4	11	110	47	63 mins
4	Francesc Fabregas	7	13	20	105	45	60 mins

PLAYER APPEARANCES

	AGE (on 01/07/08)	IN NAMED 16	APPEARANCES	COUNTING GAMES	MINUTES ON PITCH	APPEARANCES	MINUTES ON PITCH	THIS SEASON	HOME COUNTRY
Goalkeepers									
Manuel Almunia	31	32	29	29	2610	38	3420	-	Spain
Lukasz Fabianski	23	13	3	3	248	8	728	2	Poland
Jens Lehmann	38	29	7	6	562	13	1102	12	Germany
Vito Mannone	20	2	0	0	0	0	0	-	Italy
Defenders									
Gael Clichy	22	38	38	37	3330	49	4320	-	France
Johan Djourou	21	4	2	1	103	3	148	3	Switzerland
Emmanuel Eboue	25	24	23	14	1654	36	2511	6	Ivory Coast
William Gallas	30	31	31	30	2724	42	3714	9	France
Kerrea Gilbert	21	1	0	0	0	0	0	-	England
Gavin Hoyte	17	0	0	0	0	0	0	-	England
Justin Hoyte	23	12	5	1	155	15	990	-	England
Bacary Sagna	25	29	29	26	2458	40	3317	2	France
Philippe Senderos	23	27	17	12	1245	32	2549	9	Switzerland
Habib Kolo Toure	27	30	30	28	2565	41	3471	4	Ivory Coast
Armand Traore	18	5	3	1	103	11	807	-	France
Midfielders									
Nacer Barazite	18	1	0	0	0	2	26	-	Holland
Denilson	20	15	13	4	547	23	1302	-	Brazil
Vassiriki Diaby	22	16	15	5	716	28	1723	-	France
Lassana Diarra	23	10	7	3	370	13	785	-	France
Francesc Fabregas	21	32	32	32	2856	45	3885	10	Spain
Mathieu Flamini	24	30	30	30	2662	40	3416	2	France
Gilberto Silva	31	28	23	11	1189	36	2020	5	Brazil
Alexander Hleb	27	31	31	26	2430	42	3295	5	Belarus
Henri Lansbury	17	0	0	0	0	1	8	-	England
Francisco Perez	18	0	0	0	0	3	25	-	Spain
Mark Randall	18	1	1	0	10	3	90	-	England
Tomas Rosicky	27	18	18	14	1337	24	1607	3	Czech Republic
Alexandre Song	20	16	9	5	469	15	960	6	Cameroon
Theo Walcott	19	29	25	10	1256	39	2115	1	England
Forwards									
Emmanuel Adebayor	24	36	36	32	2929	48	3697	1	Togo
Nicklas Bendtner	20	32	27	6	938	40	1923	8	Denmark
Eduardo da Silva	25	18	17	7	963	31	1931	5	Croatia
Kieran Gibbs	18	1	0	0	0	2	96	-	England
Robin van Persie	24	16	15	11	1073	23	1578	8	Holland

KEY: LEAGUE ALL COMPS CAPS (MAY FIFA RANKING)

TEAM OF THE SEASON

ALMUNIA

CG 29 DR 108

EBOUE
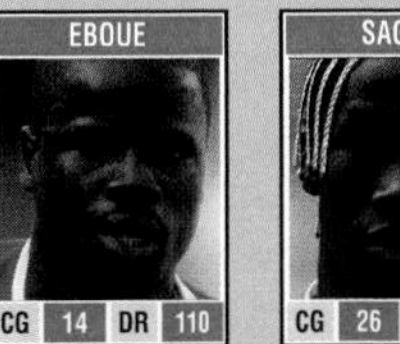
CG 14 DR 110

SAGNA

CG 26 DR 117

SENDEROS

CG 12 DR 124

CLICHY

CG 37 DR 111

HLEB

CG 26 SD +63

FLAMINI

CG 30 SD +64

FABREGAS

CG 32 SD +60

ROSICKY

CG 14 SD +101

VAN PERSIE

CG 11* AP 53

ADEBAYOR

CG 32 SR 122

KEY: DR = Defensive Rate, SD = Scoring Difference AP = Attacking Power SR = Strike Rate, CG=Counting games – League games playing at least 70 minutes

TOP POINT EARNERS

Tomas Rosicky	
Counting Games League games when player was on pitch for at least 70 minutes	14
Average points Average League points taken in Counting games	2.36
Club Average points Average points taken in League games	2.18

	PLAYER	GAMES	PTS
1	Tomas Rosicky	14	2.36
2	Philippe Senderos	12	2.33
3	Mathieu Flamini	30	2.23
4	Gael Clichy	37	2.22
5	Francesc Fabregas	32	2.19
6	Habib Kolo Toure	28	2.18
7	Emmanuel Adebayor	32	2.16
8	Manuel Almunia	29	2.10
9	Alexander Hleb	26	2.08
10	Bacary Sagna	26	2.08

KEY PLAYERS - DEFENDERS

Philippe Senderos	
Goals Conceded in the League Number of League goals conceded while the player was on the pitch	10
Goals Conceded in all competitions Total number of goals conceded while the player was on the pitch	23
League minutes played Number of minutes played in league matches	1245
Clean Sheets In games when the player was on pitch for at least 70 minutes	7
Defensive Rating Average number of mins between League goals conceded while on the pitch	124
Club Defensive Rating Average number of mins between League goals conceded by the club this season	110

Fly
Emirates

	PLAYER	CON LGE	CON ALL	MINS	C SHEETS	DEF RATE
1	Philippe Senderos	10	23	1245	7	124 mins
2	Bacary Sagna	21	28	2458	11	117 mins
3	Gael Clichy	30	35	3330	15	111 mins
4	Emmanuel Eboue	15	23	1654	4	110 mins

KEY GOALKEEPER

Manuel Almunia	
Goals Conceded in the League Number of League goals conceded while the player was on the pitch	24
Goals Conceded in all competitions Total number of goals conceded while the player was on the pitch	32
League minutes played Number of minutes played in league matches	2610
Clean Sheets In games when the player was on pitch for at least 70 minutes	11
Goals to Shots Ratio The average number of shots on target per each League goal conceded	6.63
Defensive Rating Ave mins between League goals conceded while on the pitch	108

BOOKINGS

Emmanuel Eboue	
League Yellow	6
League Red	0
All competitions Yellow	8
All competitions Red	1
League Average **275** mins between cards	

	PLAYER	LEAGUE		TOTAL		AVE
1	E Eboue	6Y	0R	8Y	1R	275
2	Nicklas Bendtner	2	1	3	1	312
3	Francesc Fabregas	9	0	10	0	317
4	Eduardo da Silva	3	0	5	0	321
5	William Gallas	6	0	7	0	454
6	Mathieu Flamini	5	0	7	0	532
7	Robin van Persie	2	0	4	0	536
8	Jens Lehmann	1	0	1	0	562
9	Alexander Hleb	4	0	6	0	607
10	Habib Kolo Toure	4	0	5	0	641
11	Gael Clichy	5	0	7	0	666
12	Vassiriki Diaby	0	1	0	1	716
13	Bacary Sagna	3	0	3	0	819
14	E Adebayor	3	0	7	0	976
15	Gilberto Silva	1	0	2	0	1189
	Other	1	1	7	2	
	TOTAL	55	3	82	5	

LIVERPOOL

Fernando Torres added a huge buzz to Liverpool fans' enjoyment of the season. While behind the scenes the US owners did their best to wreck the euphoria with battles over **Rafael Benitez**, Rick Parry, the Dubai International Consortium and ultimately each-other. However, when Torres was scoring consecutive hat-tricks, finishing second in the league scoring charts with Emmanuel Adebayor and levelling the club's record for consecutive home scoring games, it was easy to forget that once again Benitez had lost sight of the league title by mid-season. **Steven Gerrard** didn't forget though and is desperate that the ownership squabbles don't wreck the manager's transfer plans to help the side compete next season.

NICKNAME: THE REDS

KEY: Won, Drawn, Lost

1	prem	**Aston Villa**	A	W	2-1	Laursen 31 og, Gerrard 86
2	ecql1	**Toulouse**	A	W	1-0	Voronin 43
3	prem	**Chelsea**	H	D	1-1	Torres 16
4	prem	**Sunderland**	A	W	2-0	Sissoko 37, Voronin 87
5	ecql2	**Toulouse**	H	W	4-0	Crouch 19, Hyypia 49, Kuyt 87, 90
6	prem	**Derby**	H	W	6-0	Xabi Alonso 26, 69, Babel 45, Torres 56, 78, Voronin 76
7	prem	**Portsmouth**	A	D	0-0	
8	ecgpa	**Porto**	A	D	1-1	Kuyt 17
9	prem	**Birmingham**	H	D	0-0	
10	ccr3	**Reading**	A	W	4-2	Benayoun 23, Torres 50, 72, 86
11	prem	**Wigan**	A	W	1-0	Benayoun 75
12	ecgpa	**Marseille**	H	L	0-1	
13	prem	**Tottenham**	H	D	2-2	Voronin 13, Torres 90
14	prem	**Everton**	A	W	2-1	Kuyt 54 pen, 90 pen
15	ecgpa	**Besiktas**	A	L	1-2	Gerrard 85
16	prem	**Arsenal**	H	D	1-1	Gerrard 7
17	ccr4	**Cardiff**	H	W	2-1	El Zhar 48, Gerrard 66
18	prem	**Blackburn**	A	D	0-0	
19	ecgpa	**Besiktas**	H	W	8-0	Crouch 19, 89, Benayoun 32, 53, 56, Gerrard 69, Babel 78, 81
20	prem	**Fulham**	H	W	2-0	Torres 81, Gerrard 85 pen
21	prem	**Newcastle**	A	W	3-0	Gerrard 28, Kuyt 46, Babel 66
22	ecgpa	**Porto**	H	W	4-1	Torres 19, 78, Gerrard 83 pen, Crouch 87
23	prem	**Bolton**	H	W	4-0	Hyypia 18, Torres 45, Gerrard 56 pen, Babel 85
24	prem	**Reading**	A	L	1-3	Gerrard 28
25	ecgpa	**Marseille**	A	W	4-0	Gerrard 4, Torres 11, Kuyt 48, Babel 90
26	prem	**Man Utd**	H	L	0-1	
27	ccqf	**Chelsea**	A	L	0-2	
28	prem	**Portsmouth**	H	W	4-1	Benayoun 13, Distin 16 og, Torres 67, 85
29	prem	**Derby**	A	W	2-1	Torres 13, Gerrard 90
30	prem	**Man City**	A	D	0-0	
31	prem	**Wigan**	H	D	1-1	Torres 49
32	facr3	**Luton**	A	D	1-1	Crouch 74
33	prem	**Middlesbrough**	A	D	1-1	Torres 71
34	facr3r	**Luton**	H	W	5-0	Babel 45, Gerrard 52, 64, 71, Hyypia 57
35	prem	**Aston Villa**	H	D	2-2	Benayoun 19, Crouch 88
36	facr4	**Havant and W**	H	W	5-2	Leiva 27, Benayoun 44, 56, 59, Crouch 90
37	prem	**West Ham**	A	L	0-1	
38	prem	**Sunderland**	H	W	3-0	Crouch 57, Torres 69, Gerrard 89 pen
39	prem	**Chelsea**	A	D	0-0	
40	facr5	**Barnsley**	H	L	1-2	Kuyt 32
41	eckl1	**Inter Milan**	H	W	2-0	Kuyt 85, Gerrard 90
42	prem	**Middlesbrough**	H	W	3-2	Torres 28, 29, 61
43	prem	**Bolton**	A	W	3-1	Jaaskelainen 11 og, Babel 60, Aurelio 75
44	prem	**West Ham**	H	W	4-0	Torres 8, 61, 81, Gerrard 83
45	prem	**Newcastle**	H	W	3-0	Pennant 43, Torres 45, Gerrard 51
46	eckl2	**Inter Milan**	A	W	1-0	Torres 64
47	prem	**Reading**	H	W	2-1	Mascherano 19, Torres 48
48	prem	**Man Utd**	A	L	0-3	
49	prem	**Everton**	H	W	1-0	Torres 7
50	ecqfl1	**Arsenal**	A	D	1-1	Kuyt 26
51	prem	**Arsenal**	A	D	1-1	Crouch 42
52	ecqfl2	**Arsenal**	H	W	4-2	Hyypia 30, Torres 69, Gerrard 85 pen, Babel 90
53	prem	**Blackburn**	H	W	3-1	Gerrard 60, Torres 82, Voronin 90
54	prem	**Fulham**	A	W	2-0	Pennant 17, Crouch 70
55	ecsfl1	**Chelsea**	H	D	1-1	Kuyt 43
56	prem	**Birmingham**	A	D	2-2	Crouch 63, Benayoun 76
57	ecsfl2	**Chelsea**	A	L	2-3	Torres 64, Babel 117
58	prem	**Man City**	H	W	1-0	Torres 58
59	prem	**Tottenham**	A	W	2-0	Voronin 69, Torres 74

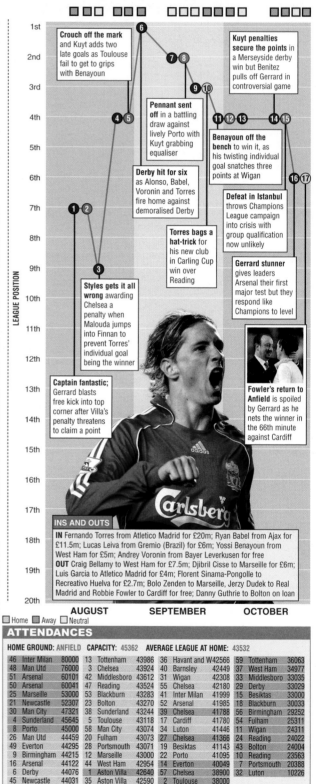

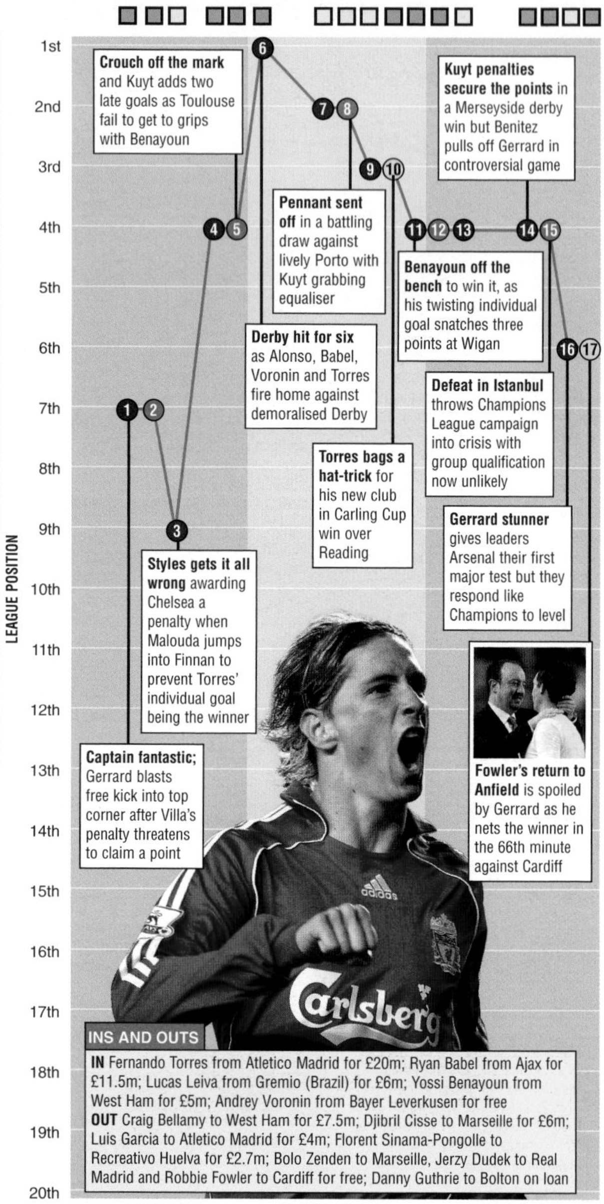

LEAGUE POSITION: 1st – 20th; AUGUST, SEPTEMBER, OCTOBER

Crouch off the mark and Kuyt adds two late goals as Toulouse fail to get to grips with Benayoun

Kuyt penalties secure the points in a Merseyside derby win but Benitez pulls off Gerrard in controversial game

Pennant sent off in a battling draw against lively Porto with Kuyt grabbing equaliser

Benayoun off the bench to win it, as his twisting individual goal snatches three points at Wigan

Derby hit for six as Alonso, Babel, Voronin and Torres fire home against demoralised Derby

Defeat in Istanbul throws Champions League campaign into crisis with group qualification now unlikely

Torres bags a hat-trick for his new club in Carling Cup win over Reading

Gerrard stunner gives leaders Arsenal their first major test but they respond like Champions to level

Styles gets it all wrong awarding Chelsea a penalty when Malouda jumps into Finnan to prevent Torres' individual goal being the winner

Captain fantastic; Gerrard blasts free kick into top corner after Villa's penalty threatens to claim a point

Fowler's return to Anfield is spoiled by Gerrard as he nets the winner in the 66th minute against Cardiff

INS AND OUTS

IN Fernando Torres from Atletico Madrid for £20m; Ryan Babel from Ajax for £11.5m; Lucas Leiva from Gremio (Brazil) for £6m; Yossi Benayoun from West Ham for £5m; Andrey Voronin from Bayer Leverkusen for free
OUT Craig Bellamy to West Ham for £7.5m; Djibril Cisse to Marseille for £6m; Luis Garcia to Atletico Madrid for £4m; Florent Sinama-Pongolle to Recreativo Huelva for £2.7m; Bolo Zenden to Marseille, Jerzy Dudek to Real Madrid and Robbie Fowler to Cardiff for free; Danny Guthrie to Bolton on loan

Home, Away, Neutral

ATTENDANCES

HOME GROUND: ANFIELD **CAPACITY:** 45362 **AVERAGE LEAGUE AT HOME:** 43532

46	Inter Milan	80000	13	Tottenham	43986	36	Havant and W	42566	59	Tottenham	36063
48	Man Utd	76000	3	Chelsea	43924	40	Barnsley	42449	37	West Ham	34977
51	Arsenal	60101	42	Middlesboro	43612	31	Wigan	42308	33	Middlesboro	33035
50	Arsenal	60041	47	Reading	43524	55	Chelsea	42180	29	Derby	33029
25	Marseille	53000	53	Blackburn	43283	41	Inter Milan	41999	15	Besiktas	33000
21	Newcastle	52307	23	Bolton	43270	52	Arsenal	41985	18	Blackburn	30033
30	Man City	47321	38	Sunderland	43244	39	Chelsea	41788	56	Birmingham	29252
4	Sunderland	45645	5	Toulouse	43118	17	Cardiff	41780	54	Fulham	25311
8	Porto	45000	58	Man City	43074	34	Luton	41446	11	Wigan	24311
26	Man Utd	44459	20	Fulham	43073	27	Chelsea	41366	24	Reading	24022
49	Everton	44295	28	Portsmouth	43071	19	Besiktas	41143	43	Bolton	24004
9	Birmingham	44215	12	Marseille	43000	22	Porto	41095	10	Reading	23563
16	Arsenal	44122	44	West Ham	42954	14	Everton	40049	7	Portsmouth	20388
6	Derby	44076	1	Aston Villa	42640	57	Chelsea	38900	32	Luton	10226
45	Newcastle	44031	35	Aston Villa	42590	2	Toulouse	38000			

Torres stars while owners fight it out

Final Position: **4th**

KEY: ● League ● Champions Lge ● UEFA Cup ● FA Cup ○ League Cup ● Other

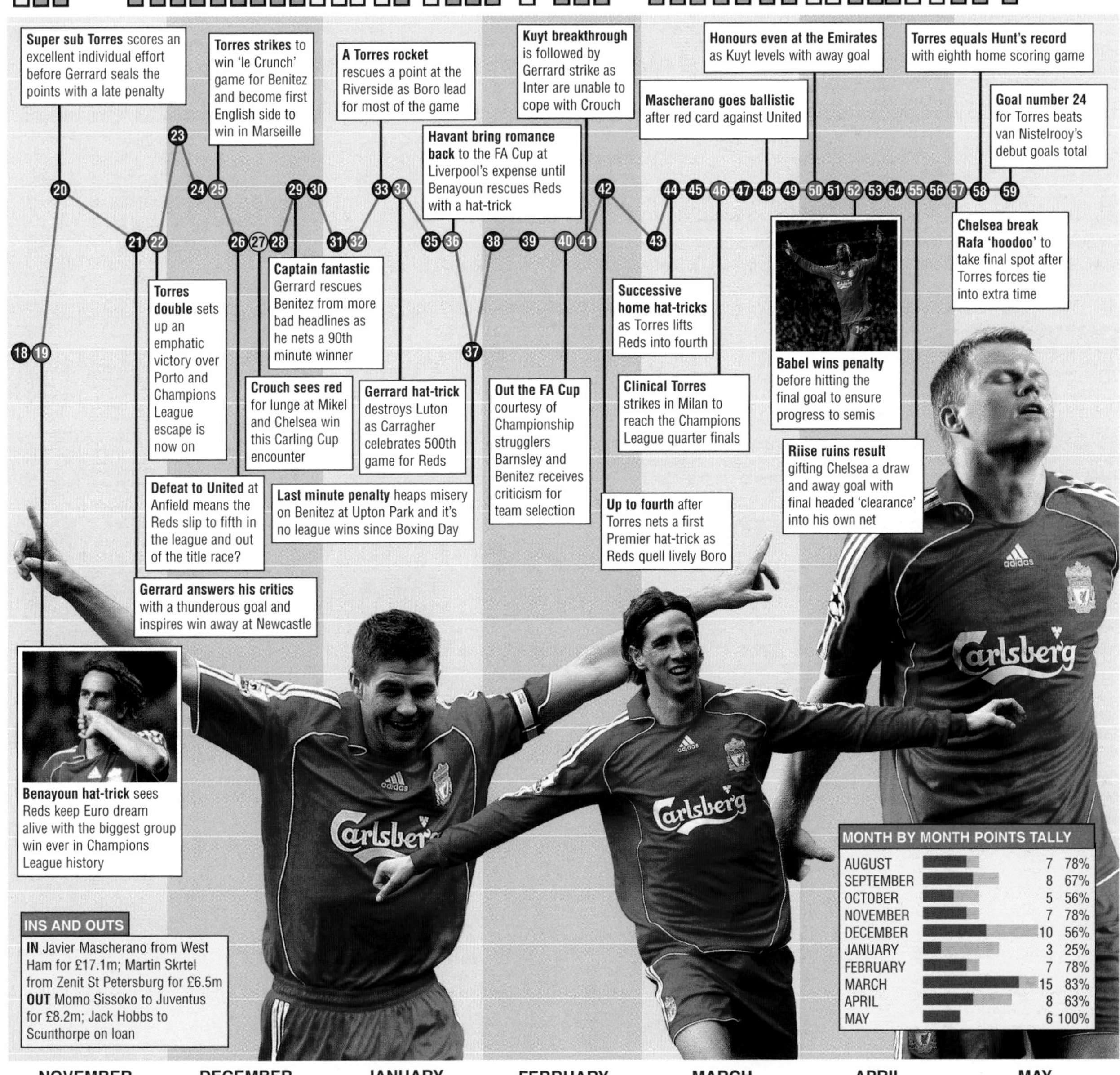

Benayoun hat-trick sees Reds keep Euro dream alive with the biggest group win ever in Champions League history
Super sub Torres scores an excellent individual effort before Gerrard seals the points with a late penalty
Gerrard answers his critics with a thunderous goal and inspires win away at Newcastle
Torres double sets up an emphatic victory over Porto and Champions League escape is now on
Torres strikes to win 'le Crunch' game for Benitez and become first English side to win in Marseille
Defeat to United at Anfield means the Reds slip to fifth in the league and out of the title race?
Crouch sees red for lunge at Mikel and Chelsea win this Carling Cup encounter
Captain fantastic Gerrard rescues Benitez from more bad headlines as he nets a 90th minute winner
Last minute penalty heaps misery on Benitez at Upton Park and it's no league wins since Boxing Day
A Torres rocket rescues a point at the Riverside as Boro lead for most of the game
Gerrard hat-trick destroys Luton as Carragher celebrates 500th game for Reds
Havant bring romance back to the FA Cup at Liverpool's expense until Benayoun rescues Reds with a hat-trick
Out the FA Cup courtesy of Championship strugglers Barnsley and Benitez receives criticism for team selection
Kuyt breakthrough is followed by Gerrard strike as Inter are unable to cope with Crouch
Up to fourth after Torres nets a first Premier hat-trick as Reds quell lively Boro
Successive home hat-tricks as Torres lifts Reds into fourth
Mascherano goes ballistic after red card against United
Clinical Torres strikes in Milan to reach the Champions League quarter finals
Honours even at the Emirates as Kuyt levels with away goal
Babel wins penalty before hitting the final goal to ensure progress to semis
Riise ruins result gifting Chelsea a draw and away goal with final headed 'clearance' into his own net
Torres equals Hunt's record with eighth home scoring game
Goal number 24 for Torres beats van Nistelrooy's debut goals total
Chelsea break Rafa 'hoodoo' to take final spot after Torres forces tie into extra time
NOVEMBER
DECEMBER
JANUARY
FEBRUARY
MARCH
APRIL
MAY

INS AND OUTS

IN Javier Mascherano from West Ham for £17.1m; Martin Skrtel from Zenit St Petersburg for £6.5m
OUT Momo Sissoko to Juventus for £8.2m; Jack Hobbs to Scunthorpe on loan

MONTH BY MONTH POINTS TALLY

Month	Points	%
AUGUST	7	78%
SEPTEMBER	8	67%
OCTOBER	5	56%
NOVEMBER	7	78%
DECEMBER	10	56%
JANUARY	3	25%
FEBRUARY	7	78%
MARCH	15	83%
APRIL	8	63%
MAY	6	100%

GOAL ATTEMPTS

FOR – Goal attempts recorded in League games

	HOME	AWAY	TOTAL	AVE
shots on target	155	134	289	7.6
shots off target	158	125	283	7.4
TOTAL	313	259	572	15.1

Ratio of goals to shots – Average number of shots on target per League goal scored: **4.3**

Accuracy rating – Average percentage of total goal attempts which were on target: **50.5**

AGAINST – Goal attempts recorded in League games

	HOME	AWAY	TOTAL	AVE
shots on target	88	89	177	4.7
shots off target	66	89	155	4.1
TOTAL	154	178	332	8.7

Ratio of goals to shots – Average number of shots on target per League goal scored: **6.3**

Accuracy rating – Average percentage of total goal attempts which were on target: **53.3**

GOALS

Torres

League	24
FA Cup	0
League Cup	3
Europe	6
Other	0
TOTAL	33

League Average **106** mins between goals

	PLAYER	LGE	FAC	LC	Euro	TOT	AVE
1	Torres	24	0	3	6	33	106
2	Gerrard	11	3	1	6	22	258
3	Crouch	5	2	0	4	11	182
4	Benayoun	4	3	1	3	11	395
5	Kuyt	3	1	0	7	11	721
6	Babel	4	1	0	5	10	354
7	Voronin	5	0	0	1	6	224
8	Hyypia	1	1	0	2	4	2025
9	Pennant	2	0	0	0	2	564
10	Alonso	2	0	0	0	2	734
11	Sissoko	1	0	0	0	1	554
12	Aurelio	1	0	0	0	1	1125
13	Mascherano	1	0	0	0	1	2154
14	El Zhar	0	0	1	0	1	
15	Leiva	0	1	0	0	1	
	Other	0	0	0	0	0	
	TOTAL	64	12	6	34	117	

SQUAD APPEARANCES

Match	1 2 3 4 5	6 7 8 9 10	11 12 13 14 15	16 17 18 19 20	21 22 23 24 25	26 27 28 29 30	31 32 33 34 35	36 37 38 39 40	41 42 43 44 45	46 47 48 49 50	51 52 53 54 55	56 57 58 59
Venue	A A H A H	H A A H A	A H H A A	H H A H H	A H H A A	H A H A A	H A A H H	H A H A H	H H A H H	A H A H A	A H H A H	A A H A
Competition	L C L L C	L L C L W	L C L L C	L W L C L	L C L L C	L W L L L	L F L F L	F L L L F	C L L L L	C L L L C	L C L L C	L C L L
Result	W W D W W	W D D D W	W L D W L	D W D W W	W W W L W	L L W W D	D D D W D	W L W D L	W W W W W	W W L W D	D W W W D	D L W W

Goalkeepers
Charles-Hubert Itandje
David Martin
Jose Reina

Defenders
Daniel Agger
Alvaro Arbeloa
Fabio Aurelio
Jamie Carragher
Steve Finnan
Jack Hobbs
Sami Hyypia
Emiliano Insua
Mikel San Jose
Martin Skrtel

Midfielders
Xabi Alonso
Yossi Benayoun
Steven Gerrard
Harry Kewell
Lucas Leiva
Sebastian Leto
Javier Mascherano
Jermaine Pennant
Damien Plessis
Ray Putterill
John Arne Riise
Momo Sissoko

Forwards
Ryan Babel
Peter Crouch
Nabil El Zhar
Dirk Kuyt
Fernando Torres
Andrey Voronin

KEY: On all match · On bench · Subbed or sent off (Counting game) · Subbed or sent off (playing less than 70 mins) · Subbed on from bench (Counting Game) · Subbed on (playing less than 70 mins) · Subbed on and then subbed or sent off (Counting Game) · Subbed on and then subbed or sent off (playing less than 70 min) · Not in 16 · Injured · ✕ Suspended

KEY PLAYERS - GOALSCORERS

Fernando Torres

Goals in the League	24
Goals in all competitions	33
Assists League goals scored by a team mate where the player delivered the final pass	4
Contribution to Attacking Power Average number of minutes between League team goals while on pitch	44
Player Strike Rate Average number of minutes between League goals scored by player	106
Club Strike Rate Average minutes between League goals scored by club	51

	PLAYER	GOALS LGE	GOALS ALL	ASSISTS	POWER	S RATE
1	Fernando Torres	24	33	4	44	106 mins
2	Andrey Voronin	5	6	4	62	224 mins
3	Steven Gerrard	11	22	13	53	258 mins
4	Yossi Benayoun	4	11	5	47	395 mins

KEY PLAYERS - MIDFIELDERS

Xabi Alonso

Goals in the League	2
Goals in all competitions	2
Assists League goals scored by a team mate where the player delivered the final pass	2
Defensive Rating Average number of mins between League goals conceded while on the pitch	146
Contribution to Attacking Power Average number of minutes between League team goals while on pitch	47
Scoring Difference Defensive Rating minus Contribution to Attacking Power	99

	PLAYER	GOALS LGE	GOALS ALL	ASSISTS	DEF RATE	POWER	SC DIFF
1	Xabi Alonso	2	2	2	146	47	99 mins
2	Javier Mascherano	1	1	2	119	53	66 mins
3	Steven Gerrard	11	22	13	113	53	60 mins
4	Yossi Benayoun	4	11	5	98	47	51 mins

PLAYER APPEARANCES

	AGE (on 01/07/08)	IN NAMED 16	APPEARANCES	COUNTING GAMES	MINUTES ON PITCH	APPEARANCES	MINUTES ON PITCH	THIS SEASON	HOME COUNTRY
Goalkeepers									
Charles-H Itandje	25	34	0	0	0	7	630	-	France
David Martin	22	4	0	0	0	0	0	-	England
Jose Reina	25	38	38	38	3420	52	4710	3	Spain
Defenders									
Daniel Agger	23	6	5	5	435	6	515	3	Denmark
Alvaro Arbeloa	25	29	28	24	2274	41	3385	3	Spain
Fabio Aurelio	28	16	16	11	1125	29	1972	-	Brazil
Jamie Carragher	30	36	35	33	3040	55	4787	-	England
Steve Finnan	32	27	24	21	1959	35	2869	4	Rep of Ireland
Jack Hobbs	19	2	2	1	130	5	312	-	England
Sami Hyypia	34	35	27	21	2025	44	3549	7	Finland
Emiliano Insua	19	3	3	2	206	3	206	-	Argentina
Mikel San Jose	19	1	0	0	0	0	0	-	Spain
Martin Skrtel	23	17	14	13	1191	20	1662	3	Slovakia
Midfielders									
Xabi Alonso	26	21	19	15	1469	27	2157	7	Spain
Yossi Benayoun	28	32	30	13	1581	47	2640	3	Israel
Steven Gerrard	28	35	34	31	2839	52	4190	10	England
Harry Kewell	28	11	10	4	601	15	755	-	Australia
Lucas Leiva	21	21	18	11	1110	32	1875	1	Brazil
Sebastian Leto	21	0	0	0	0	4	277	-	Argentina
Javier Mascherano	24	30	25	24	2154	41	3443	8	Argentina
Jermaine Pennant	25	18	18	11	1129	25	1489	-	England
Damien Plessis	20	2	2	2	180	2	180	-	France
Ray Putterill	19	0	0	0	0	0	0	-	England
John Arne Riise	27	32	29	20	1988	44	2964	6	Norway
Momo Sissoko	23	10	9	6	554	14	917	2	Mali
Forwards									
Ryan Babel	21	33	30	8	1417	49	2600	11	Holland
Peter Crouch	27	26	21	8	914	36	1948	9	England
Nabil El Zhar	21	0	0	0	0	3	106	-	Morocco
Dirk Kuyt	27	34	32	23	2163	48	3324	11	Holland
Fernando Torres	24	34	33	27	2549	46	3593	8	Spain
Andrey Voronin	28	21	19	12	1120	28	1573	7	Ukraine

KEY: LEAGUE ALL COMPS CAPS (MAY FIFA RANKING)

TEAM OF THE SEASON

REINA

CG 38 DR 122

FINNAN

CG 21 DR 130

SKRTEL

CG 13 DR 119

HYYPIA

CG 21 DR 135

CARRAGHER

CG 33 DR 126

GERRARD

CG 31 SD +60

MASCHERANO

CG 24 SD +66

ALONSO

CG 15 SD +99

BENAYOUN

CG 13 SD +51

VORONIN

CG 12 AP 62

TORRES

CG 27 SR 106

KEY: DR = Defensive Rate, SD = Scoring Difference AP = Attacking Power SR = Strike Rate, CG=Counting games – League games playing at least 70 minutes

TOP POINT EARNERS

Martin Skrtel

Counting Games League games when player was on pitch for at least 70 minutes	13
Average points Average League points taken in Counting games	2.31
Club Average points Average points taken in League games	2.00

	PLAYER	GAMES	PTS
1	Martin Skrtel	13	2.31
2	Fernando Torres	27	2.22
3	Xabi Alonso	15	2.20
4	Sami Hyypia	21	2.05
5	Alvaro Arbeloa	24	2.04
6	Dirk Kuyt	23	2.00
7	Javier Mascherano	24	2.00
8	Jose Reina	38	2.00
9	Steven Gerrard	31	1.97
10	Andrey Voronin	12	1.92

KEY PLAYERS - DEFENDERS

Sami Hyypia

Goals Conceded in the League Number of League goals conceded while the player was on the pitch	15
Goals Conceded in all competitions Total number of goals conceded while the player was on the pitch	31
League minutes played Number of minutes played in league matches	2025
Clean Sheets In games when the player was on pitch for at least 70 minutes	10
Defensive Rating Average number of mins between League goals conceded while on the pitch	135
Club Defensive Rating Average number of mins between League goals conceded by the club this season	122

Carlsberg

	PLAYER	CON LGE	CON ALL	MINS	C SHEETS	DEF RATE
1	Sami Hyypia	15	31	2025	10	135 mins
2	Steve Finnan	15	27	1959	9	130 mins
3	Jamie Carragher	24	45	3040	15	126 mins
4	Martin Skrtel	10	16	1191	7	119 mins

KEY GOALKEEPER

Jose Reina

Goals Conceded in the League Number of League goals conceded while the player was on the pitch	28
Goals Conceded in all competitions Total number of goals conceded while the player was on the pitch	41
League minutes played Number of minutes played in league matches	3420
Clean Sheets In games when the player was on pitch for at least 70 minutes	18
Goals to Shots Ratio The average number of shots on target per each League goal conceded	6.32
Defensive Rating Ave mins between League goals conceded while on the pitch	122

BOOKINGS

Momo Sissoko

League Yellow	2
League Red	0
All competitions Yellow	4
All competitions Red	0

League Average 277 mins between cards

	PLAYER	LEAGUE		TOTAL		AVE
1	Momo Sissoko	2Y	0R	4Y	0R	277
2	Javier Mascherano	6	1	7	1	307
3	Jermaine Pennant	3	0	5	1	376
4	Xabi Alonso	3	0	8	0	489
5	Fernando Torres	5	0	6	0	509
6	Andrey Voronin	2	0	2	0	560
7	Alvaro Arbeloa	4	0	6	0	568
8	John Arne Riise	3	0	4	0	662
9	Jamie Carragher	4	0	7	0	760
10	Steven Gerrard	3	0	5	0	946
11	Steve Finnan	2	0	2	0	979
12	Dirk Kuyt	2	0	3	0	1081
13	Fabio Aurelio	1	0	3	0	1125
14	Martin Skrtel	1	0	1	0	1191
15	Ryan Babel	1	0	3	0	1417
	Other	3	0	11	1	
	TOTAL	45	1	77	3	

EVERTON

David Moyes could certainly look back on his sixth season at the club as his most successful to date. The Toffees may have failed to qualify for the Champions League but a run to the semi-finals of the Carling Cup, coupled with some unforgettable European nights and a fifth placed finish in the league had Everton fans dreaming of the glory days returning to Goodison Park. For the Scot to take the club to the next level, he would need to add more depth to a squad, which looked stretched towards the end of the season, but for now Evertonians are content to savour a new band of heroes in the form of **Joleon Lescott**, **Mikel Arteta**, **Ayegbeni Yakubu** and **Phil Jagielka**.

NICKNAME: THE TOFFEES

KEY: Won / Drawn / Lost

No	Comp	Opponent	H/A	Res	Score	Scorers
1	prem	**Wigan**	H	W	2-1	Osman 26, Anichebe 75
2	prem	**Tottenham**	A	W	3-1	Lescott 3, Osman 37, Stubbs 45
3	prem	**Reading**	A	L	0-1	
4	prem	**Blackburn**	H	D	1-1	McFadden 79
5	prem	**Bolton**	A	W	2-1	Yakubu 10, Lescott 89
6	prem	**Man Utd**	H	L	0-1	
7	uc1rl1	**Metalist**	H	D	1-1	Lescott 24
8	prem	**Aston Villa**	A	L	0-2	
9	ccr3	**Sheff Wed**	A	W	3-0	McFadden 59, 84, Yakubu 85
10	prem	**Middlesbro**	H	W	2-0	Lescott 7, Pienaar 58
11	uc1rl2	**Metalist**	A	W	3-2	Lescott 48, McFadden 72, Anichebe 89
12	prem	**Newcastle**	A	L	2-3	Johnson 53, Given 90 og
13	prem	**Liverpool**	H	L	1-2	Hyypia 38 og
14	ucgpa	**Larissa**	H	W	3-1	Cahill 14, Osman 50, Anichebe 85
15	prem	**Derby**	A	W	2-0	Arteta 26, Yakubu 63
16	ccr4	**Luton**	A	W	1-0	Cahill 101
17	prem	**Birmingham**	H	W	3-1	Yakubu 10, Carsley 90, Vaughan 90
18	ucgpa	**Nurnberg**	A	W	2-0	Arteta 83 pen, Anichebe 88
19	prem	**Chelsea**	A	D	1-1	Cahill 89
20	prem	**Sunderland**	H	W	7-1	Yakubu 12, 73, Cahill 17, 62, Pienaar 43, Johnson 80, Osman 85
21	prem	**Portsmouth**	A	D	0-0	
22	ucgpa	**Zenit St Peters**	H	W	1-0	Cahill 85
23	prem	**Fulham**	H	W	3-0	Yakubu 51, 61, 79
24	ccqf	**West Ham**	A	W	2-1	Osman 40, Yakubu 88
25	prem	**West Ham**	A	W	2-0	Yakubu 45, Johnson 90
26	ucgpa	**AZ Alkmaar**	A	W	3-2	Johnson 2, Jagielka 43, Vaughan 79
27	prem	**Man Utd**	A	L	1-2	Cahill 27
28	prem	**Bolton**	H	W	2-0	P.Neville 51, Cahill 70
29	prem	**Arsenal**	H	L	1-4	Cahill 19
30	prem	**Middlesbro**	A	W	2-0	Johnson 67, McFadden 72
31	facr3	**Oldham**	H	L	0-1	
32	ccsfl1	**Chelsea**	A	L	1-2	Yakubu 64
33	prem	**Man City**	H	W	1-0	Lescott 31
34	prem	**Wigan**	A	W	2-1	Johnson 39, Lescott 42
35	ccsfl2	**Chelsea**	H	L	0-1	
36	prem	**Tottenham**	H	D	0-0	
37	prem	**Blackburn**	A	D	0-0	
38	prem	**Reading**	H	W	1-0	Jagielka 62
39	uc3rl1	**SK Brann**	A	W	2-0	Osman 59, Anichebe 88
40	uc3rl2	**SK Brann**	H	W	6-1	Yakubu 36, 54, 72, Johnson 41, 90, Arteta 70
41	prem	**Man City**	A	W	2-0	Yakubu 30, Lescott 38
42	prem	**Portsmouth**	H	W	3-1	Yakubu 1, 81, Cahill 73
43	uc4rl1	**Fiorentina**	A	L	0-2	
44	prem	**Sunderland**	A	W	1-0	Johnson 55
45	uc4rl2	**Fiorentina**	H	L	2-4*	Johnson 15, Arteta 66 (*on penalties)
46	prem	**Fulham**	A	L	0-1	
47	prem	**West Ham**	H	D	1-1	Yakubu 8
48	prem	**Liverpool**	A	L	0-1	
49	prem	**Derby**	H	W	1-0	Osman 56
50	prem	**Birmingham**	A	D	1-1	Lescott 78
51	prem	**Chelsea**	H	L	0-1	
52	prem	**Aston Villa**	H	D	2-2	P.Neville 55, Yobo 84
53	prem	**Arsenal**	A	L	0-1	
54	prem	**Newcastle**	H	W	3-1	Yakubu 28, 81 pen, Lescott 70

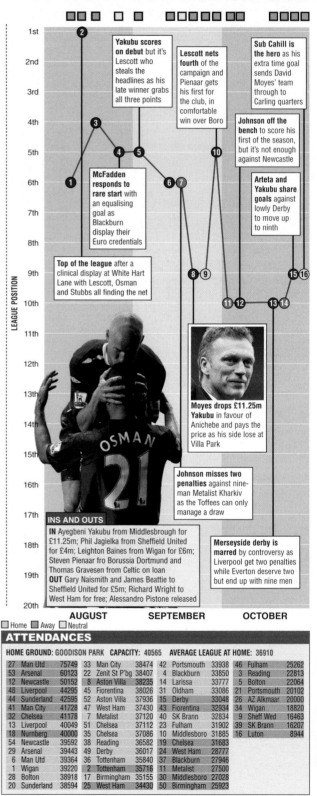

1st
2nd
3rd
4th
5th
6th
7th
8th
9th
10th
11th
12th
13th
14th
15th
16th
17th
18th
19th
20th
LEAGUE POSITION
Yakubu scores on debut but it's Lescott who steals the headlines as his late winner grabs all three points
Lescott nets fourth of the campaign and Pienaar gets his first for the club, in comfortable win over Boro
Sub Cahill is the hero as his extra time goal sends David Moyes' team through to Carling quarters
Johnson off the bench to score his first of the season, but it's not enough against Newcastle
McFadden responds to rare start with an equalising goal as Blackburn display their Euro credentials
Arteta and Yakubu share goals against lowly Derby to move up to ninth
Top of the league after a clinical display at White Hart Lane with Lescott, Osman and Stubbs all finding the net
Moyes drops £11.25m Yakubu in favour of Anichebe and pays the price as his side lose at Villa Park
Johnson misses two penalties against nine-man Metalist Kharkiv as the Toffees can only manage a draw
Merseyside derby is marred by controversy as Liverpool get two penalties while Everton deserve two but end up with nine men
OSMAN 21
AUGUST
SEPTEMBER
OCTOBER
Home Away Neutral

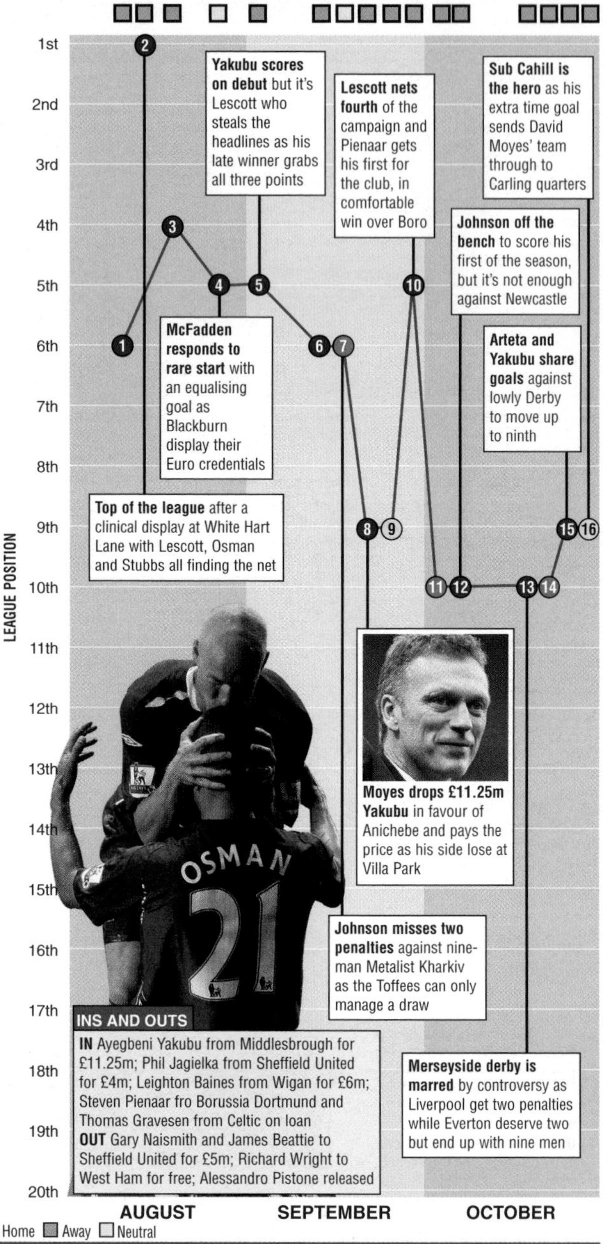

INS AND OUTS

IN Ayegbeni Yakubu from Middlesbrough for £11.25m; Phil Jagielka from Sheffield United for £4m; Leighton Baines from Wigan for £6m; Steven Pienaar fro Borussia Dortmund and Thomas Gravesen from Celtic on loan
OUT Gary Naismith and James Beattie to Sheffield United for £5m; Richard Wright to West Ham for free; Alessandro Pistone released

ATTENDANCES

HOME GROUND: GOODISON PARK **CAPACITY:** 40565 **AVERAGE LEAGUE AT HOME:** 36910

27	Man Utd	75749	33	Man City	38474	42	Portsmouth	33938	46	Fulham	25262
53	Arsenal	60123	22	Zenit St P'bg	38407	4	Blackburn	33850	3	Reading	22813
12	Newcastle	50152	8	Aston Villa	38235	14	Larissa	33777	5	Bolton	22064
48	Liverpool	44295	45	Fiorentina	38026	31	Oldham	33086	21	Portsmouth	20102
44	Sunderland	42595	52	Aston Villa	37936	15	Derby	33048	26	AZ Alkmaar	20000
41	Man City	41728	47	West Ham	37430	43	Fiorentina	32934	34	Wigan	18820
32	Chelsea	41178	7	Metalist	37120	40	SK Brann	32834	9	Sheff Wed	16463
13	Liverpool	40049	51	Chelsea	37112	23	Fulham	31902	39	SK Brann	16207
18	Nurnberg	40000	35	Chelsea	37086	10	Middlesboro	31885	16	Luton	8944
54	Newcastle	39592	38	Reading	36582	19	Chelsea	31683			
29	Arsenal	39443	49	Derby	36017	24	West Ham	28777			
6	Man Utd	39364	36	Tottenham	35840	37	Blackburn	27946			
1	Wigan	39220	2	Tottenham	35716	11	Metalist	27500			
28	Bolton	38918	17	Birmingham	35155	30	Middlesboro	27028			
20	Sunderland	38594	25	West Ham	34430	50	Birmingham	25923			

Another season of progress

Final Position: **5th**

KEY: ● League ● Champions Lge ● UEFA Cup ● FA Cup ○ League Cup ● Other

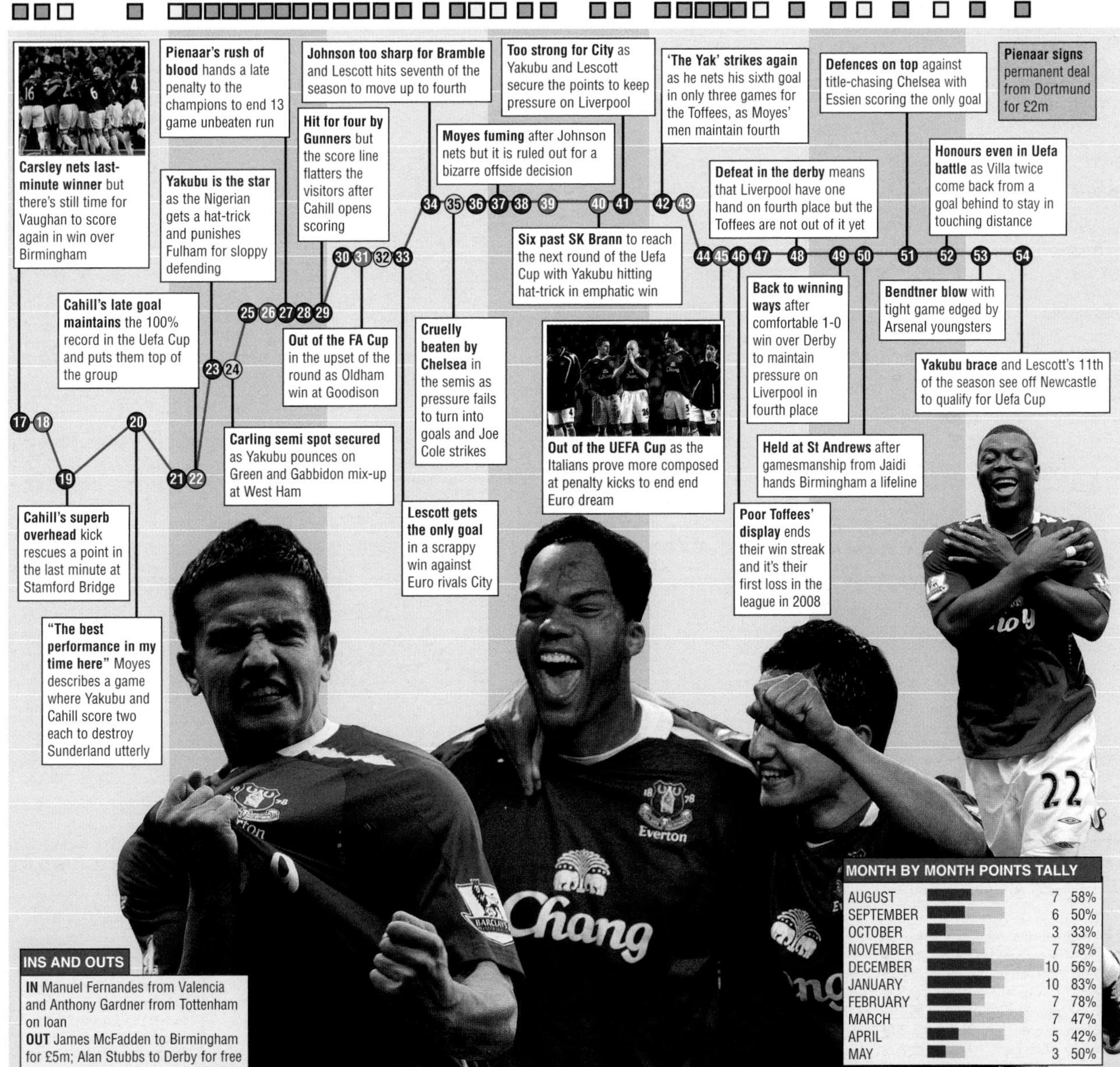

Carsley nets last-minute winner but there's still time for Vaughan to score again in win over Birmingham
Pienaar's rush of blood hands a late penalty to the champions to end 13 game unbeaten run
Johnson too sharp for Bramble and Lescott hits seventh of the season to move up to fourth
Too strong for City as Yakubu and Lescott secure the points to keep pressure on Liverpool
'The Yak' strikes again as he nets his sixth goal in only three games for the Toffees, as Moyes' men maintain fourth
Defences on top against title-chasing Chelsea with Essien scoring the only goal
Pienaar signs permanent deal from Dortmund for £2m
Hit for four by Gunners but the score line flatters the visitors after Cahill opens scoring
Moyes fuming after Johnson nets but it is ruled out for a bizarre offside decision
Honours even in Uefa battle as Villa twice come back from a goal behind to stay in touching distance
Defeat in the derby means that Liverpool have one hand on fourth place but the Toffees are not out of it yet
Yakubu is the star as the Nigerian gets a hat-trick and punishes Fulham for sloppy defending
Six past SK Brann to reach the next round of the Uefa Cup with Yakubu hitting hat-trick in emphatic win
Cahill's late goal maintains the 100% record in the Uefa Cup and puts them top of the group
Back to winning ways after comfortable 1-0 win over Derby to maintain pressure on Liverpool in fourth place
Bendtner blow with tight game edged by Arsenal youngsters
Out of the FA Cup in the upset of the round as Oldham win at Goodison
Cruelly beaten by Chelsea in the semis as pressure fails to turn into goals and Joe Cole strikes
Yakubu brace and Lescott's 11th of the season see off Newcastle to qualify for Uefa Cup
Carling semi spot secured as Yakubu pounces on Green and Gabbidon mix-up at West Ham
Out of the UEFA Cup as the Italians prove more composed at penalty kicks to end end Euro dream
Held at St Andrews after gamesmanship from Jaidi hands Birmingham a lifeline
Cahill's superb overhead kick rescues a point in the last minute at Stamford Bridge
Lescott gets the only goal in a scrappy win against Euro rivals City
Poor Toffees' display ends their win streak and it's their first loss in the league in 2008
"The best performance in my time here" Moyes describes a game where Yakubu and Cahill score two each to destroy Sunderland utterly
17 18 19 20 21 22 23 24 25 26 27 28 29 30 31 32 33 34 35 36 37 38 39 40 41 42 43 44 45 46 47 48 49 50 51 52 53 54
Chang
Everton
22

INS AND OUTS

IN Manuel Fernandes from Valencia and Anthony Gardner from Tottenham on loan
OUT James McFadden to Birmingham for £5m; Alan Stubbs to Derby for free

MONTH BY MONTH POINTS TALLY

Month	Points	%
AUGUST	7	58%
SEPTEMBER	6	50%
OCTOBER	3	33%
NOVEMBER	7	78%
DECEMBER	10	56%
JANUARY	10	83%
FEBRUARY	7	78%
MARCH	7	47%
APRIL	5	42%
MAY	3	50%

NOVEMBER DECEMBER JANUARY FEBRUARY MARCH APRIL MAY

GOAL ATTEMPTS

FOR
Goal attempts recorded in League games

	HOME	AWAY	TOTAL	AVE
shots on target	124	112	236	6.2
shots off target	123	80	203	5.3
TOTAL	247	192	439	11.6

Ratio of goals to shots — Average number of shots on target per League goal scored: **4.3**

Accuracy rating — Average percentage of total goal attempts which were on target: **53.8**

AGAINST
Goal attempts recorded in League games

	HOME	AWAY	TOTAL	AVE
shots on target	97	111	208	5.5
shots off target	96	128	224	5.9
TOTAL	193	239	432	11.4

Ratio of goals to shots — Average number of shots on target per League goal scored: **6.3**

Accuracy rating — Average percentage of total goal attempts which were on target: **48.1**

GOALS

Yakubu

League	15
FA Cup	0
League Cup	3
Europe	3
Other	0
TOTAL	21

League Average **143** mins between goals

	PLAYER	LGE	FAC	LC	Euro	TOT	AVE
1	Yakubu	15	0	3	3	21	143
2	Cahill	7	0	1	2	10	214
3	Johnson	6	0	0	4	10	307
4	Lescott	8	0	0	2	10	421
5	Osman	4	0	1	2	7	578
6	McFadden	2	0	2	1	5	236
7	Anichebe	1	0	0	4	5	1076
8	Arteta	1	0	0	3	4	2446
9	Vaughan	1	0	0	1	2	142
10	Pienaar	2	0	0	0	2	1041
11	Neville, P	2	0	0	0	2	1619
12	Jagielka	1	0	0	1	2	2654
13	Stubbs	1	0	0	0	1	561
14	Yobo	1	0	0	0	1	2609
15	Carsley	1	0	0	0	1	2866
	Other	0	0	0	0	0	
	TOTAL	53	0	7	23	83	

SQUAD APPEARANCES

Match	1	2	3	4	5	6	7	8	9	10	11	12	13	14	15	16	17	18	19	20	21	22	23	24	25	26	27
Venue	H	A	A	H	A	H	H	A	A	H	A	A	H	H	A	A	H	A	A	H	A	H	H	A	A	A	A
Competition	L	L	L	L	L	L	E	L	W	L	E	L	L	E	L	W	L	E	L	L	L	E	L	W	L	E	L
Result	W	W	L	D	W	L	D	L	W	W	W	L	L	W	W	W	W	W	D	W	D	W	W	W	W	W	L

Match	28	29	30	31	32	33	34	35	36	37	38	39	40	41	42	43	44	45	46	47	48	49	50	51	52	53	54
Venue	H	H	A	H	A	H	A	H	H	A	H	A	H	A	H	A	A	H	A	H	A	H	A	H	H	A	H
Competition	L	L	L	F	W	L	L	W	L	L	L	E	E	L	L	E	L	E	L	L	L	L	L	L	L	L	L
Result	W	L	W	L	L	W	W	L	D	D	W	W	W	W	W	L	W	L	L	D	L	W	D	L	D	L	W

Goalkeepers
- Tim Howard
- John Ruddy
- Iain Turner
- Stefan Wessels

Defenders
- Leighton Baines
- Patrick Boyle
- Dan Gosling
- Tony Hibbert
- John Irving
- Philip Jagielka
- Joleon Lescott
- Phil Neville
- Jorge Nuno Valente
- Jack Rodwell
- Alan Stubbs
- Joseph Yobo

Midfielders
- Mikel Arteta
- Tim Cahill
- Lee Carsley
- Anderson de Silva
- Thomas Gravesen
- Leon Osman
- Steven Pienaar
- Manuel Fernandes
- Andy van der Meyde
- Bjarni Thor Vidarsson

Forwards
- Victor Anichebe
- Andrew Johnson
- Lucas Jutkiewicz
- James McFadden
- James Vaughan
- Ayegbeni Yakubu

KEY: ■ On all match ■ On bench ⏮ Subbed or sent off (Counting game) « Subbed or sent off (playing less than 70 mins) ⏭ Subbed on from bench (Counting Game) » Subbed on (playing less than 70 mins) ⏭ Subbed on and then subbed or sent off (Counting Game) » Subbed on and then subbed or sent off (playing less than 70 min □ Not in 16 □ Injured ✕ Suspended

KEY PLAYERS - GOALSCORERS

Ayegbeni Yakubu

Goals in the League	15
Goals in all competitions	21
Assists League goals scored by a team mate where the player delivered the final pass	2
Contribution to Attacking Power Average number of minutes between League team goals while on pitch	55
Player Strike Rate Average number of minutes between League goals scored by player	143
Club Strike Rate Average minutes between League goals scored by club	62

	PLAYER	GOALS LGE	GOALS ALL	ASSISTS	POWER	S RATE
1	Ayegbeni Yakubu	15	21	2	55	143 mins
2	Tim Cahill	7	10	2	48	214 mins
3	Andrew Johnson	6	10	4	73	307 mins
4	Leon Osman	4	7	3	59	578 mins

KEY PLAYERS - MIDFIELDERS

Tim Cahill

Goals in the League	7
Goals in all competitions	10
Assists League goals scored by a team mate where the player delivered the final pass	2
Defensive Rating Average number of mins between League goals conceded while on the pitch	150
Contribution to Attacking Power Average number of minutes between League team goals while on pitch	48
Scoring Difference Defensive Rating minus Contribution to Attacking Power	102

	PLAYER	GOALS LGE	GOALS ALL	ASSISTS	DEF RATE	POWER	SC DIFF
1	Tim Cahill	7	10	2	150	48	102 mins
2	Mikel Arteta	1	4	5	111	59	52 mins
3	Leon Osman	4	7	3	110	59	51 mins
4	Lee Carsley	1	1	4	102	59	43 mins

PLAYER APPEARANCES

	AGE (on 01/07/08)	IN NAMED 16	APPEARANCES	COUNTING GAMES	MINUTES ON PITCH	APPEARANCES	MINUTES ON PITCH	THIS SEASON	HOME COUNTRY
Goalkeepers									
Tim Howard	29	36	36	36	3240	47	4260	1	United States
John Ruddy	21	4	0	0	0	0	0	-	England
Iain Turner	24	2	0	0	0	0	0	-	Scotland
Stefan Wessels	29	34	2	2	180	7	660	-	Germany
Defenders									
Leighton Baines	23	25	22	11	1139	29	1525	-	England
Patrick Boyle	21	0	0	0	0	0	0	-	Scotland
Dan Gosling	18	1	0	0	0	0	0	-	England
Tony Hibbert	27	30	24	19	1925	35	2541	-	England
John Irving	18	0	0	0	0	0	0	-	England
Philip Jagielka	25	38	34	29	2654	49	3878	-	England
Joleon Lescott	25	38	38	37	3375	54	4802	5	England
Phil Neville	31	37	37	36	3239	50	4424	3	England
Jorge Nuno Valente	33	21	9	8	721	15	1264	-	Portugal
Jack Rodwell	17	5	2	0	5	3	15	-	England
Alan Stubbs	36	12	8	5	561	13	954	-	England
Joseph Yobo	27	31	30	29	2609	39	3449	4	Nigeria
Midfielders									
Mikel Arteta	26	28	28	27	2446	37	3231	-	Spain
Tim Cahill	28	18	18	17	1501	28	2283	-	Australia
Lee Carsley	34	37	34	31	2866	49	4198	5	Rep of Ireland
Anderson de Silva	25	1	0	0	0	0	0	-	Brazil
Thomas Gravesen	32	16	8	1	182	13	380	-	Denmark
Leon Osman	27	28	28	26	2314	39	3329	-	England
Steven Pienaar	26	31	28	19	2082	40	3153	4	South Africa
Manuel Fernandes	22	13	12	8	845	15	1056	1	Portugal
Andy van der Meyde	28	4	0	0	0	0	0	-	Holland
Bjarni Thor Vidarsson	20	0	0	0	0	1	23	-	Iceland
Forwards									
Victor Anichebe	20	32	27	9	1076	41	1459	-	Nigeria
Andrew Johnson	27	29	29	18	1847	39	2655	2	England
Lucas Jutkiewicz	19	0	0	0	0	0	0	-	Poland
James McFadden	25	17	12	3	472	21	1208	5	Scotland
James Vaughan	19	10	8	0	142	13	299	-	England
Ayegbeni Yakubu	25	29	29	23	2153	40	3028	4	Nigeria

KEY: LEAGUE ALL COMPS CAPS (MAY FIFA RANKING)

TEAM OF THE SEASON

HOWARD

CG 36 DR 108

NEVILLE

CG 36 DR 107

JAGIELKA

CG 29 DR 110

LESCOTT

CG 37 DR 105

BAINES

CG 11* DR 94

OSMAN

CG 26 SD +51

CARSLEY

CG 31 SD +43

CAHILL

CG 17 SD +102

ARTETA

CG 27 SD +52

JOHNSON

CG 18 AP 73

YAKUBU

CG 23 SR 143

KEY: DR = Defensive Rate, SD = Scoring Difference AP = Attacking Power SR = Strike Rate, CG=Counting games – League games playing at least 70 minutes

TOP POINT EARNERS

Tim Cahill

Counting Games League games when player was on pitch for at least 70 minutes	17
Average points Average League points taken in Counting games	2.29
Club Average points Average points taken in League games	1.71

	PLAYER	GAMES	PTS
1	Tim Cahill	17	2.29
2	Steven Pienaar	19	2.00
3	Mikel Arteta	27	1.85
4	Ayegbeni Yakubu	23	1.83
5	Tim Howard	36	1.81
6	Lee Carsley	31	1.77
7	Leon Osman	26	1.73
8	Joleon Lescott	37	1.73
9	Philip Jagielka	29	1.72
10	Phil Neville	36	1.69

KEY PLAYERS - DEFENDERS

Philip Jagielka

Goals Conceded in the League Number of League goals conceded while the player was on the pitch	24
Goals Conceded in all competitions Total number of goals conceded while the player was on the pitch	36
League minutes played Number of minutes played in league matches	2654
Clean Sheets In games when the player was on pitch for at least 70 minutes	12
Defensive Rating Average number of mins between League goals conceded while on the pitch	110
Club Defensive Rating Average number of mins between League goals conceded by the club this season	103

Chang

	PLAYER	CON LGE	CON ALL	MINS	C SHEETS	DEF RATE
1	Philip Jagielka	24	36	2654	12	110 mins
2	Phil Neville	30	40	3239	13	107 mins
3	Joleon Lescott	32	45	3375	14	105 mins
4	Leighton Baines	12	15	1139	4	94 mins

KEY GOALKEEPER

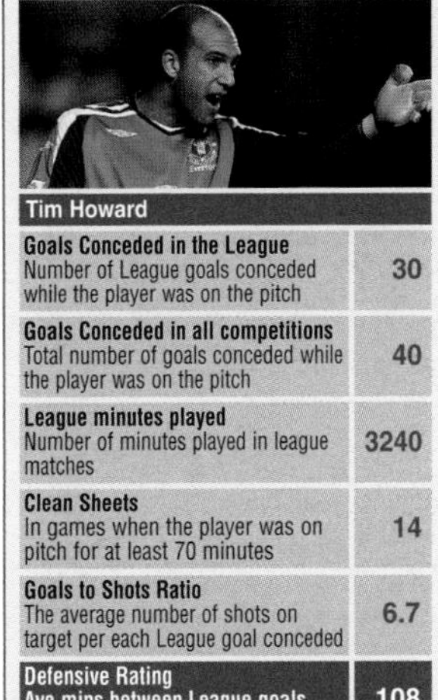

Tim Howard

Goals Conceded in the League Number of League goals conceded while the player was on the pitch	30
Goals Conceded in all competitions Total number of goals conceded while the player was on the pitch	40
League minutes played Number of minutes played in league matches	3240
Clean Sheets In games when the player was on pitch for at least 70 minutes	14
Goals to Shots Ratio The average number of shots on target per each League goal conceded	6.7
Defensive Rating Ave mins between League goals conceded while on the pitch	108

BOOKINGS

James McFadden

League Yellow	2
League Red	0
All competitions Yellow	2
All competitions Red	0
League Average	236 mins between cards

	PLAYER	LEAGUE Y	LEAGUE R	TOTAL Y	TOTAL R	AVE
1	James McFadden	2Y	0R	2Y	0R	236
2	Steven Pienaar	6	0	7	0	347
3	Tim Cahill	4	0	5	0	375
4	Lee Carsley	6	0	8	0	477
5	Tony Hibbert	3	1	6	1	481
6	Phil Neville	4	1	7	1	647
7	Nuno Valente	1	0	3	0	721
8	Mikel Arteta	2	1	2	1	815
9	Ayegbeni Yakubu	2	0	4	0	1076
10	Victor Anichebe	1	0	2	0	1076
11	Joleon Lescott	3	0	4	0	1125
12	Leighton Baines	1	0	2	0	1139
13	Philip Jagielka	2	0	3	0	1327
14	Andrew Johnson	1	0	3	0	1847
15	Tim Howard	1	0	2	0	3240
	Other	0	0	6	0	
	TOTAL	39	3	66	3	

ASTON VILLA

The tight Villa nucleus has performed wonders under the inspired management of Martin O'Neill. Fashioned out of loyalty and a hard-working budget, O'Neill has spent wisely, developed young stars and revitalised stagnating careers to challenge for a Uefa place. Now he has lost **Olof Mellberg**, has **Gareth Barry** being tempted by Liverpool's European pedigree and covetous glances focussing on **Ashley Young**, **Gabby Agbonlahor** and **Martin Laursen**. Barry's role at the club will be defended: "Liverpool talked about a £10m bid, which involved some cash and some unnamed players. That is very presumptuous of them, that the players they might be talking about, are the ones you would want - that is why I dismissed the whole thing," said O'Neill.

NICKNAME: THE VILLANS

KEY: Won / Drawn / Lost

1	prem	**Liverpool**	H	L	1-2	Barry 85 pen
2	prem	**Newcastle**	A	D	0-0	
3	prem	**Fulham**	H	W	2-1	Young 51, Maloney 90
4	ccr2	**Wrexham**	A	W	5-0	Maloney 10, 72, L.Moore 52, Reo-Coker 62, Harewood 78
5	prem	**Chelsea**	H	W	2-0	Knight 47, Agbonlahor 89
6	prem	**Man City**	A	L	0-1	
7	prem	**Everton**	H	W	2-0	Carew 14, Agbonlahor 61
8	ccr3	**Leicester**	H	L	0-1	
9	prem	**Tottenham**	A	D	4-4	Laursen 22, 33, Agbonlahor 40, Gardner 59
10	prem	**West Ham**	H	W	1-0	Gardner 24
11	prem	**Man Utd**	H	L	1-4	Agbonlahor 12
12	prem	**Bolton**	A	D	1-1	L.Moore 57
13	prem	**Derby**	H	W	2-0	Laursen 57, Young 61
14	prem	**Birmingham**	A	W	2-1	Ridgewell 10 og, Agbonlahor 87
15	prem	**Middlesbro**	A	W	3-0	Carew 45, Mellberg 48, Agbonlahor 58
16	prem	**Blackburn**	A	W	4-0	Carew 28, Barry 53 pen, Young 81, Harewood 89
17	prem	**Arsenal**	H	L	1-2	Gardner 14
18	prem	**Portsmouth**	H	L	1-3	Barry 72 pen
19	prem	**Sunderland**	A	D	1-1	Maloney 73
20	prem	**Man City**	H	D	1-1	Carew 14
21	prem	**Chelsea**	A	D	4-4	Maloney 14, 44, Laursen 72, Barry 90 pen
22	prem	**Wigan**	A	W	2-1	C.Davies 55, Agbonlahor 70
23	prem	**Tottenham**	H	W	2-1	Mellberg 40, Laursen 85
24	facr3	**Man Utd**	H	L	0-2	
25	prem	**Reading**	H	W	3-1	Carew 22, 88, Laursen 55
26	prem	**Liverpool**	A	D	2-2	Harewood 69, Aurelio 72 og
27	prem	**Blackburn**	H	D	1-1	Young 73
28	prem	**Fulham**	A	L	1-2	Hughes 69 og
29	prem	**Newcastle**	H	W	4-1	Bouma 48, Carew 51, 72, 90 pen
30	prem	**Reading**	A	W	2-1	Young 45, Harewood 84
31	prem	**Arsenal**	A	D	1-1	Senderos 27 og
32	prem	**Middlesbro**	H	D	1-1	Barry 74 pen
33	prem	**Portsmouth**	A	L	0-2	
34	prem	**Sunderland**	H	L	0-1	
35	prem	**Man Utd**	A	L	0-4	
36	prem	**Bolton**	H	W	4-0	Barry 9, 60, Agbonlahor 56, Harewood 85
37	prem	**Derby**	A	W	6-0	Young 25 , Carew 26, Petrov 36, Barry 58, Agbonlahor 76, Harewood 85
38	prem	**Birmingham**	H	W	5-1	Young 29, 63, Carew 42, 54, Agbonlahor 78
39	prem	**Everton**	A	D	2-2	Agbonlahor 80, Carew 85
40	prem	**Wigan**	H	L	0-2	
41	prem	**West Ham**	A	D	2-2	Young 14, Barry 58

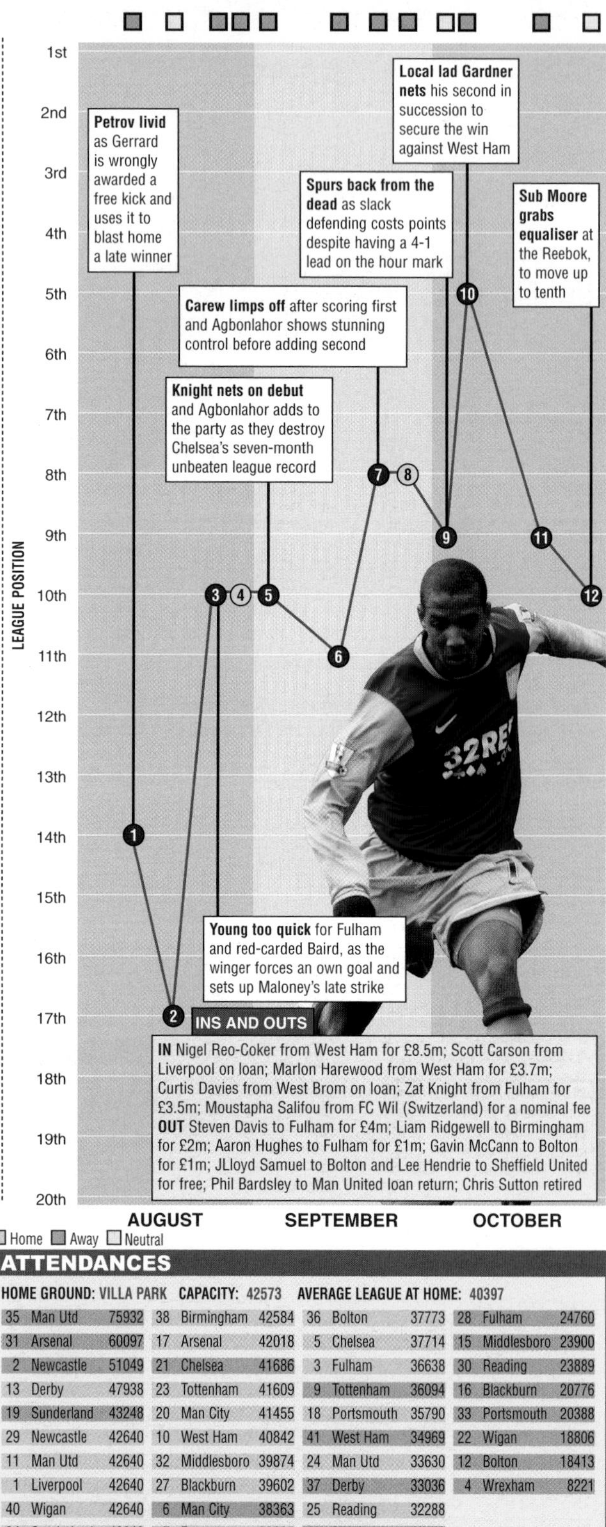

1st
2nd
3rd
4th
5th
6th
7th
8th
9th
10th
11th
12th
13th
14th
15th
16th
17th
18th
19th
20th
LEAGUE POSITION
Petrov livid as Gerrard is wrongly awarded a free kick and uses it to blast home a late winner
Local lad Gardner nets his second in succession to secure the win against West Ham
Spurs back from the dead as slack defending costs points despite having a 4-1 lead on the hour mark
Sub Moore grabs equaliser at the Reebok, to move up to tenth
Carew limps off after scoring first and Agbonlahor shows stunning control before adding second
Knight nets on debut and Agbonlahor adds to the party as they destroy Chelsea's seven-month unbeaten league record
Young too quick for Fulham and red-carded Baird, as the winger forces an own goal and sets up Maloney's late strike
1
2
3
4
5
6
7
8
9
10
11
12
AUGUST
SEPTEMBER
OCTOBER
Home
Away
Neutral

INS AND OUTS

IN Nigel Reo-Coker from West Ham for £8.5m; Scott Carson from Liverpool on loan; Marlon Harewood from West Ham for £3.7m; Curtis Davies from West Brom on loan; Zat Knight from Fulham for £3.5m; Moustapha Salifou from FC Wil (Switzerland) for a nominal fee
OUT Steven Davis to Fulham for £4m; Liam Ridgewell to Birmingham for £2m; Aaron Hughes to Fulham for £1m; Gavin McCann to Bolton for £1m; JLloyd Samuel to Bolton and Lee Hendrie to Sheffield United for free; Phil Bardsley to Man United loan return; Chris Sutton retired

ATTENDANCES

HOME GROUND: VILLA PARK **CAPACITY:** 42573 **AVERAGE LEAGUE AT HOME:** 40397

35	Man Utd	75932	38	Birmingham	42584	36	Bolton	37773	28	Fulham	24760
31	Arsenal	60097	17	Arsenal	42018	5	Chelsea	37714	15	Middlesboro	23900
2	Newcastle	51049	21	Chelsea	41686	3	Fulham	36638	30	Reading	23889
13	Derby	47938	23	Tottenham	41609	9	Tottenham	36094	16	Blackburn	20776
19	Sunderland	43248	20	Man City	41455	18	Portsmouth	35790	33	Portsmouth	20388
29	Newcastle	42640	10	West Ham	40842	41	West Ham	34969	22	Wigan	18806
11	Man Utd	42640	32	Middlesboro	39874	24	Man Utd	33630	12	Bolton	18413
1	Liverpool	42640	27	Blackburn	39602	37	Derby	33036	4	Wrexham	8221
40	Wigan	42640	6	Man City	38363	25	Reading	32288			
34	Sunderland	42640	7	Everton	38235	14	Birmingham	26539			
26	Liverpool	42590	39	Everton	37936	8	Leicester	25956			

'Neill works miracle with young squad

Final Position: 6th

KEY: ● League ● Champions Lge ● UEFA Cup ● FA Cup ○ League Cup ● Other

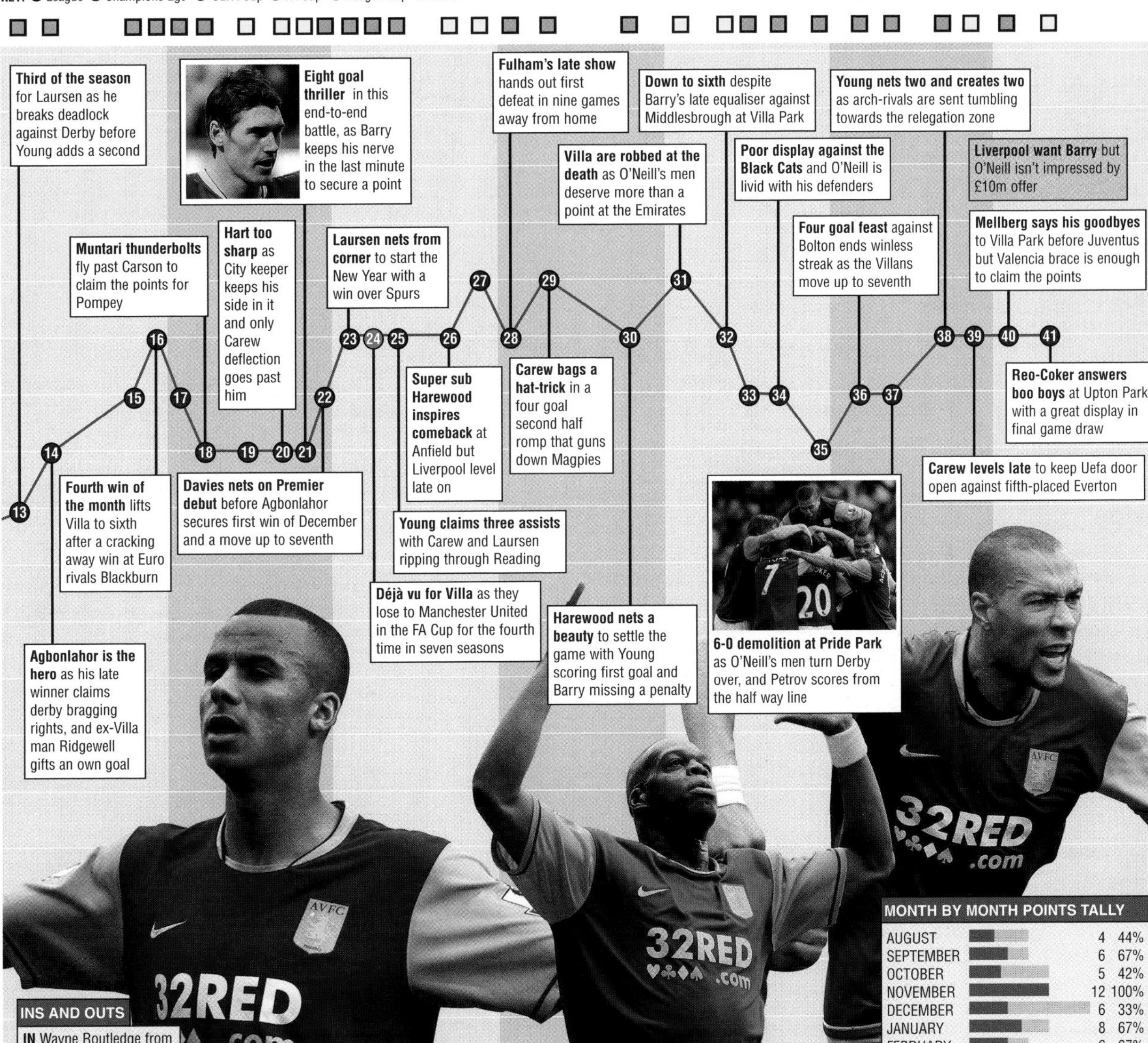

Third of the season for Laursen as he breaks deadlock against Derby before Young adds a second
Eight goal thriller in this end-to-end battle, as Barry keeps his nerve in the last minute to secure a point
Fulham's late show hands out first defeat in nine games away from home
Down to sixth despite Barry's late equaliser against Middlesbrough at Villa Park
Young nets two and creates two as arch-rivals are sent tumbling towards the relegation zone
Villa are robbed at the death as O'Neill's men deserve more than a point at the Emirates
Poor display against the Black Cats and O'Neill is livid with his defenders
Liverpool want Barry but O'Neill isn't impressed by £10m offer
Muntari thunderbolts fly past Carson to claim the points for Pompey
Hart too sharp as City keeper keeps his side in it and only Carew deflection goes past him
Laursen nets from corner to start the New Year with a win over Spurs
Four goal feast against Bolton ends winless streak as the Villans move up to seventh
Mellberg says his goodbyes to Villa Park before Juventus but Valencia brace is enough to claim the points
13 14 15 16 17 18 19 20 21 22 23 24 25 26 27 28 29 30 31 32 33 34 35 36 37 38 39 40 41
Super sub Harewood inspires comeback at Anfield but Liverpool level late on
Carew bags a hat-trick in a four goal second half romp that guns down Magpies
Reo-Coker answers boo boys at Upton Park with a great display in final game draw
Fourth win of the month lifts Villa to sixth after a cracking away win at Euro rivals Blackburn
Davies nets on Premier debut before Agbonlahor secures first win of December and a move up to seventh
Young claims three assists with Carew and Laursen ripping through Reading
Carew levels late to keep Uefa door open against fifth-placed Everton
Déjà vu for Villa as they lose to Manchester United in the FA Cup for the fourth time in seven seasons
Harewood nets a beauty to settle the game with Young scoring first goal and Barry missing a penalty
6-0 demolition at Pride Park as O'Neill's men turn Derby over, and Petrov scores from the half way line
Agbonlahor is the hero as his late winner claims derby bragging rights, and ex-Villa man Ridgewell gifts an own goal
32RED .com
AVFC

INS AND OUTS

IN Wayne Routledge from Tottenham for £1.25m **OUT** Gary Cahill to Bolton for £5m; Luke Moore to West Brom on loan

MONTH BY MONTH POINTS TALLY

Month	Points	%
AUGUST	4	44%
SEPTEMBER	6	67%
OCTOBER	5	42%
NOVEMBER	12	100%
DECEMBER	6	33%
JANUARY	8	67%
FEBRUARY	6	67%
MARCH	2	13%
APRIL	10	83%
MAY	1	17%

NOVEMBER DECEMBER JANUARY FEBRUARY MARCH APRIL MAY

GOAL ATTEMPTS

FOR – Goal attempts recorded in League games

	HOME	AWAY	TOTAL	AVE
shots on target	118	131	249	6.6
shots off target	119	93	212	5.6
TOTAL	237	224	461	12.1

Ratio of goals to shots – Average number of shots on target per League goal scored: **3.5**

Accuracy rating – Average percentage of total goal attempts which were on target: **54.0**

AGAINST – Goal attempts recorded in League games

	HOME	AWAY	TOTAL	AVE
shots on target	103	126	229	6.0
shots off target	109	120	229	6.0
TOTAL	212	246	458	12.1

Ratio of goals to shots – Average number of shots on target per League goal scored: **4.5**

Accuracy rating – Average percentage of total goal attempts which were on target: **50.0**

GOALS

Carew

League	13
FA Cup	0
League Cup	0
Europe	0
Other	0
TOTAL	13

League Average **196** mins between goals

	PLAYER	LGE	FAC	LC	Euro	TOT	AVE
1	Carew	13	0	0	0	13	196
2	Agbonlahor	11	0	0	0	11	298
3	Young	9	0	0	0	9	365
4	Barry	9	0	0	0	9	368
5	Harewood	5	0	1	0	6	102
6	Maloney	4	0	2	0	6	248
7	Laursen	6	0	0	0	6	561
8	Gardner	3	0	0	0	3	444
9	Moore, L	1	0	1	0	2	843
10	Mellberg	2	0	0	0	2	1481
11	Davies, C	1	0	0	0	1	813
12	Petrov	1	0	0	0	1	1844
13	Knight	1	0	0	0	1	2191
14	Bouma	1	0	0	0	1	3262
15	Reo-Coker	0	0	1	0	1	
	Other	0	0	0	0	0	
	TOTAL	67	0	5	0	72	

SQUAD APPEARANCES

Match	1	2	3	4	5	6	7	8	9	10	11	12	13	14	15	16	17	18	19	20
Venue	H	A	H	A	H	A	H	H	A	H	H	A	H	A	A	A	H	H	A	H
Competition	L	L	L	W	L	L	L	W	L	L	L	L	L	L	L	L	L	L	L	L
Result	L	D	W	W	W	L	W	L	D	W	L	D	W	W	W	W	L	L	D	D

Match	21	22	23	24	25	26	27	28	29	30	31	32	33	34	35	36	37	38	39	40	41
Venue	A	A	H	H	H	A	H	A	H	A	A	H	A	H	A	H	A	H	A	H	A
Competition	L	L	L	F	L	L	L	L	L	L	L	L	L	L	L	L	L	L	L	L	L
Result	D	W	W	L	W	D	D	L	W	W	D	D	L	L	L	W	W	W	D	L	D

Goalkeepers
- Scott Carson
- Thomas Sorensen
- Stuart Taylor

Defenders
- Wilfred Bouma
- Gary Cahill
- Curtis Davies
- Zatyiah Knight
- Martin Laursen
- Olof Mellberg

Midfielders
- Gareth Barry
- Patrik Berger
- Craig Gardner
- Isaiah Osbourne
- Stilian Petrov
- Nigel Reo-Coker
- Wayne Routledge
- Moustapha Salifou

Forwards
- Gabriel Agbonlahor
- John Alieu Carew
- Marlon Harewood
- Shaun Maloney
- Luke Moore
- Ashley Young

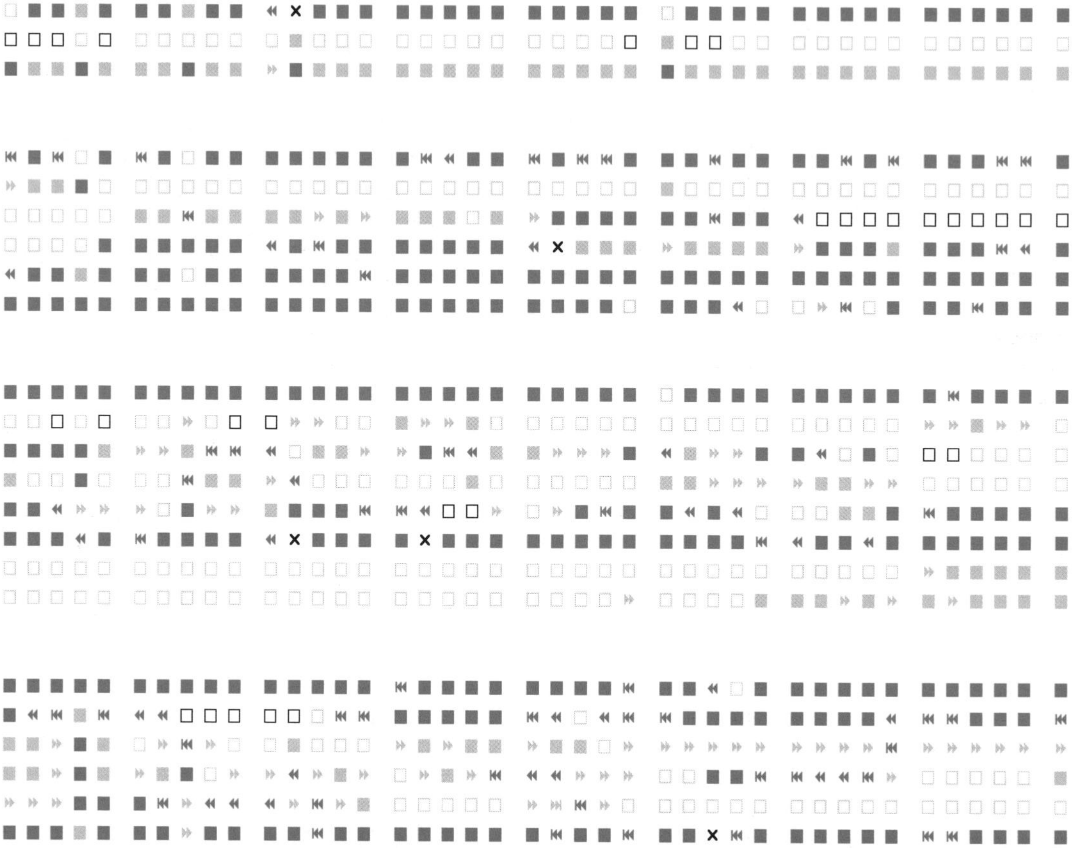

KEY: On all match / On bench / Subbed or sent off (Counting game) / Subbed or sent off (playing less than 70 mins) / Subbed on from bench (Counting Game) / Subbed on (playing less than 70 mins) / Subbed on and then subbed or sent off (Counting Game) / Subbed on and then subbed or sent off (playing less than 70 min / Not in 16 / Injured / ✕ Suspended

KEY PLAYERS - GOALSCORERS

John Alieu Carew

Goals in the League	13
Goals in all competitions	13
Assists League goals scored by a team mate where the player delivered the final pass	1
Contribution to Attacking Power Average number of minutes between League team goals while on pitch	51
Player Strike Rate Average number of minutes between League goals scored by player	196
Club Strike Rate Average minutes between League goals scored by club	48

	PLAYER	GOALS LGE	GOALS ALL	ASSISTS	POWER	S RATE
1	John Alieu Carew	13	13	1	51	196 mins
2	Gabriel Agbonlahor	11	11	6	50	298 mins
3	Ashley Young	9	9	16	49	365 mins
4	Gareth Barry	9	9	10	48	368 mins

KEY PLAYERS - MIDFIELDERS

Nigel Reo-Coker

Goals in the League	0
Goals in all competitions	1
Assists League goals scored by a team mate where the player delivered the final pass	2
Defensive Rating Average number of mins between League goals conceded while on the pitch	70
Contribution to Attacking Power Average number of minutes between League team goals while on pitch	44
Scoring Difference Defensive Rating minus Contribution to Attacking Power	26

	PLAYER	GOALS LGE	GOALS ALL	ASSISTS	DEF RATE	POWER	SC DIFF
1	Nigel Reo-Coker	0	1	2	70	44	26 mins
2	Stilian Petrov	1	1	0	70	46	24 mins
3	Gareth Barry	9	9	10	67	48	19 mins
4	Craig Gardner	3	3	0	63	53	10 mins

PLAYER APPEARANCES

	AGE (on 01/07/08)	IN NAMED 16	APPEARANCES	COUNTING GAMES	MINUTES ON PITCH	APPEARANCES	MINUTES ON PITCH	THIS SEASON	HOME COUNTRY
Goalkeepers									
Scott Carson	22	35	35	34	3125	36	3215	2	England
Thomas Sorensen	32	2	0	0	0	0	0	6	Denmark
Stuart Taylor	27	38	4	3	295	6	475	-	England
Defenders									
Wilfred Bouma	30	38	38	37	3262	39	3344	8	Holland
Gary Cahill	22	4	1	0	45	2	135	-	England
Curtis Davies	23	23	12	8	813	14	982	-	England
Zatyiah Knight	28	34	27	22	2191	28	2281	-	England
Martin Laursen	30	38	38	37	3368	39	3458	6	Denmark
Olof Mellberg	30	34	34	32	2962	37	3232	4	Sweden
Midfielders									
Gareth Barry	27	37	37	37	3319	40	3589	9	England
Patrik Berger	34	11	8	0	175	9	186	-	Czech Republic
Craig Gardner	21	29	23	11	1332	25	1430	-	England
Isaiah Osbourne	20	16	8	0	167	10	327	-	England
Stilian Petrov	28	31	28	18	1844	31	2032	6	Bulgaria
Nigel Reo-Coker	24	36	36	33	3103	39	3349	-	England
Wayne Routledge	23	6	1	0	4	1	4	-	England
Moustapha Salifou	25	13	4	0	46	4	46	-	Togo
Forwards									
Gabriel Agbonlahor	21	37	37	36	3278	40	3548	-	England
John Alieu Carew	28	32	32	27	2552	33	2615	4	Norway
Marlon Harewood	28	32	23	1	514	25	680	-	England
Shaun Maloney	25	29	22	6	993	25	1189	4	Scotland
Luke Moore	22	16	15	6	843	18	974	-	England
Ashley Young	22	37	37	36	3285	39	3395	2	England

KEY: LEAGUE ALL COMPS CAPS (MAY FIFA RANKING)

TEAM OF THE SEASON

CARSON

CG 34 DR 69

MELLBERG

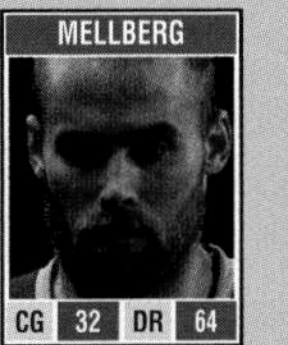

CG 32 DR 64

KNIGHT

CG 22 DR 81

LAURSEN

CG 37 DR 67

BOUMA

CG 37 DR 67

GARDNER

CG 11 SD +10

REO-COKER

CG 33 SD +26

PETROV

CG 18 SD +24

BARRY

CG 37 SD +19

AGBONLAHOR

CG 36 AP 50

CAREW

CG 27 SR 196

KEY: DR = Defensive Rate, SD = Scoring Difference AP = Attacking Power SR = Strike Rate, CG=Counting games – League games playing at least 70 minutes

TOP POINT EARNERS

Stilian Petrov	
Counting Games League games when player was on pitch for at least 70 minutes	18
Average points Average League points taken in Counting games	1.78
Club Average points Average points taken in League games	1.58

	PLAYER	GAMES	PTS
1	Stilian Petrov	18	1.78
2	Nigel Reo-Coker	33	1.76
3	Scott Carson	34	1.71
4	Zatyiah Knight	22	1.68
5	Martin Laursen	37	1.62
6	Wilfred Bouma	37	1.62
7	Gareth Barry	37	1.59
8	Gabriel Agbonlahor	36	1.58
9	Ashley Young	36	1.58
10	John Alieu Carew	27	1.56

KEY PLAYERS - DEFENDERS

Zatyiah Knight	
Goals Conceded in the League Number of League goals conceded while the player was on the pitch	27
Goals Conceded in all competitions Total number of goals conceded while the player was on the pitch	28
League minutes played Number of minutes played in league matches	2191
Clean Sheets In games when the player was on pitch for at least 70 minutes	8
Defensive Rating Average number of mins between League goals conceded while on the pitch	81
Club Defensive Rating Average number of mins between League goals conceded by the club this season	67

	PLAYER	CON LGE	CON ALL	MINS	C SHEETS	DEF RATE
1	Zatyiah Knight	27	28	2191	8	81 mins
2	Wilfred Bouma	48	49	3262	9	67 mins
3	Martin Laursen	50	52	3368	9	67 mins
4	Olof Mellberg	46	49	2962	9	64 mins

KEY GOALKEEPER

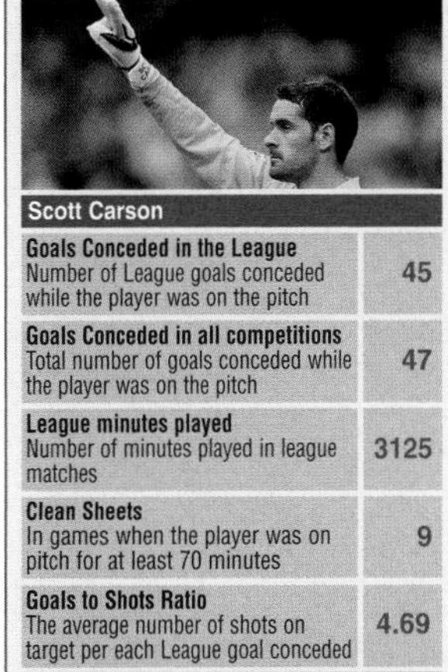

Scott Carson	
Goals Conceded in the League Number of League goals conceded while the player was on the pitch	45
Goals Conceded in all competitions Total number of goals conceded while the player was on the pitch	47
League minutes played Number of minutes played in league matches	3125
Clean Sheets In games when the player was on pitch for at least 70 minutes	9
Goals to Shots Ratio The average number of shots on target per each League goal conceded	4.69
Defensive Rating Ave mins between League goals conceded while on the pitch	69

BOOKINGS

Marlon Harewood	
League Yellow	2
League Red	0
All competitions Yellow	2
All competitions Red	0
League Average **257** mins between cards	

	PLAYER	LEAGUE		TOTAL		AVE
1	Marlon Harewood	2 Y	0R	2Y	0R	257
2	Nigel Reo-Coker	10	1	10	1	282
3	Craig Gardner	4	0	4	0	333
4	Olof Mellberg	5	1	5	1	493
5	John Alieu Carew	5	0	5	0	510
6	Ashley Young	6	0	6	0	547
7	Stilian Petrov	3	0	3	0	614
8	Wilfred Bouma	5	0	5	0	652
9	Gareth Barry	5	0	5	0	663
10	Curtis Davies	1	0	1	0	813
11	Gabriel Agbonlahor	4	0	4	0	819
12	Luke Moore	1	0	1	0	843
13	Zatyiah Knight	1	1	1	1	1095
14	Scott Carson	1	1	1	1	1562
15	Martin Laursen	1	0	1	0	3368
	Other	0	0	0	0	
	TOTAL	54	4	54	4	

BLACKBURN ROVERS

An impressive season - largely inspired by Mark Hughes' shrewd signings - saw Rovers narrowly miss out on a European place. A disappointing winter period was followed by a strong run from Christmas to the end of the season, which almost snatched sixth place from under the nose of Aston Villa. The signing of **Roque Santa Cruz** looks the best bit of business this season, with the Paraguayan netting 19 league goals. **David Bentley** has improved immeasurably, pulling most of the creative strings and Rovers have played some attractive stuff and have more strength in depth than in previous years. Heads are sure to be turning towards Bentley and Santa Cruz and with Hughes moving to City it could be a challenging season ahead for Rovers.

NICKNAME: ROVERS

KEY: Won / Drawn / Lost

No.	Comp	Opponent	H/A	Res	Score	Scorers
1	prem	**Middlesbro**	A	W	2-1	Santa Cruz 62, Derbyshire 79
2	ucql1	**MyPa-47**	A	W	1-0	Santa Cruz 5
3	prem	**Arsenal**	H	D	1-1	Dunn 72
4	prem	**Everton**	A	D	1-1	Santa Cruz 16
5	ucql2	**MyPa-47**	H	W	2-0	Bentley 48, Roberts 90
6	prem	**Man City**	H	W	1-0	McCarthy 13
7	prem	**Chelsea**	A	D	0-0	
8	uc1rl1	**Larissa**	A	L	0-2	
9	prem	**Portsmouth**	H	L	0-1	
10	ccr3	**Birmingham**	H	W	3-0	Bentley 66, Derbyshire 82 pen, Santa Cruz 90
11	prem	**Sunderland**	A	W	2-1	Bentley 53, Santa Cruz 55
12	uc1rl2	**Larissa**	H	W	2-1	Derbyshire 45 pen, Warnock 51
13	prem	**Birmingham**	H	W	2-1	Bentley 15, McCarthy 55 pen
14	prem	**Reading**	H	W	4-2	McCarthy 17, 82 pen, Santa Cruz 22, Tugay 31
15	prem	**Tottenham**	A	W	2-1	McCarthy 60, Samba 90
16	ccr4	**Portsmouth**	A	W	2-1	McCarthy 11, Pedersen 77
17	prem	**Liverpool**	H	D	0-0	
18	prem	**Man Utd**	A	L	0-2	
19	prem	**Fulham**	A	D	2-2	Emerton 57, Warnock 80
20	prem	**Aston Villa**	H	L	0-4	
21	prem	**Newcastle**	H	W	3-1	Bentley 54 , 67, Tugay 90
22	prem	**West Ham**	H	L	0-1	
23	prem	**Wigan**	A	L	3-5	Santa Cruz 45, 50, 61
24	ccqf	**Arsenal**	H	L	2-3	Santa Cruz 42, 60
25	prem	**Chelsea**	H	L	0-1	
26	prem	**Man City**	A	D	2-2	Santa Cruz 28, 83
27	prem	**Derby**	A	W	2-1	Santa Cruz 39, Bentley 42
28	prem	**Sunderland**	H	W	1-0	McCarthy 57 pen
29	facr3	**Coventry**	H	L	1-4	Bentley 85
30	prem	**Bolton**	A	W	2-1	Samba 53, Roberts 90
31	prem	**Middlesbro**	H	D	1-1	Derbyshire 75
32	prem	**Aston Villa**	A	D	1-1	Santa Cruz 67
33	prem	**Everton**	H	D	0-0	
34	prem	**Arsenal**	A	L	0-2	
35	prem	**Bolton**	H	W	4-1	McCarthy 25 pen, 67 pen, Bentley 71, Pedersen 90
36	prem	**Newcastle**	A	W	1-0	Derbyshire 90
37	prem	**Fulham**	H	D	1-1	Pedersen 59
38	prem	**West Ham**	A	L	1-2	Santa Cruz 20
39	prem	**Wigan**	H	W	3-1	Santa Cruz 11, 63, Roberts 45
40	prem	**Reading**	A	D	0-0	
41	prem	**Tottenham**	H	D	1-1	Pedersen 30
42	prem	**Liverpool**	A	L	1-3	Santa Cruz 90
43	prem	**Man Utd**	H	D	1-1	Santa Cruz 21
44	prem	**Portsmouth**	A	W	1-0	Santa Cruz 74
45	prem	**Derby**	H	W	3-1	Santa Cruz 45, 77, Roberts 47
46	prem	**Birmingham**	A	L	1-4	Pedersen 49

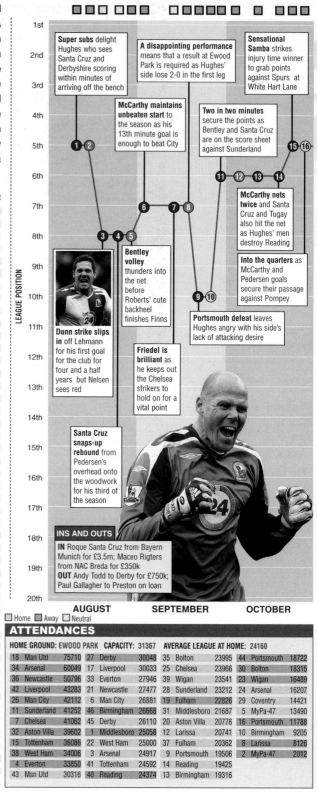

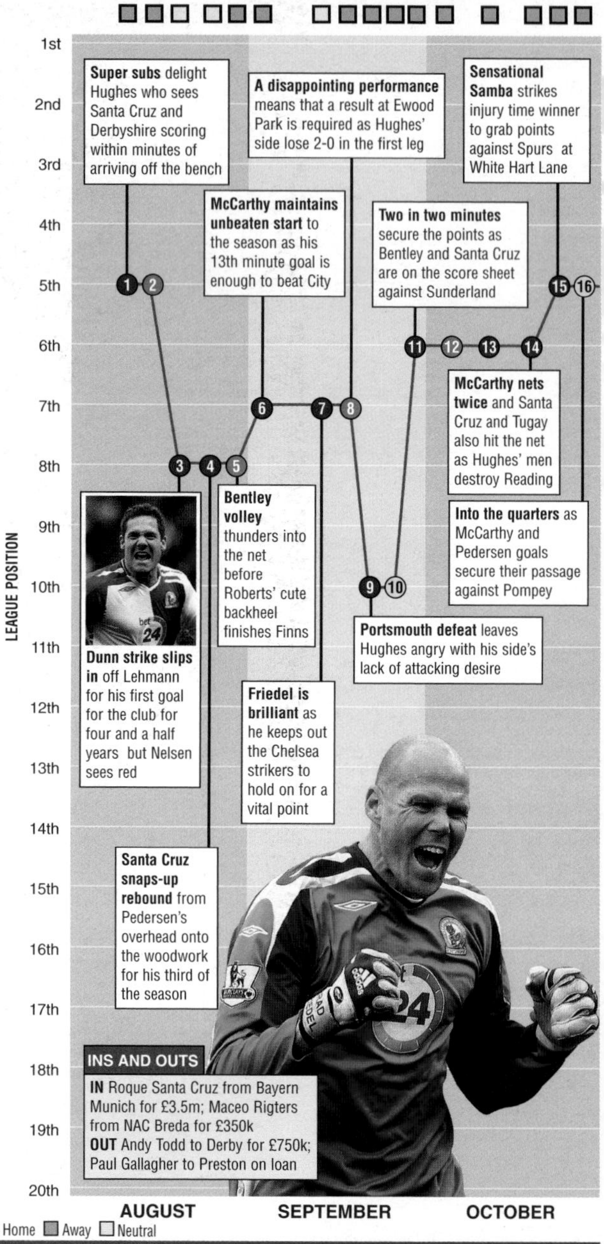

1st
2nd
3rd
4th
5th
6th
7th
8th
9th
10th
11th
12th
13th
14th
15th
16th
17th
18th
19th
20th
LEAGUE POSITION
Super subs delight Hughes who sees Santa Cruz and Derbyshire scoring within minutes of arriving off the bench
A disappointing performance means that a result at Ewood Park is required as Hughes' side lose 2-0 in the first leg
Sensational Samba strikes injury time winner to grab points against Spurs at White Hart Lane
McCarthy maintains unbeaten start to the season as his 13th minute goal is enough to beat City
Two in two minutes secure the points as Bentley and Santa Cruz are on the score sheet against Sunderland
McCarthy nets twice and Santa Cruz and Tugay also hit the net as Hughes' men destroy Reading
Bentley volley thunders into the net before Roberts' cute backheel finishes Finns
Into the quarters as McCarthy and Pedersen goals secure their passage against Pompey
Portsmouth defeat leaves Hughes angry with his side's lack of attacking desire
Dunn strike slips in off Lehmann for his first goal for the club for four and a half years but Nelsen sees red
Friedel is brilliant as he keeps out the Chelsea strikers to hold on for a vital point
Santa Cruz snaps-up rebound from Pedersen's overhead onto the woodwork for his third of the season
INS AND OUTS
IN Roque Santa Cruz from Bayern Munich for £3.5m; Maceo Rigters from NAC Breda for £350k
OUT Andy Todd to Derby for £750k; Paul Gallagher to Preston on loan
AUGUST
SEPTEMBER
OCTOBER
Home
Away
Neutral

ATTENDANCES

HOME GROUND: EWOOD PARK **CAPACITY:** 31367 **AVERAGE LEAGUE AT HOME:** 24160

18	Man Utd	75710	27	Derby	30048	35	Bolton	23995	44	Portsmouth	18722
34	Arsenal	60049	17	Liverpool	30033	25	Chelsea	23966	30	Bolton	18315
36	Newcastle	50796	33	Everton	27946	39	Wigan	23541	23	Wigan	16489
42	Liverpool	43283	21	Newcastle	27477	28	Sunderland	23212	24	Arsenal	16207
26	Man City	42112	6	Man City	26881	19	Fulham	22826	29	Coventry	14421
11	Sunderland	41252	46	Birmingham	26668	31	Middlesboro	21687	5	MyPa-47	13490
7	Chelsea	41062	45	Derby	26110	20	Aston Villa	20776	16	Portsmouth	11788
32	Aston Villa	39602	1	Middlesboro	25058	12	Larissa	20741	10	Birmingham	9205
15	Tottenham	36086	22	West Ham	25000	37	Fulham	20362	8	Larissa	8126
38	West Ham	34006	3	Arsenal	24917	9	Portsmouth	19506	2	MyPa-47	2012
4	Everton	33850	41	Tottenham	24592	14	Reading	19425			
43	Man Utd	30316	40	Reading	24374	13	Birmingham	19316			

Santa gifts Blackburn top seven finish

Final Position: **7th**

KEY: ● League ● Champions Lge ● UEFA Cup ● FA Cup ○ League Cup ● Other

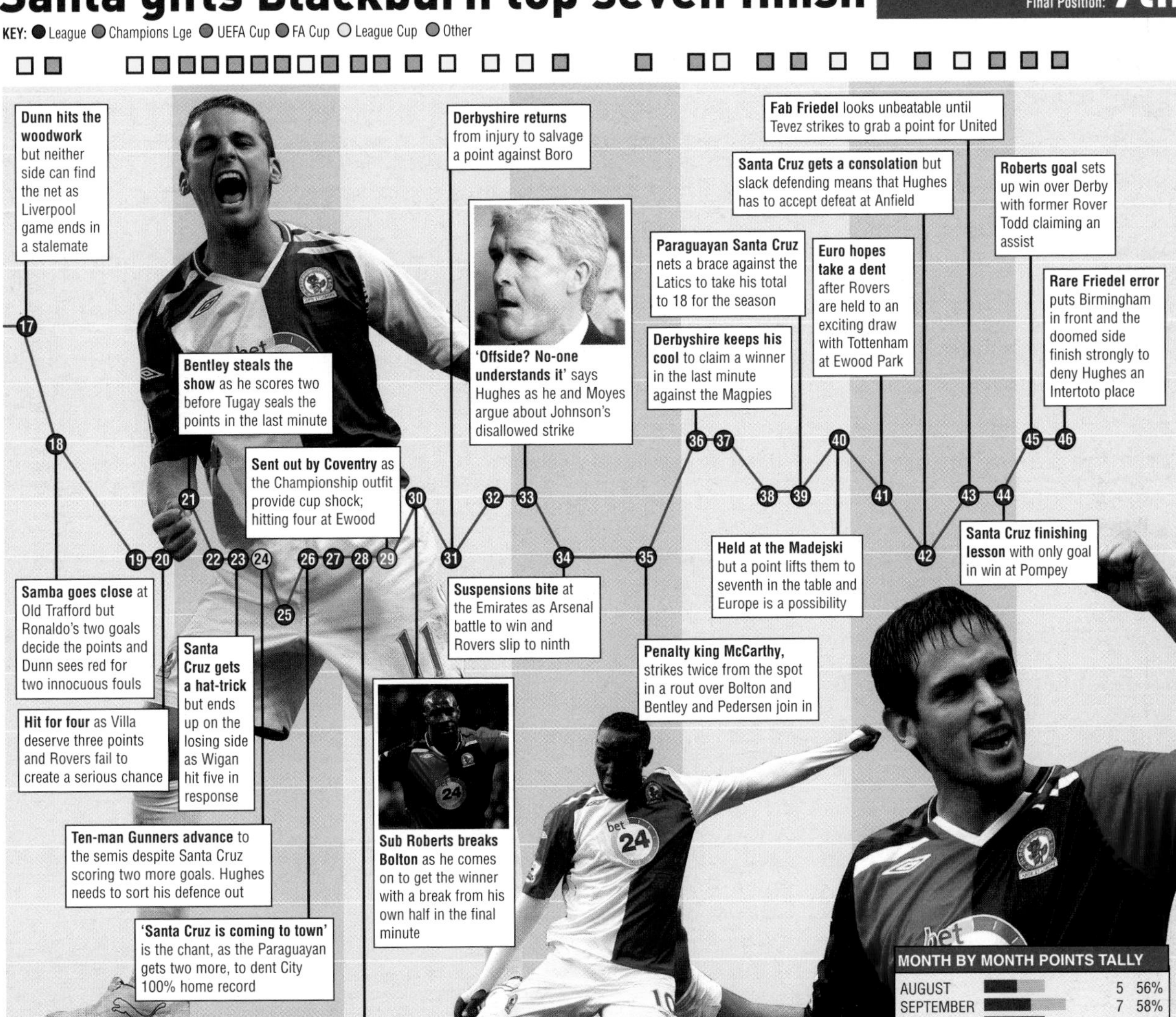

Dunn hits the woodwork but neither side can find the net as Liverpool game ends in a stalemate
Samba goes close at Old Trafford but Ronaldo's two goals decide the points and Dunn sees red for two innocuous fouls
Hit for four as Villa deserve three points and Rovers fail to create a serious chance
Bentley steals the show as he scores two before Tugay seals the points in the last minute
Santa Cruz gets a hat-trick but ends up on the losing side as Wigan hit five in response
Ten-man Gunners advance to the semis despite Santa Cruz scoring two more goals. Hughes needs to sort his defence out
Sent out by Coventry as the Championship outfit provide cup shock; hitting four at Ewood
'Santa Cruz is coming to town' is the chant, as the Paraguayan gets two more, to dent City 100% home record
McCarthy keeps his nerve to score the winner from the spot to skin the Black Cats
Sub Roberts breaks Bolton as he comes on to get the winner with a break from his own half in the final minute
Derbyshire returns from injury to salvage a point against Boro
'Offside? No-one understands it' says Hughes as he and Moyes argue about Johnson's disallowed strike
Suspensions bite at the Emirates as Arsenal battle to win and Rovers slip to ninth
Penalty king McCarthy, strikes twice from the spot in a rout over Bolton and Bentley and Pedersen join in
Paraguayan Santa Cruz nets a brace against the Latics to take his total to 18 for the season
Derbyshire keeps his cool to claim a winner in the last minute against the Magpies
Santa Cruz gets a consolation but slack defending means that Hughes has to accept defeat at Anfield
Fab Friedel looks unbeatable until Tevez strikes to grab a point for United
Euro hopes take a dent after Rovers are held to an exciting draw with Tottenham at Ewood Park
Held at the Madejski but a point lifts them to seventh in the table and Europe is a possibility
Roberts goal sets up win over Derby with former Rover Todd claiming an assist
Rare Friedel error puts Birmingham in front and the doomed side finish strongly to deny Hughes an Intertoto place
Santa Cruz finishing lesson with only goal in win at Pompey
17 18 19 20 21 22 23 24 25 26 27 28 29 30 31 32 33 34 35 36 37 38 39 40 41 42 43 44 45 46
INS AND OUTS
IN Johann Vogel from Real Betis for free
OUT Robbie Savage to Derby for £1.5m; Paul Gallagher to Stoke, Maceo Rigters to Norwich and Peter Enckelman to Cardiff on loan

MONTH BY MONTH POINTS TALLY

Month	Points	%
AUGUST	5	56%
SEPTEMBER	7	58%
OCTOBER	9	100%
NOVEMBER	2	17%
DECEMBER	7	39%
JANUARY	8	67%
FEBRUARY	4	44%
MARCH	8	53%
APRIL	5	42%
MAY	3	50%

NOVEMBER DECEMBER JANUARY FEBRUARY MARCH APRIL MAY

GOAL ATTEMPTS

FOR — Goal attempts recorded in League games

	HOME	AWAY	TOTAL	AVE
shots on target	153	117	270	7.1
shots off target	113	85	198	5.2
TOTAL	266	202	468	12.3

Ratio of goals to shots Average number of shots on target per League goal scored	5.4
Accuracy rating Average percentage of total goal attempts which were on target	57.7

AGAINST — Goal attempts recorded in League games

	HOME	AWAY	TOTAL	AVE
shots on target	141	125	266	7.0
shots off target	83	100	183	4.8
TOTAL	224	225	449	11.8

Ratio of goals to shots Average number of shots on target per League goal scored	5.5
Accuracy rating Average percentage of total goal attempts which were on target	59.2

GOALS

Santa Cruz

League	19
FA Cup	0
League Cup	3
Europe	1
Other	0
TOTAL	23

League Average **167** mins between goals

	PLAYER	LGE	FAC	LC	Euro	TOT	AVE
1	Santa Cruz	19	0	3	1	23	167
2	McCarthy	8	0	1	0	9	210
3	Bentley	6	1	1	1	9	553
4	Derbyshire	3	0	1	1	5	205
5	Pedersen	4	0	1	0	5	718
6	Roberts	3	0	0	1	4	419
7	Tugay	2	0	0	0	2	562
8	Samba	2	0	0	0	2	1445
9	Warnock	1	0	0	1	2	3284
10	Dunn	1	0	0	0	1	1952
11	Emerton	1	0	0	0	1	2752
12	Enckelman	0	0	0	0	0	
13	Friedel	0	0	0	0	0	
14	Gallagher	0	0	0	0	0	
15	Kane	0	0	0	0	0	
	Other	0	0	0	0	0	
	TOTAL	50	1	7	5	63	

SQUAD APPEARANCES

Match	1	2	3	4	5	6	7	8	9	10	11	12	13	14	15	16	17	18	19	20	21	22	23	24	25	26	27	28	29	30	31	32	33	34	35	36	37	38	39	40	41	42	43	44	45	46
Venue	A	A	H	A	H	H	A	A	H	H	A	H	H	H	A	A	H	A	A	H	H	H	A	H	H	A	A	H	H	A	H	A	H	A	H	A	H	A	H	A	H	A	H	A	H	A
Competition	L	E	L	L	E	L	L	E	L	W	L	E	L	L	L	W	L	L	L	L	L	L	L	W	L	L	L	L	F	L	L	L	L	L	L	L	L	L	L	L	L	L	L	L	L	L
Result	W	W	D	D	W	W	D	L	L	W	W	W	W	W	W	W	D	L	D	L	W	L	L	L	L	D	W	W	L	W	D	D	D	L	W	W	D	L	W	D	D	L	D	W	W	L

Goalkeepers
- Jason Brown
- Peter Enckelman
- Brad Friedel

Defenders
- Bruno Berner
- Brett Emerton
- Anthony Kane
- Zurab Khizanishvili
- Ryan Nelsen
- Martin Olsson
- Andre Ooijer
- Christopher Samba
- Stephen Warnock

Midfielders
- David Bentley
- David Dunn
- Aaron Mokoena
- Morten Gamst Pedersen
- Steven Reid
- Robbie Savage
- Keith Treacy
- Kerimoglu Tugay
- Johann Vogel

Forwards
- Matthew Derbyshire
- Paul Gallagher
- Benni McCarthy
- Maceo Rigters
- Jason Roberts
- Roque Santa Cruz

KEY: On all match · On bench · Subbed or sent off (Counting game) · Subbed or sent off (playing less than 70 mins) · Subbed on from bench (Counting Game) · Subbed on (playing less than 70 mins) · Subbed on and then subbed or sent off (Counting Game) · Subbed on and then subbed or sent off (playing less than 70 min · Not in 16 · Injured · ✕ Suspended

KEY PLAYERS - GOALSCORERS

Roque Santa Cruz

Goals in the League	19
Goals in all competitions	23
Assists League goals scored by a team mate where the player delivered the final pass	8
Contribution to Attacking Power Average number of minutes between League team goals while on pitch	70
Player Strike Rate Average number of minutes between League goals scored by player	167
Club Strike Rate Average minutes between League goals scored by club	68

	PLAYER	GOALS LGE	GOALS ALL	ASSISTS	POWER	S RATE
1	Roque Santa Cruz	19	23	8	70	167 mins
2	Benni McCarthy	8	9	0	76	210 mins
3	Jason Roberts	3	4	7	57	419 mins
4	David Bentley	6	9	9	66	553 mins

KEY PLAYERS - MIDFIELDERS

Morten Gamst Pedersen

Goals in the League	4
Goals in all competitions	5
Assists League goals scored by a team mate where the player delivered the final pass	2
Defensive Rating Average number of mins between League goals conceded while on the pitch	77
Contribution to Attacking Power Average number of minutes between League team goals while on pitch	68
Scoring Difference Defensive Rating minus Contribution to Attacking Power	9

	PLAYER	GOALS LGE	GOALS ALL	ASSISTS	DEF RATE	POWER	SC DIFF
1	Morten Gamst Pedersen	4	5	2	77	68	9 mins
2	David Bentley	6	9	9	73	66	7 mins
3	Steven Reid	0	0	0	62	64	-2 mins
4	David Dunn	1	1	5	72	75	-3 mins

PLAYER APPEARANCES

	AGE (on 01/07/08)	IN NAMED 16	APPEARANCES	COUNTING GAMES	MINUTES ON PITCH	APPEARANCES	MINUTES ON PITCH	THIS SEASON	HOME COUNTRY
Goalkeepers									
Jason Brown	26	37	0	0	0	0	0	-	Wales
Peter Enckelman	31	1	0	0	0	0	0	-	Finland
Brad Friedel	37	38	38	38	3420	46	4170	-	United States
Defenders									
Bruno Berner	30	7	2	2	180	4	360	-	Switzerland
Brett Emerton	33	33	33	28	2752	40	3253	-	Australia
Anthony Kane	20	1	0	0	0	0	0	-	N Ireland
Zurab Khizanishvili	26	21	13	9	954	17	1170	1	Georgia
Ryan Nelsen	30	23	22	21	1934	28	2410	-	New Zealand
Martin Olsson	20	4	2	0	19	4	111	-	Sweden
Andre Ooijer	33	31	27	22	2026	32	2476	5	Holland
Christopher Samba	24	33	33	32	2890	39	3460	-	Congo
Stephen Warnock	26	37	37	36	3284	43	3761	-	England
Midfielders									
David Bentley	23	37	37	37	3320	45	4016	4	England
David Dunn	28	33	31	17	1952	37	2475	-	England
Aaron Mokoena	27	27	18	5	765	24	1140	4	South Africa
Morten G Pedersen	26	37	37	30	2872	44	3362	5	Norway
Steven Reid	27	24	24	20	1865	25	1985	-	Rep of Ireland
Robbie Savage	33	16	12	7	806	16	1119	-	Wales
Keith Treacy	19	2	0	0	0	2	69	-	Rep of Ireland
Kerimoglu Tugay	37	27	20	9	1124	26	1514	-	Turkey
Johann Vogel	31	7	6	4	464	6	464	-	Switzerland
Forwards									
Matthew Derbyshire	22	29	23	3	617	31	1002	-	England
Paul Gallagher	23	0	0	0	0	0	0	-	Scotland
Benni McCarthy	30	35	31	12	1682	36	1992	-	South Africa
Maceo Rigters	24	2	2	0	16	5	158	-	Holland
Jason Roberts	30	29	26	12	1259	29	1467	-	Grenada
Roque Santa Cruz	26	37	37	35	3189	43	3706	2	Paraguay

KEY: LEAGUE ALL COMPS CAPS (MAY FIFA RANKING)

TEAM OF THE SEASON

FRIEDEL CG 38 DR 71

EMERTON CG 28 DR 70

OOIJER CG 22 DR 81

NELSEN CG 21 DR 69

WARNOCK CG 36 DR 78

BENTLEY CG 37 SD +7

REID CG 20 SD -2

DUNN CG 17 SD -3

PEDERSEN CG 30 SD +9

McCARTHY CG 12 AP 76

SANTA CRUZ CG 35 SR 167

KEY: DR = Defensive Rate, SD = Scoring Difference AP = Attacking Power SR = Strike Rate, CG=Counting games – League games playing at least 70 minutes

TOP POINT EARNERS

Benni McCarthy

Counting Games League games when player was on pitch for at least 70 minutes	12
Average points Average League points taken in Counting games	1.67
Club Average points Average points taken in League games	1.53

	PLAYER	GAMES	PTS
1	Benni McCarthy	12	1.67
2	Andre Ooijer	22	1.59
3	David Dunn	17	1.59
4	David Bentley	37	1.57
5	Christopher Samba	32	1.56
6	Brad Friedel	38	1.53
7	Brett Emerton	28	1.50
8	Morten Gamst Pedersen	30	1.50
9	Stephen Warnock	36	1.50
10	Roque Santa Cruz	35	1.46

KEY PLAYERS - DEFENDERS

Andre Ooijer

Goals Conceded in the League Number of League goals conceded while the player was on the pitch	25
Goals Conceded in all competitions Total number of goals conceded while the player was on the pitch	28
League minutes played Number of minutes played in league matches	2026
Clean Sheets In games when the player was on pitch for at least 70 minutes	4
Defensive Rating Average number of mins between League goals conceded while on the pitch	81
Club Defensive Rating Average number of mins between League goals conceded by the club this season	71

	PLAYER	CON LGE	CON ALL	MINS	C SHEETS	DEF RATE
1	Andre Ooijer	25	28	2026	4	81 mins
2	Stephen Warnock	42	48	3284	8	78 mins
3	Brett Emerton	39	44	2752	6	70 mins
4	Ryan Nelsen	28	37	1934	6	69 mins

KEY GOALKEEPER

Brad Friedel

Goals Conceded in the League Number of League goals conceded while the player was on the pitch	48
Goals Conceded in all competitions Total number of goals conceded while the player was on the pitch	59
League minutes played Number of minutes played in league matches	3420
Clean Sheets In games when the player was on pitch for at least 70 minutes	8
Goals to Shots Ratio The average number of shots on target per each League goal conceded	5.54
Defensive Rating Ave mins between League goals conceded while on the pitch	71

BOOKINGS

Kerimoglu Tugay

League Yellow	5
League Red	1
All competitions Yellow	6
All competitions Red	1

League Average 187 mins between cards

	PLAYER	LEAGUE		TOTAL		AVE
1	Kerimoglu Tugay	5Y	1R	6Y	1R	187
2	Robbie Savage	4	0	5	0	201
3	David Dunn	7	1	8	1	244
4	Chris Samba	10	1	12	1	262
5	Steven Reid	6	0	7	0	310
6	Ryan Nelsen	4	2	4	2	322
7	Aaron Mokoena	2	0	2	0	382
8	Stephen Warnock	8	0	11	0	410
9	David Bentley	8	0	10	0	415
10	Zurab Khizanishvili	2	0	3	0	477
11	Gamst Pedersen	5	0	5	0	574
12	Matt Derbyshire	1	0	1	0	617
13	Jason Roberts	2	0	2	0	629
14	Brett Emerton	3	1	3	1	688
15	Andre Ooijer	2	0	2	0	1013
	Other	4	0	4	0	
	TOTAL	73	6	85	6	

PORTSMOUTH

Arguably Portsmouth's most successful season in their history ended with an 8th place finish and an F.A. Cup triumph. Not only that, Harry Redknapp had built a side which played exciting, attractive, attacking football. A combination of staunch experience in the form of **David James**, **Sol Campbell** and **Herman Hreidarsson** perfectly complemented the youthful exuberance of **Glen Johnson**, **Nico Kranjcar** and **Lassana Diarra**. Diarra was arguably one of the buys of the season – a relative snip at £5million – and quickly became the heartbeat of a dominant midfield. Pompey gave their fans so many unforgettable memories; the 7-4 win over Reading, away days routs at Newcastle and Villa, and of course the three 1-0 wins over Man Utd, WBA and Cardiff that won the cup. Similar memories of the European variety would do just nicely next season.

NICKNAME: POMPEY

KEY: Won · Drawn · Lost

1	prem	**Derby**	A	D	2-2	Mwaruwari 27, Utaka 83
2	prem	**Man Utd**	H	D	1-1	Mwaruwari 53
3	prem	**Bolton**	H	W	3-1	Kanu 16, Utaka 30, Taylor 88 pen
4	prem	**Chelsea**	A	L	0-1	
5	ccr2	**Leeds**	H	W	3-0	Pamarot 43, 80, Nugent 84
6	prem	**Arsenal**	A	L	1-3	Kanu 60
7	prem	**Liverpool**	H	D	0-0	
8	prem	**Blackburn**	A	W	1-0	Kanu 24
9	ccr3	**Burnley**	A	W	1-0	Nugent 69
10	prem	**Reading**	H	W	7-4	Mwaruwari 6, 37, 70, Hreidarsson 55, Kranjcar 74, Ingimarsson 81 og, Muntari 90 pen
11	prem	**Fulham**	A	W	2-0	Mwaruwari 50, Hreidarsson 52
12	prem	**Wigan**	A	W	2-0	Mwaruwari 81, Johnson 86
13	prem	**West Ham**	H	D	0-0	
14	ccr4	**Blackburn**	H	L	1-2	Kanu 90
15	prem	**Newcastle**	A	W	4-1	Pamarot 8, Mwaruwari 9, Utaka 11, Kranjcar 70
16	prem	**Man City**	H	D	0-0	
17	prem	**Birmingham**	A	W	2-0	Muntari 34, Kranjcar 82
18	prem	**Everton**	H	D	0-0	
19	prem	**Aston Villa**	A	W	3-1	Gardner 9 og, Muntari 40, 61
20	prem	**Tottenham**	H	L	0-1	
21	prem	**Liverpool**	A	L	1-4	Mwaruwari 57
22	prem	**Arsenal**	H	D	0-0	
23	prem	**Middlesbrough**	H	L	0-1	
24	prem	**Reading**	A	W	2-0	Campbell 9, Utaka 66
25	facr3	**Ipswich**	A	W	1-0	Nugent 51
26	prem	**Sunderland**	A	L	0-2	
27	prem	**Derby**	H	W	3-1	Mwaruwari 38, 42, 55
28	facr4	**Plymouth**	H	W	2-1	Diarra 34, Kranjcar 45
29	prem	**Man Utd**	A	L	0-2	
30	prem	**Chelsea**	H	D	1-1	Defoe 64
31	prem	**Bolton**	A	W	1-0	Diarra 81
32	facr5	**Preston**	A	W	1-0	Carter 90 og
33	prem	**Sunderland**	H	W	1-0	Defoe 69 pen
34	prem	**Everton**	A	L	1-3	Defoe 38
35	facqf	**Man Utd**	A	W	1-0	Muntari 78 pen
36	prem	**Birmingham**	H	W	4-2	Defoe 6 pen, 8, Hreidarsson 49, Kanu 90
37	prem	**Aston Villa**	H	W	2-0	Defoe 12, Reo-Coker 38 og
38	prem	**Tottenham**	A	L	0-2	
39	prem	**Wigan**	H	W	2-0	Defoe 32, 90
40	facsf	**West Brom**	N	W	1-0	Kanu 54
41	prem	**West Ham**	A	W	1-0	Kranjcar 61
42	prem	**Newcastle**	H	D	0-0	
43	prem	**Man City**	A	L	1-3	Utaka 24
44	prem	**Blackburn**	H	L	0-1	
45	prem	**Middlesbrough**	A	L	0-2	
46	prem	**Fulham**	H	L	0-1	
47	facf	**Cardiff**	N	W	1-0	Kanu 37

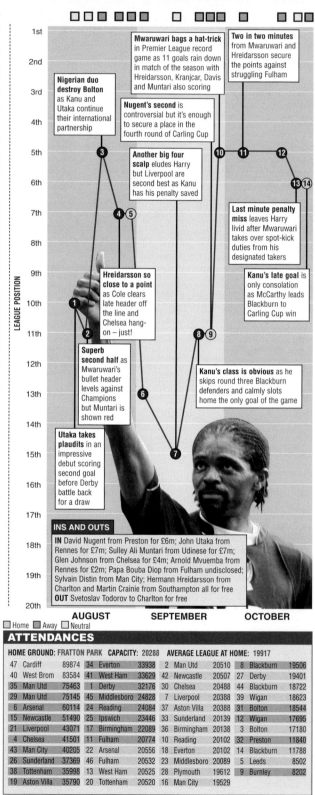

1st
2nd
3rd
4th
5th
6th
7th
8th
9th
10th
11th
12th
13th
14th
15th
16th
17th
18th
19th
20th
LEAGUE POSITION
Utaka takes plaudits in an impressive debut scoring second goal before Derby battle back for a draw
Superb second half as Mwaruwari's bullet header levels against Champions but Muntari is shown red
Nigerian duo destroy Bolton as Kanu and Utaka continue their international partnership
Hreidarsson so close to a point as Cole clears late header off the line and Chelsea hang-on – just!
Another big four scalp eludes Harry but Liverpool are second best as Kanu has his penalty saved
Nugent's second is controversial but it's enough to secure a place in the fourth round of Carling Cup
Kanu's class is obvious as he skips round three Blackburn defenders and calmly slots home the only goal of the game
Mwaruwari bags a hat-trick in Premier League record game as 11 goals rain down in match of the season with Hreidarsson, Kranjcar, Davis and Muntari also scoring
Two in two minutes from Mwaruwari and Hreidarsson secure the points against struggling Fulham
Last minute penalty miss leaves Harry livid after Mwaruwari takes over spot-kick duties from his designated takers
Kanu's late goal is only consolation as McCarthy leads Blackburn to Carling Cup win
AUGUST
SEPTEMBER
OCTOBER
Home
Away
Neutral

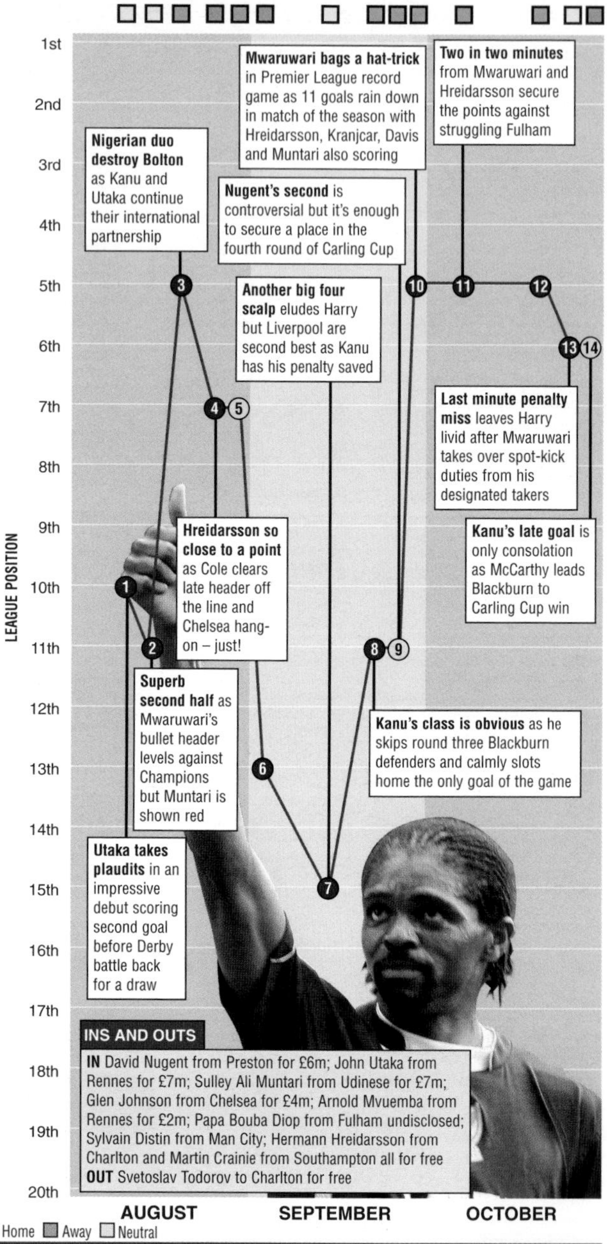

INS AND OUTS

IN David Nugent from Preston for £6m; John Utaka from Rennes for £7m; Sulley Ali Muntari from Udinese for £7m; Glen Johnson from Chelsea for £4m; Arnold Mvuemba from Rennes for £2m; Papa Bouba Diop from Fulham undisclosed; Sylvain Distin from Man City; Hermann Hreidarsson from Charlton and Martin Crainie from Southampton all for free **OUT** Svetoslav Todorov to Charlton for free

ATTENDANCES

HOME GROUND: FRATTON PARK **CAPACITY:** 20288 **AVERAGE LEAGUE AT HOME:** 19917

47	Cardiff	89874	34	Everton	33938	2	Man Utd	20510	8	Blackburn	19506
40	West Brom	83584	41	West Ham	33629	42	Newcastle	20507	27	Derby	19401
35	Man Utd	75463	1	Derby	32176	30	Chelsea	20488	44	Blackburn	18722
29	Man Utd	75145	45	Middlesboro	24828	7	Liverpool	20388	39	Wigan	18623
6	Arsenal	60114	24	Reading	24084	37	Aston Villa	20388	31	Bolton	18544
15	Newcastle	51490	25	Ipswich	23446	33	Sunderland	20139	12	Wigan	17695
21	Liverpool	43071	17	Birmingham	22089	36	Birmingham	20138	3	Bolton	17180
4	Chelsea	41501	11	Fulham	20774	10	Reading	20102	32	Preston	11840
43	Man City	40205	22	Arsenal	20556	18	Everton	20102	14	Blackburn	11788
26	Sunderland	37369	46	Fulham	20532	23	Middlesboro	20089	5	Leeds	8502
38	Tottenham	35998	13	West Ham	20525	28	Plymouth	19612	9	Burnley	8202
19	Aston Villa	35790	20	Tottenham	20520	16	Man City	19529			

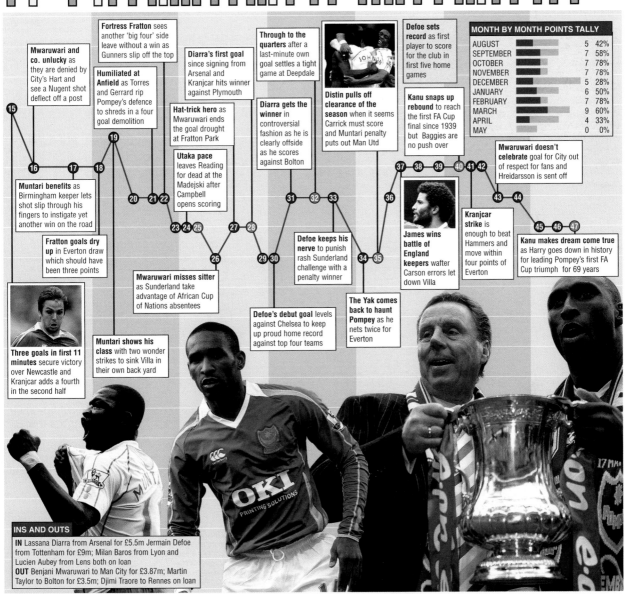

Cup win crowns dream season

Final Position: **8th**

KEY: ● League ● Champions Lge ● UEFA Cup ● FA Cup ○ League Cup ● Other

Three goals in first 11 minutes secure victory over Newcastle and Kranjcar adds a fourth in the second half

Mwaruwari and co. unlucky as they are denied by City's Hart and see a Nugent shot deflect off a post

Muntari benefits as Birmingham keeper lets shot slip through his fingers to instigate yet another win on the road

Fratton goals dry up in Everton draw which should have been three points

Muntari shows his class with two wonder strikes to sink Villa in their own back yard

Humiliated at Anfield as Torres and Gerrard rip Pompey's defence to shreds in a four goal demolition

Fortress Fratton sees another 'big four' side leave without a win as Gunners slip off the top

Hat-trick hero as Mwaruwari ends the goal drought at Fratton Park

Utaka pace leaves Reading for dead at the Madejski after Campbell opens scoring

Mwaruwari misses sitter as Sunderland take advantage of African Cup of Nations absentees

Diarra's first goal since signing from Arsenal and Kranjcar hits winner against Plymouth

Diarra gets the winner in controversial fashion as he is clearly offside as he scores against Bolton

Through to the quarters after a last-minute own goal settles a tight game at Deepdale

Defoe's debut goal levels against Chelsea to keep up proud home record against top four teams

Defoe keeps his nerve to punish rash Sunderland challenge with a penalty winner

Distin pulls off clearance of the season when it seems Carrick must score and Muntari penalty puts out Man Utd

The Yak comes back to haunt Pompey as he nets twice for Everton

Defoe sets record as first player to score for the club in first five home games

James wins battle of England keepers wafter Carson errors let down Villa

Kanu snaps up rebound to reach the first FA Cup final since 1939 but Baggies are no push over

Kranjcar strike is enough to beat Hammers and move within four points of Everton

Mwaruwari doesn't celebrate goal for City out of respect for fans and Hreidarsson is sent off

Kanu makes dream come true as Harry goes down in history for leading Pompey's first FA Cup triumph for 69 years

NOVEMBER DECEMBER JANUARY FEBRUARY MARCH APRIL MAY

MONTH BY MONTH POINTS TALLY

Month	Points	%
AUGUST	5	42%
SEPTEMBER	7	58%
OCTOBER	7	78%
NOVEMBER	7	78%
DECEMBER	5	28%
JANUARY	6	50%
FEBRUARY	7	78%
MARCH	9	60%
APRIL	4	33%
MAY	0	0%

INS AND OUTS

IN Lassana Diarra from Arsenal for £5.5m Jermain Defoe from Tottenham for £9m; Milan Baros from Lyon and Lucien Aubey from Lens both on loan

OUT Benjani Mwaruwari to Man City for £3.87m; Martin Taylor to Bolton for £3.5m; Djimi Traore to Rennes on loan

GOAL ATTEMPTS

FOR – Goal attempts recorded in League games

	HOME	AWAY	TOTAL	AVE
shots on target	114	125	239	6.3
shots off target	149	106	255	6.7
TOTAL	263	231	494	13.0

Ratio of goals to shots – Average number of shots on target per League goal scored: **5.0**

Accuracy rating – Average percentage of total goal attempts which were on target: **48.4**

AGAINST – Goal attempts recorded in League games

	HOME	AWAY	TOTAL	AVE
shots on target	114	125	239	6.3
shots off target	107	130	237	6.2
TOTAL	221	255	476	12.5

Ratio of goals to shots – Average number of shots on target per League goal scored: **6.0**

Accuracy rating – Average percentage of total goal attempts which were on target: **50.2**

GOALS

Mwaruwari

League	12
FA Cup	0
League Cup	0
Europe	0
Other	0
TOTAL	12

League Average **152** mins between goals

	PLAYER	LGE	FAC	LC	Euro	TOT	AVE
1	Mwaruwari	12	0	0	0	12	152
2	Defoe	8	0	0	0	8	133
3	Kanu	4	1	1	0	6	344
4	Utaka	5	0	0	0	5	403
5	Muntari	4	1	0	0	5	592
6	Kranjcar	4	1	0	0	5	714
7	Hreidarsson	3	0	0	0	3	863
8	Pamarot	1	0	2	0	3	1166
9	Nugent	0	1	2	0	3	
10	Diarra	1	1	0	0	2	1002
11	Taylor	1	0	0	0	1	458
12	Johnson	1	0	0	0	1	2565
13	Campbell	1	0	0	0	1	2790
14	Cranie	0	0	0	0	0	
15	Davis	0	0	0	0	0	
	Other	0	0	0	0	0	
	TOTAL	45	5	5	0	55	

SQUAD APPEARANCES

Match	1	2	3	4	5	6	7	8	9	10	11	12	13	14	15	16	17	18	19	20	21	22	23	24
Venue	A	H	H	A	H	A	H	A	A	H	A	A	H	H	A	H	A	H	A	H	A	H	H	A
Competition	L	L	L	L	W	L	L	L	W	L	L	L	L	W	L	L	L	L	L	L	L	L	L	L
Result	D	D	W	L	W	L	D	W	W	W	W	W	D	L	W	D	W	D	W	L	L	D	L	W

Match	25	26	27	28	29	30	31	32	33	34	35	36	37	38	39	40	41	42	43	44	45	46	47
Venue	A	A	H	H	A	H	A	A	H	A	A	H	H	A	H	N	A	H	A	H	A	H	N
Competition	F	L	L	F	L	L	L	F	L	L	F	L	L	L	L	F	L	L	L	L	L	L	F
Result	W	L	W	W	L	D	W	W	W	L	W	W	W	L	W	W	W	D	L	L	L	L	W

Goalkeepers
Jamie Ashdown
Asmir Begovic
David James

Defenders
Lucien Aubey
Sol Campbell
Martin Cranie
Sylvain Distin
Richard Duffy
Hermann Hreidarsson
Glen Johnson
Etame Mayer Lauren
Noe Pamarot
Djimi Traore

Midfielders
Sean Davis
Lassana Diarra
Papa Bouba Diop
Richard Hughes
Niko Kranjcar
Pedro Mendes
Sulley Ali Muntari
Arnold Mvuemba
Gary O'Neil
Franck Songo'o
Matthew Taylor
Marc Wilson

Forwards
Milan Baros
Jermain Defoe
Nwankwo Kanu
Benjani Mwaruwari
David Nugent
John Utaka

KEY: ■ On all match ■ On bench | ⏮ Subbed or sent off (Counting game) « Subbed or sent off (playing less than 70 mins) | ⏭ Subbed on from bench (Counting Game) » Subbed on (playing less than 70 mins) | Subbed on and then subbed or sent off (Counting Game) Subbed on and then subbed or sent off (playing less than 70 min | □ Not in 16 | □ Injured ✕ Suspended

KEY PLAYERS - GOALSCORERS

Jermain Defoe

Goals in the League	8
Goals in all competitions	8
Assists League goals scored by a team mate where the player delivered the final pass	1
Contribution to Attacking Power Average number of minutes between League team goals while on pitch	88
Player Strike Rate Average number of minutes between League goals scored by player	133
Club Strike Rate Average minutes between League goals scored by club	71

	PLAYER	GOALS LGE	GOALS ALL	ASSISTS	POWER	S RATE
1	Jermain Defoe	8	8	1	88	133 mins
2	Benjani Mwaruwari	12	12	1	65	152 mins
3	Nwankwo Kanu	4	7	4	114	344 mins
4	John Utaka	5	5	3	62	403 mins

KEY PLAYERS - MIDFIELDERS

Papa Bouba Diop

Goals in the League	0
Goals in all competitions	0
Assists League goals scored by a team mate where the player delivered the final pass	3
Defensive Rating Average number of mins between League goals conceded while on the pitch	97
Contribution to Attacking Power Average number of minutes between League team goals while on pitch	63
Scoring Difference Defensive Rating minus Contribution to Attacking Power	34

	PLAYER	GOALS LGE	GOALS ALL	ASSISTS	DEF RATE	POWER	SC DIFF
1	Papa Bouba Diop	0	0	3	97	63	34 mins
2	Sulley Ali Muntari	4	5	3	98	64	34 mins
3	Sean Davis	0	0	2	82	63	19 mins
4	Niko Kranjcar	4	5	4	86	69	17 mins

PLAYER APPEARANCES

	AGE (on 01/07/08)	IN NAMED 16	APPEARANCES	COUNTING GAMES	MINUTES ON PITCH	APPEARANCES	MINUTES ON PITCH	THIS SEASON	HOME COUNTRY
Goalkeepers									
Jamie Ashdown	27	27	3	3	270	5	450	-	England
Asmir Begovic	21	14	0	0	0	0	0	-	Bosnia
David James	37	35	35	35	3150	42	3780	3	England
Defenders									
Lucien Aubey	24	7	3	1	169	3	169	-	France
Sol Campbell	33	31	31	31	2790	37	3330	4	England
Martin Cranie	21	2	2	0	54	3	144	-	England
Sylvain Distin	30	36	36	35	3194	45	4000	-	France
Richard Duffy	22	1	0	0	0	0	0	1	Wales
Hermann Hreidarsson	33	36	32	26	2590	39	3134	6	Iceland
Glen Johnson	23	29	29	28	2565	36	3195	-	England
Etame Mayer Lauren	31	24	15	9	978	18	1151	-	Cameroon
Noe Pamarot	29	22	18	12	1166	22	1481	-	France
Djimi Traore	28	5	3	1	136	5	316	-	France
Midfielders									
Sean Davis	28	27	22	16	1646	25	1771	-	England
Lassana Diarra	23	12	12	11	1002	17	1452	4	France
Papa Bouba Diop	30	25	25	23	2155	32	2574	3	Senegal
Richard Hughes	29	18	13	8	770	17	952	-	Scotland
Niko Kranjcar	23	34	34	31	2857	42	3567	7	Croatia
Pedro Mendes	29	25	18	12	1221	24	1702	-	Portugal
Sulley Ali Muntari	23	29	29	26	2368	33	2713	6	Ghana
Arnold Mvuemba	23	9	8	2	316	12	549	-	France
Gary O'Neil	25	2	2	1	142	3	160	-	England
Franck Songo'o	21	2	1	0	26	1	26	-	France
Matthew Taylor	26	21	13	3	458	15	593	-	England
Marc Wilson	20	3	0	0	0	0	0	-	N Ireland
Forwards									
Milan Baros	26	13	12	4	616	16	742	5	Czech Republic
Jermain Defoe	25	12	12	12	1065	12	1065	2	England
Nwankwo Kanu	31	26	25	12	1376	31	1790	1	Nigeria
Benjani Mwaruwari	29	23	23	19	1831	27	2112	2	Zimbabwe
David Nugent	23	27	15	5	624	22	981	-	England
John Utaka	26	31	29	19	2015	36	2561	3	Nigeria

KEY: LEAGUE · ALL COMPS · CAPS · (MAY FIFA RANKING)

TEAM OF THE SEASON

JAMES — CG 35 DR 87

JOHNSON — CG 28 DR 95
CAMPBELL — CG 31 DR 90
DISTIN — CG 35 DR 81
PAMAROT — CG 12 DR 89

DAVIS — CG 16 SD +19
MUNTARI — CG 26 SD +34
DIOP — CG 23 SD +34
KRANJCAR — CG 31 SD +17

MWARUWARI — CG 19 AP 65
DEFOE — CG 12 SR 133

KEY: DR = Defensive Rate, SD = Scoring Difference AP = Attacking Power SR = Strike Rate, CG=Counting games – League games playing at least 70 minutes

TOP POINT EARNERS

Sean Davis

Counting Games League games when player was on pitch for at least 70 minutes	16
Average points Average League points taken in Counting games	1.81
Club Average points Average points taken in League games	1.50

	PLAYER	GAMES	PTS
1	Sean Davis	16	1.81
2	Papa Bouba Diop	23	1.78
3	Glen Johnson	28	1.71
4	Sulley Ali Muntari	26	1.69
5	Niko Kranjcar	31	1.65
6	Hermann Hreidarsson	26	1.65
7	David James	35	1.63
8	John Utaka	19	1.63
9	Benjani Mwaruwari	19	1.58
10	Sol Campbell	31	1.52

KEY PLAYERS - DEFENDERS

Glen Johnson

Goals Conceded in the League Number of League goals conceded while the player was on the pitch	27
Goals Conceded in all competitions Total number of goals conceded while the player was on the pitch	30
League minutes played Number of minutes played in league matches	2565
Clean Sheets In games when the player was on pitch for at least 70 minutes	14
Defensive Rating Average number of mins between League goals conceded while on the pitch	95
Club Defensive Rating Average number of mins between League goals conceded by the club this season	85

OKI
PRINTING SOLUTIONS

	PLAYER	CON LGE	CON ALL	MINS	C SHEETS	DEF RATE
1	Glen Johnson	27	30	2565	14	95 mins
2	Sol Campbell	31	33	2790	15	90 mins
3	Noe Pamarot	13	15	1166	4	89 mins
4	Sylvain Distin	39	42	3194	15	81 mins

KEY GOALKEEPER

David James

Goals Conceded in the League Number of League goals conceded while the player was on the pitch	36
Goals Conceded in all competitions Total number of goals conceded while the player was on the pitch	39
League minutes played Number of minutes played in league matches	3150
Clean Sheets In games when the player was on pitch for at least 70 minutes	16
Goals to Shots Ratio The average number of shots on target per each League goal conceded	6.28
Defensive Rating Ave mins between League goals conceded while on the pitch	87

BOOKINGS

Sean Davis

League Yellow	8
League Red	0
All competitions Yellow	9
All competitions Red	0
League Average **205** mins between cards	

	PLAYER	LEAGUE		TOTAL		AVE
1	Sean Davis	8Y	0R	9Y	0R	205
2	Etame Lauren	4	0	4	0	244
3	Sulley Ali Muntari	6	2	6	2	296
4	Papa Bouba Diop	7	0	9	0	307
5	Richard Hughes	2	0	2	0	385
6	Noe Pamarot	3	0	4	0	388
7	Matthew Taylor	1	0	1	0	458
8	Lassana Diarra	2	0	4	0	501
9	Jermain Defoe	2	0	2	0	532
10	Pedro Mendes	2	0	3	0	610
11	Glen Johnson	4	0	4	0	641
12	H Hreidarsson	3	1	5	1	647
13	Sylvain Distin	4	0	5	0	798
14	Nwankwo Kanu	1	0	1	0	1376
15	Sol Campbell	2	0	2	0	1395
	Other	6	0	8	0	
	TOTAL	57	3	69	3	

MANCHESTER CITY

The season that got underway so brightly ended with the team coming off the rails at the Riverside and the owner appalling fans by sacking Sven-Goran Eriksson. While the second half of the season was disappointing, the top half finish, the rediscovered ability to score goals and the two defiant victories over United made it one of the best seasons in recent memory. Sven spent wisely in picking up **Elano** and **Martin Petrov** but also got the best out of existing players, such as, **Richard Dunne**, **Micah Richards** and the resurgent **Didi Hamann**. We will probably never know if he could build on this platform. The vultures are now circling over Dunne and Richards but players will be impressed with the appointment of Mark Hughes for the new season.

NICKNAME: BLUES/CITIZENS

KEY: Won / Drawn / Lost

1 prem	**West Ham**	A	W	2-0	Bianchi 18, Geovanni 87
2 prem	**Derby**	H	W	1-0	Johnson 43
3 prem	**Man Utd**	H	W	1-0	Geovanni 31
4 prem	**Arsenal**	A	L	0-1	
5 ccr2	**Bristol City**	A	W	2-1	Mpenza 17, Bianchi 81
6 prem	**Blackburn**	A	L	0-1	
7 prem	**Aston Villa**	H	W	1-0	Johnson 49
8 prem	**Fulham**	A	D	3-3	Petrov 36, 60, Mpenza 50
9 ccr3	**Norwich**	H	W	1-0	Samaras 90
10 prem	**Newcastle**	H	W	3-1	Petrov 38, Mpenza 47, Elano 87
11 prem	**Middlesbro**	H	W	3-1	Riggott 9 og, Elano 33, 63
12 prem	**Birmingham**	H	W	1-0	Elano 37
13 prem	**Chelsea**	A	L	0-6	
14 ccr4	**Bolton**	A	W	1-0	Elano 86 pen
15 prem	**Sunderland**	H	W	1-0	Ireland 67
16 prem	**Portsmouth**	A	D	0-0	
17 prem	**Reading**	H	W	2-1	Petrov 11, Ireland 90
18 prem	**Wigan**	A	D	1-1	Geovanni 1
19 prem	**Tottenham**	A	L	1-2	Bianchi 61
20 prem	**Bolton**	H	W	4-2	Bianchi 7, Michalik 48 og, Vassell 77, Etuhu 90
21 ccqf	**Tottenham**	H	L	0-2	
22 prem	**Aston Villa**	A	D	1-1	Bianchi 11
23 prem	**Blackburn**	H	D	2-2	Vassell 27, Nelsen 30 og
24 prem	**Liverpool**	H	D	0-0	
25 prem	**Newcastle**	A	W	2-0	Elano 38, Fernandes 76
26 facr3	**West Ham**	A	D	0-0	
27 prem	**Everton**	A	L	0-1	
28 facr3r	**West Ham**	H	W	1-0	Elano 73
29 prem	**West Ham**	H	D	1-1	Vassell 16
30 facr4	**Sheff Utd**	A	L	1-2	Sturridge 48
31 prem	**Derby**	A	D	1-1	Sturridge 63
32 prem	**Arsenal**	H	L	1-3	Fernandes 28
33 prem	**Man Utd**	A	W	2-1	Vassell 24, Mwaruwari 45
34 prem	**Everton**	H	L	0-2	
35 prem	**Wigan**	H	D	0-0	
36 prem	**Reading**	A	L	0-2	
37 prem	**Tottenham**	H	W	2-1	Ireland 59, Onuoha 72
38 prem	**Bolton**	A	D	0-0	
39 prem	**Birmingham**	A	L	1-3	Elano 58 pen
40 prem	**Chelsea**	H	L	0-2	
41 prem	**Sunderland**	A	W	2-1	Elano 79 pen, Vassell 87
42 prem	**Portsmouth**	H	W	3-1	Vassell 11, Petrov 13, Mwaruwari 74
43 prem	**Fulham**	H	L	2-3	Ireland 10, Mwaruwari 21
44 prem	**Liverpool**	A	L	0-1	
45 prem	**Middlesbro**	A	L	1-8	Elano 87

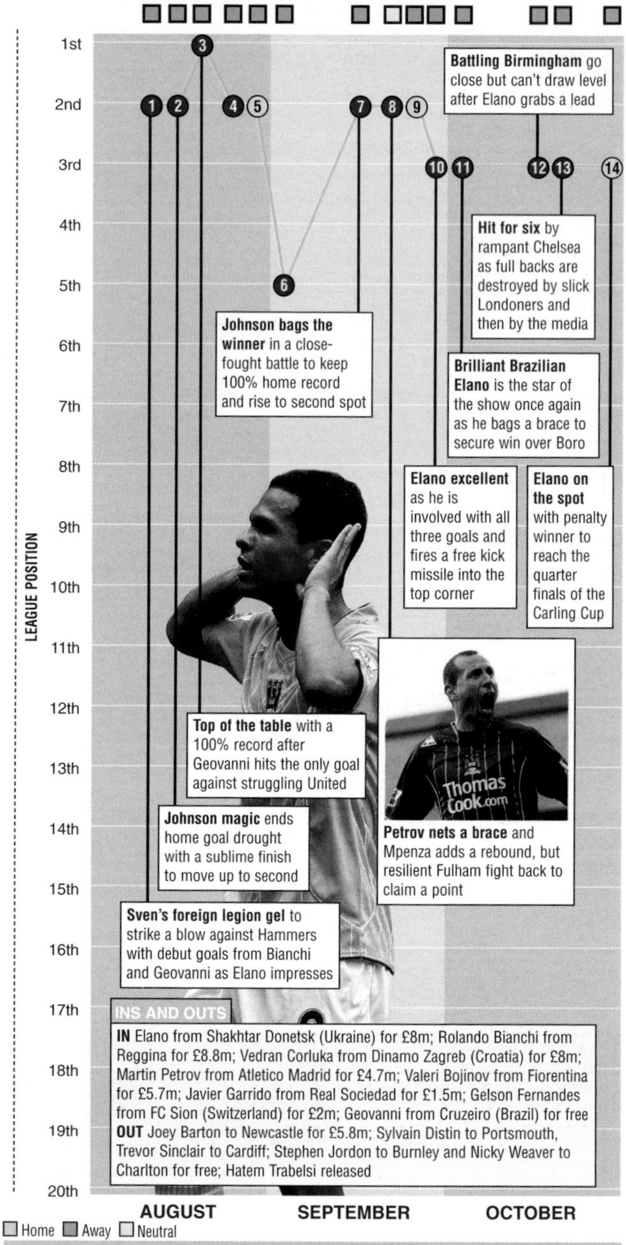

LEAGUE POSITION: 1st 2nd 3rd 4th 5th 6th 7th 8th 9th 10th 11th 12th 13th 14th 15th 16th 17th 18th 19th 20th

AUGUST SEPTEMBER OCTOBER

Home / Away / Neutral

Battling Birmingham go close but can't draw level after Elano grabs a lead

Hit for six by rampant Chelsea as full backs are destroyed by slick Londoners and then by the media

Johnson bags the winner in a close-fought battle to keep 100% home record and rise to second spot

Brilliant Brazilian Elano is the star of the show once again as he bags a brace to secure win over Boro

Elano excellent as he is involved with all three goals and fires a free kick missile into the top corner

Elano on the spot with penalty winner to reach the quarter finals of the Carling Cup

Top of the table with a 100% record after Geovanni hits the only goal against struggling United

Johnson magic ends home goal drought with a sublime finish to move up to second

Petrov nets a brace and Mpenza adds a rebound, but resilient Fulham fight back to claim a point

Sven's foreign legion gel to strike a blow against Hammers with debut goals from Bianchi and Geovanni as Elano impresses

INS AND OUTS

IN Elano from Shakhtar Donetsk (Ukraine) for £8m; Rolando Bianchi from Reggina for £8.8m; Vedran Corluka from Dinamo Zagreb (Croatia) for £8m; Martin Petrov from Atletico Madrid for £4.7m; Valeri Bojinov from Fiorentina for £5.7m; Javier Garrido from Real Sociedad for £1.5m; Gelson Fernandes from FC Sion (Switzerland) for £2m; Geovanni from Cruzeiro (Brazil) for free **OUT** Joey Barton to Newcastle for £5.8m; Sylvain Distin to Portsmouth, Trevor Sinclair to Cardiff; Stephen Jordon to Burnley and Nicky Weaver to Charlton for free; Hatem Trabelsi released

ATTENDANCES

HOME GROUND: CITY OF MANCHESTER STADIUM **CAPACITY:** 47500 **AVERAGE LEAGUE AT HOME:** 42257

33	Man Utd	75970	29	West Ham	42390	7	Aston Villa	38363	9	Norwich	20938
4	Arsenal	60114	23	Blackburn	42112	35	Wigan	38261	30	Sheff Utd	20800
25	Newcastle	50956	13	Chelsea	41832	19	Tottenham	35646	16	Portsmouth	19529
24	Liverpool	47321	34	Everton	41728	1	West Ham	34921	18	Wigan	18614
41	Sunderland	46797	22	Aston Villa	41455	26	West Ham	33806	14	Bolton	15510
32	Arsenal	46426	10	Newcastle	40606	31	Derby	31368	5	Bristol City	14541
12	Birmingham	45688	20	Bolton	40506	28	West Ham	27809			
3	Man Utd	44955	11	Middlesboro	40438	45	Middlesboro	27613			
17	Reading	43813	42	Portsmouth	40205	6	Blackburn	26881			
43	Fulham	43643	37	Tottenham	40180	8	Fulham	24674			
2	Derby	43620	15	Sunderland	40038	36	Reading	24062			
44	Liverpool	43074	21	Tottenham	38564	39	Birmingham	22962			
40	Chelsea	42594	27	Everton	38474	38	Bolton	22633			

Sven wins over fans but not the owner

Final Position: **9th**

KEY: ● League ● Champions Lge ● UEFA Cup ● FA Cup ○ League Cup ● Other

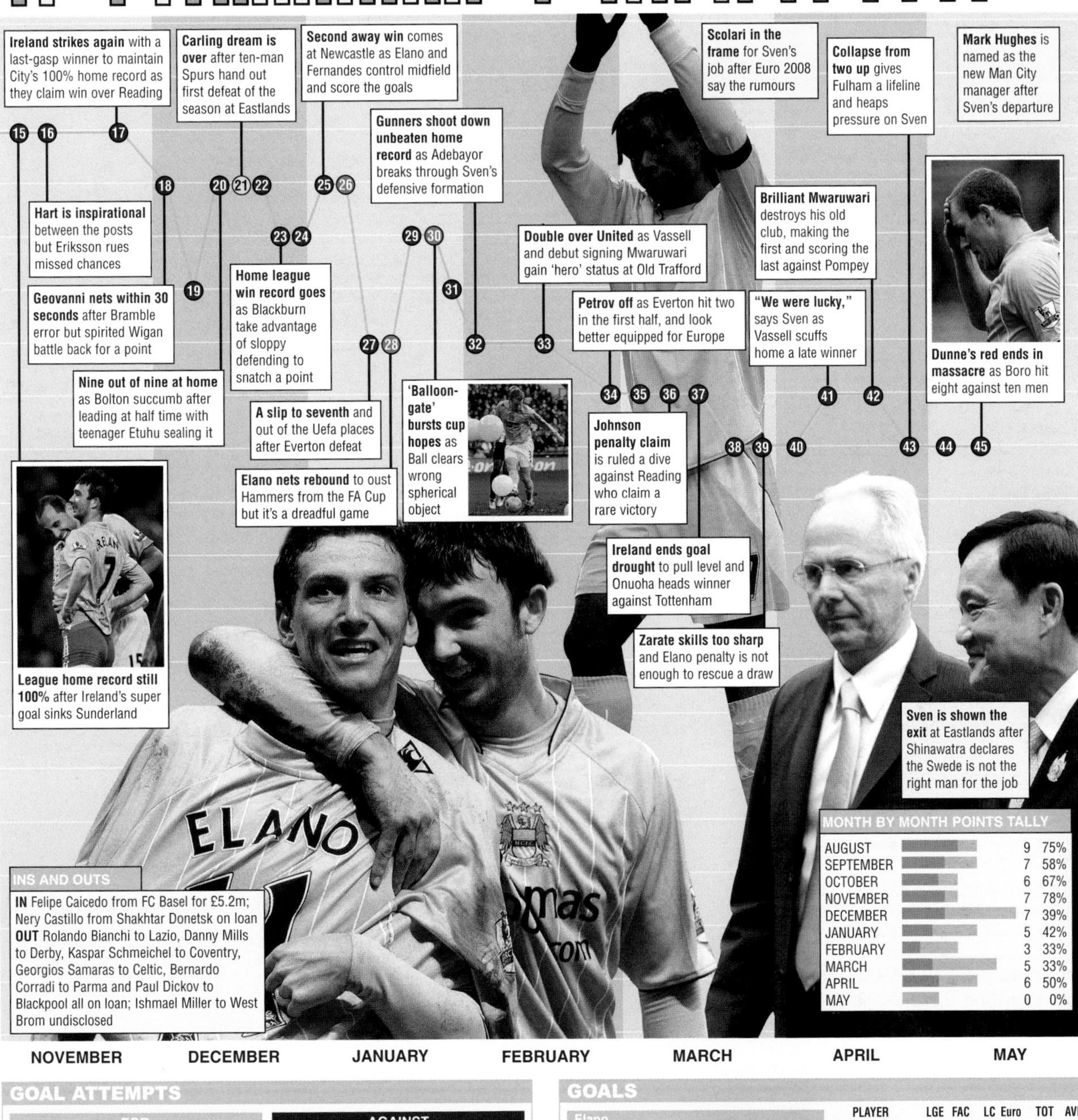

ELANO

Ireland strikes again with a last-gasp winner to maintain City's 100% home record as they claim win over Reading

Carling dream is over after ten-man Spurs hand out first defeat of the season at Eastlands

Second away win comes at Newcastle as Elano and Fernandes control midfield and score the goals

Gunners shoot down unbeaten home record as Adebayor breaks through Sven's defensive formation

Scolari in the frame for Sven's job after Euro 2008 say the rumours

Collapse from two up gives Fulham a lifeline and heaps pressure on Sven

Mark Hughes is named as the new Man City manager after Sven's departure

Hart is inspirational between the posts but Eriksson rues missed chances

Geovanni nets within 30 seconds after Bramble error but spirited Wigan battle back for a point

Nine out of nine at home as Bolton succumb after leading at half time with teenager Etuhu sealing it

Home league win record goes as Blackburn take advantage of sloppy defending to snatch a point

A slip to seventh and out of the Uefa places after Everton defeat

Elano nets rebound to oust Hammers from the FA Cup but it's a dreadful game

'Balloon-gate' bursts cup hopes as Ball clears wrong spherical object

Double over United as Vassell and debut signing Mwaruwari gain 'hero' status at Old Trafford

Brilliant Mwaruwari destroys his old club, making the first and scoring the last against Pompey

Petrov off as Everton hit two in the first half, and look better equipped for Europe

"We were lucky," says Sven as Vassell scuffs home a late winner

Dunne's red ends in massacre as Boro hit eight against ten men

Johnson penalty claim is ruled a dive against Reading who claim a rare victory

Ireland ends goal drought to pull level and Onuoha heads winner against Tottenham

Zarate skills too sharp and Elano penalty is not enough to rescue a draw

League home record still 100% after Ireland's super goal sinks Sunderland

Sven is shown the exit at Eastlands after Shinawatra declares the Swede is not the right man for the job

INS AND OUTS

IN Felipe Caicedo from FC Basel for £5.2m; Nery Castillo from Shakhtar Donetsk on loan **OUT** Rolando Bianchi to Lazio, Danny Mills to Derby, Kaspar Schmeichel to Coventry, Georgios Samaras to Celtic, Bernardo Corradi to Parma and Paul Dickov to Blackpool all on loan; Ishmael Miller to West Brom undisclosed

MONTH BY MONTH POINTS TALLY

Month	Points	%
AUGUST	9	75%
SEPTEMBER	7	58%
OCTOBER	6	67%
NOVEMBER	7	78%
DECEMBER	7	39%
JANUARY	5	42%
FEBRUARY	3	33%
MARCH	5	33%
APRIL	6	50%
MAY	0	0%

NOVEMBER DECEMBER JANUARY FEBRUARY MARCH APRIL MAY

GOAL ATTEMPTS

FOR – Goal attempts recorded in League games

	HOME	AWAY	TOTAL	AVE
shots on target	129	98	227	6.0
shots off target	109	72	181	4.8
TOTAL	238	170	408	10.7

Ratio of goals to shots – Average number of shots on target per League goal scored: **5.0**

Accuracy rating – Average percentage of total goal attempts which were on target: **55.6**

AGAINST – Goal attempts recorded in League games

	HOME	AWAY	TOTAL	AVE
shots on target	117	150	267	7.0
shots off target	106	114	220	5.8
TOTAL	223	264	487	12.8

Ratio of goals to shots – Average number of shots on target per League goal scored: **5.0**

Accuracy rating – Average percentage of total goal attempts which were on target: **54.8**

GOALS

Elano

League	8
FA Cup	1
League Cup	1
Europe	0
Other	0
TOTAL	10

League Average **305** mins between goals

	PLAYER	LGE	FAC	LC	Euro	TOT	AVE
1	Elano	8	1	1	0	10	305
2	Vassell	6	0	0	0	6	294
3	Bianchi	4	0	1	0	5	191
4	Petrov	5	0	0	0	5	594
5	Ireland	4	0	0	0	4	638
6	Geovanni	3	0	0	0	3	136
7	Mwaruwari	3	0	0	0	3	355
8	Mpenza	2	0	1	0	3	372
9	Sturridge	1	1	0	0	2	150
10	Johnson	2	0	0	0	2	965
11	Fernandes	2	0	0	0	2	979
12	Etuhu	1	0	0	0	1	204
13	Onuoha	1	0	0	0	1	1222
14	Samaras	0	0	1	0	1	
	Other	0	0	0	0	0	
	TOTAL	42	2	4	0	48	

SQUAD APPEARANCES

Match	1	2	3	4	5	6	7	8	9	10	11	12	13	14	15	16	17	18	19	20	21	22	23	24	25	26	27	28	29	30	31	32	33	34	35	36	37	38	39	40	41	42	43	44	45
Venue	A	H	H	A	A	A	H	A	H	H	H	H	A	A	H	A	H	A	A	H	H	A	H	H	A	A	A	H	H	A	A	H	A	H	H	A	H	A	A	H	A	H	H	A	A
Competition	L	L	L	L	W	L	L	L	W	L	L	L	L	W	L	L	L	L	L	L	W	L	L	L	L	F	L	F	L	F	L	L	L	L	L	L	L	L	L	L	L	L	L	L	L
Result	W	W	W	L	W	L	W	D	W	W	W	W	L	W	W	D	W	D	L	W	L	D	D	D	W	D	L	W	D	L	D	L	W	L	D	L	W	D	L	L	W	W	L	L	L

Goalkeepers
Joe Hart
Andreas Isaksson
Kasper Schmeichel

Defenders
Michael Ball
Vedran Corluka
Richard Dunne
Javier Garrido
Shaleum Logan
Danny Mills
Nedum Onuoha
Micah Richards
Sun Jihai
Sam Williamson

Midfielders
Ousmane Dabo
Blumer Elano
Kelvin Etuhu
Gelson Fernandes
Deiberson Geovanni
Dietmar Hamann
Stephen Ireland
Michael Johnson
Marc Laird
Martin Petrov

Forwards
Rolando Bianchi
Emilov Valeri Bojinov
Felipe Salvador Caicedo
Nery Alberto Castillo
Paul Dickov
Ched Evans
Emile Mpenza
Benjani Mwaruwari
Georgios Samaras
Daniel Sturridge
Darius Vassell

KEY: On all match | On bench | Subbed or sent off (Counting game) | Subbed or sent off (playing less than 70 mins) | Subbed on from bench (Counting Game) | Subbed on (playing less than 70 mins) | Subbed on and then subbed or sent off (Counting Game) | Subbed on and then subbed or sent off (playing less than 70 min | Not in 16 | Injured | ✕ Suspended

KEY PLAYERS - GOALSCORERS

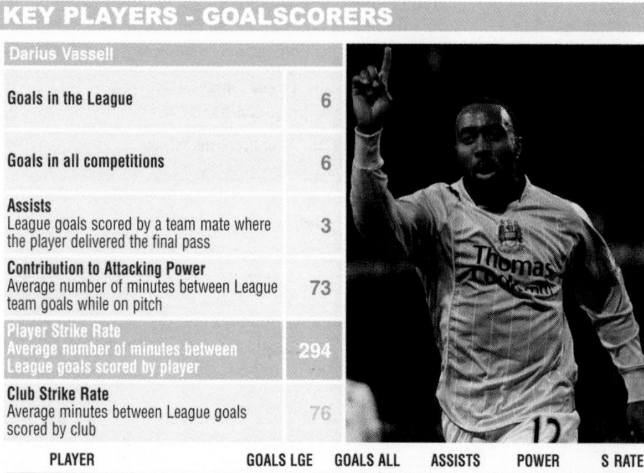

Darius Vassell

Goals in the League	6
Goals in all competitions	6
Assists League goals scored by a team mate where the player delivered the final pass	3
Contribution to Attacking Power Average number of minutes between League team goals while on pitch	73
Player Strike Rate Average number of minutes between League goals scored by player	294
Club Strike Rate Average minutes between League goals scored by club	76

	PLAYER	GOALS LGE	GOALS ALL	ASSISTS	POWER	S RATE
1	Darius Vassell	6	6	3	73	294 mins
2	Blumer Elano	8	10	9	76	305 mins
3	Benjani Mwaruwari	3	3	1	88	355 mins
4	Martin Petrov	5	5	8	74	594 mins

KEY PLAYERS - MIDFIELDERS

Dietmar Hamann

Goals in the League	0
Goals in all competitions	0
Assists League goals scored by a team mate where the player delivered the final pass	0
Defensive Rating Average number of mins between League goals conceded while on the pitch	75
Contribution to Attacking Power Average number of minutes between League team goals while on pitch	68
Scoring Difference Defensive Rating minus Contribution to Attacking Power	7

	PLAYER	GOALS LGE	GOALS ALL	ASSISTS	DEF RATE	POWER	SC DIFF
1	Dietmar Hamann	0	0	0	75	68	7 mins
2	Michael Johnson	2	2	2	71	71	0 mins
3	Blumer Elano	8	10	9	71	76	-5 mins
4	Stephen Ireland	4	4	4	67	72	-5 mins

PLAYER APPEARANCES

	AGE (on 01/07/08)	IN NAMED 16	APPEARANCES	COUNTING GAMES	MINUTES ON PITCH	APPEARANCES	MINUTES ON PITCH	THIS SEASON	HOME COUNTRY
Goalkeepers									
Joe Hart	21	38	26	26	2340	32	2880	-	England
Andreas Isaksson	26	26	5	5	450	6	540	7	Sweden
Kasper Schmeichel	21	12	7	7	630	7	630	-	Denmark
Defenders									
Michael Ball	28	32	28	19	1874	35	2428	-	England
Vedran Corluka	22	37	35	31	2971	41	3511	8	Croatia
Richard Dunne	28	36	36	32	3041	42	3581	4	Rep of Ireland
Javier Garrido	23	31	27	20	1896	29	2027	-	Spain
Shaleum Logan	19	1	0	0	0	2	180	-	England
Danny Mills	31	0	0	0	0	0	0	-	England
Nedum Onuoha	21	23	16	12	1222	21	1600	-	England
Micah Richards	20	25	25	25	2250	29	2592	7	England
Sun Jihai	30	18	14	7	811	16	991	-	China PR
Sam Williamson	20	1	1	0	37	1	37	-	England
Midfielders									
Ousmane Dabo	31	0	0	0	0	1	9	-	France
Blumer Elano	27	34	34	24	2441	38	2756	2	Brazil
Kelvin Etuhu	20	6	6	0	204	8	251	-	Nigeria
Gelson Fernandes	21	29	26	20	1959	32	2248	5	Switzerland
Deiberson Geovanni	28	27	19	2	409	23	620	-	Brazil
Dietmar Hamann	34	33	29	22	2201	34	2577	-	Germany
Stephen Ireland	21	34	33	24	2552	39	3007	1	Rep of Ireland
Michael Johnson	20	23	23	20	1931	25	2111	-	England
Marc Laird	22	0	0	0	0	0	0	-	Scotland
Martin Petrov	29	34	34	33	2973	38	3333	6	Bulgaria
Forwards									
Rolando Bianchi	25	19	19	5	767	24	1104	-	Italy
Emilov Valeri Bojinov	22	3	3	0	50	3	50	-	Bulgaria
Felipe S Caicedo	19	11	10	0	220	10	220	1	Ecuador
Nery Alberto Castillo	24	10	7	2	296	9	400	-	Mexico
Paul Dickov	35	0	0	0	0	1	2	-	Scotland
Ched Evans	19	0	0	0	0	1	12	-	England
Emile Mpenza	29	15	15	6	745	18	927	-	Belgium
Benjani Mwaruwari	29	13	13	12	1065	13	1065	2	Zimbabwe
Georgios Samaras	23	7	5	2	254	7	434	4	Greece
Daniel Sturridge	18	3	3	1	150	4	195	-	England
Darius Vassell	28	27	27	15	1769	32	2120	-	England

KEY: LEAGUE — ALL COMPS — CAPS — (MAY FIFA RANKING)

TEAM OF THE SEASON

HART — CG 26 DR 68

ONUOHA — CG 12 DR 94

RICHARDS — CG 25 DR 75

DUNNE — CG 32 DR 76

CORLUKA — CG 31 DR 66

ELANO — CG 24 SD -5

JOHNSON — CG 20 SD +0

HAMANN — CG 22 SD +7

IRELAND — CG 24 SD -5

PETROV — CG 33 AP 74

VASSELL — CG 15 SR 295

KEY: DR = Defensive Rate, SD = Scoring Difference AP = Attacking Power SR = Strike Rate, CG=Counting games – League games playing at least 70 minutes

TOP POINT EARNERS

Dietmar Hamann

Counting Games League games when player was on pitch for at least 70 minutes	22
Average points Average League points taken in Counting games	1.91
Club Average points Average points taken in League games	1.45

	PLAYER	GAMES	PTS
1	Dietmar Hamann	22	1.91
2	Javier Garrido	20	1.65
3	Michael Johnson	20	1.65
4	Micah Richards	25	1.60
5	Stephen Ireland	24	1.58
6	Blumer Elano	24	1.58
7	Martin Petrov	33	1.55
8	Richard Dunne	32	1.53
9	Nedum Onuoha	12	1.42
10	Joe Hart	26	1.35

KEY PLAYERS - DEFENDERS

Nedum Onuoha

Goals Conceded in the League Number of League goals conceded while the player was on the pitch	13
Goals Conceded in all competitions Total number of goals conceded while the player was on the pitch	16
League minutes played Number of minutes played in league matches	1222
Clean Sheets In games when the player was on pitch for at least 70 minutes	5
Defensive Rating Average number of mins between League goals conceded while on the pitch	94
Club Defensive Rating Average number of mins between League goals conceded by the club this season	64

Thomas Cook.com

	PLAYER	CON LGE	CON ALL	MINS	C SHEETS	DEF RATE
1	Nedum Onuoha	13	16	1222	5	94 mins
2	Richard Dunne	40	44	3041	10	76 mins
3	Micah Richards	30	32	2250	8	75 mins
4	Vedran Corluka	45	50	2971	10	66 mins

KEY GOALKEEPER

Joe Hart

Goals Conceded in the League Number of League goals conceded while the player was on the pitch	34
Goals Conceded in all competitions Total number of goals conceded while the player was on the pitch	39
League minutes played Number of minutes played in league matches	2340
Clean Sheets In games when the player was on pitch for at least 70 minutes	7
Goals to Shots Ratio The average number of shots on target per each League goal conceded	5.47
Defensive Rating Ave mins between League goals conceded while on the pitch	68

BOOKINGS

Dietmar Hamann

League Yellow	8
League Red	0
All competitions Yellow	9
All competitions Red	0
League Average 275 mins between cards	

	PLAYER	LEAGUE		TOTAL		AVE
1	Dietmar Hamann	8Y	0R	9Y	0R	275
2	Gelson Fernandes	5	0	6	0	391
3	Sun Jihai	2	0	2	0	405
4	Javier Garrido	4	0	4	0	474
5	Michael Johnson	4	0	5	0	482
6	Micah Richards	4	0	4	0	562
7	Richard Dunne	3	2	4	2	608
8	Vedran Corluka	4	0	6	0	742
9	Blumer Elano	3	0	4	0	813
10	Darius Vassell	2	0	3	0	884
11	Michael Ball	2	0	2	0	937
12	Martin Petrov	2	1	2	1	991
13	Stephen Ireland	1	1	2	1	1276
	Other	0	0	0	0	
	TOTAL	44	4	53	4	

WEST HAM

Although it seemed like West Ham had been in tenth position for most of the season, it was testament to Alan Curbishley's squad players that they weren't dragged into a relegation fight. The season ended up being a case of what might have been, particularly on the injury front where so many of the players who showed promise in summer 2007 never got to carry that form on past Christmas. Curbishley's future at the club hinges on trying to repeat that early form next season and carrying it through to a European finish. If the current crop of players find fitness, the club's quality youngsters continue to shine, and the promise of funds to purchase more proven quality is kept, then that will be the minimum of the Hammers fans' expectations.

NICKNAME: THE HAMMERS KEY: Won Drawn Lost

#	Comp	Opponent	Venue	Res	Score	Scorers
1	prem	Man City	H	L	0-2	
2	prem	Birmingham	A	W	1-0	Noble 70 pen
3	prem	Wigan	H	D	1-1	Bowyer 81
4	ccr2	Bristol Rovers	A	W	2-1	Bellamy 31, 45
5	prem	Reading	A	W	3-0	Bellamy 7, Etherington 49, 90
6	prem	Middlesbro	H	W	3-0	Bowyer 46, Young 51 og, Ashton 62
7	prem	Newcastle	A	L	1-3	Ashton 32
8	ccr3	Plymouth	H	W	1-0	Ashton 90
9	prem	Arsenal	H	L	0-1	
10	prem	Aston Villa	A	L	0-1	
11	prem	Sunderland	H	W	3-1	Cole 9, Gordon 78 og, Bellamy 90
12	prem	Portsmouth	A	D	0-0	
13	ccr4	Coventry	A	W	2-1	Hall 71 og, Cole 90
14	prem	Bolton	H	D	1-1	McCartney 19
15	prem	Derby	A	W	5-0	Bowyer 42, 59, Etherington 51, Lewis 54 og, Solano 69
16	prem	Tottenham	H	D	1-1	Cole 20
17	prem	Chelsea	A	L	0-1	
18	prem	Blackburn	A	W	1-0	Ashton 52
19	ccqf	Everton	H	L	1-2	Cole 12
20	prem	Everton	H	L	0-2	
21	prem	Middlesbro	A	W	2-1	Ashton 44, Parker 90
22	prem	Reading	H	D	1-1	Solano 42
23	prem	Man Utd	H	W	2-1	Ferdinand 77, Upson 82
24	prem	Arsenal	A	L	0-2	
25	facr3	Man City	H	D	0-0	
26	prem	Fulham	H	W	2-1	Ashton 28, Ferdinand 69
27	facr3r	Man City	A	L	0-1	
28	prem	Man City	A	D	1-1	Cole 8
29	prem	Liverpool	H	W	1-0	Noble 90 pen
30	prem	Wigan	A	L	0-1	
31	prem	Birmingham	H	D	1-1	Ljungberg 7
32	prem	Fulham	A	W	1-0	Solano 87
33	prem	Chelsea	H	L	0-4	
34	prem	Liverpool	A	L	0-4	
35	prem	Tottenham	A	L	0-4	
36	prem	Blackburn	H	W	2-1	Ashton 39, Sears 81
37	prem	Everton	A	D	1-1	Ashton 68
38	prem	Sunderland	A	L	1-2	Ljungberg 18
39	prem	Portsmouth	H	L	0-1	
40	prem	Bolton	A	L	0-1	
41	prem	Derby	H	W	2-1	Zamora 20, Cole 77
42	prem	Newcastle	H	D	2-2	Noble 10, Ashton 23
43	prem	Man Utd	A	L	1-4	Ashton 28
44	prem	Aston Villa	H	D	2-2	Solano 8, Ashton 88

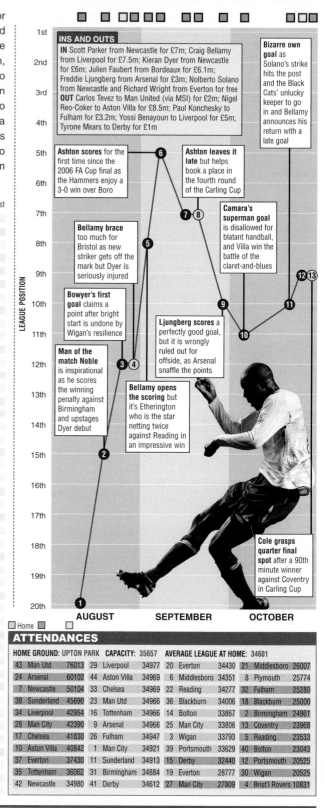

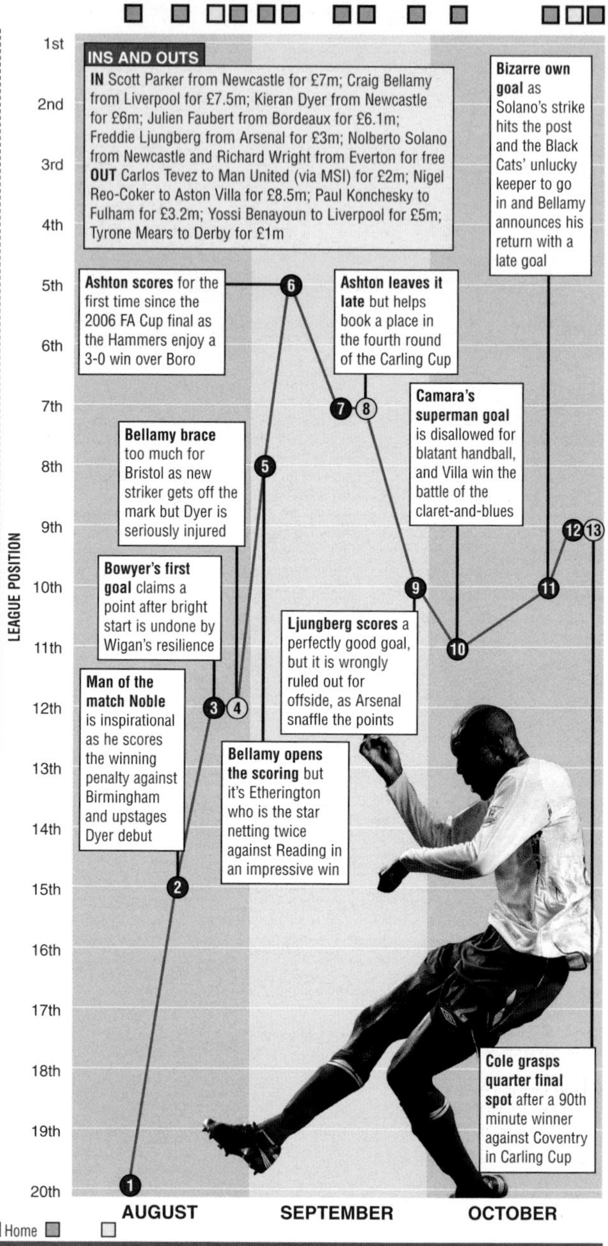

INS AND OUTS

IN Scott Parker from Newcastle for £7m; Craig Bellamy from Liverpool for £7.5m; Kieran Dyer from Newcastle for £6m; Julien Faubert from Bordeaux for £6.1m; Freddie Ljungberg from Arsenal for £3m; Nolberto Solano from Newcastle and Richard Wright from Everton for free **OUT** Carlos Tevez to Man United (via MSI) for £2m; Nigel Reo-Coker to Aston Villa for £8.5m; Paul Konchesky to Fulham for £3.2m; Yossi Benayoun to Liverpool for £5m; Tyrone Mears to Derby for £1m

LEAGUE POSITION: 1st 2nd 3rd 4th 5th 6th 7th 8th 9th 10th 11th 12th 13th 14th 15th 16th 17th 18th 19th 20th

AUGUST SEPTEMBER OCTOBER

Home

Bizarre own goal as Solano's strike hits the post and the Black Cats' unlucky keeper to go in and Bellamy announces his return with a late goal

Ashton scores for the first time since the 2006 FA Cup final as the Hammers enjoy a 3-0 win over Boro

Ashton leaves it late but helps book a place in the fourth round of the Carling Cup

Camara's superman goal is disallowed for blatant handball, and Villa win the battle of the claret-and-blues

Bellamy brace too much for Bristol as new striker gets off the mark but Dyer is seriously injured

Bowyer's first goal claims a point after bright start is undone by Wigan's resilience

Ljungberg scores a perfectly good goal, but it is wrongly ruled out for offside, as Arsenal snaffle the points

Man of the match Noble is inspirational as he scores the winning penalty against Birmingham and upstages Dyer debut

Bellamy opens the scoring but it's Etherington who is the star netting twice against Reading in an impressive win

Cole grasps quarter final spot after a 90th minute winner against Coventry in Carling Cup

ATTENDANCES

HOME GROUND: UPTON PARK **CAPACITY:** 35657 **AVERAGE LEAGUE AT HOME:** 34601

#	Opponent	Att	#	Opponent	Att	#	Opponent	Att	#	Opponent	Att
43	Man Utd	76013	29	Liverpool	34977	20	Everton	34430	21	Middlesboro	26007
24	Arsenal	60102	44	Aston Villa	34969	6	Middlesboro	34351	8	Plymouth	25774
7	Newcastle	50104	33	Chelsea	34969	22	Reading	34277	32	Fulham	25280
38	Sunderland	45690	23	Man Utd	34966	36	Blackburn	34006	18	Blackburn	25000
34	Liverpool	42954	16	Tottenham	34966	14	Bolton	33867	2	Birmingham	24961
28	Man City	42390	9	Arsenal	34966	25	Man City	33806	13	Coventry	23968
17	Chelsea	41830	26	Fulham	34947	3	Wigan	33793	5	Reading	23533
10	Aston Villa	40842	1	Man City	34921	39	Portsmouth	33629	40	Bolton	23043
37	Everton	37430	11	Sunderland	34913	15	Derby	32440	12	Portsmouth	20525
35	Tottenham	36062	31	Birmingham	34884	19	Everton	28777	30	Wigan	20525
42	Newcastle	34980	41	Derby	34612	27	Man City	27809	4	Brist'l Rovers	10831

Curbishley just wants a fit squad

Final Position: 10th

KEY: ● League ● Champions Lge ● UEFA Cup ● FA Cup ○ League Cup ● Other

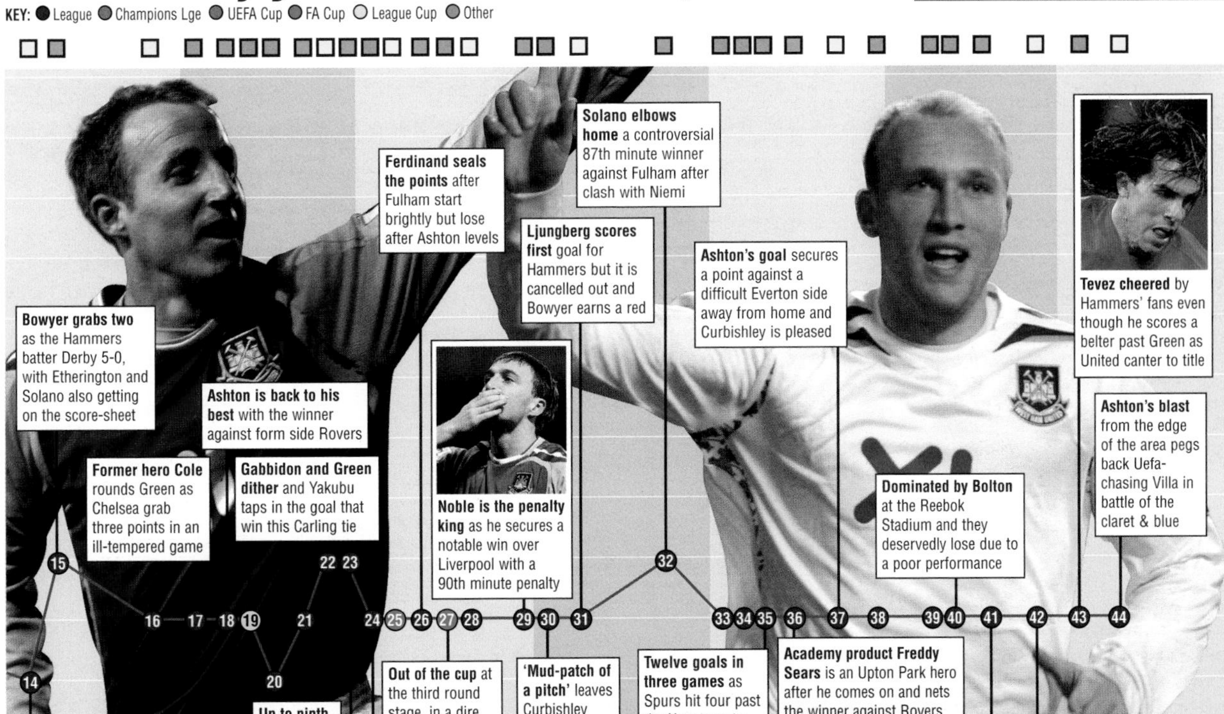
Bowyer grabs two as the Hammers batter Derby 5-0, with Etherington and Solano also getting on the score-sheet
McCartney's scissors kick cuts through Bolton but the visitors battle back for a deserved late equaliser
Former hero Cole rounds Green as Chelsea grab three points in an ill-tempered game
Ashton is back to his best with the winner against form side Rovers
Gabbidon and Green dither and Yakubu taps in the goal that win this Carling tie
Green's penalty save from old-boy Defoe salvages a point from the London derby against Spurs
Ferdinand and Upson ruin Tevez's return to Upton Park in a shock win over champions
Up to ninth even though ten-man Reading hold out for a draw
Early Arsenal goals mean it's no contest at the Emirates
Ferdinand seals the points after Fulham start brightly but lose after Ashton levels
Out of the cup at the third round stage, in a dire game at Man City
Noble is the penalty king as he secures a notable win over Liverpool with a 90th minute penalty
Ljungberg scores first goal for Hammers but it is cancelled out and Bowyer earns a red
'Mud-patch of a pitch' leaves Curbishley cursing at Latics defeat
Solano elbows home a controversial 87th minute winner against Fulham after clash with Niemi
Twelve goals in three games as Spurs hit four past the Hammers to add to thier woes
Ashton's goal secures a point against a difficult Everton side away from home and Curbishley is pleased
Academy product Freddy Sears is an Upton Park hero after he comes on and nets the winner against Rovers
Dominated by Bolton at the Reebok Stadium and they deservedly lose due to a poor performance
Cole ends three match losing streak but not before the boos ring out for Curbishley
Ljungberg added to injury list with a cracked rib and Newcastle peg back a two goal lead
Tevez cheered by Hammers' fans even though he scores a belter past Green as United canter to title
Ashton's blast from the edge of the area pegs back Uefa-chasing Villa in battle of the claret & blue

INS AND OUTS

OUT Christian Dailly to Rangers for free; Calum Davenport to Watford on loan; Hogan Ephraim to QPR undisclosed

MONTH BY MONTH POINTS TALLY

Month	Points	%
AUGUST	4	44%
SEPTEMBER	6	50%
OCTOBER	4	44%
NOVEMBER	5	56%
DECEMBER	10	56%
JANUARY	7	58%
FEBRUARY	4	44%
MARCH	4	22%
APRIL	4	33%
MAY	1	17%

NOVEMBER DECEMBER JANUARY FEBRUARY MARCH APRIL MAY

GOAL ATTEMPTS

FOR – Goal attempts recorded in League games

	HOME	AWAY	TOTAL	AVE
shots on target	122	111	233	6.1
shots off target	113	108	221	5.8
TOTAL	235	219	454	11.9

Ratio of goals to shots – Average number of shots on target per League goal scored: **5.5**

Accuracy rating – Average percentage of total goal attempts which were on target: **51.3**

AGAINST – Goal attempts recorded in League games

	HOME	AWAY	TOTAL	AVE
shots on target	123	111	234	6.2
shots off target	93	119	212	5.6
TOTAL	216	230	446	11.7

Ratio of goals to shots – Average number of shots on target per League goal scored: **4.7**

Accuracy rating – Average percentage of total goal attempts which were on target: **52.5**

GOALS

Ashton

League	10
FA Cup	0
League Cup	1
Europe	0
Other	0
TOTAL	11

League Average **200** mins between goals

	PLAYER	LGE	FAC	LC	Euro	TOT	AVE
1	Ashton	10	0	1	0	11	200
2	Cole	4	0	2	0	6	473
3	Bowyer	4	0	0	0	4	251
4	Bellamy	2	0	2	0	4	263
5	Solano	4	0	0	0	4	315
6	Etherington	3	0	0	0	3	435
7	Noble	3	0	0	0	3	759
8	Ljungberg	2	0	0	0	2	927
9	Ferdinand	2	0	0	0	2	946
10	Sears	1	0	0	0	1	213
11	Zamora	1	0	0	0	1	911
12	Parker	1	0	0	0	1	1426
13	Upson	1	0	0	0	1	2582
14	McCartney	1	0	0	0	1	3226
15	Mullins	0	0	0	0	0	
	Other	0	0	0	0	0	
	TOTAL	39	0	5	0	44	

SQUAD APPEARANCES

Match	1	2	3	4	5	6	7	8	9	10	11	12	13	14	15	16	17	18	19	20	21	22	23	24	25	26	27	28	29	30	31	32	33	34	35	36	37	38	39	40	41	42	43	44
Venue	H	A	H	A	A	H	A	H	H	A	H	A	A	H	A	H	A	A	H	H	A	H	H	A	H	H	A	A	H	A	H	A	H	A	A	H	A	A	H	A	H	H	A	H
Competition	L	L	L	W	L	L	L	W	L	L	L	L	W	L	L	L	L	L	W	L	L	L	L	L	F	L	F	L	L	L	L	L	L	L	L	L	L	L	L	L	L	L	L	L
Result	L	W	D	W	W	W	L	W	L	L	W	D	W	D	W	D	L	W	L	L	W	D	W	L	D	W	L	D	W	L	D	W	L	L	L	W	D	L	L	L	W	D	L	D

Goalkeepers
Robert Green
James Walker
Richard Wright

Defenders
James Collins
Christian Dailly
Anton Ferdinand
Daniel Gabbidon
George McCartney
Lucas Neill
John Paintsil
Jonathan Spector
James Tomkins
Matthew Upson

Midfielders
Luis Boa Morte
Lee Bowyer
Jack Collison
Kieron Dyer
Hogan Ephraim
Matthew Etherington
Julien Faubert
Fredrik Ljungberg
Hayden Mullins
Mark Noble
Scott Parker
Kyel Reid
Nolberto Solano

Forwards
Dean Ashton
Craig Bellamy
Henri Camara
Carlton Cole
Freddie Sears
Bobby Zamora

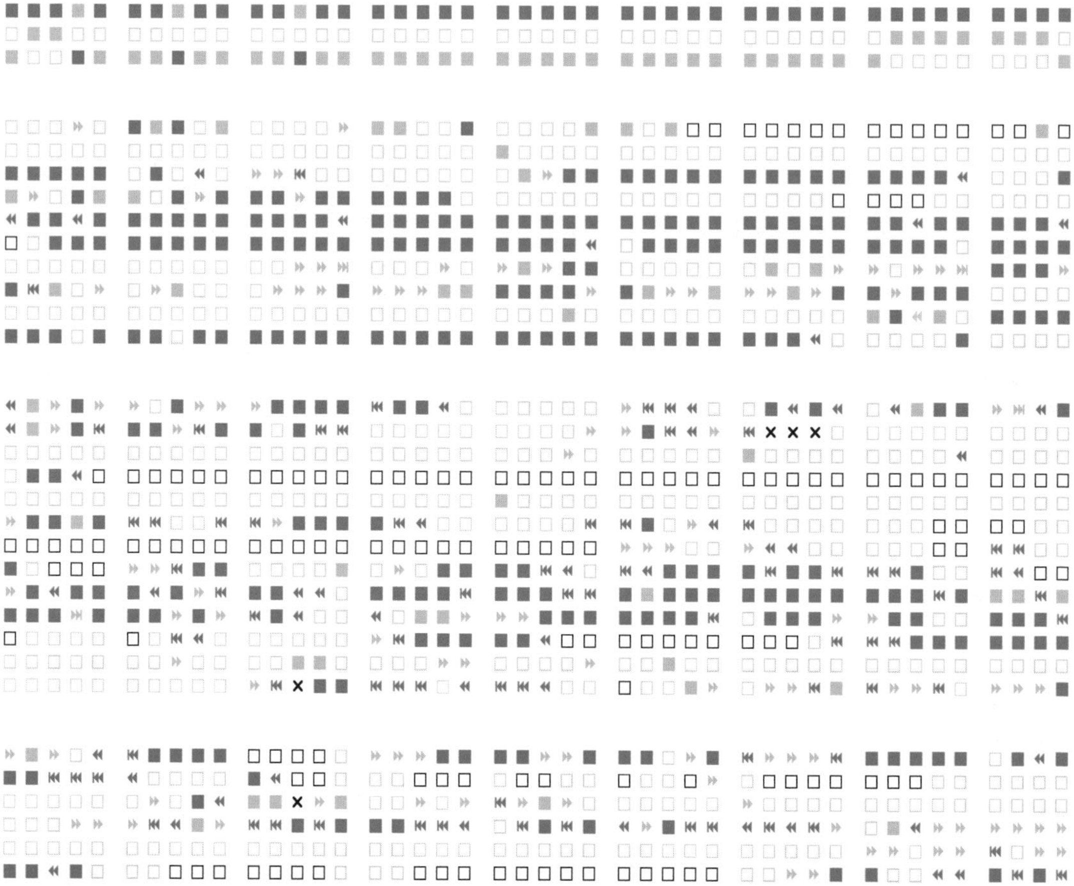

KEY: On all match · On bench · Subbed or sent off (Counting game) · Subbed or sent off (playing less than 70 mins) · Subbed on from bench (Counting Game) · Subbed on (playing less than 70 mins) · Subbed on and then subbed or sent off (Counting Game) · Subbed on and then subbed or sent off (playing less than 70 min · Not in 16 · Injured · ✕ Suspended

KEY PLAYERS - GOALSCORERS

Dean Ashton

Goals in the League	10
Goals in all competitions	11
Assists League goals scored by a team mate where the player delivered the final pass	0
Contribution to Attacking Power Average number of minutes between League team goals while on pitch	74
Player Strike Rate Average number of minutes between League goals scored by player	200
Club Strike Rate Average minutes between League goals scored by club	81

	PLAYER	GOALS LGE	GOALS ALL	ASSISTS	POWER	S RATE
1	Dean Ashton	10	11	0	74	200 mins
2	Nolberto Solano	4	4	1	78	315 mins
3	Matthew Etherington	3	3	1	62	435 mins
4	Carlton Cole	4	6	8	78	473 mins

KEY PLAYERS - MIDFIELDERS

Matthew Etherington

Goals in the League	3
Goals in all competitions	3
Assists League goals scored by a team mate where the player delivered the final pass	1
Defensive Rating Average number of mins between League goals conceded while on the pitch	100
Contribution to Attacking Power Average number of minutes between League team goals while on pitch	62
Scoring Difference Defensive Rating minus Contribution to Attacking Power	38

	PLAYER	GOALS LGE	GOALS ALL	ASSISTS	DEF RATE	POWER	SC DIFF
1	Matthew Etherington	3	3	1	100	62	38 mins
2	Nolberto Solano	4	4	1	90	78	12 mins
3	Luis Boa Morte	0	0	3	59	78	-19 mins
4	Mark Noble	3	3	3	61	81	-20 mins

PLAYER APPEARANCES

	AGE (on 01/07/08)	IN NAMED 16	APPEARANCES	COUNTING GAMES	MINUTES ON PITCH	APPEARANCES	MINUTES ON PITCH	THIS SEASON	HOME COUNTRY
Goalkeepers									
Robert Green	28	38	38	38	3420	41	3690	-	England
James Walker	34	9	0	0	0	0	0	-	England
Richard Wright	30	29	0	0	0	3	270	-	England
Defenders									
James Collins	24	10	3	2	199	5	318	5	Wales
Christian Dailly	34	1	0	0	0	0	0	1	Scotland
Anton Ferdinand	23	26	25	20	1892	29	2246	-	England
Daniel Gabbidon	28	13	10	8	768	14	1044	7	Wales
George McCartney	27	38	38	34	3226	44	3737	5	N Ireland
Lucas Neill	37	34	34	34	3060	40	3555	1	Australia
John Paintsil	27	17	14	6	681	17	816	6	Ghana
Jonathan Spector	22	30	26	13	1325	28	1415	1	United States
James Tomkins	19	9	6	5	467	6	467	-	England
Matthew Upson	29	29	29	28	2582	33	2942	-	England
Midfielders									
Luis Boa Morte	30	29	27	13	1492	32	1897	-	Portugal
Lee Bowyer	31	16	15	10	1007	20	1311	-	England
Jack Collison	19	3	2	0	103	2	103	-	Wales
Kieron Dyer	29	2	2	2	180	3	193	1	England
Hogan Ephraim	20	1	0	0	0	0	0	-	England
Matthew Etherington	26	18	18	13	1307	21	1555	-	England
Julien Faubert	24	7	7	2	344	8	373	-	France
Fredrik Ljungberg	31	26	25	20	1854	28	2078	3	Sweden
Hayden Mullins	29	37	34	29	2805	39	3193	-	England
Mark Noble	21	32	31	24	2277	36	2597	-	England
Scott Parker	27	18	18	15	1426	20	1603	-	England
Kyel Reid	20	3	1	0	11	4	85	-	England
Nolberto Solano	33	25	23	12	1260	23	1260	-	Peru
Forwards									
Dean Ashton	24	32	31	18	2000	35	2360	-	England
Craig Bellamy	28	8	8	5	526	9	601	3	Wales
Henri Camara	31	14	10	2	339	10	339	3	Senegal
Carlton Cole	24	33	31	15	1895	37	2248	-	England
Freddie Sears	18	7	7	1	213	7	213	-	England
Bobby Zamora	27	13	13	7	911	14	1001	-	England

KEY: LEAGUE ALL COMPS CAPS (MAY FIFA RANKING)

TEAM OF THE SEASON

GREEN

CG 38 DR 68

NEILL

CG 34 DR 66

SPECTOR

CG 13 DR 66

UPSON

CG 28 DR 86

McCARTNEY

CG 34 DR 68

SOLANO

CG 12 SD +12

NOBLE

CG 24 SD -20

BOA MORTE

CG 13 SD -19

ETHERINGTON

CG 13 SD +38

COLE

CG 15 AP 78

ASHTON

CG 18 SR 200

KEY: DR = Defensive Rate, SD = Scoring Difference AP = Attacking Power SR = Strike Rate, CG=Counting games – League games playing at least 70 minutes

TOP POINT EARNERS

Matthew Etherington

Counting Games League games when player was on pitch for at least 70 minutes	13
Average points Average League points taken in Counting games	1.69
Club Average points Average points taken in League games	1.29

	PLAYER	GAMES	PTS
1	Matthew Etherington	13	1.69
2	Carlton Cole	15	1.53
3	Jonathan Spector	13	1.46
4	Matthew Upson	28	1.43
5	Nolberto Solano	12	1.42
6	Mark Noble	24	1.38
7	Hayden Mullins	29	1.34
8	George McCartney	34	1.32
9	Robert Green	38	1.29
10	Lucas Neill	34	1.26

KEY PLAYERS - DEFENDERS

Matthew Upson

Goals Conceded in the League Number of League goals conceded while the player was on the pitch	30
Goals Conceded in all competitions Total number of goals conceded while the player was on the pitch	34
League minutes played Number of minutes played in league matches	2582
Clean Sheets In games when the player was on pitch for at least 70 minutes	8
Defensive Rating Average number of mins between League goals conceded while on the pitch	86
Club Defensive Rating Average number of mins between League goals conceded by the club this season	68

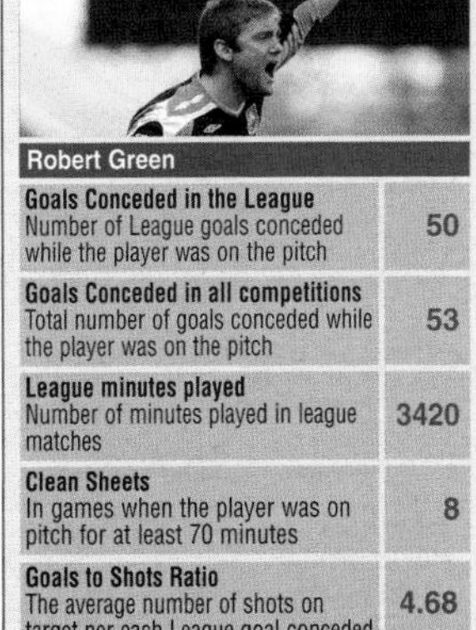

	PLAYER	CON LGE	CON ALL	MINS	C SHEETS	DEF RATE
1	Matthew Upson	30	34	2582	8	86 mins
2	George McCartney	47	51	3226	7	68 mins
3	Jonathan Spector	20	21	1325	2	66 mins
4	Lucas Neill	46	51	3060	7	66 mins

KEY GOALKEEPER

Robert Green

Goals Conceded in the League Number of League goals conceded while the player was on the pitch	50
Goals Conceded in all competitions Total number of goals conceded while the player was on the pitch	53
League minutes played Number of minutes played in league matches	3420
Clean Sheets In games when the player was on pitch for at least 70 minutes	8
Goals to Shots Ratio The average number of shots on target per each League goal conceded	4.68
Defensive Rating Ave mins between League goals conceded while on the pitch	68

BOOKINGS

Lee Bowyer

League Yellow	7
League Red	1
All competitions Yellow	7
All competitions Red	1
League Average	125 mins between cards

	PLAYER	LEAGUE 7Y	LEAGUE 1R	TOTAL 7Y	TOTAL 1R	AVE
1	Lee Bowyer	5	0	5	0	125
2	John Paintsil	5	0	5	0	136
3	Carlton Cole	9	0	9	0	210
4	Craig Bellamy	2	0	2	0	263
5	Luis Boa Morte	3	1	5	1	373
6	Mark Noble	6	0	6	0	379
7	Nolberto Solano	3	0	3	0	420
8	Scott Parker	3	0	3	0	475
9	Lucas Neill	5	0	7	0	612
10	Fredrik Ljungberg	3	0	3	0	618
11	M Etherington	2	0	2	0	653
12	Jonathan Spector	2	0	3	0	662
13	Daniel Gabbidon	1	0	2	0	768
14	George McCartney	4	0	5	0	806
15	Bobby Zamora	1	0	1	0	911
	Other	8	0	8	0	
	TOTAL	64	2	71	2	

TOTTENHAM HOTSPUR

Tottenham have had a roller-coaster ride of a season. It started with a huge down (Michael Chopra scoring the first goal of Premier 2007-08 against them), spun around the relegation places for a while, gathered up the first silverware for nine years and ended in meaningless mid-table anti-climax. Along the way the popular Martin Jol was cast off, after board shenanigans, and Juande Ramos parachuted in from serial Uefa-Cup-sters Seville. Spurs' forward line impressed with **Robbie Keane** and **Dimitar Berbatov** both hitting 15 apiece in a 'For' total better than Chelsea's and nine better than last year. The defence is still too porous without **Ledley King**, with only Newcastle and three relegated teams conceding more. Taken together Spurs' fans saw more league goals than any other Premier clubs'. And the transfer ruckus over Berbatov just gets louder.

NICKNAME: SPURS

KEY: Won / Drawn / Lost

No	Comp	Opponent	H/A	Res	Score	Scorers
1	prem	**Sunderland**	A	L	0-1	
2	prem	**Everton**	H	L	1-3	Gardner 26
3	prem	**Derby**	H	W	4-0	Malbranque 2, 6, Jenas 14, D.Bent 80
4	prem	**Man Utd**	A	L	0-1	
5	prem	**Fulham**	A	D	3-3	Kaboul 11, Berbatov 28, Bale 61
6	prem	**Arsenal**	H	L	1-3	Bale 15
7	uc1rl1	**A Famagusta**	H	W	6-1	Kaboul 5, Dawson 40, Keane 42, D.Bent 43, Defoe 65, 90
8	prem	**Bolton**	A	D	1-1	Keane 34
9	ccr3	**Middlesbro**	H	W	2-0	Bale 72, Huddlestone 75
10	prem	**Aston Villa**	H	D	4-4	Berbatov 20, Chimbonda 69, Keane 82 pen, Kaboul 90
11	uc1rl2	**A Famagusta**	A	D	1-1	Keane 78
12	prem	**Liverpool**	A	D	2-2	Keane 45, 47
13	prem	**Newcastle**	A	L	1-3	Keane 57
14	ucgpg	**Getafe**	H	L	1-2	Defoe 19
15	prem	**Blackburn**	H	L	1-2	Keane 48 pen
16	ccr4	**Blackpool**	H	W	2-0	Keane 18, Chimbonda 58
17	prem	**Middlesbro**	A	D	1-1	D.Bent 35
18	ucgpg	**Hapoel Tel-Aviv**	A	W	2-0	Keane 26, Berbatov 31
19	prem	**Wigan**	H	W	4-0	Jenas 13, 26, Lennon 35, D.Bent 72
20	prem	**West Ham**	A	D	1-1	Dawson 67
21	ucgpg	**Aalborg BK**	H	W	3-2	Berbatov 46, Malbranque 51, D.Bent 66
22	prem	**Birmingham**	H	L	2-3	Keane 50 pen, 53
23	ucgpg	**Anderlecht**	A	D	1-1	Berbatov 71 pen
24	prem	**Man City**	H	W	2-1	Chimbonda 45, Defoe 83
25	prem	**Portsmouth**	A	W	1-0	Berbatov 81
26	ccqf	**Man City**	A	W	2-0	Defoe 5, Malbranque 82
27	prem	**Arsenal**	A	L	1-2	Berbatov 66
28	prem	**Fulham**	H	W	5-1	Keane 27, 61, Huddlestone 45, 71, Defoe 90
29	prem	**Reading**	H	W	6-4	Berbatov 7, 63, 72, 83, Malbranque 75, Defoe 78
30	prem	**Aston Villa**	A	L	1-2	Defoe 79
31	facr3	**Reading**	H	D	2-2	Berbatov 28, 50 pen
32	ccsfl1	**Arsenal**	A	D	1-1	Jenas 37
33	prem	**Chelsea**	A	L	0-2	
34	facr3r	**Reading**	A	W	1-0	Keane 15
35	prem	**Sunderland**	H	W	2-0	Lennon 2, Keane 90
36	ccsfl2	**Arsenal**	H	W	5-1	Jenas 3, Bendtner 27 og, Keane 48, Lennon 60, Malbranque 90
37	facr4	**Man Utd**	A	L	1-3	Keane 24
38	prem	**Everton**	A	D	0-0	
39	prem	**Man Utd**	H	D	1-1	Berbatov 20
40	prem	**Derby**	A	W	3-0	Keane 68, Kaboul 81, Berbatov 90 pen
41	uc3rl1	**Slavia Prague**	A	W	2-1	Berbatov 4, Keane 30
42	uc3rl2	**Slavia Prague**	H	D	1-1	O'Hara 7
43	cccf	**Chelsea**	N	W	2-1	Berbatov 69 pen, Woodgate 94
44	prem	**Birmingham**	A	L	1-4	Jenas 90
45	uc4rl1	**PSV**	H	L	0-1	
46	prem	**West Ham**	H	W	4-0	Berbatov 8, 11, Gilberto 85, D.Bent 90
47	uc4rl2	**PSV**	A	W	5-6*	Berbatov 81 (*on penalties)
48	prem	**Man City**	A	L	1-2	Keane 32
49	prem	**Chelsea**	H	D	4-4	Woodgate 12, Berbatov 61, Huddlestone 75, Keane 88
50	prem	**Portsmouth**	H	W	2-0	D.Bent 80, O'Hara 82
51	prem	**Newcastle**	H	L	1-4	D.Bent 25
52	prem	**Blackburn**	A	D	1-1	Berbatov 7
53	prem	**Middlesbro**	H	D	1-1	Grounds 26 og
54	prem	**Wigan**	A	D	1-1	Berbatov 6
55	prem	**Bolton**	H	D	1-1	Malbranque 52
56	prem	**Reading**	A	W	1-0	Keane 16
57	prem	**Liverpool**	H	L	0-2	

LEAGUE POSITION: 1st, 2nd, 3rd, 4th, 5th, 6th, 7th, 8th, 9th, 10th, 11th, 12th, 13th, 14th, 15th, 16th, 17th, 18th, 19th, 20th

AUGUST — SEPTEMBER — OCTOBER

INS AND OUTS

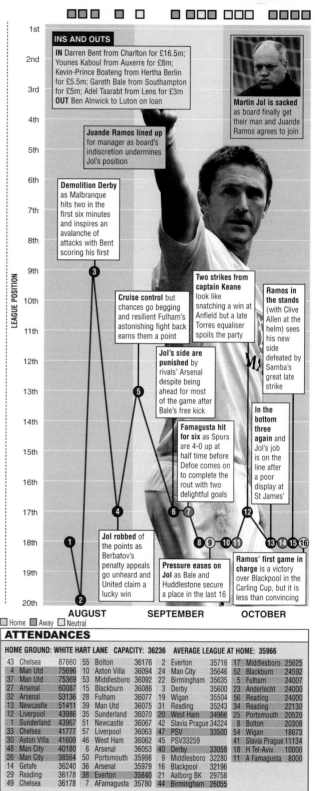

IN Darren Bent from Charlton for £16.5m; Younes Kaboul from Auxerre for £8m; Kevin-Prince Boateng from Hertha Berlin for £5.5m; Gareth Bale from Southampton for £5m; Adel Taarabt from Lens for £3m **OUT** Ben Alnwick to Luton on loan

Martin Jol is sacked as board finally get their man and Juande Ramos agrees to join

Juande Ramos lined up for manager as board's indiscretion undermines Jol's position

Demolition Derby as Malbranque hits two in the first six minutes and inspires an avalanche of attacks with Bent scoring his first

Cruise control but chances go begging and resilient Fulham's astonishing fight back earns them a point

Two strikes from captain Keane look like snatching a win at Anfield but a late Torres equaliser spoils the party

Ramos in the stands (with Clive Allen at the helm) sees his new side defeated by Samba's great late strike

Jol's side are punished by rivals' Arsenal despite being ahead for most of the game after Bale's free kick

Famagusta hit for six as Spurs are 4-0 up at half time before Defoe comes on to complete the rout with two delightful goals

In the bottom three again and Jol's job is on the line after a poor display at St James'

Jol robbed of the points as Berbatov's penalty appeals go unheard and United claim a lucky win

Pressure eases on Jol as Bale and Huddlestone secure a place in the last 16

Ramos' first game in charge is a victory over Blackpool in the Carling Cup, but it is less than convincing

Home / Away / Neutral

ATTENDANCES

HOME GROUND: WHITE HART LANE CAPACITY: 36236 AVERAGE LEAGUE AT HOME: 35966

43	Chelsea	87660	55	Bolton	36176	2	Everton	35716	17	Middlesboro	25625
4	Man Utd	75696	10	Aston Villa	36094	24	Man City	35646	52	Blackburn	24592
37	Man Utd	75369	53	Middlesboro	36092	22	Birmingham	35635	5	Fulham	24007
27	Arsenal	60087	15	Blackburn	36086	3	Derby	35600	23	Anderlecht	24000
32	Arsenal	53136	28	Fulham	36077	19	Wigan	35504	56	Reading	24000
13	Newcastle	51411	39	Man Utd	36075	31	Reading	35243	34	Reading	22130
12	Liverpool	43986	35	Sunderland	36070	20	West Ham	34966	25	Portsmouth	20520
1	Sunderland	43967	51	Newcastle	36067	42	Slavia Prague	34224	8	Bolton	20308
33	Chelsea	41777	57	Liverpool	36063	47	PSV	33500	54	Wigan	18673
30	Aston Villa	41609	46	West Ham	36062	45	PSV33259		41	Slavia Prague	11134
48	Man City	40180	6	Arsenal	36053	40	Derby	33058	18	H Tel-Aviv	10000
26	Man City	38564	50	Portsmouth	35998	9	Middlesboro	32280	11	A Famagusta	8000
14	Getafe	36240	36	Arsenal	35979	16	Blackpool	32196			
29	Reading	36178	38	Everton	35840	21	Aalborg BK	29758			
49	Chelsea	36178	7	AFamagusta	35780	44	Birmingham	26055			

Ramos jumps on board the goal-train

Final Position: 11th

KEY: ● League ● Champions Lge ● UEFA Cup ● FA Cup ○ League Cup ● Other

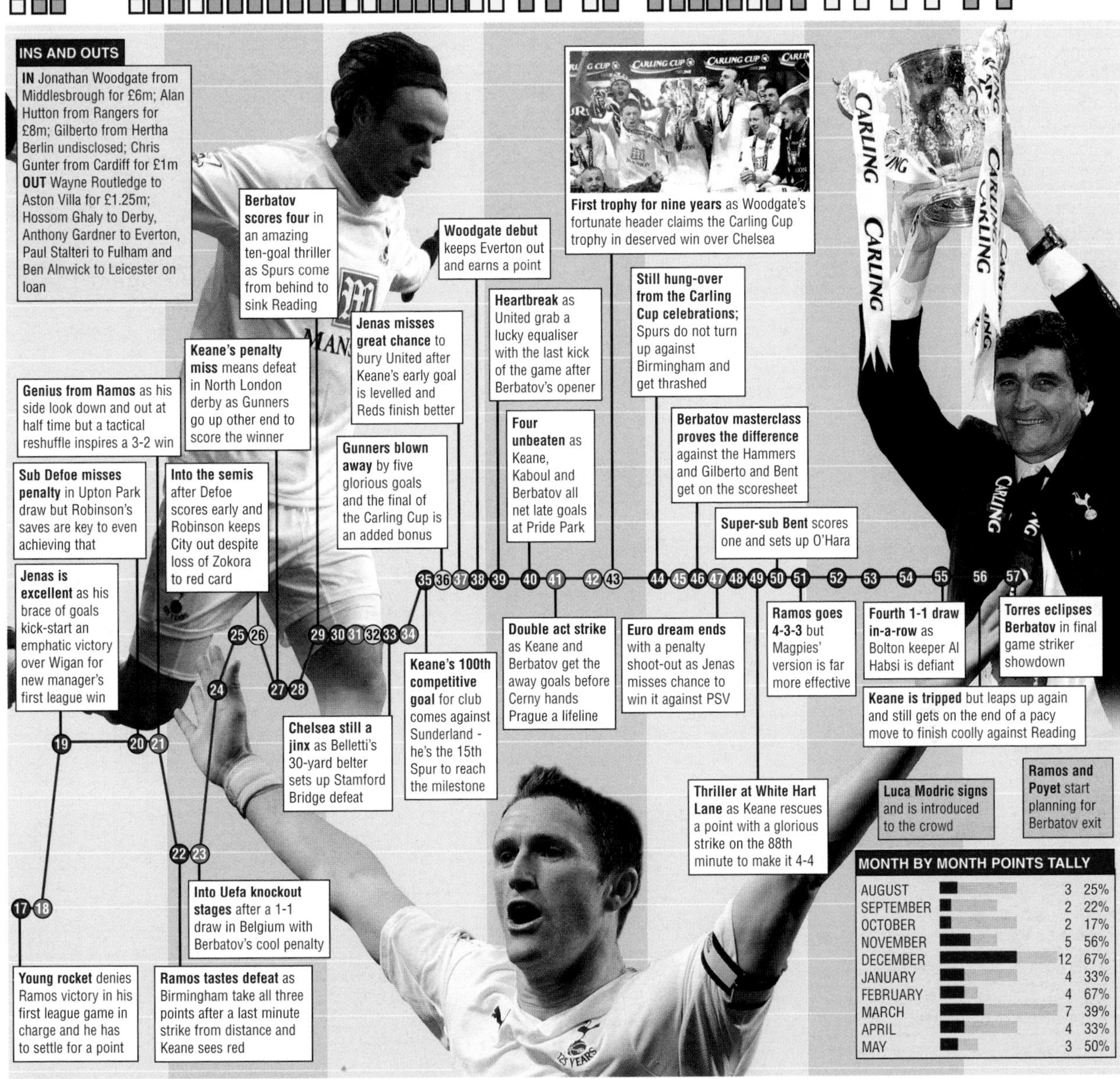

INS AND OUTS
IN Jonathan Woodgate from Middlesbrough for £6m; Alan Hutton from Rangers for £8m; Gilberto from Hertha Berlin undisclosed; Chris Gunter from Cardiff for £1m **OUT** Wayne Routledge to Aston Villa for £1.25m; Hossom Ghaly to Derby, Anthony Gardner to Everton, Paul Stalteri to Fulham and Ben Alnwick to Leicester on loan
Young rocket denies Ramos victory in his first league game in charge and he has to settle for a point
Jenas is excellent as his brace of goals kick-start an emphatic victory over Wigan for new manager's first league win
Sub Defoe misses penalty in Upton Park draw but Robinson's saves are key to even achieving that
Genius from Ramos as his side look down and out at half time but a tactical reshuffle inspires a 3-2 win
Into the semis after Defoe scores early and Robinson keeps City out despite loss of Zokora to red card
Ramos tastes defeat as Birmingham take all three points after a last minute strike from distance and Keane sees red
Into Uefa knockout stages after a 1-1 draw in Belgium with Berbatov's cool penalty
Keane's penalty miss means defeat in North London derby as Gunners go up other end to score the winner
Berbatov scores four in an amazing ten-goal thriller as Spurs come from behind to sink Reading
Chelsea still a jinx as Belletti's 30-yard belter sets up Stamford Bridge defeat
Jenas misses great chance to bury United after Keane's early goal is levelled and Reds finish better
Gunners blown away by five glorious goals and the final of the Carling Cup is an added bonus
Keane's 100th competitive goal for club comes against Sunderland - he's the 15th Spur to reach the milestone
Woodgate debut keeps Everton out and earns a point
Heartbreak as United grab a lucky equaliser with the last kick of the game after Berbatov's opener
Four unbeaten as Keane, Kaboul and Berbatov all net late goals at Pride Park
Double act strike as Keane and Berbatov get the away goals before Cerny hands Prague a lifeline
First trophy for nine years as Woodgate's fortunate header claims the Carling Cup trophy in deserved win over Chelsea
Still hung-over from the Carling Cup celebrations; Spurs do not turn up against Birmingham and get thrashed
Euro dream ends with a penalty shoot-out as Jenas misses chance to win it against PSV
Berbatov masterclass proves the difference against the Hammers and Gilberto and Bent get on the scoresheet
Super-sub Bent scores one and sets up O'Hara
Thriller at White Hart Lane as Keane rescues a point with a glorious strike on the 88th minute to make it 4-4
Ramos goes 4-3-3 but Magpies' version is far more effective
Fourth 1-1 draw in-a-row as Bolton keeper Al Habsi is defiant
Keane is tripped but leaps up again and still gets on the end of a pacy move to finish coolly against Reading
Torres eclipses Berbatov in final game striker showdown
Luca Modric signs and is introduced to the crowd
Ramos and Poyet start planning for Berbatov exit
CARLING CUP
CARLING

MONTH BY MONTH POINTS TALLY

Month	Points	%
AUGUST	3	25%
SEPTEMBER	2	22%
OCTOBER	2	17%
NOVEMBER	5	56%
DECEMBER	12	67%
JANUARY	4	33%
FEBRUARY	4	67%
MARCH	7	39%
APRIL	4	33%
MAY	3	50%

NOVEMBER DECEMBER JANUARY FEBRUARY MARCH APRIL MAY

GOAL ATTEMPTS

FOR — Goal attempts recorded in League games

	HOME	AWAY	TOTAL	AVE
shots on target	160	123	283	7.4
shots off target	120	87	207	5.4
TOTAL	280	210	490	12.9

Ratio of goals to shots — Average number of shots on target per League goal scored: **4.3**

Accuracy rating — Average percentage of total goal attempts which were on target: **57.8**

AGAINST — Goal attempts recorded in League games

	HOME	AWAY	TOTAL	AVE
shots on target	126	127	253	6.7
shots off target	80	106	186	4.9
TOTAL	206	233	439	11.6

Ratio of goals to shots — Average number of shots on target per League goal scored: **4.1**

Accuracy rating — Average percentage of total goal attempts which were on target: **57.6**

GOALS

Keane

League	15
FA Cup	2
League Cup	2
Europe	4
Other	0
TOTAL	23

League Average **181** mins between goals

	PLAYER	LGE	FAC	LC	Euro	TOT	AVE
1	Keane	15	2	2	4	**23**	181
2	Berbatov	15	2	1	5	**23**	199
3	Defoe	4	0	1	3	**8**	134
4	Bent, D	6	0	0	2	**8**	191
5	Malbranque	4	0	2	1	**7**	709
6	Jenas	4	0	2	0	**6**	618
7	Kaboul	3	0	0	1	**4**	535
8	Huddlestone	3	0	1	0	**4**	648
9	Bale	2	0	1	0	**3**	306
10	Lennon	2	0	1	0	**3**	1066
11	Chimbonda	2	0	1	0	**3**	1376
12	O'Hara	1	0	0	1	**2**	897
13	Woodgate	1	0	1	0	**2**	1066
14	Dawson	1	0	0	1	**2**	2195
15	Gilberto	1	0	0	0	**1**	343
	Other	1	0	0	0	1	
	TOTAL	**65**	**4**	**13**	**18**	**100**	

SQUAD APPEARANCES

Match: 1 2 3 4 5 | 6 7 8 9 10 | 11 12 13 14 15 | 16 17 18 19 20 | 21 22 23 24 25 | 26 27 28 29 30 | 31 32 33 34 35 | 36 37 38 39 40 | 41 42 43 44 45 | 46 47 48 49 50 | 51 52 53 54 55 | 56 57

Venue: A H H A A | H H A H H | A A A H H | H A A H A | H H A H A | A A H H A | H A A A H | H A A H A | A H N A H | H A A H H | H A H A H | A H

Competition: L L L L L | L E L W L | E L L E L | W L E L L | E L E L L | W L L L L | F W L F L | W F L L L | E E W L E | L E L L L | L L L L L | L L

Result: L L W L D | L W D W D | D D L L L | W D W W D | W L D W W | W L W W L | D D L W W | W L D D W | W D W L L | W L L D W | L D D D D | W L

Goalkeepers

Ben Alnwick
Radek Cerny
Tommy Forecast
Paul Robinson

Defenders

Troy Archibald-Henville
Benoit Assou-Ekotto
Gareth Bale
Pascal Chimbonda
Michael Dawson
Anthony Gardner
Chris Gunter
Alan Hutton
Younes Kaboul
Ledley King
Young-Pyo Lee
Ricardo S Rocha
Paul Stalteri
Jonathan Woodgate

Midfielders

Kevin-Prince Boateng
Gilberto
Tom Huddlestone
Jermaine Jenas
Aaron Lennon
Steed Malbranque
Jamie O'Hara
Danny Rose
Wayne Routledge
Adel Taarabt
Teemu Tainio
Didier Zokora

Forwards

Darren Bent
Dimitar Berbatov
Jermain Defoe
Robbie Keane

KEY: On all match · On bench · Subbed or sent off (Counting game) · Subbed or sent off (playing less than 70 mins) · Subbed on from bench (Counting Game) · Subbed on (playing less than 70 mins) · Subbed on and then subbed or sent off (Counting Game) · Subbed on and then subbed or sent off (playing less than 70 min · Not in 16 · Injured · Suspended

KEY PLAYERS - GOALSCORERS

Robbie Keane

Goals in the League	15
Goals in all competitions	23
Assists League goals scored by a team mate where the player delivered the final pass	7
Contribution to Attacking Power Average number of minutes between League team goals while on pitch	50
Player Strike Rate Average number of minutes between League goals scored by player	181
Club Strike Rate Average minutes between League goals scored by club	51

	PLAYER	GOALS LGE	GOALS ALL	ASSISTS	POWER	S RATE
1	Robbie Keane	15	23	7	50	181 mins
2	Dimitar Berbatov	15	23	12	54	199 mins
3	Jermaine Jenas	4	6	8	57	618 mins
4	Tom Huddlestone	3	4	7	40	648 mins

KEY PLAYERS - MIDFIELDERS

Aaron Lennon

Goals in the League	2
Goals in all competitions	3
Assists League goals scored by a team mate where the player delivered the final pass	6
Defensive Rating Average number of mins between League goals conceded while on the pitch	66
Contribution to Attacking Power Average number of minutes between League team goals while on pitch	52
Scoring Difference Defensive Rating minus Contribution to Attacking Power	14

	PLAYER	GOALS LGE	GOALS ALL	ASSISTS	DEF RATE	POWER	SC DIFF
1	Aaron Lennon	2	3	6	66	52	14 mins
2	Steed Malbranque	4	7	2	64	51	13 mins
3	Jermaine Jenas	4	6	8	65	57	8 mins
4	Tom Huddlestone	3	4	7	47	40	7 mins

PLAYER APPEARANCES

	AGE (on 01/07/08)	IN NAMED 16	APPEARANCES	COUNTING GAMES	MINUTES ON PITCH	APPEARANCES	MINUTES ON PITCH	THIS SEASON	HOME COUNTRY
Goalkeepers									
Ben Alnwick	21	1	0	0	0	0	0	-	England
Radek Cerny	34	38	13	13	1170	20	1800	-	Czech Republic
Tommy Forecast	21	4	0	0	0	0	0	-	England
Paul Robinson	28	33	25	25	2250	37	3390	5	England
Defenders									
T Archibald-Henville	19	2	0	0	0	0	0	-	England
Benoit Assou-Ekotto	24	1	1	1	90	2	169	-	France
Gareth Bale	18	8	8	7	612	12	825	5	Wales
Pascal Chimbonda	29	35	32	31	2753	49	4254	-	France
Michael Dawson	24	28	27	24	2195	40	3300	-	England
Anthony Gardner	27	6	4	4	360	6	492	-	England
Chris Gunter	18	4	2	0	78	4	199	3	Wales
Alan Hutton	23	14	14	13	1215	15	1335	5	Scotland
Younes Kaboul	22	22	21	16	1605	29	2210	-	France
Ledley King	27	4	4	3	290	10	813	-	England
Young-Pyo Lee	31	22	18	17	1520	30	2452	-	South Korea
Ricardo S Rocha	29	10	5	5	425	5	425	-	Portugal
Paul Stalteri	30	8	3	2	234	7	433	-	Canada
Jonathan Woodgate	28	12	12	12	1066	17	1576	-	England
Midfielders									
Kevin-Prince Boateng	21	16	13	3	590	21	936	-	Germany
Gilberto	32	7	6	3	343	7	388	4	Brazil
Tom Huddlestone	21	31	28	17	1944	43	2940	-	England
Jermaine Jenas	25	29	29	26	2475	45	3788	1	England
Aaron Lennon	21	30	29	21	2132	47	3616	-	England
Steed Malbranque	28	37	37	27	2839	55	4311	-	France
Jamie O'Hara	21	18	17	7	897	25	1314	-	England
Danny Rose	17	1	0	0	0	0	0	-	England
Wayne Routledge	23	2	2	1	95	2	95	-	England
Adel Taarabt	19	11	6	0	127	10	199	-	France
Teemu Tainio	28	23	16	4	651	26	1301	5	Finland
Didier Zokora	27	30	28	25	2252	43	3505	7	Ivory Coast
Forwards									
Darren Bent	24	28	27	7	1147	36	1670	1	England
Dimitar Berbatov	27	36	36	32	2987	52	4321	6	Bulgaria
Jermain Defoe	25	21	19	2	537	31	1025	2	England
Robbie Keane	27	36	36	26	2718	54	3883	6	Rep of Ireland

KEY: LEAGUE ALL COMPS CAPS (MAY FIFA RANKING)

TEAM OF THE SEASON

CERNY
CG 13 DR 83

HUTTON CG 13 DR 60

WOODGATE CG 12 DR 66

DAWSON CG 24 DR 56

LEE CG 17 DR 54

LENNON CG 21 SD +14

JENAS CG 26 SD +8

HUDDLESTONE CG 17 SD +7

MALBRANQUE CG 27 SD +13

BERBATOV
CG 32 AP 54

KEANE
CG 26 SR 181

KEY: DR = Defensive Rate, SD = Scoring Difference AP = Attacking Power SR = Strike Rate, CG=Counting games – League games playing at least 70 minutes

TOP POINT EARNERS

Tom Huddlestone

Counting Games League games when player was on pitch for at least 70 minutes	17
Average points Average League points taken in Counting games	1.53
Club Average points Average points taken in League games	1.21

	PLAYER	GAMES	PTS
1	Tom Huddlestone	17	1.53
2	Aaron Lennon	21	1.48
3	Young-Pyo Lee	17	1.41
4	Younes Kaboul	16	1.38
5	Jermaine Jenas	26	1.35
6	Alan Hutton	13	1.31
7	Steed Malbranque	27	1.26
8	Jonathan Woodgate	12	1.25
9	Paul Robinson	25	1.24
10	Pascal Chimbonda	31	1.23

KEY PLAYERS - DEFENDERS

Jonathan Woodgate

Goals Conceded in the League Number of League goals conceded while the player was on the pitch	16
Goals Conceded in all competitions Total number of goals conceded while the player was on the pitch	20
League minutes played Number of minutes played in league matches	1066
Clean Sheets In games when the player was on pitch for at least 70 minutes	4
Defensive Rating Average number of mins between League goals conceded while on the pitch	66
Club Defensive Rating Average number of mins between League goals conceded by the club this season	56

	PLAYER	CON LGE	CON ALL	MINS	C SHEETS	DEF RATE
1	Jonathan Woodgate	16	20	1066	4	66 mins
2	Alan Hutton	20	21	1215	4	60 mins
3	Michael Dawson	39	50	2195	5	56 mins
4	Young-Pyo Lee	28	39	1520	4	54 mins

KEY GOALKEEPER

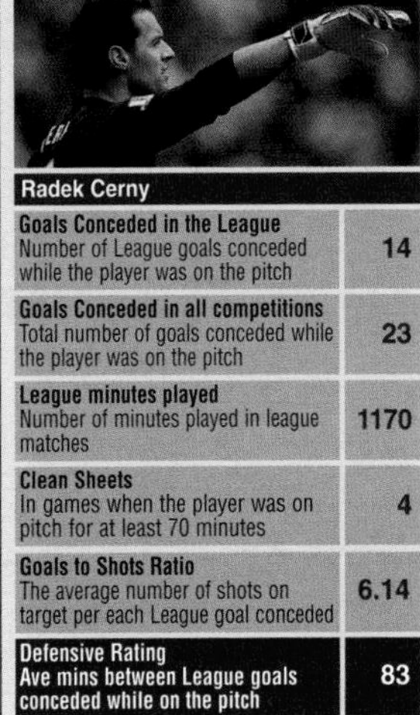

Radek Cerny

Goals Conceded in the League Number of League goals conceded while the player was on the pitch	14
Goals Conceded in all competitions Total number of goals conceded while the player was on the pitch	23
League minutes played Number of minutes played in league matches	1170
Clean Sheets In games when the player was on pitch for at least 70 minutes	4
Goals to Shots Ratio The average number of shots on target per each League goal conceded	6.14
Defensive Rating Ave mins between League goals conceded while on the pitch	83

BOOKINGS

Jermain Defoe

League Yellow	3
League Red	0
All competitions Yellow	5
All competitions Red	0

League Average **179** mins between cards

	PLAYER	LEAGUE 3Y	LEAGUE 0R	TOTAL 5Y	TOTAL 0R	AVE
1	Jermain Defoe	3	0	5	0	179
2	K-Prince Boateng	2	0	4	0	295
3	Jamie O'Hara	3	0	5	0	299
4	Didier Zokora	6	0	10	1	375
5	Tom Huddlestone	5	0	6	1	388
6	J Woodgate	2	0	2	0	533
7	Pascal Chimbonda	5	0	7	0	550
8	Gareth Bale	1	0	1	0	612
9	Teemu Tainio	1	0	5	0	651
10	Steed Malbranque	4	0	7	0	709
11	Michael Dawson	3	0	4	1	731
12	Young-Pyo Lee	2	0	2	0	760
13	Jermaine Jenas	3	0	10	0	825
14	Robbie Keane	2	1	3	1	906
15	Dimitar Berbatov	3	0	5	0	995
	Other	4	0	8	0	
	TOTAL	49	1	84	4	

NEWCASTLE UNITED

It began as a season of all change at the top for St James': new owner, new chairman, and a shiny new manager in Bolton wizard Sam Allardyce who was going to prioritise results ahead of entertaining but strangely unsuccessful football. All too soon it had slipped back into something familiar; crisis and a manager the fans hated. Newcastle needed something reassuringly old and found Kevin Keegan, the man closest to delivering a trophy to the club since the Fairs Cup. He started like a false Messiah but then hit upon a typically lavish three-forward formation, which promised a return to the old Newcastle. Of course it ended with something blue - defeats to Chelsea and Everton and a crisis meeting with the boss. Something old, something new, something blue, hmm... I suppose we couldn't borrow Ronaldinho?

NICKNAME: THE MAGPIES

KEY: Won Drawn Lost

1	prem	**Bolton**	A	W	3-1	N'Zogbia 12, Martins 22, 27
2	prem	**Aston Villa**	H	D	0-0	
3	prem	**Middlesbro**	A	D	2-2	N'Zogbia 22, Viduka 77
4	ccr2	**Barnsley**	H	W	2-0	Owen 57, Martins 86
5	prem	**Wigan**	H	W	1-0	Owen 87
6	prem	**Derby**	A	L	0-1	
7	prem	**West Ham**	H	W	3-1	Viduka 3, 41, N'Zogbia 76
8	ccr3	**Arsenal**	A	L	0-2	
9	prem	**Man City**	A	L	1-3	Martins 29
10	prem	**Everton**	H	W	3-2	Butt 42, Emre Belozoglu 86, Owen 90
11	prem	**Tottenham**	H	W	3-1	Martins 45, Cacapa 51, Milner 73
12	prem	**Reading**	A	L	1-2	Duberry 76 og
13	prem	**Portsmouth**	H	L	1-4	Campbell 15 og
14	prem	**Sunderland**	A	D	1-1	Milner 65
15	prem	**Liverpool**	H	L	0-3	
16	prem	**Blackburn**	A	L	1-3	Martins 47
17	prem	**Arsenal**	H	D	1-1	Taylor 60
18	prem	**Birmingham**	H	W	2-1	Martins 36 pen, Beye 90
19	prem	**Fulham**	A	W	1-0	Barton 90 pen
20	prem	**Derby**	H	D	2-2	Viduka 27, 86
21	prem	**Wigan**	A	L	0-1	
22	prem	**Chelsea**	A	L	1-2	Butt 55
23	prem	**Man City**	H	L	0-2	
24	facr3	**Stoke**	A	D	0-0	
25	prem	**Man Utd**	A	L	0-6	
26	facr3r	**Stoke**	H	W	4-1	Owen 8, Cacapa 31, Milner 68, Duff 76
27	prem	**Bolton**	H	D	0-0	
28	facr4	**Arsenal**	A	L	0-3	
29	prem	**Arsenal**	A	L	0-3	
30	prem	**Middlesbro**	H	D	1-1	Owen 60
31	prem	**Aston Villa**	A	L	1-4	Owen 4
32	prem	**Man Utd**	H	L	1-5	Faye 79
33	prem	**Blackburn**	H	L	0-1	
34	prem	**Liverpool**	A	L	0-3	
35	prem	**Birmingham**	A	D	1-1	Owen 56
36	prem	**Fulham**	H	W	2-0	Viduka 7, Owen 83
37	prem	**Tottenham**	A	W	4-1	Butt 45, Geremi 52 , Owen 65, Martins 82
38	prem	**Reading**	H	W	3-0	Martins 18, Owen 43, Viduka 58
39	prem	**Portsmouth**	A	D	0-0	
40	prem	**Sunderland**	H	W	2-0	Owen 4, 45 pen
41	prem	**West Ham**	A	D	2-2	Martins 42, Geremi 45
42	prem	**Chelsea**	H	L	0-2	
43	prem	**Everton**	A	L	1-3	Owen 47 pen

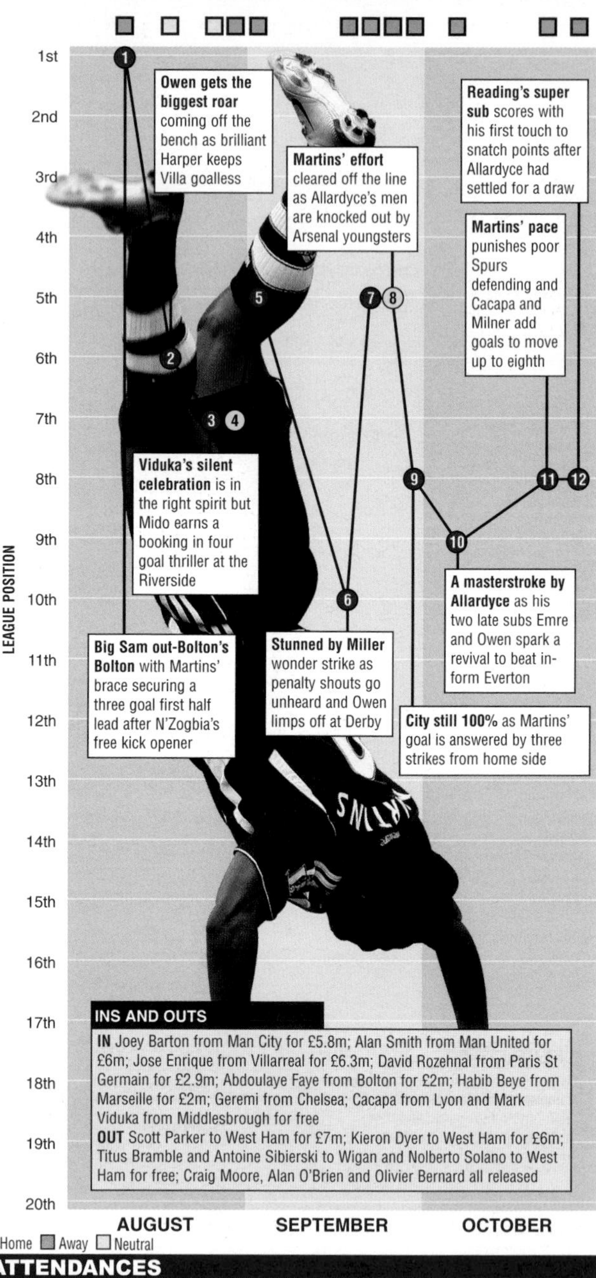

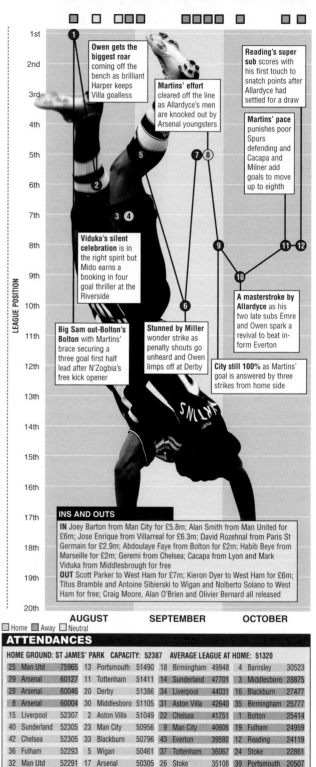

1st
2nd
3rd
4th
5th
6th
7th
8th
9th
10th
11th
12th
13th
14th
15th
16th
17th
18th
19th
20th
LEAGUE POSITION
Owen gets the biggest roar coming off the bench as brilliant Harper keeps Villa goalless
Martins' effort cleared off the line as Allardyce's men are knocked out by Arsenal youngsters
Reading's super sub scores with his first touch to snatch points after Allardyce had settled for a draw
Martins' pace punishes poor Spurs defending and Cacapa and Milner add goals to move up to eighth
Viduka's silent celebration is in the right spirit but Mido earns a booking in four goal thriller at the Riverside
A masterstroke by Allardyce as his two late subs Emre and Owen spark a revival to beat in-form Everton
Big Sam out-Bolton's Bolton with Martins' brace securing a three goal first half lead after N'Zogbia's free kick opener
Stunned by Miller wonder strike as penalty shouts go unheard and Owen limps off at Derby
City still 100% as Martins' goal is answered by three strikes from home side
AUGUST
SEPTEMBER
OCTOBER

INS AND OUTS

IN Joey Barton from Man City for £5.8m; Alan Smith from Man United for £6m; Jose Enrique from Villarreal for £6.3m; David Rozehnal from Paris St Germain for £2.9m; Abdoulaye Faye from Bolton for £2m; Habib Beye from Marseille for £2m; Geremi from Chelsea; Cacapa from Lyon and Mark Viduka from Middlesbrough for free

OUT Scott Parker to West Ham for £7m; Kieron Dyer to West Ham for £6m; Titus Bramble and Antoine Sibierski to Wigan and Nolberto Solano to West Ham for free; Craig Moore, Alan O'Brien and Olivier Bernard all released

Home Away Neutral

ATTENDANCES

HOME GROUND: ST JAMES' PARK CAPACITY: 52387 AVERAGE LEAGUE AT HOME: 51320

25	Man Utd	75965	13	Portsmouth	51490	18	Birmingham	49948	4	Barnsley	30523
29	Arsenal	60127	11	Tottenham	51411	14	Sunderland	47701	3	Middlesboro	28875
28	Arsenal	60046	20	Derby	51386	34	Liverpool	44031	16	Blackburn	27477
8	Arsenal	60004	30	Middlesboro	51105	31	Aston Villa	42640	35	Birmingham	25777
15	Liverpool	52307	2	Aston Villa	51049	22	Chelsea	41751	1	Bolton	25414
40	Sunderland	52305	23	Man City	50956	9	Man City	40606	19	Fulham	24959
42	Chelsea	52305	33	Blackburn	50796	43	Everton	39592	12	Reading	24119
36	Fulham	52293	5	Wigan	50461	37	Tottenham	36067	24	Stoke	22861
32	Man Utd	52291	17	Arsenal	50305	26	Stoke	35108	39	Portsmouth	20507
27	Bolton	52250	10	Everton	50152	41	West Ham	34980	21	Wigan	20304
38	Reading	52179	7	West Ham	50104	6	Derby	33016			

Keegan finds a new role for Owen

Final Position: 12th

KEY: ● League ● Champions Lge ● UEFA Cup ● FA Cup ○ League Cup ● Other

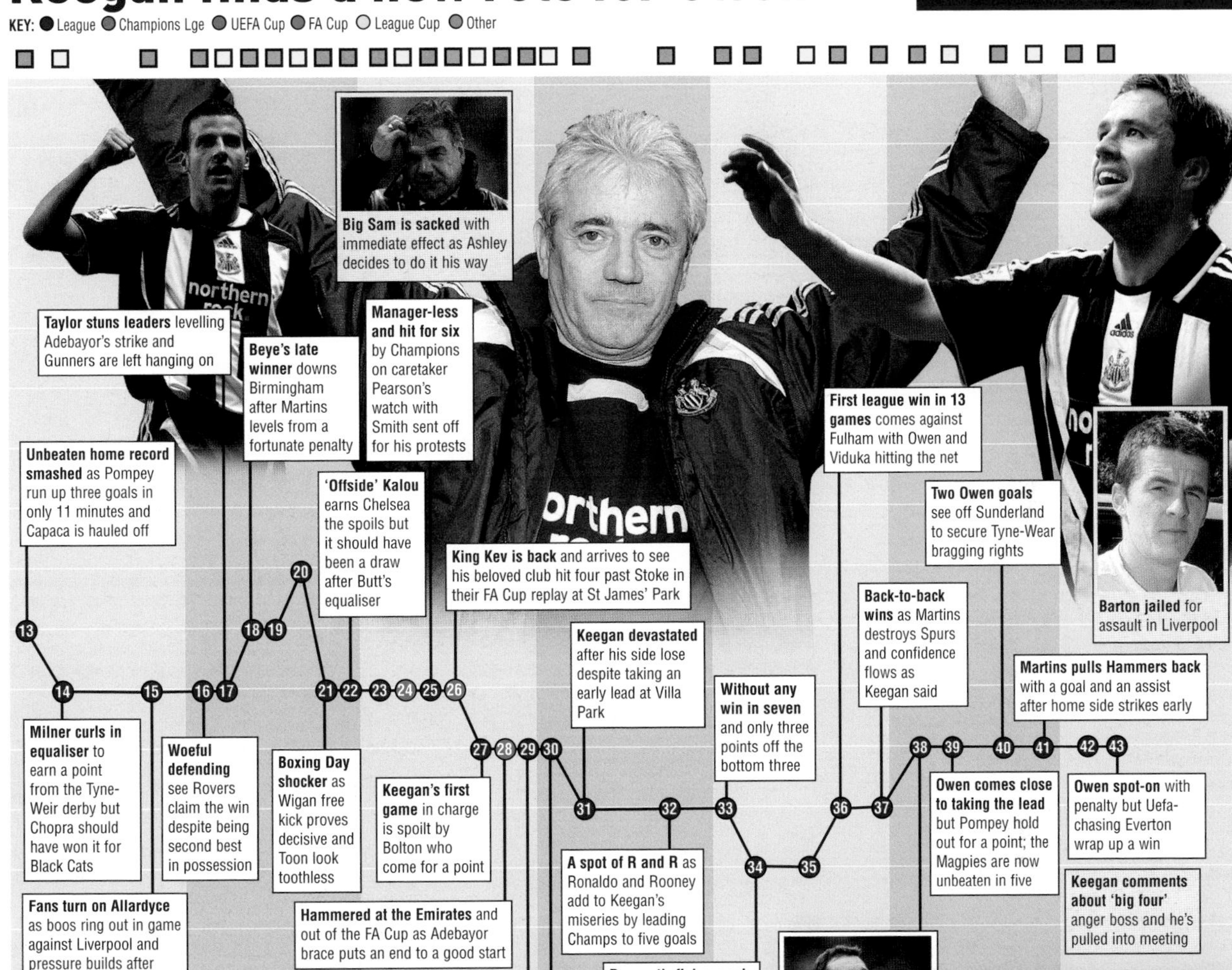
Taylor stuns leaders levelling Adebayor's strike and Gunners are left hanging on
Beye's late winner downs Birmingham after Martins levels from a fortunate penalty
Big Sam is sacked with immediate effect as Ashley decides to do it his way
Manager-less and hit for six by Champions on caretaker Pearson's watch with Smith sent off for his protests
Unbeaten home record smashed as Pompey run up three goals in only 11 minutes and Capaca is hauled off
'Offside' Kalou earns Chelsea the spoils but it should have been a draw after Butt's equaliser
King Kev is back and arrives to see his beloved club hit four past Stoke in their FA Cup replay at St James' Park
First league win in 13 games comes against Fulham with Owen and Viduka hitting the net
Two Owen goals see off Sunderland to secure Tyne-Wear bragging rights
Barton jailed for assault in Liverpool
Back-to-back wins as Martins destroys Spurs and confidence flows as Keegan said
Martins pulls Hammers back with a goal and an assist after home side strikes early
Keegan devastated after his side lose despite taking an early lead at Villa Park
Without any win in seven and only three points off the bottom three
Milner curls in equaliser to earn a point from the Tyne-Weir derby but Chopra should have won it for Black Cats
Woeful defending see Rovers claim the win despite being second best in possession
Boxing Day shocker as Wigan free kick proves decisive and Toon look toothless
Keegan's first game in charge is spoilt by Bolton who come for a point
Owen comes close to taking the lead but Pompey hold out for a point; the Magpies are now unbeaten in five
Owen spot-on with penalty but Uefa-chasing Everton wrap up a win
Keegan comments about 'big four' anger boss and he's pulled into meeting
A spot of R and R as Ronaldo and Rooney add to Keegan's miseries by leading Champs to five goals
Fans turn on Allardyce as boos ring out in game against Liverpool and pressure builds after home side can't manage one shot on target
Hammered at the Emirates and out of the FA Cup as Adebayor brace puts an end to a good start
Yet to score under Keegan as it's another 3-0 defeat at the Emirates in the league
Pennant's flukey goal beats Harper as Anfield defeat leaves Magpies too close for comfort
Third win on the spin comes against Reading at St James', as Martins, Owen and Viduka all find the net
Barton in the dock for assault on Merseyside pair
Owen's header cancelled out in the last five minutes for a point in Tyne-Tees derby
Harry says no; south coast lifestyle more important than money decides Redknapp
INS AND OUTS
IN Ben Tozer from Swindon and Fabio Zamblera from Atalanta both undisclosed
OUT Tim Krul to Fulham and David Rozehnal to Lazio on loan; Matty Patterson to Norwich undisclosed
MONTH BY MONTH POINTS TALLY
AUGUST 5 56%
SEPTEMBER 6 50%
OCTOBER 6 67%
NOVEMBER 1 11%
DECEMBER 8 38%
JANUARY 1 8%
FEBRUARY 1 11%
MARCH 7 47%
APRIL 8 67%
MAY 0 0%

NOVEMBER DECEMBER JANUARY FEBRUARY MARCH APRIL MAY

GOAL ATTEMPTS

FOR — Goal attempts recorded in League games

	HOME	AWAY	TOTAL	AVE
shots on target	121	105	226	5.9
shots off target	132	71	203	5.3
TOTAL	253	176	429	11.3

Ratio of goals to shots Average number of shots on target per League goal scored	5.0
Accuracy rating Average percentage of total goal attempts which were on target	52.7

AGAINST — Goal attempts recorded in League games

	HOME	AWAY	TOTAL	AVE
shots on target	140	159	299	7.9
shots off target	88	130	218	5.7
TOTAL	228	289	517	13.6

Ratio of goals to shots Average number of shots on target per League goal scored	4.6
Accuracy rating Average percentage of total goal attempts which were on target	57.8

GOALS

Owen

League	11
FA Cup	1
League Cup	1
Europe	0
Other	0
TOTAL	13

League Average **197** mins between goals

	PLAYER	LGE	FAC	LC	Euro	TOT	AVE
1	Owen	11	1	1	0	**13**	197
2	Martins	9	0	1	0	**10**	228
3	Viduka	7	0	0	0	**7**	236
4	N'Zogbia	3	0	0	0	**3**	812
5	Butt	3	0	0	0	**3**	999
6	Milner	2	1	0	0	**3**	1113
7	Geremi	2	0	0	0	**2**	1029
8	Cacapa	1	1	0	0	**2**	1432
9	Emre Belozoglu	1	0	0	0	**1**	593
10	Faye	1	0	0	0	**1**	1652
11	Barton	1	0	0	0	**1**	1831
12	Beye	1	0	0	0	**1**	2471
13	Taylor	1	0	0	0	**1**	2633
14	Duff	0	1	0	0	**1**	
	Other	0	0	0	0	0	
	TOTAL	**43**	**4**	**2**	**0**	**49**	

SQUAD APPEARANCES

Match	1	2	3	4	5	6	7	8	9	10	11	12	13	14	15	16	17	18	19	20	21	22	23	24	25	26	27	28	29	30	31	32	33	34	35	36	37	38	39	40	41	42	43
Venue	A	H	A	H	H	A	H	A	A	H	H	A	H	A	H	A	H	H	A	H	A	A	H	A	A	H	H	A	A	H	A	H	H	A	A	H	A	H	A	H	A	H	A
Competition	L	L	L	W	L	L	L	W	L	L	L	L	L	L	L	L	L	L	L	L	L	L	L	F	L	F	L	F	L	L	L	L	L	L	L	L	L	L	L	L	L	L	L
Result	W	D	D	W	W	L	W	L	L	W	W	L	L	D	L	L	D	W	W	D	L	L	L	D	L	W	D	L	L	D	L	L	L	L	D	W	W	W	D	W	D	L	L

Goalkeepers
- Fraser Forster
- Shay Given
- Steve Harper

Defenders
- Habib Beye
- Claudio Cacapa
- Stephen Carr
- Lamine Diatta
- David Edgar
- Jose Sanchez Enrique
- Geremi Njitap
- Paul Huntington
- Peter Ramage
- David Rozehnal
- Steven Taylor
- Ben Tozer

Midfielders
- Joey Barton
- Nicky Butt
- Damien Duff
- Emre Belozoglu
- Abdoulaye Faye
- James Milner
- Charles N'Zogbia
- Matty Pattison
- Nolberto Solano
- James Troisi

Forwards
- Shola Ameobi
- Andrew Carroll
- Kazenga LuaLua
- Obafemi Martins
- Michael Owen
- Alan Smith
- Mark Viduka

KEY: ■ On all match ■ On bench ⏮ Subbed or sent off (Counting game) « Subbed or sent off (playing less than 70 mins) » Subbed on from bench (Counting Game) » Subbed on (playing less than 70 mins) » Subbed on and then subbed or sent off (Counting Game) » Subbed on and then subbed or sent off (playing less than 70 min □ Not in 16 □ Injured ✕ Suspended

KEY PLAYERS - GOALSCORERS

Michael Owen

Goals in the League	11
Goals in all competitions	13
Assists League goals scored by a team mate where the player delivered the final pass	0
Contribution to Attacking Power Average number of minutes between League team goals while on pitch	72
Player Strike Rate Average number of minutes between League goals scored by player	197
Club Strike Rate Average minutes between League goals scored by club	76

	PLAYER	GOALS LGE	GOALS ALL	ASSISTS	POWER	S RATE
1	Michael Owen	11	13	0	72	197 mins
2	Obafemi Martins	9	10	3	68	228 mins
3	Mark Viduka	7	7	1	61	236 mins
4	Charles N'Zogbia	3	3	4	84	812 mins

KEY PLAYERS - MIDFIELDERS

Joey Barton

Goals in the League	1
Goals in all competitions	1
Assists League goals scored by a team mate where the player delivered the final pass	3
Defensive Rating Average number of mins between League goals conceded while on the pitch	59
Contribution to Attacking Power Average number of minutes between League team goals while on pitch	70
Scoring Difference Defensive Rating minus Contribution to Attacking Power	-11

	PLAYER	GOALS LGE	GOALS ALL	ASSISTS	DEF RATE	POWER	SC DIFF
1	Joey Barton	1	1	3	59	70	-11 mins
2	Abdoulaye Faye	1	1	0	59	78	-19 mins
3	Nicky Butt	3	3	1	49	74	-25 mins
4	James Milner	2	3	2	53	85	-32 mins

PLAYER APPEARANCES

	AGE (on 01/07/08)	IN NAMED 16	APPEARANCES	COUNTING GAMES	MINUTES ON PITCH	APPEARANCES	MINUTES ON PITCH	THIS SEASON	HOME COUNTRY
Goalkeepers									
Fraser Forster	20	16	0	0	0	0	0	-	England
Shay Given	32	23	19	17	1628	24	2078	6	Rep of Ireland
Steve Harper	33	37	21	19	1792	21	1792	-	England
Defenders									
Habib Beye	31	29	29	27	2471	30	2561	-	Senegal
Claudio Cacapa	32	26	19	15	1432	22	1682	-	Brazil
Stephen Carr	31	10	10	7	696	12	876	-	Rep of Ireland
Lamine Diatta	32	2	2	0	9	2	9	-	Senegal
David Edgar	21	14	5	2	188	6	192	-	Canada
Jose S Enrique	22	28	23	17	1618	28	2053	-	Spain
Geremi Njitap	29	29	27	21	2058	28	2148	6	Cameroon
Paul Huntington	20	0	0	0	0	0	0	-	England
Peter Ramage	24	4	3	0	59	3	59	-	England
David Rozehnal	27	23	21	15	1492	25	1707	7	Czech Republic
Steven Taylor	22	32	31	29	2633	36	3083	-	England
Ben Tozer	18	1	0	0	0	0	0	-	-
Midfielders									
Joey Barton	25	23	23	19	1831	23	1831	-	England
Nicky Butt	33	36	35	31	2998	39	3239	-	England
Damien Duff	29	19	16	10	1062	19	1306	1	Rep of Ireland
Emre Belozoglu	27	18	14	4	593	17	702	7	Turkey
Abdoulaye Faye	30	24	22	17	1652	24	1832	3	Senegal
James Milner	22	29	29	23	2227	32	2476	-	England
Charles N'Zogbia	22	32	32	25	2437	37	2875	-	France
Matty Pattison	21	3	0	0	0	0	0	-	South Africa
Nolberto Solano	33	1	1	0	21	2	111	-	Peru
James Troisi	19	1	0	0	0	0	0	-	Australia
Forwards									
Shola Ameobi	26	10	6	2	275	8	424	-	England
Andrew Carroll	19	12	4	1	141	6	164	-	England
Kazenga LuaLua	17	3	2	0	23	5	61	-	Congo DR
Obafemi Martins	23	31	31	20	2055	33	2153	2	Nigeria
Michael Owen	28	29	29	22	2174	33	2526	7	England
Alan Smith	27	35	33	24	2396	37	2752	2	England
Mark Viduka	32	27	26	17	1658	28	1815	-	Australia

KEY: LEAGUE ALL COMPS CAPS (MAY FIFA RANKING)

TEAM OF THE SEASON

HARPER

CG 19 DR 64

GEREMI
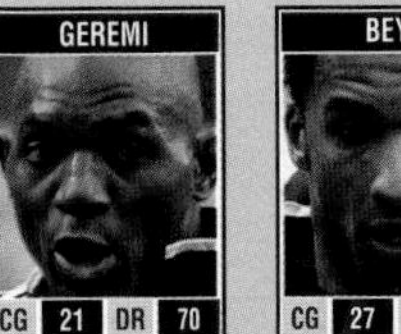
CG 21 DR 70

BEYE

CG 27 DR 53

ROZEHNAL

CG 15 DR 57

ENRIQUE

CG 17 DR 53

BARTON

CG 19 SD -11

BUTT

CG 31 SD -25

FAYE

CG 17 SD -19

MILNER

CG 23 SD -32

MARTINS

CG 20 AP 68

OWEN
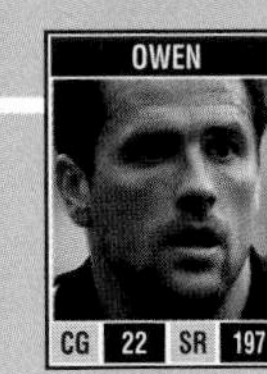
CG 22 SR 197

KEY: DR = Defensive Rate, SD = Scoring Difference AP = Attacking Power SR = Strike Rate, CG=Counting games – League games playing at least 70 minutes

TOP POINT EARNERS

Geremi Njitap

Counting Games League games when player was on pitch for at least 70 minutes	21
Average points Average League points taken in Counting games	1.71
Club Average points Average points taken in League games	1.13

	PLAYER	GAMES	PTS
1	Geremi Njitap	21	1.71
2	Obafemi Martins	20	1.65
3	Mark Viduka	17	1.47
4	Steve Harper	19	1.42
5	David Rozehnal	15	1.33
6	Joey Barton	19	1.32
7	Jose Sanchez Dias Enrique	17	1.29
8	Claudio Cacapa	15	1.20
9	Habib Beye	27	1.19
10	Nicky Butt	31	1.19

KEY PLAYERS - DEFENDERS

Geremi Njitap

Goals Conceded in the League Number of League goals conceded while the player was on the pitch	29
Goals Conceded in all competitions Total number of goals conceded while the player was on the pitch	29
League minutes played Number of minutes played in league matches	2058
Clean Sheets In games when the player was on pitch for at least 70 minutes	6
Defensive Rating Average number of mins between League goals conceded while on the pitch	70
Club Defensive Rating Average number of mins between League goals conceded by the club this season	52

	PLAYER	CON LGE	CON ALL	MINS	C SHEETS	DEF RATE
1	Geremi Njitap	29	29	2058	6	70 mins
2	David Rozehnal	26	31	1492	4	57 mins
3	Habib Beye	46	48	2471	5	53 mins
4	Jose Sanchez Dias Enrique	30	34	1618	5	53 mins

KEY GOALKEEPER

Steve Harper

Goals Conceded in the League Number of League goals conceded while the player was on the pitch	28
Goals Conceded in all competitions Total number of goals conceded while the player was on the pitch	28
League minutes played Number of minutes played in league matches	1792
Clean Sheets In games when the player was on pitch for at least 70 minutes	6
Goals to Shots Ratio The average number of shots on target per each League goal conceded	5.07
Defensive Rating Ave mins between League goals conceded while on the pitch	64

BOOKINGS

Nicky Butt

League Yellow	13
League Red	0
All competitions Yellow	14
All competitions Red	0
League Average	230 mins between cards

	PLAYER	LEAGUE		TOTAL		AVE
1	Nicky Butt	13Y	0R	14Y	0R	230
2	Alan Smith	9	1	10	1	239
3	Emre Belozoglu	2	0	2	1	296
4	Abdoulaye Faye	5	0	5	0	330
5	Damien Duff	3	0	3	0	354
6	Charles N'Zogbia	6	0	6	0	406
7	Joey Barton	4	0	4	0	457
8	Habib Beye	5	0	5	0	494
9	Geremi Njitap	3	0	3	0	686
10	James Milner	3	0	3	0	742
11	Shay Given	2	0	2	0	814
12	Steven Taylor	3	0	3	0	877
13	Michael Owen	2	0	2	0	1087
14	Claudio Cacapa	1	0	2	0	1432
15	Jose Enrique	1	0	1	0	1618
	Other	1	0	1	0	
	TOTAL	63	1	66	2	

MIDDLESBROUGH

Boro have shown two sides to their game this season: abject, as typified by the Cardiff quarter final, and scintillating, as when they regularly tested and matched the 'big four'. Champions United were lucky to get a point at the Riverside, Boro took four points off Arsenal and wouldn't have been flattered by results at Chelsea or Liverpool. The second half thrashing of Sven's City was completely at odds with a dismal second half against Bolton three games earlier. Gareth Southgate may be right in identifying his midfield as the priority with **Fabio Rochemback** already gone, **George Boateng** pondering his future and the hugely improved **Stewart Downing** in demand.

NICKNAME: BORO

KEY: Won / Drawn / Lost

1	prem	**Blackburn**	H	L	1-2	Downing 30
2	prem	**Wigan**	A	L	0-1	
3	prem	**Fulham**	A	W	2-1	Mido 55, Cattermole 89
4	prem	**Newcastle**	H	D	2-2	Mido 28, Arca 80
5	ccr2	**Northampton**	H	W	2-0	Rochemback 53, Lee Dong-Gook 66
6	prem	**Birmingham**	H	W	2-0	Wheater 12, Downing 36
7	prem	**West Ham**	A	L	0-3	
8	prem	**Sunderland**	H	D	2-2	Arca 15, Downing 67
9	ccr3	**Tottenham**	A	L	0-2	
10	prem	**Everton**	A	L	0-2	
11	prem	**Man City**	A	L	1-3	Hutchinson 89
12	prem	**Chelsea**	H	L	0-2	
13	prem	**Man Utd**	A	L	1-4	Aliadiere 6
14	prem	**Tottenham**	H	D	1-1	Young 52
15	prem	**Bolton**	A	D	0-0	
16	prem	**Aston Villa**	H	L	0-3	
17	prem	**Reading**	A	D	1-1	Tuncay Sanli 83
18	prem	**Arsenal**	H	W	2-1	Downing 4 pen, Tuncay Sanli 73
19	prem	**Derby**	A	W	1-0	Tuncay Sanli 38
20	prem	**West Ham**	H	L	1-2	Wheater 39
21	prem	**Birmingham**	A	L	0-3	
22	prem	**Portsmouth**	A	W	1-0	Tuncay Sanli 20
23	prem	**Everton**	H	L	0-2	
24	facr3	**Bristol City**	A	W	2-1	Downing 37, Wheater 72
25	prem	**Liverpool**	H	D	1-1	Boateng 26
26	prem	**Blackburn**	A	D	1-1	Wheater 13
27	facr4	**Mansfield**	A	W	2-0	Lee Dong-Gook 16, Buxton 87 og
28	prem	**Wigan**	H	W	1-0	Aliadiere 19
29	prem	**Newcastle**	A	D	1-1	Huth 87
30	prem	**Fulham**	H	W	1-0	Aliadiere 11
31	facr5	**Sheff Utd**	A	D	0-0	
32	prem	**Liverpool**	A	L	2-3	Tuncay Sanli 9, Downing 83
33	facr5r	**Sheff Utd**	H	W	1-0	Kenny 114 og
34	prem	**Reading**	H	L	0-1	
35	facqf	**Cardiff**	H	L	0-2	
36	prem	**Aston Villa**	A	D	1-1	Downing 23
37	prem	**Arsenal**	A	D	1-1	Aliadiere 23
38	prem	**Derby**	H	W	1-0	Tuncay Sanli 32
39	prem	**Chelsea**	A	L	0-1	
40	prem	**Man Utd**	H	D	2-2	Alves 35, 56
41	prem	**Tottenham**	A	D	1-1	Downing 69
42	prem	**Bolton**	H	L	0-1	
43	prem	**Sunderland**	A	L	2-3	Tuncay Sanli 4, Alves 73
44	prem	**Portsmouth**	H	W	2-0	Riggott 40, Tuncay Sanli 53
45	prem	**Man City**	H	W	8-1	Downing 15 pen, 58, Alves 37, 60, 90, Johnson 70, Rochemback 80 , Aliadiere 84

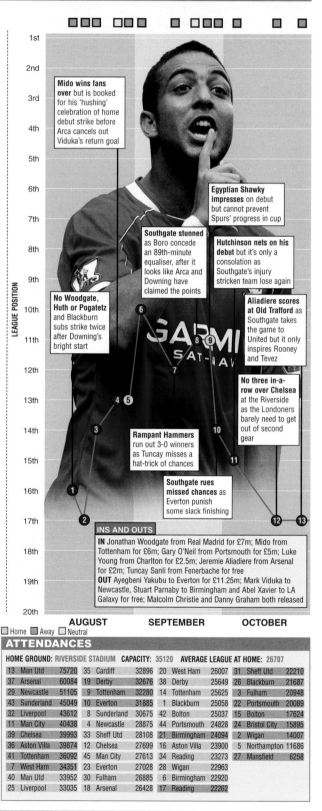

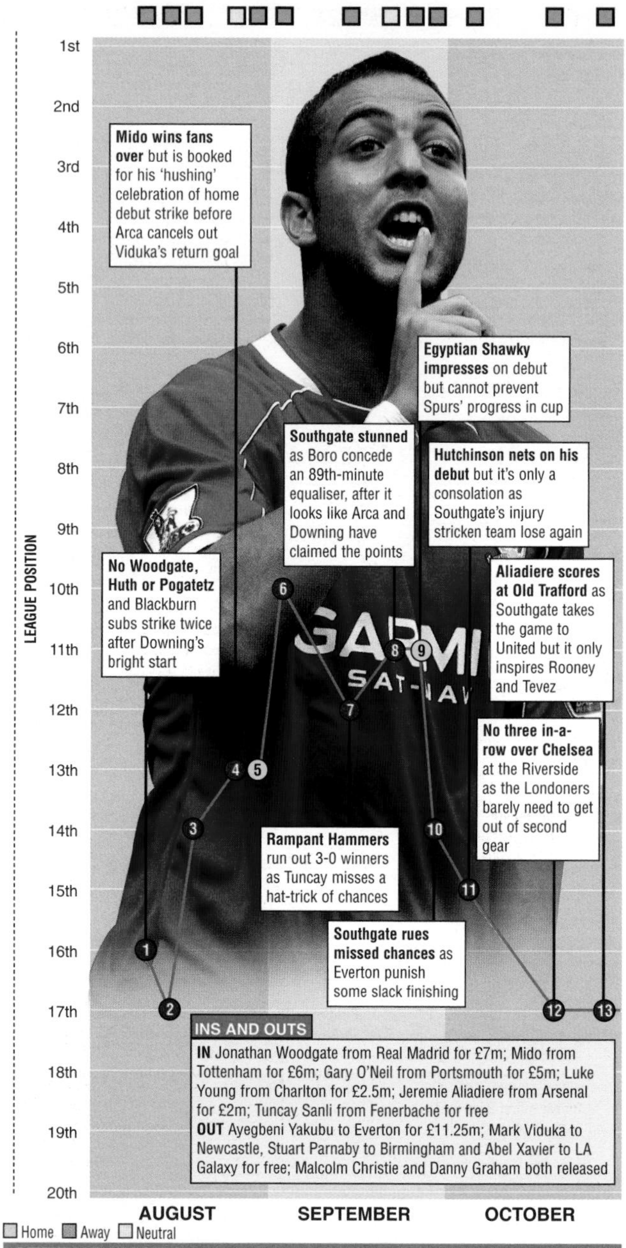

LEAGUE POSITION: 1st – 20th; AUGUST, SEPTEMBER, OCTOBER

Mido wins fans over but is booked for his 'hushing' celebration of home debut strike before Arca cancels out Viduka's return goal

Egyptian Shawky impresses on debut but cannot prevent Spurs' progress in cup

Southgate stunned as Boro concede an 89th-minute equaliser, after it looks like Arca and Downing have claimed the points

Hutchinson nets on his debut but it's only a consolation as Southgate's injury stricken team lose again

No Woodgate, Huth or Pogatetz and Blackburn subs strike twice after Downing's bright start

Aliadiere scores at Old Trafford as Southgate takes the game to United but it only inspires Rooney and Tevez

No three in-a-row over Chelsea at the Riverside as the Londoners barely need to get out of second gear

Rampant Hammers run out 3-0 winners as Tuncay misses a hat-trick of chances

Southgate rues missed chances as Everton punish some slack finishing

INS AND OUTS

IN Jonathan Woodgate from Real Madrid for £7m; Mido from Tottenham for £6m; Gary O'Neil from Portsmouth for £5m; Luke Young from Charlton for £2.5m; Jeremie Aliadiere from Arsenal for £2m; Tuncay Sanli from Fenerbache for free

OUT Ayegbeni Yakubu to Everton for £11.25m; Mark Viduka to Newcastle, Stuart Parnaby to Birmingham and Abel Xavier to LA Galaxy for free; Malcolm Christie and Danny Graham both released

Home / Away / Neutral

ATTENDANCES

HOME GROUND: RIVERSIDE STADIUM **CAPACITY:** 35120 **AVERAGE LEAGUE AT HOME:** 26707

13	Man Utd	75720	35	Cardiff	32896	20	West Ham	26007	31	Sheff Utd	22210
37	Arsenal	60084	19	Derby	32676	38	Derby	25649	26	Blackburn	21687
29	Newcastle	51105	9	Tottenham	32280	14	Tottenham	25625	3	Fulham	20948
43	Sunderland	45049	10	Everton	31885	1	Blackburn	25058	22	Portsmouth	20089
32	Liverpool	43612	8	Sunderland	30675	42	Bolton	25037	15	Bolton	17624
11	Man City	40438	4	Newcastle	28875	44	Portsmouth	24828	24	Bristol City	15895
39	Chelsea	39993	33	Sheff Utd	28108	21	Birmingham	24094	2	Wigan	14007
36	Aston Villa	39874	12	Chelsea	27699	16	Aston Villa	23900	5	Northampton	11686
41	Tottenham	36092	45	Man City	27613	34	Reading	23273	27	Mansfield	6258
7	West Ham	34351	23	Everton	27028	28	Wigan	22963			
40	Man Utd	33952	30	Fulham	26885	6	Birmingham	22920			
25	Liverpool	33035	18	Arsenal	26428	17	Reading	22262			

Eight-goal blitz papers over cracks

Final Position: **13th**

KEY: ● League ● Champions Lge ● UEFA Cup ● FA Cup ○ League Cup ● Other

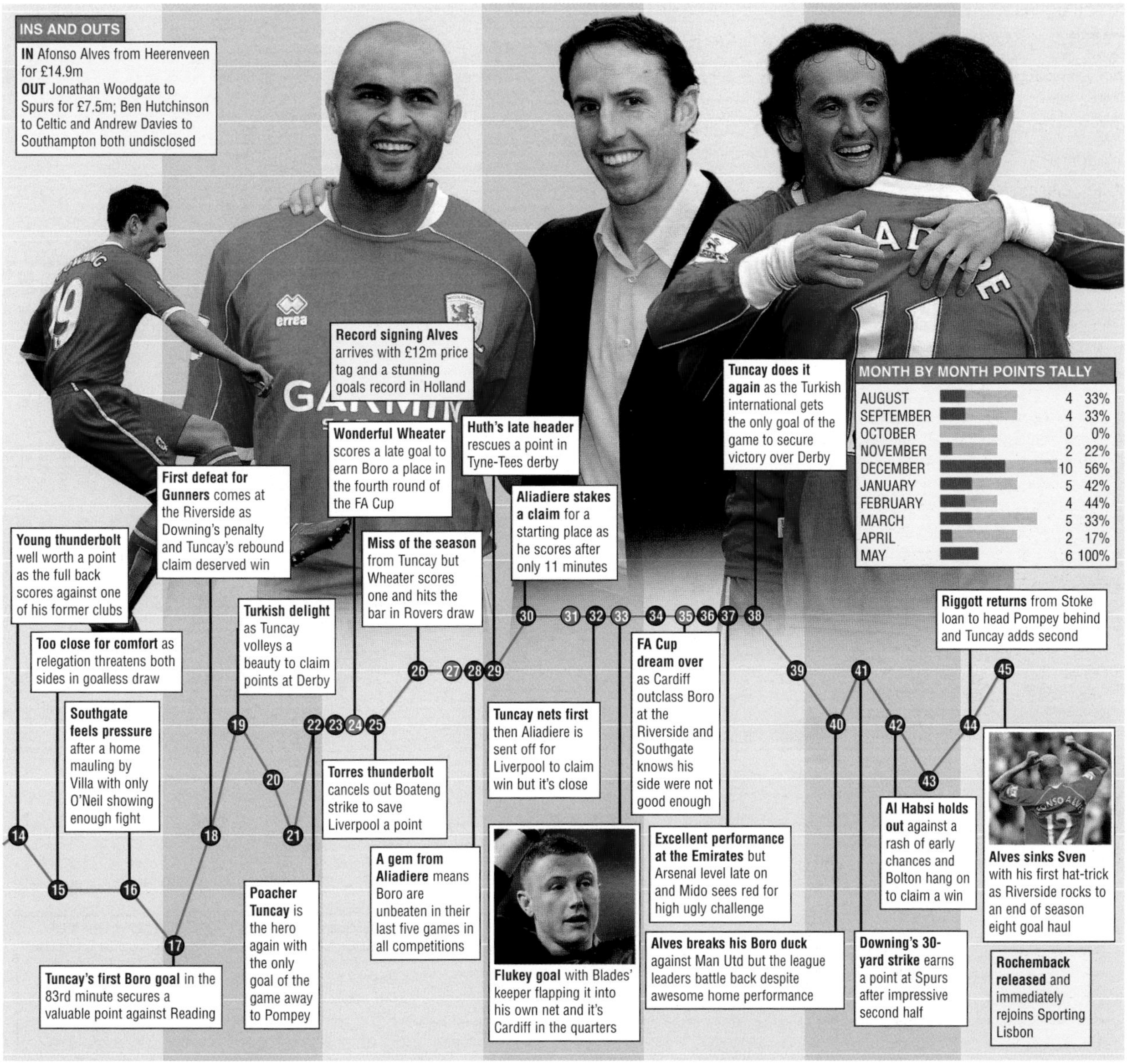

INS AND OUTS

IN Afonso Alves from Heerenveen for £14.9m
OUT Jonathan Woodgate to Spurs for £7.5m; Ben Hutchinson to Celtic and Andrew Davies to Southampton both undisclosed

Young thunderbolt well worth a point as the full back scores against one of his former clubs

Too close for comfort as relegation threatens both sides in goalless draw

Southgate feels pressure after a home mauling by Villa with only O'Neil showing enough fight

Tuncay's first Boro goal in the 83rd minute secures a valuable point against Reading

First defeat for Gunners comes at the Riverside as Downing's penalty and Tuncay's rebound claim deserved win

Turkish delight as Tuncay volleys a beauty to claim points at Derby

Poacher Tuncay is the hero again with the only goal of the game away to Pompey

Record signing Alves arrives with £12m price tag and a stunning goals record in Holland

Wonderful Wheater scores a late goal to earn Boro a place in the fourth round of the FA Cup

Torres thunderbolt cancels out Boateng strike to save Liverpool a point

Miss of the season from Tuncay but Wheater scores one and hits the bar in Rovers draw

A gem from Aliadiere means Boro are unbeaten in their last five games in all competitions

Huth's late header rescues a point in Tyne-Tees derby

Aliadiere stakes a claim for a starting place as he scores after only 11 minutes

Tuncay nets first then Aliadiere is sent off for Liverpool to claim win but it's close

Flukey goal with Blades' keeper flapping it into his own net and it's Cardiff in the quarters

FA Cup dream over as Cardiff outclass Boro at the Riverside and Southgate knows his side were not good enough

Excellent performance at the Emirates but Arsenal level late on and Mido sees red for high ugly challenge

Alves breaks his Boro duck against Man Utd but the league leaders battle back despite awesome home performance

Tuncay does it again as the Turkish international gets the only goal of the game to secure victory over Derby

Downing's 30-yard strike earns a point at Spurs after impressive second half

Al Habsi holds out against a rash of early chances and Bolton hang on to claim a win

Riggott returns from Stoke loan to head Pompey behind and Tuncay adds second

Alves sinks Sven with his first hat-trick as Riverside rocks to an end of season eight goal haul

Rochemback released and immediately rejoins Sporting Lisbon

NOVEMBER | DECEMBER | JANUARY | FEBRUARY | MARCH | APRIL | MAY

MONTH BY MONTH POINTS TALLY

Month	Points	%
AUGUST	4	33%
SEPTEMBER	4	33%
OCTOBER	0	0%
NOVEMBER	2	22%
DECEMBER	10	56%
JANUARY	5	42%
FEBRUARY	4	44%
MARCH	5	33%
APRIL	2	17%
MAY	6	100%

GOAL ATTEMPTS

FOR – Goal attempts recorded in League games

	HOME	AWAY	TOTAL	AVE
shots on target	119	113	232	6.1
shots off target	107	92	199	5.2
TOTAL	226	205	431	11.3

Ratio of goals to shots – Average number of shots on target per League goal scored: 5.4

Accuracy rating – Average percentage of total goal attempts which were on target: 53.8

AGAINST – Goal attempts recorded in League games

	HOME	AWAY	TOTAL	AVE
shots on target	100	134	234	6.2
shots off target	86	117	203	5.3
TOTAL	186	251	437	11.5

Ratio of goals to shots – Average number of shots on target per League goal scored: 4.4

Accuracy rating – Average percentage of total goal attempts which were on target: 53.5

GOALS

Downing

League	9
FA Cup	1
League Cup	0
Europe	0
Other	0
TOTAL	10

League Average 379 mins between goals

	PLAYER	LGE	FAC	LC	Euro	TOT	AVE
1	Downing	9	1	0	0	10	379
2	Tuncay Sanli	8	0	0	0	8	276
3	Alves	6	0	0	0	6	108
4	Aliadiere	5	0	0	0	5	431
5	Wheater	3	1	0	0	4	1005
6	Mido	2	0	0	0	2	374
7	Arca	2	0	0	0	2	931
8	Rochemback	1	0	1	0	2	1985
9	Lee Dong-Gook	0	1	1	0	2	
10	Hutchinson	1	0	0	0	1	190
11	Johnson	1	0	0	0	1	474
12	Riggott	1	0	0	0	1	829
13	Huth	1	0	0	0	1	922
14	Cattermole	1	0	0	0	1	1000
15	Boateng	1	0	0	0	1	2607
	Other	1	0	0	0	1	
	TOTAL	43	3	2	0	48	

SQUAD APPEARANCES

Match	1	2	3	4	5	6	7	8	9	10	11	12	13	14	15	16	17	18	19	20	21	22	23	24	25	26	27	28	29	30	31	32	33	34	35	36	37	38	39	40	41	42	43	44	45
Venue	H	A	A	H	H	H	A	H	A	A	A	H	A	H	A	H	A	H	A	H	A	A	H	A	H	A	A	H	A	H	A	A	H	H	H	A	A	H	A	H	A	H	A	H	H
Competition	L	L	L	L	W	L	L	L	W	L	L	L	L	L	L	L	L	L	L	L	L	L	L	F	L	L	F	L	L	L	F	L	F	L	F	L	L	L	L	L	L	L	L	L	L
Result	L	L	W	D	W	W	L	D	L	L	L	L	L	D	D	L	D	W	W	L	L	W	L	W	D	D	W	W	D	W	D	L	W	L	L	D	D	W	L	D	D	L	L	W	W

Goalkeepers
Brad Jones
Mark Schwarzer
Jason Steele
Ross Turnbull

Defenders
Andrew Davies
Jonathan Grounds
Seb Hines
Robert Huth
Anthony McMahon
Emanuel Pogatetz
Chris Riggott
Andrew Taylor
David Wheater
Jonathan Woodgate
Luke Young

Midfielders
Julio Arca
George Boateng
Lee Cattermole
Stewart Downing
Adam Johnson
Gary O'Neil
Graeme Owens
Fabio Rochemback
Mohamed Shawky

Forwards
Jeremie Aliadiere
Afonso Alves
Tom Craddock
Ben Hutchinson
Lee Dong-Gook
Hossam Mido
Tuncay Sanli
Ayegbeni Yakubu

KEY: On all match | On bench | Subbed or sent off (Counting game) | Subbed or sent off (playing less than 70 mins) | Subbed on from bench (Counting Game) | Subbed on (playing less than 70 mins) | Subbed on and then subbed or sent off (Counting Game) | Subbed on and then subbed or sent off (playing less than 70 min | Not in 16 | Injured | ✕ Suspended

KEY PLAYERS - GOALSCORERS

Tuncay Sanli

Goals in the League	8
Goals in all competitions	8
Assists League goals scored by a team mate where the player delivered the final pass	3
Contribution to Attacking Power Average number of minutes between League team goals while on pitch	85
Player Strike Rate Average number of minutes between League goals scored by player	276
Club Strike Rate Average minutes between League goals scored by club	79

	PLAYER	GOALS LGE	GOALS ALL	ASSISTS	POWER	S RATE
1	Tuncay Sanli	8	8	3	85	276 mins
2	Stewart Downing	9	10	6	79	379 mins
3	Jeremie Aliadiere	5	5	7	74	431 mins
4	Julio Arca	2	2	5	71	931 mins

KEY PLAYERS - MIDFIELDERS

Julio Arca

Goals in the League	2
Goals in all competitions	2
Assists League goals scored by a team mate where the player delivered the final pass	5
Defensive Rating Average number of mins between League goals conceded while on the pitch	66
Contribution to Attacking Power Average number of minutes between League team goals while on pitch	71
Scoring Difference Defensive Rating minus Contribution to Attacking Power	-5

	PLAYER	GOALS LGE	GOALS ALL	ASSISTS	DEF RATE	POWER	SC DIFF
1	Julio Arca	2	2	5	66	71	-5 mins
2	Fabio Rochemback	1	2	4	56	66	-10 mins
3	George Boateng	1	1	3	66	79	-13 mins
4	Stewart Downing	9	10	6	64	79	-15 mins

PLAYER APPEARANCES

	AGE (on 01/07/08)	IN NAMED 16	APPEARANCES	COUNTING GAMES	MINUTES ON PITCH	APPEARANCES	MINUTES ON PITCH	THIS SEASON	HOME COUNTRY
Goalkeepers									
Brad Jones	26	10	1	1	90	3	270	-	Australia
Mark Schwarzer	35	34	34	34	3060	39	3540	-	Australia
Jason Steele	17	3	0	0	0	0	0	-	England
Ross Turnbull	23	29	3	3	270	3	270	-	England
Defenders									
Andrew Davies	23	4	4	3	278	6	324	-	England
Jonathan Grounds	20	13	5	4	423	7	633	-	England
Seb Hines	20	10	1	0	1	3	176	-	England
Robert Huth	23	14	13	9	922	16	1192	-	Germany
Anthony McMahon	22	3	1	0	15	1	15	-	England
Emanuel Pogatetz	25	24	24	23	2131	29	2566	2	Austria
Chris Riggott	27	16	10	9	829	11	919	-	England
Andrew Taylor	21	22	19	17	1556	21	1736	-	England
David Wheater	21	36	34	33	3015	40	3555	-	England
Jonathan Woodgate	28	16	16	15	1373	16	1373	1	England
Luke Young	28	35	35	34	3109	42	3740	-	England
Midfielders									
Julio Arca	27	25	24	18	1862	29	2275	-	Argentina
George Boateng	32	35	33	27	2607	38	2903	-	Holland
Lee Cattermole	20	27	24	8	1000	28	1360	-	England
Stewart Downing	23	38	38	38	3416	45	3991	3	England
Adam Johnson	20	25	19	3	474	24	741	-	England
Gary O'Neil	25	26	26	24	2190	29	2383	-	England
Graeme Owens	20	0	0	0	0	1	15	-	England
Fabio Rochemback	26	27	26	20	1985	33	2613	-	Brazil
Mohamed Shawky	26	11	5	2	252	6	297	5	Egypt
Forwards									
Jeremie Aliadiere	25	29	29	23	2155	31	2335	-	France
Afonso Alves	27	11	11	5	652	14	785	3	Brazil
Tom Craddock	21	3	3	0	94	4	139	-	England
Ben Hutchinson	20	9	8	0	190	9	265	-	England
Lee Dong-Gook	29	23	14	4	548	18	813	-	South Korea
Hossam Mido	25	13	12	6	748	17	1028	-	Egypt
Tuncay Sanli	26	35	34	20	2212	38	2465	6	Turkey
Ayegbeni Yakubu	25	2	2	1	155	2	155	4	Nigeria

KEY: LEAGUE ALL COMPS CAPS (MAY FIFA RANKING)

TEAM OF THE SEASON

SCWARZER

CG 34 DR 65

YOUNG

CG 34 DR 64

WHEATER

CG 33 DR 67

POGATETZ

CG 23 DR 73

TAYLOR

CG 17 DR 50

ARCA

CG 18 SD -5

BOATENG

CG 27 SD -13

ROCHEMBACK

CG 20 SD -10

DOWNING

CG 38 SD -15

ALIADIERE

CG 23 AP 74

TUNCAY

CG 20 SR 276

KEY: DR = Defensive Rate, SD = Scoring Difference AP = Attacking Power SR = Strike Rate, CG=Counting games – League games playing at least 70 minutes

TOP POINT EARNERS

Fabio Rochemback

Counting Games League games when player was on pitch for at least 70 minutes	20
Average points Average League points taken in Counting games	1.35
Club Average points Average points taken in League games	1.11

	PLAYER	GAMES	PTS
1	Fabio Rochemback	20	1.35
2	Emanuel Pogatetz	23	1.22
3	Jeremie Aliadiere	23	1.22
4	David Wheater	33	1.18
5	Julio Arca	18	1.17
6	Gary O'Neil	24	1.17
7	Mark Schwarzer	34	1.12
8	George Boateng	27	1.11
9	Stewart Downing	38	1.11
10	Luke Young	34	1.06

KEY PLAYERS - DEFENDERS

Emanuel Pogatetz

Goals Conceded in the League Number of League goals conceded while the player was on the pitch	29
Goals Conceded in all competitions Total number of goals conceded while the player was on the pitch	32
League minutes played Number of minutes played in league matches	2131
Clean Sheets In games when the player was on pitch for at least 70 minutes	5
Defensive Rating Average number of mins between League goals conceded while on the pitch	73
Club Defensive Rating Average number of mins between League goals conceded by the club this season	64

	PLAYER	CON LGE	CON ALL	MINS	C SHEETS	DEF RATE
1	Emanuel Pogatetz	29	32	2131	5	73 mins
2	David Wheater	45	50	3015	7	67 mins
3	Luke Young	48	53	3109	8	64 mins
4	Andrew Taylor	31	33	1556	2	50 mins

KEY GOALKEEPER

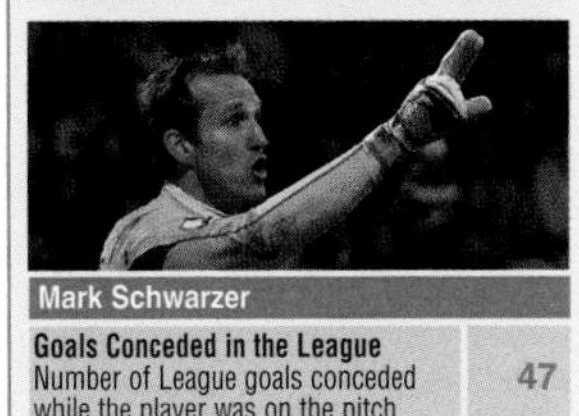

Mark Schwarzer

Goals Conceded in the League Number of League goals conceded while the player was on the pitch	47
Goals Conceded in all competitions Total number of goals conceded while the player was on the pitch	50
League minutes played Number of minutes played in league matches	3060
Clean Sheets In games when the player was on pitch for at least 70 minutes	8
Goals to Shots Ratio The average number of shots on target per each League goal conceded	4.26
Defensive Rating Ave mins between League goals conceded while on the pitch	65

BOOKINGS

Hossam Mido

League Yellow	4
League Red	1
All competitions Yellow	4
All competitions Red	1
League Average 149 mins between cards	

	PLAYER	LEAGUE Y	LEAGUE R	TOTAL Y	TOTAL R	AVE
1	Hossam Mido	4Y	1R	4Y	1R	149
2	Lee Cattermole	5	0	8	0	200
3	Adam Johnson	2	0	2	0	237
4	Gary O'Neil	8	0	9	0	273
5	Lee Dong-Gook	2	0	2	0	274
6	Fabio Rochemback	7	0	10	0	283
7	George Boateng	9	0	9	0	289
8	Robert Huth	3	0	5	0	307
9	Julio Arca	6	0	7	0	310
10	J Woodgate	4	0	4	0	343
11	Luke Young	9	0	9	0	345
12	David Wheater	8	0	9	0	376
13	Tuncay Sanli	5	0	5	0	442
14	Jeremie Aliadiere	3	1	4	1	538
15	Emanuel Pogatetz	3	0	5	0	710
	Other	6	0	7	0	
	TOTAL	84	2	99	2	

WIGAN ATHLETIC

After the turmoil of late 2007 where Chris Hutching's team were rooted in the bottom three and staring relegation in the face, the turnaround in 2008 under Steve Bruce's leadership was nothing short of astounding. Bruce turned Wigan from relegation certainties to top-half challengers in the space of a few weeks despite making hardly any alterations to the squad in the January window. The top four's hoodoo over the Latics was finally broken as **Titus Bramble** memorably gained a point at Anfield before further draws were achieved against Arsenal and Chelsea. If Bruce can keep the nucleus of the squad together and add a bit more quality to the ranks, the future looks very bright.

NICKNAME: THE LATICS

KEY: Won / Drawn / Lost

No.	Comp	Opponent	Venue	Res	Score	Scorers
1	prem	**Everton**	A	L	1-2	Sibierski 80
2	prem	**Middlesbro**	H	W	1-0	Sibierski 55
3	prem	**Sunderland**	H	W	3-0	Heskey 19, Landzaat 62 pen, Sibierski 69 pen
4	prem	**West Ham**	A	D	1-1	Scharner 79
5	ccr2	**Hull City**	H	L	0-1	
6	prem	**Newcastle**	A	L	0-1	
7	prem	**Fulham**	H	D	1-1	Koumas 79 pen
8	prem	**Reading**	A	L	1-2	Bent 50
9	prem	**Liverpool**	H	L	0-1	
10	prem	**Man Utd**	A	L	0-4	
11	prem	**Portsmouth**	H	L	0-2	
12	prem	**Birmingham**	A	L	2-3	Bent 23, 59
13	prem	**Chelsea**	H	L	0-2	
14	prem	**Tottenham**	A	L	0-4	
15	prem	**Arsenal**	A	L	0-2	
16	prem	**Man City**	H	D	1-1	Scharner 25
17	prem	**Bolton**	A	L	1-4	Landzaat 14
18	prem	**Blackburn**	H	W	5-3	Landzaat 10, Bent 12, 66, 81, Scharner 37
19	prem	**Fulham**	A	D	1-1	Bent 70
20	prem	**Newcastle**	H	W	1-0	Taylor 65
21	prem	**Aston Villa**	H	L	1-2	Bramble 28
22	prem	**Liverpool**	A	D	1-1	Bramble 80
23	facr3	**Sunderland**	A	W	3-0	Scharner 19, McShane 56 og, Cotterill 76
24	prem	**Derby**	A	W	1-0	Sibierski 82
25	prem	**Everton**	H	L	1-2	Jagielka 53 og
26	facr4	**Chelsea**	H	L	1-2	Sibierski 87
27	prem	**Middlesbro**	A	L	0-1	
28	prem	**West Ham**	H	W	1-0	Kilbane 45
29	prem	**Sunderland**	A	L	0-2	
30	prem	**Derby**	H	W	2-0	Scharner 60, Valencia 84
31	prem	**Man City**	A	D	0-0	
32	prem	**Arsenal**	H	D	0-0	
33	prem	**Bolton**	H	W	1-0	Heskey 34
34	prem	**Blackburn**	A	L	1-3	King 17 pen
35	prem	**Portsmouth**	A	L	0-2	
36	prem	**Birmingham**	H	W	2-0	Taylor 15, 55
37	prem	**Chelsea**	A	D	1-1	Heskey 90
38	prem	**Tottenham**	H	D	1-1	Heskey 12
39	prem	**Reading**	H	D	0-0	
40	prem	**Aston Villa**	A	W	2-0	Valencia 52, 63
41	prem	**Man Utd**	H	L	0-2	

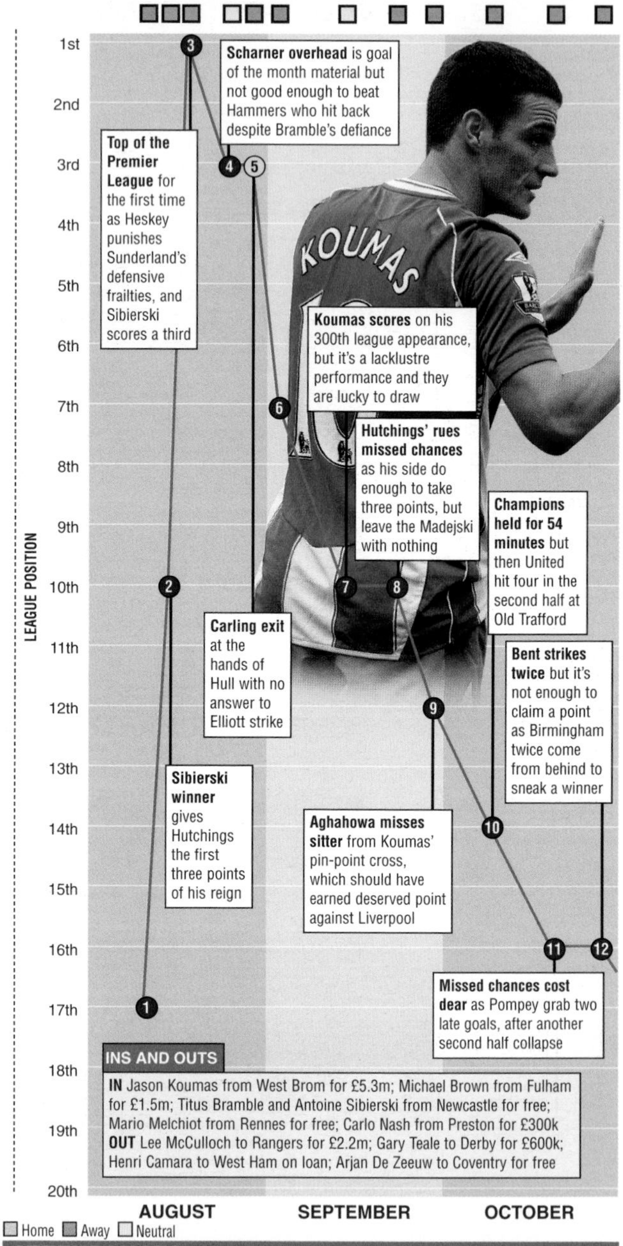

LEAGUE POSITION: 1st, 2nd, 3rd, 4th, 5th, 6th, 7th, 8th, 9th, 10th, 11th, 12th, 13th, 14th, 15th, 16th, 17th, 18th, 19th, 20th

AUGUST · SEPTEMBER · OCTOBER

Home / Away / Neutral

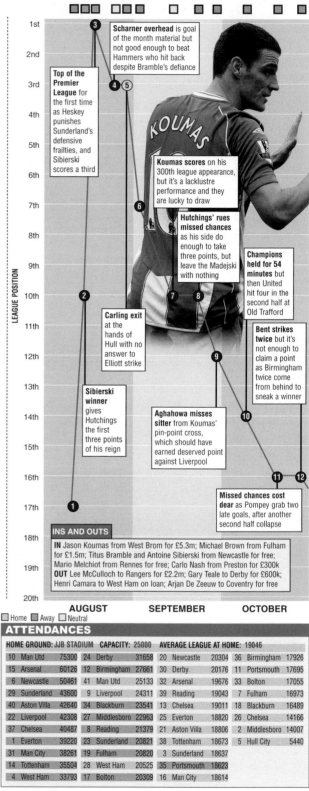

Scharner overhead is goal of the month material but not good enough to beat Hammers who hit back despite Bramble's defiance

Top of the Premier League for the first time as Heskey punishes Sunderland's defensive frailties, and Sibierski scores a third

Koumas scores on his 300th league appearance, but it's a lacklustre performance and they are lucky to draw

Hutchings' rues missed chances as his side do enough to take three points, but leave the Madejski with nothing

Champions held for 54 minutes but then United hit four in the second half at Old Trafford

Carling exit at the hands of Hull with no answer to Elliott strike

Bent strikes twice but it's not enough to claim a point as Birmingham twice come from behind to sneak a winner

Sibierski winner gives Hutchings the first three points of his reign

Aghahowa misses sitter from Koumas' pin-point cross, which should have earned deserved point against Liverpool

Missed chances cost dear as Pompey grab two late goals, after another second half collapse

INS AND OUTS

IN Jason Koumas from West Brom for £5.3m; Michael Brown from Fulham for £1.5m; Titus Bramble and Antoine Sibierski from Newcastle for free; Mario Melchiot from Rennes for free; Carlo Nash from Preston for £300k
OUT Lee McCulloch to Rangers for £2.2m; Gary Teale to Derby for £600k; Henri Camara to West Ham on loan; Arjan De Zeeuw to Coventry for free

ATTENDANCES

HOME GROUND: JJB STADIUM **CAPACITY:** 25000 **AVERAGE LEAGUE AT HOME:** 19046

10	Man Utd	75300	24	Derby	31658	20	Newcastle	20304	36	Birmingham	17926
15	Arsenal	60126	12	Birmingham	27661	30	Derby	20176	11	Portsmouth	17695
6	Newcastle	50461	41	Man Utd	25133	32	Arsenal	19676	33	Bolton	17055
29	Sunderland	43600	9	Liverpool	24311	39	Reading	19043	7	Fulham	16973
40	Aston Villa	42640	34	Blackburn	23541	13	Chelsea	19011	18	Blackburn	16489
22	Liverpool	42308	27	Middlesboro	22963	25	Everton	18820	26	Chelsea	14166
37	Chelsea	40487	8	Reading	21379	21	Aston Villa	18806	2	Middlesboro	14007
1	Everton	39220	23	Sunderland	20821	38	Tottenham	18673	5	Hull City	5440
31	Man City	38261	19	Fulham	20820	3	Sunderland	18637			
14	Tottenham	35504	28	West Ham	20525	35	Portsmouth	18623			
4	West Ham	33793	17	Bolton	20309	16	Man City	18614			

Bruce conjures stunning turnaround!

Final Position: **14th**

KEY: League Champions Lge UEFA Cup FA Cup League Cup Other
INS AND OUTS
IN Marlon King from Watford for £4m; Luis Antonio Valencia from Villarreal undisclosed; Wilson Palacios from Deportivo Olimpia (Honduras) via Birmingham undisclosed; Eric Edman from Rennes for £500k; Maynor Figueroa from D. Olimpia and Erik Hagen from Zenit St Petersburg on loan
OUT Fritz Hall to QPR undisclosed; Denny Landzaat to Feyenoord for £1m
MONTH BY MONTH POINTS TALLY
AUGUST 7 58%
SEPTEMBER 1 8%
OCTOBER 0 0%
NOVEMBER 0 0%
DECEMBER 8 44%
JANUARY 4 33%
FEBRUARY 6 67%
MARCH 5 33%
APRIL 6 50%
MAY 3 50%
Whelan picks United as his preference to win the league ahead of Chelsea on the eve of the title decider
Valuable point at Eastlands and Bruce is delighted with his side's performance away from home
Steve Bruce is appointed manager after he leaves Birmingham with sour feelings
Thankyou and goodbye – club statement recognises Hutchings' contribution but he pays the price for drop into relegation zone
Bent nets a hat-trick in eight-goal thriller as Rovers are finally overcome
Kilbane gets the only goal in the 45th minute and it's enough to escape the bottom three
Great point against league leaders and Wigan are looking safe from the drop
Valencia strikes twice to dent Villa's Uefa Cup hopes and give Bruce a total of 31 points from the turn of the year
Kirkland beaten twice in first 18 minutes as a tame defeat against Chelsea sees Latics drop into the bottom three
One-way traffic as Scharner and Cotterill get the goals that send Sunderland packing in the FA Cup
Up to 14th as Jewell returns to the JJB Stadium but leaves empty handed as Scharner and Valencia score
Taylor is the hero with two goals against Bruce's former club and relegation looks unlikely now
Heskey doubles tally for the season in just a week as he levels against Spurs
Scharner's equaliser ends eight-game losing streak, but Melchiot sees red for a two-footed challenge
Unbeaten in three as Sibierski nets vital 82nd minute winner to sink Derby
Caretaker boss Barlow struggles as his side slumps to a heavy defeat at White Hart Lane
Taylor's set piece is the difference in a confidence-boosting win over Newcastle
Bramble howler lets in Everton but Palacios promises good things ahead
No way past Hahnemann as rivals Reading scrap for a point, keeping out Brown and King
Ref sides with Champs as Bruce points to penalty decisions and Scholes booking as key points in the game
Two late goals from the Gunners means it's eight straight league defeats, but Heskey makes a return after injury
Poor display at Fratton Park as defensive mix-ups end in two easy Pompey goals
Beaten by the Black Cats but Bruce applauds a performance that was worth a win
New Year cheer as Bramble's wonder goal rescues a point at Anfield and Latics leave the drop zone
Heskey's stoppage time leveller all but ends Chelsea's title hopes and the Latics look safe from the drop
13 14 15 16 17 18 19 20 21 22 23 24 25 26 27 28 29 30 31 32 33 34 35 36 37 38 39 40 41
NOVEMBER DECEMBER JANUARY FEBRUARY MARCH APRIL MAY

GOAL ATTEMPTS

FOR – Goal attempts recorded in League games

	HOME	AWAY	TOTAL	AVE
shots on target	108	99	207	5.4
shots off target	107	105	212	5.6
TOTAL	215	204	419	11.0

Ratio of goals to shots – Average number of shots on target per League goal scored	6.1
Accuracy rating – Average percentage of total goal attempts which were on target	49.4

AGAINST – Goal attempts recorded in League games

	HOME	AWAY	TOTAL	AVE
shots on target	115	138	253	6.7
shots off target	82	126	208	5.5
TOTAL	197	264	461	12.1

Ratio of goals to shots – Average number of shots on target per League goal scored	5.0
Accuracy rating – Average percentage of total goal attempts which were on target	54.9

GOALS

Bent

League	7
FA Cup	0
League Cup	0
Europe	0
Other	0
TOTAL	7

League Average 333 mins between goals

	PLAYER	LGE	FAC	LC	Euro	TOT	AVE
1	Bent	7	0	0	0	7	333
2	Sibierski	4	1	0	0	5	255
3	Scharner	4	1	0	0	5	828
4	Heskey	4	0	0	0	4	518
5	Taylor	3	0	0	0	3	370
6	Landzaat	3	0	0	0	3	526
7	Valencia	3	0	0	0	3	904
8	Bramble	2	0	0	0	2	1170
9	King	1	0	0	0	1	667
10	Koumas	1	0	0	0	1	1983
11	Kilbane	1	0	0	0	1	2962
12	Cotterill	0	1	0	0	1	
	Other	0	0	0	0	0	
	TOTAL	33	3	0	0	36	

SQUAD APPEARANCES

Match	1	2	3	4	5	6	7	8	9	10	11	12	13	14	15	16	17	18	19	20	21	22	23	24	25	26	27	28	29	30	31	32	33	34	35	36	37	38	39	40	41
Venue	A	H	H	A	H	A	H	A	H	A	H	A	H	A	A	H	A	H	A	H	H	A	A	A	H	H	A	H	A	H	A	H	H	A	A	H	A	H	H	A	H
Competition	L	L	L	L	W	L	L	L	L	L	L	L	L	L	L	L	L	L	L	L	L	L	F	L	L	F	L	L	L	L	L	L	L	L	L	L	L	L	L	L	L
Result	L	W	W	D	L	L	D	L	L	L	L	L	L	L	L	D	L	W	D	W	L	D	W	W	L	L	L	W	L	W	D	D	W	L	L	W	D	D	D	W	L

Goalkeepers

Chris Kirkland
Carlo Nash
Mike Pollitt

Defenders

Emmerson Boyce
Titus Bramble
Erik Edman
Maynor Figueroa
Andreas Granqvist
Erik Hagen
Fitz Hall
Mario Melchiot
Paul Scharner
Ryan Taylor

Midfielders

Michael Brown
Kevin Kilbane
Jason Koumas
Denny Landzaat
Salomon Olembe
Wilson Palacios
Josip Skoko
Luis Antonio Valencia

Forwards

Julius Aghahowa
Marcus Bent
Henri Camara
David Cotterill
Caleb Folan
Emile Heskey
Marlon King
Antoine Sibierski

KEY: ■ On all match; ■ On bench; ⏮ Subbed or sent off (Counting game); ≪ Subbed or sent off (playing less than 70 mins); ⏭ Subbed on from bench (Counting Game); ≫ Subbed on (playing less than 70 mins); Subbed on and then subbed or sent off (Counting Game); Subbed on and then subbed or sent off (playing less than 70 min; □ Not in 16; □ Injured; ✕ Suspended

KEY PLAYERS - GOALSCORERS

Marcus Bent

Goals in the League	7
Goals in all competitions	7
Assists League goals scored by a team mate where the player delivered the final pass	2
Contribution to Attacking Power Average number of minutes between League team goals while on pitch	105
Player Strike Rate **Average number of minutes between League goals scored by player**	333
Club Strike Rate Average minutes between League goals scored by club	100

	PLAYER	GOALS LGE	GOALS ALL	ASSISTS	POWER	S RATE
1	Marcus Bent	7	7	2	105	**333 mins**
2	Emile Heskey	4	4	2	86	**518 mins**
3	Denny Landzaat	3	3	0	83	**526 mins**
4	Luis Antonio Valencia	3	3	4	87	**904 mins**

KEY PLAYERS - MIDFIELDERS

Wilson Palacios

Goals in the League	0
Goals in all competitions	0
Assists League goals scored by a team mate where the player delivered the final pass	1
Defensive Rating Average number of mins between League goals conceded while on the pitch	115
Contribution to Attacking Power Average number of minutes between League team goals while on pitch	115
Scoring Difference **Defensive Rating minus Contribution to Attacking Power**	0

	PLAYER	GOALS LGE	GOALS ALL	ASSISTS	DEF RATE	POWER	SC DIFF
1	Wilson Palacios	0	0	1	115	115	**0 mins**
2	Luis Antonio Valencia	3	3	4	77	87	**-10 mins**
3	Kevin Kilbane	1	1	1	63	92	**-29 mins**
4	Denny Landzaat	3	3	0	52	83	**-31 mins**

PLAYER APPEARANCES

	AGE (on 01/07/08)	IN NAMED 16	APPEARANCES	COUNTING GAMES	MINUTES ON PITCH	APPEARANCES	MINUTES ON PITCH	THIS SEASON	HOME COUNTRY
Goalkeepers									
Chris Kirkland	27	38	37	37	3330	38	3420	-	England
Carlo Nash	34	0	0	0	0	0	0	-	England
Mike Pollitt	36	38	1	1	90	3	270	-	England
Defenders									
Emmerson Boyce	28	32	25	24	2203	27	2363	-	England
Titus Bramble	26	32	26	26	2340	27	2430	-	England
Erik Edman	29	5	5	4	400	5	400	6	Sweden
Maynor Figueroa	25	2	2	1	91	2	91	-	Honduras
Andreas Granqvist	23	19	14	13	1171	16	1351	1	Sweden
Erik Hagen	32	2	1	1	73	1	73	-	Norway
Fitz Hall	27	10	1	0	40	2	130	-	England
Mario Melchiot	31	31	31	28	2635	33	2815	5	Holland
Paul Scharner	28	37	37	37	3313	39	3493	-	Austria
Ryan Taylor	23	22	17	10	1112	19	1183	-	England
Midfielders									
Michael Brown	31	32	31	27	2472	34	2671	-	England
Kevin Kilbane	31	35	35	32	2962	38	3232	6	Rep of Ireland
Jason Koumas	28	31	30	19	1983	33	2126	4	Wales
Denny Landzaat	32	20	19	17	1580	19	1580	1	Holland
Salomon Olembe	27	14	8	0	202	9	292	-	Cameroon
Wilson Palacios	23	16	16	15	1390	17	1466	-	Honduras
Josip Skoko	32	24	12	5	668	14	848	1	Australia
Luis Antonio Valencia	22	31	31	30	2712	32	2802	1	Ecuador
Forwards									
Julius Aghahowa	26	20	14	1	429	17	501	-	Nigeria
Marcus Bent	30	32	31	24	2331	32	2421	-	England
Henri Camara	31	0	0	0	0	1	73	3	Senegal
David Cotterill	20	6	2	0	98	4	264	3	Wales
Caleb Folan	25	3	2	0	79	3	169	-	England
Emile Heskey	30	28	28	20	2074	30	2229	-	England
Marlon King	28	15	15	4	667	15	667	2	Jamaica
Antoine Sibierski	33	31	30	5	1020	32	1075	-	France

KEY: LEAGUE ALL COMPS CAPS (MAY FIFA RANKING)

TEAM OF THE SEASON

KIRKLAND

CG 37 DR 67

MELCHIOT — CG 28 DR 85
BRAMBLE — CG 26 DR 55

BOYCE — CG 24 DR 71

SCHARNER — CG 37 DR 64

VALENCIA — CG 30 SD -10

PALACIOS — CG 15 SD +0

LANDZAAT — CG 17 SD -31

KILBANE — CG 32 SD -29

HESKEY — CG 20 AP 86

BENT — CG 24 SR 333

KEY: DR = Defensive Rate, SD = Scoring Difference AP = Attacking Power SR = Strike Rate, CG=Counting games – League games playing at least 70 minutes

TOP POINT EARNERS

Emile Heskey

Counting Games League games when player was on pitch for at least 70 minutes	20
Average points Average League points taken in Counting games	1.35
Club Average points Average points taken in League games	1.05

	PLAYER	GAMES	PTS
1	Emile Heskey	20	1.35
2	Wilson Palacios	15	1.33
3	Luis Antonio Valencia	30	1.30
4	Emmerson Boyce	24	1.21
5	Mario Melchiot	28	1.14
6	Denny Landzaat	17	1.12
7	Chris Kirkland	37	1.08
8	Kevin Kilbane	32	1.06
9	Michael Brown	27	1.04
10	Paul Scharner	37	1.00

KEY PLAYERS - DEFENDERS

Mario Melchiot

Goals Conceded in the League Number of League goals conceded while the player was on the pitch	31
Goals Conceded in all competitions Total number of goals conceded while the player was on the pitch	34
League minutes played Number of minutes played in league matches	2635
Clean Sheets In games when the player was on pitch for at least 70 minutes	10
Defensive Rating Average number of mins between League goals conceded while on the pitch	85
Club Defensive Rating Average number of mins between League goals conceded by the club this season	67

	PLAYER	CON LGE	CON ALL	MINS	C SHEETS	DEF RATE
1	Mario Melchiot	31	34	2635	10	85 mins
2	Emmerson Boyce	31	32	2203	9	71 mins
3	Paul Scharner	51	53	3313	11	64 mins
4	Titus Bramble	42	44	2340	5	55 mins

KEY GOALKEEPER

JJB

Chris Kirkland

Goals Conceded in the League Number of League goals conceded while the player was on the pitch	49
Goals Conceded in all competitions Total number of goals conceded while the player was on the pitch	51
League minutes played Number of minutes played in league matches	3330
Clean Sheets In games when the player was on pitch for at least 70 minutes	12
Goals to Shots Ratio The average number of shots on target per each League goal conceded	5.08
Defensive Rating Ave mins between League goals conceded while on the pitch	67

BOOKINGS

Josip Skoko

League Yellow	4
League Red	0
All competitions Yellow	4
All competitions Red	0

League Average **167** mins between cards

	PLAYER	LEAGUE 4Y	LEAGUE 0R	TOTAL 4Y	TOTAL 0R	AVE
1	Josip Skoko	4	0	4	0	167
2	Michael Brown	11	0	11	0	224
3	Wilson Palacios	5	1	6	1	231
4	Ryan Taylor	4	0	4	0	278
5	Emile Heskey	5	0	5	0	414
6	Titus Bramble	5	0	6	0	468
7	Luis A Valencia	5	0	5	0	542
8	Paul Scharner	6	0	7	0	552
9	Marlon King	1	0	1	0	667
10	Kevin Kilbane	3	1	3	1	740
11	Denny Landzaat	2	0	2	0	790
12	Mario Melchiot	2	1	2	1	878
13	Jason Koumas	1	1	1	1	991
14	Antoine Sibierski	1	0	1	0	1020
15	Andreas Granqvist	1	0	1	0	1171
	Other	2	0	2	0	
	TOTAL	58	4	61	4	

SUNDERLAND

Roy Keane's men will have at least another season amongst the English elite after finishing 15th this season. Keane was quick to admit how much it costs to establish yourself in the league, but also highlighted the need to spend another £40m-£50m this season if the Black Cats are to take the next step. Some good football was played, in particular when **Kieran Richardson** was in the side and he and **Kenwyne Jones** are perhaps the two most vital assets Sunderland own. **Andy Reid** was also a worthwhile buy. Key to their survival this year has been the results recorded against the teams below them and some good signings could see them beating some of the better sides, and boost them further up the table in 08/09.

NICKNAME: MACKEMS/BLACKCATS

KEY: Won / Drawn / Lost

#	Comp	Opponent	H/A	Res	Score	Scorers
1	prem	**Tottenham**	H	W	1-0	Chopra 90
2	prem	**Birmingham**	A	D	2-2	Chopra 75, John 90
3	prem	**Wigan**	A	L	0-3	
4	prem	**Liverpool**	H	L	0-2	
5	ccr2	**Luton**	A	L	0-3	
6	prem	**Man Utd**	A	L	0-1	
7	prem	**Reading**	H	W	2-1	Jones 29, Wallace 47
8	prem	**Middlesbro**	A	D	2-2	Leadbitter 2, L.Miller 89
9	prem	**Blackburn**	H	L	1-2	Leadbitter 90
10	prem	**Arsenal**	A	L	2-3	Wallace 25, Jones 48
11	prem	**West Ham**	A	L	1-3	Jones 52
12	prem	**Fulham**	H	D	1-1	Jones 86
13	prem	**Man City**	A	L	0-1	
14	prem	**Newcastle**	H	D	1-1	Higginbotham 52
15	prem	**Everton**	A	L	1-7	Yorke 45
16	prem	**Derby**	H	W	1-0	Stokes 90
17	prem	**Chelsea**	A	L	0-2	
18	prem	**Aston Villa**	H	D	1-1	Higginbotham 10
19	prem	**Reading**	A	L	1-2	Chopra 82 pen
20	prem	**Man Utd**	H	L	0-4	
21	prem	**Bolton**	H	W	3-1	Richardson 13, Jones 32, Murphy 90
22	prem	**Blackburn**	A	L	0-1	
23	facr3	**Wigan**	H	L	0-3	
24	prem	**Portsmouth**	H	W	2-0	Richardson 33, 44
25	prem	**Tottenham**	A	L	0-2	
26	prem	**Birmingham**	H	W	2-0	Murphy 15, Prica 65
27	prem	**Liverpool**	A	L	0-3	
28	prem	**Wigan**	H	W	2-0	Etuhu 42, Murphy 76
29	prem	**Portsmouth**	A	L	0-1	
30	prem	**Derby**	A	D	0-0	
31	prem	**Everton**	H	L	0-1	
32	prem	**Chelsea**	H	L	0-1	
33	prem	**Aston Villa**	A	W	1-0	Chopra 83
34	prem	**West Ham**	H	W	2-1	Jones 29, Reid 90
35	prem	**Fulham**	A	W	3-1	Collins 45, Chopra 54, Jones 76
36	prem	**Man City**	H	L	1-2	Whitehead 81
37	prem	**Newcastle**	A	L	0-2	
38	prem	**Middlesbro**	H	W	3-2	Higginbotham 6, Chopra 45, Murphy 90
39	prem	**Bolton**	A	L	0-2	
40	prem	**Arsenal**	H	L	0-1	

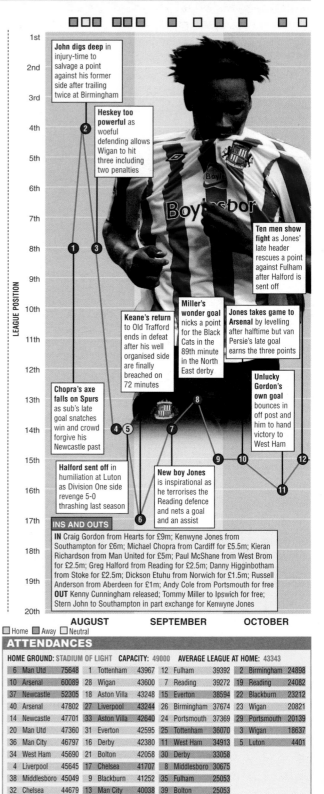

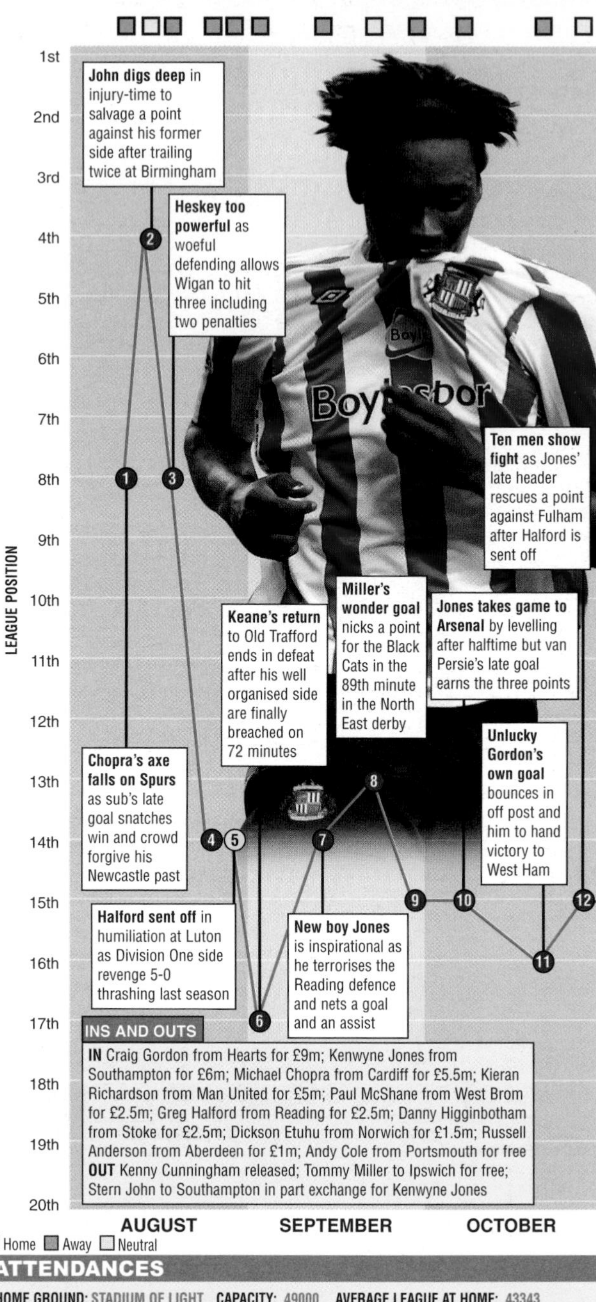
1st
2nd
3rd
4th
5th
6th
7th
8th
9th
10th
11th
12th
13th
14th
15th
16th
17th
18th
19th
20th
LEAGUE POSITION
John digs deep in injury-time to salvage a point against his former side after trailing twice at Birmingham
Heskey too powerful as woeful defending allows Wigan to hit three including two penalties
Ten men show fight as Jones' late header rescues a point against Fulham after Halford is sent off
Keane's return to Old Trafford ends in defeat after his well organised side are finally breached on 72 minutes
Miller's wonder goal nicks a point for the Black Cats in the 89th minute in the North East derby
Jones takes game to Arsenal by levelling after halftime but van Persie's late goal earns the three points
Unlucky Gordon's own goal bounces in off post and him to hand victory to West Ham
Chopra's axe falls on Spurs as sub's late goal snatches win and crowd forgive his Newcastle past
Halford sent off in humiliation at Luton as Division One side revenge 5-0 thrashing last season
New boy Jones is inspirational as he terrorises the Reading defence and nets a goal and an assist
AUGUST
SEPTEMBER
OCTOBER
Home Away Neutral

INS AND OUTS

IN Craig Gordon from Hearts for £9m; Kenwyne Jones from Southampton for £6m; Michael Chopra from Cardiff for £5.5m; Kieran Richardson from Man United for £5m; Paul McShane from West Brom for £2.5m; Greg Halford from Reading for £2.5m; Danny Higginbotham from Stoke for £2.5m; Dickson Etuhu from Norwich for £1.5m; Russell Anderson from Aberdeen for £1m; Andy Cole from Portsmouth for free
OUT Kenny Cunningham released; Tommy Miller to Ipswich for free; Stern John to Southampton in part exchange for Kenwyne Jones

ATTENDANCES

HOME GROUND: STADIUM OF LIGHT **CAPACITY:** 49000 **AVERAGE LEAGUE AT HOME:** 43343

#	Opponent	Att	#	Opponent	Att	#	Opponent	Att	#	Opponent	Att
6	Man Utd	75648	1	Tottenham	43967	12	Fulham	39392	2	Birmingham	24898
10	Arsenal	60089	28	Wigan	43600	7	Reading	39272	19	Reading	24082
37	Newcastle	52305	18	Aston Villa	43248	15	Everton	38594	22	Blackburn	23212
40	Arsenal	47802	27	Liverpool	43244	26	Birmingham	37674	23	Wigan	20821
14	Newcastle	47701	33	Aston Villa	42640	24	Portsmouth	37369	29	Portsmouth	20139
20	Man Utd	47360	31	Everton	42595	25	Tottenham	36070	3	Wigan	18637
36	Man City	46797	16	Derby	42380	11	West Ham	34913	5	Luton	4401
34	West Ham	45690	21	Bolton	42058	30	Derby	33058			
4	Liverpool	45645	17	Chelsea	41707	8	Middlesbro	30675			
38	Middlesbro	45049	9	Blackburn	41252	35	Fulham	25053			
32	Chelsea	44679	13	Man City	40038	39	Bolton	25053			

Keane says £40m is price of survival

Final Position: **15th**

KEY: ● League ● Champions Lge ● UEFA Cup ● FA Cup ○ League Cup ● Other

INS AND OUTS
IN Andy Reid from Charlton for £4m; Rade Prica from Aalborg (Denmark) for £2m; Phil Bardsley from Man United for £2m; Jonny Evans from Man United on loan
OUT Andy Cole and Stanislav Varga to Burnley and Greg Halford to Charlton on loan
MONTH BY MONTH POINTS TALLY
AUGUST 4 33%
SEPTEMBER 4 33%
OCTOBER 1 11%
NOVEMBER 1 11%
DECEMBER 7 39%
JANUARY 6 50%
FEBRUARY 3 33%
MARCH 7 47%
APRIL 6 50%
MAY 0 0%
Stokes misfires so good performance at home of 100% City goes unrewarded
Chopra header slams against the woodwork as Newcastle rustle up an equaliser and escape with a point from Tyne-and-Wear derby
In the bottom three and desperate for confidence after a 7-1 battering at Goodison Park
Stokes first Premier goal is a stoppage-time winner at the Stadium of Light against Derby
Higginbotham nets after ten minutes with Villa replying late on, then Collins' strike is ruled out for a foul
Richardson's return livens things up with first goal in victory over Bolton
Richardson; a Wearside hero after netting twice against Pompey and securing a much needed win
"The players should be ashamed" says Keane after a hammering in the FA Cup by Wigan
Debut-boy Prica nets and has another disallowed in victory over Birmingham and rise up to mid-table
Ninth straight away defeat comes at Anfield as Crouch proves too tall to handle
Gordon is brilliant as he keeps the Latics out and Reid sets up Murphy for a goal of the month strike
'Bardsley naïve' says Keane as he brings down Pompey man for decisive penalty
Chopra's 'goal' is onside but officials say different and Keane feels robbed by the referee as they have to settle for a points against the Rams
Without a goal in last four games and times are worrying at the Stadium of Light
Reid's last minute winner ensures back-to-back wins as the Mackems move closer to safety
Unlucky to be the losing team against Manchester City as they snatch a late winner
Too easy for Newcastle in 139th Tyne-Wear derby as Owen strikes twice
Murphy forces it home from 90th minute corner to help rise to 13th in the table
Bolton still scrapping and it shows as Sunderland are second best
Walcott's pace and Arsenal's quality is the difference in final game defeat
NOVEMBER
DECEMBER
JANUARY
FEBRUARY
MARCH
APRIL
MAY

GOAL ATTEMPTS

FOR — Goal attempts recorded in League games

	HOME	AWAY	TOTAL	AVE
shots on target	117	95	212	5.6
shots off target	114	92	206	5.4
TOTAL	231	187	418	11.0

Ratio of goals to shots Average number of shots on target per League goal scored	5.9
Accuracy rating Average percentage of total goal attempts which were on target	50.7

AGAINST — Goal attempts recorded in League games

	HOME	AWAY	TOTAL	AVE
shots on target	105	123	228	6.0
shots off target	91	117	208	5.5
TOTAL	196	240	436	11.5

Ratio of goals to shots Average number of shots on target per League goal scored	3.9
Accuracy rating Average percentage of total goal attempts which were on target	52.3

GOALS

Jones

League	7
FA Cup	0
League Cup	0
Europe	0
Other	0
TOTAL	7

League Average **402** mins between goals

	PLAYER	LGE	FAC	LC	Euro	TOT	AVE
1	Jones	7	0	0	0	7	402
2	Chopra	6	0	0	0	6	335
3	Murphy	4	0	0	0	4	450
4	Richardson	3	0	0	0	3	368
5	Higginbotham	3	0	0	0	3	630
6	Wallace	2	0	0	0	2	746
7	Leadbitter	2	0	0	0	2	947
8	John	1	0	0	0	1	32
9	Prica	1	0	0	0	1	210
10	Stokes	1	0	0	0	1	743
11	Reid	1	0	0	0	1	985
12	Yorke	1	0	0	0	1	1251
13	Etuhu	1	0	0	0	1	1506
14	Miller, L	1	0	0	0	1	1602
15	Whitehead	1	0	0	0	1	2398
	Other	1	0	0	0	1	
	TOTAL	36	0	0	0	36	

SQUAD APPEARANCES

Match	1	2	3	4	5	6	7	8	9	10	11	12	13	14	15	16	17	18	19	20
Venue	H	A	A	H	A	A	H	A	H	A	A	H	A	H	A	H	A	H	A	H
Competition	L	L	L	L	W	L	L	L	L	L	L	L	L	L	L	L	L	L	L	L
Result	W	D	L	L	L	L	W	D	L	L	L	D	L	D	L	W	L	D	L	L

Match	21	22	23	24	25	26	27	28	29	30	31	32	33	34	35	36	37	38	39	40
Venue	H	A	H	H	A	H	A	H	A	A	H	H	A	H	A	H	A	H	A	H
Competition	L	L	F	L	L	L	L	L	L	L	L	L	L	L	L	L	L	L	L	L
Result	W	L	L	W	L	W	L	W	L	D	L	L	W	W	W	L	L	W	L	L

Goalkeepers
- Trevor Carson
- Marton Fulop
- Craig Gordon
- Darren Ward

Defenders
- Russell Anderson
- Phillip Bardsley
- Daniel Lewis Collins
- Jonny Evans
- Greg Halford
- Ian Harte
- Danny Higginbotham
- Paul McShane
- Nayron Nosworthy

Midfielders
- Gavin Donoghue
- Carlos Edwards
- Dickson Etuhu
- Graham Kavanagh
- Michael Kay
- Grant Leadbitter
- Liam Miller
- Andrew Reid
- Kieran Richardson
- Ross Wallace
- Dean Whitehead

Forwards
- Michael Chopra
- Andy Cole
- David Connolly
- Stern John
- Kenwyne Jones
- Daryl Murphy
- Roy O'Donovan
- Rade Prica
- Anthony Stokes
- Martyn Waghorn
- Dwight Yorke

KEY: On all match · On bench · Subbed or sent off (Counting game) · Subbed or sent off (playing less than 70 mins) · Subbed on from bench (Counting Game) · Subbed on (playing less than 70 mins) · Subbed on and then subbed or sent off (Counting Game) · Subbed on and then subbed or sent off (playing less than 70 min) · Not in 16 · Injured · Suspended

KEY PLAYERS - GOALSCORERS

Michael Chopra

Goals in the League	6
Goals in all competitions	6
Assists League goals scored by a team mate where the player delivered the final pass	1
Contribution to Attacking Power Average number of mins between League team goals while on pitch	87
Player Strike Rate Average number of minutes between League goals scored by player	335
Club Strike Rate Average minutes between League goals scored by club	95

	PLAYER	GOALS LGE	GOALS ALL	ASSISTS	POWER	S RATE
1	Michael Chopra	6	6	1	87	335 mins
2	Kieran Richardson	3	3	2	100	368 mins
3	Kenwyne Jones	7	7	8	88	402 mins
4	Daryl Murphy	4	4	3	106	450 mins

KEY PLAYERS - MIDFIELDERS

Kieran Richardson

Goals in the League	3
Goals in all competitions	3
Assists League goals scored by a team mate where the player delivered the final pass	2
Defensive Rating Average number of mins between League goals conceded while on the pitch	92
Contribution to Attacking Power Average number of minutes between League team goals while on pitch	100
Scoring Difference Defensive Rating minus Contribution to Attacking Power	-8

	PLAYER	GOALS LGE	GOALS ALL	ASSISTS	DEF RATE	POWER	SC DIFF
1	Kieran Richardson	3	3	2	92	100	-8 mins
2	Liam Miller	1	1	2	51	80	-29 mins
3	Dean Whitehead	1	1	2	63	99	-36 mins
4	Dickson Etuhu	1	1	1	50	94	-44 mins

PLAYER APPEARANCES

	AGE (on 01/07/08)	IN NAMED 16	APPEARANCES	COUNTING GAMES	MINUTES ON PITCH	APPEARANCES	MINUTES ON PITCH	THIS SEASON	HOME COUNTRY
Goalkeepers									
Trevor Carson	20	0	0	0	0	0	0	-	N Ireland
Marton Fulop	25	16	1	1	90	1	90	-	Hungary
Craig Gordon	25	38	34	34	3060	35	3150	6	Scotland
Darren Ward	34	21	3	3	270	4	360	-	Wales
Defenders									
Russell Anderson	29	3	1	0	29	2	119	-	Scotland
Phillip Bardsley	23	11	11	11	990	11	990	-	England
Daniel Lewis Collins	27	36	36	32	3045	37	3135	-	Wales
Jonny Evans	20	15	15	15	1336	16	1426	5	N Ireland
Greg Halford	23	9	8	7	676	9	736	-	England
Ian Harte	30	14	8	3	311	8	311	-	Rep of Ireland
Danny Higginbotham	29	23	21	21	1890	21	1890	-	England
Paul McShane	22	29	21	19	1764	22	1854	4	Rep of Ireland
Nayron Nosworthy	27	29	29	27	2514	31	2694	-	England
Midfielders									
Gavin Donoghue	19	0	0	0	0	0	0	-	Rep of Ireland
Carlos Edwards	29	13	13	6	845	13	845	2	Trinidad & Tobago
Dickson Etuhu	26	20	20	14	1506	21	1567	-	Nigeria
Graham Kavanagh	34	2	0	0	0	1	90	-	Rep of Ireland
Michael Kay	18	1	0	0	0	0	0	-	England
Grant Leadbitter	22	32	31	17	1894	33	2017	-	England
Liam Miller	27	25	24	15	1602	25	1692	3	Rep of Ireland
Andrew Reid	25	13	13	10	985	13	985	3	Rep of Ireland
Kieran Richardson	23	17	17	11	1106	18	1179	-	England
Ross Wallace	23	21	21	14	1493	22	1583	-	Scotland
Dean Whitehead	26	27	27	26	2398	28	2455	-	England
Forwards									
Michael Chopra	24	33	33	16	2012	34	2102	-	England
Andy Cole	36	10	7	0	237	8	270	-	England
David Connolly	31	9	3	0	96	5	142	-	Rep of Ireland
Stern John	31	2	1	0	32	1	32	3	Trinidad & Tobago
Kenwyne Jones	23	33	33	30	2819	33	2819	2	Trinidad & Tobago
Daryl Murphy	25	28	28	16	1803	30	1954	2	Rep of Ireland
Roy O'Donovan	22	21	17	1	457	19	576	-	Rep of Ireland
Rade Prica	28	9	6	0	210	6	210	4	Sweden
Anthony Stokes	19	20	20	4	743	21	820	3	Rep of Ireland
Martyn Waghorn	18	5	3	1	107	4	164	-	England
Dwight Yorke	36	23	20	9	1251	21	1264	1	Trinidad & Tobago

KEY: LEAGUE ALL COMPS CAPS (MAY FIFA RANKING)

TEAM OF THE SEASON

GORDON

CG 34 DR 55

BARDSLEY

CG 11* DR 99

EVANS

CG 15 DR 89

NOSWORTHY

CG 27 DR 67

COLLINS

CG 32 DR 58

MILLER

CG 15 SD -29

WHITEHEAD

CG 26 SD -36

ETUHU

CG 14 SD -44

RICHARDSON

CG 11* SD -8

JONES

CG 30 AP 88

CHOPRA
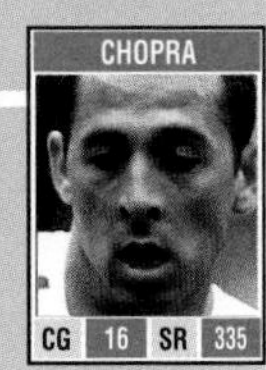
CG 16 SR 335

KEY: DR = Defensive Rate, SD = Scoring Difference AP = Attacking Power SR = Strike Rate, CG=Counting games – League games playing at least 70 minutes

TOP POINT EARNERS

Daryl Murphy

Counting Games League games when player was on pitch for at least 70 minutes	16
Average points Average League points taken in Counting games	1.44
Club Average points Average points taken in League games	1.03

	PLAYER	GAMES	PTS
1	Daryl Murphy	16	1.44
2	Jonny Evans	15	1.27
3	Dean Whitehead	26	1.23
4	Nayron Nosworthy	27	1.11
5	Kenwyne Jones	30	1.07
6	Daniel Lewis Collins	32	1.06
7	Craig Gordon	34	1.03
8	Dickson Etuhu	14	1.00
9	Michael Chopra	16	1.00
10	Liam Miller	15	0.87

KEY PLAYERS - DEFENDERS

Phillip Bardsley

Goals Conceded in the League Number of League goals conceded while the player was on the pitch	10
Goals Conceded in all competitions Total number of goals conceded while the player was on the pitch	10
League minutes played Number of minutes played in league matches	990
Clean Sheets In games when the player was on pitch for at least 70 minutes	4
Defensive Rating Average number of mins between League goals conceded while on the pitch	99
Club Defensive Rating Average number of mins between League goals conceded by the club this season	57

	PLAYER	CON LGE	CON ALL	MINS	C SHEETS	DEF RATE
1	Phillip Bardsley	10	10	990	4	99 mins
2	Jonny Evans	15	18	1336	5	89 mins
3	Nayron Nosworthy	37	43	2514	6	67 mins
4	Daniel Lewis Collins	52	55	3045	5	58 mins

KEY GOALKEEPER

Boylesports

Craig Gordon

Goals Conceded in the League Number of League goals conceded while the player was on the pitch	55
Goals Conceded in all competitions Total number of goals conceded while the player was on the pitch	58
League minutes played Number of minutes played in league matches	3060
Clean Sheets In games when the player was on pitch for at least 70 minutes	6
Goals to Shots Ratio The average number of shots on target per each League goal conceded	3.67
Defensive Rating Ave mins between League goals conceded while on the pitch	55

BOOKINGS

Dwight Yorke

League Yellow	5
League Red	1
All competitions Yellow	5
All competitions Red	1

League Average 208 mins between cards

	PLAYER	LEAGUE 5Y	LEAGUE 1R	TOTAL 5Y	TOTAL 1R	AVE
1	Dwight Yorke	5	1	5	1	208
2	Greg Halford	2	1	3	2	225
3	Roy O'Donovan	2	0	2	0	228
4	Michael Chopra	7	0	7	0	287
5	Dean Whitehead	8	0	8	0	299
6	Phillip Bardsley	3	0	3	0	330
7	Kieran Richardson	3	0	3	0	368
8	Dickson Etuhu	4	0	5	0	376
9	Grant Leadbitter	5	0	5	0	378
10	Liam Miller	3	1	3	1	400
11	Paul McShane	3	1	3	1	441
12	Andrew Reid	2	0	2	0	492
13	Ross Wallace	3	0	4	0	497
14	Daniel Collins	6	0	6	0	507
15	Anthony Stokes	1	0	1	0	743
	Other	9	0	9	0	
	TOTAL	66	4	69	5	

BOLTON WANDERERS

Bolton went through two managers but remained in the top flight, despite the expectations of many. The post 'Big Sam' Allardyce era started badly and the affectionately named 'Little Sam' was shown the door after picking up only one win in 11 matches. Gary Megson was the chairman's choice to replace him and the appointment didn't please the fans. However, the players did take to him and the results picked up... until he had to sell **Nicolas Anelka**. A lack of goals drew Bolton back into the relegation scrap, while ironically continuing a decent Uefa Cup run. It took a magnificent finish, however, to pull them clear with the Trotters unbeaten for the final five games of the season to pull off a Houdini act. For next season, Megson will need to add to his squad to cement Premier status - particularly with exits expected from **Ivan Campo**, **El Hadji Diouf** and **Stelios Giannakopoulos**.

NICKNAME: THE TROTTERS

KEY: Won Drawn Lost

No	Comp	Opponent	H/A	Res	Score	Scorers
1	prem	**Newcastle**	H	L	1-3	Anelka 50
2	prem	**Fulham**	A	L	1-2	Helguson 13
3	prem	**Portsmouth**	A	L	1-3	Anelka 13
4	prem	**Reading**	H	W	3-0	Speed 32, Anelka 54, Braaten 90
5	prem	**Everton**	H	L	1-2	Anelka 55
6	prem	**Birmingham**	A	L	0-1	
7	uc1rl1	**Rabotnicki**	A	D	1-1	Meite 85
8	prem	**Tottenham**	H	D	1-1	Campo 39
9	ccr3	**Fulham**	A	W	2-1	Guthrie 57, Giannakopoulos 112
10	prem	**Derby**	A	D	1-1	Anelka 32
11	uc1rl2	**Rabotnicki**	H	W	1-0	Anelka 68
12	prem	**Chelsea**	H	L	0-1	
13	prem	**Arsenal**	A	L	0-2	
14	ucgpf	**Braga**	H	D	1-1	Diouf 66
15	prem	**Aston Villa**	H	D	1-1	Anelka 22
16	ccr4	**Man City**	H	L	0-1	
17	prem	**West Ham**	A	D	1-1	Nolan 90
18	ucgpf	**Bayern Munich**	A	D	2-2	Gardner 8, Davies 82
19	prem	**Middlesbro**	H	D	0-0	
20	prem	**Man Utd**	H	W	1-0	Anelka 11
21	ucgpf	**Aris**	H	D	1-1	Giannakopoulos 90
22	prem	**Liverpool**	A	L	0-4	
23	ucgpf	**Crvena Zvezda**	A	W	1-0	McCann 45
24	prem	**Wigan**	H	W	4-1	Scharner 3 og, Nolan 37, Davies 70, Anelka 89
25	prem	**Man City**	A	L	2-4	Diouf 31, Nolan 40
26	prem	**Birmingham**	H	W	3-0	Diouf 72, Anelka 78, 90
27	prem	**Everton**	A	L	0-2	
28	prem	**Sunderland**	A	L	1-3	Diouf 41
29	prem	**Derby**	H	W	1-0	Giannakopoulos 90
30	facr3	**Sheff Utd**	H	L	0-1	
31	prem	**Blackburn**	H	L	1-2	Nolan 43
32	prem	**Newcastle**	A	D	0-0	
33	prem	**Fulham**	H	D	0-0	
34	prem	**Reading**	A	W	2-0	Nolan 33, Helguson 58
35	prem	**Portsmouth**	H	L	0-1	
36	uc3rl1	**Atl Madrid**	H	W	1-0	Diouf 74
37	uc3rl2	**Atl Madrid**	A	D	0-0	
38	prem	**Blackburn**	A	L	1-4	Davies 50
39	prem	**Liverpool**	H	L	1-3	Cohen 79
40	uc4rl1	**Sp Lisbon**	H	D	1-1	McCann 25
41	uc4rl2	**Sp Lisbon**	A	L	0-1	
42	prem	**Wigan**	A	L	0-1	
43	prem	**Man Utd**	A	L	0-2	
44	prem	**Man City**	H	D	0-0	
45	prem	**Arsenal**	H	L	2-3	Taylor 14, 43
46	prem	**Aston Villa**	A	L	0-4	
47	prem	**West Ham**	H	W	1-0	Davies 46
48	prem	**Middlesbro**	A	W	1-0	McCann 60
49	prem	**Tottenham**	A	D	1-1	Giannakopoulos 46
50	prem	**Sunderland**	H	W	2-0	Diouf 42, Murphy 82 og
51	prem	**Chelsea**	A	D	1-1	Taylor 90

INS AND OUTS

IN Gavin McCann from Aston Villa for £1m; JLloyd Samuel from Villa for free; Andy O'Brien from Portsmouth undisclosed; Daniel Braaten from Rosenborg for £425k; Danny Guthrie from Liverpool, Mikael Alonso from Real Sociedad and Christian Wilhelmsson from Nantes on loan; Gerald Cid from Bordeaux and Blerim Dzernaili from FC Zurich for free

OUT Tal Ben Haim to Chelsea for free; Henrik Pedersen, Quinton Fortune, David Thompson all released

LEAGUE POSITION: 1st 2nd 3rd 4th 5th 6th 7th 8th 9th 10th 11th 12th 13th 14th 15th 16th 17th 18th 19th 20th

AUGUST SEPTEMBER OCTOBER

Big Sam returns with revved up Newcastle hitting three first half goals before Anelka replies

Only club without a point after three games as Anelka's early goal is trumped by three from Portsmouth

Diouf flies to Lee's rescue with assists for Speed and Anelka in manager's crucial first win and new boy Braaten adds third

Ten years at the Reebok but party is ruined by Everton's Lescott as his last minute winner signals defeat

Anelka earns a valuable point at Pride Park but it's far from their best and they still remain in relegation zone

Giannakopoulos nets in the 112th minute to beat Fulham and secure a place in the Carling Cup last 16

Campo returns in spectacular fashion as his goal earns a draw in an evenly matched game with Spurs

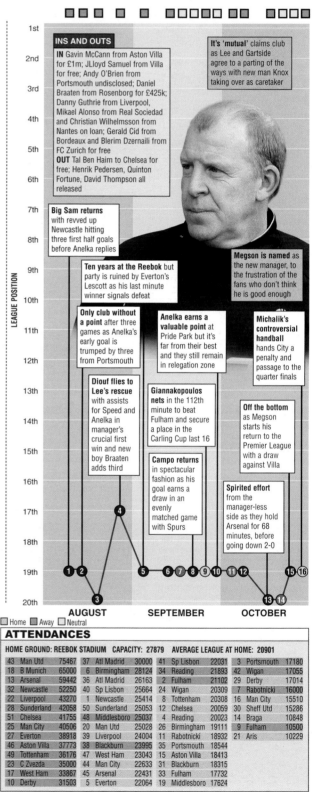

It's 'mutual' claims club as Lee and Gartside agree to a parting of the ways with new man Knox taking over as caretaker

Megson is named as the new manager, to the frustration of the fans who don't think he is good enough

Michalik's controversial handball hands City a penalty and passage to the quarter finals

Off the bottom as Megson starts his return to the Premier League with a draw against Villa

Spirited effort from the manager-less side as they hold Arsenal for 68 minutes, before going down 2-0

Home Away Neutral

ATTENDANCES

HOME GROUND: REEBOK STADIUM CAPACITY: 27879 AVERAGE LEAGUE AT HOME: 20901

43	Man Utd	75467	37	Atl Madrid	30000	41	Sp Lisbon	22031	3	Portsmouth	17180
18	B Munich	65000	6	Birmingham	28124	34	Reading	21893	42	Wigan	17055
13	Arsenal	59442	36	Atl Madrid	26163	2	Fulham	21102	29	Derby	17014
32	Newcastle	52250	40	Sp Lisbon	25664	24	Wigan	20309	7	Rabotnicki	16000
22	Liverpool	43270	1	Newcastle	25414	8	Tottenham	20308	16	Man City	15510
28	Sunderland	42058	50	Sunderland	25053	12	Chelsea	20059	30	Sheff Utd	15286
51	Chelsea	41755	48	Middlesbro	25037	4	Reading	20023	14	Braga	10848
25	Man City	40506	20	Man Utd	25028	26	Birmingham	19111	9	Fulham	10500
27	Everton	38918	39	Liverpool	24004	11	Rabotnicki	18932	21	Aris	10229
46	Aston Villa	37773	38	Blackburn	23995	35	Portsmouth	18544			
49	Tottenham	36176	47	West Ham	23043	15	Aston Villa	18413			
23	C Zvezda	35000	44	Man City	22633	31	Blackburn	18315			
17	West Ham	33867	45	Arsenal	22431	33	Fulham	17732			
10	Derby	31503	5	Everton	22064	19	Middlesboro	17624			

Megson delivers a late escape

Final Position: **16th**

KEY: ● League ● Champions Lge ● UEFA Cup ● FA Cup ○ League Cup ● Other

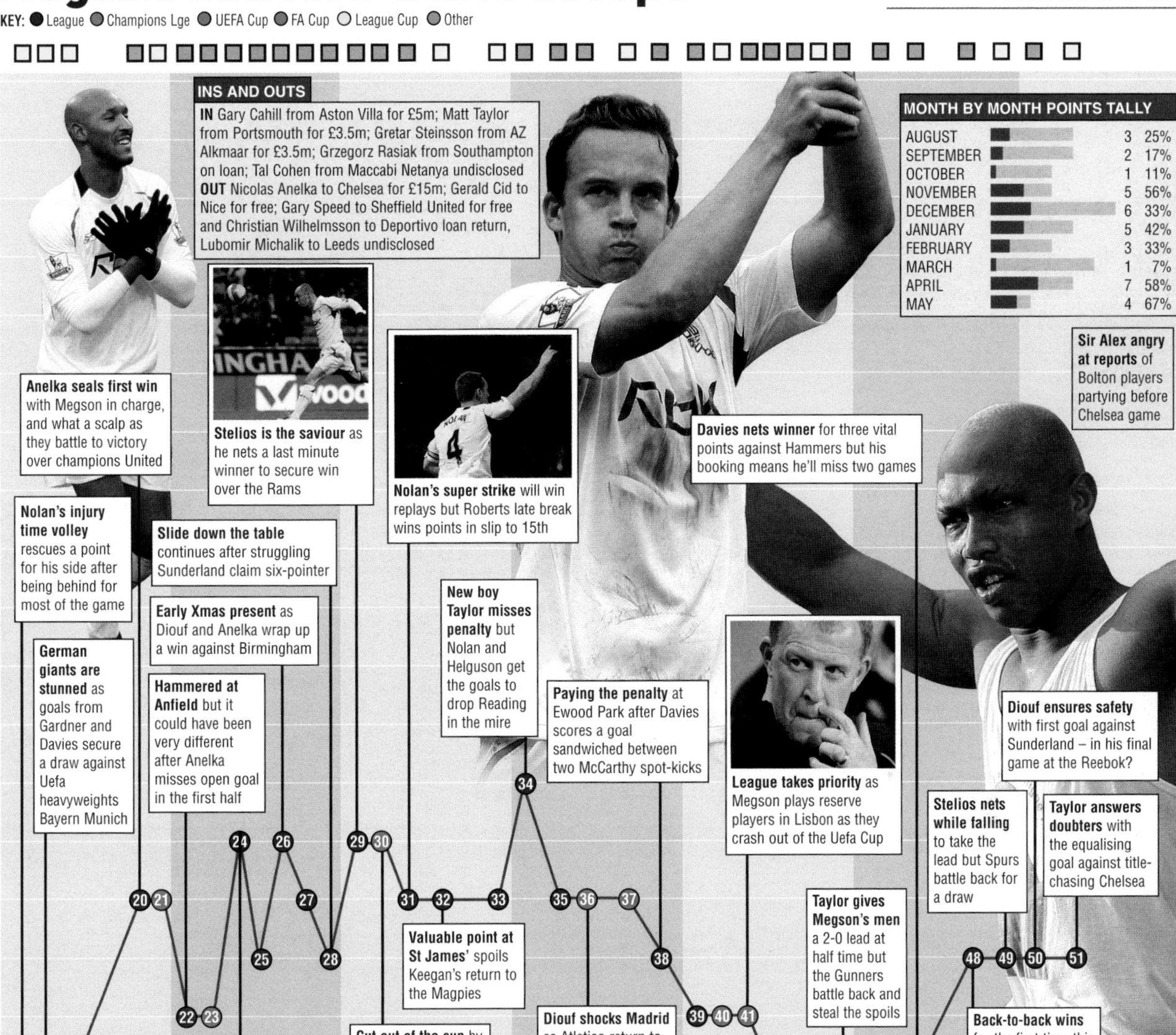
Anelka seals first win with Megson in charge, and what a scalp as they battle to victory over champions United
Nolan's injury time volley rescues a point for his side after being behind for most of the game
German giants are stunned as goals from Gardner and Davies secure a draw against Uefa heavyweights Bayern Munich
Slide down the table continues after struggling Sunderland claim six-pointer
Early Xmas present as Diouf and Anelka wrap up a win against Birmingham
Hammered at Anfield but it could have been very different after Anelka misses open goal in the first half
Stelios is the saviour as he nets a last minute winner to secure win over the Rams
Rise to 14th after a spectacular 4-1 win over Wigan, with Nolan, Davies and Anelka finding the net
Nolan's super strike will win replays but Roberts late break wins points in slip to 15th
Cut out of the cup by Blades in a dismal display by fringe players at the Reebok
New boy Taylor misses penalty but Nolan and Helguson get the goals to drop Reading in the mire
Valuable point at St James' spoils Keegan's return to the Magpies
Paying the penalty at Ewood Park after Davies scores a goal sandwiched between two McCarthy spot-kicks
Diouf shocks Madrid as Atletico return to Spain with a defeat and no away goal
Davies nets winner for three vital points against Hammers but his booking means he'll miss two games
League takes priority as Megson plays reserve players in Lisbon as they crash out of the Uefa Cup
Defeat to 10-men of Wigan as the Trotters cannot capitalise on their numerical advantage at the JJB
Taylor gives Megson's men a 2-0 lead at half time but the Gunners battle back and steal the spoils
Drubbing at Villa Park hits confidence and Megson needs a result
Sir Alex angry at reports of Bolton players partying before Chelsea game
Stelios nets while falling to take the lead but Spurs battle back for a draw
Diouf ensures safety with first goal against Sunderland – in his final game at the Reebok?
Taylor answers doubters with the equalising goal against title-chasing Chelsea
Back-to-back wins for the first time this season as McCann nets after Al Habsi repels Boro
17 18 19 20 21 22 23 24 25 26 27 28 29 30 31 32 33 34 35 36 37 38 39 40 41 42 43 44 45 46 47 48 49 50 51
NOVEMBER
DECEMBER
JANUARY
FEBRUARY
MARCH
APRIL
MAY

INS AND OUTS

IN Gary Cahill from Aston Villa for £5m; Matt Taylor from Portsmouth for £3.5m; Gretar Steinsson from AZ Alkmaar for £3.5m; Grzegorz Rasiak from Southampton on loan; Tal Cohen from Maccabi Netanya undisclosed
OUT Nicolas Anelka to Chelsea for £15m; Gerald Cid to Nice for free; Gary Speed to Sheffield United for free and Christian Wilhelmsson to Deportivo loan return, Lubomir Michalik to Leeds undisclosed

MONTH BY MONTH POINTS TALLY

Month	Points	%
AUGUST	3	25%
SEPTEMBER	2	17%
OCTOBER	1	11%
NOVEMBER	5	56%
DECEMBER	6	33%
JANUARY	5	42%
FEBRUARY	3	33%
MARCH	1	7%
APRIL	7	58%
MAY	4	67%

GOAL ATTEMPTS

FOR – Goal attempts recorded in League games

	HOME	AWAY	TOTAL	AVE
shots on target	115	107	222	5.8
shots off target	104	69	173	4.6
TOTAL	**219**	**176**	**395**	**10.4**

Ratio of goals to shots – Average number of shots on target per League goal scored: **6.2**

Accuracy rating – Average percentage of total goal attempts which were on target: **56.2**

AGAINST – Goal attempts recorded in League games

	HOME	AWAY	TOTAL	AVE
shots on target	107	137	244	6.4
shots off target	76	119	195	5.1
TOTAL	**183**	**256**	**439**	**11.6**

Ratio of goals to shots – Average number of shots on target per League goal scored: **4.5**

Accuracy rating – Average percentage of total goal attempts which were on target: **55.6**

GOALS

Anelka

League	10
FA Cup	0
League Cup	0
Europe	1
Other	0
TOTAL	11

League Average **160** mins between goals

	PLAYER	LGE	FAC	LC	Euro	TOT	AVE
1	Anelka	10	0	0	1	**11**	160
2	Diouf	4	0	0	2	**6**	660
3	Nolan	5	0	0	0	**5**	553
4	Giannakopoulos	2	0	1	1	**4**	149
5	Davies	3	0	0	1	**4**	880
6	Taylor	3	0	0	0	**3**	460
7	McCann	1	0	0	2	**3**	2017
8	Helguson	2	0	0	0	**2**	136
9	Braaten	1	0	0	0	**1**	149
10	Cohen	1	0	0	0	**1**	296
11	Speed	1	0	0	0	**1**	970
12	Campo	1	0	0	0	**1**	2061
13	Guthrie	0	0	1	0	**1**	
14	Meite	0	0	0	1	**1**	
15	Gardner	0	0	0	1	**1**	
	Other	0	0	0	0	0	
	TOTAL	**34**	**0**	**2**	**9**	**45**	

SQUAD APPEARANCES

Match	1 2 3 4 5	6 7 8 9 10	11 12 13 14 15	16 17 18 19 20	21 22 23 24 25	26 27 28 29 30	31 32 33 34 35	36 37 38 39 40	41 42 43 44 45	46 47 48 49 50	51
Venue	H A A H H	A A H A A	H H A H H	H A A H H	H A A H A	H A A H H	H A H A H	H A A H H	A A A H H	A H A A H	A
Competition	L L L L L	L E L W L	E L L E L	W L E L L	E L E L L	L L L L F	L L L L L	E E L L E	E L L L L	L L L L L	L
Result	L L L W L	L D D W D	W L L D D	L D D D W	D L W W L	W L L W L	L D D W L	W D L L D	L L L D L	L W W D W	D

Goalkeepers
- Ali Al Habsi
- Jussi Jaaskelainen
- Ian Walker

Defenders
- Gary Cahill
- Gerald Cid
- Jaroslav Fojut
- Ricardo Gardner
- Nicky Hunt
- Abdoulaye Meite
- Lubomir Michalik
- Andy O'Brien
- Joey O'Brien
- Jlloyd Samuel
- Gretar Rafn Steinsson

Midfielders
- Mikel Alonso
- Ivan Campo
- Matthew Cassidy
- Tamir Cohen
- Blerim Dzemaili
- Abdoulaye Faye
- Stelios Giannakopoulos
- Danny Guthrie
- Scott Jamieson
- Gavin McCann
- Kevin Nolan
- Robert Sissons
- Gary Speed
- Matthew Taylor
- Andranik Teymourian
- Christian Wilhelmsson
- Kevin Wolze

Forwards
- Nicolas Anelka
- Daniel Braaten
- Kevin Davies
- El Hadji Diouf
- Zoltan Harsanyi
- Heidar Helguson
- Grzegorz Rasiak
- James Sinclair
- Ricardo Vaz Te
- Nathan Woolfe

KEY: On all match | On bench | Subbed or sent off (Counting game) | Subbed or sent off (playing less than 70 mins) | Subbed on from bench (Counting Game) | Subbed on (playing less than 70 mins) | Subbed on and then subbed or sent off (Counting Game) | Subbed on and then subbed or sent off (playing less than 70 min | Not in 16 | Injured | × Suspended

KEY PLAYERS - GOALSCORERS

Nicolas Anelka

Goals in the League	10
Goals in all competitions	11
Assists League goals scored by a team mate where the player delivered the final pass	2
Contribution to Attacking Power Average number of minutes between League team goals while on pitch	73
Player Strike Rate Average number of minutes between League goals scored by player	160
Club Strike Rate Average minutes between League goals scored by club	95

	PLAYER	GOALS LGE	GOALS ALL	ASSISTS	POWER	S RATE
1	Nicolas Anelka	10	11	2	73	**160 mins**
2	Matthew Taylor	3	3	2	115	**460 mins**
3	Kevin Nolan	5	5	3	86	**553 mins**
4	El Hadji Diouf	4	6	6	85	**660 mins**

KEY PLAYERS - MIDFIELDERS

Kevin Nolan

Goals in the League	5
Goals in all competitions	5
Assists League goals scored by a team mate where the player delivered the final pass	3
Defensive Rating Average number of mins between League goals conceded while on the pitch	79
Contribution to Attacking Power Average number of minutes between League team goals while on pitch	86
Scoring Difference Defensive Rating minus Contribution to Attacking Power	-7

	PLAYER	GOALS LGE	GOALS ALL	ASSISTS	DEF RATE	POWER	SC DIFF
1	Kevin Nolan	5	5	3	79	86	**-7 mins**
2	Danny Guthrie	0	1	0	82	89	**-7 mins**
3	Ivan Campo	1	1	1	71	98	**-27 mins**
4	Gavin McCann	1	3	0	63	96	**-33 mins**

PLAYER APPEARANCES

	AGE (on 01/07/08)	IN NAMED 16	APPEARANCES	COUNTING GAMES	MINUTES ON PITCH	APPEARANCES	MINUTES ON PITCH	THIS SEASON	HOME COUNTRY
Goalkeepers									
Ali Al Habsi	26	37	10	10	900	16	1470	-	Oman
Jussi Jaaskelainen	33	29	28	28	2520	35	3150	6	Finland
Ian Walker	36	11	0	0	0	0	0	-	England
Defenders									
Gary Cahill	22	13	13	13	1148	17	1508	-	England
Gerald Cid	25	9	7	5	509	14	1141	-	France
Jaroslav Fojut	20	3	0	0	0	0	0	-	Poland
Ricardo Gardner	29	26	26	24	2223	30	2574	4	Jamaica
Nicky Hunt	24	17	14	12	1097	24	1968	-	England
Abdoulaye Meite	27	26	21	19	1800	30	2479	5	Ivory Coast
Lubomir Michalik	24	12	7	5	496	13	1034	3	Slovakia
Andy O'Brien	29	33	32	31	2821	42	3632	-	Rep of Ireland
Joey O'Brien	22	19	19	13	1320	26	1786	2	Rep of Ireland
Jlloyd Samuel	27	25	20	13	1311	25	1761	-	England
Gretar Steinsson	26	16	16	15	1391	16	1391	5	Iceland
Midfielders									
Mikel Alonso	28	8	7	3	358	12	746	-	Spain
Ivan Campo	34	29	27	19	2061	31	2281	-	Spain
Matthew Cassidy	19	0	0	0	0	0	0	-	Rep of Ireland
Tamir Cohen	24	14	10	0	296	11	386	3	Israel
Blerim Dzemaili	22	0	0	0	0	1	45	-	Switzerland
Abdoulaye Faye	30	1	1	1	90	1	90	3	Senegal
S Giannakopoulos	33	26	15	1	299	26	968	-	Greece
Danny Guthrie	21	25	25	19	1887	35	2678	-	England
Scott Jamieson	19	0	0	0	0	0	0	-	Australia
Gavin McCann	30	31	31	20	2017	41	2808	-	England
Kevin Nolan	26	33	33	29	2769	39	3309	-	England
Robert Sissons	19	0	0	0	0	0	0	-	England
Gary Speed	38	16	14	10	970	17	1240	-	Wales
Matthew Taylor	26	16	16	15	1381	19	1651	-	England
Andranik Teymourian	25	5	3	0	79	9	280	-	Iran
C Wilhelmsson	28	10	8	0	239	13	630	5	Sweden
Kevin Wolze	18	0	0	0	0	0	0	-	Germany
Forwards									
Nicolas Anelka	29	18	18	18	1607	22	1838	6	France
Daniel Braaten	26	10	6	0	149	14	630	-	Norway
Kevin Davies	31	34	32	28	2642	41	3431	-	England
El Hadji Diouf	27	34	34	26	2640	42	3077	2	Senegal
Zoltan Harsanyi	22	0	0	0	0	0	0	-	Slovakia
Heidar Helguson	30	6	6	2	273	8	402	-	Iceland
Grzegorz Rasiak	29	12	7	0	282	7	282	2	Poland
James Sinclair	20	3	0	0	0	1	4	-	England
Ricardo Vaz Te	21	1	1	0	45	2	135	-	Portugal
Nathan Woolfe	19	0	0	0	0	1	15	-	England

KEY: LEAGUE ALL COMPS CAPS (MAY FIFA RANKING)

TEAM OF THE SEASON

JAASKELAINEN

CG 28 DR 60

HUNT — CG 12 DR 68

STEINSSON — CG 15 DR 77

A O'BRIEN — CG 31 DR 76

GARDNER — CG 24 DR 65

GUTHRIE — CG 19 SD -7

CAMPO — CG 19 SD -27

NOLAN — CG 29 SD -7

MCCANN — CG 20 SD -33

DIOUF — CG 26 AP 85

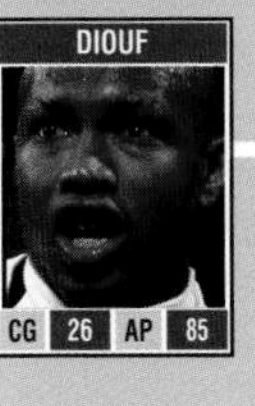

ANELKA — CG 18 SR 160

KEY: DR = Defensive Rate, SD = Scoring Difference AP = Attacking Power SR = Strike Rate, CG=Counting games – League games playing at least 70 minutes

TOP POINT EARNERS

Danny Guthrie	
Counting Games League games when player was on pitch for at least 70 minutes	19
Average points Average League points taken in Counting games	1.21
Club Average points Average points taken in League games	0.97

	PLAYER	GAMES	PTS
1	Danny Guthrie	19	1.21
2	Kevin Nolan	29	1.21
3	Ivan Campo	19	1.16
4	Gary Cahill	13	1.15
5	Gretar Rafn Steinsson	15	1.13
6	Andy O'Brien	31	1.10
7	Jlloyd Samuel	13	1.08
8	Nicky Hunt	12	1.08
9	El Hadji Diouf	26	1.04
10	Nicolas Anelka	18	1.00

KEY PLAYERS - DEFENDERS

Gretar Rafn Steinsson	
Goals Conceded in the League Number of League goals conceded while the player was on the pitch	18
Goals Conceded in all competitions Total number of goals conceded while the player was on the pitch	18
League minutes played Number of minutes played in league matches	1391
Clean Sheets In games when the player was on pitch for at least 70 minutes	7
Defensive Rating Average number of mins between League goals conceded while on the pitch	77
Club Defensive Rating Average number of mins between League goals conceded by the club this season	63

	PLAYER	CON LGE	CON ALL	MINS	C SHEETS	DEF RATE
1	Gretar Rafn Steinsson	18	18	1391	7	77 mins
2	Andy O'Brien	37	43	2821	11	76 mins
3	Nicky Hunt	16	23	1097	3	68 mins
4	Ricardo Gardner	34	38	2223	7	65 mins

KEY GOALKEEPER

Jussi Jaaskelainen	
Goals Conceded in the League Number of League goals conceded while the player was on the pitch	42
Goals Conceded in all competitions Total number of goals conceded while the player was on the pitch	46
League minutes played Number of minutes played in league matches	2520
Clean Sheets In games when the player was on pitch for at least 70 minutes	8
Goals to Shots Ratio The average number of shots on target per each League goal conceded	4.43
Defensive Rating Ave mins between League goals conceded while on the pitch	60

BOOKINGS

Nicky Hunt	
League Yellow	6
League Red	0
All competitions Yellow	8
All competitions Red	0
League Average 182 mins between cards	

	PLAYER	LEAGUE		TOTAL		AVE
		Y	R	Y	R	
1	Nicky Hunt	6	0	8	0	182
2	El Hadji Diouf	11	0	16	0	240
3	Ivan Campo	8	0	8	0	257
4	Kevin Davies	10	0	13	0	264
5	Kevin Nolan	10	0	11	0	276
6	Gavin McCann	5	0	9	0	403
7	Danny Guthrie	4	0	5	0	471
8	Gary Speed	2	0	3	0	485
9	Lubomir Michalik	1	0	1	0	496
10	Andy O'Brien	5	0	6	0	564
11	Joey O'Brien	2	0	4	0	660
12	Gretar Steinsson	2	0	2	0	695
13	Ricardo Gardner	2	0	2	0	1111
14	Jlloyd Samuel	1	0	1	0	1311
15	Matthew Taylor	1	0	1	0	1381
	Other	3	0	10	0	
	TOTAL	73	0	100	0	

FULHAM

Roy Hodgson deserves credit for saving a season, which proved it's not how much you spend, but how you spend it. Lawrie Sanchez was quick to flash the chequebook and brought in a vast number of players most of whom failed to make the grade. With Hodgson taking over the reins, £4m **Steve Davis** was not only dropped but sent out on loan to Rangers, while a number of Sanchez's other signings were also out of the team. A massive impact was made on the Cottagers' season by the return of **Jimmy Bullard** and captain **Brian McBride** from long-term injuries. Both added much needed technical ability and flare to a team struggling to score goals and Bullard's dead ball ability was priceless.

NICKNAME: THE COTTAGERS

KEY: Won, Drawn, Lost

1	prem	**Arsenal**	A	L	1-2	Healy 1
2	prem	**Bolton**	H	W	2-1	Healy 23, Cid 27 og
3	prem	**Middlesbro**	H	L	1-2	McBride 16
4	prem	**Aston Villa**	A	L	1-2	Dempsey 6
5	ccr2	**Shrewsbury**	A	W	1-0	Kamara 59
6	prem	**Tottenham**	H	D	3-3	Dempsey 42, Ricardo Rocha 77 og, Kamara 90
7	prem	**Wigan**	A	D	1-1	Dempsey 12
8	prem	**Man City**	H	D	3-3	Simon.Davies 13, Bouazza 48 , Murphy 75
9	ccr3	**Bolton**	H	L	1-2	Healy 78
10	prem	**Chelsea**	A	D	0-0	
11	prem	**Portsmouth**	H	L	0-2	
12	prem	**Derby**	H	D	0-0	
13	prem	**Sunderland**	A	D	1-1	Simon.Davies 32
14	prem	**Reading**	H	W	3-1	Simon.Davies 17, Dempsey 73, Healy 90
15	prem	**Liverpool**	A	L	0-2	
16	prem	**Blackburn**	H	D	2-2	Murphy 51 pen, Kamara 63
17	prem	**Man Utd**	A	L	0-2	
18	prem	**Everton**	A	L	0-3	
19	prem	**Newcastle**	H	L	0-1	
20	prem	**Wigan**	H	D	1-1	Dempsey 78
21	prem	**Tottenham**	A	L	1-5	Dempsey 60
22	prem	**Birmingham**	A	D	1-1	Bocanegra 8
23	prem	**Chelsea**	H	L	1-2	Murphy 10 pen
24	facr3	**Bristol Rovers**	H	D	2-2	Healy 40, Murphy 73
25	prem	**West Ham**	A	L	1-2	Davies 7
26	prem	**Arsenal**	H	L	0-3	
27	facr3	**Bristol Rovers**	A	L	3-5*	(*on penalties)
28	prem	**Bolton**	A	D	0-0	
29	prem	**Aston Villa**	H	W	2-1	Davies 72, Bullard 86
30	prem	**Middlesbro**	A	L	0-1	
31	prem	**West Ham**	H	L	0-1	
32	prem	**Man Utd**	H	L	0-3	
33	prem	**Blackburn**	A	D	1-1	Bullard 89
34	prem	**Everton**	H	W	1-0	McBride 67
35	prem	**Newcastle**	A	L	0-2	
36	prem	**Derby**	A	D	2-2	Kamara 24, Leacock 78 og
37	prem	**Sunderland**	H	L	1-3	Healy 74
38	prem	**Reading**	A	W	2-0	McBride 24, Nevland 90
39	prem	**Liverpool**	H	L	0-2	
40	prem	**Man City**	A	W	3-2	Kamara 70, 90, Murphy 79
41	prem	**Birmingham**	H	W	2-0	McBride 52, Nevland 87
42	prem	**Portsmouth**	A	W	1-0	Murphy 76

INS AND OUTS

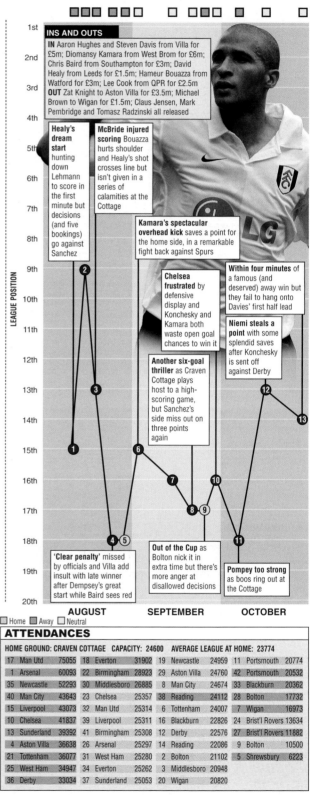

IN Aaron Hughes and Steven Davis from Villa for £5m; Diomansy Kamara from West Brom for £6m; Chris Baird from Southampton for £3m; David Healy from Leeds for £1.5m; Hameur Bouazza from Watford for £3m; Lee Cook from QPR for £2.5m **OUT** Zat Knight to Aston Villa for £3.5m; Michael Brown to Wigan for £1.5m; Claus Jensen, Mark Pembridge and Tomasz Radzinski all released

LEAGUE POSITION

1st
2nd
3rd
4th
5th
6th
7th
8th
9th
10th
11th
12th
13th
14th
15th
16th
17th
18th
19th
20th

Healy's dream start hunting down Lehmann to score in the first minute but decisions (and five bookings) go against Sanchez

McBride injured scoring Bouazza hurts shoulder and Healy's shot crosses line but isn't given in a series of calamities at the Cottage

Kamara's spectacular overhead kick saves a point for the home side, in a remarkable fight back against Spurs

Chelsea frustrated by defensive display and Konchesky and Kamara both waste open goal chances to win it

Within four minutes of a famous (and deserved) away win but they fail to hang onto Davies' first half lead

Niemi steals a point with some splendid saves after Konchesky is sent off against Derby

Another six-goal thriller as Craven Cottage plays host to a high-scoring game, but Sanchez's side miss out on three points again

'Clear penalty' missed by officials and Villa add insult with late winner after Dempsey's great start while Baird sees red

Out of the Cup as Bolton nick it in extra time but there's more anger at disallowed decisions

Pompey too strong as boos ring out at the Cottage

1 2 3 4 5 6 7 8 9 10 11 12 13

AUGUST SEPTEMBER OCTOBER

Home Away Neutral

ATTENDANCES

HOME GROUND: CRAVEN COTTAGE CAPACITY: 24600 AVERAGE LEAGUE AT HOME: 23774

17	Man Utd	75055	18	Everton	31902	19	Newcastle	24959	11	Portsmouth 20774
1	Arsenal	60093	22	Birmingham	28923	29	Aston Villa	24760	42	Portsmouth 20532
35	Newcastle	52293	30	Middlesboro	26885	8	Man City	24674	33	Blackburn 20362
40	Man City	43643	23	Chelsea	25357	38	Reading	24112	28	Bolton 17732
15	Liverpool	43073	32	Man Utd	25314	6	Tottenham	24007	7	Wigan 16973
10	Chelsea	41837	39	Liverpool	25311	16	Blackburn	22826	24	Brist'l Rovers 13634
13	Sunderland	39392	41	Birmingham	25308	12	Derby	22576	27	Brist'l Rovers 11882
4	Aston Villa	36638	26	Arsenal	25297	14	Reading	22086	9	Bolton 10500
21	Tottenham	36077	31	West Ham	25280	2	Bolton	21102	5	Shrewsbury 6223
25	West Ham	34947	34	Everton	25262	3	Middlesboro	20948		
36	Derby	33034	37	Sunderland	25053	20	Wigan	20820		

Cottagers' casualties are relegation rescuers

Final Position: 17th

KEY: League, Champions Lge, UEFA Cup, FA Cup, League Cup, Other

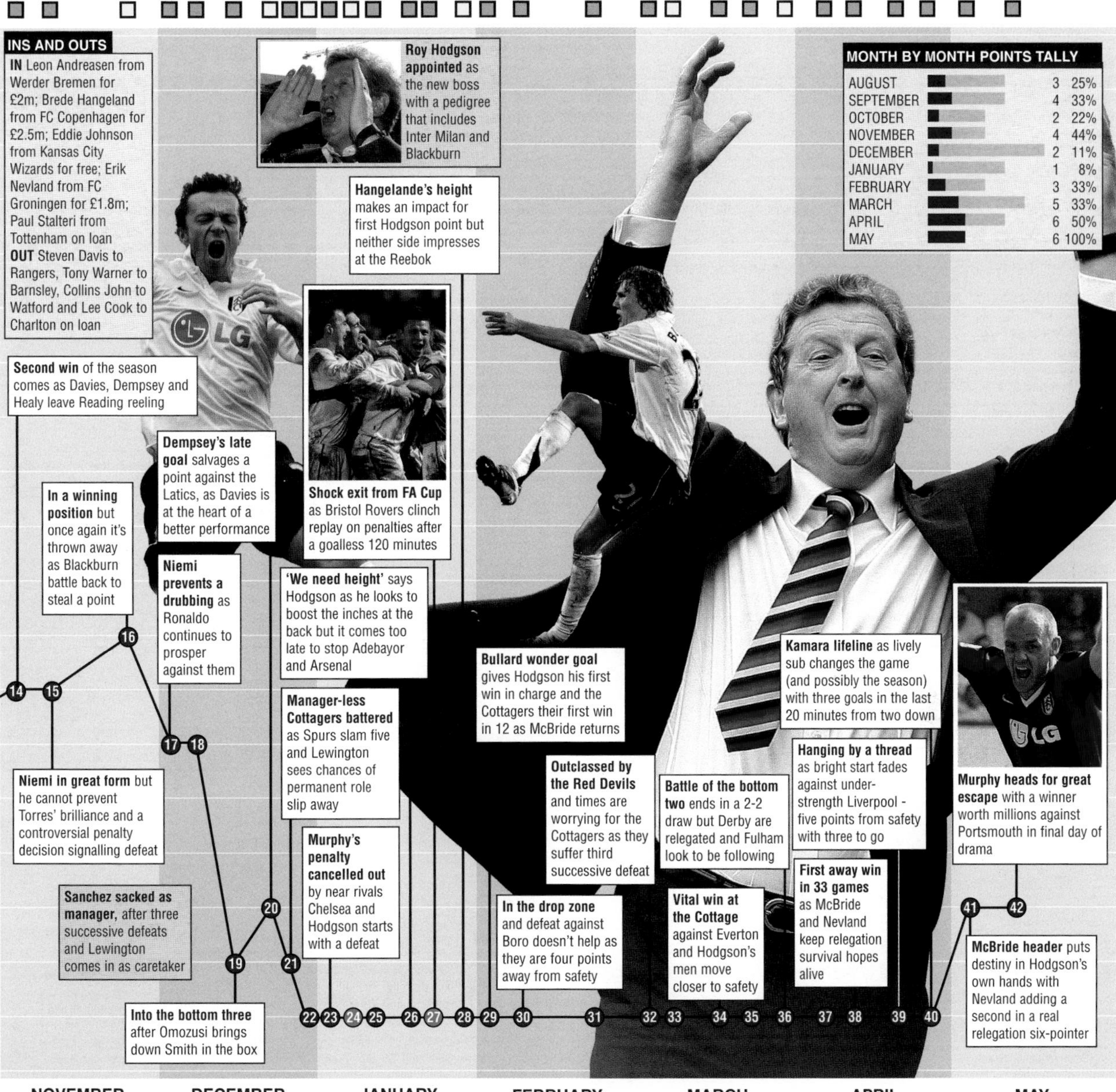

INS AND OUTS
IN Leon Andreasen from Werder Bremen for £2m; Brede Hangeland from FC Copenhagen for £2.5m; Eddie Johnson from Kansas City Wizards for free; Erik Nevland from FC Groningen for £1.8m; Paul Stalteri from Tottenham on loan
OUT Steven Davis to Rangers, Tony Warner to Barnsley, Collins John to Watford and Lee Cook to Charlton on loan
Roy Hodgson appointed as the new boss with a pedigree that includes Inter Milan and Blackburn
Hangelande's height makes an impact for first Hodgson point but neither side impresses at the Reebok
Second win of the season comes as Davies, Dempsey and Healy leave Reading reeling
In a winning position but once again it's thrown away as Blackburn battle back to steal a point
Dempsey's late goal salvages a point against the Latics, as Davies is at the heart of a better performance
Shock exit from FA Cup as Bristol Rovers clinch replay on penalties after a goalless 120 minutes
Niemi prevents a drubbing as Ronaldo continues to prosper against them
'We need height' says Hodgson as he looks to boost the inches at the back but it comes too late to stop Adebayor and Arsenal
Bullard wonder goal gives Hodgson his first win in charge and the Cottagers their first win in 12 as McBride returns
Kamara lifeline as lively sub changes the game (and possibly the season) with three goals in the last 20 minutes from two down
Manager-less Cottagers battered as Spurs slam five and Lewington sees chances of permanent role slip away
Niemi in great form but he cannot prevent Torres' brilliance and a controversial penalty decision signalling defeat
Outclassed by the Red Devils and times are worrying for the Cottagers as they suffer third successive defeat
Battle of the bottom two ends in a 2-2 draw but Derby are relegated and Fulham look to be following
Hanging by a thread as bright start fades against under-strength Liverpool - five points from safety with three to go
Murphy heads for great escape with a winner worth millions against Portsmouth in final day of drama
Murphy's penalty cancelled out by near rivals Chelsea and Hodgson starts with a defeat
Sanchez sacked as manager, after three successive defeats and Lewington comes in as caretaker
In the drop zone and defeat against Boro doesn't help as they are four points away from safety
Vital win at the Cottage against Everton and Hodgson's men move closer to safety
First away win in 33 games as McBride and Nevland keep relegation survival hopes alive
McBride header puts destiny in Hodgson's own hands with Nevland adding a second in a real relegation six-pointer
Into the bottom three after Omozusi brings down Smith in the box
14 15 16 17 18 19 20 21 22 23 24 25 26 27 28 29 30 31 32 33 34 35 36 37 38 39 40 41 42
NOVEMBER DECEMBER JANUARY FEBRUARY MARCH APRIL MAY

MONTH BY MONTH POINTS TALLY

Month	Points	%
AUGUST	3	25%
SEPTEMBER	4	33%
OCTOBER	2	22%
NOVEMBER	4	44%
DECEMBER	2	11%
JANUARY	1	8%
FEBRUARY	3	33%
MARCH	5	33%
APRIL	6	50%
MAY	6	100%

GOAL ATTEMPTS

FOR — Goal attempts recorded in League games

	HOME	AWAY	TOTAL	AVE
shots on target	118	109	227	6.0
shots off target	96	97	193	5.1
TOTAL	214	206	420	11.1

Ratio of goals to shots Average number of shots on target per League goal scored	6.0
Accuracy rating Average percentage of total goal attempts which were on target	54.0

AGAINST — Goal attempts recorded in League games

	HOME	AWAY	TOTAL	AVE
shots on target	114	145	259	6.8
shots off target	98	141	239	6.3
TOTAL	212	286	498	13.1

Ratio of goals to shots Average number of shots on target per League goal scored	4.3
Accuracy rating Average percentage of total goal attempts which were on target	52.0

GOALS

Kamara

League	5
FA Cup	0
League Cup	1
Europe	0
Other	0
TOTAL	6

League Average 322 mins between goals

	PLAYER	LGE	FAC	LC	Euro	TOT	AVE
1	Kamara	5	0	1	0	6	322
2	Healy	4	1	1	0	6	340
3	Dempsey	6	0	0	0	6	445
4	Murphy	5	1	0	0	6	494
5	Davies	5	0	0	0	5	641
6	McBride	4	0	0	0	4	300
7	Nevland	2	0	0	0	2	109
8	Bullard	2	0	0	0	2	692
9	Bouazza	1	0	0	0	1	1188
10	Bocanegra	1	0	0	0	1	1619
	Other	0	0	0	0	0	
	TOTAL	35	2	2	0	39	

SQUAD APPEARANCES

Match	1	2	3	4	5	6	7	8	9	10	11	12	13	14	15	16	17	18	19	20	21	22	23	24	25	26	27	28	29	30	31	32	33	34	35	36	37	38	39	40	41	42
Venue	A	H	H	A	A	H	A	H	H	A	H	H	A	H	A	H	A	A	H	H	A	A	H	H	A	H	A	A	H	A	H	H	A	H	A	A	H	A	H	A	H	A
Competition	L	L	L	L	W	L	L	L	W	L	L	L	L	L	L	L	L	L	L	L	L	L	L	F	L	L	F	L	L	L	L	L	L	L	L	L	L	L	L	L	L	L
Result	L	W	L	L	W	D	D	D	L	D	L	D	D	W	L	D	L	L	L	D	L	D	L	D	L	L	L	D	W	L	L	L	D	W	L	D	L	W	L	W	W	W

Goalkeepers
Ricardo Batista
Kasey Keller
Antti Niemi
Tony Warner

Defenders
Nathan Ashton
Chris Baird
Carlos Bocanegra
Philippe Christanval
Brede Paulsen Hangeland
Aaron Hughes
Zatyiah Knight
Paul Konchesky
Adrian Leijer
Elliot Omozusi
Ian Pearce
Paul Stalteri
Dejan Stefanovic
Moritz Volz
Adam Watts

Midfielders
Leon Andreasen
Wayne Brown
Jimmy Bullard
Simon Davies
Steven Davis
Papa Bouba Diop
Simon Elliott
Robert Milson
Danny Murphy
Alexei Smertin

Forwards
Hameur Bouazza
Clint Dempsey
David Healy
Collins John
Eddie Johnson
Diomansy Mehdi Kamara
Shefki Kuqi
Brian McBride
Erik Nevland
Ki-Hyeon Seol

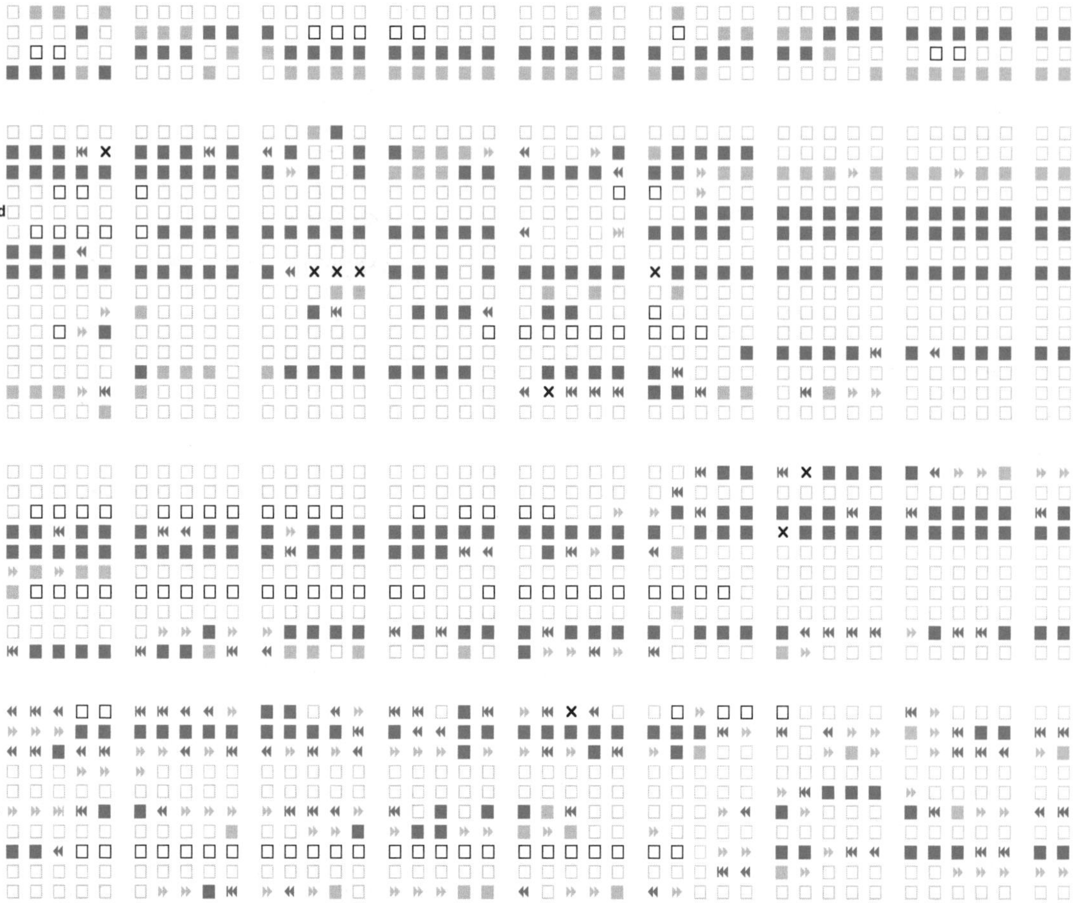

KEY: On all match / On bench / Subbed or sent off (Counting game) / Subbed or sent off (playing less than 70 mins) / Subbed on from bench (Counting Game) / Subbed on (playing less than 70 mins) / Subbed on and then subbed or sent off (Counting Game) / Subbed on and then subbed or sent off (playing less than 70 min / Not in 16 / Injured / ✕ Suspended

KEY PLAYERS - GOALSCORERS

Brian McBride

Goals in the League	4
Goals in all competitions	4
Assists League goals scored by a team mate where the player delivered the final pass	0
Contribution to Attacking Power Average number of minutes between League team goals while on pitch	70
Player Strike Rate Average number of minutes between League goals scored by player	300
Club Strike Rate Average minutes between League goals scored by club	90

	PLAYER	GOALS LGE	GOALS ALL	ASSISTS	POWER	S RATE
1	Brian McBride	4	4	0	70	300 mins
2	Diomansy Mehdi Kamara	5	6	3	73	322 mins
3	Clint Dempsey	6	6	3	99	445 mins
4	Danny Murphy	5	6	1	107	494 mins

KEY PLAYERS - MIDFIELDERS

Jimmy Bullard

Goals in the League	2
Goals in all competitions	2
Assists League goals scored by a team mate where the player delivered the final pass	3
Defensive Rating Average number of mins between League goals conceded while on the pitch	76
Contribution to Attacking Power Average number of minutes between League team goals while on pitch	92
Scoring Difference Defensive Rating minus Contribution to Attacking Power	-16

	PLAYER	GOALS LGE	GOALS ALL	ASSISTS	DEF RATE	POWER	SC DIFF
1	Jimmy Bullard	2	2	3	76	92	-16 mins
2	Steven Davis	0	0	0	54	87	-33 mins
3	Simon Davies	5	5	7	56	89	-33 mins
4	Danny Murphy	5	6	1	61	107	-46 mins

PLAYER APPEARANCES

	AGE (on 01/07/08)	IN NAMED 16	APPEARANCES	COUNTING GAMES	MINUTES ON PITCH	APPEARANCES	MINUTES ON PITCH	THIS SEASON	HOME COUNTRY
Goalkeepers									
Ricardo Batista	21	3	0	0	0	0	0	-	Portugal
Kasey Keller	38	20	13	13	1170	14	1290	-	United States
Antti Niemi	36	25	22	22	1980	23	2070	-	Finland
Tony Warner	34	27	3	3	270	5	480	-	Trinidad & Tobago
Defenders									
Nathan Ashton	21	2	1	1	90	1	90	-	England
Chris Baird	26	22	18	15	1464	21	1721	7	N Ireland
Carlos Bocanegra	29	37	22	17	1619	26	2039	2	United States
Philippe Christanval	29	1	1	0	17	1	17	-	France
Brede P Hangeland	27	15	15	15	1350	15	1350	6	Norway
Aaron Hughes	28	30	30	29	2659	32	2899	5	N Ireland
Zatyiah Knight	28	4	4	3	327	4	327	-	England
Paul Konchesky	27	33	33	32	2924	37	3344	-	England
Adrian Leijer	22	3	0	0	0	0	0	-	Australia
Elliot Omozusi	19	9	8	7	688	9	700	-	England
Ian Pearce	34	1	1	0	33	2	123	-	England
Paul Stalteri	30	13	13	12	1134	13	1134	-	Canada
Dejan Stefanovic	33	16	13	13	1170	15	1378	-	Serbia
Moritz Volz	25	16	9	4	482	12	751	-	Germany
Adam Watts	20	0	0	0	0	0	0	-	England
Midfielders									
Leon Andreasen	25	14	13	8	788	13	788	5	Denmark
Wayne Brown	19	0	0	0	0	1	90	-	England
Jimmy Bullard	29	17	17	15	1385	18	1505	-	England
Simon Davies	28	37	37	35	3208	40	3508	8	Wales
Steven Davis	23	22	22	20	1846	25	2074	8	N Ireland
Papa Bouba Diop	30	4	2	0	19	2	19	3	Senegal
Simon Elliott	34	1	0	0	0	0	0	-	New Zealand
Robert Milson	21	0	0	0	0	0	0	-	English
Danny Murphy	31	33	33	27	2474	35	2684	-	England
Alexei Smertin	33	20	15	10	988	17	1150	-	Russia
Forwards									
Hameur Bouazza	23	20	20	10	1188	22	1274	-	France
Clint Dempsey	25	37	36	26	2674	40	3094	2	United States
David Healy	28	33	30	8	1360	34	1693	8	N Ireland
Collins John	22	2	2	0	38	3	54	-	Holland
Eddie Johnson	24	6	6	4	385	6	385	1	United States
Diomansy Kamara	27	30	28	14	1613	30	1761	3	Senegal
Shefki Kuqi	31	13	10	3	410	10	410	3	Finland
Brian McBride	36	17	17	12	1203	17	1203	-	United States
Erik Nevland	30	9	8	1	218	8	218	-	Norway
Ki-Hyeon Seol	29	16	12	1	358	15	527	-	South Korea

KEY: LEAGUE ALL COMPS CAPS (MAY FIFA RANKING)

TEAM OF THE SEASON

KELLER CG 13 DR 73

STALTERI CG 12 DR 70

HUGHES CG 29 DR 60

HANGELAND CG 15 DR 75

KONCHESKY CG 32 DR 56

DAVIES CG 35 SD -33

BULLARD CG 15 SD -16

MURPHY CG 27 SD -46

DAVIS CG 20 SD -33

KAMARA CG 14 AP 73

MCBRIDE CG 12 SR 300

KEY: DR = Defensive Rate, SD = Scoring Difference AP = Attacking Power SR = Strike Rate, CG=Counting games – League games playing at least 70 minutes

TOP POINT EARNERS

Brian McBride

Counting Games League games when player was on pitch for at least 70 minutes	12
Average points Average League points taken in Counting games	1.58
Club Average points Average points taken in League games	0.95

	PLAYER	GAMES	PTS
1	Brian McBride	12	1.58
2	Paul Stalteri	12	1.42
3	Jimmy Bullard	15	1.40
4	Brede Paulsen Hangeland	15	1.40
5	Kasey Keller	13	1.38
6	Clint Dempsey	26	1.08
7	Aaron Hughes	29	1.07
8	Danny Murphy	27	1.04
9	Paul Konchesky	32	0.97
10	Simon Davies	35	0.97

KEY PLAYERS - DEFENDERS

Brede Paulsen Hangeland

Goals Conceded in the League Number of League goals conceded while the player was on the pitch	18
Goals Conceded in all competitions Total number of goals conceded while the player was on the pitch	18
League minutes played Number of minutes played in league matches	1350
Clean Sheets In games when the player was on pitch for at least 70 minutes	5
Defensive Rating Average number of mins between League goals conceded while on the pitch	75
Club Defensive Rating Average number of mins between League goals conceded by the club this season	57

	PLAYER	CON LGE	CON ALL	MINS	C SHEETS	DEF RATE
1	Brede Paulsen Hangeland	18	18	1350	5	75 mins
2	Paul Stalteri	16	16	1134	4	70 mins
3	Aaron Hughes	44	46	2659	7	60 mins
4	Paul Konchesky	52	56	2924	6	56 mins

KEY GOALKEEPER

Kasey Keller

Goals Conceded in the League Number of League goals conceded while the player was on the pitch	16
Goals Conceded in all competitions Total number of goals conceded while the player was on the pitch	18
League minutes played Number of minutes played in league matches	1170
Clean Sheets In games when the player was on pitch for at least 70 minutes	5
Goals to Shots Ratio The average number of shots on target per each League goal conceded	3.81
Defensive Rating Ave mins between League goals conceded while on the pitch	73

BOOKINGS

Moritz Volz

League Yellow	2
League Red	1
All competitions Yellow	2
All competitions Red	1

League Average 160 mins between cards

	PLAYER	LEAGUE 2Y	LEAGUE 1R	TOTAL 2Y	TOTAL 1R	AVE
1	Moritz Volz	2	1	2	1	160
2	Leon Andreasen	3	1	3	1	197
3	Elliot Omozusi	2	1	3	1	229
4	Diomansy Kamara	6	0	7	0	268
5	Dejan Stefanovic	4	0	5	1	292
6	Carlos Bocanegra	5	0	5	0	323
7	Paul Stalteri	3	0	3	0	378
8	Hameur Bouazza	2	1	2	1	396
9	David Healy	3	0	4	0	453
10	Paul Konchesky	5	1	5	1	487
11	Chris Baird	2	1	3	1	488
12	Alexei Smertin	2	0	2	0	494
13	Simon Davies	6	0	6	0	534
14	Danny Murphy	4	0	5	0	618
15	Clint Dempsey	4	0	4	0	668
	Other	4	0	4	0	
	TOTAL	57	6	63	7	

READING

Reading suffered from second season syndrome and were cruelly relegated from the league on the last day of the season – down on goal difference. The goals seemed to dry up for the team in the second half of the season. Although **Dave Kitson** finished the season with ten goals, eight of those came before Christmas and the festive period coincided with the Royals' decline as they endured a run of 11 games, in all competitions, without a win. Claiming only four points from the last seven games proved too little. Following their relegation, boss Steve Coppell's future at the club now looks in doubt, although the job he has performed has been impressive so far and owner John Madejski doesn't want to lose him.

NICKNAME: THE ROYALS

KEY: Won / Drawn / Lost

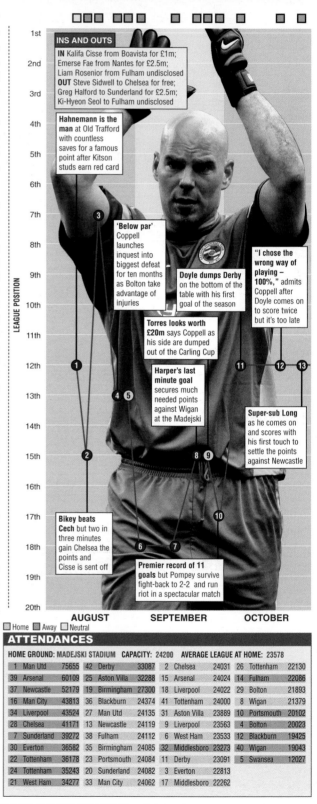

INS AND OUTS
IN Kalifa Cisse from Boavista for £1m; Emerse Fae from Nantes for £2.5m; Liam Rosenior from Fulham undisclosed
OUT Steve Sidwell to Chelsea for free; Greg Halford to Sunderland for £2.5m; Ki-Hyeon Seol to Fulham undisclosed
Hahnemann is the man at Old Trafford with countless saves for a famous point after Kitson studs earn red card
'Below par' Coppell launches inquest into biggest defeat for ten months as Bolton take advantage of injuries
Doyle dumps Derby on the bottom of the table with his first goal of the season
"I chose the wrong way of playing – 100%," admits Coppell after Doyle comes on to score twice but it's too late
Torres looks worth £20m says Coppell as his side are dumped out of the Carling Cup
Harper's last minute goal secures much needed points against Wigan at the Madejski
Super-sub Long as he comes on and scores with his first touch to settle the points against Newcastle
Bikey beats Cech but two in three minutes gain Chelsea the points and Cisse is sent off
Premier record of 11 goals but Pompey survive fight-back to 2-2 and run riot in a spectacular match
LEAGUE POSITION
AUGUST
SEPTEMBER
OCTOBER
Home Away Neutral

1	prem	**Man Utd**	A	D	0-0	
2	prem	**Chelsea**	H	L	1-2	Bikey 30
3	prem	**Everton**	H	W	1-0	Hunt 44
4	prem	**Bolton**	A	L	0-3	
5	ccr2	**Swansea**	A	W	1-0	Lita 105
6	prem	**West Ham**	H	L	0-3	
7	prem	**Sunderland**	A	L	1-2	Kitson 85
8	prem	**Wigan**	H	W	2-1	Kitson 29, Harper 90
9	ccr3	**Liverpool**	H	L	2-4	Convey 27, Halls 64
10	prem	**Portsmouth**	A	L	4-7	Hunt 45, Kitson 48, Harper 78, Campbell 90 og
11	prem	**Derby**	H	W	1-0	Doyle 63
12	prem	**Blackburn**	A	L	2-4	Doyle 80, 90
13	prem	**Newcastle**	H	W	2-1	Kitson 53, Long 83
14	prem	**Fulham**	A	L	1-3	Doyle 54
15	prem	**Arsenal**	H	L	1-3	Shorey 87
16	prem	**Man City**	A	L	1-2	Harper 43
17	prem	**Middlesbro**	H	D	1-1	Kitson 54
18	prem	**Liverpool**	H	W	3-1	Hunt 17 pen, Doyle 60, Harper 67
19	prem	**Birmingham**	A	D	1-1	Hunt 51 pen
20	prem	**Sunderland**	H	W	2-1	Ingimarsson 69, Hunt 90
21	prem	**West Ham**	A	D	1-1	Kitson 60
22	prem	**Tottenham**	A	L	4-6	Cisse 16, Ingimarsson 53, Kitson 69, 74
23	prem	**Portsmouth**	H	L	0-2	
24	facr3	**Tottenham**	A	D	2-2	Hunt 25, 78
25	prem	**Aston Villa**	A	L	1-3	Harper 90
26	facr3r	**Tottenham**	H	L	0-1	
27	prem	**Man Utd**	H	L	0-2	
28	prem	**Chelsea**	A	L	0-1	
29	prem	**Bolton**	H	L	0-2	
30	prem	**Everton**	A	L	0-1	
31	prem	**Aston Villa**	H	L	1-2	Shorey 90
32	prem	**Middlesbro**	A	W	1-0	Harper 90
33	prem	**Man City**	H	W	2-0	Long 62, Kitson 87
34	prem	**Liverpool**	A	L	1-2	Matejovsky 5
35	prem	**Birmingham**	H	W	2-1	Bikey 31, 79
36	prem	**Blackburn**	H	D	0-0	
37	prem	**Newcastle**	A	L	0-3	
38	prem	**Fulham**	H	L	0-2	
39	prem	**Arsenal**	A	L	0-2	
40	prem	**Wigan**	A	D	0-0	
41	prem	**Tottenham**	H	L	0-1	
42	prem	**Derby**	A	W	4-0	Harper 15, Kitson 60, Doyle 69, Lita 90

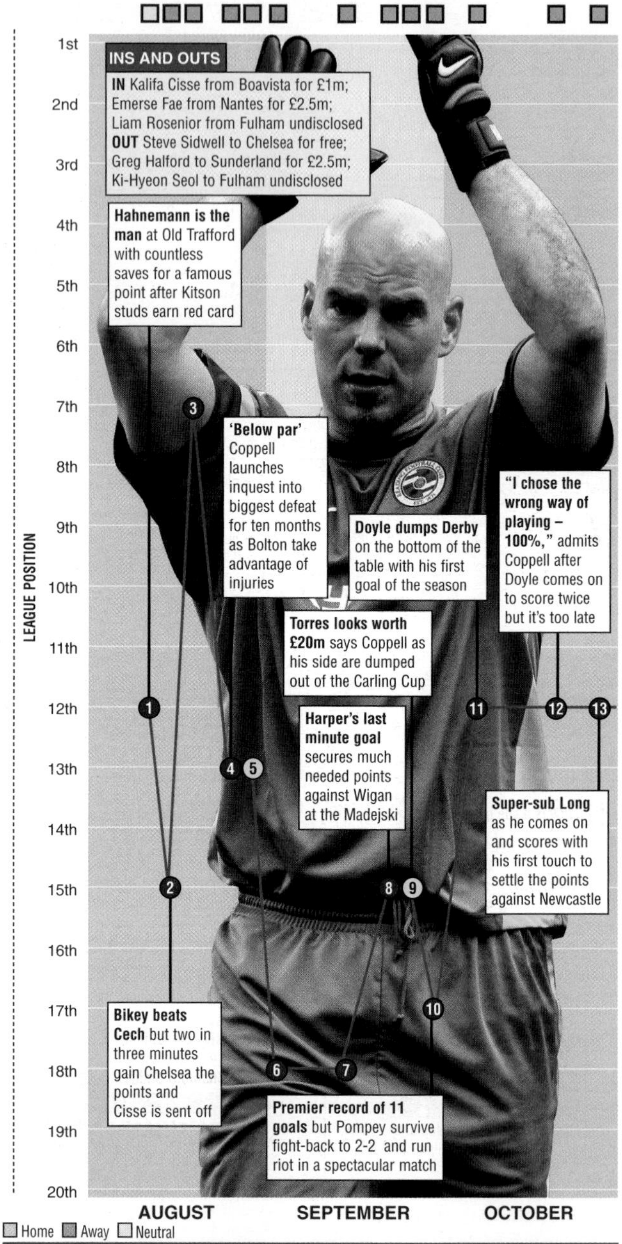

ATTENDANCES

HOME GROUND: MADEJSKI STADIUM **CAPACITY:** 24200 **AVERAGE LEAGUE AT HOME:** 23578

1	Man Utd	75655	42	Derby	33087	2	Chelsea	24031	26	Tottenham	22130
39	Arsenal	60109	25	Aston Villa	32288	15	Arsenal	24024	14	Fulham	22086
37	Newcastle	52179	19	Birmingham	27300	18	Liverpool	24022	29	Bolton	21893
16	Man City	43813	36	Blackburn	24374	41	Tottenham	24000	8	Wigan	21379
34	Liverpool	43524	27	Man Utd	24135	31	Aston Villa	23889	10	Portsmouth	20102
28	Chelsea	41171	13	Newcastle	24119	9	Liverpool	23563	4	Bolton	20023
7	Sunderland	39272	38	Fulham	24112	6	West Ham	23533	12	Blackburn	19425
30	Everton	36582	35	Birmingham	24085	32	Middlesboro	23273	40	Wigan	19043
22	Tottenham	36178	23	Portsmouth	24084	11	Derby	23091	5	Swansea	12027
24	Tottenham	35243	20	Sunderland	24082	3	Everton	22813			
21	West Ham	34277	33	Man City	24062	17	Middlesboro	22262			

...ppell future in doubt as Reading relegated

Final Position: 18th

KEY: ● League ● Champions Lge ● UEFA Cup ● FA Cup ○ League Cup ● Other

INS AND OUTS
IN Marek Matejovsky from Mlada Boleslav (Czech Republic) for £1m; Jimmy Kebe from Lens undisclosed
OUT Simon Church to Yeovil, Ben Hamer to Brentford, John Halls to Crystal Palace, James Henry and Alex Pearce to Norwich and Hal Robson-Kanu to Southend all on loan
MONTH BY MONTH POINTS TALLY
AUGUST 4 33%
SEPTEMBER 3 25%
OCTOBER 6 67%
NOVEMBER 0 0%
DECEMBER 9 50%
JANUARY 0 0%
FEBRUARY 0 0%
MARCH 10 67%
APRIL 1 8%
MAY 3 50%
Ten-goal thriller to end 2007 with Kitson scoring two against his boyhood team and still ending up on losing side
Bikey is the man of the hour as he nets two and it's enough to secure the victory against Birmingham
Harper's curler levels against City but Ireland's last minute wonder strike is third defeat of the month
Hunt pops up late to seal the points against the Black Cats after Sonko gives away a penalty
Sonko sent off for a clumsy hack after three minutes and Pompey take advantage
Harper goal ends run of eight straight league defeats and Coppell's men claim victory at the Riverside
Second string; second best as Keane puts Spurs into the next round of the cup
Villa too good but Shorey's free kick ends two month wait for a goal by the home side at the Madejski
Hahnemann on top form to deny Wigan but goalless draw doesn't help either side
Lack of firepower against the Gunners as only Shorey musters a late burst, hitting the post and scoring
Unbeaten in December as ten men hold out at Upton Park after Gunnarsson is sent off
Into the bottom three after a seventh consecutive defeat for Royals against high-flying Everton
Wasteful Gunners are still too strong, scoring two and twice hitting the woodwork
Keane opens trapdoor with a stunning finish and Reading fall into bottom three with one to go
Doyle's fourth goal of the season can't prevent defeat to fellow strugglers Fulham
Cisse inspired at centre back but United eventually breakthrough
Goals flow but it's too late to beat the drop as news comes in of Fulham win at Portsmouth
Second successive victory means that the Royals move out of the bottom three and into the dizzy heights of 13th
Fifth successive defeat in a tough January as Chelsea scrape a victory at Stamford Bridge
Famous victory at Madejski as Harper goal ensures a first Premier defeat for title contenders Liverpool
"No good enough" says Coppell as Trotters win relegation tussle despite Hanhemann penalty save
Pressure mounts on the Royals as they get closer to the relegation places after hammering at the hand of Newcastle
14 15 16 17 18 19 20 21 22 23 24 25 26 27 28 29 30 31 32 33 34 35 36 37 38 39 40 41 42
NOVEMBER DECEMBER JANUARY FEBRUARY MARCH APRIL MAY

GOAL ATTEMPTS

FOR — Goal attempts recorded in League games

	HOME	AWAY	TOTAL	AVE
shots on target	138	105	243	6.4
shots off target	91	75	166	4.4
TOTAL	229	180	409	10.8

Ratio of goals to shots — Average number of shots on target per League goal scored: **5.9**

Accuracy rating — Average percentage of total goal attempts which were on target: **59.4**

AGAINST — Goal attempts recorded in League games

	HOME	AWAY	TOTAL	AVE
shots on target	141	162	303	8.0
shots off target	107	124	231	6.1
TOTAL	248	286	534	14.1

Ratio of goals to shots — Average number of shots on target per League goal scored: **4.6**

Accuracy rating — Average percentage of total goal attempts which were on target: **56.7**

GOALS

Kitson

League	10
FA Cup	0
League Cup	0
Europe	0
Other	0
TOTAL	10

League Average **252** mins between goals

	PLAYER	LGE	FAC	LC	Euro	TOT	AVE
1	Kitson	10	0	0	0	10	252
2	Harper	7	0	0	0	7	478
3	Hunt	5	2	0	0	7	662
4	Doyle	6	0	0	0	6	501
5	Bikey	3	0	0	0	3	456
6	Long	2	0	0	0	2	385
7	Lita	1	0	1	0	2	891
8	Ingimarsson	2	0	0	0	2	1501
9	Shorey	2	0	0	0	2	1610
10	Matejovsky	1	0	0	0	1	875
11	Cisse	1	0	0	0	1	1123
12	Convey	0	0	1	0	1	
13	Halls	0	0	1	0	1	
	Other	0	0	0	0	0	
	TOTAL	40	2	3	0	45	

SQUAD APPEARANCES

Match	1	2	3	4	5	6	7	8	9	10	11	12	13	14	15	16	17	18	19	20	21	22	23	24	25	26	27	28	29	30	31	32	33	34	35	36	37	38	39	40	41	42
Venue	A	H	H	A	A	H	A	H	H	A	H	A	H	A	H	A	H	H	A	H	A	A	H	A	A	H	H	A	H	A	H	A	H	A	H	H	A	H	A	A	H	A
Competition	L	L	L	L	W	L	L	L	W	L	L	L	L	L	L	L	L	L	L	L	L	L	L	F	L	F	L	L	L	L	L	L	L	L	L	L	L	L	L	L	L	L
Result	D	L	W	L	W	L	L	W	L	L	W	L	W	L	L	L	D	W	D	W	D	L	L	D	L	L	L	L	L	L	L	W	W	L	W	D	L	L	L	D	L	W

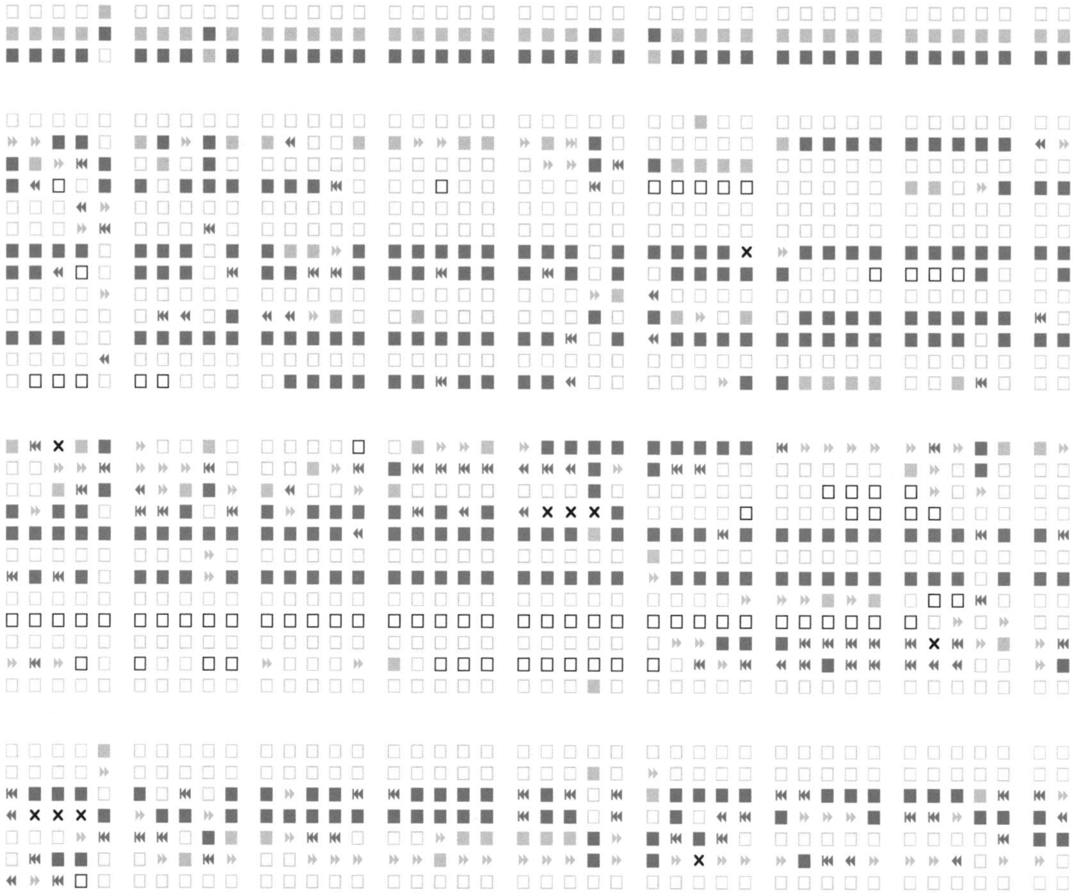

Goalkeepers

Mikkel Anderson
Adam Federici
Marcus Hahnemann

Defenders

Alan Bennett
Andre Bikey
Ulises De La Cruz
Michael Duberry
Scott Golbourne
John Halls
Ivar Ingimarsson
Graeme Murty
Alex Pearce
Liam Rosenior
Nicky Shorey
Sam Sodje
Ibrahima Sonko

Midfielders

Kalifa Cisse
Bobby Convey
Emerse Fae
Brynjar Gunnarsson
James Harper
James Henry
Stephen Hunt
Jimmy Kebe
Glen Little
Marek Matejovsky
John Oster
Hal Robson- Kanu

Forwards

Simon Church
Simon Cox
Kevin Doyle
David Kitson
Leroy Lita
Shane Long
Ki-Hyeon Seol

KEY: ■ On all match ■ On bench
⏮ Subbed or sent off (Counting game) « Subbed or sent off (playing less than 70 mins)
» Subbed on from bench (Counting Game) » Subbed on (playing less than 70 mins)
» Subbed on and then subbed or sent off (Counting Game) » Subbed on and then subbed or sent off (playing less than 70 min
□ Not in 16 □ Injured ✕ Suspended

KEY PLAYERS - GOALSCORERS

David Kitson

Goals in the League	10
Goals in all competitions	10
Assists League goals scored by a team mate where the player delivered the final pass	3
Contribution to Attacking Power Average number of minutes between League team goals while on pitch	74
Player Strike Rate Average number of minutes between League goals scored by player	252
Club Strike Rate Average minutes between League goals scored by club	83

	PLAYER	GOALS LGE	GOALS ALL	ASSISTS	POWER	S RATE
1	David Kitson	10	10	3	74	252 mins
2	James Harper	7	7	1	85	478 mins
3	Kevin Doyle	6	6	3	91	501 mins
4	Stephen Hunt	5	7	5	80	662 mins

KEY PLAYERS - MIDFIELDERS

Brynjar Gunnarsson

Goals in the League	0
Goals in all competitions	0
Assists League goals scored by a team mate where the player delivered the final pass	1
Defensive Rating Average number of mins between League goals conceded while on the pitch	49
Contribution to Attacking Power Average number of minutes between League team goals while on pitch	74
Scoring Difference Defensive Rating minus Contribution to Attacking Power	-25

	PLAYER	GOALS LGE	GOALS ALL	ASSISTS	DEF RATE	POWER	SC DIFF
1	Brynjar Gunnarsson	0	0	1	49	74	-25 mins
2	Stephen Hunt	5	7	5	51	80	-29 mins
3	James Harper	7	7	1	51	85	-34 mins
4	Kalifa Cisse	1	1	0	41	112	-71 mins

PLAYER APPEARANCES

	AGE (on 01/07/08)	IN NAMED 16	APPEARANCES	COUNTING GAMES	MINUTES ON PITCH	APPEARANCES	MINUTES ON PITCH	THIS SEASON	HOME COUNTRY
Goalkeepers									
Mikkel Anderson	19	0	0	0	0	0	0	-	Denmark
Adam Federici	23	38	0	0	0	4	390	-	Australia
Marcus Hahnemann	36	38	38	38	3420	38	3420	1	United States
Defenders									
Alan Bennett	26	1	0	0	0	0	0	-	Rep of Ireland
Andre Bikey	23	31	22	13	1370	24	1550	5	Cameroon
Ulises De La Cruz	34	12	6	3	340	10	730	2	Ecuador
Michael Duberry	32	15	13	11	1022	16	1321	-	England
Scott Golbourne	20	1	1	0	62	2	84	-	England
John Halls	26	1	1	0	9	3	186	-	England
Ivar Ingimarsson	30	37	35	33	3003	36	3093	4	Iceland
Graeme Murty	33	28	28	27	2419	28	2419	1	Scotland
Alex Pearce	19	1	0	0	0	3	47	-	England
Liam Rosenior	23	21	17	12	1243	19	1423	-	England
Nicky Shorey	27	36	36	36	3220	38	3375	1	England
Sam Sodje	29	0	0	0	0	1	57	-	England
Ibrahima Sonko	27	21	16	14	1252	16	1252	1	Senegal
Midfielders									
Kalifa Cisse	24	28	22	11	1123	25	1423	-	France
Bobby Convey	25	22	20	10	1054	24	1412	-	United States
Emerse Fae	24	12	8	1	294	11	594	4	Ivory Coast
Brynjar Gunnarsson	32	20	20	16	1498	20	1498	3	Iceland
James Harper	27	38	38	37	3349	41	3649	-	England
James Henry	19	0	0	0	0	1	12	-	England
Stephen Hunt	26	37	37	37	3314	40	3440	4	Rep of Ireland
Jimmy Kebe	24	7	5	1	146	5	146	-	Mali
Glen Little	32	2	2	0	51	2	51	-	England
Marek Matejovsky	26	15	14	10	875	14	875	5	Czech Republic
John Oster	29	19	18	9	1018	18	1018	-	Wales
Hal Robson- Kanu	27	0	0	0	0	0	0	-	England
Forwards									
Simon Cox	21	0	0	0	0	2	66	-	England
Kevin Doyle	24	37	36	34	3010	36	3010	6	Rep of Ireland
David Kitson	28	34	34	26	2524	36	2655	-	England
Leroy Lita	23	21	14	9	891	18	1280	-	England
Shane Long	21	31	29	5	770	32	1028	2	Rep of Ireland
Ki-Hyeon Seol	29	3	3	1	138	3	138	-	South Korea

KEY: LEAGUE ALL COMPS CAPS (MAY FIFA RANKING)

TEAM OF THE SEASON

HAHNEMANN

CG 38 DR 51

BIKEY

CG 13 DR 57

DUBERRY

CG 11* DR 53

INGIMARSSON

CG 33 DR 52

SHOREY

CG 36 DR 52

HARPER

CG 37 SD -34

GUNNARSSON

CG 16 SD -25

CISSE

CG 11* SD -71

HUNT

CG 37 SD -29

DOYLE

CG 34 AP 91

KITSON

CG 26 SR 252

KEY: DR = Defensive Rate, SD = Scoring Difference AP = Attacking Power SR = Strike Rate, CG=Counting games – League games playing at least 70 minutes

TOP POINT EARNERS

Brynjar Gunnarsson

Counting Games League games when player was on pitch for at least 70 minutes	16
Average points Average League points taken in Counting games	1.25
Club Average points Average points taken in League games	0.95

	PLAYER	GAMES	PTS
1	Brynjar Gunnarsson	16	1.25
2	Andre Bikey	13	1.08
3	Ivar Ingimarsson	33	1.00
4	Nicky Shorey	36	1.00
5	James Harper	37	0.97
6	Stephen Hunt	37	0.97
7	Kevin Doyle	34	0.97
8	Marcus Hahnemann	38	0.95
9	Liam Rosenior	12	0.92
10	David Kitson	26	0.88

KEY PLAYERS - DEFENDERS

Andre Bikey

Goals Conceded in the League Number of League goals conceded while the player was on the pitch	24
Goals Conceded in all competitions Total number of goals conceded while the player was on the pitch	30
League minutes played Number of minutes played in league matches	1370
Clean Sheets In games when the player was on pitch for at least 70 minutes	5
Defensive Rating Average number of mins between League goals conceded while on the pitch	57
Club Defensive Rating Average number of mins between League goals conceded by the club this season	51

	PLAYER	CON LGE	CON ALL	MINS	C SHEETS	DEF RATE
1	Andre Bikey	24	30	1370	5	57 mins
2	Michael Duberry	19	25	1022	4	53 mins
3	Ivar Ingimarsson	57	58	3003	8	52 mins
4	Nicky Shorey	61	66	3220	8	52 mins

KEY GOALKEEPER

Marcus Hahnemann

Goals Conceded in the League Number of League goals conceded while the player was on the pitch	66
Goals Conceded in all competitions Total number of goals conceded while the player was on the pitch	66
League minutes played Number of minutes played in league matches	3420
Clean Sheets In games when the player was on pitch for at least 70 minutes	8
Goals to Shots Ratio The average number of shots on target per each League goal conceded	4.59
Defensive Rating Ave mins between League goals conceded while on the pitch	51

BOOKINGS

Shane Long

League Yellow	5
League Red	0
All competitions Yellow	6
All competitions Red	0
League Average **154** mins between cards	

	PLAYER	LEAGUE		TOTAL		AVE
1	Shane Long	5Y	0R	6Y	0R	154
2	Andre Bikey	7	0	8	0	195
3	Marek Matejovsky	3	1	3	1	218
4	Kalifa Cisse	4	1	5	1	224
5	B Gunnarsson	3	1	3	1	374
6	Ibrahima Sonko	2	1	2	1	417
7	Ivar Ingimarsson	6	0	6	0	500
8	Michael Duberry	2	0	4	0	511
9	Stephen Hunt	6	0	6	0	552
10	Liam Rosenior	2	0	2	0	621
11	Nicky Shorey	5	0	5	0	644
12	Graeme Murty	3	0	3	0	806
13	David Kitson	2	1	2	1	841
14	Leroy Lita	1	0	2	0	891
15	John Oster	1	0	1	0	1018
	Other	6	0	7	0	
	TOTAL	58	5	65	5	

BIRMINGHAM CITY

Karen Brady has endured a year of police arrest without charges, relegation and fans' abuse; so where did Birmingham's board go wrong? "I have no doubt where the fault-line occurred. We allowed ourselves to believe Carson Yeung's takeover would be completed with little pain last December," Brady said. "The man from Hong Kong appeared to be a Chinese billionaire but turned out to be merely a wealthy poser." She blames Yeung for Steve Bruce's departure and feels the season would have turned out differently without the pre-Xmas distraction of changing managers. However, the players, the board and even the fans seem to believe in Alex McLeish and want him to take on the challenge of the Championship. Chairman David Gold said, "We've got great faith and we believe in Alex McLeish."

NICKNAME: THE BLUES

KEY: Won, Drawn, Lost

1	prem	**Chelsea**	A	L	2-3	Forssell 15, Kapo 36
2	prem	**Sunderland**	H	D	2-2	McShane 28 og, O'Connor 82
3	prem	**West Ham**	H	L	0-1	
4	prem	**Derby**	A	W	2-1	Jerome 1, 63
5	ccr2	**Hereford**	H	W	2-1	O'Connor 27, McSheffrey 38
6	prem	**Middlesbro**	A	L	0-2	
7	prem	**Bolton**	H	W	1-0	Kapo 37
8	prem	**Liverpool**	A	D	0-0	
9	ccr3	**Blackburn**	A	L	0-3	
10	prem	**Man Utd**	H	L	0-1	
11	prem	**Blackburn**	A	L	1-2	Jerome 68
12	prem	**Man City**	A	L	0-1	
13	prem	**Wigan**	H	W	3-2	Kapo 26 pen, 81, Ridgewell 67
14	prem	**Everton**	A	L	1-3	Kapo 79
15	prem	**Aston Villa**	H	L	1-2	Forssell 62
16	prem	**Portsmouth**	H	L	0-2	
17	prem	**Tottenham**	A	W	3-2	McSheffrey 24 pen, Jerome 62, Larsson 90
18	prem	**Newcastle**	A	L	1-2	Jerome 9
19	prem	**Reading**	H	D	1-1	Forssell 4
20	prem	**Bolton**	A	L	0-3	
21	prem	**Middlesbro**	H	W	3-0	Downing 21 og, Forssell 45, McSheffrey 90 pen
22	prem	**Fulham**	H	D	1-1	Larsson 55
23	prem	**Man Utd**	A	L	0-1	
24	facr3	**Huddersfield**	A	L	1-2	O'Connor 19
25	prem	**Arsenal**	A	D	1-1	O'Connor 48
26	prem	**Chelsea**	H	L	0-1	
27	prem	**Sunderland**	A	L	0-2	
28	prem	**Derby**	H	D	1-1	Larsson 68
29	prem	**West Ham**	A	D	1-1	McFadden 16 pen
30	prem	**Arsenal**	H	D	2-2	McFadden 28 , 90 pen
31	prem	**Tottenham**	H	W	4-1	Forssell 7, 59, 81, Larsson 55
32	prem	**Portsmouth**	A	L	2-4	Muamba 9, Larsson 39
33	prem	**Newcastle**	H	D	1-1	McFadden 33
34	prem	**Reading**	A	L	1-2	Zarate 64
35	prem	**Man City**	H	W	3-1	Zarate 40, 54, McSheffrey 76 pen
36	prem	**Wigan**	A	L	0-2	
37	prem	**Everton**	H	D	1-1	Zarate 83
38	prem	**Aston Villa**	A	L	1-5	Forssell 67
39	prem	**Liverpool**	H	D	2-2	Forssell 34, Larsson 55
40	prem	**Fulham**	A	L	0-2	
41	prem	**Blackburn**	H	W	4-1	Murphy 32, Jerome 73, 89, Muamba 90

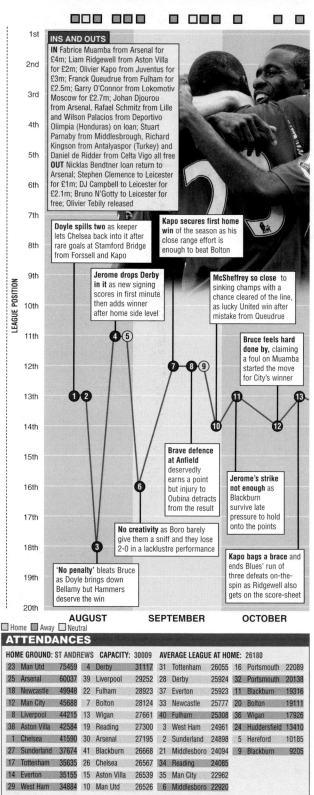

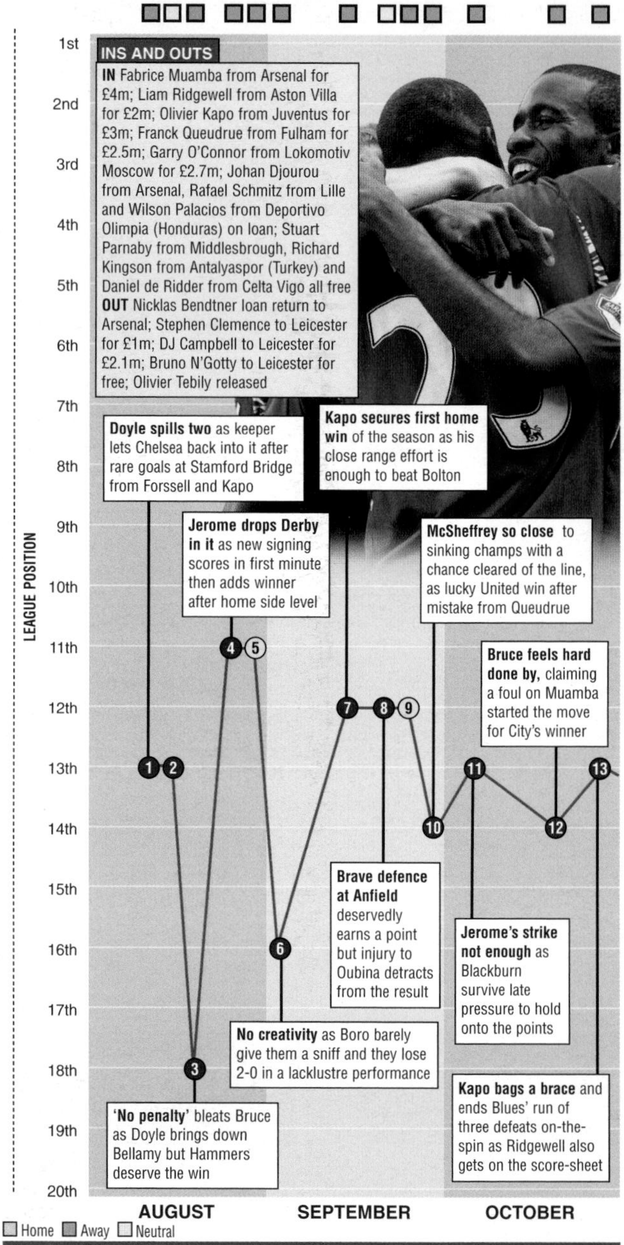

INS AND OUTS

IN Fabrice Muamba from Arsenal for £4m; Liam Ridgewell from Aston Villa for £2m; Olivier Kapo from Juventus for £3m; Franck Queudrue from Fulham for £2.5m; Garry O'Connor from Lokomotiv Moscow for £2.7m; Johan Djourou from Arsenal, Rafael Schmitz from Lille and Wilson Palacios from Deportivo Olimpia (Honduras) on loan; Stuart Parnaby from Middlesbrough, Richard Kingson from Antalyaspor (Turkey) and Daniel de Ridder from Celta Vigo all free
OUT Nicklas Bendtner loan return to Arsenal; Stephen Clemence to Leicester for £1m; DJ Campbell to Leicester for £2.1m; Bruno N'Gotty to Leicester for free; Olivier Tebily released

LEAGUE POSITION: 1st 2nd 3rd 4th 5th 6th 7th 8th 9th 10th 11th 12th 13th 14th 15th 16th 17th 18th 19th 20th

AUGUST SEPTEMBER OCTOBER

Home Away Neutral

Doyle spills two as keeper lets Chelsea back into it after rare goals at Stamford Bridge from Forssell and Kapo

'No penalty' bleats Bruce as Doyle brings down Bellamy but Hammers deserve the win

Jerome drops Derby in it as new signing scores in first minute then adds winner after home side level

No creativity as Boro barely give them a sniff and they lose 2-0 in a lacklustre performance

Kapo secures first home win of the season as his close range effort is enough to beat Bolton

Brave defence at Anfield deservedly earns a point but injury to Oubina detracts from the result

McSheffrey so close to sinking champs with a chance cleared of the line, as lucky United win after mistake from Queudrue

Jerome's strike not enough as Blackburn survive late pressure to hold onto the points

Bruce feels hard done by, claiming a foul on Muamba started the move for City's winner

Kapo bags a brace and ends Blues' run of three defeats on-the-spin as Ridgewell also gets on the score-sheet

ATTENDANCES

HOME GROUND: ST ANDREWS **CAPACITY:** 30009 **AVERAGE LEAGUE AT HOME:** 26180

23	Man Utd	75459	4	Derby	31117	31	Tottenham	26055	16	Portsmouth	22089
25	Arsenal	60037	39	Liverpool	29252	28	Derby	25924	32	Portsmouth	20138
18	Newcastle	49948	22	Fulham	28923	37	Everton	25923	11	Blackburn	19316
12	Man City	45688	7	Bolton	28124	33	Newcastle	25777	20	Bolton	19111
8	Liverpool	44215	13	Wigan	27661	40	Fulham	25308	36	Wigan	17926
38	Aston Villa	42584	19	Reading	27300	3	West Ham	24961	24	Huddersfield	13410
1	Chelsea	41590	30	Arsenal	27195	2	Sunderland	24898	5	Hereford	10185
27	Sunderland	37674	41	Blackburn	26668	21	Middlesboro	24094	9	Blackburn	9205
17	Tottenham	35635	26	Chelsea	26567	34	Reading	24085			
14	Everton	35155	15	Aston Villa	26539	35	Man City	22962			
29	West Ham	34884	10	Man Utd	26526	6	Middlesboro	22920			

'Yeung caused relegation,' says Brady

Final Position: **19th**

KEY: League, Champions Lge, UEFA Cup, FA Cup, League Cup, Other

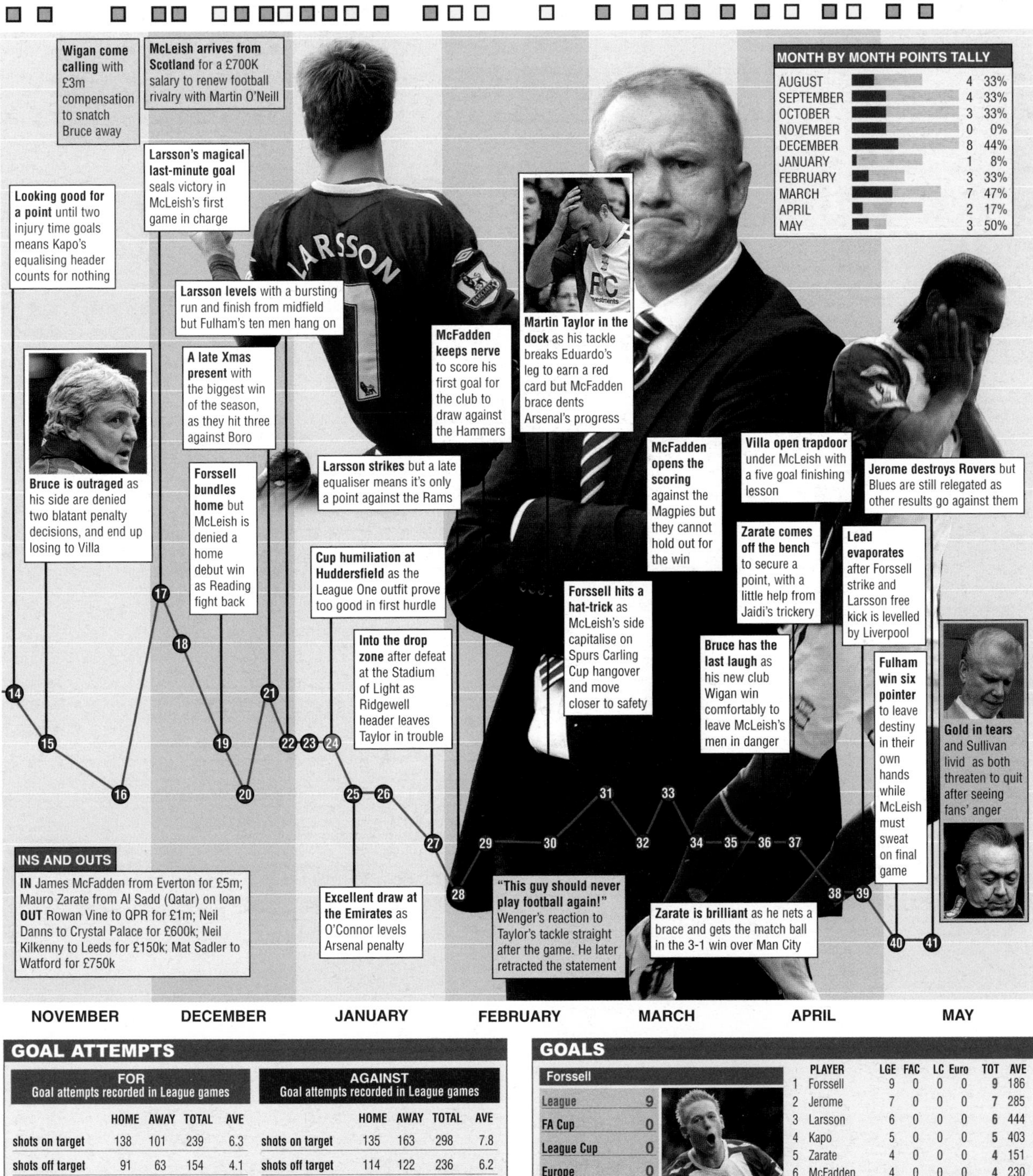

Wigan come calling with £3m compensation to snatch Bruce away
McLeish arrives from Scotland for a £700K salary to renew football rivalry with Martin O'Neill
Larsson's magical last-minute goal seals victory in McLeish's first game in charge
Looking good for a point until two injury time goals means Kapo's equalising header counts for nothing
Larsson levels with a bursting run and finish from midfield but Fulham's ten men hang on
A late Xmas present with the biggest win of the season, as they hit three against Boro
McFadden keeps nerve to score his first goal for the club to draw against the Hammers
Martin Taylor in the dock as his tackle breaks Eduardo's leg to earn a red card but McFadden brace dents Arsenal's progress
Bruce is outraged as his side are denied two blatant penalty decisions, and end up losing to Villa
Forssell bundles home but McLeish is denied a home debut win as Reading fight back
Larsson strikes but a late equaliser means it's only a point against the Rams
Cup humiliation at Huddersfield as the League One outfit prove too good in first hurdle
Into the drop zone after defeat at the Stadium of Light as Ridgewell header leaves Taylor in trouble
McFadden opens the scoring against the Magpies but they cannot hold out for the win
Villa open trapdoor under McLeish with a five goal finishing lesson
Jerome destroys Rovers but Blues are still relegated as other results go against them
Zarate comes off the bench to secure a point, with a little help from Jaidi's trickery
Lead evaporates after Forssell strike and Larsson free kick is levelled by Liverpool
Forssell hits a hat-trick as McLeish's side capitalise on Spurs Carling Cup hangover and move closer to safety
Bruce has the last laugh as his new club Wigan win comfortably to leave McLeish's men in danger
Fulham win six pointer to leave destiny in their own hands while McLeish must sweat on final game
Gold in tears and Sullivan livid as both threaten to quit after seeing fans' anger
Excellent draw at the Emirates as O'Connor levels Arsenal penalty
"This guy should never play football again!" Wenger's reaction to Taylor's tackle straight after the game. He later retracted the statement
Zarate is brilliant as he nets a brace and gets the match ball in the 3-1 win over Man City
14 15 16 17 18 19 20 21 22 23 24 25 26 27 28 29 30 31 32 33 34 35 36 37 38 39 40 41
NOVEMBER DECEMBER JANUARY FEBRUARY MARCH APRIL MAY

INS AND OUTS

IN James McFadden from Everton for £5m; Mauro Zarate from Al Sadd (Qatar) on loan **OUT** Rowan Vine to QPR for £1m; Neil Danns to Crystal Palace for £600k; Neil Kilkenny to Leeds for £150k; Mat Sadler to Watford for £750k

MONTH BY MONTH POINTS TALLY

Month	Points	%
AUGUST	4	33%
SEPTEMBER	4	33%
OCTOBER	3	33%
NOVEMBER	0	0%
DECEMBER	8	44%
JANUARY	1	8%
FEBRUARY	3	33%
MARCH	7	47%
APRIL	2	17%
MAY	3	50%

GOAL ATTEMPTS

FOR
Goal attempts recorded in League games

	HOME	AWAY	TOTAL	AVE
shots on target	138	101	239	6.3
shots off target	91	63	154	4.1
TOTAL	229	164	393	10.3

Ratio of goals to shots Average number of shots on target per League goal scored: **5.2**

Accuracy rating Average percentage of total goal attempts which were on target: **60.8**

AGAINST
Goal attempts recorded in League games

	HOME	AWAY	TOTAL	AVE
shots on target	135	163	298	7.8
shots off target	114	122	236	6.2
TOTAL	249	285	534	14.1

Ratio of goals to shots Average number of shots on target per League goal scored: **4.8**

Accuracy rating Average percentage of total goal attempts which were on target: **55.8**

GOALS

Forssell

League	9
FA Cup	0
League Cup	0
Europe	0
Other	0
TOTAL	9

League Average **186** mins between goals

	PLAYER	LGE	FAC	LC	Euro	TOT	AVE
1	Forssell	9	0	0	0	9	186
2	Jerome	7	0	0	0	7	285
3	Larsson	6	0	0	0	6	444
4	Kapo	5	0	0	0	5	403
5	Zarate	4	0	0	0	4	151
6	McFadden	4	0	0	0	4	230
7	O'Connor	2	1	1	0	4	392
8	McSheffrey	3	0	1	0	4	681
9	Muamba	2	0	0	0	2	1599
10	Murphy	1	0	0	0	1	1260
11	Ridgewell	1	0	0	0	1	3105
	Other	0	0	0	0	0	
	TOTAL	44	1	2	0	47	

SQUAD APPEARANCES

Match	1	2	3	4	5	6	7	8	9	10	11	12	13	14	15	16	17	18	19	20	21	22	23	24	25	26	27	28	29	30	31	32	33	34	35	36	37	38	39	40	41
Venue	A	H	H	A	H	A	H	A	A	H	A	A	H	A	H	H	A	A	H	A	H	H	A	A	A	H	A	H	A	H	H	A	H	A	H	A	H	A	H	A	H
Competition	L	L	L	L	W	L	L	L	W	L	L	L	L	L	L	L	L	L	L	L	L	L	L	F	L	L	L	L	L	L	L	L	L	L	L	L	L	L	L	L	L
Result	L	D	L	W	W	L	W	D	L	L	L	L	W	L	L	L	W	L	D	L	W	D	L	L	D	L	L	D	D	D	W	L	D	L	W	L	D	L	D	L	W

Goalkeepers
Colin Doyle
Richard Kingson
Maik Taylor

Defenders
Johan Djourou
Radhi Jaidi
Stephen Kelly
David Murphy
Stuart Parnaby
Krystian Pearce
Franck Queudrue
Liam Ridgewell
Matthew Sadler
Rafael Schmitz
Martin Taylor

Midfielders
Neil Danns
Daniel de Ridder
David Howland
Damien Johnson
Olivier Kapo
Sebastian Larsson
Fabrice Muamba
Jordon Mutch
Mehdi Nafti
Borja Melendez Oubina
Wilson Palacios

Forwards
Sone Aluko
Mikael Forssell
Cameron Jerome
James McFadden
Gary McSheffrey
Garry O'Connor
Rowan Vine
Mauro Matias Zarate

KEY: On all match | On bench | Subbed or sent off (Counting game) | Subbed or sent off (playing less than 70 mins) | Subbed on from bench (Counting Game) | Subbed on (playing less than 70 mins) | Subbed on and then subbed or sent off (Counting Game) | Subbed on and then subbed or sent off (playing less than 70 min | Not in 16 | Injured | ✕ Suspended

KEY PLAYERS - GOALSCORERS

Mikael Forssell

Goals in the League	9
Goals in all competitions	9
Assists League goals scored by a team mate where the player delivered the final pass	3
Contribution to Attacking Power Average number of minutes between League team goals while on pitch	62
Player Strike Rate Average number of minutes between League goals scored by player	186
Club Strike Rate Average minutes between League goals scored by club	74

	PLAYER	GOALS LGE	GOALS ALL	ASSISTS	POWER	S RATE
1	Mikael Forssell	9	9	3	62	186 mins
2	Cameron Jerome	7	7	1	86	285 mins
3	Olivier Kapo	5	5	0	91	403 mins
4	Sebastian Larsson	6	6	5	72	444 mins

KEY PLAYERS - MIDFIELDERS

Damien Johnson

Goals in the League	0
Goals in all competitions	0
Assists League goals scored by a team mate where the player delivered the final pass	0
Defensive Rating Average number of mins between League goals conceded while on the pitch	58
Contribution to Attacking Power Average number of minutes between League team goals while on pitch	70
Scoring Difference Defensive Rating minus Contribution to Attacking Power	-12

	PLAYER	GOALS LGE	GOALS ALL	ASSISTS	DEF RATE	POWER	SC DIFF
1	Damien Johnson	0	0	0	58	70	-12 mins
2	Sebastian Larsson	6	6	5	59	72	-13 mins
3	Mehdi Nafti	0	0	2	56	70	-14 mins
4	Fabrice Muamba	2	2	1	51	74	-23 mins

PLAYER APPEARANCES

	AGE (on 01/07/08)	IN NAMED 16	APPEARANCES	COUNTING GAMES	MINUTES ON PITCH	APPEARANCES	MINUTES ON PITCH	THIS SEASON	HOME COUNTRY
Goalkeepers									
Colin Doyle	23	27	3	3	270	4	315	-	Rep of Ireland
Richard Kingson	30	11	1	1	90	3	225	-	Ghana
Maik Taylor	36	38	34	34	3060	35	3150	8	N Ireland
Defenders									
Johan Djourou	21	14	13	13	1155	13	1155	3	Switzerland
Radhi Jaidi	32	20	18	18	1620	20	1765	4	Tunisia
Stephen Kelly	24	38	38	38	3420	40	3600	4	Rep of Ireland
David Murphy	24	14	14	14	1260	14	1260	-	England
Stuart Parnaby	25	25	13	5	644	15	824	-	England
Krystian Pearce	18	0	0	0	0	0	0	-	England
Franck Queudrue	29	18	16	11	1213	17	1303	-	France
Liam Ridgewell	23	35	35	34	3105	37	3285	-	England
Matthew Sadler	23	8	5	2	241	7	421	-	England
Rafael Schmitz	27	16	15	11	1075	16	1110	-	Brazil
Martin Taylor	28	5	4	3	254	5	344	-	England
Midfielders									
Neil Danns	25	5	2	0	23	4	203	-	England
Daniel de Ridder	24	12	10	5	578	12	749	-	Holland
David Howland	21	0	0	0	0	0	0	-	N Ireland
Damien Johnson	29	18	17	15	1412	18	1502	2	N Ireland
Olivier Kapo	27	26	26	20	2017	26	2017	-	France
Sebastian Larsson	23	36	35	26	2666	37	2846	1	Sweden
Fabrice Muamba	20	37	37	34	3199	38	3289	-	England
Jordon Mutch	16	0	0	0	0	0	0	-	England
Mehdi Nafti	29	32	26	19	1753	27	1826	3	Tunisia
Borja M Oubina	26	2	2	0	17	2	17	-	Spain
Wilson Palacios	23	7	7	2	338	8	347	-	Honduras
Forwards									
Sone Aluko	19	0	0	0	0	1	17	-	England
Mikael Forssell	27	33	30	15	1680	32	1831	5	Finland
Cameron Jerome	21	37	33	18	1995	34	2024	-	England
James McFadden	25	12	12	10	923	12	923	5	Scotland
Gary McSheffrey	25	34	32	18	2044	34	2224	-	England
Garry O'Connor	25	30	23	5	784	26	1054	3	Scotland
Rowan Vine	25	2	0	0	0	2	180	-	England
Mauro Matias Zarate	21	15	14	4	607	14	607	-	Argentina

KEY: LEAGUE ALL COMPS CAPS (MAY FIFA RANKING)

TEAM OF THE SEASON

TAYLOR — CG 34 DR 56

KELLY — CG 38 DR 55

RIDGEWELL — CG 34 DR 57

JAIDI — CG 18 DR 52

QUEUDRUE — CG 11 DR 71

LARSSON — CG 26 SD -13

MUAMBA — CG 34 SD -23

NAFTI — CG 19 SD -14

JOHNSON — CG 15 SD -12

JEROME — CG 18 AP 86

FORSSELL — CG 15 SR 186

KEY: DR = Defensive Rate, SD = Scoring Difference AP = Attacking Power SR = Strike Rate, CG=Counting games – League games playing at least 70 minutes

TOP POINT EARNERS

Gary McSheffrey

Counting Games League games when player was on pitch for at least 70 minutes	18
Average points Average League points taken in Counting games	1.33
Club Average points Average points taken in League games	0.92

	PLAYER	GAMES	PTS
1	Gary McSheffrey	18	1.33
2	Mikael Forssell	15	1.20
3	Damien Johnson	15	1.20
4	David Murphy	14	1.07
5	Radhi Ben Abdelmajid JaÃ¯di	18	1.06
6	Cameron Jerome	18	1.06
7	Sebastian Larsson	26	1.00
8	Maik Taylor	34	1.00
9	Liam Ridgewell	34	0.94
10	Stephen Kelly	38	0.92

KEY PLAYERS - DEFENDERS

Franck Queudrue

Goals Conceded in the League Number of League goals conceded while the player was on the pitch	17
Goals Conceded in all competitions Total number of goals conceded while the player was on the pitch	19
League minutes played Number of minutes played in league matches	1213
Clean Sheets In games when the player was on pitch for at least 70 minutes	3
Defensive Rating Average number of mins between League goals conceded while on the pitch	71
Club Defensive Rating Average number of mins between League goals conceded by the club this season	55

	PLAYER	CON LGE	CON ALL	MINS	C SHEETS	DEF RATE
1	Franck Queudrue	17	19	1213	3	71 mins
2	Liam Ridgewell	54	57	3105	3	57 mins
3	Stephen Kelly	62	65	3420	3	55 mins
4	Radhi Jaidi	31	33	1620	1	52 mins

KEY GOALKEEPER

Maik Taylor

Goals Conceded in the League Number of League goals conceded while the player was on the pitch	54
Goals Conceded in all competitions Total number of goals conceded while the player was on the pitch	56
League minutes played Number of minutes played in league matches	3060
Clean Sheets In games when the player was on pitch for at least 70 minutes	3
Goals to Shots Ratio The average number of shots on target per each League goal conceded	5.04
Defensive Rating Ave mins between League goals conceded while on the pitch	56

BOOKINGS

Mehdi Nafti

League Yellow	8
League Red	0
All competitions Yellow	8
All competitions Red	0

League Average 219 mins between cards

	PLAYER	LEAGUE		TOTAL		AVE
1	Mehdi Nafti	8Y	0R	8Y	0R	219
2	Damien Johnson	5	1	5	1	235
3	Franck Queudrue	3	1	4	1	303
4	Liam Ridgewell	10	0	11	0	310
5	Stuart Parnaby	2	0	2	0	322
6	Olivier Kapo	5	0	5	0	403
7	Radhi Jaidi	4	0	6	0	405
8	James McFadden	2	0	2	0	461
9	Gary McSheffrey	4	0	4	0	511
10	Sebastian Larsson	5	0	5	0	533
11	Rafael Schmitz	2	0	2	0	537
12	Daniel de Ridder	1	0	1	0	578
13	Mauro Zarate	1	0	1	0	607
14	David Murphy	2	0	2	0	630
15	Fabrice Muamba	5	0	5	0	639
	Other	6	0	6	0	
	TOTAL	65	2	69	2	

DERBY COUNTY

Derby endured a record-breaking season - for all the wrong reasons. Billy Davies started at the helm and back in September recorded a 1-0 victory over Newcastle, a win that would prove to be Derby's only three pointer this campaign. Paul Jewell replaced Davies, but he was unable to rescue the season and Derby ended the campaign on a record low of 11 points. Most of this season has been about planning for next with the new US owners and Jewell has been very frank about his intentions to establish Derby as a yoyo team. So money spent on players of a Championship calibre might prove better value long term. Sunderland spent £40m and stayed in the league and it may be the sad fact that Derby never had enough money available to cement top-flight football.

NICKNAME: THE RAMS

KEY: Won / Drawn / Lost

1	prem	**Portsmouth**	H	D	2-2	Oakley 5, Todd 84
2	prem	**Man City**	A	L	0-1	
3	prem	**Tottenham**	A	L	0-4	
4	prem	**Birmingham**	H	L	1-2	Oakley 52
5	ccr2	**Blackpool**	H	L	6-7*	Camara 63, Fagan 101 (*on penalties)
6	prem	**Liverpool**	A	L	0-6	
7	prem	**Newcastle**	H	W	1-0	Miller 38
8	prem	**Arsenal**	A	L	0-5	
9	prem	**Bolton**	H	D	1-1	Miller 19
10	prem	**Reading**	A	L	0-1	
11	prem	**Fulham**	A	D	0-0	
12	prem	**Everton**	H	L	0-2	
13	prem	**Aston Villa**	A	L	0-2	
14	prem	**West Ham**	H	L	0-5	
15	prem	**Chelsea**	H	L	0-2	
16	prem	**Sunderland**	A	L	0-1	
17	prem	**Man Utd**	A	L	1-4	Howard 76
18	prem	**Middlesbro**	H	L	0-1	
19	prem	**Newcastle**	A	D	2-2	Barnes 6, Miller 52
20	prem	**Liverpool**	H	L	1-2	McEveley 67
21	prem	**Blackburn**	H	L	1-2	Oakley 27
22	prem	**Bolton**	A	L	0-1	
23	facr3	**Sheff Wed**	H	D	2-2	Miller 38, Barnes 45
24	prem	**Wigan**	H	L	0-1	
25	prem	**Portsmouth**	A	L	1-3	Nyatanga 4
26	facr3	**Sheff Wed**	A	W	4-2*	Miller 47 (*on penalties)
27	facr4	**Preston**	H	L	1-4	Earnshaw 55
28	prem	**Man City**	H	D	1-1	Sun Jihai 46 og
29	prem	**Birmingham**	A	D	1-1	Villa 89
30	prem	**Tottenham**	H	L	0-3	
31	prem	**Wigan**	A	L	0-2	
32	prem	**Sunderland**	H	D	0-0	
33	prem	**Chelsea**	A	L	1-6	D.Jones 73
34	prem	**Man Utd**	H	L	0-1	
35	prem	**Middlesbro**	A	L	0-1	
36	prem	**Fulham**	H	D	2-2	Villa 10, 80
37	prem	**Everton**	A	L	0-1	
38	prem	**Aston Villa**	H	L	0-6	
39	prem	**West Ham**	A	L	1-2	Mears 65
40	prem	**Arsenal**	H	L	2-6	McEveley 31, Earnshaw 77
41	prem	**Blackburn**	A	L	1-3	Miller 19
42	prem	**Reading**	H	L	0-4	

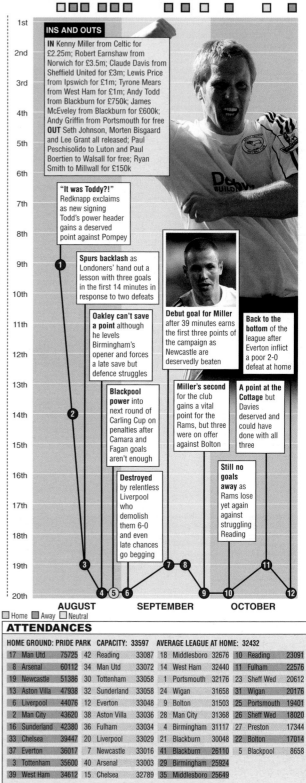

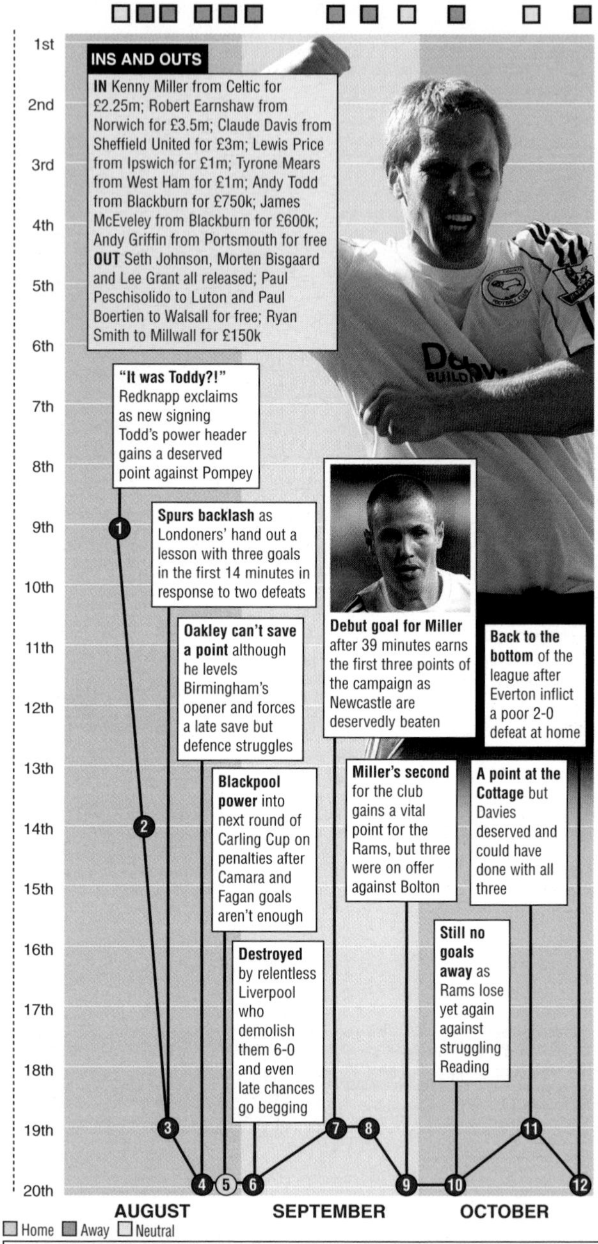

INS AND OUTS

IN Kenny Miller from Celtic for £2.25m; Robert Earnshaw from Norwich for £3.5m; Claude Davis from Sheffield United for £3m; Lewis Price from Ipswich for £1m; Tyrone Mears from West Ham for £1m; Andy Todd from Blackburn for £750k; James McEveley from Blackburn for £600k; Andy Griffin from Portsmouth for free **OUT** Seth Johnson, Morten Bisgaard and Lee Grant all released; Paul Peschisolido to Luton and Paul Boertien to Walsall for free; Ryan Smith to Millwall for £150k

1st 2nd 3rd 4th 5th 6th 7th 8th 9th 10th 11th 12th 13th 14th 15th 16th 17th 18th 19th 20th

AUGUST SEPTEMBER OCTOBER

"It was Toddy?!" Redknapp exclaims as new signing Todd's power header gains a deserved point against Pompey

Spurs backlash as Londoners' hand out a lesson with three goals in the first 14 minutes in response to two defeats

Oakley can't save a point although he levels Birmingham's opener and forces a late save but defence struggles

Blackpool power into next round of Carling Cup on penalties after Camara and Fagan goals aren't enough

Destroyed by relentless Liverpool who demolish them 6-0 and even late chances go begging

Debut goal for Miller after 39 minutes earns the first three points of the campaign as Newcastle are deservedly beaten

Miller's second for the club gains a vital point for the Rams, but three were on offer against Bolton

Still no goals away as Rams lose yet again against struggling Reading

A point at the Cottage but Davies deserved and could have done with all three

Back to the bottom of the league after Everton inflict a poor 2-0 defeat at home

Home / Away / Neutral

ATTENDANCES

HOME GROUND: PRIDE PARK CAPACITY: 33597 AVERAGE LEAGUE AT HOME: 32432

17	Man Utd	75725	42	Reading	33087	18	Middlesbro	32676	10	Reading	23091
8	Arsenal	60112	34	Man Utd	33072	14	West Ham	32440	11	Fulham	22576
19	Newcastle	51386	30	Tottenham	33058	1	Portsmouth	32176	23	Sheff Wed	20612
13	Aston Villa	47938	32	Sunderland	33058	24	Wigan	31658	31	Wigan	20176
6	Liverpool	44076	12	Everton	33048	9	Bolton	31503	25	Portsmouth	19401
2	Man City	43620	38	Aston Villa	33036	28	Man City	31368	26	Sheff Wed	18020
16	Sunderland	42380	36	Fulham	33034	4	Birmingham	31117	27	Preston	17344
33	Chelsea	39447	20	Liverpool	33029	21	Blackburn	30048	22	Bolton	17014
37	Everton	36017	7	Newcastle	33016	41	Blackburn	26110	5	Blackpool	8658
3	Tottenham	35600	40	Arsenal	33003	29	Birmingham	25924			
39	West Ham	34612	15	Chelsea	32789	35	Middlesbro	25649			

Derby hope yoyo future proves best for them

Final Position: **20th**

KEY: ● League ● Champions Lge ● UEFA Cup ● FA Cup ○ League Cup ● Other

INS AND OUTS

IN Robbie Savage from Blackburn for £1.5m; Hossam Ghaly from Tottenham, Danny Mills from Man City and Roy Carroll from Rangers on loan; Alan Stubbs from Everton and Mile Sterjovski from Genclerbirligi (Turkey) for free; Lewin Nytanga from Barnsley loan return **OUT** Mo Camara to Norwich on loan; Andy Griffin to Stoke for £300k; Steve Howard to Leicester for £1.25m; Matt Oakley to Leicester for £500k; Steven Bywater to Ipswich on loan

Savage leads new signings as Jewell goes for steel

Davies sacked after just one win as chairman Pearson is angered by 'lack of investment' comments

Howard's penalty miss, proves costly as it would have added to Oakley's early goal, instead Rovers take control

Carroll concedes three on his debut as Spurs apply late pressure

Relegated in record time as the Rams become the worst Premier team ever despite a point against Fulham

Former Wigan boss Jewell in his first game in charge as Sunderland score late on

Torres steals a late winner just as it looks as though the Rams are going to hold on

Bywater holds out for nearly an hour before Villa breakthrough and Earnshaw looks dangerous

Early away goal from Nyatanga gives hope to the away fans but Mwaruwari hits a hat-trick after Mills is injured

Price is the hero after two penalty saves earns Fagan the chance to win shoot-out in Sheffield

Carroll defies Ronaldo for eight attempts on goal but the ninth wins it in one of Jewell's best performances

Jewell suffers defeat in his first game in charge as Sunderland score late on

Hit for six at the Bridge as four-goal Lampard tears the Rams' back line apart

No goals for 521 minutes as Hammers run up five to dent Pride Park

Back from the dead as Miller and Barnes goals ensure cup recovery from two down against Wednesday

Rams end losing streak with a point against City and Jewell says 'it's much better from his players'

"Disgrace" says Jewell after his side only manage three shots at the JJB and slump against his former club

Sub Adebayor hits hat-trick in another six goal hammering but McEverley and Earnshaw both score

Miller's breakaway catches Rovers cold but home side take control second half

Miller's 'goal' ruled offside but TV replays show it was good as Chelsea take the points

Barnes and Miller find the net and only a late Viduka strike prevents a win at St James' Park

Hit for six for the third time this season as six different Villa players find the net

Fans turn on players as even Championship-bound Reading are in a different class

MONTH BY MONTH POINTS TALLY

Month	Points	%
AUGUST	1	8%
SEPTEMBER	4	33%
OCTOBER	1	11%
NOVEMBER	0	0%
DECEMBER	1	6%
JANUARY	1	8%
FEBRUARY	1	11%
MARCH	2	13%
APRIL	0	0%
MAY	0	0%

13 14 15 16 17 18 19 20 21 22 23 24 25 26 27 28 29 30 31 32 33 34 35 36 37 38 39 40 41 42

NOVEMBER DECEMBER JANUARY FEBRUARY MARCH APRIL MAY

GOAL ATTEMPTS

FOR – Goal attempts recorded in League games

	HOME	AWAY	TOTAL	AVE
shots on target	109	85	194	5.1
shots off target	88	63	151	4.0
TOTAL	197	148	345	9.1

Ratio of goals to shots Average number of shots on target per League goal scored	9.7
Accuracy rating Average percentage of total goal attempts which were on target	56.2

AGAINST – Goal attempts recorded in League games

	HOME	AWAY	TOTAL	AVE
shots on target	142	167	309	8.1
shots off target	111	144	255	6.7
TOTAL	253	311	564	14.8

Ratio of goals to shots Average number of shots on target per League goal scored	3.5
Accuracy rating Average percentage of total goal attempts which were on target	54.8

GOALS

Miller

League	4
FA Cup	2
League Cup	0
Europe	0
Other	0
TOTAL	6

League Average **641** mins between goals

	PLAYER	LGE	FAC	LC	Euro	TOT	AVE
1	Miller	4	2	0	0	6	641
2	Villa	3	0	0	0	3	305
3	Oakley	3	0	0	0	3	556
4	Earnshaw	1	1	0	0	2	939
5	McEveley	2	0	0	0	2	958
6	Barnes	1	1	0	0	2	1382
7	Nyatanga	1	0	0	0	1	180
8	Jones, D	1	0	0	0	1	864
9	Todd	1	0	0	0	1	1361
10	Howard	1	0	0	0	1	1395
11	Mears	1	0	0	0	1	2009
12	Camara	0	0	1	0	1	
13	Fagan	0	0	1	0	1	
	Other	0	0	0	0	0	
	TOTAL	19	4	2	0	25	

SQUAD APPEARANCES

Match	1	2	3	4	5	6	7	8	9	10	11	12	13	14	15	16	17	18	19	20	21	22	23	24	25	26	27	28	29	30	31	32	33	34	35	36	37	38	39	40	41	42
Venue	H	A	A	H	H	A	H	A	H	A	A	H	A	H	H	A	A	H	A	H	H	A	H	H	A	A	H	H	A	H	A	H	A	H	A	H	A	H	A	H	A	H
Competition	L	L	L	L	W	L	L	L	L	L	L	L	L	L	L	L	L	L	L	L	L	L	F	L	L	F	F	L	L	L	L	L	L	L	L	L	L	L	L	L	L	L
Result	D	L	L	L	L	L	W	L	D	L	D	L	L	L	L	L	L	L	D	L	L	L	D	L	L	W	L	D	D	L	L	D	L	L	L	D	L	L	L	L	L	L

Goalkeepers
- Stephen Bywater
- Roy Carroll
- Ben Hinchliffe
- Lewis Price

Defenders
- Miles Addison
- Jason Beardsley
- Mohammed Camara
- Claude Davis
- Marc Edworthy
- Andrew Griffin
- Michael Johnson
- Dean Leacock
- Robert Malcolm
- James McEveley
- Tyrone Mears
- Danny Mills
- Darren Moore
- Lewin Nyatanga
- Alan Stubbs
- Andy Todd

Midfielders
- Giles Barnes
- Benny Feilhaber
- Hossam Ghaly
- Lee Holmes
- David Jones
- Eddie Lewis
- Matthew Oakley
- Stephen Pearson
- Laurent Robert
- Robbie Savage
- Paris Simmons
- Mile Sterjovski
- Gary Teale

Forwards
- Robert Earnshaw
- Craig Fagan
- Steven Howard
- Jonathan Macken
- Kenny Miller
- Emanuel Alejandro Villa

KEY: On all match | On bench | Subbed or sent off (Counting game) | Subbed or sent off (playing less than 70 mins) | Subbed on from bench (Counting Game) | Subbed on (playing less than 70 mins) | Subbed on and then subbed or sent off (Counting Game) | Subbed on and then subbed or sent off (playing less than 70 min | Not in 16 | Injured | ✕ Suspended

KEY PLAYERS - GOALSCORERS

Matthew Oakley

Goals in the League	3
Goals in all competitions	3
Assists League goals scored by a team mate where the player delivered the final pass	0
Contribution to Attacking Power Average number of minutes between League team goals while on pitch	238
Player Strike Rate Average number of minutes between League goals scored by player	556
Club Strike Rate Average minutes between League goals scored by club	171

	PLAYER	GOALS LGE	GOALS ALL	ASSISTS	POWER	S RATE
1	Matthew Oakley	3	3	0	238	**556 mins**
2	Kenny Miller	4	6	3	183	**641 mins**
3	Giles Barnes	1	2	1	276	**1382 mins**
4	Steven Howard	1	1	3	139	**1395 mins**

KEY PLAYERS - MIDFIELDERS

Robbie Savage

Goals in the League	0
Goals in all competitions	0
Assists League goals scored by a team mate where the player delivered the final pass	1
Defensive Rating Average number of mins between League goals conceded while on the pitch	35
Contribution to Attacking Power Average number of minutes between League team goals while on pitch	135
Scoring Difference Defensive Rating minus Contribution to Attacking Power	-100

	PLAYER	GOALS LGE	GOALS ALL	ASSISTS	DEF RATE	POWER	SC DIFF
1	Robbie Savage	0	0	1	35	135	**-100 mins**
2	Eddie Lewis	0	0	1	38	146	**-108 mins**
3	Stephen Pearson	0	0	0	39	199	**-160 mins**
4	Matthew Oakley	3	3	0	41	238	**-197 mins**

PLAYER APPEARANCES

	AGE (on 01/07/08)	IN NAMED 16	APPEARANCES	COUNTING GAMES	MINUTES ON PITCH	APPEARANCES	MINUTES ON PITCH	THIS SEASON	HOME COUNTRY
Goalkeepers									
Stephen Bywater	27	18	18	18	1620	19	1740	-	England
Roy Carroll	30	14	14	14	1260	14	1260	-	N Ireland
Ben Hinchliffe	19	6	0	0	0	0	0	-	England
Lewis Price	23	34	6	6	540	9	840	3	Wales
Defenders									
Miles Addison	19	2	1	1	90	1	90	-	England
Jason Beardsley	18	3	0	0	0	1	60	-	England
Mohammed Camara	33	1	1	0	62	2	142	-	Guinea
Claude Davis	29	19	19	15	1533	21	1743	4	Jamaica
Marc Edworthy	35	11	9	6	659	11	869	-	England
Andrew Griffin	29	16	15	12	1148	15	1148	-	England
Michael Johnson	34	4	3	1	192	4	251	-	Jamaica
Dean Leacock	24	28	26	21	2000	28	2201	-	England
Robert Malcolm	27	1	1	0	58	2	178	-	Scotland
James McEveley	23	31	29	19	1917	30	2037	-	England
Tyrone Mears	25	28	25	21	2009	26	2040	-	England
Danny Mills	31	2	2	1	121	3	211	-	England
Darren Moore	34	33	31	25	2466	34	2715	-	Jamaica
Lewin Nyatanga	19	2	2	2	180	4	389	7	Wales
Alan Stubbs	36	8	8	7	646	8	646	-	England
Andy Todd	33	21	19	13	1361	23	1676	-	England
Midfielders									
Giles Barnes	19	21	21	13	1382	24	1558	-	England
Benny Feilhaber	23	17	10	0	298	10	298	2	United States
Hossam Ghaly	26	16	15	9	1104	16	1194	-	Egypt
Lee Holmes	21	1	0	0	0	0	0	-	England
David Jones	23	20	14	6	864	15	984	-	England
Eddie Lewis	34	27	24	19	1905	27	2097	2	United States
Matthew Oakley	30	19	19	18	1669	20	1759	-	England
Stephen Pearson	25	24	24	21	1994	27	2244	3	Scotland
Laurent Robert	33	6	4	0	180	4	180	-	France
Robbie Savage	33	16	16	14	1350	17	1440	-	Wales
Paris Simmons	18	1	1	0	28	1	28	-	England
Mile Sterjovski	29	12	12	5	689	12	689	-	Australia
Gary Teale	29	20	18	5	918	22	1294	2	Scotland
Forwards									
Robert Earnshaw	27	32	22	6	939	25	1063	4	Wales
Craig Fagan	25	23	22	13	1482	25	1812	-	England
Steven Howard	32	20	20	13	1395	21	1451	-	England
Jonathan Macken	30	4	3	0	44	4	50	-	Rep of Ireland
Kenny Miller	28	30	30	29	2567	33	2867	4	Scotland
Emanuel A Villa	26	17	16	8	917	17	962	-	Argentina

KEY: LEAGUE ALL COMPS CAPS (MAY FIFA RANKING)

TEAM OF THE SEASON

BYWATER CG 18 DR 39

DAVIS CG 15 DR 49

MOORE CG 25 DR 39

LEACOCK CG 21 DR 41

MCEVELEY CG 19 DR 39

PEARSON CG 21 SD -160

OAKLEY CG 18 SD -197

SAVAGE CG 14 SD -100

LEWIS CG 19 SD -108

HOWARD CG 13 AP 139

MILLER CG 29 SR 641

KEY: DR = Defensive Rate, SD = Scoring Difference AP = Attacking Power SR = Strike Rate, CG=Counting games – League games playing at least 70 minutes

TOP POINT EARNERS

Steven Howard

Counting Games League games when player was on pitch for at least 70 minutes	13
Average points Average League points taken in Counting games	0.46
Club Average points Average points taken in League games	0.29

	PLAYER	GAMES	PTS
1	Steven Howard	13	0.46
2	Dean Leacock	21	0.43
3	Stephen Pearson	21	0.43
4	Eddie Lewis	19	0.42
5	Claude Davis	15	0.40
6	Stephen Bywater	18	0.39
7	Matthew Oakley	18	0.33
8	Andrew Griffin	12	0.33
9	Tyrone Mears	21	0.33
10	Kenny Miller	29	0.31

KEY PLAYERS - DEFENDERS

Claude Davis

Goals Conceded in the League Number of League goals conceded while the player was on the pitch	31
Goals Conceded in all competitions Total number of goals conceded while the player was on the pitch	36
League minutes played Number of minutes played in league matches	1533
Clean Sheets In games when the player was on pitch for at least 70 minutes	1
Defensive Rating Average number of mins between League goals conceded while on the pitch	49
Club Defensive Rating Average number of mins between League goals conceded by the club this season	38

	PLAYER	CON LGE	CON ALL	MINS	C SHEETS	DEF RATE
1	Claude Davis	31	36	1533	1	49 mins
2	Dean Leacock	48	51	2000	2	41 mins
3	James McEveley	49	51	1917	2	39 mins
4	Darren Moore	62	66	2466	2	39 mins

KEY GOALKEEPER

Stephen Bywater

Goals Conceded in the League Number of League goals conceded while the player was on the pitch	41
Goals Conceded in all competitions Total number of goals conceded while the player was on the pitch	43
League minutes played Number of minutes played in league matches	1620
Clean Sheets In games when the player was on pitch for at least 70 minutes	2
Goals to Shots Ratio The average number of shots on target per each League goal conceded	3.32
Defensive Rating Ave mins between League goals conceded while on the pitch	39

BOOKINGS

David Jones

League Yellow	4
League Red	0
All competitions Yellow	4
All competitions Red	0
League Average 216 mins between cards	

	PLAYER	LEAGUE Y	LEAGUE R	TOTAL Y	TOTAL R	AVE
1	David Jones	4	0	4	0	216
2	Craig Fagan	6	0	6	0	247
3	Andrew Griffin	4	0	4	0	287
4	Emanuel Villa	3	0	3	0	305
5	James McEveley	6	0	6	0	319
6	Robbie Savage	4	0	4	0	337
7	Claude Davis	3	1	3	1	383
8	Steven Howard	3	0	3	0	465
9	Darren Moore	5	0	5	0	493
10	Hossam Ghaly	2	0	2	0	552
11	Matthew Oakley	3	0	3	0	556
12	Eddie Lewis	3	0	3	0	635
13	Kenny Miller	4	0	4	0	641
14	Alan Stubbs	1	0	1	0	646
15	Marc Edworthy	1	0	2	0	659
	Other	9	0	13	0	
	TOTAL	61	1	66	1	

THE AXA FA CUP

1ST ROUND

Hereford 0 **Leeds** 0
5,924

Accrington 2 **Huddersfield** 3
Cavanagh 12, Mullin 25 — Kamara 45, 83, Beckett 89
2,202

Altrincham 1 **Millwall** 2
Senior 45 — Dunne 53 pen, Hoskins 62
2,457

Barnet 2 **Gillingham** 1
Yakubu 61, Hatch 63 — Graham 27
2,843

Barrow 1 **Bournemouth** 1
Rapley 19 — Karacan 45
2,203

Billericay 1 **Swansea** 2
Semanshia 26 — Bauza 59, 83
2,334

Bradford 1 **Chester** 0
Thorne 28
4,069

Bury 4 **Workington** 1
Scott 22, Bishop 80, 85, 90 — Berkeley 75
2,641

Cambridge 2 **Aldershot** 1
Boylan 62, Fortune-West 85 — Dixon 31
3,457

Carlisle 1 **Grimsby** 1
Aranalde 85 pen — Bolland 28
5,128

Cheltenham 1 **Brighton** 1
Gillespie 78 — Loft 90
2,984

Chesterfield 1 **Tranmere** 2
Lester 29 — Greenacre 37 pen, Kay 84
4,296

Crewe 2 **MK Dons** 1
McCready 3, Cox 65 — Johnson 69 pen
3,049

Darlington 1 **Northampton** 1
Blundell 8 — Larkin 26
2,696

Eastbourne 0 **Weymouth** 4
2,711 — Louis 54, Beavon 81, 85, 88

Exeter 4 **Stevenage** 0
Carlisle 18, Mackie 40, Basham 60 pen, Taylor 67
3,513

Halifax 0 **Burton** 4
1,936 — Clare 26, 63, McGrath 47, 73

Hampton 0 **Dag & Red** 3
2,252 — Benson 68, Huke 83, Strevens 90

Harrogate Railway 2 **Droylsden** 0
Littlefair 65, Haigh 69
884

Horsham 4 **Maidenhead** 1
Brake 45, Carney 62, 83, Farrell 90 — Lee 64 pen
3,379

Leyton Orient 1 **Bristol Rovers** 1
Gray 16 — Lambert 81
3,157

Lincoln 1 **Nottm Forest** 1
Wilson 38 og — McGugan 25
7,361

Luton 1 **Brentford** 1
Andrew 79 — Ide 20
4,167

Mansfield 3 **Lewes** 0
M.Boulding 33, R.Boulding 40, Holmes 82
2,607

Morecambe 0 **Port Vale** 2
2,730 — Pilkington 6, Willock 22

Notts County 3 **Histon** 0
Dudfield 48, 88, Sam 73
4,344

Oldham 2 **Doncaster** 2
Trotman 32, C.Davies 49 — Hayter 63, 86
4,280

Oxford 3 **Northwich** 1
Jeannin 7, Odubade 45 pen, Anaclet 86 — C.Williams 39
2,972

Peterborough 4 **Wrexham** 1
Mackail-Smith 2, 41, 53, McLean 88 — N.Roberts 66
4,266

Rushden & D 3 **Macclesfield** 1
Jackson 6, 58, Challinor 45 — Gritton 76
1,759

Southend 2 **Rochdale** 1
Bailey 1, Harrold 24 pen — Le Fondre 12
5,180

Stockport 1 **Staines Town** 1
McNeil 47 — Charles-Smith 76
3,460

Team Bath 0 **Chasetown** 2
2,067 — Thomas 11, Holland 30

Walsall 2 **Shrewsbury** 0
Ricketts 10, Demontagnac 66
4,972

Ware 0 **Kidderminster** 2
982 — Blackwood 76, Constable 80

Wycombe 1 **Swindon** 2
Bloomfield 83 — Roberts 66, Paynter 72
3,332

York 0 **Havant & W** 1
2,001 — Harkin 24

Forest Green 2 **Rotherham** 2
Fleetwood 32, 45 — Brogan 57 pen, O'Grady 84
2,102

Gainsborough 0 **Hartlepool** 6
2,402 — Barker 8, 25, Liddle 51, Moore 70, Brown 76, Porter 82

Torquay 4 **Yeovil** 1
Todd 43, 64, Stevens 45, 89 — Stewart 20
3,718

FA 1st Round replay

Bournemouth 3 **Barrow** 2
Golbourne 43, Gradel 90 pen, Hollands 120 — Rogan 55, Walker 63
2,969

Brighton 2 **Cheltenham** 1
El-Abd 18, Hammond 69 pen — Gillespie 65
3,711

Grimsby 1 **Carlisle** 0
Jones 62
2,008

Leeds 0 **Hereford** 1
11,315 — Ainsworth 3

Northampton 2 **Darlington** 1
Kirk 36, Bradley.Johnson 41 — Wright 90
2,895

Rotherham 0 **Forest Green** 3
2,754 — Giles 28, Clist 54, Fleetwood 87

Staines Town 1 **Stockport** 1
Toppin 10 — McNeil 78
Staines win 4-3 on penalties
2,860

Brentford 0 **Luton** 2
Coyne 36, Fojut 61
2,643

Bristol Rovers 3 **Leyton Orient** 3
Hinton 2, Lambert 90 pen, Disley 111 — Boyd 28, 92 pen, Gray 55
Bristol won 6-5 on penalties
3,742

Doncaster 1 **Oldham** 2
McCammon 26 — Kilkenny 45, McDonald 49
4,340

Nottm Forest 3 **Lincoln** 1
Commons 35, Tyson 49, 61 — Forrester 71
6,783

2ND ROUND

Horsham 1 **Swansea** 1
Taylor 85 pen — Bauza 41
2,731

Bradford 0 **Tranmere** 3
6,379 — Jennings 7, Greenacre 37, 68

Bristol Rovers 5 **Rushden & D** 1
Williams 33, Disley 35, Hinton 51, Lambert 54, 87 — Kelly 11
4,816

Burton 1 **Barnet** 1
Stride 86 — Hatch 19
2,769

Bury 1 **Exeter** 0
Adams 79
2,725

Cambridge 1 **Weymouth** 0
Rendell 26 pen
4,552

Dag & Red 3 **Kidderminster** 1
Benson 33, 90, Strevens 85 — Creighton 14
1,493

Hereford 2 **Hartlepool** 0
McCombe 45, Robinson 85
3,801

Huddersfield 3 **Grimsby** 0
Jevons 52, 62, Beckett 85
6,729

Millwall 2 **Bournemouth** 1
Brkovic 50, Hoskins 55 — Cooper 74
4,495

Northampton 1 **Walsall** 1
Kirk 8 — Mooney 4
3,887

Notts County 0 **Havant & W** 1
3,810 — Taggart 87

Oldham 1 **Crewe** 0
Hughes 41
3,900

Oxford 0 **Southend** 0
5,162

Staines Town 0 **Peterborough** 5
2,460 — Mackail-Smith 10, 23, 53, 62, McLean 18

Swindon 3 **Forest Green** 2
McGovern 12, Aljofree 69, Sturrock 88 — Fleetwood 54, Beesley 66
7,588

Torquay 0 **Brighton** 2
4,010 — Forster 63, 90

Harrogate Railway 2 **Mansfield** 3
Davidson 61, 84 — Jelleyman 38, M.Boulding 51, 77
3,500

Port Vale 1 **Chasetown** 1
Rodgers 18 — Branch 44
5,875

Luton 1 **Nottm Forest** 0
Andrew 54
5,758

FA 2nd Round replay

Swansea 6 **Horsham** 2
Pratley 21, Britton 38, Scotland 42, Bodde 43, Robinson 56, Feeney 79 — Farrell 20, 23
5,911

Barnet 1 **Burton** 0
Birchall 83
1,379

Chasetown 1 **Port Vale** 0
Smith 89
1,986

Southend 3 **Oxford** 0
MacDonald 5, 90, Morgan 45 pen
2,740

Walsall 1 **Northampton** 0
Ricketts 85 pen
3,066

3RD ROUND

Aston Villa 0 **Man Utd** 2
33,630 — Ronaldo 81, Rooney 89

Barnsley 2 **Blackpool** 1
Foster 78, Coulson 81 — Fox 32
8,276

Blackburn 1 **Coventry** 4
Bentley 85 — Mifsud 34, 90, Ward 64 pen, Adebola 83
14,421

Bolton 0 **Sheff Utd** 1
15,286 — Carney 42

Brighton 1 **Mansfield** 2
Revell 23 — Hamshaw 10, Holmes 45
5,857

Expectations of an upset at Bristol proved unfounded as Boro fought back from a Liam Fontaine goal down. They needed a slice of luck when Stewart Downing's shot was spilled by Adriano Basso before David Wheater forced home a Lee Cattermole cross.

Bristol City 1 **Middlesbrough** 2
Fontaine 18 — Downing 37, Wheater 72
15,895

Charlton 1 **West Brom** 1
Z.Zheng 2 — Miller 34
12,682

Chasetown 1 **Cardiff** 3
McNaughton 17 og — Whittingham 45, Ramsey 60, Parry 73
2,420

Chelsea 1 **QPR** 0
Camp 28 og
41,289

Colchester 1 **Peterborough** 3
Sheringham 43 pen — McLean 4, Boyd 46, Lee 73
4,003

Everton 0 **Oldham** 1
33,086 — McDonald 45

Huddersfield 2 **Birmingham** 1
Beckett 4, Brandon 81 — O'Connor 19
13,410

Ipswich 0 **Portsmouth** 1
23,446 — Nugent 51

Norwich 1 **Bury** 1
Doherty 80 — Bishop 71
19,815

Plymouth 3 **Hull City** 2
Abdou 23, Halmosi 26, Ebanks-Blake 58 — Windass 51, 60
12,419

Preston 1 **Scunthorpe** 0
Whaley 47
4,616

Southampton 2 **Leicester** 0
Surman 16, Vignal 36
20,094

Southend 5 **Dag & Red** 2
MacDonald 11, Morgan 64, 90, Francis 77, Bailey 90 — Nurse 32, Strevens 58
6,393

Sunderland 0 **Wigan** 3
20,821 — Scharner 19, McShane 56 og, Cotterill 76

Swansea 1 **Havant and W** 1
Robinson 74 | Baptiste 87
8,761

Swindon 1 **Barnet** 1
Sturrock 60 | Birchall 85
5,944

Tottenham 2 **Reading** 2
Berbatov 28, 50 pen | Hunt 25, 78
35,243

Tranmere 2 **Hereford** 2
Jennings 75, G.Taylor 78 | Smith 65, Benjamin 76
6,909

Walsall 0 **Millwall** 0
4,358

Neil Warnock's Crystal Palace put the accent on youth with two 17-year-olds and 15-year-old John Bostock in the team. Danny Shittu proved too experienced with two goals from corners to put Watford through. "We're going to win at home," chanted the Watford fans.

Watford 2 **Crystal Palace** 0
Shittu 28, 65
10,480

West Ham 0 **Man City** 0
33,806

Wolverhampton 2 **Cambridge** 1
Kightly 69, N.Collins 88 | Rendell 42 pen
15,340

Burnley 0 **Arsenal** 2
16,709 | da Silva 9, Bendtner 75

Derby 2 **Sheff Wed** 2
Miller 38, Barnes 45 | Beevers 9, Tudgay 23
20,612

Struggling Fulham twice had to come from behind to snatch a draw against Bristol Rovers with Danny Murphy scoring from distance to ensure the Premier side live to fight again.

Fulham 2 **Bristol Rovers** 2
Healy 40, Murphy 73 | Coles 3, Hinton 65
13,634

Luton 1 **Liverpool** 1
Riise 77 og | Crouch 74
10,226

Stoke 0 **Newcastle** 0
22,861

FA 3rd Round replay

Barnet 1 **Swindon** 1
Paynter 53 og | Paynter 42
Barnet win 2-0 on penalties
2,810

Bristol Rovers 0 **Fulham** 0
Bristol win 5-3 on penalties
11,882

Sheff Wed 1 **Derby** 1
Watson 10 | Miller 47
Derby win 4-2 on penalties
18,020

Bury 2 **Norwich** 1
Futcher 18, Bishop 61 | Dublin 86
4,146

Liverpool 5 **Luton** 0
Babel 45, Gerrard 52, 64, 71, Hyypia 57
41,446

Millwall 2 **Walsall** 1
May 15, Alexander 49 | Nicholls 61
4,645

Reading 0 **Tottenham** 1
22,130 | Keane 15

West Brom 2 **Charlton** 2
Bednar 14, Morrison 51 | Ambrose 64, Dickson 90 pen
West Brom win 4-3 on penalties
12,691

Swansea gave Blue Square South side Havant & Waterlooville the perfect start with a Garry Monk headed own goal after four minutes. Jamie Collins' and Rocky Baptiste's close-range efforts made it 3-0 by 37 minutes and, while Swansea fought back, they never recovered.

Havant and W 4 **Swansea** 2
Monk 4 og, Collins 25, Baptiste 37, Jordan 65 | Bauza 39, Scotland 48
4,400

Hereford 1 **Tranmere** 0
Johnson 72
6,471

Man City 1 **West Ham** 0
Elano 73
27,809

The result was up-staged by the news: 'King Kev' was back at St James' Park. As he took his place alongside the directors, the crowd applauded and the Magpies were unrecognisable from the struggling side of recent weeks, with Michael Owen scoring the first of four.

Newcastle 4 **Stoke** 1
Owen 8, Cacapa 31, Milner 68, Duff 76 | Lawrence 89
35,108

4TH ROUND

Southend 0 **Barnsley** 1
Campbell-Ryce 22
7,212

Arsenal 3 **Newcastle** 0
Adebayor 51, 84, Butt 89 og
60,046

Barnet 0 **Bristol Rovers** 1
Lambert 49
5,190

Coventry 2 **Millwall** 1
S.Hughes 16, Mifsud 52 | Simpson 42
17,268

Derby 1 **Preston** 4
Earnshaw 55 | Hawley 14, 45, Whaley 33, Mellor 90 pen
17,344

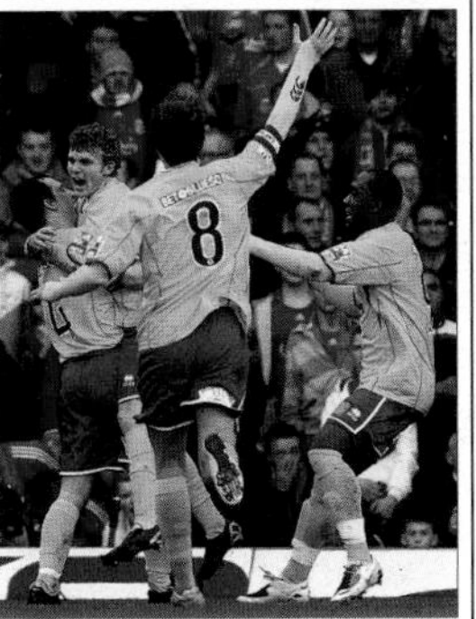

Havant & Waterlooville rocked Anfield to its foundations, going 0-1 and 1-2 ahead before Yossi Benayoun took control. The mercurial Israeli scored a rebound to make it 2-2 before halftime and completed a hat-trick in the second half as Liverpool recovered to win comfortably 5-2.

Liverpool 5 **Havant and W** 2
Leiva 27, Benayoun 44, 56, 59, Crouch 90 | Pacquette 8, Skrtel 31 og
42,566

Stags captain Jake Buxton played the game of his life yet ended up scoring the own goal that put Boro safely into the fifth round. Dong Gook Lee slotted Boro ahead but Mansfield battled on, until Buxton got ahead of Stewart Downing on the line but couldn't clear.

Mansfield 0 **Middlesbrough** 2
Dong-Gook 16, Buxton 87 og
6,258

Oldham 0 **Huddersfield** 1
Beckett 10
12,749

Peterborough 0 **West Brom** 3
Bednar 7, Koren 15, Phillips 58 pen
12,701

Portsmouth 2 **Plymouth** 1
Diarra 34, Kranjcar 45 | Clark 5
19,612

Southampton 2 **Bury** 0
Surman 71, Rasiak 80
25,449

Andy Bothroyd has decided to prioritise Watford's promotion drive and fielded a weakened side against Wolves. Andy Keogh grabbed a brace for the visitors scoring first, after four minutes, and last, on 90 minutes, as Wolves ran out comfortable 4-1 winners.

Watford 1 **Wolverhampton** 4
O'Toole 70 | Keogh 5, 90, S.Elliott 58, Bothroyd 68
12,719

Wigan 1 **Chelsea** 2
Sibierski 87 | Anelka 53, Wright-Phillips 82
14,166

Hereford 1 **Cardiff** 2
Robinson 77 | McNaughton 45, Thompson 67 pen
6,855

Robbie Keane shocked Manchester United as Spurs took the lead and almost held on until halftime at Old Trafford. However, Carlos Tevez conjured an equaliser and two from Cristiano Ronaldo in the second half ensured United's progress.

Man Utd 3 **Tottenham** 1
Tevez 38, Ronaldo 69 pen, 88 | Keane 24
75,369

Michael Ball cleared a balloon instead of a low bobbling ball and saw the Blades take advantage as Luton Shelton stabbed home. Jon Stead added a second before young sub Daniel Sturridge pulled a goal back for City but Sheffield United hung on.

Sheff Utd 2 **Man City** 1
Shelton 12, Stead 24 | Sturridge 48
20,800

5TH ROUND

Bristol Rovers	1	Southampton	0
Lambert 84			
			11,920

Cardiff City reached their first FA Cup quarter final since they won the cup in 1927. Peter Whittingham gave the Welsh club the perfect start with a goal after 90 seconds and Jimmy-Floyd Hasselbaink added a cracking curler to make sure.

Cardiff	2	Wolverhampton	0
Whittingham 2, Hasselbaink 11			
			15,339

Chelsea	3	Huddersfield	1
Lampard 18, 60, Kalou 70		Collins 45	
			41,324

Coventry	0	West Brom	5
		Brunt 12, Bednar 59, 69 pen, Miller 76, Gera 78	
			28,163

Barnsley blasted Liverpool out of the FA Cup at Anfield in the biggest shock of the season. Dirk Kuyt put the Reds ahead but the struggling Championship side struck back through Stephen Foster and reserve keeper Luke Steele kept Liverpool at bay until Brian Howard's injury time winner.

Liverpool	1	Barnsley	2
Kuyt 32		Foster 57, Howard 90	
			42,449

Man Utd	4	Arsenal	0
Rooney 16, Gallas 20 og, Nani 38, Fletcher 74			
			75,550

Preston	0	Portsmouth	1
		Carter 90 og	
			11,840

Sheff Utd	0	Middlesbrough	0
			22,210

FA 5th Round replay

A bizarre Paddy Kelly own goal in extra time saved Boro the anguish of a penalty shoot-out at the end of 210 minutes where neither side could score a goal of their own. Mido's shot hit an upright and rebounded back onto Kelly and over the line.

Middlesbrough	1	Sheff Utd	0
Kenny 114 og			
			28,108

QUARTER-FINALS

Barnsley	1	Chelsea	0
Odejayi 66			22,410

Barnsley have performed feats only dreamt of by most Premier League sides: in the space of two games they have beaten two of the 'Big Four'. Kayode Odejayi scored the header that means Chelsea join Liverpool as the Tykes' cup victims this season. Istvan Ferenczi half-volleyed onto a post for the home side while Chelsea only mustered half chances.

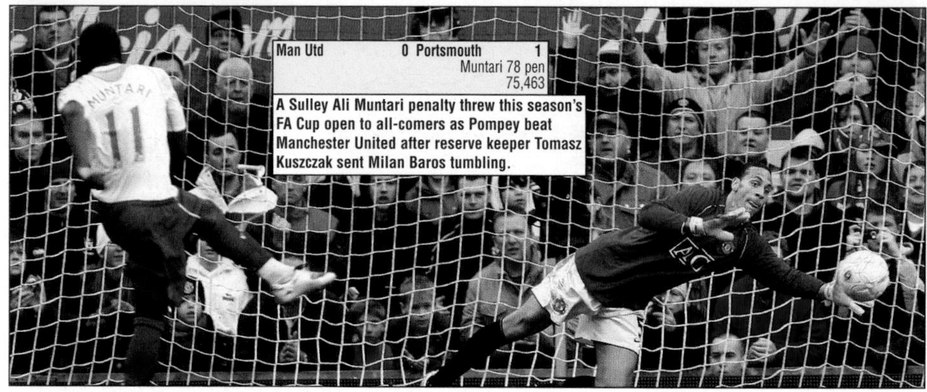

Man Utd	0	Portsmouth	1
		Muntari 78 pen	
			75,463

A Sulley Ali Muntari penalty threw this season's FA Cup open to all-comers as Pompey beat Manchester United after reserve keeper Tomasz Kuszczak sent Milan Baros tumbling.

Bristol Rovers	1	West Brom	5
Coles 32		Morrison 16, Miller 30, 69, 85, Phillips 73	
			12,011

Ishmael Miller's hat-trick kept West Brom on track for a promotion and cup double as Bristol Rovers were thumped 5-1. Further goals came from James Morrison and the revitalised Kevin Phillips.

Middlesbrough	0	Cardiff	2
		Whittingham 9, Johnson 22	
			32,896

Boro gave their worst performance of a less-than-sparkling cup run and missed a great chance of going to Wembley. Man-of-the-match Peter Whittingham scored a clever goal after nine minutes and hit the free kick for Roger Johnson's headed second.

SEMI-FINALS

West Brom	0	Portsmouth	1
			Kanu 54
			83,584

West Brom impressed in this semi-final but ended up losing to the only goal, scored by their former player, Kanu. The striker netted after Dean Kiely had made a reaction save from Milan Baros as Baggie Zoltan Gera's intervention only prevented Kiely from diving on the loose ball.

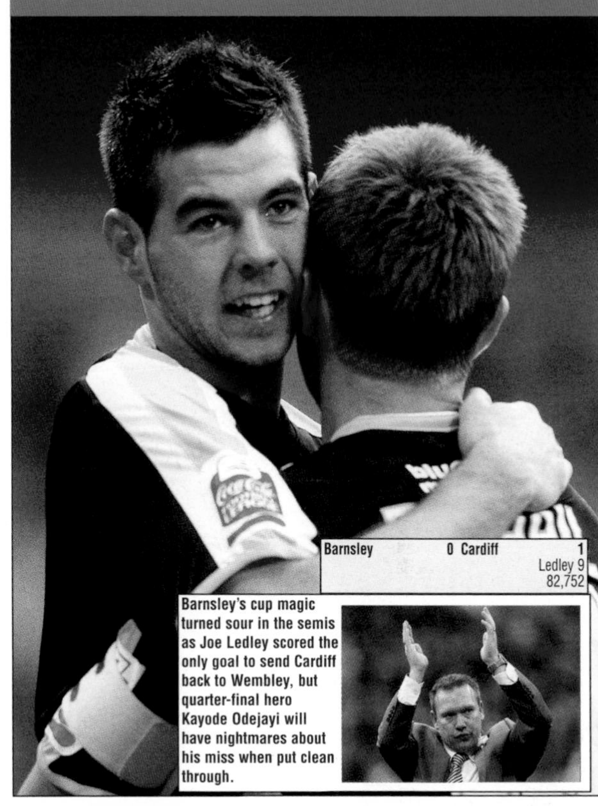

Barnsley	0	Cardiff	1
			Ledley 9
			82,752

Barnsley's cup magic turned sour in the semis as Joe Ledley scored the only goal to send Cardiff back to Wembley, but quarter-final hero Kayode Odejayi will have nightmares about his miss when put clean through.

FINAL

Portsmouth	0	Cardiff	1
Kanu 37			
			89,874

Kanu's reactions returned the FA Cup to Portsmouth for the first time in 69 years as they beat Championship Cardiff at Wembley. The tall Nigerian forward was the hero of both the semi and the final. However, he first had to endure an astonishing open-goal miss, which would have haunted him forever, had he not then hit the winner. He slipped past Cardiff's Roger Johnson and Peter Enckelman before inexplicably putting his shot against the post despite being almost on the goal line. Just 15 minutes later salvation came when John Utaka made an opening and sent a dangerous ball across the six-yard box. Enckelman pushed it out but Kanu rifled it back into the net before anyone could react.

THE CARLING FOOTBALL LEAGUE CUP

1ST ROUND

Home		Away		Home scorers	Away scorers	Note	Att
Peterborough	2	Southampton	1	Rasiak 21 og, Boyd 26	Rasiak 36		4,087
Accrington	0	Leicester	1		Wesolowski 4		2,029
Barnsley	2	Darlington	1	Ferenczi 65, P.Reid 77	Wright 70		3,780
Blackpool	1	Huddersfield	0	Burgess 75			6,395
Brentford	0	Bristol City	3		Elliott 16, Jevons 42, 86		2,213
Bristol Rovers	1	Crystal Palace	1	Disley 64	Freedman 31	Bristol Rovers win 4-1 on penalties	5,566
Bury	0	Carlisle	1		Graham 12		2,213
Cardiff	1	Brighton	0	Johnson 110			3,726
Chester	0	Nottm Forest	0			Notts Forest win 4-2 on penalties	2,720
Coventry	3	Notts County	0	Adebola 47, Best 67, Simpson 78			6,735
Dag & Red	1	Luton	2	Strevens 73	Spring 42 pen, Talbot 68		1,754
Doncaster	4	Lincoln	1	Hayter 23, Wellens 55, Heffernan 59, McCammon 73	Forrester 80		5,084
Grimsby	1	Burnley	1	North 101	Gray 108	Burnley win 4-2 on penalties	2,431
Hereford	4	Yeovil	1	Ainsworth 8, 24, 41, Easton 35	Owusu 50		2,085
Macclesfield	0	Leeds	1		Westlake 78		3,422
MK Dons	3	Ipswich	3	Knight 16, Bruce 22 og, Gallen 120 pen	Lee 45 pen, Murphy 52 og, Garvan 98	MK Dons win 5-3 on penalties	7,496
Northampton	2	Millwall	0	Bradley.Johnson 38, Kirk 62			3,735
Norwich	5	Barnet	2	Cureton 3, 16, Lappin 21, Fotheringham 25, Russell 31	Puncheon 66, Birchall 74		13,971
Oldham	4	Mansfield	1	Kilkenny 20, Kalala 27, Smalley 82, C.Davies 86	Mullins 72		3,155
Plymouth	2	Wycombe	1	Bullock 41 og, Hodges 45	Oakes 76		5,474
Port Vale	1	Wrexham	1	Rodgers 33 pen	Proctor 10	Wrexham win 5-3 on penalties	2,916
Preston	1	Morecambe	2	Pugh 73	Bentley 6, Artell 84		7,703
QPR	1	Leyton Orient	2	Rowlands 68	Demetriou 55, Boyd 64 pen		5,260
Rochdale	2	Stoke	2	Perkins 83, Prendergast 101	Shawcross 4, Cresswell 120	Rochdale win 4-2 on penalties	2,369
Scunthorpe	1	Hartlepool	2	Paterson 51	Foley 70, 85		2,965
Sheff Utd	3	Chesterfield	1	Stead 14, 45, Webber 56	Lester 16		11,170
Shrewsbury	1	Colchester	0	Kempson 106			3,069
Southend	4	Cheltenham	1	Bradbury 11, 108 pen, 117, Barrett 104	Finnigan 70		3,084
Stockport	1	Tranmere	0	McNeil 84			3,499
Swansea	2	Walsall	0	Anderson 22, Scotland 90			6,943
Swindon	0	Charlton	2		Ambrose 52, Reid 63 pen		6,175
Watford	3	Gillingham	0	Priskin 22, Rinaldi 36, Campana 71			8,166
West Brom	1	Bournemouth	0	Beattie 22			10,250
Crewe	0	Hull City	3		Bridges 44, Garcia 55, McPhee 70		2,862
Wolverhampton	2	Bradford	1	Eastwood 46, Craddock 49	Nix 77		9,625
Rotherham	1	Sheff Wed	3	Harrison 34	Whelan 45, Burton 49, Small 55		6,416

2ND ROUND

Home		Away		Home scorers	Away scorers	Note	Att
Birmingham	2	Hereford	1	O'Connor 27, McSheffrey 38	Robinson 74		10,185
Bristol Rovers	1	West Ham	2	A.Williams 72	Bellamy 31, 45		10,831
Burnley	3	Oldham	0	Gray 59, Blake 76, Akinbiyi 90			7,317
Cardiff	1	Leyton Orient	0	Whittingham 90			6,150
Carlisle	0	Coventry	2		Mifsud 21, 56		5,744
Charlton	4	Stockport	3	Todorov 35, Z.Zheng 42 pen, Sam 74, McCarthy 90	Proudlock 54, Elding 62, Blizzard 69		8,022
Derby	2	Blackpool	2	Camara 63, Fagan 101	Gorkss 86, 120	Blackpool win 7-6 on penalties	8,658
Luton	3	Sunderland	0	Bell 16, Furlong 43, 75			4,401
MK Dons	2	Sheff Utd	3	Broughton 12, McGovern 78	Lucketti 20, Law 55, Horsfield 104		7,943
Peterborough	0	West Brom	2		Gera 33, Ellington 45		4,917
Plymouth	2	Doncaster	0	Ebanks-Blake 15, Summerfield 90			5,133
Portsmouth	3	Leeds	0	Pamarot 43, 80, Nugent 84			8,502
Rochdale	1	Norwich	1	Murray 9	Dublin 49	Norwich win 4-3 on penalties	2,990
Sheff Wed	2	Hartlepool	1	Burton 68, Folly 120	Moore 55		8,751
Shrewsbury	0	Fulham	1		Kamara 59		6,223
Southend	2	Watford	0	MacDonald 20, Harrold 55			5,554
Swansea	0	Reading	1		Lita 105		12,027
Wigan	0	Hull City	1		Elliott 31		5,440
Wolverhampton	1	Morecambe	3	Keogh 84 pen	Baker 62 pen, Newby 92, Thompson 105		11,296
Wrexham	0	Aston Villa	5		Maloney 10, 72, L.Moore 52, Reo-Coker 62, Harewood 78		8,221
Bristol City	1	Man City	2	Orr 69	Mpenza 17, Bianchi 81		14,541
Middlesbrough	2	Northampton	0	Rochemback 53, Lee Dong-Gook 66			11,686
Newcastle	2	Barnsley	0	Owen 57, Martins 86			30,523
Nottm Forest	2	Leicester	3	Smith 1, Tyson 64	Sheehan 31, Stearman 88, Clemence 90		15,519

3RD ROUND

Home		Away		Home scorers	Away scorers	Att
Arsenal	2	Newcastle	0	Bendtner 83, Denilson 89		60,004
Blackpool	2	Southend	1	Hoolahan 81, Jackson 118	Harrold 7 pen	5,022
Burnley	0	Portsmouth	1		Nugent 69	8,202
Luton	3	Charlton	1	Robinson 43, Spring 105, Talbot 117	Sinclair 4	4,534
Man City	1	Norwich	0	Samaras 90		20,938
Man Utd	0	Coventry	2		Mifsud 27, 70	74,055
Reading	2	Liverpool	4	Convey 27, Halls 64	Benayoun 23, Torres 50, 72, 86	23,563
Sheff Utd	5	Morecambe	0	B.Sharp 18, 33, Shelton 52, 72, Hendrie 67		8,854
West Brom	2	Cardiff	4	Miller 33, 87 pen	Fowler 4, 27 pen, Hasselbaink 23, Sinclair 30	14,085
Aston Villa	0	Leicester	1		Fryatt 76	25,956
Blackburn	3	Birmingham	0	Bentley 66, Derbyshire 82 pen, Santa Cruz 90		9,205
Fulham	1	Bolton	2	Healy 78	Guthrie 57, Giannakopoulos 112	10,500
Hull City	0	Chelsea	4		Sinclair 37, Kalou 48, 81, Sidwell 52	23,543
Sheff Wed	0	Everton	3		McFadden 59, 84, Yakubu 85	16,463
Tottenham	2	Middlesbrough	0	Bale 72, Huddlestone 75		32,280
West Ham	1	Plymouth	0	Ashton 90		25,774

The 'Mosquito' bites twice at Old Trafford to dump Manchester United out of the Carling Cup as Misfud (nicknamed the Mosquito) sends Coventry through.

4TH ROUND

Home		Away		Home scorers	Away scorers	Att
Coventry	1	West Ham	2	Tabb 68	Hall 71 og, Cole 90	23,968
Bolton	0	Man City	1		Elano 86 pen	15,510
Chelsea	4	Leicester	3	Lampard 20, 29, 90, Shevchenko 87	McAuley 6, Campbell 69, Cort 74	40,037
Liverpool	2	Cardiff	1	El Zhar 48, Gerrard 66	Purse 65	41,780
Luton	0	Everton	1		Cahill 101	8,994
Portsmouth	1	Blackburn	2	Kanu 90	McCarthy 11, Pedersen 77	11,788
Sheff Utd	0	Arsenal	3		da Silva 8, 50, Denilson 69	32,196
Tottenham	2	Blackpool	0	Keane 18, Chimbonda 58		32,196

Goals from Keane and Chimbonda get Ramos off to a victorious start at White Hart Lane, ending Spurs' run of six matches without a win.

QUARTER-FINALS

West Ham	1	Everton	2
Cole 12		Osman 40, Yakubu 88	28,777

Everton's Yakubu averted extra time, and claimed a semi spot, by scoring with two minutes to go after Hammers' defender Gabbidon headed the ball beyond his own keeper.

Blackburn	2	Arsenal	3
Santa Cruz 42, 60		Diaby 6, da Silva 29, 104	16,207

The Young Guns are riding over more experienced opposition in the Carling Cup again. Eduardo scored the only goal in extra time despite Denilson seeing red after a two-goal lead was pulled back by Rovers.

Man City	0	Tottenham	2
38,564		Defoe 5, Malbranque 82	

Ten-man Spurs reached the Carling semis by ending Man City's 100% home record at Eastlands with goals from Defoe and Malbranque and despite losing Zokora for a lunge at Elano.

Chelsea	2	Liverpool	0
Lampard 59, Shevchenko 90			41,366

Goals from Lampard and a rare success by Shevchenko on 90 minutes gave Chelsea a Carling win over their regular cup rivals Liverpool.

SEMI-FINALS

Chelsea	2	Everton	1
Wright-Phillips 26, Lescott 90 og		Yakubu 64	41,178

Everton	(1) 0	Chelsea	(2) 1
		J.Cole 69	37,086

The key point in the tie turned out to be Lescott's 90th minute own goal at Stamford Bridge. Joe Cole scored the only goal of the second leg to help Chelsea hang onto their narrow first leg advantage. Everton flew at the holders at Goodison but could not break them down.

Arsenal	1	Tottenham	1
Walcott 79		Jenas 37	53,136

Tottenham	(1) 5	Arsenal	(1) 1
Jenas 3, Bendtner 27 og, Keane 48, Lennon 60, Malbranque 90		Adebayor 70	35,979

It took 21 games but it was worth it as Spurs finally returned a win over their local rivals – and not just a win but a rout. Arsenal narrowly averted defeat in their home leg but were found out at White Hart Lane as Jenas scored after just three minutes. Both sides had chances but Spurs took theirs.

FINAL

CARLING CUP
FINAL2008
CARLING CUP
FINAL2008

Tottenham	2	Chelsea	1
Berbatov 69 pen, Woodgate 94		Drogba 39	87,660

Within two months of his transfer from Boro Woodgate scored the winner against Chelsea at Wembley to win the Carling Cup for Spurs. The goal owed something to a missed punch by keeper Cech and came in extra time after a 1-1 score-line at full time. Drogba scored first for Chelsea from a free kick but Berbatov levelled from the penalty spot after Bridge handled in the area. Ramos' cup pedigree continues to impress but Grant's selection makes the headlines.

CHAMPIONSHIP LEAGUE ROUND-UP

FINAL LEAGUE TABLE

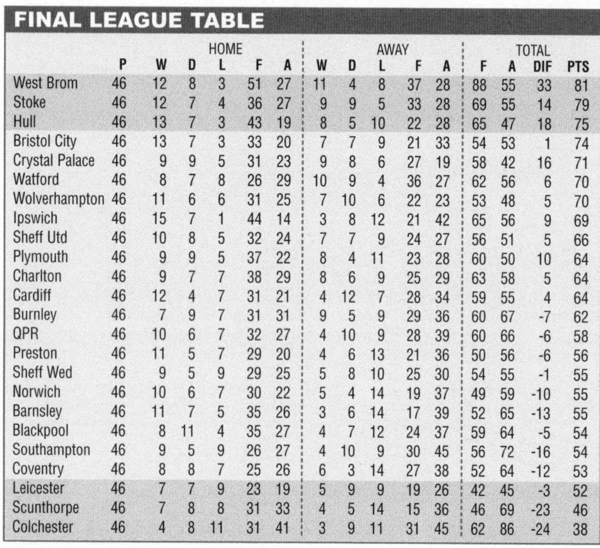

		HOME					AWAY					TOTAL			
	P	W	D	L	F	A	W	D	L	F	A	F	A	DIF	PTS
West Brom	46	12	8	3	51	27	11	4	8	37	28	88	55	33	81
Stoke	46	12	7	4	36	27	9	9	5	33	28	69	55	14	79
Hull	46	13	7	3	43	19	8	5	10	22	28	65	47	18	75
Bristol City	46	13	7	3	33	20	7	7	9	21	33	54	53	1	74
Crystal Palace	46	9	9	5	31	23	9	8	6	27	19	58	42	16	71
Watford	46	8	7	8	26	29	10	9	4	36	27	62	56	6	70
Wolverhampton	46	11	6	6	31	25	7	10	6	22	23	53	48	5	70
Ipswich	46	15	7	1	44	14	3	8	12	21	42	65	56	9	69
Sheff Utd	46	10	8	5	32	24	7	7	9	24	27	56	51	5	66
Plymouth	46	9	9	5	37	22	8	4	11	23	28	60	50	10	64
Charlton	46	9	7	7	38	29	8	6	9	25	29	63	58	5	64
Cardiff	46	12	4	7	31	21	4	12	7	28	34	59	55	4	64
Burnley	46	7	9	7	31	31	9	5	9	29	36	60	67	-7	62
QPR	46	10	6	7	32	27	4	10	9	28	39	60	66	-6	58
Preston	46	11	5	7	29	20	4	6	13	21	36	50	56	-6	56
Sheff Wed	46	9	5	9	29	25	5	8	10	25	30	54	55	-1	55
Norwich	46	10	6	7	30	22	5	4	14	19	37	49	59	-10	55
Barnsley	46	11	7	5	35	26	3	6	14	17	39	52	65	-13	55
Blackpool	46	8	11	4	35	27	4	7	12	24	37	59	64	-5	54
Southampton	46	9	5	9	26	27	4	10	9	30	45	56	72	-16	54
Coventry	46	8	8	7	25	26	6	3	14	27	38	52	64	-12	53
Leicester	46	7	7	9	23	19	5	9	9	19	26	42	45	-3	52
Scunthorpe	46	7	8	8	31	33	4	5	14	15	36	46	69	-23	46
Colchester	46	4	8	11	31	41	3	9	11	31	45	62	86	-24	38

CLUB STRIKE FORCE

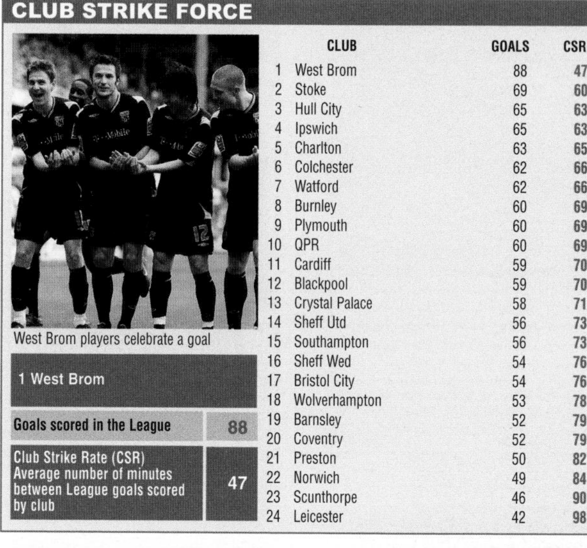

West Brom players celebrate a goal

1 West Brom

Goals scored in the League	88
Club Strike Rate (CSR) Average number of minutes between League goals scored by club	47

	CLUB	GOALS	CSR
1	West Brom	88	47
2	Stoke	69	60
3	Hull City	65	63
4	Ipswich	65	63
5	Charlton	63	65
6	Colchester	62	66
7	Watford	62	66
8	Burnley	60	69
9	Plymouth	60	69
10	QPR	60	69
11	Cardiff	59	70
12	Blackpool	59	70
13	Crystal Palace	58	71
14	Sheff Utd	56	73
15	Southampton	56	73
16	Sheff Wed	54	76
17	Bristol City	54	76
18	Wolverhampton	53	78
19	Barnsley	52	79
20	Coventry	52	79
21	Preston	50	82
22	Norwich	49	84
23	Scunthorpe	46	90
24	Leicester	42	98

CLUB DISCIPLINARY RECORDS

QPR's Martin Rowlands late tackle

1 QPR

League Yellow	83
League Red	6
League Total	89
Cards Average in League Average number of minutes between a card being shown of either colour	46

	CLUB	Y	R	TOTAL	AVE
1	QPR	83	6	89	46
2	Coventry	85	3	88	47
3	Burnley	77	8	85	48
4	Preston	75	4	79	52
5	Stoke	76	2	78	53
6	Norwich	70	7	77	53
7	Hull City	72	4	76	54
8	Barnsley	69	6	75	55
9	Charlton	69	6	75	55
10	Plymouth	71	2	73	56
11	Scunthorpe	63	10	73	56
12	Sheff Wed	69	3	72	57
13	Leicester	67	4	71	58
14	Watford	63	5	68	60
15	Sheff Utd	63	4	67	61
16	Crystal Palace	63	1	64	64
17	Bristol City	59	3	62	66
18	Colchester	57	5	62	66
19	Ipswich	52	4	56	73
20	West Brom	52	3	55	75
21	Southampton	50	4	54	76
22	Wolverhampton	53	0	53	78
23	Cardiff	45	3	48	86
24	Blackpool	43	4	47	88

CLUB DEFENCES

	CLUB	LGE	CS	CDR
1	Crystal Palace	42	13	98
2	Leicester	45	17	92
3	Hull City	47	15	88
4	Wolverhampton	48	19	86
5	Plymouth	50	14	82
6	Sheff Utd	51	15	81
7	Bristol City	53	15	78
8	Cardiff	55	13	75
9	Sheff Wed	55	11	75
10	Stoke	55	11	75
11	West Brom	55	14	75
12	Watford	56	13	73
13	Preston	56	13	73
14	Ipswich	56	12	73
15	Charlton	58	12	71
16	Norwich	59	12	70
17	Blackpool	64	11	64
18	Coventry	64	9	64
19	Barnsley	65	12	63
20	QPR	66	14	62
21	Burnley	67	10	61
22	Scunthorpe	69	10	60
23	Southampton	72	10	57
24	Colchester	86	2	48

Strong defending by Palace defender Hill

1 Crystal Palace

Goals conceded in the League	42
Clean Sheets (CS) Number of league games where no goals were conceded	13
Club Defensive Rate (CDR) Average number of minutes between League goals conceded by club	98

STADIUM CAPACITY AND HOME CROWDS

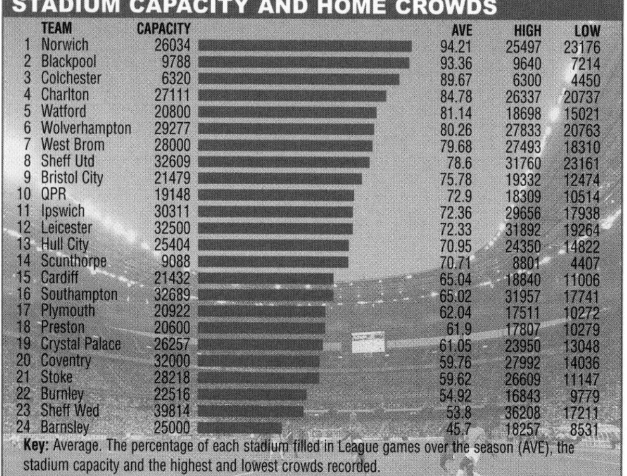

	TEAM	CAPACITY	AVE	HIGH	LOW
1	Norwich	26034	94.21	25497	23176
2	Blackpool	9788	93.36	9640	7214
3	Colchester	6320	89.67	6300	4450
4	Charlton	27111	84.78	26337	20737
5	Watford	20800	81.14	18698	15021
6	Wolverhampton	29277	80.26	27833	20763
7	West Brom	28000	79.68	27493	18310
8	Sheff Utd	32609	78.6	31760	23161
9	Bristol City	21479	75.78	19332	12474
10	QPR	19148	72.9	18309	10514
11	Ipswich	30311	72.36	29656	17938
12	Leicester	32500	72.33	31892	19264
13	Hull City	25404	70.95	24350	14822
14	Scunthorpe	9088	70.71	8801	4407
15	Cardiff	21432	65.04	18840	11006
16	Southampton	32689	65.02	31957	17741
17	Plymouth	20922	62.04	17511	10272
18	Preston	20600	61.9	17807	10279
19	Crystal Palace	26257	61.05	23950	13048
20	Coventry	32000	59.76	27992	14036
21	Stoke	28218	59.62	26609	11147
22	Burnley	22516	54.92	16843	9779
23	Sheff Wed	39814	53.8	36208	17211
24	Barnsley	25000	45.7	18257	8531

Key: Average. The percentage of each stadium filled in League games over the season (AVE), the stadium capacity and the highest and lowest crowds recorded.

AWAY ATTENDANCE

	TEAM	AVE	HIGH	LOW
1	Bristol City	73.82	29787	5423
2	Sheff Wed	73.68	31892	5086
3	Wolverhampton	72.59	27992	5989
4	Sheff Utd	72.32	31957	5695
5	West Brom	72.24	27833	5798
6	Watford	71.53	26508	5760
7	Hull City	71.14	30374	5497
8	Stoke	70.45	25373	5521
9	Ipswich	70.41	26072	6264
10	QPR	70.1	28894	5361
11	Norwich	69.81	36208	5560
12	Crystal Palace	69.65	26202	5856
13	Southampton	69.62	26206	6035
14	Blackpool	69.44	26650	4407
15	Burnley	68.88	25306	4925
16	Leicester	68.82	26609	5661
17	Barnsley	68.68	27769	4450
18	Coventry	67.73	26130	5836
19	Charlton	67.48	25327	5860
20	Scunthorpe	67.44	25668	5218
21	Plymouth	67.03	26293	4833
22	Colchester	66.57	26202	5554
23	Preston	66.09	24092	5122
24	Cardiff	65.53	27246	4699

Key: Average. How close each club has come to filling grounds in its away league matches (AVE) and the highest and lowest crowds recorded.

CHART-TOPPING MIDFIELDERS

1 Sam - Charlton	
Goals scored in the League	2
Defensive Rating Av number of mins between League goals conceded while on the pitch	94
Contribution to Attacking Power Average number of minutes between League team goals while on pitch	61
Scoring Difference Defensive Rating minus Contribution to Attacking Power	94

	PLAYER	CLUB	GOALS	DEF RATE	POWER	S DIFF
1	Lloyd Sam	Charlton	2	155	61	94
2	James Morrison	West Brom	4	99	43	56
3	Shaun Derry	Crystal Palace	0	122	67	55
4	Tom Soares	Crystal Palace	6	111	62	49
5	Danny Haynes	Ipswich	6	114	65	49
6	Ben Watson	Crystal Palace	5	110	68	42
7	Zoltan Gera	West Brom	8	84	48	36
8	Michael Kightly	Wolverhampton	4	106	74	32
9	Chris Brunt	West Brom	5	71	41	30
10	Nadjim Abdou	Plymouth	1	91	63	28
11	Jonathan Greening	West Brom	1	75	47	28
12	Peter Halmosi	Plymouth	8	89	63	26
13	Gary Speed	Sheff Utd	3	94	68	26
14	Robert Koren	West Brom	9	69	45	24
15	Richard Garcia	Hull City	5	88	65	23

CHART-TOPPING GOALSCORERS

1 Phillips - West Brom	
Goals scored in the League	22
Contribution to Attacking Power (AP) Average number of minutes between League team goals while on pitch	43
Club Strike Rate (CSR) Average minutes between League goals scored by club	47
Player Strike Rate Average number of minutes between League goals scored by player	115

	PLAYER	CLUB	GOALS: LGE	POWER	CSR	S RATE
1	Kevin Phillips	West Brom	22	43	47	115
2	Roman Bednar	West Brom	12	45	47	131
3	James Beattie	Sheff Utd	22	71	73	136
4	Sylvain Ebanks-Blake	Wolverhampton	12	63	79	142
5	Sylvain Ebanks-Blake	Plymouth	11	62	69	154
6	Stern John	Southampton	19	82	73	155
7	Fraizer Campbell	Hull City	15	59	65	177
8	Ched Evans	Norwich	10	75	84	182
9	Patrick Agyemang	QPR	8	52	70	184
10	Clinton Morrison	Crystal Palace	16	64	71	186
11	Kevin Lisbie	Colchester	17	67	68	194
12	Andy Gray	Burnley	11	66	70	200
13	Marlon King	Watford	11	54	66	203
14	Ade Akinbiyi	Burnley	8	65	70	204
15	Caleb Folan	Hull City	8	65	65	213

CHART-TOPPING DEFENDERS

1 Dickinson - Stoke	
Goals Conceded in the League The number of League goals conceded while he was on the pitch	13
Clean Sheets In games when he played at least 70 mins	7
Club Defensive Rating Average mins between League goals conceded by the club this season	75
Defensive Rating Average number of minutes between League goals conceded while on pitch	134

	PLAYER	CLUB	CON: LGE	CS	CDR	DEF RATE
1	Carl Dickinson	Stoke	13	7	75	134
2	Gary Breen	Wolverhampton	12	10	88	134
3	Jody Craddock	Wolverhampton	15	12	88	130
4	Phillip Bardsley	Sheff Utd	11	7	81	129
5	Clinton Hill	Crystal Palace	21	9	98	118
6	Alan Sheehan	Leicester	13	7	92	109
7	Danny Butterfield	Crystal Palace	23	9	98	100
8	Michael Turner	Hull City	39	15	90	100
9	Matt Lawrence	Crystal Palace	32	10	98	99
10	Patrick Kisnorbo	Leicester	35	14	92	99
11	Richard Stearman	Leicester	33	14	92	99
12	Mark Hudson	Crystal Palace	41	13	98	98
13	Mohammed Camara	Norwich	17	6	70	98
14	Krisztian Timar	Plymouth	33	14	82	96
15	George Elokobi	Wolverhampton	14	6	88	96

CHART-TOPPING GOALKEEPERS

1 Speroni - Crystal Palace	
Counting Games Games in which he played at least 70 minutes	46
Goals Conceded in the League The number of League goals conceded while he was on the pitch	42
Clean Sheets In games when he played at least 70 mins	13
Defensive Rating Average number of minutes between League goals conceded while on pitch	98

	PLAYER	CLUB	CG	CONC	CS	DEF RATE
1	Julian Speroni	Crystal Palace	46	42	13	98
2	Marton Fulop	Leicester	24	23	8	93
3	Kasper Schmeichel	Cardiff	14	14	5	90
4	Peter Enckelman	Cardiff	15	15	6	90
5	Boaz Myhill	Hull City	43	43	15	90
6	Luke McCormick	Plymouth	30	31	10	86
7	Wayne Hennessey	Wolverhampton	45	48	18	84
8	Andy Marshall	Coventry	16	18	5	80
9	Stephen Bywater	Ipswich	17	19	4	80
10	Richard Lee	Watford	34	39	11	79
11	Paul Henderson	Leicester	14	16	5	78
12	Luke Steele	Barnsley	14	16	4	78
13	Adriano Basso	Bristol City	42	50	14	77
14	Lee Grant	Sheff Wed	45	52	12	77
15	Dean Kiely	West Brom	44	52	14	76

PLAYER DISCIPLINARY RECORD

Sheffield United's Lee Hendrie: 5 cards

1. Lee Hendrie - Sheffield United	
Cards Average mins between cards	106
League Yellow	5
League Red	0
TOTAL	5

	PLAYER		LY	LR	TOT	AVE
1	Lee Hendrie	Sheff Utd	5	0	5	106
2	Kevin Kyle	Coventry	3	2	5	110
3	F Songo'o	Crystal Palace	4	0	4	136
4	J Brellier	Norwich	3	1	4	169
5	A Ostlund	Southampton	4	0	4	173
6	G Roberts	Ipswich	5	0	5	182
7	D Livermore	Hull City	5	0	5	184
8	P Gilbert	Sheff Wed	3	1	4	190
9	A Sheehan	Leicester	7	0	7	203
10	Lee Martin	Plymouth	4	0	4	203
11	R Anderson	Plymouth	6	0	6	206
12	C Byrne	Scunthorpe	8	2	10	206
13	J V Semedo	Charlton	10	1	11	207
14	G Williams	Ipswich	4	0	4	207
15	S Kabba	Watford	2	1	3	219

TEAM OF THE SEASON

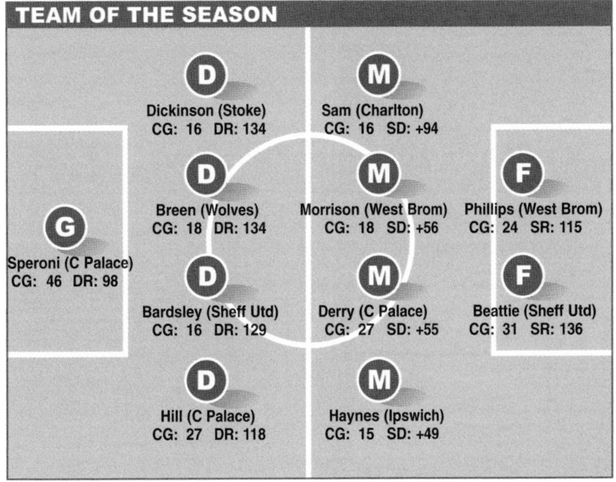
G
Speroni (C Palace)
CG: 46 DR: 98
D
Dickinson (Stoke)
CG: 16 DR: 134
D
Breen (Wolves)
CG: 18 DR: 134
D
Bardsley (Sheff Utd)
CG: 16 DR: 129
D
Hill (C Palace)
CG: 27 DR: 118
M
Sam (Charlton)
CG: 16 SD: +94
M
Morrison (West Brom)
CG: 18 SD: +56
M
Derry (C Palace)
CG: 27 SD: +55
M
Haynes (Ipswich)
CG: 15 SD: +49
F
Phillips (West Brom)
CG: 24 SR: 115
F
Beattie (Sheff Utd)
CG: 31 SR: 136

COCA-COLA LEAGUE CHAMPIONSHIP CHAMPIONS

WEST BROMWICH ALBION

Final Position: **1st**

NICKNAME: BAGGIES

KEY: ☐Won ☐Drawn ☐Lost

							Attendance
1	div1	Burnley	A	L	1-2	Phillips 18	15,337
2	ccr1	Bournemouth	H	W	1-0	Beattie 22	10,250
3	div1	Preston	H	W	2-0	Phillips 65, Miller 71	19,556
4	div1	Sheff Utd	A	L	0-1		23,491
5	ccr2	Peterborough	A	W	2-0	Gera 33, Ellington 45	4,917
6	div1	Barnsley	H	W	2-0	Teixeira 30, Beattie 38	18,310
7	div1	Ipswich	H	W	4-0	Miller 23, Teixeira 87, Phillips 89, 90	19,460
8	div1	Bristol City	A	D	1-1	Koren 74	16,571
9	div1	Scunthorpe	A	W	3-2	Barnett 49, Brunt 60, Teixeira 78	8,307
10	ccr3	Cardiff	H	L	2-4	Miller 33, 87 pen	14,085
11	div1	QPR	H	W	5-1	Phillips 17, 38, Miller 18, Koren 57, Greening 66	24,757
12	div1	Stoke	H	D	1-1	Barnett 73	20,048
13	div1	Southampton	A	L	2-3	Koren 32, 62	21,967
14	div1	Colchester	A	L	2-3	Phillips 6, Miller 39	5,798
15	div1	Blackpool	H	W	2-1	Miller 22, Morrison 79	22,030
16	div1	Norwich	H	W	2-0	Miller 16, Phillips 51	20,247
17	div1	Watford	A	W	3-0	Miller 33, Phillips 35, Albrechtsen 49	18,273
18	div1	Sheff Wed	H	D	1-1	Phillips 77	19,807
19	div1	Coventry	A	W	4-0	Robinson 56, Teixeira 58, 73, Koren 90	18,566
20	div1	Wolverhampton	H	D	0-0		27,493
21	div1	Plymouth	A	W	2-1	Bednar 9, 43	14,348
22	div1	Crystal Palace	A	D	1-1	Hudson 8 og	15,247
23	div1	Coventry	H	L	2-4	Bednar 52, Brunt 65	20,641
24	div1	Leicester	A	W	2-1	Gera 31, Beattie 88	22,088
25	div1	Charlton	H	W	4-2	Bednar 43, Gera 50, 80, Phillips 84	20,346
26	div1	Stoke	A	L	1-3	Bednar 72	18,420
27	div1	Bristol City	H	W	4-1	Bednar 48, Koren 67, Phillips 72, 75	27,314
28	div1	Scunthorpe	H	W	5-0	Phillips 35, 52, Koren 45, Gera 77, Beattie 81	25,238
29	div1	Ipswich	A	L	0-2		24,000
30	facr3	Charlton	A	D	1-1	Miller 34	12,682
31	div1	Hull City	A	W	3-1	Phillips 2, Morrison 32, Bednar 90	18,391
32	facr3r	Charlton	H	W	4-3*	Bednar 14, Morrison 51 (*on penalties)	12,691
33	div1	Cardiff	H	D	3-3	Bednar 35, Albrechtsen 72, Johnson 88 og	22,325
34	facr4	Peterborough	A	W	3-0	Bednar 7, Koren 15, Phillips 58 pen	12,701
35	div1	Preston	A	L	1-2	Gera 50	12,473
36	div1	Burnley	H	W	2-1	Cesar 26, Bednar 60	22,206
37	div1	Barnsley	A	L	1-2	Morrison 58	13,083
38	div1	Sheff Utd	H	D	0-0		22,643
39	facr5	Coventry	A	W	5-0	Brunt 12, Bednar 59, 69 pen, Miller 76, Gera 78	28,163
40	div1	Hull City	H	L	1-2	Bednar 42	22,716
41	div1	Plymouth	H	W	3-0	Gera 45, Miller 59, Bednar 67	22,503
42	div1	Sheff Wed	A	W	1-0	Phillips 90	18,805
43	facqf	Bristol Rovers	A	W	5-1	Morrison 16, Miller 30, 69, 85, Phillips 73	12,011
44	div1	Crystal Palace	H	D	1-1	Phillips 30	20,378
45	div1	Leicester	H	L	1-4	Koren 22	22,038
46	div1	Charlton	A	D	1-1	Phillips 42	23,412
47	div1	Colchester	H	W	4-3	Phillips 36, Brunt 39, Bednar 90, Morrison 90	20,433
48	div1	Cardiff	A	D	0-0		13,915
49	facsf	Portsmouth	N	L	0-1		83,584
50	div1	Blackpool	A	W	3-1	Phillips 81 pen, 84, Miller 87	9,628
51	div1	Watford	H	D	1-1	Barnett 49	26,508
52	div1	Wolverhampton	A	W	1-0	Gera 59	27,833
53	div1	Norwich	A	W	2-1	Koren 2, Gera 71	25,442
54	div1	Southampton	H	D	1-1	Brunt 84	26,167
55	div1	QPR	A	W	2-0	Kim 53, Brunt 77	18,309

LEAGUE APPEARANCES, BOOKINGS AND GOALS

	AGE (on 01/07/08)	IN NAMED 16	APPEARANCES	COUNTING GAMES	MINUTES ON PITCH	LEAGUE GOALS	Yellow	Red
Goalkeepers								
Michal Danek	24	9	0	0	0	0	0	0
Luke Daniels	20	1	0	0	0	0	0	0
Dean Kiely	37	44	44	44	3960	0	1	0
Luke Steele	23	20	2	2	180	0	0	0
Defenders								
Martin Albrechtsen	28	36	32	26	2494	2	0	0
Leon Barnett	22	38	32	30	2808	3	4	0
Bostjan Cesar	25	21	20	15	1567	1	6	0
Neil Clement	29	12	9	7	727	0	3	0
Jared Hodgkiss	21	6	4	3	315	0	0	0
Carl Hoeens	31	42	42	41	3714	0	4	0
Shelton Martis	25	9	2	2	180	0	1	0
Pedro Pele	30	36	21	9	1172	0	0	0
Paul Robinson	29	43	43	43	3791	1	7	2
Miguel Tininho	27	3	1	1	90	0	0	0
Midfielders								
Chris Brunt	23	40	34	13	1928	5	1	0
Richard Chaplow	23	8	5	2	204	0	0	0
Zoltan Gera	29	43	43	30	3119	8	4	0
Jonathan Greening	29	46	46	45	4067	1	8	0
Do-Heon Kim	25	8	4	0	172	1	1	0
Robert Koren	27	40	40	36	3340	9	2	0
James Morrison	22	37	35	18	2187	4	1	0
Felipe Teixeira	27	32	30	18	1888	5	1	0
David Worrall	17	1	0	0	0	0	0	0
Forwards								
Craig Beattie	24	25	21	1	726	3	0	0
Roman Bednar	25	32	29	13	1578	12	2	0
Nathan Ellington	26	3	3	0	78	0	0	0
Sherjili MacDonald	23	14	10	0	222	0	0	0
Ishmael Miller	21	36	34	17	2052	9	4	0
Luke Moore	22	11	10	2	336	0	0	1
Kevin Phillips	34	36	35	24	2545	22	2	0
Bartosz Slusarski	26	4	1	0	7	0	0	0

TEAM OF THE SEASON

G — Dean Kiely, CG: 44 DR: 76

D — Paul Robinson, CG: 43 DR: 84

D — Carl Hoeens, CG: 41 DR: 80

D — Leon Barnett, CG: 30 DR: 78

D — Martin Albrechtsen, CG: 26 DR: 73

M — James Morrison, CG: 18 SD: 56

M — Zoltan Gera, CG: 30 SD: 36

M — Chris Brunt, CG: 13 SD: 30

M — Jonathan Greening, CG: 45 SD: 28

F — Kevin Phillips, CG: 24 SR: 115

F — Roman Bednar, CG: 13 SR: 131

MONTHLY POINTS TALLY

Month	Points	%
AUGUST	3	33%
SEPTEMBER	13	87%
OCTOBER	7	47%
NOVEMBER	11	73%
DECEMBER	13	62%
JANUARY	4	33%
FEBRUARY	4	33%
MARCH	11	61%
APRIL	12	67%
MAY	3	100%

LEAGUE GOALS

	PLAYER	MINS	GOALS	S RATE
1	Phillips	2545	22	115
2	Bednar	1578	12	131
3	Miller	2052	9	228
4	Koren	3340	9	371
5	Gera	3119	8	389
6	Brunt	1928	5	385
7	Morrison	2187	4	546
8	Teixeira	1888	5	377
9	Beattie	726	3	242
10	Barnett	2808	3	936
11	Albrechtsen	2494	2	1247
12	Kim	172	1	172
13	Cesar	1567	1	1567
	Other		2	
	TOTAL		86	

TOP POINT EARNERS

	PLAYER	GAMES	AV PTS
1	Chris Brunt	13	2.23
2	Bostjan Cesar	15	2.07
3	Zoltan Gera	30	1.93
4	Robert Koren	36	1.83
5	Kevin Phillips	24	1.83
6	Paul Robinson	43	1.79
7	Carl Hoeens	41	1.78
8	Roman Bednar	13	1.77
9	Jonathan Greening	45	1.73
10	Ishmael Miller	17	1.71
	CLUB AVERAGE:		1.76

DISCIPLINARY RECORDS

	PLAYER	YELLOW	RED	AVE
1	Neil Clement	3	0	242
2	Bostjan Cesar	6	0	261
3	Paul Robinson	7	2	421
4	Jonathan Greening	8	0	508
5	Ishmael Miller	4	0	513
6	Leon Barnett	4	0	702
7	Zoltan Gera	4	0	779
8	Roman Bednar	2	0	789
9	Carl Hoeens	4	0	928
10	Kevin Phillips	2	0	1272
11	Robert Koren	2	0	1670
12	Felipe Teixeira	1	0	1888
13	Chris Brunt	1	0	1928
	Other	2	0	
	TOTAL	50	2	

KEY GOALKEEPER

Dean Kiely

Goals Conceded in the League	52	Counting Games League games when player was on pitch for at least 70 minutes	44
Defensive Rating Ave number of mins between League goals conceded while on the pitch	76	Clean Sheets In League games when player was on pitch for at least 70 minutes	14

KEY PLAYERS - DEFENDERS

Paul Robinson

Goals Conceded Number of League goals conceded while the player was on the pitch	45	Clean Sheets In League games when player was on pitch for at least 70 minutes	15
Defensive Rating Ave number of mins between League goals conceded while on the pitch	84	Club Defensive Rating Average number of mins between League goals conceded by the club this season	75

	PLAYER	CON LGE	CLEAN SHEETS	DEF RATE
1	Paul Robinson	45	15	84 mins
2	Carl Hoefkens	46	14	80 mins
3	Leon Barnett	36	10	78 mins
4	Martin Albrechtsen	34	9	73 mins

KEY PLAYERS - MIDFIELDERS

James Morrison

Goals in the League	4	Contribution to Attacking Power Average number of minutes between League team goals while on pitch	43
Defensive Rating Average number of mins between League goals conceded while on the pitch	99	Scoring Difference Defensive Rating minus Contribution to Attacking Power	56

	PLAYER	LGE GOALS	DEF RATE	POWER	SCORE DIFF
1	James Morrison	4	99	43	56 mins
2	Zoltan Gera	8	84	48	36 mins
3	Chris Brunt	5	71	41	30 mins
4	Jonathan Greening	1	75	47	28 mins

KEY PLAYERS - GOALSCORERS

Kevin Phillips

Goals in the League	22	Player Strike Rate Average number of minutes between League goals scored by player	115
Contribution to Attacking Power Average number of minutes between League team goals while on pitch	43	Club Strike Rate Average number of minutes between League goals scored by club	47

	PLAYER	LGE GOALS	POWER	STRIKE RATE
1	Kevin Phillips	22	43	115 mins
2	Roman Bednar	12	45	131 mins
3	Ishmael Miller	9	43	228 mins
4	Robert Koren	9	45	371 mins

T · · Mobile·
ALBION
Kevin Phillips

SQUAD APPEARANCES

Match	1	2	3	4	5	6	7	8	9	10	11	12	13	14	15	16	17	18	19	20	21	22	23	24	25	26	27	28
Venue	A	H	H	A	A	H	H	A	A	H	H	H	A	A	H	H	A	H	A	H	A	A	H	A	H	A	H	H
Competition	L	W	L	L	W	L	L	L	L	W	L	L	L	L	L	L	L	L	L	L	L	L	L	L	L	L	L	L
Result	L	W	W	L	W	W	W	D	W	L	W	D	L	L	W	W	W	D	W	D	W	D	L	W	W	L	W	W

Match	29	30	31	32	33	34	35	36	37	38	39	40	41	42	43	44	45	46	47	48	49	50	51	52	53	54	55
Venue	A	A	A	H	H	A	A	H	A	H	A	H	H	A	A	H	H	A	H	A	N	A	H	A	A	H	A
Competition	L	F	L	F	L	F	L	L	L	L	F	L	L	L	F	L	L	L	L	L	F	L	L	L	L	L	L
Result	L	D	W	W	D	W	L	W	L	D	W	L	W	W	W	D	L	D	W	D	L	W	D	W	W	D	W

Goalkeepers
Michal Danek
Luke Daniels
Dean Kiely
Luke Steele
Defenders
Martin Albrechtsen
Leon Barnett
Bostjan Cesar
Neil Clement
Jared Hodgkiss
Carl Hoeens
Shelton Martis
Pedro Pele
Paul Robinson
Miguel Tininho
Midfielders
Chris Brunt
Richard Chaplow
Zoltan Gera
Jonathan Greening
Do-Heon Kim
Robert Koren
James Morrison
Felipe Teixeira
David Worrall
Forwards
Craig Beattie
Roman Bednar
Nathan Ellington
Sherjili MacDonald
Ishmael Miller
Luke Moore
Stuart Nicholson
Kevin Phillips
Bartosz Slusarski

KEY: ■ On all match ■ On bench ⏮ Subbed or sent off (Counting game) « Subbed or sent off (playing less than 70 minutes) ⏭ Subbed on from bench (Counting Game) » Subbed on (playing less than 70 minutes) » Subbed on and then subbed or sent off (Counting Game) » Subbed on and then subbed or sent off (playing less than 70 minutes) □ Not in 16

STOKE CITY

Final Position: **2nd**

NICKNAME: THE POTTERS

KEY: ☐Won ☐Drawn ☐Lost

							Attendance
1	div1	Cardiff	A	W	1-0	Shawcross 27	18,840
2	ccr1	Rochdale	A	L	2-4*	Shawcross 4, Cresswell 120 (*on penalties)	2,369
3	div1	Charlton	H	W	2-1	Fuller 57, Parkin 78	12,649
4	div1	Southampton	A	L	2-3	Fuller 10, Parkin 82	20,300
5	div1	Wolverhampton	H	D	0-0		17,135
6	div1	Hull City	A	D	1-1	Delap 44	19,642
7	div1	Barnsley	H	D	0-0		13,071
8	div1	Plymouth	H	W	3-2	Seip 10 og, Lawrence 66, Fuller 73	12,533
9	div1	Leicester	A	D	1-1	Fuller 15	23,654
10	div1	West Brom	A	D	1-1	Shawcross 27	20,048
11	div1	Colchester	H	W	2-1	Shawcross 8, Lawrence 73	12,395
12	div1	Sheff Wed	H	L	2-4	Fuller 12, 41	14,019
13	div1	Crystal Palace	A	W	3-1	Cresswell 49, 59, Shawcross 74	14,237
14	div1	Bristol City	A	L	0-1		15,012
15	div1	Coventry	H	L	1-3	Lawrence 72 pen	13,448
16	div1	Scunthorpe	A	W	3-2	Cresswell 26, Hayes 88 og, Lawrence 90	5,521
17	div1	Sheff Utd	H	L	0-1		12,158
18	div1	Burnley	A	D	0-0		11,758
19	div1	QPR	H	W	3-1	Cresswell 5, Lawrence 19, Cort 77	11,147
20	div1	Norwich	H	W	2-1	Cort 46, Cresswell 89	19,285
21	div1	Sheff Utd	A	W	3-0	Cresswell 2, Beattie 7 og, Shawcross 19	23,378
22	div1	Watford	H	D	0-0		15,516
23	div1	Blackpool	A	W	3-2	Fuller 37, 61, Cort 41	9,123
24	div1	West Brom	H	W	3-1	Fuller 5, 38, 66	18,420
25	div1	Barnsley	A	D	3-3	Lawrence 31 pen, 84, 90 pen	12,398
26	div1	Plymouth	A	D	2-2	Cresswell 8, Shawcross 57	13,692
27	div1	Hull City	H	D	1-1	Cort 33	15,788
28	facr3	Newcastle	H	D	0-0		22,861
29	div1	Ipswich	A	D	1-1	Fuller 33	20,346
30	facr3r	Newcastle	A	L	1-4	Lawrence 89	35,108
31	div1	Preston	H	W	3-1	Cort 16, 72, Cresswell 28	15,011
32	div1	Charlton	A	L	0-1		22,108
33	div1	Cardiff	H	W	2-1	Johnson 39 og, Fuller 57 pen	15,045
34	div1	Wolverhampton	A	W	4-2	Delap 4, Lawrence 49, Cort 74, Fuller 90	25,373
35	div1	Southampton	H	W	3-2	Powell 27 og, Shawcross 35, Sidibe 44	19,481
36	div1	Scunthorpe	H	W	3-2	Lawrence 53, 67, Cresswell 63	20,979
37	div1	Ipswich	H	W	1-0	Lawrence 42	23,563
38	div1	Preston	A	L	0-2		10,347
39	div1	QPR	A	L	0-3		13,398
40	div1	Burnley	H	D	1-1	Lawrence 90 pen	18,432
41	div1	Norwich	A	W	1-0	Sidibe 58	23,471
42	div1	Watford	A	D	0-0		18,338
43	div1	Blackpool	H	D	1-1	Cort 47	20,019
44	div1	Sheff Wed	A	D	1-1	Cresswell 21	21,857
45	div1	Crystal Palace	H	L	1-2	Whelan 85	15,756
46	div1	Coventry	A	W	2-1	Fuller 55 pen, Lawrence 79	20,249
47	div1	Bristol City	H	W	2-1	Sidibe 14, 36	24,475
48	div1	Colchester	A	W	1-0	Cresswell 45	6,300
49	div1	Leicester	H	D	0-0		26,609

LEAGUE APPEARANCES, BOOKINGS AND GOALS

	AGE (on 01/07/08)	IN NAMED 16	APPEARANCES	COUNTING GAMES	MINUTES ON PITCH	LEAGUE GOALS	Yellow	Red
Goalkeepers								
Russell Hoult	35	33	1	1	81	0	0	1
Carlo Nash	34	10	10	10	900	0	0	0
Steve Simonsen	29	46	36	35	3159	0	0	0
Defenders								
Lewis Buxton	24	7	4	1	158	0	1	0
Leon Cort	28	33	33	31	2856	8	0	0
Jody Craddock	32	4	4	4	360	0	0	0
Carl Dickinson	21	34	27	16	1746	0	2	0
Andrew Griffin	29	15	15	13	1252	0	1	1
Danny Higginbotham	29	1	1	1	90	0	0	0
Clinton Hill	29	6	5	3	317	0	1	0
Dominic Matteo	34	14	14	14	1248	0	2	0
Danny Pugh	25	32	30	27	2481	0	5	0
Chris Riggott	27	9	9	9	810	0	0	0
Ryan Shawcross	20	43	41	39	3571	7	10	0
Andy Wilkinson	23	32	23	11	1394	0	3	0
Stephen Wright	28	17	16	11	1101	0	3	0
Gabriel Zakuani	22	30	19	11	1169	0	1	0
Midfielders								
Rory Delap	31	44	44	43	3896	2	5	0
Salif Diao	31	13	11	4	575	0	1	0
John Eustace	28	28	26	20	1894	0	2	0
Liam Lawrence	26	41	41	39	3527	14	12	0
Stephen Pearson	25	6	4	2	222	0	0	0
Glenn Whelan	24	14	14	13	1168	1	2	0
Forwards								
Shola Ameobi	26	6	6	2	207	0	2	0
Jay Bothroyd	26	5	4	0	117	0	0	0
Richard Cresswell	30	43	43	41	3780	11	10	0
Ricardo Fuller	28	42	42	38	3519	15	11	0
Paul Gallagher	23	11	7	1	273	0	1	0
Jonathan Parkin	26	38	29	2	720	2	0	0
Vincent Pericard	25	14	5	0	132	0	0	0
Mamady Sidibe	28	35	35	26	2660	4	1	0

TEAM OF THE SEASON

D
Carl Dickinson
CG: 16 DR: 134
M
Rory Delap
CG: 43 SD: 20
D
Dominic Matteo
CG: 14 DR: 78
M
Liam Lawrence
CG: 39 SD: 16
F
Ricardo Fuller
CG: 38 SR: 234
G
Steve Simonsen
CG: 35 DR: 68
D
Andrew Griffin
CG: 13 DR: 73
M
John Eustace
CG: 20 SD: 12
F
Richard Cresswell
CG: 41 SR: 343
D
Leon Cort
CG: 31 DR: 73
M
Glenn Whelan
CG: 13 SD: 5

MONTHLY POINTS TALLY

AUGUST	6	67%
SEPTEMBER	7	47%
OCTOBER	7	47%
NOVEMBER	7	47%
DECEMBER	15	71%
JANUARY	5	42%
FEBRUARY	15	83%
MARCH	7	39%
APRIL	9	75%
MAY	1	33%

LEAGUE GOALS

	PLAYER	MINS	GOALS	S RATE
1	Fuller	3519	15	234
2	Lawrence	3527	14	251
3	Cresswell	3780	11	343
4	Cort	2856	8	357
5	Shawcross	3571	7	510
6	Sidibe	2660	4	665
7	Parkin	720	2	360
8	Delap	3896	2	1948
9	Whelan	1168	1	1168
10	Wilkinson	1394	0	
11	Wright	1101	0	
12	Zakuani	1169	0	
13	Pearson	222	0	
	Other		0	
	TOTAL		64	

TOP POINT EARNERS

	PLAYER	GAMES	AV PTS
1	Mamady Sidibe	26	2.15
2	Carl Dickinson	16	2.13
3	Liam Lawrence	39	1.87
4	Leon Cort	31	1.84
5	Rory Delap	43	1.79
6	Ryan Shawcross	39	1.77
7	Danny Pugh	27	1.74
8	Steve Simonsen	35	1.74
9	Ricardo Fuller	38	1.74
10	Glenn Whelan	13	1.69
	CLUB AVERAGE:		1.72

DISCIPLINARY RECORDS

	PLAYER	YELLOW	RED	AVE
1	Liam Lawrence	12	0	293
2	Ricardo Fuller	11	0	319
3	Ryan Shawcross	10	0	357
4	Stephen Wright	3	0	367
5	Richard Cresswell	10	0	378
6	Andy Wilkinson	3	0	464
7	Danny Pugh	5	0	496
8	Salif Diao	1	0	575
9	Glenn Whelan	2	0	584
10	Dominic Matteo	2	0	624
11	Andrew Griffin	1	1	626
12	Rory Delap	5	0	779
13	Carl Dickinson	2	0	873
	Other	4	0	
	TOTAL	71	1	

KEY GOALKEEPER

Steve Simonsen

Goals Conceded in the League	46	Counting Games League games when player was on pitch for at least 70 minutes	35
Defensive Rating Ave number of mins between League goals conceded while on the pitch	68	Clean Sheets In League games when player was on pitch for at least 70 minutes	7

KEY PLAYERS - DEFENDERS

Carl Dickinson

Goals Conceded Number of League goals conceded while the player was on the pitch	13	Clean Sheets In League games when player was on pitch for at least 70 minutes	7
Defensive Rating Ave number of mins between League goals conceded while on the pitch	134	Club Defensive Rating Average number of mins between League goals conceded by the club this season	75

	PLAYER	CON LGE	CLEAN SHEETS	DEF RATE
1	Carl Dickinson	13	7	134 mins
2	Dominic Matteo	16	4	78 mins
3	Andrew Griffin	17	3	73 mins
4	Leon Cort	39	7	73 mins

KEY PLAYERS - MIDFIELDERS

Rory Delap

Goals in the League	2	Contribution to Attacking Power Average number of minutes between League team goals while on pitch	57
Defensive Rating Average number of mins between League goals conceded while on the pitch	77	Scoring Difference Defensive Rating minus Contribution to Attacking Power	20

	PLAYER	LGE GOALS	DEF RATE	POWER	SCORE DIFF
1	Rory Delap	2	77	57	20 mins
2	Liam Lawrence	14	71	55	16 mins
3	John Eustace	0	63	51	12 mins
4	Glenn Whelan	1	73	68	5 mins

KEY PLAYERS - GOALSCORERS

Ricardo Fuller

Goals in the League	15	Player Strike Rate Average number of minutes between League goals scored by player	234
Contribution to Attacking Power Average number of minutes between League team goals while on pitch	57	Club Strike Rate Average number of minutes between League goals scored by club	60

	PLAYER	LGE GOALS	POWER	STRIKE RATE
1	Ricardo Fuller	15	57	234 mins
2	Liam Lawrence	14	55	251 mins
3	Richard Cresswell	11	64	343 mins
4	Mamady Sidibe	4	57	665 mins

Liam Lawrence and Ricardo Fuller

SQUAD APPEARANCES

Match	1	2	3	4	5	6	7	8	9	10	11	12	13	14	15	16	17	18	19	20	21	22	23	24	25	26	27	28	29	30	31	32	33	34	35	36	37	38	39	40	41	42	43	44	45	46	47	48	49
Venue	A	A	H	A	H	A	H	H	A	A	H	H	A	A	H	A	H	A	H	H	A	H	A	H	A	A	H	H	A	A	H	A	H	A	H	H	H	A	A	H	A	A	H	A	H	A	H	A	H
Competition	L	W	L	L	L	L	L	L	L	L	L	L	L	L	L	L	L	L	L	L	L	L	L	L	L	L	L	F	L	F	L	L	L	L	L	L	L	L	L	L	L	L	L	L	L	L	L	L	L
Result	W	L	W	L	D	D	D	W	D	D	W	L	W	L	L	W	L	D	W	W	W	D	W	W	D	D	D	D	D	L	W	L	W	W	W	W	W	L	L	D	W	D	D	D	L	W	W	W	D

Goalkeepers
Russell Hoult
Carlo Nash
Steve Simonsen

Defenders
Lewis Buxton
Leon Cort
Jody Craddock
Carl Dickinson
Andrew Griffin
Danny Higginbotham
Clinton Hill
Dominic Matteo
Danny Pugh
Chris Riggott
Ryan Shawcross
Andy Wilkinson
Stephen Wright
Gabriel Zakuani

Midfielders
Rory Delap
Salif Diao
John Eustace
Liam Lawrence
Stephen Pearson
Glenn Whelan

Forwards
Shola Ameobi
Jay Bothroyd
Richard Cresswell
Ricardo Fuller
Paul Gallagher
Jonathan Parkin
Vincent Pericard
Mamady Sidibe

KEY: On all match | On bench | Subbed or sent off (Counting game) | Subbed or sent off (playing less than 70 minutes) | Subbed on from bench (Counting Game) | Subbed on (playing less than 70 minutes) | Subbed on and then subbed or sent off (Counting Game) | Subbed on and then subbed or sent off (playing less than 70 minutes) | Not in 16

HULL CITY

PROMOTED VIA THE PLAY-OFFS Final Position: **3rd**

NICKNAME: THE TIGERS

KEY: ☐Won ☐Drawn ☐Lost

#	Comp	Opponent	H/A	Res	Score	Scorers	Attendance
1	div1	Plymouth	H	L	2-3	Windass 3, Marney 49	16,633
2	ccr1	Crewe	A	W	3-0	Bridges 44, Garcia 55, McPhee 70	2,862
3	div1	Coventry	A	D	1-1	Barmby 62	21,059
4	div1	Norwich	H	W	2-1	Windass 49, Garcia 77	15,939
5	ccr2	Wigan	A	W	1-0	Elliott 31	5,440
6	div1	Blackpool	A	L	1-2	Ashbee 50	7,902
7	div1	Stoke	H	D	1-1	Livermore 87	19,642
8	div1	Wolverhampton	A	W	1-0	Windass 49 pen	21,352
9	div1	Sheff Wed	A	L	0-1		21,518
10	ccr3	Chelsea	H	L	0-4		23,543
11	div1	Ipswich	H	W	3-1	Pedersen 11, 40, Brown 45	15,456
12	div1	Charlton	H	L	1-2	McPhee 90	15,001
13	div1	Crystal Palace	A	D	1-1	Marney 90 pen	15,769
14	div1	Watford	A	L	0-1		15,803
15	div1	Barnsley	H	W	3-0	Campbell 7, 18, Marney 90	15,761
16	div1	Sheff Utd	H	D	1-1	Windass 54 pen	20,185
17	div1	QPR	A	L	0-2		12,375
18	div1	Burnley	A	W	1-0	Turner 90	9,978
19	div1	Preston	H	W	3-0	Windass 11, Campbell 21, Dawson 63	16,358
20	div1	Scunthorpe	A	W	2-1	Windass 4, 16	8,633
21	div1	Bristol City	H	D	0-0		15,768
22	div1	Cardiff	H	D	2-2	McPhee 3, Garcia 43	16,269
23	div1	Preston	A	L	0-3		11,311
24	div1	Southampton	A	L	0-4		18,125
25	div1	Leicester	H	W	2-0	Folan 17, Campbell 78	16,006
26	div1	Charlton	A	D	1-1	Campbell 37	22,040
27	div1	Wolverhampton	H	W	2-0	Garcia 47, Campbell 61	19,127
28	div1	Sheff Wed	H	W	1-0	Windass 33	21,252
29	div1	Stoke	A	D	1-1	Folan 61	15,788
30	facr3	Plymouth	A	L	2-3	Windass 51, 60	12,419
31	div1	West Brom	H	L	1-3	Garcia 71	18,391
32	div1	Coventry	H	W	1-0	Folan 90	14,822
33	div1	Plymouth	A	W	1-0	Windass 45	11,011
34	div1	Blackpool	H	D	2-2	Folan 60, Windass 71	18,407
35	div1	Norwich	A	D	1-1	Campbell 53	25,259
36	div1	Colchester	H	D	1-1	Campbell 64	15,664
37	div1	West Brom	A	W	2-1	Campbell 29, Folan 82	22,716
38	div1	Bristol City	A	L	1-2	Fontaine 45 og	15,859
39	div1	Burnley	H	W	2-0	Campbell 14, Garcia 28	15,838
40	div1	Scunthorpe	H	W	2-0	Pedersen 27, Turner 37	20,906
41	div1	Cardiff	A	L	0-1		17,555
42	div1	Southampton	H	W	5-0	Campbell 7, Pedersen 55, Turner 57, Marney 68, Hughes 90	16,829
43	div1	Colchester	A	W	3-1	Campbell 20, 33, Folan 87	5,497
44	div1	Leicester	A	W	2-0	Marney 45, Folan 76	30,374
45	div1	Watford	H	W	3-0	Turner 1, Campbell 13, Folan 73	23,501
46	div1	QPR	H	D	1-1	Turner 90	22,468
47	div1	Barnsley	A	W	3-1	Marney 24 pen, Ashbee 52, Windass 83	13,061
48	div1	Sheff Utd	A	L	0-2		28,188
49	div1	Crystal Palace	H	W	2-1	Campbell 18, Ashbee 85	24,350
50	div1	Ipswich	A	L	0-1		28,223
51	d1po1	Watford	A	W	2-0	Barmby 8, Windass 23	14,713
52	d1po2	Watford	H	W	4-1	Barmby 43, Folan 70, Garcia 88, Doyle 90	23,155
53	d1pof	Bristol City	N	W	1-0	Windass 38	86,703

LEAGUE APPEARANCES, BOOKINGS AND GOALS

	AGE (on 01/07/08)	IN NAMED 16	APPEARANCES	COUNTING GAMES	MINUTES ON PITCH	LEAGUE GOALS	Yellow	Red
Goalkeepers								
Matt Duke	30	29	3	3	270	0	0	0
Boaz Myhill	25	46	43	43	3870	0	3	0
Mark Tyler	31	12	0	0	0	0	0	0
Defenders								
Wayne Brown	30	41	41	39	3582	1	4	0
Neil Clement	29	7	5	4	427	0	0	0
Danny Coles	26	1	1	1	90	0	0	0
Sam Collins	31	1	0	0	0	0	0	0
Andrew Dawson	29	39	29	23	2249	1	4	0
Damien Delaney	26	26	22	20	1805	0	5	0
Samuel Ricketts	26	45	44	43	3926	0	8	1
Michael Turner	24	45	44	43	3915	5	6	0
Midfielders								
Ian Ashbee	31	42	42	40	3687	3	4	1
Will Atkinson	19	0	0	0	0	0	0	0
Nathan Doyle	21	11	1	0	59	0	0	0
Stuart Elliott	29	8	7	3	308	0	0	0
Craig Fagan	25	8	8	3	428	0	2	0
Ryan France	27	16	13	3	405	0	0	0
Richard Garcia	26	38	38	29	2931	5	5	0
Bryan Hughes	32	36	35	22	2314	1	1	0
David Livermore	28	24	20	9	920	1	5	0
Dean Marney	24	43	41	31	3091	6	8	0
Augustine Okocha	34	22	18	8	880	0	0	1
Simon Walton	20	18	10	3	428	0	2	0
Forwards								
Nick Barmby	34	15	15	3	513	1	2	0
Michael Bridges	29	10	7	0	209	0	0	0
Fraizer Campbell	20	34	34	28	2661	15	3	0
Nicky Featherstone	18	8	6	0	63	0	0	0
Caleb Folan	25	29	29	15	1704	8	4	1
Stephen McPhee	27	20	19	5	808	2	0	0
Henrik Pedersen	33	21	21	14	1535	4	0	0
Dean Windass	39	37	37	20	2356	11	6	0

TEAM OF THE SEASON

G
Boaz Myhill
CG: 43 DR: 90
D
Michael Turner
CG: 43 DR: 100
D
Andrew Dawson
CG: 23 DR: 93
D
Samuel Ricketts
CG: 43 DR: 89
D
Wayne Brown
CG: 39 DR: 87
M
Richard Garcia
CG: 29 SD: 23
M
Bryan Hughes
CG: 22 SD: 22
M
Dean Marney
CG: 31 SD: 21
M
Ian Ashbee
CG: 40 SD: 20
F
Fraizer Campbell
CG: 28 SR: 177
F
Caleb Folan
CG: 15 SR: 213

MONTHLY POINTS TALLY

Month	Points	%
AUGUST	4	44%
SEPTEMBER	7	47%
OCTOBER	5	33%
NOVEMBER	10	67%
DECEMBER	11	52%
JANUARY	4	44%
FEBRUARY	9	60%
MARCH	18	75%
APRIL	7	58%
MAY	0	0%

LEAGUE GOALS

	PLAYER	MINS	GOALS	S RATE
1	Campbell	2661	15	177
2	Windass	2356	11	214
3	Folan	1704	8	213
4	Garcia	2931	5	586
5	Marney	3091	6	515
6	Turner	3915	5	783
7	Pedersen	1535	4	383
8	McPhee	808	2	404
9	Barmby	513	1	513
10	Ashbee	3687	3	1229
11	Livermore	920	1	920
12	Dawson	2249	1	2249
13	Hughes	2314	1	2314
	Other		1	
	TOTAL		64	

TOP POINT EARNERS

	PLAYER	GAMES	AV PTS
1	Richard Garcia	29	1.97
2	Andrew Dawson	23	1.96
3	Fraizer Campbell	28	1.89
4	Henrik Pedersen	14	1.79
5	Michael Turner	43	1.74
6	Bryan Hughes	22	1.73
7	Dean Marney	31	1.65
8	Boaz Myhill	43	1.65
9	Samuel Ricketts	44	1.64
10	Wayne Brown	39	1.62
	CLUB AVERAGE:		1.63

DISCIPLINARY RECORDS

	PLAYER	YELLOW	RED	AVE
1	David Livermore	5	0	184
2	Nick Barmby	2	0	256
3	Caleb Folan	4	1	340
4	Damien Delaney	5	0	361
5	Dean Marney	8	0	386
6	Dean Windass	6	0	392
7	Samuel Ricketts	8	1	436
8	Andrew Dawson	4	0	562
9	Richard Garcia	5	0	586
10	Michael Turner	6	0	652
11	Ian Ashbee	4	1	737
12	Augustine Okocha	0	1	880
13	Fraizer Campbell	3	0	887
	Other	8	0	
	TOTAL	68	4	

KEY GOALKEEPER

Boaz Myhill

Goals Conceded in the League	43	**Counting Games** League games when player was on pitch for at least 70 minutes	43
Defensive Rating Ave number of mins between League goals conceded while on the pitch	90	**Clean Sheets** In League games when player was on pitch for at least 70 minutes	15

KEY PLAYERS - DEFENDERS

Michael Turner

Goals Conceded Number of League goals conceded while the player was on the pitch	39	**Clean Sheets** In League games when player was on pitch for at least 70 minutes	15
Defensive Rating Ave number of mins between League goals conceded while on the pitch	100	**Club Defensive Rating** Average number of mins between League goals conceded by the club this season	90

	PLAYER	CON LGE	CLEAN SHEETS	DEF RATE
1	Michael Turner	39	15	100 mins
2	Andrew Dawson	24	9	93 mins
3	Samuel Ricketts	44	15	89 mins
4	Wayne Brown	41	12	87 mins

KEY PLAYERS - MIDFIELDERS

Richard Garcia

Goals in the League	5	**Contribution to Attacking Power** Average number of minutes between League team goals while on pitch	65
Defensive Rating Average number of mins between League goals conceded while on the pitch	88	**Scoring Difference** Defensive Rating minus Contribution to Attacking Power	23

	PLAYER	LGE GOALS	DEF RATE	POWER	SCORE DIFF
1	Richard Garcia	5	88	65	23 mins
2	Bryan Hughes	1	96	74	22 mins
3	Dean Marney	6	85	64	21 mins
4	Ian Ashbee	3	83	63	20 mins

KEY PLAYERS - GOALSCORERS

Fraizer Campbell

Goals in the League	15	**Player Strike Rate** Average number of minutes between League goals scored by player	177
Contribution to Attacking Power Average number of minutes between League team goals while on pitch	59	**Club Strike Rate** Average number of minutes between League goals scored by club	65

	PLAYER	LGE GOALS	POWER	STRIKE RATE
1	Fraizer Campbell	15	59	177 mins
2	Caleb Folan	8	65	213 mins
3	Dean Windass	11	58	214 mins
4	Henrik Pedersen	4	51	383 mins

KAROO
Dean Windass

SQUAD APPEARANCES

Match	1	2	3	4	5	6	7	8	9	10	11	12	13	14	15	16	17	18	19	20	21	22	23	24	25	26	27	28	29	30	31	32	33	34	35	36	37	38	39	40	41	42	43	44	45	46	47	48	49	50	51	52	53
Venue	H	A	A	H	A	A	H	A	A	H	H	H	A	A	H	H	A	A	H	A	H	H	A	A	H	A	H	H	A	A	H	H	A	H	A	H	A	A	H	H	A	H	A	A	H	H	A	A	H	A	A	H	N
Competition	L	W	L	L	W	L	L	L	L	W	L	L	L	L	L	L	L	L	L	L	L	L	L	L	L	L	L	L	L	F	L	L	L	L	L	L	L	L	L	L	L	L	L	L	L	L	L	L	L	L	O	O	O
Result	L	W	D	W	W	L	D	W	L	L	W	L	D	L	W	D	L	W	W	W	D	D	L	L	W	D	W	W	D	L	L	W	W	D	D	D	W	L	W	W	L	W	W	W	W	D	W	L	W	L	W	W	W

Goalkeepers
Matt Duke
Boaz Myhill
Mark Tyler
Defenders
Wayne Brown
Neil Clement
Danny Coles
Sam Collins
Andrew Dawson
Damien Delaney
Samuel Ricketts
Michael Turner
Midfielders
Ian Ashbee
Will Atkinson
Nathan Doyle
Stuart Elliott
Craig Fagan
Ryan France
Richard Garcia
Bryan Hughes
David Livermore
Dean Marney
Augustine Okocha
Simon Walton
Forwards
Nick Barmby
Michael Bridges
Fraizer Campbell
Nicky Featherstone
Caleb Folan
Stephen McPhee
Henrik Pedersen
Dean Windass

KEY: On all match | On bench | Subbed or sent off (Counting game) | Subbed or sent off (playing less than 70 minutes) | Subbed on from bench (Counting Game) | Subbed on (playing less than 70 minutes) | Subbed on and then subbed or sent off (Counting Game) | Subbed on and then subbed or sent off (playing less than 70 minutes) | Not in 16

BRISTOL CITY

Final Position: **4th**

NICKNAME: THE ROBINS

KEY: ☐Won ☐Drawn ☐Lost

							Attendance
1	div1	QPR	H	D	2-2	Johnson 33, Murray 90	18,228
2	ccr1	Brentford	A	W	3-0	Elliott 16, Jevons 42, 86	2,213
3	div1	Blackpool	A	D	1-1	Murray 75	8,983
4	div1	Scunthorpe	H	W	2-1	Trundle 36, 45	12,474
5	ccr2	Man City	H	L	1-2	Orr 69	14,541
6	div1	Sheff Wed	A	W	1-0	Wilson 4	17,559
7	div1	Coventry	A	W	3-0	McIndoe 15, Konstantopoulos 74 og, Byfield 90	21,538
8	div1	West Brom	H	D	1-1	Orr 89	16,571
9	div1	Burnley	H	D	2-2	Byfield 80, 86	14,079
10	div1	Preston	A	D	0-0		12,098
11	div1	Barnsley	A	L	0-3		9,679
12	div1	Sheff Utd	H	W	2-0	Noble 44, McIndoe 72	13,071
13	div1	Norwich	A	W	3-1	McIndoe 48, Murray 85, Trundle 90	24,125
14	div1	Southampton	H	W	2-1	Byfield 4, Sproule 17	18,326
15	div1	Stoke	H	W	1-0	Elliott 35	15,012
16	div1	Wolverhampton	A	D	1-1	Fontaine 27	26,094
17	div1	Charlton	H	L	0-1		15,420
18	div1	Ipswich	A	L	0-6		22,020
19	div1	Leicester	H	L	0-2		15,040
20	div1	Hull City	A	D	0-0		15,768
21	div1	Watford	A	W	2-1	Showunmi 75, Byfield 90	16,689
22	div1	Ipswich	H	W	2-0	Elliott 5, Orr 32 pen	14,062
23	div1	Plymouth	A	D	1-1	Timar 71 og	16,530
24	div1	Cardiff	H	W	1-0	Elliott 57	15,753
25	div1	Barnsley	H	W	3-2	Showunmi 35, 45, Byfield 90	16,588
26	div1	West Brom	A	L	1-4	Byfield 87	27,314
27	div1	Burnley	A	W	1-0	Vasko 67	12,109
28	div1	Coventry	H	W	2-1	Byfield 5, Elliott 67	15,899
29	facr3	Middlesbrough	H	L	1-2	Fontaine 18	15,895
30	div1	Colchester	H	D	1-1	Sproule 33	16,484
31	div1	Crystal Palace	A	L	0-2		19,010
32	div1	Blackpool	H	W	1-0	Elliott 20	15,465
33	div1	QPR	A	L	0-3		16,502
34	div1	Sheff Wed	H	W	2-1	Adebola 7, Orr 56	15,520
35	div1	Scunthorpe	A	W	1-0	Orr 83	5,423
36	div1	Crystal Palace	H	D	1-1	McCombe 90	16,446
37	div1	Colchester	A	W	2-1	Adebola 52, McIndoe 58	5,609
38	div1	Hull City	H	W	2-1	Adebola 14, McCombe 46	15,859
39	div1	Charlton	A	D	1-1	McCombe 62	24,075
40	div1	Leicester	A	D	0-0		22,616
41	div1	Watford	H	D	0-0		19,026
42	div1	Plymouth	H	L	1-2	Trundle 74 pen	19,011
43	div1	Cardiff	A	L	1-2	Adebola 73	16,458
44	div1	Norwich	H	W	2-1	Adebola 41, Brooker 90	17,511
45	div1	Southampton	A	L	0-2		22,890
46	div1	Wolverhampton	H	D	0-0		19,332
47	div1	Stoke	A	L	1-2	Adebola 67	24,475
48	div1	Sheff Utd	A	L	1-2	McIndoe 25 pen	29,787
49	div1	Preston	H	W	3-0	Trundle 8, McIndoe 16, Noble 51	19,169
50	d1po1	Crystal Palace	A	W	2-1	Carey 53, Noble 90	22,869
51	d1po1	Crystal Palace	H	W	2-1	Trundle 104, McIndoe 110	18,842
52	d1pof	Hull City	N	L	0-1		86,703

LEAGUE APPEARANCES, BOOKINGS AND GOALS

	AGE (on 01/07/08)	IN NAMED 16	APPEARANCES	COUNTING GAMES	MINUTES ON PITCH	LEAGUE GOALS		
Goalkeepers								
Adriano Basso	33	46	44	42	3890	0	0	0
Stephen Henderson	20	10	1	0	45	0	0	0
Chris Weale	26	36	3	2	205	0	0	0
Defenders								
Louis Carey	31	33	33	31	2837	0	5	0
Liam Fontaine	22	44	38	31	2981	1	7	0
Richard Keogh	21	0	0	0	0	0	0	0
James McAllister	30	44	41	38	3531	0	9	1
Jamie McCombe	25	35	34	26	2441	3	3	0
Bradley Orr	25	42	42	40	3700	4	5	2
Christian Ribeiro	18	1	0	0	0	0	0	0
James Wilson	19	19	18	11	1243	1	1	0
Midfielders								
Kevin Betsy	30	1	1	0	16	0	1	0
Nick Carle	26	18	17	9	1119	0	1	0
Marvin Elliott	23	45	45	44	3938	5	2	0
Lee Johnson	27	40	40	37	3413	1	3	0
Michael McIndoe	28	45	45	44	3959	6	3	0
Scott Murray	34	21	14	3	576	3	0	0
David Noble	26	31	26	9	1194	2	2	0
Alex Russell	35	2	1	1	76	0	0	0
Cole Skuse	22	35	25	4	595	0	1	0
Ivan Sproule	27	41	40	25	2655	2	4	0
Tamas Vasko	24	26	19	5	719	1	2	0
Forwards								
Dele Adebola	33	17	17	14	1345	6	2	0
Stephen Brooker	27	4	4	1	176	1	0	0
Darren Byfield	31	37	33	14	1784	8	5	0
Phil Jevons	28	3	2	0	39	0	0	0
Enoch Showunmi	25	18	17	7	911	3	1	0
Lee Trundle	31	42	35	19	2050	5	2	0

TEAM OF THE SEASON

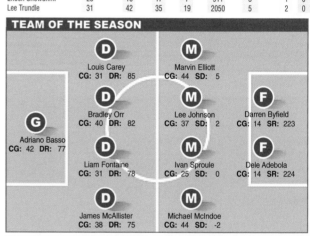

G Adriano Basso CG: 42 DR: 77

D Louis Carey CG: 31 DR: 85

D Bradley Orr CG: 40 DR: 82

D Liam Fontaine CG: 31 DR: 78

D James McAllister CG: 38 DR: 75

M Marvin Elliott CG: 44 SD: 5

M Lee Johnson CG: 37 SD: 2

M Ivan Sproule CG: 25 SD: 0

M Michael McIndoe CG: 44 SD: -2

F Darren Byfield CG: 14 SR: 223

F Dele Adebola CG: 14 SR: 224

MONTHLY POINTS TALLY

AUGUST	5	56%
SEPTEMBER	9	60%
OCTOBER	12	80%
NOVEMBER	2	13%
DECEMBER	16	76%
JANUARY	7	58%
FEBRUARY	10	67%
MARCH	9	43%
APRIL	1	8%
MAY	3	100%

LEAGUE GOALS

	PLAYER	MINS	GOALS	S RATE
1	Byfield	1784	8	223
2	McIndoe	3959	6	659
3	Adebola	1345	6	224
4	Trundle	2050	5	410
5	Elliott	3938	5	787
6	Orr	3700	4	925
7	Murray	576	3	192
8	Showunmi	911	3	303
9	Noble	1194	2	597
10	McCombe	2441	3	813
11	Sproule	2655	2	1327
12	Fontaine	2981	1	2981
13	Jevons	39	0	
	Other		4	
	TOTAL		52	

TOP POINT EARNERS

	PLAYER	GAMES	AV PTS
1	Ivan Sproule	25	1.96
2	Lee Johnson	37	1.76
3	Liam Fontaine	31	1.71
4	Jamie McCombe	26	1.69
5	Lee Trundle	19	1.63
6	Bradley Orr	41	1.61
7	Marvin Elliott	44	1.61
8	Michael McIndoe	44	1.59
9	Louis Carey	31	1.58
10	Adriano Basso	42	1.57
	CLUB AVERAGE:		1.61

DISCIPLINARY RECORDS

	PLAYER	YELLOW	RED	AVE
1	James McAllister	9	1	353
2	Darren Byfield	5	0	356
3	Tamas Vasko	2	0	359
4	Liam Fontaine	7	0	425
5	Bradley Orr	5	2	528
6	Louis Carey	5	0	567
7	Cole Skuse	1	0	595
8	David Noble	2	0	597
9	Ivan Sproule	4	0	663
10	Dele Adebola	2	0	672
11	Jamie McCombe	3	0	813
12	Enoch Showunmi	1	0	911
13	Lee Trundle	2	0	1025
	Other	10	0	
	TOTAL	58	3	

KEY GOALKEEPER

Adriano Basso

Goals Conceded in the League	50	**Counting Games** League games when player was on pitch for at least 70 minutes	42
Defensive Rating Ave number of mins between League goals conceded while on the pitch	77	**Clean Sheets** In League games when player was on pitch for at least 70 minutes	14

KEY PLAYERS - GOALSCORERS

Darren Byfield

Goals in the League	8	**Player Strike Rate** Average number of minutes between League goals scored by player	223
Contribution to Attacking Power Average number of minutes between League team goals while on pitch	77	**Club Strike Rate** Average number of minutes between League goals scored by club	76

	PLAYER	LGE GOALS	POWER	STRIKE RATE
1	Darren Byfield	8	77	223 mins
2	Dele Adebola	6	84	224 mins
3	Lee Trundle	5	64	410 mins
4	Michael McIndoe	6	79	659 mins

KEY PLAYERS - DEFENDERS

Louis Carey

Goals Conceded Number of League goals conceded while the player was on the pitch	33	**Clean Sheets** In League games when player was on pitch for at least 70 minutes	11
Defensive Rating Ave number of mins between League goals conceded while on the pitch	85	**Club Defensive Rating** Average number of mins between League goals conceded by the club this season	78

	PLAYER	CON LGE	CLEAN SHEETS	DEF RATE
1	Louis Carey	33	11	85 mins
2	Bradley Orr	45	13	82 mins
3	Liam Fontaine	38	11	78 mins
4	James McAllister	47	12	75 mins

Darren Byfield

KEY PLAYERS - MIDFIELDERS

Marvin Elliott

Goals in the League	5	**Contribution to Attacking Power** Average number of minutes between League team goals while on pitch	75
Defensive Rating Average number of mins between League goals conceded while on the pitch	80	**Scoring Difference** Defensive Rating minus Contribution to Attacking Power	5

	PLAYER	LGE GOALS	DEF RATE	POWER	SCORE DIFF
1	Marvin Elliott	5	80	75	5 mins
2	Lee Johnson	1	79	77	2 mins
3	Ivan Sproule	2	88	88	0 mins
4	Michael McIndoe	6	77	79	-2 mins

SQUAD APPEARANCES

Match	1	2	3	4	5	6	7	8	9	10	11	12	13	14	15	16	17	18	19	20	21	22	23	24	25	26	27	28	29	30	31	32	33	34	35	36	37	38	39	40	41	42	43	44	45	46	47	48	49	50	51	52
Venue	H	A	A	H	H	A	A	H	H	A	A	H	A	H	H	A	H	A	H	A	A	H	A	H	H	A	A	H	H	H	A	H	A	H	A	H	A	H	A	A	H	H	A	H	A	H	A	A	H	A	H	N
Competition	L	W	L	L	W	L	L	L	L	L	L	L	L	L	L	L	L	L	L	L	L	L	L	L	L	L	L	L	F	L	L	L	L	L	L	L	L	L	L	L	L	L	L	L	L	L	L	L	L	O	O	O
Result	D	W	D	W	L	W	W	D	D	D	L	W	W	W	W	D	L	L	L	D	W	W	D	W	W	L	W	W	L	D	L	W	L	W	W	D	W	W	D	D	D	L	L	W	L	D	L	L	W	W	W	L

Goalkeepers
- Adriano Basso
- Stephen Henderson
- Chris Weale

Defenders
- Louis Carey
- Liam Fontaine
- Richard Keogh
- James McAllister
- Jamie McCombe
- Bradley Orr
- Christian Ribeiro
- James Wilson

Midfielders
- Kevin Betsy
- Nick Carle
- Marvin Elliott
- Lee Johnson
- Michael McIndoe
- Scott Murray
- David Noble
- Alex Russell
- Cole Skuse
- Ivan Sproule
- Tamas Vasko

Forwards
- Dele Adebola
- Stephen Brooker
- Darren Byfield
- Phil Jevons
- Enoch Showunmi
- Lee Trundle

KEY: On all match | On bench | Subbed or sent off (Counting game) | Subbed or sent off (playing less than 70 minutes) | Subbed on from bench (Counting Game) | Subbed on (playing less than 70 minutes) | Subbed on and then subbed or sent off (Counting Game) | Subbed on and then subbed or sent off (playing less than 70 minutes) | Not in 16

CRYSTAL PALACE

Final Position: **5th**

NICKNAME: THE EAGLES

KEY: Won Drawn Lost

							Attendance
1	div1	Southampton	A	W	4-1	Scowcroft 30, 31, 55, Morrison 57	25,054
2	ccr1	Bristol Rovers	A	L	1-4*	Freedman 31 (*on penalties)	5,566
3	div1	Leicester	H	D	2-2	Green 33, Morrison 90	15,607
4	div1	Ipswich	A	L	0-1		19,382
5	div1	Charlton	H	L	0-1		18,556
6	div1	Norwich	A	L	0-1		24,228
7	div1	Coventry	H	D	1-1	Green 26	14,455
8	div1	Sheff Utd	H	W	3-2	Soares 60, Fletcher 70, Watson 89 pen	14,131
9	div1	Burnley	A	D	1-1	Hudson 5	10,711
10	div1	Plymouth	A	L	0-1		10,451
11	div1	Hull City	H	D	1-1	Scowcroft 81	15,769
12	div1	Blackpool	A	D	1-1	Soares 59	9,037
13	div1	Stoke	H	L	1-3	Freedman 51	14,237
14	div1	Watford	H	L	0-2		13,986
15	div1	Scunthorpe	A	D	0-0		6,778
16	div1	Cardiff	A	D	1-1	Watson 44 pen	11,781
17	div1	QPR	H	D	1-1	Morrison 88	17,010
18	div1	Colchester	A	W	2-1	Morrison 6, 74	5,856
19	div1	Preston	H	W	2-1	Morrison 40, Hill 45	13,048
20	div1	West Brom	H	D	1-1	Morrison 21	15,247
21	div1	QPR	A	W	2-1	Hill 65, Morrison 68	13,300
22	div1	Barnsley	A	D	0-0		10,298
23	div1	Sheff Wed	H	W	2-1	Morrison 37, Scannell 90	14,865
24	div1	Plymouth	H	W	2-1	Hill 8, Scowcroft 44	15,097
25	div1	Coventry	A	W	2-0	Morrison 47, Ifill 88	22,134
26	div1	Sheff Utd	A	W	1-0	Scowcroft 38	23,982
27	div1	Norwich	H	D	1-1	Morrison 51	17,199
28	facr3	Watford	A	L	0-2		10,480
29	div1	Wolverhampton	A	W	3-0	Morrison 24, Scannell 49, Scowcroft 66	22,650
30	div1	Bristol City	H	W	2-0	Morrison 6, Hudson 85	19,010
31	div1	Leicester	A	L	0-1		21,764
32	div1	Southampton	H	D	1-1	Scowcroft 73	17,967
33	div1	Charlton	A	L	0-2		26,202
34	div1	Ipswich	H	L	0-1		16,090
35	div1	Bristol City	A	D	1-1	Hills 61	16,446
36	div1	Wolverhampton	H	L	0-2		15,679
37	div1	Preston	A	W	1-0	Morrison 76	12,347
38	div1	Cardiff	H	D	0-0		13,446
39	div1	Colchester	H	W	2-1	Ifil 21 og, Watson 74	13,895
40	div1	West Brom	A	D	1-1	Moses 55	20,378
41	div1	Barnsley	H	W	2-0	Soares 46, Scowcroft 83	17,459
42	div1	Sheff Wed	A	D	2-2	Watson 40, Lawrence 90	19,875
43	div1	Blackpool	H	D	0-0		16,028
44	div1	Stoke	A	W	2-1	Soares 23, Fonte 45	15,756
45	div1	Scunthorpe	H	W	2-0	Soares 21, Morrison 39	15,975
46	div1	Watford	A	W	2-0	Ifill 72, Moses 75	17,694
47	div1	Hull City	A	L	1-2	Sinclair 38	24,350
48	div1	Burnley	H	W	5-0	Watson 8 pen, Moses 10, Soares 37, Sinclair 61, Morrison 65	23,950
49	d1po1	Bristol City	H	L	1-2	Watson 87 pen	22,869
50	d1po1	Bristol City	A	L	1-2	Watson 24	18,842

LEAGUE APPEARANCES, BOOKINGS AND GOALS

	AGE (on 01/07/08)	IN NAMED 16	APPEARANCES	COUNTING GAMES	MINUTES ON PITCH	LEAGUE GOALS	Yellow	Red
Goalkeepers								
Julian Speroni	29	46	46	46	4140	0	3	0
Defenders								
Danny Butterfield	28	34	30	24	2315	0	4	0
Leon Cort	28	12	12	12	1080	0	0	0
Tony Craig	23	14	12	12	1080	0	2	0
Jose Fonte	24	31	22	15	1612	1	2	0
John Halls	26	5	5	5	450	0	0	0
Clinton Hill	29	28	28	27	2483	3	6	0
Mark Hudson	26	45	45	45	4050	2	2	0
Jeff Hughes	23	15	10	2	335	0	0	0
Matt Lawrence	34	41	37	35	3190	1	6	0
Midfielders								
John Bostock	16	5	4	1	144	0	0	0
Neil Danns	25	4	4	2	223	0	0	0
Shaun Derry	30	30	30	27	2567	0	4	0
Carl Fletcher	28	36	27	16	1590	1	2	0
Stuart Green	27	11	10	4	593	2	1	0
Lee Hills	18	25	13	6	709	1	0	0
Paul Ifill	28	15	13	1	494	2	1	0
Mark Kennedy	32	10	8	7	659	0	1	0
David Martin	23	15	9	1	328	0	1	0
Victor Moses	19	14	13	4	651	3	1	0
Kyel Reid	20	3	2	0	80	0	0	0
Tom Soares	21	41	39	32	3134	6	6	1
Franck Songo'o	21	9	9	2	544	0	4	0
Ben Watson	22	42	42	38	3551	5	2	0
Forwards								
Paul Dickov	35	10	9	3	454	0	2	0
Dougie Freedman	34	28	19	2	655	1	0	0
Besian Idrizaj	20	10	7	0	239	0	3	0
Shefki Kuqi	31	8	7	2	253	0	1	0
Clinton Morrison	29	44	43	30	2988	16	3	0
Sean Scannell	17	29	23	9	1144	2	0	0
James Scowcroft	34	39	38	33	3117	9	4	0
Scott Sinclair	19	6	6	5	492	2	1	0

TEAM OF THE SEASON

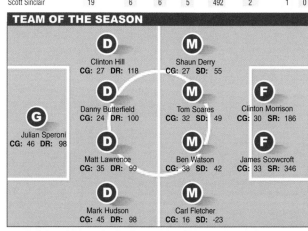

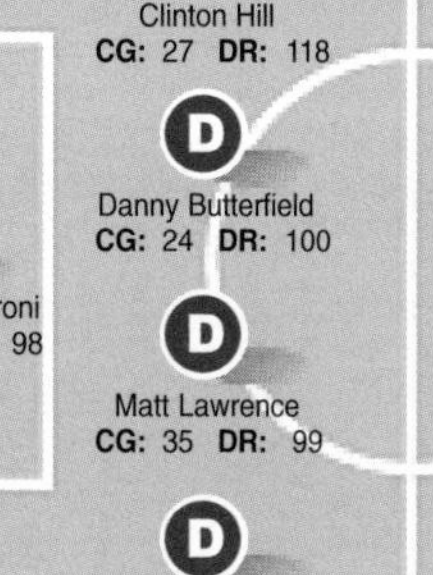
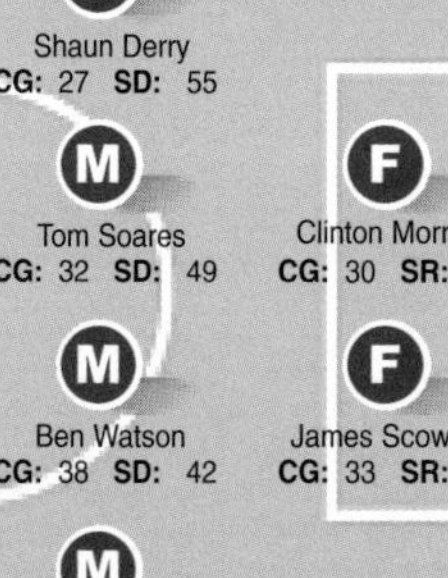

G — Julian Speroni — CG: 46 DR: 98

D — Clinton Hill — CG: 27 DR: 118

D — Danny Butterfield — CG: 24 DR: 100

D — Matt Lawrence — CG: 35 DR: 99

D — Mark Hudson — CG: 45 DR: 98

M — Shaun Derry — CG: 27 SD: 55

M — Tom Soares — CG: 32 SD: 49

M — Ben Watson — CG: 38 SD: 42

M — Carl Fletcher — CG: 16 SD: -23

F — Clinton Morrison — CG: 30 SR: 186

F — James Scowcroft — CG: 33 SR: 346

MONTHLY POINTS TALLY

AUGUST	4	44%
SEPTEMBER	5	33%
OCTOBER	2	13%
NOVEMBER	9	60%
DECEMBER	17	81%
JANUARY	7	58%
FEBRUARY	2	13%
MARCH	13	62%
APRIL	9	75%
MAY	3	100%

LEAGUE GOALS

	PLAYER	MINS	GOALS	S RATE
1	Morrison	2988	16	186
2	Scowcroft	3117	9	346
3	Watson	3551	5	710
4	Soares	3134	6	522
5	Moses	651	3	217
6	Hill	2483	3	827
7	Sinclair	492	2	246
8	Ifill	494	2	247
9	Green	593	2	296
10	Scannell	1144	2	572
11	Freedman	655	1	655
12	Hudson	4050	2	2025
13	Hills	709	1	709
	Other		3	
	TOTAL		57	

TOP POINT EARNERS

	PLAYER	GAMES	AV PTS
1	Clinton Hill	27	1.93
2	Shaun Derry	27	1.89
3	Clinton Morrison	30	1.83
4	Jose Fonte	15	1.80
5	Ben Watson	38	1.79
6	Tom Soares	32	1.78
7	Danny Butterfield	24	1.71
8	James Scowcroft	33	1.55
9	Julian Speroni	46	1.54
10	Mark Hudson	45	1.51
	CLUB AVERAGE:		1.54

DISCIPLINARY RECORDS

	PLAYER	YELLOW	RED	AVE
1	Franck Songo'o	4	0	136
2	Paul Dickov	2	0	227
3	Clinton Hill	6	0	413
4	Tom Soares	6	1	447
5	Scott Sinclair	1	0	492
6	Paul Ifill	1	0	494
7	Matt Lawrence	6	0	531
8	Tony Craig	2	0	540
9	Danny Butterfield	4	0	578
10	Stuart Green	1	0	593
11	Shaun Derry	4	0	641
12	Victor Moses	1	0	651
13	Mark Kennedy	1	0	659
	Other	18	0	
	TOTAL	57	1	

KEY GOALKEEPER

Julian Speroni

Goals Conceded in the League	42	Counting Games League games when player was on pitch for at least 70 minutes	46
Defensive Rating Ave number of mins between League goals conceded while on the pitch	98	Clean Sheets In League games when player was on pitch for at least 70 minutes	13

KEY PLAYERS - DEFENDERS

Clinton Hill

Goals Conceded Number of League goals conceded while the player was on the pitch	21	Clean Sheets In League games when player was on pitch for at least 70 minutes	9
Defensive Rating Ave number of mins between League goals conceded while on the pitch	118	Club Defensive Rating Average number of mins between League goals conceded by the club this season	98

	PLAYER	CON LGE	CLEAN SHEETS	DEF RATE
1	Clinton Hill	21	9	118 mins
2	Danny Butterfield	23	9	100 mins
3	Matt Lawrence	32	10	99 mins
4	Mark Hudson	41	13	98 mins

KEY PLAYERS - MIDFIELDERS

Shaun Derry

Goals in the League	0	Contribution to Attacking Power Average number of minutes between League team goals while on pitch	67
Defensive Rating Average number of mins between League goals conceded while on the pitch	122	Scoring Difference Defensive Rating minus Contribution to Attacking Power	55

	PLAYER	LGE GOALS	DEF RATE	POWER	SCORE DIFF
1	Shaun Derry	0	122	67	55 mins
2	Tom Soares	6	111	62	49 mins
3	Ben Watson	5	110	68	42 mins
4	Carl Fletcher	1	83	106	-23 mins

KEY PLAYERS - GOALSCORERS

Clinton Morrison

Goals in the League	16	Player Strike Rate Average number of minutes between League goals scored by player	186
Contribution to Attacking Power Average number of minutes between League team goals while on pitch	64	Club Strike Rate Average number of minutes between League goals scored by club	71

	PLAYER	LGE GOALS	POWER	STRIKE RATE
1	Clinton Morrison	16	64	186 mins
2	James Scowcroft	9	74	346 mins
3	Tom Soares	6	62	522 mins
4	Ben Watson	5	68	710 mins

GAC Logistics
Clinton Morrison and Victor Moses

SQUAD APPEARANCES

Match	Venue	Competition	Result
1	A	L	W
2	A	W	L
3	H	L	D
4	A	L	L
5	H	L	L
6	A	L	L
7	H	L	D
8	H	L	W
9	A	L	D
10	A	L	L
11	H	L	D
12	A	L	D
13	H	L	L
14	H	L	L
15	A	L	D
16	A	L	D
17	H	L	D
18	A	L	W
19	H	L	W
20	H	L	D
21	A	L	W
22	A	L	D
23	H	L	W
24	H	L	W
25	A	L	W
26	A	L	W
27	H	L	D
28	A	F	L
29	A	L	W
30	H	L	W
31	A	L	L
32	H	L	D
33	A	L	L
34	H	L	L
35	A	L	D
36	H	L	L
37	A	L	W
38	H	L	D
39	H	L	W
40	A	L	D
41	H	L	W
42	A	L	D
43	H	L	D
44	A	L	W
45	H	L	W
46	A	L	W
47	A	L	L
48	H	L	W
49	H	O	L
50	A	O	L

Goalkeepers
Julian Speroni

Defenders
Danny Butterfield
Leon Cort
Tony Craig
Jose Fonte
John Halls
Clinton Hill
Mark Hudson
Jeff Hughes
Matt Lawrence

Midfielders
John Bostock
Neil Danns
Shaun Derry
Carl Fletcher
Stuart Green
Lee Hills
Paul Ifill
Mark Kennedy
David Martin
Victor Moses
Kyel Reid
Tom Soares
Franck Songo'o
Ben Watson

Forwards
Paul Dickov
Dougie Freedman
Besian Idrizaj
Shefki Kuqi
Clinton Morrison
Sean Scannell
James Scowcroft
Scott Sinclair

KEY: On all match · On bench · Subbed or sent off (Counting game) · Subbed or sent off (playing less than 70 minutes) · Subbed on from bench (Counting Game) · Subbed on (playing less than 70 minutes) · Subbed on and then subbed or sent off (Counting Game) · Subbed on and then subbed or sent off (playing less than 70 minutes) · Not in 16

WATFORD

Final Position: **6th**

NICKNAME: THE HORNETS

KEY: ☐ Won ☐ Drawn ☐ Lost

		Opponent			Score	Scorers	Attendance
1	div1	Wolverhampton	A	W	2-1	Stewart 87, King 90 pen	23,115
2	ccr1	Gillingham	H	W	3-0	Priskin 22, Rinaldi 36, Campana 71	8,166
3	div1	Sheff Utd	H	W	1-0	Williamson 56	16,414
4	div1	Leicester	A	L	1-4	King 90 pen	21,642
5	ccr2	Southend	A	L	0-2		5,554
6	div1	Ipswich	H	W	2-0	D.Henderson 6, T.Smith 75	17,295
7	div1	Southampton	H	W	3-2	Shittu 42, D.Henderson 81, 90	15,915
8	div1	Cardiff	A	W	2-1	D.Henderson 17, 78	13,169
9	div1	QPR	A	D	1-1	Johnson 49	14,240
10	div1	Blackpool	H	D	1-1	Johnson 41	16,580
11	div1	Sheff Wed	H	W	2-1	D.Henderson 6, King 16 pen	15,473
12	div1	Scunthorpe	A	W	3-1	Johnson 10, D.Henderson 61, King 63	7,515
13	div1	Hull City	H	W	1-0	King 20	15,803
14	div1	Coventry	A	W	3-0	Johnson 30, King 42, D.Henderson 46	17,032
15	div1	Crystal Palace	A	W	2-0	T.Smith 32, King 67	13,986
16	div1	West Brom	H	L	0-3		18,273
17	div1	Norwich	A	W	3-1	D.Henderson 36, Marshall 43 og, King 88	24,192
18	div1	Colchester	H	D	2-2	Johnson 4, King 64	16,069
19	div1	Barnsley	A	L	2-3	Shittu 36, 45	10,117
20	div1	Burnley	H	L	1-2	Shittu 86	15,021
21	div1	Bristol City	H	L	1-2	O'Toole 87	16,689
22	div1	Colchester	A	W	3-2	King 40, O'Toole 42, Priskin 64	5,760
23	div1	Stoke	A	D	0-0		15,516
24	div1	Plymouth	H	L	0-1		18,532
25	div1	Sheff Wed	A	W	1-0	McAnuff 6	19,641
26	div1	Cardiff	H	D	2-2	DeMerit 49, McAnuff 90	17,014
27	div1	QPR	H	L	2-4	Francis 52, Shittu 84	18,698
28	div1	Southampton	A	W	3-0	Francis 45, King 55, D.Henderson 62	23,008
29	facr3	Crystal Palace	H	W	2-0	Shittu 28, 65	10,480
30	div1	Preston	A	L	0-1		12,347
31	div1	Charlton	H	D	1-1	Ellington 59	17,214
32	facr4	Wolverhampton	H	L	1-4	O'Toole 70	12,719
33	div1	Sheff Utd	A	D	1-1	Ellington 21	23,161
34	div1	Wolverhampton	H	W	3-0	Kabba 1, T.Smith 76, 78	18,082
35	div1	Ipswich	A	W	2-1	T.Smith 33, Ellington 56	24,227
36	div1	Leicester	H	W	1-0	D.Henderson 45	15,944
37	div1	Charlton	A	D	2-2	O'Toole 54, Shittu 55	26,337
38	div1	Preston	H	D	0-0		16,798
39	div1	Burnley	A	D	2-2	D.Henderson 23, Stewart 85	13,677
40	div1	Norwich	H	D	1-1	Shittu 11	16,537
41	div1	Bristol City	A	D	0-0		19,026
42	div1	Stoke	H	D	0-0		18,338
43	div1	Plymouth	A	D	1-1	Williamson 37	17,511
44	div1	Hull City	A	L	0-3		23,501
45	div1	Coventry	H	W	2-1	Ellington 7, T.Smith 79	17,188
46	div1	Barnsley	H	L	0-3		16,129
47	div1	West Brom	A	D	1-1	Bromby 6	26,508
48	div1	Crystal Palace	H	L	0-2		17,694
49	div1	Scunthorpe	H	L	0-1		16,454
50	div1	Blackpool	A	D	1-1	T.Smith 62	9,640
51	d1po1	Hull City	H	L	0-2		14,713
52	d1po2	Hull City	A	L	1-4	D.Henderson 12	23,155

LEAGUE APPEARANCES, BOOKINGS AND GOALS

	AGE (on 01/07/08)	IN NAMED 16	APPEARANCES	COUNTING GAMES	MINUTES ON PITCH	LEAGUE GOALS	Yellow	Red
Goalkeepers								
Richard Lee	25	45	35	34	3116	0	0	0
Mart Poom	36	33	12	11	1024	0	0	0
Defenders								
Leigh Bromby	28	16	16	16	1440	1	1	0
Calum Davenport	25	1	1	0	44	0	0	0
Jay DeMerit	28	37	35	28	2647	1	2	0
Lloyd Doyley	25	39	36	36	3223	0	4	0
Matt Jackson	36	12	6	5	477	0	2	0
Malcolm Mackay	36	0	0	0	0	0	0	0
Adrian Mariappa	21	38	25	12	1344	0	1	0
Junior Osborne	20	0	0	0	0	0	0	0
Jordan Parkes	18	0	0	0	0	0	0	0
Matthew Sadler	23	16	15	13	1224	0	2	0
Danny Shittu	27	41	39	37	3381	7	4	0
Jordan Stewart	26	44	39	33	3043	2	3	0
Midfielders								
Lionel Ainsworth	20	18	8	0	235	0	0	0
Alhassan Bangura	20	10	7	1	261	0	1	0
John Eustace	28	13	13	12	1102	0	3	1
Damian Francis	29	11	11	6	616	2	1	0
Adam Johnson	20	12	12	10	951	5	1	0
Gavin Mahon	31	19	19	18	1646	0	3	0
Jobi McAnuff	26	40	39	29	2810	2	6	0
John-Jo O'Toole	19	37	35	21	2127	3	5	1
Tommy Smith	28	44	44	43	3790	7	3	0
Lee Williamson	26	39	32	27	2574	2	5	1
Forwards								
Nathan Ellington	26	42	34	12	1602	4	1	0
Darius Henderson	26	40	40	31	2945	12	11	1
William Hoskins	22	2	1	0	8	0	0	0
Collins John	22	7	5	1	199	0	0	0
Steve Kabba	27	19	14	6	659	1	2	1
Marlon King	28	27	27	24	2237	11	2	0
Tamas Priskin	21	29	14	4	633	1	0	0

TEAM OF THE SEASON

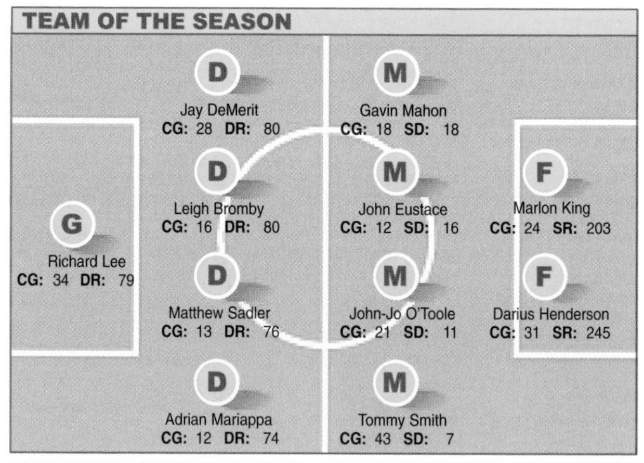

D
Jay DeMerit
CG: 28 DR: 80
M
Gavin Mahon
CG: 18 SD: 18
D
Leigh Bromby
CG: 16 DR: 80
M
John Eustace
CG: 12 SD: 16
F
Marlon King
CG: 24 SR: 203
G
Richard Lee
CG: 34 DR: 79
D
Matthew Sadler
CG: 13 DR: 76
M
John-Jo O'Toole
CG: 21 SD: 11
F
Darius Henderson
CG: 31 SR: 245
D
Adrian Mariappa
CG: 12 DR: 74
M
Tommy Smith
CG: 43 SD: 7

MONTHLY POINTS TALLY

Month	Points	%
AUGUST	6	67%
SEPTEMBER	11	73%
OCTOBER	15	100%
NOVEMBER	4	27%
DECEMBER	8	38%
JANUARY	5	42%
FEBRUARY	11	73%
MARCH	5	28%
APRIL	4	27%
MAY	1	33%

LEAGUE GOALS

	PLAYER	MINS	GOALS	S RATE
1	Henderson, D	2945	12	245
2	King	2237	11	203
3	Shittu	3381	7	483
4	Smith, T	3790	7	541
5	Johnson	951	5	190
6	Ellington	1602	4	400
7	O'Toole	2127	3	709
8	Francis	616	2	308
9	Priskin	633	1	633
10	Williamson	2574	2	1287
11	McAnuff	2810	2	1405
12	Stewart	3043	2	1521
13	Kabba	659	1	659
	Other		2	
	TOTAL		61	

TOP POINT EARNERS

	PLAYER	GAMES	AV PTS
1	Gavin Mahon	18	2.00
2	Marlon King	24	1.79
3	Nathan Ellington	12	1.67
4	Adrian Mariappa	12	1.67
5	Jay DeMerit	28	1.64
6	Danny Shittu	37	1.62
7	Lloyd Doyley	36	1.58
8	Matthew Sadler	13	1.54
9	Jordan Stewart	33	1.52
10	John-Jo O'Toole	22	1.50
	CLUB AVERAGE:		1.52

DISCIPLINARY RECORDS

	PLAYER	YELLOW	RED	AVE
1	Steve Kabba	2	1	219
2	Matt Jackson	2	0	238
3	Darius Henderson	11	1	245
4	John Eustace	3	1	275
5	John-Jo O'Toole	5	1	354
6	Lee Williamson	5	1	429
7	Jobi McAnuff	6	0	468
8	Gavin Mahon	3	0	548
9	Matthew Sadler	2	0	612
10	Damian Francis	1	0	616
11	Lloyd Doyley	4	0	805
12	Danny Shittu	4	0	845
13	Adam Johnson	1	0	951
	Other	13	0	
	TOTAL	62	5	

KEY GOALKEEPER

Richard Lee

Goals Conceded in the League	39	**Counting Games** League games when player was on pitch for at least 70 minutes	34
Defensive Rating Ave number of mins between League goals conceded while on the pitch	79	**Clean Sheets** In League games when player was on pitch for at least 70 minutes	11

KEY PLAYERS - DEFENDERS

Jay DeMerit

Goals Conceded Number of League goals conceded while the player was on the pitch	33	**Clean Sheets** In League games when player was on pitch for at least 70 minutes	9
Defensive Rating Ave number of mins between League goals conceded while on the pitch	80	**Club Defensive Rating** Average number of mins between League goals conceded by the club this season	73

	PLAYER	CON LGE	CLEAN SHEETS	DEF RATE
1	Jay DeMerit	33	9	80 mins
2	Leigh Bromby	18	5	80 mins
3	Matthew Sadler	16	5	76 mins
4	Adrian Mariappa	18	3	74 mins

KEY PLAYERS - MIDFIELDERS

Gavin Mahon

Goals in the League	0	**Contribution to Attacking Power** Average number of minutes between League team goals while on pitch	53
Defensive Rating Average number of mins between League goals conceded while on the pitch	71	**Scoring Difference** Defensive Rating minus Contribution to Attacking Power	18

	PLAYER	LGE GOALS	DEF RATE	POWER	SCORE DIFF
1	Gavin Mahon	0	71	53	18 mins
2	John Eustace	0	100	84	16 mins
3	John-Jo O'Toole	3	92	81	11 mins
4	Tommy Smith	7	72	65	7 mins

KEY PLAYERS - GOALSCORERS

Marlon King

Goals in the League	11	**Player Strike Rate** Average number of minutes between League goals scored by player	203
Contribution to Attacking Power Average number of minutes between League team goals while on pitch	54	**Club Strike Rate** Average number of minutes between League goals scored by club	66

	PLAYER	LGE GOALS	POWER	STRIKE RATE
1	Marlon King	11	54	203 mins
2	Darius Henderson	12	62	245 mins
3	Nathan Ellington	4	66	400 mins
4	Tommy Smith	7	65	541 mins

DIADORA
BEKO
SHITTU
4
BEKO
Darius Hendersen and Danny Shittu

SQUAD APPEARANCES

Match	Venue	Competition	Result
1	A	L	W
2	H	W	W
3	H	L	W
4	A	L	L
5	A	W	L
6	H	L	W
7	H	L	W
8	A	L	W
9	A	L	D
10	H	L	D
11	H	L	W
12	A	L	W
13	H	L	W
14	A	L	W
15	A	L	W
16	H	L	L
17	A	L	W
18	H	L	D
19	A	L	L
20	H	L	L
21	H	L	L
22	A	L	W
23	A	L	D
24	H	L	L
25	A	L	W
26	H	L	D
27	H	L	L
28	A	L	W
29	H	F	W
30	A	L	L
31	H	L	D
32	H	F	L
33	A	L	D
34	H	L	W
35	A	L	W
36	H	L	W
37	A	L	D
38	H	L	D
39	A	L	D
40	H	L	D
41	A	L	D
42	H	L	D
43	A	L	D
44	A	L	L
45	H	L	W
46	H	L	L
47	A	L	D
48	H	L	L
49	H	L	L
50	A	L	D
51	H	O	L
52	A	O	L

Goalkeepers
- Richard Lee
- Mart Poom

Defenders
- Leigh Bromby
- Calum Davenport
- Jay DeMerit
- Lloyd Doyley
- Matt Jackson
- Malcolm Mackay
- Adrian Mariappa
- Junior Osborne
- Jordan Parkes
- Matthew Sadler
- Danny Shittu
- Jordan Stewart

Midfielders
- Lionel Ainsworth
- Alhassan Bangura
- John Eustace
- Damian Francis
- Adam Johnson
- Gavin Mahon
- Jobi McAnuff
- Anthony McNamee
- John-Jo O'Toole
- Tommy Smith
- Lee Williamson

Forwards
- Nathan Ellington
- Darius Henderson
- William Hoskins
- Collins John
- Steve Kabba
- Marlon King
- Tamas Priskin

KEY: On all match · On bench · Subbed or sent off (Counting game) · Subbed or sent off (playing less than 70 minutes) · Subbed on from bench (Counting Game) · Subbed on (playing less than 70 minutes) · Subbed on and then subbed or sent off (Counting Game) · Subbed on and then subbed or sent off (playing less than 70 minutes) · Not in 16

WOLVERHAMPTON WANDERERS

Final Position: **7th**

NICKNAME: WOLVES

KEY: ☐Won ☐Drawn ☐Lost

	Comp	Opponent	H/A	Res	Score	Scorers	Attendance
1	div1	Watford	H	L	1-2	Olofinjana 45	23,115
2	ccr1	Bradford	H	W	2-1	Eastwood 46, Craddock 49	9,625
3	div1	Sheff Wed	A	W	3-1	Eastwood 14, Kightly 48, Bothroyd 90	22,131
4	div1	Blackpool	H	W	2-1	Eastwood 69, 78	24,294
5	ccr2	Morecambe	H	L	1-3	Keogh 84 pen	11,296
6	div1	Stoke	A	D	0-0		17,135
7	div1	Sheff Utd	A	L	1-3	S.Elliott 24	26,003
8	div1	Hull City	H	L	0-1		21,352
9	div1	Norwich	H	W	2-0	Foley 23, Keogh 35	22,564
10	div1	Plymouth	A	D	1-1	S.Elliott 41	13,638
11	div1	Leicester	A	D	0-0		21,311
12	div1	Coventry	H	W	1-0	N.Collins 90	24,338
13	div1	Charlton	H	W	2-0	Bothroyd 46, Henry 85	24,058
14	div1	Cardiff	A	W	3-2	Kightly 13, 66, Craddock 74	15,000
15	div1	Ipswich	A	L	0-3		23,308
16	div1	Bristol City	H	D	1-1	Bothroyd 22	26,094
17	div1	Southampton	A	D	0-0		19,856
18	div1	Barnsley	H	W	1-0	N.Collins 13	22,231
19	div1	West Brom	A	D	0-0		27,493
20	div1	Colchester	H	W	1-0	S.Elliott 32	20,966
21	div1	Preston	H	W	1-0	Henry 55	22,836
22	div1	Barnsley	A	L	0-1		9,956
23	div1	Burnley	H	L	2-3	Gibson 24, S.Elliott 60 pen	20,763
24	div1	QPR	A	D	0-0		13,482
25	div1	Leicester	H	D	1-1	Jarvis 73	23,477
26	div1	Hull City	A	L	0-2		19,127
27	div1	Norwich	A	D	1-1	Keogh 52	24,300
28	div1	Sheff Utd	H	D	0-0		24,791
29	facr3	Cambridge	H	W	2-1	Kightly 69, N.Collins 88	15,340
30	div1	Crystal Palace	H	L	0-3		22,650
31	div1	Scunthorpe	A	W	2-0	Edwards 8, Ebanks-Blake 46	7,465
32	facr4	Watford	A	W	4-1	Keogh 5, 90, S.Elliott 58, Bothroyd 68	12,719
33	div1	Sheff Wed	H	W	2-1	Keogh 11, Ebanks-Blake 90	22,746
34	div1	Watford	A	L	0-3		18,082
35	div1	Stoke	H	L	2-4	R.Edwards 45, Keogh 47	25,373
36	div1	Blackpool	A	D	0-0		9,413
37	facr5	Cardiff	A	L	0-2		15,339
38	div1	Crystal Palace	A	W	2-0	Gray 76, Kyle 89	15,679
39	div1	Colchester	A	W	1-0	Ebanks-Blake 30	5,989
40	div1	Southampton	H	D	2-2	Ebanks-Blake 61, 88	21,795
41	div1	Preston	A	L	1-2	Keogh 52	12,090
42	div1	Burnley	A	W	3-1	Olofinjana 14, Gray 16, Ebanks-Blake 56	12,749
43	div1	Scunthorpe	H	W	2-1	Gray 57, N.Collins 83	21,628
44	div1	QPR	H	D	3-3	Keogh 45, 90, Ebanks-Blake 67 pen	24,290
45	div1	Charlton	A	W	3-2	Ebanks-Blake 15, 81, Henry 90	23,187
46	div1	Bristol City	A	D	0-0		19,332
47	div1	West Brom	H	L	0-1		27,833
48	div1	Ipswich	H	D	1-1	Ebanks-Blake 73	26,072
49	div1	Cardiff	H	W	3-0	Keogh 8, Ebanks-Blake 44, Kightly 56	20,862
50	div1	Coventry	A	D	1-1	Ebanks-Blake 53 pen	27,992
51	div1	Plymouth	H	W	1-0	Olofinjana 87	26,293

LEAGUE APPEARANCES, BOOKINGS AND GOALS

	AGE (on 01/07/08)	IN NAMED 16	APPEARANCES	COUNTING GAMES	MINUTES ON PITCH	LEAGUE GOALS	Yellow	Red
Goalkeepers								
Wayne Hennessey	21	46	46	45	4074	0	1	0
Carl Ikeme	22	9	0	0	0	0	0	0
Graham Stack	26	37	2	0	66	0	0	0
Defenders								
Gary Breen	34	22	19	18	1614	0	3	0
Lee Collins	19	1	0	0	0	0	0	0
Neill Collins	24	43	39	34	3149	3	5	0
Jody Craddock	32	23	23	21	1959	1	2	0
Rob Edwards	25	18	8	4	417	1	2	0
George Elokobi	22	16	15	15	1350	0	3	0
Kevin Foley	23	45	44	42	3818	1	1	0
Michael Gray	33	36	33	22	2305	3	3	0
Mark Little	19	8	1	0	45	0	0	0
Darren Ward	29	31	30	29	2662	0	1	0
Midfielders								
Elliott Bennett	19	2	0	0	0	0	0	0
David Edwards	22	11	10	8	780	1	1	0
Darron Gibson	20	23	21	11	1293	1	4	0
Stephen Gleeson	19	1	0	0	0	0	0	0
Karl Henry	25	41	40	37	3449	3	7	0
Daniel Jones	21	1	1	0	19	0	0	0
Michael Kightly	22	21	21	18	1705	4	1	0
Seyi Olofinjana	28	37	36	35	3141	3	8	0
Darren Potter	23	31	18	7	943	0	3	0
Denes Rosa	31	0	0	0	0	0	0	0
Forwards								
Jay Bothroyd	26	25	22	12	1224	3	0	0
Freddy Eastwood	24	41	31	8	1273	3	0	0
Sylvain Ebanks-Blake	22	20	20	19	1712	12	2	0
Stephen Elliott	24	31	29	13	1551	4	0	0
Matthew Jarvis	22	31	26	15	1708	1	1	0
Andrew Keogh	22	43	43	29	3007	8	2	0
Kevin Kyle	27	13	12	2	326	1	0	0
Stephen Ward	22	29	29	18	1950	0	3	0

TEAM OF THE SEASON

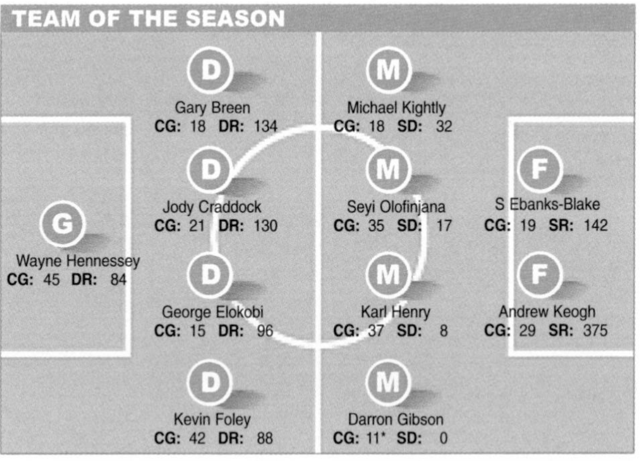

G
Wayne Hennessey
CG: 45 DR: 84
D
Gary Breen
CG: 18 DR: 134
D
Jody Craddock
CG: 21 DR: 130
D
George Elokobi
CG: 15 DR: 96
D
Kevin Foley
CG: 42 DR: 88
M
Michael Kightly
CG: 18 SD: 32
M
Seyi Olofinjana
CG: 35 SD: 17
M
Karl Henry
CG: 37 SD: 8
M
Darron Gibson
CG: 11* SD: 0
F
S Ebanks-Blake
CG: 19 SR: 142
F
Andrew Keogh
CG: 29 SR: 375

MONTHLY POINTS TALLY

Month	Points	%
AUGUST	6	67%
SEPTEMBER	5	33%
OCTOBER	10	67%
NOVEMBER	9	60%
DECEMBER	6	29%
JANUARY	7	58%
FEBRUARY	4	33%
MARCH	14	67%
APRIL	6	40%
MAY	3	100%

LEAGUE GOALS

	PLAYER	MINS	GOALS	S RATE
1	Ebanks-Blake	1712	12	142
2	Keogh	3007	8	375
3	Elliott, S	1551	4	387
4	Kightly	1705	4	426
5	Bothroyd	1224	3	408
6	Eastwood	1273	3	424
7	Collins, N	3149	3	1049
8	Gray	2305	3	768
9	Olofinjana	3141	3	1047
10	Henry	3449	3	1149
11	Craddock	1959	1	1959
12	Kyle	326	1	326
13	Edwards, R	417	1	417
	Other		4	
	TOTAL		53	

TOP POINT EARNERS

	PLAYER	GAMES	AV PTS
1	Jody Craddock	21	1.86
2	Stephen Elliott	13	1.85
3	George Elokobi	15	1.80
4	Sylvain Ebanks-Blake	19	1.74
5	Michael Kightly	18	1.67
6	Gary Breen	18	1.56
7	Karl Henry	37	1.54
8	Kevin Foley	42	1.52
9	Andrew Keogh	29	1.52
10	Seyi Olofinjana	35	1.51
	CLUB AVERAGE:		1.52

DISCIPLINARY RECORDS

	PLAYER	YELLOW	RED	AVE
1	Darren Potter	3	0	314
2	Darron Gibson	4	0	323
3	Seyi Olofinjana	8	0	392
4	George Elokobi	3	0	450
5	Karl Henry	7	0	492
6	Gary Breen	3	0	538
7	Neill Collins	5	0	629
8	Stephen Ward	3	0	650
9	Michael Gray	3	0	768
10	David Edwards	1	0	780
11	S. Ebanks-Blake	2	0	856
12	Jody Craddock	2	0	979
13	Andrew Keogh	2	0	1503
	Other	5	0	
	TOTAL	51	0	

KEY GOALKEEPER

Wayne Hennessey

Goals Conceded in the League	48	**Counting Games** League games when player was on pitch for at least 70 minutes	45
Defensive Rating Ave number of mins between League goals conceded while on the pitch	84	**Clean Sheets** In League games when player was on pitch for at least 70 minutes	18

KEY PLAYERS - DEFENDERS

Gary Breen

Goals Conceded Number of League goals conceded while the player was on the pitch	12	**Clean Sheets** In League games when player was on pitch for at least 70 minutes	10
Defensive Rating Ave number of mins between League goals conceded while on the pitch	134	**Club Defensive Rating** Average number of mins between League goals conceded by the club this season	88

	PLAYER	CON LGE	CLEAN SHEETS	DEF RATE
1	Gary Breen	12	10	134 mins
2	Jody Craddock	15	12	130 mins
3	George Elokobi	14	6	96 mins
4	Kevin Foley	43	17	88 mins

KEY PLAYERS - MIDFIELDERS

Michael Kightly

Goals in the League	4	**Contribution to Attacking Power** Average number of minutes between League team goals while on pitch	74
Defensive Rating Average number of mins between League goals conceded while on the pitch	106	**Scoring Difference** Defensive Rating minus Contribution to Attacking Power	32

	PLAYER	LGE GOALS	DEF RATE	POWER	SCORE DIFF
1	Michael Kightly	4	106	74	32 mins
2	Seyi Olofinjana	3	95	78	17 mins
3	Karl Henry	3	88	80	8 mins
4	Darron Gibson	1	99	99	0 mins

KEY PLAYERS - GOALSCORERS

Sylvain Ebanks-Blake

Goals in the League	12	**Player Strike Rate** Average number of minutes between League goals scored by player	142
Contribution to Attacking Power Average number of minutes between League team goals while on pitch	63	**Club Strike Rate** Average number of minutes between League goals scored by club	79

	PLAYER	LGE GOALS	POWER	STRIKE RATE
1	Sylvain Ebanks-Blake	12	63	142 mins
2	Andrew Keogh	8	73	375 mins
3	Stephen Elliott	4	91	387 mins
4	Jay Bothroyd	3	81	408 mins

Sylvain Ebanks-Blake

SQUAD APPEARANCES

Match	1	2	3	4	5	6	7	8	9	10	11	12	13	14	15	16	17	18	19	20	21	22	23	24	25	26	27	28	29	30	31	32	33	34	35	36	37	38	39	40	41	42	43	44	45	46	47	48	49	50	51
Venue	H	H	A	H	H	A	A	H	H	A	A	H	H	A	A	H	A	H	A	H	H	A	H	A	H	A	A	H	H	H	A	A	H	A	H	A	A	A	A	H	A	A	H	H	A	A	H	H	H	A	H
Competition	L	W	L	L	W	L	L	L	L	L	L	L	L	L	L	L	L	L	L	L	L	L	L	L	L	L	L	L	F	L	L	F	L	L	L	L	F	L	L	L	L	L	L	L	L	L	L	L	L	L	L
Result	L	W	W	W	L	D	L	L	W	D	D	W	W	W	L	D	D	W	D	W	W	L	L	D	D	L	D	D	W	L	W	W	W	L	L	D	L	W	W	D	L	W	W	D	W	D	L	D	W	D	W

Goalkeepers
Wayne Hennessey
Carl Ikeme
Graham Stack
Defenders
Gary Breen
Lee Collins
Neill Collins
Jody Craddock
Rob Edwards
George Elokobi
Kevin Foley
Michael Gray
Mark Little
Darren Ward
Midfielders
Elliott Bennett
David Edwards
Darron Gibson
Stephen Gleeson
Karl Henry
Daniel Jones
Michael Kightly
Seyi Olofinjana
Darren Potter
Denes Rosa
Forwards
Jay Bothroyd
Freddy Eastwood
Sylvain Ebanks-Blake
Stephen Elliott
Matthew Jarvis
Andrew Keogh
Kevin Kyle
Stephen Ward

KEY: On all match · On bench · Subbed or sent off (Counting game) · Subbed or sent off (playing less than 70 minutes) · Subbed on from bench (Counting Game) · Subbed on (playing less than 70 minutes) · Subbed on and then subbed or sent off (Counting Game) · Subbed on and then subbed or sent off (playing less than 70 minutes) · Not in 16

IPSWICH TOWN

Final Position: **8th**

NICKNAME: TRACTOR BOYS

KEY: ☐Won ☐Drawn ☐Lost

	Comp	Opponent	Venue	Result	Score	Scorers	Attendance
1	div1	Sheff Wed	H	W	4-1	Lee 2 pen, 25, G.Roberts 11, Counago 60	23,099
2	ccr1	MK Dons	A	L	3-5*	Lee 45 pen, Murphy 52 og, Garvan 98 (*on penalties)	7,496
3	div1	Plymouth	A	D	1-1	Lee 2	13,260
4	div1	Crystal Palace	H	W	1-0	Walters 72	19,382
5	div1	Watford	A	L	0-2		17,295
6	div1	West Brom	A	L	0-4		19,460
7	div1	Coventry	H	W	4-1	De Vos 10, Counago 24, 57, Walters 40	18,840
8	div1	Hull City	A	L	1-3	Harding 45	15,456
9	div1	Burnley	A	D	2-2	Legwinski 7, Lee 9	9,952
10	div1	Preston	H	W	2-1	Lee 34, T.Miller 74	19,243
11	div1	QPR	A	D	1-1	Legwinski 53	13,946
12	div1	Colchester	H	W	3-1	Walters 71, Trotter 81, Haynes 84	25,727
13	div1	Wolverhampton	H	W	3-0	Lee 42, Counago 52, Haynes 90	23,308
14	div1	Norwich	A	D	2-2	Lee 27, Counago 41	25,461
15	div1	Sheff Utd	A	L	1-3	Walters 54	25,033
16	div1	Bristol City	H	W	6-0	Walters 5, 55, 72, Wright 15, T.Miller 48 pen, Counago 65	22,020
17	div1	Cardiff	A	L	0-1		15,173
18	div1	Southampton	H	W	2-0	Walters 34, Counago 69	19,791
19	div1	Barnsley	H	D	0-0		19,540
20	div1	Bristol City	A	L	0-2		14,062
21	div1	Charlton	A	L	1-3	Counago 70	24,680
22	div1	Leicester	H	W	3-1	Counago 19, Lee 41 pen, Walters 65	17,938
23	div1	Scunthorpe	H	W	3-2	Counago 18, Garvan 21, T.Miller 83	19,306
24	div1	Burnley	H	D	0-0		20,077
25	div1	Leicester	A	L	0-2		24,049
26	div1	Coventry	A	L	1-2	Haynes 42	18,346
27	div1	West Brom	H	W	2-0	Wright 75, De Vos 84	24,000
28	facr3	Portsmouth	H	L	0-1		23,446
29	div1	Stoke	H	D	1-1	Haynes 19	20,346
30	div1	Blackpool	A	D	1-1	Walters 65	9,154
31	div1	Plymouth	H	D	0-0		20,095
32	div1	Sheff Wed	A	W	2-1	A.Quinn 4, Lee 71	19,092
33	div1	Watford	H	L	1-2	Walters 71	24,227
34	div1	Crystal Palace	A	W	1-0	Haynes 45	16,090
35	div1	Blackpool	H	W	2-1	Sumulikoski 50, Walters 58	21,059
36	div1	Stoke	A	L	0-1		23,563
37	div1	Southampton	A	D	1-1	Norris 56	23,299
38	div1	Sheff Utd	H	D	1-1	Lee 54	20,190
39	div1	Barnsley	A	L	1-4	Counago 20	11,333
40	div1	Charlton	H	W	2-0	Garvan 20, Haynes 53	23,539
41	div1	Scunthorpe	A	W	2-1	Counago 19, Sito 71	6,636
42	div1	QPR	H	D	0-0		24,570
43	div1	Colchester	A	L	0-2		6,264
44	div1	Cardiff	H	D	1-1	Rhodes 73	20,311
45	div1	Norwich	H	W	2-1	A.Pearce 13 og, Haynes 40	29,656
46	div1	Wolverhampton	A	D	1-1	T.Miller 90	26,072
47	div1	Preston	A	D	2-2	T.Miller 11, Walters 87	14,187
48	div1	Hull City	H	W	1-0	Lee 70	28,223

LEAGUE APPEARANCES, BOOKINGS AND GOALS

	AGE (on 01/07/08)	IN NAMED 16	APPEARANCES	COUNTING GAMES	MINUTES ON PITCH	LEAGUE GOALS	Yellow	Red
Goalkeepers								
Neil Alexander	30	29	29	29	2610	0	2	0
Stephen Bywater	27	17	17	17	1530	0	1	0
Shane Supple	21	28	0	0	0	0	0	0
Defenders								
Alex Bruce	23	43	36	32	3029	0	3	0
Chris Casement	20	9	3	2	190	0	0	0
Jason De Vos	34	46	46	46	4140	2	4	0
Dan Harding	24	31	30	28	2573	1	3	0
Richard Naylor	31	10	7	6	565	0	0	0
Matthew Richards	23	1	0	0	0	0	0	0
Danny Simpson	21	8	8	7	650	0	2	0
Luis Castro Sito	28	16	13	8	942	1	2	1
Fabian Wilnis	37	22	13	10	926	0	0	1
David Wright	28	45	41	39	3544	2	1	0
Midfielders								
Owen Garvan	20	45	43	37	3489	2	3	0
Danny Haynes	20	42	40	15	1954	7	6	0
Sylvain Legwinski	34	24	15	7	737	2	2	0
Tommy Miller	29	39	37	29	2799	5	3	1
David Norris	27	9	9	8	729	1	0	0
George O'Callaghan	28	1	1	1	90	0	0	0
Jamie Peters	21	6	5	0	109	0	0	0
Alan Quinn	29	17	17	13	1245	1	1	0
Jordan Rhodes	17	11	8	0	117	1	0	0
Gary Roberts	21	23	21	6	912	1	5	0
Velice Sumulikoski	27	16	16	9	902	1	0	0
Liam Trotter	19	13	6	2	200	1	1	0
Gavin Williams	27	15	13	7	828	0	4	0
Forwards								
Billy Clarke	20	21	20	7	805	0	1	0
Pablo Counago	28	43	43	29	2959	12	4	1
Shefki Kuqi	31	4	4	0	126	0	0	0
Alan Lee	29	45	45	32	3210	11	3	0
Jonathan Walters	24	40	40	39	3538	13	1	0

TEAM OF THE SEASON

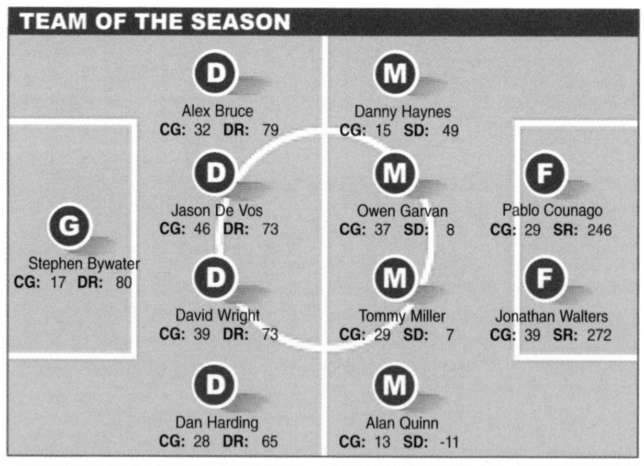

D
Alex Bruce
CG: 32 DR: 79
M
Danny Haynes
CG: 15 SD: 49
D
Jason De Vos
CG: 46 DR: 73
M
Owen Garvan
CG: 37 SD: 8
F
Pablo Counago
CG: 29 SR: 246
G
Stephen Bywater
CG: 17 DR: 80
D
David Wright
CG: 39 DR: 73
M
Tommy Miller
CG: 29 SD: 7
F
Jonathan Walters
CG: 39 SR: 272
D
Dan Harding
CG: 28 DR: 65
M
Alan Quinn
CG: 13 SD: -11

MONTHLY POINTS TALLY

Month	Points	%
AUGUST	7	78%
SEPTEMBER	3	25%
OCTOBER	11	73%
NOVEMBER	7	47%
DECEMBER	8	33%
JANUARY	6	50%
FEBRUARY	9	60%
MARCH	9	50%
APRIL	6	40%
MAY	3	100%

LEAGUE GOALS

	PLAYER	MINS	GOALS	S RATE
1	Walters	3538	**13**	272
2	Counago	2959	**12**	246
3	Lee	3210	**11**	291
4	Haynes	1954	**6**	325
5	Miller, T	2799	**5**	559
6	Garvan	3489	**2**	1744
7	Legwinski	737	**2**	368
8	Wright	3544	**2**	1772
9	De Vos	4140	**2**	2070
10	Rhodes	117	**1**	117
11	Trotter	200	**1**	200
12	Norris	729	**1**	729
13	Sumulikoski	902	**1**	902
	Other		4	
	TOTAL		**63**	

TOP POINT EARNERS

	PLAYER	GAMES	AV PTS
1	Pablo Counago	30	**1.83**
2	Alan Quinn	13	**1.77**
3	Danny Haynes	15	**1.67**
4	Stephen Bywater	17	**1.59**
5	David Wright	39	**1.56**
6	Owen Garvan	37	**1.54**
7	Jason De Vos	46	**1.50**
8	Jonathan Walters	39	**1.49**
9	Dan Harding	28	**1.46**
10	Neil Alexander	29	**1.45**
	CLUB AVERAGE:		**1.50**

DISCIPLINARY RECORDS

	PLAYER	YELLOW	RED	AVE
1	Gary Roberts	5	0	**182**
2	Gavin Williams	4	0	**207**
3	Luis Castro Sito	2	1	**314**
4	Danny Simpson	2	0	**325**
5	Sylvain Legwinski	2	0	**368**
6	Danny Haynes	5	0	**390**
7	Pablo Counago	4	1	**591**
8	Tommy Miller	3	1	**699**
9	Billy Clarke	1	0	**805**
10	Dan Harding	3	0	**857**
11	Fabian Wilnis	0	1	**926**
12	Alex Bruce	3	0	**1009**
13	Jason De Vos	4	0	**1035**
	Other	12	0	
	TOTAL	**50**	**4**	

KEY GOALKEEPER

Stephen Bywater

Goals Conceded in the League	19	Counting Games League games when player was on pitch for at least 70 minutes	17
Defensive Rating Ave number of mins between League goals conceded while on the pitch	80	Clean Sheets In League games when player was on pitch for at least 70 minutes	4

KEY PLAYERS - DEFENDERS

Alex Bruce

Goals Conceded Number of League goals conceded while the player was on the pitch	38	Clean Sheets In League games when player was on pitch for at least 70 minutes	11
Defensive Rating Ave number of mins between League goals conceded while on the pitch	79	Club Defensive Rating Average number of mins between League goals conceded by the club this season	73

	PLAYER	CON LGE	CLEAN SHEETS	DEF RATE
1	Alex Bruce	38	11	79 mins
2	Jason De Vos	56	12	73 mins
3	David Wright	48	10	73 mins
4	Dan Harding	39	7	65 mins

KEY PLAYERS - MIDFIELDERS

Danny Haynes

Goals in the League	6	Contribution to Attacking Power Average number of minutes between League team goals while on pitch	65
Defensive Rating Average number of mins between League goals conceded while on the pitch	114	Scoring Difference Defensive Rating minus Contribution to Attacking Power	49

	PLAYER	LGE GOALS	DEF RATE	POWER	SCORE DIFF
1	Danny Haynes	6	114	65	49 mins
2	Owen Garvan	2	69	61	8 mins
3	Tommy Miller	5	75	68	7 mins
4	Alan Quinn	1	77	88	-11 mins

KEY PLAYERS - GOALSCORERS

Pablo Counago

Goals in the League	12	Player Strike Rate Average number of minutes between League goals scored by player	246
Contribution to Attacking Power Average number of minutes between League team goals while on pitch	58	Club Strike Rate Average number of minutes between League goals scored by club	63

	PLAYER	LGE GOALS	POWER	STRIKE RATE
1	Pablo Counago	12	58	246 mins
2	Jonathan Walters	13	61	272 mins
3	Alan Lee	11	59	291 mins
4	Danny Haynes	6	65	325 mins

mitre
e.on

Jonathan Walters

SQUAD APPEARANCES

Match	1	2	3	4	5	6	7	8	9	10	11	12	13	14	15	16	17	18	19	20	21	22	23	24	25	26	27	28	29	30	31	32	33	34	35	36	37	38	39	40	41	42	43	44	45	46	47	48
Venue	H	A	A	H	A	A	H	A	A	H	A	H	H	A	A	H	A	H	H	A	A	H	H	H	A	A	H	H	H	A	H	A	H	A	H	A	A	H	A	H	A	H	A	H	H	A	A	H
Competition	L	W	L	L	L	L	L	L	L	L	L	L	L	L	L	L	L	L	L	L	L	L	L	L	L	L	L	F	L	L	L	L	L	L	L	L	L	L	L	L	L	L	L	L	L	L	L	L
Result	W	L	D	W	L	L	W	L	D	W	D	W	W	D	L	W	L	W	D	L	L	W	W	D	L	L	W	L	D	D	D	W	L	W	W	L	D	D	L	W	W	D	L	D	W	D	D	W

Goalkeepers
Neil Alexander
Stephen Bywater
Shane Supple

Defenders
Alex Bruce
Chris Casement
Jason De Vos
Dan Harding
Richard Naylor
Matthew Richards
Danny Simpson
Luis Castro Sito
Fabian Wilnis
David Wright

Midfielders
Owen Garvan
Danny Haynes
Sylvain Legwinski
Tommy Miller
David Norris
George O'Callaghan
Jamie Peters
Alan Quinn
Jordan Rhodes
Gary Roberts
Velice Sumulikoski
Liam Trotter
Gavin Williams

Forwards
Billy Clarke
Pablo Counago
Shefki Kuqi
Alan Lee
Jonathan Walters

KEY: On all match | On bench | Subbed or sent off (Counting game) | Subbed or sent off (playing less than 70 minutes) | Subbed on from bench (Counting Game) | Subbed on (playing less than 70 minutes) | Subbed on and then subbed or sent off (Counting Game) | Subbed on and then subbed or sent off (playing less than 70 minutes) | Not in 16

SHEFFIELD UNITED

Final Position: **9th**

NICKNAME: THE BLADES

KEY: ☐Won ☐Drawn ☐Lost

							Attendance
1	div1	Colchester	H	D	2-2	Beattie 68, Tonge 82	26,202
2	ccr1	Chesterfield	H	W	3-1	Stead 14, 45, Webber 56	11,170
3	div1	Watford	A	L	0-1		16,414
4	div1	West Brom	H	W	1-0	Beattie 37	23,491
5	ccr2	MK Dons	A	W	3-2	Lucketti 20, Law 55, Horsfield 104	7,943
6	div1	Scunthorpe	A	L	2-3	Webber 79, 83	8,801
7	div1	Wolverhampton	H	W	3-1	Beattie 57, 83 pen, Stead 90	26,003
8	div1	Blackpool	A	D	2-2	Beattie 13, 88	9,512
9	div1	Crystal Palace	A	L	2-3	Hudson 48 og, Beattie 76	14,131
10	ccr3	Morecambe	H	W	5-0	B.Sharp 18, 33, Shelton 52, 72, Hendrie 67	8,854
11	div1	Southampton	H	L	1-2	Gillespie 12	24,561
12	div1	Cardiff	H	D	3-3	Beattie 18, Armstrong 85, Morgan 90	26,186
13	div1	Bristol City	A	L	0-2		13,071
14	div1	Preston	H	D	1-1	Beattie 80 pen	23,661
15	div1	Leicester	A	W	1-0	Webber 56	21,146
16	div1	Hull City	A	D	1-1	Stead 35	20,185
17	ccr4	Arsenal	H	L	0-3		16,971
18	div1	Burnley	H	D	0-0		25,306
19	div1	Ipswich	H	W	3-1	Beattie 33, 72 pen, Gillespie 86	25,033
20	div1	Stoke	A	W	1-0	Cahill 43	12,158
21	div1	Plymouth	H	L	0-1		23,811
22	div1	Charlton	A	W	3-0	Beattie 34 pen, Cahill 75, Armstrong 89	20,737
23	div1	Coventry	A	W	1-0	Armstrong 62	20,355
24	div1	Stoke	H	L	0-3		23,378
25	div1	Norwich	A	L	0-1		24,493
26	div1	Barnsley	H	W	1-0	Kilgallon 64	26,629
27	div1	Cardiff	A	L	0-1		12,869
28	div1	Blackpool	H	D	1-1	Beattie 23	26,409
29	div1	Crystal Palace	H	L	0-1		23,982
30	div1	Wolverhampton	A	D	0-0		24,791
31	facr3	Bolton	A	W	1-0	Carney 42	15,286
32	div1	QPR	H	W	2-1	Stewart 64, Hendrie 69	28,894
33	div1	Sheff Wed	A	L	0-2		30,486
34	facr4	Man City	H	W	2-1	Shelton 12, Stead 24	20,800
35	div1	Watford	H	D	1-1	Carney 67	23,161
36	div1	Colchester	A	D	2-2	Shelton 45, Carney 66	5,695
37	div1	Scunthorpe	H	D	0-0		25,668
38	div1	West Brom	A	D	0-0		22,643
39	facr5	Middlesbrough	H	D	0-0		22,210
40	div1	QPR	A	D	1-1	Morgan 78	15,383
41	facr5r	Middlesbrough	A	L	0-1		28,108
42	div1	Charlton	H	L	0-2		23,180
43	div1	Ipswich	A	D	1-1	Beattie 32	20,190
44	div1	Plymouth	A	W	1-0	Beattie 63	13,669
45	div1	Coventry	H	W	2-1	B.Sharp 69, Speed 78	23,864
46	div1	Norwich	H	W	2-0	B.Sharp 52, Kilgallon 56	25,536
47	div1	Barnsley	A	W	1-0	B.Sharp 77	15,798
48	div1	Preston	A	L	1-3	Beattie 87 pen	14,647
49	div1	Leicester	H	W	3-0	Beattie 12, 14, 19	24,818
50	div1	Sheff Wed	H	D	2-2	Wood 62 og, Beattie 85	31,760
51	div1	Burnley	A	W	2-1	Beattie 33, B.Sharp 53	11,693
52	div1	Hull City	H	W	2-0	S.Quinn 51, Beattie 72 pen	28,188
53	div1	Bristol City	H	W	2-1	Speed 29, 55 pen	29,787
54	div1	Southampton	A	L	2-3	S.Quinn 23, Stead 65	31,957

LEAGUE APPEARANCES, BOOKINGS AND GOALS

	AGE (on 01/07/08)	IN NAMED 16	APPEARANCES	COUNTING GAMES	MINUTES ON PITCH	LEAGUE GOALS	Yellow	Red
Goalkeepers								
Ian Bennett	36	17	7	6	592	0	0	0
Patrick Kenny	30	41	40	39	3548	0	1	0
Defenders								
Chris Armstrong	25	36	32	25	2524	3	4	0
Phillip Bardsley	23	16	16	16	1428	0	4	0
Leigh Bromby	28	18	11	11	979	0	1	0
Gary Cahill	22	16	16	16	1440	2	3	0
Ugo Ehiogu	35	16	10	3	372	0	0	0
Derek Geary	28	22	21	18	1710	0	2	1
John Halls	26	9	6	5	504	0	1	0
Matthew Kilgallon	24	44	40	39	3571	2	1	0
Chris Lucketti	37	17	6	4	394	0	2	0
Chris Morgan	30	32	25	23	2170	2	7	2
Gary Naysmith	29	39	38	35	3332	0	4	0
Midfielders								
David Carney	24	26	21	12	1501	2	1	0
Keith Gillespie	33	41	35	17	2021	2	2	0
Lee Hendrie	31	12	12	2	534	1	5	0
Mikele Leigertwood	25	3	2	0	80	0	1	0
Lee Martin	21	7	6	5	452	0	0	0
Nick Montgomery	26	22	20	16	1542	0	0	0
Alan Quinn	29	13	8	4	425	0	2	0
Stephen Quinn	22	23	19	12	1345	2	0	1
Gary Speed	38	20	20	18	1702	3	3	0
Michael Tonge	25	45	45	36	3410	1	5	0
Forwards								
James Beattie	30	39	39	31	3011	22	2	0
David Cotterill	20	16	16	12	1232	0	1	0
Geoff Horsfield	34	0	0	0	0	0	0	0
Robert Hulse	28	22	21	9	1135	0	3	0
Billy Sharp	22	41	29	17	1876	4	3	0
Luton Shelton	22	18	15	5	641	1	2	0
Jonathan Stead	25	43	24	10	1225	3	2	0
Danny Webber	26	15	14	7	792	3	1	0

TEAM OF THE SEASON

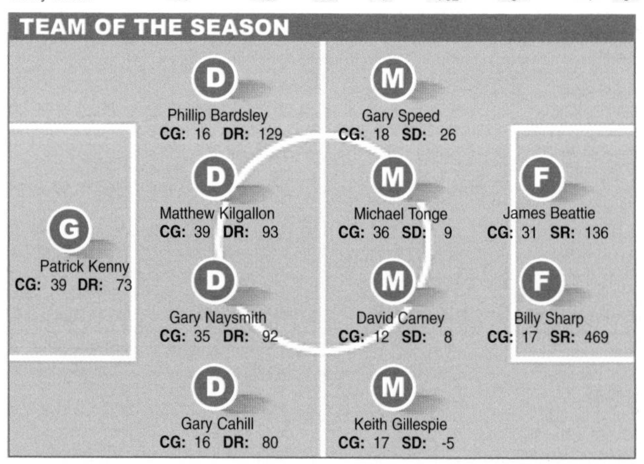

G
Patrick Kenny
CG: 39 DR: 73
D
Phillip Bardsley
CG: 16 DR: 129
D
Matthew Kilgallon
CG: 39 DR: 93
D
Gary Naysmith
CG: 35 DR: 92
D
Gary Cahill
CG: 16 DR: 80
M
Gary Speed
CG: 18 SD: 26
M
Michael Tonge
CG: 36 SD: 9
M
David Carney
CG: 12 SD: 8
M
Keith Gillespie
CG: 17 SD: -5
F
James Beattie
CG: 31 SR: 136
F
Billy Sharp
CG: 17 SR: 469

MONTHLY POINTS TALLY

AUGUST	4	44%
SEPTEMBER	4	27%
OCTOBER	6	40%
NOVEMBER	10	67%
DECEMBER	7	33%
JANUARY	5	42%
FEBRUARY	4	33%
MARCH	13	62%
APRIL	13	87%
MAY	0	0%

LEAGUE GOALS

	PLAYER	MINS	GOALS	S RATE
1	Beattie	3011	22	136
2	Stead	1225	3	408
3	Sharp, B	1876	4	469
4	Webber	792	3	264
5	Shelton	641	1	641
6	Speed	1702	3	567
7	Carney	1501	2	750
8	Armstrong	2524	3	841
9	Hendrie	534	1	534
10	Quinn, S	1345	2	672
11	Cahill	1440	2	720
12	Gillespie	2021	2	1010
13	Morgan	2170	2	1085
	Other		3	
	TOTAL		53	

TOP POINT EARNERS

	PLAYER	GAMES	AV PTS
1	David Carney	12	2.08
2	David Cotterill	12	2.08
3	Billy Sharp	17	2.06
4	Gary Speed	18	1.78
5	Gary Naysmith	35	1.69
6	Keith Gillespie	17	1.59
7	Matthew Kilgallon	39	1.59
8	Stephen Quinn	12	1.58
9	Michael Tonge	36	1.50
10	Phillip Bardsley	16	1.44
	CLUB AVERAGE:		1.43

DISCIPLINARY RECORDS

	PLAYER	YELLOW	RED	AVE
1	Lee Hendrie	5	0	106
2	Chris Morgan	7	2	241
3	Luton Shelton	2	0	320
4	Phillip Bardsley	4	0	357
5	Robert Hulse	3	0	378
6	Gary Cahill	3	0	480
7	John Halls	1	0	504
8	Gary Speed	3	0	567
9	Derek Geary	2	1	570
10	Jonathan Stead	2	0	612
11	Billy Sharp	3	0	625
12	Chris Armstrong	4	0	631
13	Michael Tonge	5	0	682
	Other	14	1	
	TOTAL	58	4	

KEY GOALKEEPER

Patrick Kenny

Goals Conceded in the League	48	**Counting Games** League games when player was on pitch for at least 70 minutes	39
Defensive Rating Ave number of mins between League goals conceded while on the pitch	73	**Clean Sheets** In League games when player was on pitch for at least 70 minutes	11

KEY PLAYERS - DEFENDERS

Phillip Bardsley

Goals Conceded Number of League goals conceded while the player was on the pitch	11	**Clean Sheets** In League games when player was on pitch for at least 70 minutes	7
Defensive Rating Ave number of mins between League goals conceded while on the pitch	129	**Club Defensive Rating** Average number of mins between League goals conceded by the club this season	81

	PLAYER	CON LGE	CLEAN SHEETS	DEF RATE
1	Phillip Bardsley	11	7	129 mins
2	Matthew Kilgallon	38	14	93 mins
3	Gary Naysmith	36	14	92 mins
4	Gary Cahill	18	6	80 mins

KEY PLAYERS - MIDFIELDERS

Gary Speed

Goals in the League	3	**Contribution to Attacking Power** Average number of minutes between League team goals while on pitch	68
Defensive Rating Average number of mins between League goals conceded while on the pitch	94	**Scoring Difference** Defensive Rating minus Contribution to Attacking Power	26

	PLAYER	LGE GOALS	DEF RATE	POWER	SCORE DIFF
1	Gary Speed	3	94	68	26 mins
2	Michael Tonge	1	81	72	9 mins
3	David Carney	2	83	75	8 mins
4	Keith Gillespie	2	69	74	-5 mins

KEY PLAYERS - GOALSCORERS

James Beattie

Goals in the League	22	**Player Strike Rate** Average number of minutes between League goals scored by player	136
Contribution to Attacking Power Average number of minutes between League team goals while on pitch	71	**Club Strike Rate** Average number of minutes between League goals scored by club	73

	PLAYER	LGE GOALS	POWER	STRIKE RATE
1	James Beattie	22	71	136 mins
2	Billy Sharp	4	64	469 mins
3	Gary Speed	3	68	567 mins
4	Stephen Quinn	2	67	672 mins

apitalOne
James Beattie

SQUAD APPEARANCES

Match	1	2	3	4	5	6	7	8	9	10	11	12	13	14	15	16	17	18	19	20	21	22	23	24	25	26	27
Venue	H	H	A	H	A	A	H	A	A	H	H	H	A	H	A	A	H	H	H	A	H	A	A	H	A	H	A
Competition	L	W	L	L	W	L	L	L	L	W	L	L	L	L	L	L	W	L	L	L	L	L	L	L	L	L	L
Result	D	W	L	W	W	L	W	D	L	W	L	D	L	D	W	D	L	D	W	W	L	W	W	L	L	W	L

Match	28	29	30	31	32	33	34	35	36	37	38	39	40	41	42	43	44	45	46	47	48	49	50	51	52	53	54
Venue	H	H	A	A	H	A	H	H	A	H	A	H	A	A	H	A	A	H	H	A	A	H	H	A	H	H	A
Competition	L	L	L	F	L	L	F	L	L	L	L	F	L	F	L	L	L	L	L	L	L	L	L	L	L	L	L
Result	D	L	D	W	W	L	W	D	D	D	D	D	D	L	L	D	W	W	W	W	L	W	D	W	W	W	L

Goalkeepers
Ian Bennett
Patrick Kenny

Defenders
Chris Armstrong
Phillip Bardsley
Leigh Bromby
Gary Cahill
Ugo Ehiogu
Derek Geary
John Halls
Matthew Kilgallon
Chris Lucketti
Chris Morgan
Gary Naysmith

Midfielders
David Carney
Keith Gillespie
Lee Hendrie
Mikele Leigertwood
Lee Martin
Nick Montgomery
Alan Quinn
Stephen Quinn
Gary Speed
Michael Tonge

Forwards
James Beattie
David Cotterill
Geoff Horsfield
Robert Hulse
Billy Sharp
Luton Shelton
Jonathan Stead
Danny Webber

KEY: On all match · On bench · Subbed or sent off (Counting game) · Subbed or sent off (playing less than 70 minutes) · Subbed on from bench (Counting Game) · Subbed on (playing less than 70 minutes) · Subbed on and then subbed or sent off (Counting Game) · Subbed on and then subbed or sent off (playing less than 70 minutes) · Not in 16

PLYMOUTH ARGYLE

Final Position: **10th**

NICKNAME: THE PILGRIMS

KEY: ☐ Won ☐ Drawn ☐ Lost

						Attendance
1	div1	Hull City	A	W	3-2 Norris 15, Fallon 45, Ebanks-Blake 81	16,633
2	ccr1	Wycombe	H	W	2-1 Bullock 41 og, Hodges 45	5,474
3	div1	Ipswich	H	D	1-1 Ebanks-Blake 85 pen	13,260
4	div1	Barnsley	A	L	2-3 Hayles 63, Chadwick 68	9,240
5	ccr2	Doncaster	H	W	2-0 Ebanks-Blake 15, Summerfield 90	5,133
6	div1	Leicester	H	D	0-0	11,850
7	div1	Cardiff	H	D	2-2 Ebanks-Blake 30, 58	11,591
8	div1	QPR	A	W	2-0 Halmosi 50, Norris 62	10,850
9	div1	Stoke	A	L	2-3 Seip 52, Fallon 59	12,533
10	ccr3	West Ham	A	L	0-1	25,774
11	div1	Wolverhampton	H	D	1-1 Chadwick 61	13,638
12	div1	Crystal Palace	H	W	1-0 Halmosi 50	10,451
13	div1	Blackpool	A	D	0-0	8,784
14	div1	Coventry	H	W	1-0 Martin 16	11,576
15	div1	Charlton	A	W	2-1 Ebanks-Blake 5, Hayles 38	22,123
16	div1	Preston	A	L	0-2	11,055
17	div1	Sheff Wed	H	L	1-2 Ebanks-Blake 47 pen	12,145
18	div1	Colchester	A	D	1-1 Norris 88	4,833
19	div1	Norwich	H	W	3-0 Martin 26, Connolly 47, Norris 49	11,222
20	div1	Sheff Utd	A	W	1-0 Halmosi 24	23,811
21	div1	West Brom	H	L	1-2 Easter 84	14,348
22	div1	Scunthorpe	H	W	3-0 Ebanks-Blake 51, Timar 64, Abdou 77	10,520
23	div1	Norwich	A	L	1-2 Timar 89	25,434
24	div1	Bristol City	H	D	1-1 Ebanks-Blake 23 pen	16,530
25	div1	Watford	A	W	1-0 Norris 89	18,532
26	div1	Crystal Palace	A	L	1-2 Easter 49	15,097
27	div1	QPR	H	W	2-1 Ebanks-Blake 50 pen, 90	16,502
28	div1	Stoke	H	D	2-2 Ebanks-Blake 44, Timar 67	13,692
29	div1	Cardiff	A	L	0-1	14,965
30	facr3	Hull City	H	W	3-2 Abdou 23, Halmosi 26, Ebanks-Blake 58	12,419
31	div1	Burnley	A	L	0-1	14,162
32	div1	Southampton	H	D	1-1 Fallon 49	14,676
33	facr4	Portsmouth	A	L	1-2 Clark 5	19,612
34	div1	Ipswich	A	D	0-0	20,095
35	div1	Hull City	H	L	0-1	11,011
36	div1	Leicester	A	W	1-0 Halmosi 34	21,264
37	div1	Barnsley	H	W	3-0 MacLean 6, Mackie 76, 85	11,346
38	div1	Southampton	A	W	2-0 Halmosi 31, Paterson 33	17,806
39	div1	Burnley	H	W	3-1 Nalis 12, Halmosi 35, 76	13,557
40	div1	West Brom	A	L	0-3	22,503
41	div1	Colchester	H	W	4-1 Ifil 11 og, Easter 57, MacLean 60 Sawyer 68	11,562
42	div1	Sheff Utd	H	L	0-1	13,669
43	div1	Scunthorpe	A	L	0-1	4,920
44	div1	Bristol City	A	W	2-1 Fallon 45, 59	19,011
45	div1	Watford	H	D	1-1 Easter 34	17,511
46	div1	Coventry	A	L	1-3 MacLean 81	18,775
47	div1	Charlton	H	L	1-2 Easter 60	14,715
48	div1	Sheff Wed	A	D	1-1 Halmosi 2	20,635
49	div1	Preston	H	D	2-2 Mackie 12, Wotton 75 pen	10,272
50	div1	Blackpool	H	W	3-0 Easter 4, Fallon 25, 55	12,911
51	div1	Wolverhampton	A	L	0-1	26,293

LEAGUE APPEARANCES, BOOKINGS AND GOALS

	AGE (on 01/07/08)	IN NAMED 16	APPEARANCES	COUNTING GAMES	MINUTES ON PITCH	LEAGUE GOALS	Yellow	Red
Goalkeepers								
Romain Larrieu	31	25	15	15	1350	0	0	0
Luke McCormick	24	40	30	30	2680	0	0	1
Defenders								
Russell Anderson	29	14	14	13	1236	0	6	0
Paul Connolly	24	43	42	42	3766	1	6	0
Mathias Doumbe	28	29	12	9	914	0	2	0
Dan Gosling	18	15	10	3	409	0	1	0
Gary Sawyer	22	40	31	27	2494	1	5	0
Marcel Seip	26	36	34	32	2918	1	3	0
Krisztian Timar	28	41	38	34	3181	3	9	0
Midfielders								
Nadjim Abdou	23	33	31	21	2103	1	1	0
Akos Buzsaky	26	12	11	5	694	0	1	0
Christopher Clark	27	14	12	6	696	0	0	0
Bojan Djordjic	26	2	1	0	45	0	0	0
Yoann Folly	23	5	4	0	96	0	0	0
Peter Halmosi	28	43	43	38	3592	8	2	1
Lee Hodges	34	32	27	20	1803	0	0	0
Lee Martin	21	12	12	7	813	2	4	0
Lilian Nalis	36	41	40	34	3168	1	7	0
David Norris	27	27	27	27	2430	5	4	0
Jim Paterson	28	8	8	7	624	1	1	0
Luke Summerfield	29	12	7	3	443	0	0	0
Gary Teale	29	12	12	6	674	0	0	0
Paul Wotton	30	13	8	5	482	1	1	0
Forwards								
Nick Chadwick	25	14	9	2	304	2	0	0
Jermaine Easter	26	34	32	18	1869	6	4	0
Sylvain Ebanks-Blake	22	26	25	16	1694	11	4	0
Rory Fallon	26	41	29	10	1264	7	1	0
Barry Hayles	36	24	23	18	1769	2	6	0
Lucas Jutkiewicz	19	7	3	1	101	0	0	0
Jamie Mackie	22	17	13	4	494	3	0	0
Steven MacLean	25	19	17	13	1277	3	2	0

TEAM OF THE SEASON

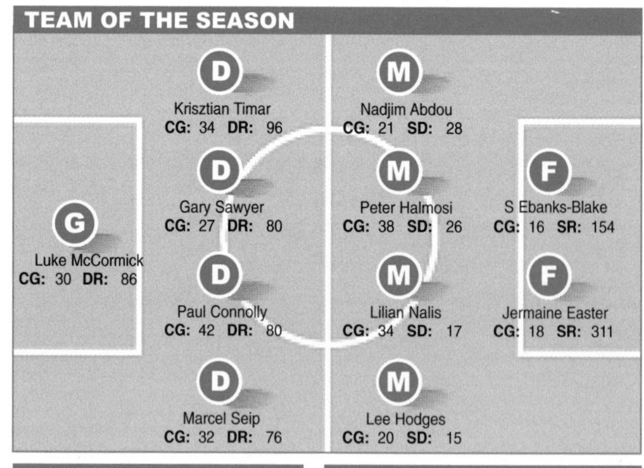
G
Luke McCormick
CG: 30 DR: 86
D
Krisztian Timar
CG: 34 DR: 96
D
Gary Sawyer
CG: 27 DR: 80
D
Paul Connolly
CG: 42 DR: 80
D
Marcel Seip
CG: 32 DR: 76
M
Nadjim Abdou
CG: 21 SD: 28
M
Peter Halmosi
CG: 38 SD: 26
M
Lilian Nalis
CG: 34 SD: 17
M
Lee Hodges
CG: 20 SD: 15
F
S Ebanks-Blake
CG: 16 SR: 154
F
Jermaine Easter
CG: 18 SR: 311

MONTHLY POINTS TALLY

Month	Points	%
AUGUST	4	44%
SEPTEMBER	6	40%
OCTOBER	10	67%
NOVEMBER	7	47%
DECEMBER	11	52%
JANUARY	2	17%
FEBRUARY	12	80%
MARCH	7	33%
APRIL	5	42%
MAY	0	0%

LEAGUE GOALS

	PLAYER	MINS	GOALS	S RATE
1	Ebanks-Blake	1694	11	154
2	Halmosi	3592	8	449
3	Fallon	1264	7	180
4	Easter	1869	6	311
5	Norris	2430	5	486
6	Mackie	494	3	164
7	MacLean	1277	3	425
8	Timar	3181	3	1060
9	Chadwick	304	2	152
10	Martin	813	2	406
11	Hayles	1769	2	884
12	Abdou	2103	1	2103
13	Wotton	482	1	482
	Other		5	
	TOTAL		59	

TOP POINT EARNERS

	PLAYER	GAMES	AV PTS
1	Sylvain Ebanks-Blake	16	1.63
2	Barry Hayles	18	1.61
3	Jermaine Easter	18	1.56
4	Krisztian Timar	34	1.56
5	Peter Halmosi	39	1.54
6	Lilian Nalis	34	1.53
7	Romain Larrieu	15	1.47
8	David Norris	27	1.44
9	Gary Sawyer	27	1.41
10	Lee Hodges	20	1.40
	CLUB AVERAGE:		1.39

DISCIPLINARY RECORDS

	PLAYER	YELLOW	RED	AVE
1	Lee Martin	4	0	203
2	Russell Anderson	6	0	206
3	Barry Hayles	6	0	294
4	Krisztian Timar	9	0	353
5	Sylvain Ebanks-Blake	4	0	423
6	Lilian Nalis	7	0	452
7	Mathias Doumbe	2	0	457
8	Jermaine Easter	4	0	467
9	Paul Wotton	1	0	482
10	Gary Sawyer	5	0	498
11	David Norris	4	0	607
12	Jim Paterson	1	0	624
13	Paul Connolly	6	0	627
	Other	10	2	
	TOTAL	69	2	

KEY GOALKEEPER

Luke McCormick

Goals Conceded in the League	31	**Counting Games** League games when player was on pitch for at least 70 minutes	30
Defensive Rating Ave number of mins between League goals conceded while on the pitch	86	**Clean Sheets** In League games when player was on pitch for at least 70 minutes	10

KEY PLAYERS - DEFENDERS

Krisztian Timar

Goals Conceded Number of League goals conceded while the player was on the pitch	33	**Clean Sheets** In League games when player was on pitch for at least 70 minutes	14
Defensive Rating Ave number of mins between League goals conceded while on the pitch	96	**Club Defensive Rating** Average number of mins between League goals conceded by the club this season	82

	PLAYER	CON LGE	CLEAN SHEETS	DEF RATE
1	Krisztian Timar	33	14	96 mins
2	Gary Sawyer	31	8	80 mins
3	Paul Connolly	47	12	80 mins
4	Marcel Seip	38	9	76 mins

KEY PLAYERS - MIDFIELDERS

Nadjim Abdou

Goals in the League	1	**Contribution to Attacking Power** Average number of minutes between League team goals while on pitch	63
Defensive Rating Average number of mins between League goals conceded while on the pitch	91	**Scoring Difference** Defensive Rating minus Contribution to Attacking Power	28

	PLAYER	LGE GOALS	DEF RATE	POWER	SCORE DIFF
1	Nadjim Abdou	1	91	63	28 mins
2	Peter Halmosi	8	89	63	26 mins
3	Lilian Nalis	1	85	68	17 mins
4	Lee Hodges	0	100	85	15 mins

KEY PLAYERS - GOALSCORERS

Sylvain Ebanks-Blake

Goals in the League	11	**Player Strike Rate** Average number of minutes between League goals scored by player	154
Contribution to Attacking Power Average number of minutes between League team goals while on pitch	62	**Club Strike Rate** Average number of minutes between League goals scored by club	69

	PLAYER	LGE GOALS	POWER	STRIKE RATE
1	Sylvain Ebanks-Blake	11	62	154 mins
2	Jermaine Easter	6	64	311 mins
3	Steven MacLean	3	75	425 mins
4	Peter Halmosi	8	63	449 mins

Paul Connolly

SQUAD APPEARANCES

Match	1	2	3	4	5	6	7	8	9	10	11	12	13	14	15	16	17	18	19	20	21	22	23	24	25
Venue	A	H	H	A	H	H	H	A	A	A	H	H	A	H	A	A	H	A	H	A	H	H	A	H	A
Competition	L	W	L	L	W	L	L	L	L	W	L	L	L	L	L	L	L	L	L	L	L	L	L	L	L
Result	W	W	D	L	W	D	D	W	L	L	D	W	D	W	W	L	L	D	W	W	L	W	L	D	W

Match	26	27	28	29	30	31	32	33	34	35	36	37	38	39	40	41	42	43	44	45	46	47	48	49	50	51
Venue	A	H	H	A	H	A	H	A	A	H	A	H	A	H	A	H	H	A	A	H	A	H	A	H	H	A
Competition	L	L	L	L	F	L	L	F	L	L	L	L	L	L	L	L	L	L	L	L	L	L	L	L	L	L
Result	L	W	D	L	W	L	D	L	D	L	W	W	W	W	L	W	L	L	W	D	L	L	D	D	W	L

Goalkeepers
Romain Larrieu
Luke McCormick

Defenders
Russell Anderson
Paul Connolly
Mathias Doumbe
Dan Gosling
Gary Sawyer
Marcel Seip
Krisztian Timar

Midfielders
Nadjim Abdou
Akos Buzsaky
Christopher Clark
Bojan Djordjic
Yoann Folly
Peter Halmosi
Lee Hodges
Lee Martin
Lilian Nalis
David Norris
Jim Paterson
Luke Summerfield
Gary Teale
Paul Wotton

Forwards
Nick Chadwick
Jermaine Easter
Sylvain Ebanks-Blake
Rory Fallon
Barry Hayles
Lucas Jutkiewicz
Jamie Mackie
Steven MacLean

KEY: ■ On all match ■ On bench ⏮ Subbed or sent off (Counting game) « Subbed or sent off (playing less than 70 minutes) ⏭ Subbed on from bench (Counting Game) » Subbed on (playing less than 70 minutes) Subbed on and then subbed or sent off (Counting Game) Subbed on and then subbed or sent off (playing less than 70 minutes) □ Not in 16

CHARLTON ATHLETIC

Final Position: **11th**

NICKNAME: THE ADDICKS

KEY: ☐Won ☐Drawn ☐Lost

	Comp	Opponent			Score	Scorers	Attendance
1	div1	Scunthorpe	H	D	1-1	M.Bent 62	23,151
2	ccr1	Swindon	A	W	2-0	Ambrose 52, Reid 63 pen	6,175
3	div1	Stoke	A	L	1-2	Reid 55	12,649
4	div1	Sheff Wed	H	W	3-2	Reid 51, Iwelumo 67, 87	22,033
5	ccr2	Stockport	H	W	4-3	Todorov 35, Z.Zheng 42 pen, Sam 74 McCarthy 90	8,022
6	div1	Crystal Palace	A	W	1-0	Todorov 74	18,556
7	div1	Colchester	A	D	2-2	Todorov 45, Z.Zheng 73	5,860
8	div1	Norwich	H	W	2-0	Reid 85 pen, 88 pen	21,543
9	div1	Leicester	H	W	2-0	Iwelumo 18, Varney 23	21,918
10	ccr3	Luton	A	L	1-3	Sinclair 4	4,534
11	div1	Coventry	A	D	1-1	Sam 15	19,021
12	div1	Hull City	A	W	2-1	Varney 41, Iwelumo 89	15,001
13	div1	Barnsley	H	D	1-1	Z.Zheng 82	21,081
14	div1	Wolverhampton	A	L	0-2		24,058
15	div1	Plymouth	H	L	1-2	McCormick 12 og	22,123
16	div1	QPR	H	L	0-1		23,671
17	div1	Southampton	A	W	1-0	Iwelumo 90	23,363
18	div1	Bristol City	A	W	1-0	Iwelumo 90	15,420
19	div1	Cardiff	H	W	3-0	Iwelumo 45, Sodje 45, Z.Zheng 80	22,866
20	div1	Preston	A	W	2-0	Z.Zheng 45, Varney 90	12,532
21	div1	Sheff Utd	H	L	0-3		20,737
22	div1	Burnley	H	L	1-3	Reid 36	21,122
23	div1	Cardiff	A	W	2-0	Holland 34, Reid 79 pen	11,874
24	div1	Ipswich	H	W	3-1	Ambrose 5, 39, Iwelumo 30	24,680
25	div1	West Brom	A	L	2-4	Iwelumo 36, McLeod 73	20,346
26	div1	Hull City	H	D	1-1	Bougherra 57	22,040
27	div1	Norwich	A	D	1-1	Z.Zheng 21	25,327
28	div1	Leicester	A	D	1-1	McCarthy 90	23,667
29	div1	Colchester	H	L	1-2	Varney 45	21,508
30	facr3	West Brom	H	D	1-1	Z.Zheng 2	12,682
31	div1	Blackpool	H	W	4-1	Bougherra 6, Varney 10, Z.Zheng 24, 52	21,412
32	facr3r	West Brom	A	L	3-4*	Ambrose 64, Dickson 90 pen (*on pens)	12,691
33	div1	Watford	A	D	1-1	Ambrose 79	17,214
34	div1	Stoke	H	W	1-0	Sam 83	22,108
35	div1	Scunthorpe	A	L	0-1		6,084
36	div1	Crystal Palace	H	W	2-0	Varney 60, 87	26,202
37	div1	Sheff Wed	A	D	0-0		17,211
38	div1	Watford	H	D	2-2	Ambrose 15, Shittu 36 og	26,337
39	div1	Blackpool	A	L	3-5	Ambrose 29, 30, Fortune 74	9,134
40	div1	Sheff Utd	A	W	2-0	Iwelumo 45, Sodje 82	23,180
41	div1	Bristol City	H	D	1-1	Ambrose 8	24,075
42	div1	Preston	H	L	1-2	McCarthy 74	21,124
43	div1	Burnley	A	L	0-1		10,700
44	div1	Ipswich	A	L	0-2		23,539
45	div1	West Brom	H	D	1-1	Halford 30	23,412
46	div1	Wolverhampton	H	L	2-3	Halford 31, Lita 90	23,187
47	div1	Plymouth	A	W	2-1	Lita 65, 76	14,715
48	div1	Southampton	H	D	1-1	Gray 69	26,206
49	div1	QPR	A	L	0-1		17,035
50	div1	Barnsley	A	L	0-3		11,228
51	div1	Coventry	H	W	4-1	Varney 4, Gray 19, Basey 48, Powell 86	26,130

LEAGUE APPEARANCES, BOOKINGS AND GOALS

	AGE (on 01/07/08)	IN NAMED 16	APPEARANCES	COUNTING GAMES	MINUTES ON PITCH	LEAGUE GOALS		
Goalkeepers								
Darren Randolph	21	33	1	1	90	0	0	0
Nicky Weaver	29	45	45	44	3962	0	0	1
Defenders								
Grant Basey	19	11	8	7	674	1	0	0
Madjid Bougherra	25	34	29	23	2189	2	7	0
Jonathan Fortune	27	32	26	23	2145	1	3	1
Greg Halford	23	16	16	16	1431	2	0	0
Patrick McCarthy	25	30	29	27	2478	2	6	0
Danny Mills	31	19	19	19	1691	0	6	1
Yassin Moutaouakil	21	12	10	6	655	0	2	0
Chris Powell	38	17	17	15	1363	1	1	0
Sam Sodje	29	32	27	17	1791	2	2	1
Ben Thatcher	32	12	11	10	944	0	1	0
Kelly Youga	22	11	11	10	944	0	2	0
Midfielders								
Darren Ambrose	24	39	37	26	2454	7	2	0
Lee Cook	25	10	9	2	275	0	1	0
Matt Holland	34	32	31	28	2593	1	2	0
Therry Racon	24	6	4	1	115	0	0	0
Andrew Reid	25	22	22	21	1891	6	3	0
Lloyd Sam	23	29	28	16	1710	2	4	1
Jose Vitor Semedo	23	42	37	20	2282	0	10	1
Jonjo Shelvey	16	2	2	2	173	0	0	0
Jerome Thomas, J	25	33	32	16	1937	0	2	0
Zhi Zheng	27	43	42	38	3455	7	3	0
Forwards								
Marcus Bent	30	3	3	2	208	1	0	0
Andy Gray	30	17	16	7	925	2	0	0
Chris Iwelumo	29	46	46	24	2940	10	3	0
Leroy Lita	23	8	8	8	691	3	1	0
Izale McLeod	23	23	18	1	431	1	2	0
Scott Sinclair	19	3	3	1	111	0	0	0
Svetoslav Todorov	29	10	7	1	301	2	1	0
Luke Varney	25	40	39	20	2233	8	4	0

TEAM OF THE SEASON

G
Nicky Weaver
CG: 44 DR: 70

D
Danny Mills
CG: 19 DR: 93

D
Chris Powell
CG: 15 DR: 75

D
Jonathan Fortune
CG: 23 DR: 73

D
Madjid Bougherra
CG: 23 DR: 70

M
Lloyd Sam
CG: 16 SD: 94

M
Andrew Reid
CG: 21 SD: 18

M
Zhi Zheng
CG: 38 SD: 11

M
Darren Ambrose
CG: 26 SD: 4

F
Luke Varney
CG: 20 SR: 279

F
Chris Iwelumo
CG: 24 SR: 294

MONTHLY POINTS TALLY

Month	Points	%
AUGUST	4	44%
SEPTEMBER	11	73%
OCTOBER	4	27%
NOVEMBER	12	80%
DECEMBER	9	43%
JANUARY	7	58%
FEBRUARY	5	33%
MARCH	5	24%
APRIL	4	33%
MAY	3	100%

LEAGUE GOALS

	PLAYER	MINS	GOALS	S RATE
1	Iwelumo	2940	10	294
2	Ambrose	2454	7	350
3	Zheng, Z	3455	7	493
4	Varney	2233	8	279
5	Reid	1891	6	315
6	Todorov	301	2	150
7	Lita	691	3	230
8	Sam	1710	2	855
9	McCarthy	2478	2	1239
10	Gray	925	2	462
11	Halford	1431	2	715
12	Sodje	1791	2	895
13	Bougherra	2189	2	1094
	Other		6	
	TOTAL		61	

TOP POINT EARNERS

	PLAYER	GAMES	AV PTS
1	Lloyd Sam	17	2.18
2	Chris Iwelumo	24	1.79
3	Danny Mills	19	1.79
4	Andrew Reid	21	1.71
5	Jonathan Fortune	23	1.61
6	Chris Powell	15	1.60
7	Jose Vitor Semedo	21	1.57
8	Zhi Zheng	38	1.47
9	Jerome Thomas, J	16	1.44
10	Nicky Weaver	45	1.40
	CLUB AVERAGE:		1.39

DISCIPLINARY RECORDS

	PLAYER	YELLOW	RED	AVE
1	Jose Vitor Semedo	10	1	207
2	Danny Mills	6	1	241
3	Madjid Bougherra	7	0	312
4	Yassin Moutaouakil	2	0	327
5	Lloyd Sam	4	1	342
6	Patrick McCarthy	6	0	413
7	Kelly Youga	2	0	472
8	Jonathan Fortune	3	1	536
9	Luke Varney	4	0	558
10	Sam Sodje	2	1	597
11	Andrew Reid	3	0	630
12	Leroy Lita	1	0	691
13	Ben Thatcher	1	0	944
	Other	13	1	
	TOTAL	64	6	

KEY GOALKEEPER

Nicky Weaver

Goals Conceded in the League	56	Counting Games League games when player was on pitch for at least 70 minutes	44
Defensive Rating Ave number of mins between League goals conceded while on the pitch	70	Clean Sheets In League games when player was on pitch for at least 70 minutes	12

KEY PLAYERS - DEFENDERS

Danny Mills

Goals Conceded Number of League goals conceded while the player was on the pitch	18	Clean Sheets In League games when player was on pitch for at least 70 minutes	8
Defensive Rating Ave number of mins between League goals conceded while on the pitch	93	Club Defensive Rating Average number of mins between League goals conceded by the club this season	71

	PLAYER	CON LGE	CLEAN SHEETS	DEF RATE
1	Danny Mills	18	8	93 mins
2	Chris Powell	18	4	75 mins
3	Jonathan Fortune	29	9	73 mins
4	Madjid Bougherra	31	4	70 mins

KEY PLAYERS - MIDFIELDERS

Lloyd Sam

Goals in the League	2	Contribution to Attacking Power Average number of minutes between League team goals while on pitch	61
Defensive Rating Average number of mins between League goals conceded while on the pitch	155	Scoring Difference Defensive Rating minus Contribution to Attacking Power	94

	PLAYER	LGE GOALS	DEF RATE	POWER	SCORE DIFF
1	Lloyd Sam	2	155	61	94 mins
2	Andrew Reid	6	85	67	18 mins
3	Zhi Zheng	7	76	65	11 mins
4	Darren Ambrose	7	68	64	4 mins

KEY PLAYERS - GOALSCORERS

Luke Varney

Goals in the League	8	Player Strike Rate Average number of minutes between League goals scored by player	279
Contribution to Attacking Power Average number of minutes between League team goals while on pitch	63	Club Strike Rate Average number of minutes between League goals scored by club	65

	PLAYER	LGE GOALS	POWER	STRIKE RATE
1	Luke Varney	8	63	279 mins
2	Chris Iwelumo	10	68	294 mins
3	Andrew Reid	6	67	315 mins
4	Darren Ambrose	7	64	350 mins

Chris Iwelumo and Jerome Thomas

SQUAD APPEARANCES

Match	1	2	3	4	5	6	7	8	9	10	11	12	13	14	15	16	17	18	19	20	21	22	23	24	25
Venue	H	A	A	H	H	A	A	H	H	A	A	A	H	A	H	H	A	A	H	A	H	H	A	H	A
Competition	L	W	L	L	W	L	L	L	L	W	L	L	L	L	L	L	L	L	L	L	L	L	L	L	L
Result	D	W	L	W	W	W	D	W	W	L	D	W	D	L	L	L	W	W	W	W	L	L	W	W	L

Match	26	27	28	29	30	31	32	33	34	35	36	37	38	39	40	41	42	43	44	45	46	47	48	49	50	51
Venue	H	A	A	H	H	H	A	A	H	A	H	A	H	A	A	H	H	A	A	H	H	A	H	A	A	H
Competition	L	L	L	L	F	L	F	L	L	L	L	L	L	L	L	L	L	L	L	L	L	L	L	L	L	L
Result	D	D	D	L	D	W	L	D	W	L	W	D	D	L	W	D	L	L	L	D	L	W	D	L	L	W

Goalkeepers
- Darren Randolph
- Nicky Weaver

Defenders
- Grant Basey
- Madjid Bougherra
- Jonathan Fortune
- Greg Halford
- Patrick McCarthy
- Danny Mills
- Yassin Moutaouakil
- Chris Powell
- Sam Sodje
- Ben Thatcher
- Kelly Youga

Midfielders
- Darren Ambrose
- Lee Cook
- Matt Holland
- Therry Racon
- Andrew Reid
- Lloyd Sam
- Jose Vitor Semedo
- Jonjo Shelvey
- Jerome Thomas, J
- Zhi Zheng

Forwards
- Marcus Bent
- Andy Gray
- Chris Iwelumo
- Leroy Lita
- Izale McLeod
- Scott Sinclair
- Svetoslav Todorov
- Luke Varney

KEY: ■ On all match · ■ On bench · ⏮ Subbed or sent off (Counting game) · « Subbed or sent off (playing less than 70 minutes) · ⏭ Subbed on from bench (Counting Game) · » Subbed on (playing less than 70 minutes) · Subbed on and then subbed or sent off (Counting Game) · Subbed on and then subbed or sent off (playing less than 70 minutes) · Not in 16

CARDIFF CITY

Final Position: **12th**

NICKNAME: THE BLUEBIRDS

KEY: ☐Won ☐Drawn ☐Lost

No	Comp	Opponent	Venue	Result	Score	Scorers	Attendance
1	div1	Stoke	H	L	0-1		18,840
2	ccr1	Brighton	H	W	1-0	Johnson 110	3,726
3	div1	QPR	A	W	2-0	Parry 29, 59	12,596
4	div1	Coventry	H	L	0-1		16,407
5	ccr2	Leyton Orient	H	W	1-0	Whittingham 90	6,150
6	div1	Norwich	A	W	2-1	Whittingham 64, Johnson 84	24,292
7	div1	Plymouth	A	D	2-2	Rae 71, Thompson 89	11,591
8	div1	Watford	H	L	1-2	Hasselbaink 61	13,169
9	div1	Preston	H	D	2-2	Fowler 28, 61	11,772
10	ccr3	West Brom	A	W	4-2	Fowler 4, 27 pen, Hasselbaink 23 Sinclair 30	14,085
11	div1	Barnsley	A	D	1-1	Hasselbaink 73	10,709
12	div1	Sheff Utd	A	D	3-3	Ledley 31, Fowler 45 pen, Rae 59	26,186
13	div1	Burnley	H	W	2-1	Ledley 36, Parry 55	12,914
14	div1	Southampton	A	L	0-1		20,796
15	div1	Wolverhampton	H	L	2-3	Fowler 25 pen, Hasselbaink 29	15,000
16	div1	Scunthorpe	H	D	1-1	McPhail 37	11,850
17	ccr4	Liverpool	A	L	1-2	Purse 65	41,780
18	div1	Crystal Palace	H	D	1-1	Purse 9	11,781
19	div1	Charlton	A	L	0-3		22,866
20	div1	Ipswich	H	W	1-0	Parry 33	15,173
21	div1	Leicester	A	D	0-0		27,246
22	div1	Hull City	A	D	2-2	Thompson 6, Johnson 90	16,269
23	div1	Charlton	H	L	0-2		11,874
24	div1	Colchester	H	W	4-1	Thompson 52, Whittingham 57 Hasselbaink 66, Virgo 70 og	11,006
25	div1	Blackpool	A	W	1-0	Thompson 14	7,214
26	div1	Bristol City	A	L	0-1		15,753
27	div1	Sheff Utd	H	W	1-0	Parry 30	12,869
28	div1	Watford	A	D	2-2	Johnson 34, Whittingham 56	17,014
29	div1	Preston	A	W	2-1	Johnson 53, Ledley 67	12,046
30	div1	Plymouth	H	W	1-0	Ledley 30	14,965
31	facr3	Chasetown	A	W	3-1	Whittingham 45, Ramsey 60, Parry 73	2,420
32	div1	Sheff Wed	H	W	1-0	Hasselbaink 36	14,015
33	div1	West Brom	A	D	3-3	Parry 1, 33, Ledley 52	22,325
34	facr4	Hereford	A	W	2-1	McNaughton 45, Thompson 67 pen	6,855
35	div1	QPR	H	W	3-1	Ledley 12, 40, Parry 57	13,602
36	div1	Stoke	A	L	1-2	Hasselbaink 63	15,045
37	div1	Norwich	H	L	1-2	Rae 45	11,937
38	div1	Coventry	A	D	0-0		15,260
39	facr5	Wolverhampton	H	W	2-0	Whittingham 2, Hasselbaink 11	15,339
40	div1	Sheff Wed	A	L	0-1		18,539
41	div1	Leicester	H	L	0-1		13,355
42	div1	Crystal Palace	A	D	0-0		13,446
43	facqf	Middlesbrough	A	W	2-0	Whittingham 9, Johnson 22	32,896
44	div1	Hull City	H	W	1-0	McPhail 1	17,555
45	div1	Colchester	A	D	1-1	Parry 11	4,699
46	div1	Bristol City	H	W	2-1	Johnson 44, Whittingham 81	16,458
47	div1	Southampton	H	W	1-0	Parry 6	12,955
48	div1	West Brom	H	D	0-0		13,915
49	facsf	Barnsley	N	W	1-0	Ledley 9	82,752
50	div1	Ipswich	A	D	1-1	Rae 37	20,311
51	div1	Blackpool	H	W	3-1	McPhail 7, Sinclair 50, Whittingham 58	14,715
52	div1	Scunthorpe	A	L	2-3	Hasselbaink 45, Ledley 59	4,727
53	div1	Wolverhampton	A	L	0-3		20,862
54	div1	Burnley	A	D	3-3	Ledley 57 pen, Ramsey 69, Thompson 89	10,694
55	div1	Barnsley	H	W	3-0	Parry 44, McNaughton 49, Ledley 63	14,469
56	facf	Portsmouth	N	L	0-1		89,874

LEAGUE APPEARANCES, BOOKINGS AND GOALS

	AGE (on 01/07/08)	IN NAMED 16	APPEARANCES	COUNTING GAMES	MINUTES ON PITCH	LEAGUE GOALS	Yellow	Red
Goalkeepers								
Peter Enckelman	31	20	16	15	1362	0	0	0
David Forde	28	3	0	0	0	0	0	0
Josh Magennis	-	0	0	0	0	0	0	0
Michael Oakes	34	45	11	11	978	0	0	0
Kasper Schmeichel	21	14	14	14	1260	0	1	0
Ross Turnbull	23	9	6	6	540	0	0	0
Defenders								
Anthony Capaldi	26	44	44	38	3701	0	3	0
Chris Gunter	18	17	13	10	1017	0	1	0
Roger Johnson	25	46	42	41	3696	5	2	0
Glenn Loovens	24	40	36	34	3133	0	10	0
Kevin McNaughton	25	40	35	31	2927	1	2	0
Darren Purse	31	41	18	13	1199	1	3	1
Midfielders								
Darcy Blake	19	19	8	4	476	0	1	0
Jonathan Brown	-	3	2	0	26	0	0	0
Joe Ledley	21	42	41	33	3325	10	3	0
Stephen McPhail	28	43	43	40	3673	3	4	0
Paul Parry	27	41	41	34	3264	11	0	0
Gavin Rae	30	46	45	40	3735	4	3	0
Aaron Ramsey	-	24	15	10	1016	1	1	0
Riccardo Scimeca	33	11	9	2	374	0	1	0
Trevor Sinclair	35	26	21	12	1307	1	1	0
Peter Whittingham	23	45	41	21	2492	5	1	0
Forwards								
Warren Feeney	27	7	5	0	82	0	0	0
Robbie Fowler	33	14	13	5	789	4	0	0
Matthew Green	21	2	0	0	0	0	0	0
Jimmy-Floyd Hasselbaink	36	38	36	29	2715	7	3	1
Steven MacLean	25	19	15	5	611	0	2	0
Steven Thompson	29	36	36	15	1736	5	3	1

TEAM OF THE SEASON

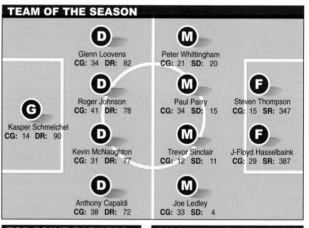

G — Kasper Schmeichel — CG: 14 DR: 90

D — Glenn Loovens — CG: 34 DR: 82

D — Roger Johnson — CG: 41 DR: 78

D — Kevin McNaughton — CG: 31 DR: 77

D — Anthony Capaldi — CG: 38 DR: 72

M — Peter Whittingham — CG: 21 SD: 20

M — Paul Parry — CG: 34 SD: 15

M — Trevor Sinclair — CG: 12 SD: 11

M — Joe Ledley — CG: 33 SD: 4

F — Steven Thompson — CG: 15 SR: 347

F — J-Floyd Hasselbaink — CG: 29 SR: 387

MONTHLY POINTS TALLY

Month	Points	%
AUGUST	3	33%
SEPTEMBER	6	40%
OCTOBER	5	33%
NOVEMBER	5	42%
DECEMBER	14	58%
JANUARY	10	83%
FEBRUARY	1	8%
MARCH	11	61%
APRIL	6	33%
MAY	3	100%

LEAGUE GOALS

	PLAYER	MINS	GOALS	S RATE
1	Parry	3264	11	296
2	Ledley	3325	10	332
3	Hasselbaink	2715	7	387
4	Whittingham	2492	5	498
5	Johnson	3696	5	739
6	Fowler	789	4	197
7	Thompson	1736	5	347
8	Rae	3735	4	933
9	McPhail	3673	3	1224
10	Ramsey	1016	1	1016
11	Purse	1199	1	1199
12	Sinclair	1307	1	1307
13	McNaughton	2927	1	2927
	Other		0	
	TOTAL		**58**	

TOP POINT EARNERS

	PLAYER	GAMES	AV PTS
1	Peter Whittingham	21	**1.90**
2	Kasper Schmeichel	14	**1.64**
3	Steven Thompson	16	**1.63**
4	Paul Parry	34	**1.50**
5	Glenn Loovens	34	**1.47**
6	Joe Ledley	33	**1.45**
7	Roger Johnson	41	**1.44**
8	Peter Enckelman	15	**1.40**
9	Stephen McPhail	40	**1.38**
10	J-Floyd Hasselbaink	30	**1.33**
	CLUB AVERAGE:		**1.39**

DISCIPLINARY RECORDS

	PLAYER	YELLOW	RED	AVE
1	Darren Purse	3	1	**299**
2	Steven MacLean	2	0	**305**
3	Glenn Loovens	10	0	**313**
4	Steven Thompson	3	1	**434**
5	Darcy Blake	1	0	**476**
6	J-Floyd Hasselbaink	3	1	**678**
7	Stephen McPhail	4	0	**918**
8	Aaron Ramsey	1	0	**1016**
9	Chris Gunter	1	0	**1017**
10	Joe Ledley	3	0	**1108**
11	Anthony Capaldi	3	0	**1233**
12	Gavin Rae	3	0	**1245**
13	Kasper Schmeichel	1	0	**1260**
	Other	6	0	
	TOTAL	**44**	**3**	

KEY GOALKEEPER

Kasper Schmeichel

Goals Conceded in the League	14	Counting Games League games when player was on pitch for at least 70 minutes	14
Defensive Rating Ave number of mins between League goals conceded while on the pitch	90	Clean Sheets In League games when player was on pitch for at least 70 minutes	5

KEY PLAYERS - DEFENDERS

Glenn Loovens

Goals Conceded Number of League goals conceded while the player was on the pitch	38	Clean Sheets In League games when player was on pitch for at least 70 minutes	12
Defensive Rating Ave number of mins between League goals conceded while on the pitch	82	Club Defensive Rating Average number of mins between League goals conceded by the club this season	75

	PLAYER	CON LGE	CLEAN SHEETS	DEF RATE
1	Glenn Loovens	38	12	82 mins
2	Roger Johnson	47	11	78 mins
3	Kevin McNaughton	38	8	77 mins
4	Anthony Capaldi	51	10	72 mins

KEY PLAYERS - MIDFIELDERS

Peter Whittingham

Goals in the League	5	Contribution to Attacking Power Average number of minutes between League team goals while on pitch	65
Defensive Rating Average number of mins between League goals conceded while on the pitch	85	Scoring Difference Defensive Rating minus Contribution to Attacking Power	20

	PLAYER	LGE GOALS	DEF RATE	POWER	SCORE DIFF
1	Peter Whittingham	5	85	65	20 mins
2	Paul Parry	11	83	68	15 mins
3	Trevor Sinclair	1	87	76	11 mins
4	Joe Ledley	10	70	66	4 mins

KEY PLAYERS - GOALSCORERS

Paul Parry

Goals in the League	11	Player Strike Rate Average number of minutes between League goals scored by player	296
Contribution to Attacking Power Average number of minutes between League team goals while on pitch	68	Club Strike Rate Average number of minutes between League goals scored by club	70

	PLAYER	LGE GOALS	POWER	STRIKE RATE
1	Paul Parry	11	68	296 mins
2	Joe Ledley	10	66	332 mins
3	Steven Thompson	5	78	347 mins
4	Jimmy-Floyd Hasselbaink	7	61	387 mins

Joma
COMMS DIRECT
Jimmy-Floyd Hasselbaink and Robbie Fowler

SQUAD APPEARANCES

Match	1	2	3	4	5	6	7	8	9	10	11	12	13	14
Venue	H	H	A	H	H	A	A	H	H	A	A	A	H	A
Competition	L	W	L	L	W	L	L	L	L	W	L	L	L	L
Result	L	W	W	L	W	W	D	L	D	W	D	D	W	L

Match	15	16	17	18	19	20	21	22	23	24	25	26	27	28
Venue	H	H	A	H	A	H	A	A	H	H	A	A	H	A
Competition	L	L	W	L	L	L	L	L	L	L	L	L	L	L
Result	L	D	L	D	L	W	D	D	L	W	W	L	W	D

Match	29	30	31	32	33	34	35	36	37	38	39	40	41	42
Venue	A	H	A	H	A	A	H	A	H	A	H	A	H	A
Competition	L	L	F	L	L	F	L	L	L	L	F	L	L	L
Result	W	W	W	W	D	W	W	L	L	D	W	L	L	D

Match	43	44	45	46	47	48	49	50	51	52	53	54	55	56
Venue	A	H	A	H	H	H	N	A	H	A	A	A	H	N
Competition	F	L	L	L	L	L	F	L	L	L	L	L	L	F
Result	W	W	D	W	W	D	W	D	W	L	L	D	W	L

Goalkeepers
Peter Enckelman
David Forde
Josh Magennis
Michael Oakes
Kasper Schmeichel
Ross Turnbull

Defenders
Anthony Capaldi
Chris Gunter
Roger Johnson
Glenn Loovens
Kevin McNaughton
Darren Purse

Midfielders
Darcy Blake
Jonathan Brown
Joe Ledley
Stephen McPhail
Paul Parry
Gavin Rae
Aaron Ramsey
Riccardo Scimeca
Trevor Sinclair
Peter Whittingham

Forwards
Warren Feeney
Robbie Fowler
Matthew Green
Jimmy-Floyd Hasselbaink
Steven MacLean
Steven Thompson

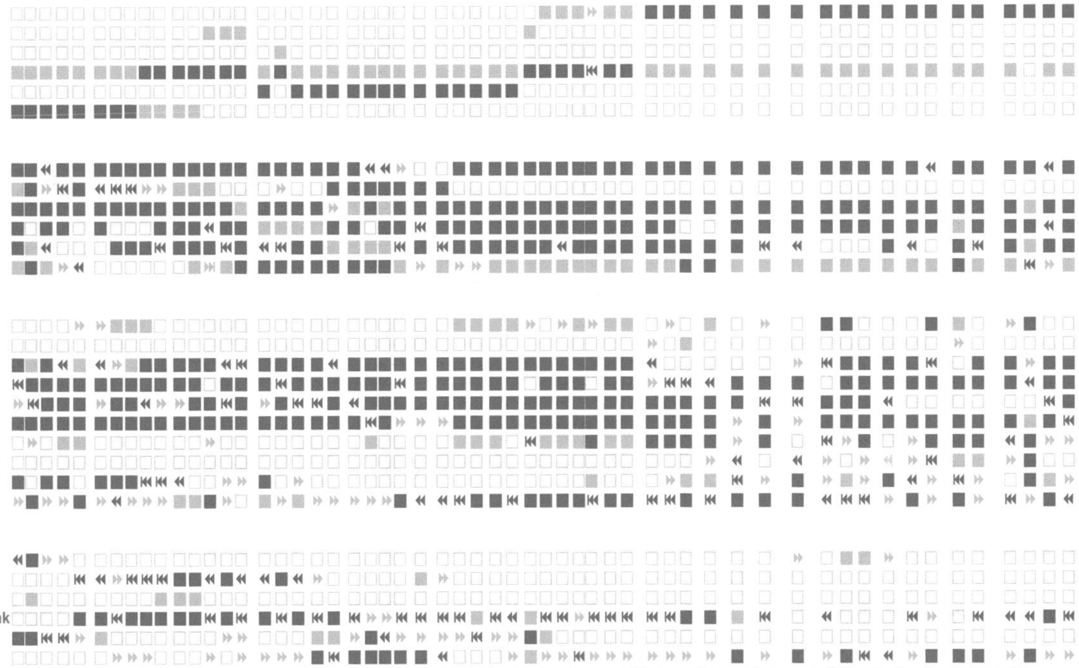

KEY: ■ On all match | ■ On bench | ⏮ Subbed or sent off (Counting game) | « Subbed or sent off (playing less than 70 minutes) | ⏭ Subbed on from bench (Counting Game) | » Subbed on (playing less than 70 minutes) | » Subbed on and then subbed or sent off (Counting Game) | » Subbed on and then subbed or sent off (playing less than 70 minutes) | □ Not in 16

BURNLEY

Final Position: **13th**

NICKNAME: THE CLARETS

KEY: Won / Drawn / Lost

#	Comp	Opponent	H/A	Res	Score	Scorers	Attendance
1	div1	West Brom	H	W	2-1	Duff 47, Gray 79 pen	15,337
2	ccr1	Grimsby	A	W	4-2*	Gray 108 (*on penalties)	2,431
3	div1	Scunthorpe	A	L	0-2		6,975
4	ccr2	Oldham	H	W	3-0	Gray 59, Blake 76, Akinbiyi 90	7,317
5	div1	Colchester	A	W	3-2	Mahon 15, Gray 29, 63 pen	4,925
6	div1	Blackpool	H	D	2-2	Jones 52, Akinbiyi 86	16,843
7	div1	Sheff Wed	A	W	2-0	Blake 15, McCann 48	18,359
8	div1	Bristol City	A	D	2-2	Gray 52, Carlisle 90	14,079
9	ccr3	Portsmouth	H	L	0-1		8,202
10	div1	Crystal Palace	H	D	1-1	Duff 13	10,711
11	div1	Ipswich	H	D	2-2	Lafferty 11, Gray 60	9,952
12	div1	Cardiff	A	L	1-2	Akinbiyi 50	12,914
13	div1	Barnsley	A	D	1-1	Gray 11	11,560
14	div1	Norwich	H	W	2-1	Blake 1, Gray 4 pen	10,133
15	div1	Southampton	H	L	2-3	McCann 31, Akinbiyi 83	10,944
16	div1	Sheff Utd	A	D	0-0		25,306
17	div1	Hull City	H	L	0-1		9,978
18	div1	Leicester	A	W	1-0	Gray 23	21,334
19	div1	Stoke	H	D	0-0		11,758
20	div1	Watford	A	W	2-1	Gray 58, Gudjonsson 80	15,021
21	div1	Charlton	A	W	3-1	Gray 8, 70 pen, McCann 13	21,122
22	div1	Leicester	H	D	1-1	Unsworth 19	10,688
23	div1	Wolverhampton	A	W	3-2	Blake 20 fk, Lafferty 30, D.Ward 42 og	20,763
24	div1	QPR	H	L	0-2		10,522
25	div1	Preston	H	L	2-3	Lafferty 31, McCann 62	14,829
26	div1	Ipswich	A	D	0-0		20,077
27	div1	Sheff Wed	H	D	1-1	Akinbiyi 31	15,326
28	div1	Bristol City	H	L	0-1		12,109
29	div1	Blackpool	A	L	0-3		9,599
30	facr3	Arsenal	H	L	0-2		16,709
31	div1	Plymouth	H	W	1-0	Blake 66	14,162
32	div1	Coventry	A	W	2-1	Akinbiyi 10, Blake 68	17,347
33	div1	Scunthorpe	H	W	2-0	Blake 9, Akinbiyi 32	14,516
34	div1	West Brom	A	L	1-2	J.O'Connor 3	22,206
35	div1	Colchester	H	D	1-1	Cole 23	15,376
36	div1	QPR	A	W	4-2	Cole 41, 56, 86, Akinbiyi 77	13,410
37	div1	Plymouth	A	L	1-3	J.O'Connor 19	13,557
38	div1	Coventry	H	W	2-0	McCann 20, Caldwell 85	9,779
39	div1	Watford	H	D	2-2	Blake 75, 88	13,677
40	div1	Hull City	A	L	0-2		15,838
41	div1	Stoke	A	D	1-1	Lafferty 3	18,432
42	div1	Charlton	H	W	1-0	Elliott 59	10,700
43	div1	Wolverhampton	H	L	1-3	Akinbiyi 76	12,749
44	div1	Preston	A	L	1-2	J.O'Connor 38	16,149
45	div1	Barnsley	H	W	2-1	Elliott 30, Lafferty 36	11,915
46	div1	Norwich	A	L	0-2		24,049
47	div1	Sheff Utd	H	L	1-2	Cole 80	11,693
48	div1	Southampton	A	W	1-0	Caldwell 45	21,762
49	div1	Cardiff	H	D	3-3	Alexander 36, Cole 54, Carlisle 86	10,694
50	div1	Crystal Palace	A	L	0-5		23,950

LEAGUE APPEARANCES, BOOKINGS AND GOALS

Player	AGE (on 01/07/08)	IN NAMED 16	APPEARANCES	COUNTING GAMES	MINUTES ON PITCH	LEAGUE GOALS	Yellow	Red
Goalkeepers								
Brian Jensen	33	45	19	19	1710	0	0	0
Gabor Kiraly	32	45	27	27	2430	0	0	0
Defenders								
Graham Alexander	36	43	43	42	3847	1	10	0
Stephen Caldwell	27	30	29	24	2264	2	6	1
Clarke Carlisle	28	33	33	30	2762	2	4	2
Mike Duff	29	11	8	7	668	2	2	0
Stephen Foster	27	0	0	0	0	0	0	0
Jon Harley	28	37	33	29	2741	0	6	0
Stephen Jordan	26	27	20	17	1683	0	2	0
Wayne Thomas	29	1	1	1	90	0	0	0
David Unsworth	34	40	29	24	2295	1	5	1
Stanislav Varga	35	11	10	9	812	0	3	0
Midfielders								
Wade Elliott	29	46	46	44	3980	2	6	0
Johannes Gudjonsson	28	29	28	11	1471	1	2	2
Adam Kay	18	1	0	0	0	0	0	0
Alan Mahon	30	27	26	7	1259	1	4	0
Christopher McCann	20	34	34	29	2746	5	6	1
Gareth O'Connor	29	7	2	1	92	0	0	0
James O'Connor	28	38	29	21	2098	3	3	0
Mark Randall	18	14	10	0	226	0	2	0
John Spicer	24	28	23	8	947	0	2	1
Forwards								
Ade Akinbiyi	33	43	39	13	1636	8	3	0
Besart Berisha	22	0	0	0	0	0	0	0
Robbie Blake	32	45	45	31	3298	8	4	0
Andy Cole	36	13	13	8	798	6	1	0
Andy Gray	30	25	25	25	2201	11	0	0
Steve Jones	31	21	18	1	463	1	0	0
Kyle Lafferty	20	37	37	28	2786	5	5	0
Alexander MacDonald	19	2	2	0	33	0	0	0
Jay Rodriguez	18	2	1	0	5	0	0	0

TEAM OF THE SEASON

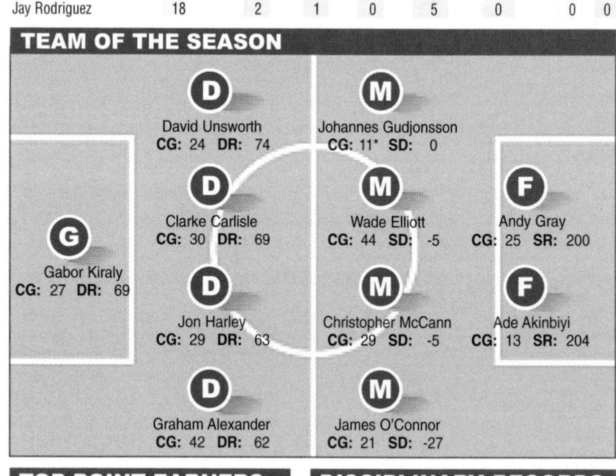

G
Gabor Kiraly
CG: 27 DR: 69
D
David Unsworth
CG: 24 DR: 74
D
Clarke Carlisle
CG: 30 DR: 69
D
Jon Harley
CG: 29 DR: 63
D
Graham Alexander
CG: 42 DR: 62
M
Johannes Gudjonsson
CG: 11* SD: 0
M
Wade Elliott
CG: 44 SD: -5
M
Christopher McCann
CG: 29 SD: -5
M
James O'Connor
CG: 21 SD: -27
F
Andy Gray
CG: 25 SR: 200
F
Ade Akinbiyi
CG: 13 SR: 204

MONTHLY POINTS TALLY

Month	Points	%
AUGUST	3	50%
SEPTEMBER	9	60%
OCTOBER	5	33%
NOVEMBER	8	53%
DECEMBER	9	38%
JANUARY	9	75%
FEBRUARY	7	47%
MARCH	8	38%
APRIL	4	33%
MAY	0	0%

LEAGUE GOALS

	PLAYER	MINS	GOALS	S RATE
1	Gray	2201	11	200
2	Akinbiyi	1636	8	204
3	Blake	3298	8	412
4	Cole	798	6	133
5	McCann	2746	5	549
6	Lafferty	2786	5	557
7	O'Connor, J	2098	3	699
8	Duff	668	2	334
9	Caldwell	2264	2	1132
10	Carlisle	2762	2	1381
11	Elliott	3980	2	1990
12	Jones	463	1	463
13	Mahon	1259	1	1259
	Other		3	
	TOTAL		59	

TOP POINT EARNERS

	PLAYER	GAMES	AV PTS
1	Christopher McCann	30	1.53
2	Robbie Blake	31	1.48
3	Jon Harley	29	1.48
4	Brian Jensen	19	1.47
5	Andy Gray	25	1.44
6	Wade Elliott	44	1.41
7	Clarke Carlisle	31	1.35
8	Graham Alexander	42	1.33
9	Kyle Lafferty	28	1.32
10	Ade Akinbiyi	13	1.31
	CLUB AVERAGE:		1.35

DISCIPLINARY RECORDS

	PLAYER	YELLOW	RED	AVE
1	Stanislav Varga	3	0	270
2	Alan Mahon	4	0	314
3	John Spicer	2	1	315
4	Stephen Caldwell	6	1	323
5	Mike Duff	2	0	334
6	J Gudjonsson	2	2	367
7	David Unsworth	5	1	382
8	Graham Alexander	10	0	384
9	Chris McCann	6	1	392
10	Jon Harley	6	0	456
11	Clarke Carlisle	4	2	460
12	Ade Akinbiyi	3	0	545
13	Kyle Lafferty	5	0	557
	Other	16	0	
	TOTAL	74	8	

KEY GOALKEEPER

Gabor Kiraly

Goals Conceded in the League	35	Counting Games League games when player was on pitch for at least 70 minutes	27
Defensive Rating Ave number of mins between League goals conceded while on the pitch	69	Clean Sheets In League games when player was on pitch for at least 70 minutes	6

KEY PLAYERS - DEFENDERS

David Unsworth

Goals Conceded Number of League goals conceded while the player was on the pitch	31	Clean Sheets In League games when player was on pitch for at least 70 minutes	6
Defensive Rating Ave number of mins between League goals conceded while on the pitch	74	Club Defensive Rating Average number of mins between League goals conceded by the club this season	63

	PLAYER	CON LGE	CLEAN SHEETS	DEF RATE
1	David Unsworth	31	6	74 mins
2	Clarke Carlisle	40	7	69 mins
3	Jon Harley	43	7	63 mins
4	Graham Alexander	62	10	62 mins

KEY PLAYERS - MIDFIELDERS

Johannes Gudjonsson

Goals in the League	1	Contribution to Attacking Power Average number of minutes between League team goals while on pitch	58
Defensive Rating Average number of mins between League goals conceded while on the pitch	58	Scoring Difference Defensive Rating minus Contribution to Attacking Power	0

	PLAYER	LGE GOALS	DEF RATE	POWER	SCORE DIFF
1	Johannes Gudjonsson	1	58	58	0 mins
2	Wade Elliott	2	63	68	-5 mins
3	Christopher McCann	5	58	63	-5 mins
4	James O'Connor	3	53	80	-27 mins

KEY PLAYERS - GOALSCORERS

Andy Gray

Goals in the League	11	Player Strike Rate Average number of minutes between League goals scored by player	200
Contribution to Attacking Power Average number of minutes between League team goals while on pitch	66	Club Strike Rate Average number of minutes between League goals scored by club	70

	PLAYER	LGE GOALS	POWER	STRIKE RATE
1	Andy Gray	11	66	200 mins
2	Ade Akinbiyi	8	65	204 mins
3	Robbie Blake	8	67	412 mins
4	Christopher McCann	5	63	549 mins

SINCE 1851
errea
Robbie Blake

SQUAD APPEARANCES

Match	1	2	3	4	5	6	7	8	9	10	11	12	13	14	15	16	17	18	19	20	21	22	23	24	25
Venue	H	A	A	H	A	H	A	A	H	H	H	A	A	H	H	A	H	A	H	A	A	H	A	H	H
Competition	L	W	L	W	L	L	L	L	W	L	L	L	L	L	L	L	L	L	L	L	L	L	L	L	L
Result	W	W	L	W	W	D	W	D	L	D	D	L	D	W	L	D	L	W	D	W	W	D	W	L	L

Match	26	27	28	29	30	31	32	33	34	35	36	37	38	39	40	41	42	43	44	45	46	47	48	49	50
Venue	A	H	H	A	H	H	A	H	A	H	A	A	H	H	A	A	H	H	A	H	A	H	A	H	A
Competition	L	L	L	L	F	L	L	L	L	L	L	L	L	L	L	L	L	L	L	L	L	L	L	L	L
Result	D	D	L	L	L	W	W	W	L	D	W	L	W	D	L	D	W	L	L	W	L	L	W	D	L

Goalkeepers
Brian Jensen
Gabor Kiraly

Defenders
Graham Alexander
Stephen Caldwell
Clarke Carlisle
Mike Duff
Stephen Foster
Jon Harley
Stephen Jordan
Wayne Thomas
David Unsworth
Stanislav Varga

Midfielders
Wade Elliott
Johannes Gudjonsson
Adam Kay
Alan Mahon
Christopher McCann
Gareth O'Connor
James O'Connor
Mark Randall
John Spicer

Forwards
Ade Akinbiyi
Besart Berisha
Robbie Blake
Andy Cole
Andy Gray
Steve Jones
Kyle Lafferty
Alexander MacDonald
Jay Rodriguez

KEY: ■ On all match · ■ On bench · ⏮ Subbed or sent off (Counting game) · « Subbed or sent off (playing less than 70 minutes) · ⏭ Subbed on from bench (Counting Game) · » Subbed on (playing less than 70 minutes) · Subbed on and then subbed or sent off (Counting Game) · Subbed on and then subbed or sent off (playing less than 70 minutes) · □ Not in 16

QUEENS PARK RANGERS

Final Position: **14th**

NICKNAME: RANGERS

KEY: ☐Won ☐Drawn ☐Lost

		Opponent			Score	Scorers	Attendance
1	div1	Bristol City	A	D	2-2	Blackstock 34, Stewart 90	18,228
2	ccr1	Leyton Orient	H	L	1-2	Rowlands 68	5,260
3	div1	Cardiff	H	L	0-2		12,596
4	div1	Southampton	H	L	0-3		15,560
5	div1	Leicester	A	D	1-1	Leigertwood 82	21,893
6	div1	Plymouth	H	L	0-2		10,850
7	div1	Watford	H	D	1-1	Moore 59	14,240
8	div1	West Brom	A	L	1-5	Ainsworth 24	24,757
9	div1	Colchester	A	L	2-4	Ephraim 29, Vine 58	5,361
10	div1	Norwich	H	W	1-0	Rowlands 67 pen	10,514
11	div1	Ipswich	H	D	1-1	Nygaard 73	13,946
12	div1	Preston	A	D	0-0		11,407
13	div1	Charlton	A	W	1-0	Bolder 72	23,671
14	div1	Hull City	H	W	2-0	Ephraim 26, Leigertwood 56	12,375
15	div1	Coventry	H	L	1-2	Buzsaky 50	11,922
16	div1	Crystal Palace	A	D	1-1	Sinclair 45	17,010
17	div1	Sheff Wed	H	D	0-0		15,241
18	div1	Stoke	A	L	1-3	Vine 63	11,147
19	div1	Blackpool	A	L	0-1		8,527
20	div1	Crystal Palace	H	L	1-2	Stewart 10	13,300
21	div1	Scunthorpe	A	D	2-2	Buzsaky 12, 42	5,612
22	div1	Burnley	A	W	2-0	Stewart 60, Vine 90	10,522
23	div1	Wolverhampton	H	D	0-0		13,482
24	div1	Colchester	H	W	2-1	Buzsaky 27, 52	12,464
25	div1	Plymouth	A	L	1-2	Ainsworth 20	16,502
26	div1	Watford	A	W	4-2	Rowlands 13 pen, 40, Stewart 29 Buzsaky 80	18,698
27	div1	Leicester	H	W	3-1	Stewart 15, Bolder 26, Blackstock 56	13,326
28	facr3	Chelsea	A	L	0-1		41,289
29	div1	Sheff Utd	A	L	1-2	Agyemang 45	28,894
30	div1	Barnsley	H	W	2-0	Agyemang 5, Vine 45	16,197
31	div1	Cardiff	A	L	1-3	Ephraim 76	13,602
32	div1	Bristol City	H	W	3-0	Agyemang 18, 33, Buzsaky 63	16,502
33	div1	Southampton	A	W	3-2	Rowlands 38, Agyemang 45, 60	22,505
34	div1	Burnley	H	L	2-4	Mahon 14, Agyemang 30	13,410
35	div1	Sheff Utd	H	D	1-1	Balanta 19	15,383
36	div1	Barnsley	A	D	0-0		9,019
37	div1	Stoke	H	W	3-0	Leigertwood 12, 21, Buzsaky 56	13,398
38	div1	Coventry	A	D	0-0		15,225
39	div1	Sheff Wed	A	L	1-2	Delaney 15	18,555
40	div1	Blackpool	H	W	3-2	Buzsaky 11, Vine 40, Rowlands 47	11,538
41	div1	Scunthorpe	H	W	3-1	Rowlands 43 pen, Agyemang 79, Vine 90	14,499
42	div1	Wolverhampton	A	D	3-3	Buzsaky 28, Blackstock 49 pen Leigertwood 79	24,290
43	div1	Ipswich	A	D	0-0		24,570
44	div1	Preston	H	D	2-2	Ainsworth 90, Blackstock 90	14,966
45	div1	Hull City	A	D	1-1	Blackstock 14	22,468
46	div1	Charlton	H	W	1-0	Blackstock 15	17,035
47	div1	Norwich	A	L	0-3		25,497
48	div1	West Brom	H	L	0-2		18,309

LEAGUE APPEARANCES, BOOKINGS AND GOALS

	AGE (on 01/07/08)	IN NAMED 16	APPEARANCES	COUNTING GAMES	MINUTES ON PITCH	LEAGUE GOALS	Yellow	Red
Goalkeepers								
Lee Camp	23	46	46	46	4140	0	3	0
Defenders								
Chris Barker	28	30	25	24	2201	0	3	0
Matthew Connolly	20	20	20	16	1539	0	4	0
Martin Cranie	21	6	6	5	469	0	0	0
Danny Cullip	31	8	6	5	457	0	2	0
John Curtis	29	7	4	3	316	0	1	0
Damien Delaney	26	17	17	17	1530	1	5	0
Fitz Hall	27	14	14	12	1126	0	2	0
Kieran Lee	20	16	7	1	191	0	0	0
Robert Malcolm	27	11	11	10	945	0	1	0
Michael Mancienne	20	30	30	24	2349	0	5	0
Zeshan Rehman	24	23	21	16	1534	0	2	0
Damion Stewart	27	42	39	34	3080	5	7	2
Sampsa Timoska	29	9	7	4	386	0	0	0
Midfielders								
Gareth Ainsworth	35	30	24	9	1238	3	2	0
Angelo Balanta	18	20	11	4	489	1	1	0
Adam Bolder	27	26	24	20	1840	2	7	0
Akos Buzsaky	26	27	27	23	2144	10	6	0
Hogan Ephraim	20	30	29	17	1869	3	1	1
Mikele Leigertwood	25	40	40	31	3081	5	8	1
Gavin Mahon	31	16	16	10	1109	1	0	0
Martin Rowlands	29	44	44	39	3668	6	10	1
Simon Walton	20	7	5	1	103	0	1	0
Forwards								
Patrick Agyemang	27	17	17	16	1475	8	0	0
Dextor Blackstock	22	36	35	24	2335	6	2	1
Stefan Moore	24	17	11	3	506	1	0	0
Daniel Nardiello	25	9	8	1	356	0	1	0
Marc Nygaard	31	19	19	5	779	1	3	0
Ben Sahar	18	11	9	2	393	0	0	0
Scott Sinclair	19	9	9	8	697	1	0	0
Rowan Vine	25	33	33	28	2721	6	6	0

TEAM OF THE SEASON

G Lee Camp CG: 46 DR: 62

D Fitz Hall CG: 12 DR: 86

D Michael Mancienne CG: 24 DR: 69

D Damion Stewart CG: 34 DR: 65

D Matthew Connolly CG: 16 DR: 64

M Akos Buzsaky CG: 23 SD: 8

M Hogan Ephraim CG: 17 SD: 7

M Martin Rowlands CG: 39 SD: -2

M Adam Bolder CG: 20 SD: -18

F Patrick Agyemang CG: 16 SR: 184

F Dextor Blackstock CG: 24 SR: 389

MONTHLY POINTS TALLY

Month	Points	%
AUGUST	1	17%
SEPTEMBER	2	13%
OCTOBER	8	53%
NOVEMBER	5	33%
DECEMBER	11	46%
JANUARY	6	50%
FEBRUARY	8	53%
MARCH	12	57%
APRIL	5	42%
MAY	0	0%

LEAGUE GOALS

	PLAYER	MINS	GOALS	S RATE
1	Buzsaky	2144	10	214
2	Agyemang	1475	8	184
3	Rowlands	3668	6	611
4	Blackstock	2335	6	389
5	Vine	2721	6	453
6	Stewart	3080	5	616
7	Leigertwood	3081	5	616
8	Ainsworth	1238	3	412
9	Ephraim	1869	3	623
10	Bolder	1840	2	920
11	Balanta	489	1	489
12	Moore, S	506	1	506
13	Sinclair	697	1	697
	Other		3	
	TOTAL		60	

TOP POINT EARNERS

	PLAYER	GAMES	AV PTS
1	Hogan Ephraim	17	1.59
2	Fitz Hall	12	1.58
3	Rowan Vine	28	1.57
4	Damien Delaney	17	1.53
5	Matthew Connolly	16	1.44
6	Patrick Agyemang	16	1.38
7	Zeshan Rehman	16	1.38
8	Akos Buzsaky	23	1.35
9	Michael Mancienne	24	1.33
10	Mikele Leigertwood	31	1.29
	CLUB AVERAGE:		1.26

DISCIPLINARY RECORDS

	PLAYER	YELLOW	RED	AVE
1	Danny Cullip	2	0	228
2	Marc Nygaard	3	0	259
3	Adam Bolder	7	0	262
4	Damien Delaney	5	0	306
5	Martin Rowlands	10	1	333
6	Mikele Leigertwood	8	1	342
7	Damion Stewart	7	2	342
8	Akos Buzsaky	6	0	357
9	Matthew Connolly	4	0	384
10	Rowan Vine	6	0	453
11	Michael Mancienne	5	0	469
12	Angelo Balanta	1	0	489
13	Fitz Hall	2	0	563
	Other	14	2	
	TOTAL	80	6	

KEY GOALKEEPER

Lee Camp

Goals Conceded in the League	66	**Counting Games** League games when player was on pitch for at least 70 minutes	46
Defensive Rating Ave number of mins between League goals conceded while on the pitch	62	**Clean Sheets** In League games when player was on pitch for at least 70 minutes	14

KEY PLAYERS - DEFENDERS

Fitz Hall

Goals Conceded Number of League goals conceded while the player was on the pitch	13	**Clean Sheets** In League games when player was on pitch for at least 70 minutes	5
Defensive Rating Ave number of mins between League goals conceded while on the pitch	86	**Club Defensive Rating** Average number of mins between League goals conceded by the club this season	64

	PLAYER	CON LGE	CLEAN SHEETS	DEF RATE
1	Fitz Hall	13	5	86 mins
2	Michael Mancienne	34	9	69 mins
3	Damion Stewart	47	11	65 mins
4	Matthew Connolly	24	7	64 mins

KEY PLAYERS - MIDFIELDERS

Akos Buzsaky

Goals in the League	10	**Contribution to Attacking Power** Average number of minutes between League team goals while on pitch	61
Defensive Rating Average number of mins between League goals conceded while on the pitch	69	**Scoring Difference** Defensive Rating minus Contribution to Attacking Power	8

	PLAYER	LGE GOALS	DEF RATE	POWER	SCORE DIFF
1	Akos Buzsaky	10	69	61	8 mins
2	Hogan Ephraim	3	81	74	7 mins
3	Martin Rowlands	6	67	69	-2 mins
4	Adam Bolder	2	55	73	-18 mins

KEY PLAYERS - GOALSCORERS

Patrick Agyemang

Goals in the League	8	**Player Strike Rate** Average number of minutes between League goals scored by player	184
Contribution to Attacking Power Average number of minutes between League team goals while on pitch	52	**Club Strike Rate** Average number of minutes between League goals scored by club	70

	PLAYER	LGE GOALS	POWER	STRIKE RATE
1	Patrick Agyemang	8	52	184 mins
2	Akos Buzsaky	10	61	214 mins
3	Dextor Blackstock	6	70	389 mins
4	Rowan Vine	6	56	453 mins

cargiant
Dextor Blackstock

SQUAD APPEARANCES

Match	1	2	3	4	5	6	7	8	9	10	11	12	13	14	15	16	17	18	19	20	21	22	23	24	25	26	27	28	29	30	31	32	33	34	35	36	37	38	39	40	41	42	43	44	45	46	47	48
Venue	A	H	H	H	A	H	H	A	A	H	H	A	A	H	H	A	H	A	A	H	A	A	H	H	A	A	H	A	A	H	A	H	A	H	H	A	H	A	A	H	H	A	A	H	A	H	A	H
Competition	L	W	L	L	L	L	L	L	L	L	L	L	L	L	L	L	L	L	L	L	L	L	L	L	L	L	L	F	L	L	L	L	L	L	L	L	L	L	L	L	L	L	L	L	L	L	L	L
Result	D	L	L	L	D	L	D	L	L	W	D	D	W	W	L	D	D	L	L	L	D	W	D	W	L	W	W	L	L	W	L	W	W	L	D	D	W	D	L	W	W	D	D	D	D	W	L	L

Goalkeepers
Lee Camp

Defenders
Chris Barker
Matthew Connolly
Martin Cranie
Danny Cullip
John Curtis
Damien Delaney
Fitz Hall
Kieran Lee
Robert Malcolm
Michael Mancienne
Zeshan Rehman
Damion Stewart
Sampsa Timoska

Midfielders
Gareth Ainsworth
Angelo Balanta
Adam Bolder
Akos Buzsaky
Hogan Ephraim
Mikele Leigertwood
Gavin Mahon
Martin Rowlands
Simon Walton

Forwards
Patrick Agyemang
Dextor Blackstock
Stefan Moore
Daniel Nardiello
Marc Nygaard
Ben Sahar
Scott Sinclair
Rowan Vine

KEY: On all match · On bench · Subbed or sent off (Counting game) · Subbed or sent off (playing less than 70 minutes) · Subbed on from bench (Counting Game) · Subbed on (playing less than 70 minutes) · Subbed on and then subbed or sent off (Counting Game) · Subbed on and then subbed or sent off (playing less than 70 minutes) · Not in 16

PRESTON NORTH END

Final Position: **15th**

NICKNAME: THE LILYWHITES

KEY: ☐Won ☐Drawn ☐Lost

	Comp	Opponent	H/A	Res	Score	Scorers	Attendance
1	div1	Norwich	H	D	0-0		13,408
2	ccr1	Morecambe	H	L	1-2	Pugh 73	7,703
3	div1	West Brom	A	L	0-2		19,556
4	div1	Colchester	H	L	0-3		11,582
5	div1	Coventry	A	L	1-2	Agyemang 16	17,551
6	div1	Sheff Wed	H	W	1-0	Gallagher 28	13,062
7	div1	Scunthorpe	A	L	1-2	Mawene 44	5,754
8	div1	Cardiff	A	D	2-2	Davidson 51, 90	11,772
9	div1	Bristol City	H	D	0-0		12,098
10	div1	Southampton	H	W	5-1	Hawley 12, Carter 58, Sedgwick 75 Agyemang 83, 90	10,279
11	div1	Ipswich	A	L	1-2	Mellor 88 pen	19,243
12	div1	Sheff Utd	A	D	1-1	Carter 35	23,661
13	div1	QPR	H	D	0-0		11,407
14	div1	Plymouth	H	W	2-0	Ormerod 11, Carter 67	11,055
15	div1	Barnsley	A	L	0-1		10,223
16	div1	Leicester	H	D	1-1	Carroll 14	10,930
17	div1	Hull City	A	L	0-3		16,358
18	div1	Charlton	H	L	0-2		12,532
19	div1	Crystal Palace	A	L	1-2	Mawene 36	13,048
20	div1	Wolverhampton	A	L	0-1		22,836
21	div1	Hull City	H	W	3-0	Agyemang 60, Whaley 68, L.Neal 89	11,311
22	div1	Blackpool	H	L	0-1		17,807
23	div1	Burnley	A	W	3-2	Sedgwick 45, Mellor 54, Whaley 82	14,829
24	div1	Southampton	A	W	1-0	L.Neal 90	23,267
25	div1	Scunthorpe	H	L	0-1		12,920
26	div1	Cardiff	H	L	1-2	Whaley 5	12,046
27	div1	Sheff Wed	A	L	1-2	Hawley 35	20,690
28	facr3	Scunthorpe	H	W	1-0	Whaley 47	4,616
29	div1	Watford	H	W	1-0	Mellor 75	12,347
30	div1	Stoke	A	L	1-3	Brown 68	15,011
31	facr4	Derby	A	W	4-1	Hawley 14, 45, Whaley 33, Mellor 90 pen	17,344
32	div1	West Brom	H	W	2-1	Mawene 6, Hawley 72	12,473
33	div1	Norwich	A	L	0-1		24,092
34	div1	Coventry	H	W	1-0	St Ledger 21	11,857
35	div1	Colchester	A	L	1-2	Mellor 81	5,122
36	facr5	Portsmouth	H	L	0-1		11,840
37	div1	Watford	A	D	0-0		16,798
38	div1	Stoke	H	W	2-0	Chaplow 22, 33	10,347
39	div1	Crystal Palace	H	L	0-1		12,347
40	div1	Leicester	A	W	1-0	Carter 90	19,264
41	div1	Charlton	A	W	2-1	Brown 15, 77	21,124
42	div1	Wolverhampton	H	W	2-1	Davidson 60 pen, Whaley 81	12,090
43	div1	Blackpool	A	D	0-0		9,629
44	div1	Burnley	H	W	2-1	Priskin 5, Brown 54	16,149
45	div1	Sheff Utd	H	W	3-1	Davidson 28 pen, Mellor 63, 90	14,647
46	div1	QPR	A	D	2-2	Mellor 37, Priskin 64	14,966
47	div1	Barnsley	H	L	1-2	Foster 67 og	13,994
48	div1	Plymouth	A	D	2-2	Mellor 77, Chaplow 90	10,272
49	div1	Ipswich	H	D	2-2	Brown 34, Mellor 79	14,187
50	div1	Bristol City	A	L	0-3		19,169

LEAGUE APPEARANCES, BOOKINGS AND GOALS

	AGE (on 01/07/08)	IN NAMED 16	APPEARANCES	COUNTING GAMES	MINUTES ON PITCH	LEAGUE GOALS	Yellow	Red
Goalkeepers								
Wayne Henderson	24	3	3	3	270	0	0	0
Andrew Lonergan	24	46	43	43	3870	0	1	0
Chris Neal	22	39	0	0	0	0	0	0
Grzegorz Szamotulski	32	1	0	0	0	0	0	0
Defenders								
Graham Alexander	36	3	3	3	270	0	0	0
Liam Chilvers	26	30	28	26	2361	0	1	0
Callum Davidson	32	42	40	37	3429	4	10	0
John Halls	26	5	4	4	359	0	1	0
Matthew Hill	27	37	26	22	1997	0	8	0
Youl Mawene	28	39	38	36	3259	3	11	1
Danny Pugh	25	8	7	4	423	0	1	0
Sean St Ledger	23	42	37	33	3050	1	5	1
Neal Trotman	21	7	3	2	240	0	0	0
Midfielders								
Darren Carter	24	42	39	28	2871	4	6	0
Richard Chaplow	23	15	12	6	635	3	1	0
Michael Hart	28	2	2	2	180	0	0	0
Billy Jones	21	33	29	25	2345	0	4	0
Paul McKenna	30	34	33	32	2927	0	5	0
Lewis Neal	26	27	17	7	776	2	0	0
Kevin Nicholls	29	20	18	16	1465	0	2	0
Chris Sedgwick	28	45	42	38	3463	2	8	0
Simon Whaley	23	43	43	26	2717	4	1	0
Forwards								
Patrick Agyemang	27	22	22	8	1101	4	0	0
Craig Beattie	24	2	2	0	71	0	0	0
Chris Brown	23	17	17	16	1473	5	3	1
Andrew Carroll	19	11	11	5	614	1	1	1
Paul Gallagher	23	19	19	8	1236	1	2	0
Karl Hawley	26	30	25	18	1641	3	0	0
Neil Mellor	25	41	36	10	1426	9	4	0
Brett Ormerod	31	21	18	5	704	1	0	0
Tamas Priskin	21	6	5	3	308	2	0	0

TEAM OF THE SEASON

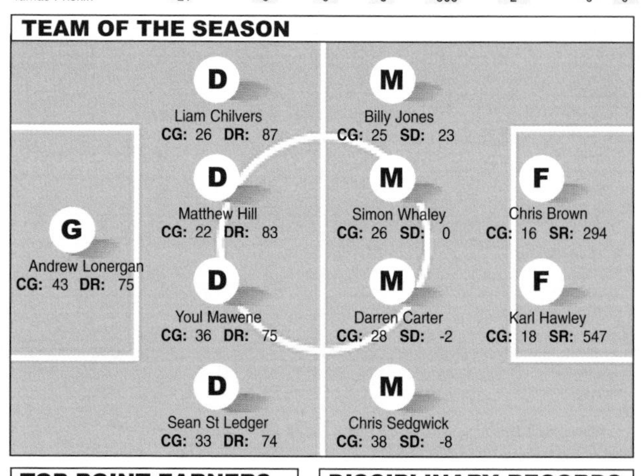

G
Andrew Lonergan
CG: 43 DR: 75
D
Liam Chilvers
CG: 26 DR: 87
D
Matthew Hill
CG: 22 DR: 83
D
Youl Mawene
CG: 36 DR: 75
D
Sean St Ledger
CG: 33 DR: 74
M
Billy Jones
CG: 25 SD: 23
M
Simon Whaley
CG: 26 SD: 0
M
Darren Carter
CG: 28 SD: -2
M
Chris Sedgwick
CG: 38 SD: -8
F
Chris Brown
CG: 16 SR: 294
F
Karl Hawley
CG: 18 SR: 547

MONTHLY POINTS TALLY

Month	Points	%
AUGUST	1	11%
SEPTEMBER	5	33%
OCTOBER	8	53%
NOVEMBER	1	7%
DECEMBER	9	43%
JANUARY	6	50%
FEBRUARY	7	47%
MARCH	16	76%
APRIL	3	25%
MAY	0	0%

LEAGUE GOALS

	PLAYER	MINS	GOALS	S RATE
1	Mellor	1426	**9**	158
2	Whaley	2717	**4**	679
3	Brown	1473	**5**	294
4	Hawley	1641	**3**	547
5	Agyemang	1101	**4**	275
6	Carter	2871	**4**	717
7	Davidson	3429	**4**	857
8	Chaplow	635	**3**	211
9	Mawene	3259	**3**	1086
10	Priskin	308	**2**	154
11	Neal, L	776	**2**	388
12	Sedgwick	3463	**2**	1731
13	Carroll	614	**1**	614
	Other		3	
	TOTAL		**49**	

TOP POINT EARNERS

	PLAYER	GAMES	AV PTS
1	Chris Brown	16	**1.94**
2	Simon Whaley	26	**1.58**
3	Billy Jones	25	**1.52**
4	Darren Carter	28	**1.39**
5	Chris Sedgwick	38	**1.37**
6	Youl Mawene	36	**1.31**
7	Andrew Lonergan	43	**1.28**
8	Karl Hawley	18	**1.28**
9	Liam Chilvers	26	**1.27**
10	Sean St Ledger	34	**1.24**
	CLUB AVERAGE:		**1.22**

DISCIPLINARY RECORDS

	PLAYER	YELLOW	RED	AVE
1	Matthew Hill	8	0	**249**
2	Youl Mawene	11	1	**271**
3	Andrew Carroll	1	1	**307**
4	Callum Davidson	10	0	**342**
5	Neil Mellor	4	0	**356**
6	Chris Brown	3	1	**368**
7	Chris Sedgwick	8	0	**432**
8	Darren Carter	6	0	**478**
9	Sean St Ledger	5	1	**508**
10	Paul McKenna	5	0	**585**
11	Billy Jones	4	0	**586**
12	Paul Gallagher	2	0	**618**
13	Richard Chaplow	1	0	**635**
	Other	5	0	
	TOTAL	**73**	**4**	

KEY GOALKEEPER

Andrew Lonergan

Goals Conceded in the League	51	**Counting Games** League games when player was on pitch for at least 70 minutes	43
Defensive Rating Ave number of mins between League goals conceded while on the pitch	75	**Clean Sheets** In League games when player was on pitch for at least 70 minutes	12

KEY PLAYERS - DEFENDERS

Liam Chilvers

Goals Conceded Number of League goals conceded while the player was on the pitch	27	**Clean Sheets** In League games when player was on pitch for at least 70 minutes	9
Defensive Rating Ave number of mins between League goals conceded while on the pitch	87	**Club Defensive Rating** Average number of mins between League goals conceded by the club this season	73

	PLAYER	CON LGE	CLEAN SHEETS	DEF RATE
1	Liam Chilvers	27	9	87 mins
2	Matthew Hill	24	7	83 mins
3	Youl Mawene	43	11	75 mins
4	Sean St Ledger	41	9	74 mins

KEY PLAYERS - MIDFIELDERS

Billy Jones

Goals in the League	0	**Contribution to Attacking Power** Average number of minutes between League team goals while on pitch	67
Defensive Rating Average number of mins between League goals conceded while on the pitch	90	**Scoring Difference** Defensive Rating minus Contribution to Attacking Power	23

	PLAYER	LGE GOALS	DEF RATE	POWER	SCORE DIFF
1	Billy Jones	0	90	67	23 mins
2	Simon Whaley	4	84	84	0 mins
3	Darren Carter	4	75	77	-2 mins
4	Chris Sedgwick	2	72	80	-8 mins

KEY PLAYERS - GOALSCORERS

Chris Brown

Goals in the League	5	**Player Strike Rate** Average number of minutes between League goals scored by player	294
Contribution to Attacking Power Average number of minutes between League team goals while on pitch	70	**Club Strike Rate** Average number of minutes between League goals scored by club	82

	PLAYER	LGE GOALS	POWER	STRIKE RATE
1	Chris Brown	5	70	294 mins
2	Karl Hawley	3	91	547 mins
3	Simon Whaley	4	84	679 mins
4	Darren Carter	4	77	717 mins

DIADORA
Enterprise
Darren Carter

SQUAD APPEARANCES

Match	1	2	3	4	5	6	7	8	9	10	11	12	13	14	15	16	17	18	19	20	21	22	23	24	25
Venue	H	H	A	H	A	H	A	A	H	H	A	A	H	H	A	H	A	H	A	A	H	H	A	A	H
Competition	L	W	L	L	L	L	L	L	L	L	L	L	L	L	L	L	L	L	L	L	L	L	L	L	L
Result	D	L	L	L	L	W	L	D	D	W	L	D	D	W	L	D	L	L	L	L	W	L	W	W	L

Match	26	27	28	29	30	31	32	33	34	35	36	37	38	39	40	41	42	43	44	45	46	47	48	49	50
Venue	H	A	H	H	A	A	H	A	H	A	H	A	H	H	A	A	H	A	H	H	A	H	A	H	A
Competition	L	L	F	L	L	F	L	L	L	L	F	L	L	L	L	L	L	L	L	L	L	L	L	L	L
Result	L	L	W	W	L	W	W	L	W	L	L	D	W	L	W	W	W	D	W	W	D	L	D	D	L

Goalkeepers
Wayne Henderson
Andrew Lonergan
Chris Neal
Grzegorz Szamotulski

Defenders
Graham Alexander
Liam Chilvers
Callum Davidson
John Halls
Matthew Hill
Youl Mawene
Danny Pugh
Sean St Ledger
Neal Trotman

Midfielders
Darren Carter
Richard Chaplow
Michael Hart
Billy Jones
Paul McKenna
Lewis Neal
Kevin Nicholls
Chris Sedgwick
Simon Whaley

Forwards
Patrick Agyemang
Craig Beattie
Chris Brown
Andrew Carroll
Paul Gallagher
Karl Hawley
Neil Mellor
Brett Ormerod
Tamas Priskin

KEY: On all match · On bench · Subbed or sent off (Counting game) · Subbed or sent off (playing less than 70 minutes) · Subbed on from bench (Counting Game) · Subbed on (playing less than 70 minutes) · Subbed on and then subbed or sent off (Counting Game) · Subbed on and then subbed or sent off (playing less than 70 minutes) · Not in 16

SHEFFIELD WEDNESDAY

Final Position: **16th**

NICKNAME: THE OWLS

KEY: □Won □Drawn □Lost

							Attendance
1	div1	Ipswich	A	L	1-4	Clarke 89	23,099
2	ccr1	Rotherham	A	W	3-1	Whelan 45, Burton 49, Small 55	6,416
3	div1	Wolverhampton	H	L	1-3	Small 45	22,131
4	div1	Charlton	A	L	2-3	O'Brien 6, Spurr 15	22,033
5	ccr2	Hartlepool	H	W	2-1	Burton 68, Folly 120	8,751
6	div1	Bristol City	H	L	0-1		17,559
7	div1	Preston	A	L	0-1		13,062
8	div1	Burnley	H	L	0-2		18,359
9	div1	Hull City	H	W	1-0	Jeffers 40	21,518
10	ccr3	Everton	H	L	0-3		16,463
11	div1	Norwich	A	W	1-0	Small 76	23,293
12	div1	Watford	A	L	1-2	Kavanagh 36	15,473
13	div1	Leicester	H	L	0-2		20,010
14	div1	Stoke	A	W	4-2	J.Johnson 16, Tudgay 23, 85, Burton 87	14,019
15	div1	Scunthorpe	H	L	1-2	Burton 23 pen	21,557
16	div1	Blackpool	H	W	2-1	Tudgay 66, Hinds 71	19,238
17	div1	Plymouth	A	W	2-1	Sodje 52, O'Brien 56	12,145
18	div1	West Brom	A	D	1-1	Watson 90	19,807
19	div1	Southampton	H	W	5-0	Whelan 41 pen, 56, Sodje 51, 62 O'Brien 65	19,442
20	div1	QPR	A	D	0-0		15,241
21	div1	Barnsley	H	W	1-0	Sodje 60	27,769
22	div1	Colchester	H	L	1-2	Sodje 36	22,331
23	div1	Southampton	A	D	0-0		17,981
24	div1	Crystal Palace	A	L	1-2	Hinds 11	14,865
25	div1	Watford	H	L	0-1		19,641
26	div1	Burnley	A	D	1-1	Burton 30 pen	15,326
27	div1	Hull City	A	L	0-1		21,252
28	div1	Preston	H	W	2-1	Sodje 51, Jeffers 82 pen	20,690
29	facr3	Derby	A	D	2-2	Beevers 9, Tudgay 23	20,612
30	div1	Cardiff	A	L	0-1		14,015
31	div1	Sheff Utd	H	W	2-0	Sodje 25, Tudgay 76	30,486
32	facr3	Derby	H	L	2-4*	Watson 10 (*on penalties)	18,020
33	div1	Wolverhampton	A	L	1-2	Tudgay 19	22,746
34	div1	Ipswich	H	L	1-2	Tudgay 13	19,092
35	div1	Bristol City	A	L	1-2	Bullen 90	15,520
36	div1	Charlton	H	D	0-0		17,211
37	div1	Cardiff	H	W	1-0	Tudgay 41	18,539
38	div1	Barnsley	A	D	0-0		18,257
39	div1	West Brom	H	L	0-1		18,805
40	div1	QPR	H	W	2-1	Kavanagh 45, Burton 52 pen	18,555
41	div1	Colchester	A	W	2-1	Burton 18, Small 44	5,086
42	div1	Coventry	A	D	0-0		19,283
43	div1	Crystal Palace	H	D	2-2	Sahar 18, Small 68	19,875
44	div1	Stoke	H	D	1-1	Songo'o 82	21,857
45	div1	Coventry	H	D	1-1	Wood 90	21,110
46	div1	Scunthorpe	A	D	1-1	Sahar 49	7,245
47	div1	Sheff Utd	A	D	2-2	Bolder 39, 56	31,760
48	div1	Plymouth	H	D	1-1	Spurr 81	20,635
49	div1	Blackpool	A	L	1-2	Wood 12	9,633
50	div1	Leicester	A	W	3-1	Slusarski 45, Watson 53, L.Clarke 89	31,892
51	div1	Norwich	H	W	4-1	Burton 23 pen, 76, Sahar 53, L.Clarke 87	36,208

LEAGUE APPEARANCES, BOOKINGS AND GOALS

	AGE (on 01/07/08)	IN NAMED 16	APPEARANCES	COUNTING GAMES	MINUTES ON PITCH	LEAGUE GOALS		
Goalkeepers								
Robert Burch	24	29	2	2	180	0	0	0
Lee Grant	25	45	44	44	3960	0	3	0
Defenders								
Mark Beevers	18	35	28	26	2397	0	1	0
Lee Bullen	37	25	22	13	1572	1	0	0
Peter Gilbert	24	19	10	8	763	0	3	1
Richard Hinds	27	40	38	27	2756	2	1	0
Michael Johnson	34	12	12	11	1019	0	1	0
Frankie Simek	23	17	17	15	1430	0	2	0
Tommy Spurr	20	41	41	39	3547	2	7	0
Steve Watson	34	25	23	17	1696	2	4	0
Richard Wood	22	31	27	25	2290	2	4	0
Midfielders								
Adam Bolder	27	15	13	11	1045	2	4	0
Chris Brunt	23	1	1	1	90	0	0	0
Yoann Folly	23	13	10	6	690	0	1	0
Jermaine Johnson	28	37	36	24	2586	1	6	2
Graham Kavanagh	34	23	23	19	1851	2	4	0
Kenny Lunt	28	20	4	3	311	0	1	0
Sean McAllister	20	10	8	4	535	0	1	0
Burton O'Brien	27	36	33	22	2271	3	3	0
Wade Small	24	30	29	15	1725	4	3	0
Franck Songo'o	21	12	12	9	932	1	3	0
Ronnie Wallwork	30	14	7	3	411	0	0	0
Glenn Whelan	24	25	25	25	2221	2	7	0
Forwards								
Luke Boden	19	7	2	0	28	0	0	0
Deon Burton	31	42	40	19	2284	7	4	0
Leon Clarke	23	8	8	2	267	3	1	0
Etienne Esajas	23	25	18	4	618	0	1	0
Francis Jeffers	27	10	10	1	431	2	0	0
Ben Sahar	18	12	12	5	716	3	1	0
Enoch Showunmi	25	10	10	5	490	0	0	0
Bartosz Slusarski	26	8	7	3	332	1	0	0
Akpo Sodje	28	21	19	9	1241	7	1	0
Marcus Tudgay	25	35	35	28	2799	7	2	0

TEAM OF THE SEASON

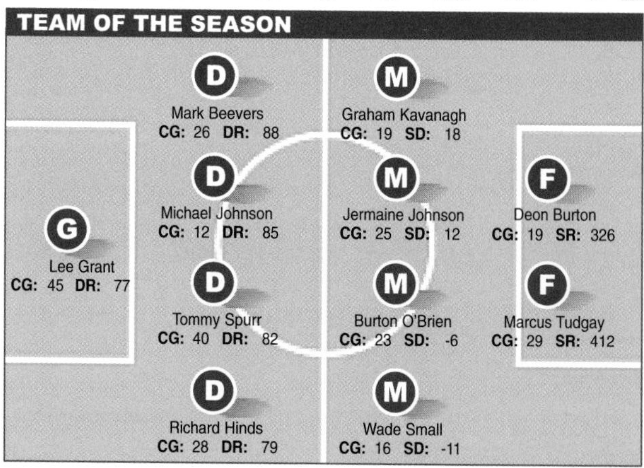
D
Mark Beevers
CG: 26 DR: 88
M
Graham Kavanagh
CG: 19 SD: 18
D
Michael Johnson
CG: 12 DR: 85
M
Jermaine Johnson
CG: 25 SD: 12
F
Deon Burton
CG: 19 SR: 326
G
Lee Grant
CG: 45 DR: 77
D
Tommy Spurr
CG: 40 DR: 82
M
Burton O'Brien
CG: 23 SD: -6
F
Marcus Tudgay
CG: 29 SR: 412
D
Richard Hinds
CG: 28 DR: 79
M
Wade Small
CG: 16 SD: -11

MONTHLY POINTS TALLY

Month	Points	%
AUGUST	0	0%
SEPTEMBER	6	40%
OCTOBER	6	40%
NOVEMBER	11	73%
DECEMBER	2	11%
JANUARY	6	50%
FEBRUARY	4	33%
MARCH	10	48%
APRIL	7	39%
MAY	3	100%

LEAGUE GOALS

	PLAYER	MINS	GOALS	S RATE
1	Burton	2284	7	326
2	Tudgay	2889	7	412
3	Sodje	1241	7	177
4	Small	1815	4	453
5	Clarke, L	267	3	89
6	Sahar	716	3	238
7	O'Brien	2361	3	787
8	Watson	1786	2	893
9	Whelan	2311	2	1155
10	Jeffers	431	2	215
11	Bolder	1045	2	522
12	Kavanagh	1851	2	925
13	Wood	2290	2	1145
	Other		8	
	TOTAL		54	

TOP POINT EARNERS

	PLAYER	GAMES	AV PTS
1	Graham Kavanagh	19	**1.42**
2	Jermaine Johnson	24	**1.38**
3	Frankie Simek	15	**1.33**
4	Richard Wood	25	**1.32**
5	Burton O'Brien	22	**1.27**
6	Lee Grant	44	**1.25**
7	Steve Watson	17	**1.24**
8	Tommy Spurr	39	**1.23**
9	Mark Beevers	26	**1.23**
10	Deon Burton	19	**1.21**
	CLUB AVERAGE:		**1.20**

DISCIPLINARY RECORDS

	PLAYER	YELLOW	RED	AVE
1	Peter Gilbert	3	1	**190**
2	Adam Bolder	4	0	**261**
3	Franck Songo'o	3	0	**310**
4	Glenn Whelan	7	0	**330**
5	Jermaine Johnson	6	2	**334**
6	Steve Watson	4	0	**446**
7	Graham Kavanagh	4	0	**462**
8	Tommy Spurr	7	0	**519**
9	Sean McAllister	1	0	**535**
10	Deon Burton	4	0	**571**
11	Richard Wood	4	0	**572**
12	Wade Small	3	0	**605**
13	Etienne Esajas	1	0	**618**
	Other	16	0	
	TOTAL	67	3	

KEY GOALKEEPER

Lee Grant

Goals Conceded in the League	52	Counting Games League games when player was on pitch for at least 70 minutes	45
Defensive Rating Ave number of mins between League goals conceded while on the pitch	77	Clean Sheets In League games when player was on pitch for at least 70 minutes	12

KEY PLAYERS - DEFENDERS

Mark Beevers

Goals Conceded Number of League goals conceded while the player was on the pitch	27	Clean Sheets In League games when player was on pitch for at least 70 minutes	6
Defensive Rating Ave number of mins between League goals conceded while on the pitch	88	Club Defensive Rating Average number of mins between League goals conceded by the club this season	78

	PLAYER	CON LGE	CLEAN SHEETS	DEF RATE
1	Mark Beevers	27	6	88 mins
2	Michael Johnson	13	5	85 mins
3	Tommy Spurr	44	9	82 mins
4	Richard Hinds	36	8	79 mins

KEY PLAYERS - MIDFIELDERS

Graham Kavanagh

Goals in the League	2	Contribution to Attacking Power Average number of minutes between League team goals while on pitch	74
Defensive Rating Average number of mins between League goals conceded while on the pitch	92	Scoring Difference Defensive Rating minus Contribution to Attacking Power	18

	PLAYER	LGE GOALS	DEF RATE	POWER	SCORE DIFF
1	Graham Kavanagh	2	92	74	18 mins
2	Jermaine Johnson	1	78	66	12 mins
3	Burton O'Brien	3	81	87	-6 mins
4	Wade Small	4	95	106	-11 mins

KEY PLAYERS - GOALSCORERS

Deon Burton

Goals in the League	7	Player Strike Rate Average number of minutes between League goals scored by player	326
Contribution to Attacking Power Average number of minutes between League team goals while on pitch	67	Club Strike Rate Average number of minutes between League goals scored by club	80

	PLAYER	LGE GOALS	POWER	STRIKE RATE
1	Deon Burton	7	67	326 mins
2	Marcus Tudgay	7	90	412 mins
3	Wade Small	4	106	453 mins
4	Burton O'Brien	3	87	787 mins

plus
Marcus Tudgay

SQUAD APPEARANCES

Match	1	2	3	4	5	6	7	8	9	10	11	12	13	14	15	16	17	18	19	20	21	22	23	24	25	26
Venue	A	A	H	A	H	H	A	H	H	H	A	A	H	A	H	H	A	A	H	A	H	H	A	A	H	A
Competition	L	W	L	L	W	L	L	L	L	W	L	L	L	L	L	L	L	L	L	L	L	L	L	L	L	L
Result	L	W	L	L	W	L	L	L	W	L	W	L	L	W	L	W	W	D	W	D	W	L	D	L	L	D

Match	27	28	29	30	31	32	33	34	35	36	37	38	39	40	41	42	43	44	45	46	47	48	49	50	51
Venue	A	H	A	A	H	H	A	H	A	H	H	A	H	H	A	A	H	H	H	A	A	H	A	A	H
Competition	L	L	F	L	L	F	L	L	L	L	L	L	L	L	L	L	L	L	L	L	L	L	L	L	L
Result	L	W	D	L	W	L	L	L	L	D	W	D	L	W	W	D	D	D	D	D	D	D	L	W	W

Goalkeepers
Robert Burch
Lee Grant

Defenders
Mark Beevers
Lee Bullen
Peter Gilbert
Richard Hinds
Michael Johnson
Frankie Simek
Tommy Spurr
Steve Watson
Richard Wood

Midfielders
Adam Bolder
Chris Brunt
Yoann Folly
Jermaine Johnson
Graham Kavanagh
Kenny Lunt
Sean McAllister
Burton O'Brien
Wade Small
Franck Songo'o
Ronnie Wallwork
Glenn Whelan

Forwards
Luke Boden
Deon Burton
Leon Clarke
Etienne Esajas
Francis Jeffers
Ben Sahar
Enoch Showunmi
Bartosz Slusarski
Akpo Sodje
Marcus Tudgay

KEY: ■ On all match ■ On bench | ⏮ Subbed or sent off (Counting game) « Subbed or sent off (playing less than 70 minutes) | ⏭ Subbed on from bench (Counting Game) » Subbed on (playing less than 70 minutes) | Subbed on and then subbed or sent off (Counting Game) Subbed on and then subbed or sent off (playing less than 70 minutes) | □ Not in 16

NORWICH CITY

Final Position: **17th**

NICKNAME: THE CANARIES

KEY: ☐Won ☐Drawn ☐Lost

						Attendance
1 div1	Preston	A	D	0-0		13,408
2 ccr1	Barnet	H	W	5-2	Cureton 3, 16, Lappin 21 Fotheringham 25, Russell 31	13,971
3 div1	Southampton	H	W	2-1	Cureton 61, 71	24,004
4 div1	Hull City	A	L	1-2	Dublin 71	15,939
5 ccr2	Rochdale	A	W	4-3*	Dublin 49 (*on penalties)	2,990
6 div1	Cardiff	H	L	1-2	Lappin 12	24,292
7 div1	Crystal Palace	H	W	1-0	Strihavka 75	24,228
8 div1	Charlton	A	L	0-2		21,543
9 div1	Wolverhampton	A	L	0-2		22,564
10 ccr3	Man City	A	L	0-1		20,938
11 div1	Sheff Wed	H	L	0-1		23,293
12 div1	Scunthorpe	H	D	0-0		23,176
13 div1	QPR	A	L	0-1		10,514
14 div1	Bristol City	H	L	1-3	Huckerby 82	24,125
15 div1	Burnley	A	L	1-2	Brown 68	10,133
16 div1	West Brom	A	L	0-2		20,247
17 div1	Ipswich	H	D	2-2	Martin.Taylor 55, Cureton 67	25,461
18 div1	Watford	H	L	1-3	Croft 65	24,192
19 div1	Plymouth	A	L	0-3		11,222
20 div1	Coventry	H	W	2-0	Chadwick 34, Cureton 77	24,590
21 div1	Blackpool	A	W	3-1	Dublin 30, 90, Martin.Taylor 74	7,759
22 div1	Stoke	A	L	1-2	Huckerby 5	19,285
23 div1	Plymouth	H	W	2-1	Evans 2, Huckerby 87 pen	25,434
24 div1	Sheff Utd	H	W	1-0	Evans 10	24,493
25 div1	Colchester	A	D	1-1	Granville 90 og	5,560
26 div1	Scunthorpe	A	W	1-0	Cureton 78	6,648
27 div1	Charlton	H	D	1-1	Russell 73	25,327
28 div1	Wolverhampton	H	D	1-1	Cureton 75	24,300
29 div1	Crystal Palace	A	D	1-1	Russell 9	17,199
30 facr3	Bury	H	D	1-1	Doherty 80	19,815
31 div1	Barnsley	A	W	3-1	Evans 48, Fotheringham 70, Dublin 74	10,117
32 facr3r	Bury	A	L	1-2	Dublin 86	4,146
33 div1	Leicester	H	D	0-0		25,462
34 div1	Southampton	A	W	1-0	Evans 45	18,004
35 div1	Preston	H	W	1-0	Russell 90	24,092
36 div1	Cardiff	A	W	2-1	Evans 15, 88	11,937
37 div1	Hull City	H	D	1-1	Dublin 19	25,259
38 div1	Leicester	A	L	0-4		25,854
39 div1	Barnsley	H	W	1-0	Cureton 26	24,197
40 div1	Blackpool	H	L	1-2	Cureton 65 pen	24,531
41 div1	Watford	A	D	1-1	Cureton 81	16,537
42 div1	Coventry	A	L	0-1		18,108
43 div1	Stoke	H	L	0-1		23,471
44 div1	Sheff Utd	A	L	0-2		25,536
45 div1	Colchester	H	W	5-1	Otsemobor 6, Cureton 36, 53 pen, 87 Dublin 90	25,215
46 div1	Bristol City	A	L	1-2	Huckerby 70	17,511
47 div1	Burnley	H	W	2-0	Dublin 2, Evans 90	24,049
48 div1	Ipswich	A	L	1-2	Evans 4	29,656
49 div1	West Brom	H	L	1-2	Evans 73 pen	25,442
50 div1	QPR	H	W	3-0	Evans 7, Fotheringham 56, Russell 83	25,497
51 div1	Sheff Wed	A	L	1-4	Huckerby 9	36,208

LEAGUE APPEARANCES, BOOKINGS AND GOALS

	AGE (on 01/07/08)	IN NAMED 16	APPEARANCES	COUNTING GAMES	MINUTES ON PITCH	LEAGUE GOALS		
Goalkeepers								
David Marshall	23	46	46	46	4140	0	1	0
Defenders								
Matthew Bates	21	3	3	1	183	0	1	0
Ryan Bertrand	18	18	18	18	1593	0	2	0
Mohammed Camara	33	24	21	19	1673	0	2	0
Gary Doherty	28	36	34	30	2822	0	7	1
Adam Drury	29	9	9	8	748	0	0	0
Rossi Jarvis	20	6	5	4	361	0	0	0
Jon Otsemobor	25	44	43	40	3671	1	2	0
Alex Pearce	19	16	11	8	823	0	0	0
Jason Shackell	24	42	39	34	3231	0	6	1
Martin Taylor	28	8	8	7	653	2	0	0
Juan Velasco	31	5	3	1	111	0	1	0
Midfielders								
Julien Brellier	26	10	10	6	679	0	3	1
Luke Chadwick	27	16	12	6	644	1	1	0
Lee Croft	23	45	41	17	2119	1	1	0
Mark Fotheringham	24	28	28	24	2286	2	7	0
James Henry	19	3	3	0	81	0	0	0
Simon Lappin	25	17	15	14	1322	1	1	0
Ian Murray	27	12	9	7	741	0	2	0
Matty Pattison	21	29	27	16	1917	0	5	0
Darel Russell	27	40	39	35	3262	4	8	2
Jimmy Smith	21	12	9	2	417	0	0	0
Michael Spillane	19	15	6	3	405	0	2	0
Forwards								
Chris Brown	23	17	14	7	785	1	0	0
Jamie Cureton	32	43	41	24	2658	12	3	0
Dion Dublin	39	38	37	22	2485	7	6	1
Ched Evans	19	30	28	17	1821	10	3	0
Kieran Gibbs	18	13	7	4	448	0	1	0
John Hartson	33	4	4	1	207	0	1	0
Darren Huckerby	32	34	34	26	2468	5	4	1
David Strihavka	25	13	10	1	318	1	0	0

TEAM OF THE SEASON

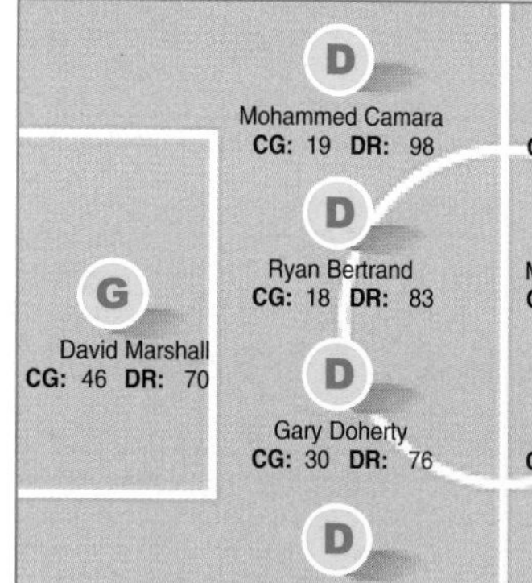

G
David Marshall
CG: 46 DR: 70
D
Mohammed Camara
CG: 19 DR: 98
D
Ryan Bertrand
CG: 18 DR: 83
D
Gary Doherty
CG: 30 DR: 76
D
Jon Otsemobor
CG: 40 DR: 71
M
Matty Pattison
CG: 16 SD: 15
M
Mark Fotheringham
CG: 24 SD: 13
M
Darel Russell
CG: 35 SD: -10
M
Lee Croft
CG: 17 SD: -22
F
Ched Evans
CG: 17 SR: 182
F
Jamie Cureton
CG: 24 SR: 221

MONTHLY POINTS TALLY

AUGUST	4	44%
SEPTEMBER	3	20%
OCTOBER	1	7%
NOVEMBER	7	47%
DECEMBER	12	57%
JANUARY	8	67%
FEBRUARY	10	67%
MARCH	4	19%
APRIL	6	50%
MAY	0	0%

LEAGUE GOALS

	PLAYER	MINS	GOALS	S RATE
1	Cureton	2658	12	221
2	Evans	1821	10	182
3	Dublin	2485	7	355
4	Huckerby	2468	5	493
5	Russell	3262	4	815
6	Fotheringham	2286	2	1143
7	Taylor	653	2	326
8	Lappin	1322	1	1322
9	Strihavka	318	1	318
10	Chadwick	644	1	644
11	Brown	785	1	785
12	Croft	2119	1	2119
13	Otsemobor	3671	1	3671
	Other		0	
	TOTAL		48	

TOP POINT EARNERS

	PLAYER	GAMES	AV PTS
1	Mohammed Camara	19	1.74
2	Ched Evans	17	1.65
3	Mark Fotheringham	24	1.58
4	Ryan Bertrand	18	1.50
5	Dion Dublin	22	1.50
6	Matty Pattison	16	1.38
7	Lee Croft	17	1.35
8	Gary Doherty	31	1.26
9	Jason Shackell	35	1.26
10	Darel Russell	36	1.25
	CLUB AVERAGE:		1.20

DISCIPLINARY RECORDS

	PLAYER	YELLOW	RED	AVE
1	Julien Brellier	3	1	169
2	Darel Russell	8	2	326
3	Mark Fotheringham	7	0	326
4	Gary Doherty	7	1	352
5	Dion Dublin	6	1	355
6	Ian Murray	2	0	370
7	Matty Pattison	5	0	383
8	Jason Shackell	6	1	461
9	Darren Huckerby	4	1	493
10	Ched Evans	3	0	607
11	Luke Chadwick	1	0	644
12	Ryan Bertrand	2	0	796
13	Mohammed Camara	2	0	836
	Other	8	0	
	TOTAL	64	7	

KEY GOALKEEPER

David Marshall

Goals Conceded in the League	59	Counting Games League games when player was on pitch for at least 70 minutes	46
Defensive Rating Ave number of mins between League goals conceded while on the pitch	70	Clean Sheets In League games when player was on pitch for at least 70 minutes	12

KEY PLAYERS - DEFENDERS

Mohammed Camara

Goals Conceded Number of League goals conceded while the player was on the pitch	17	Clean Sheets In League games when player was on pitch for at least 70 minutes	6
Defensive Rating Ave number of mins between League goals conceded while on the pitch	98	Club Defensive Rating Average number of mins between League goals conceded by the club this season	70

	PLAYER	CON LGE	CLEAN SHEETS	DEF RATE
1	Mohammed Camara	17	6	98 mins
2	Ryan Bertrand	19	6	83 mins
3	Gary Doherty	37	9	76 mins
4	Jon Otsemobor	51	11	71 mins

KEY PLAYERS - MIDFIELDERS

Matty Pattison

Goals in the League	0	Contribution to Attacking Power Average number of minutes between League team goals while on pitch	76
Defensive Rating Average number of mins between League goals conceded while on the pitch	91	Scoring Difference Defensive Rating minus Contribution to Attacking Power	15

	PLAYER	LGE GOALS	DEF RATE	POWER	SCORE DIFF
1	Matty Pattison	0	91	76	15 mins
2	Mark Fotheringham	2	78	65	13 mins
3	Darel Russell	4	69	79	-10 mins
4	Lee Croft	1	62	84	-22 mins

KEY PLAYERS - GOALSCORERS

Ched Evans

Goals in the League	10	Player Strike Rate Average number of minutes between League goals scored by player	182
Contribution to Attacking Power Average number of minutes between League team goals while on pitch	75	Club Strike Rate Average number of minutes between League goals scored by club	84

	PLAYER	LGE GOALS	POWER	STRIKE RATE
1	Ched Evans	10	75	182 mins
2	Jamie Cureton	12	83	221 mins
3	Dion Dublin	7	75	355 mins
4	Darren Huckerby	5	79	493 mins

Jamie Cureton

SQUAD APPEARANCES

Match	1	2	3	4	5	6	7	8	9	10	11	12	13	14	15	16	17	18	19	20	21	22	23	24	25
Venue	A	H	H	A	A	H	H	A	A	A	H	H	A	H	A	A	H	H	A	H	A	A	H	H	A
Competition	L	W	L	L	W	L	L	L	L	W	L	L	L	L	L	L	L	L	L	L	L	L	L	L	L
Result	D	W	W	L	W	L	W	L	L	L	L	D	L	L	L	L	D	L	L	W	W	L	W	W	D

Match	26	27	28	29	30	31	32	33	34	35	36	37	38	39	40	41	42	43	44	45	46	47	48	49	50	51
Venue	A	H	H	A	H	A	A	H	A	H	A	H	A	H	H	A	A	H	A	H	A	H	A	H	H	A
Competition	L	L	L	L	F	L	F	L	L	L	L	L	L	L	L	L	L	L	L	L	L	L	L	L	L	L
Result	W	D	D	D	D	W	L	D	W	W	W	D	L	W	L	D	L	L	L	W	L	W	L	L	W	L

Goalkeepers
David Marshall
Defenders
Matthew Bates
Ryan Bertrand
Mohammed Camara
Gary Doherty
Adam Drury
Rossi Jarvis
Jon Otsemobor
Alex Pearce
Jason Shackell
Martin Taylor
Juan Velasco
Midfielders
Julien Brellier
Luke Chadwick
Lee Croft
Mark Fotheringham
James Henry
Simon Lappin
Ian Murray
Matty Pattison
Darel Russell
Jimmy Smith
Michael Spillane
Forwards
Chris Brown
Jamie Cureton
Dion Dublin
Ched Evans
John Hartson
Darren Huckerby
Chris Martin
David Strihavka

KEY: On all match | On bench | Subbed or sent off (Counting game) | Subbed or sent off (playing less than 70 minutes) | Subbed on from bench (Counting Game) | Subbed on (playing less than 70 minutes) | Subbed on and then subbed or sent off (Counting Game) | Subbed on and then subbed or sent off (playing less than 70 minutes) | Not in 16

BARNSLEY

Final Position: **18th**

NICKNAME: THE TYKES

KEY: ☐Won ☐Drawn ☐Lost

							Attendance
1	div1	**Coventry**	H	L	1-4	Howard 9 pen	12,616
2	ccr1	**Darlington**	H	W	2-1	Ferenczi 65, P.Reid 77	3,780
3	div1	**Colchester**	A	D	2-2	Howard 28 pen, 85 pen	4,450
4	div1	**Plymouth**	H	W	3-2	Ferenczi 12, Werling 45, Howard 60	9,240
5	ccr2	**Newcastle**	A	L	0-2		30,523
6	div1	**West Brom**	A	L	0-2		18,310
7	div1	**Scunthorpe**	H	W	2-0	Williams 45 og, Odejayi 65	11,230
8	div1	**Stoke**	A	D	0-0		13,071
9	div1	**Southampton**	A	W	3-2	McCann 27, 40, Devaney 90	19,151
10	div1	**Cardiff**	H	D	1-1	Howard 84	10,709
11	div1	**Bristol City**	H	W	3-0	Howard 67, Souza Guedes 72 Devaney 88	9,679
12	div1	**Charlton**	A	D	1-1	K.Christensen 90	21,081
13	div1	**Burnley**	H	D	1-1	Mostto 71	11,560
14	div1	**Hull City**	A	L	0-3		15,761
15	div1	**Leicester**	A	L	0-2		24,133
16	div1	**Preston**	H	W	1-0	Ferenczi 42	10,223
17	div1	**Blackpool**	H	W	2-1	Howard 21 pen, Ferenczi 70	8,531
18	div1	**Wolverhampton**	A	L	0-1		22,231
19	div1	**Watford**	H	W	3-2	Howard 31, Devaney 34, Lee 66 og	10,117
20	div1	**Sheff Wed**	A	L	0-1		27,769
21	div1	**Ipswich**	A	D	0-0		19,540
22	div1	**Wolverhampton**	H	W	1-0	Ferenczi 47	9,956
23	div1	**Crystal Palace**	H	D	0-0		10,298
24	div1	**Sheff Utd**	A	L	0-1		26,629
25	div1	**Bristol City**	A	L	2-3	Macken 33, Souza Guedes 40	16,588
26	div1	**Stoke**	H	D	3-3	Howard 23 pen, Macken 66, 85	12,398
27	div1	**Southampton**	H	D	2-2	Togwell 1, Campbell-Ryce 34	10,425
28	div1	**Scunthorpe**	A	D	2-2	McCann 74, Howard 90 pen	6,897
29	facr3	**Blackpool**	H	W	2-1	Foster 78, Coulson 81	8,276
30	div1	**Norwich**	H	L	1-3	Devaney 18	10,117
31	div1	**QPR**	A	L	0-2		16,197
32	facr4	**Southend**	A	W	1-0	Campbell-Ryce 22	7,212
33	div1	**Colchester**	H	W	1-0	Macken 45	9,246
34	div1	**Coventry**	A	L	0-4		16,449
35	div1	**West Brom**	H	W	2-1	Nardiello 30, Macken 45	13,083
36	div1	**Plymouth**	A	L	0-3		11,346
37	facr5	**Liverpool**	A	W	2-1	Foster 57, Howard 90	42,449
38	div1	**Norwich**	A	L	0-1		24,197
39	div1	**QPR**	H	D	0-0		9,019
40	div1	**Sheff Wed**	H	D	0-0		18,257
41	div1	**Blackpool**	A	D	1-1	Campbell-Ryce 45	8,080
42	facqf	**Chelsea**	H	W	1-0	Odejayi 66	22,410
43	div1	**Ipswich**	H	W	4-1	Howard 27, 83 pen, Macken 50 Wright 86 og	11,333
44	div1	**Crystal Palace**	A	L	0-2		17,459
45	div1	**Sheff Utd**	H	L	0-1		15,798
46	div1	**Burnley**	A	L	1-2	Howard 43	11,915
47	facsf	**Cardiff**	H	L	0-1		82,752
48	div1	**Watford**	A	W	3-0	Odejayi 36, 54, Foster 47	16,129
49	div1	**Preston**	A	W	2-1	Leon 33, Macken 55 pen	13,994
50	div1	**Hull City**	H	L	1-3	Ferenczi 90	13,061
51	div1	**Leicester**	H	L	0-1		14,644
52	div1	**Charlton**	H	W	3-0	Campbell-Ryce 11, Nyatanga 33 Macken 85	11,228
53	div1	**Cardiff**	A	L	0-3		14,469

LEAGUE APPEARANCES, BOOKINGS AND GOALS

	AGE (on 01/07/08)	IN NAMED 16	APPEARANCES	COUNTING GAMES	MINUTES ON PITCH	LEAGUE GOALS		
Goalkeepers								
Nick Colgan	34	14	1	1	90	0	0	0
Heinz Muller	30	28	28	28	2520	0	0	0
Luke Steele	23	14	14	14	1260	0	0	0
Tony Warner	34	3	3	3	270	0	0	0
Defenders								
Robert Atkinson	21	0	0	0	0	0	0	0
Jacob Butterfield	17	5	3	1	108	0	0	0
Stephen Foster	27	41	41	41	3667	1	6	1
Bobby Hassell	28	23	20	17	1575	0	3	0
Robert Kozluk	30	32	24	23	2055	0	6	1
Lewin Nyatanga	19	42	41	39	3544	1	2	1
Paul Reid	26	11	3	1	141	0	0	1
Dennis Souza Guedes	27	45	45	44	3969	2	7	0
Miguel Tininho	27	3	3	3	270	0	0	0
Marciano van Homoet	24	21	19	17	1602	0	1	0
Dominik Werling	25	18	17	15	1356	1	5	1
Midfielders								
Jamal Campbell-Ryce	25	39	37	31	2833	3	5	1
Anderson de Silva	25	20	20	19	1725	0	7	0
Martin Devaney	28	36	34	22	2125	4	3	0
Brian Howard	25	41	41	41	3672	13	9	0
Andy Johnson	34	5	4	2	277	0	0	0
Diego Leon	24	20	18	10	1251	1	0	0
Grant McCann	28	27	19	10	1113	3	1	0
Rohan Ricketts	25	15	10	2	311	0	0	0
Sam Togwell	23	37	22	10	1127	1	2	0
Forwards								
Kim Christensen	28	14	12	0	185	1	0	0
Michael Coulson	21	20	12	0	241	0	0	0
Istvan Ferenczi	30	41	37	17	2043	5	4	0
Jonathan Macken	30	29	29	28	2492	8	5	0
Miguel Mostto	28	25	14	5	659	1	0	0
Daniel Nardiello	25	15	11	3	560	1	2	0
Kayode Odejayi	26	42	39	21	2278	3	1	0

TEAM OF THE SEASON

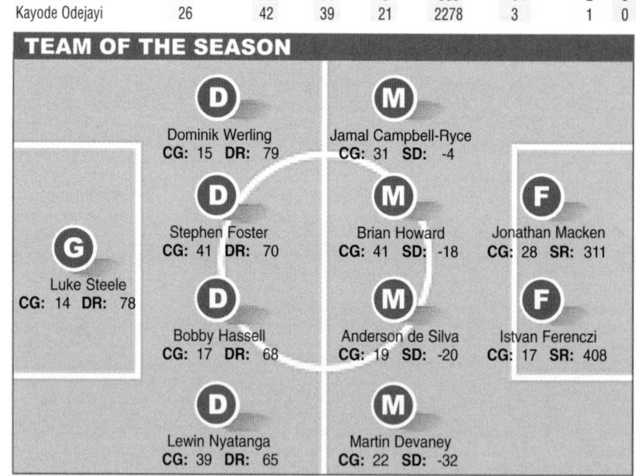

D
Dominik Werling
CG: 15 DR: 79
M
Jamal Campbell-Ryce
CG: 31 SD: -4
D
Stephen Foster
CG: 41 DR: 70
M
Brian Howard
CG: 41 SD: -18
F
Jonathan Macken
CG: 28 SR: 311
G
Luke Steele
CG: 14 DR: 78
D
Bobby Hassell
CG: 17 DR: 68
M
Anderson de Silva
CG: 19 SD: -20
F
Istvan Ferenczi
CG: 17 SR: 408
D
Lewin Nyatanga
CG: 39 DR: 65
M
Martin Devaney
CG: 22 SD: -32

MONTHLY POINTS TALLY

AUGUST	4	44%
SEPTEMBER	8	53%
OCTOBER	5	33%
NOVEMBER	9	60%
DECEMBER	7	33%
JANUARY	4	33%
FEBRUARY	4	27%
MARCH	5	28%
APRIL	9	60%
MAY	0	0%

LEAGUE GOALS

	PLAYER	MINS	GOALS	S RATE
1	Howard	3672	13	282
2	Macken	2492	8	311
3	Ferenczi	2043	5	408
4	Devaney	2125	4	531
5	Odejayi	2278	3	759
6	Campbell-Ryce	2833	3	944
7	McCann	1113	3	371
8	Foster	3667	1	3667
9	Souza Guedes	3969	2	1984
10	Christensen, K	185	1	185
11	Nardiello	560	1	560
12	Mostto	659	1	659
13	Togwell	1127	1	1127
	Other		3	
	TOTAL		49	

TOP POINT EARNERS

	PLAYER	GAMES	AV PTS
1	Dominik Werling	15	1.53
2	Istvan Ferenczi	17	1.41
3	Kayode Odejayi	21	1.38
4	Anderson de Silva	19	1.37
5	Jamal Campbell-Ryce	32	1.34
6	Heinz Muller	28	1.32
7	Robert Kozluk	23	1.30
8	Jonathan Macken	28	1.29
9	Lewin Nyatanga	40	1.23
10	Dennis Souza Guedes	44	1.23
	CLUB AVERAGE:		1.20

DISCIPLINARY RECORDS

	PLAYER	YELLOW	RED	AVE
1	Dominik Werling	5	1	226
2	Anderson de Silva	7	0	246
3	Daniel Nardiello	2	0	280
4	Robert Kozluk	6	1	293
5	Brian Howard	9	0	408
6	J Campbell-Ryce	5	1	472
7	Jonathan Macken	5	0	498
8	Istvan Ferenczi	4	0	510
9	Stephen Foster	6	1	523
10	Bobby Hassell	3	0	525
11	Sam Togwell	2	0	563
12	D Souza Guedes	7	0	567
13	Martin Devaney	3	0	708
	Other	5	1	
	TOTAL	69	5	

KEY GOALKEEPER

Luke Steele

Goals Conceded in the League	16	**Counting Games** League games when player was on pitch for at least 70 minutes	14
Defensive Rating Ave number of mins between League goals conceded while on the pitch	78	**Clean Sheets** In League games when player was on pitch for at least 70 minutes	4

KEY PLAYERS - DEFENDERS

Dominik Werling

Goals Conceded Number of League goals conceded while the player was on the pitch	17	**Clean Sheets** In League games when player was on pitch for at least 70 minutes	6
Defensive Rating Ave number of mins between League goals conceded while on the pitch	79	**Club Defensive Rating** Average number of mins between League goals conceded by the club this season	63

	PLAYER	CON LGE	CLEAN SHEETS	DEF RATE
1	Dominik Werling	17	6	79 mins
2	Stephen Foster	52	11	70 mins
3	Bobby Hassell	23	5	68 mins
4	Lewin Nyatanga	54	10	65 mins

KEY PLAYERS - MIDFIELDERS

Jamal Campbell-Ryce

Goals in the League	3	**Contribution to Attacking Power** Average number of minutes between League team goals while on pitch	80
Defensive Rating Average number of mins between League goals conceded while on the pitch	76	**Scoring Difference** Defensive Rating minus Contribution to Attacking Power	-4

	PLAYER	LGE GOALS	DEF RATE	POWER	SCORE DIFF
1	Jamal Campbell-Ryce	3	76	80	-4 mins
2	Brian Howard	13	63	81	-18 mins
3	Anderson de Silva	0	66	86	-20 mins
4	Martin Devaney	4	60	92	-32 mins

KEY PLAYERS - GOALSCORERS

Brian Howard

Goals in the League	13	**Player Strike Rate** Average number of minutes between League goals scored by player	282
Contribution to Attacking Power Average number of minutes between League team goals while on pitch	81	**Club Strike Rate** Average number of minutes between League goals scored by club	79

	PLAYER	LGE GOALS	POWER	STRIKE RATE
1	Brian Howard	13	81	282 mins
2	Jonathan Macken	8	83	311 mins
3	Istvan Ferenczi	5	78	408 mins
4	Martin Devaney	4	92	531 mins

wake smith
solicitors

Brian Howard

SQUAD APPEARANCES

Match	1	2	3	4	5	6	7	8	9	10	11	12	13	14	15	16	17	18	19	20	21	22	23	24	25	26	27	28	29	30	31	32	33	34	35	36	37	38	39	40	41	42	43	44	45	46	47	48	49	50	51	52	53
Venue	H	H	A	H	A	A	H	A	A	H	H	A	H	A	A	H	H	A	H	A	A	H	H	A	A	H	H	A	H	H	A	A	H	A	H	A	A	A	H	H	A	H	H	A	H	A	H	A	A	H	H	H	A
Competition	L	W	L	L	W	L	L	L	L	L	L	L	L	L	L	L	L	L	L	L	L	L	L	L	L	L	L	L	F	L	L	F	L	L	L	L	F	L	L	L	L	F	L	L	L	L	F	L	L	L	L	L	L
Result	L	W	D	W	L	L	W	D	W	D	W	D	D	L	L	W	W	L	W	L	D	W	D	L	L	D	D	D	W	L	L	W	W	L	W	L	W	L	D	D	D	W	W	L	L	L	L	W	W	L	L	W	L

Goalkeepers
Nick Colgan
Heinz Muller
Luke Steele
Tony Warner

Defenders
Robert Atkinson
Jacob Butterfield
Stephen Foster
Bobby Hassell
Robert Kozluk
Lewin Nyatanga
Paul Reid
Dennis Souza Guedes
Miguel Tininho
Marciano van Homoet
Dominik Werling

Midfielders
Jamal Campbell-Ryce
Anderson de Silva
Martin Devaney
Brian Howard
Andy Johnson
Diego Leon
Grant McCann
Rohan Ricketts
Sam Togwell

Forwards
Kim Christensen
Michael Coulson
Istvan Ferenczi
Jonathan Macken
Miguel Mostto
Daniel Nardiello
Kayode Odejayi

KEY: On all match | On bench | Subbed or sent off (Counting game) | Subbed or sent off (playing less than 70 minutes) | Subbed on from bench (Counting Game) | Subbed on (playing less than 70 minutes) | Subbed on and then subbed or sent off (Counting Game) | Subbed on and then subbed or sent off (playing less than 70 minutes) | Not in 16

BLACKPOOL

Final Position: **19th**

NICKNAME: THE SEASIDERS

KEY: ☐Won ☐Drawn ☐Lost

#	Comp	Opponent	H/A	Res	Score	Scorers	Attendance
1	div1	**Leicester**	A	W	1-0	Southern 63	26,650
2	ccr1	**Huddersfield**	H	W	1-0	Burgess 75	6,395
3	div1	**Bristol City**	H	D	1-1	Morrell 52	8,983
4	div1	**Wolverhampton**	A	L	1-2	Taylor-Fletcher 51	24,294
5	ccr2	**Derby**	A	W	7-6*	Gorkss 86, 120 (*on penalties)	8,658
6	div1	**Hull City**	H	W	2-1	Taylor-Fletcher 47, Burgess 90	7,902
7	div1	**Burnley**	A	D	2-2	Hoolahan 73 pen, Morrell 90	16,843
8	div1	**Sheff Utd**	H	D	2-2	Crainey 45, Burgess 87	9,512
9	div1	**Colchester**	H	D	2-2	Morrell 54, Barker 84	7,959
10	ccr3	**Southend**	H	W	2-1	Hoolahan 81, Jackson 118	5,022
11	div1	**Watford**	A	D	1-1	Hoolahan 73 pen	16,580
12	div1	**Coventry**	A	L	1-3	Morrell 32	15,803
13	div1	**Plymouth**	H	D	0-0		8,784
14	div1	**Crystal Palace**	H	D	1-1	Fox 69	9,037
15	div1	**West Brom**	A	L	1-2	Vernon 31	22,030
16	div1	**Sheff Wed**	A	L	1-2	Hoolahan 37	19,238
17	ccr4	**Tottenham**	A	L	0-2		32,196
18	div1	**Barnsley**	A	L	1-2	Southern 72	8,531
19	div1	**Scunthorpe**	H	W	1-0	Gorkss 73	8,051
20	div1	**Southampton**	A	L	0-1		21,075
21	div1	**Norwich**	H	L	1-3	Slusarski 38	7,759
22	div1	**QPR**	H	W	1-0	Burgess 90	8,527
23	div1	**Scunthorpe**	A	D	1-1	Flynn 88	4,407
24	div1	**Preston**	A	W	1-0	Hoolahan 68 pen	17,807
25	div1	**Cardiff**	H	L	0-1		7,214
26	div1	**Stoke**	H	L	2-3	Flynn 13, Barker 89	9,123
27	div1	**Coventry**	H	W	4-0	Hoolahan 28 pen, Flynn 65, Gorkss 72 Vernon 88	8,690
28	div1	**Sheff Utd**	A	D	1-1	Jorgensen 69	26,409
29	div1	**Colchester**	A	W	2-0	Vernon 26, 36	5,160
30	div1	**Burnley**	H	W	3-0	Gorkss 23, Burgess 59, Jorgensen 63	9,599
31	facr3	**Barnsley**	A	L	1-2	Fox 32	8,276
32	div1	**Charlton**	A	L	1-4	Burgess 12	21,412
33	div1	**Ipswich**	H	D	1-1	Jorgensen 39	9,154
34	div1	**Bristol City**	A	L	0-1		15,465
35	div1	**Leicester**	H	W	2-1	Taylor-Fletcher 3, Dickov 90	9,298
36	div1	**Hull City**	A	D	2-2	Dickov 39, 50	18,407
37	div1	**Wolverhampton**	H	D	0-0		9,413
38	div1	**Ipswich**	A	L	1-2	Dickov 89	21,059
39	div1	**Charlton**	H	W	5-3	McPhee 16, Gorkss 26, Taylor-Fletcher 59, 69, Dickov 62	9,134
40	div1	**Norwich**	A	W	2-1	McPhee 15, 39	24,531
41	div1	**Barnsley**	H	D	1-1	Taylor-Fletcher 20	8,080
42	div1	**Southampton**	H	D	2-2	Southern 49, Gorkss 55	9,050
43	div1	**QPR**	A	L	2-3	Burgess 60, McPhee 73	11,538
44	div1	**Preston**	H	D	0-0		9,629
45	div1	**Stoke**	A	D	1-1	Burgess 37	20,019
46	div1	**Crystal Palace**	A	D	0-0		16,028
47	div1	**West Brom**	H	L	1-3	Burgess 35	9,628
48	div1	**Cardiff**	A	L	1-3	Morrell 73	14,715
49	div1	**Sheff Wed**	H	W	2-1	Jorgensen 6, Dickov 30	9,633
50	div1	**Plymouth**	A	L	0-3		12,911
51	div1	**Watford**	H	D	1-1	Burgess 2	9,640

LEAGUE APPEARANCES, BOOKINGS AND GOALS

	AGE (on 01/07/08)	IN NAMED 16	APPEARANCES	COUNTING GAMES	MINUTES ON PITCH	LEAGUE GOALS	Yellow	Red
Goalkeepers								
Paul Gerrard	35	4	0	0	0	0	0	0
Paul Rachubka	27	46	46	46	4140	0	0	0
Defenders								
Shaun Barker	25	46	46	46	4140	2	5	0
Danny Coid	26	27	13	10	885	0	0	0
Stephen Crainey	27	40	40	38	3429	1	0	0
Phil Doughty	21	0	0	0	0	0	0	0
Ian Evatt	26	34	29	24	2227	0	4	1
Kaspar Gorkss	26	43	40	39	3543	5	5	2
John Hills	30	9	4	1	143	0	0	0
Matt Jackson	36	4	3	2	225	0	0	0
Michael Jackson	34	34	25	19	1945	0	4	1
Anthony McMahon	22	2	2	1	104	0	0	0
Midfielders								
Marcus Bean	23	1	0	0	0	0	0	0
Michael Flynn	27	33	28	18	1828	3	0	0
David Fox	24	38	28	15	1683	1	0	0
Stuart Green	27	6	6	0	170	0	0	0
Wesley Hoolahan	26	45	45	43	3864	5	4	0
Claus Jorgensen	32	40	37	26	2690	4	3	0
Joe Martin	18	2	1	1	74	0	0	0
Keith Southern	24	30	30	26	2399	3	2	0
Andrew Welsh	24	33	21	1	467	0	1	0
Forwards								
Ben Burgess	26	36	35	23	2265	9	4	0
Paul Dickov	35	11	11	6	623	6	1	0
Adrian Forbes	29	2	2	0	12	0	0	0
Grant Holt	27	4	4	0	24	0	0	0
Stephen McPhee	27	19	19	14	1385	4	1	0
Andy Morrell	33	42	38	17	1967	5	2	0
Keigan Parker	26	22	21	10	1102	0	2	0
Bartosz Slusarski	26	8	6	2	284	1	0	0
Gary Taylor-Fletcher	27	43	42	34	3193	6	5	0
Scott Vernon	24	27	15	5	589	4	0	0

TEAM OF THE SEASON

G — Paul Rachubka **CG:** 46 **DR:** 64

D — Michael Jackson **CG:** 19 **DR:** 72
D — Stephen Crainey **CG:** 38 **DR:** 67
D — Shaun Barker **CG:** 46 **DR:** 64
D — Ian Evatt **CG:** 24 **DR:** 63

M — David Fox **CG:** 15 **SD:** 6
M — Michael Flynn **CG:** 18 **SD:** -3
M — Wesley Hoolahan **CG:** 43 **SD:** -3
M — Claus Jorgensen **CG:** 26 **SD:** -4

F — Ben Burgess **CG:** 23 **SR:** 251
F — Stephen McPhee **CG:** 14 **SR:** 346

MONTHLY POINTS TALLY

Month	Points	%
AUGUST	4	44%
SEPTEMBER	7	47%
OCTOBER	2	13%
NOVEMBER	3	25%
DECEMBER	14	58%
JANUARY	4	33%
FEBRUARY	8	53%
MARCH	8	38%
APRIL	3	25%
MAY	1	33%

LEAGUE GOALS

	PLAYER	MINS	GOALS	S RATE
1	Burgess	2265	9	251
2	Gorkss	3543	5	708
3	Dickov	623	6	103
4	Taylor-Fletcher	3193	6	532
5	Hoolahan	3864	5	772
6	Morrell	1967	5	393
7	Vernon	589	4	147
8	McPhee	1385	4	346
9	Jorgensen	2690	4	672
10	Flynn	1828	3	609
11	Southern	2399	3	799
12	Fox	1683	1	1683
13	Barker	4140	2	2070
	Other		2	
	TOTAL		59	

TOP POINT EARNERS

	PLAYER	GAMES	AV PTS
1	Andy Morrell	17	1.65
2	Claus Jorgensen	26	1.54
3	Stephen McPhee	14	1.36
4	Ian Evatt	25	1.32
5	Gary Taylor-Fletcher	34	1.29
6	Wesley Hoolahan	43	1.26
7	Michael Jackson	20	1.25
8	Stephen Crainey	38	1.21
9	Kaspar Gorkss	39	1.18
10	Michael Flynn	18	1.17
	CLUB AVERAGE:		1.17

DISCIPLINARY RECORDS

	PLAYER	YELLOW	RED	AVE
1	Michael Jackson	4	1	389
2	Ian Evatt	4	1	445
3	Andrew Welsh	1	0	467
4	Kaspar Gorkss	5	2	506
5	Keigan Parker	2	0	551
6	Ben Burgess	4	0	566
7	Paul Dickov	1	0	623
8	Gary Taylor-Fletcher	5	0	638
9	Shaun Barker	5	0	828
10	Claus Jorgensen	3	0	896
11	Wesley Hoolahan	4	0	966
12	Andy Morrell	2	0	983
13	Keith Southern	2	0	1199
	Other	1	0	
	TOTAL	43	4	

KEY GOALKEEPER

Paul Rachubka

Goals Conceded in the League	64	**Counting Games** League games when player was on pitch for at least 70 minutes	46
Defensive Rating Ave number of mins between League goals conceded while on the pitch	64	**Clean Sheets** In League games when player was on pitch for at least 70 minutes	11

KEY PLAYERS - DEFENDERS

Michael Jackson

Goals Conceded Number of League goals conceded while the player was on the pitch	27	**Clean Sheets** In League games when player was on pitch for at least 70 minutes	6
Defensive Rating Ave number of mins between League goals conceded while on the pitch	72	**Club Defensive Rating** Average number of mins between League goals conceded by the club this season	64

	PLAYER	CON LGE	CLEAN SHEETS	DEF RATE
1	Michael Jackson	27	6	72 mins
2	Stephen Crainey	51	10	67 mins
3	Shaun Barker	64	11	64 mins
4	Ian Evatt	35	5	63 mins

KEY PLAYERS - MIDFIELDERS

David Fox

Goals in the League	1	**Contribution to Attacking Power** Average number of minutes between League team goals while on pitch	70
Defensive Rating Average number of mins between League goals conceded while on the pitch	76	Scoring Difference Defensive Rating minus Contribution to Attacking Power	6

	PLAYER	LGE GOALS	DEF RATE	POWER	SCORE DIFF
1	David Fox	1	76	70	6 mins
2	Michael Flynn	3	67	70	-3 mins
3	Wesley Hoolahan	5	63	66	-3 mins
4	Claus Jorgensen	4	64	68	-4 mins

KEY PLAYERS - GOALSCORERS

Ben Burgess

Goals in the League	9	Player Strike Rate Average number of minutes between League goals scored by player	251
Contribution to Attacking Power Average number of minutes between League team goals while on pitch	70	**Club Strike Rate** Average number of minutes between League goals scored by club	70

	PLAYER	LGE GOALS	POWER	STRIKE RATE
1	Ben Burgess	9	70	251 mins
2	Stephen McPhee	4	69	346 mins
3	Andy Morrell	5	78	393 mins
4	Gary Taylor-Fletcher	6	72	532 mins

Pointbet
games.com
Wes Hoolahan

SQUAD APPEARANCES

Match	1	2	3	4	5	6	7	8	9	10	11	12	13	14	15	16	17	18	19	20	21	22	23	24	25	26	27	28	29	30	31	32	33	34	35	36	37	38	39	40	41	42	43	44	45	46	47	48	49	50	51
Venue	A	H	H	A	A	H	A	H	H	H	A	A	H	H	A	A	A	A	H	A	H	H	A	A	H	H	H	A	A	H	A	A	H	A	H	A	H	A	H	A	H	H	A	H	A	A	H	A	H	A	H
Competition	L	W	L	L	W	L	L	L	L	W	L	L	L	L	L	L	W	L	L	L	L	L	L	L	L	L	L	L	L	L	F	L	L	L	L	L	L	L	L	L	L	L	L	L	L	L	L	L	L	L	L
Result	W	W	D	L	W	W	D	D	D	W	D	L	D	D	L	L	L	L	W	L	L	W	D	W	L	L	W	D	W	W	L	L	D	L	W	D	D	L	W	W	D	D	L	D	D	D	L	L	W	L	D

Goalkeepers
Scott Flinders
Paul Rachubka
Defenders
Shaun Barker
Danny Coid
Stephen Crainey
Phil Doughty
Ian Evatt
Kaspar Gorkss
John Hills
Matt Jackson
Michael Jackson
Anthony McMahon
Midfielders
Marcus Bean
Michael Flynn
David Fox
Stuart Green
Wesley Hoolahan
Claus Jorgensen
Matt Lawlor
Joe Martin
Keith Southern
Andrew Welsh
Forwards
Ben Burgess
Paul Dickov
Adrian Forbes
Grant Holt
Stephen McPhee
Andy Morrell
Keigan Parker
Bartosz Slusarski
Gary Taylor-Fletcher
Scott Vernon

KEY: ■ On all match; ■ On bench; ⏮ Subbed or sent off (Counting game); ◀◀ Subbed or sent off (playing less than 70 minutes); ⏭ Subbed on from bench (Counting Game); ▶▶ Subbed on (playing less than 70 minutes); Subbed on and then subbed or sent off (Counting Game); Subbed on and then subbed or sent off (playing less than 70 minutes); □ Not in 16

SOUTHAMPTON

Final Position: **20th**

NICKNAME: THE SAINTS

KEY: ☐Won ☐Drawn ☐Lost

							Attendance
1	div1	Crystal Palace	H	L	1-4	Saganowski 45	25,054
2	ccr1	Peterborough	A	L	1-2	Rasiak 36	4,087
3	div1	Norwich	A	L	1-2	Jones 37	24,004
4	div1	Stoke	H	W	3-2	Surman 36, Rasiak 71, Viafara 75	20,300
5	div1	QPR	A	W	3-0	Rasiak 18, 45, Wright-Phillips 49	15,560
6	div1	Watford	A	L	2-3	Rasiak 45, Dyer 69	15,915
7	div1	Colchester	H	D	1-1	Wright-Phillips 52	18,773
8	div1	Barnsley	H	L	2-3	Saganowski 45, Idiakez 90	19,151
9	div1	Sheff Utd	A	W	2-1	Rasiak 19, Viafara 31	24,561
10	div1	Preston	A	L	1-5	B.Jones 45 og	10,279
11	div1	West Brom	H	W	3-2	John 17, 64, Skacel 23	21,967
12	div1	Cardiff	H	W	1-0	John 15	20,796
13	div1	Bristol City	A	L	1-2	McAllister 54 og	18,326
14	div1	Burnley	A	W	3-2	Wright-Phillips 3, Euell 15, John 51	10,944
15	div1	Charlton	H	L	0-1		23,363
16	div1	Wolverhampton	H	D	0-0		19,856
17	div1	Sheff Wed	A	L	0-5		19,442
18	div1	Blackpool	H	W	1-0	John 35	21,075
19	div1	Ipswich	A	L	0-2		19,791
20	div1	Leicester	A	W	2-1	John 32, Surman 56 pen	20,070
21	div1	Sheff Wed	H	D	0-0		17,981
22	div1	Hull City	H	W	4-0	Wright-Phillips 43, John 58, 76, 78	18,125
23	div1	Coventry	A	D	1-1	Wright-Phillips 59	19,143
24	div1	Preston	H	L	0-1		23,267
25	div1	Colchester	A	D	1-1	Viafara 19	6,157
26	div1	Barnsley	A	D	2-2	Wright-Phillips 61, 70	10,425
27	div1	Watford	H	L	0-3		23,008
28	facr3	Leicester	H	W	2-0	Surman 16, Vignal 36 fk	20,094
29	div1	Scunthorpe	H	W	1-0	Rasiak 25	18,146
30	div1	Plymouth	A	D	1-1	Wright-Phillips 12	14,676
31	facr4	Bury	H	W	2-0	Surman 71, Rasiak 80	25,449
32	div1	Norwich	H	L	0-1		18,004
33	div1	Crystal Palace	A	D	1-1	John 84	17,967
34	div1	QPR	H	L	2-3	Powell 1, John 90	22,505
35	div1	Stoke	A	L	2-3	John 46, 54	19,481
36	facr5	Bristol Rovers	A	L	0-1		11,920
37	div1	Plymouth	H	L	0-2		17,806
38	div1	Scunthorpe	A	D	1-1	Vignal 88 pen	6,035
39	div1	Ipswich	H	D	1-1	John 51	23,299
40	div1	Wolverhampton	A	D	2-2	Vignal 75 pen, Euell 90	21,795
41	div1	Blackpool	A	D	2-2	Vignal 31 pen, John 63	9,050
42	div1	Leicester	H	W	1-0	John 76	17,741
43	div1	Hull City	A	L	0-5		16,829
44	div1	Coventry	H	D	0-0		22,014
45	div1	Cardiff	A	L	0-1		12,955
46	div1	Bristol City	H	W	2-0	John 35, Euell 84	22,890
47	div1	Charlton	A	D	1-1	McCarthy 11 og	26,206
48	div1	Burnley	H	L	0-1		21,762
49	div1	West Brom	A	D	1-1	Lallana 77	26,167
50	div1	Sheff Utd	H	W	3-2	Saganowski 42, John 53, 69	31,957

LEAGUE APPEARANCES, BOOKINGS AND GOALS

	AGE (on 01/07/08)	IN NAMED 16	APPEARANCES	COUNTING GAMES	MINUTES ON PITCH	LEAGUE GOALS	Yellow	Red
Goalkeepers								
Kelvin Davis	31	43	35	34	3105	0	0	0
Michael Poke	22	7	4	3	315	0	0	0
Richard Wright	30	7	7	7	630	0	1	0
Defenders								
Alan Bennett	26	12	10	10	900	0	0	0
Christian Dailly	34	11	11	11	990	0	0	0
Andrew Davies	23	23	23	20	1891	0	2	0
Philip Ifil	21	12	12	11	1035	0	1	0
Chris Lucketti	37	4	4	4	360	0	0	0
Chris Makin	35	6	5	5	450	0	1	0
Alexander Ostlund	29	17	12	6	693	0	4	0
Chris Perry	35	6	6	6	540	0	2	0
Darren Powell	32	13	10	8	786	1	2	0
Wayne Thomas	29	31	30	28	2563	0	2	0
Gregory Vignal	26	21	20	17	1672	3	5	1
Midfielders								
Nathan Dyer	20	17	17	14	1340	1	2	0
Adam Hammill	20	32	25	8	1164	0	1	0
Inigo Idiakez	34	24	21	12	1229	1	4	0
Adam Lallana	20	7	5	0	106	1	0	0
Mario Licka	26	14	12	8	856	0	1	0
Youssef Safri	31	37	37	36	3273	0	5	2
Rudolf Skacel	28	20	16	13	1223	1	0	0
Andrew Surman	21	42	40	30	3044	2	2	0
John Eduis Viafara	29	43	40	27	2880	3	6	0
Jermaine Wright	32	37	36	33	3009	0	0	0
Forwards								
Jason Euell	31	40	38	30	2920	3	2	0
Stern John	31	42	40	32	2962	19	2	1
David McGoldrick	20	11	8	0	200	0	0	0
Vincent Pericard	25	7	5	1	159	0	0	0
Grzegorz Rasiak	29	28	23	9	1236	6	3	0
Marek Saganowski	29	38	30	10	1340	3	1	0
Bradley Wright-Phillips	23	41	39	18	2307	8	1	0

TEAM OF THE SEASON

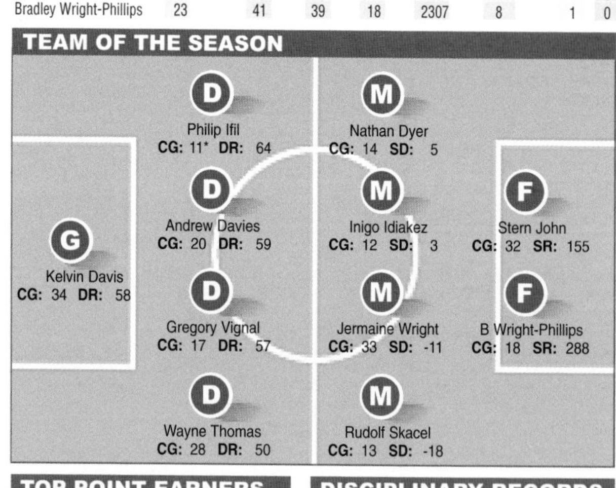

D
Philip Ifil
CG: 11* DR: 64
M
Nathan Dyer
CG: 14 SD: 5
D
Andrew Davies
CG: 20 DR: 59
M
Inigo Idiakez
CG: 12 SD: 3
F
Stern John
CG: 32 SR: 155
G
Kelvin Davis
CG: 34 DR: 58
D
Gregory Vignal
CG: 17 DR: 57
M
Jermaine Wright
CG: 33 SD: -11
F
B Wright-Phillips
CG: 18 SR: 288
D
Wayne Thomas
CG: 28 DR: 50
M
Rudolf Skacel
CG: 13 SD: -18

MONTHLY POINTS TALLY

Month	Points	%
AUGUST	3	33%
SEPTEMBER	7	47%
OCTOBER	9	60%
NOVEMBER	4	27%
DECEMBER	10	48%
JANUARY	4	33%
FEBRUARY	2	13%
MARCH	7	33%
APRIL	5	42%
MAY	3	100%

LEAGUE GOALS

	PLAYER	MINS	GOALS	S RATE
1	John	2962	19	155
2	Rasiak	1236	6	206
3	Wright-Phillips	2307	8	288
4	Vignal	1672	3	557
5	Surman	3044	2	1522
6	Saganowski	1340	3	446
7	Viafara	2880	3	960
8	Euell	2920	3	973
9	Jones	90	1	90
10	Lallana	106	1	106
11	Powell	786	1	786
12	Skacel	1223	1	1223
13	Idiakez	1229	1	1229
	Other		1	
	TOTAL		53	

TOP POINT EARNERS

	PLAYER	GAMES	AV PTS
1	Nathan Dyer	14	1.79
2	Bradley Wright-Phillips	18	1.67
3	Inigo Idiakez	12	1.58
4	Rudolf Skacel	13	1.23
5	Youssef Safri	36	1.22
6	John Eduis Viafara	27	1.22
7	Stern John	32	1.19
8	Kelvin Davis	34	1.18
9	Wayne Thomas	28	1.11
10	Jason Euell	30	1.07
	CLUB AVERAGE:		1.17

DISCIPLINARY RECORDS

	PLAYER	YELLOW	RED	AVE
1	Alexander Ostlund	4	0	173
2	Chris Perry	2	0	270
3	Gregory Vignal	5	1	278
4	Inigo Idiakez	4	0	307
5	Darren Powell	2	0	393
6	Grzegorz Rasiak	3	0	412
7	Youssef Safri	5	2	467
8	John Eduis Viafara	6	0	480
9	Richard Wright	1	0	630
10	Nathan Dyer	2	0	670
11	Mario Licka	1	0	856
12	Andrew Davies	2	0	945
13	Stern John	2	1	987
	Other	10	0	
	TOTAL	49	4	

KEY GOALKEEPER

Kelvin Davis

Goals Conceded in the League	53	**Counting Games** League games when player was on pitch for at least 70 minutes	34
Defensive Rating Ave number of mins between League goals conceded while on the pitch	58	**Clean Sheets** In League games when player was on pitch for at least 70 minutes	7

KEY PLAYERS - DEFENDERS

Philip Ifil

Goals Conceded Number of League goals conceded while the player was on the pitch	16	**Clean Sheets** In League games when player was on pitch for at least 70 minutes	3
Defensive Rating Ave number of mins between League goals conceded while on the pitch	64	**Club Defensive Rating** Average number of mins between League goals conceded by the club this season	57

	PLAYER	CON LGE	CLEAN SHEETS	DEF RATE
1	Philip Ifil	16	3	64 mins
2	Andrew Davies	32	4	59 mins
3	Gregory Vignal	29	5	57 mins
4	Wayne Thomas	51	5	50 mins

KEY PLAYERS - MIDFIELDERS

Nathan Dyer

Goals in the League	1	**Contribution to Attacking Power** Average number of minutes between League team goals while on pitch	53
Defensive Rating Average number of mins between League goals conceded while on the pitch	58	**Scoring Difference** Defensive Rating minus Contribution to Attacking Power	5

	PLAYER	LGE GOALS	DEF RATE	POWER	SCORE DIFF
1	Nathan Dyer	1	58	53	5 mins
2	Inigo Idiakez	1	61	58	3 mins
3	Jermaine Wright	0	60	71	-11 mins
4	Rudolf Skacel	1	76	94	-18 mins

KEY PLAYERS - GOALSCORERS

Stern John

Goals in the League	19	**Player Strike Rate** Average number of minutes between League goals scored by player	155
Contribution to Attacking Power Average number of minutes between League team goals while on pitch	82	**Club Strike Rate** Average number of minutes between League goals scored by club	73

	PLAYER	LGE GOALS	POWER	STRIKE RATE
1	Stern John	19	82	155 mins
2	Bradley Wright-Phillips	8	72	288 mins
3	John Eduis Viafara	3	72	960 mins
4	Jason Euell	3	83	973 mins

SKACEL
pe.com

Rudolf Skacel

SQUAD APPEARANCES

Match	1	2	3	4	5	6	7	8	9	10	11	12	13	14	15	16	17	18	19	20	21	22	23	24	25
Venue	H	A	A	H	A	A	H	H	A	A	H	H	A	A	H	H	A	H	A	A	H	H	A	H	A
Competition	L	W	L	L	L	L	L	L	L	L	L	L	L	L	L	L	L	L	L	L	L	L	L	L	L
Result	L	L	L	W	W	L	D	L	W	L	W	W	L	W	L	D	L	W	L	W	D	W	D	L	D

Match	26	27	28	29	30	31	32	33	34	35	36	37	38	39	40	41	42	43	44	45	46	47	48	49	50
Venue	A	H	H	H	A	H	H	A	H	A	A	H	A	H	A	A	H	A	H	A	H	A	H	A	H
Competition	L	L	F	L	L	F	L	L	L	L	F	L	L	L	L	L	L	L	L	L	L	L	L	L	L
Result	D	L	W	W	D	W	L	D	L	L	L	L	D	D	D	D	W	L	D	L	W	D	L	D	W

Goalkeepers
Kelvin Davis
Michael Poke
Richard Wright

Defenders
Alan Bennett
Christian Dailly
Andrew Davies
Philip Ifil
Chris Lucketti
Chris Makin
Stephen O'Halloran
Alexander Ostlund
Chris Perry
Darren Powell
Wayne Thomas
Gregory Vignal

Midfielders
Nathan Dyer
Adam Hammill
Inigo Idiakez
Adam Lallana
Mario Licka
Youssef Safri
Rudolf Skacel
Andrew Surman
John Eduis Viafara
Jermaine Wright

Forwards
Jason Euell
Stern John
David McGoldrick
Vincent Pericard
Grzegorz Rasiak
Marek Saganowski
Bradley Wright-Phillips

KEY: On all match; On bench; Subbed or sent off (Counting game); Subbed or sent off (playing less than 70 minutes); Subbed on from bench (Counting Game); Subbed on (playing less than 70 minutes); Subbed on and then subbed or sent off (Counting Game); Subbed on and then subbed or sent off (playing less than 70 minutes); Not in 16

COVENTRY CITY

Final Position: **21st**

NICKNAME: THE SKY BLUES

KEY: ☐Won ☐Drawn ☐Lost

							Attendance
1	div1	Barnsley	A	W	4-1	McKenzie 6, Kyle 50, Gray 65, Mifsud 90	12,616
2	ccr1	Notts County	H	W	3-0	Adebola 47, Best 67, Simpson 78	6,735
3	div1	Hull City	H	D	1-1	McKenzie 51	21,059
4	div1	Cardiff	A	W	1-0	Tabb 34	16,407
5	ccr2	Carlisle	A	W	2-0	Mifsud 21, 56	5,744
6	div1	Preston	H	W	2-1	Adebola 80, Doyle 85	17,551
7	div1	Bristol City	H	L	0-3		21,538
8	div1	Crystal Palace	A	D	1-1	Best 87	14,455
9	div1	Ipswich	A	L	1-4	S.Hughes 69	18,840
10	ccr3	Man Utd	A	W	2-0	Mifsud 27, 70	74,055
11	div1	Charlton	H	D	1-1	Mifsud 84	19,021
12	div1	Blackpool	H	W	3-1	Doyle 44 pen, Mifsud 69, Simpson 86	15,803
13	div1	Wolverhampton	A	L	0-1		24,338
14	div1	Plymouth	A	L	0-1		11,576
15	div1	Watford	H	L	0-3		17,032
16	div1	Colchester	H	W	1-0	Mifsud 81	23,431
17	ccr4	West Ham	H	L	1-2	Tabb 68	23,968
18	div1	Stoke	A	W	3-1	Mifsud 58, 79, Adebola 63	13,448
19	div1	QPR	A	W	2-1	Mifsud 61, Kyle 90	11,922
20	div1	West Brom	H	L	0-4		18,566
21	div1	Norwich	A	L	0-2		24,590
22	div1	Scunthorpe	H	D	1-1	Doyle 51 pen	14,036
23	div1	Sheff Utd	H	L	0-1		20,355
24	div1	West Brom	A	W	4-2	Best 6, 83, Mifsud 11, 86	20,641
25	div1	Southampton	H	D	1-1	Tabb 19	19,143
26	div1	Blackpool	A	L	0-4		8,690
27	div1	Crystal Palace	H	L	0-2		22,134
28	div1	Ipswich	H	W	2-1	Gray 11, Adebola 64	18,346
29	div1	Bristol City	A	L	1-2	Adebola 72	15,899
30	facr3	Blackburn	A	W	4-1	Mifsud 34, 90, Ward 64 pen, Adebola 83	14,421
31	div1	Leicester	A	L	0-2		23,905
32	div1	Burnley	H	L	1-2	Doyle 26	17,347
33	facr4	Millwall	H	W	2-1	S.Hughes 16, Mifsud 52	17,268
34	div1	Hull City	A	L	0-1		14,822
35	div1	Barnsley	H	W	4-0	Best 37, 84, Gray 70, Tabb 75	16,449
36	div1	Preston	A	L	0-1		11,857
37	div1	Cardiff	H	D	0-0		15,260
38	facr5	West Brom	H	L	0-5		28,163
39	div1	Leicester	H	W	2-0	Ward 32 pen, Best 79	23,129
40	div1	Burnley	A	L	0-2		9,779
41	div1	Scunthorpe	A	L	1-2	Thornton 21 pen	5,866
42	div1	QPR	H	D	0-0		15,225
43	div1	Norwich	H	W	1-0	Tabb 6	18,108
44	div1	Sheff Utd	A	L	1-2	Ward 81 pen	23,864
45	div1	Sheff Wed	H	D	0-0		19,283
46	div1	Southampton	A	D	0-0		22,014
47	div1	Plymouth	H	W	3-1	Doyle 37, 43, Tabb 65	18,775
48	div1	Sheff Wed	A	D	1-1	Hines 83	21,110
49	div1	Watford	A	L	1-2	Best 59	17,188
50	div1	Stoke	H	L	1-2	Ward 31 pen	20,249
51	div1	Colchester	A	W	5-1	Best 48, Fox 51, Ward 78 pen, 90 pen Doyle 80	5,836
52	div1	Wolverhampton	H	D	1-1	Ward 18	27,992
53	div1	Charlton	A	L	1-4	Mifsud 20	26,130

LEAGUE APPEARANCES, BOOKINGS AND GOALS

	AGE (on 01/07/08)	IN NAMED 16	APPEARANCES	COUNTING GAMES	MINUTES ON PITCH	LEAGUE GOALS	Yellow	Red
Goalkeepers								
Dimitrios Konstantopoulos	29	30	21	21	1890	0	0	0
Andy Marshall	33	40	16	16	1440	0	0	0
Kasper Schmeichel	21	9	9	9	810	0	0	0
Defenders								
Gary Borrowdale	22	24	21	19	1706	0	3	0
Scott Dann	21	18	16	14	1276	0	3	0
Arjan De Zeeuw	38	20	17	16	1499	0	6	0
Daniel Fox	22	18	18	18	1610	1	5	0
Marcus Hall	32	29	18	17	1516	0	1	0
David McNamee	27	15	13	10	966	0	3	0
Robert Page	33	3	0	0	0	0	0	0
Ben Turner	20	20	19	19	1710	0	2	0
Elliott Ward	23	45	37	35	3197	6	7	0
Midfielders								
Christopher Birchall	24	3	1	0	37	0	0	0
Liam Davis	21	9	6	2	254	0	2	0
Michael Doyle	26	42	42	41	3747	7	7	0
Julian Gray	28	35	26	18	1813	3	0	0
Zavon Hines	19	7	7	0	70	1	0	0
Michael Hughes	36	21	19	15	1458	0	2	0
Stephen Hughes	31	38	36	27	2642	1	7	0
Isaac Osbourne	22	43	42	36	3326	0	5	0
Jay Tabb	24	43	42	39	3426	5	4	0
Kevin Thornton	21	24	19	9	1026	1	2	0
Forwards								
Dele Adebola	33	27	26	13	1538	4	2	0
Wayne Andrews	30	12	7	0	94	0	0	0
Leon Best	21	35	34	25	2434	8	10	0
Ellery Cairo	29	15	7	3	382	0	2	0
Kevin Kyle	27	15	13	3	550	2	3	2
Leon McKenzie	30	11	11	8	722	2	1	0
Michael Mifsud	27	41	41	32	3040	10	4	1
Donovan Simmonds	19	2	0	0	0	0	0	0
Robbie Simpson	23	32	28	6	1051	1	3	0

TEAM OF THE SEASON

G — Andy Marshall — CG: 16 DR: 80

D — Daniel Fox — CG: 18 DR: 89

D — Scott Dann — CG: 14 DR: 79

D — Elliott Ward — CG: 35 DR: 73

D — Marcus Hall — CG: 17 DR: 63

M — Julian Gray — CG: 18 SD: 7

M — Michael Hughes — CG: 16 SD: -9

M — Jay Tabb — CG: 39 SD: -9

M — Michael Doyle — CG: 41 SD: -12

F — Michael Mifsud — CG: 32 SR: 304

F — Leon Best — CG: 25 SR: 315

MONTHLY POINTS TALLY

Month	Points	%
AUGUST	7	78%
SEPTEMBER	5	33%
OCTOBER	6	40%
NOVEMBER	7	47%
DECEMBER	7	39%
JANUARY	0	0%
FEBRUARY	7	47%
MARCH	9	43%
APRIL	5	33%
MAY	0	0%

LEAGUE GOALS

	PLAYER	MINS	GOALS	S RATE
1	Mifsud	3040	10	304
2	Best	2524	8	315
3	Ward	3287	6	547
4	Doyle	3837	7	548
5	Adebola	1538	4	384
6	Tabb	3516	5	703
7	Gray	1813	3	604
8	Kyle	550	2	275
9	McKenzie	812	2	406
10	Simpson	1051	1	1051
11	Hughes, S	2642	1	2642
12	Hines	70	1	70
13	Thornton	1026	1	1026
	Other		1	
	TOTAL		52	

TOP POINT EARNERS

	PLAYER	GAMES	AV PTS
1	Marcus Hall	17	1.41
2	Isaac Osbourne	36	1.25
3	Jay Tabb	39	1.24
4	Michael Mifsud	32	1.21
5	Michael Doyle	41	1.20
6	Stephen Hughes	27	1.19
7	D Konstantopoulos	21	1.19
8	Elliott Ward	35	1.17
9	Daniel Fox	18	1.17
10	Julian Gray	18	1.17
	CLUB AVERAGE:		1.15

DISCIPLINARY RECORDS

	PLAYER	YELLOW	RED	AVE
1	Kevin Kyle	3	2	110
2	Ellery Cairo	2	0	236
3	Arjan De Zeeuw	6	0	249
4	Leon Best	10	0	252
5	Daniel Fox	5	0	322
6	Robbie Simpson	3	0	350
7	David McNamee	3	0	352
8	Stephen Hughes	7	0	377
9	Scott Dann	3	0	425
10	Elliott Ward	7	0	469
11	Kevin Thornton	2	0	513
12	Michael Doyle	7	0	548
13	Gary Borrowdale	3	0	598
	Other	21	1	
	TOTAL	82	3	

KEY GOALKEEPER

Andy Marshall

Goals Conceded in the League	18	Counting Games League games when player was on pitch for at least 70 minutes	16
Defensive Rating Ave number of mins between League goals conceded while on the pitch	80	Clean Sheets In League games when player was on pitch for at least 70 minutes	5

KEY PLAYERS - DEFENDERS

Daniel Fox

Goals Conceded Number of League goals conceded while the player was on the pitch	18	Clean Sheets In League games when player was on pitch for at least 70 minutes	8
Defensive Rating Ave number of mins between League goals conceded while on the pitch	89	Club Defensive Rating Average number of mins between League goals conceded by the club this season	67

	PLAYER	CON LGE	CLEAN SHEETS	DEF RATE
1	Daniel Fox	18	8	89 mins
2	Scott Dann	16	5	79 mins
3	Elliott Ward	45	9	73 mins
4	Marcus Hall	24	3	63 mins

KEY PLAYERS - MIDFIELDERS

Julian Gray

Goals in the League	3	Contribution to Attacking Power Average number of minutes between League team goals while on pitch	75
Defensive Rating Average number of mins between League goals conceded while on the pitch	82	Scoring Difference Defensive Rating minus Contribution to Attacking Power	7

	PLAYER	LGE GOALS	DEF RATE	POWER	SCORE DIFF
1	Julian Gray	3	82	75	7 mins
2	Michael Hughes	0	64	73	-9 mins
3	Jay Tabb	5	67	76	-9 mins
4	Michael Doyle	7	66	78	-12 mins

KEY PLAYERS - GOALSCORERS

Michael Mifsud

Goals in the League	10	Player Strike Rate Average number of minutes between League goals scored by player	304
Contribution to Attacking Power Average number of minutes between League team goals while on pitch	74	Club Strike Rate Average number of minutes between League goals scored by club	83

	PLAYER	LGE GOALS	POWER	STRIKE RATE
1	Michael Mifsud	10	74	304 mins
2	Leon Best	8	81	315 mins
3	Dele Adebola	4	96	384 mins
4	Michael Doyle	7	78	548 mins

CASSIDY
GROUP
Michael Mifsud

SQUAD APPEARANCES

Match	1	2	3	4	5	6	7	8	9	10	11	12	13	14	15	16	17	18	19	20	21	22	23	24	25	26	27
Venue	A	H	H	A	A	H	H	A	A	A	H	H	A	A	H	H	H	A	A	H	A	H	H	A	H	A	H
Competition	L	W	L	L	W	L	L	L	L	W	L	L	L	L	L	L	W	L	L	L	L	L	L	L	L	L	L
Result	W	W	D	W	W	W	L	D	L	W	D	W	L	L	L	W	L	W	W	L	L	D	L	W	D	L	L

Match	28	29	30	31	32	33	34	35	36	37	38	39	40	41	42	43	44	45	46	47	48	49	50	51	52	53
Venue	H	A	A	A	H	H	A	H	A	H	H	H	A	A	H	H	A	H	A	H	A	A	H	A	H	A
Competition	L	L	F	L	L	F	L	L	L	L	F	L	L	L	L	L	L	L	L	L	L	L	L	L	L	L
Result	W	L	W	L	L	W	L	W	L	D	L	W	L	L	D	W	L	D	D	W	D	L	L	W	D	L

Goalkeepers
D Konstantopoulos
Andy Marshall
Kasper Schmeichel

Defenders
Gary Borrowdale
Scott Dann
Arjan De Zeeuw
Daniel Fox
Marcus Hall
David McNamee
Robert Page
Ben Turner
Elliott Ward

Midfielders
Christopher Birchall
Liam Davis
Michael Doyle
Julian Gray
Zavon Hines
Michael Hughes
Stephen Hughes
Isaac Osbourne
Jay Tabb
Kevin Thornton

Forwards
Dele Adebola
Wayne Andrews
Leon Best
Ellery Cairo
Kevin Kyle
Leon McKenzie
Michael Mifsud
Donovan Simmonds
Robbie Simpson

KEY: On all match | On bench | Subbed or sent off (Counting game) | Subbed or sent off (playing less than 70 minutes) | Subbed on from bench (Counting Game) | Subbed on (playing less than 70 minutes) | Subbed on and then subbed or sent off (Counting Game) | Subbed on and then subbed or sent off (playing less than 70 minutes) | Not in 16

LEICESTER CITY

Final Position: **22nd**

NICKNAME: THE FOXES

KEY: ☐ Won ☐ Drawn ☐ Lost

		Opponent			Score	Scorers	Attendance
1	div1	Blackpool	H	L	0-1		26,650
2	ccr1	Accrington	A	W	1-0	Wesolowski 4	2,029
3	div1	Crystal Palace	A	D	2-2	Campbell 63, Kisnorbo 87	15,607
4	div1	Watford	H	W	4-1	Hume 15, Campbell 51, Sheehan 54 de Vries 85	21,642
5	div1	Plymouth	A	D	0-0		11,850
6	div1	QPR	H	D	1-1	Hume 63 pen	21,893
7	ccr2	Nottm Forest	A	W	3-2	Sheehan 31, Stearman 88, Clemence 90	15,519
8	div1	Charlton	A	L	0-2		21,918
9	ccr3	Aston Villa	A	W	1-0	Fryatt 76	25,956
10	div1	Stoke	H	D	1-1	Fryatt 47	23,654
11	div1	Wolverhampton	H	D	0-0		21,311
12	div1	Sheff Wed	A	W	2-0	McAuley 7, Kisnorbo 14	20,010
13	div1	Scunthorpe	A	D	0-0		6,006
14	div1	Sheff Utd	H	L	0-1		21,146
15	div1	Barnsley	H	W	2-0	John 22, Kisnorbo 30	24,133
16	ccr4	Chelsea	A	L	3-4	McAuley 6, Campbell 69, Cort 74	40,037
17	div1	Colchester	A	D	1-1	John 8	5,661
18	div1	Preston	A	D	1-1	Campbell 59	10,930
19	div1	Burnley	H	L	0-1		21,334
20	div1	Bristol City	A	W	2-0	Stearman 23, Fryatt 78	15,040
21	div1	Cardiff	H	D	0-0		27,246
22	div1	Southampton	H	L	1-2	King 45	20,070
23	div1	Burnley	A	D	1-1	Hume 78	10,688
24	div1	West Brom	H	L	1-2	Hume 75	22,088
25	div1	Ipswich	A	L	1-3	Hume 27	17,938
26	div1	Hull City	A	L	0-2		16,006
27	div1	Wolverhampton	A	D	1-1	Hume 4	23,477
28	div1	Ipswich	H	W	2-0	Stearman 12, Kisnorbo 33	24,049
29	div1	Charlton	H	D	1-1	Clemence 78	23,667
30	div1	QPR	A	L	1-3	Hume 59	13,326
31	facr3	Southampton	A	L	0-2		20,094
32	div1	Coventry	H	W	2-0	Howard 11, Hayles 85	23,905
33	div1	Norwich	A	D	0-0		25,462
34	div1	Crystal Palace	H	W	1-0	Hayles 89	21,764
35	div1	Blackpool	A	L	1-2	Howard 62	9,298
36	div1	Plymouth	H	L	0-1		21,264
37	div1	Watford	A	L	0-1		15,944
38	div1	Norwich	H	W	4-0	Hume 22, Howard 57, Campbell 77 Clemence 82	25,854
39	div1	Coventry	A	L	0-2		23,129
40	div1	Cardiff	A	W	1-0	Purse 27 og	13,355
41	div1	Preston	H	L	0-1		19,264
42	div1	Bristol City	H	D	0-0		22,616
43	div1	Southampton	A	L	0-1		17,741
44	div1	West Brom	A	W	4-1	McAuley 38, Howard 59 pen, 79, 86	22,038
45	div1	Hull City	H	L	0-2		30,374
46	div1	Scunthorpe	H	W	1-0	Hendrie 41	22,165
47	div1	Sheff Utd	A	L	0-3		24,818
48	div1	Colchester	H	D	1-1	Hume 89	22,719
49	div1	Barnsley	A	W	1-0	Hume 72	14,644
50	div1	Sheff Wed	H	L	1-3	Hume 9	31,892
51	div1	Stoke	A	D	0-0		26,609

LEAGUE APPEARANCES, BOOKINGS AND GOALS

	AGE (on 01/07/08)	IN NAMED 16	APPEARANCES	COUNTING GAMES	MINUTES ON PITCH	LEAGUE GOALS	Yellow	Red
Goalkeepers								
Ben Alnwick	21	11	8	8	720	0	1	0
Marton Fulop	25	24	24	24	2160	0	1	0
Paul Henderson	32	35	14	14	1260	0	1	0
Defenders								
James Chambers	27	33	25	12	1542	0	4	0
Jamie Clapham	32	12	11	11	963	0	0	0
Darren Kenton	29	17	10	5	601	0	0	0
Patrick Kisnorbo	27	42	41	38	3487	4	6	2
Joe Mattock	18	32	31	19	2058	0	4	0
Gareth McAuley	28	45	44	41	3753	2	7	0
Bruno N'Gotty	37	46	38	27	2787	0	0	0
Alan Sheehan	21	22	20	13	1426	1	7	0
Richard Stearman	20	40	39	34	3296	2	7	0
Midfielders								
David Bell	24	6	6	6	538	0	0	0
Gabor Bori	24	6	6	2	305	0	0	0
Stephen Clemence	30	32	31	28	2604	2	6	0
Jonathan Hayes	20	11	7	2	279	0	0	0
Lee Hendrie	31	9	9	8	757	1	3	0
Andy King	19	15	11	5	603	1	0	0
Radostin Kishishev	33	10	7	1	232	0	1	0
Zsolt Laczko	21	11	9	2	429	0	2	0
Shaun Newton	32	14	10	6	645	0	0	0
Matthew Oakley	30	20	20	19	1764	0	1	0
James Wesolowski	20	27	22	11	1292	0	2	0
Forwards								
Dudley Campbell	26	31	28	12	1508	4	2	0
Carl Cort	30	15	14	5	761	0	0	0
Mark de Vries	32	7	6	2	321	1	0	0
Matty Fryatt	22	37	30	19	1964	2	0	1
Barry Hayles	36	19	18	8	928	2	4	0
Steven Howard	32	21	21	20	1817	6	4	0
Iain Hume	24	40	40	30	2979	11	3	1
Collins John	22	11	11	3	567	2	1	0

TEAM OF THE SEASON

G – Marton Fulop – CG: 24 DR: 93

D – Alan Sheehan – CG: 13 DR: 109

D – Patrick Kisnorbo – CG: 38 DR: 99

D – Richard Stearman – CG: 34 DR: 99

D – Jamie Clapham – CG: 11* DR: 96

M – Lee Hendrie – CG: 8* SD: 18

M – James Wesolowski – CG: 11* SD: 16

M – Stephen Clemence – CG: 28 SD: -7

M – Matthew Oakley – CG: 19 SD: -12

F – Iain Hume – CG: 30 SR: 270

F – Steven Howard – CG: 20 SR: 302

MONTHLY POINTS TALLY

Month	Points	%
AUGUST	4	44%
SEPTEMBER	3	25%
OCTOBER	8	53%
NOVEMBER	6	40%
DECEMBER	6	25%
JANUARY	7	58%
FEBRUARY	3	20%
MARCH	10	48%
APRIL	4	33%
MAY	1	33%

LEAGUE GOALS

	PLAYER	MINS	GOALS	S RATE
1	Hume	2979	11	270
2	Howard	1817	6	302
3	Campbell	1508	4	377
4	Kisnorbo	3487	4	871
5	Fryatt	1964	2	982
6	Clemence	2604	2	1302
7	Stearman	3296	2	1648
8	McAuley	3753	2	1876
9	John	567	2	283
10	Hayles	928	2	464
11	Sheehan	1426	1	1426
12	de Vries	321	1	321
13	King	603	1	603
	Other		1	
	TOTAL		41	

TOP POINT EARNERS

	PLAYER	GAMES	AV PTS
1	Alan Sheehan	13	1.46
2	Matthew Oakley	19	1.32
3	Steven Howard	20	1.25
4	Iain Hume	31	1.23
5	Patrick Kisnorbo	40	1.23
6	Joe Mattock	19	1.21
7	Bruno N'Gotty	27	1.19
8	Richard Stearman	34	1.18
9	Matty Fryatt	19	1.16
10	Gareth McAuley	41	1.15
	CLUB AVERAGE:		1.13

DISCIPLINARY RECORDS

	PLAYER	YELLOW	RED	AVE
1	Alan Sheehan	7	0	203
2	Barry Hayles	4	0	232
3	Lee Hendrie	3	0	252
4	James Chambers	4	0	385
5	Stephen Clemence	6	0	434
6	Patrick Kisnorbo	6	2	435
7	Steven Howard	4	0	454
8	Richard Stearman	7	0	470
9	Joe Mattock	4	0	514
10	Gareth McAuley	7	0	536
11	Collins John	1	0	567
12	James Wesolowski	2	0	646
13	Ben Alnwick	1	0	720
	Other	8	2	
	TOTAL	64	4	

KEY GOALKEEPER

Marton Fulop

Goals Conceded in the League	23	Counting Games League games when player was on pitch for at least 70 minutes	24
Defensive Rating Ave number of mins between League goals conceded while on the pitch	93	Clean Sheets In League games when player was on pitch for at least 70 minutes	8

KEY PLAYERS - DEFENDERS

Alan Sheehan

Goals Conceded Number of League goals conceded while the player was on the pitch	13	Clean Sheets In League games when player was on pitch for at least 70 minutes	7
Defensive Rating Ave number of mins between League goals conceded while on the pitch	109	Club Defensive Rating Average number of mins between League goals conceded by the club this season	92

	PLAYER	CON LGE	CLEAN SHEETS	DEF RATE
1	Alan Sheehan	13	7	109 mins
2	Patrick Kisnorbo	35	14	99 mins
3	Richard Stearman	33	14	99 mins
4	Jamie Clapham	10	4	96 mins

KEY PLAYERS - MIDFIELDERS

Lee Hendrie

Goals in the League	1	Contribution to Attacking Power Average number of minutes between League team goals while on pitch	108
Defensive Rating Average number of mins between League goals conceded while on the pitch	126	Scoring Difference Defensive Rating minus Contribution to Attacking Power	18

	PLAYER	LGE GOALS	DEF RATE	POWER	SCORE DIFF
1	Lee Hendrie	1	126	108	18 mins
2	James Wesolowski	0	92	76	16 mins
3	Stephen Clemence	2	86	93	-7 mins
4	Matthew Oakley	0	98	110	-12 mins

KEY PLAYERS - GOALSCORERS

Iain Hume

Goals in the League	11	Player Strike Rate Average number of minutes between League goals scored by player	270
Contribution to Attacking Power Average number of minutes between League team goals while on pitch	90	Club Strike Rate Average number of minutes between League goals scored by club	98

	PLAYER	LGE GOALS	POWER	STRIKE RATE
1	Iain Hume	11	90	270 mins
2	Steven Howard	6	106	302 mins
3	Dudley Campbell	4	94	377 mins
4	Barry Hayles	2	92	464 mins

Topps
Tiles
Iain Hume

SQUAD APPEARANCES

Match	1	2	3	4	5	6	7	8	9	10	11	12	13	14	15	16	17	18	19	20	21	22	23	24	25	26	27	28	29	30	31	32	33	34	35	36	37	38	39	40	41	42	43	44	45	46	47	48	49	50	51
Venue	H	A	A	H	A	H	A	A	A	H	H	A	A	H	H	A	A	A	H	A	H	H	A	H	A	A	A	H	H	A	A	H	A	H	A	H	A	H	A	A	H	H	A	A	H	H	A	H	A	H	A
Competition	L	W	L	L	L	L	W	L	W	L	L	L	L	L	L	W	L	L	L	L	L	L	L	L	L	L	L	L	L	L	F	L	L	L	L	L	L	L	L	L	L	L	L	L	L	L	L	L	L	L	L
Result	L	W	D	W	D	D	W	L	W	D	D	W	D	L	W	L	D	D	L	W	D	L	D	L	L	L	D	W	D	L	L	W	D	W	L	L	L	W	L	W	L	D	L	W	L	W	L	D	W	L	D

Goalkeepers
Ben Alnwick
Marton Fulop
Paul Henderson
Defenders
James Chambers
Jamie Clapham
Darren Kenton
Patrick Kisnorbo
Joe Mattock
Gareth McAuley
Bruno N'Gotty
Alan Sheehan
Richard Stearman
Midfielders
David Bell
Gabor Bori
Stephen Clemence
Jonathan Hayes
Lee Hendrie
Andy King
Radostin Kishishev
Shaun Newton
Matthew Oakley
James Wesolowski
Forwards
Dudley Campbell
Carl Cort
Mark de Vries
Matty Fryatt
Barry Hayles
Steven Howard
Iain Hume
Collins John

KEY: On all match | On bench | Subbed or sent off (Counting game) | Subbed or sent off (playing less than 70 minutes) | Subbed on from bench (Counting Game) | Subbed on (playing less than 70 minutes) | Subbed on and then subbed or sent off (Counting Game) | Subbed on and then subbed or sent off (playing less than 70 minutes) | Not in 16

SCUNTHORPE UNITED

Final Position: **23rd**

NICKNAME: THE IRON

KEY: ☐ Won ☐ Drawn ☐ Lost

	Comp	Opponent	H/A	Res	Score	Scorers	Attendance
1	div1	Charlton	A	D	1-1	Iriekpen 69	23,151
2	ccr1	Hartlepool	H	L	1-2	Paterson 51	2,965
3	div1	Burnley	H	W	2-0	Paterson 47, Goodwin 64	6,975
4	div1	Bristol City	A	L	1-2	Paterson 44	12,474
5	div1	Sheff Utd	H	W	3-2	Crosby 37, Paterson 61, Sparrow 90	8,801
6	div1	Barnsley	A	L	0-2		11,230
7	div1	Preston	H	W	2-1	Crosby 24, Hayes 49	5,754
8	div1	West Brom	H	L	2-3	Crosby 16 pen, Paterson 90	8,307
9	div1	Colchester	A	W	1-0	Hayes 41	5,218
10	div1	Norwich	A	D	0-0		23,176
11	div1	Watford	H	L	1-3	Forte 20	7,515
12	div1	Leicester	H	D	0-0		6,006
13	div1	Sheff Wed	A	W	2-1	Paterson 24, 40	21,557
14	div1	Cardiff	A	D	1-1	Goodwin 55	11,850
15	div1	Crystal Palace	H	D	0-0		6,778
16	div1	Stoke	H	L	2-3	Hayes 31, Goodwin 85	5,521
17	div1	Blackpool	A	L	0-1		8,051
18	div1	Hull City	H	L	1-2	Forte 45	8,633
19	div1	Coventry	A	D	1-1	Cork 68	14,036
20	div1	Plymouth	A	L	0-3		10,520
21	div1	Blackpool	H	D	1-1	Butler 19	4,407
22	div1	QPR	H	D	2-2	Paterson 24, Forte 55	5,612
23	div1	Ipswich	A	L	2-3	Paterson 16, 33	19,306
24	div1	Norwich	H	L	0-1		6,648
25	div1	Preston	A	W	1-0	Paterson 43	12,920
26	div1	West Brom	A	L	0-5		25,238
27	div1	Barnsley	H	D	2-2	Morris 45, Youga 47	6,897
28	facr3	Preston	A	L	0-1		4,616
29	div1	Southampton	A	L	0-1		18,146
30	div1	Wolverhampton	H	L	0-2		7,465
31	div1	Burnley	A	L	0-2		14,516
32	div1	Charlton	H	W	1-0	Paterson 63	6,084
33	div1	Sheff Utd	A	D	0-0		25,668
34	div1	Bristol City	H	L	0-1		5,423
35	div1	Stoke	A	L	2-3	Paterson 7, Hobbs 23	20,979
36	div1	Southampton	H	D	1-1	Crosby 41	6,035
37	div1	Coventry	H	W	2-1	Paterson 15, Cork 66	5,866
38	div1	Hull City	A	L	0-2		20,906
39	div1	Plymouth	H	W	1-0	Morris 55	4,920
40	div1	QPR	A	L	1-3	McCann 8	14,499
41	div1	Wolverhampton	A	L	1-2	Butler 5	21,628
42	div1	Ipswich	H	L	1-2	May 90	6,636
43	div1	Leicester	A	L	0-1		22,165
44	div1	Sheff Wed	H	D	1-1	Morris 18	7,245
45	div1	Crystal Palace	A	L	0-2		15,975
46	div1	Cardiff	H	W	3-2	Hayes 53, 90 pen, Hurst 56	4,727
47	div1	Watford	A	W	1-0	Hayes 69	16,454
48	div1	Colchester	H	D	3-3	Forte 15, Hayes 67, 82	5,554

LEAGUE APPEARANCES, BOOKINGS AND GOALS

	AGE (on 01/07/08)	IN NAMED 16	APPEARANCES	COUNTING GAMES	MINUTES ON PITCH	LEAGUE GOALS	Yellow	Red
Goalkeepers								
Josh Lillis	21	45	4	1	214	0	1	0
Joe Murphy	27	45	45	42	3926	0	2	1
Defenders								
Andy Butler	24	39	36	34	3128	2	7	1
Clifford Byrne	26	25	25	21	2060	0	8	2
Andrew Crosby	35	38	38	36	3310	4	5	0
Jack Hobbs	19	16	9	6	666	1	0	0
Ezomo Iriekpen	26	21	17	11	1160	1	1	0
Shaleum Logan	19	5	4	3	315	0	0	0
Shelton Martis	25	3	3	3	270	0	0	0
Mamadou Seck	28	2	1	0	1	0	0	0
Marcus Williams	22	34	34	27	2606	0	2	1
Kelly Youga	22	20	19	18	1624	1	3	2
Midfielders								
Ian Baraclough	37	28	17	13	1387	0	2	0
Jack Cork	19	40	34	31	2851	2	0	1
James Goodwin	26	40	40	38	3495	3	9	0
Kevin Horlock	35	1	0	0	0	0	0	0
Kevan Hurst	22	37	33	25	2513	1	2	0
Grant McCann	28	14	14	9	959	1	0	1
Matthew Sparrow	24	32	32	22	2287	1	7	1
Cleveland Taylor	24	24	20	9	1073	0	1	0
Curtis Weston	21	8	7	0	227	0	0	0
Andrew Wright	23	3	2	0	3	0	0	0
Forwards								
Tommy Ameobi	19	11	9	1	186	0	0	0
Jonathan Forte	21	40	38	16	1916	4	2	0
Paul Hayes	24	45	40	26	2721	8	2	0
Geoff Horsfield	34	12	12	9	892	0	3	0
Ben May	24	25	21	5	678	1	0	0
Ian Morris	21	30	25	20	1810	3	2	0
Martin Paterson	21	40	40	29	2934	13	4	0
Peter Winn	19	4	4	0	34	0	0	0

TEAM OF THE SEASON

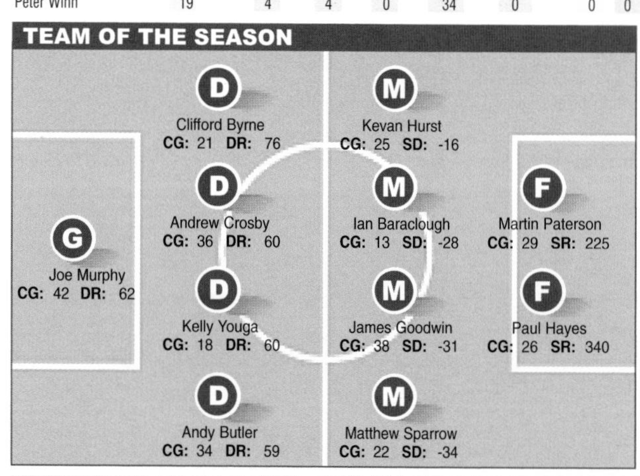

D
Clifford Byrne
CG: 21 DR: 76
M
Kevan Hurst
CG: 25 SD: -16
D
Andrew Crosby
CG: 36 DR: 60
M
Ian Baraclough
CG: 13 SD: -28
F
Martin Paterson
CG: 29 SR: 225
G
Joe Murphy
CG: 42 DR: 62
D
Kelly Youga
CG: 18 DR: 60
M
James Goodwin
CG: 38 SD: -31
F
Paul Hayes
CG: 26 SR: 340
D
Andy Butler
CG: 34 DR: 59
M
Matthew Sparrow
CG: 22 SD: -34

MONTHLY POINTS TALLY

Month	Points	%
AUGUST	4	44%
SEPTEMBER	9	60%
OCTOBER	6	40%
NOVEMBER	2	13%
DECEMBER	5	24%
JANUARY	1	8%
FEBRUARY	5	33%
MARCH	6	29%
APRIL	7	58%
MAY	1	33%

LEAGUE GOALS

	PLAYER	MINS	GOALS	S RATE
1	Paterson	2934	13	225
2	Hayes	2721	8	340
3	Forte	1916	4	479
4	Crosby	3310	4	827
5	Morris	1810	3	603
6	Goodwin	3495	3	1165
7	Cork	2851	2	1425
8	Butler	3128	2	1564
9	Hobbs	666	1	666
10	May	678	1	678
11	McCann	959	1	959
12	Iriekpen	1160	1	1160
13	Youga	1624	1	1624
	Other		2	
	TOTAL		46	

TOP POINT EARNERS

	PLAYER	GAMES	AV PTS
1	Clifford Byrne	21	1.52
2	Ian Baraclough	13	1.31
3	Paul Hayes	26	1.23
4	Kevan Hurst	25	1.16
5	Jonathan Forte	16	1.06
6	Kelly Youga	18	1.06
7	Joe Murphy	43	1.05
8	James Goodwin	38	1.03
9	Andy Butler	34	1.00
10	Martin Paterson	29	0.97
	CLUB AVERAGE:		1.00

DISCIPLINARY RECORDS

	PLAYER	YELLOW	RED	AVE
1	Clifford Byrne	8	2	206
2	Matthew Sparrow	7	1	285
3	Geoff Horsfield	3	0	297
4	Kelly Youga	3	2	324
5	James Goodwin	9	0	388
6	Andy Butler	7	1	391
7	Andrew Crosby	5	0	662
8	Ian Baraclough	2	0	693
9	Martin Paterson	4	0	733
10	Marcus Williams	2	1	868
11	Ian Morris	2	0	905
12	Jonathan Forte	2	0	958
13	Grant McCann	0	1	959
	Other	8	2	
	TOTAL	62	10	

KEY GOALKEEPER

Joe Murphy

Goals Conceded in the League	63	Counting Games League games when player was on pitch for at least 70 minutes	42
Defensive Rating Ave number of mins between League goals conceded while on the pitch	62	Clean Sheets In League games when player was on pitch for at least 70 minutes	10

KEY PLAYERS - DEFENDERS

Clifford Byrne

Goals Conceded Number of League goals conceded while the player was on the pitch	27	Clean Sheets In League games when player was on pitch for at least 70 minutes	6
Defensive Rating Ave number of mins between League goals conceded while on the pitch	76	Club Defensive Rating Average number of mins between League goals conceded by the club this season	61

	PLAYER	CON LGE	CLEAN SHEETS	DEF RATE
1	Clifford Byrne	27	6	76 mins
2	Andrew Crosby	55	7	60 mins
3	Kelly Youga	27	5	60 mins
4	Andy Butler	53	7	59 mins

KEY PLAYERS - MIDFIELDERS

Kevan Hurst

Goals in the League	1	Contribution to Attacking Power Average number of minutes between League team goals while on pitch	83
Defensive Rating Average number of mins between League goals conceded while on the pitch	67	Scoring Difference Defensive Rating minus Contribution to Attacking Power	-16

	PLAYER	LGE GOALS	DEF RATE	POWER	SCORE DIFF
1	Kevan Hurst	1	67	83	-16 mins
2	Ian Baraclough	0	53	81	-28 mins
3	James Goodwin	3	63	94	-31 mins
4	Matthew Sparrow	1	57	91	-34 mins

KEY PLAYERS - GOALSCORERS

Martin Paterson

Goals in the League	13	Player Strike Rate Average number of minutes between League goals scored by player	225
Contribution to Attacking Power Average number of minutes between League team goals while on pitch	86	Club Strike Rate Average number of minutes between League goals scored by club	91

	PLAYER	LGE GOALS	POWER	STRIKE RATE
1	Martin Paterson	13	86	225 mins
2	Paul Hayes	8	82	340 mins
3	Jonathan Forte	4	100	479 mins
4	Ian Morris	3	90	603 mins

RAINHAM
STEEL
Martin Paterson

SQUAD APPEARANCES

Match	1	2	3	4	5	6	7	8	9	10	11	12	13	14	15	16	17	18	19	20	21	22	23	24
Venue	A	H	H	A	H	A	H	H	A	A	H	H	A	A	H	H	A	H	A	A	H	H	A	H
Competition	L	W	L	L	L	L	L	L	L	L	L	L	L	L	L	L	L	L	L	L	L	L	L	L
Result	D	L	W	L	W	L	W	L	W	D	L	D	W	D	D	L	L	L	D	L	D	D	L	L

Match	25	26	27	28	29	30	31	32	33	34	35	36	37	38	39	40	41	42	43	44	45	46	47	48
Venue	A	A	H	A	A	H	A	H	A	H	A	H	H	A	H	A	A	H	A	H	A	H	A	H
Competition	L	L	L	F	L	L	L	L	L	L	L	L	L	L	L	L	L	L	L	L	L	L	L	L
Result	W	L	D	L	L	L	L	W	D	L	L	D	W	L	W	L	L	L	L	D	L	W	W	D

Goalkeepers
Josh Lillis
Joe Murphy

Defenders
Andy Butler
Clifford Byrne
Andrew Crosby
Jack Hobbs
Ezomo Iriekpen
Shaleum Logan
Shelton Martis
Mamadou Seck
Marcus Williams
Kelly Youga

Midfielders
Ian Baraclough
Jack Cork
James Goodwin
Kevin Horlock
Kevan Hurst
Grant McCann
Matthew Sparrow
Cleveland Taylor
Curtis Weston
Andrew Wright

Forwards
Tommy Ameobi
Jonathan Forte
Paul Hayes
Geoff Horsfield
Ben May
Ian Morris
Martin Paterson
Peter Winn

KEY: On all match | On bench | Subbed or sent off (Counting game) | Subbed or sent off (playing less than 70 minutes) | Subbed on from bench (Counting Game) | Subbed on (playing less than 70 minutes) | Subbed on and then subbed or sent off (Counting Game) | Subbed on and then subbed or sent off (playing less than 70 minutes) | Not in 16

COLCHESTER UNITED

Final Position: **24th**

NICKNAME: THE U'S

KEY: ☐Won ☐Drawn ☐Lost

							Attendance
1	div1	Sheff Utd	A	D	2-2	McLeod 68, Platt 89	26,202
2	ccr1	Shrewsbury	A	L	0-1		3,069
3	div1	Barnsley	H	D	2-2	Sheringham 45, Connolly 48	4,450
4	div1	Preston	A	W	3-0	Lisbie 41, Sheringham 61 pen, Yeates 72	11,582
5	div1	Burnley	H	L	2-3	Lisbie 45, Virgo 88	4,925
6	div1	Charlton	H	D	2-2	Yeates 32, Lisbie 38	5,860
7	div1	Southampton	A	D	1-1	Skacel 58 og	18,773
8	div1	Blackpool	A	D	2-2	Yeates 63, 86	7,959
9	div1	Scunthorpe	H	L	0-1		5,218
10	div1	QPR	H	W	4-2	Leigertwood 19 og, Izzet 30, Yeates 38 Platt 63	5,361
11	div1	Stoke	A	L	1-2	Platt 58	12,395
12	div1	West Brom	H	W	3-2	Yeates 8, 68 pen, Lisbie 19	5,798
13	div1	Ipswich	A	L	1-3	Platt 31	25,727
14	div1	Coventry	A	L	0-1		23,431
15	div1	Leicester	H	D	1-1	Jackson 45	5,661
16	div1	Plymouth	H	D	1-1	Lisbie 56	4,833
17	div1	Watford	A	D	2-2	Platt 20, Lisbie 46	16,069
18	div1	Crystal Palace	H	L	1-2	Jackson 69	5,856
19	div1	Wolverhampton	A	L	0-1		20,966
20	div1	Sheff Wed	A	W	2-1	Sheringham 1, Elokobi 26	22,331
21	div1	Watford	H	L	2-3	Platt 7, Connolly 28	5,760
22	div1	Cardiff	A	L	1-4	Jackson 45	11,006
23	div1	Norwich	H	D	1-1	McLeod 78	5,560
24	div1	QPR	A	L	1-2	Yeates 62	12,464
25	div1	Southampton	H	D	1-1	Platt 47	6,157
26	div1	Blackpool	H	L	0-2		5,160
27	div1	Charlton	A	W	2-1	Lisbie 16 pen, 29	21,508
28	facr3	Peterborough	H	L	1-3	Sheringham 43 pen	4,003
29	div1	Bristol City	A	D	1-1	Lisbie 6	16,484
30	div1	Barnsley	A	L	0-1		9,246
31	div1	Sheff Utd	H	D	2-2	Lisbie 46, Armstrong 64 og	5,695
32	div1	Burnley	A	D	1-1	Jackson 38	15,376
33	div1	Preston	H	W	2-1	Vernon 69 pen, Jackson 88	5,122
34	div1	Hull City	A	D	1-1	Jackson 47	15,664
35	div1	Bristol City	H	L	1-2	Platt 50	5,609
36	div1	Wolverhampton	H	L	0-1		5,989
37	div1	Plymouth	A	L	1-4	Lisbie 64	11,562
38	div1	Crystal Palace	A	L	1-2	Lisbie 23	13,895
39	div1	Sheff Wed	H	L	1-2	Lisbie 4	5,086
40	div1	Cardiff	H	D	1-1	Jackson 71	4,699
41	div1	Hull City	H	L	1-3	Lisbie 37	5,497
42	div1	Norwich	A	L	1-5	Lisbie 41	25,215
43	div1	West Brom	A	L	3-4	Coyne 14, Elito 17, Lisbie 76	20,433
44	div1	Ipswich	H	W	2-0	Vernon 29, 73	6,264
45	div1	Leicester	A	D	1-1	Lisbie 76	22,719
46	div1	Coventry	H	L	1-5	Vernon 17	5,836
47	div1	Stoke	H	L	0-1		6,300
48	div1	Scunthorpe	A	D	3-3	K.McLeod 11, 48, Vernon 47	5,554

LEAGUE APPEARANCES, BOOKINGS AND GOALS

	AGE (on 01/07/08)	IN NAMED 16	APPEARANCES	COUNTING GAMES	MINUTES ON PITCH	LEAGUE GOALS	Yellow	Red
Goalkeepers								
Mark Cousins	21	30	2	0	73	0	0	0
Aidan Davison	40	9	6	6	540	0	0	0
Dean Gerken	22	45	40	39	3526	0	1	1
Defenders								
Pat Baldwin	25	27	26	21	1967	0	2	1
Bela Balogh	23	29	16	8	980	0	3	0
Matthew Connolly	20	20	16	12	1259	2	1	1
Chris Coyne	29	17	17	15	1418	1	2	0
George Elokobi	22	20	17	17	1526	1	1	0
Danny Granville	33	27	19	13	1305	0	2	0
Matt Heath	27	5	5	5	450	0	2	0
Philip Ifil	21	20	20	18	1687	0	2	1
Adam Virgo	25	40	36	28	2694	1	6	0
John White	21	24	21	19	1754	0	1	0
Midfielders								
Karl Duguid	30	38	37	34	3159	0	3	0
Medy Elito	17	14	11	5	610	1	0	0
Luke Guttridge	26	24	14	5	624	0	2	0
Dean Hammond	25	13	13	11	1057	0	0	0
Kemal Izzet	27	43	39	31	3004	1	8	0
Johnnie Jackson	25	46	46	46	4140	7	4	0
Kevin McLeod	27	33	28	15	1843	4	3	0
Kevin Watson	34	17	7	5	568	0	0	0
Anthony Wordsworth	19	9	3	0	86	0	0	0
Mark Yeates	23	29	29	26	2479	8	4	0
Forwards								
Jamie Guy	20	20	11	0	200	0	2	0
Kevin Lisbie	29	42	42	35	3299	17	5	0
Izale McLeod	23	2	2	0	64	0	0	0
Clive Platt	30	42	41	32	3095	8	3	0
Teddy Sheringham	42	25	19	9	1006	3	0	1
Scott Vernon	24	18	17	5	864	5	0	0

TEAM OF THE SEASON

G: Dean Gerken — CG: 39 DR: 47

D: Danny Granville — CG: 13 DR: 54

D: Pat Baldwin — CG: 21 DR: 54

D: Matthew Connolly — CG: 12 DR: 52

D: John White — CG: 19 DR: 51

M: Mark Yeates — CG: 26 SD: -8

M: Karl Duguid — CG: 34 SD: -13

M: Johnnie Jackson — CG: 46 SD: -18

M: Kemal Izzet — CG: 31 SD: -19

F: Kevin Lisbie — CG: 35 SR: 194

F: Clive Platt — CG: 32 SR: 386

MONTHLY POINTS TALLY

Month	Points	%
AUGUST	5	56%
SEPTEMBER	3	20%
OCTOBER	6	40%
NOVEMBER	3	20%
DECEMBER	5	24%
JANUARY	4	44%
FEBRUARY	6	40%
MARCH	1	4%
APRIL	4	33%
MAY	1	33%

LEAGUE GOALS

	PLAYER	MINS	GOALS	S RATE
1	Lisbie	3299	17	194
2	Yeates	2479	8	309
3	Platt	3095	8	386
4	Jackson	4140	7	591
5	Vernon	864	5	172
6	Sheringham	1006	3	335
7	McLeod, K	1843	4	460
8	Connolly	1259	2	629
9	Elito	610	1	610
10	Coyne	1418	1	1418
11	Elokobi	1526	1	1526
12	Virgo	2694	1	2694
13	Izzet	3004	1	3004
	Other		0	
	TOTAL		59	

TOP POINT EARNERS

	PLAYER	GAMES	AV PTS
1	George Elokobi	17	1.18
2	Pat Baldwin	21	1.00
3	Kevin McLeod	15	1.00
4	John White	19	1.00
5	Mark Yeates	26	0.96
6	Kemal Izzet	31	0.90
7	Karl Duguid	34	0.88
8	Danny Granville	13	0.85
9	Johnnie Jackson	46	0.83
10	Kevin Lisbie	35	0.80
	CLUB AVERAGE:		0.83

DISCIPLINARY RECORDS

	PLAYER	YELLOW	RED	AVE
1	Luke Guttridge	2	0	312
2	Bela Balogh	3	0	326
3	Kemal Izzet	8	0	375
4	Adam Virgo	6	0	449
5	Philip Ifil	2	1	562
6	Kevin McLeod	3	0	614
7	Mark Yeates	4	0	619
8	Matthew Connolly	1	1	629
9	Danny Granville	2	0	652
10	Pat Baldwin	2	1	655
11	Kevin Lisbie	5	0	659
12	Chris Coyne	2	0	709
13	Teddy Sheringham	0	1	1006
	Other	13	1	
	TOTAL	53	5	

KEY GOALKEEPER

Dean Gerken

Goals Conceded in the League	75	Counting Games League games when player was on pitch for at least 70 minutes	39
Defensive Rating Ave number of mins between League goals conceded while on the pitch	47	Clean Sheets In League games when player was on pitch for at least 70 minutes	1

KEY PLAYERS - DEFENDERS

Danny Granville

Goals Conceded Number of League goals conceded while the player was on the pitch	24	Clean Sheets In League games when player was on pitch for at least 70 minutes	0
Defensive Rating Ave number of mins between League goals conceded while on the pitch	54	Club Defensive Rating Average number of mins between League goals conceded by the club this season	49

	PLAYER	CON LGE	CLEAN SHEETS	DEF RATE
1	Danny Granville	24	0	54 mins
2	Pat Baldwin	36	1	54 mins
3	Matthew Connolly	24	1	52 mins
4	John White	34	2	51 mins

KEY PLAYERS - MIDFIELDERS

Mark Yeates

Goals in the League	8	Contribution to Attacking Power Average number of minutes between League team goals while on pitch	63
Defensive Rating Average number of mins between League goals conceded while on the pitch	55	Scoring Difference Defensive Rating minus Contribution to Attacking Power	-8

	PLAYER	LGE GOALS	DEF RATE	POWER	SCORE DIFF
1	Mark Yeates	8	55	63	-8 mins
2	Karl Duguid	0	50	63	-13 mins
3	Johnnie Jackson	7	48	66	-18 mins
4	Kemal Izzet	1	47	66	-19 mins

KEY PLAYERS - GOALSCORERS

Kevin Lisbie

Goals in the League	17	Player Strike Rate Average number of minutes between League goals scored by player	194
Contribution to Attacking Power Average number of minutes between League team goals while on pitch	67	Club Strike Rate Average number of minutes between League goals scored by club	68

	PLAYER	LGE GOALS	POWER	STRIKE RATE
1	Kevin Lisbie	17	67	194 mins
2	Mark Yeates	8	63	309 mins
3	Clive Platt	8	71	386 mins
4	Kevin McLeod	4	65	460 mins

SMART energy
Kevin Lisbie

SQUAD APPEARANCES

Match	1	2	3	4	5	6	7	8	9	10	11	12	13	14	15	16	17	18	19	20	21	22	23	24
Venue	A	A	H	A	H	H	A	A	H	H	A	H	A	A	H	H	A	H	A	A	H	A	H	A
Competition	L	W	L	L	L	L	L	L	L	L	L	L	L	L	L	L	L	L	L	L	L	L	L	L
Result	D	L	D	W	L	D	D	D	L	W	L	W	L	L	D	D	D	L	L	W	L	L	D	L

Match	25	26	27	28	29	30	31	32	33	34	35	36	37	38	39	40	41	42	43	44	45	46	47	48
Venue	H	H	A	H	A	A	H	A	H	A	H	H	A	A	H	H	H	A	A	H	A	H	H	A
Competition	L	L	L	F	L	L	L	L	L	L	L	L	L	L	L	L	L	L	L	L	L	L	L	L
Result	D	L	W	L	D	L	D	D	W	D	L	L	L	L	L	D	L	L	L	W	D	L	L	D

Goalkeepers
Mark Cousins
Aidan Davison
Dean Gerken

Defenders
Pat Baldwin
Bela Balogh
Matthew Connolly
Chris Coyne
George Elokobi
Danny Granville
Matt Heath
Philip Ifil
Adam Virgo
John White

Midfielders
Karl Duguid
Medy Elito
Luke Guttridge
Dean Hammond
Kemal Izzet
Johnnie Jackson
Kevin McLeod
Kevin Watson
Anthony Wordsworth
Mark Yeates

Forwards
Jamie Guy
Kevin Lisbie
Izale McLeod
Clive Platt
Teddy Sheringham
Scott Vernon

KEY: On all match
On bench
Subbed or sent off (Counting game)
Subbed or sent off (playing less than 70 minutes)
Subbed on from bench (Counting Game)
Subbed on (playing less than 70 minutes)
Subbed on and then subbed or sent off (Counting Game)
Subbed on and then subbed or sent off (playing less than 70 minutes)
Not in 16

LEAGUE ONE ROUND-UP

FINAL LEAGUE TABLE

		HOME					AWAY					TOTAL			
	P	W	D	L	F	A	W	D	L	F	A	F	A	DIF	PTS
Swansea	46	13	5	5	38	21	14	6	3	44	21	82	42	40	92
Nottm Forest	46	13	8	2	37	13	9	8	6	27	19	64	32	32	82
Doncaster	46	14	4	5	34	18	9	7	7	31	23	65	41	24	80
Carlisle	46	17	3	3	39	16	6	8	9	25	30	64	46	18	80
Leeds	46	15	4	4	41	18	12	6	5	31	20	72	38	34	76
Southend	46	12	6	5	35	20	10	4	9	35	35	70	55	15	76
Brighton	46	12	6	5	37	25	7	6	10	21	25	58	50	8	69
Oldham	46	10	7	6	32	21	8	6	9	26	25	58	46	12	67
Northampton	46	12	6	5	38	21	5	9	9	22	34	60	55	5	66
Huddersfield	46	12	4	7	29	22	8	2	13	21	40	50	62	-12	66
Tranmere	46	13	4	6	32	18	5	7	11	20	29	52	47	5	65
Walsall	46	7	9	7	27	26	9	7	7	25	20	52	46	6	64
Swindon	46	12	5	6	41	24	4	8	11	22	32	63	56	7	61
Leyton Orient	46	9	6	8	27	29	7	6	10	22	34	49	63	-14	60
Hartlepool	46	11	5	7	40	26	4	4	15	23	40	63	66	-3	54
Bristol Rovers	46	5	10	8	25	30	7	7	9	20	23	45	53	-8	53
Millwall	46	9	4	10	30	26	5	6	12	15	34	45	60	-15	52
Yeovil	46	9	4	10	19	27	5	6	12	19	32	38	59	-21	52
Cheltenham	46	10	8	5	23	21	3	4	16	19	43	42	64	-22	51
Crewe	46	8	6	9	27	33	4	8	11	20	32	47	65	-18	50
Bournemouth	46	10	4	9	31	35	7	3	13	31	37	62	72	-10	48
Gillingham	46	9	9	5	26	22	2	4	17	18	51	44	73	-29	46
Port Vale	46	5	8	10	26	35	4	3	16	21	46	47	81	-34	38
Luton	46	10	5	8	29	25	1	5	17	14	38	43	63	-20	33

CLUB STRIKE FORCE

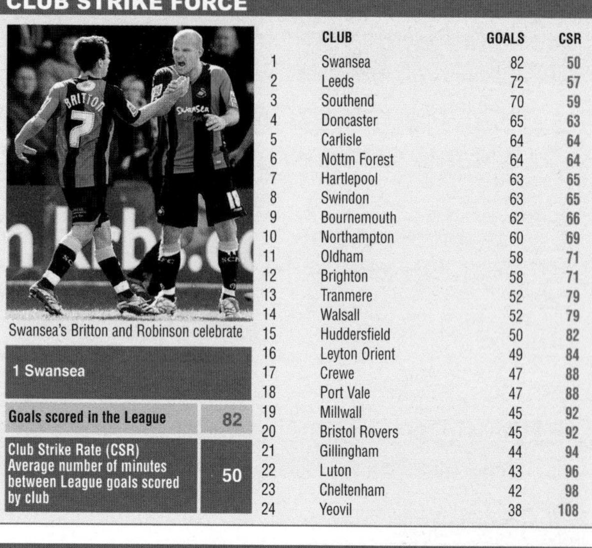

Swansea's Britton and Robinson celebrate

1 Swansea

Goals scored in the League	82
Club Strike Rate (CSR) Average number of minutes between League goals scored by club	50

	CLUB	GOALS	CSR
1	Swansea	82	50
2	Leeds	72	57
3	Southend	70	59
4	Doncaster	65	63
5	Carlisle	64	64
6	Nottm Forest	64	64
7	Hartlepool	63	65
8	Swindon	63	65
9	Bournemouth	62	66
10	Northampton	60	69
11	Oldham	58	71
12	Brighton	58	71
13	Tranmere	52	79
14	Walsall	52	79
15	Huddersfield	50	82
16	Leyton Orient	49	84
17	Crewe	47	88
18	Port Vale	47	88
19	Millwall	45	92
20	Bristol Rovers	45	92
21	Gillingham	44	94
22	Luton	43	96
23	Cheltenham	42	98
24	Yeovil	38	108

CLUB DISCIPLINARY RECORDS

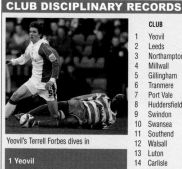

Yeovil's Terrell Forbes dives in

1 Yeovil

League Yellow	77
League Red	6
League Total	83
Cards Average in League Average number of minutes between a card being shown of either colour	49

	CLUB	Y	R	TOTAL	AVE
1	Yeovil	77	6	83	49
2	Leeds	78	4	82	50
3	Northampton	78	1	79	52
4	Millwall	71	5	76	54
5	Gillingham	67	8	75	55
6	Tranmere	67	6	73	56
7	Port Vale	67	5	72	57
8	Huddersfield	64	7	71	58
9	Swindon	62	8	70	59
10	Swansea	64	5	69	60
11	Southend	60	7	67	61
12	Walsall	63	3	66	62
13	Luton	59	6	65	63
14	Carlisle	62	2	64	64
15	Brighton	59	4	63	65
16	Bournemouth	60	2	62	66
17	Oldham	59	2	61	67
18	Nottm Forest	55	4	59	70
19	Doncaster	53	3	56	73
20	Bristol Rovers	53	2	55	75
21	Hartlepool	51	4	55	75
22	Leyton Orient	46	2	48	86
23	Cheltenham	44	4	48	86
24	Crewe	25	1	26	159

CLUB DEFENCES

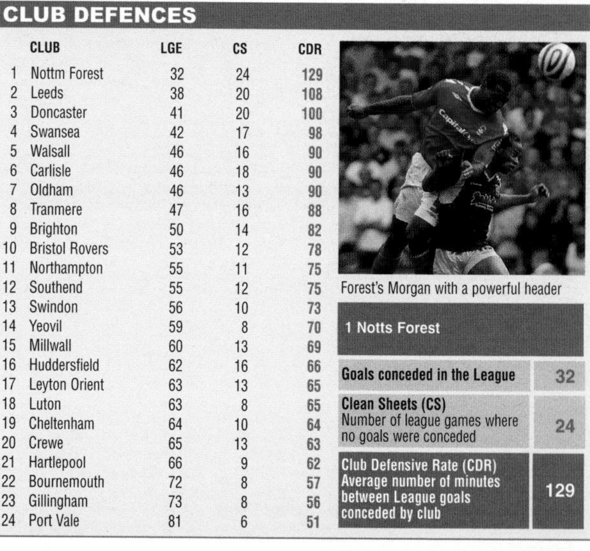

	CLUB	LGE	CS	CDR
1	Nottm Forest	32	24	129
2	Leeds	38	20	108
3	Doncaster	41	20	100
4	Swansea	42	17	98
5	Walsall	46	16	90
6	Carlisle	46	18	90
7	Oldham	46	13	90
8	Tranmere	47	16	88
9	Brighton	50	14	82
10	Bristol Rovers	53	12	78
11	Northampton	55	11	75
12	Southend	55	12	75
13	Swindon	56	10	73
14	Yeovil	59	8	70
15	Millwall	60	13	69
16	Huddersfield	62	16	66
17	Leyton Orient	63	13	65
18	Luton	63	8	65
19	Cheltenham	64	10	64
20	Crewe	65	13	63
21	Hartlepool	66	9	62
22	Bournemouth	72	8	57
23	Gillingham	73	8	56
24	Port Vale	81	6	51

Forest's Morgan with a powerful header

1 Notts Forest

Goals conceded in the League	32
Clean Sheets (CS) Number of league games where no goals were conceded	24
Club Defensive Rate (CDR) Average number of minutes between League goals conceded by club	129

STADIUM CAPACITY AND HOME CROWDS

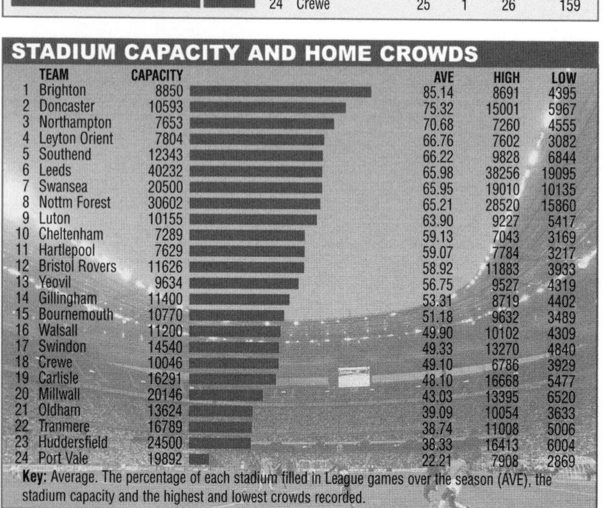

	TEAM	CAPACITY	AVE	HIGH	LOW
1	Brighton	8850	85.14	8691	4395
2	Doncaster	10593	75.32	15001	5967
3	Northampton	7653	70.68	7260	4555
4	Leyton Orient	7804	66.76	7602	3082
5	Southend	12343	66.22	9828	6844
6	Leeds	40232	65.98	38256	19095
7	Swansea	20500	65.95	19010	10135
8	Nottm Forest	30602	65.21	28520	15860
9	Luton	10155	63.90	9227	5417
10	Cheltenham	7289	59.13	7043	3169
11	Hartlepool	7629	59.07	7784	3217
12	Bristol Rovers	11626	58.92	11883	3933
13	Yeovil	9634	56.75	9527	4319
14	Gillingham	11400	53.31	8719	4402
15	Bournemouth	10770	51.18	9632	3489
16	Walsall	11200	49.90	10102	4309
17	Swindon	14540	49.33	13270	4840
18	Crewe	10046	49.10	6786	3929
19	Carlisle	16291	48.10	16668	5477
20	Millwall	20146	43.03	13395	6520
21	Oldham	13624	39.09	10054	3633
22	Tranmere	16789	38.74	11008	5006
23	Huddersfield	24500	38.33	16413	6004
24	Port Vale	19892	22.21	7908	2869

Key: Average. The percentage of each stadium filled in League games over the season (AVE), the stadium capacity and the highest and lowest crowds recorded.

AWAY ATTENDANCE

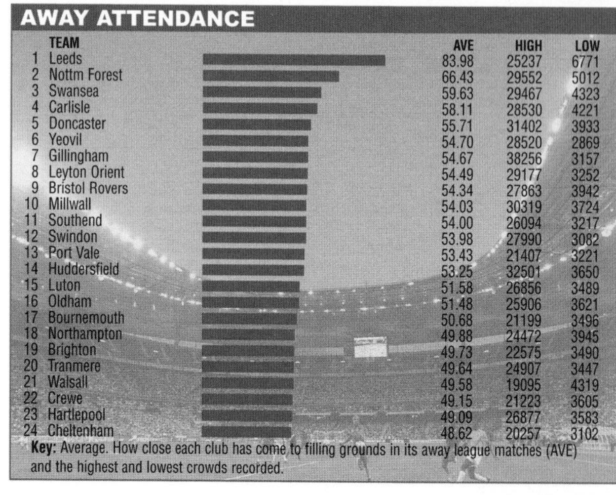

	TEAM	AVE	HIGH	LOW
1	Leeds	83.98	25237	6771
2	Nottm Forest	66.43	29552	5012
3	Swansea	59.63	29467	4323
4	Carlisle	58.11	28530	4221
5	Doncaster	55.71	31402	3933
6	Yeovil	54.70	28520	2869
7	Gillingham	54.67	38256	3157
8	Leyton Orient	54.49	29177	3252
9	Bristol Rovers	54.34	27863	3942
10	Millwall	54.03	30319	3724
11	Southend	54.00	26094	3217
12	Swindon	53.98	27990	3082
13	Port Vale	53.43	21407	3221
14	Huddersfield	53.25	32501	3650
15	Luton	51.58	26856	3489
16	Oldham	51.48	25906	3621
17	Bournemouth	50.68	21199	3496
18	Northampton	49.88	24472	3945
19	Brighton	49.73	22575	3490
20	Tranmere	49.64	24907	3447
21	Walsall	49.58	19095	4319
22	Crewe	49.15	21223	3605
23	Hartlepool	49.09	26877	3583
24	Cheltenham	48.62	20257	3102

Key: Average. How close each club has come to filling grounds in its away league matches (AVE) and the highest and lowest crowds recorded.

CHART-TOPPING MIDFIELDERS

1 Lennon - Notts Forest	
Goals scored in the League	0
Defensive Rating Av number of mins between League goals conceded while on the pitch	161
Contribution to Attacking Power Average number of minutes between League team goals while on pitch	61
Scoring Difference Defensive Rating minus Contribution to Attacking Power	100

	PLAYER	CLUB	GOALS	DEF RATE	POWER	S DIFF
1	Neil Lennon	Nottm Forest	0	161	61	100
2	Jonathan Douglas	Leeds	3	139	48	91
3	Neil Kilkenny	Leeds	1	144	62	82
4	Chris Cohen	Nottm Forest	2	142	60	82
5	Cleveland Taylor	Carlisle	0	145	72	73
6	Sammy Clingan	Nottm Forest	1	136	64	72
7	Kristian Commons	Nottm Forest	9	132	61	71
8	Paul Anderson	Swansea	6	108	39	69
9	Jonathan Howson	Leeds	3	124	56	68
10	Ferrie Bodde	Swansea	6	115	49	66
11	Paul Green, P	Doncaster	5	119	59	60
12	Bradley Johnson	Leeds	2	125	68	57
13	Jason Price	Doncaster	7	106	51	55
14	Lewis McGugan	Nottm Forest	6	113	59	54
15	Andy Robinson	Swansea	8	100	47	53

CHART-TOPPING GOALSCORERS

1 Scotland - Swansea	
Goals scored in the League	24
Contribution to Attacking Power (AP) Average number of minutes between League team goals while on pitch	53
Club Strike Rate (CSR) Average minutes between League goals scored by club	53
Player Strike Rate Average number of minutes between League goals scored by player	153

	PLAYER	CLUB	GOALS: LGE	POWER	CSR	S RATE
1	Jason Scotland	Swansea	24	53	53	153
2	Nicky Maynard	Crewe	14	77	90	154
3	Adebayo Akinfenwa	Northampton	7	51	69	160
4	Jermaine Beckford	Leeds	20	57	58	172
5	Lee Hughes	Oldham	7	73	71	178
6	Joe Garner	Carlisle	14	60	68	180
7	Junior Agogo	Nottm Forest	13	64	66	184
8	Leon Clarke	Southend	7	52	59	195
9	Phil Jevons	Huddersfield	7	84	82	204
10	Paul Heffernan	Doncaster	7	70	65	211
11	Richard Barker	Hartlepool	13	67	67	211
12	Jason Price	Doncaster	7	51	65	212
13	Alex Revell	Brighton	6	80	72	215
14	Simon Cox	Swindon	14	59	65	216
15	Stephen Gillespie	Cheltenham	14	95	100	218

CHART-TOPPING DEFENDERS

1 Bennett - Notts Forest	
Goals Conceded in the League The number of League goals conceded while he was on the pitch	21
Clean Sheets In games when he played at least 70 mins	17
Club Defensive Rating Average mins between League goals conceded by the club this season	132
Defensive Rating Average number of minutes between League goals conceded while on pitch	138

	PLAYER	CLUB	CON: LGE	CS	CDR	DEF RATE
1	Julian Bennett	Nottm Forest	21	17	132	138
2	Ian Breckin	Nottm Forest	16	12	132	128
3	Luke Chambers	Nottm Forest	28	22	132	128
4	Marcos Painter	Swansea	20	14	105	126
5	Paul Huntington	Leeds	9	6	111	125
6	Mark Little	Northampton	12	7	75	124
7	Stephen Roberts	Doncaster	14	9	103	123
8	Kelvin Wilson	Nottm Forest	29	19	132	123
9	Gary Monk	Swansea	23	13	105	123
10	Wes Morgan	Nottm Forest	27	18	132	122
11	Neal Trotman	Oldham	12	6	90	120
12	Frazer Richardson	Leeds	30	18	111	116
13	Daniel Fox	Walsall	16	9	90	116
14	Gabor Gyepes	Northampton	10	5	75	111
15	Charles Mulgrew	Southend	14	5	75	111

CHART-TOPPING GOALKEEPERS

1 Smith - Notts Forest	
Counting Games Games in which he played at least 70 minutes	46
Goals Conceded in the League The number of League goals conceded while he was on the pitch	32
Clean Sheets In games when he played at least 70 mins	24
Defensive Rating Average number of minutes between League goals conceded while on pitch	129

	PLAYER	CLUB	CG	CONC	CS	DEF RATE
1	Paul Smith	Nottm Forest	46	32	24	129
2	Casper Ankergren	Leeds	43	34	20	113
3	Neil Sullivan	Doncaster	46	41	20	100
4	Dorus de Vries	Swansea	46	42	17	98
5	Mark Crossley	Oldham	37	37	11	91
6	Rhys Evans	Millwall	20	20	6	91
7	Kieren Westwood	Carlisle	46	46	18	90
8	Clayton Ince	Walsall	46	46	16	90
9	Danny Coyne	Tranmere	41	42	15	87
10	Michel Kuipers	Brighton	46	50	14	82
11	Darryl Flahavan	Southend	26	30	7	78
12	Steve Phillips	Bristol Rovers	46	53	12	78
13	Mark Bunn	Northampton	45	54	11	75
14	Phil Smith	Swindon	15	18	2	75
15	Peter Brezovan	Swindon	31	38	8	73

PLAYER DISCIPLINARY RECORD

Bircham's on his opponent's back

1. Marc Bircham - Yeovil	
Cards Average mins between cards	115
League Yellow	6
League Red	1
TOTAL	7

	PLAYER		LY	LR	TOT	AVE
1	M Bircham	Yeovil	6	1	7	115
2	M Ricketts	Oldham	5	0	5	134
3	M Williams	Yeovil	7	0	7	137
4	Barry Corr	Swindon	3	1	4	145
5	M Richards	Port Vale	10	0	10	173
6	Worthington	Huddersfield	8	1	9	181
7	A Thompson	Leeds	4	0	4	196
8	S Robinson	Luton	9	1	10	204
9	N Trotman	Oldham	7	0	7	205
10	Steve Lomas	Gillingham	2	1	3	218
11	J Finnigan	Cheltenham	4	0	4	221
12	D Carlton	Carlisle	3	0	3	227
13	R Gilligan	Northampton	11	0	11	228
14	S Thurgood	Gillingham	3	1	4	233
15	D Howland	Port Vale	6	0	6	237

TEAM OF THE SEASON

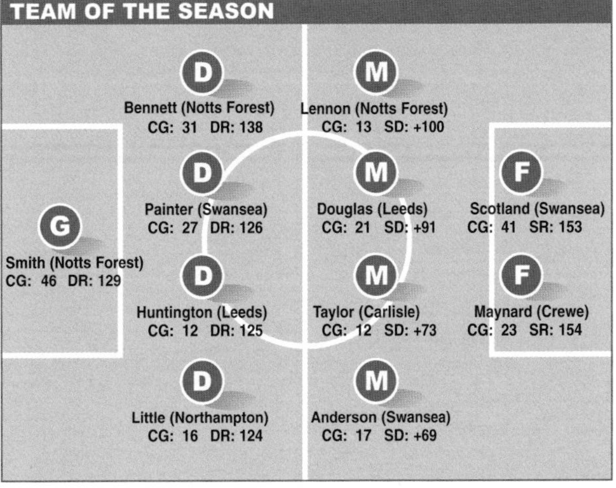
D
Bennett (Notts Forest)
CG: 31 DR: 138
M
Lennon (Notts Forest)
CG: 13 SD: +100
G
Smith (Notts Forest)
CG: 46 DR: 129
D
Painter (Swansea)
CG: 27 DR: 126
M
Douglas (Leeds)
CG: 21 SD: +91
F
Scotland (Swansea)
CG: 41 SR: 153
D
Huntington (Leeds)
CG: 12 DR: 125
M
Taylor (Carlisle)
CG: 12 SD: +73
F
Maynard (Crewe)
CG: 23 SR: 154
D
Little (Northampton)
CG: 16 DR: 124
M
Anderson (Swansea)
CG: 17 SD: +69

COCA-COLA LEAGUE ONE CHAMPIONS

SWANSEA

Final Position: **1st**

NICKNAME: THE SWANS

KEY: ☐Won ☐Drawn ☐Lost

							Attendance
1	div2	Oldham	A	L	1-2	Scotland 55	7,397
2	ccr1	Walsall	H	W	2-0	Anderson 22, Scotland 90	6,943
3	div2	Nottm Forest	H	D	0-0		17,220
4	div2	Walsall	A	W	3-1	Robinson 12, 66 pen, Scotland 26	5,673
5	ccr2	Reading	H	L	0-1		12,027
6	div2	Doncaster	H	L	1-2	Scotland 41	11,933
7	div2	Carlisle	H	W	2-1	D.Duffy 81, Anderson 83	11,354
8	div2	Cheltenham	A	W	2-1	Scotland 50, Robinson 69	4,323
9	div2	Leeds	A	L	0-2		29,467
10	div2	Brighton	H	D	0-0		11,058
11	div2	Swindon	H	W	2-1	Anderson 21, Feeney 74	10,135
12	div2	Leyton Orient	A	W	5-0	Butler 4, 51, Pratley 46, Anderson 57, Feeney 90	5,586
13	div2	Bournemouth	A	W	4-1	Bodde 15, Lawrence 28, Feeney 83 pen, 88	5,843
14	div2	Yeovil	A	W	2-1	Scotland 40, Bodde 79	6,207
15	div2	Gillingham	H	D	1-1	Anderson 79	13,452
16	div2	Millwall	A	D	2-2	Scotland 18, D.Duffy 78	6,750
17	facr1	Billericay	A	W	2-1	Bauza 59, 83	2,334
18	div2	Huddersfield	H	L	0-1		12,184
19	div2	Tranmere	A	W	1-0	Jennings 81 og	6,149
20	div2	Hartlepool	H	W	1-0	Rangel 82	11,421
21	facr2	Horsham	A	D	1-1	Bauza 41	2,731
22	div2	Northampton	H	W	3-0	Scotland 16, 66 pen, Pratley 19	10,957
23	facr2r	Horsham	H	W	6-2	Pratley 21, Britton 38, Scotland 42, Bodde 43, Robinson 56, Feeney 79	5,911
24	div2	Southend	H	W	3-0	Feeney 18, Rangel 58, Butler 83	12,629
25	div2	Cheltenham	H	W	4-1	Robinson 18, 20, Bodde 47, Scotland 78	14,049
26	div2	Leeds	H	W	3-2	Robinson 9, Monk 23, Scotland 45	19,010
27	div2	Swindon	A	D	1-1	Butler 87	9,426
28	facr3	Havant and W	H	D	1-1	Robinson 74	8,761
29	div2	Luton	A	W	3-1	Keane 5 og, Bauza 64, Scotland 73	6,756
30	facr3r	Havant and W	A	L	2-4	Bauza 39, Scotland 48	4,400
31	div2	Port Vale	H	W	2-0	Bodde 28, Pratley 47	12,310
32	div2	Crewe	H	W	2-1	Butler 14, Anderson 77	11,200
33	div2	Doncaster	A	W	4-0	Bodde 28, Bauza 52, Scotland 86 pen, Brandy 90	10,358
34	div2	Nottm Forest	A	D	0-0		21,065
35	div2	Oldham	H	W	2-1	McDonald 67 og, Brandy 85	12,458
36	div2	Crewe	A	D	2-2	Scotland 9 pen, Roberts 40 og	4,955
37	div2	Walsall	H	W	1-0	Bodde 53	13,020
38	div2	Port Vale	A	W	2-0	Scotland 63 pen, 76	4,347
39	div2	Luton	H	W	1-0	Butler 79	14,122
40	div2	Huddersfield	A	W	1-0	Scotland 45	10,471
41	div2	Millwall	H	L	1-2	Scotland 73 pen	15,561
42	div2	Tranmere	H	D	1-1	Tate 43	11,039
43	div2	Northampton	A	L	2-4	Scotland 29, 83	5,926
44	div2	Bristol Rovers	A	W	2-0	Lawrence 72, Scotland 79 pen	6,410
45	div2	Southend	A	D	1-1	Scotland 22 pen	9,797
46	div2	Bristol Rovers	H	D	2-2	Scotland 50, 84	15,048
47	div2	Hartlepool	A	W	3-1	Pratley 23, 73, Scotland 45 pen	4,484
48	div2	Bournemouth	H	L	1-2	Robinson 50	15,613
49	div2	Carlisle	A	D	0-0		10,623
50	div2	Gillingham	A	W	2-1	Bauza 44, 45	8,520
51	div2	Yeovil	H	L	1-2	Robinson 79	18,321
52	div2	Leyton Orient	H	W	4-1	Anderson 18, Bauza 25, 35, 44	16,856
53	div2	Brighton	A	W	1-0	Brandy 78	7,283

LEAGUE APPEARANCES, BOOKINGS AND GOALS

	AGE (on 01/07/08)	IN NAMED 16	APPEARANCES	COUNTING GAMES	MINUTES ON PITCH	LEAGUE GOALS	Yellow	Red
Goalkeepers								
Dorus de Vries	27	46	46	46	4140	0	2	0
Callum Hawthorne	17	2	0	0	0	0	0	0
David Knight	21	12	0	0	0	0	0	0
Defenders								
Kevin Amankwaah	26	0	0	0	0	0	0	0
Kevin Austin	35	35	19	17	1504	0	2	0
James Burgin	18	3	0	0	0	0	0	0
Dennis Lawrence	33	40	40	38	3508	2	1	0
Gary Monk	29	33	32	31	2851	1	5	0
Marcos Painter	21	32	30	27	2528	0	6	0
Angel Rangel	25	43	43	43	3870	2	7	0
Alan Tate	25	34	21	18	1716	1	2	0
Ashley Williams	23	5	3	3	270	0	0	0
Midfielders								
Joe Allen	18	10	6	0	175	0	0	0
Paul Anderson	19	31	31	17	1852	6	3	0
Ferrie Bodde	26	33	33	31	2876	6	5	2
Leon Britton	25	40	40	31	3103	0	4	0
Thomas Butler	27	44	42	26	2761	6	1	0
Ian Craney	25	2	1	0	18	0	0	0
Shaun MacDonald	20	11	1	0	18	0	0	0
Kristian O'Leary	30	25	11	3	507	0	1	0
Andrea Orlandi	23	13	8	1	166	0	1	0
Darren Pratley	23	42	42	35	3383	5	12	1
Andy Robinson	28	40	40	29	2908	8	4	0
Owain Tudur-Jones	23	7	6	2	212	0	0	0
Darren Way	28	12	2	0	38	0	0	0
Forwards								
Guillem Bauza	23	35	28	10	1213	7	5	0
Febian Brandy	19	20	19	2	486	3	1	1
Darryl Duffy	24	26	20	8	1079	2	0	0
Warren Feeney	27	12	10	3	487	5	1	1
Christopher Jones	18	3	2	0	30	0	0	0
Jason Scotland	29	45	45	41	3684	24	1	0

TEAM OF THE SEASON

G Dorus de Vries CG: 46 DR: 98

D Marcos Painter CG: 27 DR: 126

D Gary Monk CG: 31 DR: 123

D Angel Rangel CG: 43 DR: 99

D Dennis Lawrence CG: 38 DR: 92

M Paul Anderson CG: 17 SD: 69

M Ferrie Bodde CG: 31 SD: 66

M Andy Robinson CG: 29 SD: 53

M Thomas Butler CG: 26 SD: 51

F Jason Scotland CG: 41 SR: 153

F Guillem Bauza CG: 10* SR: 173

MONTHLY POINTS TALLY

AUGUST	4	44%
SEPTEMBER	7	47%
OCTOBER	12	100%
NOVEMBER	8	53%
DECEMBER	12	100%
JANUARY	14	78%
FEBRUARY	13	87%
MARCH	12	50%
APRIL	7	47%
MAY	3	100%

LEAGUE GOALS

	PLAYER	MINS	GOALS	S RATE
1	Scotland	3684	**24**	153
2	Robinson	2908	**8**	363
3	Bauza	1213	**7**	173
4	Anderson	1852	**6**	308
5	Butler	2761	**6**	460
6	Bodde	2876	**6**	479
7	Feeney	487	**5**	97
8	Pratley	3383	**5**	676
9	Brandy	486	**3**	162
10	Duffy, D	1079	**2**	539
11	Lawrence	3508	**2**	1754
12	Rangel	3870	**2**	1935
13	Tate	1716	**1**	1716
	Other		1	
	TOTAL		**78**	

TOP POINT EARNERS

	PLAYER	GAMES	AV PTS
1	Paul Anderson	17	**2.59**
2	Marcos Painter	27	**2.48**
3	Gary Monk	31	**2.26**
4	Andy Robinson	29	**2.07**
5	Ferrie Bodde	31	**2.06**
6	Angel Rangel	43	**2.05**
7	Darren Pratley	35	**2.03**
8	Dorus de Vries	46	**2.00**
9	Jason Scotland	41	**1.98**
10	Dennis Lawrence	38	**1.97**
	CLUB AVERAGE:		**2.00**

DISCIPLINARY RECORDS

	PLAYER	YELLOW	RED	AVE
1	Guillem Bauza	5	0	**242**
2	Warren Feeney	1	1	**243**
3	Febian Brandy	1	1	**243**
4	Darren Pratley	12	1	**260**
5	Ferrie Bodde	5	2	**410**
6	Marcos Painter	6	0	**421**
7	Kristian O'Leary	1	0	**507**
8	Angel Rangel	7	0	**552**
9	Gary Monk	5	0	**570**
10	Paul Anderson	3	0	**617**
11	Andy Robinson	4	0	**727**
12	Kevin Austin	2	0	**752**
13	Leon Britton	4	0	**775**
	Other	7	0	
	TOTAL	**63**	**5**	

KEY GOALKEEPER

Dorus de Vries

Goals Conceded in the League	42	Counting Games League games when player was on pitch for at least 70 minutes	46
Defensive Rating Ave number of mins between League goals conceded while on the pitch	98	Clean Sheets In League games when player was on pitch for at least 70 minutes	17

KEY PLAYERS - DEFENDERS

Marcos Painter

Goals Conceded Number of League goals conceded while the player was on the pitch	20	Clean Sheets In League games when player was on pitch for at least 70 minutes	14
Defensive Rating Ave number of mins between League goals conceded while on the pitch	126	Club Defensive Rating Average number of mins between League goals conceded by the club this season	105

	PLAYER	CON LGE	CLEAN SHEETS	DEF RATE
1	Marcos Painter	20	14	126 mins
2	Gary Monk	23	13	123 mins
3	Angel Rangel	39	16	99 mins
4	Dennis Lawrence	38	12	92 mins

KEY PLAYERS - MIDFIELDERS

Paul Anderson

Goals in the League	6	Contribution to Attacking Power Average number of minutes between League team goals while on pitch	39
Defensive Rating Average number of mins between League goals conceded while on the pitch	108	Scoring Difference Defensive Rating minus Contribution to Attacking Power	69

	PLAYER	LGE GOALS	DEF RATE	POWER	SCORE DIFF
1	Paul Anderson	6	108	39	69 mins
2	Ferrie Bodde	6	115	49	66 mins
3	Andy Robinson	8	100	47	53 mins
4	Thomas Butler	6	106	55	51 mins

KEY PLAYERS - GOALSCORERS

Jason Scotland

Goals in the League	24	Player Strike Rate Average number of minutes between League goals scored by player	153
Contribution to Attacking Power Average number of minutes between League team goals while on pitch	53	Club Strike Rate Average number of minutes between League goals scored by club	53

	PLAYER	LGE GOALS	POWER	STRIKE RATE
1	Jason Scotland	24	53	153 mins
2	Guillem Bauza	7	46	173 mins
3	Paul Anderson	6	39	308 mins
4	Andy Robinson	8	47	363 mins

macron
swansea.com
Jason Scotland

SQUAD APPEARANCES

Match	1	2	3	4	5	6	7	8	9	10	11	12	13	14	15	16	17	18	19	20	21	22	23	24	25	26	27	28	29	30	31	32	33	34	35	36	37	38	39	40	41	42	43	44	45	46	47	48	49	50	51	52	53
Venue	A	H	H	A	H	H	H	A	A	H	H	A	A	A	H	A	A	H	A	H	A	H	H	H	H	H	A	H	A	A	H	H	A	A	H	A	H	A	H	A	H	H	A	A	A	H	A	H	A	A	H	H	A
Competition	L	W	L	L	W	L	L	L	L	L	L	L	L	L	L	L	F	L	L	L	F	L	F	L	L	L	L	F	L	F	L	L	L	L	L	L	L	L	L	L	L	L	L	L	L	L	L	L	L	L	L	L	L
Result	L	W	D	W	L	L	W	W	L	D	W	W	W	W	D	D	W	L	W	W	D	W	W	W	W	W	D	D	W	L	W	W	W	D	W	D	W	W	W	W	L	D	L	W	D	D	W	L	D	W	L	W	W

Goalkeepers
Dorus de Vries
Callum Hawthorne
David Knight
Defenders
Kevin Amankwaah
Kevin Austin
James Burgin
Dennis Lawrence
Gary Monk
Marcos Painter
Angel Rangel
Alan Tate
Ashley Williams
Midfielders
Joe Allen
Paul Anderson
Ferrie Bodde
Leon Britton
Thomas Butler
Ian Craney
Shaun MacDonald
Kristian O'Leary
Andrea Orlandi
Darren Pratley
Andy Robinson
Owain Tudur-Jones
Darren Way
Forwards
Guillem Bauza
Febian Brandy
Darryl Duffy
Warren Feeney
Christopher Jones
Jason Scotland

KEY: On all match / On bench / Subbed or sent off (Counting game) / Subbed or sent off (playing less than 70 minutes) / Subbed on from bench (Counting Game) / Subbed on (playing less than 70 minutes) / Subbed on and then subbed or sent off (Counting Game) / Subbed on and then subbed or sent off (playing less than 70 minutes) / Not in 16

NOTTINGHAM FOREST

Final Position: **2nd**

NICKNAME: THE REDS

KEY: ☐Won ☐Drawn ☐Lost

							Attendance
1	div2	Bournemouth	H	D	0-0		18,791
2	ccr1	Chester	A	W	4-2*	(*on penalties)	2,720
3	div2	Swansea	A	D	0-0		17,220
4	div2	Leeds	H	L	1-2	Commons 50	25,237
5	div2	Bristol Rovers	A	D	2-2	Anthony 29 og, Grant.Holt 45	9,080
6	div2	Port Vale	A	W	2-0	P.Edwards 3 og, Chambers 86	6,521
7	ccr2	Leicester	H	L	2-3	Smith 1, Tyson 64	15,519
8	div2	Gillingham	H	W	4-0	Agogo 43, 61, 73, Sinclair 84	16,330
9	div2	Yeovil	A	W	3-0	Chambers 57, Agogo 79, Commons 84	6,818
10	div2	Huddersfield	A	D	1-1	Commons 75	10,994
11	div2	Hartlepool	H	W	2-1	Commons 11, Agogo 83	17,520
12	div2	Cheltenham	A	W	3-0	Commons 11, 45, 66	5,012
13	div2	Doncaster	H	D	0-0		23,108
14	div2	Luton	A	L	1-2	Bennett 90	8,524
15	div2	Oldham	H	D	0-0		16,423
16	div2	Tranmere	H	W	2-0	Agogo 50 pen, Tyson 78	16,825
17	div2	Southend	H	W	4-1	Breckin 41, Tyson 65, Agogo 73, 88	26,094
18	facr1	Lincoln	A	D	1-1	McGugan 25	7,361
19	div2	Crewe	H	W	2-0	Davies 45, Clingan 52	16,650
20	facr1r	Lincoln	H	W	3-1	Commons 35, Tyson 49, 61	6,783
21	div2	Walsall	A	L	0-1		6,605
22	div2	Brighton	A	W	2-0	Tyson 30, 49	6,536
23	facr2	Luton	A	L	0-1		5,758
24	div2	Northampton	H	D	2-2	McGugan 15, Agogo 90	17,081
25	div2	Port Vale	H	W	2-0	Agogo 24, McGugan 67	21,407
26	div2	Oldham	A	D	0-0		8,140
27	div2	Gillingham	A	L	0-3		7,712
28	div2	Huddersfield	H	W	2-1	Cohen 68, McGugan 90	18,762
29	div2	Leyton Orient	H	W	4-0	Grant.Holt 31, 54 pen, Commons 72, Thornhill 89	17,805
30	div2	Swindon	A	L	1-2	Chambers 63	9,815
31	div2	Millwall	A	D	2-2	Cohen 85, Tyson 88	8,436
32	div2	Swansea	H	D	0-0		21,065
33	div2	Bournemouth	A	L	0-2		7,251
34	div2	Millwall	H	W	2-0	Bennett 48, Chambers 58	17,046
35	div2	Leeds	A	D	1-1	Bennett 69	29,552
36	div2	Swindon	H	W	1-0	Tyson 50	23,439
37	div2	Leyton Orient	A	W	1-0	Agogo 61	7,136
38	div2	Carlisle	H	L	0-1		28,487
39	div2	Crewe	A	D	0-0		6,314
40	div2	Southend	A	D	1-1	Thornhill 65	8,376
41	div2	Walsall	H	D	1-1	Ormerod 49	17,177
42	div2	Northampton	A	W	2-1	Ormerod 9, Tyson 63 pen	7,244
43	div2	Brighton	H	D	0-0		18,165
44	div2	Doncaster	A	L	0-1		12,508
45	div2	Carlisle	A	W	2-0	Chambers 76, McCleary 90	9,979
46	div2	Cheltenham	H	W	3-1	Agogo 26, 47, Chambers 45	19,860
47	div2	Bristol Rovers	H	D	1-1	McGugan 33	15,860
48	div2	Tranmere	A	W	2-0	Tyson 34, Morgan 51	8,689
49	div2	Luton	H	W	1-0	Tyson 67	17,331
50	div2	Hartlepool	A	W	1-0	McGugan 84	5,206
51	div2	Yeovil	H	W	3-2	Bennett 12, Commons 18, McGugan 28	28,520

LEAGUE APPEARANCES, BOOKINGS AND GOALS

	AGE (on 01/07/08)	IN NAMED 16	APPEARANCES	COUNTING GAMES	MINUTES ON PITCH	LEAGUE GOALS	Yellow	Red
Goalkeepers								
Barry Richardson	38	5	0	0	0	0	0	0
Dale Roberts	21	25	0	0	0	0	0	0
Paul Smith	28	46	46	46	4140	0	0	0
Defenders								
Julian Bennett	23	36	34	31	2912	4	7	0
Ian Breckin	32	39	28	22	2057	1	4	0
Luke Chambers	22	43	42	40	3585	6	3	0
Matthew Lockwood	31	17	11	11	915	0	1	0
Brendan Moloney	19	2	2	0	121	0	0	0
Wes Morgan	24	45	42	36	3296	1	6	0
James Perch	22	38	30	16	1699	0	1	1
Kelvin Wilson	22	43	42	39	3572	0	3	1
Midfielders								
Felix Bastians	20	3	1	0	13	0	0	0
Mark Byrne	25	5	1	0	21	0	0	0
Sammy Clingan	24	43	43	40	3688	1	5	1
Chris Cohen	21	40	40	37	3427	2	6	0
Kristian Commons	24	39	39	26	2646	9	2	0
Aaron Davies	24	23	19	8	863	1	2	0
Neil Lennon	37	22	18	13	1291	0	4	0
Lewis McGugan	19	36	33	22	2158	6	4	0
Alan Power	20	1	0	0	0	0	0	0
Matt Thornhill	19	27	14	4	498	2	1	0
Forwards								
Junior Agogo	28	36	35	24	2392	13	0	0
Scott Dobie	29	3	2	0	70	0	0	0
Grant Holt	27	33	32	18	2069	3	4	1
William Hoskins	22	3	2	1	127	0	0	0
Garath McCleary	19	11	8	2	382	1	0	0
Brett Ormerod	31	13	13	10	996	2	0	0
Emile Sinclair	20	24	12	0	134	1	0	0
Nathan Tyson	26	34	34	20	2299	9	2	0

TEAM OF THE SEASON

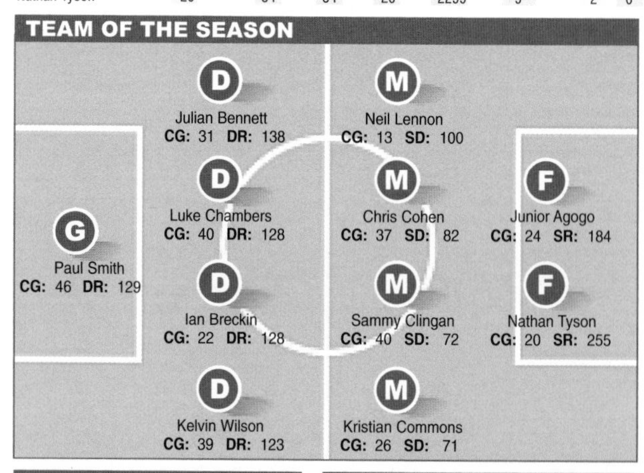

G
Paul Smith
CG: 46 DR: 129
D
Julian Bennett
CG: 31 DR: 138
D
Luke Chambers
CG: 40 DR: 128
D
Ian Breckin
CG: 22 DR: 128
D
Kelvin Wilson
CG: 39 DR: 123
M
Neil Lennon
CG: 13 SD: 100
M
Chris Cohen
CG: 37 SD: 82
M
Sammy Clingan
CG: 40 SD: 72
M
Kristian Commons
CG: 26 SD: 71
F
Junior Agogo
CG: 24 SR: 184
F
Nathan Tyson
CG: 20 SR: 255

MONTHLY POINTS TALLY

Month	Points	%
AUGUST	2	22%
SEPTEMBER	10	83%
OCTOBER	9	50%
NOVEMBER	9	100%
DECEMBER	8	44%
JANUARY	8	53%
FEBRUARY	10	67%
MARCH	7	33%
APRIL	16	89%
MAY	3	100%

LEAGUE GOALS

	PLAYER	MINS	GOALS	S RATE
1	Agogo	2392	13	184
2	Tyson	2299	9	255
3	Commons	2646	9	294
4	McGugan	2158	6	359
5	Chambers	3585	6	597
6	Bennett	2912	4	728
7	Holt, G	2069	3	689
8	Thornhill	498	2	249
9	Ormerod	996	2	498
10	Cohen	3427	2	1713
11	Sinclair	134	1	134
12	McCleary	382	1	382
13	Davies	863	1	863
	Other		3	
	TOTAL		62	

TOP POINT EARNERS

	PLAYER	GAMES	AV PTS
1	Lewis McGugan	22	1.95
2	Chris Cohen	37	1.92
3	Junior Agogo	24	1.92
4	Neil Lennon	13	1.85
5	Nathan Tyson	20	1.85
6	Luke Chambers	40	1.83
7	Julian Bennett	31	1.81
8	Sammy Clingan	40	1.78
9	Wes Morgan	36	1.78
10	Paul Smith	46	1.78
	CLUB AVERAGE:		1.78

DISCIPLINARY RECORDS

	PLAYER	YELLOW	RED	AVE
1	Neil Lennon	4	0	322
2	Grant Holt	4	1	413
3	Aaron Davies	2	0	431
4	Julian Bennett	6	0	485
5	Matt Thornhill	1	0	498
6	Ian Breckin	4	0	514
7	Lewis McGugan	4	0	539
8	Wes Morgan	6	0	549
9	Chris Cohen	6	0	571
10	Sammy Clingan	5	1	614
11	James Perch	1	1	849
12	Kelvin Wilson	3	1	893
13	Matthew Lockwood	1	0	915
	Other	7	0	
	TOTAL	54	4	

KEY GOALKEEPER

Paul Smith

Goals Conceded in the League	32	Counting Games League games when player was on pitch for at least 70 minutes	46
Defensive Rating Ave number of mins between League goals conceded while on the pitch	129	Clean Sheets In League games when player was on pitch for at least 70 minutes	24

KEY PLAYERS - DEFENDERS

Julian Bennett

Goals Conceded Number of League goals conceded while the player was on the pitch	21	Clean Sheets In League games when player was on pitch for at least 70 minutes	17
Defensive Rating Ave number of mins between League goals conceded while on the pitch	138	Club Defensive Rating Average number of mins between League goals conceded by the club this season	132

	PLAYER	CON LGE	CLEAN SHEETS	DEF RATE
1	Julian Bennett	21	17	138 mins
2	Luke Chambers	28	22	128 mins
3	Ian Breckin	16	12	128 mins
4	Kelvin Wilson	29	19	123 mins

KEY PLAYERS - MIDFIELDERS

Neil Lennon

Goals in the League	0	Contribution to Attacking Power Average number of minutes between League team goals while on pitch	61
Defensive Rating Average number of mins between League goals conceded while on the pitch	161	Scoring Difference Defensive Rating minus Contribution to Attacking Power	100

	PLAYER	LGE GOALS	DEF RATE	POWER	SCORE DIFF
1	Neil Lennon	0	161	61	100 mins
2	Chris Cohen	2	142	60	82 mins
3	Sammy Clingan	1	136	64	72 mins
4	Kristian Commons	9	132	61	71 mins

KEY PLAYERS - GOALSCORERS

Junior Agogo

Goals in the League	13	Player Strike Rate Average number of minutes between League goals scored by player	184
Contribution to Attacking Power Average number of minutes between League team goals while on pitch	64	Club Strike Rate Average number of minutes between League goals scored by club	66

	PLAYER	LGE GOALS	POWER	STRIKE RATE
1	Junior Agogo	13	64	184 mins
2	Nathan Tyson	9	63	255 mins
3	Kristian Commons	9	61	294 mins
4	Lewis McGugan	6	59	359 mins

Nathan Tyson and Junior Agogo

SQUAD APPEARANCES

Match	1	2	3	4	5	6	7	8	9	10	11	12	13	14	15	16	17	18	19	20	21	22	23	24	25
Venue	H	A	A	H	A	A	H	H	A	A	H	A	H	A	H	H	H	A	H	H	A	A	A	H	H
Competition	L	W	L	L	L	L	W	L	L	L	L	L	L	L	L	L	L	F	L	F	L	L	F	L	L
Result	D	W	D	L	D	W	L	W	W	D	W	W	D	L	D	W	W	D	W	W	L	W	L	D	W

Match	26	27	28	29	30	31	32	33	34	35	36	37	38	39	40	41	42	43	44	45	46	47	48	49	50	51
Venue	A	A	H	H	A	A	H	A	H	A	H	A	H	A	A	H	A	H	A	A	H	H	A	H	A	H
Competition	L	L	L	L	L	L	L	L	L	L	L	L	L	L	L	L	L	L	L	L	L	L	L	L	L	L
Result	D	L	W	W	L	D	D	L	W	D	W	W	L	D	D	D	W	D	L	W	W	D	W	W	W	W

Goalkeepers
Barry Richardson
Dale Roberts
Paul Smith

Defenders
Julian Bennett
Ian Breckin
Luke Chambers
Matthew Lockwood
Brendan Moloney
Wes Morgan
James Perch
Kelvin Wilson

Midfielders
Felix Bastians
Mark Byrne
Sammy Clingan
Chris Cohen
Kristian Commons
Aaron Davies
Neil Lennon
Lewis McGugan
Alan Power
James Reid
Matt Thornhill

Forwards
Junior Agogo
Scott Dobie
Grant Holt
William Hoskins
Garath McCleary
Brett Ormerod
Emile Sinclair
Nathan Tyson

KEY: On all match | Subbed or sent off (Counting game) | Subbed on from bench (Counting Game) | Subbed on and then subbed or sent off (Counting Game) | Not in 16
On bench | Subbed or sent off (playing less than 70 minutes) | Subbed on (playing less than 70 minutes) | Subbed on and then subbed or sent off (playing less than 70 minutes)

DONCASTER ROVERS

PROMOTED VIA THE PLAY-OFFS Final Position: **3rd**

NICKNAME: ROVERS

KEY: ☐ Won ☐ Drawn ☐ Lost

					Score	Scorers	Attendance
1	div2	Millwall	H	D	0-0		7,542
2	ccr1	Lincoln	H	W	4-1	Hayter 23, Wellens 55, Heffernan 59, McCammon 73	5,084
3	div2	Hartlepool	A	L	1-2	Hayter 71	5,544
4	div2	Bournemouth	H	L	1-2	Greer 24	6,476
5	ccr2	Plymouth	A	L	0-2		5,133
6	div2	Swansea	A	W	2-1	Wellens 68, 84	11,933
7	div2	Northampton	A	L	0-2		5,274
8	div2	Crewe	H	W	2-0	Heffernan 31, Woodards 48 og	6,726
9	div2	Southend	A	L	2-3	G.Roberts 28, Guy 36	8,117
10	div2	Cheltenham	H	W	2-0	Guy 18, M.Mills 58	6,150
11	div2	Walsall	H	L	2-3	M.Mills 17, Guy 40	6,038
12	div2	Luton	A	D	1-1	Hayter 26	6,513
13	div2	Huddersfield	H	W	2-0	Stock 13, Wilson 65	6,866
14	div2	Nottm Forest	A	D	0-0		23,108
15	div2	Leyton Orient	H	W	4-2	Wellens 52, 88, Price 69, Hayter 83	7,184
16	div2	Swindon	A	W	2-1	Stock 31, Guy 73	6,570
17	div2	Gillingham	A	D	1-1	Hayter 65 pen	5,030
18	facr1	Oldham	A	D	2-2	Hayter 63, 86	4,280
19	div2	Tranmere	H	D	0-0		7,070
20	div2	Port Vale	A	W	3-1	Guy 59, Hayter 68, Wellens 81	4,581
21	facr1r	Oldham	H	L	1-2	McCammon 26	4,340
22	div2	Brighton	H	D	0-0		6,215
23	div2	Oldham	A	D	1-1	Hayter 90 pen	4,776
24	div2	Yeovil	H	L	1-2	Skiverton 90 og	5,967
25	div2	Crewe	A	W	4-0	Price 38, 50, P.Green 90, Guy 90	4,122
26	div2	Northampton	H	W	2-0	McCammon 11, Lockwood 29	7,046
27	div2	Southend	H	W	3-1	Lockwood 8, P.Green 30, G.Roberts 42	7,163
28	div2	Walsall	A	D	1-1	Price 45	6,266
29	div2	Carlisle	H	W	1-0	Hayter 84	8,197
30	div2	Leeds	A	W	1-0	Stock 21	31,402
31	div2	Swansea	H	L	0-4		10,358
32	div2	Hartlepool	H	W	2-0	Wellens 34, Lockwood 54	6,442
33	div2	Millwall	A	W	3-0	Price 43, Coppinger 77, P.Green 90	8,230
34	div2	Bristol Rovers	H	W	2-0	Stock 63 pen, Heffernan 90 pen	8,168
35	div2	Bournemouth	A	W	2-0	Price 1, 70	4,947
36	div2	Carlisle	A	L	0-1		8,390
37	div2	Tranmere	A	W	1-0	Coppinger 2	7,551
38	div2	Bristol Rovers	A	W	1-0	Heffernan 3	3,933
39	div2	Port Vale	H	W	2-1	Heffernan 11, McCammon 19	8,040
40	div2	Gillingham	H	W	2-1	Coppinger 4, Heffernan 48 pen	7,867
41	div2	Brighton	A	L	0-1		6,252
42	div2	Yeovil	A	L	1-2	Heffernan 73	6,146
43	div2	Oldham	H	D	1-1	Heffernan 37	8,777
44	div2	Nottm Forest	H	W	1-0	G.Roberts 74	12,508
45	div2	Leeds	H	L	0-1		15,001
46	div2	Huddersfield	A	D	2-2	G.Taylor 52, P.Green 84	10,279
47	div2	Swindon	H	W	2-0	McDaid 39, Stock 68 pen	8,371
48	div2	Leyton Orient	A	D	1-1	McCammon 60	4,582
49	div2	Luton	H	W	2-0	M.Mills 34, McCammon 82	9,332
50	div2	Cheltenham	A	L	1-2	P.Green 76	6,787
51	d2po1	Southend	A	D	0-0		9,109
52	d2po2	Southend	H	W	5-1	Stock 11 pen, Barrett 21 og, Coppinger 39, 52, 80	13,081
53	d2pof	Leeds	N	W	1-0	Hayter 48	75,132

LEAGUE APPEARANCES, BOOKINGS AND GOALS

	AGE (on 01/07/08)	IN NAMED 16	APPEARANCES	COUNTING GAMES	MINUTES ON PITCH	LEAGUE GOALS	Yellow	Red
Goalkeepers								
Benjamin Smith	21	2	0	0	0	0	0	0
Neil Sullivan	38	46	46	46	4140	0	2	0
Defenders								
Gordon Greer	27	14	11	9	843	1	0	0
Sam Hird	19	12	4	3	300	0	1	0
Graeme Lee	30	3	1	0	6	0	0	0
Adam Lockwood	26	40	39	37	3405	3	6	0
Sean McDaid	22	41	24	11	1294	1	0	0
Matthew Mills	21	34	34	28	2654	3	6	1
Matt Noble	19	1	0	0	0	0	0	0
James O'Connor	23	40	40	40	3595	0	3	0
Gareth Roberts	30	39	37	34	3157	3	3	0
Stephen Roberts	28	29	24	16	1727	0	4	1
Midfielders								
James Coppinger	27	42	39	29	2780	3	3	0
Stuart Elliott	29	10	10	1	265	0	1	0
Paul Green	25	44	38	26	2512	5	1	0
Kevin Horlock	35	2	0	0	0	0	0	0
Craig Nelthorpe	21	10	2	0	12	0	0	0
Jason Price	31	30	28	13	1486	7	3	0
Brian Stock	26	40	40	38	3445	5	7	0
Richard Wellens	28	45	45	45	3928	6	2	0
Mark Wilson	29	36	31	20	1977	1	3	0
Martin Woods	22	23	14	6	679	0	1	0
Forwards								
Lewis Guy	22	36	30	12	1310	6	1	1
James Hayter	29	38	34	21	1945	7	1	0
Paul Heffernan	26	31	27	14	1483	7	1	0
Mark McCammon	29	34	32	21	2055	4	4	0
Gareth Taylor	35	14	12	3	386	1	0	0

TEAM OF THE SEASON

G Neil Sullivan CG: 46 DR: 100

D Stephen Roberts CG: 16 DR: 123

D Adam Lockwood CG: 37 DR: 103

D James O'Connor CG: 40 DR: 97

D Gareth Roberts CG: 34 DR: 95

M Paul Green CG: 26 SD: 60

M Jason Price CG: 13 SD: 55

M Brian Stock CG: 38 SD: 46

M James Coppinger CG: 29 SD: 42

F Paul Heffernan CG: 14 SR: 211

F Lewis Guy CG: 12 SR: 218

MONTHLY POINTS TALLY

Month	Points	%
AUGUST	1	11%
SEPTEMBER	9	60%
OCTOBER	8	53%
NOVEMBER	8	67%
DECEMBER	11	61%
JANUARY	10	67%
FEBRUARY	9	75%
MARCH	16	67%
APRIL	8	53%
MAY	0	0%

LEAGUE GOALS

	PLAYER	MINS	GOALS	S RATE
1	Heffernan	1483	7	211
2	Price	1486	7	212
3	Hayter	1945	7	277
4	Guy	1310	6	218
5	Wellens	3928	6	654
6	Green, P	2512	5	502
7	Stock	3445	5	689
8	McCammon	2055	4	513
9	Mills, M	2654	3	884
10	Coppinger	2780	3	926
11	Roberts, G	3157	3	1052
12	Lockwood	3405	3	1135
13	Taylor, G	386	1	386
	Other		3	
	TOTAL		63	

TOP POINT EARNERS

	PLAYER	GAMES	AV PTS
1	Jason Price	13	2.38
2	Stephen Roberts	16	2.13
3	Mark McCammon	21	2.10
4	Paul Green	26	2.00
5	Brian Stock	38	1.89
6	James Coppinger	29	1.86
7	Lewis Guy	12	1.83
8	Matthew Mills	28	1.82
9	Adam Lockwood	37	1.78
10	Gareth Roberts	34	1.76
	CLUB AVERAGE:		1.74

DISCIPLINARY RECORDS

	PLAYER	YELLOW	RED	AVE
1	Stephen Roberts	4	1	345
2	Matthew Mills	6	1	379
3	Brian Stock	7	0	492
4	Jason Price	3	0	495
5	Mark McCammon	4	0	513
6	Adam Lockwood	6	0	567
7	Lewis Guy	1	1	655
8	Mark Wilson	3	0	659
9	Martin Woods	1	0	679
10	James Coppinger	3	0	926
11	Gareth Roberts	3	0	1052
12	James O'Connor	3	0	1198
13	Paul Heffernan	1	0	1483
	Other	6	0	
	TOTAL	51	3	

KEY GOALKEEPER

Neil Sullivan

Goals Conceded in the League	41	**Counting Games** League games when player was on pitch for at least 70 minutes	46
Defensive Rating Ave number of mins between League goals conceded while on the pitch	100	**Clean Sheets** In League games when player was on pitch for at least 70 minutes	20

KEY PLAYERS - DEFENDERS

Stephen Roberts

Goals Conceded Number of League goals conceded while the player was on the pitch	14	**Clean Sheets** In League games when player was on pitch for at least 70 minutes	9
Defensive Rating Ave number of mins between League goals conceded while on the pitch	123	**Club Defensive Rating** Average number of mins between League goals conceded by the club this season	103

	PLAYER	CON LGE	CLEAN SHEETS	DEF RATE
1	Stephen Roberts	14	9	123 mins
2	Adam Lockwood	33	16	103 mins
3	James O'Connor	37	18	97 mins
4	Gareth Roberts	33	13	95 mins

KEY PLAYERS - MIDFIELDERS

Paul Green

Goals in the League	5	**Contribution to Attacking Power** Average number of minutes between League team goals while on pitch	59
Defensive Rating Average number of mins between League goals conceded while on the pitch	119	**Scoring Difference** Defensive Rating minus Contribution to Attacking Power	60

	PLAYER	LGE GOALS	DEF RATE	POWER	SCORE DIFF
1	Paul Green	5	119	59	60 mins
2	Jason Price	7	106	51	55 mins
3	Brian Stock	5	111	65	46 mins
4	James Coppinger	3	106	64	42 mins

KEY PLAYERS - GOALSCORERS

Paul Heffernan

Goals in the League	7	**Player Strike Rate** Average number of minutes between League goals scored by player	211
Contribution to Attacking Power Average number of minutes between League team goals while on pitch	70	**Club Strike Rate** Average number of minutes between League goals scored by club	65

	PLAYER	LGE GOALS	POWER	STRIKE RATE
1	Paul Heffernan	7	70	211 mins
2	Jason Price	7	51	212 mins
3	Lewis Guy	6	48	218 mins
4	James Hayter	7	72	277 mins

James Coppinger (left) celebrates

SQUAD APPEARANCES

Match	1	2	3	4	5	6	7	8	9	10	11	12	13	14	15	16	17	18
Venue	H	H	A	H	A	A	A	H	A	H	H	A	H	A	H	A	A	A
Competition	L	W	L	L	W	L	L	L	L	L	L	L	L	L	L	L	L	F
Result	D	W	L	L	L	W	L	W	L	W	L	D	W	D	W	W	D	D

Match	19	20	21	22	23	24	25	26	27	28	29	30	31	32	33	34	35	36
Venue	H	A	H	H	A	H	A	H	H	A	H	A	H	H	A	H	A	A
Competition	L	L	F	L	L	L	L	L	L	L	L	L	L	L	L	L	L	L
Result	D	W	L	D	D	L	W	W	W	D	W	W	L	W	W	W	W	L

Match	37	38	39	40	41	42	43	44	45	46	47	48	49	50	51	52	53
Venue	A	A	H	H	A	A	H	H	H	A	H	A	H	A	A	H	N
Competition	L	L	L	L	L	L	L	L	L	L	L	L	L	L	O	O	O
Result	W	W	W	W	L	L	D	W	L	D	W	D	W	L	D	W	W

Goalkeepers
Benjamin Smith
Neil Sullivan

Defenders
Gordon Greer
Sam Hird
Graeme Lee
Adam Lockwood
Sean McDaid
Matthew Mills
Matt Noble
James O'Connor
Gareth Roberts
Stephen Roberts

Midfielders
James Coppinger
Stuart Elliott
Paul Green, P
Kevin Horlock
Craig Nelthorpe
Jason Price
Brian Stock
Richard Wellens
Mark Wilson
Martin Woods

Forwards
Lewis Guy
James Hayter
Paul Heffernan
Mark McCammon
Gareth Taylor

KEY: On all match · On bench · Subbed or sent off (Counting game) · Subbed or sent off (playing less than 70 minutes) · Subbed on from bench (Counting Game) · Subbed on (playing less than 70 minutes) · Subbed on and then subbed or sent off (Counting Game) · Subbed on and then subbed or sent off (playing less than 70 minutes) · Not in 16

CARLISLE

Final Position: **4th**

NICKNAME: THE FOXES

KEY: ☐Won ☐Drawn ☐Lost

							Attendance
1	div2	Walsall	A	D	1-1	Gall 19	6,933
2	ccr1	Bury	A	W	1-0	Graham 12	2,213
3	div2	Oldham	H	W	1-0	Graham 42 pen	7,777
4	div2	Huddersfield	A	W	2-0	Livesey 34, Garner 44	10,022
5	ccr2	Coventry	H	L	0-2		5,744
6	div2	Cheltenham	H	W	1-0	Livesey 90	6,125
7	div2	Tranmere	H	L	0-1		6,556
8	div2	Swansea	A	L	1-2	Graham 48 pen	11,354
9	div2	Bristol Rovers	H	D	1-1	Graham 70	6,106
10	div2	Bournemouth	A	W	3-1	Garner 27, 39, Anyinsah 66	4,940
11	div2	Hartlepool	A	D	2-2	Graham 19, 45	5,359
12	div2	Millwall	H	W	4-0	Garner 15, Graham 29, 34, Bridge-Wilkinson 45	7,022
13	div2	Yeovil	A	L	1-2	Hackney 49	4,757
14	div2	Gillingham	H	W	2-0	Cox 15 og, Hackney 54	6,461
15	div2	Southend	A	W	1-0	Garner 59	9,281
16	div2	Leeds	H	W	3-1	Hackney 61, Garner 70, Bridge-Wilkinson 90	16,668
17	div2	Luton	A	D	0-0		5,462
18	facr1	Grimsby	H	D	1-1	Aranalde 85 pen	5,128
19	facr1r	Grimsby	A	L	0-1		2,008
20	div2	Brighton	A	D	2-2	Hackney 34, Garner 53	5,390
21	div2	Swindon	H	W	3-0	Anyinsah 27, 54, Garner 75	5,477
22	div2	Northampton	A	D	2-2	Bridge-Wilkinson 26, Garner 63	4,908
23	div2	Leyton Orient	H	W	1-0	Garner 50	6,843
24	div2	Tranmere	A	L	0-2		8,516
25	div2	Bristol Rovers	A	L	0-3		6,254
26	div2	Hartlepool	H	W	4-2	Garner 42, 69, Jeff.Smith 66, Hackney 90	7,496
27	div2	Port Vale	H	W	3-2	Joyce 50, Hackney 65, 69	6,313
28	div2	Doncaster	A	L	0-1		8,197
29	div2	Crewe	H	W	1-0	Garner 52	6,449
30	div2	Cheltenham	A	L	0-1		4,221
31	div2	Oldham	A	L	0-2		4,701
32	div2	Walsall	H	W	2-1	Bridge-Wilkinson 31 pen, Graham 75	6,220
33	div2	Port Vale	A	D	1-1	Garner 62	4,221
34	div2	Huddersfield	H	W	2-1	Livesey 21, Graham 76	6,196
35	div2	Doncaster	H	W	1-0	Graham 40	8,390
36	div2	Crewe	A	W	1-0	Dobie 64	4,786
37	div2	Nottm Forest	A	W	1-0	Graham 71	28,487
38	div2	Brighton	H	W	2-0	Graham 35, Livesey 59	6,793
39	div2	Luton	H	W	2-1	Livesey 22, Murphy 29	5,489
40	div2	Swindon	A	D	2-2	Bridge-Wilkinson 54, Murphy 86	6,004
41	div2	Leyton Orient	A	W	3-0	Graham 17, D.Raven 32, Smith 49	6,134
42	div2	Northampton	H	W	2-0	Livesey 50, Bridge-Wilkinson 84	9,038
43	div2	Gillingham	A	D	0-0		6,673
44	div2	Nottm Forest	H	L	0-2		9,979
45	div2	Yeovil	H	W	2-1	Murphy 77, Dobie 90	6,843
46	div2	Swansea	H	D	0-0		10,623
47	div2	Leeds	A	L	2-3	Dobie 17, Graham 60	28,530
48	div2	Southend	H	L	1-2	Hackney 52	9,122
49	div2	Millwall	A	L	0-3		10,075
50	div2	Bournemouth	H	D	1-1	Dobie 57	12,223
51	d2po1	Leeds	A	W	2-1	Graham 32, Bridge-Wilkinson 50	36,297
52	d2po2	Leeds	H	L	0-2		12,873

LEAGUE APPEARANCES, BOOKINGS AND GOALS

	AGE (on 01/07/08)	IN NAMED 16	APPEARANCES	COUNTING GAMES	MINUTES ON PITCH	LEAGUE GOALS	Yellow	Red
Goalkeepers								
Chris Howarth	22	46	0	0	0	0	0	0
Kieren Westwood	23	46	46	46	4140	0	1	0
Defenders								
Zigor Aranalde	35	29	27	27	2417	0	4	0
Paul Arnison	30	40	17	7	786	0	1	0
Darren Campion	20	2	2	1	122	0	0	0
Evan Horwood	22	19	19	19	1708	0	3	0
Richard Keogh	21	7	7	7	630	0	1	0
Danny Livesey	23	45	45	44	4015	6	3	1
Peter Murphy	27	42	36	31	2965	3	4	0
David Raven	23	44	43	42	3832	1	6	1
Paul Reid	26	2	1	0	45	0	0	0
Harry Worley	19	2	1	0	45	0	1	0
Midfielders								
Joe Anyinsah	23	12	12	9	854	3	1	0
Marc Bridge-Wilkinson	29	45	45	44	3932	6	10	0
Martin Brittain	23	2	1	0	4	0	0	0
Danny Carlton	24	41	31	4	682	0	3	0
Simon Hackney	24	46	43	36	3434	8	2	0
Luke Joyce	20	9	3	0	113	1	0	0
Dan Kirkup	20	0	0	0	0	0	0	0
Chris Lumsdon	28	43	40	37	3435	0	8	0
Neale McDermott	23	5	0	0	0	0	0	0
Grant Smith	28	18	15	11	1096	1	2	0
Jeff Smith	28	27	21	9	1130	1	0	0
Cleveland Taylor	24	19	18	12	1165	0	1	0
Paul Thirlwell	29	14	13	7	736	0	1	0
Forwards								
Scott Dobie	29	15	15	7	812	4	0	0
Kevin Gall	26	25	21	9	1012	1	1	0
Joe Garner	20	31	31	27	2530	14	8	0
Danny Graham	22	46	45	37	3558	14	1	0
Gary Madine	17	13	10	1	193	0	0	0

TEAM OF THE SEASON

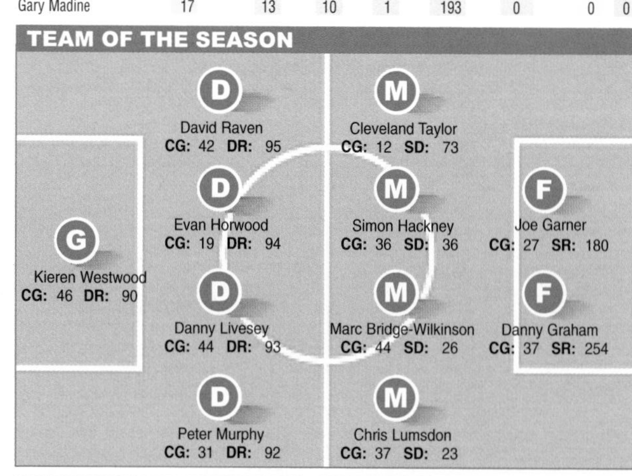

G
Kieren Westwood
CG: 46 DR: 90
D
David Raven
CG: 42 DR: 95
D
Evan Horwood
CG: 19 DR: 94
D
Danny Livesey
CG: 44 DR: 93
D
Peter Murphy
CG: 31 DR: 92
M
Cleveland Taylor
CG: 12 SD: 73
M
Simon Hackney
CG: 36 SD: 36
M
Marc Bridge-Wilkinson
CG: 44 SD: 26
M
Chris Lumsdon
CG: 37 SD: 23
F
Joe Garner
CG: 27 SR: 180
F
Danny Graham
CG: 37 SR: 254

MONTHLY POINTS TALLY

Month	Points	%
AUGUST	7	78%
SEPTEMBER	7	47%
OCTOBER	10	67%
NOVEMBER	5	56%
DECEMBER	7	47%
JANUARY	9	50%
FEBRUARY	13	87%
MARCH	17	81%
APRIL	4	22%
MAY	1	33%

LEAGUE GOALS

	PLAYER	MINS	GOALS	S RATE
1	Garner	2530	14	180
2	Graham	3558	14	254
3	Hackney	3434	8	429
4	B-Wilkinson	3932	6	655
5	Livesey	4015	6	669
6	Dobie	812	4	203
7	Anyinsah	854	3	284
8	Murphy	2965	3	988
9	Joyce	113	1	113
10	Gall	1012	1	1012
11	Smith	1096	1	1096
12	Smith, Jeff	1130	1	1130
13	Raven, D	3832	1	3832
	Other		0	
	TOTAL		63	

TOP POINT EARNERS

	PLAYER	GAMES	AV PTS
1	Cleveland Taylor	12	2.42
2	Simon Hackney	36	1.89
3	Joe Garner	27	1.85
4	Evan Horwood	19	1.84
5	Peter Murphy	31	1.81
6	David Raven	42	1.81
7	Danny Livesey	44	1.80
8	Kieren Westwood	46	1.74
9	Chris Lumsdon	37	1.73
10	Marc Bridge-Wilkinson	44	1.73
	CLUB AVERAGE:		1.74

DISCIPLINARY RECORDS

	PLAYER	YELLOW	RED	AVE
1	Danny Carlton	3	0	227
2	Joe Garner	8	0	316
3	M B-Wilkinson	10	0	393
4	Chris Lumsdon	8	0	429
5	David Raven	6	1	547
6	Grant Smith	2	0	548
7	Evan Horwood	3	0	569
8	Zigor Aranalde	4	0	604
9	Richard Keogh	1	0	630
10	Paul Thirlwell	1	0	736
11	Peter Murphy	4	0	741
12	Paul Arnison	1	0	786
13	Joe Anyinsah	1	0	854
	Other	9	1	
	TOTAL	61	2	

KEY GOALKEEPER

Kieren Westwood

Goals Conceded in the League	46	Counting Games League games when player was on pitch for at least 70 minutes	46
Defensive Rating Ave number of mins between League goals conceded while on the pitch	90	Clean Sheets In League games when player was on pitch for at least 70 minutes	18

KEY PLAYERS - DEFENDERS

David Raven

Goals Conceded Number of League goals conceded while the player was on the pitch	40	Clean Sheets In League games when player was on pitch for at least 70 minutes	18
Defensive Rating Ave number of mins between League goals conceded while on the pitch	95	Club Defensive Rating Average number of mins between League goals conceded by the club this season	95

	PLAYER	CON LGE	CLEAN SHEETS	DEF RATE
1	David Raven	40	18	95 mins
2	Evan Horwood	18	8	94 mins
3	Danny Livesey	43	18	93 mins
4	Peter Murphy	32	12	92 mins

KEY PLAYERS - MIDFIELDERS

Cleveland Taylor

Goals in the League	0	Contribution to Attacking Power Average number of minutes between League team goals while on pitch	72
Defensive Rating Average number of mins between League goals conceded while on the pitch	145	Scoring Difference Defensive Rating minus Contribution to Attacking Power	73

	PLAYER	LGE GOALS	DEF RATE	POWER	SCORE DIFF
1	Cleveland Taylor	0	145	72	73 mins
2	Simon Hackney	8	95	59	36 mins
3	Marc Bridge-Wilkinson	6	91	65	26 mins
4	Chris Lumsdon	0	83	60	23 mins

KEY PLAYERS - GOALSCORERS

Joe Garner

Goals in the League	14	Player Strike Rate Average number of minutes between League goals scored by player	180
Contribution to Attacking Power Average number of minutes between League team goals while on pitch	60	Club Strike Rate Average number of minutes between League goals scored by club	68

	PLAYER	LGE GOALS	POWER	STRIKE RATE
1	Joe Garner	14	60	180 mins
2	Danny Graham	14	67	254 mins
3	Simon Hackney	8	59	429 mins
4	Marc Bridge-Wilkinson	6	65	655 mins

Stobart
Danny Graham

SQUAD APPEARANCES

Match	1	2	3	4	5	6	7	8	9	10	11	12	13	14	15	16	17	18	19	20	21	22	23	24	25	26	27	28	29	30	31	32	33	34	35	36	37	38	39	40	41	42	43	44	45	46	47	48	49	50	51	52
Venue	A	A	H	A	H	H	H	A	H	A	A	H	A	H	A	H	A	H	A	A	H	A	H	A	A	H	H	A	H	A	A	H	A	H	H	A	A	H	H	A	A	H	A	H	H	H	A	H	A	H	A	H
Competition	L	W	L	L	W	L	L	L	L	L	L	L	L	L	L	L	L	F	F	L	L	L	L	L	L	L	L	L	L	L	L	L	L	L	L	L	L	L	L	L	L	L	L	L	L	L	L	L	L	L	O	O
Result	D	W	W	W	L	W	L	L	D	W	D	W	L	W	W	W	D	D	L	D	W	D	W	L	L	W	W	L	W	L	L	W	D	W	W	W	W	W	W	D	W	W	D	L	W	D	L	L	L	D	W	L

Goalkeepers
Chris Howarth
Kieren Westwood
Defenders
Zigor Aranalde
Paul Arnison
Darren Campion
Evan Horwood
Richard Keogh
Danny Livesey
Peter Murphy
David Raven
Paul Reid
Harry Worley
Midfielders
Joe Anyinsah
Marc Bridge-Wilkinson
Martin Brittain
Danny Carlton
Simon Hackney
Luke Joyce
Dan Kirkup
Chris Lumsdon
Neale McDermott
Grant Smith
Jeff Smith
Cleveland Taylor
Paul Thirlwell
Forwards
Scott Dobie
Kevin Gall
Joe Garner
Danny Graham
Gary Madine

KEY: On all match | On bench | Subbed or sent off (Counting game) | Subbed or sent off (playing less than 70 minutes) | Subbed on from bench (Counting Game) | Subbed on (playing less than 70 minutes) | Subbed on and then subbed or sent off (Counting Game) | Subbed on and then subbed or sent off (playing less than 70 minutes) | Not in 16

LEEDS UNITED

Final Position: **5th**

NICKNAME: UNITED

KEY: ☐Won ☐Drawn ☐Lost

		Opponent			Score	Scorers	Attendance
1	div2	Tranmere	A	W	2-1	Heath 55, Kandol 89	11,008
2	ccr1	Macclesfield	A	W	1-0	Westlake 78	3,422
3	div2	Southend	H	W	4-1	Thompson 3, Flo 85, Kandol 88, Beckford 90	24,036
4	div2	Nottm Forest	A	W	2-1	Kandol 17, Beckford 89	25,237
5	ccr2	Portsmouth	A	L	0-3		8,502
6	div2	Luton	H	W	1-0	Kandol 44	26,856
7	div2	Hartlepool	H	W	2-0	Kandol 20, Beckford 50	26,877
8	div2	Bristol Rovers	A	W	3-0	Beckford 9, 90, Kandol 77	11,883
9	div2	Swansea	H	W	2-0	Beckford 62, Prutton 67	29,467
10	div2	Gillingham	A	D	1-1	Carole 28	8,719
11	div2	Oldham	A	W	1-0	Westlake 90	10,054
12	div2	Yeovil	H	W	1-0	De Vries 89	27,808
13	div2	Leyton Orient	H	D	1-1	Carole 55	29,177
14	div2	Brighton	A	W	1-0	Kandol 79	8,691
15	div2	Millwall	H	W	4-2	Prutton 37, Beckford 53, Douglas 57, 64	30,319
16	div2	Carlisle	A	L	1-3	Beckford 28	16,668
17	div2	Bournemouth	A	W	3-1	Kandol 4, 86, Carole 54	9,632
18	facr1	Hereford	A	D	0-0		5,924
19	div2	Swindon	H	W	2-1	Beckford 32 pen, 56	27,990
20	facr1r	Hereford	H	L	0-1		11,315
21	div2	Cheltenham	A	L	0-1		7,043
22	div2	Port Vale	H	W	3-0	Prutton 18, Beckford 55, Flo 83	20,301
23	div2	Huddersfield	H	W	4-0	Douglas 24, Beckford 49, 69, Flo 87	32,501
24	div2	Walsall	A	D	1-1	Thompson 90	10,102
25	div2	Bristol Rovers	H	W	1-0	Howson 84	27,863
26	div2	Hartlepool	A	D	1-1	Beckford 90	7,784
27	div2	Swansea	A	L	2-3	Beckford 12, Thompson 46	19,010
28	div2	Oldham	H	L	1-3	Constantine 46	25,906
29	div2	Northampton	H	W	3-0	Richardson 43, Marques 52, Weston 90	24,472
30	div2	Crewe	A	W	1-0	Beckford 36	6,771
31	div2	Doncaster	H	L	0-1		31,402
32	div2	Luton	A	D	1-1	Huntington 27	9,227
33	div2	Southend	A	L	0-1		9,819
34	div2	Tranmere	H	L	0-2		24,907
35	div2	Northampton	A	D	1-1	Howson 38	7,260
36	div2	Nottm Forest	H	D	1-1	Beckford 83 pen	29,552
37	div2	Crewe	H	D	1-1	Kandol 86	21,223
38	div2	Swindon	A	W	1-0	Kandol 25	13,270
39	div2	Bournemouth	H	W	2-0	Bradley.Johnson 11, Kilkenny 63	21,199
40	div2	Cheltenham	H	L	1-2	Elding 85	20,257
41	div2	Port Vale	A	D	3-3	Marques 39, Freedman 41, 86	7,908
42	div2	Walsall	H	W	2-0	Beckford 29, 80	19,095
43	div2	Brighton	H	D	0-0		22,575
44	div2	Doncaster	A	W	1-0	Sheehan 20	15,001
45	div2	Leyton Orient	A	W	2-0	Huntington 16, Beckford 50	7,602
46	div2	Carlisle	H	W	3-2	Freedman 50, 69, Howson 59	28,530
47	div2	Huddersfield	A	L	0-1		16,413
48	div2	Millwall	A	W	2-0	Prutton 70, Hughes 79	13,395
49	div2	Yeovil	A	W	1-0	Freedman 4	9,527
50	div2	Gillingham	H	W	2-1	Bradley.Johnson 69, Kandol 88	38,256
51	d2po1	Carlisle	H	L	1-2	Freedman 90	36,297
52	d2po2	Carlisle	A	W	2-0	Howson 10, 90	12,873
53	d2pof	Doncaster	H	L	0-1		75,132

LEAGUE APPEARANCES, BOOKINGS AND GOALS

	AGE (on 01/07/08)	IN NAMED 16	APPEARANCES	COUNTING GAMES	MINUTES ON PITCH	LEAGUE GOALS	Yellow	Red
Goalkeepers								
Casper Ankergren	28	43	43	43	3870	0	2	0
David Lucas	30	27	3	3	270	0	0	0
Defenders								
Jamie Clapham	32	14	13	11	1049	0	1	0
Matt Heath	27	30	26	25	2295	1	4	0
Paul Huntington	20	37	17	12	1133	2	3	0
Darren Kenton	29	16	16	13	1319	0	3	0
Rui Manuel Marques	30	37	36	34	3067	2	4	0
Lubomir Michalik	24	17	17	17	1530	0	3	0
Frazer Richardson	25	42	39	39	3489	1	0	0
Alan Sheehan	21	11	10	9	857	1	2	1
Midfielders								
Sebastien Carole	25	33	28	14	1615	3	1	0
Jonathan Douglas	26	24	24	21	1955	3	7	1
Jonathan Howson	20	30	26	19	1868	3	3	0
Andrew Hughes	30	40	40	30	2885	1	9	0
Bradley Johnson	21	21	21	17	1502	2	1	0
Neil Kilkenny	22	16	16	16	1303	1	3	0
Radostin Kishishev	33	10	7	2	334	0	1	0
Ben Parker	20	13	9	6	577	0	0	0
David Prutton	26	44	43	35	3296	4	7	0
Peter Sweeney	23	10	9	3	503	0	1	0
Alan Thompson	34	19	13	7	785	3	4	0
Ian Westlake	24	21	20	6	935	1	3	0
Curtis Weston	21	11	7	1	145	1	0	0
Forwards								
Wayne Andrews	30	4	1	1	90	0	0	0
Jermaine Beckford	24	40	40	36	3450	20	6	1
Leon Constantine	30	7	4	1	129	1	0	0
Mark de Vries	32	6	6	1	147	1	1	0
Anthony Elding	26	17	9	2	339	1	0	0
Tore Andre Flo	35	23	22	2	601	3	0	0
Dougie Freedman	34	11	11	9	853	5	0	0
Tresor Kandol	26	43	41	31	2960	12	8	1

TEAM OF THE SEASON

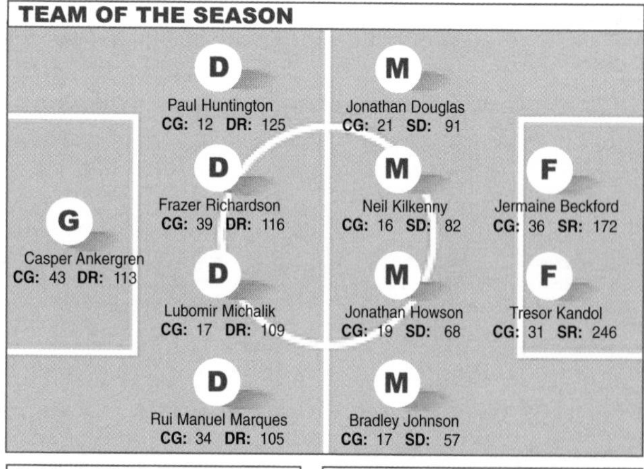
G
Casper Ankergren
CG: 43 DR: 113
D
Paul Huntington
CG: 12 DR: 125
D
Frazer Richardson
CG: 39 DR: 116
D
Lubomir Michalik
CG: 17 DR: 109
D
Rui Manuel Marques
CG: 34 DR: 105
M
Jonathan Douglas
CG: 21 SD: 91
M
Neil Kilkenny
CG: 16 SD: 82
M
Jonathan Howson
CG: 19 SD: 68
M
Bradley Johnson
CG: 17 SD: 57
F
Jermaine Beckford
CG: 36 SR: 172
F
Tresor Kandol
CG: 31 SR: 246

MONTHLY POINTS TALLY

Month	Points	%
AUGUST	9	100%
SEPTEMBER	13	87%
OCTOBER	13	87%
NOVEMBER	6	50%
DECEMBER	11	61%
JANUARY	7	39%
FEBRUARY	3	25%
MARCH	11	61%
APRIL	15	83%
MAY	3	100%

LEAGUE GOALS

	PLAYER	MINS	GOALS	S RATE
1	Beckford	3450	20	172
2	Kandol	2960	12	246
3	Freedman	853	5	170
4	Prutton	3296	4	824
5	Flo	601	3	200
6	Thompson	785	3	261
7	Carole	1615	3	538
8	Howson	1868	3	622
9	Douglas	1955	3	651
10	Huntington	1133	2	566
11	B. Johnson	1502	2	751
12	Marques	3067	2	1533
13	Constantine	129	1	129
	Other		9	
	TOTAL		72	

TOP POINT EARNERS

	PLAYER	GAMES	AV PTS
1	Jonathan Douglas	21	2.52
2	Sebastien Carole	14	2.29
3	Casper Ankergren	43	2.12
4	Paul Huntington	12	2.08
5	Matt Heath	25	2.08
6	Frazer Richardson	39	2.08
7	Jonathan Howson	19	2.05
8	Rui Manuel Marques	34	2.03
9	Neil Kilkenny	16	2.00
10	David Prutton	35	1.97
	CLUB AVERAGE:		1.65

DISCIPLINARY RECORDS

	PLAYER	YELLOW	RED	AVE
1	Alan Thompson	4	0	196
2	Jonathan Douglas	7	1	244
3	Alan Sheehan	2	1	285
4	Ian Westlake	3	0	311
5	Andrew Hughes	9	0	320
6	Tresor Kandol	8	1	328
7	Paul Huntington	3	0	377
8	Neil Kilkenny	3	0	434
9	Darren Kenton	3	0	439
10	David Prutton	7	0	470
11	Jermaine Beckford	6	1	492
12	Peter Sweeney	1	0	503
13	Lubomir Michalik	3	0	510
	Other	16	0	
	TOTAL	75	4	

KEY GOALKEEPER

Casper Ankergren

Goals Conceded in the League	34	**Counting Games** League games when player was on pitch for at least 70 minutes	43
Defensive Rating Ave number of mins between League goals conceded while on the pitch	113	**Clean Sheets** In League games when player was on pitch for at least 70 minutes	20

KEY PLAYERS - DEFENDERS

Paul Huntington

Goals Conceded Number of League goals conceded while the player was on the pitch	9	**Clean Sheets** In League games when player was on pitch for at least 70 minutes	6
Defensive Rating Ave number of mins between League goals conceded while on the pitch	125	**Club Defensive Rating** Average number of mins between League goals conceded by the club this season	111

	PLAYER	CON LGE	CLEAN SHEETS	DEF RATE
1	Paul Huntington	9	6	125 mins
2	Frazer Richardson	30	18	116 mins
3	Lubomir Michalik	14	8	109 mins
4	Rui Manuel Marques	29	15	105 mins

KEY PLAYERS - MIDFIELDERS

Jonathan Douglas

Goals in the League	3	**Contribution to Attacking Power** Average number of minutes between League team goals while on pitch	48
Defensive Rating Average number of mins between League goals conceded while on the pitch	139	**Scoring Difference** Defensive Rating minus Contribution to Attacking Power	91

	PLAYER	LGE GOALS	DEF RATE	POWER	SCORE DIFF
1	Jonathan Douglas	3	139	48	91 mins
2	Neil Kilkenny	1	144	62	82 mins
3	Jonathan Howson	3	124	56	68 mins
4	Bradley Johnson	2	125	68	57 mins

KEY PLAYERS - GOALSCORERS

Jermaine Beckford

Goals in the League	20	**Player Strike Rate** Average number of minutes between League goals scored by player	172
Contribution to Attacking Power Average number of minutes between League team goals while on pitch	57	**Club Strike Rate** Average number of minutes between League goals scored by club	58

	PLAYER	LGE GOALS	POWER	STRIKE RATE
1	Jermaine Beckford	20	57	172 mins
2	Tresor Kandol	12	53	246 mins
3	Sebastien Carole	3	46	538 mins
4	Jonathan Howson	3	56	622 mins

RedKite
Jermaine Beckford

SQUAD APPEARANCES

Match	Venue	Competition	Result
1	A	L	W
2	A	W	W
3	H	L	W
4	A	L	W
5	A	W	L
6	H	L	W
7	H	L	W
8	A	L	W
9	H	L	W
10	A	L	D
11	A	L	W
12	H	L	W
13	H	L	D
14	A	L	W
15	H	L	W
16	A	L	L
17	A	L	W
18	A	F	D
19	H	L	W
20	H	F	L
21	A	L	L
22	H	L	W
23	H	L	W
24	A	L	D
25	H	L	W
26	A	L	D
27	A	L	L
28	H	L	L
29	H	L	W
30	A	L	W
31	H	L	L
32	A	L	D
33	A	L	L
34	H	L	L
35	A	L	D
36	H	L	D
37	H	L	D
38	A	L	W
39	H	L	W
40	H	L	L
41	A	L	D
42	H	L	W
43	H	L	D
44	A	L	W
45	A	L	W
46	H	L	W
47	A	L	L
48	A	L	W
49	A	L	W
50	H	L	W
51	H	O	L
52	A	O	W
53	N	O	L

Goalkeepers
Casper Ankergren
David Lucas

Defenders
Jamie Clapham
Matt Heath
Paul Huntington
Darren Kenton
Rui Manuel Marques
Lubomir Michalik
Frazer Richardson
Alan Sheehan

Midfielders
Sebastien Carole
Jonathan Douglas
Jonathan Howson
Andrew Hughes
Bradley Johnson
Neil Kilkenny
Radostin Kishishev
Ben Parker
David Prutton
Peter Sweeney
Alan Thompson
Ian Westlake
Curtis Weston

Forwards
Wayne Andrews
Jermaine Beckford
Leon Constantine
Mark de Vries
Anthony Elding
Tore Andre Flo
Dougie Freedman
Tresor Kandol

KEY: On all match · On bench · Subbed or sent off (Counting game) · Subbed or sent off (playing less than 70 minutes) · Subbed on from bench (Counting Game) · Subbed on (playing less than 70 minutes) · Subbed on and then subbed or sent off (Counting Game) · Subbed on and then subbed or sent off (playing less than 70 minutes) · Not in 16

SOUTHEND UNITED

Final Position: **6th**

NICKNAME: THE SHRIMPERS

KEY: ☐Won ☐Drawn ☐Lost

							Attendance
1	div2	**Leyton Orient**	H	L	1-2	Gower 24	9,828
2	ccr1	**Cheltenham**	H	W	4-1	Bradbury 11, 108 pen, 117, Barrett 104	3,084
3	div2	**Leeds**	A	L	1-4	Barrett 69	24,036
4	div2	**Millwall**	H	W	1-0	Bailey 55	8,758
5	ccr2	**Watford**	H	W	2-0	MacDonald 20, Harrold 55	5,554
6	div2	**Brighton**	A	L	2-3	McCormack 40, Bailey 78	5,652
7	div2	**Gillingham**	H	W	3-0	Bailey 8, McCormack 44, L.Clarke 59	7,348
8	div2	**Oldham**	A	W	1-0	L.Clarke 28	5,151
9	div2	**Doncaster**	H	W	3-2	Barrett 25, McCormack 49, L.Clarke 59 pen	8,117
10	ccr3	**Blackpool**	A	L	1-2	Harrold 7 pen	5,022
11	div2	**Port Vale**	A	W	2-1	L.Clarke 32, McCormack 45	3,969
12	div2	**Bristol Rovers**	A	D	1-1	L.Clarke 90	5,762
13	div2	**Tranmere**	H	L	1-2	Barrett 43	7,619
14	div2	**Crewe**	H	W	3-0	Bailey 17, Hooper 63, L.Clarke 82 pen	6,927
15	div2	**Walsall**	A	W	2-0	P.Clarke 38, L.Clarke 51	5,661
16	div2	**Carlisle**	H	L	0-1		9,281
17	div2	**Northampton**	A	W	1-0	Barrett 65	6,646
18	div2	**Nottm Forest**	A	L	1-4	Gower 3	26,094
19	facr1	**Rochdale**	H	W	2-1	Bailey 1, Harrold 24 pen	5,180
20	div2	**Cheltenham**	H	D	2-2	Gower 50, Hammell 56	7,158
21	div2	**Luton**	A	L	0-1		6,820
22	facr2	**Oxford**	A	D	0-0		5,162
23	div2	**Huddersfield**	H	W	4-1	Bailey 3, McCormack 57, 90, Gower 84	6,844
24	div2	**Swindon**	H	W	2-1	Barrett 32, Gower 90	7,403
25	facr2r	**Oxford**	H	W	3-0	MacDonald 5, 90, Morgan 45 pen	2,740
26	div2	**Swansea**	A	L	0-3		12,629
27	div2	**Oldham**	H	L	0-1		7,388
28	div2	**Gillingham**	A	D	1-1	P.Clarke 54	8,268
29	div2	**Doncaster**	A	L	1-3	MacDonald 18	7,163
30	div2	**Bristol Rovers**	H	L	0-1		7,664
31	facr3	**Dag & Red**	H	W	5-2	MacDonald 11, Morgan 64, 90, Francis 77, Bailey 90	6,393
32	div2	**Yeovil**	H	D	1-1	Bailey 20	7,352
33	div2	**Bournemouth**	A	W	4-1	Gower 18, Francis 23, Black 44, Hooper 65	5,419
34	div2	**Hartlepool**	A	L	3-4	Hammell 30 pen, Gower 83, Black 90	3,217
35	facr4	**Barnsley**	H	L	0-1		7,212
36	div2	**Leeds**	H	W	1-0	Barnard 41	9,819
37	div2	**Leyton Orient**	A	D	2-2	Barnard 27, P.Clarke 56	6,886
38	div2	**Hartlepool**	H	W	2-1	McCormack 61, Bailey 66	7,436
39	div2	**Millwall**	A	L	1-2	Bailey 9	7,425
40	div2	**Bournemouth**	H	W	2-1	Barnard 10, J.Walker 79	7,474
41	div2	**Yeovil**	A	W	3-0	Barnard 20, P.Clarke 34, Gower 64	4,820
42	div2	**Cheltenham**	A	D	1-1	Bailey 74	3,859
43	div2	**Luton**	H	W	2-0	Bailey 37, J.Walker 90	8,241
44	div2	**Nottm Forest**	H	D	1-1	Robson- Kanu 20	8,376
45	div2	**Huddersfield**	A	W	2-1	Robson- Kanu 40, McCormack 90	7,823
46	div2	**Swansea**	H	D	1-1	Robson- Kanu 45	9,797
47	div2	**Swindon**	A	W	1-0	Francis 18	6,378
48	div2	**Walsall**	H	W	1-0	Barnard 47	8,145
49	div2	**Crewe**	A	W	3-1	Barnard 2, 80, J.Walker 19	4,895
50	div2	**Brighton**	H	W	2-0	Gower 24, Barrett 30	8,428
51	div2	**Northampton**	H	D	1-1	Barnard 51	9,286
52	div2	**Carlisle**	A	W	2-1	Mulgrew 7, Barnard 90	9,122
53	div2	**Tranmere**	A	L	0-1		5,842
54	div2	**Port Vale**	H	D	1-1	J.Walker 84	9,292
55	d2po1	**Doncaster**	H	D	0-0		9,109
56	d2po2	**Doncaster**	A	L	1-5	Bailey 88	13,081

LEAGUE APPEARANCES, BOOKINGS AND GOALS

	AGE (on 01/07/08)	IN NAMED 16	APPEARANCES	COUNTING GAMES	MINUTES ON PITCH	LEAGUE GOALS	Yellow	Red
Goalkeepers								
Stephen Collis	27	46	20	20	1800	0	1	0
Darryl Flahavan	29	40	26	26	2340	0	1	0
Defenders								
Adam Barrett	28	45	45	44	4009	6	3	0
Peter Clarke	26	45	45	45	4050	4	5	0
Simon Francis	23	31	27	24	2231	2	3	0
Kerrea Gilbert	21	7	5	5	440	0	1	0
Anthony Grant	21	15	10	0	142	0	1	0
Steven Hammell	26	16	16	16	1436	2	1	0
Lewis Hunt	25	32	24	23	2058	0	5	0
Charles Mulgrew	25	18	18	17	1563	1	2	0
Garry Richards	22	19	10	7	725	0	0	1
Che Wilson	29	13	6	4	409	0	0	0
Midfielders								
Nick Bailey	24	44	44	41	3799	10	9	1
Thomas Black	28	39	37	28	2476	2	2	0
Jamal Campbell-Ryce	25	2	2	2	180	0	0	0
Mark Gower	29	44	43	39	3550	9	3	0
Kevin Maher	31	26	19	18	1637	0	3	0
Alan McCormack	24	42	42	39	3575	8	9	2
Dean Morgan	24	8	8	5	487	0	0	0
Franck Moussa	18	36	16	6	636	0	1	0
Hal Robson-Kanu	27	9	9	5	548	3	0	0
Damian Scannell	23	13	9	0	93	0	0	1
Forwards								
Lee Barnard	23	15	15	10	1001	9	1	0
Lee Bradbury	32	1	1	1	81	0	0	0
Leon Clarke	23	16	16	14	1366	7	4	1
Matt Harrold	23	19	16	11	1077	0	3	1
Gary Hooper	20	20	13	7	725	2	1	0
Charlie MacDonald	27	31	25	9	1025	1	1	0
Eric Odhiambo	19	7	5	2	195	0	0	0
Alex Revell	24	9	8	5	467	0	0	0
James Walker	20	15	14	12	1151	4	0	0

TEAM OF THE SEASON

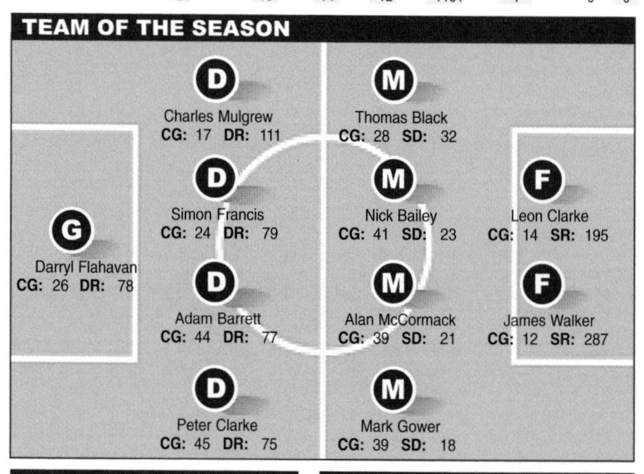

D
Charles Mulgrew
CG: 17 DR: 111
M
Thomas Black
CG: 28 SD: 32
D
Simon Francis
CG: 24 DR: 79
M
Nick Bailey
CG: 41 SD: 23
F
Leon Clarke
CG: 14 SR: 195
G
Darryl Flahavan
CG: 26 DR: 78
D
Adam Barrett
CG: 44 DR: 77
M
Alan McCormack
CG: 39 SD: 21
F
James Walker
CG: 12 SR: 287
D
Peter Clarke
CG: 45 DR: 75
M
Mark Gower
CG: 39 SD: 18

MONTHLY POINTS TALLY

AUGUST	3	33%
SEPTEMBER	12	80%
OCTOBER	7	47%
NOVEMBER	4	33%
DECEMBER	7	39%
JANUARY	7	47%
FEBRUARY	11	61%
MARCH	14	78%
APRIL	10	67%
MAY	1	33%

LEAGUE GOALS

	PLAYER	MINS	GOALS	S RATE
1	Bailey	3799	**10**	379
2	Barnard	1001	**9**	111
3	Gower	3550	**9**	394
4	McCormack	3575	**8**	446
5	Clarke, L	1366	**7**	195
6	Barrett	4009	**6**	668
7	Walker, J	1151	**4**	287
8	Clarke, P	4050	**4**	1012
9	Robson- Kanu	548	**3**	182
10	Hooper	725	**2**	362
11	Hammell	1436	**2**	718
12	Francis	2231	**2**	1115
13	Black	2476	**2**	1238
	Other		2	
	TOTAL		**70**	

TOP POINT EARNERS

	PLAYER	GAMES	AV PTS
1	James Walker	12	**2.08**
2	Thomas Black	28	**1.96**
3	Charles Mulgrew	17	**1.94**
4	Leon Clarke	15	**1.93**
5	Nick Bailey	41	**1.80**
6	Alan McCormack	39	**1.79**
7	Simon Francis	24	**1.79**
8	Darryl Flahavan	26	**1.77**
9	Adam Barrett	44	**1.66**
10	Mark Gower	39	**1.62**
	CLUB AVERAGE:		**1.65**

DISCIPLINARY RECORDS

	PLAYER	YELLOW	RED	AVE
1	Matt Harrold	3	1	**269**
2	Leon Clarke	4	1	**273**
3	Alan McCormack	9	2	**325**
4	Nick Bailey	9	1	**379**
5	Lewis Hunt	5	0	**411**
6	Kevin Maher	3	0	**545**
7	Franck Moussa	1	0	**636**
8	Garry Richards	0	1	**725**
9	Gary Hooper	1	0	**725**
10	Simon Francis	3	0	**743**
11	Charles Mulgrew	2	0	**781**
12	Peter Clarke	5	0	**810**
13	Lee Barnard	1	0	**1001**
	Other	11	0	
	TOTAL	**57**	**6**	

KEY GOALKEEPER

Darryl Flahavan

Goals Conceded in the League	30	Counting Games League games when player was on pitch for at least 70 minutes	26
Defensive Rating Ave number of mins between League goals conceded while on the pitch	78	Clean Sheets In League games when player was on pitch for at least 70 minutes	7

KEY PLAYERS - DEFENDERS

Charles Mulgrew

Goals Conceded Number of League goals conceded while the player was on the pitch	14	Clean Sheets In League games when player was on pitch for at least 70 minutes	5
Defensive Rating Ave number of mins between League goals conceded while on the pitch	111	Club Defensive Rating Average number of mins between League goals conceded by the club this season	75

	PLAYER	CON LGE	CLEAN SHEETS	DEF RATE
1	Charles Mulgrew	14	5	111 mins
2	Simon Francis	28	6	79 mins
3	Adam Barrett	52	12	77 mins
4	Peter Clarke	54	12	75 mins

KEY PLAYERS - MIDFIELDERS

Thomas Black

Goals in the League	2	Contribution to Attacking Power Average number of minutes between League team goals while on pitch	50
Defensive Rating Average number of mins between League goals conceded while on the pitch	82	Scoring Difference Defensive Rating minus Contribution to Attacking Power	32

	PLAYER	LGE GOALS	DEF RATE	POWER	SCORE DIFF
1	Thomas Black	2	82	50	32 mins
2	Nick Bailey	10	79	56	23 mins
3	Alan McCormack	8	77	56	21 mins
4	Mark Gower	9	75	57	18 mins

KEY PLAYERS - GOALSCORERS

Leon Clarke

Goals in the League	7	Player Strike Rate Average number of minutes between League goals scored by player	195
Contribution to Attacking Power Average number of minutes between League team goals while on pitch	52	Club Strike Rate Average number of minutes between League goals scored by club	59

	PLAYER	LGE GOALS	POWER	STRIKE RATE
1	Leon Clarke	7	52	195 mins
2	James Walker	4	54	287 mins
3	Nick Bailey	10	56	379 mins
4	Mark Gower	9	57	394 mins

Lee Barnard and team-mates

SQUAD APPEARANCES

Match	1	2	3	4	5	6	7	8	9	10	11	12	13	14	15	16	17	18	19	20	21	22	23	24	25	26	27	28
Venue	H	H	A	H	H	A	H	A	H	A	A	A	H	H	A	H	A	A	H	H	A	A	H	H	H	A	H	A
Competition	L	W	L	L	W	L	L	L	L	W	L	L	L	L	L	L	L	L	F	L	L	F	L	L	F	L	L	L
Result	L	W	L	W	W	L	W	W	W	L	W	D	L	W	W	L	W	L	W	D	L	D	W	W	W	L	L	D

Match	29	30	31	32	33	34	35	36	37	38	39	40	41	42	43	44	45	46	47	48	49	50	51	52	53	54	55	56
Venue	A	H	H	H	A	A	H	H	A	H	A	H	A	A	H	H	A	H	A	H	A	H	H	A	A	H	H	A
Competition	L	L	F	L	L	L	F	L	L	L	L	L	L	L	L	L	L	L	L	L	L	L	L	L	L	L	O	O
Result	L	L	W	D	W	L	L	W	D	W	L	W	W	D	W	D	W	D	W	W	W	W	D	W	L	D	D	L

Goalkeepers
- Stephen Collis
- Darryl Flahavan

Defenders
- Adam Barrett
- Peter Clarke
- Simon Francis
- Kerrea Gilbert
- Anthony Grant
- Steven Hammell
- Lewis Hunt
- Charles Mulgrew
- Garry Richards
- Che Wilson

Midfielders
- Nick Bailey
- Thomas Black
- Jamal Campbell-Ryce
- Mark Gower
- Kevin Maher
- Alan McCormack
- Dean Morgan
- Franck Moussa
- Hal Robson-Kanu
- Damian Scannell

Forwards
- Lee Barnard
- Lee Bradbury
- Leon Clarke
- Matt Harrold
- Gary Hooper
- Charlie MacDonald
- Eric Odhiambo
- Alex Revell
- James Walker

KEY: On all match; On bench; Subbed or sent off (Counting game); Subbed or sent off (playing less than 70 minutes); Subbed on from bench (Counting Game); Subbed on (playing less than 70 minutes); Subbed on and then subbed or sent off (Counting Game); Subbed on and then subbed or sent off (playing less than 70 minutes); Not in 16

BRIGHTON & HOVE ALBION

Final Position: **7th**

NICKNAME: THE SEAGULLS

KEY: ☐Won ☐Drawn ☐Lost

	Comp	Opponent	H/A	Res	Score	Scorers	Attendance
1	div2	Crewe	A	L	1-2	Cox 14	5,394
2	ccr1	Cardiff	A	L	0-1		3,726
3	div2	Northampton	H	W	2-1	Hammond 2 pen, Revell 66	5,137
4	div2	Tranmere	A	L	0-2		5,670
5	div2	Southend	H	W	3-2	Forster 75, 85, Hammond 90	5,652
6	div2	Millwall	H	W	3-0	Hammond 12 pen, Cox 19, Martot 78	6,563
7	div2	Gillingham	A	L	0-1		6,118
8	div2	Yeovil	H	L	1-2	Hammond 61 pen	5,231
9	div2	Swansea	A	D	0-0		11,058
10	div2	Bournemouth	A	W	2-0	Cox 46, Savage 66	4,638
11	div2	Bristol Rovers	H	D	0-0		5,820
12	div2	Port Vale	A	W	1-0	Revell 64	3,490
13	div2	Leeds	H	L	0-1		8,691
14	div2	Hartlepool	A	W	2-1	Nelson 14 og, Savage 90	5,619
15	div2	Luton	H	W	3-1	Savage 40, Forster 69, 85	5,317
16	div2	Walsall	H	D	1-1	Robinson 36	4,717
17	facr1	Cheltenham	A	D	1-1	Loft 90	2,984
18	div2	Leyton Orient	A	D	2-2	Forster 68, Cox 75	6,496
19	facr1r	Cheltenham	H	W	2-1	El-Abd 18, Hammond 69 pen	3,711
20	div2	Carlisle	H	D	2-2	Forster 47, 84	5,390
21	facr2	Torquay	A	W	2-0	Forster 63, 90	4,010
22	div2	Doncaster	A	D	0-0		6,215
23	div2	Nottm Forest	H	L	0-2		6,536
24	div2	Swindon	A	W	3-0	Forster 3, Robinson 45, Hammond 73	6,415
25	div2	Millwall	A	L	0-3		9,401
26	div2	Yeovil	A	L	1-2	Revell 19	6,881
27	div2	Bournemouth	H	W	3-2	Revell 15, 58, 90	5,963
28	facr3	Mansfield	H	L	1-2	Revell 23	5,857
29	div2	Oldham	A	D	1-1	Elder 90	5,168
30	div2	Huddersfield	H	D	1-1	Elphick 74	5,343
31	div2	Northampton	A	L	0-1		4,657
32	div2	Crewe	H	W	3-0	Murray 23, 45, Butters 41	4,802
33	div2	Cheltenham	A	L	1-2	Robinson 55	3,963
34	div2	Tranmere	H	D	0-0		4,797
35	div2	Cheltenham	H	W	2-1	Murray 80, Lynch 88	4,395
36	div2	Oldham	H	W	1-0	Murray 61	4,815
37	div2	Leyton Orient	H	D	1-1	Forster 90 pen	6,242
38	div2	Gillingham	H	W	4-2	Forster 23 pen, El-Abd 43, Elphick 45, Robinson 68	6,836
39	div2	Carlisle	A	L	0-2		6,793
40	div2	Walsall	A	W	2-1	Forster 34, Gerrard 79 og	4,309
41	div2	Doncaster	H	W	1-0	Forster 59	6,252
42	div2	Huddersfield	A	L	1-2	Forster 47 pen	6,004
43	div2	Swindon	H	W	2-1	Forster 12, 66	6,849
44	div2	Nottm Forest	A	D	0-0		18,165
45	div2	Leeds	A	D	0-0		22,575
46	div2	Port Vale	H	L	2-3	Cox 26, Murray 90	7,741
47	div2	Southend	A	L	0-2		8,428
48	div2	Luton	A	W	2-1	Westlake 51, Murray 59	6,652
49	div2	Hartlepool	H	W	2-1	Murray 38, Cox 89	6,178
50	div2	Bristol Rovers	A	W	2-0	Westlake 71, Murray 74	7,590
51	div2	Swansea	H	L	0-1		7,283

LEAGUE APPEARANCES, BOOKINGS AND GOALS

	AGE (on 01/07/08)	IN NAMED 16	APPEARANCES	COUNTING GAMES	MINUTES ON PITCH	LEAGUE GOALS	Yellow	Red
Goalkeepers								
Michel Kuipers	34	46	46	46	4140	0	4	0
Defenders								
Guy Butters	38	35	21	16	1528	1	0	0
Adam El-Abd	23	36	35	31	2879	1	5	0
Joel Lynch	20	25	22	18	1678	1	3	0
Kerry Mayo	30	24	15	9	975	0	1	0
Paul Reid	28	11	7	1	292	0	0	0
Sam Rents	21	15	5	4	382	0	1	0
Matthew Richards	23	28	28	27	2452	0	1	0
Andrew Whing	23	42	42	41	3734	0	11	1
Midfielders								
Dean Cox	20	42	42	37	3517	6	6	0
Tommy Elphick	20	40	39	39	3510	2	4	0
Wes Fogden	20	5	3	0	68	0	1	0
Tommy Fraser	20	32	24	9	1209	0	3	0
Sam Gargan	19	1	1	0	5	0	0	0
Dean Hammond	25	24	24	23	2069	5	3	1
Gary Hart	31	13	7	2	242	0	1	1
Douglas Loft	21	18	13	1	316	0	0	0
David Martot	27	34	26	11	1508	1	1	0
George O'Callaghan	28	14	14	12	1155	0	3	1
Therry Racon	24	8	8	8	709	0	1	0
Steven Thomson	30	20	20	20	1772	0	2	0
Ian Westlake	24	11	11	9	899	2	3	0
Forwards								
Dean Bowditch	22	5	5	3	368	0	0	0
Jonathan Dixon	24	6	4	1	137	0	0	0
Nathan Elder	20	19	9	0	131	1	1	0
Nick Forster	34	41	41	38	3443	15	0	0
Joe Gatting	20	12	9	0	34	0	0	0
Glenn Murray	24	21	21	20	1803	8	0	0
Alex Revell	24	21	21	12	1292	6	1	0
Jake Robinson	21	40	34	13	1696	4	0	0
Basir Savage	26	21	21	15	1485	3	3	0

TEAM OF THE SEASON

G — Michel Kuipers, CG: 46 DR: 82

D — Matthew Richards, CG: 27 DR: 102

D — Andrew Whing, CG: 41 DR: 86

D — Guy Butters, CG: 16 DR: 84

D — Joel Lynch, CG: 18 DR: 79

M — Tommy Elphick, CG: 39 SD: 22

M — George O'Callaghan, CG: 12 SD: 22

M — Steven Thomson, CG: 20 SD: 18

M — Dean Hammond, CG: 23 SD: 8

F — Alex Revell, CG: 12 SR: 215

F — Glenn Murray, CG: 20 SR: 225

MONTHLY POINTS TALLY

Month	Points	%
AUGUST	3	33%
SEPTEMBER	7	47%
OCTOBER	10	67%
NOVEMBER	6	50%
DECEMBER	4	27%
JANUARY	5	42%
FEBRUARY	10	67%
MARCH	15	56%
APRIL	9	60%
MAY	0	0%

LEAGUE GOALS

	PLAYER	MINS	GOALS	S RATE
1	Forster	3443	15	229
2	Murray	1803	8	225
3	Revell	1292	6	215
4	Cox	3517	6	586
5	Hammond	2069	5	413
6	Robinson	1696	4	424
7	Savage	1485	3	495
8	Westlake	899	2	449
9	Elphick	3510	2	1755
10	Elder	131	1	131
11	Martot	1508	1	1508
12	Butters	1528	1	1528
13	Lynch	1678	1	1678
	Other		1	
	TOTAL		**56**	

TOP POINT EARNERS

	PLAYER	GAMES	AV PTS
1	Glenn Murray	20	1.70
2	Tommy Elphick	39	1.64
3	Jake Robinson	13	1.62
4	Steven Thomson	20	1.60
5	George O'Callaghan	12	1.58
6	Matthew Richards	27	1.56
7	Alex Revell	12	1.50
8	Michel Kuipers	46	1.50
9	Guy Butters	16	1.50
10	Andrew Whing	41	1.49
	CLUB AVERAGE:		**1.50**

DISCIPLINARY RECORDS

	PLAYER	YELLOW	RED	AVE
1	George O'Callaghan	3	1	288
2	Ian Westlake	3	0	299
3	Andrew Whing	11	1	311
4	Tommy Fraser	3	0	403
5	Basir Savage	3	0	495
6	Dean Hammond	3	1	517
7	Joel Lynch	3	0	559
8	Adam El-Abd	5	0	575
9	Dean Cox	6	0	586
10	Therry Racon	1	0	709
11	Tommy Elphick	4	0	877
12	Steven Thomson	2	0	886
13	Kerry Mayo	1	0	975
	Other	7	0	
	TOTAL	**55**	**3**	

KEY GOALKEEPER

Michel Kuipers

Goals Conceded in the League	50	Counting Games League games when player was on pitch for at least 70 minutes	46
Defensive Rating Ave number of mins between League goals conceded while on the pitch	82	Clean Sheets In League games when player was on pitch for at least 70 minutes	14

KEY PLAYERS - DEFENDERS

Matthew Richards

Goals Conceded Number of League goals conceded while the player was on the pitch	24	Clean Sheets In League games when player was on pitch for at least 70 minutes	10
Defensive Rating Ave number of mins between League goals conceded while on the pitch	102	Club Defensive Rating Average number of mins between League goals conceded by the club this season	84

	PLAYER	CON LGE	CLEAN SHEETS	DEF RATE
1	Matthew Richards	24	10	102 mins
2	Andrew Whing	43	13	86 mins
3	Guy Butters	18	6	84 mins
4	Joel Lynch	21	7	79 mins

KEY PLAYERS - MIDFIELDERS

Tommy Elphick

Goals in the League	2	Contribution to Attacking Power Average number of minutes between League team goals while on pitch	68
Defensive Rating Average number of mins between League goals conceded while on the pitch	90	Scoring Difference Defensive Rating minus Contribution to Attacking Power	22

	PLAYER	LGE GOALS	DEF RATE	POWER	SCORE DIFF
1	Tommy Elphick	2	90	68	22 mins
2	George O'Callaghan	0	82	60	22 mins
3	Steven Thomson	0	98	80	18 mins
4	Dean Hammond	5	76	68	8 mins

KEY PLAYERS - GOALSCORERS

Alex Revell

Goals in the League	6	Player Strike Rate Average number of minutes between League goals scored by player	215
Contribution to Attacking Power Average number of minutes between League team goals while on pitch	80	Club Strike Rate Average number of minutes between League goals scored by club	72

	PLAYER	LGE GOALS	POWER	STRIKE RATE
1	Alex Revell	6	80	215 mins
2	Glenn Murray	8	69	225 mins
3	Nick Forster	15	68	229 mins
4	Dean Hammond	5	68	413 mins

SKINT
errea
Nick Forster

SQUAD APPEARANCES

Match	1	2	3	4	5	6	7	8	9	10	11	12	13	14	15	16	17	18	19	20	21	22	23	24	25	26	27	28	29	30	31	32	33	34	35	36	37	38	39	40	41	42	43	44	45	46	47	48	49	50	51
Venue	A	A	H	A	H	H	A	H	A	A	H	A	H	A	H	H	A	A	H	H	A	A	H	A	A	A	H	H	A	H	A	H	A	H	H	H	H	H	A	A	H	A	H	A	A	H	A	A	H	A	H
Competition	L	W	L	L	L	L	L	L	L	L	L	L	L	L	L	L	F	L	F	L	F	L	L	L	L	L	L	F	L	L	L	L	L	L	L	L	L	L	L	L	L	L	L	L	L	L	L	L	L	L	L
Result	L	L	W	L	W	W	L	L	D	W	D	W	L	W	W	D	D	D	W	D	W	D	L	W	L	L	W	L	D	D	L	W	L	D	W	W	D	W	L	W	W	L	W	D	D	L	L	W	W	W	L

Goalkeepers
Michel Kuipers

Defenders
Guy Butters
Adam El-Abd
Joel Lynch
Kerry Mayo
Paul Reid
Sam Rents
Matthew Richards
Andrew Whing

Midfielders
Dean Cox
Tommy Elphick
Wes Fogden
Tommy Fraser
Sam Gargan
Dean Hammond
Gary Hart
Douglas Loft
David Martot
George O'Callaghan
Therry Racon
Steven Thomson
Ian Westlake

Forwards
Dean Bowditch
Jonathan Dixon
Nathan Elder
Nick Forster
Joe Gatting
Glenn Murray
Alex Revell
Jake Robinson
Basir Savage

KEY: On all match · On bench · Subbed or sent off (Counting game) · Subbed or sent off (playing less than 70 minutes) · Subbed on from bench (Counting Game) · Subbed on (playing less than 70 minutes) · Subbed on and then subbed or sent off (Counting Game) · Subbed on and then subbed or sent off (playing less than 70 minutes) · Not in 16

OLDHAM ATHLETIC

Final Position: **8th**

NICKNAME: THE LATICS

KEY: ☐Won ☐Drawn ☐Lost

	Comp	Opponent	H/A	Res	Score	Scorers	Attendance
1	div2	**Swansea**	H	W	2-1	Ricketts 3 pen, C.Davies 90	7,397
2	ccr1	**Mansfield**	H	W	4-1	Kilkenny 20, Kalala 27, Smalley 82, C.Davies 86	3,155
3	div2	**Carlisle**	A	L	0-1		7,777
4	div2	**Bristol Rovers**	H	L	0-1		5,348
5	ccr2	**Burnley**	A	L	0-3		7,317
6	div2	**Hartlepool**	A	L	1-4	C.Davies 14	5,015
7	div2	**Southend**	H	L	0-1		5,151
8	div2	**Walsall**	A	W	3-0	Ricketts 33, Liddell 65 pen, C.Davies 90	6,202
9	div2	**Crewe**	H	W	3-2	Allott 36, Wolfenden 83, Kilkenny 90	5,082
10	div2	**Leeds**	H	L	0-1		10,054
11	div2	**Cheltenham**	A	D	1-1	Liddell 46	3,621
12	div2	**Huddersfield**	A	D	1-1	C.Davies 27	10,909
13	div2	**Northampton**	H	L	0-1		4,870
14	div2	**Nottm Forest**	A	D	0-0		16,423
15	div2	**Leyton Orient**	A	L	0-1		4,690
16	div2	**Tranmere**	A	W	1-0	C.Davies 90	5,473
17	facr1	**Doncaster**	H	D	2-2	Trotman 32, C.Davies 49	4,280
18	div2	**Port Vale**	H	D	1-1	C.Davies 23	5,097
19	div2	**Bournemouth**	A	W	3-0	Hughes 56, 87 pen, C.Taylor 70	5,261
20	facr1r	**Doncaster**	A	W	2-1	Kilkenny 45, McDonald 49	4,340
21	facr2	**Crewe**	H	W	1-0	Hughes 41	3,900
22	div2	**Luton**	H	D	1-1	C.Davies 32	4,251
23	div2	**Doncaster**	H	D	1-1	Allott 44	4,776
24	div2	**Millwall**	A	W	3-2	Hughes 32, 74 pen, 80	8,033
25	div2	**Southend**	A	W	1-0	Hughes 4	7,388
26	div2	**Nottm Forest**	H	D	0-0		8,140
27	div2	**Walsall**	H	L	0-2		5,292
28	div2	**Leeds**	A	W	3-1	Hazell 28, Trotman 36, Hughes 41 og	25,906
29	facr3	**Everton**	A	W	1-0	McDonald 45	33,086
30	div2	**Brighton**	H	D	1-1	Hughes 40	5,168
31	div2	**Yeovil**	A	D	0-0		4,905
32	div2	**Gillingham**	A	D	0-0		4,402
33	facr4	**Huddersfield**	H	L	0-1		12,749
34	div2	**Carlisle**	H	W	2-0	McDonald 21, 44	4,701
35	div2	**Swansea**	A	L	1-2	C.Davies 76 pen	12,458
36	div2	**Gillingham**	H	W	2-1	C.Taylor 42, C.Davies 67	4,866
37	div2	**Bristol Rovers**	A	L	0-1		5,778
38	div2	**Yeovil**	H	W	3-0	McDonald 15, Peltier 77 og, C.Davies 87	4,781
39	div2	**Brighton**	A	L	0-1		4,815
40	div2	**Swindon**	H	D	2-2	Livermore 50, Allott 55	3,923
41	div2	**Port Vale**	A	W	3-0	J.Robertson 23, Eardley 78, Wolfenden 90	3,715
42	div2	**Hartlepool**	H	L	0-1		3,765
43	div2	**Tranmere**	H	W	3-1	Eardley 41 pen, C.Taylor 45, Alessandra 76	5,442
44	div2	**Bournemouth**	H	W	2-0	Eardley 24 pen, 80 pen	3,633
45	div2	**Luton**	A	L	0-3		5,417
46	div2	**Millwall**	H	D	1-1	Constantine 79	4,391
47	div2	**Doncaster**	A	D	1-1	Jarrett 52	8,777
48	div2	**Huddersfield**	H	W	4-1	Jarrett 8, 45, Constantine 40, C.Taylor 61	5,637
49	div2	**Swindon**	A	L	0-3		5,384
50	div2	**Leyton Orient**	H	W	2-0	C.Taylor 22, Allott 42	4,325
51	div2	**Northampton**	A	L	0-2		5,171
52	div2	**Cheltenham**	H	W	2-1	Smalley 16, Alessandra 87	6,400
53	div2	**Crewe**	A	W	4-1	Smalley 5, Eardley 32, 59, McDonald 69	6,786

LEAGUE APPEARANCES, BOOKINGS AND GOALS

	AGE (on 01/07/08)	IN NAMED 16	APPEARANCES	COUNTING GAMES	MINUTES ON PITCH	LEAGUE GOALS	Yellow	Red
Goalkeepers								
Marlon Beresford	38	5	5	5	450	0	0	0
Mark Crossley	39	41	38	37	3389	0	0	0
Richard O'Donnell	19	9	4	3	301	0	0	0
Defenders								
Ryan Bertrand	18	21	21	21	1890	0	4	0
Paul Black	-	17	2	0	60	0	0	0
Neil Eardley	20	44	42	39	3634	6	2	1
Stuart Giddings	22	2	2	2	180	0	0	0
Sean Gregan	34	15	15	15	1338	0	5	0
Reuben Hazell	29	38	34	29	2768	1	4	1
Kelvin Lomax	21	25	21	16	1588	0	0	0
Stefan Stam	28	36	36	32	3057	0	2	0
John Thompson	26	19	7	3	432	0	1	0
Neal Trotman	21	22	17	15	1440	1	7	0
Midfielders								
Mark Allott	30	44	43	34	3307	4	1	0
Aaron Chalmers	17	2	2	0	42	0	0	0
Jason Jarrett	28	15	15	10	1004	3	1	0
J-P Kamudimba Kalala	26	32	19	10	1133	0	3	0
Ashley Kelly	19	8	1	0	12	0	1	0
Neil Kilkenny	22	20	20	19	1716	1	4	0
Andy Liddell	35	19	18	14	1445	2	0	0
David Livermore	28	10	10	10	900	1	1	0
Gary McDonald	26	41	35	25	2558	4	2	0
Chris Taylor	21	42	42	38	3546	5	6	0
Forwards								
Lewis Alessandra	19	18	15	13	1158	2	0	0
Leon Constantine	30	8	8	7	687	2	0	0
Craig Davies	22	32	32	30	2701	10	5	0
Lee Hughes	32	18	18	12	1247	7	5	0
Michael Ricketts	29	10	9	6	673	2	5	0
Jordan Robertson	20	3	3	1	139	1	0	0
Dean Smalley	19	40	37	20	2070	2	0	0
Matthew Wolfenden	20	39	25	5	610	2	0	0

TEAM OF THE SEASON

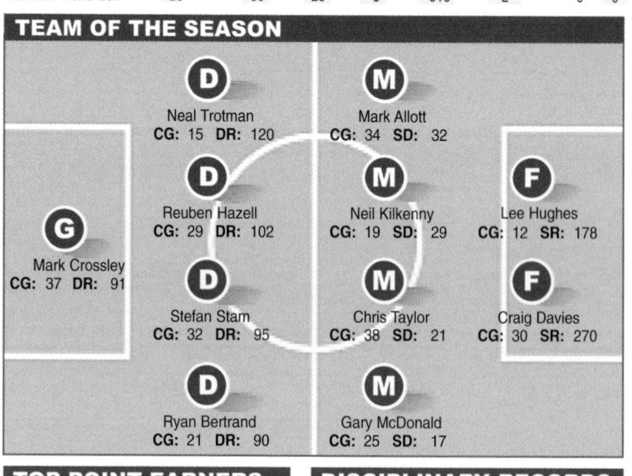

G Mark Crossley CG: 37 DR: 91
D Neal Trotman CG: 15 DR: 120
D Reuben Hazell CG: 29 DR: 102
D Stefan Stam CG: 32 DR: 95
D Ryan Bertrand CG: 21 DR: 90
M Mark Allott CG: 34 SD: 32
M Neil Kilkenny CG: 19 SD: 29
M Chris Taylor CG: 38 SD: 21
M Gary McDonald CG: 25 SD: 17
F Lee Hughes CG: 12 SR: 178
F Craig Davies CG: 30 SR: 270

MONTHLY POINTS TALLY

Month	Points	%
AUGUST	3	33%
SEPTEMBER	6	50%
OCTOBER	3	20%
NOVEMBER	7	58%
DECEMBER	9	50%
JANUARY	9	60%
FEBRUARY	7	39%
MARCH	14	58%
APRIL	6	50%
MAY	3	100%

LEAGUE GOALS

	PLAYER	MINS	GOALS	S RATE
1	Davies, C	2701	**10**	270
2	Hughes	1247	**7**	178
3	Eardley	3634	**6**	605
4	Taylor, C	3546	**5**	709
5	McDonald	2558	**4**	639
6	Allott	3307	**4**	826
7	Jarrett	1004	**3**	334
8	Wolfenden	610	**2**	305
9	Ricketts	673	**2**	336
10	Constantine	687	**2**	343
11	Alessandra	1158	**2**	579
12	Liddell	1445	**2**	722
13	Smalley	2070	**2**	1035
	Other		5	
	TOTAL		**56**	

TOP POINT EARNERS

	PLAYER	GAMES	AV PTS
1	Lewis Alessandra	13	**1.92**
2	Dean Smalley	20	**1.80**
3	Kelvin Lomax	16	**1.69**
4	Mark Allott	34	**1.62**
5	Reuben Hazell	29	**1.57**
6	Mark Crossley	37	**1.54**
7	Stefan Stam	32	**1.53**
8	Chris Taylor	38	**1.47**
9	Neal Trotman	15	**1.47**
10	Neil Eardley	39	**1.41**
	CLUB AVERAGE:		**1.46**

DISCIPLINARY RECORDS

	PLAYER	YELLOW	RED	AVE
1	Michael Ricketts	5	0	**134**
2	Neal Trotman	7	0	**205**
3	Lee Hughes	5	0	**249**
4	Sean Gregan	5	0	**267**
5	Kamudimba Kalala	3	0	**377**
6	Neil Kilkenny	4	0	**429**
7	Ryan Bertrand	4	0	**472**
8	Craig Davies	5	0	**540**
9	Reuben Hazell	4	1	**553**
10	Chris Taylor	6	0	**591**
11	David Livermore	1	0	**900**
12	Jason Jarrett	1	0	**1004**
13	Neil Eardley	2	1	**1211**
	Other	5	0	
	TOTAL	**57**	**2**	

KEY GOALKEEPER

Mark Crossley

Goals Conceded in the League	37	Counting Games League games when player was on pitch for at least 70 minutes	37
Defensive Rating Ave number of mins between League goals conceded while on the pitch	91	Clean Sheets In League games when player was on pitch for at least 70 minutes	11

KEY PLAYERS - DEFENDERS

Neal Trotman

Goals Conceded Number of League goals conceded while the player was on the pitch	12	Clean Sheets In League games when player was on pitch for at least 70 minutes	6
Defensive Rating Ave number of mins between League goals conceded while on the pitch	120	Club Defensive Rating Average number of mins between League goals conceded by the club this season	90

	PLAYER	CON LGE	CLEAN SHEETS	DEF RATE
1	Neal Trotman	12	6	120 mins
2	Reuben Hazell	27	9	102 mins
3	Stefan Stam	32	12	95 mins
4	Ryan Bertrand	21	6	90 mins

KEY PLAYERS - MIDFIELDERS

Mark Allott

Goals in the League	4	Contribution to Attacking Power Average number of minutes between League team goals while on pitch	62
Defensive Rating Average number of mins between League goals conceded while on the pitch	94	Scoring Difference Defensive Rating minus Contribution to Attacking Power	32

	PLAYER	LGE GOALS	DEF RATE	POWER	SCORE DIFF
1	Mark Allott	4	94	62	32 mins
2	Neil Kilkenny	1	114	85	29 mins
3	Chris Taylor	5	93	72	21 mins
4	Gary McDonald	4	94	77	17 mins

KEY PLAYERS - GOALSCORERS

Lee Hughes

Goals in the League	7	Player Strike Rate Average number of minutes between League goals scored by player	178
Contribution to Attacking Power Average number of minutes between League team goals while on pitch	73	Club Strike Rate Average number of minutes between League goals scored by club	71

	PLAYER	LGE GOALS	POWER	STRIKE RATE
1	Lee Hughes	7	73	178 mins
2	Craig Davies	10	84	270 mins
3	Lewis Alessandra	2	48	579 mins
4	Gary McDonald	4	77	639 mins

carlotti
HILLSTONE
Developments
Craig Davies

SQUAD APPEARANCES

Match	1	2	3	4	5	6	7	8	9	10	11	12	13	14	15	16	17	18	19	20	21	22	23	24	25	26	27
Venue	H	H	A	H	A	A	H	A	H	H	A	A	H	A	A	A	H	H	A	A	H	H	H	A	A	H	H
Competition	L	W	L	L	W	L	L	L	L	L	L	L	L	L	L	L	F	L	L	F	F	L	L	L	L	L	L
Result	W	W	L	L	L	L	L	W	W	L	D	D	L	D	L	W	D	D	W	W	W	D	D	W	W	D	L

Match	28	29	30	31	32	33	34	35	36	37	38	39	40	41	42	43	44	45	46	47	48	49	50	51	52	53
Venue	A	A	H	A	A	H	H	A	H	A	H	A	H	A	H	H	H	A	H	A	H	A	H	A	H	A
Competition	L	F	L	L	L	F	L	L	L	L	L	L	L	L	L	L	L	L	L	L	L	L	L	L	L	L
Result	W	W	D	D	D	L	W	L	W	L	W	L	D	W	L	W	W	L	D	D	W	L	W	L	W	W

Goalkeepers
Marlon Beresford
Mark Crossley
Richard O'Donnell
Defenders
Ryan Bertrand
Paul Black
Neil Eardley
Stuart Giddings
Sean Gregan
Reuben Hazell
Kelvin Lomax
Stefan Stam
John Thompson
Neal Trotman
Midfielders
Mark Allott
Aaron Chalmers
Jason Jarrett
J-P Kamudimba Kalala
Ashley Kelly
Neil Kilkenny
Andy Liddell
David Livermore
Gary McDonald
Chris Taylor
Forwards
Lewis Alessandra
Leon Constantine
Craig Davies
Lee Hughes
Michael Ricketts
Jordan Robertson
Dean Smalley
Matthew Wolfenden

KEY: On all match | On bench | Subbed or sent off (Counting game) | Subbed or sent off (playing less than 70 minutes) | Subbed on from bench (Counting Game) | Subbed on (playing less than 70 minutes) | Subbed on and then subbed or sent off (Counting Game) | Subbed on and then subbed or sent off (playing less than 70 minutes) | Not in 16

NORTHAMPTON TOWN

Final Position: **9th**

NICKNAME: THE COBBLERS

KEY: ☐Won ☐Drawn ☐Lost

							Attendance
1	div2	**Swindon**	H	D	1-1	Kirk 9	6,210
2	ccr1	**Millwall**	H	W	2-0	Bradley Johnson 38, Kirk 62	3,735
3	div2	**Brighton**	A	L	1-2	Kirk 23	5,137
4	div2	**Yeovil**	H	L	1-2	Hubertz 32	4,555
5	ccr2	**Middlesbrough**	A	L	0-2		11,686
6	div2	**Leyton Orient**	A	D	2-2	Hubertz 15, Doig 19	5,170
7	div2	**Doncaster**	H	W	2-0	Gilligan 50, Kirk 71	5,274
8	div2	**Bournemouth**	A	D	1-1	Larkin 78	5,009
9	div2	**Huddersfield**	H	W	3-0	Hubertz 44, Holt 62, Kirk 66	5,014
10	div2	**Tranmere**	A	D	2-2	Kirk 12, Hubertz 39	6,338
11	div2	**Millwall**	A	L	0-2		6,520
12	div2	**Port Vale**	H	W	2-1	Kirk 19, 33	4,755
13	div2	**Luton**	A	L	1-4	Bradley Johnson 23	5,881
14	div2	**Cheltenham**	H	W	2-1	Kirk 22, Gilligan 80	5,012
15	div2	**Oldham**	A	W	1-0	Russell 66	4,870
16	div2	**Southend**	H	L	0-1		6,646
17	div2	**Bristol Rovers**	H	L	0-1		5,126
18	facr1	**Darlington**	A	D	1-1	Larkin 26	2,696
19	div2	**Crewe**	A	L	0-1		4,531
20	facr1r	**Darlington**	H	W	2-1	Kirk 36, Bradley Johnson 41	2,895
21	div2	**Walsall**	H	L	0-2		5,767
22	facr2	**Walsall**	H	D	1-1	Kirk 8	3,887
23	div2	**Swansea**	A	L	0-3		10,957
24	div2	**Carlisle**	H	D	2-2	Crowe 28, Bradley Johnson 90	4,908
25	facr2r	**Walsall**	A	L	0-1		3,066
26	div2	**Nottm Forest**	A	D	2-2	Hubertz 59, D.Jones 65	17,081
27	div2	**Bournemouth**	H	W	4-1	Bowditch 4, Crowe 43, D.Jones 50, Bradley Johnson 67	4,806
28	div2	**Doncaster**	A	L	0-2		7,046
29	div2	**Huddersfield**	A	W	2-1	Hubertz 71, Crowe 85	8,566
30	div2	**Millwall**	H	D	1-1	Bowditch 37	5,329
31	div2	**Leeds**	A	L	0-3		24,472
32	div2	**Hartlepool**	H	D	1-1	Dolman 16	4,639
33	div2	**Gillingham**	A	W	1-0	D.Jones 3	5,579
34	div2	**Leyton Orient**	H	W	2-0	Coke 14, Hubertz 78 pen	5,405
35	div2	**Brighton**	H	W	1-0	Hughes 44	4,657
36	div2	**Swindon**	A	D	1-1	Akinfenwa 87	7,375
37	div2	**Leeds**	H	D	1-1	Akinfenwa 75	7,260
38	div2	**Yeovil**	A	L	0-1		5,001
39	div2	**Gillingham**	H	W	4-0	Crowe 44, Akinfenwa 45, 53, Coke 64	4,978
40	div2	**Hartlepool**	A	W	1-0	Coke 82	3,945
41	div2	**Crewe**	H	D	0-0		5,507
42	div2	**Walsall**	A	W	2-0	Akinfenwa 8, 71	6,844
43	div2	**Bristol Rovers**	A	D	1-1	Hubertz 55	4,657
44	div2	**Swansea**	H	W	4-2	Hubertz 14, 23 pen, Tate 20 og, Jackman 52	5,926
45	div2	**Nottm Forest**	H	L	1-2	Hubertz 32	7,244
46	div2	**Carlisle**	A	L	0-2		9,038
47	div2	**Cheltenham**	A	D	1-1	Coke 76	4,024
48	div2	**Luton**	H	W	2-1	Hubertz 34 pen, Dyer 41	5,132
49	div2	**Southend**	A	D	1-1	Larkin 24	9,286
50	div2	**Oldham**	H	W	2-0	Coke 51, Gilligan 64	5,171
51	div2	**Port Vale**	A	D	2-2	Gilligan 24, Holt 27	4,556
52	div2	**Tranmere**	H	W	2-1	Akinfenwa 3, Hubertz 69	5,088

LEAGUE APPEARANCES, BOOKINGS AND GOALS

	AGE (on 01/07/08)	IN NAMED 16	APPEARANCES	COUNTING GAMES	MINUTES ON PITCH	LEAGUE GOALS	Yellow	Red
Goalkeepers								
Mark Bunn	23	45	45	45	4050	0	5	0
Chris Dunn	20	46	1	1	90	0	0	0
Defenders								
Guy Branston	29	4	3	3	270	0	1	0
Jason Crowe	29	44	44	42	3814	4	8	0
Chris Doig	27	17	15	14	1262	1	1	0
Liam Dolman	20	41	30	26	2426	1	4	0
Gabor Gyepes	27	14	13	12	1119	0	2	0
Mark Hughes	21	35	35	32	3031	1	9	0
Danny Jackman	25	40	39	27	2954	1	1	0
Brett Johnson	22	25	16	10	992	0	1	0
Mark Little	19	17	17	16	1491	0	3	0
Danny May	19	9	2	0	29	0	0	0
Midfielders								
Sam Aiston	31	1	1	0	14	0	0	0
Joe Burnell	27	40	33	21	2181	0	3	0
Giles Coke	22	20	20	10	1142	5	3	0
Alex Dyer	18	15	6	0	209	1	0	0
Ryan Gilligan	21	39	38	24	2509	4	11	0
Jonathan Hayes	20	15	11	4	530	0	0	0
Andy Holt	30	38	36	24	2537	2	1	0
Bradley Johnson	21	23	23	22	1985	3	4	0
Daniel Jones	21	35	33	28	2596	3	7	0
Alex Russell	35	13	13	11	1020	1	0	0
Ian Taylor	40	1	0	0	0	0	0	0
Forwards								
Adebayo Akinfenwa	26	19	15	12	1125	7	2	0
Dean Bowditch	22	11	10	6	685	2	0	0
Ian Henderson	23	29	23	4	872	0	2	0
Poul Hubertz	31	41	40	32	3063	13	8	1
Andy Kirk	29	25	25	22	2089	8	2	0
Colin Larkin	26	34	33	10	1445	2	0	0

TEAM OF THE SEASON

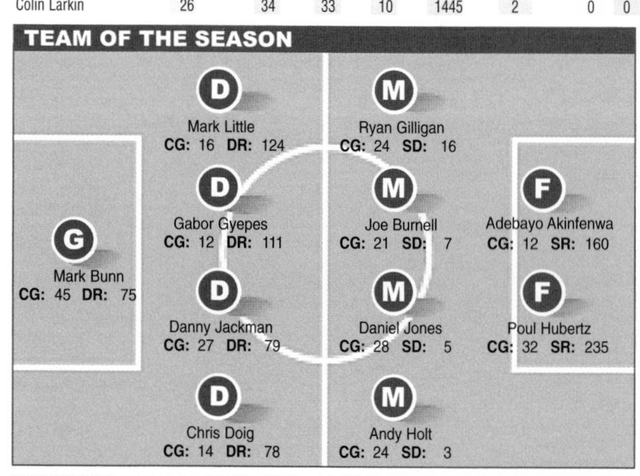

D
Mark Little
CG: 16 DR: 124
M
Ryan Gilligan
CG: 24 SD: 16
D
Gabor Gyepes
CG: 12 DR: 111
M
Joe Burnell
CG: 21 SD: 7
F
Adebayo Akinfenwa
CG: 12 SR: 160
G
Mark Bunn
CG: 45 DR: 75
D
Danny Jackman
CG: 27 DR: 79
M
Daniel Jones
CG: 28 SD: 5
F
Poul Hubertz
CG: 32 SR: 235
D
Chris Doig
CG: 14 DR: 78
M
Andy Holt
CG: 24 SD: 3

MONTHLY POINTS TALLY

Month	Points	%
AUGUST	1	11%
SEPTEMBER	9	60%
OCTOBER	9	60%
NOVEMBER	0	0%
DECEMBER	8	44%
JANUARY	11	61%
FEBRUARY	8	53%
MARCH	9	43%
APRIL	8	67%
MAY	3	100%

LEAGUE GOALS

	PLAYER	MINS	GOALS	S RATE
1	Hubertz	3063	13	235
2	Kirk	2089	8	261
3	Akinfenwa	1125	7	160
4	Coke	1142	5	228
5	Gilligan	2509	4	627
6	Crowe	3814	4	953
7	Johnson, B	1985	3	661
8	Jones, D	2596	3	865
9	Bowditch	685	2	342
10	Larkin	1445	2	722
11	Holt	2537	2	1268
12	Dyer	209	1	209
13	Russell	1020	1	1020
	Other		4	
	TOTAL		59	

TOP POINT EARNERS

	PLAYER	GAMES	AV PTS
1	Mark Little	16	1.88
2	Adebayo Akinfenwa	12	1.83
3	Gabor Gyepes	12	1.83
4	Joe Burnell	21	1.57
5	Danny Jackman	27	1.56
6	Poul Hubertz	32	1.53
7	Daniel Jones	28	1.50
8	Ryan Gilligan	24	1.50
9	Andy Holt	24	1.46
10	Mark Hughes	32	1.44
	CLUB AVERAGE:		1.43

DISCIPLINARY RECORDS

	PLAYER	YELLOW	RED	AVE
1	Ryan Gilligan	11	0	228
2	Mark Hughes	9	0	336
3	Poul Hubertz	8	1	340
4	Daniel Jones	7	0	370
5	Giles Coke	3	0	380
6	Ian Henderson	2	0	436
7	Jason Crowe	8	0	476
8	Bradley Johnson	4	0	496
9	Mark Little	3	0	497
10	Gabor Gyepes	2	0	559
11	Adebayo Akinfenwa	2	0	562
12	Liam Dolman	4	0	606
13	Joe Burnell	3	0	727
	Other	11	0	
	TOTAL	77	1	

KEY GOALKEEPER

Mark Bunn

Goals Conceded in the League	54	Counting Games League games when player was on pitch for at least 70 minutes	45
Defensive Rating Ave number of mins between League goals conceded while on the pitch	75	Clean Sheets In League games when player was on pitch for at least 70 minutes	11

KEY PLAYERS - DEFENDERS

Mark Little

Goals Conceded Number of League goals conceded while the player was on the pitch	12	Clean Sheets In League games when player was on pitch for at least 70 minutes	7
Defensive Rating Ave number of mins between League goals conceded while on the pitch	124	Club Defensive Rating Average number of mins between League goals conceded by the club this season	75

	PLAYER	CON LGE	CLEAN SHEETS	DEF RATE
1	Mark Little	12	7	124 mins
2	Gabor Gyepes	10	5	111 mins
3	Danny Jackman	37	9	79 mins
4	Chris Doig	16	3	78 mins

KEY PLAYERS - MIDFIELDERS

Ryan Gilligan

Goals in the League	4	Contribution to Attacking Power Average number of minutes between League team goals while on pitch	73
Defensive Rating Average number of mins between League goals conceded while on the pitch	89	Scoring Difference Defensive Rating minus Contribution to Attacking Power	16

	PLAYER	LGE GOALS	DEF RATE	POWER	SCORE DIFF
1	Ryan Gilligan	4	89	73	16 mins
2	Joe Burnell	0	77	70	7 mins
3	Daniel Jones	3	68	63	5 mins
4	Andy Holt	2	68	65	3 mins

KEY PLAYERS - GOALSCORERS

Adebayo Akinfenwa

Goals in the League	7	Player Strike Rate Average number of minutes between League goals scored by player	160
Contribution to Attacking Power Average number of minutes between League team goals while on pitch	51	Club Strike Rate Average number of minutes between League goals scored by club	69

	PLAYER	LGE GOALS	POWER	STRIKE RATE
1	Adebayo Akinfenwa	7	51	160 mins
2	Poul Hubertz	13	61	235 mins
3	Andy Kirk	8	74	261 mins
4	Ryan Gilligan	4	73	627 mins

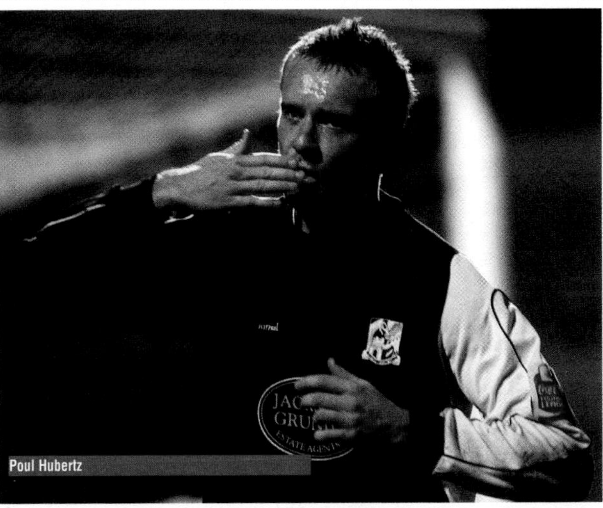

Poul Hubertz

SQUAD APPEARANCES

Match	1	2	3	4	5	6	7	8	9	10	11	12	13	14	15	16	17	18	19	20	21	22	23	24	25	26	27	28	29	30	31	32	33	34	35	36	37	38	39	40	41	42	43	44	45	46	47	48	49	50	51	52
Venue	H	H	A	H	A	A	H	A	H	A	A	H	A	H	A	H	H	A	A	H	H	H	A	H	A	A	H	A	A	H	A	H	A	H	H	A	H	A	H	A	H	A	A	H	H	A	A	H	A	H	A	H
Competition	L	W	L	L	W	L	L	L	L	L	L	L	L	L	L	L	L	F	L	F	L	F	L	L	F	L	L	L	L	L	L	L	L	L	L	L	L	L	L	L	L	L	L	L	L	L	L	L	L	L	L	L
Result	D	W	L	L	L	D	W	D	W	D	L	W	L	W	W	L	L	D	L	W	L	D	L	D	L	D	W	L	W	D	L	D	W	W	W	D	D	L	W	W	D	W	D	W	L	L	D	W	D	W	D	W

Goalkeepers
- Mark Bunn
- Chris Dunn

Defenders
- Guy Branston
- Jason Crowe
- Chris Doig
- Liam Dolman
- Gabor Gyepes
- Mark Hughes
- Danny Jackman
- Brett Johnson
- Mark Little
- Danny May

Midfielders
- Sam Aiston
- Joe Burnell
- Giles Coke
- Alex Dyer
- Ryan Gilligan
- Jonathan Hayes
- Andy Holt
- Bradley Johnson
- Daniel Jones
- Alex Russell
- Ian Taylor

Forwards
- Adebayo Akinfenwa
- Dean Bowditch
- Ian Henderson
- Poul Hubertz
- Andy Kirk
- Colin Larkin

KEY: On all match · On bench · Subbed or sent off (Counting game) · Subbed or sent off (playing less than 70 minutes) · Subbed on from bench (Counting Game) · Subbed on (playing less than 70 minutes) · Subbed on and then subbed or sent off (Counting Game) · Subbed on and then subbed or sent off (playing less than 70 minutes) · Not in 16

HUDDERSFIELD TOWN

Final Position: **10th**

NICKNAME: THE TERRIERS

KEY: ☐Won ☐Drawn ☐Lost

							Attendance
1	div2	Yeovil	H	W	1-0	Beckett 17	9,876
2	ccr1	Blackpool	A	L	0-1		6,395
3	div2	Bournemouth	A	W	1-0	Beckett 43	5,606
4	div2	Carlisle	H	L	0-2		10,022
5	div2	Millwall	A	W	2-1	Booth 44, Kamara 52	9,004
6	div2	Crewe	A	L	0-2		5,164
7	div2	Cheltenham	H	L	2-3	Kamara 48, Keogh 90	8,756
8	div2	Northampton	A	L	0-3		5,014
9	div2	Luton	H	W	2-0	Beckett 36, Cadamarteri 60	9,028
10	div2	Nottm Forest	H	D	1-1	Cadamarteri 67	10,994
11	div2	Walsall	A	L	0-4		5,112
12	div2	Doncaster	A	L	0-2		6,866
13	div2	Oldham	H	D	1-1	Wallwork 80	10,909
14	div2	Tranmere	A	L	0-3		6,008
15	div2	Port Vale	H	W	3-1	Booth 3, Wallwork 9, N.Clarke 21	8,555
16	div2	Hartlepool	H	W	2-0	Cadamarteri 12, Beckett 87	8,154
17	facr1	Accrington	A	W	3-2	Kamara 45, 83, Beckett 89	2,202
18	div2	Swansea	A	W	1-0	Kamara 54	12,184
19	div2	Leyton Orient	H	L	0-1		9,697
20	facr2	Grimsby	H	W	3-0	Jevons 52, 62, Beckett 85	6,729
21	div2	Southend	A	L	1-4	Schofield 67	6,844
22	div2	Leeds	A	L	0-4		32,501
23	div2	Bristol Rovers	H	W	2-1	Wallwork 16, Jevons 55	8,118
24	div2	Cheltenham	A	W	2-0	Booth 14, 66	3,998
25	div2	Crewe	H	D	1-1	Booth 85	9,759
26	div2	Northampton	H	L	1-2	Booth 45	8,566
27	div2	Nottm Forest	A	L	1-2	Jevons 37 pen	18,762
28	facr3	Birmingham	H	W	2-1	Beckett 4, Brandon 81	13,410
29	div2	Gillingham	H	L	1-3	Brandon 32	11,212
30	div2	Brighton	A	D	1-1	Williams 77	5,343
31	facr4	Oldham	A	W	1-0	Beckett 10	12,749
32	div2	Bournemouth	H	W	1-0	Jevons 35	7,359
33	div2	Yeovil	A	W	2-0	Beckett 25 pen, Collins 51	4,823
34	div2	Swindon	H	W	1-0	Jevons 1	9,388
35	div2	Carlisle	A	L	1-2	Page 87	6,196
36	facr5	Chelsea	A	L	1-3	Collins 45	41,324
37	div2	Millwall	H	W	1-0	Beckett 29 pen	6,326
38	div2	Gillingham	A	L	0-1		5,022
39	div2	Swansea	H	L	0-1		10,471
40	div2	Swindon	A	L	2-3	Jevons 39 pen, 77 pen	4,840
41	div2	Leyton Orient	A	W	1-0	Beckett 75	4,660
42	div2	Hartlepool	A	L	1-2	N.Clarke 64	3,650
43	div2	Southend	H	L	1-2	Booth 73	7,823
44	div2	Brighton	H	W	2-1	Holdsworth 4, Beckett 79 pen	6,004
45	div2	Bristol Rovers	A	W	3-2	Berrett 39, Brandon 70, Collins 88	6,585
46	div2	Oldham	A	L	1-4	Mirfin 90	5,637
47	div2	Doncaster	H	D	2-2	Williams 7, Holdsworth 61	10,279
48	div2	Port Vale	A	D	0-0		4,150
49	div2	Leeds	H	W	1-0	Holdsworth 76	16,413
50	div2	Tranmere	H	W	1-0	Booth 61	8,315
51	div2	Walsall	H	W	2-0	Schofield 41, Booth 56	9,969
52	div2	Luton	A	W	1-0	Jevons 77	6,539

LEAGUE APPEARANCES, BOOKINGS AND GOALS

	AGE (on 01/07/08)	IN NAMED 16	APPEARANCES	COUNTING GAMES	MINUTES ON PITCH	LEAGUE GOALS	Yellow	Red
Goalkeepers								
Simon Eastwood	19	12	0	0	0	0	0	0
Mathew Glennon	29	45	45	45	4034	0	0	1
Alex Smithies	18	32	2	1	105	0	0	0
Defenders								
Danny Adams	32	1	1	1	90	0	0	0
Tom Clarke	20	9	3	2	190	0	1	0
Nathan Clarke	24	44	44	44	3952	2	8	0
Aaron Hardy	22	12	6	5	465	0	0	0
Spencer Harris	17	1	0	0	0	0	0	0
Richard Keogh	21	9	9	9	793	1	2	0
Shane Killock	19	8	1	1	90	0	0	0
David Mirfin	23	35	29	23	2124	1	0	0
Robert Page	33	18	18	17	1569	1	3	1
Frank Sinclair	36	30	29	26	2436	0	7	2
Joe Skarz	18	35	26	21	1909	0	4	0
Robbie Williams	24	28	25	23	2124	2	3	0
Midfielders								
James Berrett	19	21	15	8	869	1	3	0
Chris Brandon	32	34	28	25	2304	2	1	1
Michael Collins	22	44	41	34	3107	2	2	0
Andy Holdsworth	24	44	44	41	3822	3	8	0
Malvin Kamara	24	45	43	29	3007	3	1	0
Danny Racchi	19	10	3	0	22	0	0	0
Danny Schofield	28	31	25	18	1721	2	1	0
Ronnie Wallwork	30	16	16	16	1392	3	2	0
John Worthington	25	27	25	15	1632	0	8	1
Matthew Young	22	14	8	4	350	0	0	0
Forwards								
Lucas Akins	19	5	3	0	18	0	0	0
Luke Beckett	31	46	37	26	2410	8	0	0
Andy Booth	34	41	37	27	2468	9	5	0
Daniel Broadbent	18	6	5	0	54	0	0	0
Danny Cadamarteri	28	12	12	9	918	3	2	1
Phil Jevons	28	21	21	15	1432	7	2	0

TEAM OF THE SEASON

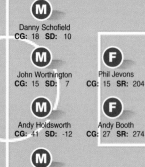

G — Mathew Glennon — CG: 45 DR: 72

D — Robert Page — CG: 17 DR: 98

D — Robbie Williams — CG: 23 DR: 70

D — Nathan Clarke — CG: 44 DR: 69

D — David Mirfin — CG: 23 DR: 68

M — Danny Schofield — CG: 18 SD: 10

M — John Worthington — CG: 15 SD: 7

M — Andy Holdsworth — CG: 41 SD: -12

M — Malvin Kamara — CG: 29 SD: -16

F — Phil Jevons — CG: 15 SR: 204

F — Andy Booth — CG: 27 SR: 274

MONTHLY POINTS TALLY

AUGUST	6	67%
SEPTEMBER	6	40%
OCTOBER	2	13%
NOVEMBER	9	75%
DECEMBER	7	39%
JANUARY	4	33%
FEBRUARY	9	60%
MARCH	9	38%
APRIL	11	73%
MAY	3	100%

LEAGUE GOALS

	PLAYER	MINS	GOALS	S RATE
1	Booth	2468	9	274
2	Beckett	2410	8	301
3	Jevons	1432	7	204
4	Cadamarteri	918	3	306
5	Wallwork	1392	3	464
6	Kamara	3007	3	1002
7	Holdsworth	3822	3	1274
8	Schofield	1721	2	860
9	Williams	2124	2	1062
10	Brandon	2304	2	1152
11	Collins	3107	2	1553
12	Clarke, N	3952	2	1976
13	Keogh	793	1	793
	Other		3	
	TOTAL		50	

TOP POINT EARNERS

	PLAYER	GAMES	AV PTS
1	Danny Schofield	18	1.94
2	Robert Page	17	1.88
3	John Worthington	15	1.73
4	Andy Booth	27	1.56
5	Michael Collins	34	1.53
6	Phil Jevons	15	1.53
7	Andy Holdsworth	41	1.51
8	Nathan Clarke	44	1.50
9	David Mirfin	23	1.48
10	Mathew Glennon	45	1.47
	CLUB AVERAGE:		1.43

DISCIPLINARY RECORDS

	PLAYER	YELLOW	RED	AVE
1	John Worthington	8	1	181
2	Frank Sinclair	7	2	270
3	James Berrett	3	0	289
4	Danny Cadamarteri	2	1	306
5	Robert Page	3	1	392
6	Richard Keogh	2	0	396
7	Andy Holdsworth	8	0	477
8	Joe Skarz	4	0	477
9	Andy Booth	5	0	493
10	Nathan Clarke	8	0	494
11	Ronnie Wallwork	2	0	696
12	Robbie Williams	3	0	708
13	Phil Jevons	2	0	716
	Other	5	2	
	TOTAL	62	7	

KEY GOALKEEPER

Mathew Glennon

Goals Conceded in the League	56	Counting Games League games when player was on pitch for at least 70 minutes	45
Defensive Rating Ave number of mins between League goals conceded while on the pitch	72	Clean Sheets In League games when player was on pitch for at least 70 minutes	16

KEY PLAYERS - DEFENDERS

Robert Page

Goals Conceded Number of League goals conceded while the player was on the pitch	16	Clean Sheets In League games when player was on pitch for at least 70 minutes	9
Defensive Rating Ave number of mins between League goals conceded while on the pitch	98	Club Defensive Rating Average number of mins between League goals conceded by the club this season	66

	PLAYER	CON LGE	CLEAN SHEETS	DEF RATE
1	Robert Page	16	9	98 mins
2	Robbie Williams	30	9	70 mins
3	Nathan Clarke	57	16	69 mins
4	David Mirfin	31	9	68 mins

KEY PLAYERS - MIDFIELDERS

Danny Schofield

Goals in the League	2	Contribution to Attacking Power Average number of minutes between League team goals while on pitch	71
Defensive Rating Average number of mins between League goals conceded while on the pitch	81	Scoring Difference Defensive Rating minus Contribution to Attacking Power	10

	PLAYER	LGE GOALS	DEF RATE	POWER	SCORE DIFF
1	Danny Schofield	2	81	71	10 mins
2	John Worthington	0	81	74	7 mins
3	Andy Holdsworth	3	74	86	-12 mins
4	Malvin Kamara	3	63	79	-16 mins

KEY PLAYERS - GOALSCORERS

Phil Jevons

Goals in the League	7	Player Strike Rate Average number of minutes between League goals scored by player	204
Contribution to Attacking Power Average number of minutes between League team goals while on pitch	84	Club Strike Rate Average number of minutes between League goals scored by club	82

	PLAYER	LGE GOALS	POWER	STRIKE RATE
1	Phil Jevons	7	84	204 mins
2	Andy Booth	9	70	274 mins
3	Luke Beckett	8	89	301 mins
4	Ronnie Wallwork	3	87	464 mins

mitre
CASINO
RED.COM

Michael Collins

SQUAD APPEARANCES

Match	1	2	3	4	5	6	7	8	9	10	11	12	13	14	15	16	17	18	19	20	21	22	23	24	25
Venue	H	A	A	H	A	A	H	A	H	H	A	A	H	A	H	H	A	A	H	H	A	A	H	A	H
Competition	L	W	L	L	L	L	L	L	L	L	L	L	L	L	L	L	F	L	L	F	L	L	L	L	L
Result	W	L	W	L	W	L	L	L	W	D	L	L	D	L	W	W	W	W	L	W	L	L	W	W	D

Match	26	27	28	29	30	31	32	33	34	35	36	37	38	39	40	41	42	43	44	45	46	47	48	49	50	51	52
Venue	H	A	H	H	A	A	H	A	H	A	A	H	A	H	A	A	A	H	H	A	A	H	A	H	H	H	A
Competition	L	L	F	L	L	F	L	L	L	L	F	L	L	L	L	L	L	L	L	L	L	L	L	L	L	L	L
Result	L	L	W	L	D	W	W	W	W	L	L	W	L	L	L	W	L	L	W	W	L	D	D	W	W	W	W

Goalkeepers
Simon Eastwood
Mathew Glennon
Alex Smithies
Defenders
Danny Adams
Tom Clarke
Nathan Clarke
Aaron Hardy
Spencer Harris
Richard Keogh
Shane Killock
David Mirfin
Robert Page
Frank Sinclair
Joe Skarz
Robbie Williams
Midfielders
James Berrett
Chris Brandon
Michael Collins
Andy Holdsworth
Malvin Kamara
Danny Racchi
Danny Schofield
Ronnie Wallwork
John Worthington
Matthew Young
Forwards
Lucas Akins
Luke Beckett
Andy Booth
Daniel Broadbent
Danny Cadamarteri
Phil Jevons

KEY: On all match | On bench | Subbed or sent off (Counting game) | Subbed or sent off (playing less than 70 minutes) | Subbed on from bench (Counting Game) | Subbed on (playing less than 70 minutes) | Subbed on and then subbed or sent off (Counting Game) | Subbed on and then subbed or sent off (playing less than 70 minutes) | Not in 16

TRANMERE ROVERS

Final Position: **11th**

NICKNAME: ROVERS

KEY: ☐Won ☐Drawn ☐Lost

							Attendance
1	div2	Leeds	H	L	1-2	Greenacre 22	11,008
2	ccr1	Stockport	A	L	0-1		3,499
3	div2	Gillingham	A	W	2-0	Greenacre 19, Davies 50	5,302
4	div2	Brighton	H	W	2-0	Greenacre 78, Shuker 90	5,670
5	div2	Yeovil	A	D	1-1	Davies 90	4,985
6	div2	Carlisle	A	W	1-0	Curran 42	6,556
7	div2	Luton	H	W	2-1	Curran 83, Kay 86	6,525
8	div2	Cheltenham	A	D	1-1	Greenacre 34	3,742
9	div2	Northampton	H	D	2-2	Shuker 69, Taylor 88	6,338
10	div2	Crewe	H	D	1-1	Shuker 65	6,155
11	div2	Southend	A	W	2-1	Chorley 30, Taylor 55	7,619
12	div2	Walsall	H	D	0-0		7,697
13	div2	Swindon	A	L	0-1		6,430
14	div2	Huddersfield	H	W	3-0	McLaren 29, Sherriff 53, Taylor 83	6,008
15	div2	Nottm Forest	A	L	0-2		16,825
16	div2	Oldham	H	L	0-1		5,473
17	facr1	Chesterfield	A	W	2-1	Greenacre 37 pen, Kay 84	4,296
18	div2	Doncaster	A	D	0-0		7,070
19	div2	Swansea	H	L	0-1		6,149
20	facr2	Bradford	A	W	3-0	Jennings 7, Greenacre 37, 68	6,379
21	div2	Hartlepool	A	L	1-3	Sherriff 54	3,583
22	div2	Bournemouth	H	W	3-1	Zola 23, Greenacre 28 pen, Jennings 63	5,043
23	div2	Port Vale	A	D	0-0		3,604
24	div2	Luton	A	L	0-1		6,070
25	div2	Carlisle	H	W	2-0	McLaren 16, Kay 45	8,516
26	div2	Cheltenham	H	W	1-0	Zola 59	6,111
27	div2	Crewe	A	L	3-4	A.Taylor 8, Greenacre 31, McLaren 74	5,137
28	facr3	Hereford	H	D	2-2	Jennings 75, G.Taylor 78	6,909
29	div2	Leyton Orient	A	L	0-3		3,447
30	div2	Bristol Rovers	H	L	0-2		5,887
31	facr3r	Hereford	A	L	0-1		6,471
32	div2	Millwall	A	W	1-0	Kay 87	8,925
33	div2	Yeovil	H	W	2-1	Zola 4, Myrie-Williams 62 pen	5,386
34	div2	Gillingham	H	W	2-0	McLaren 7, Zola 14	5,006
35	div2	Leeds	A	W	2-0	Myrie-Williams 61, Moore 69	24,907
36	div2	Leyton Orient	H	D	1-1	Zola 2	6,530
37	div2	Brighton	A	D	0-0		4,797
38	div2	Millwall	H	W	2-0	A.Taylor 10, Moore 45	6,108
39	div2	Bristol Rovers	A	D	1-1	Kay 74	7,777
40	div2	Doncaster	H	L	0-1		7,551
41	div2	Oldham	A	L	1-3	M.Jones 70	5,442
42	div2	Swansea	A	D	1-1	Greenacre 90	11,039
43	div2	Hartlepool	H	W	3-1	Greenacre 36, Nelson 64 og, Sherriff 90	5,608
44	div2	Port Vale	H	W	2-0	Greenacre 68 pen, Moore 88	6,484
45	div2	Bournemouth	A	L	1-2	Kay 87	4,118
46	div2	Swindon	H	W	2-1	Jennings 12, Greenacre 40	5,815
47	div2	Walsall	A	L	1-2	Myrie-Williams 3	5,745
48	div2	Nottm Forest	H	L	0-2		8,689
49	div2	Huddersfield	A	L	0-1		8,315
50	div2	Southend	H	W	1-0	Kay 53	5,842
51	div2	Northampton	A	L	1-2	Greenacre 43	5,088

LEAGUE APPEARANCES, BOOKINGS AND GOALS

	AGE (on 01/07/08)	IN NAMED 16	APPEARANCES	COUNTING GAMES	MINUTES ON PITCH	LEAGUE GOALS		
Goalkeepers								
John Achterberg	36	46	5	5	450	0	0	0
Danny Coyne	34	41	41	41	3690	0	0	0
Shane McWeeney	18	5	0	0	0	0	0	0
Defenders								
Ben Chorley	25	42	31	29	2674	1	4	1
Ian Goodison	35	42	42	40	3689	0	6	2
Antony Kay	25	44	38	29	2805	6	6	0
Shane Sherriff	25	44	44	41	3790	3	8	1
Robbie Stockdale	28	45	44	42	3818	0	2	0
Andy Taylor	22	30	30	29	2649	2	6	0
Carl Tremarco	22	18	8	3	397	0	1	1
Midfielders								
Adnan Ahmed	24	20	6	3	329	0	1	0
Kevin Cooper	33	4	4	2	216	0	0	0
Paul Henry	20	4	2	1	99	0	0	0
Stephen Jennings	23	42	41	37	3379	2	8	1
Mike Jones	20	21	9	4	475	1	0	0
Paul McLaren	31	43	43	41	3808	4	9	0
John Mullin	32	21	10	3	439	0	1	0
Chris Shuker	26	24	23	16	1683	3	0	0
Forwards								
Craig Curran	18	45	35	1	554	2	0	0
Steve Davies	20	11	10	7	697	2	2	0
Chris Greenacre	30	43	40	35	3192	11	5	0
Ian Moore	31	17	17	17	1482	3	0	0
Jennison Myrie-Williams	20	25	25	15	1760	3	1	0
Gareth Taylor	35	25	23	18	1605	3	5	0
Calvin Zola	23	32	30	15	1641	5	2	0

TEAM OF THE SEASON

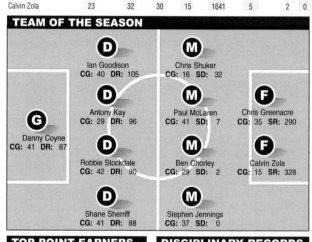

G Danny Coyne CG: 41 DR: 87

D Ian Goodison CG: 40 DR: 105

D Antony Kay CG: 29 DR: 96

D Robbie Stockdale CG: 42 DR: 90

D Shane Sherriff CG: 41 DR: 88

M Chris Shuker CG: 16 SD: 32

M Paul McLaren CG: 41 SD: 7

M Ben Chorley CG: 29 SD: 2

M Stephen Jennings CG: 37 SD: 0

F Chris Greenacre CG: 35 SR: 290

F Calvin Zola CG: 15 SR: 328

MONTHLY POINTS TALLY

Month	Points	%
AUGUST	6	67%
SEPTEMBER	9	60%
OCTOBER	8	53%
NOVEMBER	1	8%
DECEMBER	10	56%
JANUARY	9	50%
FEBRUARY	9	60%
MARCH	10	48%
APRIL	3	25%
MAY	0	0%

LEAGUE GOALS

	PLAYER	MINS	GOALS	S RATE
1	Greenacre	3192	**11**	290
2	Kay	2805	**6**	467
3	Zola	1641	**5**	328
4	McLaren	3808	**4**	952
5	Moore	1482	**3**	494
6	Taylor, G	1605	**3**	535
7	Shuker	1683	**3**	561
8	Myrie-Williams	1760	**3**	586
9	Sherriff	3790	**3**	1263
10	Curran	554	**2**	277
11	Davies	697	**2**	348
12	Taylor, A	2649	**2**	1324
13	Jennings	3379	**2**	1689
	Other		2	
	TOTAL		**51**	

TOP POINT EARNERS

	PLAYER	GAMES	AV PTS
1	J Myrie-Williams	15	**2.00**
2	Calvin Zola	15	**1.80**
3	Stephen Jennings	37	**1.59**
4	Shane Sherriff	41	**1.56**
5	Ian Goodison	40	**1.53**
6	Antony Kay	29	**1.45**
7	Robbie Stockdale	42	**1.45**
8	Chris Shuker	16	**1.44**
9	Gareth Taylor	18	**1.44**
10	Andy Taylor	29	**1.41**
	CLUB AVERAGE:		**1.41**

DISCIPLINARY RECORDS

	PLAYER	YELLOW	RED	AVE
1	Gareth Taylor	5	0	**321**
2	Steve Davies	2	0	**348**
3	Stephen Jennings	8	1	**375**
4	Shane Sherriff	8	1	**421**
5	Paul McLaren	9	0	**423**
6	Andy Taylor	6	0	**441**
7	Ian Goodison	6	2	**461**
8	Antony Kay	6	0	**467**
9	Ben Chorley	4	1	**534**
10	Chris Greenacre	5	0	**638**
11	Calvin Zola	2	0	**820**
12	J Myrie-Williams	1	0	**1760**
13	Robbie Stockdale	2	0	**1909**
	Other	0	0	
	TOTAL	**64**	**5**	

KEY GOALKEEPER

Danny Coyne

Goals Conceded in the League	42	Counting Games League games when player was on pitch for at least 70 minutes	41
Defensive Rating Ave number of mins between League goals conceded while on the pitch	87	Clean Sheets In League games when player was on pitch for at least 70 minutes	15

KEY PLAYERS - DEFENDERS

Ian Goodison

Goals Conceded Number of League goals conceded while the player was on the pitch	35	Clean Sheets In League games when player was on pitch for at least 70 minutes	16
Defensive Rating Ave number of mins between League goals conceded while on the pitch	105	Club Defensive Rating Average number of mins between League goals conceded by the club this season	88

	PLAYER	CON LGE	CLEAN SHEETS	DEF RATE
1	Ian Goodison	35	16	105 mins
2	Antony Kay	29	11	96 mins
3	Robbie Stockdale	42	15	90 mins
4	Shane Sherriff	43	15	88 mins

KEY PLAYERS - MIDFIELDERS

Chris Shuker

Goals in the League	3	Contribution to Attacking Power Average number of minutes between League team goals while on pitch	88
Defensive Rating Average number of mins between League goals conceded while on the pitch	120	Scoring Difference Defensive Rating minus Contribution to Attacking Power	32

	PLAYER	LGE GOALS	DEF RATE	POWER	SCORE DIFF
1	Chris Shuker	3	120	88	32 mins
2	Paul McLaren	4	84	77	7 mins
3	Ben Chorley	1	76	74	2 mins
4	Stephen Jennings	2	86	86	0 mins

KEY PLAYERS - GOALSCORERS

Chris Greenacre

Goals in the League	11	Player Strike Rate Average number of minutes between League goals scored by player	290
Contribution to Attacking Power Average number of minutes between League team goals while on pitch	76	Club Strike Rate Average number of minutes between League goals scored by club	79

	PLAYER	LGE GOALS	POWER	STRIKE RATE
1	Chris Greenacre	11	76	290 mins
2	Calvin Zola	5	68	328 mins
3	Ian Moore	3	87	494 mins
4	Gareth Taylor	3	114	535 mins

WIRRAL

Calvin Zola

SQUAD APPEARANCES

Match	1	2	3	4	5	6	7	8	9	10	11	12	13	14	15	16	17	18	19	20	21	22	23	24	25
Venue	H	A	A	H	A	A	H	A	H	H	A	H	A	H	A	H	A	A	H	A	A	H	A	A	H
Competition	L	W	L	L	L	L	L	L	L	L	L	L	L	L	L	L	F	L	L	F	L	L	L	L	L
Result	L	L	W	W	D	W	W	D	D	D	W	D	L	W	L	L	W	D	L	W	L	W	D	L	W

Match	26	27	28	29	30	31	32	33	34	35	36	37	38	39	40	41	42	43	44	45	46	47	48	49	50	51
Venue	H	A	H	A	H	A	A	H	H	A	H	A	H	A	H	A	A	H	H	A	H	A	H	A	H	A
Competition	L	L	F	L	L	F	L	L	L	L	L	L	L	L	L	L	L	L	L	L	L	L	L	L	L	L
Result	W	L	D	L	L	L	W	W	W	W	D	D	W	D	L	L	D	W	W	L	W	L	L	L	W	L

Goalkeepers
- John Achterberg
- Danny Coyne
- Shane McWeeney

Defenders
- Ben Chorley
- Ian Goodison
- Antony Kay
- Shane Sherriff
- Robbie Stockdale
- Andy Taylor
- Carl Tremarco

Midfielders
- Adnan Ahmed
- Kevin Cooper
- Paul Henry
- Stephen Jennings
- Mike Jones
- Paul McLaren
- John Mullin
- Chris Shuker

Forwards
- Craig Curran
- Steve Davies
- Chris Greenacre
- Ian Moore
- Jennison Myrie-Williams
- Gareth Taylor
- Calvin Zola

KEY: On all match | On bench | Subbed or sent off (Counting game) | Subbed or sent off (playing less than 70 minutes) | Subbed on from bench (Counting Game) | Subbed on (playing less than 70 minutes) | Subbed on and then subbed or sent off (Counting Game) | Subbed on and then subbed or sent off (playing less than 70 minutes) | Not in 16

WALSALL

Final Position: **12th**

NICKNAME: THE SADDLERS

KEY: ☐Won ☐Drawn ☐Lost

	Comp	Opponent	H/A	Res	Score	Scorers	Attendance
1	div2	Carlisle	H	D	1-1	Mooney 47	6,933
2	ccr1	Swansea	A	L	0-2		6,943
3	div2	Leyton Orient	A	L	0-1		4,524
4	div2	Swansea	H	L	1-3	Butler 7	5,673
5	div2	Gillingham	A	L	1-2	Fox 20	4,806
6	div2	Port Vale	H	D	0-0		4,967
7	div2	Millwall	A	W	2-1	Fox 42, Deeney 86	7,720
8	div2	Oldham	H	L	0-3		6,202
9	div2	Hartlepool	A	W	1-0	Hall 90	4,948
10	div2	Doncaster	A	W	3-2	Fox 28, Bradley 66, Mooney 71 pen	6,038
11	div2	Huddersfield	H	W	4-0	Gerrard 31, Sonko 43, Bradley 50, Mooney 67	5,112
12	div2	Tranmere	A	D	0-0		7,697
13	div2	Southend	H	L	0-2		5,661
14	div2	Bournemouth	A	D	1-1	Wrack 81	5,414
15	div2	Cheltenham	H	W	2-0	Mooney 10 pen, 56	4,810
16	div2	Brighton	A	D	1-1	Demontagnac 78	4,717
17	facr1	Shrewsbury	H	W	2-0	Ricketts 10, Demontagnac 66	4,972
18	div2	Luton	H	D	0-0		5,056
19	div2	Northampton	A	W	2-0	Bradley 45, Demontagnac 86	5,767
20	facr2	Northampton	A	D	1-1	Mooney 4	3,887
21	div2	Nottm Forest	H	W	1-0	Ricketts 48	6,605
22	div2	Crewe	A	D	0-0		4,639
23	facr2r	Northampton	H	W	1-0	Ricketts 85 pen	3,066
24	div2	Leeds	H	D	1-1	Mooney 76	10,102
25	div2	Millwall	H	W	3-0	Mooney 29, 38, Harris 45 og	5,433
26	div2	Port Vale	A	D	1-1	Ricketts 90	6,029
27	div2	Oldham	A	W	2-0	Dann 2, Ricketts 65	5,292
28	div2	Doncaster	H	D	1-1	Dann 75	6,266
29	facr3	Millwall	H	D	0-0		4,358
30	div2	Yeovil	A	W	2-0	Dann 59, Nicholls 64	4,319
31	div2	Swindon	H	D	2-2	Sonko 22, 68	5,449
32	facr3r	Millwall	A	L	1-2	Nicholls 61	4,645
33	div2	Bristol Rovers	A	D	1-1	Sonko 37	6,276
34	div2	Gillingham	H	W	2-1	Mooney 28, Sonko 72	4,914
35	div2	Leyton Orient	H	D	0-0		4,643
36	div2	Carlisle	A	L	1-2	Holmes 23	6,220
37	div2	Yeovil	H	W	2-0	Holmes 67, Betsy 90	5,034
38	div2	Swansea	A	L	0-1		13,020
39	div2	Swindon	A	W	3-0	Holmes 11, 57, Nicholls 90	6,265
40	div2	Luton	A	W	1-0	S.Moore 4	6,157
41	div2	Northampton	H	L	0-2		6,844
42	div2	Brighton	H	L	1-2	Gerrard 29	4,309
43	div2	Nottm Forest	A	D	1-1	Wilson 54 og	17,177
44	div2	Leeds	A	L	0-2		19,095
45	div2	Crewe	H	D	1-1	Roper 90	4,741
46	div2	Southend	A	L	0-1		8,145
47	div2	Tranmere	H	W	2-1	N'Dour 45, Demontagnac 59	5,745
48	div2	Cheltenham	A	W	2-1	Mooney 27 pen, Gerrard 28	4,861
49	div2	Bristol Rovers	H	L	0-1		4,500
50	div2	Bournemouth	H	L	1-3	Betsy 33	4,530
51	div2	Huddersfield	A	L	0-2		9,969
52	div2	Hartlepool	H	D	2-2	Dobson 9, Mooney 15	5,021

LEAGUE APPEARANCES, BOOKINGS AND GOALS

	AGE (on 01/07/08)	IN NAMED 16	APPEARANCES	COUNTING GAMES	MINUTES ON PITCH	LEAGUE GOALS	Yellow	Red
Goalkeepers								
Bertrand Bossu	27	41	0	0	0	0	0	0
Clayton Ince	35	46	46	46	4140	0	0	0
Defenders								
Paul Boertien	29	21	20	20	1774	0	2	0
Scott Dann	21	28	28	28	2520	3	4	0
Michael Dobson	27	26	24	15	1773	1	1	0
Daniel Fox	22	23	22	19	1858	3	5	1
Anthony Gerrard	22	46	44	43	3913	3	5	0
Alassane N'Dour	26	12	9	3	425	1	1	0
Ian Roper	31	35	19	16	1582	1	5	1
Emmanuele Smith	19	11	4	4	360	0	0	0
Richard Taundry	19	26	21	10	1273	0	0	1
Rhys Weston	27	45	44	41	3824	0	5	0
Midfielders								
Kevin Betsy	30	16	16	15	1376	2	2	0
Mark Bradley	20	36	35	23	2488	3	4	0
Martin Brittain	23	2	1	0	7	0	0	0
Ishmel Demontagnac	20	34	30	10	1289	3	4	0
Paul Hall	35	22	19	5	792	1	0	0
Lee Holmes	21	19	19	16	1542	4	2	0
Dwayne Mattis	26	4	4	3	261	0	2	0
Edrissa Sonko	28	39	37	21	2561	5	4	0
Danny Sonner	36	6	6	5	474	0	1	0
Peter Sweeney	23	7	7	6	586	0	1	0
Darren Wrack	32	37	37	31	3050	1	3	0
Forwards								
Martin Butler	33	5	5	5	450	1	2	0
Carlos Carneiro	33	4	3	2	182	0	1	0
Troy Deeney	20	42	34	9	1570	1	3	0
David McDermott	20	14	13	0	258	0	0	0
Tommy Mooney	36	36	36	34	3101	11	3	0
Stefan Moore	24	6	5	0	232	1	0	0
Alex Nicholls	20	27	19	5	864	2	0	0
Michael Ricketts	29	12	12	9	957	3	3	0

TEAM OF THE SEASON

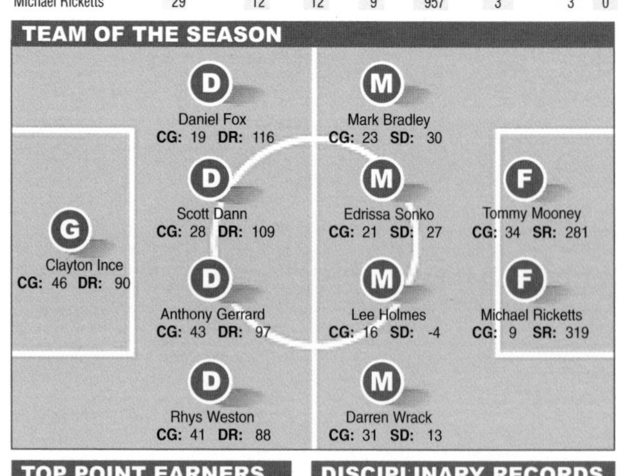

D
Daniel Fox
CG: 19 DR: 116
M
Mark Bradley
CG: 23 SD: 30
D
Scott Dann
CG: 28 DR: 109
M
Edrissa Sonko
CG: 21 SD: 27
F
Tommy Mooney
CG: 34 SR: 281
G
Clayton Ince
CG: 46 DR: 90
D
Anthony Gerrard
CG: 43 DR: 97
M
Lee Holmes
CG: 16 SD: -4
F
Michael Ricketts
CG: 9 SR: 319
D
Rhys Weston
CG: 41 DR: 88
M
Darren Wrack
CG: 31 SD: 13

MONTHLY POINTS TALLY

Month	Points	%
AUGUST	1	11%
SEPTEMBER	7	47%
OCTOBER	8	53%
NOVEMBER	8	67%
DECEMBER	12	67%
JANUARY	10	56%
FEBRUARY	6	50%
MARCH	5	24%
APRIL	6	40%
MAY	1	33%

LEAGUE GOALS

	PLAYER	MINS	GOALS	S RATE
1	Mooney	3101	11	281
2	Sonko	2561	5	512
3	Holmes	1542	4	385
4	Ricketts	957	3	319
5	Demontagnac	1289	3	429
6	Fox	1858	3	619
7	Bradley	2488	3	829
8	Dann	2520	3	840
9	Gerrard	3913	3	1304
10	Nicholls	864	2	432
11	Betsy	1376	2	688
12	Moore, S	232	1	232
13	N'Dour	425	1	425
	Other		5	
	TOTAL		49	

TOP POINT EARNERS

	PLAYER	GAMES	AV PTS
1	Daniel Fox	19	1.68
2	Edrissa Sonko	21	1.67
3	Darren Wrack	31	1.55
4	Scott Dann	28	1.54
5	Mark Bradley	23	1.52
6	Anthony Gerrard	43	1.49
7	Michael Dobson	15	1.40
8	Clayton Ince	46	1.39
9	Rhys Weston	41	1.39
10	Tommy Mooney	34	1.38
	CLUB AVERAGE:		1.39

DISCIPLINARY RECORDS

	PLAYER	YELLOW	RED	AVE
1	Ian Roper	5	1	263
2	Daniel Fox	5	1	309
3	Michael Ricketts	3	0	319
4	Ishmel Demontagnac	4	0	322
5	Danny Sonner	1	0	474
6	Troy Deeney	3	0	523
7	Peter Sweeney	1	0	586
8	Mark Bradley	4	0	622
9	Scott Dann	4	0	630
10	Edrissa Sonko	4	0	640
11	Kevin Betsy	2	0	688
12	Rhys Weston	5	0	764
13	Lee Holmes	2	0	771
	Other	14	1	
	TOTAL	57	3	

KEY GOALKEEPER

Clayton Ince

Goals Conceded in the League	46	Counting Games League games when player was on pitch for at least 70 minutes	46
Defensive Rating Ave number of mins between League goals conceded while on the pitch	90	Clean Sheets In League games when player was on pitch for at least 70 minutes	16

KEY PLAYERS - DEFENDERS

Daniel Fox

Goals Conceded Number of League goals conceded while the player was on the pitch	16	Clean Sheets In League games when player was on pitch for at least 70 minutes	9
Defensive Rating Ave number of mins between League goals conceded while on the pitch	116	Club Defensive Rating Average number of mins between League goals conceded by the club this season	90

	PLAYER	CON LGE	CLEAN SHEETS	DEF RATE
1	Daniel Fox	16	9	116 mins
2	Scott Dann	23	13	109 mins
3	Anthony Gerrard	40	16	97 mins
4	Rhys Weston	43	15	88 mins

KEY PLAYERS - MIDFIELDERS

Mark Bradley

Goals in the League	3	Contribution to Attacking Power Average number of minutes between League team goals while on pitch	65
Defensive Rating Average number of mins between League goals conceded while on the pitch	95	Scoring Difference Defensive Rating minus Contribution to Attacking Power	30

	PLAYER	LGE GOALS	DEF RATE	POWER	SCORE DIFF
1	Mark Bradley	3	95	65	30 mins
2	Edrissa Sonko	5	102	75	27 mins
3	Darren Wrack	1	95	82	13 mins
4	Lee Holmes	4	77	81	-4 mins

KEY PLAYERS - GOALSCORERS

Tommy Mooney

Goals in the League	11	Player Strike Rate Average number of minutes between League goals scored by player	281
Contribution to Attacking Power Average number of minutes between League team goals while on pitch	81	Club Strike Rate Average number of minutes between League goals scored by club	79

	PLAYER	LGE GOALS	POWER	STRIKE RATE
1	Tommy Mooney	11	81	281 mins
2	Michael Ricketts	3	73	319 mins
3	Lee Holmes	4	81	385 mins
4	Ishmel Demontagnac	3	67	429 mins

SWIFT
EASY FIT
RIES
Tommy Mooney

SQUAD APPEARANCES

Match	1	2	3	4	5	6	7	8	9	10	11	12	13	14	15	16	17	18	19	20	21	22	23	24	25	26
Venue	H	A	A	H	A	H	A	H	A	A	H	A	H	A	H	A	H	H	A	A	H	A	H	H	H	A
Competition	L	W	L	L	L	L	L	L	L	L	L	L	L	L	L	L	F	L	L	F	L	L	F	L	L	L
Result	D	L	L	L	L	D	W	L	W	W	W	D	L	D	W	D	W	D	W	D	W	D	W	D	W	D

Match	27	28	29	30	31	32	33	34	35	36	37	38	39	40	41	42	43	44	45	46	47	48	49	50	51	52
Venue	A	H	H	A	H	A	A	H	H	A	H	A	A	A	H	H	A	A	H	A	H	A	H	H	A	H
Competition	L	L	F	L	L	F	L	L	L	L	L	L	L	L	L	L	L	L	L	L	L	L	L	L	L	L
Result	W	D	D	W	D	L	D	W	D	L	W	L	W	W	L	L	D	L	D	L	W	W	L	L	L	D

Goalkeepers
Bertrand Bossu
Clayton Ince
Defenders
Paul Boertien
Scott Dann
Michael Dobson
Daniel Fox
Anthony Gerrard
Alassane N'Dour
Ian Roper
Emmanuele Smith
Richard Taundry
Rhys Weston
Midfielders
Kevin Betsy
Mark Bradley
Martin Brittain
Ishmel Demontagnac
Paul Hall
Lee Holmes
Dwayne Mattis
Edrissa Sonko
Danny Sonner
Peter Sweeney
Darren Wrack
Forwards
Martin Butler
Carlos Carneiro
Troy Deeney
David McDermott
Tommy Mooney
Stefan Moore
Alex Nicholls
Michael Ricketts

KEY: On all match | On bench | Subbed or sent off (Counting game) | Subbed or sent off (playing less than 70 minutes) | Subbed on from bench (Counting Game) | Subbed on (playing less than 70 minutes) | Subbed on and then subbed or sent off (Counting Game) | Subbed on and then subbed or sent off (playing less than 70 minutes) | Not in 16

SWINDON TOWN

Final Position: **13th**

NICKNAME: THE ROBINS

KEY: ☐Won ☐Drawn ☐Lost

							Attendance
1	div2	Northampton	A	D	1-1	Roberts 44 pen	6,210
2	ccr1	Charlton	H	L	0-2		6,175
3	div2	Luton	H	W	2-1	Peacock 56, Easton 88	7,520
4	div2	Cheltenham	A	D	1-1	Sturrock 35	5,442
5	div2	Crewe	H	D	1-1	Pook 24	6,595
6	div2	Yeovil	H	L	0-1		6,944
7	div2	Hartlepool	A	D	1-1	McGovern 31	4,943
8	div2	Bournemouth	H	W	4-1	Cox 7, Paynter 48, 64, 85	6,668
9	div2	Millwall	A	W	2-1	Cox 8, Ifil 79	8,744
10	div2	Swansea	A	L	1-2	Roberts 70	10,135
11	div2	Gillingham	H	W	5-0	McGovern 4, Cox 6, 62, Paynter 52, 84	6,345
12	div2	Tranmere	H	W	1-0	Corr 88	6,430
13	div2	Port Vale	A	L	1-2	Peacock 19	4,013
14	div2	Doncaster	H	L	1-2	Cox 47	6,570
15	div2	Leyton Orient	H	D	1-1	Aljofree 90	5,874
16	facr1	Wycombe	A	W	2-1	Roberts 66, Paynter 72	3,332
17	div2	Leeds	A	L	1-2	Peacock 47	27,990
18	div2	Bristol Rovers	H	W	1-0	Roberts 67 pen	9,342
19	facr2	Forest Green	H	W	3-2	McGovern 12, Aljofree 69, Sturrock 88	7,588
20	div2	Carlisle	A	L	0-3		5,477
21	div2	Southend	A	L	1-2	Cox 2	7,403
22	div2	Brighton	H	L	0-3		6,415
23	div2	Hartlepool	H	W	2-1	Cox 49, Corr 73 pen	5,875
24	div2	Yeovil	A	W	1-0	Corr 66	6,539
25	div2	Bournemouth	A	D	2-2	Corr 49, 83	6,540
26	div2	Swansea	H	D	1-1	Cox 90 pen	9,426
27	facr3	Barnet	H	D	1-1	Sturrock 60	5,944
28	div2	Walsall	A	D	2-2	Nicholas 65, Easton 67	5,449
29	div2	Nottm Forest	H	W	2-1	Perch 35 og, Breckin 82 og	9,815
30	facr3	Barnet	A	L	0-2*	Paynter 42 (*on penalties)	2,810
31	div2	Crewe	A	D	0-0		4,344
32	div2	Luton	A	W	1-0	Roberts 52	5,738
33	div2	Northampton	H	D	1-1	Sturrock 56	7,375
34	div2	Huddersfield	A	L	0-1		9,388
35	div2	Cheltenham	H	W	3-0	Cox 20, Paynter 41, Roberts 80	6,483
36	div2	Nottm Forest	A	L	0-1		23,439
37	div2	Walsall	H	L	0-3		6,265
38	div2	Oldham	A	D	2-2	Peacock 29, 58	3,923
39	div2	Leeds	H	L	0-1		13,270
40	div2	Huddersfield	H	W	3-2	Paynter 4, Easton 23, 31	4,840
41	div2	Leyton Orient	A	L	1-2	Thelwell 20 og	3,082
42	div2	Carlisle	H	D	2-2	Cox 61, Sturrock 80	6,004
43	div2	Brighton	A	L	1-2	Easton 8	6,849
44	div2	Southend	H	L	0-1		6,378
45	div2	Tranmere	A	L	1-2	Paynter 68	8,777
46	div2	Oldham	H	W	3-0	Peacock 49, Cox 53, 70	5,384
47	div2	Doncaster	A	L	0-2		8,371
48	div2	Port Vale	H	W	6-0	Peacock 16, Easton 21, J.Smith 33, McNamee 45, Timlin 45, Joyce 90	7,361
49	div2	Bristol Rovers	A	W	1-0	Cox 74	6,102
50	div2	Gillingham	A	D	1-1	Aljofree 88	6,334
51	div2	Millwall	H	W	2-1	Cox 31 pen, McNamee 51	7,781

LEAGUE APPEARANCES, BOOKINGS AND GOALS

	AGE (on 01/07/08)	IN NAMED 16	APPEARANCES	COUNTING GAMES	MINUTES ON PITCH	LEAGUE GOALS	Yellow	Red
Goalkeepers								
Peter Brezovan	28	40	31	31	2790	0	1	0
Phil Smith	28	27	15	15	1350	0	0	0
Defenders								
Hasney Aljofree	29	39	39	35	3232	2	3	1
Chris Blackburn	25	12	7	5	513	0	1	0
Sam Collins	31	4	4	2	235	0	0	0
Miguel Comminges	26	41	40	33	3038	0	6	0
Jerel Ifil	26	41	40	38	3494	1	6	1
Patrick Kanyuka	20	8	4	2	224	0	1	0
Sean Morrison	17	4	2	1	147	0	0	0
Andrew Nicholas	24	21	11	7	793	1	0	0
Jack Smith	24	24	20	18	1691	1	4	0
Ben Tozer	18	6	2	0	68	0	0	1
Jamie Vincent	33	34	33	32	2938	0	3	0
Midfielders								
Steve Adams	27	6	2	2	171	0	0	0
Chris Allen	19	13	8	4	518	0	0	0
Craig Easton	29	41	40	39	3516	6	3	0
John-Paul McGovern	27	41	41	32	3113	2	2	0
Anthony McNamee	23	21	19	12	1395	2	0	0
Lee Peacock	31	38	37	34	3178	7	2	1
Michael Pook	22	30	22	13	1322	1	4	0
Michael Timlin	23	10	10	8	775	1	2	0
Sofiane Zaaboub	25	31	29	17	1667	0	2	1
Forwards								
Ibon Arietea	31	4	4	0	55	0	1	0
Moses Ashikodi	21	12	10	2	351	0	2	0
Barry Corr	23	18	17	4	582	5	3	1
Simon Cox	21	36	36	32	3031	14	8	0
Ben Joyce	18	4	3	0	46	1	0	0
Kaid Mohamed	23	18	11	2	297	0	0	0
William Paynter	23	37	36	21	2239	8	4	2
Christian Roberts	28	28	27	13	1488	5	3	0
Blair Sturrock	26	37	21	10	1082	3	1	0

TEAM OF THE SEASON

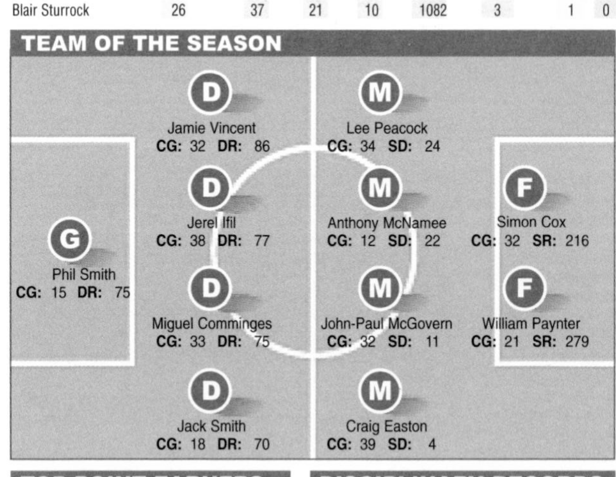
D
Jamie Vincent
CG: 32 DR: 86
M
Lee Peacock
CG: 34 SD: 24
D
Jerel Ifil
CG: 38 DR: 77
M
Anthony McNamee
CG: 12 SD: 22
F
Simon Cox
CG: 32 SR: 216
G
Phil Smith
CG: 15 DR: 75
D
Miguel Comminges
CG: 33 DR: 75
M
John-Paul McGovern
CG: 32 SD: 11
F
William Paynter
CG: 21 SR: 279
D
Jack Smith
CG: 18 DR: 70
M
Craig Easton
CG: 39 SD: 4

MONTHLY POINTS TALLY

AUGUST	5	56%
SEPTEMBER	8	53%
OCTOBER	6	50%
NOVEMBER	4	33%
DECEMBER	7	39%
JANUARY	9	60%
FEBRUARY	5	28%
MARCH	4	19%
APRIL	10	67%
MAY	3	100%

LEAGUE GOALS

	PLAYER	MINS	GOALS	S RATE
1	Cox	3031	14	216
2	Paynter	2239	8	279
3	Peacock	3178	7	454
4	Easton	3516	6	586
5	Corr	582	5	116
6	Roberts	1488	5	297
7	Sturrock	1082	3	360
8	McNamee	1395	2	697
9	McGovern	3113	2	1556
10	Aljofree	3232	2	1616
11	Joyce	46	1	46
12	Timlin	775	1	775
13	Nicholas	793	1	793
	Other		3	
	TOTAL		60	

TOP POINT EARNERS

	PLAYER	GAMES	AV PTS
1	Anthony McNamee	12	1.58
2	Jamie Vincent	32	1.56
3	Phil Smith	15	1.53
4	John-Paul McGovern	32	1.50
5	William Paynter	21	1.48
6	Lee Peacock	34	1.47
7	Jerel Ifil	38	1.39
8	Miguel Comminges	33	1.33
9	Craig Easton	39	1.31
10	Christian Roberts	13	1.31
	CLUB AVERAGE:		1.33

DISCIPLINARY RECORDS

	PLAYER	YELLOW	RED	AVE
1	Barry Corr	3	1	145
2	Michael Pook	4	0	330
3	William Paynter	4	2	373
4	Simon Cox	8	0	378
5	Michael Timlin	2	0	387
6	Jack Smith	4	0	422
7	Christian Roberts	3	0	496
8	Jerel Ifil	6	1	499
9	Miguel Comminges	6	0	506
10	Chris Blackburn	1	0	513
11	Sofiane Zaaboub	2	1	555
12	Hasney Aljofree	3	1	808
13	Jamie Vincent	3	0	979
	Other	9	1	
	TOTAL	58	7	

KEY GOALKEEPER

Phil Smith

Goals Conceded in the League	18	Counting Games League games when player was on pitch for at least 70 minutes	15
Defensive Rating Ave number of mins between League goals conceded while on the pitch	75	Clean Sheets In League games when player was on pitch for at least 70 minutes	2

KEY PLAYERS - DEFENDERS

Jamie Vincent

Goals Conceded Number of League goals conceded while the player was on the pitch	34	Clean Sheets In League games when player was on pitch for at least 70 minutes	7
Defensive Rating Ave number of mins between League goals conceded while on the pitch	86	Club Defensive Rating Average number of mins between League goals conceded by the club this season	73

	PLAYER	CON LGE	CLEAN SHEETS	DEF RATE
1	Jamie Vincent	34	7	86 mins
2	Jerel Ifil	45	9	77 mins
3	Miguel Comminges	40	9	75 mins
4	Jack Smith	24	4	70 mins

KEY PLAYERS - MIDFIELDERS

Lee Peacock

Goals in the League	7	Contribution to Attacking Power Average number of minutes between League team goals while on pitch	61
Defensive Rating Average number of mins between League goals conceded while on the pitch	85	Scoring Difference Defensive Rating minus Contribution to Attacking Power	24

	PLAYER	LGE GOALS	DEF RATE	POWER	SCORE DIFF
1	Lee Peacock	7	85	61	24 mins
2	Anthony McNamee	2	82	60	22 mins
3	John-Paul McGovern	2	75	64	11 mins
4	Craig Easton	6	67	63	4 mins

KEY PLAYERS - GOALSCORERS

Simon Cox

Goals in the League	14	Player Strike Rate Average number of minutes between League goals scored by player	216
Contribution to Attacking Power Average number of minutes between League team goals while on pitch	59	Club Strike Rate Average number of minutes between League goals scored by club	65

	PLAYER	LGE GOALS	POWER	STRIKE RATE
1	Simon Cox	14	59	216 mins
2	William Paynter	8	63	279 mins
3	Christian Roberts	5	74	297 mins
4	Lee Peacock	7	61	454 mins

Kingswood
Group
William Paynter

SQUAD APPEARANCES

Match	1	2	3	4	5	6	7	8	9	10	11	12	13	14	15	16	17	18	19	20	21	22	23	24	25
Venue	A	H	H	A	H	H	A	H	A	A	H	H	A	H	H	A	A	H	H	A	A	H	H	A	A
Competition	L	W	L	L	L	L	L	L	L	L	L	L	L	L	L	F	L	L	F	L	L	L	L	L	L
Result	D	L	W	D	D	L	D	W	W	L	W	W	L	L	D	W	L	W	W	L	L	L	W	W	D

Match	26	27	28	29	30	31	32	33	34	35	36	37	38	39	40	41	42	43	44	45	46	47	48	49	50	51
Venue	H	H	A	H	A	A	A	H	A	H	A	H	A	H	H	A	H	A	H	A	H	A	H	A	A	H
Competition	L	F	L	L	F	L	L	L	L	L	L	L	L	L	L	L	L	L	L	L	L	L	L	L	L	L
Result	D	D	D	W	L	D	W	D	L	W	L	L	D	L	W	L	D	L	L	L	W	L	W	W	D	W

Goalkeepers
- Peter Brezovan
- Phil Smith

Defenders
- Hasney Aljofree
- Chris Blackburn
- Sam Collins
- Miguel Comminges
- Jerel Ifil
- Patrick Kanyuka
- Sean Morrison
- Andrew Nicholas
- Jack Smith
- Ben Tozer
- Jamie Vincent

Midfielders
- Steve Adams
- Chris Allen
- Craig Easton
- John-Paul McGovern
- Anthony McNamee
- Lee Peacock
- Michael Pook
- Michael Timlin
- Sofiane Zaaboub

Forwards
- Ibon Arietea
- Moses Ashikodi
- Barry Corr
- Simon Cox
- Ben Joyce
- Kaid Mohamed
- William Paynter
- Christian Roberts
- Blair Sturrock

KEY: On all match · On bench · Subbed or sent off (Counting game) · Subbed or sent off (playing less than 70 minutes) · Subbed on from bench (Counting Game) · Subbed on (playing less than 70 minutes) · Subbed on and then subbed or sent off (Counting Game) · Subbed on and then subbed or sent off (playing less than 70 minutes) · Not in 16

LEYTON ORIENT

Final Position: **14th**

NICKNAME: THE O'S

KEY: ☐ Won ☐ Drawn ☐ Lost

						Attendance
1 div2	Southend	A	W	2-1	Thornton 38, Boyd 86	9,828
2 ccr1	QPR	A	W	2-1	Demetriou 55, Boyd 64 pen	5,260
3 div2	Walsall	H	W	1-0	Gray 52	4,524
4 div2	Crewe	A	W	2-0	Melligan 35, Boyd 85 pen	4,683
5 ccr2	Cardiff	A	L	0-1		6,150
6 div2	Northampton	H	D	2-2	A.Chambers 52, Mkandawire 57	5,170
7 div2	Bournemouth	H	W	1-0	Boyd 71	4,995
8 div2	Yeovil	A	W	1-0	Boyd 57	5,217
9 div2	Hartlepool	H	L	2-4	Melligan 57, Daniels 87	5,325
10 div2	Bristol Rovers	A	W	3-2	Gray 59, Mkandawire 75, Demetriou 81	7,181
11 div2	Gillingham	A	L	1-3	Ibehre 72	5,632
12 div2	Swansea	H	L	0-5		5,586
13 div2	Leeds	A	D	1-1	Thornton 9	29,177
14 div2	Port Vale	H	W	3-1	Mkandawire 53, Ibehre 55, Boyd 60 pen	4,555
15 div2	Doncaster	A	L	2-4	Ibehre 56, Purches 68	7,184
16 div2	Oldham	H	W	1-0	Daniels 8	4,690
17 div2	Swindon	A	D	1-1	Boyd 87	5,874
18 facr1	Bristol Rovers	H	D	1-1	Gray 16	3,157
19 div2	Brighton	H	D	2-2	Gray 27, Demetriou 70	6,496
20 div2	Huddersfield	A	W	1-0	Boyd 4	9,697
21 facr1r	Bristol Rovers	A	L	5-6*	Boyd 28, 92 pen, Gray 55 (*on penalties)	3,742
22 div2	Millwall	H	L	0-1		6,220
23 div2	Cheltenham	H	W	2-0	Boyd 41, Melligan 76	4,156
24 div2	Carlisle	A	L	0-1		6,843
25 div2	Yeovil	H	D	0-0		4,687
26 div2	Bournemouth	A	L	1-3	Saah 72	5,536
27 div2	Hartlepool	A	D	1-1	A.Chambers 33	4,379
28 div2	Gillingham	H	D	0-0		5,369
29 div2	Tranmere	H	W	3-0	Gray 11, Thornton 84, Demetriou 90	3,447
30 div2	Nottm Forest	A	L	0-4		17,805
31 div2	Luton	H	W	2-1	Boyd 39, Barcham 55	5,516
32 div2	Northampton	A	L	0-2		5,405
33 div2	Walsall	A	D	0-0		4,643
34 div2	Southend	H	D	2-2	Boyd 51 pen, Ibehre 90	6,886
35 div2	Tranmere	A	D	1-1	A.Chambers 87	6,530
36 div2	Crewe	H	L	0-1		3,881
37 div2	Luton	A	W	1-0	Ibehre 26	6,412
38 div2	Nottm Forest	H	L	0-1		7,136
39 div2	Brighton	A	D	1-1	Ibehre 80	6,242
40 div2	Huddersfield	H	L	0-1		4,660
41 div2	Swindon	H	W	2-1	Boyd 51 pen, 55	3,082
42 div2	Millwall	A	W	1-0	Gray 50	10,986
43 div2	Carlisle	H	L	0-3		6,134
44 div2	Cheltenham	A	L	0-1		3,988
45 div2	Port Vale	A	L	1-2	Boyd 26 pen	3,252
46 div2	Leeds	H	L	0-2		7,602
47 div2	Oldham	A	L	0-2		4,325
48 div2	Doncaster	H	D	1-1	Gray 44	4,582
49 div2	Swansea	A	L	1-4	Gray 63	16,856
50 div2	Bristol Rovers	H	W	3-1	Gray 12 pen, Boyd 81, Ibehre 90	5,132

LEAGUE APPEARANCES, BOOKINGS AND GOALS

	AGE (on 01/07/08)	IN NAMED 16	APPEARANCES	COUNTING GAMES	MINUTES ON PITCH	LEAGUE GOALS	Yellow	Red
Goalkeepers								
Glenn Morris	24	36	16	16	1440	0	2	0
Stuart Nelson	26	40	30	30	2700	0	4	0
Defenders								
Adam Chambers	27	45	45	45	4050	3	5	0
Jason Demetriou	20	45	43	28	2918	3	7	0
Clayton Fortune	25	4	1	0	54	0	0	0
Tamika Mkandawire	25	36	35	34	3083	3	3	0
Samuel Oji	22	23	13	7	849	0	2	0
Aiden Palmer	21	40	23	22	2042	0	0	0
Stephen Purches	28	37	37	33	3130	1	1	0
Chris Robson	18	1	0	0	0	0	0	0
Brian Saah	21	35	25	22	2019	1	3	0
Alton Thelwell	27	31	28	25	2369	0	1	0
Midfielders								
Wayne Corden	32	33	26	13	1489	0	1	0
Charlie Daniels	20	43	31	24	2315	2	2	0
John Melligan	26	39	32	19	2150	3	2	1
Solomon Shields	18	2	0	0	0	0	0	0
Paul Terry	29	45	43	38	3627	0	5	0
Sean Thornton	25	33	31	17	1862	3	4	1
Forwards								
Andy Barcham	21	28	25	11	1299	1	0	0
Adam Boyd	26	44	44	37	3522	14	2	0
Efe Echanomi	21	23	14	0	199	0	0	0
Wayne Gray	27	38	38	22	2491	8	1	0
Jabo Ibehre	25	31	31	16	1807	7	1	0
Loick Pires	19	1	1	0	8	0	0	0
Raphael Sylvester	19	2	0	0	0	0	0	0

TEAM OF THE SEASON

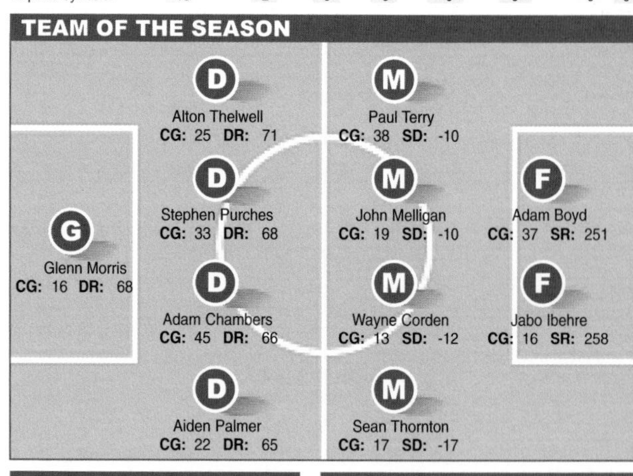

G
Glenn Morris
CG: 16 DR: 68
D
Alton Thelwell
CG: 25 DR: 71
D
Stephen Purches
CG: 33 DR: 68
D
Adam Chambers
CG: 45 DR: 66
D
Aiden Palmer
CG: 22 DR: 65
M
Paul Terry
CG: 38 SD: -10
M
John Melligan
CG: 19 SD: -10
M
Wayne Corden
CG: 13 SD: -12
M
Sean Thornton
CG: 17 SD: -17
F
Adam Boyd
CG: 37 SR: 251
F
Jabo Ibehre
CG: 16 SR: 258

MONTHLY POINTS TALLY

Month	Points	%
AUGUST	9	100%
SEPTEMBER	10	67%
OCTOBER	4	27%
NOVEMBER	8	67%
DECEMBER	5	28%
JANUARY	8	44%
FEBRUARY	5	33%
MARCH	7	33%
APRIL	1	8%
MAY	3	100%

LEAGUE GOALS

	PLAYER	MINS	GOALS	S RATE
1	Boyd	3522	14	251
2	Gray	2491	8	311
3	Ibehre	1807	7	258
4	Thornton	1862	3	620
5	Melligan	2150	3	716
6	Demetriou	2918	3	972
7	Mkandawire	3083	3	1027
8	Chambers, A	4050	3	1350
9	Daniels	2315	2	1157
10	Barcham	1299	1	1299
11	Saah	2019	1	2019
12	Purches	3130	1	3130
13	Robson	0	0	
	Other		0	
	TOTAL		49	

TOP POINT EARNERS

	PLAYER	GAMES	AV PTS
1	Wayne Corden	13	1.92
2	John Melligan	19	1.89
3	Sean Thornton	17	1.82
4	Wayne Gray	22	1.73
5	Aiden Palmer	22	1.68
6	Alton Thelwell	25	1.48
7	Stuart Nelson	30	1.43
8	Adam Boyd	37	1.38
9	Tamika Mkandawire	34	1.35
10	Paul Terry	38	1.34
	CLUB AVERAGE:		1.30

DISCIPLINARY RECORDS

	PLAYER	YELLOW	RED	AVE
1	Sean Thornton	4	1	372
2	Jason Demetriou	7	0	416
3	Samuel Oji	2	0	424
4	Brian Saah	3	0	673
5	Stuart Nelson	4	0	675
6	John Melligan	2	1	716
7	Glenn Morris	2	0	720
8	Paul Terry	5	0	725
9	Adam Chambers	5	0	810
10	Tamika Mkandawire	3	0	1027
11	Charlie Daniels	2	0	1157
12	Wayne Corden	1	0	1489
13	Adam Boyd	2	0	1761
	Other	4	0	
	TOTAL	46	2	

KEY GOALKEEPER

Glenn Morris

Goals Conceded in the League	21	Counting Games League games when player was on pitch for at least 70 minutes	16
Defensive Rating Ave number of mins between League goals conceded while on the pitch	68	Clean Sheets In League games when player was on pitch for at least 70 minutes	3

KEY PLAYERS - DEFENDERS

Alton Thelwell

Goals Conceded Number of League goals conceded while the player was on the pitch	33	Clean Sheets In League games when player was on pitch for at least 70 minutes	10
Defensive Rating Ave number of mins between League goals conceded while on the pitch	71	Club Defensive Rating Average number of mins between League goals conceded by the club this season	65

	PLAYER	CON LGE	CLEAN SHEETS	DEF RATE
1	Alton Thelwell	33	10	71 mins
2	Stephen Purches	46	9	68 mins
3	Adam Chambers	61	13	66 mins
4	Aiden Palmer	31	8	65 mins

KEY PLAYERS - MIDFIELDERS

Paul Terry

Goals in the League	0	Contribution to Attacking Power Average number of minutes between League team goals while on pitch	84
Defensive Rating Average number of mins between League goals conceded while on the pitch	74	Scoring Difference Defensive Rating minus Contribution to Attacking Power	-10

	PLAYER	LGE GOALS	DEF RATE	POWER	SCORE DIFF
1	Paul Terry	0	74	84	-10 mins
2	John Melligan	3	61	71	-10 mins
3	Wayne Corden	0	70	82	-12 mins
4	Sean Thornton	3	60	77	-17 mins

KEY PLAYERS - GOALSCORERS

Adam Boyd

Goals in the League	14	Player Strike Rate Average number of minutes between League goals scored by player	251
Contribution to Attacking Power Average number of minutes between League team goals while on pitch	83	Club Strike Rate Average number of minutes between League goals scored by club	84

	PLAYER	LGE GOALS	POWER	STRIKE RATE
1	Adam Boyd	14	83	251 mins
2	Jabo Ibehre	7	86	258 mins
3	Wayne Gray	8	85	311 mins
4	Sean Thornton	3	77	620 mins

Vandanel
Adam Boyd

SQUAD APPEARANCES

Match	1	2	3	4	5	6	7	8	9	10	11	12	13	14	15	16	17	18	19	20	21	22	23	24	25
Venue	A	A	H	A	A	H	H	A	H	A	A	H	A	H	A	H	A	H	H	A	A	H	H	A	H
Competition	L	W	L	L	W	L	L	L	L	L	L	L	L	L	L	L	L	F	L	L	F	L	L	L	L
Result	W	W	W	W	L	D	W	W	L	W	L	L	D	W	L	W	D	D	D	W	L	L	W	L	D

Match	26	27	28	29	30	31	32	33	34	35	36	37	38	39	40	41	42	43	44	45	46	47	48	49	50
Venue	A	A	H	H	A	H	A	A	H	A	H	A	H	A	H	H	A	H	A	A	H	A	H	A	H
Competition	L	L	L	L	L	L	L	L	L	L	L	L	L	L	L	L	L	L	L	L	L	L	L	L	L
Result	L	D	D	W	L	W	L	D	D	D	L	W	L	D	L	W	W	L	L	L	L	L	D	L	W

Goalkeepers
- Glenn Morris
- Stuart Nelson

Defenders
- Adam Chambers
- Jason Demetriou
- Clayton Fortune
- Tamika Mkandawire
- Samuel Oji
- Aiden Palmer
- Stephen Purches
- Chris Robson
- Brian Saah
- Alton Thelwell

Midfielders
- Wayne Corden
- Charlie Daniels
- John Melligan
- Solomon Shields
- Paul Terry
- Sean Thornton

Forwards
- Andy Barcham
- Adam Boyd
- Efe Echanomi
- Wayne Gray
- Jabo Ibehre
- Loick Pires
- Raphael Sylvester

KEY: On all match | On bench | Subbed or sent off (Counting game) | Subbed or sent off (playing less than 70 minutes) | Subbed on from bench (Counting Game) | Subbed on (playing less than 70 minutes) | Subbed on and then subbed or sent off (Counting Game) | Subbed on and then subbed or sent off (playing less than 70 minutes) | Not in 16

HARTLEPOOL

Final Position: **15th**

NICKNAME: THE POOL

KEY: ☐Won ☐Drawn ☐Lost

No	Comp	Opponent	H/A	Res	Score	Scorers	Attendance
1	div2	**Luton**	A	L	1-2	Barker 90 pen	8,013
2	ccr1	**Scunthorpe**	A	W	2-1	Foley 70, 85	2,965
3	div2	**Doncaster**	H	W	2-1	Antwi 43, Barker 81 pen	5,544
4	div2	**Port Vale**	A	W	2-0	Robson 6, Brown 88	3,978
5	ccr2	**Sheff Wed**	A	L	1-2	Moore 55	8,751
6	div2	**Oldham**	H	W	4-1	Moore 15, Brown 26, Barker 44 pen, Porter 83	5,015
7	div2	**Leeds**	A	L	0-2		26,877
8	div2	**Swindon**	H	D	1-1	Porter 68	4,943
9	div2	**Leyton Orient**	A	W	4-2	Moore 10, 90, Brown 51, Monkhouse 84	5,325
10	div2	**Walsall**	H	L	0-1		4,948
11	div2	**Carlisle**	H	D	2-2	Barker 39, Mackay 86	5,359
12	div2	**Nottm Forest**	A	L	1-2	Barker 38	17,520
13	div2	**Bristol Rovers**	H	W	1-0	Brown 39	4,963
14	div2	**Brighton**	H	L	1-2	Barker 86 pen	5,619
15	div2	**Millwall**	A	W	1-0	Sweeney 51	7,731
16	div2	**Huddersfield**	A	L	0-2		8,154
17	facr1	**Gainsborough**	A	W	6-0	Barker 8, 25, Liddle 51, Moore 70, Brown 76, Porter 82	2,402
18	div2	**Bournemouth**	H	D	1-1	Moore 41	3,496
19	div2	**Gillingham**	A	L	1-2	Brown 25	5,488
20	div2	**Swansea**	A	L	0-1		11,421
21	facr2	**Hereford**	A	L	0-2		3,801
22	div2	**Tranmere**	H	W	3-1	Liddle 3, Brown 11, Porter 58	3,583
23	div2	**Yeovil**	A	L	1-3	Mackay 10	4,694
24	div2	**Crewe**	H	W	3-0	Nelson 67, Barker 85, 88 pen	3,915
25	div2	**Swindon**	A	L	1-2	Moore 45	5,875
26	div2	**Leeds**	H	D	1-1	Nelson 21	7,784
27	div2	**Leyton Orient**	H	D	1-1	Moore 55	4,379
28	div2	**Carlisle**	A	L	2-4	Humphreys 39, 48	7,496
29	div2	**Northampton**	A	D	1-1	Clark 45	4,639
30	div2	**Cheltenham**	H	L	0-2		4,120
31	div2	**Southend**	H	W	4-3	Barker 17 pen, Brown 47, 53, Sweeney 90	3,217
32	div2	**Doncaster**	A	L	0-2		6,442
33	div2	**Luton**	H	W	4-0	Barker 30 pen, 73, Thompson 61, Porter 64	3,913
34	div2	**Southend**	A	L	1-2	Sweeney 9	7,436
35	div2	**Port Vale**	H	W	3-2	Barker 68, 90, Sweeney 87	3,630
36	div2	**Cheltenham**	A	D	1-1	Porter 53	3,583
37	div2	**Northampton**	H	L	0-1		3,945
38	div2	**Bournemouth**	A	L	0-2		3,984
39	div2	**Oldham**	A	W	1-0	Mackay 74	3,765
40	div2	**Gillingham**	H	W	4-0	Monkhouse 21, Porter 26, Collins 74, McCunnie 90	4,055
41	div2	**Huddersfield**	H	W	2-1	Collins 30, Mackay 50	3,650
42	div2	**Tranmere**	A	L	1-3	Humphreys 71	5,608
43	div2	**Crewe**	A	L	1-3	Porter 81	4,412
44	div2	**Yeovil**	H	W	2-0	Brown 28, Porter 67	3,808
45	div2	**Swansea**	H	L	1-3	Liddle 1	4,484
46	div2	**Bristol Rovers**	A	D	0-0		5,526
47	div2	**Millwall**	H	L	0-1		4,077
48	div2	**Brighton**	A	L	1-2	Porter 75	6,178
49	div2	**Nottm Forest**	H	L	0-1		5,206
50	div2	**Walsall**	A	D	2-2	Mackay 18, Clark 90	5,021

LEAGUE APPEARANCES, BOOKINGS AND GOALS

	AGE (on 01/07/08)	IN NAMED 16	APPEARANCES	COUNTING GAMES	MINUTES ON PITCH	LEAGUE GOALS	Yellow	Red
Goalkeepers								
Jan Budtz	29	35	28	28	2520	0	0	0
Arran Lee-Barrett	25	30	18	18	1620	0	1	0
Defenders								
Godwin Antwi	20	38	27	25	2338	1	2	0
Ben Clark	25	28	19	13	1319	2	3	0
Danny Coles	26	4	3	3	256	0	1	0
Sam Collins	31	11	10	7	751	2	0	1
Robbie Elliott	34	37	15	10	1091	0	1	1
Richie Humphreys	30	46	45	39	3793	3	1	0
Graeme Lee	30	4	3	3	270	0	0	0
Jamie McCunnie	25	33	29	22	2122	1	5	1
Michael Nelson	28	45	45	44	4008	2	5	0
Eddie Nolan	19	11	11	10	948	0	1	0
Matty Robson	23	24	17	5	736	1	2	0
Midfielders								
Willie Boland	32	36	34	21	2522	0	7	1
Lee Bullock	27	3	1	0	42	0	0	0
Alistair Gibb	32	14	6	4	415	0	2	0
Gary Liddle	22	41	41	40	3635	2	1	0
Andy Monkhouse	27	30	25	20	1913	2	5	0
Antony Sweeney	24	40	36	26	2520	4	2	0
Alan Thompson	34	7	7	4	489	1	1	0
Steve Turnbull	21	1	1	0	5	0	0	0
Forwards								
Richard Barker	33	36	36	29	2752	13	2	0
James Brown	21	35	35	28	2730	9	1	0
Tom Craddock	21	7	4	1	141	0	0	0
David Foley	20	42	34	8	1254	0	1	0
Michael Mackay	25	31	24	8	1094	5	0	0
Ian Moore	31	24	24	19	1886	6	4	0
Joel Porter	29	40	39	21	2233	9	3	0

TEAM OF THE SEASON

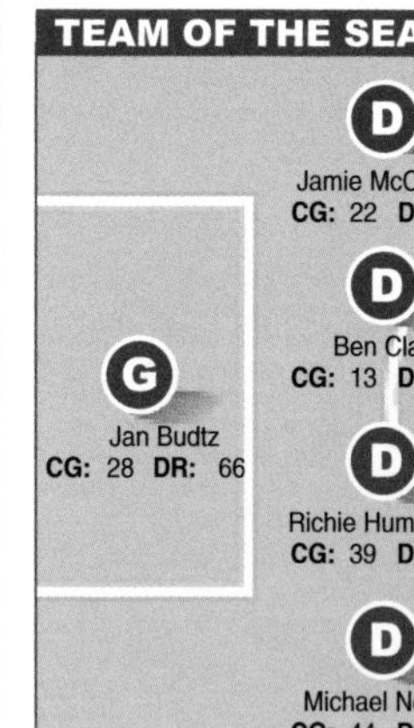

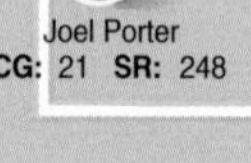

		CG	
G	Jan Budtz	CG: 28	DR: 66
D	Jamie McCunnie	CG: 22	DR: 73
D	Ben Clark	CG: 13	DR: 65
D	Richie Humphreys	CG: 39	DR: 64
D	Michael Nelson	CG: 44	DR: 61
M	Willie Boland	CG: 21	SD: 5
M	Andy Monkhouse	CG: 20	SD: 2
M	Gary Liddle	CG: 40	SD: -1
M	Antony Sweeney	CG: 26	SD: -12
F	Richard Barker	CG: 29	SR: 211
F	Joel Porter	CG: 21	SR: 248

MONTHLY POINTS TALLY

Month	Points	%
AUGUST	6	67%
SEPTEMBER	7	47%
OCTOBER	4	33%
NOVEMBER	4	27%
DECEMBER	8	44%
JANUARY	4	27%
FEBRUARY	7	47%
MARCH	12	50%
APRIL	1	8%
MAY	1	33%

LEAGUE GOALS

	PLAYER	MINS	GOALS	S RATE
1	Barker	2752	13	211
2	Porter	2233	9	248
3	Brown	2730	9	303
4	Moore	1886	6	314
5	Mackay	1094	5	218
6	Sweeney	2520	4	630
7	Humphreys	3793	3	1264
8	Collins	751	2	375
9	Clark	1319	2	659
10	Monkhouse	1913	2	956
11	Liddle	3635	2	1817
12	Nelson	4008	2	2004
13	Thompson	489	1	489
	Other		3	
	TOTAL		63	

TOP POINT EARNERS

	PLAYER	GAMES	AV PTS
1	Joel Porter	21	1.52
2	Jamie McCunnie	22	1.41
3	Willie Boland	21	1.38
4	Andy Monkhouse	20	1.35
5	Jan Budtz	28	1.29
6	Gary Liddle	40	1.28
7	Ian Moore	19	1.21
8	Michael Nelson	44	1.18
9	Richard Barker	29	1.17
10	Richie Humphreys	39	1.13
	CLUB AVERAGE:		1.17

DISCIPLINARY RECORDS

	PLAYER	YELLOW	RED	AVE
1	Willie Boland	7	1	315
2	Jamie McCunnie	5	1	353
3	Matty Robson	2	0	368
4	Andy Monkhouse	5	0	382
5	Ben Clark	3	0	439
6	Ian Moore	4	0	471
7	Alan Thompson	1	0	489
8	Robbie Elliott	1	1	545
9	Joel Porter	3	0	744
10	Sam Collins	0	1	751
11	Michael Nelson	5	0	801
12	Eddie Nolan	1	0	948
13	Godwin Antwi	2	0	1169
	Other	9	0	
	TOTAL	48	4	

KEY GOALKEEPER

Jan Budtz

Goals Conceded in the League	38	**Counting Games** League games when player was on pitch for at least 70 minutes	28
Defensive Rating Ave number of mins between League goals conceded while on the pitch	66	**Clean Sheets** In League games when player was on pitch for at least 70 minutes	5

KEY PLAYERS - DEFENDERS

Jamie McCunnie

Goals Conceded Number of League goals conceded while the player was on the pitch	29	**Clean Sheets** In League games when player was on pitch for at least 70 minutes	5
Defensive Rating Ave number of mins between League goals conceded while on the pitch	73	**Club Defensive Rating** Average number of mins between League goals conceded by the club this season	64

	PLAYER	CON LGE	CLEAN SHEETS	DEF RATE
1	Jamie McCunnie	29	5	73 mins
2	Ben Clark	20	4	65 mins
3	Richie Humphreys	59	9	64 mins
4	Michael Nelson	65	9	61 mins

KEY PLAYERS - MIDFIELDERS

Willie Boland

Goals in the League	0	**Contribution to Attacking Power** Average number of minutes between League team goals while on pitch	76
Defensive Rating Average number of mins between League goals conceded while on the pitch	81	**Scoring Difference** Defensive Rating minus Contribution to Attacking Power	5

	PLAYER	LGE GOALS	DEF RATE	POWER	SCORE DIFF
1	Willie Boland	0	81	76	5 mins
2	Andy Monkhouse	2	70	68	2 mins
3	Gary Liddle	2	59	60	-1 mins
4	Antony Sweeney	4	54	66	-12 mins

KEY PLAYERS - GOALSCORERS

Richard Barker

Goals in the League	13	**Player Strike Rate** Average number of minutes between League goals scored by player	211
Contribution to Attacking Power Average number of minutes between League team goals while on pitch	67	**Club Strike Rate** Average number of minutes between League goals scored by club	67

	PLAYER	LGE GOALS	POWER	STRIKE RATE
1	Richard Barker	13	67	211 mins
2	Joel Porter	9	57	248 mins
3	James Brown	9	70	303 mins
4	Ian Moore	6	65	314 mins

Richard Barker

SQUAD APPEARANCES

Match	1	2	3	4	5	6	7	8	9	10	11	12	13	14	15	16	17	18	19	20	21	22	23	24	25
Venue	A	A	H	A	A	H	A	H	A	H	H	A	H	H	A	A	A	H	A	A	A	H	A	H	A
Competition	L	W	L	L	W	L	L	L	L	L	L	L	L	L	L	L	F	L	L	L	F	L	L	L	L
Result	L	W	W	W	L	W	L	D	W	L	D	L	W	L	W	L	W	D	L	L	L	W	L	W	L

Match	26	27	28	29	30	31	32	33	34	35	36	37	38	39	40	41	42	43	44	45	46	47	48	49	50
Venue	H	H	A	A	H	H	A	H	A	H	A	H	A	A	H	H	A	A	H	H	A	H	A	H	A
Competition	L	L	L	L	L	L	L	L	L	L	L	L	L	L	L	L	L	L	L	L	L	L	L	L	L
Result	D	D	L	D	L	W	L	W	L	W	D	L	L	W	W	W	L	L	W	L	D	L	L	L	D

Goalkeepers
Jan Budtz
Arran Lee-Barrett

Defenders
Godwin Antwi
Ben Clark
Danny Coles
Sam Collins
Robbie Elliott
Richie Humphreys
Graeme Lee
Jamie McCunnie
Michael Nelson
Eddie Nolan
Matty Robson

Midfielders
Willie Boland
Lee Bullock
Alistair Gibb
Gary Liddle
Andy Monkhouse
Antony Sweeney
Alan Thompson
Steve Turnbull

Forwards
Richard Barker
James Brown
Tom Craddock
David Foley
Michael Mackay
Ian Moore
Joel Porter

KEY: On all match · On bench · Subbed or sent off (Counting game) · Subbed or sent off (playing less than 70 minutes) · Subbed on from bench (Counting Game) · Subbed on (playing less than 70 minutes) · Subbed on and then subbed or sent off (Counting Game) · Subbed on and then subbed or sent off (playing less than 70 minutes) · Not in 16

BRISTOL ROVERS

Final Position: **16th**

NICKNAME: THE PIRATES

KEY: ☐Won ☐Drawn ☐Lost

							Attendance
1	div2	**Port Vale**	A	D	1-1	Williams 77	6,808
2	ccr1	**Crystal Palace**	H	W	4-1*	Disley 64 (*on penalties)	5,566
3	div2	**Crewe**	H	D	1-1	Disley 32	7,750
4	div2	**Oldham**	A	W	1-0	Jacobson 38	5,348
5	ccr2	**West Ham**	H	L	1-2	A.Williams 72	10,831
6	div2	**Nottm Forest**	H	D	2-2	Anthony 25, R.Walker 28 pen	9,080
7	div2	**Luton**	A	W	2-1	Lambert 2, 82	6,131
8	div2	**Leeds**	H	L	0-3		11,883
9	div2	**Carlisle**	A	D	1-1	Elliott 14	6,106
10	div2	**Leyton Orient**	H	L	2-3	R.Walker 41 pen, 54 pen	7,181
11	div2	**Southend**	H	D	1-1	R.Walker 11 pen	5,762
12	div2	**Brighton**	A	D	0-0		5,820
13	div2	**Hartlepool**	A	L	0-1		4,963
14	div2	**Yeovil**	H	D	1-1	Elliott 90	7,726
15	div2	**Gillingham**	A	L	2-3	Lambert 27, Pipe 46	5,333
16	div2	**Bournemouth**	H	L	0-2		6,405
17	div2	**Northampton**	A	W	1-0	Lambert 70	5,126
18	facr1	**Leyton Orient**	A	D	1-1	Lambert 81	3,157
19	div2	**Millwall**	H	W	2-1	Lambert 78 pen, Haldane 90	6,991
20	div2	**Swindon**	A	L	0-1		9,342
21	facr1r	**Leyton Orient**	H	W	6-5*	Hinton 2, Lambert 90 pen, Disley 111 (*on penalties)	3,742
22	facr2	**Rushden & D**	H	W	5-1	Williams 33, Disley 35, Hinton 51, Lambert 54, 87	4,816
23	div2	**Huddersfield**	A	L	1-2	Pipe 51	8,118
24	div2	**Leeds**	A	L	0-1		27,863
25	div2	**Luton**	H	D	1-1	Lambert 17 pen	7,556
26	div2	**Carlisle**	H	W	3-0	Lines 8, Hinton 15, A.Williams 59	6,254
27	div2	**Southend**	A	W	1-0	A.Williams 57	7,664
28	facr3	**Fulham**	A	D	2-2	Coles 3, Hinton 65	13,634
29	div2	**Tranmere**	A	W	2-0	A.Williams 12, Lambert 58	5,887
30	div2	**Walsall**	H	D	1-1	Disley 87	6,276
31	facr3	**Fulham**	H	W	5-3*	(*on penalties)	11,882
32	facr4	**Barnet**	A	W	1-0	Lambert 49	5,190
33	div2	**Crewe**	A	D	1-1	B.Williams 45 og	3,942
34	div2	**Port Vale**	H	W	3-2	Coles 13, Lines 81, Lambert 87 pen	6,927
35	div2	**Cheltenham**	H	W	2-0	Hinton 40, Lambert 81	6,780
36	div2	**Doncaster**	A	L	0-2		8,168
37	div2	**Oldham**	H	W	1-0	Disley 90	5,778
38	facr5	**Southampton**	H	W	1-0	Lambert 84	11,920
39	div2	**Tranmere**	H	D	1-1	Disley 81	7,777
40	div2	**Millwall**	A	W	1-0	Disley 90	9,202
41	div2	**Doncaster**	H	L	0-1		3,933
42	facqf	**West Brom**	H	L	1-5	Coles 32	12,011
43	div2	**Northampton**	H	D	1-1	Rigg 45	4,657
44	div2	**Cheltenham**	A	L	0-1		5,187
45	div2	**Swansea**	H	L	0-2		6,410
46	div2	**Huddersfield**	H	L	2-3	Klein-Davies 20, Lines 49	6,585
47	div2	**Swansea**	A	D	2-2	Lambert 14, Disley 36	15,048
48	div2	**Yeovil**	A	D	0-0		6,654
49	div2	**Hartlepool**	H	D	0-0		5,526
50	div2	**Nottm Forest**	A	D	1-1	Lambert 64	15,860
51	div2	**Bournemouth**	A	L	1-2	Lambert 56	6,867
52	div2	**Walsall**	A	W	1-0	Lambert 34	4,500
53	div2	**Gillingham**	H	D	1-1	Elliott 84	6,614
54	div2	**Swindon**	H	L	0-1		6,102
55	div2	**Brighton**	H	L	0-2		7,590
56	div2	**Leyton Orient**	A	L	1-3	Lambert 30	5,132

LEAGUE APPEARANCES, BOOKINGS AND GOALS

	AGE (on 01/07/08)	IN NAMED 16	APPEARANCES	COUNTING GAMES	MINUTES ON PITCH	LEAGUE GOALS	Yellow	Red
Goalkeepers								
Steve Book	38	2	0	0	0	0	0	0
Mike Green	18	7	0	0	0	0	0	0
Steve Phillips	30	46	46	46	4140	0	3	0
Defenders								
Byron Anthony	23	30	20	19	1723	1	2	0
Chris Carruthers	24	33	17	14	1289	0	5	0
Danny Coles	26	25	24	22	2055	1	3	0
Steve Elliott	29	33	33	33	2963	3	0	1
Ryan Green	27	12	12	12	1054	0	3	0
Matt Groves	28	1	1	0	15	0	0	0
Craig Hinton	30	46	24	21	1922	2	3	0
Joe Jacobson	21	41	40	32	3085	1	6	0
Tom Parrinello	18	1	0	0	0	0	0	0
Midfielders								
Stuart Campbell	30	46	46	46	4140	0	7	0
Charlie Clough	17	4	1	0	23	0	0	0
Craig Disley	26	44	44	37	3575	6	6	0
Sam Igoe	32	27	21	8	1002	0	0	0
Aaron Lescott	29	36	34	34	3043	0	3	0
Chris Lines	22	33	27	24	2243	3	1	0
David Pipe	24	41	40	27	2939	2	1	0
Anthony Pulis	23	5	1	0	15	0	1	0
Charles Reece	18	4	1	0	2	0	0	0
Sean Rigg	19	41	31	8	1161	1	0	0
Forwards								
Wayne Andrews	30	1	1	0	20	0	0	0
Lewis Haldane	23	38	32	18	1826	1	5	0
Josh Klein-Davies	18	14	10	2	338	1	0	0
Rickie Lambert	26	46	46	42	3736	14	1	0
Richard Walker	30	33	24	10	1187	4	2	1
Andrew Williams	21	46	41	16	2029	4	1	0

TEAM OF THE SEASON

D
Craig Hinton
CG: 21 DR: 96
M
Chris Lines
CG: 24 SD: 0
D
Danny Coles
CG: 22 DR: 82
M
Aaron Lescott
CG: 34 SD: -6
F
Rickie Lambert
CG: 42 SR: 266
G
Steve Phillips
CG: 46 DR: 78
D
Steve Elliott
CG: 33 DR: 80
M
David Pipe
CG: 27 SD: -11
F
Andrew Williams
CG: 16 SR: 507
D
Joe Jacobson
CG: 32 DR: 79
M
Stuart Campbell
CG: 46 SD: -14

MONTHLY POINTS TALLY

AUGUST	5	56%
SEPTEMBER	5	33%
OCTOBER	3	20%
NOVEMBER	6	50%
DECEMBER	4	33%
JANUARY	8	67%
FEBRUARY	10	67%
MARCH	6	25%
APRIL	6	29%
MAY	0	0%

LEAGUE GOALS

	PLAYER	MINS	GOALS	S RATE
1	Lambert	3736	14	266
2	Disley	3575	6	595
3	Walker, R	1187	4	296
4	Williams, A	2029	4	507
5	Lines	2243	3	747
6	Elliott	2963	3	987
7	Hinton	1922	2	961
8	Pipe	2939	2	1469
9	Klein-Davies	338	1	338
10	Rigg	1161	1	1161
11	Anthony	1723	1	1723
12	Haldane	1826	1	1826
13	Coles	2055	1	2055
	Other		1	
	TOTAL		44	

TOP POINT EARNERS

	PLAYER	GAMES	AV PTS
1	Andrew Williams	16	1.69
2	Chris Lines	24	1.42
3	Craig Hinton	21	1.38
4	Chris Carruthers	14	1.29
5	Danny Coles	22	1.23
6	David Pipe	27	1.22
7	Aaron Lescott	34	1.18
8	Rickie Lambert	42	1.17
9	Joe Jacobson	32	1.16
10	Steve Elliott	33	1.15
	CLUB AVERAGE:		1.15

DISCIPLINARY RECORDS

	PLAYER	YELLOW	RED	AVE
1	Chris Carruthers	5	0	257
2	Ryan Green	3	0	351
3	Lewis Haldane	5	0	365
4	Richard Walker	2	1	395
5	Joe Jacobson	6	0	514
6	Stuart Campbell	7	0	591
7	Craig Disley	6	0	595
8	Craig Hinton	3	0	640
9	Danny Coles	3	0	685
10	Byron Anthony	2	0	861
11	Aaron Lescott	3	0	1014
12	Steve Phillips	3	0	1380
13	Andrew Williams	1	0	2029
	Other	3	1	
	TOTAL	52	2	

KEY GOALKEEPER

Steve Phillips

Goals Conceded in the League	53	Counting Games League games when player was on pitch for at least 70 minutes	46
Defensive Rating Ave number of mins between League goals conceded while on the pitch	78	Clean Sheets In League games when player was on pitch for at least 70 minutes	12

KEY PLAYERS - DEFENDERS

Craig Hinton

Goals Conceded Number of League goals conceded while the player was on the pitch	20	Clean Sheets In League games when player was on pitch for at least 70 minutes	8
Defensive Rating Ave number of mins between League goals conceded while on the pitch	96	Club Defensive Rating Average number of mins between League goals conceded by the club this season	81

	PLAYER	CON LGE	CLEAN SHEETS	DEF RATE
1	Craig Hinton	20	8	96 mins
2	Danny Coles	25	6	82 mins
3	Steve Elliott	37	9	80 mins
4	Joe Jacobson	39	10	79 mins

KEY PLAYERS - MIDFIELDERS

Chris Lines

Goals in the League	3	Contribution to Attacking Power Average number of minutes between League team goals while on pitch	86
Defensive Rating Average number of mins between League goals conceded while on the pitch	86	Scoring Difference Defensive Rating minus Contribution to Attacking Power	0

	PLAYER	LGE GOALS	DEF RATE	POWER	SCORE DIFF
1	Chris Lines	3	86	86	0 mins
2	Aaron Lescott	0	80	86	-6 mins
3	David Pipe	2	83	94	-11 mins
4	Stuart Campbell	0	78	92	-14 mins

KEY PLAYERS - GOALSCORERS

Rickie Lambert

Goals in the League	14	Player Strike Rate Average number of minutes between League goals scored by player	266
Contribution to Attacking Power Average number of minutes between League team goals while on pitch	98	Club Strike Rate Average number of minutes between League goals scored by club	96

	PLAYER	LGE GOALS	POWER	STRIKE RATE
1	Rickie Lambert	14	98	266 mins
2	Andrew Williams	4	88	507 mins
3	Craig Disley	6	105	595 mins
4	Chris Lines	3	86	747 mins

errea
COWLIN
CONSTRUCTION
Rickie Lambert

SQUAD APPEARANCES

Match	1	2	3	4	5	6	7	8	9	10	11	12	13	14	15	16	17	18	19	20	21	22	23	24	25	26	27	28	29	30	31	32	33	34	35	36	37	38	39	40	41	42	43	44	45	46	47	48	49	50	51	52	53	54	55	56
Venue	A	H	H	A	H	H	A	H	A	H	H	A	A	H	A	H	A	A	H	A	H	H	A	A	H	H	A	A	A	H	H	A	A	H	H	A	H	H	H	A	H	H	H	A	H	H	A	A	H	A	A	A	H	H	H	A
Competition	L	W	L	L	W	L	L	L	L	L	L	L	L	L	L	L	L	F	L	L	F	F	L	L	L	L	L	F	L	L	F	F	L	L	L	L	L	F	L	L	L	F	L	L	L	L	L	L	L	L	L	L	L	L	L	L
Result	D	W	D	W	L	D	W	L	D	L	D	D	L	D	L	L	W	D	W	L	W	W	L	L	D	W	W	D	W	D	W	W	D	W	W	L	W	W	D	W	L	L	D	L	L	L	D	D	D	D	L	W	D	L	L	L

Goalkeepers
Steve Book
Mike Green
Steve Phillips

Defenders
Byron Anthony
Chris Carruthers
Danny Coles
Steve Elliott
Ryan Green
Matt Groves
Craig Hinton
Joe Jacobson
Tom Parrinello

Midfielders
Stuart Campbell
Charlie Clough
Craig Disley
Sam Igoe
Aaron Lescott
Chris Lines
David Pipe
Anthony Pulis
Charles Reece
Sean Rigg

Forwards
Wayne Andrews
Lewis Haldane
Josh Klein-Davies
Rickie Lambert
Richard Walker
Andrew Williams

KEY: On all match | On bench | Subbed or sent off (Counting game) | Subbed or sent off (playing less than 70 minutes) | Subbed on from bench (Counting Game) | Subbed on (playing less than 70 minutes) | Subbed on and then subbed or sent off (Counting Game) | Subbed on and then subbed or sent off (playing less than 70 minutes) | Not in 16

MILLWALL

Final Position: **17th**

NICKNAME: THE LIONS

KEY: ☐Won ☐Drawn ☐Lost

							Attendance
1	div2	**Doncaster**	A	D	0-0		7,542
2	ccr1	**Northampton**	A	L	0-2		3,735
3	div2	**Cheltenham**	H	W	1-0	Spiller 45	8,671
4	div2	**Southend**	A	L	0-1		8,758
5	div2	**Huddersfield**	H	L	1-2	P.Robinson 41	9,004
6	div2	**Brighton**	A	L	0-3		6,563
7	div2	**Walsall**	H	L	1-2	Frampton 83	7,720
8	div2	**Crewe**	A	D	0-0		4,478
9	div2	**Swindon**	H	L	1-2	Simpson 56	8,744
10	div2	**Northampton**	H	W	2-0	Dunne 12, P.Robinson 31	6,520
11	div2	**Carlisle**	A	L	0-4		7,022
12	div2	**Gillingham**	A	D	1-1	Dunne 61	6,120
13	div2	**Bournemouth**	H	W	2-1	O'Hara 33, Hoskins 55	7,805
14	div2	**Leeds**	A	L	2-4	Hoskins 65, Brkovic 76	30,319
15	div2	**Hartlepool**	H	L	0-1		7,731
16	div2	**Swansea**	H	D	2-2	Whitbread 58, Dunne 70 pen	6,750
17	facr1	**Altrincham**	A	W	2-1	Dunne 53 pen, Hoskins 62	2,457
18	div2	**Bristol Rovers**	A	L	1-2	Fuseini 8	6,991
19	div2	**Yeovil**	H	W	2-1	O'Hara 71, Fuseini 82	8,105
20	facr2	**Bournemouth**	H	W	2-1	Brkovic 50, Hoskins 55	4,495
21	div2	**Leyton Orient**	A	W	1-0	Whitbread 9	6,220
22	div2	**Oldham**	H	L	2-3	Simpson 38, Whitbread 45	8,033
23	div2	**Walsall**	A	L	0-3		5,433
24	div2	**Brighton**	H	W	3-0	Alexander 7, 54, 71 pen	9,401
25	div2	**Crewe**	H	W	2-0	Harris 45 pen, Brkovic 53	8,068
26	div2	**Northampton**	A	D	1-1	Alexander 90	5,329
27	facr3	**Walsall**	A	D	0-0		4,358
28	div2	**Port Vale**	A	L	1-3	Alexander 14	3,724
29	facr3r	**Walsall**	H	W	2-1	May 15, Alexander 49	4,645
30	div2	**Tranmere**	H	L	0-1		8,925
31	div2	**Nottm Forest**	H	D	2-2	Harris 27, Simpson 53	8,436
32	facr4	**Coventry**	A	L	1-2	Simpson 42	17,268
33	div2	**Cheltenham**	A	W	1-0	Alexander 55	3,812
34	div2	**Doncaster**	H	L	0-3		8,230
35	div2	**Nottm Forest**	A	L	0-2		17,046
36	div2	**Southend**	H	W	2-1	Alexander 41, Martin 54	7,425
37	div2	**Tranmere**	A	L	0-2		6,108
38	div2	**Huddersfield**	A	L	0-1		6,326
39	div2	**Port Vale**	H	W	3-0	Grabban 18, Laird 44, Martin 68	7,775
40	div2	**Luton**	A	D	1-1	Grabban 39	6,417
41	div2	**Bristol Rovers**	H	L	0-1		9,202
42	div2	**Swansea**	A	W	2-1	Grabban 1, Simpson 70	15,561
43	div2	**Yeovil**	A	W	1-0	Savage 70	4,439
44	div2	**Leyton Orient**	H	L	0-1		10,986
45	div2	**Oldham**	A	D	1-1	Savage 76	4,391
46	div2	**Luton**	H	D	0-0		8,375
47	div2	**Bournemouth**	A	L	0-2		4,962
48	div2	**Gillingham**	H	D	1-1	P.Robinson 75	10,006
49	div2	**Hartlepool**	A	W	1-0	Simpson 11	4,077
50	div2	**Leeds**	H	L	0-2		13,395
51	div2	**Carlisle**	H	W	3-0	Simpson 43, Harris 56 pen, Craig 64	10,075
52	div2	**Swindon**	A	L	1-2	Senda 6	7,781

LEAGUE APPEARANCES, BOOKINGS AND GOALS

	AGE (on 01/07/08)	IN NAMED 16	APPEARANCES	COUNTING GAMES	MINUTES ON PITCH	LEAGUE GOALS	Yellow	Red
Goalkeepers								
Chris Day	32	19	5	5	450	0	0	0
Robert Douglas	36	7	7	7	630	0	0	0
Rhys Evans	26	21	21	20	1833	0	2	0
Lenny Pidgeley	24	18	13	13	1170	0	2	0
Defenders								
Zoumana Bakayogo	21	15	10	5	541	0	2	0
Scott Barron	22	26	12	6	659	0	0	0
Marcus Bignot	33	26	21	16	1493	0	4	0
Tony Craig	23	5	5	5	450	1	0	0
Alan Dunne	25	21	19	13	1349	3	3	0
Paul Robinson	26	45	45	45	4050	3	6	0
Danny Senda	27	42	40	37	3431	1	1	0
Richard Shaw	39	26	18	13	1358	0	1	1
Zak Whitbread	24	28	23	21	1955	3	6	1
Midfielders								
David Brammer	33	24	23	20	1931	0	7	0
Ahmet Brkovic	33	25	25	10	1491	2	2	0
Andrew Frampton	28	33	30	26	2510	1	6	0
Ali Fuseini	19	39	37	30	2963	2	3	0
Chris Hackett	25	6	6	1	222	0	1	0
Bryan Hodge	20	10	10	9	853	0	0	0
Jem Karacan	19	8	7	6	606	0	0	0
Marc Laird	22	19	17	15	1434	1	2	1
David Martin	23	16	11	4	618	2	1	0
Jamie O'Hara	21	14	14	8	869	2	2	0
Jay Simpson	19	41	41	30	2997	6	2	1
Ryan Smith	21	18	16	4	852	0	0	0
Daniel Spiller	26	8	6	5	485	1	0	0
Forwards								
Adebayo Akinfenwa	26	7	7	1	153	0	2	0
Gary Alexander	28	36	36	26	2793	7	8	0
Adrian Forbes	29	12	11	5	594	0	1	0
Lewis Grabban	20	14	14	6	819	3	2	0
Neil Harris	30	33	27	14	1667	3	2	1
William Hoskins	22	10	10	7	777	2	1	0
Ben May	24	9	8	4	447	0	1	0
Basir Savage	26	12	10	6	735	2	1	0

TEAM OF THE SEASON

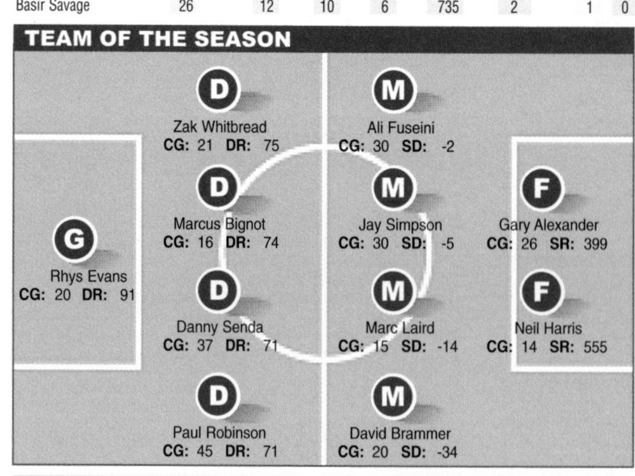

G
Rhys Evans
CG: 20 DR: 91
D
Zak Whitbread
CG: 21 DR: 75
D
Marcus Bignot
CG: 16 DR: 74
D
Danny Senda
CG: 37 DR: 71
D
Paul Robinson
CG: 45 DR: 71
M
Ali Fuseini
CG: 30 SD: -2
M
Jay Simpson
CG: 30 SD: -5
M
Marc Laird
CG: 15 SD: -14
M
David Brammer
CG: 20 SD: -34
F
Gary Alexander
CG: 26 SR: 399
F
Neil Harris
CG: 14 SR: 555

MONTHLY POINTS TALLY

AUGUST	4	44%
SEPTEMBER	1	7%
OCTOBER	7	47%
NOVEMBER	4	33%
DECEMBER	9	60%
JANUARY	5	33%
FEBRUARY	7	33%
MARCH	8	38%
APRIL	7	58%
MAY	0	0%

LEAGUE GOALS

	PLAYER	MINS	GOALS	S RATE
1	Alexander	2793	7	399
2	Simpson	2997	6	499
3	Grabban	819	3	273
4	Dunne	1349	3	449
5	Harris	1667	3	555
6	Whitbread	1955	3	651
7	Robinson, P	4050	3	1350
8	Martin	618	2	309
9	Savage	735	2	367
10	Hoskins	777	2	388
11	O'Hara	869	2	434
12	Brkovic	1491	2	745
13	Fuseini	2963	2	1481
	Other		5	
	TOTAL		**45**	

TOP POINT EARNERS

	PLAYER	GAMES	AV PTS
1	Marcus Bignot	16	**1.38**
2	Ali Fuseini	30	**1.37**
3	Neil Harris	14	**1.36**
4	Marc Laird	15	**1.33**
5	Zak Whitbread	21	**1.33**
6	Jay Simpson	30	**1.30**
7	Rhys Evans	20	**1.30**
8	Alan Dunne	13	**1.23**
9	Danny Senda	37	**1.19**
10	Paul Robinson	45	**1.16**
	CLUB AVERAGE:		**1.13**

DISCIPLINARY RECORDS

	PLAYER	YELLOW	RED	AVE
1	Zoumana Bakayogo	2	0	**270**
2	David Brammer	7	0	**275**
3	Zak Whitbread	6	1	**279**
4	Gary Alexander	8	0	**349**
5	Marcus Bignot	4	0	**373**
6	Lewis Grabban	2	0	**409**
7	Andrew Frampton	6	0	**418**
8	Jamie O'Hara	2	0	**434**
9	Alan Dunne	3	0	**449**
10	Marc Laird	2	1	**478**
11	Neil Harris	2	1	**555**
12	Lenny Pidgeley	2	0	**585**
13	Adrian Forbes	1	0	**594**
	Other	20	2	
	TOTAL	**67**	**5**	

KEY GOALKEEPER

Rhys Evans

Goals Conceded in the League	20	**Counting Games** League games when player was on pitch for at least 70 minutes	20
Defensive Rating Ave number of mins between League goals conceded while on the pitch	91	**Clean Sheets** In League games when player was on pitch for at least 70 minutes	6

KEY PLAYERS - DEFENDERS

Zak Whitbread

Goals Conceded Number of League goals conceded while the player was on the pitch	26	**Clean Sheets** In League games when player was on pitch for at least 70 minutes	6
Defensive Rating Ave number of mins between League goals conceded while on the pitch	75	**Club Defensive Rating** Average number of mins between League goals conceded by the club this season	70

	PLAYER	CON LGE	CLEAN SHEETS	DEF RATE
1	Zak Whitbread	26	6	75 mins
2	Marcus Bignot	20	5	74 mins
3	Danny Senda	48	13	71 mins
4	Paul Robinson	57	13	71 mins

KEY PLAYERS - MIDFIELDERS

Ali Fuseini

Goals in the League	2	**Contribution to Attacking Power** Average number of minutes between League team goals while on pitch	84
Defensive Rating Average number of mins between League goals conceded while on the pitch	82	**Scoring Difference** Defensive Rating minus Contribution to Attacking Power	-2

	PLAYER	LGE GOALS	DEF RATE	POWER	SCORE DIFF
1	Ali Fuseini	2	82	84	-2 mins
2	Jay Simpson	6	76	81	-5 mins
3	Marc Laird	1	75	89	-14 mins
4	David Brammer	0	62	96	-34 mins

KEY PLAYERS - GOALSCORERS

Gary Alexander

Goals in the League	7	**Player Strike Rate** Average number of minutes between League goals scored by player	399
Contribution to Attacking Power Average number of minutes between League team goals while on pitch	90	**Club Strike Rate** Average number of minutes between League goals scored by club	94

	PLAYER	LGE GOALS	POWER	STRIKE RATE
1	Gary Alexander	7	90	399 mins
2	Jay Simpson	6	81	499 mins
3	Neil Harris	3	87	555 mins
4	Marc Laird	1	89	1434 mins

CAPTAIN
Coca-Cola FOOTBALL LEAGUE
Paul Robinson

SQUAD APPEARANCES

Match: 1 2 3 4 5 | 6 7 8 9 10 | 11 12 13 14 15 | 16 17 18 19 20 | 21 22 23 24 25 | 26 27 28 29 30 | 31 32 33 34 35 | 36 37 38 39 40 | 41 42 43 44 45 | 46 47 48 49 50 | 51 52

Venue: A A H A H | A H A H H | A A H A H | H A A H H | A H A H H | A A A H H | H A A H A | H A A H A | H A A H A | H A H A H | H A

Competition: L W L L L | L L L L L | L L L L L | L F L L F | L L L L L | L F L F L | L F L L L | L L L L L | L L L L L | L L L L L | L L

Result: D L W L L | L L D L W | L D W L L | D W L W W | W L L W W | D D L W L | D L W L L | W L L W D | L W W L D | D L D W L | W L

Goalkeepers
Chris Day
Robert Douglas
Rhys Evans
Lenny Pidgeley

Defenders
Zoumana Bakayogo
Scott Barron
Marcus Bignot
Tony Craig
Alan Dunne
Paul Robinson
Danny Senda
Richard Shaw
Zak Whitbread

Midfielders
David Brammer
Ahmet Brkovic
Andrew Frampton
Ali Fuseini
Chris Hackett
Bryan Hodge
Jem Karacan
Marc Laird
David Martin
Jamie O'Hara
Jay Simpson
Ryan Smith
Daniel Spiller

Forwards
Adebayo Akinfenwa
Gary Alexander
Adrian Forbes
Lewis Grabban
Neil Harris
William Hoskins
Ben May
Basir Savage

KEY: On all match | On bench | Subbed or sent off (Counting game) | Subbed or sent off (playing less than 70 minutes) | Subbed on from bench (Counting Game) | Subbed on (playing less than 70 minutes) | Subbed on and then subbed or sent off (Counting Game) | Subbed on and then subbed or sent off (playing less than 70 minutes) | Not in 16

YEOVIL

Final Position: **18th**

NICKNAME: THE GLOVERS

KEY: ☐Won ☐Drawn ☐Lost

	Comp	Opponent	Venue	Result	Score	Scorers	Attendance
1	div2	Huddersfield	A	L	0-1		9,876
2	ccr1	Hereford	A	L	1-4	Owusu 50	2,085
3	div2	Port Vale	H	W	1-0	Cochrane 17	5,071
4	div2	Northampton	A	W	2-1	Cochrane 26, Owusu 90	4,555
5	div2	Tranmere	H	D	1-1	Stewart 57	4,985
6	div2	Swindon	A	W	1-0	Owusu 77	6,944
7	div2	Leyton Orient	H	L	0-1		5,217
8	div2	Brighton	A	W	2-1	Owusu 15, Warne 43	5,231
9	div2	Nottm Forest	H	L	0-3		6,818
10	div2	Luton	H	D	0-0		4,848
11	div2	Leeds	A	L	0-1		27,808
12	div2	Carlisle	H	W	2-1	Owusu 54, N.Jones 65	4,757
13	div2	Bristol Rovers	A	D	1-1	Rose 62	7,726
14	div2	Swansea	H	L	1-2	Betsy 48	6,207
15	div2	Crewe	A	L	0-2		4,363
16	div2	Cheltenham	A	D	1-1	Owusu 31	3,169
17	facr1	Torquay	A	L	1-4	Stewart 20	3,718
18	div2	Gillingham	H	W	2-1	Owusu 66, Walker 88	4,408
19	div2	Millwall	A	L	1-2	Walker 49	8,105
20	div2	Bournemouth	H	W	2-1	Skiverton 3, Walker 38	5,321
21	div2	Hartlepool	H	W	3-1	Skiverton 27, Stewart 31, Owusu 77	4,694
22	div2	Doncaster	A	W	2-1	Way 37, Stewart 78	5,967
23	div2	Leyton Orient	A	D	0-0		4,687
24	div2	Swindon	H	L	0-1		6,539
25	div2	Brighton	H	W	2-1	Dempsey 42, Stieber 50	6,881
26	div2	Luton	A	L	0-1		6,811
27	div2	Walsall	H	L	0-2		4,319
28	div2	Southend	A	D	1-1	Owusu 71	7,352
29	div2	Oldham	H	D	0-0		4,905
30	div2	Tranmere	A	L	1-2	Kirk 51	5,386
31	div2	Port Vale	A	D	2-2	Dempsey 6, Kirk 52	2,869
32	div2	Huddersfield	H	L	0-2		4,823
33	div2	Walsall	A	L	0-2		5,034
34	div2	Northampton	H	W	1-0	Skiverton 90	5,001
35	div2	Oldham	A	L	0-3		4,781
36	div2	Southend	H	L	0-3		4,820
37	div2	Gillingham	A	D	0-0		5,083
38	div2	Cheltenham	H	W	2-1	Wright 9 og, Kirk 73	4,588
39	div2	Millwall	H	L	0-1		4,439
40	div2	Bournemouth	A	L	0-2		4,145
41	div2	Doncaster	H	W	2-1	Skiverton 22, Owusu 31	6,146
42	div2	Hartlepool	A	L	0-2		3,808
43	div2	Bristol Rovers	H	D	0-0		6,654
44	div2	Carlisle	A	L	1-2	Stewart 38	6,843
45	div2	Crewe	H	L	0-3		4,785
46	div2	Swansea	A	W	2-1	Skiverton 23, Downes 60	18,321
47	div2	Leeds	H	L	0-1		9,527
48	div2	Nottm Forest	A	L	2-3	Peters 20, Kirk 75	28,520

LEAGUE APPEARANCES, BOOKINGS AND GOALS

	AGE (on 01/07/08)	IN NAMED 16	APPEARANCES	COUNTING GAMES	MINUTES ON PITCH	LEAGUE GOALS	Yellow	Red
Goalkeepers								
Asmir Begovic	21	2	2	2	180	0	0	0
Scott Flinders	22	9	9	9	810	0	0	0
Romain Larrieu	31	6	6	6	540	0	0	0
Steve Mildenhall	30	29	29	27	2537	0	2	0
Defenders								
Craig Alcock	20	33	8	5	540	0	0	0
Terrell Forbes	26	41	41	41	3690	0	3	0
Scott Guyett	32	44	34	34	3049	0	2	0
Nathan Jones	35	33	31	28	2562	1	5	1
Mark Lynch	26	27	14	11	1071	0	3	0
Matthew Rose	32	34	30	22	2222	1	7	0
Terry Skiverton	33	31	31	26	2430	5	4	1
Midfielders								
Anthony Barry	22	43	35	24	2397	0	4	0
Kevin Betsy	30	5	5	5	450	1	0	0
Marc Bircham	30	18	14	8	807	0	6	1
Liam Bridcutt	19	10	8	3	454	0	0	0
Jean Christophe	26	5	5	3	369	0	2	0
Justin Cochrane	26	17	12	4	560	2	2	0
Gary Dempsey	27	18	16	9	882	2	0	0
Simon Gillett	22	6	4	2	254	0	0	0
Ritchie Jones	21	15	9	6	601	0	1	0
Stephen Maher	20	7	6	2	283	0	0	1
Lee Peltier	21	34	34	31	2956	0	8	0
Jamie Peters	21	14	13	9	906	1	0	0
Nathan Smith	21	6	6	5	480	0	1	0
Zoltan Stieber	19	17	15	10	1080	1	0	0
Paul Warne	35	36	33	24	2410	1	9	1
Darren Way	28	7	7	6	588	1	0	0
Marvin Williams	20	26	22	6	961	0	7	0
Martin Woods	22	3	3	1	198	0	0	0
Forwards								
Simon Church	19	9	6	1	265	0	1	0
Aidan Downes	19	5	5	3	300	1	1	0
Andy Kirk	29	20	19	13	1365	4	0	0
Darryl Knights	20	7	3	0	93	0	0	0
Lloyd Owusu	31	46	43	27	2871	9	1	0
Marcus Stewart	35	36	36	34	3035	4	7	1
James Walker	20	14	13	11	1016	3	0	0

TEAM OF THE SEASON

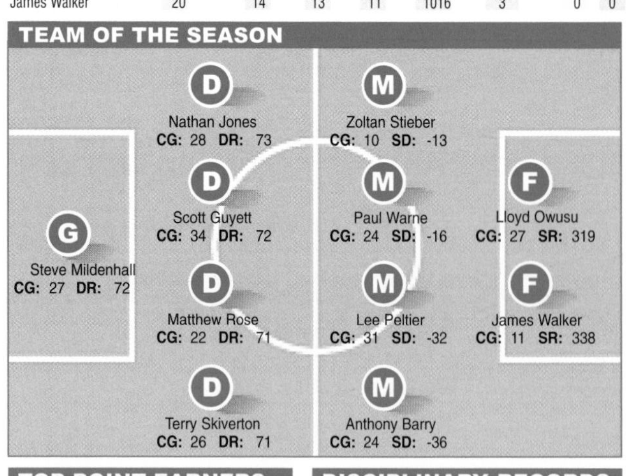

G
Steve Mildenhall
CG: 27 DR: 72
D
Nathan Jones
CG: 28 DR: 73
D
Scott Guyett
CG: 34 DR: 72
D
Matthew Rose
CG: 22 DR: 71
D
Terry Skiverton
CG: 26 DR: 71
M
Zoltan Stieber
CG: 10 SD: -13
M
Paul Warne
CG: 24 SD: -16
M
Lee Peltier
CG: 31 SD: -32
M
Anthony Barry
CG: 24 SD: -36
F
Lloyd Owusu
CG: 27 SR: 319
F
James Walker
CG: 11 SR: 338

MONTHLY POINTS TALLY

Month	Points	%
AUGUST	6	67%
SEPTEMBER	7	47%
OCTOBER	5	33%
NOVEMBER	4	33%
DECEMBER	13	72%
JANUARY	3	17%
FEBRUARY	3	20%
MARCH	8	38%
APRIL	3	25%
MAY	0	0%

LEAGUE GOALS

	PLAYER	MINS	GOALS	S RATE
1	Owusu	2871	9	319
2	Skiverton	2430	5	486
3	Kirk	1365	4	341
4	Stewart	3035	4	758
5	Walker, J	1016	3	338
6	Cochrane	560	2	280
7	Dempsey	882	2	441
8	Downes	300	1	300
9	Betsy	450	1	450
10	Way	588	1	588
11	Peters	906	1	906
12	Stieber	1080	1	1080
13	Rose	2222	1	2222
	Other		2	
	TOTAL		37	

TOP POINT EARNERS

	PLAYER	GAMES	AV PTS
1	Paul Warne	24	1.38
2	Lee Peltier	31	1.23
3	Steve Mildenhall	27	1.22
4	Terry Skiverton	26	1.19
5	Matthew Rose	22	1.18
6	Scott Guyett	34	1.18
7	Anthony Barry	24	1.17
8	Terrell Forbes	41	1.17
9	Marcus Stewart	34	1.15
10	Nathan Jones	28	1.04
	CLUB AVERAGE:		1.13

DISCIPLINARY RECORDS

	PLAYER	YELLOW	RED	AVE
1	Marc Bircham	6	1	115
2	Marvin Williams	7	0	137
3	Paul Warne	9	1	241
4	Justin Cochrane	2	0	280
5	Matthew Rose	7	0	317
6	Mark Lynch	3	0	357
7	Lee Peltier	8	0	369
8	Marcus Stewart	7	1	379
9	Nathan Jones	5	1	427
10	Nathan Smith	1	0	480
11	Terry Skiverton	4	1	486
12	Anthony Barry	4	0	599
13	Ritchie Jones	1	0	601
	Other	8	0	
	TOTAL	72	5	

KEY GOALKEEPER

Steve Mildenhall

Goals Conceded in the League	35	Counting Games League games when player was on pitch for at least 70 minutes	27
Defensive Rating Ave number of mins between League goals conceded while on the pitch	72	Clean Sheets In League games when player was on pitch for at least 70 minutes	4

KEY PLAYERS - DEFENDERS

Nathan Jones

Goals Conceded Number of League goals conceded while the player was on the pitch	35	Clean Sheets In League games when player was on pitch for at least 70 minutes	5
Defensive Rating Ave number of mins between League goals conceded while on the pitch	73	Club Defensive Rating Average number of mins between League goals conceded by the club this season	70

	PLAYER	CON LGE	CLEAN SHEETS	DEF RATE
1	Nathan Jones	35	5	73 mins
2	Scott Guyett	42	6	72 mins
3	Matthew Rose	31	5	71 mins
4	Terry Skiverton	34	6	71 mins

KEY PLAYERS - MIDFIELDERS

Zoltan Stieber

Goals in the League	1	Contribution to Attacking Power Average number of minutes between League team goals while on pitch	90
Defensive Rating Average number of mins between League goals conceded while on the pitch	77	Scoring Difference Defensive Rating minus Contribution to Attacking Power	-13

	PLAYER	LGE GOALS	DEF RATE	POWER	SCORE DIFF
1	Zoltan Stieber	1	77	90	-13 mins
2	Paul Warne	1	73	89	-16 mins
3	Lee Peltier	0	73	105	-32 mins
4	Anthony Barry	0	72	108	-36 mins

KEY PLAYERS - GOALSCORERS

Lloyd Owusu

Goals in the League	9	Player Strike Rate Average number of minutes between League goals scored by player	319
Contribution to Attacking Power Average number of minutes between League team goals while on pitch	130	Club Strike Rate Average number of minutes between League goals scored by club	108

	PLAYER	LGE GOALS	POWER	STRIKE RATE
1	Lloyd Owusu	9	130	319 mins
2	James Walker	3	84	338 mins
3	Andy Kirk	4	151	341 mins
4	Marcus Stewart	4	112	758 mins

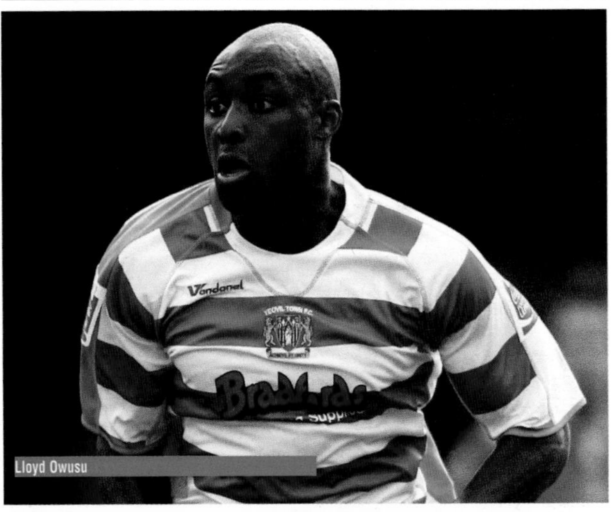
Vandanel
Bradfords
Lloyd Owusu

SQUAD APPEARANCES

Match	1	2	3	4	5	6	7	8	9	10	11	12	13	14	15	16	17	18	19	20	21	22	23	24
Venue	A	A	H	A	H	A	H	A	H	H	A	H	A	H	A	A	A	H	A	H	H	A	A	H
Competition	L	W	L	L	L	L	L	L	L	L	L	L	L	L	L	L	F	L	L	L	L	L	L	L
Result	L	L	W	W	D	W	L	W	L	D	L	W	D	L	L	D	L	W	L	W	W	W	D	L

Match	25	26	27	28	29	30	31	32	33	34	35	36	37	38	39	40	41	42	43	44	45	46	47	48
Venue	H	A	H	A	H	A	A	H	A	H	A	H	A	H	H	A	H	A	H	A	H	A	H	A
Competition	L	L	L	L	L	L	L	L	L	L	L	L	L	L	L	L	L	L	L	L	L	L	L	L
Result	W	L	L	D	D	L	D	L	L	W	L	L	D	W	L	L	W	L	D	L	L	W	L	L

Goalkeepers
Asmir Begovic
Scott Flinders
Romain Larrieu
Steve Mildenhall
Defenders
Craig Alcock
Terrell Forbes
Scott Guyett
Nathan Jones
Mark Lynch
Matthew Rose
Terry Skiverton
Midfielders
Anthony Barry
Kevin Betsy
Marc Bircham
Liam Bridcutt
Jean Christophe
Justin Cochrane
Gary Dempsey
Simon Gillett
Ritchie Jones
Stephen Maher
Lee Peltier
Jamie Peters
Nathan Smith
Zoltan Stieber
Paul Warne
Darren Way
Marvin Williams
Martin Woods
Forwards
Simon Church
Aidan Downes
Andy Kirk
Darryl Knights
Lloyd Owusu
Marcus Stewart
James Walker

KEY: On all match | On bench | Subbed or sent off (Counting game) | Subbed or sent off (playing less than 70 minutes) | Subbed on from bench (Counting Game) | Subbed on (playing less than 70 minutes) | Subbed on and then subbed or sent off (Counting Game) | Subbed on and then subbed or sent off (playing less than 70 minutes) | Not in 16

CHELTENHAM

Final Position: **19th**

NICKNAME: THE ROBINS

KEY: ☐ Won ☐ Drawn ☐ Lost

	Comp	Opponent	Venue	Result	Score	Scorers	Attendance
1	div2	Gillingham	H	W	1-0	Gillespie 24	4,008
2	ccr1	Southend	A	L	1-4	Finnigan 70	3,084
3	div2	Millwall	A	L	0-1		8,671
4	div2	Swindon	H	D	1-1	Vincent 72	5,442
5	div2	Carlisle	A	L	0-1		6,125
6	div2	Huddersfield	A	W	3-2	Spencer 62, 78, Finnigan 83	8,756
7	div2	Swansea	H	L	1-2	Vincent 4	4,323
8	div2	Tranmere	H	D	1-1	Caines 50	3,742
9	div2	Doncaster	A	L	0-2		6,150
10	div2	Port Vale	A	L	0-3		3,102
11	div2	Oldham	H	D	1-1	Townsend 45 pen	3,621
12	div2	Nottm Forest	H	L	0-3		5,012
13	div2	Northampton	A	L	1-2	Spencer 50	5,012
14	div2	Crewe	H	D	2-2	Wright 85, Bird 89	3,605
15	div2	Walsall	A	L	0-2		4,810
16	div2	Yeovil	H	D	1-1	Caines 90	3,169
17	facr1	Brighton	H	D	1-1	Gillespie 78	2,984
18	div2	Southend	A	D	2-2	Gillespie 14, Sinclair 25	7,158
19	facr1r	Brighton	A	L	1-2	Gillespie 65	3,711
20	div2	Leeds	H	W	1-0	Gillespie 86	7,043
21	div2	Leyton Orient	A	L	0-2		4,156
22	div2	Luton	H	W	1-0	Lindegaard 2	3,702
23	div2	Huddersfield	H	L	0-2		3,998
24	div2	Swansea	A	L	1-4	Gillespie 82	14,049
25	div2	Tranmere	A	L	0-1		6,111
26	div2	Port Vale	H	W	1-0	Connor 22	3,221
27	div2	Bournemouth	H	W	1-0	Bird 90	3,959
28	div2	Hartlepool	A	W	2-0	Gillespie 11, 84	4,120
29	div2	Carlisle	H	W	1-0	Gillespie 20	4,221
30	div2	Millwall	H	L	0-1		3,812
31	div2	Gillingham	A	D	0-0		4,993
32	div2	Bristol Rovers	A	L	0-2		6,780
33	div2	Brighton	H	W	2-1	Gillespie 90, Russell 90	3,963
34	div2	Swindon	A	L	0-3		6,483
35	div2	Hartlepool	H	D	1-1	Lindegaard 40	3,583
36	div2	Brighton	A	L	1-2	Brooker 3	4,395
37	div2	Bournemouth	A	D	2-2	Bird 45, Brooker 89	4,365
38	div2	Southend	H	D	1-1	Brooker 25	3,859
39	div2	Yeovil	A	L	1-2	Brooker 64	4,588
40	div2	Leeds	A	W	2-1	Bird 38, Russell 63	20,257
41	div2	Bristol Rovers	H	W	1-0	Brooker 80	5,187
42	div2	Luton	A	D	1-1	Gillespie 81	6,087
43	div2	Leyton Orient	H	W	1-0	Connor 47	3,988
44	div2	Northampton	H	D	1-1	Gillespie 39	4,024
45	div2	Nottm Forest	A	L	1-3	Gillespie 20	19,860
46	div2	Walsall	H	L	1-2	Connor 74	4,861
47	div2	Crewe	A	L	1-3	Gillespie 62	5,279
48	div2	Oldham	A	L	1-2	Gillespie 50 pen	6,400
49	div2	Doncaster	H	W	2-1	Gillespie 24, Connor 85	6,787

LEAGUE APPEARANCES, BOOKINGS AND GOALS

	AGE (on 01/07/08)	IN NAMED 16	APPEARANCES	COUNTING GAMES	MINUTES ON PITCH	LEAGUE GOALS	Yellow	Red
Goalkeepers								
Scott P Brown	23	42	0	0	0	0	0	0
Shane Higgs	31	46	46	46	4140	0	0	0
Defenders								
Gavin Caines	24	29	28	22	2117	2	3	0
Shane Duff	26	30	30	30	2691	0	3	0
Andy Gallinagh	23	39	26	22	2068	0	1	0
Jeremy Gill	37	42	42	41	3695	0	4	1
Richard Keogh	21	10	10	10	900	0	2	0
Lee Ridley	26	8	8	8	698	0	1	0
Michael Townsend	22	13	13	13	1158	1	1	0
Alan Wright	36	33	33	32	2905	1	2	0
Michael Wylde	21	8	0	0	0	0	0	0
Midfielders								
Craig Armstrong	33	17	14	13	1135	0	0	0
David Bird	23	46	46	45	4072	4	0	0
Scott Brown	23	23	20	7	854	0	0	1
Adam Connolly	22	31	15	3	493	0	0	0
Michael D'Agostino	21	29	25	9	1255	0	1	0
John Finnigan	32	10	10	10	887	1	4	0
Ben Gill	20	8	3	1	135	0	1	0
Andrew Lindegaard	27	43	42	24	2581	2	0	1
Alex Russell	35	13	13	12	1106	2	2	0
Dean Sinclair	23	12	12	11	1048	1	3	0
Sosthene Yao	20	8	4	0	43	0	1	0
Forwards								
Stephen Brooker	27	14	14	12	1125	5	0	0
Paul Connor	29	41	39	25	2374	4	2	0
Stephen Gillespie	23	37	37	33	3055	14	6	1
Guy Madjo	23	7	5	1	188	0	0	0
Jennison Myrie-Williams	20	12	12	5	629	0	1	0
Craig Reid	19	11	8	0	183	0	0	0
Damian Spencer	26	32	30	20	2082	3	4	0
Ashley Vincent	23	39	37	13	1821	2	2	0

TEAM OF THE SEASON

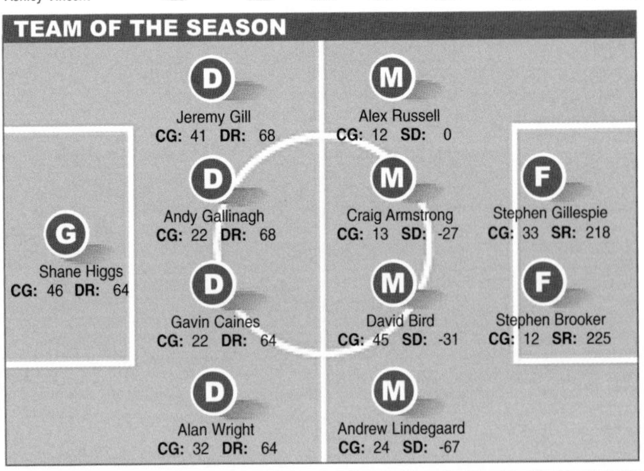

G
Shane Higgs
CG: 46 DR: 64
D
Jeremy Gill
CG: 41 DR: 68
D
Andy Gallinagh
CG: 22 DR: 68
D
Gavin Caines
CG: 22 DR: 64
D
Alan Wright
CG: 32 DR: 64
M
Alex Russell
CG: 12 SD: 0
M
Craig Armstrong
CG: 13 SD: -27
M
David Bird
CG: 45 SD: -31
M
Andrew Lindegaard
CG: 24 SD: -67
F
Stephen Gillespie
CG: 33 SR: 218
F
Stephen Brooker
CG: 12 SR: 225

MONTHLY POINTS TALLY

Month	Points	%
AUGUST	4	44%
SEPTEMBER	4	27%
OCTOBER	2	13%
NOVEMBER	5	42%
DECEMBER	3	20%
JANUARY	12	80%
FEBRUARY	7	29%
MARCH	11	61%
APRIL	0	0%
MAY	3	100%

LEAGUE GOALS

	PLAYER	MINS	GOALS	S RATE
1	Gillespie	3055	14	218
2	Brooker	1125	5	225
3	Connor	2374	4	593
4	Bird	4072	4	1018
5	Spencer	2082	3	694
6	Russell	1106	2	553
7	Vincent	1821	2	910
8	Caines	2117	2	1058
9	Lindegaard	2581	2	1290
10	Finnigan	887	1	887
11	Sinclair	1048	1	1048
12	Townsend	1158	1	1158
13	Wright	2905	1	2905
	Other		0	
	TOTAL		42	

TOP POINT EARNERS

	PLAYER	GAMES	AV PTS
1	Alex Russell	12	1.67
2	Stephen Brooker	12	1.50
3	Stephen Gillespie	33	1.33
4	Alan Wright	32	1.22
5	Andy Gallinagh	22	1.18
6	Gavin Caines	22	1.18
7	Jeremy Gill	41	1.15
8	David Bird	45	1.13
9	Shane Higgs	46	1.11
10	Shane Duff	30	1.10
	CLUB AVERAGE:		1.11

DISCIPLINARY RECORDS

	PLAYER	YELLOW	RED	AVE
1	John Finnigan	4	0	221
2	Dean Sinclair	3	0	349
3	Stephen Gillespie	6	1	436
4	Richard Keogh	2	0	450
5	Damian Spencer	4	0	520
6	Alex Russell	2	0	553
7	J Myrie-Williams	1	0	629
8	Lee Ridley	1	0	698
9	Gavin Caines	3	0	705
10	Jeremy Gill	4	1	739
11	Scott Brown	0	1	854
12	Shane Duff	3	0	897
13	Ashley Vincent	2	0	910
	Other	7	1	
	TOTAL	42	4	

KEY GOALKEEPER

Shane Higgs

Goals Conceded in the League	64	Counting Games League games when player was on pitch for at least 70 minutes	46
Defensive Rating Ave number of mins between League goals conceded while on the pitch	64	Clean Sheets In League games when player was on pitch for at least 70 minutes	10

KEY PLAYERS - DEFENDERS

Jeremy Gill

Goals Conceded Number of League goals conceded while the player was on the pitch	54	Clean Sheets In League games when player was on pitch for at least 70 minutes	9
Defensive Rating Ave number of mins between League goals conceded while on the pitch	68	Club Defensive Rating Average number of mins between League goals conceded by the club this season	66

	PLAYER	CON LGE	CLEAN SHEETS	DEF RATE
1	Jeremy Gill	54	9	68 mins
2	Andy Gallinagh	30	7	68 mins
3	Gavin Caines	33	7	64 mins
4	Alan Wright	45	8	64 mins

KEY PLAYERS - MIDFIELDERS

Alex Russell

Goals in the League	2	Contribution to Attacking Power Average number of minutes between League team goals while on pitch	92
Defensive Rating Average number of mins between League goals conceded while on the pitch	92	Scoring Difference Defensive Rating minus Contribution to Attacking Power	0

	PLAYER	LGE GOALS	DEF RATE	POWER	SCORE DIFF
1	Alex Russell	2	92	92	0 mins
2	Craig Armstrong	0	54	81	-27 mins
3	David Bird	4	65	96	-31 mins
4	Andrew Lindegaard	2	62	129	-67 mins

KEY PLAYERS - GOALSCORERS

Stephen Gillespie

Goals in the League	14	Player Strike Rate Average number of minutes between League goals scored by player	218
Contribution to Attacking Power Average number of minutes between League team goals while on pitch	95	Club Strike Rate Average number of minutes between League goals scored by club	100

	PLAYER	LGE GOALS	POWER	STRIKE RATE
1	Stephen Gillespie	14	95	218 mins
2	Stephen Brooker	5	102	225 mins
3	Alex Russell	2	92	553 mins
4	Paul Connor	4	84	593 mins

Andy Lindegaard celebrates with team-mates

SQUAD APPEARANCES

Match	1	2	3	4	5	6	7	8	9	10	11	12	13	14	15	16	17	18	19	20	21	22	23	24	25	26	27	28	29	30	31	32	33	34	35	36	37	38	39	40	41	42	43	44	45	46	47	48	49
Venue	H	A	A	H	A	A	H	H	A	A	H	H	A	H	A	H	H	A	A	H	A	H	H	A	A	H	H	A	H	H	A	A	H	A	H	A	A	H	A	A	H	A	H	H	A	H	A	A	H
Competition	L	W	L	L	L	L	L	L	L	L	L	L	L	L	L	L	F	L	F	L	L	L	L	L	L	L	L	L	L	L	L	L	L	L	L	L	L	L	L	L	L	L	L	L	L	L	L	L	L
Result	W	L	L	D	L	W	L	D	L	L	D	L	L	D	L	D	D	D	L	W	L	W	L	L	L	W	W	W	W	L	D	L	W	L	D	L	D	D	L	W	W	D	W	D	L	L	L	L	W

Goalkeepers
Scott P Brown
Shane Higgs
Defenders
Gavin Caines
Shane Duff
Andy Gallinagh
Jeremy Gill
Richard Keogh
Lee Ridley
Michael Townsend
Alan Wright
Michael Wylde
Midfielders
Craig Armstrong
David Bird
Scott Brown
Adam Connolly
Michael D'Agostino
John Finnigan
Ben Gill
Andrew Lindegaard
Alex Russell
Dean Sinclair
Sosthene Yao
Forwards
Stephen Brooker
Paul Connor
Stephen Gillespie
Guy Madjo
Jennison Myrie-Williams
Craig Reid
Damian Spencer
Ashley Vincent

KEY: On all match | On bench | Subbed or sent off (Counting game) | Subbed or sent off (playing less than 70 minutes) | Subbed on from bench (Counting Game) | Subbed on (playing less than 70 minutes) | Subbed on and then subbed or sent off (Counting Game) | Subbed on and then subbed or sent off (playing less than 70 minutes) | Not in 16

CREWE ALEXANDRA

Final Position: **20th**

NICKNAME: THE RAILWAYMEN

KEY: □Won □Drawn □Lost

						Attendance
1	div2	Brighton	H W	2-1	Roberts 22 pen, 79	5,394
2	ccr1	Hull City	H L	0-3		2,862
3	div2	Bristol Rovers	A D	1-1	Pope 34	7,750
4	div2	Leyton Orient	H L	0-2		4,683
5	div2	Swindon	A D	1-1	Schumacher 42	6,595
6	div2	Huddersfield	H W	2-0	Barnard 16, Bopp 39	5,164
7	div2	Doncaster	A L	0-2		6,726
8	div2	Millwall	H D	0-0		4,478
9	div2	Oldham	A L	2-3	Barnard 17, Moore 26	5,082
10	div2	Tranmere	A D	1-1	Roberts 56 pen	6,155
11	div2	Bournemouth	H L	1-4	Miller 89	4,799
12	div2	Southend	A L	0-3		6,927
13	div2	Luton	H W	2-0	Lowe 14, 40	4,490
14	div2	Cheltenham	A D	2-2	Church 74, Lowe 78	3,605
15	div2	Yeovil	H W	2-0	Mccready 28, Moore 40	4,363
16	div2	Port Vale	A W	1-0	Bennett 76	5,329
17	facr1	MK Dons	H W	2-1	Mccready 3, Cox 65	3,049
18	div2	Northampton	H W	1-0	Lowe 59	4,531
19	div2	Nottm Forest	A L	0-2		16,650
20	facr2	Oldham	A L	0-1		3,900
21	div2	Gillingham	H L	2-3	Moore 43, Roberts 49	3,929
22	div2	Walsall	H D	0-0		4,639
23	div2	Hartlepool	A L	0-3		3,915
24	div2	Doncaster	H L	0-4		4,122
25	div2	Huddersfield	A D	1-1	Barnard 19	9,759
26	div2	Millwall	A L	0-2		8,068
27	div2	Tranmere	H W	4-3	Roberts 30 pen, 48, Maynard 67, O'Donnell 89	5,137
28	div2	Leeds	H L	0-1		6,771
29	div2	Carlisle	A L	0-1		6,449
30	div2	Swansea	A L	1-2	Pope 90	11,200
31	div2	Swindon	H D	0-0		4,344
32	div2	Bristol Rovers	H D	1-1	Pope 47	3,942
33	div2	Brighton	A L	0-3		4,802
34	div2	Swansea	H D	2-2	Baudet 82, Pope 90	4,955
35	div2	Leyton Orient	A W	1-0	Maynard 26	3,881
36	div2	Leeds	A D	1-1	Maynard 47	21,223
37	div2	Carlisle	H L	0-1		4,786
38	div2	Northampton	A D	0-0		5,507
39	div2	Nottm Forest	H D	0-0		6,314
40	div2	Port Vale	H L	0-2		5,229
41	div2	Gillingham	A W	3-0	Pope 9, Maynard 50, Morgan 76	4,956
42	div2	Hartlepool	H W	3-1	Maynard 20, 30, Pope 85	4,412
43	div2	Walsall	A D	1-1	Maynard 61	4,741
44	div2	Luton	A L	1-2	Maynard 58	5,465
45	div2	Southend	H L	1-3	Maynard 74	4,895
46	div2	Yeovil	A W	3-0	Maynard 8, 58, Pope 90	4,785
47	div2	Cheltenham	H W	3-1	Maynard 14, 68, 76	5,279
48	div2	Bournemouth	A L	0-1		8,621
49	div2	Oldham	H L	1-4	Jones 84	6,786

LEAGUE APPEARANCES, BOOKINGS AND GOALS

	AGE (on 01/07/08)	IN NAMED 16	APPEARANCES	COUNTING GAMES	MINUTES ON PITCH	LEAGUE GOALS	Yellow	Red
Goalkeepers								
Ben Williams	25	46	46	46	4140	0	0	0
Defenders								
George Abbey	29	33	23	18	1784	0	0	0
Julien Baudet	29	35	35	31	2962	1	4	0
Patrick Boyle	21	17	17	17	1530	0	2	0
Neil Cox	36	34	27	20	1873	0	0	0
David Gray	20	2	1	1	79	0	0	0
Billy Jones	25	23	23	22	1969	1	0	0
Chris McCready	26	37	34	30	2781	1	1	0
Daniel O'Donnell	22	34	27	20	1926	1	0	0
Dan Woodards	29	37	36	35	3155	0	2	0
Midfielders								
Joe Anyinsah	23	9	8	3	455	0	0	0
Elliott Bennett	19	12	9	5	447	1	1	0
Eugen Bopp	24	17	10	3	428	1	0	0
Mark Carrington	21	15	9	3	369	0	0	0
Ryan Lowe	29	32	27	16	1600	4	0	0
Kenny Lunt	28	14	14	14	1259	0	1	0
Dean Morgan	24	10	9	6	610	1	0	0
Michael O'Connor	20	27	23	15	1507	0	3	0
Ben Rix	24	29	26	17	1841	0	2	0
Gary Roberts	21	4	4	3	294	0	0	0
Gary Roberts	21	41	41	38	3467	5	4	1
Steve Schumacher	24	29	26	24	2115	1	1	0
Forwards								
Lee Barnard	23	11	10	7	714	3	1	0
Cedric Baseya	20	4	3	1	114	0	0	0
Simon Church	19	12	12	8	851	1	0	0
Chris Dickson	23	4	3	1	159	0	0	0
Steve Jones	31	3	3	2	189	0	0	0
Nicky Maynard	21	28	27	23	2163	14	1	0
Shaun Miller	20	23	15	4	677	1	1	0
Byron Moore	19	39	33	24	2309	3	0	0
Tom Pope	22	27	26	16	1590	7	0	0

TEAM OF THE SEASON

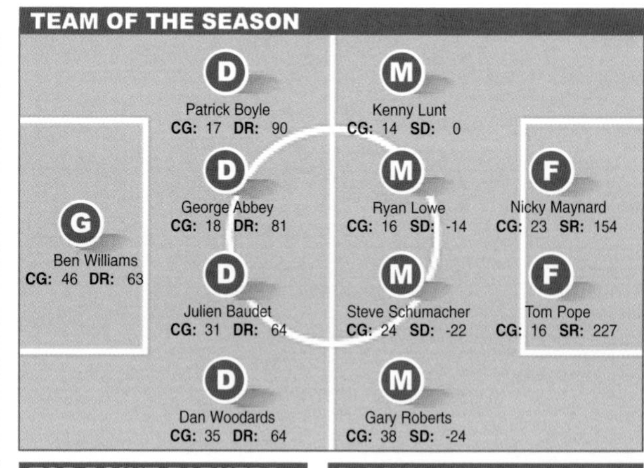

D
Patrick Boyle
CG: 17 DR: 90
M
Kenny Lunt
CG: 14 SD: 0
D
George Abbey
CG: 18 DR: 81
M
Ryan Lowe
CG: 16 SD: -14
F
Nicky Maynard
CG: 23 SR: 154
G
Ben Williams
CG: 46 DR: 63
D
Julien Baudet
CG: 31 DR: 64
M
Steve Schumacher
CG: 24 SD: -22
F
Tom Pope
CG: 16 SR: 227
D
Dan Woodards
CG: 35 DR: 64
M
Gary Roberts
CG: 38 SD: -24

MONTHLY POINTS TALLY

AUGUST	4	44%
SEPTEMBER	5	33%
OCTOBER	5	33%
NOVEMBER	9	75%
DECEMBER	2	11%
JANUARY	5	28%
FEBRUARY	5	33%
MARCH	9	43%
APRIL	6	50%
MAY	0	0%

LEAGUE GOALS

	PLAYER	MINS	GOALS	S RATE
1	Maynard	2163	14	154
2	Pope	1590	7	227
3	Roberts	3467	5	693
4	Lowe	1600	4	400
5	Barnard	714	3	238
6	Moore	2309	3	769
7	Bopp	428	1	428
8	Bennett	447	1	447
9	Morgan	610	1	610
10	Miller	677	1	677
11	Church	851	1	851
12	O'Donnell	1926	1	1926
13	Jones	1969	1	1969
	Other		3	
	TOTAL		46	

TOP POINT EARNERS

	PLAYER	GAMES	AV PTS
1	Ryan Lowe	16	1.38
2	Patrick Boyle	17	1.29
3	Neil Cox	20	1.25
4	Tom Pope	16	1.19
5	Gary Roberts	38	1.16
6	Billy Jones	22	1.14
7	Kenny Lunt	14	1.14
8	Ben Rix	17	1.12
9	Julien Baudet	31	1.10
10	Ben Williams	46	1.09
	CLUB AVERAGE:		1.09

DISCIPLINARY RECORDS

	PLAYER	YELLOW	RED	AVE
1	Michael O'Connor	3	0	502
2	Shaun Miller	1	0	677
3	Gary Roberts	4	1	693
4	Lee Barnard	1	0	714
5	Julien Baudet	4	0	740
6	Patrick Boyle	2	0	765
7	Ben Rix	2	0	920
8	Kenny Lunt	1	0	1259
9	Dan Woodards	2	0	1577
10	Steve Schumacher	1	0	2115
11	Nicky Maynard	1	0	2163
12	Chris McCready	1	0	2781
13	George Abbey	0	0	
	Other	0	0	
	TOTAL	23	1	

KEY GOALKEEPER

Ben Williams

Goals Conceded in the League	65	Counting Games League games when player was on pitch for at least 70 minutes	46
Defensive Rating Ave number of mins between League goals conceded while on the pitch	63	Clean Sheets In League games when player was on pitch for at least 70 minutes	13

KEY PLAYERS - DEFENDERS

Patrick Boyle

Goals Conceded Number of League goals conceded while the player was on the pitch	17	Clean Sheets In League games when player was on pitch for at least 70 minutes	6
Defensive Rating Ave number of mins between League goals conceded while on the pitch	90	Club Defensive Rating Average number of mins between League goals conceded by the club this season	65

	PLAYER	CON LGE	CLEAN SHEETS	DEF RATE
1	Patrick Boyle	17	6	90 mins
2	George Abbey	22	4	81 mins
3	Julien Baudet	46	7	64 mins
4	Dan Woodards	49	10	64 mins

KEY PLAYERS - MIDFIELDERS

Kenny Lunt

Goals in the League	0	Contribution to Attacking Power Average number of minutes between League team goals while on pitch	74
Defensive Rating Average number of mins between League goals conceded while on the pitch	74	Scoring Difference Defensive Rating minus Contribution to Attacking Power	0

	PLAYER	LGE GOALS	DEF RATE	POWER	SCORE DIFF
1	Kenny Lunt	0	74	74	0 mins
2	Ryan Lowe	4	66	80	-14 mins
3	Steve Schumacher	1	62	84	-22 mins
4	Gary Roberts	5	67	91	-24 mins

KEY PLAYERS - GOALSCORERS

Nicky Maynard

Goals in the League	14	Player Strike Rate Average number of minutes between League goals scored by player	154
Contribution to Attacking Power Average number of minutes between League team goals while on pitch	77	Club Strike Rate Average number of minutes between League goals scored by club	90

	PLAYER	LGE GOALS	POWER	STRIKE RATE
1	Nicky Maynard	14	77	154 mins
2	Tom Pope	7	75	227 mins
3	Ryan Lowe	4	80	400 mins
4	Gary Roberts	5	91	693 mins

DIADORA
Mornflake
Oats

Neil Cox

SQUAD APPEARANCES

Match	Venue	Competition	Result
1	H	L	W
2	H	W	L
3	A	L	D
4	H	L	L
5	A	L	D
6	H	L	W
7	A	L	L
8	H	L	D
9	A	L	L
10	A	L	D
11	H	L	L
12	A	L	L
13	H	L	W
14	A	L	D
15	H	L	W
16	A	L	W
17	H	F	W
18	H	L	W
19	A	L	L
20	A	F	L
21	H	L	L
22	H	L	D
23	A	L	L
24	H	L	L
25	A	L	D
26	A	L	L
27	H	L	W
28	H	L	L
29	A	L	L
30	A	L	L
31	H	L	D
32	H	L	D
33	A	L	L
34	H	L	D
35	A	L	W
36	A	L	D
37	H	L	L
38	A	L	D
39	H	L	D
40	H	L	L
41	A	L	W
42	H	L	W
43	A	L	D
44	A	L	L
45	H	L	L
46	A	L	W
47	H	L	W
48	A	L	L
49	H	L	L

Goalkeepers
Ben Williams
Defenders
George Abbey
Julien Baudet
Patrick Boyle
Neil Cox
David Gray
Billy Jones
Chris McCready
Daniel O'Donnell
Dan Woodards
Midfielders
Joe Anyinsah
Elliott Bennett
Eugen Bopp
Mark Carrington
Ryan Lowe
Kenny Lunt
Dean Morgan
Michael O'Connor
Ben Rix
Gary Roberts
Gary Roberts
Steve Schumacher
Forwards
Lee Barnard
Cedric Baseya
Simon Church
Chris Dickson
Steve Jones
Nicky Maynard
Shaun Miller
Byron Moore
Tom Pope

KEY: On all match · On bench · Subbed or sent off (Counting game) · Subbed or sent off (playing less than 70 minutes) · Subbed on from bench (Counting Game) · Subbed on (playing less than 70 minutes) · Subbed on and then subbed or sent off (Counting Game) · Subbed on and then subbed or sent off (playing less than 70 minutes) · Not in 16

BOURNEMOUTH

Final Position: **21st**

NICKNAME: THE CHERRIES

KEY: ☐ Won ☐ Drawn ☐ Lost

							Attendance
1	div2	Nottm Forest	A	D	0-0		18,791
2	ccr1	West Brom	A	L	0-1		10,250
3	div2	Huddersfield	H	L	0-1		5,606
4	div2	Doncaster	A	W	2-1	Gradel 28, Kuffour 46	6,476
5	div2	Port Vale	H	L	0-1		5,444
6	div2	Leyton Orient	A	L	0-1		4,995
7	div2	Northampton	H	D	1-1	Anderton 34	5,009
8	div2	Swindon	A	L	1-4	Hollands 37	6,668
9	div2	Carlisle	H	L	1-3	Kuffour 54	4,940
10	div2	Brighton	H	L	0-2		4,638
11	div2	Crewe	A	W	4-1	Bradbury 37, Gradel 61, 77, Anderton 85	4,799
12	div2	Swansea	H	L	1-4	Bradbury 31 pen	5,843
13	div2	Millwall	A	L	1-2	Bradbury 90	7,805
14	div2	Walsall	H	D	1-1	Kuffour 20	5,414
15	div2	Bristol Rovers	A	W	2-0	Henry 41, 90	6,405
16	div2	Leeds	H	L	1-3	Karacan 37	9,632
17	facr1	Barrow	A	D	1-1	Karacan 45	2,203
18	div2	Hartlepool	A	D	1-1	Henry 16	3,496
19	facr1r	Barrow	H	W	3-2	Golbourne 43, Gradel 90 pen, Hollands 120	2,969
20	div2	Oldham	H	L	0-3		5,261
21	facr2	Millwall	A	L	1-2	Cooper 74	4,495
22	div2	Yeovil	A	L	1-2	Cummings 65 pen	5,321
23	div2	Tranmere	A	L	1-3	Vokes 76	5,043
24	div2	Gillingham	H	W	1-0	Pitman 34	4,746
25	div2	Northampton	A	L	1-4	Pitman 5	4,806
26	div2	Leyton Orient	H	W	3-1	Gradel 19, Vokes 54, Henry 89	5,536
27	div2	Swindon	H	D	2-2	Kuffour 63, Vokes 78	6,540
28	div2	Brighton	A	L	2-3	Christophe 24, Pitman 79	5,963
29	div2	Cheltenham	A	L	0-1		3,959
30	div2	Southend	H	L	1-4	Cummings 50	5,419
31	div2	Luton	H	W	4-3	Gradel 2, Kuffour 31, Vokes 89, Pitman 90	3,489
32	div2	Port Vale	A	W	3-1	Vokes 10, Hollands 28, Cooper 84	4,047
33	div2	Huddersfield	A	L	0-1		7,359
34	div2	Nottm Forest	H	W	2-0	Vokes 20, 29	7,251
35	div2	Luton	A	W	4-1	Vokes 13, Kuffour 14, 84, Gradel 45	5,897
36	div2	Doncaster	H	L	0-2		4,947
37	div2	Southend	A	L	1-2	J.Pearce 40	7,474
38	div2	Cheltenham	H	D	2-2	Gradel 17 pen, Bartley 39	4,365
39	div2	Hartlepool	H	W	2-0	Vokes 6, 45	3,984
40	div2	Leeds	A	L	0-2		21,199
41	div2	Oldham	A	L	0-2		3,633
42	div2	Yeovil	H	W	2-0	Hollands 9, Vokes 32	4,145
43	div2	Gillingham	A	L	1-2	Kuffour 28	6,540
44	div2	Tranmere	H	W	2-1	Goodison 1 og, Kuffour 34	4,118
45	div2	Millwall	H	W	2-0	Gradel 75 pen, 89	4,962
46	div2	Swansea	A	W	2-1	Kuffour 90, Partington 90	15,613
47	div2	Bristol Rovers	H	W	2-1	Anderton 18, Kuffour 55	6,867
48	div2	Walsall	A	W	3-1	Hollands 10, Kuffour 35, Pitman 63 pen	4,530
49	div2	Crewe	H	W	1-0	Vokes 55	8,621
50	div2	Carlisle	A	D	1-1	Pitman 68	12,223

LEAGUE APPEARANCES, BOOKINGS AND GOALS

	AGE (on 01/07/08)	IN NAMED 16	APPEARANCES	COUNTING GAMES	MINUTES ON PITCH	LEAGUE GOALS		
Goalkeepers								
Asmir Begovic	21	10	8	8	720	0	0	0
David Forde	28	11	11	11	990	0	1	0
Neil Moss	33	15	7	7	630	0	0	0
Ryan Pryce	21	28	4	2	250	0	0	0
Gareth Stewart	28	23	17	16	1460	0	0	0
Defenders								
Warren Cummings	27	33	32	30	2772	2	5	0
Ryan Garry	24	11	8	6	543	0	2	0
Scott Golbourne	20	5	5	4	425	0	1	0
Josh Gowling	24	37	37	36	3257	0	2	0
Alex Pearce	19	11	11	11	990	0	3	0
Jason Pearce	20	45	32	28	2641	1	2	0
Russell Perrett	35	13	10	9	857	0	1	0
Paul Telfer	36	18	18	16	1511	0	1	0
Jo Tessem	36	15	11	2	465	0	0	0
Neil Young	34	25	21	18	1650	0	3	0
Midfielders								
Darren Anderton	36	20	20	17	1694	3	0	0
Marvyn Bartley	18	27	20	14	1306	1	3	0
Jean Christophe	26	11	9	3	456	1	0	0
Shaun Cooper	24	39	38	30	2862	1	5	1
Mark-Alain Gradel	20	35	34	30	2808	9	7	0
James Henry	19	11	11	8	782	4	2	0
Danny Hollands	22	39	38	38	3414	4	7	0
Jem Karacan	19	12	12	9	882	1	1	0
Adam Lallana	20	4	3	1	180	0	0	0
Josh McQuoid	18	15	5	1	176	0	0	0
Gareth O'Connor	29	8	6	2	337	0	0	0
Marc Wilson	20	7	7	7	617	0	0	0
Forwards								
Lee Bradbury	32	40	35	28	2820	3	8	1
Jonathan Osei Kuffour	26	42	42	34	3332	12	1	0
Brett Pitman	20	43	39	10	1530	6	3	0
Sam Vokes	18	43	41	26	2701	12	2	0

TEAM OF THE SEASON

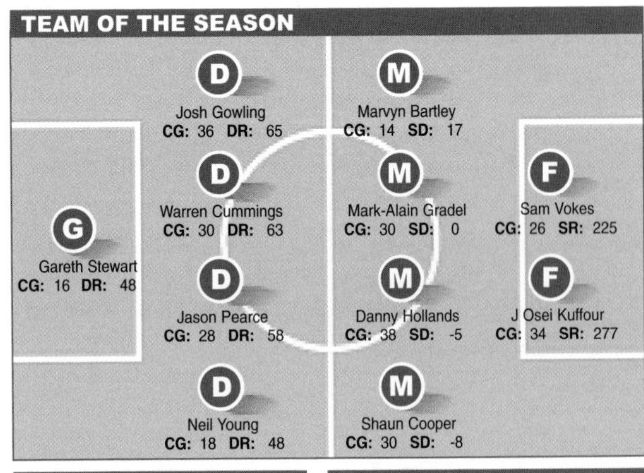

D
Josh Gowling
CG: 36 DR: 65
M
Marvyn Bartley
CG: 14 SD: 17
G
Gareth Stewart
CG: 16 DR: 48
D
Warren Cummings
CG: 30 DR: 63
M
Mark-Alain Gradel
CG: 30 SD: 0
F
Sam Vokes
CG: 26 SR: 225
D
Jason Pearce
CG: 28 DR: 58
M
Danny Hollands
CG: 38 SD: -5
F
J Osei Kuffour
CG: 34 SR: 277
D
Neil Young
CG: 18 DR: 48
M
Shaun Cooper
CG: 30 SD: -8

MONTHLY POINTS TALLY

Month	Points	%
AUGUST	4	44%
SEPTEMBER	1	7%
OCTOBER	4	27%
NOVEMBER	4	33%
DECEMBER	7	39%
JANUARY	6	33%
FEBRUARY	7	47%
MARCH	12	57%
APRIL	12	100%
MAY	1	33%

LEAGUE GOALS

	PLAYER	MINS	GOALS	S RATE
1	Vokes	2701	12	225
2	Kuffour	3332	12	277
3	Gradel	2808	9	312
4	Pitman	1530	6	255
5	Henry	782	4	195
6	Hollands	3414	4	853
7	Anderton	1694	3	564
8	Bradbury	2820	3	940
9	Cummings	2772	2	1386
10	Partington	38	1	38
11	Christophe	456	1	456
12	Karacan	882	1	882
13	Bartley	1306	1	1306
	Other		2	
	TOTAL		61	

TOP POINT EARNERS

	PLAYER	GAMES	AV PTS
1	Lee Bradbury	28	1.64
2	Sam Vokes	26	1.62
3	Marvyn Bartley	14	1.57
4	Mark-Alain Gradel	30	1.47
5	Shaun Cooper	30	1.43
6	Jason Pearce	28	1.43
7	Warren Cummings	30	1.33
8	Josh Gowling	36	1.33
9	Danny Hollands	38	1.32
10	Jonathan Osei Kuffour	34	1.32
	CLUB AVERAGE:		1.04

DISCIPLINARY RECORDS

	PLAYER	YELLOW	RED	AVE
1	Ryan Garry	2	0	271
2	Lee Bradbury	8	1	313
3	Alex Pearce	3	0	330
4	James Henry	2	0	391
5	Mark-Alain Gradel	7	0	401
6	Marvyn Bartley	3	0	435
7	Shaun Cooper	5	1	477
8	Danny Hollands	7	0	487
9	Brett Pitman	3	0	510
10	Neil Young	3	0	550
11	Warren Cummings	5	0	554
12	Russell Perrett	1	0	857
13	Jem Karacan	1	0	882
	Other	9	0	
	TOTAL	59	2	

KEY GOALKEEPER

Gareth Stewart

Goals Conceded in the League	30	Counting Games League games when player was on pitch for at least 70 minutes	16
Defensive Rating Ave number of mins between League goals conceded while on the pitch	48	Clean Sheets In League games when player was on pitch for at least 70 minutes	2

KEY PLAYERS - DEFENDERS

Josh Gowling

Goals Conceded Number of League goals conceded while the player was on the pitch	50	Clean Sheets In League games when player was on pitch for at least 70 minutes	7
Defensive Rating Ave number of mins between League goals conceded while on the pitch	65	Club Defensive Rating Average number of mins between League goals conceded by the club this season	57

	PLAYER	CON LGE	CLEAN SHEETS	DEF RATE
1	Josh Gowling	50	7	65 mins
2	Warren Cummings	44	6	63 mins
3	Jason Pearce	45	6	58 mins
4	Neil Young	34	2	48 mins

KEY PLAYERS - MIDFIELDERS

Marvyn Bartley

Goals in the League	1	Contribution to Attacking Power Average number of minutes between League team goals while on pitch	59
Defensive Rating Average number of mins between League goals conceded while on the pitch	76	Scoring Difference Defensive Rating minus Contribution to Attacking Power	17

	PLAYER	LGE GOALS	DEF RATE	POWER	SCORE DIFF
1	Marvyn Bartley	1	76	59	17 mins
2	Mark-Alain Gradel	9	65	65	0 mins
3	Danny Hollands	4	55	60	-5 mins
4	Shaun Cooper	1	54	62	-8 mins

KEY PLAYERS - GOALSCORERS

Sam Vokes

Goals in the League	12	Player Strike Rate Average number of minutes between League goals scored by player	225
Contribution to Attacking Power Average number of minutes between League team goals while on pitch	60	Club Strike Rate Average number of minutes between League goals scored by club	66

	PLAYER	LGE GOALS	POWER	STRIKE RATE
1	Sam Vokes	12	60	225 mins
2	Jonathan Osei Kuffour	12	65	277 mins
3	Mark-Alain Gradel	9	65	312 mins
4	Darren Anderton	3	80	564 mins

FOCAL
POINT
Sam Vokes

SQUAD APPEARANCES

Match	1	2	3	4	5	6	7	8	9	10	11	12	13	14	15	16	17	18	19	20	21	22	23	24	25
Venue	A	A	H	A	H	A	H	A	H	H	A	H	A	H	A	H	A	A	H	H	A	A	A	H	A
Competition	L	W	L	L	L	L	L	L	L	L	L	L	L	L	L	L	F	L	F	L	F	L	L	L	L
Result	D	L	L	W	L	L	D	L	L	L	W	L	L	D	W	L	D	D	W	L	L	L	L	W	L

Match	26	27	28	29	30	31	32	33	34	35	36	37	38	39	40	41	42	43	44	45	46	47	48	49	50
Venue	H	H	A	A	H	H	A	A	H	A	H	A	H	H	A	A	H	A	H	H	A	H	A	H	A
Competition	L	L	L	L	L	L	L	L	L	L	L	L	L	L	L	L	L	L	L	L	L	L	L	L	L
Result	W	D	L	L	L	W	W	L	W	W	L	L	D	W	L	L	W	L	W	W	W	W	W	W	D

Goalkeepers
Asmir Begovic
David Forde
Neil Moss
Ryan Pryce
Gareth Stewart

Defenders
Warren Cummings
Ryan Garry
Scott Golbourne
Josh Gowling
Alex Pearce
Jason Pearce
Russell Perrett
Paul Telfer
Jo Tessem
Neil Young

Midfielders
Darren Anderton
Marvyn Bartley
Jean Christophe
Shaun Cooper
Mark-Alain Gradel
James Henry
Danny Hollands
Jem Karacan
Adam Lallana
Josh McQuoid
Gareth O'Connor
Marc Wilson

Forwards
Lee Bradbury
Jonathan Osei Kuffour
Brett Pitman
Sam Vokes

KEY: On all match | On bench | Subbed or sent off (Counting game) | Subbed or sent off (playing less than 70 minutes) | Subbed on from bench (Counting Game) | Subbed on (playing less than 70 minutes) | Subbed on and then subbed or sent off (Counting Game) | Subbed on and then subbed or sent off (playing less than 70 minutes) | Not in 16

GILLINGHAM

Final Position: **22nd**

NICKNAME: THE GILLS

KEY: ☐ Won ☐ Drawn ☐ Lost

							Attendance
1	div2	Cheltenham	A	L	0-1		4,008
2	ccr1	Watford	A	L	0-3		8,166
3	div2	Tranmere	H	L	0-2		5,302
4	div2	Luton	A	L	1-3	Bentley 22	6,178
5	div2	Walsall	H	W	2-1	Mulligan 15, 34	4,806
6	div2	Southend	A	L	0-3		7,348
7	div2	Brighton	H	W	1-0	Facey 82	6,118
8	div2	Nottm Forest	A	L	0-4		16,330
9	div2	Leeds	H	D	1-1	Cox 90	8,719
10	div2	Leyton Orient	H	W	3-1	Graham 25, 50, Cogan 67	5,632
11	div2	Swindon	A	L	0-5		6,345
12	div2	Millwall	H	D	1-1	Dickson 16	6,120
13	div2	Carlisle	A	L	0-2		6,461
14	div2	Bristol Rovers	H	W	3-2	Brown 19, Graham 85, Dickson 89	5,333
15	div2	Swansea	A	D	1-1	Facey 10	13,452
16	div2	Doncaster	H	D	1-1	Dickson 18	5,030
17	facr1	Barnet	A	L	1-2	Graham 27	2,843
18	div2	Yeovil	A	L	1-2	Dickson 76	4,408
19	div2	Hartlepool	H	W	2-1	Oli 46, 59	5,488
20	div2	Crewe	A	W	3-2	Oli 8, Dickson 56 pen, 73	3,929
21	div2	Port Vale	H	L	1-2	Dickson 32	7,001
22	div2	Bournemouth	A	L	0-1		4,746
23	div2	Southend	H	D	1-1	Miller 89	8,268
24	div2	Nottm Forest	H	W	3-0	Mulligan 49, Miller 61, Griffiths 81	7,712
25	div2	Leyton Orient	A	D	0-0		5,369
26	div2	Huddersfield	A	W	3-1	Mulligan 45, 75 pen, Facey 82	11,212
27	div2	Northampton	H	L	0-1		5,579
28	div2	Oldham	H	D	0-0		4,402
29	div2	Walsall	A	L	1-2	Crofts 90	4,914
30	div2	Tranmere	A	L	0-2		5,006
31	div2	Cheltenham	H	D	0-0		4,993
32	div2	Oldham	A	L	1-2	Oli 25	4,866
33	div2	Northampton	A	L	0-4		4,978
34	div2	Huddersfield	H	W	1-0	Miller 88 pen	5,022
35	div2	Yeovil	H	D	0-0		5,083
36	div2	Brighton	A	L	2-4	Crofts 4, 76	6,836
37	div2	Hartlepool	A	L	0-4		4,055
38	div2	Doncaster	A	L	1-2	Crofts 56	7,867
39	div2	Crewe	H	L	0-3		4,956
40	div2	Bournemouth	H	W	2-1	Crofts 9, Jackson 26	6,540
41	div2	Port Vale	A	L	1-2	Griffiths 78	3,157
42	div2	Carlisle	H	D	0-0		6,673
43	div2	Luton	H	W	2-1	Jackson 75, 87	6,142
44	div2	Millwall	A	D	1-1	Southall 26	10,006
45	div2	Swansea	H	L	1-2	Oli 22	8,520
46	div2	Bristol Rovers	A	D	1-1	Nutter 38	6,614
47	div2	Swindon	H	D	1-1	Richards 2	6,334
48	div2	Leeds	A	L	1-2	Jackson 20	38,256

LEAGUE APPEARANCES, BOOKINGS AND GOALS

	AGE (on 01/07/08)	IN NAMED 16	APPEARANCES	COUNTING GAMES	MINUTES ON PITCH	LEAGUE GOALS	(yellow)	(red)
Goalkeepers								
Simon Royce	36	33	33	32	2917	0	0	1
Derek Stillie	34	45	14	13	1223	0	1	0
Defenders								
Adam Bygrave	19	19	15	11	1136	0	1	0
Sean Clohessy	21	30	17	15	1400	0	1	1
Ian Cox	37	20	20	16	1577	1	2	1
Danny Cullip	31	11	11	10	930	0	3	0
Marvin Hamilton	19	5	5	4	373	0	0	0
Duncan Jupp	33	4	2	1	151	0	0	0
Simon King	25	43	42	38	3458	0	1	0
John Nutter	26	24	24	22	2068	1	1	0
Garry Richards	22	16	14	11	1075	1	2	1
Efetobore Sodje	35	13	13	12	1097	0	2	0
Midfielders								
Craig Armstrong	33	14	13	9	999	0	3	0
Mark Bentley	30	34	33	28	2774	1	9	0
Aaron Brown	28	12	11	7	813	1	2	0
Barry Cogan	23	23	16	8	970	1	1	0
Andrew Crofts	24	41	41	40	3606	5	5	0
Barry Fuller	23	16	10	9	855	0	3	0
Stuart Lewis	20	11	10	5	583	0	1	0
Steve Lomas	34	11	8	7	655	0	2	1
Kevin Maher	31	8	7	6	596	0	1	1
Adam Miller	26	28	28	23	2275	3	6	1
Adam Nowland	26	5	5	3	359	0	1	0
Craig Rocastle	26	3	2	1	156	0	0	0
Nicky Southall	36	33	33	29	2796	1	3	0
Craig Stone	19	19	9	2	320	0	0	0
Stuart Thurgood	26	14	12	10	932	0	3	1
Forwards								
Georges Ba	29	5	4	0	127	0	1	0
Luis Cumbers	19	8	6	1	147	0	0	0
Chris Dickson	23	14	12	9	833	7	0	0
Delroy Facey	28	33	32	24	2376	3	1	0
David Graham	29	16	16	6	754	3	1	0
Leroy Griffiths	31	29	24	3	742	2	3	0
Simeon Jackson	21	18	18	14	1262	4	1	0
Gary Mulligan	23	31	30	9	1467	5	3	0
Dennis Oli	24	23	22	12	1377	5	3	0
Andy Pugh	19	3	2	0	23	0	0	0
Donovan Simmonds	19	4	3	0	37	0	0	0

TEAM OF THE SEASON

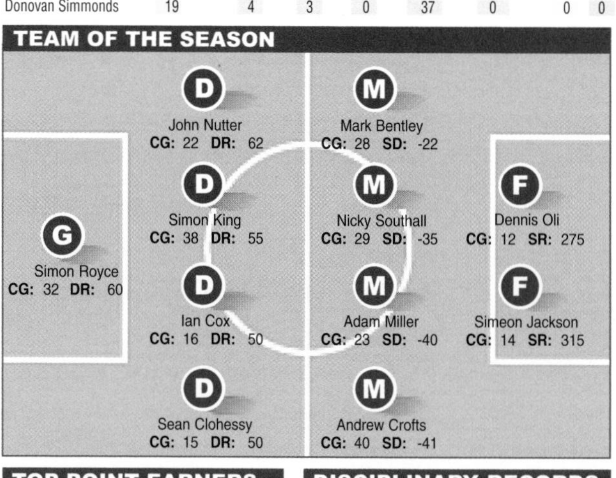

D
John Nutter
CG: 22 DR: 62
M
Mark Bentley
CG: 28 SD: -22
G
Simon Royce
CG: 32 DR: 60
D
Simon King
CG: 38 DR: 55
M
Nicky Southall
CG: 29 SD: -35
F
Dennis Oli
CG: 12 SR: 275
D
Ian Cox
CG: 16 DR: 50
M
Adam Miller
CG: 23 SD: -40
F
Simeon Jackson
CG: 14 SR: 315
D
Sean Clohessy
CG: 15 DR: 50
M
Andrew Crofts
CG: 40 SD: -41

MONTHLY POINTS TALLY

AUGUST	0	0%
SEPTEMBER	7	47%
OCTOBER	7	47%
NOVEMBER	5	42%
DECEMBER	7	47%
JANUARY	5	28%
FEBRUARY	4	33%
MARCH	5	21%
APRIL	6	40%
MAY	0	0%

LEAGUE GOALS

	PLAYER	MINS	GOALS	S RATE
1	Dickson	833	7	119
2	Oli	1377	5	275
3	Mulligan	1467	5	293
4	Crofts	3606	5	721
5	Jackson	1262	4	315
6	Graham	754	3	251
7	Miller	2275	3	758
8	Facey	2376	3	792
9	Griffiths	742	2	371
10	Brown	813	1	813
11	Cogan	970	1	970
12	Richards	1075	1	1075
13	Cox	1577	1	1577
	Other		3	
	TOTAL		44	

TOP POINT EARNERS

	PLAYER	GAMES	AV PTS
1	Sean Clohessy	15	1.33
2	Mark Bentley	28	1.25
3	Dennis Oli	12	1.17
4	Simon Royce	32	1.09
5	Efetobore Sodje	12	1.08
6	Delroy Facey	24	1.08
7	Nicky Southall	29	1.07
8	Ian Cox	16	1.06
9	Andrew Crofts	40	1.03
10	Simeon Jackson	14	1.00
	CLUB AVERAGE:		1.00

DISCIPLINARY RECORDS

	PLAYER	YELLOW	RED	AVE
1	Steve Lomas	2	1	218
2	Stuart Thurgood	3	1	233
3	Leroy Griffiths	3	0	247
4	Barry Fuller	3	0	285
5	Kevin Maher	1	1	298
6	Mark Bentley	9	0	308
7	Danny Cullip	3	0	310
8	Adam Miller	6	1	325
9	Craig Armstrong	3	0	333
10	Garry Richards	2	1	358
11	Aaron Brown	2	0	406
12	Dennis Oli	3	0	459
13	Gary Mulligan	3	0	489
	Other	22	3	
	TOTAL	65	8	

KEY GOALKEEPER

Simon Royce

Goals Conceded in the League	48	Counting Games League games when player was on pitch for at least 70 minutes	32
Defensive Rating Ave number of mins between League goals conceded while on the pitch	60	Clean Sheets In League games when player was on pitch for at least 70 minutes	6

KEY PLAYERS - DEFENDERS

John Nutter

Goals Conceded Number of League goals conceded while the player was on the pitch	33	Clean Sheets In League games when player was on pitch for at least 70 minutes	7
Defensive Rating Ave number of mins between League goals conceded while on the pitch	62	Club Defensive Rating Average number of mins between League goals conceded by the club this season	59

	PLAYER	CON LGE	CLEAN SHEETS	DEF RATE
1	John Nutter	33	7	62 mins
2	Simon King	62	6	55 mins
3	Ian Cox	31	2	50 mins
4	Sean Clohessy	28	2	50 mins

KEY PLAYERS - MIDFIELDERS

Mark Bentley

Goals in the League	1	Contribution to Attacking Power Average number of minutes between League team goals while on pitch	89
Defensive Rating Average number of mins between League goals conceded while on the pitch	67	Scoring Difference Defensive Rating minus Contribution to Attacking Power	-22

	PLAYER	LGE GOALS	DEF RATE	POWER	SCORE DIFF
1	Mark Bentley	1	67	89	-22 mins
2	Nicky Southall	1	58	93	-35 mins
3	Adam Miller	3	58	98	-40 mins
4	Andrew Crofts	5	56	97	-41 mins

KEY PLAYERS - GOALSCORERS

Dennis Oli

Goals in the League	5	Player Strike Rate Average number of minutes between League goals scored by player	275
Contribution to Attacking Power Average number of minutes between League team goals while on pitch	91	Club Strike Rate Average number of minutes between League goals scored by club	98

	PLAYER	LGE GOALS	POWER	STRIKE RATE
1	Dennis Oli	5	91	275 mins
2	Simeon Jackson	4	105	315 mins
3	Andrew Crofts	5	97	721 mins
4	Adam Miller	3	98	758 mins

Chris Dickson

SQUAD APPEARANCES

Match	1	2	3	4	5	6	7	8	9	10	11	12	13	14	15	16	17	18	19	20	21	22	23	24	25	26	27	28	29	30	31	32	33	34	35	36	37	38	39	40	41	42	43	44	45	46	47	48
Venue	A	A	H	A	H	A	H	A	H	H	A	H	A	H	A	H	A	A	H	A	H	A	H	H	A	A	H	H	A	A	H	A	A	H	H	A	A	A	H	H	A	H	H	A	H	A	H	A
Competition	L	W	L	L	L	L	L	L	L	L	L	L	L	L	L	L	F	L	L	L	L	L	L	L	L	L	L	L	L	L	L	L	L	L	L	L	L	L	L	L	L	L	L	L	L	L	L	L
Result	L	L	L	L	W	L	W	L	D	W	L	D	L	W	D	D	L	L	W	W	L	L	D	W	D	W	L	D	L	L	D	L	L	W	D	L	L	L	L	W	L	D	W	D	L	D	D	L

Goalkeepers
Simon Royce
Derek Stillie
Defenders
Adam Bygrave
Sean Clohessy
Ian Cox
Danny Cullip
Marvin Hamilton
Duncan Jupp
Simon King
John Nutter
Garry Richards
Efetobore Sodje
Midfielders
Craig Armstrong
Mark Bentley
Aaron Brown
Barry Cogan
Andrew Crofts
Barry Fuller
Stuart Lewis
Steve Lomas
Kevin Maher
Adam Miller
Adam Nowland
Craig Rocastle
Nicky Southall
Craig Stone
Stuart Thurgood
Forwards
Georges Ba
Luis Cumbers
Chris Dickson
Delroy Facey
David Graham
Leroy Griffiths
Simeon Jackson
Gary Mulligan
Dennis Oli
Andy Pugh
Donovan Simmonds

KEY: On all match | On bench | Subbed or sent off (Counting game) | Subbed or sent off (playing less than 70 minutes) | Subbed on from bench (Counting Game) | Subbed on (playing less than 70 minutes) | Subbed on and then subbed or sent off (Counting Game) | Subbed on and then subbed or sent off (playing less than 70 minutes) | Not in 16

PORT VALE

Final Position: **23rd**

NICKNAME: THE VALIANTS

KEY: Won / Drawn / Lost

						Scorers	Attendance
1	div2	Bristol Rovers	H	D	1-1	Rodgers 66 pen	6,808
2	ccr1	Wrexham	H	L	3-5*	Rodgers 33 pen (*on penalties)	2,916
3	div2	Yeovil	A	L	0-1		5,071
4	div2	Hartlepool	H	L	0-2		3,978
5	div2	Bournemouth	A	W	1-0	Rodgers 82	5,444
6	div2	Walsall	A	D	0-0		4,967
7	div2	Nottm Forest	H	L	0-2		6,521
8	div2	Luton	A	L	1-2	Rodgers 90	6,084
9	div2	Southend	H	L	1-2	Rodgers 59 pen	3,969
10	div2	Cheltenham	H	W	3-0	McGoldrick 21, P.Edwards 73, Rocastle 88	3,102
11	div2	Northampton	A	L	1-2	McGoldrick 55	4,755
12	div2	Brighton	H	L	0-1		3,490
13	div2	Leyton Orient	A	L	1-3	Rodgers 40	4,555
14	div2	Swindon	H	W	2-1	Rodgers 18 pen, Whitaker 26	4,013
15	div2	Huddersfield	A	L	1-3	Rodgers 43	8,555
16	div2	Crewe	H	L	0-1		5,329
17	facr1	Morecambe	A	W	2-0	Pilkington 6, Willock 22	2,730
18	div2	Oldham	A	D	1-1	Willock 32	5,097
19	div2	Doncaster	H	L	1-3	Pilkington 10	4,581
20	facr2	Chasetown	H	D	1-1	Rodgers 18	5,875
21	div2	Leeds	A	L	0-3		20,301
22	div2	Gillingham	A	W	2-1	Willock 34, King 45 og	7,001
23	facr2r	Chasetown	A	L	0-1		1,986
24	div2	Tranmere	H	D	0-0		3,604
25	div2	Nottm Forest	A	L	0-2		21,407
26	div2	Walsall	H	D	1-1	Laird 12	6,029
27	div2	Luton	H	L	1-2	Willock 45	4,224
28	div2	Cheltenham	A	L	0-1		3,221
29	div2	Carlisle	A	L	2-3	Harsley 27, Whitaker 38	6,313
30	div2	Millwall	H	W	3-1	Whitaker 24, Lowe 75, 90	3,724
31	div2	Swansea	A	L	0-2		12,310
32	div2	Bournemouth	H	L	1-3	Pilkington 49	4,047
33	div2	Yeovil	H	D	2-2	Eckersley 38, P.Edwards 58	2,869
34	div2	Bristol Rovers	A	L	2-3	Harsley 12 pen, Lowe 64	6,927
35	div2	Carlisle	H	D	1-1	Harsley 84 pen	4,221
36	div2	Hartlepool	A	L	2-3	Herd 3, 15	3,630
37	div2	Swansea	H	L	0-2		4,347
38	div2	Millwall	A	L	0-3		7,775
39	div2	Oldham	H	L	0-3		3,715
40	div2	Doncaster	A	L	1-2	Whitaker 34	8,040
41	div2	Crewe	A	W	2-0	Harsley 57 pen, Rodgers 81	5,229
42	div2	Leeds	H	D	3-3	Harsley 65 pen, Whitaker 67, Rodgers 90	7,908
43	div2	Tranmere	A	L	0-2		6,484
44	div2	Gillingham	H	W	2-1	Richards 19, Whitaker 53	3,157
45	div2	Leyton Orient	H	W	2-1	Richards 75, Howland 90	3,252
46	div2	Brighton	A	W	3-2	Richards 12, 19, Whitaker 87	7,741
47	div2	Huddersfield	H	D	0-0		4,150
48	div2	Swindon	A	L	0-6		7,361
49	div2	Northampton	H	D	2-2	Richards 30, Glover 49	4,556
50	div2	Southend	A	D	1-1	Mulligan 23	9,292

LEAGUE APPEARANCES, BOOKINGS AND GOALS

	AGE (on 01/07/08)	IN NAMED 16	APPEARANCES	COUNTING GAMES	MINUTES ON PITCH	LEAGUE GOALS	Yellow	Red
Goalkeepers								
Joe Anyon	21	44	44	44	3960	0	2	0
Chris Martin	17	16	2	2	180	0	0	0
Defenders								
Adam Eckersley	22	18	18	18	1582	1	3	1
Keith Lowe	22	31	28	21	2060	3	0	0
Mark McGregor	31	29	20	16	1619	0	6	0
Colin Miles	29	6	3	1	104	0	0	0
Justin Miller	27	16	14	11	1047	0	0	0
Dave Mulligan	26	18	13	8	898	1	2	0
Charlie O'Loughlin	19	4	3	0	66	0	0	0
Krystian Pearce	18	12	12	10	987	0	3	1
George Pilkington	26	45	45	44	4005	2	2	0
Luke Prosser	20	8	5	3	287	0	1	0
Mark Salmon	19	9	9	5	575	0	0	0
Chris Slater	18	12	5	1	189	0	0	0
Jason Talbot	22	32	25	18	1727	0	1	1
Michael Walsh	30	1	1	1	90	0	0	0
Ashley Westwood	31	13	12	9	930	0	1	1
Midfielders								
Will Atkinson	19	5	4	1	208	0	0	0
Joe Cardle	21	13	9	3	396	0	0	0
Ross Davidson	17	3	3	1	94	0	0	0
Paul Edwards	28	29	25	13	1564	2	3	0
Paul Harsley	30	43	41	37	3484	5	4	0
Chris Herd	19	11	11	11	988	2	3	1
David Howland	21	17	17	15	1425	1	6	0
Robin Hulbert	28	26	22	11	1342	0	4	0
Marc Laird	22	7	7	6	571	1	1	0
Simon Richman	18	6	6	5	492	0	2	0
Craig Rocastle	26	24	23	16	1635	1	4	0
Shane Tudor	26	15	14	7	784	0	1	0
Danny Whitaker	27	40	40	30	3074	7	3	0
Forwards								
Danny Glover	18	29	15	8	848	1	0	0
James Lawrie	17	17	6	0	33	0	0	0
David McGoldrick	20	18	17	13	1311	2	0	0
Tobias Mikaelsson	19	6	6	3	415	0	0	0
Kyle Perry	22	17	16	9	955	0	3	0
Marc Richards	25	31	29	15	1736	5	10	0
Luke Rodgers	26	36	36	29	2717	9	2	0
Akpo Sodje	28	3	3	2	241	0	0	0
Callum Willock	26	20	15	7	759	3	0	0

TEAM OF THE SEASON

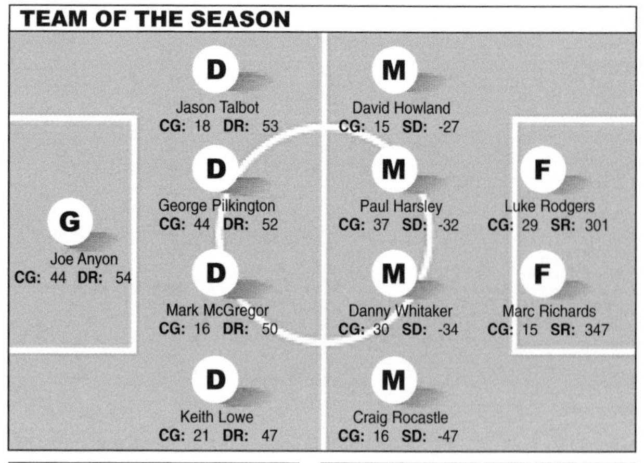

G
Joe Anyon
CG: 44 DR: 54
D
Jason Talbot
CG: 18 DR: 53
D
George Pilkington
CG: 44 DR: 52
D
Mark McGregor
CG: 16 DR: 50
D
Keith Lowe
CG: 21 DR: 47
M
David Howland
CG: 15 SD: -27
M
Paul Harsley
CG: 37 SD: -32
M
Danny Whitaker
CG: 30 SD: -34
M
Craig Rocastle
CG: 16 SD: -47
F
Luke Rodgers
CG: 29 SR: 301
F
Marc Richards
CG: 15 SR: 347

MONTHLY POINTS TALLY

Month	Points	%
AUGUST	1	11%
SEPTEMBER	4	27%
OCTOBER	6	40%
NOVEMBER	1	8%
DECEMBER	5	28%
JANUARY	4	22%
FEBRUARY	1	7%
MARCH	10	48%
APRIL	5	42%
MAY	1	33%

LEAGUE GOALS

	PLAYER	MINS	GOALS	S RATE
1	Rodgers	2717	**9**	301
2	Whitaker	3074	**7**	439
3	Richards	1736	**5**	347
4	Harsley	3484	**5**	696
5	Willock	759	**3**	253
6	Lowe	2060	**3**	686
7	Herd	988	**2**	494
8	McGoldrick	1311	**2**	655
9	Edwards, P	1564	**2**	782
10	Pilkington	4005	**2**	2002
11	Laird	571	**1**	571
12	Glover	848	**1**	848
13	Mulligan	898	**1**	898
	Other		3	
	TOTAL		**46**	

TOP POINT EARNERS

	PLAYER	GAMES	AV PTS
1	Marc Richards	15	**1.33**
2	Adam Eckersley	18	**1.11**
3	David Howland	15	**1.07**
4	Paul Harsley	37	**0.97**
5	Luke Rodgers	29	**0.93**
6	Danny Whitaker	30	**0.93**
7	George Pilkington	44	**0.86**
8	Joe Anyon	44	**0.84**
9	Craig Rocastle	16	**0.75**
10	David McGoldrick	13	**0.69**
	CLUB AVERAGE:		**0.83**

DISCIPLINARY RECORDS

	PLAYER	YELLOW	RED	AVE
1	Marc Richards	10	0	**173**
2	David Howland	6	0	**237**
3	Krystian Pearce	3	1	**246**
4	Simon Richman	2	0	**246**
5	Chris Herd	3	1	**247**
6	Mark McGregor	6	0	**269**
7	Kyle Perry	3	0	**318**
8	Robin Hulbert	4	0	**335**
9	Adam Eckersley	3	1	**395**
10	Craig Rocastle	4	0	**408**
11	Dave Mulligan	2	0	**449**
12	Ashley Westwood	1	1	**465**
13	Paul Edwards	3	0	**521**
	Other	16	1	
	TOTAL	**66**	**5**	

KEY GOALKEEPER

Joe Anyon

Goals Conceded in the League	73	**Counting Games** League games when player was on pitch for at least 70 minutes	44
Defensive Rating Ave number of mins between League goals conceded while on the pitch	54	**Clean Sheets** In League games when player was on pitch for at least 70 minutes	6

KEY PLAYERS - DEFENDERS

Jason Talbot

Goals Conceded Number of League goals conceded while the player was on the pitch	32	**Clean Sheets** In League games when player was on pitch for at least 70 minutes	2
Defensive Rating Ave number of mins between League goals conceded while on the pitch	53	**Club Defensive Rating** Average number of mins between League goals conceded by the club this season	51

	PLAYER	CON LGE	CLEAN SHEETS	DEF RATE
1	Jason Talbot	32	2	**53 mins**
2	George Pilkington	77	6	**52 mins**
3	Mark McGregor	32	2	**50 mins**
4	Keith Lowe	43	1	**47 mins**

KEY PLAYERS - MIDFIELDERS

David Howland

Goals in the League	1	**Contribution to Attacking Power** Average number of minutes between League team goals while on pitch	71
Defensive Rating Average number of mins between League goals conceded while on the pitch	44	**Scoring Difference** Defensive Rating minus Contribution to Attacking Power	-27

	PLAYER	LGE GOALS	DEF RATE	POWER	SCORE DIFF
1	David Howland	1	44	71	**-27 mins**
2	Paul Harsley	5	50	82	**-32 mins**
3	Danny Whitaker	7	49	83	**-34 mins**
4	Craig Rocastle	1	62	109	**-47 mins**

KEY PLAYERS - GOALSCORERS

Luke Rodgers

Goals in the League	9	**Player Strike Rate** Average number of minutes between League goals scored by player	301
Contribution to Attacking Power Average number of minutes between League team goals while on pitch	84	**Club Strike Rate** Average number of minutes between League goals scored by club	88

	PLAYER	LGE GOALS	POWER	STRIKE RATE
1	Luke Rodgers	9	84	**301 mins**
2	Marc Richards	5	86	**347 mins**
3	Danny Whitaker	7	83	**439 mins**
4	David McGoldrick	2	163	**655 mins**

Vandanel
SENNHE
George Pilkington

SQUAD APPEARANCES

Match	1	2	3	4	5	6	7	8	9	10	11	12	13	14	15	16	17	18	19	20	21	22	23	24	25
Venue	H	H	A	H	A	A	H	A	H	H	A	H	A	H	A	H	A	A	H	H	A	A	A	H	A
Competition	L	W	L	L	L	L	L	L	L	L	L	L	L	L	L	L	F	L	L	F	L	L	F	L	L
Result	D	L	L	L	W	D	L	L	L	W	L	L	L	W	L	L	W	D	L	D	L	W	L	D	L

Match	26	27	28	29	30	31	32	33	34	35	36	37	38	39	40	41	42	43	44	45	46	47	48	49	50
Venue	H	H	A	A	H	A	H	H	A	H	A	H	A	H	A	A	H	A	H	H	A	H	A	H	A
Competition	L	L	L	L	L	L	L	L	L	L	L	L	L	L	L	L	L	L	L	L	L	L	L	L	L
Result	D	L	L	L	W	L	L	D	L	D	L	L	L	L	L	W	D	L	W	W	W	D	L	D	D

Goalkeepers
Joe Anyon
Chris Martin
Defenders
Adam Eckersley
Keith Lowe
Mark McGregor
Colin Miles
Justin Miller
Dave Mulligan
Charlie O'Loughlin
Krystian Pearce
George Pilkington
Luke Prosser
Mark Salmon
Chris Slater
Jason Talbot
Michael Walsh
Ashley Westwood
Midfielders
Will Atkinson
Joe Cardle
Ross Davidson
Paul Edwards
Paul Harsley
Chris Herd
David Howland
Robin Hulbert
Marc Laird
Simon Richman
Craig Rocastle
Shane Tudor
Danny Whitaker
Forwards
Danny Glover
James Lawrie
David McGoldrick
Tobias Mikaelsson
Kyle Perry
Marc Richards
Luke Rodgers
Akpo Sodje
Callum Willock

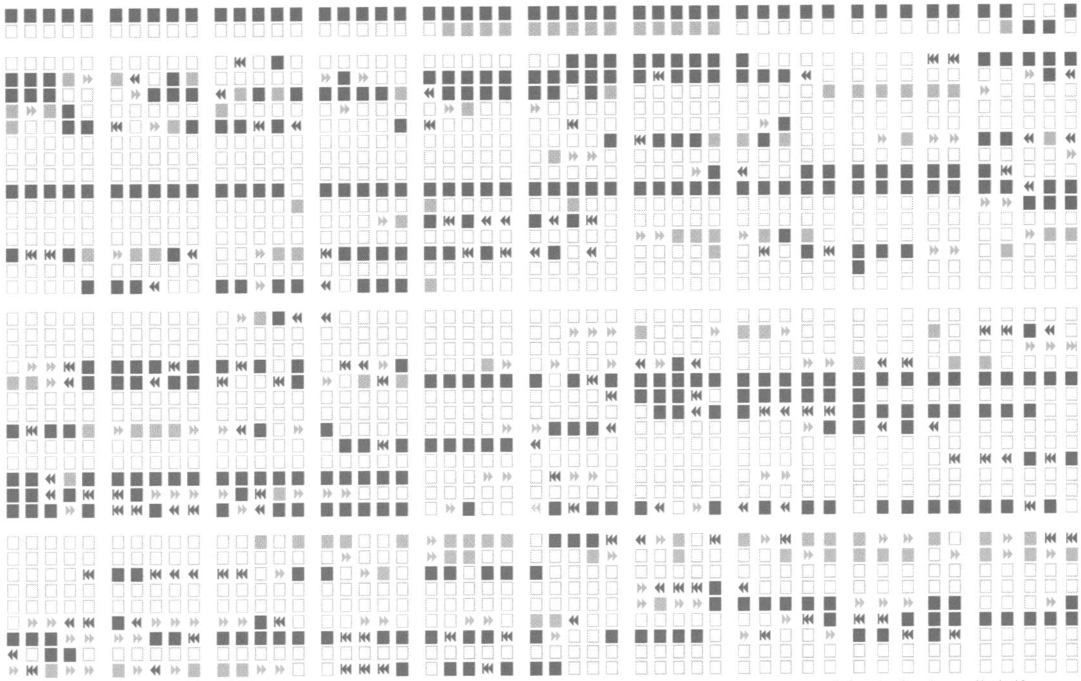

KEY: On all match | On bench | Subbed or sent off (Counting game) | Subbed or sent off (playing less than 70 minutes) | Subbed on from bench (Counting Game) | Subbed on (playing less than 70 minutes) | Subbed on and then subbed or sent off (Counting Game) | Subbed on and then subbed or sent off (playing less than 70 minutes) | Not in 16

LUTON TOWN

Final Position: **24th**

NICKNAME: THE HATTERS

KEY: ☐Won ☐Drawn ☐Lost

					Score	Scorers	Attendance
1	div2	**Hartlepool**	H	W	2-1	Currie 36, Goodall 84	8,013
2	ccr1	**Dag & Red**	A	W	2-1	Spring 42 pen, Talbot 68	1,754
3	div2	**Swindon**	A	L	1-2	Edwards 66	7,520
4	div2	**Gillingham**	H	W	3-1	Bell 17, Furlong 27, Spring 80 pen	6,178
5	ccr2	**Sunderland**	H	W	3-0	Bell 16, Furlong 43, 75	4,401
6	div2	**Leeds**	A	L	0-1		26,856
7	div2	**Bristol Rovers**	H	L	1-2	Spring 19 pen	6,131
8	div2	**Tranmere**	A	L	1-2	Furlong 5	6,525
9	div2	**Port Vale**	H	W	2-1	Furlong 30, Bell 86	6,084
10	ccr3	**Charlton**	H	W	3-1	Robinson 43, Spring 105, Talbot 117	4,534
11	div2	**Huddersfield**	A	L	0-2		9,028
12	div2	**Yeovil**	A	D	0-0		4,848
13	div2	**Doncaster**	H	D	1-1	Furlong 57	6,513
14	div2	**Northampton**	H	W	4-1	Currie 4, Spring 49 pen, 90 pen, Furlong 62	5,881
15	div2	**Crewe**	A	L	0-2		4,490
16	div2	**Nottm Forest**	H	W	2-1	Perry 52, Bell 88	8,524
17	ccr4	**Everton**	H	L	0-1		8,944
18	div2	**Brighton**	A	L	1-3	Edwards 79	5,317
19	div2	**Carlisle**	H	D	0-0		5,462
20	facr1	**Brentford**	H	D	1-1	Andrew 79	4,167
21	div2	**Walsall**	A	D	0-0		5,056
22	div2	**Southend**	H	W	1-0	Andrew 74	6,820
23	facr1r	**Brentford**	A	W	2-0	Coyne 36, Fojut 61	2,643
24	div2	**Oldham**	A	D	1-1	Fojut 34	4,251
25	facr2	**Nottm Forest**	H	W	1-0	Andrew 54	5,758
26	div2	**Cheltenham**	A	L	0-1		3,702
27	div2	**Tranmere**	H	W	1-0	Edwards 70	6,070
28	div2	**Bristol Rovers**	A	D	1-1	Edwards 49	7,556
29	div2	**Port Vale**	A	W	2-1	Fojut 3, Spring 90	4,224
30	div2	**Yeovil**	H	W	1-0	Andrew 48	6,811
31	facr3	**Liverpool**	H	D	1-1	Riise 77 og	10,226
32	div2	**Swansea**	H	L	1-3	Furlong 74	6,756
33	facr3r	**Liverpool**	A	L	0-5		41,446
34	div2	**Leyton Orient**	A	L	1-2	Keane 67	5,516
35	div2	**Bournemouth**	A	L	3-4	Spring 45 pen, Morgan 60, Furlong 78	3,489
36	div2	**Leeds**	H	D	1-1	Parkin 90	9,227
37	div2	**Swindon**	H	L	0-1		5,738
38	div2	**Hartlepool**	A	L	0-4		3,913
39	div2	**Bournemouth**	H	L	1-4	Emanuel 50	5,897
40	div2	**Leyton Orient**	H	L	0-1		6,412
41	div2	**Swansea**	A	L	0-1		14,122
42	div2	**Millwall**	H	D	1-1	Furlong 19	6,417
43	div2	**Walsall**	H	L	0-1		6,157
44	div2	**Southend**	A	L	0-2		8,241
45	div2	**Carlisle**	A	L	1-2	Bell 51	5,489
46	div2	**Oldham**	H	W	3-0	Charles 20, Spring 33 pen, Emanuel 35	5,417
47	div2	**Cheltenham**	H	D	1-1	Parkin 24	6,087
48	div2	**Millwall**	A	D	0-0		8,375
49	div2	**Crewe**	H	W	2-1	Spring 4, 78 pen	5,465
50	div2	**Gillingham**	A	L	1-2	Parkin 19	6,142
51	div2	**Northampton**	A	L	1-2	Parkin 90	5,132
52	div2	**Brighton**	H	L	1-2	Parkin 49	6,652
53	div2	**Nottm Forest**	A	L	0-1		17,331
54	div2	**Doncaster**	A	L	0-2		9,332
55	div2	**Huddersfield**	H	L	0-1		6,539

LEAGUE APPEARANCES, BOOKINGS AND GOALS

	AGE (on 01/07/08)	IN NAMED 16	APPEARANCES	COUNTING GAMES	MINUTES ON PITCH	LEAGUE GOALS	Yellow	Red
Goalkeepers								
Ben Alnwick	21	4	4	4	360	0	0	0
Dean Brill	22	37	37	37	3330	0	0	0
David Forde	28	5	5	5	450	0	0	0
Defenders								
Ed Asafu-Adjaye	21	7	7	7	630	0	1	0
Chris Coyne	29	21	18	16	1486	0	2	1
Sol Davis	28	16	15	14	1195	0	2	1
Lewis Emanuel	24	19	17	14	1322	2	1	0
Jaroslav Fojut	20	18	16	14	1308	2	1	0
Alan Goodall	26	38	29	25	2322	1	4	1
Anthony Grant	21	6	4	1	149	0	1	1
Richard Jackson	28	36	29	26	2428	0	2	0
Chris Perry	35	36	35	32	3047	1	5	0
Midfielders								
George Beavan	18	10	2	2	170	0	0	0
David Bell	24	32	32	29	2762	4	3	0
Darren Currie	33	41	31	20	2185	2	3	0
David Edwards	22	21	19	17	1568	4	1	0
Don Hutchison	37	32	21	14	1335	0	1	0
Keith Keane	21	34	28	26	2395	1	2	0
Richard Langley	28	3	1	0	16	0	0	0
Dean Morgan	24	20	16	5	770	1	0	0
Stephen O'Leary	23	21	16	10	1045	0	2	0
Steve Robinson	33	34	27	18	2042	0	9	1
Matthew Spring	28	44	44	44	3960	9	9	0
Marc Wilson	20	4	4	4	360	0	1	0
Forwards								
Calvin Andrew	21	42	39	16	1900	2	2	0
Ryan Charles	18	9	7	6	503	1	0	0
Paul Furlong	39	32	32	20	2058	8	5	1
Paul McVeigh	30	36	25	10	1259	0	1	0
Sam Parkin	27	20	19	11	1228	5	0	0
Paul Peschisolido	37	4	4	1	162	0	0	0
Drew Talbot	21	34	27	13	1553	0	1	0

TEAM OF THE SEASON

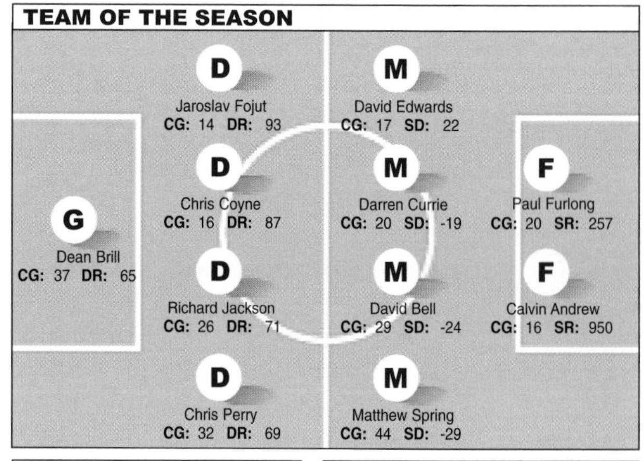

D
Jaroslav Fojut
CG: 14 DR: 93
M
David Edwards
CG: 17 SD: 22
D
Chris Coyne
CG: 16 DR: 87
M
Darren Currie
CG: 20 SD: -19
F
Paul Furlong
CG: 20 SR: 257
G
Dean Brill
CG: 37 DR: 65
D
Richard Jackson
CG: 26 DR: 71
M
David Bell
CG: 29 SD: -24
F
Calvin Andrew
CG: 16 SR: 950
D
Chris Perry
CG: 32 DR: 69
M
Matthew Spring
CG: 44 SD: -29

MONTHLY POINTS TALLY

Month	Points	%
AUGUST	6	67%
SEPTEMBER	3	20%
OCTOBER	8	53%
NOVEMBER	5	42%
DECEMBER	8	53%
JANUARY	4	22%
FEBRUARY	1	7%
MARCH	8	38%
APRIL	0	0%
MAY	0	0%

LEAGUE GOALS

	PLAYER	MINS	GOALS	S RATE
1	Spring	3960	**9**	440
2	Furlong	2058	**8**	257
3	Parkin	1228	**5**	245
4	Edwards, D	1568	**4**	392
5	Bell	2762	**4**	690
6	Fojut	1308	**2**	654
7	Emanuel	1322	**2**	661
8	Andrew	1900	**2**	950
9	Currie	2185	**2**	1092
10	Charles	503	**1**	503
11	Morgan	770	**1**	770
12	Goodall	2322	**1**	2322
13	Keane	2395	**1**	2395
	Other		1	
	TOTAL		**43**	

TOP POINT EARNERS

	PLAYER	GAMES	AV PTS
1	David Edwards	17	**1.71**
2	Jaroslav Fojut	14	**1.50**
3	Chris Coyne	16	**1.38**
4	Calvin Andrew	16	**1.19**
5	David Bell	29	**1.17**
6	Alan Goodall	25	**1.12**
7	Darren Currie	20	**1.05**
8	Chris Perry	32	**1.03**
9	Richard Jackson	26	**0.96**
10	Matthew Spring	44	**0.95**
	CLUB AVERAGE:		**0.72**

DISCIPLINARY RECORDS

	PLAYER	YELLOW	RED	AVE
1	Steve Robinson	9	1	**204**
2	Paul Furlong	5	1	**343**
3	Sol Davis	2	1	**398**
4	Matthew Spring	9	0	**440**
5	Alan Goodall	4	1	**464**
6	Chris Coyne	2	1	**495**
7	Stephen O'Leary	2	0	**522**
8	Chris Perry	5	0	**609**
9	Ed Asafu-Adjaye	1	0	**630**
10	Darren Currie	3	0	**728**
11	David Bell	3	0	**920**
12	Calvin Andrew	2	0	**950**
13	Keith Keane	2	0	**1197**
	Other	8	0	
	TOTAL	**57**	**5**	

KEY GOALKEEPER

Dean Brill

Goals Conceded in the League	51	Counting Games League games when player was on pitch for at least 70 minutes	37
Defensive Rating Ave number of mins between League goals conceded while on the pitch	65	Clean Sheets In League games when player was on pitch for at least 70 minutes	7

KEY PLAYERS - DEFENDERS

Jaroslav Fojut

Goals Conceded Number of League goals conceded while the player was on the pitch	14	Clean Sheets In League games when player was on pitch for at least 70 minutes	5
Defensive Rating Ave number of mins between League goals conceded while on the pitch	93	Club Defensive Rating Average number of mins between League goals conceded by the club this season	68

	PLAYER	CON LGE	CLEAN SHEETS	DEF RATE
1	Jaroslav Fojut	14	5	93 mins
2	Chris Coyne	17	5	87 mins
3	Richard Jackson	34	5	71 mins
4	Chris Perry	44	5	69 mins

KEY PLAYERS - MIDFIELDERS

David Edwards

Goals in the League	4	Contribution to Attacking Power Average number of minutes between League team goals while on pitch	82
Defensive Rating Average number of mins between League goals conceded while on the pitch	104	Scoring Difference Defensive Rating minus Contribution to Attacking Power	22

	PLAYER	LGE GOALS	DEF RATE	POWER	SCORE DIFF
1	David Edwards	4	104	82	22 mins
2	Darren Currie	2	68	87	-19 mins
3	David Bell	4	74	98	-24 mins
4	Matthew Spring	9	67	96	-29 mins

KEY PLAYERS - GOALSCORERS

Paul Furlong

Goals in the League	8	Player Strike Rate Average number of minutes between League goals scored by player	257
Contribution to Attacking Power Average number of minutes between League team goals while on pitch	70	Club Strike Rate Average number of minutes between League goals scored by club	100

	PLAYER	LGE GOALS	POWER	STRIKE RATE
1	Paul Furlong	8	70	257 mins
2	David Edwards	4	82	392 mins
3	Matthew Spring	9	96	440 mins
4	David Bell	4	98	690 mins

Electrolux

Sam Parkin

SQUAD APPEARANCES

Match	1	2	3	4	5	6	7	8	9	10	11	12	13	14	15	16	17	18	19	20	21	22	23	24	25	26	27	28	29	30	31	32	33	34	35	36	37	38	39	40	41	42	43	44	45	46	47	48	49	50	51	52	53	54	55
Venue	H	A	A	H	H	A	H	A	H	H	A	A	H	H	A	H	H	A	H	H	A	H	A	A	H	A	H	A	A	H	H	H	A	A	A	H	H	A	H	H	A	H	H	A	A	H	H	A	H	A	A	H	A	A	H
Competition	L	W	L	L	W	L	L	L	L	W	L	L	L	L	L	L	W	L	L	F	L	L	F	L	F	L	L	L	L	L	F	L	F	L	L	L	L	L	L	L	L	L	L	L	L	L	L	L	L	L	L	L	L	L	L
Result	W	W	L	W	W	L	L	L	W	W	L	D	D	W	L	W	L	L	D	D	D	W	W	D	W	L	W	D	W	W	D	L	L	L	L	D	L	L	L	L	L	D	L	L	L	W	D	D	W	L	L	L	L	L	L

Goalkeepers
Ben Alnwick
Dean Brill
David Forde
Defenders
Ed Asafu-Adjaye
Chris Coyne
Sol Davis
Lewis Emanuel
Jaroslav Fojut
Alan Goodall
Anthony Grant
Richard Jackson
Chris Perry
Midfielders
George Beavan
David Bell
Darren Currie
David Edwards
Don Hutchison
Keith Keane
Richard Langley
Dean Morgan
Stephen O'Leary
Steve Robinson
Matthew Spring
Marc Wilson
Forwards
Calvin Andrew
Ryan Charles
Paul Furlong
Paul McVeigh
Sam Parkin
Paul Peschisolido
Drew Talbot

KEY: On all match · On bench · Subbed or sent off (Counting game) · Subbed or sent off (playing less than 70 minutes) · Subbed on from bench (Counting Game) · Subbed on (playing less than 70 minutes) · Subbed on and then subbed or sent off (Counting Game) · Subbed on and then subbed or sent off (playing less than 70 minutes) · Not in 16

LEAGUE TWO ROUND-UP

FINAL LEAGUE TABLE

	P	HOME W	HOME D	HOME L	HOME F	HOME A	AWAY W	AWAY D	AWAY L	AWAY F	AWAY A	TOTAL F	TOTAL A	TOTAL DIF	PTS
M K Dons	46	11	7	5	39	17	18	3	2	43	20	82	37	45	97
Peterborough	46	14	4	5	46	20	14	4	5	38	23	84	43	41	92
Hereford	46	11	6	6	34	19	15	4	4	38	22	72	41	31	88
Stockport	46	11	5	7	40	30	13	5	5	32	24	72	54	18	82
Rochdale	46	11	4	8	37	28	12	7	4	40	26	77	54	23	80
Darlington	46	11	7	5	36	22	11	5	7	31	18	67	40	27	78
Wycombe	46	13	6	4	29	15	9	6	8	27	27	56	42	14	78
Chesterfield	46	9	8	6	42	29	10	4	9	34	27	76	56	20	69
Rotherham	46	12	4	7	37	29	9	7	7	25	29	62	58	4	64
Bradford	46	10	4	9	30	30	7	7	9	33	31	63	61	2	62
Morecambe	46	9	6	8	33	32	7	6	10	26	31	59	63	-4	60
Barnet	46	10	6	7	37	30	6	6	11	19	33	56	63	-7	60
Bury	46	8	6	9	30	30	8	5	10	28	31	58	61	-3	59
Brentford	46	7	5	11	25	35	10	3	10	27	35	52	70	-18	59
Lincoln City	46	9	3	11	33	38	9	1	13	28	39	61	77	-16	58
Grimsby	46	7	5	11	26	34	8	5	10	29	32	55	66	-11	55
Accrington	46	7	1	15	20	39	9	2	12	29	44	49	83	-34	51
Shrewsbury	46	9	6	8	31	22	3	8	12	25	43	56	65	-9	50
Macclesfield	46	6	8	9	27	31	5	9	9	20	33	47	64	-17	50
Dag & Red	46	6	7	10	27	32	7	3	13	22	38	49	70	-21	49
Notts County	46	8	5	10	19	23	2	13	8	18	30	37	53	-16	48
Chester	46	5	5	13	21	30	7	6	10	30	38	51	68	-17	47
Mansfield	46	6	3	14	30	39	5	6	12	18	29	48	68	-20	42
Wrexham	46	6	7	10	16	28	4	3	16	22	42	38	70	-32	40

CLUB STRIKE FORCE

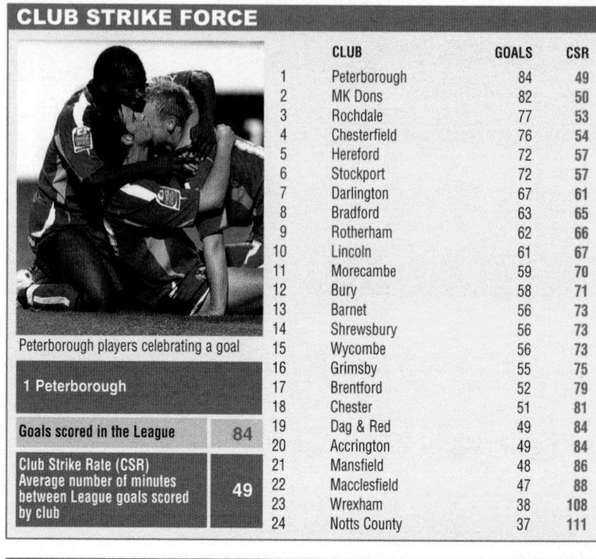

Peterborough players celebrating a goal

1 Peterborough

Goals scored in the League	84
Club Strike Rate (CSR) Average number of minutes between League goals scored by club	49

	CLUB	GOALS	CSR
1	Peterborough	84	49
2	MK Dons	82	50
3	Rochdale	77	53
4	Chesterfield	76	54
5	Hereford	72	57
6	Stockport	72	57
7	Darlington	67	61
8	Bradford	63	65
9	Rotherham	62	66
10	Lincoln	61	67
11	Morecambe	59	70
12	Bury	58	71
13	Barnet	56	73
14	Shrewsbury	56	73
15	Wycombe	56	73
16	Grimsby	55	75
17	Brentford	52	79
18	Chester	51	81
19	Dag & Red	49	84
20	Accrington	49	84
21	Mansfield	48	86
22	Macclesfield	47	88
23	Wrexham	38	108
24	Notts County	37	111

CLUB DISCIPLINARY RECORDS

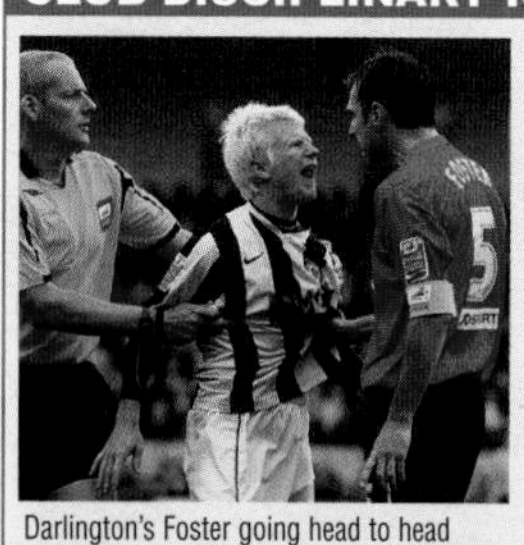

Darlington's Foster going head to head

1 Darlington

League Yellow	87
League Red	6
League Total	93
Cards Average in League Average number of minutes between a card being shown of either colour	44

	CLUB	Y	R	TOTAL	AVE
1	Darlington	87	6	93	44
2	Macclesfield	91	1	92	45
3	MK Dons	83	4	87	47
4	Wrexham	77	4	81	51
5	Accrington	75	5	80	51
6	Chesterfield	76	1	77	53
7	Chester	70	4	74	55
8	Peterborough	68	1	69	60
9	Rochdale	61	4	65	63
10	Barnet	59	6	65	63
11	Bury	58	3	61	67
12	Shrewsbury	60	1	61	67
13	Brentford	54	5	59	70
14	Wycombe	55	2	57	72
15	Grimsby	52	5	57	72
16	Morecambe	54	2	56	73
17	Lincoln	48	8	56	73
18	Notts County	53	2	55	75
19	Bradford	51	3	54	76
20	Mansfield	47	6	53	78
21	Stockport	44	3	47	88
22	Rotherham	40	0	40	103
23	Hereford	37	1	38	108
24	Dag & Red	36	2	38	108

CLUB DEFENCES

	CLUB	LGE	CS	CDR
1	MK Dons	37	20	111
2	Darlington	40	24	103
3	Hereford	41	19	100
4	Wycombe	42	19	98
5	Peterborough	43	16	96
6	Notts County	53	14	78
7	Stockport	54	17	76
8	Rochdale	54	12	76
9	Chesterfield	56	11	73
10	Rotherham	58	13	71
11	Bury	61	8	67
12	Bradford	61	9	67
13	Barnet	63	11	65
14	Morecambe	63	7	65
15	Macclesfield	64	11	64
16	Shrewsbury	65	13	63
17	Grimsby	66	10	62
18	Mansfield	68	8	60
19	Chester	68	8	60
20	Dag & Red	70	11	59
21	Brentford	70	7	59
22	Wrexham	70	12	59
23	Lincoln	77	6	53
24	Accrington	83	8	49

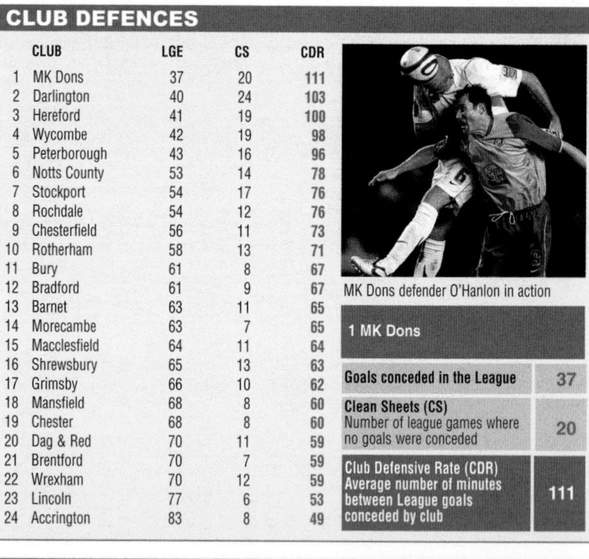

MK Dons defender O'Hanlon in action

1 MK Dons

Goals conceded in the League	37
Clean Sheets (CS) Number of league games where no goals were conceded	20
Club Defensive Rate (CDR) Average number of minutes between League goals conceded by club	111

STADIUM CAPACITY AND HOME CROWDS

	TEAM	CAPACITY	AVE	HIGH	LOW
1	Bradford	25136	54.48	15510	13072
2	Shrewsbury	10840	52.20	7707	4499
3	Stockport	10817	52.16	8838	4477
4	Chesterfield	8502	48.26	6300	3274
5	Wycombe	10000	47.46	6202	3821
6	Rotherham	9624	44.56	6709	2979
7	Morecambe	6400	43.93	4761	1634
8	MK Dons	22000	42.98	17250	6483
9	Chester	6000	41.32	3849	1566
10	Grimsby	10033	41.01	5829	2537
11	Lincoln	10127	40.27	5286	3189
12	Peterborough	15460	38.78	10400	4200
13	Barnet	5560	37.83	3074	1303
14	Macclesfield	6208	37.01	3585	1378
15	Brentford	12763	35.02	6246	3155
16	Dag & Red	6000	33.46	3451	1328
17	Accrington	5057	32.31	2898	1149
18	Rochdale	10249	29.82	4692	2278
19	Mansfield	9954	28.89	5271	1923
20	Wrexham	15500	27.32	7687	2805
21	Hereford	13777	24.83	6020	2271
22	Notts County	20300	23.31	10027	3421
23	Bury	11699	22.23	6271	1690
24	Darlington	25000	15.27	6965	2628

Key: Average. The percentage of each stadium filled in League games over the season (AVE), the stadium capacity and the highest and lowest crowds recorded.

AWAY ATTENDANCE

	TEAM	AVE	HIGH	LOW
1	MK Dons	40.21	14609	1559
2	Peterborough	39.21	14521	1484
3	Mansfield	39.18	13611	1408
4	Stockport	39.15	13837	1834
5	Darlington	38.25	14074	1678
6	Wrexham	37.93	13546	1521
7	Notts County	37.61	13494	1649
8	Hereford	37.56	13640	1262
9	Rotherham	37.39	13436	1715
10	Lincoln	37.32	15510	1281
11	Morecambe	37.24	17250	1448
12	Rochdale	37.14	14017	1621
13	Chesterfield	37.08	13825	1448
14	Bradford	36.53	7903	1566
15	Wycombe	36.07	13530	1200
16	Chester	36.05	13211	1311
17	Bury	34.82	13844	1597
18	Grimsby	34.48	13448	1350
19	Shrewsbury	34.09	13269	1410
20	Barnet	33.64	13072	1288
21	Brentford	33.53	13326	1149
22	Macclesfield	33.46	13401	1303
23	Accrington	32.69	13346	1596
24	Dag & Red	32.61	13537	1262

Key: Average. How close each club has come to filling grounds in its away league matches (AVE) and the highest and lowest crowds recorded.

CHART-TOPPING MIDFIELDERS

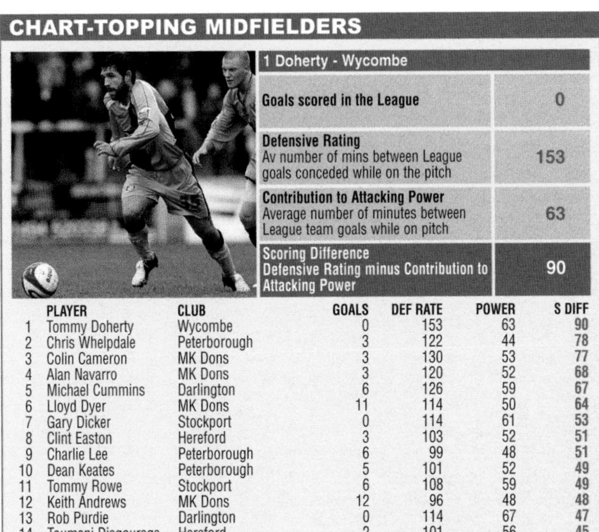

1 Doherty - Wycombe	
Goals scored in the League	0
Defensive Rating Av number of mins between League goals conceded while on the pitch	153
Contribution to Attacking Power Average number of minutes between League team goals while on pitch	63
Scoring Difference Defensive Rating minus Contribution to Attacking Power	90

	PLAYER	CLUB	GOALS	DEF RATE	POWER	S DIFF
1	Tommy Doherty	Wycombe	0	153	63	90
2	Chris Whelpdale	Peterborough	3	122	44	78
3	Colin Cameron	MK Dons	3	130	53	77
4	Alan Navarro	MK Dons	3	120	52	68
5	Michael Cummins	Darlington	6	126	59	67
6	Lloyd Dyer	MK Dons	11	114	50	64
7	Gary Dicker	Stockport	0	114	61	53
8	Clint Easton	Hereford	3	103	52	51
9	Charlie Lee	Peterborough	6	99	48	51
10	Dean Keates	Peterborough	5	101	52	49
11	Tommy Rowe	Stockport	6	108	59	49
12	Keith Andrews	MK Dons	12	96	48	48
13	Rob Purdie	Darlington	0	114	67	47
14	Toumani Diagouraga	Hereford	2	101	56	45
15	Lionel Ainsworth	Hereford	4	90	46	44

CHART-TOPPING GOALSCORERS

1 Lester - Chesterfield	
Goals scored in the League	23
Contribution to Attacking Power (AP) Average number of minutes between League team goals while on pitch	50
Club Strike Rate (CSR) Average minutes between League goals scored by club	54
Player Strike Rate Average number of minutes between League goals scored by player	130

	PLAYER	CLUB	GOALS: LGE	POWER	CSR	S RATE
1	Jack Lester	Chesterfield	23	50	54	130
2	Aaron McLean	Peterborough	29	49	50	135
3	Anthony Elding	Stockport	13	57	61	136
4	Gary Hooper	Hereford	11	62	58	147
5	Scott McGleish	Wycombe	25	78	73	151
6	Liam Dickinson	Stockport	19	54	61	164
7	Ben Wright	Lincoln	14	62	69	170
8	Kevin Gallen	MK Dons	8	50	51	176
9	Michael Boulding	Mansfield	21	79	90	178
10	Andrew Bishop	Bury	19	72	74	179
11	Rene Howe	Rochdale	9	49	59	181
12	Adam Le Fondre	Rochdale	15	52	59	185
13	Peter Thorne	Bradford	14	57	70	190
14	Danny North	Grimsby	9	72	75	200
15	Mark Wright	MK Dons	13	52	51	200

CHART-TOPPING DEFENDERS

1 Rose - Stockport	
Goals Conceded in the League The number of League goals conceded while he was on the pitch	16
Clean Sheets In games when he played at least 70 mins	14
Club Defensive Rating Average mins between League goals conceded by the club this season	81
Defensive Rating Average number of minutes between League goals conceded while on pitch	146

	PLAYER	CLUB	CON: LGE	CS	CDR	DEF RATE
1	Michael Rose	Stockport	16	14	81	146
2	Drissa Diallo	MK Dons	19	14	114	134
3	Jude Stirling	MK Dons	16	12	114	133
4	Claude Gnakpa	Peterborough	17	10	98	128
5	Chris Westwood	Peterborough	25	15	98	125
6	Danny Swailes	MK Dons	29	18	114	122
7	Craig Woodman	Wycombe	20	12	98	120
8	Sam Hird	Grimsby	11	7	62	118
9	Dean Beckwith	Hereford	28	19	103	118
10	Stephen Foster	Darlington	33	24	110	115
11	Marcus Holness	Rochdale	12	6	85	115
12	David McCracken	Wycombe	27	14	98	115
13	Dean Lewington	MK Dons	36	19	114	111
14	Ryan Valentine	Darlington	11	5	110	108
15	Richard Rose	Hereford	25	13	103	108

CHART-TOPPING GOALKEEPERS

1 Ruddy - Stockport	
Counting Games Games in which he played at least 70 minutes	13
Goals Conceded in the League The number of League goals conceded while he was on the pitch	7
Clean Sheets In games when he played at least 70 mins	9
Defensive Rating Average number of minutes between League goals conceded while on pitch	167

	PLAYER	CLUB	CG	CONC	CS	DEF RATE
1	John Ruddy	Stockport	13	7	9	167
2	Joe Lewis	Peterborough	22	15	11	131
3	Willy Gueret	MK Dons	46	37	20	111
4	Frank Fielding	Wycombe	34	31	15	100
5	Russell Hoult	Notts County	14	13	7	96
6	Darren Randolph	Bury	14	13	4	96
7	Wayne Brown	Hereford	44	41	17	96
8	David Stockdale	Darlington	39	38	19	93
9	Joe Lewis	Morecambe	19	20	6	87
10	Mark Tyler	Peterborough	17	19	3	80
11	Barry Roche	Chesterfield	45	54	11	75
12	Jonathan Brain	Macclesfield	28	35	7	73
13	Kevin Pilkington	Notts County	32	40	7	72
14	Sam Russell	Rochdale	15	19	6	71
15	Andy Warrington	Rotherham	46	58	13	71

PLAYER DISCIPLINARY RECORD

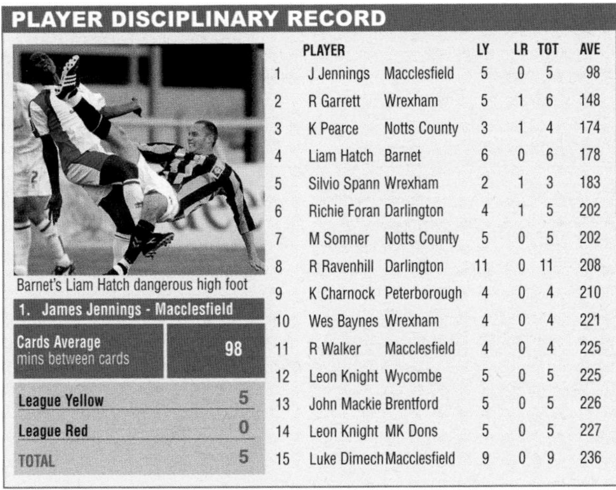

Barnet's Liam Hatch dangerous high foot

1. James Jennings - Macclesfield	
Cards Average mins between cards	98
League Yellow	5
League Red	0
TOTAL	5

	PLAYER		LY	LR	TOT	AVE
1	J Jennings	Macclesfield	5	0	5	98
2	R Garrett	Wrexham	5	1	6	148
3	K Pearce	Notts County	3	1	4	174
4	Liam Hatch	Barnet	6	0	6	178
5	Silvio Spann	Wrexham	2	1	3	183
6	Richie Foran	Darlington	4	1	5	202
7	M Somner	Notts County	5	0	5	202
8	R Ravenhill	Darlington	11	0	11	208
9	K Charnock	Peterborough	4	0	4	210
10	Wes Baynes	Wrexham	4	0	4	221
11	R Walker	Macclesfield	4	0	4	225
12	Leon Knight	Wycombe	5	0	5	225
13	John Mackie	Brentford	5	0	5	226
14	Leon Knight	MK Dons	5	0	5	227
15	Luke Dimech	Macclesfield	9	0	9	236

TEAM OF THE SEASON

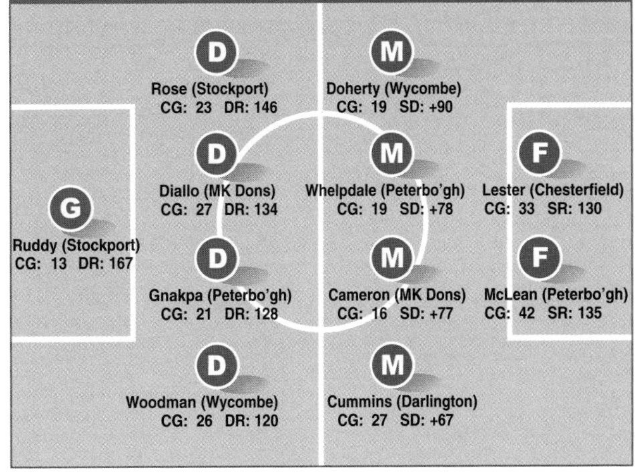
D
Rose (Stockport)
CG: 23 DR: 146
M
Doherty (Wycombe)
CG: 19 SD: +90
G
Ruddy (Stockport)
CG: 13 DR: 167
D
Diallo (MK Dons)
CG: 27 DR: 134
M
Whelpdale (Peterbo'gh)
CG: 19 SD: +78
F
Lester (Chesterfield)
CG: 33 SR: 130
D
Gnakpa (Peterbo'gh)
CG: 21 DR: 128
M
Cameron (MK Dons)
CG: 16 SD: +77
F
McLean (Peterbo'gh)
CG: 42 SR: 135
D
Woodman (Wycombe)
CG: 26 DR: 120
M
Cummins (Darlington)
CG: 27 SD: +67

COCA-COLA LEAGUE TWO CHAMPIONS

MK DONS

Final Position: **1st**

NICKNAME: THE DONS/WOMBLES

KEY: ☐Won ☐Drawn ☐Lost

	Comp	Opponent	H/A	Res	Score	Scorers	Attendance
1	div3	Bury	H	L	1-2	Andrews 21	7,740
2	ccr1	Ipswich	H	W	5-3*	Knight 16, Bruce 22 og, Gallen 120 pen (*on penalties)	7,496
3	div3	Macclesfield	A	D	3-3	Andrews 20, Knight 73, Cameron 90	2,257
4	div3	Shrewsbury	H	W	3-0	Knight 47, Dyer 78, Andrews 84	7,380
5	ccr2	Sheff Utd	H	L	2-3	Broughton 12, McGovern 78	7,943
6	div3	Rochdale	A	L	2-3	Gallen 16, 28	2,743
7	div3	Notts County	H	W	3-0	Andrews 41, Swailes 67, Wilbraham 85	7,977
8	div3	Brentford	A	W	3-0	Andrews 4, 79, Johnson 90	4,476
9	div3	Darlington	H	W	1-0	Diallo 89	7,901
10	div3	Morecambe	A	W	1-0	Dyer 21	2,688
11	div3	Mansfield	A	W	2-1	Dyer 72, Stirling 83	1,984
12	div3	Bradford	H	W	2-1	Andrews 73, Swailes 81	7,903
13	div3	Lincoln	H	W	4-0	Knight 45, 82, Dyer 70, Wilbraham 78	13,037
14	div3	Hereford	A	W	1-0	Wright 87	3,936
15	div3	Stockport	H	L	0-2		8,290
16	div3	Wycombe	A	D	1-1	Cameron 45	5,929
17	div3	Grimsby	H	W	2-0	Wilbraham 1, Wright 41	6,797
18	facr1	Crewe	A	L	1-2	Johnson 69 pen	3,049
19	div3	Chester	A	W	2-0	Wright 38, Johnson 64	3,102
20	div3	Chesterfield	H	L	1-2	Wright 10	9,638
21	div3	Dag & Red	A	W	1-0	Diallo 24	1,880
22	div3	Accrington	H	W	5-0	Andrews 9, Navarro 25, Cameron 33 Dyer 49, 77	6,917
23	div3	Peterborough	A	W	2-1	Gallen 47, Andrews 57	10,351
24	div3	Brentford	H	D	1-1	Gallen 68	8,445
25	div3	Notts County	A	W	2-1	Wright 15, Johnson 90	5,106
26	div3	Darlington	A	W	1-0	Johnson 84	5,304
27	div3	Mansfield	H	W	1-0	Andrews 58	9,583
28	div3	Rotherham	A	W	1-0	Wright 82	5,421
29	div3	Barnet	H	L	0-1		9,881
30	div3	Wrexham	A	L	0-1		4,319
31	div3	Rochdale	H	L	0-1		7,882
32	div3	Macclesfield	H	D	1-1	O'Hanlon 50	6,483
33	div3	Bury	A	W	5-1	Wright 10, 36, 68, Dyer 23, Gallen 81	2,241
34	div3	Rotherham	H	D	1-1	Gallen 16	9,455
35	div3	Shrewsbury	A	D	3-3	Wright 32, 40, Gallen 35	5,474
36	div3	Barnet	A	W	2-0	Navarro 13, Dyer 17	2,495
37	div3	Chester	H	W	1-0	Swailes 57	8,172
38	div3	Grimsby	A	W	1-0	O'Hanlon 10	4,106
39	div3	Chesterfield	A	W	2-1	Andrews 42, Dyer 70	3,834
40	div3	Dag & Red	H	W	4-0	Wilbraham 3, 37, Dyer 10, Gallen 82	9,417
41	div3	Peterborough	H	D	1-1	Wilbraham 12	14,521
42	div3	Accrington	A	W	1-0	Wright 83	1,559
43	div3	Lincoln	A	W	2-1	Regan 3, Johnson 55	3,896
44	div3	Wrexham	H	W	4-1	Swailes 2, Wilbraham 10, 90, O'Hanlon 75	8,646
45	div3	Wycombe	H	D	2-2	Wilbraham 72, O'Hanlon 90	12,747
46	div3	Hereford	H	D	0-0		11,428
47	div3	Stockport	A	W	3-2	Wright 31, Navarro 59, Andrews 74	8,838
48	div3	Bradford	A	W	2-1	Stirling 13, Dyer 18	14,609
49	div3	Morecambe	H	D	1-1	Wilbraham 41	17,250

TEAM OF THE SEASON

G — Willy Gueret — CG: 46 DR: 111

D — Drissa Diallo — CG: 27 DR: 134

D — Jude Stirling — CG: 18 DR: 133

D — Danny Swailes — CG: 39 DR: 122

D — Dean Lewington — CG: 44 DR: 111

M — Colin Cameron — CG: 16 SD: 77

M — Alan Navarro — CG: 37 SD: 68

M — Lloyd Dyer — CG: 39 SD: 64

M — Keith Andrews — CG: 39 SD: 48

F — Kevin Gallen — CG: 13 SR: 176

F — Aaron Wilbraham — CG: 24 SR: 247

KEY PLAYER APPEARANCES

	PLAYER	POS	AGE	APP	MINS ON	GOALS	CARDS(Y)	CARDS(R)
1	Willy Gueret	GK	34	46	4140	0	4	0
2	Dean Lewington	DEF	24	45	4013	0	5	0
3	Lloyd Dyer	MID	25	45	3660	11	1	1
4	Keith Andrews	MID	27	41	3587	12	12	1
5	Danny Swailes	DEF	29	40	3565	4	10	0
6	Sean O'Hanlon	DEF	25	43	3525	4	6	0
7	Alan Navarro	MID	27	39	3361	3	10	0
8	Mark Wright	MID	26	34	2604	13	2	0
9	Drissa Diallo	DEF	35	30	2549	2	4	2
10	Aaron Wilbraham	ATT	28	34	2472	10	3	0
11	Jude Stirling	DEF	26	35	2134	2	7	0
12	Jemal Johnson	ATT	23	39	1855	5	5	0
13	Colin Cameron	MID	35	29	1822	3	1	0
14	Kevin Gallen	ATT	32	24	1410	8	1	0
15	Leon Knight	ATT	25	17	1135	4	5	0
16	Luke Howell	MID	21	8	672	0	2	0
17	Carl Regan	DEF	27	9	646	1	2	0
18	John Miles	ATT	26	12	626	0	1	0

KEY PLAYERS - GOALSCORERS

Kevin Gallen

Goals in the League	8
Contribution to Attacking Power Average number of minutes between League team goals while on pitch	50
Player Strike Rate Average number of minutes between League goals scored by player	176
Club Strike Rate Average number of minutes between League goals scored by club	51

	PLAYER	GOALS LGE	POWER	STRIKE RATE
1	Kevin Gallen	8	50	176 mins
2	Mark Wright	13	52	200 mins
3	Aaron Wilbraham	10	46	247 mins
4	Keith Andrews	12	48	298 mins

KEY PLAYERS - MIDFIELDERS

Colin Cameron

Goals in the League	3
Defensive Rating Average number of mins between League goals conceded while on the pitch	130
Contribution to Attacking Power Average number of minutes between League team goals while on pitch	53
Scoring Difference Defensive Rating minus Contribution to Attacking Power	77

	PLAYER	GOALS LGE	DEF RATE	POWER	SCORE DIFF
1	Colin Cameron	3	130	53	77 mins
2	Alan Navarro	3	120	52	68 mins
3	Lloyd Dyer	11	114	50	64 mins
4	Keith Andrews	12	96	48	48 mins

KEY PLAYERS - DEFENDERS

Drissa Diallo

Goals Conceded when he was on pitch	19
Defensive Rating Ave number of mins between League goals conceded while on the pitch	134
Clean Sheets In games when he played at least 70 minutes	14
Club Defensive Rating Average number of mins between League goals conceded by the club this season.	114

	PLAYER	CON LGE	CLEAN SHEETS	DEF RATE
1	Drissa Diallo	19	14	134 mins
2	Jude Stirling	16	12	133 mins
3	Danny Swailes	29	18	122 mins
4	Dean Lewington	36	19	111 mins

KEY GOALKEEPER

Willy Gueret

Goals Conceded in the League	37
Defensive Rating Ave number of mins between League goals conceded while on the pitch.	111
Counting Games Games when he played at least 70 mins	46
Clean Sheets In games when he played at least 70 mins	20

TOP POINT EARNERS

	PLAYER	GAMES	AV PTS
1	Jude Stirling	18	2.44
2	Aaron Wilbraham	24	2.38
3	Danny Swailes	39	2.28
4	Lloyd Dyer	39	2.28
5	Alan Navarro	37	2.22
6	Drissa Diallo	27	2.15
7	Colin Cameron	16	2.13
8	Willy Gueret	46	2.11
9	Dean Lewington	44	2.07
10	Keith Andrews	39	2.05
	CLUB AVERAGE:		2.11

PETERBOROUGH UNITED

Final Position: **2nd**

NICKNAME: THE POSH

KEY: Won / Drawn / Lost

						Attendance
1	div3	Rochdale	H W	3-0	Low 10, McLean 44, Crow 90	5,575
2	ccr1	Southampton	H W	2-1	Rasiak 21 og, Boyd 26	4,087
3	div3	Rotherham	A L	1-3	McLean 88	4,291
4	div3	Chesterfield	H L	2-3	McLean 9, Lee 45	5,005
5	ccr2	West Brom	H L	0-2		4,917
6	div3	Accrington	A W	2-0	Lee 55, McLean 90	1,484
7	div3	Mansfield	H W	2-1	Low 29, Crow 75	4,721
8	div3	Bradford	A L	0-1		13,819
9	div3	Morecambe	H D	1-1	McLean 63 pen	4,473
10	div3	Darlington	A D	1-1	Mackail-Smith 90	3,974
11	div3	Shrewsbury	A W	2-0	Lee 33, Boyd 81	5,220
12	div3	Grimsby	H W	2-1	Boyd 65, McLean 80 pen	4,786
13	div3	Wycombe	H W	2-1	Boyd 48, McLean 87	4,584
14	div3	Lincoln	A D	1-1	Croft 89 og	5,036
15	div3	Hereford	H D	1-1	Mackail-Smith 43	5,008
16	div3	Stockport	A W	2-1	Mackail-Smith 15, McLean 45	5,042
17	div3	Dag & Red	H W	3-1	Keates 69, McLean 79, 82	4,200
18	facr1	Wrexham	H W	4-1	Mackail-Smith 2, 41, 53, McLean 88	4,266
19	div3	Bury	A L	0-2		2,660
20	div3	Brentford	H W	7-0	McLean 3 pen, 14, 41, Whelpdale 45 Boyd 49, Mackail-Smith 56, Howe 76	4,865
21	facr2	Staines Town	A W	5-0	Mackail-Smith 10, 23, 53, 62, McLean 18	2,460
22	div3	Notts County	A W	1-0	Mackail-Smith 52	4,412
23	div3	Chester	A W	2-1	McLean 80, Mackail-Smith 85 pen	2,291
24	div3	MK Dons	H L	1-2	McLean 75	10,351
25	div3	Bradford	H W	2-1	McLean 58, Hughes 88	5,355
26	div3	Mansfield	A L	0-2		3,107
27	div3	Morecambe	A L	2-3	Morgan 5, Lee 12	2,371
28	div3	Shrewsbury	H W	2-1	Lee 55, Morgan 57	5,062
29	facr3	Colchester	A W	3-1	McLean 4, Boyd 46, Lee 73	4,003
30	div3	Macclesfield	H L	0-1		5,238
31	div3	Accrington	H W	8-2	Mackail-Smith 12, 89, Boyd 27, 33, 76 McLean 39, 78, 82	4,257
32	facr4	West Brom	H L	0-3		12,701
33	div3	Rotherham	H W	3-1	Lee 22, McLean 81, Mackail-Smith 90	5,152
34	div3	Rochdale	A W	2-0	Boyd 57, McLean 76	3,076
35	div3	Wrexham	H D	0-0		5,505
36	div3	Chesterfield	A W	2-1	McLean 45, Boyd 47	3,973
37	div3	Barnet	H W	1-0	Hatch 73	5,520
38	div3	Macclesfield	A W	3-0	Boyd 46, Whelpdale 65, McLean 72	2,094
39	div3	Wrexham	A W	2-0	Day 65, 81	4,103
40	div3	Bury	H W	1-0	Keates 59	6,150
41	div3	Barnet	A W	2-0	Keates 32, Day 90	2,202
42	div3	Dag & Red	A W	3-2	Boyd 57, Mackail-Smith 73, McLean 86	3,130
43	div3	Brentford	A W	2-1	McLean 10, Mackail-Smith 58	4,049
44	div3	Notts County	H D	0-0		7,173
45	div3	MK Dons	A D	1-1	Whelpdale 27	14,521
46	div3	Chester	H W	1-0	Keates 71	6,457
47	div3	Lincoln	H W	4-0	McLean 18, 49, Rendell 56, 67	8,035
48	div3	Wycombe	A D	2-2	Boyd 66, Hatch 83	6,202
49	div3	Stockport	H L	0-1		10,023
50	div3	Hereford	A W	1-0	Keates 29	5,279
51	div3	Grimsby	A W	4-1	McLean 33, 49, Mackail-Smith 73 Rendell 82	4,125
52	div3	Darlington	H L	0-2		10,400

TEAM OF THE SEASON

G	Joe Lewis	CG: 22	DR: 131
D	Claude Gnakpa	CG: 21	DR: 128
D	Chris Westwood	CG: 34	DR: 125
D	Craig Morgan	CG: 40	DR: 103
D	Jamie Day	CG: 39	DR: 94
M	Chris Whelpdale	CG: 19	SD: 78
M	Charlie Lee	CG: 31	SD: 51
M	Dean Keates	CG: 32	SD: 49
M	Micah Hyde	CG: 30	SD: 28
F	Aaron McLean	CG: 42	SR: 135
F	Craig Mackail-Smith	CG: 32	SR: 239

KEY PLAYER APPEARANCES

	PLAYER	POS	AGE	APP	MINS ON	GOALS	CARDS(Y/R)	
1	Aaron McLean	ATT	25	45	3925	29	9	0
2	George Boyd	ATT	22	46	3770	12	3	0
3	Craig Morgan	DEF	23	41	3624	2	9	0
4	Jamie Day	DEF	22	42	3602	3	7	0
5	Chris Westwood	DEF	31	37	3127	0	3	0
6	Dean Keates	MID	30	40	3057	5	2	0
7	Charlie Lee	MID	21	42	2992	6	7	0
8	Micah Hyde	MID	33	37	2884	0	1	0
9	Craig Mackail-Smith	ATT	24	36	2868	12	2	0
10	Chris Whelpdale	MID	21	35	2331	3	3	0
11	Adam Newton	DEF	27	32	2310	0	1	0
12	Claude Gnakpa	DEF	25	28	2179	0	9	0
13	Joe Lewis	GK	20	22	1965	0	0	0
14	Mark Tyler	GK	31	17	1530	0	0	0
15	Kieran Charnock	DEF	23	10	843	0	4	0
16	Shane Blackett	DEF	25	11	838	0	1	0
17	Joshua Low	MID	29	15	755	2	0	0
18	Shwan Jalal	GK	24	7	630	0	0	0

KEY PLAYERS - GOALSCORERS

Aaron McLean

Goals in the League	29
Contribution to Attacking Power Average number of minutes between League team goals while on pitch	49
Player Strike Rate Average number of minutes between League goals scored by player	135
Club Strike Rate Average number of minutes between League goals scored by club	50

	PLAYER	GOALS LGE	POWER	STRIKE RATE
1	Aaron McLean	29	49	135 mins
2	Craig Mackail-Smith	12	46	239 mins
3	George Boyd	12	46	314 mins
4	Charlie Lee	6	48	498 mins

KEY PLAYERS - MIDFIELDERS

Chris Whelpdale

Goals in the League	3
Defensive Rating Average number of mins between League goals conceded while on the pitch	122
Contribution to Attacking Power Average number of minutes between League team goals while on pitch	44
Scoring Difference Defensive Rating minus Contribution to Attacking Power	78

	PLAYER	GOALS LGE	DEF RATE	POWER	SCORE DIFF
1	Chris Whelpdale	3	122	44	78 mins
2	Charlie Lee	6	99	48	51 mins
3	Dean Keates	5	101	52	49 mins
4	Micah Hyde	0	77	49	28 mins

KEY PLAYERS - DEFENDERS

Claude Gnakpa

Goals Conceded when he was on pitch	17
Defensive Rating Ave number of mins between League goals conceded while on the pitch	128
Clean Sheets In games when he played at least 70 minutes	10
Club Defensive Rating Average number of mins between League goals conceded by the club this season.	98

	PLAYER	CON LGE	CLEAN SHEETS	DEF RATE
1	Claude Gnakpa	17	10	128 mins
2	Chris Westwood	25	15	125 mins
3	Craig Morgan	35	16	103 mins
4	Jamie Day	38	13	94 mins

KEY GOALKEEPER

Joe Lewis

Goals Conceded in the League	15
Defensive Rating Ave number of mins between League goals conceded while on the pitch.	131
Counting Games Games when he played at least 70 mins	22
Clean Sheets In games when he played at least 70 mins	11

TOP POINT EARNERS

	PLAYER	GAMES	AV PTS
1	Chris Whelpdale	19	2.42
2	Craig Mackail-Smith	32	2.28
3	Claude Gnakpa	21	2.24
4	Chris Westwood	34	2.24
5	Joe Lewis	22	2.23
6	Aaron McLean	42	2.12
7	Dean Keates	32	2.09
8	Craig Morgan	40	2.08
9	George Boyd	41	2.07
10	Charlie Lee	31	2.03
	CLUB AVERAGE:		2.00

HEREFORD UNITED

Final Position: **3rd**

NICKNAME: THE BULLS

KEY: Won / Drawn / Lost

	Comp	Opponent	H/A	Res	Score	Scorers	Attendance
1	div3	Rotherham	H	D	0-0		3,566
2	ccr1	Yeovil	H	W	4-1	Ainsworth 8, 24, 41, Easton 35	2,085
3	div3	Barnet	A	W	2-1	Benjamin 44 pen, Robinson 67	1,790
4	div3	Rochdale	H	D	1-1	Robinson 27	2,732
5	ccr2	Birmingham	A	L	1-2	Robinson 74	10,185
6	div3	Wrexham	A	W	2-0	Taylor 53, Benjamin 74	4,004
7	div3	Macclesfield	H	L	0-1		2,725
8	div3	Morecambe	A	W	3-0	Benjamin 80, Ainsworth 84, Webb 90	2,949
9	div3	Bradford	H	W	4-2	Diagouraga 15, Guinan 18, Benjamin 52 pen, Robinson 84	3,275
10	div3	Grimsby	A	L	1-2	Benjamin 56	3,699
11	div3	Notts County	A	W	3-2	Smith 13, Guinan 26, 70	3,576
12	div3	Brentford	H	W	2-0	Webb 31, 34	2,942
13	div3	Chester	A	D	1-1	Diagouraga 77	3,430
14	div3	MK Dons	H	L	0-1		3,936
15	div3	Peterborough	A	D	1-1	Easton 72	5,008
16	div3	Darlington	H	W	5-1	Rose 4, Robinson 22, Smith 47, Benjamin 58, Easton 90	3,516
17	div3	Mansfield	H	W	2-1	Robinson 25, Benjamin 48	2,272
18	facr1	Leeds	H	D	0-0		5,924
19	div3	Stockport	A	W	3-2	Ainsworth 37, 54, 70	5,103
20	facr1r	Leeds	A	W	1-0	Ainsworth 3	11,315
21	div3	Accrington	H	D	0-0		2,804
22	facr2	Hartlepool	H	W	2-0	McCombe 45, Robinson 85	3,801
23	div3	Wycombe	A	D	2-2	Robinson 86, Johnson 89	4,081
24	div3	Lincoln	H	W	3-1	Robinson 10 pen, McClenahan 44, Smith 84	2,528
25	div3	Bury	A	W	1-0	Robinson 90	2,099
26	div3	Morecambe	H	L	0-3		3,058
27	div3	Macclesfield	A	W	1-0	Robinson 57	2,393
28	div3	Bradford	A	W	3-1	Robinson 17, Beckwith 39, Benjamin 45	13,640
29	div3	Notts County	H	D	0-0		3,945
30	facr3	Tranmere	A	D	2-2	Smith 65, Benjamin 76	6,909
31	div3	Shrewsbury	H	W	3-1	Benjamin 41 pen, Beckwith 73, Johnson 79	4,707
32	facr3r	Tranmere	H	W	1-0	Johnson 72	6,471
33	div3	Chesterfield	A	L	0-4		3,274
34	facr4	Cardiff	H	L	1-2	Robinson 77	6,855
35	div3	Barnet	H	L	1-2	Benjamin 64	2,271
36	div3	Rotherham	A	W	1-0	Hooper 40	4,746
37	div3	Dag & Red	H	W	4-1	MacDonald 9, 67, Hooper 21, Johnson 45 pen	2,594
38	div3	Rochdale	A	W	4-2	MacDonald 14, 21, 31, Hooper 73	2,884
39	div3	Chesterfield	H	W	2-0	MacDonald 8, Hooper 45	3,503
40	div3	Shrewsbury	A	W	2-1	Johnson 27, Hooper 67	7,402
41	div3	Dag & Red	A	L	0-1		1,929
42	div3	Stockport	H	L	0-1		3,526
43	div3	Accrington	A	W	2-0	Hooper 43, Roberts 52 og	1,262
44	div3	Mansfield	A	W	1-0	Easton 7	1,606
45	div3	Wycombe	H	W	1-0	Martin 72 og	3,126
46	div3	Bury	H	D	0-0		3,420
47	div3	Lincoln	A	L	1-2	Hooper 62	3,614
48	div3	Chester	H	D	2-2	Smith 25, Hooper 35	3,210
49	div3	Darlington	A	W	1-0	Hooper 69	4,331
50	div3	MK Dons	A	D	0-0		11,428
51	div3	Peterborough	H	L	0-1		5,279
52	div3	Wrexham	H	W	2-0	Hooper 42, Robinson 60	3,739
53	div3	Brentford	A	W	3-0	Hooper 18, Robinson 36, Johnson 90	6,246
54	div3	Grimsby	H	W	2-0	Smith 36, Robinson 42	6,020

TEAM OF THE SEASON

G — Wayne Brown, CG: 44 DR: 96

D — Dean Beckwith, CG: 37 DR: 118

D — Richard Rose, CG: 30 DR: 108

D — Trent McClenahan, CG: 38 DR: 103

D — Karl Broadhurst, CG: 20 DR: 96

M — Clint Easton, CG: 35 SD: 51

M — Toumani Diagouraga, CG: 40 SD: 45

M — Lionel Ainsworth, CG: 13 SD: 44

M — Ben Smith, CG: 42 SD: 42

F — Gary Hooper, CG: 18 SR: 147

F — Theo Robinson, CG: 30 SR: 232

KEY PLAYER APPEARANCES

	PLAYER	POS	AGE	APP	MINS ON	GOALS	CARDS(Y)	CARDS(R)
1	Wayne Brown	GK	31	44	3960	0	1	0
2	Ben Smith	MID	29	44	3767	5	4	0
3	Toumani Diagouraga	MID	21	41	3642	2	4	0
4	Trent McClenahan	DEF	23	38	3408	1	1	0
5	Dean Beckwith	DEF	24	38	3325	2	5	0
6	Clint Easton	MID	30	39	3205	3	3	0
7	Theo Robinson	ATT	19	43	3025	13	3	0
8	Richard Rose	DEF	25	31	2716	1	2	0
9	John McCombe	DEF	23	26	2131	0	3	0
10	Simon Johnson	ATT	25	33	2036	5	2	0
11	Kris Taylor	MID	24	31	1999	1	1	0
12	Karl Broadhurst	DEF	28	23	1922	0	3	0
13	Stephen Guinan	ATT	32	28	1733	3	2	1
14	Gary Hooper	ATT	20	19	1619	11	1	0
15	Trevor Benjamin	ATT	29	34	1414	10	0	0
16	Lee Collins	DEF	19	16	1308	0	0	0
17	Lionel Ainsworth	MID	20	15	1170	4	0	0
18	Sam Gwynne	MID	20	15	783	0	1	0

KEY PLAYERS - GOALSCORERS

Gary Hooper

Goals in the League	11
Contribution to Attacking Power — Average number of minutes between League team goals while on pitch	62
Player Strike Rate — Average number of minutes between League goals scored by player	147
Club Strike Rate — Average number of minutes between League goals scored by club	58

	PLAYER	GOALS LGE	POWER	STRIKE RATE
1	Gary Hooper	11	62	147 mins
2	Theo Robinson	13	65	232 mins
3	Lionel Ainsworth	4	46	292 mins
4	Simon Johnson	5	56	407 mins

KEY PLAYERS - MIDFIELDERS

Clint Easton

Goals in the League	3
Defensive Rating — Average number of mins between League goals conceded while on the pitch	103
Contribution to Attacking Power — Average number of minutes between League team goals while on pitch	52
Scoring Difference — Defensive Rating minus Contribution to Attacking Power	51

	PLAYER	GOALS LGE	DEF RATE	POWER	SCORE DIFF
1	Clint Easton	3	103	52	51 mins
2	Toumani Diagouraga	2	101	56	45 mins
3	Lionel Ainsworth	4	90	46	44 mins
4	Ben Smith	5	99	57	42 mins

KEY PLAYERS - DEFENDERS

Dean Beckwith

Goals Conceded when he was on pitch	28
Defensive Rating — Ave number of mins between League goals conceded while on the pitch	118
Clean Sheets — In games when he played at least 70 minutes	19
Club Defensive Rating — Average number of mins between League goals conceded by the club this season.	103

	PLAYER	CON LGE	CLEAN SHEETS	DEF RATE
1	Dean Beckwith	28	19	118 mins
2	Richard Rose	25	13	108 mins
3	Trent McClenahan	33	16	103 mins
4	Karl Broadhurst	20	8	96 mins

KEY GOALKEEPER

Wayne Brown

Goals Conceded in the League	41
Defensive Rating — Ave number of mins between League goals conceded while on the pitch.	96
Counting Games — Games when he played at least 70 mins	44
Clean Sheets — In games when he played at least 70 mins	17

TOP POINT EARNERS

	PLAYER	GAMES	AV PTS
1	Simon Johnson	21	2.29
2	Clint Easton	35	2.09
3	Lee Collins	14	2.07
4	Richard Rose	30	2.07
5	Lionel Ainsworth	13	2.00
6	Dean Beckwith	37	2.00
7	Gary Hooper	18	1.94
8	Theo Robinson	30	1.93
9	John McCombe	23	1.91
10	Wayne Brown	44	1.91
	CLUB AVERAGE:		1.91

STOCKPORT COUNTY

PROMOTED VIA THE PLAY-OFFS Final Position: **4th**

NICKNAME: COUNTY

KEY: ☐Won ☐Drawn ☐Lost

					Score		Attendance
1	div3	Dag & Red	H	W	1-0	Dickinson 85	5,577
2	ccr1	Tranmere	H	W	1-0	McNeil 84	3,499
3	div3	Chesterfield	A	D	1-1	Dickinson 64	4,600
4	div3	Rotherham	H	D	2-2	Elding 13, Griffin 67	5,764
5	ccr2	Charlton	A	L	3-4	Proudlock 54, Elding 62, Blizzard 69	8,022
6	div3	Mansfield	A	L	2-4	Proudlock 35, 42	2,747
7	div3	Shrewsbury	H	D	1-1	Proudlock 32	5,473
8	div3	Grimsby	A	D	1-1	McNeil 45	3,726
9	div3	Wrexham	H	W	2-1	Elding 29, Blizzard 65	5,513
10	div3	Brentford	A	W	3-1	Elding 7 pen, 44 pen, 61	4,449
11	div3	Morecambe	A	L	0-2		2,871
12	div3	Barnet	H	L	2-4	Elding 25 pen, Dickinson 90	4,751
13	div3	Darlington	A	L	0-4		3,841
14	div3	Chester	H	L	1-2	Taylor 45	5,566
15	div3	MK Dons	A	W	2-0	Elding 74, Pilkington 90	8,290
16	div3	Peterborough	H	L	1-2	McNeil 22	5,042
17	div3	Rochdale	A	W	2-1	Dickinson 28, 53	2,915
18	facr1	Staines Town	H	D	1-1	McNeil 47	3,460
19	div3	Hereford	H	L	2-3	Elding 61 pen, Brown 83 og	5,103
20	facr1r	Staines Town	A	L	3-4*	McNeil 78 (*on penalties)	2,860
21	div3	Bradford	A	D	1-1	Poole 90	13,837
22	div3	Lincoln	H	L	1-3	Dickinson 84	5,260
23	div3	Wycombe	H	W	6-0	Proudlock 34, 60, 74, Dickinson 37 Christon 64 og, Martin 78 og	4,477
24	div3	Macclesfield	A	W	2-0	Dickinson 63, Proudlock 90	3,585
25	div3	Grimsby	H	D	1-1	Rose 83	4,711
26	div3	Shrewsbury	A	L	1-3	Pilkington 72	7,707
27	div3	Wrexham	A	W	1-0	Elding 59	4,287
28	div3	Morecambe	H	W	2-1	Elding 9, Dickinson 41	5,489
29	div3	Notts County	A	W	2-1	Elding 13, Dickinson 35	4,120
30	div3	Accrington	H	W	2-0	Rose 3, Elding 45	4,714
31	div3	Chesterfield	H	D	2-2	Dickinson 34, Elding 63	5,105
32	div3	Dag & Red	A	W	1-0	McSweeney 6	1,834
33	div3	Bury	A	W	3-2	Pilkington 7, 58, Taylor 52	3,142
34	div3	Notts County	H	D	1-1	Rowe 22	5,849
35	div3	Rotherham	A	W	4-1	Rowe 8, 49, 63, Pilkington 56	4,004
36	div3	Bury	H	L	1-2	Randolph 21 og	5,704
37	div3	Accrington	A	W	2-0	Dickinson 33, 63	2,576
38	div3	Hereford	A	W	1-0	Dickinson 54 pen	3,526
39	div3	Bradford	H	W	2-1	Pilkington 69, Rose 79	5,763
40	div3	Rochdale	H	W	2-0	Dickinson 10, 56	5,530
41	div3	Lincoln	A	W	1-0	Poole 68	4,544
42	div3	Macclesfield	H	W	2-0	Taylor 10, 46	7,824
43	div3	Wycombe	A	D	0-0		5,380
44	div3	Darlington	H	W	1-0	Dickinson 37	6,460
45	div3	Mansfield	H	W	2-1	Muggleton 44 og, Dickinson 74 pen	4,982
46	div3	Peterborough	A	W	1-0	Rowe 59	10,023
47	div3	MK Dons	H	L	2-3	Dickinson 30, Proudlock 58	8,838
48	div3	Barnet	A	L	1-2	Rowe 51	3,074
49	div3	Chester	A	D	0-0		3,060
50	div3	Brentford	H	W	1-0	Havern 49	6,284
51	d3po1	Wycombe	A	D	1-1	Gleeson 82	6,371
52	d3po2	Wycombe	H	W	1-0	Dickinson 7	9,245
53	d3pof	Rochdale	H	W	3-2	Stanton 34 og, Pilkington 49 Dickinson 67	35,715

TEAM OF THE SEASON

G John Ruddy CG: 13 DR: 167

D Michael Rose CG: 22 DR: 146

D James Smith CG: 19 DR: 102

D Michael Raynes CG: 17 DR: 98

D Gareth Owen CG: 35 DR: 79

M Gary Dicker CG: 26 SD: 53

M Tommy Rowe CG: 18 SD: 49

M Paul Turnbull CG: 12 SD: 28

M Jason Taylor CG: 35 SD: 19

F Anthony Elding CG: 16 SR: 136

F Liam Dickinson CG: 31 SR: 164

KEY PLAYER APPEARANCES

	PLAYER	POS	AGE	APP	MINS ON	GOALS	CARDS(Y/R)	
1	Jason Taylor	MID	21	42	3438	4	7	0
2	Gareth Owen	DEF	25	36	3088	0	4	0
3	Liam Dickinson	ATT	22	40	3043	19	6	0
4	Conrad Logan	GK	22	34	3011	0	1	1
5	Gary Dicker	MID	0	30	2544	0	0	0
6	Ashley Williams	DEF	23	26	2295	0	2	0
7	Michael Rose	DEF	25	28	2247	3	2	0
8	Dominic Blizzard	MID	24	27	1975	1	0	0
9	Anthony Pilkington	ATT	20	29	1908	6	3	0
10	James Smith	DEF	22	23	1855	0	1	0
11	Anthony Elding	ATT	26	25	1769	13	2	0
12	Adam Griffin	MID	23	28	1737	1	2	0
13	Adam Proudlock	ATT	27	33	1710	8	4	1
14	Michael Raynes	DEF	20	27	1681	0	0	1
15	Tommy Rowe	MID	19	24	1642	6	0	0
16	Matty McNeil	ATT	31	17	1474	2	3	0
17	Paul Tierney	DEF	25	16	1375	0	1	0
18	Paul Turnbull	MID	19	19	1254	0	0	0

KEY PLAYERS - GOALSCORERS

Anthony Elding

Goals in the League	13
Contribution to Attacking Power Average number of minutes between League team goals while on pitch	57
Player Strike Rate Average number of minutes between League goals scored by player	136
Club Strike Rate Average number of minutes between League goals scored by club	61

	PLAYER	GOALS LGE	POWER	STRIKE RATE
1	Anthony Elding	13	57	136 mins
2	Liam Dickinson	19	54	164 mins
3	Tommy Rowe	6	59	288 mins
4	Anthony Pilkington	6	54	333 mins

KEY PLAYERS - MIDFIELDERS

Gary Dicker

Goals in the League	0
Defensive Rating Average number of mins between League goals conceded while on the pitch	114
Contribution to Attacking Power Average number of minutes between League team goals while on pitch	61
Scoring Difference Defensive Rating minus Contribution to Attacking Power	53

	PLAYER	GOALS LGE	DEF RATE	POWER	SCORE DIFF
1	Gary Dicker	0	114	61	53 mins
2	Tommy Rowe	6	108	59	49 mins
3	Paul Turnbull	0	78	50	28 mins
4	Jason Taylor	4	76	57	19 mins

KEY PLAYERS - DEFENDERS

Michael Rose

Goals Conceded when he was on pitch	16
Defensive Rating Ave number of mins between League goals conceded while on the pitch	146
Clean Sheets In games when he played at least 70 minutes	14
Club Defensive Rating Average number of mins between League goals conceded by the club this season.	81

	PLAYER	CON LGE	CLEAN SHEETS	DEF RATE
1	Michael Rose	16	14	146 mins
2	James Smith	19	8	102 mins
3	Michael Raynes	18	8	98 mins
4	Gareth Owen	40	14	79 mins

KEY GOALKEEPER

John Ruddy

Goals Conceded in the League	7
Defensive Rating Ave number of mins between League goals conceded while on the pitch.	167
Counting Games Games when he played at least 70 mins	13
Clean Sheets In games when he played at least 70 mins	9

TOP POINT EARNERS

	PLAYER	GAMES	AV PTS
1	Michael Rose	22	2.45
2	John Ruddy	12	2.33
3	James Smith	19	2.21
4	Gary Dicker	26	2.08
5	Anthony Pilkington	16	2.06
6	Tommy Rowe	18	2.06
7	Liam Dickinson	31	2.00
8	Jason Taylor	35	1.94
9	Paul Turnbull	12	1.92
10	Michael Raynes	17	1.82
	CLUB AVERAGE:		1.78

ROCHDALE

Final Position: **5th**

NICKNAME: THE DALE

KEY: Won / Drawn / Lost

No	Comp	Opponent	H/A	Res	Score	Scorers	Attendance
1	div3	Peterborough	A	L	0-3		5,575
2	ccr1	Stoke	H	W	4-2*	Perkins 83, Prendergast 101 (*on penalties)	2,369
3	div3	Chester	H	L	1-2	Ramsden 21	3,243
4	div3	Hereford	A	D	1-1	Dagnall 22 pen	2,732
5	ccr2	Norwich	H	L	3-4*	Murray 9 (*on penalties)	2,990
6	div3	MK Dons	H	W	3-2	Dagnall 27, 90, Le Fondre 90	2,743
7	div3	Barnet	A	D	0-0		2,040
8	div3	Macclesfield	H	D	1-1	McNulty 17 og	3,066
9	div3	Shrewsbury	A	W	4-3	Rundle 46, Murray 80, Jones 85 Flitcroft 90	6,262
10	div3	Darlington	A	D	1-1	Prendergast 88	3,031
11	div3	Bury	H	L	1-2	McArdle 61	4,692
12	div3	Grimsby	A	W	2-1	Le Fondre 12, Murray 59	5,829
13	div3	Brentford	H	D	1-1	Murray 63	2,424
14	div3	Morecambe	A	D	1-1	McArdle 55	3,651
15	div3	Dag & Red	H	W	1-0	Foster 59 og	2,278
16	div3	Stockport	H	L	1-2	Le Fondre 69 pen	2,915
17	facr1	Southend	A	L	1-2	Le Fondre 12	5,180
18	div3	Mansfield	H	W	1-0	McEvilly 67	2,431
19	div3	Wrexham	H	D	0-0		2,808
20	div3	Accrington	A	W	2-1	Higginbotham 56, Murray 75	1,621
21	div3	Rotherham	A	W	4-2	Jones 4, Le Fondre 7, Murray 48 McEvilly 90	3,808
22	div3	Wrexham	A	W	2-0	Murray 7, McEvilly 60	4,302
23	div3	Macclesfield	A	D	2-2	Rundle 63, Murray 90	2,742
24	div3	Darlington	H	W	3-1	Thompson 22, Murray 37 Le Fondre 45 pen	3,116
25	div3	Lincoln	H	L	0-2		2,721
26	div3	Wycombe	A	W	1-0	Kennedy 90 pen	4,493
27	div3	Chesterfield	A	W	4-3	Perkins 18, 39, 86, Murray 88	3,595
28	div3	MK Dons	A	W	1-0	Jones 32	7,882
29	div3	Chester	A	W	4-0	Le Fondre 29, Butler 44 og, Kennedy 60 Rundle 88	2,131
30	div3	Peterborough	H	L	0-2		3,076
31	div3	Lincoln	A	L	1-2	Howe 56	3,955
32	div3	Hereford	H	L	2-4	Ramsden 7, Howe 90	2,884
33	div3	Bradford	A	W	2-1	M.Clarke 12 og, Le Fondre 90	14,017
34	div3	Wycombe	H	L	0-1		2,616
35	div3	Chesterfield	H	L	0-1		3,108
36	div3	Mansfield	A	W	4-0	Jones 27, 55, Le Fondre 47, Howe 67	2,351
37	div3	Stockport	A	L	0-2		5,530
38	div3	Accrington	H	W	4-1	Le Fondre 45 pen, 65, 83, Jones 48	3,247
39	div3	Notts County	A	L	0-1		4,030
40	div3	Rotherham	H	W	4-1	Jones 30, Dagnall 81, 86, 90	2,985
41	div3	Brentford	A	W	2-0	Thorpe 76, Rundle 90	4,896
42	div3	Bradford	H	W	2-1	Perkins 1, Le Fondre 87	3,811
43	div3	Grimsby	H	W	3-1	Howe 47, 55, 90	2,974
44	div3	Notts County	H	W	4-2	Howe 58, Rundle 70, Le Fondre 78 M.Johnson 85 og	2,536
45	div3	Dag & Red	A	D	1-1	Higginbotham 28	2,032
46	div3	Barnet	H	W	3-0	Le Fondre 34, Howe 50, Higginbotham 72	2,925
47	div3	Morecambe	H	W	1-0	Howe 66	3,706
48	div3	Bury	A	D	1-1	Le Fondre 90 pen	6,271
49	div3	Shrewsbury	H	D	1-1	Dagnall 54	4,000
50	d3po1	Darlington	A	L	1-2	Dagnall 70	8,057
51	d3po2	Darlington	H	W	5-4*	Dagnall 43, Perkins 78 (*on penalties)	9,870
52	d3pof	Stockport	A	L	2-3	McArdle 24, Rundle 77	35,715

TEAM OF THE SEASON

- **G** Sam Russell — CG: 15 DR: 71
- **D** Marcus Holness — CG: 13 DR: 115
- **D** Thomas Kennedy — CG: 43 DR: 78
- **D** Nathan Stanton — CG: 23 DR: 78
- **D** Rory McArdle — CG: 40 DR: 74
- **M** Kallum Higginbotham — CG: 18 SD: 43
- **M** David Perkins — CG: 38 SD: 24
- **M** Gary Jones — CG: 43 SD: 23
- **M** John Doolan — CG: 14 SD: 18
- **F** Rene Howe — CG: 14 SR: 181
- **F** Adam Le Fondre — CG: 21 SR: 185

KEY PLAYER APPEARANCES

	PLAYER	POS	AGE	APP	MINS ON	GOALS	CARDS(Y)	CARDS(R)
1	Thomas Kennedy	DEF	23	43	3840	2	6	0
2	Gary Jones	MID	31	43	3810	7	3	0
3	Rory McArdle	DEF	21	43	3659	2	5	0
4	David Perkins	MID	26	40	3476	4	4	2
5	Simon Ramsden	DEF	26	35	3088	2	4	0
6	Adam Rundle	MID	23	42	2934	5	3	0
7	Adam Le Fondre	ATT	21	46	2784	15	3	0
8	Nathan Stanton	DEF	27	27	2203	0	2	2
9	Kallum Higginbotham	MID	0	32	2004	3	6	0
10	Glenn Murray	ATT	24	23	1854	9	5	0
11	James Spencer	GK	23	20	1800	0	0	0
12	Rene Howe	ATT	21	20	1637	9	0	0
13	John Doolan	MID	34	25	1623	0	3	0
14	Ben Muirhead	MID	25	31	1520	0	3	0
15	Marcus Holness	DEF	0	19	1389	0	2	0
16	Sam Russell	GK	25	15	1350	0	1	0
17	Tommy Lee	GK	22	11	990	0	0	0
18	Kelvin Lomax	DEF	21	10	892	0	1	0

KEY PLAYERS - GOALSCORERS

Rene Howe

Goals in the League	9
Contribution to Attacking Power — Average number of minutes between League team goals while on pitch	49
Player Strike Rate — Average number of minutes between League goals scored by player	181
Club Strike Rate — Average number of minutes between League goals scored by club	59

	PLAYER	GOALS LGE	POWER	STRIKE RATE
1	Rene Howe	9	49	181 mins
2	Adam Le Fondre	15	52	185 mins
3	Glenn Murray	9	56	206 mins
4	Gary Jones	7	53	544 mins

KEY PLAYERS - MIDFIELDERS

Kallum Higginbotham

Goals in the League	3
Defensive Rating — Average number of mins between League goals conceded while on the pitch	91
Contribution to Attacking Power — Average number of minutes between League team goals while on pitch	48
Scoring Difference — Defensive Rating minus Contribution to Attacking Power	43

	PLAYER	GOALS LGE	DEF RATE	POWER	SCORE DIFF
1	Kallum Higginbotham	3	91	48	43 mins
2	David Perkins	4	80	56	24 mins
3	Gary Jones	7	76	53	23 mins
4	John Doolan	0	70	52	18 mins

KEY PLAYERS - DEFENDERS

Marcus Holness

Goals Conceded when he was on pitch	12
Defensive Rating — Ave number of mins between League goals conceded while on the pitch	115
Clean Sheets — In games when he played at least 70 minutes	6
Club Defensive Rating — Average number of mins between League goals conceded by the club this season.	85

	PLAYER	CON LGE	CLEAN SHEETS	DEF RATE
1	Marcus Holness	12	6	115 mins
2	Thomas Kennedy	49	12	78 mins
3	Nathan Stanton	28	7	78 mins
4	Rory McArdle	49	10	74 mins

KEY GOALKEEPER

Sam Russell

Goals Conceded in the League	19
Defensive Rating — Ave number of mins between League goals conceded while on the pitch.	71
Counting Games — Games when he played at least 70 mins	15
Clean Sheets — In games when he played at least 70 mins	6

TOP POINT EARNERS

	PLAYER	GAMES	AV PTS
1	Kallum Higginbotham	18	2.44
2	Adam Rundle	24	2.04
3	Sam Russell	15	1.93
4	Nathan Stanton	23	1.83
5	Thomas Kennedy	43	1.81
6	Rory McArdle	40	1.80
7	Rene Howe	14	1.79
8	John Doolan	14	1.79
9	Simon Ramsden	34	1.76
10	Gary Jones	43	1.74
	CLUB AVERAGE:		1.74

DARLINGTON

Final Position: **6th**

NICKNAME: THE QUAKERS

KEY: ☐ Won ☐ Drawn ☐ Lost

							Attendance
1	div3	Wrexham	H	W	2-0	McBride 42, Joachim 72	4,408
2	ccr1	Barnsley	A	L	1-2	Wright 70	3,780
3	div3	Accrington	A	W	3-0	Wright 26, Abbott 49, 90 pen	1,805
4	div3	Notts County	H	D	2-2	Wright 40, Miller 86	3,763
5	div3	Macclesfield	A	D	0-0		2,288
6	div3	Rotherham	A	W	2-0	Abbott 10, Blundell 76	3,988
7	div3	Lincoln	H	W	2-0	Abbott 34, Ravenhill 46	4,075
8	div3	MK Dons	A	L	0-1		7,901
9	div3	Peterborough	H	D	1-1	Wright 63	3,974
10	div3	Rochdale	H	D	1-1	Wright 59	3,031
11	div3	Dag & Red	A	W	3-0	Foster 45, Blundell 67, Wright 83	1,888
12	div3	Stockport	H	W	4-0	Wright 21, 85, Joachim 28, Blundell 81	3,841
13	div3	Bradford	A	D	0-0		14,074
14	div3	Chesterfield	H	D	0-0		4,205
15	div3	Hereford	A	L	1-5	Colbeck 16	3,516
16	div3	Shrewsbury	H	W	2-0	Joachim 27, Colbeck 63	2,628
17	facr1	Northampton	H	D	1-1	Blundell 8	2,696
18	div3	Brentford	A	W	2-0	Keltie 17 pen, Wright 37	4,657
19	facr1r	Northampton	A	L	1-2	Wright 90	2,895
20	div3	Wycombe	H	W	1-0	Abbott 77	3,002
21	div3	Grimsby	A	W	4-0	White 3, Blundell 25, Foran 50 Cummins 90	3,057
22	div3	Lincoln	A	W	4-0	Foran 11, Keltie 32 pen, Cummins 45, 51	4,025
23	div3	Rotherham	H	D	1-1	Cummins 68	6,965
24	div3	MK Dons	H	L	0-1		5,304
25	div3	Rochdale	A	L	1-3	Keltie 54 pen	3,116
26	div3	Bury	H	W	3-0	Wright 12, Miller 22, Mayo 58	3,003
27	div3	Morecambe	A	W	3-0	Austin 27, Joachim 63, Blundell 70	2,773
28	div3	Mansfield	A	W	1-0	Blundell 30 pen	3,344
29	div3	Macclesfield	H	D	2-2	Wright 10, Cresswell 72 og	3,585
30	div3	Accrington	H	W	1-0	Wright 1	2,808
31	div3	Wrexham	A	L	0-2		4,013
32	div3	Barnet	H	W	1-0	Joachim 11	3,145
33	div3	Notts County	A	W	1-0	Ravenhill 45	3,421
34	div3	Mansfield	H	L	1-2	Austin 22	3,527
35	div3	Bury	A	W	2-1	Ndumbu-Nsungu 6 pen, Cummins 67	2,554
36	div3	Brentford	H	W	3-1	Ndumbu-Nsungu 48, Joachim 59 Abbott 90	3,508
37	div3	Chester	H	W	1-0	Abbott 27	3,294
38	div3	Wycombe	A	L	0-2		5,185
39	div3	Shrewsbury	A	D	0-0		4,499
40	div3	Grimsby	H	W	3-2	Abbott 33, 44, Wright 64	3,499
41	div3	Chester	A	L	1-2	Foster 84	1,759
42	div3	Morecambe	H	D	2-2	Kennedy 84, Ndumbu-Nsungu 89	3,719
43	div3	Bradford	H	L	1-3	Keltie 11 pen	4,492
44	div3	Barnet	A	D	0-0		1,678
45	div3	Stockport	A	L	0-1		6,460
46	div3	Hereford	H	L	0-1		4,331
47	div3	Chesterfield	A	D	1-1	Wright 68	3,809
48	div3	Dag & Red	H	L	2-3	Ravenhill 20, Arber 52 og	3,709
49	div3	Peterborough	A	W	2-0	Kennedy 3, Cummins 53	10,400
50	d3po1	Rochdale	H	W	2-1	Kennedy 28, Miller 90	8,057
51	d3po2	Rochdale	A	L	4-5*	Keltie 28 pen (*on penalties)	9,870

TEAM OF THE SEASON

G — David Stockdale — CG: 38 DR: 93

D — Stephen Foster — CG: 41 DR: 115

D — Ryan Valentine — CG: 12 DR: 108

D — Alan White — CG: 35 DR: 99

D — Ian Miller — CG: 17 DR: 97

M — Michael Cummins — CG: 26 SD: 67

M — Rob Purdie — CG: 28 SD: 47

M — Clark Keltie — CG: 20 SD: 33

M — Richard Ravenhill — CG: 20 SD: 33

F — Tommy Wright — CG: 29 SR: 245

F — Greg Blundell — CG: 13 SR: 293

KEY PLAYER APPEARANCES

	PLAYER	POS	AGE	APP	MINS ON	GOALS	CARDS(Y/R)	
1	Stephen Foster	DEF	33	42	3721	2	9	0
2	David Stockdale	GK	22	40	3456	0	2	0
3	Julian Joachim	ATT	33	40	3455	6	0	0
4	Tommy Wright	ATT	23	40	3096	13	11	0
5	Alan White	DEF	32	35	3087	1	7	2
6	Rob Purdie	MID	25	39	2887	0	2	0
7	Michael Cummins	MID	30	40	2810	6	4	0
8	Richard Ravenhill	MID	27	35	2201	3	11	0
9	Neil Austin	DEF	25	29	2149	2	7	0
10	Clark Keltie	MID	24	27	1919	4	7	0
11	Ian Miller	DEF	24	28	1754	2	3	0
12	Greg Blundell	ATT	30	35	1672	6	3	0
13	Pawel Abbott	ATT	26	25	1448	9	0	0
14	Ryan Valentine	DEF	25	17	1188	0	2	0
15	Jason Kennedy	MID	21	13	1146	2	2	0
16	Ben Parker	MID	20	13	1117	0	1	1
17	Tim Ryan	DEF	33	13	1082	0	2	0
18	Richie Foran	ATT	28	12	922	2	4	1

KEY PLAYERS - GOALSCORERS

Tommy Wright

Goals in the League	13
Contribution to Attacking Power Average number of minutes between League team goals while on pitch	60
Player Strike Rate Average number of minutes between League goals scored by player	245
Club Strike Rate Average number of minutes between League goals scored by club	65

	PLAYER	GOALS LGE	POWER	STRIKE RATE
1	Tommy Wright	13	60	245 mins
2	Greg Blundell	6	56	293 mins
3	Clark Keltie	4	58	479 mins
4	Michael Cummins	6	59	483 mins

KEY PLAYERS - MIDFIELDERS

Michael Cummins

Goals in the League	6
Defensive Rating Average number of mins between League goals conceded while on the pitch	126
Contribution to Attacking Power Average number of minutes between League team goals while on pitch	59
Scoring Difference Defensive Rating minus Contribution to Attacking Power	67

	PLAYER	GOALS LGE	DEF RATE	POWER	SCORE DIFF
1	Michael Cummins	6	126	59	67 mins
2	Rob Purdie	0	114	67	47 mins
3	Clark Keltie	4	91	58	33 mins
4	Richard Ravenhill	3	104	71	33 mins

KEY PLAYERS - DEFENDERS

Stephen Foster

Goals Conceded when he was on pitch	33
Defensive Rating Ave number of mins between League goals conceded while on the pitch	115
Clean Sheets In games when he played at least 70 minutes	24
Club Defensive Rating Average number of mins between League goals conceded by the club this season.	110

	PLAYER	CON LGE	CLEAN SHEETS	DEF RATE
1	Stephen Foster	33	24	115 mins
2	Ryan Valentine	11	5	108 mins
3	Alan White	32	18	99 mins
4	Ian Miller	18	9	97 mins

KEY GOALKEEPER

David Stockdale

Goals Conceded in the League	38
Defensive Rating Ave number of mins between League goals conceded while on the pitch.	93
Counting Games Games when he played at least 70 mins	39
Clean Sheets In games when he played at least 70 mins	19

TOP POINT EARNERS

	PLAYER	GAMES	AV PTS
1	Greg Blundell	13	2.08
2	Ian Miller	17	2.06
3	Michael Cummins	26	1.96
4	Stephen Foster	41	1.80
5	Julian Joachim	37	1.78
6	Clark Keltie	20	1.70
7	David Stockdale	38	1.63
8	Richard Ravenhill	20	1.60
9	Rob Purdie	28	1.57
10	Neil Austin	22	1.55
	CLUB AVERAGE:		1.70

WYCOMBE WANDERERS

Final Position: **7th**

NICKNAME: THE CHAIRBOYS

KEY: ☐Won ☐Drawn ☐Lost

							Attendance
1	div3	Accrington	H	L	0-1		4,408
2	ccr1	Plymouth	A	L	1-2	Oakes 76	5,474
3	div3	Dag & Red	A	D	2-2	Bloomfield 69, Easter 90 pen	2,280
4	div3	Bury	H	W	1-0	Torres 70	4,067
5	div3	Chesterfield	A	L	0-2		3,757
6	div3	Brentford	H	W	1-0	Easter 81 pen	4,711
7	div3	Macclesfield	A	W	2-1	McGleish 65, Reid 90	2,173
8	div3	Shrewsbury	H	D	1-1	McGleish 37	4,936
9	div3	Bradford	A	W	1-0	McGleish 7	13,530
10	div3	Barnet	A	L	1-2	Sutton 22	2,023
11	div3	Notts County	H	W	3-1	Sutton 48 pen, McGleish 71 Bloomfield 82	4,199
12	div3	Peterborough	A	L	1-2	Bloomfield 53	4,584
13	div3	Grimsby	H	W	3-0	Holt 24, McGleish 77, 90 pen	4,052
14	div3	Chester	A	D	2-2	Torres 13, Sutton 64	2,598
15	div3	MK Dons	H	D	1-1	Bloomfield 37	5,929
16	div3	Wrexham	A	D	0-0		2,805
17	facr1	Swindon	H	L	1-2	Bloomfield 83	3,332
18	div3	Lincoln	H	W	1-0	McGleish 39	4,297
19	div3	Darlington	A	L	0-1		3,002
20	div3	Hereford	H	D	2-2	Oakes 6, Holt 45	4,081
21	div3	Stockport	A	L	0-6		4,477
22	div3	Morecambe	H	W	2-0	McGleish 19, Sutton 69	3,821
23	div3	Macclesfield	H	W	2-1	McGleish 32 pen, 73	3,867
24	div3	Brentford	A	W	3-1	Torres 55, McGleish 61, Sutton 65	5,841
25	div3	Shrewsbury	A	W	1-0	Sutton 8	6,208
26	div3	Barnet	H	D	0-0		4,818
27	div3	Mansfield	A	W	4-0	McGleish 5, 69, 73, Jelleyman 58 og	1,959
28	div3	Rochdale	H	L	0-1		4,493
29	div3	Rotherham	A	D	1-1	McGleish 56	6,709
30	div3	Chesterfield	H	W	1-0	McGleish 26	5,203
31	div3	Dag & Red	H	L	0-1		3,974
32	div3	Accrington	A	W	2-0	McGleish 13, Knight 75	1,200
33	div3	Mansfield	H	L	1-2	McGleish 42	5,963
34	div3	Bury	A	D	2-2	Torres 14, McGleish 39 pen	1,895
35	div3	Rotherham	H	W	1-0	Mccracken 50	4,610
36	div3	Rochdale	A	W	1-0	Knight 13	2,616
37	div3	Lincoln	A	L	0-1		4,002
38	div3	Darlington	H	W	2-0	Knight 24, McGleish 84	5,185
39	div3	Wrexham	H	W	2-1	Knight 14, McGleish 21	4,002
40	div3	Hereford	A	L	0-1		3,126
41	div3	Morecambe	A	W	1-0	Oakes 36	2,524
42	div3	Stockport	H	D	0-0		5,380
43	div3	Peterborough	H	D	2-2	Oakes 5, McGleish 90 pen	6,202
44	div3	MK Dons	A	D	2-2	McGleish 37, 73	12,747
45	div3	Grimsby	A	W	1-0	Torres 19	2,537
46	div3	Chester	H	W	1-0	McGleish 78	5,497
47	div3	Notts County	A	L	0-1		7,327
48	div3	Bradford	H	W	2-1	Facey 6, Knight 25	5,467
49	d3po1	Stockport	H	D	1-1	Facey 37	6,371
50	d3po2	Stockport	A	L	0-1		9,245

TEAM OF THE SEASON

G — Frank Fielding, CG: 34 DR: 100

D — Craig Woodman, CG: 26 DR: 120

D — David Mccracken, CG: 34 DR: 115

D — Leon Johnson, CG: 44 DR: 99

D — Sam Stockley, CG: 13 DR: 74

M — Tommy Doherty, CG: 19 SD: 90

M — Sergio Torres, CG: 33 SD: 34

M — Stefan Oakes, CG: 19 SD: 32

M — Russell Martin, CG: 43 SD: 30

F — Scott McGleish, CG: 42 SR: 151

F — John Sutton, CG: 20 SR: 360

KEY PLAYER APPEARANCES

	PLAYER	POS	AGE	APP	MINS ON	GOALS	CARDS(Y	/R)
1	Leon Johnson	DEF	27	45	3985	0	3	0
2	Russell Martin	MID	22	44	3892	0	2	0
3	Scott McGleish	ATT	34	46	3778	25	2	0
4	Gary Holt	MID	35	43	3683	2	1	0
5	Sergio Torres	MID	24	42	3278	5	3	0
6	David Mccracken	DEF	26	37	3121	1	9	0
7	Frank Fielding	GK	20	35	3116	0	2	0
8	Matt Bloomfield	MID	24	35	2438	4	3	0
9	Craig Woodman	DEF	25	29	2405	0	2	0
10	John Sutton	ATT	24	43	2161	6	1	0
11	Stefan Oakes	MID	29	34	2038	3	4	0
12	Tommy Doherty	MID	29	24	1837	0	6	1
13	Martin Bullock	MID	33	25	1591	0	0	0
14	Sam Stockley	DEF	30	21	1420	0	4	1
15	Leon Knight	ATT	25	20	1128	5	5	0
16	Mike Williamson	DEF	24	12	751	0	0	0
17	Tommy Williams	DEF	27	11	729	0	0	0
18	Neil Lennon	MID	37	9	702	0	1	0

KEY PLAYERS - GOALSCORERS

Scott McGleish

Goals in the League	25
Contribution to Attacking Power Average number of minutes between League team goals while on pitch	78
Player Strike Rate Average number of minutes between League goals scored by player	151
Club Strike Rate Average number of minutes between League goals scored by club	73

	PLAYER	GOALS LGE	POWER	STRIKE RATE
1	Scott McGleish	25	78	151 mins
2	John Sutton	6	63	360 mins
3	Matt Bloomfield	4	76	609 mins
4	Sergio Torres	5	65	655 mins

KEY PLAYERS - MIDFIELDERS

Tommy Doherty

Goals in the League	0
Defensive Rating Average number of mins between League goals conceded while on the pitch	153
Contribution to Attacking Power Average number of minutes between League team goals while on pitch	63
Scoring Difference Defensive Rating minus Contribution to Attacking Power	90

	PLAYER	GOALS LGE	DEF RATE	POWER	SCORE DIFF
1	Tommy Doherty	0	153	63	90 mins
2	Sergio Torres	5	99	65	34 mins
3	Stefan Oakes	3	113	81	32 mins
4	Russell Martin	0	102	72	30 mins

KEY PLAYERS - DEFENDERS

Craig Woodman

Goals Conceded when he was on pitch	20
Defensive Rating Ave number of mins between League goals conceded while on the pitch	120
Clean Sheets In games when he played at least 70 minutes	12
Club Defensive Rating Average number of mins between League goals conceded by the club this season.	98

	PLAYER	CON LGE	CLEAN SHEETS	DEF RATE
1	Craig Woodman	20	12	120 mins
2	David Mccracken	27	14	115 mins
3	Leon Johnson	40	18	99 mins
4	Sam Stockley	19	4	74 mins

KEY GOALKEEPER

Frank Fielding

Goals Conceded in the League	31
Defensive Rating Ave number of mins between League goals conceded while on the pitch.	100
Counting Games Games when he played at least 70 mins	34
Clean Sheets In games when he played at least 70 mins	15

TOP POINT EARNERS

	PLAYER	GAMES	AV PTS
1	Tommy Doherty	19	2.00
2	Craig Woodman	26	1.85
3	Martin Bullock	14	1.79
4	David McCracken	34	1.79
5	Sergio Torres	33	1.76
6	Leon Johnson	44	1.75
7	Russell Martin	43	1.74
8	Matt Bloomfield	23	1.74
9	Frank Fielding	34	1.71
10	Gary Holt	41	1.71
	CLUB AVERAGE:		1.70

CHESTERFIELD

Final Position: **8th**

NICKNAME: THE SPIREITES

KEY: ☐Won ☐Drawn ☐Lost

							Attendance
1	div3	Chester	A	D	0-0		3,183
2	ccr1	Sheff Utd	A	L	1-3	Lester 16	11,170
3	div3	Stockport	H	D	1-1	Lester 79	4,600
4	div3	Peterborough	A	W	3-2	Lester 19, Lowry 60, Niven 61	5,005
5	div3	Wycombe	H	W	2-0	Niven 44, Lester 74	3,757
6	div3	Bury	H	W	3-1	Fletcher 33, 77, Lester 84	4,161
7	div3	Mansfield	A	W	3-1	Robertson 3, Lowry 45, Lester 90	4,514
8	div3	Barnet	H	L	0-1		4,088
9	div3	Notts County	A	L	0-1		5,757
10	div3	Wrexham	A	W	4-0	Lester 6, 15, Rooney 14, Leven 60	3,058
11	div3	Macclesfield	H	D	2-2	Rooney 5, 46	4,080
12	div3	Shrewsbury	A	W	3-2	Rooney 44, Lowry 49, Lester 65 pen	5,143
13	div3	Dag & Red	H	D	1-1	Downes 8	4,101
14	div3	Darlington	A	D	0-0		4,205
15	div3	Morecambe	H	D	2-2	Lester 56, 64	3,721
16	div3	Lincoln	A	W	4-2	Lester 8, 18, 42, Kovacs 65	3,893
17	facr1	Tranmere	H	L	1-2	Lester 29	4,296
18	div3	MK Dons	A	W	2-1	Bastians 33, Ward 52	9,638
19	div3	Rotherham	H	L	0-2		5,417
20	div3	Bradford	H	D	1-1	Rooney 13	3,727
21	div3	Accrington	A	L	1-2	Ward 18	1,448
22	div3	Mansfield	H	W	2-0	Lester 52, Ward 61	6,300
23	div3	Bury	A	W	1-0	Leven 45 pen	3,158
24	div3	Barnet	A	W	2-0	Rooney 21, Kovacs 80	2,346
25	div3	Wrexham	H	W	2-1	Leven 7, Lester 41	4,293
26	div3	Grimsby	H	L	1-2	Ward 83	4,540
27	div3	Brentford	A	L	1-2	Lester 41	4,882
28	div3	Rochdale	H	L	3-4	Downes 49, Lester 59, Rooney 90	3,595
29	div3	Hereford	H	W	4-0	Lowry 2, Lester 21, 40, Moloney 90	3,274
30	div3	Wycombe	A	L	0-1		5,203
31	div3	Stockport	A	D	2-2	Fletcher 16, Lester 51	5,105
32	div3	Chester	H	D	1-1	Lester 54	3,701
33	div3	Grimsby	A	L	2-4	Cooper 73, Ward 83	4,601
34	div3	Peterborough	H	L	1-2	Leven 87	3,973
35	div3	Hereford	A	L	0-2		3,503
36	div3	Brentford	H	W	1-0	Dowson 4	3,728
37	div3	Rochdale	A	W	1-0	Leven 89	3,108
38	div3	Lincoln	H	W	4-1	Kerry 39, 81, Lester 52, Leven 59	4,352
39	div3	MK Dons	H	L	1-2	Lowry 69	3,834
40	div3	Rotherham	A	L	1-2	Ward 75	4,550
41	div3	Accrington	H	W	4-2	Niven 33, Roberts 58 og, Lowry 59, Ward 85	3,274
42	div3	Bradford	A	L	0-1		13,825
43	div3	Dag & Red	A	W	3-0	Ward 37, 46, Fletcher 79	2,054
44	div3	Shrewsbury	H	W	4-1	Dowson 47, 90, Ward 50, 59	3,570
45	div3	Morecambe	A	D	1-1	Fletcher 35	2,531
46	div3	Darlington	H	D	1-1	Ward 50	3,809
47	div3	Macclesfield	A	L	0-1		2,573
48	div3	Notts County	H	D	1-1	Lester 59	4,477

TEAM OF THE SEASON

G	Barry Roche	CG: 45	DR: 75
D	Janos Kovacs	CG: 41	DR: 70
D	Phil Picken	CG: 34	DR: 81
D	Aaron Downes	CG: 37	DR: 76
D	James Lowry	CG: 35	DR: 75
M	Jamie Winter	CG: 17	SD: 40
M	Peter Leven	CG: 38	SD: 24
M	Felix Bastians	CG: 9	SD: 22
M	Derek Niven	CG: 36	SD: 18
F	Jack Lester	CG: 33	SR: 130
F	Jamie Ward	CG: 33	SR: 214

KEY PLAYER APPEARANCES

	PLAYER	POS	AGE	APP	MINS ON	GOALS	CARDS(Y	/R)
1	Barry Roche	GK	26	45	4050	0	3	0
2	Janos Kovacs	DEF	22	41	3613	2	10	0
3	Peter Leven	MID	24	42	3531	6	5	0
4	Aaron Downes	DEF	23	40	3421	2	8	0
5	James Lowry	DEF	21	42	3410	6	6	0
6	Derek Niven	MID	24	38	3316	3	5	0
7	Phil Picken	DEF	22	37	3087	0	8	0
8	Gregor Robertson	DEF	24	35	3046	1	3	0
9	Jack Lester	ATT	32	36	2993	23	6	0
10	Jamie Ward	ATT	22	35	2575	12	4	0
11	Steve Fletcher	ATT	35	38	2383	5	3	0
12	Jamie Winter	MID	22	25	1808	0	4	0
13	Adam Rooney	ATT	20	22	1111	7	0	0
14	Peter Hartley	DEF	20	12	994	0	3	0
15	Felix Bastians	MID	20	12	887	1	1	0
16	Kevin Gray	DEF	36	14	883	0	1	1
17	Lloyd Kerry	MID	20	13	867	2	3	0
18	David Dowson	ATT	19	12	765	3	1	0

KEY PLAYERS - GOALSCORERS

Jack Lester

Goals in the League	23
Contribution to Attacking Power Average number of minutes between League team goals while on pitch	50
Player Strike Rate Average number of minutes between League goals scored by player	130
Club Strike Rate Average number of minutes between League goals scored by club	54

	PLAYER	GOALS LGE	POWER	STRIKE RATE
1	Jack Lester	23	50	130 mins
2	Adam Rooney	7	44	158 mins
3	Jamie Ward	12	54	214 mins
4	Lloyd Kerry	2	72	433 mins

KEY PLAYERS - MIDFIELDERS

Jamie Winter

Goals in the League	0
Defensive Rating Average number of mins between League goals conceded while on the pitch	100
Contribution to Attacking Power Average number of minutes between League team goals while on pitch	60
Scoring Difference Defensive Rating minus Contribution to Attacking Power	40

	PLAYER	GOALS LGE	DEF RATE	POWER	SCORE DIFF
1	Jamie Winter	0	100	60	40 mins
2	Peter Leven	6	75	51	24 mins
3	Felix Bastians	1	68	46	22 mins
4	Derek Niven	3	69	51	18 mins

KEY PLAYERS - DEFENDERS

Phil Picken

Goals Conceded when he was on pitch	38
Defensive Rating Ave number of mins between League goals conceded while on the pitch	81
Clean Sheets In games when he played at least 70 minutes	9
Club Defensive Rating Average number of mins between League goals conceded by the club this season.	73

	PLAYER	CON LGE	CLEAN SHEETS	DEF RATE
1	Phil Picken	38	9	81 mins
2	Aaron Downes	45	10	76 mins
3	James Lowry	45	9	75 mins
4	Janos Kovacs	51	10	70 mins

KEY GOALKEEPER

Barry Roche

Goals Conceded in the League	54
Defensive Rating Ave number of mins between League goals conceded while on the pitch.	75
Counting Games Games when he played at least 70 mins	45
Clean Sheets In games when he played at least 70 mins	11

TOP POINT EARNERS

	PLAYER	GAMES	AV PTS
1	Jamie Winter	17	2.12
2	Jack Lester	33	1.64
3	Phil Picken	34	1.62
4	James Lowry	35	1.60
5	Peter Leven	38	1.58
6	Derek Niven	36	1.56
7	Janos Kovacs	40	1.53
8	Barry Roche	45	1.53
9	Gregor Robertson	32	1.50
10	Aaron Downes	37	1.49
	CLUB AVERAGE:		1.50

ROTHERHAM UNITED

Final Position: **9th**

NICKNAME: THE MERRY MILLERS — KEY: ☐ Won ☐ Drawn ☐ Lost

							Attendance
1	div3	Hereford	A	D	0-0		3,566
2	ccr1	Sheff Wed	H	L	1-3	Harrison 34	6,416
3	div3	Peterborough	H	W	3-1	D.Holmes 8, 35, O'Grady 33	4,291
4	div3	Stockport	A	D	2-2	Sharps 55, McNeil 72 og	5,764
5	div3	Chester	H	D	1-1	O'Grady 57	4,036
6	div3	Darlington	H	L	0-2		3,988
7	div3	Wrexham	A	W	1-0	O'Grady 78	3,711
8	div3	Notts County	H	D	1-1	P.Holmes 7	4,181
9	div3	Barnet	A	L	0-2		2,008
10	div3	Macclesfield	A	D	1-1	D.Holmes 13	1,715
11	div3	Mansfield	H	W	3-2	Bean 4, Newsham 20, Brogan 67	3,881
12	div3	Brentford	A	D	1-1	Coughlan 62	3,841
13	div3	Morecambe	H	W	3-1	Brogan 71 pen, Yates 81, 87	4,181
14	div3	Dag & Red	A	W	2-0	Harrison 45, 52	2,091
15	div3	Grimsby	H	W	2-1	Hudson 39, O'Grady 77	4,162
16	div3	Bury	H	W	2-1	Newsham 22, O'Grady 55	3,425
17	facr1	Forest Green	A	D	2-2	Brogan 57 pen, O'Grady 84	2,102
18	div3	Accrington	A	W	1-0	Hudson 52	1,918
19	facr1r	Forest Green	H	L	0-3		2,754
20	div3	Shrewsbury	H	W	2-0	Taylor 38, D.Holmes 81	3,832
21	div3	Chesterfield	A	W	2-0	D.Holmes 8, Hudson 55	5,417
22	div3	Rochdale	H	L	2-4	Sharps 14, D.Holmes 16	3,808
23	div3	Wrexham	H	W	3-0	D.Holmes 40, 72, Newsham 82	5,773
24	div3	Darlington	A	D	1-1	O'Grady 36	6,965
25	div3	Notts County	A	W	1-0	Joseph 34	5,290
26	div3	Macclesfield	H	W	3-0	Hudson 70, Taylor 80, 87	4,464
27	div3	MK Dons	H	L	0-1		5,421
28	div3	Lincoln	A	W	3-1	D.Holmes 24, 57, 84	5,016
29	div3	Wycombe	H	D	1-1	Brogan 14	6,709
30	div3	Chester	A	W	1-0	O'Grady 7	2,536
31	div3	Peterborough	A	L	1-3	Taylor 90	5,152
32	div3	Hereford	H	L	0-1		4,746
33	div3	MK Dons	A	D	1-1	Harrison 82	9,455
34	div3	Stockport	H	L	1-4	Hudson 37	4,004
35	div3	Wycombe	A	L	0-1		4,610
36	div3	Lincoln	H	W	3-2	Joseph 35, Hudson 65, Newsham 74	4,321
37	div3	Bradford	A	L	2-3	Taylor 29, O'Grady 84	13,436
38	div3	Accrington	H	L	0-1		3,683
39	div3	Shrewsbury	A	D	1-1	Mills 37	5,265
40	div3	Bury	A	L	0-3		1,957
41	div3	Chesterfield	H	W	2-1	P.Holmes 30, Joseph 45	4,550
42	div3	Bradford	H	D	1-1	O'Grady 65	4,157
43	div3	Rochdale	A	L	1-4	Joseph 7	2,985
44	div3	Morecambe	A	L	1-5	Hudson 35	2,171
45	div3	Brentford	H	L	1-2	Hudson 87	2,979
46	div3	Grimsby	A	W	1-0	Taylor 40	3,583
47	div3	Dag & Red	H	W	2-1	Hudson 6 pen, Harrison 41	3,203
48	div3	Mansfield	A	W	1-0	Yates 71	5,271
49	div3	Barnet	H	W	1-0	Green 8	4,834

TEAM OF THE SEASON

G — Andy Warrington — CG: 46 DR: 71

D — Stephen Brogan — CG: 27 DR: 89

D — Pablo Mills — CG: 31 DR: 81

D — Ian Sharps — CG: 33 DR: 73

D — Marc Joseph — CG: 33 DR: 71

M — Mark Hudson — CG: 30 SD: 5

M — Danny Harrison — CG: 43 SD: 5

M — Dale Tonge — CG: 31 SD: -2

M — Peter Holmes, P — CG: 17 SD: -8

F — Derek Holmes — CG: 23 SR: 238

F — Ryan Taylor — CG: 14 SR: 317

KEY PLAYER APPEARANCES

	PLAYER	POS	AGE	APP	MINS ON	GOALS	CARDS(Y/R)	
1	Andy Warrington	GK	32	46	4140	0	0	0
2	Graham Coughlan	DEF	33	45	4041	1	2	0
3	Danny Harrison	MID	25	44	3913	4	5	0
4	Chris O'Grady	ATT	22	38	3162	9	1	0
5	Marc Joseph	DEF	31	36	2999	4	1	0
6	Ian Sharps	DEF	27	33	2949	2	4	0
7	Dale Tonge	MID	23	37	2884	0	2	0
8	Pablo Mills	DEF	24	33	2768	1	3	0
9	Mark Hudson	MID	27	31	2717	9	3	0
10	Derek Holmes, D	ATT	29	37	2627	11	0	0
11	Stephen Brogan	DEF	20	29	2510	3	3	0
12	Ryan Taylor	ATT	20	35	1905	6	2	0
13	Peter Holmes, P	MID	27	24	1818	2	3	0
14	Marc Newsham	ATT	21	25	1248	4	1	0
15	Marcus Bean	MID	23	12	980	1	2	0
16	Andy Todd	MID	29	13	942	0	0	0
17	Ian Ross	MID	22	17	899	0	2	0
18	Paul Hurst	DEF	33	11	675	0	0	0

KEY PLAYERS - GOALSCORERS

Derek Holmes

Goals in the League: 11

Contribution to Attacking Power — Average number of minutes between League team goals while on pitch: 69

Player Strike Rate — Average number of minutes between League goals scored by player: 238

Club Strike Rate — Average number of minutes between League goals scored by club: 68

	PLAYER	GOALS LGE	POWER	STRIKE RATE
1	Derek Holmes	11	69	238 mins
2	Mark Hudson	9	61	301 mins
3	Ryan Taylor	6	61	317 mins
4	Chris O'Grady	9	70	351 mins

KEY PLAYERS - MIDFIELDERS

Mark Hudson

Goals in the League: 9

Defensive Rating — Average number of mins between League goals conceded while on the pitch: 66

Contribution to Attacking Power — Average number of minutes between League team goals while on pitch: 61

Scoring Difference — Defensive Rating minus Contribution to Attacking Power: 5

	PLAYER	GOALS LGE	DEF RATE	POWER	SCORE DIFF
1	Mark Hudson	9	66	61	5 mins
2	Danny Harrison	4	72	67	5 mins
3	Dale Tonge	0	68	70	-2 mins
4	Peter Holmes, P	2	64	72	-8 mins

KEY PLAYERS - DEFENDERS

Stephen Brogan

Goals Conceded when he was on pitch: 28

Defensive Rating — Ave number of mins between League goals conceded while on the pitch: 89

Clean Sheets — In games when he played at least 70 minutes: 10

Club Defensive Rating — Average number of mins between League goals conceded by the club this season: 72

	PLAYER	CON LGE	CLEAN SHEETS	DEF RATE
1	Stephen Brogan	28	10	89 mins
2	Pablo Mills	34	11	81 mins
3	Ian Sharps	40	9	73 mins
4	Marc Joseph	42	10	71 mins

KEY GOALKEEPER

Andy Warrington

Goals Conceded in the League: 58

Defensive Rating — Ave number of mins between League goals conceded while on the pitch: 71

Counting Games — Games when he played at least 70 mins: 46

Clean Sheets — In games when he played at least 70 mins: 13

TOP POINT EARNERS

	PLAYER	GAMES	AV PTS
1	Ryan Taylor	14	1.86
2	Stephen Brogan	27	1.81
3	Derek Holmes, D	23	1.74
4	Pablo Mills	31	1.71
5	Mark Hudson	30	1.70
6	Ian Sharps	33	1.64
7	Danny Harrison	43	1.63
8	Dale Tonge	31	1.61
9	Andy Warrington	46	1.61
10	Marc Joseph	33	1.58
	CLUB AVERAGE:		1.39

BRADFORD CITY

Final Position: **10th**

NICKNAME: THE BANTAMS

KEY: ☐Won ☐Drawn ☐Lost

							Attendance
1	div3	**Macclesfield**	H	D	1-1	Ndumbu-Nsungu 45	13,401
2	ccr1	**Wolverhampton**	A	L	1-2	Nix 77	9,625
3	div3	**Shrewsbury**	A	L	0-1		6,413
4	div3	**Wrexham**	H	W	2-1	Johnson 49, Medley 78	13,546
5	div3	**Barnet**	A	L	1-2	Johnson 52	2,412
6	div3	**Lincoln**	A	W	2-1	Ndumbu-Nsungu 35, Colbeck 79	5,286
7	div3	**Peterborough**	H	W	1-0	Bower 56	13,819
8	div3	**Hereford**	A	L	2-4	Ndumbu-Nsungu 30, 59	3,275
9	div3	**Wycombe**	H	L	0-1		13,530
10	div3	**Accrington**	H	L	0-3		13,346
11	div3	**MK Dons**	A	L	1-2	Conlon 90 pen	7,903
12	div3	**Morecambe**	A	L	1-2	Bower 43	4,761
13	div3	**Darlington**	H	D	0-0		14,074
14	div3	**Grimsby**	A	D	1-1	Ndumbu-Nsungu 90 pen	4,883
15	div3	**Brentford**	H	L	1-2	Bower 88	13,326
16	div3	**Chester**	H	W	2-1	Daley 36, Rhodes 89	13,211
17	facr1	**Chester**	H	W	1-0	Thorne 28	4,069
18	div3	**Dag & Red**	A	W	4-1	Thorne 19, Wetherall 75, Law 89, 90	2,247
19	div3	**Stockport**	H	D	1-1	Ndumbu-Nsungu 71	13,837
20	facr2	**Tranmere**	H	L	0-3		6,379
21	div3	**Mansfield**	A	D	0-0		2,308
22	div3	**Chesterfield**	A	D	1-1	Nix 77	3,727
23	div3	**Peterborough**	A	L	1-2	Nix 11	5,355
24	div3	**Lincoln**	H	W	2-1	Thorne 1, Conlon 90	15,510
25	div3	**Hereford**	H	L	1-3	Wetherall 44	13,640
26	div3	**Accrington**	A	W	2-0	M.Clarke 47, Colbeck 90	2,898
27	div3	**Notts County**	H	W	3-0	Thorne 34, 58, 90	13,494
28	div3	**Bury**	A	D	2-2	Conlon 45 pen, Nix 79	2,776
29	div3	**Wrexham**	A	D	1-1	Nix 49	4,341
30	div3	**Shrewsbury**	H	W	4-2	Nix 7, Daley 40, Thorne 57 Conlon 85 pen	13,269
31	div3	**Macclesfield**	A	W	1-0	Brown 75	2,778
32	div3	**Bury**	H	L	1-2	Thorne 23	13,844
33	div3	**Rochdale**	H	L	1-2	Thorne 45	14,017
34	div3	**Notts County**	A	W	3-1	Thorne 63, Colbeck 69, Rhodes 76	4,717
35	div3	**Rotherham**	H	W	3-2	Daley 15, Rhodes 17, Bullock 44	13,436
36	div3	**Dag & Red**	H	L	0-2		13,537
37	div3	**Stockport**	A	L	1-2	Thorne 53 pen	5,763
38	div3	**Chester**	A	W	1-0	Conlon 66	1,566
39	div3	**Mansfield**	H	L	1-2	Conlon 45	13,611
40	div3	**Rotherham**	A	D	1-1	Colbeck 48	4,157
41	div3	**Chesterfield**	H	W	1-0	Thorne 16	13,825
42	div3	**Darlington**	A	W	3-1	Penford 50, Conlon 63, Colbeck 79	4,492
43	div3	**Rochdale**	A	L	1-2	Thorne 60 pen	3,811
44	div3	**Morecambe**	H	W	1-0	Johnson 56	13,562
45	div3	**Barnet**	H	D	1-1	Johnson 76	13,072
46	div3	**Brentford**	A	D	2-2	Thorne 17, Nix 19	4,336
47	div3	**Grimsby**	H	W	2-1	Thorne 62, Colbeck 90	13,448
48	div3	**MK Dons**	H	L	1-2	Daley 45	14,609
49	div3	**Wycombe**	A	L	1-2	Medley 44 pen	5,467

TEAM OF THE SEASON

- G — Donovan Ricketts — CG: 22 DR: 68
- D — Matthew Clarke — CG: 15 DR: 75
- D — Ben Starosta — CG: 12 DR: 74
- D — Darren Williams — CG: 26 DR: 72
- D — Paul Heckingbottom — CG: 42 DR: 70
- M — Lee Bullock — CG: 12 SD: 18
- M — Paul Evans — CG: 17 SD: 14
- M — Joe Colbeck — CG: 24 SD: 9
- M — Omar Daley — CG: 35 SD: -2
- F — Peter Thorne — CG: 30 SR: 190
- F — Guylain Nsungu — CG: 14 SR: 232

KEY PLAYER APPEARANCES

	PLAYER	POS	AGE	APP	MINS ON	GOALS	CARDS(Y/R)	
1	David Wetherall	DEF	37	46	4140	2	2	0
2	Paul Heckingbottom	DEF	30	44	3851	0	5	1
3	Omar Daley	MID	27	41	3203	4	4	1
4	Karl Nix	MID	22	40	2753	6	4	0
5	Eddie Johnson	ATT	23	32	2725	4	3	0
6	Peter Thorne	ATT	35	33	2661	14	1	0
7	Joe Colbeck	MID	21	33	2428	6	2	1
8	Darren Williams	DEF	31	28	2405	0	4	0
9	Mark Bower	DEF	28	26	2251	3	2	0
10	Barry Conlon	ATT	29	42	2001	7	2	0
11	Donovan Ricketts	GK	31	22	1980	0	1	0
12	Scott Loach	GK	20	20	1800	0	0	0
13	Paul Evans	MID	33	25	1587	0	6	0
14	Matthew Clarke	DEF	27	17	1431	1	3	0
15	Guylain Ndumbu-Nsungu	ATT	25	18	1394	6	1	0
16	Alex Rhodes	ATT	26	28	1170	3	1	0
17	Ben Starosta	DEF	21	15	1110	0	0	0
18	Lee Bullock	MID	27	12	1080	1	1	0

KEY PLAYERS - GOALSCORERS

Peter Thorne

Goals in the League	14	Player Strike Rate: Average number of minutes between League goals scored by player	190
Contribution to Attacking Power Average number of minutes between League team goals while on pitch	57	**Club Strike Rate** Average number of minutes between League goals scored by club	70

	PLAYER	GOALS LGE	POWER	STRIKE RATE
1	Peter Thorne	14	57	190 mins
2	Guylain Ndumbu-Nsungu	6	107	232 mins
3	Barry Conlon	7	76	285 mins
4	Joe Colbeck	6	56	404 mins

KEY PLAYERS - MIDFIELDERS

Lee Bullock

Goals in the League	1	**Contribution to Attacking Power** Average number of minutes between League team goals while on pitch	49
Defensive Rating Average number of mins between League goals conceded while on the pitch	67	Scoring Difference: Defensive Rating minus Contribution to Attacking Power	18

	PLAYER	GOALS LGE	DEF RATE	POWER	SCORE DIFF
1	Lee Bullock	1	67	49	18 mins
2	Paul Evans	0	75	61	14 mins
3	Joe Colbeck	6	65	56	9 mins
4	Omar Daley	4	64	66	-2 mins

KEY PLAYERS - DEFENDERS

Matthew Clarke

Goals Conceded when he was on pitch	19	**Clean Sheets** In games when he played at least 70 minutes	4
Defensive Rating: Ave number of mins between League goals conceded while on the pitch	75	**Club Defensive Rating** Average number of mins between League goals conceded by the club this season.	72

	PLAYER	CON LGE	CLEAN SHEETS	DEF RATE
1	Matthew Clarke	19	4	75 mins
2	Ben Starosta	15	3	74 mins
3	Darren Williams	33	5	72 mins
4	Paul Heckingbottom	55	9	70 mins

KEY GOALKEEPER

Donovan Ricketts

Goals Conceded in the League	29
Defensive Rating: Ave number of mins between League goals conceded while on the pitch.	68
Counting Games Games when he played at least 70 mins	22
Clean Sheets In games when he played at least 70 mins	4

TOP POINT EARNERS

	PLAYER	GAMES	AV PTS
1	Joe Colbeck	24	1.88
2	Matthew Clarke	15	1.73
3	Lee Bullock	12	1.67
4	Peter Thorne	30	1.60
5	Ben Starosta	12	1.58
6	Scott Loach	20	1.50
7	Paul Evans	17	1.47
8	Barry Conlon	18	1.39
9	Paul Heckingbottom	42	1.36
10	Donovan Ricketts	22	1.36
	CLUB AVERAGE:		1.35

MORECAMBE

Final Position: **11th**

NICKNAME: THE SHRIMPS

KEY: ☐ Won ☐ Drawn ☐ Lost

							Attendance
1	div3	Barnet	H	D	0-0		3,633
2	ccr1	Preston	A	W	2-1	Bentley 6, Artell 84	7,703
3	div3	Wrexham	A	L	1-2	Newby 56	5,504
4	div3	Mansfield	H	W	3-1	White 5 og, Stanley 44, Baker 51 pen	2,980
5	ccr2	Wolverhampton	A	W	3-1	Baker 62 pen, Newby 92, Thompson 105	11,296
6	div3	Notts County	A	D	1-1	Twiss 34	4,434
7	div3	Chester	A	W	1-0	Baker 90 pen	3,199
8	div3	Hereford	H	L	0-3		2,949
9	div3	Peterborough	A	D	1-1	Thompson 83	4,473
10	ccr3	Sheff Utd	A	L	0-5		8,854
11	div3	MK Dons	H	L	0-1		2,688
12	div3	Stockport	H	W	2-0	Baker 45, 66	2,871
13	div3	Lincoln	A	D	1-1	Beevers 36 og	3,281
14	div3	Bradford	H	W	2-1	Thompson 64, Baker 90	4,761
15	div3	Rotherham	A	L	1-3	Bentley 46	4,181
16	div3	Rochdale	H	D	1-1	Artell 17	3,651
17	div3	Chesterfield	A	D	2-2	Curtis 1, Grand 90	3,721
18	div3	Accrington	H	L	0-1		2,814
19	facr1	Port Vale	H	L	0-2		2,730
20	div3	Grimsby	A	W	2-1	Newby 28, Twiss 50	4,897
21	div3	Bury	H	W	2-1	Bentley 11, Twiss 27	3,124
22	div3	Brentford	A	W	1-0	Twiss 56	3,155
23	div3	Wycombe	A	L	0-2		3,821
24	div3	Hereford	A	W	3-0	Bentley 27, Blinkhorn 38, Artell 64	3,058
25	div3	Chester	H	W	5-3	Bentley 18, 70, Thompson 20 Blinkhorn 25, Baker 45	3,419
26	div3	Peterborough	H	W	3-2	Artell 27, Baker 52, 71 pen	2,371
27	div3	Stockport	A	L	1-2	Blinkhorn 80	5,489
28	div3	Macclesfield	A	W	2-1	Blinkhorn 30, Thompson 86	2,254
29	div3	Dag & Red	H	W	1-0	Blinkhorn 90	2,754
30	div3	Darlington	H	L	0-3		2,773
31	div3	Shrewsbury	A	L	0-2		5,036
32	div3	Notts County	H	D	1-1	Baker 72	2,727
33	div3	Wrexham	H	D	2-2	Curtis 8, N.Roberts 52 og	2,421
34	div3	Barnet	A	W	1-0	Thompson 62	1,619
35	div3	Macclesfield	H	L	0-1		2,626
36	div3	Mansfield	A	W	2-1	Bentley 6, Blinkhorn 24	2,287
37	div3	Dag & Red	A	L	0-2		1,809
38	div3	Grimsby	H	L	0-4		2,303
39	div3	Bury	A	L	1-2	Drummond 53	2,596
40	div3	Accrington	A	L	2-3	Blinkhorn 14, Twiss 50	1,448
41	div3	Brentford	H	W	3-1	Drummond 31, Thompson 53, Hunter 88	2,180
42	div3	Wycombe	H	L	0-1		2,524
43	div3	Darlington	A	D	2-2	Thompson 38 pen, Newby 41	3,719
44	div3	Rotherham	H	W	5-1	Blinkhorn 8, Newby 9, 18, 42, Stanley 73	2,171
45	div3	Bradford	A	L	0-1		13,562
46	div3	Shrewsbury	H	D	1-1	Baker 32	1,634
47	div3	Chesterfield	H	D	1-1	Blinkhorn 74	2,531
48	div3	Rochdale	A	L	0-1		3,706
49	div3	Lincoln	H	L	1-2	Blinkhorn 90	2,762
50	div3	MK Dons	A	D	1-1	Twiss 78	17,250

TEAM OF THE SEASON

		CG	
G	Joe Lewis	CG: 18	DR: 87
D	Adam Yates	CG: 42	DR: 71
D	Danny Adams	CG: 42	DR: 68
D	Jim Bentley	CG: 42	DR: 68
D	David Artell	CG: 34	DR: 65
M	Craig Stanley	CG: 40	SD: 0
M	Garry Thompson	CG: 34	SD: -3
M	Gary Hunter	CG: 17	SD: -4
M	Stuart Drummond	CG: 16	SD: -6
F	Matthew Blinkhorn	CG: 34	SR: 321
F	Michael Twiss	CG: 24	SR: 416

KEY PLAYER APPEARANCES

	PLAYER	POS	AGE	APP	MINS ON	GOALS	CARDS(Y	R)
1	Adam Yates	DEF	25	44	3850	0	5	0
2	Jim Bentley	DEF	32	43	3801	6	4	0
3	Danny Adams	DEF	32	42	3731	0	10	0
4	Craig Stanley	MID	25	41	3594	2	8	0
5	Carl Baker	MID	50	42	3361	10	3	0
6	Garry Thompson	MID	27	40	3225	7	2	0
7	Matthew Blinkhorn	ATT	23	41	3215	10	2	0
8	David Artell	DEF	27	36	3069	3	4	1
9	Michael Twiss	ATT	30	36	2409	6	2	1
10	Gary Hunter	MID	23	38	1935	1	1	0
11	Joe Lewis	GK	20	19	1661	0	0	0
12	Wayne Curtis	ATT	28	36	1639	2	2	0
13	Stuart Drummond	MID	32	18	1432	2	2	0
14	Damien Allen	MID	21	20	1279	0	0	0
15	Neil Sorvel	MID	35	22	1234	0	0	0
16	Shwan Jalal	GK	24	12	1080	0	0	0
17	Jon Newby	ATT	29	32	1065	6	1	0
18	Henry McStay	DEF	0	13	1010	0	2	0

KEY PLAYERS - GOALSCORERS

Matthew Blinkhorn

Goals in the League	10	Player Strike Rate Average number of minutes between League goals scored by player	321
Contribution to Attacking Power Average number of minutes between League team goals while on pitch	71	Club Strike Rate Average number of minutes between League goals scored by club	73

	PLAYER	GOALS LGE	POWER	STRIKE RATE
1	Matthew Blinkhorn	10	71	321 mins
2	Carl Baker	10	78	345 mins
3	Michael Twiss	6	69	416 mins
4	Garry Thompson	7	63	460 mins

KEY PLAYERS - MIDFIELDERS

Craig Stanley

Goals in the League	2	Contribution to Attacking Power Average number of minutes between League team goals while on pitch	72
Defensive Rating Average number of mins between League goals conceded while on the pitch	72	Scoring Difference Defensive Rating minus Contribution to Attacking Power	0

	PLAYER	GOALS LGE	DEF RATE	POWER	SCORE DIFF
1	Craig Stanley	2	72	72	0 mins
2	Garry Thompson	7	60	63	-3 mins
3	Gary Hunter	1	63	67	-4 mins
4	Stuart Drummond	2	62	68	-6 mins

KEY PLAYERS - DEFENDERS

Adam Yates

Goals Conceded when he was on pitch	55	Clean Sheets In games when he played at least 70 minutes	8
Defensive Rating Ave number of mins between League goals conceded while on the pitch	71	Club Defensive Rating Average number of mins between League goals conceded by the club this season.	68

	PLAYER	CON LGE	CLEAN SHEETS	DEF RATE
1	Adam Yates	55	8	71 mins
2	Danny Adams	56	8	68 mins
3	Jim Bentley	57	8	68 mins
4	David Artell	48	7	65 mins

KEY GOALKEEPER

Joe Lewis

Goals Conceded in the League	20
Defensive Rating Ave number of mins between League goals conceded while on the pitch.	87
Counting Games Games when he played at least 70 mins	19
Clean Sheets In games when he played at least 70 mins	6

TOP POINT EARNERS

	PLAYER	GAMES	AV PTS
1	Joe Lewis	18	1.89
2	Michael Twiss	24	1.58
3	Gary Hunter	17	1.47
4	Carl Baker	36	1.42
5	Adam Yates	42	1.38
6	Craig Stanley	40	1.35
7	Garry Thompson	34	1.35
8	Jim Bentley	42	1.33
9	David Artell	34	1.32
10	Stuart Drummond	16	1.31
	CLUB AVERAGE:		1.30

BARNET

Final Position: **12th**

NICKNAME: THE BEES

KEY: ☐Won ☐Drawn ☐Lost

	Comp	Opponent	H/A	Res	Score	Scorers	Attendance
1	div3	**Morecambe**	A	D	0-0		3,633
2	ccr1	**Norwich**	A	L	2-5	Puncheon 66, Birchall 74	13,971
3	div3	**Hereford**	H	L	1-2	Puncheon 13	1,790
4	div3	**Brentford**	A	L	1-2	Puncheon 61	4,744
5	div3	**Bradford**	H	W	2-1	Johnson 43 og, Puncheon 90	2,412
6	div3	**Dag & Red**	A	D	1-1	Thomas 45	2,192
7	div3	**Rochdale**	H	D	0-0		2,040
8	div3	**Chesterfield**	A	W	1-0	Norville 69	4,088
9	div3	**Rotherham**	H	W	2-0	Birchall 52, Puncheon 83 pen	2,008
10	div3	**Wycombe**	H	W	2-1	Hatch 77, Puncheon 86	2,023
11	div3	**Stockport**	A	W	4-2	Birchall 14, 47, J.Wright 62, Carew 84	4,751
12	div3	**Mansfield**	H	D	1-1	Hatch 71	2,041
13	div3	**Wrexham**	A	W	2-0	Hatch 59, 69	3,591
14	div3	**Accrington**	H	D	2-2	Hatch 59, Burton 70	2,178
15	div3	**Bury**	A	L	0-3		2,121
16	div3	**Notts County**	H	D	1-1	Puncheon 39	2,089
17	facr1	**Gillingham**	H	W	2-1	Yakubu 61, Hatch 63	2,843
18	div3	**Shrewsbury**	A	L	0-1		5,197
19	div3	**Grimsby**	H	L	0-3		2,059
20	facr2	**Burton**	A	D	1-1	Hatch 19	2,769
21	div3	**Chester**	A	L	0-3		1,858
22	div3	**Macclesfield**	H	D	2-2	Hatch 9, Bishop 90	1,303
23	facr2r	**Burton**	H	W	1-0	Birchall 83	1,379
24	div3	**Lincoln**	A	L	1-4	Birchall 59	3,549
25	div3	**Dag & Red**	H	W	3-1	Puncheon 41 pen, 50, 78	2,513
26	div3	**Chesterfield**	H	L	0-2		2,346
27	div3	**Wycombe**	A	D	0-0		4,818
28	facr3	**Swindon**	A	D	1-1	Birchall 85	5,944
29	div3	**MK Dons**	A	W	1-0	Yakubu 22	9,881
30	facr3	**Swindon**	H	W	2-0*	Paynter 53 og (*on penalties)	2,810
31	facr4	**Bristol Rovers**	H	L	0-1		5,190
32	div3	**Hereford**	A	W	2-1	Adomah 52, Nicolau 85	2,271
33	div3	**Morecambe**	H	L	0-1		1,619
34	div3	**Darlington**	A	L	0-1		3,145
35	div3	**Brentford**	H	L	1-2	Birchall 90	2,522
36	div3	**Peterborough**	A	L	0-1		5,520
37	div3	**MK Dons**	H	L	0-2		2,495
38	div3	**Shrewsbury**	H	W	4-1	Akurang 16, 54, Adomah 32, 45	1,864
39	div3	**Peterborough**	H	L	0-2		2,202
40	div3	**Notts County**	A	D	0-0		3,687
41	div3	**Grimsby**	A	L	1-4	Akurang 80	3,325
42	div3	**Chester**	H	W	3-1	Adomah 50, Akurang 72 pen, 80	1,663
43	div3	**Lincoln**	H	W	5-2	Birchall 28, 46, Adomah 38 pen Thomas 44, Porter 63	2,115
44	div3	**Macclesfield**	A	L	0-3		1,718
45	div3	**Wrexham**	H	W	3-2	Yakubu 45, Thomas 51, Nicolau 62	2,286
46	div3	**Darlington**	H	D	0-0		1,678
47	div3	**Mansfield**	A	D	2-2	Thomas 70, Birchall 77	2,463
48	div3	**Bradford**	A	D	1-1	Birchall 23	13,072
49	div3	**Bury**	H	W	3-0	Birchall 57, 70, Akurang 84	2,054
50	div3	**Rochdale**	A	L	0-3		2,925
51	div3	**Accrington**	A	W	2-0	Bishop 54, Leary 82	1,288
52	div3	**Stockport**	H	W	2-1	Puncheon 47, Akurang 81	3,074
53	div3	**Rotherham**	A	L	0-1		4,834

TEAM OF THE SEASON

G — Lee Harrison, CG: 37 DR: 62

D — Sagi Burton, CG: 28 DR: 72

D — Kenny Gillet, CG: 29 DR: 71

D — Ishmail Yakubu, CG: 24 DR: 69

D — Joe Devera, CG: 41 DR: 68

M — Nicky Nicolau, CG: 27 SD: 7

M — Josh Wright, CG: 31 SD: -2

M — Max Porter, CG: 25 SD: -3

M — Ashley Carew, CG: 13 SD: -5

F — Cliff Akurang, CG: 14 SR: 211

F — Adam Birchall, CG: 35 SR: 295

KEY PLAYER APPEARANCES

	PLAYER	POS	AGE	APP	MINS ON	GOALS	CARDS(Y	/R)
1	Joe Devera	DEF	21	41	3538	0	1	1
2	Neil Bishop	MID	26	39	3468	2	3	0
3	Lee Harrison	GK	36	38	3387	0	0	0
4	Jason Puncheon	MID	22	41	3292	10	8	1
5	Adam Birchall	ATT	23	42	3247	11	0	0
6	Josh Wright	MID	18	32	2791	1	4	0
7	Nicky Nicolau	MID	24	38	2756	2	2	0
8	Kenny Gillet	DEF	22	31	2654	0	7	0
9	Sagi Burton	DEF	30	30	2599	1	5	0
10	Ishmail Yakubu	DEF	23	28	2300	2	4	1
11	Max Porter	MID	21	30	2277	1	0	0
12	Albert Adomah	MID	20	22	1870	5	1	0
13	Ashley Carew	MID	22	33	1724	1	7	0
14	Michael Leary	MID	25	22	1549	1	4	1
15	Cliff Akurang	ATT	27	21	1481	7	4	0
16	Anthony Thomas	ATT	25	26	1349	4	1	0
17	Liam Hatch	ATT	26	20	1071	6	6	0
18	Joe O'Cearuill	DEF	21	14	966	0	0	1

KEY PLAYERS - GOALSCORERS

Cliff Akurang

Goals in the League	7	**Player Strike Rate** Average number of minutes between League goals scored by player	211
Contribution to Attacking Power Average number of minutes between League team goals while on pitch	87	**Club Strike Rate** Average number of minutes between League goals scored by club	78

	PLAYER	GOALS LGE	POWER	STRIKE RATE
1	Cliff Akurang	7	87	211 mins
2	Adam Birchall	11	67	295 mins
3	Jason Puncheon	10	76	329 mins
4	Albert Adomah	5	69	374 mins

KEY PLAYERS - MIDFIELDERS

Nicky Nicolau

Goals in the League	2	**Contribution to Attacking Power** Average number of minutes between League team goals while on pitch	61
Defensive Rating Average number of mins between League goals conceded while on the pitch	68	**Scoring Difference** Defensive Rating minus Contribution to Attacking Power	7

	PLAYER	GOALS LGE	DEF RATE	POWER	SCORE DIFF
1	Nicky Nicolau	2	68	61	7 mins
2	Josh Wright	1	69	71	-2 mins
3	Max Porter	1	81	84	-3 mins
4	Ashley Carew	1	61	66	-5 mins

KEY PLAYERS - DEFENDERS

Sagi Burton

Goals Conceded when he was on pitch	36	**Clean Sheets** In games when he played at least 70 minutes	9
Defensive Rating Ave number of mins between League goals conceded while on the pitch	72	**Club Defensive Rating** Average number of mins between League goals conceded by the club this season.	70

	PLAYER	CON LGE	CLEAN SHEETS	DEF RATE
1	Sagi Burton	36	9	72 mins
2	Kenny Gillet	37	7	71 mins
3	Ishmail Yakubu	33	6	69 mins
4	Joe Devera	52	10	68 mins

KEY GOALKEEPER

Lee Harrison

Goals Conceded in the League	54
Defensive Rating Ave number of mins between League goals conceded while on the pitch.	62
Counting Games Games when he played at least 70 mins	37
Clean Sheets In games when he played at least 70 mins	8

TOP POINT EARNERS

	PLAYER	GAMES	AV PTS
1	Ashley Carew	13	1.92
2	Nicky Nicolau	27	1.63
3	Josh Wright	31	1.52
4	Sagi Burton	28	1.50
5	Cliff Akurang	14	1.43
6	Lee Harrison	37	1.41
7	Albert Adomah	20	1.40
8	Jason Puncheon	35	1.37
9	Adam Birchall	35	1.34
10	Joe Devera	41	1.32
	CLUB AVERAGE:		1.30

BURY

Final Position: **13th**

NICKNAME: THE SHAKERS

KEY: Won Drawn Lost

	Comp	Opponent	H/A	Res	Score	Scorers	Attendance
1	div3	MK Dons	A	W	2-1	Bishop 51, 58 pen	7,740
2	ccr1	Carlisle	H	L	0-1		2,213
3	div3	Grimsby	H	D	1-1	Parrish 71	2,493
4	div3	Wycombe	A	L	0-1		4,067
5	div3	Brentford	H	L	1-2	Bishop 46	2,301
6	div3	Chesterfield	A	L	1-3	Woodthorpe 75	4,161
7	div3	Chester	H	L	0-2		2,539
8	div3	Dag & Red	A	D	1-1	Scott 21	1,597
9	div3	Accrington	H	W	2-1	Mangan 71, Adams 84	2,784
10	div3	Lincoln	H	D	1-1	Scott 24	1,690
11	div3	Rochdale	A	W	2-1	Mangan 2, Adams 12	4,692
12	div3	Notts County	A	W	3-1	Haslam 35, Scott 67, Adams 90	3,710
13	div3	Shrewsbury	H	D	1-1	Scott 45	2,667
14	div3	Macclesfield	A	D	2-2	Mangan 49, Adams 64 pen	2,672
15	div3	Barnet	H	W	3-0	Hurst 31, Adams 54, 86	2,121
16	div3	Rotherham	A	L	1-2	Adams 43 pen	3,425
17	facr1	Workington	H	W	4-1	Scott 22, Bishop 80, 85, 90	2,641
18	div3	Peterborough	H	W	2-0	Baker 32, Mangan 82	2,660
19	div3	Morecambe	A	L	1-2	Bishop 76	3,124
20	facr2	Exeter	H	W	1-0	Adams 79	2,725
21	div3	Wrexham	H	L	0-1		2,248
22	div3	Hereford	H	L	0-1		2,099
23	div3	Chester	A	L	1-2	Bishop 16	2,260
24	div3	Chesterfield	H	L	0-1		3,158
25	div3	Dag & Red	H	L	0-2		1,887
26	div3	Lincoln	A	D	1-1	Bishop 85	3,327
27	facr3	Norwich	A	D	1-1	Bishop 71	19,815
28	div3	Darlington	A	L	0-3		3,003
29	facr3r	Norwich	H	W	2-1	Futcher 18, Bishop 61	4,146
30	div3	Bradford	H	D	2-2	Bishop 57, Stephens 88	2,776
31	facr4	Southampton	A	L	0-2		25,449
32	div3	Grimsby	A	L	0-1		3,445
33	div3	MK Dons	H	L	1-5	Hurst 89	2,241
34	div3	Stockport	H	L	2-3	Bishop 13, Hurst 48	3,142
35	div3	Bradford	A	W	2-1	Bishop 56 pen, 89	13,844
36	div3	Wycombe	H	D	2-2	Bishop 65 pen, Barry-Murphy 88	1,895
37	div3	Stockport	A	W	2-1	Scott 71, Adams 79	5,704
38	div3	Darlington	H	L	1-2	Sodje 88	2,554
39	div3	Mansfield	A	D	1-1	Rooney 84	1,923
40	div3	Peterborough	A	L	0-1		6,150
41	div3	Brentford	A	W	4-1	Adams 13, Hurst 15, Bishop 37, 83	3,333
42	div3	Morecambe	H	W	2-1	Bishop 45, 49 pen	2,596
43	div3	Rotherham	H	W	3-0	Bishop 16, 62, Adams 66	1,957
44	div3	Wrexham	A	L	1-2	Hurst 45	4,431
45	div3	Hereford	A	D	0-0		3,420
46	div3	Mansfield	H	W	2-0	Scott 10, Rooney 37	2,779
47	div3	Shrewsbury	A	W	1-0	Adams 71	5,213
48	div3	Notts County	H	W	2-1	Rooney 18, Hughes 87	2,463
49	div3	Barnet	A	L	0-3		2,054
50	div3	Macclesfield	H	W	1-0	Bennett 43	2,506
51	div3	Rochdale	H	D	1-1	Adams 56	6,271
52	div3	Accrington	A	W	2-0	Bishop 22 pen, 45	2,566

TEAM OF THE SEASON

G	Darren Randolph	CG: 14 DR: 96
D	Efetobore Sodje	CG: 16 DR: 102
D	Paul Scott	CG: 39 DR: 72
D	Steven Haslam	CG: 36 DR: 71
D	Ben Futcher	CG: 40 DR: 67
M	Elliott Bennett	CG: 17 SD: 18
M	David Buchanan	CG: 24 SD: 12
M	Brian Barry-Murphy	CG: 25 SD: 2
M	Nicky Adams	CG: 39 SD: -4
F	Andrew Bishop	CG: 34 SR: 179
F	Glynn Hurst	CG: 24 SR: 517

KEY PLAYER APPEARANCES

	PLAYER	POS	AGE	APP	MINS ON	GOALS	CARDS(Y)	CARDS(R)
1	Nicky Adams	MID	21	43	3649	12	2	0
2	Ben Futcher	DEF	27	40	3587	0	10	1
3	Paul Scott	DEF	28	40	3567	6	10	1
4	Andrew Bishop	ATT	25	44	3412	19	4	1
5	Steven Haslam	DEF	28	37	3268	1	1	0
6	Jim Provett	GK	25	32	2864	0	0	0
7	Colin Woodthorpe	DEF	39	31	2626	1	7	0
8	Glynn Hurst	ATT	32	41	2587	5	4	0
9	Brian Barry-Murphy	MID	29	31	2427	1	3	0
10	David Buchanan	MID	22	35	2308	0	1	0
11	David Challinor	DEF	32	26	2253	0	3	0
12	Richie Baker	MID	20	32	1998	1	8	0
13	Paul Morgan	DEF	29	20	1763	0	1	0
14	Elliott Bennett	MID	19	19	1558	1	1	0
15	Andy Parrish	DEF	20	26	1515	1	0	0
16	Efetobore Sodje	DEF	35	16	1440	1	3	0
17	Darren Randolph	GK	21	14	1260	0	0	0
18	Adam Rooney	ATT	20	16	815	3	0	0

KEY PLAYERS - GOALSCORERS

Andrew Bishop

Goals in the League	19
Contribution to Attacking Power Average number of minutes between League team goals while on pitch	72
Player Strike Rate Average number of minutes between League goals scored by player	179
Club Strike Rate Average number of minutes between League goals scored by club	74

	PLAYER	GOALS LGE	POWER	STRIKE RATE
1	Andrew Bishop	19	72	179 mins
2	Nicky Adams	12	76	304 mins
3	Glynn Hurst	5	68	517 mins
4	Elliott Bennett	1	59	1558 mins

KEY PLAYERS - MIDFIELDERS

Elliott Bennett

Goals in the League	1
Defensive Rating Average number of mins between League goals conceded while on the pitch	77
Contribution to Attacking Power Average number of minutes between League team goals while on pitch	59
Scoring Difference Defensive Rating minus Contribution to Attacking Power	18

	PLAYER	GOALS LGE	DEF RATE	POWER	SCORE DIFF
1	Elliott Bennett	1	77	59	18 mins
2	David Buchanan	0	79	67	12 mins
3	Brian Barry-Murphy	1	67	65	2 mins
4	Nicky Adams	12	72	76	-4 mins

KEY PLAYERS - DEFENDERS

Efetobore Sodje

Goals Conceded when he was on pitch	14
Defensive Rating Ave number of mins between League goals conceded while on the pitch	102
Clean Sheets In games when he played at least 70 minutes	6
Club Defensive Rating Average number of mins between League goals conceded by the club this season.	70

	PLAYER	CON LGE	CLEAN SHEETS	DEF RATE
1	Efetobore Sodje	14	6	102 mins
2	Paul Scott	49	8	72 mins
3	Steven Haslam	46	8	71 mins
4	Ben Futcher	53	8	67 mins

KEY GOALKEEPER

Darren Randolph

Goals Conceded in the League	13
Defensive Rating Ave number of mins between League goals conceded while on the pitch.	96
Counting Games Games when he played at least 70 mins	14
Clean Sheets In games when he played at least 70 mins	4

TOP POINT EARNERS

	PLAYER	GAMES	AV PTS
1	Darren Randolph	14	1.93
2	Efetobore Sodje	16	1.88
3	Elliott Bennett	17	1.65
4	Brian Barry-Murphy	25	1.48
5	Steven Haslam	36	1.42
6	Paul Scott	39	1.38
7	Nicky Adams	39	1.31
8	Ben Futcher	40	1.30
9	David Buchanan	24	1.29
10	Andrew Bishop	34	1.21
	CLUB AVERAGE:		1.28

BRENTFORD

Final Position: **14th**

NICKNAME: THE BEES

KEY: ☐Won ☐Drawn ☐Lost

							Attendance
1	div3	Mansfield	H	D	1-1	Connell 14	4,909
2	ccr1	Bristol City	H	L	0-3		2,213
3	div3	Notts County	A	D	1-1	O'Connor 63	4,670
4	div3	Barnet	H	W	2-1	O'Connor 50 pen, Mousinho 71	4,744
5	div3	Bury	A	W	2-1	Poole 21, Shakes 84	2,301
6	div3	Wycombe	A	L	0-1		4,711
7	div3	MK Dons	H	L	0-3		4,476
8	div3	Chester	A	W	2-0	Thorpe 53, Moore 90	2,453
9	div3	Stockport	H	L	1-3	Connell 80	4,449
10	div3	Dag & Red	H	L	2-3	Mousinho 62, Thorpe 75	3,662
11	div3	Hereford	A	L	0-2		2,942
12	div3	Rotherham	H	D	1-1	Thorpe 55	3,841
13	div3	Rochdale	A	D	1-1	Poole 88	2,424
14	div3	Lincoln	H	W	1-0	Moore 80	4,368
15	div3	Bradford	A	W	2-1	Poole 41, Thorpe 60	13,326
16	div3	Macclesfield	A	L	0-1		1,378
17	facr1	Luton	A	D	1-1	Ide 20	4,167
18	div3	Darlington	H	L	0-2		4,657
19	div3	Peterborough	A	L	0-7		4,865
20	facr1r	Luton	H	L	0-2		2,643
21	div3	Morecambe	H	L	0-1		3,155
22	div3	Grimsby	H	L	0-1		3,999
23	div3	Wrexham	A	W	3-1	Connell 66, 77, S.Evans 72 og	3,811
24	div3	MK Dons	A	D	1-1	Connell 16	8,445
25	div3	Wycombe	H	L	1-3	Poole 23	5,841
26	div3	Chester	H	W	3-0	Connell 4, Montague 76, Poole 79	4,323
27	div3	Dag & Red	A	W	2-1	Poole 22, 68	2,353
28	div3	Shrewsbury	A	W	1-0	Osborne 52	5,083
29	div3	Chesterfield	H	W	2-1	Smith 25, Poole 61	4,882
30	div3	Notts County	H	D	0-0		4,332
31	div3	Mansfield	A	W	3-2	O'Connor 25, Connell 56, Elder 85	2,511
32	div3	Shrewsbury	H	D	1-1	Connell 57	5,353
33	div3	Barnet	A	W	2-1	Poole 36, 79 pen	2,522
34	div3	Accrington	H	W	3-1	Poole 34, Heywood 44, Connell 63	4,635
35	div3	Chesterfield	A	L	0-1		3,728
36	div3	Accrington	A	L	0-1		1,149
37	div3	Darlington	A	L	1-3	Reid 82	3,508
38	div3	Bury	H	L	1-4	Poole 56 pen	3,333
39	div3	Macclesfield	H	W	1-0	Poole 90	3,863
40	div3	Peterborough	H	L	1-2	Connell 62	4,049
41	div3	Morecambe	A	L	1-3	Elder 42	2,180
42	div3	Wrexham	H	W	2-0	Shakes 31, 81	4,448
43	div3	Grimsby	A	W	2-1	Connell 51, Brown 82	4,620
44	div3	Rochdale	H	L	0-2		4,896
45	div3	Rotherham	A	W	2-1	Elder 39, Connell 90	2,979
46	div3	Bradford	H	D	2-2	Poole 6, Bennett 26	4,336
47	div3	Lincoln	A	L	1-3	Elder 45	3,699
48	div3	Hereford	H	L	0-3		6,246
49	div3	Stockport	A	L	0-1		6,284

TEAM OF THE SEASON

G — Simon Brown CG: 20 DR: 69

D — Ben Starosta CG: 18 DR: 77

D — Karleigh Osborne CG: 23 DR: 66

D — Matthew Heywood CG: 30 DR: 61

D — Craig Pead CG: 23 DR: 61

M — Gary Smith CG: 22 SD: -11

M — Sammy Moore CG: 12 SD: -15

M — Ryan Dickson CG: 29 SD: -17

M — Kevin O'Connor CG: 36 SD: -21

F — Alan Connell CG: 32 SR: 257

F — Nathan Elder CG: 14 SR: 349

KEY PLAYER APPEARANCES

	PLAYER	POS	AGE	APP	MINS ON	GOALS	CARDS(Y/R)	
1	Glenn Poole	MID	27	45	3681	14	1	0
2	Kevin O'Connor	MID	26	37	3237	3	3	0
3	Alan Connell	ATT	25	42	3091	12	3	0
4	Matthew Heywood	DEF	28	32	2692	1	3	0
5	Ryan Dickson	MID	21	31	2680	0	4	0
6	Ricky Shakes	ATT	23	39	2476	3	0	0
7	Craig Pead	DEF	26	32	2383	0	1	0
8	Karleigh Osborne	DEF	20	29	2271	1	5	0
9	Gary Smith	MID	24	29	2165	1	5	1
10	Simon Brown	GK	31	21	1801	0	0	1
11	Ben Hamer	GK	0	20	1800	0	3	0
12	Ben Starosta	DEF	21	21	1713	0	1	1
13	Lee Thorpe	ATT	32	19	1469	4	3	1
14	Nathan Elder	ATT	20	17	1396	4	2	0
15	John Mousinho	MID	22	23	1354	2	2	0
16	Charlie Ide	ATT	20	19	1253	0	1	0
17	Sammy Moore	MID	20	20	1198	2	3	1
18	John Mackie	DEF	31	14	1132	0	5	0

KEY PLAYERS - GOALSCORERS

Alan Connell

Goals in the League	12
Contribution to Attacking Power: Average number of minutes between League team goals while on pitch	71
Player Strike Rate: Average number of minutes between League goals scored by player	257
Club Strike Rate: Average number of minutes between League goals scored by club	81

	PLAYER	GOALS LGE	POWER	STRIKE RATE
1	Alan Connell	12	71	257 mins
2	Glenn Poole	14	81	262 mins
3	Nathan Elder	4	66	349 mins
4	Lee Thorpe	4	113	367 mins

KEY PLAYERS - MIDFIELDERS

Gary Smith

Goals in the League	1
Defensive Rating: Average number of mins between League goals conceded while on the pitch	61
Contribution to Attacking Power: Average number of minutes between League team goals while on pitch	72
Scoring Difference: Defensive Rating minus Contribution to Attacking Power	-11

	PLAYER	GOALS LGE	DEF RATE	POWER	SCORE DIFF
1	Gary Smith	1	61	72	-11 mins
2	Sammy Moore	2	70	85	-15 mins
3	Ryan Dickson	0	57	74	-17 mins
4	Kevin O'Connor	3	59	80	-21 mins

KEY PLAYERS - DEFENDERS

Ben Starosta

Goals Conceded when he was on pitch	22
Defensive Rating: Ave number of mins between League goals conceded while on the pitch	77
Clean Sheets: In games when he played at least 70 minutes	2
Club Defensive Rating: Average number of mins between League goals conceded by the club this season.	60

	PLAYER	CON LGE	CLEAN SHEETS	DEF RATE
1	Ben Starosta	22	2	77 mins
2	Karleigh Osborne	34	4	66 mins
3	Matthew Heywood	44	4	61 mins
4	Craig Pead	39	6	61 mins

KEY GOALKEEPER

Simon Brown

Goals Conceded in the League	26
Defensive Rating: Ave number of mins between League goals conceded while on the pitch.	69
Counting Games: Games when he played at least 70 mins	20
Clean Sheets: In games when he played at least 70 mins	4

TOP POINT EARNERS

	PLAYER	GAMES	AV PTS
1	Nathan Elder	14	1.64
2	Craig Pead	23	1.61
3	Ricky Shakes	23	1.61
4	Ben Hamer	20	1.40
5	Matthew Heywood	30	1.40
6	Karleigh Osborne	23	1.39
7	Alan Connell	32	1.38
8	Ryan Dickson	29	1.38
9	Kevin O'Connor	36	1.36
10	Simon Brown	20	1.35
	CLUB AVERAGE:		1.28

LINCOLN CITY

Final Position: **15th**

NICKNAME: THE RED IMPS

KEY: Won Drawn Lost

							Attendance
1	div3	Shrewsbury	H	L	0-4		3,893
2	ccr1	Doncaster	A	L	1-4	Forrester 80	5,084
3	div3	Mansfield	A	W	3-1	Dodds 2, N'Guessan 36, M.McIntosh 54 og	3,357
4	div3	Accrington	H	W	2-0	N'Guessan 31, Dodds 66	3,189
5	div3	Dag & Red	A	L	0-1		2,060
6	div3	Bradford	H	L	1-2	Dodds 26	5,286
7	div3	Darlington	A	L	0-2		4,075
8	div3	Grimsby	H	L	1-2	Forrester 38	4,428
9	div3	Wrexham	A	L	0-1		3,614
10	div3	Bury	A	D	1-1	Kerr 19	1,690
11	div3	Morecambe	H	D	1-1	Amoo 22	3,281
12	div3	MK Dons	A	L	0-4		13,037
13	div3	Peterborough	H	D	1-1	Wright 45	5,036
14	div3	Brentford	A	L	0-1		4,368
15	div3	Chester	H	L	0-1		3,960
16	div3	Chesterfield	H	L	2-4	N'Guessan 44, Bencherif 67	3,893
17	facr1	Nottm Forest	H	D	1-1	Wilson 38 og	7,361
18	div3	Wycombe	A	L	0-1		4,297
19	div3	Notts County	H	W	2-1	Wright 44, Frecklington 75	4,503
20	facr1r	Nottm Forest	A	L	1-3	Forrester 71	6,783
21	div3	Stockport	A	W	3-1	Wright 50, 53, John-Lewis 86	5,260
22	div3	Hereford	A	L	1-3	Frecklington 21	2,528
23	div3	Barnet	H	W	4-1	Wright 9, 90, Forrester 32 pen, Dodds 50	3,549
24	div3	Darlington	H	L	0-4		4,025
25	div3	Bradford	A	L	1-2	John-Lewis 51	15,510
26	div3	Grimsby	A	L	0-1		5,533
27	div3	Bury	H	D	1-1	Dodds 79	3,327
28	div3	Rochdale	A	W	2-0	Forrester 82, Frecklington 83	2,721
29	div3	Rotherham	H	L	1-3	Forrester 55	5,016
30	div3	Dag & Red	H	W	2-0	Wright 15, N'Guessan 90	3,779
31	div3	Mansfield	H	L	1-2	Forrester 60 pen	4,280
32	div3	Shrewsbury	A	W	2-1	Dodds 12, 85	4,892
33	div3	Macclesfield	A	W	2-1	N'Guessan 81, Forrester 89	1,576
34	div3	Rochdale	H	W	2-1	Forrester 45, Hone 81	3,955
35	div3	Accrington	A	W	3-0	Stallard 6, Wright 70, Beevers 75	1,281
36	div3	Macclesfield	H	W	3-1	John-Lewis 72, Forrester 81	
						N'Guessan 90	3,682
37	div3	Rotherham	A	L	2-3	Dodds 25, Wright 87	4,321
38	div3	Wycombe	H	W	1-0	Dodds 66	4,002
39	div3	Chesterfield	A	L	1-4	Wright 58	4,352
40	div3	Notts County	A	W	1-0	Forrester 16	3,858
41	div3	Stockport	H	L	0-1		4,544
42	div3	Barnet	A	L	2-5	Wright 76, 81	2,115
43	div3	Hereford	H	W	2-1	N'Guessan 31, 85 pen	3,614
44	div3	Peterborough	A	L	0-4		8,035
45	div3	MK Dons	H	L	1-2	Wright 59	3,896
46	div3	Chester	A	W	2-1	Forrester 21, 23	2,089
47	div3	Brentford	H	W	3-1	King 39, Forrester 67, Frecklington 83	3,699
48	div3	Morecambe	A	W	2-1	Wright 42, Green 70	2,762
49	div3	Wrexham	H	L	2-4	S.Evans 39 og, Wright 90	4,958

TEAM OF THE SEASON

G	Alan Marriott	CG: 33 DR: 54
D	Adrian Moses	CG: 15 DR: 72
D	Lee Ridley	CG: 15 DR: 63
D	Paul Green	CG: 34 DR: 56
D	Lee Beevers	CG: 36 DR: 55
M	Dany N'Guessan	CG: 22 SD: -16
M	Scott Kerr	CG: 31 SD: -18
M	Lee Frecklington	CG: 27 SD: -19
M	Jamie Hand	CG: 17 SD: -27
F	Ben Wright	CG: 22 SR: 170
F	Jamie Forrester	CG: 33 SR: 263

KEY PLAYER APPEARANCES

	PLAYER	POS	AGE	APP	MINS ON	GOALS	CARDS(Y)	CARDS(R)
1	Lee Beevers	DEF	24	37	3267	1	1	0
2	Jamie Forrester	ATT	33	40	3156	12	0	0
3	Paul Green	DEF	21	36	3134	1	4	0
4	Louis Dodds	ATT	21	41	3129	9	5	0
5	Alan Marriott	GK	29	34	2985	0	1	0
6	Scott Kerr	MID	26	36	2887	1	9	2
7	Lee Frecklington	MID	22	34	2685	4	1	0
8	Ben Wright	ATT	28	34	2386	14	0	0
9	Dany N'Guessan	MID	20	37	2176	8	4	1
10	Nathaniel Brown	DEF	27	27	2150	0	2	0
11	Daniel Hone	DEF	18	23	1895	1	3	0
12	Jamie Hand	MID	24	25	1730	0	6	0
13	Gary Croft	DEF	34	20	1592	0	2	2
14	Adrian Moses	DEF	33	18	1443	0	1	0
15	Mark Stallard	ATT	33	25	1404	1	3	1
16	Lee Ridley	DEF	26	15	1335	0	0	0
17	Lenell John-Lewis	ATT	19	21	1295	3	1	0
18	Shane Clarke	MID	20	16	1115	0	1	1

KEY PLAYERS - GOALSCORERS

Ben Wright

Goals in the League	14
Contribution to Attacking Power Average number of minutes between League team goals while on pitch	62
Player Strike Rate Average number of minutes between League goals scored by player	170
Club Strike Rate Average number of minutes between League goals scored by club	69

	PLAYER	GOALS LGE	POWER	STRIKE RATE
1	Ben Wright	14	62	170 mins
2	Jamie Forrester	12	63	263 mins
3	Dany N'Guessan	8	58	272 mins
4	Louis Dodds	9	65	347 mins

KEY PLAYERS - MIDFIELDERS

Dany N'Guessan

Goals in the League	8
Defensive Rating Average number of mins between League goals conceded while on the pitch	42
Contribution to Attacking Power Average number of minutes between League team goals while on pitch	58
Scoring Difference Defensive Rating minus Contribution to Attacking Power	-16

	PLAYER	GOALS LGE	DEF RATE	POWER	SCORE DIFF
1	Dany N'Guessan	8	42	58	-16 mins
2	Scott Kerr	1	52	70	-18 mins
3	Lee Frecklington	4	55	74	-19 mins
4	Jamie Hand	0	64	91	-27 mins

KEY PLAYERS - DEFENDERS

Adrian Moses

Goals Conceded when he was on pitch	20
Defensive Rating Ave number of mins between League goals conceded while on the pitch	72
Clean Sheets In games when he played at least 70 minutes	1
Club Defensive Rating Average number of mins between League goals conceded by the club this season.	54

	PLAYER	CON LGE	CLEAN SHEETS	DEF RATE
1	Adrian Moses	20	1	72 mins
2	Lee Ridley	21	4	63 mins
3	Paul Green	55	5	56 mins
4	Lee Beevers	59	6	55 mins

KEY GOALKEEPER

Alan Marriott

Goals Conceded in the League	55
Defensive Rating Ave number of mins between League goals conceded while on the pitch.	54
Counting Games Games when he played at least 70 mins	33
Clean Sheets In games when he played at least 70 mins	6

TOP POINT EARNERS

	PLAYER	GAMES	AV PTS
1	Lee Ridley	15	2.00
2	Daniel Hone	20	1.65
3	Lenell John-Lewis	12	1.58
4	Mark Stallard	12	1.50
5	Jamie Forrester	33	1.48
6	Paul Green	34	1.44
7	Louis Dodds	33	1.42
8	Ben Wright	22	1.32
9	Lee Frecklington	27	1.22
10	Lee Beevers	36	1.19
	CLUB AVERAGE:		1.26

GRIMSBY TOWN

Final Position: **16th**

NICKNAME: THE MARINERS

KEY: ☐ Won ☐ Drawn ☐ Lost

							Attendance
1	div3	**Notts County**	H	D	1-1	Bennett 12	5,483
2	ccr1	**Burnley**	H	L	2-4*	North 101 (*on penalties)	2,431
3	div3	**Bury**	A	D	1-1	Bolland 10	2,493
4	div3	**Macclesfield**	H	D	1-1	Taylor 74	3,701
5	div3	**Shrewsbury**	A	L	1-2	Toner 68 pen	5,490
6	div3	**Accrington**	A	L	1-4	Bolland 57	1,350
7	div3	**Stockport**	H	D	1-1	Bolland 51	3,726
8	div3	**Lincoln**	A	W	2-1	Whittle 19, Toner 52 pen	4,428
9	div3	**Hereford**	H	W	2-1	Boshell 20, Newey 52	3,699
10	div3	**Chester**	H	L	1-2	Boshell 25	3,479
11	div3	**Peterborough**	A	L	1-2	Toner 59 pen	4,786
12	div3	**Rochdale**	H	L	1-2	Logan 18	5,829
13	div3	**Wycombe**	A	L	0-3		4,052
14	div3	**Bradford**	H	D	1-1	Logan 49	4,883
15	div3	**Rotherham**	A	L	1-2	Fenton 53	4,162
16	div3	**MK Dons**	A	L	0-2		6,797
17	facr1	**Carlisle**	A	D	1-1	Bolland 28	5,128
18	div3	**Morecambe**	H	L	1-2	Taylor 53	4,897
19	facr1r	**Carlisle**	H	W	1-0	Jones 62	2,008
20	div3	**Barnet**	A	W	3-0	North 11, 44, Taylor 89	2,059
21	facr2	**Huddersfield**	A	L	0-3		6,729
22	div3	**Darlington**	H	L	0-4		3,057
23	div3	**Brentford**	A	W	1-0	Jones 57	3,999
24	div3	**Mansfield**	H	W	1-0	Jones 62	3,836
25	div3	**Stockport**	A	D	1-1	Butler 25	4,711
26	div3	**Accrington**	H	L	1-2	Hegarty 8	4,240
27	div3	**Lincoln**	H	W	1-0	Jones 85	5,533
28	div3	**Chester**	A	W	2-0	Boshell 65 pen, Atkinson 84	2,255
29	div3	**Chesterfield**	A	W	2-1	North 45, 78 pen	4,540
30	div3	**Wrexham**	H	W	1-0	North 68	4,084
31	div3	**Dag & Red**	A	D	0-0		2,216
32	div3	**Shrewsbury**	H	D	1-1	North 90	3,785
33	div3	**Bury**	H	W	1-0	Clarke 40	3,445
34	div3	**Notts County**	A	D	1-1	Fenton 61	4,902
35	div3	**Chesterfield**	H	W	4-2	Boshell 19 pen, 86 pen, North 31 Hegarty 53	4,601
36	div3	**Macclesfield**	A	W	2-1	North 5, Clarke 82	2,194
37	div3	**Dag & Red**	H	L	1-4	Jones 90	4,060
38	div3	**Wrexham**	A	D	0-0		4,217
39	div3	**Morecambe**	A	W	4-0	Bore 22, 25, Hegarty 59, Butler 81	2,303
40	div3	**MK Dons**	H	L	0-1		4,106
41	div3	**Barnet**	H	W	4-1	Hegarty 29, Butler 43, Bolland 55 Taylor 85	3,325
42	div3	**Darlington**	A	L	2-3	Butler 29, 30	3,499
43	div3	**Mansfield**	A	W	2-1	Till 32, Boshell 74	2,616
44	div3	**Brentford**	H	L	1-2	North 19	4,620
45	div3	**Rochdale**	A	L	1-3	Taylor 85	2,974
46	div3	**Rotherham**	H	L	0-1		3,583
47	div3	**Wycombe**	H	L	0-1		2,537
48	div3	**Bradford**	A	L	1-2	Till 9	13,448
49	div3	**Peterborough**	H	L	1-4	Butler 63	4,125
50	div3	**Hereford**	A	L	0-2		6,020

TEAM OF THE SEASON

G — Philip Barnes — CG: 42 DR: 64

D — Sam Hird — CG: 13 DR: 118

D — Robert Atkinson — CG: 23 DR: 73

D — Ryan Bennett — CG: 25 DR: 62

D — Tom Newey — CG: 41 DR: 60

M — Nick Hegarty — CG: 26 SD: 3

M — James Hunt — CG: 26 SD: -1

M — Danny Boshell — CG: 32 SD: -8

M — Paul Bolland — CG: 28 SD: -12

F — Danny North — CG: 14 SR: 200

F — Martin Butler — CG: 13 SR: 231

KEY PLAYER APPEARANCES

	PLAYER	POS	AGE	APP	MINS ON	GOALS	CARDS(Y/R)	
1	Philip Barnes	GK	29	42	3779	0	0	1
2	Tom Newey	DEF	25	42	3713	1	6	0
3	Nicky Fenton	DEF	28	42	3512	2	9	1
4	Danny Boshell	MID	27	40	3203	6	4	1
5	Paul Bolland	MID	28	35	2821	4	4	0
6	James Hunt	MID	31	37	2766	0	2	0
7	Ryan Bennett	DEF	18	40	2741	1	5	1
8	Nick Hegarty	MID	22	30	2531	4	3	0
9	Peter Till	MID	22	34	2355	2	1	0
10	Jamie Clarke	DEF	25	29	2249	2	1	0
11	Ciaran Toner	MID	27	29	2125	2	3	0
12	Robert Atkinson	DEF	21	24	2123	1	2	0
13	Danny North	ATT	20	27	1801	9	2	0
14	Gary Jones	ATT	33	35	1759	4	2	0
15	Martin Butler	ATT	33	21	1391	6	2	0
16	Justin Whittle	DEF	37	18	1333	1	0	0
17	Sam Hird	DEF	19	17	1298	0	2	0
18	Isaiah Rankin	ATT	30	17	897	0	1	0

KEY PLAYERS - GOALSCORERS

Danny North

Goals in the League	9
Contribution to Attacking Power Average number of minutes between League team goals while on pitch	72
Player Strike Rate Average number of minutes between League goals scored by player	200
Club Strike Rate Average number of minutes between League goals scored by club	75

	PLAYER	GOALS LGE	POWER	STRIKE RATE
1	Danny North	9	72	200 mins
2	Martin Butler	6	86	231 mins
3	Gary Jones	4	60	439 mins
4	Danny Boshell	6	76	533 mins

KEY PLAYERS - MIDFIELDERS

Nick Hegarty

Goals in the League	4
Defensive Rating Average number of mins between League goals conceded while on the pitch	79
Contribution to Attacking Power Average number of minutes between League team goals while on pitch	76
Scoring Difference Defensive Rating minus Contribution to Attacking Power	3

	PLAYER	GOALS LGE	DEF RATE	POWER	SCORE DIFF
1	Nick Hegarty	4	79	76	3 mins
2	James Hunt	0	69	70	-1 mins
3	Danny Boshell	6	68	76	-8 mins
4	Paul Bolland	4	64	76	-12 mins

KEY PLAYERS - DEFENDERS

Sam Hird

Goals Conceded when he was on pitch	11
Defensive Rating Ave number of mins between League goals conceded while on the pitch	118
Clean Sheets In games when he played at least 70 minutes	7
Club Defensive Rating Average number of mins between League goals conceded by the club this season.	62

	PLAYER	CON LGE	CLEAN SHEETS	DEF RATE
1	Sam Hird	11	7	118 mins
2	Robert Atkinson	29	9	73 mins
3	Ryan Bennett	44	7	62 mins
4	Tom Newey	61	8	60 mins

KEY GOALKEEPER

Philip Barnes

Goals Conceded in the League	59
Defensive Rating Ave number of mins between League goals conceded while on the pitch.	64
Counting Games Games when he played at least 70 mins	42
Clean Sheets In games when he played at least 70 mins	9

TOP POINT EARNERS

	PLAYER	GAMES	AV PTS
1	Sam Hird	13	2.31
2	Gary Jones	14	2.07
3	Danny North	14	1.86
4	Robert Atkinson	23	1.61
5	Nick Hegarty	26	1.46
6	James Hunt	26	1.38
7	Jamie Clarke	22	1.23
8	Paul Bolland	28	1.18
9	Philip Barnes	42	1.17
10	Danny Boshell	32	1.16
	CLUB AVERAGE:		1.20

ACCRINGTON STANLEY

Final Position: **17th**

NICKNAME: THE STANS

KEY: ☐Won ☐Drawn ☐Lost

							Attendance
1	div3	Wycombe	A	W	1-0	Mullin 58	4,408
2	ccr1	Leicester	H	L	0-1		2,029
3	div3	Darlington	H	L	0-3		1,805
4	div3	Lincoln	A	L	0-2		3,189
5	div3	Peterborough	H	L	0-2		1,484
6	div3	Grimsby	H	W	4-1	Proctor 29 pen, 90, Mullin 48, 69	1,350
7	div3	Shrewsbury	A	L	0-2		5,789
8	div3	Mansfield	H	W	1-0	Mullin 26	1,408
9	div3	Bury	A	L	1-2	Mullin 46	2,784
10	div3	Bradford	A	W	3-0	D'Sane 2, 32, Proctor 61	13,346
11	div3	Wrexham	H	L	0-2		1,822
12	div3	Dag & Red	A	W	3-1	McGivern 16, Proctor 27, Mullin 78	1,596
13	div3	Macclesfield	H	W	3-2	D'Sane 51, 74, Mullin 54	1,792
14	div3	Barnet	A	D	2-2	Craney 51, D'Sane 83	2,178
15	div3	Notts County	H	L	0-2		1,722
16	div3	Morecambe	A	W	1-0	Craney 13	2,814
17	facr1	Huddersfield	H	L	2-3	Cavanagh 12, Mullin 25	2,202
18	div3	Rotherham	H	L	0-1		1,918
19	div3	Hereford	A	D	0-0		2,804
20	div3	Rochdale	H	L	1-2	Craney 23	1,621
21	div3	MK Dons	A	L	0-5		6,917
22	div3	Chesterfield	H	W	2-1	Proctor 74 pen, D'Sane 89	1,448
23	div3	Shrewsbury	H	L	1-2	Mullin 39	1,410
24	div3	Grimsby	A	W	2-1	Mullin 48, Proctor 58	4,240
25	div3	Mansfield	A	W	2-1	Mullin 75, Proctor 90 pen	2,494
26	div3	Bradford	H	L	0-2		2,898
27	div3	Chester	H	D	3-3	Proctor 37, Craney 63, D'Sane 74	1,311
28	div3	Stockport	A	L	0-2		4,714
29	div3	Peterborough	A	L	2-8	Mullin 46, Whalley 62	4,257
30	div3	Darlington	A	L	0-1		2,808
31	div3	Wycombe	H	L	0-2		1,200
32	div3	Chester	A	W	3-2	A.Thomas 14, 68, Craney 90	1,957
33	div3	Lincoln	H	L	0-3		1,281
34	div3	Brentford	A	L	1-3	Craney 39	4,635
35	div3	Stockport	H	L	0-2		2,576
36	div3	Brentford	H	W	1-0	Richardson 31	1,149
37	div3	Rotherham	A	W	1-0	Craney 64	3,683
38	div3	Hereford	H	L	0-2		1,262
39	div3	Morecambe	H	W	3-2	Kempson 43, Mangan 72, Mullin 73	1,448
40	div3	Rochdale	A	L	1-4	Whalley 34	3,247
41	div3	Chesterfield	A	L	2-4	Proctor 23, 31 pen	3,274
42	div3	MK Dons	H	L	0-1		1,559
43	div3	Macclesfield	A	L	1-2	Craney 31	1,853
44	div3	Dag & Red	H	W	1-0	Edwards 47	1,262
45	div3	Notts County	A	L	0-1		5,525
46	div3	Barnet	H	L	0-2		1,288
47	div3	Wrexham	A	W	3-1	Pejic 7 og, Cavanagh 28, Whalley 72	3,657
48	div3	Bury	H	L	0-2		2,566

TEAM OF THE SEASON

G — Kenny Arthur CG: 23 DR: 55

D — Peter Cavanagh CG: 18 DR: 72

D — Graham Branch CG: 18 DR: 64

D — Mark Roberts CG: 30 DR: 54

D — Leam Richardson CG: 33 DR: 51

M — Andrew Proctor CG: 40 SD: -35

M — Jay Harris CG: 33 SD: -35

M — Shaun Whalley CG: 12 SD: -38

M — Ian Craney CG: 32 SD: -44

F — Roscoe D'Sane CG: 15 SR: 219

F — Paul Mullin CG: 43 SR: 319

KEY PLAYER APPEARANCES

	PLAYER	POS	AGE	APP	MINS ON	GOALS	CARDS(Y/R)	
1	Paul Mullin	ATT	34	43	3830	12	4	0
2	Andrew Proctor	MID	25	43	3618	10	3	0
3	Jay Harris	MID	21	41	3246	0	10	1
4	Leam Richardson	DEF	28	37	2961	1	7	1
5	Ian Craney	MID	25	34	2906	8	5	0
6	Mark Roberts	DEF	24	34	2798	0	3	0
7	Phil Edwards	DEF	22	31	2538	1	4	0
8	Robbie Williams	DEF	29	26	2126	0	2	0
9	Kenny Arthur	GK	29	24	2096	0	2	0
10	Ian Dunbavin	GK	28	23	2044	0	0	0
11	Graham Branch	DEF	36	22	1682	0	5	1
12	Peter Cavanagh	DEF	26	19	1669	1	5	0
13	Shaun Whalley	MID	20	31	1667	3	7	0
14	Sean Webb	DEF	25	18	1595	0	5	0
15	Roscoe D'Sane	ATT	27	22	1537	7	1	0
16	Andy Todd	MID	29	21	1244	0	2	0
17	Aswad Thomas, A	DEF	0	13	1149	2	3	1
18	John Miles	ATT	26	16	934	0	0	0

KEY PLAYERS - GOALSCORERS

Roscoe D'Sane

Goals in the League	7
Contribution to Attacking Power Average number of minutes between League team goals while on pitch	64
Player Strike Rate Average number of minutes between League goals scored by player	219
Club Strike Rate Average number of minutes between League goals scored by club	86

	PLAYER	GOALS LGE	POWER	STRIKE RATE
1	Roscoe D'Sane	7	64	219 mins
2	Paul Mullin	12	81	319 mins
3	Andrew Proctor	10	84	361 mins
4	Ian Craney	8	90	363 mins

KEY PLAYERS - MIDFIELDERS

Andrew Proctor

Goals in the League	10
Defensive Rating Average number of mins between League goals conceded while on the pitch	49
Contribution to Attacking Power Average number of minutes between League team goals while on pitch	84
Scoring Difference Defensive Rating minus Contribution to Attacking Power	-35

	PLAYER	GOALS LGE	DEF RATE	POWER	SCORE DIFF
1	Andrew Proctor	10	49	84	-35 mins
2	Jay Harris	0	46	81	-35 mins
3	Shaun Whalley	3	49	87	-38 mins
4	Ian Craney	8	46	90	-44 mins

KEY PLAYERS - DEFENDERS

Peter Cavanagh

Goals Conceded when he was on pitch	23
Defensive Rating Ave number of mins between League goals conceded while on the pitch	72
Clean Sheets In games when he played at least 70 minutes	6
Club Defensive Rating Average number of mins between League goals conceded by the club this season.	50

	PLAYER	CON LGE	CLEAN SHEETS	DEF RATE
1	Peter Cavanagh	23	6	72 mins
2	Graham Branch	26	3	64 mins
3	Mark Roberts	51	7	54 mins
4	Leam Richardson	58	5	51 mins

KEY GOALKEEPER

Kenny Arthur

Goals Conceded in the League	38
Defensive Rating Ave number of mins between League goals conceded while on the pitch.	55
Counting Games Games when he played at least 70 mins	23
Clean Sheets In games when he played at least 70 mins	5

TOP POINT EARNERS

	PLAYER	GAMES	AV PTS
1	Roscoe D'Sane	15	1.73
2	Peter Cavanagh	18	1.56
3	Graham Branch	18	1.39
4	Mark Roberts	30	1.30
5	Sean Webb	17	1.29
6	Paul Mullin	43	1.19
7	Robbie Williams	22	1.18
8	Jay Harris	33	1.18
9	Leam Richardson	33	1.18
10	Ian Dunbavin	22	1.09
	CLUB AVERAGE:		1.11

SHREWSBURY TOWN

Final Position: **18th**

NICKNAME: THE SHREWS

KEY: □Won □Drawn □Lost

	Comp	Opponent	H/A	Res	Score	Scorers	Attendance
1	div3	Lincoln	A	W	4-0	Cooke 52, 81, Hibbert 57, Leslie 82	3,893
2	ccr1	Colchester	H	W	1-0	Kempson 106	3,069
3	div3	Bradford	H	W	1-0	Hibbert 9 pen	6,413
4	div3	MK Dons	A	L	0-3		7,380
5	ccr2	Fulham	H	L	0-1		6,223
6	div3	Grimsby	H	W	2-1	Hibbert 50, Symes 59	5,490
7	div3	Stockport	A	D	1-1	Hibbert 25	5,473
8	div3	Accrington	H	W	2-0	Nicholson 3, Hibbert 52 pen	5,789
9	div3	Wycombe	A	D	1-1	Murdock 27	4,936
10	div3	Rochdale	H	L	3-4	Hibbert 38, Drummond 62, Hunt 88	6,262
11	div3	Peterborough	H	L	0-2		5,220
12	div3	Chester	A	L	1-3	Moss 69	3,057
13	div3	Chesterfield	H	L	2-3	Hibbert 5, Murdock 68	5,143
14	div3	Bury	A	D	1-1	Drummond 82	2,667
15	div3	Mansfield	H	D	0-0		5,347
16	div3	Wrexham	A	W	1-0	Symes 59	4,305
17	div3	Darlington	A	L	0-2		2,628
18	facr1	Walsall	A	L	0-2		4,972
19	div3	Barnet	H	W	1-0	Symes 90	5,197
20	div3	Rotherham	A	L	0-2		3,832
21	div3	Macclesfield	H	W	2-0	Drummond 33, Hunt 65	4,763
22	div3	Notts County	A	L	1-2	Hibbert 41 pen	3,819
23	div3	Dag & Red	H	W	4-0	Davies 54, 69, Pugh 78, Tierney 81	4,597
24	div3	Accrington	A	W	2-1	Davies 64, Hibbert 68	1,410
25	div3	Stockport	H	W	3-1	Cooke 22, Davies 76, Hibbert 86 pen	7,707
26	div3	Wycombe	H	L	0-1		6,208
27	div3	Peterborough	A	L	1-2	Cooke 27	5,062
28	div3	Brentford	H	L	0-1		5,083
29	div3	Hereford	A	L	1-3	Briggs 31	4,707
30	div3	Morecambe	H	W	2-0	Hall 4, Madjo 31	5,036
31	div3	Grimsby	A	D	1-1	Madjo 75	3,785
32	div3	Bradford	A	L	2-4	Hibbert 48, Pugh 65	13,269
33	div3	Lincoln	H	L	1-2	Davies 76	4,892
34	div3	Brentford	A	D	1-1	Constable 79	5,353
35	div3	MK Dons	H	D	3-3	Langmead 44, Constable 70, 90	5,474
36	div3	Hereford	H	L	1-2	Hall 6	7,402
37	div3	Barnet	A	L	1-4	Madjo 10	1,864
38	div3	Rotherham	H	D	1-1	Davies 43	5,265
39	div3	Darlington	H	D	0-0		4,499
40	div3	Macclesfield	A	L	1-2	Hibbert 65	2,473
41	div3	Dag & Red	A	D	1-1	Cooke 34	1,686
42	div3	Notts County	H	D	0-0		5,673
43	div3	Bury	H	L	0-1		5,213
44	div3	Chesterfield	A	L	1-4	McIntyre 81	3,570
45	div3	Morecambe	A	D	1-1	Pugh 70	1,634
46	div3	Wrexham	H	W	3-0	McIntyre 7, Moss 58, Constable 68	7,065
47	div3	Mansfield	A	L	1-3	Pugh 2	3,334
48	div3	Chester	H	D	0-0		6,417
49	div3	Rochdale	A	D	1-1	Hall 34	4,000

TEAM OF THE SEASON

G — Glyn Garner CG: 41 DR: 61

D — Colin Murdock CG: 24 DR: 91

D — Marc Tierney CG: 40 DR: 67

D — Darren Moss CG: 22 DR: 64

D — Ben Herd CG: 38 DR: 62

M — Stuart Drummond CG: 22 SD: 12

M — Marc Pugh CG: 22 SD: 0

M — David Hunt CG: 17 SD: -3

M — Ben Davies CG: 25 SD: -11

F — Dave Hibbert CG: 29 SR: 259

F — Kelvin Langmead CG: 39 SR: 3510

KEY PLAYER APPEARANCES

	PLAYER	POS	AGE	APP	MINS ON	GOALS	CARDS(Y)	CARDS(R)
1	Ben Herd	DEF	23	45	3741	0	6	0
2	Marc Tierney	DEF	22	43	3730	1	2	0
3	Glyn Garner	GK	31	41	3690	0	0	0
4	Kelvin Langmead	ATT	23	39	3510	1	3	0
5	Dave Hibbert	ATT	22	44	3115	12	8	0
6	Marc Pugh	MID	21	37	2487	4	3	0
7	Colin Murdock	DEF	32	29	2376	2	4	1
8	Darren Moss	DEF	27	31	2268	2	3	0
9	Ben Davies	MID	27	27	2262	6	2	0
10	Stuart Drummond	MID	32	23	2004	3	3	0
11	Kevin McIntyre	MID	30	22	1949	2	4	0
12	David Hunt	MID	25	27	1808	2	6	0
13	Darren Kempson	DEF	23	23	1713	0	1	0
14	Asa Hall	MID	21	15	1159	3	1	0
15	Michael Symes	ATT	24	21	1064	3	3	0
16	Chris Humphrey	MID	19	25	963	0	0	0
17	Guy Madjo	ATT	0	15	933	3	0	0
18	Steven Leslie	MID	20	17	919	1	0	0

KEY PLAYERS - GOALSCORERS

Dave Hibbert

Goals in the League	12
Contribution to Attacking Power Average number of minutes between League team goals while on pitch	74
Player Strike Rate Average number of minutes between League goals scored by player	259
Club Strike Rate Average number of minutes between League goals scored by club	75

	PLAYER	GOALS LGE	POWER	STRIKE RATE
1	Dave Hibbert	12	74	259 mins
2	Ben Davies	6	75	377 mins
3	Asa Hall	3	72	386 mins
4	Marc Pugh	4	63	621 mins

KEY PLAYERS - MIDFIELDERS

Stuart Drummond

Goals in the League	3
Defensive Rating Average number of mins between League goals conceded while on the pitch	74
Contribution to Attacking Power Average number of minutes between League team goals while on pitch	62
Scoring Difference Defensive Rating minus Contribution to Attacking Power	12

	PLAYER	GOALS LGE	DEF RATE	POWER	SCORE DIFF
1	Stuart Drummond	3	74	62	12 mins
2	Marc Pugh	4	63	63	0 mins
3	David Hunt	2	66	69	-3 mins
4	Ben Davies	6	64	75	-11 mins

KEY PLAYERS - DEFENDERS

Colin Murdock

Goals Conceded when he was on pitch	26
Defensive Rating Ave number of mins between League goals conceded while on the pitch	91
Clean Sheets In games when he played at least 70 minutes	9
Club Defensive Rating Average number of mins between League goals conceded by the club this season.	65

	PLAYER	CON LGE	CLEAN SHEETS	DEF RATE
1	Colin Murdock	26	9	91 mins
2	Marc Tierney	55	12	67 mins
3	Darren Moss	35	8	64 mins
4	Ben Herd	60	10	62 mins

KEY GOALKEEPER

Glyn Garner

Goals Conceded in the League	60
Defensive Rating Ave number of mins between League goals conceded while on the pitch.	61
Counting Games Games when he played at least 70 mins	41
Clean Sheets In games when he played at least 70 mins	11

TOP POINT EARNERS

	PLAYER	GAMES	AV PTS
1	Stuart Drummond	22	1.55
2	Colin Murdock	24	1.50
3	Darren Moss	22	1.41
4	David Hunt	17	1.41
5	Dave Hibbert	29	1.31
6	Marc Pugh	22	1.18
7	Marc Tierney	40	1.15
8	Kelvin Langmead	39	1.13
9	Ben Davies	25	1.08
10	Ben Herd	38	1.08
	CLUB AVERAGE:		1.09

MACCLESFIELD

Final Position: **19th**

NICKNAME: THE SILKMEN

KEY: ☐ Won ☐ Drawn ☐ Lost

		Opponent			Score	Scorers	Attendance
1	div3	Bradford	A	D	1-1	Green 9	13,401
2	ccr1	Leeds	H	L	0-1		3,422
3	div3	MK Dons	H	D	3-3	Green 33, 63, Gritton 57	2,257
4	div3	Grimsby	A	D	1-1	Gritton 63	3,701
5	div3	Darlington	H	D	0-0		2,288
6	div3	Hereford	A	W	1-0	Green 82	2,725
7	div3	Wycombe	H	L	1-2	Evans 90	2,173
8	div3	Rochdale	A	D	1-1	McIntyre 22 pen	3,066
9	div3	Chester	H	L	1-2	Dunfield 53	2,647
10	div3	Rotherham	H	D	1-1	Gritton 61	1,715
11	div3	Chesterfield	A	D	2-2	Gritton 29, Green 73	4,080
12	div3	Wrexham	H	W	3-2	Gritton 36, Morley 90, Thomas 90	2,256
13	div3	Accrington	A	L	2-3	McIntyre 71 pen, Evans 73	1,792
14	div3	Bury	H	D	2-2	Thomas 21, Gritton 45	2,672
15	div3	Mansfield	A	L	0-5		2,853
16	div3	Brentford	H	W	1-0	Thomas 76	1,378
17	facr1	Rushden & D	A	L	1-3	Gritton 76	1,759
18	div3	Notts County	A	W	1-0	Green 63	4,390
19	div3	Dag & Red	H	D	1-1	Blackman 90	1,781
20	div3	Shrewsbury	A	L	0-2		4,763
21	div3	Barnet	A	D	2-2	McNulty 3, L.Reid 7	1,303
22	div3	Stockport	H	L	0-2		3,585
23	div3	Wycombe	A	L	1-2	Green 17	3,867
24	div3	Hereford	H	L	0-1		2,393
25	div3	Rochdale	H	D	2-2	L.Reid 20, Evans 30	2,742
26	div3	Rotherham	A	L	0-3		4,464
27	div3	Morecambe	H	L	1-2	Gritton 25	2,254
28	div3	Peterborough	A	W	1-0	I.Reid 37	5,238
29	div3	Darlington	A	D	2-2	Gritton 60, Cresswell 64	3,585
30	div3	MK Dons	A	D	1-1	Symes 3	6,483
31	div3	Bradford	H	L	0-1		2,778
32	div3	Lincoln	H	L	1-2	Evans 90	1,576
33	div3	Morecambe	A	W	1-0	Green 87	2,626
34	div3	Grimsby	H	L	1-2	Evans 79	2,194
35	div3	Lincoln	A	L	1-3	Evans 8	3,682
36	div3	Peterborough	H	L	0-3		2,094
37	div3	Notts County	H	D	1-1	I.Reid 22	2,193
38	div3	Brentford	A	L	0-1		3,863
39	div3	Dag & Red	A	W	1-0	Green 72	1,350
40	div3	Shrewsbury	H	W	2-1	Tolley 82, Green 85	2,473
41	div3	Stockport	A	L	0-2		7,824
42	div3	Barnet	H	W	3-0	Thomas 31, Ashton 41, Green 48	1,718
43	div3	Accrington	H	W	2-1	Brisley 15, 38	1,853
44	div3	Wrexham	A	D	1-1	Tolley 52	3,993
45	div3	Mansfield	H	D	0-0		3,250
46	div3	Bury	A	L	0-1		2,506
47	div3	Chesterfield	H	W	1-0	Evans 42	2,573
48	div3	Chester	A	D	0-0		2,396

TEAM OF THE SEASON

G — Jonathan Brain CG: 28 DR: 73

D — Neil Ashton CG: 19 DR: 89

D — Ryan Cresswell CG: 17 DR: 76

D — Sean Hessey CG: 22 DR: 75

D — Luke Dimech CG: 22 DR: 60

M — Terry Dunfield CG: 38 SD: -8

M — Danny Thomas CG: 40 SD: -17

M — Adam Murray CG: 22 SD: -23

M — Kevin McIntyre CG: 22 SD: -26

F — Martin Gritton CG: 19 SR: 265

F — Francis Green CG: 30 SR: 276

KEY PLAYER APPEARANCES

	PLAYER	POS	AGE	APP	MINS ON	GOALS	CARDS(Y/R)	
1	Danny Thomas	MID	21	43	3670	4	5	0
2	Terry Dunfield	MID	26	41	3543	1	12	0
3	Francis Green	ATT	28	40	3044	11	3	0
4	Jonathan Brain	GK	25	29	2558	0	1	0
5	Sean Hessey	DEF	29	26	2196	0	7	0
6	Luke Dimech	DEF	31	26	2130	0	9	0
7	Martin Gritton	ATT	30	31	2120	8	6	0
8	Gary Evans	ATT	25	42	2111	7	1	1
9	Adam Murray	MID	26	23	2010	0	4	0
10	Kevin McIntyre	MID	30	23	1991	2	5	0
11	Levi Reid	MID	25	28	1943	2	5	0
12	Izak Reid	MID	18	27	1910	2	0	0
13	Jamie Tolley	MID	25	24	1755	2	4	0
14	Neil Ashton	DEF	23	19	1701	1	2	0
15	Carl Regan	DEF	27	20	1680	0	5	0
16	Ryan Cresswell	DEF	20	19	1616	1	1	0
17	Tommy Lee	GK	22	18	1582	0	2	0
18	Jim McNulty	DEF	19	19	1251	1	4	0

KEY PLAYERS - GOALSCORERS

Martin Gritton

Goals in the League	8
Contribution to Attacking Power Average number of minutes between League team goals while on pitch	73
Player Strike Rate Average number of minutes between League goals scored by player	265
Club Strike Rate Average number of minutes between League goals scored by club	90

	PLAYER	GOALS LGE	POWER	STRIKE RATE
1	Martin Gritton	8	73	265 mins
2	Francis Green	11	84	276 mins
3	Gary Evans	7	84	301 mins
4	Jamie Tolley	2	92	877 mins

KEY PLAYERS - MIDFIELDERS

Terry Dunfield

Goals in the League	1
Defensive Rating Average number of mins between League goals conceded while on the pitch	72
Contribution to Attacking Power Average number of minutes between League team goals while on pitch	80
Scoring Difference Defensive Rating minus Contribution to Attacking Power	-8

	PLAYER	GOALS LGE	DEF RATE	POWER	SCORE DIFF
1	Terry Dunfield	1	72	80	-8 mins
2	Danny Thomas	4	66	83	-17 mins
3	Adam Murray	0	54	77	-23 mins
4	Kevin McIntyre	2	53	79	-26 mins

KEY PLAYERS - DEFENDERS

Neil Ashton

Goals Conceded when he was on pitch	19
Defensive Rating Ave number of mins between League goals conceded while on the pitch	89
Clean Sheets In games when he played at least 70 minutes	7
Club Defensive Rating Average number of mins between League goals conceded by the club this season.	66

	PLAYER	CON LGE	CLEAN SHEETS	DEF RATE
1	Neil Ashton	19	7	89 mins
2	Ryan Cresswell	21	4	76 mins
3	Sean Hessey	29	6	75 mins
4	Luke Dimech	35	5	60 mins

KEY GOALKEEPER

Jonathan Brain

Goals Conceded in the League	35
Defensive Rating Ave number of mins between League goals conceded while on the pitch.	73
Counting Games Games when he played at least 70 mins	28
Clean Sheets In games when he played at least 70 mins	7

TOP POINT EARNERS

	PLAYER	GAMES	AV PTS
1	Gary Evans	16	1.38
2	Jamie Tolley	17	1.29
3	Neil Ashton	19	1.26
4	Tommy Lee	17	1.24
5	Richard Edghill	13	1.23
6	Sean Hessey	22	1.18
7	Terry Dunfield	38	1.16
8	Danny Thomas	40	1.15
9	Jonathan Brain	28	1.04
10	Francis Green	30	1.03
	CLUB AVERAGE:		1.09

DAGENHAM & REDBRIDGE

Final Position: **20th**

NICKNAME: THE DAGGERS

KEY: Won / Drawn / Lost

#	Comp	Opponent	H/A	Res	Score	Scorers	Attendance
1	div3	Stockport	A	L	0-1		5,577
2	ccr1	Luton	H	L	1-2	Strevens 73	1,754
3	div3	Wycombe	H	D	2-2	Sloma 33, Moore 49	2,280
4	div3	Chester	A	L	0-4		2,098
5	div3	Lincoln	H	W	1-0	Benson 88	2,060
6	div3	Barnet	H	D	1-1	Strevens 20	2,192
7	div3	Notts County	A	L	0-1		3,926
8	div3	Bury	H	D	1-1	Rainford 39	1,597
9	div3	Mansfield	A	W	1-0	Huke 63	2,048
10	div3	Brentford	A	W	3-2	Strevens 23, Rainford 47 pen, Moore 60	3,662
11	div3	Darlington	H	L	0-3		1,888
12	div3	Accrington	H	L	1-3	Cavanagh 26 og	1,596
13	div3	Chesterfield	A	D	1-1	Benson 56	4,101
14	div3	Rotherham	H	L	0-2		2,091
15	div3	Rochdale	A	L	0-1		2,278
16	div3	Peterborough	A	L	1-3	Benson 30	4,200
17	facr1	Hampton	A	W	3-0	Benson 68, Huke 83, Strevens 90	2,252
18	div3	Bradford	H	L	1-4	Benson 77	2,247
19	div3	Macclesfield	A	D	1-1	Southam 7 pen	1,781
20	facr2	Kidderminster	H	W	3-1	Benson 33, 90, Strevens 85	1,493
21	div3	MK Dons	H	L	0-1		1,880
22	div3	Wrexham	H	W	3-0	S.Evans 24 og, Strevens 86, Taylor 90	1,521
23	div3	Shrewsbury	A	L	0-4		4,597
24	div3	Notts County	H	D	1-1	Southam 50 pen	1,649
25	div3	Barnet	A	L	1-3	Huke 88	2,513
26	div3	Bury	A	W	2-0	Strevens 21, 62	1,887
27	div3	Brentford	H	L	1-2	Strevens 49	2,353
28	facr3	Southend	A	L	2-5	Nurse 32, Strevens 58	6,393
29	div3	Morecambe	A	L	0-1		2,754
30	div3	Grimsby	H	D	0-0		2,216
31	div3	Lincoln	A	L	0-2		3,779
32	div3	Wycombe	A	W	1-0	Rainford 45 pen	3,974
33	div3	Stockport	H	L	0-1		1,834
34	div3	Hereford	A	L	1-4	Strevens 33	2,594
35	div3	Chester	H	W	6-2	Strevens 13, 60, Uddin 15, Rainford 23 Nurse 83, Hall 90	1,328
36	div3	Grimsby	A	W	4-1	Smith 16, Rainford 31 pen, 85 Strevens 82	4,060
37	div3	Morecambe	H	W	2-0	Gain 20, Strevens 90	1,809
38	div3	Hereford	H	W	1-0	Foster 45	1,929
39	div3	Bradford	A	W	2-0	Arber 30, Strevens 79	13,537
40	div3	Peterborough	H	L	2-3	Rainford 83 pen, Hall 90	3,130
41	div3	Macclesfield	H	L	0-1		1,350
42	div3	MK Dons	A	L	0-4		9,417
43	div3	Shrewsbury	H	D	1-1	Benson 70	1,686
44	div3	Wrexham	A	D	0-0		4,692
45	div3	Chesterfield	H	L	0-3		2,054
46	div3	Accrington	A	L	0-1		1,262
47	div3	Rochdale	H	D	1-1	Strevens 33	2,032
48	div3	Rotherham	A	L	1-2	Strevens 52	3,203
49	div3	Darlington	A	W	3-2	Sloma 63, Rainford 66 pen, Keltie 74 og	3,709
50	div3	Mansfield	H	W	2-0	Strevens 50, Benson 53 pen	3,451

TEAM OF THE SEASON

G — Tony Roberts, CG: 43 DR: 57

D — Ross Smith, CG: 21 DR: 71
D — Mark Arber, CG: 16 DR: 68
D — Scott Griffiths, CG: 40 DR: 63
D — Danny Foster, CG: 31 DR: 60

M — David Rainford, CG: 25 SD: -7
M — Sam Saunders, CG: 19 SD: -8
M — Sam Sloma, CG: 16 SD: -10
M — Peter Gain, CG: 18 SD: -13

F — Ben Strevens, CG: 38 SR: 239
F — Paul Benson, CG: 18 SR: 286

KEY PLAYER APPEARANCES

	PLAYER	POS	AGE	APP	MINS ON	GOALS	CARDS(Y)	CARDS(R)
1	Tony Roberts	GK	38	43	3870	0	1	0
2	Glen Southam	MID	28	45	3848	2	3	0
3	Scott Griffiths	DEF	22	41	3640	0	0	0
4	Anwar Uddin	DEF	26	41	3618	1	1	0
5	Ben Strevens	ATT	28	46	3585	15	4	0
6	Danny Foster	DEF	23	32	2783	1	2	0
7	Shane Huke	MID	22	36	2755	2	2	0
8	David Rainford	MID	29	29	2421	8	1	0
9	Jon Nurse	ATT	27	30	2093	1	3	0
10	Jonathan Boardman	DEF	27	27	1996	0	3	0
11	Ross Smith	DEF	27	23	1935	1	1	0
12	Sam Sloma	MID	25	29	1891	2	2	0
13	Sam Saunders	MID	24	22	1785	0	2	0
14	Paul Benson	ATT	28	22	1716	6	2	0
15	Peter Gain	MID	31	18	1608	1	5	0
16	Mark Arber	DEF	30	16	1440	1	0	0
17	Chris Moore	ATT	28	26	1176	2	4	0
18	Magnus Okuonghae	DEF	22	10	815	0	0	0

KEY PLAYERS - GOALSCORERS

Ben Strevens

Goals in the League	15	Player Strike Rate Average number of minutes between League goals scored by player	239
Contribution to Attacking Power Average number of minutes between League team goals while on pitch	83	Club Strike Rate Average number of minutes between League goals scored by club	84

	PLAYER	GOALS LGE	POWER	STRIKE RATE
1	Ben Strevens	15	83	239 mins
2	Paul Benson	6	95	286 mins
3	David Rainford	8	78	302 mins
4	Sam Sloma	2	65	945 mins

KEY PLAYERS - MIDFIELDERS

David Rainford

Goals in the League	8	Contribution to Attacking Power Average number of minutes between League team goals while on pitch	78
Defensive Rating Average number of mins between League goals conceded while on the pitch	71	Scoring Difference Defensive Rating minus Contribution to Attacking Power	-7

	PLAYER	GOALS LGE	DEF RATE	POWER	SCORE DIFF
1	David Rainford	8	71	78	-7 mins
2	Sam Saunders	0	66	74	-8 mins
3	Sam Sloma	2	55	65	-10 mins
4	Peter Gain	1	67	80	-13 mins

KEY PLAYERS - DEFENDERS

Ross Smith

Goals Conceded when he was on pitch	27	Clean Sheets In games when he played at least 70 minutes	6
Defensive Rating Ave number of mins between League goals conceded while on the pitch	71	Club Defensive Rating Average number of mins between League goals conceded by the club this season.	59

	PLAYER	CON LGE	CLEAN SHEETS	DEF RATE
1	Ross Smith	27	6	71 mins
2	Mark Arber	21	5	68 mins
3	Scott Griffiths	57	10	63 mins
4	Danny Foster	46	7	60 mins

KEY GOALKEEPER

Tony Roberts

Goals Conceded in the League	67
Defensive Rating Ave number of mins between League goals conceded while on the pitch.	57
Counting Games Games when he played at least 70 mins	43
Clean Sheets In games when he played at least 70 mins	10

TOP POINT EARNERS

	PLAYER	GAMES	AV PTS
1	Mark Arber	16	1.50
2	Sam Saunders	19	1.37
3	David Rainford	25	1.36
4	Peter Gain	18	1.33
5	Ross Smith	21	1.24
6	Jon Nurse	21	1.19
7	Ben Strevens	38	1.16
8	Scott Griffiths	40	1.13
9	Tony Roberts	43	1.12
10	Glen Southam	40	1.08
	CLUB AVERAGE:		1.07

NOTTS COUNTY

Final Position: **21st**

NICKNAME: THE MAGPIES

KEY: ☐Won ☐Drawn ☐Lost

							Attendance
1	div3	Grimsby	A	D	1-1	MacKenzie 29	5,483
2	ccr1	Coventry	A	L	0-3		6,735
3	div3	Brentford	H	D	1-1	Butcher 82	4,670
4	div3	Darlington	A	D	2-2	Butcher 72, 90	3,763
5	div3	Morecambe	H	D	1-1	Butcher 87	4,434
6	div3	MK Dons	A	L	0-3		7,977
7	div3	Dag & Red	H	W	1-0	MacKenzie 83	3,926
8	div3	Rotherham	A	D	1-1	Weir-Daley 36	4,181
9	div3	Chesterfield	H	W	1-0	Hunt 21	5,757
10	div3	Hereford	H	L	2-3	Silk 64, Sam 74	3,576
11	div3	Wycombe	A	L	1-3	Butcher 68	4,199
12	div3	Bury	H	L	1-3	MacKenzie 64 pen	3,710
13	div3	Mansfield	A	L	0-2		4,002
14	div3	Wrexham	H	W	2-1	Weir-Daley 17, MacKenzie 90	4,359
15	div3	Accrington	A	W	2-0	Lindfield 23, Dudfield 87	1,722
16	div3	Barnet	A	D	1-1	Butcher 49	2,089
17	facr1	Histon	H	W	3-0	Dudfield 48, 88, Sam 73	4,344
18	div3	Macclesfield	H	L	0-1		4,390
19	div3	Lincoln	A	L	1-2	Silk 50	4,503
20	facr2	Havant & W	H	L	0-1		3,810
21	div3	Peterborough	H	L	0-1		4,412
22	div3	Shrewsbury	H	W	2-1	Pearce 69, MacKenzie 75	3,819
23	div3	Dag & Red	A	D	1-1	Butcher 6	1,649
24	div3	MK Dons	H	L	1-2	Butcher 9	5,106
25	div3	Rotherham	H	L	0-1		5,290
26	div3	Hereford	A	D	0-0		3,945
27	div3	Stockport	H	L	1-2	Hunt 7	4,120
28	div3	Bradford	A	L	0-3		13,494
29	div3	Chester	H	W	1-0	Tann 58	3,774
30	div3	Morecambe	A	D	1-1	Butcher 28	2,727
31	div3	Brentford	A	D	0-0		4,332
32	div3	Grimsby	H	D	1-1	Butcher 59	4,902
33	div3	Stockport	A	D	1-1	Edwards 9	5,849
34	div3	Darlington	H	L	0-1		3,421
35	div3	Chester	A	W	1-0	Crow 69	1,798
36	div3	Bradford	H	L	1-3	Ryan.Jarvis 59	4,717
37	div3	Macclesfield	A	D	1-1	Butcher 72	2,193
38	div3	Barnet	H	D	0-0		3,687
39	div3	Lincoln	H	L	0-1		3,858
40	div3	Peterborough	A	D	0-0		7,173
41	div3	Rochdale	H	W	1-0	M.Johnson 28	4,030
42	div3	Shrewsbury	A	D	0-0		5,673
43	div3	Mansfield	H	D	0-0		10,027
44	div3	Bury	A	L	1-2	Crow 71	2,463
45	div3	Rochdale	A	L	2-4	Lee 72, MacKenzie 90 pen	2,536
46	div3	Accrington	H	W	1-0	Ryan.Jarvis 37	5,525
47	div3	Wrexham	A	L	0-1		4,076
48	div3	Wycombe	H	W	1-0	Butcher 66	7,327
49	div3	Chesterfield	A	D	1-1	Weir-Daley 45	4,477

TEAM OF THE SEASON

G – Russell Hoult, CG: 14 DR: 96

D – Gary Silk, CG: 22 DR: 98
D – Michael Edwards, CG: 18 DR: 97
D – Paul Mayo, CG: 26 DR: 86
D – Lee Canoville, CG: 29 DR: 82

M – Neil MacKenzie, CG: 24 SD: -5
M – Myles Weston, CG: 12 SD: -33
M – Richard Butcher, CG: 44 SD: -37
M – Austin McCann, CG: 13 SD: -55

F – Ryan Jarvis, CG: 16 SR: 716
F – Jason Lee, CG: 20 SR: 2061

KEY PLAYER APPEARANCES

	PLAYER	POS	AGE	APP	MINS ON	GOALS	CARDS(Y/R)	
1	Richard Butcher	MID	27	46	4015	12	2	0
2	Adam Tann	DEF	26	41	3608	1	4	0
3	Stephen Hunt	DEF	23	37	3154	2	2	0
4	Kevin Pilkington	GK	34	32	2880	0	0	0
5	Lee Canoville	DEF	27	35	2805	0	5	0
6	Paul Mayo	DEF	26	29	2434	0	2	1
7	Lawrie Dudfield	ATT	28	33	2330	1	3	0
8	Neil MacKenzie	MID	32	29	2205	6	1	0
9	Gary Silk	DEF	23	33	2161	2	3	0
10	Jason Lee	ATT	37	31	2061	1	3	0
11	Michael Edwards	DEF	28	19	1665	1	2	0
12	Ryan Jarvis	ATT	21	17	1433	2	0	0
13	Myles Weston	MID	20	25	1424	0	1	0
14	Jay Smith	MID	26	20	1413	0	3	0
15	Austin McCann	MID	28	22	1352	0	3	0
16	Spencer Weir-Daley	ATT	22	30	1264	3	0	0
17	Russell Hoult	GK	35	14	1260	0	0	0
18	Andy Parkinson	MID	29	23	1058	0	1	0

KEY PLAYERS - GOALSCORERS

Richard Butcher

Goals in the League	12
Contribution to Attacking Power Average number of minutes between League team goals while on pitch	114
Player Strike Rate Average number of minutes between League goals scored by player	334
Club Strike Rate Average number of minutes between League goals scored by club	116

	PLAYER	GOALS LGE	POWER	STRIKE RATE
1	Richard Butcher	12	114	334 mins
2	Neil MacKenzie	6	78	367 mins
3	Ryan Jarvis	2	143	716 mins
4	Jason Lee	1	121	2061 mins

KEY PLAYERS - MIDFIELDERS

Neil MacKenzie

Goals in the League	6
Defensive Rating Average number of mins between League goals conceded while on the pitch	73
Contribution to Attacking Power Average number of minutes between League team goals while on pitch	78
Scoring Difference Defensive Rating minus Contribution to Attacking Power	-5

	PLAYER	GOALS LGE	DEF RATE	POWER	SCORE DIFF
1	Neil MacKenzie	6	73	78	-5 mins
2	Myles Weston	0	61	94	-33 mins
3	Richard Butcher	12	77	114	-37 mins
4	Austin McCann	0	67	122	-55 mins

KEY PLAYERS - DEFENDERS

Gary Silk

Goals Conceded when he was on pitch	22
Defensive Rating Ave number of mins between League goals conceded while on the pitch	98
Clean Sheets In games when he played at least 70 minutes	8
Club Defensive Rating Average number of mins between League goals conceded by the club this season.	81

	PLAYER	CON LGE	CLEAN SHEETS	DEF RATE
1	Gary Silk	22	8	98 mins
2	Michael Edwards	17	7	97 mins
3	Paul Mayo	28	9	86 mins
4	Lee Canoville	34	9	82 mins

KEY GOALKEEPER

Russell Hoult

Goals Conceded in the League	13
Defensive Rating Ave number of mins between League goals conceded while on the pitch.	96
Counting Games Games when he played at least 70 mins	14
Clean Sheets In games when he played at least 70 mins	7

TOP POINT EARNERS

	PLAYER	GAMES	AV PTS
1	Myles Weston	12	1.50
2	Jason Lee	20	1.20
3	Ryan Jarvis	16	1.19
4	Paul Mayo	26	1.15
5	Lee Canoville	29	1.14
6	Richard Butcher	44	1.09
7	Stephen Hunt	34	1.09
8	Russell Hoult	14	1.07
9	Jay Smith	15	1.07
10	Neil MacKenzie	24	1.04
	CLUB AVERAGE:		1.04

CHESTER CITY

Final Position: **22nd**

NICKNAME: THE BLUES

KEY: ☐ Won ☐ Drawn ☐ Lost

						Attendance
1	div3	Chesterfield	H	D	0-0		3,183
2	ccr1	Nottm Forest	H	L	2-4*	(*on penalties)	2,720
3	div3	Rochdale	A	W	2-1	Grant 58, Ellison 90	3,243
4	div3	Dag & Red	H	W	4-0	Yeo 50, 58, Murphy 71, 81	2,098
5	div3	Rotherham	A	D	1-1	Roberts 72	4,036
6	div3	Morecambe	H	L	0-1		3,199
7	div3	Bury	A	W	2-0	Butler 32, Hughes 52	2,539
8	div3	Brentford	H	L	0-2		2,453
9	div3	Macclesfield	A	W	2-1	Murphy 12, Wilson 41	2,647
10	div3	Grimsby	A	W	2-1	Murphy 10, Ellison 47	3,479
11	div3	Shrewsbury	H	W	3-1	Partridge 62, Murphy 72, Yeo 73	3,057
12	div3	Hereford	H	D	1-1	Yeo 58	3,430
13	div3	Stockport	A	W	2-1	Partridge 53, 81	5,566
14	div3	Wycombe	H	D	2-2	Holroyd 16, Murphy 40	2,598
15	div3	Lincoln	A	W	1-0	Dinning 57 pen	3,960
16	div3	Bradford	A	L	1-2	Ellison 90	13,211
17	facr1	Bradford	A	L	0-1		4,069
18	div3	MK Dons	H	L	0-2		3,102
19	div3	Wrexham	A	D	2-2	Roberts 27, Linwood 45	7,687
20	div3	Barnet	H	W	3-0	Partridge 6, Ellison 40, 76	1,858
21	div3	Peterborough	H	L	1-2	Hughes 45	2,291
22	div3	Bury	H	W	2-1	Hughes 45, Ellison 79	2,260
23	div3	Morecambe	A	L	3-5	Ellison 5, 73, Holroyd 76	3,419
24	div3	Brentford	A	L	0-3		4,323
25	div3	Grimsby	H	L	0-2		2,255
26	div3	Accrington	A	D	3-3	Holroyd 8, 78, Wilson 68	1,311
27	div3	Mansfield	H	L	0-1		2,092
28	div3	Notts County	A	L	0-1		3,774
29	div3	Rotherham	H	L	0-1		2,536
30	div3	Rochdale	H	L	0-4		2,131
31	div3	Chesterfield	A	D	1-1	Murphy 59	3,701
32	div3	Accrington	H	L	2-3	Butler 20, Murphy 34	1,957
33	div3	Dag & Red	A	L	2-6	Roberts 51, Murphy 90	1,328
34	div3	Notts County	H	L	0-1		1,798
35	div3	Mansfield	A	W	3-1	Ellison 56, 90, Dinning 72 pen	2,362
36	div3	MK Dons	A	L	0-1		8,172
37	div3	Darlington	A	L	0-1		3,294
38	div3	Wrexham	H	L	0-2		3,849
39	div3	Bradford	H	L	0-1		1,566
40	div3	Barnet	A	L	1-3	Hughes 90	1,663
41	div3	Darlington	H	W	2-1	Rutherford 6, Partridge 36	1,759
42	div3	Peterborough	A	L	0-1		6,457
43	div3	Hereford	A	D	2-2	Sandwith 68, Ellison 90 pen	3,210
44	div3	Lincoln	H	L	1-2	McManus 20	2,089
45	div3	Wycombe	A	L	0-1		5,497
46	div3	Shrewsbury	A	D	0-0		6,417
47	div3	Stockport	H	D	0-0		3,060
48	div3	Macclesfield	H	D	0-0		2,396

TEAM OF THE SEASON

G — John Danby CG: 46 DR: 62

D — Lawrence Wilson CG: 37 DR: 69

D — Kevin Sandwith CG: 12 DR: 65

D — Paul Linwood CG: 38 DR: 65

D — James Vaughan CG: 29 DR: 63

M — Tony Grant CG: 13 SD: -4

M — Ritchie Partridge CG: 29 SD: -5

M — Mark Hughes CG: 38 SD: -11

M — Kevin Ellison CG: 34 SD: -12

F — Chris Holroyd CG: 11* SR: 324

F — John Murphy CG: 37 SR: 384

KEY PLAYER APPEARANCES

	PLAYER	POS	AGE	APP	MINS ON	GOALS	CARDS(Y/R)	
1	John Danby	GK	26	46	4118	0	2	0
2	Paul Linwood	DEF	24	42	3583	1	7	1
3	Mark Hughes	MID	24	43	3499	4	14	0
4	Lawrence Wilson	DEF	21	40	3471	2	3	1
5	John Murphy	ATT	31	39	3372	9	2	0
6	Kevin Ellison	MID	29	36	3119	11	7	1
7	Paul Butler	DEF	35	35	3015	2	7	0
8	Kevin Roberts	DEF	18	37	2894	3	6	0
9	Ritchie Partridge	MID	27	36	2793	5	0	0
10	James Vaughan	DEF	21	30	2574	0	2	0
11	Tony Dinning	MID	33	20	1732	2	4	1
12	Simon Marples	DEF	32	16	1428	0	2	0
13	Kevin Sandwith	DEF	30	22	1381	1	1	0
14	Tony Grant	MID	33	19	1346	1	1	0
15	Chris Holroyd	ATT	21	25	1297	4	3	0
16	Paul Rutherford	MID	20	23	1105	1	3	0
17	Paul McManus	ATT	18	19	881	1	0	0
18	Simon Yeo	ATT	34	21	847	4	0	0

KEY PLAYERS - GOALSCORERS

Kevin Ellison

Goals in the League	11
Contribution to Attacking Power Average number of minutes between League team goals while on pitch	76
Player Strike Rate Average number of minutes between League goals scored by player	283
Club Strike Rate Average number of minutes between League goals scored by club	86

	PLAYER	GOALS LGE	POWER	STRIKE RATE
1	Kevin Ellison	11	76	283 mins
2	Chris Holroyd	4	86	324 mins
3	John Murphy	9	84	384 mins
4	Ritchie Partridge	5	73	576 mins

KEY PLAYERS - MIDFIELDERS

Tony Grant

Goals in the League	1
Defensive Rating Average number of mins between League goals conceded while on the pitch	70
Contribution to Attacking Power Average number of minutes between League team goals while on pitch	74
Scoring Difference Defensive Rating minus Contribution to Attacking Power	-4

	PLAYER	GOALS LGE	DEF RATE	POWER	SCORE DIFF
1	Tony Grant	1	70	74	-4 mins
2	Ritchie Partridge	5	68	73	-5 mins
3	Mark Hughes	4	60	71	-11 mins
4	Kevin Ellison	11	64	76	-12 mins

KEY PLAYERS - DEFENDERS

Lawrence Wilson

Goals Conceded when he was on pitch	51
Defensive Rating Ave number of mins between League goals conceded while on the pitch	69
Clean Sheets In games when he played at least 70 minutes	8
Club Defensive Rating Average number of mins between League goals conceded by the club this season.	64

	PLAYER	CON LGE	CLEAN SHEETS	DEF RATE
1	Lawrence Wilson	51	8	69 mins
2	Kevin Sandwith	21	3	65 mins
3	Paul Linwood	56	8	65 mins
4	James Vaughan	42	7	63 mins

KEY GOALKEEPER

John Danby

Goals Conceded in the League	67
Defensive Rating Ave number of mins between League goals conceded while on the pitch.	62
Counting Games Games when he played at least 70 mins	47
Clean Sheets In games when he played at least 70 mins	10

TOP POINT EARNERS

	PLAYER	GAMES	AV PTS
1	Simon Marples	16	1.50
2	Paul Butler	32	1.22
3	Mark Hughes	38	1.21
4	Ritchie Partridge	29	1.21
5	Kevin Ellison	34	1.15
6	Tony Grant	13	1.15
7	John Murphy	37	1.14
8	Lawrence Wilson	37	1.14
9	Paul Linwood	38	1.11
10	John Danby	46	1.02
	CLUB AVERAGE:		1.02

MANSFIELD TOWN

Final Position: **23rd**

NICKNAME: THE STAGS

KEY: ☐ Won ☐ Drawn ☐ Lost

		Opponent	H/A	Res	Score	Scorers	Attendance
1	div3	Brentford	A	D	1-1	M.Boulding 23	4,909
2	ccr1	Oldham	A	L	1-4	Mullins 72	3,155
3	div3	Lincoln	H	L	1-3	M.Boulding 36 pen	3,357
4	div3	Morecambe	A	L	1-3	M.Boulding 40	2,980
5	div3	Stockport	H	W	4-2	McAliskey 3, M.McIntosh 9 Buxton 25, M.Boulding 32 pen	2,747
6	div3	Peterborough	A	L	1-2	McAliskey 53	4,721
7	div3	Chesterfield	H	L	1-3	Dawson 9	4,514
8	div3	Accrington	A	L	0-1		1,408
9	div3	Dag & Red	H	L	0-1		2,048
10	div3	MK Dons	H	L	1-2	M.Boulding 29	1,984
11	div3	Rotherham	A	L	2-3	M.Boulding 76, Arnold 83	3,881
12	div3	Barnet	A	D	1-1	Brown 47	2,041
13	div3	Notts County	H	W	2-0	M.Boulding 57 pen, 61	4,002
14	div3	Shrewsbury	A	D	0-0		5,347
15	div3	Macclesfield	H	W	5-0	Si.Brown 8, 19, 22, Arnold 21 M.Boulding 54	2,853
16	div3	Hereford	A	L	1-2	M.Boulding 66	2,272
17	facr1	Lewes	H	W	3-0	M.Boulding 33, R.Boulding 40, Holmes 82	2,607
18	div3	Rochdale	A	L	0-1		2,431
19	facr2	Harrogate Rail	A	W	3-2	Jelleyman 38, M.Boulding 51, 77	3,500
20	div3	Bradford	H	D	0-0		2,308
21	div3	Grimsby	A	L	0-1		3,836
22	div3	Chesterfield	A	L	0-2		6,300
23	div3	Peterborough	H	W	2-0	M.Boulding 35, 61	3,107
24	div3	Accrington	H	L	1-2	Holmes 90	2,494
25	div3	MK Dons	A	L	0-1		9,583
26	facr3	Brighton	A	W	2-1	Hamshaw 10, Holmes 45	5,857
27	div3	Wycombe	H	L	0-4		1,959
28	div3	Chester	A	W	1-0	Hamshaw 49	2,092
29	div3	Darlington	H	L	0-1		3,344
30	facr4	Middlesbrough	H	L	0-2		6,258
31	div3	Lincoln	A	W	2-1	M.Boulding 49, 90	4,280
32	div3	Brentford	H	L	2-3	Elder 15 og, Louis 64	2,511
33	div3	Wycombe	A	W	2-1	M.Boulding 9 pen, Louis 90	5,963
34	div3	Morecambe	H	L	1-2	Bell 48	2,287
35	div3	Darlington	A	W	2-1	Louis 56, Dawson 64	3,527
36	div3	Chester	H	L	1-3	Mullins 45	2,362
37	div3	Bury	H	D	1-1	Buxton 56	1,923
38	div3	Wrexham	A	D	1-1	M.Boulding 53	4,865
39	div3	Rochdale	H	L	0-4		2,351
40	div3	Hereford	H	L	0-1		-
41	div3	Bradford	A	W	2-1	Arnold 14, M.Boulding 51	13,611
42	div3	Grimsby	H	L	1-2	Arnold 49	2,616
43	div3	Bury	A	L	0-2		2,779
44	div3	Notts County	A	D	0-0		10,027
45	div3	Wrexham	H	W	2-1	Louis 51 pen, Mullins 54	3,435
46	div3	Barnet	H	D	2-2	M.Boulding 14, Hamshaw 55	2,463
47	div3	Stockport	A	L	1-2	Dicker 39 og	4,982
48	div3	Macclesfield	A	D	0-0		3,250
49	div3	Shrewsbury	H	W	3-1	M.Boulding 22, 37, 87	3,334
50	div3	Rotherham	H	L	0-1		5,271
51	div3	Dag & Red	A	L	0-2		3,451

TEAM OF THE SEASON

G — Carl Muggleton, CG: 33 DR: 63

D — Daniel Martin, CG: 18 DR: 73

D — Alex Baptiste, CG: 24 DR: 69

D — Gareth Jelleyman, CG: 32 DR: 63

D — John Mullins, CG: 40 DR: 60

M — Lee Bell, CG: 19 SD: -13

M — Nathan Arnold, CG: 18 SD: -15

M — Jonathan D'Laryea, CG: 21 SD: -23

M — Matthew Hamshaw, CG: 42 SD: -25

F — Michael Boulding, CG: 41 SR: 178

F — Jefferson Louis, CG: 13 SR: 317

KEY PLAYER APPEARANCES

	PLAYER	POS	AGE	APP	MINS ON	GOALS	CARDS(Y	/R)
1	Matthew Hamshaw	MID	26	45	3846	2	2	0
2	Stephen Dawson	MID	22	43	3830	2	7	0
3	Michael Boulding	ATT	32	43	3745	21	0	0
4	John Mullins	DEF	22	43	3706	2	7	1
5	Jake Buxton	DEF	23	40	3512	2	9	3
6	Carl Muggleton	GK	39	36	3111	0	1	0
7	Gareth Jelleyman	DEF	27	39	3096	0	4	0
8	Alex Baptiste	DEF	22	25	2224	0	3	0
9	Jonathan D'Laryea	MID	22	29	2157	0	0	0
10	Nathan Arnold	MID	20	32	1995	4	0	0
11	Lee Bell	MID	25	23	1892	1	1	1
12	Daniel Martin	DEF	21	26	1849	0	2	0
13	Simon Brown	ATT	24	29	1565	4	3	0
14	Jefferson Louis	ATT	29	18	1271	4	1	0
15	Jason White	GK	22	13	1029	0	0	0
16	Keith Briggs	DEF	26	13	905	0	2	0
17	Will Atkinson	MID	19	12	885	0	0	0
18	Chris Wood	DEF	21	13	857	0	0	0

KEY PLAYERS - GOALSCORERS

Michael Boulding

Goals in the League	21	**Player Strike Rate** Average number of minutes between League goals scored by player	178
Contribution to Attacking Power Average number of minutes between League team goals while on pitch	79	**Club Strike Rate** Average number of minutes between League goals scored by club	90

	PLAYER	GOALS LGE	POWER	STRIKE RATE
1	Michael Boulding	21	79	178 mins
2	Jefferson Louis	4	74	317 mins
3	Simon Brown	4	111	391 mins
4	Nathan Arnold	4	79	498 mins

KEY PLAYERS - MIDFIELDERS

Lee Bell

Goals in the League	1	**Contribution to Attacking Power** Average number of minutes between League team goals while on pitch	72
Defensive Rating Average number of mins between League goals conceded while on the pitch	59	**Scoring Difference** Defensive Rating minus Contribution to Attacking Power	-13

	PLAYER	GOALS LGE	DEF RATE	POWER	SCORE DIFF
1	Lee Bell	1	59	72	-13 mins
2	Nathan Arnold	4	64	79	-15 mins
3	Jonathan D'Laryea	0	63	86	-23 mins
4	Matthew Hamshaw	2	62	87	-25 mins

KEY PLAYERS - DEFENDERS

Daniel Martin

Goals Conceded when he was on pitch	25	**Clean Sheets** In games when he played at least 70 minutes	6
Defensive Rating Ave number of mins between League goals conceded while on the pitch	73	**Club Defensive Rating** Average number of mins between League goals conceded by the club this season.	63

	PLAYER	CON LGE	CLEAN SHEETS	DEF RATE
1	Daniel Martin	25	6	73 mins
2	Alex Baptiste	32	6	69 mins
3	Gareth Jelleyman	49	4	63 mins
4	John Mullins	61	6	60 mins

KEY GOALKEEPER

Carl Muggleton

Goals Conceded in the League	49
Defensive Rating Ave number of mins between League goals conceded while on the pitch.	63
Counting Games Games when he played at least 70 mins	33
Clean Sheets In games when he played at least 70 mins	7

TOP POINT EARNERS

	PLAYER	GAMES	AV PTS
1	Jefferson Louis	13	1.31
2	Nathan Arnold	18	1.22
3	Lee Bell	19	1.11
4	Jonathan D'Laryea	21	1.10
5	Daniel Martin	18	1.06
6	Carl Muggleton	33	1.03
7	Simon Brown	14	1.00
8	Matthew Hamshaw	42	0.95
9	Gareth Jelleyman	32	0.94
10	John Mullins	40	0.93
	CLUB AVERAGE:		0.91

WREXHAM

Final Position: **24th**

NICKNAME: THE ROBINS

KEY: Won Drawn Lost

							Attendance
1	div3	Darlington	A	L	0-2		4,408
2	ccr1	Port Vale	A	W	5-3*	Proctor 10 (*on penalties)	2,916
3	div3	Morecambe	H	W	2-1	Proctor 6, 22	5,504
4	div3	Bradford	A	L	1-2	N.Roberts 54	13,546
5	ccr2	Aston Villa	H	L	0-5		8,221
6	div3	Hereford	H	L	0-2		4,004
7	div3	Rotherham	H	L	0-1		3,711
8	div3	Stockport	A	L	1-2	Marc.Williams 26	5,513
9	div3	Lincoln	H	W	1-0	Marc.Williams 51	3,614
10	div3	Chesterfield	H	L	0-4		3,058
11	div3	Accrington	A	W	2-0	N.Roberts 37, 66	1,822
12	div3	Macclesfield	A	L	2-3	Proctor 6 pen, Llewellyn 22	2,256
13	div3	Barnet	H	L	0-2		3,591
14	div3	Notts County	A	L	1-2	Spann 70	4,359
15	div3	Shrewsbury	H	L	0-1		4,305
16	div3	Wycombe	H	D	0-0		2,805
17	facr1	Peterborough	A	L	1-4	N.Roberts 66	4,266
18	div3	Chester	H	D	2-2	Proctor 37, 75	7,687
19	div3	Rochdale	A	D	0-0		2,808
20	div3	Bury	A	W	1-0	E.Williams 31	2,248
21	div3	Dag & Red	A	L	0-3		1,521
22	div3	Brentford	H	L	1-3	Llewellyn 41	3,811
23	div3	Rotherham	A	L	0-3		5,773
24	div3	Rochdale	H	L	0-2		4,302
25	div3	Stockport	H	L	0-1		4,287
26	div3	Chesterfield	A	L	1-2	S.Evans 68	4,293
27	div3	Grimsby	A	L	0-1		4,084
28	div3	MK Dons	H	W	1-0	N.Roberts 71	4,319
29	div3	Bradford	H	D	1-1	N.Roberts 38	4,341
30	div3	Morecambe	A	D	2-2	Sonner 30 pen, Proctor 79 pen	2,421
31	div3	Darlington	H	W	2-0	S.Evans 21, Proctor 86	4,013
32	div3	Peterborough	A	D	0-0		5,505
33	div3	Grimsby	H	D	0-0		4,217
34	div3	Peterborough	H	L	0-2		4,103
35	div3	Mansfield	H	D	1-1	Proctor 70	4,865
36	div3	Chester	A	W	2-0	Hall 22, Proctor 65	3,849
37	div3	Wycombe	A	L	1-2	Proctor 53	4,002
38	div3	Bury	H	W	2-1	Broughton 25, Proctor 77	4,431
39	div3	Brentford	A	L	0-2		4,448
40	div3	Dag & Red	H	D	0-0		4,692
41	div3	Barnet	A	L	2-3	Broughton 55, Spender 66	2,286
42	div3	Mansfield	A	L	1-2	Marc.Williams 78	3,435
43	div3	Macclesfield	H	D	1-1	S.Evans 79	3,993
44	div3	MK Dons	A	L	1-4	N.Roberts 59 pen	8,646
45	div3	Shrewsbury	A	L	0-3		7,065
46	div3	Notts County	H	W	1-0	N.Roberts 77	4,076
47	div3	Hereford	A	L	0-2		3,739
48	div3	Accrington	H	L	1-3	N.Roberts 90 pen	3,657
49	div3	Lincoln	A	W	4-2	Mackin 11, Baynes 33, 88, Llewellyn 90	4,958

TEAM OF THE SEASON

G — Gavin Ward CG: 22 DR: 68

D — Mike Williams CG: 12 DR: 69
D — Simon Spender CG: 31 DR: 68
D — Philip Bolland CG: 16 DR: 67
D — Stephen Evans CG: 27 DR: 62

M — Danny Williams CG: 9 SD: -37
M — Robert Garrett CG: 9 SD: -48
M — Sam Aiston CG: 11 SD: -64
M — Matt Done CG: 11 SD: -89

F — Mike Proctor CG: 19 SR: 207
F — Marc Williams CG: 9 SR: 360

KEY PLAYER APPEARANCES

	PLAYER	POS	AGE	APP	MINS ON	GOALS	CARDS(Y)	CARDS(R)
1	Chris Llewellyn	ATT	28	40	3431	3	6	0
2	Neil Roberts	ATT	30	36	3012	8	6	0
3	Richard Hope	DEF	30	33	2879	0	5	1
4	Simon Spender	DEF	22	34	2856	1	4	0
5	Stephen Evans	DEF	29	32	2644	3	4	0
6	Mike Proctor	ATT	27	40	2277	11	4	0
7	Neil Taylor	DEF	0	26	2013	0	4	0
8	Anthony Williams	GK	30	22	1980	0	0	0
9	Gavin Ward	GK	38	22	1980	0	0	0
10	Shaun Pejic	DEF	25	19	1593	0	3	0
11	Philip Bolland	DEF	31	18	1548	0	3	0
12	Matt Done	MID	19	24	1357	0	2	0
13	Drewe Broughton	ATT	29	16	1344	2	3	0
14	Mike Williams	DEF	21	17	1317	0	0	0
15	Ryan Valentine	DEF	25	14	1260	0	2	0
16	Sam Aiston	MID	31	19	1243	0	1	0
17	Mark Jones	MID	24	16	1083	0	3	0
18	Marc Williams	ATT	19	20	1080	3	1	0

KEY PLAYERS - GOALSCORERS

Mike Proctor

Goals in the League	11
Contribution to Attacking Power — Average number of minutes between League team goals while on pitch	94
Player Strike Rate — Average number of minutes between League goals scored by player	207
Club Strike Rate — Average number of minutes between League goals scored by club	116

	PLAYER	GOALS LGE	POWER	STRIKE RATE
1	Mike Proctor	11	94	207 mins
2	Marc Williams	3	98	360 mins
3	Neil Roberts	8	125	376 mins
4	Drewe Broughton	2	96	672 mins

KEY PLAYERS - MIDFIELDERS

Danny Williams

Goals in the League	0
Defensive Rating — Average number of mins between League goals conceded while on the pitch	49
Contribution to Attacking Power — Average number of minutes between League team goals while on pitch	86
Scoring Difference — Defensive Rating minus Contribution to Attacking Power	-37

	PLAYER	GOALS LGE	DEF RATE	POWER	SCORE DIFF
1	Danny Williams	0	49	86	-37 mins
2	Robert Garrett	0	63	111	-48 mins
3	Sam Aiston	0	49	113	-64 mins
4	Matt Done	0	46	135	-89 mins

KEY PLAYERS - DEFENDERS

Mike Williams

Goals Conceded when he was on pitch	19
Defensive Rating — Ave number of mins between League goals conceded while on the pitch	69
Clean Sheets — In games when he played at least 70 minutes	5
Club Defensive Rating — Average number of mins between League goals conceded by the club this season.	63

	PLAYER	CON LGE	CLEAN SHEETS	DEF RATE
1	Mike Williams	19	5	69 mins
2	Simon Spender	42	8	68 mins
3	Philip Bolland	23	6	67 mins
4	Stephen Evans	42	8	62 mins

KEY GOALKEEPER

Gavin Ward

Goals Conceded in the League	29
Defensive Rating — Ave number of mins between League goals conceded while on the pitch.	68
Counting Games — Games when he played at least 70 mins	22
Clean Sheets — In games when he played at least 70 mins	7

TOP POINT EARNERS

	PLAYER	GAMES	AV PTS
1	Gavin Ward	22	1.14
2	Philip Bolland	16	1.06
3	Drewe Broughton	15	1.00
4	Shaun Pejic	17	1.00
5	Mike Proctor	19	1.00
6	Neil Taylor	19	1.00
7	Stephen Evans	27	0.93
8	Mike Williams	12	0.92
9	Simon Spender	31	0.90
10	Chris Llewellyn	37	0.89
	CLUB AVERAGE:		0.87

SCOTTISH PREMIERSHIP ROUND-UP

FINAL LEAGUE TABLE

		HOME					AWAY					TOTAL			
	P	W	D	L	F	A	W	D	L	F	A	F	A	DIF	PTS
Celtic	38	14	4	1	42	7	14	1	4	42	19	84	26	58	89
Rangers	38	18	0	1	50	10	9	5	5	34	23	84	33	51	86
Motherwell	38	9	4	6	30	26	9	2	8	20	20	50	46	4	60
Aberdeen	38	11	5	4	33	21	4	3	11	17	37	50	58	-8	53
Dundee Utd	38	9	6	4	26	14	5	4	10	27	33	53	47	6	52
Hibernian	38	10	5	4	34	22	4	5	10	15	23	49	45	4	52
Falkirk	38	8	6	5	21	16	5	4	10	24	33	45	49	-4	49
Hearts	38	8	4	7	27	26	5	5	9	20	29	47	55	-8	48
Inverness CT	38	9	2	8	32	28	4	2	13	19	34	51	62	-11	43
St Mirren	38	7	4	8	17	27	3	7	9	9	27	26	54	-28	41
Kilmarnock	38	7	5	7	26	23	3	5	11	13	29	39	52	-13	40
Gretna	38	4	3	11	18	34	1	5	14	14	49	32	83	-51	13

CLUB STRIKE FORCE

Celtic players celebrate a McDonald goal

1 Celtic

Goals scored in the League	84
Club Strike Rate (CSR) Average number of minutes between League goals scored by club	40

	CLUB	GOALS	CSR
1	Celtic	84	40
2	Rangers	84	40
3	Dundee Utd	53	64
4	Inverness CT	51	67
5	Aberdeen	50	68
6	Motherwell	50	68
7	Hibernian	49	69
8	Hearts	47	72
9	Falkirk	45	76
10	Kilmarnock	39	87
11	Gretna	32	106
12	St Mirren	26	131

CLUB DISCIPLINARY RECORDS

Hearts' Neilson tackles from behind

1 Hearts

League Yellow	76
League Red	9
League Total	85
Cards Average in League Average number of minutes between a card being shown of either colour	40

	CLUB	Y	R	TOTAL	AVE
1	Hearts	76	9	85	40
2	Hibernian	74	10	84	40
3	Gretna	69	4	73	46
4	St Mirren	67	5	72	47
5	Kilmarnock	65	4	69	49
6	Celtic	63	0	63	54
7	Motherwell	62	1	63	54
8	Dundee Utd	54	9	63	54
9	Aberdeen	57	0	57	60
10	Inverness CT	50	6	56	61
11	Falkirk	47	6	53	64
12	Rangers	48	4	52	65

CLUB DEFENCES

	CLUB	LGE	CS	CDR
1	Celtic	26	19	131
2	Rangers	33	17	103
3	Hibernian	45	11	76
4	Motherwell	46	10	74
5	Dundee Utd	47	13	72
6	Falkirk	49	15	69
7	Kilmarnock	52	7	65
8	St Mirren	54	12	63
9	Hearts	55	10	62
10	Aberdeen	58	9	58
11	Inverness CT	62	7	55
12	Gretna	83	5	41

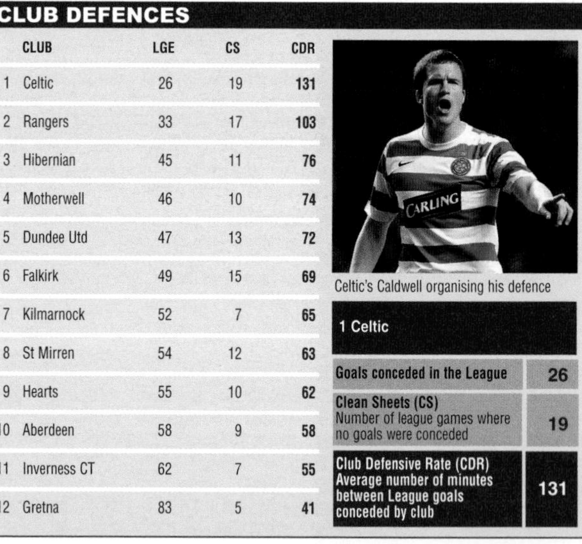

Celtic's Caldwell organising his defence

1 Celtic

Goals conceded in the League	26
Clean Sheets (CS) Number of league games where no goals were conceded	19
Club Defensive Rate (CDR) Average number of minutes between League goals conceded by club	131

STADIUM CAPACITY AND HOME CROWDS

TEAM	CAPACITY	AVE	HIGH	LOW
1 Rangers	51082	94.14	50440	30293
2 Celtic	60506	93.73	60000	45000
3 Hearts	18300	86.89	17131	10512
4 Hibernian	17458	80.58	16872	11692
5 Inverness CT	7711	63.27	7753	3420
6 Dundee Utd	14223	60.91	13613	5845
7 Falkirk	10000	55.27	6803	4490
8 Aberdeen	22199	51.31	17798	1284
9 Motherwell	13742	48.63	10445	4259
10 St Mirren	10752	42.29	7840	3163
11 Kilmarnock	18220	33.93	11544	4086
12 Gretna	13742	19.64	7031	431

Key: Average. The percentage of each stadium filled in League games over the season (AVE), the stadium capacity and the highest and lowest crowds recorded.

AWAY ATTENDANCE

TEAM	AVE	HIGH	LOW
1 Rangers	84.25	58964	6137
2 Celtic	79.29	50428	3561
3 Aberdeen	78.87	58000	1730
4 Hibernian	75.01	58515	2666
5 Motherwell	73.98	58624	2877
6 Kilmarnock	71.92	60000	1545
7 Hearts	69.68	57300	1090
8 St Mirren	69.29	55747	1284
9 Gretna	68.78	57171	3163
10 Falkirk	66.23	54291	1609
11 Dundee Utd	64.71	57006	507
12 Inverness CT	62.41	56787	431

Key: Average. How close each club has come to filling grounds in its away league matches (AVE) and the highest and lowest crowds recorded.

CHART-TOPPING MIDFIELDERS

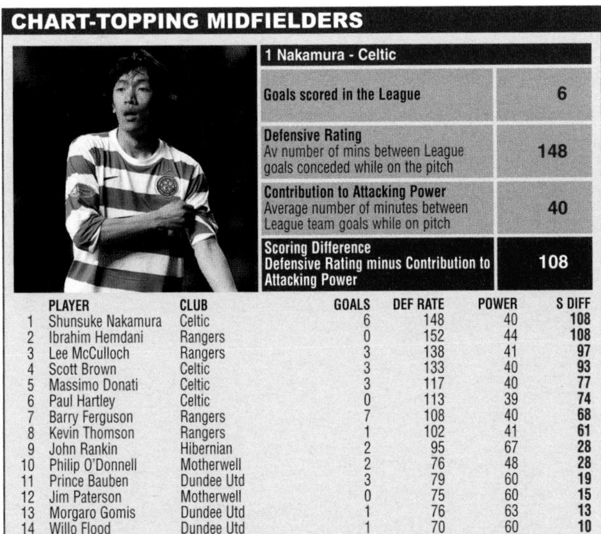

1 Nakamura - Celtic	
Goals scored in the League	6
Defensive Rating Av number of mins between League goals conceded while on the pitch	148
Contribution to Attacking Power Average number of minutes between League team goals while on pitch	40
Scoring Difference Defensive Rating minus Contribution to Attacking Power	108

	PLAYER	CLUB	GOALS	DEF RATE	POWER	S DIFF
1	Shunsuke Nakamura	Celtic	6	148	40	**108**
2	Ibrahim Hemdani	Rangers	0	152	44	**108**
3	Lee McCulloch	Rangers	3	138	41	**97**
4	Scott Brown	Celtic	3	133	40	**93**
5	Massimo Donati	Celtic	3	117	40	**77**
6	Paul Hartley	Celtic	0	113	39	**74**
7	Barry Ferguson	Rangers	7	108	40	**68**
8	Kevin Thomson	Rangers	1	102	41	**61**
9	John Rankin	Hibernian	2	95	67	**28**
10	Philip O'Donnell	Motherwell	2	76	48	**28**
11	Prince Bauben	Dundee Utd	3	79	60	**19**
12	Jim Paterson	Motherwell	0	75	60	**15**
13	Morgaro Gomis	Dundee Utd	1	76	63	**13**
14	Willo Flood	Dundee Utd	1	70	60	**10**
15	Eggert Jonsson	Hearts	1	72	63	**9**

CHART-TOPPING GOALSCORERS

1 Boyd - Rangers	
Goals scored in the League	14
Contribution to Attacking Power (AP) Average number of minutes between League team goals while on pitch	41
Club Strike Rate (CSR) Average minutes between League goals scored by club	43
Player Strike Rate Average number of minutes between League goals scored by player	105

	PLAYER	CLUB	GOALS: LGE	POWER	CSR	S RATE
1	Kris Boyd	Rangers	14	41	43	**105**
2	Scott McDonald	Celtic	25	39	45	**117**
3	Daniel Cousin	Rangers	10	46	43	**158**
4	Jan V of Hesselink	Celtic	15	38	45	**163**
5	Barry Robson	Dundee Utd	11	61	67	**167**
6	Steven Fletcher	Hibernian	13	62	73	**186**
7	Dean Shiels	Hibernian	7	64	73	**211**
8	Chris Porter	Motherwell	14	69	77	**218**
9	Noel Hunt	Dundee Utd	13	61	67	**233**
10	David Clarkson	Motherwell	12	64	77	**240**
11	Lee Miller	Aberdeen	12	69	68	**242**
12	Carl Finnigan	Falkirk	7	66	76	**247**
13	Michael Higdon	Falkirk	8	72	76	**252**
14	Colin Nish	Kilmarnock	7	80	87	**263**
15	Colin Nish	Hibernian	4	64	73	**275**

CHART-TOPPING DEFENDERS

1 Hinkel - Celtic	
Goals Conceded in the League The number of League goals conceded while he was on the pitch	9
Clean Sheets In games when he played at least 70 mins	6
Club Defensive Rating Average mins between League goals conceded by the club this season	145
Defensive Rating Average number of minutes between League goals conceded while on pitch	146

	PLAYER	CLUB	CON: LGE	CS	CDR	DEF RATE
1	Andreas Hinkel	Celtic	9	6	145	**146**
2	Lee Naylor	Celtic	20	17	145	**144**
3	Stephen McManus	Celtic	23	18	145	**140**
4	Gary Caldwell	Celtic	25	17	145	**126**
5	Kirk Broadfoot	Rangers	10	7	111	**122**
6	Christian Kalvenes	Dundee Utd	13	10	76	**121**
7	Gary Kenneth	Dundee Utd	12	8	76	**118**
8	Alan Hutton	Rangers	16	9	111	**112**
9	Carlos Cuellar	Rangers	29	16	111	**111**
10	David Weir	Rangers	32	16	111	**102**
11	Gerard Aafjes	Falkirk	24	10	69	**91**
12	David Lilley	Kilmarnock	23	7	65	**89**
13	Sasa Papac	Rangers	23	9	111	**85**
14	Steven Whittaker	Rangers	30	11	111	**85**
15	Steven Hammell	Motherwell	15	3	84	**81**

CHART-TOPPING GOALKEEPERS

1 Boruc - Celtic	
Counting Games Games in which he played at least 70 minutes	30
Goals Conceded in the League The number of League goals conceded while he was on the pitch	20
Clean Sheets In games when he played at least 70 mins	15
Defensive Rating Average number of minutes between League goals conceded while on pitch	135

	PLAYER	CLUB	CG	CONC	CS	DEF RATE
1	Artur Boruc	Celtic	30	20	15	**135**
2	Robert Olejnik	Falkirk	12	9	7	**120**
3	Allan McGregor	Rangers	31	25	14	**111**
4	Lukasz Zaluska	Dundee Utd	15	17	4	**79**
5	Yves Ma-Kalambay	Hibernian	28	34	8	**75**
6	Graeme Smith	Motherwell	36	44	9	**73**
7	Alan Combe	Kilmarnock	37	48	7	**69**
8	Grzegorz Szamotulski	Dundee Utd	18	24	8	**67**
9	James Langfield	Aberdeen	25	36	7	**62**
10	Steve Banks	Hearts	28	41	8	**61**
11	Chris Smith	St Mirren	28	42	7	**60**
12	Mike Fraser	Inverness CT	36	59	7	**54**
13	Derek Soutar	Aberdeen	13	22	2	**53**
14	Tim Krul	Falkirk	22	37	7	**53**
15	Greg Fleming	Gretna	27	61	3	**40**

PLAYER DISCIPLINARY RECORD

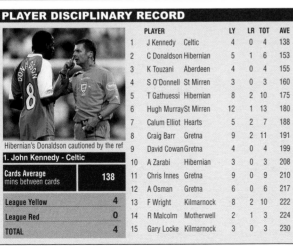

Hibernian's Donaldson cautioned by the ref

1. John Kennedy - Celtic	
Cards Average mins between cards	138
League Yellow	4
League Red	0
TOTAL	4

	PLAYER		LY	LR	TOT	AVE
1	J Kennedy	Celtic	4	0	4	138
2	C Donaldson	Hibernian	5	1	6	153
3	K Touzani	Aberdeen	4	0	4	155
4	S O'Donnell	St Mirren	3	0	3	160
5	T Gathuessi	Hibernian	8	2	10	175
6	Hugh Murray	St Mirren	12	1	13	180
7	Calum Elliot	Hearts	5	2	7	188
8	Craig Barr	Gretna	9	2	11	191
9	David Cowan	Gretna	4	0	4	199
10	A Zarabi	Hibernian	3	0	3	208
11	Chris Innes	Gretna	9	0	9	210
12	A Osman	Gretna	6	0	6	217
13	F Wright	Kilmarnock	8	2	10	222
14	R Malcolm	Motherwell	2	1	3	224
15	Gary Locke	Kilmarnock	3	0	3	230

TEAM OF THE SEASON

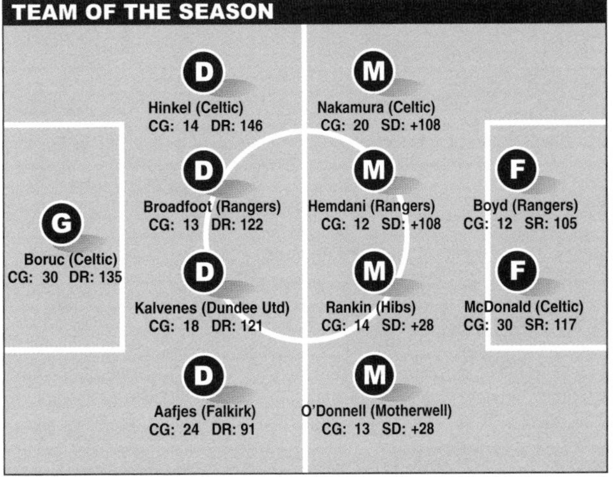

G
Boruc (Celtic)
CG: 30 DR: 135
D
Hinkel (Celtic)
CG: 14 DR: 146
D
Broadfoot (Rangers)
CG: 13 DR: 122
D
Kalvenes (Dundee Utd)
CG: 18 DR: 121
D
Aafjes (Falkirk)
CG: 24 DR: 91
M
Nakamura (Celtic)
CG: 20 SD: +108
M
Hemdani (Rangers)
CG: 12 SD: +108
M
Rankin (Hibs)
CG: 14 SD: +28
M
O'Donnell (Motherwell)
CG: 13 SD: +28
F
Boyd (Rangers)
CG: 12 SR: 105
F
McDonald (Celtic)
CG: 30 SR: 117

The race for the Scottish Premiership 2007 - 2008

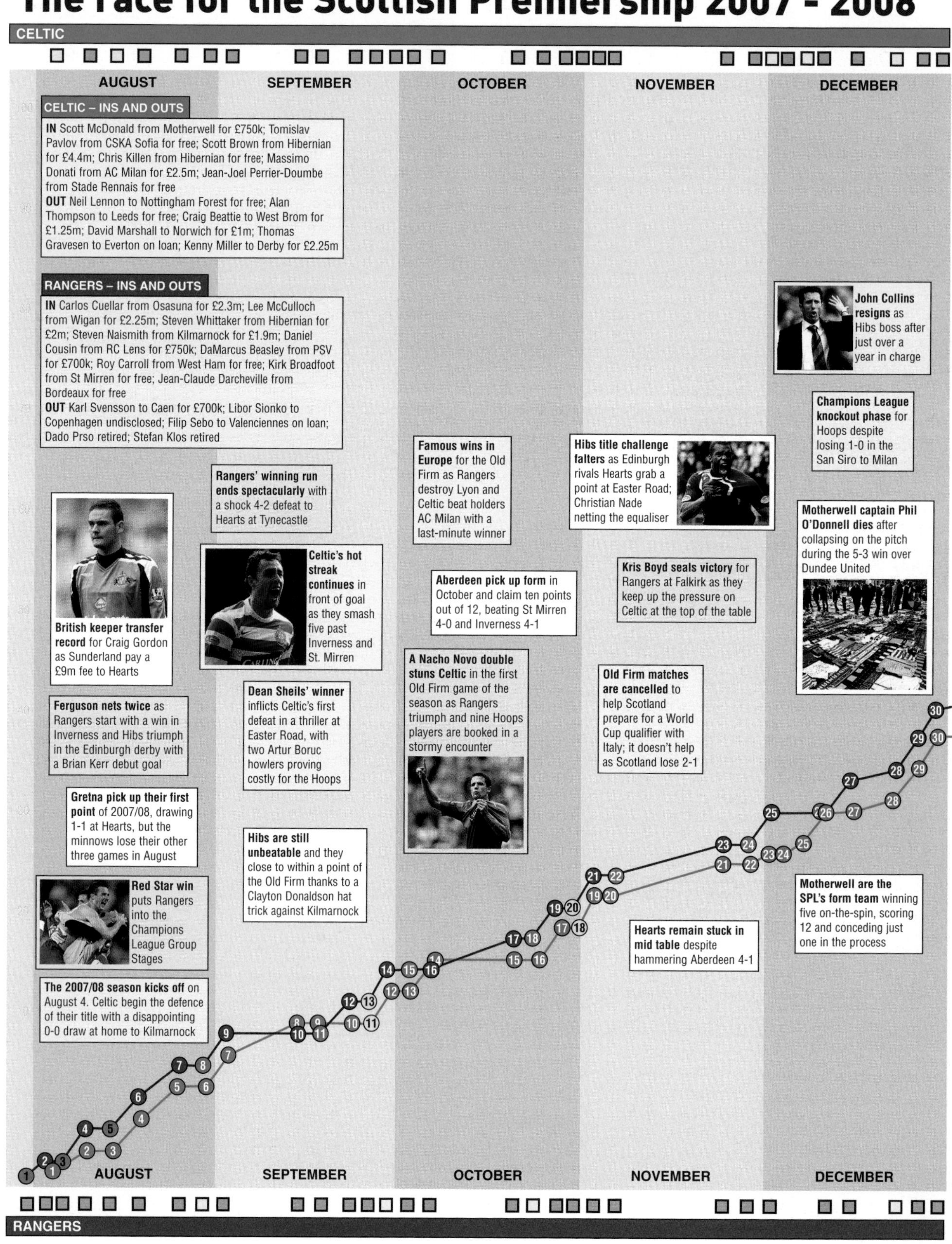
CELTIC
AUGUST
SEPTEMBER
OCTOBER
NOVEMBER
DECEMBER
CELTIC – INS AND OUTS
IN Scott McDonald from Motherwell for £750k; Tomislav Pavlov from CSKA Sofia for free; Scott Brown from Hibernian for £4.4m; Chris Killen from Hibernian for free; Massimo Donati from AC Milan for £2.5m; Jean-Joel Perrier-Doumbe from Stade Rennais for free
OUT Neil Lennon to Nottingham Forest for free; Alan Thompson to Leeds for free; Craig Beattie to West Brom for £1.25m; David Marshall to Norwich for £1m; Thomas Gravesen to Everton on loan; Kenny Miller to Derby for £2.25m
RANGERS – INS AND OUTS
IN Carlos Cuellar from Osasuna for £2.3m; Lee McCulloch from Wigan for £2.25m; Steven Whittaker from Hibernian for £2m; Steven Naismith from Kilmarnock for £1.9m; Daniel Cousin from RC Lens for £750k; DaMarcus Beasley from PSV for £700k; Roy Carroll from West Ham for free; Kirk Broadfoot from St Mirren for free; Jean-Claude Darcheville from Bordeaux for free
OUT Karl Svensson to Caen for £700k; Libor Sionko to Copenhagen undisclosed; Filip Sebo to Valenciennes on loan; Dado Prso retired; Stefan Klos retired
British keeper transfer record for Craig Gordon as Sunderland pay a £9m fee to Hearts
Ferguson nets twice as Rangers start with a win in Inverness and Hibs triumph in the Edinburgh derby with a Brian Kerr debut goal
Gretna pick up their first point of 2007/08, drawing 1-1 at Hearts, but the minnows lose their other three games in August
Red Star win puts Rangers into the Champions League Group Stages
The 2007/08 season kicks off on August 4. Celtic begin the defence of their title with a disappointing 0-0 draw at home to Kilmarnock
Rangers' winning run ends spectacularly with a shock 4-2 defeat to Hearts at Tynecastle
Celtic's hot streak continues in front of goal as they smash five past Inverness and St. Mirren
Dean Sheils' winner inflicts Celtic's first defeat in a thriller at Easter Road, with two Artur Boruc howlers proving costly for the Hoops
Hibs are still unbeatable and they close to within a point of the Old Firm thanks to a Clayton Donaldson hat trick against Kilmarnock
Famous wins in Europe for the Old Firm as Rangers destroy Lyon and Celtic beat holders AC Milan with a last-minute winner
Aberdeen pick up form in October and claim ten points out of 12, beating St Mirren 4-0 and Inverness 4-1
A Nacho Novo double stuns Celtic in the first Old Firm game of the season as Rangers triumph and nine Hoops players are booked in a stormy encounter
Hibs title challenge falters as Edinburgh rivals Hearts grab a point at Easter Road; Christian Nade netting the equaliser
Kris Boyd seals victory for Rangers at Falkirk as they keep up the pressure on Celtic at the top of the table
Old Firm matches are cancelled to help Scotland prepare for a World Cup qualifier with Italy; it doesn't help as Scotland lose 2-1
Hearts remain stuck in mid table despite hammering Aberdeen 4-1
John Collins resigns as Hibs boss after just over a year in charge
Champions League knockout phase for Hoops despite losing 1-0 in the San Siro to Milan
Motherwell captain Phil O'Donnell dies after collapsing on the pitch during the 5-3 win over Dundee United
Motherwell are the SPL's form team winning five on-the-spin, scoring 12 and conceding just one in the process
AUGUST
SEPTEMBER
OCTOBER
NOVEMBER
DECEMBER
RANGERS

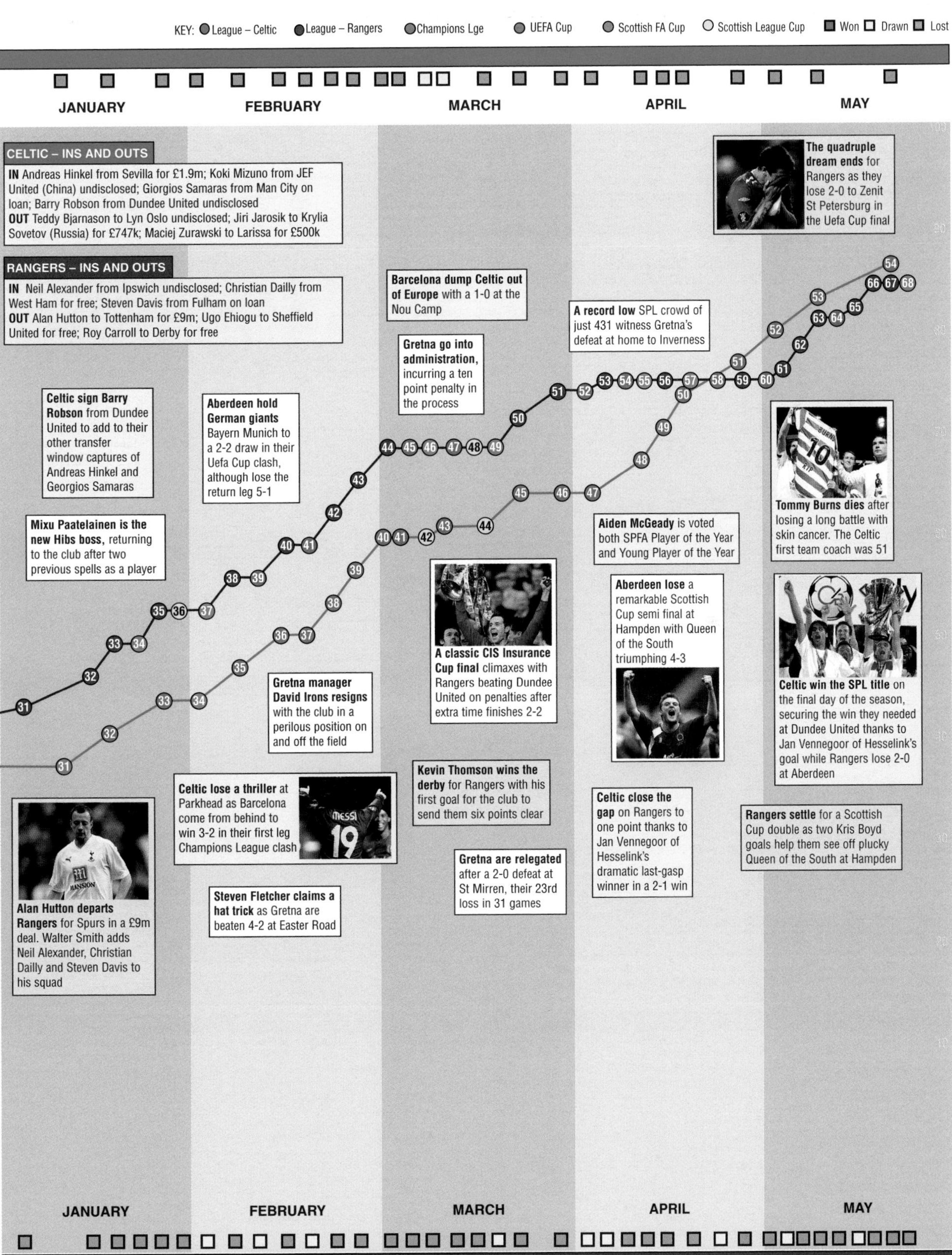
KEY: League – Celtic League – Rangers Champions Lge UEFA Cup Scottish FA Cup Scottish League Cup Won Drawn Lost
JANUARY
FEBRUARY
MARCH
APRIL
MAY
CELTIC – INS AND OUTS
IN Andreas Hinkel from Sevilla for £1.9m; Koki Mizuno from JEF United (China) undisclosed; Giorgios Samaras from Man City on loan; Barry Robson from Dundee United undisclosed
OUT Teddy Bjarnason to Lyn Oslo undisclosed; Jiri Jarosik to Krylia Sovetov (Russia) for £747k; Maciej Zurawski to Larissa for £500k
RANGERS – INS AND OUTS
IN Neil Alexander from Ipswich undisclosed; Christian Dailly from West Ham for free; Steven Davis from Fulham on loan
OUT Alan Hutton to Tottenham for £9m; Ugo Ehiogu to Sheffield United for free; Roy Carroll to Derby for free
Celtic sign Barry Robson from Dundee United to add to their other transfer window captures of Andreas Hinkel and Georgios Samaras
Mixu Paatelainen is the new Hibs boss, returning to the club after two previous spells as a player
Alan Hutton departs Rangers for Spurs in a £9m deal. Walter Smith adds Neil Alexander, Christian Dailly and Steven Davis to his squad
Aberdeen hold German giants Bayern Munich to a 2-2 draw in their Uefa Cup clash, although lose the return leg 5-1
Gretna manager David Irons resigns with the club in a perilous position on and off the field
Celtic lose a thriller at Parkhead as Barcelona come from behind to win 3-2 in their first leg Champions League clash
MESSI 19
Steven Fletcher claims a hat trick as Gretna are beaten 4-2 at Easter Road
Barcelona dump Celtic out of Europe with a 1-0 at the Nou Camp
Gretna go into administration, incurring a ten point penalty in the process
A classic CIS Insurance Cup final climaxes with Rangers beating Dundee United on penalties after extra time finishes 2-2
Kevin Thomson wins the derby for Rangers with his first goal for the club to send them six points clear
Gretna are relegated after a 2-0 defeat at St Mirren, their 23rd loss in 31 games
A record low SPL crowd of just 431 witness Gretna's defeat at home to Inverness
Aiden McGeady is voted both SPFA Player of the Year and Young Player of the Year
Aberdeen lose a remarkable Scottish Cup semi final at Hampden with Queen of the South triumphing 4-3
Celtic close the gap on Rangers to one point thanks to Jan Vennegoor of Hesselink's dramatic last-gasp winner in a 2-1 win
The quadruple dream ends for Rangers as they lose 2-0 to Zenit St Petersburg in the Uefa Cup final
Tommy Burns dies after losing a long battle with skin cancer. The Celtic first team coach was 51
Celtic win the SPL title on the final day of the season, securing the win they needed at Dundee United thanks to Jan Vennegoor of Hesselink's goal while Rangers lose 2-0 at Aberdeen
Rangers settle for a Scottish Cup double as two Kris Boyd goals help them see off plucky Queen of the South at Hampden
JANUARY
FEBRUARY
MARCH
APRIL
MAY

CELTIC

Final Position: **1st**

NICKNAME: THE BHOYS

KEY: ☐Won ☐Drawn ☐Lost

							Attendance
1	spl	Kilmarnock	H	D	0-0		60,000
2	spl	Falkirk	A	W	4-1	Milne 30 og, Miller 76, Nakamura 79 Vennegoor 81	6,329
3	ecql1	S Moscow	A	D	1-1	Hartley 22	50,000
4	spl	Aberdeen	A	W	3-1	Donati 61, Miller 85, 90	16,232
5	spl	Hearts	H	W	5-0	Berra 9 og, Donati 22, Brown 61 Vennegoor 63 pen, Nakamura 79	57,300
6	ecql2	S Moscow	H	W	4-3*	McDonald 27 (*on penalties)	65,000
7	spl	St Mirren	A	W	5-1	Brown 22, McDonald 25, Vennegoor 53 Miranda 56 og, McManus 74	7,840
8	spl	Inverness CT	H	W	5-0	Vennegoor 15, 59, Donati 41, Nakamura 56 McGuire 70 og	56,020
9	ecgpd	Shakhtar	A	L	0-2		28,000
10	spl	Hibernian	A	L	2-3	McGeady 26, Caldwell 66	16,125
11	sccc3	Dundee	A	W	2-1	McDonald 27, Vennegoor 60	8,203
12	spl	Dundee Utd	H	W	3-0	McDonald 7, 67, 72	57,006
13	ecgpd	AC Milan	H	W	2-1	McManus 62, McDonald 90	60,000
14	spl	Gretna	A	W	2-1	Killen 86, McDonald 90	6,011
15	spl	Rangers	A	L	0-3		50,428
16	ecgpd	Benfica	A	L	0-1		55,000
17	spl	Motherwell	H	W	3-0	McDonald 42, 59, 88 pen	57,633
18	sccqf	Hearts	H	L	0-2		21,492
19	spl	Kilmarnock	A	W	2-1	McDonald 34, 36	8,260
20	ecgpd	Benfica	H	W	1-0	McGeady 45	52,000
21	spl	Aberdeen	H	W	3-0	Vennegoor 14, McGeady 27 McDonald 49	58,000
22	ecgpd	Shakhtar	H	W	2-1	Jarosik 45, Donati 90	59,146
23	spl	Hearts	A	D	1-1	McDonald 73	16,454
24	ecgpd	AC Milan	A	L	0-1		38,409
25	spl	St Mirren	H	D	1-1	Riordan 85	55,747
26	spl	Falkirk	H	W	4-0	McDonald 9 pen, McGeady 41, 67, 82	54,291
27	spl	Inverness CT	A	L	2-3	Vennegoor 24, 26	7,004
28	spl	Hibernian	H	D	1-1	Jarosik 78	58,016
29	spl	Dundee Utd	A	W	2-0	Vennegoor 68, McManus 74	12,357
30	spl	Gretna	H	W	3-0	McDonald 35, Brown 49, McGeady 89	57,171
31	scr4	Stirling	H	W	3-0	Vennegoor 37, McDonald 70 Nakamura 75	27,923
32	spl	Kilmarnock	H	W	1-0	Corrigan 64 og	56,618
33	spl	Falkirk	A	W	1-0	McDonald 45	6,803
34	scr5	Kilmarnock	A	W	5-1	McDonald 22, 67, Caldwell 52, Vennegoor 58 Samaras 85	6,491
35	spl	Aberdeen	A	W	5-1	Nakamura 17, McGeady 34, McDonald 43 pen 48, Robson 74	14,651
36	spl	Hearts	H	W	3-0	Vennegoor 14, McDonald 51 Hinkel 76	56,738
37	eckl1	Barcelona	H	L	2-3	Vennegoor 16, Robson 38	58,345
38	spl	St Mirren	A	W	1-0	Nakamura 87	7,213
39	spl	Inverness CT	H	W	2-1	McDonald 45, Samaras 61	56,787
40	spl	Hibernian	A	W	2-0	Naylor 64, Samaras 75	15,735
41	eckl2	Barcelona	A	L	0-1		75,002
42	scpqf	Aberdeen	A	D	1-1	Vennegoor 90	10,909
43	spl	Dundee Utd	H	D	0-0		45,000
44	scqfr	Aberdeen	H	L	0-1		33,506
45	spl	Gretna	A	W	3-0	McDonald 42, Vennegoor 70, Samaras 88	3,561
46	spl	Rangers	A	L	0-1		50,325
47	spl	Motherwell	H	L	0-1		58,624
48	spl	Motherwell	A	W	4-1	McManus 17, Scott.McDonald 30 Vennegoor 43, 57	9,771
49	spl	Rangers	H	W	2-1	Nakamura 20, Vennegoor 90	58,964
50	spl	Aberdeen	H	W	1-0	Samaras 56	55,766
51	spl	Rangers	H	W	3-2	McDonald 4, 43, Robson 70 pen	58,662
52	spl	Motherwell	A	W	2-1	McDonald 62, Samaras 79	9,158
53	spl	Hibernian	H	W	2-0	McManus 37, McDonald 87	58,515
54	spl	Dundee Utd	A	W	1-0	Vennegoor 72	13,613

LEAGUE APPEARANCES, BOOKINGS AND CAPS

	AGE (on 01/07/08)	IN NAMED 18	APPEARANCES	COUNTING GAMES	MINUTES ON PITCH	YELLOW CARDS	RED CARDS	CAPS THIS SEASON	NATIONAL SIDE
Goalkeepers									
Artur Boruc	28	30	30	30	2700	4	0	10	Poland
Mark Brown	27	38	8	8	720	0	0	-	Scotland
Defenders									
Dianbobo Balde	32	9	4	4	360	0	0	-	France
Paul Caddis	20	11	2	0	62	0	0	-	Scotland
Gary Caldwell	26	36	35	35	3150	1	0	1	Scotland
Andreas Hinkel	26	16	16	14	1318	0	0	-	Germany
John Kennedy	24	8	7	5	553	4	0	-	Scotland
Stephen McManus	25	37	37	34	3222	4	0	7	Scotland
Lee Naylor	28	33	33	32	2894	4	0	-	England
Darren O'Dea	21	32	6	3	325	1	0	-	Rep of Ireland
Jean Perrier-Doumbe	29	2	2	2	180	0	0	-	Cameroon
Steven Pressley	34	8	5	5	410	0	0	-	Scotland
Mark Wilson	24	14	11	8	796	1	0	-	Scotland
Midfielders									
Scott Brown	23	35	34	30	2799	7	0	5	Scotland
Ryan Conroy	21	4	2	2	180	0	0	-	Scotland
Massimo Donati	28	34	25	20	1879	8	0	-	Italy
Paul Hartley	31	35	27	22	2034	4	0	4	Scotland
Jiri Jarosik	30	11	8	5	524	1	0	-	Czech Republic
Shunsuke Nakamura	30	27	26	20	2073	2	0	5	Japan
Barry Robson	29	16	15	8	855	2	0	2	Scotland
Evander Sno	21	34	12	1	342	0	0	-	Holland
Forwards									
Ben Hutchinson	20	4	2	0	8	0	0	-	England
Christopher Killen	26	27	20	3	517	0	0	-	New Zealand
Scott McDonald	24	36	36	31	2936	5	0	2	Australia
Aiden McGeady	22	37	36	35	3161	9	0	8	Rep of Ireland
Kenny Miller	28	3	2	1	105	0	0	5	Scotland
Derek Riordan	25	24	8	2	297	0	0	-	Scotland
Georgios Samaras	23	16	16	4	630	1	0	6	Greece
Jan Vennegoor	29	32	32	25	2449	5	0	5	Holland
Maciej Zurawski	31	12	5	0	105	0	0	8	Poland

TEAM OF THE SEASON

D
Andreas Hinkel
CG: 14 DR: 146
M
Shunsuke Nakamura
CG: 20 SD: 108
D
Lee Naylor
CG: 32 DR: 144
M
Scott Brown
CG: 30 SD: 93
F
Scott McDonald
CG: 31 SR: 117
G
Artur Boruc
CG: 30 DR: 135
D
Stephen McManus
CG: 34 DR: 140
M
Massimo Donati
CG: 20 SD: 77
F
Jan Vennegoor
CG: 25 SR: 163
D
Gary Caldwell
CG: 35 DR: 126
M
Paul Hartley
CG: 22 SD: 74

MONTHLY POINTS TALLY

AUGUST	10	83%
SEPTEMBER	9	75%
OCTOBER	6	67%
NOVEMBER	6	100%
DECEMBER	12	57%
JANUARY	6	100%
FEBRUARY	12	100%
MARCH	7	58%
APRIL	12	80%
MAY	9	100%

LEAGUE GOALS

	PLAYER	MINS	GOALS	S RATE
1	McDonald	2936	25	117
2	Vennegoor	2449	15	163
3	McGeady	3161	7	451
4	Nakamura	2073	6	345
5	Samaras	630	5	126
6	McManus	3222	4	805
7	Miller	105	3	35
8	Donati	1879	3	626
9	Brown	2799	3	933
10	Robson	855	2	427
11	Riordan	297	1	297
12	Killen	517	1	517
13	Jarosik	524	1	524
	Other		3	
	TOTAL		79	

TOP POINT EARNERS

	PLAYER	GAMES	AV PTS
1	Shunsuke Nakamura	20	2.60
2	Scott McDonald	31	2.55
3	Artur Boruc	30	2.47
4	Lee Naylor	32	2.44
5	Andreas Hinkel	14	2.43
6	Massimo Donati	20	2.40
7	Aiden McGeady	35	2.37
8	Stephen McManus	34	2.35
9	Gary Caldwell	35	2.34
10	Paul Hartley	22	2.23
	CLUB AVERAGE:		2.34

DISCIPLINARY RECORDS

	PLAYER	YELLOW	RED	AVE
1	John Kennedy	4	0	138
2	Massimo Donati	8	0	234
3	Aiden McGeady	9	0	351
4	Scott Brown	7	0	399
5	Barry Robson	2	0	427
6	Jan Vennegoor	5	0	489
7	Paul Hartley	4	0	508
8	Jiri Jarosik	1	0	524
9	Scott McDonald	5	0	587
10	Georgios Samaras	1	0	630
11	Artur Boruc	4	0	675
12	Lee Naylor	4	0	723
13	Mark Wilson	1	0	796
	Other	7	0	
	TOTAL	62	0	

KEY GOALKEEPER

Artur Boruc

Goals Conceded in the League	20	Counting Games League games when player was on pitch for at least 70 minutes	30
Defensive Rating Ave number of mins between League goals conceded while on the pitch	135	Clean Sheets In League games when player was on pitch for at least 70 minutes	15

KEY PLAYERS - DEFENDERS

Andreas Hinkel

Goals Conceded Number of League goals conceded while the player was on the pitch	9	Clean Sheets In League games when player was on pitch for at least 70 minutes	6
Defensive Rating Ave number of mins between League goals conceded while on the pitch	146	Club Defensive Rating Average number of mins between League goals conceded by the club this season	145

	PLAYER	CON LGE	CLEAN SHEETS	DEF RATE
1	Andreas Hinkel	9	6	146 mins
2	Lee Naylor	20	17	144 mins
3	Stephen McManus	23	18	140 mins
4	Gary Caldwell	25	17	126 mins

KEY PLAYERS - MIDFIELDERS

Shunsuke Nakamura

Goals in the League	6	Contribution to Attacking Power Average number of minutes between League team goals while on pitch	40
Defensive Rating Average number of mins between League goals conceded while on the pitch	148	Scoring Difference Defensive Rating minus Contribution to Attacking Power	108

	PLAYER	LGE GOALS	DEF RATE	POWER	SCORE DIFF
1	Shunsuke Nakamura	6	148	40	108 mins
2	Scott Brown	3	133	40	93 mins
3	Massimo Donati	3	117	40	77 mins
4	Paul Hartley	0	113	39	74 mins

KEY PLAYERS - GOALSCORERS

Scott McDonald

Goals in the League	25	Player Strike Rate Average number of minutes between League goals scored by player	117
Contribution to Attacking Power Average number of minutes between League team goals while on pitch	39	Club Strike Rate Average number of minutes between League goals scored by club	45

	PLAYER	LGE GOALS	POWER	STRIKE RATE
1	Scott McDonald	25	39	117 mins
2	Jan Vennegoor of Hesselink	15	38	163 mins
3	Shunsuke Nakamura	6	40	345 mins
4	Aiden McGeady	7	41	451 mins

CARLING
CARLING
Scott McDonald and Georgios Samaras

SQUAD APPEARANCES

Match	1	2	3	4	5	6	7	8	9	10	11	12	13	14	15	16	17	18	19	20	21	22	23	24	25	26	27	28	29	30	31	32	33	34	35	36	37	38	39	40	41	42	43	44	45	46	47	48	49	50	51	52	53	54
Venue	H	A	A	A	H	H	A	H	A	A	A	H	H	A	A	A	H	H	A	H	H	H	A	A	H	H	A	H	A	H	H	H	A	A	A	H	H	A	H	A	A	A	H	H	A	A	H	A	H	H	H	A	H	A
Competition	L	L	C	L	L	C	L	L	C	L	O	L	C	L	L	C	L	O	L	C	L	C	L	C	L	L	L	L	L	L	O	L	L	O	L	L	C	L	L	L	C	O	L	O	L	L	L	L	L	L	L	L	L	L
Result	D	W	D	W	W	W	W	W	L	L	W	W	W	W	L	L	W	L	W	W	W	W	D	L	D	W	L	D	W	W	W	W	W	W	W	W	L	W	W	W	L	D	D	L	W	L	L	W	W	W	W	W	W	W

Goalkeepers
Artur Boruc
Mark Brown

Defenders
Dianbobo Balde
Paul Caddis
Gary Caldwell
Andreas Hinkel
John Kennedy
Stephen McManus
Lee Naylor
Darren O'Dea
Jean Perrier-Doumbe
Steven Pressley
Mark Wilson

Midfielders
Scott Brown
Ryan Conroy
Massimo Donati
Paul Hartley
Jiri Jarosik
Shunsuke Nakamura
Barry Robson
Evander Sno

Forwards
Ben Hutchinson
Christopher Killen
Scott McDonald
Aiden McGeady
Kenny Miller
Derek Riordan
Georgios Samaras
Jan Vennegoor
Maciej Zurawski

KEY: On all match; On bench; Subbed or sent off (Counting game); Subbed or sent off (playing less than 70 minutes); Subbed on from bench (Counting Game); Subbed on (playing less than 70 minutes); Subbed on and then subbed or sent off (Counting Game); Subbed on and then subbed or sent off (playing less than 70 minutes); Not in 16

RANGERS

Final Position: **2nd**

NICKNAME: THE GERS

KEY: Won Drawn Lost

	Comp	Opponent	Venue	Result	Score	Scorers	Attendance
1	ecql1	Zeta	H	W	2-0	Weir 55, McCulloch 73	33,000
2	spl	Inverness CT	A	W	3-0	Ferguson 16, 90, Novo 64	7,711
3	ecql2	Zeta	A	W	1-0	Beasley 81	11,000
4	spl	St Mirren	H	W	2-0	Ferguson 52, Cousin 80	47,772
5	ecql1	Crvena Zvezda	H	W	1-0	Novo 90	45,000
6	spl	Falkirk	H	W	7-2	Cousin 2, 54, Whittaker 34, Boyd 75 Darcheville 88, 90, Broadfoot 90	47,419
7	spl	Kilmarnock	A	W	2-1	Beasley 52, Darcheville 76	11,544
8	ecql2	Crvena Zvezda	A	D	0-0		47,012
9	spl	Gretna	H	W	4-0	Boyd 38, Webster 63, Cuellar 81 Collin 83 og	49,689
10	spl	Hearts	A	L	2-4	Cousin 49 pen, Beasley 74	15,948
11	ecgpe	Stuttgart	H	W	2-1	Adam 62, Darcheville 74 pen	49,795
12	spl	Aberdeen	H	W	3-0	McCulloch 46, Naismith 65, Boyd 88	49,046
13	sccc3	East Fife	A	W	4-0	Novo 14, Boyd 35, 66 pen, Cuellar 54	7,413
14	spl	Motherwell	A	D	1-1	Boyd 67 pen	10,009
15	ecgpe	Lyon	A	W	3-0	McCulloch 23, Cousin 47, Beasley 53	38,000
16	spl	Hibernian	H	L	0-1		50,440
17	spl	Celtic	H	W	3-0	Novo 28, 79 pen, Ferguson 56	50,428
18	ecgpe	Barcelona	H	D	0-0		49,957
19	spl	Dundee Utd	A	L	1-2	Cousin 51 pen	12,129
20	sccqf	Motherwell	A	W	2-1	Novo 23, Boyd 54	10,009
21	spl	Inverness CT	H	W	2-0	Boyd 1, Cuellar 63	48,898
22	ecgpe	Barcelona	A	L	0-2		80,000
23	spl	Falkirk	A	W	3-1	Cuellar 20, Darcheville 55, Boyd 90	6,627
24	ecgpe	Stuttgart	A	L	2-3	Adam 27, Ferguson 69	51,300
25	spl	Kilmarnock	H	W	2-0	Darcheville 4, Whittaker 55	48,055
26	ecgpe	Lyon	H	L	0-3		50,062
27	spl	Hearts	H	W	2-1	McCulloch 18, 87	48,392
28	spl	Aberdeen	A	D	1-1	Adam 30	17,798
29	spl	Motherwell	H	W	3-1	Cousin 42, Porter 70 og, Boyd 90	49,823
30	spl	Hibernian	A	W	2-1	Naismith 12, Cousin 59	16,217
31	spl	Dundee Utd	H	W	2-0	Naismith 9, Ferguson 40	48,559
32	spl	Gretna	A	W	2-1	Ferguson 45, Cousin 74	6,137
33	spl	Inverness CT	A	W	1-0	Darcheville 89	7,753
34	scr4	East Stirling	H	W	6-0	McCulloch 25, 50, Hutton 28 Boyd 30, 45, 62 pen	34,024
35	spl	St Mirren	H	W	4-0	Burke 27, Boyd 33, Whittaker 37, 81	49,198
36	slc5	Hearts	H	W	2-0	Ferguson 50, Darcheville 69	31,980
37	scr5	Hibernian	A	D	0-0		11,513
38	spl	Falkirk	H	W	2-0	Boyd 23, Naismith 89	48,590
39	uc3rl1	Panathinaikos	H	D	0-0		45,203
40	spl	Kilmarnock	A	W	2-0	Cuellar 25, Boyd 63 pen	10,546
41	uc3rl2	Panathinaikos	A	D	1-1	Novo 81	14,452
42	spl	Gretna	H	W	4-2	Cousin 13, Naismith 22, Burke 60 Boyd 88	48,375
43	spl	Hearts	A	W	4-0	Darcheville 25, 44, Novo 53, 70	16,173
44	spl	Aberdeen	H	W	3-1	Dailly 38, Adam 50, Boyd 83	50,066
45	uc4rl1	W Bremen	H	W	2-0	Cousin 45, Davis 48	45,959
46	scr5r	Hibernian	H	W	1-0	Burke 39	33,837
47	uc4rl2	W Bremen	A	L	0-1		33,000
48	sccсf	Dundee Utd	A	W	3-2*	Boyd 85, 113 (*on penalties)	50,019
49	scpqf	Partick	H	D	1-1	Boyd 69	36,724
50	spl	Hibernian	H	W	2-1	Darcheville 40, Novo 79	50,117
51	spl	Celtic	H	W	1-0	Thomson 45	50,325
52	ucqfl1	Sp Lisbon	H	D	0-0		48,923
53	spl	Dundee Utd	A	D	3-3	Weir 44, Novo 58, Boyd 67	11,214
54	ucqfl2	Sp Lisbon	A	W	2-0	Darcheville 59, Whittaker 90	31,155
55	scqfr	Partick	A	W	2-0	Novo 27, Burke 40	9,909
56	spl	Celtic	A	L	1-2	Novo 55	58,964
57	scsf	St Johnstone	A	W	4-3*	Novo 103 pen (*on penalties)	26,180
58	ucsfl1	Fiorentina	H	D	0-0		49,199
59	spl	Celtic	A	L	2-3	Weir 17, Cousin 29	58,662
60	ucsfl2	Fiorentina	A	W	4-2*	(*on penalties)	39,130
61	spl	Hibernian	A	D	0-0		16,872
62	spl	Motherwell	H	W	1-0	Ferguson 74	48,238
63	spl	Dundee Utd	H	W	3-1	Novo 7, 18, Darcheville 90	30,293
64	ucfin	Z St Petersburg	A	L	0-2		47,726
65	spl	Motherwell	A	D	1-1	Dailly 29	10,445
66	spl	St Mirren	A	W	3-0	Boyd 4, Darcheville 24, 69	7,439
67	spl	Aberdeen	A	L	0-2		17,509
68	scfin	Queen of South	A	W	3-2	Boyd 33, 72, Beasley 43	48,821

LEAGUE APPEARANCES, BOOKINGS AND CAPS

	AGE (on 01/07/08)	IN NAMED 18	APPEARANCES	COUNTING GAMES	MINUTES ON PITCH	YELLOW CARDS	RED CARDS	CAPS THIS SEASON	NATIONAL SIDE
Goalkeepers									
Neil Alexander	30	16	8	7	644	0	0	-	Scotland
Roy Carroll	30	19	0	0	0	0	0	-	N Ireland
Allan McGregor	26	31	31	31	2776	2	0	-	Scotland
Defenders									
Kirk Broadfoot	23	25	15	13	1222	2	0	-	Scotland
Carlos Cuellar	26	36	36	36	3219	5	1	-	Spain
Christian Dailly	34	16	12	12	1080	2	0	2	Scotland
Alan Hutton	23	20	20	20	1800	7	0	5	Scotland
Sasa Papac	28	25	22	22	1966	0	0	-	Bosnia
Andy Webster	26	1	1	1	90	0	0	-	Scotland
David Weir	38	37	37	36	3290	2	0	5	Scotland
Steven Whittaker	24	33	30	27	2551	4	1	-	Scotland
Midfielders									
Charlie Adam	22	18	16	11	1106	1	0	-	Scotland
DaMarcus Beasley	26	13	11	8	776	2	0	4	United States
Thomas Buffel	27	1	1	0	27	0	0	-	Belgium
Chris Burke	24	11	11	9	833	2	0	-	Scotland
Steven Davis	23	15	12	11	998	0	0	8	N Ireland
Paul Emslie	20	10	0	0	0	0	0	-	Scotland
Amdy Faye	31	9	4	0	134	0	0	-	Senegal
Barry Ferguson	30	38	38	37	3375	0	0	4	Scotland
Dean Furman	20	22	1	0	39	0	0	-	South Africa
Ibrahim Hemdani	30	15	12	12	1068	1	0	-	France
Steven Lennon	20	18	0	0	0	0	0	-	Scotland
Lee McCulloch	30	23	22	17	1666	4	1	4	Scotland
Kevin Thomson	25	26	26	23	2160	8	0	-	Scotland
Forwards									
Kris Boyd	24	37	28	12	1479	2	0	4	Scotland
Daniel Cousin	31	29	26	16	1588	1	0	-	Gabon
Jean C Darcheville	32	31	30	6	1267	0	0	-	France
John Fleck	16	12	1	0	15	0	0	-	Scotland
Steven Naismith	21	27	21	9	1083	2	0	-	Scotland
Nacho Novo	29	29	28	9	1280	1	1	-	Spain

TEAM OF THE SEASON

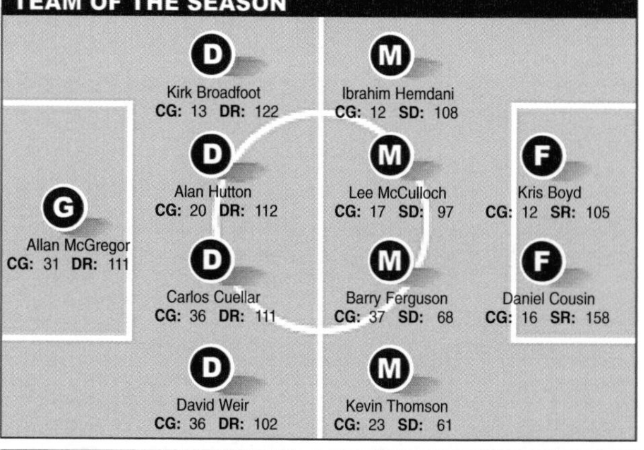

G
Allan McGregor
CG: 31 DR: 111
D
Kirk Broadfoot
CG: 13 DR: 122
D
Alan Hutton
CG: 20 DR: 112
D
Carlos Cuellar
CG: 36 DR: 111
D
David Weir
CG: 36 DR: 102
M
Ibrahim Hemdani
CG: 12 SD: 108
M
Lee McCulloch
CG: 17 SD: 97
M
Barry Ferguson
CG: 37 SD: 68
M
Kevin Thomson
CG: 23 SD: 61
F
Kris Boyd
CG: 12 SR: 105
F
Daniel Cousin
CG: 16 SR: 158

MONTHLY POINTS TALLY

Month	Points	%
AUGUST	12	100%
SEPTEMBER	7	58%
OCTOBER	3	33%
NOVEMBER	6	100%
DECEMBER	13	87%
JANUARY	12	100%
FEBRUARY	12	100%
MARCH	9	100%
APRIL	1	11%
MAY	11	61%

LEAGUE GOALS

	PLAYER	MINS	GOALS	S RATE
1	Boyd	1479	**14**	105
2	Darcheville	1267	**12**	105
3	Novo	1280	**10**	128
4	Cousin	1588	**10**	158
5	Ferguson	3375	**7**	482
6	Naismith	1083	**5**	216
7	Whittaker	2551	**4**	637
8	Cuellar	3219	**4**	804
9	McCulloch	1666	**3**	555
10	Beasley	776	**2**	388
11	Burke	833	**2**	416
12	Dailly	1080	**2**	540
13	Adam	1106	**2**	553
	Other		5	
	TOTAL		**82**	

TOP POINT EARNERS

	PLAYER	GAMES	AV PTS
1	Ibrahim Hemdani	12	**2.50**
2	Kirk Broadfoot	13	**2.46**
3	Kris Boyd	12	**2.42**
4	Allan McGregor	31	**2.42**
5	Lee McCulloch	17	**2.41**
6	Alan Hutton	20	**2.35**
7	Steven Whittaker	27	**2.33**
8	Barry Ferguson	37	**2.32**
9	Carlos Cuellar	36	**2.31**
10	David Weir	36	**2.31**
	CLUB AVERAGE:		**2.26**

DISCIPLINARY RECORDS

	PLAYER	YELLOW	RED	AVE
1	Alan Hutton	7	0	**257**
2	Kevin Thomson	8	0	**270**
3	Lee McCulloch	4	1	**333**
4	DaMarcus Beasley	2	0	**388**
5	Chris Burke	2	0	**416**
6	Steven Whittaker	4	1	**510**
7	Carlos Cuellar	5	1	**536**
8	Christian Dailly	2	0	**540**
9	Kirk Broadfoot	2	0	**611**
10	Nacho Novo	1	1	**640**
11	Kris Boyd	2	0	**739**
12	Ibrahim Hemdani	1	0	**1068**
13	Steven Naismith	1	0	**1083**
	Other	6	0	
	TOTAL	**47**	**4**	

KEY GOALKEEPER

Allan McGregor

Goals Conceded in the League	25	Counting Games League games when player was on pitch for at least 70 minutes	31
Defensive Rating Ave number of mins between League goals conceded while on the pitch	111	Clean Sheets In League games when player was on pitch for at least 70 minutes	14

KEY PLAYERS - DEFENDERS

Kirk Broadfoot

Goals Conceded Number of League goals conceded while the player was on the pitch	10	Clean Sheets In League games when player was on pitch for at least 70 minutes	7
Defensive Rating Ave number of mins between League goals conceded while on the pitch	122	Club Defensive Rating Average number of mins between League goals conceded by the club this season	111

	PLAYER	CON LGE	CLEAN SHEETS	DEF RATE
1	Kirk Broadfoot	10	7	122 mins
2	Alan Hutton	16	9	112 mins
3	Carlos Cuellar	29	16	111 mins
4	David Weir	32	16	102 mins

KEY PLAYERS - MIDFIELDERS

Ibrahim Hemdani

Goals in the League	0	Contribution to Attacking Power Average number of minutes between League team goals while on pitch	44
Defensive Rating Average number of mins between League goals conceded while on the pitch	152	Scoring Difference Defensive Rating minus Contribution to Attacking Power	108

	PLAYER	LGE GOALS	DEF RATE	POWER	SCORE DIFF
1	Ibrahim Hemdani	0	152	44	108 mins
2	Lee McCulloch	3	138	41	97 mins
3	Barry Ferguson	7	108	40	68 mins
4	Kevin Thomson	1	102	41	61 mins

KEY PLAYERS - GOALSCORERS

Kris Boyd

Goals in the League	14	Player Strike Rate Average number of minutes between League goals scored by player	105
Contribution to Attacking Power Average number of minutes between League team goals while on pitch	41	Club Strike Rate Average number of minutes between League goals scored by club	43

	PLAYER	LGE GOALS	POWER	STRIKE RATE
1	Kris Boyd	14	41	105 mins
2	Daniel Cousin	10	46	158 mins
3	Barry Ferguson	7	40	482 mins
4	Lee McCulloch	3	41	555 mins

Kris Boyd

SQUAD APPEARANCES

Match	1	2	3	4	5	6	7	8	9	10	11	12	13	14	15	16	17	18	19	20	21	22	23	24	25	26	27	28	29	30	31	32	33	34
Venue	H	A	A	H	H	H	A	A	H	A	H	H	A	A	A	H	H	H	A	A	H	A	A	A	H	H	H	A	H	A	H	A	A	H
Competition	C	L	C	L	C	L	L	C	L	L	C	L	O	L	C	L	L	C	L	O	L	C	L	C	L	C	L	L	L	L	L	L	L	O
Result	W	W	W	W	W	W	W	D	W	L	W	W	W	D	W	L	W	D	L	W	W	L	W	L	W	L	W	D	W	W	W	W	W	W

Match	35	36	37	38	39	40	41	42	43	44	45	46	47	48	49	50	51	52	53	54	55	56	57	58	59	60	61	62	63	64	65	66	67	68
Venue	H	H	A	H	H	A	A	H	A	H	H	H	A	A	H	H	H	H	A	A	A	A	A	H	A	A	A	H	H	A	A	A	A	A
Competition	L	O	O	L	E	L	E	L	L	L	E	O	E	O	O	L	L	E	L	E	O	L	O	E	L	E	L	L	L	E	L	L	L	O
Result	W	W	D	W	D	W	D	W	W	W	W	W	L	W	D	W	W	D	D	W	W	L	W	D	L	W	D	W	W	L	D	W	L	W

Goalkeepers
- Neil Alexander
- Roy Carroll
- Allan McGregor

Defenders
- Kirk Broadfoot
- Carlos Cuellar
- Christian Dailly
- Alan Hutton
- Sasa Papac
- Andy Webster
- David Weir
- Steven Whittaker

Midfielders
- Charlie Adam
- DaMarcus Beasley
- Thomas Buffel
- Chris Burke
- Steven Davis
- Paul Emslie
- Amdy Faye
- Barry Ferguson
- Dean Furman
- Ibrahim Hemdani
- Steven Lennon
- Lee McCulloch
- Kevin Thomson

Forwards
- Kris Boyd
- Daniel Cousin
- Jean C Darcheville
- John Fleck
- Steven Naismith
- Nacho Novo

KEY: On all match · On bench · Subbed or sent off (Counting game) · Subbed or sent off (playing less than 70 minutes) · Subbed on from bench (Counting Game) · Subbed on (playing less than 70 minutes) · Subbed on and then subbed or sent off (Counting Game) · Subbed on and then subbed or sent off (playing less than 70 minutes) · Not in 16

MOTHERWELL

Final Position: **3rd**

NICKNAME: THE WELL

KEY: ☐Won ☐Drawn ☐Lost

							Attendance
1	spl	**St Mirren**	A	W	1-0	McGarry 3	5,257
2	spl	**Inverness CT**	H	W	2-1	O'Donnell 85, R.McCormack 90 pen	4,259
3	spl	**Kilmarnock**	H	L	1-2	Clarkson 23	4,985
4	spl	**Gretna**	A	W	2-1	Lasley 8, Porter 62	3,758
5	sccc2	**Raith**	H	W	3-1	McLean 45, R.McCormack 74, Porter 90	3,571
6	spl	**Hearts**	H	L	0-2		5,081
7	spl	**Aberdeen**	A	W	2-1	P.Quinn 34, Porter 37	10,154
8	spl	**Falkirk**	A	L	0-1		5,245
9	sccc3	**Hibernian**	A	W	4-2	Clarkson 17, Lasley 20, R.McCormack 24 Porter 83	7,000
10	spl	**Rangers**	H	D	1-1	Porter 24	10,009
11	spl	**Dundee Utd**	A	L	0-1		6,286
12	spl	**Hibernian**	H	W	2-1	R.McCormack 35, 37	7,071
13	spl	**Celtic**	A	L	0-3		57,633
14	sccqf	**Rangers**	H	L	1-2	P.Quinn 90	10,009
15	spl	**St Mirren**	H	D	1-1	Porter 29	5,123
16	spl	**Inverness CT**	A	W	3-0	Clarkson 15, 53, Darren L.Smith 87	3,608
17	spl	**Kilmarnock**	A	W	1-0	O'Donnell 46	5,016
18	spl	**Gretna**	H	W	3-0	Clarkson 44, 74, Porter 61	6,431
19	spl	**Hearts**	A	W	2-1	Porter 53, Zaliukas 67 og	16,633
20	spl	**Aberdeen**	H	W	3-0	R.McCormack 8 pen, 45, McGarry 12	5,326
21	spl	**Falkirk**	H	L	0-3		5,241
22	spl	**Rangers**	A	L	1-3	P.Quinn 65	49,823
23	spl	**Dundee Utd**	H	W	5-3	Hughes 11, Porter 14, R.McCormack 17 Clarkson 55, 56	5,227
24	scr4	**Hearts**	A	D	2-2	Porter 64, 78	13,651
25	spl	**St Mirren**	A	L	1-3	Clarkson 11	4,291
26	scr4r	**Hearts**	H	W	1-0	R.McCormack 23 pen	8,300
27	spl	**Kilmarnock**	H	W	1-0	Clarkson 90	6,618
28	scr5	**Dundee**	H	L	1-2	Darren L.Smith 61	5,733
29	spl	**Gretna**	A	W	3-1	Porter 25, R.McCormack 47, 90	2,877
30	spl	**Inverness CT**	H	W	3-1	Clarkson 7, 42, Porter 10	4,526
31	spl	**Hearts**	H	L	0-1		5,925
32	spl	**Aberdeen**	A	D	1-1	Darren L.Smith 83	8,240
33	spl	**Falkirk**	A	D	0-0		5,108
34	spl	**Hibernian**	A	L	0-1		11,692
35	spl	**Dundee Utd**	A	L	0-2		6,779
36	spl	**Hibernian**	H	W	1-0	Clarkson 3	6,580
37	spl	**Celtic**	A	W	1-0	Lappin 33	58,624
38	spl	**Celtic**	H	L	1-4	McManus 24 og	9,771
39	spl	**Dundee Utd**	H	D	2-2	Porter 17, 50	5,027
40	spl	**Celtic**	H	L	1-2	Porter 60	9,158
41	spl	**Rangers**	A	L	0-1		48,238
42	spl	**Aberdeen**	H	W	2-1	Darren L.Smith 61, Porter 81	8,574
43	spl	**Rangers**	H	D	1-1	Porter 50	10,445
44	spl	**Hibernian**	A	W	2-0	Lappin 4, J.Murphy 50 pen	7,650

LEAGUE APPEARANCES, BOOKINGS AND CAPS

	AGE (on 01/07/08)	IN NAMED 18	APPEARANCES	COUNTING GAMES	MINUTES ON PITCH	YELLOW CARDS	RED CARDS	CAPS THIS SEASON	NATIONAL SIDE
Goalkeepers									
Luke Daniels	20	17	2	2	180	0	0	-	England
Graeme Smith	25	37	36	36	3240	2	0	-	Scotland
Defenders									
Stephen Craigan	31	38	38	38	3403	6	0	6	N Ireland
Steven Hammell	26	16	15	13	1228	2	0	-	Scotland
William Kinniburgh	23	8	1	0	10	0	0	-	Scotland
Robert Malcolm	27	10	8	7	672	2	1	-	Scotland
Brian McLean	23	31	9	6	564	0	0	-	N Ireland
Danny Murphy	25	7	4	0	13	0	0	-	England
Paul Quinn	22	31	31	30	2762	7	0	-	Scotland
Mark Reynolds	21	38	38	38	3420	1	0	-	Scotland
Midfielders									
Marc Fitzpatrick	22	38	30	18	1920	3	0	-	Scotland
Stephen Hughes	25	31	31	26	2452	4	0	-	Scotland
Simon Lappin	25	17	14	5	780	3	0	-	Scotland
Keith Lasley	28	38	32	22	2192	5	0	-	Scotland
Stephen Maguire	21	4	1	0	18	0	0	-	Scotland
Robert McHugh	16	1	1	0	15	0	0	-	Scotland
Simon Mensing	26	11	2	0	59	1	0	-	England
Jamie Murphy	18	27	14	0	185	0	0	-	Scotland
Philip O'Donnell	36	18	18	13	1297	3	0	-	Scotland
Jim Paterson	28	20	20	19	1741	6	0	-	Scotland
Forwards									
David Clarkson	22	36	35	31	2881	6	0	-	Scotland
Lewis Grabban	20	10	5	0	61	0	0	-	England
Martin Grehan	23	1	1	0	6	0	0	-	Scotland
Ross McCormack	21	37	36	29	2648	5	0	1	Scotland
Steven McGarry	28	34	30	17	2132	0	0	-	Scotland
Chris Porter	24	37	37	33	3058	6	0	-	England
Darren Lee Smith	20	35	23	2	643	0	0	-	Scotland

TEAM OF THE SEASON

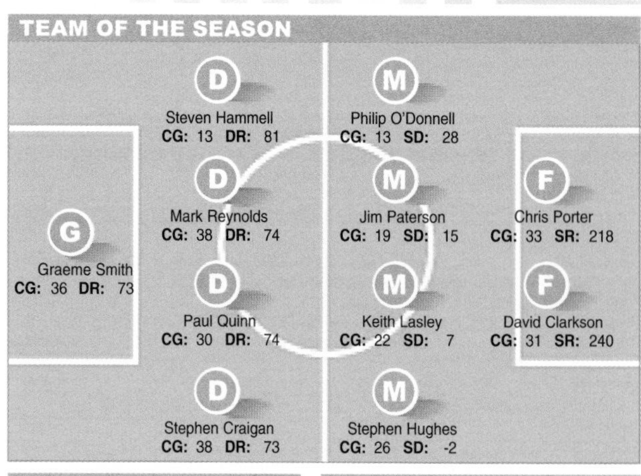

D
Steven Hammell
CG: 13 DR: 81
M
Philip O'Donnell
CG: 13 SD: 28
D
Mark Reynolds
CG: 38 DR: 74
M
Jim Paterson
CG: 19 SD: 15
F
Chris Porter
CG: 33 SR: 218
G
Graeme Smith
CG: 36 DR: 73
D
Paul Quinn
CG: 30 DR: 74
M
Keith Lasley
CG: 22 SD: 7
F
David Clarkson
CG: 31 SR: 240
D
Stephen Craigan
CG: 38 DR: 73
M
Stephen Hughes
CG: 26 SD: -2

MONTHLY POINTS TALLY

AUGUST	9	75%
SEPTEMBER	4	33%
OCTOBER	3	33%
NOVEMBER	7	78%
DECEMBER	12	67%
JANUARY	0	0%
FEBRUARY	10	67%
MARCH	4	33%
APRIL	4	44%
MAY	7	47%

LEAGUE GOALS

	PLAYER	MINS	GOALS	S RATE
1	Porter	3058	14	218
2	Clarkson	2881	12	240
3	McCormack	2648	8	331
4	Smith	643	3	214
5	Lappin	780	2	390
6	O'Donnell	1297	2	648
7	McGarry	2132	2	1066
8	Quinn	2762	2	1381
9	Murphy	185	1	185
10	Lasley	2192	1	2192
11	Hughes	2452	1	2452
	Other			0
	TOTAL		48	

TOP POINT EARNERS

	PLAYER	GAMES	AV PTS
1	Philip O'Donnell	13	1.92
2	Jim Paterson	19	1.84
3	Paul Quinn	30	1.77
4	Steven McGarry	17	1.76
5	David Clarkson	31	1.65
6	Keith Lasley	22	1.59
7	Stephen Craigan	38	1.58
8	Mark Reynolds	38	1.58
9	Graeme Smith	36	1.58
10	Chris Porter	33	1.55
	CLUB AVERAGE:		1.58

DISCIPLINARY RECORDS

	PLAYER	YELLOW	RED	AVE
1	Robert Malcolm	2	1	224
2	Simon Lappin	3	0	260
3	Jim Paterson	6	0	290
4	Paul Quinn	7	0	394
5	Philip O'Donnell	3	0	432
6	Keith Lasley	5	0	438
7	David Clarkson	6	0	480
8	Chris Porter	6	0	509
9	Ross McCormack	5	0	529
10	Stephen Craigan	6	0	567
11	Stephen Hughes	4	0	613
12	Steven Hammell	2	0	614
13	Marc Fitzpatrick	3	0	640
	Other	3	0	
	TOTAL	61	1	

KEY GOALKEEPER

Graeme Smith

Goals Conceded in the League	44	**Counting Games** League games when player was on pitch for at least 70 minutes	36
Defensive Rating Ave number of mins between League goals conceded while on the pitch	73	**Clean Sheets** In League games when player was on pitch for at least 70 minutes	9

KEY PLAYERS - DEFENDERS

Steven Hammell

Goals Conceded Number of League goals conceded while the player was on the pitch	15	**Clean Sheets** In League games when player was on pitch for at least 70 minutes	3
Defensive Rating Ave number of mins between League goals conceded while on the pitch	81	**Club Defensive Rating** Average number of mins between League goals conceded by the club this season	84

	PLAYER	CON LGE	CLEAN SHEETS	DEF RATE
1	Steven Hammell	15	3	81 mins
2	Mark Reynolds	46	10	74 mins
3	Paul Quinn	37	9	74 mins
4	Stephen Craigan	46	10	73 mins

KEY PLAYERS - MIDFIELDERS

Philip O'Donnell

Goals in the League	2	**Contribution to Attacking Power** Average number of minutes between League team goals while on pitch	48
Defensive Rating Average number of mins between League goals conceded while on the pitch	76	**Scoring Difference** Defensive Rating minus Contribution to Attacking Power	28

	PLAYER	LGE GOALS	DEF RATE	POWER	SCORE DIFF
1	Philip O'Donnell	2	76	48	28 mins
2	Jim Paterson	0	75	60	15 mins
3	Keith Lasley	1	91	84	7 mins
4	Stephen Hughes	1	72	74	-2 mins

KEY PLAYERS - GOALSCORERS

Chris Porter

Goals in the League	14	**Player Strike Rate** Average number of minutes between League goals scored by player	218
Contribution to Attacking Power Average number of minutes between League team goals while on pitch	69	**Club Strike Rate** Average number of minutes between League goals scored by club	77

	PLAYER	LGE GOALS	POWER	STRIKE RATE
1	Chris Porter	14	69	218 mins
2	David Clarkson	12	64	240 mins
3	Ross McCormack	8	64	331 mins
4	Philip O'Donnell	2	48	648 mins

ngian

Philip O'Donnell - R.I.P (1972 - 2007)

SQUAD APPEARANCES

Match	1	2	3	4	5	6	7	8	9	10	11	12	13	14	15	16	17	18	19	20	21	22	23	24	25	26	27	28	29	30	31	32	33	34	35	36	37	38	39	40	41	42	43	44
Venue	A	H	H	A	H	H	A	A	A	H	A	H	A	H	H	A	A	H	A	H	H	A	H	A	A	H	H	H	A	H	H	A	A	A	A	H	A	H	H	H	A	H	H	A
Competition	L	L	L	L	O	L	L	L	O	L	L	L	L	O	L	L	L	L	L	L	L	L	L	O	L	O	L	O	L	L	L	L	L	L	L	L	L	L	L	L	L	L	L	L
Result	W	W	L	W	W	L	W	L	W	D	L	W	L	L	D	W	W	W	W	W	L	L	W	D	L	W	W	L	W	W	L	D	D	L	L	W	W	L	D	L	L	W	D	W

Goalkeepers
Luke Daniels
Graeme Smith

Defenders
Stephen Craigan
Steven Hammell
William Kinniburgh
Robert Malcolm
Brian McLean
Danny Murphy
Paul Quinn
Mark Reynolds

Midfielders
Marc Fitzpatrick
Stephen Hughes
Simon Lappin
Keith Lasley
Stephen Maguire
Robert McHugh
Simon Mensing
Jamie Murphy
Philip O'Donnell
Jim Paterson

Forwards
David Clarkson
Lewis Grabban
Martin Grehan
Ross McCormack
Steven McGarry
Chris Porter
Darren Lee Smith

KEY: On all match · On bench · Subbed or sent off (Counting game) · Subbed or sent off (playing less than 70 minutes) · Subbed on from bench (Counting Game) · Subbed on (playing less than 70 minutes) · Subbed on and then subbed or sent off (Counting Game) · Subbed on and then subbed or sent off (playing less than 70 minutes) · Not in 16

ABERDEEN

Final Position: **4th**

NICKNAME: THE DONS

KEY: ☐ Won ☐ Drawn ☐ Lost

	Comp	Opponent	H/A	Res	Score	Scorers	Attendance
1	spl	Dundee Utd	A	L	0-1		12,496
2	spl	Hearts	H	D	1-1	Nicholson 19	13,134
3	spl	Celtic	H	L	1-3	Brewster 24	16,232
4	spl	Hibernian	A	D	3-3	Brewster 18, 37, Smith 57	15,280
5	spl	Kilmarnock	A	W	1-0	Miller 54	5,814
6	spl	Motherwell	H	L	1-2	Smith 65	10,154
7	ucrl1	Dnipro	H	D	0-0		15,431
8	spl	Rangers	A	L	0-3		49,046
9	sccc3	Partick	A	W	2-0	Young 42, Considine 64	3,337
10	spl	Gretna	H	W	2-0	Diamond 16, Smith 18	10,279
11	ucrl2	Dnipro	A	D	1-1	Mackie 28	26,275
12	spl	St Mirren	H	W	4-0	Severin 43 pen, 71 pen, Miller 63, 88	1,284
13	spl	Inverness CT	A	W	2-1	Young 8, Tokely 62 og	6,023
14	ucgpb	Panathinaikos	A	L	0-3		8,154
15	spl	Falkirk	H	D	1-1	Severin 45 pen	10,399
16	sccqf	Inverness CT	H	W	4-1	Nicholson 11 pen, 22 pen, 79, Miller 45	7,270
17	spl	Dundee Utd	H	W	2-0	Aluko 45, Miller 90	11,964
18	ucgpb	L Moscow	H	D	1-1	Diamond 27	15,000
19	spl	Hearts	A	L	1-4	de Visscher 38	17,122
20	spl	Celtic	A	L	0-3		58,000
21	ucgpb	Atl Madrid	A	L	0-2		25,000
22	spl	Hibernian	H	W	3-1	Miller 33, Clark 47, Young 86	10,110
23	spl	Kilmarnock	H	W	2-1	Nicholson 63 pen, Miller 75	10,207
24	spl	Motherwell	A	L	0-3		5,326
25	ucgpb	Copenhagen	H	W	4-0	Smith 47, 55, Antonsson 71 og Foster 83	20,446
26	spl	Rangers	H	D	1-1	Miller 45	17,798
27	spl	Gretna	A	D	1-1	Lovell 86	1,730
28	spl	St Mirren	A	W	1-0	Lovell 85	5,025
29	spl	Inverness CT	H	W	1-0	Nicholson 83 pen	13,372
30	spl	Falkirk	A	D	0-0		5,457
31	scr4	Falkirk	A	D	2-2	Jamie.Smith 4, Lovell 10	5,798
32	spl	Dundee Utd	A	L	0-3		8,579
33	scr4r	Falkirk	H	W	3-1	Jamie.Smith 19, 55, de Visscher 43	8,547
34	spl	Hearts	H	L	0-1		14,000
35	scr5	Hamilton	H	W	1-0	Diamond 62	6,441
36	slc5	Dundee Utd	H	L	1-4	Considine 19	12,046
37	spl	Celtic	H	L	1-5	Miller 62	14,651
38	uc3rl1	Bayern Munich	H	D	2-2	Walker 24, Aluko 41	20,047
39	spl	Hibernian	A	L	1-3	Diamond 18	13,825
40	uc3rl2	Bayern Munich	A	L	1-5	Lovell 83	66,000
41	spl	Kilmarnock	A	L	1-3	Mackie 86	6,113
42	spl	Motherwell	H	D	1-1	Diamond 28	8,240
43	spl	Rangers	A	L	1-3	Lovell 28	50,066
44	scpqf	Celtic	H	D	1-1	de Visscher 79	10,909
45	spl	Gretna	H	W	3-0	Maguire 40, Miller 71 pen, Nicholson 73	9,025
46	scqfr	Celtic	A	W	1-0	Mackie 69	33,506
47	spl	St Mirren	H	D	1-1	Mair 29	9,779
48	spl	Inverness CT	A	W	4-3	Aluko 7, Nicholson 45, Miller 53 Maguire 90	5,655
49	spl	Falkirk	H	W	2-1	Maguire 22, 82	11,484
50	scsf	Queen of South	A	L	3-4	Considine 36, 59, Nicholson 53	24,008
51	spl	Celtic	A	L	0-1		55,766
52	spl	Hibernian	H	W	2-1	Mackie 63, Miller 70 pen	8,387
53	spl	Dundee Utd	H	W	2-1	Foster 30, Touzani 48	10,312
54	spl	Motherwell	A	L	1-2	Aluko 67	8,574
55	spl	Rangers	H	W	2-0	Miller 63, Mackie 77	17,509

LEAGUE APPEARANCES, BOOKINGS AND CAPS

	AGE (on 01/07/08)	IN NAMED 18	APPEARANCES	COUNTING GAMES	MINUTES ON PITCH	YELLOW CARDS	RED CARDS	CAPS THIS SEASON	NATIONAL SIDE
Goalkeepers									
James Langfield	28	38	25	25	2250	0	0	-	Scotland
Derek Soutar	27	34	13	13	1170	0	0	-	Scotland
Defenders									
Dave Bus	30	13	6	3	333	0	0	-	Holland
Richie Byrne	26	14	13	11	1051	1	0	-	Rep of Ireland
Andrew Considine	21	28	22	19	1785	5	0	-	Scotland
Alexander Diamond	23	27	26	24	2247	6	0	-	Scotland
Richard Foster	22	35	33	28	2713	5	0	-	Scotland
Lee Mair	27	25	18	12	1248	1	0	-	Scotland
Alan Maybury	29	13	13	12	1102	1	0	-	Rep of Ireland
Jackie McNamara	34	18	17	10	1075	1	0	-	Scotland
Daniel Smith	21	14	3	0	82	0	0	-	Scotland
Midfielders									
Christopher Clark	27	18	18	16	1475	2	0	-	Scotland
Stuart Duff	26	12	10	6	632	0	0	-	Scotland
Michael Hart	28	18	18	18	1612	1	0	-	Scotland
Barry Nicholson	29	38	38	36	3265	1	0	-	Scotland
Scott Severin	29	35	35	30	2839	4	0	-	Scotland
Karim Touzani	27	28	14	4	622	4	0	-	Holland
Josh Walker	19	13	8	1	274	1	0	-	England
Derek Young	28	24	24	15	1686	6	0	-	Scotland
Forwards									
Sone Aluko	19	27	20	5	1069	0	0	-	England
Craig Brewster	41	3	3	1	145	0	0	-	Scotland
Jeffrey de Visscher	27	28	22	11	1171	3	0	-	Holland
Steve Lovell	27	30	22	6	1013	0	0	-	England
Darren Mackie	26	22	19	9	1169	3	0	-	Scotland
Christopher Maguire	19	36	28	6	1307	2	0	-	Scotland
Lee Miller	25	37	36	32	2907	9	0	-	Scotland
Jamie Smith	27	17	17	13	1373	1	0	-	Scotland

TEAM OF THE SEASON

G
James Langfield
CG: 25 DR: 62
D
Andrew Considine
CG: 19 DR: 71
D
Lee Mair
CG: 12 DR: 65
D
Richard Foster
CG: 28 DR: 63
D
Alexander Diamond
CG: 24 DR: 53
M
Barry Nicholson
CG: 36 SD: -4
M
Michael Hart
CG: 18 SD: -11
M
Derek Young
CG: 15 SD: -13
M
Scott Severin
CG: 30 SD: -13
F
Lee Miller
CG: 32 SR: 242
F
Jamie Smith
CG: 13 SR: 457

MONTHLY POINTS TALLY

Month	Points	%
AUGUST	2	17%
SEPTEMBER	6	50%
OCTOBER	7	78%
NOVEMBER	3	33%
DECEMBER	11	61%
JANUARY	4	33%
FEBRUARY	1	8%
MARCH	7	58%
APRIL	6	67%
MAY	6	67%

LEAGUE GOALS

	PLAYER	MINS	GOALS	S RATE
1	Miller	2907	12	242
2	Nicholson	3265	5	653
3	Maguire	1307	4	326
4	Brewster	145	3	48
5	Lovell	1013	3	337
6	Aluko	1069	3	356
7	Mackie	1169	3	389
8	Smith	1373	3	457
9	Diamond	2247	3	749
10	Severin	2839	3	946
11	Young	1686	2	843
12	Touzani	622	1	622
13	de Visscher	1171	1	1171
	Other		3	
	TOTAL		49	

TOP POINT EARNERS

	PLAYER	GAMES	AV PTS
1	Derek Young	15	1.93
2	Lee Mair	12	1.67
3	Richard Foster	28	1.61
4	Andrew Considine	19	1.58
5	James Langfield	25	1.48
6	Lee Miller	32	1.47
7	Barry Nicholson	36	1.47
8	Christopher Clark	16	1.44
9	Alan Maybury	12	1.42
10	Jamie Smith	13	1.31
	CLUB AVERAGE:		1.39

DISCIPLINARY RECORDS

	PLAYER	YELLOW	RED	AVE
1	Karim Touzani	4	0	155
2	Derek Young	6	0	281
3	Lee Miller	9	0	323
4	Andrew Considine	5	0	357
5	Alexander Diamond	6	0	374
6	Darren Mackie	3	0	389
7	Jeffrey de Visscher	3	0	390
8	Richard Foster	5	0	542
9	C Maguire	2	0	653
10	Scott Severin	4	0	709
11	Christopher Clark	2	0	737
12	Richie Byrne	1	0	1051
13	Jackie McNamara	1	0	1075
	Other	5	0	
	TOTAL	56	0	

KEY GOALKEEPER

James Langfield

Goals Conceded in the League	36	**Counting Games** League games when player was on pitch for at least 70 minutes	25
Defensive Rating Ave number of mins between League goals conceded while on the pitch	62	**Clean Sheets** In League games when player was on pitch for at least 70 minutes	7

KEY PLAYERS - DEFENDERS

Andrew Considine

Goals Conceded Number of League goals conceded while the player was on the pitch	25	**Clean Sheets** In League games when player was on pitch for at least 70 minutes	5
Defensive Rating Ave number of mins between League goals conceded while on the pitch	71	**Club Defensive Rating** Average number of mins between League goals conceded by the club this season	58

	PLAYER	CON LGE	CLEAN SHEETS	DEF RATE
1	Andrew Considine	25	5	71 mins
2	Lee Mair	19	4	65 mins
3	Richard Foster	43	7	63 mins
4	Alexander Diamond	42	5	53 mins

KEY PLAYERS - MIDFIELDERS

Barry Nicholson

Goals in the League	5	**Contribution to Attacking Power** Average number of minutes between League team goals while on pitch	68
Defensive Rating Average number of mins between League goals conceded while on the pitch	64	**Scoring Difference** Defensive Rating minus Contribution to Attacking Power	-4

	PLAYER	LGE GOALS	DEF RATE	POWER	SCORE DIFF
1	Barry Nicholson	5	64	68	-4 mins
2	Michael Hart	0	59	70	-11 mins
3	Derek Young	2	60	73	-13 mins
4	Scott Severin	3	54	67	-13 mins

KEY PLAYERS - GOALSCORERS

Lee Miller

Goals in the League	12	**Player Strike Rate** Average number of minutes between League goals scored by player	242
Contribution to Attacking Power Average number of minutes between League team goals while on pitch	69	**Club Strike Rate** Average number of minutes between League goals scored by club	68

	PLAYER	LGE GOALS	POWER	STRIKE RATE
1	Lee Miller	12	69	242 mins
2	Jamie Smith	3	98	457 mins
3	Barry Nicholson	5	68	653 mins
4	Derek Young	2	73	843 mins

APEX
TUBULARS
Lee Miller

SQUAD APPEARANCES

Match	1	2	3	4	5	6	7	8	9	10	11	12	13	14	15	16	17	18	19	20	21	22	23	24	25	26	27	28
Venue	A	H	H	A	A	H	H	A	A	H	A	H	A	A	H	H	H	H	A	A	A	H	H	A	H	H	A	A
Competition	L	L	L	L	L	L	E	L	O	L	E	L	L	E	L	O	L	E	L	L	E	L	L	L	E	L	L	L
Result	L	D	L	D	W	L	D	L	W	W	D	W	W	L	D	W	W	D	L	L	L	W	W	L	W	D	D	W

Match	29	30	31	32	33	34	35	36	37	38	39	40	41	42	43	44	45	46	47	48	49	50	51	52	53	54	55
Venue	H	A	A	A	H	H	H	H	H	H	A	A	A	H	A	H	H	A	H	A	H	A	A	H	H	A	H
Competition	L	L	O	L	O	L	O	O	L	E	L	E	L	L	L	O	L	O	L	L	L	O	L	L	L	L	L
Result	W	D	D	L	W	L	W	L	L	D	L	L	L	D	L	D	W	W	D	W	W	L	L	W	W	L	W

Goalkeepers
James Langfield
Derek Soutar

Defenders
Dave Bus
Richie Byrne
Andrew Considine
Alexander Diamond
Richard Foster
Lee Mair
Alan Maybury
Jackie McNamara
Daniel Smith

Midfielders
Christopher Clark
Stuart Duff
Michael Hart
Barry Nicholson
Scott Severin
Karim Touzani
Josh Walker
Derek Young

Forwards
Sone Aluko
Craig Brewster
Jeffrey de Visscher
Steve Lovell
Darren Mackie
Christopher Maguire
Lee Miller
Jamie Smith

KEY: On all match | On bench | Subbed or sent off (Counting game) | Subbed or sent off (playing less than 70 minutes) | Subbed on from bench (Counting Game) | Subbed on (playing less than 70 minutes) | Subbed on and then subbed or sent off (Counting Game) | Subbed on and then subbed or sent off (playing less than 70 minutes) | Not in 16

DUNDEE UNITED

Final Position: **5th**

NICKNAME: THE TERRORS/ ARABS

KEY: ☐ Won ☐ Drawn ☐ Lost

							Attendance
1	spl	Aberdeen	H	W	1-0	Robertson 90	12,496
2	spl	Kilmarnock	A	L	1-2	Hunt 50	5,557
3	spl	Hibernian	H	D	0-0		8,405
4	spl	Inverness CT	A	W	3-0	Dillon 47, Robson 58 pen, 81 pen	4,178
5	sccc2	Ross County	H	W	2-1	Hunt 65 pen, J.Robertson 88	3,114
6	spl	Falkirk	H	W	2-0	Hunt 58, Robson 84	6,864
7	spl	St Mirren	H	W	2-0	Hunt 38, J.Robertson 68	6,128
8	spl	Gretna	A	L	2-3	Bauben 9, Wilkie 65	1,624
9	sccc3	Falkirk	A	W	1-0	Wilkie 60	2,804
10	spl	Celtic	A	L	0-3		57,006
11	spl	Motherwell	H	W	1-0	Dods 78	6,286
12	spl	Hearts	A	W	3-1	J.Robertson 14, 25, Robson 89 pen	16,661
13	spl	Rangers	H	W	2-1	Wilkie 28, Robson 54 pen	12,129
14	sccqf	Hamilton	H	W	3-1	Hunt 11, 78, 86	4,567
15	spl	Aberdeen	A	L	0-2		11,964
16	spl	Kilmarnock	H	W	2-0	Hunt 8, Bauben 90	6,065
17	spl	Hibernian	A	D	2-2	D.Robertson 66, 74	14,440
18	spl	Inverness CT	H	L	0-1		5,845
19	spl	Falkirk	A	L	0-3		4,803
20	spl	St Mirren	A	W	3-0	D.Robertson 49, Hunt 77, Flood 90	3,490
21	spl	Gretna	H	L	1-2	Hunt 29	6,304
22	spl	Celtic	H	L	0-2		12,357
23	spl	Motherwell	A	L	3-5	D.Robertson 36, Hunt 75, 90	5,227
24	spl	Hearts	H	W	4-1	Robson 23, 70 pen, 88 pen, Hunt 84	12,100
25	spl	Rangers	A	L	0-2		48,559
26	scr4	Clyde	A	W	1-0	Robson 57	1,550
27	spl	Aberdeen	H	W	3-0	Hunt 50, Robson 77, 84	8,579
28	spl	Kilmarnock	A	W	2-1	Robson 30, Conway 66	4,803
29	scr5	St Mirren	A	D	0-0		3,945
30	slc5	Aberdeen	A	W	4-1	Dods 23, Kalvenes 60, Conway 65 Gomis 77	12,046
31	spl	Hibernian	H	D	1-1	Hunt 13 pen	6,635
32	scr5r	St Mirren	H	L	0-1		3,723
33	spl	Inverness CT	A	D	1-1	Bauben 68	4,087
34	spl	Falkirk	H	D	0-0		6,835
35	spl	St Mirren	H	D	1-1	Dillon 69	6,037
36	spl	Gretna	A	W	3-0	Kenneth 16, Gomis 51, D.Robertson 64	507
37	spl	Celtic	A	D	0-0		45,000
38	scccf	Rangers	H	L	2-3*	Hunt 34, de Vries 96 (*on penalties)	50,019
39	spl	Motherwell	H	W	2-0	Swanson 76, de Vries 89	6,779
40	spl	Hearts	A	L	0-1		16,871
41	spl	Rangers	H	D	3-3	Kalvenes 37, Hunt 51, Cuellar 65 og	11,214
42	spl	Hibernian	H	D	1-1	Hunt 60 pen	7,404
43	spl	Motherwell	A	D	2-2	Craigan 45 og, Wilkie 86	5,027
44	spl	Aberdeen	A	L	1-2	Swanson 49	10,312
45	spl	Rangers	A	L	1-3	de Vries 76	30,293
46	spl	Celtic	H	L	0-1		13,613

LEAGUE APPEARANCES, BOOKINGS AND CAPS

	AGE (on 01/07/08)	IN NAMED 18	APPEARANCES	COUNTING GAMES	MINUTES ON PITCH	YELLOW CARDS	RED CARDS	CAPS THIS SEASON	NATIONAL SIDE
Goalkeepers									
Euan McLean	22	36	6	5	451	0	0	-	Scotland
Grzegorz Szamotulski	32	20	18	18	1619	1	1	-	Poland
Lukasz Zaluska	26	18	15	15	1350	0	0	-	Poland
Defenders									
Sean Dillon	24	37	33	32	2911	1	1	-	Rep of Ireland
Darren Dods	43	35	33	33	2970	8	0	-	Scotland
Danny Grainger	21	18	14	12	1119	1	0	-	England
Christian Kalvenes	31	19	19	18	1585	1	0	-	Norway
Gary Kenneth	21	32	19	14	1418	5	1	-	Scotland
Lee Wilkie	28	32	31	30	2716	9	1	-	Scotland
Midfielders									
Prince Bauben	20	31	24	19	1823	3	0	1	Ghana
Greg Cameron	20	12	3	1	130	0	0	-	Scotland
Craig Conway	23	22	15	5	706	0	0	-	Scotland
Stuart Duff	26	19	9	4	486	0	0	-	Scotland
Willo Flood	23	37	36	26	2741	4	1	-	Rep of Ireland
Morgaro Gomis	22	36	36	32	3042	5	1	-	France
Mark Kerr	26	37	30	23	2151	4	0	-	Scotland
Mihael Kovacevic	20	9	4	4	347	0	0	-	Switzerland
Fraser Milligan	19	6	1	0	12	0	0	-	Scotland
Stephen Robb	26	15	12	1	316	0	0	-	Scotland
David Robertson	21	32	20	11	1339	1	0	-	Scotland
Barry Robson	29	21	21	21	1845	2	1	2	Scotland
Danny Swanson	21	15	12	2	532	1	1	-	Scotland
Forwards									
Jon Daly	25	15	9	2	284	1	0	-	Rep of Ireland
Mark de Vries	32	15	14	8	905	1	0	-	Holland
David Goodwillie	19	8	2	0	70	0	0	-	Scotland
Noel Hunt	25	36	36	33	3030	4	0	-	Rep of Ireland
James O'Brien	20	14	10	4	481	1	0	-	Scotland
Eric Odhiambo	19	12	4	0	61	0	0	-	England
Jordan Robertson	20	17	14	11	1020	1	1	-	England
Johnny Russell	28	11	2	0	56	0	0	-	Scotland

TEAM OF THE SEASON

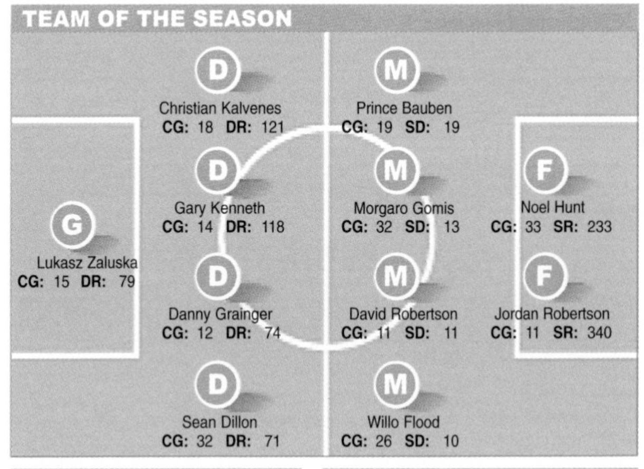

G
Lukasz Zaluska
CG: 15 DR: 79
D
Christian Kalvenes
CG: 18 DR: 121
D
Gary Kenneth
CG: 14 DR: 118
D
Danny Grainger
CG: 12 DR: 74
D
Sean Dillon
CG: 32 DR: 71
M
Prince Bauben
CG: 19 SD: 19
M
Morgaro Gomis
CG: 32 SD: 13
M
David Robertson
CG: 11 SD: 11
M
Willo Flood
CG: 26 SD: 10
F
Noel Hunt
CG: 33 SR: 233
F
Jordan Robertson
CG: 11 SR: 340

MONTHLY POINTS TALLY

AUGUST	7	58%
SEPTEMBER	6	50%
OCTOBER	9	100%
NOVEMBER	4	44%
DECEMBER	3	17%
JANUARY	9	75%
FEBRUARY	4	33%
MARCH	7	58%
APRIL	3	33%
MAY	0	0%

LEAGUE GOALS

	PLAYER	MINS	GOALS	S RATE
1	Hunt	3030	13	233
2	Robson	1845	11	167
3	Robertson, D	1339	6	223
4	Robertson, J	1020	3	340
5	Bauben	1823	3	607
6	Wilkie	2716	3	905
7	Swanson	532	2	266
8	de Vries	905	2	452
9	Dillon	2911	2	1455
10	Conway	706	1	706
11	Kenneth	1418	1	1418
12	Kalvenes	1585	1	1585
13	Flood	2741	1	2741
	Other		2	
	TOTAL		51	

TOP POINT EARNERS

	PLAYER	GAMES	AV PTS
1	Christian Kalvenes	18	1.94
2	Gary Kenneth	14	1.86
3	Prince Bauben	19	1.63
4	Barry Robson	21	1.62
5	Sean Dillon	32	1.50
6	Willo Flood	26	1.50
7	Noel Hunt	33	1.48
8	Grzegorz Szamotulski	18	1.44
9	Morgaro Gomis	32	1.41
10	Darren Dods	33	1.33
	CLUB AVERAGE:		1.37

DISCIPLINARY RECORDS

	PLAYER	YELLOW	RED	AVE
1	Gary Kenneth	5	1	236
2	Danny Swanson	1	1	266
3	Lee Wilkie	9	1	271
4	Darren Dods	8	0	371
5	James O'Brien	1	0	481
6	Morgaro Gomis	5	1	507
7	Jordan Robertson	1	1	510
8	Mark Kerr	4	0	537
9	Willo Flood	4	1	548
10	Prince Bauben	3	0	607
11	Barry Robson	2	1	615
12	Noel Hunt	4	0	757
13	G Szamotulski	1	1	809
	Other	5	1	
	TOTAL	53	9	

KEY GOALKEEPER

Lukasz Zaluska

Goals Conceded in the League	17	**Counting Games** League games when player was on pitch for at least 70 minutes	15
Defensive Rating Ave number of mins between League goals conceded while on the pitch	79	**Clean Sheets** In League games when player was on pitch for at least 70 minutes	4

KEY PLAYERS - DEFENDERS

Christian Kalvenes

Goals Conceded Number of League goals conceded while the player was on the pitch	13	**Clean Sheets** In League games when player was on pitch for at least 70 minutes	10
Defensive Rating Ave number of mins between League goals conceded while on the pitch	121	**Club Defensive Rating** Average number of mins between League goals conceded by the club this season	76

	PLAYER	CON LGE	CLEAN SHEETS	DEF RATE
1	Christian Kalvenes	13	10	121 mins
2	Gary Kenneth	12	8	118 mins
3	Danny Grainger	15	2	74 mins
4	Sean Dillon	41	11	71 mins

KEY PLAYERS - MIDFIELDERS

Prince Bauben

Goals in the League	3	**Contribution to Attacking Power** Average number of minutes between League team goals while on pitch	60
Defensive Rating Average number of mins between League goals conceded while on the pitch	79	**Scoring Difference** Defensive Rating minus Contribution to Attacking Power	19

	PLAYER	LGE GOALS	DEF RATE	POWER	SCORE DIFF
1	Prince Bauben	3	79	60	19 mins
2	Morgaro Gomis	1	76	63	13 mins
3	David Robertson	6	74	63	11 mins
4	Willo Flood	1	70	60	10 mins

KEY PLAYERS - GOALSCORERS

Barry Robson

Goals in the League	11	**Player Strike Rate** Average number of minutes between League goals scored by player	167
Contribution to Attacking Power Average number of minutes between League team goals while on pitch	61	**Club Strike Rate** Average number of minutes between League goals scored by club	67

	PLAYER	LGE GOALS	POWER	STRIKE RATE
1	Barry Robson	11	61	167 mins
2	David Robertson	6	63	223 mins
3	Noel Hunt	13	61	233 mins
4	Jordan Robertson	3	85	340 mins

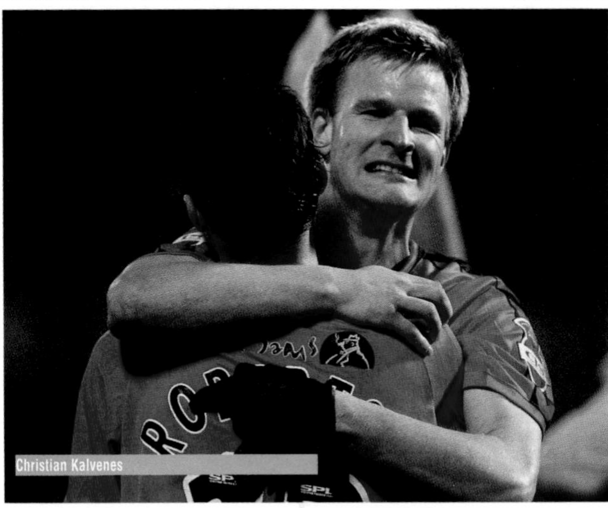
Christian Kalvenes

SQUAD APPEARANCES

Match	1	2	3	4	5	6	7	8	9	10	11	12	13	14	15	16	17	18	19	20	21	22	23	24	25	26	27	28	29	30	31	32	33	34	35	36	37	38	39	40	41	42	43	44	45	46
Venue	H	A	H	A	H	H	H	A	A	A	H	A	H	H	A	H	A	H	A	A	H	H	A	H	A	A	H	A	A	A	H	H	A	H	H	A	A	H	H	A	H	H	A	A	A	H
Competition	L	L	L	L	O	L	L	L	O	L	L	L	L	O	L	L	L	L	L	L	L	L	L	L	L	O	L	L	O	O	L	O	L	L	L	L	L	O	L	L	L	L	L	L	L	L
Result	W	L	D	W	W	W	W	L	W	L	W	W	W	W	L	W	D	L	L	W	L	L	L	W	L	W	W	W	D	W	D	L	D	D	D	W	D	L	W	L	D	D	D	L	L	L

Goalkeepers
Euan McLean
Grzegorz Szamotulski
Lukasz Zaluska
Defenders
Sean Dillon
Darren Dods
Danny Grainger
Christian Kalvenes
Gary Kenneth
Lee Wilkie
Midfielders
Prince Bauben
Greg Cameron
Craig Conway
Stuart Duff
Willo Flood
Morgaro Gomis
Mark Kerr
Mihael Kovacevic
Fraser Milligan
Stephen Robb
David Robertson
Barry Robson
Danny Swanson
Forwards
Jon Daly
Mark de Vries
David Goodwillie
Noel Hunt
James O'Brien
Eric Odhiambo
Jordan Robertson
Johnny Russell

KEY: On all match; On bench; Subbed or sent off (Counting game); Subbed or sent off (playing less than 70 minutes); Subbed on from bench (Counting Game); Subbed on (playing less than 70 minutes); Subbed on and then subbed or sent off (Counting Game); Subbed on and then subbed or sent off (playing less than 70 minutes); Not in 16

HIBERNIAN

Final Position: **6th**

NICKNAME: THE HIBEES

KEY: ☐ Won ☐ Drawn ☐ Lost

							Attendance
1	spl	Hearts	A	W	1-0	Kerr 2	16,436
2	spl	Gretna	H	W	4-2	Zemmama 64, 82, Fletcher 66 McCann 90	13,795
3	spl	Dundee Utd	A	D	0-0		8,405
4	spl	Aberdeen	H	D	3-3	Zemmama 5, Fletcher 70, D.Shiels 84	15,280
5	sccc2	Queens Park	A	W	2-1	Morais 56, Fletcher 58	2,343
6	spl	Inverness CT	H	W	1-0	Fletcher 2 pen	13,258
7	spl	Falkirk	A	D	1-1	Donaldson 5 pen	6,298
8	spl	Celtic	H	W	3-2	Fletcher 5, Gathuessi 41, D.Shiels 87	16,125
9	sccc3	Motherwell	H	L	2-4	Donaldson 11, Antoine-Curier 85	7,000
10	spl	Kilmarnock	H	W	4-1	Donaldson 12, 31 pen, 78 pen Antoine-Curier 65	14,500
11	spl	Rangers	A	W	1-0	Murphy 61	50,440
12	spl	Motherwell	A	L	1-2	Fletcher 31 pen	7,071
13	spl	St Mirren	H	L	0-1		13,884
14	spl	Hearts	H	D	1-1	Berra 18 og	17,015
15	spl	Gretna	A	W	1-0	Fletcher 52	2,666
16	spl	Dundee Utd	H	D	2-2	Benjelloun 77, Antoine-Curier 82 pen	14,440
17	spl	Aberdeen	A	L	1-3	Fletcher 24	10,110
18	spl	Inverness CT	A	L	0-2		4,224
19	spl	Falkirk	H	D	1-1	Donaldson 21 pen	12,391
20	spl	Celtic	A	D	1-1	Murphy 20	58,016
21	spl	Kilmarnock	A	L	1-2	D.Shiels 90 pen	6,372
22	spl	Rangers	H	L	1-2	Zemmama 88	16,217
23	spl	St Mirren	A	L	1-2	Antoine-Curier 89	4,212
24	scr4	Inverness CT	H	W	3-0	D.Shiels 5, 53, 84	12,578
25	spl	Hearts	A	L	0-1		17,131
26	scr5	Rangers	H	D	0-0		11,513
27	spl	Dundee Utd	A	D	1-1	Rankin 46	6,635
28	spl	Gretna	H	W	4-2	Nish 10, Fletcher 19, 58, 90 pen	12,087
29	spl	Aberdeen	H	W	3-1	Zemmama 49, D.Shiels 55, Fletcher 90	13,825
30	spl	Inverness CT	H	W	2-0	Nish 3, Fletcher 5	12,552
31	spl	Falkirk	A	W	2-0	Ross 12 og, Rankin 52	5,928
32	spl	Celtic	H	L	0-2		15,735
33	scr5r	Rangers	A	L	0-1		33,837
34	spl	Motherwell	H	W	1-0	Nish 52	11,692
35	spl	Kilmarnock	H	W	2-0	Morais 29, Fletcher 73	12,486
36	spl	Rangers	A	L	1-2	D.Shiels 90	50,117
37	spl	Motherwell	A	L	0-1		6,580
38	spl	St Mirren	H	W	2-0	Nish 4, Zemmama 5	14,000
39	spl	Dundee Utd	A	D	1-1	D.Shiels 57	7,404
40	spl	Aberdeen	A	L	1-2	D.Shiels 54	8,387
41	spl	Rangers	H	D	0-0		16,872
42	spl	Celtic	A	L	0-2		58,515
43	spl	Motherwell	H	L	0-2		7,650

LEAGUE APPEARANCES, BOOKINGS AND CAPS

	AGE (on 01/07/08)	IN NAMED 18	APPEARANCES	COUNTING GAMES	MINUTES ON PITCH	YELLOW CARDS	RED CARDS	CAPS THIS SEASON	NATIONAL SIDE
Goalkeepers									
Yves M Ma-Kalambay	22	34	29	28	2577	0	0	-	Belgium
Andrew McNeil	21	37	10	9	843	0	0	-	Scotland
Defenders									
Martin Canning	26	13	11	11	983	1	1	-	Scotland
Thierry Gathuessi	26	31	23	18	1750	8	2	-	Cameroon
Paul Hanlon	18	10	7	5	465	1	0	-	Scotland
Chris Hogg	23	34	34	33	3030	6	0	-	England
Robert Jones	28	30	30	29	2647	7	0	-	England
Kevin McCann	20	24	19	17	1620	2	0	-	Scotland
Darren McCormack	19	15	4	2	223	0	0	-	Scotland
David Murphy	24	17	17	16	1438	1	0	-	England
Abderaouf Zarabi	29	11	7	7	624	3	0	-	Algeria
Midfielders									
Guillaume Beuzelin	29	28	27	20	2046	6	0	-	France
Ross Chisholm	20	31	18	11	1305	3	0	-	Scotland
Brian Kerr	26	31	25	21	1999	2	0	-	Scotland
Ian Murray	27	15	15	14	1264	2	2	-	Scotland
Patrick Noubissie	25	7	4	2	258	0	1	-	France
John Rankin	25	17	17	14	1340	5	0	-	Scotland
Lewis Stevenson	20	28	21	14	1503	3	0	-	Scotland
Merouane Zemmama	24	33	28	11	1522	4	0	-	Morocco
Forwards									
M Antoine-Curier	25	15	13	4	633	2	0	-	France
A Benjelloun	23	20	15	3	654	2	0	5	Morocco
Ross Campbell	20	10	5	2	240	0	0	-	Scotland
Clayton Donaldson	24	26	18	6	922	5	1	-	England
Steven Fletcher	21	32	32	23	2418	3	0	-	Scotland
Filipe Morais	22	36	28	11	1532	1	1	-	Portugal
Colin Nish	27	15	15	12	1102	3	1	-	Scotland
Alan O'Brien	23	30	23	5	869	0	0	-	England
Dean Shiels	23	32	22	15	1479	4	1	-	N Ireland

TEAM OF THE SEASON

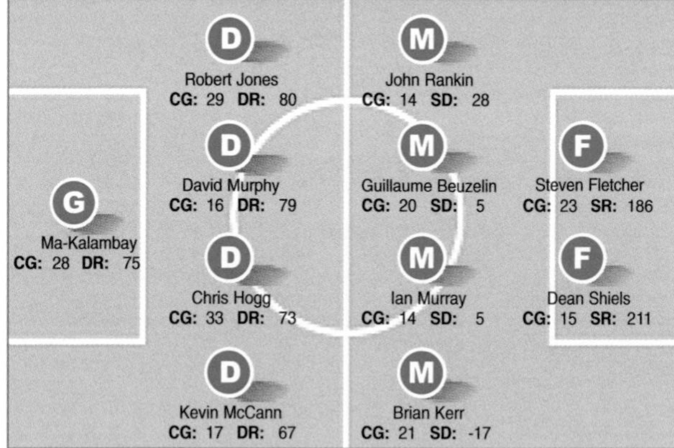
D
Robert Jones
CG: 29 DR: 80
M
John Rankin
CG: 14 SD: 28
D
David Murphy
CG: 16 DR: 79
M
Guillaume Beuzelin
CG: 20 SD: 5
F
Steven Fletcher
CG: 23 SR: 186
G
Ma-Kalambay
CG: 28 DR: 75
D
Chris Hogg
CG: 33 DR: 73
M
Ian Murray
CG: 14 SD: 5
F
Dean Shiels
CG: 15 SR: 211
D
Kevin McCann
CG: 17 DR: 67
M
Brian Kerr
CG: 21 SD: -17

MONTHLY POINTS TALLY

AUGUST	8	67%
SEPTEMBER	10	83%
OCTOBER	3	33%
NOVEMBER	5	56%
DECEMBER	2	11%
JANUARY	0	0%
FEBRUARY	13	87%
MARCH	6	40%
APRIL	4	44%
MAY	1	11%

LEAGUE GOALS

	PLAYER	MINS	GOALS	S RATE
1	Fletcher	2418	13	186
2	Shiels, D	1479	7	211
3	Zemmama	1522	6	253
4	Donaldson	922	5	184
5	Nish	1102	4	275
6	Antoine-Curier	633	3	211
7	Rankin	1340	2	670
8	Murphy	1438	2	719
9	Benjelloun	654	1	654
10	Morais	1532	1	1532
11	McCann	1620	1	1620
12	Gathuessi	1750	1	1750
13	Kerr	1999	1	1999
	Other		0	
	TOTAL		47	

TOP POINT EARNERS

	PLAYER	GAMES	AV PTS
1	Thierry Gathuessi	18	1.72
2	John Rankin	14	1.71
3	Colin Nish	12	1.67
4	Steven Fletcher	23	1.61
5	Yves M Ma-Kalambay	28	1.54
6	David Murphy	16	1.50
7	Kevin McCann	17	1.41
8	Dean Shiels	15	1.40
9	Chris Hogg	33	1.33
10	Robert Jones	29	1.31
	CLUB AVERAGE:		1.37

DISCIPLINARY RECORDS

	PLAYER	YELLOW	RED	AVE
1	Clayton Donaldson	5	1	153
2	Thierry Gathuessi	8	2	175
3	Abderaouf Zarabi	3	0	208
4	John Rankin	5	0	268
5	Colin Nish	3	1	275
6	Dean Shiels	4	1	295
7	Ian Murray	2	2	316
8	M Antoine-Curier	2	0	316
9	A Benjelloun	2	0	327
10	Guillaume Beuzelin	6	0	341
11	Robert Jones	7	0	378
12	M Zemmama	4	0	380
13	Ross Chisholm	3	0	435
	Other	20	2	
	TOTAL	74	9	

KEY GOALKEEPER

Yves Makabu Ma-Kalambay

Goals Conceded in the League	34	**Counting Games** League games when player was on pitch for at least 70 minutes	28
Defensive Rating Ave number of mins between League goals conceded while on the pitch	75	**Clean Sheets** In League games when player was on pitch for at least 70 minutes	8

KEY PLAYERS - DEFENDERS

Robert Jones

Goals Conceded Number of League goals conceded while the player was on the pitch	33	**Clean Sheets** In League games when player was on pitch for at least 70 minutes	9
Defensive Rating Ave number of mins between League goals conceded while on the pitch	80	**Club Defensive Rating** Average number of mins between League goals conceded by the club this season	80

	PLAYER	CON LGE	CLEAN SHEETS	DEF RATE
1	Robert Jones	33	9	80 mins
2	David Murphy	18	5	79 mins
3	Chris Hogg	41	9	73 mins
4	Kevin McCann	24	5	67 mins

KEY PLAYERS - MIDFIELDERS

John Rankin

Goals in the League	2	**Contribution to Attacking Power** Average number of minutes between League team goals while on pitch	67
Defensive Rating Average number of mins between League goals conceded while on the pitch	95	**Scoring Difference** Defensive Rating minus Contribution to Attacking Power	28

	PLAYER	LGE GOALS	DEF RATE	POWER	SCORE DIFF
1	John Rankin	2	95	67	28 mins
2	Guillaume Beuzelin	0	73	68	5 mins
3	Ian Murray	0	84	79	5 mins
4	Brian Kerr	1	62	79	-17 mins

KEY PLAYERS - GOALSCORERS

Steven Fletcher

Goals in the League	13	**Player Strike Rate** Average number of minutes between League goals scored by player	186
Contribution to Attacking Power Average number of minutes between League team goals while on pitch	62	**Club Strike Rate** Average number of minutes between League goals scored by club	73

	PLAYER	LGE GOALS	POWER	STRIKE RATE
1	Steven Fletcher	13	62	186 mins
2	Dean Shiels	7	64	211 mins
3	Colin Nish	4	64	275 mins
4	John Rankin	2	67	670 mins

Dean Shiels

SQUAD APPEARANCES

Match	1	2	3	4	5	6	7	8	9	10	11	12	13	14	15	16	17	18	19	20	21	22	23	24	25	26	27	28	29	30	31	32	33	34	35	36	37	38	39	40	41	42	43
Venue	A	H	A	H	A	H	A	H	H	H	A	A	H	H	A	H	A	A	H	A	A	H	A	H	A	H	A	H	H	H	A	H	A	H	H	A	A	H	A	A	H	A	H
Competition	L	L	L	L	O	L	L	L	O	L	L	L	L	L	L	L	L	L	L	L	L	L	L	O	L	O	L	L	L	L	L	L	O	L	L	L	L	L	L	L	L	L	L
Result	W	W	D	D	W	W	D	W	L	W	W	L	L	D	W	D	L	L	D	D	L	L	L	W	L	D	D	W	W	W	W	L	L	W	W	L	L	W	D	L	D	L	L

Goalkeepers

Yves M Ma-Kalambay
Andrew McNeil

Defenders

Martin Canning
Thierry Gathuessi
Paul Hanlon
Chris Hogg
Robert Jones
Kevin McCann
Darren McCormack
David Murphy
Abderaouf Zarabi

Midfielders

Guillaume Beuzelin
Ross Chisholm
Brian Kerr
Ian Murray
Patrick Noubissie
John Rankin
Lewis Stevenson
Merouane Zemmama

Forwards

Mickael Antoine-Curier
Abdessalam Benjelloun
Ross Campbell
Clayton Donaldson
Steven Fletcher
Filipe Morais
Colin Nish
Alan O'Brien
Dean Shiels

KEY: ■ On all match ■ On bench ⏮ Subbed or sent off (Counting game) « Subbed or sent off (playing less than 70 minutes) ⏭ Subbed on from bench (Counting Game) » Subbed on (playing less than 70 minutes) Subbed on and then subbed or sent off (Counting Game) Subbed on and then subbed or sent off (playing less than 70 minutes) □ Not in 16

FALKIRK

Final Position: **7th**

NICKNAME: THE BAIRNS

KEY: ☐Won ☐Drawn ☐Lost

							Attendance
1	spl	Gretna	A	W	4-0	Higdon 14, 24, Moutinho 66, Latapy 74	2,731
2	spl	Celtic	H	L	1-4	Higdon 5	6,329
3	spl	Rangers	A	L	2-7	Riera 44, G.Barrett 72	47,419
4	spl	St Mirren	H	L	0-1		5,626
5	sccc2	Montrose	A	W	2-1	Higdon 17, S.Thomson 60	642
6	spl	Dundee Utd	A	L	0-2		6,864
7	spl	Hibernian	H	D	1-1	Moutinho 47	6,298
8	spl	Motherwell	H	W	1-0	Latapy 74	5,245
9	sccc3	Dundee Utd	H	L	0-1		2,804
10	spl	Inverness CT	A	L	2-4	Milne 28, Arfield 47	4,011
11	spl	Hearts	A	L	2-4	G.Barrett 87, Moutinho 89	15,800
12	spl	Kilmarnock	H	D	1-1	Finnigan 2	5,143
13	spl	Aberdeen	A	D	1-1	Cregg 68	10,399
14	spl	Gretna	H	W	2-0	Barr 41, G.Barrett 50	4,843
15	spl	Rangers	H	L	1-3	Moutinho 62	6,627
16	spl	St Mirren	A	W	5-1	Moutinho 5, 41, S.Thomson 14, G.Barrett 82 Finnigan 85	4,133
17	spl	Dundee Utd	H	W	3-0	Moutinho 5, G.Barrett 41, Higdon 66	4,803
18	spl	Celtic	A	L	0-4		54,291
19	spl	Hibernian	A	D	1-1	G.Barrett 80	12,391
20	spl	Motherwell	A	W	3-0	Higdon 49, 60, Cregg 65	5,241
21	spl	Inverness CT	H	W	1-0	Aafjes 35	5,265
22	spl	Hearts	H	W	2-1	Finnigan 78, Higdon 81	6,614
23	spl	Kilmarnock	A	W	1-0	Finnigan 11	5,956
24	spl	Aberdeen	H	D	0-0		5,457
25	scr4	Aberdeen	H	D	2-2	Barr 5, Riera 73	5,798
26	spl	Gretna	A	L	0-2		1,609
27	scr4r	Aberdeen	A	L	1-3	G.Barrett 61	8,547
28	spl	Celtic	H	L	0-1		6,803
29	spl	Rangers	A	L	0-2		48,590
30	spl	St Mirren	H	W	4-0	Arfield 6, 58, Cregg 61, 71	5,803
31	spl	Dundee Utd	A	D	0-0		6,835
32	spl	Hibernian	H	L	0-2		5,928
33	spl	Motherwell	H	D	0-0		5,108
34	spl	Inverness CT	A	W	1-0	Clarke 86	4,012
35	spl	Hearts	A	D	0-0		16,682
36	spl	Kilmarnock	H	D	0-0		5,134
37	spl	Aberdeen	A	L	1-2	Finnigan 49	11,484
38	spl	Gretna	H	D	0-0		4,490
39	spl	St Mirren	A	L	0-1		3,500
40	spl	Hearts	H	W	2-1	Scobbie 45, Finnigan 52	4,638
41	spl	Inverness CT	H	W	2-1	Higdon 28, Finnigan 68	5,631
42	spl	Kilmarnock	A	L	1-2	Moutinho 11	5,475

LEAGUE APPEARANCES, BOOKINGS AND CAPS

	AGE (on 01/07/08)	IN NAMED 18	APPEARANCES	COUNTING GAMES	MINUTES ON PITCH	YELLOW CARDS	RED CARDS	CAPS THIS SEASON	NATIONAL SIDE
Goalkeepers									
Tim Krul	20	22	22	22	1979	1	1	-	Holland
Robert Olejnik	21	38	13	12	1081	1	0	-	Austria
Shane Supple	21	14	4	4	360	0	0	-	Rep of Ireland
Defenders									
Gerard Aafjes	23	35	26	24	2206	3	0	-	Netherlands
Brian Allison	20	14	2	0	66	0	0	-	Scotland
Darren Barr	23	33	33	31	2907	7	2	-	Scotland
Dean Holden	28	22	20	19	1703	1	0	-	England
Kenny Milne	28	30	28	21	2156	5	0	-	Scotland
Jack Ross	32	27	23	20	1886	4	0	-	Scotland
Thomas Scobbie	20	37	32	29	2617	2	0	-	Scotland
Midfielders									
Scott Arfield	19	37	35	27	2718	3	1	-	England
Stephen Bradley	23	17	3	1	131	0	0	-	Rep of Ireland
Liam Craig	21	13	6	0	98	0	0	-	Scotland
Patrick Cregg	22	37	36	31	3055	3	1	-	Rep of Ireland
Michael Higdon	24	29	28	20	2020	4	0	-	England
Russell Latapy	39	38	32	9	1391	0	0	-	Trinidad & Tobago
Kevin McBride	27	16	15	15	1330	2	0	-	Scotland
Chris Mitchell	19	15	5	3	272	0	0	-	Scotland
Kevin Moffat	19	11	3	0	26	0	0	-	Scotland
Arnau Riera	26	29	19	8	1060	2	1	-	Spain
Steven Thomson	30	18	18	16	1516	0	0	-	Scotland
Forwards									
Graham Barrett	26	36	33	21	2263	4	0	-	Rep of Ireland
Billy Clarke	20	12	8	1	220	2	0	-	Rep of Ireland
Carl Finnigan	21	33	31	17	1730	1	0	-	England
Pedro Moutinho	28	37	37	25	2546	1	0	-	Portugal
Mark Stewart	20	12	3	0	20	0	0	-	Scotland
Roman Wallner	26	9	2	0	35	1	0	-	Austria

TEAM OF THE SEASON

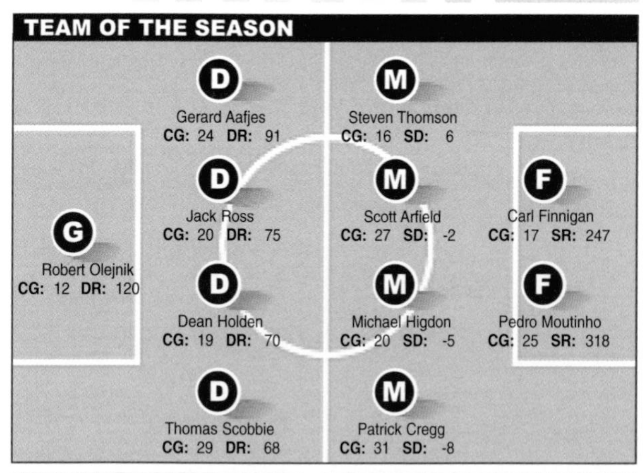

G
Robert Olejnik
CG: 12 DR: 120
D
Gerard Aafjes
CG: 24 DR: 91
D
Jack Ross
CG: 20 DR: 75
D
Dean Holden
CG: 19 DR: 70
D
Thomas Scobbie
CG: 29 DR: 68
M
Steven Thomson
CG: 16 SD: 6
M
Scott Arfield
CG: 27 SD: -2
M
Michael Higdon
CG: 20 SD: -5
M
Patrick Cregg
CG: 31 SD: -8
F
Carl Finnigan
CG: 17 SR: 247
F
Pedro Moutinho
CG: 25 SR: 318

MONTHLY POINTS TALLY

AUGUST	3	25%
SEPTEMBER	4	33%
OCTOBER	2	22%
NOVEMBER	3	50%
DECEMBER	16	76%
JANUARY	4	33%
FEBRUARY	4	33%
MARCH	6	50%
APRIL	1	11%
MAY	6	67%

LEAGUE GOALS

	PLAYER	MINS	GOALS	S RATE
1	Higdon	2020	8	252
2	Moutinho	2546	8	318
3	Finnigan	1730	7	247
4	Barrett, G	2263	6	377
5	Cregg	3055	4	763
6	Arfield	2718	3	906
7	Latapy	1391	2	695
8	Clarke	220	1	220
9	Riera	1060	1	1060
10	Thomson, S	1516	1	1516
11	Milne	2156	1	2156
12	Aafjes	2206	1	2206
13	Scobbie	2617	1	2617
	Other		1	
	TOTAL		**45**	

TOP POINT EARNERS

	PLAYER	GAMES	AV PTS
1	Steven Thomson	16	**1.69**
2	Dean Holden	19	**1.53**
3	Pedro Moutinho	25	**1.52**
4	Michael Higdon	20	**1.50**
5	Gerard Aafjes	24	**1.46**
6	Tim Krul	22	**1.41**
7	Scott Arfield	27	**1.37**
8	Thomas Scobbie	29	**1.28**
9	Patrick Cregg	31	**1.26**
10	Graham Barrett	21	**1.24**
	CLUB AVERAGE:		**1.29**

DISCIPLINARY RECORDS

	PLAYER	YELLOW	RED	AVE
1	Darren Barr	7	2	**323**
2	Arnau Riera	2	1	**353**
3	Kenny Milne	5	0	**431**
4	Jack Ross	4	0	**471**
5	Michael Higdon	4	0	**505**
6	Graham Barrett	4	0	**565**
7	Kevin McBride	2	0	**665**
8	Scott Arfield	3	1	**679**
9	Gerard Aafjes	3	0	**735**
10	Patrick Cregg	3	1	**763**
11	Tim Krul	1	1	**989**
12	Robert Olejnik	1	0	**1081**
13	Thomas Scobbie	2	0	**1308**
	Other	3	0	
	TOTAL	**44**	**6**	

KEY GOALKEEPER

Robert Olejnik

Goals Conceded in the League	9	Counting Games League games when player was on pitch for at least 70 minutes	12
Defensive Rating Ave number of mins between League goals conceded while on the pitch	120	Clean Sheets In League games when player was on pitch for at least 70 minutes	7

KEY PLAYERS - DEFENDERS

Gerard Aafjes

Goals Conceded Number of League goals conceded while the player was on the pitch	24	Clean Sheets In League games when player was on pitch for at least 70 minutes	10
Defensive Rating Ave number of mins between League goals conceded while on the pitch	91	Club Defensive Rating Average number of mins between League goals conceded by the club this season	69

	PLAYER	CON LGE	CLEAN SHEETS	DEF RATE
1	Gerard Aafjes	24	10	91 mins
2	Jack Ross	25	10	75 mins
3	Dean Holden	24	7	70 mins
4	Thomas Scobbie	38	13	68 mins

KEY PLAYERS - MIDFIELDERS

Steven Thomson

Goals in the League	1	Contribution to Attacking Power Average number of minutes between League team goals while on pitch	52
Defensive Rating Average number of mins between League goals conceded while on the pitch	58	Scoring Difference Defensive Rating minus Contribution to Attacking Power	6

	PLAYER	LGE GOALS	DEF RATE	POWER	SCORE DIFF
1	Steven Thomson	1	58	52	6 mins
2	Scott Arfield	3	73	75	-2 mins
3	Michael Higdon	8	67	72	-5 mins
4	Patrick Cregg	4	66	74	-8 mins

KEY PLAYERS - GOALSCORERS

Carl Finnigan

Goals in the League	7	Player Strike Rate Average number of minutes between League goals scored by player	247
Contribution to Attacking Power Average number of minutes between League team goals while on pitch	66	Club Strike Rate Average number of minutes between League goals scored by club	76

	PLAYER	LGE GOALS	POWER	STRIKE RATE
1	Carl Finnigan	7	66	247 mins
2	Michael Higdon	8	72	252 mins
3	Pedro Moutinho	8	67	318 mins
4	Graham Barrett	6	78	377 mins

enta

Michael Higdon

SQUAD APPEARANCES

Match	1	2	3	4	5	6	7	8	9	10	11	12	13	14	15	16	17	18	19	20	21	22	23	24	25	26	27	28	29	30	31	32	33	34	35	36	37	38	39	40	41	42
Venue	A	H	A	H	A	A	H	H	H	A	A	H	A	H	H	A	H	A	A	A	H	H	A	H	H	A	A	H	A	H	A	H	H	A	A	H	A	H	A	H	H	A
Competition	L	L	L	L	O	L	L	L	O	L	L	L	L	L	L	L	L	L	L	L	L	L	L	L	O	L	O	L	L	L	L	L	L	L	L	L	L	L	L	L	L	L
Result	W	L	L	L	W	L	D	W	L	L	L	D	D	W	L	W	W	L	D	W	W	W	W	D	D	L	L	L	L	W	D	L	D	W	D	D	L	D	L	W	W	L

Goalkeepers
Tim Krul
Robert Olejnik
Shane Supple

Defenders
Gerard Aafjes
Brian Allison
Darren Barr
Dean Holden
Kenny Milne
Jack Ross
Thomas Scobbie

Midfielders
Scott Arfield
Stephen Bradley
Liam Craig
Patrick Cregg
Michael Higdon
Russell Latapy
Kevin McBride
Chris Mitchell
Kevin Moffat
Arnau Riera
Steven Thomson

Forwards
Graham Barrett
Billy Clarke
Carl Finnigan
Pedro Moutinho
Mark Stewart
Roman Wallner

KEY: On all match · On bench · Subbed or sent off (Counting game) · Subbed or sent off (playing less than 70 minutes) · Subbed on from bench (Counting Game) · Subbed on (playing less than 70 minutes) · Subbed on and then subbed or sent off (Counting Game) · Subbed on and then subbed or sent off (playing less than 70 minutes) · Not in 16

HEART OF MIDLOTHIAN

Final Position: **8th**

NICKNAME: THE JAM TARTS

KEY: ☐ Won ☐ Drawn ☐ Lost

							Attendance
1	spl	Hibernian	H	L	0-1		16,436
2	spl	Aberdeen	A	D	1-1	Stewart 45	13,134
3	spl	Gretna	H	D	1-1	Driver 73	16,407
4	spl	Celtic	A	L	0-5		57,300
5	sccc2	Stirling	A	W	2-0	Ellis 39 og, L.Kingston 53	2,059
6	spl	Motherwell	A	W	2-0	L.Kingston 24, Velicka 90	5,081
7	spl	Rangers	H	W	4-2	Driver 13, Tall 27, Stewart 66 pen Ivaskevicius 70	15,948
8	spl	Inverness CT	A	L	1-2	Black 34 og	4,918
9	sccc3	Dunfermline	H	W	4-1	Nade 34 pen, Berra 97, Elliot 100, 102	10,500
10	spl	St Mirren	A	W	3-1	Driver 40, Stewart 56, Velicka 83	4,233
11	spl	Falkirk	H	W	4-2	Ksanavicius 5, Zaliukas 27, Velicka 58 Nade 68	15,800
12	spl	Dundee Utd	H	L	1-3	L.Kingston 90	16,661
13	spl	Kilmarnock	A	L	1-3	Tall 90	6,373
14	sccqf	Celtic	A	W	2-0	Velicka 78, 87	21,492
15	spl	Hibernian	A	D	1-1	Nade 46	17,015
16	spl	Aberdeen	H	W	4-1	Driver 3, Velicka 14, Tall 54, Nade 62	17,122
17	spl	Gretna	A	D	1-1	L.Kingston 27	1,544
18	spl	Celtic	H	D	1-1	Velicka 90 pen	16,454
19	spl	Motherwell	H	L	1-2	Driver 12	16,633
20	spl	Rangers	A	L	1-2	Velicka 56	48,392
21	spl	Inverness CT	H	L	2-3	Berra 62, Velicka 90 pen	16,202
22	spl	St Mirren	H	L	0-1		16,476
23	spl	Falkirk	A	L	1-2	Palazuelos 28	6,614
24	spl	Dundee Utd	A	L	1-4	Berra 37	12,100
25	spl	Kilmarnock	H	D	1-1	Velicka 63	14,346
26	scr4	Motherwell	H	D	2-2	Cesnauskis 10, Velicka 52	13,651
27	spl	Hibernian	H	W	1-0	Velicka 20	17,131
28	scr4r	Motherwell	A	L	0-1		8,300
29	spl	Aberdeen	A	W	1-0	Nade 55	14,000
30	slc5	Rangers	A	L	0-2		31,980
31	spl	Gretna	H	W	2-0	Velicka 3, 42 pen	16,138
32	spl	Celtic	A	L	0-3		56,738
33	spl	Motherwell	A	W	1-0	Craigan 12 og	5,925
34	spl	Rangers	H	L	0-4		16,173
35	spl	Inverness CT	A	W	3-0	Karipidis 22, Elliot 33, 47	4,489
36	spl	St Mirren	A	D	1-1	Mikoliunas 87	4,557
37	spl	Falkirk	H	D	0-0		16,682
38	spl	Dundee Utd	H	W	1-0	L.Kingston 27	16,871
39	spl	Kilmarnock	A	D	0-0		5,901
40	spl	St Mirren	H	W	3-2	Jonsson 28, Glen 42, L.Kingston 81	15,269
41	spl	Inverness CT	H	W	1-0	Glen 80	15,423
42	spl	Falkirk	A	L	1-2	Cesnauskis 77	4,638
43	spl	Kilmarnock	H	L	0-2		10,512
44	spl	Gretna	A	L	0-1		1,090

LEAGUE APPEARANCES, BOOKINGS AND CAPS

	AGE (on 01/07/08)	IN NAMED 18	APPEARANCES	COUNTING GAMES	MINUTES ON PITCH	YELLOW CARDS	RED CARDS	CAPS THIS SEASON	NATIONAL SIDE
Goalkeepers									
Steve Banks	36	33	28	28	2520	0	0	-	England
Anthony Basso	28	24	7	7	630	0	0	-	France
Eduardas Kurskis	31	11	3	3	266	1	1	-	Lithuania
Defenders									
Christophe Berra	23	35	35	35	3150	4	0	-	Scotland
Jose Goncalves	22	33	23	21	1972	4	0	-	Portugal
Tomas Kancelskis	32	4	1	1	90	0	0	-	Lithuania
Christos Karipidis	25	21	16	15	1395	1	0	-	Greece
Robbie Neilson	28	33	33	32	2918	7	0	-	Scotland
Ibrahim Tall	27	19	12	11	1048	2	0	-	Senegal
Jason Thomson	20	10	5	5	450	1	0	-	Scotland
Lee Wallace	20	32	21	16	1578	2	1	-	Scotland
Marius Zaliukas	24	33	26	21	1910	6	1	-	Lithuania
Midfielders									
Ricardas Beniussis	28	12	8	1	177	1	0	-	Lithuania
Deividas Cesnauskis	27	17	13	6	765	1	0	-	Lithuania
Andrew Driver	20	25	25	16	1848	3	0	-	Scotland
Gary Glen	18	8	6	3	358	0	1	-	Scotland
Kestutis Ivaskevicius	23	26	17	4	756	3	0	-	Lithuania
Eggert Jonsson	19	31	28	20	2107	5	0	1	Iceland
Laryea Kingston	27	18	18	13	1423	2	0	-	Ghana
Ruben Palazuelos	25	36	29	23	2173	6	0	-	Spain
Fernando Screpis	29	8	5	3	264	0	0	-	Argentina
Michael Stewart	27	28	27	19	2032	5	2	-	Scotland
Forwards									
Calum Elliot	21	29	24	10	1316	5	2	-	Scotland
Audrius Ksanavicius	31	26	22	14	1525	5	0	2	Lithuania
Juho Makela	25	5	5	0	131	0	0	-	Finland
Saulius Mikoliunas	24	29	25	10	1331	5	0	5	Lithuania
Jamie Mole	20	7	6	1	266	1	0	-	England
Christian Nade	23	24	24	9	1361	2	1	-	France
Michal Pospisil	29	11	8	0	135	1	0	-	Czech Republic
Andrius Velicka	29	21	20	11	1326	3	0	2	Lithuania

TEAM OF THE SEASON

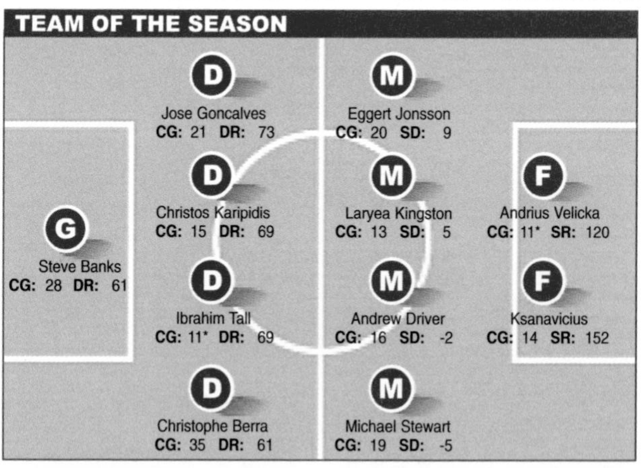
D
Jose Goncalves
CG: 21 DR: 73
M
Eggert Jonsson
CG: 20 SD: 9
D
Christos Karipidis
CG: 15 DR: 69
M
Laryea Kingston
CG: 13 SD: 5
F
Andrius Velicka
CG: 11* SR: 120
G
Steve Banks
CG: 28 DR: 61
D
Ibrahim Tall
CG: 11* DR: 69
M
Andrew Driver
CG: 16 SD: -2
F
Ksanavicius
CG: 14 SR: 152
D
Christophe Berra
CG: 35 DR: 61
M
Michael Stewart
CG: 19 SD: -5

MONTHLY POINTS TALLY

AUGUST	2	17%
SEPTEMBER	9	75%
OCTOBER	3	33%
NOVEMBER	5	56%
DECEMBER	1	6%
JANUARY	7	58%
FEBRUARY	6	50%
MARCH	8	67%
APRIL	7	78%
MAY	0	0%

LEAGUE GOALS

	PLAYER	MINS	GOALS	S RATE
1	Velicka	1326	11	120
2	Kingston, L	1423	5	284
3	Driver	1848	5	369
4	Nade	1361	4	340
5	Tall	1048	3	349
6	Stewart	2032	3	677
7	Glen	358	2	179
8	Elliot	1316	2	658
9	Berra	3150	2	1575
10	Ivaskevicius	756	1	756
11	Cesnauskis	765	1	765
12	Mikoliunas	1331	1	1331
13	Karipidis	1395	1	1395
	Other		4	
	TOTAL		45	

TOP POINT EARNERS

	PLAYER	GAMES	AV PTS
1	Eggert Jonsson	20	1.70
2	Jose Goncalves	21	1.67
3	Christos Karipidis	15	1.53
4	Laryea Kingston	13	1.38
5	Christophe Berra	35	1.37
6	Steve Banks	28	1.36
7	Michael Stewart	19	1.32
8	Ruben Palazuelos	23	1.30
9	Robbie Neilson	32	1.22
10	Audrius Ksanavicius	14	1.21
	CLUB AVERAGE:		1.26

DISCIPLINARY RECORDS

	PLAYER	YELLOW	RED	AVE
1	Calum Elliot	5	2	188
2	Kestutis Ivaskevicius	3	0	252
3	Saulius Mikoliunas	5	0	266
4	Marius Zaliukas	6	1	272
5	Michael Stewart	5	2	290
6	Audrius Ksanavicius	5	0	305
7	Ruben Palazuelos	6	0	362
8	Robbie Neilson	7	0	416
9	Eggert Jonsson	5	0	421
10	Andrius Velicka	3	0	442
11	Christian Nade	2	1	453
12	Jose Goncalves	4	0	493
13	Ibrahim Tall	2	0	524
	Other	13	1	
	TOTAL	71	7	

KEY GOALKEEPER

Steve Banks

Goals Conceded in the League	41	Counting Games League games when player was on pitch for at least 70 minutes	28
Defensive Rating Ave number of mins between League goals conceded while on the pitch	61	Clean Sheets In League games when player was on pitch for at least 70 minutes	8

KEY PLAYERS - DEFENDERS

Jose Goncalves

Goals Conceded Number of League goals conceded while the player was on the pitch	27	Clean Sheets In League games when player was on pitch for at least 70 minutes	8
Defensive Rating Ave number of mins between League goals conceded while on the pitch	73	Club Defensive Rating Average number of mins between League goals conceded by the club this season	62

	PLAYER	CON LGE	CLEAN SHEETS	DEF RATE
1	Jose Goncalves	27	8	73 mins
2	Christos Karipidis	20	6	69 mins
3	Ibrahim Tall	15	2	69 mins
4	Christophe Berra	51	10	61 mins

KEY PLAYERS - MIDFIELDERS

Eggert Jonsson

Goals in the League	1	Contribution to Attacking Power Average number of minutes between League team goals while on pitch	63
Defensive Rating Average number of mins between League goals conceded while on the pitch	72	Scoring Difference Defensive Rating minus Contribution to Attacking Power	9

	PLAYER	LGE GOALS	DEF RATE	POWER	SCORE DIFF
1	Eggert Jonsson	1	72	63	9 mins
2	Laryea Kingston	5	64	59	5 mins
3	Andrew Driver	5	57	59	-2 mins
4	Michael Stewart	3	65	70	-5 mins

KEY PLAYERS - GOALSCORERS

Andrius Velicka

Goals in the League	11	Player Strike Rate Average number of minutes between League goals scored by player	120
Contribution to Attacking Power Average number of minutes between League team goals while on pitch	60	Club Strike Rate Average number of minutes between League goals scored by club	72

	PLAYER	LGE GOALS	POWER	STRIKE RATE
1	Andrius Velicka	11	60	120 mins
2	Laryea Kingston	5	59	284 mins
3	Andrew Driver	5	59	369 mins
4	Michael Stewart	3	70	677 mins

Christian Nade

SQUAD APPEARANCES

Match	1	2	3	4	5	6	7	8	9	10	11	12	13	14	15	16	17	18	19	20	21	22
Venue	H	A	H	A	A	A	H	A	H	A	H	H	A	A	A	H	A	H	H	A	H	H
Competition	L	L	L	L	O	L	L	L	O	L	L	L	L	O	L	L	L	L	L	L	L	L
Result	L	D	D	L	W	W	W	L	W	W	W	L	L	W	D	W	D	D	L	L	L	L

Match	23	24	25	26	27	28	29	30	31	32	33	34	35	36	37	38	39	40	41	42	43	44
Venue	A	A	H	H	H	A	A	A	H	A	A	H	A	A	H	H	A	H	H	A	H	A
Competition	L	L	L	O	L	O	L	O	L	L	L	L	L	L	L	L	L	L	L	L	L	L
Result	L	L	D	D	W	L	W	L	W	L	W	L	W	D	D	W	D	W	W	L	L	L

Goalkeepers
Steve Banks
Anthony Basso
Eduardas Kurskis

Defenders
Christophe Berra
Jose Goncalves
Tomas Kancelskis
Christos Karipidis
Robbie Neilson
Ibrahim Tall
Jason Thomson
Lee Wallace
Marius Zaliukas

Midfielders
Ricardas Beniussis
Deividas Cesnauskis
Andrew Driver
Gary Glen
Kestutis Ivaskevicius
Eggert Jonsson
Laryea Kingston
Ruben Palazuelos
Fernando Screpis
Michael Stewart

Forwards
Calum Elliot
Audrius Ksanavicius
Juho Makela
Saulius Mikoliunas
Jamie Mole
Christian Nade
Michal Pospisil
Andrius Velicka

KEY: On all match | On bench | Subbed or sent off (Counting game) | Subbed or sent off (playing less than 70 minutes) | Subbed on from bench (Counting Game) | Subbed on (playing less than 70 minutes) | Subbed on and then subbed or sent off (Counting Game) | Subbed on and then subbed or sent off (playing less than 70 minutes) | Not in 16

INVERNESS CALEDONIAN THISTLE

Final Position: **9th**

NICKNAME: CALEY THISTLE

KEY: ☐Won ☐Drawn ☐Lost

No	Comp	Opponent	H/A	Res	Score	Scorers	Attendance
1	spl	Rangers	H	L	0-3		7,711
2	spl	Motherwell	A	L	1-2	Tokely 82	4,259
3	spl	St Mirren	A	L	1-2	Cowie 58	3,309
4	spl	Dundee Utd	H	L	0-3		4,178
5	sccc2	Arbroath	H	W	3-1	Niculae 34, 74, Wyness 64	1,246
6	spl	Hibernian	A	L	0-1		13,258
7	spl	Celtic	A	L	0-5		56,020
8	spl	Hearts	H	W	2-1	Wyness 64, Brewster 90	4,918
9	sccc3	Gretna	H	W	3-0	Bayne 21, Wilson 67, Wyness 80	1,717
10	spl	Falkirk	H	W	4-2	Wyness 7, 54, Duncan 18, Black 32	4,011
11	spl	Kilmarnock	A	D	2-2	Ford 22 og, Cowie 61	4,456
12	spl	Aberdeen	H	L	1-2	Wyness 58	6,023
13	spl	Gretna	A	W	4-0	Wyness 2 pen, Cowie 31, Wilson 73 McBain 75	1,020
14	sccqf	Aberdeen	A	L	1-4	Bayne 69	7,270
15	spl	Rangers	A	L	0-2		48,898
16	spl	Motherwell	H	L	0-3		3,608
17	spl	St Mirren	H	W	1-0	Cowie 6	3,699
18	spl	Dundee Utd	A	W	1-0	Black 20	5,845
19	spl	Hibernian	H	W	2-0	Niculae 42, 78	4,224
20	spl	Celtic	H	W	3-2	Rankin 42 pen, Proctor 57, Cowie 61	7,004
21	spl	Hearts	A	W	3-2	Duncan 22, Rankin 53 pen, Bayne 90	16,202
22	spl	Falkirk	A	L	0-1		5,265
23	spl	Kilmarnock	H	W	3-1	Niculae 42, 76, Cowie 52	4,169
24	spl	Aberdeen	A	L	0-1		13,372
25	spl	Gretna	H	W	3-0	Niculae 34, 43, Rankin 40 pen	3,919
26	scr4	Hibernian	A	L	0-3		12,578
27	spl	Rangers	H	L	0-1		7,753
28	spl	St Mirren	A	D	1-1	Munro 28	3,609
29	spl	Dundee Utd	H	D	1-1	Markus.Paatelainen 84	4,087
30	spl	Motherwell	A	L	1-3	Cowie 19	4,526
31	spl	Hibernian	A	L	0-2		12,552
32	spl	Celtic	A	L	1-2	Niculae 70	56,787
33	spl	Hearts	H	L	0-3		4,489
34	spl	Falkirk	H	L	0-1		4,012
35	spl	Kilmarnock	A	L	1-4	Black 14 pen	5,100
36	spl	Aberdeen	H	L	3-4	Bus 21 og, Duncan 40, McBain 57	5,655
37	spl	Gretna	A	W	2-1	McBain 71, Cowie 73	431
38	spl	Kilmarnock	H	W	3-0	Imrie 10, Lilley 71 og, Niculae 79	3,420
39	spl	Hearts	A	L	0-1		15,423
40	spl	Gretna	H	W	6-1	Imrie 1, McAllister 24, Wilson 51, Cowie 70 Tokely 89, Vigurs 90	3,639
41	spl	Falkirk	A	L	1-2	Wilson 90 pen	5,631
42	spl	St Mirren	H	D	0-0		3,783

LEAGUE APPEARANCES, BOOKINGS AND CAPS

	AGE (on 01/07/08)	IN NAMED 18	APPEARANCES	COUNTING GAMES	MINUTES ON PITCH	YELLOW CARDS	RED CARDS	CAPS THIS SEASON	NATIONAL SIDE
Goalkeepers									
Mike Fraser	24	38	36	36	3240	0	0	-	Scotland
Zibigniew Malkowski	30	34	2	2	180	0	0	-	Poland
Defenders									
Richard Hastings	31	35	33	31	2760	4	0	5	Canada
Stuart McCaffrey	29	12	7	6	592	0	0	-	Scotland
Philip McGuire	28	24	24	22	2069	8	0	-	Scotland
Grant Munro	27	33	33	33	2964	2	1	-	Scotland
David Proctor	24	26	21	13	1393	3	2	-	Scotland
Ross Tokely	29	35	35	33	3043	6	1	-	Scotland
Midfielders									
Ian Black	23	35	33	27	2592	6	0	-	Scotland
Don Cowie	25	38	37	33	3098	1	0	-	Scotland
Russell Duncan	27	36	34	32	2944	5	1	-	Scotland
Richard Hart	30	9	7	0	117	0	0	-	Scotland
Guy Kerr	20	24	1	0	5	0	0	-	Scotland
Roy McBain	33	36	33	30	2652	4	0	-	Scotland
Alan Morgan	24	4	3	0	15	0	0	-	Scotland
Markus Paatelainen	25	11	11	3	375	0	0	-	Finland
John Rankin	25	16	15	11	1023	0	0	-	Scotland
Iain Vigurs	20	32	4	0	83	0	0	-	Scotland
Barry Wilson	36	27	25	12	1285	1	0	-	Scotland
Forwards									
Graham Bayne	28	28	26	8	1090	3	1	-	Scotland
Craig Brewster	41	3	2	1	95	0	0	-	Scotland
Douglas Imrie	24	15	15	12	1122	2	0	-	Scotland
Alexander MacDonald	19	5	1	0	5	0	0	-	Scotland
Rory McAllister	21	24	10	1	251	2	0	-	Scotland
Dean McDonald	22	11	4	0	47	0	0	-	England
Marius Niculae	27	35	35	31	2785	2	0	3	Romania
Dennis Wyness	31	31	24	15	1619	1	0	-	Scotland

TEAM OF THE SEASON

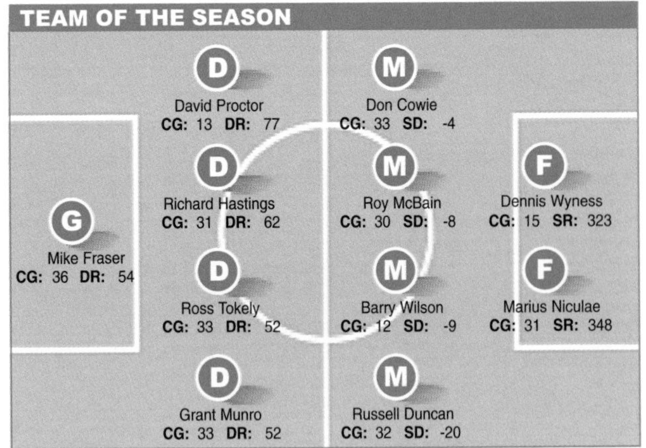

D
David Proctor
CG: 13 DR: 77
M
Don Cowie
CG: 33 SD: -4
D
Richard Hastings
CG: 31 DR: 62
M
Roy McBain
CG: 30 SD: -8
F
Dennis Wyness
CG: 15 SR: 323
G
Mike Fraser
CG: 36 DR: 54
D
Ross Tokely
CG: 33 DR: 52
M
Barry Wilson
CG: 12 SD: -9
F
Marius Niculae
CG: 31 SR: 348
D
Grant Munro
CG: 33 DR: 52
M
Russell Duncan
CG: 32 SD: -20

MONTHLY POINTS TALLY

Month	Points	%
AUGUST	0	0%
SEPTEMBER	6	50%
OCTOBER	4	44%
NOVEMBER	3	33%
DECEMBER	15	83%
JANUARY	3	33%
FEBRUARY	2	13%
MARCH	0	0%
APRIL	6	67%
MAY	4	44%

LEAGUE GOALS

	PLAYER	MINS	GOALS	S RATE
1	Cowie	3098	9	344
2	Niculae	2785	8	348
3	Wyness	1619	5	323
4	Rankin	1023	3	341
5	Wilson	1285	3	428
6	Black	2592	3	864
7	McBain	2652	3	884
8	Duncan	2944	3	981
9	Imrie	1122	2	561
10	Tokely	3043	2	1521
11	Vigurs	83	1	83
12	Brewster	95	1	95
13	McAllister	251	1	251
	Other		4	
	TOTAL		48	

TOP POINT EARNERS

	PLAYER	GAMES	AV PTS
1	David Proctor	13	1.62
2	Dennis Wyness	15	1.53
3	Philip McGuire	22	1.45
4	Barry Wilson	12	1.42
5	Roy McBain	30	1.23
6	Marius Niculae	31	1.23
7	Don Cowie	33	1.21
8	Richard Hastings	31	1.16
9	Ian Black	27	1.11
10	Mike Fraser	36	1.11
	CLUB AVERAGE:		1.13

DISCIPLINARY RECORDS

	PLAYER	YELLOW	RED	AVE
1	Philip McGuire	8	0	258
2	Graham Bayne	3	1	272
3	David Proctor	3	2	278
4	Ian Black	6	0	432
5	Ross Tokely	6	1	434
6	Russell Duncan	5	1	490
7	Douglas Imrie	2	0	561
8	Roy McBain	4	0	663
9	Richard Hastings	4	0	690
10	Grant Munro	2	1	988
11	Barry Wilson	1	0	1285
12	Marius Niculae	2	0	1392
13	Dennis Wyness	1	0	1619
	Other	1	0	
	TOTAL	48	6	

KEY GOALKEEPER

Mike Fraser

Goals Conceded in the League	59	**Counting Games** League games when player was on pitch for at least 70 minutes	36
Defensive Rating Ave number of mins between League goals conceded while on the pitch	54	**Clean Sheets** In League games when player was on pitch for at least 70 minutes	7

KEY PLAYERS - DEFENDERS

David Proctor

Goals Conceded Number of League goals conceded while the player was on the pitch	18	**Clean Sheets** In League games when player was on pitch for at least 70 minutes	5
Defensive Rating Ave number of mins between League goals conceded while on the pitch	77	**Club Defensive Rating** Average number of mins between League goals conceded by the club this season	56

	PLAYER	CON LGE	CLEAN SHEETS	DEF RATE
1	David Proctor	18	5	77 mins
2	Richard Hastings	44	7	62 mins
3	Ross Tokely	58	4	52 mins
4	Grant Munro	56	6	52 mins

KEY PLAYERS - MIDFIELDERS

Don Cowie

Goals in the League	9	**Contribution to Attacking Power** Average number of minutes between League team goals while on pitch	61
Defensive Rating Average number of mins between League goals conceded while on the pitch	57	**Scoring Difference** Defensive Rating minus Contribution to Attacking Power	-4

	PLAYER	LGE GOALS	DEF RATE	POWER	SCORE DIFF
1	Don Cowie	9	57	61	-4 mins
2	Roy McBain	3	56	64	-8 mins
3	Barry Wilson	3	55	64	-9 mins
4	Russell Duncan	3	55	75	-20 mins

KEY PLAYERS - GOALSCORERS

Dennis Wyness

Goals in the League	5	**Player Strike Rate** Average number of minutes between League goals scored by player	323
Contribution to Attacking Power Average number of minutes between League team goals while on pitch	67	**Club Strike Rate** Average number of minutes between League goals scored by club	68

	PLAYER	LGE GOALS	POWER	STRIKE RATE
1	Dennis Wyness	5	67	323 mins
2	Don Cowie	9	61	344 mins
3	Marius Niculae	8	66	348 mins
4	Barry Wilson	3	64	428 mins

flybe.com
Marius Niculae

SQUAD APPEARANCES

Match	1	2	3	4	5	6	7	8	9	10	11	12	13	14	15	16	17	18	19	20	21	22	23	24	25	26	27	28	29	30	31	32	33	34	35	36	37	38	39	40	41	42
Venue	H	A	A	H	H	A	A	H	H	H	A	H	A	A	A	H	H	A	H	H	A	A	H	A	H	A	H	A	H	A	A	A	H	H	A	H	A	H	A	H	A	H
Competition	L	L	L	L	O	L	L	L	O	L	L	L	L	O	L	L	L	L	L	L	L	L	L	L	L	O	L	L	L	L	L	L	L	L	L	L	L	L	L	L	L	L
Result	L	L	L	L	W	L	L	W	W	W	D	L	W	L	L	L	W	W	W	W	W	L	W	L	W	L	L	D	D	L	L	L	L	L	L	L	W	W	L	W	L	D

Goalkeepers
Mike Fraser
Zibigniew Malkowski

Defenders
Richard Hastings
Stuart McCaffrey
Philip McGuire
Grant Munro
David Proctor
Ross Tokely

Midfielders
Ian Black
Don Cowie
Russell Duncan
Richard Hart
Guy Kerr
Roy McBain
Alan Morgan
Markus Paatelainen
John Rankin
Iain Vigurs
Barry Wilson

Forwards
Graham Bayne
Craig Brewster
Douglas Imrie
Alexander MacDonald
Rory McAllister
Dean McDonald
Marius Niculae
Dennis Wyness

KEY: On all match · On bench · Subbed or sent off (Counting game) · Subbed or sent off (playing less than 70 minutes) · Subbed on from bench (Counting Game) · Subbed on (playing less than 70 minutes) · Subbed on and then subbed or sent off (Counting Game) · Subbed on and then subbed or sent off (playing less than 70 minutes) · Not in 16

ST MIRREN

Final Position: **10th**

NICKNAME: BUDDIES/SAINTS

KEY: ☐Won ☐Drawn ☐Lost

							Attendance
1	spl	Motherwell	H	L	0-1		5,257
2	spl	Rangers	A	L	0-2		47,772
3	spl	Inverness CT	H	W	2-1	Miranda 19, Corcoran 55	3,309
4	spl	Falkirk	A	W	1-0	Mehmet 90	5,626
5	sccc2	East Fife	H	L	0-1		1,782
6	spl	Celtic	H	L	1-5	Miranda 75	7,840
7	spl	Dundee Utd	A	L	0-2		6,128
8	spl	Kilmarnock	A	D	0-0		5,596
9	spl	Hearts	H	L	1-3	Corcoran 78	4,233
10	spl	Aberdeen	A	L	0-4		1,284
11	spl	Gretna	H	W	1-0	Mehmet 35	3,646
12	spl	Hibernian	A	W	1-0	Mehmet 13	13,884
13	spl	Motherwell	A	D	1-1	Kean 45	5,123
14	spl	Inverness CT	A	L	0-1		3,699
15	spl	Falkirk	H	L	1-5	Mehmet 50	4,133
16	spl	Celtic	A	D	1-1	McGinn 74	55,747
17	spl	Dundee Utd	H	L	0-3		3,490
18	spl	Kilmarnock	H	D	0-0		4,216
19	spl	Hearts	A	W	1-0	McGinn 17	16,476
20	spl	Aberdeen	H	L	0-1		5,025
21	spl	Hibernian	H	W	2-1	Maxwell 4, Mason 43	4,212
22	scr4	Dumbarton	H	W	3-0	Corcoran 17, Barron 38, Mehmet 70	2,814
23	spl	Motherwell	H	W	3-1	Corcoran 9, Maxwell 38, 49	4,291
24	spl	Rangers	A	L	0-4		49,198
25	scr5	Dundee Utd	H	D	0-0		3,945
26	spl	Inverness CT	H	D	1-1	Mehmet 74	3,609
27	scr5r	Dundee Utd	A	W	1-0	Dorman 48	3,723
28	spl	Falkirk	A	L	0-4		5,803
29	spl	Celtic	H	L	0-1		7,213
30	spl	Dundee Utd	A	D	1-1	Dorman 88	6,037
31	spl	Kilmarnock	A	L	0-1		5,352
32	scpqf	St Johnstone	A	D	1-1	Dorman 73	6,094
33	spl	Hearts	H	D	1-1	Hamilton 59	4,557
34	scqfr	St Johnstone	H	L	1-3	Mehmet 70 pen	4,596
35	spl	Aberdeen	A	D	1-1	Dorman 10	9,779
36	spl	Gretna	H	W	2-0	Dargo 27, Mehmet 49	3,577
37	spl	Hibernian	A	L	0-2		14,000
38	spl	Gretna	A	D	0-0		7,031
39	spl	Hearts	A	L	2-3	McCay 20, Mason 78	15,269
40	spl	Falkirk	H	W	1-0	Dorman 82	3,500
41	spl	Kilmarnock	H	W	1-0	Haining 90	3,690
42	spl	Gretna	H	D	0-0		3,163
43	spl	Inverness CT	A	D	0-0		3,783
44	spl	Rangers	H	L	0-3		7,439

LEAGUE APPEARANCES, BOOKINGS AND CAPS

	AGE (on 01/07/08)	IN NAMED 18	APPEARANCES	COUNTING GAMES	MINUTES ON PITCH	YELLOW CARDS	RED CARDS	CAPS THIS SEASON	NATIONAL SIDE
Goalkeepers									
Mark Howard	21	37	10	10	900	0	0	-	England
Chris Smith	22	36	28	28	2520	3	0	-	Scotland
Defenders									
David Barron	20	28	18	17	1561	4	1	-	Scotland
Will Haining	25	29	29	27	2481	4	2	-	Scotland
Ian Maxwell	33	19	17	16	1483	1	0	-	Scotland
John-Paul Potter	28	38	31	30	2720	4	0	-	Scotland
David van Zanten	26	29	29	29	2610	4	0	-	Rep of Ireland
Midfielders									
Christopher Birchall	24	10	9	3	519	0	0	-	Trinidad & Tobago
Garry Brady	31	30	18	8	1180	1	0	-	Scotland
Richard Brittain	24	15	6	1	251	0	0	-	Scotland
Mark Corcoran	27	33	26	16	1682	2	0	-	Scotland
Andy Dorman	26	19	18	18	1599	2	0	-	Wales
Craig Malloy	22	4	2	0	45	0	0	-	Scotland
Gary Mason	28	31	31	30	2716	5	0	-	Scotland
Ryan McCay	22	32	12	9	867	1	0	-	Scotland
Stephen McGinn	19	38	25	6	1010	3	0	-	Scotland
Andy Millen	43	12	9	8	782	0	0	-	Scotland
Franco Miranda	23	30	24	17	1803	5	1	-	Argentina
Craig Molloy	22	4	3	0	49	0	0	-	Scotland
Hugh Murray	29	30	29	25	2343	12	1	-	Scotland
Stephen O'Donnell	24	15	10	4	481	3	0	-	Scotland
Alan Reid	27	14	12	9	896	0	0	-	Scotland
Forwards									
Alex Burke	30	16	10	4	521	1	0	-	Scotland
Craig Dargo	30	20	16	14	1238	3	0	-	Scotland
Jim Hamilton	32	16	15	6	755	3	0	-	Scotland
Stewart Kean	25	36	32	14	1629	1	0	-	Scotland
Billy Mehmet	24	37	37	28	2815	5	0	-	Rep of Ireland

TEAM OF THE SEASON

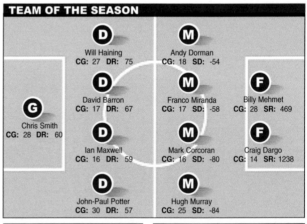

G — Chris Smith — CG: 28 DR: 60

D — Will Haining — CG: 27 DR: 75

D — David Barron — CG: 17 DR: 67

D — Ian Maxwell — CG: 16 DR: 59

D — John-Paul Potter — CG: 30 DR: 57

M — Andy Dorman — CG: 18 SD: -54

M — Franco Miranda — CG: 17 SD: -58

M — Mark Corcoran — CG: 16 SD: -80

M — Hugh Murray — CG: 25 SD: -84

F — Billy Mehmet — CG: 28 SR: 469

F — Craig Dargo — CG: 14 SR: 1238

MONTHLY POINTS TALLY

AUGUST	6	50%
SEPTEMBER	1	8%
OCTOBER	6	67%
NOVEMBER	1	17%
DECEMBER	5	28%
JANUARY	6	67%
FEBRUARY	2	17%
MARCH	5	42%
APRIL	4	33%
MAY	5	42%

LEAGUE GOALS

	PLAYER	MINS	GOALS	S RATE
1	Mehmet	2815	**6**	469
2	Maxwell	1483	**3**	494
3	Dorman	1599	**3**	533
4	Corcoran	1682	**3**	560
5	McGinn	1010	**2**	505
6	Miranda	1803	**2**	901
7	Mason	2716	**2**	1358
8	Hamilton	755	**1**	755
9	McCay	867	**1**	867
10	Dargo	1238	**1**	1238
11	Kean	1629	**1**	1629
12	Haining	2481	**1**	2481
	Other		0	
	TOTAL		**26**	

TOP POINT EARNERS

	PLAYER	GAMES	AV PTS
1	Craig Dargo	14	**1.29**
2	Will Haining	27	**1.26**
3	Billy Mehmet	28	**1.21**
4	Franco Miranda	17	**1.18**
5	Stewart Kean	14	**1.14**
6	David Barron	17	**1.12**
7	Chris Smith	28	**1.11**
8	Gary Mason	30	**1.10**
9	Andy Dorman	18	**1.06**
10	John-Paul Potter	30	**1.03**
	CLUB AVERAGE:		**1.08**

DISCIPLINARY RECORDS

	PLAYER	YELLOW	RED	AVE
1	Stephen O'Donnell	3	0	**160**
2	Hugh Murray	12	1	**180**
3	Jim Hamilton	3	0	**251**
4	Franco Miranda	5	1	**300**
5	David Barron	4	1	**312**
6	Stephen McGinn	3	0	**336**
7	Craig Dargo	3	0	**412**
8	Will Haining	4	2	**413**
9	Alex Burke	1	0	**521**
10	Gary Mason	5	0	**543**
11	Billy Mehmet	5	0	**563**
12	David van Zanten	4	0	**652**
13	John-Paul Potter	4	0	**680**
	Other	11	0	
	TOTAL	**67**	**5**	

KEY GOALKEEPER

Chris Smith

Goals Conceded in the League	42	Counting Games League games when player was on pitch for at least 70 minutes	28
Defensive Rating Ave number of mins between League goals conceded while on the pitch	60	Clean Sheets In League games when player was on pitch for at least 70 minutes	7

KEY PLAYERS - DEFENDERS

Will Haining

Goals Conceded Number of League goals conceded while the player was on the pitch	33	Clean Sheets In League games when player was on pitch for at least 70 minutes	10
Defensive Rating Ave number of mins between League goals conceded while on the pitch	75	Club Defensive Rating Average number of mins between League goals conceded by the club this season	70

	PLAYER	CON LGE	CLEAN SHEETS	DEF RATE
1	Will Haining	33	10	75 mins
2	David Barron	23	5	67 mins
3	Ian Maxwell	25	2	59 mins
4	John-Paul Potter	47	9	57 mins

KEY PLAYERS - MIDFIELDERS

Andy Dorman

Goals in the League	3	Contribution to Attacking Power Average number of minutes between League team goals while on pitch	123
Defensive Rating Average number of mins between League goals conceded while on the pitch	69	Scoring Difference Defensive Rating minus Contribution to Attacking Power	-54

	PLAYER	LGE GOALS	DEF RATE	POWER	SCORE DIFF
1	Andy Dorman	3	69	123	-54 mins
2	Franco Miranda	2	62	120	-58 mins
3	Mark Corcoran	3	49	129	-80 mins
4	Hugh Murray	0	53	137	-84 mins

KEY PLAYERS - GOALSCORERS

Billy Mehmet

Goals in the League	6	Player Strike Rate Average number of minutes between League goals scored by player	469
Contribution to Attacking Power Average number of minutes between League team goals while on pitch	127	Club Strike Rate Average number of minutes between League goals scored by club	145

	PLAYER	LGE GOALS	POWER	STRIKE RATE
1	Billy Mehmet	6	127	469 mins
2	Andy Dorman	3	123	533 mins
3	Mark Corcoran	3	129	560 mins
4	Franco Miranda	2	120	901 mins

hummel
Braehead
SHOPPING CENTRE
Billy Mehmet

SQUAD APPEARANCES

Match	1	2	3	4	5	6	7	8	9	10	11	12	13	14	15	16	17	18	19	20	21	22	23	24	25	26	27	28	29	30	31	32	33	34	35	36	37	38	39	40	41	42	43	44
Venue	H	A	H	A	H	H	A	A	H	A	H	A	A	A	H	A	H	H	A	H	H	H	H	A	H	H	A	A	H	A	A	A	H	H	A	H	A	A	A	H	H	H	A	H
Competition	L	L	L	L	O	L	L	L	L	L	L	L	L	L	L	L	L	L	L	L	L	O	L	L	O	L	O	L	L	L	L	O	L	O	L	L	L	L	L	L	L	L	L	L
Result	L	L	W	W	L	L	L	D	L	L	W	W	D	L	L	D	L	D	W	L	W	W	W	L	D	D	W	L	L	D	L	D	D	L	D	W	L	D	L	W	W	D	D	L

Goalkeepers
Mark Howard
Chris Smith

Defenders
David Barron
Will Haining
Ian Maxwell
John-Paul Potter
David van Zanten

Midfielders
Christopher Birchall
Garry Brady
Richard Brittain
Mark Corcoran
Andy Dorman
Craig Malloy
Gary Mason
Ryan McCay
Stephen McGinn
Andy Millen
Franco Miranda
Craig Molloy
Hugh Murray
Stephen O'Donnell
Alan Reid

Forwards
Alex Burke
Craig Dargo
Jim Hamilton
Stewart Kean
Billy Mehmet

KEY: On all match | Subbed or sent off (Counting game) | Subbed on from bench (Counting Game) | Subbed on and then subbed or sent off (Counting Game) | Not in 16
On bench | Subbed or sent off (playing less than 70 minutes) | Subbed on (playing less than 70 minutes) | Subbed on and then subbed or sent off (playing less than 70 minutes)

KILMARNOCK

Final Position: **11th**

NICKNAME: KILLIE

KEY: ☐Won ☐Drawn ☐Lost

							Attendance
1	spl	Celtic	A	D	0-0		60,000
2	spl	Dundee Utd	H	W	2-1	Gibson 79, Nish 87	5,557
3	spl	Motherwell	A	W	2-1	Lilley 60, Dodds 90	4,985
4	spl	Rangers	H	L	1-2	Invincibile 61	11,544
5	sccc2	Peterhead	A	W	3-0	Nish 30, F.Wright 48, Naismith 55	1,118
6	spl	Aberdeen	H	L	0-1		5,814
7	spl	Gretna	A	W	2-1	Gibson 4, Ryan.Jarvis 36	1,516
8	spl	St Mirren	H	D	0-0		5,596
9	sccc3	Hamilton	A	L	0-2		2,627
10	spl	Hibernian	A	L	1-4	Nish 76	14,500
11	spl	Inverness CT	H	D	2-2	Koudou 1, Nish 56	4,456
12	spl	Falkirk	A	D	1-1	F.Wright 10	5,143
13	spl	Hearts	H	W	3-1	Wales 55, Nish 72 pen, Gibson 77	6,373
14	spl	Celtic	H	L	1-2	F.Wright 55	8,260
15	spl	Dundee Utd	A	L	0-2		6,065
16	spl	Motherwell	H	L	0-1		5,016
17	spl	Rangers	A	L	0-2		48,055
18	spl	Aberdeen	A	L	1-2	Fernandez 27	10,207
19	spl	Gretna	H	D	3-3	Invincibile 27, Fernandez 53, Nish 73	5,122
20	spl	St Mirren	A	D	0-0		4,216
21	spl	Hibernian	H	W	2-1	Nish 36, Taouil 75	6,372
22	spl	Inverness CT	A	L	1-3	Nish 87 pen	4,169
23	spl	Falkirk	H	L	0-1		5,956
24	spl	Hearts	A	D	1-1	Di Giacomo 45	14,346
25	spl	Celtic	A	L	0-1		56,618
26	spl	Dundee Utd	H	L	1-2	Wales 83	4,803
27	scr4	Airdrie Utd	A	W	2-0	Hamill 25, Nish 37 pen	3,258
28	scr5	Celtic	H	L	1-5	Hamill 66	6,491
29	spl	Motherwell	A	L	0-1		6,618
30	spl	Rangers	H	L	0-2		10,546
31	spl	Aberdeen	H	W	3-1	Bryson 14, 75, F.Wright 41	6,113
32	spl	Gretna	A	L	2-4	Ford 72, Gibson 83	1,545
33	spl	St Mirren	H	W	1-0	Invincibile 25	5,352
34	spl	Hibernian	A	L	0-2		12,486
35	spl	Inverness CT	H	W	4-1	F.Wright 38, Bryson 50, 56, Flannigan 64	5,100
36	spl	Falkirk	A	D	0-0		5,134
37	spl	Hearts	H	D	0-0		5,901
38	spl	Inverness CT	A	L	0-3		3,420
39	spl	Gretna	H	D	1-1	Fernandez 57	4,086
40	spl	St Mirren	A	L	0-1		3,690
41	spl	Hearts	A	W	2-0	G.Murray 74, Di Giacomo 83	10,512
42	spl	Falkirk	H	W	2-1	Taouil 24, Di Giacomo 81	5,475

LEAGUE APPEARANCES, BOOKINGS AND CAPS

	AGE (on 01/07/08)	IN NAMED 18	APPEARANCES	COUNTING GAMES	MINUTES ON PITCH	YELLOW CARDS	RED CARDS	CAPS THIS SEASON	NATIONAL SIDE
Goalkeepers									
Alan Combe	34	37	37	37	3330	3	0	-	Scotland
Chad Harpur	25	27	1	1	90	0	0	-	South Africa
Defenders									
Tim Clancy	24	21	11	8	851	2	0	-	Rep of Ireland
Martyn Corrigan	30	8	7	5	548	0	0	-	Scotland
Simon Ford	26	29	28	26	2428	3	0	-	England
James Fowler	27	34	34	33	3000	3	0	-	Scotland
Jamie Hamill	21	38	32	26	2528	6	0	-	Scotland
Garry Hay	30	26	26	25	2299	5	0	-	Scotland
David Lilley	30	25	24	22	2069	3	1	-	Scotland
Grant Murray	32	16	11	9	859	1	0	-	Scotland
Ryan O'Leary	20	31	19	15	1454	2	1	-	Scotland
Fraser Wright	28	26	25	24	2222	8	2	-	Scotland
Midfielders									
Craig Bryson	21	27	19	14	1432	2	0	-	Scotland
Rhian Dodds	28	11	9	3	514	1	0	-	Canada
Iain Flannigan	20	21	8	5	555	0	0	-	Scotland
William Gibson	23	31	23	7	1029	1	0	-	Scotland
Danny Invincibile	29	28	27	25	2352	4	0	-	Australia
Allan Johnston	34	25	22	11	1155	1	0	-	Scotland
Gary Locke	33	26	17	3	690	3	0	-	Scotland
Mehdi Taouil	25	25	22	18	1673	3	0	-	Morocco
Forwards									
Paul Dalglish	31	9	6	2	304	0	0	-	Scotland
Paul Di Giacomo	26	18	10	3	407	1	0	-	Scotland
David Fernandez	32	32	29	12	1486	3	0	-	Spain
Ryan Jarvis	21	12	9	1	314	0	0	-	England
Aime Koudou	31	14	6	1	162	0	0	-	Ivory Coast
Steven Naismith	21	4	4	4	360	1	0	-	Scotland
Colin Nish	27	22	22	19	1845	6	0	-	Scotland
Gary Wales	29	25	24	15	1564	3	0	-	Scotland

TEAM OF THE SEASON

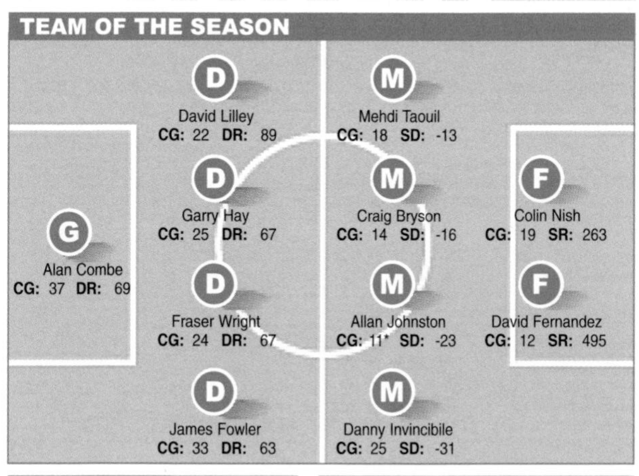

D
David Lilley
CG: 22 DR: 89
M
Mehdi Taouil
CG: 18 SD: -13
D
Garry Hay
CG: 25 DR: 67
M
Craig Bryson
CG: 14 SD: -16
F
Colin Nish
CG: 19 SR: 263
G
Alan Combe
CG: 37 DR: 69
D
Fraser Wright
CG: 24 DR: 67
M
Allan Johnston
CG: 11* SD: -23
F
David Fernandez
CG: 12 SR: 495
D
James Fowler
CG: 33 DR: 63
M
Danny Invincibile
CG: 25 SD: -31

MONTHLY POINTS TALLY

AUGUST	7	58%
SEPTEMBER	4	33%
OCTOBER	5	56%
NOVEMBER	0	0%
DECEMBER	5	28%
JANUARY	1	8%
FEBRUARY	3	25%
MARCH	7	58%
APRIL	2	22%
MAY	6	67%

LEAGUE GOALS

	PLAYER	MINS	GOALS	S RATE
1	Nish	1845	7	263
2	Gibson	1029	4	257
3	Bryson	1432	4	358
4	Wright, F	2222	4	555
5	Di Giacomo	407	3	135
6	Fernandez	1486	3	495
7	Invincibile	2352	3	784
8	Wales	1564	2	782
9	Taouil	1673	2	836
10	Koudou	162	1	162
11	Jarvis, Ryan	314	1	314
12	Dodds	514	1	514
13	Flannigan	555	1	555
	Other		3	
	TOTAL		39	

TOP POINT EARNERS

	PLAYER	GAMES	AV PTS
1	David Lilley	22	1.36
2	David Fernandez	12	1.33
3	Jamie Hamill	26	1.19
4	Colin Nish	19	1.16
5	Craig Bryson	14	1.14
6	Fraser Wright	24	1.13
7	Alan Combe	37	1.08
8	Garry Hay	25	1.08
9	Mehdi Taouil	18	1.06
10	James Fowler	33	1.00
	CLUB AVERAGE:		1.05

DISCIPLINARY RECORDS

	PLAYER	YELLOW	RED	AVE
1	Fraser Wright	8	2	222
2	Gary Locke	3	0	230
3	Colin Nish	6	0	307
4	Jamie Hamill	6	0	421
5	Tim Clancy	2	0	425
6	Garry Hay	5	0	459
7	Ryan O'Leary	2	1	484
8	David Fernandez	3	0	495
9	Rhian Dodds	1	0	514
10	David Lilley	3	1	517
11	Gary Wales	3	0	521
12	Mehdi Taouil	3	0	557
13	Danny Invincibile	4	0	588
	Other	14	0	
	TOTAL	63	4	

KEY GOALKEEPER

Alan Combe

Goals Conceded in the League	48	Counting Games League games when player was on pitch for at least 70 minutes	37
Defensive Rating Ave number of mins between League goals conceded while on the pitch	69	Clean Sheets In League games when player was on pitch for at least 70 minutes	7

KEY PLAYERS - DEFENDERS

David Lilley

Goals Conceded Number of League goals conceded while the player was on the pitch	23	Clean Sheets In League games when player was on pitch for at least 70 minutes	7
Defensive Rating Ave number of mins between League goals conceded while on the pitch	89	Club Defensive Rating Average number of mins between League goals conceded by the club this season	65

	PLAYER	CON LGE	CLEAN SHEETS	DEF RATE
1	David Lilley	23	7	89 mins
2	Garry Hay	34	5	67 mins
3	Fraser Wright	33	5	67 mins
4	James Fowler	47	6	63 mins

KEY PLAYERS - MIDFIELDERS

Mehdi Taouil

Goals in the League	2	Contribution to Attacking Power Average number of minutes between League team goals while on pitch	79
Defensive Rating Average number of mins between League goals conceded while on the pitch	66	Scoring Difference Defensive Rating minus Contribution to Attacking Power	-13

	PLAYER	LGE GOALS	DEF RATE	POWER	SCORE DIFF
1	Mehdi Taouil	2	66	79	-13 mins
2	Craig Bryson	4	68	84	-16 mins
3	Allan Johnston	0	82	105	-23 mins
4	Danny Invincibile	3	63	94	-31 mins

KEY PLAYERS - GOALSCORERS

Colin Nish

Goals in the League	7	Player Strike Rate Average number of minutes between League goals scored by player	263
Contribution to Attacking Power Average number of minutes between League team goals while on pitch	80	Club Strike Rate Average number of minutes between League goals scored by club	87

	PLAYER	LGE GOALS	POWER	STRIKE RATE
1	Colin Nish	7	80	263 mins
2	Craig Bryson	4	84	358 mins
3	David Fernandez	3	74	495 mins
4	Gary Wales	2	97	782 mins

SMALLWORLD
lotto
Danny Invincibile

SQUAD APPEARANCES

Match	1	2	3	4	5	6	7	8	9	10	11	12	13	14	15	16	17	18	19	20	21	22	23	24	25	26	27	28	29	30	31	32	33	34	35	36	37	38	39	40	41	42
Venue	A	H	A	H	A	H	A	H	A	A	H	A	H	H	A	H	A	A	H	A	H	A	H	A	A	H	A	H	A	H	H	A	H	A	H	A	H	A	H	A	A	H
Competition	L	L	L	L	O	L	L	L	O	L	L	L	L	L	L	L	L	L	L	L	L	L	L	L	L	L	O	O	L	L	L	L	L	L	L	L	L	L	L	L	L	L
Result	D	W	W	L	W	L	W	D	L	L	D	D	W	L	L	L	L	L	D	D	W	L	L	D	L	L	W	L	L	L	W	L	W	L	W	D	D	L	D	L	W	W

Goalkeepers
Alan Combe
Chad Harpur

Defenders
Tim Clancy
Martyn Corrigan
Simon Ford
James Fowler
Jamie Hamill
Garry Hay
David Lilley
Grant Murray
Ryan O'Leary
Fraser Wright

Midfielders
Craig Bryson
Rhian Dodds
Iain Flannigan
William Gibson
Danny Invincibile
Allan Johnston
Gary Locke
Mehdi Taouil

Forwards
Paul Dalglish
Paul Di Giacomo
David Fernandez
Ryan Jarvis
Aime Koudou
Steven Naismith
Colin Nish
Gary Wales

KEY: On all match | On bench | Subbed or sent off (Counting game) | Subbed or sent off (playing less than 70 minutes) | Subbed on from bench (Counting Game) | Subbed on (playing less than 70 minutes) | Subbed on and then subbed or sent off (Counting Game) | Subbed on and then subbed or sent off (playing less than 70 minutes) | Not in 16

GRETNA

Final Position: **12th**

NICKNAME: BLACK & WHITES

KEY: ☐Won ☐Drawn ☐Lost

					Result	Scorers	Attendance
1	spl	Falkirk	H	L	0-4		2,731
2	spl	Hibernian	A	L	2-4	Yantorno 17, McMenamin 49	13,795
3	spl	Hearts	A	D	1-1	Barr 79	16,407
4	spl	Motherwell	H	L	1-2	Osman 18	3,758
5	sccc2	Cowdenbeath	H	W	3-1	Barr 52, Yantorno 85, Jenkins 88	342
6	spl	Rangers	A	L	0-4		49,689
7	spl	Kilmarnock	H	L	1-2	Skelton 90	1,516
8	spl	Dundee Utd	H	W	3-2	Cowan 14, 36, Jenkins 86	1,624
9	sccc3	Inverness CT	A	L	0-3		1,717
10	spl	Aberdeen	A	L	0-2		10,279
11	spl	Celtic	H	L	1-2	Yantorno 37	6,011
12	spl	St Mirren	A	L	0-1		3,646
13	spl	Inverness CT	H	L	0-4		1,020
14	spl	Falkirk	A	L	0-2		4,843
15	spl	Hibernian	H	L	0-1		2,666
16	spl	Hearts	H	D	1-1	L.Kingston 49 og	1,544
17	spl	Motherwell	A	L	0-3		6,431
18	spl	Kilmarnock	A	D	3-3	Skelton 5, Grainger 51 pen, Horwood 57	5,122
19	spl	Dundee Utd	A	W	2-1	Deuchar 12, Deverdics 42	6,304
20	spl	Aberdeen	H	D	1-1	Jenkins 90	1,730
21	spl	Celtic	A	L	0-3		57,171
22	spl	Inverness CT	A	L	0-3		3,919
23	scr4	G Morton	A	D	2-2	Yantorno 13, Horwood 49	2,848
24	spl	Rangers	H	L	1-2	Deuchar 46	6,137
25	spl	Falkirk	H	W	2-0	Deuchar 33, P.Murray 50	1,609
26	scr4r	G Morton	H	L	0-3		1,167
27	spl	Hearts	A	L	0-2		16,138
28	spl	Hibernian	A	L	2-4	Skelton 81, Deuchar 88	12,087
29	spl	Motherwell	H	L	1-3	McGill 50	2,877
30	spl	Rangers	A	L	2-4	Deuchar 71, 89	48,375
31	spl	Kilmarnock	H	W	4-2	Deverdics 27, Meynell 39, Barr 44 Buscher 59	1,545
32	spl	Dundee Utd	H	L	0-3		507
33	spl	Aberdeen	A	L	0-3		9,025
34	spl	Celtic	H	L	0-3		3,561
35	spl	St Mirren	A	L	0-2		3,577
36	spl	Inverness CT	H	L	1-2	Barr 80	431
37	spl	St Mirren	H	D	0-0		7,031
38	spl	Falkirk	A	D	0-0		4,490
39	spl	Kilmarnock	A	D	1-1	Barr 74	4,086
40	spl	Inverness CT	A	L	1-6	Hogg 27	3,639
41	spl	St Mirren	A	D	0-0		3,163
42	spl	Hearts	H	W	1-0	Skelton 90	1,090

LEAGUE APPEARANCES, BOOKINGS AND CAPS

	AGE (on 01/07/08)	IN NAMED 18	APPEARANCES	COUNTING GAMES	MINUTES ON PITCH	YELLOW CARDS	RED CARDS	CAPS THIS SEASON	NATIONAL SIDE
Goalkeepers									
Tony Caig	34	12	7	7	630	0	0	-	England
Greg Fleming	21	36	28	27	2492	0	1	-	Scotland
Artur Krysiak	18	13	4	3	297	0	0	-	Poland
Defenders									
Craig Barr	21	31	26	22	2104	9	2	-	Scotland
Aurelien Collin	22	19	19	16	1497	4	0	-	France
David Cowan	26	16	11	7	796	4	0	-	England
Danny Grainger	21	13	10	10	867	2	0	-	England
Daniel Hall	24	15	15	11	1184	2	1	-	England
Evan Horwood	22	15	15	15	1349	3	0	-	England
Chris Innes	31	22	21	21	1890	9	0	-	Scotland
Rhys Meynell	19	16	16	13	1261	2	0	-	England
Kyle Naughton	19	18	18	18	1611	2	0	-	England
Midfielders									
Ryan Baldacchino	27	13	8	3	369	0	0	-	England
Nicky Deverdics	20	33	25	15	1602	0	0	-	England
Rostyn Griffiths	20	16	12	7	797	1	0	-	England
Allan Jenkins	26	22	20	14	1365	0	0	-	Scotland
John Kissock	18	11	11	8	798	0	0	-	Scotland
Brendan McGill	27	31	20	13	1360	0	0	-	Rep of Ireland
Ryan McGuffie	27	9	9	4	534	1	0	-	Scotland
Paul Murray	31	35	32	28	2622	4	0	-	England
Abdul Osman	21	19	18	12	1302	6	0	-	England
Erik Paartalu	22	16	9	3	379	0	0	-	Australia
Gavin Skelton	27	38	38	37	3372	6	0	-	England
Ben Wilkinson	21	15	13	5	606	0	0	-	England
Fabian Yantorno	25	21	21	19	1818	6	0	-	Uruguay
Forwards									
Mickael Buscher	21	20	17	6	823	2	0	-	France
Kenny Deuchar	27	15	15	11	1084	1	0	-	Scotland
James Grady	37	10	8	3	443	1	0	-	Scotland
Henry Makinwa	30	17	13	4	590	0	0	-	Nigeria
Colin McMenamin	27	12	12	7	735	3	0	-	Scotland

TEAM OF THE SEASON

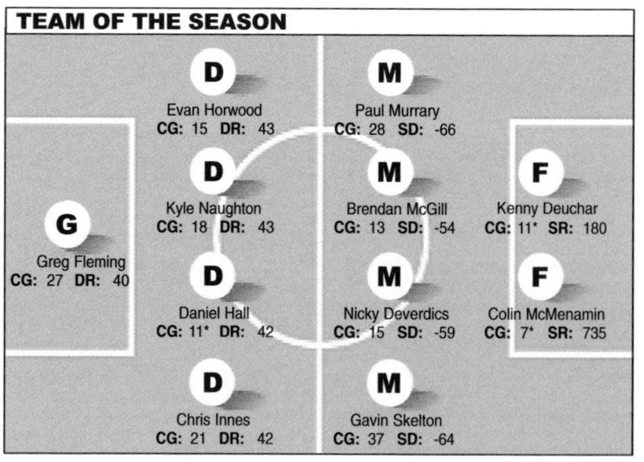

G
Greg Fleming
CG: 27 DR: 40
D
Evan Horwood
CG: 15 DR: 43
D
Kyle Naughton
CG: 18 DR: 43
D
Daniel Hall
CG: 11* DR: 42
D
Chris Innes
CG: 21 DR: 42
M
Paul Murray
CG: 28 SD: -66
M
Brendan McGill
CG: 13 SD: -54
M
Nicky Deverdics
CG: 15 SD: -59
M
Gavin Skelton
CG: 37 SD: -64
F
Kenny Deuchar
CG: 11* SR: 180
F
Colin McMenamin
CG: 7* SR: 735

MONTHLY POINTS TALLY

Month	Points	%
AUGUST	1	8%
SEPTEMBER	3	25%
OCTOBER	0	0%
NOVEMBER	1	11%
DECEMBER	5	33%
JANUARY	3	33%
FEBRUARY	3	20%
MARCH	0	0%
APRIL	3	25%
MAY	4	44%

LEAGUE GOALS

	PLAYER	MINS	GOALS	S RATE
1	Deuchar	1084	**6**	180
2	Barr	2104	**4**	526
3	Skelton	3372	**4**	843
4	Cowan	796	**2**	398
5	Jenkins	1365	**2**	682
6	Deverdics	1602	**2**	801
7	Yantorno	1818	**2**	909
8	Hogg	373	**1**	373
9	McMenamin	735	**1**	735
10	Buscher	823	**1**	823
11	Grainger	867	**1**	867
12	Meynell	1261	**1**	1261
13	Osman	1302	**1**	1302
	Other		3	
	TOTAL		**31**	

TOP POINT EARNERS

	PLAYER	GAMES	AV PTS
1	Nicky Deverdics	15	**1.13**
2	Aurelien Collin	16	**0.81**
3	Chris Innes	21	**0.76**
4	Kyle Naughton	18	**0.72**
5	Brendan McGill	13	**0.69**
6	Rhys Meynell	13	**0.69**
7	Fabian Yantorno	19	**0.63**
8	Gavin Skelton	37	**0.62**
9	Evan Horwood	15	**0.60**
10	Abdul Osman	12	**0.50**
	CLUB AVERAGE:		**0.34**

DISCIPLINARY RECORDS

	PLAYER	YELLOW	RED	AVE
1	Craig Barr	9	2	**191**
2	David Cowan	4	0	**199**
3	Chris Innes	9	0	**210**
4	Abdul Osman	6	0	**217**
5	Colin McMenamin	3	0	**245**
6	Fabian Yantorno	6	0	**303**
7	Aurelien Collin	4	0	**374**
8	Daniel Hall	2	1	**394**
9	Mickael Buscher	2	0	**411**
10	Danny Grainger	2	0	**433**
11	Evan Horwood	3	0	**449**
12	Ryan McGuffie	1	0	**534**
13	Gavin Skelton	6	0	**562**
	Other	10	1	
	TOTAL	**67**	**4**	

KEY GOALKEEPER

Greg Fleming

Goals Conceded in the League	62	Counting Games League games when player was on pitch for at least 70 minutes	27
Defensive Rating Ave number of mins between League goals conceded while on the pitch	40	Clean Sheets In League games when player was on pitch for at least 70 minutes	3

KEY PLAYERS - DEFENDERS

Evan Horwood

Goals Conceded Number of League goals conceded while the player was on the pitch	31	Clean Sheets In League games when player was on pitch for at least 70 minutes	0
Defensive Rating Ave number of mins between League goals conceded while on the pitch	43	Club Defensive Rating Average number of mins between League goals conceded by the club this season	46

	PLAYER	CON LGE	CLEAN SHEETS	DEF RATE
1	Evan Horwood	31	0	43 mins
2	Kyle Naughton	37	5	43 mins
3	Daniel Hall	28	3	42 mins
4	Chris Innes	44	1	42 mins

KEY PLAYERS - MIDFIELDERS

John Kissock

Goals in the League	0	Contribution to Attacking Power Average number of minutes between League team goals while on pitch	88
Defensive Rating Average number of mins between League goals conceded while on the pitch	53	Scoring Difference Defensive Rating minus Contribution to Attacking Power	-35

	PLAYER	LGE GOALS	DEF RATE	POWER	SCORE DIFF
1	John Kissock	0	53	88	-35 mins
2	Brendan McGill	1	43	97	-54 mins
3	Nicky Deverdics	2	47	106	-59 mins
4	Gavin Skelton	4	41	105	-64 mins

KEY PLAYERS - GOALSCORERS

Kenny Deuchar

Goals in the League	6	Player Strike Rate Average number of minutes between League goals scored by player	180
Contribution to Attacking Power Average number of minutes between League team goals while on pitch	72	Club Strike Rate Average number of minutes between League goals scored by club	120

	PLAYER	LGE GOALS	POWER	STRIKE RATE
1	Kenny Deuchar	6	72	180 mins
2	Allan Jenkins	2	105	682 mins
3	Colin McMenamin	1	105	735 mins
4	Nicky Deverdics	2	106	801 mins

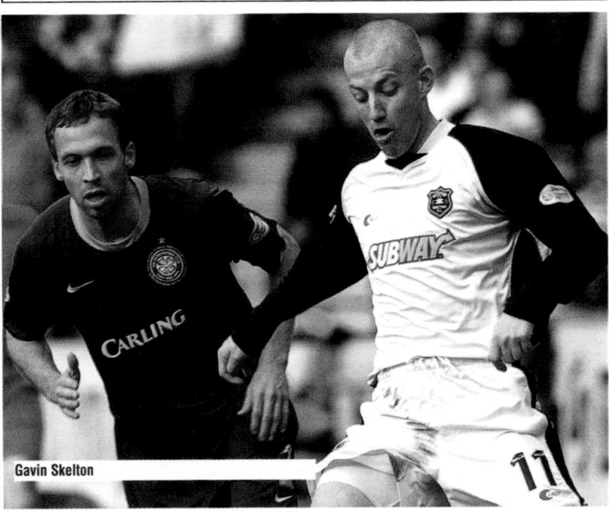
SUBWAY
CARLING
11
Gavin Skelton

SQUAD APPEARANCES

Match	1	2	3	4	5	6	7	8	9	10	11	12	13	14	15	16	17	18	19	20	21	22	23	24	25	26	27	28	29	30	31	32	33	34	35	36	37	38	39	40	41	42
Venue	H	A	A	H	H	A	H	H	A	A	H	A	H	A	H	H	A	A	A	H	A	A	A	H	H	H	A	A	H	A	H	H	A	H	A	H	H	A	A	A	A	H
Competition	L	L	L	L	O	L	L	L	O	L	L	L	L	L	L	L	L	L	L	L	L	L	O	L	L	O	L	L	L	L	L	L	L	L	L	L	L	L	L	L	L	L
Result	L	L	D	L	W	L	L	W	L	L	L	L	L	L	L	D	L	D	W	D	L	L	D	L	W	L	L	L	L	L	W	L	L	L	L	L	D	D	D	L	D	W

Goalkeepers
- Tony Caig
- Greg Fleming
- Artur Krysiak

Defenders
- Craig Barr
- Aurelien Collin
- David Cowan
- Danny Grainger
- Daniel Hall
- Evan Horwood
- Chris Innes
- Rhys Meynell
- Kyle Naughton

Midfielders
- Ryan Baldacchino
- Nicky Deverdics
- Rostyn Griffiths
- Allan Jenkins
- John Kissock
- Brendan McGill
- Ryan McGuffie
- Paul Murray
- Abdul Osman
- Erik Paartalu
- Gavin Skelton
- Ben Wilkinson
- Fabian Yantorno

Forwards
- Mickael Buscher
- Kenny Deuchar
- James Grady
- Henry Makinwa
- Colin McMenamin

KEY: On all match · On bench · Subbed or sent off (Counting game) · Subbed or sent off (playing less than 70 minutes) · Subbed on from bench (Counting Game) · Subbed on (playing less than 70 minutes) · Subbed on and then subbed or sent off (Counting Game) · Subbed on and then subbed or sent off (playing less than 70 minutes) · Not in 16

SPANISH LEAGUE ROUND-UP

FINAL LEAGUE TABLE

		HOME					AWAY					TOTAL			
	P	W	D	L	F	A	W	D	L	F	A	F	A	DIF	PTS
Real Madrid	38	17	0	2	53	18	10	4	5	31	18	84	36	48	85
Villarreal	38	12	5	2	33	15	12	0	7	30	25	63	40	23	77
Barcelona	38	14	2	3	46	12	5	8	6	30	31	76	43	33	67
Atlético Madrid	38	12	2	5	45	26	7	5	7	21	21	66	47	19	64
Sevilla FC	38	13	1	5	46	20	7	3	9	29	29	75	49	26	64
R Santander	38	11	3	5	24	18	6	6	7	18	23	42	41	1	60
Mallorca	38	9	6	4	35	22	6	8	5	34	32	69	54	15	59
Almeria	38	9	5	5	18	14	5	5	9	24	31	42	45	-3	52
Deportivo	38	9	3	7	24	23	6	4	9	22	24	46	47	-1	52
Valencia	38	7	3	9	24	31	8	3	8	24	31	48	62	-14	51
Athletic Bilbao	38	7	8	4	22	14	6	3	10	18	29	40	43	-3	50
Espanyol	38	8	3	8	21	23	5	6	8	22	30	43	53	-10	48
Real Betis	38	7	4	8	27	26	5	7	7	18	25	45	51	-6	47
Getafe	38	7	7	5	24	22	5	4	10	20	26	44	48	-4	47
Valladolid	38	6	9	4	19	18	5	3	11	23	39	42	57	-15	45
Recreativo	38	6	7	6	24	25	5	4	10	16	35	40	60	-20	44
Osasuna	38	8	4	7	25	21	4	3	12	12	23	37	44	-7	43
Real Zaragoza	38	9	7	3	36	24	1	5	13	14	37	50	61	-11	42
Murcia	38	6	4	9	21	26	1	5	13	15	39	36	65	-29	30
Levante	38	5	4	10	22	34	2	1	16	11	41	33	75	-42	26

CLUB STRIKE FORCE

Madrid's Raul and his team celebrate

1 Real Madrid

Goals scored in the League	84
Club Strike Rate (CSR) Average number of minutes between League goals scored by club	40

	CLUB	GOALS	CSR
1	Real Madrid	84	40
2	Sevilla	75	45
3	Barcelona	76	45
4	Mallorca	69	49
5	Atl Madrid	66	51
6	Villarreal	63	54
7	Real Zaragoza	50	68
8	Valencia	48	71
9	Deportivo	46	74
10	Real Betis	45	76
11	Getafe	44	77
12	Espanyol	43	79
13	Almeria	42	81
14	R Santander	42	81
15	Valladolid	42	81
16	Recreativo Huelva	40	85
17	Athl Bilbao	40	85
18	Osasuna	37	92
19	Murcia	36	95
20	Levante	33	103

CLUB DISCIPLINARY RECORDS

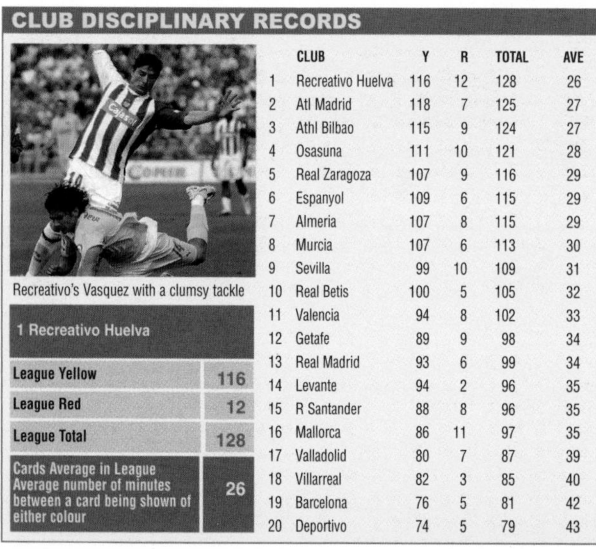

Recreativo's Vasquez with a clumsy tackle

1 Recreativo Huelva

League Yellow	116
League Red	12
League Total	128
Cards Average in League Average number of minutes between a card being shown of either colour	26

	CLUB	Y	R	TOTAL	AVE
1	Recreativo Huelva	116	12	128	26
2	Atl Madrid	118	7	125	27
3	Athl Bilbao	115	9	124	27
4	Osasuna	111	10	121	28
5	Real Zaragoza	107	9	116	29
6	Espanyol	109	6	115	29
7	Almeria	107	8	115	29
8	Murcia	107	6	113	30
9	Sevilla	99	10	109	31
10	Real Betis	100	5	105	32
11	Valencia	94	8	102	33
12	Getafe	89	9	98	34
13	Real Madrid	93	6	99	34
14	Levante	94	2	96	35
15	R Santander	88	8	96	35
16	Mallorca	86	11	97	35
17	Valladolid	80	7	87	39
18	Villarreal	82	3	85	40
19	Barcelona	76	5	81	42
20	Deportivo	74	5	79	43

CLUB DEFENCES

	CLUB	LGE	CS	CDR
1	Real Madrid	36	14	95
2	Villarreal	40	18	85
3	R Santander	41	18	83
4	Athl Bilbao	43	11	79
5	Barcelona	43	14	79
6	Osasuna	44	10	77
7	Almeria	45	13	76
8	Deportivo	47	12	72
9	Atl Madrid	47	16	72
10	Getafe	48	12	71
11	Sevilla	49	11	69
12	Real Betis	51	8	67
13	Espanyol	53	8	64
14	Mallorca	54	7	63
15	Valladolid	57	11	60
16	Recreativo Huelva	60	8	57
17	Real Zaragoza	61	7	56
18	Valencia	62	9	55
19	Murcia	65	8	52
20	Levante	75	4	45

Madrid's Spanish defender Sergio Ramos

1 Real Madrid

Goals conceded in the League	36
Clean Sheets (CS) Number of league games where no goals were conceded	14
Club Defensive Rate (CDR) Average number of minutes between League goals conceded by club	95

PLAYER NATIONALITIES

Overseas country with the most player appearances in the Spanish League - Argentina

864 league appearances by Argentinian players

	COUNTRY	PLAYERS	IN SQUAD	LGE APP	% LGE ACT	CAPS	MOST APP	APP
	Spain	372	8108	6259	60.03	173	Ricardo Lopez Felipe	97.0
1	Argentina	39	1054	864	8.88	55	Fabricio Coloccini	100.0
2	Brazil	30	724	592	5.62	23	Daniel Alves da Silva	86.2
3	France	19	471	389	3.74	40	F Sinama-Pongolle	80.9
4	Uruguay	18	456	328	3.12	4	Jose Caceres	88.1
5	Portugal	17	360	299	2.83	37	J Carlos de Araujo	92.1
6	Italy	12	322	264	2.82	19	Stefano Sorrentino	100.0
7	Mexico	4	118	110	0.89	0	Carlos Alberto Vela	58.5
8	Holland	5	106	89	0.82	30	Wesley Sneijder	66.1
9	Cameroon	4	84	78	0.78	12	Idriss Carlos Kameni	78.9
10	Serbia	4	104	72	0.66	5	Ivica Dragutinovic	58.8
11	Mali	2	65	61	0.64	2	Seydou Keita	73.8
12	Colombia	3	76	60	0.63	1	Luis Amaranto Perea	76.2
13	Germany	4	80	57	0.56	21	Timo Hildebrand	68.4
14	Nigeria	4	109	80	0.48	0	Ikechukwu Uche	46.8
15	Greece	2	53	45	0.42	17	Angelos Basinas	59.6
16	Switzerland	3	79	42	0.40	2	Fabio Celestini	47.4
17	Venezuela	1	38	38	0.40	0	J Fernando Arango	87.7
18	Canada	1	37	35	0.39	0	Julian De Guzman	85.7
19	Sweden	2	50	45	0.38	7	Henok Goitom	51.5
20	Ivory Coast	2	57	46	0.38	0	Yaya Gnegneri Toure	59.9

CLUB MAKE-UP – HOME AND OVERSEAS PLAYERS

1 Sevilla

63.9% of appearances by overseas players

	CLUB	OVERSEAS	HOME	% OVERSEAS	% LGE ACT	MOST APP	APP
1	Sevilla	23	13	63.9	73.00	Daniel Alves	86.2
2	Atl Madrid	19	20	48.7	71.69	Sergio Aguero	86.7
3	Barcelona	17	16	51.5	63.29	Eric Abidal	73.7
4	Real Madrid	16	9	64.0	62.78	Fabio Cannavaro	82.6
5	Villarreal	14	11	56.0	51.79	Robert Pires	63.5
6	Levante	20	15	57.1	50.78	Mustapha Riga	76.7
7	Real Zaragoza	9	21	30.0	46.25	Roberto Ayala	85.6
8	Mallorca	12	16	42.9	45.08	J C de Araujo	92.1
9	Recreativo Huelva	13	14	48.1	44.69	S Sorrentino	100.0
10	Deportivo	9	23	28.1	43.84	F Coloccini	100.0
11	Real Betis	11	19	36.7	41.58	Ricardo	73.7
12	Getafe	9	23	28.1	39.80	R Abbondanzieri	89.5
13	Murcia	10	19	34.5	31.94	Daniel Alonso	57.7
14	Valencia	11	21	34.4	31.30	Emiliano Moretti	72.2
15	R Santander	10	24	29.4	26.08	Aldo Duscher	85.5
16	Osasuna	10	20	33.3	24.97	Jaroslav Plasil	74.4
17	Espanyol	7	21	25.0	24.67	Pablo Zabaleta	79.8
18	Almeria	9	17	34.6	20.49	Felipe Carvalho	76.1
19	Valladolid	7	20	25.9	7.26	Daniel Kome	26.6
20	Athl Bilbao	0	31	-	0.00		0.0

CHART-TOPPING MIDFIELDERS

1 Eguren - Villarreal	
Goals scored in the League	0
Defensive Rating Av number of mins between League goals conceded while on the pitch	245
Contribution to Attacking Power Average number of minutes between League team goals while on pitch	64
Scoring Difference Defensive Rating minus Contribution to Attacking Power	181

	PLAYER	CLUB	GOALS	DEF RATE	POWER	S DIFF
1	Sebastian Eguren	Villarreal	0	245	64	**181**
2	Wesley Sneijder	Real Madrid	9	107	45	**62**
3	Guti	Real Madrid	3	89	37	**52**
4	Andres Iniesta	Barcelona	3	96	49	**47**
5	Mahamadou Diarra	Real Madrid	0	90	43	**47**
6	Fernando Gago	Real Madrid	0	82	35	**47**
7	Xavier Hernandez	Barcelona	7	81	41	**40**
8	Enzo Maresca	Sevilla	1	74	34	**40**
9	Santiago Cazorla	Villarreal	5	96	59	**37**
10	Nuno Ricardo Oliveira	Atl Madrid	2	77	42	**35**
11	Diego Capel Trinidad	Sevilla	3	79	44	**35**
12	Yaya Gnegneri Toure	Barcelona	1	81	49	**32**
13	Miguel Angel (Corona)	Almeria	1	94	63	**31**
14	Simao Sabrosa	Atl Madrid	7	75	45	**30**
15	Jorge Lopez Montana	R Santander	6	108	78	**30**

CHART-TOPPING GOALSCORERS

1 Eto'o - Barcelona	
Goals scored in the League	16
Contribution to Attacking Power (AP) Average number of minutes between League team goals while on pitch	38
Club Strike Rate (CSR) Average minutes between League goals scored by club	45
Player Strike Rate Average number of minutes between League goals scored by player	93

	PLAYER	CLUB	GOALS: LGE	POWER	CSR	S RATE
1	Samuel Eto'o	Barcelona	16	38	45	**93**
2	Luis Fabiano	Sevilla	24	45	46	**96**
3	Daniel Guiza	Mallorca	27	49	49	**111**
4	Nihat Kahveci	Villarreal	18	51	54	**111**
5	Ruud Van Nistelrooy	Real Madrid	16	41	40	**117**
6	David Villa	Valencia	18	60	71	**117**
7	Frederic Kanoute	Sevilla	16	41	46	**136**
8	Ricardo Oliveira	Real Zaragoza	19	66	68	**142**
9	Sergio Aguero	Atl Madrid	20	46	51	**144**
10	Bojan Krkic	Barcelona	10	47	45	**147**
11	Giuseppe Rossi	Villarreal	11	48	54	**160**
12	Raul Gonzalez	Real Madrid	18	42	40	**172**
13	Raul Tamudo	Espanyol	10	82	79	**182**
14	Diego Forlan	Atl Madrid	16	52	51	**183**
15	Diego Milito	Real Zaragoza	15	71	68	**189**

CHART-TOPPING DEFENDERS

1 Rodriguez - Villarreal	
Goals Conceded in the League The number of League goals conceded while he was on the pitch	6
Clean Sheets In games when he played at least 70 mins	11
Club Defensive Rating Average mins between League goals conceded by the club this season	85
Defensive Rating Average number of minutes between League goals conceded while on pitch	254

	PLAYER	CLUB	CON: LGE	CS	CDR	DEF RATE
1	Gonzalo Rodriguez	Villarreal	6	11	85	**254**
2	Rafael Marquez	Barcelona	11	6	79	**136**
3	Gabriel Ivan Heinze	Real Madrid	12	6	95	**122**
4	Santiago Acasiete	Almeria	13	6	76	**115**
5	Pepe	Real Madrid	14	7	95	**109**
6	Alberto Lopo Garcia	Deportivo	18	8	72	**102**
7	Gabriel Milito	Barcelona	22	10	79	**100**
8	Ezequiel Marcelo Garay	R Santander	19	12	83	**100**
9	Pablo Amo Uguado	Deportivo	17	7	72	**99**
10	Oriol Lozano Ferran	R Santander	19	8	83	**97**
11	Sergio Ramos Garcia	Real Madrid	29	11	95	**97**
12	Fabio Cannavaro	Real Madrid	29	12	95	**95**
13	Cesar Cruchaga	Osasuna	25	9	79	**94**
14	Diego Godin Leal	Villarreal	21	10	85	**94**
15	Javier Rodriguez Venta	Villarreal	23	13	85	**94**

CHART-TOPPING GOALKEEPERS

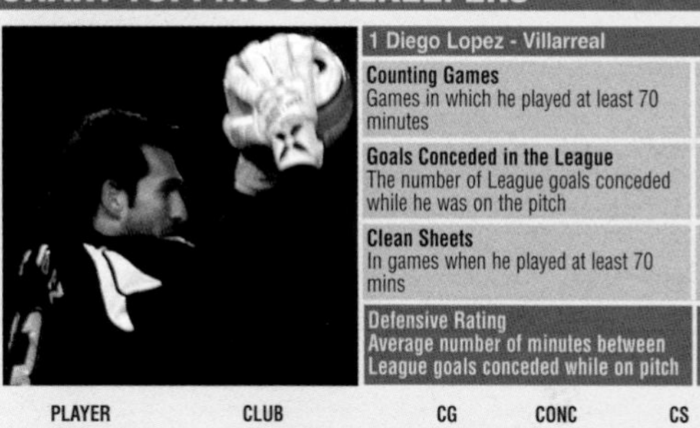

1 Diego Lopez - Villarreal	
Counting Games Games in which he played at least 70 minutes	19
Goals Conceded in the League The number of League goals conceded while he was on the pitch	12
Clean Sheets In games when he played at least 70 mins	11
Defensive Rating Average number of minutes between League goals conceded while on pitch	143

	PLAYER	CLUB	CG	CONC	CS	DEF RATE
1	Diego Lopez	Villarreal	19	12	11	**143**
2	Iker Casillas	Real Madrid	36	32	14	**101**
3	Victor Valdes	Barcelona	35	34	15	**92**
4	Antonio Tono	R Santander	31	31	16	**90**
5	Leo Franco	Atl Madrid	18	18	9	**89**
6	Ricardo Lopez	Osasuna	36	38	11	**85**
7	Dudu Aouate	Deportivo	28	31	10	**81**
8	Gorka Iraizoz Moreno	Athl Bilbao	12	14	3	**80**
9	Diego Alves Carreira	Almeria	21	25	8	**78**
10	Miguel Moya	Mallorca	28	34	6	**75**
11	Sergio Asenjo	Valladolid	24	29	9	**73**
12	David Cobeno	Almeria	16	20	5	**73**
13	Roberto Abbondanzieri	Getafe	34	42	11	**72**
14	Andres Palop	Sevilla	31	41	9	**68**
15	Armando Riveiro	Athl Bilbao	16	21	4	**68**

PLAYER DISCIPLINARY RECORD

Barcelona's Deco pleading with the referee

1. Lopez Gerrard - Recreativo	
Cards Average mins between cards	92
League Yellow	5
League Red	12
TOTAL	6

	PLAYER		LY	LR	TOT	AVE
1	L Gerard	Recreativo	5	1	6	92
2	Deco	Barcelona	11	0	11	112
3	J Urtasun	Osasuna	13	2	15	116
4	Ivan Soto	Deportivo	8	1	9	120
5	Fran Rufete	Espanyol	4	0	4	121
6	E Alvarez	Recreativo	5	1	6	121
7	R Gaspar	Recreativo	12	2	14	122
8	D Camacho	Valladolid	4	0	4	136
9	I de la Pena	Espanyol	5	0	5	140
10	J M Poyan	Real Betis	4	0	4	141
11	M Berson	Levante	10	1	11	147
12	I Barnola	Atl Madrid	5	0	5	149
13	J V Espin	Atl Madrid	2	1	3	150
14	M Salgado	Real Madrid	4	0	4	150
15	Edmilson	Barcelona	2	1	3	151

TEAM OF THE SEASON

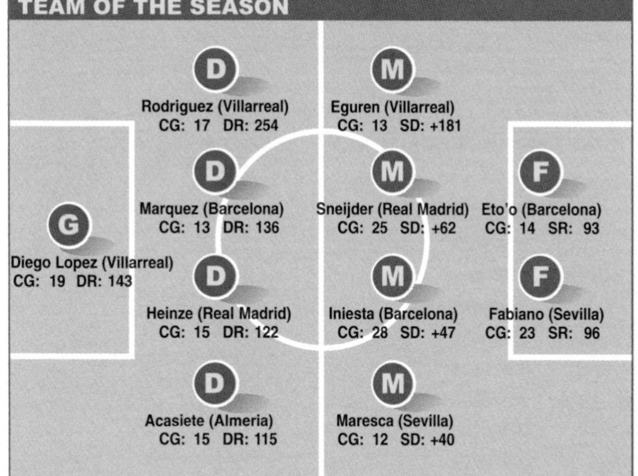
D
Rodriguez (Villarreal)
CG: 17 DR: 254
M
Eguren (Villarreal)
CG: 13 SD: +181
G
Diego Lopez (Villarreal)
CG: 19 DR: 143
D
Marquez (Barcelona)
CG: 13 DR: 136
M
Sneijder (Real Madrid)
CG: 25 SD: +62
F
Eto'o (Barcelona)
CG: 14 SR: 93
D
Heinze (Real Madrid)
CG: 15 DR: 122
M
Iniesta (Barcelona)
CG: 28 SD: +47
F
Fabiano (Sevilla)
CG: 23 SR: 96
D
Acasiete (Almeria)
CG: 15 DR: 115
M
Maresca (Sevilla)
CG: 12 SD: +40

REAL MADRID

Position **1st**

NICKNAME: LOS BLANCOS

KEY: ☐Won ☐Drawn ☐Lost

							Attendance
1	sppr1	**Atl Madrid**	H	W	2-1	Raul 15, Sneijder 80	80,000
2	sppr1	**Villarreal**	A	W	5-0	Raul 38, Sneijder 48, 72, Van Nistelrooy 49 Guti 78	21,000
3	sppr1	**Almeria**	H	W	3-1	Saviola 34, Sneijder 68, Higuain 86	75,000
4	ecgpc	**W Bremen**	H	W	2-1	Raul 16, Van Nistelrooy 74	70,000
5	sppr1	**Valladolid**	A	D	1-1	Saviola 86	27,000
6	sppr1	**Real Betis**	H	W	2-0	Raul 66 pen, Baptista 83	70,400
7	sppr1	**Getafe**	A	W	1-0	Ramos 65	16,150
8	ecgpc	**Lazio**	A	D	2-2	Van Nistelrooy 9, 61	60,000
9	sppr1	**Recreativo**	H	W	2-0	Van Nistelrooy 72, Higuain 90	76,000
10	sppr1	**Espanyol**	A	L	1-2	Ramos 90	50,400
11	ecgpc	**Olympiakos**	H	W	4-2	Raul 2, Robinho 68, 83, Balboa 90	60,000
12	sppr1	**Deportivo**	H	W	3-1	Van Nistelrooy 8 pen, Raul 79 Robinho 89	69,600
13	sppr1	**Valencia**	A	W	5-1	Raul 1, Van Nistelrooy 24, 36 Ramos 29, Robinho 61	40,000
14	sppr1	**Sevilla**	A	L	0-2		45,532
15	ecgpc	**Olympiakos**	A	D	0-0		33,000
16	sppr1	**Mallorca**	H	W	4-3	Robinho 11, 16, Raul 62 Van Nistelrooy 72	77,600
17	sppr1	**Murcia**	A	D	1-1	Robinho 9	31,100
18	ecgpc	**W Bremen**	A	L	2-3	Robinho 14, Van Nistelrooy 71	36,350
19	sppr1	**R Santander**	H	W	3-1	Raul 4, 70, Sanchez Ortega 10 og	68,000
20	sppr1	**Athl Bilbao**	A	W	1-0	Van Nistelrooy 55	40,000
21	ecgpc	**Lazio**	H	W	3-1	Baptista 13, Raul 15, Robinho 36	76,000
22	sppr1	**Osasuna**	H	W	2-0	Van Nistelrooy 16, Sneijder 76	70,400
23	sppr1	**Barcelona**	A	W	1-0	Baptista 36	98,700
24	sppr1	**Real Zaragoza**	H	W	2-0	Van Nistelrooy 66, Robinho 77	72,800
25	sppr1	**Levante**	A	W	2-0	Van Nistelrooy 75 pen, 87	15,000
26	sppr1	**Atl Madrid**	A	W	2-0	Raul 1, Van Nistelrooy 41	56,001
27	sppr1	**Villarreal**	H	W	3-2	Robinho 9, 53, Sneijder 77	79,200
28	sppr1	**Almeria**	A	L	0-2		20,900
29	sppr1	**Valladolid**	H	W	7-0	Baptista 8, Raul 30, 38 pen, Robben 33 Guti 43, 62, Drenthe 80	78,400
30	sppr1	**Real Betis**	A	L	1-2	Drenthe 7	47,850
31	eckl1	**Roma**	A	L	1-2	Gonzalez Blanco 8	52,000
32	sppr1	**Getafe**	H	L	0-1		69,600
33	sppr1	**Recreativo**	A	W	3-2	Raul 27, Robinho 74, 90	20,600
34	eckl2	**Roma**	H	L	1-2	Raul 75	75,000
35	sppr1	**Espanyol**	H	W	2-1	Higuain 43, Raul 72 pen	72,000
36	sppr1	**Deportivo**	A	L	0-1		31,140
37	sppr1	**Valencia**	H	L	2-3	Raul 34, 55	70,000
38	sppr1	**Sevilla**	H	W	3-1	Heinze 8, Raul 39, Higuain 65	76,000
39	sppr1	**Mallorca**	A	D	1-1	Sneijder 43	19,635
40	sppr1	**Murcia**	H	W	1-0	Sneijder 59	76,000
41	sppr1	**R Santander**	A	W	2-0	Raul 13, Higuain 90	22,251
42	sppr1	**Athl Bilbao**	H	W	3-0	Saviola 14, Robben 74, Higuain 76	76,000
43	sppr1	**Osasuna**	A	W	2-1	Robben 87, Higuain 89	19,750
44	sppr1	**Barcelona**	H	W	4-1	Raul 12, Robben 20, Higuain 63 Van Nistelrooy 77 pen	80,000
45	sppr1	**Real Zaragoza**	A	D	2-2	Van Nistelrooy 26, Robinho 77	34,155
46	sppr1	**Levante**	H	W	5-2	Van Nistelrooy 23, 41, Ramos 28, 78 Sneijder 54	72,000

LEAGUE APPEARANCES, BOOKINGS AND CAPS

	AGE (on 01/07/08)	IN NAMED 18	APPEARANCES	COUNTING GAMES	MINUTES ON PITCH	YELLOW CARDS	RED CARDS	CAPS THIS SEASON	NATIONAL SIDE
Goalkeepers									
Iker Casillas	27	36	36	36	3240	2	0	10	Spain
Jordi Codina	26	7	1	1	90	0	0	-	Spain
Jerzy Dudek	35	33	1	1	90	0	0	-	Poland
Defenders									
Fabio Cannavaro	34	33	33	28	2781	6	1	8	Italy
Royston Drenthe	21	26	18	3	739	1	0	-	Holland
Gabriel Ivan Heinze	30	25	20	15	1469	6	0	4	Argentina
Pepe	25	20	19	16	1535	5	0	6	Portugal
Christoph Metzelder	27	14	9	7	704	1	0	12	Germany
Sergio Ramos Garcia	22	33	33	29	2815	14	3	12	Spain
Miguell Salgado	32	19	8	6	603	4	0	-	Spain
Miguel Torres Gomez	22	27	20	13	1285	3	1	-	Spain
Marcelo	20	33	24	23	2109	8	0	-	Brazil
Midfielders									
Javier Balboa Osa	23	15	5	0	58	0	0	-	Guinea
Julio Cesar Baptista	26	35	27	8	1163	2	0	4	Brazil
Mahamadou Diarra	27	34	30	24	2255	4	0	2	Mali
Fernando Gago	22	36	31	20	1976	6	0	8	Argentina
Guti	31	33	32	27	2493	8	1	-	Spain
Arjen Robben	24	24	21	10	1182	4	0	6	Holland
Wesley Sneijder	24	31	30	25	2262	8	0	12	Holland
Forwards									
Robinho	24	34	32	20	2148	3	0	7	Brazil
Raul Gonzalez	31	37	37	34	3110	3	0	-	Spain
Gonzalo Higuain	20	31	25	5	886	2	0	-	France
Javier Saviola	26	27	9	2	388	0	0	1	Argentina
Roberto Soldado	23	14	5	0	125	0	0	2	Spain
Ruud Van Nistelrooy	32	25	24	20	1886	2	0	9	Holland

TEAM OF THE SEASON

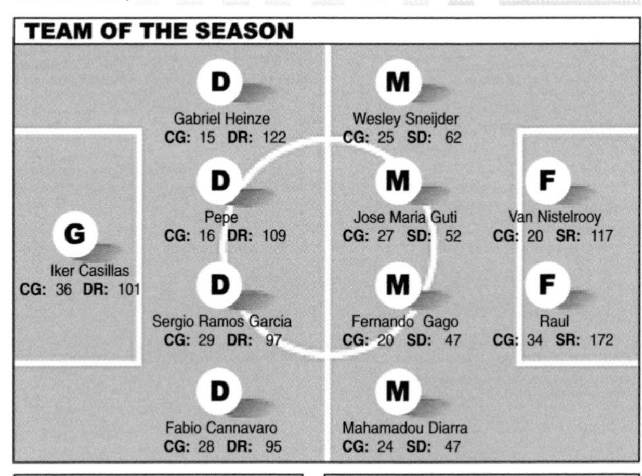

G
Iker Casillas
CG: 36 DR: 101
D
Gabriel Heinze
CG: 15 DR: 122
D
Pepe
CG: 16 DR: 109
D
Sergio Ramos Garcia
CG: 29 DR: 97
D
Fabio Cannavaro
CG: 28 DR: 95
M
Wesley Sneijder
CG: 25 SD: 62
M
Jose Maria Guti
CG: 27 SD: 52
M
Fernando Gago
CG: 20 SD: 47
M
Mahamadou Diarra
CG: 24 SD: 47
F
Van Nistelrooy
CG: 20 SR: 117
F
Raul
CG: 34 SR: 172

MONTHLY POINTS TALLY

AUGUST	3	100%
SEPTEMBER	13	87%
OCTOBER	9	75%
NOVEMBER	4	44%
DECEMBER	12	100%
JANUARY	12	100%
FEBRUARY	3	25%
MARCH	9	60%
APRIL	10	83%
MAY	10	83%

LEAGUE GOALS

	PLAYER	MINS	GOALS	S RATE
1	Raul	3110	**18**	172
2	Van Nistelrooy	1886	**16**	117
3	Robinho	2148	**11**	195
4	Sneijder	2262	**9**	251
5	Higuain	886	**8**	110
6	Sergio Ramos	2815	**5**	563
7	Robben	1182	**4**	295
8	Saviola	388	**3**	129
9	Baptista	1163	**3**	387
10	Jose Maria Guti	2493	**3**	831
11	Drenthe	739	**2**	369
12	Heinze	1469	**1**	1469
	Other		0	
	TOTAL		**83**	

TOP POINT EARNERS

	PLAYER	GAMES	AV PTS
1	Pepe	16	**2.50**
2	Wesley Sneijder	25	**2.48**
3	Gabriel Ivan Heinze	15	**2.47**
4	Fernando Ruben Gago	20	**2.35**
5	Robinho	20	**2.35**
6	Miguel Torres Gomez	13	**2.31**
7	Sergio Ramos	29	**2.28**
8	Mahamadou Diarra	24	**2.25**
9	Iker Casillas Fernandez	36	**2.25**
10	Ruud Van Nistelrooy	20	**2.25**
	CLUB AVERAGE:		**2.24**

DISCIPLINARY RECORDS

	PLAYER	YELLOW	RED	AVE
1	Miguel Salgado	4	0	**150**
2	Sergio Ramos	14	3	**165**
3	Gabriel Ivan Heinze	6	0	**244**
4	Marcelo	8	0	**263**
5	Jose Maria Guti	8	1	**277**
6	Wesley Sneijder	8	0	**282**
7	Arjen Robben	4	0	**295**
8	Pepe	5	0	**307**
9	Miguel Torres	3	1	**321**
10	Fernando R Gago	6	0	**329**
11	Fabio Cannavaro	6	1	**397**
12	Gonzalo G Higuain	2	0	**443**
13	Mahamadou Diarra	4	0	**563**
	Other	14	0	
	TOTAL	**92**	**6**	

KEY GOALKEEPER

Iker Casillas

Goals Conceded in the League	32	Counting Games League games when player was on pitch for at least 70 minutes	36
Defensive Rating Ave number of mins between League goals conceded while on the pitch	101	Clean Sheets In League games when player was on pitch for at least 70 minutes	14

KEY PLAYERS - DEFENDERS

Gabriel Ivan Heinze

Goals Conceded Number of League goals conceded while the player was on the pitch	12	Clean Sheets In League games when player was on pitch for at least 70 minutes	6
Defensive Rating Ave number of mins between League goals conceded while on the pitch	122	Club Defensive Rating Average number of mins between League goals conceded by the club this season	95

	PLAYER	CON LGE	CLEAN SHEETS	DEF RATE
1	Gabriel Ivan Heinze	12	6	**122 mins**
2	Pepe	14	7	**109 mins**
3	Sergio Ramos	29	11	**97 mins**
4	Fabio Cannavaro	29	12	**95 mins**

KEY PLAYERS - MIDFIELDERS

Wesley Sneijder

Goals in the League	9	Contribution to Attacking Power Average number of minutes between League team goals while on pitch	45
Defensive Rating Average number of mins between League goals conceded while on the pitch	107	Scoring Difference Defensive Rating minus Contribution to Attacking Power	62

	PLAYER	LGE GOALS	DEF RATE	POWER	SCORE DIFF
1	Wesley Sneijder	9	107	45	**62 mins**
2	Jose Maria Gutierrez	3	89	37	**52 mins**
3	Fernando Ruben Gago	0	82	35	**47 mins**
4	Mahamadou Diarra	0	90	43	**47 mins**

KEY PLAYERS - GOALSCORERS

Ruud Van Nistelrooy

Goals in the League	16	Player Strike Rate Average number of minutes between League goals scored by player	117
Contribution to Attacking Power Average number of minutes between League team goals while on pitch	41	Club Strike Rate Average number of minutes between League goals scored by club	40

	PLAYER	LGE GOALS	POWER	STRIKE RATE
1	Ruud Van Nistelrooy	16	41	**117 mins**
2	Raul	18	42	**172 mins**
3	Robinho	11	39	**195 mins**
4	Wesley Sneijder	9	45	**251 mins**

bwin.com
Gonzalez Raul

SQUAD APPEARANCES

Match	1	2	3	4	5	6	7	8	9	10	11	12	13	14	15	16	17	18	19	20	21	22	23	24	25	26	27	28	29	30	31	32	33	34	35	36	37	38	39	40	41	42	43	44	45	46
Venue	H	A	H	H	A	H	A	A	H	A	H	H	A	A	A	H	A	A	H	A	H	H	A	H	A	A	H	A	H	A	A	H	A	H	H	A	H	H	A	H	A	H	A	H	A	H
Competition	L	L	L	C	L	L	L	C	L	L	C	L	L	L	C	L	L	C	L	L	C	L	L	L	L	L	L	L	L	L	C	L	L	C	L	L	L	L	L	L	L	L	L	L	L	L
Result	W	W	W	W	D	W	W	D	W	L	W	W	W	L	D	W	D	L	W	W	W	W	W	W	W	W	W	L	W	L	L	L	W	L	W	L	L	W	D	W	W	W	W	W	D	W
Goalkeepers																																														
Iker Casillas																																														
Jordi Codina																																														
Jerzy Dudek																																														
Defenders																																														
Fabio Cannavaro																																														
Royston Drenthe																																														
Gabriel Ivan Heinze																																														
Pepe																																														
Christoph Metzelder																																														
Sergio Ramos Garcia																																														
Miguel Salgado																																														
Miguel Torres Gomez																																														
Marcelo																																														
Midfielders																																														
Javier Balboa Osa																																														
Julio Cesar Baptista																																														
Mahamadou Diarra																																														
Fernando Gago																																														
Jose Maria Guti																																														
Arjen Robben																																														
Wesley Sneijder																																														
Forwards																																														
Robinho																																														
Raul Gonzalez Blanco																																														
Gonzalo Higuain																																														
Javier Saviola																																														
Roberto Soldado																																														
Ruud Van Nistelrooy																																														

KEY: ■ On all match ◀◀ Subbed or sent off (Counting game) ▶▶ Subbed on from bench (Counting Game) ▶▶ Subbed on and then subbed or sent off (Counting Game) □ Not in 16
■ On bench ◀◀ Subbed or sent off (playing less than 70 minutes) ▶▶ Subbed on (playing less than 70 minutes) ▶▶ Subbed on and then subbed or sent off (playing less than 70 minutes)

VILLARREAL

Final Position: **2nd**

NICKNAME: YELLOW SUBMARINES

KEY: ☐Won ☐Drawn ☐Lost

		Opponent	H/A	Res	Score	Scorers	Attendance
1	sppr1	**Valencia**	A	W	3-0	Tomasson 16, Rossi 62 pen, Cazorla 70	52,500
2	sppr1	**Real Madrid**	H	L	0-5		21,000
3	sppr1	**Mallorca**	A	W	1-0	Kahveci 84	15,015
4	ucrl1	**BATE Borisov**	H	W	4-1	Kahveci 5, 50, Senna da Silva 18 Tomasson 53	15,000
5	sppr1	**Murcia**	H	W	2-0	Rossi 85, 89	20,398
6	sppr1	**R Santander**	A	W	2-0	Kahveci 39, Rossi 77	11,100
7	sppr1	**Athl Bilbao**	H	W	1-0	Fuentes 63	18,000
8	ucrl2	**BATE Borisov**	A	W	2-0	Garcia Calmache 24, Angel 77	6,000
9	sppr1	**Osasuna**	A	L	2-3	Rossi 20, Godin Leal 36	15,840
10	sppr1	**Barcelona**	H	W	3-1	Cazorla Rodriguez 2, Senna 13 pen, 35 pen	19,096
11	ucgpc	**Fiorentina**	H	D	1-1	Capdevila Mendez 85	15,000
12	sppr1	**Real Zaragoza**	A	L	1-4	Pires 81	24,150
13	sppr1	**Levante**	H	W	3-0	Franco 3, Rossi 15 pen, Cygan 37	11,501
14	sppr1	**Atl Madrid**	A	W	4-3	Rossi 31, Fuentes 42, Kahveci 69, 89	54,800
15	ucgpc	**Mlada Boleslav**	A	W	2-1	Kahveci 33, Cazorla Rodriguez 56	5,000
16	sppr1	**Sevilla**	H	W	3-2	Franco 31, 68, Fernandez 86 pen	18,445
17	sppr1	**Almeria**	H	D	1-1	Kahveci 14	15,400
18	sppr1	**Valladolid**	A	L	0-2		18,550
19	ucgpc	**Elfsborg**	H	W	2-0	Tomasson 2, 51	18,231
20	sppr1	**Real Betis**	H	L	0-1		15,190
21	sppr1	**Getafe**	A	W	3-1	Kahveci 16, 79, Cazorla Rodriguez 84	11,050
22	ucgpc	**AEK Athens**	A	W	2-1	Antonio Mavuba 40, Tomasson 69	24,328
23	sppr1	**Recreativo**	H	D	1-1	Kahveci 38	14,539
24	sppr1	**Espanyol**	A	L	0-3		38,640
25	sppr1	**Deportivo**	H	W	4-3	Rossi 30 pen, Kahveci 64, 67 Tomasson 81 pen	19,747
26	sppr1	**Valencia**	H	W	3-0	Pires 6, Capdevila Mendez 63 Kahveci 70	15,190
27	sppr1	**Real Madrid**	A	L	2-3	Rossi 16, Capdevila Mendez 76	79,200
28	sppr1	**Mallorca**	H	D	1-1	Rossi 27 pen	17,794
29	sppr1	**Murcia**	A	W	1-0	Franco 90	23,150
30	ucrl1	**Z St Petersburg**	A	L	0-1		21,500
31	sppr1	**R Santander**	H	D	0-0		15,190
32	ucrl2	**Z St Petersburg**	H	W	2-1	Franco 75, Tomasson 90	15,000
33	sppr1	**Athl Bilbao**	A	W	2-1	Franco 65, Capdevila Mendez 83	28,000
34	sppr1	**Osasuna**	H	D	0-0		19,530
35	sppr1	**Barcelona**	A	W	2-1	Senna 31 pen, Tomasson 81	78,950
36	sppr1	**Real Zaragoza**	H	W	2-0	Kahveci 11, Rossi 65 pen	20,181
37	sppr1	**Levante**	A	W	2-1	Fernandez 27, Franco 83	22,770
38	sppr1	**Atl Madrid**	H	W	3-0	Cazorla Rodriguez 39, Kahveci 43, 66	19,530
39	sppr1	**Sevilla**	A	L	0-2		45,500
40	sppr1	**Almeria**	A	L	0-1		20,680
41	sppr1	**Valladolid**	H	W	2-0	Kahveci 16, Cazorla Rodriguez 47	15,624
42	sppr1	**Real Betis**	A	W	1-0	Senna da Silva 16	44,000
43	sppr1	**Getafe**	H	W	2-0	Kahveci 36, 43	19,530
44	sppr1	**Recreativo**	A	W	2-0	Kahveci 53, Franco 82	19,500
45	sppr1	**Espanyol**	H	W	2-0	Rodriguez Venta 30, Pires 42	15,624
46	sppr1	**Deportivo**	A	W	2-0	Fernandez 34, Franco 90	24,500

LEAGUE APPEARANCES, BOOKINGS AND CAPS

	AGE (on 01/07/08)	IN NAMED 18	APPEARANCES	COUNTING GAMES	MINUTES ON PITCH	YELLOW CARDS	RED CARDS	CAPS THIS SEASON	NATIONAL SIDE
Goalkeepers									
Diego L Rodriguez	26	37	20	19	1725	2	1	-	Spain
Juan Carlos Martinez	20	3	1	1	75	0	0	-	Spain
Sebastian Viera	25	36	18	18	1620	1	0	-	Uruguay
Defenders									
Joan Capdevila	30	36	36	36	3239	6	1	2	Spain
Pascal Cygan	34	33	22	19	1765	3	0	-	France
Fabricio Fuentes	31	19	18	17	1572	3	1	-	Argentina
Diego Godin Leal	22	35	23	22	1978	4	0	8	Uruguay
Jose Miguel Rey	28	26	1	1	90	0	0	-	Spain
Angel D Ruano	27	31	19	16	1504	6	0	1	Spain
Gonzalo J Rodriguez	24	19	18	17	1528	3	0	1	Argentina
Javier Rodriguez	32	34	26	23	2162	2	0	-	Spain
Midfielders									
Santiago Cazorla	23	37	36	25	2609	3	0	2	Spain
Sebastian Eguren	27	16	15	13	1226	8	0	-	Uruguay
Matias Fernandez	22	34	30	7	1251	1	0	6	Chile
Ruben G Calmache	26	35	32	12	1573	6	0	-	Spain
Rio Antonio Mavuba	24	13	5	1	222	0	0	-	France
Jose Joaquin Verdu	33	20	13	7	823	0	0	-	Spain
Robert Pires	34	37	32	21	2170	1	0	-	France
Marcos Senna	31	35	34	32	2917	9	0	4	Spain
Bruno Soriano Llido	24	33	21	10	1255	5	0	-	Spain
Forwards									
Guillermo Franco	31	28	23	11	1442	7	0	-	Mexico
Nihat Kahveci	28	36	33	19	2008	3	0	8	Turkey
Antonio M Nunes	21	0	0	0	0	0	0	-	Portugal
Giuseppe Rossi	21	30	27	15	1763	7	0	-	Italy
Jon Dahl Tomasson	31	33	25	2	934	2	0	7	Denmark

TEAM OF THE SEASON

G Diego L Rodriguez — CG: 19 DR: 143

D Gonzalo Rodriguez — CG: 17 DR: 254

D Diego Godin Leal — CG: 22 DR: 94

D Javier Rodriguez Venta — CG: 23 DR: 94

D Juan Capdevila — CG: 36 DR: 83

M Sebastian Eguren — CG: 13 SD: 181

M Santiago Cazorla — CG: 25 SD: 37

M Robert Pires — CG: 21 SD: 26

M Marcos Senna — CG: 32 SD: 24

F Nihat Kahveci — CG: 19 SR: 111

F Giuseppe Rossi — CG: 15 SR: 160

MONTHLY POINTS TALLY

Month	Points	%
AUGUST	3	100%
SEPTEMBER	12	80%
OCTOBER	6	50%
NOVEMBER	7	78%
DECEMBER	4	33%
JANUARY	6	50%
FEBRUARY	8	67%
MARCH	13	87%
APRIL	6	50%
MAY	12	100%

LEAGUE GOALS

	PLAYER	MINS	GOALS	S RATE
1	Kahveci	2008	**18**	111
2	Rossi	1763	**11**	160
3	Franco	1442	**8**	180
4	Cazorla	2609	**5**	521
5	Marcos Senna	2917	**4**	729
6	Tomasson	934	**3**	311
7	Fernandez	1251	**3**	417
8	Pires	2170	**3**	723
9	Capdevila	3239	**3**	1079
10	Fuentes	1572	**2**	786
11	Cygan	1765	**1**	1765
12	Godin Leal	1978	**1**	1978
13	Rodriguez	2162	**1**	2162
	Other		0	
	TOTAL		**63**	

TOP POINT EARNERS

	PLAYER	GAMES	AV PTS
1	Sebastian Eguren	13	**2.62**
2	Gonzalo Rodriguez	17	**2.29**
3	Diego Lopez Rodriguez	19	**2.26**
4	Ruben Garcia Calmache	12	**2.25**
5	Nihat	19	**2.21**
6	Giuseppe Rossi	15	**2.13**
7	Juan Capdevila	36	**2.11**
8	Robert Pires	21	**2.10**
9	Marcos Senna	32	**2.06**
10	Santiago Cazorla	25	**2.04**
	CLUB AVERAGE:		**2.03**

DISCIPLINARY RECORDS

	PLAYER	YELLOW	RED	AVE
1	Sebastian Eguren	8	0	**153**
2	Guillermo Franco	7	0	**206**
3	Angel D Ruano	6	0	**250**
4	Giuseppe Rossi	7	0	**251**
5	Bruno S Llido	5	0	**251**
6	Ruben G Calmache	6	0	**262**
7	Marcos Senna	9	0	**324**
8	Fabricio Fuentes	3	1	**393**
9	Juan Capdevila	6	1	**462**
10	Jon Dahl Tomasson	2	0	**467**
11	Diego Godin Leal	4	0	**494**
12	Gonzalo Rodriguez	3	0	**509**
13	Diego Lopez	2	1	**575**
	Other	14	0	
	TOTAL	**82**	**3**	

KEY GOALKEEPER

Diego Lopez Rodriguez

Goals Conceded in the League	12	**Counting Games** League games when player was on pitch for at least 70 minutes	19
Defensive Rating Ave number of mins between League goals conceded while on the pitch	143	**Clean Sheets** In League games when player was on pitch for at least 70 minutes	11

KEY PLAYERS - DEFENDERS

Gonzalo Javier Rodriguez

Goals Conceded Number of League goals conceded while the player was on the pitch	6	**Clean Sheets** In League games when player was on pitch for at least 70 minutes	11
Defensive Rating Ave number of mins between League goals conceded while on the pitch	254	**Club Defensive Rating** Average number of mins between League goals conceded by the club this season	85

	PLAYER	CON LGE	CLEAN SHEETS	DEF RATE
1	Gonzalo Javier Rodriguez	6	11	254 mins
2	Diego Godin Leal	21	10	94 mins
3	Javier Rodriguez Venta	23	13	94 mins
4	Juan Capdevila	39	17	83 mins

KEY PLAYERS - MIDFIELDERS

Sebastian Eguren

Goals in the League	0	**Contribution to Attacking Power** Average number of minutes between League team goals while on pitch	64
Defensive Rating Average number of mins between League goals conceded while on the pitch	245	**Scoring Difference** Defensive Rating minus Contribution to Attacking Power	181

	PLAYER	LGE GOALS	DEF RATE	POWER	SCORE DIFF
1	Sebastian Eguren	0	245	64	181 mins
2	Santiago Cazorla	5	96	59	37 mins
3	Robert Pires	3	77	51	26 mins
4	Marcos Senna	4	76	52	24 mins

KEY PLAYERS - GOALSCORERS

Nihat Kahveci

Goals in the League	18	**Player Strike Rate** Average number of minutes between League goals scored by player	111
Contribution to Attacking Power Average number of minutes between League team goals while on pitch	51	**Club Strike Rate** Average number of minutes between League goals scored by club	54

	PLAYER	LGE GOALS	POWER	STRIKE RATE
1	Nihat Kahveci	18	51	111 mins
2	Giuseppe Rossi	11	48	160 mins
3	Santiago Cazorla	5	59	521 mins
4	Robert Pires	3	51	723 mins

AEROPORT
CASTELLO
Marcos Senna and Joan Capdevila

SQUAD APPEARANCES

Match	1	2	3	4	5	6	7	8	9	10	11	12	13	14	15	16	17	18	19	20	21	22	23	24	25	26	27	28	29	30	31	32	33	34	35	36	37	38	39	40	41	42	43	44	45	46
Venue	A	H	A	H	H	A	H	A	A	H	H	A	H	A	A	H	H	A	H	H	A	A	H	A	H	H	A	H	A	A	H	H	A	H	A	H	A	H	A	A	H	A	H	A	H	A
Competition	L	L	L	E	L	L	L	E	L	L	E	L	L	L	E	L	L	L	E	L	L	E	L	L	L	L	L	L	L	E	L	E	L	L	L	L	L	L	L	L	L	L	L	L	L	L
Result	W	L	W	W	W	W	W	W	L	W	D	L	W	W	W	W	D	L	W	L	W	W	D	L	W	W	L	D	W	L	D	W	W	D	W	W	W	W	L	L	W	W	W	W	W	W

Goalkeepers
Diego L Rodriguez
Juan Carlos Martinez
Sebastian Viera

Defenders
Joan Capdevila
Pascal Cygan
Fabricio Fuentes
Diego Godin Leal
Jose Miguel Rey
Angel Domingo Ruano
Gonzalo Javier Rodriguez
Javier Rodriguez

Midfielders
Santiago Cazorla
Sebastian Eguren
Matias Fernandez
Ruben Garcia Calmache
Rio Antonio Mavuba
Jose Joaquin Verdu
Robert Pires
Marcos Senna
Bruno Soriano Llido

Forwards
Guillermo Franco
Nihat Kahveci
Antonio Manuel Ferreira
Giuseppe Rossi
Jon Dahl Tomasson

KEY: On all match | On bench | Subbed or sent off (Counting game) | Subbed or sent off (playing less than 70 minutes) | Subbed on from bench (Counting Game) | Subbed on (playing less than 70 minutes) | Subbed on and then subbed or sent off (Counting Game) | Subbed on and then subbed or sent off (playing less than 70 minutes) | Not in 16

BARCELONA

Final Position: **3rd**

NICKNAME: BARCA

KEY: ☐Won ☐Drawn ☐Lost

							Attendance
1	sppr1	**R Santander**	A	D	0-0		22,100
2	sppr1	**Athl Bilbao**	H	W	3-1	De Assis Moreira 8, 34 pen, Toure 72	76,817
3	sppr1	**Osasuna**	A	D	0-0		17,820
4	ecgpe	**Lyon**	H	W	3-0	Clerc 21 og, Messi 82, Henry 90	90,000
5	sppr1	**Sevilla**	H	W	2-1	Messi 73, 79 pen	98,772
6	sppr1	**Real Zaragoza**	H	W	4-1	Messi 5, 10, Iniesta 21 Marquez 45	75,000
7	sppr1	**Levante**	A	W	4-1	Henry 16, 23, 48, Messi 50	25,360
8	ecgpe	**Stuttgart**	A	W	2-0	Puyol 53, Messi 68	51,300
9	sppr1	**Atl Madrid**	H	W	3-0	Deco 15, Messi 19, Xavi 89	89,876
10	sppr1	**Villarreal**	A	L	1-3	Bojan 25	19,096
11	ecgpe	**Rangers**	A	D	0-0		49,957
12	sppr1	**Almeria**	H	W	2-0	Henry 37, Messi 80 pen	92,778
13	sppr1	**Valladolid**	A	D	1-1	Ronaldinho 42	22,525
14	sppr1	**Real Betis**	H	W	3-0	Henry 32, Ronaldinho 52, 91	83,895
15	ecgpe	**Rangers**	H	W	2-0	Henry 6, Messi 43	80,000
16	sppr1	**Getafe**	A	L	0-2		17,000
17	sppr1	**Recreativo**	H	W	3-0	Milito 64, Bojan 66, Messi 82 pen	88,830
18	ecgpe	**Lyon**	A	D	2-2	Iniesta 3, Messi 58 pen	38,000
19	sppr1	**Espanyol**	A	D	1-1	Iniesta 6	44,800
20	sppr1	**Deportivo**	H	W	2-1	Ronaldinho 40 pen, Xavi 71	64,155
21	ecgpe	**Stuttgart**	H	W	3-1	Dos Santos 36, Eto'o 58, Ronaldinho 67	60,000
22	sppr1	**Valencia**	A	W	3-0	Eto'o 13, 27, Gudjohnsen 61	55,000
23	sppr1	**Real Madrid**	H	L	0-1		98,700
24	sppr1	**Mallorca**	A	W	2-0	Marquez 63, Eto'o 90	23,100
25	sppr1	**Murcia**	H	W	4-0	Gudjohnsen 27, Bojan 52, Eto'o 77, 87	88,830
26	sppr1	**R Santander**	H	W	1-0	Henry 30	88,830
27	sppr1	**Athl Bilbao**	A	D	1-1	Bojan 34	39,200
28	sppr1	**Osasuna**	H	W	1-0	Xavi 88	90,804
29	sppr1	**Sevilla**	A	D	1-1	Xavi 76	45,500
30	sppr1	**Real Zaragoza**	A	W	2-1	Henry 35, Ronaldinho 83 pen	34,500
31	eckl1	**Celtic**	A	W	3-2	Messi 18, 79, Henry 52	58,345
32	sppr1	**Levante**	H	W	5-1	Xavi 13, Messi 44, Eto'o 55, 61, 87	98,772
33	sppr1	**Atl Madrid**	A	L	2-4	Ronaldinho 30, Eto'o 74	54,800
34	eckl2	**Celtic**	H	W	1-0	Xavi 2	75,002
35	sppr1	**Villarreal**	H	L	1-2	Xavi 67	78,950
36	sppr1	**Almeria**	A	D	2-2	Bojan 17, Eto'o 57	19,800
37	sppr1	**Valladolid**	H	W	4-1	Eto'o 24, Iniesta 47, Bojan 62, 84	88,830
38	sppr1	**Real Betis**	A	L	2-3	Bojan 13, Eto'o 16	51,150
39	ecqfl1	**Schalke**	A	W	1-0	Bojan 12	53,951
40	sppr1	**Getafe**	H	D	0-0		69,090
41	ecqfl2	**Schalke**	H	W	1-0	Toure 43	88,000
42	sppr1	**Recreativo**	A	D	2-2	Eto'o 2, 46	20,600
43	sppr1	**Espanyol**	H	D	0-0		69,090
44	ecsfl1	**Man Utd**	H	D	0-0		96,330
45	sppr1	**Deportivo**	A	L	0-2		27,680
46	ecsfl2	**Man Utd**	A	L	0-1		75,061
47	sppr1	**Valencia**	H	W	6-0	Messi 5 pen, Xavi 8, Henry 14, 57 Bojan 71, 78	71,064
48	sppr1	**Real Madrid**	A	L	1-4	Henry 87	80,000
49	sppr1	**Mallorca**	H	L	2-3	Henry 17, Eto'o Fils 57	65,142
50	sppr1	**Murcia**	A	W	5-3	Eto'o Fils 23, Henry 26 Dos Santos 33, 52, 67	27,990

LEAGUE APPEARANCES, BOOKINGS AND CAPS

	AGE (on 01/07/08)	IN NAMED 18	APPEARANCES	COUNTING GAMES	MINUTES ON PITCH	YELLOW CARDS	RED CARDS	CAPS THIS SEASON	NATIONAL SIDE
Goalkeepers									
Jose M Colorado	32	19	3	3	270	0	0	-	Spain
Victor Valdes	26	38	35	35	3150	2	0	-	Spain
Defenders									
Eric Abidal	28	35	30	27	2520	2	0	11	France
Gabriel Milito	27	29	27	23	2219	6	1	4	Argentina
Rafael Marquez	29	25	23	13	1500	6	1	8	Mexico
Sylvinho	34	29	14	10	960	1	0	-	Brazil
Oleguer Presas	28	23	12	7	736	0	0	-	Spain
Carles Puyol	30	30	30	26	2516	7	0	5	Spain
Lilian Thuram	36	33	18	15	1424	3	0	11	France
Gianluca Zambrotta	31	32	29	20	2113	7	1	8	Italy
Midfielders									
Deco	30	23	18	11	1232	11	0	8	Portugal
Giovani dos Santos	19	33	28	7	1269	2	0	5	Mexico
Yaya Toure	25	27	26	20	2048	7	0	8	Ivory Coast
Jose Edmilson	31	17	11	1	453	2	1	-	Brazil
Xavi Hernandez	28	36	35	31	2927	2	1	9	Spain
Andres Iniesta	24	32	31	28	2615	6	0	9	Spain
Victor Sanchez Mata	20	4	1	0	1	0	0	-	Spain
Forwards									
Ronaldinho	28	19	17	11	1167	1	0	4	Brazil
Samuel Eto'o	27	18	18	14	1495	3	0	6	Cameroon
Santiago Ezquerro	31	15	2	1	96	0	0	-	Spain
Eidur Gudjohnsen	29	33	23	5	996	2	0	9	Iceland
Thierry Henry	30	32	30	22	2338	2	0	7	France
Bojan Krkic	17	33	31	12	1477	1	0	-	Spain
Lionel Andres Messi	21	28	28	18	2001	2	0	6	Argentina
Pedro R Ledesma	20	4	2	0	7	0	0	-	Spain
Victor V Solsona	21	3	1	0	13	0	0	-	Spain

TEAM OF THE SEASON

D
Rafael Marquez
CG: 13 DR: 136
M
Deco
CG: 11* SD: 91
D
Gabriel Milito
CG: 23 DR: 100
M
Andres Iniesta
CG: 28 SD: 47
F
Samuel Eto'o
CG: 14 SR: 93
G
Victor Valdes
CG: 35 DR: 92
D
Gianluca Zambrotta
CG: 20 DR: 91
M
Xavi Hernandez
CG: 31 SD: 40
F
Ronaldinho
CG: 11* SR: 145
D
Lilian Thuram
CG: 15 DR: 79
M
Yaya Toure
CG: 20 SD: 32

MONTHLY POINTS TALLY

AUGUST	1	33%
SEPTEMBER	13	87%
OCTOBER	6	67%
NOVEMBER	7	58%
DECEMBER	7	58%
JANUARY	10	83%
FEBRUARY	10	83%
MARCH	4	27%
APRIL	3	25%
MAY	6	50%

LEAGUE GOALS

	PLAYER	MINS	GOALS	S RATE
1	Eto'o	1495	16	93
2	Henry	2338	12	194
3	Bojan	1477	10	147
4	Messi	2001	10	200
5	Ronaldinho	1167	8	145
6	Xavi	2927	7	418
7	Dos Santos	1269	3	423
8	Iniesta	2615	3	871
9	Gudjohnsen	996	2	498
10	Marquez	1500	2	750
11	Deco	1232	1	1232
12	Toure	2048	1	2048
13	Milito	2219	1	2219
	Other		0	
	TOTAL		76	

TOP POINT EARNERS

	PLAYER	GAMES	AV PTS
1	Rafael Marquezez	13	2.38
2	Lionel Messi	18	2.06
3	Thierry Henry	22	1.91
4	Victor Valdes	35	1.83
5	Xavi Hernandez	31	1.81
6	Andres Iniesta	28	1.79
7	Gianluca Zambrotta	20	1.75
8	Gabriel A Milito	23	1.74
9	Eric Abidal	27	1.67
10	Lilian Thuram	15	1.67
	CLUB AVERAGE:		1.76

DISCIPLINARY RECORDS

	PLAYER	YELLOW	RED	AVE
1	Deco	11	0	112
2	Edmilson	2	1	151
3	Rafael Marquez	6	1	214
4	Gianluca Zambrotta	7	1	264
5	Yaya Toure	7	0	292
6	Gabriel Milito	6	1	317
7	Carles Puyol	7	0	359
8	Andres Iniesta	6	0	435
9	Lilian Thuram	3	0	474
10	Samuel Eto'o	3	0	498
11	Eidur Gudjohnsen	2	0	498
12	Giovani dos Santos	2	0	634
13	Sylvinho	1	0	960
	Other	12	1	
	TOTAL	75	5	

KEY GOALKEEPER

Victor Valdes

Goals Conceded in the League	34	Counting Games League games when player was on pitch for at least 70 minutes	35
Defensive Rating Ave number of mins between League goals conceded while on the pitch	92	Clean Sheets In League games when player was on pitch for at least 70 minutes	15

KEY PLAYERS - DEFENDERS

Rafael Marquez

Goals Conceded Number of League goals conceded while the player was on the pitch	11	Clean Sheets In League games when player was on pitch for at least 70 minutes	6
Defensive Rating Ave number of mins between League goals conceded while on the pitch	136	Club Defensive Rating Average number of mins between League goals conceded by the club this season	79

	PLAYER	CON LGE	CLEAN SHEETS	DEF RATE
1	Rafael Marquez	11	6	136 mins
2	Gabriel Milito	22	10	100 mins
3	Gianluca Zambrotta	23	10	91 mins
4	Lilian Thuram	18	6	79 mins

KEY PLAYERS - MIDFIELDERS

Deco

Goals in the League	1	Contribution to Attacking Power Average number of minutes between League team goals while on pitch	45
Defensive Rating Average number of mins between League goals conceded while on the pitch	136	Scoring Difference Defensive Rating minus Contribution to Attacking Power	91

	PLAYER	LGE GOALS	DEF RATE	POWER	SCORE DIFF
1	Deco	1	136	45	91 mins
2	Andres Iniesta	3	96	49	47 mins
3	Xavi Hernandez	7	81	41	40 mins
4	Yaya Toure	1	81	49	32 mins

KEY PLAYERS - GOALSCORERS

Samuel Eto'o Fils

Goals in the League	16	Player Strike Rate Average number of minutes between League goals scored by player	93
Contribution to Attacking Power Average number of minutes between League team goals while on pitch	38	Club Strike Rate Average number of minutes between League goals scored by club	45

	PLAYER	LGE GOALS	POWER	STRIKE RATE
1	Samuel Eto'o	16	38	93 mins
2	Ronaldinho	8	55	145 mins
3	Bojan Krkic	10	47	147 mins
4	Thierry Henry	12	44	194 mins

Ronaldinho and Samuel Eto'o

SQUAD APPEARANCES

Match	1	2	3	4	5	6	7	8	9	10	11	12	13	14	15	16	17	18	19	20	21	22	23	24	25
Venue	A	H	A	H	H	H	A	A	H	A	A	H	A	H	H	A	H	A	A	H	H	A	H	A	H
Competition	L	L	L	C	L	L	L	C	L	L	C	L	L	L	C	L	L	C	L	L	C	L	L	L	L
Result	D	W	D	W	W	W	W	W	W	L	D	W	D	W	W	L	W	D	D	W	W	W	L	W	W

Match	26	27	28	29	30	31	32	33	34	35	36	37	38	39	40	41	42	43	44	45	46	47	48	49	50
Venue	H	A	H	A	A	A	H	A	H	H	A	H	A	A	H	H	A	H	H	A	A	H	A	H	A
Competition	L	L	L	L	L	C	L	L	C	L	L	L	L	C	L	C	L	L	C	L	C	L	L	L	L
Result	W	D	W	D	W	W	W	L	W	L	D	W	L	W	D	W	D	D	D	L	L	W	L	L	W

Goalkeepers
Jose Manuel Colorado
Victor Valdes

Defenders
Eric Abidal
Gabriel Milito
Rafael Marquez
Sylvinho
Oleguer Presas
Carles Puyol
Lilian Thuram
Gianluca Zambrotta

Midfielders
Deco
Giovani dos Santos
Yaya Toure
Jose Edmilson
Xavi Hernandez
Andres Iniesta
Victor Sanchez Mata

Forwards
Ronaldinho
Samuel Eto'o
Santiago Ezquerro
Eidur Gudjohnsen
Thierry Henry
Bojan Krkic
Lionel Andres Messi
Pedro R Ledesma
Victor V Solsona

KEY: On all match · On bench · Subbed or sent off (Counting game) · Subbed or sent off (playing less than 70 minutes) · Subbed on from bench (Counting Game) · Subbed on (playing less than 70 minutes) · Subbed on and then subbed or sent off (Counting Game) · Subbed on and then subbed or sent off (playing less than 70 minutes) · Not in 16

ATLETICO MADRID

Final Position: **4th**

NICKNAME: LOS INDIOS

KEY: Won / Drawn / Lost

#	Comp	Opponent	Venue	Res	Score	Scorers	Attendance
1	ucql1	**Vojvodina**	H	W	3-0	Rodriguez 38, Forlan 61, Aguero 70	42,000
2	sppr1	**Real Madrid**	A	L	1-2	Aguero 1	80,000
3	ucql2	**Vojvodina**	A	W	2-1	Garcia Sanz 54, Garcia Escudero 75	5,000
4	sppr1	**Mallorca**	H	D	1-1	Andres Pernia 78	40,000
5	sppr1	**Murcia**	A	D	1-1	Leonel Aguero 14	25,000
6	ucrl1	**Erciyesspor**	H	W	4-0	Ferrer Martinez 12, Forlan 17 Garcia Sanz 82, 88	27,500
7	sppr1	**R Santander**	H	W	4-0	Garcia Escudero 12, Aguero 69 Forlan 76, Simao 86	46,580
8	sppr1	**Athl Bilbao**	A	W	2-0	Aguero 12, Forlan 78	38,000
9	sppr1	**Osasuna**	H	W	2-0	Garcia Escudero 38, Aguero 82	40,000
10	ucrl2	**Erciyesspor**	A	W	5-0	Aguero 5, 43, Jurado Marin 12 Rodriguez 52 pen, Forlan 78	27,500
11	sppr1	**Barcelona**	A	L	0-3		89,876
12	sppr1	**Real Zaragoza**	H	W	4-0	Garcia Sanz 10, Forlan 35 Rodriguez 63 pen, 90	43,840
13	ucgpb	**L Moscow**	A	D	3-3	Aguero 16, 85, Forlan 47	10,000
14	sppr1	**Levante**	A	W	1-0	Forlan 26	15,000
15	sppr1	**Sevilla**	H	W	4-3	Oliveira Ribeiro 1, Aguero 17 Rodriguez 69, Jurado Marin 90	41,100
16	sppr1	**Villarreal**	H	L	3-4	Ibanez Tebar 10, Simao 25 Aguero 62	54,800
17	sppr1	**Almeria**	A	D	0-0		19,800
18	sppr1	**Valladolid**	H	W	4-3	Oliveira Ribeiro 2, Rodriguez 49, 55 Lopez Munoz 90 og	45,484
19	ucgpb	**Aberdeen**	H	W	2-0	Forlan 45 pen, Langfield 61 og	25,000
20	sppr1	**Real Betis**	A	W	2-0	Forlan 34, Garcia Escudero 90	46,750
21	ucgpb	**Copenhagen**	A	W	2-0	Simao 21, Aguero 62	33,034
22	sppr1	**Getafe**	H	W	1-0	Forlan 20	52,060
23	sppr1	**Recreativo**	A	D	0-0		16,480
24	ucgpb	**Panathinaikos**	H	W	2-1	Garcia Sanz 74, Simao 90	10,000
25	sppr1	**Espanyol**	H	L	1-2	Simao 37	49,320
26	sppr1	**Deportivo**	A	W	3-0	Forlan 39, Aguero 52, Jurado Marin 64	20,760
27	sppr1	**Valencia**	H	W	1-0	Aguero 28	43,840
28	sppr1	**Real Madrid**	H	L	0-2		56,001
29	sppr1	**Mallorca**	A	L	0-1		19,635
30	sppr1	**Murcia**	H	D	1-1	Garcia Sanz 62	49,320
31	sppr1	**R Santander**	A	W	2-0	Forlan 56, 73	20,646
32	ucrl1	**Bolton**	A	L	0-1		26,163
33	sppr1	**Athl Bilbao**	H	L	1-2	Aguero 5	43,080
34	ucrl2	**Bolton**	H	D	0-0		30,000
35	sppr1	**Osasuna**	A	L	1-3	Forlan 26	11,880
36	sppr1	**Barcelona**	H	W	4-2	Aguero 36, 71, Rodriguez 42 Forlan 62 pen	54,800
37	sppr1	**Real Zaragoza**	A	L	1-2	Simao 25	34,000
38	sppr1	**Levante**	H	W	3-0	Simao 23, Forlan 38, 52	47,676
39	sppr1	**Sevilla**	A	W	2-1	Rodriguez 19, Aguero 58	45,500
40	sppr1	**Villarreal**	A	L	0-3		19,530
41	sppr1	**Almeria**	H	W	6-3	Lopez Guerrero 2, Forlan 5 pen Simao 33, 45, Aguero 54, 70	43,840
42	sppr1	**Valladolid**	A	D	1-1	Rodriguez 70	23,055
43	sppr1	**Real Betis**	H	L	1-3	Aguero 26	46,580
44	sppr1	**Getafe**	A	D	1-1	Aguero 39	14,960
45	sppr1	**Recreativo**	H	W	3-0	Camacho Barnola 22, 74, Aguero 54	52,060
46	sppr1	**Espanyol**	A	W	2-0	Aguero 27, Forlan 30	30,800
47	sppr1	**Deportivo**	H	W	1-0	Forlan 45	53,418
48	sppr1	**Valencia**	A	L	1-3	Aguero 74	41,250

LEAGUE APPEARANCES, BOOKINGS AND CAPS

	AGE (on 01/07/08)	IN NAMED 18	APPEARANCES	COUNTING GAMES	MINUTES ON PITCH	YELLOW CARDS	RED CARDS	CAPS THIS SEASON	NATIONAL SIDE
Goalkeepers									
Christian Abbiati	30	36	21	20	1804	1	0	-	Italy
Ismael G Falcon	24	15	0	0	0	0	0	-	Spain
Leonardo N Franco	31	23	18	18	1616	1	0	-	Argentina
Defenders									
Luis A Perea	29	32	30	28	2607	14	0	1	Colombia
Mariano A Pernia	31	36	29	24	2380	14	1	4	Spain
Fabiano dos Santos	30	25	18	11	1281	4	0	-	Brazil
Pablo Ibanez Tebar	26	35	34	34	3060	13	0	-	Spain
Antonio Lopez	26	37	24	23	2102	9	0	-	Spain
Jose Eduardo Vale	25	23	8	4	553	0	0	-	Portugal
Giourkas Seitaridis	27	18	14	10	1113	6	0	5	Greece
Juan Valera Espin	23	16	8	4	451	2	1	-	Spain
Midfielders									
Ignacio C Barnola	18	14	10	7	747	5	0	-	Spain
Francisco Costinha	33	0	0	0	0	0	0	-	Portugal
Miguel Angel	22	20	13	1	298	1	0	-	Spain
Simao Sabrosa	28	31	30	14	1879	2	0	7	Portugal
Raul Garcia	21	35	35	31	2946	11	1	-	Spain
Luis Javier Garcia	30	37	30	7	1234	0	0	4	Spain
Jose Manuel Jurado	22	23	16	3	418	0	0	-	Spain
Peter B Luccin	29	0	0	0	0	0	0	-	France
Thiago Motta	25	6	5	3	287	3	0	-	Brazil
Maniche	30	15	14	14	1246	5	0	7	Portugal
Jose Antonio Reyes	24	29	25	6	1108	5	2	-	Spain
Maxi Rodriguez	27	35	35	30	2860	9	0	5	Argentina
Cleber Santana	27	35	23	9	1159	2	0	-	Brazil
Forwards									
Sergio Leonel Aguero	20	37	36	29	2880	9	2	4	Argentina
Miguel A Martinez	29	24	5	0	170	0	0	-	Spain
Diego Forlan	29	36	35	32	2938	1	0	2	Uruguay

TEAM OF THE SEASON

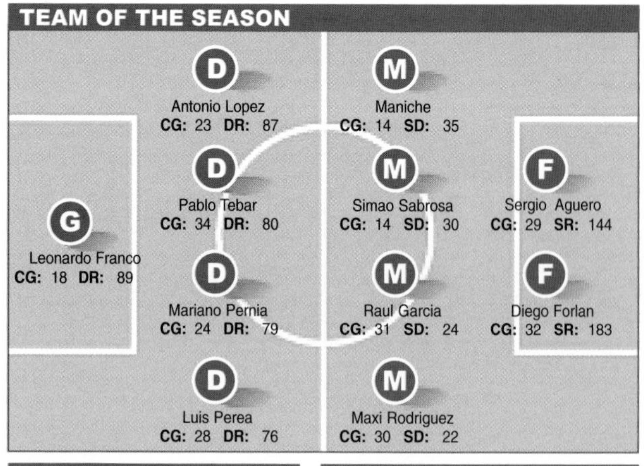

G
Leonardo Franco
CG: 18 DR: 89
D
Antonio Lopez
CG: 23 DR: 87
D
Pablo Tebar
CG: 34 DR: 80
D
Mariano Pernia
CG: 24 DR: 79
D
Luis Perea
CG: 28 DR: 76
M
Maniche
CG: 14 SD: 35
M
Simao Sabrosa
CG: 14 SD: 30
M
Raul Garcia
CG: 31 SD: 24
M
Maxi Rodriguez
CG: 30 SD: 22
F
Sergio Aguero
CG: 29 SR: 144
F
Diego Forlan
CG: 32 SR: 183

MONTHLY POINTS TALLY

Month	Points	%
AUGUST	0	0%
SEPTEMBER	11	73%
OCTOBER	9	75%
NOVEMBER	4	44%
DECEMBER	7	58%
JANUARY	6	50%
FEBRUARY	4	33%
MARCH	9	60%
APRIL	5	42%
MAY	9	75%

LEAGUE GOALS

	PLAYER	MINS	GOALS	S RATE
1	Aguero	2880	20	144
2	Forlan	2938	16	183
3	Rodriguez	2860	8	357
4	Simao	1879	7	268
5	Escudero	2946	3	982
6	Jurado Marin	418	2	209
7	C Barnola	747	2	373
8	Garcia Sanz	1234	2	617
9	Maniche	1246	2	623
10	Lopez Guerrero	2102	1	2102
11	Pernia	2380	1	2380
12	Tebar	3060	1	3060
	Other		0	
	TOTAL		65	

TOP POINT EARNERS

	PLAYER	GAMES	AV PTS
1	Maniche	14	2.07
2	Antonio L Guerrero	23	1.96
3	Leonardo N Franco	18	1.94
4	Sergio Aguero	29	1.93
5	Mariano Andres Pernia	24	1.88
6	Raul Garcia Escudero	31	1.74
7	Maxi Rodriguez	30	1.73
8	Pablo Tebar	34	1.71
9	Simao Sabrosa	14	1.71
10	Diego Forlan	32	1.66
	CLUB AVERAGE:		1.68

DISCIPLINARY RECORDS

	PLAYER	YELLOW	RED	AVE
1	Ignacio C Barnola	5	0	149
2	Juan Valera Espin	2	1	150
3	Mariano A Pernia	14	1	158
4	Jose A Reyes	5	2	158
5	Giourkas Seitaridis	6	0	185
6	Luis A Perea	14	0	186
7	Antonio L Guerrero	9	0	233
8	Pablo Tebar	13	0	235
9	Raul G Escudero	11	1	245
10	Maniche	5	0	249
11	Sergio L Aguero	9	2	261
12	Maxi Rodriguez	9	0	317
13	Fabiano dos Santos	4	0	320
	Other	7	0	
	TOTAL	113	7	

KEY GOALKEEPER

Leonardo Franco

Goals Conceded in the League	18	Counting Games League games when player was on pitch for at least 70 minutes	18
Defensive Rating Ave number of mins between League goals conceded while on the pitch	89	Clean Sheets In League games when player was on pitch for at least 70 minutes	9

KEY PLAYERS - DEFENDERS

Antonio Lopez

Goals Conceded Number of League goals conceded while the player was on the pitch	24	Clean Sheets In League games when player was on pitch for at least 70 minutes	12
Defensive Rating Ave number of mins between League goals conceded while on the pitch	87	Club Defensive Rating Average number of mins between League goals conceded by the club this season	72

	PLAYER	CON LGE	CLEAN SHEETS	DEF RATE
1	Antonio Lopez	24	12	87 mins
2	Pablo Tebar	38	15	80 mins
3	Mariano Andres Pernia	30	10	79 mins
4	Luis Amaranto Perea	34	11	76 mins

KEY PLAYERS - MIDFIELDERS

Maniche

Goals in the League	2	Contribution to Attacking Power Average number of minutes between League team goals while on pitch	42
Defensive Rating Average number of mins between League goals conceded while on the pitch	77	Scoring Difference Defensive Rating minus Contribution to Attacking Power	35

	PLAYER	LGE GOALS	DEF RATE	POWER	SCORE DIFF
1	Maniche	2	77	42	35 mins
2	Simao Pedro Fonseca Sabrosa	7	75	45	30 mins
3	Raul Garcia	3	70	46	24 mins
4	Maximiliano R Rodriguez	8	73	51	22 mins

KEY PLAYERS - GOALSCORERS

Sergio Leonel Aguero

Goals in the League	20	Player Strike Rate Average number of minutes between League goals scored by player	144
Contribution to Attacking Power Average number of minutes between League team goals while on pitch	46	Club Strike Rate Average number of minutes between League goals scored by club	51

	PLAYER	LGE GOALS	POWER	STRIKE RATE
1	Sergio Leonel Aguero	20	46	144 mins
2	Diego Forlan	16	52	183 mins
3	Simao Sabrosa	7	45	268 mins
4	Maximiliano R Rodriguez	8	51	357 mins

Diego Forlan

SQUAD APPEARANCES

Match	1	2	3	4	5	6	7	8	9	10	11	12	13	14	15	16	17	18	19	20	21	22	23	24	25	26	27	28	29	30	31	32	33	34	35	36	37	38	39	40	41	42	43	44	45	46	47	48
Venue	H	A	A	H	A	H	H	A	H	A	A	H	A	A	H	H	A	H	H	A	A	H	A	H	H	A	H	H	A	H	A	A	H	H	A	H	A	H	A	A	H	A	H	A	H	A	H	A
Competition	E	L	E	L	L	E	L	L	L	E	L	L	E	L	L	L	L	L	E	L	E	L	L	E	L	L	L	L	L	L	L	E	L	E	L	L	L	L	L	L	L	L	L	L	L	L	L	L
Result	W	L	W	D	D	W	W	W	W	W	L	W	D	W	W	L	D	W	W	W	W	W	D	W	L	W	W	L	L	D	W	L	L	D	L	W	L	W	W	L	W	D	L	D	W	W	W	L

Goalkeepers
- Christian Abbiati
- Ismael Gomez Falcon
- Leonardo Franco

Defenders
- Luis Amaranto Perea
- Mariano Andres Pernia
- Fabiano dos Santos
- Pablo Ibanez Tebar
- Antonio Lopez Guerrero
- Jose Eduardo Rosa Vale
- Giourkas Seitaridis
- Juan Valera Espin

Midfielders
- Ignacio C Barnola
- Francisco Costinha
- Miguel Angel
- Simao Sabrosa
- Raul Garcia
- Luis Javier Garcia
- Jose Manuel Marin
- Peter Bernard Luccin
- Thiago Motta
- Maniche
- Jose Antonio Reyes
- Maximiliano Rodriguez
- Cleber Santana

Forwards
- Sergio Leonel Aguero
- Miguel Angel Martinez
- Diego Forlan

KEY: On all match · On bench · Subbed or sent off (Counting game) · Subbed or sent off (playing less than 70 minutes) · Subbed on from bench (Counting Game) · Subbed on (playing less than 70 minutes) · Subbed on and then subbed or sent off (Counting Game) · Subbed on and then subbed or sent off (playing less than 70 minutes) · Not in 16

SEVILLA

Final Position: **5th**

NICKNAME: SEVILLISTAS

KEY: □Won □Drawn □Lost

	Comp	Opponent			Score	Scorers	Attendance
1	ecql1	**AEK Athens**	H	W	2-0	Fabiano 48, Kanoute 68	35,000
2	sppr1	**Getafe**	H	W	4-1	Navas Gonzalez 45, Fabiano 68 Kanoute 70, Kerzhakov 83	40,000
3	escup	**AC Milan**	A	L	1-3	Florencio Santos 14	20,000
4	ecql2	**AEK Athens**	A	W	4-1	Fabiano 30 pen, 45, Keita 41 Kerzhakov 53	37,800
5	sppr1	**Recreativo**	H	W	4-1	Kerzhakov 11, 74, Kanoute 30, 53	45,000
6	ecgph	**Arsenal**	A	L	0-3		60,000
7	sppr1	**Barcelona**	A	L	1-2	Kanoute 91	98,772
8	sppr1	**Espanyol**	H	L	2-3	Navas Gonzalez 60, Kone 66	45,000
9	sppr1	**Real Zaragoza**	A	L	0-2		30,000
10	ecgph	**Slavia Prague**	H	W	4-2	Kanoute 8, Fabiano 27, Escude 58 Kone 69	40,000
11	sppr1	**Deportivo**	H	L	0-1		40,040
12	sppr1	**Levante**	A	W	2-0	Fabiano 7, 14 pen	12,650
13	ecgph	**S Bucharest**	H	W	2-1	Kanoute 5, Fabiano 17	40,000
14	sppr1	**Valencia**	H	W	3-0	Kanoute 10, Poulsen 74, Fabiano 86	40,950
15	sppr1	**Atl Madrid**	A	L	3-4	Fabiano 14, 92 Rosa Vale de Castro 45 og	41,100
16	sppr1	**Real Madrid**	H	W	2-0	Keita 18, Fabiano Clemente 21	45,532
17	ecgph	**S Bucharest**	A	W	2-0	Florencio Santos 25, 65	20,000
18	sppr1	**Villarreal**	A	L	2-3	Kanoute 35, Fabiano 50	18,445
19	sppr1	**Mallorca**	H	L	1-2	Kanoute 50	45,500
20	ecgph	**Arsenal**	H	W	3-1	Keita 24, Fabiano 34, Kanoute 89 pen	40,000
21	sppr1	**Almeria**	A	L	0-1		18,000
22	sppr1	**Osasuna**	A	D	1-1	Navas Gonzalez 48	17,820
23	sppr1	**Murcia**	H	W	3-1	Fabiano 4, 90, Maresca 58 pen	36,400
24	ecgph	**Slavia Prague**	A	W	3-0	Fabiano 66, Kanoute 69 Alves da Silva 87	11,689
25	sppr1	**Valladolid**	A	D	0-0		18,550
26	sppr1	**R Santander**	H	W	4-1	Kanoute 26, Chevanton Espinoza 66 Navas Gonzalez 85, Correira Claro 90	38,675
27	sppr1	**Real Betis**	H	W	3-0	Fabiano 25, 41, Alves da Silva 62	55,000
28	sppr1	**Athl Bilbao**	A	L	0-2		38,400
29	sppr1	**Getafe**	A	L	2-3	Fabiano 16, Dragutinovic 89	12,920
30	sppr1	**Osasuna**	H	W	2-1	Poulsen 55, Fabiano 90 pen	34,580
31	sppr1	**Recreativo**	A	W	2-1	Fabiano 45, 83	19,500
32	sppr1	**Barcelona**	H	D	1-1	Capel Trinidad 35	45,500
33	sppr1	**Espanyol**	A	W	4-2	Fabiano 6, Kanoute 10, Poulsen 73 Capel Trinidad 77	39,200
34	eckl1	**Fenerbahce**	A	L	2-3	Abonizio de Souza 23 og, Escude 66	46,000
35	sppr1	**Real Zaragoza**	H	W	5-0	Fabiano 20, 25, Ayala 43 og Diogo Ensenat 50 og, Keita 68	25,000
36	sppr1	**Deportivo**	A	L	1-2	Kanoute 24	25,950
37	eckl2	**Fenerbahce**	H	L	2-3*	Alves da Silva 5, Keita 9 Kanoute 41 (*on penalties)	45,000
38	sppr1	**Levante**	H	W	2-1	Keita 27, Fabiano 47	31,850
39	sppr1	**Valencia**	A	W	2-1	Fabiano 11, 22	49,500
40	sppr1	**Atl Madrid**	H	L	1-2	Capel Trinidad 49	45,500
41	sppr1	**Real Madrid**	A	L	1-3	Kanoute 38	76,000
42	sppr1	**Villarreal**	H	W	2-0	Fabiano 19, Kanoute 87 pen	45,500
43	sppr1	**Mallorca**	A	W	3-2	Florencio Santos 43, Kanoute 67 Alves da Silva 76	18,480
44	sppr1	**Almeria**	H	L	1-4	Kanoute 71	34,125
45	sppr1	**Murcia**	A	D	0-0		24,880
46	sppr1	**Valladolid**	H	W	2-0	Florencio Santos 10, 40	35,000
47	sppr1	**R Santander**	A	W	3-0	Fazio 29, 65, Florencio Santos 90	22,250
48	sppr1	**Real Betis**	A	W	2-0	Fabiano Clemente 31, Fazio 50	54,500
49	sppr1	**Athl Bilbao**	H	W	4-1	Kanoute 40, 80, Keita 78 Navas Gonzalez 85	36,855

LEAGUE APPEARANCES, BOOKINGS AND CAPS

	AGE (on 01/07/08)	IN NAMED 18	APPEARANCES	COUNTING GAMES	MINUTES ON PITCH	YELLOW CARDS	RED CARDS	CAPS THIS SEASON	NATIONAL SIDE
Goalkeepers									
Morgan De Sanctis	31	36	8	7	632	0	0	-	Italy
Andres Palop	34	32	31	31	2788	4	0	-	Spain
Defenders									
Daniel Alves da Silva	25	33	33	30	2822	12	3	1	Brazil
Khalid Boulahrouz	26	12	6	5	513	3	0	7	Holland
Jose Manuel Casado	21	2	2	0	49	0	0	-	Spain
Jose Crespo Rincon	21	18	13	9	947	2	0	-	Spain
Ivica Dragutinovic	32	25	23	22	2011	7	0	5	Serbia
Julien Escude	28	16	16	14	1328	2	1	4	France
Federico Fazio	21	31	22	15	1576	5	1	1	Argentina
Andreas Hinkel	26	6	2	2	180	1	0	-	Germany
Aquivaldo Mosquera	27	29	24	19	1966	6	1	-	Colombia
Manuel Ortiz Toribio	23	6	2	1	111	1	0	-	Spain
David Prieto Galvez	25	11	9	8	772	2	0	-	Spain
Midfielders									
Sergio Valente	28	29	17	2	615	1	0	2	Portugal
Diego Capel Trinidad	20	36	31	17	2070	2	0	-	Spain
Adriano Correia Claro	23	28	27	13	1775	4	1	-	Brazil
Tom de Mul	22	25	6	1	284	0	0	2	Belgium
Renato	29	36	28	14	1674	0	0	-	Brazil
Seydou Keita	28	31	31	27	2512	8	1	2	Mali
Enzo Maresca	28	25	21	12	1197	2	1	-	Italy
Josep Lluis Marti	33	16	9	4	438	2	0	-	Spain
Jesus Navas Gonzalez	22	36	36	29	2915	8	0	-	Spain
Christian Poulsen	28	33	29	18	1953	9	0	6	Denmark
Antonio Puerta Perez	23	1	1	0	30	0	0	-	Deceased
Forwards									
Ernesto Chevanton	27	9	7	0	257	4	0	-	Uruguay
Juan Jose Exposito	22	1	1	0	34	0	0	-	Spain
Luis Fabiano	27	31	30	23	2313	8	1	5	Brazil
Frederic Kanoute	30	30	30	20	2182	5	0	3	Mali
Alexander Kerzhakov	25	14	11	4	560	0	0	-	Russia
Arouna Kone	24	30	20	3	777	0	0	1	Ivory Coast

TEAM OF THE SEASON

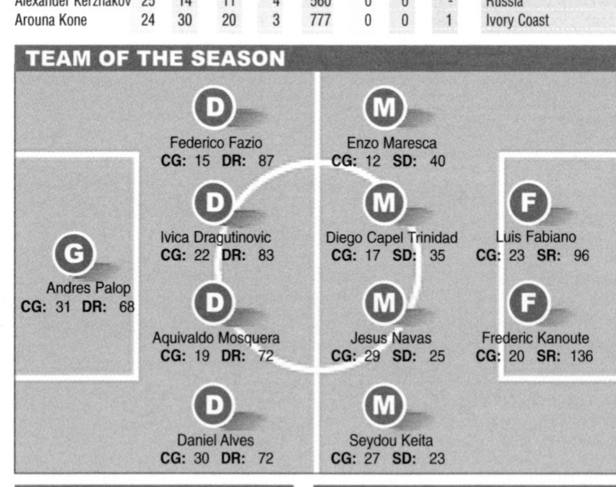

G
Andres Palop
CG: 31 DR: 68
D
Federico Fazio
CG: 15 DR: 87
D
Ivica Dragutinovic
CG: 22 DR: 83
D
Aquivaldo Mosquera
CG: 19 DR: 72
D
Daniel Alves
CG: 30 DR: 72
M
Enzo Maresca
CG: 12 SD: 40
M
Diego Capel Trinidad
CG: 17 SD: 35
M
Jesus Navas
CG: 29 SD: 25
M
Seydou Keita
CG: 27 SD: 23
F
Luis Fabiano
CG: 23 SR: 96
F
Frederic Kanoute
CG: 20 SR: 136

MONTHLY POINTS TALLY

Month	Points	%
AUGUST	3	100%
SEPTEMBER	3	25%
OCTOBER	6	50%
NOVEMBER	3	33%
DECEMBER	8	53%
JANUARY	6	50%
FEBRUARY	10	83%
MARCH	6	40%
APRIL	7	58%
MAY	12	100%

LEAGUE GOALS

	PLAYER	MINS	GOALS	S RATE
1	Fabiano	2313	24	96
2	Kanoute	2182	16	136
3	Navas	2915	5	583
4	F Santos	1674	4	418
5	Keita	2512	4	628
6	Kerzhakov	560	3	186
7	Fazio	1576	3	525
8	Poulsen	1953	3	651
9	Capel Trinidad	2070	3	690
10	Alves da Silva	2822	2	1411
11	Chevanton	257	1	257
12	Kone	777	1	777
13	Maresca	1197	1	1197
	Other		2	
	TOTAL		72	

TOP POINT EARNERS

	PLAYER	GAMES	AV PTS
1	Enzo Maresca	12	2.25
2	Diego Capel Trinidad	17	2.12
3	Aquivaldo Mosquera	19	2.11
4	Ivica Dragutinovic	22	2.00
5	Renato	14	2.00
6	Kanoute	20	1.95
7	Adriano Correia Claro	13	1.92
8	Luis Fabiano	23	1.74
9	Federico Fazio	15	1.73
10	Daniel Alves	30	1.70
	CLUB AVERAGE:		1.68

DISCIPLINARY RECORDS

	PLAYER	YELLOW	RED	AVE
1	Khalid Boulahrouz	3	0	171
2	Daniel Alves	12	3	188
3	Christian Poulsen	9	0	217
4	Luis Fabiano	8	1	257
5	Federico Fazio	5	1	262
6	Seydou Keita	8	1	279
7	Mosquera	6	1	280
8	Ivica Dragutinovic	7	0	287
9	Adriano	4	1	355
10	Jesus Navas	8	0	364
11	David Prieto Galvez	2	0	386
12	Enzo Maresca	2	1	399
13	Frederic Kanoute	5	0	436
	Other	11	1	
	TOTAL	90	10	

KEY GOALKEEPER

Andres Palop

Goals Conceded in the League	41	**Counting Games** League games when player was on pitch for at least 70 minutes	31
Defensive Rating Ave number of mins between League goals conceded while on the pitch	68	**Clean Sheets** In League games when player was on pitch for at least 70 minutes	9

KEY PLAYERS - DEFENDERS

Federico Fazio

Goals Conceded Number of League goals conceded while the player was on the pitch	18	**Clean Sheets** In League games when player was on pitch for at least 70 minutes	6
Defensive Rating Ave number of mins between League goals conceded while on the pitch	87	**Club Defensive Rating** Average number of mins between League goals conceded by the club this season	71

	PLAYER	CON LGE	CLEAN SHEETS	DEF RATE
1	Federico Fazio	18	6	87 mins
2	Ivica Dragutinovic	24	7	83 mins
3	Aquivaldo Mosquera	27	5	72 mins
4	Daniel Alves	39	10	72 mins

KEY PLAYERS - MIDFIELDERS

Enzo Maresca

Goals in the League	1	**Contribution to Attacking Power** Average number of minutes between League team goals while on pitch	34
Defensive Rating Average number of mins between League goals conceded while on the pitch	74	**Scoring Difference** Defensive Rating minus Contribution to Attacking Power	40

	PLAYER	LGE GOALS	DEF RATE	POWER	SCORE DIFF
1	Enzo Maresca	1	74	34	40 mins
2	Diego Capel Trinidad	3	79	44	35 mins
3	Jesus Navas	5	71	46	25 mins
4	Seydou Keita	4	69	46	23 mins

KEY PLAYERS - GOALSCORERS

Luis Fabiano Clemente

Goals in the League	24	**Player Strike Rate** Average number of minutes between League goals scored by player	96
Contribution to Attacking Power Average number of minutes between League team goals while on pitch	45	**Club Strike Rate** Average number of minutes between League goals scored by club	46

	PLAYER	LGE GOALS	POWER	STRIKE RATE
1	Luis Fabiano	24	45	96 mins
2	Frederic Kanoute	16	41	136 mins
3	Renato Dirnei Florencio Santos	4	54	418 mins
4	Jesus Navas	5	46	583 mins

Joma
388
Luis Fabiano

SQUAD APPEARANCES

Match	1	2	3	4	5	6	7	8	9	10	11	12	13	14	15	16	17	18	19	20	21	22	23	24	25	26	27	28	29	30	31	32	33	34	35	36	37	38	39	40	41	42	43	44	45	46	47	48	49	50
Venue	H	A	H	A	A	H	A	A	H	A	H	H	A	H	H	A	H	A	A	H	H	A	A	H	A	A	H	H	A	A	H	A	H	A	A	H	A	H	H	A	H	A	H	A	H	A	H	A	A	H
Competition	C	O	L	O	C	L	C	L	L	L	C	L	L	C	L	L	L	C	L	L	C	L	L	L	C	L	L	L	L	L	L	L	L	L	C	L	L	C	L	L	L	L	L	L	L	L	L	L	L	L
Result	W	W	W	L	W	W	L	L	L	L	W	L	W	W	W	L	W	W	L	L	W	L	D	W	W	D	W	W	L	L	W	W	D	W	L	W	L	L	W	W	L	L	W	W	L	D	W	W	W	W

Goalkeepers
Morgan De Sanctis
Andres Palop
Defenders
Daniel Alves da Silva
Khalid Boulahrouz
Jose Manuel Casado
Jose Crespo Rincon
Ivica Dragutinovic
Julien Escude
Federico Fazio
Andreas Hinkel
Aquivaldo Mosquera
Manuel Ortiz Toribio
David Prieto Galvez
Midfielders
Sergio Valente
Diego Capel Trinidad
Adriano Correia Claro
Tom de Mul
Renato
Seydou Keita
Enzo Maresca
Josep Lluis Marti
Jesus Navas Gonzalez
Christian Poulsen
Antonio Puerta Perez
Forwards
Ernesto Chevanton
Juan Jose Exposito
Luis Fabiano Clemente
Frederic Kanoute
Alexander Kerzhakov
Arouna Kone

KEY: On all match | Subbed or sent off (Counting game) | Subbed on from bench (Counting Game) | Subbed on and then subbed or sent off (Counting Game) | Not in 16
On bench | Subbed or sent off (playing less than 70 minutes) | Subbed on (playing less than 70 minutes) | Subbed on and then subbed or sent off (playing less than 70 minutes)

RACING SANTANDER

Final Position: **6th**

NICKNAME: RACING

KEY: ☐Won ☐Drawn ☐Lost

						Attendance
1	sppr1	**Barcelona**	H D	0-0		22,100
2	sppr1	**Real Zaragoza**	A D	1-1	Serrano Rodriguez 55	33,000
3	sppr1	**Levante**	H W	1-0	Munitis Alvarez 27	19,536
4	sppr1	**Atl Madrid**	A L	0-4		46,580
5	sppr1	**Villarreal**	H L	0-2		11,100
6	sppr1	**Almeria**	A W	1-0	Marcelo Garay 6	15,000
7	sppr1	**Valladolid**	H W	2-0	Smolarek 54, Tchite 90	15,540
8	sppr1	**Real Betis**	A D	1-1	Lopez Montana 85	44,000
9	sppr1	**Getafe**	H W	2-0	Serrano Rodriguez 39	
					Lopez Montana 75	19,980
10	sppr1	**Recreativo**	A D	0-0		20,000
11	sppr1	**Espanyol**	H D	1-1	Tchite 55	22,251
12	sppr1	**Deportivo**	A W	1-0	Tchite 67	28,026
13	sppr1	**Valencia**	H W	1-0	Lopez Montana 69	20,000
14	sppr1	**Real Madrid**	A L	1-3	Munitis Alvarez 73	68,000
15	sppr1	**Mallorca**	H W	3-1	Lopez Montana 18, Pedro Duscher 29	
					Munitis Alvarez 83	17,760
16	sppr1	**Murcia**	A L	1-2	Smolarek 62	23,325
17	sppr1	**Sevilla**	A L	1-4	Marcelo Garay 50	38,675
18	sppr1	**Athl Bilbao**	H W	1-0	Tchite 42	19,092
19	sppr1	**Osasuna**	A W	2-0	Colsa Albendea 81, Alvarez 83	12,000
20	sppr1	**Barcelona**	A L	0-1		88,830
21	sppr1	**Real Zaragoza**	H D	2-2	Bolado 4, Tchite 90	21,090
22	sppr1	**Levante**	A D	1-1	Pedro Duscher 75 pen	19,987
23	sppr1	**Atl Madrid**	H L	0-2		20,646
24	sppr1	**Villarreal**	A D	0-0		15,190
25	sppr1	**Almeria**	H W	1-0	Tchite 61	20,650
26	sppr1	**Valladolid**	A W	1-0	Pedro Duscher 85	21,500
27	sppr1	**Real Betis**	H W	3-0	Pedro Duscher 50, Marcelo Garay 58	
					Tchite 87	19,980
28	sppr1	**Getafe**	A L	1-2	Smolarek 54	10,200
29	sppr1	**Recreativo**	H W	2-0	Orteman 81, Smolarek 90	19,314
30	sppr1	**Espanyol**	A W	3-0	Serrano Rodriguez 14, Munitis Alvarez 24	
					Bolado 90	32,480
31	sppr1	**Deportivo**	H L	1-3	Lopez Montana 37	20,646
32	sppr1	**Valencia**	A W	2-1	Colsa Albendea 60, Tchite 82	47,850
33	sppr1	**Real Madrid**	H L	0-2		22,251
34	sppr1	**Mallorca**	A L	1-3	Pedro Duscher 86 pen	14,784
35	sppr1	**Murcia**	H W	3-2	Gutierrez 36 og, Lopez Montana 46	
					Munitis Alvarez 58	19,980
36	sppr1	**Sevilla**	H L	0-3		22,250
37	sppr1	**Athl Bilbao**	A D	0-0		40,000
38	sppr1	**Osasuna**	H W	1-0	Bolado 85	22,000

LEAGUE APPEARANCES, BOOKINGS AND CAPS

	AGE (on 01/07/08)	IN NAMED 18	APPEARANCES	COUNTING GAMES	MINUTES ON PITCH	YELLOW CARDS	RED CARDS	CAPS THIS SEASON	NATIONAL SIDE
Goalkeepers									
Fabio Coltorti	27	33	7	6	590	0	0	2	Switzerland
Antonio Tono	28	33	32	31	2816	3	1	-	Spain
Defenders									
Ayoze Diaz Diaz	26	34	30	20	2090	6	1	-	Spain
Cristian F Sales	22	4	2	0	22	0	0	-	Spain
Luis F Gutierrez	35	28	17	15	1386	3	0	-	Spain
Cesar Gonzalez Navas	28	21	19	17	1588	0	0	-	Spain
Oriol Lozano Ferran	27	29	24	19	1845	10	0	-	Spain
Ivan Marcano Sierra	21	17	2	2	166	0	0	-	Spain
Ezequiel M Garay	21	24	22	22	1906	2	1	1	Argentina
Jose Moraton Taeno	28	23	18	9	1043	6	0	-	Spain
Pablo Pinillos Caro	33	37	32	30	2717	9	0	-	Spain
Sergio S Ortega	22	28	18	13	1290	5	0	-	Spain
Samuel SJ Fernandez	24	9	1	0	14	0	0	-	Spain
Midfielders									
Pablo Alvarez Nunez	28	18	18	7	976	3	1	-	Spain
Gonzalo C Albendea	29	38	38	33	3067	3	0	-	Spain
Jordi Lopez Felpeto	27	17	13	4	506	2	1	-	Spain
Jorge Lopez Montana	29	36	35	27	2813	5	0	-	Spain
Sergio D Orteman	29	12	5	1	229	2	0	-	Uruguay
Aldo Pedro Duscher	29	35	34	31	2896	4	1	-	Argentina
Oscar Serrano	26	35	34	18	2273	12	1	-	Spain
Jonathan V Trueba	23	13	8	0	173	0	0	-	Spain
Luis Manuel Villa	18	1	1	0	4	0	0	-	Spain
Forwards									
Ivan Bolado	18	33	15	3	677	2	0	-	Spain
Damian I Saravia	19	3	1	0	1	0	0	-	Peru
Pedro M Munitis	33	31	31	22	2248	5	0	-	Spain
Euzebiusz Smolarek	27	34	34	18	2081	2	1	9	Poland
Mohamed Tchite	24	35	33	18	2031	4	0	-	Congo DR

TEAM OF THE SEASON

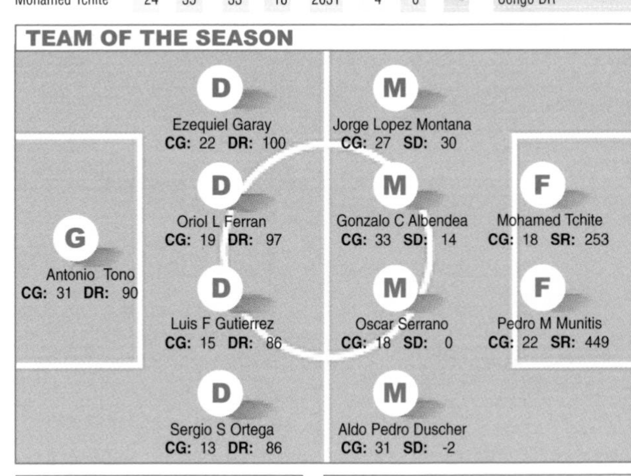

D
Ezequiel Garay
CG: 22 DR: 100
M
Jorge Lopez Montana
CG: 27 SD: 30
D
Oriol L Ferran
CG: 19 DR: 97
M
Gonzalo C Albendea
CG: 33 SD: 14
F
Mohamed Tchite
CG: 18 SR: 253
G
Antonio Tono
CG: 31 DR: 90
D
Luis F Gutierrez
CG: 15 DR: 86
M
Oscar Serrano
CG: 18 SD: 0
F
Pedro M Munitis
CG: 22 SR: 449
D
Sergio S Ortega
CG: 13 DR: 86
M
Aldo Pedro Duscher
CG: 31 SD: -2

MONTHLY POINTS TALLY

	Points	%
AUGUST	1	33%
SEPTEMBER	7	47%
OCTOBER	8	67%
NOVEMBER	7	78%
DECEMBER	3	25%
JANUARY	7	58%
FEBRUARY	5	42%
MARCH	12	80%
APRIL	3	25%
MAY	7	58%

LEAGUE GOALS

	PLAYER	MINS	GOALS	S RATE
1	Tchite	2031	8	253
2	Lopez Montana	2813	6	468
3	Munitis Alvarez	2248	5	449
4	Pedro Duscher	2896	5	579
5	Smolarek	2081	4	520
6	Bolado	677	3	225
7	Marcelo Garay	1906	3	635
8	S Rodriguez	2273	3	757
9	Colsa Albendea	3067	2	1533
10	Orteman	229	1	229
11	Alvarez	976	1	976
	Other		0	
	TOTAL		41	

TOP POINT EARNERS

	PLAYER	GAMES	AV PTS
1	Jorge Lopez Montana	27	1.81
2	Gonzalo Colsa Albendea	33	1.73
3	Mohamed Tchite	18	1.72
4	Ayoze Diaz Diaz	20	1.70
5	Ezequiel M Garay	22	1.68
6	Antonio Martinez Tono	31	1.68
7	Pablo Pinillos Caro	30	1.63
8	Sergio Sanchez Ortega	13	1.62
9	Luis F Gutierrez	15	1.60
10	Cesar Gonzalez Navas	17	1.59
	CLUB AVERAGE:		1.58

DISCIPLINARY RECORDS

	PLAYER	YELLOW	RED	AVE
1	Jordi Lopez Felpeto	2	1	168
2	Jose M Taeno	6	0	173
3	Oscar Rodriguez	12	1	174
4	Oriol L Ferran	10	0	184
5	Pablo A Nunez	3	1	244
6	Sergio S Ortega	5	0	258
7	Ayoze Diaz Diaz	6	1	298
8	Pablo Pinillos Caro	9	0	301
9	Ivan Bolado	2	0	338
10	Pedro M Munitis	5	0	449
11	Luis F Gutierrez	3	0	462
12	Mohamed Tchite	4	0	507
13	Jorge L Montana	5	0	562
	Other	14	4	
	TOTAL	86	8	

KEY GOALKEEPER

Antonio Rodriguez Martinez Tono

Goals Conceded in the League	31	Counting Games League games when player was on pitch for at least 70 minutes	31
Defensive Rating Ave number of mins between League goals conceded while on the pitch	90	Clean Sheets In League games when player was on pitch for at least 70 minutes	16

KEY PLAYERS - GOALSCORERS

Mohamed Tchite

Goals in the League	8	Player Strike Rate Average number of minutes between League goals scored by player	253
Contribution to Attacking Power Average number of minutes between League team goals while on pitch	63	Club Strike Rate Average number of minutes between League goals scored by club	81

	PLAYER	LGE GOALS	POWER	STRIKE RATE
1	Mohamed Tchite	8	63	253 mins
2	Pedro Manuel Munitis Alvarez	5	86	449 mins
3	Jorge Lopez Montana	6	78	468 mins
4	Euzebiusz Smolarek	4	99	520 mins

KEY PLAYERS - DEFENDERS

Ezequiel Marcelo Garay

Goals Conceded Number of League goals conceded while the player was on the pitch	19	Clean Sheets In League games when player was on pitch for at least 70 minutes	12
Defensive Rating Ave number of mins between League goals conceded while on the pitch	100	Club Defensive Rating Average number of mins between League goals conceded by the club this season	83

	PLAYER	CON LGE	CLEAN SHEETS	DEF RATE
1	Ezequiel Marcelo Garay	19	12	100 mins
2	Oriol Lozano Ferran	19	8	97 mins
3	Luis Fernandez Gutierrez	16	6	86 mins
4	Sergio Sanchez Ortega	15	6	86 mins

Oscar Serrano

KEY PLAYERS - MIDFIELDERS

Jorge Lopez Montana

Goals in the League	6	Contribution to Attacking Power Average number of minutes between League team goals while on pitch	78
Defensive Rating Average number of mins between League goals conceded while on the pitch	108	Scoring Difference Defensive Rating minus Contribution to Attacking Power	30

	PLAYER	LGE GOALS	DEF RATE	POWER	SCORE DIFF
1	Jorge Lopez Montana	6	108	78	30 mins
2	Gonzalo Colsa Albendea	2	92	78	14 mins
3	Oscar Serrano Rodriguez	3	81	81	0 mins
4	Aldo Pedro Duscher	5	76	78	-2 mins

SQUAD APPEARANCES

Match	1	2	3	4	5	6	7	8	9	10	11	12	13	14	15	16	17	18	19	20	21	22	23	24	25	26	27	28	29	30	31	32	33	34	35	36	37	38
Venue	H	A	H	A	H	A	H	A	H	A	H	A	H	A	H	A	A	H	A	A	H	A	H	A	H	A	H	A	H	A	H	A	H	A	H	H	A	H
Competition	L	L	L	L	L	L	L	L	L	L	L	L	L	L	L	L	L	L	L	L	L	L	L	L	L	L	L	L	L	L	L	L	L	L	L	L	L	L
Result	D	D	W	L	L	W	W	D	W	D	D	W	W	L	W	L	L	W	W	L	D	D	L	D	W	W	W	L	W	W	L	W	L	L	W	L	D	W

Goalkeepers
Fabio Coltorti
Antonio Tono

Defenders
Ayoze Diaz Diaz
Cristian Fernandez Sales
Luis Fernandez Gutierrez
Cesar Gonzalez Navas
Oriol Lozano Ferran
Ivan Marcano Sierra
Ezequiel Marcelo Garay
Jose Moraton Taeno
Pablo Pinillos Caro
Sergio Sanchez Ortega
Samuel SJ Fernandez

Midfielders
Pablo Alvarez Nunez
Gonzalo Colsa Albendea
Jordi Lopez Felpeto
Jorge Lopez Montana
Sergio Daniel Orteman
Aldo Pedro Duscher
Cristian Portilla Rodriguez
Oscar Serrano Rodriguez
Jonathan Valle Trueba
Luis Manuel Villa Lopez

Forwards
Ivan Bolado
Damian Ismodes Saravia
Pedro Manuel Munitis
Euzebiusz Smolarek
Mohamed Tchite

KEY: On all match · On bench · Subbed or sent off (Counting game) · Subbed or sent off (playing less than 70 minutes) · Subbed on from bench (Counting Game) · Subbed on (playing less than 70 minutes) · Subbed on and then subbed or sent off (Counting Game) · Subbed on and then subbed or sent off (playing less than 70 minutes) · Not in 16

MALLORCA

Final Position: **7th**

NICKNAME: BARRALETS

KEY: ☐Won ☐Drawn ☐Lost

#		Opponent	H/A	Res	Score	Scorers	Attendance
1	sppr1	**Levante**	H	W	3-0	Ibagaza 23 pen, 72, Guiza 56	22,400
2	sppr1	**Atl Madrid**	A	D	1-1	Guiza 18	40,000
3	sppr1	**Villarreal**	H	L	0-1		15,015
4	sppr1	**Almeria**	A	D	1-1	Gonzalez Guiza 78	14,960
5	sppr1	**Valladolid**	H	W	4-2	De Araujo Nunes 49, Arango Saenz 52, 87, Cassadesus Castano 83	11,550
6	sppr1	**Real Betis**	A	L	0-3		35,000
7	sppr1	**Getafe**	H	W	4-2	Santiago Ibagaza 53 pen Arango Saenz 69, 78, Ramis Barrios 90	16,863
8	sppr1	**Recreativo**	A	W	2-0	Gonzalez Guiza 2, Adrove Colom 78	15,450
9	sppr1	**Espanyol**	H	D	2-2	Arango Saenz 2, Gonzalez Guiza 69	23,142
10	sppr1	**Deportivo**	A	D	1-1	Gonzalez Guiza 12	17,300
11	sppr1	**Valencia**	H	L	0-2		20,790
12	sppr1	**Real Madrid**	A	L	3-4	Varela Ramos 13, 36 Gonzalez Guiza 57	77,600
13	sppr1	**Sevilla**	A	W	2-1	Santiago Ibagaza 17, Varela Ramos 38	45,500
14	sppr1	**Murcia**	H	D	1-1	Webo Kouamo 69	18,480
15	sppr1	**R Santander**	A	L	1-3	Webo Kouamo 11	17,760
16	sppr1	**Athl Bilbao**	H	D	0-0		16,170
17	sppr1	**Osasuna**	A	L	1-3	Gonzalez Guiza 49	28,900
18	sppr1	**Barcelona**	H	L	0-2		23,100
19	sppr1	**Real Zaragoza**	A	D	2-2	Varela Ramos 17, Gonzalez Guiza 61	27,600
20	sppr1	**Levante**	A	D	2-2	Gonzalez Guiza 30, 77	12,400
21	sppr1	**Atl Madrid**	H	W	1-0	Arango Saenz 21	19,635
22	sppr1	**Villarreal**	A	D	1-1	Basinas 39 pen	17,794
23	sppr1	**Almeria**	H	D	0-0		16,170
24	sppr1	**Valladolid**	A	D	1-1	Santiago Ibagaza 79 pen	15,600
25	sppr1	**Real Betis**	H	D	1-1	Varela Ramos 57	19,635
26	sppr1	**Getafe**	A	D	3-3	Gonzalez Guiza 14, Arango Saenz 75 Ramis Barrios 79	12,750
27	sppr1	**Recreativo**	H	W	7-1	Arango Saenz 18, 47, 50, Guiza 22, 31 Valero Iglesias 38, 41	17,325
28	sppr1	**Espanyol**	A	L	1-2	Gonzalez Guiza 12	39,200
29	sppr1	**Deportivo**	H	W	1-0	Arango Saenz 23	11,550
30	sppr1	**Valencia**	A	W	3-0	Gonzalez Guiza 12, 57 Ramis Barrios 20	51,700
31	sppr1	**Real Madrid**	H	D	1-1	Valero Iglesias 73	19,635
32	sppr1	**Sevilla**	H	L	2-3	Gonzalez Guiza 47, Webo Kouamo 90	18,480
33	sppr1	**Murcia**	A	W	4-1	Gonzalez Guiza 8, 46, 85 Arango Saenz 18	23,325
34	sppr1	**R Santander**	H	W	3-1	De Arauijo Nunes 48, Guido Trejo 82 Gonzalez Guiza 88	14,784
35	sppr1	**Athl Bilbao**	A	W	2-1	Gonzalez Guiza 3, 71	40,000
36	sppr1	**Osasuna**	H	W	2-1	Gonzalez Guiza 31, Guido Trejo 90	10,395
37	sppr1	**Barcelona**	A	W	3-2	Valero Iglesias 67, Webo Kouamo 70 Gonzalez Guiza 90	65,142
38	sppr1	**Real Zaragoza**	H	W	3-2	Gonzalez Guiza 14, Webo Kouamo 64 Castro Irizabal 90	16,170

LEAGUE APPEARANCES, BOOKINGS AND CAPS

	AGE (on 01/07/08)	IN NAMED 18	APPEARANCES	COUNTING GAMES	MINUTES ON PITCH	YELLOW CARDS	RED CARDS	CAPS THIS SEASON	NATIONAL SIDE
Goalkeepers									
German Dario Lux	26	33	10	9	861	2	0	-	Argentina
Miguel Moya	24	30	29	28	2558	1	1	-	Spain
Defenders									
Hector	33	33	29	28	2541	9	0	-	Spain
Jose Nunes	31	36	35	34	3087	4	2	-	Portugal
Antonio Valeriano	21	1	0	0	0	0	0	-	Spain
Sergio Ballesteros	32	24	17	15	1409	4	3	-	Spain
Francisco Calderon	22	23	5	3	306	0	0	-	Spain
Fernando Navarro	26	36	36	36	3213	8	0	1	Spain
David Navarro	28	27	18	15	1461	7	0	-	Spain
Ivan Ramis Barrios	23	22	13	10	942	3	0	-	Spain
Lionel Scaloni	30	6	6	4	404	2	1	-	Argentina
Fernando V Ramos	28	34	33	21	2243	9	1	-	Spain
Midfielders									
Tuni	26	33	16	4	670	0	0	-	Spain
Juan F Arango	28	38	38	31	3000	1	0	-	Venezuela
Guillermo Pereyra	28	18	18	13	1445	4	1	-	Argentina
Angelos Basinas	32	35	31	20	2038	6	0	9	Greece
Gonzalo C Irizabal	23	16	8	0	166	0	0	-	Uruguay
Jonas M Gutierrez	24	31	30	22	2212	5	0	1	Argentina
Alberto Arteseros	20	4	1	0	12	0	0	-	Spain
Borja V Iglesias	23	37	34	16	1888	5	0	-	Spain
Forwards									
Ariel Ibagaza	31	33	32	27	2482	5	0	-	Argentina
Victor	23	14	10	1	306	1	0	-	Spain
Daniel G Guiza	27	37	37	31	3010	5	1	3	Spain
Oscar Guido Trejo	20	26	17	1	358	3	0	-	Argentina
Emilio Nsue	18	3	2	0	6	0	0	-	Spain
Pierre Achille Webo	26	16	15	4	683	2	1	-	Cameroon

TEAM OF THE SEASON

D
Sergio Ballesteros
CG: 14 DR: 69
M
Angelos Basinas
CG: 20 SD: 20
D
Berenguel del Pino
CG: 28 DR: 66
M
Borla Valero Iglesias
CG: 16 SD: 18
F
Daniel Guiza
CG: 31 SR: 111
G
Miguel Moya
CG: 28 DR: 75
D
Fernando Varela Ramos
CG: 21 DR: 65
M
Juan Arango
CG: 31 SD: 13
F
Ariel Ibagaza
CG: 27 SR: 496
D
Fernando Navarro
CG: 36 DR: 64
M
Jonas Gutierrez
CG: 22 SD: 4

MONTHLY POINTS TALLY

Month	Points	%
AUGUST	3	100%
SEPTEMBER	5	33%
OCTOBER	8	67%
NOVEMBER	3	33%
DECEMBER	2	17%
JANUARY	5	42%
FEBRUARY	4	33%
MARCH	10	67%
APRIL	7	58%
MAY	12	100%

LEAGUE GOALS

	PLAYER	MINS	GOALS	S RATE
1	Daniel Guiza	3010	27	111
2	Arango Saenz	3000	12	250
3	Webo Kouamo	683	5	136
4	Varela Ramos	2243	5	448
5	S Ibagaza	2482	5	496
6	Valero Iglesias	1888	4	472
7	Ramis Barrios	942	3	314
8	Guido Trejo	358	2	179
9	Arauijo Nunes	3087	2	1543
10	Castro Irizabal	166	1	166
11	Victor	306	1	306
12	Adrove Colom	670	1	670
13	Basinas	2038	1	2038
	Other		0	
	TOTAL		69	

TOP POINT EARNERS

	PLAYER	GAMES	AV PTS
1	David Navarro	15	2.00
2	Borla Valero Iglesias	16	2.00
3	Fernando Varela	21	1.95
4	Miguel Angel Moya	28	1.86
5	Angelos Basinas	20	1.75
6	Jose Nunes	34	1.65
7	Fernando Navarro	36	1.58
8	Daniel G Guiza	31	1.55
9	Juan Fernando Arango	31	1.55
10	Hector Berenguel	28	1.50
	CLUB AVERAGE:		1.55

DISCIPLINARY RECORDS

	PLAYER	YELLOW	RED	AVE
1	David Navarro	7	0	208
2	Sergio Ballesteros	4	2	220
3	Fernando Varela	9	1	224
4	Pierre Achille Webo	2	1	227
5	Hector Berenguel	9	0	282
6	Guillermo Pereyra	4	1	289
7	Ivan Ramis Barrios	3	0	314
8	Angelos Basinas	6	0	339
9	Borla V Iglesias	5	0	377
10	Fernando Navarro	8	0	401
11	German Dario Lux	2	0	430
12	Jonas M Gutierrez	5	0	442
13	Ariel Ibagaza	5	0	496
	Other	11	4	
	TOTAL	80	9	

KEY GOALKEEPER

Miguel Moya

Goals Conceded in the League	34	Counting Games League games when player was on pitch for at least 70 minutes	28
Defensive Rating Ave number of mins between League goals conceded while on the pitch	75	Clean Sheets In League games when player was on pitch for at least 70 minutes	6

KEY PLAYERS - DEFENDERS

Sergio Martinez Ballesteros

Goals Conceded Number of League goals conceded while the player was on the pitch	19	Clean Sheets In League games when player was on pitch for at least 70 minutes	3
Defensive Rating Ave number of mins between League goals conceded while on the pitch	69	Club Defensive Rating Average number of mins between League goals conceded by the club this season	63

	PLAYER	CON LGE	CLEAN SHEETS	DEF RATE
1	Sergio Martinez Ballesteros	19	3	69 mins
2	Hector Berenguel del Pino	38	6	66 mins
3	Fernando Varela Ramos	34	6	65 mins
4	Fernando Navarro Corbacho	50	7	64 mins

KEY PLAYERS - MIDFIELDERS

Angelos Basinas

Goals in the League	1	Contribution to Attacking Power Average number of minutes between League team goals while on pitch	41
Defensive Rating Average number of mins between League goals conceded while on the pitch	61	Scoring Difference Defensive Rating minus Contribution to Attacking Power	20

	PLAYER	LGE GOALS	DEF RATE	POWER	SCORE DIFF
1	Angelos Basinas	1	61	41	20 mins
2	Borla Valero Iglesias	4	57	39	18 mins
3	Juan Fernando Arango	12	61	48	13 mins
4	Jonas Manuel Gutierrez	0	73	69	4 mins

KEY PLAYERS - GOALSCORERS

Daniel Guiza

Goals in the League	27	Player Strike Rate Average number of minutes between League goals scored by player	111
Contribution to Attacking Power Average number of minutes between League team goals while on pitch	49	Club Strike Rate Average number of minutes between League goals scored by club	49

	PLAYER	LGE GOALS	POWER	STRIKE RATE
1	Daniel Guiza	27	49	111 mins
2	Juan Fernando Arango	12	48	250 mins
3	Borla Valero Iglesias	4	39	472 mins
4	Ariel Miguel Santiago Ibagaza	5	51	496 mins

Daniel Guiza

SQUAD APPEARANCES

Match	1	2	3	4	5	6	7	8	9	10	11	12	13	14	15	16	17	18	19	20	21	22	23	24	25	26	27	28	29	30	31	32	33	34	35	36	37	38
Venue	H	A	H	A	H	A	H	A	H	A	H	A	A	H	A	H	A	H	A	A	H	A	H	A	H	A	H	A	H	A	H	H	A	H	A	H	A	H
Competition	L	L	L	L	L	L	L	L	L	L	L	L	L	L	L	L	L	L	L	L	L	L	L	L	L	L	L	L	L	L	L	L	L	L	L	L	L	L
Result	W	D	L	D	W	L	W	W	D	D	L	L	W	D	L	D	L	L	D	D	W	D	D	D	D	D	W	L	W	W	D	L	W	W	W	W	W	W

Goalkeepers
German Dario Lux
Miguel Moya

Defenders
Hector
Jose Nunes
Antonio Valeriano
Sergio Ballesteros
Francisco Calderon
Fernando Navarro
David Navarro
Ivan Ramis Barrios
Lionel Scaloni
Fernando Varela Ramos

Midfielders
Antoni Lluis Adrove
Juan Fernando Arango
Guillermo Ariel Pereyra
Angelos Basinas
Jonas Manuel Gutierrez
Alberto Lopez Arteseros
Borla Valero Iglesias

Forwards
Ariel Ibagaza
Victor C Castano
Gonzalo Castro Irizabal
Daniel Gonzalez Guiza
Oscar Guido Trejo
Emilio Nsue
Pierre Achille Webo

KEY: On all match · On bench · Subbed or sent off (Counting game) · Subbed or sent off (playing less than 70 minutes) · Subbed on from bench (Counting Game) · Subbed on (playing less than 70 minutes) · Subbed on and then subbed or sent off (Counting Game) · Subbed on and then subbed or sent off (playing less than 70 minutes) · Not in 16

ALMERIA

Final Position: **8th**

KEY: ☐ Won ☐ Drawn ☐ Lost

	Comp	Opponent	Venue	Result	Score	Scorers	Attendance
1	sppr1	**Deportivo**	A	W	3-0	Negredo Sanchez 18, Soriano 33	
						Crusat 50	25,200
2	sppr1	**Valencia**	H	L	1-2	Negredo Sanchez 63	10,000
3	sppr1	**Real Madrid**	A	L	1-3	Uche 73	75,000
4	sppr1	**Mallorca**	H	D	1-1	Jimenez Ortiz 34	14,960
5	sppr1	**Murcia**	A	W	1-0	de Carvalho 42	17,105
6	sppr1	**R Santander**	H	L	0-1		15,000
7	sppr1	**Athl Bilbao**	A	D	1-1	de Carvalho 61	36,000
8	sppr1	**Osasuna**	H	W	2-0	de Carvalho 50 pen	
						Negredo Sanchez 70	17,600
9	sppr1	**Barcelona**	A	L	0-2		92,778
10	sppr1	**Real Zaragoza**	H	L	0-1		16,000
11	sppr1	**Levante**	A	L	0-3		15,180
12	sppr1	**Atl Madrid**	H	D	0-0		19,800
13	sppr1	**Villarreal**	A	D	1-1	Negredo Sanchez 53	15,400
14	sppr1	**Sevilla**	H	W	1-0	Acasiete Ariadela 87	18,000
15	sppr1	**Valladolid**	H	W	1-0	Negredo Sanchez 73	25,000
16	sppr1	**Real Betis**	A	L	1-3	Negredo Sanchez 10 pen	41,250
17	sppr1	**Getafe**	H	L	0-2		19,800
18	sppr1	**Recreativo**	A	D	1-1	Jimenez Ortiz 20	14,420
19	sppr1	**Espanyol**	H	W	1-0	Uche 87	16,500
20	sppr1	**Deportivo**	H	W	1-0	Martin Pulido 89	19,500
21	sppr1	**Valencia**	A	W	1-0	de Carvalho 20	49,500
22	sppr1	**Real Madrid**	H	W	2-0	Gutierrez Robles 16	
						Negredo Sanchez 47 pen	20,900
23	sppr1	**Mallorca**	A	D	0-0		16,170
24	sppr1	**Murcia**	H	W	1-0	Negredo Sanchez 43	12,100
25	sppr1	**R Santander**	A	L	0-1		20,650
26	sppr1	**Athl Bilbao**	H	D	1-1	Negredo Sanchez 59 pen	15,400
27	sppr1	**Osasuna**	A	L	1-2	Garcia Perez 20	17,820
28	sppr1	**Barcelona**	H	D	2-2	Martin Pulido 33, Uche 85	19,800
29	sppr1	**Real Zaragoza**	A	D	1-1	Negredo Sanchez 88	30,000
30	sppr1	**Levante**	H	W	2-1	Soriano Marcos 2, de Carvalho 36	16,500
31	sppr1	**Atl Madrid**	A	L	3-6	de Carvalho 10, Ortiz Palazon 17	
						Negredo Sanchez 36	43,840
32	sppr1	**Villarreal**	H	W	1-0	Acasiete Ariadela 84	20,680
33	sppr1	**Sevilla**	A	W	4-1	Alves da Silva 23 og, Negredo Sanchez 46, 65	
						Ortiz Palazon 61	34,125
34	sppr1	**Valladolid**	A	L	0-1		25,970
35	sppr1	**Real Betis**	H	D	1-1	Martin Pulido 47	18,040
36	sppr1	**Getafe**	A	L	2-4	Crusat Domene 5, Paunovic 11	11,390
37	sppr1	**Recreativo**	H	L	0-2		15,400
38	sppr1	**Espanyol**	A	W	3-1	de Carvalho 44, Crusat Domene 54	
						Paunovic 90	9,500

LEAGUE APPEARANCES, BOOKINGS AND CAPS

	AGE (on 01/07/08)	IN NAMED 18	APPEARANCES	COUNTING GAMES	MINUTES ON PITCH	YELLOW CARDS	RED CARDS	CAPS THIS SEASON	NATIONAL SIDE
Goalkeepers									
Diego Alves	23	33	22	21	1956	3	0	-	Brazil
David Cobeno Iglesias	26	34	17	16	1461	0	1	-	Spain
Defenders									
Santiago Acasiete	30	31	21	15	1497	3	1	4	Peru
Domingo Cisma	26	28	11	8	772	3	1	-	Spain
Carlos Garcia Badias	24	36	34	34	3060	9	0	-	Spain
Juanito	28	35	31	21	2235	10	1	-	Spain
Jose Manuel Ortiz	26	36	36	33	3123	8	0	-	Spain
Aitor Lopez Rekarte	32	27	12	7	762	2	0	-	Spain
Ruben Martin Pulido	29	31	25	21	2015	7	1	-	Spain
Guilherme Santos	20	9	2	0	33	0	0	-	Brazil
Bruno Saltor Grau	27	34	32	29	2722	11	0	-	Spain
Midfielders									
Jose Luis Cabrera	26	11	2	1	103	0	0	-	Spain
Felipe Melo	24	34	34	27	2604	11	0	-	Brazil
Corona	27	34	32	15	1981	5	0	-	Spain
Santos da Silva Iriney	27	13	8	2	281	0	0	-	Brazil
Juan Manuel Palazon	26	32	29	15	2032	10	0	-	Spain
Veljko Paunovic	30	10	7	0	200	1	1	-	Serbia
Fernando Soriano	28	36	34	20	2226	9	0	-	Spain
Kalu Uche	25	34	29	3	1060	1	0	-	Nigeria
Mathias Leonardo	21	1	0	0	0	0	0	-	Chile
Forwards									
Albert C Domene	26	35	34	29	2707	8	2	-	Spain
Natalio Lorenzo	23	19	13	1	409	0	0	-	Spain
Alvaro Negredo	22	36	36	29	2852	3	0	-	Spain
Jose Ortiz Bernal	30	34	27	4	1103	2	0	-	Spain

TEAM OF THE SEASON

D Santiago Acasiete CG: 15 DR: 115
M Corona CG: 15 SD: 31
D Bruno CG: 29 DR: 82
M Juan Palazon CG: 15 SD: 17
F Ãlvaro Negredo CG: 29 SR: 219
G Diego Alves CG: 21 DR: 78
D Juanito CG: 21 DR: 79
M Felipe Melo CG: 27 SD: -3
F Albert Domene CG: 29 SR: 902
D Jose Manuel Ortiz CG: 33 DR: 78
M Fernando Soriano CG: 20 SD: -13

MONTHLY POINTS TALLY

Month	Points	%
AUGUST	3	100%
SEPTEMBER	4	27%
OCTOBER	4	33%
NOVEMBER	2	22%
DECEMBER	6	50%
JANUARY	10	83%
FEBRUARY	7	58%
MARCH	6	40%
APRIL	6	50%
MAY	4	33%

LEAGUE GOALS

	PLAYER	MINS	GOALS	S RATE
1	Negredo	2852	13	219
2	Felipe Melo	2604	7	372
3	Uche	1060	3	353
4	Martin Pulido	2015	3	671
5	Crusat Domene	2707	3	902
6	Paunovic	200	2	100
7	A Ariadela	1497	2	748
8	S Marcos	2226	2	1113
9	Jimenez Ortiz	3123	2	1561
10	Garcia Perez	1981	1	1981
11	Ortiz Palazon	2032	1	2032
12	G Robles	2235	1	2235
	Other		0	
	TOTAL		40	

TOP POINT EARNERS

	PLAYER	GAMES	AV PTS
1	Diego Alves Carreira	21	1.57
2	Corona	15	1.53
3	Juan Palazon	15	1.53
4	Gutierrez Robles	21	1.52
5	Felipe Melo	27	1.52
6	Ruben Martin Pulido	21	1.48
7	Santiago Acasiete	15	1.47
8	Alvaro Negredo	29	1.45
9	Carlos Garcia Badias	34	1.41
10	Albert Crusat Domene	29	1.38
	CLUB AVERAGE:		1.37

DISCIPLINARY RECORDS

	PLAYER	YELLOW	RED	AVE
1	Domingo Cisma	3	1	193
2	Juanito	10	1	203
3	Juan Palazon	9	0	225
4	Felipe Melo	11	0	236
5	Fernando Soriano	9	0	247
6	Ruben M Pulido	7	1	251
7	Albert C Domene	8	2	270
8	Bruno Saltor Grau	10	0	272
9	Carlos G Badias	9	0	340
10	Santiago Acasiete	3	1	374
11	Aitor L Rekarte	2	0	381
12	Mane	8	0	390
13	Corona	5	0	396
	Other	9	1	
	TOTAL	103	7	

KEY GOALKEEPER

Diego Alves Carreira

Goals Conceded in the League	25	**Counting Games** League games when player was on pitch for at least 70 minutes	21
Defensive Rating Ave number of mins between League goals conceded while on the pitch	78	**Clean Sheets** In League games when player was on pitch for at least 70 minutes	8

KEY PLAYERS - DEFENDERS

Wilmer Santiago Acasiete Ariadela

Goals Conceded Number of League goals conceded while the player was on the pitch	13	**Clean Sheets** In League games when player was on pitch for at least 70 minutes	6
Defensive Rating Ave number of mins between League goals conceded while on the pitch	115	**Club Defensive Rating** Average number of mins between League goals conceded by the club this season	76

	PLAYER	CON LGE	CLEAN SHEETS	DEF RATE
1	Wilmer Santiago Acasiete Ariadela	13	6	115 mins
2	Bruno Saltor Grau	33	10	82 mins
3	Juanito	28	9	79 mins
4	Jose Manuel Ortiz	40	10	78 mins

KEY PLAYERS - MIDFIELDERS

Corona

Goals in the League	1	**Contribution to Attacking Power** Average number of minutes between League team goals while on pitch	63
Defensive Rating Average number of mins between League goals conceded while on the pitch	94	**Scoring Difference** Defensive Rating minus Contribution to Attacking Power	31

	PLAYER	LGE GOALS	DEF RATE	POWER	SCORE DIFF
1	Corona	1	94	63	31 mins
2	Juan Ortiz	1	92	75	17 mins
3	Felipe Melo	7	81	84	-3 mins
4	Fernando Soriano Marcos	2	76	89	-13 mins

KEY PLAYERS - GOALSCORERS

Alvaro Negredo Sanchez

Goals in the League	13	**Player Strike Rate** Average number of minutes between League goals scored by player	219
Contribution to Attacking Power Average number of minutes between League team goals while on pitch	77	**Club Strike Rate** Average number of minutes between League goals scored by club	81

	PLAYER	LGE GOALS	POWER	STRIKE RATE
1	Alvaro Negredo Sanchez	13	77	219 mins
2	Felipe Melo de Carvalho	7	84	372 mins
3	Albert Crusat Domene	3	90	902 mins
4	Fernando Soriano Marcos	2	89	1113 mins

bwin.com
OBRASCAMPO
Alvaro Negredo

SQUAD APPEARANCES

Match	1	2	3	4	5	6	7	8	9	10	11	12	13	14	15	16	17	18	19	20	21	22	23	24	25	26	27	28	29	30	31	32	33	34	35	36	37	38
Venue	A	H	A	H	A	H	A	H	A	H	A	H	A	H	H	A	H	A	H	H	A	H	A	H	A	H	A	H	A	H	A	H	A	A	H	A	H	A
Competition	L	L	L	L	L	L	L	L	L	L	L	L	L	L	L	L	L	L	L	L	L	L	L	L	L	L	L	L	L	L	L	L	L	L	L	L	L	L
Result	W	L	L	D	W	L	D	W	L	L	L	D	D	W	W	L	L	D	W	W	W	W	D	W	L	D	L	D	D	W	L	W	W	L	D	L	L	W

Goalkeepers
Diego Alves
David Cobeno Iglesias

Defenders
Santiago Acasiete
Domingo Cisma
Carlos Garcia Badias
Juanito
Jose Manuel Orti
Aitor Lopez Rekarte
Pedro Mairata Gual
Ruben Martin Pulido
Guilherme Santos
Bruno Saltor Grau

Midfielders
Jose Luis Cabrera
Felipe Melo
Corona
Santos da Silva Iriney
Juan Manuel Palazon
Veljko Paunovic
Fernando Soriano
Kalu Uche
Mathias Leonardo

Forwards
Albert Crusat Domene
Natalio Lorenzo
Alvaro Negredo
Jose Ortiz Bernal

KEY: On all match | On bench | Subbed or sent off (Counting game) | Subbed or sent off (playing less than 70 minutes) | Subbed on from bench (Counting Game) | Subbed on (playing less than 70 minutes) | Subbed on and then subbed or sent off (Counting Game) | Subbed on and then subbed or sent off (playing less than 70 minutes) | Not in 16

DEPORTIVO LA CORUNA

Final Position: **9th**

NICKNAME: DEPOR

KEY: ☐Won ☐Drawn ☐Lost

		Opponent	H/A	Result	Score	Scorers	Attendance
1	sppr1	**Almeria**	H	L	0-3		25,200
2	sppr1	**Valladolid**	A	D	2-2	Taborda Ramos 54, Rico Soto 78	20,000
3	sppr1	**Real Betis**	H	W	1-0	Guardado 8	22,490
4	sppr1	**Getafe**	A	D	0-0		11,900
5	sppr1	**Recreativo**	H	L	0-2		20,760
6	sppr1	**Espanyol**	A	L	0-1		50,400
7	sppr1	**Sevilla**	A	W	1-0	Rico Soto 72	40,040
8	sppr1	**Valencia**	H	L	2-4	Jimenez Tejada 29, Bodipo 87	24,220
9	sppr1	**Real Madrid**	A	L	1-3	Jimenez Tejada 2	69,600
10	sppr1	**Mallorca**	H	D	1-1	Guardado 42 pen	17,300
11	sppr1	**Murcia**	A	W	2-0	Jimenez Tejada 56, Guardado 72	24,880
12	sppr1	**R Santander**	H	L	0-1		28,026
13	sppr1	**Athl Bilbao**	A	D	2-2	Rico Soto 61, Taborda Ramos 89	36,000
14	sppr1	**Osasuna**	H	L	1-2	Castro Martin 79	15,000
15	sppr1	**Barcelona**	A	L	1-2	Hidalgo Gonzalez 2	64,155
16	sppr1	**Real Zaragoza**	H	D	1-1	Coloccini 8	22,000
17	sppr1	**Levante**	A	W	1-0	Gonzalez Soriano 85 pen	25,354
18	sppr1	**Atl Madrid**	H	L	0-3		20,760
19	sppr1	**Villarreal**	A	L	3-4	Gonzalez Soriano 27 pen, Amo Uguado 59 Guardado 90	19,747
20	sppr1	**Almeria**	A	L	0-1		19,500
21	sppr1	**Valladolid**	H	W	3-1	Lopo Garcia 7, Jimenez Tejada 46 Guardado 71	28,500
22	sppr1	**Real Betis**	A	W	1-0	Amo Uguado 35	41,200
23	sppr1	**Getafe**	H	D	1-1	Alvarez Abrante 44 og	27,334
24	sppr1	**Recreativo**	A	L	2-3	Verdu Fernandez 9 pen, Rico Soto 81	15,450
25	sppr1	**Espanyol**	H	W	2-0	Coloccini 17, Lafita Castillo 23	24,220
26	sppr1	**Sevilla**	H	W	2-1	Wilhelmsson 34 pen, Lafita Castillo 64	25,950
27	sppr1	**Valencia**	A	D	2-2	Gonzalez Soriano 36, Lafita Castillo 44	44,550
28	sppr1	**Real Madrid**	H	W	1-0	Laveran Lima 57 og	31,140
29	sppr1	**Mallorca**	A	L	0-1		11,550
30	sppr1	**Murcia**	H	W	3-1	Jimenez Tejada 22, 46, 48	18,000
31	sppr1	**R Santander**	A	W	3-1	Jimenez Tejada 1, 43, Coloccini 25	20,646
32	sppr1	**Athl Bilbao**	H	W	3-0	Coloccini 31, Gonzalez Soriano 63 pen Luis Kasmirski 79	26,780
33	sppr1	**Osasuna**	A	W	1-0	Gonzalez Soriano 64 pen	15,840
34	sppr1	**Barcelona**	H	W	2-0	Rodriguez Villamuela 54, Amo Uguado 76	27,680
35	sppr1	**Real Zaragoza**	A	L	0-1		34,500
36	sppr1	**Levante**	H	W	1-0	Rico Soto 87	12,110
37	sppr1	**Atl Madrid**	A	L	0-1		53,418
38	sppr1	**Villarreal**	H	L	0-2		24,500

LEAGUE APPEARANCES, BOOKINGS AND CAPS

	AGE (on 01/07/08)	IN NAMED 18	APPEARANCES	COUNTING GAMES	MINUTES ON PITCH	YELLOW CARDS	RED CARDS	CAPS THIS SEASON	NATIONAL SIDE
Goalkeepers									
Fabricio A Ramirez	20	7	6	6	540	2	0	-	Spain
Dudu Aouate	30	31	28	28	2520	1	0	4	Israel
Gustavo Munua	30	31	4	4	360	1	0	-	Uruguay
Defenders									
Pablo Amo Uguado	30	21	19	19	1690	3	1	-	Spain
Aythami Artiles Oliva	22	10	1	1	90	0	0	-	Spain
Antonio B Fernandez	21	17	9	6	616	2	0	-	Spain
Fabricio Coloccini	26	38	38	38	3420	3	0	1	Argentina
Manuel Diaz	32	35	34	33	2984	4	0	-	Spain
Adrian L Rodriguez	21	22	15	15	1350	3	0	-	Spain
Alberto Lopo Garcia	29	24	21	20	1838	5	0	-	Spain
Filipe Luis Kasmirski	22	35	33	32	2873	3	1	-	Brazil
Sergio R Garcia	23	1	1	1	90	0	0	-	Spain
Laureano S Ruiz	23	5	1	1	90	0	0	-	Spain
David Chapi Vazquez	23	8	1	0	49	1	1	-	Spain
Midfielders									
Julian De Guzman	27	37	35	32	2932	9	0	8	Canada
Sergio Gonzalez	31	34	32	28	2574	5	1	-	Spain
Jose Guardado	21	26	26	21	1935	3	0	-	Mexico
Cristian Hidalgo	24	17	14	6	689	2	0	-	Spain
Angel Lafita Castillo	23	29	24	11	1425	5	0	-	Spain
Juan R Villamuela	26	36	25	13	1518	3	0	-	Spain
Antonio Tomas	23	17	12	7	655	2	0	-	Spain
Juan Carlos Valeron	33	11	5	0	85	0	0	-	Spain
Joan Verdu Fernandez	25	29	24	13	1514	0	0	-	Spain
Christian Wilhelmsson	28	15	15	11	1109	3	0	7	Sweden
Forwards									
Rodolfo Bodipo Diaz	30	25	19	6	878	1	0	-	Guinea
Ruben Castro Martin	27	11	7	0	247	0	0	-	Spain
Xisco	22	28	25	7	1576	3	0	-	Spain
Adrian Lopez Alvarez	20	17	7	1	294	1	0	-	Spain
Ivan Rico Soto	27	34	32	5	1086	8	1	-	Spain
Sebastian Taborda	27	26	15	3	465	1	0	-	Uruguay

TEAM OF THE SEASON

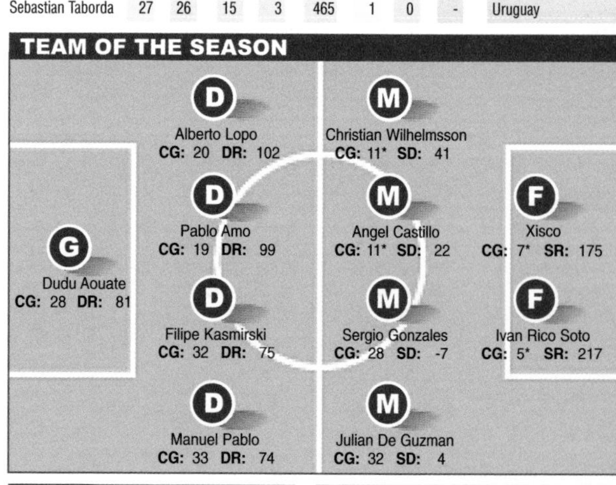

D
Alberto Lopo
CG: 20 DR: 102
M
Christian Wilhelmsson
CG: 11* SD: 41
D
Pablo Amo
CG: 19 DR: 99
M
Angel Castillo
CG: 11* SD: 22
F
Xisco
CG: 7* SR: 175
G
Dudu Aouate
CG: 28 DR: 81
D
Filipe Kasmirski
CG: 32 DR: 75
M
Sergio Gonzales
CG: 28 SD: -7
F
Ivan Rico Soto
CG: 5* SR: 217
D
Manuel Pablo
CG: 33 DR: 74
M
Julian De Guzman
CG: 32 SD: 4

MONTHLY POINTS TALLY

Month	Points	%
AUGUST	0	0%
SEPTEMBER	5	33%
OCTOBER	4	33%
NOVEMBER	4	44%
DECEMBER	4	33%
JANUARY	3	25%
FEBRUARY	7	58%
MARCH	10	67%
APRIL	12	100%
MAY	3	25%

LEAGUE GOALS

	PLAYER	MINS	GOALS	S RATE
1	Xisco	1576	9	175
2	Rico Soto	1086	5	217
3	Guardado	1935	5	387
4	Soriano	2574	5	514
5	Coloccini	3420	4	855
6	Lafita Castillo	1425	3	475
7	Amo Uguado	1690	3	563
8	Taborda Ramos	465	2	232
9	Castro Martin	247	1	247
10	Hidalgo	689	1	689
11	Bodipo	878	1	878
12	Wilhelmsson	1109	1	1109
13	Verdu	1514	1	1514
	Other		3	
	TOTAL		44	

TOP POINT EARNERS

	PLAYER	GAMES	AV PTS
1	Pablo Amo Uguado	19	**1.84**
2	Alberto Lopo Garcia	20	**1.70**
3	Juan R Villamuela	13	**1.62**
4	Julian De Guzman	32	**1.47**
5	Dudu Aouate	28	**1.46**
6	Filipe Luis Kasmirski	32	**1.44**
7	Fabricio Coloccini	38	**1.37**
8	Manuel Diaz	33	**1.36**
9	Sergio G Soriano	28	**1.32**
10	Joan Verdu	13	**1.23**
	CLUB AVERAGE:		**1.37**

DISCIPLINARY RECORDS

	PLAYER	YELLOW	RED	AVE
1	Ivan Rico Soto	8	1	**120**
2	Fabricio A Ramirez	2	0	**270**
3	Angel Lafita Castillo	5	0	**285**
4	Antonio Barragan	2	0	**308**
5	Julian De Guzman	9	0	**325**
6	Antonio Tomas	2	0	**327**
7	Cristian Hidalgo	2	0	**344**
8	Alberto Lopo	5	0	**367**
9	Wilhelmsson	3	0	**369**
10	Pablo Amo Uguado	3	1	**422**
11	Sergio G Soriano	5	1	**429**
12	Adrian Lopez	3	0	**450**
13	Sebastian Taborda	1	0	**465**
	Other	21	1	
	TOTAL	71	4	

KEY GOALKEEPER

Dudu Aouate

Goals Conceded in the League	31	Counting Games League games when player was on pitch for at least 70 minutes	28
Defensive Rating Ave number of mins between League goals conceded while on the pitch	81	Clean Sheets In League games when player was on pitch for at least 70 minutes	10

KEY PLAYERS - DEFENDERS

Alberto Lopo Garcia

Goals Conceded Number of League goals conceded while the player was on the pitch	18	Clean Sheets In League games when player was on pitch for at least 70 minutes	8
Defensive Rating Ave number of mins between League goals conceded while on the pitch	102	Club Defensive Rating Average number of mins between League goals conceded by the club this season	72

	PLAYER	CON LGE	CLEAN SHEETS	DEF RATE
1	Alberto Lopo Garcia	18	8	102 mins
2	Pablo Amo Uguado	17	7	99 mins
3	Filipe Luis Kasmirski	38	10	75 mins
4	Manuel Pablo Garcia Diaz	40	10	74 mins

KEY PLAYERS - MIDFIELDERS

Christian Wilhelmsson

Goals in the League	1	Contribution to Attacking Power Average number of minutes between League team goals while on pitch	69
Defensive Rating Average number of mins between League goals conceded while on the pitch	110	Scoring Difference Defensive Rating minus Contribution to Attacking Power	41

	PLAYER	LGE GOALS	DEF RATE	POWER	SCORE DIFF
1	Christian Wilhelmsson	1	110	69	41 mins
2	Angel Lafita Castillo	3	89	67	22 mins
3	Julian De Guzman	0	73	69	4 mins
4	Sergio Gonzales	5	73	80	-7 mins

KEY PLAYERS - GOALSCORERS

Xisco

Goals in the League	9	Player Strike Rate Average number of minutes between League goals scored by player	175
Contribution to Attacking Power Average number of minutes between League team goals while on pitch	60	Club Strike Rate Average number of minutes between League goals scored by club	74

	PLAYER	LGE GOALS	POWER	STRIKE RATE
1	Xisco	9	60	175 mins
2	Ivan Sanchez Rico Soto	5	77	217 mins
3	Jose Andres Guardado	5	92	387 mins
4	Angel Lafita Castillo	3	67	475 mins

MARTINSA
FADESA

Andres Guardado

SQUAD APPEARANCES

Match	1	2	3	4	5	6	7	8	9	10	11	12	13	14	15	16	17	18	19	20	21	22	23	24	25	26	27	28	29	30	31	32	33	34	35	36	37	38
Venue	H	A	H	A	H	A	A	H	A	H	A	H	A	H	A	H	A	H	A	A	H	A	H	A	H	H	A	H	A	H	A	H	A	H	A	H	A	H
Competition	L	L	L	L	L	L	L	L	L	L	L	L	L	L	L	L	L	L	L	L	L	L	L	L	L	L	L	L	L	L	L	L	L	L	L	L	L	L
Result	L	D	W	D	L	L	W	L	L	D	W	L	D	L	L	D	W	L	L	L	W	W	D	L	W	W	D	W	L	W	W	W	W	W	L	W	L	L

Goalkeepers
Fabricio Agosto Ramirez
Dudu Aouate
Gustavo Munua

Defenders
Pablo Amo Uguado
Aythami Artiles Oliva
Antonio B Fernandez
Fabricio Coloccini
Manuel Diaz
Adrian Lopez Rodriguez
Alberto Lopo Garcia
Filipe Luis Kasmirski
Sergio Rodrigues Garcia
Laureano Sanabria Ruiz
David Vazquez

Midfielders
Julian De Guzman
Sergio Gonzalez Soriano
Jose Guardado
Cristian Hidalgo
Angel Lafita Castillo
Juan R Villamuela
Antonio Tomas
Juan Carlos Valeron
Joan Verdu Fernandez
Christian Wilhelmsson

Forwards
Rodolfo Bodipo Diaz
Ruben Castro Martin
Xisco
Adrian Lopez Alvarez
Ivan Rico Soto
Sebastian Taborda

KEY: On all match · On bench · Subbed or sent off (Counting game) · Subbed or sent off (playing less than 70 minutes) · Subbed on from bench (Counting Game) · Subbed on (playing less than 70 minutes) · Subbed on and then subbed or sent off (Counting Game) · Subbed on and then subbed or sent off (playing less than 70 minutes) · Not in 16

VALENCIA

Final Position: **10th**

NICKNAME: THE BATS

KEY: ☐ Won ☐ Drawn ☐ Lost

	Comp	Opponent			Score	Scorers	Attendance
1	ecql1	**Elfsborg**	H	W	3-0	Vicente 7, Silva 59, Morientes 71	30,000
2	sppr1	**Villarreal**	H	L	0-3		52,500
3	ecql2	**Elfsborg**	A	W	2-1	Helguera Bujia 3, Villa Sanchez 90	13,148
4	sppr1	**Almeria**	A	W	2-1	Morientes Sanchez 46, Moretti 81	10,000
5	sppr1	**Valladolid**	H	W	2-1	Morientes Sanchez 23, Jimenez Silva 89	40,150
6	ecgpb	**Schalke**	A	W	1-0	Villa Sanchez 63	53,951
7	sppr1	**Real Betis**	A	W	2-1	Garcia Monteiro 68, Sanchez Rodriguez 82	41,250
8	sppr1	**Getafe**	H	W	2-1	Jimenez Silva 15, Villa Sanchez 31	44,000
9	sppr1	**Recreativo**	A	W	1-0	Villa Sanchez 5	20,694
10	ecgpb	**Chelsea**	H	L	1-2	Villa Sanchez 9	50,000
11	sppr1	**Espanyol**	H	L	1-2	Baraja Vegas 5	45,100
12	sppr1	**Deportivo**	A	W	4-2	Sanchez Rodriguez 9 pen, Baraja Vegas 15 Morientes Sanchez 38, 74	24,220
13	ecgpb	**Rosenborg BK**	A	L	0-2		21,119
14	sppr1	**Sevilla**	A	L	0-3		40,950
15	sppr1	**Real Madrid**	H	L	1-5	Angulo Valderrey 14	40,000
16	sppr1	**Mallorca**	A	W	2-0	Morientes Sanchez 45, 62	20,790
17	ecgpb	**Rosenborg BK**	H	L	0-2		28,341
18	sppr1	**Murcia**	H	W	3-0	Helguera 11, Villa Sanchez 25, 50	41,250
19	sppr1	**R Santander**	A	L	0-1		20,000
20	ecgpb	**Schalke**	H	D	0-0		30,000
21	sppr1	**Athl Bilbao**	H	L	0-3		49,500
22	sppr1	**Osasuna**	A	D	0-0		18,612
23	ecgpb	**Chelsea**	A	D	0-0		41,139
24	sppr1	**Barcelona**	H	L	0-3		55,000
25	sppr1	**Real Zaragoza**	A	D	2-2	Zigic 75, Jimenez Silva 81	34,596
26	sppr1	**Levante**	H	D	0-0		46,750
27	sppr1	**Atl Madrid**	A	L	0-1		43,840
28	sppr1	**Villarreal**	A	L	0-3		15,190
29	sppr1	**Almeria**	H	L	0-1		49,500
30	sppr1	**Valladolid**	A	W	2-0	Mata Garcia 59, Villa Sanchez 71	19,875
31	sppr1	**Real Betis**	H	W	3-1	Villa Sanchez 15, 88, Jimenez Silva 27	50,050
32	sppr1	**Getafe**	A	D	0-0		12,750
33	sppr1	**Recreativo**	H	D	1-1	Mata Garcia 38	41,250
34	sppr1	**Espanyol**	A	L	0-2		39,200
35	sppr1	**Deportivo**	H	D	2-2	Mata Garcia 16, Villa Sanchez 23	44,550
36	sppr1	**Sevilla**	H	L	1-2	Albiol Tortajada 90	49,500
37	sppr1	**Real Madrid**	A	W	3-2	Villa Sanchez 33, 66 pen Arizmendi de Lucas 88	70,000
38	sppr1	**Mallorca**	H	L	0-3		51,700
39	sppr1	**Murcia**	A	L	0-1		24,880
40	sppr1	**R Santander**	H	L	1-2	Villa Sanchez 64 pen	47,850
41	sppr1	**Athl Bilbao**	A	L	1-5	Villa Sanchez 75	36,000
42	sppr1	**Osasuna**	H	W	3-0	Villa Sanchez 19 pen, Mata Garcia 51 Sanchez Rodriguez 83	55,000
43	sppr1	**Barcelona**	A	L	0-6		71,064
44	sppr1	**Real Zaragoza**	H	W	1-0	Jimenez Silva 20	38,500
45	sppr1	**Levante**	A	W	5-1	Villa Sanchez 13, 28, 66 Mata Garcia 34, Angulo Valderrey 65	14,421
46	sppr1	**Atl Madrid**	H	W	3-1	Seitaridis 11, Villa Sanchez 39, 54	41,250

LEAGUE APPEARANCES, BOOKINGS AND CAPS

	AGE (on 01/07/08)	IN NAMED 18	APPEARANCES	COUNTING GAMES	MINUTES ON PITCH	YELLOW CARDS	RED CARDS	CAPS THIS SEASON	NATIONAL SIDE
Goalkeepers									
Santiago Canizares	38	16	10	10	900	1	0	-	Spain
Timo Hildebrand	29	35	26	26	2340	1	0	2	Germany
Juan Palacios	34	22	2	2	180	1	0	-	Spain
Defenders									
Raul Albiol	22	35	32	32	2873	6	1	4	Spain
Luis Monteiro	28	29	26	22	2121	7	0	7	Portugal
Ivan Helguera	33	33	24	21	2047	7	1	-	Spain
David Lomban	21	11	3	1	150	0	0	-	Spain
Carlos Marchena	28	32	28	24	2277	12	0	9	Spain
Emiliano Moretti	27	29	28	27	2470	5	0	-	Italy
Alexis R Delgado	22	18	14	10	1028	1	0	-	Spain
Marco A Caneira	29	25	19	15	1557	8	0	-	Portugal
Midfielders									
David Albelda	30	17	15	10	1023	6	0	6	Spain
Ever Banega	20	17	12	3	681	2	0	1	Argentina
Ruben Baraja	32	25	25	18	1889	8	0	-	Spain
Eduardo C Daude	30	22	13	2	442	1	0	-	Brazil
Jaime G Martinez	23	4	3	1	198	0	0	-	Spain
David Jimenez Silva	22	35	34	31	2774	6	1	8	Spain
Hedwiges Maduro	23	12	11	7	776	2	1	-	Holland
Angel Montoso	20	8	4	2	229	1	0	-	Spain
Vicente Rodriguez	26	21	17	3	718	1	0	-	Spain
Joaquin Sanchez	26	36	34	23	2478	3	1	6	Spain
Stephen Sunday	19	26	10	3	447	0	0	-	Spain
Manuel Fernandes	22	9	6	2	392	1	0	-	Portugal
Forwards									
Miguel Angel Angulo	31	17	15	8	822	1	0	-	Spain
Javier Arizmendi	24	34	28	12	1450	5	0	-	Spain
Juan Manuel Mata	20	28	24	12	1390	1	0	-	Spain
Fernando Morientes	32	24	22	7	1178	3	0	-	Spain
David Villa Sanchez	26	28	28	22	2115	2	2	7	Spain
Nikola Zigic	27	25	16	1	533	2	1	6	Serbia

TEAM OF THE SEASON

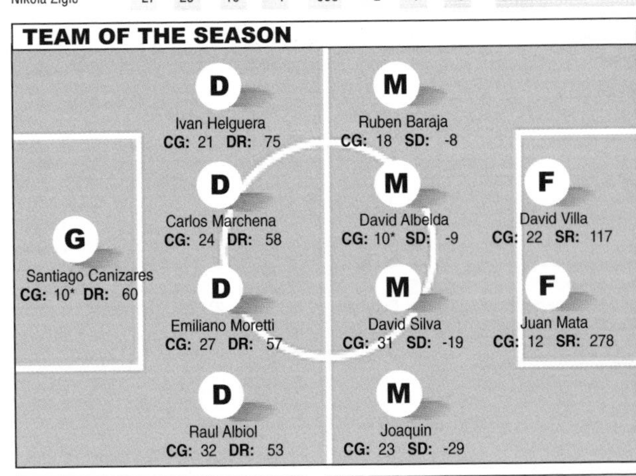

G
Santiago Canizares
CG: 10* DR: 60
D
Ivan Helguera
CG: 21 DR: 75
D
Carlos Marchena
CG: 24 DR: 58
D
Emiliano Moretti
CG: 27 DR: 57
D
Raul Albiol
CG: 32 DR: 53
M
Ruben Baraja
CG: 18 SD: -8
M
David Albelda
CG: 10* SD: -9
M
David Silva
CG: 31 SD: -19
M
Joaquin
CG: 23 SD: -29
F
David Villa
CG: 22 SR: 117
F
Juan Mata
CG: 12 SR: 278

MONTHLY POINTS TALLY

Month	Points	%
AUGUST	0	0%
SEPTEMBER	15	100%
OCTOBER	3	25%
NOVEMBER	6	67%
DECEMBER	2	17%
JANUARY	1	8%
FEBRUARY	8	67%
MARCH	4	27%
APRIL	3	25%
MAY	9	75%

LEAGUE GOALS

	PLAYER	MINS	GOALS	S RATE
1	Villa	2115	**18**	117
2	Morientes	1178	**6**	196
3	Mata	1390	**5**	278
4	Silva	2774	**5**	554
5	Rodriguez	2478	**3**	826
6	Angulo	822	**2**	411
7	Baraja	1889	**2**	944
8	Zigic	533	**1**	533
9	Arizmendi	1450	**1**	1450
10	Helguera	2047	**1**	2047
11	Monteiro	2121	**1**	2121
12	Moretti	2470	**1**	2470
13	Albiol	2873	**1**	2873
	Other		0	
	TOTAL		**47**	

TOP POINT EARNERS

	PLAYER	GAMES	AV PTS
1	David Villa	22	**1.77**
2	Ivan Helguera	21	**1.76**
3	Juan Manuel Mata	12	**1.67**
4	Marco Antonio Caneira	15	**1.60**
5	Luis Monteiro	22	**1.45**
6	Joaquin	23	**1.35**
7	Raul Albiol	32	**1.34**
8	Timo Hildebrand	26	**1.31**
9	Ruben Baraja	18	**1.28**
10	David Silva	31	**1.26**
	CLUB AVERAGE:		**1.34**

DISCIPLINARY RECORDS

	PLAYER	YELLOW	RED	AVE
1	David Albelda	6	0	**170**
2	Nikola Zigic	2	1	**177**
3	Carlos Marchena	12	0	**189**
4	Marco A Caneira	8	0	**194**
5	Ruben Baraja	8	0	**236**
6	Ivan Helguera	7	1	**255**
7	Hedwiges Maduro	2	1	**258**
8	Javier Arizmendi	5	0	**290**
9	Luis Monteiro	7	0	**303**
10	Ever Banega	2	0	**340**
11	Fernando Morientes	3	0	**392**
12	David Jiminez Silva	6	1	**396**
13	Raul Albiol	6	1	**410**
	Other	16	3	
	TOTAL	**90**	**8**	

KEY GOALKEEPER

Santiago Canizares

Goals Conceded in the League	15	Counting Games League games when player was on pitch for at least 70 minutes	10
Defensive Rating Ave number of mins between League goals conceded while on the pitch	60	Clean Sheets In League games when player was on pitch for at least 70 minutes	2

KEY PLAYERS - DEFENDERS

Ivan Helguera

Goals Conceded Number of League goals conceded while the player was on the pitch	27	Clean Sheets In League games when player was on pitch for at least 70 minutes	8
Defensive Rating Ave number of mins between League goals conceded while on the pitch	75	Club Defensive Rating Average number of mins between League goals conceded by the club this season	55

	PLAYER	CON LGE	CLEAN SHEETS	DEF RATE
1	Ivan Helguera	27	8	75 mins
2	Carlos Marchena	39	8	58 mins
3	Emiliano Moretti	43	6	57 mins
4	Raul Albiol	54	6	53 mins

KEY PLAYERS - MIDFIELDERS

Ruben Baraja

Goals in the League	2	Contribution to Attacking Power Average number of minutes between League team goals while on pitch	65
Defensive Rating Average number of mins between League goals conceded while on the pitch	57	Scoring Difference Defensive Rating minus Contribution to Attacking Power	-8

	PLAYER	LGE GOALS	DEF RATE	POWER	SCORE DIFF
1	Ruben Baraja	2	57	65	-8 mins
2	David Albelda	0	44	53	-9 mins
3	David J Silva	5	55	74	-19 mins
4	Joaquin Sanchez	3	53	82	-29 mins

KEY PLAYERS - GOALSCORERS

David Villa

Goals in the League	18	Player Strike Rate Average number of minutes between League goals scored by player	117
Contribution to Attacking Power Average number of minutes between League team goals while on pitch	60	Club Strike Rate Average number of minutes between League goals scored by club	71

	PLAYER	LGE GOALS	POWER	STRIKE RATE
1	David Villa	18	60	117 mins
2	Juan Manuel Mata Garcia	5	73	278 mins
3	David J Silva	5	74	554 mins
4	Joaquin Sanchez	3	82	826 mins

David Villa

SQUAD APPEARANCES

Match	1	2	3	4	5	6	7	8	9	10	11	12	13	14	15	16	17	18	19	20	21	22	23
Venue	H	H	A	A	H	A	A	H	A	H	H	A	A	A	H	A	H	H	A	H	H	A	A
Competition	C	L	C	L	L	C	L	L	L	C	L	L	C	L	L	L	C	L	L	C	L	L	C
Result	W	L	W	W	W	W	W	W	W	L	L	W	L	L	L	W	L	W	L	D	L	D	D

Match	24	25	26	27	28	29	30	31	32	33	34	35	36	37	38	39	40	41	42	43	44	45	46
Venue	H	A	H	A	A	H	A	H	A	H	A	H	H	A	H	A	H	A	H	A	H	A	H
Competition	L	L	L	L	L	L	L	L	L	L	L	L	L	L	L	L	L	L	L	L	L	L	L
Result	L	D	D	L	L	L	W	W	D	D	L	D	L	W	L	L	L	L	W	L	W	W	W

Goalkeepers
Santiago Canizares
Timo Hildebrand
Juan Luis Mora

Defenders
Raul Albiol
Luis Monteiro
Ivan Helguera
David Lomban
Carlos Marchena
Emiliano Moretti
Alexis Ruano Delgado
Marco Antonio Caneira

Midfielders
David Albelda
Ever Banega
Ruben Baraja
Eduardo Cesar Daude
Jaime Gavilan Martinez
David Jimenez Silva
Hedwiges Maduro
Angel Montoso
Vicente Rodriguez
Joaquin Sanchez
Stephen Sunday
Manuel Fernandes

Forwards
Miguel Angel Angulo
Javier Arizmendi
Juan Manuel Mata
Fernando Morientes
David Villa Sanchez
Nikola Zigic

KEY: On all match | Subbed or sent off (Counting game) | Subbed on from bench (Counting Game) | Subbed on and then subbed or sent off (Counting Game) | Not in 16
On bench | Subbed or sent off (playing less than 70 minutes) | Subbed on (playing less than 70 minutes) | Subbed on and then subbed or sent off (playing less than 70 minutes)

ATHLETIC BILBAO

Final Position: **11th**

NICKNAME: LIONS

KEY: ☐Won ☐Drawn ☐Lost

							Attendance
1	sppr1	**Osasuna**	H	D	0-0		40,000
2	sppr1	**Barcelona**	A	L	1-3	Susaeta 71	76,817
3	sppr1	**Real Zaragoza**	H	D	1-1	Susaeta 9	40,000
4	sppr1	**Levante**	A	W	2-1	Aduriz 8, 72	17,710
5	sppr1	**Atl Madrid**	H	L	0-2		38,000
6	sppr1	**Villarreal**	A	L	0-1		18,000
7	sppr1	**Almeria**	H	D	1-1	Etxeberria Lizardi 30	36,000
8	sppr1	**Valladolid**	A	W	2-1	Aduriz 10, 32	22,790
9	sppr1	**Real Betis**	H	D	0-0		40,000
10	sppr1	**Getafe**	A	L	0-2		12,750
11	sppr1	**Recreativo**	H	W	2-0	Etxeberria Lizardi 52, 62	36,000
12	sppr1	**Espanyol**	A	L	1-2	Gabilondo 3	48,720
13	sppr1	**Deportivo**	H	D	2-2	Barragan 22 og, Lopez 53	36,000
14	sppr1	**Valencia**	A	W	3-0	Yeste 32, Llorente 60, 90	49,500
15	sppr1	**Real Madrid**	H	L	0-1		40,000
16	sppr1	**Mallorca**	A	D	0-0		16,170
17	sppr1	**Murcia**	H	D	1-1	Koikili 45 pen	30,400
18	sppr1	**R Santander**	A	L	0-1		19,092
19	sppr1	**Sevilla**	H	W	2-0	Yeste 26, Susaeta 67	38,400
20	sppr1	**Osasuna**	A	L	0-2		17,820
21	sppr1	**Barcelona**	H	D	1-1	Llorente 78	39,200
22	sppr1	**Real Zaragoza**	A	L	0-1		25,875
23	sppr1	**Levante**	H	W	1-0	Llorente 55	39,200
24	sppr1	**Atl Madrid**	A	W	2-1	Susaeta 38, Llorente 45	43,080
25	sppr1	**Villarreal**	H	L	1-2	Llorente 3	28,000
26	sppr1	**Almeria**	A	D	1-1	Llorente 73	15,400
27	sppr1	**Valladolid**	H	W	2-0	Gabilondo 5, 68	30,000
28	sppr1	**Real Betis**	A	W	2-1	Yeste 7, Lopez 64 pen	25,000
29	sppr1	**Getafe**	H	W	1-0	Etxeberria Lizardi 29	34,000
30	sppr1	**Recreativo**	A	D	1-1	Aduriz 82	15,450
31	sppr1	**Espanyol**	H	W	1-0	Garmendia 13	35,000
32	sppr1	**Deportivo**	A	L	0-3		26,780
33	sppr1	**Valencia**	H	W	5-1	Martinez 19, Llorente 49, 66, Iraola 85 Aduriz 90	36,000
34	sppr1	**Real Madrid**	A	L	0-3		76,000
35	sppr1	**Mallorca**	H	L	1-2	Llorente 8	40,000
36	sppr1	**Murcia**	A	W	2-1	Llorente 32, Gabilondo 83	12,000
37	sppr1	**R Santander**	H	D	0-0		40,000
38	sppr1	**Sevilla**	A	L	1-4	Aduriz 3 pen	36,855

LEAGUE APPEARANCES, BOOKINGS AND CAPS

	AGE (on 01/07/08)	IN NAMED 18	APPEARANCES	COUNTING GAMES	MINUTES ON PITCH	YELLOW CARDS	RED CARDS	CAPS THIS SEASON	NATIONAL SIDE
Goalkeepers									
Daniel Aranzubia	28	35	10	9	859	1	0	-	Spain
Gorka Moreno	27	14	13	12	1121	3	0	-	Spain
Armando Riveiro	37	16	16	16	1440	2	0	-	Spain
Defenders									
U Aldekoaotalora	25	31	20	14	1344	6	0	-	Spain
Fernando Amorebieta	23	34	34	33	2972	13	2	-	Spain
Asier Del Horno	27	23	16	11	1177	5	1	-	Spain
Unai Exposito	28	10	3	2	200	0	0	-	Spain
Lertxundi Koikili	27	35	27	23	2205	7	1	-	Spain
Ander Murillo	24	19	5	0	79	1	0	-	Spain
Aitor Ocio Carrion	31	27	27	26	2380	9	3	-	Spain
Luis Prieto	29	10	3	1	96	0	0	-	Spain
Iban Z Urrutia	25	5	1	1	90	0	0	-	Spain
Midfielders									
David Cuellar Tainta	28	10	6	0	182	0	0	-	Spain
Joseba Etxeberria	30	30	25	10	1526	6	0	-	Spain
Igor Gabilondo	29	30	26	16	1770	3	0	-	Spain
Joseba Garmendia	22	20	18	3	783	4	0	-	Spain
Carlos G Nausia	27	5	5	5	450	1	0	-	Spain
Andoni I Sagarra	26	36	36	34	3161	5	0	-	Spain
David Moreno	25	37	31	17	1936	3	0	-	Spain
Roberto M Ripodas	31	5	2	0	121	0	0	-	Spain
Javier M Aguinaga	19	35	34	28	2816	13	0	-	Spain
Inaki Munoz Oroz	29	28	11	2	462	1	0	-	Spain
Pablo Orbaiz Lesaka	29	24	23	16	1748	8	0	-	Spain
Markel S Laskurain	20	31	28	20	1942	10	0	-	Spain
Francisco J Yeste	28	24	24	15	1670	6	2	-	Spain
Forwards									
Aritz Aduriz Zubeldia	27	38	33	15	1924	4	0	-	Spain
Urko Arroyo Rivas	21	1	1	0	45	0	0	-	Spain
Fernando Llorente	23	37	34	22	2299	3	0	-	Spain
Aitor Ramos Leniz	23	6	5	0	177	1	0	-	Spain
Ion Velez Martinez	23	11	7	0	259	0	0	-	Spain

TEAM OF THE SEASON

D
Aitor Ocio
CG: 26 DR: 79
M
Francisco Javier Yeste
CG: 15 SD: 17
D
Aldekoaotalora
CG: 14 DR: 79
M
Pablo Orbaiz
CG: 16 SD: 14
F
Fernando Llorente
CG: 22 SR: 209
G
Gorka Morena
CG: 12 DR: 80
D
Fernando Amorebieta
CG: 33 DR: 78
M
Markel Susaeta
CG: 20 SD: -3
F
Aritz Zubeldia
CG: 15 SR: 274
D
Lertxundi Koikili
CG: 23 DR: 73
M
Andoni Iraola
CG: 34 SD: -6

MONTHLY POINTS TALLY

AUGUST	1	33%
SEPTEMBER	4	27%
OCTOBER	5	42%
NOVEMBER	4	44%
DECEMBER	5	42%
JANUARY	4	33%
FEBRUARY	6	50%
MARCH	11	73%
APRIL	6	50%
MAY	4	33%

LEAGUE GOALS

	PLAYER	MINS	GOALS	S RATE
1	Llorente	2299	11	209
2	Aduriz	1924	7	274
3	Etxeberria	1526	4	381
4	Gabilondo	1770	4	442
5	Susaeta	1942	4	485
6	Yeste	1670	3	556
7	Lopez	1936	2	968
8	Garmendia	783	1	783
9	Koikili	2205	1	2205
10	Martinez	2816	1	2816
11	Iraola	3161	1	3161
	Other		0	
	TOTAL		39	

TOP POINT EARNERS

	PLAYER	GAMES	AV PTS
1	Ustaritz Aldekoaotalora	14	1.71
2	Fernando Llorente	22	1.55
3	Pablo Orbaiz Lesaka	16	1.50
4	Armando Riveiro	16	1.50
5	Igor Gabilondo	16	1.44
6	Javier Aguinaga	28	1.39
7	Andoni Iraola Sagarra	34	1.38
8	Markel Susaeta	20	1.35
9	Francisco Javier Yeste	15	1.33
10	Aitor Ocio	26	1.27
	CLUB AVERAGE:		1.32

DISCIPLINARY RECORDS

	PLAYER	YELLOW	RED	AVE
1	Markel Susaeta	10	0	194
2	Joseba Garmendia	4	0	195
3	Asier Del Horno	5	1	196
4	F Amorebieta	13	2	198
5	Aitor Ocio	9	3	198
6	Francisco J Yeste	6	2	208
7	Javier Aguinaga	13	0	216
8	Pablo Orbaiz	8	0	218
9	U Aldekoaotalora	6	0	224
10	Joseba Etxeberria	6	0	254
11	Lertxundi Koikili	7	1	275
12	Gorka Iraizoz	3	0	373
13	Munoz Oroz	1	0	462
	Other	20	0	
	TOTAL	111	9	

KEY GOALKEEPER

Gorka Iraizoz Moreno

Goals Conceded in the League	14	Counting Games League games when player was on pitch for at least 70 minutes	12
Defensive Rating Ave number of mins between League goals conceded while on the pitch	80	Clean Sheets In League games when player was on pitch for at least 70 minutes	3

KEY PLAYERS - GOALSCORERS

Fernando Llorente Torres

Goals in the League	11	Player Strike Rate Average number of minutes between League goals scored by player	209
Contribution to Attacking Power Average number of minutes between League team goals while on pitch	79	Club Strike Rate Average number of minutes between League goals scored by club	85

	PLAYER	LGE GOALS	POWER	STRIKE RATE
1	Fernando Llorente	11	79	209 mins
2	Aritz Aduriz Zubeldia	7	83	274 mins
3	Igor Gabilondo del Campo	4	76	442 mins
4	Markel Susaeta	4	77	485 mins

KEY PLAYERS - DEFENDERS

Aitor Ocio

Goals Conceded Number of League goals conceded while the player was on the pitch	30	Clean Sheets In League games when player was on pitch for at least 70 minutes	7
Defensive Rating Ave number of mins between League goals conceded while on the pitch	79	Club Defensive Rating Average number of mins between League goals conceded by the club this season	79

	PLAYER	CON LGE	CLEAN SHEETS	DEF RATE
1	Aitor Ocio	30	7	79 mins
2	Ustaritz Aldekoaotalora	17	5	79 mins
3	Fernando Amorebieta Mardaras	38	10	78 mins
4	Lertxundi Koikili	30	6	73 mins

15
8

Andoni Iraola and David Lopez

KEY PLAYERS - MIDFIELDERS

Francisco Javier Yeste

Goals in the League	3	Contribution to Attacking Power Average number of minutes between League team goals while on pitch	87
Defensive Rating Average number of mins between League goals conceded while on the pitch	104	Scoring Difference Defensive Rating minus Contribution to Attacking Power	17

	PLAYER	LGE GOALS	DEF RATE	POWER	SCORE DIFF
1	Francisco Javier Yeste	3	104	87	17 mins
2	Pablo Orbaiz Lesaka	0	97	83	14 mins
3	Markel Susaeta	4	74	77	-3 mins
4	Andoni Iraola	1	77	83	-6 mins

SQUAD APPEARANCES

Match	1	2	3	4	5	6	7	8	9	10	11	12	13	14	15	16	17	18	19	20	21	22	23	24	25	26	27	28	29	30	31	32	33	34	35	36	37	38
Venue	H	A	H	A	H	A	H	A	H	A	H	A	H	A	H	A	H	A	H	A	H	A	H	A	H	A	H	A	H	A	H	A	H	A	H	A	H	A
Competition	L	L	L	L	L	L	L	L	L	L	L	L	L	L	L	L	L	L	L	L	L	L	L	L	L	L	L	L	L	L	L	L	L	L	L	L	L	L
Result	D	L	D	W	L	L	D	W	D	L	W	L	D	W	L	D	D	L	W	L	D	L	W	W	L	D	W	W	W	D	W	L	W	L	L	W	D	L

Goalkeepers
- Daniel Aranzubia
- Gorka Moreno
- Armando Riveiro

Defenders
- Ustaritz Aldekoaotalora
- Fernando Amorebieta
- Asier Del Horno
- Unai Exposito
- Lertxundi Koikili
- Ander Murillo
- Aitor Ocio Carrion
- Luis Prieto
- Iban Zubiaurre Urrutia

Midfielders
- David Cuellar Tainta
- Joseba Etxeberria
- Igor Gabilondo
- Joseba Garmendia
- Carlos Gurpegui Nausia
- Andoni Iraola Sagarra
- David Moreno
- Roberto M Ripodas
- Javier Martinez Aguinaga
- Inaki Munoz Oroz
- Pablo Orbaiz Lesaka
- Markel Susaeta Laskurain
- Francisco Javier Yeste

Forwards
- Aritz Aduriz Zubeldia
- Urko Arroyo Rivas
- Fernando Llorente
- Aitor Ramos Leniz
- Ion Velez Martinez

KEY: On all match; On bench; Subbed or sent off (Counting game); Subbed or sent off (playing less than 70 minutes); Subbed on from bench (Counting Game); Subbed on (playing less than 70 minutes); Subbed on and then subbed or sent off (Counting Game); Subbed on and then subbed or sent off (playing less than 70 minutes); Not in 16

ESPANYOL

Final Position: **12th**

NICKNAME: PARAKEETS

KEY: Won / Drawn / Lost

						Attendance
1	sppr1	**Valladolid**	H	L	0-1		20,000
2	sppr1	**Real Betis**	A	D	2-2	Garcia Fernandez 33, 41	45,000
3	sppr1	**Getafe**	H	W	1-0	Soriano Casas 88	18,000
4	sppr1	**Recreativo**	A	L	1-2	Riera Ortega 4	19,000
5	sppr1	**Sevilla**	A	W	3-2	Garcia Fernandez 29, 55 Tamudo Montero 87	45,000
6	sppr1	**Deportivo**	H	W	1-0	Tamudo Montero 45	50,400
7	sppr1	**Valencia**	A	W	2-1	Riera Ortega 20, Garcia Fernandez 80	45,100
8	sppr1	**Real Madrid**	H	W	2-1	Riera Ortega 1, Tamudo Montero 53	50,400
9	sppr1	**Mallorca**	A	D	2-2	Arango Saenz 21 og Tamudo Montero 26 pen	23,142
10	sppr1	**Murcia**	H	D	0-0		29,860
11	sppr1	**R Santander**	A	D	1-1	Tamudo Montero 90 pen	22,251
12	sppr1	**Athl Bilbao**	H	W	2-1	Tamudo Montero 39, Ocio 90 og	48,720
13	sppr1	**Osasuna**	A	W	2-1	Martinez Cervera 30, Lopez Rocha 33	14,850
14	sppr1	**Barcelona**	H	D	1-1	Corominas Telechea 69	44,800
15	sppr1	**Real Zaragoza**	A	D	3-3	Tamudo Montero 7, Lopez Rocha 10 Zabaleta Girod 14	31,050
16	sppr1	**Levante**	H	W	1-0	Jarque Gonzalez 8	22,400
17	sppr1	**Atl Madrid**	A	W	2-1	Tamudo Montero 52 Garcia Fernandez 85	49,320
18	sppr1	**Villarreal**	H	W	3-0	Tamudo Montero 8, 35, Lopez Rocha 13	38,640
19	sppr1	**Almeria**	A	L	0-1		16,500
20	sppr1	**Valladolid**	A	L	1-2	Torrejon Moya 58	23,055
21	sppr1	**Real Betis**	H	L	1-2	Garcia Fernandez 51	39,200
22	sppr1	**Getafe**	A	W	1-0	Soriano Casas 16	11,900
23	sppr1	**Recreativo**	H	L	1-2	de Souza 39	21,280
24	sppr1	**Sevilla**	H	L	2-4	Garcia Fernandez 40 Corominas Telechea 75	39,200
25	sppr1	**Deportivo**	A	L	0-2		24,220
26	sppr1	**Valencia**	H	W	2-0	Garcia Fernandez 4, 51 pen	39,200
27	sppr1	**Real Madrid**	A	L	1-2	Lopez Rocha 29	72,000
28	sppr1	**Mallorca**	H	W	2-1	Garcia Fernandez 58 pen, 88	39,200
29	sppr1	**Murcia**	A	L	0-4		20,215
30	sppr1	**R Santander**	H	L	0-3		32,480
31	sppr1	**Athl Bilbao**	A	L	0-1		35,000
32	sppr1	**Osasuna**	H	L	0-1		21,150
33	sppr1	**Barcelona**	A	D	0-0		69,090
34	sppr1	**Real Zaragoza**	H	D	1-1	Riera Ortega 60	25,150
35	sppr1	**Levante**	A	D	1-1	Garcia Fernandez 90 pen	10,120
36	sppr1	**Atl Madrid**	H	L	0-2		30,800
37	sppr1	**Villarreal**	A	L	0-2		15,624
38	sppr1	**Almeria**	H	L	1-3	Garcia Fernandez 59 pen	9,500

LEAGUE APPEARANCES, BOOKINGS AND CAPS

	AGE (on 01/07/08)	IN NAMED 18	APPEARANCES	COUNTING GAMES	MINUTES ON PITCH	YELLOW CARDS	RED CARDS	CAPS THIS SEASON	NATIONAL SIDE
Goalkeepers									
Francisco Casilla	21	7	4	3	313	1	0	-	Spain
Idriss Carlos Kameni	24	30	30	30	2700	2	0	6	Cameroon
Inaki Lafuente	32	27	5	4	407	0	0	-	Spain
Defenders									
Francisco C Torres	23	31	17	11	1171	5	0	-	Spain
David Garcia	27	22	17	15	1398	3	0	-	Spain
Clemente Rodriguez	26	25	17	10	1162	3	1	-	Argentina
Jesus Maria Lacruz	30	25	18	12	1152	4	0	-	Spain
Albert Serran	23	10	1	1	90	0	0	-	Spain
Marc Torrejon	22	36	36	35	3208	5	1	-	Spain
Pablo Javier Zabaleta	23	33	32	29	2703	13	1	1	Argentina
Midfielders									
Ivan de la Pena	32	13	12	6	704	5	0	-	Spain
Jonatas Domingo	25	10	9	1	264	0	0	-	Brazil
Mohammed Yaagoubi	30	25	9	1	343	0	0	-	Morocco
Jordi Gomez Penche	23	5	3	0	87	0	0	-	Spain
Moises Hurtado	27	35	34	26	2618	12	0	-	Spain
Daniel Jarque	25	32	31	30	2744	10	1	-	Spain
Angel M Cervera	22	31	28	15	1928	8	0	-	Spain
Francisco Rufete	31	19	10	3	486	4	0	-	Spain
Albert Riera	26	36	36	25	2533	8	0	5	Spain
Milan Smiljanic	21	35	29	14	1598	4	0	5	Serbia
Forwards									
Ferran C Telechea	25	35	26	12	1439	1	1	-	Spain
Henrique Ewerthon	27	15	8	2	448	0	0	-	Brazil
Luis Garcia	27	37	37	35	3155	9	0	1	Spain
Valmiro Rocha	27	36	31	20	2246	5	0	-	Spain
Jonathan Soriano	22	35	24	2	797	3	0	-	Spain
Raul Tamudo	30	25	25	18	1820	4	1	4	Spain

TEAM OF THE SEASON

D
Marc Torrejan
CG: 35 DR: 69
M
Albert Riera
CG: 25 SD: -5
D
Pablo Zabaleta
CG: 29 DR: 67
M
Moises Hurtado
CG: 26 SD: -14
F
Raul Tamudo
CG: 18 SR: 182
G
Idriss Carlos Kameni
CG: 30 DR: 64
D
David Garcia
CG: 15 DR: 58
M
Daniel Jarque
CG: 30 SD: -19
F
Luis Garcia
CG: 35 SR: 225
D
Jesus Maria Lacruz
CG: 12 DR: 52
M
Angel Martinez Cervera
CG: 15 SD: -23

MONTHLY POINTS TALLY

AUGUST	0	0%
SEPTEMBER	10	67%
OCTOBER	7	78%
NOVEMBER	8	67%
DECEMBER	8	67%
JANUARY	3	25%
FEBRUARY	3	25%
MARCH	6	40%
APRIL	2	17%
MAY	1	8%

LEAGUE GOALS

	PLAYER	MINS	GOALS	S RATE
1	G Fernandez	3155	14	225
2	Tamudo	1820	10	182
3	Lopez Rocha	2246	4	561
4	Riera Ortega	2533	4	633
5	Soriano Casas	797	2	398
6	C Telechea	1439	2	719
7	Ewerthon	448	1	448
8	M Cervera	1928	1	1928
9	Zabaleta Girod	2703	1	2703
10	Jarque	2744	1	2744
11	Torrejon Moya	3208	1	3208
	Other		0	
	TOTAL		41	

TOP POINT EARNERS

	PLAYER	GAMES	AV PTS
1	Valmiro Lopez Rocha	20	1.55
2	Raul Tamudo	18	1.50
3	Jesus Maria Lacruz	12	1.42
4	Moises Hurtado Perez	26	1.42
5	Daniel Jarque Gonzalez	30	1.37
6	Idriss Carlos Kameni	30	1.37
7	Marc Torrejon Moya	35	1.34
8	Albert Riera Ortega	25	1.32
9	Pablo Javier Zabaleta	29	1.31
10	Luis Garcia Fernandez	35	1.23
	CLUB AVERAGE:		1.26

DISCIPLINARY RECORDS

	PLAYER	YELLOW	RED	AVE
1	Francisco Rufete	4	0	121
2	Ivan de la Pena	5	0	140
3	Pablo J Zabaleta	13	1	193
4	Moises Hurtado	12	0	218
5	Francisco J Chica	5	0	234
6	Angel M Cervera	8	0	241
7	Daniel Jarque	10	1	249
8	Jonathan Soriano	3	0	265
9	Jesus Maria Lacruz	4	0	288
10	Clemente Rodriguez	3	1	290
11	Albert Riera Ortega	8	0	316
12	Luis Garcia	9	0	350
13	Raul Tamudo	4	1	364
	Other	20	2	
	TOTAL	108	6	

KEY GOALKEEPER

Idriss Carlos Kameni

Goals Conceded in the League	42	**Counting Games** League games when player was on pitch for at least 70 minutes	30
Defensive Rating Ave number of mins between League goals conceded while on the pitch	64	**Clean Sheets** In League games when player was on pitch for at least 70 minutes	7

KEY PLAYERS - DEFENDERS

Marc Torrejon Moya

Goals Conceded Number of League goals conceded while the player was on the pitch	46	**Clean Sheets** In League games when player was on pitch for at least 70 minutes	8
Defensive Rating Ave number of mins between League goals conceded while on the pitch	69	**Club Defensive Rating** Average number of mins between League goals conceded by the club this season	64

	PLAYER	CON LGE	CLEAN SHEETS	DEF RATE
1	Marc Torrejon	46	8	69 mins
2	Pablo Javier Zabaleta	40	8	67 mins
3	David Garcia de la Cruz	24	4	58 mins
4	Jesus Maria Lacruz Gomez	22	2	52 mins

KEY PLAYERS - MIDFIELDERS

Albert Riera Ortega

Goals in the League	4	**Contribution to Attacking Power** Average number of minutes between League team goals while on pitch	79
Defensive Rating Average number of mins between League goals conceded while on the pitch	74	**Scoring Difference** Defensive Rating minus Contribution to Attacking Power	-5

	PLAYER	LGE GOALS	DEF RATE	POWER	SCORE DIFF
1	Albert Riera Ortega	4	74	79	-5 mins
2	Moises Hurtado Perez	0	70	84	-14 mins
3	Daniel Jarque Gonzalez	1	66	85	-19 mins
4	Angel Martinez Cervera	1	64	87	-23 mins

KEY PLAYERS - GOALSCORERS

Raul Tamudo

Goals in the League	10	**Player Strike Rate** Average number of minutes between League goals scored by player	182
Contribution to Attacking Power Average number of minutes between League team goals while on pitch	82	**Club Strike Rate** Average number of minutes between League goals scored by club	79

	PLAYER	LGE GOALS	POWER	STRIKE RATE
1	Raul Tamudo	10	82	182 mins
2	Luis Garcia Fernandez	14	76	225 mins
3	Valmiro Lopez Rocha	4	70	561 mins
4	Albert Riera	4	79	633 mins

uhlsport
QU
AT
Raul Tamudo

SQUAD APPEARANCES

Match	1	2	3	4	5	6	7	8	9	10	11	12	13	14	15	16	17	18	19	20	21	22	23	24	25	26	27	28	29	30	31	32	33	34	35	36	37	38
Venue	H	A	H	A	A	H	A	H	A	H	A	H	A	H	A	H	A	H	A	A	H	A	H	H	A	H	A	H	A	H	A	H	A	H	A	H	A	H
Competition	L	L	L	L	L	L	L	L	L	L	L	L	L	L	L	L	L	L	L	L	L	L	L	L	L	L	L	L	L	L	L	L	L	L	L	L	L	L
Result	L	D	W	L	W	W	W	W	D	D	D	W	W	D	D	W	W	W	L	L	L	W	L	L	L	W	L	W	L	L	L	L	D	D	D	L	L	L

Goalkeepers
Francisco Casilla
Idriss Carlos Kameni
Inaki Lafuente

Defenders
Francisco Chica Torres
David Garcia
Clemente Rodriguez
Jesus Maria Lacruz
Albert Serran
Marc Torrejon
Pablo Javier Zabaleta

Midfielders
Ivan de la Pena
Jonatas Domingo
Mohammed Yaagoubi
Jordi Gomez Penche
Moises Hurtado
Daniel Jarque
Angel Martinez Cervera
Francisco Rufete
Albert Riera
Milan Smiljanic

Forwards
Ferran C Telechea
Henrique Ewerthon
Luis Garcia
Valmiro Rocha
Jonathan Soriano
Raul Tamudo

KEY: On all match · On bench · Subbed or sent off (Counting game) · Subbed or sent off (playing less than 70 minutes) · Subbed on from bench (Counting Game) · Subbed on (playing less than 70 minutes) · Subbed on and then subbed or sent off (Counting Game) · Subbed on and then subbed or sent off (playing less than 70 minutes) · Not in 16

REAL BETIS

Final Position: **13th**

NICKNAME: BETICOS

KEY: Won Drawn Lost

						Attendance
1	sppr1	**Recreativo**	A D	1-1	Rivas Alvaro 39	17,000
2	sppr1	**Espanyol**	H D	2-2	Fernandez Escribano 82, Sobis 83	45,000
3	sppr1	**Deportivo**	A L	0-1		22,490
4	sppr1	**Valencia**	H L	1-2	Sobis 86	41,250
5	sppr1	**Real Madrid**	A L	0-2		70,400
6	sppr1	**Mallorca**	H W	3-0	Xisco 59, Sobis 77, Schmidt 91	35,000
7	sppr1	**Murcia**	A D	0-0		25,195
8	sppr1	**R Santander**	H D	1-1	Vega 63	44,000
9	sppr1	**Athl Bilbao**	A D	0-0		40,000
10	sppr1	**Osasuna**	H L	0-3		43,450
11	sppr1	**Barcelona**	A L	0-3		83,895
12	sppr1	**Real Zaragoza**	H W	2-1	Pavone 81, 90	29,000
13	sppr1	**Levante**	A L	3-4	Garcia Munoz 10, Schmidt 24 pen	
					Pavone 51	22,770
14	sppr1	**Atl Madrid**	H L	0-2		46,750
15	sppr1	**Villarreal**	A W	1-0	Capitan Prado 9	15,190
16	sppr1	**Almeria**	H W	3-1	Schmidt 28 pen, Pavone 50 og, 82 og	41,250
17	sppr1	**Valladolid**	A D	0-0		16,200
18	sppr1	**Sevilla**	A L	0-3		55,000
19	sppr1	**Getafe**	H W	3-2	Pavone 3 fk, 59, Schmidt 33	36,300
20	sppr1	**Recreativo**	H D	1-1	Schmidt 56	13,000
21	sppr1	**Espanyol**	A W	2-1	Rivera 45, Schmidt 90	39,200
22	sppr1	**Deportivo**	H L	0-1		41,200
23	sppr1	**Valencia**	A L	1-3	Schmidt 47	50,050
24	sppr1	**Real Madrid**	H W	2-1	Schmidt 33, Gonzalez Hoffmann 36	47,850
25	sppr1	**Mallorca**	A D	1-1	Schmidt 70	19,635
26	sppr1	**Murcia**	H W	4-0	Arzo Amposta 14, Schmidt 41	
					Pavone 56, Sobis 74 pen	38,000
27	sppr1	**R Santander**	A L	0-3		19,980
28	sppr1	**Athl Bilbao**	H L	1-2	Gonzalez Hoffmann 34	25,000
29	sppr1	**Osasuna**	A W	1-0	Gonzalez Hoffmann 53	15,840
30	sppr1	**Barcelona**	H W	3-2	Schmidt 63, 79, Gutierrez Moreno 76	51,150
31	sppr1	**Real Zaragoza**	A W	3-0	Gonzalez Hoffmann 8, 16, Pavone 63	24,150
32	sppr1	**Levante**	H L	0-1		55,000
33	sppr1	**Atl Madrid**	A W	3-1	Juande 15, Xisco 49, Capitan Prado 66	46,580
34	sppr1	**Villarreal**	H L	0-1		44,000
35	sppr1	**Almeria**	A D	1-1	Odonkor 44	18,040
36	sppr1	**Valladolid**	H D	1-1	Gonzalez Hoffmann 50 pen	42,000
37	sppr1	**Sevilla**	H L	0-2		54,500
38	sppr1	**Getafe**	A D	1-1	Rivas Alvaro 68	13,600

LEAGUE APPEARANCES, BOOKINGS AND CAPS

	AGE (on 01/07/08)	IN NAMED 18	APPEARANCES	COUNTING GAMES	MINUTES ON PITCH	YELLOW CARDS	RED CARDS	CAPS THIS SEASON	NATIONAL SIDE
Goalkeepers									
Casto Espinosa	26	23	9	9	810	1	0	-	Spain
Ricardo	32	32	28	28	2520	0	0	11	Portugal
Defenders									
Damia Abella Perez	26	29	26	24	2238	6	1	-	Spain
Juan A Alvarado	24	29	26	21	2075	11	1	-	Spain
Marko Babic	27	20	10	3	485	3	0	4	Croatia
Branko Ilic	25	30	18	16	1512	5	0	-	Slovenia
William Lanes Lima	23	16	9	5	485	1	0	-	Brazil
Juan G Moreno	31	34	33	33	2949	9	2	3	Spain
Alejandro Ortiz	22	1	1	1	90	0	0	-	Spain
David Rivas	29	13	11	8	801	1	0	-	Spain
Victoriano R Alvaro	28	10	6	4	402	2	0	-	Spain
Fernando Vega	23	32	30	27	2551	7	0	-	Spain
Alejandro Zamora	24	1	1	1	90	0	0	-	Spain
Midfielders									
Juan Pablo Caffa	23	28	19	6	926	1	0	-	Argentina
Jesus Capi	31	30	27	19	2083	5	0	-	Spain
Edu	29	30	30	28	2509	3	0	-	Brazil
Fernando Escribano	29	26	10	4	482	1	0	-	Spain
Arturo Munoz	27	26	25	21	2057	8	1	-	Spain
Mark Gonzalez	23	25	24	12	1495	3	0	-	Chile
Juan de Dios Juande	22	31	21	15	1521	7	0	-	Spain
David Odonkor	24	25	20	5	977	1	0	6	Germany
Alberto Rivera	30	28	26	18	1891	3	0	-	Spain
Leandro Somoza	27	27	16	10	1057	4	0	-	Argentina
Forwards									
Mariano Pavone	26	34	29	22	2130	7	0	-	Argentina
Jose Poyon	29	16	13	4	565	4	0	-	Spain
Rafael Sobis	23	34	26	13	1546	2	0	1	Brazil
Francisco Xisco	27	25	22	7	1110	5	0	-	Spain

TEAM OF THE SEASON

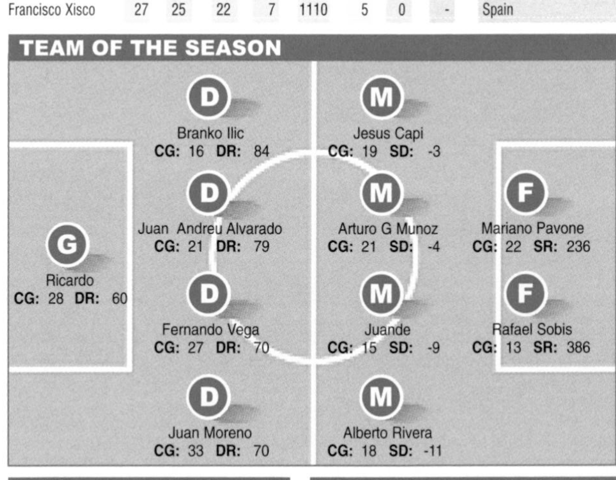

G
Ricardo
CG: 28 DR: 60
D
Branko Ilic
CG: 16 DR: 84
D
Juan Andreu Alvarado
CG: 21 DR: 79
D
Fernando Vega
CG: 27 DR: 70
D
Juan Moreno
CG: 33 DR: 70
M
Jesus Capi
CG: 19 SD: -3
M
Arturo G Munoz
CG: 21 SD: -4
M
Juande
CG: 15 SD: -9
M
Alberto Rivera
CG: 18 SD: -11
F
Mariano Pavone
CG: 22 SR: 236
F
Rafael Sobis
CG: 13 SR: 386

MONTHLY POINTS TALLY

AUGUST	1	33%
SEPTEMBER	4	27%
OCTOBER	3	25%
NOVEMBER	3	33%
DECEMBER	7	58%
JANUARY	7	58%
FEBRUARY	4	33%
MARCH	9	60%
APRIL	6	50%
MAY	3	25%

LEAGUE GOALS

	PLAYER	MINS	GOALS	S RATE
1	Edu	2509	12	209
2	Pavone	2130	9	236
3	Hoffmann	1495	6	249
4	Sobis	1546	4	386
5	Rivas Alvaro	402	2	201
6	Xisco	1110	2	555
7	Capitan Prado	2083	2	1041
8	Escribano	482	1	482
9	Odonkor	977	1	977
10	Juande	1521	1	1521
11	Rivera	1891	1	1891
12	Garcia Munoz	2057	1	2057
13	Vega	2551	1	2551
	Other		1	
	TOTAL		44	

TOP POINT EARNERS

	PLAYER	GAMES	AV PTS
1	Alberto Rivera	18	1.56
2	Branko Ilic	16	1.44
3	Hugo Mariano Pavone	22	1.41
4	Melli	21	1.38
5	Luis Schmidt	28	1.36
6	Juan G Moreno	33	1.33
7	Damia Abella Perez	24	1.29
8	Arturo Garcia Munoz	21	1.24
9	Jesus Capi	19	1.21
10	Rafael Sobis	13	1.08
	CLUB AVERAGE:		1.24

DISCIPLINARY RECORDS

	PLAYER	YELLOW	RED	AVE
1	Jose Maria Poyan	4	0	141
2	Marko Babic	3	0	161
3	Juan Alvarado	11	1	172
4	Juande	7	0	217
5	Francisco Xisco	5	0	222
6	Arturo G Munoz	8	1	228
7	Leandro Somoza	4	0	264
8	Juan G Moreno	9	2	268
9	Branko Ilic	5	0	302
10	Hugo M Pavone	7	0	304
11	Damia Abella Perez	6	1	319
12	Jesus Capi	5	0	416
13	Fernando Vega	6	0	425
	Other	15	0	
	TOTAL	95	5	

KEY GOALKEEPER

Ricardo

Goals Conceded in the League	42	**Counting Games** League games when player was on pitch for at least 70 minutes	28
Defensive Rating Ave number of mins between League goals conceded while on the pitch	60	**Clean Sheets** In League games when player was on pitch for at least 70 minutes	5

KEY PLAYERS - DEFENDERS

Branko Ilic

Goals Conceded Number of League goals conceded while the player was on the pitch	18	**Clean Sheets** In League games when player was on pitch for at least 70 minutes	4
Defensive Rating Ave number of mins between League goals conceded while on the pitch	84	**Club Defensive Rating** Average number of mins between League goals conceded by the club this season	67

	PLAYER	CON LGE	CLEAN SHEETS	DEF RATE
1	Branko Ilic	18	4	84 mins
2	Juan A Alvarado	26	4	79 mins
3	Fernando Vega	36	7	70 mins
4	Juan G Moreno	42	8	70 mins

KEY PLAYERS - MIDFIELDERS

Jesus Capi

Goals in the League	2	**Contribution to Attacking Power** Average number of minutes between League team goals while on pitch	77
Defensive Rating Average number of mins between League goals conceded while on the pitch	74	**Scoring Difference** Defensive Rating minus Contribution to Attacking Power	-3

	PLAYER	LGE GOALS	DEF RATE	POWER	SCORE DIFF
1	Jesus Capi	2	74	77	-3 mins
2	Arturo Garcia Munoz	1	66	70	-4 mins
3	Juan de Dios Juande	1	80	89	-9 mins
4	Alberto Rivera	1	61	72	-11 mins

KEY PLAYERS - GOALSCORERS

Edu

Goals in the League	12	**Player Strike Rate** Average number of minutes between League goals scored by player	209
Contribution to Attacking Power Average number of minutes between League team goals while on pitch	76	**Club Strike Rate** Average number of minutes between League goals scored by club	76

	PLAYER	LGE GOALS	POWER	STRIKE RATE
1	Edu	12	76	209 mins
2	Hugo Mariano Pavone	9	64	236 mins
3	Mark Gonzalez	6	99	249 mins
4	Rafael Sobis	4	70	386 mins

Andalucía
Edu

SQUAD APPEARANCES

Match	1	2	3	4	5	6	7	8	9	10	11	12	13	14	15	16	17	18	19	20	21	22	23	24	25	26	27	28	29	30	31	32	33	34	35	36	37	38
Venue	A	H	A	H	A	H	A	H	A	H	A	H	A	H	A	H	A	A	H	H	A	H	A	H	A	H	A	H	A	H	A	H	A	H	A	H	H	A
Competition	L	L	L	L	L	L	L	L	L	L	L	L	L	L	L	L	L	L	L	L	L	L	L	L	L	L	L	L	L	L	L	L	L	L	L	L	L	L
Result	D	D	L	L	L	W	D	D	D	L	L	W	L	L	W	W	D	L	W	D	W	L	L	W	D	W	L	L	W	W	W	L	W	L	D	D	L	D

Goalkeepers
Casto Espinosa
Ricardo

Defenders
Damia Abella Perez
Juan Andreu Alvarado
Marko Babic
Branko Ilic
William Lanes Lima
Juan Gutierrez Moreno
Alejandro Ortiz
David Rivas
Victoriano Rivas
Fernando Vega
Alejandro Zamora

Midfielders
Juan Pablo Caffa
Jesus Capi
Edu
Fernando Escribano
Arturo Munoz
Mark Gonzalez
Juan de Dios Juande
David Odonkor
Alberto Rivera
Leandro Somoza

Forwards
Mariano Pavone
Jose Poyon
Rafael Sobis
Francisco Xisco

KEY: On all match | On bench | Subbed or sent off (Counting game) | Subbed or sent off (playing less than 70 minutes) | Subbed on from bench (Counting Game) | Subbed on (playing less than 70 minutes) | Subbed on and then subbed or sent off (Counting Game) | Subbed on and then subbed or sent off (playing less than 70 minutes) | Not in 16

GETAFE

Final Position: **14th**

NICKNAME: LOS AZULONES

KEY: ☐Won ☐Drawn ☐Lost

							Attendance
1	sppr1	**Sevilla**	A	L	1-4	Hernandez 3	40,000
2	sppr1	**Recreativo**	H	D	1-1	Del Moral Fernandez 94	12,000
3	sppr1	**Espanyol**	A	L	0-1		18,000
4	ucrl1	**Twente**	H	W	1-0	Uche 90	10,000
5	sppr1	**Deportivo**	H	D	0-0		11,900
6	sppr1	**Valencia**	A	L	1-2	Braulio Nobrega 76	44,000
7	sppr1	**Real Madrid**	H	L	0-1		16,150
8	ucrl2	**Twente**	A	L	2-3	Belenguer Reverte 100 Granero Molina 102	13,200
9	sppr1	**Mallorca**	A	L	2-4	Sousa Franquelo 2, 47	16,863
10	sppr1	**Murcia**	H	W	2-0	Blanco Gonzalez 55 Casquero Paredes 59	11,050
11	ucgpg	**Tottenham**	A	W	2-1	De la Red Gutierrez 21 Nobrega Rodriguez 70	36,240
12	sppr1	**R Santander**	A	L	0-2		19,980
13	sppr1	**Athl Bilbao**	H	W	2-0	Casquero Paredes 9, Uche 29	12,750
14	sppr1	**Osasuna**	A	W	2-0	Hernandez 81 pen, Granero Molina 82	17,622
15	sppr1	**Barcelona**	H	W	2-0	Del Moral Fernandez 28, Albin Leites 90	17,000
16	sppr1	**Real Zaragoza**	A	D	1-1	Sousa Franquelo 64	22,425
17	ucgpg	**Hapoel Tel-Aviv**	H	L	1-2	Hernandez 90 pen	500
18	sppr1	**Levante**	H	W	2-1	Nobrega Rodriguez 61, 90	13,600
19	ucgpg	**Aalborg BK**	A	W	2-1	Hernandez 11, Granero Molina 78	10,000
20	sppr1	**Atl Madrid**	A	L	0-1		52,060
21	sppr1	**Villarreal**	H	L	1-3	Blanco Gonzalez 86	11,050
22	ucgpg	**Anderlecht**	H	W	2-1	Hernandez 6, Celestini 50	7,000
23	sppr1	**Almeria**	A	W	2-0	Licht 38, De la Red Gutierrez 86	19,800
24	sppr1	**Valladolid**	H	L	0-3		13,770
25	sppr1	**Real Betis**	A	L	2-3	De la Red Gutierrez 61 pen Del Moral Fernandez 77	36,300
26	sppr1	**Sevilla**	H	W	3-2	Casquero Paredes 33, Albin Leites 58 Marius Contra 90	12,920
27	sppr1	**Recreativo**	A	W	3-1	Albin Leites 2, Granero Molina 43 Del Moral Fernandez 90	16,480
28	sppr1	**Espanyol**	H	L	0-1		11,900
29	sppr1	**Deportivo**	A	D	1-1	Uche 69	27,334
30	ucrl1	**AEK Athens**	A	D	1-1	De la Red Gutierrez 86	13,080
31	sppr1	**Valencia**	H	D	0-0		12,750
32	ucrl2	**AEK Athens**	H	W	3-0	Granero Molina 45, Marius Contra 82 pen Nobrega Rodriguez 84	8,000
33	sppr1	**Real Madrid**	A	W	1-0	Uche 64	69,600
34	sppr1	**Mallorca**	H	D	3-3	Gutierrez Cotelo 2, Albin Leites 11 Ramis Barrios 58 og	12,750
35	ucrl1	**Benfica**	A	W	2-1	De la Red Gutierrez 25, Hernandez 67	25,000
36	sppr1	**Murcia**	A	W	3-0	Hernandez 56, Albin Leites 84 Casquero Paredes 87	20,215
37	ucrl2	**Benfica**	H	W	1-0	Albin Leites 77	14,000
38	sppr1	**R Santander**	H	W	2-1	Uche 66, Gavilan Martinez 75	10,200
39	sppr1	**Athl Bilbao**	A	L	0-1		34,000
40	sppr1	**Osasuna**	H	L	0-2		10,200
41	ucqfl1	**Bayern Munich**	A	D	1-1	Marius Contra 90	62,000
42	sppr1	**Barcelona**	A	D	0-0		69,090
43	ucqfl2	**Bayern Munich**	H	D	3-3	Marius Contra 44, Casquero Paredes 91 Nobrega Rodriguez 93	16,300
44	sppr1	**Real Zaragoza**	H	D	0-0		15,300
45	sppr1	**Levante**	A	L	1-3	De la Red Gutierrez 59 pen	7,843
46	sppr1	**Atl Madrid**	H	D	1-1	Albin Leites 13	14,960
47	sppr1	**Villarreal**	A	L	0-2		19,530
48	sppr1	**Almeria**	H	W	4-2	Albin Leites 31, Del Moral Fernandez 61, 67 Granero Molina 74 pen	11,390
49	sppr1	**Valladolid**	A	D	0-0		26,235
50	sppr1	**Real Betis**	H	D	1-1	Del Moral Fernandez 4	13,600

LEAGUE APPEARANCES, BOOKINGS AND CAPS

	AGE (on 01/07/08)	IN NAMED 18	APPEARANCES	COUNTING GAMES	MINUTES ON PITCH	YELLOW CARDS	RED CARDS	CAPS THIS SEASON	NATIONAL SIDE
Goalkeepers									
R Abbondanzieri	35	36	34	34	3046	3	1	6	Argentina
Oscar Alfredo Ustari	21	28	4	4	360	0	0	-	Argentina
Defenders									
Pedro Mario Abrante	26	16	13	7	843	3	0	-	Spain
David B Reverte	35	32	24	21	2016	3	0	-	Spain
Cosmin M Contra	32	23	13	6	666	3	1	3	Romania
David C Caballero	28	33	33	26	2587	3	1	-	Spain
Daniel Alberto Diaz	29	31	30	30	2700	5	0	-	Argentina
Lucas Matias Licht	27	35	33	32	2920	7	1	-	Argentina
Franck Signorino	26	6	5	3	348	1	0	-	France
Manuel Tena Lopez	30	22	12	9	951	4	0	-	Spain
Midfielders									
Alberto Aguilar Leiva	23	4	2	0	31	0	0	-	Spain
Juan Albin Leites	21	31	30	13	1616	3	0	-	Uruguay
Francisco C Paredes	32	35	33	23	2392	5	0	-	Spain
Fabio Celestini	32	26	22	16	1621	7	0	-	Switzerland
Ruben De la Red	23	31	31	27	2557	8	0	1	Spain
Jaime G Martinez	23	18	16	5	759	2	0	-	Spain
Esteban Granero	20	28	27	17	1786	7	1	-	Spain
Mario Cotelo	33	24	15	7	1021	2	1	-	Spain
Pablo H Dominguez	23	28	28	19	1991	5	0	-	Spain
Ignacio P Santamaria	28	8	7	2	282	1	0	-	Spain
Miguel Pallardo	21	21	13	4	585	3	0	-	Spain
Francisco Franquelo	28	20	12	8	802	4	1	-	Spain
Forwards									
Kepa Blanco	24	25	15	1	431	3	1	-	Spain
Manuel Del Moral	24	36	33	20	2213	3	0	-	Spain
Juan Moreno Fuertes	19	2	1	0	7	1	0	-	Spain
Braulio Nobrega	22	28	19	9	1093	3	1	-	Spain
Ikechukwu Uche	24	23	22	15	1601	0	0	6	Nigeria

TEAM OF THE SEASON

G Abbondanzieri CG: 34 DR: 72

D David Caballero CG: 26 DR: 86

D Daniel Alberto Diaz CG: 30 DR: 79

D Lucas Matias Licht CG: 32 DR: 69

D David Reverte CG: 21 DR: 63

M Francisco Paredes CG: 23 SD: 16

M Juan Leites CG: 13 SD: 3

M Ruben De la Red CG: 27 SD: 0

M Pablo Dominguez CG: 19 SD: -8

F Del Moral CG: 20 SR: 316

F Ikechukwu Uche CG: 15 SR: 400

MONTHLY POINTS TALLY

AUGUST	0	0%
SEPTEMBER	2	13%
OCTOBER	6	50%
NOVEMBER	7	78%
DECEMBER	6	50%
JANUARY	6	50%
FEBRUARY	5	42%
MARCH	7	47%
APRIL	3	25%
MAY	5	42%

LEAGUE GOALS

	PLAYER	MINS	GOALS	S RATE
1	Albin Leites	1616	7	230
2	Del Moral	2213	7	316
3	Uche	1601	4	400
4	Paredes	2392	4	598
5	Sousa Franquelo	802	3	267
6	Nabrega	1093	3	364
7	Granero Molina	1786	3	595
8	Hernandez	1991	3	663
9	De la Red	2557	3	852
10	Blanco Gonzalez	431	2	215
11	Contra	666	1	666
12	Gavilan	759	1	759
13	Cotelo	1021	1	1021
	Other		1	
	TOTAL		43	

TOP POINT EARNERS

	PLAYER	GAMES	AV PTS
1	Francisco Paredes	23	1.39
2	Roberto Abbondanzieri	34	1.35
3	David C Caballero	26	1.35
4	Daniel Alberto Diaz	30	1.33
5	Pablo H Dominguez	19	1.32
6	Lucas Matias Licht	32	1.31
7	Juan Alban Leites	13	1.23
8	Ruben De la Red	27	1.19
9	Ikechukwu Uche	15	1.13
10	Esteban G Molina	17	1.12
	CLUB AVERAGE:		1.24

DISCIPLINARY RECORDS

	PLAYER	YELLOW	RED	AVE
1	Franquelo	4	1	160
2	Cosmin M Contra	3	1	166
3	Miguel Pallardo	3	0	195
4	Esteban G Molina	7	1	223
5	Fabio Celestini	7	0	231
6	Manuel Tena	4	0	237
7	Braulio Nabrega	3	1	273
8	Pedro M Abrante	3	0	281
9	Ruben De la Red	8	0	319
10	Lucas Matias Licht	7	1	365
11	Jaime Gavilan	2	0	379
12	Pablo Dominguez	5	0	398
13	Francisco Paredes	5	0	478
	Other	21	3	
	TOTAL	82	8	

KEY GOALKEEPER

Roberto Carlos Abbondanzieri

Goals Conceded in the League	42	**Counting Games** League games when player was on pitch for at least 70 minutes	34
Defensive Rating Ave number of mins between League goals conceded while on the pitch	72	**Clean Sheets** In League games when player was on pitch for at least 70 minutes	11

KEY PLAYERS - DEFENDERS

David Cortas Caballero

Goals Conceded Number of League goals conceded while the player was on the pitch	30	**Clean Sheets** In League games when player was on pitch for at least 70 minutes	9
Defensive Rating Ave number of mins between League goals conceded while on the pitch	86	**Club Defensive Rating** Average number of mins between League goals conceded by the club this season	71

	PLAYER	CON LGE	CLEAN SHEETS	DEF RATE
1	David Cortas Caballero	30	9	86 mins
2	Daniel Alberto Diaz	34	10	79 mins
3	Lucas Matias Licht	42	9	69 mins
4	David Belenguer Reverte	32	4	63 mins

KEY PLAYERS - MIDFIELDERS

Francisco Casquero Paredes

Goals in the League	4	**Contribution to Attacking Power** Average number of minutes between League team goals while on pitch	79
Defensive Rating Average number of mins between League goals conceded while on the pitch	95	**Scoring Difference** Defensive Rating minus Contribution to Attacking Power	16

	PLAYER	LGE GOALS	DEF RATE	POWER	SCORE DIFF
1	Francisco Casquero Paredes	4	95	79	16 mins
2	Juan Albin Leites	7	76	73	3 mins
3	Ruben De la Red	3	67	67	0 mins
4	Pablo Hernandez Dominguez	3	82	90	-8 mins

KEY PLAYERS - GOALSCORERS

Juan Albin Leites

Goals in the League	7	**Player Strike Rate** Average number of minutes between League goals scored by player	230
Contribution to Attacking Power Average number of minutes between League team goals while on pitch	73	**Club Strike Rate** Average number of minutes between League goals scored by club	77

	PLAYER	LGE GOALS	POWER	STRIKE RATE
1	Juan Albin Leites	7	73	230 mins
2	Manuel Del Moral	7	67	316 mins
3	Ikechukwu Uche	4	100	400 mins
4	Esteban Granero Molina	3	68	595 mins

Braulio Nobrega and Cosmin Contra

SQUAD APPEARANCES

Match	1	2	3	4	5	6	7	8	9	10	11	12	13	14	15	16	17	18	19	20	21	22	23	24	25	26	27	28	29	30	31	32	33	34	35	36	37	38	39	40	41	42	43	44	45	46	47	48	49	50
Venue	A	H	A	H	H	A	H	A	A	H	A	A	H	A	H	A	H	H	A	A	H	H	A	H	A	H	A	H	A	A	H	H	A	H	A	A	H	H	A	H	A	A	H	H	A	H	A	H	A	H
Competition	L	L	L	E	L	L	L	E	L	L	E	L	L	L	L	L	E	L	E	L	L	E	L	L	L	L	L	L	L	E	L	E	L	L	E	L	E	L	L	L	E	L	E	L	L	L	L	L	L	L
Result	L	D	L	W	D	L	L	L	L	W	W	L	W	W	W	D	L	W	W	L	L	W	W	L	L	W	W	L	D	D	D	W	W	D	W	W	W	W	L	L	D	D	D	D	L	D	L	W	D	D

Goalkeepers
Roberto Abbondanzieri
Oscar Alfredo Ustari

Defenders
Pedro Mario Abrante
David Belenguer Reverte
Cosmin Marius Contra
David Cortes Caballero
Daniel Alberto Diaz
Lucas Matias Licht
Franck Signorino
Manuel Tena Lopez

Midfielders
Alberto Aguilar Leiva
Juan Albin Leites
Francisco C Paredes
Fabio Celestini
Ruben De la Red
Jaime Gavilan Martinez
Esteban Granero Molina
Mario Cotelo
Pablo H Dominguez
Ignacio Perez Santamaria
Miguel Pallardo
Francisco Franquelo

Forwards
Kepa Blanco
Manuel Del Moral
Juan Moreno Fuertes
Braulio Nobrega
Ikechukwu Uche

KEY: On all match | On bench | Subbed or sent off (Counting game) | Subbed or sent off (playing less than 70 minutes) | Subbed on from bench (Counting Game) | Subbed on (playing less than 70 minutes) | Subbed on and then subbed or sent off (Counting Game) | Subbed on and then subbed or sent off (playing less than 70 minutes) | Not in 16

REAL VALLADOLID

Final Position: **15th**

NICKNAME: PUCELA

KEY: ☐Won ☐Drawn ☐Lost

						Attendance
1 sppr1	**Espanyol**	A	W	1-0	Llorente 56	20,000
2 sppr1	**Deportivo**	H	D	2-2	Garcia Calvo 45, Sisi 72	20,000
3 sppr1	**Valencia**	A	L	1-2	Mgom Kome 10	40,150
4 sppr1	**Real Madrid**	H	D	1-1	Lopez Munoz 69	27,000
5 sppr1	**Mallorca**	A	L	2-4	Ogbeche 6, Fernandez Gutierrez 27	11,550
6 sppr1	**Murcia**	H	L	1-4	Llorente Etxarri 50	14,521
7 sppr1	**R Santander**	A	L	0-2		15,540
8 sppr1	**Athl Bilbao**	H	L	1-2	Fernandez Gutierrez 70 pen	22,790
9 sppr1	**Osasuna**	A	D	2-2	Rubio Robres 36, Sesma Gonzalez 51	14,850
10 sppr1	**Barcelona**	H	D	1-1	Llorente Etxarri 16	22,525
11 sppr1	**Real Zaragoza**	A	W	3-2	Fernandez Gutierrez 27, 30	
					Rubio Robres 33	20,000
12 sppr1	**Levante**	H	W	1-0	Sesma Gonzalez 64	17,755
13 sppr1	**Atl Madrid**	A	L	3-4	Fernandez Gutierrez 39, Gonzalez Martinez 47	
					Llorente Etxarri 54	45,484
14 sppr1	**Villarreal**	H	W	2-0	Llorente Etxarri 19	
					Fernandez Gutierrez 57	18,550
15 sppr1	**Almeria**	A	L	0-1		25,000
16 sppr1	**Sevilla**	H	D	0-0		18,550
17 sppr1	**Real Betis**	H	D	0-0		16,200
18 sppr1	**Getafe**	A	W	3-0	Vivar Dorado 54, 76, Rubio Robres 67	13,770
19 sppr1	**Recreativo**	H	W	3-1	Llorente Etxarri 7, 22, 87	18,550
20 sppr1	**Espanyol**	H	W	2-1	Llorente Etxarri 1, 33	23,055
21 sppr1	**Deportivo**	A	L	1-3	Fernandez Gutierrez 82	28,500
22 sppr1	**Valencia**	H	L	0-2		19,875
23 sppr1	**Real Madrid**	A	L	0-7		78,400
24 sppr1	**Mallorca**	H	D	1-1	Llorente Etxarri 37	15,600
25 sppr1	**Murcia**	A	W	1-0	Llorente Etxarri 42	18,660
26 sppr1	**R Santander**	H	L	0-1		21,500
27 sppr1	**Athl Bilbao**	A	L	0-2		30,000
28 sppr1	**Osasuna**	H	D	0-0		14,575
29 sppr1	**Barcelona**	A	L	1-4	Sesma Gonzalez 31 pen	88,830
30 sppr1	**Real Zaragoza**	H	W	2-1	Fernandez Gutierrez 52 pen	
					Llorente Etxarri 74	15,000
31 sppr1	**Levante**	A	W	3-0	Llorente Etxarri 23, Fernandez Gutierrez 58	
					Borja 88	14,421
32 sppr1	**Atl Madrid**	H	D	1-1	Ogbeche 90	23,055
33 sppr1	**Villarreal**	A	L	0-2		15,624
34 sppr1	**Almeria**	H	W	1-0	Sesma Gonzalez 90	25,970
35 sppr1	**Sevilla**	A	L	0-2		35,000
36 sppr1	**Real Betis**	A	D	1-1	Fernandez Gutierrez 62	42,000
37 sppr1	**Getafe**	H	D	0-0		26,235
38 sppr1	**Recreativo**	A	D	1-1	Llorente Etxarri 41	18,540

LEAGUE APPEARANCES, BOOKINGS AND CAPS

	AGE (on 01/07/08)	IN NAMED 18	APPEARANCES	COUNTING GAMES	MINUTES ON PITCH	YELLOW CARDS	RED CARDS	CAPS THIS SEASON	NATIONAL SIDE
Goalkeepers									
Alberto	39	33	7	6	597	0	0	-	Spain
Sergio Asenjo	19	26	24	24	2142	2	1	-	Spain
Ludovic Butelle	24	14	8	7	661	1	1	-	France
Defenders									
Javier Vegas Baraja	27	32	17	11	1124	5	0	-	Spain
Daniel Cifuentes	27	14	9	7	643	2	2	-	Spain
Jose Garcia Calvo	33	33	33	32	2882	6	1	-	Spain
Enrique L Delgado	20	7	3	0	37	0	0	-	Spain
Alberto Marcos Rey	34	33	30	27	2574	11	0	-	Spain
Oscar Sanchez	28	30	21	12	1264	5	0	-	Spain
Jose Alejandro Martin	34	22	12	6	664	2	0	-	Spain
Midfielders									
Marcos S Aguirre	24	13	8	3	339	0	0	-	Argentina
Inaki Bea Jauregui	30	11	7	5	554	0	0	-	Spain
Diego Camacho	31	14	9	6	546	4	0	-	Spain
Jose Luis Capdevila	27	23	13	5	643	0	0	-	Spain
Borja	27	36	31	12	1519	8	0	-	Spain
Sisinio	22	37	36	24	2472	3	0	-	Spain
Rafael Lopez	23	28	20	19	1753	2	0	-	Spain
Pedro Lopez Munoz	25	29	28	27	2461	5	1	-	Spain
Fabian L Estoyanoff	25	7	4	1	102	0	0	-	Uruguay
Daniel Armand Kome	28	20	15	6	910	1	0	-	Cameroon
Rubio Alvaro Robres	29	37	37	34	3131	2	0	-	Spain
Manuel Vivar Dorado	31	35	30	22	2236	4	0	-	Spain
Forwards									
Victor	34	34	32	24	2293	3	0	-	Spain
Joseba Llorente	28	36	36	33	3025	8	1	-	Spain
Vladimir Manchev	30	10	5	1	146	0	0	-	Bulgaria
B Ogbeche	23	26	19	2	476	2	0	-	Nigeria
Jonathan Sesma	29	35	33	22	2215	4	0	-	Spain

TEAM OF THE SEASON

G — Sergio Asenjo — CG: 24 DR: 73

D — Oscar Sanchez — CG: 12 DR: 66

D — Jose Garcia Calvo — CG: 32 DR: 65

D — Alberto Marcos Rey — CG: 27 DR: 58

D — Javier Vegas Baraja — CG: 11 DR: 51

M — Rafael Lopez — CG: 19 SD: -11

M — Pedro Lopez Munoz — CG: 27 SD: -12

M — Angel Vivar Dorado — CG: 22 SD: -14

M — Sisinio — CG: 24 SD: -15

F — Joseba Llorente — CG: 33 SR: 201

F — Victor — CG: 24 SR: 229

MONTHLY POINTS TALLY

AUGUST	3	100%
SEPTEMBER	2	13%
OCTOBER	1	11%
NOVEMBER	7	58%
DECEMBER	5	42%
JANUARY	9	75%
FEBRUARY	4	33%
MARCH	4	27%
APRIL	7	58%
MAY	3	25%

LEAGUE GOALS

	PLAYER	MINS	GOALS	S RATE
1	J Llorente	3025	15	201
2	Victor	2293	10	229
3	Sesma	2215	4	553
4	Rubio Robres	3131	3	1043
5	Ogbeche	476	2	238
6	Vivar Dorado	2236	2	1118
7	Gonzalez	2472	2	1236
8	Mgom Kome	910	1	910
9	Borja	1519	1	1519
10	Lopez Munoz	2461	1	2461
11	Garcia Calvo	2882	1	2882
	Other		0	
	TOTAL		42	

TOP POINT EARNERS

	PLAYER	GAMES	AV PTS
1	Angel Vivar Dorado	22	1.45
2	Jonathan Sesma	22	1.41
3	Alberto Marcos Rey	27	1.37
4	Pedro Lopez Munoz	27	1.33
5	Joseba Llorente Etxarri	33	1.33
6	Sergio Asenjo Andres	24	1.33
7	Jose Garcia Calvo	32	1.31
8	Sisinio	24	1.25
9	Victor M Fernandez	24	1.25
10	Rafael Lopez Gomez	19	1.16
	CLUB AVERAGE:		1.18

DISCIPLINARY RECORDS

	PLAYER	YELLOW	RED	AVE
1	Diego Camacho	4	0	136
2	Daniel Cifuentes	2	2	160
3	Borja	8	0	189
4	Baraja	5	0	224
5	Alberto Marcos	11	0	234
6	Ogbeche	2	0	238
7	Oscar Sanchez	5	0	252
8	Ludovic Butelle	1	1	330
9	Jose Alejandro	2	0	332
10	Joseba Llorente	8	1	336
11	Pedro Lopez	5	1	410
12	Jose Garcia Calvo	6	1	411
13	J Sesma Gonzalez	4	0	553
	Other	17	1	
	TOTAL	80	7	

KEY GOALKEEPER

Sergio Asenjo

Goals Conceded in the League	29	Counting Games League games when player was on pitch for at least 70 minutes	24
Defensive Rating Ave number of mins between League goals conceded while on the pitch	73	Clean Sheets In League games when player was on pitch for at least 70 minutes	9

KEY PLAYERS - DEFENDERS

Oscar Sanchez

Goals Conceded Number of League goals conceded while the player was on the pitch	19	Clean Sheets In League games when player was on pitch for at least 70 minutes	3
Defensive Rating Ave number of mins between League goals conceded while on the pitch	66	Club Defensive Rating Average number of mins between League goals conceded by the club this season	60

	PLAYER	CON LGE	CLEAN SHEETS	DEF RATE
1	Oscar Sanchez	19	3	66 mins
2	Jose Garcia Calvo	44	10	65 mins
3	Alberto Marcos Rey	44	8	58 mins
4	Javier Vegas Baraja	22	2	51 mins

KEY PLAYERS - MIDFIELDERS

Rafael Lopez

Goals in the League	0	Contribution to Attacking Power Average number of minutes between League team goals while on pitch	67
Defensive Rating Average number of mins between League goals conceded while on the pitch	56	Scoring Difference Defensive Rating minus Contribution to Attacking Power	-11

	PLAYER	LGE GOALS	DEF RATE	POWER	SCORE DIFF
1	Rafael Lopez	0	56	67	-11 mins
2	Pedro Lopez Munoz	1	58	70	-12 mins
3	Angel Vivar Dorado	2	53	67	-14 mins
4	Sisinio	2	70	85	-15 mins

KEY PLAYERS - GOALSCORERS

Joseba Llorente

Goals in the League	15	Player Strike Rate Average number of minutes between League goals scored by player	201
Contribution to Attacking Power Average number of minutes between League team goals while on pitch	81	Club Strike Rate Average number of minutes between League goals scored by club	81

	PLAYER	LGE GOALS	POWER	STRIKE RATE
1	Joseba Llorente Etxarri	15	81	201 mins
2	Victor	10	81	229 mins
3	Jonathan Sesma	4	82	553 mins
4	Rubio Alvaro Robres	3	84	1043 mins

Caja Duero
Joseba Llorente

SQUAD APPEARANCES

Match	1	2	3	4	5	6	7	8	9	10	11	12	13	14	15	16	17	18	19	20	21	22	23	24	25	26	27	28	29	30	31	32	33	34	35	36	37	38
Venue	A	H	A	H	A	H	A	H	A	H	A	H	A	H	A	H	H	A	H	H	A	H	A	H	A	H	A	H	A	H	A	H	A	H	A	A	H	A
Competition	L	L	L	L	L	L	L	L	L	L	L	L	L	L	L	L	L	L	L	L	L	L	L	L	L	L	L	L	L	L	L	L	L	L	L	L	L	L
Result	W	D	L	D	L	L	L	L	D	D	W	W	L	W	L	D	D	W	W	W	L	L	L	D	W	L	L	D	L	W	W	D	L	W	L	D	D	D

Goalkeepers
Alberto
Sergio Asenjo
Ludovic Butelle

Defenders
Javier Vegas Baraja
Daniel Cifuentes
Jose Garcia Calvo
Enrique Lopez Delgado
Alberto Marcos Rey
Oscar Sanchez
Jose Alejandro Martin

Midfielders
Marcos S Aguirre
Inaki Bea Jauregui
Diego Camacho
Jose Luis Capdevila
Borja
Sisinio
Rafael Lopez
Pedro Lopez Munoz
Fabian Larry Estoyanoff
Daniel Armand Kome
Rubio Alvaro Robres
Angel Vivar Dorado

Forwards
Victor
Joseba Llorente
Vladimir Manchev
Bartholomew Ogbeche
Jonathan Sesma

KEY: On all match · On bench · Subbed or sent off (Counting game) · Subbed or sent off (playing less than 70 minutes) · Subbed on from bench (Counting Game) · Subbed on (playing less than 70 minutes) · Subbed on and then subbed or sent off (Counting Game) · Subbed on and then subbed or sent off (playing less than 70 minutes) · Not in 16

RECREATIVO HUELVA

Final Position: **16th**

NICKNAME: RECRE

KEY: ☐Won ☐Drawn ☐Lost

							Attendance
1	sppr1	**Real Betis**	H	D	1-1	Sinama-Pongolle 25	17,000
2	sppr1	**Getafe**	A	D	1-1	Sinama-Pongolle 85	12,000
3	sppr1	**Sevilla**	A	L	1-4	Tornavaca Fernandez 54	45,000
4	sppr1	**Espanyol**	H	W	2-1	Garcia Guerrero 53, 60	19,000
5	sppr1	**Deportivo**	A	W	2-0	Nieto Martins 12, Garcia Guerrero 46	20,760
6	sppr1	**Valencia**	H	L	0-1		20,694
7	sppr1	**Real Madrid**	A	L	0-2		76,000
8	sppr1	**Mallorca**	H	L	0-2		15,450
9	sppr1	**Murcia**	A	L	0-1		25,191
10	sppr1	**R Santander**	H	D	0-0		20,000
11	sppr1	**Athl Bilbao**	A	L	0-2		36,000
12	sppr1	**Osasuna**	H	W	1-0	Nieto Martins 69	14,420
13	sppr1	**Barcelona**	A	L	0-3		88,830
14	sppr1	**Real Zaragoza**	H	W	2-1	Nieto Martins 25, 40	18,540
15	sppr1	**Levante**	A	W	2-0	Camunas Gallego 38	
						Tornavaca Fernandez 54	12,650
16	sppr1	**Atl Madrid**	H	D	0-0		16,480
17	sppr1	**Villarreal**	A	D	1-1	Camunas Gallego 37	14,539
18	sppr1	**Almeria**	H	D	1-1	Sinama-Pongolle 14	14,420
19	sppr1	**Valladolid**	A	L	1-3	Camunas Gallego 44	18,550
20	sppr1	**Real Betis**	A	D	1-1	Garcia Guerrero 58	13,000
21	sppr1	**Getafe**	H	L	1-3	Camunas Gallego 15	16,480
22	sppr1	**Sevilla**	H	L	1-2	Gaspar Deus Severo 89	19,500
23	sppr1	**Espanyol**	A	W	2-1	Sinama-Pongolle 17, 25	21,280
24	sppr1	**Deportivo**	H	W	3-2	Gaspar Deus Severo 53	
						Sinama-Pongolle 56, Martin Caceres 87	15,450
25	sppr1	**Valencia**	A	D	1-1	Nieto Martins 51	41,250
26	sppr1	**Real Madrid**	H	L	2-3	Martin Caceres 16, Nieto Martins 90	20,600
27	sppr1	**Mallorca**	A	L	1-7	Ruben 40	17,325
28	sppr1	**Murcia**	H	W	4-2	Sinama-Pongolle 18, 71, Ruben 59	
						Garcia Barreno 85	17,510
29	sppr1	**R Santander**	A	L	0-2		19,314
30	sppr1	**Athl Bilbao**	H	D	1-1	Amorebieta 14 og	15,450
31	sppr1	**Osasuna**	A	W	1-0	Sinama-Pongolle 36	19,000
32	sppr1	**Barcelona**	H	D	2-2	Ruben 41, 71	20,600
33	sppr1	**Real Zaragoza**	A	L	0-3		31,740
34	sppr1	**Levante**	H	W	2-0	Martin 10, Camunas Gallego 42	14,420
35	sppr1	**Atl Madrid**	A	L	0-3		52,060
36	sppr1	**Villarreal**	H	L	0-2		19,500
37	sppr1	**Almeria**	A	W	2-0	Vasquez 23, Sinama-Pongolle 42	15,400
38	sppr1	**Valladolid**	H	D	1-1	Garcia Guerrero 90	18,540

LEAGUE APPEARANCES, BOOKINGS AND CAPS

	AGE (on 01/07/08)	IN NAMED 18	APPEARANCES	COUNTING GAMES	MINUTES ON PITCH	YELLOW CARDS	RED CARDS	CAPS THIS SEASON	NATIONAL SIDE
Goalkeepers									
Mariano Barbosa	23	25	0	0	0	0	0	-	Argentina
Jose Ramirez	34	10	0	0	0	0	0	-	Spain
Stefano Sorrentino	29	38	38	38	3420	2	0	-	Italy
Defenders									
Enrique Sanjuan	32	28	11	6	730	5	1	-	Spain
Dani Bautista Pina	27	30	16	12	1133	3	0	-	Spain
Iago Amoedo Bouzon	25	33	27	24	2251	11	2	-	Spain
Jose Maria Calvo	26	17	14	11	1088	3	0	-	Argentina
Hipolito Serrano	31	34	26	25	2215	10	0	-	Spain
Roberto Luis Gaspar	32	25	23	16	1717	12	2	-	Portugal
Jose Martin Caceres	21	34	34	32	2988	10	1	-	Uruguay
Eduardo Castillo	27	19	16	13	1302	6	1	-	Spain
Pablo Serrano	21	4	3	2	216	0	0	-	Spain
Midfielders									
Javier Camunas	27	37	37	34	3141	6	0	-	Spain
Rafael Rodriguez	27	27	18	4	573	2	0	-	Spain
Marcos Barreno	21	32	19	8	925	1	0	-	Spain
Lopez Segu Gerard	29	27	18	3	556	5	1	-	Spain
Carlos Martins	26	32	32	24	2410	4	1	1	Portugal
Aitor Tornavaca	32	38	36	24	2652	4	0	-	Spain
Jesus Vasquez	27	34	34	34	3052	13	0	-	Spain
Silvestre Varela	23	28	22	6	1031	0	0	-	Portugal
Jose Ignacio Zahinos	30	19	11	3	482	2	0	-	Spain
Forwards									
Edwin Congo	31	15	6	0	125	1	0	-	Colombia
Francisco Guerrero	31	28	26	13	1490	3	0	-	Spain
Ersen Martin	29	13	9	0	229	3	1	-	Turkey
Dimitru Rosu	32	10	4	0	66	0	0	-	Romania
Marco Gaston Ruben	21	16	14	6	801	4	1	-	Argentina
F Sinama-Pongolle	23	35	34	30	2772	6	1	-	France

TEAM OF THE SEASON

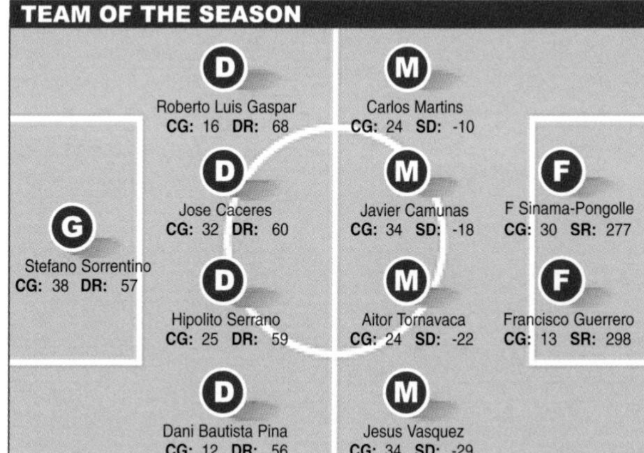

G
Stefano Sorrentino
CG: 38 DR: 57
D
Roberto Luis Gaspar
CG: 16 DR: 68
D
Jose Caceres
CG: 32 DR: 60
D
Hipolito Serrano
CG: 25 DR: 59
D
Dani Bautista Pina
CG: 12 DR: 56
M
Carlos Martins
CG: 24 SD: -10
M
Javier Camunas
CG: 34 SD: -18
M
Aitor Tornavaca
CG: 24 SD: -22
M
Jesus Vasquez
CG: 34 SD: -29
F
F Sinama-Pongolle
CG: 30 SR: 277
F
Francisco Guerrero
CG: 13 SR: 298

MONTHLY POINTS TALLY

AUGUST	1	33%
SEPTEMBER	7	47%
OCTOBER	1	8%
NOVEMBER	3	33%
DECEMBER	8	67%
JANUARY	2	17%
FEBRUARY	7	58%
MARCH	4	27%
APRIL	7	58%
MAY	4	33%

LEAGUE GOALS

	PLAYER	MINS	GOALS	S RATE
1	S-Pongolle	2772	**10**	277
2	Nieto Martins	2410	**6**	401
3	F. Guerrero	1490	**5**	298
4	Camunas	3141	**5**	628
5	Ruben	801	**4**	200
6	Gaspar Deus	1717	**2**	858
7	Tornavaca	2652	**2**	1326
8	Caceres	2988	**2**	1494
9	Martin	229	**1**	229
10	Garcia Barreno	925	**1**	925
11	Vasquez	3052	**1**	3052
	Other		0	
	TOTAL		**39**	

TOP POINT EARNERS

	PLAYER	GAMES	AV PTS
1	Fernandez Serrano	25	**1.40**
2	Carlos Martins	24	**1.38**
3	Aitor Tornavaca	24	**1.33**
4	Jose Caceres	32	**1.28**
5	Javier Camunas	34	**1.26**
6	Roberto Luis Gaspar	16	**1.19**
7	Stefano Sorrentino	38	**1.16**
8	Francisco Guerrero	13	**1.15**
9	F Sinama-Pongolle	30	**1.13**
10	Jesus Vasquez	34	**1.12**
	CLUB AVERAGE:		**1.16**

DISCIPLINARY RECORDS

	PLAYER	YELLOW	RED	AVE
1	Lopez Gerard	5	1	**92**
2	Enrique Alvarez	5	1	**121**
3	Roberto Gaspar	12	2	**122**
4	Marco Ruben	4	1	**160**
5	Iago Bouzon	11	2	**173**
6	Eduardo Castillo	6	1	**186**
7	Hipolito Serrano	10	0	**221**
8	Jesus Vasquez	13	0	**234**
9	JIgnacio Zahinos	2	0	**241**
10	Jose Caceres	10	1	**271**
11	Rafael Rodriguez	2	0	**286**
12	Jose Calvo	3	0	**362**
13	Dani Bautista Pina	3	0	**377**
	Other	26	2	
	TOTAL	**112**	**11**	

KEY GOALKEEPER

Stefano Sorrentino

Goals Conceded in the League	59	Counting Games League games when player was on pitch for at least 70 minutes	38
Defensive Rating Ave number of mins between League goals conceded while on the pitch	57	Clean Sheets In League games when player was on pitch for at least 70 minutes	9

KEY PLAYERS - DEFENDERS

Roberto Luis Gaspar

Goals Conceded Number of League goals conceded while the player was on the pitch	25	Clean Sheets In League games when player was on pitch for at least 70 minutes	4
Defensive Rating Ave number of mins between League goals conceded while on the pitch	68	Club Defensive Rating Average number of mins between League goals conceded by the club this season	57

	PLAYER	CON LGE	CLEAN SHEETS	DEF RATE
1	Roberto Luis Gaspar	25	4	68 mins
2	Jose Caceres	49	9	60 mins
3	Hipolito Serrano	37	7	59 mins
4	Dani Bautista Pina	20	2	56 mins

KEY PLAYERS - MIDFIELDERS

Carlos Jorge Nieto Martins

Goals in the League	6	Contribution to Attacking Power Average number of minutes between League team goals while on pitch	68
Defensive Rating Average number of mins between League goals conceded while on the pitch	58	Scoring Difference Defensive Rating minus Contribution to Attacking Power	-10

	PLAYER	LGE GOALS	DEF RATE	POWER	SCORE DIFF
1	Carlos Jorge Nieto Martins	6	58	68	-10 mins
2	Javier Camunas	5	64	82	-18 mins
3	Aitor Tornavaca	2	63	85	-22 mins
4	Jesus Vasquez	1	66	95	-29 mins

KEY PLAYERS - GOALSCORERS

Florent Sinama-Pongolle

Goals in the League	10	Player Strike Rate Average number of minutes between League goals scored by player	277
Contribution to Attacking Power Average number of minutes between League team goals while on pitch	89	Club Strike Rate Average number of minutes between League goals scored by club	85

	PLAYER	LGE GOALS	POWER	STRIKE RATE
1	Florent Sinama-Pongolle	10	89	277 mins
2	Francisco Guerrero	5	93	298 mins
3	Carlos Jorge Nieto Martins	6	68	401 mins
4	Javier Camunas	5	82	628 mins

Cajasol
Florent Sinama-Pongolle

SQUAD APPEARANCES

Match	1	2	3	4	5	6	7	8	9	10	11	12	13	14	15	16	17	18	19	20	21	22	23	24	25	26	27	28	29	30	31	32	33	34	35	36	37	38
Venue	H	A	A	H	A	H	A	H	A	H	A	H	A	H	A	H	A	H	A	A	H	H	A	H	A	H	A	H	A	H	A	H	A	H	A	H	A	H
Competition	L	L	L	L	L	L	L	L	L	L	L	L	L	L	L	L	L	L	L	L	L	L	L	L	L	L	L	L	L	L	L	L	L	L	L	L	L	L
Result	D	D	L	W	W	L	L	L	L	D	L	W	L	W	W	D	D	D	L	D	L	L	W	W	D	L	L	W	L	D	W	D	L	W	L	L	W	D

Goalkeepers
Mariano Damian Barbosa
Jose Ramirez
Stefano Sorrentino

Defenders
Enrique Alvarez Sanjuan
Dani Bautista Pina
Iago Amoedo Bouzon
Jose Maria Calvo
Hipolito Serrano
Roberto Luis Gaspar
Jose Martin Caceres
Eduardo Moya Castillo
Pablo Oliveira Serrano

Midfielders
Javier Camunas
Rafael Barber Rodriguez
Marcos Garcia Barreno
Lopez Segu Gerard
Carlos Martins
Aitor Tornavaca
Jesus Vasquez
Silvestre Varela
Jose Ignacio Zahinos

Forwards
Edwin Congo
Francisco Guerrero
Ersen Martin
Dimitru Laurentiu Rosu
Marco Gaston Ruben
Florent Sinama-Pongolle

KEY: On all match · On bench · Subbed or sent off (Counting game) · Subbed or sent off (playing less than 70 minutes) · Subbed on from bench (Counting Game) · Subbed on (playing less than 70 minutes) · Subbed on and then subbed or sent off (Counting Game) · Subbed on and then subbed or sent off (playing less than 70 minutes) · Not in 16

OSASUNA

Final Position: **17th**

NICKNAME: LOS ROJILLOS

KEY: ☐ Won ☐ Drawn ☐ Lost

	Match	Opponent	H/A	Result	Score	Scorers	Attendance
1	sppr1	**Athl Bilbao**	A	D	0-0		40,000
2	sppr1	**Barcelona**	H	D	0-0		17,820
3	sppr1	**Real Zaragoza**	A	L	1-2	Torres Belen 24	27,600
4	sppr1	**Levante**	H	W	4-1	Pandiani Urquiza 31, 51, Torres Belen 57, Garcia Fernandez 76	12,870
5	sppr1	**Atl Madrid**	A	L	0-2		40,000
6	sppr1	**Villarreal**	H	W	3-2	Rodriguez Venta 21 og, Fernandes Pereira 34, Garcia Fernandez 79	15,840
7	sppr1	**Almeria**	A	L	0-2		17,600
8	sppr1	**Valladolid**	H	D	2-2	Fernandes Pereira 73, 78	14,850
9	sppr1	**Real Betis**	A	W	3-0	Andreu Alvarado 42 og, Fernandes Pereira 51, Vela Garrido 55	43,450
10	sppr1	**Getafe**	H	L	0-2		17,622
11	sppr1	**Recreativo**	A	L	0-1		14,420
12	sppr1	**Espanyol**	H	L	1-2	Portillo 75	14,850
13	sppr1	**Deportivo**	A	W	2-1	Plasil 47, Fernandes Pereira 87	15,000
14	sppr1	**Sevilla**	H	D	1-1	Plasil 19	17,820
15	sppr1	**Valencia**	H	D	0-0		18,612
16	sppr1	**Real Madrid**	A	L	0-2		70,400
17	sppr1	**Mallorca**	H	W	3-1	Font 8, Plasil 47, Ferreira Viana 94	28,900
18	sppr1	**Murcia**	A	L	0-2		21,770
19	sppr1	**R Santander**	H	L	0-2		12,000
20	sppr1	**Athl Bilbao**	H	W	2-0	Fernandes Pereira 66 fk, Vela Garrido 68	17,820
21	sppr1	**Sevilla**	A	L	1-2	Sola Clemente 69	34,580
22	sppr1	**Barcelona**	A	L	0-1		90,804
23	sppr1	**Real Zaragoza**	H	W	1-0	Plasil 45	16,830
24	sppr1	**Levante**	A	L	1-2	Monreal Eraso 21 fk	14,927
25	sppr1	**Atl Madrid**	H	W	3-1	Sola Clemente 1, Vela Garrido 4, Font 75	11,880
26	sppr1	**Villarreal**	A	D	0-0		19,530
27	sppr1	**Almeria**	H	W	2-1	Sola Clemente 6, Cruchaga 29	17,820
28	sppr1	**Valladolid**	A	D	0-0		14,575
29	sppr1	**Real Betis**	H	L	0-1		15,840
30	sppr1	**Getafe**	A	W	2-0	Flano Bezunartea 40, Punal Martinez 68 pen	10,200
31	sppr1	**Recreativo**	H	L	0-1		19,000
32	sppr1	**Espanyol**	A	W	1-0	Astudillo 31	21,150
33	sppr1	**Deportivo**	H	L	0-1		15,840
34	sppr1	**Valencia**	A	L	0-3		55,000
35	sppr1	**Real Madrid**	H	L	1-2	Punal Martinez 83 pen	19,750
36	sppr1	**Mallorca**	A	L	1-2	Portillo 72	10,395
37	sppr1	**Murcia**	H	W	2-1	Fernandes Pereira 2, Torres Belen 53	19,800
38	sppr1	**R Santander**	A	L	0-1		22,000

LEAGUE APPEARANCES, BOOKINGS AND CAPS

	AGE (on 01/07/08)	IN NAMED 18	APPEARANCES	COUNTING GAMES	MINUTES ON PITCH	YELLOW CARDS	RED CARDS	CAPS THIS SEASON	NATIONAL SIDE
Goalkeepers									
Juan Elia Vallejo	29	32	3	1	134	1	1	-	Spain
Andres Moreno	21	2	1	0	41	0	0	-	Spain
Ricardo Lopez	36	37	37	36	3242	6	2	-	Spain
Defenders									
Jokin Arcaya Esparza	20	2	2	0	51	0	0	-	Spain
Enrique Martin	26	12	12	11	980	2	1	-	Spain
Cesar Cruchaga	34	32	28	26	2362	6	1	-	Spain
Ion Echaide Sola	22	3	1	0	20	0	0	-	Spain
Miguel Flano	23	31	28	27	2475	8	0	-	Spain
Javier Flano	23	27	4	2	267	0	0	-	Spain
Jose Izquierdo	27	17	9	9	810	2	0	-	Spain
Nacho Monreal	22	28	27	27	2430	6	0	-	Spain
Jose Romero Urtasun	33	28	21	18	1747	13	2	-	Spain
Midfielders									
Martin Mauricio	30	17	13	9	908	2	0	-	Argentina
Ludovic Delporte	28	10	9	1	235	0	0	-	France
Jon Erice Dominguez	21	7	4	1	159	1	0	-	Spain
Hugo Viana	25	14	9	1	233	2	0	-	Portugal
Romero Hector Font	24	36	32	14	1684	4	0	-	Spain
Francisco Fernandez	21	27	24	19	1821	7	2	-	Spain
Xavier Margairaz	24	20	13	4	762	2	0	-	Switzerland
Javad Nekounam	27	3	2	0	26	0	0	-	Iran
Jaroslav Plasil	26	35	33	28	2546	4	0	10	Czech Republic
Francisco Punal	32	35	35	33	2980	13	0	-	Spain
Juanfran	23	34	34	26	2597	7	0	-	Spain
Forwards									
Cesar Azpilicueta	18	32	29	28	2584	8	0	-	Spain
Eduardo Fernandes	26	32	30	12	1802	6	0	-	Portugal
Walter Pandiani	32	20	17	5	723	3	0	-	Uruguay
Javier Garcia Portillo	26	27	18	4	787	0	1	-	Spain
Enrique Clemente	22	28	19	7	1052	2	0	-	Spain
Carlos Vela Garrido	19	34	33	18	2000	6	0	-	Mexico

TEAM OF THE SEASON

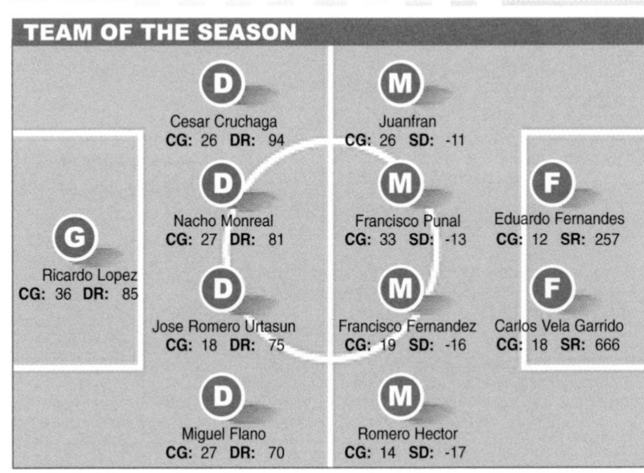

G
Ricardo Lopez
CG: 36 DR: 85
D
Cesar Cruchaga
CG: 26 DR: 94
D
Nacho Monreal
CG: 27 DR: 81
D
Jose Romero Urtasun
CG: 18 DR: 75
D
Miguel Flano
CG: 27 DR: 70
M
Juanfran
CG: 26 SD: -11
M
Francisco Punal
CG: 33 SD: -13
M
Francisco Fernandez
CG: 19 SD: -16
M
Romero Hector
CG: 14 SD: -17
F
Eduardo Fernandes
CG: 12 SR: 257
F
Carlos Vela Garrido
CG: 18 SR: 666

MONTHLY POINTS TALLY

Month	Points	%
AUGUST	1	33%
SEPTEMBER	4	33%
OCTOBER	7	58%
NOVEMBER	0	0%
DECEMBER	8	53%
JANUARY	3	25%
FEBRUARY	6	50%
MARCH	8	53%
APRIL	3	25%
MAY	3	25%

LEAGUE GOALS

	PLAYER	MINS	GOALS	S RATE
1	E. Fernandes	1802	7	257
2	Plasil	2546	4	636
3	Sola Clemente	1052	3	350
4	Vela Garrido	2000	3	666
5	Juanfran	2597	3	865
6	Pandiani	723	2	361
7	Portillo	787	2	393
8	Font	1684	2	842
9	G Fernandez	1821	2	910
10	Punal Martinez	2980	2	1490
11	Ferreira Viana	233	1	233
12	Astudillo	908	1	908
13	Cruchaga	2362	1	2362
	Other		2	
	TOTAL		35	

TOP POINT EARNERS

	PLAYER	GAMES	AV PTS
1	Jose Romero Urtasun	18	1.33
2	Carlos Vela Garrido	18	1.33
3	Nacho Monreal Eraso	27	1.22
4	Cesar Cruchaga	26	1.19
5	Ricardo Lopez Felipe	36	1.19
6	Fran Punal Martinez	33	1.18
7	Francisco Fernandez	19	1.16
8	Cesar Azpilicueta	28	1.14
9	Juan Torres Belen	26	1.12
10	Eduardo Fernandes	12	1.08
	CLUB AVERAGE:		1.13

DISCIPLINARY RECORDS

	PLAYER	YELLOW	RED	AVE
1	Jose Urtasun	13	2	116
2	Franc Fernandez	7	2	202
3	Francisco Punal	13	0	229
4	Walter Pandiani	3	0	241
5	Eduardo Fernandes	6	0	300
6	Miguel Flano	8	0	309
7	Cesar Azpilicueta	8	0	323
8	Enrique Corrales	2	1	326
9	Carlos Vela Garrido	6	0	333
10	Cesar Cruchaga	6	1	337
11	Juan Torres Belen	7	0	371
12	Xavier Margairaz	2	0	381
13	Nacho Monreal	6	0	405
	Other	20	3	
	TOTAL	107	9	

KEY GOALKEEPER

Ricardo Lopez Felipe

Goals Conceded in the League	38	**Counting Games** League games when player was on pitch for at least 70 minutes	36
Defensive Rating Ave number of mins between League goals conceded while on the pitch	85	**Clean Sheets** In League games when player was on pitch for at least 70 minutes	11

KEY PLAYERS - DEFENDERS

Cesar Cruchaga

Goals Conceded Number of League goals conceded while the player was on the pitch	25	**Clean Sheets** In League games when player was on pitch for at least 70 minutes	9
Defensive Rating Ave number of mins between League goals conceded while on the pitch	94	**Club Defensive Rating** Average number of mins between League goals conceded by the club this season	79

	PLAYER	CON LGE	CLEAN SHEETS	DEF RATE
1	Cesar Cruchaga	25	9	94 mins
2	Nacho Monreal Eraso	30	7	81 mins
3	Jose Romero Urtasun	23	3	75 mins
4	Miguel Flano Bezunartea	35	7	70 mins

KEY PLAYERS - MIDFIELDERS

Juanfran

Goals in the League	3	**Contribution to Attacking Power** Average number of minutes between League team goals while on pitch	92
Defensive Rating Average number of mins between League goals conceded while on the pitch	81	**Scoring Difference** Defensive Rating minus Contribution to Attacking Power	-11

	PLAYER	LGE GOALS	DEF RATE	POWER	SCORE DIFF
1	Juanfran	3	81	92	-11 mins
2	Francisco Punal	2	80	93	-13 mins
3	Francisco Javier Fernandez	2	79	95	-16 mins
4	Romero Hector Font	2	88	105	-17 mins

KEY PLAYERS - GOALSCORERS

Eduardo Fernandes Pereira

Goals in the League	7	**Player Strike Rate** Average number of minutes between League goals scored by player	257
Contribution to Attacking Power Average number of minutes between League team goals while on pitch	85	**Club Strike Rate** Average number of minutes between League goals scored by club	94

	PLAYER	LGE GOALS	POWER	STRIKE RATE
1	Eduardo Fernandes Pereira	7	85	257 mins
2	Jaroslav Plasil	4	106	636 mins
3	Carlos Alberto Vela Garrido	3	83	666 mins
4	Romero Hector Font	2	105	842 mins

RESTAURA
Juanfran

SQUAD APPEARANCES

Match	1	2	3	4	5	6	7	8	9	10	11	12	13	14	15	16	17	18	19	20	21	22	23	24	25	26	27	28	29	30	31	32	33	34	35	36	37	38
Venue	A	H	A	H	A	H	A	H	A	H	A	H	A	H	H	A	H	A	H	H	A	A	H	A	H	A	H	A	H	A	H	A	H	A	H	A	H	A
Competition	L	L	L	L	L	L	L	L	L	L	L	L	L	L	L	L	L	L	L	L	L	L	L	L	L	L	L	L	L	L	L	L	L	L	L	L	L	L
Result	D	D	L	W	L	W	L	D	W	L	L	L	W	D	D	L	W	L	L	W	L	L	W	L	W	D	W	D	L	W	L	W	L	L	L	L	W	L

Goalkeepers
Juan Elia Vallejo
Andres Moreno
Ricardo Lopez Felipe
Defenders
Jokin Arcaya Esparza
Enrique Corrales Martin
Cesar Cruchaga
Ion Echaide Sola
Miguel Flano
Javier Flano
Jose Izquierdo Martinez
Nacho Monreal Eraso
Jose Romero Urtasun
Midfielders
Martin Mauricio
Ludovic Delporte
Jon Erice Dominguez
HugoViana
Romero Hector Font
Francisco Javier Garcia
Xavier Margairaz
Javad Nekounam
Jaroslav Plasil
Francisco Puna
Juanfran
Forwards
Cesar Azpilicueta
Eduardo Fernandes
Walter Pandiani
Javier Garcia Portillo
Enrique Sola Clemente
Carlos Vela Garrido

KEY: On all match | On bench | Subbed or sent off (Counting game) | Subbed or sent off (playing less than 70 minutes) | Subbed on from bench (Counting Game) | Subbed on (playing less than 70 minutes) | Subbed on and then subbed or sent off (Counting Game) | Subbed on and then subbed or sent off (playing less than 70 minutes) | Not in 16

REAL ZARAGOZA

Final Position: **18th**

NICKNAME: LOS BLANQUILLOS

KEY: ☐Won ☐Drawn ☐Lost

							Attendance
1	sppr1	**Murcia**	A	L	1-2	Oliveira 30	22,000
2	sppr1	**R Santander**	H	D	1-1	Oliveira 75	33,000
3	sppr1	**Athl Bilbao**	A	D	1-1	D.Milito 15	40,000
4	ucrl1	**Aris**	A	L	0-1		20,000
5	sppr1	**Osasuna**	H	W	2-1	Oliveira 17, Milito 70 pen	27,600
6	sppr1	**Barcelona**	A	L	1-4	Zapater Arjol 9	75,000
7	sppr1	**Sevilla**	H	W	2-0	D'Alessandro 53, Garcia de la Fuente 87 og	30,000
8	ucrl2	**Aris**	H	W	2-1	Oliveira 18, Garcia de la Fuente 73	16,208
9	sppr1	**Levante**	H	W	3-0	Garcia de la Fuente 63, Oliveira 72, 80	24,840
10	sppr1	**Atl Madrid**	A	L	0-4		43,840
11	sppr1	**Villarreal**	H	W	4-1	Oliveira 36, Gonzalez Marcos 49, Milito 67 pen, Garcia de la Fuente 78	24,150
12	sppr1	**Almeria**	A	W	1-0	Milito 73 pen	16,000
13	sppr1	**Valladolid**	H	L	2-3	Oliveira 14, Milito 90	20,000
14	sppr1	**Real Betis**	A	L	1-2	D'Alessandro 34	29,000
15	sppr1	**Getafe**	H	D	1-1	D'Alessandro 80	22,425
16	sppr1	**Recreativo**	A	L	1-2	Milito 22	18,540
17	sppr1	**Espanyol**	H	D	3-3	Milito 5, Oliveira 83, 87	31,050
18	sppr1	**Deportivo**	A	D	1-1	Milito 17	22,000
19	sppr1	**Valencia**	H	D	2-2	Milito 17 pen, Mora Palacios 30 og	34,596
20	sppr1	**Real Madrid**	A	L	0-2		72,800
21	sppr1	**Mallorca**	H	D	2-2	Milito 23, 37	27,600
22	sppr1	**Murcia**	H	W	3-1	Oliveira 34, Milito 61, 82	31,050
23	sppr1	**R Santander**	A	D	2-2	Milito 60, Celades Lopez 84	21,090
24	sppr1	**Athl Bilbao**	H	W	1-0	Oliveira 28	25,875
25	sppr1	**Osasuna**	A	L	0-1		16,830
26	sppr1	**Barcelona**	H	L	1-2	Oliveira 53	34,500
27	sppr1	**Sevilla**	A	L	0-5		25,000
28	sppr1	**Levante**	A	L	1-2	Gonzalez Marcos 65	16,445
29	sppr1	**Atl Madrid**	H	W	2-1	Ibanez Tebar 33 og, Milito 72 pen	34,000
30	sppr1	**Villarreal**	A	L	0-2		20,181
31	sppr1	**Almeria**	H	D	1-1	Oliveira 68	30,000
32	sppr1	**Valladolid**	A	L	1-2	Zapater Arjol 28	15,000
33	sppr1	**Real Betis**	H	L	0-3		24,150
34	sppr1	**Getafe**	A	D	0-0		15,300
35	sppr1	**Recreativo**	H	W	3-0	Garcia de la Fuente 2, Oliveira 20, 78	31,740
36	sppr1	**Espanyol**	A	D	1-1	Oliveira 85 pen	25,150
37	sppr1	**Deportivo**	H	W	1-0	Ayala 90	34,500
38	sppr1	**Valencia**	A	L	0-1		38,500
39	sppr1	**Real Madrid**	H	D	2-2	Oliveira 20, Fernandez Gonzalez 86	34,155
40	sppr1	**Mallorca**	A	L	2-3	Oliveira 56, 90	16,170

LEAGUE APPEARANCES, BOOKINGS AND CAPS

	AGE (on 01/07/08)	IN NAMED 18	APPEARANCES	COUNTING GAMES	MINUTES ON PITCH	YELLOW CARDS	RED CARDS	CAPS THIS SEASON	NATIONAL SIDE
Goalkeepers									
Javier Lopez Vallejo	32	28	2	2	164	1	0	-	Spain
Cesar Sanchez	36	37	37	36	3256	2	0	-	Spain
Defenders									
Roberto Ayala	35	33	33	32	2925	15	1	-	Argentina
Victor Laguardia	20	2	0	0	0	0	0	-	Spain
Luis Carlos Cuartero	33	6	2	1	144	0	0	-	Spain
Carlos Andres Diogo	24	32	29	26	2461	8	1	1	Uruguay
Sergio Gonzalez	31	26	24	23	2074	7	0	-	Spain
Juan Garcia Garcia	31	33	28	24	2244	6	1	-	Spain
Jesus Maria Gomez	24	24	10	5	608	3	0	-	Spain
Javier Paredes	25	26	24	18	1728	5	0	-	Spain
Francisco Pavon	28	26	8	7	618	0	1	-	Spain
Midfielders									
Pablo Cesar Aimar	28	24	22	10	1374	3	0	5	Argentina
Albert Celades Lopez	32	29	24	13	1362	7	0	-	Spain
Andres D'Alessandro	27	17	13	2	465	2	0	-	Argentina
Fran Matuzalem	28	19	14	9	951	3	2	-	Brazil
Gabriel Fernandez	24	34	31	16	1850	11	1	-	Spain
David Miranda	25	10	4	0	59	0	0	-	Spain
Raul Goni Bayo	18	10	2	1	109	0	0	-	Spain
Oscar	25	34	32	12	1628	3	0	-	Spain
Guillermo Grande	22	2	0	0	0	0	0	-	Spain
Peter Luccin	29	33	30	21	2188	11	1	-	France
Alberto Ganan	20	1	1	0	11	0	0	-	Spain
Vicente Collados	21	1	1	0	29	1	1	-	Spain
Oscar Valero Navarro	22	12	4	1	184	0	0	-	Spain
Alberto Zapater Arjol	23	37	36	29	2712	6	0	-	Spain
Forwards									
Sergio Garcia	25	38	38	25	2666	5	0	-	Spain
Diego Alberto Milito	29	36	35	29	2841	4	0	3	Argentina
Ricardo Oliveira	28	37	36	28	2709	4	0	-	Brazil

TEAM OF THE SEASON

G
Cesar Sanchez
CG: 36 DR: 57

D
Sergio Gonzalez
CG: 23 DR: 64

D
Javier Paredes
CG: 18 DR: 61

D
Roberto Ayala
CG: 32 DR: 56

D
J Garcia Garcia
CG: 24 DR: 53

M
Oscar
CG: 12 SD: 2

M
Alberto Zapaterl
CG: 29 SD: -13

M
Peter Luccin
CG: 21 SD: -16

M
Albert Celades
CG: 13 SD: -21

F
Ricardo Oliveira
CG: 28 SR: 142

F
Diego Alberto Milito
CG: 29 SR: 189

MONTHLY POINTS TALLY

AUGUST	0	0%
SEPTEMBER	8	53%
OCTOBER	9	75%
NOVEMBER	1	11%
DECEMBER	3	25%
JANUARY	5	42%
FEBRUARY	3	25%
MARCH	4	27%
APRIL	5	42%
MAY	4	33%

LEAGUE GOALS

	PLAYER	MINS	GOALS	S RATE
1	Oliveira	2709	**19**	142
2	Milito	2841	**15**	189
3	Sergo Garcia	2666	**4**	666
4	D'Alessandro	465	**3**	155
5	Gonzalez M	1628	**2**	814
6	Zapater Arjol	2712	**2**	1356
7	Celades	1362	**1**	1362
8	Gonzalez F	2074	**1**	2074
9	Ayala	2925	**1**	2925
	Other		**0**	
	TOTAL		**48**	

TOP POINT EARNERS

	PLAYER	GAMES	AV PTS
1	Oscar	12	**1.33**
2	Peter Luccin	21	**1.33**
3	Sergio Gonzalez	23	**1.30**
4	Sergio G de la Fuente	25	**1.20**
5	Ricardo Oliveira	28	**1.14**
6	Cesar Sanchez	36	**1.14**
7	Diego Alberto Milito	29	**1.10**
8	Juan Francisco Garcia	24	**1.08**
9	Carlos Andres Diogo	26	**1.08**
10	Alberto Zapater Arjol	29	**1.07**
	CLUB AVERAGE:		**1.11**

DISCIPLINARY RECORDS

	PLAYER	YELLOW	RED	AVE
1	Gab Fernandez	11	1	**154**
2	Roberto Ayala	15	1	**182**
3	Peter Luccin	11	1	**182**
4	Fran Matuzalem	3	2	**190**
5	Albert Celades	7	0	**194**
6	Jesus Gomez	3	0	**202**
7	A D'Alessandro	2	0	**232**
8	Carlos Diogo	8	1	**273**
9	Sergio Gonzalez	7	0	**296**
10	Juan Francisco	6	1	**320**
11	Javier Paredes	5	0	**345**
12	Alberto Arjol	6	0	**452**
13	Pablo Aimar	3	0	**458**
	Other	18	1	
	TOTAL	105	8	

KEY GOALKEEPER

Cesar Sanchez

Goals Conceded in the League	57	Counting Games League games when player was on pitch for at least 70 minutes	36
Defensive Rating Ave number of mins between League goals conceded while on the pitch	57	Clean Sheets In League games when player was on pitch for at least 70 minutes	7

KEY PLAYERS - DEFENDERS

Sergio Gonzalez

Goals Conceded Number of League goals conceded while the player was on the pitch	32	Clean Sheets In League games when player was on pitch for at least 70 minutes	6
Defensive Rating Ave number of mins between League goals conceded while on the pitch	64	Club Defensive Rating Average number of mins between League goals conceded by the club this season	56

	PLAYER	CON LGE	CLEAN SHEETS	DEF RATE
1	Sergio Gonzalez	32	6	64 mins
2	Javier Paredes	28	4	61 mins
3	Roberto Ayala	52	6	56 mins
4	Juan Garcia Garcia	42	3	53 mins

KEY PLAYERS - MIDFIELDERS

Oscar

Goals in the League	2	Contribution to Attacking Power Average number of minutes between League team goals while on pitch	54
Defensive Rating Average number of mins between League goals conceded while on the pitch	56	Scoring Difference Defensive Rating minus Contribution to Attacking Power	2

	PLAYER	LGE GOALS	DEF RATE	POWER	SCORE DIFF
1	Oscar	2	56	54	2 mins
2	Alberto Zapater	2	53	66	-13 mins
3	Peter Luccin	0	50	66	-16 mins
4	Albert Celades	1	54	75	-21 mins

KEY PLAYERS - GOALSCORERS

Ricardo Oliveira

Goals in the League	19	Player Strike Rate Average number of minutes between League goals scored by player	142
Contribution to Attacking Power Average number of minutes between League team goals while on pitch	66	Club Strike Rate Average number of minutes between League goals scored by club	68

	PLAYER	LGE GOALS	POWER	STRIKE RATE
1	Ricardo Oliveira	19	66	142 mins
2	Diego Alberto Milito	15	71	189 mins
3	Sergio Garcia de la Fuente	4	65	666 mins
4	Oscar	2	54	814 mins

LFP
EXPOZARAGOZA2008
Telefonica
Francisco Pavon, Diego Milito & Sergio Garcia

SQUAD APPEARANCES

Match	1	2	3	4	5	6	7	8	9	10	11	12	13	14	15	16	17	18	19	20
Venue	A	H	A	A	H	A	H	H	H	A	H	A	H	A	H	A	H	A	H	A
Competition	L	L	L	E	L	L	L	E	L	L	L	L	L	L	L	L	L	L	L	L
Result	L	D	D	L	W	L	W	W	W	L	W	W	L	L	D	L	D	D	D	L

Match	21	22	23	24	25	26	27	28	29	30	31	32	33	34	35	36	37	38	39	40
Venue	H	H	A	H	A	H	A	A	H	A	H	A	H	A	H	A	H	A	H	A
Competition	L	L	L	L	L	L	L	L	L	L	L	L	L	L	L	L	L	L	L	L
Result	D	W	D	W	L	L	L	L	W	L	D	L	L	D	W	D	W	L	D	L

Goalkeepers
Javier Lopez Vallejo
Cesar Sanchez

Defenders
Roberto Ayala
Victor Laguardia
Luis Carlos Cuartero
Carlos Andres Diogo
Sergio Gonzalez
Juan Garcia Garcia
Jesus Maria Gomez
Javier Paredes
Francisco Pavon

Midfielders
Pablo Cesar Aimar
Albert Celades
Andres D'Alessandro
Francelino Matuzalem
Gabriel Fernandez Arenas
David Generelo Miranda
Raul Goni Bayo
Oscar
Guillermo Grande Escosa
Peter Bernard Luccin
Alberto Montejo Ganan
Vicente Pascual Collados
Oscar Valero Navarro
Alberto Zapater Arjol

Forwards
Sergio Garcia
Diego Alberto Milito
Ricardo Oliveira

KEY: ■ On all match ■ On bench ⏮ Subbed or sent off (Counting game) « Subbed or sent off (playing less than 70 minutes) ⏭ Subbed on from bench (Counting Game) » Subbed on (playing less than 70 minutes) Subbed on and then subbed or sent off (Counting Game) Subbed on and then subbed or sent off (playing less than 70 minutes) □ Not in 16

MURCIA

Final Position: **19th**

NICKNAME: LOS PIMENTONEROS

KEY: ☐Won ☐Drawn ☐Lost

							Attendance
1	sppr1	**Real Zaragoza**	H	W	2-1	Mejia 18, Baiano 63	22,000
2	sppr1	**Levante**	A	D	0-0		12,000
3	sppr1	**Atl Madrid**	H	D	1-1	Gallardo Leon 81	25,000
4	sppr1	**Villarreal**	A	L	0-2		20,398
5	sppr1	**Almeria**	H	L	0-1		17,105
6	sppr1	**Valladolid**	A	W	4-1	De Lucas Martinez 29, Fernando Baiano 77, Alonso Vallejo 81, Gomez Moreno 88	14,521
7	sppr1	**Real Betis**	H	D	0-0		25,195
8	sppr1	**Getafe**	A	L	0-2		11,050
9	sppr1	**Recreativo**	H	W	1-0	Regueiro Pintos 46	25,191
10	sppr1	**Espanyol**	A	D	0-0		29,860
11	sppr1	**Deportivo**	H	L	0-2		24,880
12	sppr1	**Valencia**	A	L	0-3		41,250
13	sppr1	**Real Madrid**	H	D	1-1	De Lucas Martinez 48	31,100
14	sppr1	**Mallorca**	A	D	1-1	de Mendizabal 23	18,480
15	sppr1	**Sevilla**	A	L	1-3	Fernando Baiano 65	36,400
16	sppr1	**R Santander**	H	W	2-1	Goitom 56, Fernando Baiano 81 pen	23,325
17	sppr1	**Athl Bilbao**	A	D	1-1	Fernando Baiano 54 pen	30,400
18	sppr1	**Osasuna**	H	W	2-0	Goitom 73, Gomez Moreno 90 pen	21,770
19	sppr1	**Barcelona**	A	L	0-4		88,830
20	sppr1	**Real Zaragoza**	A	L	1-3	Alonso Vallejo 90	31,050
21	sppr1	**Levante**	H	L	2-3	Alonso Vallejo 46, Adolfo Nascimento 89	15,861
22	sppr1	**Atl Madrid**	A	D	1-1	Mateu Gonzalez 51 pen	49,320
23	sppr1	**Villarreal**	H	L	0-1		23,150
24	sppr1	**Almeria**	A	L	0-1		12,100
25	sppr1	**Valladolid**	H	L	0-1		18,660
26	sppr1	**Real Betis**	A	L	0-4		38,000
27	sppr1	**Getafe**	H	L	0-3		20,215
28	sppr1	**Recreativo**	A	L	2-4	De Lucas Martinez 15, Alonso Vallejo 75 pen	17,510
29	sppr1	**Espanyol**	H	W	4-0	Alonso Vallejo 35 pen, 46, Gomez Moreno 62 pen, de Zabalza 86	20,215
30	sppr1	**Deportivo**	A	L	1-3	De Lucas Martinez 2	18,000
31	sppr1	**Valencia**	H	W	1-0	Alonso Vallejo 35	24,880
32	sppr1	**Real Madrid**	A	L	0-1		76,000
33	sppr1	**Mallorca**	H	L	1-4	Fernando Baiano 88	23,325
34	sppr1	**Sevilla**	H	D	0-0		24,880
35	sppr1	**R Santander**	A	L	2-3	Aquino Pintos 13, Alonso Vallejo 28	19,980
36	sppr1	**Athl Bilbao**	H	L	1-2	Alonso Vallejo 19	12,000
37	sppr1	**Osasuna**	A	L	1-2	Gomez Moreno 90	19,800
38	sppr1	**Barcelona**	H	L	3-5	Ochoa Lopez 17, Alonso Vallejo 81 pen, Gomez Moreno 85	27,990

LEAGUE APPEARANCES, BOOKINGS AND CAPS

	AGE (on 01/07/08)	IN NAMED 18	APPEARANCES	COUNTING GAMES	MINUTES ON PITCH	YELLOW CARDS	RED CARDS	CAPS THIS SEASON	NATIONAL SIDE
Goalkeepers									
Alberto Cabrera	23	3	1	1	90	0	0	-	Spain
Fabian Carini	28	33	11	11	990	0	0	-	Uruguay
Antonio Notario	35	34	26	26	2340	1	0	-	Spain
Defenders									
Cesar Arzo	22	29	29	26	2454	9	1	-	Spain
Ivan Javier Cuadrado	29	20	10	9	854	1	0	-	Spain
Stephane Pignol	31	22	18	13	1334	7	1	-	France
David Gutierrez	28	21	20	19	1773	7	0	-	Spain
Alejandro Perez	28	13	6	3	437	2	0	-	Spain
Alvaro Mejia Perez	26	32	29	28	2556	11	2	-	Spain
Juan Ochoa Lopez	29	28	16	15	1330	5	0	-	Spain
Paco Pena Romero	29	36	35	35	3150	7	0	-	Spain
Juan Pedro Martinez	23	4	3	2	208	2	0	-	Spain
Cristobal Emilio Ruiz	31	3	2	2	180	0	0	-	Spain
Midfielders									
Rosinei Nascimento	25	14	11	2	477	0	0	-	Brazil
Enrique De Lucas	29	32	30	19	2148	7	0	-	Spain
Ricardo de Zabalza	31	34	26	14	1534	3	0	-	Spain
Abel Gomez Moreno	26	35	29	13	1582	5	0	-	Spain
Francisco Gallardo	28	17	8	2	314	1	0	-	Spain
Abderrahman Kabous	25	7	6	5	455	2	0	-	Morocco
Jofre Gonzalez	28	24	14	1	647	0	0	-	Spain
Jose Maria Movilla	33	33	25	14	1728	3	0	-	Spain
Gabriel Perez Garcia	31	24	22	21	1893	7	0	-	Uruguay
Mario Pintos	29	25	23	9	1391	7	1	2	Uruguay
Forwards									
Ivan Alonso Vallejo	29	33	28	19	1972	6	0	-	Uruguay
Daniel Aquino Pintos	17	13	13	9	933	1	0	-	Spain
Inigo Velez	26	27	24	6	1032	4	0	-	Spain
Joao Fernando Baiano	29	32	27	15	1704	3	0	-	Brazil
Henok Goitom	23	35	30	14	1761	5	0	-	Sweden

TEAM OF THE SEASON

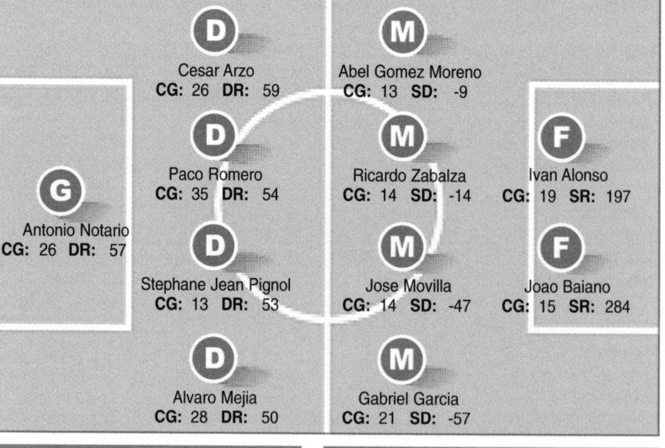

G
Antonio Notario
CG: 26 DR: 57
D
Cesar Arzo
CG: 26 DR: 59
D
Paco Romero
CG: 35 DR: 54
D
Stephane Jean Pignol
CG: 13 DR: 53
D
Alvaro Mejia
CG: 28 DR: 50
M
Abel Gomez Moreno
CG: 13 SD: -9
M
Ricardo Zabalza
CG: 14 SD: -14
M
Jose Movilla
CG: 14 SD: -47
M
Gabriel Garcia
CG: 21 SD: -57
F
Ivan Alonso
CG: 19 SR: 197
F
Joao Baiano
CG: 15 SR: 284

MONTHLY POINTS TALLY

Month	Points	%
AUGUST	3	100%
SEPTEMBER	5	33%
OCTOBER	4	44%
NOVEMBER	2	17%
DECEMBER	5	42%
JANUARY	3	25%
FEBRUARY	1	8%
MARCH	3	20%
APRIL	4	33%
MAY	0	0%

LEAGUE GOALS

	PLAYER	MINS	GOALS	S RATE
1	Alonso	1972	10	197
2	J. Baiano	1704	6	284
3	Gomez Moreno	1582	5	316
4	De Lucas M	2148	4	537
5	Goitom	1761	2	880
6	Gallardo Lean	314	1	314
7	A Nascimento	477	1	477
8	Mateu Gonzalez	647	1	647
9	Aquino Pintos	933	1	933
10	de Mendizabal	1032	1	1032
11	Ochoa Lopez	1330	1	1330
12	Regueiro Pintos	1391	1	1391
13	de Zabalza	1534	1	1534
	Other		1	
	TOTAL		36	

TOP POINT EARNERS

	PLAYER	GAMES	AV PTS
1	Abel Gomez Moreno	13	1.00
2	Gabriel Pablo Garcia	21	0.95
3	Jose Movilla Cubero	14	0.93
4	Joao Fernando Baiano	15	0.93
5	Paco Pena Romero	35	0.86
6	Alvaro Mejia Perez	28	0.86
7	Antonio Notario Caro	26	0.85
8	Cesar Arzo Amposta	26	0.85
9	Enrique De Lucas	19	0.79
10	Ricardo de Zabalza	14	0.79
	CLUB AVERAGE:		0.79

DISCIPLINARY RECORDS

	PLAYER	YELLOW	RED	AVE
1	S Jean Pignol	7	1	166
2	Mario Pintos	7	1	173
3	Alvaro Meija	11	2	196
4	A Kabous	2	0	227
5	Cesar Arzo	9	1	245
6	David Gutierrez	7	0	253
7	Inigo Velez	4	0	258
8	Juan Ochoa	5	0	266
9	Pablo Garcia	7	0	270
10	Enrique De Lucas	7	0	306
11	A Gomez Moreno	5	0	316
12	Ivan Alonso	6	0	328
13	Henok Goitom	5	0	352
	Other	19	0	
	TOTAL	101	5	

KEY GOALKEEPER

Antonio Notario Caro

Goals Conceded in the League	41	**Counting Games** League games when player was on pitch for at least 70 minutes	26
Defensive Rating Ave number of mins between League goals conceded while on the pitch	57	**Clean Sheets** In League games when player was on pitch for at least 70 minutes	4

KEY PLAYERS - DEFENDERS

Cesar Arzo Amposta

Goals Conceded Number of League goals conceded while the player was on the pitch	41	**Clean Sheets** In League games when player was on pitch for at least 70 minutes	5
Defensive Rating Ave number of mins between League goals conceded while on the pitch	59	**Club Defensive Rating** Average number of mins between League goals conceded by the club this season	52

	PLAYER	CON LGE	CLEAN SHEETS	DEF RATE
1	Cesar Arzo Amposta	41	5	59 mins
2	Paco Romero	58	8	54 mins
3	Stephane Jean Francois Pignol	25	4	53 mins
4	Alvaro Mejia	51	8	50 mins

KEY PLAYERS - MIDFIELDERS

Abel Gomez Moreno

Goals in the League	5	**Contribution to Attacking Power** Average number of minutes between League team goals while on pitch	60
Defensive Rating Average number of mins between League goals conceded while on the pitch	51	**Scoring Difference** Defensive Rating minus Contribution to Attacking Power	-9

	PLAYER	LGE GOALS	DEF RATE	POWER	SCORE DIFF
1	Abel Gomez Moreno	5	51	60	-9 mins
2	Ricardo Perez de Zabalza	1	76	90	-14 mins
3	Jose Movilla Cubero	0	54	101	-47 mins
4	Gabriel Perez Pablo Garcia	0	61	118	-57 mins

KEY PLAYERS - GOALSCORERS

Ivan Daniel Alonso Vallejo

Goals in the League	10	**Player Strike Rate** Average number of minutes between League goals scored by player	197
Contribution to Attacking Power Average number of minutes between League team goals while on pitch	75	**Club Strike Rate** Average number of minutes between League goals scored by club	95

	PLAYER	LGE GOALS	POWER	STRIKE RATE
1	Ivan Daniel Alonso Vallejo	10	75	197 mins
2	Joao Fernando Baiano	6	94	284 mins
3	Abel Gomez Moreno	5	60	316 mins
4	Enrique De Lucas Martinez	4	113	537 mins

LFP
CM
CAJAMUR
Enrique De Lucas

SQUAD APPEARANCES

Match	1	2	3	4	5	6	7	8	9	10	11	12	13	14	15	16	17	18	19	20	21	22	23	24	25	26	27	28	29	30	31	32	33	34	35	36	37	38
Venue	H	A	H	A	H	A	H	A	H	A	H	A	H	A	A	H	A	H	A	A	H	A	H	A	H	A	H	A	H	A	H	A	H	H	A	H	A	H
Competition	L	L	L	L	L	L	L	L	L	L	L	L	L	L	L	L	L	L	L	L	L	L	L	L	L	L	L	L	L	L	L	L	L	L	L	L	L	L
Result	W	D	D	L	L	W	D	L	W	D	L	L	D	D	L	W	D	W	L	L	L	D	L	L	L	L	L	L	W	L	W	L	L	D	L	L	L	L

Goalkeepers
Alberto Garcia Cabrera
Fabian Hector Carini
Antonio Notario Caro

Defenders
Cesar Arzo Amposta
Ivan Javier Cuadrado
Stephane Pignol
David Gutierrez De Coz
Alejandro Maranon Perez
Alvaro Mejia Perez
Juan Cruz Ochoa Lopez
Paco Pena Romero
Juan Pedro Pina Martinez
Cristobal Emilio Ruiz

Midfielders
Rosinei Nascimento
Enrique De Lucas
Ricardo Perez de Zabalza
Abel Gomez Moreno
Francisco Gallardo Leon
Abderrahman Kabous
Jofre Mateu Gonzalez
Jose Maria Movilla Cubero
Gabriel Perez Pablo Garcia
Mario Regueiro Pintos

Forwards
Ivan Alonso Vallejo
Daniel Aquino Pintos
Inigo Velez
Joao Fernando Baiano
Henok Goitom

KEY: On all match · On bench · Subbed or sent off (Counting game) · Subbed or sent off (playing less than 70 minutes) · Subbed on from bench (Counting Game) · Subbed on (playing less than 70 minutes) · Subbed on and then subbed or sent off (Counting Game) · Subbed on and then subbed or sent off (playing less than 70 minutes) · Not in 16

LEVANTE

Final Position: **20th**

NICKNAME: GRANOTES (FROGS)

KEY: ☐Won ☐Drawn ☐Lost

							Attendance
1	sppr1	**Mallorca**	A	L	0-3		22,400
2	sppr1	**Murcia**	H	D	0-0		12,000
3	sppr1	**R Santander**	A	L	0-1		19,536
4	sppr1	**Athl Bilbao**	H	L	1-2	Rigano 78	17,710
5	sppr1	**Osasuna**	A	L	1-4	Ettien 34	12,870
6	sppr1	**Barcelona**	H	L	1-4	Viqueira Moure 71 pen	25,360
7	sppr1	**Real Zaragoza**	A	L	0-3		24,840
8	sppr1	**Sevilla**	H	L	0-2		12,650
9	sppr1	**Atl Madrid**	H	L	0-1		15,000
10	sppr1	**Villarreal**	A	L	0-3		11,501
11	sppr1	**Almeria**	H	W	3-0	Rigano 1, 16, 34	15,180
12	sppr1	**Valladolid**	A	L	0-1		17,755
13	sppr1	**Real Betis**	H	W	4-3	Tommasi 39, Riga 40, 50, Fuego Martinez 80	22,770
14	sppr1	**Getafe**	A	L	1-2	Riga 14 pen	13,600
15	sppr1	**Recreativo**	H	L	0-2		12,650
16	sppr1	**Espanyol**	A	L	0-1		22,400
17	sppr1	**Deportivo**	H	L	0-1		25,354
18	sppr1	**Valencia**	A	D	0-0		46,750
19	sppr1	**Real Madrid**	H	L	0-2		15,000
20	sppr1	**Mallorca**	H	D	2-2	Geijo Pazos 18, Luiz Maior de Aquino 88	12,400
21	sppr1	**Murcia**	A	W	3-2	Luiz Maior de Aquino 73, Riga 81 pen, Sanchez Gil 90	15,861
22	sppr1	**R Santander**	H	D	1-1	Riga 57	19,987
23	sppr1	**Athl Bilbao**	A	L	0-1		39,200
24	sppr1	**Osasuna**	H	W	2-1	Luiz Maior de Aquino 54, Geijo Pazos 58	14,927
25	sppr1	**Barcelona**	A	L	1-5	Riga 40 pen	98,772
26	sppr1	**Real Zaragoza**	H	W	2-1	Geijo Pazos 21, Riga 60	16,445
27	sppr1	**Sevilla**	A	L	1-2	Riga 4	31,850
28	sppr1	**Atl Madrid**	A	L	0-3		47,676
29	sppr1	**Villarreal**	H	L	1-2	Lozano Ayala 64	22,770
30	sppr1	**Almeria**	A	L	1-2	Iborra 90	16,500
31	sppr1	**Valladolid**	H	L	0-3		14,421
32	sppr1	**Real Betis**	A	W	1-0	Sanchez Gil 53	55,000
33	sppr1	**Getafe**	H	W	3-1	Gomez Sanchez 41, Berson 44, Sanchez Gil 54	7,843
34	sppr1	**Recreativo**	A	L	0-2		14,420
35	sppr1	**Espanyol**	H	D	1-1	Gomez Sanchez 77	10,120
36	sppr1	**Deportivo**	A	L	0-1		12,110
37	sppr1	**Valencia**	H	L	1-5	Serrano Arenas 31	14,421
38	sppr1	**Real Madrid**	A	L	2-5	Geijo Pazos 52, 63	72,000

LEAGUE APPEARANCES, BOOKINGS AND CAPS

	AGE (on 01/07/08)	IN NAMED 18	APPEARANCES	COUNTING GAMES	MINUTES ON PITCH	YELLOW CARDS	RED CARDS	CAPS THIS SEASON	NATIONAL SIDE
Goalkeepers									
Vladan Kujovic	29	34	13	13	1170	1	0	-	Serbia
Manuel Reina	24	14	8	8	720	1	0	-	Spain
Marco Storari	31	17	16	16	1440	1	0	-	Italy
Defenders									
David Castedo	34	21	18	18	1620	2	0	-	Spain
Bruno Cirillo	31	16	15	14	1320	6	0	-	Italy
Inaki Retegui	31	32	29	24	2297	6	0	-	Spain
Manuel Gaspar Haro	27	22	14	10	961	4	0	-	Spain
Armando Lozano	23	18	12	7	734	4	0	-	-
Alvaro Luiz Maior	29	31	28	25	2368	10	1	-	Brazil
Miquel Robuste	23	14	4	3	311	1	0	-	Spain
Luis Rubiales	30	31	20	17	1669	4	0	-	Spain
Jose Manuel Serrano	27	33	29	29	2602	6	0	-	Spain
Midfielders									
Mathieu Berson	28	30	22	15	1618	10	1	-	France
Savio Bortolini	34	12	12	9	938	2	0	-	Brazil
Laurent Courtois	29	27	25	16	1739	0	0	-	France
Felix Dja Ettien	28	23	13	1	397	1	0	-	Ivory Coast
Javier Fuego Martinez	24	30	24	16	1607	5	0	-	Spain
Juan Manuel Gomez	27	35	34	27	2659	6	0	-	Spain
Vicente Iborra	20	21	14	4	529	0	0	-	Spanish
Miguel Angel	29	26	23	16	1679	6	0	-	Spain
Pedro Leon Gil	21	30	22	7	1126	2	0	-	Spain
Damiano Tommasi	34	17	15	11	1221	5	0	-	Italy
Emilio Jose Viqueira	33	11	8	0	326	0	0	-	Spain
Forwards									
Shota Arveladze	35	4	4	0	44	0	0	-	Georgia
Saul Fernandez Garcia	23	24	19	2	581	2	0	-	Spain
A Geijo Pazos	26	32	30	18	1934	3	0	-	Switzerland
Albert Meyong Ze	27	1	1	0	11	0	0	-	Cameroon
Mustapha Riga	26	35	33	27	2622	2	0	-	Ghana
Christian Rigano	34	13	13	10	969	4	0	-	Italy

TEAM OF THE SEASON

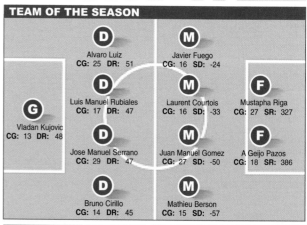

G — Vladan Kujovic, CG: 13 DR: 48

D — Alvaro Luiz, CG: 25 DR: 51

D — Luis Manuel Rubiales, CG: 17 DR: 47

D — Jose Manuel Serrano, CG: 29 DR: 47

D — Bruno Cirillo, CG: 14 DR: 45

M — Javier Fuego, CG: 16 SD: -24

M — Laurent Courtois, CG: 16 SD: -33

M — Juan Manuel Gomez, CG: 27 SD: -50

M — Mathieu Berson, CG: 15 SD: -57

F — Mustapha Riga, CG: 27 SR: 327

F — A Geijo Pazos, CG: 18 SR: 386

MONTHLY POINTS TALLY

AUGUST	0	0%
SEPTEMBER	1	7%
OCTOBER	0	0%
NOVEMBER	6	67%
DECEMBER	0	0%
JANUARY	5	42%
FEBRUARY	4	33%
MARCH	3	20%
APRIL	6	50%
MAY	1	8%

LEAGUE GOALS

	PLAYER	MINS	GOALS	S RATE
1	Riga	2622	8	327
2	Geijo Pazos	1934	5	386
3	Rigano	969	4	242
4	Sanchez Gil	1126	3	375
5	L M de Aquino	2368	3	789
6	Gomez Sanchez	2659	2	1329
7	Viqueira Moure	326	1	326
8	Ettien	397	1	397
9	Iborra	529	1	529
10	Tommasi	1221	1	1221
11	Fuego Martinez	1607	1	1607
12	Berson	1618	1	1618
13	Lozano Ayala	1679	1	1679
	Other		1	
	TOTAL		33	

TOP POINT EARNERS

	PLAYER	GAMES	AV PTS
1	Javier Fuego Martinez	16	0.94
2	Vladan Kujovic	13	0.92
3	Alvaro L M de Aquino	25	0.92
4	Jose Serrano Arenas	29	0.86
5	Luis Manuel Rubiales	17	0.82
6	Laurent Courtois	16	0.81
7	Juan Manuel Gomez	27	0.78
8	Alexandre Geijo Pazos	18	0.78
9	Inaki Descarga Retegui	24	0.67
10	Mathieu Berson	15	0.67
	CLUB AVERAGE:		0.68

DISCIPLINARY RECORDS

	PLAYER	YELLOW	RED	AVE
1	Mathieu Berson	10	1	147
2	Armando Lozano	4	0	183
3	A L M de Aquino	10	1	215
4	Manuel Gaspar	4	0	240
5	Christian Rigano	4	0	242
6	Damiano Tommasi	5	0	244
7	Bruno Cirillo	5	0	264
8	Miguel Angel	6	0	279
9	Saul Fernandez	2	0	290
10	Javier Fuego	5	0	321
11	Inaki Descarga	6	0	382
12	Luis Rubiales	4	0	417
13	Juan Gomez	6	0	443
	Other	19	0	
	TOTAL	90	2	

KEY GOALKEEPER

Vladan Kujovic

Goals Conceded in the League	24	Counting Games League games when player was on pitch for at least 70 minutes	13
Defensive Rating Ave number of mins between League goals conceded while on the pitch	48	Clean Sheets In League games when player was on pitch for at least 70 minutes	1

KEY PLAYERS - DEFENDERS

Alvaro Luiz Maior de Aquino

Goals Conceded Number of League goals conceded while the player was on the pitch	46	Clean Sheets In League games when player was on pitch for at least 70 minutes	4
Defensive Rating Ave number of mins between League goals conceded while on the pitch	51	Club Defensive Rating Average number of mins between League goals conceded by the club this season	45

	PLAYER	CON LGE	CLEAN SHEETS	DEF RATE
1	Alvaro Luiz Maior de Aquino	46	4	51 mins
2	Luis Manuel Rubiales	35	4	47 mins
3	Jose Manuel Serrano	55	3	47 mins
4	Bruno Cirillo	29	1	45 mins

KEY PLAYERS - MIDFIELDERS

Javier Fuego

Goals in the League	1	Contribution to Attacking Power Average number of minutes between League team goals while on pitch	69
Defensive Rating Average number of mins between League goals conceded while on the pitch	45	Scoring Difference Defensive Rating minus Contribution to Attacking Power	-24

	PLAYER	LGE GOALS	DEF RATE	POWER	SCORE DIFF
1	Javier Fuego	1	45	69	-24 mins
2	Laurent Courtois	0	42	75	-33 mins
3	Juan Manuel Gomez	2	44	94	-50 mins
4	Mathieu Berson	1	44	101	-57 mins

KEY PLAYERS - GOALSCORERS

Mustapha Riga

Goals in the League	8	Player Strike Rate Average number of minutes between League goals scored by player	327
Contribution to Attacking Power Average number of minutes between League team goals while on pitch	104	Club Strike Rate Average number of minutes between League goals scored by club	103

	PLAYER	LGE GOALS	POWER	STRIKE RATE
1	Mustapha Riga	8	104	327 mins
2	Alexandre Geijo Pazos	5	77	386 mins
3	Juan Manuel Gomez	2	94	1329 mins
4	Javier Fuego	1	69	1607 mins

COMUNITAT
VALENCIANA
Mustapha Riga

SQUAD APPEARANCES

Match	1	2	3	4	5	6	7	8	9	10	11	12	13	14	15	16	17	18	19	20	21	22	23	24	25	26	27	28	29	30	31	32	33	34	35	36	37	38
Venue	A	H	A	H	A	H	A	H	H	A	H	A	H	A	H	A	H	A	H	H	A	H	A	H	A	H	A	A	H	A	H	A	H	A	H	A	H	A
Competition	L	L	L	L	L	L	L	L	L	L	L	L	L	L	L	L	L	L	L	L	L	L	L	L	L	L	L	L	L	L	L	L	L	L	L	L	L	L
Result	L	D	L	L	L	L	L	L	L	L	W	L	W	L	L	L	L	D	L	D	W	D	L	W	L	W	L	L	L	L	L	W	W	L	D	L	L	L

Goalkeepers
Vladan Kujovic
Manuel Reina Rodriguez
Marco Storari
Defenders
David Castedo Escudero
Bruno Cirillo
Inaki Descarga Retegui
Manuel Gaspar Haro
Armando Lozano Sanchez
Alvaro Luiz Maior
Miquel Robuste Colomer
Luis Manuel Rubiales
Jose Manuel Serrano
Midfielders
Mathieu Berson
Savio Bortolini Pimentel
Laurent Courtois
Felix Dja Ettien
Javier Fuego Martinez
Juan Manuel Gomez
Vicente Iborra
Miguel Angel
Pedro Leon Sanchez Gil
Damiano Tommasi
Emilio Jose Viqueira
Forwards
Shota Arveladze
Saul Fernandez Garcia
Alexandre Geijo Pazos
Albert Meyong Ze
Mustapha Riga
Christian Rigano

KEY: On all match | On bench | Subbed or sent off (Counting game) | Subbed or sent off (playing less than 70 minutes) | Subbed on from bench (Counting Game) | Subbed on (playing less than 70 minutes) | Subbed on and then subbed or sent off (Counting Game) | Subbed on and then subbed or sent off (playing less than 70 minutes) | Not in 16

ITALIAN LEAGUE ROUND-UP

FINAL LEAGUE TABLE

		HOME					AWAY					TOTAL			
	P	W	D	L	F	A	W	D	L	F	A	F	A	DIF	PTS
Inter Milan	38	15	3	1	41	14	10	7	2	28	12	69	26	43	85
Roma	38	15	3	1	43	20	9	7	3	29	17	72	37	35	82
Juventus	38	12	5	2	39	12	8	7	4	33	25	72	37	35	72
Fiorentina	38	12	4	3	35	18	7	5	7	20	21	55	39	16	66
AC Milan	38	8	7	4	31	18	10	3	6	35	20	66	38	28	64
Sampdoria	38	10	7	2	35	18	7	2	10	21	28	56	46	10	60
Udinese	38	9	4	6	30	29	7	5	7	18	24	48	53	-5	57
Napoli	38	11	4	4	27	16	3	4	12	23	37	50	53	-3	50
Atalanta	38	8	7	4	36	28	4	5	10	16	28	52	56	-4	48
Genoa	38	8	4	7	23	22	5	5	9	21	32	44	54	-10	48
Palermo	38	8	7	4	25	21	4	4	11	22	36	47	57	-10	47
Lazio	38	9	4	6	28	23	2	9	8	19	28	47	51	-4	46
Siena	38	6	9	4	24	17	3	8	8	16	28	40	45	-5	44
Cagliari	38	8	5	6	22	20	3	4	12	18	36	40	56	-16	42
Torino	38	5	7	7	19	19	3	9	7	17	30	36	49	-13	40
Reggina	38	8	5	6	24	19	1	8	10	13	37	37	56	-19	40
Catania Calcio	38	8	6	5	21	14	0	7	12	12	31	33	45	-12	37
Empoli	38	5	7	7	18	21	4	2	13	11	31	29	52	-23	36
Parma	38	7	6	6	28	26	0	7	12	14	36	42	62	-20	34
Livorno	38	3	8	8	18	28	3	4	12	17	32	35	60	-25	30

CLUB STRIKE FORCE

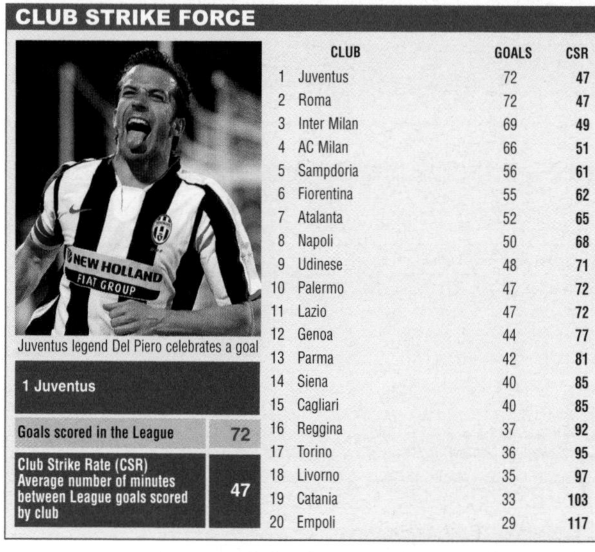
NEW HOLLAND
FIAT GROUP

Juventus legend Del Piero celebrates a goal

1 Juventus

Goals scored in the League	72
Club Strike Rate (CSR) Average number of minutes between League goals scored by club	47

	CLUB	GOALS	CSR
1	Juventus	72	47
2	Roma	72	47
3	Inter Milan	69	49
4	AC Milan	66	51
5	Sampdoria	56	61
6	Fiorentina	55	62
7	Atalanta	52	65
8	Napoli	50	68
9	Udinese	48	71
10	Palermo	47	72
11	Lazio	47	72
12	Genoa	44	77
13	Parma	42	81
14	Siena	40	85
15	Cagliari	40	85
16	Reggina	37	92
17	Torino	36	95
18	Livorno	35	97
19	Catania	33	103
20	Empoli	29	117

CLUB DISCIPLINARY RECORDS

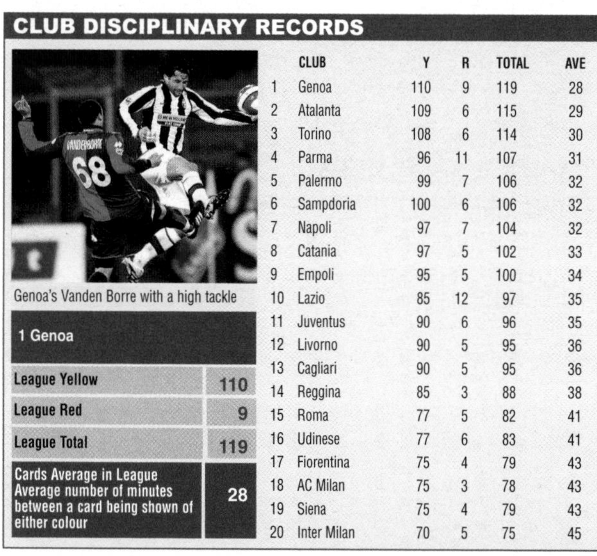

Genoa's Vanden Borre with a high tackle

1 Genoa

League Yellow	110
League Red	9
League Total	119
Cards Average in League Average number of minutes between a card being shown of either colour	28

	CLUB	Y	R	TOTAL	AVE
1	Genoa	110	9	119	28
2	Atalanta	109	6	115	29
3	Torino	108	6	114	30
4	Parma	96	11	107	31
5	Palermo	99	7	106	32
6	Sampdoria	100	6	106	32
7	Napoli	97	7	104	32
8	Catania	97	5	102	33
9	Empoli	95	5	100	34
10	Lazio	85	12	97	35
11	Juventus	90	6	96	35
12	Livorno	90	5	95	36
13	Cagliari	90	5	95	36
14	Reggina	85	3	88	38
15	Roma	77	5	82	41
16	Udinese	77	6	83	41
17	Fiorentina	75	4	79	43
18	AC Milan	75	3	78	43
19	Siena	75	4	79	43
20	Inter Milan	70	5	75	45

CLUB DEFENCES

	CLUB	LGE	CS	CDR
1	Inter Milan	26	18	131
2	Juventus	37	16	92
3	Roma	37	16	92
4	AC Milan	38	11	90
5	Fiorentina	39	13	87
6	Siena	45	12	76
7	Catania	45	10	76
8	Sampdoria	46	16	74
9	Torino	49	10	69
10	Lazio	51	10	67
11	Empoli	52	9	65
12	Genoa	52	9	65
13	Napoli	53	11	64
14	Udinese	53	12	64
15	Atalanta	56	6	61
16	Cagliari	56	8	61
17	Reggina	56	8	61
18	Palermo	57	8	60
19	Livorno	60	5	57
20	Parma	62	7	55

Inter Milan's animated defender Materazzi

1 Inter Milan

Goals conceded in the League	26
Clean Sheets (CS) Number of league games where no goals were conceded	18
Club Defensive Rate (CDR) Average number of minutes between League goals conceded by club	131

PLAYER NATIONALITIES

Overseas country with the most player appearances in the Italian League - Brazil — **734 league appearances by Brazilian players**

	COUNTRY	PLAYERS	IN SQUAD	LGE APP	% LGE ACT	CAPS	MOST APP	APP
	Italy	390	9208	7137	68.73	148	Ferdinando Coppola	100
1	Brazil	45	904	734	7.23	25	Doni	96.1
2	Argentina	32	734	579	5.53	31	Javier Zanetti	94.8
3	Uruguay	17	409	304	2.58	0	Walter A G Gargano	88.0
4	France	16	317	272	2.53	9	Abdoulay Konko	91.7
5	Czech Republic	11	200	154	1.54	40	Tomas Ujfalusi	71.1
6	Croatia	5	132	108	1.04	18	Dario Kneevic	91.6
7	Romania	5	107	97	1.00	27	Adrian Mutu	70.4
8	Switzerland	5	112	91	0.83	17	Gokhan Inler	96.9
9	Serbia	3	80	75	0.80	10	Aleksandar Lukovic	76.3
10	Portugal	9	169	104	0.78	9	Fernando Couto	41.8
11	Australia	4	103	80	0.76	0	Zeljko Kalac	68.4
12	Colombia	3	70	58	0.63	0	Cristian E Zapata	66.9
13	Denmark	5	103	68	0.61	8	Per B Kroldrup	50.0
14	Chile	4	98	71	0.59	0	David Pizarro	71.2
15	Austria	2	66	52	0.53	15	Alex Manninger	68.4
16	Honduras	4	105	72	0.48	0	Julio Cesar Leon	57.0
17	Slovenia	2	47	35	0.42	0	Samir Handanovic	92.1
18	Paraguay	3	49	43	0.41	6	Edgar Barreto	83.1
19	Peru	2	52	36	0.40	0	Juan Manuel Vargas	88.8
20	Senegal	5	79	53	0.40	0	Ferdinand Coly	49.8

CLUB MAKE-UP – HOME AND OVERSEAS PLAYERS

1 Inter Milan — **93.56% of appearances by overseas players**

	CLUB	OVERSEAS	HOME	% OVERSEAS	% LGE ACT	MOST APP	APP
1	Inter Milan	26	7	78.8	93.56	Javier Zanetti	94.8
2	Lazio	19	18	51.4	57.78	Cristian Ledesma	82.0
3	Roma	15	14	51.7	53.97	Doni	96.1
4	AC Milan	15	14	51.7	44.61	Clarence Seedorf	80.0
5	Genoa	15	18	45.5	44.42	Abdoulay Konko	91.7
6	Udinese	16	15	51.6	44.24	Gokhan Inler	96.9
7	Fiorentina	13	19	40.6	43.08	Sebastian Frey	91.1
8	Napoli	11	18	37.9	41.03	Walter Gargano	88.0
9	Juventus	13	20	39.4	39.85	David Trezeguet	89.8
10	Palermo	8	23	25.8	32.49	Amauri	88.0
11	Siena	17	17	50.0	32.06	Alex Manninger	68.4
12	Catania	11	19	36.7	30.11	Juan M Vargas	88.8
13	Reggina	12	18	40.0	26.90	Edgar Barreto	83.1
14	Atalanta	11	23	32.4	23.93	Adriano F Pinto	91.1
15	Livorno	11	21	34.4	22.75	Dario Kneevic	91.6
16	Parma	8	26	23.5	20.30	Reginaldo	75.8
17	Torino	9	26	25.7	19.88	Herman Dellafiore	69.0
18	Cagliari	7	24	22.6	14.84	Diego Luis Lopez	63.6
19	Sampdoria	7	23	23.3	7.36	H Campagnaro	52.9
20	Empoli	3	27	10.0	2.82	G Giacomazzi	31.0

CHART-TOPPING MIDFIELDERS

1 Cesar - Inter Milan

Goals scored in the League	1
Defensive Rating Av number of mins between League goals conceded while on the pitch	188
Contribution to Attacking Power Average number of minutes between League team goals while on pitch	45
Scoring Difference Defensive Rating minus Contribution to Attacking Power	143

	PLAYER	CLUB	GOALS	DEF RATE	POWER	S DIFF
1	Cesar	Inter Milan	1	188	45	143
2	Dejan Stankovic	Inter Milan	1	157	52	105
3	Andrade Maxwell	Inter Milan	0	151	49	102
4	Esteban Cambiasso	Inter Milan	6	133	46	87
5	Rodrigo Taddei	Roma	6	113	45	68
6	Hasan Salihamidzic	Juventus	4	115	48	67
7	Cristiano Zanetti	Juventus	0	105	42	63
8	Pavel Nedved	Juventus	2	106	49	57
9	Patrick Vieira	Inter Milan	3	108	54	54
10	Antonio Nocerino	Juventus	0	102	51	51
11	Daniele De Rossi	Roma	5	92	47	45
12	Andrea Pirlo	AC Milan	3	92	48	44
13	Ricardo Kaka	AC Milan	15	91	47	44
14	Clarence Seedorf	AC Milan	7	91	51	40
15	Mauro Camoranesi	Juventus	5	80	41	39

CHART-TOPPING GOALSCORERS

1 Ibrahimovic - Inter Milan

Goals scored in the League	17
Contribution to Attacking Power Average number of minutes between League team goals while on pitch	46
Club Strike Rate (CSR) Average minutes between League goals scored by club	50
Player Strike Rate Average number of minutes between League goals scored by player	115

	PLAYER	CLUB	GOALS: LGE	POWER	CSR	S RATE
1	Zlatan Ibrahimovic	Inter Milan	17	46	50	115
2	Filippo Inzaghi	AC Milan	11	50	53	128
3	Alessandro Del Piero	Juventus	21	49	48	130
4	Alexandre Pato	AC Milan	9	45	53	141
5	Adrian Mutu	Fiorentina	17	63	62	141
6	Francesco Totti	Roma	14	48	48	148
7	Julio Ricardo Cruz	Inter Milan	13	42	50	150
8	Marco Borriello	Genoa	19	72	77	152
9	David Trezeguet	Juventus	20	45	48	153
10	Antonio Cassano	Sampdoria	10	53	61	154
11	Robert Acquafresca	Cagliari	10	76	87	169
12	Ricardo Kaka	AC Milan	15	47	53	176
13	Antonio Di Natale	Udinese	17	66	71	179
14	Goran Pandev	Lazio	14	72	74	181
15	Tommaso Rocchi	Lazio	14	70	74	192

CHART-TOPPING DEFENDERS

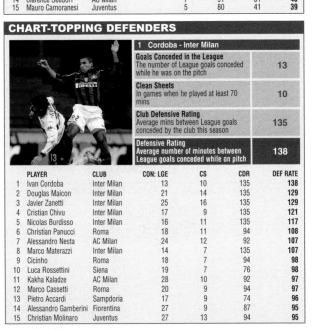

1 Cordoba - Inter Milan

Goals Conceded in the League The number of League goals conceded while he was on the pitch	13
Clean Sheets In games when he played at least 70 mins	10
Club Defensive Rating Average mins between League goals conceded by the club this season	135
Defensive Rating Average number of minutes between League goals conceded while on pitch	138

	PLAYER	CLUB	CON: LGE	CS	CDR	DEF RATE
1	Ivan Cordoba	Inter Milan	13	10	135	138
2	Douglas Maicon	Inter Milan	21	14	135	129
3	Javier Zanetti	Inter Milan	25	16	135	129
4	Cristian Chivu	Inter Milan	17	9	135	121
5	Nicolas Burdisso	Inter Milan	16	11	135	117
6	Christian Panucci	Roma	18	11	94	108
7	Alessandro Nesta	AC Milan	24	12	92	107
8	Marco Materazzi	Inter Milan	14	7	135	107
9	Cicinho	Roma	18	7	94	98
10	Luca Rossettini	Siena	19	7	76	98
11	Kakha Kaladze	AC Milan	28	10	92	97
12	Marco Cassetti	Roma	20	9	94	97
13	Pietro Accardi	Sampdoria	17	9	74	96
14	Alessandro Gamberini	Fiorentina	27	9	87	95
15	Christian Molinaro	Juventus	27	13	94	95

CHART-TOPPING GOALKEEPERS

1 Julio Cesar - Inter Milan

Counting Games Games in which he played at least 70 minutes	31
Goals Conceded in the League The number of League goals conceded while he was on the pitch	24
Clean Sheets In games when he played at least 70 mins	13
Defensive Rating Average number of minutes between League goals conceded while on pitch	120

	PLAYER	CLUB	CG	CONC	CS	DEF RATE
1	Julio Cesar	Inter Milan	31	24	13	120
2	Nelson Silva Dida	AC Milan	13	10	5	117
3	Gianluigi Buffon	Juventus	34	30	16	101
4	Doni	Roma	36	33	15	99
5	Sebastian Frey	Fiorentina	34	35	12	88
6	Marco Storari	Cagliari	20	21	5	85
7	Luca Castellazzi	Sampdoria	23	26	10	84
8	Alex Manninger	Siena	26	28	10	83
9	Zeljko Kalac	AC Milan	26	28	7	83
10	Ciro Polito	Catania	32	36	9	80
11	Matteo Sereni	Torino	30	37	10	75
12	Daniele Balli	Empoli	20	24	5	75
13	Matteo Gianello	Napoli	16	20	5	72
14	Marco Ballotta	Lazio	29	36	9	72
15	Samir Handanovic	Udinese	35	45	12	70

PLAYER DISCIPLINARY RECORD

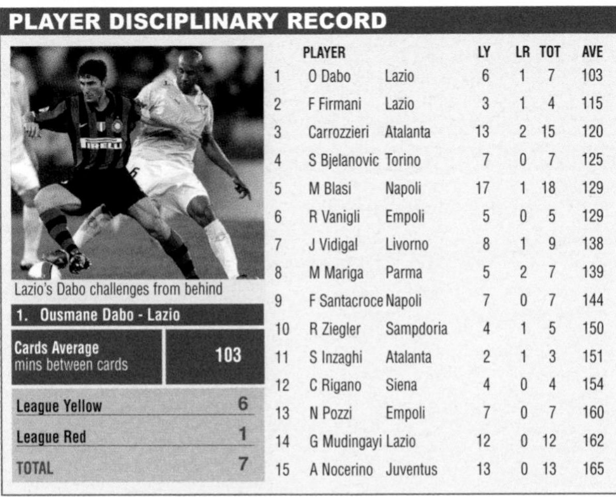

Lazio's Dabo challenges from behind

1. Ousmane Dabo - Lazio

Cards Average mins between cards	103
League Yellow	6
League Red	1
TOTAL	7

	PLAYER		LY	LR	TOT	AVE
1	O Dabo	Lazio	6	1	7	103
2	F Firmani	Lazio	3	1	4	115
3	Carrozzieri	Atalanta	13	2	15	120
4	S Bjelanovic	Torino	7	0	7	125
5	M Blasi	Napoli	17	1	18	129
6	R Vanigli	Empoli	5	0	5	129
7	J Vidigal	Livorno	8	1	9	138
8	M Mariga	Parma	5	2	7	139
9	F Santacroce	Napoli	7	0	7	144
10	R Ziegler	Sampdoria	4	1	5	150
11	S Inzaghi	Atalanta	2	1	3	151
12	C Rigano	Siena	4	0	4	154
13	N Pozzi	Empoli	7	0	7	160
14	G Mudingayi	Lazio	12	0	12	162
15	A Nocerino	Juventus	13	0	13	165

TEAM OF THE SEASON

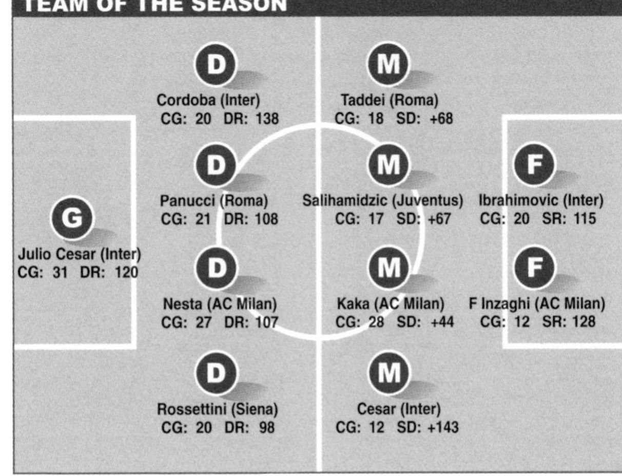
G
Julio Cesar (Inter)
CG: 31 DR: 120
D
Cordoba (Inter)
CG: 20 DR: 138
D
Panucci (Roma)
CG: 21 DR: 108
D
Nesta (AC Milan)
CG: 27 DR: 107
D
Rossettini (Siena)
CG: 20 DR: 98
M
Taddei (Roma)
CG: 18 SD: +68
M
Salihamidzic (Juventus)
CG: 17 SD: +67
M
Kaka (AC Milan)
CG: 28 SD: +44
M
Cesar (Inter)
CG: 12 SD: +143
F
Ibrahimovic (Inter)
CG: 20 SR: 115
F
F Inzaghi (AC Milan)
CG: 12 SR: 128

INTER MILAN

Final Position: **1st**

NICKNAME: NERAZZURRI. IL BISCIONE.

KEY: ☐ Won ☐ Drawn ☐ Lost

No	Comp	Opponent	H/A	Res	Score	Scorers	Attendance
1	itpr1	Udinese	H	D	1-1	D.Stankovic 9	42,797
2	itpr1	Empoli	A	W	2-0	Ibrahimovic 13, 83	16,326
3	itpr1	Catania	H	W	2-0	Crespo 14, AR.Cesar 79	40,000
4	ecgpg	Fenerbahce	A	L	0-1		45,000
5	itpr1	Livorno	A	D	2-2	Ibrahimovic 35, 74 pen	14,000
6	itpr1	Sampdoria	H	W	3-0	Ibrahimovic 23, 49, Figo 58	42,013
7	itpr1	Roma	A	W	4-1	Ibrahimovic 29 pen, Crespo 57 Cruz 60, Cordoba 68	60,000
8	ecgpg	PSV Eindhoven	H	W	2-0	Ibrahimovic 15 pen, 31	40,000
9	itpr1	Napoli	H	W	2-1	Cruz 20, 36	45,000
10	itpr1	Reggina	A	W	1-0	Adriano 18	16,965
11	ecgpg	CSKA Moscow	A	W	2-1	Crespo 52, Samuel 80	24,000
12	itpr1	Palermo	A	D	0-0		33,972
13	itpr1	Genoa	H	W	4-1	Cordoba 8, Cambiasso 50, Suazo 74 Cruz 86 pen	47,230
14	itpr1	Juventus	A	D	1-1	Cruz 41	25,000
15	ecgpg	CSKA Moscow	H	W	4-2	Ibrahimovic 33, 75, Cambiasso 34, 68	40,000
16	itpr1	Atalanta	H	W	2-1	Suazo 10, Cruz 30	45,000
17	ecgpg	Fenerbahce	H	W	3-0	Cruz 55, Ibrahimovic 66, Jimenez 90	25,000
18	itpr1	Fiorentina	A	W	2-0	Jimenez 10, Cruz 44	35,000
19	itpr1	Lazio	H	W	3-0	Ibrahimovic 22 pen, Maicon 33 Suazo 54	45,000
20	itpr1	Torino	H	W	4-0	Ibrahimovic 38 pen, Cruz 50 Jimenez 52, Cordoba 76	45,000
21	ecgpg	PSV Eindhoven	A	W	1-0	Cruz 64	34,500
22	itpr1	Cagliari	A	W	2-0	Cruz 57, Suazo 78	23,000
23	itpr1	AC Milan	H	W	2-1	Cruz 36, Cambiasso 63	70,000
24	itpr1	Siena	A	W	3-2	Ibrahimovic 26 pen, 52, Cambiasso 45	13,000
25	itpr1	Parma	H	W	3-2	Cambiasso 30, Ibrahimovic 89 pen, 90	43,413
26	itpr1	Udinese	A	D	0-0		24,000
27	itpr1	Empoli	H	W	1-0	Ibrahimovic 34 pen	43,946
28	itpr1	Catania	A	W	2-0	Cambiasso 64, Suazo 67	21,068
29	itpr1	Livorno	H	W	2-0	Suazo 14, 18	45,276
30	eckl1	Liverpool	A	L	0-2		41,999
31	itpr1	Sampdoria	A	D	1-1	Crespo 76	26,306
32	itpr1	Roma	H	D	1-1	J.Zanetti 88	48,717
33	itpr1	Napoli	A	L	0-1		53,818
34	itpr1	Reggina	H	W	2-0	Ibrahimovic 14 pen, Burdisso 34	64,575
35	eckl2	Liverpool	H	L	0-1		80,000
36	itpr1	Palermo	H	W	2-1	Vieira 5, Jimenez 36	49,360
37	itpr1	Genoa	A	D	1-1	Suazo 11	27,624
38	itpr1	Juventus	H	L	1-2	Oliveira Ribeiro 83	58,049
39	itpr1	Lazio	A	D	1-1	Crespo 11	32,802
40	itpr1	Atalanta	A	W	2-0	Vieira 21, Balotelli Barwuah 74	19,081
41	itpr1	Fiorentina	H	W	2-0	Cambiasso 55, Balotelli Barwuah 62	53,483
42	itpr1	Torino	A	W	1-0	Cruz 30	21,865
43	itpr1	Cagliari	H	W	2-1	Cruz 22, Materazzi 82	56,676
44	itpr1	AC Milan	A	L	1-2	Cruz 76	81,766
45	itpr1	Siena	H	D	2-2	Vieira 11, Balotelli Barwuah 45	76,633
46	itpr1	Parma	A	W	2-0	Ibrahimovic 62, 79	25,149

LEAGUE APPEARANCES, BOOKINGS AND CAPS

	AGE (on 01/07/08)	IN NAMED 18	APPEARANCES	COUNTING GAMES	MINUTES ON PITCH	YELLOW CARDS	RED CARDS	CAPS THIS SEASON	NATIONAL SIDE
Goalkeepers									
Soares Julio Cesar	28	35	33	31	2891	3	1	5	Brazil
Paolo Orlandoni	35	12	2	1	135	0	0	-	Italy
Francesco Toldo	36	27	3	2	213	0	0	-	Italy
Defenders									
Nicolas A Burdisso	27	32	24	20	1878	7	0	3	Argentina
Cristian Chivu	27	29	27	21	2067	7	0	8	Romania
Ivan R Cordoba	31	21	20	20	1800	3	0	-	Colombia
Ivan Fatic	19	1	0	0	0	0	0	-	Serbia
Douglas S Maicon	26	31	31	30	2711	3	1	4	Brazil
Marco Materazzi	34	26	23	15	1506	5	0	2	Italy
Nelson E L Rivas	25	22	11	5	618	3	0	-	Colombia
Walter Samuel	30	15	12	11	1026	4	0	-	Argentina
Javier Zanetti	34	38	38	35	3243	0	0	6	Argentina
Midfielders									
Esteban Cambiasso	27	33	32	30	2800	3	0	4	Argentina
Aparecido R Cesar	33	22	19	12	1316	3	1	-	Brazil
Olivier Dacourt	33	12	9	4	451	0	0	-	France
Luis Filipe Figo	35	19	17	6	871	3	0	-	Portugal
Vitor Pele	20	28	15	3	524	2	1	-	Portugal
Antonio Luis Jimenez	24	23	15	6	836	3	0	-	Chile
Maxwell	26	34	31	25	2428	2	0	-	Brazil
Maniche	30	16	8	0	310	0	0	7	Portugal
Santiago H Solari	31	19	5	0	146	0	0	-	Argentina
Dejan Stankovic	29	23	21	14	1573	2	0	3	Serbia
Patrick Vieira	32	17	17	13	1193	5	1	3	France
Forwards									
Leite Adriano	26	6	4	1	239	0	0	-	Brazil
Mario B Barwuah	17	14	11	5	567	3	0	-	Italy
Hernan Jorge Crespo	32	37	19	7	986	1	0	2	Argentina
Julio Ricardo Cruz	33	34	28	18	1953	4	0	2	Argentina
Zlatan Ibrahimovic	26	28	26	20	1967	4	0	6	Sweden
David Suazo	28	32	27	8	1156	0	0	-	Honduras

TEAM OF THE SEASON

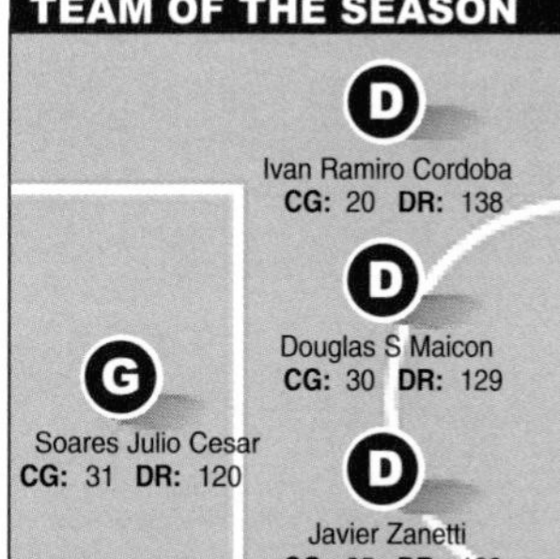

D
Ivan Ramiro Cordoba
CG: 20 DR: 138
M
Aparecido R Cesar
CG: 12 SD: 143
D
Douglas S Maicon
CG: 30 DR: 129
M
Dejan Stankovic
CG: 14 SD: 105
F
Zlatan Ibrahimovic
CG: 20 SR: 115
G
Soares Julio Cesar
CG: 31 DR: 120
D
Javier Zanetti
CG: 35 DR: 129
M
Maxwell
CG: 25 SD: 102
F
Julio R Cruz
CG: 18 SR: 150
D
Cristian Chivu
CG: 21 DR: 121
M
Esteban Cambiasso
CG: 30 SD: 87

MONTHLY POINTS TALLY

Month	Points	%
AUGUST	1	33%
SEPTEMBER	13	87%
OCTOBER	10	83%
NOVEMBER	4	67%
DECEMBER	15	100%
JANUARY	7	78%
FEBRUARY	11	73%
MARCH	8	44%
APRIL	12	100%
MAY	4	44%

LEAGUE GOALS

	PLAYER	MINS	GOALS	S RATE
1	Ibrahimovic	1967	**17**	115
2	Cruz	1953	**13**	150
3	Suazo	1156	**8**	144
4	Cambiasso	2800	**6**	466
5	Crespo	986	**4**	246
6	B Barwuah	567	**3**	189
7	Jimenez	836	**3**	278
8	Vieira	1193	**3**	397
9	Cordoba	1800	**3**	600
10	Adriano	239	**1**	239
11	Maniche	310	**1**	310
12	Figo	871	**1**	871
13	Cesar, AR	1316	**1**	1316
	Other		5	
	TOTAL		**69**	

TOP POINT EARNERS

	PLAYER	GAMES	AV PTS
1	Julio Ricardo Cruz	18	**2.61**
2	Maxwell	25	**2.52**
3	Ivan Ramiro Cordoba	20	**2.50**
4	Aparecido R Cesar	12	**2.50**
5	Esteban M Cambiasso	30	**2.43**
6	Javier Zanetti	35	**2.26**
7	Nicolas A Burdisso	20	**2.25**
8	Cristian Chivu	21	**2.24**
9	Soares Julio Cesar	31	**2.19**
10	Zlatan Ibrahimovic	20	**2.15**
	CLUB AVERAGE:		**2.24**

DISCIPLINARY RECORDS

	PLAYER	YELLOW	RED	AVE
1	Vitor Pele	2	1	**174**
2	Mario B Barwuah	3	0	**189**
3	Patrick Vieira	5	1	**198**
4	Nelson E L Rivas	3	0	**206**
5	Walter Samuel	4	0	**256**
6	Nicolas A Burdisso	7	0	**268**
7	Antonio L Jimenez	3	0	**278**
8	Luis Filipe Figo	3	0	**290**
9	Cristian Chivu	7	0	**295**
10	Marco Materazzi	5	0	**301**
11	Aparecido R Cesar	3	1	**329**
12	Julio Ricardo Cruz	4	0	**488**
13	Zlatan Ibrahimovic	4	0	**491**
	Other	17	2	
	TOTAL	**70**	**5**	

KEY GOALKEEPER

Soares Julio Cesar

Goals Conceded in the League	24	Counting Games League games when player was on pitch for at least 70 minutes	31
Defensive Rating Ave number of mins between League goals conceded while on the pitch	120	Clean Sheets In League games when player was on pitch for at least 70 minutes	13

KEY PLAYERS - DEFENDERS

Ivan Ramiro Cordoba

Goals Conceded Number of League goals conceded while the player was on the pitch	13	Clean Sheets In League games when player was on pitch for at least 70 minutes	10
Defensive Rating Ave number of mins between League goals conceded while on the pitch	138	Club Defensive Rating Average number of mins between League goals conceded by the club this season	135

	PLAYER	CON LGE	CLEAN SHEETS	DEF RATE
1	Ivan Ramiro Cordoba	13	10	138 mins
2	Douglas Sisenando Maicon	21	14	129 mins
3	Javier Zanetti	25	16	129 mins
4	Cristian Chivu	17	9	121 mins

KEY PLAYERS - MIDFIELDERS

Aparecido Rodrigues Cesar

Goals in the League	1	Contribution to Attacking Power Average number of minutes between League team goals while on pitch	45
Defensive Rating Average number of mins between League goals conceded while on the pitch	188	Scoring Difference Defensive Rating minus Contribution to Attacking Power	143

	PLAYER	LGE GOALS	DEF RATE	POWER	SCORE DIFF
1	Aparecido Rodrigues Cesar	1	188	45	143 mins
2	Dejan Stankovic	1	157	52	105 mins
3	Maxwell	0	151	49	102 mins
4	Esteban M Cambiasso	6	133	46	87 mins

KEY PLAYERS - GOALSCORERS

Zlatan Ibrahimovic

Goals in the League	17	Player Strike Rate Average number of minutes between League goals scored by player	115
Contribution to Attacking Power Average number of minutes between League team goals while on pitch	46	Club Strike Rate Average number of minutes between League goals scored by club	50

	PLAYER	LGE GOALS	POWER	STRIKE RATE
1	Zlatan Ibrahimovic	17	46	115 mins
2	Julio Ricardo Cruz	13	42	150 mins
3	Patrick Vieira	3	54	397 mins
4	Esteban Matias Cambiasso	6	46	466 mins

Zlatan Ibrahimovic

SQUAD APPEARANCES

Match	1	2	3	4	5	6	7	8	9	10	11	12	13	14	15	16	17	18	19	20	21	22	23	24	25	26	27	28	29	30	31	32	33	34	35	36	37	38	39	40	41	42	43	44	45	46
Venue	H	A	H	A	A	H	A	H	H	A	A	A	H	A	H	H	H	A	H	H	A	A	H	A	H	A	H	A	H	A	A	H	A	H	H	H	A	H	A	A	H	A	H	A	H	A
Competition	L	L	L	C	L	L	L	C	L	L	C	L	L	L	C	L	C	L	L	L	C	L	L	L	L	L	L	L	L	C	L	L	L	L	C	L	L	L	L	L	L	L	L	L	L	L
Result	D	W	W	L	D	W	W	W	W	W	W	D	W	D	W	W	W	W	W	W	W	W	W	W	W	D	W	W	W	L	D	D	L	W	L	W	D	L	D	W	W	W	W	L	D	W

Goalkeepers
Soares Julio Cesar
Paolo Orlandoni
Francesco Toldo

Defenders
Nicolas A Burdisso
Cristian Chivu
Ivan Ramiro Cordoba
Ivan Fatic
Douglas S Maicon
Marco Materazzi
Nelson E L Rivas
Walter Adrian Samuel
Javier Zanetti

Midfielders
Esteban M Cambiasso
Aparecido R Cesar
Olivier Dacourt
Luis Filipe Figo
Vitor Pele
Antonio Luis Jimenez
Maxwell
R Oliveira (Maniche)
Santiago Hernan Solari
Dejan Stankovic
Patrick Vieira

Forwards
Leite Adriano
Mario Balotelli Barwuah
Hernan Jorge Crespo
Julio Ricardo Cruz
Zlatan Ibrahimovic
David Suazo

KEY: On all match · On bench · Subbed or sent off (Counting game) · Subbed or sent off (playing less than 70 minutes) · Subbed on from bench (Counting Game) · Subbed on (playing less than 70 minutes) · Subbed on and then subbed or sent off (Counting Game) · Subbed on and then subbed or sent off (playing less than 70 minutes) · Not in 16

AS ROMA

Final Position: **2nd**

NICKNAME: LA MAGICA. I LUPI.

KEY: ☐ Won ☐ Drawn ☐ Lost

							Attendance
1	itpr1	**Palermo**	A	W	2-0	Mexes 3, Aquilani 22	32,202
2	itpr1	**Siena**	H	W	3-0	Aquilani 17, Giuly 82, Totti 89	44,037
3	itpr1	**Reggina**	A	W	2-0	Dos Santos 50, Totti 84	15,000
4	ecgpf	**Dinamo Kiev**	H	W	2-0	Perrotta 9, Totti 70	60,000
5	itpr1	**Juventus**	H	D	2-2	Totti 30, 36	55,000
6	itpr1	**Fiorentina**	A	D	2-2	Amantino 19, Giuly 37	36,056
7	itpr1	**Inter Milan**	H	L	1-4	Perrotta 53	60,000
8	ecgpf	**Man Utd**	A	L	0-1		73,652
9	itpr1	**Parma**	A	W	3-0	Totti 2, 82, Mancini 21	18,000
10	itpr1	**Napoli**	H	D	4-4	Totti 30 pen, Perrotta 42, De Rossi 52	
						Pizarro 80	27,313
11	ecgpf	**Sp Lisbon**	H	W	2-1	Dos Santos 15, Vucinic 70	60,000
12	itpr1	**AC Milan**	A	W	1-0	Vucinic 72	60,205
13	itpr1	**Lazio**	H	W	3-2	Vucinic 19, Mancini 42, Perrotta 56	54,860
14	itpr1	**Empoli**	A	D	2-2	Giuly 13, Brighi 32	15,000
15	ecgpf	**Sp Lisbon**	A	D	2-2	Cassetti 4, Anderson Polga 89 og	35,000
16	itpr1	**Genoa**	A	W	1-0	Panucci 90	24,106
17	ecgpf	**Dinamo Kiev**	A	W	4-1	Panucci 4, Giuly 32, Vucinic 36, 78	15,000
18	itpr1	**Udinese**	H	W	2-1	Dos Santos 11, Taddei 26	30,000
19	itpr1	**Cagliari**	H	W	2-0	Taddei 28, 36	30,000
20	itpr1	**Livorno**	A	D	1-1	De Rossi 5	10,000
21	ecgpf	**Man Utd**	H	D	1-1	Mancini 71	50,000
22	itpr1	**Torino**	A	D	0-0		18,501
23	itpr1	**Sampdoria**	H	W	2-0	Totti 18 pen, 90	35,000
24	itpr1	**Atalanta**	A	W	2-1	Totti 38, Mancini 44	15,000
25	itpr1	**Catania**	H	W	2-0	Giuly 8, De Rossi 57 pen	33,378
26	itpr1	**Palermo**	H	W	1-0	Amantino 59	33,000
27	itpr1	**Siena**	A	L	0-3		10,158
28	itpr1	**Reggina**	H	W	2-0	Panucci 21, Amantino 76	31,635
29	itpr1	**Juventus**	A	L	0-1		21,139
30	eckl1	**Real Madrid**	H	W	2-1	Pizarro 24, Amantino 58	52,000
31	itpr1	**Fiorentina**	H	W	1-0	De Cezare Cicinho 54	34,254
32	itpr1	**Inter Milan**	A	D	1-1	Totti 38	48,717
33	itpr1	**Parma**	H	W	4-0	Aquilani 27, Falcone 51 og, Totti 80	
						Vucinic 90	31,788
34	eckl2	**Real Madrid**	A	W	2-1	Taddei 73, Vucinic 90	75,000
35	itpr1	**Napoli**	A	W	2-0	Perrotta 2, Totti 49 pen	59,272
36	itpr1	**AC Milan**	H	W	2-1	Giuly 79, Vucinic 81	48,447
37	itpr1	**Lazio**	A	L	2-3	Taddei 31, Perrotta 62	78,000
38	itpr1	**Empoli**	H	W	2-1	Tonetto 36, Panucci 63	31,392
39	itpr1	**Cagliari**	A	D	1-1	Totti 45	22,000
40	ecqfl1	**Man Utd**	H	L	0-2		80,023
41	itpr1	**Genoa**	H	W	3-2	Taddei 14, Vucinic 17, De Rossi 80 pen	36,366
42	ecqfl2	**Man Utd**	A	L	0-1		74,423
43	itpr1	**Udinese**	A	W	3-1	Vucinic 64, Taddei 70, Giuly 90	20,405
44	itpr1	**Livorno**	H	D	1-1	Vucinic 54	34,061
45	itpr1	**Torino**	H	W	4-1	Pizarro 18 pen, Vucinic 20	
						Amantino 26, 32	34,001
46	itpr1	**Sampdoria**	A	W	3-0	Panucci 75, Pizarro 79	
						De Cezare Cicinho 85	24,311
47	itpr1	**Atalanta**	H	W	2-1	Panucci 23, De Rossi 68	36,416
48	itpr1	**Catania**	A	D	1-1	Vucinic 8	21,148

LEAGUE APPEARANCES, BOOKINGS AND CAPS

	AGE (on 01/07/08)	IN NAMED 18	APPEARANCES	COUNTING GAMES	MINUTES ON PITCH	YELLOW CARDS	RED CARDS	CAPS THIS SEASON	NATIONAL SIDE
Goalkeepers									
Julio S Bertagnoli	29	5	0	0	0	0	0	-	Brazil
Gianluca Curci	22	30	2	1	135	0	0	-	Italy
Doni	28	38	37	36	3285	1	0	-	Brazil
Carlo Zotti	25	3	0	0	0	0	0	-	Italy
Defenders									
Vitorino G P Antunes	21	18	5	0	69	0	0	-	Portugal
Marco Cassetti	31	27	27	18	1942	5	0	-	Italy
Cicinho	28	37	30	17	1765	3	1	-	Brazil
Juan	29	27	22	19	1691	2	1	4	Brazil
Matteo Ferrari	28	26	15	15	1350	4	0	-	Italy
Philippe Mexes	26	33	32	30	2744	9	1	-	France
Christian Panucci	35	32	27	21	1958	5	0	7	Italy
Max Tonetto	33	37	35	31	2950	4	0	1	Italy
Midfielders									
Edgar A R Alvarez	28	1	1	0	6	0	0	-	Honduras
Alberto Aquilani	23	22	21	11	1152	4	0	4	Italy
Ahmed A Barusso	23	15	3	0	27	1	0	-	Ghana
Matteo Brighi	27	37	24	4	739	2	0	-	Italy
Daniele De Rossi	24	35	34	34	3045	12	0	6	Italy
Ludovic Giuly	31	35	32	11	1609	1	1	-	France
Simone Perrotta	30	30	29	18	2065	2	1	5	Italy
Adrian Florin Pit	24	5	0	0	0	0	0	-	Romania
David M C Pizarro	28	34	31	25	2435	4	0	-	Chile
Aleandro Rosi	21	1	0	0	0	0	0	-	Italy
Rodrigo F Taddei	28	26	26	18	1929	6	0	-	Brazil
Daniel Unal	18	3	0	0	0	0	0	-	Switzerland
Forwards									
Mancini	27	35	31	19	2185	5	0	-	Brazil
Claudio Della Penna	19	1	0	0	0	0	0	-	Italy
Mauro Esposito	29	30	8	0	99	0	0	-	Italy
Francesco Totti	31	26	25	23	2084	2	0	-	Italy
Mirko Vucinic	24	34	33	20	2236	5	0	4	Montenegro

TEAM OF THE SEASON

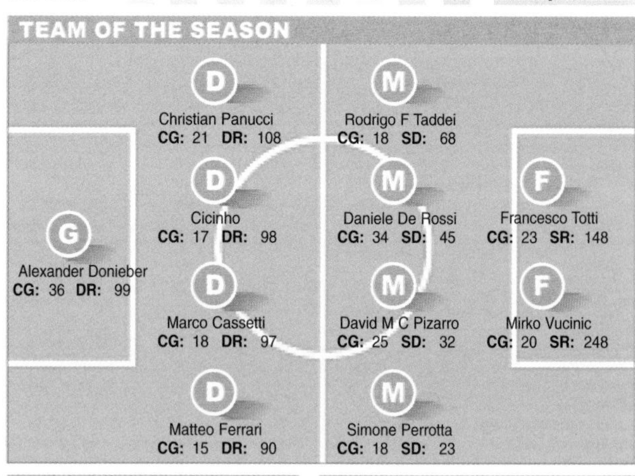

G
Alexander Donieber
CG: 36 DR: 99
D
Christian Panucci
CG: 21 DR: 108
D
Cicinho
CG: 17 DR: 98
D
Marco Cassetti
CG: 18 DR: 97
D
Matteo Ferrari
CG: 15 DR: 90
M
Rodrigo F Taddei
CG: 18 SD: 68
M
Daniele De Rossi
CG: 34 SD: 45
M
David M C Pizarro
CG: 25 SD: 32
M
Simone Perrotta
CG: 18 SD: 23
F
Francesco Totti
CG: 23 SR: 148
F
Mirko Vucinic
CG: 20 SR: 248

MONTHLY POINTS TALLY

AUGUST	3	100%
SEPTEMBER	8	53%
OCTOBER	10	83%
NOVEMBER	4	67%
DECEMBER	11	73%
JANUARY	9	100%
FEBRUARY	7	47%
MARCH	13	72%
APRIL	10	83%
MAY	7	78%

LEAGUE GOALS

	PLAYER	MINS	GOALS	S RATE
1	Totti	2084	14	148
2	Vucinic	2236	9	248
3	Amantino	2185	8	273
4	Giuly	1609	6	268
5	Taddei	1929	6	321
6	Panucci	1958	5	391
7	Perrotta	2065	5	413
8	De Rossi	3045	5	609
9	Aquilani	1152	3	384
10	Pizarro	2435	3	811
11	Dos Santos	1691	2	845
12	Cicinho	1765	2	882
13	Brighi	739	1	739
	Other		2	
	TOTAL		71	

TOP POINT EARNERS

	PLAYER	GAMES	AV PTS
1	Christian Panucci	21	2.57
2	Rodrigo F Taddei	18	2.44
3	Cicinho	17	2.35
4	Mirko Vucinic	20	2.25
5	Mancini	19	2.21
6	Max Tonetto	31	2.19
7	Daniele De Rossi	34	2.18
8	Alexander M Donieber	36	2.17
9	Marco Cassetti	18	2.17
10	Juan	19	2.16
	CLUB AVERAGE:		2.16

DISCIPLINARY RECORDS

	PLAYER	YELLOW	RED	AVE
1	Daniele De Rossi	12	0	253
2	Philippe Mexes	9	1	274
3	Alberto Aquilani	4	0	288
4	Rodrigo F Taddei	6	0	321
5	Matteo Ferrari	4	0	337
6	Matteo Brighi	2	0	369
7	Marco Cassetti	5	0	388
8	Christian Panucci	5	0	391
9	Mancini	5	0	437
10	Cicinho	3	1	441
11	Mirko Vucinic	5	0	447
12	Juan	2	1	563
13	David M C Pizarro	4	0	608
	Other	10	2	
	TOTAL	76	5	

KEY GOALKEEPER

Alexander Marangon Doniebér

Goals Conceded in the League	33	**Counting Games** League games when player was on pitch for at least 70 minutes	36
Defensive Rating Ave number of mins between League goals conceded while on the pitch	99	**Clean Sheets** In League games when player was on pitch for at least 70 minutes	15

KEY PLAYERS - GOALSCORERS

Francesco Totti

Goals in the League	14	**Player Strike Rate** Average number of minutes between League goals scored by player	148
Contribution to Attacking Power Average number of minutes between League team goals while on pitch	48	**Club Strike Rate** Average number of minutes between League goals scored by club	48

	PLAYER	LGE GOALS	POWER	STRIKE RATE
1	Francesco Totti	14	48	148 mins
2	Mirko Vucinic	9	44	248 mins
3	Mancini	8	49	273 mins
4	Rodrigo Ferrante Taddei	6	45	321 mins

KEY PLAYERS - DEFENDERS

Christian Panucci

Goals Conceded Number of League goals conceded while the player was on the pitch	18	**Clean Sheets** In League games when player was on pitch for at least 70 minutes	11
Defensive Rating Ave number of mins between League goals conceded while on the pitch	108	**Club Defensive Rating** Average number of mins between League goals conceded by the club this season	94

	PLAYER	CON LGE	CLEAN SHEETS	DEF RATE
1	Christian Panucci	18	11	108 mins
2	Cicinho	18	7	98 mins
3	Marco Cassetti	20	9	97 mins
4	Matteo Ferrari	15	7	90 mins

Mauro Esposito and Francesco Totti

KEY PLAYERS - MIDFIELDERS

Rodrigo Ferrante Taddei

Goals in the League	6	**Contribution to Attacking Power** Average number of minutes between League team goals while on pitch	45
Defensive Rating Average number of mins between League goals conceded while on the pitch	113	**Scoring Difference** Defensive Rating minus Contribution to Attacking Power	68

	PLAYER	LGE GOALS	DEF RATE	POWER	SCORE DIFF
1	Rodrigo Ferrante Taddei	6	113	45	68 mins
2	Daniele De Rossi	5	92	47	45 mins
3	David Marcelo Cortes Pizarro	3	83	51	32 mins
4	Simone Perrotta	5	71	48	23 mins

SQUAD APPEARANCES

Match	1	2	3	4	5	6	7	8	9	10	11	12	13	14	15	16	17	18	19	20	21	22	23	24	25	26	27	28	29	30	31	32	33	34	35	36	37	38	39	40	41	42	43	44	45	46	47	48
Venue	A	H	A	H	H	A	H	A	A	H	H	A	H	A	A	A	A	H	H	A	H	A	H	A	H	H	A	H	A	H	H	A	H	A	A	H	A	H	A	H	H	A	A	H	H	A	H	A
Competition	L	L	L	C	L	L	L	C	L	L	C	L	L	L	C	L	C	L	L	L	C	L	L	L	L	L	L	L	L	C	L	L	L	C	L	L	L	L	L	C	L	C	L	L	L	L	L	L
Result	W	W	W	W	D	D	L	L	W	D	W	W	W	D	D	W	W	W	W	D	D	D	W	W	W	W	L	W	L	W	W	D	W	W	W	W	L	W	D	L	W	L	W	D	W	W	W	D

Goalkeepers
Julio Sergio Bertagnoli
Gianluca Curci
Doni
Carlo Zotti

Defenders
Vitorino G P Antunes
Marco Cassetti
Cicinho
Juan
Matteo Ferrari
Philippe Mexes
Christian Panucci
Max Tonetto

Midfielders
Edgar A R Alvarez
Alberto Aquilani
Ahmed Apimah Barusso
Matteo Brighi
Daniele De Rossi
Ludovic Giuly
Simone Perrotta
Adrian Florin Pit
David M C Pizarro
Aleandro Rosi
Rodrigo F Taddei
Daniel Unal

Forwards
Mancini
Claudio Della Penna
Mauro Esposito
Francesco Totti
Mirko Vucinic

KEY: On all match — On bench — Subbed or sent off (Counting game) — Subbed or sent off (playing less than 70 minutes) — Subbed on from bench (Counting Game) — Subbed on (playing less than 70 minutes) — Subbed on and then subbed or sent off (Counting Game) — Subbed on and then subbed or sent off (playing less than 70 minutes) — Not in 16

JUVENTUS

Final Position: **3rd**

LA VECCHIA SIGNORA (THE OLD LADY) KEY: ☐Won ☐Drawn ☐Lost

	Comp	Opponent	H/A	Res	Score	Scorers	Attendance
1	itpr1	**Livorno**	H	W	5-1	Trezeguet 25, 86, 90	
						Iaquinta 70 pen, 85	21,414
2	itpr1	**Cagliari**	A	W	3-2	Trezeguet 54, Del Piero 77, Chiellini 90	23,000
3	itpr1	**Udinese**	H	L	0-1		20,000
4	itpr1	**Roma**	A	D	2-2	Trezeguet 17, Iaquinta 87	55,000
5	itpr1	**Reggina**	H	W	4-0	Legrottaglie 48, Salihamidzic 50	
						Trezeguet 70, Palladino 90	19,050
6	itpr1	**Torino**	A	W	1-0	Trezeguet 90	27,000
7	itpr1	**Fiorentina**	A	D	1-1	Iaquinta 23	40,000
8	itpr1	**Genoa**	H	W	1-0	Del Piero 36	20,000
9	itpr1	**Napoli**	A	L	1-3	Del Piero 46	63,000
10	itpr1	**Empoli**	H	W	3-0	Trezeguet 51 pen, 63, 70	15,000
11	itpr1	**Inter Milan**	H	D	1-1	Camoranesi 77	25,000
12	itpr1	**Parma**	A	D	2-2	Legrottaglie 75, Iaquinta 81	16,000
13	itpr1	**Palermo**	H	W	5-0	Trezeguet 29, Iaquinta 41,	
						Del Piero 71, 90 pen, Marchionni 74	25,000
14	itpr1	**AC Milan**	A	D	0-0		60,000
15	itpr1	**Atalanta**	H	W	1-0	Nedved 86	20,000
16	itpr1	**Lazio**	A	W	3-2	Trezeguet 28, Del Piero 47, 69	30,000
17	itpr1	**Siena**	H	W	2-0	Salihamidzic 32, Trezeguet 59	20,000
18	itpr1	**Catania**	A	D	1-1	Del Piero 90 pen	16,000
19	itpr1	**Sampdoria**	H	D	0-0		22,379
20	itpr1	**Livorno**	A	W	3-1	Trezeguet 30, 63, Del Piero 49	14,630
21	itpr1	**Cagliari**	H	D	1-1	Nedved 56	19,412
22	itpr1	**Udinese**	A	W	2-1	Camoranesi 60, Iaquinta 76	25,152
23	itpr1	**Roma**	H	W	1-0	Del Piero 45	21,139
24	itpr1	**Reggina**	A	L	1-2	Del Piero 71	21,884
25	itpr1	**Torino**	H	D	0-0		23,000
26	itpr1	**Fiorentina**	H	L	2-3	Sissoko 29, Camoranesi 57	20,993
27	itpr1	**Genoa**	A	W	2-0	Grygera 25, Trezeguet 33	28,151
28	itpr1	**Napoli**	H	W	1-0	Iaquinta 88	21,095
29	itpr1	**Empoli**	A	D	0-0		11,000
30	itpr1	**Inter Milan**	A	W	2-1	Camoranesi 49, Trezeguet 63	58,049
31	itpr1	**Palermo**	A	L	2-3	Del Piero 52, 71	34,271
32	itpr1	**AC Milan**	H	W	3-2	Del Piero 12, Salihamidzic 45, 80	21,605
33	itpr1	**Parma**	H	W	3-0	Trezeguet 16, Palladino 30	
						Morrone 77 og	21,406
34	itpr1	**Atalanta**	A	W	4-0	Legrottaglie 1, Del Piero 6, 34, 65	21,323
35	itpr1	**Lazio**	H	W	5-2	Chiellini 15, 88, Camoranesi 21	
						Del Piero 32, Trezeguet 34	20,588
36	itpr1	**Siena**	A	L	0-1		15,419
37	itpr1	**Catania**	H	D	1-1	Del Piero 89	20,638
38	itpr1	**Sampdoria**	A	D	3-3	Del Piero 7, 65 pen, Trezeguet 16 pen	26,954

LEAGUE APPEARANCES, BOOKINGS AND CAPS

	AGE (on 01/07/08)	IN NAMED 18	APPEARANCES	COUNTING GAMES	MINUTES ON PITCH	YELLOW CARDS	RED CARDS	CAPS THIS SEASON	NATIONAL SIDE
Goalkeepers									
Emanuele Belardi	30	35	5	4	370	0	0	-	Italy
Gianluigi Buffon	30	34	34	34	3050	1	0	8	Italy
Defenders									
Jorge M Andrade	30	4	4	3	323	0	0	1	Portugal
Lorenzo Ariaudo	19	3	0	0	0	0	0	-	Italy
Alessandro Birindelli	33	28	7	4	421	0	0	-	Italy
Jean-Alain Boumsong	28	2	0	0	0	0	0	1	France
Giorgio Chiellini	23	31	30	30	2687	9	1	5	Italy
Domenico Criscito	21	14	8	6	630	3	0	-	Italy
Zdenek Grygera	28	31	24	19	1935	4	0	4	Czech Republic
Nicola Legrottaglie	31	35	33	29	2804	9	0	-	Italy
Christian Molinaro	24	34	30	28	2580	3	0	-	Italy
Guglielmo Stendardo	27	14	5	3	346	1	0	-	Italy
Jonathan Zebina	29	21	17	14	1325	5	1	-	France
Midfielders									
Sergio B Almiron	27	14	9	5	489	0	0	-	Argentina
Mauro Camoranesi	31	24	22	14	1537	8	0	7	Italy
Luca Castiglia	19	7	2	0	3	0	0	-	Italy
Marco Marchionni	27	18	11	1	299	0	0	-	Italy
Pavel Nedved	35	32	31	25	2348	6	2	-	Czech Republic
Antonio Nocerino	23	34	32	20	2154	13	0	-	Italy
Ruben Ariel Olivera	25	5	1	0	12	0	0	-	Uruguay
Christian Pasquato	18	3	1	0	1	0	0	-	Italy
Hasan Salihamidzic	31	37	26	17	1854	3	0	-	Bosnia
Momo Sissoko	23	16	15	10	1051	3	1	2	Mali
Tiago C Mendes	27	38	20	6	1005	3	0	1	Portugal
Cristiano Zanetti	31	28	26	24	2225	8	1	-	Italy
Forwards									
Alessandro Del Piero	33	38	37	28	2735	1	0	4	Italy
Vincenzo Iaquinta	28	25	24	7	1068	4	0	4	Italy
Raffaele Palladino	24	37	26	11	1241	3	0	-	Italy
David Trezeguet	30	36	36	34	3071	2	0	2	France

TEAM OF THE SEASON

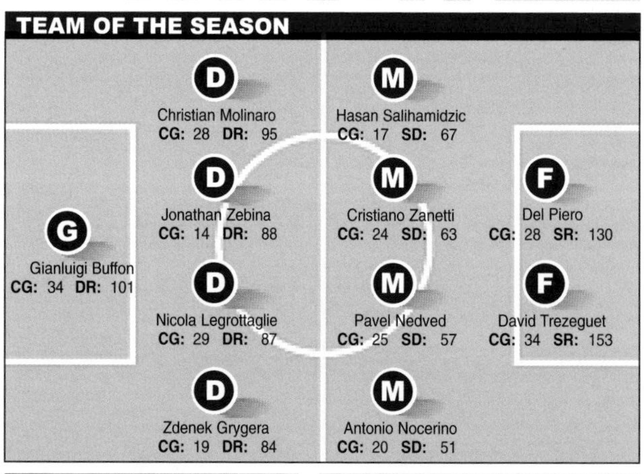

G
Gianluigi Buffon
CG: 34 DR: 101
D
Christian Molinaro
CG: 28 DR: 95
D
Jonathan Zebina
CG: 14 DR: 88
D
Nicola Legrottaglie
CG: 29 DR: 87
D
Zdenek Grygera
CG: 19 DR: 84
M
Hasan Salihamidzic
CG: 17 SD: 67
M
Cristiano Zanetti
CG: 24 SD: 63
M
Pavel Nedved
CG: 25 SD: 57
M
Antonio Nocerino
CG: 20 SD: 51
F
Del Piero
CG: 28 SR: 130
F
David Trezeguet
CG: 34 SR: 153

MONTHLY POINTS TALLY

Month	Points	%
AUGUST	3	100%
SEPTEMBER	10	67%
OCTOBER	7	58%
NOVEMBER	5	56%
DECEMBER	10	83%
JANUARY	5	56%
FEBRUARY	8	53%
MARCH	10	67%
APRIL	12	80%
MAY	2	22%

LEAGUE GOALS

	PLAYER	MINS	GOALS	S RATE
1	Del Piero	2735	**21**	130
2	Trezeguet	3071	**20**	153
3	Iaquinta	1068	**8**	133
4	Camoranesi	1537	**5**	307
5	Salihamidzic	1854	**4**	463
6	Chiellini	2687	**3**	895
7	Legrottaglie	2804	**3**	934
8	Palladino	1241	**2**	620
9	Nedved	2348	**2**	1174
10	Marchionni	299	**1**	299
11	Sissoko	1051	**1**	1051
12	Grygera	1935	**1**	1935
13	Vanstrattan	0	**0**	
	Other		0	
	TOTAL		**71**	

TOP POINT EARNERS

	PLAYER	GAMES	AV PTS
1	Antonio Nocerino	20	**2.15**
2	Cristiano Zanetti	24	**2.13**
3	Jonathan Zebina	14	**2.07**
4	David Trezeguet	34	**2.06**
5	Zdenek Grygera	19	**2.05**
6	Pavel Nedved	25	**2.00**
7	Hasan Salihamidzic	17	**2.00**
8	Gianluigi Buffon	34	**1.97**
9	Christian Molinaro	28	**1.89**
10	Giorgio Chiellini	30	**1.83**
	CLUB AVERAGE:		**1.89**

DISCIPLINARY RECORDS

	PLAYER	YELLOW	RED	AVE
1	Antonio Nocerino	13	0	**165**
2	Mauro Camoranesi	8	0	**192**
3	Domenico Criscito	3	0	**210**
4	Jonathan Zebina	5	1	**220**
5	Cristiano Zanetti	8	1	**247**
6	Momo Sissoko	3	1	**262**
7	Vincenzo Iaquinta	4	0	**267**
8	Giorgio Chiellini	9	1	**268**
9	Pavel Nedved	6	2	**293**
10	Nicola Legrottaglie	9	0	**311**
11	Tiago C Mendes	3	0	**335**
12	Raffaele Palladino	3	0	**413**
13	Zdenek Grygera	4	0	**483**
	Other	10	0	
	TOTAL	**88**	**6**	

KEY GOALKEEPER

Gianluigi Buffon

Goals Conceded in the League	30	Counting Games League games when player was on pitch for at least 70 minutes	34
Defensive Rating Ave number of mins between League goals conceded while on the pitch	101	Clean Sheets In League games when player was on pitch for at least 70 minutes	16

KEY PLAYERS - DEFENDERS

Christian Molinaro

Goals Conceded Number of League goals conceded while the player was on the pitch	27	Clean Sheets In League games when player was on pitch for at least 70 minutes	13
Defensive Rating Ave number of mins between League goals conceded while on the pitch	95	Club Defensive Rating Average number of mins between League goals conceded by the club this season	94

	PLAYER	CON LGE	CLEAN SHEETS	DEF RATE
1	Christian Molinaro	27	13	95 mins
2	Jonathan Zebina	15	7	88 mins
3	Nicola Legrottaglie	32	13	87 mins
4	Zdenek Grygera	23	8	84 mins

KEY PLAYERS - MIDFIELDERS

Hasan Salihamidzic

Goals in the League	4	Contribution to Attacking Power Average number of minutes between League team goals while on pitch	48
Defensive Rating Average number of mins between League goals conceded while on the pitch	115	Scoring Difference Defensive Rating minus Contribution to Attacking Power	67

	PLAYER	LGE GOALS	DEF RATE	POWER	SCORE DIFF
1	Hasan Salihamidzic	4	115	48	67 mins
2	Cristiano Zanetti	0	105	42	63 mins
3	Pavel Nedved	2	106	49	57 mins
4	Antonio Nocerino	0	102	51	51 mins

KEY PLAYERS - GOALSCORERS

Alessandro Del Piero

Goals in the League	21	Player Strike Rate Average number of minutes between League goals scored by player	130
Contribution to Attacking Power Average number of minutes between League team goals while on pitch	49	Club Strike Rate Average number of minutes between League goals scored by club	48

	PLAYER	LGE GOALS	POWER	STRIKE RATE
1	Alessandro Del Piero	21	49	130 mins
2	David Trezeguet	20	45	153 mins
3	Mauro German Camoranesi	5	41	307 mins
4	Hasan Salihamidzic	4	48	463 mins

Nicola Legrottaglie, David Trezeguet and Vincenzo Iaquinta

SQUAD APPEARANCES

Match	1	2	3	4	5	6	7	8	9	10	11	12	13	14	15	16	17	18	19	20	21	22	23	24	25	26	27	28	29	30	31	32	33	34	35	36	37	38
Venue	H	A	H	A	H	A	A	H	A	H	H	A	H	A	H	A	H	A	H	A	H	A	H	A	H	H	A	H	A	A	A	H	H	A	H	A	H	A
Competition	L	L	L	L	L	L	L	L	L	L	L	L	L	L	L	L	L	L	L	L	L	L	L	L	L	L	L	L	L	L	L	L	L	L	L	L	L	L
Result	W	W	L	D	W	W	D	W	L	W	D	D	W	D	W	W	W	D	D	W	D	W	W	L	D	L	W	W	D	W	L	W	W	W	W	L	D	D

Goalkeepers
- Emanuele Belardi
- Gianluigi Buffon

Defenders
- Jorge Manuel Andrade
- Lorenzo Ariaudo
- Alessandro Birindelli
- Jean-Alain Boumsong
- Giorgio Chiellini
- Domenico Criscito
- Zdenek Grygera
- Nicola Legrottaglie
- Christian Molinaro
- Guglielmo Stendardo
- Jonathan Zebina

Midfielders
- Sergio Bernardo Almiron
- Mauro G Camoranesi
- Luca Castiglia
- Marco Marchionni
- Pavel Nedved
- Antonio Nocerino
- Ruben Ariel Olivera
- Christian Pasquato
- Hasan Salihamidzic
- Momo Sissoko
- Tiago Cardoso Mendes
- Cristiano Zanetti

Forwards
- Alessandro Del Piero
- Vincenzo Iaquinta
- Raffaele Palladino
- David Trezeguet

KEY: On all match; On bench; Subbed or sent off (Counting game); Subbed or sent off (playing less than 70 minutes); Subbed on from bench (Counting Game); Subbed on (playing less than 70 minutes); Subbed on and then subbed or sent off (Counting Game); Subbed on and then subbed or sent off (playing less than 70 minutes); Not in 16

FIORENTINA

Final Position: **4th**

NICKNAME: LA VIOLA. GIGLIATI (LILIES)

KEY: Won / Drawn / Lost

							Attendance
1	itpr1	Empoli	H	W	3-1	Pazzini 56, Mutu 62, Montolivo 70	31,280
2	itpr1	AC Milan	A	D	1-1	Mutu 56	53,559
3	itpr1	Atalanta	H	D	2-2	Rivalta 25 og, Vieri 74	30,000
4	uc1rl1	Groningen	A	D	1-1	Semioli 66	19,703
5	itpr1	Catania	A	W	1-0	Mutu 4	18,000
6	itpr1	Roma	H	D	2-2	Gamberini 24, Mutu 81 pen	36,056
7	itpr1	Livorno	A	W	3-0	Osvaldo 45, 67, Santana 69	10,000
8	uc1rl2	Groningen	H	W	4-3*	Mutu 59 (*on penalties)	26,925
9	itpr1	Juventus	H	D	1-1	Mutu 89 pen	40,000
10	itpr1	Siena	H	W	3-0	Pazzini 15, Mutu 31, Vieri 71	27,361
11	ucgpc	Villarreal	A	D	1-1	Vieri 48	15,000
12	itpr1	Genoa	A	D	0-0		23,000
13	itpr1	Napoli	H	W	1-0	Vieri 60	33,000
14	itpr1	Lazio	A	W	1-0	Pazzini 19	25,687
15	ucgpc	Elfsborg	H	W	6-1	Jorgensen 4, 77, Vieri 5, Donadel 62	
						Kroldrup 65, Di Carmine 87	25,000
16	itpr1	Udinese	H	L	1-2	Pazzini 28	30,000
17	itpr1	Reggina	A	D	0-0		10,000
18	ucgpc	AEK Athens	A	D	1-1	Osvaldo 29	26,386
19	itpr1	Inter Milan	H	L	0-2		35,000
20	itpr1	Palermo	A	L	0-2		22,823
21	itpr1	Sampdoria	A	D	2-2	Mutu 39, Donadel 57	21,000
22	ucgpc	Mlada Boleslav	H	W	2-1	Mutu 44 pen, Vieri 67	11,140
23	itpr1	Cagliari	H	W	5-1	Montolivo 3, Mutu 41, 45 pen	
						Santana 47, 79	30,000
24	itpr1	Parma	A	W	2-1	Mutu 43, 85 pen	12,000
25	itpr1	Torino	H	W	2-1	Vieri 45 pen, Mutu 75 pen	27,992
26	itpr1	Empoli	A	W	2-0	Mutu 85, Pazzini 90	6,000
27	itpr1	AC Milan	H	L	0-1		38,977
28	itpr1	Atalanta	A	D	2-2	Pazzini 29, Semioli 60	10,822
29	uc3rl1	Rosenborg BK	A	W	1-0	Mutu 16	16,000
30	itpr1	Catania	H	W	2-1	Kuzmanovic 40, Mutu 70	26,648
31	uc3rl2	Rosenborg BK	H	W	2-1	Liverani 38, D.Cacia 81	23,139
32	itpr1	Roma	A	L	0-1		34,254
33	itpr1	Livorno	H	W	1-0	Papa Waigo 62	26,291
34	itpr1	Juventus	A	W	3-2	Gobbi 19, Papa Waigo 75, Osvaldo 90	20,993
35	uc4rl1	Everton	H	W	2-0	Kuzmanovic 70, Montolivo 81	32,934
36	itpr1	Siena	A	L	0-1		12,785
37	uc4rl2	Everton	A	W	4-2*	(*on penalties)	38,026
38	itpr1	Genoa	H	W	3-1	Santana 19, Mutu 30, Pazzini 56	28,728
39	itpr1	Napoli	A	L	0-2		47,500
40	itpr1	Lazio	H	W	1-0	Pazzini 77	26,579
41	itpr1	Udinese	A	L	1-3	Vieri 63	15,374
42	ucqfl1	PSV Eindhoven	H	D	1-1	Mutu 56	34,317
43	itpr1	Reggina	H	W	2-0	Pazzini 23, Mutu 90	27,321
44	ucqfl2	PSV Eindhoven	A	W	2-0	Mutu 38, 53	36,200
45	itpr1	Inter Milan	A	L	0-2		53,483
46	itpr1	Palermo	H	W	1-0	Donadel 29	28,827
47	ucsfl1	Rangers	A	D	0-0		49,199
48	itpr1	Sampdoria	H	D	2-2	Vieri 78, Mutu 84 pen	36,627
49	ucsfl2	Rangers	H	L	2-4*	(*on penalties)	39,130
50	itpr1	Cagliari	A	L	1-2	Santana 53	18,000
51	itpr1	Parma	H	W	3-1	Santana 39, Semioli 77, Osvaldo 86	36,289
52	itpr1	Torino	A	W	1-0	Osvaldo 76	23,771

LEAGUE APPEARANCES, BOOKINGS AND CAPS

	AGE (on 01/07/08)	IN NAMED 18	APPEARANCES	COUNTING GAMES	MINUTES ON PITCH	YELLOW CARDS	RED CARDS	CAPS THIS SEASON	NATIONAL SIDE
Goalkeepers									
Vlada Avramov	29	20	2	1	126	0	0	2	Serbia
Sebastian Frey	28	35	35	34	3114	0	0	2	France
Cristiano Lupatelli	30	20	2	2	180	0	0	-	Italy
Defenders									
Federico Balzaretti	26	11	6	4	388	1	0	-	Italy
Manuel C Trindade	22	11	0	0	0	0	0	-	Portugal
Dario Dainelli	29	33	22	18	1819	3	0	-	Italy
Alessandro Gamberini	26	31	30	28	2575	3	0	2	Italy
Per B Kroldrup	28	32	19	19	1710	2	0	4	Denmark
Ondrej Mazuch	19	2	0	0	0	0	0	-	Czech Republic
Manuel Pasqual	26	34	29	23	2234	4	1	-	Italy
Alessandro Potenza	24	23	14	10	971	2	0	-	Italy
Tomas Ujfalusi	30	29	28	26	2432	6	0	8	Czech Republic
Anthony V Borre	20	3	2	0	36	0	0	1	Belgium
Midfielders									
Marco Donadel	25	32	31	21	2349	11	1	-	Italy
Massimo Gobbi	27	31	22	11	1269	5	0	-	Italy
Martin Jorgensen	32	29	26	10	1448	0	0	4	Denmark
Zdravko Kuzmanovic	20	37	34	17	2188	3	0	7	Serbia
Fabio Liverani	32	30	27	12	1761	3	0	-	Italy
Riccardo Montolivo	23	34	34	23	2574	7	0	1	Italy
Michele Pazienza	25	12	8	1	330	1	0	-	Italy
Mario A Santana	26	26	26	17	1948	3	0	-	Argentina
Franco Semioli	28	28	22	10	1256	3	0	1	Italy
Forwards									
Daniele Cacia	24	8	3	0	77	0	0	-	Italy
Samuele Di Carmine	19	0	0	0	0	0	0	-	Italy
Lorenzo Morelli	20	0	0	0	0	0	0	-	Italy
Adrian Mutu	29	29	29	26	2406	5	1	6	Romania
Pablo Daniel Osvaldo	22	25	14	6	724	3	1	-	Italy
Ndiaye Papa Waigo	24	13	7	0	322	2	0	-	Senegal
Giampaolo Pazzini	23	35	31	21	2277	4	0	-	Italy
Christian Vieri	34	28	26	6	1090	4	0	-	Italy

TEAM OF THE SEASON

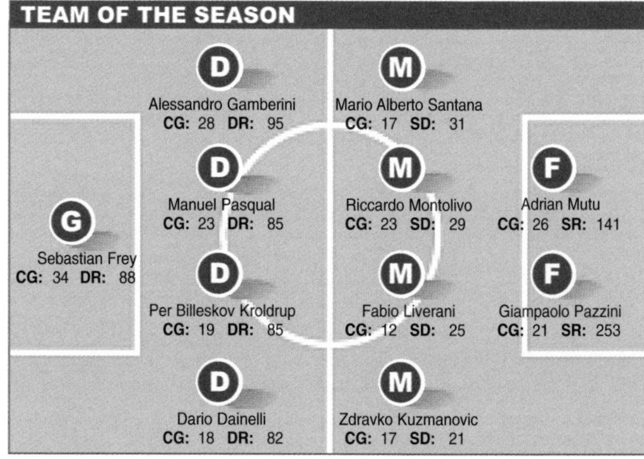
G
Sebastian Frey
CG: 34 DR: 88
D
Alessandro Gamberini
CG: 28 DR: 95
D
Manuel Pasqual
CG: 23 DR: 85
D
Per Billeskov Kroldrup
CG: 19 DR: 85
D
Dario Dainelli
CG: 18 DR: 82
M
Mario Alberto Santana
CG: 17 SD: 31
M
Riccardo Montolivo
CG: 23 SD: 29
M
Fabio Liverani
CG: 12 SD: 25
M
Zdravko Kuzmanovic
CG: 17 SD: 21
F
Adrian Mutu
CG: 26 SR: 141
F
Giampaolo Pazzini
CG: 21 SR: 253

MONTHLY POINTS TALLY

AUGUST	3	100%
SEPTEMBER	9	60%
OCTOBER	8	67%
NOVEMBER	4	44%
DECEMBER	4	33%
JANUARY	9	100%
FEBRUARY	7	47%
MARCH	9	50%
APRIL	7	58%
MAY	6	67%

LEAGUE GOALS

	PLAYER	MINS	GOALS	S RATE
1	Mutu	2406	17	141
2	Pazzini	2277	9	253
3	Vieri	1090	6	181
4	Santana	1948	6	324
5	Osvaldo	724	5	144
6	Papa Waigo	322	2	161
7	Semioli	1256	2	628
8	Donadel	2349	2	1174
9	Montolivo	2574	2	1287
10	Gobbi	1269	1	1269
11	Kuzmanovic	2188	1	2188
	Other		0	
	TOTAL		53	

TOP POINT EARNERS

	PLAYER	GAMES	AV PTS
1	Fabio Liverani	12	2.17
2	Giampaolo Pazzini	21	1.95
3	Mario Alberto Santana	17	1.94
4	Manuel Pasqual	23	1.87
5	Zdravko Kuzmanovic	17	1.82
6	Alessandro Gamberini	28	1.75
7	Adrian Mutu	26	1.73
8	Riccardo Montolivo	23	1.70
9	Sebastian Frey	34	1.65
10	Per Billeskov Kroldrup	19	1.63
	CLUB AVERAGE:		1.74

DISCIPLINARY RECORDS

	PLAYER	YELLOW	RED	AVE
1	Pablo D Osvaldo	3	1	181
2	Marco Donadel	11	1	195
3	Massimo Gobbi	5	0	253
4	Christian Vieri	4	0	272
5	Riccardo Montolivo	7	0	367
6	Adrian Mutu	5	1	401
7	Tomas Ujfalusi	6	0	405
8	Franco Semioli	3	0	418
9	Manuel Pasqual	4	1	446
10	Giampaolo Pazzini	4	0	569
11	Fabio Liverani	3	0	587
12	Dario Dainelli	3	0	606
13	Mario A Santana	3	0	649
	Other	9	0	
	TOTAL	70	4	

KEY GOALKEEPER

Sebastian Frey

Goals Conceded in the League	35	Counting Games League games when player was on pitch for at least 70 minutes	34
Defensive Rating Ave number of mins between League goals conceded while on the pitch	88	Clean Sheets In League games when player was on pitch for at least 70 minutes	12

KEY PLAYERS - DEFENDERS

Alessandro Gamberini

Goals Conceded Number of League goals conceded while the player was on the pitch	27	Clean Sheets In League games when player was on pitch for at least 70 minutes	9
Defensive Rating Ave number of mins between League goals conceded while on the pitch	95	Club Defensive Rating Average number of mins between League goals conceded by the club this season	87

	PLAYER	CON LGE	CLEAN SHEETS	DEF RATE
1	Alessandro Gamberini	27	9	95 mins
2	Manuel Pasqual	26	8	85 mins
3	Per Billeskov Kroldrup	20	7	85 mins
4	Dario Dainelli	22	6	82 mins

KEY PLAYERS - MIDFIELDERS

Mario Alberto Santana

Goals in the League	6	Contribution to Attacking Power Average number of minutes between League team goals while on pitch	57
Defensive Rating Average number of mins between League goals conceded while on the pitch	88	Scoring Difference Defensive Rating minus Contribution to Attacking Power	31

	PLAYER	LGE GOALS	DEF RATE	POWER	SCORE DIFF
1	Mario Alberto Santana	6	88	57	31 mins
2	Riccardo Montolivo	2	91	62	29 mins
3	Fabio Liverani	0	80	55	25 mins
4	Zdravko Kuzmanovic	1	81	60	21 mins

KEY PLAYERS - GOALSCORERS

Adrian Mutu

Goals in the League	17	Player Strike Rate Average number of minutes between League goals scored by player	141
Contribution to Attacking Power Average number of minutes between League team goals while on pitch	63	Club Strike Rate Average number of minutes between League goals scored by club	62

	PLAYER	LGE GOALS	POWER	STRIKE RATE
1	Adrian Mutu	17	63	141 mins
2	Giampaolo Pazzini	9	63	253 mins
3	Mario Alberto Santana	6	57	324 mins
4	Marco Donadel	2	69	1174 mins

Adrian Mutu

SQUAD APPEARANCES

Match	1	2	3	4	5	6	7	8	9	10	11	12	13	14	15	16	17	18	19	20	21	22	23	24	25	26
Venue	H	A	H	A	A	H	A	H	H	H	A	A	H	A	H	H	A	A	H	A	A	H	H	A	H	A
Competition	L	L	L	E	L	L	L	E	L	L	E	L	L	L	E	L	L	E	L	L	L	E	L	L	L	L
Result	W	D	D	D	W	D	W	W	D	W	D	D	W	W	W	L	D	D	L	L	D	W	W	W	W	W

Match	27	28	29	30	31	32	33	34	35	36	37	38	39	40	41	42	43	44	45	46	47	48	49	50	51	52
Venue	H	A	A	H	H	A	H	A	H	A	A	H	A	H	A	H	H	A	A	H	A	H	H	A	H	A
Competition	L	L	E	L	E	L	L	L	E	L	E	L	L	L	L	E	L	E	L	L	E	L	E	L	L	L
Result	L	D	W	W	W	L	W	W	W	L	W	W	L	W	L	D	W	W	L	W	D	D	L	L	W	W

Goalkeepers
Vlada Avramov
Sebastian Frey
Cristiano Lupatelli

Defenders
Federico Balzaretti
Manuel C Trindade
Dario Dainelli
Alessandro Gamberini
Per Billeskov Kroldrup
Ondrej Mazuch
Manuel Pasqual
Alessandro Potenza
Tomas Ujfalusi
Anthony Vanden Borre

Midfielders
Marco Donadel
Massimo Gobbi
Martin Jorgensen
Zdravko Kuzmanovic
Fabio Liverani
Riccardo Montolivo
Michele Pazienza
Mario Alberto Santana
Franco Semioli

Forwards
Daniele Cacia
Samuele Di Carmine
Lorenzo Morelli
Adrian Mutu
Pablo Daniel Osvaldo
Ndiaye Papa Waigo
Giampaolo Pazzini
Christian Vieri

KEY: On all match | On bench | Subbed or sent off (Counting game) | Subbed or sent off (playing less than 70 minutes) | Subbed on from bench (Counting Game) | Subbed on (playing less than 70 minutes) | Subbed on and then subbed or sent off (Counting Game) | Subbed on and then subbed or sent off (playing less than 70 minutes) | Not in 16

AC MILAN

Final Position: **5th**

NICKNAME: LA ROSSONERI

KEY: ☐Won ☐Drawn ☐Lost

#	Comp	Opponent	H/A	Res	Score	Scorers	Attendance
1	itpr1	Genoa	A	W	3-0	Ambrosini 21, Kaka 44, 45 pen	23,533
2	escup	Sevilla	H	W	3-1	Inzaghi 56, Jankulovski 61, Kaka 87	20,000
3	itpr1	Fiorentina	H	D	1-1	Kaka 27	53,559
4	itpr1	Siena	A	D	1-1	Nesta 90	14,084
5	ecgpd	Benfica	H	W	2-1	Pirlo 9 fk, Inzaghi 24	35,000
6	itpr1	Parma	H	D	1-1	Seedorf 44	50,000
7	itpr1	Palermo	A	L	1-2	Seedorf 10	30,761
8	itpr1	Catania	H	D	1-1	Kaka 48 pen	50,000
9	ecgpd	Celtic	A	L	1-2	Kaka 68 pen	60,000
10	itpr1	Lazio	A	W	5-1	Ambrosini 16, Kaka 33 pen, 52 Gilardino 70, 79	40,000
11	itpr1	Empoli	H	L	0-1		48,953
12	ecgpd	Shakhtar D	H	W	4-1	Gilardino 6, 14, Seedorf 63, 69	40,000
13	itpr1	Roma	H	L	0-1		60,205
14	itpr1	Sampdoria	A	W	5-0	Kaka 47, Gilardino 53, 62, Gourcuff 76 Seedorf 81	20,000
15	itpr1	Torino	H	D	0-0		54,980
16	ecgpd	Shakhtar D	A	W	3-0	Inzaghi 67, 90, Kaka 71	35,000
17	itpr1	Cagliari	A	W	2-1	Gilardino 61, Pirlo 86	20,000
18	ecgpd	Benfica	A	D	1-1	Pirlo 15	40,000
19	itpr1	Juventus	H	D	0-0		60,000
20	ecgpd	Celtic	H	W	1-0	Inzaghi 70	38,409
21	itpr1	Inter Milan	A	L	1-2	Pirlo 18	70,000
22	itpr1	Napoli	H	W	5-2	Ronaldo 14, 46, Seedorf 30, Kaka 67 Pato 73	60,000
23	itpr1	Udinese	A	W	1-0	Gilardino 90	12,095
24	itpr1	Atalanta	A	L	1-2	Gattuso 16	24,567
25	itpr1	Genoa	H	W	2-0	Pato 69, 82	70,000
26	itpr1	Reggina	A	W	1-0	Gilardino 18	17,426
27	itpr1	Fiorentina	A	W	1-0	Pato 77	38,977
28	itpr1	Siena	H	W	1-0	Paloschi 63	51,552
29	itpr1	Livorno	H	D	1-1	Pirlo 61 pen	50,000
30	itpr1	Parma	A	D	0-0		19,361
31	eckl1	Arsenal	A	D	0-0		60,082
32	itpr1	Palermo	H	W	2-1	Ambrosini 24, Inzaghi 90	50,643
33	itpr1	Catania	A	D	1-1	Pato 55	21,000
34	itpr1	Lazio	H	D	1-1	Oddo 66 pen	52,016
35	eckl2	Arsenal	H	L	0-2		81,879
36	itpr1	Empoli	A	W	3-1	Pato 19, Ambrosini 86, Kaka 89	9,532
37	itpr1	Roma	A	L	1-2	Kaka 56	48,447
38	itpr1	Sampdoria	H	L	1-2	Paloschi 71	60,000
39	itpr1	Torino	A	W	1-0	Pato 66	21,009
40	itpr1	Atalanta	H	L	1-2	Maldini 85	50,990
41	itpr1	Cagliari	H	W	3-1	Kaka 8, Inzaghi 31, 69	52,422
42	itpr1	Juventus	A	L	2-3	Inzaghi 14, 31	21,605
43	itpr1	Reggina	H	W	5-1	Kaka 8 pen, 34 pen, 68, Inzaghi 73 Pato 89	55,274
44	itpr1	Livorno	A	W	4-1	Inzaghi 23, 52, 59, Seedorf 71	14,504
45	itpr1	Inter Milan	H	W	2-1	Inzaghi 51, Kaka 56	81,766
46	itpr1	Napoli	A	L	1-3	Seedorf 90	55,874
47	itpr1	Udinese	H	W	4-1	Pato 48, Inzaghi 59, Cafu 79, Seedorf 88	65,829

LEAGUE APPEARANCES, BOOKINGS AND CAPS

	AGE (on 01/07/08)	IN NAMED 18	APPEARANCES	COUNTING GAMES	MINUTES ON PITCH	YELLOW CARDS	RED CARDS	CAPS THIS SEASON	NATIONAL SIDE
Goalkeepers									
Nelson Silva Dida	34	22	12	12	1080	1	0	-	Brazil
Valerio Fiori	39	17	0	0	0	0	0	-	Italy
Zeljko Kalac	35	37	26	26	2340	0	0	-	Australia
Defenders									
Dario Simic	32	21	4	1	131	0	0	7	Croatia
Daniele Bonera	27	31	21	16	1620	4	1	-	Italy
Cafu	38	25	15	6	804	4	0	-	Brazil
Rodrigo Digao	22	6	1	0	45	0	0	-	Brazil
Giuseppe Favalli	36	32	26	13	1602	7	0	-	Italy
Marek Jankulovski	31	16	14	8	918	2	0	5	Czech Republic
Kakha Kaladze	30	33	32	29	2731	4	0	-	Georgia
Paolo Maldini	40	19	17	13	1306	1	0	-	Italy
Alessandro Nesta	32	29	29	27	2487	4	1	-	Italy
Massimo Oddo	32	30	25	17	1796	3	0	5	Italy
Midfielders									
Massimo Ambrosini	31	34	33	28	2698	10	1	8	Italy
Christian Brocchi	32	36	24	6	999	1	0	-	Italy
Emerson	32	24	15	4	612	2	0	-	Brazil
Gennaro Gattuso	30	32	31	21	2316	11	0	7	Italy
Giorgio Gianola	18	1	0	0	0	0	0	-	Italy
Yoann Gourcuff	21	30	15	3	498	1	0	-	France
Ricardo Kaka	26	30	30	28	2551	3	0	4	Brazil
Andrea Pirlo	29	33	33	32	2878	8	0	9	Italy
Clarence Seedorf	32	33	32	28	2646	2	0	6	Holland
Sergio Serginho	37	13	11	2	474	1	0	-	Brazil
Forwards									
Willy Aubameyang	21	1	0	0	0	0	0	-	France
Alberto Gilardino	25	37	30	16	1857	4	0	2	Italy
Filippo Inzaghi	34	26	21	12	1321	1	0	1	Italy
Alberto Paloschi	18	11	7	1	279	0	0	-	Italy
Alexandre Pato	18	19	18	12	1276	1	0	2	Brazil
Ronaldo	31	6	6	2	315	0	0	-	Brazil

TEAM OF THE SEASON

G — Nelson Silva Dida, CG: 12 DR: 117

D — Alessandro Nesta, CG: 27 DR: 107

D — Kakha Kaladze, CG: 29 DR: 97

D — Massimo Oddo, CG: 17 DR: 89

D — Paolo Maldini, CG: 13 DR: 82

M — Andrea Pirlo, CG: 32 SD: 44

M — Ricardo Kaka, CG: 28 SD: 44

M — Clarence Seedorf, CG: 28 SD: 40

M — Gennaro Ivan Gattuso, CG: 21 SD: 31

F — Filippo Inzaghi, CG: 12 SR: 128

F — Alexandre Pato, CG: 12 SR: 141

MONTHLY POINTS TALLY

Month	Points	%
AUGUST	3	100%
SEPTEMBER	4	27%
OCTOBER	6	50%
NOVEMBER	4	67%
DECEMBER	1	17%
JANUARY	12	80%
FEBRUARY	12	67%
MARCH	7	39%
APRIL	9	75%
MAY	6	67%

LEAGUE GOALS

	PLAYER	MINS	GOALS	S RATE
1	Kaka	2641	15	176
2	Inzaghi	1411	11	128
3	Pato	1276	9	141
4	Gilardino	1857	7	265
5	Seedorf	2736	7	390
6	Ambrosini	2788	4	697
7	Pirlo	2968	3	989
8	Paloschi	279	2	139
9	Ronaldo	315	2	157
10	Gourcuff	498	1	498
11	Cafu	804	1	804
12	Maldini	1396	1	1396
13	Oddo	1886	1	1886
	Other		2	
	TOTAL		66	

TOP POINT EARNERS

	PLAYER	GAMES	AV PTS
1	Daniele Bonera	16	2.00
2	Alexandre Pato	12	1.92
3	Alberto Gilardino	16	1.88
4	Giuseppe Favalli	13	1.85
5	Filippo Inzaghi	12	1.83
6	Ricardo Kaka	28	1.82
7	Kakha Kaladze	29	1.79
8	Andrea Pirlo	32	1.78
9	Massimo Ambrosini	28	1.75
10	Paolo Maldini	13	1.69
	CLUB AVERAGE:		1.68

DISCIPLINARY RECORDS

	PLAYER	YELLOW	RED	AVE
1	Cafu	4	0	201
2	Gennaro I Gattuso	11	0	218
3	Giuseppe Favalli	7	0	228
4	M Ambrosini	10	1	253
5	Emerson	2	0	306
6	Daniele Bonera	4	1	324
7	Andrea Pirlo	8	0	371
8	Marek Jankulovski	2	0	459
9	Alberto Gilardino	4	0	464
10	Yoann Gourcuff	1	0	498
11	Alessandro Nesta	4	1	515
12	Sergio Serginho	1	0	564
13	Massimo Oddo	3	0	628
	Other	14	0	
	TOTAL	75	3	

KEY GOALKEEPER

Nelson Silva Dida

Goals Conceded in the League	10	**Counting Games** League games when player was on pitch for at least 70 minutes	13
Defensive Rating Ave number of mins between League goals conceded while on the pitch	117	**Clean Sheets** In League games when player was on pitch for at least 70 minutes	5

KEY PLAYERS - DEFENDERS

Alessandro Nesta

Goals Conceded Number of League goals conceded while the player was on the pitch	24	**Clean Sheets** In League games when player was on pitch for at least 70 minutes	12
Defensive Rating Ave number of mins between League goals conceded while on the pitch	107	**Club Defensive Rating** Average number of mins between League goals conceded by the club this season	92

	PLAYER	CON LGE	CLEAN SHEETS	DEF RATE
1	Alessandro Nesta	24	12	107 mins
2	Kakha Kaladze	28	10	97 mins
3	Massimo Oddo	21	7	89 mins
4	Paolo Maldini	17	5	82 mins

KEY PLAYERS - MIDFIELDERS

Andrea Pirlo

Goals in the League	3	**Contribution to Attacking Power** Average number of minutes between League team goals while on pitch	48
Defensive Rating Average number of mins between League goals conceded while on the pitch	92	**Scoring Difference** Defensive Rating minus Contribution to Attacking Power	44

	PLAYER	LGE GOALS	DEF RATE	POWER	SCORE DIFF
1	Andrea Pirlo	3	92	48	44 mins
2	Ricardo Kaka	15	91	47	44 mins
3	Clarence Seedorf	7	91	51	40 mins
4	Gennaro Ivan Gattuso	1	89	58	31 mins

KEY PLAYERS - GOALSCORERS

Filippo Inzaghi

Goals in the League	11	**Player Strike Rate** Average number of minutes between League goals scored by player	128
Contribution to Attacking Power Average number of minutes between League team goals while on pitch	50	**Club Strike Rate** Average number of minutes between League goals scored by club	53

	PLAYER	LGE GOALS	POWER	STRIKE RATE
1	Filippo Inzaghi	11	50	128 mins
2	Alexandre Pato	9	45	141 mins
3	Ricardo Kaka	15	47	176 mins
4	Alberto Gilardino	7	66	265 mins

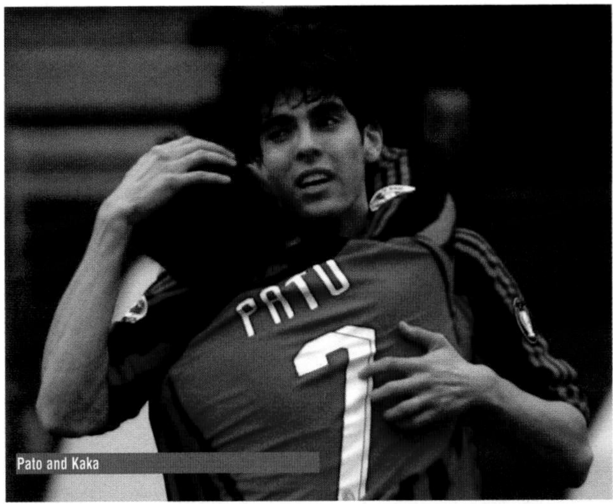

Pato and Kaka

SQUAD APPEARANCES

Match	1	2	3	4	5	6	7	8	9	10	11	12	13	14	15	16	17	18	19	20	21	22	23	24
Venue	A	H	H	A	H	H	A	H	A	A	H	H	H	A	H	A	A	A	H	H	A	H	A	A
Competition	L	O	L	L	C	L	L	L	C	L	L	C	L	L	L	C	L	C	L	C	L	L	L	L
Result	W	W	D	D	W	D	L	D	L	W	L	W	L	W	D	W	W	D	D	W	L	W	W	L

Match	25	26	27	28	29	30	31	32	33	34	35	36	37	38	39	40	41	42	43	44	45	46	47
Venue	H	A	A	H	H	A	A	H	A	H	H	A	A	H	A	H	H	A	H	A	H	A	H
Competition	L	L	L	L	L	L	C	L	L	L	C	L	L	L	L	L	L	L	L	L	L	L	L
Result	W	W	W	W	D	D	D	W	D	D	L	W	L	L	W	L	W	L	W	W	W	L	W

Goalkeepers
Nelson Silva Dida
Valerio Fiori
Zeljko Kalac

Defenders
Dario Simic
Daniele Bonera
Cafu
Rodrigo Digao
Giuseppe Favalli
Marek Jankulovski
Kakha Kaladze
Paolo Maldini
Alessandro Nesta
Massimo Oddo

Midfielders
Massimo Ambrosini
Christian Brocchi
Emerson
Gennaro Ivan Gattuso
Giorgio Gianola
Yoann Gourcuff
Ricardo Kaka
Andrea Pirlo
Clarence Seedorf
Sergio Serginho

Forwards
Willy Aubameyang
Alberto Gilardino
Filippo Inzaghi
Alberto Paloschi
Alexandre Pato
Ronaldo

KEY: On all match | On bench | Subbed or sent off (Counting game) | Subbed or sent off (playing less than 70 minutes) | Subbed on from bench (Counting Game) | Subbed on (playing less than 70 minutes) | Subbed on and then subbed or sent off (Counting Game) | Subbed on and then subbed or sent off (playing less than 70 minutes) | Not in 16

SAMPDORIA

Final Position: **6th**

NICKNAME: BLUCERCHIATI. DORIA.

KEY: ☐Won ☐Drawn ☐Lost

#	Comp	Opponent	H/A	Res	Score	Scorers	Attendance
1	ucql1	**Hajduk Split**	A	W	1-0	Campagnaro 44	35,000
2	itpr1	**Siena**	A	W	2-1	Bellucci 33, Montella 86	10,768
3	ucql2	**Hajduk Split**	H	D	1-1	Montella 31 pen	32,000
4	itpr1	**Lazio**	H	D	0-0		20,564
5	itpr1	**Napoli**	A	L	0-2		40,000
6	uc1rl1	**Aalborg BK**	H	D	2-2	Delvecchio 18, Bellucci 59	16,768
7	itpr1	**Genoa**	H	D	0-0		33,060
8	itpr1	**Inter Milan**	A	L	0-3		42,013
9	itpr1	**Atalanta**	H	W	3-0	Bellucci 3, Sammarco 57, Cassano 83	20,000
10	uc1rl2	**Aalborg BK**	A	D	0-0		21,000
11	itpr1	**Torino**	A	L	0-1		18,000
12	itpr1	**Parma**	H	W	3-0	Montella 25, Bellucci 46, 58	19,852
13	itpr1	**Catania**	A	L	0-2		16,276
14	itpr1	**AC Milan**	H	L	0-5		20,000
15	itpr1	**Cagliari**	A	W	3-0	Volpi 33, Caracciolo 39, Maggio 44	10,000
16	itpr1	**Empoli**	H	W	3-0	Giacomazzi 5 og, Montella 40 Sammarco 89	19,000
17	itpr1	**Livorno**	A	L	1-3	Bellucci 79	10,000
18	itpr1	**Reggina**	H	W	3-0	Bellucci 5, 75, Sammarco 55	22,058
19	itpr1	**Udinese**	A	L	2-3	Bellucci 31 pen, Maggio 40	13,000
20	itpr1	**Fiorentina**	H	D	2-2	Gastaldello 18, Cassano 69	21,000
21	itpr1	**Roma**	A	L	0-2		35,000
22	itpr1	**Palermo**	H	W	3-0	Bellucci 20, Sammarco 45, Cassano 77	19,574
23	itpr1	**Juventus**	A	D	0-0		22,379
24	itpr1	**Siena**	H	W	1-0	Cassano 44	19,562
25	itpr1	**Lazio**	A	L	1-2	Cassano 45	18,683
26	itpr1	**Napoli**	H	W	2-0	Delvecchio 76, Franceschini 81	19,592
27	itpr1	**Genoa**	A	W	1-0	Maggio 87	37,508
28	itpr1	**Inter Milan**	H	D	1-1	Cassano 65	26,306
29	itpr1	**Atalanta**	A	L	1-4	Volpi 3	10,244
30	itpr1	**Torino**	H	D	2-2	Sala 45, Cassano 52	19,032
31	itpr1	**Parma**	A	W	2-1	Maggio 12, Bonazzoli 57	16,328
32	itpr1	**Catania**	H	W	3-1	Palombo 68, Accardi 76, Bellucci 86	19,409
33	itpr1	**AC Milan**	A	W	2-1	Maggio 12, Delvecchio 25	52,477
34	itpr1	**Cagliari**	H	D	1-1	Franceschini 90	19,877
35	itpr1	**Empoli**	A	W	2-0	Sammarco 7, Marzoratti 16 og	7,066
36	itpr1	**Livorno**	H	W	2-0	Maggio 67, Bonazzoli 85	21,426
37	itpr1	**Reggina**	A	L	0-1		11,082
38	itpr1	**Udinese**	H	W	3-0	Cassano 24, Bellucci 44, 55 pen	25,181
39	itpr1	**Fiorentina**	A	D	2-2	Maggio 63, Gastaldello 90	36,627
40	itpr1	**Roma**	H	L	0-3		24,311
41	itpr1	**Palermo**	A	W	2-0	Cassano 61, Maggio 76	23,929
42	itpr1	**Juventus**	H	D	3-3	Cassano 22, Maggio 39, Montella 80	26,954

LEAGUE APPEARANCES, BOOKINGS AND CAPS

	AGE (on 01/07/08)	IN NAMED 18	APPEARANCES	COUNTING GAMES	MINUTES ON PITCH	YELLOW CARDS	RED CARDS	CAPS THIS SEASON	NATIONAL SIDE
Goalkeepers									
Luca Castellazzi	32	31	25	23	2201	0	0	-	Italy
Vincenzo Fiorillo	18	9	1	0	25	0	0	-	Italy
Antonio Mirante	24	35	14	13	1194	1	0	-	Italy
Defenders									
Pietro Accardi	25	22	22	18	1641	5	0	-	Italy
Alessandro Bastrini	21	9	3	1	156	0	0	-	Italy
Hugo A Campagnaro	28	22	22	19	1810	5	0	-	Argentina
Daniele Gastaldello	25	33	29	25	2405	8	0	-	Italy
Stefano Lucchini	27	30	26	19	1875	8	1	-	Italy
Christian Maggio	26	30	29	28	2539	6	0	-	Italy
Leonardo Miglionico	28	12	4	1	131	0	0	-	Uruguay
Mirko Pieri	29	34	32	27	2548	5	1	-	Italy
Luigi Sala	34	34	26	21	2085	4	0	-	Italy
Cristian Zenoni	31	35	16	12	1155	6	0	-	Italy
Midfielders									
Gennaro Delvecchio	30	28	26	14	1653	5	0	-	Italy
Daniele Franceschini	32	37	30	20	2152	6	0	-	Italy
Nikola Gulan	19	1	0	0	0	0	0	-	Serbia
Vladimir Koman	19	1	0	0	0	0	0	-	Hungary
Angelo Palombo	26	35	33	33	2948	9	0	1	Italy
Andrea Poli	18	8	1	0	2	0	0	-	Italy
Paolo Sammarco	25	33	30	20	2168	8	0	-	Italy
Sergio Volpi	34	30	28	16	1725	6	2	-	Italy
Reto Ziegler	22	34	20	6	751	4	1	-	Switzerland
Forwards									
Claudio Bellucci	33	32	32	20	2310	3	0	-	Italy
Emiliano Bonazzoli	29	31	30	9	1157	1	0	-	Italy
Andrea Caracciolo	26	16	12	4	517	2	0	-	Italy
Antonio Cassano	25	23	22	14	1541	7	1	3	Italy
Gabriel Enzo Ferrari	19	3	0	0	0	0	0	-	United States
Salvatore Foti	19	0	0	0	0	0	0	-	Italy
Ikechukwu Kalu	24	19	5	0	69	0	0	-	Nigeria
Vincenzo Montella	34	15	13	7	746	1	0	-	Italy

TEAM OF THE SEASON

G: Luca Castellazzi — CG: 23 DR: 84

D: Pietro Accardi — CG: 18 DR: 96
D: Mirko Pieri — CG: 27 DR: 91
D: Cristian Zenoni — CG: 12 DR: 88
D: Hugo Campagnaro — CG: 19 DR: 86

M: Gennaro Delvecchio — CG: 14 SD: 32
M: Angelo Palombo — CG: 33 SD: 16
M: Daniele Franceschini — CG: 20 SD: 16
M: Paolo Sammarco — CG: 20 SD: 7

F: Antonio Cassano — CG: 14 SR: 154
F: Claudio Bellucci — CG: 20 SR: 192

MONTHLY POINTS TALLY

Month	Points	%
AUGUST	3	100%
SEPTEMBER	5	33%
OCTOBER	3	25%
NOVEMBER	6	67%
DECEMBER	4	33%
JANUARY	7	78%
FEBRUARY	7	47%
MARCH	14	78%
APRIL	7	58%
MAY	4	44%

LEAGUE GOALS

	PLAYER	MINS	GOALS	S RATE
1	Bellucci	2310	12	192
2	Cassano	1541	10	154
3	Maggio	2539	9	282
4	Montella	746	4	186
5	Sammarco	2168	5	433
6	Delvecchio	1653	2	826
7	Bonazzoli	1157	2	578
8	Volpi	1725	2	862
9	Franceschini	2152	2	1076
10	Gastaldello	2405	2	1202
11	Caracciolo	517	1	517
12	Accardi	1641	1	1641
13	Sala	2085	1	2085
	Other		1	
	TOTAL		**54**	

TOP POINT EARNERS

	PLAYER	GAMES	AV PTS
1	Pietro Accardi	18	2.11
2	Gennaro Delvecchio	14	1.86
3	Daniele Franceschini	20	1.80
4	Luca Castellazzi	23	1.78
5	Christian Maggio	28	1.75
6	Paolo Sammarco	20	1.70
7	Angelo Palombo	33	1.64
8	Antonio Cassano	14	1.64
9	Stefano Lucchini	19	1.63
10	Daniele Gastaldello	25	1.60
	CLUB AVERAGE:		**1.58**

DISCIPLINARY RECORDS

	PLAYER	YELLOW	RED	AVE
1	Reto Ziegler	4	1	150
2	Antonio Cassano	7	1	192
3	Cristian Zenoni	6	0	192
4	Stefano Lucchini	8	1	208
5	Sergio Volpi	6	2	215
6	Andrea Caracciolo	2	0	258
7	Paolo Sammarco	8	0	271
8	Daniele Gastaldello	8	0	300
9	Angelo Palombo	9	0	327
10	Pietro Accardi	5	0	328
11	G Delvecchio	5	0	330
12	D Franceschini	6	0	358
13	Hugo Campagnaro	5	0	362
	Other	21	1	
	TOTAL	**100**	**6**	

KEY GOALKEEPER

Luca Castellazzi

Goals Conceded in the League	26	Counting Games League games when player was on pitch for at least 70 minutes	23
Defensive Rating Ave number of mins between League goals conceded while on the pitch	84	Clean Sheets In League games when player was on pitch for at least 70 minutes	10

KEY PLAYERS - DEFENDERS

Pietro Accardi

Goals Conceded Number of League goals conceded while the player was on the pitch	17	Clean Sheets In League games when player was on pitch for at least 70 minutes	9
Defensive Rating Ave number of mins between League goals conceded while on the pitch	96	Club Defensive Rating Average number of mins between League goals conceded by the club this season	74

	PLAYER	CON LGE	CLEAN SHEETS	DEF RATE
1	Pietro Accardi	17	9	96 mins
2	Mirko Pieri	28	12	91 mins
3	Cristian Zenoni	13	6	88 mins
4	Hugo Armando Campagnaro	21	10	86 mins

KEY PLAYERS - MIDFIELDERS

Gennaro Delvecchio

Goals in the League	2	Contribution to Attacking Power Average number of minutes between League team goals while on pitch	71
Defensive Rating Average number of mins between League goals conceded while on the pitch	103	Scoring Difference Defensive Rating minus Contribution to Attacking Power	32

	PLAYER	LGE GOALS	DEF RATE	POWER	SCORE DIFF
1	Gennaro Delvecchio	2	103	71	32 mins
2	Angelo Palombo	1	77	61	16 mins
3	Daniele Franceschini	2	79	63	16 mins
4	Paolo Sammarco	5	61	54	7 mins

KEY PLAYERS - GOALSCORERS

Antonio Cassano

Goals in the League	10	Player Strike Rate Average number of minutes between League goals scored by player	154
Contribution to Attacking Power Average number of minutes between League team goals while on pitch	53	Club Strike Rate Average number of minutes between League goals scored by club	61

	PLAYER	LGE GOALS	POWER	STRIKE RATE
1	Antonio Cassano	10	53	154 mins
2	Claudio Bellucci	12	57	192 mins
3	Paolo Sammarco	5	54	433 mins
4	Gennaro Delvecchio	2	71	826 mins

Kappa
ERG
Antonio Cassano

SQUAD APPEARANCES

Match	1	2	3	4	5	6	7	8	9	10	11	12	13	14	15	16	17	18	19	20	21
Venue	A	A	H	H	A	H	H	A	H	A	A	H	A	H	A	H	A	H	A	H	A
Competition	E	L	E	L	L	E	L	L	L	E	L	L	L	L	L	L	L	L	L	L	L
Result	W	W	D	D	L	D	D	L	W	D	L	W	L	L	W	W	L	W	L	D	L

Match	22	23	24	25	26	27	28	29	30	31	32	33	34	35	36	37	38	39	40	41	42
Venue	H	A	H	A	H	A	H	A	H	A	H	A	H	A	H	A	H	A	H	A	H
Competition	L	L	L	L	L	L	L	L	L	L	L	L	L	L	L	L	L	L	L	L	L
Result	W	D	W	L	W	W	D	L	D	W	W	W	D	W	W	L	W	D	L	W	D

Goalkeepers
Luca Castellazzi
Vincenzo Fiorillo
Antonio Mirante
Defenders
Pietro Accardi
Alessandro Bastrini
Hugo Campagnaro
Daniele Gastaldello
Stefano Lucchini
Christian Maggio
Leonardo Miglionico
Mirko Pieri
Luigi Sala
Cristian Zenoni
Midfielders
Gennaro Delvecchio
Daniele Franceschini
Nikola Gulan
Vladimir Koman
Angelo Palombo
Andrea Poli
Paolo Sammarco
Sergio Volpi
Reto Ziegler
Forwards
Claudio Bellucci
Emiliano Bonazzoli
Andrea Caracciolo
Antonio Cassano
Gabriel Enzo Ferrari
Salvatore Foti
Ikechukwu Kalu
Vincenzo Montella

KEY: On all match | On bench | Subbed or sent off (Counting game) | Subbed or sent off (playing less than 70 minutes) | Subbed on from bench (Counting Game) | Subbed on (playing less than 70 minutes) | Subbed on and then subbed or sent off (Counting Game) | Subbed on and then subbed or sent off (playing less than 70 minutes) | Not in 16

UDINESE

Final Position: **7th**

BIANCONERI. ZEBRETTE (LITTLE ZEBRAS) KEY: ☐Won ☐Drawn ☐Lost

							Attendance
1	itpr1	Inter Milan	A	D	1-1	Cordoba 90 og	42,797
2	itpr1	Napoli	H	L	0-5		16,197
3	itpr1	Juventus	A	W	1-0	Di Natale 47	20,000
4	itpr1	Reggina	H	W	2-0	Di Natale 6, 62	15,000
5	itpr1	Genoa	A	L	2-3	Asamoah 50, Mesto 88	22,253
6	itpr1	Parma	H	W	2-1	Quagliarella 79, Zapata 90	12,000
7	itpr1	Atalanta	A	D	0-0		10,000
8	itpr1	Palermo	H	D	1-1	Asamoah 65	14,851
9	itpr1	Lazio	A	W	1-0	Asamoah 78	17,536
10	itpr1	Torino	H	W	2-1	Floro Flores 25, Inler 52	14,000
11	itpr1	Livorno	A	D	0-0		8,500
12	itpr1	Fiorentina	A	W	2-1	Quagliarella 23, Di Natale 63	30,000
13	itpr1	Siena	H	W	2-0	Quagliarella 43, Di Natale 80	12,000
14	itpr1	Roma	A	L	1-2	Quagliarella 12	30,000
15	itpr1	Sampdoria	H	W	3-2	Di Natale 23, Quagliarella 70, 86	13,000
16	itpr1	Catania	A	L	0-2		17,000
17	itpr1	Empoli	H	D	2-2	Dossena 21, Di Natale 85	13,000
18	itpr1	Cagliari	A	W	1-0	Quagliarella 32	8,000
19	itpr1	AC Milan	H	L	0-1		12,095
20	itpr1	Inter Milan	H	D	0-0		24,000
21	itpr1	Napoli	A	L	1-3	Pepe 8	36,034
22	itpr1	Juventus	H	L	1-2	Dossena 6	25,152
23	itpr1	Reggina	A	W	3-1	Pepe 8, Di Natale 63, 90	9,917
24	itpr1	Genoa	H	L	3-5	Di Natale 28 pen, 39 pen Floro Flores 72	13,640
25	itpr1	Parma	A	L	0-2		12,457
26	itpr1	Atalanta	H	W	2-0	Quagliarella 30, Di Natale 32	13,245
27	itpr1	Palermo	A	D	1-1	Felipe Dal Belo 64	24,833
28	itpr1	Lazio	H	D	2-2	Ferronetti 56, Di Natale 86	13,084
29	itpr1	Torino	A	W	1-0	Pepe 25	17,599
30	itpr1	Livorno	H	W	2-0	Quagliarella 19, Di Natale 47	12,594
31	itpr1	Fiorentina	H	W	3-1	Inler 13, Di Natale 72, Quagliarella 76	15,374
32	itpr1	Siena	A	D	1-1	Floro Flores 77	8,652
33	itpr1	Roma	H	L	1-3	Di Natale 51	20,405
34	itpr1	Sampdoria	A	L	0-3		25,181
35	itpr1	Catania	H	W	2-1	Di Natale 6, Quagliarella 38	13,958
36	itpr1	Empoli	A	W	1-0	Quagliarella 17	7,257
37	itpr1	Cagliari	H	L	0-2		16,689
38	itpr1	AC Milan	A	L	1-4	Mesto 32	65,829

LEAGUE APPEARANCES, BOOKINGS AND CAPS

	AGE (on 01/07/08)	IN NAMED 18	APPEARANCES	COUNTING GAMES	MINUTES ON PITCH	YELLOW CARDS	RED CARDS	CAPS THIS SEASON	NATIONAL SIDE
Goalkeepers									
Antonio Chimenti	38	33	3	3	270	0	0	-	Italy
Samir Handanovic	23	37	35	35	3150	2	0	-	Slovenia
Saulo S Rodrigues	22	6	0	0	0	0	0	-	Brazil
Defenders									
Andrea Coda	23	37	20	17	1626	1	0	-	Italy
Riccardo Colombo	25	13	4	0	44	0	0	-	Italy
Andrea Dossena	26	35	35	33	3037	8	1	1	Italy
Felipe Dal Belo	23	24	22	19	1804	8	2	-	Brazil
Damiano Ferronetti	23	22	16	11	989	2	0	-	Italy
Aleksandar Lukovic	25	35	32	28	2611	3	0	-	Serbia
Moreno Aoas Vidal	25	5	0	0	0	0	0	-	Brazil
Cristian Zapata	21	27	27	25	2287	7	0	-	Colombia
Tomas Zapotocny	27	30	21	13	1539	5	1	-	Czech Republic
Midfielders									
Viktor Boudianski	24	9	1	0	45	0	0	2	Ukraine
Antonio Candreva	21	14	3	0	12	0	0	-	Italy
Gaetano D'Agostino	26	35	35	30	2844	7	0	-	Italy
Raffaele De Martino	22	2	0	0	0	0	0	-	Italy
Roman Eremenko	21	27	7	2	282	0	0	4	Finland
Gokhan Inler	24	37	37	37	3313	6	0	9	Switzerland
Mauricio Anibal Isla	20	18	10	2	356	1	0	1	Chile
Giandomenico Mesto	26	29	28	26	2362	5	0	-	Italy
Christian Obodo	24	3	1	0	40	0	0	-	Nigeria
Simone Pepe	24	35	33	20	2050	8	1	-	Italy
Giampiero Pinzi	27	19	13	1	249	2	1	-	Italy
Guilherme Siqueira	22	9	4	2	242	1	0	-	Brazil
Tomas Sivok	24	8	2	0	100	1	0	2	Czech Republic
Forwards									
Gyan Asamoah	22	13	13	5	734	1	0	6	Ghana
Antonio Di Natale	30	36	36	34	3048	4	0	9	Italy
Antonio Floro Flores	25	38	37	9	1283	1	0	-	Italy
Michele Paolucci	22	9	2	0	11	0	0	-	Italy
Fabio Quagliarella	25	37	37	34	3073	4	0	4	Italy

TEAM OF THE SEASON

G – Samir Handanovic – CG: 35 DR: 70

D – Felipe Dal Belo – CG: 19 DR: 90

D – Aleksandar Lukovic – CG: 28 DR: 68

D – Andrea Dossena – CG: 33 DR: 64

D – Cristian Eduardo Zapata – CG: 25 DR: 60

M – Simone Pepe – CG: 20 SD: 7

M – Gaetano D'Agostino – CG: 30 SD: 0

M – Giandomenico Mesto – CG: 26 SD: 0

M – Gokhan Inler – CG: 37 SD: -6

F – Antonio Di Natale – CG: 34 SR: 179

F – Fabio Quagliarella – CG: 34 SR: 256

MONTHLY POINTS TALLY

AUGUST	1	33%
SEPTEMBER	9	60%
OCTOBER	8	67%
NOVEMBER	7	78%
DECEMBER	4	33%
JANUARY	4	44%
FEBRUARY	3	20%
MARCH	14	78%
APRIL	4	33%
MAY	3	33%

LEAGUE GOALS

	PLAYER	MINS	GOALS	S RATE
1	Di Natale	3048	17	179
2	Quagliarella	3073	12	256
3	Asamoah	734	3	244
4	Floro Flores	1283	3	427
5	Pepe	2050	3	683
6	Mesto	2362	2	1181
7	Dossena	3037	2	1518
8	Inler	3313	2	1656
9	Ferronetti	989	1	989
10	Felipe Dal Belo	1804	1	1804
11	Zapata	2287	1	2287
	Other		0	
	TOTAL		**47**	

TOP POINT EARNERS

	PLAYER	GAMES	AV PTS
1	Tomas Zapotocny	13	2.00
2	Felipe Dal Belo	19	1.79
3	Giandomenico Mesto	26	1.65
4	Samir Handanovic	35	1.60
5	Gaetano D'Agostino	30	1.57
6	Gokhan Inler	37	1.54
7	Antonio Di Natale	34	1.53
8	Andrea Dossena	33	1.48
9	Simone Pepe	20	1.45
10	Aleksandar Lukovic	28	1.43
	CLUB AVERAGE:		**1.50**

DISCIPLINARY RECORDS

	PLAYER	YELLOW	RED	AVE
1	Felipe Dal Belo	8	2	180
2	Simone Pepe	8	1	227
3	Tomas Zapotocny	5	1	256
4	Cristian Zapata	7	0	326
5	Andrea Dossena	8	1	337
6	G D'Agostino	7	0	406
7	G Mesto	5	0	472
8	Damiano Ferronetti	2	0	494
9	Gokhan Inler	6	0	552
10	Gyan Asamoah	1	0	734
11	Antonio Di Natale	4	0	762
12	Fabio Quagliarella	4	0	768
13	Aleksandar Lukovic	3	0	870
	Other	4	0	
	TOTAL	**72**	**5**	

KEY GOALKEEPER

Samir Handanovic

Goals Conceded in the League	45	Counting Games League games when player was on pitch for at least 70 minutes	35
Defensive Rating Ave number of mins between League goals conceded while on the pitch	70	Clean Sheets In League games when player was on pitch for at least 70 minutes	12

KEY PLAYERS - DEFENDERS

Felipe Dal Belo

Goals Conceded Number of League goals conceded while the player was on the pitch	20	Clean Sheets In League games when player was on pitch for at least 70 minutes	7
Defensive Rating Ave number of mins between League goals conceded while on the pitch	90	Club Defensive Rating Average number of mins between League goals conceded by the club this season	64

	PLAYER	CON LGE	CLEAN SHEETS	DEF RATE
1	Felipe Dal Belo	20	7	90 mins
2	Aleksandar Lukovic	38	8	68 mins
3	Andrea Dossena	47	11	64 mins
4	Cristian Eduardo Zapata	38	7	60 mins

KEY PLAYERS - MIDFIELDERS

Simone Pepe

Goals in the League	3	Contribution to Attacking Power Average number of minutes between League team goals while on pitch	66
Defensive Rating Average number of mins between League goals conceded while on the pitch	73	Scoring Difference Defensive Rating minus Contribution to Attacking Power	7

	PLAYER	LGE GOALS	DEF RATE	POWER	SCORE DIFF
1	Simone Pepe	3	73	66	7 mins
2	Gaetano D'Agostino	0	71	71	0 mins
3	Giandomenico Mesto	2	81	81	0 mins
4	Gokhan Inler	2	64	70	-6 mins

KEY PLAYERS - GOALSCORERS

Antonio Di Natale

Goals in the League	17	Player Strike Rate Average number of minutes between League goals scored by player	179
Contribution to Attacking Power Average number of minutes between League team goals while on pitch	66	Club Strike Rate Average number of minutes between League goals scored by club	71

	PLAYER	LGE GOALS	POWER	STRIKE RATE
1	Antonio Di Natale	17	66	179 mins
2	Fabio Quagliarella	12	71	256 mins
3	Simone Pepe	3	66	683 mins
4	Giandomenico Mesto	2	81	1181 mins

Antonio Di Natale and Fabio Quagliarella

SQUAD APPEARANCES

Match	1	2	3	4	5	6	7	8	9	10	11	12	13	14	15	16	17	18	19	20	21	22	23	24	25	26	27	28	29	30	31	32	33	34	35	36	37	38
Venue	A	H	A	H	A	H	A	H	A	H	A	A	H	A	H	A	H	A	H	H	A	H	A	H	A	H	A	H	A	H	H	A	H	A	H	A	H	A
Competition	L	L	L	L	L	L	L	L	L	L	L	L	L	L	L	L	L	L	L	L	L	L	L	L	L	L	L	L	L	L	L	L	L	L	L	L	L	L
Result	D	L	W	W	L	W	D	D	W	W	D	W	W	L	W	L	D	W	L	D	L	L	W	L	L	W	D	D	W	W	W	D	L	L	W	W	L	L

Goalkeepers
Antonio Chimenti
Samir Handanovic
Saulo S Rodrigues

Defenders
Andrea Coda
Riccardo Colombo
Andrea Dossena
Felipe Dal Belo
Damiano Ferronetti
Aleksandar Lukovic
Giandomenico Mesto
Moreno Aoas Vidal
Cristian Eduardo Zapata
Tomas Zapotocny

Midfielders
Viktor Boudianski
Antonio Candreva
Gaetano D'Agostino
Raffaele De Martino
Roman Eremenko
Gokhan Inler
Mauricio Anibal Isla
Christian Obodo
Simone Pepe
Giampiero Pinzi
Guilherme Siqueira
Tomas Sivok

Forwards
Gyan Asamoah
Antonio Di Natale
Antonio Floro Flores
Michele Paolucci
Fabio Quagliarella

KEY: On all match · On bench · Subbed or sent off (Counting game) · Subbed or sent off (playing less than 70 minutes) · Subbed on from bench (Counting Game) · Subbed on (playing less than 70 minutes) · Subbed on and then subbed or sent off (Counting Game) · Subbed on and then subbed or sent off (playing less than 70 minutes) · Not in 16

NAPOLI

Final Position: **8th**

NICKNAME: AZZURRI

KEY: ☐Won ☐Drawn ☐Lost

							Attendance
1	itpr1	**Cagliari**	H	L	0-2		39,026
2	itpr1	**Udinese**	A	W	5-0	Zalayeta 16, 70, Domizzi 41, Lavezzi 65	
						Sosa 81	16,197
3	itpr1	**Sampdoria**	H	W	2-0	Zalayeta 43, Hamsik 76	40,000
4	itpr1	**Empoli**	A	D	0-0		5,000
5	itpr1	**Livorno**	H	W	1-0	Sosa 85	37,163
6	itpr1	**Genoa**	H	L	1-2	Domizzi 52 pen	0
7itpr1		**Inter Milan**	A	L	1-2	Sosa 85	45,000
8	itpr1	**Roma**	A	D	4-4	Lavezzi 2, Hamsik 46, Gargano 64	
						Zalayeta 84	27,313
9	itpr1	**Juventus**	H	W	3-1	Gargano 49, Domizzi 62 pen, 70 pen	63,000
10	itpr1	**Fiorentina**	A	L	0-1		33,000
11	itpr1	**Reggina**	H	D	1-1	Lavezzi 90	40,000
12	itpr1	**Palermo**	A	L	1-2	Bogliacino 54	25,138
13	itpr1	**Catania**	H	W	2-0	Zalayeta 43, 65	30,000
14	itpr1	**Atalanta**	A	L	1-5	Sosa 60	15,000
15	itpr1	**Parma**	H	W	1-0	Zalayeta 17	30,000
16	itpr1	**Siena**	A	D	1-1	Bogliacino 64	9,000
17	itpr1	**Torino**	H	D	1-1	Hamsik 80	35,000
18	itpr1	**AC Milan**	A	L	2-5	Sosa 27, Domizzi 37 pen	60,000
19	itpr1	**Lazio**	H	D	2-2	Hamsik 5, 90	34,480
20	itpr1	**Cagliari**	A	L	1-2	Hamsik 57	8,000
21	itpr1	**Udinese**	H	W	3-1	Zapata 3 og, Lavezzi 74, 75	36,034
22	itpr1	**Sampdoria**	A	L	0-2		19,592
23	itpr1	**Empoli**	H	L	1-3	Mannini 37	46,946
24	itpr1	**Livorno**	A	W	2-1	Calaio 58, 90	8,495
25	itpr1	**Genoa**	A	L	0-2		26,417
26	itpr1	**Inter Milan**	H	W	1-0	Zalayeta 3	53,818
27	itpr1	**Roma**	H	L	0-2		59,272
28	itpr1	**Juventus**	A	L	0-1		21,095
29	itpr1	**Fiorentina**	H	W	2-0	Lavezzi 23, 31	42,661
30	itpr1	**Reggina**	A	D	1-1	Sosa 76	12,383
31	itpr1	**Palermo**	H	W	1-0	Hamsik 90	49,341
32	itpr1	**Catania**	A	L	0-3		14,246
33	itpr1	**Atalanta**	H	W	2-0	Hamsik 62, Lavezzi 64	38,688
34	itpr1	**Parma**	A	W	2-1	Domizzi 45 pen, Bogliacino 72	17,996
35	itpr1	**Siena**	H	D	0-0		39,086
36	itpr1	**Torino**	A	L	1-2	Contini 53	21,112
37	itpr1	**AC Milan**	H	W	3-1	Hamsik 36, Domizzi 69 pen, Garics 90	55,874
38	itpr1	**Lazio**	A	L	1-2	Domizzi 83	14,891

LEAGUE APPEARANCES, BOOKINGS AND CAPS

	AGE (on 01/07/08)	IN NAMED 18	APPEARANCES	COUNTING GAMES	MINUTES ON PITCH	YELLOW CARDS	RED CARDS	CAPS THIS SEASON	NATIONAL SIDE
Goalkeepers									
Biagio Del Giudice	19	4	0	0	0	0	0	-	Italy
Matteo Gianello	32	32	16	16	1440	1	0	-	Italy
Gennaro Iezzo	35	23	19	19	1710	0	0	-	Italy
Nicolas Navarro	23	17	3	3	270	0	0	-	Argentina
Defenders									
Paolo Cannavaro	27	34	34	33	3005	7	1	-	Italy
Matteo Contini	28	34	28	19	1929	9	0	-	Italy
Andrea Cupi	32	21	16	11	1187	1	0	-	Italy
Maurizio Domizzi	28	29	29	27	2523	10	2	-	Italy
Gyorgy Garics	24	29	26	16	1668	2	0	8	Austria
Gianluca Grava	31	34	19	11	1213	1	0	-	Italy
Ruben Maldonado	29	3	2	1	141	1	0	-	Paraguay
Erminio Rullo	24	13	4	1	156	2	0	-	Italy
Fabiano Santacroce	21	13	13	11	1013	7	0	-	Italy
Mirko Savini	29	29	29	25	2378	8	0	-	Italy
Midfielders									
Manuele Blasi	27	27	27	26	2322	17	1	-	Italy
Mariano A Bogliacino	28	38	35	11	1555	1	0	-	Uruguay
Marco Capparella	33	7	2	0	32	0	0	-	Italy
Mario D'Urso	18	1	0	0	0	0	0	-	Italy
Samuele Dalla Bona	27	16	2	0	50	0	0	-	Italy
Walter Gargano	23	35	34	33	2993	6	2	11	Uruguay
Marek Hamsik	20	37	37	28	2874	3	0	11	Slovakia
Daniele Mannini	24	15	15	12	1205	6	0	-	Italy
Francesco Montervino	30	38	9	0	204	0	0	-	Italy
Michele Pazienza	25	14	13	8	807	4	0	-	Italy
Forwards									
Emanuele Calaio	26	37	26	4	835	1	0	-	Italy
Roberto De Zerbi	29	13	3	0	119	1	0	-	Italy
Ezequiel Ivan Lavezzi	23	35	35	33	2964	6	0	-	Argentina
Roberto Carlos Sosa	33	35	30	8	1146	3	0	-	Argentina
Marcelo Zalayeta	29	22	22	17	1731	0	1	-	Uruguay

TEAM OF THE SEASON

G – Matteo Gianello, CG: 16 DR: 72

D – Matteo Contini, CG: 19 DR: 80

D – Paolo Cannavaro, CG: 33 DR: 66

D – Mirko Savini, CG: 25 DR: 62

D – Maurizio Domizzi, CG: 27 DR: 61

M – Marek Hamsik, CG: 28 SD: 8

M – Manuele Blasi, CG: 26 SD: 2

M – Walter Gargano, CG: 33 SD: -2

M – Daniele Mannini, CG: 12 SD: -5

F – Marcelo Zalayeta, CG: 17 SR: 216

F – Ezequiel Lavezzi, CG: 33 SR: 370

MONTHLY POINTS TALLY

AUGUST	0	0%
SEPTEMBER	10	67%
OCTOBER	4	33%
NOVEMBER	4	44%
DECEMBER	5	42%
JANUARY	1	11%
FEBRUARY	6	40%
MARCH	10	56%
APRIL	7	58%
MAY	3	33%

LEAGUE GOALS

	PLAYER	MINS	GOALS	S RATE
1	Hamsik	2874	9	319
2	Zalayeta	1731	8	216
3	Domizzi	2523	8	315
4	Lavezzi	2964	8	370
5	Sosa	1146	6	191
6	Bogliacino	1555	3	518
7	Calaio	835	2	417
8	Gargano	2993	2	1496
9	Mannini	1205	1	1205
10	Garics	1668	1	1668
11	Contini	1929	1	1929
	Other		0	
	TOTAL		49	

TOP POINT EARNERS

	PLAYER	GAMES	AV PTS
1	Daniele Mannini	12	1.83
2	Marek Hamsik	28	1.64
3	Manuele Blasi	26	1.50
4	Matteo Contini	19	1.47
5	Marcelo D Zalayeta	17	1.47
6	Paolo Cannavaro	33	1.42
7	Gennaro Iezzo	19	1.42
8	Mirko Savini	25	1.40
9	Walter A G Gargano	33	1.36
10	Ezequiel Ivan Lavezzi	33	1.27
	CLUB AVERAGE:		1.32

DISCIPLINARY RECORDS

	PLAYER	YELLOW	RED	AVE
1	Manuele Blasi	17	1	129
2	Fabiano Santacroce	7	0	144
3	Daniele Mannini	6	0	200
4	Michele Pazienza	4	0	201
5	Maurizio Domizzi	10	2	210
6	Matteo Contini	9	0	214
7	Mirko Savini	8	0	297
8	Walter A G Gargano	6	2	374
9	Paolo Cannavaro	7	1	375
10	Roberto C Sosa	3	0	382
11	Ezequiel I Lavezzi	6	0	494
12	Gyorgy Garics	2	0	834
13	Emanuele Calaio	1	0	835
	Other	7	1	
	TOTAL	93	7	

KEY GOALKEEPER

Matteo Gianello

Goals Conceded in the League	20	Counting Games League games when player was on pitch for at least 70 minutes	16
Defensive Rating Ave number of mins between League goals conceded while on the pitch	72	Clean Sheets In League games when player was on pitch for at least 70 minutes	5

KEY PLAYERS - DEFENDERS

Matteo Contini

Goals Conceded Number of League goals conceded while the player was on the pitch	24	Clean Sheets In League games when player was on pitch for at least 70 minutes	6
Defensive Rating Ave number of mins between League goals conceded while on the pitch	80	Club Defensive Rating Average number of mins between League goals conceded by the club this season	64

	PLAYER	CON LGE	CLEAN SHEETS	DEF RATE
1	Matteo Contini	24	6	80 mins
2	Paolo Cannavaro	45	11	66 mins
3	Mirko Savini	38	10	62 mins
4	Maurizio Domizzi	41	8	61 mins

KEY PLAYERS - MIDFIELDERS

Marek Hamsik

Goals in the League	9	Contribution to Attacking Power Average number of minutes between League team goals while on pitch	65
Defensive Rating Average number of mins between League goals conceded while on the pitch	73	Scoring Difference Defensive Rating minus Contribution to Attacking Power	8

	PLAYER	LGE GOALS	DEF RATE	POWER	SCORE DIFF
1	Marek Hamsik	9	73	65	8 mins
2	Manuele Blasi	0	68	66	2 mins
3	Walter Gargano	2	63	65	-2 mins
4	Daniele Mannini	1	70	75	-5 mins

KEY PLAYERS - GOALSCORERS

Marcelo Danubio Zalayeta

Goals in the League	8	Player Strike Rate Average number of minutes between League goals scored by player	216
Contribution to Attacking Power Average number of minutes between League team goals while on pitch	66	Club Strike Rate Average number of minutes between League goals scored by club	68

	PLAYER	LGE GOALS	POWER	STRIKE RATE
1	Marcelo Zalayeta	8	66	216 mins
2	Marek Hamsik	9	65	319 mins
3	Ezequiel Ivan Lavezzi	8	67	370 mins
4	Daniele Mannini	1	75	1205 mins

Lete
Marcelo Zalayeta and Ivan Lavezzi

SQUAD APPEARANCES

Match	1	2	3	4	5	6	7	8	9	10	11	12	13	14	15	16	17	18	19	20	21	22	23	24	25	26	27	28	29	30	31	32	33	34	35	36	37	38
Venue	H	A	H	A	H	H	A	A	H	A	H	A	H	A	H	A	H	A	H	A	H	A	H	A	A	H	H	A	H	A	H	A	H	A	H	A	H	A
Competition	L	L	L	L	L	L	L	L	L	L	L	L	L	L	L	L	L	L	L	L	L	L	L	L	L	L	L	L	L	L	L	L	L	L	L	L	L	L
Result	L	W	W	D	W	L	L	D	W	L	D	L	W	L	W	D	D	L	D	L	W	L	L	W	L	W	L	L	W	D	W	L	W	W	D	L	W	L

Goalkeepers
- Biagio Del Giudice
- Matteo Gianello
- Gennaro Iezzo
- Nicolas Navarro

Defenders
- Paolo Cannavaro
- Matteo Contini
- Andrea Cupi
- Maurizio Domizzi
- Gyorgy Garics
- Gianluca Grava
- Ruben Maldonado
- Erminio Rullo
- Fabiano Santacroce
- Mirko Savini

Midfielders
- Manuele Blasi
- Mariano A Bogliacino
- Marco Capparella
- Mario D'Urso
- Samuele Dalla Bona
- Walter Gargano
- Marek Hamsik
- Daniele Mannini
- Francesco Montervino
- Michele Pazienza

Forwards
- Emanuele Calaio
- Roberto De Zerbi
- Ezequiel Ivan Lavezzi
- Roberto Carlos Sosa
- Marcelo Zalayeta

KEY: On all match; On bench; Subbed or sent off (Counting game); Subbed or sent off (playing less than 70 minutes); Subbed on from bench (Counting Game); Subbed on (playing less than 70 minutes); Subbed on and then subbed or sent off (Counting Game); Subbed on and then subbed or sent off (playing less than 70 minutes); Not in 16

ATALANTA

Final Position: **9th**

NICKNAME: LA DEA

KEY: ☐Won ☐Drawn ☐Lost

						Attendance
1	itpr1	Reggina	A D	1-1	Doni 84 pen	12,963
2	itpr1	Parma	H W	2-0	Zampagna 21 pen, Carrozzieri 65	10,141
3	itpr1	Fiorentina	A D	2-2	Doni 51, Zampagna 86	30,000
4	itpr1	Lazio	H W	2-1	Langella 43, Zampagna 90	12,000
5	itpr1	Siena	A D	1-1	Doni 61	8,377
6	itpr1	Sampdoria	A L	0-3		20,000
7	itpr1	Udinese	H D	0-0		10,000
8	itpr1	Torino	H D	2-2	Ferreira Pinto 45, Doni 67 pen	8,955
9	itpr1	Empoli	A W	1-0	Doni 75	5,616
10	itpr1	Cagliari	H D	2-2	Capelli 55, Doni 80	10,000
11	itpr1	Catania	A W	2-1	Langella 57, 59	16,000
12	itpr1	Inter Milan	A L	1-2	Floccari 39	45,000
13	itpr1	Napoli	H W	5-1	Floccari 6, Langella 20, Doni 36 Carrozzieri 47, Ferreira Pinto 73	15,000
14	itpr1	Juventus	A L	0-1		20,000
15	itpr1	Palermo	H L	1-3	Amauri 62 og	10,000
16	itpr1	Livorno	A D	1-1	Tissone 33	8,500
17	itpr1	Roma	H L	1-2	Ferreira Pinto 17	15,000
18	itpr1	Genoa	A L	1-2	Doni 67 pen	23,743
19	itpr1	AC Milan	H W	2-1	Langella 42, Tissone 68	0
20	itpr1	Reggina	H D	2-2	Rivalta 18, Langella 46	7,000
21	itpr1	Parma	A W	3-2	Pellegrino 18, Bellini 55, Floccari 68	13,089
22	itpr1	Fiorentina	H D	2-2	Muslimovic 30, 90	10,822
23	itpr1	Lazio	A L	0-3		19,003
24	itpr1	Siena	H D	2-2	Floccari 42, 45	9,226
25	itpr1	Sampdoria	H W	4-1	Doni 13, 31, Floccari 36, Capelli 53	10,244
26	itpr1	Udinese	A L	0-2		13,245
27	itpr1	Torino	A L	0-1		18,208
28	itpr1	Empoli	H W	4-1	Langella 19, Doni 27, Padoin 77, 84	9,220
29	itpr1	Cagliari	A L	0-1		10,000
30	itpr1	Catania	H D	0-0		9,414
31	itpr1	AC Milan	A W	2-1	Floccari 32, Langella 42	50,990
32	itpr1	Inter Milan	H L	0-2		19,081
33	itpr1	Napoli	A L	0-2		38,688
34	itpr1	Juventus	H L	0-4		21,323
35	itpr1	Palermo	A D	0-0		23,288
36	itpr1	Livorno	H W	3-2	Doni 56, Ferreira Pinto 59, Padoin 89	8,999
37	itpr1	Roma	A L	1-2	Bellini 88	36,416
38	itpr1	Genoa	H W	2-0	Floccari 32, Marconi 90	10,925

LEAGUE APPEARANCES, BOOKINGS AND CAPS

	AGE (on 01/07/08)	IN NAMED 18	APPEARANCES	COUNTING GAMES	MINUTES ON PITCH	YELLOW CARDS	RED CARDS	CAPS THIS SEASON	NATIONAL SIDE
Goalkeepers									
Ferdinando Coppola	30	38	38	38	3420	2	0	-	Italy
Andrea Ivan	35	21	0	0	0	0	0	-	Italy
Defenders									
Pereira da Silva	26	1	1	0	52	1	0	-	Brazil
Manuel Belleri	30	32	20	12	1347	1	0	-	Italy
Gianpaolo Bellini	28	23	23	22	2037	8	0	-	Italy
Daniele Capelli	22	32	23	19	1855	4	0	-	Italy
Morris Carrozzieri	27	20	20	18	1710	13	2	-	Italy
Riccardo Fissore	28	12	2	1	129	1	0	-	Italy
Thomas Manfredini	28	25	18	15	1421	6	0	-	Italy
Maximilano Pellegrino	28	33	26	20	1980	7	1	-	Argentina
Claudio Rivalta	30	31	30	28	2587	3	0	-	Italy
Leonardo Talamonti	26	9	9	5	650	4	0	-	Argentina
Midfielders									
Antonio Bernardini	34	15	6	2	247	1	0	-	Italy
Giacomo Bonaventura	18	2	1	0	14	0	0	-	Italy
Francisco Costinha	33	1	1	0	53	0	0	-	Portugal
Diego De Ascentis	31	33	30	19	2018	8	0	-	Italy
Cristiano Doni	35	30	30	27	2532	13	1	-	Italy
Adriano F Pinto	28	38	38	29	3026	1	0	-	Brazil
Tiberio Guarente	22	32	26	18	1887	6	0	-	Italy
Simone Padoin	24	38	30	10	1529	3	0	-	Italy
Ivan Radovanovic	19	5	0	0	0	0	0	-	Serbia
Fernando D Tissone	21	36	35	25	2583	8	0	-	Argentina
Forwards									
Marino Defendi	22	12	6	0	166	0	0	-	Italy
Sergio Floccari	26	37	34	28	2580	3	0	-	Italy
Simone Inzaghi	32	26	19	0	455	2	1	-	Italy
Antonio Langella	31	29	27	7	1551	8	0	-	Italy
Michele Marconi	19	6	4	0	98	0	0	-	Italy
Zlatan Muslimovic	27	22	10	2	409	2	0	-	Bosnia
Michele Paolucci	22	16	9	0	255	0	0	-	Italy
Riccardo Zampagna	33	10	10	8	825	4	1	-	Italy

TEAM OF THE SEASON

G — Ferdinando Coppola CG: 38 DR: 62

D — Morris Carrozzieri CG: 18 DR: 66

D — Claudio Rivalta CG: 28 DR: 66

D — Daniele Capelli CG: 19 DR: 62

D — Thomas Manfredini CG: 15 DR: 61

M — Cristiano Doni CG: 27 SD: 7

M — Fernando D Tissone CG: 25 SD: 1

M — Adriano Ferreira Pinto CG: 29 SD: 0

M — Tiberio Guarente CG: 18 SD: -7

F — Antonio Langella CG: 17 SR: 205

F — Sergio Floccari CG: 28 SR: 333

MONTHLY POINTS TALLY

AUGUST	1	33%
SEPTEMBER	8	53%
OCTOBER	6	50%
NOVEMBER	3	50%
DECEMBER	4	33%
JANUARY	4	33%
FEBRUARY	8	53%
MARCH	7	39%
APRIL	1	8%
MAY	6	67%

LEAGUE GOALS

	PLAYER	MINS	GOALS	S RATE
1	Doni	2622	12	218
2	Langella	1641	8	205
3	Floccari	2670	8	333
4	Ferreira Pinto	3116	4	779
5	Zampagna	825	3	275
6	Padoin	1529	3	509
7	Bellini	2127	2	1063
8	Muslimovic	409	2	204
9	Carrozzieri	1800	2	900
10	Capelli	1945	2	972
11	Tissone	2673	2	1336
12	Marconi	98	1	98
13	Pellegrino	1980	1	1980
	Other		1	
	TOTAL		51	

TOP POINT EARNERS

	PLAYER	GAMES	AV PTS
1	Claudio Rivalta	28	1.57
2	Fernando D Tissone	25	1.48
3	Adriano Ferreira Pinto	29	1.48
4	Daniele Capelli	19	1.37
5	Cristiano Doni	27	1.33
6	Sergio Floccari	28	1.29
7	Thomas Manfredini	15	1.27
8	Ferdinando Coppola	38	1.26
9	Tiberio Guarente	18	1.22
10	Diego De Ascentis	19	1.21
	CLUB AVERAGE:		1.26

DISCIPLINARY RECORDS

	PLAYER	YELLOW	RED	AVE
1	Morris Carrozzieri	13	2	120
2	Simone Inzaghi	2	1	151
3	L Talamonti	4	0	162
4	R Zampagna	4	1	165
5	Cristiano Doni	13	1	187
6	Antonio Langella	8	0	205
7	Thomas Manfredini	6	0	236
8	M Pellegrino	7	1	247
9	Diego De Ascentis	8	0	252
10	Gianpaolo Bellini	8	0	265
11	Tiberio Guarente	6	0	329
12	Fernando Tissone	8	0	334
13	Daniele Capelli	4	0	486
	Other	13	0	
	TOTAL	104	6	

KEY GOALKEEPER

Ferdinando Coppola

Goals Conceded in the League	56	Counting Games League games when player was on pitch for at least 70 minutes	39
Defensive Rating Ave number of mins between League goals conceded while on the pitch	62	Clean Sheets In League games when player was on pitch for at least 70 minutes	7

KEY PLAYERS - DEFENDERS

Morris Carrozzieri

Goals Conceded Number of League goals conceded while the player was on the pitch	27	Clean Sheets In League games when player was on pitch for at least 70 minutes	4
Defensive Rating Ave number of mins between League goals conceded while on the pitch	66	Club Defensive Rating Average number of mins between League goals conceded by the club this season	62

	PLAYER	CON LGE	CLEAN SHEETS	DEF RATE
1	Morris Carrozzieri	27	4	66 mins
2	Claudio Rivalta	40	6	66 mins
3	Daniele Capelli	31	5	62 mins
4	Thomas Manfredini	23	3	61 mins

KEY PLAYERS - MIDFIELDERS

Cristiano Doni

Goals in the League	12	Contribution to Attacking Power Average number of minutes between League team goals while on pitch	62
Defensive Rating Average number of mins between League goals conceded while on the pitch	69	Scoring Difference Defensive Rating minus Contribution to Attacking Power	7

	PLAYER	LGE GOALS	DEF RATE	POWER	SCORE DIFF
1	Cristiano Doni	12	69	62	7 mins
2	Fernando Damian Tissone	2	63	62	1 mins
3	Adriano Ferreira Pinto	4	64	64	0 mins
4	Tiberio Guarente	0	54	61	-7 mins

KEY PLAYERS - GOALSCORERS

Antonio Langella

Goals in the League	8	Player Strike Rate Average number of minutes between League goals scored by player	205
Contribution to Attacking Power Average number of minutes between League team goals while on pitch	60	Club Strike Rate Average number of minutes between League goals scored by club	67

	PLAYER	LGE GOALS	POWER	STRIKE RATE
1	Antonio Langella	8	60	205 mins
2	Cristiano Doni	12	62	218 mins
3	Riccardo Zampagna	3	68	275 mins
4	Sergio Floccari	8	66	333 mins

DAIHATSU
SPORT
Cristiano Doni

SQUAD APPEARANCES

Match	1	2	3	4	5	6	7	8	9	10	11	12	13	14	15	16	17	18	19	20	21	22	23	24	25	26	27	28	29	30	31	32	33	34	35	36	37	38
Venue	A	H	A	H	A	A	H	H	A	H	A	A	H	A	H	A	H	A	H	H	A	H	A	H	H	A	A	H	A	H	A	H	A	H	A	H	A	H
Competition	L	L	L	L	L	L	L	L	L	L	L	L	L	L	L	L	L	L	L	L	L	L	L	L	L	L	L	L	L	L	L	L	L	L	L	L	L	L
Result	D	W	D	W	D	L	D	D	W	D	W	L	W	L	L	D	L	L	W	D	W	D	L	D	W	L	L	W	L	D	W	L	L	L	D	W	L	W

Goalkeepers
Ferdinando Coppola
Andrea Ivan

Defenders
Pereira da Silva Adriano
Manuel Belleri
Gianpaolo Bellini
Daniele Capelli
Morris Carrozzieri
Riccardo Fissore
Thomas Manfredini
Maximilano Pellegrino
Claudio Rivalta
Leonardo Talamonti

Midfielders
Antonio Bernardini
Giacomo Bonaventura
Francisco Costinha
Diego De Ascentis
Cristiano Doni
Adriano Ferreira Pinto
Tiberio Guarente
Simone Padoin
Ivan Radovanovic
Fernando D Tissone

Forwards
Marino Defendi
Sergio Floccari
Simone Inzaghi
Antonio Langella
Michele Marconi
Zlatan Muslimovic
Michele Paolucci
Riccardo Zampagna

KEY: On all match · On bench · Subbed or sent off (Counting game) · Subbed or sent off (playing less than 70 minutes) · Subbed on from bench (Counting Game) · Subbed on (playing less than 70 minutes) · Subbed on and then subbed or sent off (Counting Game) · Subbed on and then subbed or sent off (playing less than 70 minutes) · Not in 16

GENOA

Final Position: **10th**

NICKNAME: IL GRIFONE (THE GRIFFIN)

KEY: ☐Won ☐Drawn ☐Lost

							Attendance
1	itpr1	**AC Milan**	H	L	0-3		23,533
2	itpr1	**Catania**	A	D	0-0		16,000
3	itpr1	**Livorno**	H	D	1-1	Borriello 56	18,000
4	itpr1	**Sampdoria**	A	D	0-0		33,060
5	itpr1	**Udinese**	H	W	3-2	Borriello 20, 47, 74 pen	22,253
6	itpr1	**Napoli**	A	W	2-1	Cannavaro 12 og, Sculli 89	-
7	itpr1	**Cagliari**	H	W	2-0	Borriello 59, Di Vaio 73	24,000
8	itpr1	**Juventus**	A	L	0-1		20,000
9	itpr1	**Fiorentina**	H	D	0-0		23,000
10	itpr1	**Inter Milan**	A	L	1-4	Konko 73	47,230
11	itpr1	**Palermo**	H	D	3-3	Leon 59, 66, Borriello 82	32,503
12	itpr1	**Reggina**	A	L	0-2		11,000
13	itpr1	**Roma**	H	L	0-1		24,106
14	itpr1	**Torino**	A	D	1-1	Borriello 47	18,000
15	itpr1	**Siena**	H	L	1-3	Figueroa 89	23,000
16	itpr1	**Empoli**	A	D	1-1	Masiello 86	6,483
17	itpr1	**Parma**	H	W	1-0	Borriello 42 pen	23,000
18	itpr1	**Lazio**	A	W	2-1	Borriello 51 pen, 55	18,964
19	itpr1	**Atalanta**	H	W	2-1	Borriello 71, Figueroa 84	23,743
20	itpr1	**AC Milan**	A	L	0-2		70,000
21	itpr1	**Catania**	H	W	2-1	Sacramento 13, Borriello 71 pen	22,935
22	itpr1	**Livorno**	A	D	1-1	Di Vaio 83	9,445
23	itpr1	**Sampdoria**	H	L	0-1		37,508
24	itpr1	**Udinese**	A	W	5-3	Leon 9, Sculli 43, Borriello 54, 78, 85	13,640
25	itpr1	**Napoli**	H	W	2-0	Sculli 41, Borriello 75	26,417
26	itpr1	**Cagliari**	A	L	1-2	Lucarelli 15	13,000
27	itpr1	**Juventus**	H	L	0-2		28,151
28	itpr1	**Fiorentina**	A	L	1-3	Masiero 82	28,728
29	itpr1	**Inter Milan**	H	D	1-1	Borriello 85	27,624
30	itpr1	**Palermo**	A	W	3-2	Figueroa 29, Milanetto 50, Konko 61	23,260
31	itpr1	**Reggina**	H	W	2-0	Borriello 59, M.Rossi 90	23,349
32	itpr1	**Roma**	A	L	2-3	M.Rossi 58, Leon 59	36,366
33	itpr1	**Torino**	H	W	3-0	Di Vaio 51, Borriello 61, Sculli 69	25,751
34	itpr1	**Siena**	A	W	1-0	Konko 24	12,228
35	itpr1	**Empoli**	H	L	0-1		23,885
36	itpr1	**Parma**	A	L	0-1		17,693
37	itpr1	**Lazio**	H	L	0-2		25,077
38	itpr1	**Atalanta**	A	L	0-2		10,925

LEAGUE APPEARANCES, BOOKINGS AND CAPS

	AGE (on 01/07/08)	IN NAMED 18	APPEARANCES	COUNTING GAMES	MINUTES ON PITCH	YELLOW CARDS	RED CARDS	CAPS THIS SEASON	NATIONAL SIDE
Goalkeepers									
Rubens F Moedim	24	31	30	26	2544	5	2	-	Brazil
Alessio Scarpi	35	37	13	8	874	0	0	-	Italy
Defenders									
Francesco Bega	33	13	10	8	763	4	0	-	Italy
Cesare Bovo	25	29	27	25	2290	10	0	-	Italy
Manuel Coppola	26	12	3	1	138	1	0	-	Italy
Domenico Criscito	21	16	16	15	1400	5	0	-	Italy
Gaetano De Rosa	35	30	16	13	1245	1	1	-	Italy
Gleison P Santos	26	22	16	8	988	2	1	-	Brazil
Tommaso Ghinassi	21	10	1	0	21	0	0	-	Italy
Fabiano L Rodrigues	29	33	28	15	1707	4	0	-	Brazil
Alessandro Lucarelli	30	36	29	22	2120	9	0	-	Italy
Andrea Masiello	22	8	4	2	193	1	0	-	Italy
Anthony V Borre	20	15	6	0	147	0	0	1	Belgium
Midfielders									
Ivan Juric	32	34	34	32	2859	11	1	-	Croatia
Abdoulay Konko	24	37	37	33	3137	6	0	-	France
Julio Cesar Leon	28	33	29	15	1949	8	0	-	Honduras
Omar Milanetto	32	34	29	21	2177	9	1	-	Italy
Matteo Paro	25	22	20	13	1351	6	0	-	Italy
Silvano R Garibaldi	19	4	2	0	25	0	0	-	Italy
Marco Rossi	30	34	33	24	2525	3	0	-	Italy
Danilo V Sacramento	25	25	22	16	1636	6	2	-	Brazil
Forwards									
Marco Borriello	26	35	35	31	2904	9	0	3	Italy
Marco Di Vaio	31	30	22	3	992	2	1	-	Italy
Luciano G Figueroa	27	32	20	3	739	2	0	-	Argentina
Mirco Gasparetto	28	1	1	1	90	0	0	-	Italy
Matias N Masiero	20	8	2	0	47	0	0	-	Uruguay
Ndiaye Papa Waigo	24	11	9	2	327	0	0	-	Senegal
Richard Porta	24	0	0	0	0	0	0	-	Uruguay
Wilson R Fonseca	23	6	3	1	108	0	0	-	Brazil
Giuseppe Sculli	27	36	34	15	2118	6	0	-	Italy

TEAM OF THE SEASON

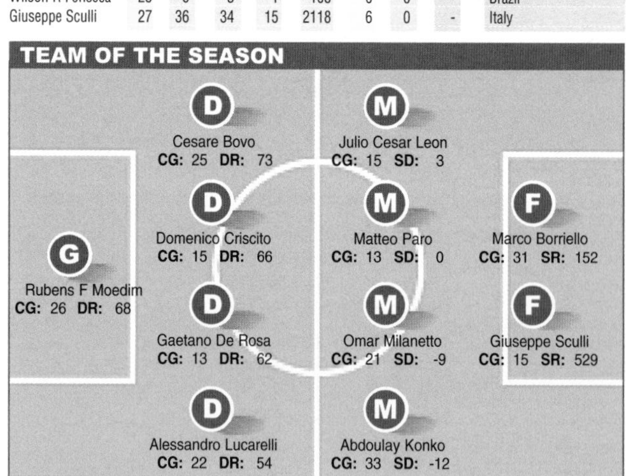

D
Cesare Bovo
CG: 25 DR: 73
M
Julio Cesar Leon
CG: 15 SD: 3
G
Rubens F Moedim
CG: 26 DR: 68
D
Domenico Criscito
CG: 15 DR: 66
M
Matteo Paro
CG: 13 SD: 0
F
Marco Borriello
CG: 31 SR: 152
D
Gaetano De Rosa
CG: 13 DR: 62
M
Omar Milanetto
CG: 21 SD: -9
F
Giuseppe Sculli
CG: 15 SR: 529
D
Alessandro Lucarelli
CG: 22 DR: 54
M
Abdoulay Konko
CG: 33 SD: -12

MONTHLY POINTS TALLY

AUGUST	0	0%
SEPTEMBER	9	60%
OCTOBER	4	33%
NOVEMBER	1	11%
DECEMBER	5	42%
JANUARY	6	67%
FEBRUARY	10	67%
MARCH	7	39%
APRIL	6	50%
MAY	0	0%

LEAGUE GOALS

	PLAYER	MINS	GOALS	S RATE
1	Borriello	2904	19	152
2	Leon	1949	4	487
3	Sculli	2118	4	529
4	Figueroa	739	3	246
5	Di Vaio	992	3	330
6	Konko	3137	3	1045
7	Rossi, M	2525	2	1262
8	Masiero	47	1	47
9	Masiello	193	1	193
10	Sacramento	1636	1	1636
11	Lucarelli	2120	1	2120
12	Milanetto	2177	1	2177
	Other		0	
	TOTAL		43	

TOP POINT EARNERS

	PLAYER	GAMES	AV PTS
1	Giuseppe Sculli	15	1.60
2	Cesare Bovo	25	1.56
3	Domenico Criscito	15	1.47
4	Matteo Paro	13	1.46
5	Marco Borriello	31	1.39
6	Abdoulay Konko	33	1.39
7	Fabiano L Rodrigues	15	1.33
8	Omar Milanetto	21	1.33
9	Gaetano De Rosa	13	1.31
10	Ivan Juric	32	1.25
	CLUB AVERAGE:		1.26

DISCIPLINARY RECORDS

	PLAYER	YELLOW	RED	AVE
1	Francesco Bega	4	0	190
2	Danilo Sacramento	6	2	204
3	Omar Milanetto	9	1	217
4	Matteo Paro	6	0	225
5	Cesare Bovo	10	0	229
6	A Lucarelli	9	0	235
7	Ivan Juric	11	1	238
8	Julio Cesar Leon	8	0	243
9	Domenico Criscito	5	0	280
10	Marco Borriello	9	0	322
11	Gleison P Santos	2	1	329
12	Marco Di Vaio	2	1	330
13	Giuseppe Sculli	6	0	353
	Other	21	3	
	TOTAL	108	9	

KEY GOALKEEPER

Rubens Fernando Moedim

Goals Conceded in the League	37	Counting Games League games when player was on pitch for at least 70 minutes	26
Defensive Rating Ave number of mins between League goals conceded while on the pitch	68	Clean Sheets In League games when player was on pitch for at least 70 minutes	7

KEY PLAYERS - DEFENDERS

Cesare Bovo

Goals Conceded Number of League goals conceded while the player was on the pitch	31	Clean Sheets In League games when player was on pitch for at least 70 minutes	7
Defensive Rating Ave number of mins between League goals conceded while on the pitch	73	Club Defensive Rating Average number of mins between League goals conceded by the club this season	65

	PLAYER	CON LGE	CLEAN SHEETS	DEF RATE
1	Cesare Bovo	31	7	73 mins
2	Domenico Criscito	21	3	66 mins
3	Gaetano De Rosa	20	2	62 mins
4	Alessandro Lucarelli	39	5	54 mins

KEY PLAYERS - MIDFIELDERS

Julio Cesar Leon

Goals in the League	4	Contribution to Attacking Power Average number of minutes between League team goals while on pitch	59
Defensive Rating Average number of mins between League goals conceded while on the pitch	62	Scoring Difference Defensive Rating minus Contribution to Attacking Power	3

	PLAYER	LGE GOALS	DEF RATE	POWER	SCORE DIFF
1	Julio Cesar Leon	4	62	59	3 mins
2	Matteo Paro	0	61	61	0 mins
3	Omar Milanetto	1	68	77	-9 mins
4	Abdoulay Konko	3	66	78	-12 mins

KEY PLAYERS - GOALSCORERS

Marco Borriello

Goals in the League	19	Player Strike Rate Average number of minutes between League goals scored by player	152
Contribution to Attacking Power Average number of minutes between League team goals while on pitch	72	Club Strike Rate Average number of minutes between League goals scored by club	77

	PLAYER	LGE GOALS	POWER	STRIKE RATE
1	Marco Borriello	19	72	152 mins
2	Julio Cesar Leon	4	59	487 mins
3	Giuseppe Sculli	4	84	529 mins
4	Abdoulay Konko	3	78	1045 mins

HOLLAND
AT GROUP
Abdoulay Konko

SQUAD APPEARANCES

Match	1	2	3	4	5	6	7	8	9	10	11	12	13	14	15	16	17	18	19	20	21	22	23	24	25	26	27	28	29	30	31	32	33	34	35	36	37	38
Venue	H	A	H	A	H	A	H	A	H	A	H	A	H	A	H	A	H	A	H	A	H	A	H	A	H	A	H	A	H	A	H	A	H	A	H	A	H	A
Competition	L	L	L	L	L	L	L	L	L	L	L	L	L	L	L	L	L	L	L	L	L	L	L	L	L	L	L	L	L	L	L	L	L	L	L	L	L	L
Result	L	D	D	D	W	W	W	L	D	L	D	L	L	D	L	D	W	W	W	L	W	D	L	W	W	L	L	L	D	W	W	L	W	W	L	L	L	L

Goalkeepers
Rubens Fernando Moedim
Alessio Scarpi

Defenders
Francesco Bega
Cesare Bovo
Manuel Coppola
Domenico Criscito
Gaetano De Rosa
Gleison Pinto dos Santos
Tommaso Ghinassi
Fabiano Lima Rodrigues
Alessandro Lucarelli
Andrea Masiello
Anthony Vanden Borre

Midfielders
Ivan Juric
Abdoulay Konko
Julio Cesar Leon
Omar Milanetto
Matteo Paro
Silvano Raggio Garibaldi
Marco Rossi
Danilo Valerio Sacramento

Forwards
Marco Borriello
Marco Di Vaio
Luciano Gabriel Figueroa
Mirco Gasparetto
Matias Nicolas Masiero
Ndiaye Papa Waigo
Richard Porta
Wilson R Fonseca
Giuseppe Sculli

KEY: On all match / On bench / Subbed or sent off (Counting game) / Subbed or sent off (playing less than 70 minutes) / Subbed on from bench (Counting Game) / Subbed on (playing less than 70 minutes) / Subbed on and then subbed or sent off (Counting Game) / Subbed on and then subbed or sent off (playing less than 70 minutes) / Not in 16

PALERMO

Final Position: **11th**

NICKNAME: ROSANERO

KEY: ☐Won ☐Drawn ☐Lost

							Attendance
1	itpr1	Roma	H	L	0-2		32,202
2	itpr1	Livorno	A	W	4-2	Rinaudo 9, Miccoli 23, 37, Amauri 41	8,475
3	itpr1	Torino	H	D	1-1	Simplicio 4	30,000
4	ucrl1	Mlada Boleslav	A	W	1-0	Jankovic 90	4,110
5	itpr1	Cagliari	A	W	1-0	Zaccardo 14	18,000
6	itpr1	AC Milan	H	W	2-1	Diana 73, Miccoli 90	30,761
7	itpr1	Empoli	A	L	1-3	Cavani 39	5,000
8	ucrL2	Mlada Boleslav	H	L	2-4*	(*on penalties)	6,335
9	itpr1	Reggina	H	D	1-1	Amauri 90	22,845
10	itpr1	Udinese	A	D	1-1	Amauri 17	14,851
11	itpr1	Inter Milan	H	D	0-0		33,972
12	itpr1	Parma	H	D	1-1	Amauri 87 pen	30,000
13	itpr1	Genoa	A	D	3-3	Cavani 8, Brienza 76, Amauri 90	32,503
14	itpr1	Napoli	H	W	2-1	Tedesco 57, 66	25,138
15	itpr1	Juventus	A	L	0-5		25,000
16	itpr1	Catania	A	L	1-3	Caserta 63	16,000
17	itpr1	Fiorentina	H	W	2-0	Miccoli 17, Simplicio 83	22,823
18	itpr1	Atalanta	A	W	3-1	Cavani 13, Langella 35 og, Amauri 54	10,000
19	itpr1	Lazio	H	D	2-2	Simplicio 34, Amauri 46	24,184
20	itpr1	Sampdoria	A	L	0-3		19,574
21	itpr1	Siena	H	L	2-3	Amauri 4, Miccoli 75 pen	22,542
22	itpr1	Roma	A	L	0-1		33,000
23	itpr1	Livorno	H	W	1-0	Miccoli 76	23,000
24	itpr1	Torino	A	L	1-3	Amauri 36	17,914
25	itpr1	Cagliari	H	W	2-1	Cavani 23, Jankovic 45	21,829
26	itpr1	AC Milan	A	L	1-2	Bresciano 9	50,643
27	itpr1	Empoli	H	W	2-0	Simplicio 14, Rinaudo 38	22,000
28	itpr1	Reggina	A	D	0-0		10,316
29	itpr1	Udinese	H	D	1-1	Simplicio 32	24,833
30	itpr1	Inter Milan	A	L	1-2	Materazzi 25 og	49,360
31	itpr1	Parma	A	L	1-2	Cavani 68	12,599
32	itpr1	Genoa	H	L	2-3	Amauri 24 pen, 90	23,260
33	itpr1	Napoli	A	L	0-1		49,341
34	itpr1	Juventus	H	W	3-2	Amauri 11, 45, Cassani 89	34,271
35	itpr1	Catania	H	W	1-0	Miccoli 84	24,847
36	itpr1	Fiorentina	A	L	0-1		28,827
37	itpr1	Atalanta	H	D	0-0		23,288
38	itpr1	Lazio	A	W	2-1	Amauri 82, 90	20,786
39	itpr1	Sampdoria	H	L	0-2		23,929
40	itpr1	Siena	A	D	2-2	Jankovic 24, Miccoli 30	9,339

LEAGUE APPEARANCES, BOOKINGS AND CAPS

	AGE (on 01/07/08)	IN NAMED 18	APPEARANCES	COUNTING GAMES	MINUTES ON PITCH	YELLOW CARDS	RED CARDS	CAPS THIS SEASON	NATIONAL SIDE
Goalkeepers									
Federico Agliardi	25	38	10	9	856	0	0	-	Italy
Alberto Fontana	41	35	30	28	2564	1	0	-	Italy
Defenders									
Federico Balzaretti	26	16	16	16	1422	6	0	-	Italy
Andrea Barzagli	27	36	34	33	2980	5	1	9	Italy
Giuseppe Biava	31	31	24	22	2041	6	1	-	Italy
Ciro Capuano	26	18	12	8	849	3	0	-	Italy
Mattia Cassani	24	33	25	15	1546	6	0	-	Italy
Alberto Cossentino	19	12	1	1	80	0	0	-	Italy
Herman P Dellafiore	23	1	0	0	0	0	0	-	Argentina
Marco Pisano	26	6	5	3	301	2	0	-	Italy
Leandro Rinaudo	25	34	22	18	1722	5	2	-	Italy
Samuele Romeo	19	2	0	0	0	0	0	-	Italy
Francesco Velardi	20	1	0	0	0	0	0	-	Italy
Cristian Zaccardo	26	36	36	32	2945	8	0	1	Italy
Midfielders									
Mark Bresciano	28	31	26	6	1269	4	0	6	Australia
Fabio Caserta	29	32	27	16	1875	4	2	-	Italy
Luca Di Matteo	20	9	2	0	49	0	0	-	Italy
Stefano Aimo Diana	30	15	14	10	999	1	0	-	Italy
Roberto Guana	27	34	32	23	2357	12	0	-	Italy
Bosko Jankovic	24	34	26	9	1279	2	0	7	Serbia
Giulio Migliaccio	27	33	31	22	2298	7	0	-	Italy
Fabio E Simplicio	28	34	32	24	2512	6	0	-	Brazil
Giovanni Tedesco	36	33	16	3	694	1	0	-	Italy
Forwards									
Carvalho Amauri	28	34	34	33	2992	9	1	-	Brazil
Franco Brienza	29	13	8	2	334	0	0	-	Italy
Edgar Cani	18	8	1	0	18	0	0	-	Albania
Paolo Carbonaro	19	3	1	0	12	0	0	-	Italy
Edison Cavani	21	34	33	13	1776	3	0	2	Uruguay
Davide Matteini	26	1	0	0	0	0	0	-	Italy
Fabrizio Miccoli	29	28	22	13	1591	6	0	-	Italy

TEAM OF THE SEASON

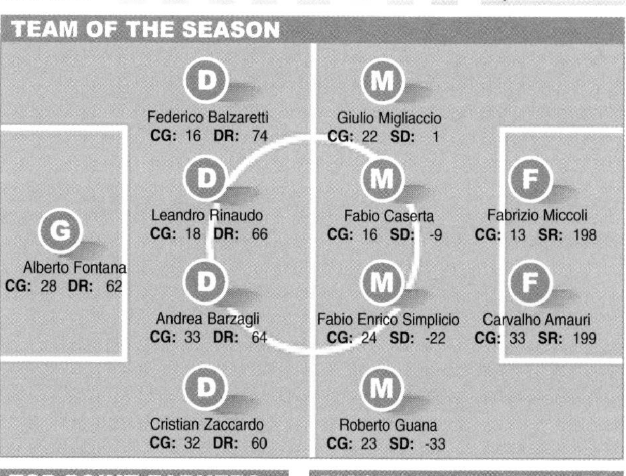

G
Alberto Fontana
CG: 28 DR: 62
D
Federico Balzaretti
CG: 16 DR: 74
D
Leandro Rinaudo
CG: 18 DR: 66
D
Andrea Barzagli
CG: 33 DR: 64
D
Cristian Zaccardo
CG: 32 DR: 60
M
Giulio Migliaccio
CG: 22 SD: 1
M
Fabio Caserta
CG: 16 SD: -9
M
Fabio Enrico Simplicio
CG: 24 SD: -22
M
Roberto Guana
CG: 23 SD: -33
F
Fabrizio Miccoli
CG: 13 SR: 198
F
Carvalho Amauri
CG: 33 SR: 199

MONTHLY POINTS TALLY

AUGUST	0	0%
SEPTEMBER	10	67%
OCTOBER	4	33%
NOVEMBER	4	44%
DECEMBER	7	58%
JANUARY	0	0%
FEBRUARY	9	60%
MARCH	2	11%
APRIL	7	58%
MAY	4	44%

LEAGUE GOALS

	PLAYER	MINS	GOALS	S RATE
1	Amauri	2992	15	199
2	Miccoli	1591	8	198
3	Cavani	1776	5	355
4	Simplicio	2512	5	502
5	Tedesco	694	2	347
6	Jankovic	1279	2	639
7	Rinaudo	1722	2	861
8	Brienza	334	1	334
9	Diana	999	1	999
10	Bresciano	1269	1	1269
11	Cassani	1546	1	1546
12	Caserta	1875	1	1875
13	Zaccardo	2945	1	2945
	Other		0	
	TOTAL		45	

TOP POINT EARNERS

	PLAYER	GAMES	AV PTS
1	Giulio Migliaccio	22	1.64
2	Edison Cavani	13	1.62
3	Andrea Barzagli	33	1.39
4	Alberto Fontana	28	1.32
5	Leandro Rinaudo	18	1.28
6	Mattia Cassani	15	1.27
7	Fabio Caserta	16	1.25
8	Federico Balzaretti	16	1.25
9	Cristian Zaccardo	32	1.25
10	Fabrizio Miccoli	13	1.23
	CLUB AVERAGE:		1.24

DISCIPLINARY RECORDS

	PLAYER	YELLOW	RED	AVE
1	Roberto Guana	12	0	196
2	Federico Balzaretti	6	0	237
3	Leandro Rinaudo	5	2	246
4	Mattia Cassani	6	0	257
5	Fabrizio Miccoli	6	0	265
6	Ciro Capuano	3	0	283
7	Giuseppe Biava	6	1	291
8	Carvalho Amauri	9	1	299
9	Fabio Caserta	4	2	312
10	Mark Bresciano	4	0	317
11	Giulio Migliaccio	7	0	328
12	Cristian Zaccardo	8	0	368
13	Fabio E Simplicio	6	0	418
	Other	13	1	
	TOTAL	95	7	

KEY GOALKEEPER

Alberto Fontana

Goals Conceded in the League	41	**Counting Games** League games when player was on pitch for at least 70 minutes	28
Defensive Rating Ave number of mins between League goals conceded while on the pitch	62	**Clean Sheets** In League games when player was on pitch for at least 70 minutes	5

KEY PLAYERS - DEFENDERS

Federico Balzaretti

Goals Conceded Number of League goals conceded while the player was on the pitch	19	**Clean Sheets** In League games when player was on pitch for at least 70 minutes	5
Defensive Rating Ave number of mins between League goals conceded while on the pitch	74	**Club Defensive Rating** Average number of mins between League goals conceded by the club this season	60

	PLAYER	CON LGE	CLEAN SHEETS	DEF RATE
1	Federico Balzaretti	19	5	74 mins
2	Leandro Rinaudo	26	4	66 mins
3	Andrea Barzagli	46	8	64 mins
4	Cristian Zaccardo	49	8	60 mins

KEY PLAYERS - MIDFIELDERS

Giulio Migliaccio

Goals in the League	0	**Contribution to Attacking Power** Average number of minutes between League team goals while on pitch	62
Defensive Rating Average number of mins between League goals conceded while on the pitch	63	**Scoring Difference** Defensive Rating minus Contribution to Attacking Power	1

	PLAYER	LGE GOALS	DEF RATE	POWER	SCORE DIFF
1	Giulio Migliaccio	0	63	62	1 mins
2	Fabio Caserta	1	69	78	-9 mins
3	Fabio Enrico Simplicio	5	54	76	-22 mins
4	Roberto Guana	0	54	87	-33 mins

KEY PLAYERS - GOALSCORERS

Fabrizio Miccoli

Goals in the League	8	**Player Strike Rate** Average number of minutes between League goals scored by player	198
Contribution to Attacking Power Average number of minutes between League team goals while on pitch	66	**Club Strike Rate** Average number of minutes between League goals scored by club	72

	PLAYER	LGE GOALS	POWER	STRIKE RATE
1	Fabrizio Miccoli	8	66	198 mins
2	Carvalho De Oliveira Amauri	15	72	199 mins
3	Edison Cavani	5	49	355 mins
4	Fabio Enrico Simplicio	5	76	502 mins

Amauri

SQUAD APPEARANCES

Match	1	2	3	4	5	6	7	8	9	10	11	12	13	14	15	16	17	18	19	20	21	22	23	24	25	26	27	28	29	30	31	32	33	34	35	36	37	38	39	40
Venue	H	A	H	A	A	H	A	H	H	A	H	H	A	H	A	A	H	A	H	A	H	A	H	A	H	A	H	A	H	A	A	H	A	H	H	A	H	A	H	A
Competition	L	L	L	E	L	L	L	E	L	L	L	L	L	L	L	L	L	L	L	L	L	L	L	L	L	L	L	L	L	L	L	L	L	L	L	L	L	L	L	L
Result	L	W	D	W	W	W	L	L	D	D	D	D	D	W	L	L	W	W	D	L	L	L	W	L	W	L	W	D	D	L	L	L	L	W	W	L	D	W	L	D

Goalkeepers
Federico Agliardi
Alberto Fontana

Defenders
Federico Balzaretti
Andrea Barzagli
Giuseppe Biava
Ciro Capuano
Mattia Cassani
Alberto Cossentino
Herman Paolo Dellafiore
Marco Pisano
Leandro Rinaudo
Samuele Romeo
Francesco Velardi
Cristian Zaccardo

Midfielders
Mark Bresciano
Fabio Caserta
Luca Di Matteo
Stefano Aimo Diana
Roberto Guana
Bosko Jankovic
Giulio Migliaccio
Fabio Enrico Simplicio
Giovanni Tedesco

Forwards
Carvalho Amauri
Franco Brienza
Edgar Cani
Paolo Carbonaro
Edison Cavani
Davide Matteini
Fabrizio Miccoli

KEY: On all match · On bench · Subbed or sent off (Counting game) · Subbed or sent off (playing less than 70 minutes) · Subbed on from bench (Counting Game) · Subbed on (playing less than 70 minutes) · Subbed on and then subbed or sent off (Counting Game) · Subbed on and then subbed or sent off (playing less than 70 minutes) · Not in 16

LAZIO

Final Position: **12th**

NICKNAME: AQUILOTTI (YOUNG EAGLES) KEY: ☐Won ☐Drawn ☐Lost

							Attendance
1	ecql1	**D Bucharest**	H	D	1-1	Mutarelli 53	50,000
2	itpr1	**Torino**	H	D	2-2	Pandev 56, Rocchi 61	21,495
3	ecql2	**D Bucharest**	A	W	3-1	Rocchi 47 pen, 65, Pandev 54	50,000
4	itpr1	**Sampdoria**	A	D	0-0		20,564
5	itpr1	**Empoli**	H	D	0-0		19,460
6	ecgpc	**Olympiakos**	A	D	1-1	Zauri 77	0
7	itpr1	**Atalanta**	A	L	1-2	Mutarelli 69	12,000
8	itpr1	**Cagliari**	H	W	3-1	Rocchi 48, 85, Pandev 60	17,652
9	itpr1	**Reggina**	A	D	1-1	Kolarov 73	12,000
10	ecgpc	**Real Madrid**	H	D	2-2	Pandev 32, 75	60,000
11	itpr1	**AC Milan**	H	L	1-5	Mauri 23	40,000
12	itpr1	**Livorno**	A	W	1-0	Pandev 45	9,934
13	ecgpc	**W Bremen**	A	L	1-2	Manfredini Sisostri 82	36,587
14	itpr1	**Udinese**	H	L	0-1		17,536
15	itpr1	**Roma**	A	L	2-3	Rocchi 12, CD.Ledesma 70	54,860
16	itpr1	**Fiorentina**	H	L	0-1		25,687
17	ecgpc	**W Bremen**	H	W	2-1	Rocchi 57, 68	35,045
18	itpr1	**Parma**	H	W	1-0	Firmani 90	20,000
19	ecgpc	**Olympiakos**	H	L	1-2	Pandev 30	30,000
20	itpr1	**Siena**	A	D	1-1	Pandev 23	8,000
21	itpr1	**Inter Milan**	A	L	0-3		45,000
22	itpr1	**Catania**	H	W	2-0	Rocchi 8, Pandev 89	15,000
23	ecgpc	**Real Madrid**	A	L	1-3	Pandev 80	76,000
24	itpr1	**Juventus**	H	L	2-3	Pandev 36, 90	30,000
25	itpr1	**Palermo**	A	D	2-2	Firmani 59, Tare 80	24,184
26	itpr1	**Genoa**	H	L	1-2	Mauri 23	18,964
27	itpr1	**Napoli**	A	D	2-2	CD.Ledesma 26, Pandev 31	34,480
28	itpr1	**Torino**	A	D	0-0		18,000
29	itpr1	**Sampdoria**	H	W	2-1	Mauri 37, Rocchi 77	18,683
30	itpr1	**Empoli**	A	L	0-1		7,232
31	itpr1	**Atalanta**	H	W	3-0	Rocchi 26 pen, 88 pen, Pandev 56	19,003
32	itpr1	**Cagliari**	A	L	0-1		12,000
33	itpr1	**Reggina**	H	W	1-0	Bianchi 45 pen	17,663
34	itpr1	**AC Milan**	A	D	1-1	Bianchi 54	52,016
35	itpr1	**Livorno**	H	W	2-0	Rocchi 15, Pandev 25	19,110
36	itpr1	**Udinese**	A	D	2-2	Rocchi 11, CD.Ledesma 80	13,084
37	itpr1	**Roma**	H	W	3-2	Pandev 44, Rocchi 58 pen, Behrami 90	49,284
38	itpr1	**Fiorentina**	A	L	0-1		26,579
39	itpr1	**Inter Milan**	H	D	1-1	Rocchi 59	32,802
40	itpr1	**Parma**	A	D	2-2	Pandev 35, Bianchi 38	13,370
41	itpr1	**Siena**	H	D	1-1	Mutarelli 45	18,996
42	itpr1	**Catania**	A	L	0-1		16,000
43	itpr1	**Juventus**	A	L	2-5	Bianchi 55, Siviglia 61	20,588
44	itpr1	**Palermo**	H	L	1-2	Pandev 25 pen	20,786
45	itpr1	**Genoa**	A	W	2-0	Pandev 31, Rocchi 45	25,077
46	itpr1	**Napoli**	H	W	2-1	Rocchi 14, Firmani 71	14,891

LEAGUE APPEARANCES, BOOKINGS AND CAPS

	AGE (on 01/07/08)	IN NAMED 18	APPEARANCES	COUNTING GAMES	MINUTES ON PITCH	YELLOW CARDS	RED CARDS	CAPS THIS SEASON	NATIONAL SIDE
Goalkeepers									
Marco Ballotta	44	37	29	29	2610	0	0	-	Italy
Nestor F Muslera	22	37	9	9	810	1	0	-	Uruguay
Defenders									
Ivan Artipoli	22	5	1	0	66	0	0	-	Italy
Emilson S Cribari	28	34	31	29	2684	1	0	-	Brazil
Lorenzo De Silvestri	20	31	24	15	1570	5	2	-	Italy
Mobido Diakite	21	1	1	0	40	0	0	-	France
Aleksandar Kolarov	22	34	24	15	1495	4	1	-	Serbia
Stefan Daniel Radu	21	14	11	10	948	1	0	2	Romania
David Rozehnal	27	17	10	7	652	1	0	10	Czech Republic
Lionel Scaloni	30	19	12	7	793	0	0	-	Argentina
Sebastiano Siviglia	35	20	19	19	1678	5	2	-	Italy
Guglielmo Stendardo	27	16	13	11	1083	2	1	-	Italy
Midfielders									
Roberto Baronio	30	13	7	4	481	2	0	-	Italy
Valon Behrami	23	22	22	19	1816	5	0	6	Switzerland
Ousmane Dabo	31	14	13	4	724	6	1	-	France
Fabio Firmani	30	10	7	5	460	3	1	-	Italy
Cristian D Ledesma	25	33	32	31	2805	8	0	-	Argentina
Christian Sisostri	33	34	23	13	1337	2	0	-	Ivory Coast
Stefano Mauri	28	28	24	15	1583	1	0	2	Italy
Mourad Meghni	24	22	19	1	701	0	0	-	France
Gaby Mudingayi	26	30	27	18	1955	12	0	4	Belgium
Massimo Mutarelli	30	24	24	19	1866	6	2	-	Italy
Luciano Zauri	30	19	18	16	1512	7	1	-	Italy
Forwards									
Rolando Bianchi	25	17	15	8	809	3	1	-	Italy
Simone Del Nero	26	13	5	1	178	1	0	-	Italy
Stephen A Makinwa	24	16	14	4	573	0	0	-	Nigeria
Goran Pandev	24	33	32	27	2534	7	0	5	Macedonia
Tommaso Rocchi	30	36	36	27	2690	0	0	-	Italy
Igli Tare	34	30	18	3	539	2	0	-	Albania
Fabio Vignaroli	32	17	9	2	392	0	0	-	Italy

TEAM OF THE SEASON

G — Marco Ballotta CG: 29 DR: 72

D — Sebastiano Siviglia CG: 19 DR: 76

D — Aleksandar Kolarov CG: 15 DR: 62

D — Emilson S Cribari CG: 29 DR: 61

D — Lorenzo De Silvestri CG: 15 DR: 50

M — Valon Behrami CG: 19 SD: 17

M — Cristian D Ledesma CG: 31 SD: 14

M — Stefano Mauri CG: 15 SD: 0

M — Christian Sisostri CG: 13 SD: 0

F — Goran Pandev CG: 27 SR: 181

F — Tommaso Rocchi CG: 27 SR: 192

MONTHLY POINTS TALLY

AUGUST	1	33%
SEPTEMBER	6	40%
OCTOBER	3	25%
NOVEMBER	3	50%
DECEMBER	5	33%
JANUARY	2	22%
FEBRUARY	9	60%
MARCH	9	50%
APRIL	2	17%
MAY	6	67%

LEAGUE GOALS

	PLAYER	MINS	GOALS	S RATE
1	Pandev	2534	14	181
2	Rocchi	2690	14	192
3	Bianchi	809	4	202
4	Mauri	1583	3	527
5	Firmani	460	3	153
6	Mutarelli	1866	2	933
7	Ledesma, CD	2805	3	935
8	Tare	539	1	539
9	Kolarov	1495	1	1495
10	Siviglia	1678	1	1678
11	Behrami	1816	1	1816
	Other		0	
	TOTAL		47	

TOP POINT EARNERS

	PLAYER	GAMES	AV PTS
1	Valon Behrami	19	1.53
2	Sebastiano Siviglia	19	1.47
3	Tommaso Rocchi	27	1.41
4	Cristian Daniel Ledesma	31	1.32
5	Goran Pandev	27	1.30
6	Marco Ballotta	29	1.24
7	Christian J Sisostri	13	1.23
8	Stefano Mauri	15	1.20
9	Luciano Zauri	16	1.19
10	Gaby Mudingayi	18	1.11
	CLUB AVERAGE:		1.21

DISCIPLINARY RECORDS

	PLAYER	YELLOW	RED	AVE
1	Ousmane Dabo	6	1	103
2	Fabio Firmani	3	1	115
3	Gaby Mudingayi	12	0	162
4	Luciano Zauri	7	1	189
5	Rolando Bianchi	3	1	202
6	L De Silvestri	5	2	224
7	Massimo Mutarelli	6	2	233
8	Sebastiano Siviglia	5	2	239
9	Roberto Baronio	2	0	240
10	Igli Tare	2	0	269
11	Aleksandar Kolarov	4	1	299
12	Cristian D Ledesma	8	0	350
13	G Stendardo	2	1	361
	Other	19	0	
	TOTAL	84	12	

KEY GOALKEEPER

Marco Ballotta

Goals Conceded in the League	36	**Counting Games** League games when player was on pitch for at least 70 minutes	29
Defensive Rating Ave number of mins between League goals conceded while on the pitch	72	**Clean Sheets** In League games when player was on pitch for at least 70 minutes	9

KEY PLAYERS - DEFENDERS

Sebastiano Siviglia

Goals Conceded Number of League goals conceded while the player was on the pitch	22	**Clean Sheets** In League games when player was on pitch for at least 70 minutes	6
Defensive Rating Ave number of mins between League goals conceded while on the pitch	76	**Club Defensive Rating** Average number of mins between League goals conceded by the club this season	68

	PLAYER	CON LGE	CLEAN SHEETS	DEF RATE
1	Sebastiano Siviglia	22	6	76 mins
2	Aleksandar Kolarov	24	2	62 mins
3	Emilson Sanchez Cribari	44	7	61 mins
4	Lorenzo De Silvestri	31	4	50 mins

KEY PLAYERS - MIDFIELDERS

Valon Behrami

Goals in the League	1	**Contribution to Attacking Power** Average number of minutes between League team goals while on pitch	58
Defensive Rating Average number of mins between League goals conceded while on the pitch	75	**Scoring Difference** Defensive Rating minus Contribution to Attacking Power	17

	PLAYER	LGE GOALS	DEF RATE	POWER	SCORE DIFF
1	Valon Behrami	1	75	58	17 mins
2	Cristian Daniel Ledesma	3	82	68	14 mins
3	Stefano Mauri	3	63	63	0 mins
4	Christian Jose' Manfredini Sisostri	0	78	78	0 mins

KEY PLAYERS - GOALSCORERS

Goran Pandev

Goals in the League	14	**Player Strike Rate** Average number of minutes between League goals scored by player	181
Contribution to Attacking Power Average number of minutes between League team goals while on pitch	72	**Club Strike Rate** Average number of minutes between League goals scored by club	74

	PLAYER	LGE GOALS	POWER	STRIKE RATE
1	Goran Pandev	14	72	181 mins
2	Tommaso Rocchi	14	70	192 mins
3	Stefano Mauri	3	63	527 mins
4	Massimo Mutarelli	2	71	933 mins

PUMA
Goran Pandev

SQUAD APPEARANCES

Match	1	2	3	4	5	6	7	8	9	10	11	12	13	14	15	16	17	18	19	20	21	22	23
Venue	H	H	A	A	H	A	A	H	A	H	H	A	A	H	A	H	H	H	H	A	A	H	A
Competition	C	L	C	L	L	C	L	L	L	C	L	L	C	L	L	L	C	L	C	L	L	L	C
Result	D	D	W	D	D	D	L	W	D	D	L	W	L	L	L	L	W	W	L	D	L	W	L

Match	24	25	26	27	28	29	30	31	32	33	34	35	36	37	38	39	40	41	42	43	44	45	46
Venue	H	A	H	A	A	H	A	H	A	H	A	H	A	H	A	H	A	H	A	A	H	A	H
Competition	L	L	L	L	L	L	L	L	L	L	L	L	L	L	L	L	L	L	L	L	L	L	L
Result	L	D	L	D	D	W	L	W	L	W	D	W	D	W	L	D	D	D	L	L	L	W	W

Goalkeepers
Marco Ballotta
Nestor F Muslera
Defenders
Ivan Artipoli
Emilson Sanchez Cribari
Lorenzo De Silvestri
Mobido Diakite
Aleksandar Kolarov
Stefan Daniel Radu
David Rozehnal
Lionel Scaloni
Sebastiano Siviglia
Guglielmo Stendardo
Midfielders
Roberto Baronio
Valon Behrami
Ousmane Dabo
Fabio Firmani
Cristian Daniel Ledesma
Christian Sisostri
Stefano Mauri
Mourad Meghni
Gaby Mudingayi
Massimo Mutarelli
Luciano Zauri
Forwards
Rolando Bianchi
Simone Del Nero
Stephen Ayodele Makinwa
Goran Pandev
Tommaso Rocchi
Igli Tare
Fabio Vignaroli

KEY: On all match | On bench | Subbed or sent off (Counting game) | Subbed or sent off (playing less than 70 minutes) | Subbed on from bench (Counting Game) | Subbed on (playing less than 70 minutes) | Subbed on and then subbed or sent off (Counting Game) | Subbed on and then subbed or sent off (playing less than 70 minutes) | Not in 16

SIENA

Final Position: **13th**

NICKNAME: BIANCONERI. ROBUR.

KEY: ☐ Won ☐ Drawn ☐ Lost

					Score	Scorers	Attendance
1	itpr1	Sampdoria	H	L	1-2	Corvia 68	10,768
2	itpr1	Roma	A	L	0-3		44,037
3	itpr1	AC Milan	H	D	1-1	Maccarone 24	14,084
4	itpr1	Torino	A	D	1-1	Maccarone 53	20,000
5	itpr1	Atalanta	H	D	1-1	Loria 31	8,377
6	itpr1	Cagliari	A	L	0-1		12,000
7	itpr1	Empoli	H	W	3-0	Maccarone 70 pen, Locatelli 79 Galloppa 82	8,377
8	itpr1	Fiorentina	A	L	0-3		27,361
9	itpr1	Reggina	H	D	0-0		8,435
10	itpr1	Catania	H	D	1-1	De Ceglie 80	8,000
11	itpr1	Parma	A	D	2-2	De Ceglie 33, Galloppa 90	13,172
12	itpr1	Livorno	H	L	2-3	Maccarone 18, Loria 90	8,000
13	itpr1	Udinese	A	L	0-2		12,000
14	itpr1	Lazio	H	D	1-1	Maccarone 32	8,000
15	itpr1	Genoa	A	W	3-1	Frick 11, 24, Loria 20	23,000
16	itpr1	Napoli	H	D	1-1	Frick 63	9,000
17	itpr1	Juventus	A	L	0-2		20,000
18	itpr1	Inter Milan	H	L	2-3	Cordoba 31 og, Forestieri 90	13,000
19	itpr1	Palermo	A	W	3-2	Locatelli 5, Maccarone 11, Loria 78	22,542
20	itpr1	Sampdoria	A	L	0-1		19,562
21	itpr1	Roma	H	W	3-0	Vergassola 11, Tonetto 43 og, Frick 83	10,158
22	itpr1	AC Milan	A	L	0-1		51,552
23	itpr1	Torino	H	D	0-0		8,913
24	itpr1	Atalanta	A	D	2-2	Bertotto 32, Locatelli 40	9,226
25	itpr1	Cagliari	H	W	1-0	Maccarone 88	8,913
26	itpr1	Empoli	A	W	2-0	Portanova 33, RiganÃ? 90	6,139
27	itpr1	Fiorentina	H	W	1-0	Maccarone 80	12,785
28	itpr1	Reggina	A	L	0-4		10,300
29	itpr1	Catania	A	D	0-0		16,655
30	itpr1	Parma	H	W	2-0	Maccarone 87 pen, 90	8,000
31	itpr1	Livorno	A	D	0-0		10,207
32	itpr1	Udinese	H	D	1-1	Kharja 69	8,652
33	itpr1	Lazio	A	D	1-1	Loria 88	18,996
34	itpr1	Genoa	H	L	0-1		12,228
35	itpr1	Napoli	A	D	0-0		39,086
36	itpr1	Juventus	H	W	1-0	Kharja 7	15,419
37	itpr1	Inter Milan	A	D	2-2	Maccarone 30, Kharja 69	76,633
38	itpr1	Palermo	H	D	2-2	Maccarone 2, 58	9,339

LEAGUE APPEARANCES, BOOKINGS AND CAPS

	AGE (on 01/07/08)	IN NAMED 18	APPEARANCES	COUNTING GAMES	MINUTES ON PITCH	YELLOW CARDS	RED CARDS	CAPS THIS SEASON	NATIONAL SIDE
Goalkeepers									
D Eleftheropoulos	31	38	12	12	1060	1	0	-	Greece
Alex Manninger	31	37	26	26	2340	2	0	5	Austria
Defenders									
Valerio Bertotto	35	25	16	15	1337	4	0	-	Italy
Manuel Coppola	26	14	12	10	972	4	0	-	Italy
Daniele Ficagna	27	17	7	5	497	2	0	-	Italy
Leandro Grimi	23	16	13	12	1118	1	0	-	Argentina
Simone Loria	31	36	36	36	3240	6	0	-	Italy
Daniele Portanova	29	37	37	36	3285	5	0	-	Italy
Luca Rossettini	23	35	25	20	1870	4	0	-	Italy
Andrea Rossi	21	24	15	11	1058	3	0	-	Italy
Midfielders									
Do C Neto Alberto	33	31	15	0	366	2	0	-	Brazil
Prosperi C Caetano	24	5	2	0	50	0	0	-	Brazil
Paul C Codrea	27	30	30	21	2125	9	1	5	Romania
Paolo De Ceglie	21	34	29	24	2281	1	0	-	Italy
Daniele Galloppa	23	33	30	22	2223	6	0	-	Italy
Mirko Guadalupi	21	1	1	0	28	0	0	-	-
David Jarolim	29	2	2	1	86	0	0	6	Czech Republic
Lukas Jarolim	31	31	22	15	1553	1	0	-	Czech Republic
Houssine Kharja	25	16	15	9	1016	3	0	3	Morocco
Tomas Locatelli	32	31	30	10	1823	2	0	-	Italy
Ricardo Matias Veron	27	5	0	0	0	0	0	-	Argentina
Simone Vergassola	32	30	29	24	2396	5	1	-	Italy
Forwards									
Christian Bucchi	31	13	10	3	491	0	0	-	Italy
Enrico Chiesa	37	3	2	0	60	0	0	-	Italy
Daniele Corvia	23	19	14	0	374	2	0	-	Italy
Fernando Forestieri	18	27	17	3	600	1	0	-	Argentina
Mario Frick	33	28	27	11	1656	4	1	-	Liechtenstein
Massimo Maccarone	28	35	35	33	3014	3	1	-	Italy
Richard Porta	24	8	1	0	29	0	0	-	Uruguay
Christian Rigano	34	18	17	3	618	4	0	-	Italy

TEAM OF THE SEASON

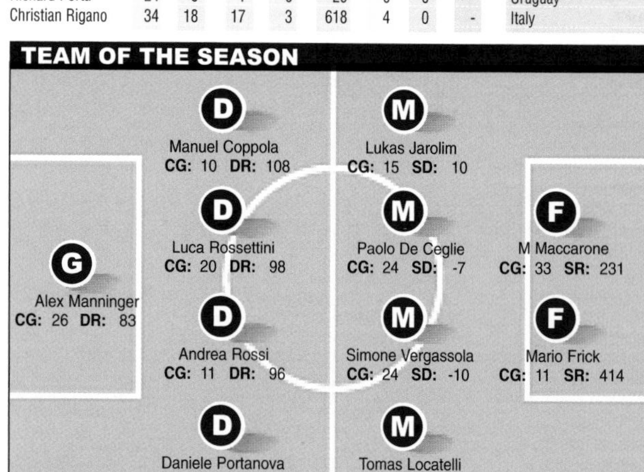

D
Manuel Coppola
CG: 10 DR: 108
M
Lukas Jarolim
CG: 15 SD: 10
D
Luca Rossettini
CG: 20 DR: 98
M
Paolo De Ceglie
CG: 24 SD: -7
F
M Maccarone
CG: 33 SR: 231
G
Alex Manninger
CG: 26 DR: 83
D
Andrea Rossi
CG: 11 DR: 96
M
Simone Vergassola
CG: 24 SD: -10
F
Mario Frick
CG: 11 SR: 414
D
Daniele Portanova
CG: 36 DR: 76
M
Tomas Locatelli
CG: 10 SD: -12

MONTHLY POINTS TALLY

Month	Points	%
AUGUST	0	0%
SEPTEMBER	3	20%
OCTOBER	5	42%
NOVEMBER	1	11%
DECEMBER	5	42%
JANUARY	3	33%
FEBRUARY	8	53%
MARCH	11	61%
APRIL	3	25%
MAY	5	56%

LEAGUE GOALS

	PLAYER	MINS	GOALS	S RATE
1	Maccarone	3014	**13**	231
2	Loria	3240	**5**	648
3	Frick	1656	**4**	414
4	Kharja	1016	**3**	338
5	Locatelli	1823	**3**	607
6	Galloppa	2223	**2**	1111
7	De Ceglie	2281	**2**	1140
8	Corvia	374	**1**	374
9	Forestieri	600	**1**	600
10	Rigano	618	**1**	618
11	Bertotto	1337	**1**	1337
12	Vergassola	2396	**1**	2396
13	Portanova	3285	**1**	3285
	Other		0	
	TOTAL		**38**	

TOP POINT EARNERS

	PLAYER	GAMES	AV PTS
1	Lukas Jarolim	15	**1.33**
2	Alex Manninger	26	**1.31**
3	Massimo Maccarone	33	**1.27**
4	Paul Constantin Codrea	21	**1.24**
5	Daniele Portanova	36	**1.22**
6	Luca Rossettini	20	**1.20**
7	Simone Loria	36	**1.17**
8	Daniele Galloppa	22	**1.14**
9	Simone Vergassola	24	**1.13**
10	Paolo De Ceglie	24	**1.04**
	CLUB AVERAGE:		**1.16**

DISCIPLINARY RECORDS

	PLAYER	YELLOW	RED	AVE
1	Christian Rigano	4	0	**154**
2	Paul C Codrea	9	1	**212**
3	Manuel Coppola	4	0	**243**
4	Daniele Ficagna	2	0	**248**
5	Mario Frick	4	1	**331**
6	Valerio Bertotto	4	0	**334**
7	Houssine Kharja	3	0	**338**
8	Andrea Rossi	3	0	**352**
9	Daniele Galloppa	6	0	**370**
10	Simone Vergassola	5	1	**399**
11	Luca Rossettini	4	0	**467**
12	Simone Loria	6	0	**540**
13	Fernando Forestieri	1	0	**600**
	Other	16	1	
	TOTAL	**71**	**4**	

KEY GOALKEEPER

Alex Manninger

Goals Conceded in the League	28	Counting Games League games when player was on pitch for at least 70 minutes	26
Defensive Rating Ave number of mins between League goals conceded while on the pitch	83	Clean Sheets In League games when player was on pitch for at least 70 minutes	10

KEY PLAYERS - GOALSCORERS

Massimo Maccarone

Goals in the League	13	Player Strike Rate Average number of minutes between League goals scored by player	231
Contribution to Attacking Power Average number of minutes between League team goals while on pitch	83	Club Strike Rate Average number of minutes between League goals scored by club	85

	PLAYER	LGE GOALS	POWER	STRIKE RATE
1	Massimo Maccarone	13	83	231 mins
2	Mario Frick	4	103	414 mins
3	Tomas Locatelli	3	79	607 mins
4	Daniele Galloppa	2	101	1111 mins

KEY PLAYERS - DEFENDERS

Manuel Coppola

Goals Conceded Number of League goals conceded while the player was on the pitch	9	Clean Sheets In League games when player was on pitch for at least 70 minutes	5
Defensive Rating Ave number of mins between League goals conceded while on the pitch	108	Club Defensive Rating Average number of mins between League goals conceded by the club this season	76

	PLAYER	CON LGE	CLEAN SHEETS	DEF RATE
1	Manuel Coppola	9	5	108 mins
2	Luca Rossettini	19	7	98 mins
3	Andrea Rossi	11	4	96 mins
4	Daniele Portanova	43	12	76 mins

MONTE PASCHI

Massimo Maccarone and Daniele Galloppa

KEY PLAYERS - MIDFIELDERS

Lukas Jarolim

Goals in the League	0	Contribution to Attacking Power Average number of minutes between League team goals while on pitch	81
Defensive Rating Average number of mins between League goals conceded while on the pitch	91	Scoring Difference Defensive Rating minus Contribution to Attacking Power	10

	PLAYER	LGE GOALS	DEF RATE	POWER	SCORE DIFF
1	Lukas Jarolim	0	91	81	10 mins
2	Paolo De Ceglie	2	71	78	-7 mins
3	Simone Vergassola	1	72	82	-10 mins
4	Tomas Locatelli	3	67	79	-12 mins

SQUAD APPEARANCES

Match	1	2	3	4	5	6	7	8	9	10	11	12	13	14	15	16	17	18	19	20	21	22	23	24	25	26	27	28	29	30	31	32	33	34	35	36	37	38
Venue	H	A	H	A	H	A	H	A	H	H	A	H	A	H	A	H	A	H	A	A	H	A	H	A	H	A	H	A	A	H	A	H	A	H	A	H	A	H
Competition	L	L	L	L	L	L	L	L	L	L	L	L	L	L	L	L	L	L	L	L	L	L	L	L	L	L	L	L	L	L	L	L	L	L	L	L	L	L
Result	L	L	D	D	D	L	W	L	D	D	D	L	L	D	W	D	L	L	W	L	W	L	D	D	W	W	W	L	D	W	D	D	D	L	D	W	D	D

Goalkeepers
Dimitrios Eleftheropoulos
Alex Manninger

Defenders
Valerio Bertotto
Manuel Coppola
Daniele Ficagna
Leandro Grimi
Simone Loria
Daniele Portanova
Luca Rossettini
Andrea Rossi

Midfielders
Do Carmo Neto Alberto
Prosperi Calil Caetano
Paul Constantin Codrea
Paolo De Ceglie
Daniele Galloppa
Mirko Guadalupi
David Jarolim
Lukas Jarolim
Houssine Kharja
Tomas Locatelli
Ricardo Matias Veron
Simone Vergassola

Forwards
Christian Bucchi
Enrico Chiesa
Daniele Corvia
Fernando Martin Forestieri
Mario Frick
Massimo Maccarone
Richard Porta
Christian Rigano

KEY: On all match · On bench · Subbed or sent off (Counting game) · Subbed or sent off (playing less than 70 minutes) · Subbed on from bench (Counting Game) · Subbed on (playing less than 70 minutes) · Subbed on and then subbed or sent off (Counting Game) · Subbed on and then subbed or sent off (playing less than 70 minutes) · Not in 16

CAGLIARI

Final Position: **14th**

NICKNAME: ROSSOBLU. ISOLANI.

KEY: ☐Won ☐Drawn ☐Lost

		Opponent	H/A	Res	Score	Scorers	Attendance
1	itpr1	Napoli	A	W	2-0	Matri 49, Foggia 59 pen	39,026
2	itpr1	Juventus	H	L	2-3	Foggia 56 pen, 81 pen	23,000
3	itpr1	Parma	A	D	1-1	Matri 40	12,853
4	itpr1	Palermo	H	L	0-1		18,000
5	itpr1	Lazio	A	L	1-3	Acquafresca 70	17,652
6	itpr1	Siena	H	W	1-0	Foggia 7 pen	12,000
7	itpr1	Genoa	A	L	0-2		24,000
8	itpr1	Catania	H	D	1-1	Matri 46	9,759
9	itpr1	Torino	A	L	0-2		18,000
10	itpr1	Atalanta	A	D	2-2	Fini 39 pen, Matri 70	10,000
11	itpr1	Sampdoria	H	L	0-3		10,000
12	itpr1	AC Milan	H	L	1-2	Acquafresca 4	20,000
13	itpr1	Livorno	H	D	0-0		10,000
14	itpr1	Roma	A	L	0-2		30,000
15	itpr1	Empoli	A	L	1-4	Conti 77	5,000
16	itpr1	Inter Milan	H	L	0-2		23,000
17	itpr1	Fiorentina	A	L	1-5	Fini 5	30,000
18	itpr1	Udinese	H	L	0-1		8,000
19	itpr1	Reggina	A	L	0-2		10,122
20	itpr1	Napoli	H	W	2-1	Conti 90, Matri 90	8,000
21	itpr1	Juventus	A	D	1-1	Bianco 55	19,412
22	itpr1	Parma	H	D	1-1	Jeda 34	15,000
23	itpr1	Palermo	A	L	1-2	Cavani 51 og	21,829
24	itpr1	Lazio	H	W	1-0	Matri 88	12,000
25	itpr1	Siena	A	L	0-1		8,913
26	itpr1	Genoa	H	W	2-1	Acquafresca 29, Rubinho 45 og	13,000
27	itpr1	Catania	A	L	1-2	Conti 21	30,643
28	itpr1	Torino	H	W	3-0	Jeda 11, Acquafresca 23 pen, 57	12,000
29	itpr1	Atalanta	H	W	1-0	Acquafresca 18 pen	10,000
30	itpr1	Sampdoria	A	D	1-1	Foggia 41	19,877
31	itpr1	Roma	H	D	1-1	Ferrari 2 og	22,000
32	itpr1	AC Milan	A	L	1-3	Conti 49	52,422
33	itpr1	Livorno	A	W	2-1	Acquafresca 10, 54	13,941
34	itpr1	Empoli	H	W	2-0	Acquafresca 9, Fini 64	15,000
35	itpr1	Inter Milan	A	L	1-2	Biondini 90	56,676
36	itpr1	Fiorentina	H	W	2-1	Jeda 20, Conti 52	18,000
37	itpr1	Udinese	A	W	2-0	Acquafresca 48, Cossu 55	16,689
38	itpr1	Reggina	H	D	2-2	Larrivey 18, Bianco 81	20,000

LEAGUE APPEARANCES, BOOKINGS AND CAPS

	AGE (on 01/07/08)	IN NAMED 18	APPEARANCES	COUNTING GAMES	MINUTES ON PITCH	YELLOW CARDS	RED CARDS	CAPS THIS SEASON	NATIONAL SIDE
Goalkeepers									
Luca Capecchi	33	19	1	1	90	0	0	-	Italy
Marco Fortin	33	13	12	12	1080	0	0	-	Italy
Jan Koprivec	20	10	0	0	0	0	0	-	Slovenia
Vincenzo Marruocco	29	14	5	5	450	0	0	-	Italy
Marco Storari	31	20	20	20	1800	1	0	-	Italy
Defenders									
Alessandro Agostini	28	36	29	28	2472	8	0	-	Italy
Paolo Bianco	30	31	30	30	2700	5	0	-	Italy
Joe Bizera	28	14	8	6	562	1	0	-	Uruguay
Michele Canini	23	30	19	18	1634	4	0	-	Italy
Cristiano Del Grosso	25	35	16	11	1087	2	1	-	Italy
Michele Ferri	27	31	27	19	1984	4	0	-	Italy
Diego Luis Lopez	33	26	26	24	2175	6	0	-	Uruguay
Daniele Magliocchetti	22	17	2	2	180	1	0	-	Italy
Francesco Pisano	22	22	17	12	1232	4	1	-	Italy
Midfielders									
Rafael Cammarota	19	1	0	0	0	0	0	-	Venezuela
Davide Biondini	25	34	28	19	1958	7	0	-	Italy
Alessandro Budel	27	15	8	2	389	1	0	-	Italy
Daniele Conti	29	33	32	30	2781	14	0	-	Italy
Antonino D'Agostino	29	12	11	2	393	0	0	-	Italy
Michele Fini	34	32	32	15	1867	5	2	-	Italy
Pasquale Foggia	25	34	33	18	2122	4	0	-	Italy
Marco Mancosu	19	17	9	0	237	0	0	-	Italy
Davide Marchini	27	3	1	0	13	0	0	-	Italy
Andrea Parola	29	33	33	26	2609	8	0	-	Italy
Forwards									
Robert Acquafresca	20	36	32	12	1693	4	0	-	Italy
Andrea Cossu	28	16	16	10	1077	5	0	-	Italy
Enrico Cotza	19	9	4	1	118	0	0	-	Italy
Neves C J Jeda	29	21	20	18	1636	1	0	-	Brazil
Joaquin Larrivey	23	33	27	7	1210	3	1	-	Argentina
Allessandro Matri	23	37	34	15	1994	2	0	-	Italy

TEAM OF THE SEASON

- **G** Marco Storari — CG: 20 DR: 85
- **D** Francesco Pisano — CG: 12 DR: 82
- **D** Diego Luis Lopez — CG: 24 DR: 75
- **D** Alessandro Agostini — CG: 28 DR: 65
- **D** Michele Canini — CG: 18 DR: 65
- **M** Michele Fini — CG: 15 SD: -7
- **M** Davide Biondini — CG: 19 SD: -24
- **M** Andrea Parola — CG: 26 SD: -24
- **M** Daniele Conti — CG: 30 SD: -29
- **F** Robert Acquafresca — CG: 12 SR: 169
- **F** Allessandro Matri — CG: 15 SR: 332

MONTHLY POINTS TALLY

Month	Points	%
AUGUST	3	100%
SEPTEMBER	4	27%
OCTOBER	2	17%
NOVEMBER	0	0%
DECEMBER	1	7%
JANUARY	3	33%
FEBRUARY	5	33%
MARCH	11	61%
APRIL	6	50%
MAY	7	78%

LEAGUE GOALS

	PLAYER	MINS	GOALS	S RATE
1	Acquafresca	1693	10	169
2	Matri	1994	6	332
3	Foggia	2122	5	424
4	Conti	2781	5	556
5	Jeda	1636	3	545
6	Fini	1867	3	622
7	Bianco	2700	2	1350
8	Cossu	1077	1	1077
9	Larrivey	1210	1	1210
10	Biondini	1958	1	1958
	Other		0	
	TOTAL		37	

TOP POINT EARNERS

	PLAYER	GAMES	AV PTS
1	Francesco Pisano	12	1.67
2	Marco Storari	20	1.60
3	Neves C Jedous Jeda	18	1.56
4	Michele Canini	18	1.39
5	Robert Acquafresca	12	1.33
6	Michele Fini	15	1.27
7	Diego Luis Lopez	24	1.25
8	Davide Biondini	19	1.21
9	Alessandro Agostini	28	1.11
10	Andrea Parola	26	1.08
	CLUB AVERAGE:		1.11

DISCIPLINARY RECORDS

	PLAYER	YELLOW	RED	AVE
1	Daniele Conti	14	0	198
2	Andrea Cossu	5	0	215
3	Francesco Pisano	4	1	246
4	Michele Fini	5	2	266
5	Davide Biondini	7	0	279
6	Joaquin Larrivey	3	1	302
7	Alessandro Agostini	8	0	309
8	Andrea Parola	8	0	326
9	Diego Luis Lopez	6	0	362
10	Cristiano Del Grosso	2	1	362
11	Michele Canini	4	0	408
12	Robert Acquafresca	4	0	423
13	Michele Ferri	4	0	496
	Other	14	0	
	TOTAL	88	5	

KEY GOALKEEPER

Marco Storari

Goals Conceded in the League	21	**Counting Games** League games when player was on pitch for at least 70 minutes	20
Defensive Rating Ave number of mins between League goals conceded while on the pitch	85	**Clean Sheets** In League games when player was on pitch for at least 70 minutes	5

KEY PLAYERS - DEFENDERS

Francesco Pisano

Goals Conceded Number of League goals conceded while the player was on the pitch	15	**Clean Sheets** In League games when player was on pitch for at least 70 minutes	4
Defensive Rating Ave number of mins between League goals conceded while on the pitch	82	**Club Defensive Rating** Average number of mins between League goals conceded by the club this season	62

	PLAYER	CON LGE	CLEAN SHEETS	DEF RATE
1	Francesco Pisano	15	4	82 mins
2	Diego Luis Lopez	29	6	75 mins
3	Alessandro Agostini	38	7	65 mins
4	Michele Canini	25	4	65 mins

KEY PLAYERS - MIDFIELDERS

Michele Fini

Goals in the League	3	**Contribution to Attacking Power** Average number of minutes between League team goals while on pitch	69
Defensive Rating Average number of mins between League goals conceded while on the pitch	62	**Scoring Difference** Defensive Rating minus Contribution to Attacking Power	-7

	PLAYER	LGE GOALS	DEF RATE	POWER	SCORE DIFF
1	Michele Fini	3	62	69	-7 mins
2	Davide Biondini	1	65	89	-24 mins
3	Andrea Parola	0	62	86	-24 mins
4	Daniele Conti	5	55	84	-29 mins

KEY PLAYERS - GOALSCORERS

Robert Acquafresca

Goals in the League	10	**Player Strike Rate** Average number of minutes between League goals scored by player	169
Contribution to Attacking Power Average number of minutes between League team goals while on pitch	76	**Club Strike Rate** Average number of minutes between League goals scored by club	87

	PLAYER	LGE GOALS	POWER	STRIKE RATE
1	Robert Acquafresca	10	76	169 mins
2	Allessandro Matri	6	99	332 mins
3	Pasquale Foggia	5	117	424 mins
4	Neves Capucho Jedous Jeda	3	71	545 mins

Allessandro Matri, Pasquale Foggia and Cristiano Del Grosso

SQUAD APPEARANCES

Match	1	2	3	4	5	6	7	8	9	10	11	12	13	14	15	16	17	18	19	20	21	22	23	24	25	26	27	28	29	30	31	32	33	34	35	36	37	38
Venue	A	H	A	H	A	H	A	H	A	A	H	H	H	A	A	H	A	H	A	H	A	H	A	H	A	H	A	H	H	A	H	A	A	H	A	H	A	H
Competition	L	L	L	L	L	L	L	L	L	L	L	L	L	L	L	L	L	L	L	L	L	L	L	L	L	L	L	L	L	L	L	L	L	L	L	L	L	L
Result	W	L	D	L	L	W	L	D	L	D	L	L	D	L	L	L	L	L	L	W	D	D	L	W	L	W	L	W	W	D	D	L	W	W	L	W	W	D

Goalkeepers
Luca Capecchi
Marco Fortin
Jan Koprivec
Vincenzo Marruocco
Marco Storari

Defenders
Alessandro Agostini
Paolo Bianco
Joe Bizera
Michele Canini
Cristiano Del Grosso
Michele Ferri
Diego Luis Lopez
Daniele Magliocchetti
Francesco Pisano

idfielders
Rafael Cammarota
Davide Biondini
Alessandro Budel
Daniele Conti
Antonino D'Agostino
Michele Fini
Pasquale Foggia
Marco Mancosu
Davide Marchini
Andrea Parola

Forwards
Robert Acquafresca
Andrea Cossu
Enrico Cotza
Neves C J Jeda
Joaquin Larrivey
Allessandro Matri

KEY: ■ On all match ■ On bench
⏮ Subbed or sent off (Counting game)
« Subbed or sent off (playing less than 70 minutes)
» Subbed on from bench (Counting Game)
» Subbed on (playing less than 70 minutes)
» Subbed on and then subbed or sent off (Counting Game)
» Subbed on and then subbed or sent off (playing less than 70 minutes)
Not in 16

TORINO

Final Position: **15th**

NICKNAME: GRANATA. IL TORO.

KEY: ☐Won ☐Drawn ☐Lost

							Attendance
1	itpr1	Lazio	A	D	2-2	Rosina 34, Vailatti 68	21,495
2	itpr1	Reggina	H	D	2-2	Rosina 45, Ventola 58	2,403
3	itpr1	Palermo	A	D	1-1	Recoba 54	30,000
4	itpr1	Siena	H	D	1-1	Dellafiore 24	20,000
5	itpr1	Parma	A	L	0-2		12,932
6	itpr1	Juventus	H	L	0-1		27,000
7	itpr1	Sampdoria	H	W	1-0	Corini 87	18,000
8	itpr1	Atalanta	A	D	2-2	Ventola 75, Motta 87	8,955
9	itpr1	Cagliari	H	W	2-0	Rosina 71, Ferri 86 og	18,000
10	itpr1	Udinese	A	L	1-2	Ventola 62	14,000
11	itpr1	AC Milan	A	D	0-0		54,980
12	itpr1	Catania	H	D	1-1	Malonga 15	18,000
13	itpr1	Empoli	A	D	0-0		7,000
14	itpr1	Genoa	H	D	1-1	Lanna 55	18,000
15	itpr1	Inter Milan	A	L	0-4		45,000
16	itpr1	Roma	H	D	0-0		18,501
17	itpr1	Napoli	A	D	1-1	Rosina 36 pen	35,000
18	itpr1	Livorno	H	L	1-2	Bottone 78	18,000
19	itpr1	Fiorentina	A	L	1-2	Grella 57	27,992
20	itpr1	Lazio	H	D	0-0		18,000
21	itpr1	Reggina	A	W	3-1	Rosina 23 pen, 66 pen, Stellone 35	10,300
22	itpr1	Palermo	H	W	3-1	Diana 60, Di Michele 71, 81	17,914
23	itpr1	Siena	A	D	0-0		8,913
24	itpr1	Parma	H	D	4-4	Stellone 11, 69, Natali 45, Di Michele 82	17,999
25	itpr1	Juventus	A	D	0-0		23,000
26	itpr1	Sampdoria	A	D	2-2	Comotto 18, Di Michele 51 pen	19,032
27	itpr1	Atalanta	H	W	1-0	Barone 36	18,208
28	itpr1	Cagliari	A	L	0-3		12,000
29	itpr1	Udinese	H	L	0-1		17,599
30	itpr1	AC Milan	H	L	0-1		21,009
31	itpr1	Catania	A	W	2-1	Diana 4, Di Michele 63	16,955
32	itpr1	Empoli	H	L	0-1		18,750
33	itpr1	Genoa	A	L	0-3		25,751
34	itpr1	Inter Milan	H	L	0-1		21,865
35	itpr1	Roma	A	L	1-4	Ventola 50	34,001
36	itpr1	Napoli	H	W	2-1	Rosina 27 pen, Di Michele 56	21,112
37	itpr1	Livorno	A	W	1-0	Rosina 41	8,813
38	itpr1	Fiorentina	H	L	0-1		23,771

LEAGUE APPEARANCES, BOOKINGS AND CAPS

	AGE (on 01/07/08)	IN NAMED 18	APPEARANCES	COUNTING GAMES	MINUTES ON PITCH	YELLOW CARDS	RED CARDS	CAPS THIS SEASON	NATIONAL SIDE
Goalkeepers									
Alberto Maria Fontana	33	35	8	6	613	0	0	-	Italy
Lys Gomis	18	6	0	0	0	0	0	-	Senegal
Matteo Sereni	33	32	32	30	2807	2	0	-	Italy
Defenders									
Gianluca Comotto	29	23	23	21	1929	6	2	-	Italy
Herman P Dellafiore	23	31	28	25	2361	6	0	-	Argentina
Marco Di Loreto	33	34	28	26	2394	0	0	-	Italy
Ivan Franceschini	31	3	1	0	14	0	0	-	Italy
Salvatore Lanna	31	36	29	25	2386	8	0	-	Italy
Marco Motta	22	32	24	9	1311	6	0	-	Italy
Cesare Natali	29	25	25	22	2104	4	1	-	Italy
Angelo O Ogbonna	20	1	0	0	0	0	0	-	Italy
Marco Pisano	26	14	14	14	1260	4	0	-	Italy
Matteo Rubin	20	11	6	2	242	1	0	-	Italy
Midfielders									
Simone Barone	30	28	22	19	1811	7	1	-	Italy
Davide Bottone	22	20	7	1	264	4	0	-	Italy
Eugenio Corini	37	35	32	23	2313	9	0	-	Italy
Stefano Aimo Diana	30	17	17	15	1412	5	0	-	Italy
Vincenzo Grella	28	29	28	20	2054	9	1	4	Australia
Nikola Lazetic	30	19	15	6	847	4	0	-	Serbia
Vincenzo Nitride	18	4	0	0	0	0	0	-	Italy
Alessandro Rosina	23	35	35	23	2532	3	0	1	Italy
Tommaso Vailatti	22	10	7	1	308	0	1	-	Italy
Paolo Zanetti	25	28	25	19	1839	6	0	-	Italy
Forwards									
Sasa Bjelanovic	29	24	19	7	879	7	0	-	Croatia
David Di Michele	32	26	25	16	1753	4	0	-	Italy
Dominic Malonga	19	18	9	0	235	0	0	-	France
Masashi Oguro	28	13	3	0	39	0	0	-	Japan
Alvaro Recoba	32	27	22	5	1016	4	0	4	Uruguay
Roberto Stellone	30	22	21	16	1607	7	0	-	Italy
Nicola Ventola	30	27	21	8	1116	2	0	-	Italy

TEAM OF THE SEASON

G — Matteo Sereni — CG: 30 DR: 75

D — Salvatore Lanna — CG: 25 DR: 74

D — Marco Pisano — CG: 14 DR: 70

D — Herman Paolo Dellafiore — CG: 25 DR: 67

D — Marco Di Loreto — CG: 26 DR: 66

M — Alessandro Rosina — CG: 23 SD: -6

M — Paolo Zanetti — CG: 19 SD: -15

M — Stefano Aimo Diana — CG: 15 SD: -22

M — Vincenzo Grella — CG: 20 SD: -32

F — David Di Michele — CG: 16 SR: 292

F — Roberto Stellone — CG: 16 SR: 535

MONTHLY POINTS TALLY

SEPTEMBER	3	20%
OCTOBER	7	58%
NOVEMBER	3	33%
DECEMBER	3	25%
JANUARY	1	11%
FEBRUARY	9	60%
MARCH	7	39%
APRIL	0	0%
MAY	6	67%

LEAGUE GOALS

	PLAYER	MINS	GOALS	S RATE
1	Rosina	2532	8	316
2	Di Michele	1753	6	292
3	Ventola	1116	4	279
4	Stellone	1607	3	535
5	Diana	1412	2	706
6	Malonga	235	1	235
7	Bottone	264	1	264
8	Vailatti	308	1	308
9	Recoba	1016	1	1016
10	Motta	1311	1	1311
11	Barone	1811	1	1811
12	Comotto	1929	1	1929
13	Grella	2054	1	2054
	Other		4	
	TOTAL		35	

TOP POINT EARNERS

	PLAYER	GAMES	AV PTS
1	Marco Pisano	14	**1.36**
2	Alessandro Rosina	23	**1.35**
3	Stefano Aimo Diana	15	**1.33**
4	Roberto Stellone	16	**1.31**
5	Paolo Zanetti	19	**1.21**
6	Salvatore Lanna	25	**1.20**
7	Matteo Sereni	30	**1.17**
8	Vincenzo Grella	20	**1.10**
9	Eugenio Corini	23	**1.09**
10	Marco Di Loreto	26	**1.08**
	CLUB AVERAGE:		**1.05**

DISCIPLINARY RECORDS

	PLAYER	YELLOW	RED	AVE
1	Sasa Bjelanovic	7	0	**125**
2	Vincenzo Grella	9	1	**205**
3	Nikola Lazetic	4	0	**211**
4	Marco Motta	6	0	**218**
5	Simone Barone	7	1	**226**
6	Roberto Stellone	7	0	**229**
7	Gianluca Comotto	6	2	**241**
8	Alvaro Recoba	4	0	**254**
9	Eugenio Corini	9	0	**257**
10	Stefano Aimo Diana	5	0	**282**
11	Salvatore Lanna	8	0	**298**
12	Paolo Zanetti	6	0	**306**
13	Marco Pisano	4	0	**315**
	Other	21	1	
	TOTAL	103	5	

KEY GOALKEEPER

Matteo Sereni

Goals Conceded in the League	37	Counting Games League games when player was on pitch for at least 70 minutes	30
Defensive Rating Ave number of mins between League goals conceded while on the pitch	75	Clean Sheets In League games when player was on pitch for at least 70 minutes	10

KEY PLAYERS - DEFENDERS

Salvatore Lanna

Goals Conceded Number of League goals conceded while the player was on the pitch	32	Clean Sheets In League games when player was on pitch for at least 70 minutes	8
Defensive Rating Ave number of mins between League goals conceded while on the pitch	74	Club Defensive Rating Average number of mins between League goals conceded by the club this season	69

	PLAYER	CON LGE	CLEAN SHEETS	DEF RATE
1	Salvatore Lanna	32	8	74 mins
2	Marco Pisano	18	3	70 mins
3	Herman Paolo Dellafiore	35	6	67 mins
4	Marco Di Loreto	36	7	66 mins

KEY PLAYERS - MIDFIELDERS

Alessandro Rosina

Goals in the League	8	Contribution to Attacking Power Average number of minutes between League team goals while on pitch	87
Defensive Rating Average number of mins between League goals conceded while on the pitch	81	Scoring Difference Defensive Rating minus Contribution to Attacking Power	-6

	PLAYER	LGE GOALS	DEF RATE	POWER	SCORE DIFF
1	Alessandro Rosina	8	81	87	-6 mins
2	Paolo Zanetti	0	87	102	-15 mins
3	Stefano Aimo Diana	2	56	78	-22 mins
4	Vincenzo Grella	1	70	102	-32 mins

KEY PLAYERS - GOALSCORERS

David Di Michele

Goals in the League	6	Player Strike Rate Average number of minutes between League goals scored by player	292
Contribution to Attacking Power Average number of minutes between League team goals while on pitch	97	Club Strike Rate Average number of minutes between League goals scored by club	95

	PLAYER	LGE GOALS	POWER	STRIKE RATE
1	David Di Michele	6	97	292 mins
2	Alessandro Rosina	8	87	316 mins
3	Roberto Stellone	3	76	535 mins
4	Stefano Aimo Diana	2	78	706 mins

Gianluca Comotto

SQUAD APPEARANCES

Match	1	2	3	4	5	6	7	8	9	10	11	12	13	14	15	16	17	18	19	20	21	22	23	24	25	26	27	28	29	30	31	32	33	34	35	36	37	38
Venue	A	H	A	H	A	H	H	A	H	A	A	H	A	H	A	H	A	H	A	H	A	H	A	H	A	A	H	A	H	H	A	H	A	H	A	H	A	H
Competition	L	L	L	L	L	L	L	L	L	L	L	L	L	L	L	L	L	L	L	L	L	L	L	L	L	L	L	L	L	L	L	L	L	L	L	L	L	L
Result	D	D	D	D	L	L	W	D	W	L	D	D	D	D	L	D	D	L	L	D	W	W	D	D	D	D	W	L	L	L	W	L	L	L	L	W	W	L

Goalkeepers
Alberto Maria Fontana
Lys Gomis
Matteo Sereni
Defenders
Gianluca Comotto
Herman Paolo Dellafiore
Marco Di Loreto
Ivan Franceschini
Salvatore Lanna
Marco Motta
Cesare Natali
Angelo Obinze Ogbonna
Marco Pisano
Matteo Rubin
Midfielders
Simone Barone
Davide Bottone
Eugenio Corini
Stefano Aimo Diana
Vincenzo Grella
Nikola Lazetic
Vincenzo Nitride
Alessandro Rosina
Tommaso Vailatti
Paolo Zanetti
Forwards
Sasa Bjelanovic
David Di Michele
Dominic Malonga
Masashi Oguro
Alvaro Recoba
Roberto Stellone
Nicola Ventola

KEY: On all match; On bench; Subbed or sent off (Counting game); Subbed or sent off (playing less than 70 minutes); Subbed on from bench (Counting Game); Subbed on (playing less than 70 minutes); Subbed on and then subbed or sent off (Counting Game); Subbed on and then subbed or sent off (playing less than 70 minutes); Not in 16

REGGINA

Final Position: **16th**

NICKNAME: AMARANTO

KEY: ☐ Won ☐ Drawn ☐ Lost

							Attendance
1	itpr1	Atalanta	H	D	1-1	Amoruso 77	12,963
2	itpr1	Torino	A	D	2-2	Amoruso 31, Cozza 90	2,403
3	itpr1	Roma	H	L	0-2		15,000
4	itpr1	Udinese	A	L	0-2		15,000
5	itpr1	Juventus	A	L	0-4		19,050
6	itpr1	Lazio	H	D	1-1	Cozza 7	12,000
7	itpr1	Palermo	A	D	1-1	Amoruso 90	22,845
8	itpr1	Inter Milan	H	L	0-1		16,965
9	itpr1	Siena	A	D	0-0		8,435
10	itpr1	Livorno	H	L	1-3	Amoruso 37	11,000
11	itpr1	Napoli	A	D	1-1	Vigiani 54	40,000
12	itpr1	Genoa	H	W	2-0	Amoruso 31, Joelson 81	11,000
13	itpr1	Fiorentina	H	D	0-0		10,000
14	itpr1	Sampdoria	A	L	0-3		22,058
15	itpr1	Parma	A	L	0-3		12,000
16	itpr1	Catania	H	W	3-1	Vigiani 34, 78, 90	10,000
17	itpr1	Empoli	A	D	1-1	Ceravolo 2	5,349
18	itpr1	Cagliari	H	W	2-0	Brienza 66, Cozza 80	10,122
19	itpr1	Atalanta	A	D	2-2	Vigiani 61, Barreto 67	7,000
20	itpr1	AC Milan	H	L	0-1		17,426
21	itpr1	Torino	H	L	1-3	Amoruso 59	10,300
22	itpr1	Roma	A	L	0-2		31,635
23	itpr1	Udinese	H	L	1-3	Modesto 76	9,917
24	itpr1	Juventus	H	W	2-1	Brienza 32, Amoruso 90 pen	21,884
25	itpr1	Lazio	A	L	0-1		17,663
26	itpr1	Palermo	H	D	0-0		10,316
27	itpr1	Inter Milan	A	L	0-2		64,575
28	itpr1	Siena	H	W	4-0	Brienza 9, 39, Cozza 19, Missiroli 68	10,300
29	itpr1	Livorno	A	D	1-1	Brienza 33	9,027
30	itpr1	Napoli	H	D	1-1	Brienza 90	12,383
31	itpr1	Genoa	A	L	0-2		23,349
32	itpr1	Fiorentina	A	L	0-2		27,321
33	itpr1	Sampdoria	H	W	1-0	Brienza 35	11,082
34	itpr1	AC Milan	A	L	1-5	Barreto 40	55,274
35	itpr1	Parma	H	W	2-1	Cozza 56, 65	16,117
36	itpr1	Catania	A	W	2-1	Amoruso 40, 90 pen	18,177
37	itpr1	Empoli	H	W	2-0	Barreto 68, Amoruso 79	23,248
38	itpr1	Cagliari	A	D	2-2	Amoruso 55, 86 pen	20,000

LEAGUE APPEARANCES, BOOKINGS AND CAPS

	AGE (on 01/07/08)	IN NAMED 18	APPEARANCES	COUNTING GAMES	MINUTES ON PITCH	YELLOW CARDS	RED CARDS	CAPS THIS SEASON	NATIONAL SIDE
Goalkeepers									
Andrea Campagnolo	30	36	36	36	3240	3	0	-	Italy
Nenad Novakovic	25	37	2	2	180	0	0	-	Serbia
Giuseppe Sarao	20	2	0	0	0	0	0	-	Italy
Defenders									
Pablo A Menendez	23	27	12	3	475	2	0	1	Uruguay
Salvatore Aronica	30	36	35	33	3067	8	0	-	Italy
Nicolo Cherubin	21	19	6	4	423	0	0	-	Italy
Bruno Cirillo	31	21	18	17	1579	7	0	-	Italy
Andrea Costa	22	15	10	4	505	0	0	-	Italy
Maurizio Lanzaro	26	33	33	33	2908	11	1	-	Italy
Francesco Modesto	26	33	32	28	2697	3	1	-	Italy
Kris Stadsgaard	22	14	5	3	308	0	0	-	Denmark
Carlos Valdez Suarez	25	33	33	30	2782	7	1	-	Uruguay
Midfielders									
Pablo Alvarez Nunez	28	1	0	0	0	0	0	-	Spain
Edgar Barreto	23	37	36	30	2841	6	0	5	Paraguay
Emmanuel Cascione	24	34	30	23	2212	9	0	-	Italy
Francesco Cozza	34	33	26	11	1476	7	0	-	Italy
Emil Hallfredsson	24	28	21	11	1340	2	0	-	Iceland
Simone Missiroli	22	30	24	12	1409	4	0	-	Italy
Leonardo Pettinari	21	4	0	0	0	0	0	-	Italy
Luca Tognozzi	30	28	21	11	1271	3	0	-	Italy
Luca Vigiani	31	30	29	19	2026	3	0	-	Italy
Forwards									
Nicola Amoruso	33	33	33	29	2745	6	0	-	Italy
Franco Brienza	29	20	20	15	1531	1	0	-	Italy
Fabio Ceravolo	21	25	20	2	965	2	0	-	Italy
Inacio Jose Joelson	24	24	13	2	556	0	0	-	Brazil
Stephen A Makinwa	24	11	9	3	461	0	0	9	Nigeria
Jose A M Nunez	19	9	5	0	91	0	0	-	Paraguay
Christian Curbelo	21	18	12	0	249	0	0	-	Uruguay
Mike Tullberg	23	14	5	1	226	1	0	-	Denmark
Alessio Viola	17	1	0	0	0	0	0	-	Italy

TEAM OF THE SEASON

G Andrea Campagnolo CG: 36 DR: 58

D Maurizio Lanzaro CG: 33 DR: 70

D Carlos Valdez Suarez CG: 30 DR: 64

D Bruno Cirillo CG: 17 DR: 63

D Salvatore Aronica CG: 33 DR: 60

M Edgar Barreto CG: 30 SD: -9

M Emmanuel Cascione CG: 23 SD: -39

M Luca Vigiani CG: 19 SD: -40

M Simone Missiroli CG: 12 SD: -65

F Franco Brienza CG: 15 SR: 218

F Nicola Amoruso CG: 29 SR: 228

MONTHLY POINTS TALLY

AUGUST	1	33%
SEPTEMBER	2	13%
OCTOBER	2	17%
NOVEMBER	5	56%
DECEMBER	3	33%
JANUARY	5	42%
FEBRUARY	3	20%
MARCH	6	33%
APRIL	6	50%
MAY	7	78%

LEAGUE GOALS

	PLAYER	MINS	GOALS	S RATE
1	Amoruso	2745	12	228
2	Brienza	1531	7	218
3	Cozza	1476	6	246
4	Vigiani	2026	5	405
5	Barreto	2841	3	947
6	Joelson	556	1	556
7	Ceravolo	965	1	965
8	Missiroli	1409	1	1409
9	Modesto	2697	1	2697
	Other		0	
	TOTAL		37	

TOP POINT EARNERS

	PLAYER	GAMES	AV PTS
1	Edgar Barreto	30	1.30
2	Bruno Cirillo	17	1.29
3	Francesco Modesto	28	1.29
4	Franco Brienza	15	1.27
5	Nicola Amoruso	29	1.21
6	Maurizio Lanzaro	33	1.12
7	Luca Vigiani	19	1.05
8	Salvatore Aronica	33	1.03
9	Andrea Campagnolo	36	1.00
10	Carlos Valdez Suarez	30	1.00
	CLUB AVERAGE:		1.05

DISCIPLINARY RECORDS

	PLAYER	YELLOW	RED	AVE
1	Francesco Cozza	7	0	210
2	Bruno Cirillo	7	0	225
3	Pablo A Menendez	2	0	237
4	Maurizio Lanzaro	11	1	242
5	E Cascione	9	0	245
6	Carlos V Suarez	7	1	347
7	Simone Missiroli	4	0	352
8	Salvatore Aronica	8	0	383
9	Luca Tognozzi	3	0	423
10	Nicola Amoruso	6	0	457
11	Edgar Barreto	6	0	473
12	Fabio Ceravolo	2	0	482
13	Emil Hallfredsson	2	0	670
	Other	10	1	
	TOTAL	84	3	

KEY GOALKEEPER

Andrea Campagnolo

Goals Conceded in the League	55	Counting Games League games when player was on pitch for at least 70 minutes	36
Defensive Rating Ave number of mins between League goals conceded while on the pitch	58	Clean Sheets In League games when player was on pitch for at least 70 minutes	7

KEY PLAYERS - DEFENDERS

Maurizio Lanzaro

Goals Conceded Number of League goals conceded while the player was on the pitch	41	Clean Sheets In League games when player was on pitch for at least 70 minutes	8
Defensive Rating Ave number of mins between League goals conceded while on the pitch	70	Club Defensive Rating Average number of mins between League goals conceded by the club this season	61

	PLAYER	CON LGE	CLEAN SHEETS	DEF RATE
1	Maurizio Lanzaro	41	8	70 mins
2	Carlos Valdez Suarez	43	7	64 mins
3	Bruno Cirillo	25	4	63 mins
4	Salvatore Aronica	51	6	60 mins

KEY PLAYERS - MIDFIELDERS

Edgar Barreto

Goals in the League	3	Contribution to Attacking Power Average number of minutes between League team goals while on pitch	78
Defensive Rating Average number of mins between League goals conceded while on the pitch	69	Scoring Difference Defensive Rating minus Contribution to Attacking Power	-9

	PLAYER	LGE GOALS	DEF RATE	POWER	SCORE DIFF
1	Edgar Barreto	3	69	78	-9 mins
2	Emmanuel Cascione	0	71	110	-39 mins
3	Luca Vigiani	5	61	101	-40 mins
4	Simone Missiroli	1	52	117	-65 mins

KEY PLAYERS - GOALSCORERS

Franco Brienza

Goals in the League	7	Player Strike Rate Average number of minutes between League goals scored by player	218
Contribution to Attacking Power Average number of minutes between League team goals while on pitch	80	Club Strike Rate Average number of minutes between League goals scored by club	92

	PLAYER	LGE GOALS	POWER	STRIKE RATE
1	Franco Brienza	7	80	218 mins
2	Nicola Amoruso	12	88	228 mins
3	Luca Vigiani	5	101	405 mins
4	Edgar Barreto	3	78	947 mins

Franco Brienza, Nicola Amoruso and Emmanuel Cascione

SQUAD APPEARANCES

Match	1	2	3	4	5	6	7	8	9	10	11	12	13	14	15	16	17	18	19	20	21	22	23	24	25	26	27	28	29	30	31	32	33	34	35	36	37	38
Venue	H	A	H	A	A	H	A	H	A	H	A	H	H	A	A	H	A	H	A	H	H	A	H	H	A	H	A	H	A	H	A	A	H	A	H	A	H	A
Competition	L	L	L	L	L	L	L	L	L	L	L	L	L	L	L	L	L	L	L	L	L	L	L	L	L	L	L	L	L	L	L	L	L	L	L	L	L	L
Result	D	D	L	L	L	D	D	L	D	L	D	W	D	L	L	W	D	W	D	L	L	L	L	W	L	D	L	W	D	D	L	L	W	L	W	W	W	D

Goalkeepers
Andrea Campagnolo
Nenad Novakovic
Giuseppe Sarao

Defenders
Pablo A Menendez
Salvatore Aronica
Nicolo Cherubin
Bruno Cirillo
Andrea Costa
Maurizio Lanzaro
Francesco Modesto
Kris Stadsgaard
Carlos Valdez Suarez

Midfielders
Pablo Alvarez Nunez
Edgar Barreto
Emmanuel Cascione
Francesco Cozza
Emil Hallfredsson
Simone Missiroli
Leonardo Pettinari
Luca Tognozzi
Luca Vigiani

Forwards
Nicola Amoruso
Franco Brienza
Fabio Ceravolo
Inacio Jose Joelson
Stephen A Makinwa
Jose Arnulfo Nunez
Christian R Curbelo
Mike Tullberg
Alessio Viola

KEY: On all match | On bench | Subbed or sent off (Counting game) | Subbed or sent off (playing less than 70 minutes) | Subbed on from bench (Counting Game) | Subbed on (playing less than 70 minutes) | Subbed on and then subbed or sent off (Counting Game) | Subbed on and then subbed or sent off (playing less than 70 minutes) | Not in 16

CATANIA

Final Position: **17th**

NICKNAME: GLI ELEFENTI (THE ELEPHANTS) KEY: ☐Won ☐Drawn ☐Lost

							Attendance
1	itpr1	Parma	A	D	2-2	Morimoto 12, Baiocco 44	12,579
2	itpr1	Genoa	H	D	0-0		16,000
3	itpr1	Inter Milan	A	L	0-2		40,000
4	itpr1	Fiorentina	H	L	0-1		18,000
5	itpr1	Empoli	H	W	1-0	Martinez 48	15,887
6	itpr1	AC Milan	A	D	1-1	Martinez 25	50,000
7	itpr1	Livorno	H	W	1-0	Sardo 20	16,000
8	itpr1	Cagliari	A	D	1-1	Terlizzi 11	9,759
9	itpr1	Sampdoria	H	W	2-0	Mascara 2, Martinez 43	16,276
10	itpr1	Siena	A	D	1-1	Vargas 89	8,000
11	itpr1	Atalanta	H	L	1-2	Spinesi 83	16,000
12	itpr1	Torino	A	D	1-1	Martinez 63	18,000
13	itpr1	Napoli	A	L	0-2		30,000
14	itpr1	Palermo	H	W	3-1	Mascara 29, Spinesi 41, Martinez 89	16,000
15	itpr1	Lazio	A	L	0-2		15,000
16	itpr1	Udinese	H	W	2-0	Mascara 7, 86	17,000
17	itpr1	Reggina	A	L	1-3	Vargas 90	10,000
18	itpr1	Juventus	H	D	1-1	Spinesi 15	16,000
19	itpr1	Roma	A	L	0-2		33,378
20	itpr1	Parma	H	D	0-0		16,287
21	itpr1	Genoa	A	L	1-2	Bovo 59 og	22,935
22	itpr1	Inter Milan	H	L	0-2		21,068
23	itpr1	Fiorentina	A	L	1-2	Vargas 60	26,648
24	itpr1	Empoli	A	L	0-2		5,712
25	itpr1	AC Milan	H	D	1-1	Spinesi 63	20,021
26	itpr1	Livorno	A	L	0-1		9,759
27	itpr1	Cagliari	H	W	2-1	Silvestri 44, Canini 47 og	30,643
28	itpr1	Sampdoria	A	L	1-3	Stovini 73	19,409
29	itpr1	Siena	H	D	0-0		16,655
30	itpr1	Atalanta	A	D	0-0		9,414
31	itpr1	Torino	H	L	1-2	Spinesi 3	16,955
32	itpr1	Napoli	H	W	3-0	Colucci 4, Spinesi 16, Vargas 48	14,246
33	itpr1	Palermo	A	L	0-1		24,847
34	itpr1	Lazio	H	W	1-0	Spinesi 34 pen	16,000
35	itpr1	Udinese	A	L	1-2	Vargas 34	13,958
36	itpr1	Reggina	H	L	1-2	Martinez 90	18,177
37	itpr1	Juventus	A	D	1-1	Martinez 48	20,638
38	itpr1	Roma	H	D	1-1	Martinez 85	21,148

LEAGUE APPEARANCES, BOOKINGS AND CAPS

	AGE (on 01/07/08)	IN NAMED 18	APPEARANCES	COUNTING GAMES	MINUTES ON PITCH	YELLOW CARDS	RED CARDS	CAPS THIS SEASON	NATIONAL SIDE
Goalkeepers									
Albano B Bizzarri	30	23	6	6	540	0	0	-	Argentina
Ciro Polito	29	38	32	32	2880	0	0	-	Italy
Generoso Rossi	29	14	0	0	0	0	0	-	Italy
Defenders									
Pablo S Alvarez	24	9	6	2	213	0	0	-	Argentina
Marcello Gazzola	23	15	3	2	217	0	0	-	Italy
Mauro Minelli	27	1	0	0	0	0	0	-	Italy
Riccardo Nardini	25	5	1	0	33	0	0	-	Italy
Rocco Sabato	26	29	19	10	1072	1	0	-	Italy
Gennaro Sardo	29	30	22	19	1811	7	1	-	Italy
Matias A Silvestre	23	16	11	9	835	1	0	-	Argentina
Cristian Silvestri	33	34	21	16	1637	6	0	-	Italy
Andrea Sottil	34	19	7	4	421	1	0	-	Italy
Lorenzo Stovini	31	36	36	36	3240	10	0	-	Italy
Christian Terlizzi	28	28	25	23	2088	10	0	-	Italy
Juan Manuel Vargas	24	36	36	31	2970	7	1	3	Peru
Midfielders									
Davide Baiocco	33	34	33	29	2712	10	1	-	Italy
Marco Biagianti	24	29	19	10	1330	4	0	-	Italy
Fabio Caserta	29	1	1	0	33	0	0	-	Italy
Giuseppe Colucci	27	31	25	12	1544	5	0	-	Italy
Mark Edusei	31	32	26	19	1930	5	0	-	Ghana
Mariano Julio Izco	25	37	33	18	2074	4	0	-	Argentina
Cristian E Llama	22	6	1	0	45	0	0	-	Argentina
Francesco Millesi	27	5	2	1	91	0	0	-	Italy
Giacomo Tedesco	32	34	28	16	1744	6	1	-	Italy
Forwards									
Anderson O Babu	27	9	2	0	32	0	0	-	Brazil
Joao Batista Pia'	26	15	8	3	356	0	0	-	Brazil
Jorge A B Martinez	25	31	30	16	1860	6	0	-	Uruguay
Guiseppe Mascara	29	35	35	31	2867	7	0	-	Italy
Takayuki Morimoto	20	22	14	0	408	3	0	-	Japan
Gionatha Spinesi	30	32	32	28	2545	4	1	-	Italy

TEAM OF THE SEASON

G — Ciro Polito, CG: 32 DR: 80

D — Christian Terlizzi, CG: 23 DR: 83

D — Juan Manuel Vargas, CG: 31 DR: 80

D — Lorenzo Stovini, CG: 36 DR: 79

D — Gennaro Sardo, CG: 19 DR: 75

M — Giuseppe Colucci, CG: 12 SD: -23

M — Mariano Julio Izco, CG: 18 SD: -24

M — Giacomo Tedesco, CG: 16 SD: -29

M — Mark Edusei, CG: 19 SD: -37

F — Jorge Martinez, CG: 16 SR: 232

F — Gionatha Spinesi, CG: 28 SR: 363

MONTHLY POINTS TALLY

AUGUST	1	33%
SEPTEMBER	5	33%
OCTOBER	8	67%
NOVEMBER	1	11%
DECEMBER	6	50%
JANUARY	2	22%
FEBRUARYaa	1	7%
MARCH	5	28%
APRIL	6	50%
MAY	2	22%

LEAGUE GOALS

	PLAYER	MINS	GOALS	S RATE
1	Martinez	1860	8	232
2	Spinesi	2545	7	363
3	Vargas	2970	5	594
4	Mascara	2867	4	716
5	Morimoto	408	1	408
6	Colucci	1544	1	1544
7	Silvestri	1637	1	1637
8	Sardo	1811	1	1811
9	Terlizzi	2088	1	2088
10	Baiocco	2712	1	2712
11	Stovini	3240	1	3240
	Other		0	
	TOTAL		31	

TOP POINT EARNERS

	PLAYER	GAMES	AV PTS
1	Mariano Julio Izco	18	1.22
2	Jorge A B Martinez	16	1.19
3	Giacomo Tedesco	16	1.13
4	Gionatha Spinesi	28	1.07
5	Juan Manuel Vargas	31	1.06
6	Gennaro Sardo	19	1.05
7	Lorenzo Stovini	36	1.03
8	Christian Terlizzi	23	1.00
9	Giuseppe Colucci	12	1.00
10	Mark Edusei	19	1.00
	CLUB AVERAGE:		0.97

DISCIPLINARY RECORDS

	PLAYER	YELLOW	RED	AVE
1	Christian Terlizzi	10	0	208
2	Gennaro Sardo	7	1	226
3	Davide Baiocco	10	1	246
4	Giacomo Tedesco	6	1	249
5	Cristian Silvestri	6	0	272
6	Giuseppe Colucci	5	0	308
7	Jorge A B Martinez	6	0	310
8	Lorenzo Stovini	10	0	324
9	Marco Biagianti	4	0	332
10	Juan M Vargas	7	1	371
11	Mark Edusei	5	0	386
12	Guiseppe Mascara	7	0	409
13	Gionatha Spinesi	4	1	509
	Other	6	0	
	TOTAL	93	5	

KEY GOALKEEPER

Ciro Polito

Goals Conceded in the League	36	**Counting Games** League games when player was on pitch for at least 70 minutes	32
Defensive Rating Ave number of mins between League goals conceded while on the pitch	80	**Clean Sheets** In League games when player was on pitch for at least 70 minutes	9

KEY PLAYERS - DEFENDERS

Christian Terlizzi

Goals Conceded Number of League goals conceded while the player was on the pitch	25	**Clean Sheets** In League games when player was on pitch for at least 70 minutes	6
Defensive Rating Ave number of mins between League goals conceded while on the pitch	83	**Club Defensive Rating** Average number of mins between League goals conceded by the club this season	76

	PLAYER	CON LGE	CLEAN SHEETS	DEF RATE
1	Christian Terlizzi	25	6	83 mins
2	Juan Manuel Vargas	37	10	80 mins
3	Lorenzo Stovini	41	10	79 mins
4	Gennaro Sardo	24	5	75 mins

KEY PLAYERS - MIDFIELDERS

Giuseppe Colucci

Goals in the League	1	**Contribution to Attacking Power** Average number of minutes between League team goals while on pitch	90
Defensive Rating Average number of mins between League goals conceded while on the pitch	67	**Scoring Difference** Defensive Rating minus Contribution to Attacking Power	-23

	PLAYER	LGE GOALS	DEF RATE	POWER	SCORE DIFF
1	Giuseppe Colucci	1	67	90	-23 mins
2	Mariano Julio Izco	0	74	98	-24 mins
3	Giacomo Tedesco	0	87	116	-29 mins
4	Mark Edusei	0	83	120	-37 mins

KEY PLAYERS - GOALSCORERS

Jorge Andreas Barrios Martinez

Goals in the League	8	**Player Strike Rate** Average number of minutes between League goals scored by player	232
Contribution to Attacking Power Average number of minutes between League team goals while on pitch	103	**Club Strike Rate** Average number of minutes between League goals scored by club	103

	PLAYER	LGE GOALS	POWER	STRIKE RATE
1	Jorge Andreas Barrios Martinez	8	103	232 mins
2	Gionatha Spinesi	7	101	363 mins
3	Guiseppe Mascara	4	106	716 mins
4	Giuseppe Colucci	1	90	1544 mins

Gionatha Spinesi

SQUAD APPEARANCES

Match	1	2	3	4	5	6	7	8	9	10	11	12	13	14	15	16	17	18	19	20	21	22	23	24	25	26	27	28	29	30	31	32	33	34	35	36	37	38
Venue	A	H	A	H	H	A	H	A	H	A	H	A	A	H	A	H	A	H	A	H	A	H	A	A	H	A	H	A	H	A	H	H	A	H	A	H	A	H
Competition	L	L	L	L	L	L	L	L	L	L	L	L	L	L	L	L	L	L	L	L	L	L	L	L	L	L	L	L	L	L	L	L	L	L	L	L	L	L
Result	D	D	L	L	W	D	W	D	W	D	L	D	L	W	L	W	L	D	L	D	L	L	L	L	D	L	W	L	D	D	L	W	L	W	L	L	D	D

Goalkeepers
Albano Benjamin Bizzarri
Ciro Polito
Generoso Rossi
Defenders
Pablo Sebastian Alvarez
Marcello Gazzola
Mauro Minelli
Riccardo Nardini
Rocco Sabato
Gennaro Sardo
Matias Agustin Silvestre
Cristian Silvestri
Andrea Sottil
Lorenzo Stovini
Christian Terlizzi
Juan Manuel Vargas
Midfielders
Davide Baiocco
Marco Biagianti
Fabio Caserta
Giuseppe Colucci
Mark Edusei
Mariano Julio Izco
Cristian Ezequiel Llama
Francesco Millesi
Giacomo Tedesco
Forwards
Anderson Babu
Joao Batista Pia'
Jorge A B Martinez
Guiseppe Mascara
Takayuki Morimoto
Gionatha Spinesi

KEY: On all match · On bench · Subbed or sent off (Counting game) · Subbed or sent off (playing less than 70 minutes) · Subbed on from bench (Counting Game) · Subbed on (playing less than 70 minutes) · Subbed on and then subbed or sent off (Counting Game) · Subbed on and then subbed or sent off (playing less than 70 minutes) · Not in 16

EMPOLI

Final Position: **18th**

NICKNAME: AZZURRI

KEY: Won Drawn Lost

							Attendance
1	itpr1	Fiorentina	A	L	1-3	Saudati 90	31,280
2	itpr1	Inter Milan	H	L	0-2		16,326
3	itpr1	Lazio	A	D	0-0		19,460
4	ucrl1	Zurich	H	W	2-1	Piccolo 44, Antonini 49 pen	2,000
5	itpr1	Napoli	H	D	0-0		5,000
6	itpr1	Catania	A	L	0-1		15,887
7	itpr1	Palermo	H	W	3-1	Pozzi 47, Giovinco 82, Vannucchi 90 pen	5,000
8	ucrl2	Zurich	A	L	0-3		13,600
9	itpr1	Siena	A	L	0-3		8,377
10	itpr1	AC Milan	A	W	1-0	Saudati 55	48,953
11	itpr1	Atalanta	H	L	0-1		5,616
12	itpr1	Juventus	A	L	0-3		15,000
13	itpr1	Roma	H	D	2-2	Vannucchi 67, Giovinco 89	15,000
14	itpr1	Sampdoria	A	L	0-3		19,000
15	itpr1	Torino	H	D	0-0		7,000
16	itpr1	Parma	A	L	0-1		12,238
17	itpr1	Cagliari	H	W	4-1	Pozzi 2, 10, 50, 64	5,000
18	itpr1	Genoa	H	D	1-1	Giovinco 45	6,483
19	itpr1	Udinese	A	D	2-2	Raggi 50, Marzoratti 90	13,000
20	itpr1	Reggina	H	D	1-1	Saudati 5 pen	5,349
21	itpr1	Livorno	A	L	0-1		8,428
22	itpr1	Fiorentina	H	L	0-2		6,000
23	itpr1	Inter Milan	A	L	0-1		43,946
24	itpr1	Lazio	H	W	1-0	Vannucchi 7	7,232
25	itpr1	Napoli	A	W	3-1	Pozzi 21, 65, Budel 81	46,946
26	itpr1	Catania	H	W	2-0	Giovinco 36, Budel 78	5,712
27	itpr1	Palermo	A	L	0-2		22,000
28	itpr1	Siena	H	L	0-2		6,139
29	itpr1	AC Milan	H	L	1-3	Busce 23	9,532
30	itpr1	Atalanta	A	L	1-4	Vannucchi 83	9,220
31	itpr1	Juventus	H	D	0-0		8,719
32	itpr1	Roma	A	L	1-2	Giovinco 50	31,392
33	itpr1	Sampdoria	H	L	0-2		7,066
34	itpr1	Torino	A	W	1-0	Vannucchi 88	18,750
35	itpr1	Parma	H	D	1-1	Giovinco 30	5,938
36	itpr1	Cagliari	A	L	0-2		15,000
37	itpr1	Genoa	A	W	1-0	Abate 15	23,885
38	itpr1	Udinese	H	L	0-1		7,257
39	itpr1	Reggina	A	L	0-2		23,248
40	itpr1	Livorno	H	W	2-1	Busce 10, Saudati 56	6,858

LEAGUE APPEARANCES, BOOKINGS AND CAPS

	AGE (on 01/07/08)	IN NAMED 18	APPEARANCES	COUNTING GAMES	MINUTES ON PITCH	YELLOW CARDS	RED CARDS	CAPS THIS SEASON	NATIONAL SIDE
Goalkeepers									
Daniele Balli	40	35	20	20	1800	2	0	-	Italy
Davide Bassi	21	37	18	18	1620	0	0	-	Italy
Alberto Pelagotti	19	3	0	0	0	0	0	-	Italy
Defenders									
Daniele Adani	33	14	6	4	427	1	1	-	Italy
Nicola Ascoli	28	6	1	0	30	0	0	-	Italy
Simone Iacoponi	21	1	0	0	0	0	0	-	Italy
Lino Marzoratti	21	36	32	25	2553	5	1	-	Italy
Davide Moro	26	35	32	20	2188	9	1	-	Italy
Felice Piccolo	24	27	20	14	1477	5	1	-	Italy
Francesco Pratali	29	18	15	12	1179	5	1	-	Italy
Andrea Raggi	24	33	33	30	2825	4	0	-	Italy
Lourenco C E Rincon	21	10	0	0	0	0	0	-	Brazil
Vittorio Tosto	34	37	32	24	2337	3	0	-	Italy
Richard Vanigli	37	27	13	4	648	5	0	-	Italy
Midfielders									
Ignazio Abate	21	36	24	6	1183	5	0	-	Italy
Luca Antonini	26	38	32	21	2379	1	0	-	Italy
Alessandro Budel	27	19	19	15	1450	4	0	-	Italy
Antonio Busce	32	30	30	28	2616	2	0	-	Italy
Guillermo Giacomazzi	30	31	20	7	1061	6	0	-	Uruguay
Sebastian Giovinco	21	35	35	16	2056	6	0	-	Italy
Claudio Marchisio	22	30	26	18	1893	8	0	-	Italy
Francesco Marianini	29	31	25	12	1463	2	0	-	Italy
Gianluca Musacci	21	2	2	1	91	0	0	-	Italy
Felice Prevete	21	1	0	0	0	0	0	-	Italy
Ighli Vannucchi	30	35	34	24	2593	7	0	-	Italy
Forwards									
Salvatore Caturano	17	2	0	0	0	0	0	-	Italy
Eder Citadin Martins	21	0	0	0	0	0	0	-	Brazil
Nicola Pozzi	22	19	17	8	1122	7	0	-	Italy
Luca Saudati	30	31	30	19	2090	8	0	-	Italy
Rej Volpato	21	24	13	2	436	0	0	-	Italy

TEAM OF THE SEASON

D
Vittorio Tosto
CG: 24 DR: 73
M
Sebastian Giovinco
CG: 16 SD: -27
D
Francesco Pratali
CG: 12 DR: 69
M
Antonio BuscÃ©
CG: 28 SD: -32
F
Nicola Pozzi
CG: 8 SR: 160
G
Daniele Balli
CG: 20 DR: 75
D
Davide Moro
CG: 20 DR: 68
M
Claudio Marchisio
CG: 18 SD: -36
F
Luca Saudati
CG: 19 SR: 522
D
Lino Marzoratti
CG: 25 DR: 67
M
Alessandro Budel
CG: 15 SD: -40

MONTHLY POINTS TALLY

AUGUST	0	0%
SEPTEMBER	5	33%
OCTOBER	3	25%
NOVEMBER	2	22%
DECEMBER	5	42%
JANUARY	1	11%
FEBRUARY	9	60%
MARCH	1	6%
APRIL	7	58%
MAY	3	33%

LEAGUE GOALS

	PLAYER	MINS	GOALS	S RATE
1	Pozzi	1122	7	160
2	Giovinco	2056	6	342
3	Vannucchi	2593	5	518
4	Saudati	2090	4	522
5	Budel	1450	2	725
6	Busce	2616	2	1308
7	Abate	1183	1	1183
8	Marzoratti	2553	1	2553
9	Raggi	2825	1	2825
10	Rincon	0	0	
11	Pratali	1179	0	
12	Prevete	0	0	
13	Tosto	2337	0	
	Other		0	
	TOTAL		29	

TOP POINT EARNERS

	PLAYER	GAMES	AV PTS
1	Vittorio Tosto	24	1.13
2	Francesco Marianini	12	1.08
3	Alessandro Budel	15	1.07
4	Antonio Busce	28	1.07
5	Claudio Marchisio	18	1.06
6	Daniele Balli	20	1.05
7	Luca Antonini	21	1.00
8	Lino Marzoratti	25	1.00
9	Ighli Vannucchi	24	1.00
10	Felice Piccolo	14	1.00
	CLUB AVERAGE:		0.95

DISCIPLINARY RECORDS

	PLAYER	YELLOW	RED	AVE
1	Richard Vanigli	5	0	129
2	Nicola Pozzi	7	0	160
3	G Giacomazzi	6	0	176
4	Francesco Pratali	5	1	196
5	Davide Moro	9	1	218
6	Claudio Marchisio	8	0	236
7	Ignazio Abate	5	0	236
8	Felice Piccolo	5	1	246
9	Luca Saudati	8	0	261
10	Sebastian Giovinco	6	0	342
11	Alessandro Budel	4	0	362
12	Ighli Vannucchi	7	0	370
13	Lino Marzoratti	5	1	425
	Other	14	0	
	TOTAL	94	4	

KEY GOALKEEPER

Daniele Balli

Goals Conceded in the League	24	**Counting Games** League games when player was on pitch for at least 70 minutes	20
Defensive Rating Ave number of mins between League goals conceded while on the pitch	75	**Clean Sheets** In League games when player was on pitch for at least 70 minutes	5

KEY PLAYERS - DEFENDERS

Vittorio Tosto

Goals Conceded Number of League goals conceded while the player was on the pitch	32	**Clean Sheets** In League games when player was on pitch for at least 70 minutes	7
Defensive Rating Ave number of mins between League goals conceded while on the pitch	73	**Club Defensive Rating** Average number of mins between League goals conceded by the club this season	65

	PLAYER	CON LGE	CLEAN SHEETS	DEF RATE
1	Vittorio Tosto	32	7	73 mins
2	Francesco Pratali	17	3	69 mins
3	Davide Moro	32	6	68 mins
4	Lino Marzoratti	38	7	67 mins

KEY PLAYERS - MIDFIELDERS

Sebastian Giovinco

Goals in the League	6	**Contribution to Attacking Power** Average number of minutes between League team goals while on pitch	93
Defensive Rating Average number of mins between League goals conceded while on the pitch	66	**Scoring Difference** Defensive Rating minus Contribution to Attacking Power	-27

	PLAYER	LGE GOALS	DEF RATE	POWER	SCORE DIFF
1	Sebastian Giovinco	6	66	93	-27 mins
2	Antonio BuscÃ©	2	72	104	-32 mins
3	Claudio Marchisio	0	63	99	-36 mins
4	Alessandro Budel	2	63	103	-40 mins

KEY PLAYERS - GOALSCORERS

Nicola Pozzi

Goals in the League	7	**Player Strike Rate** Average number of minutes between League goals scored by player	160
Contribution to Attacking Power Average number of minutes between League team goals while on pitch	80	**Club Strike Rate** Average number of minutes between League goals scored by club	117

	PLAYER	LGE GOALS	POWER	STRIKE RATE
1	Nicola Pozzi	7	80	160 mins
2	Sebastian Giovinco	6	93	342 mins
3	Ighli Vannucchi	5	117	518 mins
4	Luca Saudati	4	139	522 mins

asics
navigare
Ighli Vannucchi

SQUAD APPEARANCES

Match	1	2	3	4	5	6	7	8	9	10	11	12	13	14	15	16	17	18	19	20	21	22	23	24	25	26	27	28	29	30	31	32	33	34	35	36	37	38	39	40
Venue	A	H	A	H	H	A	H	A	A	A	H	A	H	A	H	A	H	H	A	H	A	H	A	H	A	H	A	H	H	A	H	A	H	A	H	A	A	H	A	H
Competition	L	L	L	E	L	L	L	E	L	L	L	L	L	L	L	L	L	L	L	L	L	L	L	L	L	L	L	L	L	L	L	L	L	L	L	L	L	L	L	L
Result	L	L	D	W	D	L	W	L	L	W	L	L	D	L	D	L	W	D	D	D	L	L	L	W	W	W	L	L	L	L	D	L	L	W	D	L	W	L	L	W

Goalkeepers
Daniele Balli
Davide Bassi
Alberto Pelagotti
Defenders
Daniele Adani
Nicola Ascoli
Simone Iacoponi
Lino Marzoratti
Davide Moro
Felice Piccolo
Francesco Pratali
Andrea Raggi
Lourenco C E Rincon
Vittorio Tosto
Richard Vanigli
Midfielders
Ignazio Abate
Luca Antonini
Alessandro Budel
Antonio Busce
Guillermo Giacomazzi
Sebastian Giovinco
Claudio Marchisio
Francesco Marianini
Gianluca Musacci
Felice Prevete
Ighli Vannucchi
Forwards
Salvatore Caturano
Eder Citadin Martins
Nicola Pozzi
Luca Saudati
Rej Volpato

KEY: On all match · On bench · Subbed or sent off (Counting game) · Subbed or sent off (playing less than 70 minutes) · Subbed on from bench (Counting Game) · Subbed on (playing less than 70 minutes) · Subbed on and then subbed or sent off (Counting Game) · Subbed on and then subbed or sent off (playing less than 70 minutes) · Not in 16

PARMA

Final Position: **19th**

NICKNAME: DUCALI

KEY: ☐Won ☐Drawn ☐Lost

							Attendance
1	itpr1	**Catania**	H	D	2-2	Pisanu 28, Rossi 43	12,579
2	itpr1	**Atalanta**	A	L	0-2		10,141
3	itpr1	**Cagliari**	H	D	1-1	Corradi 72	12,853
4	itpr1	**AC Milan**	A	D	1-1	Pisanu 73	50,000
5	itpr1	**Torino**	H	W	2-0	Reginaldo 61, Corradi 63	12,932
6	itpr1	**Udinese**	A	L	1-2	Corradi 72	12,000
7	itpr1	**Roma**	H	L	0-3		18,000
8	itpr1	**Sampdoria**	A	L	0-3		19,852
9	itpr1	**Livorno**	H	W	3-2	Morrone 10, Paci 54, Morfeo 74	11,890
10	itpr1	**Palermo**	A	D	1-1	Morrone 3	30,000
11	itpr1	**Siena**	H	D	2-2	Corradi 24, Matteini 80	13,172
12	itpr1	**Juventus**	H	D	2-2	Gasbarroni 43 pen, Pisanu 57	16,000
13	itpr1	**Lazio**	A	L	0-1		20,000
14	itpr1	**Empoli**	H	W	1-0	Paci 21	12,238
15	itpr1	**Napoli**	A	L	0-1		30,000
16	itpr1	**Reggina**	H	W	3-0	Corradi 26, Pisanu 49, Paci 66	12,000
17	itpr1	**Genoa**	A	L	0-1		23,000
18	itpr1	**Fiorentina**	H	L	1-2	Coly 69	12,000
19	itpr1	**Inter Milan**	A	L	2-3	Cigarini 40, Gasbarroni 70	43,413
20	itpr1	**Catania**	A	D	0-0		16,287
21	itpr1	**Atalanta**	H	L	2-3	C.Lucarelli 39, Gasbarroni 90 pen	13,089
22	itpr1	**Cagliari**	A	D	1-1	Reginaldo 35	15,000
23	itpr1	**AC Milan**	H	D	0-0		19,361
24	itpr1	**Torino**	A	D	4-4	Gasbarroni 29, 32, Morrone 42, Budan 43	17,999
25	itpr1	**Udinese**	H	W	2-0	C.Lucarelli 78, Cigarini 87 pen	12,457
26	itpr1	**Roma**	A	L	0-4		31,788
27	itpr1	**Sampdoria**	H	L	1-2	Budan 67	16,328
28	itpr1	**Livorno**	A	D	1-1	Reginaldo 61	11,008
29	itpr1	**Palermo**	H	W	2-1	Budan 52, 90 pen	12,599
30	itpr1	**Siena**	A	L	0-2		8,000
31	itpr1	**Lazio**	H	D	2-2	Budan 17, Paci 43	13,370
32	itpr1	**Empoli**	A	D	1-1	C.Lucarelli 7	5,938
33	itpr1	**Juventus**	A	L	0-3		21,403
34	itpr1	**Napoli**	H	L	1-2	Budan 23 pen	17,996
35	itpr1	**Reggina**	A	L	1-2	Cigarini 25 pen	16,117
36	itpr1	**Genoa**	H	W	1-0	C.Lucarelli 58	17,693
37	itpr1	**Fiorentina**	A	L	1-3	Budan 11	36,289
38	itpr1	**Inter Milan**	H	L	0-2		25,149

LEAGUE APPEARANCES, BOOKINGS AND CAPS

	AGE (on 01/07/08)	IN NAMED 18	APPEARANCES	COUNTING GAMES	MINUTES ON PITCH	YELLOW CARDS	RED CARDS	CAPS THIS SEASON	NATIONAL SIDE
Goalkeepers									
Luca Bucci	39	36	32	30	2760	0	0	-	Italy
Nicola Pavarini	34	38	8	7	660	4	0	-	Italy
Defenders									
Cristian Anelli	19	2	1	0	1	0	0	-	Italy
Luca Antonelli	21	13	8	3	302	0	0	-	Italy
Paolo Castellini	29	34	34	33	3008	5	0	-	Italy
Ferdinand Coly	34	24	21	18	1702	3	1	-	Senegal
Fernando Couto	38	25	17	15	1416	3	2	-	Portugal
Giulio Falcone	34	29	27	24	2182	5	1	-	Italy
Massimo Paci	30	27	23	21	1957	6	1	-	Italy
Marco Rossi	20	26	15	12	1177	3	1	-	Italy
Alessio Tombesi	26	5	2	0	36	0	0	-	Italy
Damiano Zenoni	31	37	31	25	2383	4	0	-	Italy
Midfielders									
Luca Cigarini	22	34	31	24	2286	8	0	-	Italy
Daniele Dessena	21	34	28	14	1571	6	0	-	Italy
Andrea Gasbarroni	26	27	26	13	1656	6	1	-	Italy
McDonald Mariga	21	26	18	9	976	5	2	-	Kenya
Frederico Moretti	19	3	1	0	3	0	0	-	Italy
Domenico Morfeo	32	19	11	0	307	3	1	-	Italy
Stefano Morrone	29	36	36	35	3208	6	0	-	Italy
Francesco Parravicini	26	34	17	7	942	5	0	-	Italy
Andrea Pisanu	26	27	26	20	2019	6	0	-	Italy
Forwards									
Igor Budan	28	16	15	5	803	1	0	2	Croatia
Bernardo Corradi	32	30	27	18	1838	4	1	-	Italy
Pietro Lorenzini	19	2	1	0	8	0	0	-	Italy
Cristiano Lucarelli	32	18	16	10	1072	5	0	2	Italy
Leandro Martinez	19	6	1	0	13	0	0	-	Argentina
Davide Matteini	26	17	12	0	251	0	0	-	Italy
Daniele Paponi	20	13	7	1	206	0	0	-	Italy
Aleksandr Prijovic	18	2	1	0	8	0	0	-	Serbia
Reginaldo F Da Silva	24	36	35	27	2592	8	0	-	Brazil

TEAM OF THE SEASON

D
Ferdinand Coly
CG: 18 DR: 68
M
Luca Cigarini
CG: 24 SD: -15
D
Giulio Falcone
CG: 24 DR: 64
M
Andrea Pisanu
CG: 20 SD: -16
F
Bernardo Corradi
CG: 18 SR: 367
G
Luca Bucci
CG: 30 DR: 54
D
Massimo Paci
CG: 21 DR: 57
M
Andrea Gasbarroni
CG: 13 SD: -23
F
Reginaldo Silva
CG: 27 SR: 864
D
Fernando Couto
CG: 15 DR: 52
M
Stefano Morrone
CG: 35 SD: -24

MONTHLY POINTS TALLY

AUGUST	1	33%
SEPTEMBER	5	33%
OCTOBER	4	33%
NOVEMBER	2	22%
DECEMBER	6	50%
JANUARY	1	11%
FEBRUARY	6	40%
MARCH	4	27%
APRIL	2	13%
MAY	3	33%

LEAGUE GOALS

	PLAYER	MINS	GOALS	S RATE
1	Budan	803	7	114
2	Gasbarroni	1656	5	331
3	Corradi	1838	5	367
4	Lucarelli, C	1072	4	268
5	Paci	1957	4	489
6	Pisanu	2019	4	504
7	Cigarini	2286	3	762
8	Reginaldo	2592	3	864
9	Morrone	3208	3	1069
10	Matteini	251	1	251
11	Morfeo	307	1	307
12	Rossi	1177	1	1177
13	Coly	1702	1	1702
	Other		0	
	TOTAL		42	

TOP POINT EARNERS

	PLAYER	GAMES	AV PTS
1	Ferdinand Coly	18	**1.22**
2	Bernardo Corradi	18	**1.22**
3	Andrea Pisanu	20	**1.15**
4	Stefano Morrone	35	**0.97**
5	Massimo Paci	21	**0.95**
6	Paolo Castellini	33	**0.94**
7	Reginaldo F Da Silva	27	**0.93**
8	Marco Rossi	12	**0.92**
9	Giulio Falcone	24	**0.92**
10	Andrea Gasbarroni	13	**0.92**
	CLUB AVERAGE:		**0.89**

DISCIPLINARY RECORDS

	PLAYER	YELLOW	RED	AVE
1	McDonald Mariga	5	2	**139**
2	Nicola Pavarini	4	0	**165**
3	F Parravicini	5	0	**188**
4	Cristiano Lucarelli	5	0	**214**
5	Andrea Gasbarroni	6	1	**236**
6	Daniele Dessena	6	0	**261**
7	Massimo Paci	6	1	**279**
8	Fernando Couto	3	2	**283**
9	Marco Rossi	3	1	**294**
10	Reginaldo F Silva	8	0	**324**
11	Luca Cigarini	7	0	**326**
12	Andrea Pisanu	6	0	**336**
13	Giulio Falcone	5	1	**363**
	Other	23	2	
	TOTAL	92	10	

KEY GOALKEEPER

Luca Bucci			
Goals Conceded in the League	51	**Counting Games** League games when player was on pitch for at least 70 minutes	30
Defensive Rating Ave number of mins between League goals conceded while on the pitch	54	**Clean Sheets** In League games when player was on pitch for at least 70 minutes	5

KEY PLAYERS - DEFENDERS

Ferdinand Coly			
Goals Conceded Number of League goals conceded while the player was on the pitch	25	**Clean Sheets** In League games when player was on pitch for at least 70 minutes	5
Defensive Rating Ave number of mins between League goals conceded while on the pitch	68	**Club Defensive Rating** Average number of mins between League goals conceded by the club this season	56

	PLAYER	CON LGE	CLEAN SHEETS	DEF RATE
1	Ferdinand Coly	25	5	68 mins
2	Giulio Falcone	34	6	64 mins
3	Massimo Paci	34	3	57 mins
4	Fernando Couto	27	2	52 mins

KEY PLAYERS - MIDFIELDERS

Luca Cigarini			
Goals in the League	3	**Contribution to Attacking Power** Average number of minutes between League team goals while on pitch	76
Defensive Rating Average number of mins between League goals conceded while on the pitch	61	**Scoring Difference** Defensive Rating minus Contribution to Attacking Power	-15

	PLAYER	LGE GOALS	DEF RATE	POWER	SCORE DIFF
1	Luca Cigarini	3	61	76	-15 mins
2	Andrea Pisanu	4	61	77	-16 mins
3	Andrea Gasbarroni	5	55	78	-23 mins
4	Stefano Morrone	3	56	80	-24 mins

KEY PLAYERS - GOALSCORERS

Andrea Gasbarroni			
Goals in the League	5	**Player Strike Rate** Average number of minutes between League goals scored by player	331
Contribution to Attacking Power Average number of minutes between League team goals while on pitch	78	**Club Strike Rate** Average number of minutes between League goals scored by club	83

	PLAYER	LGE GOALS	POWER	STRIKE RATE
1	Andrea Gasbarroni	5	78	331 mins
2	Bernardo Corradi	5	73	367 mins
3	Andrea Pisanu	4	77	504 mins
4	Luca Cigarini	3	76	762 mins

Andres Gasbarroni

SQUAD APPEARANCES

Match	1	2	3	4	5	6	7	8	9	10	11	12	13	14	15	16	17	18	19	20	21	22	23	24	25	26	27	28	29	30	31	32	33	34	35	36	37	38
Venue	H	A	H	A	H	A	H	A	H	A	H	H	A	H	A	H	A	H	A	A	H	A	H	A	H	A	H	A	H	A	H	A	A	H	A	H	A	H
Competition	L	L	L	L	L	L	L	L	L	L	L	L	L	L	L	L	L	L	L	L	L	L	L	L	L	L	L	L	L	L	L	L	L	L	L	L	L	L
Result	D	L	D	D	W	L	L	L	W	D	D	D	L	W	L	W	L	L	L	D	L	D	D	D	W	L	L	D	W	L	D	D	L	L	L	W	L	L

Goalkeepers
Luca Bucci
Nicola Pavarini
Defenders
Cristian Anelli
Luca Antonelli
Paolo Castellini
Ferdinand Coly
Fernando Couto
Giulio Falcone
Massimo Paci
Marco Rossi
Alessio Tombesi
Damiano Zenoni
Midfielders
Luca Cigarini
Daniele Dessena
Andrea Gasbarroni
McDonald Mariga
Frederico Moretti
Domenico Morfeo
Stefano Morrone
Francesco Parravicini
Andrea Pisanu
Forwards
Igor Budan
Bernardo Corradi
Stefano Crisci
Pietro Lorenzini
Cristiano Lucarelli
Leandro Martinez
Davide Matteini
Daniele Paponi
Aleksandr Prijovic
Reginaldo F Da Silva

KEY: On all match / On bench / Subbed or sent off (Counting game) / Subbed or sent off (playing less than 70 minutes) / Subbed on from bench (Counting Game) / Subbed on (playing less than 70 minutes) / Subbed on and then subbed or sent off (Counting Game) / Subbed on and then subbed or sent off (playing less than 70 minutes) / Not in 16

LIVORNO

Final Position: **20th**

NICKNAME: AMARANTO (DARK RED)

KEY: ☐Won ☐Drawn ☐Lost

							Attendance
1	itpr1	**Juventus**	A	L	1-5	Loviso 90	21,414
2	itpr1	**Palermo**	H	L	2-4	Rossini 54, Grandoni 74	8,475
3	itpr1	**Genoa**	A	D	1-1	Tavano 51 pen	18,000
4	itpr1	**Inter Milan**	H	D	2-2	De Vezze 1, Loviso 62	14,000
5	itpr1	**Napoli**	A	L	0-1		37,163
6	itpr1	**Fiorentina**	H	L	0-3		10,000
7	itpr1	**Catania**	A	L	0-1		16,000
8	itpr1	**Lazio**	H	L	0-1		9,934
9	itpr1	**Parma**	A	L	2-3	Tavano 23, 50 pen	11,890
10	itpr1	**Reggina**	A	W	3-1	Pulzetti 34, Valdez Suarez 78 og	
						Rossini 90	11,000
11	itpr1	**Udinese**	H	D	0-0		8,500
12	itpr1	**Siena**	A	W	3-2	Tavano 16, Bergvold 30, Knezevic 41	8,000
13	itpr1	**Sampdoria**	H	W	3-1	Knezevic 9, Tavano 10, 88	10,000
14	itpr1	**Cagliari**	A	D	0-0		10,000
15	itpr1	**Roma**	H	D	1-1	Tristan 6	10,000
16	itpr1	**Atalanta**	H	D	1-1	Galante 26	8,500
17	itpr1	**Torino**	A	W	2-1	Tavano 21, 45	18,000
18	itpr1	**Empoli**	H	W	1-0	Tavano 51 pen	8,428
19	itpr1	**Juventus**	H	L	1-3	Bogdani 79	14,630
20	itpr1	**Palermo**	A	L	0-1		23,000
21	itpr1	**Genoa**	H	D	1-1	Tavano 15	9,445
22	itpr1	**AC Milan**	A	D	1-1	Pulzetti 50	50,000
23	itpr1	**Inter Milan**	A	L	0-2		45,276
24	itpr1	**Napoli**	H	L	1-2	Diamanti 74	8,495
25	itpr1	**Fiorentina**	A	L	0-1		26,291
26	itpr1	**Catania**	H	W	1-0	Diamanti 62	9,759
27	itpr1	**Lazio**	A	L	0-2		19,110
28	itpr1	**Parma**	H	D	1-1	Vidigal 41	11,008
29	itpr1	**Reggina**	H	D	1-1	Bogdani 61	9,027
30	itpr1	**Udinese**	A	L	0-2		12,594
31	itpr1	**Siena**	H	D	0-0		10,207
32	itpr1	**Sampdoria**	A	L	0-2		21,426
33	itpr1	**Cagliari**	H	L	1-2	Galante 2	13,941
34	itpr1	**Roma**	A	D	1-1	Diamanti 83	34,061
35	itpr1	**AC Milan**	H	L	1-4	Knezevic 73	14,504
36	itpr1	**Atalanta**	A	L	2-3	Rossini 64, Pavan 81	8,999
37	itpr1	**Torino**	H	L	0-1		8,813
38	itpr1	**Empoli**	A	L	1-2	Diamanti 84	6,858

LEAGUE APPEARANCES, BOOKINGS AND CAPS

	AGE (on 01/07/08)	IN NAMED 18	APPEARANCES	COUNTING GAMES	MINUTES ON PITCH	YELLOW CARDS	RED CARDS	CAPS THIS SEASON	NATIONAL SIDE
Goalkeepers									
Marco Amelia	26	35	33	33	2957	2	0	3	Italy
Alfonso De Lucia	24	38	6	5	463	0	0	-	Italy
Defenders									
David Balleri	39	31	28	20	2123	8	1	-	Italy
Sidney F dos Santos	26	2	2	1	150	0	0	-	Brazil
Fabio Galante	34	34	34	32	2959	4	0	-	Italy
Alessandro Grandoni	30	34	34	33	2993	7	0	-	Italy
Dario Knezevic	26	37	36	34	3132	5	0	6	Croatia
Filip Krstic	19	2	1	0	33	0	0	-	Serbia
Matteo Melara	29	8	4	4	360	1	0	-	Italy
Giovanni Pasquale	26	35	35	34	3099	7	0	-	Italy
Simone Pavan	34	33	16	7	784	4	0	-	Italy
Midfielders									
Edgar A R Alvarez	28	19	7	0	238	0	0	-	Honduras
Martin Bergvold	24	14	13	7	863	1	0	-	Denmark
Daniele De Vezze	28	29	27	18	1941	10	2	-	Italy
Vikash Dhorasoo	34	2	0	0	0	0	0	-	France
Emanuele Filippini	34	33	17	8	984	6	0	-	Italy
Antonio Filippini	34	30	27	17	1913	3	0	-	Italy
Guiliano Giannichedda	33	11	8	3	423	1	0	-	Italy
Massimo Loviso	24	29	20	13	1450	6	1	-	Italy
Massimo Piscopo	19	2	0	0	0	0	0	-	-
Nico Pulzetti	24	26	26	20	2007	3	0	-	Italy
Rahman Rezaei	33	14	4	0	130	0	0	-	Iran
Tommaso Vailatti	22	7	4	0	74	1	0	-	Italy
Jose Luis Vidigal	35	20	17	12	1248	8	1	-	Portugal
Francesco M Volpe	22	5	2	0	61	0	0	-	Italy
Forwards									
Erjon Bogdani	31	33	28	9	1440	4	0	3	Albania
Alessandro Diamanti	25	34	26	10	1425	2	0	-	Italy
Fausto Rossini	30	23	20	3	737	3	0	-	Italy
Francesco Tavano	29	32	30	22	2328	1	0	-	Italy
Diego Tristan	32	27	21	11	1314	2	0	-	Spain

TEAM OF THE SEASON

G
Marco Amelia
CG: 33 DR: 61
D
David Balleri
CG: 20 DR: 70
D
Fabio Galante
CG: 32 DR: 59
D
Dario Knezevic
CG: 34 DR: 58
D
Giovanni Pasquale
CG: 34 DR: 56
M
Massimo Loviso
CG: 13 SD: -29
M
Nico Pulzetti
CG: 20 SD: -39
M
Jose Luis Vidigal
CG: 12 SD: -60
M
Daniele De Vezze
CG: 17 SD: -60
F
Francesco Tavano
CG: 22 SR: 232
F
A Diamanti
CG: 10* SR: 356

MONTHLY POINTS TALLY

SEPTEMBER	2	13%
OCTOBER	3	25%
NOVEMBER	7	78%
DECEMBER	3	33%
JANUARY	6	67%
FEBRUARY	2	11%
MARCH	6	33%
APRIL	1	8%
MAY	0	0%

LEAGUE GOALS

	PLAYER	MINS	GOALS	S RATE
1	Tavano	2328	10	232
2	Diamanti	1425	4	356
3	Rossini	737	3	245
4	Knezevic	3132	3	1044
5	Bogdani	1440	2	720
6	Loviso	1450	2	725
7	Pulzetti	2007	2	1003
8	Galante	2959	2	1479
9	Pavan	784	1	784
10	Bergvold	863	1	863
11	Vidigal	1248	1	1248
12	Tristan	1314	1	1314
13	De Vezze	1849	1	1849
	Other		1	
	TOTAL		34	

TOP POINT EARNERS

	PLAYER	GAMES	AV PTS
1	David Balleri	20	1.25
2	Francesco Tavano	22	1.09
3	Daniele De Vezze	17	1.00
4	Fabio Galante	32	0.94
5	Alessandro Grandoni	33	0.85
6	Dario Knezevic	34	0.85
7	Marco Amelia	33	0.85
8	Giovanni Pasquale	34	0.79
9	Jose Luis Vidigal	12	0.75
10	Antonio Filippini	17	0.71
	CLUB AVERAGE:		0.79

DISCIPLINARY RECORDS

	PLAYER	YELLOW	RED	AVE
1	Jose Luis Vidigal	8	1	138
2	Emanuele Filippini	6	0	164
3	Daniele De Vezze	9	1	184
4	Simone Pavan	4	0	196
5	Massimo Loviso	6	1	207
6	David Balleri	8	1	235
7	Fausto Rossini	3	0	245
8	Erjon Bogdani	4	0	360
9	A Grandoni	7	0	427
10	Giovanni Pasquale	7	0	442
11	Dario Knezevic	5	0	626
12	Antonio Filippini	3	0	637
13	Diego Tristan	2	0	657
	Other	13	0	
	TOTAL	85	4	

KEY GOALKEEPER

Marco Amelia

Goals Conceded in the League	48	**Counting Games** League games when player was on pitch for at least 70 minutes	33
Defensive Rating Ave number of mins between League goals conceded while on the pitch	61	**Clean Sheets** In League games when player was on pitch for at least 70 minutes	5

KEY PLAYERS - DEFENDERS

David Balleri

Goals Conceded Number of League goals conceded while the player was on the pitch	30	**Clean Sheets** In League games when player was on pitch for at least 70 minutes	4
Defensive Rating Ave number of mins between League goals conceded while on the pitch	70	**Club Defensive Rating** Average number of mins between League goals conceded by the club this season	57

	PLAYER	CON LGE	CLEAN SHEETS	DEF RATE
1	David Balleri	30	4	70 mins
2	Fabio Galante	50	6	59 mins
3	Dario Knezevic	54	5	58 mins
4	Giovanni Pasquale	55	5	56 mins

KEY PLAYERS - MIDFIELDERS

Massimo Loviso

Goals in the League	2	**Contribution to Attacking Power** Average number of minutes between League team goals while on pitch	80
Defensive Rating Average number of mins between League goals conceded while on the pitch	51	**Scoring Difference** Defensive Rating minus Contribution to Attacking Power	-29

	PLAYER	LGE GOALS	DEF RATE	POWER	SCORE DIFF
1	Massimo Loviso	2	51	80	-29 mins
2	Nico Pulzetti	2	48	87	-39 mins
3	Jose Luis Vidigal	1	78	138	-60 mins
4	Daniele De Vezze	1	63	123	-60 mins

KEY PLAYERS - GOALSCORERS

Francesco Tavano

Goals in the League	10	**Player Strike Rate** Average number of minutes between League goals scored by player	232
Contribution to Attacking Power Average number of minutes between League team goals while on pitch	89	**Club Strike Rate** Average number of minutes between League goals scored by club	97

	PLAYER	LGE GOALS	POWER	STRIKE RATE
1	Francesco Tavano	10	89	232 mins
2	Alessandro Diamanti	4	118	356 mins
3	Massimo Loviso	2	80	725 mins
4	Nico Pulzetti	2	87	1003 mins

LEGEA
GRUPPO CARIGE
BANCA e ASSICURAZIONE
Daniele De Vezze

SQUAD APPEARANCES

Match	1	2	3	4	5	6	7	8	9	10	11	12	13	14	15	16	17	18	19	20	21	22	23	24	25	26	27	28	29	30	31	32	33	34	35	36	37	38
Venue	A	H	A	H	A	H	A	H	A	A	H	A	H	A	H	H	A	H	H	A	H	A	A	H	A	H	A	H	H	A	H	A	H	A	H	A	H	A
Competition	L	L	L	L	L	L	L	L	L	L	L	L	L	L	L	L	L	L	L	L	L	L	L	L	L	L	L	L	L	L	L	L	L	L	L	L	L	L
Result	L	L	D	D	L	L	L	L	L	W	D	W	W	D	D	D	W	W	L	L	D	D	L	L	L	W	L	D	D	L	D	L	L	D	L	L	L	L
Goalkeepers																																						
Marco Amelia																																						
Alfonso De Lucia																																						
Defenders																																						
David Balleri																																						
Sidney F dos Santos																																						
Fabio Galante																																						
Alessandro Grandoni																																						
Dario Knezevic																																						
Filip Krstic																																						
Matteo Melara																																						
Giovanni Pasquale																																						
Simone Pavan																																						
Midfielders																																						
Edgar A Reyes Alvarez																																						
Martin Bergvold																																						
Daniele De Vezze																																						
Vikash Dhorasoo																																						
Emanuele Filippini																																						
Antonio Filippini																																						
Guiliano Giannichedda																																						
Massimo Loviso																																						
Massimo Piscopo																																						
Nico Pulzetti																																						
Rahman Rezaei																																						
Tommaso Vailatti																																						
Jose Luis Vidigal																																						
Francesco M Volpe																																						
Forwards																																						
Erjon Bogdani																																						
Alessandro Diamanti																																						
Fausto Rossini																																						
Francesco Tavano																																						
Diego Tristan																																						

KEY: On all match · On bench · Subbed or sent off (Counting game) · Subbed or sent off (playing less than 70 minutes) · Subbed on from bench (Counting Game) · Subbed on (playing less than 70 minutes) · Subbed on and then subbed or sent off (Counting Game) · Subbed on and then subbed or sent off (playing less than 70 minutes) · Not in 16

DUTCH LEAGUE ROUND-UP

FINAL LEAGUE TABLE

	HOME					AWAY					TOTAL			
	P	W	D	L	F	A	W	D	L	F	A	F	A	DIF	PTS
PSV Eindhoven	34	12	4	1	41	12	9	5	3	24	12	65	24	41	72
Ajax Amsterdam	34	12	3	2	57	20	8	6	3	37	25	94	45	49	69
NAC Breda	34	8	3	6	24	22	11	3	3	24	18	48	40	8	63
Twente E	34	11	4	2	29	14	6	7	4	23	18	52	32	20	62
Heerenveen	34	9	3	5	56	26	9	3	5	32	22	88	48	40	60
Feyenoord	34	12	3	2	40	12	6	3	8	24	29	64	41	23	60
FC Groningen	34	9	2	6	23	19	6	4	7	30	35	53	54	-1	51
NEC Nijmegen	34	8	5	4	30	17	6	2	9	19	33	49	50	-1	49
Roda JC Kerk	34	8	5	4	31	24	4	6	7	24	31	55	55	0	47
FC Utrecht	34	8	3	6	35	27	5	4	8	24	28	59	55	4	46
AZ Alkmaar	34	8	4	5	25	14	3	6	8	23	39	48	53	-5	43
Vitesse Arnhem	34	7	5	5	24	19	5	2	10	22	36	46	55	-9	43
S Rotterdam	34	7	5	5	33	26	2	2	13	19	50	52	76	-24	34
SC Heracles	34	6	5	6	19	20	2	3	12	15	44	34	64	-30	32
Willem II Tilburg	34	7	2	8	33	24	1	5	11	7	25	40	49	-9	31
De Graafschap	34	3	6	8	17	30	4	3	10	16	34	33	64	-31	30
VVV Venlo	34	4	4	9	24	36	3	4	10	20	40	44	76	-32	29
Excelsior	34	5	4	8	21	32	2	2	13	11	43	32	75	-43	27

CLUB STRIKE FORCE

Ajax players celebrate their goal

1 Ajax

Goals scored in the League	94
Club Strike Rate (CSR) Average number of minutes between League goals scored by club	32

	CLUB	GOALS	CSR
1	Ajax	94	32
2	Heerenveen	88	34
3	Feyenoord	64	47
4	PSV Eindhoven	65	47
5	Utrecht	59	51
6	Roda JC Kerk	55	55
7	Groningen	53	57
8	S Rotterdam	52	58
9	Twente	52	58
10	NEC Nijmegen	49	62
11	NAC Breda	48	63
12	AZ Alkmaar	48	63
13	Vitesse Arnhem	46	66
14	VVV	44	69
15	Willem II Tilb	40	76
16	Heracles	34	90
17	De Graafschap	33	92
18	Excelsior	32	95

CLUB DISCIPLINARY RECORDS

Heracles' Emanuel Boakye; 9 cards

1 Heracles

League Yellow	77
League Red	2
League Total	79
Cards Average in League Average number of minutes between a card being shown of either colour	38

	CLUB	Y	R	TOTAL	AVE
1	Heracles	77	2	79	38
2	Roda JC Kerk	74	3	77	39
3	S Rotterdam	73	3	76	40
4	Utrecht	67	4	71	43
5	Excelsior	64	3	67	45
6	Vitesse Arnhem	62	5	67	45
7	VVV	61	4	65	47
8	Twente	58	3	61	50
9	Ajax	58	2	60	51
10	AZ Alkmaar	55	4	59	51
11	Feyenoord	54	1	55	55
12	NAC Breda	50	3	53	57
13	Willem II Tilb	50	3	53	57
14	NEC Nijmegen	49	3	52	58
15	Heerenveen	48	4	52	58
16	Groningen	49	2	51	60
17	PSV Eindhoven	48	2	50	61
18	De Graafschap	40	2	42	72

CLUB DEFENCES

	CLUB	LGE	CS	CDR
1	PSV Eindhoven	24	17	127
2	Twente	32	13	95
3	NAC Breda	40	16	76
4	Feyenoord	41	14	74
5	Ajax	45	7	68
6	Heerenveen	48	12	63
7	Willem II Tilb	49	8	62
8	NEC Nijmegen	50	8	61
9	AZ Alkmaar	53	8	57
10	Groningen	54	6	56
11	Roda JC Kerk	55	5	55
12	Utrecht	55	4	55
13	Vitesse Arnhem	55	8	55
14	Heracles	64	8	47
15	De Graafschap	64	6	47
16	Excelsior	75	4	40
17	VVV	76	6	40
18	S Rotterdam	76	2	40

PSV's Dutch defender Dirk Marcellis

1 PSV Eindhoven

Goals conceded in the League	24
Clean Sheets (CS) Number of league games where no goals were conceded	17
Club Defensive Rate (CDR) Average number of minutes between League goals conceded by club	127

PLAYER NATIONALITIES

Overseas country with the most player appearances in the Dutch League - Belgium

575 league appearances by Belgian players

	COUNTRY	PLAYERS	IN SQUAD	LGE APP	% LGE ACT	CAPS	MOST APP	APP
	Holland	342	7000	5203	62.98	100	Brian van Loo	100.0
1	Belgium	31	754	575	6.96	23	Timmy Simons	97.1
2	Denmark	14	338	294	3.44	11	Lasse Schone	90.5
3	Brazil	16	285	215	2.37	0	Heurelho Gomes	100.0
4	Sweden	7	190	177	2.23	3	Rasmus Lindgren	87.4
5	Ghana	8	176	144	1.83	0	Francis Dickoh	86.9
6	Hungary	5	143	110	1.42	0	Gabor Babos	100.0
7	Switzerland	3	92	92	1.32	0	Blaise N'Kufo	97.8
8	Uruguay	3	94	94	1.31	0	Bruno Barone	88.2
9	Croatia	3	96	95	1.23	10	Danijel Pranjic	94.2
10	Australia	4	102	90	1.09	0	Luke Wilkshire	79.5
11	Serbia	4	125	99	1.05	6	Miralem Sulejmani	78.7
12	Spain	6	134	91	0.99	0	G Garcia de la Torre	67.9
13	France	4	95	86	0.96	0	Sebastien Sansoni	71.2
14	Germany	3	86	75	0.92	0	M Pieckenhagen	100.0
15	Sierra Leone	2	61	60	0.89	0	Gibril Sankoh	94.1
16	Turkey	4	85	67	0.74	0	Nuri Sahin	72.8
17	Iceland	4	61	51	0.66	4	Arnar Vidarsson	86.5
18	Canada	4	69	59	0.63	0	Jonathan de Guzman	95.9
19	Ivory Coast	3	53	51	0.62	0	Cheik Ismael Tiote	73.6
22	Finland	4	79	64	0.61	0	Joonas Kolkka	76.2

CLUB MAKE-UP – HOME AND OVERSEAS PLAYERS

1 Heracles

51.7% of appearances by overseas players

	CLUB	OVERSEAS	HOME	% OVERSEAS	% LGE ACT	MOST APP	APP
1	Heracles	15	14	51.7	70.54	M Pieckenhagen	100.0
2	Roda JC Kerk	17	10	63.0	67.61	Bram Castro	97.1
3	PSV Eindhoven	19	11	63.3	67.41	Heurelho Gomes	100.0
4	Ajax	16	22	42.1	64.32	Bruno Barone	88.2
5	Groningen	15	18	45.5	59.70	Gibril Sankoh	94.1
6	Heerenveen	17	14	54.8	51.71	Danijel Pranjic	94.2
7	Vitesse Arnhem	15	17	46.9	46.36	Gill Swerts	94.7
8	VVV	9	19	32.1	43.77	Mike Mampuya	92.6
9	AZ Alkmaar	14	17	45.2	41.99	Moussa Dembele	93.4
10	NEC Nijmegen	11	21	34.4	38.11	Gabor Babos	100.0
11	De Graafschap	8	21	27.6	36.82	Lasse Schone	90.5
12	NAC Breda	6	24	20.0	34.83	Patrick Mtiliga	86.8
13	Willem II Tilb	13	21	38.2	30.97	Thomas Baelum	82.9
14	Utrecht	10	25	28.6	30.86	Francis Dickoh	86.9
15	S Rotterdam	6	23	20.7	25.92	Nourdin Boukhari	84.1
16	Feyenoord	7	24	22.6	24.46	J de Guzman	95.9
17	Twente	10	17	37.0	23.98	Blaise N'Kufo	97.8
18	Excelsior	4	24	14.3	9.85	Sebastien Pardo	46.9

CHART-TOPPING MIDFIELDERS

1 Dzsudzsak - PSV Eindhoven

Goals scored in the League	3
Defensive Rating Av number of mins between League goals conceded while on the pitch	181
Contribution to Attacking Power Average number of minutes between League team goals while on pitch	60
Scoring Difference Defensive Rating minus Contribution to Attacking Power	121

	PLAYER	CLUB	GOALS	DEF RATE	POWER	S DIFF
1	Balazs Dzsudzsak	PSV Eindhoven	3	181	60	**121**
2	Otman Bakkal	PSV Eindhoven	8	153	44	**109**
3	Geert Arend Roorda	Heerenveen	2	125	30	**95**
4	Timmy Simons	PSV Eindhoven	4	129	48	**81**
5	Ibrahim Afellay	PSV Eindhoven	2	126	53	**73**
6	Csaba Feher	NAC Breda	2	110	58	**52**
7	Nuri Sahin	Feyenoord	6	89	40	**49**
8	Edgar Davids	Ajax	0	85	36	**49**
9	Kenneth Perez	Ajax	7	71	32	**39**
10	Bas Sibum	NEC Nijmegen	1	83	44	**39**
11	Orlando Engelaar	Twente	4	93	55	**38**
12	Stein Huysegems	Twente	5	81	46	**35**
13	Theo Lucius	Feyenoord	1	79	45	**34**
14	Jan Vertonghen	Ajax	2	70	37	**33**
15	Rogier Molhoek	NAC Breda	3	99	66	**33**

CHART-TOPPING GOALSCORERS

1 Huntelaar - Ajax

Goals scored in the League	33
Contribution to Attacking Power (AP) Average number of minutes between League team goals while on pitch	33
Club Strike Rate (CSR) Average minutes between League goals scored by club	35
Player Strike Rate Average number of minutes between League goals scored by player	95

	PLAYER	CLUB	GOALS: LGE	POWER	CSR	S RATE
1	Klaas-Jan Huntelaar	Ajax	33	33	35	**95**
2	Marcus Berg	Groningen	15	47	59	**127**
3	Blaise N'Kufo	Twente	22	57	60	**136**
4	Luis Suarez	Ajax	17	34	35	**148**
5	Jhon van Beukering	NEC Nijmegen	11	54	62	**169**
6	Miralem Sulejmani	Heerenveen	14	33	34	**172**
7	Matthew Amoah	NAC Breda	11	63	65	**172**
8	Robin Nelisse	Utrecht	16	52	51	**172**
9	Kenneth Perez	Ajax	7	32	35	**174**
10	Frank Demouge	Willem II Tilb	8	64	76	**178**
11	Roy Makaay	Feyenoord	13	49	50	**186**
12	Michael Bradley	Heerenveen	15	37	34	**191**
13	Danko Lazovic	PSV Eindhoven	11	46	49	**197**
14	Marvin Emnes	S Rotterdam	8	63	60	**197**
15	Geert den Ouden	Excelsior	12	121	95	**201**

CHART-TOPPING DEFENDERS

1 Salcido - PSV Eindhoven

Goals Conceded in the League The number of League goals conceded while he was on the pitch	20
Clean Sheets In games when he played at least 70 mins	17
Club Defensive Rating Average mins between League goals conceded by the club this season	135
Defensive Rating Average number of minutes between League goals conceded while on pitch	146

	PLAYER	CLUB	CON: LGE	CS	CDR	DEF RATE
1	Carlos Salcido	PSV Eindhoven	20	17	135	**146**
2	Jan Kromkamp	PSV Eindhoven	17	12	135	**137**
3	Mendes Alves	PSV Eindhoven	15	9	135	**112**
4	Dirk Marcellis	PSV Eindhoven	20	10	135	**109**
5	Mike Zonneveld	PSV Eindhoven	15	9	135	**108**
6	Edson Braafheid	Twente	28	11	98	**100**
7	Thomas Vermaelen	Ajax	15	6	74	**97**
8	Luke Wilkshire	Twente	25	9	98	**97**
9	Jeroen Heubach	Twente	28	12	98	**96**
10	Patrick Zwaanswijk	NAC Breda	27	15	78	**95**
11	Rob Wielaert	Twente	31	12	98	**92**
12	Rob Penders	NAC Breda	26	13	78	**90**
13	Patrick Mtiliga	NAC Breda	31	14	78	**84**
14	Henrico Drost	Heerenveen	14	4	63	**79**
15	Gretar Rafn Steinsson	AZ Alkmaar	17	5	62	**77**

CHART-TOPPING GOALKEEPERS

1 Gomes - PSV Eindhoven

Counting Games Games in which he played at least 70 minutes	34
Goals Conceded in the League The number of League goals conceded while he was on the pitch	24
Clean Sheets In games when he played at least 70 mins	17
Defensive Rating Average number of minutes between League goals conceded while on pitch	127

	PLAYER	CLUB	CG	CONC	CS	DEF RATE
1	Heurelho Gomes	PSV Eindhoven	34	24	17	**127**
2	Sander Boschker	Twente	34	32	13	**95**
3	Maikel Aerts	Willem II Tilb	18	18	6	**91**
4	Jelle ten Rouwelaar	NAC Breda	32	34	16	**84**
5	Sergio Romero	AZ Alkmaar	12	14	3	**77**
6	Henk Timmer	Feyenoord	32	38	13	**75**
7	Maarten Stekelenburg	Ajax	30	42	5	**66**
8	Brian Vandenbussche	Heerenveen	19	27	6	**64**
9	Rob van Dijk	Heerenveen	14	21	6	**63**
10	Gabor Babos	NEC Nijmegen	34	50	8	**61**
11	Piet Velthuizen	Vitesse Arnhem	31	49	8	**59**
12	Brian van Loo	Groningen	35	54	7	**58**
13	Franck Grandel	Utrecht	13	22	1	**56**
14	Bram Castro	Roda JC Kerk	33	55	4	**54**
15	Danny Wintjens	VVV	20	35	5	**51**

PLAYER DISCIPLINARY RECORD

Gaaouiri pulling his opponent's shirt

1. Samir el Gaaouiri - VVV

Cards Average mins between cards	134
League Yellow	5
League Red	1
TOTAL	6

	PLAYER		LY	LR	TOT	AVE
1	S Gaaouiri	VVV	5	1	6	134
2	E v Bueren	S Rotterdam	8	0	8	157
3	J Broerse	Utrecht	3	0	3	168
4	E V Mendez	PSV Eindhoven	5	1	6	172
5	A Yakubu	Vitesse Arnhem	5	0	5	183
6	Wellenberg	Twente	7	0	7	187
7	F Sonkaya	Roda JC Kerk	4	0	4	203
8	D Tornhout	Roda JC Kerk	3	0	3	205
9	Nick Hofs	Feyenoord	5	1	6	210
10	N Rutjes	S Rotterdam	5	1	6	211
11	H Maduro	Ajax	5	0	5	215
12	Rick Kruys	Utrecht	5	0	5	218
13	I Moreno	S Rotterdam	4	0	4	219
14	R Ouedraogo	Heracles	6	1	7	220
15	Danny Holla	Groningen	2	0	2	228

TEAM OF THE SEASON

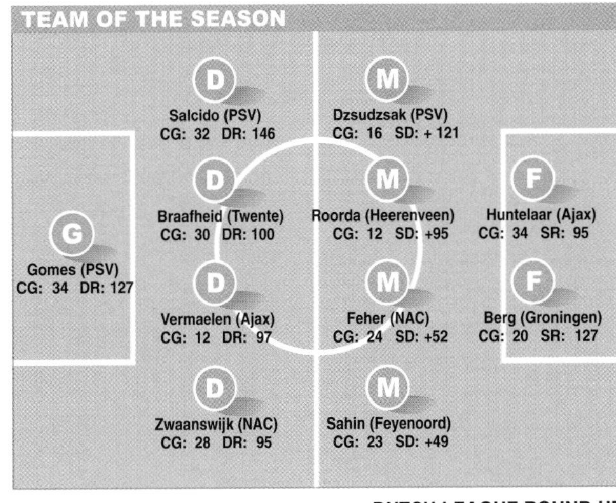

G
Gomes (PSV)
CG: 34 DR: 127
D
Salcido (PSV)
CG: 32 DR: 146
D
Braafheid (Twente)
CG: 30 DR: 100
D
Vermaelen (Ajax)
CG: 12 DR: 97
D
Zwaanswijk (NAC)
CG: 28 DR: 95
M
Dzsudzsak (PSV)
CG: 16 SD: + 121
M
Roorda (Heerenveen)
CG: 12 SD: +95
M
Feher (NAC)
CG: 24 SD: +52
M
Sahin (Feyenoord)
CG: 23 SD: +49
F
Huntelaar (Ajax)
CG: 34 SR: 95
F
Berg (Groningen)
CG: 20 SR: 127

PSV EINDHOVEN

Final Position: **1st**

NICKNAME: BOEREN

KEY: ☐Won ☐Drawn ☐Lost

	Comp	Opponent	Venue	Res	Score	Scorers	Attendance
1	hopr1	**Heracles**	A	W	2-0	Afellay 83, Zonneveld 90	8,500
2	hopr1	**NEC Nijmegen**	H	W	5-0	Lazovic 6, 82, Addo 44, Fagner 87, Bakkal 89	33,000
3	hopr1	**Twente**	A	D	0-0		13,150
4	hopr1	**Vitesse Arnhem**	H	W	1-0	Koevermans 7	34,000
5	ecgpg	**CSKA Moscow**	H	W	2-1	Lazovic 60, Perez 81	32,500
6	hopr1	**Feyenoord**	H	W	4-0	Perez 36, 43, Mendez 39, Koevermans 88	33,000
7	hopr1	**NAC Breda**	A	D	1-1	Perez 76	15,089
8	ecgpg	**Inter Milan**	A	L	0-2		40,000
9	hopr1	**Willem II Tilb**	H	W	3-0	Koevermans 23, 45, Farfan 77	33,258
10	hopr1	**VVV**	H	W	3-1	Bakkal 24, Koevermans 51, 77	33,600
11	ecgpg	**Fenerbahce**	H	D	0-0		35,000
12	hopr1	**S Rotterdam**	A	W	4-1	Lazovic 1, Zonneveld 11, Farfan 26, Perez 70	10,450
13	hopr1	**Heerenveen**	A	L	1-2	Lazovic 29	25,500
14	ecgpg	**Fenerbahce**	A	L	0-2		45,000
15	hopr1	**AZ Alkmaar**	H	D	1-1	Farfan 59	33,600
16	hopr1	**Excelsior**	A	W	4-1	Bakkal 23, Koevermans 57, Lazovic 58, Perez 76 pen	2,500
17	ecgpg	**CSKA Moscow**	A	W	1-0	Farfan 39	25,000
18	hopr1	**De Graafschap**	A	W	1-0	Farfan 45	12,000
19	hopr1	**Roda JC Kerk**	H	L	2-4	Saeijs 81 og, Koevermans 83	33,000
20	ecgpg	**Inter Milan**	H	L	0-1		34,500
21	hopr1	**Utrecht**	H	W	4-1	Perez 16, 67, Lazovic 64, Koevermans 85	33,500
22	hopr1	**Groningen**	A	L	1-2	De Araujo Alves 21	18,273
23	hopr1	**NAC Breda**	H	W	2-0	Koevermans 45, Perez 90	33,000
24	hopr1	**Feyenoord**	A	W	1-0	Bakkal 40	45,000
25	hopr1	**VVV**	A	D	1-1	Dzsudzsak 12	6,000
26	hopr1	**S Rotterdam**	H	W	3-1	Lazovic 25, Kromkamp 56, Culina 90	33,000
27	hopr1	**Excelsior**	H	W	2-1	Dzsudzsak 7, Koevermans 90	33,000
28	hopr1	**Ajax**	A	W	2-0	Dzsudzsak 41, Bakkal 73	49,822
29	hopr1	**AZ Alkmaar**	A	W	2-0	Lazovic 13, Afellay 25	16,457
30	hopr1	**Heerenveen**	H	D	1-1	Bakkal 1	33,600
31	ucrl1	**Helsingborg**	H	W	2-0	Simons 7 pen, Lazovic 32	21,500
32	hopr1	**Willem II Tilb**	A	W	1-0	Simons 84 pen	14,192
33	ucrl2	**Helsingborg**	A	W	2-1	Bakkal 47, Lazovic 65	10,194
34	hopr1	**De Graafschap**	H	W	4-1	Lazovic 8, 90, Bakkal 51, Simons 82 pen	33,200
35	hopr1	**Utrecht**	A	L	1-3	Simons 29 pen	21,700
36	ucrl1	**Tottenham**	A	W	1-0	Farfan 34	33,259
37	ucrl2	**Tottenham**	H	W	6-5*	(*on penalties)	33,500
38	hopr1	**Roda JC Kerk**	A	D	1-1	Farfan 67	17,000
39	hopr1	**Ajax**	H	D	0-0		35,000
40	hopr1	**Groningen**	H	W	3-0	Koevermans 33, 84, Bakkal 47	33,000
41	hopr1	**NEC Nijmegen**	A	D	0-0		12,500
42	ucqfl1	**Fiorentina**	A	D	1-1	Koevermans 63	34,317
43	hopr1	**Heracles**	H	W	2-0	Simons 12, Farfan 80	33,000
44	ucqfl2	**Fiorentina**	H	L	0-2		36,200
45	hopr1	**Twente**	H	D	1-1	Farfan 68	34,000
46	hopr1	**Vitesse Arnhem**	A	W	1-0	Lazovic 47	25,420

LEAGUE APPEARANCES, BOOKINGS AND CAPS

	AGE (on 01/07/08)	IN NAMED 18	APPEARANCES	COUNTING GAMES	MINUTES ON PITCH	YELLOW CARDS	RED CARDS	CAPS THIS SEASON	NATIONAL SIDE
Goalkeepers									
Heurelho Gomes	27	34	34	34	3060	1	0	-	Brazil
Cassio Ramos	21	2	0	0	0	0	0	-	Brazil
Bas Roorda	35	32	0	0	0	0	0	-	Holland
Defenders									
Eric Addo	29	22	12	11	1056	1	0	12	Ghana
Fagner C Lemos	19	8	3	0	79	0	0	-	Brazil
Manuel da Costa	22	7	1	0	2	0	0	-	Portugal
Mendes de A Alves	23	28	21	19	1692	4	0	-	Brazil
Jan Kromkamp	27	26	26	26	2340	1	0	-	Holland
Dirk Marcellis	20	29	26	24	2184	3	0	-	Holland
Slobodan Rajkovic	19	25	13	5	560	1	0	-	Serbia
Carlos Salcido	28	33	33	32	2929	5	0	1	Mexico
Rens van Eijden	20	1	0	0	0	0	0	-	Holland
Mike Zonneveld	27	31	21	17	1627	3	0	-	Holland
Midfielders									
Ibrahim Afellay	22	24	24	21	2018	7	0	7	Holland
Ismael Aissati	19	31	16	5	635	0	0	-	Holland
Otman Bakkal	23	32	31	18	1994	4	0	-	Holland
Jason Culina	27	28	18	8	937	4	0	5	Australia
John de Jong	31	1	0	0	0	0	0	-	Holland
Balazs Dzsudzsak	21	17	17	16	1455	3	0	-	Hungary
Edison V Mendez	29	28	20	6	1037	5	1	-	Ecuador
Kenneth Perez	33	16	14	10	1071	1	0	-	Denmark
Timmy Simons	31	33	33	33	2970	0	0	6	Belgium
Mika Vayrynen	26	7	1	0	4	0	0	-	Finland
T van der Leegte	31	11	2	0	25	0	0	-	Holland
Forwards									
Jefferson Farfan	23	31	29	23	2319	1	0	4	Peru
Danny Koevermans	29	31	29	9	1343	0	0	3	Holland
Arouna Kone	24	1	1	1	85	0	0	1	Ivory Coast
Danko Lazovic	25	32	31	20	2171	4	1	6	Serbia
Jonathan Reis	19	10	3	0	24	0	0	-	Brazil
Genero Zeefuik	18	2	2	0	23	0	0	-	Holland

TEAM OF THE SEASON

G
Gomes
CG: 34 DR: 127

D
Carlos Salcido
CG: 32 DR: 146

D
Jan Kromkamp
CG: 26 DR: 137

D
Alcides
CG: 19 DR: 112

D
Dirk Marcellis
CG: 24 DR: 109

M
Balazs Dzsudzsak
CG: 16 SD: 121

M
Otman Bakkal
CG: 18 SD: 109

M
Timmy Simons
CG: 33 SD: 81

M
Ibrahim Afellay
CG: 21 SD: 73

F
Danko Lazovic
CG: 20 SR: 197

F
Jefferson Farfan
CG: 23 SR: 331

MONTHLY POINTS TALLY

Month	Points	%
AUGUST	6	100%
SEPTEMBER	8	67%
OCTOBER	9	100%
NOVEMBER	4	44%
DECEMBER	9	60%
JANUARY	13	87%
FEBRUARY	10	83%
MARCH	6	40%
APRIL	7	78%

LEAGUE GOALS

	PLAYER	MINS	GOALS	S RATE
1	Koevermans	1343	13	103
2	Lazovic	2171	11	197
3	Perez	1071	8	133
4	Bakkal	1994	8	249
5	Farfan	2319	7	331
6	Simons	2970	4	742
7	Dzsudzsak	1455	3	485
8	Zonneveld	1627	2	813
9	Afellay	2018	2	1009
10	Conserva Lemos	79	1	79
11	Culina	937	1	937
12	Mendez	1037	1	1037
13	Addo	1056	1	1056
	Other		2	
	TOTAL		64	

TOP POINT EARNERS

	PLAYER	GAMES	AV PTS
1	Otman Bakkal	18	2.39
2	Ibrahim Afellay	21	2.24
3	Danko Lazovic	20	2.20
4	Balazs Dzsudzsak	16	2.19
5	Carlos Salcido	32	2.16
6	Gomes	34	2.12
7	Timmy Simons	33	2.09
8	Jan Kromkamp	26	2.08
9	Dirk Marcellis	24	2.04
10	Alcides	19	2.00
	CLUB AVERAGE:		2.12

DISCIPLINARY RECORDS

	PLAYER	YELLOW	RED	AVE
1	Edison Mendez	5	1	172
2	Jason Culina	4	0	234
3	Ibrahim Afellay	7	0	288
4	Eduardo Alcides	4	0	423
5	Danko Lazovic	4	1	434
6	Balazs Dzsudzsak	3	0	485
7	Otman Bakkal	4	0	498
8	Mike Zonneveld	3	0	542
9	Slobodan Rajkovic	1	0	560
10	Carlos Salcido	5	0	585
11	Dirk Marcellis	3	0	728
12	Eric Addo	1	0	1056
13	Kenneth Perez	1	0	1071
	Other	3	0	
	TOTAL	48	2	

KEY GOALKEEPER

Heurelho da Silva Gomes

Goals Conceded in the League	24	**Counting Games** League games when player was on pitch for at least 70 minutes	34
Defensive Rating Ave number of mins between League goals conceded while on the pitch	127	**Clean Sheets** In League games when player was on pitch for at least 70 minutes	17

KEY PLAYERS - DEFENDERS

Carlos Salcido

Goals Conceded Number of League goals conceded while the player was on the pitch	20	**Clean Sheets** In League games when player was on pitch for at least 70 minutes	17
Defensive Rating Ave number of mins between League goals conceded while on the pitch	146	**Club Defensive Rating** Average number of mins between League goals conceded by the club this season	135

	PLAYER	CON LGE	CLEAN SHEETS	DEF RATE
1	Carlos Salcido	20	17	146 mins
2	Jan Kromkamp	17	12	137 mins
3	Eduardo Alcides	15	9	112 mins
4	Dirk Marcellis	20	10	109 mins

KEY PLAYERS - MIDFIELDERS

Balazs Dzsudzsak

Goals in the League	3	**Contribution to Attacking Power** Average number of minutes between League team goals while on pitch	60
Defensive Rating Average number of mins between League goals conceded while on the pitch	181	**Scoring Difference** Defensive Rating minus Contribution to Attacking Power	121

	PLAYER	LGE GOALS	DEF RATE	POWER	SCORE DIFF
1	Balazs Dzsudzsak	3	181	60	121 mins
2	Otman Bakkal	8	153	44	109 mins
3	Timmy Simons	4	129	48	81 mins
4	Ibrahim Afellay	2	126	53	73 mins

KEY PLAYERS - GOALSCORERS

Danko Lazovic

Goals in the League	11	**Player Strike Rate** Average number of minutes between League goals scored by player	197
Contribution to Attacking Power Average number of minutes between League team goals while on pitch	46	**Club Strike Rate** Average number of minutes between League goals scored by club	49

	PLAYER	LGE GOALS	POWER	STRIKE RATE
1	Danko Lazovic	11	46	197 mins
2	Otman Bakkal	8	44	249 mins
3	Jefferson Farfan	7	53	331 mins
4	Balazs Dzsudzsak	3	60	485 mins

PHILIP
Jefferson Farfan

SQUAD APPEARANCES

Match	1	2	3	4	5	6	7	8	9	10	11	12	13	14	15	16	17	18	19	20	21	22	23
Venue	A	H	A	H	H	H	A	A	H	H	H	A	A	A	H	A	A	A	H	H	H	A	H
Competition	L	L	L	L	C	L	L	C	L	L	C	L	L	C	L	L	C	L	L	C	L	L	L
Result	W	W	D	W	W	W	D	L	W	W	D	W	L	L	D	W	W	W	L	L	W	L	W

Match	24	25	26	27	28	29	30	31	32	33	34	35	36	37	38	39	40	41	42	43	44	45	46
Venue	A	A	H	H	A	A	H	H	A	A	H	A	A	H	A	H	H	A	A	H	H	H	A
Competition	L	L	L	L	L	L	L	E	L	E	L	L	E	E	L	L	L	L	E	L	E	L	L
Result	W	D	W	W	W	W	D	W	W	W	W	L	W	W	D	D	W	D	D	W	L	D	W

Goalkeepers
- Heurelho Gomes
- Cassio Ramos
- Bas Roorda

Defenders
- Eric Addo
- Fagner Conserva Lemos
- Manuel da Costa
- Mendes de Araujo Alves
- Jan Kromkamp
- Dirk Marcellis
- Slobodan Rajkovic
- Carlos Salcido
- Rens van Eijden
- Mike Zonneveld

Midfielders
- Ibrahim Afellay
- Ismaal Aissati
- Otman Bakkal
- Jason Culina
- John de Jong
- Balazs Dzsudzsak
- Edison Vincente Mendez
- Kenneth Perez
- Timmy Simons
- Mika Vayrynen
- Tommie van der Leegte

Forwards
- Jefferson Farfan
- Danny Koevermans
- Arouna Kone
- Danko Lazovic
- Jonathan Reis
- Genero Zeefuik

KEY: On all match | On bench | Subbed or sent off (Counting game) | Subbed or sent off (playing less than 70 minutes) | Subbed on from bench (Counting Game) | Subbed on (playing less than 70 minutes) | Subbed on and then subbed or sent off (Counting Game) | Subbed on and then subbed or sent off (playing less than 70 minutes) | Not in 16

AJAX

Final Position: **2nd**

NICKNAME: GODENZONEN

KEY: ☐Won ☐Drawn ☐Lost

#	Comp	Opponent	Venue	Res	Score	Scorers	Attendance
1	hopr1	**De Graafschap**	A	W	8-1	Huntelaar 36, 70, 90, 90 pen, Suarez 43, Maduro 54, 57, Bakircioglu 60	11,000
2	hopr1	**Heerenveen**	H	W	4-1	Suarez 44, 58, Vermaelen 45, Schilder 53	48,988
3	ecql2	**Slavia Prague**	A	L	1-2	Suarez 33	17,500
4	hopr1	**Groningen**	H	D	2-2	Suarez 33, Huntelaar 83	45,000
5	hopr1	**Heracles**	A	W	1-0	Huntelaar 76	8,500
6	ucrl1	**Dinamo Zagreb**	A	W	1-0	Rommedahl 62	30,000
7	hopr1	**AZ Alkmaar**	A	W	3-2	Huntelaar 33 fk, Suarez 43, 65	16,556
8	hopr1	**VVV**	H	W	6-1	Martos 16, 19, Maduro 27, Rommedahl 32, Delorge 77, Huntelaar 89	49,126
9	ucrl2	**Dinamo Zagreb**	H	L	2-3	Huntelaar 101, 121	51,000
10	hopr1	**S Rotterdam**	A	D	2-2	Huntelaar 68, De Jong 90	10,800
11	hopr1	**NEC Nijmegen**	H	D	0-0		48,123
12	hopr1	**Utrecht**	A	W	1-0	Huntelaar 68	23,300
13	hopr1	**Roda JC Kerk**	H	W	4-2	Huntelaar 22, Suarez 42, Martos 46, Rommedahl 90	48,621
14	hopr1	**Feyenoord**	A	D	2-2	Rommedahl 52, De Jong 67	42,500
15	hopr1	**Vitesse Arnhem**	H	W	4-1	Suarez 17, Garcia de la Torre 27, Martos 44 pen, Huntelaar 82	49,566
16	hopr1	**NAC Breda**	H	L	1-3	Huntelaar 90	47,588
17	hopr1	**Willem II Tilb**	A	W	3-2	Bakircioglu 2, Suarez 29, Vertonghen 45	14,044
18	hopr1	**Excelsior**	A	L	1-2	Maduro 63	3,500
19	hopr1	**Twente**	H	D	2-2	Huntelaar 31, Braafheid 76 og	50,523
20	hopr1	**VVV**	A	D	2-2	Suarez 37, Huntelaar 77	6,000
21	hopr1	**AZ Alkmaar**	H	W	6-1	Vertonghen 23, Perez 44 pen, Huntelaar 61, 89, Bakircioglu 67, Vitor Santiago 87	50,639
22	hopr1	**NEC Nijmegen**	A	D	1-1	Huntelaar 74	12,400
23	hopr1	**Utrecht**	H	W	2-0	Huntelaar 68, Heitinga 77	45,537
24	hopr1	**Vitesse Arnhem**	A	D	2-2	Emanuelson 46, Suarez 51	22,700
25	hopr1	**PSV Eindhoven**	H	L	0-2		49,822
26	hopr1	**Feyenoord**	H	W	3-0	Heitinga 8, Huntelaar 45, 90	49,893
27	hopr1	**Roda JC Kerk**	A	L	1-2	Huntelaar 38	17,800
28	hopr1	**S Rotterdam**	H	W	6-2	Heitinga 14, 39, Huntelaar 29, Lindgren 31, Perez 40, 81	49,260
29	hopr1	**NAC Breda**	A	W	3-2	Huntelaar 21, Emanuelson 76, Heitinga 82	16,500
30	hopr1	**Excelsior**	H	W	4-0	Huntelaar 26, 40, Emanuelson 55, Vitor Santiago 85	49,313
31	hopr1	**Willem II Tilb**	H	W	4-1	Huntelaar 29, Suarez 45, 51, 89	49,918
32	hopr1	**PSV Eindhoven**	A	D	0-0		35,000
33	hopr1	**Twente**	A	L	1-2	Teixeira 63 og	13,250
34	hopr1	**Heerenveen**	A	W	4-2	Suarez 44, Perez 55 pen, Huntelaar 61, 89	25,000
35	hopr1	**De Graafschap**	H	W	4-1	Huntelaar 4, 9, 41, Perez 63	50,057
36	hopr1	**Groningen**	A	W	2-1	Lindgren 18, Suarez 66	19,700
37	hopr1	**Heracles**	H	W	5-1	Suarez 4, Perez 18, 73, Huntelaar 29, Heitinga 80	50,139
38	erepo	**Heerenveen**	A	W	2-1	Suarez 61, Heitinga 76	23,000
39	erepo	**Heerenveen**	H	W	3-1	Perez 45 pen, 55, Rommedahl 48	49,144
40	erepo	**Twente**	A	L	1-2	Suarez 44	8,000
41	erepo	**Twente**	H	D	0-0		49,764

LEAGUE APPEARANCES, BOOKINGS AND CAPS

	AGE (on 01/07/08)	IN NAMED 18	APPEARANCES	COUNTING GAMES	MINUTES ON PITCH	YELLOW CARDS	RED CARDS	CAPS THIS SEASON	NATIONAL SIDE
Goalkeepers									
Dennis Gentenaar	32	34	5	3	360	0	0	-	Holland
Maarten Stekelenburg	25	31	31	29	2700	1	0	6	Holland
Defenders									
Jurgen Colin	27	24	12	5	654	1	0	-	Holland
Urby Emanuelson	22	33	31	27	2499	4	0	5	Holland
John Heitinga	24	33	33	32	2939	6	0	11	Holland
Samuel Osei Kuffour	31	9	2	0	34	1	0	-	Ghana
George Ogararu	28	26	16	13	1276	1	1	6	Romania
Bruno Silva	28	12	12	12	1080	4	0	-	Uruguay
Jaap Stam	35	6	6	5	473	1	0	-	Holland
Gregory van der Wiel	20	10	6	3	424	0	0	-	Holland
Thomas Vermaelen	22	19	19	12	1367	4	0	2	Belgium
Midfielders									
Edgar Davids	35	15	14	11	1104	2	1	-	Holland
Siem De Jong	19	26	22	11	1236	1	0	-	Holland
Laurent Delorge	28	4	4	2	226	0	0	-	Belgium
Mitchell Donald	19	11	3	0	42	0	0	-	Holland
G Garcia de la Torre	29	27	26	21	2079	8	0	-	Spain
Michael Krohn-Dehli	25	2	1	0	15	0	0	-	Denmark
Rasmus Lindgren	23	12	11	8	794	2	0	-	Sweden
Hedwiges Maduro	23	16	15	9	1075	5	0	-	Holland
Kenneth Perez	33	16	16	11	1130	2	0	-	Denmark
Jeffrey Sarpong	19	6	1	0	19	0	0	-	Holland
Robbert Schilder	22	16	8	0	290	0	0	-	Holland
Jan Vertonghen	21	32	31	27	2574	3	0	-	Belgium
Forwards									
Kennedy Bakircioglu	27	26	18	6	876	1	0	3	Sweden
Klaas-Jan Huntelaar	24	34	34	34	3056	4	0	5	Holland
Albert Luque	30	23	16	6	762	1	0	-	Spain
Dennis Rommedahl	29	33	30	10	1704	0	0	9	Denmark
Luis Suarez	21	33	33	23	2436	5	0	7	Uruguay
Ismael Urzaiz	36	19	3	0	77	1	0	-	Spain
Leonardo V Santigo	25	11	8	1	283	0	0	-	Brazil

TEAM OF THE SEASON

G — Maarten Stekelenburg — CG: 29 DR: 66

D — Thomas Vermaelen — CG: 12 DR: 97

D — Urby Emanuelson — CG: 28 DR: 69

D — John Heitinga — CG: 32 DR: 68

D — Bruno Silva — CG: 12 DR: 68

M — Edgar Davids — CG: 11* SD: 49

M — Kenneth Perez — CG: 11* SD: 39

M — Jan Vertonghen — CG: 27 SD: 33

M — Garcia de la Torre — CG: 21 SD: 29

F — Klaas-Jan Huntelaar — CG: 34 SR: 95

F — Luis Suarez — CG: 23 SR: 148

MONTHLY POINTS TALLY

Month	Points	%
AUGUST	6	100%
SEPTEMBER	10	83%
OCTOBER	5	56%
NOVEMBER	7	78%
DECEMBER	5	33%
JANUARY	8	53%
FEBRUARY	9	75%
MARCH	10	67%
APRIL	9	100%

LEAGUE GOALS

	PLAYER	MINS	GOALS	S RATE
1	Huntelaar	3146	33	95
2	Suarez	2526	17	148
3	Perez	1220	7	174
4	Heitinga	3029	6	504
5	Martos	762	4	190
6	Maduro	1075	4	268
7	Bakircioglu	876	3	292
8	Rommedahl	1704	3	568
9	Emanuelson	2589	3	863
10	Vitor Santiago	283	2	141
11	Lindgren	884	2	442
12	De Jong	1236	2	618
13	Vertonghen	2664	2	1332
	Other		4	
	TOTAL		92	

TOP POINT EARNERS

	PLAYER	GAMES	AV PTS
1	Thomas Vermaelen	12	2.17
2	Maarten Stekelenburg	29	2.10
3	Luis Suarez	23	2.09
4	John Heitinga	32	2.03
5	Klaas-Jan Huntelaar	34	2.03
6	George Ogararu	13	2.00
7	Urby Emanuelson	27	2.00
8	Jan Vertonghen	27	2.00
9	Bruno Silva	12	1.92
10	Garcia de la Torre	21	1.67
	CLUB AVERAGE:		2.03

DISCIPLINARY RECORDS

	PLAYER	YELLOW	RED	AVE
1	Hedwiges Maduro	5	0	215
2	Garcia de la Torre	8	0	259
3	Bruno Silva	4	0	292
4	Thomas Vermaelen	4	0	364
5	Edgar Davids	2	1	398
6	Rasmus Lindgren	2	0	442
7	Jaap Stam	1	0	473
8	John Heitinga	6	0	504
9	Luis Suarez	5	0	505
10	Kenneth Perez	2	0	610
11	George Ogararu	1	1	638
12	Urby Emanuelson	4	0	647
13	Jurgen Colin	1	0	654
	Other	11	0	
	TOTAL	56	2	

KEY GOALKEEPER

Maarten Stekelenburg

Goals Conceded in the League	42	**Counting Games** League games when player was on pitch for at least 70 minutes	29
Defensive Rating Ave number of mins between League goals conceded while on the pitch	66	**Clean Sheets** In League games when player was on pitch for at least 70 minutes	5

KEY PLAYERS - DEFENDERS

Thomas Vermaelen

Goals Conceded Number of League goals conceded while the player was on the pitch	15	**Clean Sheets** In League games when player was on pitch for at least 70 minutes	6
Defensive Rating Ave number of mins between League goals conceded while on the pitch	97	**Club Defensive Rating** Average number of mins between League goals conceded by the club this season	74

	PLAYER	CON LGE	CLEAN SHEETS	DEF RATE
1	Thomas Vermaelen	15	6	97 mins
2	Urby Emanuelson	37	7	69 mins
3	John Heitinga	44	7	68 mins
4	Bruno Silva	17	3	68 mins

KEY PLAYERS - MIDFIELDERS

Edgar Davids

Goals in the League	0	**Contribution to Attacking Power** Average number of minutes between League team goals while on pitch	36
Defensive Rating Average number of mins between League goals conceded while on the pitch	85	**Scoring Difference** Defensive Rating minus Contribution to Attacking Power	49

	PLAYER	LGE GOALS	DEF RATE	POWER	SCORE DIFF
1	Edgar Davids	0	85	36	49 mins
2	Kenneth Perez	7	71	32	39 mins
3	Jan Vertonghen	2	70	37	33 mins
4	Gabriel Garcia de la Torre	1	63	34	29 mins

KEY PLAYERS - GOALSCORERS

Klaas-Jan Huntelaar

Goals in the League	33	**Player Strike Rate** Average number of minutes between League goals scored by player	95
Contribution to Attacking Power Average number of minutes between League team goals while on pitch	33	**Club Strike Rate** Average number of minutes between League goals scored by club	35

	PLAYER	LGE GOALS	POWER	STRIKE RATE
1	Klaas-Jan Huntelaar	33	33	95 mins
2	Luis Suarez	17	34	148 mins
3	Kenneth Perez	7	32	174 mins
4	Jan Vertonghen	2	37	1332 mins

Klaas-Jan Huntelaar

SQUAD APPEARANCES

Match	1	2	3	4	5	6	7	8	9	10	11	12	13	14	15	16	17	18	19	20	21	22	23	24	25	26	27	28	29	30	31	32	33	34	35	36	37	38	39	40	41	42	43	44	45	46
Venue	H	H	A	H	A	H	A	A	A	A	H	H	A	H	A	H	H	A	H	H	A	A	H	A	H	A	A	H	A	H	H	A	H	A	H	H	A	A	A	H	A	H	A	H	A	H
Competition	O	C	L	L	C	L	L	E	L	O	L	E	L	L	L	O	L	L	L	L	L	L	L	L	L	O	L	L	L	L	L	L	L	L	L	L	L	L	L	L	L	L	O	O	O	O
Result	W	L	W	W	L	D	W	W	W	W	W	L	D	D	W	W	W	D	W	L	W	L	D	D	W	L	D	W	D	L	W	L	W	W	W	W	D	L	W	W	W	W	W	W	L	D

Goalkeepers
Dennis Gentenaar
Maarten Stekelenburg
Defenders
Jurgen Colin
Urby Emanuelson
John Heitinga
Samuel Osei Kuffour
George Ogararu
Bruno Silva
Jaap Stam
Gregory van der Wiel
Thomas Vermaelen
Midfielders
Edgar Davids
Siem De Jong
Laurent Delorge
Mitchell Donald
Gabriel Garcia de la Torre
Michael Krohn-Dehli
Rasmus Lindgren
Hedwiges Maduro
Kenneth Perez
Jeffrey Sarpong
Robbert Schilder
Jan Vertonghen
Forwards
Kennedy Bakircioglu
Klaas-Jan Huntelaar
Albert Luque
Dennis Rommedahl
Luis Suarez
Ismael Urzaiz
Leonardo Vitor Santigo

KEY: ■ On all match ■ On bench | ⏮ Subbed or sent off (Counting game) « Subbed or sent off (playing less than 70 minutes) | ⏭ Subbed on from bench (Counting Game) » Subbed on (playing less than 70 minutes) | Subbed on and then subbed or sent off (Counting Game) Subbed on and then subbed or sent off (playing less than 70 minutes) | □ Not in 16

NAC BREDA

Final Position: **3rd**

NICKNAME: PEARL OF THE SOUTH

KEY: ☐Won ☐Drawn ☐Lost

		Opponent	H/A	Res	Score	Scorers	Attendance
1	hopr1	**Groningen**	H	L	0-3		15,104
2	hopr1	**Feyenoord**	A	L	0-5		41,000
3	hopr1	**Heracles**	H	W	4-1	Kolkka 58, Feher 63 fk, Amoah 81, 88	14,000
4	hopr1	**NEC Nijmegen**	A	W	1-0	de Graaf 44	11,750
5	hopr1	**VVV**	A	W	3-1	Lurling 1, Zwaanswijk 68, de Graaf 88 pen	6,000
6	hopr1	**PSV Eindhoven**	H	D	1-1	Amoah 66	15,089
7	hopr1	**De Graafschap**	H	W	1-0	Sikora 5	14,845
8	hopr1	**Willem II Tilb**	A	D	0-0		13,500
9	hopr1	**AZ Alkmaar**	H	L	2-3	Lurling 19, 56 pen	15,000
10	hopr1	**Utrecht**	A	W	1-0	Amoah 75	20,000
11	hopr1	**Twente**	A	D	1-1	Amoah 16	13,000
12	hopr1	**Roda JC Kerk**	H	D	0-0		15,000
13	hopr1	**Ajax**	A	W	3-1	Vertonghen 24 og, Amoah 69, Ammi 88	47,588
14	hopr1	**Excelsior**	A	W	3-0	Zwaanswijk 56, Amoah 74, Elshot 88	2,500
15	hopr1	**Heerenveen**	H	L	1-5	Tamerus 75	15,500
16	hopr1	**Vitesse Arnhem**	H	L	1-2	de Graaf 90 pen	15,000
17	hopr1	**PSV Eindhoven**	A	L	0-2		33,000
18	hopr1	**VVV**	H	D	0-0		15,000
19	hopr1	**Willem II Tilb**	H	W	1-0	Baelum 47 og	15,000
20	hopr1	**AZ Alkmaar**	A	W	2-1	Idabdelhay 85, 89	16,312
21	hopr1	**Roda JC Kerk**	A	W	2-0	Sikora 38, Idabdelhay 68	14,800
22	hopr1	**Twente**	H	W	1-0	Zwaanswijk 22 pen	14,450
23	hopr1	**S Rotterdam**	A	W	1-0	Idabdelhay 63	9,876
24	hopr1	**Utrecht**	H	W	1-0	Penders 2	15,000
25	hopr1	**De Graafschap**	A	W	1-0	Molhoek 75	12,000
26	hopr1	**Ajax**	H	L	2-3	Amoah 49, Penders 58	16,500
27	hopr1	**S Rotterdam**	H	W	3-0	Feher 9, Lurling 57, 81	15,000
28	hopr1	**Heerenveen**	A	L	0-3		25,000
29	hopr1	**Excelsior**	H	W	2-0	Idabdelhay 45, Kolkka 60	16,000
30	hopr1	**Vitesse Arnhem**	A	D	3-3	Idabdelhay 4, Van der Schaaf 16 og, Molhoek 39	22,780
31	hopr1	**Feyenoord**	H	W	3-1	Elshot 32, Molhoek 40, Amoah 72	15,873
32	hopr1	**Groningen**	A	W	2-1	Ammi 17, Amoah 42	19,000
33	hopr1	**Heracles**	A	W	1-0	de Graaf 59	8,500
34	hopr1	**NEC Nijmegen**	H	L	1-3	Amoah 27	16,450
35	erepo	**Twente**	A	L	0-3		6,080
36	erepo	**Twente**	H	L	1-5	Feher 54	16,000
37	erepo	**Heerenveen**	A	L	0-2		20,000
38	erepo	**Heerenveen**	H	D	2-2	Idabdelhay 28, Veenstra 85	8,200
39	erepo	**NEC Nijmegen**	A	L	0-6		11,500
40	erepo	**NEC Nijmegen**	H	L	0-1		5,200

LEAGUE APPEARANCES, BOOKINGS AND CAPS

	AGE (on 01/07/08)	IN NAMED 18	APPEARANCES	COUNTING GAMES	MINUTES ON PITCH	YELLOW CARDS	RED CARDS	CAPS THIS SEASON	NATIONAL SIDE
Goalkeepers									
Johan Jansen	19	9	1	1	90	0	0	-	Holland
Jelle ten Rouwelaar	27	33	32	32	2880	0	0	-	Holland
Bas van Wegen	23	21	0	0	0	0	0	-	Holland
Edwin Zoetebier	38	5	1	1	90	0	0	-	Holland
Defenders									
Ahmed Ammi	27	33	24	11	1340	3	0	-	Morocco
Aykut Demir	19	7	0	0	0	0	0	-	Turkey
Kurt Elshot	30	31	31	31	2790	4	0	-	Surinam
Sander Fischer	19	2	1	1	77	0	0	-	Holland
Tyrone Loran	27	24	14	10	1021	2	0	-	Holland
Patrick Mtiliga	27	30	30	28	2614	5	1	-	Denmark
Rob Penders	32	27	27	26	2360	5	0	-	Holland
Patrick Zwaanswijk	33	31	30	28	2588	3	0	-	Holland
Midfielders									
Ali Benomar	20	2	0	0	0	0	0	-	Holland
Edwin de Graaf	28	13	12	10	969	1	0	-	Holland
Csaba Feher	32	30	30	24	2326	6	0	-	Hungary
Tim Gilissen	26	34	21	9	1065	3	0	-	Holland
Donny Gorter	20	21	1	0	60	0	0	-	Holland
Rogier Molhoek	26	26	26	21	1996	6	1	-	Holland
Ronnie Stam	24	29	29	26	2387	1	1	-	Holland
B van den Broek	20	6	0	0	0	0	0	-	Holland
Sander van Gessel	31	26	15	3	406	0	0	-	Holland
Forwards									
Matthew Amoah	27	25	25	20	1896	0	0	-	Ghana
Andro Franca	20	3	0	0	0	0	0	-	Holland
Fouad Idabdelhay	20	22	17	0	657	0	0	-	Holland
Joonas Kolkka	33	32	32	22	2332	3	0	7	Finland
Michiel Kramer	19	0	0	0	0	0	0	-	Holland
Anthony Lurling	31	29	29	24	2409	3	0	-	Holland
Victor Sikora	30	25	21	5	965	4	0	-	Holland
Gertjan Tamerus	27	15	10	1	209	1	0	-	Holland
Rogier Veenstra	20	19	5	0	70	0	0	-	Holland

TEAM OF THE SEASON

G
Jelle ten Rouwelaar
CG: 32 DR: 84

D
Patrick Zwaanswijk
CG: 28 DR: 95

D
Rob Penders
CG: 26 DR: 90

D
Patrick Mtiliga
CG: 28 DR: 84

D
Ahmed Ammi
CG: 11 DR: 83

M
Csaba Feher
CG: 24 SD: 52

M
Rogier Molhoek
CG: 21 SD: 33

M
Ronnie Stam
CG: 26 SD: 8

M
Edwin de Graaf
CG: 10 SD: 4

F
Matthew Amoah
CG: 20 SR: 172

F
Anthony Lurling
CG: 24 SR: 481

MONTHLY POINTS TALLY

Month	Points	%
AUGUST	0	0%
SEPTEMBER	10	83%
OCTOBER	4	44%
NOVEMBER	5	56%
DECEMBER	6	40%
JANUARY	10	83%
FEBRUARY	12	80%
MARCH	10	67%
APRIL	6	67%

LEAGUE GOALS

	PLAYER	MINS	GOALS	S RATE
1	Amoah	1896	**11**	172
2	Idabdelhay	657	**6**	109
3	Lurling	2409	**5**	481
4	de Graaf	969	**4**	242
5	Molhoek	1996	**3**	665
6	Zwaanswijk	2588	**3**	862
7	Sikora	965	**2**	482
8	Ammi	1340	**2**	670
9	Feher	2326	**2**	1163
10	Kolkka	2332	**2**	1166
11	Penders	2360	**2**	1180
12	Elshot	2790	**2**	1395
13	Tamerus	209	**1**	209
	Other		0	
	TOTAL		**45**	

TOP POINT EARNERS

	PLAYER	GAMES	AV PTS
1	Joonas Kolkka	22	**2.14**
2	Rogier Molhoek	21	**2.10**
3	Csaba Feher	24	**2.08**
4	Patrick Zwaanswijk	28	**2.04**
5	Anthony Lurling	24	**2.04**
6	Jelle ten Rouwelaar	32	**1.97**
7	Patrick Mtiliga	28	**1.93**
8	Rob Penders	26	**1.88**
9	Ronnie Stam	26	**1.77**
10	Kurt Elshot	31	**1.74**
	CLUB AVERAGE:		**1.85**

DISCIPLINARY RECORDS

	PLAYER	YELLOW	RED	AVE
1	Victor Sikora	4	0	**241**
2	Rogier Molhoek	6	1	**285**
3	Tim Gilissen	3	0	**355**
4	Csaba Feher	6	0	**387**
5	Patrick Mtiliga	5	1	**435**
6	Ahmed Ammi	3	0	**446**
7	Rob Penders	5	0	**472**
8	Tyrone Loran	2	0	**510**
9	Kurt Elshot	4	0	**697**
10	Joonas Kolkka	3	0	**777**
11	Anthony Lurling	3	0	**803**
12	Patrick Zwaanswijk	3	0	**862**
13	Edwin de Graaf	1	0	**969**
	Other	1	1	
	TOTAL	**49**	**3**	

KEY GOALKEEPER

Jelle ten Rouwelaar

Goals Conceded in the League	34	Counting Games League games when player was on pitch for at least 70 minutes	32
Defensive Rating Ave number of mins between League goals conceded while on the pitch	84	Clean Sheets In League games when player was on pitch for at least 70 minutes	16

KEY PLAYERS - DEFENDERS

Patrick Zwaanswijk

Goals Conceded Number of League goals conceded while the player was on the pitch	27	Clean Sheets In League games when player was on pitch for at least 70 minutes	15
Defensive Rating Ave number of mins between League goals conceded while on the pitch	95	Club Defensive Rating Average number of mins between League goals conceded by the club this season	78

	PLAYER	CON LGE	CLEAN SHEETS	DEF RATE
1	Patrick Zwaanswijk	27	15	95 mins
2	Rob Penders	26	13	90 mins
3	Patrick Mtiliga	31	14	84 mins
4	Ahmed Ammi	16	7	83 mins

KEY PLAYERS - MIDFIELDERS

Csaba Feher

Goals in the League	2	Contribution to Attacking Power Average number of minutes between League team goals while on pitch	58
Defensive Rating Average number of mins between League goals conceded while on the pitch	110	Scoring Difference Defensive Rating minus Contribution to Attacking Power	52

	PLAYER	LGE GOALS	DEF RATE	POWER	SCORE DIFF
1	Csaba Feher	2	110	58	52 mins
2	Rogier Molhoek	3	99	66	33 mins
3	Ronnie Stam	0	70	62	8 mins
4	Edwin de Graaf	4	64	60	4 mins

KEY PLAYERS - GOALSCORERS

Matthew Amoah

Goals in the League	11	Player Strike Rate Average number of minutes between League goals scored by player	172
Contribution to Attacking Power Average number of minutes between League team goals while on pitch	63	Club Strike Rate Average number of minutes between League goals scored by club	65

	PLAYER	LGE GOALS	POWER	STRIKE RATE
1	Matthew Amoah	11	63	172 mins
2	Edwin de Graaf	4	60	242 mins
3	Anthony Lurling	5	63	481 mins
4	Rogier Molhoek	3	66	665 mins

NAC
Sunweb
VAKANTIES
Matthew Amoah

SQUAD APPEARANCES

Match	1	2	3	4	5	6	7	8	9	10	11	12	13	14	15	16	17	18	19	20	21	22	23	24	25	26	27	28	29	30	31	32	33	34	35	36	37	38	39	40
Venue	H	A	H	A	A	H	H	A	H	A	A	H	A	A	H	H	A	H	H	A	A	H	A	H	A	H	H	A	H	A	H	A	A	H	A	H	A	H	A	H
Competition	L	L	L	L	L	L	L	L	L	L	L	L	L	L	L	L	L	L	L	L	L	L	L	L	L	L	L	L	L	L	L	L	L	L	O	O	O	O	O	O
Result	L	L	W	W	W	D	W	D	L	W	D	D	W	W	L	L	L	D	W	W	W	W	W	W	W	L	W	L	W	D	W	W	W	L	L	L	L	D	L	L

Goalkeepers
Johan Jansen
Jelle ten Rouwelaar
Bas van Wegen
Edwin Zoetebier
Defenders
Ahmed Ammi
Aykut Demir
Kurt Elshot
Sander Fischer
Tyrone Loran
Patrick Mtiliga
Rob Penders
Patrick Zwaanswijk
Midfielders
Ali Benomar
Edwin de Graaf
Csaba Feher
Tim Gilissen
Donny Gorter
Rogier Molhoek
Ronnie Stam
Benjamin van den Broek
Sander van Gessel
Forwards
Matthew Amoah
Andro Franca
Fouad Idabdelhay
Joonas Kolkka
Michiel Kramer
Anthony Lurling
Victor Sikora
Gertjan Tamerus
Rogier Veenstra

KEY: On all match | On bench | Subbed or sent off (Counting game) | Subbed or sent off (playing less than 70 minutes) | Subbed on from bench (Counting Game) | Subbed on (playing less than 70 minutes) | Subbed on and then subbed or sent off (Counting Game) | Subbed on and then subbed or sent off (playing less than 70 minutes) | Not in 16

TWENTE

Final Position: **4th**

NICKNAME: THE TUKKERS

KEY: ☐ Won ☐ Drawn ☐ Lost

	Comp	Opponent			Score	Scorers	Attendance
1	hopr1	**Excelsior**	A	W	2-0	N'Kufo 10, 71 pen	3,000
2	hopr1	**Utrecht**	H	D	2-2	N'Kufo 40 pen, Engelaar 46	13,000
3	hopr1	**PSV Eindhoven**	H	D	0-0		13,150
4	hopr1	**Willem II Tilb**	A	W	3-1	N'Kufo 31, Demouge 45 og Denneboom 57	12,000
5	ucrl1	**Getafe**	A	L	0-1		10,000
6	hopr1	**NEC Nijmegen**	H	W	3-0	Wielaert 7, N'Kufo 14, Wilkshire 58	13,000
7	hocr1	**NEC Nijmegen**	H	L	1-2	Engelaar 47	8,500
8	hopr1	**De Graafschap**	A	D	0-0		12,300
9	ucrl2	**Getafe**	H	W	3-2	Wielaert 29, Engelaar 117, Zijler 120	13,200
10	hopr1	**Roda JC Kerk**	H	L	0-1		13,000
11	hopr1	**Groningen**	A	L	0-1		18,971
12	hopr1	**Feyenoord**	H	W	2-0	N'Kufo 11, Huysegems 57	13,250
13	hopr1	**Heracles**	A	W	3-0	Denneboom 24, N'Kufo 81, Engelaar 90	8,500
14	hopr1	**NAC Breda**	H	D	1-1	Wilkshire 24	13,000
15	hopr1	**S Rotterdam**	A	D	1-1	Engelaar 71	10,000
16	hopr1	**AZ Alkmaar**	H	W	2-1	N'Kufo 43, 60	13,000
17	hopr1	**Vitesse**	A	D	2-2	Denneboom 39, Hersi 82	18,973
18	hopr1	**VVV**	H	D	1-1	N'Kufo 16 pen	13,250
19	hopr1	**Heerenveen**	A	W	2-1	N'Kufo 33 pen, Denneboom 66	25,000
20	hopr1	**Ajax**	A	D	2-2	Huysegems 60, N'Kufo 90	50,523
21	hopr1	**De Graafschap**	H	W	2-0	Huysegems 20, N'Kufo 34	13,250
22	hopr1	**NEC Nijmegen**	A	D	2-2	N'Kufo 17, Engelaar 90	12,000
23	hopr1	**Groningen**	H	W	3-1	N'Kufo 29, 86, Huysegems 53	13,250
24	hopr1	**Feyenoord**	A	L	1-3	N'Kufo 22 pen	45,000
25	hopr1	**S Rotterdam**	H	L	1-2	Denneboom 38	13,000
26	hopr1	**NAC Breda**	A	L	0-1		14,450
27	hopr1	**Heracles**	H	W	2-1	Elia 77, N'Kufo 86	13,250
28	hopr1	**Roda JC Kerk**	A	L	1-3	N'Kufo 33	14,300
29	hopr1	**AZ Alkmaar**	A	D	0-0		16,535
30	hopr1	**Heerenveen**	H	W	1-0	Hersi 78	13,100
31	hopr1	**VVV**	A	W	2-0	Teixeira 18, Hersi 77	6,000
32	hopr1	**Vitesse**	H	W	4-3	Denneboom 4, N'Kufo 48, 85, Hersi 77	13,200
33	hopr1	**Ajax**	H	W	2-1	Wilkshire 70, Elia 90	13,250
34	hopr1	**Utrecht**	A	W	1-0	Huysegems 90	22,731
35	hopr1	**Excelsior**	H	W	1-0	Hersi 58	13,100
36	hopr1	**PSV Eindhoven**	A	D	1-1	N'Kufo 35	34,000
37	hopr1	**Willem II Tilb**	H	W	2-0	Hersi 52, 80	13,250
38	erepo	**NAC Breda**	H	W	3-0	Wielaert 32, Denneboom 80 Huysegems 90	6,080
39	erepo	**NAC Breda**	A	W	5-1	Huysegems 52, 77, N'Kufo 56, Hersi 66 Braafheid 90	16,000
40	erepo	**Ajax**	H	W	2-1	N'Kufo 66 pen, 77	8,000
41	erepo	**Ajax**	A	D	0-0		49,764

LEAGUE APPEARANCES, BOOKINGS AND CAPS

	AGE (on 01/07/08)	IN NAMED 18	APPEARANCES	COUNTING GAMES	MINUTES ON PITCH	YELLOW CARDS	RED CARDS	CAPS THIS SEASON	NATIONAL SIDE
Goalkeepers									
Sander Boschker	37	34	34	34	3060	4	0	-	Holland
Nikolay Mihaylov	20	2	0	0	0	0	0	-	Bulgaria
Cees Paauwe	30	32	0	0	0	0	0	-	Holland
Defenders									
Edson Braafheid	25	32	32	30	2817	6	0	-	Holland
Wout Droste	19	2	0	0	0	0	0	-	Holland
Jeroen Heubach	33	32	32	30	2707	7	0	-	Holland
Douglas F Teixeira	20	17	12	7	725	1	1	-	Brazil
Niels Wellenberg	25	28	26	9	1310	7	0	-	Holland
Rob Wielaert	29	32	32	32	2860	4	1	-	Holland
Luke Wilkshire	26	31	31	23	2431	7	1	6	Australia
Ramon Zomer	25	33	11	4	552	1	0	-	Holland
Midfielders									
Wout Brama	21	34	26	5	1055	1	0	-	Holland
Karim El Ahmadi	23	33	33	32	2909	5	0	-	Holland
Orlando Engelaar	28	26	26	23	2159	4	0	8	Holland
Youssouf Hersi	25	34	25	9	1282	0	0	-	Holland
Stein Huysegems	26	29	27	13	1630	3	0	3	Belgium
Andrej Rendla	17	2	1	0	23	0	0	-	Slovakia
Alfred Schreuder	35	27	3	0	30	0	0	-	Holland
Forwards									
Marko Arnautovic	19	29	14	1	219	1	0	-	Austria
Romano Denneboom	27	34	34	29	2697	3	0	-	Holland
Eljero Elia	21	32	30	21	2090	3	0	-	Holland
Patrick Gerritsen	21	3	0	0	0	0	0	-	Holland
Ibrahim Maaroufi	19	4	0	0	0	0	0	-	Belgium
Blaise N'Kufo	33	34	34	33	2992	1	0	8	Switzerland
Jules Reimerink	18	2	0	0	0	0	0	-	Holland
Sergio Zijler	20	7	1	0	61	0	0	-	Holland

TEAM OF THE SEASON

G
Sander Boschker
CG: 34 DR: 95
D
Edson Braafheid
CG: 30 DR: 100
D
Niels Wellenberg
CG: 9* DR: 100
D
Luke Wilkshire
CG: 23 DR: 97
D
Jeroen Heubach
CG: 30 DR: 96
M
Youssouf Hersi
CG: 9* SD: 67
M
Orlando Engelaar
CG: 23 SD: 38
M
Stein Huysegems
CG: 13 SD: 35
M
Karim El Ahmadi
CG: 32 SD: 33
F
Blaise N'Kufo
CG: 33 SR: 136
F
Denneboom
CG: 29 SR: 449

MONTHLY POINTS TALLY

Month	Points	%
AUGUST	4	67%
SEPTEMBER	8	67%
OCTOBER	3	33%
NOVEMBER	5	56%
DECEMBER	12	67%
JANUARY	4	33%
FEBRUARY	4	33%
MARCH	15	100%
APRIL	7	78%

LEAGUE GOALS

	PLAYER	MINS	GOALS	S RATE
1	N'Kufo	2992	22	136
2	Hersi	1282	7	183
3	Denneboom	2697	6	449
4	Huysegems	1630	5	326
5	Engelaar	2159	4	539
6	Wilkshire	2431	3	810
7	Elia	2090	2	1045
8	Teixeira	725	1	725
9	Wielaert	2860	1	2860
	Other		0	
	TOTAL		51	

TOP POINT EARNERS

	PLAYER	GAMES	AV PTS
1	Eljero Elia	21	2.10
2	Romano Denneboom	29	1.93
3	Stein Huysegems	13	1.92
4	Jeroen Heubach	30	1.90
5	Luke Wilkshire	23	1.87
6	Edson Braafheid	30	1.83
7	Sander Boschker	34	1.82
8	Blaise N'Kufo	33	1.79
9	Rob Wielaert	32	1.75
10	Karim El Ahmadi	32	1.75
	CLUB AVERAGE:		1.82

DISCIPLINARY RECORDS

	PLAYER	YELLOW	RED	AVE
1	Niels Wellenberg	7	0	187
2	Luke Wilkshire	7	1	303
3	Douglas F Teixeira	1	1	362
4	Jeroen Heubach	7	0	386
5	Edson Braafheid	6	0	469
6	Orlando Engelaar	4	0	539
7	Stein Huysegems	3	0	543
8	Ramon Zomer	1	0	552
9	Rob Wielaert	4	1	572
10	Karim El Ahmadi	5	0	581
11	Eljero Elia	3	0	696
12	Sander Boschker	4	0	765
13	R Denneboom	3	0	899
	Other	2	0	
	TOTAL	57	3	

KEY GOALKEEPER

Sander Boschker

Goals Conceded in the League	32	**Counting Games** League games when player was on pitch for at least 70 minutes	34
Defensive Rating Ave number of mins between League goals conceded while on the pitch	95	**Clean Sheets** In League games when player was on pitch for at least 70 minutes	13

KEY PLAYERS - DEFENDERS

Edson Braafheid

Goals Conceded Number of League goals conceded while the player was on the pitch	28	**Clean Sheets** In League games when player was on pitch for at least 70 minutes	11
Defensive Rating Ave number of mins between League goals conceded while on the pitch	100	**Club Defensive Rating** Average number of mins between League goals conceded by the club this season	98

	PLAYER	CON LGE	CLEAN SHEETS	DEF RATE
1	Edson Braafheid	28	11	100 mins
2	Niels Wellenberg	13	4	100 mins
3	Luke Wilkshire	25	9	97 mins
4	Jeroen Heubach	28	12	96 mins

KEY PLAYERS - MIDFIELDERS

Youssouf Hersi

Goals in the League	7	**Contribution to Attacking Power** Average number of minutes between League team goals while on pitch	61
Defensive Rating Average number of mins between League goals conceded while on the pitch	128	**Scoring Difference** Defensive Rating minus Contribution to Attacking Power	67

	PLAYER	LGE GOALS	DEF RATE	POWER	SCORE DIFF
1	Youssouf Hersi	7	128	61	67 mins
2	Orlando Engelaar	4	93	55	38 mins
3	Stein Huysegems	5	81	46	35 mins
4	Karim El Ahmadi	0	93	60	33 mins

KEY PLAYERS - GOALSCORERS

Blaise N'Kufo

Goals in the League	22	**Player Strike Rate** Average number of minutes between League goals scored by player	136
Contribution to Attacking Power Average number of minutes between League team goals while on pitch	57	**Club Strike Rate** Average number of minutes between League goals scored by club	60

	PLAYER	LGE GOALS	POWER	STRIKE RATE
1	Blaise N'Kufo	22	57	136 mins
2	Youssouf Hersi	7	61	183 mins
3	Stein Huysegems	5	46	326 mins
4	Romano Denneboom	6	61	449 mins

Orlando Engelaar

SQUAD APPEARANCES

Match	1	2	3	4	5	6	7	8	9	10	11	12	13	14	15	16	17	18	19	20	21	22	23	24	25	26	27	28	29	30	31	32	33	34	35	36	37	38	39	40
Venue	A	H	H	A	A	H	A	H	H	A	H	A	H	A	H	A	H	A	A	H	A	H	A	H	A	H	A	A	H	A	H	H	A	H	A	H	H	A	H	A
Competition	L	L	L	L	E	L	L	E	L	L	L	L	L	L	L	L	L	L	L	L	L	L	L	L	L	L	L	L	L	L	L	L	L	L	L	L	O	O	O	O
Result	W	D	D	W	L	W	D	W	L	L	W	W	D	D	W	D	D	W	D	W	D	W	L	L	L	W	L	D	W	W	W	W	W	W	D	W	W	W	W	D

Goalkeepers
- Sander Boschker
- Nikolay Mihaylov
- Cees Paauwe

Defenders
- Edson Braafheid
- Wout Droste
- Jeroen Heubach
- Douglas Franco Teixeira
- Niels Wellenberg
- Rob Wielaert
- Luke Wilkshire
- Ramon Zomer

Midfielders
- Wout Brama
- Karim El Ahmadi
- Orlando Engelaar
- Youssouf Hersi
- Stein Huysegems
- Andrej Rendla
- Alfred Schreuder

Forwards
- Marko Arnautovic
- Romano Denneboom
- Eljero Elia
- Patrick Gerritsen
- Ibrahim Maaroufi
- Blaise N'Kufo
- Jules Reimerink
- Sergio Zijler

KEY: On all match; On bench; Subbed or sent off (Counting game); Subbed or sent off (playing less than 70 minutes); Subbed on from bench (Counting Game); Subbed on (playing less than 70 minutes); Subbed on and then subbed or sent off (Counting Game); Subbed on and then subbed or sent off (playing less than 70 minutes); Not in 16

HEERENVEEN

Final Position: **5th**

KEY: ☐ Won ☐ Drawn ☐ Lost

	Comp	Opponent	H/A	Res	Score	Scorers	Attendance
1	hopr1	**Willem II Tilb**	H	D	0-0		26,000
2	hopr1	**Ajax**	A	L	1-4	Sulejmani 27	48,988
3	hopr1	**S Rotterdam**	H	D	3-3	Sibon 32, Pranjic 59, Roberts 88 og	22,000
4	hopr1	**Excelsior**	A	W	5-2	Sulejmani 39, Sibon 45, 52, Zuiverloon 45 Bradley 54	2,864
5	ucrl1	**Helsingborg**	H	W	5-3	Bradley 20, 60, Sibon 30, 35 Bak Nielsen 59	18,000
6	hopr1	**Utrecht**	H	L	2-3	Bradley 50, Sulejmani 85	24,000
7	hopr1	**Feyenoord**	A	L	0-2		47,000
8	ucrl2	**Helsingborg**	A	L	1-5	Sibon 89	6,500
9	hopr1	**Heracles**	H	W	9-0	Alves 10, 17, 18, 68, 70, 75, 77 Sibon 60, 81	24,700
10	hopr1	**AZ Alkmaar**	A	W	1-0	Alves 90	16,644
11	hopr1	**VVV**	A	W	4-0	Bak Nielsen 3, Alves 12, 71, Matusiak 86	5,930
12	hopr1	**PSV Eindhoven**	H	W	2-1	Bak Nielsen 32, Kromkamp 70 og	25,500
13	hopr1	**Vitesse**	A	W	1-0	Bradley 50	19,221
14	hopr1	**De Graafschap**	H	L	2-3	Dingsdag 25, Pranjic 74 pen	23,000
15	hopr1	**NEC Nijmegen**	A	W	1-0	Poulsen 41	12,000
16	hopr1	**Groningen**	H	W	4-2	Lovre 2 og, Bradley 7, 22, 41	26,000
17	hopr1	**NAC Breda**	A	W	5-1	Sibon 24, 56, Sulejmani 50 Corneiro Filho 69, 73	15,500
18	hopr1	**Twente**	H	L	1-2	Alves 41	25,000
19	hopr1	**Roda JC Kerk**	A	L	0-1		13,000
20	hopr1	**Feyenoord**	H	D	1-1	Sibon 87	26,500
21	hopr1	**Utrecht**	A	D	2-2	Pranjic 1, Bradley 27	20,100
22	hopr1	**AZ Alkmaar**	H	W	4-0	Pranjic 3 pen, Poulsen 21, Sulejmani 39 Bradley 56	25,000
23	hopr1	**VVV**	H	W	5-1	Bradley 23, Sulejmani 28, Poulsen 39 Sibon 60, Pranjic 89	24,000
24	hopr1	**De Graafschap**	A	W	3-0	Bradley 21, 81, Sulejmani 64	12,600
25	hopr1	**Vitesse**	H	W	7-0	Sulejmani 10, Pranjic 14, Bradley 50 Zuiverloon 58, Beerens 66, 80 Prager 82	25,000
26	hopr1	**PSV Eindhoven**	A	D	1-1	Bradley 52	33,600
27	hopr1	**Heracles**	A	D	2-2	Beerens 18, Sulejmani 30	8,500
28	hopr1	**NEC Nijmegen**	H	L	2-3	Beerens 2, Roorda 29	25,000
29	hopr1	**Twente**	A	L	0-1		13,100
30	hopr1	**NAC Breda**	H	W	3-0	Mtiliga 32 og, Sulejmani 38, 78	25,000
31	hopr1	**Groningen**	A	W	1-0	Sulejmani 85	19,700
32	hopr1	**Roda JC Kerk**	H	W	4-3	Bradley 34, 61, Corneiro Filho 48 Beerens 51	25,000
33	hopr1	**Ajax**	H	L	2-4	Sulejmani 60, Pranjic 90	25,000
34	hopr1	**Willem II Tilb**	A	W	3-2	Pranjic 29 pen, Beerens 31, Sibon 74	14,000
35	hopr1	**S Rotterdam**	A	L	2-4	Pranjic 13, Sibon 44	10,463
36	hopr1	**Excelsior**	H	W	5-0	Sibon 8, 78, Sulejmani 45, Bandjar 54 og Roorda 79	25,000
37	erepo	**Ajax**	H	L	1-2	Sibon 71	23,000
38	erepo	**Ajax**	A	L	1-3	Pranjic 63	49,144
39	erepo	**NAC Breda**	H	W	2-0	Corneiro Filho 75, 83	20,000
40	erepo	**NAC Breda**	A	D	2-2	Sibon 42, 74	8,200

LEAGUE APPEARANCES, BOOKINGS AND CAPS

	AGE (on 01/07/08)	IN NAMED 18	APPEARANCES	COUNTING GAMES	MINUTES ON PITCH	YELLOW CARDS	RED CARDS	CAPS THIS SEASON	NATIONAL SIDE
Goalkeepers									
Rob van Dijk	39	34	15	14	1326	0	0	-	Holland
Brian Vandenbussche	26	31	20	19	1732	2	1	-	Belgium
Defenders									
Kristian Bak Nielsen	25	15	15	14	1256	2	0	-	Denmark
Michel Breuer	28	31	31	30	2760	2	1	-	Holland
Michael Dingsdag	25	32	32	29	2754	7	0	-	Holland
Jeroen Drost	21	7	0	0	0	0	0	-	Holland
Henrico Drost	21	26	15	12	1116	0	0	-	Holland
Timmi Johansen	21	32	7	3	379	0	0	-	Denmark
Calvin Jong-a-Pin	21	26	19	11	1292	3	0	-	Holland
Gianni Zuiverloon	21	30	30	27	2522	9	1	-	Holland
Midfielders									
Arjan Bergsma	19	2	0	0	0	0	0	-	Holland
Michael S Bradley	20	33	33	30	2872	6	0	5	United States
Christian Grindheim	24	11	9	6	609	2	0	-	Norway
Niek Loohuis	22	10	1	1	71	0	0	-	Holland
Jakob Poulsen	24	32	30	11	1672	1	0	-	Denmark
Thomas Prager	22	28	15	3	540	1	0	-	Austria
Danijel Pranjic	26	33	33	32	2882	1	0	10	Croatia
Geert Arend Roorda	20	24	22	12	1382	2	0	-	Holland
Michal Svec	21	9	5	0	217	1	0	-	Czech Republic
Forwards									
Afonso Alves	27	8	8	6	616	1	1	3	Brazil
Roy Beerens	20	29	28	13	1583	3	0	-	Holland
Paulo Henrique Filho	19	17	13	0	277	1	0	-	Brazil
Gonzalo G Garcia	24	9	5	0	117	0	0	-	Spain
Radoslaw Matusiak	26	16	10	1	339	0	0	3	Poland
Gerald Sibon	34	34	34	29	2736	3	0	-	Holland
Arnar Smarason	19	9	2	0	30	0	0	-	Iceland
Miralem Sulejmani	19	34	34	23	2409	1	0	-	Serbia

TEAM OF THE SEASON

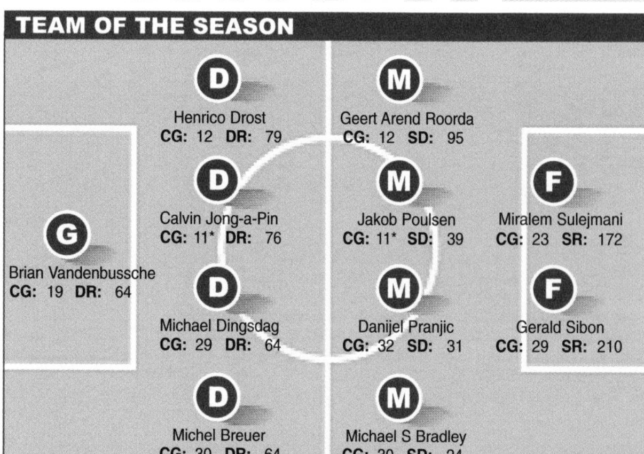

G
Brian Vandenbussche
CG: 19 DR: 64
D
Henrico Drost
CG: 12 DR: 79
D
Calvin Jong-a-Pin
CG: 11* DR: 76
D
Michael Dingsdag
CG: 29 DR: 64
D
Michel Breuer
CG: 30 DR: 64
M
Geert Arend Roorda
CG: 12 SD: 95
M
Jakob Poulsen
CG: 11* SD: 39
M
Danijel Pranjic
CG: 32 SD: 31
M
Michael S Bradley
CG: 30 SD: 24
F
Miralem Sulejmani
CG: 23 SR: 172
F
Gerald Sibon
CG: 29 SR: 210

MONTHLY POINTS TALLY

Month	Points	%
AUGUST	1	17%
SEPTEMBER	4	33%
OCTOBER	9	100%
NOVEMBER	6	67%
DECEMBER	10	56%
JANUARY	10	83%
FEBRUARY	5	42%
MARCH	9	60%
APRIL	6	67%

LEAGUE GOALS

	PLAYER	MINS	GOALS	S RATE
1	Bradley	2872	15	191
2	Sulejmani	2409	14	172
3	Sibon	2736	13	210
4	Alves	616	11	56
5	Pranjic	2882	9	320
6	Beerens	1583	6	263
7	Corneiro Filho	277	3	92
8	Poulsen	1672	3	557
9	Bak Nielsen	1256	2	628
10	Roorda	1382	2	691
11	Zuiverloon	2522	2	1261
12	Matusiak	339	1	339
13	Prager	540	1	540
	Other		1	
	TOTAL		83	

TOP POINT EARNERS

	PLAYER	GAMES	AV PTS
1	Geert Arend Roorda	12	2.33
2	Michel Breuer	30	1.93
3	Rob van Dijk	14	1.93
4	Kristian Bak Nielsen	14	1.86
5	Gerald Sibon	29	1.86
6	Michael Dingsdag	29	1.83
7	Brian Vandenbussche	19	1.74
8	Danijel Pranjic	32	1.69
9	Michael S Bradley	30	1.67
10	Gianni Zuiverloon	27	1.67
	CLUB AVERAGE:		1.76

DISCIPLINARY RECORDS

	PLAYER	YELLOW	RED	AVE
1	Gianni Zuiverloon	9	1	252
2	C Grindheim	2	0	304
3	Afonso Alves	1	1	308
4	Michael Dingsdag	7	0	393
5	Calvin Jong-a-Pin	3	0	430
6	Michael S Bradley	6	0	478
7	Roy Beerens	3	0	527
8	Thomas Prager	1	0	540
9	Vandenbussche	2	1	577
10	Kristian Nielsen	2	0	628
11	Geert A Roorda	2	0	691
12	Gerald Sibon	3	0	912
13	Michel Breuer	2	1	920
	Other	3	0	
	TOTAL	46	4	

KEY GOALKEEPER

Brian Vandenbussche

Goals Conceded in the League	27	Counting Games League games when player was on pitch for at least 70 minutes	19
Defensive Rating Ave number of mins between League goals conceded while on the pitch	64	Clean Sheets In League games when player was on pitch for at least 70 minutes	6

KEY PLAYERS - DEFENDERS

Henrico Drost

Goals Conceded Number of League goals conceded while the player was on the pitch	14	Clean Sheets In League games when player was on pitch for at least 70 minutes	4
Defensive Rating Ave number of mins between League goals conceded while on the pitch	79	Club Defensive Rating Average number of mins between League goals conceded by the club this season	63

	PLAYER	CON LGE	CLEAN SHEETS	DEF RATE
1	Henrico Drost	14	4	79 mins
2	Calvin Jong-a-Pin	17	4	76 mins
3	Michael Dingsdag	43	11	64 mins
4	Michel Breuer	43	12	64 mins

KEY PLAYERS - MIDFIELDERS

Geert Arend Roorda

Goals in the League	2	Contribution to Attacking Power Average number of minutes between League team goals while on pitch	30
Defensive Rating Average number of mins between League goals conceded while on the pitch	125	Scoring Difference Defensive Rating minus Contribution to Attacking Power	95

	PLAYER	LGE GOALS	DEF RATE	POWER	SCORE DIFF
1	Geert Arend Roorda	2	125	30	95 mins
2	Jakob Poulsen	3	69	30	39 mins
3	Danijel Pranjic	9	64	33	31 mins
4	Michael Sheenan Bradley	15	61	37	24 mins

KEY PLAYERS - GOALSCORERS

Miralem Sulejmani

Goals in the League	14	Player Strike Rate Average number of minutes between League goals scored by player	172
Contribution to Attacking Power Average number of minutes between League team goals while on pitch	33	Club Strike Rate Average number of minutes between League goals scored by club	34

	PLAYER	LGE GOALS	POWER	STRIKE RATE
1	Miralem Sulejmani	14	33	172 mins
2	Michael Sheenan Bradley	15	37	191 mins
3	Gerald Sibon	13	36	210 mins
4	Roy Beerens	6	41	263 mins

Gerald Sibon and Kristian Bak Nielsen

SQUAD APPEARANCES

Match	1	2	3	4	5	6	7	8	9	10	11	12	13	14	15	16	17	18	19	20	21	22	23	24	25	26	27	28	29	30	31	32	33	34	35	36	37	38	39	40
Venue	H	A	H	A	H	H	A	A	H	A	A	H	A	H	A	H	A	H	A	H	A	H	H	A	H	A	A	H	A	H	A	H	H	A	A	H	H	A	H	A
Competition	L	L	L	L	E	L	L	E	L	L	L	L	L	L	L	L	L	L	L	L	L	L	L	L	L	L	L	L	L	L	L	L	L	L	L	L	O	O	O	O
Result	D	L	D	W	W	L	L	L	W	W	W	W	W	L	W	W	W	L	L	D	D	W	W	W	W	D	D	L	L	W	W	W	L	W	L	W	L	L	W	D

Goalkeepers
Rob van Dijk
Brian Vandenbussche

Defenders
Kristian Bak Nielsen
Michel Breuer
Michael Dingsdag
Jeroen Drost
Henrico Drost
Timmi Johansen
Calvin Jong-a-Pin
Gianni Zuiverloon

Midfielders
Arjan Bergsma
Michael Sheenan Bradley
Christian Grindheim
Niek Loohuis
Jakob Poulsen
Thomas Prager
Danijel Pranjic
Geert Arend Roorda
Michal Svec

Forwards
Afonso Alves
Roy Beerens
Paulo Henrique Filho
Gonzalo Garcia Garcia
Radoslaw Matusiak
Gerald Sibon
Arnar Smarason
Miralem Sulejmani

KEY: On all match · On bench · Subbed or sent off (Counting game) · Subbed or sent off (playing less than 70 minutes) · Subbed on from bench (Counting Game) · Subbed on (playing less than 70 minutes) · Subbed on and then subbed or sent off (Counting Game) · Subbed on and then subbed or sent off (playing less than 70 minutes) · Not in 16

FEYENOORD

Final Position: **6th**

NICKNAME: DE CLUB VAN ZUID

KEY: ☐ Won ☐ Drawn ☐ Lost

							Attendance
1	hopr1	**Utrecht**	A	W	3-0	Bruins 25, Hofs 62, Makaay 86	23,000
2	hopr1	**NAC Breda**	H	W	5-0	Makaay 21 pen, Vlaar 49, Sahin 56, 72 de Guzman 69	41,000
3	hopr1	**Willem II Tilb**	H	W	2-0	Bruins 26, Makaay 43	42,000
4	hopr1	**Roda JC Kerk**	A	W	3-1	Makaay 47 pen, De Guzman 62, 71	17,000
5	hopr1	**PSV Eindhoven**	A	L	0-4		33,000
6	hopr1	**Heerenveen**	H	W	2-0	Makaay 22, Hofs 27	47,000
7	hopr1	**Vitesse**	A	W	1-0	Hofs 55	18,450
8	hopr1	**Excelsior**	H	W	1-0	Van Bronckhorst 77	47,000
9	hopr1	**Twente**	A	L	0-2		13,250
10	hopr1	**De Graafschap**	H	W	2-0	De Guzman 54, Makaay 58 pen	45,000
11	hopr1	**Ajax**	H	D	2-2	Van Bronckhorst 28, De Guzman 74	42,500
12	hopr1	**Groningen**	A	L	2-3	Makaay 11, Sahin 77	19,000
13	hopr1	**Heracles**	H	W	6-0	Makaay 1, 27, Hofland 41, Slory 67 Van Bronckhorst 73, Wijnaldum 74	44,500
14	hopr1	**VVV**	A	D	0-0		6,000
15	hopr1	**NEC Nijmegen**	A	W	2-0	De Guzman 48, 60	12,500
16	hopr1	**S Rotterdam**	H	W	2-0	Makaay 4, 74	46,783
17	hopr1	**Heerenveen**	A	D	1-1	Slory 17	26,500
18	hopr1	**PSV Eindhoven**	H	L	0-1		45,000
19	hopr1	**Excelsior**	A	L	1-2	Buijs 80	3,500
20	hopr1	**Twente**	H	W	3-1	Bruins 40, Makaay 56, De Cler 63	45,000
21	hopr1	**Groningen**	H	D	1-1	Fledderus 45 og	42,500
22	hopr1	**AZ Alkmaar**	H	D	2-2	Van Bronckhorst 50, Bahia 75	46,500
23	hopr1	**Ajax**	A	L	0-3		49,893
24	hopr1	**De Graafschap**	A	W	3-1	Makaay 45, Hofs 56, 63	12,600
25	hopr1	**Vitesse**	H	W	1-0	De Guzman 45	45,000
26	hopr1	**Heracles**	A	D	3-3	Bahia 17, Landzaat 31, Hofs 57	8,500
27	hopr1	**NEC Nijmegen**	H	L	1-3	Van Bronckhorst 39	45,000
28	hopr1	**AZ Alkmaar**	A	W	1-0	De Guzman 20	16,652
29	hopr1	**VVV**	H	W	4-1	Bruins 5, Van Bronckhorst 33, Mols 44 Sahin 58	46,000
30	hopr1	**S Rotterdam**	A	L	2-3	Lucius 12, Van Bronckhorst 62	10,894
31	hopr1	**NAC Breda**	A	L	1-3	Fer 10	15,873
32	hopr1	**Utrecht**	H	W	3-1	Bruins 34, Landzaat 38, Sahin 56	46,000
33	hopr1	**Willem II Tilb**	A	L	1-3	Bahia 74	14,700
34	hopr1	**Roda JC Kerk**	H	W	3-0	Bruins 55, Sahin 77, Mols 88	46,000

LEAGUE APPEARANCES, BOOKINGS AND CAPS

	AGE (on 01/07/08)	IN NAMED 18	APPEARANCES	COUNTING GAMES	MINUTES ON PITCH	YELLOW CARDS	RED CARDS	CAPS THIS SEASON	NATIONAL SIDE
Goalkeepers									
Sherif Ekramy	25	13	1	1	90	0	0	-	Egypt
Erwin Mulder	19	21	1	1	90	0	0	-	Holland
Henk Timmer	36	32	32	32	2880	0	0	1	Holland
Defenders									
Andre Bahia	24	34	29	27	2528	3	0	-	Brazil
Jordy Buijs	19	18	0	0	0	0	0	-	Holland
Tim de Cler	29	32	32	32	2873	8	0	-	Holland
Serginho Greene	26	30	22	12	1236	2	0	-	Holland
Kevin Hofland	29	28	27	25	2336	6	0	-	Holland
Ron Vlaar	23	4	4	3	310	1	0	-	Holland
Midfielders									
Danny Buijs	26	30	23	5	834	0	0	-	Holland
Jonathan de Guzman	20	33	33	33	2934	2	0	-	Canada
Leroy Fer	18	17	13	7	659	2	0	-	Holland
Nick Hofs	25	25	23	10	1264	5	1	-	Holland
Denny Landzaat	32	12	11	11	971	2	0	2	Holland
Jacob Lensky	19	3	0	0	0	0	0	-	Canada
Theo Lucius	31	29	29	28	2539	6	0	-	Holland
Nuri Sahin	19	34	29	23	2227	3	0	-	Turkey
Gio van Bronckhorst	33	32	32	31	2838	7	0	14	Holland
Georginio Wijnaldum	17	30	10	2	309	0	0	-	Holland
Forwards									
Diego Biseswar	20	15	1	0	8	0	0	-	Holland
Luigi Bruins	21	27	27	22	2092	2	0	-	Holland
Hanne Hagary	19	2	0	0	0	0	0	-	Holland
Chun-Soo Lee	26	17	12	1	454	1	0	-	South Korea
Roy Makaay	33	29	28	26	2427	0	0	-	Holland
Michael Mols	37	30	22	7	875	1	0	-	Holland
Luis Pedro	18	1	0	0	0	0	0	-	Holland
Andwele Slory	25	19	17	7	858	3	0	-	Holland

TEAM OF THE SEASON

D
Tim de Cler
CG: 32 DR: 77
M
Nuri Sahin
CG: 23 SD: 49
G
Henk Timmer
CG: 32 DR: 75
D
Kevin Hofland
CG: 25 DR: 75
M
Theo Lucius
CG: 28 SD: 34
F
Roy Makaay
CG: 26 SR: 186
D
Andre Bahia
CG: 27 DR: 74
M
Gio van Bronckhorst
CG: 31 SD: 31
F
Luigi Bruins
CG: 22 SR: 348
D
Serginho Greene
CG: 12 DR: 58
M
Jonathan de Guzman
CG: 33 SD: 23

MONTHLY POINTS TALLY

Month	Points	%
AUGUST	6	100%
SEPTEMBER	9	75%
OCTOBER	6	67%
NOVEMBER	4	44%
DECEMBER	11	73%
JANUARY	5	33%
FEBRUARY	7	58%
MARCH	6	40%
APRIL	6	67%

LEAGUE GOALS

	PLAYER	MINS	GOALS	S RATE
1	Makaay	2427	13	186
2	De Guzman	2934	9	326
3	V Bronckhorst	2838	7	405
4	Hofs	1264	6	210
5	Bruins	2092	6	348
6	Sahin	2227	6	371
7	Bahia	2528	3	842
8	Slory	858	2	429
9	Mols	875	2	437
10	Landzaat	971	2	485
11	Wijnaldum	309	1	309
12	Vlaar	310	1	310
13	Fer	659	1	659
	Other		4	
	TOTAL		63	

TOP POINT EARNERS

	PLAYER	GAMES	AV PTS
1	Nuri Sahin	23	2.17
2	Luigi Bruins	22	1.91
3	Theo Lucius	28	1.89
4	Roy Makaay	26	1.81
5	Gio van Bronckhorst	31	1.81
6	Henk Timmer	32	1.78
7	Tim de Cler	32	1.75
8	Jonathan de Guzman	33	1.73
9	Kevin Hofland	25	1.68
10	Andre Bahia	27	1.67
	CLUB AVERAGE:		1.76

DISCIPLINARY RECORDS

	PLAYER	YELLOW	RED	AVE
1	Nick Hofs	5	1	210
2	Andwele Slory	3	0	286
3	Leroy Fer	2	0	329
4	Tim de Cler	8	0	359
5	Kevin Hofland	6	0	389
6	Gio v Bronckhorst	7	0	405
7	Theo Lucius	6	0	423
8	Chun-Soo Lee	1	0	454
9	Denny Landzaat	2	0	485
10	Serginho Greene	2	0	618
11	Nuri Sahin	3	0	742
12	Andre Bahia	3	0	842
13	Michael Mols	1	0	875
	Other	4	0	
	TOTAL	53	1	

KEY GOALKEEPER

Henk Timmer

Goals Conceded in the League	38	Counting Games League games when player was on pitch for at least 70 minutes	32
Defensive Rating Ave number of mins between League goals conceded while on the pitch	75	Clean Sheets In League games when player was on pitch for at least 70 minutes	13

KEY PLAYERS - DEFENDERS

Tim de Cler

Goals Conceded Number of League goals conceded while the player was on the pitch	37	Clean Sheets In League games when player was on pitch for at least 70 minutes	14
Defensive Rating Ave number of mins between League goals conceded while on the pitch	77	Club Defensive Rating Average number of mins between League goals conceded by the club this season	79

	PLAYER	CON LGE	CLEAN SHEETS	DEF RATE
1	Tim de Cler	37	14	77 mins
2	Kevin Hofland	31	11	75 mins
3	Andre Bahia	34	11	74 mins
4	Serginho Greene	21	3	58 mins

KEY PLAYERS - MIDFIELDERS

Nuri Sahin

Goals in the League	6	Contribution to Attacking Power Average number of minutes between League team goals while on pitch	40
Defensive Rating Average number of mins between League goals conceded while on the pitch	89	Scoring Difference Defensive Rating minus Contribution to Attacking Power	49

	PLAYER	LGE GOALS	DEF RATE	POWER	SCORE DIFF
1	Nuri Sahin	6	89	40	49 mins
2	Theo Lucius	1	79	45	34 mins
3	Giovanni van Bronckhorst	7	76	45	31 mins
4	Jonathan de Guzman	9	71	48	23 mins

KEY PLAYERS - GOALSCORERS

Roy Makaay

Goals in the League	13	Player Strike Rate Average number of minutes between League goals scored by player	186
Contribution to Attacking Power Average number of minutes between League team goals while on pitch	49	Club Strike Rate Average number of minutes between League goals scored by club	50

	PLAYER	LGE GOALS	POWER	STRIKE RATE
1	Roy Makaay	13	49	186 mins
2	Jonathan de Guzman	9	48	326 mins
3	Luigi Bruins	6	46	348 mins
4	Nuri Sahin	6	40	371 mins

Roy Makaay

SQUAD APPEARANCES

Match	1	2	3	4	5	6	7	8	9	10	11	12	13	14	15	16	17	18	19	20	21	22	23	24	25	26	27	28	29	30	31	32	33	34
Venue	A	H	H	A	A	H	A	H	A	H	H	A	H	A	A	H	A	H	A	H	H	H	A	A	H	A	H	A	H	A	A	H	A	H
Competition	L	L	L	L	L	L	L	L	L	L	L	L	L	L	L	L	L	L	L	L	L	L	L	L	L	L	L	L	L	L	L	L	L	L
Result	W	W	W	W	L	W	W	W	L	W	D	L	W	D	W	W	D	L	L	W	D	D	L	W	W	D	L	W	W	L	L	W	L	W

Goalkeepers
- Sherif Ekramy
- Erwin Mulder
- Henk Timmer

Defenders
- Andre Bahia
- Jordy Buijs
- Tim de Cler
- Serginho Greene
- Kevin Hofland
- Ron Vlaar

Midfielders
- Danny Buijs
- Jonathan de Guzman
- Leroy Fer
- Nick Hofs
- Denny Landzaat
- Jacob Lensky
- Theo Lucius
- Nuri Sahin
- Gio van Bronckhorst
- Georginio Wijnaldum

Forwards
- Diego Biseswar
- Luigi Bruins
- Hanne Hagary
- Chun-Soo Lee
- Roy Makaay
- Michael Mols
- Luis Pedro
- Andwele Slory

KEY: On all match · On bench · Subbed or sent off (Counting game) · Subbed or sent off (playing less than 70 minutes) · Subbed on from bench (Counting Game) · Subbed on (playing less than 70 minutes) · Subbed on and then subbed or sent off (Counting Game) · Subbed on and then subbed or sent off (playing less than 70 minutes) · Not in 16

FC GRONINGEN

Final Position: **7th**

NICKNAME: PRIDE OF THE NORTH

KEY: ☐Won ☐Drawn ☐Lost

							Attendance
1	hopr1	NAC Breda	A	W	3-0	Lovre 45, Nevland 73, Fledderus 90	15,104
2	hopr1	De Graafschap	H	L	0-2		19,300
3	hopr1	Ajax	A	D	2-2	Berg 36, 60	45,000
4	hopr1	Utrecht	H	L	0-2		19,000
5	ucrl1	Fiorentina	H	D	1-1	Lovre 26	19,703
6	hopr1	Excelsior	A	W	3-1	Nevland 45, Berg 55, Levchenko 63 pen	2,500
7	hopr1	S Rotterdam	H	W	1-0	Lovre 50	19,304
8	ucrl2	Fiorentina	A	L	3-4*	Nevland 56 (*on penalties)	26,925
9	hopr1	AZ Alkmaar	A	D	2-2	Berg 70, Svejdik 90	16,378
10	hopr1	Twente	H	W	1-0	Meerdink 56	18,971
11	hopr1	NEC Nijmegen	A	L	1-5	van de Laak 7 pen	12,000
12	hopr1	Vitesse	H	D	0-0		19,175
13	hopr1	Roda JC Kerk	A	L	1-5	Nevland 20	12,800
14	hopr1	Feyenoord	H	W	3-2	Berg 73, 90, Nevland 76	19,000
15	hopr1	VVV	H	W	1-0	Berg 53	19,500
16	hopr1	Heerenveen	A	L	2-4	Nevland 9, 14	26,000
17	hopr1	Willem II Tilb	H	W	1-0	Silva 53	19,000
18	hopr1	Heracles	A	W	2-1	Nijland 24, van de Laak 47	8,011
19	hopr1	PSV Eindhoven	H	W	2-1	Lindgren 61, Berg 77	18,273
20	hopr1	S Rotterdam	A	W	3-1	Nijland 30, 53, Lovre 81	10,612
21	hopr1	Excelsior	H	W	3-2	Lovre 58, 90, Berg 64	19,300
22	hopr1	Twente	A	L	1-3	Lovre 47	13,250
23	hopr1	NEC Nijmegen	H	W	5-1	Fledderus 33 pen, 35, Berg 68, Lovre 82 Hiariej 90	19,200
24	hopr1	Feyenoord	A	D	1-1	Berg 32	42,500
25	hopr1	Roda JC Kerk	H	D	1-1	Powel 14	19,294
26	hopr1	Vitesse	A	L	1-2	Meerdink 56	20,105
27	hopr1	AZ Alkmaar	H	W	2-1	Berg 30, 86 pen	19,400
28	hopr1	VVV	A	W	5-2	Lovre 16, Berg 45, 85, Powel 47 Nijland 89	6,000
29	hopr1	Heracles	H	L	1-2	Powel 10	19,000
30	hopr1	Willem II Tilb	A	W	2-1	Baelum 82 og, de Roover 85	13,500
31	hopr1	Heerenveen	H	L	0-1		19,700
32	hopr1	PSV Eindhoven	A	L	0-3		33,000
33	hopr1	De Graafschap	A	D	1-1	Powel 45	12,600
34	hopr1	NAC Breda	H	L	1-2	Lovre 46	19,000
35	hopr1	Ajax	H	L	1-2	Cahais 45	19,700
36	hopr1	Utrecht	A	L	0-1		21,000
37	erepo	Utrecht	A	D	2-2	Lovre 52, Levchenko 90	11,250
38	erepo	Utrecht	H	W	3-1	Berg 54, 76, Svejdik 73	19,000
39	erepo	NEC Nijmegen	A	L	0-1		8,250
40	erepo	NEC Nijmegen	H	L	1-3	Berg 60	19,000

LEAGUE APPEARANCES, BOOKINGS AND CAPS

	AGE (on 01/07/08)	IN NAMED 18	APPEARANCES	COUNTING GAMES	MINUTES ON PITCH	YELLOW CARDS	RED CARDS	CAPS THIS SEASON	NATIONAL SIDE
Goalkeepers									
Brian van Loo	33	34	34	34	3060	1	0	-	Holland
Defenders									
Matias Cahais	20	13	10	4	460	0	0	-	Argentina
Sepp De Roover	23	13	11	7	764	1	0	-	Belgium
Tom Hiariej	19	23	21	17	1607	1	0	-	Holland
Arnold Kruiswijk	23	30	30	29	2649	4	0	-	Holland
Gibril Sankoh	25	32	31	31	2790	7	0	-	Sierra Leone
Bruno Silva	28	17	17	17	1529	4	0	-	Uruguay
Fredrik Stenman	25	28	28	25	2377	2	0	-	Sweden
Ondrej Svejdik	25	16	9	3	403	1	1	-	Czech Republic
Jeroen Veldmate	19	19	4	0	45	0	0	-	Holland
Midfielders									
Mark-Jan Fledderus	25	32	29	19	1868	3	0	-	Belgium
Danny Holla	20	6	6	5	456	2	0	-	Holland
Evgeniy Levchenko	30	16	15	10	1061	3	0	-	Ukraine
Rasmus Lindgren	23	20	20	20	1791	2	0	-	Sweden
Goran Lovre	26	33	33	29	2684	2	0	-	Serbia
Paul Matthijs	31	4	3	2	205	1	0	-	Holland
Martijn Meerdink	31	24	22	14	1557	3	1	-	Holland
Shkodran Metaj	20	33	21	11	1203	1	0	-	Serbia
Koen van de Laak	25	18	18	11	1130	2	0	-	Holland
Martijn van der Laan	19	15	2	0	40	0	0	-	Holland
Forwards									
Marcus Berg	21	25	25	20	1908	1	0	-	Sweden
Marnix Kolder	27	9	6	4	378	0	0	-	Holland
Rogier Krohne	21	4	1	0	15	0	0	-	Holland
Tim Matavz	19	28	15	1	394	0	0	-	Slovenia
Erik Nevland	30	15	15	10	1006	2	0	-	Norway
Stefan Nijland	19	28	23	9	1141	3	0	-	Holland
Berry Powel	28	12	12	10	996	3	0	-	Holland

TEAM OF THE SEASON

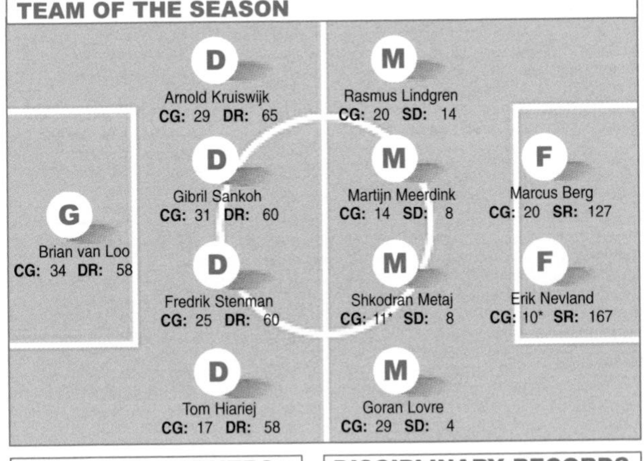

D
Arnold Kruiswijk
CG: 29 DR: 65
M
Rasmus Lindgren
CG: 20 SD: 14
D
Gibril Sankoh
CG: 31 DR: 60
M
Martijn Meerdink
CG: 14 SD: 8
F
Marcus Berg
CG: 20 SR: 127
G
Brian van Loo
CG: 34 DR: 58
D
Fredrik Stenman
CG: 25 DR: 60
M
Shkodran Metaj
CG: 11* SD: 8
F
Erik Nevland
CG: 10* SR: 167
D
Tom Hiariej
CG: 17 DR: 58
M
Goran Lovre
CG: 29 SD: 4

MONTHLY POINTS TALLY

AUGUST	3	50%
SEPTEMBER	7	58%
OCTOBER	4	44%
NOVEMBER	4	44%
DECEMBER	15	83%
JANUARY	7	58%
FEBRUARY	7	58%
MARCH	4	27%
APRIL	0	0%

LEAGUE GOALS

	PLAYER	MINS	GOALS	S RATE
1	Berg	1908	15	127
2	Lovre	2774	9	308
3	Nevland	1006	6	167
4	Powel	1086	4	271
5	Nijland	1141	4	285
6	Fledderus	1958	3	652
7	van de Laak	1130	2	565
8	Meerdink	1557	2	778
9	Svejdik	403	1	403
10	Cahais	550	1	550
11	de Roover	854	1	854
12	Levchenko	1151	1	1151
13	Silva	1529	1	1529
	Other		2	
	TOTAL		52	

TOP POINT EARNERS

	PLAYER	GAMES	AV PTS
1	Rasmus Lindgren	20	2.00
2	Bruno Silva	17	1.76
3	Fredrik Stenman	25	1.76
4	Marcus Berg	20	1.75
5	Gibril Sankoh	31	1.65
6	Arnold Kruiswijk	29	1.62
7	Martijn Meerdink	14	1.50
8	Brian van Loo	34	1.50
9	Goran Lovre	29	1.48
10	Tom Hiariej	17	1.29
	CLUB AVERAGE:		1.50

DISCIPLINARY RECORDS

	PLAYER	YELLOW	RED	AVE
1	Danny Holla	2	0	228
2	Berry Powel	3	0	362
3	Stefan Nijland	3	0	380
4	Bruno Silva	4	0	382
5	Evgeniy Levchenko	3	0	383
6	Martijn Meerdink	3	1	389
7	Gibril Sankoh	7	0	411
8	Erik Nevland	2	0	503
9	Koen van de Laak	2	0	565
10	Mark-Jan Fledderus	3	0	652
11	Arnold Kruiswijk	4	0	684
12	Sepp De Roover	1	0	854
13	Rasmus Lindgren	2	0	895
	Other	8	0	
	TOTAL	47	1	

KEY GOALKEEPER

Brian van Loo

Goals Conceded in the League	54	Counting Games League games when player was on pitch for at least 70 minutes	34
Defensive Rating Ave number of mins between League goals conceded while on the pitch	58	Clean Sheets In League games when player was on pitch for at least 70 minutes	7

KEY PLAYERS - DEFENDERS

Arnold Kruiswijk

Goals Conceded Number of League goals conceded while the player was on the pitch	42	Clean Sheets In League games when player was on pitch for at least 70 minutes	6
Defensive Rating Ave number of mins between League goals conceded while on the pitch	65	Club Defensive Rating Average number of mins between League goals conceded by the club this season	58

	PLAYER	CON LGE	CLEAN SHEETS	DEF RATE
1	Arnold Kruiswijk	42	6	65 mins
2	Gibril Sankoh	48	7	60 mins
3	Fredrik Stenman	39	6	60 mins
4	Tom Hiariej	29	2	58 mins

KEY PLAYERS - MIDFIELDERS

Rasmus Lindgren

Goals in the League	1	Contribution to Attacking Power Average number of minutes between League team goals while on pitch	49
Defensive Rating Average number of mins between League goals conceded while on the pitch	63	Scoring Difference Defensive Rating minus Contribution to Attacking Power	14

	PLAYER	LGE GOALS	DEF RATE	POWER	SCORE DIFF
1	Rasmus Lindgren	1	63	49	14 mins
2	Martijn Meerdink	2	55	47	8 mins
3	Goran Lovre	9	64	60	4 mins
4	Mark-Jan Fledderus	3	51	69	-18 mins

KEY PLAYERS - GOALSCORERS

Marcus Berg

Goals in the League	15	Player Strike Rate Average number of minutes between League goals scored by player	127
Contribution to Attacking Power Average number of minutes between League team goals while on pitch	47	Club Strike Rate Average number of minutes between League goals scored by club	59

	PLAYER	LGE GOALS	POWER	STRIKE RATE
1	Marcus Berg	15	47	127 mins
2	Goran Lovre	9	60	308 mins
3	Mark-Jan Fledderus	3	69	652 mins
4	Martijn Meerdink	2	47	778 mins

lease
amer
9
Goran Lovre

SQUAD APPEARANCES

Match	1	2	3	4	5	6	7	8	9	10	11	12	13	14	15	16	17	18	19	20	21	22	23	24	25	26	27	28	29	30	31	32	33	34	35	36	37	38	39	40
Venue	A	H	A	H	H	A	H	A	A	H	A	H	A	H	H	A	H	A	H	A	H	A	H	A	H	A	H	A	H	A	H	A	A	H	H	A	A	H	A	H
Competition	L	L	L	L	E	L	L	E	L	L	L	L	L	L	L	L	L	L	L	L	L	L	L	L	L	L	L	L	L	L	L	L	L	L	L	L	O	O	O	O
Result	W	L	D	L	D	W	W	L	D	W	L	D	L	W	W	L	W	W	W	W	W	L	W	D	D	L	W	W	L	W	L	L	D	L	L	L	D	W	L	L

Goalkeepers
Brian van Loo

Defenders
Matias Cahais
Sepp De Roover
Tom Hiariej
Arnold Kruiswijk
Gibril Sankoh
Bruno Silva
Fredrik Stenman
Ondrej Svejdik
Jeroen Veldmate

Midfielders
Mark-Jan Fledderus
Danny Holla
Evgeniy Levchenko
Rasmus Lindgren
Goran Lovre
Paul Matthijs
Martijn Meerdink
Shkodran Metaj
Koen van de Laak
Martijn van der Laan

Forwards
Marcus Berg
Marnix Kolder
Rogier Krohne
Tim Matavz
Erik Nevland
Stefan Nijland
Berry Powel

KEY: On all match · On bench · Subbed or sent off (Counting game) · Subbed or sent off (playing less than 70 minutes) · Subbed on from bench (Counting Game) · Subbed on (playing less than 70 minutes) · Subbed on and then subbed or sent off (Counting Game) · Subbed on and then subbed or sent off (playing less than 70 minutes) · Not in 16

NEC NIJMEGEN

Final Position: **8th**

NICKNAME: NEC

KEY: ☐Won ☐Drawn ☐Lost

		Opponent	H/A	Res	Score	Scorers	Attendance
1	hopr1	**Roda JC Kerk**	H	D	1-1	van Beukering 39	11,300
2	hopr1	**PSV Eindhoven**	A	L	0-5		33,000
3	hopr1	**Vitesse**	A	L	0-1		18,515
4	hopr1	**NAC Breda**	H	L	0-1		11,750
5	hopr1	**Twente**	A	L	0-3		13,000
6	hopr1	**Willem II Tilb**	H	W	1-0	Worm 68 pen	12,000
7	hopr1	**Excelsior**	A	L	0-2		2,583
8	hopr1	**Ajax**	A	D	0-0		48,123
9	hopr1	**Groningen**	H	W	5-1	El-Akchaoui 5 pen, Davids 63 van Beukering 74, 87, Olsson 78	12,000
10	hopr1	**AZ Alkmaar**	A	L	0-4		16,333
11	hopr1	**Heracles**	H	W	3-0	van Beukering 33, Lens 82 Nalbantoglu 90	12,000
12	hopr1	**Utrecht**	A	L	2-3	Olsson 17, Davids 57	20,000
13	hopr1	**Heerenveen**	H	L	0-1		12,000
14	hopr1	**S Rotterdam**	A	L	0-1		9,083
15	hopr1	**De Graafschap**	A	D	1-1	El-Akchaoui 90	12,000
16	hopr1	**Feyenoord**	H	L	0-2		12,500
17	hopr1	**VVV**	H	D	2-2	Janssen 12, 55	12,300
18	hopr1	**Willem II Tilb**	A	L	0-3		12,000
19	hopr1	**Twente**	H	D	2-2	El-Akchaoui 36 pen, van Beukering 67	12,000
20	hopr1	**Ajax**	H	D	1-1	Lens 16	12,400
21	hopr1	**Groningen**	A	L	1-5	van Beukering 56	19,200
22	hopr1	**Utrecht**	H	W	2-0	van Beukering 68, Holman 78	11,800
23	hopr1	**Heracles**	A	W	2-0	Lens 26, 69	8,500
24	hopr1	**AZ Alkmaar**	H	W	5-2	Bobson 10, Holman 13, van Beukering 20 pen Wisgerhof 24, Drost 68	12,000
25	hopr1	**Excelsior**	H	L	0-1		12,150
26	hopr1	**Heerenveen**	A	W	3-2	Lens 63, Holman 73, El-Akchaoui 90	25,000
27	hopr1	**Feyenoord**	A	W	3-1	Holman 17, Olsson 79, Lens 90	45,000
28	hopr1	**De Graafschap**	H	W	3-1	Holman 33, 75, Vadocz 48	12,500
29	hopr1	**S Rotterdam**	H	W	4-2	Bobson 61, Pothuizen 82, 86 El-Akchaoui 90	12,500
30	hopr1	**VVV**	A	W	2-1	van Beukering 79, Sibum 90	6,000
31	hopr1	**PSV Eindhoven**	H	D	0-0		12,500
32	hopr1	**Roda JC Kerk**	A	W	2-0	van Beukering 32, Lens 68	15,100
33	hopr1	**Vitesse**	H	W	1-0	Vadocz 28	12,500
34	hopr1	**NAC Breda**	A	W	3-1	Lens 32, 87, van Beukering 65	16,450
35	erepo	**Roda JC Kerk**	A	W	1-0	Holman 6	11,000
36	erepo	**Roda JC Kerk**	H	W	2-0	van Beukering 40, Kivuvu 84	7,500
37	erepo	**Groningen**	H	W	1-0	Lens 71	8,250
38	erepo	**Groningen**	A	W	3-1	Holman 5, Vadocz 45, Davids 72	19,000
39	erepo	**NAC Breda**	H	W	6-0	Olsson 14, 27, Holman 50, Lens 63, 67 El-Akchaoui 71 pen	11,500
40	erepo	**NAC Breda**	A	W	1-0	Lens 61	5,200

LEAGUE APPEARANCES, BOOKINGS AND CAPS

	AGE (on 01/07/08)	IN NAMED 18	APPEARANCES	COUNTING GAMES	MINUTES ON PITCH	YELLOW CARDS	RED CARDS	CAPS THIS SEASON	NATIONAL SIDE
Goalkeepers									
Rein Baart	36	33	0	0	0	0	0	-	Holland
Gabor Babos	33	34	34	34	3060	2	0	-	Hungary
Defenders									
Jeroen Drost	21	15	5	2	292	0	0	-	Holland
Youssef El-Akchaoui	27	34	34	34	3060	3	0	-	Holland
Daniel F Artola	25	14	4	1	151	0	0	-	Spain
Muslu Nalbantoglu	24	32	32	27	2534	7	0	-	Holland
Jonas Olsson	25	27	27	22	2191	6	1	-	Sweden
Ferne Snoyl	23	5	4	3	301	0	0	-	Holland
Bob Verweij	21	8	1	0	9	0	0	-	Holland
Peter Wisgerhof	28	32	32	30	2809	6	1	-	Holland
Midfielders									
Naim Aarab	21	21	6	1	248	1	0	-	Belgium
Lorenzo Davids	21	32	29	21	2128	2	1	-	Holland
Brett Holman	24	27	27	22	2159	2	0	-	Australia
Dominique Kivuvu	20	34	22	15	1389	2	0	-	Holland
Patrick Pothuizen	36	28	13	7	756	1	0	-	Holland
Bas Sibum	25	14	14	14	1253	5	0	-	Holland
Krisztian Vadocz	23	29	27	24	2265	1	0	4	Hungary
Bart van Brakel	21	14	4	1	113	0	0	-	Holland
Forwards									
Kevin Bobson	27	14	14	13	1176	1	0	-	Holland
Karim Fachtali	20	13	4	0	41	0	0	-	Holland
Adam Hrepka	21	11	7	0	196	0	0	-	Hungary
Tim Janssen	22	16	15	7	888	0	0	-	Holland
Jeremain Lens	20	31	31	27	2571	3	0	-	Holland
Saidi Ntibazonkiza	21	9	6	3	339	0	0	-	Burundi
Alexander Prent	25	16	13	2	521	0	0	-	Holland
Jhon van Beukering	24	29	28	17	1862	4	0	-	Holland
Rutger Worm	22	34	24	10	1272	3	0	-	Holland

TEAM OF THE SEASON

D
Jonas Olsson
CG: 22 DR: 68
M
Bas Sibum
CG: 14 SD: 39
D
Muslu Nalbantoglu
CG: 27 DR: 64
M
Krisztian Vadocz
CG: 24 SD: 16
F
Jhon van Beukering
CG: 17 SR: 169
G
Gabor Babos
CG: 34 DR: 61
D
Peter Wisgerhof
CG: 30 DR: 62
M
Brett Holman
CG: 22 SD: 9
F
Jeremain Lens
CG: 27 SR: 285
D
Youssef El-Akchaoui
CG: 34 DR: 61
M
Lorenzo Davids
CG: 21 SD: -23

MONTHLY POINTS TALLY

Month	Points	%
AUGUST	1	17%
SEPTEMBER	3	25%
OCTOBER	4	44%
NOVEMBER	3	33%
DECEMBER	2	11%
JANUARY	5	42%
FEBRUARY	9	75%
MARCH	13	87%
APRIL	9	100%

LEAGUE GOALS

	PLAYER	MINS	GOALS	S RATE
1	van Beukering	1862	11	169
2	Lens	2571	9	285
3	Holman	2159	6	359
4	El-Akchaoui	3060	5	612
5	Olsson	2191	3	730
6	Pothuizen	756	2	378
7	Janssen	888	2	444
8	Bobson	1176	2	588
9	Davids	2128	2	1064
10	Vadocz	2265	2	1132
11	Drost	292	1	292
12	Sibum	1253	1	1253
13	Worm	1272	1	1272
	Other		2	
	TOTAL		49	

TOP POINT EARNERS

	PLAYER	GAMES	AV PTS
1	Bas Sibum	14	2.29
2	Kevin Bobson	13	2.23
3	Krisztian Vadocz	24	1.83
4	Brett Holman	22	1.73
5	Jhon van Beukering	17	1.71
6	Jeremain Lens	27	1.70
7	Muslu Nalbantoglu	27	1.48
8	Jonas Olsson	22	1.45
9	Gabor Babos	34	1.44
10	Youssef El-Akchaoui	34	1.44
	CLUB AVERAGE:		1.44

DISCIPLINARY RECORDS

	PLAYER	YELLOW	RED	AVE
1	Bas Sibum	5	0	250
2	Jonas Olsson	6	1	313
3	Muslu Nalbantoglu	7	0	362
4	Peter Wisgerhof	6	1	401
5	Rutger Worm	3	0	424
6	J van Beukering	4	0	465
7	Dominique Kivuvu	2	0	694
8	Lorenzo Davids	2	1	709
9	Patrick Pothuizen	1	0	756
10	Jeremain Lens	3	0	857
11	Y El-Akchaoui	3	0	1020
12	Brett Holman	2	0	1079
13	Kevin Bobson	1	0	1176
	Other	3	0	
	TOTAL	48	3	

KEY GOALKEEPER

GÃ¡bor Babos

Goals Conceded in the League	50	**Counting Games** League games when player was on pitch for at least 70 minutes	34
Defensive Rating Ave number of mins between League goals conceded while on the pitch	61	**Clean Sheets** In League games when player was on pitch for at least 70 minutes	8

KEY PLAYERS - DEFENDERS

Jonas Olsson

Goals Conceded Number of League goals conceded while the player was on the pitch	32	**Clean Sheets** In League games when player was on pitch for at least 70 minutes	5
Defensive Rating Ave number of mins between League goals conceded while on the pitch	68	**Club Defensive Rating** Average number of mins between League goals conceded by the club this season	61

	PLAYER	CON LGE	CLEAN SHEETS	DEF RATE
1	Jonas Olsson	32	5	68 mins
2	Muslu Nalbantoglu	39	8	64 mins
3	Peter Wisgerhof	45	7	62 mins
4	Youssef El-Akchaoui	50	8	61 mins

KEY PLAYERS - MIDFIELDERS

Bas Sibum

Goals in the League	1	**Contribution to Attacking Power** Average number of minutes between League team goals while on pitch	44
Defensive Rating Average number of mins between League goals conceded while on the pitch	83	**Scoring Difference** Defensive Rating minus Contribution to Attacking Power	39

	PLAYER	LGE GOALS	DEF RATE	POWER	SCORE DIFF
1	Bas Sibum	1	83	44	39 mins
2	Krisztian Vadocz	2	66	50	16 mins
3	Brett Holman	6	67	58	9 mins
4	Lorenzo Davids	2	53	76	-23 mins

KEY PLAYERS - GOALSCORERS

Jhon van Beukering

Goals in the League	11	**Player Strike Rate** Average number of minutes between League goals scored by player	169
Contribution to Attacking Power Average number of minutes between League team goals while on pitch	54	**Club Strike Rate** Average number of minutes between League goals scored by club	62

	PLAYER	LGE GOALS	POWER	STRIKE RATE
1	Jhon van Beukering	11	54	169 mins
2	Jeremain Lens	9	53	285 mins
3	Brett Holman	6	58	359 mins
4	Kevin Bobson	2	39	588 mins

NEC
Jiba
Vakanties.
Jeremain Lens

SQUAD APPEARANCES

Match	1	2	3	4	5	6	7	8	9	10	11	12	13	14	15	16	17	18	19	20	21	22	23	24	25	26	27	28	29	30	31	32	33	34	35	36	37	38	39	40
Venue	H	A	A	H	A	H	A	A	H	A	H	A	H	A	A	H	H	A	H	H	A	H	A	H	H	A	A	H	H	A	H	A	H	A	A	H	H	A	H	A
Competition	L	L	L	L	L	L	L	L	L	L	L	L	L	L	L	L	L	L	L	L	L	L	L	L	L	L	L	L	L	L	L	L	L	L	O	O	O	O	O	O
Result	D	L	L	L	L	W	L	D	W	L	W	L	L	L	D	L	D	L	D	D	L	W	W	W	L	W	W	W	W	W	D	W	W	W	W	W	W	W	W	W

Goalkeepers
Rein Baart
Gabor Babos

Defenders
Jeroen Drost
Youssef El-Akchaoui
Daniel Fernandez Artola
Muslu Nalbantoglu
Jonas Olsson
Ferne Snoyl
Bob Verweij
Peter Wisgerhof

Midfielders
Naim Aarab
Lorenzo Davids
Brett Holman
Dominique Kivuvu
Patrick Pothuizen
Bas Sibum
Krisztian Vadocz
Bart van Brakel

Forwards
Kevin Bobson
Karim Fachtali
Adam Hrepka
Tim Janssen
Jeremain Lens
Saidi Ntibazonkiza
Alexander Prent
Jhon van Beukering
Rutger Worm

KEY: On all match; On bench; Subbed or sent off (Counting game); Subbed or sent off (playing less than 70 minutes); Subbed on from bench (Counting Game); Subbed on (playing less than 70 minutes); Subbed on and then subbed or sent off (Counting Game); Subbed on and then subbed or sent off (playing less than 70 minutes); Not in 16

RODA JC KERK

Final Position: **9th**

NICKNAME: DE KOEMPELS

KEY: ☐Won ☐Drawn ☐Lost

						Attendance
1	hopr1 **NEC Nijmegen**	A	D	1-1	Lamah 85	11,300
2	hopr1 **Heracles**	H	W	2-1	Lamah 4, Kah 80	13,000
3	hopr1 **VVV**	A	W	5-3	Oper 12, 50, Yulu-Matondo 41, 60	
					Van Tornhout 90	6,000
4	hopr1 **Feyenoord**	H	L	1-3	Tiote 40	17,000
5	hopr1 **Willem II Tilb**	A	L	0-1		12,000
6	hopr1 **Excelsior**	H	D	3-3	Janssen 9, Lamah 13, Saeijs 49	13,000
7	hopr1 **Twente**	A	W	1-0	De Fauw 71	13,000
8	hopr1 **Utrecht**	H	D	1-1	Bodor 27	12,800
9	hopr1 **De Graafschap**	H	W	1-0	Meeuwis 61 pen	13,000
10	hopr1 **Ajax**	A	L	2-4	Lamah 38, Hadouir 76	48,621
11	hopr1 **Groningen**	H	W	5-1	Hadouir 1, Lamah 23, Oper 35, 50	
					Cisse 65	12,800
12	hopr1 **NAC Breda**	A	D	0-0		15,000
13	hopr1 **Vitesse**	H	W	3-2	Lamah 45, 46, Saeijs 69	12,000
14	hopr1 **PSV Eindhoven**	A	W	4-2	De Fauw 19, Meeuwis 45, Oper 48	
					Hadouir 64	33,000
15	hopr1 **S Rotterdam**	H	L	2-3	Schenkel 67 og, Meeuwis 79 pen	14,425
16	hopr1 **AZ Alkmaar**	A	D	1-1	Yulu-Matondo 53	16,413
17	hopr1 **Heerenveen**	H	W	1-0	Tiote 1	13,000
18	hopr1 **Excelsior**	A	W	2-1	Cisse 28, Bodor 74	2,500
19	hopr1 **Willem II Tilb**	H	D	1-1	Meeuwis 83 pen	13,700
20	hopr1 **Utrecht**	A	L	1-3	Oper 53	20,000
21	hopr1 **De Graafschap**	A	L	1-2	Bodor 32 pen	12,000
22	hopr1 **NAC Breda**	H	L	0-2		14,800
23	hopr1 **Groningen**	A	D	1-1	Oper 81	19,294
24	hopr1 **Ajax**	H	W	2-1	Lamah 22, Hadouir 79	17,800
25	hopr1 **Twente**	H	W	3-1	Lamah 24, Janssen 31, Van Tornhout 67	14,300
26	hopr1 **Vitesse**	A	D	1-1	Saeijs 87	19,475
27	hopr1 **AZ Alkmaar**	H	D	1-1	Janssen 4	14,800
28	hopr1 **S Rotterdam**	A	L	1-4	Yulu-Matondo 64	9,846
29	hopr1 **PSV Eindhoven**	H	D	1-1	Meeuwis 90	17,000
30	hopr1 **Heerenveen**	A	L	3-4	Lamah 25, Yulu-Matondo 27, Janssen 37	25,000
31	hopr1 **Heracles**	A	D	0-0		8,500
32	hopr1 **NEC Nijmegen**	H	L	0-2		15,100
33	hopr1 **VVV**	H	W	4-1	Meeuwis 36 pen, Lamah 50, Bodor 53, Hadouir	
7818,500						
34	hopr1 **Feyenoord**	A	L	0-3		46,000
35	erepo **NEC Nijmegen**	H	L	0-1		11,000
36	erepo **NEC Nijmegen**	A	L	0-2		7,500

LEAGUE APPEARANCES, BOOKINGS AND CAPS

	AGE (on 01/07/08)	IN NAMED 18	APPEARANCES	COUNTING GAMES	MINUTES ON PITCH	YELLOW CARDS	RED CARDS	CAPS THIS SEASON	NATIONAL SIDE
Goalkeepers									
Bram Castro	25	33	33	33	2970	0	0	-	Belgium
Cliff Mardulier	25	2	0	0	0	0	0	-	Belgium
Przemyslaw Tyton	21	32	1	1	90	0	0	-	Poland
Defenders									
Davy de Fauw	26	33	33	33	2938	5	0	-	Belgium
Marcel de Jong	21	33	25	20	1888	6	1	-	Holland
Pa-Modou Kah	27	33	29	23	2239	6	0	-	Norway
Kjell Knops	20	7	0	0	0	0	0	-	Holland
Jan-Paul Saeijs	30	30	30	26	2450	9	0	-	Holland
Ger Senden	36	13	3	0	16	0	0	-	Holland
Fatih Sonkaya	27	23	15	7	813	4	0	-	Turkey
Frank van Kouwen	27	33	8	1	290	0	0	-	Holland
Nuelson Wau	27	15	10	6	609	1	0	-	Holland
Midfielders									
Boldizsar Bodor	26	32	27	16	1705	3	0	1	Hungary
Elbekay Bouchiba	29	5	2	1	119	0	0	-	Morocco
Willem Janssen	21	34	31	18	1802	1	0	-	Holland
Marcel Meeuwis	27	32	31	30	2722	5	1	-	Holland
Bas Sibum	25	19	7	5	482	2	0	-	Holland
Cheik Ismael Tiote	22	28	26	22	2194	6	1	-	Ivory Coast
Forwards									
Sekou Cisse	23	24	24	13	1438	2	0	-	Ivory Coast
Anouar Hadouir	25	30	30	29	2527	6	0	-	Holland
Roland Lamah	20	32	32	26	2613	5	0	-	Belgium
Andres Oper	30	20	20	9	1193	4	0	-	Estonia
Slama Solou	19	2	0	0	0	0	0	-	Holland
Dieter van Tornhout	23	26	19	2	616	3	0	-	Belgium
J Vandamme	22	5	2	0	55	1	0	-	Belgium
J Yulu-Matondo	22	30	30	15	1801	5	0	-	Zaire

TEAM OF THE SEASON

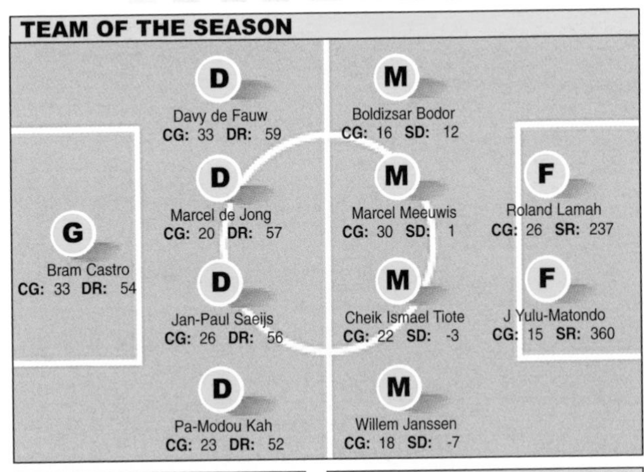
G
Bram Castro
CG: 33 DR: 54
D
Davy de Fauw
CG: 33 DR: 59
D
Marcel de Jong
CG: 20 DR: 57
D
Jan-Paul Saeijs
CG: 26 DR: 56
D
Pa-Modou Kah
CG: 23 DR: 52
M
Boldizsar Bodor
CG: 16 SD: 12
M
Marcel Meeuwis
CG: 30 SD: 1
M
Cheik Ismael Tiote
CG: 22 SD: -3
M
Willem Janssen
CG: 18 SD: -7
F
Roland Lamah
CG: 26 SR: 237
F
J Yulu-Matondo
CG: 15 SR: 360

MONTHLY POINTS TALLY

AUGUST	4	67%
SEPTEMBER	4	33%
OCTOBER	7	78%
NOVEMBER	4	44%
DECEMBER	13	72%
JANUARY	1	8%
FEBRUARY	8	67%
MARCH	3	20%
APRIL	3	33%

LEAGUE GOALS

	PLAYER	MINS	GOALS	S RATE
1	Lamah	2613	**11**	237
2	Oper	1193	**7**	170
3	Meeuwis	2722	**6**	453
4	Yulu-Matondo	1801	**5**	360
5	Hadouir	2527	**5**	505
6	Bodor	1705	**4**	426
7	Janssen	1802	**4**	450
8	Saeijs	2450	**3**	816
9	Van Tornhout	616	**2**	308
10	Cisse	1438	**2**	719
11	Tiote	2194	**2**	1097
12	De Fauw	2938	**2**	1469
13	Kah	2239	**1**	2239
	Other		0	
	TOTAL		**54**	

TOP POINT EARNERS

	PLAYER	GAMES	AV PTS
1	Boldizsar Bodor	16	**1.69**
2	Roland Lamah	26	**1.62**
3	Pa-Modou Kah	23	**1.57**
4	Jeanvion Yulu-Matondo	15	**1.53**
5	Marcel Meeuwis	30	**1.50**
6	Jan-Paul Saeijs	26	**1.50**
7	Davy de Fauw	33	**1.42**
8	Bram Castro	33	**1.39**
9	Willem Janssen	18	**1.39**
10	Cheik Ismael Tiote	22	**1.32**
	CLUB AVERAGE:		**1.38**

DISCIPLINARY RECORDS

	PLAYER	YELLOW	RED	AVE
1	Fatih Sonkaya	4	0	**203**
2	Dieter van Tornhout	3	0	**205**
3	Bas Sibum	2	0	**241**
4	Marcel de Jong	6	1	**269**
5	Jan-Paul Saeijs	9	0	**272**
6	Andres Oper	4	0	**298**
7	Cheik Ismael Tiote	6	1	**313**
8	J Yulu-Matondo	5	0	**360**
9	Pa-Modou Kah	6	0	**373**
10	Anouar Hadouir	6	0	**421**
11	Marcel Meeuwis	5	1	**453**
12	Roland Lamah	5	0	**522**
13	Boldizsar Bodor	3	0	**568**
	Other	9	0	
	TOTAL	**73**	**3**	

KEY GOALKEEPER

Bram Castro

Goals Conceded in the League	55	**Counting Games** League games when player was on pitch for at least 70 minutes	33
Defensive Rating **Ave number of mins between League goals conceded while on the pitch**	54	**Clean Sheets** In League games when player was on pitch for at least 70 minutes	4

KEY PLAYERS - DEFENDERS

Davy de Fauw

Goals Conceded Number of League goals conceded while the player was on the pitch	49	**Clean Sheets** In League games when player was on pitch for at least 70 minutes	6
Defensive Rating **Ave number of mins between League goals conceded while on the pitch**	59	**Club Defensive Rating** Average number of mins between League goals conceded by the club this season	55

	PLAYER	CON LGE	CLEAN SHEETS	DEF RATE
1	Davy de Fauw	49	6	59 mins
2	Marcel de Jong	33	2	57 mins
3	Jan-Paul Saeijs	43	3	56 mins
4	Pa-Modou Kah	43	4	52 mins

KEY PLAYERS - MIDFIELDERS

Boldizsar Bodor

Goals in the League	4	**Contribution to Attacking Power** Average number of minutes between League team goals while on pitch	48
Defensive Rating Average number of mins between League goals conceded while on the pitch	60	**Scoring Difference** **Defensive Rating minus Contribution to Attacking Power**	12

	PLAYER	LGE GOALS	DEF RATE	POWER	SCORE DIFF
1	Boldizsar Bodor	4	60	48	12 mins
2	Marcel Meeuwis	6	56	55	1 mins
3	Cheik Ismael Tiote	2	48	51	-3 mins
4	Willem Janssen	4	51	58	-7 mins

KEY PLAYERS - GOALSCORERS

Roland Lamah

Goals in the League	11	**Player Strike Rate** **Average number of minutes between League goals scored by player**	237
Contribution to Attacking Power Average number of minutes between League team goals while on pitch	52	**Club Strike Rate** Average number of minutes between League goals scored by club	55

	PLAYER	LGE GOALS	POWER	STRIKE RATE
1	Roland Lamah	11	52	237 mins
2	Jeanvion Yulu-Matondo	5	60	360 mins
3	Boldizsar Bodor	4	48	426 mins
4	Willem Janssen	4	58	450 mins

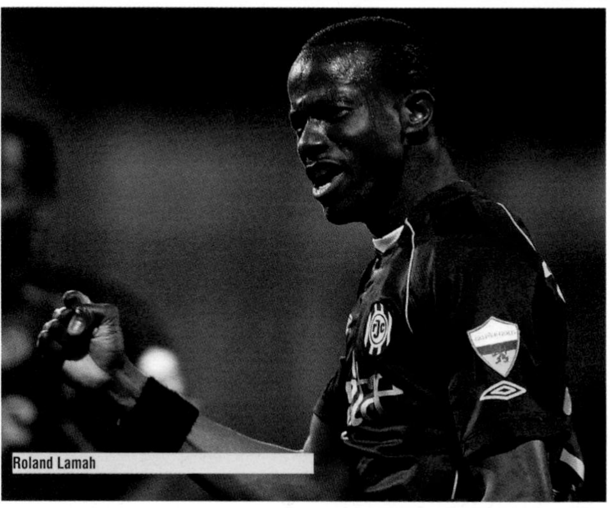
Roland Lamah

SQUAD APPEARANCES

Match	1	2	3	4	5	6	7	8	9	10	11	12	13	14	15	16	17	18	19	20	21	22	23	24	25	26	27	28	29	30	31	32	33	34	35	36
Venue	A	H	A	H	A	H	A	H	H	A	H	A	H	A	H	A	H	A	H	A	A	H	A	H	H	A	H	A	H	A	A	H	H	A	H	A
Competition	L	L	L	L	L	L	L	L	L	L	L	L	L	L	L	L	L	L	L	L	L	L	L	L	L	L	L	L	L	L	L	L	L	L	O	O
Result	D	W	W	L	L	D	W	D	W	L	W	D	W	W	L	D	W	W	D	L	L	L	D	W	W	D	D	L	D	L	D	L	W	L	L	L

Goalkeepers
Bram Castro
Cliff Mardulier
Przemyslaw Tyton

Defenders
Davy de Fauw
Marcel de Jong
Pa-Modou Kah
Kjell Knops
Jan-Paul Saeijs
Ger Senden
Fatih Sonkaya
Frank van Kouwen
Nuelson Wau

Midfielders
Boldizsar Bodor
Elbekay Bouchiba
Willem Janssen
Marcel Meeuwis
Bas Sibum
Cheik Ismael Tiote

Forwards
Sekou Cisse
Anouar Hadouir
Roland Lamah
Andres Oper
Slama Solou
Dieter van Tornhout
Jamaique Vandamme
Jeanvion Yulu-Matondo

KEY: On all match | On bench | Subbed or sent off (Counting game) | Subbed or sent off (playing less than 70 minutes) | Subbed on from bench (Counting Game) | Subbed on (playing less than 70 minutes) | Subbed on and then subbed or sent off (Counting Game) | Subbed on and then subbed or sent off (playing less than 70 minutes) | Not in 16

UTRECHT

Final Position: **10th**

NICKNAME: UTREG

KEY: ☐Won ☐Drawn ☐Lost

	Comp	Opponent	H/A	Res	Score	Scorers	Attendance
1	hopr1	**Feyenoord**	H	L	0-3		23,000
2	hopr1	**Twente**	A	D	2-2	Broerse 27, Caluwe 56	13,000
3	hopr1	**De Graafschap**	H	D	2-2	Nelisse 45, 53	19,000
4	hopr1	**Groningen**	A	W	2-0	van Dijk 58 pen, Somers 86	19,000
5	hopr1	**Heerenveen**	A	W	3-2	Nelisse 2, 83, Rossini 90	24,000
6	hopr1	**Vitesse**	H	L	2-4	van Dijk 62 pen, Nelisse 85	18,000
7	hopr1	**VVV**	A	W	2-1	Nelisse 5, Vandenbergh 75	5,850
8	hopr1	**Roda JC Kerk**	A	D	1-1	Somers 61	12,800
9	hopr1	**Ajax**	H	L	0-1		23,300
10	hopr1	**NAC Breda**	H	L	0-1		20,000
11	hopr1	**Willem II Tilb**	A	W	4-1	Nelisse 34, George 42, Pieters 79 Broerse 89	12,000
12	hopr1	**NEC Nijmegen**	H	W	3-2	van Dijk 19, George 53, Rossini 89	20,000
13	hopr1	**S Rotterdam**	H	W	7-1	Loval 7, 29, 88, Nelisse 31, 60 George 36, Dickoh 43	20,000
14	hopr1	**AZ Alkmaar**	A	L	1-2	Keller 90	16,441
15	hopr1	**Heracles**	H	W	3-1	van Dijk 45, 70 pen, George 85	20,000
16	hopr1	**PSV Eindhoven**	A	L	1-4	George 46	33,500
17	hopr1	**Excelsior**	H	W	4-1	Nelisse 9, George 37, Dickoh 64 Loval 86	20,000
18	hopr1	**Vitesse**	A	D	2-2	Nelisse 16, Loval 65	18,733
19	hopr1	**Heerenveen**	H	D	2-2	Schut 50, Keller 69	20,100
20	hopr1	**Roda JC Kerk**	H	W	3-1	Nelisse 31, 34, van Dijk 37 pen	20,000
21	hopr1	**Ajax**	A	L	0-2		45,537
22	hopr1	**NEC Nijmegen**	A	L	0-2		11,800
23	hopr1	**Willem II Tilb**	H	W	2-0	Van der Gun 4, Nelisse 56	20,000
24	hopr1	**NAC Breda**	A	L	0-1		15,000
25	hopr1	**VVV**	H	L	1-4	Wolters 89	20,000
26	hopr1	**S Rotterdam**	A	L	1-2	Kruys 56	10,095
27	hopr1	**PSV Eindhoven**	H	W	3-1	Nelisse 35, Cornelisse 44 van Dijk 76 pen	21,700
28	hopr1	**Heracles**	A	L	1-2	Cornelisse 68	8,500
29	hopr1	**AZ Alkmaar**	H	D	2-2	Van der Gun 62, Vandenbergh 84	21,000
30	hopr1	**Excelsior**	A	W	2-0	van Dijk 12, Nelisse 84	3,000
31	hopr1	**Twente**	H	L	0-1		22,731
32	hopr1	**Feyenoord**	A	L	1-3	George 74	46,000
33	hopr1	**De Graafschap**	A	D	1-1	Van der Gun 76	12,600
34	hopr1	**Groningen**	H	W	1-0	Pieters 46	21,000
35	erepo	**Groningen**	H	D	2-2	Schaken 24, Nelisse 27	11,250
36	erepo	**Groningen**	A	L	1-3	Vandenbergh 68	19,000

LEAGUE APPEARANCES, BOOKINGS AND CAPS

	AGE (on 01/07/08)	IN NAMED 18	APPEARANCES	COUNTING GAMES	MINUTES ON PITCH	YELLOW CARDS	RED CARDS	CAPS THIS SEASON	NATIONAL SIDE
Goalkeepers									
Wesley de Ruiter	22	20	11	10	938	0	0	-	Holland
Franck Grandel	30	32	15	13	1246	1	0	-	France
Michel Vorm	24	15	11	8	876	0	0	-	Holland
Defenders									
Tim Cornelisse	30	29	29	28	2535	7	1	-	Holland
Francis Dickoh	25	33	32	28	2658	3	0	-	Ghana
Sander Keller	28	26	26	23	2216	4	1	-	Holland
Nick Kuipers	19	12	5	2	261	0	0	-	Holland
Erik Pieters	19	31	31	29	2681	9	0	-	Holland
Alje Schut	27	27	18	9	995	2	0	-	Holland
Jahri Valentijn	23	1	1	1	90	0	0	-	Holland
Kees van Buuren	21	10	4	4	351	1	0	-	Holland
Mike van der Kooy	19	13	5	3	304	0	0	-	Holland
Midfielders									
Joost Broerse	29	16	9	3	504	3	0	-	Holland
Tom Caluwe	30	29	28	23	2169	0	0	-	Belgium
Rick Kruys	23	32	21	8	1094	5	0	-	Holland
Gianluca Nijholt	18	7	1	0	4	0	0	-	Holland
Lucian Sanmartean	28	14	14	8	850	1	0	-	Romania
Gregory Schaken	19	6	3	3	262	0	0	-	Holland
Hans Somers	30	30	22	6	940	4	0	-	Belgium
Gregoor van Dijk	26	31	31	29	2729	7	1	-	Holland
Forwards									
Irfan Bachdim	19	2	1	1	90	0	0	-	Holland
Leroy George	21	33	33	32	2911	5	0	-	Holland
Peter Kopteff	29	11	3	0	59	0	0	-	Finland
Loic Loval	26	20	20	19	1680	4	0	-	France
Ingmar Maayen	20	1	1	0	26	0	0	-	Holland
Robin Nelisse	30	33	33	31	2764	5	0	-	Holland
Guiseppe Rossini	21	29	21	1	413	1	0	-	Italy
Cedric van der Gun	29	13	13	10	1055	2	0	-	Holland
Kevin Vandenbergh	25	30	13	2	370	0	1	-	Belgium
Randy Wolters	18	9	7	2	369	3	0	-	Holland

TEAM OF THE SEASON

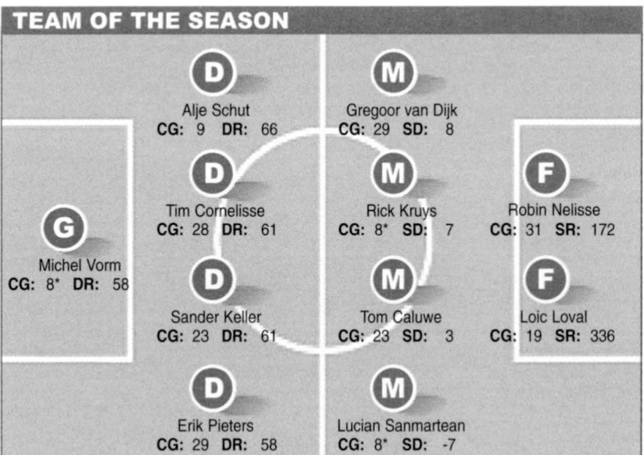

D Alje Schut CG: 9 DR: 66
M Gregoor van Dijk CG: 29 SD: 8
G Michel Vorm CG: 8* DR: 58
D Tim Cornelisse CG: 28 DR: 61
M Rick Kruys CG: 8* SD: 7
F Robin Nelisse CG: 31 SR: 172
D Sander Keller CG: 23 DR: 61
M Tom Caluwe CG: 23 SD: 3
F Loic Loval CG: 19 SR: 336
D Erik Pieters CG: 29 DR: 58
M Lucian Sanmartean CG: 8* SD: -7

MONTHLY POINTS TALLY

Month	Points	%
AUGUST	1	17%
SEPTEMBER	7	58%
OCTOBER	4	44%
NOVEMBER	9	75%
DECEMBER	7	47%
JANUARY	4	33%
FEBRUARY	3	25%
MARCH	7	47%
APRIL	4	44%

LEAGUE GOALS

	PLAYER	MINS	GOALS	S RATE
1	Nelisse	2764	16	172
2	van Dijk	2729	8	341
3	George	2911	7	415
4	Loval	1680	5	336
5	Van der Gun	1055	3	351
6	Vandenbergh	370	2	185
7	Rossini	413	2	206
8	Broerse	504	2	252
9	Somers	940	2	470
10	Keller	2216	2	1108
11	Cornelisse	2535	2	1267
12	Dickoh	2658	2	1329
13	Pieters	2681	2	1340
	Other		4	
	TOTAL		59	

TOP POINT EARNERS

	PLAYER	GAMES	AV PTS
1	Loic Loval	19	1.58
2	Franck Grandel	13	1.54
3	Tim Cornelisse	28	1.50
4	Sander Keller	23	1.48
5	Robin Nelisse	31	1.45
6	Francis Dickoh	28	1.36
7	Leroy George	32	1.34
8	Erik Pieters	29	1.34
9	Tom Caluwe	23	1.30
10	Gregoor van Dijk	29	1.28
	CLUB AVERAGE:		1.35

DISCIPLINARY RECORDS

	PLAYER	YELLOW	RED	AVE
1	Joost Broerse	3	0	168
2	Rick Kruys	5	0	218
3	Hans Somers	4	0	235
4	Erik Pieters	9	0	297
5	Tim Cornelisse	7	1	316
6	Gregoor van Dijk	7	1	341
7	Loic Loval	4	0	420
8	Sander Keller	4	1	443
9	Alje Schut	2	0	497
10	Cedric van der Gun	2	0	527
11	Robin Nelisse	5	0	552
12	Leroy George	5	0	582
13	Lucian Sanmartean	1	0	850
	Other	4	0	
	TOTAL	62	3	

KEY GOALKEEPER

Michel Vorm

Goals Conceded in the League	15	**Counting Games** League games when player was on pitch for at least 70 minutes	8
Defensive Rating Ave number of mins between League goals conceded while on the pitch	58	**Clean Sheets** In League games when player was on pitch for at least 70 minutes	1

KEY PLAYERS - DEFENDERS

Alje Schut

Goals Conceded Number of League goals conceded while the player was on the pitch	15	**Clean Sheets** In League games when player was on pitch for at least 70 minutes	2
Defensive Rating Ave number of mins between League goals conceded while on the pitch	66	**Club Defensive Rating** Average number of mins between League goals conceded by the club this season	55

	PLAYER	CON LGE	CLEAN SHEETS	DEF RATE
1	Alje Schut	15	2	66 mins
2	Tim Cornelisse	41	4	61 mins
3	Sander Keller	36	3	61 mins
4	Erik Pieters	46	4	58 mins

KEY PLAYERS - MIDFIELDERS

Gregoor van Dijk

Goals in the League	8	**Contribution to Attacking Power** Average number of minutes between League team goals while on pitch	48
Defensive Rating Average number of mins between League goals conceded while on the pitch	56	**Scoring Difference** Defensive Rating minus Contribution to Attacking Power	8

	PLAYER	LGE GOALS	DEF RATE	POWER	SCORE DIFF
1	Gregoor van Dijk	8	56	48	8 mins
2	Rick Kruys	1	54	47	7 mins
3	Tom Caluwe	1	51	48	3 mins
4	Lucian Sanmartean	0	53	60	-7 mins

KEY PLAYERS - GOALSCORERS

Robin Nelisse

Goals in the League	16	**Player Strike Rate** Average number of minutes between League goals scored by player	172
Contribution to Attacking Power Average number of minutes between League team goals while on pitch	52	**Club Strike Rate** Average number of minutes between League goals scored by club	51

	PLAYER	LGE GOALS	POWER	STRIKE RATE
1	Robin Nelisse	16	52	172 mins
2	Loic Loval	5	48	336 mins
3	Gregoor van Dijk	8	48	341 mins
4	Cedric van der Gun	3	58	351 mins

PHANOS

Robin Nelisse

SQUAD APPEARANCES

Match	1	2	3	4	5	6	7	8	9	10	11	12	13	14	15	16	17	18	19	20	21	22	23	24	25	26	27	28	29	30	31	32	33	34	35	36
Venue	H	A	H	A	A	H	A	A	H	H	A	H	H	A	H	A	H	A	H	H	A	A	H	A	H	A	H	A	H	A	H	A	A	H	H	A
Competition	L	L	L	L	L	L	L	L	L	L	L	L	L	L	L	L	L	L	L	L	L	L	L	L	L	L	L	L	L	L	L	L	L	L	O	O
Result	L	D	D	W	W	L	W	D	L	L	W	W	W	L	W	L	W	D	D	W	L	L	W	L	L	L	W	L	D	W	L	L	D	W	D	L

Goalkeepers
Wesley de Ruiter
Franck Grandel
Michel Vorm

Defenders
Tim Cornelisse
Francis Dickoh
Sander Keller
Nick Kuipers
Erik Pieters
Alje Schut
Jahri Valentijn
Kees van Buuren
Mike van der Kooy

Midfielders
Joost Broerse
Tom Caluwe
Rick Kruys
Gianluca Nijholt
Lucian Sanmartean
Gregory Schaken
Hans Somers
Gregoor van Dijk

Forwards
Irfan Bachdim
Leroy George
Peter Kopteff
Loic Loval
Ingmar Maayen
Robin Nelisse
Guiseppe Rossini
Cedric van der Gun
Kevin Vandenbergh
Randy Wolters

KEY: On all match | On bench | Subbed or sent off (Counting game) | Subbed or sent off (playing less than 70 minutes) | Subbed on from bench (Counting Game) | Subbed on (playing less than 70 minutes) | Subbed on and then subbed or sent off (Counting Game) | Subbed on and then subbed or sent off (playing less than 70 minutes) | Not in 16

AZ ALKMAAR

Final Position: **11th**

NICKNAME: AZ

KEY: ☐ Won ☐ Drawn ☐ Lost

						Attendance
1	hopr1	**VVV**	H	W	4-0	Agustien 7, De Silva Ferreira 32, 58 pen
						Medunjanin 79	16,496
2	hopr1	**Vitesse**	A	L	0-1		17,581
3	hopr1	**Excelsior**	H	W	3-0	Agustien 24, Steinsson 45, de Zeeuw 62	16,153
4	hopr1	**S Rotterdam**	A	D	2-2	Jenner 68, El Hamdaoui 77	9,000
5	ucrl1	**Pacos Ferreira**	A	W	1-0	Pocognoli 89	3,000
6	hopr1	**Ajax**	H	L	2-3	de Zeeuw 45, Dembele 90	16,556
7	hopr1	**Heracles**	A	L	1-2	Dembele 14	8,500
8	ucrl2	**Pacos Ferreira**	H	D	0-0		13,418
9	hopr1	**Groningen**	H	D	2-2	De Silva Ferreira 17, de Zeeuw 84	16,378
10	hopr1	**Heerenveen**	H	L	0-1		16,644
11	ucgpa	**Z St Petersburg**	A	D	1-1	De Silva Ferreira 20	21,000
12	hopr1	**NAC Breda**	A	W	3-2	Opdam 5, De Silva Ferreira 39	
						Jenner 47	15,000
13	hopr1	**NEC Nijmegen**	H	W	4-0	Cziommer 13, Jaliens 19, De Silva Ferreira 33	
						de Zeeuw 67	16,333
14	hopr1	**PSV Eindhoven**	A	D	1-1	De Silva Ferreira 37	33,600
15	hopr1	**Willem II Tilb**	H	W	2-0	De Silva Ferreira 25, Dembele 44	16,000
16	ucgpa	**Larissa**	H	W	1-0	Dembele 77	15,762
17	hopr1	**Twente**	A	L	1-2	Pelle 72	13,000
18	ucgpa	**Nurnberg**	A	L	1-2	de Zeeuw 29	35,020
19	hopr1	**Utrecht**	H	W	2-1	Pocognoli 19, de Zeeuw 25	16,441
20	ucgpa	**Everton**	H	L	2-3	Pelle 16, Jaliens 65	20,000
21	hopr1	**Roda JC Kerk**	H	D	1-1	Pelle 5	16,413
22	hopr1	**Heracles**	H	W	1-0	Steinsson 71	16,313
23	hopr1	**Ajax**	A	L	1-6	De Silva Ferreira 5	50,639
24	hopr1	**De Graafschap**	A	W	2-1	Mendes Da Silva 45, Dembele 50	12,600
25	hopr1	**Heerenveen**	A	L	0-4		25,000
26	hopr1	**NAC Breda**	H	L	1-2	Pocognoli 24	16,312
27	hopr1	**Willem II Tilb**	A	L	0-3		12,800
28	hopr1	**Feyenoord**	A	D	2-2	Pelle 40, El Hamdaoui 72	46,500
29	hopr1	**PSV Eindhoven**	H	L	0-2		16,457
30	hopr1	**NEC Nijmegen**	A	L	2-5	Mendes Da Silva 3, El Hamdaoui 88	12,000
31	hopr1	**Groningen**	A	L	1-2	Jaliens 84	19,400
32	hopr1	**Twente**	H	D	0-0		16,535
33	hopr1	**Roda JC Kerk**	A	D	1-1	Cziommer 80	14,800
34	hopr1	**Feyenoord**	H	L	0-1		16,652
35	hopr1	**Utrecht**	A	D	2-2	de Zeeuw 53, El Hamdaoui 90	21,000
36	hopr1	**De Graafschap**	H	D	0-0		16,322
37	hopr1	**Vitesse Arnhem**	H	W	2-1	Moreno 21, Jenner 72	16,403
38	hopr1	**VVV**	A	W	3-2	De Silva Ferreira 23, El Hamdaoui 65, 72	6,000
39	hopr1	**Excelsior**	A	D	1-1	Donk 69	3,500
40	hopr1	**S Rotterdam**	H	W	1-0	El Hamdaoui 15	16,653

LEAGUE APPEARANCES, BOOKINGS AND CAPS

	AGE (on 01/07/08)	IN NAMED 18	APPEARANCES	COUNTING GAMES	MINUTES ON PITCH	YELLOW CARDS	RED CARDS	CAPS THIS SEASON	NATIONAL SIDE
Goalkeepers									
Kevin Rijnvis	20	1	0	0	0	0	0	-	Holland
Sergio Romero	21	34	12	12	1080	3	0	-	Argentina
Boy Waterman	24	32	22	22	1980	0	0	-	Holland
Defenders									
Ryan Donk	22	34	24	17	1747	3	0	-	Holland
Aron Gunnarsson	18	2	1	0	14	0	0	-	Iceland
Kew Jaliens	29	30	30	29	2644	8	1	3	Holland
Milano Koenders	20	25	13	5	627	1	0	-	Holland
Hector Al Moreno	20	14	8	8	720	3	0	2	Mexico
Barry Opdam	32	32	32	29	2716	2	1	-	Holland
Sebastien Pocognoli	20	32	28	17	1840	4	0	-	Belgium
Gretar Rafn Steinsson	26	16	16	14	1318	2	0	5	Iceland
Midfielders									
Kemy Agustien	21	30	25	17	1773	4	0	-	Holland
Simon Cziommer	27	27	20	10	1265	3	0	-	Germany
Demy de Zeeuw	25	31	31	22	2417	4	1	13	Holland
Maarten Martens	23	7	7	6	577	1	0	-	Belgium
Haris Medunjanin	23	24	12	4	579	0	0	-	Holland
D Mendes Da Silva	25	28	27	24	2289	4	0	-	Holland
Rogier Molhoek	26	3	0	0	0	0	0	-	Holland
Kiki Musampa	30	5	5	1	161	0	0	-	Holland
Simon Poulsen	23	12	8	3	420	1	0	2	Denmark
Ruud Vormer	20	25	16	11	1170	3	0	-	Holland
Forwards									
Ariclenes Ferreira	22	32	29	8	1689	0	0	-	Brazil
Moussa Dembele	20	33	33	31	2859	2	0	8	Belgium
Mounir el Hamdaoui	23	28	23	7	1272	4	0	-	Holland
Julian Jenner	24	30	21	4	810	1	1	-	Holland
Gregory Nelson	20	1	1	0	25	0	0	-	Holland
Graziano Pelle	22	32	27	13	1587	2	0	-	Italy

TEAM OF THE SEASON

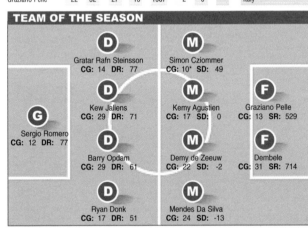

G — Sergio Romero — CG: 12 DR: 77

D — Gratar Rafn Steinsson — CG: 14 DR: 77

D — Kew Jaliens — CG: 29 DR: 71

D — Barry Opdam — CG: 29 DR: 61

D — Ryan Donk — CG: 17 DR: 51

M — Simon Cziommer — CG: 10* SD: 49

M — Kemy Agustien — CG: 17 SD: 0

M — Demy de Zeeuw — CG: 22 SD: -2

M — Mendes Da Silva — CG: 24 SD: -13

F — Graziano Pelle — CG: 13 SR: 529

F — Dembele — CG: 31 SR: 714

MONTHLY POINTS TALLY

AUGUST	6	67%
SEPTEMBER	1	11%
OCTOBER	4	44%
NOVEMBER	7	78%
DECEMBER	7	58%
JANUARY	4	22%
FEBRUARY	1	8%
MARCH	6	40%
APRIL	7	78%

LEAGUE GOALS

	PLAYER	MINS	GOALS	S RATE
1	De S Ferreira	1689	9	187
2	El Hamdaoui	1272	7	181
3	de Zeeuw	2417	6	402
4	Dembele	2859	4	714
5	Jenner	810	3	270
6	Pelle	1587	3	529
7	Cziommer	1265	2	632
8	Steinsson	1318	2	659
9	Agustien	1773	2	886
10	Pocognoli	1840	2	920
11	M Da Silva	2289	2	1144
12	Jaliens	2644	2	1322
13	Medunjanin	579	1	579
	Other		3	
	TOTAL		48	

TOP POINT EARNERS

	PLAYER	GAMES	AV PTS
1	Gratar Rafn Steinsson	14	1.57
2	Kew Jaliens	29	1.45
3	Barry Opdam	29	1.38
4	Demy de Zeeuw	22	1.32
5	Boy Waterman	22	1.32
6	David Mendes Da Silva	24	1.29
7	Kemy Agustien	17	1.24
8	Moussa Dembele	31	1.23
9	Ryan Donk	17	1.18
10	Sebastien Pocognoli	17	1.18
	CLUB AVERAGE:		1.26

DISCIPLINARY RECORDS

	PLAYER	YELLOW	RED	AVE
1	Hector Al Moreno	3	0	240
2	Kew Jaliens	8	1	293
3	M el Hamdaoui	4	0	318
4	Sergio Romero	3	0	360
5	Ruud Vormer	3	0	390
6	Julian Jenner	1	1	405
7	Simon Cziommer	3	0	421
8	Kemy Agustien	4	0	443
9	Sebastien Pocognoli	4	0	460
10	Demy de Zeeuw	4	1	483
11	D Mendes Da Silva	4	0	572
12	Maarten Martens	1	0	577
13	Ryan Donk	3	0	582
	Other	9	1	
	TOTAL	54	4	

KEY GOALKEEPER

Sergio Romero

Goals Conceded in the League	14	Counting Games League games when player was on pitch for at least 70 minutes	12
Defensive Rating Ave number of mins between League goals conceded while on the pitch	77	Clean Sheets In League games when player was on pitch for at least 70 minutes	3

KEY PLAYERS - GOALSCORERS

Demy de Zeeuw

Goals in the League	6	Player Strike Rate Average number of minutes between League goals scored by player	402
Contribution to Attacking Power Average number of minutes between League team goals while on pitch	63	Club Strike Rate Average number of minutes between League goals scored by club	69

	PLAYER	LGE GOALS	POWER	STRIKE RATE
1	Demy de Zeeuw	6	63	402 mins
2	Graziano Pelle	3	75	529 mins
3	Simon Cziommer	2	66	632 mins
4	Moussa Dembele	4	62	714 mins

KEY PLAYERS - DEFENDERS

GrÃ©tar Rafn Steinsson

Goals Conceded Number of League goals conceded while the player was on the pitch	17	Clean Sheets In League games when player was on pitch for at least 70 minutes	5
Defensive Rating Ave number of mins between League goals conceded while on the pitch	77	Club Defensive Rating Average number of mins between League goals conceded by the club this season	62

	PLAYER	CON LGE	CLEAN SHEETS	DEF RATE
1	Gratar Rafn Steinsson	17	5	77 mins
2	Kew Jaliens	37	8	71 mins
3	Barry Opdam	44	9	61 mins
4	Ryan Donk	34	5	51 mins

Demy de Zeeuw

KEY PLAYERS - MIDFIELDERS

Simon Cziommer

Goals in the League	2	Contribution to Attacking Power Average number of minutes between League team goals while on pitch	66
Defensive Rating Average number of mins between League goals conceded while on the pitch	115	Scoring Difference Defensive Rating minus Contribution to Attacking Power	49

	PLAYER	LGE GOALS	DEF RATE	POWER	SCORE DIFF
1	Simon Cziommer	2	115	66	49 mins
2	Kemy Agustien	2	61	61	0 mins
3	Demy de Zeeuw	6	61	63	-2 mins
4	David Mendes Da Silva	2	54	67	-13 mins

SQUAD APPEARANCES

Match	1	2	3	4	5	6	7	8	9	10	11	12	13	14	15	16	17	18	19	20
Venue	H	A	H	A	A	H	A	H	H	H	A	A	H	A	H	H	A	A	H	H
Competition	L	L	L	L	E	L	L	E	L	L	E	L	L	L	L	E	L	E	L	E
Result	W	L	W	D	W	L	L	D	D	L	D	W	W	D	W	W	L	L	W	L

Match	21	22	23	24	25	26	27	28	29	30	31	32	33	34	35	36	37	38	39	40
Venue	H	H	A	A	A	H	A	A	H	A	A	H	A	H	A	H	H	A	A	H
Competition	L	L	L	L	L	L	L	L	L	L	L	L	L	L	L	L	L	L	L	L
Result	D	W	L	W	L	L	L	D	L	L	L	D	D	L	D	D	W	W	D	W

Goalkeepers
Kevin Rijnvis
Sergio Romero
Boy Waterman

Defenders
Ryan Donk
Aron Gunnarsson
Kew Jaliens
Milano Koenders
Hector Alfredo Moreno
Barry Opdam
Sebastien Pocognoli
Gretar Rafn Steinsson

Midfielders
Kemy Agustien
Simon Cziommer
Demy de Zeeuw
Maarten Martens
Haris Medunjanin
David Mendes Da Silva
Rogier Molhoek
Kiki Musampa
Simon Poulsen
Ruud Vormer

Forwards
Ariclenes Ferreira
Moussa Dembele
Mounir el Hamdaoui
Julian Jenner
Gregory Nelson
Graziano Pelle

KEY: On all match · On bench · Subbed or sent off (Counting game) · Subbed or sent off (playing less than 70 minutes) · Subbed on from bench (Counting Game) · Subbed on (playing less than 70 minutes) · Subbed on and then subbed or sent off (Counting Game) · Subbed on and then subbed or sent off (playing less than 70 minutes) · Not in 16

VITESSE ARNHEM

Final Position: **12th**

NICKNAME: GEEL EN ZWART

KEY: ☐ Won ☐ Drawn ☐ Lost

							Attendance
1	hopr1	**S Rotterdam**	A	W	2-1	Van der Schaaf 79, Swerts 82	10,000
2	hopr1	**AZ Alkmaar**	H	W	1-0	Kolk 26	17,581
3	hopr1	**NEC Nijmegen**	H	W	1-0	Gommans 17	18,515
4	hopr1	**PSV Eindhoven**	A	L	0-1		34,000
5	hopr1	**De Graafschap**	H	L	0-2		17,000
6	hopr1	**Utrecht**	A	W	4-2	Swerts 4, Sprockel 16, Junker 50 Magralishvili 80	18,000
7	hopr1	**Feyenoord**	H	L	0-1		18,450
8	hopr1	**Heracles**	A	D	2-2	Due 56, Sprockel 58	8,500
9	hopr1	**Willem II Tilb**	H	W	1-0	Kolk 76	19,586
10	hopr1	**Groningen**	A	D	0-0		19,175
11	hopr1	**Heerenveen**	H	L	0-1		19,221
12	hopr1	**Ajax**	A	L	1-4	Junker 45	49,566
13	hopr1	**Roda JC Kerk**	A	L	2-3	Sansoni 77, Gommans 84	12,000
14	hopr1	**Twente**	H	D	2-2	Junker 25, 43	18,973
15	hopr1	**Excelsior**	H	W	3-0	Kolk 50, 90, Gommans 88 pen	17,175
16	hopr1	**VVV**	A	L	0-2		5,806
17	hopr1	**NAC Breda**	A	W	2-1	Kolk 42, Gommans 51	15,000
18	hopr1	**Utrecht**	H	D	2-2	Gommans 3, Junker 48	18,733
19	hopr1	**De Graafschap**	A	W	3-0	Kolk 41, 79, Takak 56	12,000
20	hopr1	**Heracles**	H	W	2-0	Van der Schaaf 44, Kolk 53	19,411
21	hopr1	**Willem II Tilb**	A	L	0-4		11,800
22	hopr1	**Ajax**	H	D	2-2	Junker 8, Gommans 56	22,700
23	hopr1	**Heerenveen**	A	L	0-7		25,000
24	hopr1	**Groningen**	H	W	2-1	Gommans 34, Van der Schaaf 75	20,105
25	hopr1	**Feyenoord**	A	L	0-1		45,000
26	hopr1	**Roda JC Kerk**	H	D	1-1	Janssen 68	19,475
27	hopr1	**VVV**	H	L	1-3	Kolk 61	18,500
28	hopr1	**Excelsior**	A	W	2-1	Pryor 36, Lorca 86	3,240
29	hopr1	**Twente**	A	L	3-4	Lorca 39, Kolk 47, Domingues 90	13,200
30	hopr1	**NAC Breda**	H	D	3-3	Domingues de Souza 35, Kolk 52, 57	22,780
31	hopr1	**AZ Alkmaar**	A	L	1-2	Swerts 29	16,403
32	hopr1	**S Rotterdam**	H	W	3-0	Junker 58, Janssen 78, Domingues 80	21,209
33	hopr1	**NEC Nijmegen**	A	L	0-1		12,500
34	hopr1	**PSV Eindhoven**	H	L	0-1		25,420

LEAGUE APPEARANCES, BOOKINGS AND CAPS

	AGE (on 01/07/08)	IN NAMED 18	APPEARANCES	COUNTING GAMES	MINUTES ON PITCH	YELLOW CARDS	RED CARDS	CAPS THIS SEASON	NATIONAL SIDE
Goalkeepers									
Balazs Raboczki	30	30	2	0	67	0	0	-	Hungary
Stephan Veenboer	20	2	1	1	90	0	0	-	Holland
Piet Velthuizen	21	33	33	31	2902	2	1	-	Holland
Defenders									
Haim Megrelishvili	26	33	24	17	1733	4	0	-	Israel
Sebastien Sansoni	30	29	27	22	2164	6	2	-	France
Civard Sprockel	25	32	32	31	2853	7	0	-	Holland
Gill Swerts	25	34	34	31	2898	4	0	4	Belgium
Kevin van Diermen	18	27	5	1	239	2	0	-	Holland
Paul Verhaegh	24	33	33	28	2799	4	1	-	Holland
Midfielders									
Jaime Bruinier	21	12	1	0	27	1	0	-	Holland
Domingues de Souza	20	9	9	6	580	2	0	-	Brazil
Anders Due	26	9	8	3	431	0	0	-	Denmark
Giovanny P Espinoza	31	17	17	15	1422	1	0	-	Ecuador
Theo Janssen	26	19	19	15	1521	1	0	-	Holland
Onur Kaya	22	26	11	0	174	1	0	-	Belgium
Cees Keizer	22	3	2	1	97	0	0	-	Holland
Santi Kolk	26	32	32	28	2660	2	0	-	Holland
Anduele Pryor	23	21	15	5	718	0	0	-	Holland
Jasar Takak	26	26	23	13	1427	5	0	-	Turkey
Remco van der Schaaf	29	29	29	28	2569	6	0	-	Holland
Abubakari Yakubu	26	29	17	8	917	5	0	-	Ghana
Forwards									
Fred Benson	24	1	1	0	7	0	0	-	Holland
Harrie Gommans	25	28	26	11	1460	3	0	-	Netherlands
Mads Junker	27	29	28	19	1904	1	0	-	Denmark
Juan Gonzalo Lorca	23	30	26	13	1484	2	0	-	Chili
Ricky van Wolfswinkel	19	3	1	0	7	0	0	-	Holland
Yu Hai	21	22	8	1	297	2	0	-	China PR

TEAM OF THE SEASON

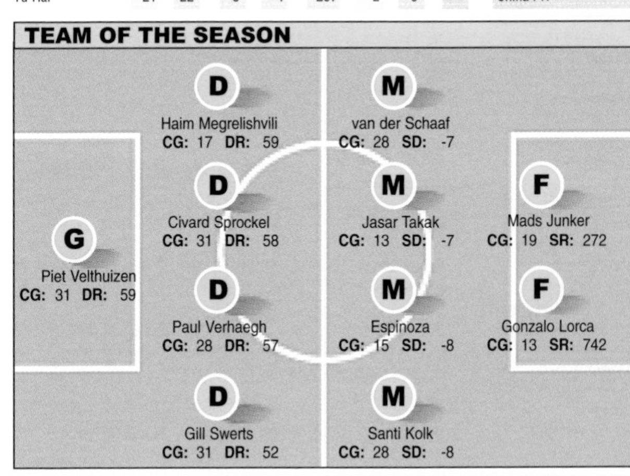

D
Haim Megrelishvili
CG: 17 DR: 59
M
van der Schaaf
CG: 28 SD: -7
D
Civard Sprockel
CG: 31 DR: 58
M
Jasar Takak
CG: 13 SD: -7
F
Mads Junker
CG: 19 SR: 272
G
Piet Velthuizen
CG: 31 DR: 59
D
Paul Verhaegh
CG: 28 DR: 57
M
Espinoza
CG: 15 SD: -8
F
Gonzalo Lorca
CG: 13 SR: 742
D
Gill Swerts
CG: 31 DR: 52
M
Santi Kolk
CG: 28 SD: -8

MONTHLY POINTS TALLY

AUGUST	6	100%
SEPTEMBER	6	50%
OCTOBER	4	44%
NOVEMBER	1	11%
DECEMBER	8	44%
JANUARY	7	58%
FEBRUARY	4	27%
MARCH	4	33%
APRIL	3	33%

LEAGUE GOALS

	PLAYER	MINS	GOALS	S RATE
1	Kolk	2660	**12**	221
2	Gommans	1460	**7**	208
3	Junker	1904	**7**	272
4	Domingues	580	**3**	193
5	Van der Schaaf	2569	**3**	856
6	Swerts	2898	**3**	966
7	Lorca	1484	**2**	742
8	Janssen	1521	**2**	760
9	Sprockel	2853	**2**	1426
10	Due	431	**1**	431
11	Pryor	718	**1**	718
12	Takak	1427	**1**	1427
13	Megrelishvili	1733	**1**	1733
	Other		1	
	TOTAL		**46**	

TOP POINT EARNERS

	PLAYER	GAMES	AV PTS
1	Jasar Takak	13	**1.62**
2	Haim Megrelishvili	17	**1.47**
3	G Patricio Espinoza	15	**1.40**
4	Mads Junker	19	**1.37**
5	Gill Swerts	31	**1.35**
6	Remco van der Schaaf	28	**1.32**
7	Piet Velthuizen	31	**1.29**
8	Santi Kolk	28	**1.29**
9	Theo Janssen	15	**1.27**
10	Civard Sprockel	31	**1.26**
	CLUB AVERAGE:		**1.26**

DISCIPLINARY RECORDS

	PLAYER	YELLOW	RED	AVE
1	Abubakari Yakubu	5	0	**183**
2	Sebastien Sansoni	6	2	**270**
3	Jasar Takak	5	0	**285**
4	C Domingues	2	0	**290**
5	Civard Sprockel	7	0	**407**
6	R van der Schaaf	6	0	**428**
7	Haim Megrelishvili	4	0	**433**
8	Harrie Gommans	3	0	**486**
9	Paul Verhaegh	4	1	**559**
10	Gill Swerts	4	0	**724**
11	J Gonzalo Lorca	2	0	**742**
12	Piet Velthuizen	2	1	**967**
13	Santi Kolk	2	0	**1330**
	Other	3	0	
	TOTAL	**55**	**4**	

KEY GOALKEEPER

Piet Velthuizen

Goals Conceded in the League	49	**Counting Games** League games when player was on pitch for at least 70 minutes	31
Defensive Rating **Ave number of mins between League goals conceded while on the pitch**	59	**Clean Sheets** In League games when player was on pitch for at least 70 minutes	8

KEY PLAYERS - DEFENDERS

Haim Megrelishvili

Goals Conceded Number of League goals conceded while the player was on the pitch	29	**Clean Sheets** In League games when player was on pitch for at least 70 minutes	5
Defensive Rating **Ave number of mins between League goals conceded while on the pitch**	59	**Club Defensive Rating** Average number of mins between League goals conceded by the club this season	55

	PLAYER	CON LGE	CLEAN SHEETS	DEF RATE
1	Haim Megrelishvili	29	5	59 mins
2	Civard Sprockel	49	8	58 mins
3	Paul Verhaegh	49	7	57 mins
4	Gill Swerts	55	7	52 mins

KEY PLAYERS - MIDFIELDERS

Remco van der Schaaf

Goals in the League	3	**Contribution to Attacking Power** Average number of minutes between League team goals while on pitch	65
Defensive Rating Average number of mins between League goals conceded while on the pitch	58	**Scoring Difference** **Defensive Rating minus Contribution to Attacking Power**	-7

	PLAYER	LGE GOALS	DEF RATE	POWER	SCORE DIFF
1	Remco van der Schaaf	3	58	65	-7 mins
2	Jasar Takak	1	50	57	-7 mins
3	Giovanny Patricio Espinoza	0	71	79	-8 mins
4	Santi Kolk	12	56	64	-8 mins

KEY PLAYERS - GOALSCORERS

Santi Kolk

Goals in the League	12	**Player Strike Rate** **Average number of minutes between League goals scored by player**	221
Contribution to Attacking Power Average number of minutes between League team goals while on pitch	64	**Club Strike Rate** Average number of minutes between League goals scored by club	66

	PLAYER	LGE GOALS	POWER	STRIKE RATE
1	Santi Kolk	12	64	221 mins
2	Mads Junker	7	65	272 mins
3	Juan Gonzalo Lorca	2	61	742 mins
4	Theo Janssen	2	56	760 mins

AFAB
LEGEA
VITESSE

Santi Kolk

SQUAD APPEARANCES

Match	1	2	3	4	5	6	7	8	9	10	11	12	13	14	15	16	17	18	19	20	21	22	23	24	25	26	27	28	29	30	31	32	33	34
Venue	A	H	H	A	H	A	H	A	H	A	H	A	A	H	H	A	A	H	A	H	A	H	A	H	A	H	H	A	A	H	A	H	A	H
Competition	L	L	L	L	L	L	L	L	L	L	L	L	L	L	L	L	L	L	L	L	L	L	L	L	L	L	L	L	L	L	L	L	L	L
Result	W	W	W	L	L	W	L	D	W	D	L	L	L	D	W	L	W	D	W	W	L	D	L	W	L	D	L	W	L	D	L	W	L	L

Goalkeepers
Balazs Rabozcki
Stephan Veenboer
Piet Velthuizen

Defenders
Haim Megrelishvili
Sebastien Sansoni
Civard Sprockel
Gill Swerts
Kevin van Diermen
Paul Verhaegh

Midfielders
Jaime Bruinier
Domingues de Souza
Anders Due
G Patricio Espinoza
Theo Janssen
Onur Kaya
Cees Keizer
Santi Kolk
Anduele Pryor
Jasar Takak
Remco van der Schaaf
Abubakari Yakubu

Forwards
Fred Benson
Harrie Gommans
Mads Junker
Juan Gonzalo Lorca
Ricky van Wolfswinkel
Yu Hai

KEY: On all match / On bench / Subbed or sent off (Counting game) / Subbed or sent off (playing less than 70 minutes) / Subbed on from bench (Counting Game) / Subbed on (playing less than 70 minutes) / Subbed on and then subbed or sent off (Counting Game) / Subbed on and then subbed or sent off (playing less than 70 minutes) / Not in 16

SPARTA ROTTERDAM

Final Position: **13th**

NICKNAME: SPARTA

KEY: ☐Won ☐Drawn ☐Lost

						Attendance
1	hopr1 **Vitesse**	H	L	1-2	Dissels 19	10,000
2	hopr1 **Willem II Tilb**	A	D	2-2	Dissels 40, Roberts 88	12,750
3	hopr1 **Heerenveen**	A	D	3-3	Rose 44, Polak 56 pen, Slot 60	22,000
4	hopr1 **AZ Alkmaar**	H	D	2-2	Medunjanin 6 og, Boukhari 51	9,000
5	hopr1 **Heracles**	H	D	1-1	Boukhari 31	10,121
6	hopr1 **Groningen**	A	L	0-1		19,304
7	hopr1 **Ajax**	H	D	2-2	Dissels 52, de Roover 80	10,800
8	hopr1 **De Graafschap**	A	L	0-4		12,300
9	hopr1 **PSV Eindhoven**	H	L	1-4	Polak 77 pen	10,450
10	hopr1 **Excelsior**	A	L	3-4	Rose 18, Roberts 40, Boukhari 66	3,651
11	hopr1 **VVV**	A	L	0-2		5,842
12	hopr1 **Twente**	H	D	1-1	Polak 21	10,000
13	hopr1 **Utrecht**	A	L	1-7	Rose 77	20,000
14	hopr1 **NEC Nijmegen**	H	W	1-0	Rose 38	9,083
15	hopr1 **Roda JC Kerk**	A	W	3-2	Polak 22 fk, Roberts 48, 58	14,425
16	hopr1 **Feyenoord**	A	L	0-2		46,783
17	hopr1 **Groningen**	H	L	1-3	de Roover 44	10,612
18	hopr1 **Heracles**	A	L	0-2		8,426
19	hopr1 **De Graafschap**	H	W	6-1	Rose 7, Dissels 11, 57, 60, de Roover 26 Boukhari 69	9,814
20	hopr1 **PSV Eindhoven**	A	L	1-3	Roberts 90	33,000
21	hopr1 **Twente**	A	W	2-1	Rose 28, Dissels 53	13,000
22	hopr1 **VVV**	H	W	2-0	Promes 45, Rose 49	10,208
23	hopr1 **NAC Breda**	H	L	0-1		9,876
24	hopr1 **Excelsior**	H	L	0-1		10,528
25	hopr1 **Ajax**	A	L	2-6	Roberts 34, Emnes 82	49,260
26	hopr1 **Utrecht**	H	W	2-1	Emnes 39, Boukhari 57	10,095
27	hopr1 **NAC Breda**	A	L	0-3		15,000
28	hopr1 **Roda JC Kerk**	H	W	4-1	Roberts 18, Rutjes 23, Emnes 51, 60	9,846
29	hopr1 **NEC Nijmegen**	A	L	2-4	Emnes 3, 64	12,500
30	hopr1 **Feyenoord**	H	W	3-2	Boukhari 15, 50, Emnes 90	10,894
31	hopr1 **Willem II Tilb**	H	D	2-2	Rose 69, Baelum 73 og	9,922
32	hopr1 **Vitesse**	A	L	0-3		21,209
33	hopr1 **Heerenveen**	H	W	4-2	Dissels 55, Boukhari 62, Polak 73 pen Emnes 80	10,463
34	hopr1 **AZ Alkmaar**	A	L	0-1		16,653

LEAGUE APPEARANCES, BOOKINGS AND CAPS

	AGE (on 01/07/08)	IN NAMED 18	APPEARANCES	COUNTING GAMES	MINUTES ON PITCH	YELLOW CARDS	RED CARDS	CAPS THIS SEASON	NATIONAL SIDE
Goalkeepers									
Cor Varkevisser	26	18	3	3	270	0	0	-	Holland
Harald Wapenaar	38	17	3	2	192	0	0	-	Holland
Sander Westerveld	33	30	29	29	2598	1	0	-	Holland
Defenders									
Ayodele Adeleye	19	27	22	15	1571	5	1	-	Nigeria
Sepp De Roover	23	19	19	19	1692	1	0	-	Belgium
Wouter Gudde	23	12	4	3	321	2	0	-	Holland
Kim Jaggy	25	27	27	25	2254	5	0	-	Switzerland
Olaf Lindenbergh	34	18	18	17	1564	5	0	-	Holland
Jerold Promes	24	31	17	14	1306	5	0	-	Holland
Danny Schenkel	30	29	28	26	2428	6	0	-	Holland
Dwight Tiendalli	22	13	13	12	1125	2	0	-	Holland
Cees Toet	20	18	7	1	207	1	1	-	Holland
Midfielders									
Sani Kaita	22	16	8	2	350	1	0	1	Nigeria
I Moreno Freire	23	21	12	8	879	4	0	-	Holland
Sjaak Polak	32	33	25	18	1717	3	0	-	Holland
Nathan Rutjes	24	18	17	12	1270	5	1	-	Holland
Arne Slot	29	30	23	16	1601	2	0	-	Holland
Kevin Strootman	18	6	3	1	138	1	0	-	Holland
Edwin van Bueren	28	23	19	12	1257	8	0	-	Holland
Forwards									
Rachid Bouaouzan	24	2	2	2	180	0	0	-	Holland
Nourdin Boukhari	28	33	32	26	2573	6	0	1	Morocco
Charles Dissels	23	32	31	27	2525	2	0	-	Holland
Edouard Duplan	25	15	11	2	444	0	0	-	France
Marvin Emnes	20	34	29	14	1582	0	0	-	Holland
Joshua John	19	19	12	0	279	0	0	-	Holland
Darryl Roberts	24	34	29	11	1523	1	0	-	Trinidad & Tobago
Yuri Rose	29	25	25	18	1770	7	0	-	Holland

TEAM OF THE SEASON

G — Sander Westerveld CG: 29 DR: 40

D — Dwight Tiendalli CG: 12 DR: 46
D — Danny Schenkel CG: 26 DR: 45
D — Jerold Promes CG: 14 DR: 43
D — Olaf Lindenbergh CG: 17 DR: 41

M — Edwin van Bueren CG: 12 SD: -10
M — Nathan Rutjes CG: 12 SD: -15
M — Arne Slot CG: 16 SD: -17
M — Sjaak Polak CG: 18 SD: -38

F — Marvin Emnes CG: 14 SR: 197
F — Yuri Rose CG: 18 SR: 221

MONTHLY POINTS TALLY

AUGUST	1	17%
SEPTEMBER	3	25%
OCTOBER	1	11%
NOVEMBER	1	8%
DECEMBER	6	50%
JANUARY	6	50%
FEBRUARY	6	40%
MARCH	7	47%
APRIL	3	33%

LEAGUE GOALS

	PLAYER	MINS	GOALS	S RATE
1	Emnes	1582	8	197
2	Rose	1770	8	221
3	Dissels	2525	8	315
4	Boukhari	2573	8	321
5	Roberts	1523	7	217
6	Polak	1717	5	343
7	de Roover	1692	3	564
8	Rutjes	1270	1	1270
9	Promes	1306	1	1306
10	Slot	1601	1	1601
	Other		0	
	TOTAL		50	

TOP POINT EARNERS

	PLAYER	GAMES	AV PTS
1	Dwight Tiendalli	12	1.58
2	Danny Schenkel	26	1.27
3	Charles Dissels	27	1.19
4	Yuri Rose	18	1.17
5	Edwin van Bueren	12	1.17
6	Jerold Promes	14	1.14
7	Sander Westerveld	29	1.10
8	Ayodele Adeleye	15	1.07
9	Marvin Emnes	14	1.07
10	Nourdin Boukhari	26	1.04
	CLUB AVERAGE:		1.00

DISCIPLINARY RECORDS

	PLAYER	YELLOW	RED	AVE
1	Edwin van Bueren	8	0	157
2	Nathan Rutjes	5	1	211
3	I Moreno Freire	4	0	219
4	Yuri Rose	7	0	252
5	Jerold Promes	5	0	261
6	Ayodele Adeleye	5	1	261
7	Olaf Lindenbergh	5	0	312
8	Danny Schenkel	6	0	404
9	Nourdin Boukhari	6	0	428
10	Kim Jaggy	5	0	450
11	Dwight Tiendalli	2	0	562
12	Sjaak Polak	3	0	572
13	Arne Slot	2	0	800
	Other	5	0	
	TOTAL	68	2	

KEY GOALKEEPER

Sander Westerveld

Goals Conceded in the League	64	Counting Games League games when player was on pitch for at least 70 minutes	29
Defensive Rating Ave number of mins between League goals conceded while on the pitch	40	Clean Sheets In League games when player was on pitch for at least 70 minutes	2

KEY PLAYERS - DEFENDERS

Dwight Tiendalli

Goals Conceded Number of League goals conceded while the player was on the pitch	24	Clean Sheets In League games when player was on pitch for at least 70 minutes	1
Defensive Rating Ave number of mins between League goals conceded while on the pitch	46	Club Defensive Rating Average number of mins between League goals conceded by the club this season	41

	PLAYER	CON LGE	CLEAN SHEETS	DEF RATE
1	Dwight Tiendalli	24	1	46 mins
2	Danny Schenkel	53	2	45 mins
3	Jerold Promes	30	1	43 mins
4	Olaf Lindenbergh	38	0	41 mins

KEY PLAYERS - MIDFIELDERS

Edwin van Bueren

Goals in the League	0	Contribution to Attacking Power Average number of minutes between League team goals while on pitch	54
Defensive Rating Average number of mins between League goals conceded while on the pitch	44	Scoring Difference Defensive Rating minus Contribution to Attacking Power	-10

	PLAYER	LGE GOALS	DEF RATE	POWER	SCORE DIFF
1	Edwin van Bueren	0	44	54	-10 mins
2	Nathan Rutjes	1	40	55	-15 mins
3	Arne Slot	1	40	57	-17 mins
4	Sjaak Polak	5	33	71	-38 mins

KEY PLAYERS - GOALSCORERS

Marvin Emnes

Goals in the League	8	Player Strike Rate Average number of minutes between League goals scored by player	197
Contribution to Attacking Power Average number of minutes between League team goals while on pitch	63	Club Strike Rate Average number of minutes between League goals scored by club	60

	PLAYER	LGE GOALS	POWER	STRIKE RATE
1	Marvin Emnes	8	63	197 mins
2	Yuri Rose	8	53	221 mins
3	Charles Dissels	8	53	315 mins
4	Nourdin Boukhari	8	64	321 mins

KELME
SINCE 1888
SPARTA
Charles Dissels

SQUAD APPEARANCES

Match	1	2	3	4	5	6	7	8	9	10	11	12	13	14	15	16	17	18	19	20	21	22	23	24	25	26	27	28	29	30	31	32	33	34
Venue	H	A	A	H	H	A	H	A	H	A	A	H	A	H	A	A	H	A	H	A	A	H	H	H	A	H	A	H	A	H	H	A	H	A
Competition	L	L	L	L	L	L	L	L	L	L	L	L	L	L	L	L	L	L	L	L	L	L	L	L	L	L	L	L	L	L	L	L	L	L
Result	L	D	D	D	D	L	D	L	L	L	L	D	L	W	W	L	L	L	W	L	W	W	L	L	L	W	L	W	L	W	D	L	W	L

Goalkeepers
Cor Varkevisser
Harald Wapenaar
Sander Westerveld

Defenders
Ayodele Adeleye
Sepp De Roover
Wouter Gudde
Kim Jaggy
Olaf Lindenbergh
Jerold Promes
Danny Schenkel
Dwight Tiendalli
Cees Toet

Midfielders
Sani Kaita
Iderlindo Moreno Freire
Sjaak Polak
Nathan Rutjes
Arne Slot
Kevin Strootman
Edwin van Bueren

Forwards
Rachid Bouaouzan
Nourdin Boukhari
Charles Dissels
Edouard Duplan
Marvin Emnes
Joshua John
Darryl Roberts
Yuri Rose

KEY: On all match; On bench; Subbed or sent off (Counting game); Subbed or sent off (playing less than 70 minutes); Subbed on from bench (Counting Game); Subbed on (playing less than 70 minutes); Subbed on and then subbed or sent off (Counting Game); Subbed on and then subbed or sent off (playing less than 70 minutes); Not in 16

SC HERACLES

Final Position: **14th**

NICKNAME: HERACLIEDEN

KEY: ☐Won ☐Drawn ☐Lost

						Attendance
1	hopr1 **PSV Eindhoven**	H	L	0-2		8,500
2	hopr1 **Roda JC Kerk**	A	L	1-2	Klavan 76	13,000
3	hopr1 **NAC Breda**	A	L	1-4	Ramos da Silva 50	14,000
4	hopr1 **Ajax**	H	L	0-1		8,500
5	hopr1 **S Rotterdam**	A	D	1-1	Ramos da Silva 63	10,121
6	hopr1 **AZ Alkmaar**	H	W	2-1	Ramos da Silva 26, Maas 57 pen	8,500
7	hopr1 **Heerenveen**	A	L	0-9		24,700
8	hopr1 **Vitesse**	H	D	2-2	Ramos da Silva 33, Maas 88 pen	8,500
9	hopr1 **Excelsior**	A	D	1-1	Gluscevic 5	2,500
10	hopr1 **Twente**	H	L	0-3		8,500
11	hopr1 **NEC Nijmegen**	A	L	0-3		12,000
12	hopr1 **VVV**	H	D	0-0		8,420
13	hopr1 **Feyenoord**	A	L	0-6		44,500
14	hopr1 **De Graafschap**	H	W	2-0	Gluscevic 57, Quansah 66	7,950
15	hopr1 **Utrecht**	A	L	1-3	Bosnar 90	20,000
16	hopr1 **Groningen**	H	L	1-2	Quansah 12	8,011
17	hopr1 **Willem II Tilb**	H	W	1-0	Quansah 86	8,000
18	hopr1 **AZ Alkmaar**	A	L	0-1		16,313
19	hopr1 **S Rotterdam**	H	W	2-0	Quansah 13, van den Bergh 53	8,426
20	hopr1 **Vitesse**	A	L	0-2		19,411
21	hopr1 **Excelsior**	H	W	2-0	Lakic 12, Ramos da Silva 73	8,320
22	hopr1 **VVV**	A	W	5-0	Looms 11, Garcia Garcia 33, Lakic 42, 51 Gluscevic 83	6,000
23	hopr1 **NEC Nijmegen**	H	L	0-2		8,500
24	hopr1 **Twente**	A	L	1-2	Garcia Garcia 73	13,250
25	hopr1 **Heerenveen**	H	D	2-2	Garcia Garcia 20, Schilder 80	8,500
26	hopr1 **Feyenoord**	H	D	3-3	Ramos da Silva 1, Lakic 23, 60 pen	8,500
27	hopr1 **Groningen**	A	W	2-1	Ramos da Silva 14, Lakic 72	19,000
28	hopr1 **Utrecht**	H	W	2-1	Ramos da Silva 29, Lakic 73	8,500
29	hopr1 **De Graafschap**	A	D	0-0		12,000
30	hopr1 **Willem II Tilb**	A	L	1-2	Schilder 71	13,500
31	hopr1 **Roda JC Kerk**	H	D	0-0		8,500
32	hopr1 **PSV Eindhoven**	A	L	0-2		33,000
33	hopr1 **NAC Breda**	H	L	0-1		8,500
34	hopr1 **Ajax**	A	L	1-5	Klavan 54	50,139

LEAGUE APPEARANCES, BOOKINGS AND CAPS

	AGE (on 01/07/08)	IN NAMED 18	APPEARANCES	COUNTING GAMES	MINUTES ON PITCH	YELLOW CARDS	RED CARDS	CAPS THIS SEASON	NATIONAL SIDE
Goalkeepers									
Remko Pasveer	24	33	0	0	0	0	0	-	Holland
Martin Pieckenhagen	36	34	34	34	3060	0	0	-	Germany
Defenders									
Emmanuel Boakye	23	25	25	21	2062	8	1	-	Ghana
Eddy Bosnar	28	16	14	11	1084	4	0	-	Australia
Bjorn Daelemans	30	29	9	2	341	1	0	-	Belgium
Ragnar Klavan	22	30	29	22	2131	3	0	-	Estonia
Mark Looms	27	30	30	26	2540	6	0	-	Holland
John Lubbers	20	2	0	0	0	0	0	-	Holland
Rahim Ouedraogo	27	20	19	16	1540	6	1	-	Burkina Faso
Marnix Smit	32	34	10	4	522	2	0	-	Holland
Jan Wuytens	23	30	30	28	2632	6	0	-	Belgium
Midfielders									
Tim Breukers	20	11	6	3	356	0	0	-	Holland
Martin Christensen	20	12	11	3	488	2	0	-	Denmark
Nick de Graaf	21	7	1	0	20	0	0	-	Holland
Remon de Vries	28	26	14	10	1001	3	0	-	Holland
Rob Maas	38	27	26	25	2294	9	0	-	Holland
Kai Michalke	32	25	21	9	1274	2	0	-	Germany
Robbert Schilder	22	12	11	7	742	2	0	-	Holland
Ricky van den Bergh	27	26	24	14	1531	5	0	-	Holland
Forwards									
Nino Beukert	20	6	3	0	57	0	0	-	Holland
Karim Bridji	26	18	14	9	971	2	0	-	Holland
Gonzalo Garcia Garcia	24	16	16	14	1344	4	0	-	Spain
Igor Gluscevic	34	32	26	10	1194	1	0	-	Montenegro
Srdjan Lakic	24	29	28	18	1775	2	0	-	Croatia
Kwame Quansah	25	31	30	24	2420	7	0	-	Ghana
Ramos da Silva	25	33	33	21	2239	2	0	-	Brazil
Sander Weenk	22	4	0	0	0	0	0	-	Holland

TEAM OF THE SEASON

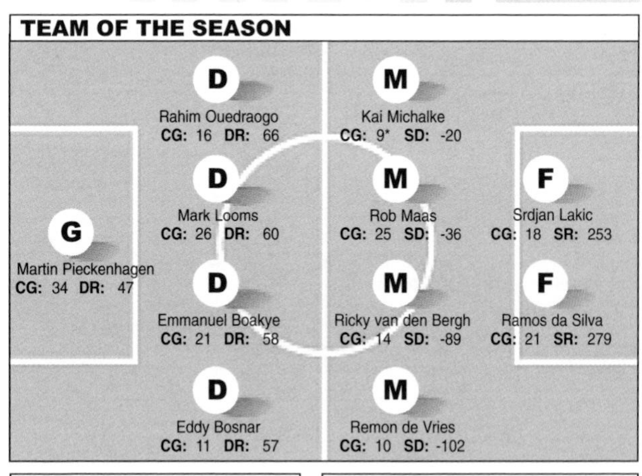
D
Rahim Ouedraogo
CG: 16 DR: 66
M
Kai Michalke
CG: 9* SD: -20
D
Mark Looms
CG: 26 DR: 60
M
Rob Maas
CG: 25 SD: -36
F
Srdjan Lakic
CG: 18 SR: 253
G
Martin Pieckenhagen
CG: 34 DR: 47
D
Emmanuel Boakye
CG: 21 DR: 58
M
Ricky van den Bergh
CG: 14 SD: -89
F
Ramos da Silva
CG: 21 SR: 279
D
Eddy Bosnar
CG: 11 DR: 57
M
Remon de Vries
CG: 10 SD: -102

MONTHLY POINTS TALLY

AUGUST	0	0%
SEPTEMBER	4	33%
OCTOBER	2	22%
NOVEMBER	1	11%
DECEMBER	6	33%
JANUARY	9	75%
FEBRUARY	2	17%
MARCH	8	53%
APRIL	0	0%

LEAGUE GOALS

	PLAYER	MINS	GOALS	S RATE
1	Ramos da Silva	2239	**8**	279
2	Lakic	1775	**7**	253
3	Quansah	2420	**4**	605
4	Gluscevic	1194	**3**	398
5	Garcia Garcia	1344	**3**	448
6	Schilder	742	**2**	371
7	Klavan	2131	**2**	1065
8	Maas	2294	**2**	1147
9	Bosnar	1084	**1**	1084
10	van den Bergh	1531	**1**	1531
11	Looms	2540	**1**	2540
	Other		0	
	TOTAL		**34**	

TOP POINT EARNERS

	PLAYER	GAMES	AV PTS
1	Gonzalo Garcia Garcia	14	**1.36**
2	Rahim Ouedraogo	16	**1.13**
3	Srdjan Lakic	18	**1.11**
4	Kwame Quansah	24	**1.08**
5	Mark Looms	26	**1.00**
6	Jan Wuytens	28	**0.96**
7	Ramos da Silva	21	**0.95**
8	Martin Pieckenhagen	34	**0.94**
9	Rob Maas	25	**0.92**
10	Ragnar Klavan	22	**0.86**
	CLUB AVERAGE:		**0.94**

DISCIPLINARY RECORDS

	PLAYER	YELLOW	RED	AVE
1	Rahim Ouedraogo	6	1	**220**
2	Emmanuel Boakye	8	1	**229**
3	Martin Christensen	2	0	**244**
4	Rob Maas	9	0	**254**
5	Eddy Bosnar	4	0	**271**
6	R van den Bergh	5	0	**306**
7	Remon de Vries	3	0	**333**
8	Gonzalo G Garcia	4	0	**336**
9	Kwame Quansah	7	0	**345**
10	Robbert Schilder	2	0	**371**
11	Mark Looms	6	0	**423**
12	Jan Wuytens	6	0	**438**
13	Karim Bridji	2	0	**485**
	Other	11	0	
	TOTAL	**75**	**2**	

KEY GOALKEEPER

Martin Pieckenhagen

Goals Conceded in the League	64	Counting Games League games when player was on pitch for at least 70 minutes	34
Defensive Rating Ave number of mins between League goals conceded while on the pitch	47	Clean Sheets In League games when player was on pitch for at least 70 minutes	8

KEY PLAYERS - DEFENDERS

Rahim Ouedraogo

Goals Conceded Number of League goals conceded while the player was on the pitch	23	Clean Sheets In League games when player was on pitch for at least 70 minutes	5
Defensive Rating Ave number of mins between League goals conceded while on the pitch	66	Club Defensive Rating Average number of mins between League goals conceded by the club this season	47

	PLAYER	CON LGE	CLEAN SHEETS	DEF RATE
1	Rahim Ouedraogo	23	5	66 mins
2	Mark Looms	42	8	60 mins
3	Emmanuel Boakye	35	4	58 mins
4	Eddy Bosnar	19	3	57 mins

KEY PLAYERS - MIDFIELDERS

Kai Michalke

Goals in the League	0	Contribution to Attacking Power Average number of minutes between League team goals while on pitch	63
Defensive Rating Average number of mins between League goals conceded while on the pitch	43	Scoring Difference Defensive Rating minus Contribution to Attacking Power	-20

	PLAYER	LGE GOALS	DEF RATE	POWER	SCORE DIFF
1	Kai Michalke	0	43	63	-20 mins
2	Rob Maas	2	52	88	-36 mins
3	Ricky van den Bergh	1	38	127	-89 mins
4	Remon de Vries	0	41	143	-102 mins

KEY PLAYERS - GOALSCORERS

Srdjan Lakic

Goals in the League	7	Player Strike Rate Average number of minutes between League goals scored by player	253
Contribution to Attacking Power Average number of minutes between League team goals while on pitch	73	Club Strike Rate Average number of minutes between League goals scored by club	90

	PLAYER	LGE GOALS	POWER	STRIKE RATE
1	Srdjan Lakic	7	73	253 mins
2	Ramos da Silva	8	93	279 mins
3	Igor Gluscevic	3	119	398 mins
4	Gonzalo Garcia Garcia	3	64	448 mins

TENCATE
Ramos Da Silva

SQUAD APPEARANCES

Match	1	2	3	4	5	6	7	8	9	10	11	12	13	14	15	16	17
Venue	H	A	A	H	A	H	A	H	A	H	A	H	A	H	A	H	H
Competition	L	L	L	L	L	L	L	L	L	L	L	L	L	L	L	L	L
Result	L	L	L	L	D	W	L	D	D	L	L	D	L	W	L	L	W

Match	18	19	20	21	22	23	24	25	26	27	28	29	30	31	32	33	34
Venue	A	H	A	H	A	H	A	H	H	A	H	A	A	H	A	H	A
Competition	L	L	L	L	L	L	L	L	L	L	L	L	L	L	L	L	L
Result	L	W	L	W	W	L	L	D	D	W	W	D	L	D	L	L	L

Goalkeepers
Remko Pasveer
Martin Pieckenhagen

Defenders
Emmanuel Boakye
Eddy Bosnar
Bjorn Daelemans
Ragnar Klavan
Mark Looms
John Lubbers
Rahim Ouedraogo
Marnix Smit
Jan Wuytens

Midfielders
Tim Breukers
Martin Christensen
Nick de Graaf
Remon de Vries
Rob Maas
Kai Michalke
Robbert Schilder
Ricky van den Bergh

Forwards
Nino Beukert
Karim Bridji
Gonzalo Garcia Garcia
Igor Gluscevic
Srdjan Lakic
Kwame Quansah
Ramos da Silva
Sander Weenk

KEY: On all match · On bench · Subbed or sent off (Counting game) · Subbed or sent off (playing less than 70 minutes) · Subbed on from bench (Counting Game) · Subbed on (playing less than 70 minutes) · Subbed on and then subbed or sent off (Counting Game) · Subbed on and then subbed or sent off (playing less than 70 minutes) · Not in 16

WILLEM II TILBURG

Final Position: **15th**

NICKNAME: KING'S ARMY

KEY: ☐Won ☐Drawn ☐Lost

						Attendance
1	hopr1 **Heerenveen**	A	D	0-0		26,000
2	hopr1 **S Rotterdam**	H	D	2-2	Hadouir 20, Boutahar 34	12,750
3	hopr1 **Feyenoord**	A	L	0-2		42,000
4	hopr1 **Twente**	H	L	1-3	Messoudi 25 pen	12,000
5	hopr1 **Roda JC Kerk**	H	W	1-0	Kargbo 45	12,000
6	hopr1 **NEC Nijmegen**	A	L	0-1		12,000
7	hopr1 **PSV Eindhoven**	A	L	0-3		33,258
8	hopr1 **NAC Breda**	H	D	0-0		13,500
9	hopr1 **Vitesse**	A	L	0-1		19,586
10	hopr1 **VVV**	H	L	1-2	Kargbo 10 fk	11,833
11	hopr1 **Utrecht**	H	L	1-4	Poepon 67	12,000
12	hopr1 **AZ Alkmaar**	A	L	0-2		16,000
13	hopr1 **Excelsior**	H	W	6-0	Poepon 9, 88, Demouge 29, 80, Boutahar 59 Van der Struijk 78 pen	11,995
14	hopr1 **Ajax**	H	L	2-3	Bobson 6, Swinkels 75	14,044
15	hopr1 **Groningen**	A	L	0-1		19,000
16	hopr1 **De Graafschap**	H	L	1-2	Van der Struijk 20 pen	11,528
17	hopr1 **Heracles**	A	L	0-1		8,000
18	hopr1 **NEC Nijmegen**	H	W	3-0	Poepon 14, 51, 84	12,000
19	hopr1 **Roda JC Kerk**	A	D	1-1	Poepon 37	13,700
20	hopr1 **NAC Breda**	A	L	0-1		15,000
21	hopr1 **Vitesse**	H	W	4-0	Swinkels 60, Poepon 61, Boutahar 88 Douglas 90	11,800
22	hopr1 **AZ Alkmaar**	H	W	3-0	Messoudi 37, Boutahar 61 Van der Struijk 87 pen	12,800
23	hopr1 **Utrecht**	A	L	0-2		20,000
24	hopr1 **VVV**	A	D	1-1	dos Santos Rodrigues 77	6,000
25	hopr1 **PSV Eindhoven**	H	L	0-1		14,192
26	hopr1 **Excelsior**	A	D	0-0		3,000
27	hopr1 **De Graafschap**	A	W	2-1	Poepon 40, Demouge 58	12,000
28	hopr1 **Groningen**	H	L	1-2	Van der Struijk 38 pen	13,500
29	hopr1 **Ajax**	A	L	1-4	Demouge 18	49,918
30	hopr1 **Heracles**	H	W	2-1	Mourad 46, Demouge 69	13,500
31	hopr1 **S Rotterdam**	A	D	2-2	Messoudi 50, Demouge 54	9,922
32	hopr1 **Heerenveen**	H	L	2-3	Boutahar 3, Poepon 65	14,000
33	hopr1 **Feyenoord**	H	W	3-1	Demouge 7, 19, Boutahar 36	14,700
34	hopr1 **Twente**	A	L	0-2		13,250

LEAGUE APPEARANCES, BOOKINGS AND CAPS

	AGE (on 01/07/08)	IN NAMED 18	APPEARANCES	COUNTING GAMES	MINUTES ON PITCH	YELLOW CARDS	RED CARDS	CAPS THIS SEASON	NATIONAL SIDE
Goalkeepers									
Maikel Aerts	32	19	19	18	1643	1	0	-	Holland
Kenneth Vermeer	22	33	16	15	1417	1	0	-	Holland
Defenders									
Thomas Baelum	30	31	30	27	2537	1	0	-	Denmark
Delano Hill	33	25	21	12	1309	1	0	-	Holland
Jens Janse	22	32	32	28	2685	4	0	-	Holland
Angelo Martha	26	6	0	0	0	0	0	-	Holland
Arjan Swinkels	23	33	31	25	2389	5	0	-	Holland
Frank van der Struijk	23	33	33	30	2863	2	0	-	Holland
Daan van Dinter	19	2	1	1	90	0	0	-	Holland
Nuelson Wau	27	16	7	3	379	1	0	-	Holland
Midfielders									
Mehmet Akgun	21	7	6	5	458	0	0	-	Germany, Turkey
Said Boutahar	25	31	31	29	2631	2	0	-	Morocco
Christophe Gregoire	28	15	14	12	1155	3	0	-	Belgium
Ibrahim Kargbo	26	28	28	28	2519	6	0	-	Sierra Leone
Danny Mathijssen	25	29	23	16	1618	6	0	-	Holland
Mohamed Messoudi	24	33	26	17	1849	4	0	-	Belgium
Steef Nieuwendaal	22	22	11	3	380	1	0	-	Holland
Niels Vorthoren	20	27	19	1	427	1	0	-	Holland
Forwards									
Kevin Bobson	27	15	15	12	1116	2	1	-	Holland
Frank Demouge	26	23	23	14	1429	2	1	-	Holland
Cristiano S Rodrigues	27	20	12	4	485	1	1	-	Brazil
Darl Douglas	28	22	16	4	641	0	0	-	Holland
Mounir el Hamdaoui	23	2	2	2	173	0	0	-	Holland
Anouar Hadouir	25	2	2	1	97	0	0	-	Holland
George Mourad	25	16	15	7	781	0	0	-	Sweden
Rydell Poepon	20	33	32	21	2218	6	0	-	Holland
Sergio Zijler	20	12	5	1	214	0	0	-	Holland

TEAM OF THE SEASON

G — Maikel Aerts — CG: 18 DR: 91

D — Arjan Swinkels — CG: 25 DR: 68

D — Jens Janse — CG: 28 DR: 65

D — Frank van der Struijk — CG: 30 DR: 63

D — Thomas Baelum — CG: 27 DR: 63

M — Christophe Gregoire — CG: 12 SD: 18

M — Mohamed Messoudi — CG: 17 SD: -4

M — Said Boutahar — CG: 29 SD: -5

M — Ibrahim Kargbo — CG: 28 SD: -17

F — Frank Demouge — CG: 14 SR: 178

F — Rydell Poepon — CG: 21 SR: 221

MONTHLY POINTS TALLY

AUGUST	2	33%
SEPTEMBER	3	25%
OCTOBER	1	11%
NOVEMBER	0	0%
DECEMBER	6	33%
JANUARY	7	58%
FEBRUARY	2	17%
MARCH	7	47%
APRIL	3	33%

LEAGUE GOALS

	PLAYER	MINS	GOALS	S RATE
1	Poepon	2218	10	221
2	Demouge	1429	8	178
3	Boutahar	2631	6	438
4	Van der Struijk	2863	4	715
5	Messoudi	1849	3	616
6	Swinkels	2389	2	1194
7	Kargbo	2519	2	1259
8	Hadouir	97	1	97
9	Rodrigues	485	1	485
10	Douglas	641	1	641
11	Mourad	781	1	781
12	Bobson	1116	1	1116
	Other		0	
	TOTAL		40	

TOP POINT EARNERS

	PLAYER	GAMES	AV PTS
1	Christophe Gregoire	12	1.50
2	Mohamed Messoudi	17	1.24
3	Maikel Aerts	18	1.17
4	Frank Demouge	14	1.07
5	Thomas Baelum	27	1.00
6	Jens Janse	28	0.96
7	Arjan Swinkels	25	0.92
8	Rydell Poepon	21	0.90
9	Said Boutahar	29	0.90
10	Ibrahim Kargbo	28	0.86
	CLUB AVERAGE:		0.91

DISCIPLINARY RECORDS

	PLAYER	YELLOW	RED	AVE
1	C Rodrigues	1	1	242
2	Danny Mathijssen	6	0	269
3	Rydell Poepon	6	0	369
4	Kevin Bobson	2	1	372
5	C Gregoire	3	0	385
6	Ibrahim Kargbo	6	0	419
7	M Messoudi	4	0	462
8	Frank Demouge	2	1	476
9	Arjan Swinkels	5	0	477
10	Jens Janse	4	0	671
11	Delano Hill	1	0	1309
12	Said Boutahar	2	0	1315
13	Kenneth Vermeer	1	0	1417
	Other	4	0	
	TOTAL	47	3	

KEY GOALKEEPER

Maikel Aerts

Goals Conceded in the League	18	**Counting Games** League games when player was on pitch for at least 70 minutes	18
Defensive Rating Ave number of mins between League goals conceded while on the pitch	91	**Clean Sheets** In League games when player was on pitch for at least 70 minutes	6

KEY PLAYERS - DEFENDERS

Arjan Swinkels

Goals Conceded Number of League goals conceded while the player was on the pitch	35	**Clean Sheets** In League games when player was on pitch for at least 70 minutes	7
Defensive Rating Ave number of mins between League goals conceded while on the pitch	68	**Club Defensive Rating** Average number of mins between League goals conceded by the club this season	62

	PLAYER	CON LGE	CLEAN SHEETS	DEF RATE
1	Arjan Swinkels	35	7	68 mins
2	Jens Janse	41	8	65 mins
3	Frank van der Struijk	45	6	63 mins
4	Thomas Baelum	40	7	63 mins

KEY PLAYERS - MIDFIELDERS

Christophe Gregoire

Goals in the League	0	**Contribution to Attacking Power** Average number of minutes between League team goals while on pitch	64
Defensive Rating Average number of mins between League goals conceded while on the pitch	82	**Scoring Difference** Defensive Rating minus Contribution to Attacking Power	18

	PLAYER	LGE GOALS	DEF RATE	POWER	SCORE DIFF
1	Christophe Gregoire	0	82	64	18 mins
2	Mohamed Messoudi	3	59	63	-4 mins
3	Said Boutahar	6	62	67	-5 mins
4	Ibrahim Kargbo	2	64	81	-17 mins

KEY PLAYERS - GOALSCORERS

Frank Demouge

Goals in the League	8	**Player Strike Rate** Average number of minutes between League goals scored by player	178
Contribution to Attacking Power Average number of minutes between League team goals while on pitch	64	**Club Strike Rate** Average number of minutes between League goals scored by club	76

	PLAYER	LGE GOALS	POWER	STRIKE RATE
1	Frank Demouge	8	64	178 mins
2	Rydell Poepon	10	79	221 mins
3	Said Boutahar	6	67	438 mins
4	Mohamed Messoudi	3	63	616 mins

9
MASITA
Interpolis

Frank Demouge

SQUAD APPEARANCES

Match	1	2	3	4	5	6	7	8	9	10	11	12	13	14	15	16	17	18	19	20	21	22	23	24	25	26	27	28	29	30	31	32	33	34
Venue	A	H	A	H	H	A	A	H	A	H	H	A	H	H	A	H	A	H	A	A	H	H	A	A	H	A	A	H	A	H	A	H	H	A
Competition	L	L	L	L	L	L	L	L	L	L	L	L	L	L	L	L	L	L	L	L	L	L	L	L	L	L	L	L	L	L	L	L	L	L
Result	D	D	L	L	W	L	L	D	L	L	L	L	W	L	L	L	L	W	D	L	W	W	L	D	L	D	W	L	L	W	D	L	W	L

Goalkeepers
Maikel Aerts
Kenneth Vermeer

Defenders
Thomas Baelum
Delano Hill
Jens Janse
Angelo Martha
Arjan Swinkels
Frank van der Struijk
Daan van Dinter
Nuelson Wau

Midfielders
Mehmet Akgun
Said Boutahar
Christophe Gregoire
Ibrahim Kargbo
Danny Mathijssen
Mohamed Messoudi
Steef Nieuwendaal
Niels Vorthoren

Forwards
Kevin Bobson
Frank Demouge
Cristiano S Rodrigues
Darl Douglas
Mounir el Hamdaoui
Anouar Hadouir
George Mourad
Rydell Poepon
Sergio Zijler

KEY: On all match; On bench; Subbed or sent off (Counting game); Subbed or sent off (playing less than 70 minutes); Subbed on from bench (Counting Game); Subbed on (playing less than 70 minutes); Subbed on and then subbed or sent off (Counting Game); Subbed on and then subbed or sent off (playing less than 70 minutes); Not in 16

DE GRAAFSCHAP

Final Position: **16th**

NICKNAME: SUPERBOEREN

KEY: ☐ Won ☐ Drawn ☐ Lost

	Comp	Opponent	H/A	Res	Score	Scorers	Attendance
1	hopr1	**Ajax**	H	L	1-8	de Groot 71	11,000
2	hopr1	**Groningen**	A	W	2-0	de Groot 47, Powel 63	19,300
3	hopr1	**Utrecht**	A	D	2-2	de Groot 77, 88	19,000
4	hopr1	**VVV**	H	W	3-2	de Groot 8, Fung A Wing 26, Keller 83	11,000
5	hopr1	**Vitesse**	A	W	2-0	Frankel 68, Powel 90	17,000
6	hopr1	**Twente**	H	D	0-0		12,300
7	hopr1	**NAC Breda**	A	L	0-1		14,845
8	hopr1	**S Rotterdam**	H	W	4-0	Schone 66, Powel 77, Hese 83 de Groot 86	12,300
9	hopr1	**Roda JC Kerk**	A	L	0-1		13,000
10	hopr1	**Feyenoord**	A	L	0-2		45,000
11	hopr1	**Excelsior**	H	D	1-1	Fung A Wing 18	12,000
12	hopr1	**Heerenveen**	A	W	3-2	de Groot 12, Schone 42, Powel 68	23,000
13	hopr1	**PSV Eindhoven**	H	L	0-1		12,000
14	hopr1	**Heracles**	A	L	0-2		7,950
15	hopr1	**NEC Nijmegen**	H	D	1-1	Schone 65	12,000
16	hopr1	**Willem II Tilb**	A	W	2-1	Powel 25, de Groot 35	11,528
17	hopr1	**Twente**	A	L	0-2		13,250
18	hopr1	**Vitesse**	H	L	0-3		12,000
19	hopr1	**AZ Alkmaar**	H	L	1-2	Schone 29	12,600
20	hopr1	**S Rotterdam**	A	L	1-6	Vidarsson 36	9,814
21	hopr1	**Roda JC Kerk**	H	W	2-1	Schone 44 pen, Powel 50	12,000
22	hopr1	**Heerenveen**	H	L	0-3		12,600
23	hopr1	**Excelsior**	A	D	1-1	Tarvajarvi 23	3,000
24	hopr1	**Feyenoord**	H	L	1-3	Schone 18	12,600
25	hopr1	**NAC Breda**	H	L	0-1		12,000
26	hopr1	**PSV Eindhoven**	A	L	1-4	Schone 7	33,200
27	hopr1	**Willem II Tilb**	H	L	1-2	Tarvajarvi 3	12,000
28	hopr1	**NEC Nijmegen**	A	L	1-3	Tarvajarvi 61	12,500
29	hopr1	**Heracles**	H	D	0-0		12,000
30	hopr1	**AZ Alkmaar**	A	D	0-0		16,322
31	hopr1	**Groningen**	H	D	1-1	Johnson 83	12,600
32	hopr1	**Ajax**	A	L	1-4	Tarvajarvi 32	50,057
33	hopr1	**Utrecht**	H	D	1-1	Johnson 72	12,600
34	hopr1	**VVV**	A	L	0-3		6,000
35	honac	**Helmond Sport**	A	W	3-2	Schone 16, 58, 65	3,698
36	honac	**Helmond Sport**	H	W	3-1	Hese 34, Tarvajarvi 36, 90	9,983
37	honac	**Zwolle**	A	W	3-1	Tarvajarvi 27, 31, Biseswar 90	4,753
38	honac	**Zwolle**	H	D	0-0		8,000

LEAGUE APPEARANCES, BOOKINGS AND CAPS

	AGE (on 01/07/08)	IN NAMED 18	APPEARANCES	COUNTING GAMES	MINUTES ON PITCH	YELLOW CARDS	RED CARDS	CAPS THIS SEASON	NATIONAL SIDE
Goalkeepers									
Nicolas Cinalli	28	33	0	0	0	0	0	-	Argentina
Jim van Fessem	32	34	34	34	3060	0	0	-	Holland
Defenders									
Rene Bot	30	30	10	4	450	1	0	-	Holland
Jordy Buijs	19	12	6	6	540	1	0	-	Holland
Dave Bus	30	5	0	0	0	0	0	-	Holland
Purrel Frankel	31	29	24	19	1850	5	0	-	Surinam
Cerezo Fung A Wing	24	33	32	29	2785	3	0	-	Holland
Michael Jansen	24	12	5	2	295	1	0	-	Holland
Stephan Keller	29	31	31	30	2729	9	1	-	Switzerland
Resit Schuurman	29	34	34	33	3024	4	0	-	Holland
Ard van Peppen	23	15	2	1	105	0	0	-	Holland
Joost Volmer	34	13	12	10	969	0	0	-	Holland
Midfielders									
Leon Hese	27	32	29	22	2122	4	1	-	Holland
Rogier Meijer	26	31	26	23	2132	4	0	-	Holland
Sjoerd Overgoor	19	2	0	0	0	0	0	-	Holland
Reinier Robbemond	36	32	23	6	961	2	0	-	Holland
Lasse Schone	22	34	34	28	2769	0	0	-	Denmark
Rik Sebens	20	4	1	0	3	0	0	-	Holland
J van den Ouweland	24	22	12	2	413	0	0	-	Holland
Arnar Vidarsson	30	34	32	28	2646	1	0	-	Iceland
Forwards									
Diego Biseswar	20	11	11	5	587	1	0	-	Holland
Donny de Groot	28	29	28	19	1941	2	0	-	Holland
Will Johnson	21	32	26	4	875	1	0	-	Canada
Girts Karlsons	27	5	5	2	200	1	0	-	Latvia
Berry Powel	28	22	22	19	1852	0	0	-	Holland
Kevin Sissing	22	4	2	0	18	0	0	-	Holland
Niklas Tarvajarvi	25	29	28	10	1317	0	0	-	Finland

TEAM OF THE SEASON

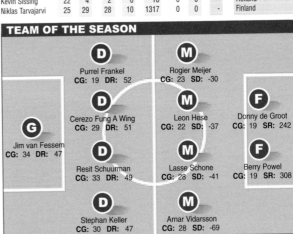

G — Jim van Fessem — CG: 34 DR: 47

D — Purrel Frankel — CG: 19 DR: 52

D — Cerezo Fung A Wing — CG: 29 DR: 51

D — Resit Schuurman — CG: 33 DR: 49

D — Stephan Keller — CG: 30 DR: 47

M — Rogier Meijer — CG: 23 SD: -30

M — Leon Hese — CG: 22 SD: -37

M — Lasse Schone — CG: 28 SD: -41

M — Arnar Vidarsson — CG: 28 SD: -69

F — Donny de Groot — CG: 19 SR: 242

F — Berry Powel — CG: 19 SR: 308

MONTHLY POINTS TALLY

Month	Points	%
AUGUST	3	50%
SEPTEMBER	8	67%
OCTOBER	3	33%
NOVEMBER	4	44%
DECEMBER	4	27%
JANUARY	3	20%
FEBRUARY	1	8%
MARCH	3	20%
APRIL	1	11%

LEAGUE GOALS

	PLAYER	MINS	GOALS	S RATE
1	de Groot	1941	8	242
2	Schone	2769	7	395
3	Powel	1852	6	308
4	Tarvajarvi	1317	4	329
5	Johnson	875	2	437
6	Fung A Wing	2785	2	1392
7	Frankel	1850	1	1850
8	Hese	2122	1	2122
9	Vidarsson	2646	1	2646
10	Keller	2729	1	2729
	Other		0	
	TOTAL		33	

TOP POINT EARNERS

	PLAYER	GAMES	AV PTS
1	Donny de Groot	19	1.26
2	Berry Powel	19	1.26
3	Rogier Meijer	23	1.13
4	Leon Hese	22	1.05
5	Stephan Keller	30	0.97
6	Resit Schuurman	33	0.91
7	Cerezo Fung A Wing	29	0.90
8	Lasse Schone	28	0.89
9	Jim van Fessem	34	0.88
10	Purrel Frankel	19	0.84
	CLUB AVERAGE:		0.88

DISCIPLINARY RECORDS

	PLAYER	YELLOW	RED	AVE
1	Stephan Keller	9	1	272
2	Purrel Frankel	5	0	370
3	Leon Hese	4	1	424
4	R Robbemond	2	0	480
5	Rogier Meijer	4	0	533
6	Jordy Buijs	1	0	540
7	Diego Biseswar	1	0	587
8	Resit Schuurman	4	0	756
9	Will Johnson	1	0	875
10	C Fung A Wing	3	0	928
11	Donny de Groot	2	0	970
12	Arnar Vidarsson	1	0	2646
13	Jim van Fessem	0	0	
	Other	0	0	
	TOTAL	37	2	

KEY GOALKEEPER

Jim van Fessem

Goals Conceded in the League	64	Counting Games League games when player was on pitch for at least 70 minutes	34
Defensive Rating Ave number of mins between League goals conceded while on the pitch	47	Clean Sheets In League games when player was on pitch for at least 70 minutes	6

KEY PLAYERS - DEFENDERS

Purrel Frankel

Goals Conceded Number of League goals conceded while the player was on the pitch	35	Clean Sheets In League games when player was on pitch for at least 70 minutes	2
Defensive Rating Ave number of mins between League goals conceded while on the pitch	52	Club Defensive Rating Average number of mins between League goals conceded by the club this season	49

	PLAYER	CON LGE	CLEAN SHEETS	DEF RATE
1	Purrel Frankel	35	2	52 mins
2	Cerezo Fung A Wing	54	5	51 mins
3	Resit Schuurman	61	6	49 mins
4	Stephan Keller	57	5	47 mins

KEY PLAYERS - MIDFIELDERS

Rogier Meijer

Goals in the League	0	Contribution to Attacking Power Average number of minutes between League team goals while on pitch	78
Defensive Rating Average number of mins between League goals conceded while on the pitch	48	Scoring Difference Defensive Rating minus Contribution to Attacking Power	-30

	PLAYER	LGE GOALS	DEF RATE	POWER	SCORE DIFF
1	Rogier Meijer	0	48	78	-30 mins
2	Leon Hese	1	55	92	-37 mins
3	Lasse Schone	7	48	89	-41 mins
4	Arnar Vidarsson	1	46	115	-69 mins

KEY PLAYERS - GOALSCORERS

Donny de Groot

Goals in the League	8	Player Strike Rate Average number of minutes between League goals scored by player	242
Contribution to Attacking Power Average number of minutes between League team goals while on pitch	80	Club Strike Rate Average number of minutes between League goals scored by club	95

	PLAYER	LGE GOALS	POWER	STRIKE RATE
1	Donny de Groot	8	80	242 mins
2	Berry Powel	6	84	308 mins
3	Lasse Schone	7	89	395 mins
4	Leon Hese	1	92	2122 mins

kwd
CENTRIC
IT SOLUTIONS
Lasse Schone

SQUAD APPEARANCES

Match	1	2	3	4	5	6	7	8	9	10	11	12	13	14	15	16	17	18	19	20	21	22	23	24	25	26	27	28	29	30	31	32	33	34	35	36	37	38
Venue	H	A	A	H	A	H	A	H	A	A	H	A	H	A	H	A	A	H	H	A	H	H	A	H	H	A	H	A	H	A	H	A	H	A	A	H	A	H
Competition	L	L	L	L	L	L	L	L	L	L	L	L	L	L	L	L	L	L	L	L	L	L	L	L	L	L	L	L	L	L	L	L	L	L	O	O	O	O
Result	L	W	D	W	W	D	L	W	L	L	D	W	L	L	D	W	L	L	L	L	W	L	D	L	L	L	L	L	D	D	D	L	D	L	W	W	W	D

Goalkeepers
Nicolas Cinalli
Jim van Fessem

Defenders
Rene Bot
Jordy Buijs
Dave Bus
Purrel Frankel
Cerezo Fung A Wing
Michael Jansen
Stephan Keller
Resit Schuurman
Ard van Peppen
Joost Volmer

Midfielders
Leon Hese
Rogier Meijer
Sjoerd Overgoor
Reinier Robbemond
Lasse Schone
Rik Sebens
Joep van den Ouweland
Arnar Vidarsson

Forwards
Diego Biseswar
Donny de Groot
Will Johnson
Girts Karlsons
Berry Powel
Kevin Sissing
Niklas Tarvajarvi

KEY: On all match / On bench / Subbed or sent off (Counting game) / Subbed or sent off (playing less than 70 minutes) / Subbed on from bench (Counting Game) / Subbed on (playing less than 70 minutes) / Subbed on and then subbed or sent off (Counting Game) / Subbed on and then subbed or sent off (playing less than 70 minutes) / Not in 16

VVV-VENLO

Final Position: 17th

NICKNAME: THE GOOD OLD

KEY: Won Drawn Lost

#	Comp	Opponent	H/A	Res	Score	Scorers	Attendance
1	hopr1	**AZ Alkmaar**	A	L	0-4		16,496
2	hopr1	**Excelsior**	H	W	3-1	Blondelle 38, Amrabat 51, El Gaaouiri 90	5,650
3	hopr1	**Roda JC Kerk**	H	L	3-5	Kantelberg 17, Linssen 23, Amrabat 30	6,000
4	hopr1	**De Graafschap**	A	L	2-3	Leemans 88, Kantelberg 90	11,000
5	hopr1	**NAC Breda**	H	L	1-3	Linssen 82	6,000
6	hopr1	**Ajax**	A	L	1-6	Soltani 4	49,126
7	hopr1	**Utrecht**	H	L	1-2	Leemans 75	5,850
8	hopr1	**PSV Eindhoven**	A	L	1-3	El Gaaouiri 66	33,600
9	hopr1	**Heerenveen**	H	L	0-4		5,930
10	hopr1	**Willem II Tilb**	A	W	2-1	Auassar 73, Kahya 83	11,833
11	hopr1	**S Rotterdam**	H	W	2-0	Oost 59, Amrabat 87	5,842
12	hopr1	**Heracles**	A	D	0-0		8,420
13	hopr1	**Groningen**	A	L	0-1		19,500
14	hopr1	**Feyenoord**	H	D	0-0		6,000
15	hopr1	**Twente**	A	D	1-1	Amrabat 13	13,250
16	hopr1	**Vitesse**	H	W	2-0	Amrabat 54, 68	5,806
17	hopr1	**NEC Nijmegen**	A	D	2-2	Kantelberg 70, Calabro 83	12,300
18	hopr1	**Ajax**	H	D	2-2	Ofrany 57, Calabro 89	6,000
19	hopr1	**NAC Breda**	A	D	0-0		15,000
20	hopr1	**PSV Eindhoven**	H	D	1-1	Ofrany 2	6,000
21	hopr1	**Heerenveen**	A	L	1-5	Calabro 81	24,000
22	hopr1	**Heracles**	H	L	0-5		6,000
23	hopr1	**S Rotterdam**	A	L	0-2		10,208
24	hopr1	**Willem II Tilb**	H	D	1-1	Reekers 45	6,000
25	hopr1	**Utrecht**	A	W	4-1	Calabro 17 pen, 80, Oost 39, 49	20,000
26	hopr1	**Groningen**	H	L	2-5	Leemans 50, Oost 59	6,000
27	hopr1	**Vitesse**	A	W	3-1	Oost 2 pen, Amrabat 6, 45	18,500
28	hopr1	**Twente**	H	L	0-2		6,000
29	hopr1	**Feyenoord**	A	L	1-4	Honda 13	46,000
30	hopr1	**NEC Nijmegen**	H	L	1-2	Honda 34	6,000
31	hopr1	**Excelsior**	A	L	1-2	Soltani 10	3,500
32	hopr1	**AZ Alkmaar**	H	L	2-3	Oost 3, Amrabat 64 pen	6,000
33	hopr1	**Roda JC Kerk**	A	L	1-4	Soltani 21	18,500
34	hopr1	**De Graafschap**	H	W	3-0	Volmer 56 og, Amrabat 64, Ofrany 84	6,000
35	honac	**Den Haag**	A	L	0-1		5,121
36	honac	**Den Haag**	H	W	1-0	Linssen 59	5,893
37	honac	**Den Haag**	A	L	0-2		5,023

LEAGUE APPEARANCES, BOOKINGS AND CAPS

	AGE (on 01/07/08)	IN NAMED 18	APPEARANCES	COUNTING GAMES	MINUTES ON PITCH	YELLOW CARDS	RED CARDS	CAPS THIS SEASON	NATIONAL SIDE
Goalkeepers									
Kevin Begois	26	28	13	13	1170	1	0	-	Belgium
Raymond van Driel	24	14	1	1	90	0	0	-	Holland
Danny Wintjens	24	24	20	20	1800	0	0	-	Holland
Defenders									
Adil Auassar	21	26	21	13	1325	2	0	-	Holland
Siebe Blondelle	22	33	16	9	990	2	0	-	Belgium
Ferry De Regt	19	17	2	1	98	0	0	-	Holland
Niels Fleuren	21	33	33	33	2970	3	0	-	Holland
Ken Leemans	25	25	19	12	1238	2	0	-	Belgium
Mike Mampuya	25	33	33	31	2833	1	0	-	Belgium
Peter Reekers	27	31	25	22	2107	7	1	-	Holland
Michael Timisela	22	19	3	1	161	0	0	-	Holland
Sjors Verdellen	26	28	28	26	2428	5	0	-	Holland
Robert Willemse	19	2	0	0	0	0	0	-	Holland
Midfielders									
Keisuke Honda	22	14	14	12	1136	2	0	-	Japan
Robin Janssen	21	6	0	0	0	0	0	-	Holland
Peter Jungschlager	24	7	7	6	532	1	0	-	Holland
Ekrem Kahya	30	31	24	21	2000	6	0	-	Holland, Turkey
Leon Kantelberg	29	25	16	4	699	0	0	-	Holland
Edwin Linssen	27	30	30	29	2649	8	0	-	Netherlands
Rick Verbeek	19	1	0	0	0	0	0	-	Holland
Forwards									
Nordin Amrabat	21	33	33	29	2763	6	0	-	Holland
Sandro Calabro	25	17	12	3	431	3	0	-	Holland
Samir el Gaaouiri	24	25	22	3	806	5	1	-	Holland
Paul Jans	26	15	10	3	507	1	0	-	Holland
Rachid Ofrany	21	30	26	8	1183	4	1	-	Holland, Morocco
Jason Oost	25	32	31	20	2127	0	0	-	Holland
Karim Soltani	23	31	28	13	1523	2	1	-	France

TEAM OF THE SEASON

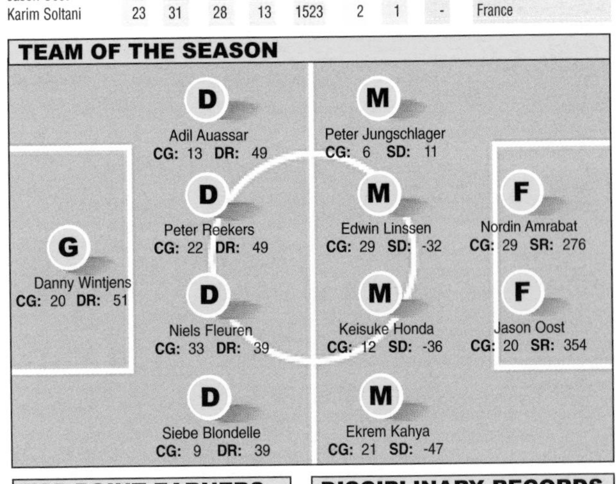

D
Adil Auassar
CG: 13 DR: 49
M
Peter Jungschlager
CG: 6 SD: 11
D
Peter Reekers
CG: 22 DR: 49
M
Edwin Linssen
CG: 29 SD: -32
F
Nordin Amrabat
CG: 29 SR: 276
G
Danny Wintjens
CG: 20 DR: 51
D
Niels Fleuren
CG: 33 DR: 39
M
Keisuke Honda
CG: 12 SD: -36
F
Jason Oost
CG: 20 SR: 354
D
Siebe Blondelle
CG: 9 DR: 39
M
Ekrem Kahya
CG: 21 SD: -47

MONTHLY POINTS TALLY

Month	Points	%
AUGUST	3	50%
SEPTEMBER	0	0%
OCTOBER	0	0%
NOVEMBER	7	78%
DECEMBER	7	39%
JANUARY	2	17%
FEBRUARY	7	47%
MARCH	0	0%
APRIL	3	33%

LEAGUE GOALS

	PLAYER	MINS	GOALS	S RATE
1	Amrabat	2763	**10**	276
2	Oost	2127	**6**	354
3	Calabro	431	**5**	86
4	Kantelberg	699	**3**	233
5	Ofrany	1183	**3**	394
6	Leemans	1238	**3**	412
7	Soltani	1523	**3**	507
8	El Gaaouiri	806	**2**	403
9	Honda	1136	**2**	568
10	Linssen	2649	**2**	1324
11	Blondelle	990	**1**	990
12	Auassar	1325	**1**	1325
13	Kahya	2000	**1**	2000
	Other		1	
	TOTAL		**43**	

TOP POINT EARNERS

	PLAYER	GAMES	AV PTS
1	Adil Auassar	13	**1.23**
2	Danny Wintjens	20	**1.15**
3	Peter Reekers	22	**1.00**
4	Nordin Amrabat	29	**1.00**
5	Edwin Linssen	29	**0.90**
6	Mike Mampuya	31	**0.90**
7	Sjors Verdellen	26	**0.88**
8	Niels Fleuren	33	**0.85**
9	Jason Oost	20	**0.80**
10	Ken Leemans	12	**0.75**
	CLUB AVERAGE:		**0.85**

DISCIPLINARY RECORDS

	PLAYER	YELLOW	RED	AVE
1	Samir el Gaaouiri	5	1	**134**
2	Rachid Ofrany	4	1	**236**
3	Peter Reekers	7	1	**263**
4	Edwin Linssen	8	0	**331**
5	Ekrem Kahya	6	0	**333**
6	Nordin Amrabat	6	0	**460**
7	Sjors Verdellen	5	0	**485**
8	Siebe Blondelle	2	0	**495**
9	Karim Soltani	2	1	**507**
10	Paul Jans	1	0	**507**
11	Peter Jungschlager	1	0	**532**
12	Keisuke Honda	2	0	**568**
13	Ken Leemans	2	0	**619**
	Other	7	0	
	TOTAL	**58**	**4**	

KEY GOALKEEPER

Danny Wintjens

Goals Conceded in the League	**35**	**Counting Games** League games when player was on pitch for at least 70 minutes	**20**
Defensive Rating **Ave number of mins between League goals conceded while on the pitch**	**51**	**Clean Sheets** In League games when player was on pitch for at least 70 minutes	**5**

KEY PLAYERS - DEFENDERS

Adil Auassar

Goals Conceded Number of League goals conceded while the player was on the pitch	**27**	**Clean Sheets** In League games when player was on pitch for at least 70 minutes	**6**
Defensive Rating **Ave number of mins between League goals conceded while on the pitch**	**49**	**Club Defensive Rating** Average number of mins between League goals conceded by the club this season	**41**

	PLAYER	CON LGE	CLEAN SHEETS	DEF RATE
1	Adil Auassar	27	6	**49 mins**
2	Peter Reekers	43	5	**49 mins**
3	Niels Fleuren	76	5	**39 mins**
4	Siebe Blondelle	25	2	**39 mins**

KEY PLAYERS - MIDFIELDERS

Peter Jungschlager

Goals in the League	**0**	**Contribution to Attacking Power** Average number of minutes between League team goals while on pitch	**48**
Defensive Rating Average number of mins between League goals conceded while on the pitch	**59**	**Scoring Difference** **Defensive Rating minus Contribution to Attacking Power**	**11**

	PLAYER	LGE GOALS	DEF RATE	POWER	SCORE DIFF
1	Peter Jungschlager	0	59	48	**11 mins**
2	Edwin Linssen	2	41	73	**-32 mins**
3	Keisuke Honda	2	35	71	**-36 mins**
4	Ekrem Kahya	1	39	86	**-47 mins**

KEY PLAYERS - GOALSCORERS

Nordin Amrabat

Goals in the League	**10**	**Player Strike Rate** **Average number of minutes between League goals scored by player**	**276**
Contribution to Attacking Power Average number of minutes between League team goals while on pitch	**69**	**Club Strike Rate** Average number of minutes between League goals scored by club	**71**

	PLAYER	LGE GOALS	POWER	STRIKE RATE
1	Nordin Amrabat	10	69	**276 mins**
2	Jason Oost	6	73	**354 mins**
3	Rachid Ofrany	3	91	**394 mins**
4	Karim Soltani	3	66	**507 mins**

Nordin Amrabat

SQUAD APPEARANCES

Match	1	2	3	4	5	6	7	8	9	10	11	12	13	14	15	16	17	18	19	20	21	22	23	24	25	26	27	28	29	30	31	32	33	34	35	36	37
Venue	A	H	H	A	H	A	H	A	H	A	H	A	A	H	A	H	A	H	A	H	A	H	A	H	A	H	A	H	A	H	A	H	A	H	A	H	A
Competition	L	L	L	L	L	L	L	L	L	L	L	L	L	L	L	L	L	L	L	L	L	L	L	L	L	L	L	L	L	L	L	L	L	L	O	O	O
Result	L	W	L	L	L	L	L	L	L	W	W	D	L	D	D	W	D	D	D	D	L	L	L	D	W	L	W	L	L	L	L	L	L	W	L	W	L

Goalkeepers
Kevin Begois
Raymond van Driel
Danny Wintjens

Defenders
Adil Auassar
Siebe Blondelle
Ferry De Regt
Niels Fleuren
Ken Leemans
Mike Mampuya
Peter Reekers
Michael Timisela
Sjors Verdellen
Robert Willemse

Midfielders
Keisuke Honda
Robin Janssen
Peter Jungschlager
Ekrem Kahya
Leon Kantelberg
Edwin Linssen
Rick Verbeek

Forwards
Nordin Amrabat
Sandro Calabro
Samir el Gaaouiri
Paul Jans
Rachid Ofrany
Jason Oost
Karim Soltani

KEY: On all match | On bench | Subbed or sent off (Counting game) | Subbed or sent off (playing less than 70 minutes) | Subbed on from bench (Counting Game) | Subbed on (playing less than 70 minutes) | Subbed on and then subbed or sent off (Counting Game) | Subbed on and then subbed or sent off (playing less than 70 minutes) | Not in 16

EXCELSIOR

Final Position: **18th**

NICKNAME: THE KRALINGERS

KEY: ☐Won ☐Drawn ☐Lost

							Attendance
1	hopr1	**Twente**	H	L	0-2		3,000
2	hopr1	**VVV**	A	L	1-3	den Ouden 19	5,650
3	hopr1	**AZ Alkmaar**	A	L	0-3		16,153
4	hopr1	**Heerenveen**	H	L	2-5	den Ouden 20, 28	2,864
5	hopr1	**Groningen**	H	L	1-3	den Ouden 40	2,500
6	hopr1	**Roda JC Kerk**	A	D	3-3	den Ouden 57 pen, Voskamp 79, 90	13,000
7	hopr1	**NEC Nijmegen**	H	W	2-0	Steur 82, Voskamp 90	2,583
8	hopr1	**Feyenoord**	A	L	0-1		47,000
9	hopr1	**Heracles**	H	D	1-1	Korf 13	2,500
10	hopr1	**S Rotterdam**	H	W	4-3	den Ouden 34 pen, 44, Voskamp 88	
						Luijckx 90	3,651
11	hopr1	**De Graafschap**	A	D	1-1	van Guldener 87	12,000
12	hopr1	**PSV Eindhoven**	H	L	1-4	Pardo 71	2,500
13	hopr1	**Willem II Tilb**	A	L	0-6		11,995
14	hopr1	**NAC Breda**	H	L	0-3		2,500
15	hopr1	**Vitesse**	A	L	0-3		17,175
16	hopr1	**Ajax**	H	W	2-1	Pique 1, den Ouden 49	3,500
17	hopr1	**Utrecht**	A	L	1-4	van Guldener 62	20,000
18	hopr1	**Roda JC Kerk**	H	L	1-2	Voskamp 86	2,500
19	hopr1	**Groningen**	A	L	2-3	den Ouden 59, Guijo-Velasco 73	19,300
20	hopr1	**Feyenoord**	H	W	2-1	van Guldener 5, den Ouden 12	3,500
21	hopr1	**Heracles**	A	L	0-2		8,320
22	hopr1	**PSV Eindhoven**	A	L	1-2	den Ouden 81	33,000
23	hopr1	**De Graafschap**	H	D	1-1	Luijckx 83	3,000
24	hopr1	**S Rotterdam**	A	W	1-0	van Steensel 58	10,528
25	hopr1	**NEC Nijmegen**	A	W	1-0	den Ouden 71	12,150
26	hopr1	**Willem II Tilb**	H	D	0-0		3,000
27	hopr1	**Ajax**	A	L	0-4		49,313
28	hopr1	**Vitesse**	H	L	1-2	Voskamp 70 pen	3,240
29	hopr1	**NAC Breda**	A	L	0-2		16,000
30	hopr1	**Utrecht**	H	L	0-2		3,000
31	hopr1	**VVV**	H	W	2-1	van Steensel 78, Braber 80	3,500
32	hopr1	**Twente**	A	L	0-1		13,100
33	hopr1	**AZ Alkmaar**	H	D	1-1	Luijckx 61	3,500
34	hopr1	**Heerenveen**	A	L	0-5		25,000

LEAGUE APPEARANCES, BOOKINGS AND CAPS

	AGE (on 01/07/08)	IN NAMED 18	APPEARANCES	COUNTING GAMES	MINUTES ON PITCH	YELLOW CARDS	RED CARDS	CAPS THIS SEASON	NATIONAL SIDE
Goalkeepers									
Ronald Graafland	29	30	30	29	2655	3	0	-	Holland
Arjan van Dijk	21	4	0	0	0	0	0	-	Holland
Jorg van Nieuwenhuijzen	29	34	5	4	405	0	0	-	Holland
Defenders									
Jeffrey Altheer	21	26	20	16	1604	4	0	-	Holland
Sigourney Bandjar	24	30	30	29	2642	10	0	-	Holland
Daan Bovenberg	19	16	2	1	91	0	0	-	Holland
Aykut Demir	19	15	15	12	1174	5	0	-	Turkey
Ryan Koolwijk	22	15	7	7	609	0	0	-	Holland
Mitchell Pique	28	29	28	24	2333	2	0	-	Holland
Koen Stam	21	11	7	4	421	1	0	-	Holland
Jos van Nieuwstadt	28	32	32	31	2845	6	0	-	Holland
Ard van Peppen	23	12	8	4	489	2	0	-	Holland
Leen van Steensel	24	26	24	18	1807	4	0	-	Holland
Sieme Zijm	30	21	13	6	724	3	0	-	Holland
Midfielders									
Adnan Alisic	24	33	11	7	792	1	0	-	Holland
Daniel Guijo-Velasco	24	19	10	5	609	1	1	-	Belgium
Kees Luijckx	22	32	32	30	2788	3	0	-	Holland
Sebastian Pardo	26	19	18	14	1409	2	1	-	Chile
Jarda Simr	29	3	3	0	79	0	0	-	Czech Republic
Rene van Dieren	27	8	8	8	720	0	0	-	Holland
Forwards									
Robert Braber	25	29	23	18	1765	6	0	-	Holland
Geert den Ouden	31	34	34	22	2422	3	1	-	Holland
Tjeerd Korf	25	34	29	11	1569	2	0	-	Holland
Eldridge Rojer	24	4	4	3	328	0	0	-	Holland
Sebastiaan Steur	24	19	19	9	1073	2	0	-	Holland
Michel van Guldener	22	34	24	4	902	2	0	-	Holland
Johan Voskamp	23	32	28	9	1321	2	0	-	Holland

TEAM OF THE SEASON

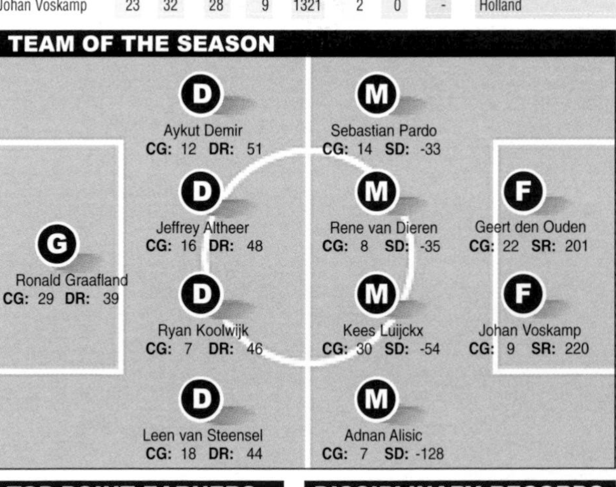

D
Aykut Demir
CG: 12 DR: 51
M
Sebastian Pardo
CG: 14 SD: -33
D
Jeffrey Altheer
CG: 16 DR: 48
M
Rene van Dieren
CG: 8 SD: -35
F
Geert den Ouden
CG: 22 SR: 201
G
Ronald Graafland
CG: 29 DR: 39
D
Ryan Koolwijk
CG: 7 DR: 46
M
Kees Luijckx
CG: 30 SD: -54
F
Johan Voskamp
CG: 9 SR: 220
D
Leen van Steensel
CG: 18 DR: 44
M
Adnan Alisic
CG: 7 SD: -128

MONTHLY POINTS TALLY

AUGUST	0	0%
SEPTEMBER	1	11%
OCTOBER	4	44%
NOVEMBER	4	44%
DECEMBER	3	17%
JANUARY	3	25%
FEBRUARY	8	67%
MARCH	3	20%
APRIL	1	11%

LEAGUE GOALS

	PLAYER	MINS	GOALS	S RATE
1	den Ouden	2422	**12**	201
2	Voskamp	1321	**6**	220
3	van Guldener	902	**3**	300
4	Luijckx	2788	**3**	929
5	van Steensel	1807	**2**	903
6	Guijo-Velasco	609	**1**	609
7	Steur	1073	**1**	1073
8	Pardo	1409	**1**	1409
9	Korf	1569	**1**	1569
10	Braber	1765	**1**	1765
11	Pique	2333	**1**	2333
12	Rojer	328	**0**	
13	Simr	79	**0**	
	Other		0	
	TOTAL		**32**	

TOP POINT EARNERS

	PLAYER	GAMES	AV PTS
1	Sebastian Pardo	14	**1.14**
2	Jeffrey Altheer	16	**1.13**
3	Geert den Ouden	22	**1.00**
4	Leen van Steensel	18	**0.89**
5	Jos van Nieuwstadt	31	**0.87**
6	Mitchell Pique	24	**0.83**
7	Robert Braber	18	**0.83**
8	Kees Luijckx	30	**0.80**
9	Ronald Graafland	29	**0.79**
10	Sigourney Bandjar	29	**0.72**
	CLUB AVERAGE:		**0.79**

DISCIPLINARY RECORDS

	PLAYER	YELLOW	RED	AVE
1	Aykut Demir	5	0	**234**
2	Sieme Zijm	3	0	**241**
3	Ard van Peppen	2	0	**244**
4	Sigourney Bandjar	10	0	**264**
5	Robert Braber	6	0	**294**
6	D Guijo-Velasco	1	1	**304**
7	Jeffrey Altheer	4	0	**401**
8	Leen van Steensel	4	0	**451**
9	M van Guldener	2	0	**451**
10	Sebastian Pardo	2	1	**469**
11	J van Nieuwstadt	6	0	**474**
12	Sebastiaan Steur	2	0	**536**
13	Geert den Ouden	3	1	**605**
	Other	13	0	
	TOTAL	**63**	**3**	

KEY GOALKEEPER

Ronald Graafland

Goals Conceded in the League	68	Counting Games League games when player was on pitch for at least 70 minutes	29
Defensive Rating Ave number of mins between League goals conceded while on the pitch	39	Clean Sheets In League games when player was on pitch for at least 70 minutes	4

KEY PLAYERS - DEFENDERS

Aykut Demir

Goals Conceded Number of League goals conceded while the player was on the pitch	23	Clean Sheets In League games when player was on pitch for at least 70 minutes	3
Defensive Rating Ave number of mins between League goals conceded while on the pitch	51	Club Defensive Rating Average number of mins between League goals conceded by the club this season	40

	PLAYER	CON LGE	CLEAN SHEETS	DEF RATE
1	Aykut Demir	23	3	51 mins
2	Jeffrey Altheer	33	2	48 mins
3	Ryan Koolwijk	13	0	46 mins
4	Leen van Steensel	41	2	44 mins

KEY PLAYERS - MIDFIELDERS

Sebastian Pardo

Goals in the League	1	Contribution to Attacking Power Average number of minutes between League team goals while on pitch	78
Defensive Rating Average number of mins between League goals conceded while on the pitch	45	Scoring Difference Defensive Rating minus Contribution to Attacking Power	-33

	PLAYER	LGE GOALS	DEF RATE	POWER	SCORE DIFF
1	Sebastian Pardo	1	45	78	-33 mins
2	Rene van Dieren	0	37	72	-35 mins
3	Kees Luijckx	3	42	96	-54 mins
4	Adnan Alisic	0	30	158	-128 mins

KEY PLAYERS - GOALSCORERS

Geert den Ouden

Goals in the League	12	Player Strike Rate Average number of minutes between League goals scored by player	201
Contribution to Attacking Power Average number of minutes between League team goals while on pitch	121	Club Strike Rate Average number of minutes between League goals scored by club	95

	PLAYER	LGE GOALS	POWER	STRIKE RATE
1	Geert den Ouden	12	121	201 mins
2	Johan Voskamp	6	69	220 mins
3	Kees Luijckx	3	96	929 mins
4	Sebastiaan Steur	1	76	1073 mins

MASITA
S.B.V. EXCELSIOR
ZORGVERZEKERAAR
DSW
Geert den Ouden

SQUAD APPEARANCES

Match	1	2	3	4	5	6	7	8	9	10	11	12	13	14	15	16	17	18	19	20	21	22	23	24	25	26	27	28	29	30	31	32	33	34
Venue	H	A	A	H	H	A	H	A	H	H	A	H	A	H	A	H	A	H	A	H	A	A	H	A	A	H	A	H	A	H	H	A	H	A
Competition	L	L	L	L	L	L	L	L	L	L	L	L	L	L	L	L	L	L	L	L	L	L	L	L	L	L	L	L	L	L	L	L	L	L
Result	L	L	L	L	L	D	W	L	D	W	D	L	L	L	L	W	L	L	L	W	L	L	D	W	W	D	L	L	L	L	W	L	D	L

Goalkeepers
Ronald Graafland
Arjan van Dijk
Jorg van Nieuwenhuijzen

Defenders
Jeffrey Altheer
Sigourney Bandjar
Daan Bovenberg
Aykut Demir
Ryan Koolwijk
Mitchell Pique
Koen Stam
Jos van Nieuwstadt
Ard van Peppen
Leen van Steensel
Sieme Zijm

Midfielders
Adnan Alisic
Daniel Guijo-Velasco
Kees Luijckx
Sebastian Pardo
Jarda Simr
Rene van Dieren

Forwards
Robert Braber
Geert den Ouden
Tjeerd Korf
Eldridge Rojer
Sebastiaan Steur
Michel van Guldener
Johan Voskamp

KEY: On all match · On bench · Subbed or sent off (Counting game) · Subbed or sent off (playing less than 70 minutes) · Subbed on from bench (Counting Game) · Subbed on (playing less than 70 minutes) · Subbed on and then subbed or sent off (Counting Game) · Subbed on and then subbed or sent off (playing less than 70 minutes) · Not in 16

GERMAN LEAGUE ROUND-UP

FINAL LEAGUE TABLE

		HOME					AWAY					TOTAL			
	P	W	D	L	F	A	W	D	L	F	A	F	A	DIF	PTS
Bayern Munich	34	12	5	0	41	8	10	5	2	27	13	68	21	47	76
Werder Bremen	34	13	0	4	48	19	7	6	4	27	26	75	45	30	66
Schalke 04	34	10	4	3	29	13	8	6	3	26	19	55	32	23	64
Hamburg SV	34	9	5	3	30	11	5	7	5	17	15	47	26	21	54
VfL Wolfsburg	34	7	6	4	28	17	8	3	6	30	29	58	46	12	54
VfB Stuttgart	34	12	2	3	39	19	4	2	11	18	38	57	57	0	52
B Leverkusen	34	9	4	4	32	13	6	2	9	25	27	57	40	17	51
Hannover 96	34	8	5	4	32	27	5	5	7	22	29	54	56	-2	49
E Frankfurt	34	8	4	5	24	24	4	6	7	19	26	43	50	-7	46
Hertha Berlin	34	9	3	5	21	18	3	5	9	18	26	39	44	-5	44
Karlsruhe	34	6	6	5	23	22	5	4	8	15	31	38	53	-15	43
VfL Bochum	34	5	9	3	32	28	5	2	10	16	26	48	54	-6	41
B Dortmund	34	7	5	5	29	24	3	5	9	21	38	50	62	-12	40
Energie Cottbus	34	8	2	7	25	20	1	7	9	10	36	35	56	-21	36
Arminia B	34	7	4	6	21	18	1	6	10	14	42	35	60	-25	34
Nurnberg	34	5	7	5	21	18	2	3	12	14	33	35	51	-16	31
Hansa Rostock	34	5	4	8	17	21	3	2	12	13	31	30	52	-22	30
MSV Duisburg	34	3	3	11	19	29	5	2	10	17	26	36	55	-19	29

CLUB STRIKE FORCE

Werder Bremen's Markus Rosenberg

1 Werder Bremen

Goals scored in the League	75
Club Strike Rate (CSR) Average number of minutes between League goals scored by club	40

	CLUB	GOALS	CSR
1	W Bremen	75	40
2	Bayern Munich	68	45
3	Wolfsburg	58	52
4	Stuttgart	57	53
5	B Leverkusen	57	53
6	Schalke	55	55
7	Hannover 96	54	56
8	B Dortmund	50	61
9	Bochum	48	63
10	Hamburg	47	65
11	Eintr Frankfurt	43	71
12	Hertha Berlin	39	78
13	Karlsruhe	38	80
14	Duisburg	36	85
15	Cottbus	35	87
16	Arminia B	35	87
17	Nurnberg	35	87
18	Hansa Rostock	30	102

CLUB DISCIPLINARY RECORDS

Duisburg's aggressive defender Caceres

1 Duisburg

League Yellow	87
League Red	5
League Total	92
Cards Average in League Average number of minutes between a card being shown of either colour	33

	CLUB	Y	R	TOTAL	AVE
1	Duisburg	87	5	92	33
2	W Bremen	70	7	77	39
3	Hannover 96	70	5	75	40
4	Cottbus	72	1	73	41
5	Stuttgart	64	6	70	43
6	B Dortmund	65	5	70	43
7	Bochum	67	1	68	45
8	Nurnberg	63	3	66	46
9	B Leverkusen	63	2	65	47
10	Wolfsburg	62	3	65	47
11	Hansa Rostock	63	0	63	48
12	Schalke	57	2	59	51
13	Karlsruhe	57	1	58	52
14	Arminia B	57	1	58	52
15	Hamburg	54	3	57	53
16	Eintr Frankfurt	57	0	57	53
17	Hertha Berlin	55	0	55	55
18	Bayern Munich	48	3	51	60

CLUB DEFENCES

	CLUB	LGE	CS	CDR
1	Bayern Munich	21	17	145
2	Hamburg	26	13	117
3	Schalke	32	12	95
4	B Leverkusen	40	10	76
5	Hertha Berlin	44	10	69
6	W Bremen	45	9	68
7	Wolfsburg	46	9	66
8	Eintr Frankfurt	50	10	61
9	Nurnberg	51	5	60
10	Hansa Rostock	52	5	58
11	Karlsruhe	53	10	57
12	Bochum	54	5	56
13	Duisburg	55	5	55
14	Hannover 96	56	7	54
15	Cottbus	56	9	54
16	Stuttgart	57	9	53
17	Arminia B	60	6	51
18	B Dortmund	62	7	49

Bayern Munich defender Lucio

1 Bayern Munich

Goals conceded in the League	21
Clean Sheets (CS) Number of league games where no goals were conceded	17
Club Defensive Rate (CDR) Average number of minutes between League goals conceded by club	145

PLAYER NATIONALITIES

Overseas country with the most player appearances in the German League - Brazil — 522 league appearances by Brazilian players

	COUNTRY	PLAYERS	IN SQUAD	LGE APP	% LGE ACT	CAPS	MOST APP	APP
	Germany	251	4914	3568	43.96	160	Robert Enke	100.0
1	Brazil	29	632	522	6.54	17	Naldo	94.1
2	Czech Republic	13	336	292	3.82	24	Jaroslav Drobny	100.0
3	Switzerland	11	270	222	2.90	38	Mario Eggimann	97.1
4	Croatia	13	266	198	2.17	27	Mario Cvitanovic	90.0
5	France	13	241	167	2.02	16	Marc Pfertzel	78.8
6	Holland	5	151	142	1.90	36	Joris Mathijsen	91.2
7	Denmark	11	221	180	1.78	17	Dennis S√ørensen	87.7
8	Poland	11	200	147	1.57	24	Artur Wichniarek	90.1
9	Greece	6	158	128	1.46	35	Ioannis Amanatidis	89.2
10	Romania	8	175	132	1.39	7	Mihai Tararache	90.1
11	Slovakia	4	112	103	1.25	3	Stanislav Sestak	93.5
12	Bulgaria	5	108	96	1.14	0	Stanislav Angelov	88.8
13	Hungary	4	97	89	1.13	0	Tamas Hajnal	91.9
14	Serbia	6	117	88	1.06	8	Marko Pantelic	74.2
15	Mexico	3	86	73	1.03	0	Pavel Pardo	83.1
18	Portugal	4	77	72	0.93	16	Fernando Meira	80.1
18	Bosnia & Herzegovina	3	79	70	0.83	0	Zvjezdan Misimovic	70.5
19	Cameroon	8	97	75	0.81	0	Joel Epalle	58.6
20	Sweden	4	91	71	0.75	9	Markus Rosenberg	65.0

CLUB MAKE-UP – HOME AND OVERSEAS PLAYERS

1 Cottbus — 71.4% of appearances by overseas players

	CLUB	OVERSEAS	HOME	% OVERSEAS	% LGE ACT	MOST APP	APP
1	Cottbus	25	10	71.4	79.18	Ervin Skela	97.6
2	Nurnberg	19	10	65.5	75.38	Tomas Galasek	90.1
3	Hertha Berlin	22	10	68.8	70.22	Jaroslav Drobny	100.0
4	Hamburg	20	10	66.7	69.80	Joris Mathijsen	91.2
5	Bochum	17	12	58.6	68.75	Stanislav Sestak	93.5
6	Wolfsburg	21	13	61.8	67.69	Marcelinho	93.0
7	Duisburg	22	12	64.7	66.44	Mihai Tararache	90.1
8	B Dortmund	17	16	51.5	62.88	Tinga	90.7
9	Stuttgart	16	16	50.0	60.60	Pavel Pardo	83.1
10	Bayern Munich	13	15	46.4	59.42	Luca Toni	85.9
11	W Bremen	15	17	46.9	55.64	Naldo	94.1
12	Eintr Frankfurt	20	14	58.8	54.27	Ioannis Amanatidis	89.2
13	Schalke	18	13	58.1	52.09	Rafinha	91.4
14	Hannover 96	15	15	50.0	50.62	Steve Cherundolo	95.8
15	B Leverkusen	16	16	50.0	47.98	Tranquillo Barnetta	87.7
16	Karlsruhe	13	14	48.1	44.80	Mario Eggimann	97.1
17	Arminia B	10	20	33.3	38.26	Radim Kucera	91.2
18	Hansa Rostock	14	18	43.8	29.11	Orestes	92.6

CHART-TOPPING MIDFIELDERS

1 Schweinsteiger - Bayern Munich	
Goals scored in the League	1
Defensive Rating Av number of mins between League goals conceded while on the pitch	168
Contribution to Attacking Power Average number of minutes between League team goals while on pitch	42
Scoring Difference Defensive Rating minus Contribution to Attacking Power	126

	PLAYER	CLUB	GOALS	DEF RATE	POWER	S DIFF
1	Bastian Schweinsteiger	Bayern Munich	1	168	42	126
2	Mark van Bommel	Bayern Munich	2	165	47	118
3	Franck Ribery	Bayern Munich	11	156	45	111
4	Jose Ze Roberto	Bayern Munich	5	144	48	96
5	Hamit Altintop	Bayern Munich	3	126	48	78
6	David Jarolim	Hamburg	2	123	55	68
7	Piotr Trochowski	Hamburg	1	123	67	56
8	Ivan Rakitic	Schalke	3	108	54	54
9	Nigel de Jong	Hamburg	1	118	71	47
10	Jermaine Jones	Schalke	1	102	56	46
11	Rafael Van der Vaart	Hamburg	12	109	68	41
12	Fabian Ernst	Schalke	1	91	56	35
13	Diego	W Bremen	13	70	39	31
14	Tim Borowski	W Bremen	2	74	45	29
15	Tranquillo Barnetta	B Leverkusen	6	81	55	26

CHART-TOPPING GOALSCORERS

1 Gomez - Stuttgart	
Goals scored in the League	19
Contribution to Attacking Power Average number of minutes between League team goals while on pitch	52
Club Strike Rate (CSR) Average minutes between League goals scored by club	55
Player Strike Rate Average number of minutes between League goals scored by player	103

	PLAYER	CLUB	GOALS: LGE	POWER	CSR	S RATE
1	Mario Gomez	Stuttgart	19	52	55	103
2	Luca Toni	Bayern Munich	24	44	45	109
3	Miguel Hugo Almeida	W Bremen	11	41	40	125
4	Markus Rosenberg	W Bremen	14	36	40	142
5	Theofanis Gekas	B Leverkusen	11	49	53	161
6	Boubacar Sanogo	W Bremen	9	43	40	170
7	Ivica Olic	Hamburg	14	60	65	172
8	Libano Batista Grafite	Wolfsburg	11	51	54	172
9	Marko Pantelic	Hertha Berlin	13	78	78	174
10	Mladen Petric	B Dortmund	13	64	61	182
11	Kevin Kuranyi	Schalke	15	57	55	182
12	Manaseh Ishiaku	Duisburg	10	80	85	185
13	Diego	W Bremen	13	39	40	196
14	Franck Ribery	Bayern Munich	11	45	45	199
15	Miroslav Klose	Bayern Munich	10	53	45	199

CHART-TOPPING DEFENDERS

1 Van Buyten - Bayern Munich	
Goals Conceded in the League The number of League goals conceded while he was on the pitch	10
Clean Sheets In games when he played at least 70 mins	10
Club Defensive Rating Average mins between League goals conceded by the club this season	145
Defensive Rating Average number of minutes between League goals conceded while on pitch	162

	PLAYER	CLUB	CON: LGE	CS	CDR	DEF RATE
1	Daniel Van Buyten	Bayern Munich	10	10	145	162
2	Marcell Jansen	Bayern Munich	9	7	145	159
3	Martin Demichelis	Bayern Munich	16	15	145	157
4	Christian Lell	Bayern Munich	15	14	145	153
5	Lucio	Bayern Munich	16	11	145	133
6	Philipp Lahm	Bayern Munich	14	10	145	132
7	Jerome Boateng	Hamburg	17	7	117	126
8	Bastian Reinhardt	Hamburg	22	11	117	122
9	Joris Mathijsen	Hamburg	23	13	117	121
10	Guy Demel	Hamburg	19	9	117	111
11	Vincent Kompany	Hamburg	14	6	117	109
12	Heiko Westermann	Schalke	26	12	95	107
13	Christian Pander	Schalke	14	6	95	103
14	Karim Haggui	B Leverkusen	20	9	76	102
15	Rafinha	Schalke	29	10	95	96

CHART-TOPPING GOALKEEPERS

1 Kahn - Bayern Munich	
Counting Games Games in which he played at least 70 minutes	25
Goals Conceded in the League The number of League goals conceded while he was on the pitch	18
Clean Sheets In games when he played at least 70 mins	11
Defensive Rating Average number of minutes between League goals conceded while on pitch	127

	PLAYER	CLUB	CG	CONC	CS	DEF RATE
1	Oliver Kahn	Bayern Munich	25	18	11	127
2	Frank Rost	Hamburg	34	26	13	117
3	Diego Benaglio	Wolfsburg	18	17	7	95
4	Manuel Neuer	Schalke	34	32	12	95
5	Rene Adler	B Leverkusen	33	40	9	74
6	Jaroslav Drobny	Hertha Berlin	34	44	10	69
7	Marc Ziegler	B Dortmund	14	20	5	65
8	Tim Wiese	W Bremen	31	43	8	64
9	Stefan Wachter	Hansa Rostock	28	40	4	63
10	Gerhard Tremmel	Cottbus	24	36	7	60
11	Tom Starke	Duisburg	31	47	5	59
12	Rowen Fernandez	Arminia B	13	21	4	58
13	Markus Miller	Karlsruhe	28	43	9	58
14	Jaromir Blazek	Nurnberg	25	41	2	56
15	Robert Enke	Hannover 96	34	56	7	54

PLAYER DISCIPLINARY RECORD

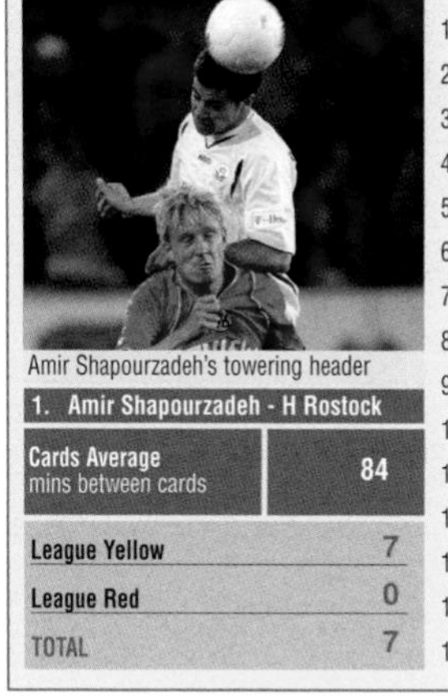

Amir Shapourzadeh's towering header

1. Amir Shapourzadeh - H Rostock	
Cards Average mins between cards	84
League Yellow	7
League Red	0
TOTAL	7

	PLAYER		LY	LR	TOT	AVE
1	Shap'zadeh	Hansa Rostock	7	0	7	84
2	T Frings	W Bremen	6	0	6	156
3	T Zdebel	Bochum	11	0	11	168
4	Stefan Buck	Karlsruhe	3	0	3	169
5	Aaron Hunt	W Bremen	5	0	5	175
6	M Tararache	Duisburg	14	1	15	183
7	D Klimowicz	B Dortmund	7	0	7	186
8	L Grafite	Wolfsburg	9	1	10	189
9	Fe Santos	Duisburg	5	0	5	193
10	J Bohme	Arminia B	6	1	7	195
11	van Bommel	Bayern Munich	9	2	11	195
12	C Bassila	Cottbus	9	0	9	199
13	I Filipescu	Duisburg	7	0	7	205
14	M Bollmann	Arminia B	7	0	7	206
15	M Idrissou	Duisburg	3	1	4	210

TEAM OF THE SEASON

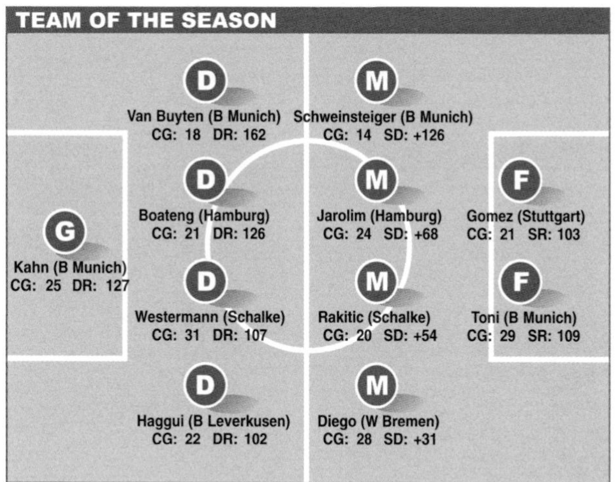
D
Van Buyten (B Munich)
CG: 18 DR: 162
M
Schweinsteiger (B Munich)
CG: 14 SD: +126
G
Kahn (B Munich)
CG: 25 DR: 127
D
Boateng (Hamburg)
CG: 21 DR: 126
M
Jarolim (Hamburg)
CG: 24 SD: +68
F
Gomez (Stuttgart)
CG: 21 SR: 103
D
Westermann (Schalke)
CG: 31 DR: 107
M
Rakitic (Schalke)
CG: 20 SD: +54
F
Toni (B Munich)
CG: 29 SR: 109
D
Haggui (B Leverkusen)
CG: 22 DR: 102
M
Diego (W Bremen)
CG: 28 SD: +31

BAYERN MUNICH

Final Position: **1st**

NICKNAME: DIE ROTEN

KEY: ☐Won ☐Drawn ☐Lost

	Comp	Opponent	H/A	Res	Score	Scorers	Attendance
1	grpr1	**Hansa Rostock**	H	W	3-0	Toni 13, Klose 65, 84	69,000
2	grpr1	**W Bremen**	A	W	4-0	Ribery 30 pen, Toni 51, Ham.Altintop 79, Ottl 87	42,000
3	grpr1	**Hannover 96**	H	W	3-0	Toni 28, van Bommel 69, Ham.Altintop 86	69,000
4	grpr1	**Hamburg**	A	D	1-1	Klose 70	57,000
5	grpr1	**Schalke**	H	D	1-1	Klose 54	69,000
6	ucrl1	**Belenenses**	H	W	1-0	Toni 35	64,000
7	grpr1	**Karlsruhe**	A	W	4-1	Toni 4, Klose 20, Ham.Altintop 49, Ze Roberto 74	30,702
8	grpr1	**Cottbus**	H	W	5-0	Klose 60, 75, 89, Demichelis 63, Toni 69	68,000
9	grpr1	**B Leverkusen**	A	W	1-0	Toni 40	22,500
10	ucrl2	**Belenenses**	A	W	2-0	Toni 59, Ham.Altintop 77	4,000
11	grpr1	**Nurnberg**	H	W	3-0	Toni 32, 81, Ze Roberto 40	69,000
12	grpr1	**Bochum**	A	W	2-1	Ribery 35, Schweinsteiger 78	31,328
13	ucgpf	**Crvena Zvezda**	A	W	3-2	Klose 20, 86, Kroos 90	50,000
14	grpr1	**B Dortmund**	A	D	0-0		80,708
15	grpr1	**Eintr Frankfurt**	H	D	0-0		69,000
16	ucgpf	**Bolton**	H	D	2-2	Podolski 30, 49	65,000
17	grpr1	**Stuttgart**	A	L	1-3	Toni 85	55,000
18	grpr1	**Wolfsburg**	H	W	2-1	Klose 35, Ribery 50	69,000
19	ucgpf	**Braga**	A	D	1-1	Klose 47	15,000
20	grpr1	**Arminia B**	A	W	1-0	Ribery 22	23,800
21	grpr1	**Duisburg**	H	D	0-0		69,000
22	grpr1	**Hertha Berlin**	A	D	0-0		74,220
23	ucgpf	**Aris**	H	W	6-0	Toni 25, 38, 64, 66, Lell 78, Lahm 81	64,000
24	grpr1	**Hansa Rostock**	A	W	2-1	Ribery 11, Toni 43	29,000
25	grpr1	**W Bremen**	H	D	1-1	Ze Roberto 32	69,000
26	ucrl1	**Aberdeen**	A	D	2-2	Klose 29, Ham.Altintop 54	20,047
27	grpr1	**Hannover 96**	A	W	3-0	Toni 58, 64, 82	49,000
28	ucrl2	**Aberdeen**	H	W	5-1	da Silva Ferreira 12, Van Buyten 36, Podolski 71, 77, van Bommel 85	66,000
29	grpr1	**Hamburg**	H	D	1-1	Ze Roberto 66	69,000
30	grpr1	**Schalke**	A	W	1-0	Klose 14	61,482
31	ucrl1	**Anderlecht**	A	W	5-0	Ham.Altintop 9, Toni 45, Podolski 57, Klose 67, Ribery 86	21,750
32	grpr1	**Karlsruhe**	H	W	2-0	Toni 41, Ribery 64	69,000
33	ucrl2	**Anderlecht**	H	L	1-2	da Silva Ferreira 8	63,000
34	grpr1	**Cottbus**	A	L	0-2		22,700
35	grpr1	**B Leverkusen**	H	W	2-1	Toni 17, 59	69,000
36	grpr1	**Nurnberg**	A	D	1-1	Podolski 81	47,000
37	ucqfl1	**Getafe**	H	D	1-1	Toni 26	62,000
38	grpr1	**Bochum**	H	W	3-1	da Silva Ferreira 31, Ribery 74 pen, Lell 88	69,000
39	ucqfl2	**Getafe**	A	D	3-3	Ribery 89, Toni 115, 120	16,300
40	grpr1	**B Dortmund**	H	W	5-0	Podolski 3, Ze Roberto 8, Toni 18, 22, Ottl 67	69,000
41	grpr1	**Eintr Frankfurt**	A	W	3-1	Van Buyten 60, Toni 74, 85	51,500
42	ucsfl1	**Z St Petersburg**	H	D	1-1	Ribery 18	66,000
43	grpr1	**Stuttgart**	H	W	4-1	Toni 8, van Bommel 55, Ribery 75, 76	69,000
44	ucsfl2	**Z St Petersburg**	A	L	0-4		22,000
45	grpr1	**Wolfsburg**	A	D	0-0		30,000
46	grpr1	**Arminia B**	H	W	2-0	Ribery 26, Podolski 47	69,000
47	grpr1	**Duisburg**	A	W	3-2	Ottl 3, Podolski 18, 20	31,500
48	grpr1	**Hertha Berlin**	H	W	4-1	Toni 3, 27, 61, Ribery 33	69,000

LEAGUE APPEARANCES, BOOKINGS AND CAPS

	AGE (on 01/07/08)	IN NAMED 18	APPEARANCES	COUNTING GAMES	MINUTES ON PITCH	YELLOW CARDS	RED CARDS	CAPS THIS SEASON	NATIONAL SIDE
Goalkeepers									
Bernd Dreher	43	7	0	0	0	0	0	-	Germany
Oliver Kahn	39	26	26	25	2292	1	0	-	Germany
Michael Rensing	24	31	10	8	768	0	0	-	Germany
Defenders									
Lucio	30	26	24	24	2138	2	1	3	Brazil
Martin Demichelis	27	30	28	28	2514	3	0	6	Argentina
Matts Hummels	19	1	0	0	0	0	0	-	Germany
Valerien Ismael	32	3	0	0	0	0	0	-	France
Marcell Jansen	22	21	17	15	1431	1	0	9	Germany
Philipp Lahm	24	26	22	20	1858	0	0	9	Germany
Christian Lell	23	32	29	23	2296	6	0	-	Germany
Willy Sagnol	31	11	9	6	632	1	0	4	France
Daniel Van Buyten	30	30	19	18	1621	1	0	4	Belgium
Breno	18	9	1	0	18	0	0	-	Brazil
Midfielders									
Hamit Altintop	25	23	23	16	1642	3	0	10	Turkey
Stephan Furstner	20	1	0	0	0	0	0	-	Germany
Toni Kroos	18	25	12	2	357	0	0	-	Germany
Andreas Ottl	23	33	19	8	807	0	0	-	Germany
Franck Ribery	25	28	28	23	2196	2	0	9	France
Jan Schlaudraff	24	24	8	1	157	0	0	-	Germany
B Schweinsteiger	23	30	30	14	1850	7	0	10	Germany
Jose Ernesto Sosa	23	28	15	6	738	0	0	-	Argentina
Mark van Bommel	31	28	27	23	2150	9	2	-	Holland
Jose Ze Roberto	33	31	30	27	2457	5	0	-	Brazil
Forwards									
Miroslav Klose	30	27	27	21	1992	2	0	8	Germany
Lukas Podolski	23	28	25	5	961	3	0	12	Germany
Luca Toni	31	31	31	29	2630	1	0	8	Italy
Sandro Wagner	20	6	4	0	68	1	0	-	Germany

TEAM OF THE SEASON

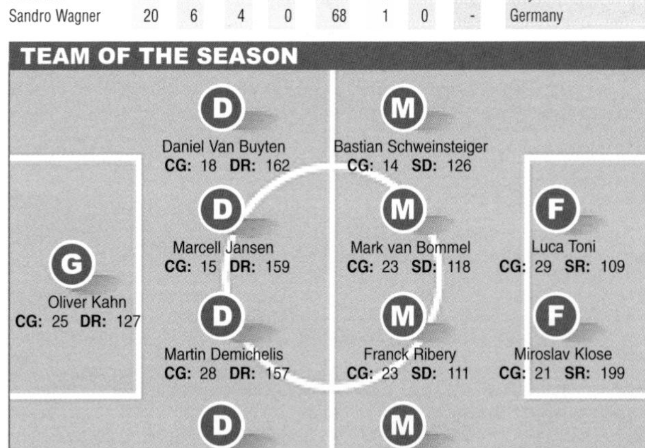

G
Oliver Kahn
CG: 25 DR: 127
D
Daniel Van Buyten
CG: 18 DR: 162
D
Marcell Jansen
CG: 15 DR: 159
D
Martin Demichelis
CG: 28 DR: 157
D
Christian Lell
CG: 23 DR: 153
M
Bastian Schweinsteiger
CG: 14 SD: 126
M
Mark van Bommel
CG: 23 SD: 118
M
Franck Ribery
CG: 23 SD: 111
M
Jose Ze Roberto
CG: 27 SD: 96
F
Luca Toni
CG: 29 SR: 109
F
Miroslav Klose
CG: 21 SR: 199

MONTHLY POINTS TALLY

Month	Points	%
AUGUST	9	100%
SEPTEMBER	11	73%
OCTOBER	7	78%
NOVEMBER	4	44%
DECEMBER	5	56%
NO LEAGUE GAMES PLAYED IN JANUARY		
FEBRUARY	8	67%
MARCH	10	67%
APRIL	12	100%
MAY	10	83%

LEAGUE GOALS

	PLAYER	MINS	GOALS	S RATE
1	Toni	2630	24	109
2	Ribery	2196	11	199
3	Klose	1992	10	199
4	Podolski	961	5	192
5	Ze Roberto	2457	5	491
6	Ottl	807	3	269
7	Altintop, Ham	1642	3	547
8	van Bommel	2150	2	1075
9	Van Buyten	1621	1	1621
10	Schweinsteiger	1850	1	1850
11	Silva Ferreira	2138	1	2138
12	Lell	2296	1	2296
13	Demichelis	2514	1	2514
	Other		0	
	TOTAL		68	

TOP POINT EARNERS

	PLAYER	GAMES	AV PTS
1	Bastian Schweinsteiger	14	2.71
2	Marcell Jansen	15	2.60
3	Christian Lell	23	2.39
4	Martin Demichelis	28	2.32
5	Daniel Van Buyten	18	2.28
6	Hamit Altintop	16	2.25
7	Luca Toni	29	2.24
8	Mark van Bommel	23	2.22
9	Franck Ribery	23	2.22
10	Oliver Kahn	25	2.20
	CLUB AVERAGE:		2.24

DISCIPLINARY RECORDS

	PLAYER	YELLOW	RED	AVE
1	Mark van Bommel	9	2	195
2	B Schweinsteiger	7	0	264
3	Lukas Podolski	3	0	320
4	Christian Lell	6	0	382
5	Jose Ze Roberto	5	0	491
6	Hamit Altintop	3	0	547
7	Willy Sagnol	1	0	632
8	Lucio	2	1	712
9	Martin Demichelis	3	0	838
10	Miroslav Klose	2	0	996
11	Franck Ribery	2	0	1098
12	Marcell Jansen	1	0	1431
13	Daniel Van Buyten	1	0	1621
	Other	2	0	
	TOTAL	47	3	

KEY GOALKEEPER

Oliver Kahn

Goals Conceded in the League	18	**Counting Games** League games when player was on pitch for at least 70 minutes	25
Defensive Rating Ave number of mins between League goals conceded while on the pitch	127	**Clean Sheets** In League games when player was on pitch for at least 70 minutes	11

KEY PLAYERS - GOALSCORERS

Luca Toni

Goals in the League	24	**Player Strike Rate** Average number of minutes between League goals scored by player	109
Contribution to Attacking Power Average number of minutes between League team goals while on pitch	44	**Club Strike Rate** Average number of minutes between League goals scored by club	45

	PLAYER	LGE GOALS	POWER	STRIKE RATE
1	Luca Toni	24	44	109 mins
2	Franck Ribery	11	45	199 mins
3	Miroslav Klose	10	53	199 mins
4	Jose Ze Roberto	5	48	491 mins

KEY PLAYERS - DEFENDERS

Daniel Van Buyten

Goals Conceded Number of League goals conceded while the player was on the pitch	10	**Clean Sheets** In League games when player was on pitch for at least 70 minutes	10
Defensive Rating Ave number of mins between League goals conceded while on the pitch	162	**Club Defensive Rating** Average number of mins between League goals conceded by the club this season	145

	PLAYER	CON LGE	CLEAN SHEETS	DEF RATE
1	Daniel Van Buyten	10	10	162 mins
2	Marcell Jansen	9	7	159 mins
3	Martin Demichelis	16	15	157 mins
4	Christian Lell	15	14	153 mins

BAYERN MÜNC
LIGA
Miroslav Klose and Luca Toni

KEY PLAYERS - MIDFIELDERS

Bastian Schweinsteiger

Goals in the League	1	**Contribution to Attacking Power** Average number of minutes between League team goals while on pitch	42
Defensive Rating Average number of mins between League goals conceded while on the pitch	168	**Scoring Difference** Defensive Rating minus Contribution to Attacking Power	126

	PLAYER	LGE GOALS	DEF RATE	POWER	SCORE DIFF
1	Bastian Schweinsteiger	1	168	42	126 mins
2	Mark van Bommel	2	165	47	118 mins
3	Franck Ribery	11	156	45	111 mins
4	Jose Ze Roberto	5	144	48	96 mins

SQUAD APPEARANCES

Match	1	2	3	4	5	6	7	8	9	10	11	12	13	14	15	16	17	18	19	20	21	22	23	24
Venue	H	A	H	A	H	H	A	H	A	A	H	A	A	A	H	H	A	H	A	A	H	A	H	A
Competition	L	L	L	L	L	E	L	L	L	E	L	L	E	L	L	E	L	L	E	L	L	L	E	L
Result	W	W	W	D	D	W	W	W	W	W	W	W	W	D	D	D	L	W	D	W	D	D	W	W

Match	25	26	27	28	29	30	31	32	33	34	35	36	37	38	39	40	41	42	43	44	45	46	47	48
Venue	H	A	A	H	H	A	A	H	H	A	H	A	H	H	A	H	A	H	H	A	A	H	A	H
Competition	L	E	L	E	L	L	E	L	E	L	L	L	E	L	E	L	L	E	L	E	L	L	L	L
Result	D	D	W	W	D	W	W	W	L	L	W	D	D	W	D	W	W	D	W	L	D	W	W	W

Goalkeepers
Bernd Dreher
Oliver Kahn
Michael Rensing

Defenders
Lucio
Martin Demichelis
Matts Hummels
Valerien Ismael
Marcell Jansen
Philipp Lahm
Christian Lell
Willy Sagnol
Daniel Van Buyten
Breno

Midfielders
Hamit Altintop
Stephan Furstner
Toni Kroos
Andreas Ottl
Franck Ribery
Jan Schlaudraff
Bastian Schweinsteiger
Jose Ernesto Sosa
Mark van Bommel
Jose Ze Roberto

Forwards
Miroslav Klose
Lukas Podolski
Luca Toni
Sandro Wagner

KEY: On all match | On bench | Subbed or sent off (Counting game) | Subbed or sent off (playing less than 70 minutes) | Subbed on from bench (Counting Game) | Subbed on (playing less than 70 minutes) | Subbed on and then subbed or sent off (Counting Game) | Subbed on and then subbed or sent off (playing less than 70 minutes) | Not in 16

WERDER BREMEN

Final Position: **2nd**

NICKNAME: FISCHKOPPE

KEY: ☐Won ☐Drawn ☐Lost

							Attendance
1	grpr1	**Bochum**	A	D	2-2	Diego 38 pen, Sanogo 45	29,037
2	ecql1	**Dinamo Zagreb**	H	W	2-1	Hugo Almeida 46, D.Jensen 85	33,000
3	grpr1	**Bayern Munich**	H	L	0-4		42,000
4	grpr1	**Nurnberg**	A	W	1-0	Harnik 69	45,200
5	ecql2	**Dinamo Zagreb**	A	W	3-2	Diego 13 pen, 70 pen, Sanogo 38	34,000
6	grpr1	**Eintr Frankfurt**	H	W	2-1	Sanogo 35, Pasanen 80	40,983
7	grpr1	**B Dortmund**	A	L	0-3		79,030
8	ecgpc	**Real Madrid**	A	L	1-2	Sanogo 17	70,000
9	grpr1	**Stuttgart**	H	W	4-1	Hugo Almeida 3, 4, Sanogo 15, Diego 89	40,000
10	grpr1	**Wolfsburg**	A	D	1-1	Diego 48	25,533
11	grpr1	**Arminia B**	H	W	8-1	Niemeyer 17, Hugo Almeida 35, 88, Sanogo 41, 44, Mertesacker 59, Rosenberg 66, Diego 85	40,120
12	ecgpc	**Olympiakos**	H	L	1-3	Hugo Almeida 32	35,000
13	grpr1	**Duisburg**	A	W	3-1	D.Jensen 8, Sanogo 57, Andreasen 87	31,005
14	grpr1	**Hertha Berlin**	H	W	3-2	Hugo Almeida 57, Rosenberg 62, Andreasen 74	40,278
15	ecgpc	**Lazio**	H	W	2-1	Sanogo 28, Hugo Almeida 54	36,587
16	grpr1	**Schalke**	A	D	1-1	Naldo 35	61,428
17	grpr1	**Hansa Rostock**	H	W	1-0	Hugo Almeida 39	41,738
18	ecgpc	**Lazio**	A	L	1-2	Diego 87 pen	35,045
19	grpr1	**Karlsruhe**	H	W	4-0	Diego 25, 45, Hugo Almeida 66, Naldo 76	39,669
20	grpr1	**Cottbus**	A	W	2-0	Diego 63 pen, Mosquera 83	15,000
21	ecgpc	**Real Madrid**	H	W	3-2	Rosenberg 4, Sanogo 40, Hunt 58	36,350
22	grpr1	**Hamburg**	H	W	2-1	Sanogo 16, Pasanen 65	42,100
23	grpr1	**Hannover 96**	A	L	3-4	Rosenberg 10, 53, Diego 39 pen	49,000
24	ecgpc	**Olympiakos**	A	L	0-3		33,500
25	grpr1	**B Leverkusen**	H	W	5-2	Klasnic 30, 63, Diego 49, Fritz 57, Rosenberg 69	39,308
26	grpr1	**Bochum**	H	L	1-2	D.Jensen 44	37,149
27	grpr1	**Bayern Munich**	A	D	1-1	Diego 6	69,000
28	ucrl1	**Braga**	H	W	3-0	Naldo 5, D.Jensen 27, Hugo Almeida 90 pen	25,690
29	grpr1	**Nurnberg**	H	W	2-0	Rosenberg 30, Klasnic 81	37,073
30	ucrl2	**Braga**	A	W	1-0	Klasnic 78	5,706
31	grpr1	**Eintr Frankfurt**	A	L	0-1		51,500
32	grpr1	**B Dortmund**	H	W	2-0	Rosenberg 45, 63	42,100
33	ucrl1	**Rangers**	A	L	0-2		45,959
34	grpr1	**Stuttgart**	A	L	3-6	Hugo Almeida 9, Boenisch 60, Rosenberg 77	55,000
35	ucrl2	**Rangers**	H	W	1-0	Diego 58	33,000
36	grpr1	**Wolfsburg**	H	L	0-1		39,831
37	grpr1	**Arminia B**	A	D	1-1	Diego 70 pen	27,000
38	grpr1	**Duisburg**	H	L	1-2	Diego 58	39,615
39	grpr1	**Hertha Berlin**	A	W	2-1	Rosenberg 1, Borowski 73	59,728
40	grpr1	**Schalke**	H	W	5-1	Baumann 19, Sanogo 32, Rosenberg 59, Klasnic 76, 89	42,100
41	grpr1	**Hansa Rostock**	A	W	2-1	Frings 57, Klasnic 82	22,000
42	grpr1	**Karlsruhe**	A	D	3-3	Diego 23, Ozil 29, Sanogo 86	29,470
43	grpr1	**Cottbus**	H	W	2-0	Rosenberg 67, Hugo Almeida 79	39,687
44	grpr1	**Hamburg**	A	W	1-0	Hugo Almeida 50	57,000
45	grpr1	**Hannover 96**	H	W	6-1	Hugo Almeida 14, Naldo 27, Borowski 73, Klasnic 80, Rosenberg 82, Hunt 87	42,100
46	grpr1	**B Leverkusen**	A	W	1-0	Rosenberg 80	22,500

LEAGUE APPEARANCES, BOOKINGS AND CAPS

	AGE (on 01/07/08)	IN NAMED 18	APPEARANCES	COUNTING GAMES	MINUTES ON PITCH	YELLOW CARDS	RED CARDS	CAPS THIS SEASON	NATIONAL SIDE
Goalkeepers									
Nico Pellatz	21	4	0	0	0	0	0	-	Germany
Christian Vander	27	32	3	3	270	0	0	-	Germany
Tim Wiese	26	31	31	31	2790	4	0	-	Germany
Defenders									
Sebastian Boenisch	21	11	9	5	541	0	0	-	Germany
Clemens Fritz	27	23	23	18	1780	3	0	9	Germany
Per Mertesacker	23	32	32	31	2833	4	1	12	Germany
Naldo	25	32	32	32	2859	3	1	1	Brazil
Patrick Owomoyela	28	17	9	1	362	0	0	-	Germany
Petri Pasanen	27	32	28	23	2300	1	0	-	Finland
Christian Schulz	25	3	3	3	270	1	0	-	Germany
Dusko Tosic	23	26	12	11	1045	4	0	6	Serbia
Midfielders									
Mesut Ozil	19	16	12	5	620	0	0	-	Germany
Leon Andreasen	25	11	10	3	402	1	1	6	Denmark
Frank Baumann	32	25	23	16	1769	4	1	-	Germany
Tim Borowski	28	22	21	17	1649	7	0	2	Germany
Carlos Alberto	23	4	2	0	44	0	0	-	Brazil
Diego	23	30	30	28	2550	4	1	2	Brazil
Torsten Frings	31	11	11	11	941	6	0	6	Germany
Daniel Jensen	29	27	27	23	2239	8	0	5	Denmark
Max Kruse	20	8	1	0	29	0	0	-	Germany
Peter Niemeyer	24	13	3	0	90	0	0	-	Germany
Jurica Vranjes	28	32	22	9	1130	3	1	1	Croatia
Forwards									
Martin Harnik	21	22	9	1	300	0	0	9	Austria
Miguel Hugo Almeida	24	26	23	12	1377	4	1	5	Portugal
Aaron Hunt	21	16	14	6	875	5	0	-	Germany
Ivan Klasnic	28	17	16	4	830	0	0	2	Croatia
John Jairo Mosquera	20	11	3	0	47	0	0	-	Colombia
Markus Rosenberg	25	33	30	17	1989	6	0	5	Sweden
Boubacar Sanogo	25	24	21	14	1531	2	0	3	Ivory Coast
Kevin Schindler	20	12	4	0	76	0	0	-	Germany

TEAM OF THE SEASON

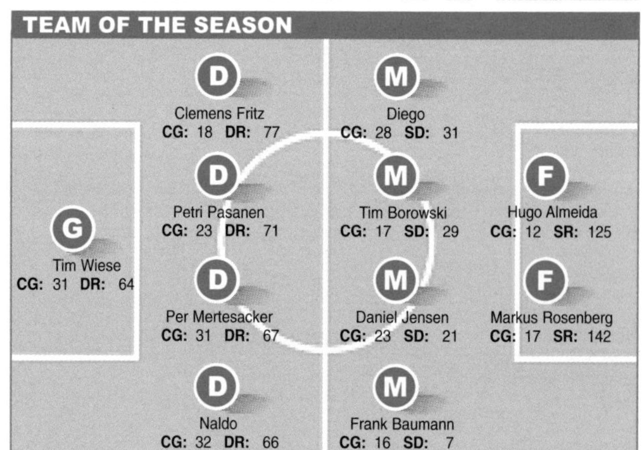

D
Clemens Fritz
CG: 18 DR: 77
M
Diego
CG: 28 SD: 31
D
Petri Pasanen
CG: 23 DR: 71
M
Tim Borowski
CG: 17 SD: 29
F
Hugo Almeida
CG: 12 SR: 125
G
Tim Wiese
CG: 31 DR: 64
D
Per Mertesacker
CG: 31 DR: 67
M
Daniel Jensen
CG: 23 SD: 21
F
Markus Rosenberg
CG: 17 SR: 142
D
Naldo
CG: 32 DR: 66
M
Frank Baumann
CG: 16 SD: 7

MONTHLY POINTS TALLY

AUGUST	4	44%
SEPTEMBER	10	67%
OCTOBER	7	78%
NOVEMBER	9	100%
DECEMBER	6	67%
NO LEAGUE GAMES PLAYED IN JANUARY		
FEBRUARY	4	33%
MARCH	4	27%
APRIL	10	83%
MAY	12	100%

LEAGUE GOALS

	PLAYER	MINS	GOALS	S RATE
1	Rosenberg	1989	14	142
2	Diego	2550	13	196
3	Hugo Almeida	1377	11	125
4	Sanogo	1531	9	170
5	Klasnic	830	7	118
6	Naldo	2859	3	953
7	Andreasen	402	2	201
8	Borowski	1649	2	824
9	Jensen	2239	2	1119
10	Pasanen	2300	2	1150
11	Mosquera	47	1	47
12	Niemeyer	90	1	90
13	Harnik	300	1	300
	Other		7	
	TOTAL		75	

TOP POINT EARNERS

	PLAYER	GAMES	AV PTS
1	Clemens Fritz	18	2.50
2	Petri Pasanen	23	2.35
3	Markus Rosenberg	17	2.18
4	Diego	28	2.14
5	Per Mertesacker	31	2.10
6	Tim Borowski	17	2.00
7	Naldo	32	1.94
8	Miguel Hugo Almeida	12	1.92
9	Daniel Jensen	23	1.87
10	Tim Wiese	31	1.84
	CLUB AVERAGE:		1.94

DISCIPLINARY RECORDS

	PLAYER	YELLOW	RED	AVE
1	Torsten Frings	6	0	156
2	Aaron Hunt	5	0	175
3	Tim Borowski	7	0	235
4	Dusko Tosic	4	0	261
5	Hugo Almeida	4	1	275
6	Daniel Jensen	8	0	279
7	Jurica Vranjes	3	1	282
8	Markus Rosenberg	6	0	331
9	Frank Baumann	4	1	353
10	Diego	4	1	510
11	Per Mertesacker	4	1	566
12	Clemens Fritz	3	0	593
13	Tim Wiese	4	0	697
	Other	6	1	
	TOTAL	68	6	

KEY GOALKEEPER

Tim Wiese

Goals Conceded in the League	43	**Counting Games** League games when player was on pitch for at least 70 minutes	31
Defensive Rating Ave number of mins between League goals conceded while on the pitch	64	**Clean Sheets** In League games when player was on pitch for at least 70 minutes	8

KEY PLAYERS - DEFENDERS

Clemens Fritz

Goals Conceded Number of League goals conceded while the player was on the pitch	23	**Clean Sheets** In League games when player was on pitch for at least 70 minutes	7
Defensive Rating Ave number of mins between League goals conceded while on the pitch	77	**Club Defensive Rating** Average number of mins between League goals conceded by the club this season	68

	PLAYER	CON LGE	CLEAN SHEETS	DEF RATE
1	Clemens Fritz	23	7	77 mins
2	Petri Pasanen	32	7	71 mins
3	Per Mertesacker	42	9	67 mins
4	Naldo	43	8	66 mins

KEY PLAYERS - MIDFIELDERS

Diego

Goals in the League	13	**Contribution to Attacking Power** Average number of minutes between League team goals while on pitch	39
Defensive Rating Average number of mins between League goals conceded while on the pitch	70	**Scoring Difference** Defensive Rating minus Contribution to Attacking Power	31

	PLAYER	LGE GOALS	DEF RATE	POWER	SCORE DIFF
1	Diego	13	70	39	31 mins
2	Tim Borowski	2	74	45	29 mins
3	Daniel Jensen	2	60	39	21 mins
4	Frank Baumann	1	65	58	7 mins

KEY PLAYERS - GOALSCORERS

Miguel Hugo Almeida

Goals in the League	11	**Player Strike Rate** Average number of minutes between League goals scored by player	125
Contribution to Attacking Power Average number of minutes between League team goals while on pitch	41	**Club Strike Rate** Average number of minutes between League goals scored by club	40

	PLAYER	LGE GOALS	POWER	STRIKE RATE
1	Miguel Hugo Almeida	11	41	125 mins
2	Markus Rosenberg	14	36	142 mins
3	Boubacar Sanogo	9	43	170 mins
4	Diego	13	39	196 mins

BAUMANN
6
WERDER BREMEN
bank
Diego and Frank Baumann

SQUAD APPEARANCES

Match	1	2	3	4	5	6	7	8	9	10	11	12	13	14	15	16	17	18	19	20	21	22	23	24	25	26	27	28	29	30	31	32	33	34	35	36	37	38	39	40	41	42	43	44	45	46
Venue	A	H	H	A	A	H	A	A	H	A	H	H	A	H	H	A	H	A	H	A	H	H	A	A	H	H	A	H	H	A	A	H	A	A	H	H	A	H	A	H	A	A	H	A	H	A
Competition	L	C	L	L	C	L	L	C	L	L	L	C	L	L	C	L	L	C	L	L	C	L	L	C	L	L	L	E	L	E	L	L	E	L	E	L	L	L	L	L	L	L	L	L	L	L
Result	D	W	L	W	W	W	L	L	W	D	W	L	W	W	W	D	W	L	W	W	W	W	L	L	W	L	D	W	W	W	L	W	L	L	W	L	D	L	W	W	W	D	W	W	W	W

Goalkeepers
- Nico Pellatz
- Christian Vander
- Tim Wiese

Defenders
- Sebastian Boenisch
- Clemens Fritz
- Per Mertesacker
- Naldo
- Patrick Owomoyela
- Petri Pasanen
- Christian Schulz
- Dusko Tosic

Midfielders
- Mesut Ozil
- Leon Andreasen
- Frank Baumann
- Tim Borowski
- Carlos Alberto
- Diego
- Torsten Frings
- Daniel Jensen
- Max Kruse
- Peter Niemeyer
- Jurica Vranjes

Forwards
- Martin Harnik
- Miguel Hugo Almeida
- Aaron Hunt
- Ivan Klasnic
- John Jairo Mosquera
- Markus Rosenberg
- Boubacar Sanogo
- Kevin Schindler

KEY: On all match | On bench | Subbed or sent off (Counting game) | Subbed or sent off (playing less than 70 minutes) | Subbed on from bench (Counting Game) | Subbed on (playing less than 70 minutes) | Subbed on and then subbed or sent off (Counting Game) | Subbed on and then subbed or sent off (playing less than 70 minutes) | Not in 16

SCHALKE 04

Final Position: **3rd**

NICKNAME: KONIGSBLAUE

KEY: ☐ Won ☐ Drawn ☐ Lost

#	Comp	Opponent	H/A	Res	Score	Scorers	Attendance
1	grpr1	**Stuttgart**	A	D	2-2	Kobiashvili 25, Rakitic 76	55,800
2	grpr1	**B Dortmund**	H	W	4-1	Bordon 11, Pander 31, Asamoah 59, Kuranyi 78	61,482
3	grpr1	**Wolfsburg**	A	D	1-1	Hal.Altintop 86	28,000
4	grpr1	**B Leverkusen**	H	D	1-1	Kuranyi 45	61,482
5	grpr1	**Bayern Munich**	A	D	1-1	Rakitic 36	69,000
6	ecgpb	**Valencia**	H	L	0-1		53,951
7	grpr1	**Arminia B**	H	W	3-0	Kuranyi 24, Asamoah 54, Rafinha 65 pen	61,482
8	grpr1	**Duisburg**	A	W	2-0	Hal.Altintop 3, Kuranyi 75	31,500
9	grpr1	**Hertha Berlin**	H	W	1-0	Rafinha 44 pen	61,482
10	ecgpb	**Rosenborg BK**	A	W	2-0	Jones 62, Kuranyi 89	22,000
11	grpr1	**Karlsruhe**	H	L	0-2		61,000
12	grpr1	**Hansa Rostock**	A	D	1-1	Asamoah 33	29,000
13	ecgpb	**Chelsea**	A	L	0-2		35,000
14	grpr1	**W Bremen**	H	D	1-1	Grossmuller 14	61,428
15	grpr1	**Cottbus**	A	L	0-1		17,012
16	ecgpb	**Chelsea**	H	D	0-0		53,951
17	grpr1	**Hamburg**	H	D	1-1	Krstajic 12	61,482
18	grpr1	**Hannover 96**	A	W	3-2	Kuranyi 41, 50, Hal.Altintop 61	49,000
19	ecgpb	**Valencia**	A	D	0-0		30,000
20	grpr1	**Bochum**	H	W	1-0	Bordon 32	61,482
21	grpr1	**Eintr Frankfurt**	A	D	2-2	Westermann 78, 90	51,500
22	ecgpb	**Rosenborg BK**	H	W	3-1	Asamoah 12, Rafinha 19, Kuranyi 36	53,951
23	grpr1	**Nurnberg**	H	W	2-1	Asamoah 14, Engelhardt 35 og	61,500
24	grpr1	**Stuttgart**	H	W	4-1	Kuranyi 32, 52, Westermann 76, de Oliveira 90	61,482
25	grpr1	**B Dortmund**	A	W	3-2	Asamoah 19, Amedick 30 og, Ernst 82	80,708
26	grpr1	**Wolfsburg**	H	L	1-2	Sanchez Bragunde 65	60,387
27	eckl1	**Porto**	H	W	1-0	Kuranyi 4	53,951
28	grpr1	**B Leverkusen**	A	L	0-1		22,500
29	grpr1	**Bayern Munich**	H	L	0-1		61,482
30	eckl2	**Porto**	A	W	4-1*	(*on penalties)	45,316
31	grpr1	**Arminia B**	A	W	2-0	Varela 24, Hal.Altintop 74	26,100
32	grpr1	**Duisburg**	H	W	2-1	Kuranyi 60, Westermann 74	61,482
33	grpr1	**Hertha Berlin**	A	W	2-1	Asamoah 12, Jones 23	60,000
34	grpr1	**Karlsruhe**	A	D	0-0		29,477
35	ecqfl1	**Barcelona**	H	L	0-1		53,951
36	grpr1	**Hansa Rostock**	H	W	1-0	Hal.Altintop 52	61,482
37	ecqfl2	**Barcelona**	A	L	0-1		88,000
38	grpr1	**W Bremen**	A	L	1-5	Kuranyi 42	42,100
39	grpr1	**Cottbus**	H	W	5-0	da Silva 31 og, Kuranyi 37, 41, 59, 80	60,018
40	grpr1	**Hamburg**	A	W	1-0	Kuranyi 2	57,000
41	grpr1	**Hannover 96**	H	D	1-1	Hal.Altintop 40	61,482
42	grpr1	**Bochum**	A	W	3-0	Asamoah 34, Rakitic 67, Bordon 85	31,328
43	grpr1	**Eintr Frankfurt**	H	W	1-0	Krstajic 65	61,482
44	grpr1	**Nurnberg**	A	W	2-0	Bordon 19, 61	46,800

LEAGUE APPEARANCES, BOOKINGS AND CAPS

	AGE (on 01/07/08)	IN NAMED 18	APPEARANCES	COUNTING GAMES	MINUTES ON PITCH	YELLOW CARDS	RED CARDS	CAPS THIS SEASON	NATIONAL SIDE
Goalkeepers									
Manuel Neuer	22	34	34	34	3060	2	0	-	Germany
Matthias Schober	32	34	0	0	0	1	0	-	Germany
Defenders									
Mathias Abel	27	3	0	0	0	0	0	-	Germany
Sebastian Boenisch	21	1	0	0	0	0	0	-	Germany
Marcelo Jose Bordon	32	31	31	31	2767	8	0	-	Brazil
Benedikt Howedes	20	27	6	3	297	0	0	-	Germany
Mladen Krstajic	34	24	23	22	1999	5	0	2	Serbia
Christian Pander	24	17	17	15	1451	0	0	-	Germany
Rafinha	22	32	32	31	2796	6	0	1	Brazil
Dario Rodriguez	33	9	3	2	184	0	0	1	Uruguay
Heiko Westermann	24	34	32	31	2784	1	0	3	Germany
Carlos Zambrano	18	1	0	0	0	0	0	-	Peru
Midfielders									
Mesut Ozil	19	13	11	3	560	0	0	-	Germany
Mimoun Azaouagh	25	13	5	0	51	0	0	-	Germany
Zlatan Bajramovic	28	17	12	8	753	3	0	2	Bosnia
J Roberto de Oliveira	27	5	3	0	35	0	0	-	Brazil
Fabian Ernst	29	33	33	32	2931	5	0	-	Germany
Carlos Grossmuller	25	25	12	6	580	2	1	-	Uruguay
Jermaine Jones	26	31	30	27	2557	10	1	2	Germany
Levan Kobiashvili	30	17	13	8	767	1	0	-	Georgia
Ivan Rakitic	20	29	29	20	1959	1	0	8	Croatia
Albert Streit	28	15	10	5	540	1	0	-	Germany
Gustavo A Varela	30	8	2	0	90	0	0	-	Uruguay
Forwards									
Halil Altintop	25	28	25	10	1326	0	0	3	Turkey
Gerald Asamoah	29	33	31	16	1894	4	0	-	Germany
Kevin Kuranyi	26	32	32	30	2744	6	0	9	Germany
Peter Lovenkrands	28	30	20	4	820	1	0	3	Denmark
Soren Larsen	26	16	10	1	230	0	0	1	Denmark
Vicente Bragunde	28	16	14	3	568	0	0	-	Uruguay
Dominique Wassi	18	1	0	0	0	0	0	-	Cameroon

TEAM OF THE SEASON

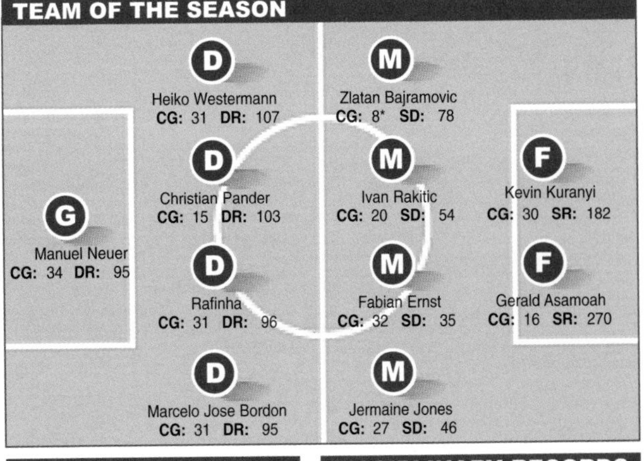

D
Heiko Westermann
CG: 31 DR: 107
M
Zlatan Bajramovic
CG: 8* SD: 78
D
Christian Pander
CG: 15 DR: 103
M
Ivan Rakitic
CG: 20 SD: 54
F
Kevin Kuranyi
CG: 30 SR: 182
G
Manuel Neuer
CG: 34 DR: 95
D
Rafinha
CG: 31 DR: 96
M
Fabian Ernst
CG: 32 SD: 35
F
Gerald Asamoah
CG: 16 SR: 270
D
Marcelo Jose Bordon
CG: 31 DR: 95
M
Jermaine Jones
CG: 27 SD: 46

MONTHLY POINTS TALLY

Month	Points	%
AUGUST	6	50%
SEPTEMBER	10	83%
OCTOBER	2	22%
NOVEMBER	4	44%
DECEMBER	7	78%
NO LEAGUE GAMES PLAYED IN JANUARY		
FEBRUARY	6	50%
MARCH	10	67%
APRIL	9	75%
MAY	10	83%

LEAGUE GOALS

	PLAYER	MINS	GOALS	S RATE
1	Kuranyi	2744	15	182
2	Asamoah	1894	7	270
3	Altintop, Hal	1326	6	221
4	Bordon	2767	5	553
5	Westermann	2784	4	696
6	Rakitic	1959	3	653
7	Krstajic	1999	2	999
8	Rafinha	2796	2	1398
9	de Oliveira	35	1	35
10	Varela	90	1	90
11	Grossmuller	496	1	496
12	S Bragunde	568	1	568
13	Kobiashvili	767	1	767
	Other		3	
	TOTAL		52	

TOP POINT EARNERS

	PLAYER	GAMES	AV PTS
1	Ivan Rakitic	20	2.20
2	Christian Pander	15	2.13
3	Jermaine Jones	27	2.04
4	Marcelo Jose Bordon	31	1.90
5	Kevin Kuranyi	30	1.90
6	Heiko Westermann	31	1.90
7	Manuel Neuer	34	1.88
8	Fabian Ernst	32	1.88
9	Rafinha	31	1.87
10	Mladen Krstajic	22	1.77
	CLUB AVERAGE:		1.88

DISCIPLINARY RECORDS

	PLAYER	YELLOW	RED	AVE
1	Jermaine Jones	10	1	232
2	Carlos Grossmuller	2	0	248
3	Zlatan Bajramovic	3	0	251
4	Marcelo J Bordon	8	0	345
5	Mladen Krstajic	5	0	399
6	Kevin Kuranyi	6	0	457
7	Rafinha	6	0	466
8	Gerald Asamoah	4	0	473
9	Albert Streit	1	0	540
10	Fabian Ernst	5	0	586
11	Levan Kobiashvili	1	0	767
12	Peter Lovenkrands	1	0	820
13	Manuel Neuer	2	0	1530
	Other	2	0	
	TOTAL	56	1	

KEY GOALKEEPER

Manuel Neuer

Goals Conceded in the League	32	**Counting Games** League games when player was on pitch for at least 70 minutes	34
Defensive Rating Ave number of mins between League goals conceded while on the pitch	95	**Clean Sheets** In League games when player was on pitch for at least 70 minutes	12

KEY PLAYERS - DEFENDERS

Heiko Westermann

Goals Conceded Number of League goals conceded while the player was on the pitch	26	**Clean Sheets** In League games when player was on pitch for at least 70 minutes	12
Defensive Rating Ave number of mins between League goals conceded while on the pitch	107	**Club Defensive Rating** Average number of mins between League goals conceded by the club this season	95

	PLAYER	CON LGE	CLEAN SHEETS	DEF RATE
1	Heiko Westermann	26	12	107 mins
2	Christian Pander	14	6	103 mins
3	Rafinha	29	10	96 mins
4	Marcelo Jose Bordon	29	12	95 mins

KEY PLAYERS - MIDFIELDERS

Zlatan Bajramovic

Goals in the League	0	**Contribution to Attacking Power** Average number of minutes between League team goals while on pitch	47
Defensive Rating Average number of mins between League goals conceded while on the pitch	125	**Scoring Difference** Defensive Rating minus Contribution to Attacking Power	78

	PLAYER	LGE GOALS	DEF RATE	POWER	SCORE DIFF
1	Zlatan Bajramovic	0	125	47	78 mins
2	Ivan Rakitic	3	108	54	54 mins
4	Jermaine Jones	1	102	56	46 mins
5	Fabian Ernst	1	91	56	35 mins

KEY PLAYERS - GOALSCORERS

Kevin Kuranyi

Goals in the League	15	**Player Strike Rate** Average number of minutes between League goals scored by player	182
Contribution to Attacking Power Average number of minutes between League team goals while on pitch	57	**Club Strike Rate** Average number of minutes between League goals scored by club	55

	PLAYER	LGE GOALS	POWER	STRIKE RATE
1	Kevin Kuranyi	15	57	182 mins
2	Gerald Asamoah	7	55	270 mins
3	Ivan Rakitic	3	54	653 mins
4	Jermaine Jones	1	56	2557 mins

GAZPROM
Rafinha and Kevin Kuranyi

SQUAD APPEARANCES

Match	1	2	3	4	5	6	7	8	9	10	11	12	13	14	15	16	17	18	19	20	21	22	23	24	25	26	27	28	29	30	31	32	33	34	35	36	37	38	39	40	41	42	43	44
Venue	A	H	A	H	A	H	H	A	H	A	H	A	A	H	A	H	H	A	A	H	A	H	H	H	A	H	H	A	H	A	A	H	A	A	H	H	A	A	H	A	H	A	H	A
Competition	L	L	L	L	L	C	L	L	L	C	L	L	C	L	L	C	L	L	C	L	L	C	L	L	L	L	C	L	L	C	L	L	L	L	C	L	C	L	L	L	L	L	L	L
Result	D	W	D	D	D	L	W	W	W	W	L	D	L	D	L	D	D	W	D	W	D	W	W	W	W	L	W	L	L	W	W	W	W	D	L	W	L	L	W	W	D	W	W	W

Goalkeepers
Manuel Neuer
Matthias Schober

Defenders
Mathias Abel
Sebastian Boenisch
Marcelo Jose Bordon
Benedikt Howedes
Mladen Krstajic
Christian Pander
Rafinha
Dario Rodriguez
Heiko Westermann
Carlos Zambrano

Midfielders
Mesut Ozil
Mimoun Azaouagh
Zlatan Bajramovic
Jose Roberto de Oliveira
Fabian Ernst
Carlos Grossmuller
Jermaine Jones
Levan Kobiashvili
Ivan Rakitic
Albert Streit
Gustavo Antonio Varela

Forwards
Halil Altintop
Gerald Asamoah
Kevin Kuranyi
Peter Lovenkrands
Soren Larsen
Vicente Bragunde
Dominique Wassi

KEY: On all match | On bench | ⏮ Subbed or sent off (Counting game) | « Subbed or sent off (playing less than 70 minutes) | Subbed on from bench (Counting Game) | » Subbed on (playing less than 70 minutes) | Subbed on and then subbed or sent off (Counting Game) | Subbed on and then subbed or sent off (playing less than 70 minutes) | Not in 16

HAMBURG SV

Final Position: **4th**

NICKNAME: HSV

KEY: ☐ Won ☐ Drawn ☐ Lost

	Comp	Opponent	Venue	Res	Score	Scorers	Attendance
1	grpr1	Hannover 96	A	W	1-0	Benjamin 23	49,000
2	ucql1	Budapest H	A	D	0-0		9,000
3	grpr1	B Leverkusen	H	W	1-0	Van der Vaart 64 pen	52,000
4	grpr1	Bochum	A	L	1-2	Van der Vaart 86 pen	27,000
5	ucql2	Budapest H	H	W	4-0	Guerrero 10, 39, Smiljanic 50 og, Choupo-Moting 90	42,090
6	grpr1	Bayern Munich	H	D	1-1	Zidan 87	57,000
7	grpr1	Eintr Frankfurt	A	L	1-2	Van der Vaart 82 pen	51,500
8	ucrl1	Liteks Lovetch	A	W	1-0	Castelen 75	7,000
9	grpr1	Nurnberg	H	W	1-0	Van der Vaart 53	52,365
10	grpr1	B Dortmund	A	W	3-0	Guerrero 7, Van der Vaart 42, Olic 64	70,000
11	grpr1	Wolfsburg	H	D	2-2	Reinhardt 17, Van der Vaart 71	54,000
12	ucrl2	Liteks Lovetch	H	W	3-1	Guerrero 40, 52, Van der Vaart 72	43,000
13	grpr1	Arminia B	A	W	1-0	Van der Vaart 49	22,800
14	grpr1	Stuttgart	H	W	4-1	Olic 7, 22, 35, Mathijsen 60	57,000
15	ucgpd	SK Brann	A	W	1-0	Kompany 62	16,000
16	grpr1	Duisburg	A	W	1-0	Kompany 37	30,160
17	grpr1	Hertha Berlin	H	W	2-1	Guerrero 4, Reinhardt 80	56,493
18	grpr1	Schalke	A	D	1-1	Olic 35	61,482
19	grpr1	Hansa Rostock	H	W	2-0	Van der Vaart 19, Olic 62	57,000
20	ucgpd	Rennes	H	W	3-0	Van der Vaart 30, Choupo-Moting 83, Zidan 90 pen	36,472
21	grpr1	W Bremen	A	L	1-2	Van der Vaart 61	42,100
22	ucgpd	Dinamo Zagreb	A	W	2-0	de Jong 88, Trochowski 90 pen	27,388
23	grpr1	Cottbus	H	D	0-0		56,000
24	grpr1	Karlsruhe	A	D	1-1	Olic 90	30,300
25	ucgpd	Basel	H	D	1-1	Olic 73	48,917
26	grpr1	Hannover 96	H	D	1-1	Olic 70	57,000
27	grpr1	B Leverkusen	A	D	1-1	Van der Vaart 27	22,500
28	ucrl1	Zurich	A	W	3-1	Jarolim 49, Olic 67, Trochowski 77	16,800
29	grpr1	Bochum	H	W	3-0	Olic 40, Jarolim 64, 71	50,069
30	ucrl2	Zurich	H	D	0-0		33,586
31	grpr1	Bayern Munich	A	D	1-1	Olic 60	69,000
32	grpr1	Eintr Frankfurt	H	W	4-1	Guerrero 5, 79, de Jong 57, Zidan 83	53,787
33	ucrl1	B Leverkusen	A	L	0-1		22,500
34	grpr1	Nurnberg	A	D	0-0		44,900
35	ucrl2	B Leverkusen	H	W	3-2	Trochowski 53, Guerrero 64, Van der Vaart 80	38,083
36	grpr1	B Dortmund	H	W	1-0	Guerrero 63	57,000
37	grpr1	Wolfsburg	A	D	1-1	Reinhardt 14	30,000
38	grpr1	Arminia B	H	D	1-1	Guerrero 82	56,398
39	grpr1	Stuttgart	A	L	0-1		55,800
40	grpr1	Duisburg	H	L	0-1		54,218
41	grpr1	Hertha Berlin	A	D	0-0		40,289
42	grpr1	Schalke	H	L	0-1		57,000
43	grpr1	Hansa Rostock	A	W	3-1	Olic 18, 51, Van der Vaart 27	28,000
44	grpr1	W Bremen	H	L	0-1		57,000
45	grpr1	Cottbus	A	L	0-2		22,746
46	grpr1	Karlsruhe	H	W	7-0	Van der Vaart 23 pen, Guerrero 34, 43, 49, Trochowski 57, Olic 78, 89	57,000

LEAGUE APPEARANCES, BOOKINGS AND CAPS

	AGE (on 01/07/08)	IN NAMED 18	APPEARANCES	COUNTING GAMES	MINUTES ON PITCH	YELLOW CARDS	RED CARDS	CAPS THIS SEASON	NATIONAL SIDE
Goalkeepers									
Wolfgang Hesl	22	34	1	0	17	0	0	-	Germany
Frank Rost	35	34	34	34	3043	1	0	-	Germany
Defenders									
Timothee Atouba	26	23	22	15	1574	6	0	-	Cameroon
Jerome Boateng	19	29	27	21	2148	5	0	-	Germany
Miso Brecko	24	31	14	4	610	1	0	-	Slovenia
Guy Demel	27	26	26	21	2121	2	0	1	Ivory Coast
Vincent Kompany	22	24	22	14	1529	3	1	8	Belgium
Sebastian Langkamp	20	4	0	0	0	0	0	-	Germany
Joris Mathijsen	28	31	31	31	2789	4	1	11	Holland
Bastian Reinhardt	32	34	32	29	2686	2	0	-	Germany
Volker Schmidt	29	2	0	0	0	0	0	-	Germany
Juan Pablo Sorin	32	7	5	0	118	0	0	-	Argentina
Midfielders									
Otto Addo	33	11	4	0	24	1	0	-	Ghana
Anis Ben-Hatira	19	19	3	1	114	0	0	-	Germany
Collin Benjamin	29	22	17	10	1079	0	0	-	Namibia
Romeo Castelen	25	13	13	6	695	2	0	-	Holland
Nigel de Jong	23	31	29	27	2488	6	0	7	Holland
Mario Fillinger	23	4	1	0	1	0	0	-	Germany
David Jarolim	29	28	28	24	2216	8	1	6	Czech Republic
Vadis Odjidja-Ofoe	19	6	2	0	10	0	0	-	Belgium
Anton Putsilo	21	13	3	0	18	0	0	-	Belarus
Kosi Saka	22	1	0	0	0	0	0	-	Congo DR
Piotr Trochowski	24	34	32	19	2103	0	0	8	Germany
Rafael Van der Vaart	25	29	29	28	2522	6	0	12	Holland
Forwards									
E M Choupo-Moting	19	21	13	0	326	0	0	-	Germany
Jose Paolo Guerrero	24	29	29	20	2060	3	0	-	Peru
Ivica Olic	28	32	32	26	2421	3	0	10	Croatia
Sidney Sam	20	9	4	0	55	0	0	-	Germany
Mohammed Zidan	26	25	21	6	836	1	0	3	Egypt

TEAM OF THE SEASON

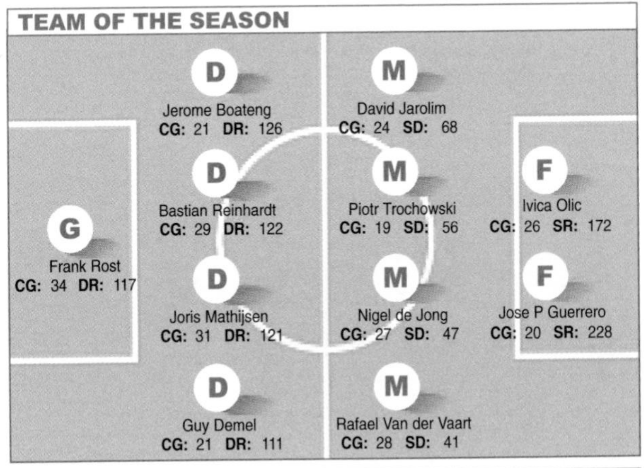
D
Jerome Boateng
CG: 21 DR: 126
M
David Jarolim
CG: 24 SD: 68
D
Bastian Reinhardt
CG: 29 DR: 122
M
Piotr Trochowski
CG: 19 SD: 56
F
Ivica Olic
CG: 26 SR: 172
G
Frank Rost
CG: 34 DR: 117
D
Joris Mathijsen
CG: 31 DR: 121
M
Nigel de Jong
CG: 27 SD: 47
F
Jose P Guerrero
CG: 20 SR: 228
D
Guy Demel
CG: 21 DR: 111
M
Rafael Van der Vaart
CG: 28 SD: 41

MONTHLY POINTS TALLY

Month	Points	%
AUGUST	6	67%
SEPTEMBER	8	53%
OCTOBER	9	100%
NOVEMBER	7	78%
DECEMBER	2	22%
NO LEAGUE GAMES PLAYED IN JANUARY		
FEBRUARY	6	50%
MARCH	9	60%
APRIL	1	8%
MAY	6	50%

LEAGUE GOALS

	PLAYER	MINS	GOALS	S RATE
1	Olic	2421	14	172
2	Van der Vaart	2522	12	210
3	Guerrero	2060	9	228
4	Reinhardt	2686	3	895
5	Zidan	836	2	418
6	Jarolim	2216	2	1108
7	Benjamin	1079	1	1079
8	Kompany	1529	1	1529
9	Trochowski	2103	1	2103
10	de Jong	2488	1	2488
11	Mathijsen	2789	1	2789
	Other		0	
	TOTAL		47	

TOP POINT EARNERS

	PLAYER	GAMES	AV PTS
1	David Jarolim	24	1.79
2	Guy Demel	21	1.76
3	Piotr Trochowski	19	1.74
4	Joris Mathijsen	31	1.71
5	Ivica Olic	26	1.65
6	Vincent Kompany	14	1.64
7	Bastian Reinhardt	29	1.62
8	Frank Rost	34	1.59
9	Rafael Van der Vaart	28	1.50
10	Jerome Boateng	21	1.48
	CLUB AVERAGE:		1.59

DISCIPLINARY RECORDS

	PLAYER	YELLOW	RED	AVE
1	David Jarolim	8	1	246
2	Timothee Atouba	6	0	262
3	Romeo Castelen	2	0	347
4	Vincent Kompany	3	1	382
5	Nigel de Jong	6	0	414
6	R Van der Vaart	6	0	420
7	Jerome Boateng	5	0	429
8	Joris Mathijsen	4	1	557
9	Miso Brecko	1	0	610
10	Jose P Guerrero	3	0	686
11	Ivica Olic	3	0	807
12	Mohammed Zidan	1	0	836
13	Guy Demel	2	0	1060
	Other	3	0	
	TOTAL	53	3	

KEY GOALKEEPER

Frank Rost

Goals Conceded in the League	26	**Counting Games** League games when player was on pitch for at least 70 minutes	34
Defensive Rating Ave number of mins between League goals conceded while on the pitch	117	**Clean Sheets** In League games when player was on pitch for at least 70 minutes	13

KEY PLAYERS - DEFENDERS

Jerome Boateng

Goals Conceded Number of League goals conceded while the player was on the pitch	17	**Clean Sheets** In League games when player was on pitch for at least 70 minutes	7
Defensive Rating Ave number of mins between League goals conceded while on the pitch	126	**Club Defensive Rating** Average number of mins between League goals conceded by the club this season	117

	PLAYER	CON LGE	CLEAN SHEETS	DEF RATE
1	Jerome Boateng	17	7	126 mins
2	Bastian Reinhardt	22	11	122 mins
3	Joris Mathijsen	23	13	121 mins
4	Guy Demel	19	9	111 mins

KEY PLAYERS - MIDFIELDERS

David Jarolim

Goals in the League	2	**Contribution to Attacking Power** Average number of minutes between League team goals while on pitch	55
Defensive Rating Average number of mins between League goals conceded while on the pitch	123	**Scoring Difference** Defensive Rating minus Contribution to Attacking Power	68

	PLAYER	LGE GOALS	DEF RATE	POWER	SCORE DIFF
1	David Jarolim	2	123	55	68 mins
2	Piotr Trochowski	1	123	67	56 mins
3	Nigel de Jong	1	118	71	47 mins
4	Rafael Van der Vaart	12	109	68	41 mins

KEY PLAYERS - GOALSCORERS

Ivica Olic

Goals in the League	14	**Player Strike Rate** Average number of minutes between League goals scored by player	172
Contribution to Attacking Power Average number of minutes between League team goals while on pitch	60	**Club Strike Rate** Average number of minutes between League goals scored by club	65

	PLAYER	LGE GOALS	POWER	STRIKE RATE
1	Ivica Olic	14	60	172 mins
2	Rafael Van der Vaart	12	68	210 mins
3	Jose Paolo Guerrero	9	60	228 mins
4	David Jarolim	2	55	1108 mins

adidas
Rafael Van der Vaart

SQUAD APPEARANCES

Match	1	2	3	4	5	6	7	8	9	10	11	12	13	14	15	16	17	18	19	20	21	22	23	24	25	26	27	28	29	30	31	32	33	34	35	36	37	38	39	40	41	42	43	44	45	46
Venue	A	A	H	A	H	H	A	A	H	A	H	H	A	H	A	A	H	A	H	H	A	A	H	A	H	H	A	A	H	H	A	H	A	A	H	H	A	H	A	H	A	H	A	H	A	H
Competition	L	E	L	L	E	L	L	E	L	L	L	E	L	L	E	L	L	L	L	E	L	E	L	L	E	L	L	E	L	E	L	L	E	L	E	L	L	L	L	L	L	L	L	L	L	L
Result	W	D	W	L	W	D	L	W	W	W	D	W	W	W	W	W	W	D	W	W	L	W	D	D	D	D	D	W	W	D	D	W	L	D	W	W	D	D	L	L	D	L	W	L	L	W

Goalkeepers
- Wolfgang Hesl
- Frank Rost

Defenders
- Timothee Atouba
- Jerome Boateng
- Miso Brecko
- Guy Demel
- Vincent Kompany
- Sebastian Langkamp
- Joris Mathijsen
- Bastian Reinhardt
- Volker Schmidt
- Juan Pablo Sorin

Midfielders
- Otto Addo
- Anis Ben-Hatira
- Collin Benjamin
- Romeo Castelen
- Macauley Chrisantus
- Nigel de Jong
- Mario Fillinger
- David Jarolim
- Vadis Odjidja-Ofoe
- Anton Putsilo
- Kosi Saka
- Piotr Trochowski
- Rafael Van der Vaart

Forwards
- Eric Choupo-Moting
- Jose Paolo Guerrero
- Ivica Olic
- Sidney Sam
- Mohammed Zidan

KEY: On all match · On bench · Subbed or sent off (Counting game) · Subbed or sent off (playing less than 70 minutes) · Subbed on from bench (Counting Game) · Subbed on (playing less than 70 minutes) · Subbed on and then subbed or sent off (Counting Game) · Subbed on and then subbed or sent off (playing less than 70 minutes) · Not in 16

VfL WOLFSBURG

Final Position: **5th**

NICKNAME: DIE WOLFE

KEY: ☐Won ☐Drawn ☐Lost

							Attendance
1	grpr1	**Arminia B**	H	L	1-3	Radu 84	20,000
2	grpr1	**Duisburg**	A	W	3-1	Marcelinho 41, Madlung 52, Radu 72	18,000
3	grpr1	**Schalke**	H	D	1-1	Krzynowek 36	28,000
4	grpr1	**Hertha Berlin**	A	L	1-2	Dejagah 60	40,000
5	grpr1	**Karlsruhe**	H	L	1-2	Krzynowek 21	21,600
6	grpr1	**Cottbus**	A	W	2-1	Dzeko 22, Krzynowek 81	15,269
7	grpr1	**W Bremen**	H	D	1-1	Josue 65	25,533
8	grpr1	**Hamburg**	A	D	2-2	Grafite 57 pen, Dejagah 89	54,000
9	grpr1	**Hansa Rostock**	H	W	1-0	Dzeko 88	26,100
10	grpr1	**Hannover 96**	A	D	2-2	Marcelinho 21, Dejagah 30	37,812
11	grpr1	**Nurnberg**	H	W	3-1	Charisteas 30 og, Grafite 34, Dejagah 67	19,798
12	grpr1	**Bochum**	A	L	3-5	Schafer 49, Grafite 56, 72	20,940
13	grpr1	**B Leverkusen**	H	L	1-2	Friedrich 70 og	20,000
14	grpr1	**Bayern Munich**	A	L	1-2	Dejagah 71	69,000
15	grpr1	**Eintr Frankfurt**	H	D	2-2	Gentner 7, Dzeko 48	20,656
16	grpr1	**Stuttgart**	A	L	1-3	Dzeko 51	53,000
17	grpr1	**B Dortmund**	H	W	4-0	Schafer 9, Ricardo Costa 11, Gentner 60, Dzeko 78	29,000
18	grpr1	**Arminia B**	A	W	1-0	Grafite 27	17,000
19	grpr1	**Duisburg**	H	W	2-1	Schafer 36, Grafite 54	18,000
20	grpr1	**Schalke**	A	W	2-1	Grafite 73, 84 pen	60,387
21	grpr1	**Hertha Berlin**	H	D	0-0		23,659
22	grpr1	**Karlsruhe**	A	L	1-3	Schafer 28	27,871
23	grpr1	**Cottbus**	H	W	3-0	Gentner 17, Marcelinho 19, 76	21,460
24	grpr1	**W Bremen**	A	W	1-0	Grafite 50	39,831
25	grpr1	**Hamburg**	H	D	1-1	Ljuboja 52	30,000
26	grpr1	**Hansa Rostock**	A	W	1-0	Krzynowek 90	15,000
27	grpr1	**Hannover 96**	H	W	3-2	Dejagah 20, 71, Marcelinho 29	29,322
28	grpr1	**Bochum**	H	L	0-1		18,101
29	grpr1	**Nurnberg**	A	L	0-1		45,100
30	grpr1	**B Leverkusen**	A	D	2-2	Dzeko 13, Hasebe 43	22,500
31	grpr1	**Bayern Munich**	H	D	0-0		30,000
32	grpr1	**Eintr Frankfurt**	A	W	3-2	Grafite 4, Schafer 28, Dzeko 79	45,300
33	grpr1	**Stuttgart**	H	W	4-0	Marcelinho 16, Dzeko 22, Ricardo Costa 55, Dejagah 75	28,001
34	grpr1	**B Dortmund**	A	W	4-2	Riether 3, Marcelinho 6, Schafer 62, Grafite 76	75,000

LEAGUE APPEARANCES, BOOKINGS AND CAPS

	AGE (on 01/07/08)	IN NAMED 18	APPEARANCES	COUNTING GAMES	MINUTES ON PITCH	YELLOW CARDS	RED CARDS	CAPS THIS SEASON	NATIONAL SIDE
Goalkeepers									
Diego Benaglio	24	17	17	17	1530	1	0	5	Switzerland
Simon Jentzsch	32	15	15	14	1305	1	0	-	Germany
Andre Lenz	34	33	3	3	255	0	0	-	Germany
Defenders									
Sergej Karimov	21	5	4	3	284	0	0	-	Germany
Uwe Mohrle	28	1	1	1	90	0	0	-	Germany
Alexander Madlung	25	31	27	22	2139	5	1	-	Germany
Facundo Quiroga	30	16	12	6	809	2	0	-	Argentina
Ricardo Costa	27	20	20	18	1725	8	0	-	Portugal
Marcel Schafer	24	34	29	26	2471	3	0	-	Germany
Jan Simunek	21	31	30	25	2374	4	0	-	Czech Republic
Peter van der Heyden	31	2	1	1	90	0	0	-	Belgium
Midfielders									
Daniel Baier	24	31	15	7	919	2	0	-	Germany
Christian Gentner	22	32	31	22	2280	2	0	-	Germany
Makoto Hasebe	24	16	16	10	1113	2	0	-	Japan
Josue	28	30	30	24	2423	7	1	-	Brazil
Jacek Krzynowek	32	25	19	6	920	0	0	9	Poland
Alexander Laas	24	12	4	0	88	1	0	-	Germany
Marcelinho	33	34	33	31	2755	2	0	-	Brazil
Vlad Munteanu	27	13	10	1	323	0	0	-	Romania
Sascha Riether	25	32	27	23	2169	1	0	-	Germany
Jonathan Santana	26	12	10	5	653	2	0	2	Paraguay
Pablo Thiam	34	15	10	4	625	1	0	-	Guinea
Forwards									
Isaac Boakye	26	9	2	0	98	0	0	-	Ghana
Ashkan Dejagah	21	33	31	15	1883	5	0	-	Iran
Edin Dzeko	22	31	28	17	1840	3	0	3	Bosnia
Libano Batista Grafite	21	25	24	18	1896	9	1	-	Brazil
Danijel Ljuboja	30	14	8	3	373	3	0	-	Serbia
Mame Cheikh Niang	24	13	4	0	79	1	0	-	Senegal
Sergiu Marian Radu	30	16	11	2	430	0	0	-	Romania

TEAM OF THE SEASON

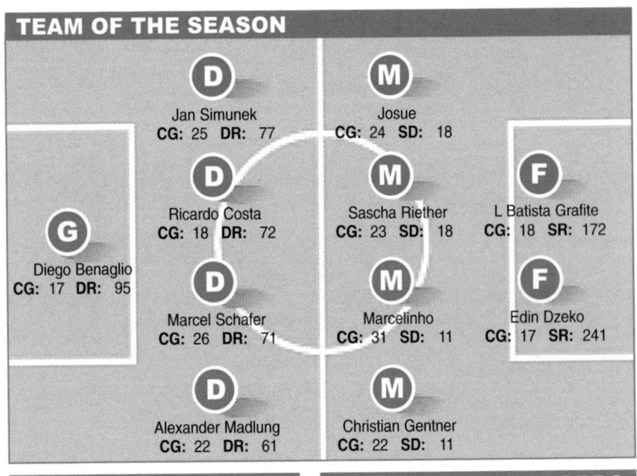

G
Diego Benaglio
CG: 17 DR: 95
D
Jan Simunek
CG: 25 DR: 77
D
Ricardo Costa
CG: 18 DR: 72
D
Marcel Schafer
CG: 26 DR: 71
D
Alexander Madlung
CG: 22 DR: 61
M
Josue
CG: 24 SD: 18
M
Sascha Riether
CG: 23 SD: 18
M
Marcelinho
CG: 31 SD: 11
M
Christian Gentner
CG: 22 SD: 11
F
L Batista Grafite
CG: 18 SR: 172
F
Edin Dzeko
CG: 17 SR: 241

MONTHLY POINTS TALLY

AUGUST	4	44%
SEPTEMBER	5	33%
OCTOBER	7	78%
NOVEMBER	0	0%
DECEMBER	4	44%
NO LEAGUE GAMES PLAYED IN JANUARY		
FEBRUARY	10	83%
MARCH	10	67%
APRIL	4	33%
MAY	10	83%

LEAGUE GOALS

	PLAYER	MINS	GOALS	S RATE
1	Grafite	1896	11	172
2	Dzeko	1930	8	241
3	Dejagah	1973	8	246
4	Marcelinho	2845	7	406
5	Schafer	2561	6	426
6	Krzynawek	920	4	230
7	Gentner	2370	3	790
8	Radu	430	2	215
9	Ricardo Costa	1815	2	907
10	Ljuboja	373	1	373
11	Hasebe	1203	1	1203
12	Madlung	2139	1	2139
13	Riether	2212	1	2212
	Other		1	
	TOTAL		56	

TOP POINT EARNERS

	PLAYER	GAMES	AV PTS
1	Diego Benaglio	17	2.00
2	Josue	24	1.92
3	Edin Dzeko	17	1.82
4	Sascha Riether	23	1.74
5	Libano Batista Grafite	18	1.72
6	Marcel Schffer	26	1.69
7	Christian Gentner	22	1.68
8	Jan Simunek	25	1.64
9	Ricardo Costa	18	1.56
10	Marcelinho	31	1.55
	CLUB AVERAGE:		1.59

DISCIPLINARY RECORDS

	PLAYER	YELLOW	RED	AVE
1	L Batista Grafite	9	1	189
2	Ricardo Costa	8	0	226
3	Josue	7	1	314
4	Jonathan Santana	2	0	326
5	Alexander Madlung	5	1	356
6	Ashkan Dejagah	5	0	394
7	Facundo Quiroga	2	0	404
8	Daniel Baier	2	0	459
9	Makoto Hasebe	2	0	601
10	Jan Simunek	4	0	616
11	Pablo Thiam	1	0	625
12	Edin Dzeko	3	0	643
13	Christian Gentner	3	0	790
	Other	8	0	
	TOTAL	61	3	

KEY GOALKEEPER

Diego Benaglio

Goals Conceded in the League	17	**Counting Games** League games when player was on pitch for at least 70 minutes	18
Defensive Rating Ave number of mins between League goals conceded while on the pitch	95	**Clean Sheets** In League games when player was on pitch for at least 70 minutes	7

KEY PLAYERS - GOALSCORERS

Libano Batista Grafite

Goals in the League	11	**Player Strike Rate** Average number of minutes between League goals scored by player	172
Contribution to Attacking Power Average number of minutes between League team goals while on pitch	51	**Club Strike Rate** Average number of minutes between League goals scored by club	54

	PLAYER	LGE GOALS	POWER	STRIKE RATE
1	Libano Batista Grafite	11	51	172 mins
2	Edin Dzeko	8	50	241 mins
3	Ashkan Dejagah	8	53	246 mins
4	Marcelinho	7	56	406 mins

KEY PLAYERS - DEFENDERS

Jan Simunek

Goals Conceded Number of League goals conceded while the player was on the pitch	32	**Clean Sheets** In League games when player was on pitch for at least 70 minutes	7
Defensive Rating Ave number of mins between League goals conceded while on the pitch	77	**Club Defensive Rating** Average number of mins between League goals conceded by the club this season	67

	PLAYER	CON LGE	CLEAN SHEETS	DEF RATE
1	Jan Simunek	32	7	77 mins
2	Ricardo Costa	25	5	72 mins
3	Marcel Schafer	36	9	71 mins
4	Alexander Madlung	35	6	61 mins

TIGUAN
Grafite

KEY PLAYERS - MIDFIELDERS

Josue

Goals in the League	1	**Contribution to Attacking Power** Average number of minutes between League team goals while on pitch	51
Defensive Rating Average number of mins between League goals conceded while on the pitch	69	**Scoring Difference** Defensive Rating minus Contribution to Attacking Power	18

	PLAYER	LGE GOALS	DEF RATE	POWER	SCORE DIFF
1	Josue	1	69	51	18 mins
2	Sascha Riether	1	65	47	18 mins
3	Marcelinho	7	67	56	11 mins
4	Christian Gentner	3	64	53	11 mins

SQUAD APPEARANCES

Match	1	2	3	4	5	6	7	8	9	10	11	12	13	14	15	16	17	18	19	20	21	22	23	24	25	26	27	28	29	30	31	32	33	34
Venue	H	A	H	A	H	A	H	A	H	A	H	A	H	A	H	A	H	A	H	A	H	A	H	A	H	A	H	H	A	A	H	A	H	A
Competition	L	L	L	L	L	L	L	L	L	L	L	L	L	L	L	L	L	L	L	L	L	L	L	L	L	L	L	L	L	L	L	L	L	L
Result	L	W	D	L	L	W	D	D	W	D	W	L	L	L	D	L	W	W	W	W	D	L	W	W	D	W	W	L	L	D	D	W	W	W

Goalkeepers
Diego Benaglio
Simon Jentzsch
Andre Lenz
Defenders
Sergej Karimov
Uwe Mohrle
Alexander Madlung
Facundo Quiroga
Ricardo Costa
Marcel Schafer
Jan Simunek
Peter van der Heyden
Midfielders
Daniel Baier
Christian Gentner
Makoto Hasebe
Josue
Jacek Krzynowek
Alexander Laas
Marcelinho
Vlad Munteanu
Sascha Riether
Jonathan Santana
Pablo Thiam
Forwards
Isaac Boakye
Ashkan Dejagah
Edin Dzeko
Libano Batista Grafite
Danijel Ljuboja
Mame Cheikh Niang
Sergiu Marian Radu

KEY: On all match | On bench | Subbed or sent off (Counting game) | Subbed or sent off (playing less than 70 minutes) | Subbed on from bench (Counting Game) | Subbed on (playing less than 70 minutes) | Subbed on and then subbed or sent off (Counting Game) | Subbed on and then subbed or sent off (playing less than 70 minutes) | Not in 16

VfB STUTTGART

Final Position: **6th**

NICKNAME: DIE SCHWABEN

KEY: ☐ Won ☐ Drawn ☐ Lost

No	Comp	Opponent	H/A	Res	Score	Scorers	Attendance
1	grpr1	**Schalke**	H	D	2-2	Khedira 63, Pardo 67 pen	55,800
2	grpr1	**Hertha Berlin**	A	L	1-3	Hitzlsperger 15	50,000
3	grpr1	**Duisburg**	H	W	1-0	Gomez 35	40,000
4	grpr1	**Karlsruhe**	A	L	0-1		27,800
5	grpr1	**Cottbus**	H	W	3-0	Cacau 53, Ewerthon 79, Gomez 82	41,000
6	ecgpe	**Rangers**	A	L	1-2	Gomez 56	49,795
7	grpr1	**W Bremen**	A	L	1-4	Gomez 15	40,000
8	grpr1	**Bochum**	H	W	1-0	Hilbert 50	36,000
9	grpr1	**Hansa Rostock**	A	L	1-2	Gomez 73	18,000
10	ecgpe	**Barcelona**	H	L	0-2		51,300
11	grpr1	**Hannover 96**	H	L	0-2		50,000
12	grpr1	**Hamburg**	A	L	1-4	Tasci 73	57,000
13	ecgpe	**Lyon**	H	L	0-2		51,300
14	grpr1	**B Leverkusen**	H	W	1-0	Beck 72	51,000
15	grpr1	**Nurnberg**	A	W	1-0	Gomez 25	45,565
16	ecgpe	**Lyon**	A	L	2-4	Gomez 16, 56	38,000
17	grpr1	**Bayern Munich**	H	W	3-1	Gomez 10, 41, Basturk 29	55,000
18	grpr1	**Eintr Frankfurt**	A	W	4-1	Hilbert 45, Marica 48, Hitzlsperger 57, Claudemir da Silva 90	51,500
19	ecgpe	**Rangers**	H	W	3-2	Claudemir da Silva 45, Pardo Segura 62, Marica 85	51,300
20	grpr1	**B Dortmund**	H	L	1-2	Meira 35	55,800
21	grpr1	**Wolfsburg**	H	W	3-1	Marica 26, Claudemir da Silva 48, Hitzlsperger 86	53,000
22	ecgpe	**Barcelona**	A	L	1-3	da Silva 3	60,000
23	grpr1	**Arminia B**	A	L	0-2		20,000
24	grpr1	**Schalke**	A	L	1-4	da Silva 61	61,482
25	grpr1	**Hertha Berlin**	H	L	1-3	Gomez 41	50,000
26	grpr1	**Duisburg**	A	W	3-2	Gomez 16, 41, Hitzlsperger 90	21,562
27	grpr1	**Karlsruhe**	H	W	3-1	Gomez 5, Hilbert 26, Claudemir da Silva 88	55,000
28	grpr1	**W Bremen**	H	W	6-3	Gomez 20, 43, 65, Claudemir da Silva 66, 87, Mertesacker 83 og	55,000
29	grpr1	**Cottbus**	A	W	1-0	Meira 30	13,150
30	grpr1	**Bochum**	A	D	1-1	Hitzlsperger 47	25,086
31	grpr1	**Hansa Rostock**	H	W	4-1	Pardo Segura 52 pen, Claudemir da Silva 54, Gomez 87, Basturk 90	48,000
32	grpr1	**Hannover 96**	A	D	0-0		45,176
33	grpr1	**Hamburg**	H	W	1-0	Hilbert 20	55,800
34	grpr1	**B Leverkusen**	A	L	0-3		22,500
35	grpr1	**Nurnberg**	H	W	3-0	Claudemir da Silva 4, da Silva 13, Meira 31	45,000
36	grpr1	**Bayern Munich**	A	L	1-4	da Silva 19	69,000
37	grpr1	**Eintr Frankfurt**	H	W	4-1	Basturk 3, 18, Gomez 6, Claudemir da Silva 47	55,500
38	grpr1	**B Dortmund**	A	L	2-3	Gomez 55, 83	64,400
39	grpr1	**Wolfsburg**	A	L	0-4		28,001
40	grpr1	**Arminia B**	H	D	2-2	Gomez 75 pen, Fischer 85	55,500

LEAGUE APPEARANCES, BOOKINGS AND CAPS

	AGE (on 01/07/08)	IN NAMED 18	APPEARANCES	COUNTING GAMES	MINUTES ON PITCH	YELLOW CARDS	RED CARDS	CAPS THIS SEASON	NATIONAL SIDE
Goalkeepers									
Michael Langer	23	16	0	0	0	0	0	-	Austria
Raphael Schafer	29	32	23	23	2070	2	0	-	Germany
Sven Ulreich	19	17	11	11	990	0	0	-	Germany
Defenders									
Andreas Beck	21	29	18	10	1074	2	0	-	Germany
Arthur Boka	25	23	17	8	1046	3	0	6	Ivory Coast
Mathieu Delpierre	27	22	22	22	1956	5	1	-	France
Ludovic Magnin	29	30	27	19	1912	4	0	7	Switzerland
Fernando Meira	30	28	28	25	2294	3	2	9	Portugal
Gledson	28	4	0	0	0	0	0	-	Brazil
Ricardo Osorio	28	27	22	18	1741	1	1	-	Mexico
Marco Pischorn	22	16	4	1	117	0	0	-	Germany
Serdar Tasci	21	24	21	17	1677	5	0	-	Germany
Midfielders									
Yildiray Basturk	29	26	26	21	2092	2	0	1	Turkey
Antonio da Silva	30	27	20	7	1004	2	0	-	Brazil
Alexander Farnerud	24	17	10	2	407	2	0	-	Sweden
Roberto Hilbert	23	32	32	24	2531	7	0	6	Germany
Thomas Hitzlsperger	26	25	25	20	1983	3	0	8	Germany
Sami Khedira	21	26	24	17	1725	4	0	-	Germany
Silvio Meißner	35	17	8	0	111	1	0	-	Germany
Pavel Pardo	31	29	29	26	2480	5	2	1	Mexico
Peter Perchtold	23	3	2	0	40	1	0	-	Germany
David Pisot	20	2	1	1	90	0	0	-	Germany
Julian Schuster	23	8	2	0	49	0	0	-	Germany
Christian Trasch	20	2	1	0	58	0	0	-	Germany
Forwards									
Cacau	27	28	27	21	2056	6	0	-	Brazil
Ewerthon de Souza	27	17	11	2	381	1	0	-	Brazil
Manuel Fischer	18	6	2	0	30	0	0	-	Germany
Mario Gomez	22	26	25	21	1958	1	0	9	Germany
Ciprian Marica	22	31	28	11	1469	4	0	7	Romania
Sergiu Marian Radu	30	12	2	1	84	0	0	-	Romania

TEAM OF THE SEASON

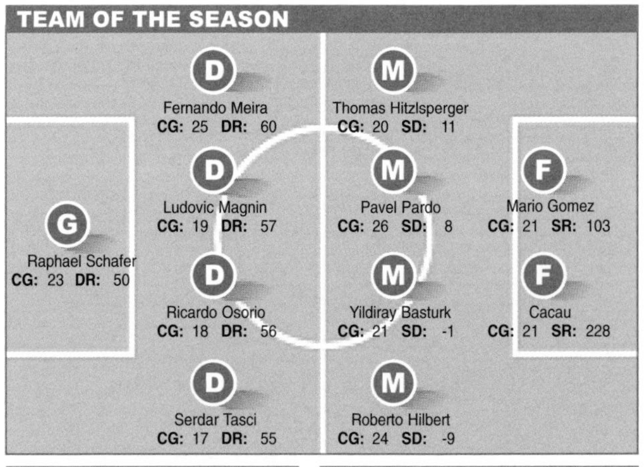

D
Fernando Meira
CG: 25 DR: 60
M
Thomas Hitzlsperger
CG: 20 SD: 11
D
Ludovic Magnin
CG: 19 DR: 57
M
Pavel Pardo
CG: 26 SD: 8
F
Mario Gomez
CG: 21 SR: 103
G
Raphael Schafer
CG: 23 DR: 50
D
Ricardo Osorio
CG: 18 DR: 56
M
Yildiray Basturk
CG: 21 SD: -1
F
Cacau
CG: 21 SR: 228
D
Serdar Tasci
CG: 17 DR: 55
M
Roberto Hilbert
CG: 24 SD: -9

MONTHLY POINTS TALLY

Month	Points	%
AUGUST	4	44%
SEPTEMBER	6	40%
OCTOBER	3	33%
NOVEMBER	9	100%
DECEMBER	3	33%
NO LEAGUE GAMES PLAYED IN JANUARY		
FEBRUARY	6	50%
MARCH	11	73%
APRIL	6	50%
MAY	4	33%

LEAGUE GOALS

	PLAYER	MINS	GOALS	S RATE
1	Gomez	1958	19	103
2	Cacau	2056	9	228
3	Hitzlsperger	1983	5	396
4	Basturk	2092	4	523
5	Hilbert	2531	4	632
6	da Silva	1004	3	334
7	Meira	2294	3	764
8	Marica	1469	2	734
9	Pardo Segura	2480	2	1240
10	Fischer	30	1	30
11	de Souza	381	1	381
12	Beck	1074	1	1074
13	Tasci	1677	1	1677
	Other		1	
	TOTAL		56	

TOP POINT EARNERS

	PLAYER	GAMES	AV PTS
1	Thomas Hitzlsperger	20	1.95
2	Ricardo Osorio	18	1.78
3	Pavel Pardo	26	1.73
4	Serdar Tasci	17	1.65
5	Mathieu Delpierre	22	1.64
6	Ludovic Magnin	19	1.63
7	Roberto Hilbert	24	1.63
8	Fernando Meira	25	1.56
9	Yildiray Basturk	21	1.52
10	Cacau	21	1.48
	CLUB AVERAGE:		1.53

DISCIPLINARY RECORDS

	PLAYER	YELLOW	RED	AVE
1	Mathieu Delpierre	5	1	326
2	Serdar Tasci	5	0	335
3	Cacau	6	0	342
4	Arthur Boka	3	0	348
5	Pavel Pardo	5	2	354
6	Roberto Hilbert	7	0	361
7	Ciprian Marica	4	0	367
8	Sami Khedira	4	0	431
9	Fernando Meira	3	2	458
10	Ludovic Magnin	4	0	478
11	Antonio da Silva	2	0	502
12	Andreas Beck	2	0	537
13	T Hitzlsperger	3	0	661
	Other	6	1	
	TOTAL	59	6	

KEY GOALKEEPER

Raphael Schafer

Goals Conceded in the League	41	**Counting Games** League games when player was on pitch for at least 70 minutes	23
Defensive Rating Ave number of mins between League goals conceded while on the pitch	50	**Clean Sheets** In League games when player was on pitch for at least 70 minutes	6

KEY PLAYERS - DEFENDERS

Fernando Meira

Goals Conceded Number of League goals conceded while the player was on the pitch	38	**Clean Sheets** In League games when player was on pitch for at least 70 minutes	7
Defensive Rating Ave number of mins between League goals conceded while on the pitch	60	**Club Defensive Rating** Average number of mins between League goals conceded by the club this season	55

	PLAYER	CON LGE	CLEAN SHEETS	DEF RATE
1	Fernando Meira	38	7	60 mins
2	Ludovic Magnin	33	5	57 mins
3	Ricardo Osorio	31	6	56 mins
4	Serdar Tasci	30	5	55 mins

KEY PLAYERS - MIDFIELDERS

Thomas Hitzlsperger

Goals in the League	5	**Contribution to Attacking Power** Average number of minutes between League team goals while on pitch	49
Defensive Rating Average number of mins between League goals conceded while on the pitch	60	**Scoring Difference** Defensive Rating minus Contribution to Attacking Power	11

	PLAYER	LGE GOALS	DEF RATE	POWER	SCORE DIFF
1	Thomas Hitzlsperger	5	60	49	11 mins
2	Pavel Pardo	2	57	49	8 mins
3	Yildiray Basturk	4	51	52	-1 mins
4	Roberto Hilbert	4	52	61	-9 mins

KEY PLAYERS - GOALSCORERS

Mario Gomez

Goals in the League	19	**Player Strike Rate** Average number of minutes between League goals scored by player	103
Contribution to Attacking Power Average number of minutes between League team goals while on pitch	52	**Club Strike Rate** Average number of minutes between League goals scored by club	55

	PLAYER	LGE GOALS	POWER	STRIKE RATE
1	Mario Gomez	19	52	103 mins
2	Cacau	9	47	228 mins
3	Thomas Hitzlsperger	5	49	396 mins
4	Yildiray Basturk	4	52	523 mins

Mario Gomez, Pavel Pardo and Roberto Hilbert

SQUAD APPEARANCES

Match	1	2	3	4	5	6	7	8	9	10	11	12	13	14	15	16	17	18	19	20	21	22	23	24	25	26	27	28	29	30	31	32	33	34	35	36	37	38	39	40
Venue	H	A	H	A	H	A	A	H	A	H	H	A	H	H	A	A	H	A	H	H	H	A	A	A	H	A	H	H	A	A	H	A	H	A	H	A	H	A	A	H
Competition	L	L	L	L	L	C	L	L	L	C	L	L	C	L	L	C	L	L	C	L	L	C	L	L	L	L	L	L	L	L	L	L	L	L	L	L	L	L	L	L
Result	D	L	W	L	W	L	L	W	L	L	L	L	L	W	W	L	W	W	W	L	W	L	L	L	L	W	W	W	W	D	W	D	W	L	W	L	W	L	L	D

Goalkeepers
Michael Langer
Raphael Schafer
Sven Ulreich

Defenders
Andreas Beck
Arthur Boka
Mathieu Delpierre
Ludovic Magnin
Fernando Meira
Gledson
Ricardo Osorio
Marco Pischorn
Serdar Tasci

Midfielders
Yildiray Basturk
Antonio da Silva
Alexander Farnerud
Roberto Hilbert
Thomas Hitzlsperger
Sami Khedira
Silvio Meißner
Pavel Pardo
Peter Perchtold
David Pisot
Julian Schuster
Christian Trasch

Forwards
Cacau
Ewerthon de Souza
Manuel Fischer
Mario Gomez
Ciprian Marica
Sergiu Marian Radu

KEY: On all match · On bench · Subbed or sent off (Counting game) · Subbed or sent off (playing less than 70 minutes) · Subbed on from bench (Counting Game) · Subbed on (playing less than 70 minutes) · Subbed on and then subbed or sent off (Counting Game) · Subbed on and then subbed or sent off (playing less than 70 minutes) · Not in 16

BAYER LEVERKUSEN

Final Position: **7th**

NICKNAME: BAYER-LOWEN

KEY: ☐Won ☐Drawn ☐Lost

No	Comp	Opponent	Venue	Res	Score	Scorers	Attendance
1	grpr1	**Cottbus**	H	D	0-0		22,500
2	grpr1	**Hamburg**	A	L	0-1		52,000
3	grpr1	**Karlsruhe**	H	W	3-0	Franz 19 og, Friedrich 26, Gekas 35	22,000
4	grpr1	**Schalke**	A	D	1-1	Gekas 53	61,482
5	grpr1	**Bochum**	H	W	2-0	Haggui 62, Friedrich 88	22,500
6	ucrl1	**Leiria**	H	W	3-1	Kiessling 19, 78, Rolfes 31	16,331
7	grpr1	**Hannover 96**	A	W	3-0	Kiessling 50, Vidal 68, Gekas 73 pen	32,000
8	grpr1	**Nurnberg**	A	W	2-1	Kiessling 40, Barnetta 76	38,000
9	grpr1	**Bayern Munich**	H	L	0-1		22,500
10	ucrl2	**Leiria**	A	L	2-3	Papadopulos 11, Kiessling 88	1,800
11	grpr1	**Eintr Frankfurt**	A	L	1-2	Russ 72 og	47,600
12	grpr1	**B Dortmund**	H	D	2-2	Gekas 52, Kiessling 87	22,500
13	ucgpe	**Toulouse**	H	W	1-0	Kiessling 35	20,000
14	grpr1	**Stuttgart**	A	L	0-1		51,000
15	grpr1	**Arminia B**	H	W	4-0	Barbarez 9, 80, Gekas 29, 34	22,500
16	ucgpe	**S Moscow**	A	L	1-2	Freier 90	22,000
17	grpr1	**Wolfsburg**	A	W	2-1	Barnetta 36, Kiessling 52	20,000
18	grpr1	**Duisburg**	H	W	4-1	Barbarez 47, Rolfes 66, Freier 75 pen, Gekas 81	22,500
19	grpr1	**Hertha Berlin**	A	W	3-0	Ramelow 30, Barnetta 49, Barbarez 90	40,527
20	ucgpe	**Sparta Prague**	H	W	1-0	Friedrich 71	22,500
21	grpr1	**Hansa Rostock**	H	W	3-0	Rolfes 4, Freier 55 pen, Gekas 72	22,500
22	grpr1	**W Bremen**	A	L	2-5	Barnetta 5, Kiessling 76	39,308
23	ucgpe	**Zurich**	A	W	5-0	Gresko 19, Bulykin 23, 57, Barnetta 50, Kiessling 80	12,000
24	grpr1	**Cottbus**	A	W	3-2	Rolfes 59, 86 pen, Bulykin 69	14,966
25	grpr1	**Hamburg**	H	D	1-1	Friedrich 60	22,500
26	ucrl1	**Galatasaray**	A	D	0-0		20,006
27	grpr1	**Karlsruhe**	A	D	2-2	Rolfes 6, Kiessling 58	28,500
28	ucrl2	**Galatasaray**	H	W	5-1	Barbarez 12, 22, Kiessling 13, Haggui 55, Schneider 61 pen	22,500
29	grpr1	**Schalke**	H	W	1-0	Friedrich 85	22,500
30	grpr1	**Bochum**	A	L	0-2		23,781
31	ucrl1	**Hamburg**	H	W	1-0	Gekas 77	22,500
32	grpr1	**Hannover 96**	H	W	2-0	Gekas 30, Barnetta 39	22,500
33	ucrl2	**Hamburg**	A	L	2-3	Barbarez 19, Gekas 55	38,083
34	grpr1	**Nurnberg**	H	W	4-1	Haggui 6, Glauber 56 og, Gekas 59, Kiessling 82	22,500
35	grpr1	**Bayern Munich**	A	L	1-2	Bulykin 83	69,000
36	grpr1	**Eintr Frankfurt**	H	L	0-2		22,500
37	ucqfl1	**Z St Petersburg**	H	L	1-4	Kiessling 33	19,500
38	grpr1	**B Dortmund**	A	L	1-2	Kiessling 51	69,400
39	ucqfl2	**Z St Petersburg**	A	W	1-0	Bulykin 18	21,500
40	grpr1	**Stuttgart**	H	W	3-0	Rolfes 41, 70, Kiessling 45	22,500
41	grpr1	**Arminia B**	A	L	0-1		19,400
42	grpr1	**Wolfsburg**	H	D	2-2	Gekas 33, Ricardo Costa 73 og	22,500
43	grpr1	**Duisburg**	A	L	2-3	Sinkiewicz 18, Barnetta 74	25,275
44	grpr1	**Hertha Berlin**	H	L	1-2	Sinkiewicz 90	22,500
45	grpr1	**Hansa Rostock**	A	W	2-1	Rolfes 40 pen, Castro 58 pen	22,000
46	grpr1	**W Bremen**	H	L	0-1		22,500

LEAGUE APPEARANCES, BOOKINGS AND CAPS

	AGE (on 01/07/08)	IN NAMED 18	APPEARANCES	COUNTING GAMES	MINUTES ON PITCH	YELLOW CARDS	RED CARDS	CAPS THIS SEASON	NATIONAL SIDE
Goalkeepers									
Rene Adler	23	33	33	33	2970	4	0	-	Germany
Erik Domaschke	22	12	0	0	0	0	0	-	Germany
Benedikt Fernandez	23	22	1	1	90	0	0	-	Germany
Fabian Giefer	18	1	0	0	0	0	0	-	Germany
Defenders									
J-I Callsen-Bracker	23	23	10	6	549	2	0	-	Germany
Gonzalo Castro	21	33	33	32	2925	8	0	4	Germany
Manuel Friedrich	28	34	32	31	2848	4	0	3	Germany
Vratislav Gresko	30	28	21	14	1456	5	0	-	Slovakia
Karim Haggui	24	26	24	22	2050	5	0	4	Tunisia
Jens Hegeler	20	3	1	0	33	1	1	-	Germany
Hans Sarpei	32	31	27	19	1874	2	0	6	Ghana
Lukas Sinkiewicz	22	29	19	11	1100	0	0	-	Germany
Assimou Toure	20	1	0	0	0	0	0	-	Togo
Arturo Vidal	21	30	24	14	1556	6	0	4	Chile
Midfielders									
Sergei Barbarez	36	32	29	21	2122	7	0	-	Bosnia
Tranquillo Barnetta	23	32	32	29	2684	3	0	9	Switzerland
Sascha Dum	21	24	17	0	388	2	0	-	Germany
Ricardo Faty	21	6	2	0	14	0	0	-	France
Paul Freier	28	24	19	5	798	2	0	-	Germany
Carsten Ramelow	34	9	4	3	260	2	0	-	Germany
Marcel Risse	18	5	3	1	96	0	0	-	Germany
Simon Rolfes	26	34	34	34	3057	0	0	7	Germany
Bernd Schneider	34	17	15	11	1098	1	0	3	Germany
Pirmin Schwegler	21	22	11	3	513	0	0	-	Switzerland
Forwards									
Dmitri Bulykin	28	27	14	2	525	2	0	-	Russia
Theofanis Gekas	28	33	29	17	1775	1	0	10	Greece
Stefan Kiessling	24	31	31	30	2695	6	1	-	Germany
Michal Papadopulos	23	10	7	0	146	0	0	-	Czech Republic
Dennis Schmidt	20	1	0	0	0	0	0	-	Germany

TEAM OF THE SEASON

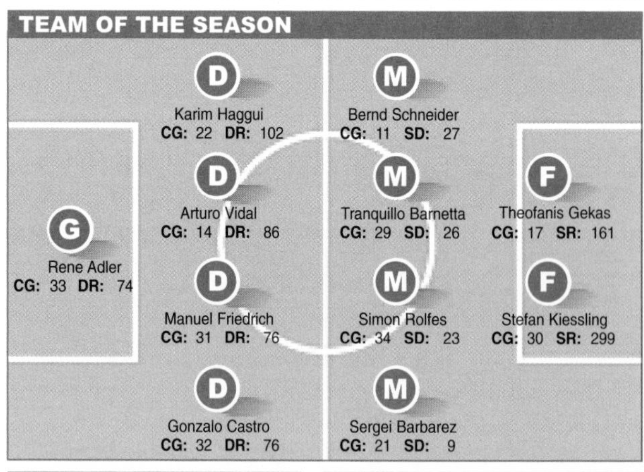

G
Rene Adler
CG: 33 DR: 74
D
Karim Haggui
CG: 22 DR: 102
D
Arturo Vidal
CG: 14 DR: 86
D
Manuel Friedrich
CG: 31 DR: 76
D
Gonzalo Castro
CG: 32 DR: 76
M
Bernd Schneider
CG: 11 SD: 27
M
Tranquillo Barnetta
CG: 29 SD: 26
M
Simon Rolfes
CG: 34 SD: 23
M
Sergei Barbarez
CG: 21 SD: 9
F
Theofanis Gekas
CG: 17 SR: 161
F
Stefan Kiessling
CG: 30 SR: 299

MONTHLY POINTS TALLY

Month	Points	%
AUGUST	5	42%
SEPTEMBER	9	75%
OCTOBER	1	11%
NOVEMBER	9	100%
DECEMBER	6	67%
NO LEAGUE GAMES PLAYED IN JANUARY		
FEBRUARY	8	67%
MARCH	6	40%
APRIL	4	33%
MAY	3	25%

LEAGUE GOALS

	PLAYER	MINS	GOALS	S RATE
1	Gekas	1775	11	161
2	Kiessling	2695	9	299
3	Rolfes	3057	8	382
4	Barnetta	2684	6	447
5	Barbarez	2122	4	530
6	Friedrich	2848	4	712
7	Bulykin	525	2	262
8	Freier	798	2	399
9	Sinkiewicz	1100	2	550
10	Haggui	2050	2	1025
11	Ramelow	260	1	260
12	Vidal	1556	1	1556
13	Castro	2925	1	2925
	Other		0	
	TOTAL		53	

TOP POINT EARNERS

	PLAYER	GAMES	AV PTS
1	A Erasmo Vidal Pardo	14	2.00
2	Theofanis Gekas	17	1.82
3	Karim Haggui	22	1.77
4	Vratislav Gresko	14	1.71
5	Tranquillo Barnetta	29	1.62
6	Gonzalo Castro	32	1.56
7	Manuel Friedrich	31	1.55
8	Stefan Kiessling	30	1.50
9	Simon Rolfes	34	1.50
10	Rene Adler	33	1.45
	CLUB AVERAGE:		1.50

DISCIPLINARY RECORDS

	PLAYER	YELLOW	RED	AVE
1	A-E Vidal Pardo	6	0	259
2	Dmitri Bulykin	2	0	262
3	J-I Callsen-Bracker	2	0	274
4	Vratislav Gresko	5	0	291
5	Sergei Barbarez	7	0	303
6	Gonzalo Castro	8	0	365
7	Stefan Kiessling	6	1	385
8	Paul Freier	2	0	399
9	Karim Haggui	5	0	410
10	Manuel Friedrich	4	0	712
11	Rene Adler	4	0	742
12	Tranquillo Barnetta	3	0	894
13	Hans Sarpei	2	0	937
	Other	2	0	
	TOTAL	58	1	

KEY GOALKEEPER

Rene Adler

Goals Conceded in the League	40	Counting Games League games when player was on pitch for at least 70 minutes	33
Defensive Rating Ave number of mins between League goals conceded while on the pitch	74	Clean Sheets In League games when player was on pitch for at least 70 minutes	9

KEY PLAYERS - DEFENDERS

Karim Haggui

Goals Conceded Number of League goals conceded while the player was on the pitch	20	Clean Sheets In League games when player was on pitch for at least 70 minutes	9
Defensive Rating Ave number of mins between League goals conceded while on the pitch	102	Club Defensive Rating Average number of mins between League goals conceded by the club this season	76

	PLAYER	CON LGE	CLEAN SHEETS	DEF RATE
1	Karim Haggui	20	9	102 mins
2	Arturo Vidal	18	5	86 mins
3	Manuel Friedrich	37	10	76 mins
4	Gonzalo Castro	38	10	76 mins

KEY PLAYERS - MIDFIELDERS

Bernd Schneider

Goals in the League	0	Contribution to Attacking Power Average number of minutes between League team goals while on pitch	64
Defensive Rating Average number of mins between League goals conceded while on the pitch	91	Scoring Difference Defensive Rating minus Contribution to Attacking Power	27

	PLAYER	LGE GOALS	DEF RATE	POWER	SCORE DIFF
1	Bernd Schneider	0	91	64	27 mins
2	Tranquillo Barnetta	6	81	55	26 mins
3	Simon Rolfes	8	76	53	23 mins
4	Sergei Barbarez	4	62	53	9 mins

KEY PLAYERS - GOALSCORERS

Theofanis Gekas

Goals in the League	11	Player Strike Rate Average number of minutes between League goals scored by player	161
Contribution to Attacking Power Average number of minutes between League team goals while on pitch	49	Club Strike Rate Average number of minutes between League goals scored by club	53

	PLAYER	LGE GOALS	POWER	STRIKE RATE
1	Theofanis Gekas	11	49	161 mins
2	Stefan Kiessling	9	53	299 mins
3	Simon Rolfes	8	53	382 mins
4	Tranquillo Barnetta	6	55	447 mins

Gonzalo Castro and Theofanis Gekas

SQUAD APPEARANCES

Match	1	2	3	4	5	6	7	8	9	10	11	12	13	14	15	16	17	18	19	20	21	22	23
Venue	H	A	H	A	H	H	A	A	H	A	A	H	H	A	H	A	A	H	A	H	H	A	A
Competition	L	L	L	L	L	E	L	L	L	E	L	L	E	L	L	E	L	L	L	E	L	L	E
Result	D	L	W	D	W	W	W	W	L	L	L	D	W	L	W	L	W	W	W	W	W	L	W

Match	24	25	26	27	28	29	30	31	32	33	34	35	36	37	38	39	40	41	42	43	44	45	46
Venue	A	H	A	A	H	H	A	H	H	A	H	A	H	H	A	A	H	A	H	A	H	A	H
Competition	L	L	E	L	E	L	L	E	L	E	L	L	L	E	L	E	L	L	L	L	L	L	L
Result	W	D	D	D	W	W	L	W	W	L	W	L	L	L	L	W	W	L	D	L	L	W	L

Goalkeepers
Rene Adler
Erik Domaschke
Benedikt Fernandez
Fabian Giefer

Defenders
J-I Callsen-Bracker
Gonzalo Castro
Manuel Friedrich
Vratislav Gresko
Karim Haggui
Jens Hegeler
Hans Sarpei
Lukas Sinkiewicz
Assimou Toure
Arturo Vidal

Midfielders
Sergei Barbarez
Tranquillo Barnetta
Sascha Dum
Ricardo Faty
Paul Freier
Carsten Ramelow
Marcel Risse
Simon Rolfes
Bernd Schneider
Pirmin Schwegler

Forwards
Dmitri Bulykin
Theofanis Gekas
Stefan Kiessling
Michal Papadopulos
Dennis Schmidt

KEY: On all match · On bench · Subbed or sent off (Counting game) · Subbed or sent off (playing less than 70 minutes) · Subbed on from bench (Counting Game) · Subbed on (playing less than 70 minutes) · Subbed on and then subbed or sent off (Counting Game) · Subbed on and then subbed or sent off (playing less than 70 minutes) · Not in 16

HANNOVER 96

Final Position: **8th**

NICKNAME: DIE ROTEN

KEY: ☐Won ☐Drawn ☐Lost

							Attendance
1	grpr1	**Hamburg**	H	L	0-1		49,000
2	grpr1	**Karlsruhe**	A	W	2-1	Hanke 55, Balitsch 75	30,000
3	grpr1	**Bayern Munich**	A	L	0-3		69,000
4	grpr1	**Bochum**	H	W	3-2	Hanke 12, Rosenthal 36, Hashemian 71	30,794
5	grpr1	**Nurnberg**	A	D	2-2	Hanke 12, 39	42,000
6	grpr1	**B Leverkusen**	H	L	0-3		32,000
7	grpr1	**Arminia B**	A	W	2-0	Huszti 54 pen, Pinto 85	21,000
8	grpr1	**Duisburg**	H	W	2-1	Schulz 7, 64	30,000
9	grpr1	**Stuttgart**	A	W	2-0	Huszti 8 pen, 52	50,000
10	grpr1	**Wolfsburg**	H	D	2-2	Pinto 28, Tarnat 35	37,812
11	grpr1	**Eintr Frankfurt**	A	D	0-0		44,700
12	grpr1	**B Dortmund**	H	W	2-1	Huszti 54 pen, Schulz 74	45,087
13	grpr1	**Hertha Berlin**	A	L	0-1		34,213
14	grpr1	**Schalke**	H	L	2-3	Huszti 17 pen, 53	49,000
15	grpr1	**Hansa Rostock**	A	W	3-0	Fahrenhorst 84, Hanke 86, Stajner 88	17,000
16	grpr1	**W Bremen**	H	W	4-3	Hanke 12, 21, 76, Baumann 20 og	49,000
17	grpr1	**Cottbus**	A	L	1-5	Kleine 68	14,026
18	grpr1	**Hamburg**	A	D	1-1	Huszti 40 pen	57,000
19	grpr1	**Karlsruhe**	H	D	2-2	Balitsch 44, Rosenthal 87	41,112
20	grpr1	**Bayern Munich**	H	L	0-3		49,000
21	grpr1	**Bochum**	A	L	1-2	Hanke 47	19,902
22	grpr1	**Nurnberg**	H	W	2-1	Bruggink 29, Huszti 65	31,282
23	grpr1	**B Leverkusen**	A	L	0-2		22,500
24	grpr1	**Arminia B**	H	D	2-2	Bruggink 16, Stajner 56	35,104
25	grpr1	**Duisburg**	A	D	1-1	Stajner 42	20,747
26	grpr1	**Stuttgart**	H	D	0-0		45,176
27	grpr1	**Wolfsburg**	A	L	2-3	Bruggink 27, Stajner 79	29,322
28	grpr1	**Eintr Frankfurt**	H	W	2-1	Pinto 35, C..Schulz 89	38,104
29	grpr1	**B Dortmund**	A	W	3-1	Bruggink 38, Fahrenhorst 41, Huszti 79	61,400
30	grpr1	**Hertha Berlin**	H	D	2-2	Hanke 19, Stajner 26	41,473
31	grpr1	**Schalke**	A	D	1-1	Bruggink 8	61,482
32	grpr1	**Hansa Rostock**	H	W	3-0	Balitsch 19, Rosenthal 47, 87	35,453
33	grpr1	**W Bremen**	A	L	1-6	Huszti 90	42,100
34	grpr1	**Cottbus**	H	W	4-0	Bruggink 23, Stajner 45, Vinicius 59, Balitsch 89	46,632

LEAGUE APPEARANCES, BOOKINGS AND CAPS

	AGE (on 01/07/08)	IN NAMED 18	APPEARANCES	COUNTING GAMES	MINUTES ON PITCH	YELLOW CARDS	RED CARDS	CAPS THIS SEASON	NATIONAL SIDE
Goalkeepers									
Robert Enke	30	34	34	34	3060	2	0	-	Germany
Richard Golz	40	29	0	0	0	0	0	-	Germany
Morten Jensen	20	2	0	0	0	0	0	-	Germany
Frank Juric	34	3	0	0	0	0	0	-	Australia
Defenders									
Steve Cherundolo	29	33	33	32	2930	4	0	5	United States
Frank Fahrenhorst	30	27	23	19	1863	3	0	-	Germany
Soren Halfar	21	3	2	2	180	0	0	-	Germany
Valerien Ismael	32	16	14	12	1178	2	0	-	France
Thomas Kleine	30	17	9	8	721	1	0	-	Germany
Christian Schulz	25	29	29	25	2381	4	1	-	Germany
Michael Tarnat	38	16	16	15	1379	3	0	-	Germany
Bergantin Vinicius	27	29	28	26	2421	4	0	-	Brazil
Dariusz Zuraw	35	24	5	2	220	0	0	-	Poland
Midfielders									
Hanno Balitsch	27	29	29	23	2279	10	0	-	Germany
Ferhat Bikmaz	19	5	1	0	15	0	0	-	Turkey
Arnold Jan Bruggink	30	32	26	13	1516	6	0	-	Holland
Szabolcs Huszti	25	33	33	28	2678	4	0	-	Hungary
Gaetan Krebs	22	22	10	2	351	0	0	-	France
Altin Lala	32	29	27	18	1937	6	1	5	Albania
Sergio Pinto	27	22	20	11	1269	4	2	-	Portugal
Konstantin Rausch	18	5	2	0	68	0	0	-	Denmark
Jan Rosenthal	22	23	23	11	1390	5	0	-	Germany
Bastian Schulz	22	6	2	0	68	0	0	-	Germany
Chavdar Yankov	24	12	8	2	281	2	0	-	Bulgaria
Salvatore Zizzo	21	6	2	0	66	1	0	-	United States
Forwards									
Mike Hanke	24	31	31	27	2518	3	1	1	Germany
Vahid Hashemian	31	28	20	1	546	0	0	2	Iran
Benjamin Lauth	26	30	21	4	672	2	0	-	Germany
Fabian Montabell	23	1	0	0	0	0	0	-	Germany
Jiri Stajner	32	30	26	13	1500	4	0	-	Czech Republic

TEAM OF THE SEASON

G Robert Enke CG: 34 DR: 54

D Christian Schulz CG: 25 DR: 58

D Valerien Ismael CG: 12 DR: 58

D Frank Fahrenhorst CG: 19 DR: 58

D Steve Cherundolo CG: 32 DR: 56

M Szabolcs Huszti CG: 28 SD: 2

M Arnold Jan Bruggink CG: 13 SD: 0

M Hanno Balitsch CG: 23 SD: 0

M Altin Lala CG: 18 SD: -2

F Jiri Stajner CG: 13 SR: 250

F Mike Hanke CG: 27 SR: 251

MONTHLY POINTS TALLY

AUGUST	3	33%
SEPTEMBER	10	67%
OCTOBER	5	56%
NOVEMBER	6	50%
DECEMBER	3	50%
NO LEAGUE GAMES PLAYED IN JANUARY		
FEBRUARY	2	17%
MARCH	6	40%
APRIL	7	58%
MAY	7	58%

LEAGUE GOALS

	PLAYER	MINS	GOALS	S RATE
1	Hanke	2518	10	251
2	Huszti	2678	10	267
3	Stajner	1500	6	250
4	Bruggink	1516	6	252
5	Rosenthal	1390	4	347
6	Balitsch	2279	4	569
7	Schulz	2381	4	595
8	Pinto	1269	3	423
9	Fahrenhorst	1863	2	931
10	Hashemian	546	1	546
11	Kleine	721	1	721
12	Tarnat	1379	1	1379
13	Vinicius	2421	1	2421
	Other		0	
	TOTAL		53	

TOP POINT EARNERS

	PLAYER	GAMES	AV PTS
1	Arnold Jan Bruggink	13	1.77
2	Jiri Stajner	13	1.62
3	Altin Lala	18	1.61
4	Christian Schulz	25	1.60
5	Szabolcs Huszti	28	1.54
6	Steve Cherundolo	32	1.53
7	Mike Hanke	27	1.52
8	Michael Tarnat	15	1.47
9	Bergantin Vinicius	26	1.46
10	Robert Enke	34	1.44
	CLUB AVERAGE:		1.44

DISCIPLINARY RECORDS

	PLAYER	YELLOW	RED	AVE
1	Sergio Pinto	4	2	211
2	Hanno Balitsch	10	0	227
3	A Jan Bruggink	6	0	252
4	Altin Lala	6	1	276
5	Jan Rosenthal	5	0	278
6	Benjamin Lauth	2	0	336
7	Jiri Stajner	4	0	375
8	Michael Tarnat	3	0	459
9	Christian Schulz	4	1	476
10	Valerien Ismael	2	0	589
11	Bergantin Vinicius	4	0	605
12	Frank Fahrenhorst	3	0	621
13	Mike Hanke	3	1	629
	Other	11	0	
	TOTAL	67	5	

KEY GOALKEEPER

Robert Enke

Goals Conceded in the League	56	Counting Games League games when player was on pitch for at least 70 minutes	34
Defensive Rating Ave number of mins between League goals conceded while on the pitch	54	Clean Sheets In League games when player was on pitch for at least 70 minutes	7

KEY PLAYERS - DEFENDERS

Christian Schulz

Goals Conceded Number of League goals conceded while the player was on the pitch	41	Clean Sheets In League games when player was on pitch for at least 70 minutes	5
Defensive Rating Ave number of mins between League goals conceded while on the pitch	58	Club Defensive Rating Average number of mins between League goals conceded by the club this season	54

	PLAYER	CON LGE	CLEAN SHEETS	DEF RATE
1	Christian Schulz	41	5	58 mins
2	Valerien Ismael	20	2	58 mins
3	Frank Fahrenhorst	32	4	58 mins
4	Steve Cherundolo	52	7	56 mins

KEY PLAYERS - MIDFIELDERS

Szabolcs Huszti

Goals in the League	10	Contribution to Attacking Power Average number of minutes between League team goals while on pitch	54
Defensive Rating Average number of mins between League goals conceded while on the pitch	56	Scoring Difference Defensive Rating minus Contribution to Attacking Power	2

	PLAYER	LGE GOALS	DEF RATE	POWER	SCORE DIFF
1	Szabolcs Huszti	10	56	54	2 mins
2	Arnold Jan Bruggink	6	65	65	0 mins
3	Hanno Balitsch	4	56	56	0 mins
4	Altin Lala	0	56	58	-2 mins

KEY PLAYERS - GOALSCORERS

Jiri Stajner

Goals in the League	6	Player Strike Rate Average number of minutes between League goals scored by player	250
Contribution to Attacking Power Average number of minutes between League team goals while on pitch	45	Club Strike Rate Average number of minutes between League goals scored by club	56

	PLAYER	LGE GOALS	POWER	STRIKE RATE
1	Jiri Stajner	6	45	250 mins
2	Mike Hanke	10	54	251 mins
3	Arnold Jan Bruggink	6	65	252 mins
4	Szabolcs Huszti	10	54	267 mins

DIADORA
96
TUI
Mike Hanke

SQUAD APPEARANCES

Match	1	2	3	4	5	6	7	8	9	10	11	12	13	14	15	16	17	18	19	20	21	22	23	24	25	26	27	28	29	30	31	32	33	34
Venue	H	A	A	H	A	H	A	H	A	H	A	H	A	H	A	H	A	A	H	H	A	H	A	H	A	H	A	H	A	H	A	H	A	H
Competition	L	L	L	L	L	L	L	L	L	L	L	L	L	L	L	L	L	L	L	L	L	L	L	L	L	L	L	L	L	L	L	L	L	L
Result	L	W	L	W	D	L	W	W	W	D	D	W	L	L	W	W	L	D	D	L	L	W	L	D	D	D	L	W	W	D	D	W	L	W

Goalkeepers
Robert Enke
Richard Golz
Morten Jensen
Frank Juric

Defenders
Steve Cherundolo
Frank Fahrenhorst
Soren Halfar
Valerien Ismael
Thomas Kleine
Christian Schulz
Michael Tarnat
Bergantin Vinicius
Dariusz Zuraw

Midfielders
Hanno Balitsch
Ferhat Bikmaz
Arnold Jan Bruggink
Szabolcs Huszti
Gaetan Krebs
Altin Lala
Sergio Pinto
Konstantin Rausch
Jan Rosenthal
Bastian Schulz
Chavdar Yankov
Salvatore Zizzo

Forwards
Mike Hanke
Vahid Hashemian
Benjamin Lauth
Fabian Montabell
Jiri Stajner

KEY: ■ On all match ■ On bench ⏮ Subbed or sent off (Counting game) ⏪ Subbed or sent off (playing less than 70 minutes) ⏭ Subbed on from bench (Counting Game) ⏩ Subbed on (playing less than 70 minutes) Subbed on and then subbed or sent off (Counting Game) Subbed on and then subbed or sent off (playing less than 70 minutes) □ Not in 16

EINTRACHT FRANKFURT

Final Position: **9th**

NICKNAME: DIE EINTRACHT

KEY: ☐ Won ☐ Drawn ☐ Lost

							Attendance
1	grpr1	**Hertha Berlin**	H	W	1-0	Amanatidis 30	46,000
2	grpr1	**Arminia B**	A	D	2-2	Meier 87, Russ 89	22,000
3	grpr1	**Hansa Rostock**	H	W	1-0	Meier 2	44,000
4	grpr1	**W Bremen**	A	L	1-2	Thurk 85	40,983
5	grpr1	**Hamburg**	H	W	2-1	Meier 8, 87	51,500
6	grpr1	**Bochum**	A	D	0-0		25,586
7	grpr1	**Karlsruhe**	H	L	0-1		48,500
8	grpr1	**Cottbus**	A	D	2-2	Amanatidis 49, 79 pen	12,400
9	grpr1	**B Leverkusen**	H	W	2-1	Kyrgiakos 54, 79	47,600
10	grpr1	**Nurnberg**	A	L	1-5	Takahara 12	45,050
11	grpr1	**Hannover 96**	H	D	0-0		44,700
12	grpr1	**Bayern Munich**	A	D	0-0		69,000
13	grpr1	**B Dortmund**	A	D	1-1	Amanatidis 55	75,300
14	grpr1	**Stuttgart**	H	L	1-4	Kohler 41	51,500
15	grpr1	**Wolfsburg**	A	D	2-2	Chris 35, Fink 53	20,656
16	grpr1	**Schalke**	H	D	2-2	Toski 49, Amanatidis 82	51,500
17	grpr1	**Duisburg**	A	W	1-0	Amanatidis 40	26,557
18	grpr1	**Hertha Berlin**	A	W	3-0	Fenin 39, 60, 90	35,930
19	grpr1	**Arminia B**	H	W	2-1	Amanatidis 37, Fenin 47	43,300
20	grpr1	**Hansa Rostock**	A	L	0-1		15,500
21	grpr1	**W Bremen**	H	W	1-0	Amanatidis 56	51,500
22	grpr1	**Hamburg**	A	L	1-4	Kyrgiakos 70	53,787
23	grpr1	**Bochum**	H	D	1-1	Toski 49	46,700
24	grpr1	**Karlsruhe**	A	W	1-0	Fink 25	29,348
25	grpr1	**Cottbus**	H	W	2-1	Alves dos Santos 59, Russ 64	45,100
26	grpr1	**B Leverkusen**	A	W	2-0	Kiessling 24 og, Mantzios 90	22,500
27	grpr1	**Nurnberg**	H	L	1-3	Fink 3	51,500
28	grpr1	**Hannover 96**	A	L	1-2	Russ 27	38,104
29	grpr1	**Bayern Munich**	H	L	1-3	Kohler 29	51,500
30	grpr1	**B Dortmund**	H	D	1-1	Kohler 46	51,500
31	grpr1	**Stuttgart**	A	L	1-4	Amanatidis 62	55,500
32	grpr1	**Wolfsburg**	H	L	2-3	Amanatidis 22 pen, Weissenberger 62	45,300
33	grpr1	**Schalke**	A	L	0-1		61,482
34	grpr1	**Duisburg**	H	W	4-2	Amanatidis 13, Fenin 15, 38, Heller 78	49,500

LEAGUE APPEARANCES, BOOKINGS AND CAPS

	AGE (on 01/07/08)	IN NAMED 18	APPEARANCES	COUNTING GAMES	MINUTES ON PITCH	YELLOW CARDS	RED CARDS	CAPS THIS SEASON	NATIONAL SIDE
Goalkeepers									
Oka Nikolov	34	31	12	11	1035	0	0	-	Macedonia
Markus Proll	28	25	23	22	2055	1	0	-	Germany
Jan Zimmermann	23	11	0	0	0	0	0	-	Germany
Defenders									
Mounir Chaftar	22	17	6	0	51	0	0	-	Germany
C M Hening Chris	29	12	10	9	862	4	0	-	Brazil
Aaron Galindo	26	30	22	21	1962	2	0	-	Mexico
Sotirios Kyrgiakos	28	26	24	23	2070	8	0	9	Greece
Mehdi Mahdavikia	30	25	20	12	1218	1	0	-	Iran
Patrick Ochs	24	30	29	28	2572	8	0	-	Germany
Marco Russ	22	32	29	25	2339	3	0	-	Germany
Christoph Spycher	30	30	30	29	2699	2	0	7	Switzerland
Aleksandar Vasoski	28	15	5	3	313	0	0	-	Macedonia
Midfielders									
C Alves dos Santos	22	17	10	0	249	0	0	-	Brazil
Michael Fink	26	34	32	31	2766	3	0	-	Germany
Junichi Inamoto	28	29	24	16	1750	5	0	1	Japan
Kreso Ljubicic	19	7	1	0	41	0	0	-	Croatia
Alexander Meier	25	12	11	11	990	2	0	-	Germany
Christoph Preuss	26	10	7	2	283	1	0	-	Germany
Albert Streit	28	11	11	10	941	1	0	-	Germany
Faton Toski	21	22	12	5	751	1	0	-	Germany
M Weissenberger	33	29	22	9	1161	2	0	4	Austria
Forwards									
Ioannis Amanatidis	26	32	32	28	2730	3	0	4	Greece
Martin Fenin	21	17	17	15	1369	4	0	4	Czech Republic
Marcel Heller	22	9	4	0	103	0	0	-	Germany
Martin Hess	21	1	1	0	44	0	0	-	Germany
Benjamin Kohler	27	34	29	24	2244	2	0	-	Germany
Evangelos Mantzios	25	17	10	2	312	1	0	-	Greece
Naohiro Takahara	29	10	8	3	446	1	0	-	Japan
Michael Thurk	32	14	12	6	634	2	0	-	Germany
Juvhel Tsoumou	17	2	0	0	0	0	0	-	Congo

TEAM OF THE SEASON

G
Markus Proll
CG: 22 DR: 52
D
Mehdi Mahdavikia
CG: 12* DR: 67
D
Patrick Ochs
CG: 28 DR: 62
D
Marco Russ
CG: 25 DR: 61
D
Aaron Galindo
CG: 21 DR: 59
M
Michael Fink
CG: 31 SD: -10
M
Alexander Meier
CG: 11* SD: -12
M
Albert Streit
CG: 10* SD: -27
M
Junichi Inamoto
CG: 16 SD: -45
F
Martin Fenin
CG: 15 SR: 228
F
Ioannis Amanatidis
CG: 28 SR: 248

MONTHLY POINTS TALLY

AUGUST	7	78%
SEPTEMBER	5	33%
OCTOBER	4	44%
NOVEMBER	2	22%
DECEMBER	5	56%
NO LEAGUE GAMES PLAYED IN JANUARY		
FEBRUARY	9	75%
MARCH	10	67%
APRIL	1	8%
MAY	3	25%

LEAGUE GOALS

	PLAYER	MINS	GOALS	S RATE
1	Amanatidis	2730	**11**	248
2	Fenin	1369	**6**	228
3	Meier	990	**4**	247
4	Kyrgiakos	2070	**3**	690
5	Kohler	2244	**3**	748
6	Russ	2339	**3**	779
7	Fink	2766	**3**	922
8	Toski	751	**2**	375
9	Heller	103	**1**	103
10	A dos Santos	249	**1**	249
11	Mantzios	312	**1**	312
12	Takahara	446	**1**	446
13	Thurk	634	**1**	634
	Other		2	
	TOTAL		**42**	

TOP POINT EARNERS

	PLAYER	GAMES	AV PTS
1	Martin Fenin	15	**1.53**
2	Christoph Spycher	29	**1.45**
3	Aaron Galindo	21	**1.43**
4	Michael Fink	31	**1.42**
5	Patrick Ochs	28	**1.39**
6	Benjamin Kohler	24	**1.38**
7	Sotirios Kyrgiakos	23	**1.35**
8	Mehdi Mahdavikia	12	**1.33**
9	Marco Russ	25	**1.32**
10	Ioannis Amanatidis	28	**1.25**
	CLUB AVERAGE:		**1.35**

DISCIPLINARY RECORDS

	PLAYER	YELLOW	RED	AVE
1	C-M Hening Chris	4	0	**215**
2	Sotirios Kyrgiakos	8	0	**258**
3	Michael Thurk	2	0	**317**
4	Patrick Ochs	8	0	**321**
5	Martin Fenin	4	0	**342**
6	Junichi Inamoto	5	0	**350**
7	Alexander Meier	2	0	**495**
8	M Weissenberger	2	0	**580**
9	Faton Toski	1	0	**751**
10	Marco Russ	3	0	**779**
11	Ioannis Amanatidis	3	0	**910**
12	Michael Fink	3	0	**922**
13	Albert Streit	1	0	**941**
	Other	8	0	
	TOTAL	**54**	**0**	

KEY GOALKEEPER

Markus Proll

Goals Conceded in the League	39	Counting Games League games when player was on pitch for at least 70 minutes	22
Defensive Rating Ave number of mins between League goals conceded while on the pitch	52	Clean Sheets In League games when player was on pitch for at least 70 minutes	4

KEY PLAYERS - GOALSCORERS

Martin Fenin

Goals in the League	6	Player Strike Rate Average number of minutes between League goals scored by player	228
Contribution to Attacking Power Average number of minutes between League team goals while on pitch	65	Club Strike Rate Average number of minutes between League goals scored by club	71

	PLAYER	LGE GOALS	POWER	STRIKE RATE
1	Martin Fenin	6	65	228 mins
2	Ioannis Amanatidis	11	73	248 mins
3	Benjamin Kohler	3	66	748 mins
4	Michael Fink	3	74	922 mins

KEY PLAYERS - DEFENDERS

Mehdi Mahdavikia

Goals Conceded Number of League goals conceded while the player was on the pitch	18	Clean Sheets In League games when player was on pitch for at least 70 minutes	4
Defensive Rating Ave number of mins between League goals conceded while on the pitch	67	Club Defensive Rating Average number of mins between League goals conceded by the club this season	61

	PLAYER	CON LGE	CLEAN SHEETS	DEF RATE
1	Mehdi Mahdavikia	18	4	67 mins
2	Patrick Ochs	41	9	62 mins
3	Marco Russ	38	7	61 mins
4	Aaron Galindo	33	6	59 mins

JAKO
Ioannis Amanatidis

KEY PLAYERS - MIDFIELDERS

Michael Fink

Goals in the League	3	Contribution to Attacking Power Average number of minutes between League team goals while on pitch	74
Defensive Rating Average number of mins between League goals conceded while on the pitch	64	Scoring Difference Defensive Rating minus Contribution to Attacking Power	-10

	PLAYER	LGE GOALS	DEF RATE	POWER	SCORE DIFF
1	Michael Fink	3	64	74	-10 mins
2	Alexander Meier	4	70	82	-12 mins
3	Albert Streit	0	67	94	-27 mins
4	Junichi Inamoto	0	64	109	-45 mins

SQUAD APPEARANCES

Match	1	2	3	4	5	6	7	8	9	10	11	12	13	14	15	16	17	18	19	20	21	22	23	24	25	26	27	28	29	30	31	32	33	34
Venue	H	A	H	A	H	A	H	A	H	A	H	A	A	H	A	H	A	A	H	A	H	A	H	A	H	A	H	A	H	H	A	H	A	H
Competition	L	L	L	L	L	L	L	L	L	L	L	L	L	L	L	L	L	L	L	L	L	L	L	L	L	L	L	L	L	L	L	L	L	L
Result	W	D	W	L	W	D	L	D	W	L	D	D	D	L	D	D	W	W	W	L	W	L	D	W	W	W	L	L	L	D	L	L	L	W

Goalkeepers
Oka Nikolov
Markus Proll
Jan Zimmermann

Defenders
Mounir Chaftar
C M Hening Chris
Aaron Galindo
Sotirios Kyrgiakos
Mehdi Mahdavikia
Patrick Ochs
Marco Russ
Christoph Spycher
Aleksandar Vasoski

Midfielders
Cesar Alves dos Santos
Michael Fink
Junichi Inamoto
Kreso Ljubicic
Alexander Meier
Christoph Preuss
Albert Streit
Faton Toski
Markus Weissenberger

Forwards
Ioannis Amanatidis
Martin Fenin
Marcel Heller
Martin Hess
Benjamin Kohler
Evangelos Mantzios
Naohiro Takahara
Michael Thurk
Juvhel Tsoumou

KEY: On all match | On bench | Subbed or sent off (Counting game) | Subbed or sent off (playing less than 70 minutes) | Subbed on from bench (Counting Game) | Subbed on (playing less than 70 minutes) | Subbed on and then subbed or sent off (Counting Game) | Subbed on and then subbed or sent off (playing less than 70 minutes) | Not in 16

HERTHA BERLIN

Final Position: **10th**

NICKNAME: FROSCHE

KEY: Won / Drawn / Lost

No	Comp	Opponent	H/A	Res	Score	Scorers	Attendance
1	grpr1	Eintr Frankfurt	A	L	0-1		46,000
2	grpr1	Stuttgart	H	W	3-1	Chahed 51 pen, Fathi 64, Okoronkwo 80	50,000
3	grpr1	Arminia B	A	L	0-2		20,000
4	grpr1	Wolfsburg	H	W	2-1	Pantelic 38, Okoronkwo 88	40,000
5	grpr1	Duisburg	A	W	2-1	Pantelic 60, 70	20,000
6	grpr1	B Dortmund	H	W	3-2	Pantelic 43, Lucio 54, Okoronkwo 76	45,000
7	grpr1	Hansa Rostock	H	L	1-3	Pantelic 2	40,000
8	grpr1	Schalke	A	L	0-1		61,482
9	grpr1	Cottbus	H	D	0-0		48,719
10	grpr1	W Bremen	A	L	2-3	Gilberto 60, Okoronkwo 90	40,278
11	grpr1	Bochum	H	W	2-0	Maltritz 26 og, Pantelic 35	34,580
12	grpr1	Hamburg	A	L	1-2	Ebert 59	56,493
13	grpr1	Hannover 96	H	W	1-0	Andre Lima 87	34,213
14	grpr1	Karlsruhe	A	L	1-2	Pantelic 35	29,000
15	grpr1	B Leverkusen	H	L	0-3		40,527
16	grpr1	Nurnberg	A	L	1-2	F.Lustenberger 65	41,000
17	grpr1	Bayern Munich	H	D	0-0		74,220
18	grpr1	Eintr Frankfurt	H	L	0-3		35,930
19	grpr1	Stuttgart	A	W	3-1	Pantelic 7, 45, Raffael De Araujo 49	50,000
20	grpr1	Arminia B	H	W	1-0	Raffael De Araujo 90	33,031
21	grpr1	Wolfsburg	A	D	0-0		23,659
22	grpr1	Duisburg	H	W	2-0	Raffael De Araujo 34, Pantelic 37	32,382
23	grpr1	B Dortmund	A	D	1-1	Pantelic 50	69,400
24	grpr1	Hansa Rostock	A	D	0-0		22,500
25	grpr1	Schalke	H	L	1-2	Chahed 67 pen	60,000
26	grpr1	Cottbus	A	L	1-2	Mineiro 21	20,746
27	grpr1	W Bremen	H	L	1-2	Andre Lima 10	59,728
28	grpr1	Bochum	A	D	1-1	Skacel 28	20,883
29	grpr1	Hamburg	H	D	0-0		40,289
30	grpr1	Hannover 96	A	D	2-2	Chahed 55 pen, Piszczek 66	41,473
31	grpr1	Karlsruhe	H	W	3-1	Kacar 25, Pantelic 31, Skacel 87	49,595
32	grpr1	B Leverkusen	A	W	2-1	Pantelic 26, Chahed 68 pen	22,500
33	grpr1	Nurnberg	H	W	1-0	Raffael De Araujo 74	47,072
34	grpr1	Bayern Munich	A	L	1-4	Domovchiyski 84	69,000

LEAGUE APPEARANCES, BOOKINGS AND CAPS

	AGE (on 01/07/08)	IN NAMED 18	APPEARANCES	COUNTING GAMES	MINUTES ON PITCH	YELLOW CARDS	RED CARDS	CAPS THIS SEASON	NATIONAL SIDE
Goalkeepers									
Jaroslav Drobny	28	34	34	34	3060	1	0	-	Czech Republic
Christian Fiedler	33	34	0	0	0	0	0	-	Germany
Defenders									
Josip Simunic	30	29	29	29	2610	7	0	10	Croatia
Pascal Bieler	22	24	6	1	138	1	0	-	Germany
Dennis Cagara	23	1	0	0	0	0	0	-	Denmark
Sofian Chahed	25	34	33	30	2692	4	0	-	Germany
Malik Fathi	24	22	22	21	1935	3	0	-	Germany
Arne Friedrich	29	30	30	29	2624	6	0	8	Germany
Steve von Bergen	25	26	25	21	1983	3	0	-	Switzerland
Midfielders									
Bryan Arguez	19	9	1	0	28	0	0	-	United States
Pal Dardai	32	31	23	11	1285	4	0	-	Hungary
Patrick Ebert	21	27	26	19	1982	4	0	-	Germany
Gilberto	32	15	15	13	1233	1	0	4	Brazil
Tobias Grahn	28	16	13	3	620	2	0	-	Sweden
Gojko Kacar	21	17	17	14	1436	3	0	-	Serbia
Lucio	29	8	8	6	605	2	0	-	Brazil
Fabian Lustenberger	20	29	23	14	1396	1	0	-	Switzerland
Christian Muller	24	3	1	1	90	0	0	-	Germany
Mineiro	32	33	26	17	1651	3	0	4	Brazil
Andreas Schmidt	34	16	6	3	389	0	0	-	Germany
Rudolf Skacel	28	16	16	13	1298	4	0	1	Czech Republic
Ibrahima Traore	20	2	1	0	18	0	0	-	France
Forwards									
Andre Lima	23	25	16	7	969	1	0	-	Brazil
Valeri Domovchiyski	22	10	4	0	57	0	0	-	Bulgaria
Chinedu Ede	21	10	4	0	83	0	0	-	Germany
Srdjan Lakic	24	1	1	0	18	0	0	-	Croatia
Solomon Okoronkwo	21	33	22	2	586	2	0	-	Nigeria
Marko Pantelic	29	28	28	25	2271	1	0	5	Serbia
Lukasz Piszczek	23	31	24	10	1214	1	0	2	Poland
C Raffael De Araujo	23	15	15	14	1299	1	0	-	Brazil

TEAM OF THE SEASON

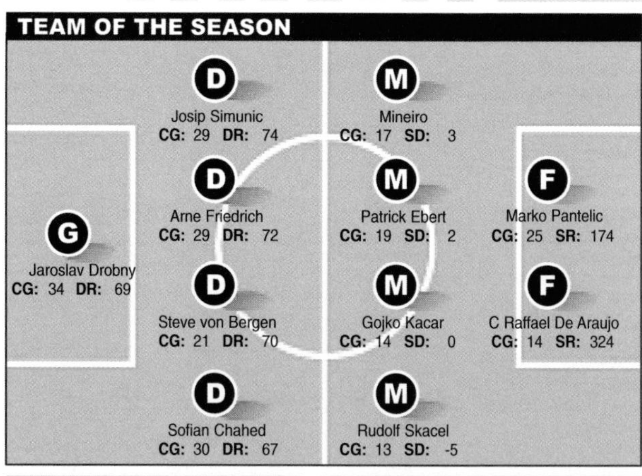

G
Jaroslav Drobny
CG: 34 DR: 69
D
Josip Simunic
CG: 29 DR: 74
D
Arne Friedrich
CG: 29 DR: 72
D
Steve von Bergen
CG: 21 DR: 70
D
Sofian Chahed
CG: 30 DR: 67
M
Mineiro
CG: 17 SD: 3
M
Patrick Ebert
CG: 19 SD: 2
M
Gojko Kacar
CG: 14 SD: 0
M
Rudolf Skacel
CG: 13 SD: -5
F
Marko Pantelic
CG: 25 SR: 174
F
C Raffael De Araujo
CG: 14 SR: 324

MONTHLY POINTS TALLY

Month	Points	%
AUGUST	3	33%
SEPTEMBER	9	60%
OCTOBER	4	44%
NOVEMBER	3	33%
DECEMBER	1	11%
NO LEAGUE GAMES PLAYED IN JANUARY		
FEBRUARY	10	67%
MARCH	2	17%
APRIL	3	25%
MAY	9	75%

LEAGUE GOALS

	PLAYER	MINS	GOALS	S RATE
1	Pantelic	2271	**13**	174
2	Okoronkwo	586	**4**	146
3	R De Araujo	1299	**4**	324
4	Chahed	2692	**4**	673
5	Andre Lima	969	**2**	484
6	Skacel	1298	**2**	649
7	Domovchiyski	57	**1**	57
8	Lucio	605	**1**	605
9	Piszczek	1214	**1**	1214
10	Gilberto	1233	**1**	1233
11	Lustenberger	1396	**1**	1396
12	Kacar	1436	**1**	1436
13	Mineiro	1651	**1**	1651
	Other		2	
	TOTAL		**38**	

TOP POINT EARNERS

	PLAYER	GAMES	AV PTS
1	C Raffael De Araujo	14	**1.57**
2	Rudolf Skacel	13	**1.54**
3	Marko Pantelic	25	**1.48**
4	Patrick Ebert	19	**1.42**
5	Josip Simunic	29	**1.41**
6	Mineiro	17	**1.35**
7	Sofian Chahed	30	**1.30**
8	Jaroslav Drobny	34	**1.29**
9	Gojko Kacar	14	**1.29**
10	Malik Fathi	21	**1.29**
	CLUB AVERAGE:		**1.29**

DISCIPLINARY RECORDS

	PLAYER	YELLOW	RED	AVE
1	S Okoronkwo	2	0	**293**
2	Lucio	2	0	**302**
3	Tobias Grahn	2	0	**310**
4	Pal Dardai	4	0	**321**
5	Rudolf Skacel	4	0	**324**
6	Josip Simunic	7	0	**372**
7	Arne Friedrich	6	0	**437**
8	Gojko Kacar	3	0	**478**
9	Patrick Ebert	4	0	**495**
10	Mineiro	3	0	**550**
11	Malik Fathi	3	0	**645**
12	Steve von Bergen	3	0	**661**
13	Sofian Chahed	4	0	**673**
	Other	7	0	
	TOTAL	**54**	**0**	

KEY GOALKEEPER

Jaroslav Drobny

Goals Conceded in the League	44	Counting Games League games when player was on pitch for at least 70 minutes	34
Defensive Rating Ave number of mins between League goals conceded while on the pitch	69	Clean Sheets In League games when player was on pitch for at least 70 minutes	10

KEY PLAYERS - DEFENDERS

Josip Simunic

Goals Conceded Number of League goals conceded while the player was on the pitch	35	Clean Sheets In League games when player was on pitch for at least 70 minutes	10
Defensive Rating Ave number of mins between League goals conceded while on the pitch	74	Club Defensive Rating Average number of mins between League goals conceded by the club this season	69

	PLAYER	CON LGE	CLEAN SHEETS	DEF RATE
1	Josip Simunic	35	10	74 mins
2	Arne Friedrich	36	10	72 mins
3	Steve von Bergen	28	7	70 mins
4	Sofian Chahed	40	7	67 mins

KEY PLAYERS - MIDFIELDERS

Mineiro

Goals in the League	1	Contribution to Attacking Power Average number of minutes between League team goals while on pitch	75
Defensive Rating Average number of mins between League goals conceded while on the pitch	78	Scoring Difference Defensive Rating minus Contribution to Attacking Power	3

	PLAYER	LGE GOALS	DEF RATE	POWER	SCORE DIFF
1	Mineiro	1	78	75	3 mins
2	Patrick Ebert	1	70	68	2 mins
3	Gojko Kacar	1	75	75	0 mins
4	Rudolf Skacel	2	81	86	-5 mins

KEY PLAYERS - GOALSCORERS

Marko Pantelic

Goals in the League	13	Player Strike Rate Average number of minutes between League goals scored by player	174
Contribution to Attacking Power Average number of minutes between League team goals while on pitch	78	Club Strike Rate Average number of minutes between League goals scored by club	78

	PLAYER	LGE GOALS	POWER	STRIKE RATE
1	Marko Pantelic	13	78	174 mins
2	Caetano Raffael De Araujo	4	68	324 mins
3	Rudolf Skacel	2	86	649 mins
4	Gilberto	1	82	1233 mins

DB
Marko Pantelic

SQUAD APPEARANCES

Match	1	2	3	4	5	6	7	8	9	10	11	12	13	14	15	16	17	18	19	20	21	22	23	24	25	26	27	28	29	30	31	32	33	34
Venue	A	H	A	H	A	H	H	A	H	A	H	A	H	A	H	A	H	H	A	H	A	H	A	A	H	A	H	A	H	A	H	A	H	A
Competition	L	L	L	L	L	L	L	L	L	L	L	L	L	L	L	L	L	L	L	L	L	L	L	L	L	L	L	L	L	L	L	L	L	L
Result	L	W	L	W	W	W	L	L	D	L	W	L	W	L	L	L	D	L	W	W	D	W	D	D	L	L	L	D	D	D	W	W	W	L

Goalkeepers
Jaroslav Drobny
Christian Fiedler

Defenders
Josip Simunic
Pascal Bieler
Dennis Cagara
Sofian Chahed
Malik Fathi
Arne Friedrich
Steve von Bergen

Midfielders
Bryan Arguez
Pal Dardai
Patrick Ebert
Gilberto
Tobias Grahn
Gojko Kacar
Lucio
Fabian Lustenberger
Christian Muller
Mineiro
Andreas Schmidt
Rudolf Skacel
Ibrahima Traore

Forwards
Andre Lima
Valeri Domovchiyski
Chinedu Ede
Srdjan Lakic
Solomon Okoronkwo
Marko Pantelic
Lukasz Piszczek
C Raffael De Araujo

KEY: On all match / On bench / Subbed or sent off (Counting game) / Subbed or sent off (playing less than 70 minutes) / Subbed on from bench (Counting Game) / Subbed on (playing less than 70 minutes) / Subbed on and then subbed or sent off (Counting Game) / Subbed on and then subbed or sent off (playing less than 70 minutes) / Not in 16

KARLSRUHE

Final Position: **11th**

NICKNAME: KSC

KEY: ☐Won ☐Drawn ☐Lost

		Opponent			Score	Scorers	Attendance
1	grpr1	**Nurnberg**	A	W	2-0	Hajnal 44, 74	40,000
2	grpr1	**Hannover 96**	H	L	1-2	Franz 37	30,000
3	grpr1	**B Leverkusen**	A	L	0-3		22,000
4	grpr1	**Stuttgart**	H	W	1-0	Hajnal 54	27,800
5	grpr1	**Wolfsburg**	A	W	2-1	Eggimann 63, Eichner 79	21,600
6	grpr1	**Bayern Munich**	H	L	1-4	Porcello 51	30,702
7	grpr1	**Eintr Frankfurt**	A	W	1-0	Franz 51	48,500
8	grpr1	**B Dortmund**	H	W	3-1	Porcello 25, Eggimann 64, Freis 75	30,500
9	grpr1	**Schalke**	A	W	2-0	Timm 69, 83	61,000
10	grpr1	**Arminia B**	H	D	0-0		27,361
11	grpr1	**Hansa Rostock**	A	D	0-0		14,000
12	grpr1	**Duisburg**	H	W	1-0	Eggimann 29	27,714
13	grpr1	**W Bremen**	A	L	0-4		39,669
14	grpr1	**Hertha Berlin**	H	W	2-1	Hajnal 56, Freis 66	29,000
15	grpr1	**Cottbus**	A	L	0-2		10,900
16	grpr1	**Bochum**	A	D	2-2	Hajnal 25, Freis 56	25,000
17	grpr1	**Hamburg**	H	D	1-1	Timm 46	30,300
18	grpr1	**Nurnberg**	H	W	2-0	Eichner 66, Kennedy 74	29,300
19	grpr1	**Hannover 96**	A	D	2-2	Kennedy 61, Hajnal 64	41,112
20	grpr1	**B Leverkusen**	H	D	2-2	Freis 60, Kennedy 78	28,500
21	grpr1	**Stuttgart**	A	L	1-3	Hajnal 81	55,000
22	grpr1	**Wolfsburg**	H	W	3-1	Eggimann 23, Kennedy 73, Ricardo Costa 90 og	27,871
23	grpr1	**Bayern Munich**	A	L	0-2		69,000
24	grpr1	**Eintr Frankfurt**	H	L	0-1		29,348
25	grpr1	**B Dortmund**	A	D	1-1	Freis 63	74,300
26	grpr1	**Schalke**	H	D	0-0		29,477
27	grpr1	**Arminia B**	A	L	0-1		19,600
28	grpr1	**Hansa Rostock**	H	L	1-2	Freis 70	27,714
29	grpr1	**Duisburg**	A	W	1-0	Hajnal 81	20,255
30	grpr1	**W Bremen**	H	D	3-3	Freis 15, 59, Kapllani 66	29,470
31	grpr1	**Hertha Berlin**	A	L	1-3	Kapllani 53	49,595
32	grpr1	**Cottbus**	H	D	1-1	Buck 65	28,000
33	grpr1	**Bochum**	H	L	1-3	Eggimann 87	27,920
34	grpr1	**Hamburg**	A	L	0-7		57,000

LEAGUE APPEARANCES, BOOKINGS AND CAPS

	AGE (on 01/07/08)	IN NAMED 18	APPEARANCES	COUNTING GAMES	MINUTES ON PITCH	YELLOW CARDS	RED CARDS	CAPS THIS SEASON	NATIONAL SIDE
Goalkeepers									
J-F Kornetzky	25	34	6	6	540	0	0	-	France
Markus Miller	26	28	28	28	2520	1	0	-	Germany
Defenders									
Stefan Buck	27	26	12	4	508	3	0	-	Germany
Florian Dick	23	15	3	1	163	0	0	-	Germany
Mario Eggimann	27	33	33	33	2970	5	0	3	Switzerland
Christian Eichner	25	33	33	32	2935	4	0	-	Germany
Maik Franz	26	29	29	29	2594	9	0	-	Germany
Andreas Gorlitz	26	31	31	29	2710	4	1	-	Germany
Christopher Reinhard	23	7	0	0	0	0	0	-	Germany
Martin Stoll	25	34	8	6	564	2	0	-	Germany
Midfielders									
Godfried Aduobe	32	27	24	11	1378	5	0	-	Ghana
Benjamin Barg	23	3	0	0	0	0	0	-	Germany
Daniel Brosinski	19	2	0	0	0	0	0	-	Germany
Bradley Carnell	31	21	17	8	1015	2	0	-	South Africa
Tamas Hajnal	27	32	32	32	2813	6	0	4	Hungary
Michael Mutzel	28	29	29	28	2498	5	0	-	Germany
Massimo Porcello	28	28	25	16	1723	2	0	-	Italy
Timo Staffeldt	24	34	16	2	391	1	0	-	Germany
Lars Stindl	19	8	2	0	18	0	0	-	Germany
Forwards									
Sebastian Freis	23	33	31	21	2154	1	0	-	Germany
Alexander Iashvili	30	33	28	16	1820	0	0	-	Georgia
Edmund Kapllani	25	33	28	11	1379	1	0	5	Albania
Joshua Kennedy	25	10	10	10	838	1	0	-	Australia
Sanibal Orahovac	29	8	4	0	93	0	0	-	Montenegro
Haluk Turkeri	21	2	0	0	0	0	0	-	Turkey
Christian Timm	29	31	30	18	2031	5	0	-	Germany

TEAM OF THE SEASON

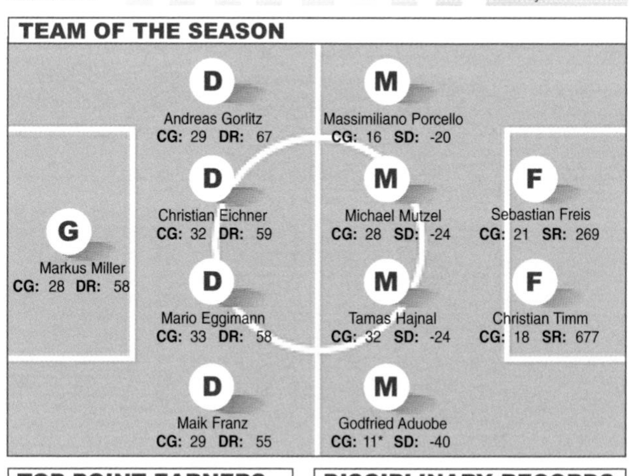

D
Andreas Gorlitz
CG: 29 DR: 67
M
Massimiliano Porcello
CG: 16 SD: -20
D
Christian Eichner
CG: 32 DR: 59
M
Michael Mutzel
CG: 28 SD: -24
F
Sebastian Freis
CG: 21 SR: 269
G
Markus Miller
CG: 28 DR: 58
D
Mario Eggimann
CG: 33 DR: 58
M
Tamas Hajnal
CG: 32 SD: -24
F
Christian Timm
CG: 18 SR: 677
D
Maik Franz
CG: 29 DR: 55
M
Godfried Aduobe
CG: 11* SD: -40

MONTHLY POINTS TALLY

AUGUST	3	33%
SEPTEMBER	12	80%
OCTOBER	5	56%
NOVEMBER	6	67%
DECEMBER	2	22%
NO LEAGUE GAMES PLAYED IN JANUARY		
FEBRUARY	5	42%
MARCH	5	33%
APRIL	4	33%
MAY	1	8%

LEAGUE GOALS

	PLAYER	MINS	GOALS	S RATE
1	Freis	2154	**8**	269
2	Hajnal	2813	**8**	351
3	Eggimann	2970	**5**	594
4	Kennedy	838	**4**	209
5	Timm	2031	**3**	677
6	Kapllani	1379	**2**	689
7	Porcello	1723	**2**	861
8	Franz	2594	**2**	1297
9	Eichner	2935	**2**	1467
10	Buck	508	**1**	508
11	Carnell	1015	**0**	
12	Dick	163	**0**	
13	Aduobe	1378	**0**	
	Other		0	
	TOTAL		**37**	

TOP POINT EARNERS

	PLAYER	GAMES	AV PTS
1	Christian Timm	18	**1.72**
2	Sebastian Freis	21	**1.38**
3	Andreas Gorlitz	29	**1.38**
4	Christian Eichner	32	**1.31**
5	Mario Eggimann	33	**1.30**
6	Maik Franz	29	**1.28**
7	Markus Miller	28	**1.25**
8	Michael Mutzel	28	**1.25**
9	Massimiliano Porcello	16	**1.25**
10	Tamas Hajnal	32	**1.25**
	CLUB AVERAGE:		**1.26**

DISCIPLINARY RECORDS

	PLAYER	YELLOW	RED	AVE
1	Stefan Buck	3	0	**169**
2	Godfried Aduobe	5	0	**275**
3	Martin Stoll	2	0	**282**
4	Maik Franz	9	0	**288**
5	Christian Timm	5	0	**406**
6	Tamas Hajnal	6	0	**468**
7	Michael Mutzel	5	0	**499**
8	Bradley Carnell	2	0	**507**
9	Andreas GÃ¶rlitz	4	1	**542**
10	Mario Eggimann	5	0	**594**
11	Christian Eichner	4	0	**733**
12	Joshua Kennedy	1	0	**838**
13	M Porcello	2	0	**861**
	Other	3	0	
	TOTAL	**56**	**1**	

KEY GOALKEEPER

Markus Miller			
Goals Conceded in the League	43	Counting Games League games when player was on pitch for at least 70 minutes	28
Defensive Rating Ave number of mins between League goals conceded while on the pitch	58	Clean Sheets In League games when player was on pitch for at least 70 minutes	9

KEY PLAYERS - DEFENDERS

Andreas Gorlitz			
Goals Conceded Number of League goals conceded while the player was on the pitch	40	Clean Sheets In League games when player was on pitch for at least 70 minutes	10
Defensive Rating Ave number of mins between League goals conceded while on the pitch	67	Club Defensive Rating Average number of mins between League goals conceded by the club this season	57

	PLAYER	CON LGE	CLEAN SHEETS	DEF RATE
1	Andreas Gorlitz	40	10	67 mins
2	Christian Eichner	49	10	59 mins
3	Mario Eggimann	51	10	58 mins
4	Maik Franz	47	9	55 mins

KEY PLAYERS - MIDFIELDERS

Massimiliano Porcello			
Goals in the League	2	Contribution to Attacking Power Average number of minutes between League team goals while on pitch	86
Defensive Rating Average number of mins between League goals conceded while on the pitch	66	Scoring Difference Defensive Rating minus Contribution to Attacking Power	-20

	PLAYER	LGE GOALS	DEF RATE	POWER	SCORE DIFF
1	Massimiliano Porcello	2	66	86	-20 mins
2	Michael Mutzel	0	54	78	-24 mins
3	Tamas Hajnal	8	58	82	-24 mins
4	Godfried Aduobe	0	51	91	-40 mins

KEY PLAYERS - GOALSCORERS

Sebastian Freis			
Goals in the League	8	Player Strike Rate Average number of minutes between League goals scored by player	69
Contribution to Attacking Power Average number of minutes between League team goals while on pitch	76	Club Strike Rate Average number of minutes between League goals scored by club	80

	PLAYER	LGE GOALS	POWER	STRIKE RATE
1	Sebastian Freis	8	76	269 mins
2	Tamas Hajnal	8	82	351 mins
3	Christian Timm	3	72	677 mins
4	Massimiliano Porcello	2	86	861 mins

JAKO
KSC
EnBW
Tamas Hajnal

SQUAD APPEARANCES

Match	1	2	3	4	5	6	7	8	9	10	11	12	13	14	15	16	17	18	19	20	21	22	23	24	25	26	27	28	29	30	31	32	33	34
Venue	A	H	A	H	A	H	A	H	A	H	A	H	A	H	A	A	H	H	A	H	A	H	A	H	A	H	A	H	A	H	A	H	H	A
Competition	L	L	L	L	L	L	L	L	L	L	L	L	L	L	L	L	L	L	L	L	L	L	L	L	L	L	L	L	L	L	L	L	L	L
Result	W	L	L	W	W	L	W	W	W	D	D	W	L	W	L	D	D	W	D	D	L	W	L	L	D	D	L	L	W	D	L	D	L	L

Goalkeepers
Jean-Francois Kornetzky
Markus Miller

Defenders
Stefan Buck
Florian Dick
Mario Eggimann
Christian Eichner
Maik Franz
Andreas Gorlitz
Christopher Reinhard
Martin Stoll

Midfielders
Godfried Aduobe
Benjamin Barg
Daniel Brosinski
Bradley Carnell
Tamas Hajnal
Michael Mutzel
Massimiliano Porcello
Timo Staffeldt
Lars Stindl

Forwards
Sebastian Freis
Alexander Iashvili
Edmund Kapllani
Joshua Kennedy
Sanibal Orahovac
Haluk Turkeri
Christian Timm

KEY: On all match | On bench | Subbed or sent off (Counting game) | Subbed or sent off (playing less than 70 minutes) | Subbed on from bench (Counting Game) | Subbed on (playing less than 70 minutes) | Subbed on and then subbed or sent off (Counting Game) | Subbed on and then subbed or sent off (playing less than 70 minutes) | Not in 16

VfL BOCHUM

Final Position: **12th**

NICKNAME: VFL

KEY: ☐Won ☐Drawn ☐Lost

							Attendance
1	grpr1	**W Bremen**	H	D	2-2	Sestak 46, Bechmann 49	29,037
2	grpr1	**Cottbus**	A	W	2-1	Bechmann 14, 42	20,000
3	grpr1	**Hamburg**	H	W	2-1	Sestak 45, Imhof 83	27,000
4	grpr1	**Hannover 96**	A	L	2-3	Bechmann 44, Maltritz 66 pen	30,794
5	grpr1	**B Leverkusen**	A	L	0-2		22,500
6	grpr1	**Eintr Frankfurt**	H	D	0-0		25,586
7	grpr1	**Stuttgart**	A	L	0-1		36,000
8	grpr1	**Nurnberg**	H	D	3-3	Sestak 43, 65, Mieciel 62	20,000
9	grpr1	**B Dortmund**	A	L	1-2	Mieciel 34	72,200
10	grpr1	**Bayern Munich**	H	L	1-2	Grote 11	31,328
11	grpr1	**Hertha Berlin**	A	L	0-2		34,580
12	grpr1	**Wolfsburg**	H	W	5-3	Sestak 3, 44, Maltritz 20 pen, Fuchs 39, Epalle 63	20,940
13	grpr1	**Duisburg**	A	W	2-0	Imhof 30, Bechmann 84	24,359
14	grpr1	**Arminia B**	H	W	3-0	Mieciel 12, 15, Dabrowski 56	20,478
15	grpr1	**Schalke**	A	L	0-1		61,482
16	grpr1	**Karlsruhe**	H	D	2-2	Sestak 19, 59	25,000
17	grpr1	**Hansa Rostock**	A	L	0-2		16,000
18	grpr1	**W Bremen**	A	W	2-1	Auer 69, Yahia 84	37,149
19	grpr1	**Cottbus**	H	D	3-3	Ipsa 7 og, Sestak 42, Auer 68	21,000
20	grpr1	**Hamburg**	A	L	0-3		50,069
21	grpr1	**Hannover 96**	H	W	2-1	Cherundolo 30 og, Auer 52	19,902
22	grpr1	**B Leverkusen**	H	W	2-0	Zdebel 66, Dabrowski 88	23,781
23	grpr1	**Eintr Frankfurt**	A	D	1-1	Azaouagh 67 fk	46,700
24	grpr1	**Stuttgart**	H	D	1-1	Dabrowski 20	25,086
25	grpr1	**Nurnberg**	A	D	1-1	Sestak 5	43,547
26	grpr1	**B Dortmund**	H	D	3-3	Dabrowski 3, Auer 9, 42	31,328
27	grpr1	**Bayern Munich**	A	L	1-3	Azaouagh 4	69,000
28	grpr1	**Hertha Berlin**	H	D	1-1	Yahia 42	20,883
29	grpr1	**Wolfsburg**	A	W	1-0	Sestak 88	18,101
30	grpr1	**Duisburg**	H	D	1-1	Sestak 84	24,339
31	grpr1	**Arminia B**	A	L	0-2		23,800
32	grpr1	**Schalke**	H	L	0-3		31,328
33	grpr1	**Karlsruhe**	A	W	3-1	Azaouagh 45, Dabrowski 47, Sestak 50	27,920
34	grpr1	**Hansa Rostock**	H	L	1-2	Mavraj 36	18,883

LEAGUE APPEARANCES, BOOKINGS AND CAPS

	AGE (on 01/07/08)	IN NAMED 18	APPEARANCES	COUNTING GAMES	MINUTES ON PITCH	YELLOW CARDS	RED CARDS	CAPS THIS SEASON	NATIONAL SIDE
Goalkeepers									
Philipp Heerwagen	25	14	0	0	0	0	0	-	Germany
Jan Lastuvka	25	31	25	25	2228	3	0	-	Czech Republic
Rene Renno	29	23	10	9	832	0	0	-	Germany
Defenders									
Phillip Bonig	28	30	25	23	2144	3	0	-	Germany
Matias Concha	28	25	18	16	1504	3	0	3	Sweden
Pavel Drsek	31	31	12	2	254	0	0	-	Czech Republic
Patrick Fabian	20	3	0	0	0	0	0	-	Germany
Daniel Imhof	30	28	24	17	1772	3	0	-	Canada
Marcel Maltritz	29	31	31	30	2749	4	0	-	Germany
Mergim Mavraj	22	2	2	1	112	0	0	-	Germany
Martin Meichelbeck	31	16	5	3	307	0	0	-	Germany
Marc Pfertzel	27	33	28	25	2374	5	1	-	France
Anthar Yahia	26	33	33	30	2844	4	0	2	Algeria
Midfielders									
Mimoun Azaouagh	25	15	14	8	899	0	0	-	Germany
Christophe Dabrowski	30	29	28	24	2355	8	0	-	Germany
Joel Epalle	30	29	26	19	1794	2	0	-	Cameroon
Danny Fuchs	32	28	17	11	942	4	0	-	Germany
Dennis Grote	21	23	18	5	710	2	0	-	Germany
Ivo Ilicevic	21	10	6	3	272	1	0	-	Croatia
Shinji Ono	28	13	12	4	597	0	0	-	Japan
Heinrich Schmidtgal	22	1	0	0	0	0	0	-	Germany
Oliver Schroder	28	19	15	6	745	0	0	-	Germany
Tomasz Zdebel	35	27	26	16	1852	11	0	-	Poland
Forwards									
Benjamin Auer	27	26	17	10	1192	3	0	-	Germany
Tommy Bechmann	26	20	20	7	950	1	0	-	Denmark
Oleksiy Bielik	27	6	4	0	96	1	0	-	Ukraine
Marcin Mieciel	32	31	25	11	1238	3	0	-	Poland
Marc Sand	20	1	0	0	0	0	0	-	Austria
Stanislav Sestak	25	33	33	31	2861	6	0	5	Slovakia

TEAM OF THE SEASON

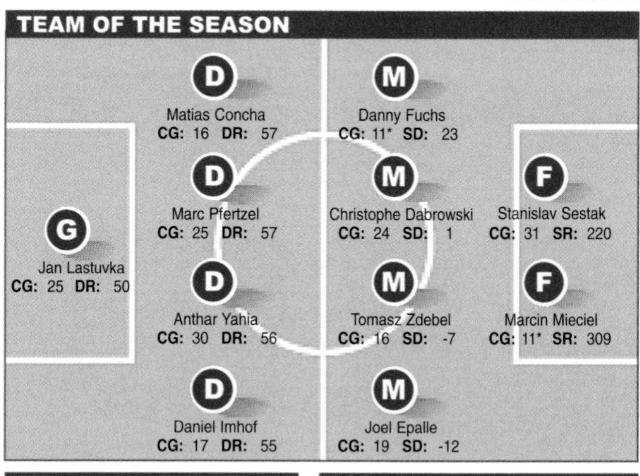

G
Jan Lastuvka
CG: 25 DR: 50
D
Matias Concha
CG: 16 DR: 57
D
Marc Pfertzel
CG: 25 DR: 57
D
Anthar Yahia
CG: 30 DR: 56
D
Daniel Imhof
CG: 17 DR: 55
M
Danny Fuchs
CG: 11* SD: 23
M
Christophe Dabrowski
CG: 24 SD: 1
M
Tomasz Zdebel
CG: 16 SD: -7
M
Joel Epalle
CG: 19 SD: -12
F
Stanislav Sestak
CG: 31 SR: 220
F
Marcin Mieciel
CG: 11* SR: 309

MONTHLY POINTS TALLY

AUGUST	7	78%
SEPTEMBER	2	13%
OCTOBER	0	0%
NOVEMBER	9	100%
DECEMBER	1	11%
NO LEAGUE GAMES PLAYED IN JANUARY		
FEBRUARY	7	58%
MARCH	7	47%
APRIL	5	42%
MAY	3	25%

LEAGUE GOALS

	PLAYER	MINS	GOALS	S RATE
1	Sestak	2861	**13**	220
2	Bechmann	950	**5**	190
3	Auer	1192	**5**	238
4	Dabrowski	2355	**5**	471
5	Mieciel	1238	**4**	309
6	Azaouagh	899	**3**	299
7	Imhof	1772	**2**	886
8	Maltritz	2749	**2**	1374
9	Yahia	2844	**2**	1422
10	Mavraj	112	**1**	112
11	Grote	710	**1**	710
12	Fuchs	942	**1**	942
13	Epalle	1794	**1**	1794
	Other		1	
	TOTAL		**46**	

TOP POINT EARNERS

	PLAYER	GAMES	AV PTS
1	Daniel Imhof	17	**1.47**
2	Christophe Dabrowski	24	**1.38**
3	Marc Pfertzel	25	**1.28**
4	Anthar Yahia	30	**1.23**
5	Marcel Maltritz	30	**1.23**
6	Tomasz Zdebel	16	**1.19**
7	Stanislav Sestak	31	**1.19**
8	Matias Concha	16	**1.19**
9	Joel Epalle	19	**1.11**
10	Jan Lastuvka	25	**1.08**
	CLUB AVERAGE:		**1.21**

DISCIPLINARY RECORDS

	PLAYER	YELLOW	RED	AVE
1	Tomasz Zdebel	11	0	**168**
2	Danny Fuchs	4	0	**235**
3	Chris Dabrowski	8	0	**294**
4	Dennis Grote	2	0	**355**
5	Marc Pfertzel	5	1	**395**
6	Benjamin Auer	3	0	**397**
7	Marcin Mieciel	3	0	**412**
8	Stanislav Sestak	6	0	**476**
9	Matias Concha	3	0	**501**
10	Daniel Imhof	3	0	**590**
11	Marcel Maltritz	4	0	**687**
12	Anthar Yahia	4	0	**711**
13	Phillip Bonig	3	0	**714**
	Other	6	0	
	TOTAL	**65**	**1**	

KEY GOALKEEPER

Jan Lastuvka

Goals Conceded in the League	44	Counting Games League games when player was on pitch for at least 70 minutes	25
Defensive Rating Ave number of mins between League goals conceded while on the pitch	50	Clean Sheets In League games when player was on pitch for at least 70 minutes	2

KEY PLAYERS - DEFENDERS

Matias Concha

Goals Conceded Number of League goals conceded while the player was on the pitch	26	Clean Sheets In League games when player was on pitch for at least 70 minutes	4
Defensive Rating Ave number of mins between League goals conceded while on the pitch	57	Club Defensive Rating Average number of mins between League goals conceded by the club this season	55

	PLAYER	CON LGE	CLEAN SHEETS	DEF RATE
1	Matias Concha	26	4	57 mins
2	Marc Pfertzel	41	3	57 mins
3	Anthar Yahia	50	5	56 mins
4	Daniel Imhof	32	3	55 mins

KEY PLAYERS - MIDFIELDERS

Danny Fuchs

Goals in the League	1	Contribution to Attacking Power Average number of minutes between League team goals while on pitch	55
Defensive Rating Average number of mins between League goals conceded while on the pitch	78	Scoring Difference Defensive Rating minus Contribution to Attacking Power	23

	PLAYER	LGE GOALS	DEF RATE	POWER	SCORE DIFF
1	Danny Fuchs	1	78	55	23 mins
2	Christophe Dabrowski	5	58	57	1 mins
3	Tomasz Zdebel	1	56	63	-7 mins
4	Joel Epalle	1	57	69	-12 mins

KEY PLAYERS - GOALSCORERS

Stanislav Sestak

Goals in the League	13	Player Strike Rate Average number of minutes between League goals scored by player	220
Contribution to Attacking Power Average number of minutes between League team goals while on pitch	62	Club Strike Rate Average number of minutes between League goals scored by club	63

	PLAYER	LGE GOALS	POWER	STRIKE RATE
1	Stanislav Sestak	13	62	220 mins
2	Marcin Mieciel	4	65	309 mins
3	Christophe Dabrowski	5	57	471 mins
4	Danny Fuchs	1	55	942 mins

kik
VfL Bochum
Thomas Zdebel and Marcel Maltritz

SQUAD APPEARANCES

Match	1	2	3	4	5	6	7	8	9	10	11	12	13	14	15	16	17	18	19	20	21	22	23	24	25	26	27	28	29	30	31	32	33	34
Venue	H	A	H	A	A	H	A	H	A	H	A	H	A	H	A	H	A	A	H	A	H	H	A	H	A	H	A	H	A	H	A	H	A	H
Competition	L	L	L	L	L	L	L	L	L	L	L	L	L	L	L	L	L	L	L	L	L	L	L	L	L	L	L	L	L	L	L	L	L	L
Result	D	W	W	L	L	D	L	D	L	L	L	W	W	W	L	D	L	W	D	L	W	W	D	D	D	D	L	D	W	D	L	L	W	L

Goalkeepers
Philipp Heerwagen
Jan Lastuvka
Rene Renno

Defenders
Phillip Bonig
Matias Concha
Pavel Drsek
Patrick Fabian
Daniel Imhof
Marcel Maltritz
Mergim Mavraj
Martin Meichelbeck
Marc Pfertzel
Anthar Yahia

Midfielders
Mimoun Azaouagh
Christophe Dabrowski
Joel Epalle
Danny Fuchs
Dennis Grote
Ivo Ilicevic
Shinji Ono
Heinrich Schmidtgal
Oliver Schroder
Tomasz Zdebel

Forwards
Benjamin Auer
Tommy Bechmann
Oleksiy Bielik
Marcin Mieciel
Marc Sand
Stanislav Sestak

KEY: On all match | On bench | Subbed or sent off (Counting game) | Subbed or sent off (playing less than 70 minutes) | Subbed on from bench (Counting Game) | Subbed on (playing less than 70 minutes) | Subbed on and then subbed or sent off (Counting Game) | Subbed on and then subbed or sent off (playing less than 70 minutes) | Not in 16

BORUSSIA DORTMUND

Final Position: **13th**

NICKNAME: DIE SCHWARZ-GELBEN

KEY: ☐ Won ☐ Drawn ☐ Lost

							Attendance
1	grpr1	**Duisburg**	H	L	1-3	Kringe 86	75,400
2	grpr1	**Schalke**	A	L	1-4	Valdez 66	61,482
3	grpr1	**Cottbus**	H	W	3-0	Kringe 44, Klimowicz 70, 84	65,000
4	grpr1	**Hansa Rostock**	A	W	1-0	Federico 75	20,000
5	grpr1	**W Bremen**	H	W	3-0	Petric 22, 33, Klimowicz 29	79,030
6	grpr1	**Hertha Berlin**	A	L	2-3	Petric 31, 88	45,000
7	grpr1	**Hamburg**	H	L	0-3		70,000
8	grpr1	**Karlsruhe**	A	L	1-3	Worns 41	30,500
9	grpr1	**Bochum**	H	W	2-1	Tinga 17, Federico 70	72,200
10	grpr1	**B Leverkusen**	A	D	2-2	Petric 41, 54	22,500
11	grpr1	**Bayern Munich**	H	D	0-0		80,708
12	grpr1	**Hannover 96**	A	L	1-2	Kringe 79	45,087
13	grpr1	**Eintr Frankfurt**	H	D	1-1	Kringe 81	75,300
14	grpr1	**Nurnberg**	A	L	0-2		45,000
15	grpr1	**Stuttgart**	A	W	2-1	Valdez 11, Petric 79	55,800
16	grpr1	**Arminia B**	H	W	6-1	Tinga 13, Schuler 19 og, Petric 47, Valdez 56 pen, Kringe 61, Federico 67	78,000
17	grpr1	**Wolfsburg**	A	L	0-4		29,000
18	grpr1	**Duisburg**	A	D	3-3	Kehl 51, Klimowicz 68, 90	30,000
19	grpr1	**Schalke**	H	L	2-3	Federico 21, Petric 50	80,708
20	grpr1	**Cottbus**	A	W	2-0	Petric 8, 85	17,842
21	grpr1	**Hansa Rostock**	H	W	1-0	Klimowicz 67	70,700
22	grpr1	**W Bremen**	A	L	0-2		42,100
23	grpr1	**Hertha Berlin**	H	D	1-1	Kehl 45	69,400
24	grpr1	**Hamburg**	A	L	0-1		57,000
25	grpr1	**Karlsruhe**	H	D	1-1	Petric 24	74,300
26	grpr1	**Bochum**	A	D	3-3	Kehl 37, Petric 39, Tinga 65	31,328
27	grpr1	**B Leverkusen**	H	W	2-1	Frei 87, Dede 90	69,400
28	grpr1	**Bayern Munich**	A	L	0-5		69,000
29	grpr1	**Hannover 96**	H	L	1-3	Frei 65	61,400
30	grpr1	**Eintr Frankfurt**	A	D	1-1	Blaszczykowski 51	51,500
31	grpr1	**Nurnberg**	H	D	0-0		70,500
32	grpr1	**Stuttgart**	H	W	3-2	Tinga 35, Frei 59, 79	64,400
33	grpr1	**Arminia B**	A	D	2-2	Buckley 28, Fernandez 83 og	27,400
34	grpr1	**Wolfsburg**	H	L	2-4	Frei 25, 69	75,000

LEAGUE APPEARANCES, BOOKINGS AND CAPS

	AGE (on 01/07/08)	IN NAMED 18	APPEARANCES	COUNTING GAMES	MINUTES ON PITCH	YELLOW CARDS	RED CARDS	CAPS THIS SEASON	NATIONAL SIDE
Goalkeepers									
Alexander Bade	37	17	1	0	45	0	0	-	Germany
Marcel Hottecke	21	10	5	5	450	0	0	-	Germany
Roman Weidenfeller	27	14	14	14	1260	2	0	-	Germany
Marc Ziegler	32	28	15	14	1305	0	0	-	Germany
Defenders									
Martin Amedick	25	32	16	11	1032	1	0	-	Germany
Markus Brzenska	24	25	12	11	997	3	0	-	Germany
Leonardo Dede	30	30	30	28	2624	3	1	-	Brazil
Philipp Degen	25	13	10	9	846	3	0	3	Switzerland
Nico Hillenbrand	21	5	1	0	25	0	0	-	Germany
Matts Hummels	19	17	13	8	880	1	0	-	Germany
Robert Kovac	34	30	22	19	1818	6	1	10	Croatia
Antonio Rukavina	24	14	14	13	1225	0	0	-	Serbia
Christian Worns	36	28	20	18	1722	7	1	-	Germany
Midfielders									
Mehmet Akgun	21	3	1	1	90	0	0	-	Turkey
Jakub Blaszczykowski	22	24	24	18	1805	4	0	3	Poland
Giovanni Federico	27	33	30	17	1975	1	0	-	Italy
Daniel Gordon	23	7	3	0	31	0	0	-	Germany
Sebastian Kehl	28	16	14	13	1220	4	0	-	Germany
Florian Kringe	25	27	27	22	2092	1	1	-	Germany
Marc-Andre Kruska	21	32	23	9	1247	4	1	-	Germany
Frank Patrick Njambe	20	4	2	0	104	1	0	-	Cameroon
Sahr Senesie	23	6	3	0	81	0	0	-	Sierra Leone
Tinga	28	33	33	29	2775	6	0	-	Brazil
Forwards									
Delron Buckley	30	33	31	10	1428	0	0	1	South Africa
Alexander Frei	28	15	13	10	944	2	0	3	Switzerland
Diego F Klimowicz	33	28	28	8	1307	7	0	-	Argentina
Christopher Nothe	20	12	3	0	101	0	0	-	Germany
Mladen Petric	27	29	29	23	2378	2	0	9	Croatia
Euzebiusz Smolarek	27	2	2	1	105	1	0	9	Poland
Nelson Valdez	24	32	27	14	1631	6	0	1	Paraguay

TEAM OF THE SEASON

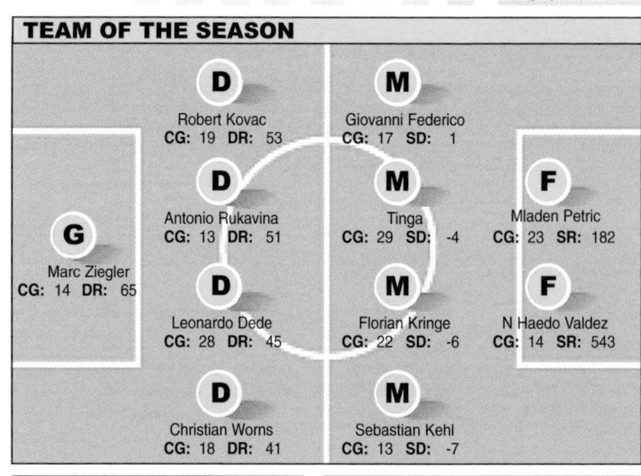

G
Marc Ziegler
CG: 14 DR: 65
D
Robert Kovac
CG: 19 DR: 53
D
Antonio Rukavina
CG: 13 DR: 51
D
Leonardo Dede
CG: 28 DR: 45
D
Christian Worns
CG: 18 DR: 41
M
Giovanni Federico
CG: 17 SD: 1
M
Tinga
CG: 29 SD: -4
M
Florian Kringe
CG: 22 SD: -6
M
Sebastian Kehl
CG: 13 SD: -7
F
Mladen Petric
CG: 23 SR: 182
F
N Haedo Valdez
CG: 14 SR: 543

MONTHLY POINTS TALLY

AUGUST	3	33%
SEPTEMBER	6	40%
OCTOBER	5	56%
NOVEMBER	1	11%
DECEMBER	6	67%
NO LEAGUE GAMES PLAYED IN JANUARY		
FEBRUARY	7	58%
MARCH	3	20%
APRIL	4	33%
MAY	5	42%

LEAGUE GOALS

	PLAYER	MINS	GOALS	S RATE
1	Petric	2378	**13**	182
2	Frei	944	**6**	157
3	Klimowicz	1307	**6**	217
4	Kringe	2092	**5**	418
5	Federico	1975	**4**	493
6	Tinga	2775	**4**	693
7	Kehl	1220	**3**	406
8	Valdez	1631	**3**	543
9	Buckley	1428	**1**	1428
10	Worns	1722	**1**	1722
11	Blaszczykowski	1805	**1**	1805
12	Dede	2624	**1**	2624
	Other		0	
	TOTAL		**48**	

TOP POINT EARNERS

	PLAYER	GAMES	AV PTS
1	Marc Ziegler	14	**1.64**
2	Giovanni Federico	17	**1.59**
3	Florian Kringe	22	**1.41**
4	Nelson Haedo Valdez	14	**1.36**
5	Tinga	29	**1.34**
6	Antonio Rukavina	13	**1.15**
7	Sebastian Kehl	13	**1.15**
8	Robert Kovac	19	**1.11**
9	Jakub Blaszczykowski	18	**1.11**
10	Mladen Petric	23	**1.09**
	CLUB AVERAGE:		**1.18**

DISCIPLINARY RECORDS

	PLAYER	YELLOW	RED	AVE
1	Diego F Klimowicz	7	0	**186**
2	Christian Worns	7	1	**215**
3	Marc-Andre Kruska	4	1	**249**
4	Robert Kovac	6	1	**259**
5	N Haedo Valdez	6	0	**271**
6	Philipp Degen	3	0	**282**
7	Sebastian Kehl	4	0	**305**
8	Markus Brzenska	3	0	**332**
9	J Blaszczykowski	4	0	**451**
10	Tinga	6	0	**462**
11	Alexander Frei	2	0	**472**
12	R Weidenfeller	2	0	**630**
13	Leonardo Dede	3	1	**656**
	Other	6	1	
	TOTAL	**63**	**5**	

KEY GOALKEEPER

Marc Ziegler

Goals Conceded in the League	20	Counting Games League games when player was on pitch for at least 70 minutes	14
Defensive Rating **Ave number of mins between League goals conceded while on the pitch**	65	Clean Sheets In League games when player was on pitch for at least 70 minutes	5

KEY PLAYERS - DEFENDERS

Robert Kovac

Goals Conceded Number of League goals conceded while the player was on the pitch	34	Clean Sheets In League games when player was on pitch for at least 70 minutes	3
Defensive Rating **Ave number of mins between League goals conceded while on the pitch**	53	Club Defensive Rating Average number of mins between League goals conceded by the club this season	49

	PLAYER	CON LGE	CLEAN SHEETS	DEF RATE
1	Robert Kovac	34	3	**53 mins**
2	Antonio Rukavina	24	2	**51 mins**
3	Leonardo Dede	58	4	**45 mins**
4	Christian Worns	42	3	**41 mins**

KEY PLAYERS - MIDFIELDERS

Giovanni Federico

Goals in the League	4	Contribution to Attacking Power Average number of minutes between League team goals while on pitch	49
Defensive Rating Average number of mins between League goals conceded while on the pitch	50	**Scoring Difference** **Defensive Rating minus Contribution to Attacking Power**	1

	PLAYER	LGE GOALS	DEF RATE	POWER	SCORE DIFF
1	Giovanni Federico	4	50	49	**1 mins**
2	Tinga	4	55	59	**-4 mins**
3	Florian Kringe	5	52	58	**-6 mins**
4	Sebastian Kehl	3	43	50	**-7 mins**

KEY PLAYERS - GOALSCORERS

Mladen Petric

Goals in the League	13	**Player Strike Rate** **Average number of minutes between League goals scored by player**	182
Contribution to Attacking Power Average number of minutes between League team goals while on pitch	64	Club Strike Rate Average number of minutes between League goals scored by club	61

	PLAYER	LGE GOALS	POWER	STRIKE RATE
1	Mladen Petric	13	64	**182 mins**
2	Sebastian Kehl	3	50	**406 mins**
3	Florian Kringe	5	58	**418 mins**
4	Giovanni Federico	4	49	**493 mins**

EVONIK
BVB 09
Mladen Petric

SQUAD APPEARANCES

Match	1	2	3	4	5	6	7	8	9	10	11	12	13	14	15	16	17	18	19	20	21	22	23	24	25	26	27	28	29	30	31	32	33	34
Venue	H	A	H	A	H	A	H	A	H	A	H	A	H	A	A	H	A	A	H	A	H	A	H	A	H	A	H	A	H	A	H	H	A	H
Competition	L	L	L	L	L	L	L	L	L	L	L	L	L	L	L	L	L	L	L	L	L	L	L	L	L	L	L	L	L	L	L	L	L	L
Result	L	L	W	W	W	L	L	L	W	D	D	L	D	L	W	W	L	D	L	W	W	L	D	L	D	D	W	L	L	D	D	W	D	L

Goalkeepers
- Alexander Bade
- Marcel Hottecke
- Roman Weidenfeller
- Marc Ziegler

Defenders
- Martin Amedick
- Markus Brzenska
- Leonardo Dede
- Philipp Degen
- Nico Hillenbrand
- Matts Hummels
- Robert Kovac
- Antonio Rukavina
- Christian Worns

Midfielders
- Mehmet Akgun
- Jakub Blaszczykowski
- Giovanni Federico
- Daniel Gordon
- Sebastian Kehl
- Florian Kringe
- Marc-Andre Kruska
- Frank Patrick Njambe
- Sahr Senesie
- Tinga

Forwards
- Delron Buckley
- Alexander Frei
- Diego Fernando Klimowicz
- Christopher Nothe
- Mladen Petric
- Euzebiusz Smolarek
- Nelson Haedo Valdez

KEY: On all match; On bench; Subbed or sent off (Counting game); Subbed or sent off (playing less than 70 minutes); Subbed on from bench (Counting Game); Subbed on (playing less than 70 minutes); Subbed on and then subbed or sent off (Counting Game); Subbed on and then subbed or sent off (playing less than 70 minutes); Not in 16

ENERGIE COTTBUS

Final Position: **14th**

NICKNAME: ENERGIE

KEY: ☐Won ☐Drawn ☐Lost

							Attendance
1	grpr1	**B Leverkusen**	A	D	0-0		22,500
2	grpr1	**Bochum**	H	L	1-2	Skela 49, 49	20,000
3	grpr1	**B Dortmund**	A	L	0-3		65,000
4	grpr1	**Nurnberg**	H	D	1-1	Sorensen 15 pen	15,089
5	grpr1	**Stuttgart**	A	L	0-3		41,000
6	grpr1	**Wolfsburg**	H	L	1-2	Sorensen 32	15,269
7	grpr1	**Bayern Munich**	A	L	0-5		68,000
8	grpr1	**Eintr Frankfurt**	H	D	2-2	Rangelov 8, 18	12,400
9	grpr1	**Hertha Berlin**	A	D	0-0		48,719
10	grpr1	**Duisburg**	H	L	1-2	Rost 66	12,000
11	grpr1	**Arminia B**	A	D	1-1	Sorensen 93	17,600
12	grpr1	**Schalke**	H	W	1-0	Bassila 46	17,012
13	grpr1	**Hansa Rostock**	A	L	2-3	da Silva 59, Skela 89	20,000
14	grpr1	**W Bremen**	H	L	0-2		15,000
15	grpr1	**Karlsruhe**	H	W	2-0	Angelov 62, Rangelov 75	10,900
16	grpr1	**Hamburg**	A	D	0-0		56,000
17	grpr1	**Hannover 96**	H	W	5-1	Bassila 11, Sorensen 30, Rangelov 44, 70, Ziebig 65	14,026
18	grpr1	**B Leverkusen**	H	L	2-3	Papadopulos 14, Bassila 77	14,966
19	grpr1	**Bochum**	A	D	3-3	Papadopulos 45, Skela 69, Jelic 79	21,000
20	grpr1	**B Dortmund**	H	L	0-2		17,842
21	grpr1	**Nurnberg**	A	D	1-1	Sorensen 59	40,900
22	grpr1	**Wolfsburg**	A	L	0-3		21,460
23	grpr1	**Stuttgart**	H	L	0-1		13,150
24	grpr1	**Bayern Munich**	H	W	2-0	Jelic 18, 38	22,700
25	grpr1	**Eintr Frankfurt**	A	L	1-2	Rost 48	45,100
26	grpr1	**Hertha Berlin**	H	W	2-1	Skela 41, 63 pen	20,746
27	grpr1	**Duisburg**	A	W	1-0	Skela 4	24,016
28	grpr1	**Arminia B**	H	W	1-0	Skela 51 pen	16,103
29	grpr1	**Schalke**	A	L	0-5		60,018
30	grpr1	**Hansa Rostock**	H	W	2-1	Rost 81, Rangelov 90	21,357
31	grpr1	**W Bremen**	A	L	0-2		39,687
32	grpr1	**Karlsruhe**	A	D	1-1	Rivic 60	28,000
33	grpr1	**Hamburg**	H	W	2-0	Rivic 29, Sorensen 84	22,746
34	grpr1	**Hannover 96**	A	L	0-4		46,632

LEAGUE APPEARANCES, BOOKINGS AND CAPS

	AGE (on 01/07/08)	IN NAMED 18	APPEARANCES	COUNTING GAMES	MINUTES ON PITCH	YELLOW CARDS	RED CARDS	CAPS THIS SEASON	NATIONAL SIDE
Goalkeepers									
Tomislav Piplica	39	34	10	10	900	0	0	-	Bosnia
Gerhard Tremmel	29	34	24	24	2160	0	0	-	Germany
Defenders									
Stanislav Angelov	30	31	31	30	2717	11	0	5	Bulgaria
Ovidiu Burca	28	5	0	0	0	0	0	-	Romania
Mario Cvitanovic	33	33	31	31	2754	5	0	-	Croatia
Vragel da Silva	34	21	21	19	1750	4	0	-	Brazil
Arne Feick	20	14	0	0	0	0	0	-	Germany
Kristijan Ipsa	22	22	4	2	186	0	0	-	Croatia
Mariusz Kukielka	31	18	14	14	1260	1	0	-	Poland
Igor Mitreski	29	32	32	30	2764	8	1	4	Macedonia
Ivan Radeljic	27	17	16	9	945	2	0	-	Croatia
Zoltan Szelesi	26	1	1	1	90	0	0	-	Hungary
Midfielders									
Efstathios Aloneftis	25	25	12	2	333	0	0	5	Cyprus
Tomasz Bandrowski	23	4	0	0	0	0	0	-	Poland
Christian Bassila	30	28	23	18	1794	9	0	-	France
Christian Muller	24	5	1	0	1	0	0	-	Germany
Timo Rost	29	33	33	33	2935	7	0	-	Germany
Sebastian Schuppan	21	4	0	0	0	0	0	-	Germany
Jiayi Shao	28	22	14	0	347	0	0	-	China PR
Ervin Skela	31	34	34	34	2988	3	0	5	Albania
Dusan Vasiljevic	26	17	12	1	370	2	0	-	Serbia
Daniel Ziebig	25	31	25	19	1796	5	0	-	Germany
Forwards									
Steffen Baumgart	36	9	8	2	263	2	0	-	Germany
Branko Jelic	31	17	15	1	599	0	0	-	Serbia
Francis Kioyo	28	15	11	5	508	1	0	-	Cameroon
Michal Papadopulos	23	16	14	5	636	1	0	-	Czech Republic
Dimitar Rangelov	25	22	22	12	1445	3	0	-	Bulgaria
Stiven Rivic	22	30	28	7	1375	3	0	-	Croatia
Dennis Sorensen	27	33	33	29	2685	5	0	1	Denmark
Przemyslaw Trytko	20	6	1	0	10	0	0	-	Poland

TEAM OF THE SEASON

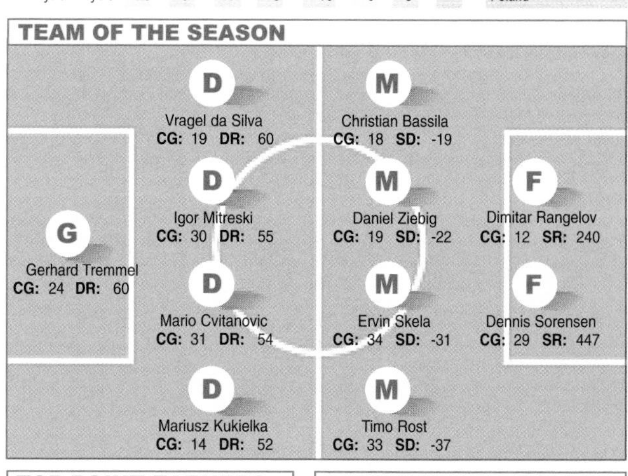

D
Vragel da Silva
CG: 19 DR: 60
M
Christian Bassila
CG: 18 SD: -19
D
Igor Mitreski
CG: 30 DR: 55
M
Daniel Ziebig
CG: 19 SD: -22
F
Dimitar Rangelov
CG: 12 SR: 240
G
Gerhard Tremmel
CG: 24 DR: 60
D
Mario Cvitanovic
CG: 31 DR: 54
M
Ervin Skela
CG: 34 SD: -31
F
Dennis Sorensen
CG: 29 SR: 447
D
Mariusz Kukielka
CG: 14 DR: 52
M
Timo Rost
CG: 33 SD: -37

MONTHLY POINTS TALLY

AUGUST	1	11%
SEPTEMBER	2	13%
OCTOBER	2	22%
NOVEMBER	3	33%
DECEMBER	7	78%
NO LEAGUE GAMES PLAYED IN JANUARY		
FEBRUARY	2	17%
MARCH	6	40%
APRIL	9	75%
MAY	4	33%

LEAGUE GOALS

	PLAYER	MINS	GOALS	S RATE
1	Skela	2988	8	373
2	Rangelov	1445	6	240
3	Sorensen	2685	6	447
4	Jelic	599	3	199
5	Bassila	1794	3	598
6	Rost	2935	3	978
7	Papadopulos	636	2	318
8	Rivic	1375	2	687
9	da Silva	1750	1	1750
10	Ziebig	1796	1	1796
11	Angelov	2717	1	2717
	Other		0	
	TOTAL		36	

TOP POINT EARNERS

	PLAYER	GAMES	AV PTS
1	Dimitar Rangelov	12	1.42
2	Vragel da Silva	19	1.37
3	Gerhard Tremmel	24	1.33
4	Daniel Ziebig	19	1.32
5	Christian Bassila	18	1.17
6	Igor Mitreski	30	1.10
7	Ervin Skela	34	1.06
8	Dennis Sorensen	29	1.03
9	Stanislav Angelov	30	1.03
10	Mario Cvitanovic	31	1.03
	CLUB AVERAGE:		1.06

DISCIPLINARY RECORDS

	PLAYER	YELLOW	RED	AVE
1	Christian Bassila	9	0	199
2	Stanislav Angelov	11	0	247
3	Igor Mitreski	8	1	307
4	Daniel Ziebig	5	0	359
5	Timo Rost	7	0	419
6	Vragel da Silva	4	0	437
7	Stiven Rivic	3	0	458
8	Ivan Radeljic	2	0	472
9	Dimitar Rangelov	3	0	481
10	Francis Kioyo	1	0	508
11	Dennis Sorensen	5	0	537
12	Mario Cvitanovic	5	0	550
13	Michal Papadopulos	1	0	636
	Other	4	0	
	TOTAL	68	1	

KEY GOALKEEPER

Gerhard Tremmel

Goals Conceded in the League	36	**Counting Games** League games when player was on pitch for at least 70 minutes	24
Defensive Rating Ave number of mins between League goals conceded while on the pitch	60	**Clean Sheets** In League games when player was on pitch for at least 70 minutes	7

KEY PLAYERS - DEFENDERS

Vragel da Silva

Goals Conceded Number of League goals conceded while the player was on the pitch	29	**Clean Sheets** In League games when player was on pitch for at least 70 minutes	7
Defensive Rating Ave number of mins between League goals conceded while on the pitch	60	**Club Defensive Rating** Average number of mins between League goals conceded by the club this season	56

	PLAYER	CON LGE	CLEAN SHEETS	DEF RATE
1	Vragel da Silva	29	7	60 mins
2	Igor Mitreski	50	9	55 mins
3	Mario Cvitanovic	51	8	54 mins
4	Mariusz Kukielka	24	4	52 mins

KEY PLAYERS - MIDFIELDERS

Christian Bassila

Goals in the League	3	**Contribution to Attacking Power** Average number of minutes between League team goals while on pitch	78
Defensive Rating Average number of mins between League goals conceded while on the pitch	59	**Scoring Difference** Defensive Rating minus Contribution to Attacking Power	-19

	PLAYER	LGE GOALS	DEF RATE	POWER	SCORE DIFF
1	Christian Bassila	3	59	78	-19 mins
2	Daniel Ziebig	1	56	78	-22 mins
3	Ervin Skela	8	54	85	-31 mins
4	Timo Rost	3	54	91	-37 mins

KEY PLAYERS - GOALSCORERS

Dimitar Rangelov

Goals in the League	6	**Player Strike Rate** Average number of minutes between League goals scored by player	240
Contribution to Attacking Power Average number of minutes between League team goals while on pitch	72	**Club Strike Rate** Average number of minutes between League goals scored by club	87

	PLAYER	LGE GOALS	POWER	STRIKE RATE
1	Dimitar Rangelov	6	72	240 mins
2	Ervin Skela	8	85	373 mins
3	Dennis Sorensen	6	83	447 mins
4	Christian Bassila	3	78	598 mins

Mario Cvitanovic

SQUAD APPEARANCES

Match	1	2	3	4	5	6	7	8	9	10	11	12	13	14	15	16	17	18	19	20	21	22	23	24	25	26	27	28	29	30	31	32	33	34
Venue	A	H	A	H	A	H	A	H	A	H	A	H	A	H	H	A	H	H	A	H	A	A	H	H	A	H	A	H	A	H	A	A	H	A
Competition	L	L	L	L	L	L	L	L	L	L	L	L	L	L	L	L	L	L	L	L	L	L	L	L	L	L	L	L	L	L	L	L	L	L
Result	D	L	L	D	L	L	L	D	D	L	D	W	L	L	W	D	W	L	D	L	D	L	L	W	L	W	W	W	L	W	L	D	W	L

Goalkeepers
Tomislav Piplica
Gerhard Tremmel
Defenders
Stanislav Angelov
Ovidiu Burca
Mario Cvitanovic
Vragel da Silva
Arne Feick
Kristijan Ipsa
Mariusz Kukielka
Igor Mitreski
Ivan Radeljic
Zoltan Szelesi
Midfielders
Efstathios Aloneftis
Tomasz Bandrowski
Christian Bassila
Christian Muller
Timo Rost
Sebastian Schuppan
Jiayi Shao
Ervin Skela
Dusan Vasiljevic
Daniel Ziebig
Forwards
Steffen Baumgart
Branko Jelic
Francis Kioyo
Michal Papadopulos
Dimitar Rangelov
Stiven Rivic
Dennis Sorensen
Przemyslaw Trytko

KEY: On all match | On bench | Subbed or sent off (Counting game) | Subbed or sent off (playing less than 70 minutes) | Subbed on from bench (Counting Game) | Subbed on (playing less than 70 minutes) | Subbed on and then subbed or sent off (Counting Game) | Subbed on and then subbed or sent off (playing less than 70 minutes) | Not in 16

ARMINIA BIELEFELD

Final Position: **15th**

NICKNAME: DIE BLAUEN

KEY: ☐Won ☐Drawn ☐Lost

							Attendance
1	grpr1	**Wolfsburg**	A	W	3-1	Wichniarek 38, Eigler 51, Kirch 80	20,000
2	grpr1	**Eintr Frankfurt**	H	D	2-2	Kucera 68, Wichniarek 80	22,000
3	grpr1	**Hertha Berlin**	H	W	2-0	Masmanidis 52, Wichniarek 90	20,000
4	grpr1	**Duisburg**	A	L	0-3		21,000
5	grpr1	**Hansa Rostock**	H	W	4-2	Agali 31 og, Eigler 50, 55, Wichniarek 59	20,600
6	grpr1	**Schalke**	A	L	0-3		61,482
7	grpr1	**Hannover 96**	H	L	0-2		21,000
8	grpr1	**W Bremen**	A	L	1-8	Wichniarek 37	40,120
9	grpr1	**Hamburg**	H	L	0-1		22,800
10	grpr1	**Karlsruhe**	A	D	0-0		27,361
11	grpr1	**Cottbus**	H	D	1-1	Kamper 77	17,600
12	grpr1	**B Leverkusen**	A	L	0-4		22,500
13	grpr1	**Nurnberg**	H	W	3-1	Kauf 64, Wichniarek 76, Zuma 90	18,000
14	grpr1	**Bochum**	A	L	0-3		20,478
15	grpr1	**Bayern Munich**	H	L	0-1		23,800
16	grpr1	**B Dortmund**	A	L	1-6	Kirch 81	78,000
17	grpr1	**Stuttgart**	H	W	2-0	Kamper 79, Wichniarek 90	20,000
18	grpr1	**Wolfsburg**	H	L	0-1		17,000
19	grpr1	**Eintr Frankfurt**	A	L	1-2	Wichniarek 74	43,300
20	grpr1	**Hertha Berlin**	A	L	0-1		33,031
21	grpr1	**Duisburg**	H	L	0-2		19,200
22	grpr1	**Hansa Rostock**	A	D	1-1	Eigler 84	14,000
23	grpr1	**Schalke**	H	L	0-2		26,100
24	grpr1	**Hannover 96**	A	D	2-2	Mijatovic 14, Eigler 38	35,104
25	grpr1	**W Bremen**	H	D	1-1	Kirch 14	27,000
26	grpr1	**Hamburg**	A	D	1-1	Bollmann 72	56,398
27	grpr1	**Karlsruhe**	H	W	1-0	Kampantais 90	19,600
28	grpr1	**Cottbus**	A	L	0-1		16,103
29	grpr1	**B Leverkusen**	H	W	1-0	Mijatovic 51	19,400
30	grpr1	**Nurnberg**	A	D	2-2	Wichniarek 47, Bollmann 59	46,300
31	grpr1	**Bochum**	H	W	2-0	Mijatovic 70, Kamper 90	23,800
32	grpr1	**Bayern Munich**	A	L	0-2		69,000
33	grpr1	**B Dortmund**	H	D	2-2	Marx 24 pen, Wichniarek 34	27,400
34	grpr1	**Stuttgart**	A	D	2-2	Tesche 10, Eigler 87	55,500

LEAGUE APPEARANCES, BOOKINGS AND CAPS

	AGE (on 01/07/08)	IN NAMED 18	APPEARANCES	COUNTING GAMES	MINUTES ON PITCH	YELLOW CARDS	RED CARDS	CAPS THIS SEASON	NATIONAL SIDE
Goalkeepers									
Rowen Fernandez	30	30	15	13	1236	0	0	-	South Africa
Mathias Hain	35	27	20	19	1755	1	0	-	Germany
Dirk Heinen	37	8	1	1	69	0	0	-	Germany
Daniel Riemer	21	3	0	0	0	0	0	-	Germany
Defenders									
Markus Bollmann	27	30	21	14	1443	7	0	-	Germany
Nils Fischer	21	6	2	0	3	0	0	-	Germany
Petr Gabriel	35	19	12	7	864	3	0	-	Czech Republic
Oliver Kirch	25	29	25	22	2029	1	0	-	Germany
Bernd Korzynietz	28	28	15	8	999	2	0	-	Germany
Radim Kucera	34	31	31	31	2790	2	0	-	Czech Republic
Matthias Langkamp	24	13	13	11	1080	2	0	-	Germany
Andre Mijatovic	18	24	24	22	2065	3	0	-	Croatia
Tobias Rau	26	19	10	7	673	1	0	-	Germany
Markus Schuler	30	32	29	27	2517	5	0	-	Germany
Marcel Stadel	21	2	0	0	0	0	0	-	Germany
Midfielders									
Stefan Aigner	20	1	0	0	0	0	0	-	Germany
Jorg Bohme	34	27	22	13	1369	6	1	-	Germany
Jonas Kamper	25	34	31	9	1374	1	0	-	Denmark
Rudiger Kauf	33	29	29	28	2564	9	0	-	Germany
David Kobylik	27	6	2	0	20	0	0	-	Czech Republic
Thorben Marx	27	29	24	18	1856	3	0	-	Germany
Ioannis Masmanidis	25	12	8	2	480	1	0	-	Germany
Siyabonga Nkosi	26	17	8	3	407	0	0	-	South Africa
Robert Tesche	21	26	15	8	1035	0	0	-	Germany
Forwards									
Christian Eigler	24	30	29	20	1989	4	0	-	Germany
Daniel Halfar	20	21	16	6	881	1	0	-	Germany
Leonidas Kampantais	26	21	8	0	192	0	0	-	Greece
Thilo Versick	22	2	1	0	33	0	0	-	Germany
Artur Wichniarek	31	33	33	27	2756	3	0	-	Poland
Sibusiso Zuma	33	22	20	10	1175	2	0	-	South Africa

TEAM OF THE SEASON

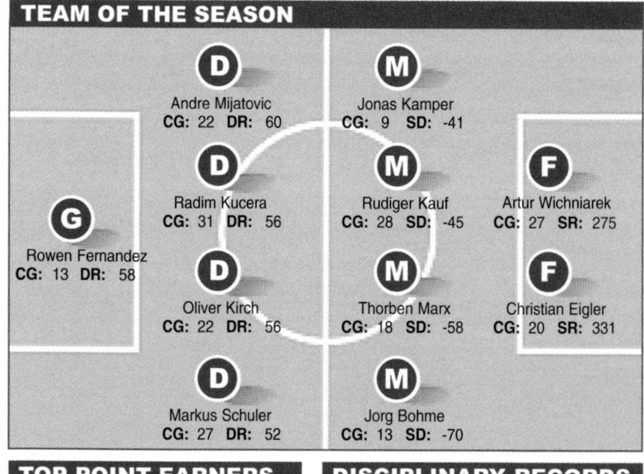

D
Andre Mijatovic
CG: 22 DR: 60
M
Jonas Kamper
CG: 9 SD: -41
D
Radim Kucera
CG: 31 DR: 56
M
Rudiger Kauf
CG: 28 SD: -45
F
Artur Wichniarek
CG: 27 SR: 275
G
Rowen Fernandez
CG: 13 DR: 58
D
Oliver Kirch
CG: 22 DR: 56
M
Thorben Marx
CG: 18 SD: -58
F
Christian Eigler
CG: 20 SR: 331
D
Markus Schuler
CG: 27 DR: 52
M
Jorg Bohme
CG: 13 SD: -70

MONTHLY POINTS TALLY

AUGUST	7	78%
SEPTEMBER	3	20%
OCTOBER	2	22%
NOVEMBER	3	33%
DECEMBER	3	33%
NO LEAGUE GAMES PLAYED IN JANUARY		
FEBRUARY	0	0%
MARCH	4	27%
APRIL	7	58%
MAY	5	42%

LEAGUE GOALS

	PLAYER	MINS	GOALS	S RATE
1	Wichniarek	2756	**10**	275
2	Eigler	1989	**6**	331
3	Kamper	1374	**3**	458
4	Kirch	2029	**3**	676
5	Mijatovic	2065	**3**	688
6	Bollmann	1443	**2**	721
7	Kampantais	192	**1**	192
8	Masmanidis	480	**1**	480
9	Tesche	1035	**1**	1035
10	Zuma	1175	**1**	1175
11	Marx	1856	**1**	1856
12	Kauf	2564	**1**	2564
13	Kucera	2790	**1**	2790
	Other		**0**	
	TOTAL		**34**	

TOP POINT EARNERS

	PLAYER	GAMES	AV PTS
1	Rowen Fernandez	13	**1.31**
2	Oliver Kirch	22	**1.18**
3	Andre Mijatovic	22	**1.18**
4	Christian Eigler	20	**1.15**
5	Jorg Bohme	13	**1.08**
6	Thorben Marx	18	**1.06**
7	Markus Schuler	27	**1.04**
8	Artur Wichniarek	27	**1.04**
9	Radim Kucera	31	**1.03**
10	Markus Bollmann	14	**0.93**
	CLUB AVERAGE:		**1.00**

DISCIPLINARY RECORDS

	PLAYER	YELLOW	RED	AVE
1	Jorg Bohme	6	1	**195**
2	Markus Bollmann	7	0	**206**
3	Rudiger Kauf	9	0	**284**
4	Petr Gabriel	3	0	**288**
5	Ioannis Masmanidis	1	0	**480**
6	Christian Eigler	4	0	**497**
7	Bernd Korzynietz	2	0	**499**
8	Markus Schuler	5	0	**503**
9	Matthias Langkamp	2	0	**540**
10	Sibusiso Zuma	2	0	**587**
11	Thorben Marx	3	0	**618**
12	Tobias Rau	1	0	**673**
13	Andre Mijatovic	3	0	**688**
	Other	8	0	
	TOTAL	**56**	**1**	

KEY GOALKEEPER

Rowen Fernandez

Goals Conceded in the League	21	**Counting Games** League games when player was on pitch for at least 70 minutes	13
Defensive Rating Ave number of mins between League goals conceded while on the pitch	58	**Clean Sheets** In League games when player was on pitch for at least 70 minutes	4

KEY PLAYERS - DEFENDERS

Andre Mijatovic

Goals Conceded Number of League goals conceded while the player was on the pitch	34	**Clean Sheets** In League games when player was on pitch for at least 70 minutes	4
Defensive Rating Ave number of mins between League goals conceded while on the pitch	60	**Club Defensive Rating** Average number of mins between League goals conceded by the club this season	51

	PLAYER	CON LGE	CLEAN SHEETS	DEF RATE
1	Andre Mijatovic	34	4	60 mins
2	Radim Kucera	49	7	56 mins
3	Oliver Kirch	36	7	56 mins
4	Markus Schuler	48	6	52 mins

KEY PLAYERS - MIDFIELDERS

Jonas Kamper

Goals in the League	3	**Contribution to Attacking Power** Average number of minutes between League team goals while on pitch	80
Defensive Rating Average number of mins between League goals conceded while on the pitch	39	**Scoring Difference** Defensive Rating minus Contribution to Attacking Power	-41

	PLAYER	LGE GOALS	DEF RATE	POWER	SCORE DIFF
1	Jonas Kamper	3	39	80	-41 mins
2	Rudiger Kauf	1	49	94	-45 mins
3	Thorben Marx	1	51	109	-58 mins
4	Jorg Bohme	0	44	114	-70 mins

KEY PLAYERS - GOALSCORERS

Artur Wichniarek

Goals in the League	10	**Player Strike Rate** Average number of minutes between League goals scored by player	275
Contribution to Attacking Power Average number of minutes between League team goals while on pitch	88	**Club Strike Rate** Average number of minutes between League goals scored by club	87

	PLAYER	LGE GOALS	POWER	STRIKE RATE
1	Artur Wichniarek	10	88	275 mins
2	Christian Eigler	6	79	331 mins
3	Jonas Kamper	3	80	458 mins
4	Sibusiso Zuma	1	97	1175 mins

Sibusiso Zuma, Rudiger Kauf and Petr Gabriel

SQUAD APPEARANCES

Match	1	2	3	4	5	6	7	8	9	10	11	12	13	14	15	16	17	18	19	20	21	22	23	24	25	26	27	28	29	30	31	32	33	34
Venue	A	H	H	A	H	A	H	A	H	A	H	A	H	A	H	A	H	H	A	A	H	A	H	A	H	A	H	A	H	A	H	A	H	A
Competition	L	L	L	L	L	L	L	L	L	L	L	L	L	L	L	L	L	L	L	L	L	L	L	L	L	L	L	L	L	L	L	L	L	L
Result	W	D	W	L	W	L	L	L	L	D	D	L	W	L	L	L	W	L	L	L	L	D	L	D	D	D	W	L	W	D	W	L	D	D

Goalkeepers
Rowen Fernandez
Mathias Hain
Dirk Heinen
Daniel Riemer

Defenders
Markus Bollmann
Nils Fischer
Petr Gabriel
Oliver Kirch
Bernd Korzynietz
Radim Kucera
Matthias Langkamp
Andre Mijatovic
Tobias Rau
Markus Schuler
Marcel Stadel

Midfielders
Stefan Aigner
Jorg Bohme
Jonas Kamper
Rudiger Kauf
David Kobylik
Thorben Marx
Ioannis Masmanidis
Siyabonga Nkosi
Robert Tesche

Forwards
Christian Eigler
Daniel Halfar
Leonidas Kampantais
Thilo Versick
Artur Wichniarek
Sibusiso Zuma

KEY: On all match · On bench · Subbed or sent off (Counting game) · Subbed or sent off (playing less than 70 minutes) · Subbed on from bench (Counting Game) · Subbed on (playing less than 70 minutes) · Subbed on and then subbed or sent off (Counting Game) · Subbed on and then subbed or sent off (playing less than 70 minutes) · Not in 16

NUREMBURG

Final Position: **16th**

KNOWN AS NURNBERG IN GERMANY

KEY: ☐Won ☐Drawn ☐Lost

						Attendance
1	grpr1	**Karlsruhe**	H	L	0-2		40,000
2	grpr1	**Hansa Rostock**	A	W	2-1	Galasek 17, Kluge 25	25,000
3	grpr1	**W Bremen**	H	L	0-1		45,200
4	grpr1	**Cottbus**	A	D	1-1	Wolf 85	15,089
5	grpr1	**Hannover 96**	H	D	2-2	Misimovic 60, Mintal 89	42,000
6	ucrl1	**R Bucharest**	H	D	0-0		40,066
7	grpr1	**Hamburg**	A	L	0-1		52,365
8	grpr1	**B Leverkusen**	H	L	1-2	Mintal 73 pen	38,000
9	grpr1	**Bochum**	A	D	3-3	Kluge 41, 60, Misimovic 81	20,000
10	ucrl2	**R Bucharest**	A	D	2-2	Kluge 22, Misimovic 55	11,000
11	grpr1	**Bayern Munich**	A	L	0-3		69,000
12	grpr1	**Eintr Frankfurt**	H	W	5-1	Charisteas 20, Mintal 50, 64, Misimovic 54 pen, Kennedy 82	45,050
13	grpr1	**Wolfsburg**	A	L	1-3	Misimovic 54 pen	19,798
14	grpr1	**Stuttgart**	H	L	0-1		45,565
15	ucgpa	**Everton**	H	L	0-2		40,000
16	grpr1	**Arminia B**	A	L	1-3	Wolf 43	18,000
17	grpr1	**B Dortmund**	H	W	2-0	Galasek 9, Charisteas 90	45,000
18	ucgpa	**Z St Petersburg**	A	D	2-2	Charisteas 25, Benko 83	21,500
19	grpr1	**Duisburg**	A	L	0-1		18,000
20	ucgpa	**AZ Alkmaar**	H	W	2-1	Mintal 83, 85	35,020
21	grpr1	**Hertha Berlin**	H	W	2-1	Charisteas 5, Misimovic 39	41,000
22	grpr1	**Schalke**	A	L	1-2	Charisteas 55	61,500
23	ucgpa	**Larissa**	A	W	3-1	Saenko 45, Mintal 57, Charisteas 73	2,863
24	grpr1	**Karlsruhe**	A	L	0-2		29,300
25	grpr1	**Hansa Rostock**	H	D	1-1	Koller 19	36,470
26	ucrl1	**Benfica**	A	L	0-1		27,378
27	grpr1	**W Bremen**	A	L	0-2		37,073
28	ucrl2	**Benfica**	H	D	2-2	Charisteas 58, Saenko 66	42,846
29	grpr1	**Cottbus**	H	D	1-1	Engelhardt 57	40,900
30	grpr1	**Hannover 96**	A	L	1-2	Misimovic 52	31,282
31	grpr1	**Hamburg**	H	D	0-0		44,900
32	grpr1	**B Leverkusen**	A	L	1-4	Misimovic 12	22,500
33	grpr1	**Bochum**	H	D	1-1	Misimovic 9	43,547
34	grpr1	**Bayern Munich**	H	D	1-1	Misimovic 44	47,000
35	grpr1	**Eintr Frankfurt**	A	W	3-1	Charisteas 18, Vittek 49, Misimovic 83	51,500
36	grpr1	**Stuttgart**	A	L	0-3		45,000
37	grpr1	**Wolfsburg**	H	W	1-0	Koller 79	45,100
38	grpr1	**Arminia B**	H	D	2-2	Mintal 29, Saenko 39	46,300
39	grpr1	**B Dortmund**	A	D	0-0		70,500
40	grpr1	**Duisburg**	H	W	2-0	Charisteas 9, Pinola 32	44,300
41	grpr1	**Hertha Berlin**	A	L	0-1		47,072
42	grpr1	**Schalke**	H	L	0-2		46,800

LEAGUE APPEARANCES, BOOKINGS AND CAPS

	AGE (on 01/07/08)	IN NAMED 18	APPEARANCES	COUNTING GAMES	MINUTES ON PITCH	YELLOW CARDS	RED CARDS	CAPS THIS SEASON	NATIONAL SIDE
Goalkeepers									
Jaromir Blazek	35	28	25	24	2217	0	0	2	Czech Republic
Daniel Klewer	31	32	10	9	843	0	0	-	Germany
Alexander Stephan	21	8	0	0	0	0	0	-	Germany
Defenders									
Jacques Abardonado	30	16	10	9	819	0	0	-	France
Michael Beauchamp	27	25	12	9	924	1	0	-	Australia
Leandro Glauber	24	28	19	14	1348	3	0	-	Brazil
Lars Jacobsen	28	10	7	6	585	0	0	2	Denmark
Javier Horacio Pinola	25	19	19	19	1669	7	0	-	Argentina
Dominik Reinhardt	23	25	25	24	2153	3	0	-	Germany
Ralf Schmidt	22	14	8	3	448	2	0	-	Germany
Matthew Spiranovic	20	22	7	5	466	2	0	-	Australia
Andreas Wolf	26	30	30	28	2604	8	1	-	Germany
Midfielders									
Marco Engelhardt	27	29	22	15	1594	7	0	-	Germany
Tomas Galasek	35	31	31	29	2668	7	0	9	Czech Republic
Peer Kluge	27	27	22	18	1777	7	0	-	Germany
Jan Kristiansen	26	33	19	12	1319	0	0	-	Denmark
Marek Mintal	30	32	31	19	1992	2	0	3	Slovakia
Zvjezdan Misimovic	26	29	28	19	2068	2	0	5	Bosnia
Jaouhar Mnari	31	31	21	8	1138	2	0	4	Tunisia
Dario Vidosic	21	9	4	0	61	0	0	-	Australia
Forwards									
Nicky Adler	23	18	13	2	473	1	0	-	Germany
Leon Benko	24	13	3	0	33	0	0	-	Croatia
Angelos Charisteas	28	28	24	15	1664	1	0	6	Greece
Joshua Kennedy	25	12	12	1	493	0	0	-	Australia
Jan Koller	35	16	14	14	1260	2	0	9	Czech Republic
Chhunly Pagenburg	21	3	1	0	9	0	0	-	Germany
Ivan Saenko	24	28	26	16	1777	3	1	1	Russia
Robert Vittek	26	17	17	10	1125	3	1	-	Slovakia

TEAM OF THE SEASON

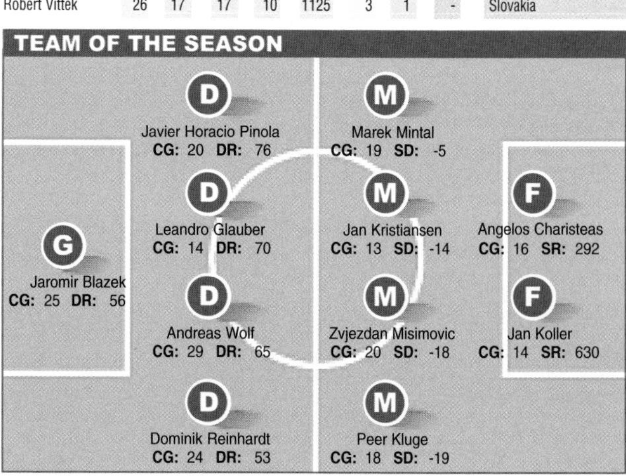
D
Javier Horacio Pinola
CG: 20 DR: 76
M
Marek Mintal
CG: 19 SD: -5
D
Leandro Glauber
CG: 14 DR: 70
M
Jan Kristiansen
CG: 13 SD: -14
F
Angelos Charisteas
CG: 16 SR: 292
G
Jaromir Blazek
CG: 25 DR: 56
D
Andreas Wolf
CG: 29 DR: 65
M
Zvjezdan Misimovic
CG: 20 SD: -18
F
Jan Koller
CG: 14 SR: 630
D
Dominik Reinhardt
CG: 24 DR: 53
M
Peer Kluge
CG: 18 SD: -19

MONTHLY POINTS TALLY

AUGUST	3	33%
SEPTEMBER	3	20%
OCTOBER	3	33%
NOVEMBER	3	33%
DECEMBER	3	33%
NO LEAGUE GAMES PLAYED IN JANUARY		
FEBRUARY	2	17%
MARCH	3	20%
APRIL	7	58%
MAY	4	33%

LEAGUE GOALS

	PLAYER	MINS	GOALS	S RATE
1	Misimovic	2158	10	215
2	Charisteas	1754	6	292
3	Mintal	1992	5	398
4	Kluge	1777	3	592
5	Koller	1260	2	630
6	Saenko	1867	2	933
7	Wolf	2694	2	1347
8	Galasek	2758	2	1379
9	Kennedy	493	1	493
10	Vittek	1215	1	1215
11	Engelhardt	1684	1	1684
12	Pinola	1759	1	1759
	Other		0	
	TOTAL		**36**	

TOP POINT EARNERS

	PLAYER	GAMES	AV PTS
1	Marek Mintal	19	1.21
2	Marco Engelhardt	15	1.13
3	Peer Kluge	18	1.06
4	Tomas Galasek	29	1.00
5	Leandro Glauber	14	1.00
6	Angelos Charisteas	15	1.00
7	Ivan Saenko	16	0.94
8	Zvjezdan Misimovic	19	0.89
9	Javier Horacio Pinola	19	0.89
10	Jaromir Blazek	24	0.88
	CLUB AVERAGE:		**0.91**

DISCIPLINARY RECORDS

	PLAYER	YELLOW	RED	AVE
1	Matt Spiranovic	2	0	233
2	Marco Engelhardt	7	0	240
3	Javier H Pinola	7	0	251
4	Peer Kluge	7	0	253
5	Andreas Wolf	9	1	269
6	Robert Vittek	3	1	303
7	Tomas Galasek	7	0	394
8	Leandro Glauber	3	0	449
9	Ivan Saenko	3	1	466
10	Nicky Adler	1	0	473
11	Jaouhar Mnari	2	0	569
12	Jan Koller	2	0	630
13	Dominik Reinhardt	3	0	717
	Other	6	0	
	TOTAL	**62**	**3**	

KEY GOALKEEPER

Jaromir Blazek

Goals Conceded in the League	41	Counting Games League games when player was on pitch for at least 70 minutes	25
Defensive Rating Ave number of mins between League goals conceded while on the pitch	56	Clean Sheets In League games when player was on pitch for at least 70 minutes	2

KEY PLAYERS - DEFENDERS

Javier Horacio Pinola

Goals Conceded Number of League goals conceded while the player was on the pitch	23	Clean Sheets In League games when player was on pitch for at least 70 minutes	5
Defensive Rating Ave number of mins between League goals conceded while on the pitch	76	Club Defensive Rating Average number of mins between League goals conceded by the club this season	61

	PLAYER	CON LGE	CLEAN SHEETS	DEF RATE
1	Javier Horacio Pinola	23	5	76 mins
2	Leandro Glauber	19	2	70 mins
3	Andreas Wolf	41	6	65 mins
4	Dominik Reinhardt	40	2	53 mins

KEY PLAYERS - MIDFIELDERS

Marek Mintal

Goals in the League	5	Contribution to Attacking Power Average number of minutes between League team goals while on pitch	73
Defensive Rating Average number of mins between League goals conceded while on the pitch	68	Scoring Difference Defensive Rating minus Contribution to Attacking Power	-5

	PLAYER	LGE GOALS	DEF RATE	POWER	SCORE DIFF
1	Marek Mintal	5	68	73	-5 mins
2	Jan Kristiansen	0	56	70	-14 mins
3	Zvjezdan Misimovic	10	56	74	-18 mins
4	Peer Kluge	3	52	71	-19 mins

KEY PLAYERS - GOALSCORERS

Zvjezdan Misimovic

Goals in the League	10	Player Strike Rate Average number of minutes between League goals scored by player	215
Contribution to Attacking Power Average number of minutes between League team goals while on pitch	74	Club Strike Rate Average number of minutes between League goals scored by club	87

	PLAYER	LGE GOALS	POWER	STRIKE RATE
1	Zvjezdan Misimovic	10	74	215 mins
2	Angelos Charisteas	6	76	292 mins
3	Marek Mintal	5	73	398 mins
4	Peer Kluge	3	71	592 mins

CHARISTEAS
9
NÜRNBERG
Angelos Charisteas, Marek Mintal and Zvjezdan Misimovic

SQUAD APPEARANCES

Match	1	2	3	4	5	6	7	8	9	10	11	12	13	14	15	16	17	18	19	20	21	22	23	24	25	26	27	28	29	30	31	32	33	34	35	36	37	38	39	40	41	42
Venue	H	A	H	A	H	H	A	H	A	A	A	H	A	H	H	A	H	A	A	H	H	A	A	A	H	A	A	H	H	A	H	A	H	H	A	A	H	H	A	H	A	H
Competition	L	L	L	L	L	E	L	L	L	E	L	L	L	L	E	L	L	E	L	E	L	L	E	L	L	E	L	E	L	L	L	L	L	L	L	L	L	L	L	L	L	L
Result	L	W	L	D	D	D	L	L	D	D	L	W	L	L	L	L	W	D	L	W	W	L	W	L	D	L	L	D	D	L	D	L	D	D	W	L	W	D	D	W	L	L

Goalkeepers
Jaromir Blazek
Daniel Klewer
Alexander Stephan

Defenders
Jacques Abardonado
Michael Beauchamp
Leandro Glauber
Lars Jacobsen
Javier Horacio Pinola
Dominik Reinhardt
Ralf Schmidt
Matthew Spiranovic
Andreas Wolf

Midfielders
Marco Engelhardt
Tomas Galasek
Lukas Kling
Peer Kluge
Jan Kristiansen
Marek Mintal
Zvjezdan Misimovic
Jaouhar Mnari
Dario Vidosic

Forwards
Nicky Adler
Leon Benko
Angelos Charisteas
Joshua Kennedy
Jan Koller
Chhunly Pagenburg
Ivan Saenko
Robert Vittek

KEY: ■ On all match ■ On bench | ⏮ Subbed or sent off (Counting game) ⏪ Subbed or sent off (playing less than 70 minutes) | ⏭ Subbed on from bench (Counting Game) ⏩ Subbed on (playing less than 70 minutes) | Subbed on and then subbed or sent off (Counting Game) Subbed on and then subbed or sent off (playing less than 70 minutes) | □ Not in 16

HANSA ROSTOCK

Final Position: **17th**

NICKNAME: DIE JUNGS VON DER OSTSEE   KEY: ☐ Won ☐ Drawn ☐ Lost

							Attendance
1	grpr1	**Bayern Munich**	A	L	0-3		69,000
2	grpr1	**Nurnberg**	H	L	1-2	Orestes 62	25,000
3	grpr1	**Eintr Frankfurt**	A	L	0-1		44,000
4	grpr1	**B Dortmund**	H	L	0-1		20,000
5	grpr1	**Arminia B**	A	L	2-4	Kern 47, Bulow 63	20,600
6	grpr1	**Duisburg**	H	W	2-0	Hahnge 34, Kern 53 pen	15,000
7	grpr1	**Hertha Berlin**	A	W	3-1	Rahn 40, Hahnge 54, Dorn 71	40,000
8	grpr1	**Stuttgart**	H	W	2-1	Rathgeb 16, Orestes 18	18,000
9	grpr1	**Wolfsburg**	A	L	0-1		26,100
10	grpr1	**Schalke**	H	D	1-1	Stein 56	29,000
11	grpr1	**Karlsruhe**	H	D	0-0		14,000
12	grpr1	**W Bremen**	A	L	0-1		41,738
13	grpr1	**Cottbus**	H	W	3-2	Kern 18, 60, 74	20,000
14	grpr1	**Hamburg**	A	L	0-2		57,000
15	grpr1	**Hannover 96**	H	L	0-3		17,000
16	grpr1	**B Leverkusen**	A	L	0-3		22,500
17	grpr1	**Bochum**	H	W	2-0	Bulow 7, Hahnge 43	16,000
18	grpr1	**Bayern Munich**	H	L	1-2	Kern 52	29,000
19	grpr1	**Nurnberg**	A	D	1-1	Rahn 27	36,470
20	grpr1	**Eintr Frankfurt**	H	W	1-0	Rahn 76	15,500
21	grpr1	**B Dortmund**	A	L	0-1		70,700
22	grpr1	**Arminia B**	H	D	1-1	Bartels 86	14,000
23	grpr1	**Duisburg**	A	D	1-1	Agali 20	20,206
24	grpr1	**Hertha Berlin**	H	D	0-0		22,500
25	grpr1	**Stuttgart**	A	L	1-4	Gomez 56 og	48,000
26	grpr1	**Wolfsburg**	H	L	0-1		15,000
27	grpr1	**Schalke**	A	L	0-1		61,482
28	grpr1	**Karlsruhe**	A	W	2-1	Bartels 30, 84	27,714
29	grpr1	**W Bremen**	H	L	1-2	Hahnge 76	22,000
30	grpr1	**Cottbus**	A	L	1-2	Cetkovic 16	21,357
31	grpr1	**Hamburg**	H	L	1-3	Mathijsen 76 og	28,000
32	grpr1	**Hannover 96**	A	L	0-3		35,453
33	grpr1	**B Leverkusen**	H	L	1-2	Menga 67	22,000
34	grpr1	**Bochum**	A	W	2-1	Kern 40, Bartels 77	18,883

LEAGUE APPEARANCES, BOOKINGS AND CAPS

	AGE (on 01/07/08)	IN NAMED 18	APPEARANCES	COUNTING GAMES	MINUTES ON PITCH	YELLOW CARDS	RED CARDS	CAPS THIS SEASON	NATIONAL SIDE
Goalkeepers									
Jorg Hahnel	26	32	7	6	545	0	0	-	Germany
Stefan Wachter	30	29	28	28	2520	0	0	-	Germany
Defenders									
Dexter Langen	27	28	25	22	2056	4	0	-	Germany
Benjamin Lense	29	11	7	4	393	0	0	-	Germany
Assani Lukimya	22	17	7	2	294	1	0	-	Congo
Gledson	28	11	10	8	810	0	0	-	Brazil
Diego Morais	25	24	7	2	243	0	0	-	Brazil
Orestes	27	32	32	31	2835	7	0	-	Brazil
Heath Pearce	23	24	19	6	903	1	0	-	United States
Tim Sebastian	24	34	31	30	2736	0	0	-	Germany
Marc Stein	22	31	29	27	2546	6	0	-	Germany
Midfielders									
Kai Bulow	22	33	29	23	2264	3	0	-	Germany
Fin Bartels	21	21	19	14	1368	5	0	-	Germany
Stefan Beinlich	36	12	9	4	538	1	0	-	Germany
Djordjije Cetkovic	25	17	13	5	669	0	0	-	Montenegro
Ryan Gyaki	22	1	0	0	0	0	0	-	Canada
Christian Rahn	29	32	28	20	2166	7	0	-	Germany
Tobias Rathgeb	26	32	30	30	2645	2	0	-	Germany
Rene Rydlewicz	34	16	5	0	184	0	0	-	Germany
Simon Tuting	21	2	1	0	28	0	0	-	Germany
Zafer Yelen	21	28	20	7	1031	0	0	-	Germany
Forwards									
Victor Agali	29	26	23	12	1509	6	0	-	Nigeria
Regis Dorn	28	19	15	2	459	1	0	-	France
Sebastian Hahnge	30	24	17	6	948	2	0	-	Germany
Enrico Kern	29	32	32	31	2805	10	0	-	Germany
Addy-Waku Menga	24	13	12	3	455	0	0	-	Congo
Marcel Schied	24	7	2	1	119	0	0	-	Germany
Amir Shapourzadeh	25	22	15	3	591	7	0	-	Iran

TEAM OF THE SEASON

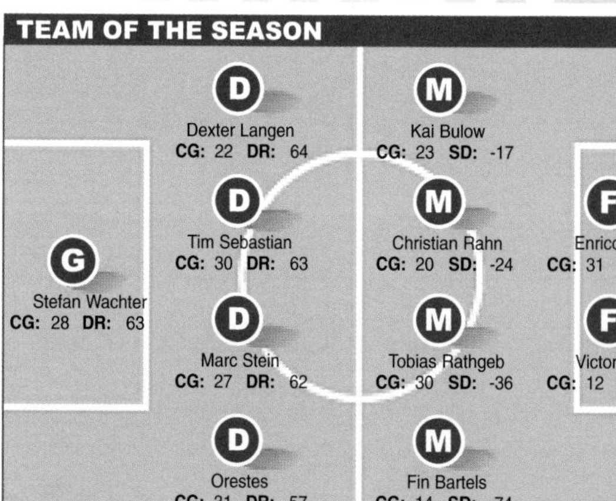

G
Stefan Wachter
CG: 28 DR: 63
D
Dexter Langen
CG: 22 DR: 64
D
Tim Sebastian
CG: 30 DR: 63
D
Marc Stein
CG: 27 DR: 62
D
Orestes
CG: 31 DR: 57
M
Kai Bulow
CG: 23 SD: -17
M
Christian Rahn
CG: 20 SD: -24
M
Tobias Rathgeb
CG: 30 SD: -36
M
Fin Bartels
CG: 14 SD: -74
F
Enrico Kern
CG: 31 SR: 400
F
Victor Agali
CG: 12 SR: 1509

MONTHLY POINTS TALLY

AUGUST	0	0%
SEPTEMBER	9	60%
OCTOBER	2	22%
NOVEMBER	3	25%
DECEMBER	3	50%
NO LEAGUE GAMES PLAYED IN JANUARY		
FEBRUARY	4	33%
MARCH	3	20%
APRIL	3	25%
MAY	3	25%

LEAGUE GOALS

	PLAYER	MINS	GOALS	S RATE
1	Kern	2805	7	400
2	Hahnge	948	4	237
3	Bartels	1368	4	342
4	Rahn	2166	3	722
5	Bulow	2264	2	1132
6	Orestes	2835	2	1417
7	Menga	455	1	455
8	Dorn	459	1	459
9	Cetkovic	669	1	669
10	Agali	1509	1	1509
11	Stein	2546	1	2546
12	Rathgeb	2645	1	2645
	Other		0	
	TOTAL		**28**	

TOP POINT EARNERS

	PLAYER	GAMES	AV PTS
1	Christian Rahn	20	**1.30**
2	Kai Bulow	23	**1.17**
3	Dexter Langen	22	**1.00**
4	Marc Stein	27	**1.00**
5	Tobias Rathgeb	30	**0.90**
6	Tim Sebastian	30	**0.90**
7	Stefan Wachter	28	**0.86**
8	Orestes	31	**0.84**
9	Enrico Kern	31	**0.84**
10	Victor Agali	12	**0.83**
	CLUB AVERAGE:		**0.88**

DISCIPLINARY RECORDS

	PLAYER	YELLOW	RED	AVE
1	Amir Shapourzadeh	7	0	**84**
2	Victor Agali	6	0	**251**
3	Fin Bartels	5	0	**273**
4	Enrico Kern	10	0	**280**
5	Christian Rahn	7	0	**309**
6	Orestes	7	0	**405**
7	Marc Stein	6	0	**424**
8	Regis Dorn	1	0	**459**
9	Sebastian Hahnge	2	0	**474**
10	Dexter Langen	4	0	**514**
11	Stefan Beinlich	1	0	**538**
12	Kai Bulow	3	0	**754**
13	Heath Pearce	1	0	**903**
	Other	2	0	
	TOTAL	**62**	**0**	

KEY GOALKEEPER

Stefan Wachter

Goals Conceded in the League	40	Counting Games League games when player was on pitch for at least 70 minutes	28
Defensive Rating Ave number of mins between League goals conceded while on the pitch	63	Clean Sheets In League games when player was on pitch for at least 70 minutes	4

KEY PLAYERS - DEFENDERS

Dexter Langen

Goals Conceded Number of League goals conceded while the player was on the pitch	32	Clean Sheets In League games when player was on pitch for at least 70 minutes	5
Defensive Rating Ave number of mins between League goals conceded while on the pitch	64	Club Defensive Rating Average number of mins between League goals conceded by the club this season	58

	PLAYER	CON LGE	CLEAN SHEETS	DEF RATE
1	Dexter Langen	32	5	64 mins
2	Tim Sebastian	43	5	63 mins
3	Marc Stein	41	5	62 mins
4	Orestes	49	5	57 mins

KEY PLAYERS - MIDFIELDERS

Kai Bulow

Goals in the League	2	Contribution to Attacking Power Average number of minutes between League team goals while on pitch	90
Defensive Rating Average number of mins between League goals conceded while on the pitch	73	Scoring Difference Defensive Rating minus Contribution to Attacking Power	-17

	PLAYER	LGE GOALS	DEF RATE	POWER	SCORE DIFF
1	Kai Bulow	2	73	90	-17 mins
2	Christian Rahn	3	74	98	-24 mins
3	Tobias Rathgeb	1	61	97	-36 mins
4	Fin Bartels	4	50	124	-74 mins

KEY PLAYERS - GOALSCORERS

Fin Bartels

Goals in the League	4	Player Strike Rate Average number of minutes between League goals scored by player	342
Contribution to Attacking Power Average number of minutes between League team goals while on pitch	124	Club Strike Rate Average number of minutes between League goals scored by club	102

	PLAYER	LGE GOALS	POWER	STRIKE RATE
1	Fin Bartels	4	124	342 mins
2	Enrico Kern	7	107	400 mins
3	Christian Rahn	3	98	722 mins
4	Kai Bulow	2	90	1132 mins

MASITA
kik
MASITA
RATHGEB
17
Tobias Rathgeb and team-mates celebrate

SQUAD APPEARANCES

Match	1	2	3	4	5	6	7	8	9	10	11	12	13	14	15	16	17	18	19	20	21	22	23	24	25	26	27	28	29	30	31	32	33	34
Venue	A	H	A	H	A	H	A	H	A	H	H	A	H	A	H	A	H	H	A	H	A	H	A	H	A	H	A	A	H	A	H	A	H	A
Competition	L	L	L	L	L	L	L	L	L	L	L	L	L	L	L	L	L	L	L	L	L	L	L	L	L	L	L	L	L	L	L	L	L	L
Result	L	L	L	L	L	W	W	W	L	D	D	L	W	L	L	L	W	L	D	W	L	D	D	D	L	L	L	W	L	L	L	L	L	W

Goalkeepers
Jorg Hahnel
Stefan Wachter

Defenders
Dexter Langen
Benjamin Lense
Assani Lukimya
Gledson
Diego Morais
Orestes
Heath Pearce
Tim Sebastian
Marc Stein

Midfielders
Kai Bulow
Fin Bartels
Stefan Beinlich
Djordjije Cetkovic
Ryan Gyaki
Christian Rahn
Tobias Rathgeb
Rene Rydlewicz
Simon Tuting
Zafer Yelen

Forwards
Victor Agali
Regis Dorn
Sebastian Hahnge
Enrico Kern
Addy-Waku Menga
Marcel Schied
Amir Shapourzadeh

KEY: On all match · On bench · Subbed or sent off (Counting game) · Subbed or sent off (playing less than 70 minutes) · Subbed on from bench (Counting Game) · Subbed on (playing less than 70 minutes) · Subbed on and then subbed or sent off (Counting Game) · Subbed on and then subbed or sent off (playing less than 70 minutes) · Not in 16

MSV DUISBURG

Final Position: **18th**

NICKNAME: ZEBRAS

KEY: ☐ Won ☐ Drawn ☐ Lost

							Attendance
1	grpr1	**B Dortmund**	A	W	**3-1**	Ishiaku 8, 64, Tararache 61 pen	75,400
2	grpr1	**Wolfsburg**	H	L	**1-3**	Lavric 88	18,000
3	grpr1	**Stuttgart**	A	L	**0-1**		40,000
4	grpr1	**Arminia B**	H	W	**3-0**	Maicon 64, Ishiaku 68, 70	21,000
5	grpr1	**Hertha Berlin**	H	L	**1-2**	Lavric 78	20,000
6	grpr1	**Hansa Rostock**	A	L	**0-2**		15,000
7	grpr1	**Schalke**	H	L	**0-2**		31,500
8	grpr1	**Hannover 96**	A	L	**1-2**	Ishiaku 20	30,000
9	grpr1	**W Bremen**	H	L	**1-3**	Ailton 18	31,005
10	grpr1	**Cottbus**	A	W	**2-1**	Schlicke 7 fk, Grlic 74	12,000
11	grpr1	**Hamburg**	H	L	**0-1**		30,160
12	grpr1	**Karlsruhe**	A	L	**0-1**		27,714
13	grpr1	**Bochum**	H	L	**0-2**		24,359
14	grpr1	**B Leverkusen**	A	L	**1-4**	Mokhtari 10	22,500
15	grpr1	**Nurnberg**	H	W	**1-0**	Grlic 72	18,000
16	grpr1	**Bayern Munich**	A	D	**0-0**		69,000
17	grpr1	**Eintr Frankfurt**	H	L	**0-1**		26,557
18	grpr1	**B Dortmund**	H	D	**3-3**	Filipescu 18, Willi 30, Tararache 59 pen	30,000
19	grpr1	**Wolfsburg**	A	L	**1-2**	Niculescu 26	18,000
20	grpr1	**Stuttgart**	H	L	**2-3**	Niculescu 49, Ishiaku 57	21,562
21	grpr1	**Arminia B**	A	W	**2-0**	Schroter 8, Ishiaku 48	19,200
22	grpr1	**Hertha Berlin**	A	L	**0-2**		32,382
23	grpr1	**Hansa Rostock**	H	D	**1-1**	Grlic 7	20,206
24	grpr1	**Schalke**	A	L	**1-2**	Georgiev 21	61,482
25	grpr1	**Hannover 96**	H	D	**1-1**	Lamey 77	20,747
26	grpr1	**W Bremen**	A	W	**2-1**	Grlic 32, Ishiaku 41	39,615
27	grpr1	**Cottbus**	H	L	**0-1**		24,016
28	grpr1	**Hamburg**	A	W	**1-0**	Grlic 54	54,218
29	grpr1	**Karlsruhe**	H	L	**0-1**		20,255
30	grpr1	**Bochum**	A	D	**1-1**	Niculescu 26	24,339
31	grpr1	**B Leverkusen**	H	W	**3-2**	Ishiaku 14, 36, Georgiev 90	25,275
32	grpr1	**Nurnberg**	A	L	**0-2**		44,300
33	grpr1	**Bayern Munich**	H	L	**2-3**	Tararache 48, Daun 54	31,500
34	grpr1	**Eintr Frankfurt**	A	L	**2-4**	Niculescu 59, Daun 86	49,500

LEAGUE APPEARANCES, BOOKINGS AND CAPS

	AGE (on 01/07/08)	IN NAMED 18	APPEARANCES	COUNTING GAMES	MINUTES ON PITCH	YELLOW CARDS	RED CARDS	CAPS THIS SEASON	NATIONAL SIDE
Goalkeepers									
Sven Beuckert	34	14	3	3	270	0	0	-	Germany
Tom Starke	27	31	31	31	2790	2	0	-	Germany
Defenders									
F Horacio Avalos	30	12	10	9	855	2	0	-	Argentina
Adam Bodzek	22	9	7	5	496	1	0	-	Germany
Pablo Caceres	23	24	18	15	1471	3	1	-	Uruguay
Iulian Filipescu	34	22	20	15	1440	7	0	-	Romania
Michael Lamey	28	26	25	18	1869	4	0	-	Holland
Roque Junior	31	4	4	3	316	0	0	-	Brazil
Fernando Santos	28	28	14	10	969	5	0	-	Brazil
Bjorn Schlicke	27	27	27	24	2305	5	1	-	Germany
Olivier Veigneau	22	9	7	4	396	1	0	-	France
Christian Weber	24	18	11	8	865	1	0	-	Germany
Midfielders									
Blagoy Georgiev	26	33	31	27	2407	5	1	-	Bulgaria
Ivica Grlic	32	28	28	24	2300	8	0	-	Bosnia
Youssef Mokhtari	29	7	7	4	456	0	0	2	Morocco
Georges Ndoum	22	6	2	1	91	0	0	-	Cameroon
Markus Neumayr	22	8	3	0	16	0	0	-	Germany
Maicon	22	27	20	12	1309	1	0	-	Brazil
Silvio Schroter	29	5	3	1	162	1	0	-	Germany
Mihai Tararache	30	31	31	30	2753	14	1	-	Romania
Christian Tiffert	26	28	25	14	1693	6	0	-	Germany
Tobias Willi	28	29	25	16	1763	5	0	-	Germany
Forwards									
Markus Daun	27	25	19	3	553	2	0	-	Germany
Ailton	34	14	8	2	436	0	0	-	Brazil
Mohamadou Idrissou	28	16	12	8	843	3	1	-	Cameroon
Manaseh Ishiaku	25	26	25	19	1856	3	0	-	Nigeria
Klemen Lavric	27	23	18	7	964	1	0	-	Slovenia
Sascha Molders	23	20	11	3	378	1	0	-	Germany
Claudiu Niculescu	32	17	17	15	1377	4	0	-	Romania
Bojan Vrucina	23	14	8	1	191	2	0	-	Croatia

TEAM OF THE SEASON

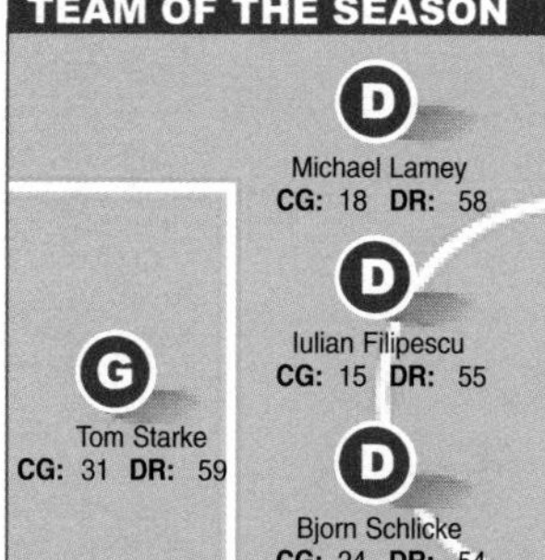
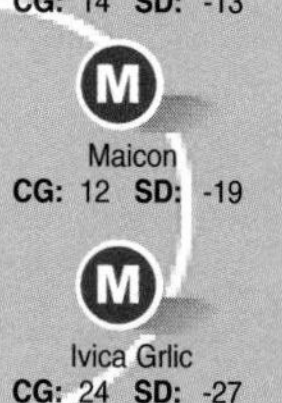
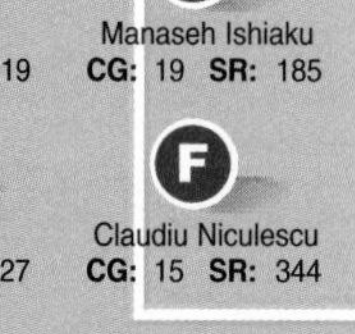

G — Tom Starke — CG: 31 DR: 59

D — Michael Lamey — CG: 18 DR: 58

D — Iulian Filipescu — CG: 15 DR: 55

D — Bjorn Schlicke — CG: 24 DR: 54

D — Pablo Caceres — CG: 15 DR: 54

M — Christian Tiffert — CG: 14 SD: -13

M — Maicon — CG: 12 SD: -19

M — Ivica Grlic — CG: 24 SD: -27

M — Mihai Tararache — CG: 30 SD: -31

F — Manaseh Ishiaku — CG: 19 SR: 185

F — Claudiu Niculescu — CG: 15 SR: 344

MONTHLY POINTS TALLY

AUGUST	3	33%
SEPTEMBER	3	20%
OCTOBER	3	33%
NOVEMBER	0	0%
DECEMBER	4	44%
NO LEAGUE GAMES PLAYED IN JANUARY		
FEBRUARY	4	27%
MARCH	5	42%
APRIL	4	33%
MAY	3	25%

LEAGUE GOALS

	PLAYER	MINS	GOALS	S RATE
1	Ishiaku	1856	10	185
2	Grlic	2300	5	460
3	Niculescu	1377	4	344
4	Tararache	2753	3	917
5	Daun	553	2	276
6	Lavric	964	2	482
7	Georgiev	2407	2	1203
8	Schrater	162	1	162
9	G da Silva	436	1	436
10	Mokhtari	456	1	456
11	P de Souza	1309	1	1309
12	Filipescu	1440	1	1440
13	Willi	1763	1	1763
	Other		2	
	TOTAL		36	

TOP POINT EARNERS

	PLAYER	GAMES	AV PTS
1	Maicon	12	1.17
2	Christian Tiffert	14	1.14
3	Michael Lamey	18	1.11
4	Claudiu Niculescu	15	1.07
5	Manaseh Ishiaku	19	1.00
6	Iulian Filipescu	15	1.00
7	Bjorn Schlicke	24	0.96
8	Ivica Grlic	24	0.92
9	Tom Starke	31	0.90
10	Tobias Willi	16	0.88
	CLUB AVERAGE:		0.85

DISCIPLINARY RECORDS

	PLAYER	YELLOW	RED	AVE
1	Mihai Tararache	14	1	183
2	Fernando Santos	5	0	193
3	Iulian Filipescu	7	0	205
4	M Idrissou	3	1	210
5	Markus Daun	2	0	276
6	Christian Tiffert	6	0	282
7	Ivica Grlic	8	0	287
8	Claudiu Niculescu	4	0	344
9	Tobias Willi	5	0	352
10	Pablo Caceres	3	1	367
11	Bjorn Schlicke	5	1	384
12	Blagoy Georgiev	5	1	401
13	F Horacio Avalos	2	0	427
	Other	13	0	
	TOTAL	82	5	

KEY GOALKEEPER

Tom Starke

Goals Conceded in the League	47	Counting Games League games when player was on pitch for at least 70 minutes	31
Defensive Rating Ave number of mins between League goals conceded while on the pitch	59	Clean Sheets In League games when player was on pitch for at least 70 minutes	5

KEY PLAYERS - DEFENDERS

Michael Lamey

Goals Conceded Number of League goals conceded while the player was on the pitch	32	Clean Sheets In League games when player was on pitch for at least 70 minutes	2
Defensive Rating Ave number of mins between League goals conceded while on the pitch	58	Club Defensive Rating Average number of mins between League goals conceded by the club this season	55

	PLAYER	CON LGE	CLEAN SHEETS	DEF RATE
1	Michael Lamey	32	2	58 mins
2	Iulian Filipescu	26	2	55 mins
3	BjÃ¶rn Schlicke	42	3	54 mins
4	Pablo Caceres	27	1	54 mins

KEY PLAYERS - MIDFIELDERS

Christian Tiffert

Goals in the League	0	Contribution to Attacking Power Average number of minutes between League team goals while on pitch	73
Defensive Rating Average number of mins between League goals conceded while on the pitch	60	Scoring Difference Defensive Rating minus Contribution to Attacking Power	-13

	PLAYER	LGE GOALS	DEF RATE	POWER	SCORE DIFF
1	Christian Tiffert	0	60	73	-13 mins
2	Maicon	1	62	81	-19 mins
3	Ivica Grlic	5	65	92	-27 mins
4	Mihai Tararache	3	55	86	-31 mins

KEY PLAYERS - GOALSCORERS

Manaseh Ishiaku

Goals in the League	10	Player Strike Rate Average number of minutes between League goals scored by player	85
Contribution to Attacking Power Average number of minutes between League team goals while on pitch	80	Club Strike Rate Average number of minutes between League goals scored by club	85

	PLAYER	LGE GOALS	POWER	STRIKE RATE
1	Manaseh Ishiaku	10	80	185 mins
2	Claudiu Niculescu	4	72	344 mins
3	Ivica Grlic	5	92	460 mins
4	Mihai Tararache	3	86	917 mins

Manaseh Ishiaku and Georges Ndoum

SQUAD APPEARANCES

Match	1	2	3	4	5	6	7	8	9	10	11	12	13	14	15	16	17	18	19	20	21	22	23	24	25	26	27	28	29	30	31	32	33	34
Venue	A	H	A	H	H	A	H	A	H	A	H	A	H	A	H	A	H	H	A	H	A	A	H	A	H	A	H	A	H	A	H	A	H	A
Competition	L	L	L	L	L	L	L	L	L	L	L	L	L	L	L	L	L	L	L	L	L	L	L	L	L	L	L	L	L	L	L	L	L	L
Result	W	L	L	W	L	L	L	L	L	W	L	L	L	L	W	D	L	D	L	L	W	L	D	L	D	W	L	W	L	D	W	L	L	L

Goalkeepers
Sven Beuckert
Tom Starke
Defenders
Fernando Horacio Avalos
Adam Bodzek
Pablo Caceres
Iulian Filipescu
Michael Lamey
Roque Junior
Fernando Santos
Bjorn Schlicke
Olivier Veigneau
Christian Weber
Midfielders
Blagoy Georgiev
Ivica Grlic
Youssef Mokhtari
Georges Ndoum
Markus Neumayr
Maicon
Silvio Schroter
Mihai Tararache
Christian Tiffert
Tobias Willi
Forwards
Markus Daun
Ailton
Mohamadou Idrissou
Manaseh Ishiaku
Klemen Lavric
Sascha Molders
Claudiu Niculescu
Bojan Vrucina

KEY: On all match | On bench | Subbed or sent off (Counting game) | Subbed or sent off (playing less than 70 minutes) | Subbed on from bench (Counting Game) | Subbed on (playing less than 70 minutes) | Subbed on and then subbed or sent off (Counting Game) | Subbed on and then subbed or sent off (playing less than 70 minutes) | Not in 16

FRENCH LEAGUE ROUND-UP

FINAL LEAGUE TABLE

		HOME					AWAY					TOTAL			
	P	W	D	L	F	A	W	D	L	F	A	F	A	DIF	PTS
Lyon	38	14	4	1	44	16	10	3	6	30	21	74	37	37	79
Bordeaux	38	13	4	2	38	17	9	5	5	27	21	65	38	27	75
Marseille	38	11	3	5	34	21	6	8	5	24	24	58	45	13	62
AS Nancy	38	13	5	1	31	11	2	10	7	13	20	44	31	13	60
St Etienne	38	12	6	1	30	4	4	4	11	17	30	47	34	13	58
Rennes	38	10	2	7	27	19	6	8	5	20	25	47	44	3	58
Lille	38	8	7	4	29	18	5	11	3	16	14	45	32	13	57
Nice	38	8	7	4	20	14	5	9	5	15	16	35	30	5	55
Le Mans	38	9	6	4	23	16	5	5	9	23	33	46	49	-3	53
Lorient	38	9	7	3	18	12	3	9	7	14	23	32	35	-3	52
Caen	38	10	5	4	31	19	3	7	9	17	34	48	53	-5	51
Monaco	38	7	5	7	22	24	6	3	10	18	24	40	48	-8	47
Valenciennes	38	11	4	4	33	13	1	5	13	9	27	42	40	2	45
Sochaux	38	3	9	7	13	21	7	5	7	21	22	34	43	-9	44
Auxerre	38	8	4	7	20	17	4	4	11	13	35	33	52	-19	44
PSG	38	4	8	7	22	23	6	5	8	15	22	37	45	-8	43
Toulouse	38	4	11	4	14	15	5	4	10	22	27	36	42	-6	42
Lens	38	5	11	3	26	22	4	2	13	17	30	43	52	-9	40
Strasbourg	38	5	5	9	19	20	4	3	12	15	40	34	60	-26	35
Metz	38	3	3	13	18	34	2	6	11	10	30	28	64	-36	24

CLUB STRIKE FORCE

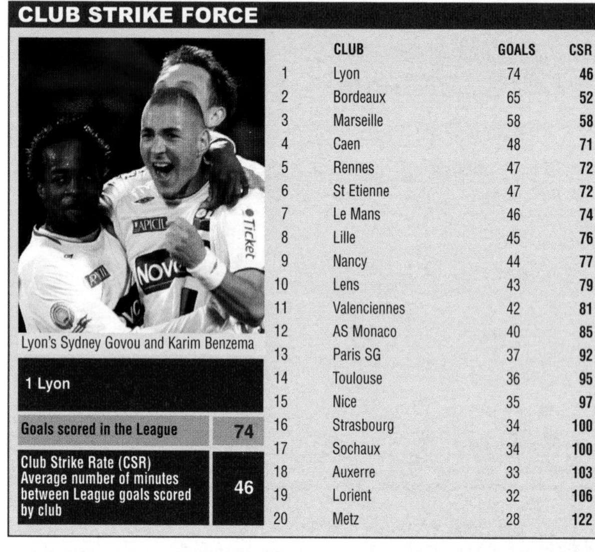

Lyon's Sydney Govou and Karim Benzema

1 Lyon

Goals scored in the League	74
Club Strike Rate (CSR) Average number of minutes between League goals scored by club	46

	CLUB	GOALS	CSR
1	Lyon	74	46
2	Bordeaux	65	52
3	Marseille	58	58
4	Caen	48	71
5	Rennes	47	72
6	St Etienne	47	72
7	Le Mans	46	74
8	Lille	45	76
9	Nancy	44	77
10	Lens	43	79
11	Valenciennes	42	81
12	AS Monaco	40	85
13	Paris SG	37	92
14	Toulouse	36	95
15	Nice	35	97
16	Strasbourg	34	100
17	Sochaux	34	100
18	Auxerre	33	103
19	Lorient	32	106
20	Metz	28	122

CLUB DISCIPLINARY RECORDS

Yellow card for Monaco's Camel Meriem

1 AS Monaco

League Yellow	83
League Red	4
League Total	87
Cards Average in League Average number of minutes between a card being shown of either colour	39

	CLUB	Y	R	TOTAL	AVE
1	AS Monaco	83	4	87	39
2	Toulouse	77	6	83	41
3	Metz	79	4	83	41
4	Bordeaux	74	5	79	43
5	Sochaux	73	1	74	46
6	Nice	72	2	74	46
7	St Etienne	70	4	74	46
8	Le Mans	66	6	72	47
9	Nancy	67	4	71	48
10	Caen	64	2	66	51
11	Auxerre	63	3	66	51
12	Strasbourg	61	5	66	51
13	Lille	61	4	65	52
14	Lyon	60	3	63	54
15	Rennes	60	2	62	55
16	Lens	59	3	62	55
17	Valenciennes	55	7	62	55
18	Marseille	58	3	61	56
19	Paris SG	57	0	57	60
20	Lorient	39	0	39	87

CLUB DEFENCES

	CLUB	LGE	CS	CDR
1	Nancy	30	17	114
2	Nice	30	16	114
3	Lille	32	12	106
4	St Etienne	34	17	100
5	Lorient	35	16	97
6	Lyon	37	13	92
7	Bordeaux	38	17	90
8	Valenciennes	40	14	85
9	Toulouse	42	12	81
10	Sochaux	43	12	79
11	Rennes	44	12	77
12	Paris SG	45	13	76
13	Marseille	45	10	76
14	AS Monaco	48	16	71
15	Le Mans	49	12	69
16	Lens	52	9	65
17	Auxerre	52	14	65
18	Caen	53	13	64
19	Strasbourg	55	11	62
20	Metz	64	6	53

Nancy's Macaluso battling with Lyon's Fred

1 Nancy

Goals conceded in the League	30
Clean Sheets (CS) Number of league games where no goals were conceded	17
Club Defensive Rate (CDR) Average number of minutes between League goals conceded by club	114

PLAYER NATIONALITIES

Overseas country with the most player appearances in the French League - Brazil

736 league appearances by Brazilian players

	COUNTRY	PLAYERS	IN SQUAD	LGE APP	% LGE ACT	CAPS	MOST APP	APP
	France	372	8718	6502	62.84	76	Jeremy Sorbon	100.0
1	Brazil	39	867	736	7.11	0	Andre do Nascimento	92.1
2	Senegal	23	461	373	3.72	2	Mouhamadou Dabo	80.0
3	Ivory Coast	12	291	276	2.42	16	Ndri Romaric	81.4
4	Cameroon	13	253	172	1.63	0	Achille Emana	81.0
5	Mali	11	254	173	1.55	0	Adama Coulibaly	80.4
6	Algeria	9	220	179	1.47	0	Rafik Saifi	92.9
7	Sweden	8	167	131	1.37	39	Petter Hansson	91.7
8	Argentina	9	179	148	1.29	0	Juan E Eluchans	72.1
9	Italy	5	132	113	1.23	10	Fabio Grosso	77.2
10	Morocco	7	133	124	1.23	0	Michael√Chretien	78.9
12	Nigeria	7	123	99	1.07	0	Onyekachi Apam	81.3
13	Colombia	7	157	125	1.06	0	Carlos Sanchez	79.4
14	Congo	3	109	101	0.93	0	Herita Nkolongo	83.0
15	Switzerland	5	106	92	0.92	22	Stephan Lichtsteiner	77.7
16	Croatia	4	90	80	0.79	11	Vedran Runje	100.0
17	Guinea	3	83	73	0.67	0	Pascal Feindouno	74.7
18	Serbia	3	59	54	0.63	0	Marko Basa	71.5
19	Algeria	2	72	56	0.55	0	Nadir Belhadj	60.8
20	Greece	1	34	34	0.40	0	Efstathios Tavlaridis	88.8

CLUB MAKE-UP – HOME AND OVERSEAS PLAYERS

1 Lens

57.6% of appearances by overseas players

	CLUB	OVERSEAS	HOME	% OVERSEAS	% LGE ACT	MOST APP	APP
1	Lens	19	14	57.6	62.63	Vedran Runje	100.0
2	AS Monaco	22	13	62.9	61.45	Flavio Roma	75.4
3	Le Mans	15	16	48.4	55.43	Ndri Romaric	81.4
4	Auxerre	14	16	46.7	49.92	Daniel Niculae	79.3
5	Metz	23	21	52.3	46.59	Papa Malik Diop	72.1
6	Bordeaux	13	18	41.9	44.58	Geraldo Wendel	90.0
7	Lyon	13	17	43.3	43.93	Fabio Grosso	77.2
8	St Etienne	14	12	53.8	43.42	Efstathios Tavlaridis	88.8
9	Marseille	16	22	42.1	42.30	Lorik Cana	86.1
10	Toulouse	12	19	38.7	40.82	Herita Nkolongo	83.0
11	Sochaux	12	20	37.5	38.83	Guirane N'Daw	75.3
12	Lille	15	19	44.1	37.49	Tony Mario Sylva	78.9
13	Strasbourg	12	21	36.4	35.28	Rodrigo Lacerba	89.5
14	Nancy	8	16	33.3	35.19	A do Nascimento	92.1
15	Paris SG	12	18	40.0	32.16	M V A Ceara	73.6
16	Nice	10	20	33.3	26.06	Honorato Ederson	91.9
17	Valenciennes	7	18	28.0	25.02	Abdeslam Ouaddou	83.2
18	Rennes	9	26	25.7	24.02	Petter Hansson	91.7
19	Lorient	6	24	20.0	18.98	Rafik Saifi	92.9
20	Caen	5	23	17.9	13.57	Juan E Eluchans	72.1

CHART-TOPPING MIDFIELDERS

1 Mavuba - Lille	
Goals scored in the League	1
Defensive Rating Av number of mins between League goals conceded while on the pitch	148
Contribution to Attacking Power Average number of minutes between League team goals while on pitch	64
Scoring Difference Defensive Rating minus Contribution to Attacking Power	84

	PLAYER	CLUB	GOALS	DEF RATE	POWER	S DIFF
1	Rio Antonio Mavuba	Lille	1	148	64	**84**
2	Ulrich Le Pen	Lorient	2	187	112	**75**
3	Loic Perrin	St Etienne	2	131	65	**66**
4	Jeremy Toulalan	Lyon	0	109	44	**65**
5	Landry N'Guemo	Nancy	0	130	70	**60**
6	Kim Kallstrom	Lyon	5	97	44	**53**
7	Pernambucano Juninho	Lyon	8	95	45	**50**
8	Yohan Cabaye	Lille	7	118	72	**46**
9	Christophe Landrin	St Etienne	2	111	65	**46**
10	Ludovic Obraniak	Lille	2	114	69	**45**
11	Jeremy Morel	Lorient	0	138	95	**43**
12	Chris Malonga	Nancy	5	108	65	**43**
13	Alou Diarra	Bordeaux	4	95	53	**42**
14	Alejandro Alonso	Bordeaux	0	94	52	**42**
15	Hatem Ben Arfa	Lyon	6	95	53	**42**

CHART-TOPPING GOALSCORERS

1 Cavenaghi - Bordeaux	
Goals scored in the League	15
Contribution to Attacking Power Average number of minutes between League team goals while on pitch	39
Club Strike Rate (CSR) Average minutes between League goals scored by club	52
Player Strike Rate Average number of minutes between League goals scored by player	93

	PLAYER	CLUB	GOALS: LGE	POWER	CSR	S RATE
1	Fernando Cavenaghi	Bordeaux	15	39	52	**93**
2	Mamadou Niang	Marseille	18	63	58	**120**
3	Karim Benzema	Lyon	20	44	46	**128**
4	Johan Audel	Valenciennes	9	90	81	**151**
5	Bafetibis Gomis	St Etienne	16	64	72	**158**
6	Mickael Pagis	Rennes	12	63	72	**164**
7	Djibril Cisse	Marseille	16	55	58	**170**
8	Bakary Kone	Nice	14	82	97	**171**
9	Mevl√ºt Erdinc	Sochaux	11	78	100	**178**
10	Vinicius De Melo	Le Mans	13	68	74	**190**
11	David Bellion	Bordeaux	12	54	52	**204**
12	Steve Savidan	Valenciennes	13	77	81	**209**
13	Wason Renteria	Strasbourg	9	99	100	**210**
14	Pauleta	Paris SG	8	91	92	**217**
15	Rafik Saifi	Lorient	14	102	106	**226**

CHART-TOPPING DEFENDERS

1 Sauget - Nancy	
Goals Conceded in the League The number of League goals conceded while he was on the pitch	14
Clean Sheets In games when he played at least 70 mins	11
Club Defensive Rating Average mins between League goals conceded by the club this season	114
Defensive Rating Average number of minutes between League goals conceded while on pitch	136

	PLAYER	CLUB	CON: LGE	CS	CDR	DEF RATE
1	David Sauget	Nancy	14	11	114	**136**
2	Adil Rami	Lille	16	9	109	**132**
3	Francois Clerc	Lyon	15	10	92	**129**
4	Samuel Bouhours	Le Mans	10	6	69	**125**
5	Sebastien Puygrenier	Nancy	23	16	114	**125**
6	Gregory Tafforeau	Lille	21	10	109	**122**
7	Cedric Kante	Nice	24	14	114	**120**
8	Peter Franquart	Lille	13	7	109	**119**
9	Michael Chretien	Nancy	23	14	114	**117**
10	Cris	Lyon	10	5	92	**114**
11	Onyekachi Apam	Nice	25	13	114	**111**
12	Vincent Hognon	Nice	13	6	114	**111**
13	Mouhamadou Dabo	St Etienne	25	14	100	**109**
14	A L S do Nascimento	Nancy	29	15	114	**108**
15	Frederic Biancalani	Nancy	18	8	114	**108**

CHART-TOPPING GOALKEEPERS

1 Viviani - St Etienne	
Counting Games Games in which he played at least 70 minutes	17
Goals Conceded in the League The number of League goals conceded while he was on the pitch	12
Clean Sheets In games when he played at least 70 mins	8
Defensive Rating Average number of minutes between League goals conceded while on pitch	127

	PLAYER	CLUB	CG	CONC	CS	DEF RATE
1	Jody Viviani	St Etienne	17	12	8	**127**
2	Gennaro Bracigliano	Nancy	38	30	17	**114**
3	Hugo Lloris	Nice	29	24	12	**109**
4	Remy Vercoutre	Lyon	19	16	7	**106**
5	Tony Mario Sylva	Lille	30	27	9	**100**
6	Fabien Audard	Lorient	38	35	16	**97**
7	Patrice Luzi	Rennes	19	19	6	**90**
8	Ulrich Rame	Bordeaux	34	35	15	**89**
9	Jeremie Janot	St Etienne	21	22	9	**86**
10	Nicolas Penneteau	Valenciennes	37	40	13	**83**
11	Gregory Coupet	Lyon	19	21	6	**81**
12	Nicolas Douchez	Toulouse	35	39	11	**81**
13	Teddy Richert	Sochaux	38	43	12	**79**
14	Mickael Landreau	Paris SG	38	45	13	**76**
15	Vincent Plante	Caen	31	37	11	**75**

PLAYER DISCIPLINARY RECORD

Lens' Keita with a strong tackle from behind

1. S. Keita - Lens	
Cards Average mins between cards	154
League Yellow	6
League Red	1
TOTAL	7

	PLAYER		LY	LR	TOT	AVE
1	S Keita	Lens	6	1	7	154
2	F Vasquez	St Etienne	3	1	4	159
3	N Pokrivac	AS Monaco	2	1	3	160
4	Tremoulinas	Bordeaux	3	0	3	168
5	Omar Daf	Sochaux	3	0	3	170
6	C Kabore	Marseille	3	0	3	171
7	A Kader	Lens	7	1	8	175
8	F Santos	Lyon	3	0	3	177
9	Bergougn'x	Toulouse	4	0	4	186
10	I Jemaa	Caen	5	0	5	188
11	Nivaldo	St Etienne	6	0	6	188
12	D Traore	Valenciennes	3	0	3	188
13	Jerko Leko	AS Monaco	10	0	10	193
14	Adriano	AS Monaco	9	1	10	195
15	J Berthod	AS Monaco	4	0	4	205

TEAM OF THE SEASON

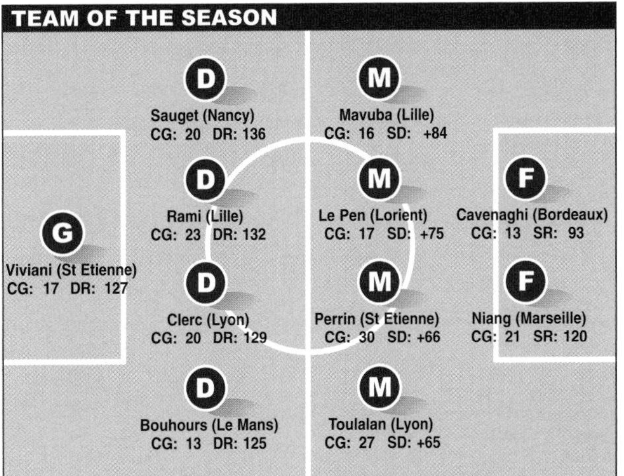
G
Viviani (St Etienne)
CG: 17 DR: 127
D
Sauget (Nancy)
CG: 20 DR: 136
D
Rami (Lille)
CG: 23 DR: 132
D
Clerc (Lyon)
CG: 20 DR: 129
D
Bouhours (Le Mans)
CG: 13 DR: 125
M
Mavuba (Lille)
CG: 16 SD: +84
M
Le Pen (Lorient)
CG: 17 SD: +75
M
Perrin (St Etienne)
CG: 30 SD: +66
M
Toulalan (Lyon)
CG: 27 SD: +65
F
Cavenaghi (Bordeaux)
CG: 13 SR: 93
F
Niang (Marseille)
CG: 21 SR: 120

LYON

Final Position: **1st**

NICKNAME: LE GONES

KEY: ☐Won ☐Drawn ☐Lost

							Attendance
1	frpr1	Auxerre	H	W	2-0	Baros 32, Benzema 69	35,537
2	frpr1	Toulouse	A	L	0-1		24,980
3	frpr1	Lorient	A	L	1-2	Benzema 31	14,612
4	frpr1	St Etienne	H	W	1-0	Benzema 52	38,438
5	frpr1	Sochaux	A	W	2-1	Benzema 18, Bodmer 56	15,488
6	frpr1	Le Mans	H	W	3-2	Govou 70, Benzema 74, Baros 77	35,042
7	frpr1	Metz	A	W	5-1	Benzema 3, 36, 38, Ben Arfa 58 Juninho 87	21,988
8	ecgpe	Barcelona	A	L	0-3		90,000
9	frpr1	Lille	H	D	1-1	Govou 58	32,658
10	frpr1	Lens	H	W	3-0	Santos 41, Kallstrom 80, Benzema 89	38,420
11	ecgpe	Rangers	H	L	0-3		38,000
12	frpr1	Bordeaux	A	W	3-1	Anderson 5, Benzema 22, Kallstrom 59	31,919
13	frpr1	AS Monaco	H	W	3-1	Juninho 12 pen, Reveillere 18 Benzema 50	36,254
14	ecgpe	Stuttgart	A	W	2-0	Santos 54, Benzema 78	51,300
15	frpr1	Paris SG	A	W	3-2	Ben Arfa 41, 43, Govou 85	39,787
16	frpr1	Valenciennes	H	W	2-0	Juninho 39, Govou 85	38,631
17	ecgpe	Stuttgart	H	W	4-2	Ben Arfa 6, 37, Kallstrom 15, Juninho 90	38,000
18	frpr1	Marseille	H	L	1-2	Juninho 7	38,818
19	frpr1	Rennes	A	W	2-0	Juninho 5 pen, Ben Arfa 23	28,596
20	ecgpe	Barcelona	H	D	2-2	Juninho 7 fk, 80 pen	38,000
21	frpr1	Strasbourg	H	W	5-0	Kallstrom 13, 81 pen, Juninho 19 Benzema 66, Clerc 74	34,595
22	frpr1	Caen	A	L	0-1		20,664
23	ecgpe	Rangers	A	W	3-0	Govou 16, Benzema 85, 88	50,062
24	frpr1	Nice	H	D	0-0		37,280
25	frpr1	Nancy	A	D	1-1	Baros 79	19,898
26	frpr1	Toulouse	H	W	3-2	Ben Arfa 16, Juninho 57, Benzema 66	36,587
27	frpr1	Lens	A	L	0-3		32,734
28	frpr1	Lorient	H	W	2-0	Ben Arfa 28, Benzema 73	38,106
29	frpr1	St Etienne	A	D	1-1	Benzema 90	31,537
30	frpr1	Sochaux	H	W	4-1	Bodmer 2, 76, Benzema 90, Govou 90	35,904
31	frpr1	Le Mans	A	L	0-1		14,015
32	eckl1	Man Utd	H	D	1-1	Benzema 53	42,000
33	frpr1	Metz	H	W	2-0	Fred 9, 68	37,281
34	frpr1	Lille	A	W	1-0	Fred 32	77,840
35	eckl2	Man Utd	A	L	0-1		75,521
36	frpr1	Bordeaux	H	W	4-2	Bodmer 12, 22, Benzema 50, Keita 90	40,381
37	frpr1	AS Monaco	A	W	3-0	Keita 20, 38, Fred 35	12,321
38	frpr1	Paris SG	H	W	4-2	Fred 8, 36, Govou 65, Juninho 72	37,895
39	frpr1	Valenciennes	A	W	2-1	Keita 8, Govou 66	15,313
40	frpr1	Marseille	A	L	1-3	Cana 45 og	55,000
41	frpr1	Rennes	H	D	1-1	Cris 16	39,900
42	frpr1	Strasbourg	A	W	2-1	Bodmer 61, Grosso 68	26,008
43	frpr1	Caen	H	D	2-2	Benzema 34, 54	39,068
44	frpr1	Nice	A	D	0-0		14,206
45	frpr1	Nancy	H	W	1-0	Andre Luiz 61 og	38,190
46	frpr1	Auxerre	A	W	3-1	Benzema 1, Fred 10, Kallstrom 53	19,796

LEAGUE APPEARANCES, BOOKINGS AND CAPS

	AGE (on 01/07/08)	IN NAMED 18	APPEARANCES	COUNTING GAMES	MINUTES ON PITCH	YELLOW CARDS	RED CARDS	CAPS THIS SEASON	NATIONAL SIDE
Goalkeepers									
Gregory Coupet	35	19	19	19	1710	0	0	4	France
Johan Hartock	21	5	0	0	0	0	0	-	France
Frederic Roux	35	14	0	0	0	0	0	-	France
Remy Vercoutre	28	38	19	19	1710	1	0	-	France
Defenders									
Nadir Belhadj	26	17	9	4	428	0	0	-	Algeria
Jean A Boumsong	28	14	8	8	720	0	0	1	France
Cleber Anderson	28	12	12	10	962	3	1	-	Brazil
Francois Clerc	25	35	27	20	1935	2	0	5	France
Cristiano M Cris	31	13	13	12	1142	3	0	-	Brazil
Fabio Grosso	30	33	30	28	2594	5	1	6	Italy
Patrick Muller	31	1	1	1	90	0	0	1	Switzerland
Sandy Paillot	21	12	1	0	20	0	0	-	France
Anthony Reveillere	28	37	28	21	2067	6	0	-	France
Sebastien Squillaci	27	36	34	32	2958	3	0	2	France
Midfielders									
Hatem Ben Arfa	21	33	30	15	1617	0	0	6	France
Romain Beynie	21	5	0	0	0	0	0	-	France
Mathieu Bodmer	25	38	37	27	2669	4	0	1	France
Marc Crosas	20	17	8	2	289	0	0	-	Spain
Juninho	33	32	32	26	2392	4	0	-	Brazil
Kim Kallstrom	25	37	37	25	2537	1	1	8	Sweden
Fabio Santos	27	14	8	5	531	3	0	-	Brazil
Jeremy Toulalan	24	31	30	27	2508	6	0	8	France
Forwards									
Milan Baros	26	20	12	5	667	2	0	5	Czech Republic
Karim Benzema	20	36	36	26	2575	1	0	8	France
Cesar Fabian Delgado	26	14	7	0	222	1	0	-	Argentina
Fred	24	23	21	8	1210	5	0	-	Brazil
Sydney Govou	28	32	32	21	2178	5	0	5	France
Abdul Kader Keita	26	31	30	12	1669	4	0	6	Ivory Coast
Anthony Mounier	20	16	1	0	11	0	0	-	France
Loic Remy	21	15	6	0	68	1	0	-	France

TEAM OF THE SEASON

G
Remy Vercoutre
CG: 19 DR: 106
D
Francois Clerc
CG: 20 DR: 129
D
Cristiano Marques Cris
CG: 12 DR: 114
D
Fabio Grosso
CG: 28 DR: 89
D
Sebastien Squillaci
CG: 32 DR: 84
M
Jeremy Toulalan
CG: 27 SD: 65
M
Kim Kallstrom
CG: 25 SD: 53
M
Juninho
CG: 26 SD: 50
M
Hatem Ben Arfa
CG: 15 SD: 42
F
Karim Benzema
CG: 26 SR: 128
F
Sydney Govou
CG: 21 SR: 311

MONTHLY POINTS TALLY

AUGUST	9	60%
SEPTEMBER	10	83%
OCTOBER	9	100%
NOVEMBER	6	67%
DECEMBER	5	42%
JANUARY	7	58%
FEBRUARY	6	67%
MARCH	15	100%
APRIL	5	42%
MAY	7	78%

LEAGUE GOALS

	PLAYER	MINS	GOALS	S RATE
1	Benzema	2575	20	128
2	Juninho	2392	8	299
3	Fred	1210	7	172
4	Govou	2178	7	311
5	Ben Arfa	1617	6	269
6	Bodmer	2669	6	444
7	Kallstrom	2537	5	507
8	Keita	1669	4	417
9	Baros	667	3	222
10	Santos	531	1	531
11	Cleber Anderson	962	1	962
12	Cris	1142	1	1142
13	Clerc	1935	1	1935
	Other		2	
	TOTAL		72	

TOP POINT EARNERS

	PLAYER	GAMES	AV PTS
1	Cristiano Marques Cris	12	2.50
2	Anthony Reveillere	21	2.24
3	Fabio Grosso	28	2.21
4	Pernambucano Juninho	26	2.19
5	Jeremy Toulalan	27	2.19
6	Abdul Kader Keita	12	2.17
7	Kim Kallstrom	25	2.16
8	Karim Benzema	26	2.12
9	Gregory Coupet	19	2.11
10	Sebastien Squillaci	32	2.06
	CLUB AVERAGE:		2.08

DISCIPLINARY RECORDS

	PLAYER	YELLOW	RED	AVE
1	Fabio Santos	3	0	177
2	Cleber Anderson	3	1	240
3	Fred	5	0	242
4	Milan Baros	2	0	333
5	Anthony Reveillere	6	0	344
6	Cristiano M Cris	3	0	380
7	Abdul Kader Keita	4	0	417
8	Jeremy Toulalan	6	0	418
9	Fabio Grosso	5	1	432
10	Sydney Govou	5	0	435
11	Juninho	4	0	598
12	Mathieu Bodmer	4	0	667
13	Francois Clerc	2	0	967
	Other	6	1	
	TOTAL	58	3	

KEY GOALKEEPER

Remy Vercoutre

Goals Conceded in the League	16	**Counting Games** League games when player was on pitch for at least 70 minutes	19
Defensive Rating Ave number of mins between League goals conceded while on the pitch	106	**Clean Sheets** In League games when player was on pitch for at least 70 minutes	7

KEY PLAYERS - DEFENDERS

Francois Clerc

Goals Conceded Number of League goals conceded while the player was on the pitch	15	**Clean Sheets** In League games when player was on pitch for at least 70 minutes	10
Defensive Rating Ave number of mins between League goals conceded while on the pitch	129	**Club Defensive Rating** Average number of mins between League goals conceded by the club this season	92

	PLAYER	CON LGE	CLEAN SHEETS	DEF RATE
1	Francois Clerc	15	10	129 mins
2	Cristiano Marques Cris	10	5	114 mins
3	Fabio Grosso	29	10	89 mins
4	Sebastien Squillaci	35	10	84 mins

KEY PLAYERS - MIDFIELDERS

Jeremy Toulalan

Goals in the League	0	**Contribution to Attacking Power** Average number of minutes between League team goals while on pitch	44
Defensive Rating Average number of mins between League goals conceded while on the pitch	109	**Scoring Difference** Defensive Rating minus Contribution to Attacking Power	65

	PLAYER	LGE GOALS	DEF RATE	POWER	SCORE DIFF
1	Jeremy Toulalan	0	109	44	65 mins
2	Kim Kallstrom	5	97	44	53 mins
3	Pernambucano Juninho	8	95	45	50 mins
4	Hatem Ben Arfa	6	95	53	42 mins

KEY PLAYERS - GOALSCORERS

Karim Benzema

Goals in the League	20	**Player Strike Rate** Average number of minutes between League goals scored by player	128
Contribution to Attacking Power Average number of minutes between League team goals while on pitch	44	**Club Strike Rate** Average number of minutes between League goals scored by club	46

	PLAYER	LGE GOALS	POWER	STRIKE RATE
1	Karim Benzema	20	44	128 mins
2	Hatem Ben Arfa	6	53	269 mins
3	Juninho	8	45	299 mins
4	Sydney Govou	7	40	311 mins

NOVOTEL
APICIL
OL

Karim Benzema

SQUAD APPEARANCES

Match	1	2	3	4	5	6	7	8	9	10	11	12	13	14	15	16	17	18	19	20	21	22	23
Venue	H	A	A	H	A	H	A	A	H	H	H	A	H	A	A	H	H	H	A	H	H	A	A
Competition	L	L	L	L	L	L	L	C	L	L	C	L	L	C	L	L	C	L	L	C	L	L	C
Result	W	L	L	W	W	W	W	L	D	W	L	W	W	W	W	W	W	L	W	D	W	L	W

Match	24	25	26	27	28	29	30	31	32	33	34	35	36	37	38	39	40	41	42	43	44	45	46
Venue	H	A	H	A	H	A	H	A	H	H	A	A	H	A	H	A	A	H	A	H	A	H	A
Competition	L	L	L	L	L	L	L	L	C	L	L	C	L	L	L	L	L	L	L	L	L	L	L
Result	D	D	W	L	W	D	W	L	D	W	W	L	W	W	W	W	L	D	W	D	D	W	W

Goalkeepers
Gregory Coupet
Johan Hartock
Frederic Roux
Remy Vercoutre

Defenders
Nadir Belhadj
Jean-Alain Boumsong
Cleber Anderson
Francois Clerc
Cristiano Marques Cris
Fabio Grosso
Patrick Muller
Sandy Paillot
Anthony Reveillere
Sebastien Squillaci

Midfielders
Hatem Ben Arfa
Romain Beynie
Mathieu Bodmer
Marc Crosas
Pernambucano Juninho
Kim Kallstrom
Fabio Santos
Jeremy Toulalan

Forwards
Milan Baros
Karim Benzema
Cesar Fabian Delgado
Frederico Fred
Sydney Govou
Abdul Kader Keita
Anthony Mounier
Loic Remy

KEY: On all match · On bench · Subbed or sent off (Counting game) · Subbed or sent off (playing less than 70 minutes) · Subbed on from bench (Counting Game) · Subbed on (playing less than 70 minutes) · Subbed on and then subbed or sent off (Counting Game) · Subbed on and then subbed or sent off (playing less than 70 minutes) · Not in 16

BORDEAUX

Final Position: **2nd**

NICKNAME: GIRONDINS

KEY: ☐Won ☐Drawn ☐Lost

							Attendance
1	frpr1	Lens	H	W	1-0	Bellion 30	30,667
2	frpr1	Auxerre	A	W	2-0	Wendel 45, 52	11,512
3	frpr1	Le Mans	H	L	1-2	Bellion 14	30,438
4	frpr1	St Etienne	A	D	0-0		32,630
5	frpr1	Lorient	H	D	2-2	Bellion 10, 68	23,392
6	frpr1	Metz	A	W	1-0	Diarra 66	15,744
7	frpr1	AS Monaco	H	W	2-1	Chamakh 60, Wendel 75	23,390
8	frpr1	Lille	A	D	1-1	Bellion 40	13,770
9	uc1rl1	Tampere Utd	A	W	3-2	Cavenaghi 47, 90, Micoud 90	10,000
10	frpr1	Paris SG	A	W	2-0	Micoud 9, Bellion 46	37,108
11	uc1rl2	Tampere Utd	H	D	1-1	Chamakh 48	7,000
12	frpr1	Lyon	H	L	1-3	Jussie 84	31,919
13	frpr1	Strasbourg	A	D	1-1	Bellion 62	18,865
14	ucgph	Galatasaray	H	W	2-1	Cavenaghi 51, Chamakh 62	20,000
15	frpr1	Valenciennes	H	W	2-1	Jussie 37 pen, Bellion 45	18,521
16	frpr1	Nancy	A	L	0-1		19,686
17	ucgph	Austria Vienna	A	W	2-1	Chamakh 45, Wendel 88 pen	5,000
18	frpr1	Rennes	H	W	3-0	Bellion 18 pen, 49, Obertan 83	21,759
19	frpr1	Caen	A	L	0-5		20,047
20	frpr1	Toulouse	H	W	4-3	Wendel 6, 39, 87, Diarra 32	21,928
21	ucgph	Helsingborg	H	W	2-1	Chamakh 12, Jussie 69	10,000
22	frpr1	Nice	A	D	1-1	Micoud 17	11,988
23	frpr1	Marseille	H	D	2-2	Chamakh 32, Jussie 70	32,286
24	ucgph	Panionios	A	W	3-2	Cavenaghi 40, 75, Moimbe 87	10,000
25	frpr1	Sochaux	A	W	1-0	Jussie 85	12,646
26	frpr1	Auxerre	H	W	4-1	Cavenaghi 13 pen, 52, Planus 40 Bellion 90	21,223
27	frpr1	Le Mans	A	W	2-1	Cavenaghi 13, Fernando Menegazzo 21	10,656
28	frpr1	St Etienne	H	W	1-0	Cavenaghi 55	25,000
29	frpr1	Lorient	A	L	0-1		11,182
30	frpr1	Metz	H	W	3-0	Cavenaghi 26 pen, 73, Diarra 88	19,673
31	uc3rl1	Anderlecht	A	L	1-2	Jussie 69 pen	17,000
32	frpr1	AS Monaco	A	W	6-0	Cavenaghi 51, 64, Micoud 60, 87 Chamakh 81, Obertan 90	10,018
33	uc3rl2	Anderlecht	H	D	1-1	Cavenaghi 71	20,127
34	frpr1	Lille	H	D	0-0		21,761
35	frpr1	Paris SG	H	W	3-0	Wendel 32, 48, 49	30,309
36	frpr1	Lyon	A	L	2-4	Wendel 35, Cavenaghi 60 pen	40,381
37	frpr1	Strasbourg	H	W	3-0	Henrique 27, 41, Cavenaghi 75	19,474
38	frpr1	Valenciennes	A	L	1-3	Wendel 14	13,657
39	frpr1	Nancy	H	W	2-1	Cavenaghi 53, 83 pen	24,308
40	frpr1	Rennes	A	W	2-0	Diarra 17, Fernando Menegazzo 83	28,124
41	frpr1	Caen	H	W	2-1	Cavenaghi 52, 76 pen	27,686
42	frpr1	Toulouse	A	W	1-0	Micoud 90	27,247
43	frpr1	Nice	H	D	0-0		29,097
44	frpr1	Marseille	A	W	2-1	Wendel 80 fk, Ducasse 90	55,778
45	frpr1	Sochaux	H	W	2-0	Fernando Menegazzo 45, Chamakh 58	32,487
46	frpr1	Lens	A	D	2-2	Cavenaghi 65, Bellion 82	40,068

LEAGUE APPEARANCES, BOOKINGS AND CAPS

	AGE (on 01/07/08)	IN NAMED 18	APPEARANCES	COUNTING GAMES	MINUTES ON PITCH	YELLOW CARDS	RED CARDS	CAPS THIS SEASON	NATIONAL SIDE
Goalkeepers									
Gilles Meslien	19	1	0	0	0	0	0	-	France
Ulrich Rame	35	36	36	34	3121	0	1	-	France
Mathieu Valverde	25	38	5	2	298	0	0	-	France
Defenders									
Romain Bregerie	21	11	0	0	0	0	0	-	France
Mathieu Chalme	27	36	34	30	2872	11	1	-	France
Souleymane Diawara	29	32	28	28	2520	6	0	3	Senegal
Bruno Ecuele Manga	19	0	0	0	0	0	0	-	Gabon
Carlos Henrique	25	20	17	17	1530	5	0	-	Brazil
David Jemmali	33	22	8	6	566	2	0	-	Tunisia
Franck Jurietti	33	32	32	28	2648	2	1	-	France
Florian Marange	22	19	7	4	487	2	0	-	France
Marc Planus	26	28	24	24	2141	3	1	-	France
Benoit Tremoulinas	22	31	9	4	506	3	0	-	France
Midfielders									
Alejandro Alonso	26	33	32	21	2083	7	0	-	Argentina
Alou Diarra	26	36	36	35	3167	7	0	3	France
Pierre Ducasse	21	35	15	1	367	1	0	-	France
Fernando Menegazzo	27	32	32	26	2468	5	0	-	Brazil
Juan-Pablo Francia	23	1	0	0	0	0	0	-	Argentina
Ted Lavie	22	0	0	0	0	0	0	-	France
Johan Micoud	34	33	29	16	1877	1	0	-	France
Wilfried Moimbe	19	1	0	0	0	0	0	-	France
Abdou Traore	20	6	0	0	0	0	0	-	Mali
Geraldo Wendel	26	36	36	33	3077	8	0	-	Brazil
Forwards									
David Bellion	25	38	37	22	2448	2	0	-	France
Fernando Cavenaghi	24	30	23	13	1396	4	0	1	Argentina
Marouane Chamakh	24	32	32	15	1751	3	1	-	Morocco
Ferreira Vieira Jussie	24	24	22	13	1346	0	0	-	Brazil
Gabriel Obertan	19	36	25	5	716	2	0	-	France
Edixon Perea	24	0	0	0	0	0	0	-	Colombia
Henri Saivet	17	3	1	0	13	0	0	-	France

TEAM OF THE SEASON

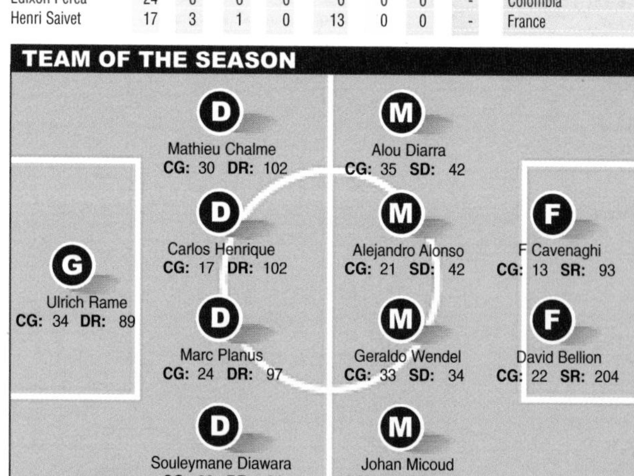
G
Ulrich Rame
CG: 34 DR: 89
D
Mathieu Chalme
CG: 30 DR: 102
D
Carlos Henrique
CG: 17 DR: 102
D
Marc Planus
CG: 24 DR: 97
D
Souleymane Diawara
CG: 28 DR: 84
M
Alou Diarra
CG: 35 SD: 42
M
Alejandro Alonso
CG: 21 SD: 42
M
Geraldo Wendel
CG: 33 SD: 34
M
Johan Micoud
CG: 16 SD: 31
F
F Cavenaghi
CG: 13 SR: 93
F
David Bellion
CG: 22 SR: 204

MONTHLY POINTS TALLY

AUGUST	11	61%
SEPTEMBER	7	78%
OCTOBER	4	44%
NOVEMBER	3	33%
DECEMBER	8	67%
JANUARY	9	75%
FEBRUARY	7	78%
MARCH	9	60%
APRIL	10	83%
MAY	7	78%

LEAGUE GOALS

	PLAYER	MINS	GOALS	S RATE
1	Cavenaghi	1396	**15**	93
2	Bellion	2448	**12**	204
3	Wendel	3077	**12**	256
4	Micoud	1877	**5**	375
5	Jussie	1346	**4**	336
6	Chamakh	1751	**4**	437
7	Diarra	3167	**4**	791
8	F Menegazzo	2468	**3**	822
9	Obertan	716	**2**	358
10	Henrique	1530	**2**	765
11	Ducasse	367	**1**	367
12	Planus	2141	**1**	2141
	Other		0	
	TOTAL		**65**	

TOP POINT EARNERS

	PLAYER	GAMES	AV PTS
1	Fernando Cavenaghi	13	**2.31**
2	Carlos Henrique	17	**2.24**
3	Marouane Chamakh	15	**2.20**
4	Alejandro Alonso	21	**2.19**
5	David Bellion	22	**2.05**
6	Mathieu Chalme	30	**2.03**
7	Alou Diarra	35	**2.03**
8	Souleymane Diawara	28	**2.00**
9	Ulrich Rame	34	**2.00**
10	Geraldo Wendel	33	**2.00**
	CLUB AVERAGE:		**1.97**

DISCIPLINARY RECORDS

	PLAYER	YELLOW	RED	AVE
1	Benoit Tremoulinas	3	0	**168**
2	Mathieu Chalme	11	1	**239**
3	Florian Marange	2	0	**243**
4	David Jemmali	2	0	**283**
5	Alejandro Alonso	7	0	**297**
6	Carlos Henrique	5	0	**306**
7	F Cavenaghi	4	0	**349**
8	Gabriel Obertan	2	0	**358**
9	Geraldo Wendel	8	0	**384**
10	S Diawara	6	0	**420**
11	M Chamakh	3	1	**437**
12	Alou Diarra	7	0	**452**
13	F Menegazzo	5	0	**493**
	Other	8	3	
	TOTAL	**73**	**5**	

KEY GOALKEEPER

Ulrich Rame

Goals Conceded in the League	35	Counting Games League games when player was on pitch for at least 70 minutes	34
Defensive Rating Ave number of mins between League goals conceded while on the pitch	89	Clean Sheets In League games when player was on pitch for at least 70 minutes	15

KEY PLAYERS - DEFENDERS

Mathieu Chalme

Goals Conceded Number of League goals conceded while the player was on the pitch	28	Clean Sheets In League games when player was on pitch for at least 70 minutes	16
Defensive Rating Ave number of mins between League goals conceded while on the pitch	102	Club Defensive Rating Average number of mins between League goals conceded by the club this season	90

	PLAYER	CON LGE	CLEAN SHEETS	DEF RATE
1	Mathieu Chalme	28	16	102 mins
2	Carlos Henrique	15	8	102 mins
3	Marc Planus	22	9	97 mins
4	Souleymane Diawara	30	13	84 mins

KEY PLAYERS - MIDFIELDERS

Alou Diarra

Goals in the League	4	Contribution to Attacking Power Average number of minutes between League team goals while on pitch	53
Defensive Rating Average number of mins between League goals conceded while on the pitch	95	Scoring Difference Defensive Rating minus Contribution to Attacking Power	42

	PLAYER	LGE GOALS	DEF RATE	POWER	SCORE DIFF
1	Alou Diarra	4	95	53	42 mins
2	Alejandro Alonso	0	94	52	42 mins
3	Geraldo Wendel	12	87	53	34 mins
4	Johan Micoud	5	81	50	31 mins

KEY PLAYERS - GOALSCORERS

Fernando Cavenaghi

Goals in the League	15	Player Strike Rate Average number of minutes between League goals scored by player	93
Contribution to Attacking Power Average number of minutes between League team goals while on pitch	39	Club Strike Rate Average number of minutes between League goals scored by club	52

	PLAYER	LGE GOALS	POWER	STRIKE RATE
1	Fernando Cavenaghi	15	39	93 mins
2	David Bellion	12	54	204 mins
3	Geraldo Wendel	12	53	256 mins
4	Ferreira Vieira Jussie	4	67	336 mins

KIA
Wendel

SQUAD APPEARANCES

Match	1	2	3	4	5	6	7	8	9	10	11	12	13	14	15	16	17	18	19	20	21	22	23
Venue	H	A	H	A	H	A	H	A	A	A	H	H	A	H	H	A	A	H	A	H	H	A	H
Competition	L	L	L	L	L	L	L	L	E	L	E	L	L	E	L	L	E	L	L	L	E	L	L
Result	W	W	L	D	D	W	W	D	W	W	D	L	D	W	W	L	W	W	L	W	W	D	D

Match	24	25	26	27	28	29	30	31	32	33	34	35	36	37	38	39	40	41	42	43	44	45	46
Venue	A	A	H	A	H	A	H	A	A	H	H	H	A	H	A	H	A	H	A	H	A	H	A
Competition	E	L	L	L	L	L	L	E	L	E	L	L	L	L	L	L	L	L	L	L	L	L	L
Result	W	W	W	W	W	L	W	L	W	D	D	W	L	W	L	W	W	W	W	D	W	W	D

Goalkeepers
Gilles Meslien
Ulrich Rame
Mathieu Valverde
Defenders
Romain Bregerie
Mathieu Chalme
Souleymane Diawara
Bruno Ecuele Manga
Carlos Henrique
David Jemmali
Franck Jurietti
Florian Marange
Marc Planus
Benoit Tremoulinas
Midfielders
Alejandro Alonso
Alou Diarra
Pierre Ducasse
Fernando Menegazzo
Juan-Pablo Francia
Ted Lavie
Johan Micoud
Wilfried Moimbe
Abdou Traore
Geraldo Wendel
Forwards
David Bellion
Fernando Cavenaghi
Marouane Chamakh
Ferreira Vieira Jussie
Gabriel Obertan
Edixon Perea
Henri Saivet

KEY: On all match | On bench | Subbed or sent off (Counting game) | Subbed or sent off (playing less than 70 minutes) | Subbed on from bench (Counting Game) | Subbed on (playing less than 70 minutes) | Subbed on and then subbed or sent off (Counting Game) | Subbed on and then subbed or sent off (playing less than 70 minutes) | Not in 16

MARSEILLE

Final Position: **3rd**

NICKNAME: I'OM

KEY: ☐ Won ☐ Drawn ☐ Lost

							Attendance
1	frpr1	**Strasbourg**	A	D	0-0		26,397
2	frpr1	**Rennes**	H	D	0-0		55,896
3	frpr1	**Valenciennes**	A	L	1-2	Ziani 57	16,018
4	frpr1	**Nancy**	H	D	2-2	Niang 22, Cisse 49	55,732
5	frpr1	**Caen**	A	W	2-1	Rodriguez 43, Niang 53	20,790
6	frpr1	**Nice**	H	L	0-2		55,490
7	frpr1	**Paris SG**	A	D	1-1	Cisse 10	43,491
8	frpr1	**Toulouse**	H	L	1-2	Zubar 90	53,650
9	ecgpa	**Besiktas**	H	W	2-0	Rodriguez 76, Cisse 90	50,000
10	frpr1	**Auxerre**	A	L	0-2		18,510
11	ecgpa	**Liverpool**	A	W	1-0	Valbuena 78	43,000
12	frpr1	**St Etienne**	A	L	0-1		32,004
13	frpr1	**Lens**	H	W	1-0	Zenden 73	49,245
14	ecgpa	**Porto**	H	D	1-1	Niang 69	50,000
15	frpr1	**Sochaux**	A	L	1-2	Niang 9	19,957
16	frpr1	**Lorient**	H	D	0-0		51,864
17	ecgpa	**Porto**	A	L	1-2	Niang 47	42,217
18	frpr1	**Lyon**	A	W	2-1	Niang 10 pen, 43	38,818
19	frpr1	**Metz**	H	W	3-1	Zenden 29, Niang 37, 70	48,035
20	ecgpa	**Besiktas**	A	L	1-2	Taiwo 65	20,000
21	frpr1	**Lille**	A	D	1-1	Niang 30	17,618
22	frpr1	**AS Monaco**	H	W	2-0	Rodriguez 52, Cana 69	47,000
23	ecgpa	**Liverpool**	H	L	0-4		53,000
24	frpr1	**Bordeaux**	A	D	2-2	Niang 1, Cheyrou 26	32,286
25	frpr1	**Le Mans**	H	W	1-0	Niang 14	48,886
26	frpr1	**Rennes**	A	L	1-3	Cisse 16	29,278
27	frpr1	**Valenciennes**	H	W	3-1	Cisse 27, 74, Rodriguez 50	48,152
28	frpr1	**Nancy**	A	D	1-1	Nasri 86	19,901
29	frpr1	**Caen**	H	W	6-1	Cisse 28, 54, 56, Valbuena 42, 44 Nasri 81	48,481
30	frpr1	**Nice**	A	W	2-0	Niang 24, Cisse 76	15,804
31	uc3rl1	**S Moscow**	H	W	3-0	Cheyrou 62, Taiwo 68, Niang 79	25,000
32	frpr1	**Paris SG**	H	W	2-1	Taiwo 37, Niang 45	57,000
33	uc3rl2	**S Moscow**	A	L	0-2		15,000
34	frpr1	**Toulouse**	A	D	0-0		34,502
35	frpr1	**Auxerre**	H	W	2-1	Cana 7, Cisse 22	53,100
36	uc4rl1	**Z St Petersburg**	H	W	3-1	Cisse 37, 55, Niang 48	45,000
37	frpr1	**St Etienne**	H	W	2-0	Valbuena 58, Taiwo 64	53,565
38	uc4rl2	**Z St Petersburg**	A	L	0-2		21,500
39	frpr1	**Lens**	A	D	3-3	Nasri 24, Cheyrou 28, Cisse 89	40,477
40	frpr1	**Sochaux**	H	L	0-1		51,435
41	frpr1	**Lorient**	A	W	2-1	Akale 53, Niang 80	15,436
42	frpr1	**Lyon**	H	W	3-1	Cisse 26, Niang 28, 54	55,000
43	frpr1	**Metz**	A	W	2-1	Cisse 14, Nasri 57	25,694
44	frpr1	**Lille**	H	L	1-3	Niang 13	40,000
45	frpr1	**AS Monaco**	A	W	3-2	Nasri 28, Taiwo 61, Cisse 83	17,368
46	frpr1	**Bordeaux**	H	L	1-2	Niang 45	55,778
47	frpr1	**Le Mans**	A	D	0-0		16,361
48	frpr1	**Strasbourg**	H	W	4-3	Niang 6, Cisse 45, 78, Nasri 45	57,000

LEAGUE APPEARANCES, BOOKINGS AND CAPS

	AGE (on 01/07/08)	IN NAMED 18	APPEARANCES	COUNTING GAMES	MINUTES ON PITCH	YELLOW CARDS	RED CARDS	CAPS THIS SEASON	NATIONAL SIDE
Goalkeepers									
Cedric Carrasso	26	18	4	4	360	0	0	-	France
Steve Mandanda	23	38	34	34	3060	0	0	1	France
Defenders									
Habib Beye	31	4	4	4	360	1	0	-	Senegal
Laurent Bonnart	28	38	35	34	3121	4	0	-	France
Hassoun Camara	24	1	1	1	90	0	0	-	France
Jacques Faty	24	29	9	8	763	2	0	-	France
Gael Givet	26	34	29	25	2332	4	0	-	France
Juan Angel Krupoviesa	29	11	6	4	378	1	1	-	Argentina
Leyti N'Diaye	22	6	2	1	135	0	0	-	Senegal
Julien Rodriguez	30	21	21	18	1732	5	1	-	France
Taye Ismaila Taiwo	23	32	28	25	2377	2	1	-	Nigeria
Ronald Zubar	22	30	21	13	1345	1	0	-	France
Midfielders									
Kanga Akale	27	19	19	4	867	0	0	-	Ivory Coast
Salim Arrache	25	11	7	0	203	0	0	-	Algeria
Lorik Cana	24	33	33	32	2943	11	0	-	Albania
Benoit Cheyrou	27	35	35	31	2863	8	0	-	France
Vincent Gragnic	25	6	3	0	70	0	0	-	France
Charles Kabore	20	16	12	3	515	3	0	-	Burkina Faso
Modeste Mbami	25	31	24	17	1670	2	0	-	Cameroon
Samir Nasri	21	30	30	28	2543	0	0	7	France
Wilson Oruma	31	17	7	0	171	0	0	-	Nigeria
Mathieu Valbuena	23	34	29	16	1819	2	0	-	France
Boudewijn Zenden	31	37	27	7	1049	3	0	-	Holland
Karim Ziani	25	23	21	10	1240	1	0	-	Algeria
Forwards									
Andre Ayew	19	14	9	1	248	1	0	-	Ghana
Djibril Cisse	26	36	35	29	2729	5	0	2	France
Elliot Grandin	20	11	8	1	255	0	0	-	France
Guy Kassa Gnabouyou	18	1	1	0	13	0	0	-	France
Matt Moussilou	26	8	4	0	128	0	0	-	France
Mamadou Niang	28	29	29	21	2168	2	0	-	Senegal

TEAM OF THE SEASON

G — Steve Mandanda CG: 34 DR: 74

D — Taye Ismaila Taiwo CG: 25 DR: 84

D — Laurent Bonnart CG: 34 DR: 80

D — Gael Givet CG: 25 DR: 72

D — Julien Rodriguez CG: 18 DR: 69

M — Mathieu Valbuena CG: 16 SD: 24

M — Samir Nasri CG: 28 SD: 21

M — Benoit Cheyrou CG: 31 SD: 19

M — Lorik Cana CG: 32 SD: 17

F — Mamadou Niang CG: 21 SR: 120

F — Djibril Cisse CG: 29 SR: 170

MONTHLY POINTS TALLY

AUGUST	6	33%
SEPTEMBER	1	11%
OCTOBER	3	33%
NOVEMBER	7	78%
DECEMBER	8	67%
JANUARY	7	58%
FEBRUARY	7	78%
MARCH	10	67%
APRIL	9	75%
MAY	4	44%

LEAGUE GOALS

	PLAYER	MINS	GOALS	S RATE
1	Niang	2168	18	120
2	Cisse	2729	16	170
3	Nasri	2543	6	423
4	Rodriguez	1732	3	577
5	Valbuena	1819	3	606
6	Taiwo	2377	3	792
7	Zenden	1049	2	524
8	Cheyrou	2863	2	1431
9	Cana	2943	2	1471
10	Akale	867	1	867
11	Ziani	1240	1	1240
12	Zubar	1345	1	1345
	Other		0	
	TOTAL		58	

TOP POINT EARNERS

	PLAYER	GAMES	AV PTS
1	Mathieu Valbuena	16	2.06
2	Modeste Mbami	17	1.88
3	Samir Nasri	28	1.79
4	Mamadou Niang	21	1.76
5	Laurent Bonnart	34	1.76
6	Steve Mandanda	34	1.74
7	Ronald Zubar	13	1.69
8	Julien Rodriguez	18	1.67
9	Djibril Cisse	29	1.62
10	Benoit Cheyrou	31	1.58
	CLUB AVERAGE:		1.63

DISCIPLINARY RECORDS

	PLAYER	YELLOW	RED	AVE
1	Charles Kabore	3	0	171
2	Lorik Cana	11	0	267
3	Julien Rodriguez	5	1	288
4	Boudewijn Zenden	3	0	349
5	Benoit Cheyrou	8	0	357
6	Jacques Faty	2	0	381
7	Djibril Cisse	5	0	545
8	Gael Givet	4	0	583
9	Laurent Bonnart	4	0	780
10	Taye Ismaila Taiwo	2	1	792
11	Modeste Mbami	2	0	835
12	Mathieu Valbuena	2	0	909
13	Mamadou Niang	2	0	1084
	Other	2	0	
	TOTAL	55	2	

KEY GOALKEEPER

Steve Mandanda

Goals Conceded in the League	41	**Counting Games** League games when player was on pitch for at least 70 minutes	34
Defensive Rating Ave number of mins between League goals conceded while on the pitch	74	**Clean Sheets** In League games when player was on pitch for at least 70 minutes	8

KEY PLAYERS - DEFENDERS

Taye Ismaila Taiwo

Goals Conceded Number of League goals conceded while the player was on the pitch	28	**Clean Sheets** In League games when player was on pitch for at least 70 minutes	10
Defensive Rating Ave number of mins between League goals conceded while on the pitch	84	**Club Defensive Rating** Average number of mins between League goals conceded by the club this season	76

	PLAYER	CON LGE	CLEAN SHEETS	DEF RATE
1	Taye Ismaila Taiwo	28	10	84 mins
2	Laurent Bonnart	39	9	80 mins
3	Gael Givet	32	7	72 mins
4	Julien Rodriguez	25	3	69 mins

KEY PLAYERS - MIDFIELDERS

Mathieu Valbuena

Goals in the League	3	**Contribution to Attacking Power** Average number of minutes between League team goals while on pitch	55
Defensive Rating Average number of mins between League goals conceded while on the pitch	79	**Scoring Difference** Defensive Rating minus Contribution to Attacking Power	24

	PLAYER	LGE GOALS	DEF RATE	POWER	SCORE DIFF
1	Mathieu Valbuena	3	79	55	24 mins
2	Samir Nasri	6	70	49	21 mins
3	Benoit Cheyrou	2	77	58	19 mins
4	Lorik Cana	2	77	60	17 mins

KEY PLAYERS - GOALSCORERS

Mamadou Niang

Goals in the League	18	**Player Strike Rate** Average number of minutes between League goals scored by player	120
Contribution to Attacking Power Average number of minutes between League team goals while on pitch	63	**Club Strike Rate** Average number of minutes between League goals scored by club	58

	PLAYER	LGE GOALS	POWER	STRIKE RATE
1	Mamadou Niang	18	63	120 mins
2	Djibril Cisse	16	55	170 mins
3	Samir Nasri	6	49	423 mins
4	Mathieu Valbuena	3	55	606 mins

adidas
Djibril Cisse

SQUAD APPEARANCES

Match	1	2	3	4	5	6	7	8	9	10	11	12	13	14	15	16	17	18	19	20	21	22	23	24
Venue	A	H	A	H	A	H	A	H	H	A	A	A	H	H	A	H	A	A	H	A	A	H	H	A
Competition	L	L	L	L	L	L	L	L	C	L	C	L	L	C	L	L	C	L	L	C	L	L	C	L
Result	D	D	L	D	W	L	D	L	W	L	W	L	W	D	L	D	L	W	W	L	D	W	L	D

Match	25	26	27	28	29	30	31	32	33	34	35	36	37	38	39	40	41	42	43	44	45	46	47	48
Venue	H	A	H	A	H	A	H	H	A	A	H	H	H	A	A	H	A	H	A	H	A	H	A	H
Competition	L	L	L	L	L	L	E	L	E	L	L	E	L	E	L	L	L	L	L	L	L	L	L	L
Result	W	L	W	D	W	W	W	W	L	D	W	W	W	L	D	L	W	W	W	L	W	L	D	W

Goalkeepers
Cedric Carrasso
Steve Mandanda
Defenders
Habib Beye
Laurent Bonnart
Hassoun Camara
Jacques Faty
Gael Givet
Juan Angel Krupoviesa
Julien Rodriguez
Taye Ismaila Taiwo
Ronald Zubar
Midfielders
Kanga Akale
Salim Arrache
Lorik Cana
Benoit Cheyrou
Vincent Gragnic
Charles Kabore
Modeste Mbami
Samir Nasri
Wilson Oruma
Mathieu Valbuena
Boudewijn Zenden
Karim Ziani
Forwards
Andre Ayew
Djibril Cisse
Elliot Grandin
Guy Kassa Gnabouyou
Matt Moussilou
Mame N'Diaye
Mamadou Niang

KEY: On all match | Subbed or sent off (Counting game) | Subbed on from bench (Counting Game) | Subbed on and then subbed or sent off (Counting Game) | Not in 16
On bench | Subbed or sent off (playing less than 70 minutes) | Subbed on (playing less than 70 minutes) | Subbed on and then subbed or sent off (playing less than 70 minutes)

NANCY

Final Position: **4th**

NICKNAME: ASNL

KEY: ☐Won ☐Drawn ☐Lost

#		Opponent	H/A	Res	Score	Scorers	Attendance
1	frpr1	Rennes	A	W	2-0	Fortune 36, Hadji 40	23,601
2	frpr1	Caen	H	W	1-0	Kim 7	17,545
3	frpr1	Nice	H	W	2-1	Puygrenier 50, Berenguer 66	18,389
4	frpr1	Marseille	A	D	2-2	Gavanon 63 pen, Hadji 79	55,732
5	frpr1	Auxerre	H	W	4-1	Malonga 35, Kim 37, Biancalani 48 Fortune 54	18,132
6	frpr1	St Etienne	H	W	2-0	Kim 11, Fortune 84	19,332
7	frpr1	Lens	A	L	0-1		32,774
8	frpr1	Lorient	H	W	2-0	Hadji 80, 86	18,151
9	frpr1	AS Monaco	A	W	3-1	Kim 31, 46, Dia 38	8,851
10	frpr1	Sochaux	H	D	1-1	Kim 26	18,689
11	frpr1	Metz	A	D	0-0		19,585
12	frpr1	Bordeaux	H	W	1-0	Malonga 28	19,686
13	frpr1	Paris SG	A	D	0-0		36,495
14	frpr1	Lille	H	W	2-0	Puygrenier 66, Brison 77	18,029
15	frpr1	Le Mans	A	L	1-2	Gavanon 9 pen	9,938
16	frpr1	Toulouse	A	D	1-1	Malonga 89	10,000
17	frpr1	Valenciennes	H	D	0-0		17,712
18	frpr1	Strasbourg	A	D	0-0		19,087
19	frpr1	Lyon	H	D	1-1	Malonga 87	19,898
20	frpr1	Caen	A	D	0-0		20,327
21	frpr1	Nice	A	L	0-1		11,813
22	frpr1	Marseille	H	D	1-1	Brison 48	19,901
23	frpr1	Auxerre	A	D	0-0		6,548
24	frpr1	Toulouse	H	W	1-0	Puygrenier 90 pen	18,151
25	frpr1	St Etienne	A	L	0-4		26,629
26	frpr1	Lens	H	W	2-1	Berenguer 72, Hadji 75	17,951
27	frpr1	Lorient	A	D	0-0		10,275
28	frpr1	AS Monaco	H	W	2-0	Modesto 5 og, Hadji 20	18,541
29	frpr1	Sochaux	A	D	1-1	Zerka 81	16,487
30	frpr1	Metz	H	W	2-1	Hadji 50, Zerka 88	18,768
31	frpr1	Bordeaux	A	L	1-2	Zerka 28	24,308
32	frpr1	Paris SG	H	W	1-0	Fortune 68	19,474
33	frpr1	Lille	A	L	1-2	Andre Luiz 45	12,242
34	frpr1	Le Mans	H	D	1-1	Fortune 68	18,672
35	frpr1	Valenciennes	A	D	1-1	Berenguer 10	13,972
36	frpr1	Strasbourg	H	W	3-0	Berenguer 39, Fortune 45, Zerka 58	19,507
37	frpr1	Lyon	A	L	0-1		38,190
38	frpr1	Rennes	H	L	2-3	Malonga 7, Andre Luiz 54	19,563

LEAGUE APPEARANCES, BOOKINGS AND CAPS

	AGE (on 01/07/08)	IN NAMED 18	APPEARANCES	COUNTING GAMES	MINUTES ON PITCH	YELLOW CARDS	RED CARDS	CAPS THIS SEASON	NATIONAL SIDE
Goalkeepers									
Gennaro Bracigliano	28	38	38	38	3420	2	0	-	France
Damien Gregorini	29	38	0	0	0	0	0	-	France
Defenders									
Andre Luiz	28	35	35	35	3148	9	1	-	Brazil
Frederic Biancalani	33	35	24	20	1958	4	1	-	France
Yamoudou Camara	20	16	0	0	0	0	0	-	France
Michael Chretien	24	31	30	30	2699	3	1	-	Morocco
Damian Macaluso	28	12	10	4	428	1	0	-	Italy
Sebastien Puygrenier	26	33	33	32	2897	8	0	-	France
David Sauget	28	31	23	20	1915	4	0	-	France
Midfielders									
Pascal Berenguer	27	38	35	28	2843	6	0	-	France
Jonathan Brison	25	35	26	11	1457	4	1	-	France
Benjamin Gavanon	27	38	36	29	2760	4	0	-	France
Ludovic Guerriero	23	27	8	2	221	2	0	-	France
Chris Malonga	20	35	32	12	1630	3	0	-	Congo
Alfred N'Diaye	18	2	0	0	0	0	0	-	France
Landry N'Guemo	22	30	25	15	1696	4	0	-	Cameroon
Adrian Sarkisian	29	8	2	0	28	0	0	-	Uruguay
Forwards									
Basile Camerling	21	3	1	0	6	0	0	-	France
Gaston Curbelo	32	37	32	7	1093	3	0	-	France
Issiar Dia	21	33	31	17	2102	2	0	-	France
Marc-Antoine Fortune	26	37	37	31	2943	1	0	-	France
Youssouf Hadji	28	25	25	21	2025	2	0	-	Morocco
Carlos Henrique Dias	28	25	24	14	1580	2	0	-	Brazil
Moncef Zerka	26	20	15	6	728	3	0	-	France

TEAM OF THE SEASON

G — Gennaro Bracigliano CG: 38 DR: 114

D — David Sauget CG: 20 DR: 136

D — Sebastien Puygrenier CG: 32 DR: 125

D — Michael Chretien CG: 30 DR: 117

D — Frederic Biancalani CG: 20 DR: 108

M — Landry N'Guemo CG: 15 SD: 60

M — Chris Malonga CG: 12 SD: 43

M — Pascal Berenguer CG: 28 SD: 32

M — Benjamin Gavanon CG: 29 SD: 17

F — Carlos H Kim CG: 14 SR: 263

F — Youssouf Hadji CG: 21 SR: 289

MONTHLY POINTS TALLY

Month	Points	%
AUGUST	13	87%
SEPTEMBER	6	67%
OCTOBER	5	56%
NOVEMBER	7	78%
DECEMBER	4	27%
JANUARY	3	25%
FEBRUARY	6	67%
MARCH	8	53%
APRIL	5	42%
MAY	3	33%

LEAGUE GOALS

	PLAYER	MINS	GOALS	S RATE
1	Hadji	2025	7	289
2	Kim	1580	6	263
3	Fortune	2943	6	490
4	Malonga	1630	5	326
5	Zerka	728	4	182
6	Berenguer	2843	4	710
7	Puygrenier	2897	3	965
8	Brison	1457	2	728
9	Gavanon	2760	2	1380
10	Andre Luiz	3148	2	1574
11	Biancalani	1958	1	1958
12	Dia	2102	1	2102
	Other		0	
	TOTAL		43	

TOP POINT EARNERS

	PLAYER	GAMES	AV PTS
1	C Henrique Dias Kim	14	1.93
2	Youssouf Hadji	21	1.81
3	Michael Chretien	30	1.77
4	Pascal Berenguer	28	1.64
5	Sebastien Puygrenier	32	1.63
6	David Sauget	20	1.60
7	Benjamin Gavanon	29	1.59
8	Gennaro Bracigliano	38	1.58
9	Andre Luiz Silva do N	35	1.57
10	Landry N'Guemo	15	1.53
	CLUB AVERAGE:		1.58

DISCIPLINARY RECORDS

	PLAYER	YELLOW	RED	AVE
1	Moncef Zerka	3	0	242
2	Jonathan Brison	4	1	291
3	Andre Nascimento	9	1	314
4	S Puygrenier	8	0	362
5	Gaston Curbelo	3	0	364
6	Frederic Biancalani	4	1	391
7	Landry N'Guemo	4	0	424
8	Pascal Berenguer	6	0	473
9	David Sauget	4	0	478
10	Chris Malonga	3	0	543
11	Michael Chretien	3	1	674
12	Benjamin Gavanon	4	0	690
13	Carlos H Kim	2	0	790
	Other	7	0	
	TOTAL	64	4	

KEY GOALKEEPER

Gennaro Bracigliano

Goals Conceded in the League	30	**Counting Games** League games when player was on pitch for at least 70 minutes	38
Defensive Rating Ave number of mins between League goals conceded while on the pitch	114	**Clean Sheets** In League games when player was on pitch for at least 70 minutes	17

KEY PLAYERS - DEFENDERS

David Sauget

Goals Conceded Number of League goals conceded while the player was on the pitch	14	**Clean Sheets** In League games when player was on pitch for at least 70 minutes	11
Defensive Rating Ave number of mins between League goals conceded while on the pitch	136	**Club Defensive Rating** Average number of mins between League goals conceded by the club this season	114

	PLAYER	CON LGE	CLEAN SHEETS	DEF RATE
1	David Sauget	14	11	136 mins
2	Sebastien Puygrenier	23	16	125 mins
3	Michael Chretien	23	14	117 mins
4	Frederic Biancalani	18	8	108 mins

KEY PLAYERS - MIDFIELDERS

Landry N'Guemo

Goals in the League	0	**Contribution to Attacking Power** Average number of minutes between League team goals while on pitch	70
Defensive Rating Average number of mins between League goals conceded while on the pitch	130	**Scoring Difference** Defensive Rating minus Contribution to Attacking Power	60

	PLAYER	LGE GOALS	DEF RATE	POWER	SCORE DIFF
1	Landry N'Guemo	0	130	70	60 mins
2	Chris Malonga	5	108	65	43 mins
3	Pascal Berenguer	4	113	81	32 mins
4	Benjamin Gavanon	2	106	89	17 mins

KEY PLAYERS - GOALSCORERS

Carlos Henrique Dias Kim

Goals in the League	6	**Player Strike Rate** Average number of minutes between League goals scored by player	263
Contribution to Attacking Power Average number of minutes between League team goals while on pitch	79	**Club Strike Rate** Average number of minutes between League goals scored by club	77

	PLAYER	LGE GOALS	POWER	STRIKE RATE
1	Carlos Henrique Dias Kim	6	79	263 mins
2	Youssouf Hadji	7	81	289 mins
3	Chris Malonga	5	65	326 mins
4	Marc-Antoine Fortune	6	75	490 mins

Grand Nancy
GEODIS
calberson
Clairefontaine
Regina

Andre Luiz

SQUAD APPEARANCES

Match	1	2	3	4	5	6	7	8	9	10	11	12	13	14	15	16	17	18	19	20	21	22	23	24	25	26	27	28	29	30	31	32	33	34	35	36	37	38
Venue	A	H	H	A	H	H	A	H	A	H	A	H	A	H	A	A	H	A	H	A	A	H	A	H	A	H	A	H	A	H	A	H	A	H	A	H	A	H
Competition	L	L	L	L	L	L	L	L	L	L	L	L	L	L	L	L	L	L	L	L	L	L	L	L	L	L	L	L	L	L	L	L	L	L	L	L	L	L
Result	W	W	W	D	W	W	L	W	W	D	D	W	D	W	L	D	D	D	D	D	L	D	D	W	L	W	D	W	D	W	L	W	L	D	D	W	L	L

Goalkeepers
Gennaro Bracigliano
Damien Gregorini

Defenders
Andre Luiz
Frederic Biancalani
Yamoudou Camara
Michael Chretien
Damian Macaluso
Sebastien Puygrenier
David Sauget

Midfielders
Pascal Berenguer
Jonathan Brison
Benjamin Gavanon
Ludovic Guerriero
Chris Malonga
Alfred N'Diaye
Landry N'Guemo
Adrian Sarkisian

Forwards
Basile Camerling
Gaston Curbelo
Issiar Dia
Marc-Antoine Fortune
Youssouf Hadji
Carlos Henrique Dias
Moncef Zerka

KEY: On all match | On bench | Subbed or sent off (Counting game) | Subbed or sent off (playing less than 70 minutes) | Subbed on from bench (Counting Game) | Subbed on (playing less than 70 minutes) | Subbed on and then subbed or sent off (Counting Game) | Subbed on and then subbed or sent off (playing less than 70 minutes) | Not in 16

St ETIENNE

Final Position: **5th**

NICKNAME: LES VERTS

KEY: Won / Drawn / Lost

					Result	Scorers	Attendance
1	frpr1	AS Monaco	A	D	1-1	Feindouno 47 pen	17,134
2	frpr1	Valenciennes	H	W	3-1	Gomis 18, Feindouno 69, 90	30,143
3	frpr1	Rennes	A	L	0-1		28,316
4	frpr1	Bordeaux	H	D	0-0		32,630
5	frpr1	Lyon	A	L	0-1		38,438
6	frpr1	Strasbourg	H	W	2-0	Ilan 35 pen, Abdessadki 68 og	25,694
7	frpr1	Nancy	A	L	0-2		19,332
8	frpr1	Caen	H	W	3-0	Ilan 9, 21, Gomis 48	25,638
9	frpr1	Nice	A	L	0-3		11,252
10	frpr1	Marseille	H	W	1-0	Dernis 90	32,004
11	frpr1	Toulouse	A	W	2-0	Gomis 29, 37	20,114
12	frpr1	Auxerre	H	D	0-0		30,448
13	frpr1	Lens	A	L	2-3	Gigliotti 16, Landrin 21	33,877
14	frpr1	Le Mans	A	L	2-3	Varrault 21, Gigliotti 41 pen	12,434
15	frpr1	Sochaux	H	W	1-0	Ilan 81	26,015
16	frpr1	Lorient	A	D	1-1	Gomis 58	11,833
17	frpr1	Metz	H	W	2-0	Bassong 64 og, Feindouno 90	20,000
18	frpr1	Lille	A	L	0-3		11,808
19	frpr1	Paris SG	H	L	0-1		31,219
20	frpr1	Valenciennes	A	L	0-2		13,516
21	frpr1	Rennes	H	W	2-0	Dernis 11, Gomis 82	21,666
22	frpr1	Bordeaux	A	L	0-1		25,000
23	frpr1	Lyon	H	D	1-1	Gomis 45	31,537
24	frpr1	Strasbourg	A	L	0-3		16,766
25	frpr1	Nancy	H	W	4-0	L.Perrin 18, Gomis 42, 72 Feindouno 71 pen	26,629
26	frpr1	Caen	A	W	3-1	Dernis 18, 35, Gomis 26	20,713
27	frpr1	Nice	H	D	0-0		28,037
28	frpr1	Marseille	A	L	0-2		53,565
29	frpr1	Toulouse	H	D	0-0		25,991
30	frpr1	Auxerre	A	W	3-1	Landrin 63, Ilan 70, Feindouno 80	13,137
31	frpr1	Le Mans	H	W	4-1	Dernis 42, 64, Gomis 56, Feindouno 86	30,006
32	frpr1	Lens	H	W	2-0	Gomis 12, 14	30,000
33	frpr1	Sochaux	A	D	1-1	Ilan 12	19,921
34	frpr1	Lorient	H	W	1-0	Jallet 51 og	33,751
35	frpr1	Metz	A	W	1-0	Gomis 47	11,520
36	frpr1	Lille	H	D	0-0		33,223
37	frpr1	Paris SG	A	D	1-1	L.Perrin 45	45,350
38	frpr1	AS Monaco	H	W	4-0	Gomis 4, 5, Dernis 32, Feindouno 81	34,237

LEAGUE APPEARANCES, BOOKINGS AND CAPS

	AGE (on 01/07/08)	IN NAMED 18	APPEARANCES	COUNTING GAMES	MINUTES ON PITCH	YELLOW CARDS	RED CARDS	CAPS THIS SEASON	NATIONAL SIDE
Goalkeepers									
Jeremie Janot	30	27	22	21	1896	0	0	-	France
Jessy Moulin	22	11	0	0	0	0	0	-	France
Jody Viviani	26	38	17	17	1524	1	0	-	France
Defenders									
Yohan Benalouane	21	14	6	5	484	0	1	-	France
Mouhamadou Dabo	21	32	32	29	2737	4	0	-	Senegal
Fousseni Diawara	27	7	4	2	217	0	0	-	Mali
Nivaldo	28	29	14	11	1128	6	0	-	Brazil
Efstathios Tavlaridis	28	34	34	33	3037	14	0	-	Greece
Cedric Varrault	28	32	24	16	1694	4	0	-	France
Midfielders									
Moustapha Bayal Sall	22	32	31	29	2632	6	1	-	Senegal
Geoffrey Dernis	27	30	29	17	1888	6	1	-	France
Fred Guarin	22	28	18	3	638	3	1	-	Colombia
Christophe Landrin	31	36	35	32	3002	6	0	-	France
Boubacar Mansaly	20	3	0	0	0	0	0	-	Senegal
Blaise Matuidi	21	37	35	29	2800	5	0	-	France
Loic Perrin	22	37	35	30	2902	3	0	-	France
Siaka Tiene	26	24	19	9	957	3	0	3	Ivory Coast
Forwards									
Rudolph M Douala	29	34	12	2	367	1	0	-	Cameroon
Maodomalick Faye	20	9	3	0	8	0	0	-	Senegal
Pascal Feindouno	27	33	33	26	2554	1	0	-	Guinea
David Gigliotti	23	34	17	2	634	2	0	-	France
Bafetimbi Gomis	23	35	35	24	2529	3	0	3	France
Marek Heinz	30	1	0	0	0	0	0	-	Czech Republic
Aruajo Ilan	27	34	31	18	1943	2	0	-	Brazil
Lasse Nilsson	26	15	5	0	109	0	0	1	Sweden
Dimitri Payet	21	37	31	13	1872	0	0	-	France

TEAM OF THE SEASON

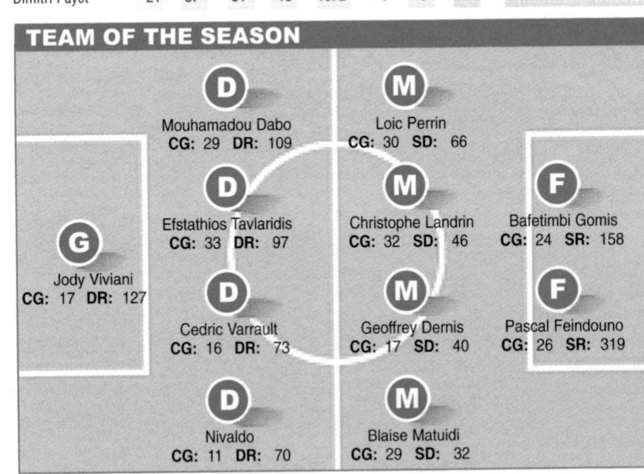

D
Mouhamadou Dabo
CG: 29 DR: 109
M
Loic Perrin
CG: 30 SD: 66
D
Efstathios Tavlaridis
CG: 33 DR: 97
M
Christophe Landrin
CG: 32 SD: 46
F
Bafetimbi Gomis
CG: 24 SR: 158
G
Jody Viviani
CG: 17 DR: 127
D
Cedric Varrault
CG: 16 DR: 73
M
Geoffrey Dernis
CG: 17 SD: 40
F
Pascal Feindouno
CG: 26 SR: 319
D
Nivaldo
CG: 11 DR: 70
M
Blaise Matuidi
CG: 29 SD: 32

MONTHLY POINTS TALLY

Month	Points	%
AUGUST	8	44%
SEPTEMBER	3	33%
OCTOBER	7	78%
NOVEMBER	3	33%
DECEMBER	4	33%
JANUARY	4	33%
FEBRUARY	6	67%
MARCH	5	42%
APRIL	13	87%
MAY	5	56%

LEAGUE GOALS

	PLAYER	MINS	GOALS	S RATE
1	Gomis	2529	16	158
2	Feindouno	2554	8	319
3	Dernis	1888	7	269
4	Ilan	1943	6	323
5	Gigliotti	634	2	317
6	Perrin	2902	2	1451
7	Landrin	3002	2	1501
8	Varrault	1694	1	1694
	Other		0	
	TOTAL		44	

TOP POINT EARNERS

	PLAYER	GAMES	AV PTS
1	Bafetimbi Gomis	24	2.00
2	Pascal Feindouno	26	1.92
3	Dimitri Payet	13	1.85
4	Jody Viviani	17	1.76
5	Christophe Landrin	32	1.69
6	Loic Perrin	30	1.67
7	Blaise Matuidi	29	1.66
8	Mouhamadou Dabo	29	1.59
9	Moustapha Bayal Sall	29	1.52
10	Efstathios Tavlaridis	33	1.48
	CLUB AVERAGE:		1.53

DISCIPLINARY RECORDS

	PLAYER	YELLOW	RED	AVE
1	Fredy A Guarin	3	1	159
2	Nivaldo	6	0	188
3	E Tavlaridis	14	0	216
4	Geoffrey Dernis	6	1	269
5	David Gigliotti	2	0	317
6	Siaka Tiene	3	0	319
7	Moustapha B Sall	6	1	376
8	Cedric Varrault	4	0	423
9	Yohan Benalouane	0	1	484
10	Christophe Landrin	6	0	500
11	Blaise Matuidi	5	0	560
12	Mouhamadou Dabo	4	0	684
13	Bafetimbi Gomis	3	0	843
	Other	7	0	
	TOTAL	69	4	

KEY GOALKEEPER

Jody Viviani

Goals Conceded in the League	12	Counting Games League games when player was on pitch for at least 70 minutes	17
Defensive Rating Ave number of mins between League goals conceded while on the pitch	127	Clean Sheets In League games when player was on pitch for at least 70 minutes	8

KEY PLAYERS - DEFENDERS

Mouhamadou Dabo

Goals Conceded Number of League goals conceded while the player was on the pitch	25	Clean Sheets In League games when player was on pitch for at least 70 minutes	14
Defensive Rating Ave number of mins between League goals conceded while on the pitch	109	Club Defensive Rating Average number of mins between League goals conceded by the club this season	100

	PLAYER	CON LGE	CLEAN SHEETS	DEF RATE
1	Mouhamadou Dabo	25	14	109 mins
2	Efstathios Tavlaridis	31	15	97 mins
3	Cedric Varrault	23	3	73 mins
4	Nivaldo	16	4	70 mins

KEY PLAYERS - MIDFIELDERS

Loic Perrin

Goals in the League	2	Contribution to Attacking Power Average number of minutes between League team goals while on pitch	65
Defensive Rating Average number of mins between League goals conceded while on the pitch	131	Scoring Difference Defensive Rating minus Contribution to Attacking Power	66

	PLAYER	LGE GOALS	DEF RATE	POWER	SCORE DIFF
1	Loic Perrin	2	131	65	66 mins
2	Christophe Landrin	2	111	65	46 mins
3	Geoffrey Dernis	7	99	59	40 mins
4	Blaise Matuidi	0	103	71	32 mins

KEY PLAYERS - GOALSCORERS

Bafetimbi Gomis

Goals in the League	16	Player Strike Rate Average number of minutes between League goals scored by player	158
Contribution to Attacking Power Average number of minutes between League team goals while on pitch	64	Club Strike Rate Average number of minutes between League goals scored by club	72

	PLAYER	LGE GOALS	POWER	STRIKE RATE
1	Bafetimbi Gomis	16	64	158 mins
2	Geoffrey Dernis	7	59	269 mins
3	Pascal Feindouno	8	63	319 mins
4	Aruajo Ilan	6	77	323 mins

adidas
Conseil général
LOIRE
KONICA
MINOLTA
INVICTA
Bafetimbi Gomis

SQUAD APPEARANCES

Match	1	2	3	4	5	6	7	8	9	10	11	12	13	14	15	16	17	18	19	20	21	22	23	24	25	26	27	28	29	30	31	32	33	34	35	36	37	38
Venue	A	H	A	H	A	H	A	H	A	H	A	H	A	A	H	A	H	A	H	A	H	A	H	A	H	A	H	A	H	A	H	H	A	H	A	H	A	H
Competition	L	L	L	L	L	L	L	L	L	L	L	L	L	L	L	L	L	L	L	L	L	L	L	L	L	L	L	L	L	L	L	L	L	L	L	L	L	L
Result	D	W	L	D	L	W	L	W	L	W	W	D	L	L	W	D	W	L	L	L	W	L	D	L	W	W	D	L	D	W	W	W	D	W	W	D	D	W

Goalkeepers
Jeremie Janot
Jessy Moulin
Jody Viviani

Defenders
Yohan Benalouane
Mouhamadou Dabo
Fousseni Diawara
Nivaldo
Efstathios Tavlaridis
Cedric Varrault

Midfielders
Moustapha Bayal Sall
Geoffrey Dernis
Fredy Guarin
Christophe Landrin
Boubacar Mansaly
Blaise Matuidi
Loic Perrin
Siaka Tiene

Forwards
Rudolph M Douala
Maodomalick Faye
Pascal Feindouno
David Gigliotti
Bafetimbi Gomis
Marek Heinz
Aruajo Ilan
Lasse Nilsson
Dimitri Payet

KEY: ■ On all match ■ On bench ⏮ Subbed or sent off (Counting game) « Subbed or sent off (playing less than 70 minutes) ⏭ Subbed on from bench (Counting Game) » Subbed on (playing less than 70 minutes) Subbed on and then subbed or sent off (Counting Game) Subbed on and then subbed or sent off (playing less than 70 minutes) □ Not in 16

RENNES

Final Position: **6th**

NICKNAME: LES ROUGES ET NOIRS

KEY: ☐Won ☐Drawn ☐Lost

							Attendance
1	frpr1	Nancy	H	L	0-2		23,601
2	frpr1	Marseille	A	D	0-0		55,896
3	frpr1	St Etienne	H	W	1-0	Hansson 3	28,316
4	frpr1	Nice	A	D	1-1	Briand 84	10,858
5	frpr1	Metz	H	W	2-0	Thomert 45, 54	24,078
6	frpr1	Auxerre	A	W	2-0	M'Bia 17, Briand 33	7,896
7	frpr1	Lille	H	D	2-2	Leroy 48, Didot 54	23,934
8	frpr1	Lorient	A	W	1-0	Didot 34	13,674
9	uc1rl1	Lokomotiv S	A	W	3-1	Leroy 38, 90, Cheyrou 73	4,000
10	frpr1	Sochaux	H	L	0-2		22,589
11	uc1rl2	Lokomotiv S	H	L	1-2	Marveaux 25	15,000
12	frpr1	Paris SG	A	W	3-1	Leroy 18, Briand 73, Wiltord 83	35,436
13	frpr1	Le Mans	H	W	3-0	Pagis 11, Wiltord 53, Esteban 90	23,349
14	ucgpd	Basel	A	L	0-1		11,407
15	frpr1	Lens	A	W	2-1	Wiltord 57, Leroy 76	30,441
16	frpr1	AS Monaco	H	L	0-1		27,754
17	ucgpd	SK Brann	H	D	1-1	Cheyrou 88 pen	15,000
18	frpr1	Bordeaux	A	L	0-3		21,759
19	frpr1	Lyon	H	L	0-2		28,596
20	ucgpd	Hamburg	A	L	0-3		36,472
21	frpr1	Valenciennes	A	L	0-3		12,161
22	frpr1	Strasbourg	A	L	0-3		20,000
23	frpr1	Caen	H	L	1-2	Pagis 89	26,081
24	ucgpd	Dinamo Zagreb	H	D	1-1	M'Bia 90	11,846
25	frpr1	Toulouse	A	D	0-0		21,183
26	frpr1	Marseille	H	W	3-1	Pagis 39, Wiltord 82, 88	29,278
27	frpr1	St Etienne	A	L	0-2		21,666
28	frpr1	Nice	H	D	1-1	Briand 49	23,241
29	frpr1	Metz	A	D	1-1	Thomert 28	9,823
30	frpr1	Auxerre	H	L	1-2	Pagis 49	22,733
31	frpr1	Lille	A	L	1-3	Pagis 89	13,396
32	frpr1	Lorient	H	W	2-0	Briand 43, Leroy 65	24,133
33	frpr1	Sochaux	A	D	0-0		14,564
34	frpr1	Paris SG	H	W	2-0	Sakho 44 og, Briand 49	25,723
35	frpr1	Le Mans	A	D	1-1	Thomert 38	10,329
36	frpr1	Lens	H	W	3-1	Leroy 12, Pagis 43, Thomert 54	24,411
37	frpr1	AS Monaco	A	W	2-1	Hansson 19, Pagis 90	5,000
38	frpr1	Bordeaux	H	L	0-2		28,124
39	frpr1	Lyon	A	D	1-1	M'Bia 90	39,900
40	frpr1	Valenciennes	H	W	1-0	Wiltord 76	26,532
41	frpr1	Strasbourg	H	W	3-0	Pagis 33, 45, Lemoine 35	24,318
42	frpr1	Caen	A	D	2-2	Leroy 30, Briand 90	20,627
43	frpr1	Toulouse	H	W	2-1	Pagis 54, Mensah 72	28,078
44	frpr1	Nancy	A	W	3-2	M'Bia 32, Pagis 48, 56	19,563

LEAGUE APPEARANCES, BOOKINGS AND CAPS

	AGE (on 01/07/08)	IN NAMED 18	APPEARANCES	COUNTING GAMES	MINUTES ON PITCH	YELLOW CARDS	RED CARDS	CAPS THIS SEASON	NATIONAL SIDE
Goalkeepers									
Patrice Luzi	27	33	19	19	1710	1	0	-	France
Simon Pouplin	23	30	19	19	1710	0	0	-	France
Defenders									
Guillaume Borne	20	17	5	3	338	0	0	-	France
Bira Dembele	20	17	7	3	361	0	0	-	France
Elderson Uwa Echiejile	20	9	4	3	312	2	0	-	Nigeria
Erik Edman	29	15	13	13	1110	2	0	6	Sweden
Rod Fanni	26	28	28	27	2494	2	0	-	France
Petter Hansson	31	37	35	35	3135	6	0	7	Sweden
Cyril Jeunechamp	32	13	5	3	314	0	0	-	France
John Mensah	25	24	24	23	2103	3	0	-	Ghana
Djimi Traore	28	15	15	13	1237	3	0	-	France
Midfielders									
Bruno Cheyrou	30	31	27	22	2154	4	0	-	France
Romain Danze	21	16	9	7	685	1	0	-	France
Etienne Didot	24	28	24	14	1490	1	0	-	France
Fabien Lemoine	21	18	18	16	1459	2	0	-	France
Jerome Leroy	33	32	32	26	2624	5	0	-	France
Stephane M'Bia	22	26	25	23	2129	8	1	2	Cameroon
Sylvain Marveaux	22	34	23	8	1031	3	0	-	France
Yann Mvila	18	2	0	0	0	0	0	-	France
Oliver Sorlin	29	37	33	22	2269	5	0	-	France
Forwards									
Lhadji Badiane	21	13	5	0	118	0	0	-	France
Jimmy Briand	23	37	36	31	2960	3	0	-	France
Marcio Emerson	29	3	3	0	31	1	0	-	Brazil
Julian Esteban	21	10	3	0	30	0	0	-	Switzerland
Jires Kembo-Ekoko	20	18	7	0	172	0	0	-	Congo DR
Daniel Moreira	30	14	9	1	258	0	0	-	France
Mickael Pagis	34	36	31	15	1968	3	0	-	France
Moussa Sow	22	4	2	0	32	0	0	-	France
Olivier Thomert	28	25	25	18	1839	4	0	-	France
Sylvain Wiltord	34	31	25	13	1444	0	0	-	France

TEAM OF THE SEASON

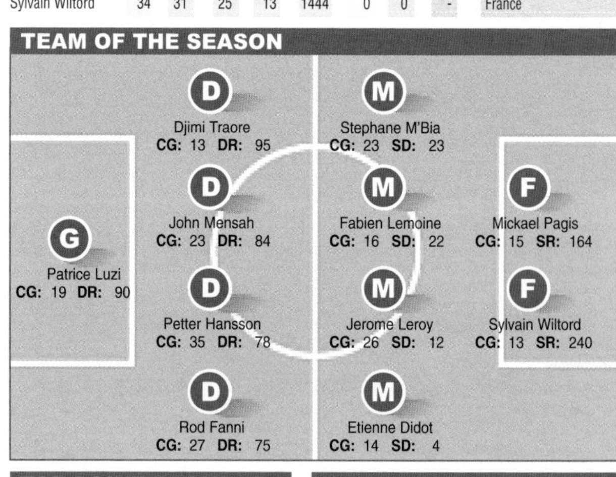

D
Djimi Traore
CG: 13 DR: 95
D
John Mensah
CG: 23 DR: 84
G
Patrice Luzi
CG: 19 DR: 90
D
Petter Hansson
CG: 35 DR: 78
D
Rod Fanni
CG: 27 DR: 75
M
Stephane M'Bia
CG: 23 SD: 23
M
Fabien Lemoine
CG: 16 SD: 22
M
Jerome Leroy
CG: 26 SD: 12
M
Etienne Didot
CG: 14 SD: 4
F
Mickael Pagis
CG: 15 SR: 164
F
Sylvain Wiltord
CG: 13 SR: 240

MONTHLY POINTS TALLY

AUGUST	11	61%
SEPTEMBER	4	44%
OCTOBER	9	100%
NOVEMBER	0	0%
DECEMBER	1	8%
JANUARY	5	42%
FEBRUARY	3	33%
MARCH	11	73%
APRIL	7	58%
MAY	7	78%

LEAGUE GOALS

	PLAYER	MINS	GOALS	S RATE
1	Pagis	1968	12	164
2	Briand	2960	7	422
3	Wiltord	1444	6	240
4	Leroy	2624	6	437
5	Thomert	1839	5	367
6	M'Bia	2129	3	709
7	Didot	1490	2	745
8	Hansson	3135	2	1567
9	Esteban	30	1	30
10	Lemoine	1459	1	1459
11	Mensah	2103	1	2103
	Other		0	
	TOTAL		46	

TOP POINT EARNERS

	PLAYER	GAMES	AV PTS
1	Djimi Traore	13	2.15
2	Mickael Pagis	15	2.07
3	Patrice Luzi	19	1.95
4	Fabien Lemoine	16	1.81
5	Jerome Leroy	26	1.77
6	Stephane M'Bia	23	1.74
7	John Mensah	23	1.74
8	Petter Hansson	35	1.57
9	Sylvain Wiltord	13	1.54
10	Jimmy Briand	31	1.48
	CLUB AVERAGE:		1.53

DISCIPLINARY RECORDS

	PLAYER	YELLOW	RED	AVE
1	Stephane M'Bia	8	1	236
2	Sylvain Marveaux	3	0	343
3	Djimi Traore	3	0	412
4	Oliver Sorlin	5	0	453
5	Olivier Thomert	4	0	459
6	Petter Hansson	6	0	522
7	Jerome Leroy	5	0	524
8	Bruno Cheyrou	4	0	538
9	Erik Edman	2	0	555
10	Mickael Pagis	3	0	656
11	Romain Danze	1	0	685
12	John Mensah	3	0	701
13	Fabien Lemoine	2	0	729
	Other	7	0	
	TOTAL	56	1	

KEY GOALKEEPER

Patrice Luzi

Goals Conceded in the League	19	**Counting Games** League games when player was on pitch for at least 70 minutes	19
Defensive Rating Ave number of mins between League goals conceded while on the pitch	90	**Clean Sheets** In League games when player was on pitch for at least 70 minutes	6

KEY PLAYERS - GOALSCORERS

Mickael Pagis

Goals in the League	12	**Player Strike Rate** Average number of minutes between League goals scored by player	164
Contribution to Attacking Power Average number of minutes between League team goals while on pitch	63	**Club Strike Rate** Average number of minutes between League goals scored by club	72

	PLAYER	LGE GOALS	POWER	STRIKE RATE
1	Mickael Pagis	12	63	164 mins
2	Sylvain Wiltord	6	72	240 mins
3	Olivier Thomert	5	79	367 mins
4	Jimmy Briand	7	74	422 mins

KEY PLAYERS - DEFENDERS

Djimi Traore

Goals Conceded Number of League goals conceded while the player was on the pitch	13	**Clean Sheets** In League games when player was on pitch for at least 70 minutes	5
Defensive Rating Ave number of mins between League goals conceded while on the pitch	95	**Club Defensive Rating** Average number of mins between League goals conceded by the club this season	77

	PLAYER	CON LGE	CLEAN SHEETS	DEF RATE
1	Djimi Traore	13	5	95 mins
2	John Mensah	25	8	84 mins
3	Petter Hansson	40	11	78 mins
4	Rod Fanni	33	10	75 mins

Michael Pagis and Fabien Lemoine

KEY PLAYERS - MIDFIELDERS

Stephane M'Bia

Goals in the League	3	**Contribution to Attacking Power** Average number of minutes between League team goals while on pitch	73
Defensive Rating Average number of mins between League goals conceded while on the pitch	96	**Scoring Difference** Defensive Rating minus Contribution to Attacking Power	23

	PLAYER	LGE GOALS	DEF RATE	POWER	SCORE DIFF
1	Stephane M'Bia	3	96	73	23 mins
2	Fabien Lemoine	1	85	63	22 mins
3	Jerome Leroy	6	79	67	12 mins
4	Etienne Didot	2	74	70	4 mins

SQUAD APPEARANCES

Match	1	2	3	4	5	6	7	8	9	10	11	12	13	14	15	16	17	18	19	20	21	22
Venue	H	A	H	A	H	A	H	A	A	H	H	A	H	A	A	H	H	A	H	A	A	A
Competition	L	L	L	L	L	L	L	L	E	L	E	L	L	E	L	L	E	L	L	E	L	L
Result	L	D	W	D	W	W	D	W	W	L	L	W	W	L	W	L	D	L	L	L	L	L

Match	23	24	25	26	27	28	29	30	31	32	33	34	35	36	37	38	39	40	41	42	43	44
Venue	H	H	A	H	A	H	A	H	A	H	A	H	A	H	A	H	A	H	H	A	H	A
Competition	L	E	L	L	L	L	L	L	L	L	L	L	L	L	L	L	L	L	L	L	L	L
Result	L	D	D	W	L	D	D	L	L	W	D	W	D	W	W	L	D	W	W	D	W	W

Goalkeepers
Patrice Luzi
Simon Pouplin
Defenders
Guillaume Borne
Bira Dembele
Elderson Uwa Echiejile
Erik Edman
Rod Fanni
Petter Hansson
Cyril Jeunechamp
John Mensah
Djimi Traore
Midfielders
Bruno Cheyrou
Romain Danze
Etienne Didot
Fabien Lemoine
Jerome Leroy
Stephane M'Bia
Sylvain Marveaux
Yann Mvila
Oliver Sorlin
Forwards
Lhadji Badiane
Jimmy Briand
Marcio Emerson
Julian Esteban
Jires Kembo-Ekoko
Daniel Moreira
Mickael Pagis
Moussa Sow
Olivier Thomert
Sylvain Wiltord

KEY: On all match; On bench; Subbed or sent off (Counting game); Subbed or sent off (playing less than 70 minutes); Subbed on from bench (Counting Game); Subbed on (playing less than 70 minutes); Subbed on and then subbed or sent off (Counting Game); Subbed on and then subbed or sent off (playing less than 70 minutes); Not in 16

LILLE

Final Position: **7th**

NICKNAME: THE MASTIFFS

KEY: ☐Won ☐Drawn ☐Lost

							Attendance
1	frpr1	**Lorient**	H	D	0-0		14,215
2	frpr1	**Metz**	A	W	2-1	Bastos 20, Maric 88	15,591
3	frpr1	**Sochaux**	H	D	1-1	Dumont 27	12,029
4	frpr1	**Le Mans**	A	D	1-1	Fauverge 33	10,724
5	frpr1	**Paris SG**	A	D	1-1	Makoun 41	31,634
6	frpr1	**AS Monaco**	H	L	0-1		13,849
7	frpr1	**Rennes**	A	D	2-2	Franquart 20, Bastos 75	23,934
8	frpr1	**Bordeaux**	H	D	1-1	Cabaye 2	13,770
9	frpr1	**Lyon**	A	D	1-1	Bastos 17	32,658
10	frpr1	**Valenciennes**	H	W	3-0	Kluivert 5 pen, Lichtsteiner 43 Plestan 65	13,739
11	frpr1	**Caen**	A	L	0-1		18,275
12	frpr1	**Strasbourg**	H	L	0-3		12,147
13	frpr1	**Auxerre**	A	W	1-0	Fauvergue 75	8,856
14	frpr1	**Nice**	H	D	1-1	Fauvergue 17	12,286
15	frpr1	**Nancy**	A	L	0-2		18,029
16	frpr1	**Marseille**	H	D	1-1	Kluivert 26	17,618
17	frpr1	**Toulouse**	A	L	0-1		15,586
18	frpr1	**St Etienne**	H	W	3-0	Lichtsteiner 20, Plestan 32 Cabaye 49 pen	11,808
19	frpr1	**Metz**	H	D	1-1	Cabaye 90	12,602
20	frpr1	**Sochaux**	A	D	1-1	Obraniak 52	25,862
21	frpr1	**Le Mans**	H	W	3-1	Mirallas 14, Obraniak 39, Cabaye 52	10,000
22	frpr1	**Paris SG**	H	D	0-0		14,887
23	frpr1	**AS Monaco**	A	D	0-0		7,679
24	frpr1	**Rennes**	H	W	3-1	Kluivert 43 pen, 53, Bastos 56	13,396
25	frpr1	**Bordeaux**	A	D	0-0		21,761
26	frpr1	**Lyon**	H	L	0-1		77,840
27	frpr1	**Valenciennes**	A	D	0-0		13,955
28	frpr1	**Lens**	A	W	2-1	Bastos 17, Beria 83	36,533
29	frpr1	**Caen**	H	W	5-0	Lichtsteiner 34, 90, Cabaye 43, 62 pen Frau 88	13,668
30	frpr1	**Strasbourg**	A	W	1-0	Mavuba 85	16,418
31	frpr1	**Auxerre**	H	L	0-2		16,017
32	frpr1	**Nice**	A	D	0-0		9,861
33	frpr1	**Nancy**	H	W	2-1	Bastos 16 pen, Mirallas 39	12,242
34	frpr1	**Marseille**	A	W	3-1	Mirallas 37, 40, Makoun 67	40,000
35	frpr1	**Toulouse**	H	W	3-2	Mirallas 30, 42, Bastos 40 pen	16,759
36	frpr1	**St Etienne**	A	D	0-0		33,223
37	frpr1	**Lens**	H	W	2-1	Cabaye 43, Frau 67	17,670
38	frpr1	**Lorient**	A	D	1-1	Bastos 57	12,939

LEAGUE APPEARANCES, BOOKINGS AND CAPS

	AGE (on 01/07/08)	IN NAMED 18	APPEARANCES	COUNTING GAMES	MINUTES ON PITCH	YELLOW CARDS	RED CARDS	CAPS THIS SEASON	NATIONAL SIDE
Goalkeepers									
Gregory Malicki	34	38	8	8	720	0	0	-	France
Tony Mario Sylva	33	34	30	30	2700	0	0	2	Senegal
Defenders									
Franck Beria	25	38	38	37	3366	6	0	-	France
Emerson	22	20	8	6	617	0	0	-	Brazil
Henri Ewane-Elong	22	4	2	0	16	0	0	-	Cameroon
Peter Franquart	23	30	19	16	1553	4	0	-	France
Badis Lebbihi	18	1	1	1	74	0	0	-	Algeria
Stephan Lichtsteiner	24	35	34	25	2624	5	1	7	Switzerland
Nicolas Plestan	27	23	23	23	2044	5	0	-	France
Adil Rami	22	24	24	23	2123	4	0	-	France
Gregory Tafforeau	31	31	31	27	2566	5	0	-	France
Midfielders									
Michel Bastos	24	35	35	24	2376	2	0	-	Brazil
Aurelien Chedjou	23	9	2	1	126	1	0	-	Cameroon
Mathieu Debuchy	22	29	16	8	894	1	1	-	France
Stephane Dumont	25	37	21	12	1277	4	0	-	France
Eden Hazard	17	3	3	0	25	0	0	-	Belgium
Jean Makoun	25	26	26	25	2243	3	0	-	Cameroon
Marko Maric	25	8	4	0	140	0	0	-	Croatia
Rio Antonio Mavuba	24	17	17	16	1485	2	0	-	France
Ludovic Obraniak	23	36	35	26	2624	4	1	-	France
Luis Yanes	25	9	2	1	97	0	0	-	Colombia
Forwards									
Yohan Cabaye	22	36	36	28	2832	5	0	-	France
Nicolas Fauvergue	23	27	21	6	953	4	0	-	France
Pierre-Alain Frau	28	12	12	2	570	0	1	-	France
Patrick Kluivert	32	25	13	4	591	0	0	-	Holland
Cris Makiese	20	9	2	0	31	0	0	-	France
Kevin Mirallas	20	37	35	15	1876	2	0	7	Belgium
Emra Tahirovic	20	6	2	0	88	1	0	-	Sweden
Larsen Toure	23	11	9	2	304	1	0	-	France
Souleymane Youla	26	23	15	1	491	2	0	-	Guinea

TEAM OF THE SEASON

G — Tony Mario Sylva, CG: 30 DR: 100

D — Adil Rami, CG: 23 DR: 132

D — Gregory Tafforeau, CG: 27 DR: 122

D — Peter Franquart, CG: 16 DR: 119

D — Nicolas Plestan, CG: 23 DR: 107

M — Rio Antonio Mavuba, CG: 16 SD: 84

M — Ludovic Obraniak, CG: 26 SD: 45

M — Michel Bastos, CG: 24 SD: 18

M — Jean Makoun, CG: 25 SD: 15

F — Kevin Mirallas, CG: 15 SR: 312

F — Yohan Cabaye, CG: 28 SR: 404

MONTHLY POINTS TALLY

AUGUST	7	39%
SEPTEMBER	3	33%
OCTOBER	3	33%
NOVEMBER	4	44%
DECEMBER	4	44%
JANUARY	6	50%
FEBRUARY	5	56%
MARCH	10	56%
APRIL	10	83%
MAY	5	56%

LEAGUE GOALS

	PLAYER	MINS	GOALS	S RATE
1	Bastos	2376	8	297
2	Cabaye	2832	7	404
3	Mirallas	1876	6	312
4	Kluivert	591	4	147
5	Lichtsteiner	2624	4	656
6	Fauvergue	953	3	317
7	Frau	570	2	285
8	Plestan	2044	2	1022
9	Makoun	2243	2	1121
10	Obraniak	2624	2	1312
11	Maric	140	1	140
12	Dumont	1277	1	1277
13	Mavuba	1485	1	1485
	Other		2	
	TOTAL		45	

TOP POINT EARNERS

	PLAYER	GAMES	AV PTS
1	Rio Antonio Mavuba	16	1.94
2	Peter Franquart	16	1.88
3	Kevin Mirallas	15	1.87
4	Ludovic Obraniak	26	1.85
5	Adil Rami	23	1.74
6	Gregory Tafforeau	27	1.56
7	Tony Mario Sylva	30	1.50
8	Michel Bastos	24	1.50
9	Franck Beria	37	1.46
10	Yohan Cabaye	28	1.46
	CLUB AVERAGE:		1.50

DISCIPLINARY RECORDS

	PLAYER	YELLOW	RED	AVE
1	Nicolas Fauvergue	4	0	238
2	Souleymane Youla	2	0	245
3	Stephane Dumont	4	0	319
4	Peter Franquart	4	0	388
5	Nicolas Plestan	5	0	408
6	S Lichtsteiner	5	1	437
7	Mathieu Debuchy	1	1	447
8	Gregory Tafforeau	5	0	513
9	Ludovic Obraniak	4	1	524
10	Adil Rami	4	0	530
11	Franck Beria	6	0	561
12	Yohan Cabaye	5	0	566
13	Pierre-Alain Frau	0	1	570
	Other	9	0	
	TOTAL	58	4	

KEY GOALKEEPER

Tony Mario Sylva

Goals Conceded in the League	27	**Counting Games** League games when player was on pitch for at least 70 minutes	30
Defensive Rating Ave number of mins between League goals conceded while on the pitch	100	**Clean Sheets** In League games when player was on pitch for at least 70 minutes	9

KEY PLAYERS - DEFENDERS

Adil Rami

Goals Conceded Number of League goals conceded while the player was on the pitch	16	**Clean Sheets** In League games when player was on pitch for at least 70 minutes	9
Defensive Rating Ave number of mins between League goals conceded while on the pitch	132	**Club Defensive Rating** Average number of mins between League goals conceded by the club this season	109

	PLAYER	CON LGE	CLEAN SHEETS	DEF RATE
1	Adil Rami	16	9	132 mins
2	Gregory Tafforeau	21	10	122 mins
3	Peter Franquart	13	7	119 mins
4	Nicolas Plestan	19	7	107 mins

KEY PLAYERS - MIDFIELDERS

Rio Antonio Mavuba

Goals in the League	1	**Contribution to Attacking Power** Average number of minutes between League team goals while on pitch	64
Defensive Rating Average number of mins between League goals conceded while on the pitch	148	**Scoring Difference** Defensive Rating minus Contribution to Attacking Power	84

	PLAYER	LGE GOALS	DEF RATE	POWER	SCORE DIFF
1	Rio Antonio Mavuba	1	148	64	84 mins
2	Ludovic Obraniak	2	114	69	45 mins
3	Michel Bastos	8	99	81	18 mins
4	Jean Makoun	2	89	74	15 mins

KEY PLAYERS - GOALSCORERS

Michel Bastos

Goals in the League	8	**Player Strike Rate** Average number of minutes between League goals scored by player	297
Contribution to Attacking Power Average number of minutes between League team goals while on pitch	81	**Club Strike Rate** Average number of minutes between League goals scored by club	78

	PLAYER	LGE GOALS	POWER	STRIKE RATE
1	Michel Bastos	8	81	297 mins
2	Kevin Mirallas	6	58	312 mins
3	Yohan Cabaye	7	72	404 mins
4	Jean Makoun	2	74	1121 mins

LOSC
ARTOUCHE
CASINO
Michel Fernandes Bastos

SQUAD APPEARANCES

Match	1	2	3	4	5	6	7	8	9	10	11	12	13	14	15	16	17	18	19	20	21	22	23	24	25	26	27	28	29	30	31	32	33	34	35	36	37	38
Venue	H	A	H	A	A	H	A	H	A	H	A	H	A	H	A	H	A	H	H	A	H	H	A	H	A	H	A	A	H	A	H	A	H	A	H	A	H	A
Competition	L	L	L	L	L	L	L	L	L	L	L	L	L	L	L	L	L	L	L	L	L	L	L	L	L	L	L	L	L	L	L	L	L	L	L	L	L	L
Result	D	W	D	D	D	L	D	D	D	W	L	L	W	D	L	D	L	W	D	D	W	D	D	W	D	L	D	W	W	W	L	D	W	W	W	D	W	D

Goalkeepers
Gregory Malicki
Tony Mario Sylva

Defenders
Franck Beria
Emerson
Henri Ewane-Elong
Peter Franquart
Badis Lebbihi
Stephan Lichtsteiner
Nicolas Plestan
Adil Rami
Gregory Tafforeau

Midfielders
Michel Bastos
Aurelien Chedjou
Mathieu Debuchy
Stephane Dumont
Eden Hazard
Jean Makoun
Marko Maric
Rio Antonio Mavuba
Ludovic Obraniak
Luis Alfredo Padilla Yanes

Forwards
Yohan Cabaye
Nicolas Fauvergue
Pierre-Alain Frau
Patrick Kluivert
Cris Makiese
Kevin Mirallas
Emra Tahirovic
Larsen Toure
Souleymane Youla

KEY: On all match | On bench | Subbed or sent off (Counting game) | Subbed or sent off (playing less than 70 minutes) | Subbed on from bench (Counting Game) | Subbed on (playing less than 70 minutes) | Subbed on and then subbed or sent off (Counting Game) | Subbed on and then subbed or sent off (playing less than 70 minutes) | Not in 16

NICE

Final Position: **8th**

NICKNAME: THE EAGLETS

KEY: ☐Won ☐Drawn ☐Lost

							Attendance
1	frpr1	Caen	A	L	0-1		19,405
2	frpr1	Strasbourg	H	W	1-0	Hognon 86	11,815
3	frpr1	Nancy	A	L	1-2	Bamogo 60 pen	18,389
4	frpr1	Rennes	H	D	1-1	Kone 25	10,858
5	frpr1	Toulouse	H	D	1-1	Ederson 42	9,969
6	frpr1	Marseille	A	W	2-0	Hognon 51, Hellebuyck 86	55,490
7	frpr1	Lens	H	W	1-0	Kone 50	10,858
8	frpr1	Auxerre	A	L	0-2		7,591
9	frpr1	St Etienne	H	W	3-0	Kone 7, 19, Hellebuyck 83	11,252
10	frpr1	Le Mans	A	L	0-2		9,604
11	frpr1	Metz	H	W	3-1	Kone 11, 58 pen, Kante 65	9,525
12	frpr1	Lorient	A	D	0-0		10,868
13	frpr1	Sochaux	H	D	0-0		10,221
14	frpr1	Lille	A	D	1-1	Plestan 43 og	12,286
15	frpr1	Paris SG	H	W	2-1	Laslandes 8, Kone 37	11,776
16	frpr1	AS Monaco	A	D	1-1	Laslandes 90	15,394
17	frpr1	Bordeaux	H	D	1-1	Kone 12	11,988
18	frpr1	Lyon	A	D	0-0		37,280
19	frpr1	Valenciennes	H	W	1-0	Hellebuyck 43	9,640
20	frpr1	Strasbourg	A	W	1-0	Ederson 51	15,047
21	frpr1	Nancy	H	W	1-0	Hellebuyck 69	11,813
22	frpr1	Rennes	A	D	1-1	Modeste 52	23,241
23	frpr1	Toulouse	A	D	1-1	Ederson 89	15,408
24	frpr1	Marseille	H	L	0-2		15,804
25	frpr1	Lens	A	D	0-0		31,799
26	frpr1	Auxerre	H	L	1-2	Kone 46	10,114
27	frpr1	St Etienne	A	D	0-0		28,037
28	frpr1	Le Mans	H	D	0-0		9,713
29	frpr1	Metz	A	W	2-1	Bamogo 40, Ederson 53 pen	10,683
30	frpr1	Lorient	H	L	1-2	Kone 50	9,878
31	frpr1	Sochaux	A	L	0-1		19,303
32	frpr1	Lille	H	D	0-0		9,861
33	frpr1	Paris SG	A	W	3-2	Kone 36, 83, Ederson 86	35,918
34	frpr1	AS Monaco	H	L	0-2		13,455
35	frpr1	Bordeaux	A	D	0-0		29,097
36	frpr1	Lyon	H	D	0-0		14,206
37	frpr1	Valenciennes	A	W	2-1	Ederson 50, Kone 59	14,546
38	frpr1	Caen	H	W	3-1	Hellebuyck 25, Ederson 57 pen, Kone 84	11,540

LEAGUE APPEARANCES, BOOKINGS AND CAPS

	AGE (on 01/07/08)	IN NAMED 18	APPEARANCES	COUNTING GAMES	MINUTES ON PITCH	YELLOW CARDS	RED CARDS	CAPS THIS SEASON	NATIONAL SIDE
Goalkeepers									
Lionel Letizi	35	36	10	8	784	0	0	-	France
Hugo Lloris	21	30	30	29	2636	2	0	-	France
Jeremie Moreau	27	10	0	0	0	0	0	-	France
Defenders									
Jacques Abardonado	30	17	10	4	431	0	0	-	France
Onyekachi Apam	21	31	31	31	2781	7	0	-	Nigeria
Patrick Barul	30	23	8	3	395	0	0	-	France
Gerald Cid	25	15	9	5	480	0	0	-	France
Ismael Gace	21	11	5	3	316	0	0	-	France
Vincent Hognon	33	23	17	16	1446	1	0	-	France
Cyril Jeunechamp	32	23	21	16	1518	3	1	-	France
Cedric Kante	28	33	32	32	2880	2	0	-	France
Mohammed Yahaya	20	3	0	0	0	0	0	-	Ghana
Alaeddine Yahia	26	19	7	4	406	0	0	-	Tunisia
Midfielders									
Florent Balmont	28	36	36	35	3112	8	0	-	France
Drissa Diakite	23	29	21	8	1062	3	1	-	Mali
Olivier Echouafni	35	36	36	28	2842	7	0	-	France
Honorato C Ederson	22	36	36	35	3144	4	0	-	Brazil
David Hellebuyck	29	36	36	33	3048	3	0	-	France
Cyril Rool	33	32	32	29	2717	14	0	-	France
A Scaramozzino	23	7	1	0	34	0	0	-	France
Mahamane Traore	19	27	10	0	132	1	0	-	Mali
Forwards									
Derek Asamoah	27	3	0	0	0	0	0	-	Ghana
Habib Bamogo	26	36	35	14	1946	4	0	-	France
Joseph-Desire Job	30	19	8	1	264	1	0	-	Cameroon
Bakary Kone	26	30	30	25	2404	4	0	4	Ivory Coast
Kamel Larbi	23	10	1	0	2	0	0	-	Algeria
Lilian Laslandes	36	24	24	17	1767	7	0	-	France
Anthony Modeste	20	32	20	7	998	1	0	-	France
Matt Moussilou	26	1	0	0	0	0	0	-	France
Nduka M Ozokwo	19	5	0	0	0	0	0	-	Nigeria

TEAM OF THE SEASON

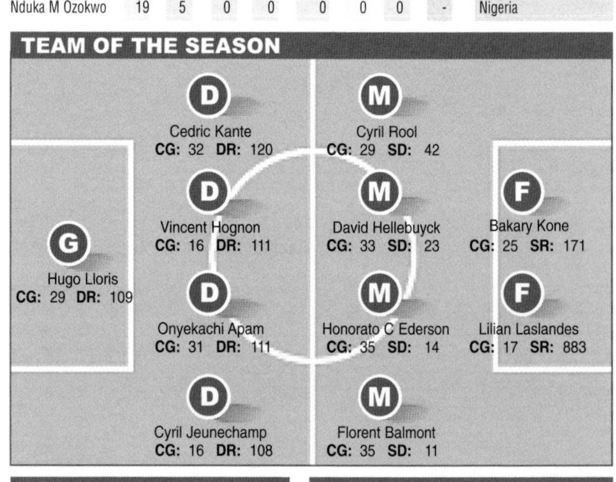

D
Cedric Kante
CG: 32 DR: 120
M
Cyril Rool
CG: 29 SD: 42
D
Vincent Hognon
CG: 16 DR: 111
M
David Hellebuyck
CG: 33 SD: 23
F
Bakary Kone
CG: 25 SR: 171
G
Hugo Lloris
CG: 29 DR: 109
D
Onyekachi Apam
CG: 31 DR: 111
M
Honorato C Ederson
CG: 35 SD: 14
F
Lilian Laslandes
CG: 17 SR: 883
D
Cyril Jeunechamp
CG: 16 DR: 108
M
Florent Balmont
CG: 35 SD: 11

MONTHLY POINTS TALLY

AUGUST	8	44%
SEPTEMBER	6	67%
OCTOBER	4	44%
NOVEMBER	5	56%
DECEMBER	6	50%
JANUARY	8	67%
FEBRUARY	1	11%
MARCH	5	33%
APRIL	5	42%
MAY	7	78%

LEAGUE GOALS

	PLAYER	MINS	GOALS	S RATE
1	Kone	2404	14	171
2	Ederson	3144	7	449
3	Hellebuyck	3048	5	609
4	Hognon	1446	2	723
5	Laslandes	1767	2	883
6	Bamogo	1946	2	973
7	Modeste	998	1	998
8	Kante	2880	1	2880
	Other		0	
	TOTAL		34	

TOP POINT EARNERS

	PLAYER	GAMES	AV PTS
1	Lilian Laslandes	17	1.71
2	Bakary Kone	25	1.60
3	Cyril Rool	29	1.59
4	Cyril Jeunechamp	16	1.56
5	David Hellebuyck	33	1.52
6	Vincent Hognon	16	1.50
7	Onyekachi Apam	31	1.48
8	Cedric Kante	32	1.47
9	Florent Balmont	35	1.46
10	Campos Ederson	35	1.43
	CLUB AVERAGE:		1.45

DISCIPLINARY RECORDS

	PLAYER	YELLOW	RED	AVE
1	Cyril Rool	14	0	194
2	Lilian Laslandes	7	0	252
3	Drissa Diakite	3	1	265
4	Cyril Jeunechamp	3	1	379
5	Florent Balmont	8	0	389
6	Onyekachi Apam	7	0	397
7	Olivier Echouafni	7	0	406
8	Habib Bamogo	4	0	486
9	Bakary Kone	4	0	601
10	Honorato Ederson	4	0	786
11	Anthony Modeste	1	0	998
12	David Hellebuyck	3	0	1016
13	Hugo Lloris	2	0	1318
	Other	3	0	
	TOTAL	70	2	

KEY GOALKEEPER

Hugo Lloris

Goals Conceded in the League	24	Counting Games League games when player was on pitch for at least 70 minutes	29
Defensive Rating Ave number of mins between League goals conceded while on the pitch	109	Clean Sheets In League games when player was on pitch for at least 70 minutes	12

KEY PLAYERS - DEFENDERS

Cedric Kante

Goals Conceded Number of League goals conceded while the player was on the pitch	24	Clean Sheets In League games when player was on pitch for at least 70 minutes	14
Defensive Rating Ave number of mins between League goals conceded while on the pitch	120	Club Defensive Rating Average number of mins between League goals conceded by the club this season	114

	PLAYER	CON LGE	CLEAN SHEETS	DEF RATE
1	Cedric Kante	24	14	120 mins
2	Vincent Hognon	13	6	111 mins
3	Onyekachi Apam	25	13	111 mins
4	Cyril Jeunechamp	14	7	108 mins

KEY PLAYERS - MIDFIELDERS

Cyril Rool

Goals in the League	0	Contribution to Attacking Power Average number of minutes between League team goals while on pitch	87
Defensive Rating Average number of mins between League goals conceded while on the pitch	129	Scoring Difference Defensive Rating minus Contribution to Attacking Power	42

	PLAYER	LGE GOALS	DEF RATE	POWER	SCORE DIFF
1	Cyril Rool	0	129	87	42 mins
2	David Hellebuyck	5	121	98	23 mins
3	Honorato Campos Ederson	7	112	98	14 mins
4	Florent Balmont	0	111	100	11 mins

KEY PLAYERS - GOALSCORERS

Bakary Kone

Goals in the League	14	Player Strike Rate Average number of minutes between League goals scored by player	171
Contribution to Attacking Power Average number of minutes between League team goals while on pitch	82	Club Strike Rate Average number of minutes between League goals scored by club	97

	PLAYER	LGE GOALS	POWER	STRIKE RATE
1	Bakary Kone	14	82	171 mins
2	Honorato Campos Ederson	7	98	449 mins
3	David Hellebuyck	5	98	609 mins
4	Lilian Laslandes	2	80	883 mins

Takara
City Sport
lotto

Bakari Kone

SQUAD APPEARANCES

Match	1	2	3	4	5	6	7	8	9	10	11	12	13	14	15	16	17	18	19	20	21	22	23	24	25	26	27	28	29	30	31	32	33	34	35	36	37	38
Venue	A	H	A	H	H	A	H	A	H	A	H	A	H	A	H	A	H	A	H	A	H	A	A	H	A	H	A	H	A	H	A	H	A	H	A	H	A	H
Competition	L	L	L	L	L	L	L	L	L	L	L	L	L	L	L	L	L	L	L	L	L	L	L	L	L	L	L	L	L	L	L	L	L	L	L	L	L	L
Result	L	W	L	D	D	W	W	L	W	L	W	D	D	D	W	D	D	D	W	W	W	D	D	L	D	L	D	D	W	L	L	D	W	L	D	D	W	W

Goalkeepers
Lionel Letizi
Hugo Lloris
Jeremie Moreau

Defenders
Jacques Abardonado
Onyekachi Apam
Patrick Barul
Gerald Cid
Ismael Gace
Vincent Hognon
Cyril Jeunechamp
Cedric Kante
Mohammed Yahaya
Alaeddine Yahia

Midfielders
Florent Balmont
Drissa Diakite
Olivier Echouafni
Honorato C Ederson
David Hellebuyck
Cyril Rool
Anthony Scaramozzino
Mahamane Traore

Forwards
Derek Asamoah
Habib Bamogo
Joseph-Desire Job
Bakary Kone
Kamel Larbi
Lilian Laslandes
Anthony Modeste
Matt Moussilou
Nduka M Ozokwo

KEY: On all match · On bench · Subbed or sent off (Counting game) · Subbed or sent off (playing less than 70 minutes) · Subbed on from bench (Counting Game) · Subbed on (playing less than 70 minutes) · Subbed on and then subbed or sent off (Counting Game) · Subbed on and then subbed or sent off (playing less than 70 minutes) · Not in 16

LE MANS

Final Position: **9th**

KEY: ☐Won ☐Drawn ☐Lost

1	frpr1	**Metz**	H	W	1-0	Basa 26	9,831
2	frpr1	**Sochaux**	A	W	3-1	De Melo 29 pen, 51, 60	14,033
3	frpr1	**Bordeaux**	A	W	2-1	De Melo 48, Grafite 72	30,438
4	frpr1	**Lille**	H	D	1-1	Grafite 56	10,724
5	frpr1	**AS Monaco**	A	L	1-3	Matsui 31	11,033
6	frpr1	**Paris SG**	H	L	0-2		13,072
7	frpr1	**Lyon**	A	L	2-3	Sessegnon 43, 54	35,042
8	frpr1	**Valenciennes**	H	W	2-0	Sessegnon 40, De Melo 47	9,570
9	frpr1	**Strasbourg**	A	W	1-0	Romaric 36	17,971
10	frpr1	**Nice**	H	W	2-0	De Melo 30, Matsui 60	9,604
11	frpr1	**Rennes**	A	L	0-3		23,349
12	frpr1	**Toulouse**	H	D	1-1	Sessegnon 61	9,841
13	frpr1	**Caen**	A	L	2-3	Basa 47, De Melo 72	20,286
14	frpr1	**St Etienne**	H	W	3-2	De Melo 18 pen, 68 pen, Romaric 42	12,434
15	frpr1	**Auxerre**	A	L	0-3		7,222
16	frpr1	**Nancy**	H	W	2-1	Yebda 58, Gervais Gervinho 78	9,938
17	frpr1	**Lens**	A	W	3-1	De Melo 24, Gervais Gervinho 50 Le Tallec 88	29,083
18	frpr1	**Lorient**	H	D	0-0		10,095
19	frpr1	**Marseille**	A	L	0-1		48,886
20	frpr1	**Sochaux**	H	L	0-2		9,714
21	frpr1	**Bordeaux**	H	L	1-2	Douillard 34	10,656
22	frpr1	**Lille**	A	L	1-3	Yebda 85	10,000
23	frpr1	**AS Monaco**	H	W	1-0	Matsui 23	9,417
24	frpr1	**Paris SG**	A	D	0-0		39,970
25	frpr1	**Lyon**	H	W	1-0	De Melo 70	14,015
26	frpr1	**Valenciennes**	A	W	2-1	Basa 1, Le Tallec 15	12,684
27	frpr1	**Strasbourg**	H	L	0-1		9,101
28	frpr1	**Nice**	A	D	0-0		9,713
29	frpr1	**Rennes**	H	D	1-1	De Melo 48	10,329
30	frpr1	**Toulouse**	A	D	1-1	Yebda 28	17,262
31	frpr1	**Caen**	H	D	1-1	Basa 33	11,045
32	frpr1	**St Etienne**	A	L	1-4	Le Tallec 32	30,006
33	frpr1	**Auxerre**	H	W	3-0	Samassa 27, Le Tallec 59 Sessegnon 72	12,339
34	frpr1	**Nancy**	A	D	1-1	Le Tallec 51	18,672
35	frpr1	**Lens**	H	W	3-2	Matsui 21, 25, Basa 49	12,125
36	frpr1	**Lorient**	A	D	0-0		13,947
37	frpr1	**Marseille**	H	D	0-0		16,361
38	frpr1	**Metz**	A	L	3-4	De Melo 51, Coutadeur 55, Baal 86	12,263

LEAGUE APPEARANCES, BOOKINGS AND CAPS

	AGE (on 01/07/08)	IN NAMED 18	APPEARANCES	COUNTING GAMES	MINUTES ON PITCH	YELLOW CARDS	RED CARDS	CAPS THIS SEASON	NATIONAL SIDE
Goalkeepers									
Thibault Ferrand	22	6	0	0	0	0	0	-	France
Yohann Pele	25	32	31	30	2734	2	0	-	France
Rodolphe Roche	29	38	9	7	686	0	0	-	France
Defenders									
Marko Basa	25	28	28	26	2446	3	0	-	Serbia
Saber Ben Frej	28	9	5	3	313	1	0	-	Tunisia
Samuel Bouhours	21	17	15	13	1257	3	1	-	France
Jean Calve	24	36	34	31	2862	6	1	-	France
Ibrahima Camara	23	27	25	21	1963	4	0	-	Guinea
Gregory Cerdan	25	27	23	21	1969	1	2	-	France
Antonio Geder	30	15	15	15	1350	5	0	-	Brazil
Cyriaque Louvion	20	32	17	8	846	1	0	-	France
Paulo Andre	24	1	0	0	0	0	0	-	Brazil
Clement Pinault	23	21	5	1	115	0	0	-	France
Midfielders									
Ludovic Baal	22	17	12	7	670	1	0	-	France
Mathieu Coutadeur	22	36	33	24	2487	3	0	-	France
Matthieu Dossevi	20	3	0	0	0	0	0	-	France
Martin Douillard	23	28	17	4	625	2	0	-	France
Brahim El Bahri	22	3	3	0	64	0	0	-	Morocco
Alphousseyni Keita	21	12	2	0	107	0	0	-	Mali
Guillaume Loriot	22	25	13	1	348	2	0	-	France
Daisuke Matsui	27	35	34	23	2455	3	0	2	Japan
Ndri Romaric	25	33	33	29	2783	9	0	3	Ivory Coast
Stephane Sessegnon	24	30	30	28	2486	7	1	-	Benin
Hassan Yebda	24	31	23	16	1563	3	0	-	Algeria
Forwards									
Vinicius De Melo	23	31	31	26	2482	2	0	-	Brazil
Yao K G Gervinho	21	28	26	20	1910	0	0	-	Ivory Coast
Libano Batista Grafite	21	6	6	4	404	1	0	-	Brazil
Anthony Le Tallec	23	29	26	11	1312	2	1	-	France
Modibo Maiga	21	32	18	2	461	2	0	-	Mali
Mamadou Samassa	22	15	15	3	674	3	0	-	France

TEAM OF THE SEASON

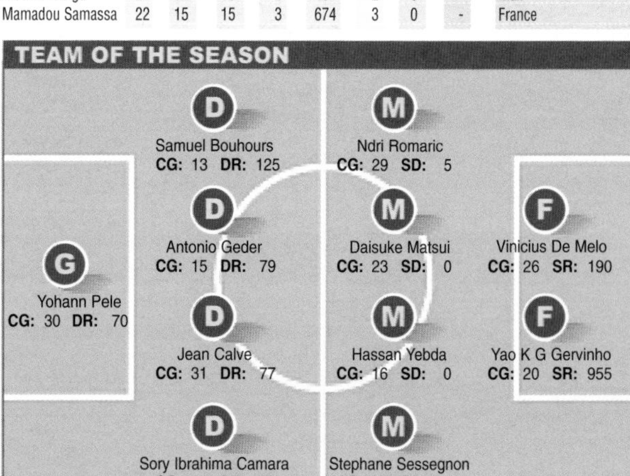
D
Samuel Bouhours
CG: 13 DR: 125
M
Ndri Romaric
CG: 29 SD: 5
D
Antonio Geder
CG: 15 DR: 79
M
Daisuke Matsui
CG: 23 SD: 0
F
Vinicius De Melo
CG: 26 SR: 190
G
Yohann Pele
CG: 30 DR: 70
D
Jean Calve
CG: 31 DR: 77
M
Hassan Yebda
CG: 16 SD: 0
F
Yao K G Gervinho
CG: 20 SR: 955
D
Sory Ibrahima Camara
CG: 21 DR: 70
M
Stephane Sessegnon
CG: 28 SD: -4

MONTHLY POINTS TALLY

AUGUST	10	56%
SEPTEMBER	6	67%
OCTOBER	4	44%
NOVEMBER	3	33%
DECEMBER	7	58%
JANUARY	3	25%
FEBRUARY	7	78%
MARCH	4	27%
APRIL	7	58%
MAY	2	22%

LEAGUE GOALS

	PLAYER	MINS	GOALS	S RATE
1	De Melo	2482	13	190
2	Le Tallec	1312	5	262
3	Basa	2446	5	489
4	Matsui	2455	5	491
5	Sessegnon	2486	5	497
6	Yebda	1563	3	521
7	Grafite	404	2	202
8	G Gervinho	1910	2	955
9	Romaric	2783	2	1391
10	Douillard	625	1	625
11	Baal	670	1	670
12	Samassa	674	1	674
13	Coutadeur	2487	1	2487
	Other		0	
	TOTAL		46	

TOP POINT EARNERS

	PLAYER	GAMES	AV PTS
1	Sory Ibrahima Camara	21	1.67
2	Gregory Cerdan	21	1.62
3	Ndri Romaric	29	1.59
4	Marko Basa	26	1.58
5	Jean Calve	31	1.55
6	Mathieu Coutadeur	24	1.54
7	Daisuke Matsui	23	1.52
8	Vinicius De Melo	26	1.46
9	Hassan Yebda	16	1.44
10	Yohann Pele	30	1.43
	CLUB AVERAGE:		1.39

DISCIPLINARY RECORDS

	PLAYER	YELLOW	RED	AVE
1	M Samassa	3	0	224
2	Modibo Maiga	2	0	230
3	Antonio Geder	5	0	270
4	Ndri Romaric	9	0	309
5	S Sessegnon	7	1	310
6	Martin Douillard	2	0	312
7	Samuel Bouhours	3	1	314
8	Jean Calve	6	1	408
9	Anthony Le Tallec	2	1	437
10	Sory Camara	4	0	490
11	Hassan Yebda	3	0	521
12	Gregory Cerdan	1	2	656
13	Ludovic Baal	1	0	670
	Other	14	0	
	TOTAL	62	6	

KEY GOALKEEPER

Yohann Pele

Goals Conceded in the League	39	**Counting Games** League games when player was on pitch for at least 70 minutes	30
Defensive Rating Ave number of mins between League goals conceded while on the pitch	70	**Clean Sheets** In League games when player was on pitch for at least 70 minutes	10

KEY PLAYERS - DEFENDERS

Samuel Bouhours

Goals Conceded Number of League goals conceded while the player was on the pitch	10	**Clean Sheets** In League games when player was on pitch for at least 70 minutes	6
Defensive Rating Ave number of mins between League goals conceded while on the pitch	125	**Club Defensive Rating** Average number of mins between League goals conceded by the club this season	69

	PLAYER	CON LGE	CLEAN SHEETS	DEF RATE
1	Samuel Bouhours	10	6	125 mins
2	Antonio Geder	17	7	79 mins
3	Jean Calve	37	10	77 mins
4	Sory Ibrahima Camara	28	7	70 mins

KEY PLAYERS - MIDFIELDERS

Ndri Romaric

Goals in the League	2	**Contribution to Attacking Power** Average number of minutes between League team goals while on pitch	66
Defensive Rating Average number of mins between League goals conceded while on the pitch	71	**Scoring Difference** Defensive Rating minus Contribution to Attacking Power	5

	PLAYER	LGE GOALS	DEF RATE	POWER	SCORE DIFF
1	Ndri Romaric	2	71	66	5 mins
2	Daisuke Matsui	5	76	76	0 mins
3	Hassan Yebda	3	104	104	0 mins
4	Stephane Sessegnon	5	69	73	-4 mins

KEY PLAYERS - GOALSCORERS

Vinicius De Melo

Goals in the League	13	**Player Strike Rate** Average number of minutes between League goals scored by player	190
Contribution to Attacking Power Average number of minutes between League team goals while on pitch	68	**Club Strike Rate** Average number of minutes between League goals scored by club	74

	PLAYER	LGE GOALS	POWER	STRIKE RATE
1	Vinicius De Melo	13	68	190 mins
2	Daisuke Matsui	5	76	491 mins
3	Stephane Sessegnon	5	73	497 mins
4	Hassan Yebda	3	104	521 mins

Kappa
gorenje

Vinicius (Tulio) De Melo

SQUAD APPEARANCES

Match	1	2	3	4	5	6	7	8	9	10	11	12	13	14	15	16	17	18	19	20	21	22	23	24	25	26	27	28	29	30	31	32	33	34	35	36	37	38
Venue	H	A	A	H	A	H	A	H	A	H	A	H	A	H	A	H	A	H	A	H	H	A	H	A	H	A	H	A	H	A	H	A	H	A	H	A	H	A
Competition	L	L	L	L	L	L	L	L	L	L	L	L	L	L	L	L	L	L	L	L	L	L	L	L	L	L	L	L	L	L	L	L	L	L	L	L	L	L
Result	W	W	W	D	L	L	L	W	W	W	L	D	L	W	L	W	W	D	L	L	L	L	W	D	W	W	L	D	D	D	D	L	W	D	W	D	D	L

Goalkeepers
Thibault Ferrand
Yohann Pele
Rodolphe Roche
Defenders
Marko Basa
Saber Ben Frej
Samuel Bouhours
Jean Calve
Ibrahima Camara
Gregory Cerdan
Antonio Geder
Cyriaque Louvion
Paulo Andre
Clement Pinault
Midfielders
Ludovic Baal
Mathieu Coutadeur
Matthieu Dossevi
Martin Douillard
Brahim El Bahri
Alphousseyni Keita
Guillaume Loriot
Daisuke Matsui
Ndri Romaric
Stephane Sessegnon
Hassan Yebda
Forwards
Vinicius De Melo
Yao K G Gervinho
Libano Batista Grafite
Anthony Le Tallec
Modibo Maiga
Mamadou Samassa

KEY: On all match; On bench; Subbed or sent off (Counting game); Subbed or sent off (playing less than 70 minutes); Subbed on from bench (Counting Game); Subbed on (playing less than 70 minutes); Subbed on and then subbed or sent off (Counting Game); Subbed on and then subbed or sent off (playing less than 70 minutes); Not in 16

LORIENT

Final Position: **10th**

NICKNAME: LES MERLUS (CODFISH)

KEY: Won, Drawn, Lost

							Attendance
1	frpr1	Lille	A	D	0-0		14,215
2	frpr1	AS Monaco	H	W	2-1	Saifi 12, 28	11,981
3	frpr1	Paris SG	A	W	3-1	Vahirua 69, 74, Saifi 90 pen	32,227
4	frpr1	Lyon	H	W	2-1	Vahirua 14, 64	14,612
5	frpr1	Bordeaux	A	D	2-2	Saifi 15, Namouchi 88	23,392
6	frpr1	Valenciennes	H	L	1-3	Marchal 43	12,588
7	frpr1	Strasbourg	A	D	0-0		20,260
8	frpr1	Rennes	H	L	0-1		13,674
9	frpr1	Nancy	A	L	0-2		18,151
10	frpr1	Caen	H	D	0-0		10,215
11	frpr1	Auxerre	A	L	3-5	Saifi 6, 58, Bourhani 90	8,157
12	frpr1	Nice	H	D	0-0		10,868
13	frpr1	Marseille	A	D	0-0		51,864
14	frpr1	Toulouse	H	W	1-0	Abriel 51	9,575
15	frpr1	Lens	A	D	1-1	Vahirua 12	30,126
16	frpr1	St Etienne	H	D	1-1	Saifi 74	11,833
17	frpr1	Sochaux	H	W	2-1	Vahirua 3, Le Pen 47	12,000
18	frpr1	Le Mans	A	D	0-0		10,095
19	frpr1	Metz	H	W	2-0	Saifi 57, Marin 90	12,677
20	frpr1	AS Monaco	A	L	0-1		7,434
21	frpr1	Paris SG	H	W	1-0	Bourillon 19 og	12,385
22	frpr1	Lyon	A	L	0-2		38,106
23	frpr1	Bordeaux	H	W	1-0	Jallet 77	11,182
24	frpr1	Valenciennes	A	L	0-3		12,667
25	frpr1	Strasbourg	H	W	1-0	Le Pen 45	12,153
26	frpr1	Rennes	A	L	0-2		24,133
27	frpr1	Nancy	H	D	0-0		10,275
28	frpr1	Caen	A	D	0-0		18,493
29	frpr1	Auxerre	H	D	1-1	Saifi 73	12,881
30	frpr1	Nice	A	W	2-1	Vahirua 11, Saifi 71	9,878
31	frpr1	Marseille	H	L	1-2	Saifi 43 pen	15,436
32	frpr1	Toulouse	A	D	0-0		20,585
33	frpr1	Lens	H	W	1-0	Saifi 85	13,279
34	frpr1	St Etienne	A	L	0-1		33,751
35	frpr1	Sochaux	A	D	1-1	Jouffre 44	17,361
36	frpr1	Le Mans	H	D	0-0		13,947
37	frpr1	Metz	A	W	2-1	Saifi 45, Abriel 65	14,000
38	frpr1	Lille	H	D	1-1	Saifi 43	12,939

LEAGUE APPEARANCES, BOOKINGS AND CAPS

	AGE (on 01/07/08)	IN NAMED 18	APPEARANCES	COUNTING GAMES	MINUTES ON PITCH	YELLOW CARDS	RED CARDS	CAPS THIS SEASON	NATIONAL SIDE
Goalkeepers									
Fabien Audard	30	38	38	38	3420	2	0	-	France
Lionel Cappone	29	31	0	0	0	0	0	-	France
Romain Salin	23	7	0	0	0	0	0	-	France
Defenders									
Mehdi Benatia	21	12	0	0	0	0	0	-	Morocco
Marc Boutruche	31	25	9	2	376	0	0	-	France
Alain Cantareil	24	35	19	10	1023	0	0	-	France
Mickael Ciani	24	36	36	36	3240	5	0	-	France
Claude Dielna	20	9	0	0	0	0	0	-	France
Benjamin Genton	28	31	10	9	788	1	0	-	France
Sylvain Marchal	28	29	28	28	2509	7	0	-	France
Midfielders									
Fabrice Abriel	28	38	38	38	3420	3	0	-	France
Oscar Ewolo	29	38	34	24	2523	3	0	-	Congo
Yohan Hautcoeur	26	37	33	22	2232	1	0	-	France
Andrew Jacobson	22	1	0	0	0	0	0	-	United States
Christophe Jallet	24	37	37	37	3330	3	0	-	France
Yann Jouffre	23	18	18	8	1024	2	0	-	France
Ulrich Le Pen	34	23	23	17	1690	0	0	-	France
Yazid Mansouri	30	34	28	12	1429	2	0	-	Algeria
Nicolas Marin	27	34	30	8	1279	1	0	-	France
Hamed Namouchi	24	14	14	10	951	0	0	-	Tunisia
Bertrand Robert	24	6	2	0	50	0	0	-	France
Rafik Saifi	33	37	37	35	3176	3	0	-	Algeria
Ricardo Sophie	20	2	0	0	0	0	0	-	France
Forwards									
Kemal Bourhani	26	17	11	2	289	0	0	-	France
Amadou D M'Bodji	23	1	1	0	16	0	0	-	France
Jeremy Morel	24	29	29	27	2487	3	0	-	France
Rafael Moura	25	12	2	0	14	0	0	-	Brazil
Frederic Nimani	19	7	2	0	44	0	0	-	France
Fabien Robert	19	19	14	0	394	1	0	-	France
Marama Vahirua	28	27	26	19	1916	1	0	-	France

TEAM OF THE SEASON

G: Fabien Audard — CG: 38 DR: 97

D: Mickael Ciani — CG: 36 DR: 104

D: Sylvain Marchal — CG: 28 DR: 96

D: Benjamin Genton — CG: 9* DR: 71

D: Alain Cantareil — CG: 10* DR: 60

M: Ulrich Le Pen — CG: 17 SD: 75

M: Rafik Saifi — CG: 35 SD: 3

M: Yohan Hautcoeur — CG: 22 SD: 0

M: Christophe Jallet — CG: 37 SD: -3

F: Marama Vahirua — CG: 19 SR: 273

F: Jeremy Morel — CG: 27 SR: 0

MONTHLY POINTS TALLY

AUGUST	11	61%
SEPTEMBER	1	11%
OCTOBER	2	22%
NOVEMBER	5	56%
DECEMBER	8	67%
JANUARY	6	50%
FEBRUARY	3	33%
MARCH	6	40%
APRIL	5	42%
MAY	5	56%

LEAGUE GOALS

	PLAYER	MINS	GOALS	S RATE
1	Saifi	3176	14	226
2	Vahirua	1916	7	273
3	Le Pen	1690	2	845
4	Abriel	3420	2	1710
5	Bourhani	289	1	289
6	Namouchi	951	1	951
7	Jouffre	1024	1	1024
8	Marin	1279	1	1279
9	Marchal	2509	1	2509
10	Jallet	3330	1	3330
	Other		0	
	TOTAL		31	

TOP POINT EARNERS

	PLAYER	GAMES	AV PTS
1	Yohan Hautcoeur	22	1.59
2	Jeremy Morel	27	1.56
3	Ulrich Le Pen	17	1.53
4	Rafik Saifi	35	1.46
5	Yazid Mansouri	12	1.42
6	Oscar Ewolo	24	1.42
7	Christophe Jallet	37	1.41
8	Fabrice Abriel	38	1.37
9	Fabien Audard	38	1.37
10	Mickael Ciani	36	1.36
	CLUB AVERAGE:		1.37

DISCIPLINARY RECORDS

	PLAYER	YELLOW	RED	AVE
1	Sylvain Marchal	7	0	358
2	Yann Jouffre	2	0	512
3	Mickael Ciani	5	0	648
4	Yazid Mansouri	2	0	714
5	Benjamin Genton	1	0	788
6	Jeremy Morel	3	0	829
7	Oscar Ewolo	3	0	841
8	Rafik Saifi	3	0	1058
9	Christophe Jallet	3	0	1110
10	Fabrice Abriel	3	0	1140
11	Nicolas Marin	1	0	1279
12	Fabien Audard	2	0	1710
13	Marama Vahirua	1	0	1916
	Other	1	0	
	TOTAL	37	0	

KEY GOALKEEPER

Fabien Audard

Goals Conceded in the League	35	Counting Games League games when player was on pitch for at least 70 minutes	38
Defensive Rating Ave number of mins between League goals conceded while on the pitch	97	Clean Sheets In League games when player was on pitch for at least 70 minutes	16

KEY PLAYERS - DEFENDERS

Mickael Ciani

Goals Conceded Number of League goals conceded while the player was on the pitch	31	Clean Sheets In League games when player was on pitch for at least 70 minutes	16
Defensive Rating Ave number of mins between League goals conceded while on the pitch	104	Club Defensive Rating Average number of mins between League goals conceded by the club this season	97

	PLAYER	CON LGE	CLEAN SHEETS	DEF RATE
1	Mickael Ciani	31	16	104 mins
2	Sylvain Marchal	26	12	96 mins
3	Benjamin Genton	11	3	71 mins
4	Alain Cantareil	17	4	60 mins

KEY PLAYERS - MIDFIELDERS

Ulrich Le Pen

Goals in the League	2	Contribution to Attacking Power Average number of minutes between League team goals while on pitch	112
Defensive Rating Average number of mins between League goals conceded while on the pitch	187	Scoring Difference Defensive Rating minus Contribution to Attacking Power	75

	PLAYER	LGE GOALS	DEF RATE	POWER	SCORE DIFF
1	Ulrich Le Pen	2	187	112	75 mins
2	Rafik Saifi	14	105	102	3 mins
3	Yohan Hautcoeur	0	111	111	0 mins
4	Christophe Jallet	1	104	107	-3 mins

KEY PLAYERS - GOALSCORERS

Rafik Saifi

Goals in the League	14	Player Strike Rate Average number of minutes between League goals scored by player	226
Contribution to Attacking Power Average number of minutes between League team goals while on pitch	102	Club Strike Rate Average number of minutes between League goals scored by club	106

	PLAYER	LGE GOALS	POWER	STRIKE RATE
1	Rafik Saifi	14	102	226 mins
2	Marama Vahirua	7	100	273 mins
3	Ulrich Le Pen	2	112	845 mins
4	Jeremy Morel	0	95	0 mins

FCL
errea
Cap l'Orient
agglomération

Marama Vahirua

SQUAD APPEARANCES

Match	1	2	3	4	5	6	7	8	9	10	11	12	13	14	15	16	17	18	19	20	21	22	23	24	25	26	27	28	29	30	31	32	33	34	35	36	37	38
Venue	A	H	A	H	A	H	A	H	A	H	A	H	A	H	A	H	H	A	H	A	H	A	H	A	H	A	H	A	H	A	H	A	H	A	A	H	A	H
Competition	L	L	L	L	L	L	L	L	L	L	L	L	L	L	L	L	L	L	L	L	L	L	L	L	L	L	L	L	L	L	L	L	L	L	L	L	L	L
Result	D	W	W	W	D	L	D	L	L	D	L	D	D	W	D	D	W	D	W	L	W	L	W	L	W	L	D	D	D	W	L	D	W	L	D	D	W	D

Goalkeepers
Fabien Audard
Lionel Cappone
Romain Salin

Defenders
Mehdi Benatia
Marc Boutruche
Alain Cantareil
Mickael Ciani
Claude Dielna
Benjamin Genton
Sylvain Marchal

Midfielders
Fabrice Abriel
Oscar Ewolo
Yohan Hautcoeur
Andrew Jacobson
Christophe Jallet
Yann Jouffre
Ulrich Le Pen
Yazid Mansouri
Nicolas Marin
Hamed Namouchi
Bertrand Robert
Rafik Saifi
Ricardo Sophie

Forwards
Kemal Bourhani
Amadou David M'Bodji
Jeremy Morel
Rafael Moura
Frederic Nimani
Fabien Robert
Marama Vahirua

KEY: On all match; On bench; Subbed or sent off (Counting game); Subbed or sent off (playing less than 70 minutes); Subbed on from bench (Counting Game); Subbed on (playing less than 70 minutes); Subbed on and then subbed or sent off (Counting Game); Subbed on and then subbed or sent off (playing less than 70 minutes); Not in 16

CAEN

Final Position: **11th**

KEY: Won Drawn Lost

							Attendance
1	frpr1	Nice	H	W	1-0	Compan 80	19,405
2	frpr1	Nancy	A	L	0-1		17,545
3	frpr1	Auxerre	A	L	0-1		7,439
4	frpr1	Marseille	H	L	1-2	Samson 90	20,790
5	frpr1	Sochaux	H	D	2-2	Eluchans 32, Proment 65	18,099
6	frpr1	St Etienne	A	L	0-3		25,638
7	frpr1	Metz	H	L	1-2	Gouffran 9	17,883
8	frpr1	Toulouse	H	W	2-1	Compan 12, Nivet 55	17,568
9	frpr1	Lorient	A	D	0-0		10,215
10	frpr1	Lille	H	W	1-0	Tafforeau 60 og	18,275
11	frpr1	AS Monaco	A	D	0-0		8,986
12	frpr1	Le Mans	H	W	3-2	Gouffran 32, 65, Eluchans 57	20,286
13	frpr1	Valenciennes	A	L	0-3		12,449
14	frpr1	Bordeaux	H	W	5-0	Gouffran 10, Sorbon 29	
						Grandin 74 pen, Eluchans 84, Gomis 86	20,047
15	frpr1	Lens	A	D	1-1	Sorbon 86	36,409
16	frpr1	Paris SG	A	W	1-0	Florentin 74	37,148
17	frpr1	Lyon	H	W	1-0	Gouffran 19	20,664
18	frpr1	Rennes	A	W	2-1	Deroin 61 pen, Eluchans 79	26,081
19	frpr1	Strasbourg	H	W	2-0	Eluchans 40, Hengbart 80 pen	20,391
20	frpr1	Nancy	H	D	0-0		20,327
21	frpr1	Toulouse	A	D	1-1	Deroin 69	14,102
22	frpr1	Auxerre	H	D	0-0		20,000
23	frpr1	Marseille	A	L	1-6	Toudic 2	48,481
24	frpr1	Lens	H	L	1-4	Lemaitre 69	20,289
25	frpr1	Sochaux	A	D	1-1	Gouffran 56	26,629
26	frpr1	St Etienne	H	L	1-3	Compan 62	20,713
27	frpr1	Metz	A	L	1-2	Jemaa 78	10,767
28	frpr1	Lorient	H	D	0-0		18,493
29	frpr1	Lille	A	L	0-5		13,668
30	frpr1	AS Monaco	H	W	4-1	Hengbart 62 pen, Sorbon 76	
						Gouffran 86 pen, Jemaa 90	20,082
31	frpr1	Le Mans	A	D	1-1	Gouffran 13	11,045
32	frpr1	Valenciennes	H	W	1-0	Jemaa 20	19,477
33	frpr1	Bordeaux	A	L	1-2	Sorbon 89	27,686
34	frpr1	Paris SG	H	W	3-0	Deroin 52, Lemaitre 75, Gouffran 89	20,933
35	frpr1	Lyon	A	D	2-2	Eluchans 38, Compan 45	39,068
36	frpr1	Rennes	H	D	2-2	Compan 54, Nivet 85	20,627
37	frpr1	Strasbourg	A	W	4-1	Toudic 6, 84, Dos Santos 11 og	
						Gouffran 31	17,311
38	frpr1	Nice	A	L	1-3	Toudic 45	11,540

LEAGUE APPEARANCES, BOOKINGS AND CAPS

	AGE (on 01/07/08)	IN NAMED 18	APPEARANCES	COUNTING GAMES	MINUTES ON PITCH	YELLOW CARDS	RED CARDS	CAPS THIS SEASON	NATIONAL SIDE
Goalkeepers									
Benoit Costil	20	33	5	4	419	0	1	-	France
Vincent Plante	27	32	31	31	2790	3	0	-	France
Alexis Thebaux	23	10	2	2	180	0	0	-	France
Defenders									
Florian Boucansaud	27	15	4	2	235	0	0	-	France
Cedric Hengbart	27	36	33	31	2856	5	0	-	France
Omour N'Diaye	22	13	5	2	296	0	0	-	France
Nicolas Seube	28	28	28	26	2463	9	0	-	France
Jeremy Sorbon	24	38	38	38	3420	3	0	-	France
Karl Svensson	24	14	6	5	475	0	0	4	Sweden
Ibrahim Thiam	34	21	16	12	1224	6	0	-	Mali
Stephane Zubar	21	1	0	0	0	0	0	-	Guadelope
Midfielders									
Anthony Deroin	29	31	29	23	2169	3	0	-	France
Juan E Eluchans	28	38	36	19	2465	2	0	-	Argentina
Nicolas Florentin	30	34	33	11	1598	4	0	-	France
Remy Gomis	24	33	24	13	1575	3	0	-	France
Gregory Leca	27	21	18	14	1340	1	0	-	France
Reynald Lemaitre	25	24	18	14	1360	1	0	-	France
Benjamin Nivet	31	35	34	26	2688	5	1	-	France
Gregory Proment	29	36	34	30	2816	7	0	-	France
Guillaume Quellier	22	12	3	0	52	0	0	-	France
Alexandre Raineau	22	3	1	0	34	0	0	-	France
Forwards									
Lilian Compan	31	31	28	11	1489	2	0	-	France
Yoan Gouffran	22	36	36	32	2980	3	0	-	France
Elliot Grandin	20	18	12	2	385	0	0	-	France
Issam Jemaa	24	27	20	5	941	6	0	4	Tunisia
Sebastien Mazure	29	11	10	2	420	0	0	-	France
Stephane Samson	33	16	8	0	288	1	0	-	France
Julien Toudic	22	31	18	1	593	0	0	-	France

TEAM OF THE SEASON

G: Vincent Plante, CG: 31 DR: 75

D: Cedric Hengbart, CG: 31 DR: 69
D: Ibrahim Thiam, CG: 12 DR: 64
D: Jeremy Sorbon, CG: 38 DR: 64
D: Nicolas Seube, CG: 26 DR: 61

M: Nicolas Florentin, CG: 11* SD: 20
M: Remy Gomis, CG: 13 SD: 15
M: Gregory Leca, CG: 14 SD: 3
M: Juan E Eluchans, CG: 19 SD: -4

F: Lilian Compan, CG: 11* SR: 297
F: Yoan Gouffran, CG: 32 SR: 298

MONTHLY POINTS TALLY

Month	Points	%
AUGUST	3	25%
SEPTEMBER	4	33%
OCTOBER	5	56%
NOVEMBER	7	58%
DECEMBER	12	100%
JANUARY	3	25%
FEBRUARY	1	11%
MARCH	5	33%
APRIL	7	58%
MAY	4	44%

LEAGUE GOALS

	PLAYER	MINS	GOALS	S RATE
1	Gouffran	2980	10	298
2	Eluchans	2465	6	410
3	Compan	1489	5	297
4	Toudic	593	4	148
5	Sorbon	3420	4	855
6	Jemaa	941	3	313
7	Deroin	2169	3	723
8	Lemaitre	1360	2	680
9	Nivet	2688	2	1344
10	Hengbart	2856	2	1428
11	Samson	288	1	288
12	Grandin	385	1	385
13	Gomis	1575	1	1575
	Other		2	
	TOTAL		46	

TOP POINT EARNERS

	PLAYER	GAMES	AV PTS
1	Gregory Leca	14	1.64
2	Remy Gomis	13	1.54
3	Juan Eduardo Eluchans	19	1.53
4	Cedric Hengbart	31	1.45
5	Vincent Plante	31	1.45
6	Ibrahim Thiam	12	1.42
7	Benjamin Nivet	26	1.42
8	Yoan Gouffran	32	1.38
9	Anthony Deroin	23	1.35
10	Jeremy Sorbon	38	1.34
	CLUB AVERAGE:		1.34

DISCIPLINARY RECORDS

	PLAYER	YELLOW	RED	AVE
1	Issam Jemaa	5	0	188
2	Ibrahim Thiam	6	0	204
3	Nicolas Seube	9	0	273
4	Nicolas Florentin	4	0	399
5	Gregory Proment	7	0	402
6	Benjamin Nivet	5	1	448
7	Remy Gomis	3	0	525
8	Cedric Hengbart	5	0	571
9	Anthony Deroin	3	0	723
10	Lilian Compan	2	0	744
11	Vincent Plante	3	0	930
12	Yoan Gouffran	3	0	993
13	Jeremy Sorbon	3	0	1140
	Other	4	0	
	TOTAL	62	1	

KEY GOALKEEPER

Vincent Plante

Goals Conceded in the League	37	**Counting Games** League games when player was on pitch for at least 70 minutes	31
Defensive Rating Ave number of mins between League goals conceded while on the pitch	75	**Clean Sheets** In League games when player was on pitch for at least 70 minutes	11

KEY PLAYERS - DEFENDERS

Cedric Hengbart

Goals Conceded Number of League goals conceded while the player was on the pitch	41	**Clean Sheets** In League games when player was on pitch for at least 70 minutes	11
Defensive Rating Ave number of mins between League goals conceded while on the pitch	69	**Club Defensive Rating** Average number of mins between League goals conceded by the club this season	64

	PLAYER	CON LGE	CLEAN SHEETS	DEF RATE
1	Cedric Hengbart	41	11	69 mins
2	Ibrahim Thiam	19	5	64 mins
3	Jeremy Sorbon	53	13	64 mins
4	Nicolas Seube	40	10	61 mins

KEY PLAYERS - MIDFIELDERS

Nicolas Florentin

Goals in the League	1	**Contribution to Attacking Power** Average number of minutes between League team goals while on pitch	59
Defensive Rating Average number of mins between League goals conceded while on the pitch	79	**Scoring Difference** Defensive Rating minus Contribution to Attacking Power	20

	PLAYER	LGE GOALS	DEF RATE	POWER	SCORE DIFF
1	Nicolas Florentin	1	79	59	20 mins
2	Remy Gomis	1	75	60	15 mins
3	Gregory Leca	0	70	67	3 mins
4	Juan Eduardo Eluchans	6	64	68	-4 mins

KEY PLAYERS - GOALSCORERS

Lilian Compan

Goals in the League	5	**Player Strike Rate** Average number of minutes between League goals scored by player	297
Contribution to Attacking Power Average number of minutes between League team goals while on pitch	74	**Club Strike Rate** Average number of minutes between League goals scored by club	71

	PLAYER	LGE GOALS	POWER	STRIKE RATE
1	Lilian Compan	5	74	297 mins
2	Yoan Gouffran	10	69	298 mins
3	Juan Eduardo Eluchans	6	68	410 mins
4	Reynald Lemaitre	2	56	680 mins

Yoan Gouffran

SQUAD APPEARANCES

Match	1	2	3	4	5	6	7	8	9	10	11	12	13	14	15	16	17	18	19
Venue	H	A	A	H	H	A	H	H	A	H	A	H	A	H	A	A	H	A	H
Competition	L	L	L	L	L	L	L	L	L	L	L	L	L	L	L	L	L	L	L
Result	W	L	L	L	D	L	L	W	D	W	D	W	L	W	D	W	W	W	W

Match	20	21	22	23	24	25	26	27	28	29	30	31	32	33	34	35	36	37	38
Venue	H	A	H	A	H	A	H	A	H	A	H	A	H	A	H	A	H	A	A
Competition	L	L	L	L	L	L	L	L	L	L	L	L	L	L	L	L	L	L	L
Result	D	D	D	L	L	D	L	L	D	L	W	D	W	L	W	D	D	W	L

Goalkeepers
Benoit Costil
Vincent Plante
Alexis Thebaux

Defenders
Florian Boucansaud
Cedric Hengbart
Omour N'Diaye
Nicolas Seube
Jeremy Sorbon
Karl Svensson
Ibrahim Thiam
Stephane Zubar

Midfielders
Anthony Deroin
Juan E Eluchans
Nicolas Florentin
Remy Gomis
Gregory Leca
Reynald Lemaitre
Benjamin Nivet
Gregory Proment
Guillaume Quellier
Alexandre Raineau

Forwards
Lilian Compan
Yoan Gouffran
Elliot Grandin
Issam Jemaa
Sebastien Mazure
Stephane Samson
Julien Toudic

KEY: ■ On all match ■ On bench | ⏮ Subbed or sent off (Counting game) ≪ Subbed or sent off (playing less than 70 minutes) | ≫ Subbed on from bench (Counting Game) ≫ Subbed on (playing less than 70 minutes) | ≫ Subbed on and then subbed or sent off (Counting Game) ≫ Subbed on and then subbed or sent off (playing less than 70 minutes) | □ Not in 16

MONACO

Final Position: **12th**

NICKNAME: LE ROUGE ET BLANC

KEY: Won / Drawn / Lost

#	Comp	Opponent	H/A	Res	Score	Scorers	Attendance
1	frpr1	St Etienne	H	D	1-1	Piquionne 44	17,134
2	frpr1	Lorient	A	L	1-2	Gakpe 65	11,981
3	frpr1	Metz	H	W	2-0	Modesto 31, Piquionne 85	11,392
4	frpr1	Sochaux	A	W	3-0	Koller 1, 88, Menez 56	14,091
5	frpr1	Le Mans	H	W	3-1	Cufre 49 pen, Piquionne 64, Menez 66	11,033
6	frpr1	Lille	A	W	1-0	Piquionne 20	13,849
7	frpr1	Bordeaux	A	L	1-2	Nene 89	23,390
8	frpr1	Paris SG	H	L	1-2	Menez 85	12,694
9	frpr1	Valenciennes	A	L	0-1		14,225
10	frpr1	Nancy	H	L	1-3	Koller 73	8,851
11	frpr1	Lyon	A	L	1-3	Monsoreau 42	36,254
12	frpr1	Caen	H	D	0-0		8,986
13	frpr1	Rennes	A	W	1-0	Piquionne 46	27,754
14	frpr1	Strasbourg	H	W	3-0	Gakpe 43, Nene 61, 90	9,448
15	frpr1	Toulouse	A	D	0-0		15,434
16	frpr1	Nice	H	D	1-1	Koller 86	15,394
17	frpr1	Marseille	A	L	0-2		47,000
18	frpr1	Lens	H	W	2-0	Menez 52, 82	14,578
19	frpr1	Auxerre	A	L	0-1		8,952
20	frpr1	Lorient	H	W	1-0	Sambou 90	7,434
21	frpr1	Metz	A	W	4-1	Menez 29, 62, Piquionne 31, Gakpe 84	12,202
22	frpr1	Sochaux	H	W	1-0	Piquionne 77	2,500
23	frpr1	Le Mans	A	L	0-1		9,417
24	frpr1	Lille	H	D	0-0		7,679
25	frpr1	Bordeaux	H	L	0-6		10,018
26	frpr1	Paris SG	A	D	1-1	Almiron 71	32,000
27	frpr1	Valenciennes	H	D	0-0		7,912
28	frpr1	Nancy	A	L	0-2		18,541
29	frpr1	Lyon	H	L	0-3		12,321
30	frpr1	Caen	A	L	1-4	Sambou 7	20,082
31	frpr1	Rennes	H	L	1-2	Sambou 36	5,000
32	frpr1	Strasbourg	A	W	2-0	Nene 66, Santos Romeu 82	19,106
33	frpr1	Toulouse	H	L	0-2		9,499
34	frpr1	Nice	A	W	2-0	Meriem 36, Almiron 90	13,455
35	frpr1	Marseille	H	L	2-3	Gonzalez 57, Leko 64	17,368
36	frpr1	Lens	A	D	0-0		39,399
37	frpr1	Auxerre	H	W	3-0	Bakar 48, Nene 75, Meriem 83	9,839
38	frpr1	St Etienne	A	L	0-4		34,237

LEAGUE APPEARANCES, BOOKINGS AND CAPS

	AGE (on 01/07/08)	IN NAMED 18	APPEARANCES	COUNTING GAMES	MINUTES ON PITCH	YELLOW CARDS	RED CARDS	CAPS THIS SEASON	NATIONAL SIDE
Goalkeepers									
Flavio Roma	34	30	29	28	2579	4	0	-	Italy
Stephane Ruffier	21	35	10	9	841	0	0	-	France
Defenders									
Adriano Pereira	26	26	24	21	1953	9	1	-	Brazil
Jeremy Berthod	24	29	12	9	820	4	0	-	France
Fabian Guedes Bolivar	27	35	22	20	1878	1	0	-	Brazil
Leandro Cufre	30	35	25	22	2072	5	0	-	Argentina
Francois Modesto	29	35	27	25	2284	8	0	-	France
Sylvain Monsoreau	27	30	26	20	1981	1	0	-	France
Vincent Muratori	20	26	22	21	1935	5	0	-	France
Massamba L Sambou	22	26	12	12	1080	1	0	-	Senegal
Fabio Santos Romeu	22	9	5	2	254	0	0	-	Brazil
Midfielders									
Sergio B Almiron	27	11	11	7	805	1	0	-	Argentina
Djamel Bakar	19	20	17	7	875	0	0	-	France
Lucas Bernardi	30	22	19	16	1501	4	0	-	Argentina
Ignacio Gonzalez	26	8	5	1	204	1	0	1	Uruguay
Jerko Leko	28	32	29	18	1931	10	0	5	Croatia
Malaury Martin	19	12	7	2	374	0	0	-	France
Jeremy Menez	21	26	25	17	1841	6	1	-	France
Camel Meriem	28	28	27	22	2075	4	0	-	France
Cedric Mongongu	19	13	5	1	213	0	0	-	Congo DR
Anderson Luiz Nene	26	31	28	20	2148	4	0	-	Brazil
Diego Fernando Perez	28	27	25	16	1825	6	1	-	Uruguay
Jaroslav Plasil	26	4	4	3	273	2	0	9	Czech Republic
Nikola Pokrivac	22	12	9	4	481	2	1	-	Croatia
Forwards									
Serge Gakpe	21	30	30	8	1436	1	0	-	France
Mohammed Kallon	28	2	2	1	136	0	0	-	Sierra Leone
Jan Koller	35	19	18	9	1116	1	0	8	Czech Republic
Juan Pablo Pino	21	21	16	1	438	0	0	-	Colombia
Frederic Piquionne	29	32	32	18	2171	3	0	-	France

TEAM OF THE SEASON

G Flavio Roma CG: 28 DR: 71

D Vincent Muratori CG: 21 DR: 101

D Francois Modesto CG: 25 DR: 91

D Sylvain Monsoreau CG: 20 DR: 79

D Adriano Pereira CG: 21 DR: 75

M Jerko Leko CG: 18 SD: 14

M Jeremy Menez CG: 17 SD: 7

M Diego F Perez CG: 16 SD: -17

M Anderson Luiz Nene CG: 20 SD: -19

F Jan Koller CG: 9* SR: 279

F Frederic Piquionne CG: 18 SR: 310

MONTHLY POINTS TALLY

Month	Points	%
AUGUST	13	72%
SEPTEMBER	0	0%
OCTOBER	1	11%
NOVEMBER	7	78%
DECEMBER	4	33%
JANUARY	9	75%
FEBRUARY	2	22%
MARCH	1	7%
APRIL	6	50%
MAY	4	44%

LEAGUE GOALS

	PLAYER	MINS	GOALS	S RATE
1	Menez	1841	7	263
2	Piquionne	2171	7	310
3	Nene	2148	5	429
4	Koller	1116	4	279
5	Sambou	1080	3	360
6	Gakpe	1436	3	478
7	Almiron	805	2	402
8	Meriem	2075	2	1037
9	Gonzalez	204	1	204
10	Santos Romeu	254	1	254
11	Bakar	875	1	875
12	Leko	1931	1	1931
13	Monsoreau	1981	1	1981
	Other		2	
	TOTAL		40	

TOP POINT EARNERS

	PLAYER	GAMES	AV PTS
1	Jeremy Menez	17	1.59
2	Diego Fernando Perez	16	1.56
3	Jerko Leko	18	1.56
4	Vincent Muratori	21	1.43
5	Lucas Bernardi	16	1.38
6	Frederic Piquionne	18	1.33
7	Massamba Lo Sambou	12	1.33
8	Anderson Luiz Nene	20	1.30
9	Camel Meriem	22	1.27
10	Francois Modesto	25	1.24
	CLUB AVERAGE:		1.24

DISCIPLINARY RECORDS

	PLAYER	YELLOW	RED	AVE
1	Nikola Pokrivac	2	1	160
2	Jerko Leko	10	0	193
3	Adriano Pereira	9	1	195
4	Jeremy Berthod	4	0	205
5	Diego F Perez	6	1	260
6	Jeremy Menez	6	1	263
7	Francois Modesto	8	0	285
8	Lucas Bernardi	4	0	375
9	Vincent Muratori	5	0	387
10	Leandro Cufre	5	0	414
11	Camel Meriem	4	0	518
12	Anderson Luiz Nene	4	0	537
13	Flavio Roma	4	0	644
	Other	9	0	
	TOTAL	80	4	

KEY GOALKEEPER

Flavio Roma

Goals Conceded in the League	36	**Counting Games** League games when player was on pitch for at least 70 minutes	28
Defensive Rating Ave number of mins between League goals conceded while on the pitch	71	**Clean Sheets** In League games when player was on pitch for at least 70 minutes	11

KEY PLAYERS - DEFENDERS

Vincent Muratori

Goals Conceded Number of League goals conceded while the player was on the pitch	19	**Clean Sheets** In League games when player was on pitch for at least 70 minutes	10
Defensive Rating Ave number of mins between League goals conceded while on the pitch	101	**Club Defensive Rating** Average number of mins between League goals conceded by the club this season	71

	PLAYER	CON LGE	CLEAN SHEETS	DEF RATE
1	Vincent Muratori	19	10	101 mins
2	Francois Modesto	25	11	91 mins
3	Sylvain Monsoreau	25	9	79 mins
4	Adriano Pereira	26	11	75 mins

KEY PLAYERS - MIDFIELDERS

Jerko Leko

Goals in the League	1	**Contribution to Attacking Power** Average number of minutes between League team goals while on pitch	66
Defensive Rating Average number of mins between League goals conceded while on the pitch	80	**Scoring Difference** Defensive Rating minus Contribution to Attacking Power	14

	PLAYER	LGE GOALS	DEF RATE	POWER	SCORE DIFF
1	Jerko Leko	1	80	66	14 mins
2	Jeremy Menez	7	80	73	7 mins
3	Diego Fernando Perez	0	79	96	-17 mins
4	Anderson Luiz Nene	5	74	93	-19 mins

KEY PLAYERS - GOALSCORERS

Jeremy Menez

Goals in the League	7	**Player Strike Rate** Average number of minutes between League goals scored by player	263
Contribution to Attacking Power Average number of minutes between League team goals while on pitch	73	**Club Strike Rate** Average number of minutes between League goals scored by club	85

	PLAYER	LGE GOALS	POWER	STRIKE RATE
1	Jeremy Menez	7	73	263 mins
2	Jan Koller	4	74	279 mins
3	Frederic Piquionne	7	94	310 mins
4	Anderson Luiz Nene	5	93	429 mins

HSBC
FEDCOM
Frederic Piquionne

SQUAD APPEARANCES

Match	1	2	3	4	5	6	7	8	9	10	11	12	13	14	15	16	17	18	19	20	21	22	23	24	25	26	27	28	29	30	31	32	33	34	35	36	37	38
Venue	H	A	H	A	H	A	A	H	A	H	A	H	A	H	A	H	A	H	A	H	A	H	A	H	H	A	H	A	H	A	H	A	H	A	H	A	H	A
Competition	L	L	L	L	L	L	L	L	L	L	L	L	L	L	L	L	L	L	L	L	L	L	L	L	L	L	L	L	L	L	L	L	L	L	L	L	L	L
Result	D	L	W	W	W	W	L	L	L	L	L	D	W	W	D	D	L	W	L	W	W	W	L	D	L	D	D	L	L	L	L	W	L	W	L	D	W	L

Goalkeepers
Flavio Roma
Stephane Ruffier

Defenders
Adriano Pereira
Jeremy Berthod
Fabian Guedes Bolivar
Leandro Cufre
Francois Modesto
Sylvain Monsoreau
Vincent Muratori
Massamba Lo Sambou
Fabio Santos Romeu

Midfielders
Sergio Bernardo Almiron
Djamel Bakar
Lucas Bernardi
Ignacio Gonzalez
Jerko Leko
Malaury Martin
Jeremy Menez
Camel Meriem
Cedric Mongongu
Anderson Luiz Nene
Diego Fernando Perez
Jaroslav Plasil
Nikola Pokrivac

Forwards
Serge Gakpe
Mohammed Kallon
Jan Koller
Juan Pablo Pino
Frederic Piquionne

KEY: On all match / On bench / Subbed or sent off (Counting game) / Subbed or sent off (playing less than 70 minutes) / Subbed on from bench (Counting Game) / Subbed on (playing less than 70 minutes) / Subbed on and then subbed or sent off (Counting Game) / Subbed on and then subbed or sent off (playing less than 70 minutes) / Not in 16

VALENCIENNES

Final Position: **13th**

NICKNAME: LES ATHENIANS

KEY: ☐ Won ☐ Drawn ☐ Lost

							Attendance
1	frpr1	**Toulouse**	H	W	3-1	Audel 5, 28, 57	12,153
2	frpr1	**St Etienne**	A	L	1-3	Audel 88	30,143
3	frpr1	**Marseille**	H	W	2-1	Savidan 62, 87	16,018
4	frpr1	**Lens**	A	D	0-0		37,194
5	frpr1	**Sochaux**	H	W	3-1	Bezzaz 10, Chelle 44, Savidan 74	13,566
6	frpr1	**Lorient**	A	W	3-1	Pujol 27, 39, Roudet 87	12,588
7	frpr1	**Metz**	H	D	0-0		13,811
8	frpr1	**Le Mans**	A	L	0-2		9,570
9	frpr1	**AS Monaco**	H	W	1-0	Audel 11	14,225
10	frpr1	**Lille**	A	L	0-3		13,739
11	frpr1	**Paris SG**	H	D	0-0		15,037
12	frpr1	**Bordeaux**	A	L	1-2	Diawara 45 og	18,521
13	frpr1	**Lyon**	A	L	0-2		38,631
14	frpr1	**Caen**	H	W	3-0	Sebo 16, 43, Savidan 59	12,449
15	frpr1	**Strasbourg**	A	D	0-0		15,889
16	frpr1	**Rennes**	H	W	3-0	Savidan 11, Pujol 65, 75	12,161
17	frpr1	**Nancy**	A	D	0-0		17,712
18	frpr1	**Auxerre**	H	W	3-0	Savidan 13 pen, Chelle 30, Audel 79	13,057
19	frpr1	**Nice**	A	L	0-1		9,640
20	frpr1	**St Etienne**	H	W	2-0	Doumeng 9, Pujol 89	13,516
21	frpr1	**Marseille**	A	L	1-3	Audel 81	48,152
22	frpr1	**Lens**	H	L	1-2	Savidan 33	14,583
23	frpr1	**Sochaux**	A	L	0-1		12,518
24	frpr1	**Lorient**	H	W	3-0	Savidan 40, Roudet 56, Sebo 86	12,667
25	frpr1	**Metz**	A	L	1-2	Belmadi 42	10,185
26	frpr1	**Le Mans**	H	L	1-2	Savidan 45	12,684
27	frpr1	**AS Monaco**	A	D	0-0		7,912
28	frpr1	**Lille**	H	D	0-0		13,955
29	frpr1	**Paris SG**	A	D	1-1	Ceara 52 og	32,368
30	frpr1	**Bordeaux**	H	W	3-1	Roudet 10, Sebo 64, Savidan 77	13,657
31	frpr1	**Lyon**	H	L	1-2	Chelle 27	15,313
32	frpr1	**Caen**	A	L	0-1		19,477
33	frpr1	**Strasbourg**	H	W	2-0	Savidan 26, 42	14,276
34	frpr1	**Rennes**	A	L	0-1		26,532
35	frpr1	**Nancy**	H	D	1-1	Audel 50	13,972
36	frpr1	**Auxerre**	A	L	0-2		19,000
37	frpr1	**Nice**	H	L	1-2	Savidan 88 pen	14,546
38	frpr1	**Toulouse**	A	L	1-2	Audel 38	26,492

LEAGUE APPEARANCES, BOOKINGS AND CAPS

	AGE (on 01/07/08)	IN NAMED 18	APPEARANCES	COUNTING GAMES	MINUTES ON PITCH	YELLOW CARDS	RED CARDS	CAPS THIS SEASON	NATIONAL SIDE
Goalkeepers									
Stephane Coque	26	1	0	0	0	0	0	-	France
Willy Grondin	33	38	1	1	90	0	0	-	France
Nicolas Penneteau	27	37	37	37	3330	0	0	-	France
Defenders									
Eric Chelle	30	24	21	20	1839	3	0	-	Mali
David Ducourtioux	30	36	31	25	2423	3	0	-	France
Williams G Martinez	25	16	7	4	503	1	1	-	Uruguay
Rudy Mater	27	32	31	22	2333	6	0	-	France
Abdeslam Ouaddou	29	33	32	31	2847	5	0	4	Morocco
Guillaume Rippert	23	26	18	9	1082	1	2	-	France
David Sommeil	33	32	19	16	1520	2	0	-	France
Dame Traore	22	21	11	5	566	3	0	-	France
Mody Traore	27	23	13	10	921	3	0	-	France
Midfielders									
Djamel Belmadi	32	29	26	17	1776	0	0	-	France
Yacine Bezzaz	26	24	20	5	891	1	1	-	Algeria
Geoffrey Doumeng	27	33	27	19	1879	7	0	-	France
Jeovanio	30	15	13	8	826	3	0	-	Brazil
Khaled Kharroubi	24	10	3	0	29	0	0	-	France
Sebastien Roudet	27	32	30	23	2237	3	0	-	France
Jose Saez	26	33	29	23	2270	6	3	-	France
Carlos Sanchez	22	35	34	28	2716	2	0	4	Colombia
Forwards									
Johan Audel	24	26	23	13	1361	1	0	-	France
Gregory Pujol	28	30	29	16	1755	1	0	-	France
Steve Savidan	30	38	38	29	2728	0	0	-	France
Filip Sebo	24	34	32	13	1508	4	0	1	Slovakia
Dia Tidiane	23	1	0	0	0	0	0	-	Senegal

TEAM OF THE SEASON

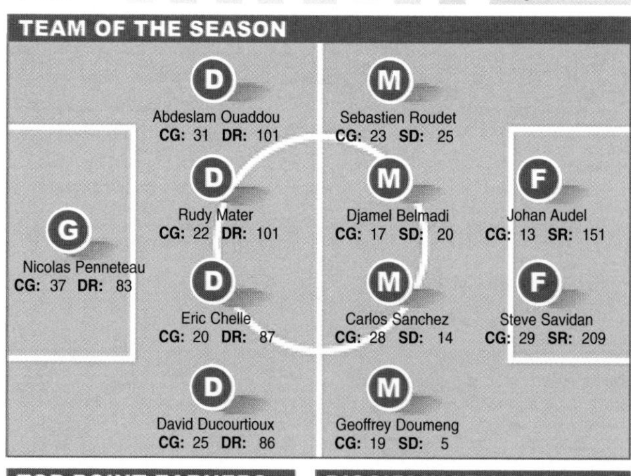

G
Nicolas Penneteau
CG: 37 DR: 83
D
Abdeslam Ouaddou
CG: 31 DR: 101
D
Rudy Mater
CG: 22 DR: 101
D
Eric Chelle
CG: 20 DR: 87
D
David Ducourtioux
CG: 25 DR: 86
M
Sebastien Roudet
CG: 23 SD: 25
M
Djamel Belmadi
CG: 17 SD: 20
M
Carlos Sanchez
CG: 28 SD: 14
M
Geoffrey Doumeng
CG: 19 SD: 5
F
Johan Audel
CG: 13 SR: 151
F
Steve Savidan
CG: 29 SR: 209

MONTHLY POINTS TALLY

AUGUST	13	72%
SEPTEMBER	4	44%
OCTOBER	1	11%
NOVEMBER	4	44%
DECEMBER	7	58%
JANUARY	3	25%
FEBRUARY	3	33%
MARCH	6	40%
APRIL	4	33%
MAY	0	0%

LEAGUE GOALS

	PLAYER	MINS	GOALS	S RATE
1	Savidan	2728	13	209
2	Audel	1361	9	151
3	Pujol	1755	5	351
4	Sebo	1508	4	377
5	Chelle	1839	3	613
6	Roudet	2237	3	745
7	Bezzaz	891	1	891
8	Belmadi	1776	1	1776
9	Doumeng	1879	1	1879
	Other		0	
	TOTAL		**40**	

TOP POINT EARNERS

	PLAYER	GAMES	AV PTS
1	Djamel Belmadi	17	1.47
2	Eric Chelle	20	1.45
3	Rudy Mater	22	1.41
4	Steve Savidan	29	1.41
5	Carlos Sanchez	28	1.36
6	Sebastien Roudet	23	1.35
7	Abdeslam Ouaddou	31	1.35
8	Filip Sebo	13	1.15
9	Nicolas Penneteau	37	1.14
10	Gregory Pujol	16	1.13
	CLUB AVERAGE:		**1.18**

DISCIPLINARY RECORDS

	PLAYER	YELLOW	RED	AVE
1	Dame Traore	3	0	188
2	Williams Martinez	1	1	251
3	Jose Saez	6	3	252
4	Geoffrey Doumeng	7	0	268
5	Jeovanio	3	0	275
6	Mody Traore	3	0	307
7	Guillaume Rippert	1	2	360
8	Filip Sebo	4	0	377
9	Rudy Mater	6	0	388
10	Yacine Bezzaz	1	1	445
11	Abdeslam Ouaddou	5	0	569
12	Eric Chelle	3	0	613
13	Sebastien Roudet	3	0	745
	Other	9	0	
	TOTAL	**55**	**7**	

KEY GOALKEEPER

Nicolas Penneteau

Goals Conceded in the League	40	**Counting Games** League games when player was on pitch for at least 70 minutes	37
Defensive Rating Ave number of mins between League goals conceded while on the pitch	83	**Clean Sheets** In League games when player was on pitch for at least 70 minutes	13

KEY PLAYERS - DEFENDERS

Abdeslam Ouaddou

Goals Conceded Number of League goals conceded while the player was on the pitch	28	**Clean Sheets** In League games when player was on pitch for at least 70 minutes	14
Defensive Rating Ave number of mins between League goals conceded while on the pitch	101	**Club Defensive Rating** Average number of mins between League goals conceded by the club this season	85

	PLAYER	CON LGE	CLEAN SHEETS	DEF RATE
1	Abdeslam Ouaddou	28	14	101 mins
2	Rudy Mater	23	9	101 mins
3	Eric Chelle	21	6	87 mins
4	David Ducourtioux	28	9	86 mins

KEY PLAYERS - MIDFIELDERS

Sebastien Roudet

Goals in the League	3	**Contribution to Attacking Power** Average number of minutes between League team goals while on pitch	86
Defensive Rating Average number of mins between League goals conceded while on the pitch	111	**Scoring Difference** Defensive Rating minus Contribution to Attacking Power	25

	PLAYER	LGE GOALS	DEF RATE	POWER	SCORE DIFF
1	Sebastien Roudet	3	111	86	25 mins
2	Djamel Belmadi	1	88	68	20 mins
3	Carlos Sanchez	0	93	79	14 mins
4	Geoffrey Doumeng	1	72	67	5 mins

KEY PLAYERS - GOALSCORERS

Johan Audel

Goals in the League	9	**Player Strike Rate** Average number of minutes between League goals scored by player	151
Contribution to Attacking Power Average number of minutes between League team goals while on pitch	90	**Club Strike Rate** Average number of minutes between League goals scored by club	81

	PLAYER	LGE GOALS	POWER	STRIKE RATE
1	Johan Audel	9	90	151 mins
2	Steve Savidan	13	77	209 mins
3	Gregory Pujol	5	79	351 mins
4	Filip Sebo	4	94	377 mins

gorenje

Rudy Mater & Filip Sebo

SQUAD APPEARANCES

Match	1	2	3	4	5	6	7	8	9	10	11	12	13	14	15	16	17	18	19	20	21	22	23	24	25	26	27	28	29	30	31	32	33	34	35	36	37	38
Venue	H	A	H	A	H	A	H	A	H	A	H	A	A	H	A	H	A	H	A	H	A	H	A	H	A	H	A	H	A	H	H	A	H	A	H	A	H	A
Competition	L	L	L	L	L	L	L	L	L	L	L	L	L	L	L	L	L	L	L	L	L	L	L	L	L	L	L	L	L	L	L	L	L	L	L	L	L	L
Result	W	L	W	D	W	W	D	L	W	L	D	L	L	W	D	W	D	W	L	W	L	L	L	W	L	L	D	D	D	W	L	L	W	L	D	L	L	L

Goalkeepers
- Stephane Coque
- Willy Grondin
- Nicolas Penneteau

Defenders
- Eric Chelle
- David Ducourtioux
- Williams G Martinez
- Rudy Mater
- Abdeslam Ouaddou
- Guillaume Rippert
- David Sommeil
- Dame Traore
- Mody Traore

Midfielders
- Djamel Belmadi
- Yacine Bezzaz
- Geoffrey Doumeng
- Jeovanio
- Khaled Kharroubi
- Sebastien Roudet
- Jose Saez
- Carlos Sanchez

Forwards
- Johan Audel
- Gregory Pujol
- Steve Savidan
- Filip Sebo
- Dia Tidiane

KEY: On all match · On bench · Subbed or sent off (Counting game) · Subbed or sent off (playing less than 70 minutes) · Subbed on from bench (Counting Game) · Subbed on (playing less than 70 minutes) · Subbed on and then subbed or sent off (Counting Game) · Subbed on and then subbed or sent off (playing less than 70 minutes) · Not in 16

SOCHAUX

Final Position: **14th**

NICKNAME: THE LION CUBS

KEY: ☐Won ☐Drawn ☐Lost

							Attendance
1	frpr1	Paris SG	A	D	0-0		37,400
2	frpr1	Le Mans	H	L	1-3	Birsa 17	14,033
3	frpr1	Lille	A	D	1-1	Dalmat 45	12,029
4	frpr1	AS Monaco	H	L	0-3		14,091
5	frpr1	Valenciennes	A	L	1-3	Quercia 6	13,566
6	frpr1	Lyon	H	L	1-2	Birsa 20 pen	15,488
7	frpr1	Caen	A	D	2-2	N'Daw 59, Birsa 74 pen	18,099
8	frpr1	Strasbourg	H	D	0-0		16,078
9	uc1rl1	Panionios	H	L	0-2		9,469
10	frpr1	Rennes	A	W	2-0	Dalmat 36, Isabey 57	22,589
11	uc1rl2	Panionios	A	W	1-0	Kumordzi 53	9,000
12	frpr1	Toulouse	H	L	0-1		12,783
13	frpr1	Nancy	A	D	1-1	Erding 56	18,689
14	frpr1	Marseille	H	W	2-1	Zubar 29 og, Bonnart 50 og	19,957
15	frpr1	Nice	A	D	0-0		10,221
16	frpr1	Auxerre	H	D	1-1	Pitau 89	18,442
17	frpr1	St Etienne	A	L	0-1		26,015
18	frpr1	Lens	H	L	0-2		13,950
19	frpr1	Lorient	A	L	1-2	Erding 81	12,000
20	frpr1	Metz	A	W	2-1	Erding 10, Dalmat 82 pen	10,370
21	frpr1	Bordeaux	H	L	0-1		12,646
22	frpr1	Le Mans	A	W	2-0	Erding 45, Isabey 54	9,714
23	frpr1	Lille	H	D	1-1	Erding 37	25,862
24	frpr1	AS Monaco	A	L	0-1		2,500
25	frpr1	Valenciennes	H	W	1-0	Brechet 22	12,518
26	frpr1	Lyon	A	L	1-4	Pancrate 52	35,904
27	frpr1	Caen	H	D	1-1	Maurice-Belay 40	26,629
28	frpr1	Strasbourg	A	W	2-0	Isabey 13, Erding 35	17,084
29	frpr1	Rennes	H	D	0-0		14,564
30	frpr1	Toulouse	A	W	2-1	Erding 5, 20	19,109
31	frpr1	Nancy	H	D	1-1	Erding 53	16,487
32	frpr1	Marseille	A	W	1-0	N'Daw 3	51,435
33	frpr1	Nice	H	W	1-0	Pitau 88	19,303
34	frpr1	Auxerre	A	W	1-0	Perquis 44	10,282
35	frpr1	St Etienne	H	D	1-1	Grax 68	19,921
36	frpr1	Lens	A	L	2-3	Erding 49, Brechet 78	39,478
37	frpr1	Lorient	H	D	1-1	Erding 79	17,361
38	frpr1	Metz	H	D	0-0		17,680
39	frpr1	Bordeaux	A	L	0-2		32,487
40	frpr1	Paris SG	H	L	1-2	N'Daw 74	19,873

LEAGUE APPEARANCES, BOOKINGS AND CAPS

	AGE (on 01/07/08)	IN NAMED 18	APPEARANCES	COUNTING GAMES	MINUTES ON PITCH	YELLOW CARDS	RED CARDS	CAPS THIS SEASON	NATIONAL SIDE
Goalkeepers									
Mathieu Dreyer	19	11	0	0	0	0	0	-	France
Jeremy Gavanon	24	26	0	0	0	0	0	-	France
Teddy Richert	33	38	38	38	3420	1	0	-	France
Defenders									
Rabiu Afolabi	28	27	27	26	2387	10	0	-	Nigeria
Jeremie Brechet	28	21	21	21	1890	1	0	-	France
Omar Daf	31	17	8	5	512	3	0	-	Senegal
Boukary Drame	22	22	10	7	726	2	0	-	Senegal
Hakim El Bounadi	21	6	0	0	0	0	0	-	France
Bojan Jokic	22	24	17	12	1291	2	0	8	Slovenia
Maxime Josse	21	19	12	9	910	1	0	-	France
Damien Perquis	24	30	23	22	2017	6	0	-	France
Stephane Pichot	31	35	34	32	2937	7	0	-	France
Midfielders									
Stephane Dalmat	29	35	35	29	2847	4	1	-	France
Mickael Isabey	33	38	37	24	2623	2	0	-	France
Lionel Mathis	26	28	16	8	907	3	0	-	France
Nicolas Maurice-Belay	23	28	25	13	1573	2	0	-	France
Guirane N'Daw	24	32	30	28	2575	8	0	-	Senegal
Vincent Nogueira	20	7	3	0	73	0	0	-	France
Romain Pitau	30	35	32	25	2494	6	0	-	France
Badara Sene	23	25	13	10	1016	3	0	-	Senegal
Forwards									
Alvaro Santos	28	5	3	0	55	0	0	-	Brazil
Valter Birsa	21	27	22	8	1186	0	0	-	Slovenia
Moumouni Dagano	27	23	21	8	1028	1	0	-	Burkina Faso
Mevlut Erdinc	21	34	29	17	1965	6	0	3	Turkey
Sebastien Grax	24	15	12	5	607	0	0	-	France
Fabrice Pancrate	28	23	18	8	963	0	0	-	France
Sloan Privat	18	2	1	0	1	0	0	-	France
Julien Quercia	21	22	18	6	917	2	0	-	France
Kandia Traore	27	13	13	2	569	2	0	-	Ivory Coast
Gonzalo Vargas	26	8	4	0	103	1	0	-	Uruguay

TEAM OF THE SEASON

G — Teddy Richert, CG: 38 DR: 79

D — Damien Perquis, CG: 22 DR: 100

D — Rabiu Afolabi, CG: 26 DR: 88

D — Stephane Pichot, CG: 32 DR: 83

D — Bojan Jokic, CG: 12 DR: 75

M — Stephane Dalmat, CG: 29 SD: -7

M — Mickael Isabey, CG: 24 SD: -11

M — Guirane N'Daw, CG: 28 SD: -13

M — Nicolas Maurice-Belay, CG: 13 SD: -21

F — Mevlut Erdinc, CG: 17 SR: 178

F — Valter Birsa, CG: 8* SR: 395

MONTHLY POINTS TALLY

AUGUST	2	11%
SEPTEMBER	5	56%
OCTOBER	4	44%
NOVEMBER	2	22%
DECEMBER	3	25%
JANUARY	7	58%
FEBRUARY	4	44%
MARCH	11	73%
APRIL	5	42%
MAY	1	11%

LEAGUE GOALS

	PLAYER	MINS	GOALS	S RATE
1	Erdinc	1965	11	178
2	Birsa	1186	3	395
3	N'Daw	2575	3	858
4	Isabey	2623	3	874
5	Dalmat	2847	3	949
6	Brechet	1890	2	945
7	Pitau	2494	2	1247
8	Grax	607	1	607
9	Quercia	917	1	917
10	Pancrate	963	1	963
11	Maurice-Belay	1573	1	1573
12	Perquis	2017	1	2017
	Other		0	
	TOTAL		**32**	

TOP POINT EARNERS

	PLAYER	GAMES	AV PTS
1	Damien Perquis	22	**1.55**
2	Mevlut Erdinc	17	**1.29**
3	Guirane N'Daw	28	**1.29**
4	Stephane Dalmat	29	**1.28**
5	Bojan Jokic	12	**1.25**
6	Nicolas Maurice-Belay	13	**1.23**
7	Rabiu Afolabi	26	**1.19**
8	Mickael Isabey	24	**1.17**
9	Romain Pitau	25	**1.16**
10	Teddy Richert	38	**1.16**
	CLUB AVERAGE:		**1.16**

DISCIPLINARY RECORDS

	PLAYER	YELLOW	RED	AVE
1	Omar Daf	3	0	**170**
2	Rabiu Afolabi	10	0	**238**
3	Kandia Traore	2	0	**284**
4	Lionel Mathis	3	0	**302**
5	Guirane N'Daw	8	0	**321**
6	Mevlut Erdinc	6	0	**327**
7	Damien Perquis	6	0	**336**
8	Badara Sene	3	0	**338**
9	Boukary Drame	2	0	**363**
10	Romain Pitau	6	0	**415**
11	Stephane Pichot	7	0	**419**
12	Julien Quercia	2	0	**458**
13	Stephane Dalmat	4	1	**569**
	Other	10	0	
	TOTAL	**72**	**1**	

KEY GOALKEEPER

Teddy Richert

Goals Conceded in the League	43	**Counting Games** League games when player was on pitch for at least 70 minutes	38
Defensive Rating Ave number of mins between League goals conceded while on the pitch	79	**Clean Sheets** In League games when player was on pitch for at least 70 minutes	12

KEY PLAYERS - DEFENDERS

Damien Perquis

Goals Conceded Number of League goals conceded while the player was on the pitch	20	**Clean Sheets** In League games when player was on pitch for at least 70 minutes	9
Defensive Rating Ave number of mins between League goals conceded while on the pitch	100	**Club Defensive Rating** Average number of mins between League goals conceded by the club this season	79

	PLAYER	CON LGE	CLEAN SHEETS	DEF RATE
1	Damien Perquis	20	9	100 mins
2	Rabiu Afolabi	27	10	88 mins
3	Stephane Pichot	35	10	83 mins
4	Bojan Jokic	17	5	75 mins

KEY PLAYERS - MIDFIELDERS

Stephane Dalmat

Goals in the League	3	**Contribution to Attacking Power** Average number of minutes between League team goals while on pitch	88
Defensive Rating Average number of mins between League goals conceded while on the pitch	81	**Scoring Difference** Defensive Rating minus Contribution to Attacking Power	-7

	PLAYER	LGE GOALS	DEF RATE	POWER	SCORE DIFF
1	Stephane Dalmat	3	81	88	-7 mins
2	Mickael Isabey	3	93	104	-11 mins
3	Guirane N'Daw	3	75	88	-13 mins
4	Nicolas Maurice-Belay	1	71	92	-21 mins

KEY PLAYERS - GOALSCORERS

Mevlut Erdinc

Goals in the League	11	**Player Strike Rate** Average number of minutes between League goals scored by player	178
Contribution to Attacking Power Average number of minutes between League team goals while on pitch	78	**Club Strike Rate** Average number of minutes between League goals scored by club	100

	PLAYER	LGE GOALS	POWER	STRIKE RATE
1	Mevlut Erdinc	11	78	178 mins
2	Valter Birsa	3	118	395 mins
3	Guirane N'Daw	3	88	858 mins
4	Mickael Isabey	3	104	874 mins

lotto
Franche-Comté
Mobil 1
Stephane Dalmat

SQUAD APPEARANCES

Match	1	2	3	4	5	6	7	8	9	10	11	12	13	14	15	16	17	18	19	20	21	22	23	24	25	26	27	28	29	30	31	32	33	34	35	36	37	38	39	40
Venue	A	H	A	H	A	H	A	H	H	A	A	H	A	H	A	H	A	H	A	A	H	A	H	A	H	A	H	A	H	A	H	A	H	A	H	A	H	H	A	H
Competition	L	L	L	L	L	L	L	L	E	L	E	L	L	L	L	L	L	L	L	L	L	L	L	L	L	L	L	L	L	L	L	L	L	L	L	L	L	L	L	L
Result	D	L	D	L	L	L	D	D	L	W	W	L	D	W	D	D	L	L	L	W	L	W	D	L	W	L	D	W	D	W	D	W	W	W	D	L	D	D	L	L

Goalkeepers
Mathieu Dreyer
Jeremy Gavanon
Teddy Richert
Defenders
Rabiu Afolabi
Jeremie Brechet
Omar Daf
Boukary Drame
Hakim El Bounadi
Bojan Jokic
Maxime Josse
Damien Perquis
Stephane Pichot
Midfielders
Stephane Dalmat
Mickael Isabey
Lionel Mathis
Nicolas Maurice-Belay
Guirane N'Daw
Vincent Nogueira
Romain Pitau
Badara Sene
Forwards
Alvaro Santos
Valter Birsa
Moumouni Dagano
Mevlut Erdinc
Sebastien Grax
Fabrice Pancrate
Sloan Privat
Julien Quercia
Kandia Traore
Gonzalo Vargas

KEY: On all match; On bench; Subbed or sent off (Counting game); Subbed or sent off (playing less than 70 minutes); Subbed on from bench (Counting Game); Subbed on (playing less than 70 minutes); Subbed on and then subbed or sent off (Counting Game); Subbed on and then subbed or sent off (playing less than 70 minutes); Not in 16

AUXERRE

Final Position: **15th**

NICKNAME: AJA

KEY: ☐ Won ☐ Drawn ☐ Lost

							Attendance
1	frpr1	**Lyon**	A	L	0-2		35,537
2	frpr1	**Bordeaux**	H	L	0-2		11,512
3	frpr1	**Strasbourg**	A	L	0-3		20,045
4	frpr1	**Caen**	H	W	1-0	Maoulida 33	7,439
5	frpr1	**Nancy**	A	L	1-4	Lejeune 59	18,132
6	frpr1	**Rennes**	H	L	0-2		7,896
7	frpr1	**Toulouse**	A	L	0-2		14,795
8	frpr1	**Nice**	H	W	2-0	Lejeune 4, Niculae 90	7,591
9	frpr1	**Marseille**	H	W	2-0	Niculae 18, 24	18,510
10	frpr1	**Lens**	A	L	0-2		31,139
11	frpr1	**Lorient**	H	W	5-3	Niculae 55, 82, Jelen 73, 75, 90	8,157
12	frpr1	**St Etienne**	A	D	0-0		30,448
13	frpr1	**Lille**	H	L	0-1		8,856
14	frpr1	**Sochaux**	A	D	1-1	Kahlenberg 7 pen	18,442
15	frpr1	**Le Mans**	H	W	3-0	Chafni 34, Niculae 80, Jelen 87	7,222
16	frpr1	**Metz**	A	W	1-0	Kahlenberg 54	10,281
17	frpr1	**Paris SG**	H	L	0-1		11,015
18	frpr1	**Valenciennes**	A	L	0-3		13,057
19	frpr1	**AS Monaco**	H	W	1-0	S.Traore 67	8,952
20	frpr1	**Bordeaux**	A	L	1-4	Niculae 2	21,223
21	frpr1	**Strasbourg**	H	D	1-1	Niculae 5	6,550
22	frpr1	**Caen**	A	D	0-0		20,000
23	frpr1	**Nancy**	H	D	0-0		6,548
24	frpr1	**Rennes**	A	W	2-1	Oliech 45, 90	22,733
25	frpr1	**Toulouse**	H	W	1-0	Niculae 52	9,106
26	frpr1	**Nice**	A	W	2-1	Niculae 66, Chafni 69	10,114
27	frpr1	**Marseille**	A	L	1-2	Pedretti 89	53,100
28	frpr1	**Lens**	H	D	0-0		10,591
29	frpr1	**Lorient**	A	D	1-1	Jaures 72 pen	12,881
30	frpr1	**St Etienne**	H	L	1-3	Benalouane 5 og	13,137
31	frpr1	**Lille**	A	W	2-0	Oliech 41, Niculae 56	16,017
32	frpr1	**Sochaux**	H	L	0-1		10,282
33	frpr1	**Le Mans**	A	L	0-3		12,339
34	frpr1	**Metz**	H	D	0-0		8,620
35	frpr1	**Paris SG**	A	L	1-3	Mignot 78	37,671
36	frpr1	**Valenciennes**	H	W	2-0	Lejeune 16, Jelen 90	19,000
37	frpr1	**AS Monaco**	A	L	0-3		9,839
38	frpr1	**Lyon**	H	L	1-3	F.Thomas 78	19,796

LEAGUE APPEARANCES, BOOKINGS AND CAPS

	AGE (on 01/07/08)	IN NAMED 18	APPEARANCES	COUNTING GAMES	MINUTES ON PITCH	YELLOW CARDS	RED CARDS	CAPS THIS SEASON	NATIONAL SIDE
Goalkeepers									
Denis Petric	20	4	0	0	0	0	0	-	Slovenia
Remy Riou	20	34	19	19	1710	0	0	-	France
Olivier Sorin	27	24	19	19	1710	0	0	-	France
Stephane Veron	22	14	0	0	0	0	0	-	France
Defenders									
Marcos E A Santos	25	29	10	6	624	0	0	-	Brazil
Stephane Grichting	29	35	29	25	2402	5	0	4	Switzerland
Jean-Sebastien Jaures	30	36	34	33	2992	8	0	-	France
Baptiste Martin	23	12	6	4	375	0	0	-	France
Jean-Pascal Mignot	27	33	27	22	2206	5	1	-	France
Robert Popov	26	14	6	4	349	1	0	-	Macedonia
Gabriel Tamas	24	30	26	20	2005	7	1	8	Romania
Sammy Traore	32	26	25	24	2212	3	0	-	Mali
Midfielders									
Issa Ba	26	7	3	0	50	0	0	-	Senegal
Kamel Chafni	26	31	31	27	2546	6	0	-	Morocco
Maxime Jasse	20	12	2	0	9	0	0	-	France
Thomas Kahlenberg	25	30	29	23	2224	2	0	8	Denmark
Steeven Langil	20	2	0	0	0	0	0	-	France
Jean-Michel Lesage	31	19	11	2	286	0	0	-	France
Vlad Munteanu	27	15	9	2	325	1	0	-	Romania
Benoit Pedretti	27	37	37	36	3281	5	0	-	France
Frederic Thomas	27	30	27	21	2098	2	0	-	France
Alain Traore	19	2	1	0	3	0	0	-	Burkina Faso
Forwards									
Ludovic Genest	20	6	2	0	51	0	0	-	France
Ireneusz Jelen	27	34	32	11	1570	0	0	1	Poland
Lynel Kitambala	19	6	0	0	0	0	0	-	France
Kevin Lejeune	23	38	38	29	2861	7	1	-	France
Toifilou Maoulida	29	17	15	9	873	2	0	-	France
Daniel Niculae	25	35	35	29	2711	2	0	6	Romania
Dennis Oliech	23	31	26	12	1674	5	0	-	Kenya
Julien Quercia	21	14	13	0	447	2	0	-	France

TEAM OF THE SEASON

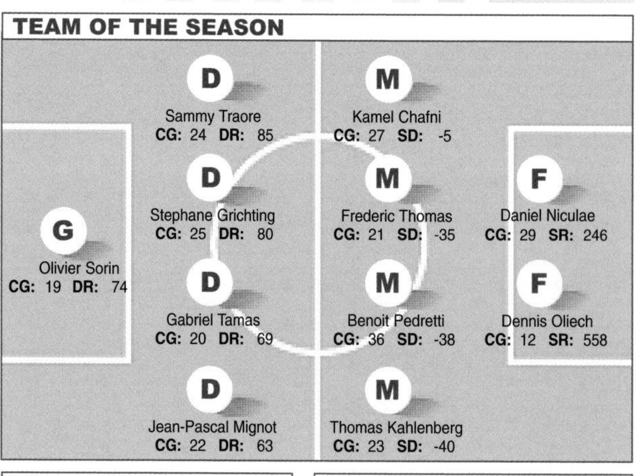
G
Olivier Sorin
CG: 19 DR: 74
D
Sammy Traore
CG: 24 DR: 85
D
Stephane Grichting
CG: 25 DR: 80
D
Gabriel Tamas
CG: 20 DR: 69
D
Jean-Pascal Mignot
CG: 22 DR: 63
M
Kamel Chafni
CG: 27 SD: -5
M
Frederic Thomas
CG: 21 SD: -35
M
Benoit Pedretti
CG: 36 SD: -38
M
Thomas Kahlenberg
CG: 23 SD: -40
F
Daniel Niculae
CG: 29 SR: 246
F
Dennis Oliech
CG: 12 SR: 558

MONTHLY POINTS TALLY

AUGUST	3	17%
SEPTEMBER	6	67%
OCTOBER	4	44%
NOVEMBER	4	44%
DECEMBER	6	50%
JANUARY	3	25%
FEBRUARY	9	100%
MARCH	5	33%
APRIL	1	8%
MAY	3	33%

LEAGUE GOALS

	PLAYER	MINS	GOALS	S RATE
1	Niculae	2711	11	246
2	Jelen	1570	5	314
3	Oliech	1674	3	558
4	Lejeune	2861	3	953
5	Kahlenberg	2224	2	1112
6	Chafni	2546	2	1273
7	Maoulida	873	1	873
8	Thomas	2098	1	2098
9	Mignot	2206	1	2206
10	Traore, S	2212	1	2212
11	Jaures	2992	1	2992
12	Pedretti	3281	1	3281
	Other		0	
	TOTAL		32	

TOP POINT EARNERS

	PLAYER	GAMES	AV PTS
1	Sammy Traore	24	**1.54**
2	Dennis Oliech	12	**1.50**
3	Kevin Lejeune	29	**1.41**
4	Kamel Chafni	27	**1.41**
5	Stephane Grichting	25	**1.32**
6	Olivier Sorin	19	**1.21**
7	Daniel Niculae	29	**1.21**
8	Benoit Pedretti	36	**1.17**
9	Jean-Sebastien Jaures	33	**1.15**
10	Frederic Thomas	21	**1.14**
	CLUB AVERAGE:		**1.16**

DISCIPLINARY RECORDS

	PLAYER	YELLOW	RED	AVE
1	Gabriel Tamas	7	1	**250**
2	Dennis Oliech	5	0	**334**
3	Kevin Lejeune	7	1	**357**
4	Jean-Pascal Mignot	5	1	**367**
5	Jean-Seb' Jaures	8	0	**374**
6	Kamel Chafni	6	0	**424**
7	Toifilou Maoulida	2	0	**436**
8	Stephane Grichting	5	0	**480**
9	Benoit Pedretti	5	0	**656**
10	Sammy Traore	3	0	**737**
11	Frederic Thomas	2	0	**1049**
12	Thomas Kahlenberg	2	0	**1112**
13	Daniel Niculae	2	0	**1355**
	Other	0	0	
	TOTAL	59	3	

KEY GOALKEEPER

Olivier Sorin

Goals Conceded in the League	23	Counting Games League games when player was on pitch for at least 70 minutes	19
Defensive Rating Ave number of mins between League goals conceded while on the pitch	74	Clean Sheets In League games when player was on pitch for at least 70 minutes	8

KEY PLAYERS - DEFENDERS

Sammy Traore

Goals Conceded Number of League goals conceded while the player was on the pitch	26	Clean Sheets In League games when player was on pitch for at least 70 minutes	10
Defensive Rating Ave number of mins between League goals conceded while on the pitch	85	Club Defensive Rating Average number of mins between League goals conceded by the club this season	65

	PLAYER	CON LGE	CLEAN SHEETS	DEF RATE
1	Sammy Traore	26	10	85 mins
2	Stephane Grichting	30	11	80 mins
3	Gabriel Tamas	29	7	69 mins
4	Jean-Pascal Mignot	35	10	63 mins

KEY PLAYERS - MIDFIELDERS

Kamel Chafni

Goals in the League	2	Contribution to Attacking Power Average number of minutes between League team goals while on pitch	87
Defensive Rating Average number of mins between League goals conceded while on the pitch	82	Scoring Difference Defensive Rating minus Contribution to Attacking Power	-5

	PLAYER	LGE GOALS	DEF RATE	POWER	SCORE DIFF
1	Kamel Chafni	2	82	87	-5 mins
2	Frederic Thomas	1	56	91	-35 mins
3	Benoit Pedretti	1	64	102	-38 mins
4	Thomas Kahlenberg	2	61	101	-40 mins

KEY PLAYERS - GOALSCORERS

Daniel Niculae

Goals in the League	11	Player Strike Rate Average number of minutes between League goals scored by player	246
Contribution to Attacking Power Average number of minutes between League team goals while on pitch	96	Club Strike Rate Average number of minutes between League goals scored by club	103

	PLAYER	LGE GOALS	POWER	STRIKE RATE
1	Daniel Niculae	11	96	246 mins
2	Dennis Oliech	3	98	558 mins
3	Kevin Lejeune	3	105	953 mins
4	Thomas Kahlenberg	2	101	1112 mins

INVICTA
PREST OIL
Daniel Niculae

SQUAD APPEARANCES

Match	1	2	3	4	5	6	7	8	9	10	11	12	13	14	15	16	17	18	19
Venue	A	H	A	H	A	H	A	H	H	A	H	A	H	A	H	A	H	A	H
Competition	L	L	L	L	L	L	L	L	L	L	L	L	L	L	L	L	L	L	L
Result	L	L	L	W	L	L	L	W	W	L	W	D	L	D	W	W	L	L	W

Match	20	21	22	23	24	25	26	27	28	29	30	31	32	33	34	35	36	37	38
Venue	A	H	A	H	A	H	A	A	H	A	H	A	H	A	H	A	H	A	H
Competition	L	L	L	L	L	L	L	L	L	L	L	L	L	L	L	L	L	L	L
Result	L	D	D	D	W	W	W	L	D	D	L	W	L	L	D	L	W	L	L

Goalkeepers
Denis Petric
Remy Riou
Olivier Sorin
Stephane Veron

Defenders
Marcos E A Santos
Stephane Grichting
Jean-Sebastien Jaures
Baptiste Martin
Jean-Pascal Mignot
Robert Popov
Gabriel Tamas
Sammy Traore

Midfielders
Issa Ba
Kamel Chafni
Maxime Jasse
Thomas Kahlenberg
Steeven Langil
Jean-Michel Lesage
Vlad Munteanu
Benoit Pedretti
Frederic Thomas
Alain Traore

Forwards
Ludovic Genest
Ireneusz Jelen
Lynel Kitambala
Kevin Lejeune
Toifilou Maoulida
Daniel Niculae
Dennis Oliech
Julien Quercia

KEY: On all match · On bench · Subbed or sent off (Counting game) · Subbed or sent off (playing less than 70 minutes) · Subbed on from bench (Counting Game) · Subbed on (playing less than 70 minutes) · Subbed on and then subbed or sent off (Counting Game) · Subbed on and then subbed or sent off (playing less than 70 minutes) · Not in 16

PARIS St GERMAIN

Final Position: **16th**

NICKNAME: PSG

KEY: ☐Won ☐Drawn ☐Lost

							Attendance
1	frpr1	**Sochaux**	H	D	0-0		37,400
2	frpr1	**Lens**	A	D	0-0		38,836
3	frpr1	**Lorient**	H	L	1-3	Pauleta 35	32,227
4	frpr1	**Metz**	A	D	0-0		19,018
5	frpr1	**Lille**	H	D	1-1	Frau 86	31,634
6	frpr1	**Le Mans**	A	W	2-0	Armand 36, Diane 52	13,072
7	frpr1	**Marseille**	H	D	1-1	Luyindula 19	43,491
8	frpr1	**AS Monaco**	A	W	2-1	Armand 38, Diane 52	12,694
9	frpr1	**Bordeaux**	H	L	0-2		37,108
10	frpr1	**Rennes**	H	L	1-3	Ceara 56	35,436
11	frpr1	**Valenciennes**	A	D	0-0		15,037
12	frpr1	**Lyon**	H	L	2-3	Pauleta 62, 90	39,787
13	frpr1	**Strasbourg**	A	W	2-1	Rodrigo 6 og, Arnaud 18	25,770
14	frpr1	**Nancy**	H	D	0-0		36,495
15	frpr1	**Nice**	A	L	1-2	N'Gog 32	11,776
16	frpr1	**Caen**	H	L	0-1		37,148
17	frpr1	**Auxerre**	A	W	1-0	Luyindula 50	11,015
18	frpr1	**Toulouse**	H	L	1-2	Pauleta 90 pen	34,095
19	frpr1	**St Etienne**	A	W	1-0	Luyindula 51	31,219
20	frpr1	**Lens**	H	W	3-0	Pauleta 59, Diane 65, 67	35,658
21	frpr1	**Lorient**	A	L	0-1		12,385
22	frpr1	**Metz**	H	W	3-0	Luyindula 4, Rothen 35, Diane 54	38,862
23	frpr1	**Lille**	A	D	0-0		14,887
24	frpr1	**Le Mans**	H	D	0-0		39,970
25	frpr1	**Marseille**	A	L	1-2	Rothen 29 pen	57,000
26	frpr1	**AS Monaco**	H	D	1-1	Diane 41	32,000
27	frpr1	**Bordeaux**	A	L	0-3		30,309
28	frpr1	**Rennes**	A	L	0-2		25,723
29	frpr1	**Valenciennes**	H	D	1-1	Pauleta 81	32,368
30	frpr1	**Lyon**	A	L	2-4	Camara 45, Rothen 52 pen	37,895
31	frpr1	**Strasbourg**	H	W	1-0	Diane 73	33,000
32	frpr1	**Nancy**	A	L	0-1		19,474
33	frpr1	**Nice**	H	L	2-3	Luyindula 50, Pauleta 75	35,918
34	frpr1	**Caen**	A	L	0-3		20,933
35	frpr1	**Auxerre**	H	W	3-1	Pauleta 3, Diane 13, 86	37,671
36	frpr1	**Toulouse**	A	D	1-1	Mendy 62	31,646
37	frpr1	**St Etienne**	H	D	1-1	Clement 59	45,350
38	frpr1	**Sochaux**	A	W	2-1	Diane 22, 83	19,873

LEAGUE APPEARANCES, BOOKINGS AND CAPS

	AGE (on 01/07/08)	IN NAMED 18	APPEARANCES	COUNTING GAMES	MINUTES ON PITCH	YELLOW CARDS	RED CARDS	CAPS THIS SEASON	NATIONAL SIDE
Goalkeepers									
Jerome Alonzo	35	38	0	0	0	0	0	-	France
Mickael Landreau	29	38	38	38	3420	0	0	5	France
Defenders									
Sylvain Armand	27	37	35	34	3103	6	0	-	France
Gregory Bourillon	24	30	22	19	1758	2	0	-	France
Zoumana Camara	29	38	38	38	3420	3	0	-	France
Ceara	27	31	30	27	2516	2	0	-	Brazil
Larrys Mabiala	20	5	1	0	22	0	0	1	Congo DR
Bernard Mendy	26	29	23	14	1432	1	0	-	France
Mamadou Sakho	18	28	12	6	741	1	0	-	France
Sammy Traore	32	4	1	1	79	1	0	-	Mali
Mario Yepes	32	34	27	24	2219	5	0	-	Colombia
Midfielders									
Clement Chantome	20	29	28	17	1788	3	0	-	France
Jeremy Clement	23	38	38	37	3340	6	0	-	France
Didier Digard	21	19	16	11	1050	1	0	-	France
Marcelo Gallardo	32	13	9	1	224	2	0	-	Argentina
Youssouf Mulumbu	21	3	1	0	45	0	0	-	Congo DR
Granddi Ngoyi	20	23	7	2	410	0	0	-	France
Jerome Rothen	30	32	32	28	2743	7	0	2	France
Willamis Souza	29	15	12	3	529	1	0	-	Brazil
Forwards									
Loris Arnaud	21	31	18	5	800	0	0	-	France
Yannick Boli	20	3	1	0	17	0	0	-	France
Amara Diane	25	37	37	24	2506	2	0	-	Ivory Coast
Everton Santos	21	4	1	0	4	0	0	-	Brazil
Pierre-Alain Frau	28	14	11	5	656	1	0	-	France
Peguy Luyindula	29	34	31	19	2079	2	0	-	France
David N'Gog	19	25	13	6	690	0	0	-	France
Pauleta	35	33	27	16	1741	8	0	-	Portugal
Younousse Sankhare	18	17	9	2	288	2	0	-	France

TEAM OF THE SEASON

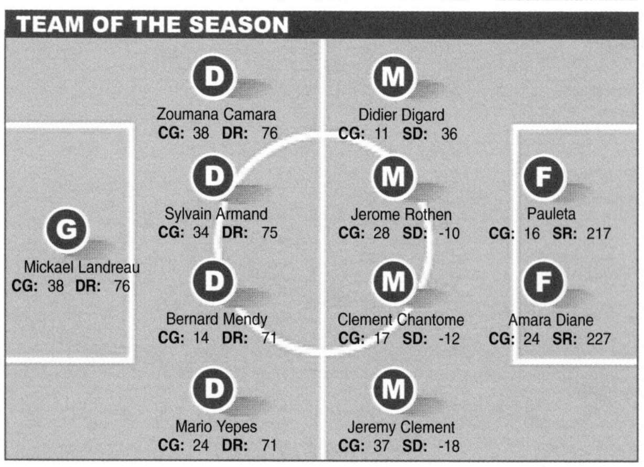

D
Zoumana Camara
CG: 38 DR: 76
M
Didier Digard
CG: 11 SD: 36
D
Sylvain Armand
CG: 34 DR: 75
M
Jerome Rothen
CG: 28 SD: -10
F
Pauleta
CG: 16 SR: 217
G
Mickael Landreau
CG: 38 DR: 76
D
Bernard Mendy
CG: 14 DR: 71
M
Clement Chantome
CG: 17 SD: -12
F
Amara Diane
CG: 24 SR: 227
D
Mario Yepes
CG: 24 DR: 71
M
Jeremy Clement
CG: 37 SD: -18

MONTHLY POINTS TALLY

AUGUST	7	39%
SEPTEMBER	4	44%
OCTOBER	1	11%
NOVEMBER	4	44%
DECEMBER	6	50%
JANUARY	7	58%
FEBRUARY	2	22%
MARCH	1	8%
APRIL	6	40%
MAY	5	56%

LEAGUE GOALS

	PLAYER	MINS	GOALS	S RATE
1	Diane	2506	11	227
2	Pauleta	1741	8	217
3	Luyindula	2079	5	415
4	Rothen	2743	3	914
5	Armand	3103	2	1551
6	Frau	656	1	656
7	N'Gog	690	1	690
8	Arnaud	800	1	800
9	Mendy	1432	1	1432
10	Ceara	2516	1	2516
11	Clement	3340	1	3340
12	Camara	3420	1	3420
	Other		0	
	TOTAL		36	

TOP POINT EARNERS

	PLAYER	GAMES	AV PTS
1	Clement Chantome	17	1.41
2	Peguy Luyindula	19	1.37
3	Jerome Rothen	28	1.25
4	Mario Yepes	24	1.21
5	Sylvain Armand	34	1.18
6	Amara Diane	24	1.17
7	Jeremy Clement	37	1.16
8	Gregory Bourillon	19	1.16
9	Zoumana Camara	38	1.13
10	Mickael Landreau	38	1.13
	CLUB AVERAGE:		1.13

DISCIPLINARY RECORDS

	PLAYER	YELLOW	RED	AVE
1	Pauleta	8	0	217
2	Jerome Rothen	7	0	391
3	Mario Yepes	5	0	443
4	Sylvain Armand	6	0	517
5	Willamis Souza	1	0	529
6	Jeremy Clement	6	0	556
7	Clement Chantome	3	0	596
8	Pierre-Alain Frau	1	0	656
9	Mamadou Sakho	1	0	741
10	Gregory Bourillon	2	0	879
11	Peguy Luyindula	2	0	1039
12	Didier Digard	1	0	1050
13	Zoumana Camara	3	0	1140
	Other	5	0	
	TOTAL	51	0	

KEY GOALKEEPER

Mickael Landreau

Goals Conceded in the League	45	Counting Games League games when player was on pitch for at least 70 minutes	38
Defensive Rating Ave number of mins between League goals conceded while on the pitch	76	Clean Sheets In League games when player was on pitch for at least 70 minutes	13

KEY PLAYERS - DEFENDERS

Zoumana Camara

Goals Conceded Number of League goals conceded while the player was on the pitch	45	Clean Sheets In League games when player was on pitch for at least 70 minutes	13
Defensive Rating Ave number of mins between League goals conceded while on the pitch	76	Club Defensive Rating Average number of mins between League goals conceded by the club this season	76

	PLAYER	CON LGE	CLEAN SHEETS	DEF RATE
1	Zoumana Camara	45	13	76 mins
2	Sylvain Armand	41	11	75 mins
3	Bernard Mendy	20	5	71 mins
4	Mario Yepes	31	8	71 mins

KEY PLAYERS - MIDFIELDERS

Didier Digard

Goals in the League	0	Contribution to Attacking Power Average number of minutes between League team goals while on pitch	95
Defensive Rating Average number of mins between League goals conceded while on the pitch	131	Scoring Difference Defensive Rating minus Contribution to Attacking Power	36

	PLAYER	LGE GOALS	DEF RATE	POWER	SCORE DIFF
1	Didier Digard	0	131	95	36 mins
2	Jerome Rothen	3	78	88	-10 mins
3	Clement Chantome	0	77	89	-12 mins
4	Jeremy Clement	1	74	92	-18 mins

KEY PLAYERS - GOALSCORERS

Pauleta

Goals in the League	8	Player Strike Rate Average number of minutes between League goals scored by player	217
Contribution to Attacking Power Average number of minutes between League team goals while on pitch	91	Club Strike Rate Average number of minutes between League goals scored by club	92

	PLAYER	LGE GOALS	POWER	STRIKE RATE
1	Pauleta	8	91	217 mins
2	Amara Diane	11	80	227 mins
3	Peguy Luyindula	5	99	415 mins
4	Jerome Rothen	3	88	914 mins

Amara Diane and Jerome Rothen

SQUAD APPEARANCES

Match	1	2	3	4	5	6	7	8	9	10	11	12	13	14	15	16	17	18	19	20	21	22	23	24	25	26	27	28	29	30	31	32	33	34	35	36	37	38
Venue	H	A	H	A	H	A	H	A	H	H	A	H	A	H	A	H	A	H	A	H	A	H	A	H	A	H	A	A	H	A	H	A	H	A	H	A	H	A
Competition	L	L	L	L	L	L	L	L	L	L	L	L	L	L	L	L	L	L	L	L	L	L	L	L	L	L	L	L	L	L	L	L	L	L	L	L	L	L
Result	D	D	L	D	D	W	D	W	L	L	D	L	W	D	L	L	W	L	W	W	L	W	D	D	L	D	L	L	D	L	W	L	L	L	W	D	D	W

Goalkeepers
Jerome Alonzo
Mickael Landreau

Defenders
Sylvain Armand
Gregory Bourillon
Zoumana Camara
Ceara
Larrys Mabiala
Bernard Mendy
Mamadou Sakho
Sammy Traore
Mario Yepes

Midfielders
Clement Chantome
Jeremy Clement
Didier Digard
Marcelo Gallardo
Youssouf Mulumbu
Granddi Ngoyi
Jerome Rothen
Willamis Souza

Forwards
Loris Arnaud
Yannick Boli
Amara Diane
Everton Santos
Pierre-Alain Frau
Peguy Luyindula
David N'Gog
Pauleta
Younousse Sankhare

KEY: On all match · On bench · Subbed or sent off (Counting game) · Subbed or sent off (playing less than 70 minutes) · Subbed on from bench (Counting Game) · Subbed on (playing less than 70 minutes) · Subbed on and then subbed or sent off (Counting Game) · Subbed on and then subbed or sent off (playing less than 70 minutes) · Not in 16

TOULOUSE

Final Position: **17th**

NICKNAME: LE TEF

KEY: ☐Won ☐Drawn ☐Lost

#	Comp	Opponent	Venue	Result	Score	Scorers	Attendance
1	frpr1	**Valenciennes**	A	L	1-3	Dieuze 11	12,153
2	frpr1	**Lyon**	H	W	1-0	Elmander 89	24,980
3	ecql1	**Liverpool**	H	L	0-1		38,000
4	frpr1	**Strasbourg**	H	L	1-3	Gignac 35	16,263
5	frpr1	**Nice**	A	D	1-1	Gignac 87	9,969
6	ecql2	**Liverpool**	A	L	0-4		43,118
7	frpr1	**Auxerre**	H	W	2-0	Elmander 67, Sisoko 90	14,795
8	frpr1	**Marseille**	A	W	2-1	Emana 10, Elmander 36	53,650
9	uc1rl1	**CSKA Sofia**	H	D	0-0		15,000
10	frpr1	**Lens**	H	D	1-1	Bergougnoux 23	15,036
11	frpr1	**Caen**	A	L	1-2	Emana 90	17,568
12	uc1rl2	**CSKA Sofia**	A	D	1-1	Gignac 90	18,000
13	frpr1	**Sochaux**	A	W	1-0	Emana 73	12,783
14	frpr1	**St Etienne**	H	L	0-2		20,114
15	ucgpe	**B Leverkusen**	A	L	0-1		20,000
16	frpr1	**Le Mans**	A	D	1-1	Dieuze 81	9,841
17	frpr1	**Metz**	H	D	0-0		16,546
18	ucgpe	**Sparta Prague**	H	L	2-3	Elmander 14, Mansare 80	14,000
19	frpr1	**Lorient**	A	L	0-1		9,575
20	frpr1	**AS Monaco**	H	D	0-0		15,434
21	ucgpe	**Zurich**	A	L	0-2		10,600
22	frpr1	**Bordeaux**	A	L	3-4	Elmander 63 pen, 72, 76	21,928
23	frpr1	**Nancy**	H	D	1-1	Elmander 17	10,000
24	frpr1	**Lille**	H	W	1-0	Elmander 68	15,586
25	frpr1	**Paris SG**	A	W	2-1	Elmander 41, 48	34,095
26	ucgpe	**S Moscow**	H	W	2-1	Santos 41, 53	14,608
27	frpr1	**Rennes**	H	D	0-0		21,183
28	frpr1	**Lyon**	A	L	2-3	Reveillere 9 og, Fabinho 90	36,587
29	frpr1	**Caen**	H	D	1-1	Dieuze 35	14,102
30	frpr1	**Strasbourg**	A	L	0-2		15,065
31	frpr1	**Nice**	H	D	1-1	Arribage 34	15,408
32	frpr1	**Nancy**	A	L	0-1		18,151
33	frpr1	**Auxerre**	A	L	0-1		9,106
34	frpr1	**Marseille**	H	D	0-0		34,502
35	frpr1	**Lens**	A	D	1-1	Emana 74	30,786
36	frpr1	**Sochaux**	H	L	1-2	Emana 84	19,109
37	frpr1	**St Etienne**	A	D	0-0		25,991
38	frpr1	**Le Mans**	H	D	1-1	Geder 62 og	17,262
39	frpr1	**Metz**	A	W	2-0	Emana 79, 81	8,960
40	frpr1	**Lorient**	H	D	0-0		20,585
41	frpr1	**AS Monaco**	A	W	2-0	Battles 3, Elmander 46	9,499
42	frpr1	**Bordeaux**	H	L	0-1		27,247
43	frpr1	**Lille**	A	L	2-3	Dieuze 25, Mansare 61	16,759
44	frpr1	**Paris SG**	H	D	1-1	Fofana 88	31,646
45	frpr1	**Rennes**	A	L	1-2	Sirieix 11	28,078
46	frpr1	**Valenciennes**	H	W	2-1	Mathieu 4, Sirieix 75	26,492

LEAGUE APPEARANCES, BOOKINGS AND CAPS

	AGE (on 01/07/08)	IN NAMED 18	APPEARANCES	COUNTING GAMES	MINUTES ON PITCH	YELLOW CARDS	RED CARDS	CAPS THIS SEASON	NATIONAL SIDE
Goalkeepers									
Nicolas Douchez	28	36	36	35	3196	0	1	-	France
Alan Mermillod	20	6	0	0	0	0	0	-	France
Rudy Riou	28	34	3	2	223	0	0	-	France
Defenders									
Dominique Arribage	37	30	27	25	2269	2	1	-	France
Mauro Cetto	26	28	24	23	2096	5	0	-	Argentina
Daniel Congre	23	11	9	8	735	0	0	-	France
Eduardo Ratinho	20	1	0	0	0	0	0	-	Brazil
Issou Malia Dao	24	1	0	0	0	0	0	-	Ivory Coast
Albin Ebondo	24	34	34	32	2982	3	0	-	France
Mohamed Fofana	23	36	19	17	1603	1	0	-	France
Herita N Ilunga	26	36	35	30	2822	8	1	-	Congo
Jon Jonsson	24	11	1	1	90	0	0	-	Sweden
Cheikh M'Bengue	19	7	3	1	140	1	0	-	France
Midfielders									
Salim Arrache	25	18	16	8	935	1	0	-	Algeria
Laurent Battles	32	36	22	13	1244	5	0	-	France
Etienne Capoue	19	14	5	0	37	0	0	-	France
Kevin Constant	21	9	2	0	23	1	0	-	France
Nicolas Dieuze	29	34	33	32	2894	6	2	-	France
Achille Emana	26	31	31	31	2771	9	0	-	Cameroon
Fabinho	28	13	9	5	534	1	0	-	Brazil
Jeremy Mathieu	24	14	14	10	967	2	0	-	France
Paulo Cesar	29	25	19	7	979	1	0	-	Brazil
Francois Sirieix	27	30	28	21	2012	6	0	-	France
Moussa Sissoko	18	36	30	15	1870	4	0	-	France
Forwards									
Bryan Bergougnoux	25	23	18	5	745	4	0	-	France
Kevin Dupuis	21	10	0	0	0	0	0	-	France
Johan Elmander	27	32	32	29	2729	7	0	5	Sweden
Pierre-Andre Gignac	23	34	28	12	1455	4	0	-	France
Fode Mansare	26	29	29	21	2031	6	1	1	Guinea
Francileudo Santos	29	15	3	1	100	0	0	3	Tunisia

TEAM OF THE SEASON

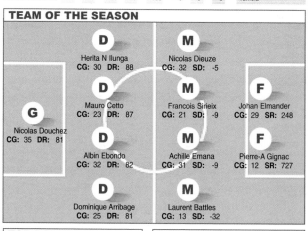

G — Nicolas Douchez — CG: 35 DR: 81

D — Herita N Ilunga — CG: 30 DR: 88

D — Mauro Cetto — CG: 23 DR: 87

D — Albin Ebondo — CG: 32 DR: 82

D — Dominique Arribage — CG: 25 DR: 81

M — Nicolas Dieuze — CG: 32 SD: -5

M — Francois Sirieix — CG: 21 SD: -9

M — Achille Emana — CG: 31 SD: -9

M — Laurent Battles — CG: 13 SD: -32

F — Johan Elmander — CG: 29 SR: 248

F — Pierre-A Gignac — CG: 12 SR: 727

MONTHLY POINTS TALLY

Month	Points	%
AUGUST	4	33%
SEPTEMBER	7	58%
OCTOBER	4	44%
NOVEMBER	2	22%
DECEMBER	8	53%
JANUARY	2	17%
FEBRUARY	1	11%
MARCH	6	40%
APRIL	4	33%
MAY	4	44%

LEAGUE GOALS

	PLAYER	MINS	GOALS	S RATE
1	Elmander	2729	11	248
2	Emana	2771	7	395
3	Dieuze	2894	4	723
4	Gignac	1455	2	727
5	Sirieix	2012	2	1006
6	Fabinho	534	1	534
7	Bergougnoux	745	1	745
8	Mathieu	967	1	967
9	Battles	1244	1	1244
10	Fofana	1603	1	1603
11	Sissoko	1870	1	1870
12	Mansare	2031	1	2031
13	Arribage	2269	1	2269
	Other		0	
	TOTAL		34	

TOP POINT EARNERS

	PLAYER	GAMES	AV PTS
1	Fode Mansare	21	**1.29**
2	Nicolas Dieuze	32	**1.28**
3	Mohamed Fofana	17	**1.24**
4	Mauro Cetto	23	**1.22**
5	Francois Sirieix	21	**1.19**
6	Achille Emana	31	**1.16**
7	Johan Elmander	29	**1.14**
8	Nicolas Douchez	35	**1.09**
9	Laurent Battles	13	**1.08**
10	Herita Nkolongo Ilunga	30	**1.07**
	CLUB AVERAGE:		**1.11**

DISCIPLINARY RECORDS

	PLAYER	YELLOW	RED	AVE
1	B Bergougnoux	4	0	**186**
2	Laurent Battles	5	0	**248**
3	Fode Mansare	6	1	**290**
4	Achille Emana	9	0	**307**
5	Herita N Ilunga	8	1	**313**
6	Francois Sirieix	6	0	**335**
7	Nicolas Dieuze	6	2	**361**
8	Pierre-A Gignac	4	0	**363**
9	Johan Elmander	7	0	**389**
10	Mauro Cetto	5	0	**419**
11	Moussa Sissoko	4	0	**467**
12	Jeremy Mathieu	2	0	**483**
13	Fabio A F Fabinho	1	0	**534**
	Other	8	2	
	TOTAL	75	6	

KEY GOALKEEPER

Nicolas Douchez

Goals Conceded in the League	39	Counting Games League games when player was on pitch for at least 70 minutes	35
Defensive Rating Ave number of mins between League goals conceded while on the pitch	81	Clean Sheets In League games when player was on pitch for at least 70 minutes	11

KEY PLAYERS - DEFENDERS

Herita Nkolongo Ilunga

Goals Conceded Number of League goals conceded while the player was on the pitch	32	Clean Sheets In League games when player was on pitch for at least 70 minutes	11
Defensive Rating Ave number of mins between League goals conceded while on the pitch	88	Club Defensive Rating Average number of mins between League goals conceded by the club this season	81

	PLAYER	CON LGE	CLEAN SHEETS	DEF RATE
1	Herita Nkolongo Ilunga	32	11	88 mins
2	Mauro Cetto	24	8	87 mins
3	Albin Ebondo	36	11	82 mins
4	Dominique Arribage	28	7	81 mins

KEY PLAYERS - MIDFIELDERS

Nicolas Dieuze

Goals in the League	4	Contribution to Attacking Power Average number of minutes between League team goals while on pitch	87
Defensive Rating Average number of mins between League goals conceded while on the pitch	82	Scoring Difference Defensive Rating minus Contribution to Attacking Power	-5

	PLAYER	LGE GOALS	DEF RATE	POWER	SCORE DIFF
1	Nicolas Dieuze	4	82	87	-5 mins
2	Francois Sirieix	2	91	100	-9 mins
3	Achille Emana	7	86	95	-9 mins
4	Laurent Battles	1	56	88	-32 mins

KEY PLAYERS - GOALSCORERS

Johan Elmander

Goals in the League	11	Player Strike Rate Average number of minutes between League goals scored by player	248
Contribution to Attacking Power Average number of minutes between League team goals while on pitch	85	Club Strike Rate Average number of minutes between League goals scored by club	95

	PLAYER	LGE GOALS	POWER	STRIKE RATE
1	Johan Elmander	11	85	248 mins
2	Achille Emana	7	95	395 mins
3	Nicolas Dieuze	4	87	723 mins
4	Pierre-Andre Gignac	2	111	727 mins

lotto
ISS
TFC
MONNE-DECROIX
IDEC
GROUPE
Johan Elmander

SQUAD APPEARANCES

Match	1	2	3	4	5	6	7	8	9	10	11	12	13	14	15	16	17	18	19	20	21	22	23
Venue	A	H	H	H	A	A	H	A	H	H	A	A	A	H	A	A	H	H	A	H	A	A	H
Competition	L	L	C	L	L	C	L	L	E	L	L	E	L	L	E	L	L	E	L	L	E	L	L
Result	L	W	L	L	D	L	W	W	D	D	L	D	W	L	L	D	D	L	L	D	L	L	D

Match	24	25	26	27	28	29	30	31	32	33	34	35	36	37	38	39	40	41	42	43	44	45	46
Venue	H	A	H	H	A	H	A	H	A	A	H	A	H	A	H	A	H	A	H	A	H	A	H
Competition	L	L	E	L	L	L	L	L	L	L	L	L	L	L	L	L	L	L	L	L	L	L	L
Result	W	W	W	D	L	D	L	D	L	L	D	D	L	D	D	W	D	W	L	L	D	L	W

Goalkeepers
Nicolas Douchez
Alan Mermillod
Rudy Riou

Defenders
Dominique Arribage
Mauro Cetto
Daniel Congre
Eduardo Ratinho
Issou Malia Dao
Albin Ebondo
Mohamed Fofana
Herita N Ilunga
Jon Jonsson
Cheikh M'Bengue

Midfielders
Salim Arrache
Laurent Battles
Etienne Capoue
Kevin Constant
Nicolas Dieuze
Achille Emana
Fabinho
Jeremy Mathieu
Paulo Cesar
Francois Sirieix
Moussa Sissoko

Forwards
Bryan Bergougnoux
Kevin Dupuis
Johan Elmander
Pierre-Andre Gignac
Fode Mansare
Francileudo Santos

KEY: On all match · On bench · Subbed or sent off (Counting game) · Subbed or sent off (playing less than 70 minutes) · Subbed on from bench (Counting Game) · Subbed on (playing less than 70 minutes) · Subbed on and then subbed or sent off (Counting Game) · Subbed on and then subbed or sent off (playing less than 70 minutes) · Not in 16

LENS

Final Position: **18th**

NICKNAME: LE SANG ET OR

KEY: ☐Won ☐Drawn ☐Lost

							Attendance
1	frpr1	**Bordeaux**	A	L	0-1		30,667
2	frpr1	**Paris SG**	H	D	0-0		38,836
3	ucqL1	**Young Boys**	A	D	1-1	Monterrubio 74	13,411
4	frpr1	**Valenciennes**	H	D	0-0		37,194
5	frpr1	**Strasbourg**	A	L	1-2	Sidi.Keita 70	24,668
6	ucqL2	**Young Boys**	H	W	5-1	Dindane 12, 54, Akale 15	
						Carriere 67, Feindouno 88	31,055
7	frpr1	**Nice**	A	L	0-1		10,858
8	frpr1	**Nancy**	H	W	1-0	Dindane 69 pen	32,774
9	uc1rl1	**Copenhagen**	H	D	1-1	Dindane 70	24,593
10	frpr1	**Toulouse**	A	D	1-1	Monterrubio 38	15,036
11	frpr1	**Lyon**	A	L	0-3		38,420
12	uc1rl2	**Copenhagen**	A	D	1-1	Carriere 14	23,861
13	frpr1	**Auxerre**	H	W	2-0	Pieroni 23 pen, Mangane 77	31,139
14	frpr1	**Marseille**	A	L	0-1		49,245
15	frpr1	**Rennes**	H	L	1-2	Monterrubio 49	30,441
16	frpr1	**St Etienne**	H	W	3-2	Coulibaly 62, Demont 64, Dindane 84	33,877
17	frpr1	**Metz**	A	W	2-1	Monterrubio 56, Khiter 86	12,268
18	frpr1	**Lorient**	H	D	1-1	Pieroni 19	30,126
19	frpr1	**Caen**	H	D	1-1	Dindane 78	36,409
20	frpr1	**Sochaux**	A	W	2-0	Dindane 20, Monterrubio 58	13,950
21	frpr1	**Le Mans**	H	L	1-3	Dindane 45	29,083
22	frpr1	**AS Monaco**	A	L	0-2		14,578
23	frpr1	**Paris SG**	A	L	0-3		35,658
24	frpr1	**Lyon**	H	W	3-0	Maoulida 55, Bisevac 70, Mangane 90	32,734
25	frpr1	**Valenciennes**	A	W	2-1	Hilton 43, Monnet-Paquet 63	14,583
26	frpr1	**Strasbourg**	H	D	2-2	Monterrubio 5 pen, 82	31,326
27	frpr1	**Caen**	A	W	4-1	Maoulida 1, Mangane 32, Remy 65	
						Seube 75 og	20,289
28	frpr1	**Nice**	H	D	0-0		31,799
29	frpr1	**Nancy**	A	L	1-2	Mangane 40	17,951
30	frpr1	**Toulouse**	H	D	1-1	Remy 8	30,786
31	frpr1	**Auxerre**	A	D	0-0		10,591
32	frpr1	**Lille**	H	L	1-2	Hilton 86	36,533
33	frpr1	**Marseille**	H	D	3-3	Maoulida 56, Mangane 65, Remy 74	40,477
34	frpr1	**Rennes**	A	L	1-3	Maoulida 32	24,411
35	frpr1	**Metz**	H	D	1-1	Monterrubio 32 pen	35,952
36	frpr1	**St Etienne**	A	L	0-2		30,000
37	frpr1	**Lorient**	A	L	0-1		13,279
38	frpr1	**Sochaux**	H	W	3-2	Coulibaly 6, Dindane 51, 69	39,478
39	frpr1	**Le Mans**	A	L	2-3	Dindane 34, Monnet-Paquet 84	12,125
40	frpr1	**AS Monaco**	H	D	0-0		39,399
41	frpr1	**Lille**	A	L	1-2	Monterrubio 69 pen	17,670
42	frpr1	**Bordeaux**	H	D	2-2	Monterrubio 69 pen, Maoulida 83	40,068

LEAGUE APPEARANCES, BOOKINGS AND CAPS

	AGE (on 01/07/08)	IN NAMED 18	APPEARANCES	COUNTING GAMES	MINUTES ON PITCH	YELLOW CARDS	RED CARDS	CAPS THIS SEASON	NATIONAL SIDE
Goalkeepers									
Ronan Le Crom	33	37	0	0	0	0	0	-	France
Vedran Runje	32	38	38	38	3420	1	0	2	Croatia
Defenders									
Lucien Aubey	24	15	12	9	942	2	0	-	France
Nadir Belhadj	26	19	19	18	1652	4	0	-	Algeria
Milan Bisevac	24	30	26	26	2305	2	0	-	Serbia
Adama Coulibaly	27	34	31	30	2748	1	0	-	Mali
Yohan Demont	30	37	31	26	2385	3	0	-	France
Vitorino Hilton	30	23	23	22	2013	7	0	-	Brazil
Fabien Laurenti	25	35	29	23	2302	3	0	-	France
Marco Ramos	25	24	13	9	948	2	0	-	Portugal
Midfielders									
Kanga Akale	27	12	9	5	627	0	0	-	Ivory Coast
Abdoulrazak Boukari	21	26	19	8	899	1	0	-	France
Eric Carriere	35	32	22	9	1138	1	0	-	France
Mounir Diane	26	10	3	1	150	0	0	-	Morocco
Sidi Yaya Keita	23	26	19	11	1082	6	1	-	Mali
Nenad Kovacevic	27	34	34	32	2912	7	0	6	Serbia
Jonathan Lacourt	21	27	17	11	1071	2	0	-	France
Kader Mangane	25	29	21	13	1402	7	1	-	Senegal
Olivier Monterrubio	31	37	34	25	2577	2	0	-	France
Julien Sable	27	31	16	12	1129	1	0	-	France
Forwards									
Daniel Cousin	31	1	1	0	23	0	0	-	Gabon
Aruna Dindane	27	28	28	22	2138	4	1	4	Ivory Coast
Simon Feindouno	22	1	1	0	25	0	0	-	Guinea
Bonaventure Kalou	30	4	4	3	283	0	0	-	Ivory Coast
Seid Khiter	23	13	9	0	232	0	0	-	France
Toifilou Maoulida	29	19	16	12	1177	2	0	-	France
Kevin Monnet-Paquet	19	30	18	4	781	0	0	-	France
Luigi Pieroni	27	16	11	2	498	1	0	2	Belgium
David Pollet	19	2	1	0	13	0	0	-	Belgium
Loic Remy	21	10	10	6	722	0	0	-	France

TEAM OF THE SEASON

G	Vedran Runje	CG: 38	DR: 65
D	Vitorino Hilton	CG: 22	DR: 71
D	Fabien Laurenti	CG: 23	DR: 69
D	Milan Bisevac	CG: 26	DR: 64
D	Adama Coulibaly	CG: 30	DR: 63
M	Olivier Monterrubio	CG: 25	SD: -8
M	Nenad Kovacevic	CG: 32	SD: -13
M	Kader Mangane	CG: 13	SD: -15
M	Julien Sable	CG: 12	SD: -159
F	Toifilou Maoulida	CG: 12	SR: 235
F	Aruna Dindane	CG: 22	SR: 267

MONTHLY POINTS TALLY

AUGUST	2	17%
SEPTEMBER	4	33%
OCTOBER	3	33%
NOVEMBER	8	67%
DECEMBER	3	33%
JANUARY	7	58%
FEBRUARY	4	44%
MARCH	3	20%
APRIL	4	27%
MAY	2	22%

LEAGUE GOALS

	PLAYER	MINS	GOALS	S RATE
1	Monterrubio	2577	9	286
2	Dindane	2138	8	267
3	Maoulida	1177	5	235
4	Mangane	1402	5	280
5	Remy	722	3	240
6	Pieroni	498	2	249
7	Monnet-Paquet	781	2	390
8	Hilton	2013	2	1006
9	Coulibaly	2748	2	1374
10	Khiter	232	1	232
11	Keita	1082	1	1082
12	Bisevac	2305	1	2305
13	Demont	2385	1	2385
	Other		0	
	TOTAL		42	

TOP POINT EARNERS

	PLAYER	GAMES	AV PTS
1	Toifilou Maoulida	12	1.33
2	Milan Bisevac	26	1.27
3	Fabien Laurenti	23	1.26
4	Olivier Monterrubio	25	1.20
5	Nadir Belhadj	18	1.11
6	Vedran Runje	38	1.05
7	Nenad Kovacevic	32	1.03
8	Kader Mangane	13	1.00
9	Yohan Demont	26	1.00
10	Aruna Dindane	22	0.95
	CLUB AVERAGE:		1.05

DISCIPLINARY RECORDS

	PLAYER	YELLOW	RED	AVE
1	Sidi Yaya Keita	6	1	154
2	Abdou K Mangane	7	1	175
3	Vitorino Hilton	7	0	287
4	Nadir Belhadj	4	0	413
5	Nenad Kovacevic	7	0	416
6	Aruna Dindane	4	1	427
7	Lucien Aubey	2	0	471
8	Marco Ramos	2	0	474
9	Luigi Pieroni	1	0	498
10	Jonathan Lacourt	2	0	535
11	Toifilou Maoulida	2	0	588
12	Fabien Laurenti	3	0	767
13	Yohan Demont	3	0	795
	Other	9	0	
	TOTAL	59	3	

KEY GOALKEEPER

Vedran Runje

Goals Conceded in the League	52	Counting Games League games when player was on pitch for at least 70 minutes	38
Defensive Rating Ave number of mins between League goals conceded while on the pitch	65	Clean Sheets In League games when player was on pitch for at least 70 minutes	9

KEY PLAYERS - DEFENDERS

Vitorino Hilton

Goals Conceded Number of League goals conceded while the player was on the pitch	28	Clean Sheets In League games when player was on pitch for at least 70 minutes	6
Defensive Rating Ave number of mins between League goals conceded while on the pitch	71	Club Defensive Rating Average number of mins between League goals conceded by the club this season	67

	PLAYER	CON LGE	CLEAN SHEETS	DEF RATE
1	Vitorino Hilton	28	6	71 mins
2	Fabien Laurenti	33	5	69 mins
3	Milan Bisevac	36	6	64 mins
4	Adama Coulibaly	43	6	63 mins

KEY PLAYERS - MIDFIELDERS

Olivier Monterrubio

Goals in the League	9	Contribution to Attacking Power Average number of minutes between League team goals while on pitch	75
Defensive Rating Average number of mins between League goals conceded while on the pitch	67	Scoring Difference Defensive Rating minus Contribution to Attacking Power	-8

	PLAYER	LGE GOALS	DEF RATE	POWER	SCORE DIFF
1	Olivier Monterrubio	9	67	75	-8 mins
2	Nenad Kovacevic	0	67	80	-13 mins
3	Kader Mangane	5	51	66	-15 mins
4	Julien Sable	0	66	225	-159 mins

KEY PLAYERS - GOALSCORERS

Toifilou Maoulida

Goals in the League	5	Player Strike Rate Average number of minutes between League goals scored by player	235
Contribution to Attacking Power Average number of minutes between League team goals while on pitch	61	Club Strike Rate Average number of minutes between League goals scored by club	81

	PLAYER	LGE GOALS	POWER	STRIKE RATE
1	Toifilou Maoulida	5	61	235 mins
2	Aruna Dindane	8	92	267 mins
3	Kader Mangane	5	66	280 mins
4	Olivier Monterrubio	9	75	286 mins

LFP

Milan Bisevac and Vitorino Hilton

SQUAD APPEARANCES

Match	1	2	3	4	5	6	7	8	9	10	11	12	13	14	15	16	17	18	19	20	21
Venue	A	H	A	H	A	H	A	H	H	A	A	A	H	A	H	H	A	H	H	A	H
Competition	L	L	E	L	L	E	L	L	E	L	L	E	L	L	L	L	L	L	L	L	L
Result	L	D	D	D	L	W	L	W	D	D	L	D	W	L	L	W	W	D	D	W	L

Match	22	23	24	25	26	27	28	29	30	31	32	33	34	35	36	37	38	39	40	41	42
Venue	A	A	H	A	H	A	H	A	H	A	H	H	A	H	A	A	H	A	H	A	H
Competition	L	L	L	L	L	L	L	L	L	L	L	L	L	L	L	L	L	L	L	L	L
Result	L	L	W	W	D	W	D	L	D	D	L	D	L	D	L	L	W	L	D	L	D

Goalkeepers
- Ronan Le Crom
- Vedran Runje

Defenders
- Lucien Aubey
- Nadir Belhadj
- Milan Bisevac
- Adama Coulibaly
- Yohan Demont
- Adil Hermach
- Vitorino Hilton
- Fabien Laurenti
- Jonathan Martins Pereira
- Marco Ramos

Midfielders
- Kanga Akale
- Abdoulrazak Boukari
- Eric Carriere
- Mounir Diane
- Sidi Yaya Keita
- Nenad Kovacevic
- Jonathan Lacourt
- Abdou Kader Mangane
- Olivier Monterrubio
- Julien Sable

Forwards
- Daniel Cousin
- Aruna Dindane
- Simon Feindouno
- Bonaventure Kalou
- Seid Khiter
- Toifilou Maoulida
- Kevin Monnet-Paquet
- Luigi Pieroni
- David Pollet
- Loic Remy

KEY: On all match · On bench · Subbed or sent off (Counting game) · Subbed or sent off (playing less than 70 minutes) · Subbed on from bench (Counting Game) · Subbed on (playing less than 70 minutes) · Subbed on and then subbed or sent off (Counting Game) · Subbed on and then subbed or sent off (playing less than 70 minutes) · Not in 16

STRASBOURG

Final Position: **19th**

NICKNAME: RACING

KEY: ☐Won ☐Drawn ☐Lost

							Attendance
1	frpr1	**Marseille**	H	D	0-0		26,397
2	frpr1	**Nice**	A	L	0-1		11,815
3	frpr1	**Auxerre**	H	W	3-0	Renteria 23, 67, Gameiro 90	20,045
4	frpr1	**Toulouse**	A	W	3-1	Mouloungui 18, Fanchone 54	
						Gameiro 72	16,263
5	frpr1	**Lens**	H	W	2-1	Renteria 55, Cohade 64	24,668
6	frpr1	**St Etienne**	A	L	0-2		25,694
7	frpr1	**Lorient**	H	D	0-0		20,260
8	frpr1	**Sochaux**	A	D	0-0		16,078
9	frpr1	**Le Mans**	H	L	0-1		17,971
10	frpr1	**Metz**	A	W	2-1	Mouloungui 41, Renteria 51	15,140
11	frpr1	**Bordeaux**	H	D	1-1	Gameiro 15	18,865
12	frpr1	**Lille**	A	W	3-0	Mouloungui 35, Rodrigo 41, Johansen 68	12,147
13	frpr1	**Paris SG**	H	L	1-2	Renteria 49	25,770
14	frpr1	**AS Monaco**	A	L	0-3		9,448
15	frpr1	**Valenciennes**	H	D	0-0		15,889
16	frpr1	**Lyon**	A	L	0-5		34,595
17	frpr1	**Rennes**	H	W	3-0	Alvaro Santos 8, 86, Renteria 65	20,000
18	frpr1	**Nancy**	H	D	0-0		19,087
19	frpr1	**Caen**	A	L	0-2		20,391
20	frpr1	**Nice**	H	L	0-1		15,047
21	frpr1	**Auxerre**	A	D	1-1	Fanchone 84	6,550
22	frpr1	**Toulouse**	H	W	2-0	Gameiro 21, Cohade 90	15,065
23	frpr1	**Lens**	A	D	2-2	Renteria 3, Alvaro Santos 77	31,326
24	frpr1	**St Etienne**	H	W	3-0	Cohade 38 pen, Alvaro Santos 85	
						Mulenga 90	16,766
25	frpr1	**Lorient**	A	L	0-1		12,153
26	frpr1	**Sochaux**	H	L	0-2		17,084
27	frpr1	**Le Mans**	A	W	1-0	Renteria 21	9,101
28	frpr1	**Metz**	H	L	2-3	Diop 35 og, Alvaro Santos 83 pen	18,545
29	frpr1	**Bordeaux**	A	L	0-3		19,474
30	frpr1	**Lille**	H	L	0-1		16,418
31	frpr1	**Paris SG**	A	L	0-1		33,000
32	frpr1	**AS Monaco**	H	L	0-2		19,106
33	frpr1	**Valenciennes**	A	L	0-2		14,276
34	frpr1	**Lyon**	H	L	1-2	Renteria 20	26,008
35	frpr1	**Rennes**	A	L	0-3		24,318
36	frpr1	**Nancy**	A	L	0-3		19,507
37	frpr1	**Caen**	H	L	1-4	Gameiro 22	17,311
38	frpr1	**Marseille**	A	L	3-4	Fanchone 10, Gameiro 19, Zenke 72	57,000

LEAGUE APPEARANCES, BOOKINGS AND CAPS

	AGE (on 01/07/08)	IN NAMED 18	APPEARANCES	COUNTING GAMES	MINUTES ON PITCH	YELLOW CARDS	RED CARDS	CAPS THIS SEASON	NATIONAL SIDE
Goalkeepers									
Stephane Cassard	35	38	38	37	3374	0	0	-	France
Nicolas Puydebois	27	35	1	0	46	0	0	-	France
Defenders									
Habib Bellaid	22	35	32	32	2880	7	0	-	France
Manuel Dos Santos	34	37	37	35	3240	2	1	-	France
Pierre Ducrocq	31	29	16	15	1371	1	0	-	France
Ahmed Kantari	23	3	0	0	0	0	0	-	Morocco
Ahmed Abou M Farag	26	7	2	1	91	0	0	-	Egypt
Gregory Paisley	31	36	36	36	3234	7	1	-	France
Yann Schneider	22	3	0	0	0	0	0	-	France
Zoltan Szelesi	26	30	22	21	1901	2	0	-	Hungary
Anthony Weber	21	5	0	0	0	0	0	-	France
Midfielders									
Yacine Abdessadki	27	25	23	14	1549	2	0	-	Morocco
Mamadou Bah	20	14	5	1	294	0	0	-	Guinea
Pascal Camadini	36	9	3	0	68	1	0	-	France
Renaud Cohade	23	26	26	21	2134	5	0	-	France
James Fanchone	28	30	29	12	1730	1	0	-	France
Rodrigo L Ramos	27	34	34	33	3023	9	1	-	Brazil
Emil Gargorov	27	7	2	0	20	0	0	-	Bulgaria
Romain Gasmi	21	12	1	0	22	0	0	-	France
Pascal Johansen	29	24	21	14	1479	4	0	-	France
Guillaume Lacour	27	26	26	25	2283	4	1	-	France
Quentin Othon	20	21	4	3	306	0	0	-	France
Morgan Schneiderlin	18	16	3	1	182	1	0	-	France
Forwards									
Alvaro Santos	28	30	28	8	1194	3	0	-	Brazil
Kevin Gameiro	21	37	34	15	1902	0	0	-	France
Ali Mathlouthi	21	4	3	0	43	1	0	-	France
Eric Mouloungui	24	33	33	21	2290	4	1	-	Gabon
Jacob Mulenga	24	27	22	6	840	2	0	-	Zambia
Wason Renteria	22	30	28	18	1897	5	0	-	Colombia
Simon Zenke	19	2	2	0	36	0	0	-	Nigeria

TEAM OF THE SEASON

G — Stephane Cassard — CG: 37 DR: 64

D — Habib Bellaid — CG: 32 DR: 64
D — Manuel Dos Santos — CG: 35 DR: 61
D — Gregory Paisley — CG: 36 DR: 61
D — Zoltan Szelesi — CG: 21 DR: 57

M — Renaud Cohade — CG: 21 SD: 3
M — Yacine Abdessadki — CG: 14 SD: -14
M — Rodrigo Ferrugem — CG: Lac SD: erba
M — F Ramos — CG: 33 SD: -34

F — James Fanchone — CG: 12 SR: -37
F — Wason Renteria — CG: 18 SR: 210

MONTHLY POINTS TALLY

AUGUST	10	56%
SEPTEMBER	2	22%
OCTOBER	7	78%
NOVEMBER	1	11%
DECEMBER	4	33%
JANUARY	5	42%
FEBRUARY	3	33%
MARCH	3	25%
APRIL	0	0%
MAY	0	0%

LEAGUE GOALS

	PLAYER	MINS	GOALS	S RATE
1	Renteria	1897	9	210
2	Gameiro	1902	6	317
3	Alvaro Santos	1194	5	238
4	Fanchone	1730	3	576
5	Cohade	2134	3	711
6	Mouloungui	2290	3	763
7	Zenke	36	1	36
8	Mulenga	840	1	840
9	Johansen	1479	1	1479
10	Lacerba Ram	3023	1	3023
	Other		0	
	TOTAL		33	

TOP POINT EARNERS

	PLAYER	GAMES	AV PTS
1	James Fanchone	12	1.58
2	Renaud Cohade	21	1.33
3	Yacine Abdessadki	14	1.29
4	Wason Renteria	18	1.22
5	Habib Bellaid	32	0.97
6	Stephane Cassard	37	0.95
7	Eric Mouloungui	21	0.95
8	Lacerba Ramos	33	0.94
9	Pascal Johansen	14	0.93
10	Guillaume Lacour	25	0.92
	CLUB AVERAGE:		0.92

DISCIPLINARY RECORDS

	PLAYER	YELLOW	RED	AVE
1	F Ramos	9	1	302
2	Pascal Johansen	4	0	369
3	Wason Renteria	5	0	379
4	Alvaro Santos	3	0	398
5	Gregory Paisley	7	1	404
6	Habib Bellaid	7	0	411
7	Jacob Mulenga	2	0	420
8	Renaud Cohade	5	0	426
9	Guillaume Lacour	4	1	456
10	Eric Mouloungui	4	1	458
11	Yacine Abdessadki	2	0	774
12	Zoltan Szelesi	2	0	950
13	Manuel Dos Santos	2	1	1080
	Other	2	0	
	TOTAL	58	5	

KEY GOALKEEPER

Stephane Cassard

Goals Conceded in the League	52	**Counting Games** League games when player was on pitch for at least 70 minutes	37
Defensive Rating Ave number of mins between League goals conceded while on the pitch	64	**Clean Sheets** In League games when player was on pitch for at least 70 minutes	11

KEY PLAYERS - DEFENDERS

Habib Bellaid

Goals Conceded Number of League goals conceded while the player was on the pitch	45	**Clean Sheets** In League games when player was on pitch for at least 70 minutes	9
Defensive Rating Ave number of mins between League goals conceded while on the pitch	64	**Club Defensive Rating** Average number of mins between League goals conceded by the club this season	62

	PLAYER	CON LGE	CLEAN SHEETS	DEF RATE
1	Habib Bellaid	45	9	64 mins
2	Manuel Dos Santos	53	10	61 mins
3	Gregory Paisley	53	10	61 mins
4	Zoltan Szelesi	33	6	57 mins

KEY PLAYERS - MIDFIELDERS

Renaud Cohade

Goals in the League	3	**Contribution to Attacking Power** Average number of minutes between League team goals while on pitch	85
Defensive Rating Average number of mins between League goals conceded while on the pitch	88	**Scoring Difference** Defensive Rating minus Contribution to Attacking Power	3

	PLAYER	LGE GOALS	DEF RATE	POWER	SCORE DIFF
1	Renaud Cohade	3	88	85	3 mins
2	Yacine Abdessadki	0	77	91	-14 mins
3	F Ramos	1	60	94	-34 mins
4	James Fanchone	3	59	96	-37 mins

KEY PLAYERS - GOALSCORERS

Wason Renteria

Goals in the League	9	**Player Strike Rate** Average number of minutes between League goals scored by player	210
Contribution to Attacking Power Average number of minutes between League team goals while on pitch	99	**Club Strike Rate** Average number of minutes between League goals scored by club	100

	PLAYER	LGE GOALS	POWER	STRIKE RATE
1	Wason Renteria	9	99	210 mins
2	Kevin Gameiro	6	111	317 mins
3	James Fanchone	3	96	576 mins
4	Renaud Cohade	3	85	711 mins

france
PARE-BRI
15

Wason Renteria, Kevin Gamerio and Zoltan Szelesi

SQUAD APPEARANCES

Match	1	2	3	4	5	6	7	8	9	10	11	12	13	14	15	16	17	18	19
Venue	H	A	H	A	H	A	H	A	H	A	H	A	H	A	H	A	H	H	A
Competition	L	L	L	L	L	L	L	L	L	L	L	L	L	L	L	L	L	L	L
Result	D	L	W	W	W	L	D	D	L	W	D	W	L	L	D	L	W	D	L

Match	20	21	22	23	24	25	26	27	28	29	30	31	32	33	34	35	36	37	38
Venue	H	A	H	A	H	A	H	A	H	A	H	A	H	A	H	A	A	H	A
Competition	L	L	L	L	L	L	L	L	L	L	L	L	L	L	L	L	L	L	L
Result	L	D	W	D	W	L	L	W	L	L	L	L	L	L	L	L	L	L	L

Goalkeepers
Stephane Cassard
Nicolas Puydebois
Defenders
Habib Bellaid
Manuel Dos Santos
Pierre Ducrocq
Ahmed Kantari
Ahmed Abou M Farag
Gregory Paisley
Yann Schneider
Zoltan Szelesi
Anthony Weber
Midfielders
Yacine Abdessadki
Mamadou Bah
Pascal Camadini
Renaud Cohade
James Fanchone
Rodrigo Lacerba Ramos
Emil Gargorov
Romain Gasmi
Pascal Johansen
Guillaume Lacour
Quentin Othon
Morgan Schneiderlin
Forwards
Alvaro Santos
Kevin Gameiro
Ali Mathlouthi
Eric Mouloungui
Jacob Mulenga
Wason Renteria
Simon Zenke

KEY: On all match · On bench · Subbed or sent off (Counting game) · Subbed or sent off (playing less than 70 minutes) · Subbed on from bench (Counting Game) · Subbed on (playing less than 70 minutes) · Subbed on and then subbed or sent off (Counting Game) · Subbed on and then subbed or sent off (playing less than 70 minutes) · Not in 16

METZ

Final Position: **20th**

NICKNAME: THE GARNETS

KEY: ☐Won ☐Drawn ☐Lost

#	Comp	Opponent	H/A	Res	Score	Scorers	Attendance
1	frpr1	Le Mans	A	L	0-1		9,831
2	frpr1	Lille	H	L	1-2	N'Diaye 83	15,591
3	frpr1	AS Monaco	A	L	0-2		11,392
4	frpr1	Paris SG	H	D	0-0		19,018
5	frpr1	Rennes	A	L	0-2		24,078
6	frpr1	Bordeaux	H	L	0-1		15,744
7	frpr1	Valenciennes	A	D	0-0		13,811
8	frpr1	Lyon	H	L	1-5	B.Gueye 46	21,988
9	frpr1	Caen	A	W	2-1	N'Diaye 36, Gygax 66	17,883
10	frpr1	Strasbourg	H	L	1-2	Francois 62	15,140
11	frpr1	Nice	A	L	1-3	Barbosa 68	9,525
12	frpr1	Nancy	H	D	0-0		19,585
13	frpr1	Toulouse	A	D	0-0		16,546
14	frpr1	Lens	H	L	1-2	Aguirre 69	12,268
15	frpr1	Marseille	A	L	1-3	C.Gueye 87	48,035
16	frpr1	Auxerre	H	L	0-1		10,281
17	frpr1	St Etienne	A	L	0-2		20,000
18	frpr1	Sochaux	H	L	1-2	Pjanic 87 pen	10,370
19	frpr1	Lorient	A	L	0-2		12,677
20	frpr1	Lille	A	D	1-1	Gygax 25	12,602
21	frpr1	AS Monaco	H	L	1-4	Aguirre 56	12,202
22	frpr1	Paris SG	A	L	0-3		38,862
23	frpr1	Rennes	H	D	1-1	N'Diaye 80	9,823
24	frpr1	Bordeaux	A	L	0-3		19,673
25	frpr1	Valenciennes	H	W	2-1	Gueye 51, Martinez 66 og	10,185
26	frpr1	Lyon	A	L	0-2		37,281
27	frpr1	Caen	H	W	2-1	Diop 35, Gueye 83 pen	10,767
28	frpr1	Strasbourg	A	W	3-2	Gueye 56, Barbosa 75, N'Diaye 89	18,545
29	frpr1	Nice	H	L	1-2	Pjanic 47 pen	10,683
30	frpr1	Nancy	A	L	1-2	Bessat 86	18,768
31	frpr1	Toulouse	H	L	0-2		8,960
32	frpr1	Lens	A	D	1-1	Pjanic 90	35,952
33	frpr1	Marseille	H	L	1-2	Barbosa 3	25,694
34	frpr1	Auxerre	A	D	0-0		8,620
35	frpr1	St Etienne	H	L	0-1		11,520
36	frpr1	Sochaux	A	D	0-0		17,680
37	frpr1	Lorient	H	L	1-2	Gueye 32	14,000
38	frpr1	Le Mans	H	W	4-3	Barbosa 4, Pjanic 13, Gueye 34 Bessat 83	12,263

LEAGUE APPEARANCES, BOOKINGS AND CAPS

	AGE (on 01/07/08)	IN NAMED 18	APPEARANCES	COUNTING GAMES	MINUTES ON PITCH	YELLOW CARDS	RED CARDS	CAPS THIS SEASON	NATIONAL SIDE
Goalkeepers									
Christophe Marichez	33	37	36	36	3239	0	0	-	France
Richard Trivino	31	5	2	2	180	0	0	-	France
Defenders									
Sebastien Bassong	21	21	19	16	1549	1	1	-	France
Gaetan Bong	20	16	11	6	670	1	0	-	Cameroon
Matheus C Vivian	26	18	11	8	743	2	0	-	Brazil
Eric Cubilier	29	26	22	20	1914	5	1	-	France
Luis Delgado	28	9	3	3	270	0	0	-	Angola
Pascal Delhommeau	29	35	25	19	1870	6	0	-	France
Papa Malik Diop	33	30	28	27	2465	4	0	-	Senegal
Julien Francois	28	35	33	32	2838	8	0	-	France
Cheikh Gueye	22	30	30	24	2336	9	0	-	Senegal
Stephane Leoni	32	16	11	9	897	4	0	-	France
Jeff Strasser	33	23	17	16	1469	3	0	6	Luxembourg
Midfielders									
Laurent Agouazi	24	35	32	22	2374	3	0	-	France
Cedric Barbosa	32	20	20	17	1617	5	1	-	France
Flavien Belson	21	12	6	2	320	4	0	-	France
Vincent Bessat	22	28	18	5	840	1	0	-	France
Manuel Corrales	25	9	4	2	275	2	0	-	Peru
Dino Djiba	22	9	6	1	191	1	0	-	Senegal
Daniel Gygax	26	25	25	15	1741	2	0	3	Switzerland
Miralem Pjanic	18	34	32	25	2390	5	0	-	Bosnia
Oumar Pouye	20	5	3	1	122	0	0	-	Senegal
Sebastien Renouard	24	25	17	10	1073	3	0	-	France
Forwards									
Wilmer Aguirre	25	24	17	10	1134	3	0	-	Peru
Cyril Chapuis	29	10	7	1	284	0	0	-	France
Papiss Demba Cisse	23	10	9	5	485	0	1	-	Senegal
Rudy Gestede	19	12	12	6	688	0	0	-	France
Babacar Gueye	22	27	26	16	1667	2	0	-	Senegal
Momar N'Diaye	20	34	28	7	1083	2	0	-	Senegal
Jean-E Owona	24	7	5	3	297	0	0	-	Cameroon

TEAM OF THE SEASON

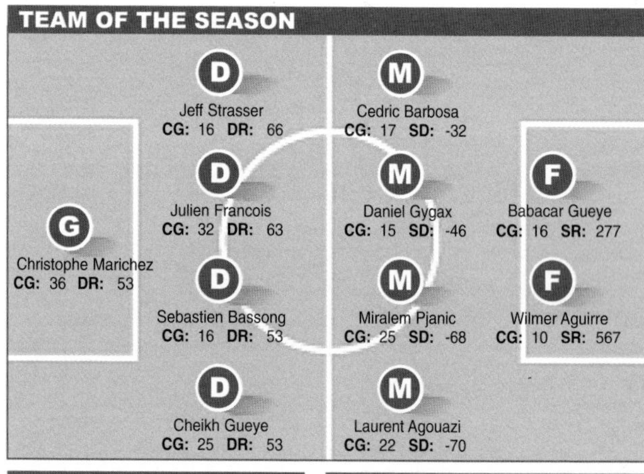

D
Jeff Strasser
CG: 16 DR: 66
M
Cedric Barbosa
CG: 17 SD: -32
D
Julien Francois
CG: 32 DR: 63
M
Daniel Gygax
CG: 15 SD: -46
F
Babacar Gueye
CG: 16 SR: 277
G
Christophe Marichez
CG: 36 DR: 53
D
Sebastien Bassong
CG: 16 DR: 53
M
Miralem Pjanic
CG: 25 SD: -68
F
Wilmer Aguirre
CG: 10 SR: 567
D
Cheikh Gueye
CG: 25 DR: 53
M
Laurent Agouazi
CG: 22 SD: -70

MONTHLY POINTS TALLY

Month	Points	%
AUGUST	1	6%
SEPTEMBER	4	44%
OCTOBER	1	11%
NOVEMBER	1	11%
DECEMBER	0	0%
JANUARY	2	17%
FEBRUARY	3	33%
MARCH	6	40%
APRIL	2	17%
MAY	4	44%

LEAGUE GOALS

	PLAYER	MINS	GOALS	S RATE
1	Gueye	1667	6	277
2	N'Diaye	1083	4	270
3	Barbosa	1617	4	404
4	Pjanic	2390	4	597
5	Bessat	840	2	420
6	Aguirre	1134	2	567
7	Gygax	1741	2	870
8	Gueye	2426	1	2426
9	Diop	2465	1	2465
10	Francois	2838	1	2838
	Other		0	
	TOTAL		27	

TOP POINT EARNERS

	PLAYER	GAMES	AV PTS
1	Babacar Gueye	16	1.13
2	Cedric Barbosa	17	1.06
3	Daniel Gygax	15	0.87
4	Julien Francois	32	0.75
5	Pascal Delhommeau	19	0.74
6	Laurent Agouazi	22	0.68
7	Christophe Marichez	36	0.67
8	Miralem Pjanic	25	0.64
9	Papa Malik Diop	27	0.63
10	Cheikh Gueye	25	0.56
	CLUB AVERAGE:		0.61

DISCIPLINARY RECORDS

	PLAYER	YELLOW	RED	AVE
1	Stephane Leoni	4	0	224
2	Cheikh Gueye	9	0	269
3	Cedric Barbosa	5	1	269
4	P Delhommeau	6	0	311
5	Eric Cubilier	5	1	319
6	Julien Francois	8	0	354
7	S Renouard	3	0	357
8	Matheus C Vivian	2	0	371
9	Wilmer Aguirre	3	0	378
10	Miralem Pjanic	5	0	478
11	Papiss D Cisse	0	1	485
12	Jeff Strasser	3	0	489
13	Momar N'Diaye	2	0	541
	Other	14	1	
	TOTAL	69	4	

KEY GOALKEEPER

Christophe Marichez

Goals Conceded in the League	61	**Counting Games** League games when player was on pitch for at least 70 minutes	36
Defensive Rating Ave number of mins between League goals conceded while on the pitch	53	**Clean Sheets** In League games when player was on pitch for at least 70 minutes	6

KEY PLAYERS - DEFENDERS

Jeff Strasser

Goals Conceded Number of League goals conceded while the player was on the pitch	22	**Clean Sheets** In League games when player was on pitch for at least 70 minutes	4
Defensive Rating Ave number of mins between League goals conceded while on the pitch	66	**Club Defensive Rating** Average number of mins between League goals conceded by the club this season	53

	PLAYER	CON LGE	CLEAN SHEETS	DEF RATE
1	Jeff Strasser	22	4	66 mins
2	Julien Francois	45	6	63 mins
3	Sebastien Bassong	29	2	53 mins
4	Cheikh Gueye	45	3	53 mins

KEY PLAYERS - MIDFIELDERS

Cedric Barbosa

Goals in the League	4	**Contribution to Attacking Power** Average number of minutes between League team goals while on pitch	85
Defensive Rating Average number of mins between League goals conceded while on the pitch	53	**Scoring Difference** Defensive Rating minus Contribution to Attacking Power	-32

	PLAYER	LGE GOALS	DEF RATE	POWER	SCORE DIFF
1	Cedric Barbosa	4	53	85	-32 mins
2	Daniel Gygax	2	56	102	-46 mins
3	Miralem Pjanic	4	51	119	-68 mins
4	Laurent Agouazi	0	48	118	-70 mins

KEY PLAYERS - GOALSCORERS

Babacar Gueye

Goals in the League	6	**Player Strike Rate** Average number of minutes between League goals scored by player	277
Contribution to Attacking Power Average number of minutes between League team goals while on pitch	83	**Club Strike Rate** Average number of minutes between League goals scored by club	122

	PLAYER	LGE GOALS	POWER	STRIKE RATE
1	Babacar Gueye	6	83	277 mins
2	Cedric Barbosa	4	85	404 mins
3	Wilmer Aguirre	2	162	567 mins
4	Miralem Pjanic	4	119	597 mins

Kappa
FC METZ
Moselle
Eric Cubilier

SQUAD APPEARANCES

Match	1	2	3	4	5	6	7	8	9	10	11	12	13	14	15	16	17	18	19
Venue	A	H	A	H	A	H	A	H	A	H	A	H	A	H	A	H	A	H	A
Competition	L	L	L	L	L	L	L	L	L	L	L	L	L	L	L	L	L	L	L
Result	L	L	L	D	L	L	D	L	W	L	L	D	D	L	L	L	L	L	L

Match	20	21	22	23	24	25	26	27	28	29	30	31	32	33	34	35	36	37	38
Venue	A	H	A	H	A	H	A	H	A	H	A	H	A	H	A	H	A	H	H
Competition	L	L	L	L	L	L	L	L	L	L	L	L	L	L	L	L	L	L	L
Result	D	L	L	D	L	W	L	W	W	L	L	L	D	L	D	L	D	L	W

Goalkeepers
Christophe Marichez
Richard Trivino

Defenders
Sebastien Bassong
Gaetan Bong
Matheus Coradini Vivian
Eric Cubilier
Luis Delgado
Pascal Delhommeau
Papa Malik Diop
Julien Francois
Cheikh Gueye
Stephane Leoni
Jeff Strasser

Midfielders
Laurent Agouazi
Cedric Barbosa
Flavien Belson
Vincent Bessat
Manuel Corrales
Dino Djiba
Daniel Gygax
Miralem Pjanic
Sebastien Renouard

Forwards
Wilmer Aguirre
Cyril Chapuis
Papiss Demba Cisse
Rudy Gestede
Babacar Gueye
Momar N'Diaye
Jean-E Effa Owona
Milan Thomas

KEY: On all match | On bench | Subbed or sent off (Counting game) | Subbed or sent off (playing less than 70 minutes) | Subbed on from bench (Counting Game) | Subbed on (playing less than 70 minutes) | Subbed on and then subbed or sent off (Counting Game) | Subbed on and then subbed or sent off (playing less than 70 minutes) | Not in 16

Champions League Group A

GROUP A TABLE

	P	W	D	L	F	A	DIF	PTS
Porto	6	3	2	1	8	7	1	11
Liverpool	6	3	1	2	18	5	13	10
Marseille	6	2	1	3	6	9	-3	7
Besiktas	6	2	0	4	4	15	-11	6

QUALIFYING - second round			L1	L2
Besiktas	4-0	Sheriff	1-0	3-0
QUALIFYING - third round				
Toulouse	0-5	Liverpool	0-1	0-4
Zürich	1-3	Besiktas	1-1	0-2

Marseille 2 Besiktas 0
Rodriguez 76, Cisse 90 — 50,000

Porto 1 Liverpool 1
Lucho Gonzalez 8 pen — Kuyt 17
45,000

Besiktas 0 Porto 1
25,000 — Quaresma 90

Liverpool 0 Marseille 1
43,000 — Valbuena 78

Former Champions and last season's losing finalists Liverpool were surprisingly beaten at home by Marseille as Mathieu Valbuena's curling strike from 20 yards flew in off Pepe Reina's crossbar.

Besiktas 2 Liverpool 1
Hyypia 13 og, Bobo 82 — Gerrard 85
33,000

Marseille 1 Porto 1
Niang 69 — Lucho Gonzalez 79 pen
50,000

Liverpool 8 Besiktas 0
Crouch 19, 89, Benayoun 32, 53, 56, Gerrard 69, Babel 78, 81 — 41,143

Yossi Benayoun and Peter Crouch tore Besiktas apart as Liverpool ran up a record Champions League winning margin of eight goals. Benayoun scored a hat-trick; Crouch netted the first and last while sub Ryan Babel claimed a brace.

Porto 2 Marseille 1
Sektioui 27, Lopez 78 — Niang 47
42,217

Besiktas 2 Marseille 1
Tello 26, Bobo 88 — Taiwo 65
20,000

Liverpool 4 Porto 1
Torres 19, 78, Gerrard 83 pen, Crouch 87 — Lopez 33
41,095

Marseille 0 Liverpool 4
53,000 — Gerrard 4, Torres 11, Kuyt 48, Babel 90

Porto 2 Besiktas 0
Lucho Gonzalez 44, Quaresma 62 — 40,000

Liverpool put in Jekyll and Hyde performances; seemingly out of the running after taking only one point from their first three games, they romped through their last three scoring 16 goals. Porto topped the group with only one defeat, while early pace-setters Marseille fell into the Uefa Cup after losing to Liverpool in the last game – the first time they had lost to an English club at home.

MARSEILLE

	PLAYER	POS	AGE	APP	MINS ON	GOALS	CARDS(Y/R)		HOME COUNTRY
1	Laurent Bonnart	DEF	28	6	540	0	0	0	France
2	Lorik Cana	MID	24	6	540	0	1	0	Albania
3	Steve Mandanda	GK	23	6	540	0	1	0	France
4	Mamadou Niang	ATT	28	6	486	2	2	0	Senegal
5	Mathieu Valbuena	MID	23	6	459	1	1	0	France
6	Julien Rodriguez	DEF	30	5	450	1	1	0	France
7	Taye Ismaila Taiwo	DEF	23	6	429	1	0	0	Nigeria
8	Gael Givet	DEF	26	5	380	0	0	0	France
9	Djibril Cisse	ATT	26	6	335	1	2	0	France
10	Boudewijn Zenden	MID	31	5	312	0	1	0	Holland
11	Benoit Cheyrou	MID	27	5	310	0	1	0	France
12	Karim Ziani	MID	25	3	270	0	0	0	Algeria
13	Samir Nasri	MID	21	4	259	0	1	0	France
14	Jacques Faty	DEF	24	3	226	0	1	0	France
15	Ronald Zubar	DEF	22	2	135	0	0	0	France
16	Andre Ayew	ATT	19	3	117	0	1	0	Ghana
17	Modeste Mbami	MID	25	2	86	0	0	0	Cameroon
18	Salim Arrache	MID	25	3	54	0	0	0	Algeria
19	Wilson Oruma	MID	31	1	7	0	0	0	Nigeria
20	Vincent Gragnic	MID	25	1	5	0	0	0	France

BESIKTAS

	PLAYER	POS	AGE	APP	MINS ON	GOALS	CARDS(Y/R)		HOME COUNTRY
1	Ibrahim Toraman	DEF	26	8	720	0	0	0	Turkey
2	Ibrahim Uzulmez	MID	34	8	720	0	0	0	Turkey
3	Serdar Ozkan	MID	21	8	659	0	2	0	Turkey
4	Deivson Rogerio da Silva	ATT	23	8	650	2	1	0	Brazil
5	Edouard Cisse	MID	30	8	649	0	1	0	France
6	Matias Emilio Delgado	MID	25	8	646	3	0	0	Argentina
7	Hakan Arikan	GK	25	6	540	0	1	0	Turkey
8	Rodrigo Alvaro Tello	MID	28	6	533	1	1	0	Chile
9	Ali Tandogan	MID	30	7	396	0	3	0	Turkey
10	Serdar Kurtulus	MID	20	6	375	0	0	0	Turkey
11	Gokhan Zan	DEF	26	4	360	0	0	0	Turkey
12	Mustafa Koray Avci	MID	29	5	286	0	1	0	Turkey
13	R Luis Pozzi Rodrigues	MID	32	5	260	0	0	0	Brazil
14	Ibrahim Akin	MID	24	5	193	0	2	0	Turkey
15	Lamine Diatta	DEF	32	3	185	0	0	0	Senegal
16	Baki Mercimek	DEF	25	2	180	0	1	0	Turkey
17	Rustu Recber	GK	35	2	180	0	1	0	Turkey
18	Federico Higuain	ATT	23	5	105	0	0	0	Argentina
19	M F Perreira Nobre	ATT	27	2	80	0	1	0	Turkey
20	Mehmet Sedef	DEF	20	1	77	0	0	0	Turkey
21	Ibrahim Kas	DEF	21	1	67	0	1	0	Turkey
22	Burak Yilmaz	MID	22	2	58	0	0	0	Turkey
23	Batuhan Karadeniz	ATT	17	1	1	0	0	0	Turkey

Champions League Group B

GROUP B TABLE

	P	W	D	L	F	A	DIF	PTS
Chelsea	6	3	3	0	9	2	7	12
Schalke	6	2	2	2	5	4	1	8
Rosenborg	6	2	1	3	6	10	-4	7
Valencia	6	1	2	3	2	6	-4	5

ROSENBORG

	PLAYER	POS	AGE	APP	MINS ON	GOALS	CARDS(Y/R)		HOME COUNTRY
1	Alexander Tettey	MID	22	8	720	0	2	0	Ghana
2	Lars Hirschfeld	GK	29	8	720	0	0	0	Canada
3	Vidar Riseth	DEF	36	8	720	1	1	0	Norway
4	Marek Sapara	MID	25	8	674	1	2	0	Slovakia
5	Abdou Razack Traore	ATT	19	8	624	0	1	0	Ivory Coast
6	Mikael Dorsin	DEF	26	7	607	0	1	0	Sweden
7	Yssouf Kone	ATT	26	8	600	4	1	0	Burkina Faso
8	Per Ciljan Skjelbred	MID	20	7	543	0	0	0	Norway
9	Steffen Iversen	ATT	32	8	496	2	0	0	Norway
10	Fredrik Stoor	DEF	24	6	438	0	0	0	Sweden
11	Bjorn Tore Kvarme	DEF	36	6	411	0	0	0	Norway
12	Christer Basma	DEF	35	6	410	0	0	0	Norway
13	Roar Strand	MID	38	6	377	0	1	0	Norway
14	Miika Koppinen	DEF	29	4	315	2	0	0	Finland
15	Didier Yah Konan	ATT	24	7	176	1	0	0	Ivory Coast
16	Oyvind Storflor	ATT	28	3	89	0	0	0	Norway

VALENCIA

	PLAYER	POS	AGE	APP	MINS ON	GOALS	CARDS(Y/R)		HOME COUNTRY
1	Ivan Helguera	DEF	33	7	630	1	1	0	Spain
2	Carlos Marchena	DEF	28	7	606	0	2	0	Spain
3	Emiliano Moretti	DEF	27	7	594	0	1	0	Italy
4	Raul Albiol	DEF	22	7	589	0	0	0	Spain
5	David Jimenez Silva	MID	22	7	529	0	0	0	Spain
6	David Villa	ATT	26	7	516	3	1	0	Spain
7	Joaquin Sanchez	MID	26	7	514	0	0	0	Spain
8	Luis Miguel	DEF	28	6	501	0	0	0	Portugal
9	Fernando Morientes	ATT	32	8	490	1	1	0	Spain
10	David Albelda	MID	30	6	465	0	1	1	Spain
11	Santiago Canizares	GK	38	5	450	0	1	0	Spain
12	Marco Antonio Caneira	DEF	29	4	311	0	0	0	Portugal
13	Timo Hildebrand	GK	29	3	270	0	0	0	Germany
14	Vicente Rodriguez	MID	26	4	250	1	0	0	Spain
15	Stephen Sunday Obayan	MID	19	3	181	0	0	0	Spain
16	Manuel Fernandes	MID	22	3	172	0	0	0	Portugal
17	Jaime Gavilan Martinez	MID	23	3	168	0	0	0	Spain
18	Ruben Baraja Vegas	MID	32	3	130	0	0	0	Spain
19	Miguel Valderrey	ATT	31	4	126	0	1	0	Spain
20	Javier Arizmendi	ATT	24	4	91	0	0	0	Spain
21	David Silva	ATT	22	1	90	1	0	0	Spain
22	Eduardo Cesar Gaspar	MID	30	1	90	0	0	0	Brazil
23	Nikola Zigic	ATT	27	3	75	0	0	0	Serbia
24	Juan Manuel Garcia	ATT	20	1	16	0	0	0	Spain
25	Alexis Ruano Delgado	DEF	22	1	7	0	0	0	Spain

QUALIFYING - second round

			L1	L2
Astana	2-10	Rosenborg	1-3	1-7

QUALIFYING - third round

			L1	L2
Tampere United	0-5	Rosenborg	0-3	0-2

Chelsea 1 **Rosenborg BK** 1
Shevchenko 53 — Koppinen 24
24,973

Schalke 0 **Valencia** 1
53,951 — Villa Sanchez 63

Rosenborg BK 0 **Schalke** 2
22,000 — Jones 62, Kuranyi 89

Valencia 1 **Chelsea** 2
Villa Sanchez 9 — J.Cole 21, Drogba 71
50,000

Chelsea 2 **Schalke** 0
Malouda 5, Drogba 47 — 35,000

Didier Drogba and Florent Malouda, former team-mates and top scorers at tiny French club Guingamp in 2003, netted the Chelsea goals that overcame Schalke and put the Blues top of their group at the halfway stage.

Rosenborg BK 2 **Valencia** 0
Kone 53, Riseth 61 — 21,119

Schalke 0 **Chelsea** 0
53,951

Valencia 0 **Rosenborg BK** 2
28,341 — Iversen 31, 57

Rosenborg BK 0 **Chelsea** 4
21,582 — Drogba 7, 20, Alex 40, J.Cole 73

Valencia 0 **Schalke** 0
30,000

Chelsea 0 **Valencia** 0
41,139

Schalke 3 **Rosenborg BK** 1
Asamoah 12, Rafinha 19, Kuranyi 36 — Kone 23
53,951

The battle for runners-up spot in Group B came down to a final match between Schalke and Norwegian champions, Rosenborg. German internationals Gerald Asamoah and Kevin Kuranyi each scored in Schalke's 3-1 win.

Spanish strugglers Valencia won their first game but lost the next three. Chelsea stuttered to a draw against Rosenborg, which cost Jose Mourinho his job, but still recovered to top the group and stay unbeaten. It left Rosenborg and Schalke to contest the runners-up spot and Schalke won both games against their rivals to go through, Kevin Kuranyi scoring in each game.

Champions League Group C

QUALIFYING - third round			L1	L2
Lazio	4-2	Dinamo Bucuresti	1-1	3-1
W Bremen	5-3	Dinamo Zagreb	2-1	3-2

Olympiakos 1 Lazio 1
Galletti 56 — Zauri 77
Played behind closed doors

Real Madrid 2 W Bremen 1
Raul 16, Van Nistelrooy 74 — Sanogo 17
70,000

Lazio 2 Real Madrid 2
Pandev 32, 75 — Van Nistelrooy 9, 61
60,000

W Bremen 1 Olympiakos 3
Hugo Almeida 32 — Stoltidis 72, Patsatzoglou 82, Kovacevic 87
35,000

Real Madrid 4 Olympiakos 2
Raul 2, Robinho 68, 83, Balboa Osa 90 — Galletti 7, Santos Correa 47
60,000

Two goals by the Brazilian star Robinho earned Real a win over Olympiakos, despite Ruud van Nistelrooy's penalty miss. Real were 2-1 down just after halftime despite Raul's early goal before Robinho's brace. The Greeks nearly levelled in injury time before Javier Balboa added a final gloss.

W Bremen 2 Lazio 1
Sanogo 28, Hugo Almeida 54 — Manfredini Sisostri 82
36,587

Lazio 2 W Bremen 1
Rocchi 57, 68 — Diego 87 pen
35,045

Olympiakos 0 Real Madrid 0
33,000

Lazio 1 Olympiakos 2
Pandev 30 — Galletti 35, Kovacevic 64
30,000

W Bremen 3 Real Madrid 2
Rosenberg 4, Sanogo 40, Hunt 58 — Robinho 14, Van Nistelrooy 71
36,350

Olympiakos 3 W Bremen 0
Stoltidis 12, 74, Kovacevic 70 — 33,500

Two rare goals by Ieroklis Stoltidis helped Olympiakos reach the Last 16 for the first time in their history with a final game win over Werder Bremen.

Real Madrid 3 Lazio 1
Baptista 13, Raul 15, Robinho 36 — Pandev 80
76,000

Greek champions Olympiakos gave Real a run for their money in Group C. The Greeks only defeat came in a closer-than-it-sounds 4-2 game in Madrid. They beat German challengers Bremen home and away, with defensive midfielder Ieroklis Stoltidis scoring three times in the two games, and took four points off mid-table Serie A side Lazio. Real's only hiccup came in a defeat to Bremen.

GROUP C TABLE

	P	W	D	L	F	A	DIF	PTS
Real Madrid	6	3	2	1	13	9	4	11
Olympiacos	6	3	2	1	11	7	4	11
W Bremen	6	2	0	4	8	13	-5	6
Lazio	6	1	2	3	8	11	-7	5

WERDER BREMEN

	PLAYER	POS	AGE	APP	MINS ON	GOALS	CARDS(Y/R)		HOME COUNTRY
1	Naldo	DEF	25	8	720	0	1	0	Brazil
2	Petri Pasanen	DEF	27	8	675	0	1	0	Finland
3	Daniel Jensen	MID	29	8	644	1	1	0	Denmark
4	Per Mertesacker	DEF	23	7	630	0	0	0	Germany
5	Diego	MID	23	7	629	3	2	1	Brazil
6	Tim Wiese	GK	26	6	540	0	0	0	Germany
7	Boubacar Sanogo	ATT	25	7	486	4	1	0	Ivory Coast
8	Frank Baumann	MID	32	6	472	0	0	0	Germany
9	Markus Rosenberg	ATT	25	7	455	1	1	0	Sweden
10	Miguel Hugo Almeida	ATT	24	7	428	3	1	0	Portugal
11	Dusko Tosic	DEF	23	6	329	0	0	0	Serbia
12	Jurica Vranjes	MID	28	4	327	0	1	0	Croatia
13	Clemens Fritz	DEF	27	5	322	0	0	0	Germany
14	Tim Borowski	MID	28	4	280	0	0	0	Germany
15	Christian Vander	GK	27	2	180	0	0	0	Germany
16	Torsten Frings	MID	31	2	180	0	0	0	Germany
17	Christian Schulz	DEF	25	2	170	0	1	0	Germany
18	Leon Andreasen	MID	25	3	153	0	1	0	Denmark
19	Aaron Hunt	ATT	21	2	109	1	1	0	Germany
20	G de J Carlos Alberto	MID	23	2	76	0	0	0	Brazil
21	Martin Harnik	ATT	21	4	69	0	0	0	Austria
22	Kevin Schindler	ATT	20	1	45	0	0	0	Germany

LAZIO

	PLAYER	POS	AGE	APP	MINS ON	GOALS	CARDS(Y/R)		HOME COUNTRY
1	Marco Ballotta	GK	44	8	720	0	0	0	Italy
2	Tommaso Rocchi	ATT	30	8	686	4	1	0	Italy
3	Gaby Mudingayi	MID	26	7	630	0	2	0	Belgium
4	Goran Pandev	ATT	24	7	598	5	2	0	Macedonia
5	Cristian Daniel Ledesma	MID	29	7	585	0	0	0	Argentina
6	Luciano Zauri	MID	30	7	557	1	2	0	Italy
7	Massimo Mutarelli	MID	30	7	545	1	3	1	Italy
8	Guglielmo Stendardo	DEF	27	7	529	0	2	0	Italy
9	Emilson Sanchez Cribari	DEF	28	6	468	0	1	1	Brazil
10	Valon Behrami	MID	23	5	394	0	0	1	Switzerland
11	Lorenzo De Silvestri	DEF	20	5	316	0	1	0	Italy
12	Christian Manfredini	MID	33	5	294	1	0	0	Italy
13	Stefano Mauri	MID	28	4	289	0	0	0	Italy
14	Lionel Scaloni	DEF	30	7	288	0	0	0	Argentina
15	Aleksandar Kolarov	DEF	22	3	219	0	1	0	Serbia
16	Mourad Meghni	MID	24	4	205	0	0	0	France
17	Simone Del Nero	ATT	26	5	188	0	0	0	Italy
18	Sebastiano Siviglia	DEF	35	2	180	0	0	0	Italy
19	Stephen A Makinwa	ATT	24	4	142	0	0	0	Nigeria
20	Roberto Baronio	MID	30	1	45	0	0	0	Italy
21	Igli Tare	ATT	34	2	10	0	0	0	Albania
22	Manuel Belleri	DEF	30	1	4	0	0	0	Italy

Champions League Group D

GROUP D TABLE

	P	W	D	L	F	A	DIF	PTS
AC Milan	6	4	1	1	12	5	7	13
Celtic	6	3	0	3	5	6	-1	9
Benfica	6	2	1	3	5	6	-1	7
Shakhtar Donetsk	6	2	0	4	6	11	-5	6

BENFICA

	PLAYER	POS	AGE	APP	MINS ON	GOALS	CARDS(Y/R)		HOME COUNTRY
1	Joaquim Manuel Silva	GK	32	8	720	0	0	0	Portugal
2	Konstantinos Katsouranis	MID	29	8	720	1	2	0	Greece
3	Leo	DEF	22	8	720	0	0	0	Brazil
4	Rui Costa	MID	36	8	702	2	1	0	Portugal
5	Oscar Rene Cardozo	ATT	25	8	604	3	3	0	Paraguay
6	Maxi Pereira Paez	MID	24	6	502	1	1	0	Uruguay
7	Anderson Luis da Silva	DEF	27	6	487	0	0	0	Brazil
8	Luis Filipe	DEF	29	7	448	0	2	0	Portugal
9	Cristian Rodriguez	MID	22	5	443	0	1	0	Uruguay
10	Angel Fabian Di Maria	MID	20	7	367	0	1	0	Argentina
11	Petit	MID	31	4	360	0	2	0	Portugal
12	Nuno Gomes	ATT	31	7	271	1	0	0	Portugal
13	Edcarlos	DEF	23	3	270	0	0	0	Brazil
14	David Luiz	DEF	21	3	267	0	2	0	Brazil
15	Gilles Augustin Binya	MID	23	4	222	0	0	1	Cameroon
16	Nuno Assis	MID	30	5	206	0	0	0	Portugal
17	Nelson Marcos	DEF	25	3	179	0	0	0	Portugal
18	Miguel Vitor	DEF	19	2	162	0	1	0	Portugal
19	Gonzalo Bergessio	ATT	23	3	117	0	0	0	Argentina
20	Freddy Adu	ATT	19	3	86	0	0	0	America
21	Fabio Coentrao	MID	20	1	45	0	0	0	Portugal
22	Romeu Ribeiro	MID	18	1	17	0	0	0	Portugal

SHAKHTAR DONETSK

	PLAYER	POS	AGE	APP	MINS ON	GOALS	CARDS(Y/R)		HOME COUNTRY
1	Andri Pyatov	GK	23	8	720	0	0	0	Ukraine
2	Darijo Srna	MID	26	8	720	0	3	0	Croatia
3	Razvan Rat	DEF	27	8	702	0	0	0	Romania
4	Ilsinho	DEF	22	8	649	0	2	0	Brazil
5	Rodrigues Jadson	MID	24	8	631	1	0	0	Brazil
6	Dmytro Chygrynskiy	DEF	21	7	630	0	1	0	Ukraine
7	Brandao	ATT	28	8	627	3	4	0	Brazil
8	Fernandinho	MID	23	7	625	0	3	0	Brazil
9	Cristiano Lucarelli	ATT	32	8	594	4	2	0	Italy
10	Oleksandr Kucher	DEF	25	7	556	0	1	0	Ukraine
11	Mariusz Lewandowski	MID	29	7	477	0	1	0	Poland
12	Tomas Hubschman	DEF	26	6	382	0	0	0	Czech Republic
13	Olexandr Glatkyi	ATT	20	7	206	0	0	0	Ukraine
14	Igor Duljaj	MID	28	4	126	0	0	0	Serbia
15	Nery Alberto Castillo	ATT	24	5	115	1	2	0	Mexico
16	Volodymyr Yezerskyy	DEF	31	2	97	0	0	0	Ukraine
17	Willian	MID	19	2	42	0	0	0	Brazil
18	Zvonimir Vukic	MID	28	1	21	0	0	0	Serbia

QUALIFYING - second round			L1	L2
Pyunik	1-4	Shakhtar	0-2	1-2
QUALIFYING - third round			**L1**	**L2**
S Moskva	2-2	Celtic (3-4p)	1-1	1-1
Benfica	3-1	København	2-1	1-0
Salzburg	2-3	Shakhtar	1-0	1-3

AC Milan 2 Benfica 1
Pirlo 9, Inzaghi 24 — Soares Ribeiro 90
35,000

Shakhtar Donetsk 2 Celtic 0
Brandao 6, C.Lucarelli 8
28,000

Benfica 0 Shakhtar Donetsk 1
50,000 — Jadson 42

Celtic 2 AC Milan 1
McManus 62, S McDonald 90 — Kaka 68 pen
60,000

Scottish Premier League top scorer Scott McDonald shocked holders Milan with a last minute winner at Celtic Park. The Aussie struck in the 89th minute after a Kaka penalty had levelled Stephen McManus' scruffy opener.

AC Milan 4 Shakhtar Donetsk 1
Gilardino 6, 14, Seedorf 63, 69 — C.Lucarelli 51
40,000

Benfica 1 Celtic 0
Cardozo 87
55,000

Celtic 1 Benfica 0
McGeady 45
52,000

Shakhtar Donetsk 0 AC Milan 3
35,000 — Inzaghi 67, 90, Kaka 71

Benfica 1 AC Milan 1
Pereira Paez 20 — Pirlo 15
40,000

Celtic 2 Shakhtar Donetsk 1
Jarosik 45, Donati 90 — Brandao 4
59,146

AC Milan 1 Celtic 0
Inzaghi 70
38,409

Shakhtar Donetsk 1 Benfica 2
C.Lucarelli 30 pen — Cardozo 6, 22
25,000

Benfica did Celtic a huge favour as two early Oscar Cardozo goals gave the Portuguese side a lead they didn't surrender in the Ukraine. Although Celtic lost tamely in Milan it meant they still went through to the Last 16.

DI MARIA
20

Holders Milan sailed serenely through Group D with only a defeat at Celtic Park to trouble them, but a scrap developed for the runners-up spot, eventually decided by Celtic's three home wins. However, Ukrainians Shakhtar looked favourites with a game to go as a home win over struggling Benfica would have put them through. Instead Benfica won to claim the Uefa Cup spot.

Champions League Group E

GROUP E TABLE	P	W	D	L	F	A	DIF	PTS
Barcelona	6	4	2	0	12	3	9	14
Lyon	6	3	1	2	11	10	1	10
Rangers	6	2	1	3	7	9	-2	7
Stuttgart	6	1	0	5	7	15	-8	3

QUALIFYING - second round			L1	L2
Rangers	3-0	Zeta	2-0	1-0

QUALIFYING - third round			L1	L2
Rangers	1-0	Crvena Zvezda	1-0	0-0

Barcelona 3 Lyon 0
Clerc 21 og, Messi 82, Henry 90 — 90,000

Rangers 2 Stuttgart 1
Adam 62, Darcheville 74 pen — Gomez 56 — 49,795

Lyon 0 Rangers 3
38,000 — McCulloch 23, Cousin 47, Beasley 53

Lee McCulloch headed Rangers into the lead against French champions Lyon and two further goals in five minutes from DaMarcus Beasley and Daniel Cousin provided the shock result of the night in Europe.

Stuttgart 0 Barcelona 2
51,300 — Puyol 53, Messi 68

Rangers 0 Barcelona 0
49,957

Stuttgart 0 Lyon 2
51,300 — Santos 54, Benzema 78

Barcelona 2 Rangers 0
Henry 6, Messi 43 — 80,000

Lyon 4 Stuttgart 2
Ben Arfa 6, 37, Kallstrom 15, Juninho 90 — Gomez 16, 56 — 38,000

Lyon 2 Barcelona 2
Juninho 7, 80 pen — Iniesta 3, Messi 58 pen — 38,000

Free kick supremo Juninho struck twice from dead ball situations to claim a confidence-boosting point against Barcelona. Lyon twice came from behind with Juninho's free kick levelling Andres Iniesta's early strike before he and Lionel Messi traded penalties.

Stuttgart 3 Rangers 2
Claudemir da Silva 45, Pardo Segura 62, Marica 85 — Adam 27, Ferguson 69 — 51,300

Barcelona 3 Stuttgart 1
Dos Santos 36, Eto'o 58, De Assis Moreira 67 — da Silva 3 — 60,000

Rangers 0 Lyon 3
50,062 — Govou 16, Benzema 85, 88

Rangers were the surprise package in Group E, beating both German and French champions in their first two games and drawing at home to favourites Barca. However, they lost their last three and had to make do with a Uefa place with French hot-shot Karim Benzema scoring twice in Glasgow to ensure that Lyon took the runners-up spot. Barca won the group, only conceding three goals.

RANGERS

	PLAYER	POS	AGE	APP	MINS ON	GOALS	CARDS(Y/R)		HOME COUNTRY
1	Allan McGregor	GK	26	9	810	0	0	0	Scotland
2	Barry Ferguson	MID	30	9	810	1	1	0	Scotland
3	Carlos Cuellar	DEF	26	9	810	0	1	0	Spain
4	David Weir	DEF	38	9	810	0	2	0	Scotland
5	Alan Hutton	DEF	23	8	720	0	4	0	Scotland
6	Kevin Thomson	MID	25	8	720	0	4	0	Scotland
7	Ibrahim Hemdani	MID	30	8	713	0	0	0	France
8	Sasa Papac	DEF	28	8	700	0	1	0	Bosnia
9	Lee McCulloch	MID	30	8	643	1	2	0	Scotland
10	DaMarcus Beasley	MID	26	8	413	2	0	0	United States
11	Jean-Claude Darcheville	ATT	32	7	408	1	0	1	France
12	Daniel Cousin	ATT	31	7	331	1	0	0	Gabon
13	Charlie Adam	MID	22	5	284	2	1	0	Scotland
14	Steven Whittaker	DEF	24	4	278	0	0	0	Scotland
15	Kirk Broadfoot	DEF	23	2	180	0	1	0	Scotland
16	Nacho Novo	ATT	29	6	167	1	0	0	Spain
17	Steven Naismith	ATT	21	3	100	0	0	0	Scotland
18	Kris Boyd	ATT	24	1	7	0	0	0	Scotland
19	Amdy Faye	MID	31	1	5	0	1	0	Senegal

STUTTGART

	PLAYER	POS	AGE	APP	MINS ON	GOALS	CARDS(Y/R)		HOME COUNTRY
1	Fernando Meira	DEF	30	6	540	0	2	0	Portugal
2	Raphael Schafer	GK	29	6	540	0	1	0	Germany
3	Serdar Tasci	DEF	21	6	454	0	1	0	Germany
4	Cacau	ATT	27	5	414	1	1	0	Brazil
5	Roberto Hilbert	MID	23	5	384	0	1	0	Germany
6	Mario Gomez	ATT	22	4	360	3	0	0	Germany
7	Pavel Pardo	MID	31	4	360	1	1	0	Mexico
8	Ricardo Osorio	DEF	28	5	346	0	0	0	Mexico
9	Sami Khedira	MID	21	5	317	0	1	0	Germany
10	Arthur Boka	DEF	25	3	270	0	0	0	Ivory Coast
11	Mathieu Delpierre	DEF	27	3	270	0	0	0	France
12	Yildiray Basturk	MID	29	4	243	0	1	0	Turkey
13	Alexander Farnerud	MID	24	4	233	0	0	0	Sweden
14	Ciprian Marica	ATT	22	4	221	1	0	0	Romania
15	Antonio da Silva	MID	30	3	204	1	0	0	Brazil
16	Ludovic Magnin	DEF	29	3	185	0	1	0	Switzerland
17	Thomas Hitzlsperger	MID	26	2	180	0	0	0	Germany
18	Andreas Beck	DEF	21	2	166	0	0	0	Germany
19	Ewerthon	ATT	27	4	140	0	0	0	Brazil
20	Silvio Meissner	MID	35	3	94	0	0	0	Germany
21	Manuel Fischer	ATT	18	1	19	0	0	0	Germany

Champions League Group F

GROUP F TABLE

	P	W	D	L	F	A	DIF	PTS
Man Utd	6	5	1	0	13	4	9	16
Roma	6	3	2	1	11	6	5	11
Sporting Lisbon	6	2	1	3	9	8	1	7
Dynamo Kiev	6	0	0	6	4	19	-15	0

SPORTING LISBON

	PLAYER	POS	AGE	APP	MINS ON	GOALS	CARDS(Y/R)		HOME COUNTRY
1	Abel Ferreira	DEF	29	6	540	1	1	0	Portugal
2	Joao Moutinho	MID	21	6	540	1	1	0	Portugal
3	Liedson	ATT	30	6	540	4	0	0	Brazil
4	Tonel	DEF	28	6	540	1	1	0	Portugal
5	Miguel Veloso	MID	22	6	480	0	1	0	Portugal
6	Anderson Polga	DEF	29	5	450	2	2	0	Brazil
7	Marat Izmailov	MID	25	6	417	0	0	0	Russia
8	Leandro Romagnoli	MID	27	5	390	0	1	0	Argentina
9	Ronny Heberson	DEF	22	5	389	0	0	0	Brazil
10	Yannick Djalo	ATT	22	4	330	0	0	0	Portugal
11	Simon Vukcevic	MID	22	6	247	0	1	0	Montenegro
12	Milan Purovic	ATT	23	4	203	0	0	0	Montenegro
13	Rui Patricio	GK	20	2	180	0	0	0	Portugal
14	Tiago Alexandre Ferreira	GK	33	2	180	0	0	0	Portugal
15	Vladimir Stojkovic	GK	24	2	180	0	0	0	Serbia
16	Adrien Silva	MID	19	1	90	0	0	0	Portugal
17	Marian Had	DEF	25	1	90	0	1	0	Slovakia
18	Pontus Farnerud	MID	28	2	76	0	0	0	Sweden
19	Carlos Paredes	MID	31	2	34	0	0	0	Paraguay
20	Bruno Pereirinha	MID	20	3	28	0	0	0	Portugal
21	Luis Celsinho	MID	19	1	10	0	0	0	Brazil
22	Luis Paez	ATT	18	1	5	0	0	0	Paraguay
23	Pereira Della Gladstone	DEF	23	1	1	0	0	0	Brazil

DYNAMO KIEV

	PLAYER	POS	AGE	APP	MINS ON	GOALS	CARDS(Y/R)		HOME COUNTRY
1	Goran Gavrancic	DEF	29	7	630	0	1	0	Serbia
2	Oleg Gusev	MID	25	8	573	0	0	0	Ukraine
3	Oleksander Shovkovskyi	GK	33	6	540	0	0	0	Ukraine
4	Maksim Shatskikh	ATT	29	7	507	1	0	0	Uzbekistan
5	Tiberiu Ghioane	MID	27	6	459	0	1	0	Romania
6	Carlos Correa	DEF	27	6	451	0	2	0	Brazil
7	Marjan Markovic	DEF	26	5	450	0	0	0	Serbia
8	Ismael Bangoura	ATT	23	6	378	3	0	0	Guinea
9	Andriy Nesmachniy	DEF	29	4	360	0	0	0	Ukraine
10	Badr El Kaddouri	MID	27	4	360	0	0	0	Morocco
11	Pape Diakhate	DEF	24	4	360	0	4	0	Senegal
12	Diogo Rincon	ATT	28	5	339	1	0	0	Brazil
13	Atanda Ayila Yussuf	MID	23	3	270	0	1	0	Nigeria
14	Taras Mykhalik	MID	24	3	270	0	1	0	Ukraine
15	Vladislav Vashchuk	DEF	33	3	270	1	1	0	Ukraine
16	Sergei Rebrov	ATT	34	5	256	1	0	0	Ukraine
17	Michael	MID	25	3	226	0	0	0	Brazil
18	Artem Milevskiy	ATT	23	4	198	0	0	0	Ukraine
19	Oleh Dopilka	DEF	22	2	180	0	0	0	Ukraine
20	Serhiy Fedorov	DEF	33	2	180	0	0	0	Ukraine
21	Milos Ninkovic	MID	23	3	172	0	0	0	Serbia
22	Valentin Belkevich	MID	35	4	112	0	0	0	Belarus
23	Ruslan Rotan	MID	26	4	107	0	0	0	Ukraine
24	Oleksandr Rybka	GK	21	1	90	0	0	0	Ukraine
25	Taras Lutsenko	GK	34	1	90	0	0	0	Ukraine
26	Giacomace Freitas Kleber	ATT	24	2	57	0	1	0	Brazil
27	Artem Kravets	ATT	19	1	35	0	0	0	Ukraine

QUALIFYING - third round

			L1	L2
Sarajevo	0-4	Dynamo Kiev	0-1	0-3

Roma 2 **Dinamo Kiev** 0
Perrotta 9, Totti 70 — 60,000

Sp Lisbon 0 **Man Utd** 1
39,514 — Ronaldo 62

Dinamo Kiev 1 **Sp Lisbon** 2
Vashchuk 28 — Tonel 14, Anderson Polga 38
40,000

Man Utd 1 **Roma** 0
Rooney 70 — 73,652

Dinamo Kiev 2 **Man Utd** 4
Rincon 34, Bangoura 78 — Ferdinand 10, Rooney 18, Ronaldo 41, 68 pen
35,000

Roma 2 **Sp Lisbon** 1
Dos Santos 15, Vucinic 70 — Liedson 18
60,000

Roma beat rivals Sporting thanks to sub Mirko Vucinic's strike. A replacement for talisman Francesco Totti, the Montenegrin's goal settled a game started by Juan's header with a Sporting reply from his fellow Brazilian Liedson.

Man Utd 4 **Dinamo Kiev** 0
Pique 31, Tevez 37, Rooney 76, Ronaldo 88 — 73,000

Gerard Pique scored a goal in a rare start and Carlos Tevez made it two before the Wayne Rooney and Cristiano Ronaldo double act shot United to one of an amazing series of four-goal wins.

Sp Lisbon 2 **Roma** 2
Liedson 22, 63 — Cassetti 4, Anderson Polga 89 og
35,000

Dinamo Kiev 1 **Roma** 4
Bangoura 63 — Panucci 4, Giuly 32, Vucinic 36, 78
15,000

Man Utd 2 **Sp Lisbon** 1
Tevez 61, Ronaldo 90 — Abel 21
75,000

Roma 1 **Man Utd** 1
Mancini 71 — Pique 34
50,000

Sp Lisbon 3 **Dinamo Kiev** 0
Anderson Polga 35 pen, Moutinho 67, Liedson 88 — 19,402

United look the form side in Europe, taking 16 points from Group F. They qualified after four games and took four points off high-flying Roma. Cristiano Ronaldo hit five goals. Roma found it easy to finish in the runners-up spot but had to rely on a 90th minute own goal by Anderson Polga in Lisbon to claim a draw against Sporting. Kiev were the group's whipping boys, conceding 19.

Champions League Group G

GROUP G TABLE

	P	W	D	L	F	A	DIF	PTS
Inter Milan	6	5	0	1	12	4	8	15
Fenerbahçe	6	3	2	1	8	6	2	11
PSV	6	2	1	3	3	6	-3	7
CSKA Moscow	6	0	1	5	7	14	-7	1

QUALIFYING - third round

			L1	L2
Fenerbahçe	3-0	Anderlecht	1-0	2-0

Fenerbahce 1 **Inter Milan** 0
Deivid 43 — 45,000

Brazilian midfielder Deivid de Souza gave Inter a wake-up call in Istanbul. Alex slipped to the by-line and his cross was volleyed fiercely home by Deivid. "We had nine players missing tonight," moaned Inter coach Roberto Mancini.

PSV Eindhoven 2 **CSKA Moscow** 1
Lazovic 60, Perez 81 — Love 89
32,500

CSKA Moscow 2 **Fenerbahce** 2
Krasic 49, Love 53 pen — de Souza 9, Deivid 85
25,000

Inter Milan 2 **PSV Eindhoven** 0
Ibrahimovic 15 pen, 31 — 40,000

CSKA Moscow 1 **Inter Milan** 2
de Assis Silva 32 — Crespo 52, Samuel 80
24,000

PSV Eindhoven 0 **Fenerbahce** 0
35,000

Fenerbahce 2 **PSV Eindhoven** 0
Marcellis 28 og, Semih Senturk 30 — 45,000

Inter Milan 4 **CSKA Moscow** 2
Ibrahimovic 33, 75, Cambiasso 34, 68 — de Assis Silva 23, Love 31
40,000

CSKA astonished themselves by taking a two goal lead in the San Siro. But three minutes after Vagner Love had made it 2-0, goals by Zlatan Ibrahimovic and Esteban Cambiasso had levelled. Both scored again for a final 4-2 score-line.

CSKA Moscow 0 **PSV Eindhoven** 1
25,000 — Farfan 39

Inter Milan 3 **Fenerbahce** 0
Cruz 55, Ibrahimovic 66, Jimenez 90 — 25,000

Fenerbahce 3 **CSKA Moscow** 1
de Souza 32, Boral 45, 90 — Abon de Souza 30 og
45,745

PSV Eindhoven 0 **Inter Milan** 1
34,500 — Cruz 64

Inter had a few surprises but recovered to dominate Group G with five wins. Fenerbahce were good value for a win over the Italian giants and were clear runners-up despite going down to three second half goals in the San Siro where in-form Julio Cruz opened the scoring. PSV may have been favourites for second but only took one point off Fenerbahce to slip into the Uefa spot.

PSV EINDHOVEN

	PLAYER	POS	AGE	APP	MINS ON	GOALS	CARDS(Y/R)		HOME COUNTRY
1	Carlos Salcido	DEF	28	6	540	0	1	0	Mexico
2	Heurelho da Silva Gomes	GK	27	6	540	0	0	0	Brazil
3	Danko Lazovic	ATT	25	6	526	1	2	0	Serbia
4	Mendes de Araujo Alves	DEF	23	5	450	0	0	0	Brazil
5	Timmy Simons	MID	31	5	450	0	0	0	Belgium
6	Jefferson Farfan	ATT	23	6	410	1	2	0	Peru
7	Edison Vincente Mendez	MID	29	6	389	0	1	1	Ecuador
8	Dirk Marcellis	DEF	20	4	360	0	2	0	Holland
9	Kenneth Perez	MID	33	6	341	1	0	0	Denmark
10	Jason Culina	MID	27	4	284	0	1	0	Australia
11	Mike Zonneveld	DEF	27	4	258	0	0	0	Holland
12	Eric Addo	DEF	29	3	237	0	0	0	Ghana
13	Jan Kromkamp	DEF	27	4	223	0	0	0	Holland
14	Otman Bakkal	MID	23	4	186	0	0	0	Holland
15	Danny Koevermans	ATT	29	5	181	0	0	0	Holland
16	Ibrahim Afellay	MID	22	3	181	0	0	0	Holland
17	Manuel da Costa	DEF	22	1	90	0	0	0	Portugal
18	Slobodan Rajkovic	DEF	19	1	90	0	0	0	Serbia
19	Tommie van der Leegte	MID	31	1	79	0	0	0	Holland
20	Ismail Aissati	MID	19	3	55	0	0	0	Holland
21	Jonathan Reis	ATT	19	1	7	0	0	0	Brazil

CSKA MOSCOW

	PLAYER	POS	AGE	APP	MINS ON	GOALS	CARDS(Y/R)		HOME COUNTRY
1	Alexei Berezutsky	DEF	26	6	540	0	1	0	Russia
2	Yuri Zhirkov	MID	24	6	540	0	3	0	Russia
3	Sergei Ignashevitch	DEF	28	5	450	0	0	0	Russia
4	Elvir Rahimic	MID	32	5	432	0	3	0	Bosnia
5	Vasili Berezutsky	DEF	26	5	383	0	1	0	Russia
6	Dudu Cearense	MID	25	5	375	0	3	0	Brazil
7	Deividas Semberas	DEF	29	4	360	0	1	0	Lithuania
8	Milos Krasic	MID	23	4	360	1	1	0	Serbia
9	Yevgeny Aldonin	MID	28	5	316	0	0	0	Russia
10	Jo	ATT	21	4	315	2	0	0	Brazil
11	Igor Akinfeev	GK	22	3	270	0	0	0	Russia
12	Vagner Love	ATT	24	3	270	3	0	0	Brazil
13	Veniamin Mandrikin	GK	26	3	270	0	0	0	Russia
14	Anton Grigoriev	DEF	22	4	231	0	0	0	Russia
15	David Janczyk	ATT	20	3	195	0	0	0	Poland
16	Daniel Carvalho	MID	25	2	180	0	1	0	Brazil
17	Eduardo Ratinho	DEF	20	4	144	0	0	0	Brazil
18	Moreira Ramon Osni	MID	20	2	105	0	0	0	Brazil
19	Caner Erkin	MID	19	2	75	0	1	0	Turkey
20	Chidi Odiah	DEF	24	2	62	0	0	0	Nigeria
21	Pavel Mamaev	MID	19	1	45	0	0	0	Russia
22	Ivan Taranov	ATT	21	2	22	0	0	0	Russia
23	Evgeni Pomazan	GK	19	0	0	0	0	0	Russian
24	Rolan Gusev	MID	30	0	0	0	0	0	Russia

Champions League Group H

GROUP H TABLE

	P	W	D	L	F	A	DIF	PTS
Sevilla	6	5	0	1	14	7	7	15
Arsenal	6	4	1	1	14	4	10	13
Slavia Prague	6	1	2	3	5	16	-11	5
Steaua Bucharest	6	0	1	5	4	10	-6	1

SLAVIA PRAGUE

	PLAYER	POS	AGE	APP	MINS ON	GOALS	CARDS(Y/R)		HOME COUNTRY
1	Marek Suchy	MID	20	8	720	0	0	0	Czech Republic
2	Matej Krajcik	MID	30	8	720	0	3	0	Czech Republic
3	Martin Vaniak	GK	37	7	630	0	0	0	Czech Republic
4	Mickael Tavares	MID	25	7	601	0	2	0	Cape Verde
5	Daniel Pudil	MID	22	6	522	1	1	0	Czech Republic
6	David Hubacek	DEF	31	6	495	0	1	0	Czech Republic
7	Erich Brabec	DEF	31	6	491	0	0	0	Czech Republic
8	Michal Svec	MID	21	6	478	0	1	0	Czech Republic
9	Stanislav Vlcek	ATT	32	5	449	2	1	0	Czech Republic
10	Zdenek Senkerik	ATT	27	5	436	2	1	0	Czech Republic
11	Frantisek Drizdal	DEF	29	5	405	0	0	0	Czech Republic
12	Tjani Belaid	MID	20	6	335	1	0	0	Tunisia
13	Petr Janda	MID	21	4	286	0	0	0	Czech Republic
14	Milan Ivana	MID	24	5	281	0	0	0	Slovakia
15	David Kalivoda	MID	25	5	253	2	0	0	Czech Republic
16	Ladislav Volesak	MID	24	7	209	0	4	0	Czech Republic
17	Vladimir Smicer	MID	35	3	121	0	0	0	Czech Republic
18	Ondrej Sourek	DEF	21	2	120	0	2	0	Czech Republic
19	Rogerio Botelho Gaucho	ATT	28	3	94	0	0	0	Brazil
20	Tomas Jablonsky	MID	20	3	91	0	0	0	Czech Republic
21	Michal Vorel	GK	33	1	90	0	0	0	Czech Republic
22	Tomas Necid	ATT	18	3	48	0	0	0	Czech Republic
23	Martin Latka	DEF	23	1	45	0	0	0	Czech Republic

STEAUA BUCHAREST

	PLAYER	POS	AGE	APP	MINS ON	GOALS	CARDS(Y/R)		HOME COUNTRY
1	Robinson Zapata	GK	29	8	720	0	0	0	Columbia
2	Ionut Rada	DEF	25	8	690	0	2	0	Romania
3	Constantin Nicolae Dica	MID	28	7	630	1	1	0	Romania
4	Nicolae Dorin Goian	DEF	27	7	630	2	1	0	Romania
5	Ovidiu Petre	MID	26	7	630	1	0	0	Romania
6	Banel Nicolita	DEF	23	6	523	0	0	0	Romania
7	Ifeanyi Emeghara	DEF	24	5	450	0	1	0	Nigeria
8	Petre Marin	DEF	34	5	450	0	2	0	Romania
9	Adrian Neaga	ATT	29	6	432	1	1	0	Romania
10	Florin Lovin	MID	26	6	390	0	1	0	Romania
11	Mihai Mircea Nesu	DEF	25	4	360	0	1	0	Romania
12	Marius Marian Croitoru	MID	27	6	323	0	3	0	Romania
13	Valentin Badea	ATT	25	5	293	1	0	0	Romania
14	Romeo Surdu	ATT	24	6	237	0	0	0	Romania
15	Victoras Iacob	ATT	27	4	230	0	0	0	Romania
16	Emanoil Valentin Badoi	MID	32	3	134	0	0	0	Romania
17	Dorel Zaharia	ATT	30	5	129	2	1	0	Romania
18	Vasilica Cristocea	MID	27	3	111	0	0	0	Romania
19	Pawel Golanski	DEF	25	2	100	0	1	0	Poland
20	Eric Cosmin Bicfalvi	DEF	20	3	98	0	0	0	Romania
21	Catalin Eugen Baciu	DEF	26	1	90	0	0	0	Romania
22	Mihaita Plesan	MID	26	1	90	0	1	0	Romania
23	Mirel Matei Radoi	DEF	27	1	90	0	1	0	Romania

ADEBAYOR

QUALIFYING - second round			L1	L2
Zilina	0-0	Slavia (3-4p)	0-0	0-0
Zaglebie Lubin	1-3	Steaua	0-1	1-2

QUALIFYING - third round			L1	L2
Sevilla	6-1	AEK	2-0	4-1
Sparta	0-5	Arsenal	0-2	0-3
Ajax	1-3	Slavia	0-1	1-2
BATE	2-4	Steaua	2-2	0-2

Arsenal 3 Sevilla 0
Fabregas 27, van Persie 60, da Silva 90
60,000

Slavia Prague 2 Steaua Bucharest 1
Senkerik 13, Belaid 63 — Goian 33
18,000

Sevilla 4 Slavia Prague 2
Kanoute 8, Fabiano 27, Escude 58, Kone 69 — Pudil 19, Kalivoda 90
40,000

Steaua Bucharest 0 Arsenal 1
28,000 — van Persie 76

Arsenal 7 Slavia Prague 0
Fabregas 5, 58, Hubacek 24 og, Walcott 41, 55, Hleb 51, Bendtner 89
59,621

Arsenal's 100% record was emphatically underlined with this thrashing of Slavia Prague. It included Theo Walcott's first and second Champions League goals as the form side of Europe took the Czechs apart.

Sevilla 2 Steaua Bucharest 1
Kanoute 5, Fabiano 17 — Petre 63
40,000

Slavia Prague 0 Arsenal 0
17,000

Steaua Bucharest 0 Sevilla 2
20,000 — Florencio Santos 25, 65

Sevilla 3 Arsenal 1
Keita 24, Fabiano 34, Kanoute 89 pen — da Silva 11
40,000

Arsene Wenger took too many liberties with his starting line-up in Spain and new Seville coach Manuel Jimenez took advantage. Luis Fabiano and Frederic Kanoute are scoring freely this season and both did so here.

Steaua Bucharest 1 Slavia Prague 1
Badea 12 — Senkerik 78
10,000

Arsenal 2 Steaua Bucharest 1
Diaby 8, Bendtner 42 — Zaharia 69
59,786

Slavia Prague 0 Sevilla 3
11,689 — Fabiano 66, Kanoute 69, Alves da Silva 87

Arsenal started like a train, winning their first three games and scoring 11 goals. Seville did a good job of derailing them though, with a 3-1 win against a weakened Gunners line-up in Spain. Luis Fabiano and Frederic Kanoute hit four goals apiece in qualifying top of the group, with a three goal defeat at the Emirates in their first game the only real blemish. Slavia grabbed the Uefa spot.

Champions League Last 16

1. LIVERPOOL V INTER MILAN

CORDOBA
2
5

Inter Milan had claims to be the form side in Europe as they ran away with Serie A but a Marco Materazzi sending off cost them dear on Merseyside.
The Milanese had to survive an hour with ten men but the steadfast Ivan Cordoba made it look easy despite missing his centre back partner. When he was carried off injured, Liverpool scented blood and Dirk Kuyt scored with a fortunate deflection on 85 minutes. Steven Gerrard's low shot from the corner of the area beat Julio Cesar to give Liverpool breathing space. The tie was over after Nicolas Burdisso saw red in Milan and Fernando Torres netted.

Liverpool 2 **Inter Milan** 0
Kuyt 85, Gerrard 90 — 41,999

Inter Milan (0) 0 **Liverpool** (2) 1
80,000 — Torres 64

2. OLYMPIAKOS V CHELSEA

MAKELELE

Avram Grant was accused of losing the plot in his selection for the Greek game but a 0-0 draw was far from a tragedy.
Petr Cech was hardly tested and Olympiakos were outclassed back at the Bridge. Michael Ballack, still missing a Champions League-winners' medal from his collection, headed Chelsea into an early lead from Frank Lampard's cross. Ballack's shot wasn't held by Antonios Nikopolidis in the 25th minutes and Lampard snapped up the rebound for 2-0 and it was game over before Salomon Kalou brought his Ivory Coast scoring form to bear with a strike from a Lampard corner.

Olympiakos 0 **Chelsea** 0
29,500

Chelsea (0) 3 **Olympiakos** (0) 0
Ballack 5, Lampard 25, Kalou 48 — 37,721

INTER MILAN

	PLAYER	POS	AGE	APP	MINS ON	GOALS	CARDS(Y/R)		HOME COUNTRY
1	Esteban Cambiasso	MID	27	8	653	2	0	0	Argentina
2	Javier Zanetti	DEF	34	8	635	0	0	0	Argentina
3	Soares Julio Cesar	GK	28	7	630	0	0	0	Brazil
4	Zlatan Ibrahimovic	ATT	26	7	599	5	2	0	Sweden
5	Maxwell	MID	26	7	582	0	0	0	Brazil
6	Dejan Stankovic	MID	29	6	515	0	1	0	Serbia
7	Cristian Chivu	DEF	27	6	491	0	3	1	Romania
8	Walter Adrian Samuel	DEF	30	5	450	1	3	0	Argentina
9	Ivan Ramiro Cordoba	DEF	31	5	435	0	0	0	Colombia
10	Julio Ricardo Cruz	ATT	33	6	365	2	0	0	Argentina
11	Douglas Maicon	DEF	26	4	360	0	0	0	Brazil
12	Hernan Jorge Crespo	ATT	32	5	292	1	0	0	Argentina
13	Nelson Rivas	DEF	25	3	270	0	1	0	Columbia
14	Santiago Hernan Solari	MID	31	5	253	0	1	0	Argentina
15	Olivier Dacourt	MID	33	3	235	0	1	0	France
16	David Suazo	ATT	28	6	222	0	0	0	Honduras
17	Luis Filipe Figo	MID	35	3	214	0	1	0	Portugal
18	Patrick Vieira	MID	32	3	128	0	0	0	France
19	Marco Materazzi	DEF	34	3	121	0	1	1	Italy
20	Francesco Bolzoni	MID	19	2	112	0	0	0	Italy
21	Cesar	MID	33	1	90	0	0	0	Brazil
22	Nicolas Andres Burdisso	DEF	27	2	64	0	1	1	Argentina
23	Antonio Luis Jimenez	MID	24	3	46	1	1	0	Italy
24	Gabriele Puccio	MID	18	1	16	0	0	0	Italy
25	Vitor Hugo Gomes Pele	MID	20	1	14	0	0	0	Portugal

OLYMPIAKOS

	PLAYER	POS	AGE	APP	MINS ON	GOALS	CARDS(Y/R)		HOME COUNTRY
1	Antonios Nikopolidis	GK	37	8	720	0	0	0	Greece
2	Ieroklis Stoltidis	MID	33	8	720	3	1	0	Greece
3	Paraskevas Antzas	DEF	31	7	630	0	2	0	Greece
4	Luciano Galletti	MID	28	7	597	3	1	0	Argentina
5	Cristian Raul Ledesma	MID	29	7	587	0	2	0	Argentina
6	Predrag Djordjevic	MID	35	7	580	0	3	0	Serbia
7	Michal Zewlakow	DEF	32	7	556	0	0	0	Poland
8	Christos Patsatzoglou	DEF	29	7	536	1	2	0	Greece
9	Vassillis Torosidis	DEF	23	7	531	0	1	1	Greece
10	Lomana LuaLua	ATT	27	6	489	0	0	0	Congo DR
11	Anastasios Pantos	DEF	32	6	455	0	2	0	Greece
12	Darko Kovacevic	ATT	34	8	416	3	1	0	Serbia
13	Julio Cesar Correa	DEF	29	5	415	1	0	0	Brazil
14	Raul Bravo	DEF	27	3	215	0	0	0	Spain
15	Didier Domi	DEF	30	2	108	0	0	0	France
16	Kostas Mendrinos	MID	23	3	100	0	0	0	Greece
17	Fernando Belluschi	MID	24	2	53	0	1	0	Argentina
18	Leonardo Geraldo	DEF	22	2	42	0	0	0	Brazil
19	Rodrigo Javier Archubi	MID	23	1	39	0	0	0	Argentina
20	Mirnes Sisic	MID	26	1	16	0	0	0	Slovenia
21	Leonel Jorge Nunez	ATT	23	3	15	0	0	0	Argentina
22	Michalis Konstantinou	ATT	30	1	12	0	0	0	Cyprus
23	Konstantinos Mitroglou	MID	20	2	10	0	1	0	Greece
24	Kyriakos Papadopoulos	DEF	17	0	0	0	0	0	Greece
25	Marco Ne	MID	24	0	0	0	0	0	Ivory Coast
26	Michalis Sifakis	GK	23	0	0	0	0	0	Greece

Champions League Last 16

3. ROMA V REAL MADRID

Kappa
WIND

Raul got Real off to a perfect start with an Arjen Robben run leading to the rejuvenated Spanish striker scoring an eighth minute away goal.
It was the last time Real had anything to celebrate though, as Serie A's second-placed team won home and away legs – both 2-1. Chilean midfielder David Pizarro levelled with a deflected shot and Mancini beat Iker Casillas in a one-on-one to win the home leg. It was tight at the Bernabeu until Real's Pepe saw red on 71 minutes and Taddei's headed goal two minutes later effectively won it. Raul gave Real hope before Vucinic's injury time goal.

Roma	2	Real Madrid	1
Pizarro 24, Amantino 58			Raul 8
			52,00
Real Madrid	(1) **1**	**Roma**	(2) **2**
Raul 75			Taddei 73, Vucinic 90
			75,000

Roma win on away goals

4. SCHALKE V PORTO

adidas
GAZPROM

Schalke goalkeeper Manuel Neuer was the penalty shoot-out hero who denied Porto a place in the quarter finals.
Poacher Kevin Kuranyi snapped up a rebound from Rafinha's parried shot to claim a narrow one goal win in Germany with Lisandro Lopez missing Porto's best chance for an away goal. The second leg was a story of Porto pressure and Neuer was busy from the start with one terrific save from Tarik Sektouri. Fucile was sent off late for Porto as Schalke held out until the 86th minute when Lopez rifled home. Porto's energy had drained away by the time penalties came and they went down 4-1.

Schalke	1	Porto	0
Kuranyi 4			53,951
Porto	(0) **1**	**Schalke**	(1) **0**
Lopez 86			45,316

Schalke win 4-1 on penalties

REAL MADRID

	PLAYER	POS	AGE	APP	MINS ON	GOALS	CARDS(Y/R)		HOME COUNTRY
1	Iker Casillas	GK	27	8	720	0	1	0	Spain
2	Raul	ATT	31	8	692	5	0	0	Spain
3	Sergio Ramos	DEF	22	7	630	0	3	0	Spain
4	Ruud Van Nistelrooy	ATT	32	7	612	4	1	0	Holland
5	Jose Maria Gutierrez	MID	31	7	571	0	1	0	Spain
6	Fabio Cannavaro	DEF	34	6	540	0	0	0	Italy
7	Marcelo Vieira da Silva	DEF	20	6	540	0	0	0	Brazil
8	Fernando Ruben Gago	MID	22	6	510	0	0	0	Argentina
9	Mahamadou Diarra	MID	27	6	498	0	2	0	Mali
10	Robinho	ATT	24	6	403	4	2	0	Brazil
11	Wesley Sneijder	MID	24	5	393	0	0	0	Holland
12	Gabriel Ivan Heinze	DEF	30	4	360	0	2	0	Argentina
13	Christoph Metzelder	DEF	27	3	270	0	0	0	Germany
14	Pepe	DEF	25	3	250	0	2	1	Portugal
15	Arjen Robben	MID	24	5	222	0	0	0	Holland
16	Julio Cesar Baptista	MID	26	3	186	1	0	0	Brazil
17	Gonzalo Gerardo Higuain	ATT	20	5	157	0	0	0	France
18	Miguel Salgado	DEF	32	2	126	0	1	0	Spain
19	Miguel Torres Gomez	DEF	22	3	120	0	1	0	Spain
20	Royston Drenthe	DEF	21	4	59	0	0	0	Holland
21	Javier Balboa Osa	MID	23	2	18	1	0	0	Spain
22	Javier Saviola	ATT	26	2	17	0	0	0	Argentina
23	Roberto Soldado	ATT	23	1	6	0	0	0	Spain

PORTO

	PLAYER	POS	AGE	APP	MINS ON	GOALS	CARDS(Y/R)		HOME COUNTRY
1	Bruno Alves	DEF	26	8	750	0	1	0	Portugal
2	Ricardo Quaresma	ATT	24	8	750	2	2	0	Portugal
3	Paulo Assuncao da Silva	MID	28	8	740	0	1	0	Brazil
4	Lisandro Lopez	ATT	25	8	734	3	0	0	Argentina
5	Helton da Silva Arruda	GK	30	7	660	0	1	0	Brazil
6	Lucho Gonzalez	MID	27	7	650	3	1	0	Portugal
7	Jorge Fucile	DEF	23	7	601	0	1	1	Uruguay
8	Jose Bosingwa	DEF	25	7	593	0	1	0	Portugal
9	Raul Meireles	MID	25	8	590	0	1	0	Portugal
10	Tarik Sektioui	ATT	31	7	392	1	0	0	Morocco
11	Milan Stepanov	DEF	25	4	360	0	2	0	Serbia
12	Pedro Emanuel	DEF	33	3	300	0	0	0	Portugal
13	Mariano Gonzalez	MID	27	6	224	0	0	0	Argentina
14	Marek Cech	DEF	25	5	211	0	0	0	Slovakia
15	Joao Paulo Andrade	DEF	27	2	180	0	0	0	Portugal
16	Ernesto Antonio Farias	ATT	28	3	146	0	0	0	Argentina
17	Helder Postiga	ATT	25	4	105	0	0	0	Portugal
18	Nuno	GK	34	1	90	0	0	0	Portugal
19	Przemyslaw Kazmierczak	MID	26	1	64	0	0	0	Poland
20	Mario Ariel Bolatti	MID	23	2	33	0	0	0	Argentina
21	Leandro Lima	MID	20	2	23	0	0	0	Brazil
22	Adriano Vieira Louzada	ATT	29	1	16	0	0	0	Brazil

Champions League Last 16

5. ARSENAL V AC MILAN

Fly
Emirates

Arsenal were kept at bay by Zelijko Kalac at the Emirates but turned the holders over at the San Siro in one of the most impressive performances in the competition.
Arsene Wenger told his young side to enjoy the occasion but they revelled in playing in one of the World's great stadia and man-of-the-match Cesc Fabregas announced his class with a 30-yarder to beat Kalac. Arsenal deserved to be ahead and emphasised the point when Theo Walcott raced onto a late pass, bounced up from a poor challenge to reach the by-line and squared for Emmanuel Adebayor to add the second goal. The Milanese applauded their opponents.

Arsenal		**0 AC Milan**	**0**
			60,082
AC Milan	(0) **0 Arsenal**		(0) **2**
			Fabregas 84, Adebayor 90
			81,879

6. CELTIC V BARCELONA

Gordon Strachan wanted goals from Celtic's home tie against Spanish giants Barca. Jan Vennegoor and Barry Robson obliged with a Lionel Messi goal sandwiched in-between.
A 2-1 lead was beyond Celtic Park expectations with novice Paul Caddis marking legend Ronaldinho, but they held out until half-time. The second half started with Thierry Henry profiting from a poor pass by Gary Caldwell and Messi ensured Barca got the win they deserved with ten minutes to go. Xavi scored after three minutes in the Nou Camp, which meant Celtic had to score three, and they barely threatened after that.

Celtic	**2 Barcelona**	**3**
Vennegoor 16, Robson 38		Messi 18, 79, Henry 52
		58,345
Barcelona	(3) **1 Celtic**	(2) **0**
Xavi Hernandez 2		75,002

AC MILAN

	PLAYER	POS	AGE	APP	MINS ON	GOALS	CARDS(Y/R)		HOME COUNTRY
1	Gennaro Ivan Gattuso	MID	30	8	720	0	2	0	Italy
2	Ricardo Kaka	MID	26	8	720	2	2	0	Brazil
3	Andrea Pirlo	MID	29	8	704	2	1	0	Italy
4	Massimo Ambrosini	MID	31	7	622	0	3	0	Italy
5	Kakha Kaladze	DEF	30	7	602	0	1	0	Georgia
6	Alessandro Nesta	DEF	32	7	589	0	1	0	Italy
7	Clarence Seedorf	MID	32	7	521	2	0	0	Holland
8	Massimo Oddo	DEF	32	6	458	0	0	0	Italy
9	Daniele Bonera	DEF	27	6	400	0	0	0	Italy
10	Zeljko Kalac	GK	35	5	361	0	0	0	Australia
11	Nelson Silva Dida	GK	34	4	359	0	0	0	Brazil
12	Filippo Inzaghi	ATT	34	5	344	4	2	0	Italy
13	Alberto Gilardino	ATT	25	7	284	2	0	0	Italy
14	Paolo Maldini	DEF	40	4	237	0	1	0	Italy
15	Marek Jankulovski	DEF	31	3	221	0	0	0	Czech Republic
16	Alexandre Pato	ATT	18	2	166	0	1	0	Brazil
17	Giuseppe Favalli	DEF	36	2	150	0	0	0	Italy
18	Sergio Serginho	MID	37	3	145	0	1	0	Brazil
19	Yoann Gourcuff	MID	21	3	98	0	0	0	France
20	Cafu	DEF	38	1	90	0	0	0	Brazil
21	Christian Brocchi	MID	32	3	72	0	0	0	Italy
22	Emerson	MID	32	3	29	0	0	0	Brazil
23	Dario Simic	DEF	32	1	28	0	0	0	Croatia

CELTIC

	PLAYER	POS	AGE	APP	MINS ON	GOALS	CARDS(Y/R)		HOME COUNTRY
1	Stephen McManus	DEF	25	10	930	1	0	0	Scotland
2	Gary Caldwell	DEF	26	10	851	0	2	0	Scotland
3	Artur Boruc	GK	28	9	840	0	0	0	Poland
4	Scott Brown	MID	23	9	838	0	5	0	Scotland
5	Paul Hartley	MID	31	9	772	1	2	0	Scotland
6	Aiden McGeady	ATT	22	10	761	1	1	0	Rep of Ireland
7	Lee Naylor	DEF	28	9	754	0	1	0	England
8	Scott McDonald	ATT	24	10	695	2	1	0	Australia
9	Massimo Donati	MID	28	10	677	1	1	0	Italy
10	Jan V of Hesselink	ATT	29	8	562	1	1	0	Holland
11	Shunsuke Nakamura	MID	30	6	461	0	0	0	Japan
12	Mark Wilson	DEF	24	5	420	0	0	0	Scotland
13	Jiri Jarosik	MID	30	5	405	1	1	0	Czech Republic
14	John Kennedy	DEF	24	5	322	0	0	0	Scotland
15	Christopher Killen	ATT	26	5	140	0	1	0	New Zealand
16	Steven Pressley	DEF	34	2	140	0	0	0	Scotland
17	Evander Sno	MID	21	5	111	0	0	0	Holland
18	Darren O'Dea	DEF	21	2	101	0	0	0	Rep of Ireland
19	Barry Robson	MID	29	1	90	1	1	0	Scotland
20	Mark Brown	GK	27	1	90	0	0	0	Scotland
21	J-J Perrier-Doumbe	DEF	29	1	78	0	0	0	Cameroon
22	Georgios Samaras	ATT	23	2	72	0	1	0	Greece
23	Paul Caddis	DEF	20	1	60	0	0	0	Scotland
24	Maciej Zurawski	ATT	31	3	43	0	0	0	Poland
25	Derek Riordan	ATT	25	1	17	0	1	0	Scotland

Champions League Last 16

7. FENERBAHCE V SEVILLA

avea

Penalties looked an unlikely way to resolve this tie after Fenerbahce won the first leg 3-2. However, the score was reversed in Spain and it took spot-kicks to separate the sides. Sub Semih Senturk netted a winner in Istanbul after Mateja Kezman and Lugano's strikes where levelled by Edu's own goal and a Julien Escude volley. Sevilla raced into a 2-0 lead through Daniel Alves and Seydou Keita at home. After Deivid pulled one back, Freddie Kanoute made it 3-1 but Deivid struck the post and then followed up to level the tie. Turkish keeper Volkan Demirel had started the game badly but saved three penalties to go home the hero.

Fenerbahce	**3**	**Sevilla**	**2**
Kezman 17, Lugano 57, Semih Senturk 87		A de Souza 23 og, Escude 66	46,000

Sevilla	(2) **3**	**Fenerbahce**	(3) **2**
Alves da Silva 5, Keita 9, Kanoute 41		Deivid 20, 79	45,000

Fenerbahce win 3-2 on penalties

8. LYON V MANCHESTER UNITED

NOVOTEL

Lyon	**1**	**Man Utd**	**1**
Benzema 53		Tevez 87	42,000

Man Utd	(1) **1**	**Lyon**	(1) **0**
Ronaldo 41			75,521

An 87th minute goal from Carlos Tevez completely changed the complexion of this tie with United grabbing both a draw and away goal to take back to Old Trafford. Karim Benzema, the French Wayne Rooney, gave Lyon the chance of their first win over English opposition for 40 years with his 54th minute goal, while United struggled to beat Gregory Coupet until Tevez struck. Cristiano Ronaldo netted the only goal of the second leg to see United through but it was never comfortable as the French champions hit the post through sub Kader Keita when they finally decided to take the game to United.

SEVILLA

	PLAYER	POS	AGE	APP	MINS ON	GOALS	CARDS(Y/R)		HOME COUNTRY
1	Ivica Dragutinovic	DEF	32	10	930	0	1	0	Serbia
2	Jesus Navas	MID	22	10	896	0	0	0	Spain
3	Andres Palop	GK	34	9	840	0	2	0	Spain
4	Daniel Alves	DEF	25	9	840	2	2	0	Brazil
5	Christian Poulsen	MID	28	9	781	0	0	0	Denmark
6	Frederic Kanoute	ATT	30	9	776	6	1	0	Mali
7	Seydou Keita	MID	28	8	685	3	4	0	Mali
8	Luis Fabiano	ATT	27	10	602	7	0	0	Brazil
9	Diego Capel	MID	20	8	595	0	0	0	Spain
10	Adriano Correia Claro	MID	23	6	559	0	3	0	Brazil
11	Julien Escude	DEF	28	5	448	2	0	0	France
12	Federico Fazio	DEF	21	4	360	0	0	0	Argentina
13	Aquivaldo Mosquera	DEF	27	5	330	0	0	0	Colombia
14	Renato	MID	29	6	286	2	0	0	Brazil
15	Josep Lluis Marti Soler	MID	33	5	187	0	0	0	Spain
16	Alexander Kerzhakov	ATT	25	3	152	1	0	0	Russia
17	Khalid Boulahrouz	DEF	26	2	135	0	0	0	Holland
18	Enzo Maresca	MID	28	4	131	0	1	0	Italy
19	Tom de Mul	MID	22	2	107	0	0	0	Belgium
20	Andreas Hinkel	DEF	26	3	102	0	0	0	Germany
21	Arouna Kone	ATT	24	3	102	1	0	0	Ivory Coast
22	Duda	MID	28	3	99	0	0	0	Portugal
23	Manuel Ortiz Toribio	DEF	23	1	90	0	0	0	Spain
24	Morgan De Sanctis	GK	31	1	90	0	0	0	Italy
25	Jose Rincon	DEF	21	1	62	0	1	0	Spain
26	Seydou Keita	ATT	28	1	45	0	0	0	Mali

LYON

	PLAYER	POS	AGE	APP	MINS ON	GOALS	CARDS(Y/R)		HOME COUNTRY
1	Sebastien Squillaci	DEF	27	8	720	0	2	0	France
2	Pernambucano Juninho	MID	33	8	697	3	2	0	Brazil
3	Sydney Govou	ATT	28	8	675	1	2	0	France
4	Kim Kallstrom	MID	25	8	632	1	2	0	Sweden
5	Fabio Grosso	DEF	30	7	630	0	2	0	Italy
6	Karim Benzema	ATT	20	7	588	4	0	0	France
7	Anthony Reveillere	DEF	28	7	546	0	3	0	France
8	Remy Vercoutre	GK	28	6	540	0	1	0	France
9	Cleber Anderson	DEF	28	5	450	0	0	0	Brazil
10	Jeremy Toulalan	MID	24	5	450	0	0	0	France
11	Hatem Ben Arfa	MID	21	8	440	2	0	0	France
12	Francois Clerc	DEF	25	7	362	0	0	0	France
13	Fabio Santos	MID	27	3	247	1	1	0	Brazil
14	Mathieu Bodmer	MID	25	5	197	0	0	0	France
15	Gregory Coupet	GK	35	2	180	0	0	0	France
16	Abdul Kader Keita	ATT	26	6	134	0	1	0	Ivory Coast
17	Milan Baros	ATT	26	3	94	0	0	0	Czech Republic
18	Cristiano Marques Cris	DEF	31	1	90	0	0	0	Brazil
19	Jean-Alain Boumsong	DEF	28	1	90	0	1	0	France
20	Fred	ATT	24	3	79	0	0	0	Brazil
21	Nadir Belhadj	DEF	26	2	70	0	0	0	Algeria
22	Loic Remy	ATT	21	1	9	0	0	0	France

Champions League Quarter Finals

1. ROMA V MANCHESTER UNITED

AIG

Wayne Rooney and Cristiano Ronaldo proved too potent a strike force for a Roma side missing their key player Francesco Totti.
The pair each scored in a 2-0 away leg win that decided the tie. First Rooney broke clear of the defence and fed Paul Scholes, who threw up an inviting chipped cross for the on-rushing Ronaldo to power home his seventh of the campaign. Rooney stole onto a Ji-Sung Park far-post header to tap home number two in the second half. The result flattered United but they looked good value as Carlos Tevez scored the only goal at Old Trafford to ensure a semi-final place.

Roma	**0**	**Man Utd**	**2**
		Ronaldo 39, Rooney 66	80,023
Man Utd	(2) **1**	**Roma**	(0) **0**
Tevez 70			74,423

2. SCHALKE V BARCELONA

unicef

Barcelona's new 17-year-old find Bojan Krkic scored the solitary goal to win the away leg at Schalke and effectively book a semi spot.
Krkic, who is the son of a Red Star Belgrade footballer and Barca scout, scored after 12 minutes. He was set up by Thierry Henry, who had just seen his shot rebound off the Schalke keeper, and flicked it across for Krkic to tap in. When the tie moved to the Nou Camp it was Yaya Toure who scored the only goal despite Schalke having much the better of the start. Kolo's brother scored his first goal in the competition after a run down the right and cross by Krkic caused panic in the German defence.

Schalke	**0**	**Barcelona**	**1**
53,951		Krkic Perez 12	
Barcelona	(1) **1**	**Schalke**	(0) **0**
Yaya Toure 43			88,000

ROMA

	PLAYER	POS	AGE	APP	MINS ON	GOALS	CARDS(Y/R)		HOME COUNTRY
1	Daniele De Rossi	MID	24	10	825	0	2	0	Italy
2	Doni	GK	28	9	810	0	0	0	Brazil
3	Philippe Mexes	DEF	26	9	765	0	2	0	France
4	Mancini	ATT	27	9	732	2	0	0	Brazil
5	Juan	DEF	29	8	696	1	1	0	Brazil
6	David Pizarro	MID	28	10	633	1	1	0	Chile
7	Marco Cassetti	DEF	31	7	596	1	4	0	Italy
8	Max Tonetto	DEF	33	8	576	0	2	0	Italy
9	Ludovic Giuly	MID	31	9	533	1	0	0	France
10	Simone Perrotta	MID	30	6	514	1	4	0	Italy
11	Francesco Totti	ATT	31	6	484	1	0	0	Italy
12	Mirko Vucinic	ATT	24	8	481	4	2	0	Montenegro
13	Christian Panucci	DEF	35	6	430	1	0	0	Italy
14	Rodrigo Ferrante Taddei	MID	28	6	408	1	1	0	Brazil
15	Cicinho	DEF	28	7	390	0	2	0	Brazil
16	Alberto Aquilani	MID	23	5	336	0	1	0	Italy
17	Matteo Ferrari	DEF	28	5	249	0	0	0	Italy
18	Mauro Esposito	ATT	29	6	152	0	0	0	Italy
19	Ahmed Apimah Barusso	MID	23	2	91	0	1	0	Ghana
20	Gianluca Curci	GK	22	1	90	0	0	0	Italy
21	Vitorino Antunes	DEF	21	1	90	0	0	0	Portugal
22	Matteo Brighi	MID	27	2	19	0	0	0	Italy

SCHALKE

	PLAYER	POS	AGE	APP	MINS ON	GOALS	CARDS(Y/R)		HOME COUNTRY
1	Heiko Westermann	DEF	24	10	930	0	2	0	Germany
2	Manuel Neuer	GK	22	10	930	0	1	0	Germany
3	Marcelo Jose Bordon	DEF	32	10	923	0	2	0	Brazil
4	Rafinha	DEF	22	10	899	1	3	0	Brazil
5	Fabian Ernst	MID	29	9	840	0	3	0	Germany
6	Jermaine Jones	MID	26	8	723	1	5	0	Germany
7	Kevin Kuranyi	ATT	26	8	672	3	2	0	Germany
8	Gerald Asamoah	ATT	29	10	599	1	0	0	Germany
9	Mladen Krstajic	DEF	34	6	570	0	1	0	Serbia
10	Halil Altintop	ATT	25	7	463	0	0	0	Turkey
11	Ivan Rakitic	MID	20	7	432	0	1	0	Croatia
12	Carlos Grossmuller	MID	25	8	409	0	2	0	Uruguay
13	Levan Kobiashvili	MID	30	5	336	0	1	0	Georgia
14	Zlatan Bajramovic	MID	28	5	299	0	0	0	Bosnia
15	Mesut Ozil	MID	19	4	264	0	1	0	Germany
16	Soren Larsen	ATT	26	4	212	0	1	0	Denmark
17	Peter Lovenkrands	ATT	28	5	203	0	0	0	Denmark
18	Christian Pander	DEF	24	2	180	0	1	0	Germany
19	Dario Rodriguez	DEF	33	2	171	0	1	0	Uruguay
20	Benedikt Howedes	DEF	20	3	98	0	0	0	Germany
21	Vicente Sanchez	ATT	28	3	55	0	0	0	Uruguay
22	Mimoun Azaouagh	MID	25	1	15	0	0	0	Germany
23	Gustavo Antonio Varela	MID	30	1	7	0	0	0	Uruguay

Champions League Quarter Finals

3. ARSENAL V LIVERPOOL

Arsenal	1	Liverpool	1
Adebayor 23			Kuyt 26
			60,041

Liverpool	(1) 4	Arsenal	(1) 2
Hyypia 30, Torres 69, Gerrard 85 pen, Babel 90		Diaby 13, Adebayor 84	41,985

Theo Walcott thought he had written his name into one of the key moments of the season when his mazy run set up Arsenal for an away goal win at Anfield.
He started deep in his own half and ended with a pass for Emmanuel Adebayor to tap in. With six minutes to go, the sides were level but Arsenal had scored two away, to Liverpool's one. However, Liverpool struck back instantly with Kolo Toure called for a penalty, converted by Steven Gerrard and Ryan Babel's injury time goal put a final gloss on the win. The tie swung on two penalty decisions, one at the Emirates not given and Toure's at Anfield, which was.

4. FENERBAHCE V CHELSEA

Several commentators underestimated Fenerbahce, who kept up their 100% home record against Chelsea in the first leg.
Brazilian midfielder Deivid scored at both ends of the park, first with an own goal on 13 minutes from Florent Malouda's cut back. Chelsea continued to dominate but couldn't add to their goal and Colin Kazim-Richards (known as Kazim Kazim in Turkey) broke clear to level. Finally Deivid's swerving shot from 30 yards flew past Carlo Cudicini to win it. An early Michael Ballack header put Chelsea in the driving seat at Stamford Bridge and Frank Lampard's late tap-in made sure.

Fenerbahce	2	Chelsea	1
Kazim-Richards 65, Deivid 81			Deivid 13 og
			46,000

Chelsea	(1) 2	Fenerbahce	(2) 0
Ballack 4, Lampard 87			38,369

ARSENAL

	PLAYER	POS	AGE	APP	MINS ON	GOALS	CARDS(Y/R)		HOME COUNTRY
1	Gael Clichy	DEF	22	10	900	0	2	0	France
2	Manuel Almunia	GK	31	9	810	0	0	0	Spain
3	Philippe Senderos	DEF	23	9	804	0	2	0	Switzerland
4	Francesc Fabregas	MID	21	10	798	6	1	0	Spain
5	Habib Kolo Toure	DEF	27	9	726	0	1	0	Ivory Coast
6	William Gallas	DEF	30	8	720	0	0	0	France
7	Alexander Hleb	MID	27	8	691	2	2	0	Belarus
8	Emmanuel Eboue	DEF	25	10	656	0	2	0	Ivory Coast
9	Mathieu Flamini	MID	24	8	643	0	2	0	France
10	Bacary Sagna	DEF	25	8	634	0	0	0	France
11	Emmanuel Adebayor	ATT	24	9	631	3	2	0	Togo
12	Robin van Persie	ATT	24	7	460	2	1	0	Holland
13	Theo Walcott	MID	19	9	459	2	1	0	England
14	Vassiriki Diaby	MID	22	6	429	2	0	0	France
15	Eduardo da Silva	ATT	25	6	368	3	0	0	Croatia
16	Gilberto Silva	MID	31	7	365	0	0	0	Brazil
17	Nicklas Bendtner	ATT	20	6	325	2	1	0	Denmark
18	Denilson	MID	20	4	288	0	2	0	Brazil
19	Jens Lehmann	GK	38	3	270	0	0	0	Germany
20	Tomas Rosicky	MID	27	5	262	1	0	0	Czech Republic
21	Alexandre Song	MID	20	3	191	0	0	0	Cameroon
22	Armand Traore	DEF	18	2	180	0	0	0	France
23	Justin Hoyte	DEF	23	2	155	0	1	0	England
24	Lassana Diarra	MID	23	3	115	0	1	0	France

FENERBAHCE

	PLAYER	POS	AGE	APP	MINS ON	GOALS	CARDS(Y/R)		HOME COUNTRY
1	Mehmet Aurelio	MID	30	12	1081	0	2	0	Turkey
2	Volkan Demirel	GK	26	11	1020	0	0	0	Turkey
3	Diego Lugano	DEF	27	11	1006	1	4	0	Uruguay
4	Alex de Souza	MID	30	12	1004	4	1	0	Brazil
5	Deivid de Souza	ATT	28	11	984	5	3	1	Brazil
6	Edu Dracana	DEF	27	10	910	0	1	0	Greece
7	Roberto Carlos	DEF	35	9	785	0	1	0	Brazil
8	Gokcek Vederson	DEF	26	11	774	0	1	0	Brazil
9	Gokhan Gonul	DEF	23	8	671	0	3	0	Turkey
10	Mateja Kezman	ATT	29	8	552	1	2	0	Serbia
11	Deniz Baris	DEF	30	6	520	0	2	0	Turkey
12	Semih Senturk	ATT	25	9	480	2	0	0	Turkey
13	Ugur Boral	MID	26	6	369	2	1	0	Turkey
14	Selcuk Sahin	MID	27	5	345	0	2	0	Turkey
15	Colin Kazim-Richards	ATT	21	10	340	1	0	0	Turkey
16	Onder Turaci	DEF	26	4	273	0	1	0	Belgium
17	Claudio Maldonado	MID	28	2	149	0	0	0	Chile
18	Tumer Metin	MID	33	3	141	0	0	0	Turkey
19	Yasin Cakmak	DEF	23	2	110	0	0	0	Turkey
20	Ali Bilgin	MID	26	5	95	0	0	0	Turkey
21	Serdar Kulbilge	GK	27	1	90	0	0	0	Turkey
23	Stephen Appiah	MID	27	2	34	0	0	0	Ghana

Champions League Semi-Final

Liverpool v Chelsea

John Arne Riise headed into his own net after 95 minutes to give Chelsea a crucial away goal from their Champions League semi-final first leg against Liverpool.

The Blues had the best chance when Frank Lampard put Joe Cole through but he mis-controlled. Didier Drogba appeared to have been hauled down by Jamie Carragher but it would have been a harsh penalty. Liverpool recovered to lead when Dirk Kuyt got the better of Claude Makelele to slot past Petr Cech. Cech produced a string of top saves, before Riise's nightmare, which makes Chelsea slight favourites for the final.

Liverpool	**1**	**Chelsea 1**
Kuyt 43		Riise 90 og
		42,180
	STATS	
6	Shots off target	4
6	Shots on target	3
6	Corners	5
20	Fouls	17
1	Offside	6
0	Yellows	1
0	Reds	0
55%	Possession	45%
Referee:		Konrad Plautz (AUS)

Chelsea's Russian owner Roman Abramovich will get his dream of seeing his side compete in a Champions League final in Moscow.

They dominated the first half with Jose Reina busy saving from Didier Drogba, Michael Essien, Michael Ballack and Salomon Kalou. However, the last save rebounded to Drogba, who lashed home. Fernando Torres levelled to cancel out the away goal as Liverpool had the better of the second half. In extra time Chelsea took over and a Frank Lampard penalty and Drogba, again, settled the tie before Ryan Babel added a consolation.

Chelsea	**(1) 3**	**Liverpool (1) 2**
Drogba 33, 105,		Torres 64, Babel 117
Lampard 98 pen		38,900
	STATS	
8	Shots off target	10
11	Shots on target	5
5	Corners	9
20	Fouls	19
8	Offside	4
0	Yellows	2
0	Reds	0
45%	Possession	55%
Referee:		Roberto Rosetti (ITA)

LIVERPOOL

	PLAYER	POS	AGE	APP	MINS ON	GOALS	CARDS(Y/R)		HOME COUNTRY
1	Jose Reina	GK	25	14	1290	0	0	0	Spain
2	Jamie Carragher	DEF	30	13	1200	0	2	0	England
3	Javier Mascherano	MID	24	13	1182	0	1	0	Argentina
4	Sami Hyypia	DEF	34	13	1171	2	1	0	Finland
5	Steven Gerrard	MID	28	13	1155	6	2	0	England
6	Dirk Kuyt	ATT	27	12	936	7	1	0	Holland
7	Fernando Torres	ATT	24	11	882	6	1	0	Spain
8	Alvaro Arbeloa	DEF	25	9	751	0	1	0	Spain
9	Ryan Babel	ATT	21	13	704	5	1	0	Holland
10	Yossi Benayoun	MID	28	11	676	3	1	0	Israel
11	John Arne Riise	MID	27	10	594	0	0	0	Norway
12	Fabio Aurelio	DEF	28	9	581	0	2	0	Brazil
13	Steve Finnan	DEF	32	7	550	0	0	0	Rep of Ireland
14	Peter Crouch	ATT	27	8	476	4	0	0	England
15	Martin Skrtel	DEF	23	5	381	0	0	0	Slovakia
16	Xabi Alonso	MID	26	4	376	0	1	0	Spain
17	Andrey Voronin	ATT	28	7	342	1	0	0	Ukraine
18	Lucas Leiva	MID	21	7	229	0	0	0	Brazil
19	Momo Sissoko	MID	23	3	183	0	1	0	Mali
20	Jermaine Pennant	MID	25	5	180	0	1	1	England
21	Sebastian Leto	MID	21	2	125	0	0	0	Argentina
22	Harry Kewell	MID	28	3	113	0	0	0	Australia
23	Daniel Agger	DEF	23	1	80	0	0	0	Denmark

Champions League Semi-Final

Barcelona v Manchester United

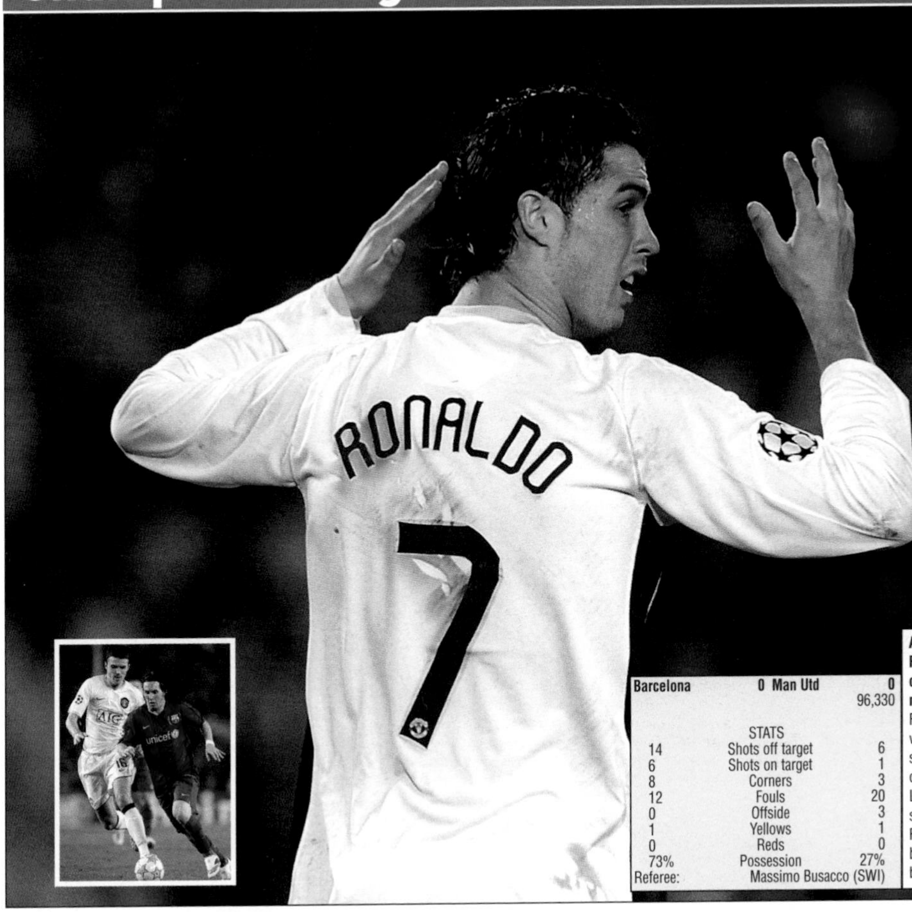

A second minute penalty miss by Cristiano Ronaldo really got to United as they were outplayed by their Spanish hosts, but managed to escape with a goalless draw.
From Wayne Rooney's corner Ronaldo's header was handled in the area by Gabriel Milito. Up stepped Ronaldo but he inexplicably drove wide of the mark. From then on it was all Barcelona; Lionel Messi dictated the pace of the game and seemingly opened United up at will. Rio Ferdinand and Wes Brown had to be at their best as Barca were in control until the final third but Edwin van der Sar was rarely troubled

Barcelona 0		Man Utd 0
		96,330
	STATS	
14	Shots off target	6
6	Shots on target	1
8	Corners	3
12	Fouls	20
0	Offside	3
1	Yellows	1
0	Reds	0
73%	Possession	27%
Referee:	Massimo Busacco (SWI)	

BARCELONA

	PLAYER	POS	AGE	APP	MINS ON	GOALS	CARDS(Y/R)		HOME COUNTRY
1	Victor Valdes	GK	26	11	990	0	0	0	Spain
2	Xavier Hernandez	MID	28	12	973	1	1	0	Spain
3	Eric Abidal	DEF	28	10	900	0	1	0	France
4	Carles Puyol	DEF	30	10	861	1	3	0	Spain
5	Andres Iniesta	MID	24	11	812	1	0	0	Spain
6	Gabriel Milito	DEF	27	9	810	0	2	0	Argentina
7	Yaya Toure	MID	25	9	757	1	3	0	Ivory Coast
8	Lionel Messi	ATT	21	9	725	6	2	0	Argentina
9	Thierry Henry	ATT	30	10	715	3	1	0	France
10	Gianluca Zambrotta	DEF	31	7	621	0	1	0	Italy
11	Ronaldinho	ATT	28	8	583	1	0	0	Brazil
12	Lilian Thuram	DEF	36	6	540	0	0	0	France
13	Samuel Eto'o	ATT	27	7	502	1	0	0	Cameroon
14	Deco	MID	30	6	501	0	2	0	Portugal
15	Rafael Marquez	DEF	29	8	402	0	3	0	Mexico
16	Bojan Krkic	ATT	17	9	360	1	0	0	Spain
17	Eidur Gudjohnsen	ATT	29	8	248	0	0	0	Iceland
18	Sylvinho	DEF	34	4	212	0	0	0	Brazil
19	Giovani dos Santos	ATT	19	5	138	1	1	0	Mexico
20	Oleguer	DEF	28	2	96	0	0	0	Spain
21	Albert Jorquera Fortia	GK	29	1	90	0	0	0	Spain
22	Jose Edmilson	MID	31	1	23	0	0	0	Brazil
23	Marc Crosas	MID	20	1	21	0	0	0	Spain

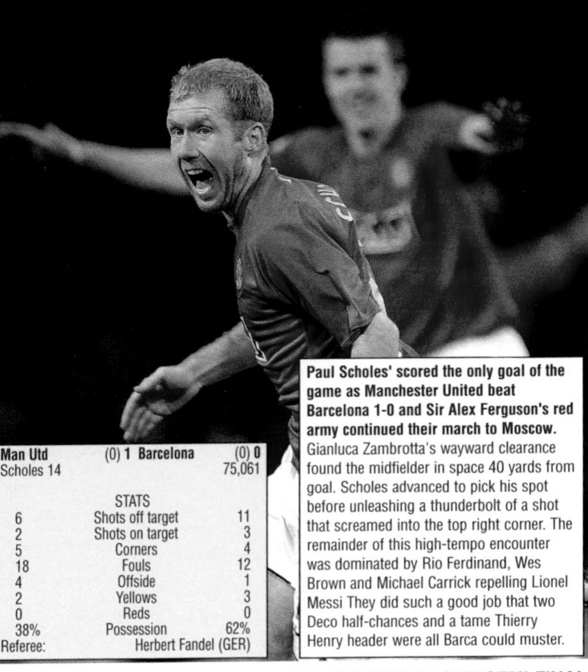

Paul Scholes' scored the only goal of the game as Manchester United beat Barcelona 1-0 and Sir Alex Ferguson's red army continued their march to Moscow.
Gianluca Zambrotta's wayward clearance found the midfielder in space 40 yards from goal. Scholes advanced to pick his spot before unleashing a thunderbolt of a shot that screamed into the top right corner. The remainder of this high-tempo encounter was dominated by Rio Ferdinand, Wes Brown and Michael Carrick repelling Lionel Messi They did such a good job that two Deco half-chances and a tame Thierry Henry header were all Barca could muster.

Man Utd (0) 1		Barcelona (0) 0
Scholes 14		75,061
	STATS	
6	Shots off target	11
2	Shots on target	3
5	Corners	4
18	Fouls	12
4	Offside	1
2	Yellows	3
0	Reds	0
38%	Possession	62%
Referee:	Herbert Fandel (GER)	

CHAMPIONS LEAGUE FINAL

Manchester United v Chelsea

Man Utd	**1**	**Chelsea**	**1**
Ronaldo 26		Lampard 45	
		74,000	

Man Utd win 6-5 on penalties

	STATS	
8	Shots off target	24
5	Shots on target	1
5	Corners	8
22	Fouls	25
1	Offside	2
4	Yellows	4
0	Reds	1
56%	Possession	44%
Referee:	Lubos Michel (SLO)	

Edwin van der Sar's big hands beat away Nicolas Anelka's spot kick and the red half of Moscow erupted.
Minutes earlier, they couldn't watch as John Terry had the chance to crown Chelsea's remarkable season with the Champions League trophy, only to slip as he took the kick and hit the post. United could have gone into halftime 3-1 ahead. First Paul Scholes engineered space for Wes Brown to curl a cross to the far post where Ronaldo leapt to head home with Michael Essien still on the ground and Petr Cech stationary.. Wayne Rooney led a breakout from deep and hit a massive pass to Ronaldo, who turned back a short cross for Carlos Tevez. His diving header from short range was parried by Cech, who had barely got back to his feet before he was fisting away Michael Carrick's drive from the rebound. Then Rooney broke with a searching low cross that Tevez glanced wide. Chelsea levelled through Frank Lampard when Essien's shot took a double deflection and fell to him to pass home just before halftime. In the second half Michael Ballack and Lampard took control of midfield. Chelsea's best chance came when Didier Drogba fired in an unexpected shot and hit the woodwork. Lampard did the same early in extra time, while Ryan Giggs came on to claim a record United appearance and mis-hit a chance to win it, allowing Terry to clear.

As the game approached penalties Drogba saw red for slapping Vidic.

MANCHESTER UNITED

	PLAYER	POS	AGE	APP	MINS ON	GOALS	CARDS(Y/R)		HOME COUNTRY
1	Rio Ferdinand	DEF	29	11	1020	1	1	0	England
2	Michael Carrick	MID	26	12	1016	0	1	0	England
3	Cristiano Ronaldo	MID	23	11	1014	8	2	0	Portugal
4	Patrice Evra	DEF	27	10	929	0	2	0	France
5	Wes Brown	DEF	28	10	876	0	0	0	England
6	Edwin van der Sar	GK	37	10	875	0	1	0	Holland
7	Wayne Rooney	ATT	22	11	860	4	1	0	England
8	Nemanja Vidic	DEF	26	9	782	0	1	0	Serbia
9	Carlos Tevez	ATT	24	12	651	4	1	0	Argentina
10	Nani	MID	21	11	639	0	2	0	Portugal
11	Paul Scholes	MID	33	7	586	1	1	0	England
12	Owen Hargreaves	MID	27	8	515	0	2	0	England
13	Luis Anderson	MID	20	9	497	0	1	0	Brazil
14	Darren Fletcher	MID	24	6	419	0	1	0	Scotland
15	Ryan Giggs	MID	34	9	402	0	0	0	Wales
16	John O'Shea	DEF	27	6	398	0	0	0	Rep of Ireland
17	Ji-Sung Park	MID	27	4	360	0	0	0	South Korea
18	Tomasz Kuszczak	GK	26	5	325	0	0	0	Poland
19	Louis Saha	ATT	29	5	276	0	0	0	France
20	Gerard Pique	DEF	21	3	252	2	0	0	Spain
21	Danny Simpson	DEF	21	3	190	0	0	0	England
22	Jonny Evans	DEF	20	2	108	0	0	0	N Ireland
23	Mikael Silvestre	DEF	30	2	91	0	0	0	France
24	Chris Eagles	MID	22	1	90	0	0	0	England
25	Dong Fanghuo	ATT	23	1	19	0	0	0	China PR
26	Gary Neville	DEF	33	1	10	0	0	0	England

CHELSEA

	PLAYER	POS	AGE	APP	MINS ON	GOALS	CARDS(Y/R)		HOME COUNTRY
1	Claude Makelele	MID	35	13	1184	0	2	0	France
2	Michael Essien	MID	25	12	1037	0	4	0	Ghana
3	Joe Cole	MID	26	13	1030	2	0	0	England
4	Didier Drogba	ATT	30	11	1022	6	0	1	Ivory Coast
5	John Terry	DEF	27	10	960	0	2	0	England
6	Ricardo Carvalho	DEF	30	10	960	0	2	0	Portugal
7	Ashley Cole	DEF	27	10	943	0	1	0	England
8	Frank Lampard	MID	30	11	888	4	1	0	England
9	Petr Cech	GK	26	9	825	0	0	0	Czech Republic
10	Florent Malouda	MID	28	11	755	1	0	0	France
11	Michael Ballack	MID	31	7	681	2	1	0	Germany
12	Salomon Kalou	ATT	22	11	485	1	0	0	Ivory Coast
13	Alex	DEF	26	6	452	1	1	0	Brazil
14	Paulo Ferreira	DEF	29	5	431	0	1	0	Portugal
15	Juliano Belletti	DEF	32	7	386	0	1	0	Brazil
16	Carlo Cudicini	GK	34	5	340	0	0	0	Italy
17	Wayne Bridge	DEF	27	3	270	0	0	0	England
18	Shaun Wright-Phillips	MID	26	5	200	0	0	0	England
19	Andriy Shevchenko	ATT	29	5	163	1	0	0	Ukraine
20	John Obi Mikel	MID	21	4	151	0	1	0	Nigeria
21	Tal Ben Haim	DEF	26	2	107	0	0	0	Israel
22	Claudio Pizarro	ATT	29	2	105	0	0	0	Peru
23	Nicolas Anelka	ATT	29	5	78	0	0	0	France
24	Henrique Hilario	GK	32	1	65	0	0	0	Portugal
25	Steven Sidwell	MID	25	1	7	0	0	0	England

CHAMPIONS LEAGUE FINAL

Manchester United v Chelsea

AIG
COUPE DES CLUBS CHAMPIONS EUROPEENS
LEAGUE 200

The penalty shoot-out swung Chelsea's way as Ronaldo only tricked himself in a stop-start run up and shot tamely against Cech, but Terry's slip and Anelka's poor effort took the trophy to United.

Sir Alex's Red Devils win Europe's biggest prize for the second time in the Scot's reign and Fergie says "it's the best team he's ever had".

THE UEFA CUP

1ST ROUND

	AGG		LEG1	LEG2
Litex	1-4	Hamburg	0-1	1-3
Lens	2-3	Kobenhavn (aet)	1-1	1-2
Artmedia	1-5	Panathinaikos	1-2	0-3
Sparta (4-3p)	0-0	OB	0-0	0-0
Empoli	2-4	Zurich	2-1	0-3
Sochaux	1-2	Panionios	0-2	1-0
Anderlecht	2-1	Rapid Wien	1-1	1-0
P de Ferreira	0-1	AZ	0-1	0-0
Zenit	4-1	Standard	3-0	1-1
Leverkusen	5-4	Leiria	3-1	2-3
Villarreal	6-1	BATE	4-1	2-0
Sion	4-7	Galatasaray	3-2	1-5
Atletico	9-0	Erciyesspor	4-0	5-0
Tampere United	3-4	Bordeaux	2-3	1-1
Getafe (ag)	3-3	Twente	1-0	2-3
Groclin	0-2	Crvena Zvezda	0-1	0-1
Midtjylland	1-5	Lokomotiv M	1-3	0-2
Groningen	2-2	Fiorentina (3-4p)	1-1	1-1
Rabotnicki	1-2	Bolton	1-1	0-1
AEK	3-1	Salzburg	3-0	0-1
Nurnberg (ag)	2-2	Rapid Bucuresti	0-0	2-2
Everton	4-3	Metalist	1-1	3-2
Sarajevo	1-8	Basel	1-2	0-6
Austria Wien	4-2	Valerenga	2-0	2-2
H. Tel-Aviv	1-0	AIK	0-0	1-0
Aris (ag)	2-2	Zaragoza	1-0	1-2
Tottenham	7-2	Anorthosis	6-1	1-1

Greek striker Dimitrios Papadopoulos got Panathinaikos off to a flyer scoring four of his side's five goals against Artmedia. He got one away in Slovakia and his first Uefa hat-trick at home.

Jermain Defoe came off the bench to score twice and put this tie way beyond Cypriot side Anorthosis Famagusta. Four other Spurs players had already scored in the first half.

GROUP A

Everton 3 Larissa 1
Cahill 14, Osman 50, Anichebe 85 — Clayton 65
33,777

Zenit St Petersburg 1 AZ Alkmaar 1
Tymoschuk 41 pen — De Silva Ferreira 20
21,000

Larissa 2 Zenit St Petersburg 3
Alexandrou 58, Fotakis 62 — Pogrebnyak 39, Zyryanov 70, Tekke 78
8,000

Nurnberg 0 Everton 2
40,000 — Arteta 83 pen, Anichebe 88

Victor Anichebe made the difference in Germany as he won a penalty and scored one.

AZ Alkmaar 1 Larissa 0
Dembele 77
15,762

Zenit St Petersburg 2 Nurnberg 2
Pogrebnyak 76, Ionov 78 — Charisteas 25, Benko 83
21,500

Everton 1 Zenit St Petersburg 0
Cahill 85
38,407

Nurnberg 2 AZ Alkmaar 1
Mintal 83, 85 — de Zeeuw 29
35,020

AZ Alkmaar 2 Everton 3
Pelle 16, Jaliens 65 — Johnson 2, Jagielka 43, Vaughan 79
20,000

Larissa 1 Nurnberg 3
Kozlej 11 — Saenko 45, Mintal 57, Charisteas 73
2,863

AZ Alkmaar were the surprise non-qualifiers in the Group as Everton took maximum points, Nurnberg beat Dutch side AZ at home to clinch second place, while Zenit scraped through with two draws and a 3-2 win away over Greek side Larissa, who finished pointless.

GROUP A TABLE

	P	W	D	L	DIF	PTS
Everton	4	4	0	0	6	12
Nurnberg	4	2	1	1	1	7
Zenit	4	1	2	1	0	5
AZ	4	1	1	2	-1	4
Larissa	4	0	0	4	-6	0

GROUP B

Lokomotiv Moscow 3 Atl Madrid 3
Bilyaletdinov 27, Odemwingie 61, 64 — Aguero 16, 85, Forlan Corazo 47
10,000

Panathinaikos 3 Aberdeen 0
Goumas 11, Papadopoulos 73, Salpigidis 77
8,154

Aberdeen 1 Lokomotiv Moscow 1
Diamond 27 — Ivanovic 45
15,000

FC Copenhagen 0 Panathinaikos 1
30,000 — N'Doye 16

Atl Madrid 2 Aberdeen 0
Forlan Corazo 45 pen, Langfield 61 og
25,000

Lokomotiv Moscow 0 FC Copenhagen 1
11,000 — Nordstrand 62 pen

FC Copenhagen 0 Atl Madrid 2
Simao Sabrosa 21, Aguero 62
33,034

Panathinaikos 2 Lokomotiv Moscow 0
Salpigidis 70, 74
10,000

Aberdeen 4 FC Copenhagen 0
Jamie.Smith 47, 55, Antonsson 71 og, Foster 83
20,446

Atl Madrid 2 Panathinaikos 1
Garcia Sanz 74, Simao Sabrosa 90 — Salpigidis 34
10,000

New Atletico recruit, Simao scored the winner against Panathinaikos six minutes into injury time. Earlier former Liverpool midfielder Luis Garcia had brought the scores level.

Atletico Madrid may have lost their favourite son, Fernando Torres but are thriving in both La Liga and Europe. They pipped rivals Panathinaikos to top spot with Simoa's last-gasp winner in the final game. Aberdeen's 4-0 win over Copenhagen gave them the third qualifying spot.

GROUP B TABLE

	P	W	D	L	DIF	PTS
A Madrid	4	3	1	0	5	10
Panathinaikos	4	3	0	1	5	9
Aberdeen	4	1	1	2	-1	4
Copenhagen	4	1	0	3	-6	3
Lokomotiv M	4	0	2	2	-3	2

GROUP C

Elfsborg 1 AEK Athens 1
Mobaeck 16 — Blanco 49
7,000

Villarreal 1 Fiorentina 1
Capdevila Mendez 85 — Vieri 48
15,000

Fiorentina 6 Elfsborg 1
Jorgensen 4, 77, Vieri 5, Donadel 62, Kroldrup 65, Di Carmine 87 — Ishizaki 41
25,000

Mlada Boleslav 1 Villarreal 2
Mendy 90 — Kahveci 33, C. Rodriguez 56
5,000

AEK Athens 1 Fiorentina 1
Balzaretti 34 og — Osvaldo 29
26,386

Elfsborg 1 Mlada Boleslav 3
M.Svensson 31 — Taborsky 67, Mendy 79, Vorisek 90
3,631

Mlada Boleslav 0 AEK Athens 1
Nsaliwa 46
4,670

Villarreal 2 Elfsborg 0
Tomasson 2, 51
18,231

AEK Athens 1 Villarreal 2
Rivaldo 68 — Antonio Mavuba 40, Tomasson 69
24,328

Fiorentina 2 Mlada Boleslav 1
Mutu 44 pen, Vieri 67 — Rajnoch 60
11,140

Adrian Mutu and Christian Vieri were the formidable strike duo powering Fiorentina to a final game win.

Favourites Villarreal and Fiorentina met early with veteran Christian Vieri scoring for the Viola. Full back Joan Capdevila's set-piece header levelled. Villarreal won the rest of their games to top the group, Fiorentina included a 6-1 thrashing of Elfsborg to take second and AEK Athens grabbed third.

GROUP C TABLE

	P	W	D	L	DIF	PTS
Villarreal	4	3	1	0	4	10
Fiorentina	4	2	2	0	6	8
AEK	4	1	2	1	0	5
M. Boleslav	4	1	0	3	-1	3
Elfsborg	4	0	1	3	-9	1

GROUP D

Basel 1 Rennes 0
Streller 55
11,407

SK Brann 0 Hamburg 1
16,000 — Kompany 62

Dinamo Zagreb 0 Basel 0
35,000

Rennes 1 SK Brann 1
Cheyrou 88 pen — Karadas 24
15,000

Hamburg 3 Rennes 0
Van der Vaart 30, Choupo-Moting 83, Zidan 90 pen
36,472

SK Brann 2 Dinamo Zagreb 1
Bjarnason 45 pen, Bakke 72 — Vukojevic 49
9,962

Basel 1 SK Brann 0
Carlitos 40
13,731

Dinamo Zagreb 0 Hamburg 2
27,388 — de Jong 88, Trochowski 90 pen

Hamburg leave it late against Zagreb with Dutch midfielder Nigel de Jong heading an 88th minute opener in Croatia.

Hamburg 1 Basel 1
Olic 73 — Ergic 58
48,917

Rennes 1 Dinamo Zagreb 1
M'Bia 90 — Vukojevic 57
11,846

Hamburg's good Bundesliga season extends to Europe with three wins taking them top of the group before they drew the final game with runners-up Basel. Eirik Bakke scored Brann's winner in the Norwegian side's one victory against Dinamo Zagreb and four points earned them third spot.

GROUP D TABLE

	P	W	D	L	DIF	PTS
Hamburg	4	3	1	0	6	10
Basel	4	2	2	0	2	8
Brann	4	1	1	2	-1	4
Dinamo Zagreb	4	0	2	2	-3	2
Rennes	4	0	2	2	-4	2

FIRST ROUND AND GROUP STAGE

D Bucuresti	2-2	Elfsborg (ag)	1-2	1-0
Lokomotiv Sofia	3-4	Rennes	1-3	2-1
Brann (ag)	2-2	Club Brugge	0-1	2-1
Bayern	3-0	Belenenses	1-0	2-0
Aberdeen (ag)	1-1	Dnipro	0-0	1-1

A good week for Scottish clubs in Europe saw Aberdeen into the Uefa Group stage on away goals. Darren Mackie's header ensured progress against experienced Ukrainian outfit, Dnipro.

Toulouse (ag)	1-1	CSKA Sofia	0-0	1-1
Spartak Moskva	8-1	Hacken	5-0	3-1
Heerenveen	6-8	Helsingborg	5-3	1-5

Heerenveen scored five at home with a brace each from Gerald Sibon and Michael Bradley but still went out in Sweden as Helsingborg won 5-1.

Sampdoria	2-2	AaB (ag)	2-2	0-0

Sunderland's Swedish signing Rade Prica caught the eye playing for Danish side Aalborg BK as he scored one of two away goals in Italy to gain a draw.

Hammarby	2-5	Braga	2-1	0-4
Larissa	3-2	Blackburn	2-0	1-2
M Boleslav (ag)	1-1	Palermo	0-1	1-0
D Zagreb (ag)	3-3	Ajax	0-1	3-2

aet - After extra time
(ag) - Won on away goals
(*-* p) - Penalties

Competition rules:
40 clubs go through to the Group Stage in eight groups of five teams, each playing two home and two away games. The top three clubs in each group go through to the Round of 32, joined by the eight third-placed clubs from the Champions League Group Stage.

GROUP E

B Leverkusen 1 **Toulouse** 0
Kiessling 35 — 20,000

Sparta Prague 1 **Zurich** 2
Slepicka 24 — Konde 38, Alphonse 63 — 6,070

Spartak Moscow 2 **B Leverkusen** 1
Pavlyuchenko 63 pen, Mozart 77 pen — Freier 90 — 22,000

Toulouse 2 **Sparta Prague** 3
Elmander 14, Mansare 80 — Kisel 67, 88, L.Dosek 68 — 14,000

Sparta Prague 0 **Spartak Moscow** 0
6,307

Zurich 2 **Toulouse** 0
Tihinen 42, Raffael De Araujo 69 — 10,600

B Leverkusen 1 **Sparta Prague** 0
Friedrich 71 — 22,500

Spartak Moscow 1 **Zurich** 0
Titov 57 — 25,000

Toulouse 2 **Spartak Moscow** 1
Santos 41, 53 — Dzyuba 61 pen — 14,608

Tunisian international striker Santos scores a brace to put Toulouse ahead against Spartak, who only muster an Artem Dzyuba penalty in reply.

Zurich 0 **B Leverkusen** 5
12,000 — Gresko 19, Bulykin 23, 57, Barnetta 50, Klessling 80

Bayer Leverkusen's European pedigree helped them to three wins to top Group E with a five goal hammering of fellow qualifiers Zurich in the last game. The German's one defeat came in Moscow against runners-up Spartak, who had already qualified before their final game defeat to Toulouse.

GROUP E TABLE

	P	W	D	L	DIF	PTS
Leverkusen	4	3	0	1	6	9
Spartak Mosk.	4	2	1	1	7	7
Zürich	4	2	0	2	-3	6
Sparta	4	1	1	2	-1	4
Toulouse	4	1	0	3	-3	3

GROUP F

Bolton 1 **Braga** 1
Diouf 66 — Jailson 88 — 10,848

Crvena Zvezda 2 **Bayern Munich** 3
Koroman 16, Milijas 75 — Klose 20, 86, Kroos 90 — 50,000

Aris 3 **Crvena Zvezda** 0
Papazoglou 77, 90, Koke 90 — 20,000

Bayern Munich 2 **Bolton** 2
Podolski 30, 49 — Gardner 8, Davies 82 — 65,000

Bolton 1 **Aris** 1
Giannakopoulos 90 — Calvo 44 — 10,229

Stelios Giannakopoulos struck a vital 92nd minute goal to level against his fellow Greeks, Aris, at the Reebok.

Braga 1 **Bayern Munich** 1
Linz 66 — Klose 47 — 15,000

Aris 1 **Braga** 1
Ronaldo 26 — Linz 6 — 15,000

Crvena Zvezda 0 **Bolton** 1
35,000 — McCann 45

Bayern Munich 6 **Aris** 0
Toni 25, 38, 64, 66, Lell 78, Lahm 81 — 64,000

Braga 2 **Crvena Zvezda** 0
Linz 11, Wender 66 — 15,000

German giants Bayern Munich's striking talent was on show in Group F. Lukas Podolski scored two, Miroslav Klose three and Luca Toni four (all against Aris) as the Bundesliga side topped the group. They dropped points against fellow qualifiers Bolton and Portuguese side Braga, though.

GROUP F TABLE

	P	W	D	L	DIF	PTS
Bayern	4	2	2	0	7	8
Braga	4	1	3	0	2	6
Bolton	4	1	3	0	1	6
Aris	4	1	2	1	-3	5
Crvena Zvezda	4	0	0	4	-7	0

GROUP G

Anderlecht 2 **Hapoel Tel-Aviv** 0
Frutos 36, 70 — 15,000

Tottenham 1 **Getafe** 2
Defoe 19 — Gutierrez 21, Nobrega Rodriguez 70
36,240

Aalborg BK 1 **Anderlecht** 1
Lindstrom 86 — Wasilewski 59 — 10,000

Hapoel Tel-Aviv 0 **Tottenham** 2
10,000 — Keane 26, Berbatov 31

Getafe 1 **Hapoel Tel-Aviv** 2
Hernandez 90 pen — Badir 5, B.Dego 31 — 500

Tottenham 3 **Aalborg BK** 2
Berbatov 46, Malbranque 51, D.Bent 66 — Enevoldsen 2, Risgard 37 — 29,758

Spurs were two behind to the Danes at halftime but Dimitar Berbatov netted in the first minute of the second half to lead a winning comeback.

Aalborg BK 1 **Getafe** 2
Prica 90 — Hernandez 11, Granero Molina 78
10,000

Anderlecht 1 **Tottenham** 1
Goor 68 — Berbatov 71 pen — 24,000

Getafe 2 **Anderlecht** 1
Hernandez 6, Celestini 50 — Thereau 90 — 7,000

Hapoel Tel-Aviv 1 **Aalborg BK** 3
Fabio Junior 45 — Risgard 27, Jakobsen 50 pen, Enevoldsen 66 — 10,000

Getafe handed out a home defeat to Spurs to end Martin Jol's reign at White Hart Lane and finished top of the group with midfielder Pablo Hernandez scoring in three games. Spurs recovered to second and Anderlecht pipped Aalborg to third after drawing with them in Denmark.

GROUP G TABLE

	P	W	D	L	DIF	PTS
Getafe	4	3	0	1	2	9
Tottenham	4	2	1	1	2	7
Anderlecht	4	1	2	1	1	5
AaB	4	1	1	2	0	4
H. Tel-Aviv	4	1	0	3	-5	3

GROUP H

Bordeaux 2 **Galatasaray** 1
Cavenaghi 51, Chamakh 62 — Nonda 22 pen — 20,000

Helsingborg 1 **Panionios** 1
Larsson 83 — Goundoulakis 45 — 6,450

Austria Vienna 1 **Bordeaux** 2
Kuljic 5 — Chamakh 45, Wendel 88 pen — 5,000

Galatasaray 2 **Helsingborg** 3
Nonda 44, 90 — Larsson 30, Omotoyossi 39, C.Andersson 75
20,000

Helsingborg 3 **Austria Vienna** 0
Skulason 47, Omotoyossi 66, 70 — 8,243

Panionios 0 **Galatasaray** 3
7,500 — Calik 50, Song 63 pen, Sukur 82

Pointless Galatasaray turned to veteran Hakan Sukur to help them win in Athens. He made one and scored one, with Rigobert Song adding a penalty for the Turks.

Austria Vienna 0 **Panionios** 1
20,000 — Majstorovic 90

Bordeaux 2 **Helsingborg** 1
Chamakh 12, Jussie 69 — Larsson 17 — 10,000

Galatasaray 0 **Austria Vienna** 0
25,000

Panionios 2 **Bordeaux** 3
Djebbour 6 pen, Makos 20 — Cavenaghi 40, 75, Moimbe 87 — 10,000

Bordeaux are giving Lyon a battle in Ligue 1 and won all four games in Group H. Argentinian striker Fernando Cavenaghi and Moroccan Marouane Chamakh each scored three times. Henrik Larsson's goals led Swedes Helsingborg into second spot and Galatasaray squeaked into third.

GROUP H TABLE

	P	W	D	L	DIF	PTS
Bordeaux	4	4	0	0	4	12
Helsingborg	4	2	1	1	3	7
Galatasaray	4	1	1	2	1	4
Panionios	4	1	1	2	-3	4
Austria Wien	4	0	1	3	-5	1

ROUND OF 32

The eight third-placed clubs from the Champions League Groups to join the 24 Uefa Cup sides through from the Group Stage are: PSV, Marseille, Rosenborg, Werder Bremen, Benfica, Rangers, Sporting and Slavia

AEK Athens 1 **Getafe** 1
Blanco 90 — De la Red Gutierrez 86
13,080

Getafe (1) 3 **AEK Athens** (1) 0
Granero Molina 45, Marius Contra 82 pen, Nobrega Rodriguez 84
8,000

Anderlecht 2 **Bordeaux** 1
Polak 79, Mpenza 90 — Jussie 69 pen
17,000

Bordeaux (1) 1 **Anderlecht** (2) 1
Cavenaghi 71 — Chatelle 34
20,127

Galatasaray 0 **B Leverkusen** 0
20,006

Galatasaray's toe-hold on Uefa Cup survival was dealt a crushing 5-1 blow by Bayer. Goalless in Turkey, Bosnian Sergej Barbarez hit two in the opening 22 minutes and the Germans had five on the board before the Turks scored.

B Leverkusen (0) 5 **Galatasaray** (0) 1
Barbarez 12, 22, Klessling 13, Haggui 55, Schneider 61 pen — Barusso 87 pen
22,500

Marseille 3 **Spartak Moscow** 0
Cheyrou 62, Taiwo 68, Niang 79
25,000

Spartak Moscow (0) 2 **Marseille** (3) 0
Pavlenko 39, Pavlyuchenko 85
15,000

PSV Eindhoven 2 **Helsingborg** 0
Simons 7 pen, Lazovic 32
21,500

Helsingborg (0) 1 **PSV Eindhoven** (2) 2
Castan 81 — Bakkal 47, Lazovic 65
10,194

Rangers 0 **Panathinaikos** 0
45,203

Panathinaikos (0) 1 **Rangers** (0) 1
Goumas 12 — Novo 81
14,452

SK Brann 0 **Everton** 2
16,207 — Osman 59, Anichebe 88

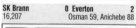

A 2-0 win in Bergen made life easy for Everton in their second leg against Brann. The Norwegians were blown away by Ayegbeni Yakubu's hat-trick, while Andrew Johnson also hit two.

Everton (2) 6 **SK Brann** (0) 1
Yakubu 36, 54, 72, Johnson 41, 90, Arteta 70 — Moen 60
32,834

Sp Lisbon 2 **Basel** 0
Vukcevic 8, 58
16,639

A brace from Simon Vukcevic gave Sporting a confident start against Basel in Lisbon. Bruno Pereirinha's goal after two minutes effectively ended Swiss hopes in their home leg even before Liedson scored another two.

Basel (0) 0 **Sp Lisbon** (2) 3
16,360 — Pereirinha 2, Liedson 41, 51

W Bremen 3 **Braga** 0
Naldo 5, D.Jensen 27, Hugo Almeida 90 pen
25,690

Braga (0) 0 **W Bremen** (3) 1
5,706 — Klasnic 78

Zenit St Petersburg 1 **Villarreal** 0
Pogrebnyak 63
21,500

Villarreal (0) 2 **Zenit St Petersburg** (1) 1
Franco 75, Tomasson 90 — Pogrebnyak 30
15,000

Aberdeen 2 **Bayern Munich** 2
Walker 24, Aluko 41 — Klose 29, Ham.Altintop 54
20,047

Bayern Munich (2) 5 **Aberdeen** (2) 1
da Silva Ferreira 12, Van Buyten 36, Podolski 71, 77, van Bommel 85 — Lovell 83
66,000

Benfica 1 **Nurnberg** 0
Makukula 43
28,378

Nurnberg (0) 2 **Benfica** (1) 2
Charisteas 58, Saenko 66 — Cardozo 89, Di Maria 90
42,846

Bolton 1 **Atl Madrid** 0
Diouf 74
26,163

El Hadji Diouf scored the only goal of the tie between fancied Atletico and struggling Bolton. Matthew Taylor was inspired on his Uefa debut though and Bolton deserved to progress

Atl Madrid (0) 0 **Bolton** (1) 0
30,000

Rosenborg BK 0 **Fiorentina** 1
16,000 — Mutu 16

Fiorentina (1) 2 **Rosenborg BK** (0) 1
Liverani 38, D.Cacia 81 — Kone 88
23,139

Slavia Prague 1 **Tottenham** 2
Strihavka 69 — Berbatov 4, Keane 30
11,134

Tottenham (2) 1 **Slavia Prague** (1) 1
O'Hara 7 — Krajcik 51
34,224

Zurich 1 **Hamburg** 3
Hassli 88 — Jarolim 49, Olic 67, Trochowski 77
16,800

Hamburg (3) 0 **Zurich** (1) 0
33,586

LAST 16

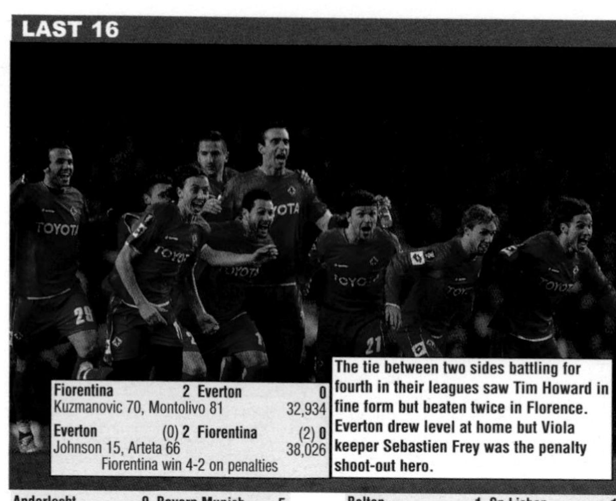

Fiorentina 2 **Everton** 0
Kuzmanovic 70, Montolivo 81
32,934

Everton (0) 2 **Fiorentina** (2) 0
Johnson 15, Arteta 66
38,026
Fiorentina win 4-2 on penalties

The tie between two sides battling for fourth in their leagues saw Tim Howard in fine form but beaten twice in Florence. Everton drew level at home but Viola keeper Sebastien Frey was the penalty shoot-out hero.

Anderlecht 0 **Bayern Munich** 5
21,750 — H.Altintop 9, Toni 45, Podolski 57, Klose 67, Ribery 86

Bayern Munich (5) 1 **Anderlecht** (0) 2
da Silva Ferreira 8 — Akin 19, Iakovenko 35
63,000

Bayern's big guns saw off Anderlecht in the first leg. Luca Toni, Lukas Podolski, Miroslav Klose and Franck Ribery all hit the net as the Belgians succumbed 5-0 at home. Marcel Wasilewski saw red for Anderlecht.

B Leverkusen 1 **Hamburg** 0
Gekas 77
22,500

Hamburg (0) 3 **B Leverkusen** (1) 2
Trochowski 53, Guerrero 64, Van der Vaart 80 — Barbarez 19, Gekas 55
38,083

Bayer Leverkusen lost 3-2 in the second leg to Bundesliga rivals Hamburg but progressed thanks to the away goals by Sergej Barbarez and Theofanis Gekas - allied to a home win.

Benfica 1 **Getafe** 2
Mantorras 76 — La Red Gutierrez 25, Hernandez 67
25,000

Getafe (2) 1 **Benfica** (1) 0
Albin Leites 77
14,000

Getafe won home and away against Benfica, who had Oscar Cardozo sent off after nine minutes of their home leg. Pablo Hernandez scored his fourth goal of the competition.

Bolton 1 **Sp Lisbon** 1
McCann 25 — Vukcevic 69
25,664

Sp Lisbon (1) 1 **Bolton** (1) 0
Pereirinha 85
22,031

Gavin McCann's goal from a rebound was not enough as Sporting's Simon Vukcevic gave the ecstatic Portuguese an away goal equaliser. Bolton played a reserve XI in the away tie.

Marseille 3 **Zenit St Petersburg** 1
Cisse 37, 55, Niang 48 — Arshavin 82
45,000

Zenit St Petersburg (1) 2 **Marseille** (3) 0
Pogrebnyak 39, 78
21,500

Andrei Arshavin's away goal at the Stade Vélodrome in the first leg proves vital as Pavel Pogrebnyak nets twice at home for the Russian side to secure Zenit's route to the quarter-final on the away goals rule

Rangers 2 **W Bremen** 0
Cousin 45, Davis 48
45,959

W Bremen (0) 1 **Rangers** (2) 0
Diego 58
33,000

Keeper Tim Wiese's two mistakes gifted Rangers a crucial lead in the first leg: Daniel Cousin and Steven Davis benefited. While Allan McGregor kept Bremen to one goal in Germany.

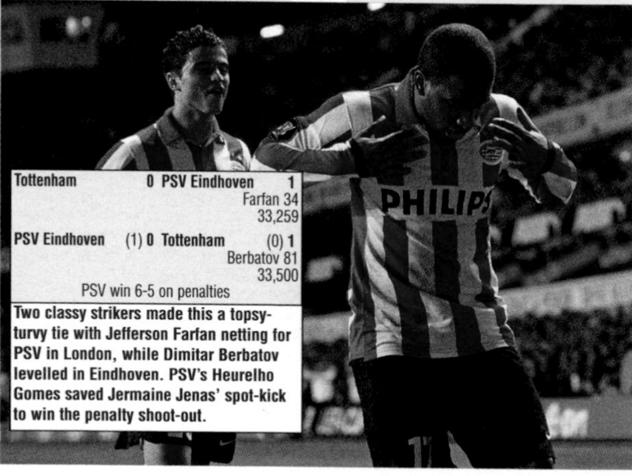

Tottenham 0 **PSV Eindhoven** 1
Farfan 34
33,259

PSV Eindhoven (1) 0 **Tottenham** (0) 1
Berbatov 81
33,500
PSV win 6-5 on penalties

Two classy strikers made this a topsy-turvy tie with Jefferson Farfan netting for PSV in London, while Dimitar Berbatov levelled in Eindhoven. PSV's Heurelho Gomes saved Jermaine Jenas' spot-kick to win the penalty shoot-out.

QUARTER-FINALS

Fiorentina	1	PSV Eindhoven	1
Mutu 56		Koevermans 63	34,317

PSV Eindhoven	(1) 0	Fiorentina	(1) 2
36,200		Mutu 38, 53	

PSV's Danny Koevermans levelled Adrian Mutu's opener in Florence to put the Dutch side in the driving seat. It didn't last as Mutu hit a brace in the away leg to put the Serie A side through.

B Leverkusen	1	Zenit St Petersburg	4
Klessling 33		Arshavin 20, Pogrebnyak 52, Anyukov 61, Denisov 64	19,500

Zenit St Petersburg	(4) 0	B Leverkusen	(1) 1
21,500		Bulykin 18	

Andrei Arshavin led Zenit to a remarkable win in Germany, scoring after 20 minutes and setting up a second for Pavel Pogrebnyak after Stefan Kiessling equalised. Zenit hit two more to win their away leg 4-1 and settle the tie despite Bayer winning in St Petersburg.

Rangers	0	Sp Lisbon	0
48,923			

Sp Lisbon	(0) 0	Rangers	(0) 2
31,155		Darcheville 59, Whittaker 90	

Steven Whittaker's astonishing solo run will be one of the most YouTube-d Uefa goals ever. It didn't win the tie though; Jean-Claude Darcheville's 60th minute away goal had already done that after a goalless draw at Ibrox.

Bayern Munich	1	Getafe	1
Toni 26		Marius Contra 90	62,000

Getafe	(1) 3	Bayern Munich	(1) 3
Marius Contra 44, Casquero Paredes 91, Nobrega Rodriguez 93		Ribery 89, Toni 115, 120	16,300

Extra time and then away goals were required for Bayern to beat Getafe. After sub Cosmin Contra's 90th minute equaliser in Munich, Franck Ribery did the same in the 89th minute in Spain. Luca Toni scored twice to pull Bayern back from 3-1 down in extra time and the Germans progress.

SEMI-FINALS

German champions-elect Bayern were everyone's Uefa favourites but they were dumped out emphatically by Zenit. A Lucio own goal drew Zenit level in Munich but the Russians hit four past Oliver Kahn in St Petersburg to claim their first European final.

Bayern Munich	1	Zenit St Petersburg	1
Ribery 18		da Silva Ferreira 60 og	66,000

Zenit St Petersburg	(1) 4	Bayern Munich	(1) 0
Pogrebnyak 4, 73, Zyryanov 39, Faizulin 54			22,000

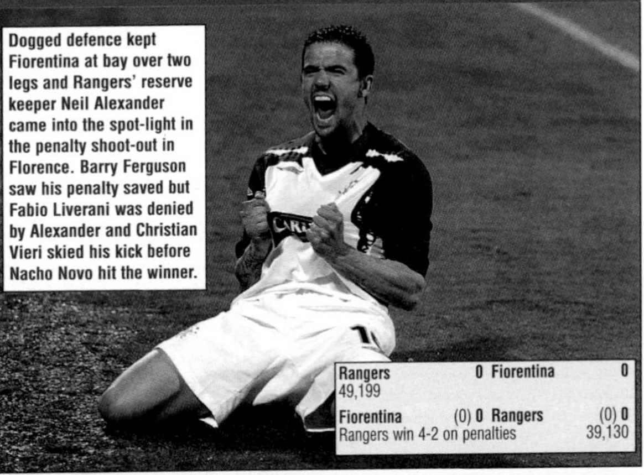

Dogged defence kept Fiorentina at bay over two legs and Rangers' reserve keeper Neil Alexander came into the spot-light in the penalty shoot-out in Florence. Barry Ferguson saw his penalty saved but Fabio Liverani was denied by Alexander and Christian Vieri skied his kick before Nacho Novo hit the winner.

Rangers	0	Fiorentina	0
49,199			

Fiorentina	(0) 0	Rangers	(0) 0
Rangers win 4-2 on penalties			39,130

THE FINAL

Zenit St Petersburg	2	Rangers	0
Denisov 72, Zyryanov 90			47,726

Rangers struggled to get hold of the ball but restricted Zenit to long-range efforts, which rarely troubled Neil Alexander. Steven Whittaker wasted Rangers' only chance of the half, heading over from Steven Davis' pinpoint cross. After the break, Jean-Claude Darcheville forced a fine save but Zenit scored two late goals by Igor Denisov and Konstantin Zyrianov. Walter Smith threw on talismanic striker Nacho Novo and Kris Boyd but man of the match Andrei Ashavin led his side to a deserved triumph.

EUROPEAN LEAGUES ROUND-UP

FINAL PREMIERSHIP LEAGUE TABLE - TOP THREE

		HOME					AWAY					TOTAL			
	P	W	D	L	F	A	W	D	L	F	A	F	A	DIF	PTS
Man Utd	38	17	1	1	47	7	10	5	4	33	15	80	22	58	87
Chelsea	38	12	7	0	36	13	13	3	3	29	13	65	26	39	85
Arsenal	38	14	5	0	37	11	10	6	3	37	20	74	31	43	83

FINAL DUTCH LEAGUE TABLE - TOP THREE

		HOME					AWAY					TOTAL			
	P	W	D	L	F	A	W	D	L	F	A	F	A	DIF	PTS
PSV Eindhoven	34	12	4	1	41	12	9	5	3	24	12	65	24	41	72
Ajax	34	12	3	2	57	20	8	6	3	37	25	94	45	49	69
NAC Breda	34	8	3	6	24	22	11	3	3	24	18	48	40	8	63

FINAL FRENCH LEAGUE TABLE - TOP THREE

		HOME					AWAY					TOTAL			
	P	W	D	L	F	A	W	D	L	F	A	F	A	DIF	PTS
Lyon	38	14	4	1	44	16	10	3	6	30	21	74	37	37	79
Bordeaux	38	13	4	2	38	17	9	5	5	27	21	65	38	27	75
Marseille	38	11	3	5	34	21	6	8	5	24	24	58	45	13	62

FINAL GERMAN LEAGUE TABLE - TOP THREE

		HOME					AWAY					TOTAL			
	P	W	D	L	F	A	W	D	L	F	A	F	A	DIF	PTS
Bayern Munich	34	12	5	0	41	8	10	5	2	27	13	68	21	47	76
Werder Bremen	34	13	0	4	48	19	7	6	4	27	26	75	45	30	66
Schalke 04	34	10	4	3	29	13	8	6	3	26	19	55	32	23	64

FINAL ITALIAN LEAGUE TABLE - TOP THREE

		HOME					AWAY					TOTAL			
	P	W	D	L	F	A	W	D	L	F	A	F	A	DIF	PTS
Inter Milan	38	15	3	1	41	14	10	7	2	28	12	69	26	43	85
Roma	38	15	3	1	43	20	9	7	3	29	17	72	37	35	82
Juventus	38	12	5	2	39	12	8	7	4	33	25	72	37	35	72

FINAL SPANISH LEAGUE TABLE - TOP THREE

		HOME					AWAY					TOTAL			
	P	W	D	L	F	A	W	D	L	F	A	F	A	DIF	PTS
Real Madrid	38	17	0	2	53	18	10	4	5	31	18	84	36	48	85
Villarreal	38	12	5	2	33	15	12	0	7	30	25	63	40	23	77
Barcelona	38	14	2	3	46	12	5	8	6	30	31	76	43	33	67

CLUB STRIKE FORCE

ABN·AMRO

Ajax's top goal-scorer Huntelaar in action

Goals scored in the League	94

1 Ajax

Club Strike Rate (CSR) Average number of minutes between League goals scored by club	32

	CLUB	LEAGUE GOALS	CSR
1	Ajax	94	32
2	Heerenveen	88	34
3	W Bremen	75	40
4	Real Madrid	84	40
5	Man Utd	80	42
6	Bayern Munich	68	45
7	Sevilla	75	45
8	Barcelona	76	45
9	Lyon	74	46
10	Arsenal	74	46
11	Feyenoord	64	47
12	PSV Eindhoven	65	47
13	Juventus	72	47
14	Roma	72	47
15	Aston Villa	71	48
16	Inter Milan	69	49
17	Mallorca	69	49
18	Utrecht	59	51
19	AC Milan	66	51
20	Liverpool	67	51

CLUB DEFENCES

1 Man Utd

Club Defensive Rate (CDR) Average number of minutes between League goals conceded by club	155

	CLUB	CONCEDED	CLEAN SH	CDR
1	Man Utd	22	21	155
2	Bayern Munich	21	17	145
3	Chelsea	26	21	131
4	Inter Milan	26	18	131
5	PSV Eindhoven	24	17	127
6	Liverpool	28	18	122
7	Hamburg	26	13	117
8	Nancy	30	17	114
9	Nice	30	16	114
10	Arsenal	31	15	110
11	Lille	32	12	106
12	Everton	33	14	103
13	St Etienne	34	17	100
14	Lorient	35	16	97
15	Real Madrid	36	14	95
16	Twente	32	13	95
17	Schalke	32	12	95
18	Juventus	37	16	92
19	Roma	37	16	92
20	Lyon	37	13	92

AIG

United's Serbian defender Nemanja Vidic

Goals conceded Number of goals conceded in League games	22
Clean Sheets (CS) Number of league games where no goals were conceded	21

PLAYER NATIONALITIES

1 Country with the most player representation across major European leagues - Italy

Number of players	413	International appearances 06-07	188
Number of occasions in squad	9807	Total minutes played	553835
Actual League appearances	7622	% of European League action	13.15

	COUNTRY	NO OF PLAYERS	CAPS	IN SQUAD	LGE APP	MINS PLAYED	% LGE ACT
1	Italy	413	188	9807	7622	553835	13.15
2	France	421	198	9447	7246	524860	12.46
3	Spain	397	212	8652	6715	486269	11.55
4	Holland	370	246	7678	5812	426881	10.14
5	Germany	266	202	5242	3791	282495	6.71
6	England	234	153	4394	3752	282212	6.70
7	Brazil	169	77	3564	2926	211085	5.01
8	Argentina	92	98	2234	1769	130540	3.10
9	Uruguay	48	4	1093	810	55957	1.33
10	Belgium	41	41	959	718	50695	1.20
11	Denmark	41	88	878	723	47613	1.13
12	Switzerland	32	99	740	595	46367	1.10
13	Rep of Ireland	30	86	707	626	45406	1.08
14	Portugal	42	90	835	650	45389	1.08
15	Czech Republic	37	106	731	587	44176	1.05
16	Sweden	31	113	695	584	43170	1.03
17	Ivory Coast	26	58	618	559	39065	0.93
18	Croatia	27	92	637	522	37250	0.88
19	Nigeria	29	22	696	577	35717	0.85
20	Senegal	31	22	602	478	35329	0.84

CLUB MAKE-UP – HOME AND OVERSEAS PLAYERS

1 Club which used the most overseas players in league action - Arsenal

Overseas players in named 16s	28	Home country players in named 16s	7
Percent of overseas players	80.0	Percent of League action	100.00
Most appearances	Gael Clichy	% of match time played	97.4

	CLUB	OVERSEAS	HOME	% OVERSEAS	% LGE ACT	MOST APP	% APP
1	Arsenal	28	7	80.0	100.0	Gael Clichy	97.4
2	Inter Milan	26	7	78.8	93.56	Javier Zanetti	94.8
3	Fulham	29	10	74.4	85.54	Simon Davies	93.8
4	Birmingham	21	12	63.6	79.62	Stephen Kelly	100.0
5	Cottbus	25	10	71.4	70.84	Ervin Skela	87.4
6	Blackburn	21	6	77.8	79.10	Brad Friedel	100.0
7	Liverpool	24	7	77.4	78.60	Jose Reina	100.0
8	Chelsea	22	10	68.8	76.18	Nicolas Anelka	75.3
9	Nurnberg	19	10	65.5	67.45	Tomas Galasek	80.6
10	Man City	23	11	67.6	74.10	Richard Dunne	91.9
11	Sevilla	23	13	63.9	73.00	Daniel Alves da Silva	86.2
12	Atl Madrid	19	20	48.7	71.69	Sergio Leonel Aguero	86.7
13	Heracles	15	14	51.7	63.11	Martin Pieckenhagen	89.5
14	Reading	23	12	65.7	70.39	Marcus Hahnemann	100.0
15	Hertha Berlin	22	10	68.8	62.83	Jaroslav Drobny	89.5
16	Portsmouth	21	10	67.7	69.94	Sylvain Distin	93.4
17	Man Utd	22	14	61.1	69.88	Patrice Evra	82.5
18	Hamburg	20	10	66.7	62.45	Joris Mathijsen	81.6
19	Bolton	29	13	69.0	69.08	Andy O'Brien	82.5
20	Bochum	17	12	58.6	61.51	Stanislav Sestak	83.7

CLUB DISCIPLINARY RECORDS

Recreativo players surround the referee

Yellow cards	116
Red cards	12
Total	128

1 Recreativo Huelva

Cards Average in League Average number of minutes between a card being shown of either colour	26

	CLUB	Y	R	TOTAL	AVE
1	Recreativo Huelva	116	12	128	26
2	Atl Madrid	118	7	125	27
3	Athl Bilbao	115	9	124	27
4	Genoa	110	9	119	28
5	Osasuna	111	10	121	28
6	Atalanta	109	6	115	29
7	Real Zaragoza	107	9	116	29
8	Espanyol	109	6	115	29
9	Almeria	107	8	115	29
10	Torino	108	6	114	30
11	Murcia	107	6	113	30
12	Parma	96	11	107	31
13	Sevilla	99	10	109	31
14	Palermo	99	7	106	32
15	Sampdoria	100	6	106	32
16	Napoli	97	7	104	32
17	Real Betis	100	5	105	32
18	Catania	97	5	102	33
19	Duisburg	87	5	92	33
20	Valencia	94	8	102	33

TEAM OF THE SEASON

LOPEZ

VILLARREAL
CG 19 DR 190

BELLETTI

CHELSEA
CG 21 DR 239

VAN BUYTEN

BAYERN MUNICH
CG 18 DR 162

VIDIC

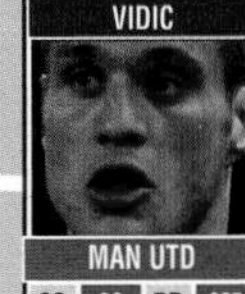

MAN UTD
CG 29 DR 205

SALCIDO

PSV EINDHOVEN
CG 32 DR 146

RONALDO

MAN UTD
CG 28 SD +121

MIKEL

CHELSEA
CG 18 SD +190

VAN BOMMEL

BAYERN MUNICH
CG 23 SD +118

BAKKAL

PSV EINDHOVEN
CG 18 SD +109

FABIANO

SEVILLA
CG 23 SR 96

HUNTELAAR

AJAX
CG 34 SR 95

The European Team of the Season shows a 4-4-2 of the best players in the major European Leagues based upon the selection criteria used for the chart-toppers. The players selected are taken from the lists for each club except that to get into this Team of the Season you must have played at least 17 Counting Games in league matches (roughly half the league season) and not 12 as is the case in the club lists. The other restriction is that we are only allowing one player from each club in each position.

- **The Top team's goalkeeper** is the player with the highest *Defensive Rating*
- **The Top team's defenders** are also tested by *Defensive Rating*, i.e. the average number of minutes between league goals conceded while on the pitch.
- **The Top team's midfield** are selected on their *Scoring Difference*, i.e. their *Defensive Rating* minus their *Contribution to Attacking Power* (average number of minutes between league goals scored while on the pitch.) It takes no account of assists.
- **The Top team strikeforce** is made up of the striker with the highest *Strike Rate* (his average number of minutes between league goals scored while on the pitch) together with the striker with the second highest.

PLAYER DISCIPLINARY RECORD

Deco commits to another mistimed tackle

1 Deco - Barcelona

Cards Average mins between cards	112
League Yellow	11
League Red	0
TOTAL	11

	PLAYER	CLUB	Y	R	TOTAL	AVE
1	Deco	Barcelona	11	0	11	112
2	J Urtasun	Osasuna	13	2	15	116
3	Carrozzieri	Atalanta	13	2	15	120
4	Ivan Soto	Deportivo	8	1	9	120
5	R Gaspar	Recreativo	12	2	14	122
6	Bowyer	West Ham	7	1	8	125
7	M Blasi	Napoli	17	1	18	129
8	J Vidigal	Livorno	8	1	9	138
9	M Berson	Levante	10	1	11	147
10	Mudingayi	Lazio	12	0	12	162
11	A Nocerino	Juventus	13	0	13	165
12	T Zdebel	Bochum	11	0	11	168
13	M Tararache	Duisburg	14	1	15	183
14	L Grafite	Wolfsburg	9	1	10	189
15	Jerko Leko	AS Monaco	10	0	10	193
16	v. Bommel	Bayern Munich	9	2	11	195
17	Adriano	AS Monaco	9	1	10	195
18	Brown	Wigan	11	0	11	224
19	Butt	Newcastle	13	0	13	230
20	Smith	Newcastle	9	1	10	239

CHART-TOPPING POINT EARNERS

	PLAYER	TEAM	GAMES	POINTS	AVE
1	Schweinst'ger	Bayern Munich	14	38	2.71
2	R Carvalho	Chelsea	19	51	2.68
3	W Rooney	Man Utd	23	61	2.65
4	S Eguren	Villarreal	13	34	2.62
5	Julio Cruz	Inter Milan	18	47	2.61
6	C Panucci	Roma	21	54	2.57
7	Cris	Lyon	12	30	2.5
8	Clemens Fritz	W Bremen	18	45	2.5
9	Pepe	Real Madrid	16	40	2.5
10	Otman Bakkal	PSV Eindhoven	18	43	2.39
11	R Marquez	Barcelona	13	31	2.38
12	T Rosicky	Arsenal	14	33	2.36
13	Geert Roorda	Heerenveen	12	28	2.33
14	Martin Skrtel	Liverpool	13	30	2.31
15	F Cavenaghi	Bordeaux	13	30	2.31
16	Tim Cahill	Everton	17	39	2.29
17	Bas Sibum	NEC Nijmegen	14	32	2.29
18	Enzo Maresca	Sevilla	12	27	2.25
19	Ivan Rakitic	Schalke	20	44	2.2
20	T Vermaelen	Ajax	12	26	2.17

(Selection limited to top player per club)

1 Schweinsteiger - Bayern Munich

Counting Games Played at least 70mins.	14
Total Points Taken in Counting Games	38
Average points per game Taken in Counting Games	2.71

MOST MISSED PLAYERS

	PLAYER	TEAM	AVERAGE	CLUB	DIFF
1	Bas Sibum	NEC Nijmegen	2.29	1.44	0.85
2	Kevin Bobson	NEC Nijmegen	2.23	1.44	0.79
3	J Fanchone	Strasbourg	1.58	0.92	0.66
4	Brian McBride	Fulham	1.58	0.95	0.63
5	Djimi Traore	Rennes	2.15	1.53	0.62
6	Rafael Marquez	Barcelona	2.38	1.76	0.62
7	C Gregoire	Willem II Tilb	1.5	0.91	0.59
8	S Eguren	Villarreal	2.62	2.03	0.59
9	D Tiendalli	S Rotterdam	1.58	1	0.58
10	Tim Cahill	Everton	2.29	1.71	0.58
11	Geremi Njitap	Newcastle	1.71	1.13	0.58
12	Geert Roorda	Heerenveen	2.33	1.76	0.57
13	Enzo Maresca	Sevilla	2.25	1.68	0.57
14	Clemens Fritz	W Bremen	2.5	1.94	0.56
15	F Pisano	Cagliari	1.67	1.11	0.56
16	Mickael Pagis	Rennes	2.07	1.53	0.54
17	Pietro Accardi	Sampdoria	2.11	1.58	0.53
18	Babacar Gueye	Metz	1.13	0.61	0.52
19	O Martins	Newcastle	1.65	1.13	0.52
20	Daniele Mannini	Napoli	1.83	1.32	0.51

(No limit on the number of players per club selected)

Jiba
Vakanties

1 Bas Sibum - NEC Nijmegen

Average points	2.29
Club average	144
Difference	0.85

CHART-TOPPING GOALSCORERS

1 Cristiano Ronaldo - Man Utd

Goals scored in the League	31
Contribution to Attacking Power Average number of minutes between League team goals while on pitch	40
Player Strike Rate Average number of minutes between League goals scored by player	88
Club Strike Rate (CSR) Average minutes between League goals scored by club	42

	PLAYER	CLUB	GOALS	POWER	CSR	S RATE
1	Cristiano Ronaldo	Man Utd	31	40	42	88
2	Samuel Eto'o	Barcelona	16	38	45	93
3	Fernando Cavenaghi	Bordeaux	15	39	52	93
4	Klaas-Jan Huntelaar	Ajax	33	33	35	95
5	Luis Fabiano	Sevilla	24	45	46	96
6	Mario Gomez	Stuttgart	19	52	55	103
7	Fernando Torres	Liverpool	24	44	51	106
8	Luca Toni	Bayern Munich	24	44	45	109
9	Daniel Guiza	Mallorca	27	49	49	111
10	Nihat Kahveci	Villarreal	18	51	54	111
11	Zlatan Ibrahimovic	Inter Milan	17	46	50	115
12	Ruud Van Nistelrooy	Real Madrid	16	41	40	117
13	David Villa	Valencia	18	60	71	117
14	Mamadou Niang	Marseille	18	63	58	120
15	Emmanuel Adebayor	Arsenal	24	45	46	122
16	Miguel Hugo Almeida	W Bremen	11	41	40	125
17	Marcus Berg	Groningen	15	47	59	127
18	Karim Benzema	Lyon	20	44	46	128
19	Filippo Inzaghi	AC Milan	11	50	53	128
20	Alessandro Del Piero	Juventus	21	49	48	130

The Chart-topping Goalscorers measures the players by Strike Rate. They are most likely to be Forwards but Midfield players and even Defenders do come through the club tables. It is not a measure of the number of League goals scored - although that is also noted - but how often on average they have scored.

CHART-TOPPING MIDFIELDERS

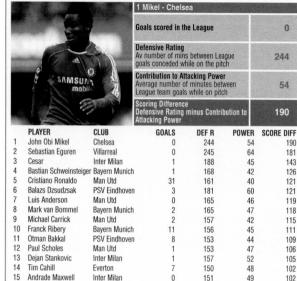

1 Mikel - Chelsea

Goals scored in the League	0
Defensive Rating Av number of mins between League goals conceded while on the pitch	244
Contribution to Attacking Power Average number of minutes between League team goals while on pitch	54
Scoring Difference Defensive Rating minus Contribution to Attacking Power	190

	PLAYER	CLUB	GOALS	DEF R	POWER	SCORE DIFF
1	John Obi Mikel	Chelsea	0	244	54	190
2	Sebastian Eguren	Villarreal	0	245	64	181
3	Cesar	Inter Milan	1	188	45	143
4	Bastian Schweinsteiger	Bayern Munich	1	168	42	126
5	Cristiano Ronaldo	Man Utd	31	161	40	121
6	Balazs Dzsudzsak	PSV Eindhoven	3	181	60	121
7	Luis Anderson	Man Utd	0	165	46	119
8	Mark van Bommel	Bayern Munich	2	165	47	118
9	Michael Carrick	Man Utd	2	157	42	115
10	Franck Ribery	Bayern Munich	11	156	45	111
11	Otman Bakkal	PSV Eindhoven	8	153	44	109
12	Paul Scholes	Man Utd	1	153	47	106
13	Dejan Stankovic	Inter Milan	1	157	52	105
14	Tim Cahill	Everton	7	150	48	102
15	Andrade Maxwell	Inter Milan	0	151	49	102
16	Tomas Rosicky	Arsenal	6	148	47	101
17	Frank Lampard	Chelsea	10	143	43	100
18	Xabi Alonso	Liverpool	2	146	47	99
19	Jose Ze Roberto	Bayern Munich	5	144	48	96
20	Nani	Man Utd	3	131	36	95

The Divisional Round-up charts combine the records of chart-topping keepers, defenders, midfield players and forwards, from every club in the division.. The one above is for **the Chart-topping Midfielders**. The players are ranked by their Scoring Difference although other attributes are shown for you to compare.

TOP LEAGUES IN EUROPE

	UEFA Cup Group Phase	Pts	Champions League Group Phase	Pts	UEFA Cup Round of 32	Pts	Champions League last 16	Pts
England	**Everton Bolton Tottenham**	3	**Man Utd Liverpool Chelsea Arsenal**	8	Everton Bolton Tottenham	3	**Man Utd Liverpool Chelsea Arsenal**	8
Spain	**Atletico Villarreal Getafe**	3	**Real Madrid Barcelona Sevilla** Valencia	8	**Getafe** Atletico Villarreal	3	**Barcelona** Real Madrid Sevilla	6
Germany	**Nuremburg Hamburg Leverkusen Bayern M**	4	**Schalke** W Bremen (U) Stuttgart	6	**H'burg Leverkusen Bayern Bremen** (U) Nuremburg	5	**Schalke**	2
Italy	**Fiorentina**	1	**AC Milan Inter Roma** Lazio	8	**Fiorentina**	1	**Roma** AC Milan Inter	6
Portugal	**Braga**	1	**Porto** Benfica (U) Sporting (U)	6	**Benfica** (U) **Sporting** (U) Braga	3	Porto	2
France	**Bordeaux** Rennes Toulouse	3	**Lyon** Marseille (U)	4	**Marseille** (U) Bordeaux	2	Lyon	2
Scotland	**Aberdeen**	1	**Celtic** Rangers (U)	4	**Rangers** (U) Aberdeen	2	Celtic	2
Greece	**Panathinaikos AEK** Aris Panionios Larissa	5	**Olympiakos**	2	Panathaniakos AEK	2	Olympiakos	2
Turkey	**Galatasaray**	1	**Fenerbahce** Besiktas	4	Galatasaray	1	**Fenerbahce**	2
Russia	**Zenit St Petersburg Spartak M** Lokomotiv M	3	CSKA Moscow	2	**Zenit St Petersburg** Spartak Moscow	2		
Holland	AZ Alkmaar	1	PSV (U)	2	**PSV** (U)	1		
Norway	**Brann**	1	Rosenborg (U)	2	Brann Rosenborg (U)	2		
Czech Republic	Sparta Prague Mlada Bloeslav	2	Slavia Prague (U)	2	Slavia Prague (U)	1		
Ukraine			Shakhtar Donetsk Dinamo Kiev	4				
Switzerland	**Basel Zurich**	2			Basel Zurich	2		
Sweden	**Helsingborg** Elfsborg	2			Helsingborg	1		
Belgium	**Anderlecht**	1			**Anderlecht**	1		
Romania			Steaua Bucharest	2				
Denmark	Aalborg FC Copenhagen	2						
Croatia	Dinamo Zagreb	1						
Serbia	Crvena Zvevda	1						
Israel	Hapoel Tel-Aviv	1						
Austria	Austria Vienna	1						

(U) shows clubs qualifying for the Uefa Cup Round of 32 from Champions League Group Phase
Teams in Bold are those going through

CHART-TOPPING DEFENDERS

1 Rodriguez - Villarreal	
Goals conceded in the League	6
Clean Sheets In games when he played at least 70 mins	11
Defensive Rating Average number of minutes between League goals conceded while on pitch	85
Club Defensive Rating Average mins between League goals conceded by the club this season	254

	PLAYER	CLUB	CON: LGE	CS	CDR	DEF RATE
1	Gonzalo Rodriguez	Villarreal	6	11	85	254
2	Juliano Belletti	Chelsea	8	14	131	239
3	Nemanja Vidic	Man Utd	13	19	155	205
4	Patrice Evra	Man Utd	16	16	155	176
5	Daniel Van Buyten	Bayern Munich	10	10	145	162
6	Marcell Jansen	Bayern Munich	9	7	145	159
7	Martin Demichelis	Bayern Munich	16	15	145	157
8	Christian Lell	Bayern Munich	15	14	145	153
9	Rio Ferdinand	Man Utd	20	19	155	152
10	Carlos Salcido	PSV Eindhoven	20	17	135	146
11	John Terry	Chelsea	13	12	131	145
12	Wes Brown	Man Utd	21	17	155	144
13	Ivan Cordoba	Inter Milan	13	10	135	138
14	Alex	Chelsea	15	13	131	138
15	Jan Kromkamp	PSV Eindhoven	17	12	135	137
16	David Sauget	Nancy	14	11	114	136
17	Rafael Marquez	Barcelona	11	6	79	136
18	Sami Hyypia	Liverpool	15	10	122	135
19	Ricardo Carvalho	Chelsea	13	13	131	134
20	Lucio	Bayern Munich	16	11	145	133

The Chart-topping Defenders are resolved by their Defensive Rating, how often their team concedes a goal while they are playing. All these rightly favour players at the best performing clubs because good players win matches. However, good players in lower-table clubs will chart where they have lifted the team's performance.

CHART-TOPPING GOALKEEPERS

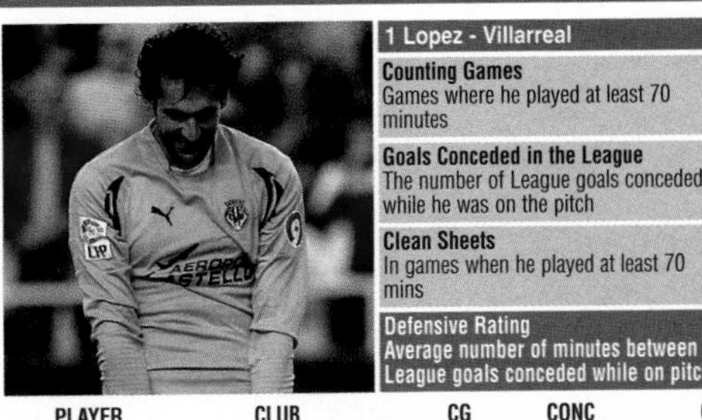

1 Lopez - Villarreal	
Counting Games Games where he played at least 70 minutes	19
Goals Conceded in the League The number of League goals conceded while he was on the pitch	12
Clean Sheets In games when he played at least 70 mins	11
Defensive Rating Average number of minutes between League goals conceded while on pitch	143

	PLAYER	CLUB	CG	CONC	CS	DEF RATE
1	Diego Lopez	Villarreal	19	12	11	143
2	Edwin van der Sar	Man Utd	28	18	14	142
3	Petr Cech	Chelsea	25	17	14	136
4	Heurelho Gomes	PSV Eindhoven	34	24	17	127
5	Oliver Kahn	Bayern Munich	25	18	11	127
6	Jody Viviani	St Etienne	17	12	8	127
7	Jose Reina	Liverpool	38	28	18	122
8	Julio Cesar	Inter Milan	31	24	13	120
9	Frank Rost	Hamburg	34	26	13	117
10	Nelson Silva Dida	AC Milan	13	10	5	117
11	Gennaro Bracigliano	Nancy	38	30	17	114
12	Hugo Lloris	Nice	29	24	12	109
13	Tim Howard	Everton	36	30	14	108
14	Manuel Almunia	Arsenal	29	24	11	108
15	Remy Vercoutre	Lyon	19	16	7	106
16	Iker Casillas	Real Madrid	36	32	14	101
17	Gianluigi Buffon	Juventus	34	30	16	101
18	Tony Mario Sylva	Lille	30	27	9	100
19	Doni	Roma	36	33	15	99
20	Fabien Audard	Lorient	38	35	16	97

The Chart-topping Goalkeepers are positioned by their Defensive Rating. We also show Clean Sheets where the team has not conceded and the Keeper has played all or most (at least 70 minutes) of the game. Only one keeper is selected from each club unless they have played the requisite number of counting games.

UEFA last 16	Pts	Champ's L. Q-finals	Pts	UEFA Q. finals	Pts	Champ's L.S-finals	Pts	UEFA Semi-finals	Pts	Champ's L.Final Winners	Pts	UEFA Final Winners	Pts
Everton Bolton Tottenham	3	**Man U L'pool Ch'sea Ars'**	18			**Man U** Liverpool **Chelsea**	6			**Man Utd** Chelsea	6		
Getafe	1	**Barcelona**	2	Getafe	1	Barca	2						
Leverk'n Bayern Hamb'g Bremen	4	Shalke	2	Leverkusen **Bayern**	2			Bayern Munich	1				
Fiorentina	1	Roma	2	Fiorentina	1			Fiorentina	1				
Sporting Benfica	2			Sporting	1								
Marseille	1												
Rangers	1			**Rangers**	1			**Rangers**	1			Rangers	1
		Fenerbahce	2										
Zenit St Petersburg	1			**Zenit St Petersburg**	1			**Zenit St Petersburg**	1			**Zenit St Petersburg**	2
PSV	1			PSV	1								
Anderlecht	1												

TOTAL		
45	England	(1)
25	Spain	(2)
23	Germany	(4=)
19	Italy	(3)
14	Portugal	(7)
12	France	(4=)
11	Scotland	(8=)
11	Greece	(8=)
10	Turkey	(13=)
10	Russia	(10=)
5	Holland	(6)
5	Norway	(-)
5	Czech Rep	(17=)
4	Ukraine	(10=)
4	Switzerland	(17=)
3	Sweden	(-)
3	Belgium	(13=)
2	Romania	(10=)
2	Denmark	(16)
1	Croatia	(-)
1	Serbia	(20=)
1	Israel	(13=)
1	Austria	(20=)

Top Leagues in Europe
This chart sees how different country's leagues fared in cross-border rivalries. Picking up from the Champions League and UEFA Cup Group Phases we've noted every surviving club. 23 leagues feature initially and it's gradually whittled down to two winners.
Each league wins one point for every survivor in the UEFA Cup each round and two points in the Champions League.

EURO 2008 GROUP A

The group stages

1. SWITZERLAND v CZECH REPUBLIC

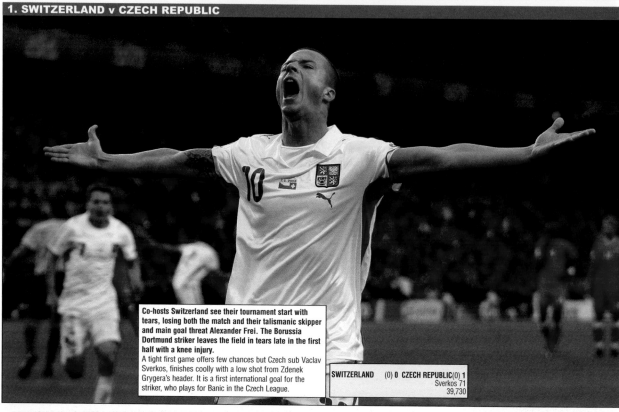

Co-hosts Switzerland see their tournament start with tears, losing both the match and their talismanic skipper and main goal threat Alexander Frei. The Borussia Dortmund striker leaves the field in tears late in the first half with a knee injury.

A tight first game offers few chances but Czech sub Vaclav Sverkos, finishes coolly with a low shot from Zdenek Grygera's header. It is a first international goal for the striker, who plays for Banic in the Czech League.

SWITZERLAND	(0) 0	CZECH REPUBLIC	(0) 1
			Sverkos 71
			39,730

2. PORTUGAL v TURKEY

15

Real Madrid centre back Pepe makes the breakthrough for fancied Portugal in their first game.

The finalists from 2004 dominate the chances in this game with Pepe having an early header disallowed and Nuno Gomes hitting the woodwork twice. These same two players combine with a one-two on the edge of the box for Pepe to slot home on 61 minutes. Cristiano Ronaldo lays a simple pass through to Porto midfielder Joao Moutinho to set up sub Paul Meireles for a late second.

PORTUGAL	(0) 0	TURKEY	(0) 2
Pepe 61, Raul Meireles 90			29,106

3. CZECH REPUBLIC v PORTUGAL

DECO
20

Europe's player-of-the-season Cristiano Ronaldo scores one and has a hand in two more as Portugal qualify for the quarter-finals with a 3-1 win over the Czech Republic.

Barca's Deco is looking for a new club and impresses after Ronaldo is thwarted by Petr Cech and the ball falls to the Brazilian-born midfielder to slot home. The Czechs level through Libor Sionko's diving header from a corner. In the second half Deco's pass sets up a fierce low drive from Ronaldo to regain the lead for Portugal. The final goal comes when Ronaldo breaks the offside trap and runs in on Cech before unselfishly squaring the ball for sub Ricardo Quaresma to score.

CZECH REPUBLIC	(0) 1	PORTUGAL	(1) 3
Sionko 17			Deco 8, Ronaldo 63, Quaresma 90
			29,016

PORTUGAL – TURKEY – CZECH REPUBLIC – SWITZERLAND

4. SWITZERLAND v TURKEY

SWITZERLAND	(1) 1	TURKEY	(0) 2
Yakin 32		Semih 57, Arda 90	
			39,730

Arda Turan gives Turkey a chance of reaching the quarter-finals and ends Swiss hopes when his shot deflects in deep in injury time. In the absence of injured Alexander Frei, Hakan Yakin continues up front for the Swiss and scores when the ball holds up on the wet pitch and he reacts to slot home. Fenerbahce striker Semih Senturk levels with a header early in the second half. The game looks to be heading for a draw when Arda strikes two minutes into injury time.

5. SWITZERLAND v PORTUGAL

Switzerland leave their own tournament on a high note after Hakan Yakin strikes twice against a below strength Portuguese side. Big Phil Scolari rests seven players but has the better of the first half with Nani and Ricardo Quaresma providing the invention. Nani hits the woodwork in the second half before Yakin slips behind the Portuguese defence and rifles home. He adds a second from the penalty spot after Fernando Meira is judged to have fouled Tranquillo Barnetta. It is popular Swiss coach Kobi Kuhn's final game in charge and he goes out on a win.

SWITZERLAND	(0) 2	PORTUGAL	(0) 0
Yakin 71, 83 pen			
			39,730

6. TURKEY v CZECH REPUBLIC

TURKEY	(0) 3	CZECH REPUBLIC	(1) 2
Arda 75,		Koller 34, Plasil 62	
Nihat 87, 89			29,016

A rare mistake from the usually immaculate Petr Cech lets in Turkey for a late late turn-around in the most thrilling game of the tournament so far.
Going 2-0 down the Turks look to be heading out of Euro 2008 in the 62nd minute when Jaroslav Plasil volleys a second to add to Jan Koller's first half power header. With Jan Polak striking the post it seems just a case of how many the Czechs will score until Arda Turan nets at the far post on 75 minutes. With three minutes remaining Cech misjudges a cross to present Nihat Kahveci with a tap-in and, just as the Czechs steal themselves for extra time, Nihat strikes again, this time with a sublime finish from the edge of the area.

GROUP A TABLE

	P	W	D	L	F	A	DIF	PTS
Portugal	3	2	0	1	5	3	+2	6
Turkey	3	2	0	1	5	5	0	6
Czech Republic	3	1	0	2	4	6	-2	3
Switzerland	3	1	0	2	3	3	0	3

CZECH REPUBLIC

PLAYER	POS	AGE	APP	MINS ON	GOALS	CARDS(Y/R)	
David Rozehnal	DEF	27	3	270	0	0	0
Jan Polak	MID	27	3	270	0	1	0
Marek Jankulovski	DEF	31	3	270	0	0	0
Petr Cech	GK	26	3	270	0	0	0
Tomas Ujfalusi	DEF	30	3	270	0	1	0
Zdenek Grygera	DEF	28	3	270	0	0	0
Jaroslav Plasil	MID	26	3	254	1	0	0
Libor Sionko	MID	31	3	254	1	0	0
Tomas Galasek	MID	35	3	252	0	1	0
Jan Koller	ATT	35	3	163	1	0	0
David Jarolim	MID	29	3	142	0	0	0
Marek Matejovsky	MID	26	2	105	0	0	0
Milan Baros	ATT	26	1	90	0	1	0
Stanislav Vlcek	ATT	32	3	39	0	0	0
Vaclav Sverkos	ATT	24	1	35	1	0	0
Michal Kadlec	DEF	23	1	11	0	0	0
Radoslav Kovac	DEF	28	1	5	0	0	0
Daniel Zitka	GK	33	0	0	0	0	0
Jaromir Blazek	GK	35	0	0	0	0	0
Martin Fenin	ATT	21	0	0	0	0	0
Rudolf Skacel	MID	28	0	0	0	0	0
Tomas Sivok	MID	24	0	0	0	0	0
Zdenek Pospech	DEF	29	0	0	0	0	0

SWITZERLAND

PLAYER	POS	AGE	APP	MINS ON	GOALS	CARDS(Y/R)	
Gokhan Inler	MID	24	3	270	0	0	0
Ludovic Magnin	DEF	29	3	270	0	1	0
Patrick Muller	DEF	31	3	270	0	0	0
Philippe Senderos	DEF	23	3	270	0	0	0
Valon Behrami	MID	23	3	262	0	0	0
Gelson Fernandes	MID	21	3	255	0	1	0
Stephan Lichtsteiner	DEF	24	3	245	0	0	0
Hakan Yakin	MID	31	3	214	3	1	0
Eren Derdiyok	ATT	20	3	188	0	1	0
Tranquillo Barnetta	MID	23	3	185	0	2	0
Diego Benaglio	GK	24	2	180	0	0	0
Johan Vonlanthen	ATT	22	3	102	0	2	0
Marco Streller	ATT	27	1	90	0	0	0
Pascal Zuberbuhler	GK	37	1	90	0	0	0
Alexander Frei	ATT	28	1	45	0	0	0
Ricardo Cabanas	MID	29	2	20	0	0	0
Stephane Grichting	DEF	29	1	8	0	0	0
Daniel Gygax	MID	26	1	6	0	0	0
Benjamin Huggel	MID	30	0	0	0	0	0
Christoph Spycher	DEF	30	0	0	0	0	0
Eldin Jakupovic	GK	23	0	0	0	0	0
Johan Djourou	DEF	21	0	0	0	0	0
Philipp Degen	DEF	25	0	0	0	0	0

EURO 2008 GROUP B

The group stages

1. AUSTRIA V CROATIA

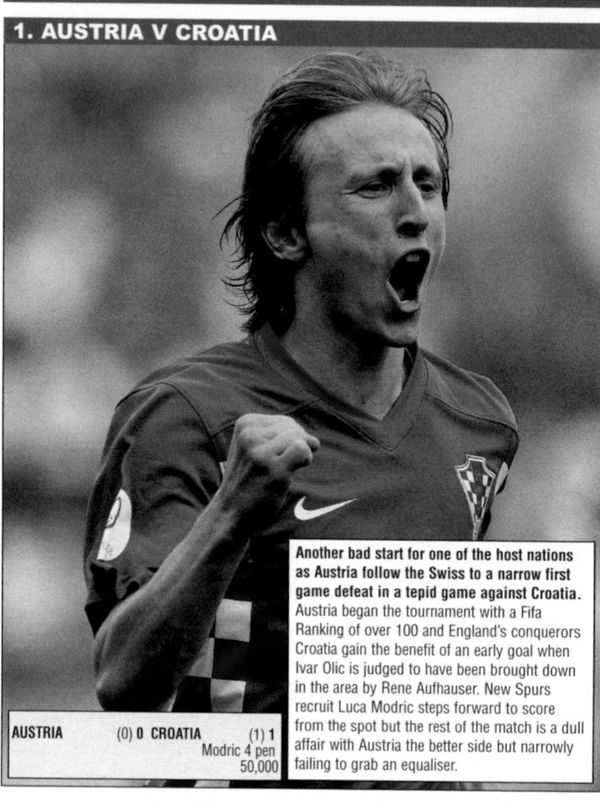

Another bad start for one of the host nations as Austria follow the Swiss to a narrow first game defeat in a tepid game against Croatia.
Austria began the tournament with a Fifa Ranking of over 100 and England's conquerors Croatia gain the benefit of an early goal when Ivar Olic is judged to have been brought down in the area by Rene Aufhauser. New Spurs recruit Luca Modric steps forward to score from the spot but the rest of the match is a dull affair with Austria the better side but narrowly failing to grab an equaliser.

AUSTRIA	(0) **0**	CROATIA	(1) **1**
			Modric 4 pen
			50,000

2. GERMANY V POLAND

Polish-born Lukas Podolski turns on his former countrymen to score twice as a confident-looking German side beat their neighbours.
The star of the World Cup, has struggled to impress since his move to Bayern Munich but is an accomplished finisher in the international arena. The Polish offside trap is regularly sprung and Miroslav Klose botches one chance before unselfishly setting up Podolski for the opener on 20 minutes. Germany continue to dominate the chances before Podolski makes it two after good work by sub Bastian Schweinsteiger and despite an air-shot by Klose.

GERMANY	(1) **2**	POLAND	(0) **0**
Podolski 20, 72			30,000

3. CROATIA V GERMANY

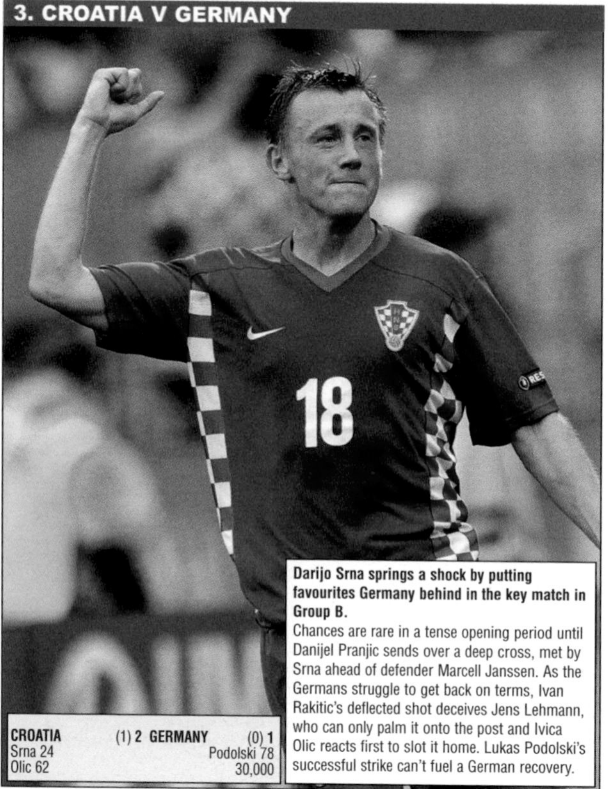

Darijo Srna springs a shock by putting favourites Germany behind in the key match in Group B.
Chances are rare in a tense opening period until Danijel Pranjic sends over a deep cross, met by Srna ahead of defender Marcell Janssen. As the Germans struggle to get back on terms, Ivan Rakitic's deflected shot deceives Jens Lehmann, who can only palm it onto the post and Ivica Olic reacts first to slot it home. Lukas Podolski's successful strike can't fuel a German recovery.

CROATIA	(1) **2**	GERMANY	(0) **1**
Srna 24			Podolski 78
Olic 62			30,000

4. AUSTRIA V POLAND

The large Polish community in England start issuing threats towards English ref Howard Webb when he awards a late penalty for Austria to level this game in injury time, leaving both sides' unlikely to progress.
Webb rules that Marcin Wasilewski is pulling Sebastian Prodi's shirt and Ivica Vastic scores from the spot to make it 1-1. Earlier, Roger Guerreiro taps home against the run of play after Marek Saganowski's shot is half-blocked by Emanuel Pogatetz. Celtic keeper Artur Boruc is in fine form for the Poles to keep out Austria until the final minute.

AUSTRIA	(0) **1**	POLAND	(1) **1**
Vastic 90 pen			Guerreiro Roger 30
			51,000

AUSTRIA

PLAYER	POS	AGE	APP	MINS ON	GOALS	CARDS(Y/R)	
Emanuel Pogatetz	DEF	25	3	270	0	1	0
Jurgen Macho	GK	30	3	270	0	0	0
Martin Stranzl	DEF	28	3	270	0	1	0
Martin Harnik	ATT	21	3	246	0	0	0
Andreas Ivanschitz	MID	24	3	243	0	1	0
Rene Aufhauser	MID	32	3	225	0	0	0
Umit Korkmaz	MID	22	3	202	0	1	0
Gyorgy Garics	DEF	24	2	180	0	0	0
Sebastian Prodl	DEF	21	2	180	0	2	0
Roland Linz	ATT	26	2	136	0	0	0
Christoph Leitgeb	MID	23	2	126	0	0	0
Jurgen Saumel	MID	23	3	105	0	1	0
Christian Fuchs	DEF	22	1	90	0	0	0
Erwin Hoffer	ATT	21	1	90	0	1	0
Joachim Standfest	DEF	28	1	90	0	0	0
Roman Kienast	MID	24	3	68	0	0	0
Ronald Gercaliu	DEF	22	1	68	0	0	0
Ivica Vastic	ATT	38	2	57	1	0	0
Martin Hiden	DEF	35	1	54	0	0	0
Alex Manninger	GK	31	0	0	0	0	0
Jurgen Patocka	DEF	30	0	0	0	0	0
Markus Katzer	DEF	28	0	0	0	0	0
Ramazan Ozcan	GK	24	0	0	0	0	0

GROUP B TABLE

	P	W	D	L	F	A	DIF	PTS
Croatia	3	3	0	0	4	1	+3	9
Germany	3	2	0	1	4	2	+2	6
Austria	3	0	1	2	1	3	-2	1
Poland	3	0	1	2	1	4	-3	1

POLAND

PLAYER	POS	AGE	APP	MINS ON	GOALS	CARDS(Y/R)	
Artur Boruc	GK	28	3	270	0	0	0
Dariusz Dudka	DEF	24	3	270	0	0	0
Jacek Krzynowek	MID	32	3	270	0	1	0
Marcin Wasilewski	DEF	28	3	270	0	1	0
Michal Zewlakow	DEF	32	3	270	0	0	0
Mariusz Lewandowski	DEF	29	3	225	0	2	0
Roger Guerreiro	MID	26	3	219	1	0	0
Euzebiusz Smolarek	ATT	27	3	216	0	1	0
Jacek Bak	DEF	35	2	180	0	1	0
Marek Saganowski	ATT	29	3	165	0	0	0
Wojciech Lobodzinski	MID	25	3	126	0	0	0
Pawel Golanski	DEF	25	2	119	0	0	0
Rafal Murawski	MID	26	2	96	0	0	0
Jakub Wawrzyniak	DEF	24	1	90	0	0	0
Adam Kokoszka	DEF	21	1	45	0	0	0
Maciej Zurawski	ATT	31	1	45	0	0	0
Mariusz Jop	DEF	29	1	45	0	0	0
Lukasz Piszczek	ATT	23	1	26	0	0	0
Tomas Zahorski	MID	23	1	23	0	1	0
Lukasz Fabianski	GK	23	0	0	0	0	0
Lukasz Gargula	MID	27	0	0	0	0	0
Michal Pazdan	MID	20	0	0	0	0	0
Wojciech Kowalewski	GK	31	0	0	0	0	0

5. AUSTRIA V GERMANY

13
DFB

Michael Ballack salvages an uncharacteristically stuttering Germany from embarrassment in their final group game.
Austria need a win to progress ahead of the Germans and another strong performance makes a mockery of their low Fifa ranking but their lack of a cutting edge tells against them again. Ballack's fierce free kick is still rising as it hits the net from 25 metres to take the Germans through. Lukas Podolski and Per Mertesacker have chances to add to the score but Germany are off form and Austria keep it tight to the end.

AUSTRIA (0) 0 GERMANY (0) 1
Ballack 49
51,000

6. POLAND V CROATIA

POLAND (0) 0 CROATIA (0) 1
Klasnic 53
30,000

Ivan Klasnic gives Croatia's second string team a victory over the disappointing Poles and a 100% record going into the quarter-finals.
Poland go into the game needing to win big and hope Austria beat Germany and are given hope by Slaven Bilic's decision to rest his first team. However, Artur Boruc is the busier keeper and even he is finally beaten by the Werder Bremen striker's whipped shot.

EURO 2008 GROUP C

The group stages

1. ROMANIA v FRANCE

The Romanians know they are supposed to be the whipping boys in the 'group of death' but are well organised and France never really look like getting through their defence in Zurich.
Thierry Henry misses the game through injury and Nicolas Anelka misses the only real opportunity of the match when he heads wide from man-of-the-match Franck Ribery's cross.

ROMANIA	(0) 0	FRANCE	(0) 0
			30,000

2. HOLLAND v ITALY

Stunning goals from Wesley Sneijder and Gio van Bronckhorst set the tournament alight as the Dutch complete a first win over Italy for 30 years.
Ruud van Nistelrooy is controversially ruled onside, due to Christian Panucci's being off the pitch, and stabs home a first goal after 26 minutes. Italy's attacks are repelled by the in-form Dutch, who break through van Bronckhorst for Dirk Kuyt to set up a sharp volleyed finish from Sneijder. And when van Bronckhorst adds a third in the 79th minute it's Italy's heaviest European Championships defeat.

HOLLAND	(2) 3	ITALY	(0) 0
van Nistelrooy 26, Sneijder 31, van Bronckhorst 80			31,500

3. ITALY v ROMANIA

Gianluigi Buffon is the hero of another poor Italian performance as he saves Adrian Mutu's penalty with just nine minutes to go and keeps his side's hopes alive.
Mutu previously gave Romania the lead before back-in-favour Italian fullback Christian Panucci levelled at a corner. The game's pivotal point comes when Panucci is judged to have held Daniel Nicolae back but Buffon gets hands and foot to Mutu's spot-kick to complete the save.

ITALY	(0) 1	ROMANIA	(0) 1
Panucci 56			Mutu 55
			30,000

HOLLAND – ITALY – ROMANIA – FRANCE

4. HOLLAND v FRANCE

The Dutch ensure they will top the 'group of death' after another famous win over one of the pre-tournament favourites – again by a three goal margin.
Dirk Kuyt heads Holland in front but France, led by the invention of Franck Ribery, have the better of the first half possession. Arjen Robben and Robin van Persie arrive after the interval and combine as Robben flies down the right wing and crosses low for van Persie to volley home. Thierry Henry glances in a goal for France before Robben blasts in over the head of Gregory Coupet from a tight angle. Wesley Sneijder finishes the game in style with a fierce shot from just outside the area which goes in off the bar.

HOLLAND	(1) 4	FRANCE	(0) 1
Kuyt 10, van Persie 59 Robben 72 Sneijder 90			Henry 71
			30,000

5. HOLLAND v ROMANIA

With Marco van Basten sending out a second string side, Romania fancy their chances of earning a result that will earn qualification from Group C; a win will be good enough and a draw might be.
However, they can't break down the Dutch defence and Ajax hot-shot Klaas-Jan Huntelaar fires the Dutch ahead from Ibrahim Afellay's low cross to shatter Romanian hopes. Robin van Persie ensures Holland's 100% record remains intact, driving home three minutes from time.

HOLLAND	(0) 2	ROMANIA	(0) 0
Huntelaar 54, van Persie 87			30,000

6. FRANCE v ITALY

The embattled French side are given a mountain to climb when Raymond Domenech's decision to drop Lilian Thuram and play Eric Abidal out of position at centre back is exploited by Italy.
Luca Toni is put through for one of a string of first half chances and Abidal is caught on the wrong side and trips the tall Italian. Andrea Pirlo converts the penalty, while Abidal is shown red, leaving France to play more than two thirds of the game with ten men. They have already lost Franck Ribery to injury and, although Jeremy Toulalan and Karim Benzema impress, there is no way back. Daniele De Rossi's free kick deflects in off Thierry Henry to end French interest in the tournament.

FRANCE	(0) 0	ITALY	(1) 2
			Pirlo 25 pen, De Rossi 62
			30,000

GROUP C TABLE

	P	W	D	L	F	A	DIF	PTS
Netherlands	3	3	0	0	9	1	+8	9
Italy	3	1	1	1	3	4	-1	4
Romania	3	0	2	1	1	3	-2	2
France	3	0	1	2	1	6	-5	1

ROMANIA

PLAYER	POS	AGE	APP	MINS ON	GOALS	CARDS(Y/R)	
Bogdan Lonut Lobont	GK	30	3	270	0	0	0
Cosmin Marius Contra	DEF	32	3	270	0	1	0
Cristian Chivu	DEF	27	3	270	0	2	0
Gabriel Tamas	DEF	24	3	270	0	0	0
Razvan Rat	DEF	27	3	270	0	0	0
Adrian Mutu	ATT	29	3	255	1	1	0
Daniel Niculae	ATT	25	3	212	0	1	0
Banel Nicolita	MID	23	3	202	0	0	0
Paul Constantin Codrea	MID	27	3	188	0	0	0
Dorin Goian	DEF	27	2	180	0	2	0
Razvan Cocis	MID	25	3	156	0	0	0
Mirel Matei Radoi	MID	27	2	113	0	0	0
Sorin Ghionea	DEF	29	1	90	0	0	0
Nicolae Dica	MID	28	3	86	0	0	0
Marius Niculae	ATT	27	2	70	0	0	0
Florentin Petre	MID	32	2	68	0	0	0
Adrian Cristea	MID	24	0	0	0	0	0
Ciprian Marica	ATT	22	0	0	0	0	0
Cosmin Moti	DEF	23	0	0	0	0	0
Cristian Sapunaru	DEF	24	0	0	0	0	0
Eduard Stanciou	GK	27	0	0	0	0	0
Marius Popa	GK	29	0	0	0	0	0
Stefan Daniel Radu	DEF	21	0	0	0	0	0

FRANCE

PLAYER	POS	AGE	APP	MINS ON	GOALS	CARDS(Y/R)	
Claude Makelele	MID	35	3	270	0	1	0
Gregory Coupet	GK	35	3	270	0	0	0
Jeremy Toulalan	MID	24	3	270	0	1	0
William Gallas	DEF	30	3	270	0	0	0
Franck Ribery	MID	25	3	189	0	0	0
Lilian Thuram	DEF	36	2	180	0	0	0
Patrice Evra	DEF	27	2	180	0	1	0
Thierry Henry	ATT	30	2	180	1	1	0
Willy Sagnol	DEF	31	2	180	0	1	0
Karim Benzema	ATT	20	2	167	0	0	0
Florent Malouda	ATT	28	2	149	0	0	0
Sydney Govou	ATT	28	2	139	0	1	0
Eric Abidal	DEF	28	2	113	0	0	1
Nicolas Anelka	ATT	29	3	112	0	0	0
Francois Clerc	DEF	25	1	90	0	0	0
Jean-Alain Boumsong	DEF	28	1	65	0	1	0
Bafetimbi Gomis	ATT	23	2	50	0	0	0
Samir Nasri	MID	21	2	29	0	0	0
Lassana Diarra	MID	23	0	0	0	0	0
Mathieu Flamini	MID	24	0	0	0	0	0
Patrick Vieira	MID	32	0	0	0	0	0
Sebastian Frey	GK	28	0	0	0	0	0
Sebastien Squillaci	DEF	27	0	0	0	0	0
Steve Mandanda	GK	23	0	0	0	0	0

EURO 2008 GROUP D

The group stages

1. SPAIN v RUSSIA

David Villa collects a sharp hat-trick to get Spain's tournament off to the best start against a game but out-classed Russia.
It was felt that Villa and Fernando Torres could not play together but the first goal puts paid to that theory as Torres' strength and persistence sends him in behind Denis Kolodin and he unselfishly squares for his partner to finish. Russia's Konstantin Zyryanov hits a post before a quick-fire Spanish move creates Villa's second and he makes the third himself. Roman Pavlyuchenko pulls a goal back before sub Cesc Fabregas completes the scoring with his first international goal.

SPAIN	(2) **4**	**RUSSIA**	(0) **1**
Villa 20,45,75, Fabregas 90			Pavluchenko 86
			30,000

2. GREECE v SWEDEN

A wondrous strike by Zlatan Ibrahimovic looks out of place in this dour game in Salzburg.
Ibrahimovic has the best strike rate in Serie A this season and is one of very few top table talents on show here. Holders Greece are pedestrian and unambitious as they try to conjure the same hard-to-beat demeanour that took them through Portugal 2004. Eventually Ibrahimovic finds space on the right, plays a one-two with Henrik Larsson and thumps his shot in by the far post. Petter Hanson scrambles home a fortunate second for Sweden before the end.

GREECE	(0) **0**	**SWEDEN**	(0) **2**
			Ibrahimovic 67, Hansson 73
			30,000

3. SWEDEN v SPAIN

David Villa strikes in injury time to pull a win out of nowhere for Spain in this game.
Sweden have worked hard to stifle opponents they know well from the qualifying competition. They fall behind to Fernando Torres opener as he latches onto a David Silva pass and turns it home. Zlatan Ibrahimovic levels with his second international strike in two games (after going 13 fixtures without a goal for Sweden), although Iker Casillas may have done better with the low shot. After that the game seems likely to end in a draw until Villa's late winner.

SWEDEN	(1) **1**	**SPAIN**	(1) **2**
Ibrahimovic 34			Torres 15, Villa 90
			30,000

4. RUSSIA v GREECE

Otto Rehhagel and holders Greece give up their Euro Championship defence with barely a murmur as Russia win through a scrappy Konstantin Zyryanov goal.
The Greek keeper Antonis Nikopolidis chases a cross that is already way past his goal in the 33rd minute only for Sergei Semak to beat the Olympiakos goalie to the ball and cross it back for Zyrianov to score. Greece have no cutting edge and Russia deserve their win.

RUSSIA	(1) **1**	**GREECE**	(0) **0**
Zyrianov 33			
			31,000

SPAIN – RUSSIA – SWEDEN – GREECE

SWEDEN

PLAYER	POS	AGE	APP	MINS ON	GOALS	CARDS(Y/R)	
Anders Svensson	MID	31	3	270	0	1	0
Andreas Isaksson	GK	26	3	270	0	1	0
Fredrik Ljungberg	MID	31	3	270	0	0	0
Olof Mellberg	DEF	30	3	270	0	0	0
Petter Hansson	DEF	31	3	270	1	0	0
Henrik Larsson	ATT	36	3	266	0	0	0
Mikael Nilsson	DEF	30	3	258	0	0	0
Daniel Andersson	MID	30	3	235	0	0	0
Zlatan Ibrahimovic	ATT	26	3	205	2	0	0
Fredrik Stoor	DEF	24	3	197	0	0	0
Johan Elmander	ATT	27	3	188	0	1	0
Christian Wilhelmsson	MID	28	1	77	0	0	0
Niclas Alexandersson	MID	36	1	73	0	0	0
Markus Rosenberg	ATT	25	2	58	0	0	0
Kim Kallstrom	MID	25	2	39	0	0	0
Marcus Allback	ATT	34	1	12	0	0	0
Sebastian Larsson	MID	23	1	12	0	0	0
Andreas Granqvist	DEF	23	0	0	0	0	0
Daniel Majstorovic	DEF	31	0	0	0	0	0
Johan Wiland	GK	27	0	0	0	0	0
Mikael Dorsin	DEF	26	0	0	0	0	0
Rami Shaaban	GK	33	0	0	0	0	0
Tobias Linderoth	MID	29	0	0	0	0	0

GROUP D TABLE

	P	W	D	L	F	A	DIF	PTS
Spain	3	3	0	0	8	3	+5	9
Russia	3	2	0	1	4	4	0	6
Sweden	3	1	0	2	3	4	-1	3
Greece	3	0	0	3	1	5	-4	0

GREECE

PLAYER	POS	AGE	APP	MINS ON	GOALS	CARDS(Y/R)		HOME COUNTRY
Angelos Basinas	MID	32	3	270	0	1	0	
Angelos Charisteas	ATT	28	3	270	1	1	0	
Antonios Nikopolidis	GK	37	3	270	0	0	0	
Konstantinos Katsouranis	MID	29	3	270	0	0	0	
Traianos Dellas	DEF	32	3	249	0	0	0	
Sotirios Kyrgiakos	DEF	28	3	242	0	0	0	
Giorgos Karagounis	MID	31	3	214	0	2	0	
Ioannis Amanatidis	ATT	26	3	190	0	0	0	
Vassillis Torosidis	DEF	23	2	180	0	1	0	
Giourkas Seitaridis	DEF	27	2	129	0	1	0	
Paraskevas Antzas	DEF	31	2	118	0	0	0	
Christos Patsatzoglou	DEF	29	1	90	0	0	0	
Loukas Vyntra	MID	27	1	90	0	1	0	
Nikolaos Spiropoulos	DEF	24	1	90	0	0	0	
Dimitrios Salpigidis	ATT	26	1	85	0	0	0	
Theofanis Gekas	ATT	28	2	75	0	0	0	
Nikolaos Liberopoulos	ATT	32	1	60	0	1	0	
Georgios Samaras	ATT	23	1	45	0	0	0	
Alexandros Tziolis	MID	23	1	17	0	0	0	
Stelios Giannakopoulos	MID	33	2	16	0	0	0	
Alexandroz Tzorvas	GK	25	0	0	0	0	0	
Konstantinos Chalkias	GK	34	0	0	0	0	0	
Yannis Goumas	DEF	33	0	0	0	0	0	

5. GREECE v SPAIN

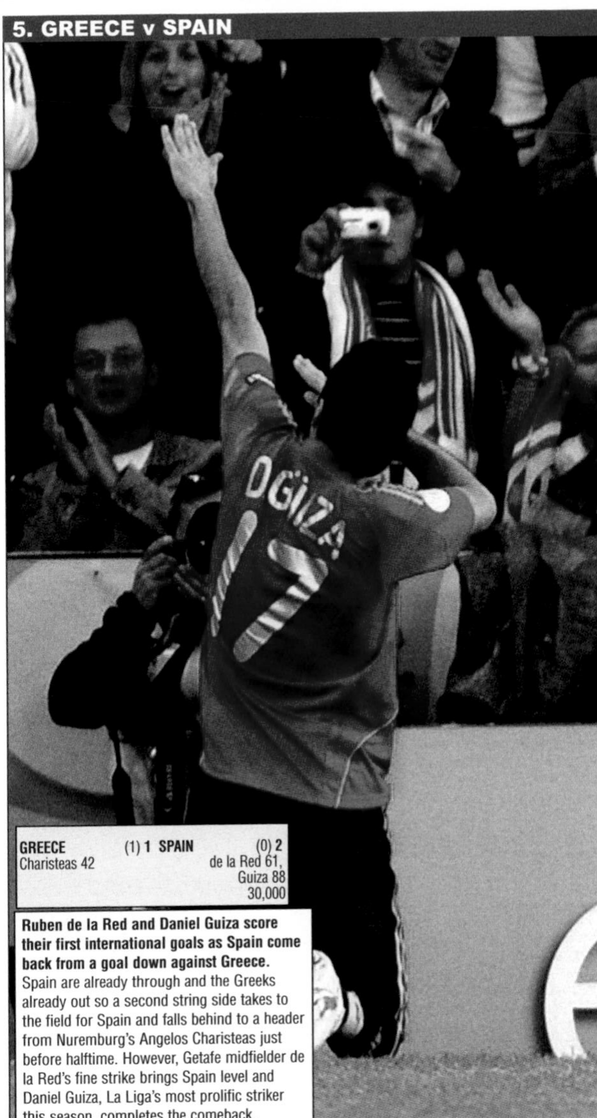

GREECE	(1) 1	SPAIN	(0) 2
Charisteas 42			de la Red 61, Guiza 88
			30,000

Ruben de la Red and Daniel Guiza score their first international goals as Spain come back from a goal down against Greece.
Spain are already through and the Greeks already out so a second string side takes to the field for Spain and falls behind to a header from Nuremburg's Angelos Charisteas just before halftime. However, Getafe midfielder de la Red's fine strike brings Spain level and Daniel Guiza, La Liga's most prolific striker this season, completes the comeback.

6. RUSSIA V SWEDEN

RUSSIA	(1) 2	SWEDEN	(0) 0
Pavluchenko 24			
Arshavin 50			30,000

Guus Hiddink's side shows unexpected attacking quality to take up the second qualifying spot behind Spain and eliminate rivals Sweden.
Previously suspended Andrei Arshavin acts as the catalyst to some fluid football and a good move ends with Roman Pavlyuchenko's strike to put Russia ahead. Henrik Larsson goes closest for Sweden with a header against the bar before the baby-faced Arshavin adds a cool finish to Yuri Zhirkov's run to ease Russia through.

EURO 2008

Quarter-finals

GERMANY v PORTUGAL

Joachim Low's Germany offer a reminder of their flamboyant attacking at the last World Cup as they run at Portugal from the start. Blond Bayern midfielder Bastian Schweinsteiger leaves his marker for dead, racing onto a Lukas Podolski cross to fire home after some crisp German inter-passing on 22 minutes. Schweisteiger turns provider four minutes later as his free kick floats beyond Portugal's back line and an unmarked Miroslav Klose heads home. Cristiano Ronaldo provides a lifeline with a fine run and shot that Jens Lehmann can only parry out to Nuno Gomes and the Portuguese skipper turns it home. Michael Ballack restores Germany's two-goal lead with a header and, although subs Nani and Helder Postiga combine to pull one back, Portugal are on their way home.

PORTUGAL (1) **2** **GERMANY** (2) **3**
Gomes 41, Postiga 87 — Schweinsteiger 22, Klose 26, Ballack 62
39,000

TURKEY v CROATIA

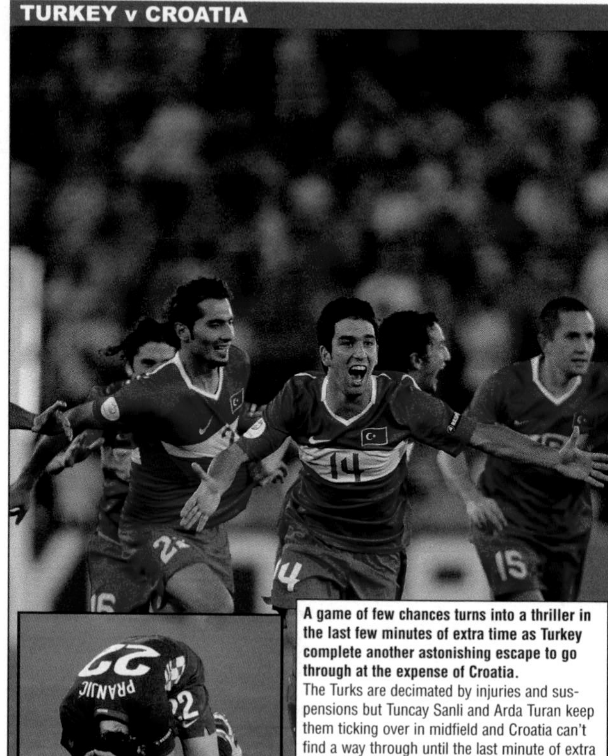

TURKEY (0) **1** **CROATIA** (0) **1**
Semih 120 — Klasnic 119
aet - Turkey won 3-1 on penalties
51,000

A game of few chances turns into a thriller in the last few minutes of extra time as Turkey complete another astonishing escape to go through at the expense of Croatia.
The Turks are decimated by injuries and suspensions but Tuncay Sanli and Arda Turan keep them ticking over in midfield and Croatia can't find a way through until the last minute of extra time when Ivan Klasnic heads in Luca Modric's cross. At which point Turkey look beaten yet somehow Semih Semturk's final kick of the game deflects in to take the game to penalties. Croatia only score one of their four and Turkey's three successful kicks are enough.

PORTUGAL

PLAYER	POS	AGE	APP	MINS ON	GOALS	CARDS(Y/R)	
Pepe	DEF	25	4	360	1	1	0
Ricardo	GK	32	4	360	0	0	0
Paulo Ferreira	DEF	29	4	310	0	1	0
Cristiano Ronaldo	ATT	23	3	270	1	0	0
Jose Bosingwa	DEF	25	3	270	0	1	0
Ricardo Carvalho	DEF	30	3	270	0	0	0
Deco	MID	30	3	269	1	0	0
Petit	MID	31	3	252	0	1	0
Simao Sabrosa	MID	28	3	251	0	0	0
Joao Moutinho	MID	21	4	214	0	0	0
Nuno Gomes	ATT	31	3	213	1	0	0
Raul Meireles	MID	25	3	158	1	0	0
Nani	ATT	21	3	136	0	0	0
Fernando Meira	DEF	30	3	107	0	1	0
Ricardo Quaresma	ATT	24	2	101	1	0	0
Helder Postiga	ATT	25	2	91	1	1	0
Bruno Alves	DEF	26	1	90	0	0	0
Luis Miguel	DEF	28	1	90	0	1	0
Miguel Veloso	MID	22	1	70	0	0	0
Jorge Ribeiro	DEF	26	1	50	0	1	0
Hugo Almeida	ATT	24	2	28	0	0	0
Quim	GK	34	0	0	0	0	0
Rui Patricio	GK	20	0	0	0	0	0

CROATIA

PLAYER	POS	AGE	APP	MINS ON	GOALS	CARDS(Y/R)	
Danijel Pranjic	MID	26	4	390	0	0	0
Vedran Corluka	DEF	22	4	364	0	0	0
Ivan Rakitic	MID	20	3	300	0	0	0
Josip Simunic	DEF	30	3	300	0	1	0
Luka Modric	MID	22	3	300	1	1	0
Niko Kovac	MID	36	3	300	0	0	0
Robert Kovac	DEF	34	3	300	0	1	0
Stipe Pletikosa	GK	29	3	300	0	0	0
Darijo Srna	MID	26	3	289	1	1	0
Ivica Olic	ATT	28	3	249	1	0	0
Niko Kranjcar	MID	23	4	226	0	0	0
Mladen Petric	ATT	27	4	219	0	0	0
Jerko Leko	MID	28	2	101	0	1	0
Ognjen Vukojevic	MID	24	2	98	0	1	0
Ivan Klasnic	ATT	28	2	97	2	0	0
Dario Simic	DEF	32	1	90	0	0	0
Hrvoje Vejic	DEF	31	1	90	0	1	0
Nikola Pokrivac	MID	22	1	90	0	0	0
Vedran Runje	GK	32	1	90	0	0	0
Dario Knezevic	DEF	26	3	61	0	0	0
Igor Budan	ATT	28	1	19	0	0	0
Nikola Kalinic	ATT	20	1	17	0	0	0
Mario Galinovic	GK	31	0	0	0	0	0

HOLLAND v RUSSIA

Guus Hiddink claims he wants to be 'a big traitor' and gets his wish as his lively Russian side put his native Holland to the sword.
The Dutch never look like the team that beat France and Italy so comprehensively as Edwin van der Sar is regularly called into action before Russia take a 56th minute lead through Roman Pavlyuchenko's volley. The Dutch are reduced to shooting from distance until a Wesley Sneijder free kick is headed home by Ruud van Nistelrooy to take the game into extra time. Far from being an escape for Holland, it just subjects them to a dominant display from the Russians who score twice, through Dmitri Torbinski and Andrei Arshavin, to progress.

HOLLAND (0) **1** **RUSSIA (aet)** (0) **3**
van Nistelrooy 86 — Pavlyuchenko 56, Torbinski 112, Arshavin 116
38,000

SPAIN v ITALY

Spain have lost major tournament penalty shoot-outs on three occasions on June 22nd but the hoodoo is finally beaten by Iker Casillas.
After a dull quarter-final, the Spanish skipper and goalkeeper is up against another of the world's best in Italian keeper Gianluigi Buffon. Casillas saves two penalties; the first from Daniel De Rossi and the second from Antonio Di Natale, after Spain's Daniel Guiza has also missed. At 3-2, Arsenal's Cesc Fabregas steps up and fires Spain into the semis with his first professional penalty kick.

SPAIN (0) **0** **ITALY** (0) **0**
aet - Spain win 4-2 on penalties
48,000

HOLLAND

PLAYER	POS	AGE	APP	MINS ON	GOALS	CARDS(Y/R)	
Andre Ooijer	DEF	33	3	300	0	1	0
Edwin van der Sar	GK	37	3	300	0	0	0
Giovanni Van Bronckhorst	MID	33	3	300	1	0	0
Joris Mathijsen	DEF	28	3	300	0	0	0
Nigel de Jong	MID	23	3	300	0	1	0
Wesley Sneijder	MID	24	3	300	2	0	0
Rafael van der Vaart	MID	25	3	287	0	1	0
Orlando Engelaar	MID	28	4	286	0	0	0
Ruud van Nistelrooy	ATT	32	3	279	2	0	0
Khalid Boulahrouz	DEF	26	4	276	0	1	0
Robin van Persie	ATT	24	4	221	2	1	0
Dirk Kuyt	ATT	27	4	209	1	0	0
John Heitinga	DEF	24	3	171	0	0	0
Ibrahim Afellay	MID	22	3	159	0	0	0
Arjen Robben	ATT	24	2	106	1	0	0
Wilfred Bouma	DEF	30	2	103	0	0	0
Demy de Zeeuw	MID	25	1	90	0	0	0
Maarten Stekelenburg	GK	25	1	90	0	0	0
Tim de Cler	DEF	29	1	90	0	0	0
Klaas-Jan Huntelaar	ATT	24	1	82	1	0	0
Mario Melchiot	DEF	31	1	33	0	0	0
Jan Vennegoor of Hesselink	ATT	29	1	8	0	0	0
Henk Timmer	GK	36	0	0	0	0	0

ITALY

PLAYER	POS	AGE	APP	MINS ON	GOALS	CARDS(Y/R)	
Christian Panucci	DEF	35	4	390	1	0	0
Gianluca Zambrotta	DEF	31	4	390	0	1	0
Gianluigi Buffon	GK	30	4	390	0	0	0
Luca Toni	ATT	31	4	390	0	1	0
Fabio Grosso	DEF	30	4	337	0	0	0
Daniele De Rossi	MID	24	3	300	1	1	0
Giorgio Chiellini	DEF	23	3	300	0	1	0
Massimo Ambrosini	MID	31	4	252	0	1	0
Mauro German Camoranesi	MID	31	4	248	0	0	0
Andrea Pirlo	MID	29	3	234	1	2	0
Antonio Cassano	ATT	25	4	213	0	0	0
Simone Perrotta	MID	30	3	177	0	0	0
Gennaro Ivan Gattuso	MID	30	2	171	0	2	0
Alberto Aquilani	MID	23	2	116	0	0	0
Alessandro Del Piero	ATT	33	3	116	0	0	0
Antonio Di Natale	ATT	30	2	109	0	0	0
Andrea Barzagli	DEF	27	1	90	0	0	0
Marco Materazzi	DEF	34	1	53	0	0	0
Fabio Quagliarella	ATT	25	1	14	0	0	0
Alessandro Gamberini	DEF	26	0	0	0	0	0
Marco Amelia	GK	26	0	0	0	0	0
Marco Borriello	ATT	26	0	0	0	0	0
Morgan De Sanctis	GK	31	0	0	0	0	0

EURO 2008

Semi-finals

GERMANY v TURKEY

German full back Philipp Lahm finally deals a killer blow to Turkish hopes and spirit in the 90th minute of this low quality but exciting semi. Manager Fatih Terim is without nine injured and suspended Turkish stars, yet his side take the game to Germany and score first through Ugur Borel. Germany's Bastian Schweinsteiger taps in against the run of play and they go ahead when Miroslav Klose heads home, taking advantage of Rustu Recber's poor attempt to claim a Lahm cross. Cue another late Turkish comeback with Semih Senturk again the scorer, this time turning in a Sabri Sarioglu cross. With extra time looming and Turkish confidence high, Germany need something special and Lahm provides the stunning finish to Thomas Hitzlsperger's pass.

GERMANY (1) **3** **TURKEY** (1) **2**
Schweinsteiger 26, Klose 79, Lahm 90 — Boral 22, Semih 86
39,000

TURKEY

PLAYER	POS	AGE	APP	MINS ON	GOALS	CARDS(Y/R)	
Hakan Kadir Balta	DEF	25	5	480	0	1	0
Hamit Altintop	MID	25	5	465	0	0	0
Tuncay Sanli	ATT	26	4	390	0	2	0
Nihat Kahveci	ATT	28	4	380	2	0	0
Mehmet Aurelio	MID	30	4	360	0	2	0
Arda Turan	MID	21	3	300	2	2	0
Sabri Sarioglu	MID	23	4	300	0	1	0
Colin Kazim-Richards	MID	21	5	279	0	1	0
Emre Asik	DEF	34	4	274	0	2	0
Servet Cetin	DEF	27	3	270	0	0	0
Volkan Demirel	GK	26	3	269	0	0	1
Mehmet Topal	MID	22	4	266	0	1	0
Gokhan Zan	DEF	26	3	264	0	1	0
Semih Senturk	ATT	25	5	240	3	1	0
Rustu Recber	GK	35	2	210	0	0	0
Ugur Boral	MID	26	2	143	1	1	0
Emre Belozoglu	MID	27	1	90	0	0	0
Ayhan Akman	MID	31	1	80	0	0	0
Fehmi Emre Gungor	DEF	23	1	62	0	0	0
Gokdeniz Karadeniz	MID	28	3	56	0	0	0
Mevlut Erdinc	ATT	21	2	55	0	0	0
Tumer Metin	MID	33	2	46	0	0	0
Tolga Zengin	GK	24	0	0	0	0	0

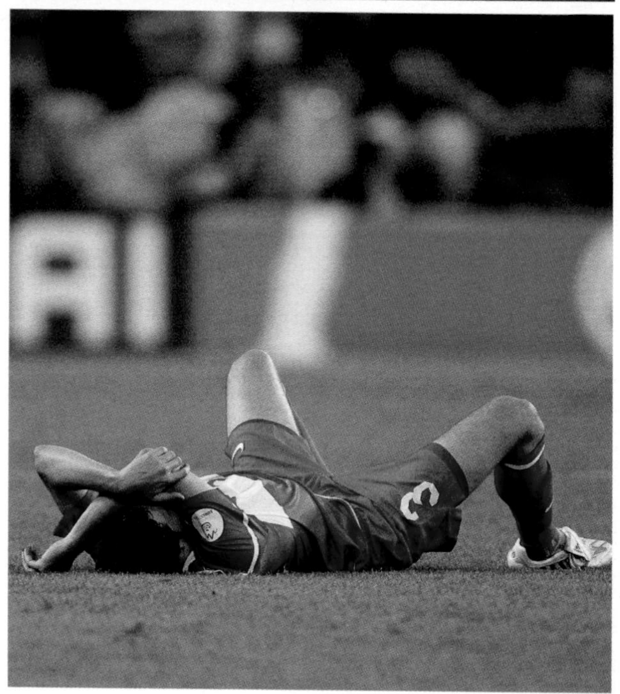

SPAIN v RUSSIA

Slick-passing Spain beat Russia by a three goal margin for the second time in the tournament to claim a final place.

Strange scheduling means Russia have to play Spain a second time and they can't cope with the sharp interplay of Spain's five-man midfield once Cesc Fabregas has replaced injured striker David Villa. Russia barely get a kick in the second half with Andres Iniesta combining with his Barca team-mate Xavi who fires Spain ahead on 50 minutes. With David Silva, one of the finds of the tournament, working tirelessly down the right, Spain's neat triangles always look like adding a second. It comes from sub Daniel Guiza after an inventive flick pass from Fabregas puts him through for an adept finish. Fabregas surely claims a starting place in the final with his incisive creativity and makes the third goal for Silva with a low pin-point cross to put the Valencia midfielder in on goal.

RUSSIA (0) **0** **SPAIN** (0) **3**
Xavi 50, Guiza 73, Silva 82
51,000

RUSSIA

PLAYER	POS	AGE	APP	MINS ON	GOALS	CARDS(Y/R)	
Aleksandr Anyukov	DEF	25	5	480	0	0	0
Igor Akinfeev	GK	22	5	480	0	0	0
Konstatnin Zyryanov	MID	30	5	480	1	0	0
Sergei Semak	MID	32	5	480	0	1	0
Yuri Zhirkov	MID	24	5	476	0	2	0
Roman Pavlyuchenko	ATT	26	5	473	3	0	0
Denis Kolodin	DEF	26	4	390	0	2	0
Sergei Ignashevitch	DEF	28	4	390	0	0	0
Igor Semshov	MID	30	5	359	0	0	0
Diniyar Bilyaletdinov	MID	23	5	311	0	1	0
Andrei Arshavin	ATT	27	3	300	2	1	0
Ivan Saenko	ATT	24	4	182	0	1	0
Dmitry Torbinsky	MID	24	3	164	1	2	0
Vasili Berezutsky	DEF	26	2	94	0	0	0
Roman Shirokov	DEF	26	1	90	0	0	0
Dmitri Sychev	ATT	24	3	85	0	0	0
Vladimir Bystrov	MID	24	2	25	0	0	0
Roman Adamov	ATT	26	1	21	0	0	0
Alexei Berezutsky	DEF	26	0	0	0	0	0
Oleg Ivanov	ATT	21	0	0	0	0	0
Renat Yanbayev	MID	24	0	0	0	0	0
Vladimir Gabulov	GK	24	0	0	0	0	0
Vyacheslav Malafeev	GK	29	0	0	0	0	0

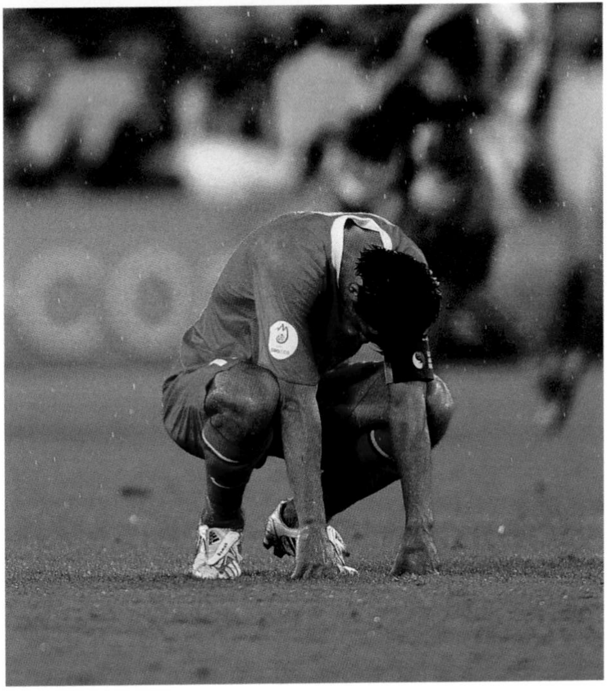

EURO 2008

GERMANY v SPAIN

GERMANY	(0) 0	SPAIN	(1) 1
			Torres 33
			51,000

Fernando Torres completes his marvellous season with the winning goal as Spain end 44 years of waiting to win a major tournament.

While fellow finalists Germany stuttered and struggled against other teams, Spain had reached the final firing goals and playing devastating one touch football through the middle. They won every game, boast the tournament top scorer in David Villa, who was injured for the final, and hit 12 goals. Germany are flattered by the 1-0 defeat as a combination of shocking defending and quick-fire Spanish breaks continue to keep Jens Lehmann busy.

Torres heads a Sergio Ramos cross against the post on 23 minutes and goes one better on 33, outstripping Philipp Lahm to a Xavi through ball and clipping a decisive finish over Lehmann. The Barca duo of Andres Iniesta and Xavi control the pace and the game in the second half and, while Spain fail to add to their goal, Germany barely threaten.

GERMANY

PLAYER	POS	AGE	APP	MINS ON	GOALS	CARDS(Y/R)	
Christoph Metzelder	DEF	27	6	540	0	0	0
Jens Lehmann	GK	38	6	540	0	1	0
Michael Ballack	MID	31	6	540	2	2	0
Per Mertesacker	DEF	23	6	540	0	0	0
Lukas Podolski	ATT	23	6	532	3	0	0
Miroslav Klose	ATT	30	6	524	2	0	0
Philipp Lahm	DEF	24	6	495	1	1	0
Torsten Frings	MID	31	5	405	0	0	0
Arne Friedrich	DEF	29	4	360	0	1	0
Bastian Schweinsteiger	MID	23	5	323	2	1	1
Thomas Hitzlsperger	MID	26	5	266	0	0	0
Clemens Fritz	DEF	27	4	232	0	0	0
Mario Gomez	ATT	22	4	209	0	0	0
Marcell Jansen	DEF	22	5	183	0	0	0
Simon Rolfes	MID	26	2	135	0	0	0
David Odonkor	MID	24	1	45	0	0	0
Kevin Kuranyi	ATT	26	3	43	0	1	0
Tim Borowski	MID	28	2	19	0	0	0
Oliver Neuville	ATT	35	1	8	0	0	0
Heiko Westermann	DEF	24	0	0	0	0	0
Piotr Trochowski	MID	24	0	0	0	0	0
Rene Adler	GK	23	0	0	0	0	0
Robert Enke	GK	30	0	0	0	0	0

SPAIN

PLAYER	POS	AGE	APP	MINS ON	GOALS	CARDS(Y/R)	
Carlos Marchena	DEF	28	5	480	0	1	0
Iker Casillas	GK	27	5	480	0	1	0
Joan Capdevila	DEF	30	5	480	0	0	0
Marcos Senna	MID	31	5	480	0	0	0
Sergio Ramos	DEF	22	5	480	0	0	0
David Silva	MID	22	5	442	1	0	0
Andres Iniesta	MID	24	6	415	0	1	0
Carles Puyol	DEF	30	5	413	0	0	0
Fernando Torres	ATT	24	5	372	2	1	0
Xavi	MID	28	5	364	1	0	0
Francesc Fabregas	MID	21	6	339	1	0	0
David Villa	ATT	26	4	334	4	1	0
Santiago Cazorla	MID	23	5	180	0	1	0
Daniel Guiza	ATT	27	4	161	2	1	0
Raul Albiol	DEF	22	2	157	0	0	0
Xabi Alonso	MID	26	4	153	0	0	0
Alvaro Arbeloa	DEF	25	1	90	0	1	0
Fernando Navarro	DEF	26	1	90	0	0	0
Jose Reina	GK	25	1	90	0	0	0
Juan Gutierrez Moreno	DEF	31	1	90	0	0	0
Ruben De la Red	MID	23	1	90	1	0	0
Sergio Garcia de la Fuente	ATT	25	1	90	0	0	0
Andres Palop	GK	34	0	0	0	0	0

GERMANY v SPAIN

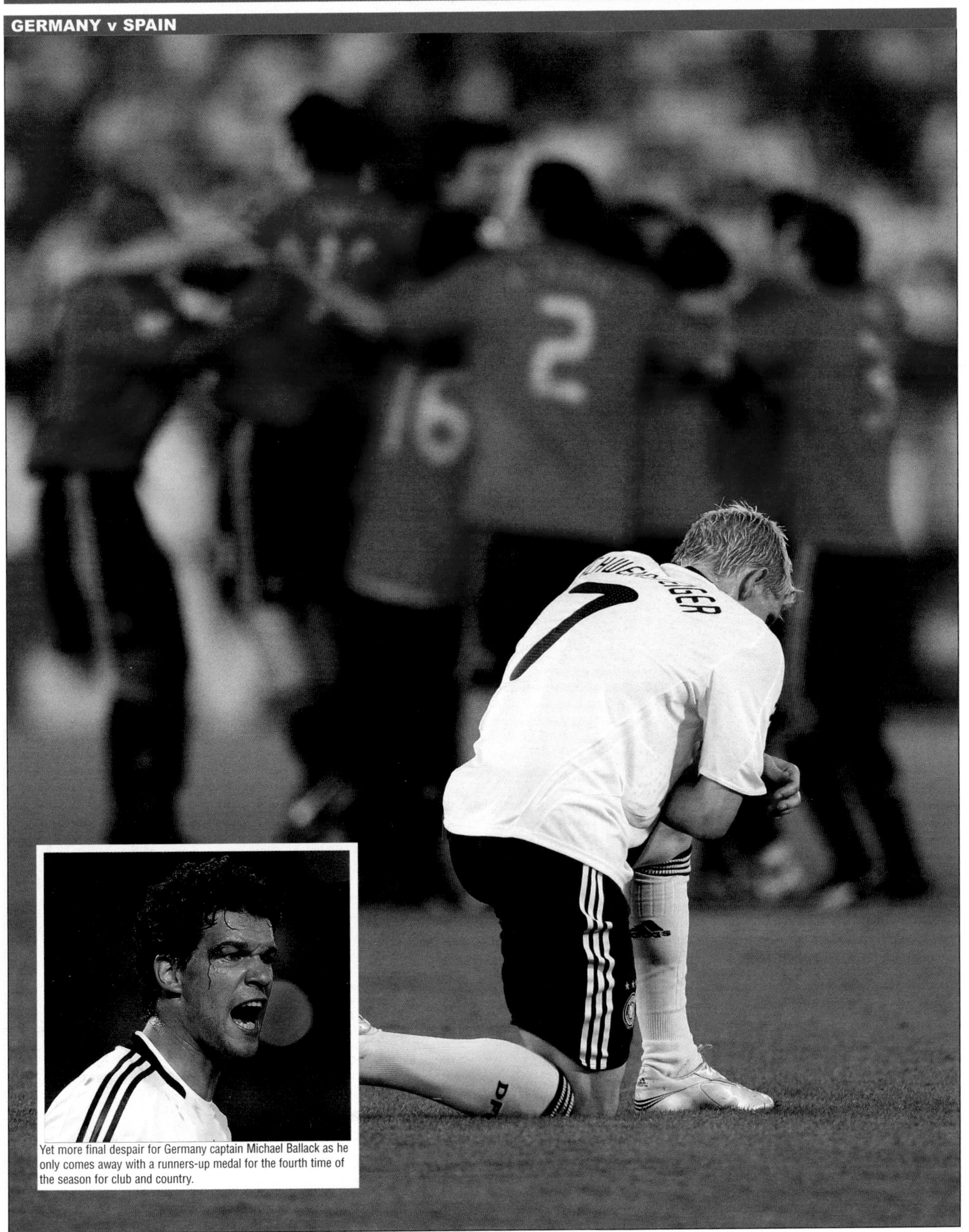

Yet more final despair for Germany captain Michael Ballack as he only comes away with a runners-up medal for the fourth time of the season for club and country.

African Nations Cup Group Stages

GROUP A

Ghana 2 **Guinea** 1
A.Gyan 55 pen, Muntari 90 — Kalabane 65
35,000

A stunning strike by Portsmouth's midfielder Sulley Ali Muntari gives hosts Ghana a welcome win in the cup opener in Accra. Asamoah Gyan of Udinese in Serie A scores first with a penalty after Junior Agogo is brought down by Oumar Kalabane. The defender makes amends by equalising for Guinea with a header from a corner but home crowd nerves are settled when Muntari strikes with a rising drive from 20 yards in the final minute.

Namibia 1 **Morocco** 5
Brendell 24 — Alloudi 1, 5, 28, Sektioui 40 pen, Zerka 74
2,000

Moroccan striker Soufane Alloudi plays his football in the United Arab Emirates but he will have come to European attention with a first half hat-trick to set the African Nations Cup alight. It comes against Namibia in Morocco's opening game and although Brian Brendell pulls one back, further goals from Porto's Tarik Sektioui and Monsef Zerka give the Moroccans a 5-1 win.

Ghana 1 **Namibia** 0
Agogo 41
45,000

Guinea 3 **Morocco** 2
Feindouno 11, 63 pen, Is.Bangoura 59 — Aboucharouane 60, Ouaddou 90
15,000

Ghana 2 **Morocco** 0
Essien 26, Muntari 45
40,000

Guinea 1 **Namibia** 1
Youla 62 — Brendell 81
1,000

Hosts Ghana kept a 100% record in Group A of their tournament with Chelsea's Michael Essien and Muntari scoring the goals in the final win over Morocco. Second spot turned on the game between Guinea and Morocco with St Etienne midfielder Pascal Feindouno scoring twice as he led his side to a 3-2 victory.

GROUP A TABLE

	P	W	D	L	DIF	PTS
Ghana	3	3	0	0	+4	9
Guinea	3	1	1	1	0	4
Morocco	3	1	0	2	+1	3
Namibia	3	0	1	2	-5	1

GROUP B

Mali 1 **Benin** 0
Kanoute 49 pen
20,000

Nigeria 0 **Ivory Coast** 1
S.Kalou 66
20,000

Salomon Kalou scores the only goal as African Nations Cup favourites Ivory Coast confirm their status with a first match victory over major rivals Nigeria. Both sides field six players from the Premier League in their starting line-ups with Kanu and Obafemi Martins creating early problems for the Ivory Coast defence, while Kolo Toure forces a good save in the 59th minute. However, there is no stopping Kalou's goal as he beats three defenders before thrashing home.

Ivory Coast 4 **Benin** 1
Drogba 41, Yaya.Toure 44, AK.Keita 52, Dindane 62 — Omotoyossi 90
13,000

Nigeria 0 **Mali** 0
16,000

Ivory Coast 3 **Mali** 0
Drogba 10, Zoro 50, Sanogo 85
20,000

Nigeria 2 **Benin** 0
Mikel 53, Yakubu 86
4,000

John Obi Mikel scores one and grabs an assist to help the Super Eagles progress from Group B in their final game. After a defeat and a goalless draw, Nigeria need to beat Benin and hope the Ivory Coast do them a favour against Mali. Under pressure coach Bertie Vogts leaves out Kanu and Martins. Benin are already eliminated but resist until Mikel's 53rd minute header. The Chelsea ball-winner then sets up Yakubu to make sure of the win.

With Ivory Coast winning narrowly over Nigeria and thrashing Benin to be sure of qualification, Mali and Nigeria were battling for the second qualifying spot. In the final games Mali fell behind to an early Didier Drogba goal against the Ivory Coast. A narrow defeat could still have put Mali through but they lost by three goals and Nigeria won by two.

GROUP B TABLE

	P	W	D	L	DIF	PTS
Ivory Coast	3	3	0	0	+7	9
Nigeria	3	1	1	1	+1	4
Mali	3	1	1	1	-2	4
Benin	3	0	0	3	-6	0

GROUP C

Egypt 4 **Cameroon** 2
Rabou 14 pen, 82, Zidan 17, 45 — Eto'o 51, 90
42,000

Holders Egypt unleash their own Zidan - Hamburg's Mohamed Zidan – to beat major Group C rivals Cameroon in their opening game. Holding midfielder Hosni Abd Rabou scores from the spot before Zidan strikes twice in the first half to go in 3-0 up. Samuel Eto'o pulls one back early in the second half before Hosni fires home again to restore the three goal lead. Eto'o's late penalty is only consolation.

Sudan 0 **Zambia** 3
Chamanga 3, J.Mulenga 51, F.Katongo 59
30,000

Cameroon 5 **Zambia** 1
Geremi 26, Job 32, 80, Emana 43, Eto'o 66 pen — C.Katongo 89
10,000

Former Boro team-mates Geremi and Joseph Desire Job score the goals to put Cameroon back on track in Group C. Geremi starts a 5-1 rout with a powerful free kick before Job nets a second four minutes later. Eto'o hits a penalty to equal the African Cup finals scoring record and Job adds a fifth before Zambian skipper Chris Katongo forces home a late reply.

Egypt 3 **Sudan** 0
Rabou 28 pen, Aboutraika 57, 83
15,000

Cameroon 3 **Sudan** 0
Eto'o 27 pen, 90, Ali Elkhidir 34 og
10,000

Egypt 1 **Zambia** 1
Zaki 15 — C.Katongo 88
2,000

Group C favourites Cameroon and Egypt qualified easily for the quarter finals ahead of Zambia and Sudan. Holders Egypt hit four against to beat their rivals before smashing Sudan. They can afford to relax against Zambia while Cameroon's Barcelona striker Eto'o strikes four goals as he helps his side ease into second spot.

GROUP C TABLE

	P	W	D	L	DIF	PTS
Egypt	3	2	1	0	+5	7
Cameroon	3	2	0	1	+5	6
Zambia	3	1	1	1	-1	4
Sudan	3	0	0	3	-9	0

GROUP D

South Africa 1 **Angola** 1
Van Heerden 87 — Manucho 29
15,000

Tunisia 2 **Senegal** 2
Jomaa 9, Traoui 82 — Sall 45, Kamara 66
12,000

Senegal 1 **Angola** 3
Ab.Faye 18 — Manucho 50, 67, Flavio 77
10,000

New Manchester United recruit Manucho looks a good acquisition as he nets twice against a powerful Senegal side to make Angola favourites to progress from Group D. Abdoulaye Faye heads Senegal into an interval lead before United's new striker - currently on loan with Panathinaikos – nods home an equaliser and scores his third of the tournament in a goalmouth scramble. Another header by team-mate Flavio completes Angola's victory.

Tunisia 3 **South Africa** 1
Dos Santos 8, 33, Ben Saada 30 — Mphela 87
15,000

Brazilian-born Tunisian striker Francileudo Silva dos Santos moves his team into a strong position in Group D with a brace of goals against South Africa. After two draws in the first round of matches in the group, Santos strikes twice, either side of a Chaouki Ben Saada goal to give the north African side a 3-0 interval lead. Katlego Mphela replies for Bafana Bafana in the 87th minute but it's all over by then.

Senegal 1 **South Africa** 1
H.Camara 37 — Van Heerden 13
15,000

Tunisia 0 **Angola** 0
10,000

Four draws in Group D but the top striking talents of Tunisian import Francileudo Silva dos Santos and emerging Angolan star Manucho resolve the qualification issue in the third and fourth fixtures. Their respective teams go into the final fixture against each-other, knowing that a draw will be enough – and it is.

GROUP D TABLE

	P	W	D	L	DIF	PTS
Tunisia	3	1	2	0	+2	5
Angola	3	1	2	0	+2	5
Senegal	3	0	2	1	-2	2
South Africa	3	0	2	1	-2	2

African Nations Cup Quarter Finals

1. GHANA v NIGERIA

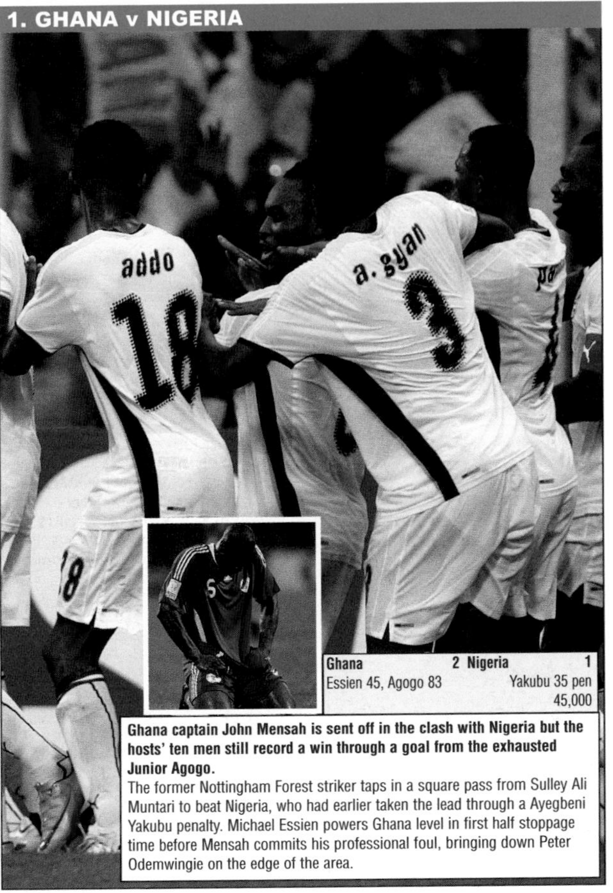
addo
18
a.gyan
3

Ghana	2	Nigeria	1
Essien 45, Agogo 83		Yakubu 35 pen	
			45,000

Ghana captain John Mensah is sent off in the clash with Nigeria but the hosts' ten men still record a win through a goal from the exhausted Junior Agogo.
The former Nottingham Forest striker taps in a square pass from Sulley Ali Muntari to beat Nigeria, who had earlier taken the lead through a Ayegbeni Yakubu penalty. Michael Essien powers Ghana level in first half stoppage time before Mensah commits his professional foul, bringing down Peter Odemwingie on the edge of the area.

2. IVORY COAST v GUINEA

Chelsea team-mates Salomon Kalou and Didier Drogba help blast the Elephants of the Ivory Coast into the semis with a five goal thrashing of Guinea.
Lyon's Abdul Kader Keïta hits the only goal of the first half before Kalou sets up Drogba for a 70th minute second. Then Kalou hits a brace in nine minutes before sub Bacary Kone adds a final flourish four minutes from the end.

Ivory Coast	5	Guinea	0
Keita 25, Drogba 70, Kalou 72, 81, B. Kone 85			20,000

NIGERIA APPEARANCES

	Appearances	Started	Subbed on	Subbed off	Mins played	% played	Goals	Yellow	Red
Match 1 2 3 4 / Result L D W L									
Goalkeepers									
Austin Ejide	4	4	0	0	360	100.0	0	0	0
Defenders									
Rabiu Afolabi	1	0	1	0	1	0.3	0	0	0
Onyekachi Apam	1	1	0	0	90	25.0	0	0	0
Obinna Nwaneri	3	3	0	0	270	75.0	0	1	0
Danny Shittu	4	4	0	0	360	100.0	0	0	0
Taye Taiwo	4	4	0	0	360	100.0	0	1	0
Joseph Yobo	4	4	0	0	360	100.0	0	0	0
Midfielders									
Richard Eromoigbe	2	0	2	0	37	10.3	0	0	0
Dickson Etuhu	2	2	0	2	143	39.7	0	0	0
John Obi Mikel	4	4	0	1	354	98.3	1	1	0
Onyekachi Okonkwo	1	0	1	0	35	9.7	0	0	0
Seyi Olofinjana	3	3	0	0	270	75.0	0	2	0
Forwards									
Nwankwo Kanu	1	1	0	1	55	15.3	0	0	0
Stephen Makinwa	2	0	2	0	19	5.3	0	0	0
Obafemi Martins	2	2	0	2	123	34.2	0	1	0
Victor Nsofor Obinna	3	1	2	1	128	35.6	0	0	0
Peter Odemwingie	4	3	1	2	253	70.3	0	1	0
Ikechukwu Uche	3	2	1	0	213	59.2	0	0	0
John Utaka	3	2	1	2	169	46.9	0	0	0
Ayegbeni Yakubu	4	4	0	0	360	100.0	2	0	0

GUINEA APPEARANCES

	Appearances	Started	Subbed on	Subbed off	Mins played	% played	Goals	Yellow	Red
Match 1 2 3 4 / Result L W D L									
Goalkeepers									
Kemoko Camara	4	4	0	0	360	100.0	0	0	0
Defenders									
Dianbobo Balde	3	3	0	0	270	75.0	0	0	0
Alseny Camara	1	1	0	0	90	25.0	0	0	0
Ibrahima Camara	3	3	0	1	260	72.2	0	1	0
Mohamed Alimou Diallo	1	1	0	0	90	25.0	0	0	0
Daouda Jabi	4	4	0	0	360	100.0	0	1	0
Kamil Zayette	2	1	1	1	92	25.6	0	1	0
Midfielders									
Mamadou Bah	3	2	1	0	181	50.3	0	0	0
Ismael Bangoura	4	4	0	0	360	100.0	1	0	0
Mohamed Cisse	1	1	0	0	90	25.0	0	1	0
Victor Corria	2	1	1	1	67	18.6	0	0	0
Pascal Feindouno	2	2	0	0	156	43.3	2	1	1
Samuel Johnson	1	1	0	1	71	19.7	0	0	0
Fode Mansare	3	3	0	2	252	70.0	0	0	0
Mohamed Sacko	4	3	1	0	282	78.3	0	0	0
Naby Soumah	3	1	2	0	138	38.3	0	0	0
Kanfory Sylla	3	2	1	1	201	55.8	0	1	0
Forwards									
Karamoko Cisse	4	0	4	0	89	24.7	0	0	0
Oumar Kalabane	4	3	1	1	256	71.1	1	1	0
Souleymane Youla	4	4	0	4	271	75.3	1	1	0

African Nations Cup Quarter Finals

3. EGYPT v ANGOLA

The Pharoahs narrowly win through against a fired up Angolan team thanks to a lucky bounce off the knees of striker Amr Zaky.
First Hosni Abd Rabou nets his fourth of the tournament in the 23rd minute after a penalty for handball. Angola reply within four minutes with Manucho also scoring his fourth – a classic left-footed thunderbolt from outside the area. The winner couldn't have been more different with the ball spinning into the net off Zaky.

Egypt	2	Angola	1
Hosny 23 pen, Zaky 38		Manucho 27	
		40,000	

4. TUNISIA v CAMEROON

Cameroon need extra time and a brace of goals from Stephane Mbia to put out Tunisia and reach the semis.
The Rennes midfielder opens the scoring with an 18th minute strike and Geremi shows his free kick skills again to add a second on 27. Tunisia's Chaouki Ben Saada replies with a free kick of his own before halftime and Yassine Chikhaoui sends the game into extra time, sweeping home a cross with 11 minutes to go. Mbai's winner comes three minutes into the added period as he fires home from 12 yards.

Tunisia	2	Cameroon (aet)	3
Ben Saada 34, Chikhaoui 81		Mbia 18, 93 Geremi 27	
		20,000	

ANGOLA APPEARANCES

Match	1 2 3 4	Appearances	Started	Subbed on	Subbed off	Mins played	% played	Goals	Yellow	Red
Result	D W D L									
Goalkeepers										
Joao Mamona Lama	■ ■ ■ ■	4	4	0	0	360	100.0	0	0	0
Defenders										
Marcos Airosa	« ■ « ■	4	4	0	2	336	93.3	0	1	0
Carlos Kali	■ ■ ■ ■	4	4	0	0	360	100.0	0	0	0
Manuel Loco	» » » □	3	0	3	0	27	7.5	0	0	0
Rui Manuel Marques	■ ■ ■ ■	4	4	0	0	360	100.0	0	0	0
da Costa Mateus	□ » » »	3	0	3	0	56	15.6	0	0	0
Joao Yamba Asha	■ ■ ■ ■	4	4	0	0	360	100.0	0	0	0
Midfielders										
Aderito Dede	□ » □ □	1	0	1	0	18	5.0	0	0	0
Nobre Edson	» □ □ »	2	0	2	0	25	6.9	0	0	0
Paulo Figueiredo	« □ □ □	1	1	0	1	51	14.2	0	0	0
Sebastiao Gilberto	■ « ■ ■	4	4	0	1	352	97.8	0	0	0
Andre Macanga	■ ■ ■ ■	4	4	0	0	360	100.0	0	2	0
Alberto Manucho	■ « ■ ■	4	4	0	1	357	99.2	4	0	0
Antonio Viana Mendonca	« □ » »	3	1	2	1	124	34.4	0	0	0
Jose Ze Kalanga	» ■ « «	4	3	1	2	284	78.9	0	0	0
Forwards										
Amado Flavio	■ ■ ■ «	4	4	0	1	353	98.1	1	2	0
Norberto Maurito	□ « « «	3	3	0	3	177	49.2	0	0	0

TUNISIA APPEARANCES

Match	1 2 3 4	Appearances	Started	Subbed on	Subbed off	Mins played	% played	Goals	Yellow	Red
Result	D W D L									
Goalkeepers										
Hamdi Kasraoui	■ ■ ■ ■	4	4	0	0	390	100.0	0	0	0
Defenders										
Wissem Bekri	■ □ □ ■	2	2	0	0	210	53.8	0	0	0
Sabeur Ben Frej	□ ■ ■ »	3	2	1	0	262	67.2	0	1	0
Radhouane Felhi	■ □ » ■	3	2	1	0	227	58.2	0	0	0
Karim Hagui	■ ■ ■ «	4	4	0	1	308	79.0	0	0	0
Radhi Jaidi	■ ■ « ■	4	4	0	1	373	95.6	0	2	0
Chaker Zouaghi	« » ■ □	3	2	1	1	185	47.4	0	0	0
Midfielders										
Chaouki Ben Saada	□ ■ □ ■	2	2	0	0	210	53.8	2	0	0
Yassine Mikari	» ■ ■ □	3	2	1	0	185	47.4	0	0	0
Joahar Mnari	■ « ■ ■	4	4	0	1	375	96.2	0	0	0
Mehdi Nafti	□ ■ ■ «	3	3	0	1	250	64.1	0	1	0
Mejdi Traoui	■ ■ □ ■	3	3	0	0	300	76.9	1	1	0
Kamel Zaiem	» □ « □	2	1	1	1	104	26.7	0	1	0
Forwards										
Mehdi Ben Dhifallah	» » » □	3	0	3	0	49	12.6	0	0	0
Amine Chermiti	□ □ ■ »	2	1	1	0	125	32.1	0	0	0
Yassine Chikhaoui	■ « » ■	4	3	1	1	301	77.2	1	0	0
Francileudo Dos Santos	« « □ «	3	3	0	3	212	54.4	2	1	0
Issam Jomaa	« » « »	4	2	2	2	224	57.4	1	1	0

African Nations Cup Semi Finals

GHANA v CAMEROON

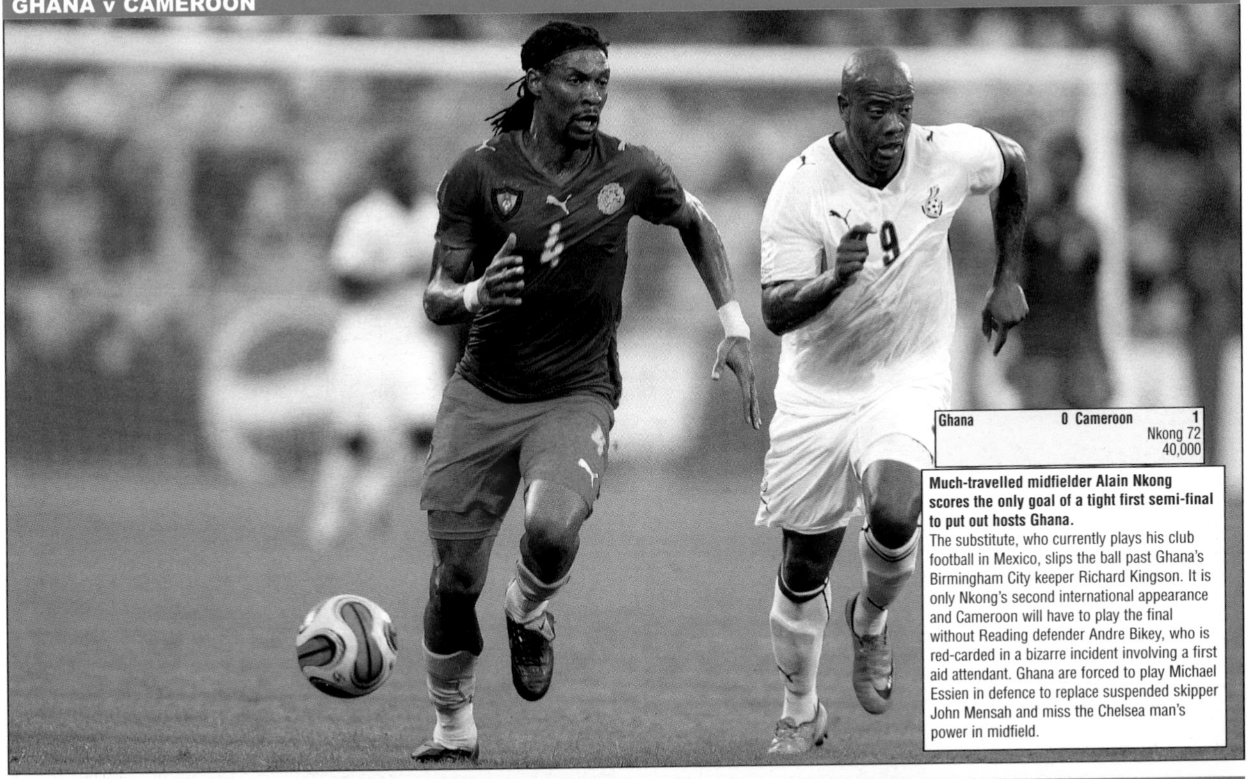

Ghana	0	Cameroon	1
		Nkong 72	
		40,000	

Much-travelled midfielder Alain Nkong scores the only goal of a tight first semi-final to put out hosts Ghana.
The substitute, who currently plays his club football in Mexico, slips the ball past Ghana's Birmingham City keeper Richard Kingson. It is only Nkong's second international appearance and Cameroon will have to play the final without Reading defender Andre Bikey, who is red-carded in a bizarre incident involving a first aid attendant. Ghana are forced to play Michael Essien in defence to replace suspended skipper John Mensah and miss the Chelsea man's power in midfield.

IVORY COAST v EGYPT

Pharoahs' keeper Essam Al Hadari puts in a defiant performance to deny Ivory Coast's Didier Drogba three times at a crucial stage of the match and the holders go through at the expense of the favourites.
Ahmed Faty gives Egypt the lead with a deflected shot after 12 minutes and Al Hadari keeps the Elephants out until Zaky heads a second for Egypt in the 62nd minute. Abdul Kader Keita pulls a goal back almost immediately before Zaki's long range shot restores a two goal margin and Mohamed Aboutreika adds a late gloss as Egypt set up a final with Cameroon.

Ivory Coast	1	Egypt	4
Keita 63		Fathi 12, Zaky 61, 67, Aboutreika 90	
		45,000	

African Nations Cup third place play-off

GHANA v IVORY COAST

Ghana	4	Ivory Coast	2
Muntari 63, Owusu-Abeyie 70, Agogo 80, Dramani 84		Sanago 24, 32	
			45,000

Ghana finish their tournament in third spot with three late goals to beat Ivory Coast. Sulley Ali Muntari belts home a free kick from 25 yards to give Ghana a lead but Boubacar Sanogo of Werder Bremen hits a brace to give the Elephants a halftime lead. As a swarm of moths fly into the Baba Yara stadium Owusu-Abeyie Quincy levels on 70 minutes and goals from Junior Agogo and Haminu Draman earn Ghana the win.

GHANA APPEARANCES

Match: 1 2 3 4 5 6 — Result: W W W W L W

Player	Appearances	Started	Subbed on	Subbed off	Mins played	% played	Goals	Yellow	Red
Goalkeepers									
Richard Kingson	6	6	0	0	540	100.0	0	0	0
Defenders									
Harrison Afful	1	0	1	0	2	0.4	0	0	0
John Mensah	5	5	0	0	418	77.4	0	0	1
John Paintsil	6	6	0	0	540	100.0	0	1	0
Hans Sarpei	6	6	0	0	540	100.0	0	0	0
Midfielders									
Eric Addo	6	6	0	1	539	99.8	0	1	0
Anthony Annan	4	4	0	0	360	66.7	0	0	0
Andre Ayew	4	1	3	1	135	25.0	0	0	0
Ahmed Barruso	1	0	1	0	4	0.7	0	0	0
Haminu Draman	4	2	2	1	197	36.5	1	0	0
Michael Essien	6	6	0	0	540	100.0	2	0	0
Asamoah Gyan	4	4	0	4	296	54.8	1	1	0
Laryea Kingston	3	2	1	1	182	33.7	0	2	0
Sulley Muntari	6	6	0	0	540	100.0	3	1	0
Forwards									
Junior Agogo	6	6	0	1	533	98.7	3	1	0
Kwadwo Asamoah	1	0	1	0	1	0.2	0	0	0
Baffour Gyan	5	1	4	1	83	15.4	0	0	0
Quincy Owusu-Abeyie	6	5	1	4	458	84.8	1	0	0

IVORY COAST APPEARANCES

Match: 1 2 3 4 5 6 — Result: W W W W L L

Player	Appearances	Started	Subbed on	Subbed off	Mins played	% played	Goals	Yellow	Red
Goalkeepers									
Boubacar Barry	5	5	0	1	398	73.7	0	0	0
Tiasse Kone	1	1	0	0	90	16.7	0	0	0
Stephan Loboue	1	0	1	0	52	9.6	0	0	0
Defenders									
Arthur Boka	6	6	0	0	540	100.0	0	1	0
Emmanuel Eboue	5	5	0	0	450	83.3	0	0	0
Steve Gohouri	2	1	1	1	96	17.8	0	1	0
Abdoulaye Meite	4	4	0	0	360	66.7	0	1	0
Habib Kolo Toure	3	3	0	1	219	40.6	0	0	0
Marco Zoro	2	2	0	0	180	33.3	1	0	0
Midfielders									
Emerse Fae	3	2	1	1	188	34.8	0	0	0
Christian Koffi Ndri	3	3	0	0	270	50.0	0	0	0
Siaka Tiene	2	2	0	0	180	33.3	0	0	0
Yaya Toure	5	4	1	0	387	71.7	1	0	0
Didier Zokora	6	6	0	0	540	100.0	0	0	0
Forwards									
Aruna Dindane	5	4	1	2	335	62.0	1	0	0
Didier Drogba	6	6	0	4	480	88.9	3	0	0
Salomon Kalou	5	5	0	2	401	74.3	3	1	0
Abdul Kader Keita	6	5	1	4	406	75.2	3	0	0
Arouna Kone	3	1	2	0	123	22.8	0	0	0
Bakary Kone	4	0	4	0	84	15.6	1	0	0
Gervais Yao Kouassi	2	0	2	0	32	5.9	0	1	0
Boubacar Sanogo	1	2	0	1	29	23.9	3	0	0